Hoover Institution Publications

# Yearbook on International Communist Affairs

## 1968

# YEARBOOK ON INTERNATIONAL COMMUNIST AFFAIRS

## 1968

*Editor:* Richard V. Allen
*Assistant Editor:* Milorad Popov

HOOVER INSTITUTION PRESS
Stanford University
Stanford, California
1969

The Hoover Institution on War, Revolution and Peace, founded at Stanford University in 1919 by the late President Herbert Hoover, is a center for advanced study and research on public and international affairs in the twentieth century. The views expressed in its publications are entirely those of the authors and do not necessarily reflect the views of the Hoover Institution.

An undertaking of the scope and nature of the YEARBOOK project requires a permanent staff and research potential of substantial size. The Hoover Institution is greatly indebted to the following foundations for their financial support of this project.

> The Carthage Foundation
> William H. Donner Foundation, Inc.
> Esso Education Foundation
> Lilly Endowment, Inc.
> Mary Reynolds Babcock Foundation, Inc.
> Relm Foundation

Hoover Institution Publications 80
Standard Book Number 8179-1801-9
Library of Congress Card Number 67-31024
Printed in the United States of America
©1969 by the Board of Trustees of the Leland Stanford Junior University

# YEARBOOK ON INTERNATIONAL
# COMMUNIST AFFAIRS
## 1968

## Advisory Board

# CONTENTS

Preface . . . . . . . . . . . . . . . . . . . . . . . . . . . . . . . . . . . . . . . . . . . . . . . . . . .xiii

PROFILES OF INDIVIDUAL COMMUNIST PARTIES

Albania . . . . . . . . . . . . . . . . . . . . . . . . . . . . . . . . . . . . . . . . . . . . . . . . 3
Algeria . . . . . . . . . . . . . . . . . . . . . . . . . . . . . . . . . . . . . . . . . . . . . . . . 12
Argentina . . . . . . . . . . . . . . . . . . . . . . . . . . . . . . . . . . . . . . . . . . . . . . 16
Australia . . . . . . . . . . . . . . . . . . . . . . . . . . . . . . . . . . . . . . . . . . . . . . 21
Austria . . . . . . . . . . . . . . . . . . . . . . . . . . . . . . . . . . . . . . . . . . . . . . . 27
Belgium . . . . . . . . . . . . . . . . . . . . . . . . . . . . . . . . . . . . . . . . . . . . . . . 34
Bolivia . . . . . . . . . . . . . . . . . . . . . . . . . . . . . . . . . . . . . . . . . . . . . . . 40
Brazil . . . . . . . . . . . . . . . . . . . . . . . . . . . . . . . . . . . . . . . . . . . . . . . . 45
Bulgaria . . . . . . . . . . . . . . . . . . . . . . . . . . . . . . . . . . . . . . . . . . . . . . 51
Burma . . . . . . . . . . . . . . . . . . . . . . . . . . . . . . . . . . . . . . . . . . . . . . . . 60
Cambodia . . . . . . . . . . . . . . . . . . . . . . . . . . . . . . . . . . . . . . . . . . . . . 67
Cameroun . . . . . . . . . . . . . . . . . . . . . . . . . . . . . . . . . . . . . . . . . . . . . 75
Canada . . . . . . . . . . . . . . . . . . . . . . . . . . . . . . . . . . . . . . . . . . . . . . . 77
Ceylon . . . . . . . . . . . . . . . . . . . . . . . . . . . . . . . . . . . . . . . . . . . . . . . 82
Chile . . . . . . . . . . . . . . . . . . . . . . . . . . . . . . . . . . . . . . . . . . . . . . . . 89
China . . . . . . . . . . . . . . . . . . . . . . . . . . . . . . . . . . . . . . . . . . . . . . . . 98
Colombia . . . . . . . . . . . . . . . . . . . . . . . . . . . . . . . . . . . . . . . . . . . . . 122
Costa Rica . . . . . . . . . . . . . . . . . . . . . . . . . . . . . . . . . . . . . . . . . . . . 133
Cuba . . . . . . . . . . . . . . . . . . . . . . . . . . . . . . . . . . . . . . . . . . . . . . . . 136
Cyprus . . . . . . . . . . . . . . . . . . . . . . . . . . . . . . . . . . . . . . . . . . . . . . . 162
Czechoslovakia . . . . . . . . . . . . . . . . . . . . . . . . . . . . . . . . . . . . . . . . . 166
Denmark . . . . . . . . . . . . . . . . . . . . . . . . . . . . . . . . . . . . . . . . . . . . . . 180
Dominican Republic . . . . . . . . . . . . . . . . . . . . . . . . . . . . . . . . . . . . . . 185
Ecuador . . . . . . . . . . . . . . . . . . . . . . . . . . . . . . . . . . . . . . . . . . . . . . 192
El Salvador . . . . . . . . . . . . . . . . . . . . . . . . . . . . . . . . . . . . . . . . . . . . 197
Finland . . . . . . . . . . . . . . . . . . . . . . . . . . . . . . . . . . . . . . . . . . . . . . . 200
France . . . . . . . . . . . . . . . . . . . . . . . . . . . . . . . . . . . . . . . . . . . . . . . 208
Germany: German Democratic Republic . . . . . . . . . . . . . . . . . . . . . . . . 223
Germany: Federal Republic of Germany . . . . . . . . . . . . . . . . . . . . . . . . 234
Germany: West Berlin . . . . . . . . . . . . . . . . . . . . . . . . . . . . . . . . . . . . 239
Great Britain . . . . . . . . . . . . . . . . . . . . . . . . . . . . . . . . . . . . . . . . . . 243
Greece . . . . . . . . . . . . . . . . . . . . . . . . . . . . . . . . . . . . . . . . . . . . . . . 252
Guadeloupe . . . . . . . . . . . . . . . . . . . . . . . . . . . . . . . . . . . . . . . . . . . . 259
Guatemala . . . . . . . . . . . . . . . . . . . . . . . . . . . . . . . . . . . . . . . . . . . . . 263
Guyana . . . . . . . . . . . . . . . . . . . . . . . . . . . . . . . . . . . . . . . . . . . . . . . 270
Haiti . . . . . . . . . . . . . . . . . . . . . . . . . . . . . . . . . . . . . . . . . . . . . . . . . 273
Honduras . . . . . . . . . . . . . . . . . . . . . . . . . . . . . . . . . . . . . . . . . . . . . . 278
Hungary . . . . . . . . . . . . . . . . . . . . . . . . . . . . . . . . . . . . . . . . . . . . . . . 282
Iceland . . . . . . . . . . . . . . . . . . . . . . . . . . . . . . . . . . . . . . . . . . . . . . . 295
India . . . . . . . . . . . . . . . . . . . . . . . . . . . . . . . . . . . . . . . . . . . . . . . . . 297
Indonesia . . . . . . . . . . . . . . . . . . . . . . . . . . . . . . . . . . . . . . . . . . . . . . 308

Iran . . . . . . . . . . . . . . . . . . . . . . . . . . . . . . . . . . . . . . . . . . . . . . . . . . 321
Iraq . . . . . . . . . . . . . . . . . . . . . . . . . . . . . . . . . . . . . . . . . . . . . . . . . . 324
Ireland . . . . . . . . . . . . . . . . . . . . . . . . . . . . . . . . . . . . . . . . . . . . . . . . 328
Israel . . . . . . . . . . . . . . . . . . . . . . . . . . . . . . . . . . . . . . . . . . . . . . . . . 330
Italy . . . . . . . . . . . . . . . . . . . . . . . . . . . . . . . . . . . . . . . . . . . . . . . . . . 335
Japan . . . . . . . . . . . . . . . . . . . . . . . . . . . . . . . . . . . . . . . . . . . . . . . . . 348
Jordan . . . . . . . . . . . . . . . . . . . . . . . . . . . . . . . . . . . . . . . . . . . . . . . . . 358
Laos . . . . . . . . . . . . . . . . . . . . . . . . . . . . . . . . . . . . . . . . . . . . . . . . . . 362
Lebanon . . . . . . . . . . . . . . . . . . . . . . . . . . . . . . . . . . . . . . . . . . . . . . . . 373
Lesotho . . . . . . . . . . . . . . . . . . . . . . . . . . . . . . . . . . . . . . . . . . . . . . . . 377
Luxembourg . . . . . . . . . . . . . . . . . . . . . . . . . . . . . . . . . . . . . . . . . . . . . 380
Malaysia . . . . . . . . . . . . . . . . . . . . . . . . . . . . . . . . . . . . . . . . . . . . . . . 383
Martinique . . . . . . . . . . . . . . . . . . . . . . . . . . . . . . . . . . . . . . . . . . . . . . 393
Mexico . . . . . . . . . . . . . . . . . . . . . . . . . . . . . . . . . . . . . . . . . . . . . . . . 396
Mongolia . . . . . . . . . . . . . . . . . . . . . . . . . . . . . . . . . . . . . . . . . . . . . . . 401
Morocco . . . . . . . . . . . . . . . . . . . . . . . . . . . . . . . . . . . . . . . . . . . . . . . 409
Nepal . . . . . . . . . . . . . . . . . . . . . . . . . . . . . . . . . . . . . . . . . . . . . . . . . 414
Netherlands . . . . . . . . . . . . . . . . . . . . . . . . . . . . . . . . . . . . . . . . . . . . . 417
New Zealand . . . . . . . . . . . . . . . . . . . . . . . . . . . . . . . . . . . . . . . . . . . . . 422
Nicaragua . . . . . . . . . . . . . . . . . . . . . . . . . . . . . . . . . . . . . . . . . . . . . . . 427
Nigeria . . . . . . . . . . . . . . . . . . . . . . . . . . . . . . . . . . . . . . . . . . . . . . . . 431
North Korea . . . . . . . . . . . . . . . . . . . . . . . . . . . . . . . . . . . . . . . . . . . . . 434
Norway . . . . . . . . . . . . . . . . . . . . . . . . . . . . . . . . . . . . . . . . . . . . . . . . 448
Pakistan . . . . . . . . . . . . . . . . . . . . . . . . . . . . . . . . . . . . . . . . . . . . . . . . 455
Panama . . . . . . . . . . . . . . . . . . . . . . . . . . . . . . . . . . . . . . . . . . . . . . . . 460
Paraguay . . . . . . . . . . . . . . . . . . . . . . . . . . . . . . . . . . . . . . . . . . . . . . . 463
Peru . . . . . . . . . . . . . . . . . . . . . . . . . . . . . . . . . . . . . . . . . . . . . . . . . . 467
Philippines . . . . . . . . . . . . . . . . . . . . . . . . . . . . . . . . . . . . . . . . . . . . . . 477
Poland . . . . . . . . . . . . . . . . . . . . . . . . . . . . . . . . . . . . . . . . . . . . . . . . . 484
Portugal . . . . . . . . . . . . . . . . . . . . . . . . . . . . . . . . . . . . . . . . . . . . . . . . 497
Puerto Rico . . . . . . . . . . . . . . . . . . . . . . . . . . . . . . . . . . . . . . . . . . . . . . 502
Réunion . . . . . . . . . . . . . . . . . . . . . . . . . . . . . . . . . . . . . . . . . . . . . . . . 506
Rumania . . . . . . . . . . . . . . . . . . . . . . . . . . . . . . . . . . . . . . . . . . . . . . . . 508
San Marino . . . . . . . . . . . . . . . . . . . . . . . . . . . . . . . . . . . . . . . . . . . . . . 520
Singapore . . . . . . . . . . . . . . . . . . . . . . . . . . . . . . . . . . . . . . . . . . . . . . . 521
South Africa . . . . . . . . . . . . . . . . . . . . . . . . . . . . . . . . . . . . . . . . . . . . . 525
Spain . . . . . . . . . . . . . . . . . . . . . . . . . . . . . . . . . . . . . . . . . . . . . . . . . . 529
Sudan . . . . . . . . . . . . . . . . . . . . . . . . . . . . . . . . . . . . . . . . . . . . . . . . . . 537
Sweden . . . . . . . . . . . . . . . . . . . . . . . . . . . . . . . . . . . . . . . . . . . . . . . . . 542
Switzerland . . . . . . . . . . . . . . . . . . . . . . . . . . . . . . . . . . . . . . . . . . . . . . 551
Syria . . . . . . . . . . . . . . . . . . . . . . . . . . . . . . . . . . . . . . . . . . . . . . . . . . 559
Thailand . . . . . . . . . . . . . . . . . . . . . . . . . . . . . . . . . . . . . . . . . . . . . . . . 566
Tunisia . . . . . . . . . . . . . . . . . . . . . . . . . . . . . . . . . . . . . . . . . . . . . . . . . 574
Turkey . . . . . . . . . . . . . . . . . . . . . . . . . . . . . . . . . . . . . . . . . . . . . . . . . 576
Union of Soviet Socialist Republics . . . . . . . . . . . . . . . . . . . . . . . . . . . . . . 579
United Arab Republic . . . . . . . . . . . . . . . . . . . . . . . . . . . . . . . . . . . . . . . 607
United States of America . . . . . . . . . . . . . . . . . . . . . . . . . . . . . . . . . . . . . 609
Uruguay . . . . . . . . . . . . . . . . . . . . . . . . . . . . . . . . . . . . . . . . . . . . . . . . 624
Venezuela . . . . . . . . . . . . . . . . . . . . . . . . . . . . . . . . . . . . . . . . . . . . . . . 629
Vietnam: Democratic Republic of Vietnam . . . . . . . . . . . . . . . . . . . . . . . . . . 638

Vietnam: Republic of Vietnam . . . . . . . . . . . . . . . . . . . . . . . . . . . . 663
Yugoslavia . . . . . . . . . . . . . . . . . . . . . . . . . . . . . . . . . . . . . . . 681

INTERNATIONAL COMMUNIST FRONT ORGANIZATIONS . . . . . . . . . . . . . . . 695

World Council of Peace . . . . . . . . . . . . . . . . . . . . . . . . . . . . . . . . 696
World Federation of Trade Unions . . . . . . . . . . . . . . . . . . . . . . . . . 706
World Federation of Democratic Youth . . . . . . . . . . . . . . . . . . . . . . 713
International Union of Students . . . . . . . . . . . . . . . . . . . . . . . . . . . 720
Women's International Democratic Federation . . . . . . . . . . . . . . . . . . . 726
International Organization of Journalists . . . . . . . . . . . . . . . . . . . . . . 731
World Federation of Scientific Workers . . . . . . . . . . . . . . . . . . . . . . 735
International Federation of Resistance Fighters . . . . . . . . . . . . . . . . . . 739
International Association of Democratic Lawyers . . . . . . . . . . . . . . . . . . 742
International Radio and Television Organization . . . . . . . . . . . . . . . . . . 745
Pro-Chinese International Communist Front Organizations . . . . . . . . . . . . 747

INTERNATIONAL COMMUNIST CONFERENCES AND EVENTS

Conference of Communist and Workers' Parties of Europe, Karlovy Vary (24-26 April) . . . . 753
First Conference of the Latin American Solidarity Organization, Havana
(31 July—10 August) . . . . . . . . . . . . . . . . . . . . . . . . . . . . . . . . 758
The Soviet Union's Fiftieth Anniversary of the October Revolution . . . . . . . . . . . . . . 764

DOCUMENTS

Albania

1. "Long Live the Great Chinese Proletarian Cultural Revolution" (*Rruga e Partisë*,
   Tirana, February 1967) (complete text) . . . . . . . . . . . . . . . . . . . . . . 773

2. On the Further Revolutionization of the Party and Regime, Speech by Enver Hoxha at
   a Joint Meeting of Tirana Basic Party Organizations, 6 February 1967 (excerpts) . . . . 777

Chile

3. "Alliance of Anti-Imperialist Forces in Latin America," Article by Luis Corvalán,
   General Secretary, Communist Party of Chile (*World Marxist Review*, July 1967)
   (complete text) . . . . . . . . . . . . . . . . . . . . . . . . . . . . . . . . . . 781

4. "A Strong Communist Party—A Guarantee For The People," Report of Luis Corvalán,
   General Secretary, Communist Party of Chile, at the National Conference of the CP
   Chile, September 1967 (*Information Bulletin*, No. 110, 1967) (abridged text) . . . . . 787

China

5. "Carry the Great Proletarian Cultural Revolution Through to the End" (*People's Daily*
   and *Red Flag* Editorial, 1 January 1967) (complete text) . . . . . . . . . . . . . . . . . . 793

6. "On the Proletarian Revolutionaries' Struggle to Seize Power" (*Red Flag* Editorial,
   No. 3, 1967) (complete text) . . . . . . . . . . . . . . . . . . . . . . . . . . . . 800

7. "On the Revolutionary 'Three-in-One' Combination" (*Hung Ch'i* Editorial, No. 5,
   1967) (complete text) . . . . . . . . . . . . . . . . . . . . . . . . . . . . . . . 805

8. Liu Shao-ch'i's Confession at the Peking Civil Engineering College, 9 July 1967
   (complete text) . . . . . . . . . . . . . . . . . . . . . . . . . . . . . . . . . . 808

9. Summaries of Speeches Made by Members of the Central Cultural Revolutionary Group
   at an Enlarged Meeting of the Peking Revolutionary Committee, 1 September 1967
   (from Red Guard newspapers) . . . . . . . . . . . . . . . . . . . . . . . . . . . . 812

10. Speech of Chiang Ch'ing (Mme. Mao Tse-tung) to Representatives of Mass Organizations in Anhwei Province Visiting Peking, 5 September 1967 (complete text) . 815

11. Speech of Lin Piao at the Rally Celebrating the 18th Anniversary of the Founding of the People's Republic of China (*Peking Review*, No. 41, 6 October 1967) (complete text) . . . . . . . . . . . . . . . . . . . . . . . . . . . . . . . . . . . . . . . . . 818

12. Speech of Chou En-lai at Wuhan Mass Rally to Welcome Albanian Party and Government Delegation, 9 October 1967 (*Peking Review*, No. 43, 20 October 1967) (abridged text) . . . . . . . . . . . . . . . . . . . . . . . . . . . . . . . . . 820

13. "Advance Along the Road Opened Up by the Great October Socialist Revolution" (by the Editorial Departments of *People's Daily*, *Red Flag*, and *Liberation Army Daily*, 6 November 1967) (complete text) . . . . . . . . . . . . . . . . . . . . . 823

14. Speech of Lin Piao at the Peking Rally Commemorating the 50th Anniversary of the October Revolution (*Peking Review*, No. 46, 10 November 1967) (complete text) . . . 829

15. "Basic Differences Between the Proletarian and Bourgeois Military Lines," Written by "Proletarian Revolutionaries" in the Offices of the Headquarters of the General Staff of the People's Liberation Army (*Peking Review*, No. 48, 24 November 1967) (complete text) . . . . . . . . . . . . . . . . . . . . . . . . . . . . . . . . . 832

Cuba

16. Speech of 13 March 1967 by Fidel Castro at the Commemoration of the 10th Anniversary of the Attack on the Presidential Palace (*Granma*, Havana, 19 March 1967, English edition) (complete text) . . . . . . . . . . . . . . . . . . . . . . . 837

17. Major Ernesto "Che" Guevara's "Message to the Peoples of the World," April 1967 (*Granma*, Havana, 23 April 1967, English edition) (complete text) . . . . . . . . . . . 855

Czechoslovakia

18. Speech by Ludvík Vaculík at the Fourth Congress of Czechoslovak Writers, 27-29 June 1967 (*IV Sjezd Svazu Ceskoslovenskych Spisovatelu [Protokol]*, Prague, 1968) (complete text) . . . . . . . . . . . . . . . . . . . . . . . . . . . . . . . . . 861

19. Communique of the Plenary Session of the Central Committee of the Communist Party of Czechoslovakia, 26-27 September 1967 (*Rudé Právo*, 28 September 1967) (excerpt) 868

Finland

20. On the Party Program, Speech of Aarne Saarinen, Chairman, Communist Party of Finland, at the June 1967 Meeting of the Central Committee (*Kansan Uutiset*, Helsinki, 12-13 September 1967) (abridged) . . . . . . . . . . . . . . . . . . . . . . . 870

France

21. Four Documents of the French Communist Party on the General Elections: A. Joint Communique by the PCF and the FGDS, 20 December 1966 (*Le Monde*, 22 December 1966) (complete text); B. Joint Communique by the PCF and PSU, 7 January 1967 (*L'Humanité*, 9 January 1967) (complete text); C. 30 March Resolution of the Central Committee, PCF (*L'Humanité*, 1 April 1967) (abridged text); D. Remarks by Waldeck Rochet at the Central Committee Meeting (*L'Humanité*, 3 April 1967) (abridged text) 872

22. "Marxism Is Not a Catechism," Article by Jean Kanapa, Member of the Central Committee, French Communist Party (*L'Humanité*, Paris, 6 February 1967) (complete text) . . . . . . . . . . . . . . . . . . . . . . . . . . . . . . . . . . . . . . . . . 878

23. "What Being a Revolutionary Means in France Today," Paper Delivered by Waldeck Rochet, Secretary-General, PCF, at the Maurice Thorez Institute, October 1967 (*Information Bulletin*, No. 93, 1967) (abridged text) . . . . . . . . . . . . . . . . 880

Great Britain

24. "Questions of Ideology and Culture," Statement adopted by the Executive Committee, CP of Great Britain, 11 March 1967 (complete text) . . . . . . . . . . . . . . . . . . . . 885

Greece

25. Resolution of the 11th Plenary Meeting, Communist Party of Greece (*Information Bulletin*, No. 104, 1967) (complete text) . . . . . . . . . . . . . . . . . . . . . . . . . 890

Hungary

26. "The Budapest Meeting," Article by Zoltán Komocsin, Member of the Politburo, Hungarian Socialist Workers' Party (*Népszabadság*, Budapest, 24 December 1967) (complete text) . . . . . . . . . . . . . . . . . . . . . . . . . . . . . . . . . 893

Indonesia

27. "Build the PKI Along the Marxist-Leninist Line to Lead the People's Democratic Revolution in Indonesia," Self-Criticism of the Political Bureau of the Central Committee of the Indonesian Communist Party (PKI) (*Indonesian Tribune*, Vol. 1, No. 3, January 1967) (complete text) . . . . . . . . . . . . . . . . . . . . . . . . . 896

28. For a Sound Indonesian Revolution (*Information Bulletin*, No. 106, 1967) (complete text) . . . . . . . . . . . . . . . . . . . . . . . . . . . . . . . . . . . . . . . . 908

Israel

29. Three Documents of the Communist Party of Israel: A. Speech by Meir Vilner in the Knesset, 22 May 1967; B. Statement of the Central Committee, CP of Israel, 26 May 1967; C. Decisions of the Central Committee 16th Plenary Session, 22 June 1967 (*Information Bulletin*, Nos. 99-100, 102, 1967) (complete texts) . . . . . . . . . . . . 920

Italy

30. "New United Efforts by Communist Parties Needed," Resolution of the Leadership of the Italian CP on the Events in China and Problems of the World Working-Class Movement (*L'Unità*, 10 February 1967) (complete text) . . . . . . . . . . . . . . . . 924

31. "The Fight for Peace and Freedom in Vietnam, Tasks of the ICP in the Struggle for World Communist Unity," Report to the CC, Italian CP by Enrico Berlinguer (*L'Unità*, 24 February 1967) (abridged text) . . . . . . . . . . . . . . . . . . . . . . . . . . 925

32. Statement of Luigi Longo, General Secretary of the Italian CP, at a Meeting of the Central Committee and CCC in July 1967 (*L'Unità*, 13 July 1967) (abridged text) . . . 931

33. Luigi Longo on the International Communist Movement, Four Articles by the Secretary-General of the Italian Communist Party (*Rinascita*, Rome, 20 October, 27 October, 3 November, 10 November 1967; *Foreign Bulletin* [CC, PCI — Foreign Section], September-December 1967) (complete texts) . . . . . . . . . . . . . . . . . 934

Japan

34. "The Mao Tse-tung Line of Today and the International Communist Movement" (*Akahata*, Tokyo, 10 October 1967) (excerpts) . . . . . . . . . . . . . . . . . . . . 940

Jordan

35. Statement by the Jordanian Communist Party (*Information Bulletin*, No. 105, 1967) (abridged text) . . . . . . . . . . . . . . . . . . . . . . . . . . . . . . . . . . . . 947

Poland

36. "On the Current Tasks in the Political Work of the Party," Report of Zenon Kliszko, Secretary of the Central Committee, Polish United Workers' Party, 16 May 1967 (*Trybuna Ludu*, Warsaw, 17 May 1967) (abridged text) . . . . . . . . . . . . . . . . 949

Rumania

37. Statement on the Establishment of Diplomatic Relations Between the Rumanian Socialist Republic and the German Federal Republic (Agerpres, 1 February 1967) (complete text) . . . . . . . . . . . . . . . . . . . . . . . . . . . . . . . . 953

38. "The Leading Role of the Party in the Stage of the Completion of Building Socialism," Article by Nicolae Ceauşescu, Secretary-General of the Rumanian Communist Party Central Committee (*Scînteia*, 7 May 1967) (excerpts) . . . . . . . . . . . . . . . . . . 954

39. Resolution of the National Conference of the Rumanian Communist Party (Agerpres, 9 December 1967) (complete text) . . . . . . . . . . . . . . . . . . . . . . . . 959

Spain

40. Political Statement by the Executive Committee, CP of Spain (*Information Bulletin*, No. 102, 1967) (complete text) . . . . . . . . . . . . . . . . . . . . . . . . . . 961

Syria

41. Statement by the Political Bureau of the Central Committee, Syrian CP (*Information Bulletin*, No. 102, 1967) (abridged text) . . . . . . . . . . . . . . . . . . . . . . . 964

USSR

42. Speech by Leonid I. Brezhnev in Gorky on 13 January 1967 (*Pravda,* 14 January 1967) (excerpts) . . . . . . . . . . . . . . . . . . . . . . . . . . . . . . . . . . . . 965

43. Statement of the Soviet Government on the Federal Republic of Germany (*Pravda*, 29 January 1967) (complete text) . . . . . . . . . . . . . . . . . . . . . . . . . 968

44. "On the Anti-Soviet Policy of Mao Tse-tung and His Group" (*Pravda*, 16 February 1967) (complete text) . . . . . . . . . . . . . . . . . . . . . . . . . . . . . . . 972

45. "On the Policy of the Soviet Union in Connection with the Israeli Aggression in the Near East," Resolution of the Plenary Meeting of the CPSU Central Committee, Adopted 21 June 1967 (*Pravda*, 22 June 1967) (complete text) . . . . . . . . . . . . . . 977

46. "The Great October Socialist Revolution and the World Revolutionary Process," Section III of the Theses of the Central Committee of the CPSU on the Fiftieth Anniversary of the Great October Socialist Revolution (*Pravda*, 25 June 1967) (complete text) . . . . . . . . . . . . . . . . . . . . . . . . . . . . . . . . . . . . 979

47. Letter by A.I. Solzhenitsyn to the Congress of the Union of Soviet Writers (*Posev*, Frankfurt-am-Main, No. 8 [August] 1968) (complete text) . . . . . . . . . . . . . . 985

48. "To The Soviet People, To All Working People Of The USSR," Message of the Central Committee of the CPSU, the Presidium of the USSR Supreme Soviet, and the Council of Ministers of the USSR, 4 November 1967 (*Pravda*, 5 November 1967) (complete text) 988

49. "Fifty Years on Guard of the Soviet Union's Security," Report by I.V. Andropov, Chairman of the State Security Committee (KGB) (*Moscow News*, Supplement to issue 52 [887], 1967, and *Pravda*, 21 December 1967; portions in brackets were omitted from the English version in *Moscow News* Supplement) (abridged text) . . . . . . . . . 992

50. Open Letter from Soviet Scientist Pavel M. Litvinov, Sent to four Soviet newspapers and the *L'Humanité* and *L'Unità,* newspapers of the French and Italian Communist parties (Text of the plea by author Vladimir I. Bukovsky at his trial in Moscow, 1 September 1967, was attached to the letter.) (*The New York Times*, 27 December 1967) (excerpts) . . . . . . . . . . . . . . . . . . . . . . . . . . . . . . . . . . . 996

51. Documents on the A.I. Solzhenitsyn Case: A. Letter from the Union of Soviet Writers to A.I. Solzhenitsyn; B. Reply by Solzhenitsyn to the Secretariat of the USSR Writers' Union; C. Remarks by *Pravda* Editor M.V. Zimianin at The House of the Press, Leningrad, 5 October 1967; D. Letter from Pavel Antokolsky to P.N. Demichev (Radio Liberty dispatch, 29 January 1968) . . . . . . . . . . . . . . . . . 1000

Venezuela

52. "The Internal Situation and the Communist Party," Statement by the Political Bureau of the Central Committee, CP of Venezuela, January 1967 (*Information Bulletin*, No. 94, 1967) (complete text) . . . . . . . . . . . . . . . . . . . . . . . . . . . . 1003

Vietnam

53. Political Program of the South Vietnam National Front for Liberation, Adopted by the Central Committee, Mid-August 1967 (Vietnam News Agency International Service, Hanoi, 1 September 1967) (complete text) . . . . . . . . . . . . . . . . . . 1006

54. "The Great October Revolution Shows the Peoples the Road to Liberation," Article by Ho Chi Minh on the Occasion of the 50th Anniversary of the October Revolution (*Pravda*, 28 October 1967) (complete text) . . . . . . . . . . . . . . . . . . . . . . 1014

Yugoslavia

55. "Conclusions From the July 1 Plenum of the Central Committee of the League of Communists of Yugoslavia on Current International Problems" (*Review of International Affairs*, Belgrade, 5-20 July 1967) (complete text) . . . . . . . . . . . . . . 1018

Conferences, Area Documents

56. "The Duty of Every Revolutionary Is to Make Revolution," Call to the First Conference of Solidarity of the Peoples of Latin America (OLAS), 15 February 1967 (*Granma*, Havana, 26 February 1967, English edition) (complete text) . . . . . . . . . 1021

57. "What is OLAS?" Pamphlet Published by the Organizing Committee of the Latin American Solidarity Organization, 24 May 1967 (complete text) . . . . . . . . . . . 1023

58. Statement of the Communist Parties and Governments on the Situation in the Middle East, 9 June 1967 (*Pravda*, 10 June 1967) (complete text) . . . . . . . . . . . . . . 1026

59. General Declaration of the First Conference of the Organization of Latin American Solidarity (Conference Document, Havana) (complete text) . . . . . . . . . . . . . . 1028

60. Four Documents of the Conference of European Communist and Workers' Parties on Problems of European Security Held in Karlovy Vary, Czechoslovakia, April 24-26, 1967: A. Opening Communique; B. Speech by Leonid I. Brezhnev; C. Statement, "For Peace and Security in Europe"; D. Final Communique (*Information Bulletin*, Nos. 8-10, 1967, Prague edition) (complete text) . . . . . . . . . . . . . . . . . . 1034

61. Statement by the Fifth Meeting of the Communist Parties of Mexico, Central America and Panama, May 1967 (*Information Bulletin*, No. 102, 1967) (complete text) . . . . 1047

62. Two Documents of the Arab Communist Meeting, May 1967: A. Statement on the Situation in the Arab Countries; B. Resolution on the Situation in the World Communist Movement (*Information Bulletin*, No. 99-100, 1967) (complete texts) . . 1049

CHRONOLOGY . . . . . . . . . . . . . . . . . . . . . . . . . . . . . . . . . . . . . . . 1057

BIBLIOGRAPHY . . . . . . . . . . . . . . . . . . . . . . . . . . . . . . . . . . . . . . . 1097

INDEXES . . . . . . . . . . . . . . . . . . . . . . . . . . . . . . . . . . . . . . . . . . 1107

# PREFACE

This volume of the *Yearbook on International Communist Affairs*, covering events and developments in 1967, continues within the general framework set by the first, 1966, *Yearbook*, edited by Dr. Milorad M. Drachkovitch. Its aim is to provide a comprehensive annual survey describing the organizational structures, internal developments, and domestic and foreign policies and activities of all the communist parties in the world. As in the previous year's edition, the *Yearbook*'s primary sources are from communist publications of a broad variety, ranging from regular periodicals such as the *World Marxist Review* to ephemeral pamphlets and newssheets.

The *Yearbook on International Communist Affairs* was conceived with the idea of assembling, in several sections, data concerning the individual communist parties and their activities, together with material pertaining to the international communist movement and its problems. This means that policies of the individual communist states, and particularly their diplomacy, are not treated systematically; rather, policies are mentioned essentially in illustration of the positions and activities of the communist parties of these countries. The selection is made with the intention of offering a global picture of the international communist movement in action, thereby displaying the internal and external elements of strength and vulnerability in the movement as a whole and in its component parties and fronts.

The coverage of the *Yearbook* in its seven sections is as follows:

(1) The *Profiles of Individual Communist Parties* provide information on all communist parties in those countries where they exist. This largest single section is organized so that each survey follows, as far as possible, the same pattern. The party profiles provide, with few exceptions, the following information: date of founding of the party; description, whenever necessary, of the specific conditions under which the party works, its legal status, and so on; statistical data on party membership; the most recent electoral returns, and the party's parliamentary strength and participation in government, if any; description of the party organization, with emphasis on leading bodies and personalities, and its auxiliary organizations and role in trade unions, student and youth groups, and other bodies; concise analysis of the most recent party program and its domestic political line, passing under review the party's decisions and statements on key problems of communist ideology, strategy, and tactics; survey of the most significant communist domestic activities; international views and positions with regard to both the party's foreign policy program and to its attitudes on major issues of the international communist movement; party activities in connection with foreign affairs; enumeration of international party contacts; listing of the most important official organs of each party. Wherever applicable, special sections are devoted to a survey of contending communist parties or movements of different alignment, primarily pro-Chinese, Castroist or Trotskyist, or, in a few instances, pro-Soviet.

(2) *International Communist Front Organizations* offers data on the historical background, structure, policy lines, and internal issues and developments of the major organizations falling under this category.

(3) The section on *International Communist Conferences and Events* is devoted to brief factual analyses of the most important international gatherings or events during the year, which were of significance to the international communist movement.

(4) The *Documents* section contains important materials (such as resolutions of international communist meetings, official pronouncements of national communist parties, key articles, and speeches of prominent communist leaders) which illustrate communist attitudes on basic international issues or reflect local problems of international importance. The selection of documents has

taken into account the desirability of a widespread geographical coverage. All the important documents dealing with five continents and all the parties could not, of course, be reproduced, but effort has been made to select the most significant material reflecting communist plans, positions, internal feuds, and problems in all key regions of the world.

(5) The *Chronology* has as its purpose to record, on a monthly basis, the most important facts related to the communist movement throughout the world. The chronology is selective in the sense that it tries to list those events and facts (with dates of international communist gatherings, top-level meetings, national communist party congresses and important conferences, and events of great significance for international communist affairs or individual communist parties) which reflect the dynamism of the movement, and also its problems. The chronology deals essentially with the affairs of the communist parties and not with communist states as such, although main diplomatic moves are also noted.

(6) The *Bibliography* lists selected books (not articles) on international communist affairs published in 1967 in four languages: English, Russian, French, and German. It is divided into two main sections — books pertaining to ruling communist parties and those on nonruling communist parties.

(7) The *Index* is intended to facilitate the finding of specific items of interest.

\*     \*     \*     \*     \*

One of the major problems that faced the editorial staff in 1966 and which, if anything, increased in 1967, was that of selectivity as to which parties or organizations should be included in the *Yearbook on International Communist Affairs*. At the outset it was decided to "treat as communist parties only those formally constituted organizations which describe themselves as Marxist-Leninist and which are so recognized by authoritative communist publications (for example, the *World Marxist Review*)." It was also deemed necessary to include "international mass organizations which are under communist leadership." In 1967 the editorial staff adhered to these limitations. Thus, although certain procommunist parties and movements are referred to (insofar as they affect the policies and activities of communist parties), their organizational structure and policies are not treated systematically. Within this category are certain guerrilla movements — particularly in Latin America and Africa — and the broad, heterogeneous area of the so-called New Left. The "challenge from the left" which these movements often represent to "orthodox" communist parties is a significant one, however, and wherever necessary it is documented. In a somewhat different context, in the general area of international front organizations, the role of such groups as the Havana-based Afro-Asian Latin American Peoples' Solidarity Organization, which is essentially one of propaganda, is noted although no special section is devoted to them.

\*     \*     \*     \*     \*

The compiling of this edition of the *Yearbook* was primarily the responsibility of a small, full-time team, working at the Hoover Institution and using as its principal source material the holdings of the Hoover Institution's library. The editor expresses his appreciation and thanks to the curators of the Hoover Institution and the staff of the Reference and Serials departments for their assistance. The editor also wishes to thank other persons connected with the Hoover Institution for their contributions in the production of the *Yearbook* including: Mr. Dimitry Pospielovsky and Mr. Thomas Weiss for their research on the Soviet Union and China respectively, the late Miss Susan Kaufmann for assisting in the coordination of source material and typing of manuscripts, and Mrs. Carole Norton and Miss Michelle Hogan of the Institution's Publications Department for their advice and assistance in preparing the volume for publication. Particularly cordial thanks are due Miss Liselotte Hofmann for her painstaking work on the *Yearbook*'s index.

The editor would also like to thank the members of the *Yearbook*'s Advisory Board who offered their advice and suggestions. In addition, a number of persons contributed their time and research in assisting the project. The editor extends his thanks and appreciation to Dr. Branko Lazitch, Mr. José Antonio Lanuza, Miss Carol Stokes, Mr. Daniel Tretiak, Mrs. Ella Wolfe, and Mrs. Natalie Wraga.

The editor is grateful also to Mr. Ralph E. Walter, policy director of Radio Free Europe; Mr. Howland H. Sargeant, president of Radio Liberty; Dr. Eric Willenz, editor of the U.S. State Department's annual report *World Strength of the Communist Party Organizations;* and Mr. C. C. van den Heuvel, director of the International Documentation and Information Center in the Hague, for their kind permission to consult and use for the purposes of the *Yearbook* some material from the publications of their institutions.

In a book such as the *Yearbook on International Communist Affairs* the function of the copy editor is of particular importance. The editor wishes to express his appreciation to Miss Nancy Clarke and special gratitude to Mr. Jesse M. Phillips for putting the manuscript in its final linguistic form.

Finally, the editor would like to thank the staff of Stanford University's Photo-Reproduction Services, in particular Miss Grace Bartholomew, Mrs. Beverly Hendricks, and Mrs. Marie Price, for their cooperation in meeting the demanding publication schedules.

## Note on Abbreviations

The meanings of the abbreviations used in the *Yearbook* are self-evident or are explained in primary contexts. For the *World Marxist Review* both the full title and the abbreviation *WMR* are used, as is the case also with the *Information Bulletin* issued by the WMR, which is often shortened to *IB*. The initials of news agencies (such as TASS, NCNA, MTI, and ATA) are used rather than their full titles. Likewise, *The New York Times* is sometimes abbreviated to *NYT*. The *Yearbook on International Communist Affairs* is abbreviated to *YICA*.

# PROFILES OF INDIVIDUAL
# COMMUNIST PARTIES

# ALBANIA

The Albanian Workers' Party (Partija e Punës të Shqiperisë; AWP) was founded 8 November 1941, at which time it was called the Communist Party of Albania. The party assumed its present name in 1948. As the only legal political party in Albania, the AWP exercises a monopoly of power. All 240 seats in the National Assembly are held by candidates of the Albanian Democratic Front, the party-controlled political alliance between the AWP and mass organizations.

There are 63,016 full and 3,310 candidate members of the AWP. The population of Albania is 1,914,000 (estimated, 1966). The ratio of party members to population is 1 to 12 in urban areas and 1 to 66 in rural areas (November 1966).

**Organization and Leadership.** The AWP is composed of 2,852 primary cells, of which 1,586 are in the towns and 1,266 in the countryside, and is headed by a Central Committee of 61 full members and 36 candidate members. The First Secretary of the AWP and head of the Politburo is Enver Hoxha. The Politburo is composed of 10 additional members: Ramiz Alia, Beqir Balluku, Adil Carcani, Hysni Kapo, Spiro Koleka, Rita Marko, Manush Myftiu, Gogo Nushi, Mehmet Shehu, and Haki Toska. The Secretariat comprises three members in addition to the First Secretary: Ramiz Alia, Hysni Kapo, and Xhafer Spahiu.

The youth organization of the party is the Union of Albanian Working Youth, whose membership as of July 1967 was 210,000. The First Secretary of the Central Committee of the Youth Union is Agim Mero.

**The Albanian "Cultural Revolution."** In 1967 the AWP continued its campaign for the "further revolutionization" of the party and the masses which was begun in early 1966. The aims of the movement were based on conclusions drawn from the Soviet "revisionist" experience and the contributions to Marxist-Leninist theory and experience made by the Chinese Communist Party and the AWP in the past year. Special emphasis was placed on the struggle against bureaucratism, the problems of the elimination of religious superstitions and backward customs and habits, the emancipation of women, and the ideological education of members of the armed forces. At the same time, the AWP stressed the acceleration of production and technological progress, the equalization of income, development of the countryside, and especially the electrification of villages.

The events of 1967 were inspired by the documents of the November 1966 Fifth Congress of the AWP, First Secretary Enver Hoxha's speech on 6 February 1967 on the "further revolutionization of the party and regime," and the proclamation of the Central Committee and the Council of Ministers of 29 April on "the further development and intensification of the revolutionary movement and working masses' creative initiative."

The Albanian "cultural revolution" was launched on 6 February 1967 by First Secretary Hoxha in a speech before a collective meeting of basic party organizations of the city and district of Tirana. With respect to party affairs, Hoxha spoke of the changes in statutes tightening admissions requirements for new party members, emphasizing the need to raise the revolutionary consciousness of party members and to assist in maintaining a tightly knit, disciplined, and ideologically pure organization. He devoted the major portion of his speech to the need for a struggle against bureaucratization in the party and administrative ranks. "Bureaucrats are the worst and cunning enemies of the Marxist-Leninist Party," he said, and to be successful in the "life and death" struggle against them party members must resolutely implement the principle of "rule belongs to the masses." Hoxha also declared that the "current very ridiculous wall newspapers should be abolished and turned into revolutionary wall newspapers to serve a revolutionary purpose."

Within the party ranks emphasis was put on the duties and responsibilities of party members and

3

the elimination of all profits and privileges. This, in addition to the stricter admissions procedures for party members, caused a serious drop in new membership in 1967. The AWP also sought to strengthen the quality of its membership by recruiting from the "revolutionary" youth. Extensive purges of party ranks were conducted to eliminate the careerists and the other undesirable elements who were unable to keep up with the times (see Sadik Bocaj and Vangjo Bocka, "More Attention Must Be Given to New Members Joining the Party," *Rruga e Partisë,* June 1967).

Other party cadres were drawn into the revolutionization movement and sent to work at the grass-roots level, assigned manual tasks, and required to rotate jobs to acquire varied experiences. These cadres, accompanied by experts, agronomists, workers, and young people, left the towns and villages of the plains and went to newly established cooperative farms in the mountain villages. In the busy farming season alone 150,000 workers and cadres reportedly went to the countryside to aid agriculture, putting in 850,000 workdays (NCNA, 20 December 1967).

The vanguard of the revolutionary movement were the young people. According to a report from Peking (NCNA, 13 October), more than 60,000 young intellectuals, workers, and peasants throughout the country joined the revolutionary movement as volunteer laborers during the preceding year. It was reported at the Union of Albanian Working Youth congress on 26-29 June 1967 that more than 20,000 youths had been engaged in the opening of new farmland in the mountain regions of the country, and additional "hundreds" of young people had resettled there to work for a period of one to five years. It was reported at the congress that during the year 150,000 young people were expected to have worked on two major transportation projects, the Malesija e Madhe highway and the Rrogozhine-Fieri railway line.

The young people were also in the vanguard of the campaign against old traditions and religion. Responding to Hoxha's call for the use of wall posters, the young revolutionaries adopted "flash bulletins" to condemn evidence of "bourgeois mentality" and criticized leaders, teachers, and even entire ministries for "nonrevolutionary activity."

Religion was a focal point of the struggle to revolutionize the party and masses. Churches were burned, closed, or in many instances converted into "houses of culture." An editorial in the Albanian literary monthly *Nendori* declared that "by May 1967 religion was forced to turn over to the young people 2,169 churches, mosques, monasteries, and other religious institutions," and claimed that "under their [the party and Hoxha] shining guidance together with the entire populace, youth has created the first atheist state in the world" (*Nendori,* September 1967). However, at the Fourth Congress of the Democratic Front (14-16 September 1967) Hoxha stressed that although religious institutions are disappearing, religion and religious influence will not automatically disappear: "This is a long, complicated and difficult struggle."

The emancipation of women and their participation in production was also an important event in Albania. At the Second Plenum of the Central Committee (15-16 June 1967), held primarily to discuss the question of women, Secretary and Politburo member Ramiz Alia noted that the full emancipation of women was "decisive for the development and further progress of our socialist country" and "one of the fundamental tasks of our Party." Enver Hoxha called for the admission of women to the party under the same conditions as those for men. Accordingly, during 1967 a substantial number of women assumed leading party, state, and social and economic positions.

The ideological education of the armed forces was an important part of the Albanian "cultural revolution." Mehmet Shehu, Politburo member and Chairman of the Council of Ministers, stressed at a meeting of the party organization of a tank unit of the Albanian People's Army that in order to revolutionize the armed forces it is necessary to proceed from two basic principles: (1) the factor that decides the outcome of a war is people, not weapons, and (2) in the armed units ideological work must be placed above technical work and education of men above technical training.

Another means of revolutionizing the party and masses by drawing the masses and party leaders closer together included an original feature, the public exchange of messages between Enver Hoxha and individuals or representatives of various social groups. The expressions of solidarity with the leader and accounts of the implementation of his directives were answered by Hoxha personally with praise and further encouragement. Also unusual was Hoxha's attendance at electoral meetings of basic party organizations (Radio Tirana, 4 March 1967). Still another means was the development of the press "as a weapon to build socialism." As a result, numerous new local party papers began publication. In December Hoxha urged the country's teachers "to cleanse the school program and textbooks from unnecessary material." Congresses of four major social-political organizations were held for the purpose of bringing their activities into the mainstream of the revolutionization process: the Albanian Trade Union (24-26 April), the Union of Albanian Working Youth (26-29 June), the Albanian Democratic Front (14-16 September), and the Sixth Congress of the Union of Albanian Women (25-28 October 1967). The Second Congress of the Union of Writers and Artists, scheduled for November, was postponed until 1968.

The Albanian "cultural revolution" was similar in many of its ideological aspects and methods to the Chinese cultural revolution and the Red Guard movement (the use of wall posters, the struggle led by young people against the ideological lethargy of their elders, the heavy concentration on destroying traditions). As Hoxha launched the movement, an article appeared in the party theoretical organ hailing the successes of the Chinese cultural revolution as "a valuable contribution to the theory and practice of scientific socialism" and enumerating the "historical lessons" to be drawn from it: (1) that class struggle is inevitable (and desirable) even in a socialist society, (2) that the proletarian party must keep its ranks pure and never lose its revolutionary characteristics, (3) that the state regime, or the question of political power, continues to be important in a socialist society, (4) that the furtherance of the revolution and socialist construction can be made only by the broad masses led by a Marxist-Leninist party, and (5) that the education of the new generation through their active participation in revolutionary activities is vitally necessary (*Rruga e Partisë*, February 1967).

The Albanian mass movement, although it was based on lessons drawn from the Chinese experience, was not a mechanical repetition of the Chinese model. In fact, the events in China were not publicized for mass consumption in Albania, and neither the communist classics nor Chairman Mao was quoted to inspire the Albanian movement (*Quotations from Chairman Mao Tse-tung* was not translated into Albanian until October 1967). Thus the Albanian "revolution" appeared to be directed entirely by the Albanian leadership. Chinese approval of this state of affairs was evidenced in the Chinese-Albanian communique of 14 October, in which Chinese leaders "highly appraised" the Albanian mass movement and noted that "this movement for revolutionization is graphic evidence of the creative application of Marxism-Leninism by the Albanian Workers' Party headed by Comrade Enver Hoxha to the revolutionary practice in Albania."

The repercussions of the Albanian movement were also different from those of the Chinese cultural revolution. The scale of the Albanian events was of minor proportions in comparison with the upheaval in China: the educational and production systems were not affected, foreign diplomats were not harrassed, and despite rumors of a possible purge in the top ranks of the party, the Albanian leadership remained intact. The Albanian movement was instead aimed primarily at the middle and lower party ranks, and in particular at the basic party organizations. Thus the Albanian "cultural revolution" was widely regarded as a struggle for the consolidation of power, and not as a struggle for power, as was the case in China (see *Rudé Právo*, Prague, 28 April 1967).

**Economic Tasks.** One of the aims of the cultural revolution, especially in its aspects of granting aid to the countryside and of raising of the collective consciousness of the people, was to increase production by relying on Albania's own forces in order to help solve the grave economic crisis. An editorial in *Zëri i Popullit* on 5 March, commemorating the first anniversary of the "open letter" which launched the campaign against bureaucratization, stated that "the consolidation and revolutionizing of the Party and of life will help the solution of economic tasks, the fulfillment of the state plan, and the improvement of the quality and reduction of prices of production."

Among the chief economic tasks were the development of the countryside, the opening up of new farmland, and the modernizing of agricultural methods. Economic measures passed during the year showed strong favoritism toward the rural areas, and the revolutionizing of the party cadres and youth involved, for the most part, work and resettlement in outlying districts.

The first quarter of 1967 marked the completion of collectivization in Albania, when some 500 farms in the mountainous regions were organized into collective farm operations. The AWP characterized this feat as a "revolutionary process which is a direct result of the Fifth Party Congress and Hoxha's directives" but admitted that it was not a smooth operation and that much ideological work was still needed among the new collective farmers (*Zëri i Popullit*, 7 April 1967).

The 29 April proclamation of the Albanian party and Council of Ministers "on the further development and intensification of the revolutionary movement and the working masses," combined "revolutionizing" measures with others aimed at raising the gross national product. It called for the reduction in size of members' plots in the agricultural cooperatives and the abolition of personal plots on state farms, the reduction of higher wages, the abolition of various incentives, and intensification of the cadres' direct participation in production. However, the proclamation also announced some measures favoring agricultural cooperatives and an eventual drop in the prices of consumer goods for all people and raised the target figure for electrification of the villages from 500 to 625 by 1970.

The 15 June Central Committee plenum heard a report from Pirro Dodbiba, member of the Central Committee and Minister of Agriculture, on the goals of the Fourth Five Year Plan regarding increased production. Dodbiba reported that collectives represent 80.5 per cent and state farms 18.1 per cent of the total land under cultivation. He emphasized the need for advanced technological education in the rural areas to raise the technical and professional level of agricultural workers.

On 19 June the National Assembly adopted a new tax law which lowered the tax on incomes of persons working in the socialized sector and eliminated taxes for those working in agriculture. Thus all wage earners and salaried workers with an income of less than 680 lek per month were no longer to pay a tax on earnings; other salaried employees with a monthly income of 680 lek or more would pay reduced income taxes. The tax on income from collective farmers' private plots, as well as on the income of members of the new collective farms in the mountainous regions, was eliminated.

The Third Plenum of the Central Committee (13-14 October) was concerned primarily with the technological revolution in the country and the development of the engineering industry. In his speech to the Central Committee Enver Hoxha emphasized repeatedly that the technological revolution is a component part of the proletarian revolution and noted the differences between the Albanian system and economic reforms of other East European states. He denounced the Yugoslav self-management system as opening the road to colonization of Yugoslavia by US capital and that of other capitalist states: "In the final analysis, this radical transformation in Yugoslavia has created unprecedented anarchy in economy, trade, politics, and ideology which we see daily in the capitalist Titoite hell." He condemned COMECON as "nothing but a kind of Common Market . . . based on the principle of exploitation and oppression of the small by the large." The basic principle of the Albanian system, according to Hoxha, is the "harmonious cooperation" among various sectors of the economy, and the vital task is that of "fully utilizing every capacity and every possibility at our disposal" and concurrently "expanding these capacities and creating new possibilities." He stressed that in fulfilling this task Albania must rely on its own forces and then called for a scientific-technical revolution, with the "systematic and massive education of cadres in all sectors" as the first step.

The Fourth Plenum of the Central Committee (12-14 December 1967) also dealt with the economy. The Central Committee discussed and adopted decisions on "the fulfillment of the state plan and budget for 1967 and the tasks of the draft plan and the draft budget for 1968," and "for the acceleration of electrification of all the country's villages." A goal was set for the country's power industry, calling for total rural electrification by 8 November 1971, the party's thirtieth anniversary—14 years ahead of schedule.

An evaluation of the economic progress of 1967 showed favorable results of the Albanian drive for acceleration of production. Above-average increases in industrial and agricultural production were recorded. According to Deputy Premier Haki Toska, industrial production for 1967 was 11 per cent higher than in 1966; this exceeded the target outlined in the Fourth Five Year Plan, which called for an average annual growth rate of 8.7 per cent. Toska also predicted a 20.7 per cent growth rate in 1968. Turning to agriculture, he declared that production was 12 per cent higher than in the previous year and called for a 12 per cent increase again in 1968. Specific industrial projects in 1967 included the completion of two large chemical plants in February and inauguration of the first section of a

Chinese-built textile plant. Currently, construction is progressing on the Vari i Dejes hydroelectric power plant, the largest industrial project undertaken by Albania to date.

**Relations with China.** The foreign policy of the AWP is based, on one hand, on friendship with China and Chairman Mao Tse-tung and, on the other, on a struggle against "imperialism" headed by the United States and "revisionism" headed by the Soviet party and state.

In January and February, during an extended visit to China by two Albanian delegations—a military delegation headed by Beqir Balluku, Defense Minister, Vice-Chairman of the Council of Ministers, and member of the AWP Politburo, and a delegation including Hysni Kapo, Politburo member and Central Committee Secretary, and Central Committee member Behar Shtylla—the AWP for the first time fully endorsed the Chinese cultural revolution and the Red Guard movement. A 14 January editorial in *Zëri i Popullit* expounded the theses of the cultural revolution, and this was followed by an article in the February issue of *Rruga e Partisë* entitled "Long Live the Great Proletarian Cultural Revolution," hailing the cultural revolution as a "valuable contribution to the theory and practice of scientific socialism." At the same time, the two Albanian delegations in China conferred with Chairman Mao on 3 February. On the same day Defense Minister Beqir Balluku, addressing a mass rally in Peking, hailed the Red Guards as "outstanding representatives of China's youth" and declared that "the Albanian young people stand forever with the Red Guards and all the young people of China." The Albanian Youth Union followed up the Defense Minister's statement on 6 February with a telegram to the Red Guards proclaiming the latter's initiative and great achievements.* On 18 July Albanian Foreign Minister Nesti Nase emphatically reaffirmed Albanian-Chinese friendship in his foreign-policy address to the National Assembly: "Regardless of the storms and great waves which may sweep the world, our two fraternal peoples and our two countries will always be side by side," he said, and warned that "there is no force in the world that can halt our march forward, or in any way weaken our alliance and friendship."

Friendship between the two countries was further evidenced in speeches and in the communique resulting from the visit to China (26 September-12 October) of an Albanian party and government delegation headed by Mehmet Shehu, member of the AWP Politburo and Chairman of the Council of Ministers of the People's Republic of Albania. The communique reported that both sides reaffirm the principles and stand set forth in the 11 May 1966 joint statement of China and Albania (the communique following Shehu's visit to China in 1966). The 1967 communique reported that the two sides had discussed socialist development in their respective countries, the international situation, and the world communist movement, and that the two sides were "completely identical in their stand and views on the questions discussed." The Albanians hailed Mao Tse-tung as the "worthy successor and heir to the undertakings of Marx, Engels, Lenin and Stalin." "Today, the attitude towards China's cultural revolution is a touchstone to distinguish Marxist-Leninists from revisionists, and genuine revolutionaries from counter-revolutionaries," they declared, and vowed that "the Albanian Workers' Party and the Albanian People will give firm support to China's Great Proletarian Cultural Revolution and will continue to do so to the very end." The Chinese praised Albania as "a great beacon of socialism in Europe" and vowed that should anyone—"imperialism, modern revisionism and all reaction"—dare to attack Albania, "the Chinese people will definitely provide a powerful backing for the Albanian people."

Albanian relations with China were reinforced by heavy trade and payments commitments. It is estimated that trade with China amounts to 60 or 70 per cent of the total of Albanian foreign trade and that current Albanian indebtedness to China amounts to about $200 million in respect to commodity trade (Jan S. Prybyla, "Albania's Economic Vassalage," *East Europe,* January 1967). On 9 December 1967 a protocol was signed in Tirana covering goods exchange and payments for 1968 between the two countries. A second protocol was signed at the same time, this one covering the use by Albania of the credit granted by the Chinese People's Republic on the basis of the agreements signed in Peking on 8 June 1965 and 20 October 1966. Albanian sources reported that the two

---

*The Red Guards returned the favor by attending the Fifth Congress of the Union of Albanian Working Youth (26-29 June). This was the first time a Red Guard delegation had traveled abroad.

documents "provide for a considerable growth of the volume of commodities compared with the 1967 volume" (ATA, 9 December 1967).

**Relations with the Soviet Union.** Albanian attacks on "imperialism" continued unabated in 1967, but were linked more frequently with the struggle against "revisionism." "The struggle against American imperialism, a struggle which cannot be separated from the struggle against the Khrushchevite revisionists, has become today the most imperative duty of all the revolutionary peoples and forces of the world," declared Nesti Nase to the National Assembly on 18 July. Nase charged that the United States, aided by the "Khrushchevite revisionists," in addition to their neocolonialist policy of penetration and economic subjugation, engage in armed aggression to promote their goal of world domination. He charged that the "American imperialists are creating new centers of local war which are to emerge as part of the world war they are hurriedly preparing" and added that they are aided in this by the "Khrushchevite Soviet revisionists."

The Soviet government and party were attacked by the Albanian leadership for "collusion" with the United States and for "adopting the shameful role of a fire brigade with regard to the national liberation struggles," especially with respect to Vietnam and the Middle East. The Soviet "revisionists" were further charged with "working to sabotage the struggle of the Vietnamese people, to perpetuate the division of Vietnam into two parts, to keep South Vietnam under occupation and to transform it into a permanent United States base and an important link in the imperialist-revisionist 'ring of iron' around the Chinese People's Republic." Albania strongly denounced Soviet "treachery" in the June 1967 Middle East conflict, describing Soviet behavior as a "stab in the back" for the Arab countries. Albania emphasized its own "principled" and "consistent" position in support of the Arab peoples. It recorded its disapproval of the various proposals offered in the U.N. debates, pointing out that the Albanian draft resolution condemned Israel, the United States, and Britain for their armed aggression, and demanded the immediate and unconditional withdrawal of all Israeli troops from the occupied Arab territories.

The Soviet Union also came under attack for "betraying the socialist revolution" and for "the restoration of capitalism in the USSR." Intensive propaganda barrages emanating from Tirana condemned the attempts of the "revisionist" leaders to cause the "spiritual degeneration" of the Soviet people by introducing Western jazz and other forms of "degenerate bourgeois art." Economic reforms under way in the Soviet Union and in other East European states were decried as a return to capitalism, and in military matters the Soviet Union was attacked for attributing the primary role in war to technology rather than to the people.

The Fiftieth Anniversary of the October Revolution was marked in Albania by festivities and press articles aimed at discrediting the present Soviet leadership. In a 7 November rally speech Hysni Kapo declared, "the October Revolution was a triumph for the ideas of Marxism-Leninism over the opportunism and treachery of the Second International" and proceeded to describe the opportunism and treachery of the present-day Soviet "revisionist" leadership.

The November celebrations in Tirana also marked a new high point in the Albanian campaign to incite the Soviet people to revolt against the present leadership. Hysni Kapo called upon the Soviet people to undertake "bold revolutionary actions . . . as soon as possible . . . before it is too late" in order to overthrow the "renegade Khrushchevite clique in its very lair." The 7 November mass rally approved a "message addressed to all the workers, peasants, soldiers, and Soviet intellectuals, to all Bolsheviks and real revolutionaries of the Soviet Union," calling on them "to rise, to found a new Bolshevik Party and to give the signal for the crushing of the revisionist counter-revolution. . . .The world is waiting with hopes that you will fulfill with honor this great historical task, that you will revive once again the glorious days of October by upsetting the new bourgeoisie which has caught the fraternal Soviet people by the throat." An editorial in *Zëri i Popullit* on 7 November 1967 stated that the AWP "is fully convinced that the Soviet brothers and the Bolsheviks of Lenin-Stalin will not long tolerate the Khrushchev revisionist treachery, but will rise up again in revolution, just as in the days of the Great October, to smash and put into the grave their arch-enemies, to save the homeland of the Soviets, and to justify the hopes of revolutionaries throughout the world."

**Attitude toward West Germany.** The Soviet and East European "revisionists" were also attacked by the Albanians for their attitude toward the West German initiatives for improving relations with East European states. On 20 January an article in *Zëri i Popullit* warned against any rapprochement with the Kiesinger government without the fulfillment of one condition: the Federal Republic must accept and finally recognize the Oder-Neisse frontier. The article claimed that the Albanians are "solidly to the end" with the "sacred" right of the Polish people on the question of the Oder-Neisse line, in contrast to the Soviet "revisionist" leaders and their followers in "certain countries of Eastern Europe." Following the establishment of diplomatic relations between Bonn and Bucharest, the Albanians upheld the position of the German Democratic Republic and condemned the Rumanian action but also declared that, "in fact, Rumania is only doing what the Soviet Union has done and continues to do on a larger scale." The Albanians also condemned the East German leadership for blindly following the Soviet revisionists and expressed their solidarity with only the East German people, calling upon them to "save their republic" and "courageously destroy the revisionist Soviet clutches" (*Zëri i Popullit*, 8 February 1967).

In addition to close friendship with China and North Vietnam (in their struggle against United States "imperialism"), favorable development of relations between Albania and Italy, France, the United Arab Republic, Pakistan, Rumania, Korea, Cambodia, Cuba, and Turkey, as well as many countries of Asia and Latin America, were noted in 1967 (Nesti Nase, 18 July 1967).*

**Relations with the Balkan States.** In a foreign-policy address to the National Assembly, Nase claimed that the Albanian government has been and is presently in favor of normal relations and neighborliness with the surrounding Balkan countries but viewed with skepticism those "who speak on the one hand of developing relations with our country and on the other hand hold a dagger under their cloaks." He also claimed that the government of Albania is in favor of the development of interstate relations and of neighborliness with Yugoslavia and added that "if this has not been achieved it is not our fault."

Thus relations between Albania and Yugoslavia remained tense. The Albanians extensively exploited the nationality issue in Yugoslavia, stating that a "great multilateral, national-chauvinistic row has broken out within the ruling circles of the Titoite gang." Referring to Yugoslav President Tito's visit to the largely Albanian-populated region of Kosovo-Metohija, the Albanians charged that the "Titoite gang is determined to continue to pursue—with regard to the Albanians of Kosovo, the Dukagjini plateau, Macedonia, and Montenegro—the old Great Serbian chauvinistic policy of denationalization, the policy of maintaining in these regions the colonial situation and their exploitation as a source of raw materials and cheap labor" (*Zëri i Popullit*, 5 April 1967). Nevertheless, the volume of trade between Albania and Yugoslavia increased by 26 per cent over the volume of 1966 (according to a trade protocol signed at the end of 1966), indicating a significant rise in the economic cooperation between the two countries despite continuing political and national differences.

On the occasion of the twentieth anniversary of the Albanian-Bulgarian friendship treaty on 16 December, the Albanian press hailed the treaty and the "traditional friendship with the Bulgarian people." *Zëri i Popullit* declared that Albania remains firm on the Marxist-Leninist road that united the two peoples in the treaty signed by Enver Hoxha and Georgi Dimitrov and vowed that the Bulgarian people continue to have a "sincere and faithful friend" in the Albanian people. The article did not mention either Todor Zhivkov or the present Bulgarian leadership.

**Other International Issues.** Albania repeatedly expressed support for the national liberation movements throughout the "third world" and fully endorsed armed struggle as "the only correct way to insure victory." "Spontaneous" protest meetings and slogans of solidarity with the "heroic people of Vietnam" in their struggle against the "barbaric aggression by American imperialism" were widely publicized. On 14 September, at the Fourth Congress of the Democratic Front, Enver Hoxha declared, "The Albanian people, Party, and government will support fully and to the end the

*With respect to France, a trade agreement signed in December 1966 and released in Paris in January 1967 called for an increase of 500 per cent in French exports to Albania, which amounts to a total of $3.6 million and an increase in projected French imports from Albania of about 350 per cent, or about $1.7 million.

Vietnamese people's liberation struggle—which we regard as our own struggle, as the struggle for the common cause of revolution and socialism."

On 11 October Albania and North Vietnam signed an agreement in Hanoi covering trade between the two countries and nonrefundable economic aid to Vietnam from Albania in 1968. Details of the agreement were not reported.

Albanian relations with the "progressive" countries of Africa, Asia, and Latin America continued to develop through an exchange of trade-and-friendship delegations; for example, a delegation of the Albanian trade unions which attended the Second Congress of the Tanganyika Workers' National Union and then paid a friendship visit to the Congo (Brazzaville) in August. On 26 October-7 November an Albanian government delegation, headed by Foreign Minister Nesti Nase, visited Algeria to participate in celebrations for Algeria's National Day. In return, foreign delegations attended the congresses held in 1967 of the Albanian Trade Unions, the Youth Union, and the Union of Women. In the "reactionary" Latin American, African, and Southeast Asian states, and in South Arabia the Albanian leadership called for insurrection, and in this connection Hoxha hailed the fact that "in the very lair of imperialism, the anger and armed rebellion of the US negroes has exploded" (speech at the Fourth Congress of the Democratic Front).

**The International Communist Movement.** The AWP maintained contacts with numerous Marxist-Leninist parties during 1967. On 10 May, and again in August, Enver Hoxha received Franz Strobl, First Secretary of the Marxist-Leninist Party of Austria; on 12 July he received a delegation of the Marxist-Leninist faction of the Sudanese party headed by First Secretary Muhammad. Also in July, a delegation of the Bolivian party visited Albania. In August a delegation of the French Communist Movement (Marxist-Leninist) headed by Jacques Jurquet, Political Secretary of the Central Committee, arrived, and Jacques Grippa, First Secretary of the Belgian party made a visit. Other visitors to Albania included a delegation of the Italian Marxist-Leninist party headed by Secretary-General Fosco Dinucci in September, and on 3-10 October Nagalingan Sanmugathasan, Politburo member and Secretary of the Ceylonese party. Tirana continued to be the seat of the "Communist Party of Poland," from which the Polish "Marxist-Leninists" beamed propaganda broadcasts to Poland.

The AWP vehemently condemned the Karlovy Vary meeting of European communist parties (24-26 April 1967) and the proposed international consultative meeting to be held in Budapest in February 1968. An editorial in *Zëri i Popullit* (5 May) entitled "What Does the Karlovy Vary Meeting of the Renegades Show?" evaluated the conference as "exposing before the world public the depths to which the Khruschchev revisionists have degenerated, their complete capitulation to the bourgeoisie and other reactionary forces, and their eventual turning into a handful of social reformists serving capitalism and counter-revolution heart and soul." A second *Zëri i Popullit* editorial (13 May) reiterated these charges and also, by strong implication, condemned the Rumanian "neutralist" position. It referred to "certain so-called communist parties" which are trying to keep their "freedom of maneuver" by not participating in the conference while opposing the Marxist-Leninist parties. "In their own two-faced way," the editorial stated, "they are trying to make deals with the imperialists without enraging Washington, Moscow, or Bonn."

With regard to the international communist party conference scheduled for February 1968, the AWP charged that the Soviet Union is seeking a way out of its present internal and international difficulties by gaining the "nominal approval" of other parties for its policies. The AWP also charged that one of the goals of the conference would be to "isolate China and Albania from the world communist movement" and to abolish the declarations of 1957 and 1960, which are an "obstacle on their anti-Marxist and counter-revolutionary road" (*Zëri i Popullit*, 3 December and 26 December 1967).

In the struggle against "revisionism," and in answer to the Soviet efforts to call an international communist party meeting, the Albanian leadership, since the Fifth Party Congress, has been the strongest advocate of the idea of creating a Marxist-Leninist international movement. Almost duplicating Enver Hoxha's words at the congress, an article in *Rruga e Partisë* of March 1967 declared:

The creation of close international ties of cooperation and joint action among Marxist-Leninist parties and organizations and the elaboration of the forms of cooperation and organization in accordance with present historical conditions are urgent tasks of our time which are of great importance to the fate of the revolution and socialism and the total victory of Marxism-Leninism over revisionism. The united imperialism-revisionism counter-revolutionary front must be opposed by a united front of the Marxist-Leninist revolutionary forces of all countries. (Hajro Zeneli, "The True Revolutionary Unity of the World Proletariat Will Be Achieved Without Revisionists and by a Relentless Struggle Against Revisionism," *Rruga e Partisë,* March 1967.)

The unity of the movement is to be forged through the struggle against revisionism as well as the struggle against "Centrism," the "hidden opportunism which preaches 'neutrality' in the struggle between Marxism-Leninism and Revisionism." "The ranks of the Marxist-Leninist parties and organizations must be closely united and well organized; they must be ideologically and politically educated and ready for any struggle at any time," according to the AWP. The party stressed, however, that the "Marxist-Leninist parties and organizations are independent and equal; they make their own policies based on the general principles of Marxism-Leninism and in accordance with the concrete conditions of each country" (*ibid.*). No comment was made concerning the center of such an international movement.

**Publications.** The central organ of the AWP is the daily *Zëri i Popullit,* and its monthly theoretical organ is *Rruga e Partisë.* The organ of the Union of Albanian Working Youth is *Zëri i Rinise.*

# ALGERIA

The Algerian Communist Party (Parti Communiste Algérien; PCA) was founded in 1920 at the same time as the French Communist Party, of which it was initially a part. After October 1936 it existed independently. The party was banned in December 1962 by the Algerian government and in 1964 seemingly disappeared as an autonomous organization; its members were instructed to adhere individually to the only official political organization, the National Liberation Front (Front de Liberation Nationale; FLN), with the aim of constituting a clandestine communist faction which would eventually assume direction of the governmental party. The objective was to try to accomplish with respect to the FLN what had succeeded in Cuba with the July 26 movement. On 19 June 1965 Colonel Houari Boumediène, with the aid of the army, accomplished a coup against President Ahmed Ben Bella. One reason for the coup was to stem rapidly growing leftist influence in the FLN to head off a complete takeover by the left. The communist militants then joined with some extreme left-wing members of the FLN to form a clandestine opposition group called the Popular Resistance Organization (Organization de la Résistance Populaire; ORP), sometimes referred to as the Avant Guard Party (Parti d'Avant-guard) or the Socialist Tali'ah Party.

**Organization and Leadership.** Leading Algerian Communists include Henri Alleg and Boualem Khalfa, former editors of the PCA daily *Alger Républicain*; Abdelhamid Benzine, former editor-in-chief of *Alger Républicain*; Bachir Hadj Ali, one of the former secretaries of the PCA; and Larbi Boukhali, former Secretary-General of the PCA. Despite the adherence of former PCA leaders to the ORP, the PCA has not been officially disbanded, and the Communist press and official announcements refer to these men as "representatives of the Algerian communists," rather than as members of the ORP.

Communist strength in Algeria is difficult to determine, since many of the former communists and ORP leaders were jailed in August and September 1965 and are still in the El Harrach prison. Membership in the PCA is estimated at less than 1,000 (including Europeans) out of a total Algerian population of 12,150,000 (estimated, 1966). The Communists and the ORP exercise some influence in the Algerian trade union organization, L'Union Generale des Travailleurs Algeriens (UGTA), and the Student Union, L'Union Nationale des Etudiants d'Algerie (UNEA). Their influence is also evident among the Algerian workers and students living abroad, especially those in France.

**Domestic Policies.** The complex situation and divergent forces in the Algerian leadership were the subject of an article by Henri Alleg in the British Communist Party organ, *Morning Star* (19 April 1967), entitled "Algeria after Ben Bella." The article was reprinted in various foreign party organs, including *The Canadian Tribune* (15 May 1967) and *Thunder* (Guyana, May 1967). Alleg attributed to the influence of the leftist elements the "successes" of the Boumediène regime—the prevention of the total liquidation of the self-managed enterprises, the liberation of certain political prisoners, and the maintenance and development of political and economic relations with the socialist countries, especially the Soviet Union. He also stated that Boumediène is maintaining an "unstable equilibrium" which satisfies no one. According to Alleg, the situation is made more complex by the fact that the demarcation line between "the forces of progress and the forces of reaction" is not merely between the regime in power and the opposition; there are revolutionaries within the official circles, and there are men within the opposition who seek to overthrow the regime through a new coup and replace it with a regime even further to the right.* Alleg called for support of the ORP and the ORP's program of grouping together in a single Democratic and Popular Front all democratic and anti-imperialist

---

*Alleg is probably referring to the rightist elements in three other opposition groups, the Clandestine Organization of the Algerian Revolution, the Socialist Forces Front, and the Committee for the Defense of the Revolution. In

forces, whether they are in the regime or in the opposition. "By isolating the reactionary and proimperialist elements of the regime," Alleg stated, "this Front will enable Algeria to find a democratic and peaceful solution to the crisis in which it now finds itself and to enjoy a new revolutionary advance for the benefit of its people and for the people of the whole of Africa."

In a declaration issued in Algiers at the beginning of February the ORP pointed out that, although there has been some "progress" in Algeria, the "continuing antidemocratic atmosphere" requires that greater efforts be made to utilize all the potentials of the revolution. The ORP called on "all the healthy revolutionary forces, from whatever sphere of the present power structure they might come," to join the struggle. The ORP emphasized that it did not wish to possess the "monopoly of the defense of democratic and socialist objectives or to play off against each other the revolutionary forces which declare themselves for these objectives," but said it would work through a process of "democratic confrontations" among all revolutionaries to develop a common program for a united front against "reaction and imperialism" and for the development of Algeria according to the principles of scientific socialism. While strengthening its own ranks, the declaration continued, the ORP would work to unite and mobilize the masses in favor of the "immediate legitimate objectives," among them a "communal reorganization" and a "profound agrarian reform." (*L'Humanité*, 6 February 1967.)

A new orientation of the ORP in 1967 was to grant partial support to some policies of the FLN in the face of the dangers threatening Algeria by American "imperialism" and by the "reactionary forces" within the Maghreb. The ORP charged that "American imperialism" is trying to expropriate the rights of the Maghreb states, to establish strategic bases, and to suffocate the Algerian revolution, which, "despite its weaknesses," still has great possibilities for development. The ORP charged that American imperialism has infiltrated the bureaucracy of the state, encouraging the repression of "progressives" and ensuring that the revolutionary forces do not unite. The ORP called on the masses to support actively "every initiative of the power structure favoring the strengthening of the anti-imperialist struggle" (*L'Humanité*, 22 March 1967).

Thus the ORP supported the Algerian stand on the June Middle East crisis. However, in the September issue of its organ *Muqawamah* the ORP called for the exposure of the reactionary representatives in the Algerian regime and charged that the "silence of the revolutionary elements on the antirevolutionary activity of some Ministers" makes the revolutionary elements "appear as collaborators or as content with the status quo." According to the ORP, the touchstone of the true revolutionary is his attitude to the progressive political detainees. "Our people will never believe those who declare their hatred for imperialism and their adherence to socialism while at the same time persecuting revolutionary strugglers," the ORP declared.

Following the crisis in the FLN in November and December, which culminated in the unsuccessful coup attempted by Colonel Tahar Zbiri at El Affroun on 14 December, the ORP concentrated attention on the Boumediène regime's harsh measures to put down the revolt and on the arrests of members of "progressive circles," the trade unions and former officers of the FLN. The ORP expressed its concern over the fate of Ben Bella, who had been imprisoned in the area and whose guard, Said Abid, had committed suicide or had been killed during the uprising. Emphasizing that in the present situation the government "rests solely on the apparatus of repression," the ORP declared that "all revolutionary and progressive forces, wherever they may be should continue the struggle in all forms and should unite their efforts" (ORP Bulletin of 21 December, reported in *L'Humanité*, 27 December 1967).

The ORP, the Algerian Communists, and the world communist press gave special attention to the campaign for the liberation or at least guarantees for the safety of political prisoners in Algeria, particularly Hocine Zahouane (ORP leader and former member of the FLN), Bachir Hadj Ali, and

December 1966 these three opposition groups agreed to merge, partly because of the efforts of Mohammed Khider, a former FLN member who was assassinated on 3 January 1967 in Madrid, allegedly by Boumediène agents. It was thought that Mohammed Khider retained control of more than $16 million in FLN funds, which he was ready to turn over to the opposition forces on condition that they merge. There was also speculation that the opposition forces were hoping the ORP would also merge with them and eliminate the extreme leftist elements in its ranks. The merger was finally effected minus the ORP in February 1967.

Mohammed Harbi (ORP member and former member of the FLN). On 3 November, *Le Monde* published a commentary on Algerian National Day by Henri Alleg in which he noted that "Algerians and French who had made their common cause that of identifying themselves with the rights and dignity of man, thinking of past struggles, will ask themselves with anxiety and bitterness if the picture presented today by justice in Algeria is that for which they fought and for which so many lives had been sacrificed." Alleg went on to describe the imprisonment of Ahmed Ben Bella, Hadj Ben Bella, and the ORP leaders and the September 1967 secret trial of 21 political prisoners charged with participation in an "association of criminals." He expressed hope that the Algerian government would follow the example of various Arab countries, such as Syria and Jordan, and, for the sake of patriotic unity, would liberate the political prisoners and allay fears for their lives, especially in the case of Ahmed Ben Bella, the "most illustrious and most threatened of them all."

**The National Liberation Front.** The Algerian communists are in the difficult position of working in opposition to a government which has been recognized by the international communist movement as a "progressive" regime which has "embarked on the road to socialism." Relations with the Soviet Union have been increasingly friendly, and the Soviet Union has extended substantial amounts of economic and military aid to Algeria. In February Leonid Brezhnev was scheduled to visit Algeria; the visit was postponed, and instead, on 12 June, Houari Boumediène made a sudden visit to Moscow to discuss the Soviet stand on the Arab-Israeli war. The reluctance of the Soviet Union to give total support for the continuation of the struggle, in contrast to Boumediène's adamant opposition to the cease-fire, marred the relations between the two countries but did not seriously damage them.

Relations with China have been cordial and marked by the exchange of a large number of friendship delegations. The FLN hailed the explosion of the Chinese hydrogen bomb as a great political event which "cannot but advance the course of history, and hasten the process of national liberation" (*Révolution Africaine*, 26 June 1967).

The leading role of the FLN in supporting national-liberation movements throughout the world, both morally and materially, has been a major factor in promoting friendly relations between Algeria and the communist states. A Cuban Communist Party delegation visited Algeria on 28 October—14 November. A communique signed on 9 November by representatives of the FLN and the Cuban Communist Party spoke of strengthening links between the two and noted that a program for that purpose was to be drawn up át a meeting of the representatives of the two parties to be held in Havana in the near future. The communique noted agreement by the two parties on their assessment of the world situation. It reiterated their solidarity with the people of Vietnam, expressed full support for the liberation movements in Africa and called for increased aid to them. The communique also condemned "American imperialism" in Latin America, declared support for the position of Latin American revolutionaries who have chosen the road of armed struggle, and paid homage to the memory of Ernesto "Che" Guevara.

Neither the FLN nor the Algerian communists were represented at the Eighteenth Congress of the French Communist Party in January 1967. Both groups were represented, however, at the Fiftieth Anniversary celebrations of the October Revolution in Moscow. The FLN representatives, led by Kaid Ahmed, member of the Council of the Revolution and Minister of Finance and Planning, were given the limelight in Moscow, while the official account of the celebrations merely mentioned the presence of "representatives of the Algerian communists." A similar situation occurred at the Twenty-Third Congress of the Communist Party of the Soviet Union in 1966; at that time the FLN delegation walked out of the congress because it had not been informed of the presence of the Algerian communists.

In the latter part of 1967 especially cordial talks were held between the FLN and the Italian Communist Party, both in Rome and in Algiers, and with the League of Communists of Yugoslavia in Algiers, (24 October—6 November) to discuss the consolidation of "progressive forces" in the Mediterranean area.

Participants and observers from a number of East European socialist states and West European communist parties, such as the Communist Party of Italy, attended the Seminar on Arab Socialism held in Algiers in May and the Algerian National Day celebrations on 1 November.

**The International Communist Movement.** Larbi Boukhali, former Secretary-General of the PCA contributed an article on the October Revolution to the October issue of the *World Marxist Review.* Boukhali rejected and attempted to disprove the claims by "some petty bourgeois ideologists" that Arab socialism "is merely the logical sequence to centuries of struggle for freedom and social justice and is in no way connected with external factors." With special reference to Algeria, Boukhali attributed the building of socialism to the experience of the October Revolution, to aid granted by the Soviet Union, to the guidance of the French Communist Party, and to the Algerian working class. He then expressed the gratitude of the Algerian communists to the French Communist Party for its role in building the Algerian workers' movement.

Boukhali's article contained no criticism of the FLN or "reactionary" forces in Algeria, except for an indirect reference to Algerian nonacceptance of the cease fire ordered by the UN Security Council in the Arab-Israeli war:

> Some Arab leaders do not accept the cease fire ordered by the Security Council, though it has been accepted by the countries most directly involved in the conflict, the United Arab Republic, Syria, and Jordan. That attitude, we think, is wrong. . . . If the struggle is to be continued in new forms, then the Arab countries should draw the necessary conclusions from the military defeat and revise some aspects of their anti-imperialist strategy and tactics.

Turning to the international communist movement, Boukhali noted that the "progressive" Arab and African countries are entitled to more support from the international communist and workers' movement. However, he objected to some "erroneous views," such as those opposing the peasantry to the proletariat or the people of the third world to the proletariat of the industrialized countries. "There is even the contention that the underdeveloped countries are being exploited by the advanced countries, by all of them, and that peaceful coexistence is at the expense of these underdeveloped countries." He called for the formation of a uniform attitude by the communist and workers' parties on these issues and added that "at the same time, we believe that it is the international duty of the communist and workers' parties to promote closer solidarity with the more consistent revolutionaries in order to facilitate the rise of genuine vanguard parties."

Boukhali concluded his article with a strong statement of support for the convening of an international communist party meeting which would unite and solidify the entire "international revolutionary and workers' movement."

**Publications.** The organ of the PCA, *Alger Républicain,* was absorbed by *El Moudjahid,* the FLN organ, in 1964. The views of the Algerian communists are published in the *World Marxist Review* and in various foreign communist party organs. The ORP has a monthly organ, *Muqawamah,* and ORP declarations are frequently carried in the French Communist Party organ *L'Humanité. El Moudjahid* and *Révolution Africaine* reflect the range of views within the FLN.

# ARGENTINA

The Communist Party of Argentina (Partido Comunista de Argentina; PCA) originated from the International Socialist Party (Partido Socialista Internacional), founded in 1918. Its present name was adopted in 1920.

The PCA, banned at present, is considered the largest communist party in Latin America outside Cuba. It claims to have a membership of more than 100,000. Western estimates, however, place the number at no more than 60,000. Contending communist factions within Argentina appear to have only small memberships (see below). The population of Argentina is 22,691,000 (estimated, July 1966).

Under the government of Arturo U. Illia (1963-1966), the PCA was legal but did not enjoy "juridical-political recognition" and was thus ineligible to participate in elections. It played an influential role in Argentine political life, partly because of its wealth, the result of its controlling position in the cooperative credit movement and indirect participation in various commercial and banking enterprises. Following the coup d'état of 28 June 1966, the new President, Lieutenant General Juan Carlos Onganía, dissolved all political parties by decree. On 25 August 1967 a 22-article law was promulgated, providing for the registration of Communists in Argentina and imposing severe restrictions on their activities. These include a ban on the holding by Communists of any public office or any official position in professional, employers', or trade-union organizations, and on teaching in state and private schools. The law also prohibits the entry into Argentina of any foreigners, other than diplomats, who are known to be Communists.

**Organization and Leadership.** The PCA's current leadership was elected in February 1966. A clandestine Seventh National Conference was held 14-16 April 1967. There do not appear to have been any changes in the party's hierarchy. Victorio Codovilla is President of the PCA and of its Central Committee and Executive Committee. Gerónimo Arnedo Alvarez is Secretary-General. The Executive Committee is composed of Victorio Codovilla, Gerónimo Arnedo Alvarez, Rodolfo Ghioldi, Alcira de la Peña, Florindo A. Moretti, Pedro Tadioli, Orestes Ghioldi, Vicente Marischi, Athos Fava, Rubens Iscaro, and Héctor Santarén. The Secretariat consists of Victorio Codovilla, Gerónimo Arnedo Alvarez, Orestes Ghioldi, Vicente Marischi, and Alcira de la Peña. In addition to the above, the following are members of the Central Committee: Ernesto Giúdici, Benito Marianetti, Paulino González Alberdi, Emilio Troise, Alfredo Varela, Fanny J. de Edelman, Jorge Bergstein, José María García, Héctor Pablo Agostí, Irma Carmen Othar, and Angel Araoz. Candidate members of the Central Committee are Juan Occhipinti, Armando Arjones, Severo Cerro, Arnoldo Piñera, Felipe Besrodnik, Irene F. Rodríguez and Oscar Arévalo.

The PCA's youth movement is the Federation of Communist Youth (Federación Juvenil Comunista; FJC), whose Secretary-General is Héctor Santarén. There are no reliable estimates of membership. The total of 8,000 which is sometimes quoted would appear to be no longer valid in view of the numerous defections from the FJC during 1967. A "conflict of generations" has been an important internal problem facing the PCA, both within the party and in the PCA's relations with the FJC (the ages of the PCA's leaders average about 60 years, and the founder of the party and still its President, Victorio Codovilla, was born in 1894). During 1967, conflict between the PCA leadership and segments of the FJC was accentuated. The Havana conference of the Latin American Solidarity Organization (OLAS) on 31 July to 10 August—which the PCA did not attend and whose advocacy of armed struggle the party rejected (see below)—was followed by the expulsion of a number of young PCA members, including leaders of the FJC, who opposed the PCA leadership's stand (*El Nacional*, Santo Domingo, 1 October). By the end of the year the PCA appeared to have lost control over most of the FJC membership. A number of the FJC dissidents formed the Revolutionary Communist

Movement (Movimiento Comunista Revolucionario; MCR), which appears to have a Castroist orientation.

The PCA was also confronted with loss of influence within the Argentine University Federation (Federacion Universitaria Argentina; FUA). At the FUA's cladestinely held Eighth Congress (8-10 December), dissident Communists, in alliance with the National Popular Student Movement (Movimiento Estudiantil Nacional Popular—previously under the influence of the PCA), gained control of 108 of the 155 voting delegates. Jorge Rocha, a former FJC leader expelled from the PCA, was elected Chairman of the FUA's Directing Committee.

**Trade-Union Movement.** Although the party is relatively large, it has not been able to penetrate or influence to any serious extent either the traditional political organizations or organized labor. The PCA's failure to gain more support among the labor unions is due largely to the influence of Peronism, which controls the major trade-union body, the General Workers' Confederation (Confederación General de Trabajadores; CGT). The PCA controls the Movement for Trade-Union Unity and Coordination (Movimiento por la Unidad y la Coordinación Sindical; MUCS), whose Secretary-General, Rubens Iscaro, is a member of the PCA Executive Committee. The MUCS, however, is illegal, and following the promulgation of the anti-Communist law of 25 August, its influence, together with the PCA's general influence within the trade-union movement, deteriorated appreciably. By the end of the year the only MUCS national affiliate, the Chemical Workers' Federation, had withdrawn its membership.

Relations between the PCA and the Peronist CGT, which earlier in the year had been governed by the party's advocacy of united-front policy, appeared to be deteriorating by the end of December. A communique distributed by the MUCS accused the CGT leaders of believing in a "utopian relationship between the exploiters and the exploited, which amounts to a brotherhood of the wolf and the sheep."

**Domestic Views and Policies.** The PCA's domestic policy at the beginning of the year was reflected in a posthumous article by Alberto Ferrari, a Central Committee member, published by the *World Marxist Review* (January 1967) and entitled "Lessons of the Popular Front and Latin America." Ferrari stressed the importance of the "unity of all forces dedicated to peace and national independence." While claiming that the "problem of working-class unity" hinged on "close cooperation between the Peronists and Communists," he went on to say: "[Because] the majority of the Peronist leaders are against unity, we have adopted the slogan advanced at one time by Maurice Thorez: *'Etre unitaire pour deux.'* "

The advocacy of a broad united front of opposition forces was reiterated at the PCA's Seventh National Conference (14-16 April). In his report to the conference, Victorio Codovilla, reviewing the failure of "patriots and anti-imperialists" to "resist the new dictatorial power so as to prevent its consolidation," concluded that "what was not done yesterday can and should be done today by uniting all the democratic and progressive forces of the country in a single front without any restrictions whatever, in order to resist the reactionary measures of the dictatorship and to fight for a government based on a broad democratic and popular coalition." Pointing out that the "links between Left Peronists and Communists, in both the lower and upper echelons, [were] becoming stronger in the course of the struggle against the dictatorship," Codovilla emphasized the importance of an alliance between the working class and the peasants, and declaring that the party had "long been committed to the policy of proffering its hand to the Catholics," welcomed the development of "antagonisms between reactionaries and progressives" within the Catholic Church.

Codovilla's conclusions as to the PCA's domestic policy portrayed a broad spectrum of tactical options and ultimate aims:

> The time has come for everyone to realize that we must look for what unites us and reject what keeps us apart, that our country cannot be developed on a new basis by one party or one social group, and that unity of action must not be temporary nor aimed at accomplishing a definite task, but must be a long-term factor, since what is needed is not to replace one government by another but to bring about—by peaceful or non-peaceful means, depending on the resistance of the reactionary forces to the combined forces of

the people—the formation of a government that will carry out fundamental changes in the economic, political, social and cultural life of the nation. It is necessary to convince present or potential allies that unity of action within a common front does not imply that all parties or social forces will lose their identity and have to discard their program, political conceptions and ideologies.

On specific program issues, Codovilla emphasized that a "genuinely democratic regime" could be "brought about solely through abolishing the latifundium and its semi-feudal survivals, and by ending foreign monopoly domination in the principal spheres of the national economy" (*IB*, no. 102, 1967).

The domestic policy lines spelled out at the Seventh National Conference were reiterated during the year. However, after the arrest on 20 April of Régis Debray, author of *Revolucion en la Revolución?* (see *Bolivia* and *Cuba*), the subsequent publicity given his revolutionary theories, and the OLAS conference, the PCA's espousal of both peaceful and nonpeaceful revolutionary means was modified somewhat in favor of the former. At an international communist seminar in Prague (22-24 June), the PCA's representative, Central Committee member Ernesto Giúdici, declared: "While we accept the concept of the two paths it is most important to recognize the historical possibility of the peaceful path. In relation to this general dominant fact, the non-peaceful way is particular. The general does not rule out the particular. However, there is no need to accentuate the particular." Giúdici's speech (published in *WMR*, August), went on to criticize a number of the basic tenets of Debray's theories on revolution and the primacy of the guerrilla movement.

In September the PCA issued a pamphlet entitled *No Puede Haber Revolución en la Revolución* (There Cannot Be a Revolution within the Revolution), reiterating its earlier critique of Debray and emphasizing the importance of mass support and the role of the proletariat and the communist party. At the end of November, the PCA's weekly organ, *Nuestra Palabra*, noted that armed struggle was "not always the answer, even when certain conditions seem to recommend it," and added: "[The PCA] is oriented toward the conquest of power by the movement of the masses, and for this purpose it accepts all paths. However, the party prefers that path that does not compel the working people to pay the dear, bloody price of a civil war."

The PCA's reluctance to commit itself to armed struggle engendered controversy between it and the more militant revolutionary elements within Argentina, particularly within the Peronist movement. One of the more outspoken critics of the party was John William Cooke, leader of the Revolutionary Peronist Movement (Movimiento Revolucionario Peronista) and Chairman of the Argentine delegation to the OLAS Conference. In *No Puede Haber Revólucion en la Revólucion,* the PCA commented: "In keeping with the caudillo concept, in Argentina the various sectors of the national left subordinate everything to Peron. In Cooke's case this Peronista messianism takes the guise of a pseudo-Marxism-Leninism." In the first week of October *Neustra Palabra* identified Peronism with Maoism, stating that both served "imperialism" in its aim to "introduce a wedge in the world socialist camp." By the end of the year it was not clear to what extent the PCA had reneged on its earlier espousal of a policy of *"unitaire pour deux"* vis-à-vis the Peronists.

**International Views and Policies.** The PCA continued during the year to voice strong support for the Soviet Union, both with regard to general issues of foreign policy and to those related to international communist affairs. Codovilla's speech at the party's Seventh National Conference stressed the importance of united "anti-imperialist solidarity." Referring to Vietnam, he termed the operations of the National Liberation Front and its supporters a "gallant fight of world significance [which enjoys]the solidarity of the world, in particular the solidarity of the socialist countries and, above all, the mighty Soviet Union." Codovilla added, however: "Mao Tse-tung and his nationalist group have sabotaged the united front of effective solidarity with Vietnam, thus doing a great service to the US imperialists that is no less effective for being cloaked in ultrarevolutionary verbiage." Following a lengthy attack on the leaders of the Chinese Communist Party, whom he accused of following the "nationalist, jingoist, great-power line advanced by Mao Tse-tung," Codovilla declared: "[The PCA], which has been carefully following the evolution of the Chinese leaders and condemns the deviations of Mao and his group, cannot but express its indignation and voice its emphatic protest against these provocations. It confirms its support of the correct policy of the CPSU and its Marxist-Leninist leadership." He then went on to say:

To contribute to greater cohesion of the world Communist and working class movement and to establish without qualification that the 'revolutionary' policy of Mao Tse-tung and his group . . . is incompatible with the principles of Marxism-Leninism and proletarian internationalism, we say once again that we think the conditions are ripe for an international meeting and the adoption by it of decisions showing the working class and the peoples of all countries who stands where at present and so helping to expose the intrigues of bourgeois governments and press. . . . This view is undoubtedly shared by every member and every leader of our party, who have been educated in the spirit of the principles of Marxism-Leninism and proletarian internationalism, of love of the Soviet Union and the CPSU. (*IB*, no. 102.)

The PCA's alignment with the Soviet Union in the Sino-Soviet dispute and its advocacy of an international communist meeting were reiterated on a number of occasions during the year. In early October the PCA issued a communique which stated: "The glorious and beloved Soviet Union, the homeland of socialism born in October has been, is, and will be the greatest and most triumphal example for the proletariat of the world in its struggle to emancipate itself and to emancipate all of humanity." At the same time, *Nuestra Palabra* berated the "Mao Tse-tung group, with its systematic opposition to coordinated action by the socialist countries," and reiterated the party's call for a world communist conference.

Relations between the PCA and the Cuban Communist Party deteriorated appreciably over the year. In April, at the PCA's Seventh National Conference, Codovilla affirmed his party's solidarity with Cuba and supported the concept of organizing "solidarity and mutual support on a continental scale, within the Latin American Solidarity Organization." His comments, however, were qualified with criticism of the "camp of the 'knights of ultra-revolutionary phrasemongering' [who] advance the idea that the proletariat does not need a Marxist-Leninist political party in order to play the leading role in the anti-imperialist agrarian and democratic revolution aimed at achieving socialism"—a reference to Debray's theories. Furthermore, with regard to OLAS, Codovilla declared: "It is well known that the revolutionary movement developing in various Latin American countries uses different forms of struggle according to the actual historical conditions, the degree of socio-economic and political development and the degree of the organization, militance and political consciousness of the working class and the people of the countries concerned." (*IB*, no. 102.)

At the Prague seminar of communist parties, in June, Ernesto Giúdici elaborated on Codovilla's remarks, implicitly refuting the Cuban view that revolution on a continental scale and following the Cuban pattern was inevitable in Latin America. The PCA was not represented at the July-August OLAS conference in Havana and on 25 October *Pravda* carried an article by PCA Executive Committee member Rodolfo Ghioldi, who while not naming Castro or Cuba, referred to "petty bourgeois nationalists" creating a "concept of local or continental exclusiveness with the aim of justifying deviation from Marxist-Leninist teaching."

The PCA's relations with other orthodox pro-Soviet communist parties in Latin America underwent a certain degree of consolidation. Following a meeting of representatives of the PCA Central Committee and the Brazilian Communist Party at Buenos Aires in early July, a joint statement committed the two parties to "still greater effort to promote the unity of the Communist and working-class movement in Latin America on the principles of Marxism-Leninism and in accordance with the resolution of the Conference of the Communist and Workers' Parties of Latin America held in Havana at the end of 1964." In this spirit the two parties declared: "The unity of each party is a necessary condition for the further development of the revolutionary process in the country concerned. Consequently, all factional activity, whatever its nature and origin, should be emphatically condemned." (*IB*, no. 103, 1967.) Earlier in the year, at the PCA's Seventh National Conference, resolutions were adopted supporting the communist parties of Colombia and Venezuela, both faced with Castroist dissident factions and, in the case of the latter, public Cuban attacks (see *Venezuela*).

On issues related to the Arab-Israeli war of June 1967, the PCA gave full support to the "activity of the Soviet delegation and the delegations of other socialist countries in the UN in defense of the attacked Arab peoples, regarding that activity as indication of their consistent policy of peace and support for the national liberation movements." The party considered it "necessary to promote solidarity with the Arab peoples," whom it termed "victims of the cowardly aggression of the US and British imperialists and their Zionist agents," and to "support the struggle to recover the territory overrun by Israeli troops and safeguard their economic and political independence." (*Ibid.*)

Despite the PCA's estrangement from Cuba, *Nuestra Palabra* carried a eulogy of Ernesto "Che" Guevara following his death in Bolivia, stating: "The Latin American revolutionary movement has just had a great, an enormous, loss. We Argentine Communists dip our combat banner to the death of the hero."

The PCA was represented by Victorio Codovilla at the Moscow celebrations of the Fiftieth Anniversary of the October Revolution.

**Publications.** Both the PCA press and the publications of the party's collateral organizations are forbidden in Argentina. The principal PCA publications that continue to appear regularly, although clandestinely, are *Nuestra Palabra,* the weekly organ of the party and *Nueva Era,* its monthly theoretical review. The FJC's irregular publications *Juventud* and *Linea* appear to have been taken over by the MCR. There are some twenty additional clandestine and irregular newspapers and journals following the PCA line.

*   *   *

Defections from the PCA and the appearance of new communist and noncommunist revolutionary groups advocating Castroist guerrilla strategy contributed to a fluid political situation among revolutionary movements. By the end of the year it was not possible to make any reliable delineation of the forces in question. These included such groups as the Revolutionary Peronist Movement (Movimiento Revolucionario Peronista; MRP), led by John William Cooke and Joe Baxter; the Camilo Torres Group; the National Liberation Movement (Movimiento de Liberación Nacional); and a very small number of guerrillas, whose political affiliation, if any, was not apparent, operating primarily in Tucumán Province. Of these groups the most prominent appeared to be the MRP, whose leader Cooke led the Argentine delegation to the OLAS conference. There are no reliable estimates of the membership of the MRP or the other groups.

The pro-Chinese element in Argentine communism is very small. Its adherents are mostly young persons, especially students; influence is insignificant among farm larborers and practically nonexistent among industrial workers. Organized pro-Chinese groups that were publicized during the year included: the Communist Vanguard Party, which appears to be led by Elías Seman and publishes an irregular, clandestine journal *No Transar*; a group referred to by the pro-Chinese US Progressive Labor Party (PLP) as the "Party of Labor of Argentina," which publishes a clandestine monthly, *Democracia Popular* (see *World Revolution,* a PLP quarterly, Spring 1968); and a somewhat nebulous youth group which publishes an irregular, clandestine journal, *Vanguardia Comunista.* The organ of the pro-Chinese Communist Party of Belgium in its listing of pro-Chinese parties of the world (*La Voix du Peuple,* 28 April 1967) referred only to "the Marxist-Leninist organization . . . in Argentina," without indicating its name. The New China News Agency in broadcasts during 1967 referred to the Communist Vanguard Party.

The only Trotskyist group on which published information was available in 1967 was the Workers' Party—Trotskyist (Partido Obrero—Trotzkista), which is affiliated with the International Secretariat of the Fourth International (the Posadas movement). It publishes a clandestine weekly, *Voz Proletaria.* The party leaders appear to be Angel Lazaro Fanjul, Roberto Muñiz, Hugo Villa, Dora Ida Colendsky de Fanjul, José Oscar Lungarzo, Guillermo Marcello Almeyra, and Roque Regubaldo Moyano. There are no reliable estimates of the membership of this group, which appears to be very small.

# AUSTRALIA

The Communist Party of Australia (CPA) was founded in October 1920. The party is at present split into two main factions: the parent party, which calls itself the Communist Party of Australia and is generally Moscow-oriented, and its offshoot the Australian Communist Party (Marxist-Leninist), established 15 March 1964, which aligns itself with Peking.

The CPA claims a membership of 5,000 (*WMR*, June 1967), which is the estimate given in *World Strength of Communist Party Organizations* (1968 ed.). The population of Australia is about 12 million.

The CPA was not able to field any winning candidates in the national elections in 1966; its candidates received only 0.4 per cent of the total vote. In the November 1967 Senate elections, the CPA ran candidates in the three states of New South Wales, Victoria, and South Australia, but none were elected. The communist vote in this election was about 20,000 (about 0.4 per cent of the total), down slightly from the 1964 Senate elections (*Tribune*, 29 November 1967). The CPA has some influence in the trade unions, although the party claims that the merger of the Australian Council of Trade Unions and the Australian Workers' Union has resulted in a "shift to the right" by the labor movement and thus has made it more difficult for the party to extend its influence among organized labor. The head of the Seamen's Union of Australia, E. V. Elliot, is a member of the party's National Committee, and a Communist, W. Smart, was elected chairman of the Australian Miners Federation in 1967.

**Organization and Leadership**. A 42-member National Committee and a 12-member National Executive elected from it are the leading bodies of the CPA (these bodies were formerly called the Central Committee and the Political Committee). The National Executive elected in June 1967 consists of National Chairman Richard Dixon, National Secretary Laurie Aarons, National Vice-Presidents Claude Jones and John Alan Sendy, and Eric Aarons, E. A. Bacon, William J. Brown, Pat Clancy, W. E. Gollan, J. Moss, Alec Robertson, and Bernard Taft.

The remaining members of the National Committee are A. Aarons, Hal Alexander, M. Bound, F. Brown, W. John Brown, L. Carmichel, G. Curthoys, D. Dawson, N. Docker, E. V. Elliot, P. George, Ralph Gibson, C. Gifford, Henry Hatfield, A. Hughes, J. R. Hughes, A. Macdonald, K. T. Macdonald, J. Mitchell, Rex Mortimer, M. Ogden, J. Palmada, M. Robertson, E. Ross, Malcolm Salmon, E. Thornton, J. Waten, R. Wilding, T. Wright, and G. Zangalis.

**Policy Trends**. A continuing problem for the CPA has been how to cope with steadily declining influence and membership from their World War II peak, when the party had more than 20,000 members. This decline in CPA fortunes has in recent years reached the proportions of a crisis threatening the very existence of the party; also, as the CPA declines it shifts to the right and as a result the threat to the party from the left increases, with the Australian Communist Party (Marxist-Leninist) now claiming to be the only truly Marxist party in Australia.

Charges that the CPA is "revisionist" have become increasingly difficult for the party to refute, and in 1967 the CPA even considered giving up the attempt to do so (see below). This situation was reflected in the following five trends in the CPA's policies and behavior in 1967: (1) away from the policy of a political alliance led by one Marxist party, and toward a policy of coalition with other parties and groups on specific issues, in which coalitions the CPA would be merely a participating rather than the leading member; (2) toward greater quantity and range of published debate within the party; (3) toward a position on international issues somewhat to the right of the Soviet Union; (4) away from identification with an international communist movement, and toward greater Australian national identification for the party; (5) away from the organizational principles of "democratic centralism" and toward greater intraparty democracy.

Thus, in any ideological spectrum of the communist parties of the world, the CPA would have to occupy a position rather far to the right. This trend, however, has been the subject of extensive disagreement and debate within the party. The party finds it very difficult to take an unequivocal stand on most issues, except for such specific reformist-type questions as treatment of the Aborigines, improved workers' benefits, and industrialization of the northern part of Australia, on which the Australian Labor Party takes stands similar to the CPA.

At the end of 1966 the then current CPA party program was discarded as a policy guide, and extensive discussion and debate within the party began concerning the draft documents which would be submitted to the party congress to be held in June 1967. In November 1966 the Central Committee (now the National Committee) published a statement of CPA ideas on Australia's future. Also, articles solicited from CPA members and others of the Australian political left were published in the form of a "discussion journal." According to committee member W. John Brown, the response was very good; by April 130 contributions had been received, requiring publication of two 96-page editions of the journal (*WMR,* June 1967). Brown described this extensive discussion within the CPA as an effort "to develop a correct creative Marxist policy to work toward socialist transition in the particular conditions of modern Australia." He also saw the discussion journal and the general movement toward greater public intraparty debate as a "basically new way" of approaching the question of the CPA's strategy and tactics.

The CPA is in truth hard put to find any suitable issues on the basis of which it might agitate for sweeping political and social changes. In 1967 the main issues the party tried to capitalize on were Australian involvement in the Vietnam war and the alleged control of Australia's wealth by "monopoly capitalism." On the Vietnam issue, however, the CPA was but a flea on the back of the Australian Labor Party elephant and did not appear to benefit much from its opposition to the Holt government's war policy. The party even tried to excuse its poor showing in the November Senatorial elections by saying that the Australian Labor Party and the Australian Reform Movement had preempted the antiwar vote (*Tribune,* 29 November 1967).

The three draft documents around which discussion centered up to the June congress dealt respectively with tactics, theory, and organization. They were: "Towards a Coalition of the Left," "Communists and the Battle of Ideas," and "Proposed Amendments to the Rules and Constitution." The first document advocated working for alliance with other parties and groups on such issues as Vietnam, the demand for a national Australian shipping line, and foreign capital's threat to Australian independence. Recognizing that this might seem to be a kind of "dishwater communism," Brown admitted that such issues were "at the level of united action for more limited aims" and did not "involve the question of basic social change"; but, he maintained, "within them can be found the kernel of class forces that could continue to develop cooperation around wider and more fundamental class issues in the fight against monopoly up to and including the end of monopoly rule itself." This, of course, is seen by the CPA as a very distant prospect.

The second document tackled the problem of simultaneously maintaining the party's Marxist character and establishing the relevance of Marxism to the Australian economic and political context. This attempt to "Aussify" Marxism was necessary both to establish the Marxist legitimacy of the CPA's tactics and to maintain some theoretical guides to policy. The document included an attempt to show that monopoly capital was retarding the economic growth of Australia. It also tried to show that wages as a per cent of the value of total production in Australia declined from 59 per cent in 1952 to 50 per cent in 1965.

The third document advocated organizational reform for the party, with the object, according to Brown, of retaining "basic Communist party political and organizational principles while taking into account democratic traditions and customs common to the Australian labor movement."

**CPA Congress.** The Twenty-first Congress of the CPA was held in Sydney 9-12 June. Present were 48 delegates from all states of Australia. Greetings were received from 14 communist parties, including that of the Soviet Union; the only Asian parties to send greetings were the Mongolian party and the pro-Moscow Ceylon Communist Party. The CPA had intended to invite foreign observers, but the Australian government indicated that any such invitees would be refused visas.

The proceedings of the congress and the extensive debate which marked it were reported in detail in the 14 and 21 June issues of the *Tribune*. The congress "broadly endorsed" the three main documents and the major reports, according to the 21 June *Tribune,* but there were a number of issues on which minority views were "firmly put." Numerous other resolutions were passed by the congress dealing with such matters as the Arab-Israeli war, Vietnam, the Aborigines, the Australian National Health Service, capital punishment, and conscription.

The most important subject of discussion at the congress was the policy expressed in the document title and slogan "Towards a Coalition of the Left." This policy's primary immediate objective, it was clear, would be to increase the party's influence in the labor movement, meaning both the Australian Labor Party and the trade unions. The *Tribune* described the policy as a departure from "the old concept of an alliance led by one Marxist party." It had, however, critics both on the right and on the left within the CPA. At a West Australia state party conference on 28-30 April, the state organization had proposed that the slogan "Towards a Coalition of the Left" be changed to "Towards an Independent Australia." Some speakers at this state conference had also urged that the phrase "towards unity of the left" be replaced with "towards national unity." (*Tribune,* 17 May.) At the Congress itself the view was put forward that there were people of "progressive views" who would join with the party in support of such specific objectives as withdrawal from Vietnam, but who would object to being identified as "left." On the other hand, the CPA left criticized the new policy as tantamount to reformism; it seemed to them that the party was giving up the struggle for revolution or any fundamental social changes.

The view that prevailed, however, was that the name of the new policy should not imply that the coalition's objectives would be limited to the struggle for democratic goals, and that such a policy was the optimal creative application of Marxism to Australian conditions. The 21 June *Tribune* explained: "Left coalition implies a program for strengthening the basis of democracy in Australia, for peace and a new and independent foreign policy and for basic social reforms that open the way for a socialist transformation. It goes beyond the fight for democracy." The party recognized that to expect that such a coalition was an immediate possibility would be unrealistic; rather, it was to be regarded as an "object to be worked for": "It is a long-range perspective and yet it has important practical implications for the activities of the party and for the left as a whole."

In the same vein, National Executive member Eric Aarons, in a speech to the congress, defended the trend of CPA policy against its left-wing critics within the party by insisting that the party was not sacrificing revolutionary principles by concentrating on such limited demands as the left coalition policy involved. "We cannot divide demands into some which are inherently revolutionary and some which are inherently reformist," he said. Rather than explicitly to disavow revolution as a policy goal of the CPA, the party chose to redefine it merely as change in a social system. On this point Aarons said:

> There has been some criticism of a statement that the essence of revolution is a change in social system. But is this "watered down" any more than the statement that the majority would resort to violence only if the reactionary minority did so? Neither is acceptable to the bourgeoisie. The criticism misses the whole point, which is aimed to make our position, *without conceding principle,* more acceptable to people in Australia. (*Tribune,* 21 June; italics in original.)

Related to this issue were proposals made at the congress to drop the word "communist" from the name of the party, and even to dissolve the party and turn it into a political-education group, with CPA members joining the Australian Labor Party. The Congress, however, resolved: "The title 'communist' best expresses the objective of our party and should be retained. Any proposal to change the name should proceed from deeper political considerations than an attempt to overcome immediate tactical difficulties." (*Ibid.*) "Pursuit of a radical change in the Australian Labor Party by mass entry of Marxists is illusory," the congress declared.

The organizational changes and reforms approved at the congress were significant, if not sweeping. In an effort to bring more young people into the party, the minimum age requirement of 18 years for party membership was dropped. The congress also stipulated that all elections, including those of officers and executives, must be by secret ballot, and gave each national congress the authority to decide whether national officers should be elected by the congress or by the National Committee. A network of special appeals committees to hear disciplinary cases was created, from the national level on down. These committees, elected by the national or local congresses, are to be composed of members who do not belong to the equivalent-level party committee. Finally, the congress increased control over party workers by elected bodies and stated the obligation of the National Committee to refer to the whole party policy questions on which there was substantial disagreement within the committee. Regarding these organizational reforms, the 21 June *Tribune* reported that Vice-President John Sendy had said: "In the present Australian conditions the party did not need to base its organizational forms on those of parties created secretly to function in conditions of tsarist terror." Accordingly, the terms "democratic centralism" and "factionalism," as well as the names "central committee" and "central executive," were dropped from official CPA usage.

**International Views and Positions.** Throughout the year, but especially at the June congress, the CPA took public positions on international issues generally following, but not always coinciding with, those of the Soviet Union. The CPA made Australian participation in the Vietnam war its major international issue in 1967, hoping to benefit from joining the labor opposition to the government on this issue. The CPA congress resolution on Vietnam stated:

> We pledge ourselves to raise to new levels the struggle against the war policy of the Holt Government, bringing people of Australia into stronger and more effective action to secure the withdrawal of Australian armed forces from the war, and restore peace . . . . Peace in Vietnam can be won only by withdrawal of foreign troops, return to the Geneva Agreements and the full establishment of sovereignty and self-determination for the Vietnamese people as the basis for the peaceful reunification of the country.

National Committee member Malcolm Salmon toured North Vietnam in May and on his return to Australia on 25 May reported that Pham Van Dong, Premier of the Democratic Republic of Vietnam, had told him that North Vietnam would begin talks with the US if the bombing of the north ceased unconditionally.

On the question of the Arab-Israeli war, the CPA followed the general line of the Moscow-oriented European communist parties, stopping short, however, of the explicit condemnation of Israeli aggression which characterized the Soviet position. The first reaction by the CPA to the war was to say that in the midst of conflicting claims by both sides the true sequence of events was not clear. The 7 June *Tribune* described the outbreak of hostilities as taking place "in a situation of long-standing tension and nationalist threats on both sides," and called for "mutual respect of sovereignty" between the Arab states and Israel. A resolution adopted at the congress and published in the 14 June *Tribune* set forth the following conditions which the CPA felt were requisite to a settlement in the Middle East:

(1) A peaceful and permanent solution to the differences between Israel and the Arab countries

(2) The renunciation by all powers of the use of military force or threats in the Middle East

(3) Recognition of: (a) the rights of the evicted Palestinian Arabs to choose return to Israel with full citizen rights or adequate compensation that will enable them to be rehabilitated in Arab countries, and (b) the just national rights of both the Jews and the Palestinian Arab people in Israel

(4) The right of the state of Israel to an independent national existence

(5) The necessity for liquidating imperialist military bases and economic interests (particularly oil) in the area, so that the people of these countries may have the opportunity to achieve genuine national independence and to use their national assets for their own welfare.

The CPA paid much attention to developments in China in 1967. A plenum of the National Committee met in Sydney 10-12 February to discuss Vietnam and China, and adopted an official statement on events in China. It appeared in the 22 February *Tribune* and was reprinted in the *Information Bulletin,* No. 94 (1967). Declaring that the Chinese Great Proletarian Cultural

Revolution was "neither proletarian, nor cultural, nor a revolution," the statement said: "Developments in China are extremely serious and dangerous, threatening the very basis of socialism in China, disrupting unity of the socialist countries and aid to Vietnam, harming the struggle for national liberation and the work of communist parties everywhere." Criticizing the excesses of the cult of personality centered on Mao, the CPA statement observed: "These absurdities, far removed from Marxism-Leninism, are unfortunately only fantastic reflections of the harsh reality that party and socialist democracy have been suppressed [in China]." With regard to relations between the Soviet Union and China it said: "The Communist Party of Australia fully supports Premier Kosygin's rejection of any possibility of conflict between the USSR and China and hopes for a similar statement by the Chinese People's Republic."

The Fiftieth Anniversary of the October Revolution was observed with due ceremony by the CPA. A delegation headed by Laurie Aarons was sent to Moscow, and the *Tribune* on 1 November published a special supplement of articles about the USSR to mark the occasion. Among these articles was one critical of certain aspects of the Soviet political system. Lloyd Churchward, a professor at the University of Melbourne, in an article titled "Soviet Democracy" frankly criticized antidemocratic tendencies of the Soviet leadership, saying:

> Shortcomings and anti-democratic elements tend to be minimized or excused by such phrases as "the personality cult," or (to quote the post-Khrushchev version), by the errors of "voluntarism" and "bureaucratism."
>
> Clearly this is inadequate and Australian communists should be more forthright in their criticism of the shortcomings of the Soviet political system.
>
> Why, for instance, are competitive elections not permitted after all these years? Why are individual rights so often ignored? Why are the rights of national and religious minorities not more firmly safeguarded? . . . Even today Soviet democracy is an unfinished and even an uncertain condition of Soviet public life.
>
> It depends for its existence far too much on the willingness and ability of the Communist Party to operate under a self-denying ordinance. This is too slender a basis for democracy in any regime.

Immediately below this article, however, was an item, "The Credit Side of the Balance Sheet," by Rupert Lockwood, the *Tribune*'s Moscow correspondent, which argued that the democratic aspects of the Soviet social and political system far outweighed the antidemocratic aspects.

**Australian Communist Party (Marxist-Leninist) [ACP(ML)].** The ACP(ML) was established by a group of former CPA members led by E. F. (Ted) Hill, a Melbourne attorney (see *YICA*, 1966, pp. 353-355). Membership is quite small. The party gives little publicity to its leadership; the few names communicated by the party press include E. F. Hill, Chairman; Frank Johnson, Secretary; Herman Edward O'Sullivan and Gerald Patrick O'Day, members of the Central Committee; and C. L. O'Shea and P. Malone, party leaders in the trade-union movement.

The ACP(ML) maintains extensive contacts with Communist China, and its statements faithfully reflect Peking's views. Chairman Hill visited Peking in late November 1967, accompanied by N. L. Gallagher, and met with Mao Tse-tung on 27 November. Frank Johnson and his wife appear to have spent much time in China during the year and were present both at the May Day celebrations in Peking and at the airport sendoff for Hill and Gallagher on 29 November. Praise for China's cultural revolution and anti-Soviet statements appear regularly in the party paper *Vanguard*. One article by E. F. Hill (quoted in *Peking Review*, 19 January 1968) said:

> Recognition of Chairman Mao's outstanding genius as a Marxist-Leninist right now is a vital question of Marxism-Leninism and the revolutionary struggle. The capitalist class and modern revisionists spare no effort to destroy Chairman Mao's greatness. The workers and working people do the reverse. Australian Marxist-Leninists must raise even higher the great red banner of Marxism-Leninism, Mao Tse-tung's thought.

In another *Vanguard* article (quoted in *Peking Review*, 8 September 1967) Hill praised Mao's theory of contradiction as the key to understanding dialectical materialism. Hill said that Mao's essays *On Practice* and *On Contradiction* "contain the most comprehensive and systematic treatment of the theory of knowledge and the laws of development." He said further:

> Chairman Mao demonstrated in masterly fashion the fundamental role of contradiction in dialectics. Wherever there is Marxism-Leninism there is revisionism. Marxism-Leninism grows strong in the struggle against revisionism. So, today the struggle against China's Khrushchev shows the generality and particularity of contradiction.

Communist China's quarrel with North Korea was also reflected in ACP(ML) comments on the papers *Pyongyang Times* and *People's Korea,* which are distributed in Australia and other English-speaking countries. The 21 December 1967 *Vanguard* attacked the North Koreans as subtle and devious accomplices of the Soviet Union and enemies of Communist China. Another *Vanguard* article (reprinted in the USA in the Progressive Labor Party periodical *World Revolution,* Spring 1968) said that while the North Korean *Pyongyang Times* and *People's Korea* contained "correct general statements" against revisionism, they slyly failed to criticize the Soviet Union as the bastion of the revisionists and attacked the Chinese Communist Party by implication and innuendo. In what amounted to a Chinese attack by proxy against the North Koreans, the article said:

> This North Korean clique lends itself to all the calls of the Soviet revisionist clique for so-called united socialist action in Vietnam. This so-called united socialist action is aimed at helping the Soviet revisionist clique more effectively to sell out the Vietnamese people. It is a fraud pure and simple. It is to let the chief collaborator with US imperialism have a bigger say in the Vietnam question. It is to let one conspirator right into the house of the victim of the conspiracy so that he can let the other conspirator in.
>
> Under the cover of general words against revisionism these persons in North Korea are actually serving the Soviet revisionist clique and the US imperialists.

**Publications.** The *Tribune* is the CPA's weekly newspaper; it is published in Sydney by the National Committee of the CPA under the editorship of Alec Robertson. The *Australian Left Review* (a "Marxist journal of information, analysis, and discussion on economics, politics, trade unionism, history, philosophy, science, and art, for the promotion of socialist ideas") appears every two months; it is published in Sydney and edited by Richard Dixon, assisted by Eric Aarons. In addition, during 1967 there were at least four issues of the CPA's publication informally designated as the "discussion journal." The party planned to continue this publication in 1968.

The ACP(ML) publishes a weekly newspaper, *Vanguard,* and a monthly review, *The Australian Communist.*

# AUSTRIA

The Communist Party of Austria (Kommunistische Partei Österreichs; KPÖ), founded 3 November 1918, is legal and has an estimated membership of 35,000. (The population of Austria is 7,290,000 [1966 estimate].) Besides the long-established Moscow-oriented KPÖ, there is a new Marxist-Leninist Party of Austria with a pro-Chinese orientation which was founded in 1967, mainly by dissident KPÖ members.

Since 1959, the KPÖ has not been represented in the Austrian Parliament. In the last Parliamentary elections, 6 March 1966, the party gained 18,638 votes (0.4 per cent of the total) for its only candidate, party Chairman Franz Muhri. Throughout the rest of the country Communist voters were asked by the party to support the Socialist Party ticket. The Austrian People's Party (ÖVP), however, emerged the strongest party, with 48.4 per cent of the vote, which gave it a majority in Parliament; the Socialist Party (SPÖ) received 42.6 per cent of the vote, a loss compared with previous election results.

The Nineteenth Congress of the KPÖ, 27-30 May 1965, elected a Central Committee of 86 members and a Politburo of 11 members. The following leaders were elected: Honorary Chairman Johann Koplenig, Chairman Franz Muhri, and Politburo members Robert Dubovsky, Friedl Fürnberg, Otto Horn (died 31 March 1967), Egon Kodicek, Josef Lauscher, Franz Marek, Franz Muhri, Alfred Ruschitzka, Erwin Scharf, Maria Urban, and Franz West. Friedl Fürnberg and Erwin Scharf were elected Central Committee Secretaries. The new Central Committee Secretariat consisted of Franz Muhri, Friedl Fürnberg, Erwin Scharf, Egon Kodicek, and Franz West.

The Communist Party of Austria has a youth organization, the Free Austrian Youth (Freie Österreichische Jugend); a small trade-union organization, Trade-Union Unity (Gewerkschaftliche Einheit), which publishes *Die Arbeit* and operates within the independent and influential Austrian Trade-Union League; and a number of auxiliary organizations most of which are national sections of international front organizations, such as the Austrian Peace Council, the League of Democratic Women of Austria, and the Federation of Austrian Resistance Fighters and Victims of Fascism. A very important friendship society for the KPÖ is the Austrian-Soviet Society (Österreichisch-sowjetische Gesellschaft). Its President, Hugo Glaser, was a visitor to the Fiftieth Anniversary celebrations in Moscow in 1967.

Lively discussion within the KPÖ concerning its political orientation in 1967 reconfirmed the policy of a "peaceful road to socialism" which the party adopted and laid down in the resolutions of its Nineteenth Congress in May 1965. In the light of this espousal of a parliamentary approach to a socialist "transformation," the poor results for the party in the national elections of March 1966 still overshadowed the political discussion in 1967. In October the state elections (*Landtagswahlen*) in Upper Austria and communal elections in Salzburg and Klagenfurt further weakened the Communist position and gave an unexpected gain to the Socialist Party. The KPÖ admitted that the results were "disappointing" and a "severe setback." The Socialist Party's gain, however, was interpreted by the Communists less as a voters' show of approval of the Socialists' trend to the right than as an alarming sign of deep discontent with the way in which the Austrian People's Party had run the government since the 1966 elections. Consequently, the KPÖ intensified its attacks upon the policies of the People's Party and at the same time urged the Socialists not to forget their obligations as elements of the working class. In numerous editorials in *Volksstimme*, in discussions and commentaries, a recurring theme of the KPÖ was that the strong Socialist Party did not offer a "genuine alternative" to the People's Party. The polemics against the Socialist Party and its new Chairman Bruno Kreisky (elected by the SPÖ Congress early in 1967) took up more space in the Communist press and its debates throughout the year than any other issue. This, of course, is not surprising in view of the fact that Bruno Kreisky drew a very sharp line between democratic socialism and the Communists, thus virtually blocking any cooperation or dialogue between the KPÖ and the noncommunist left.

Discussing the Austrian situation in *World Marxist Review* (May), Chairman Muhri wrote: "In personal and political terms alike, Bruno Kreisky's election to the chairmanship marked a turn to the right." The SPÖ Congress was analyzed by Politburo member Erwin Scharf at a Central Committee session 13 February and discussed by the Central Committee. The KPÖ Conference on 10 June again dealt largely with the political orientation of the KPÖ vis-à-vis the SPÖ. "The unity front remains our orientation," said Chairman Muhri in his report to the Conference, adding: "In spite of the increased anticommunist reaction of the Socialist Party leadership, in spite of their attempt to construct a wall between Socialists and Communists, the word of our Nineteenth Congress remains correct that we consider our efforts to reach an understanding with Socialist comrades our primary political task" (*Volksstimme*, 11 June).

A Central Committee plenary session on 21-22 September took up the ideological challenge of the Socialist Party when it prepared a discussion paper on "Democracy and Socialism" to be distributed as a supplement to the party daily *Volksstimme* in October and subsequently to be discussed by party cadres and in the press. Significant in this document is the way in which the terminological problem of the "dictatorship" of the proletariat is discussed. Arguing that the term has an unfavorable connotation in everyday language because of Fascist and Stalinist aberrations, the document proposed two alternative terms which would better correspond to the actual goals of the Communist Party: "workers' power" (*Arbeitermacht*) or "socialist democracy." The meaning of a "socialist transformation," accordingly, would be that "democratic achievements" reached by the Austrian society today would not be destroyed, a plurality of parties would be preserved, and parties opposed to the socialist orientation would be preserved "as long as they should follow the laws decided upon by the people's representatives." In a commentary on the document, Politburo member Fürnberg explicitly took up the charge of those critics who argued that an alliance between Communist parties and socialists is only a tactical maneuver. (Chairman Muhri had already explained at the Nineteenth Congress that the new orientation of a "peaceful road to socialism" was not tactical, but was a new strategy.) Discussion with Socialists and "democratic" Catholics had become necessary for the Communists in order to find a base for united action, according to Fürnberg.

The "dialogue" with Catholics received wide publicity in the party organs *Volksstimme* and *Weg und Ziel*. The coverage, in itself an integral part of the "dialogue," ranged from Podgorny's visit to the Vatican to analyses and discussion of the papal encyclical "Populorum Progressio" and to the Christian-Marxist meeting at Marienbad, Czechoslovakia. In unusually harsh words *Volksstimme* (26 August) criticized a book by a Soviet author (Mchedlov), *The Evolution of Modern Catholicism*, which viewed recent developments in the Catholic Church as an adaptation of clerical tactics to new situations. Similar charges were raised in *Weg und Zeil* (September) against another Soviet publication, *Crisis of Modern Catholicism*, by Velikovitch.

Throughout the year, indirect appeals for unity of the left were channeled through the party press by way of extensive reporting on united-left "successes" in other countries. In view of the rather selective news coverage in a paper like *Volksstimme* this indicates a carefully measured approach. Broadest coverage was given to the various events in France which could be considered milestones on the road to unity between the French Communist Party and socialist groups, especially the election agreements for the national elections in March and the cantonal elections in the fall. *Volksstimme* hailed the united-front developments in India early in the year, from *L'Unità* it reprinted a long story on socialist-communist relations in Finland, and on 19 November it published Finnish Socialist leader Raatikainen's call for cooperation between Socialists and Communists; it also carried reports on popular-front tendencies in Chile and reprinted a series of articles on Scandinavian trends to the left. Detailed coverage was given to the Communist Party of Great Britain and its "road to socialism."

In the fall, the patriarch of the KPÖ, Honorary Chairman Johann Koplenig, discussed in *Kommunist* (Moscow) Lenin's attitude toward other political parties in Russia and argued that Lenin's policy of eliminating all other parties had been a reluctant concession to necessity: the other parties, in Lenin's view, did not conform to the new type of social order. This argument was plainly intended to fend off any suspicion that the KPÖ's official adoption of a plurality of parties as part of the "peaceful road to socialism" was only a short-term tactical maneuver. The KPÖ's problem of gaining credibility for its willingness to adopt a multiparty system was also discussed in the KPÖ's contribution to the celebration of the Fiftieth Anniversary of the October Revolution, Politburo member Friedl Fürnberg's book *50 Jahre. Die Sozialistische Oktoberrevolution und Österreich* (Vienna, 1967). Koplenig's article was reprinted in *Volksstimme* on 3 October; on 8 November the paper printed an article of September 14, 1917, by Lenin under the title "Lenin on the Peaceful Road to Socialism," with an introductory comment by Koplenig saying that not to take advantage of the peaceful road if circumstances should permit would "contradict not only the spirit of Lenin, but even his words." At the end of the year *Volksstimme* reported in detail on the election agreement between the Italian Communist Party and left socialists (PSIUP).

The KPÖ actively supported the opposition to the war in Vietnam. On 28 February Chairman Muhri addressed a telegram to Federal Chancellor Klaus demanding that the Austrian Government, as an expression of genuine "neutrality," ask the United States to stop the bombing and all other acts of aggression (*Volksstimme*, 1 March). In October the Central Committee published a *Vietnam Appeal* addressed to the Government, to the Parliament, and to the leadership of the Socialist Party of Austria. This document pointed out that the governments of many countries, including neutral countries and even NATO members, had asked for a bombing pause; that the Parliament in Holland had taken a stand against the bombing, while the Austrian Parliament was silent; and that many socialist parties had clearly opposed the US policies (e.g., the Labor Party of Great Britain), while the SPÖ and its Chairman Kreisky had remained vague.

On the Sino-Soviet rift the KPÖ continued its consistently pro-Soviet line. Muhri condemned the "splitting activity of the leaders of the Communist Party of China" at the Eighteenth Congress of the French Communist Party in January; in an interview shortly afterward Muhri accused the Chinese of slowing down effective help for North Vietnam and characterized the events within China as contradictory to "the principles of inner-party democracy" (*Volksstimme*, 19 January). Politburo Member Erwin Scharf repeated this charge in an article in *Volksstimme* on 5 February and added a second charge of "anti-Sovietism" and "defamation of the Soviet Union as an accomplice of American imperialism." A KPÖ declaration of 8 February "most resolutely" condemned the "recent aggravation of relations with the Soviet Union caused by the actions of the Chinese leaders" which could "benefit only US imperialism." The Soviet Union, the declaration stated further, was the "chief bulwark securing China itself against the US imperialists' plans to spread their aggression to China," while China's "adventuristic policy" was obstructing all attempts to unite the socialist camp behind the struggle in Vietnam (*Volksstimme*, 9 February; also *IB*,, No. 93, 1967). Shortly before invitations were issued for the Budapest consultative conference (February 1968), Politburo member Franz West discussed the international communist conference in a *Volksstimme* editorial (22 November) and described polemics, defamation, and factionalism—"the way the leaders of the Communist Party of China do it"—as methods of debate "destructive and harmful to the movement as a whole."

The KPÖ demonstrated its orientation toward Moscow within the international communist movement by its participation in the preparatory meeting at Warsaw, 22-26 February, and the Karlovy Vary conference in April, and, later, by neglecting the OLAS Conference and attending and glorifying the Fiftieth Anniversary of the October Revolution. At the end of November the KPÖ welcomed the plans for the Budapest meeting in February 1968 and accepted its invitation immediately. Valuable also to the Soviet Union was the KPÖ's consistent backing in the campaign against NATO (especially in connection with Greece, Cyprus, and the Middle East), its criticism of West Germany's new "policy toward the east," and West German opposition to the text of the nonproliferation treaty. Excerpts from the Soviet note of 8 December to the Federal Republic of Germany on neo-Nazi activities appeared in *Volksstimme* on 13 December. In addition, the KPÖ repeatedly demanded recognition of the German Democratic Republic by Austria as proof of Austrian "neutrality." The argument of neutrality was also used, again fully in accordance with Moscow's wishes, to warn against any attempt by the Austrian Government to seek admission to the

European Economic Community.* On the other hand, the Austrian Communists reacted favorably to Chancellor Klaus's intensified "eastern politics," highlighted by state visits to Moscow in March, Hungary in May, Rumania in July, and Bulgaria in October, which aimed at improving East-West trade relations.

**Middle East Crisis.** A few hours after the beginning of fighting in the Middle East in June, the KPÖ issued a declaration asking for an immediate cease-fire (*Volksstimme*, 6 June). At the party conference of 10 June Chairman Muhri condemned the preemptive war of Israel. The 360 delegates adopted a resolution which linked Vietnam, the coup in Greece, and the Middle East crisis with the aims of "American imperialists." Except for excerpts from a declaration of the Mikunis group of the Israeli Communist Party (*ibid.*, 2 June) and a declaration of the Mikunis group on the outbreak of the war (*ibid.*, 7 June), the Austrian communist press gave publicity only to the Meir Vilner pro-Moscow group in the Israeli Communist Party. Generally, the position of the KPÖ has been that of a moderator. There were no indications of anti-Semitism; analyses in the press and expressions at meetings dealt with the alleged international forces behind the conflict, for instance the US-British oil interests. Noteworthy in this connection is a letter by Central Committee member Ernst Fischer, a leading intellectual of the KPÖ, to the Swiss newspaper *Die Weltwoche* (23 June) in which he said that he did not share the official communist view that Israel was the aggressor and that the Arabs were fighting a war of liberation—what mattered was the right of the Jewish people to have their own state and a guarantee of its existence.

**International Communist Relations.** Chairman Muhri attended the Eighteenth Congress of the French Communist Party on 4-8 January; Politburo member Franz West represented the party at the Warsaw preparatory meeting on 22-26 February; in March a KPÖ delegation headed by Politburo Member Josef Lauscher visited Czechoslovakia for four days; on 6-13 April a Rumanian party delegation under the direction of Executive Committee and Permanent Presidium member Alexandru Drăghici visited Austria and met with several KPÖ Politburo members. Lauscher attended the Seventh Congress of the SED on 17-22 April. Chairman Muhri and Central Committee Secretary Erwin Scharf went to the Karlovy Vary conference of European communist parties, where Muhri assailed West Germany and NATO and asked for recognition of East Germany. Muhri presented his impressions of Karlovy Vary afterward on Austrian television (see *Volksstimme*, 28 April). In an interview with *Volksstimme* 30 April, Scharf distinguished the present policies of the communist parties (adopted at Karlovy Vary) from the historical "popular front" by saying that today's front of unity would be much broader.

Chairman Muhri paid an "unofficial friendship visit" to Hungary 12-16 May, and met with First Secretary of the Hungarian Socialist Workers' Party János Kádár and Politburo member Zoltán Komocsin to exchange views on the international situation and on questions concerning the international communist movement. During his vacation in the Soviet Union, Muhri met early in August with Suslov and Ponomarev in Moscow to discuss the "international situation of the world movement" (*ibid.*, 6 August). Also early in August, Israeli Communist Party Politburo members Toufik Toubi and David Henin passed through Vienna and had talks with members of the KPÖ Central Committee. Central Committee Secretaries Fürnberg and Scharf visited the Central Committee of the Communist Party of Czechoslovakia and were received on 20 October by First Secretary Antonín Novotný.

Although the politically significant OLAS conference in Havana was given scant attention by the KPÖ, on the death of "Che" Guevara the KPÖ sent a telegram of condolence to Castro. (*Volksstimme*, 17 October 1967.)

Chairman Muhri, Central Committee Secretary Fürnberg, and Central Committee member Josef Progsch were guests at the Moscow celebrations of the Fiftieth Anniversary of the October Revolution. A Soviet delegation headed by CPSU Central Committee member Kabin toured Austria 9-17 November and participated in a number of anniversary events. Honorary Chairman Koplenig was awarded the Lenin Order on the occasion of the fiftieth anniversary.

*See A. Ruschitzka, "Bilanz der EWG-Politik der österreichischen Regierung," in the party theoretical monthly *Weg und Ziel*, no. 10 (October 1967) pp. 474-477, and F. West, "Umwege statt Auswege," *Volksstimme*, 13 October 1967.

In November Muhri, Scharf, and Central Committee member Johann Schmid visited Yugoslavia for several days. A Hungarian party delegation visited Austria on 4-9 December and "informed [the KPÖ] about the preparations for the consultative meeting" (*ibid.*, 12 December) in talks with Politburo members Fürnberg, Scharf, and Dubovsky and Central Committee members Heinrich Fritz and Rudolph Richter. Then, at a Central Committee plenary session on 19 December, Secretary Scharf reported on the exchanges of views with other parties during previous months and on the talks with the Hungarians about the forthcoming Budapest consultative meeting in February 1968. The Central Committee of the KPÖ unanimously approved the report and accepted the invitation to Budapest (*ibid.*, 20 December).

**Marxist-Leninist Party of Austria.** The Marxist-Leninist Party of Austria (Marxistisch-Leninistische Partei Österreichs; MLPÖ) was founded 12 February 1967 by a conference of the organization of the Marxist-Leninists of Austria (MLÖ)* and subsequently was welcomed by *Peking Review* (10 March) as a party which "will, together with the Chinese Communist Party, the Albanian Party of Labor and other Marxist-Leninist Parties, fight against imperialism and revisionism." The constitutive congress of the MLPÖ elected a First Secretary, Franz Strobl, and a Central Committee of eleven members (whose names were not given in the new party's organ *Rote Fahne*), together with Karl Horn as Second Secretary and Viktor Varga as Third Secretary (*Rote Fahne*, 15 February). With a Control Commission and Arbitration Commission, the Central Committee and the secretaries form the "Bureau" of the MLPÖ. Membership is perhaps about 500; a report by the MLÖ said that in the 6 March 1966 elections the MLÖ workers' lists received a little under 500 votes in those Vienna districts where MLÖ candidates were entered. In addition, the MLÖ claimed that some 3,000 persons throughout the country indicated their preference for the Marxist-Leninists of Austria by writing "MLÖ" across the voting ticket. This figure shows discontent with the official KPÖ line of support for the Socialist Party in those elections, but is not necessarily an indication of membership.

The constitutive conference of 12 February adopted a number of documents: (1) a telegram to the Central Committee of the Chinese Communist Party, (2) a message of solidarity to the activists of the Great Proletarian Cultural Revolution, (3) a message to the Albanian Party of Labor, (4) a resolution on Vietnam, (5) a resolution on Indonesia, and (6) a message to more than 30 Marxist-Leninist parties, organizations, and groups (text of this message in *Rote Fahne*, 15 March; also *La Voix du Peuple*, 10 March). Messages from abroad on the occasion of the formation of the party and reports in Marxist-Leninist publications were reproduced in the MLPÖ organ. Enver Hoxha, for instance, sent congratulations on behalf of the Albanian Party of Labor; the Organization of Communists of Switzerland and the Marxist-Leninist Center of the Netherlands sent letters; *Vanguardia Obrera*, the theoretical organ of the illegal Communist Party of Spain (Marxist-Leninist), reported on the founding conference in its April issue; the Communist Party of New Zealand sent congratulations; the "Ad Hoc Committee for a Marxist-Leninist Party USA" sent a message.

The new Austrian party is violently opposed to the united-left policies emanating from Moscow and adopted by the Communist Party of Austria. A document called "Explanations to the Statutes" of the MLPÖ and adopted at the founding conference states that the Marxist-Leninist Party of Austria "stands for the proletarian revolution, that is to say, it recognizes the need for revolutionary force, and definitely rejects all bourgeois and revisionist illusions about parliamentary, peaceful, nonviolent development to socialism" (*Rote Fahne*, 15 February). The MLPÖ considers itself the "direct successor to the Communist Party of Austria founded 3 November 1918" and wishes to be

---

*The Marxist-Leninists of Austria, established 1 May 1966, had as its publication *Rote Fahne*, which was begun in 1963 as a dissident journal within circles of the KPÖ. In 1965 the *Rote Fahne* group formed the Preparatory Committee for the Reconstitution of the Communist Party in Austria. At its constitutive meeting the MLÖ elected a "core leadership" (*engere Leitung*) which consisted of Franz Strobl (as Chairman), Josef Friedler, Helmut Hronek, and Alfred Jocha. The latter three were purged from the organization during 1966—Jocha and Hronek at the end of November and Friedler on 21 December. The extraordinary conference (Vertrauensmännerkonferenz) of 21 December elected Karl Horn as Deputy Chairman and adopted a resolution on "Unlimited Solidarity with the Proletarian Cultural Revolution in China" (*Rote Fahne*, 1 January 1967).

Hronek, editor of *Funke*, an organ of "Young Revolutionary Marxists," published since 1965, continued the irregular publication of *Funke* in 1967, like *Rote Fahne* taking a pro-Chinese position, but attacking Strobl's group.

seen as part of the "world-wide movement" led by the communist parties of China and Albania. The MLPÖ is not willing to "forego the dictatorship of the proletariat or the militant leadership of a consistent Marxist-Leninist party." This document focuses on ideological differences between the new Marxist-Leninist party and the reformist KPÖ. Throughout the year, polemics against the views and activities of the KPÖ were a major occupation of the MLPO. A series of articles by Secretary Karl Horn in *Rote Fahne* "exposed" the alleged involvement of the KPÖ in big business and banking. The KPÖ, on the other hand, ignored in its publications the existence of the new party, unless the stepped-up ideological campaign for a united left in Austria is to be interpreted as an indirect answer to MLPÖ attacks. More likely, the "peaceful road to socialism" line of the KPÖ is an attempt to gain electoral support from left socialists rather than a response to criticism from the Marxist-Leninists.

To some extent, however, the Marxist-Leninist Party of Austria has indeed become an ideological receiver of those elements among Austrian Communists who were unwilling to adopt the nonviolent road to socialism. Especially since the Austrian Socialist Party leadership so far has shown very little interest in joining forces with the KPÖ and entering a dialogue on a united-left basis, the politically insignificant MLPÖ has drawn some strength from the KPÖ and could weaken it. An example of transfer from the old-established Communist Party to the new Marxist-Leninist Party is given in the political declaration of a high-ranking regional KPÖ leader with ideological training at a Moscow party school who resigned after a long party career. *Rote Fahne* devoted the whole issue of 15 October to his statement of resignation which concluded: "I shall use all my strength to support the courageous fight of those Communists who joined the Marxist-Leninist Party of Austria. Because I am, and wish to remain, a Communist, I part from the revisionist leaders of the Communist Party of Austria."

On 28 May the Central Committee of the MLPÖ held a plenary session which dealt with the political and economic situation in Austria. Secretary Viktor Varga delivered the report. First Secretary Franz Strobl presented plans for the further development of the party organ *Rote Fahne*.

With regard to the international communist movement and international political events, the MLPÖ closely followed the line of Peking. Coverage was offered in *Rote Fahne* to developments among pro-Chinese parties. In 1967 the party organ published the message of a "recently founded" Communist Party of Poland to the Albanian Party of Labor Congress (November 1966) as well as documents of a Marxist-Leninist group in the Soviet Union. A special issue of *Rote Fahne* in March carried the complete text of a Central Committee declaration of the Communist Party of Indonesia. Instead of reporting on the Karlovy Vary conference in April, *Rote Fahne* reprinted a long letter in which the Communist Party of Holland explained to the French Communist Party why it could not attend the conference. On the Middle East crisis, the MLPÖ took a clear stand against Israel because of the support Israel received from the "forces of imperialism." The Arabs, on the other hand, insofar as they were victims of world-wide reaction and imperialism, deserved support, according to *Rote Fahne*. The whole 15 June issue of *Rote Fahne* was devoted to "Israel—Vanguard of International Monopoly Capital." An anti-Moscow orientation was also expressed in the position taken vis-à-vis Greece. Manolis Glezos, the hero of the Moscow press, was accused of having contributed, by his "revisionist politics," to the death "of hundreds, if not thousands of real communists and patriots" (*Rote Fahne* 15 May). In August the party organ reprinted excerpts from the Greek revolutionary paper *Metanastis* which not only pictured "imperialists" as responsible for the events in Greece, but also condemned the united-left front of the United Democratic Left (EDA) as a servant of the bourgeois classes and as "revisionist." The Glassboro meeting between Kosygin and President Johnson provoked outrage in the MLPÖ. "The history of mankind knows of no example of a dirtier treason," said *Rote Fahne,* on 1 July.

International activities of the MLPÖ in 1967 included talks at the end of February between First Secretary Strobl and Jacques Grippa, First Secretary of the pro-Chinese Communist Party of Belgium. These talks revealed "complete agreement." At the end of March, a MLPÖ delegation departed for a trip of several weeks to China. Late in April, Stefanie Helfert represented the MLPÖ at the Albanian trade-union congress; and early in May, Franz Strobl and two Central Committee members traveled to Albania to meet with party leader Enver Hoxha, Central Committee Secretary Ramiz Alia, and others. In June three members of the MLPÖ youth department attended the Fifth Congress of the

Youth League of Albania. On 23 June, MLPÖ functionaries met with members of the "Preparatory Committee for a Conference of Marxist-Leninist Unity of Great Britain" for talks in which there was "complete agreement in all questions discussed" (*ibid.*, 1 July). More than thirty activists of the MLPÖ, including seven members of the Central Committee, visited Albania in August for two weeks, under the leadership of First Secretary Strobl. There they not only met Central Committee Secretary Ramiz Alia of the Albanian Party of Labor on 21 August, but also had an opportunity for an exchange of views with delegations of the Communist Party of Belgium (Marxist-Leninist) under Jacques Grippa, the Communist Party of Italy (M-L), and the French Communist Movement (M-L) under Political Secretary Jacques Jurquet.

When Communist China detonated its first successful H-bomb explosion on 17 June, the MLPÖ sent a message of congratulations to the Chinese Communist Party; congratulations were sent also on the occasion of the eighteenth anniversary of the founding of the People's Republic of China in October.

**Publications.** The Communist Party of Austria publishes a daily organ, *Volksstimme,* whose editor in chief is Franz West, and a theoretical monthly, *Weg und Ziel,* whose editor in chief is Franz Marek.

The Marxist-Leninist Party of Austria publishes *Rote Fahne* twice a month; the editor is Franz Strobl. A rival splinter group publishes *Funke*, edited by Helmut Hronek.

# BELGIUM

The Belgian Communist Party (Le Parti Communiste Belge/Belgische Kommunistische Partij; PCB) was founded 3-4 September 1921. Its present membership has been estimated by Western sources at between 11,000 and 13,000. The population of Belgium is 9,528,000 (estimated 1966).

**Organization and Leadership.** The leadership of the PCB, elected following the party's 18th Congress (Brussels, 16-17 December 1967) by a Central Committee plenum of 27 January 1968 includes: President, Ernest Burnelle; Vice-Presidents, Frans Van den Branden and Marc Drumaux; Politburo: Jean Blume, Ernest Burnelle, Urbain Coussement, Jan Debrouwere, Marc Drumaux, Georges Glineur, Marcel Levaux, Gaston Moulin, Jean Terfve, Jef Turf, Frans Van den Branden, Louis Van Geyt; National Secretariat: Jean Blume, Ernest Burnelle, Urbain Coussement, Albert De Coninck, Jef Turf, Frans Van den Branden.

In spite of a gradual decline in party membership, the electoral strength of the PCB has slowly increased over recent years. In the last parliamentary elections (May 1965) the PCB obtained 236,333 votes, or 4.56 per cent of the total (as compared with 3.11 per cent in 1961) and six seats out of a total of 212 in the Belgian Chamber of Representatives and four seats out of 178 in the Senate. The Communists' success was largely attributed to the support they received from the left wing of the Belgian Socialist Party (Parti Socialiste Belge/Belgische Socialistiche Partij; PSB) who protested their party's collaboration with the more conservative Christian Social Party (Parti Social Chrétien/Kristelijk-Volkspartij; PSC). (In this election the PSB lost 460,000 votes and 20 seats in the Chamber of Representatives.) The PCB remains, however, comparatively weak, and on the municipal level holds only 165 out of a total of almost 24,000 posts.

Since 1966 the PCB has been divided into two branches, Walloon and Flemish, each of which directs the application of the party line in its own region. The two branches meet every year to make joint decisions and each has the right of veto. (In 1967 one branch, the Congress of the Wallonian Federations, convened on 19 March, and the other, the Congress of Flemish Regional Federations, on 2 April.) The ratio of Walloon members to Flemish in the party is five to one, however, and all six parliamentary representatives are Walloons. The limited influence of the party in the country is concentrated in the rather stagnant, traditional industrial and mining provinces of Hainaut and Liège, where economic conditions are unsatisfactory and adaptation to modern technology is slow, and in Brussels; influence in the Flemish part of the country is largely confined to Antwerp dockworkers.

The PCB directs a communist youth organization, the Communist Youth (Jeunesse Communiste), headed by Roger Dorsimond, which held a congress in Brussels on 18-19 November 1967. The party does not have its own trade union, but exerts some influence in the country's largest trade union, the General Workers' Federation of Belgium (Fédération Générale de Travail du Belgique/Algemeen Belgisch Vakverband; FGTB). The PCB also has some influence and leadership in the peace movement and in student organizations.

**Domestic Views and Activities.** According to the party program of 1963, which is still in effect today, the PCB aims at the destruction of the capitalist society and its replacement by a socialist society as a transitional stage toward communism. It claims to draw its inspiration from Marxist-Leninist doctrine and the experience of the international workers' movement.

The concept of the popular front is the central theme in the PCB's strategy against the present system in Belgium. In the view of the PCB, expressed near the end of 1967, the country is in a new period of political crisis and the main tasks of the Communists is to consolidate and expand the united action of workers and to develop "democratic political action." "The movement of the workers and of democracy must have governmental power," declared the resolution of the 18th

Congress of the PCB.

The opposition of the Belgian Socialist Party to the Liberal Christian coalition government since early 1966 is viewed by the Communists as a "promise of more significant changes, given well organized work among the masses and consistent struggle for democracy in the trade union" (*WMR,* March 1967).* In Parliament, the PCB's efforts were directed first of all at the government's request for special powers in view of the incipient economic crisis. The Communist parliamentary fraction repeatedly offered the Socialists its cooperation for an attack on the government, while reproaching the Socialists for being too mild in their acts of opposition. Lack of success in this endeavor was reflected in the resolution of the 18th Congress in which the PCB summed up the Christian Democrats' political activity of the liberal wing of the Christian Social Party as being "devoted to leaving the initiative to the representatives of monopoly" and charged that the Socialist Party "restricts its activity to a traditional opposition."

Communist political activity, notably in the attempt to create a permanent front for common action of Communists, Socialists and Christian Socialists has tended to shift from the parties to the trade unions, since all three parties have often defended the same interests on the local level or on the level of the enterprises. Such a front would be of unprecedented scope and could be created, according to the communists, "irrespective of ideological differences and organizational pluralism." The PCB declares that the trade unions must abandon the policy of peace with the "monopoly capitalist imperialists" and persuade the Belgian Socialist Party in particular as well as the liberal wing of the Christian Social Party to follow a more leftist course.

A second area of attention of the PCB is the problem of nationalities in Belgium and the issue of the federalization of the Flemish and Walloon sections of the country. In Wallonia the PCB promotes federalism as a remedy against economic regression. It blames the European Coal and Steel Community for making unprofitable many of the southern mines which have been closed. The European Economic Community, according to the Communists, now threatens what remains of heavy industry in the southern coal basins of Liège and Charleroi. In the Flemish section all initiatives connected with the Flemish movement are also supported by the PCB, which has attempted to put aside the traditional view of the movement as a "cultural movement" that the movement should be essentially economic and should bring the Flemish people their emancipation in the socioeconomic field. The Flemish movement as a whole has come to focus on the difficulties affecting the Catholic University of Louvain. Education in the regional language is made compulsory by law, and Louvain is in the Flemish section of the country. The university, where lectures were originally given only in French, still has a complete French speaking curriculum besides a complete Flemish one. In 1966 and 1967 the Communist press as a whole continually proclaimed that the university ought to be divided and the French part moved to Wallonia. Catholics regard this proposal as a communist attempt to destroy the university by splitting it. In November 1967, Communists incited some students to take part in a demonstration by protesting farmers in which the farmers' grievance (expropriation of land) was mingled with other themes, including the proposed dividing of the university. The ringleaders were members of the Students Trade Union (l'Union Etudiante Syndicale) in which the influence of communist ideas is strong.

Also during 1967 the PCB sought to intensify its "dialogue" with Catholics, and invited "progressive" priests to engage in public debate with prominent Communists. The PCB strongly propagandized the fact that a cardinal of the Roman Catholic Church, Jozef Cardijn, headed the organizing committee for a public demonstration for peace in Vietnam in Brussels on 4 March. The PCB was further active in organizing strikes and demonstrations in factories in protest of rising living costs, dismissals, closures of enterprises, and emergency powers of the government. The Communists demanded that factories threatened with closure should be placed under sequestration.

**International Views and Policies.** At the center of the PCB's activities, as decided by the 17th

---

*In early 1966 the Christian Social/Socialist coalition government of Pierre Harmel was replaced by a coalition of the Christian Socialists and the Liberals (Party of Liberty and Progress headed by Paul Vanden Boeynants), while the Socialists went into opposition.

Congress of the party, in December 1966, was the policy of struggle for peace in Vietnam and for Belgium's withdrawal from the NATO military alliance. In his report to a Central Committee plenum on 16 September, Ernest Burnelle stated: "We must devote ourselves to the task of promoting the realization of the idea of the need to liquidate military blocs, the solution of the disarmament problem and recognition of the German Democratic Republic, and also to the idea put forward at the Karlovy Vary Conference for holding a meeting of European states, devoting all our energy to the cause of halting the evil US aggression in Vietnam, of letting Vietnam achieve peace and freedom." (TASS, 29 September 1967.)

Countless demonstrations and propaganda campaigns against the Vietnam war were organized or strongly supported by the PCB. Participants in the most important demonstrations, on 4 March in Brussels, were estimated to number between 2,000 and 10,000. Another large demonstration was held on 23 April, protesting atomic weapons and calling for disarmament.

The PCB attitude on the Middle East conflict of mid-1967 was one of strong support for the Arab cause. Fearful of alienating Jewish opinion in Belgium, the PCB judged it necessary to announce this pro-Arab stand only gradually and to draw a clear distinction between "Jews in Belgium" and "Jews in Israel."

Looking ahead to 1968, the PCB set itself four major tasks:

1. Work for withdrawal from NATO, for a wide political debate on this issue, for European security, for the dissolving of military blocs. Combat the aggressive acts of US imperialism and develop the campaign to call an immediate halt to the American bombing of North Vietnam.

2. Action for guaranteeing employment and the standard of living, against the shutdowns, for the application of the system of controlled industrial management, for planning development and investment, for the establishment of Flemish and Walloon societies endowed with powers of initiative enabling them to create new industry. Suspension in 1968 of all dismissals and shutdowns and a rapid convocation of a national conference on employment. Increased wages.

3. Use of the state budget to combat the big firms and banks and application of a social, fiscal, and financial policy adapted to the interests of the country. Reduction of the military budget.

4. Democratization of public life by creating federalist organs of orientation and by applying labor control at all levels of the public and private sectors. Recourse to a referendum of popular initiative. (Resolution of the 18th Congress, *Le Drapeau Rouge*, no. 51, Brussels, 22 December 1967.)

**The International Communist Movement.** In the international communist movement, the PCB firmly supports the Communist Party of the Soviet Union, and the policy of peaceful coexistence, which, as Ernest Burnelle remarked to the Central Committee plenum in September 1967, "makes it possible to rally the masses around the idea of peace and to isolate the enemies of the people, the imperialists." (TASS, 29 September 1967.)

The PCB was one of the earliest supporters of the idea of convening an international conference of communist parties. Ernest Burnelle endorsed the proposal at the PCB's 17th Congress, in late 1966, noting that six years had passed since the 1960 conference and that it was necessary to meet to review the international situation and rally the ranks of the communist movement.

The PCB condemned events in China and their effect on the international scene in the harshest terms. "It is a giant drama which is taking place in China." *Drapeau Rouge* stated on 13 January 1967, "Drama which, by disfiguring socialism and dividing the forces of peace, constitutes an unexpected windfall for the imperialists."

In April the PCB was represented at the Conference of European Communist and Workers' Parties in Karlovy Vary by its National Secretary, Jean Blume. In his speech to the assembly Blume proposed a pan-European conference, in which all countries of Europe would take part and to which all political and trade union organizations, communist as well as socialist and Christian, would be invited. Such a gathering, according to Blume, ought to take place before the re-forming of NATO in order to furnish a possible contribution to the simultaneous dissolution of NATO and the Warsaw Pact. Although the PCB requested that this proposal be included in the conference resolution, it did not appear there. Blume also opposed the establishment of NATO on Belgian territory.

The PCB held a number of bilateral meetings with other communist parties. On 18-20 January a PCB delegation visited Czechoslovakia and held talks with representatives of the Communist Party of Czechoslovakia on problems of European security. In August, during a vacation in the Soviet Union, Ernest Burnelle held talks with Soviet party leaders on the international situation and the communist and workers' movement. Reports on the talks affirmed "the identity of views of the two parties on the problems discussed." Burnelle returned to the Soviet Union in November to participate in the celebrations of the fiftieth anniversary of the October Revolution.

On 20-29 September a PCB delegation visited Rumania and held talks with Rumanian party leaders including Secretary-General Nicolae Ceauşescu.

* * *

The Communist Party of Belgium, Marxist-Leninist (PCB-ML) was founded in 1963 by PCB dissidents who opposed the party's alignment with the "revisionism" of the Soviet Communists. Jacques Grippa, a former member of the central committee of the PCB heads the group. In January 1962, the dissidents took the side of the Chinese Communists, forming the first pro-Peking movement among European communist bodies. On December 22, 1963, a national conference established the breakaway group as the PCB-ML.

Estimates suggest that as much as 20 per cent of the PCB membership in Brussels and 30 per cent in Liège have switched to the new party, but no precise figures as to its strength are known. Election returns show that the PCB-ML controls 10 per cent of the communist vote. The party is not represented in Parliament.

In 1966 and 1967 the PCB-ML was plagued with factions, splits, and expulsions, and by the end of 1967 the original Grippa group appeared to be a minority. Earlier, in September 1965, Maurice Massoz, a Politburo member and second in importance to Grippa, was expelled for "irregularities." (His group subsequently split.) In June 1966 about 15 persons, including Politburo members M. Delogne and A. Moerenhout from Brussels and a Flanders group headed by Von Turnhout were expelled. In June 1967 in an extensive purge the principal leaders of four of the five of the Walloon federations were dismissed, including Jacques Trifaux, secretary of the Charleroi Federation, along with a body known as the "Central Committee of the Walloon Communist Party." Also dismissed were Arnold Hauwaert, an editor of the party organ, *La Voix du Peuple,* and Jeanne Vercheval-Vervoort, secretary of the PCR-ML front organization APIP (Action pour la Paix et L'Independence des Peuples) and chief instigator of the "Committee of Young Anti-Imperialists" affiliated with APIP. Jeanne Vervoort was subsequently expelled from the Trifaux-Hauwaerts faction also, in December.

Differences between Jacques Grippa and the Trifaux-Hauwaert faction appeared to be with reference to the communist Chinese "cultural revolution" and to reflect the conflict between Mao Tse-tung and Liu Shao-ch'i. The expelled faction addressed a letter to party militants on 21 June stating that Grippa had "stopped approving of the cultural revolution" when he attacked the theory of "servile submission." They also intimated that *La Voix du Peuple* had followed orders from Grippa in refusing to follow Mao and his partisans and attack Liu Shao-ch'i. The Trifaux-Hauwaert faction has the support of "Walloon Communist Party" activists and has perhaps 100 members in Hainaut, principally in Charleroi, and about six in Liège. It publishes the weekly *L'Exploité.*

Grippa's support for the Liu Shao-ch'i line was criticized by the Communist Youth Movement leader Michel Graindorge in a wall poster which provoked Grippa, supported by the PCB-ML Central Committee, to condemn him. Expelled on 29 September, Graindorge and another Politburo member Jules Vanderlinden took with them Central Committee members Fernand Lefebvre, Emile Remy, and Henri Glineur, thus leaving behind a Politburo of three members: Jacques Grippa, René Raindorf, and Stéphane Struelens. The dissidents, "suspended" by the remaining Politburo members, also included Julius Relecom Xavier, Jean-Claude Cols, and Marthe Huysmans, secretary of the "Association Belgique-Chine." The dissidents are supported by what was left of the

Walloon Communist Party and a group of communist students at the Free University of Brussels, called the "Union of Majority Communist Students."

The Graindorge-Vanderlinden group summoned a national conference on 19 November at Louvière which, according to the group's organ *Clarté* (22 December) was attended by 117 delegates. The conference condemned Jacques Grippa and his faction as "followers of the Chinese Khrushchev" and as "activists of another variety of modern revisionism." The conference decided that the group take on the name Communist Party (Marxist-Leninist) of Belgium. The newly elected Central Committee met on 3 December and expelled Jacques Grippa, René Raindorf, and Stéphane Struelens.

The Jacques Grippa group, numbering about 70, continues to edit *La Voix du Peuple,* controls the party offices in Brussels and Charleroi and those belonging to Livre International, the party-owned publishing house. Its militant base is reduced to the promoters of two theatrical troups—the "Theatre Populaire de Belgique" in Brussles and the "Bateau Ivre" in Liège—and some young Communists in those cities. According to a dissident socialist group in Belgium, Grippa stopped receiving funds from Peking in the summer of 1967 and has sought support from the North Korean communist leader Kim Il-song (*La Gauche* [organ of dissident socialist group] 16 December).

The Grippa group carried on an intense and vicious campaign against an American Communist in Peking named Sidney Rittenberg, who allegedly had criticized Jacques Grippa. A series of long articles appearing in *La Voix du Peuple* in November and December accused Rittenberg of leading a "cosmopolitan" communist faction and also denounced the Graindorge-Vanderlinden dissidents as "puppets of an international band, having as its center an anti-revolutionary cosmopolitan group headed by an American named Sidney Rittenberg." (*La Voix du Peuple,* 15 December.) (The word "cosmopolitan" has often been used in communist terminology to denote Jewish members; in this case, Graindorge had earlier been charged with insisting that the PCB-ML revise its position of total support for the Arabs in the Middle East crisis and recognize the "rights" of Israel. [*La Voix du Peuple,* 3 November].)

In addition to issuing polemics against factions within the PCB-ML membership, the Grippa group continued to denounce the "revisionist traitors" of the pro-Moscow PCB. Commenting on the 18th Congress of the PCB, *La Voix du Peuple* (29 December) declared:

Following the international Khrushchevite lead, this group approved two parallel courses of action: on the international level, collaboration with American imperialism and, on the national level, a policy reflecting their desire to revive the faltering capitalist system and administer it to their own advantage.

The "Khrushchevite revisionists" were also subject to severe denunciation. On the occasion of the fiftieth anniversary of the October Revolution Jacques Grippa declared:

Who are these Khrushchevite revisionist representatives of a privileged stratum, of a new bourgeoisie. They have destroyed the Communist Party of the Soviet Union as a Marxist-Leninist Party. They had destroyed the dictatorship of the proletariat and installed a police state of bourgeois dictatorship. In the countries of revisionist orientation one can see all the blemishes of the capitalist regime reappearing—the exploitation of man by man, unemployment, prostitution, etc. (*La Voix du Peuple,* 15 December.)

The Grippa group continues to be highly vocal despite its minority status, since it retains the newspaper *La Voix du Peuple,* the party office premises, and the bulk of the party funds.

On the domestic front the PCB-ML waged campaigns protesting the settling of SHAPE on Belgian territory and Belgian participation in NATO. It also denounced the assumption of special powers by the government, the closure of factories, the dismissal of workers, and the rising cost of living. The party participated in numerous demonstrations together with the PCB and other left-wing groups, but without compromising their views on the Socialists and the Moscow-oriented Communists. In the 4 March demonstrations of solidarity with Vietnam PCB-ML participants carried banners condemning US-Soviet efforts to negotiate in the Vietnamese conflict.

The Grippa group held the 15th Congress of the PCB-ML on 28-30 October (the National Conference of December 1963 which established the PCB-ML was considered the 14th Congress). The congress assessed with great optimism what it termed the deepening crisis of capitalism, the suffocating of imperialism by revolutionary peoples, and the coming victory of the proletarian revolution. The congress reaffirmed "solidarity with the Vietnamese people," repeated earlier pledges that the party was ready to respond to any appeal by the Vietnamese people for volunteers, and declared that it "considered itself mobilized locally in the struggle against the Yankee-Nazis." The congress also declared support for the "Congolese resistance," Negroes in the USA, and the "revolutionary fighters" of Spain, Greece, Portugal, Indonesia, and India. The congress reaffirmed solidarity with the Chinese people, the Chinese Communist Party, and "the revolutionary Chinese people engaged in a gigantic and complex class struggle enlightened by the thought of Comrade Mao Tse-tung." Solidarity with Albania was also reasserted. (*La Voix du Peuple,* 3 November 1967.)

**Publications.** The PCB publishes the weekly *Le Drapeau Rouge* and three times a week the four page bulletin *PCB Information.* The party also publishes a weekly in Flemish, *De Rode Vaan.*

The central organs of the PCB-ML are the weekly *La Voix du Peuple* and a Flemish monthly *De Strijd.* Organs of the Communist Youth Movement are *L'Etoile Rouge, En Avant* and *Que Faire.* Among the PCB-ML's other publications are those of party cells in the various enterprises: *La Vérité, Le Radar, L'Eclaireur, A L'Action,* and *Au Combat.* The PCB-ML directs a publishing house in Brussels, Livre International.

The Trifaux-Hauwaert faction publishes the weekly *L'Exploité.* The Graindorge-Vanderlinden faction publishes the weekly *Clarté.*

# BOLIVIA

The communist movement in Bolivia, which encompasses a number of rival parties and factions, includes organized parties adhering to Soviet, Chinese, and Trotskyist alignments: the Communist Party of Bolivia (Partido Comunista de Bolivia; PCB), founded in 1950, and its pro-Chinese counterpart, also called the Communist Party of Bolivia (PCB-II) founded in 1965; and the Trotskyist Revolutionary Workers' Party (Partido Obrero Revolucionario; POR), founded in 1940, which is split into two rival factions (see below). Party membership is estimated at 4,000 and 1,000 for the PCB and the PCB-II respectively; the two POR factions are believed to have a combined membership of 1,000. As a result of disturbances in the Bolivian mining sector and outbreaks of guerrilla activity, all the above parties were banned on 11 April 1967 and a number of their leaders were arrested. Communist influence and support is not confined, however, to these parties (see below). Furthermore, the ruling Bolivian Revolutionary Front (Frente de la Revolución Boliviana; FRB) includes the Party of the Revolutionary Left (Partido de la Izquierda Revolucionaria; PIR), a party of "Marxist intellectuals," with an estimated membership of 1,000. The population of Bolivia is 3,801,000 (estimated 1967).

Even before April 1967, none of the outlawed parties appeared to have significant national support. During the elections of 1966 communist candidacy was confined to the PCB, which presented itself in the coalition of the National Liberation Front (Frente de Liberación Nacional; FLIN), which obtained 33,054 votes out of a total of 1,012,448 and came second from last with 3.3 per cent of the poll and no representation in the Congress (see *YICA*, 1966, pp. 184-85).

The major sources of support for the various communist groups appear to be within the mining sector and among students. By the end of 1967, however, the complex but relatively discernible characteristics of political alignment of the extreme left in 1966 (see *YICA*, 1966, pp. 184-89) were no longer evident in 1967, nor were the scope of the support and its delineation with regard to the different parties. The failure of the extreme left to provide active support to the guerrilla movement led by Ernesto "Che" Guevara (see below), with the resultant alienation of Castroist-oriented sectors, particularly among students, engendered controversy within the parties and between them and their supporters. Furthermore, the outlawing of most of the communist groups and the arrest of a number of their leaders compounded the fluidity of the political scene on the extreme left. Party pronouncements, in view of the irregular appearance of party publications, most of which were banned in the spring, resulted in a plethora of contradictory statements from unreliable sources. Finally, some parties' stands tended to change during the course of the year with concomitant repudiation of earlier pronouncements—particularly in connection with the development of guerrilla activity and the parties' respective involvement in it.

**PCB.** The pro-Soviet Communist Party of Bolivia, led by First Secretary Mario Monje Molina until his resignation in late 1967 and replacement by Jorge Kolle Cueto, underwent a series of apparent organizational changes during 1967 and by the end of the year no reliable published information was available regarding the party's leadership or structure. Two other prominent members of the party are Aldo Flores and Ramiro Otero, both of whom represented the PCB at the Havana conference of the Latin American Solidarity Organization (Organización Lationoamericana de Solidaridad; OLAS), 31 July-10 August, with Flores acting as Chairman of the Bolivian delegation.

The PCB's principal front organization, the aforementioned FLIN, was launched in the mining area of Siglo Veinte in April 1964. The FLIN is intimately linked to the pro-Soviet PCB camp, but endeavors to represent itself as an "alternative" party of national "anti-imperialist" unity. So far, only the PCB is aligned with it, and it is faced with "competition" from a similar Democratic

Committee of the People (Comité Democrático del Pueblo; CODEP), which encompasses most of the other extreme left-wing groups. Support for the FLIN is very limited, despite communist assertions that it is a "vast, single front movement . . . the pole of attraction for the forces that are fighting in Bolivia for national liberation" (*Unidad,* 27 August 1966). No membership figures are known. The leaders of the FLIN are Fernando Siñani Baldivieso (Secretary-General), Mario Miranda Pacheco (Executive Secretary), and Dr. Humberto Rhea (Secretary for Organization). In contrast to the PCB, the FLIN was not outlawed in 1967.

PCB relations with the Revolutionary Party of the Nationalist Left (Partido Revolucionario de Izquierda Nacionalista; PRIN) are somewhat more complex. Founded in 1964 as a left-wing splinter group of the National Revolutionary Movement (Movimiento Nacionalista Revolucionario; MNR), which was the governing party in Bolivia between 1952 and 1964, the PRIN is headed by Juan Lechin Oquendo, a prominent labor leader and former Vice-President of Bolivia. PCB interests in the PRIN have been focused on the person of Lechin Oquendo, who, though in exile, has had considerable influence within Bolivian labor, particularly among the mineworkers, being Secretary of the communist-oriented Trade Union Federation of Mineworkers of Bolivia (Federación Sindical de Trabajadores Mineros de Bolivia; FSTMB). Controversy between the PCB and PRIN was already evident in 1965 when the PRIN joined CODEP, with its pro-Chinese and Trotskyist elements, and tended to support the latter's stands among the mineworkers. In 1967 the PRIN, with the advent of guerrilla activity, serious disturbances in the mines, and a leader in exile, underwent a series of organizational crises which were precipitated in part by the PRIN leadership's failure to respond effectively to the year's events and compounded by the outlawing of the party in April. PCB relations were thus with an organization that appeared to be uncertain as to its own policies. In early 1968 Mario Monje admitted that it had been necessary to clear up "some misunderstandings," but claimed that the PCB was resuming "fruitful dialogues with the leaders of PRIN and progressive groups of the MNR in order to be able to consolidate the anti-imperialist national political front" (*El Diario,* La Paz, 5 February).

The PCB has its own youth organization, the Bolivian Communist Youth (Juventud Comunista Boliviana; JCB), which works in cooperation with the FLIN's youth movement, the National Liberation University Front (Frente Universitario de Liberación Nacional; FULN). The degree of control exercised by the PCB and FLIN on their respective youth movements appeared in 1967 to be on the decline.

**Domestic Views and Policies.** During 1967 the party's stand on domestic policy oscillated between the advocacy of a broad "anti-imperialist front" that would attain power peacefully by the mobilization of the masses, and whose "most important instrument for achieving unity" would be the FLIN (see R. Otero in *WMR,* April 1967), and the expressing of verbal support for the guerrillas in southern Bolivia, as in statements that in Bolivia "there is no possibility for peaceful changes" and that "the most important thing now is to convince the people that the arduous way offers no other alternative but the struggle" (speech of the Bolivian delegation at the OLAS conference, in Conference Documents).

Otero's article in the *World Marxist Review* claimed that, in cooperation with the PRIN, the PCB had succeeded in averting the " 'leftism' of Trotskyites and other splitters," who were jeopardizing "the process of unity in the lower trade union organizations." He went on to point out, however, that "work to achieve unity in the countryside, to reorganize the peasant movement," was proceeding "much more slowly and with greater difficulty," adding: "This is due to the fact that the more important rural areas are controlled by the bureaucracy and the military, to the illusions harbored by the peasantry that their gains which are threatened by the ex-latifundists will be preserved, to the demagogy of the military around the so-called 'civil action' plan."

Referring to the 1966 elections, Otero claimed that its results had "confirmed the soundess of the Party's position, that the Front [FLIN] is a real force in the political life of the country." Thus the PCB appeared to be oriented toward electoral politics, but Otero added:

> After correctly assessing the scale and importance of the work accomplished, the Party decided that it would use every opportunity to extend its work among the masses. At the

same time, it has no illusions that the enemy will renounce the brutal measures employed to maintain the regime of exploitation and foreign dependence. The Party knows from experience that simply to proclaim one's readiness to use all forms of struggle—peaceful and nonpeaceful—is not enough. We have to be prepared when the time arrives to assume revolutionary responsibility.

It would appear, however, that the PCB viewed the appearance of guerrilla activity in 1967 and its own outlawing as insufficient evidence that the time had come to "assume revolutionary responsibility." Despite numerous verbal expressions of solidarity with the cause of the guerrillas led by Guevara and its own initial involvement in the preparatory stages of the guerrilla operation,* the PCB offered no active support to Guevara. According to Fidel Castro, the PCB, under Monje's orders, went even further and "began to sabotage the movement, intercepting well-trained communist militants in La Paz who were going to join the guerrilla" (Fidel Castro's "Necessary Introduction" to *The Diary of Che Guevara,* as published by *Ramparts,* San Francisco, 27 July 1968).

Following the death of "Che" Guevara on 9 October and the elimination of guerrilla activity, Jorge Kolle Cueto granted an interview to the organ of the Communist Party of Chile, *El Siglo* (25 October). While paying tribute to Guevara, he stated that guerrilla activity had been premature and had not been based on a correct evaluation of the "political and social factors necessary for [its] development." The PCB, according to Kolle, had supported the guerrillas in principle, but, as the party had foreseen, it had not been possible to organize "active, concrete support" for them. Kolle's remarks in October contrasted somewhat with his statements to *El Siglo* on 14 May, when he said that the PCB believed that guerrilla warfare had broken out in Bolivia "at the right moment" and claimed that the party was giving the guerrillas "full support."

**International Views and Policies.** The PCB is not known to have made any significant statements on international affairs during 1967. It appeared to continue to align itself steadfastly with the Soviet Union on matters concerning the international communist movement. Its relations with Cuba, though outwardly friendly during the course of the year, are likely to have been affected unfavorably by the revelations of Guevara's diaries.

The PCB was represented by an unnamed delegation at the celebrations in the Soviet Union of the fiftieth anniversary of the October Revolution.

**Publications.** The PCB's central organ is the weekly *Unidad,* which, banned in April 1967, appeared irregularly during the rest of the year. The views of FLIN are carried by the weekly *El Pueblo,* which remained legal.

**PCB-II.** The pro-Chinese Communist Party of Bolivia originated from dissident elements of the PCB during the period from 1952 to 1964, when the PCB collaborated extensively with the MNR government. It was not officially founded, however, until April 1965, when a "First Extraordinary National Congress" of the PCB-II was held in the mining area of Siglo Veinte. The meeting united various dissident pro-Chinese elements with the already formed (1962) Espartaco youth group of Federico Escobar, who died in November 1966.

Very little reliable information was available in 1967 on the leadership and organization of the PCB-II. Most of the prominent leaders of the party at the time of the 1965 congress, whose names were made public (see *YICA,* 1966, p. 187), were not referred to during the course of the year. The series of arrests by the Bolivian government of pro-Chinese militants in early 1967 appeared to include only a few of the 1965 leadership. It is known, however, that the First Secretary of the PCB-II is Oscar Zamora Medinacelli. Following Zamora's arrest in January 1967, party communiques were signed by National Secretary Justiniano Ninavia; following his arrest in March, communiques were signed by Ricardo Romero. Daniel Campos was reported by NCNA on 3 January as being a member of the party's Secretariat.

---

*For a detailed account of the guerrilla operation in Bolivia and the preparations that preceeded it, including the complete diaries of "Che" Guevara and three of his lieutenants, see *The Complete Bolivian Diaries of Ché Guevara and Other Captured Documents,* edited and with an introduction by Daniel James, New York, Stein and Day, 1968. For a Soviet version see *New Times,* Moscow (Russian edition only), 18 October 1968.

The PCB-II has its own youth movement, known under the same name as its pro-Soviet counterpart, the Juventud Comunista de Bolivia (JCB). The leader of this JCB is believed to be Antonio Alurralde. The pro-Chinese Bolivian communists sponsored the creation in the summer of 1966 of a "United Anti-Imperialist Youth Front," whose President appears to be Dulfredo Rua.

The party concentrates its activities in the Bolivian mining sector. As a consequence, its alignments with other parties and groups are determined by the influence of such "allies" in this sector. Following unrest in the mines in June 1967, however, most of the prominent pro-Chinese (and pro-Soviet) miners' leaders were arrested. Indications as to the PCB-II's relative support in the mines as compared to other political groups in terms of local electoral returns (available in 1966, *YICA*, 1966, p. 188) could in 1967 no longer be considered valid.

**Domestic Views and Policies.** The PCB-II follows pro-Chinese theory with regard to revolutionary strategy. Although advocating armed struggle, it feels that preparatory work among the masses must preceed any armed action. The party was reported to have interpreted the appearance of guerrillas in Bolivia as signifying that the Bolivian people "can stand [repression] no longer," but while reiterating that "revolution by armed struggle is the only way to the people's liberation," the PCB-II, unlike its pro-Soviet counterpart, did not claim that it was offering its active support to the guerrillas (*Peking Review,* 28 April). Following the death of "Che" Guevara, an article in the PCB-II organ *Liberación* (reported by *Peking Review,* 19 January 1968) stated: "If we depart from Mao Tse-tung's thought and try to wage an armed struggle without the masses, standing above them and looking down upon them, we will court severe and utter defeats." The article concluded:

> The armed struggle waged for the victory of the revolution, the revolutionary people's war, is not a question to be treated lightly. Heroic acts alone, no matter how magnificent they may be, will not suffice. First of all, it is necessary to bring the masses of the people on to this road and mobilize them politically and militarily, and then lead them with courage, with a new kind of heroism, revolutionary proletarian heroism. We must not waste needful energy on wrong actions. Above all, it is necessary for all revolutionaries, particularly those in our country, to understand that it is impossible to have "united action" with the revisionist in the armed struggle, because they are the sworn enemy of the revolution, who are always ready to sell it out, betray the fighters and shatter their morale as they have done before, and then in the face of "the defeat of the armed struggle," try to re-sell the dirty stock of "peaceful road" to us.

The PCB-II did not participate in "Che" Guevara's guerrilla group and thus, like its pro-Soviet counterpart, incurred the displeasure of Fidel Castro, who referred to Oscar Zamora (in the aforementioned "Necessary Introduction" to Guevara's diaries) as "another Monje, who . . . cowardly folded his arms when the hour for action arrived, becoming one of the most poisonous critics in the name of 'Marxism-Leninism' after Che's death."

**International Views and Policies.** The PCB-II adheres steadfastly to a pro-Chinese alignment. A party delegation was reported as having visited Albania in July (*La Voix du Peuple,* Brussels, 18 August).

**Publications.** The central organ of the PCB-II is the clandestine fortnightly newspaper *Liberación*. The party's JCB publishes an irregular, clandestine journal, *Venceremos.*

**POR.** The Trotskyist movement in Bolivia is divided into two factions, both claiming the name of Partido Obrero Revolucionario. One faction is led by Guillermo Lora and publishes a clandestine fortnightly newspaper, *Masas.* The other faction, led by Hugo Gonzales Moscoso and Amadeo Vargas Arze, adheres to the Fourth International—United Secretariat and publishes a clandestine fortnightly, *Lucha Obrera.* Both factions appear to cooperate with the pro-Chinese forces in Bolivia, and to give qualified support to the Chinese Communist Party in the Sino-Soviet conflict. While expressing verbal support of the guerrilla movement led by "Che" Guevara, neither of the two parties offered active support to the guerrillas.

\* \* \*

The guerrilla movement that operated in Bolivia during 1967 was led by Ernesto "Che" Guevara. At its maximum strength it counted only 51 participants: 18 Cubans, 29 Bolivians, three Peruvians, and one East German. By the end of the year only five guerrillas had survived (three Cubans and two Bolivians); all the rest had been killed or captured, or had deserted. The three Cubans escaped to Cuba via Chile. The two Bolivians—Guido Peredo Leigue and David Adriazola Veizaga—are believed to be in hiding in Bolivia.

The guerrilla operation, which was apparently planned in its initial stages as early as January 1966 (at the time of the "Tricontinental" Conference in Havana, 3-15 January), entered a new phase with the arrival of "Che" Guevara in La Paz on 3 November 1966. The first encounter between guerrillas and Bolivian troops took place on 23 March 1967, following which the guerrillas adopted the name "National Liberation Army of Bolivia" (Ejercito de Liberación Nacional de Bolivia; ELNB or ELN).

The campaign, which geographically was limited to southwestern Bolivia, near the town of Camiri, lasted till 8 October, ending with the capture of "Che" Guevara and his death (9 October). During the period of actual combat, "Che" Guevara's group included individual participants from various sectors of the Bolivian extreme left, but did not have the active support of their respective parties.

The guerrilla operation engendered considerable repercussions, both domestic and international. It was brought to the world's attention—before the revelation that "Che" Guevara was leading it—by the capture on 20 April of Jules Régis Debray, the French author of *Revolution in the Revolution?* (see *Cuba*). Debray, who had been present in the guerrilla group, was sentenced on 17 November to thirty years' imprisonment.

# BRAZIL

The original Communist Party of Brazil (Partido Comunista do Brasil; PCdoB) was founded in 1922. In 1960 its name was changed to the Brazilian Communist Party (Partido Comunista Brasileiro; PCB). In 1961 a pro-Chinese faction broke away from the PCB. Adopting the party's original name, in February 1962 this faction founded a rival Communist Party of Brazil. During 1967 the PCB was confronted with further dissidence, this time of a Castroist variety (see below).

With the overthrow of President João Goulart in April 1964, the PCB, which though illegal had been operating freely, suffered a severe setback, accentuated by the new government's seizure of notebooks giving the party's organization and structure. PCB membership, estimated to be about 40,000 at that time, is believed to have dropped to 15,000 or 20,000 by 1967. Estimates as to the membership of the pro-Chinese PCdoB range between 1,000 and 3,000. No reliable membership estimates were available in 1967 for the Castroist dissidents, a number of whom were instrumental in the founding of a Revolutionary Brazilian Communist Party in April 1968. The population of Brazil is 84,679,000 (estimated 1966).

**Organization and Leadership.** There is little information available as to the composition of the leadership of the PCB. The party's Secretary-General is Luís Carlos Prestes, and the following appear to be prominent members: José Santos, Armando Ziller, Giocondo Dias, Lucas Romao, Alfredo Castro, J. B. Tavares de Sa, Augusto Bento, Iracama Ribeiro, Olga Maranhao, Jorge Vila, Sabino Bahia, Felipe Rodrigues, Maria Segovia, Abel Chermont, Luis Tenorio de Lima, Gentil Correa, Firmino de Lima, Marcel Braz, Luis Menesse, and Valerio Kondor. At the PCB's Sixth Congress, held clandestinely in early December 1967, Executive Committee member Carlos Marighella and Central Committee members Jover Teles, Mario Alves de Souza Vieira, Jacob Gorender, Camara Ferreira, Apolonio de Carvalho, and Miguel Batista were expelled from the party for engaging in "factional activities" (see below).

Whereas under Goulart the PCB had succeeded in infiltrating and even controlling important labor, student, political, and bureaucratic groups, the Castelo Branco regime on coming into office after Goulart's overthrow either abolished or rendered powerless the organizations led by Communists or by their sympathizers. Repressive measures applied against the PCB by Castelo Branco and his successor, Costa e Silva, in 1966-67, were compounded in 1967 by a challenge to the party from the Castroist left. By the end of the year the PCB appeared to have lost all its influence in the banned National Union of Students (União Nacional dos Estudantes; UNE), one of the party's few remaining sources of qualified support. The Twenty-ninth Congress of the UNE took place clandestinely in São Paulo in late July and early August. Dominated by the extremist Christian-Marxist organization Ação Popular (AP), which advocates revolutionary violence, the congress condemned both the PCB and the Soviet-controlled International Union of Students. The PCB attacked the UNE leaders in the July 1967 issue of its organ *A Voz Operaria*, complaining that many members of the student organization had been won over to the "erroneous policy" of its leadership. The UNE, headed by AP member Luis Gonsaga Travassos, advocated a student-worker-peasant alliance, the eventual goal being to set up a "workers' state." In contrast to PCB policy, the UNE excluded the middle classes from its "united front."

**Domestic Views and Policies.** The confrontation between Cuban and Soviet views of Latin American revolutionary strategy was reflected vividly in the PCB's internal party life and its approach to domestic issues. During 1967 the challenge to veteran pro-Soviet Luís Carlos Prestes' advocacy of a broad "united front" policy of "peaceful change" confronted the PCB with an internal crisis of major proportion. Opposition to Prestes appeared to be primarily centered around Castroist-oriented Carlos

45

Marighella, whose resignations and exclusions from the PCB hierarchy during the course of the year (Marighella's original letter of resignation from the PCB's Executive Committee was dated 10 December 1966—see *Pensamiento Critico,* Havana, August 1967) culminated in the aforementioned formal expulsion from the party in December. Marighella's attendance, as an observer, at the Havana conference of the Latin American Solidarity Organization (OLAS) in the summer of 1967, in defiance of PCB directives, resulted in recriminations between the party and Marighella and his followers.

Although the extent of anti-Prestes dissidence could not be clearly delineated, a document entitled "For the Unity of the Party"—published in the October issue of *A Voz Operaria*—indicated that opposition to party policy was to be found in the PCB state committees of São Paulo, Rio Grande do Sul, and Rio de Janeiro. In Guanabara a dissident group had established a separate PCB State Committee and their own newspaper from which they attacked the Central Committee. In October a meeting of representatives of these four state committees, enlarged by the participation of delegates from Espirito Santo, Ceará, and the Federal District of Brasilia, released a statement denouncing the "opportunist orientation" of the PCB's Central Committee. The participants at the meeting committed themselves to "simultaneous struggle against revisionist and opportunist tendencies and dogmatic and sectarian tendencies." While claiming that the "immediate and fundamental task" was the "unleashing of armed struggle—guerrilla warfare," and that the "Brazilian revolution . . . should join, under the OLAS banner, the revolutionary struggle that the fraternal peoples of Latin America are waging against the common enemy," the dissidents qualified their Castroist orientation by stating:

> In view of the differences in the world communist movement, we consider it necessary to maintain an independent position, refusing to follow any fraternal party uncritically. Our role consists in planning in an independent manner revolutionary guidance adapted to the conditions in Brazil, taking into consideration conditions in the world, but especially in our country.

In an attempt to counteract dissidence within its ranks, the PCB held its Sixth Congress in early December. Althought reports on the congress, which was held clandestinely, were available in December and in the early months of 1968 (see *Jornal do Brasil,* Rio de Janeiro, 31 December 1967), a full PCB analysis and evaluation only appeared belatedly in the June issue of *World Marxist Review*, in an article written by Prestes.

Commenting on the fact that the congress was preceeded by predictions of a split in the party, Prestes claimed: "The Congress was a big success for the Party. [It] rejected the anti-Marxist concepts concerning the character of the Brazilian revolution, condemned the splitters and upheld the Leninist organizational principles. . . . The Congress was also a striking manifestation of the inner-Party democracy in our ranks and of the Party's viability which has not been undermined by the blows of reaction, by the differences in the international Communist movement." Further, the PCB Secretary-General stated:

> The Congress was preceeded by long discussion in the course of which our members freely expressed critical views about the Central Committee's "Theses" and its work as the Party's leading body. The Central Committee put out 17 issues of *Tribuna de Debates,* a fortnightly supplement to its central paper, on whose pages over a hundred comrades expressed their views. Hundreds of branch meetings were held; these were followed by district, municipal and state-level conferences. This free discussion, lasting eight months, proceeded in complex conditions, conditions when the Party and its unity were imperiled from without and in its own ranks.

According to Prestes, the discussion before the congress "evolved in the final analysis as a struggle between two opposite concepts of revolution":

> the Marxist-Leninist concept which regards revolution as part of the mass movement that arises whenever the necessary objective and subjective conditions are created, even though these are shaped by the character of the historical period and place, and the non-Marxist, petty-bourgeois concept of the "guerrilla center" which regards revolution as an impulsive act by a courageous minority, able by the example of its armed actions to enlist the

masses in revolutionary struggle, irrespective of the concrete situation.

Following a lengthy analysis of the PCB's failure to respond effectively to the 1964 coup, Prestes noted that the Sixth Congress "rejected the view that the main mistakes made by the Party were the consequence of a Right deviation and noted that they were, on the contrary, mistakes of a Leftist, putschist and petty-bourgeois character." Prestes claimed that the Brazilian "dictatorship" had lost most of its followers: "Its sole political supporters are the reactionary bourgeoisie and the big landowners, while the armed forces are its sole material support." According to the PCB, therefore:

> The most important political task is to build a front of political and mass action embracing all [the opposition] forces. . . . All trends and groups, all political and public leaders willing to fight against the dictatorship should be enlisted, regardless of their having collaborated with or supported the regime in the past. How consistent their opposition to the regime may be at present is also irrelevant. The main thing is to enlist all who are prepared to do something, no matter how little, against the dictatorship.

Turning to a more specific delineation of the nature of the PCB's desired "united front" of opposition forces, Prestes warned:

> The anti-dictator front is an alliance of heterogeneous sociopolitical forces. Therefore, its member groups cannot have the same ultimate aim or tendency. The only forces interested in totally uprooting the dictatorship and restoring democracy are the working class, the small urban bourgeoisie and the peasants. Hence, it is up to the Communists to weld into the anti-dictator movement the political trends representing these classes and groups, notably the various trends of the Left movement, the political, public and religious groups and leaders championing peasant interests, those of the small urban bourgeoisie and all people of labor. This integration of the Left may produce a center that will unite all the anti-dictator forces.

The role of the left forces within the broad coalition of the "anti-dictator" movement would, according to Prestes, be of importance, also, following the overthrow of the regime, which might "be followed by a further advance: abolition of the regime of capitalists and landowners subservient to the imperialists."

In an apparent attempt to appease its own left-wing militants the PCB declared:

> Democratic action can compel the reactionary and defeatist minority to retreat and restore democratic rights. But events may turn out differently: the dictatorship may resort to force, precipitating an armed rising or civil war. It is therefore essential for the Communists to prepare the Party and the masses for this contingency. . . . It may turn out, too, that the Party and the people will be compelled to resort to other, more elementary and particular forms of armed struggle, or to self-defense. In that case, non-violent legal or underground forms of struggle should supplement armed struggles for limited aims. Therefore the Party must also be prepared for this eventuality.

While accepting the possibility of "armed struggle," the congress "took issue with those in Brazil who [would] reduce the work of revolution to forming 'guerrilla centers,' laying more stress on topography than on studying the correlation of socio-political forces."

"A revolution cannot win," the PCB emphasized, "until it becomes the cause of the millions." Attempting to appeal to as wide a sector of the public as possible, the party went so far as to reject the contention that "at present our revolution is a socialist revolution." The congress, Prestes said, rejected this thesis and gave its reason: "The present stage of the Brazil revolution is national-democratic. If the Party were to issue the call for an immediate struggle for socialism, it would go against the objective process and isolate itself from the patriotic and democratic movement."

By the end of the year it was not apparent that the PCB had succeeded in either appeasing its militant dissidents or making any significant progress in its "united front" strategy. With regard to the latter, potential noncommunist, antigovernment support was presented with the possibility of joining the "Broad Front" (Frente Ampla), established in September-October 1967 with the support of the former governor of the state of Guanabara, Carlos Lacerda, and former Presidents Juscelino

Kubitschek and João Goulart. Some observers claimed that the domestic programs of the PCB and the Front were, in many respects, identical (e.g. *Le Monde,* Paris, 6 January 1968).

**International Views and Policies.** PCB pronouncements on foreign policy and on matters relating to the international communist movement reflected the party's alignment with the CPSU and with the communist parties of Argentina, Chile, and Uruguay—the most prominent advocates among the larger communist parties in Latin America of the possibility of "peaceful change" within their respective countries.

During July 1967 the PCB participated in bilateral meetings with representatives of these three Latin American Communist parties. The joint statement published following the meeting between the PCB and the Communist Party of Argentina (see *Argentina*) reflected the preoccupation of the "orthodox" pro-Soviet Latin American parties with preserving the "unity of the world Communist movement" and the "unity of each party" (*IB*, no. 103, September 1967). With regard to unity of the movement, Prestes (in the aforementioned contribution to the *WMR*) stressed that his party's December congress—while reaffirming the "national character" of the party, with its origins in the "historical growth" of Brazilian society—had "struck a crushing blow at nationalism and raised high the banner of proletarian internationalism" and declared itself to be "part of the world Communist and working-class movement, to which it is attached by numerous fraternal bonds."

At its congress the PCB adopted a "political resolution" which included coverage of international affairs. An abridged version of this resolution was carried by the *World Marxist Review's Information Bulletin* (no. 115, March 1968). Whereas the resolution included two sections pertaining to international affairs ("The International Situation" and "The Party and the International Communist Movement"), the *IB* report only carried the first of the two, with a passing reference to the second, excerpts from which were published in *Jornal do Brasil* (31 December 1967). In this section the PCB reiterated the fact that it considered itself "an integral part of the international Communist movement," a party "based on Marxist-Leninist theory and on the principle of proletarian internationalism, common to that movement."

In its comments on Communist China, the PCB declared itself against the "erroneous theses defended by the leaders of the Communist Party of China." These theses, it said "conflict, in important matters, with the orientation worked out collectively by the international Communist movement and . . . break with Marxism-Leninism and the action norms of the Communist parties." Reaffirming its "loyalty to the humanist ideals" of the founders of communist doctrine, the PCB stated its refusal to "believe that war, which would hurl the peoples into a nuclear catastrophe, is the only way to make socialism triumph": "We repudiate this thesis and other similarly erroneous theses defended by Mao Tse-tung and his group, [and] we cannot hide the concern that we feel with regard to certain aspects of the events taking place today in People's China, under the designation of 'great proletarian cultural revolution.' Both the negation of the whole Nation's culture, of classical and modern culture, and the military conception with which an attempt is being made to orient the life of the Party and the cult of Mao Tse-tung are completely foreign to Marxism." The PCB expressed its "certainty," moreover, that "the great Chinese people and the truly proletarian core of the Chinese Communist Party will be able to find the forces that will enable them to restore the bonds of solidarity and unity with the world Communist movement."

With regard to Cuba, the PCB congress declared:

> [We are] amazed by the gratuitious attacks on our Party occurring in the Cuban press, even in the daily newspaper *Granma*. . . . It is of the opinion that the unity of the Communist and worker parties is based on the mutual respect and recognition of the independence of each party and that solidarity among Communists consists, fundamentally, in support by the other parties of the revolutionary struggle being carried on by each one in its own country, assisting it in the application of its policy line.

In this context the congress stated its belief that the PCB was correct in not sending representatives to the OLAS conference in Havana:

> [The conference's] decisions conflict fundamentally with the policy line and the tactics of our Party. In addition to that, [the congress] does not believe that the establishment of a

revolutionary leadership center in Latin America is either suitable or well-advised. The solidarity that is indispensable to the struggle against the common enemy—US imperialism—cannot obscure the differences in the national development of each Latin American country, the different levels of economic development and the differences in the composition and correlation of the social forces, all of which are factors that make an attempt to dictate the same course and identical forms of struggle for the revolution in various Latin American countries impracticable.

Despite divergent views between the PCB and Cuba, the political resolution of the congress (in the section on "The International Situation") declared: "Solidarity with the Cuban revolution and the government building socialism in America is more important than ever before in view of the imperialists' increasing attempts to isolate Cuba, tighten the trade blockade and begin armed intervention. Our duty is to launch a broad movement of solidarity with the Cuban revolution. By defending this revolution, we are defending our own interests, the freedom, dignity and future of our people." (*IB*, no. 115, March 1968.)

On other matters of international concern the PCB congress expressed its "fraternal and active solidarity with the people of Vietnam"; advocated a condemnation of "the policy of the Brazilian government, which backs the Portuguese colonialists" and the launching of a "campaign of solidarity with the peoples of Angola, Mozambique and Portuguese Guinea"; and accused "US imperialists" of trying to "check and crush the Arab peoples' fight for freedom and independence" by "instigating Israel and fomenting war in the Middle East." The party also charged the USA with engineering "military coups, as in the case of Indonesia, Brazil, Argentina, Greece and other countries," and with encouraging the "revival of Nazism" and seeking to "arm Federal Germany with nuclear weapons." (*ibid.*)

During its bilateral meetings with the communist parties of Argentina, Chile, and Uruguay, and again at its congress, the PCB expressed support for the convocation of a world conference of communist and workers' parties.

A delegation of the PCB attended the celebrations in Moscow of the fiftieth anniversary of the October Revolution.

**Publication.** The PCB publishes an irregular clandestine newspaper, *A Voz Operaria.*

\* \* \*

As noted earlier, there is a pro-Chinese breakaway communist party in Brazil, the PCdoB. This party is illegal, like the PCB.

**Organization and Leadership.** Very little published information was available in 1967 on the organizational structure and leadership of the PCdoB. There was no evidence that the pro-Chinese party had succeeded in attracting any significant element of PCB dissidence to its ranks. The leadership of the PCdoB in 1967 was believed to include Mauricio Grabois, João Amazonas, Benedito de Carvalho, Guido Enders, Manoel Ferreira, Calil Chade, Walter Martins, Lincoln Oeste, Alcira Grabois, and Ari Gonçalves.

**Domestic Views and Policies.** In internal matters the PCdoB supports the pro-Chinese pattern of violent revolution, asserting that "armed struggle" is "the highest form of mass struggle" (*Peking Review,* no. 51, 16 December 1966). It is, however, critical of the Castroist variety of armed struggle. At the PCdoB's Sixth Congress, held in June 1966, emphasis was laid on the necessity for the party to "exert its every effort to realize in concrete form the united front of patriots," because: "As the situation stands today in Brazil, the question of the united front is of primary importance" (*ibid.*). The party also advocated the concept of "people's war" and stressed the importance of the role of the proletariat—"Only a class like the proletariat can successfully lead the revolution"—while repudiating "the proposition advanced by certain people that only the national bourgeoisie can lead the revolution" (*ibid.*). In addition to underscoring the role of the proletariat, the PCdoB congress was reported to have pointed out that "full attention must be paid to mobilizing the peasant masses as a powerful force" (*ibid.*).

While advocating a "united front," the PCdoB also declared: "Any union between the Marxist-Leninist Parties and the revisionist parties is impossible.... It is equally impracticable for the Marxist-Leninist Parties to form any united front with the revisionist parties." (*Ibid.*).

The PCdoB's advocacy of "people's war" and a "united front" (which would exclude the PCB) do not appear to have registered any success in 1967. According to the *Jornal do Brasil* (20 January 1967), however, police in São Paulo arrested ten members of the PCdoB for planning to blow up several factories.

**International Views and Policies.** The PCdoB follows a steadfast pro-Chinese course in its statements on international affairs. Thus in 1966, in the wake of Sino-Cuban controversy, the party contrasted its former support of Castro with its current disillusionment, claiming that Castro had sided up with the "revisionists" (see *YICA*, 1966, p. 191). In 1967, paralleling a modest rapprochement in Sino-Cuban relations, PCdoB criticism of Cuba appeared to abate.

The PCdoB's comments on the policies of the Soviet Union remained highly invective, following the stand adopted at the party's Sixth Congress:

> The Soviet revisionist leading group has adopted a policy which goes against the interests of the people of the various countries, a policy which has evil effects on the entire international situation. The Soviet Government pursues a policy of collaborating with the United States, with a view to dividing the world into their spheres of influence (*Peking Review,* no. 51, 16 December 1966.)

In 1967 the PCdoB reiterated its accusations of US-Soviet collusion (see Benedito de Carvalho, as quoted by NCNA, 12 May). At the same time Chinese policy and activity were favorably acclaimed (see, on the "cultural revolution," *Peking Review,* no. 27, 30 June, and on the Chinese explosion of a hydrogen bomb, NCNA, 9 August).

**Publications.** The PCdoB publishes an irregular clandestine newspaper, *A Classe Operaria*.

# BULGARIA

The Bulgarian Communist Party (Bulgarska Kommunisticheska Partiia; BCP) was founded 27 May 1919. From 1938 to December 1948 it was called the Bulgarian Workers' Party. The BCP has been the ruling party in Bulgaria since December 1947, when the National Assembly adopted a new constitution establishing the People's Republic of Bulgaria. It is the dominant element in the Fatherland Front (Otechestven Front), which consists of the BCP, the Bulgarian Agrarian Union, and various mass social organizations. The Fatherland Front sponsors all 416 deputies to the National Assembly, 275 of which belong to the BCP. The BCP has 613,393 members (31 December 1966) out of a total population of 8,258,000 (estimated 1966), or about 11 per cent of the adult population.

**Organization and Leadership.** The BCP is headed by a Central Committee composed of 137 members and 87 candidates. The leading organs of the party include an 11-member Politburo and a Secretariat composed of a First Secretary, five Secretaries, and three members. The First Secretary is Todor Zhivkov, who also holds the position of Premier of the People's Republic of Bulgaria. The Secretaries are Boyan Bulgaranov, Venelin Kotsev, Ivan Prunov, Stanko Todorov, and Boris Velchev; the members are Vladimir Bonev, Stoyan Gyaurov, and Stefan Vasilev. The members of the Politburo are Boyan Bulgaranov, Tsola Dragoycheva, Pencho Kubadinski, Ivan Mikhaylov, Todor Pavlov, Ivan Popov, Stanko Todorov, Tano Tsolov, Boris Velchev, Todor Zhivkov, and Zhivko Zhivkov.

**Domestic Issues and Activities.** The Central Committee of the BCP met on numerous occasions during 1967 to discuss economic problems and other domestic- and foreign-policy issues: on 9 January a meeting to discuss questions arising from the directives of the Ninth Congress (which had taken place on 14-19 November 1966) and to draw up the plan and budget for the coming year; on 16-17 March a joint meeting with the Council of Ministers to discuss acceleration of technical progress in the country; on 23 March a plenary session to discuss the working plan of the Central Committee on "some basic problems of Bulgaria's development," preparations for the Congress of Collective Farms, and information about talks with Soviet party leaders during the visit to Moscow in March of Todor Zhivkov and other BCP leaders; on 5 May a plenary session to discuss the Karlovy Vary Conference; on 14 June a plenum to discuss the Middle East crisis; on 31 July a joint meeting with the Council of Ministers to hear Zhivkov's report on the international situation; on 13 December a plenary session to examine the economic plan and budget for 1968; on 26-27 December a special plenum to discuss problems of youth; and on 28 December a joint session with the Council of Ministers was held to discuss economic and social matters.

Several Bulgarian mass organizations held congresses during 1967: on 28-30 March the First Congress of Collective Farms, on 24-27 April the Thirty-First Congress of the Bulgarian Agrarian Union, on 15-17 May the Sixth Congress of the Fatherland Front, on 18-20 May the First Congress of Culture, and on 30-31 May the Third Congress of Journalists.

The Ninth Congress of the BCP (November 1966) had defined the present stage in the country's development as one of building a "developed socialist society." The main tasks in this stage were outlined as (1) the further enlarging of the material and technical bases of society, (2) "perfecting of social relationships," and (3) enhancing the "socialist consciousness" of the people.

The development of the Bulgarian economy, with special emphasis on agriculture, was the major domestic issue in 1967. The principle defect of the economy had been (and continued to be in 1967) the inefficiency and the consequent critical lag in productivity. The BCP had attacked this problem at the Ninth Congress by introducing a change in the orientation of the economy from extensive to intensive development, by calling for more extensive economic research as a basis of production, and greater use of "economic" methods to inspire productivity. A new organizational model called for the decentralization of planning through the creation of 35 "trusts" covering various branches of the economy. Each trust is responsible for the over-all development of an entire branch of the economy—the requirements of production and the domestic and foreign trade of their goods—while the central authorities draw up only the long range generalized indices for the work of the trust. The trust is also given the independence and funds to solve problems connected with the intensification and development of production. Another organizational innovation was the creation of "production committees" and "economic councils" to promote better forms of workers' participation in guiding production and economic activity.

While the principles and aims of the Bulgarian economic reform are essentially similar to those currently being applied in Yugoslavia, Czechoslovakia, and Hungary, they are being much more cautiously implemented in Bulgaria. In the third year of transition to the new system, only 70 per cent of all enterprises were affected by it; final transition is not due until the end of 1968. Administrative methods continue to be used extensively in Bulgaria in influencing production; managers are subject to control by central authorities and by workers' committees; material incentives are used but are generally qualified by emphasis on moral stimuli; and finally, the party continues to permeate economic activity on all levels. At the great Kremikovtsi Iron and Steel Combine, for example, most of the managerial and administrative personnel are party members, and at the same time, the party committee of the project and party committees of individual enterprises have, and use, authority to control administrative action. In addition, no one can be appointed to an executive position (or dismissed from one) without the consent of the party committee, thus bringing the work of leading cadres under party control (Ivan Todorov, "Kremikovtsi," *WMR*, December 1967).

The economic development of the country was the subject of the great majority of government decrees and party and mass organization decisions. Wage increases effective 1 January 1967 amounted to 10 to 12 per cent for some 850,000 workers in various branches of the economy (those who did not receive a pay raise in 1966). Also on 1 January, a merger was effected between the National Bank and the Investments Bank under the control of the new National Bank, a move designed to integrate the financing of the economic model. Retail-trade enterprises were transformed into organizations permitted to engage in wholesale as well as retail operations, a move aimed at stimulating competition. A center for management training was opened, and by a 17 March decree all ministries, enterprises, and institutions were obliged to enroll unskilled personnel in training courses. The same decree provided for a revision in pay scales to give employees an incentive to raise technical and organizational levels of production and to provide for the establishment of an institute for the organization of management. A decree aimed at stiffening labor discipline and encouraging workers to stay on the job was adopted in June. In December a series of decrees on price increases, pension increases, increased family allowances, and a reduction of the work week were published. However, a price reform scheduled for completion in mid-1967 was now announced to be due in 1968, and other pressing problems connected with the reform remained unsolved.

The new economic system was applied in agriculture through the development of a new form of contractual rather than directive relationships between the producer (the cooperative or state farm) and the buyer (the government procurement agency). Additional favored treatment was given to collective farms through increased material incentives to the collective farmers to speed up agricultural production.

The Congress of Collective Farms, held on 28-30 March 1967, adopted draft statutes for collective farms putting agriculture on the level of industry by granting equivalent economic and social benefits for farmers and industrial workers (the plan was then approved at the 22 June meeting of the Presidium of the National Assembly). However, the statutes also reduced the private ownership of land in the collective farms. All farmers are now to be paid solely on the basis of their work and are to receive no dividends for the land brought into the collective. In addition, restrictions were imposed on the size and use of the private plots. The Congress also set up a Union of Collective Farms, which later in the year merged with the Central Cooperative Union to form the United Central Cooperative

Union.

Production figures showed that industries working under the new system were significantly more productive than those under the old system and that the growth rate of agricultural production rose 15 per cent in 1966—the highest rate of the East European countries. However, the reforms were not implemented without obstacles. Party and state officials complained of a "tenacious conservatism" and "over-simplified view of the new system," and that people "are prone to cling to the old methods with all their bureaucracy and management by administrative fiat" (see Stefan Vasilev, "Party Work in Bulgaria," *WMR*, December 1967). At the same time, there were charges that inadequate use was being made of economic and sociological studies, and that machinery was not being used to capacity.

The shortcomings in the nation's economy were dealt with in a government decree of November 1967, which declared that the economic results have "not come close to exhausting the immense possibilities and advantages of the socialist order and do not correspond to the conditions created by the new economic system for the further development of the economy." The decree outlined extensive measures to increase the profitability of the economy, and ordered that the various organizations, including the party, "should urgently and decisively overcome inertia and conservatism and entirely reorganize their work."

In comparison with Yugoslavia and Czechoslovakia, there was little talk in Bulgaria about the social and political implications of the reform. However, Todor Zhivkov and other leaders conceded that the switch to the reforms involved not only economic but also important political, ideological, sociological, and legal changes, and that changes were already beginning in the sphere of culture.

The "democratization" of Bulgaria's political and social life, outlined at the Ninth Party Congress, entailed the strengthening of the functions of mass organizations, the role of the National Assembly, and that of the Youth Union. Discussions on legislative reform began in March 1967 with promises for a new penal code and a new family law, while work continued on the drafting of a new constitution. However, the extensive new legislation called for by Todor Zhivkov at the April 1966 plenum—such as a new labor code, a new civil code, and a new civil procedure code—had not been realized by the end of 1967. On the idological and cultural front the BCP showed greater flexibility in allowing publication of "dissident" works by Bulgarian artists and writers, and accordingly adopted methods of "persuasion" in exerting influence on culture to replace the "old brutal methods" (Atanas Stoyanov at a meeting of the Bulgarian Writers' Union, *Literaturen Front*, 2 March 1967).

Limits to "democratization" were, however, clearly defined by the BCP. According to Politburo member and Central Committee Secretary Stanko Todorov, "the Party takes exception to petty-bourgeois spontaneity, attempts to counterpose democracy to the dictatorship of the proletariat and social discipline, to all kinds of abstract talks about democracy and freedom in general, and the preaching of bourgeois pseudo-humanism" (Stanko Todorov, "Towards a Developed Socialist Society," *WMR*, April 1967).

The BCP was aided in the dissemination of its policy line by the Fatherland Front. At its Sixth Congress (15-17 May 1967), the Fatherland Front approved the appraisals of the BCP on its functions and tasks, which are primarily to explain the party policies and to promote the communist education of the people through an extensive mass-explanatory and political-educational campaign. The Sixth Congress replaced the Fatherland Front Chairman Encho Staykov with Boyan Bulgaranov.

The BCP declared its pride in the fact that, in contrast to other East European states (see *Czechoslovakia, Yugoslavia,* and *Poland*), the Bulgarian intelligentsia can never be proclaimed an "unsound element," but that it wholeheartedly supports party policies. Bulgaria's "cultural revolution" is thus a determined effort on the part of the BCP to educate all strata of the population to the level of its "loyal" intelligentsia (see Velcho Chankov, "The Roots of the Cultural Revolution," *Bulgaria Today,* no. 3, 1967). The principles of "party-mindedness" and "socialist realism" remain firmly entrenched in the BCP's cultural policy.

The First Congress of Culture (18-20 May 1967), sponsored by the Committee for Culture and Art, was a demonstration of the "unity" of the nation's intelligentsia with the BCP.*Pavel Mateev,

---

*The Committee for Culture and Art was established in 1966 as a measure toward the "democratization" of Bulgarian life. Directly responsible to the Chairman of the Council of Ministers, the Committee controls all culture in Bulgaria.

Chairman of the Committee, hailed the party's role, influence, and guidance in cultural life. "We do not have any other road except the road of the Party, no other fate except the fate of the Party, no other future except the future of the Party," he declared. He also stated that culture would be reorganized on the basis of "socialist democracy," and that the state's cultural and education programs would be perfected and intensified. The discussions at the congress showed no divergence of views, and Todor Zhivkov summed up the three-day meeting with the declaration that the congress had clearly shown "the unity and cohesion of the cultural workers with the CC of the Party."

Despite the BCP's claims of a loyal intelligentsia, signs of dissidence were evident. Complaints of "deviations and manifestations of modernism" in literature were aired in the Bulgarian press and in various speeches. At a February 1967 meeting of the Bulgarian Writers' Union, Bogomil Raynov, who in July replaced Emil Manov as head of the Writers' Union, declared "freedom of debate" and "unity" to be incompatible.* Relations among the writers are such, he declared, that "polemics will not help unity, but on the contrary, will speed up centrifugal tendencies. We have arrived at the point where we must renounce unity if we want discussions. If we want unity, we must give up the thought of discussions." (*Literaturen Front*, 2 March 1967. See Emil Popoff, "Bulgaria's Literary 'Mini-thaw'," *East Europe*, February 1968.)

Another issue on the cultural scene was the party's concern with more effective atheistic propaganda, as reflected in a Secretariat decision of 27 December 1966; "for the further improvement of the atheistic education of the Bulgarian people." The major defect of atheistic propaganda was declared to be its "spottiness." The present task was thus to attack religion in all its aspects and to do this by referring to the newest scientific discoveries. It was emphasized that the work must be oriented to reach the entire community of believers, particularly the women, Pomaks (Bulgarian Moslems), Turks, and gypsies. "For all practical purposes," complained Mircho Dimitrov, Deputy Head of the BCP Agitprop Department, "atheistic work is carried out among the atheists . . ." (see "For a Further Improvement of the Atheistic Education of the Bulgarian People," *Politischeska Prosveta*, no. 4, 1967, and Mircho Dimitrov, "For a Systematic and Active Atheistic Propaganda," *Politicheska Prosveta*, no. 11, 1967).

**The Youth Union.** The party-controlled Dimitrov Communist Youth Union headed by First Secretary Georgi Atanassov, promotes the BCP's policies among Bulgarian young people. Work with youth was particularly intensive in 1967 in view of the economic and social changes in Bulgaria and the forthcoming congress of the Youth Union (originally scheduled for November 1967 and postponed to February 1968). The party press deplored political apathy, tendencies toward "nihilism," and "worship of everything foreign" among the youth. The problems of combating "bourgeois ideological subversion," the education of youth in "socialist patriotism," and the "patriotic-military education" of youth received maximum attention.

Party efforts to educate the young people in the "spirit of socialist patriotism" were characterized by intense propaganda on the close friendship between Bulgaria and the Soviet Union. "The most characteristic and significant point about our socialist patriotism," according to Fatherland Front Chairman Boyan Bulgaranov, "is our strong love for the Soviet Union and its Leninist party" (*Rabotnichesko Delo*, 9 July 1967). At the December plenum of the Youth Union Central Committee this point was repeatedly emphasized. The plenum's resolution declared that educating the young "in deep love for and gratitude to the Soviet people and the Soviet Union" was an important part of patriotic education. Patriotic military education was the principal subject discussed at another plenary session on 11 July. The speeches emphasized the need for untiring vigilance against the enemy and for guarding against the enemy's attempt to "mellow the ideological struggle" and thus disarm the Bulgarian youth. The speakers emphasized that communist youth must be ready to

*Emil Manov resigned as Chairman of the Writers' Union for "reasons of health." Earlier he had been sharply criticized for his contributions to a running debate on the "contemporary hero" in Bulgarian literature. Manov's last published article called for the creation of a "communist-democrat" in literature, whose "affinity with the people" would be coupled with "humanism," and also welcomed the fact that "laws of social and literary development," which cannot be easily canceled, "have found their way into the consciousness of writers and readers" (*Literaturen Front*, 29 September 1966).

give their lives for the cause of socialism and must be ready "to defend their socialist motherland with weapons in their hands."

In October 1967 Todor Zhivkov presented to the Politburo of the BCP Central Committee theses on the subject of work with youth and the upcoming congress of the Youth Union. The gist of the lengthy theses was that the Youth Union must become a true representative of the all-round interests and strivings of Bulgarian youth. Zhivkov deplored the fact that the Youth Union today is a "copy of the Party" and that it is to a great extent void of content, noting that "there is a sharp contrast between the inactivity and dull life in the Komsomol and the great activity and creative work carried out by youth in various spheres outside the Komsomol." Zhivkov proposed that the Youth Union extend its range of activities to organize and control all activities and organizations which satisfy the interests of the young people. At the same time, it must "modernize youth and inspire them in the name of communism for the progress and upsurge of the mother country and in defense of its socialist gains." The essential task at the moment, according to Zhivkov, is to secure the necessary conditions under which the Youth Union can function effectively. It must be given greater freedom of action and must in turn "democratize" its organization. The theses were reaffirmed in the resolution of the BCP Central Committee plenary session of 27 December 1967.

**Relations with the Soviet Union.** During 1967 the foreign policy of Bulgaria and the BCP was based on close friendship and solidarity with the Soviet party and state. The BCP decree on the celebration of the Fiftieth Anniversary of the October Revolution strongly reaffirmed loyalty to the Soviet Union, calling the Bulgarian friendship with the Soviet Union "life-giving" and "our most valuable alliance." "Bulgarian-Soviet friendship is one of the main motive forces in Bulgaria's development towards communism, a guarantee of the blossoming out and independence of our socialist motherland," stated the decree. The BCP went further than any other ruling communist party in its decision to celebrate the anniversary as Bulgaria's "own native Bulgarian holiday," and the month-long celebrations were the most conspicuous and intense of all the East European countries.

On the eve of the anniversary Stanko Todorov, speaking in Sofia in place of Todor Zhivkov (who was attending the celebrations in Moscow), attributed Bulgaria's achievements to the "creative application" of the experience of the Soviet party and to assistance from the Soviet Union. The Soviet Union "has been and will be always for us the vanguard of the world communist movement and the most influential force in the world revolutionary process," he stated, and hailed Bulgarian-Soviet relations as an example of relations of equality between a large and a small socialist country.

Ideologically, politically, militarily, and economically the Bulgarians reaffirmed their solidarity with the Soviet party and state. Todor Zhivkov led Bulgarian party delegations to Moscow in March on an "unofficial friendly" visit, and signed a communique expressing "full unanimity of views" on the international situation, the problems of the international communist movement and unanimity in their efforts to assure European security. During the visit by Leonid Brezhnev to Sofia (10-13 May), Bulgaria signed a 20-year Treaty of Friendship, Cooperation, and Mutual Assistance with the Soviet government, 10 months before the expiration of the existing treaty concluded in Moscow 18 March 1948. On the occasion of the signing of the treaty, Zhivkov again pledged Bulgaria's devotion to the Soviet Union: "The past, the present, and the future, our feelings and ideas, our interests and aspirations—everything unites our peoples and nothing separates them," he declared. "If we were asked what socialist internationalism means," Leonid Brezhnev replied, "we would answer: look at the relations between Bulgaria and the Soviet Union; this is socialist internationalism in operation." (*Rabotnichesko Delo,* 15 May 1967.)

Militarily, the Bulgarian leaders also affirmed close harmony with the Soviet Union. On the occasion of the twenty-third anniversary of the organization of the Bulgarian People's Army on 22 September, Colonel-General Slavcho Transky, speaking over Radio Sofia, declared: "We consider our army to be a part of the Soviet armed forces and if someone ever dares to strike at our borders, he will be met not only by the Bulgarian soldier, but by the Soviet army."

The Soviet Union was Bulgaria's largest trading partner and in 1968 is expected to account for more than 50 per cent of Bulgaria's foreign trade. The annual rate of increase in Soviet-Bulgarian trade from 1961 to 1965 was 14 per cent; this figure was 16.5 per cent for 1966 and 1967. The amount of trade in 1967 was about 1.37 billion rubles. On 2 December Foreign Trade Minister Ivan Budinov and his Soviet counterpart Nikolai Patolichev signed a protocol for Bulgarian-Soviet trade turnover in 1968; the sum involved is to be in excess of 1.5 billion rubles. "Mutual advantage and fraternal assistance" were emphasized as the two major characteristics in the development of foreign-trade relations between the two countries.* The Bulgarians attribute the recent development of the machine industry to be due to the stable Soviet market and report that one-third of the total Bulgarian exports to the Soviet Union is machines and equipment. Foreign Trade Minister Budinov welcomed the closer rapprochement of the two economies and declared: "I do not pretend to originality when I say that Bulgarian-Soviet trade is particularly stable and prospective, that it is untouched by any crisis situations or competitive tremors, and that its tendency toward a steady development in qualitative and quantitative respects is regular."

**Relations with China.** The BCP stood firmly at the side of the Soviet state and party in rebutting attacks by the Chinese state and party leadership. According to an article in *Rabotnichesko Delo*: "The Mao Tse-tung group is intentionally proceeding on the road of split and slanders; it is sinking into the swamp of nationalism, adventurism, and anti-Sovietism. In regard to the hatred and malice against the CPSU and against the other fraternal parties this group has outdone the fascists and Chiang Kai-shekists." The article also charged that the Peking leaders were impeding by all means the assistance which the Soviet Union and the other socialist countries were offering the Vietnamese people in their struggle against American "imperialism." (Georgi Bokov, "An Urgent Necessity," *Rabotnichesko Delo,* 7 March 1967.)

On the occasion of the eighteenth anniversary of the Chinese People's Republic, a *Rabotnichesko Delo* editorial noted the "disgusting anti-Soviet campaign" being waged in China and declared that the "cultural revolution" taking place there is in fact "assisting the enemies of progress" in their efforts to discredit the ideas of socialism and communism. The editorial addressed only the "Chinese working people" in asserting Bulgarian friendship. (*Rabotnichesko Delo,* 1 October 1967.)

However, according to the Chinese, there is a group of Bulgarian Communists "who uphold Mao Tse-tung's thoughts." On May Day this group reportedly sent a letter to Chairman Mao, praising him as "the wise and courageous supreme commander of genius" of the Chinese people and "the oldest Revolutionary" (*NCNA* 1 May 1967). The group hailed Mao Tse-tung as "not only guiding the Chinese workers and peasants forward, but also leading all the oppressed people and the proletariat of the world on their way to progress." In conclusion, the Bulgarian group pledged itself to "fight to liquidate imperialism and revisionism and uproot them as completely as one uproots weeds." The *Hsinhua* report on the May Day letter was unconfirmed by other sources.

**Relations with Eastern Europe.** The BCP also maintained a critical stand on Albania. On the occasion of the Albanian National Day anniversary on 29 November the BCP brought attention to the fact that Albania "could not have dealt with the centuries-long backwardness and the serious devastation inflicted by enemy occupation had it not been for the enormous aid rendered by the socialist countries, primarily the Soviet Union," and called on the Albanian people to remember what they owe to the Soviet Union. "The anti-Soviet hysteria which is rife in Tirana is against the interests of the Albanian people and socialism," the BCP declared (*Rabotnichesko Delo,* 28 November 1967).

However, on the positive side, Albanian sources reported that a delegation of "an Albanian colony in Bulgaria" attended the Sixth Congress of the Albanian Women's Union. Bulgaria and Rumania were the only two countries reported to have sent representatives.

Relations with other East European parties and governments continued to develop successfully as Bulgaria signed 20-year friendship, cooperation, and mutual assistance treaties with Poland and the German Democratic Republic. In addition, a friendship treaty with the People's Republic of Mongolia was signed in Ulan Bator on 23 July.

The treaty with Poland, signed during a visit to Bulgaria of a Polish party and government delegation headed by First Secretary of the Central Committee of the Polish United Workers' Party

---

*The most important project financed by the Soviet Union was the Kremikovtsi metallurgical combine, the second part of which was inaugurated on 5 November 1967.

Wladyslaw Gomulka and Chairman of the Polish People's Republic Józef Cyrankiewicz on 3-6 April, was a prolongation of the existing treaty signed by the two countries on 18 May 1948 and was renewed a full year before its expiration date. The treaty with East Germany, signed on 7 September, represents the eighth treaty of friendship signed by Bulgaria with socialist countries. The Bulgarians especially welcomed the economic exchange provisions of the treaty, and noted that East Germany is Bulgaria's second-ranking trading partner.

The stated purpose of the treaties was to contribute to the development of bilateral relations between the contracting countries. More important, however, was the desire to promote "European security" against the threat to peace by the "West German militarist and revanchist forces." Todor Zhivkov, speaking on the Bulgarian-East German treaty, declared that "it expresses our decision to defend peace in Europe, to strengthen the power of our defense organizations, the Warsaw Pact, to help resist everyone who intends to infringe upon the sovereignty of our states . . . and to block the road of West German forces which are trying to change the borders in Europe by force and to swallow the GDR" (Radio Sofia, 7 September 1967).

In addition to the Bulgarian consultations with the Soviet party and state leaders and consultations with Poland, East Germany, and Mongolia during the visits connected with the signing of the friendship treaties, Todor Zhivkov led a Bulgarian party and government delegation to Bucharest on 17-21 April. The final communique affirmed the desire of the two parties to establish closer economic and technical collaboration. It also stressed noninterference in the internal affairs of each state and declared that when differences appear, they must be discussed "in a sincere and comradely manner by the respective leaderships in a spirit of mutual respect, and persevering efforts must be made to achieve mutual understanding in order to achieve unity of action."

The BCP reconfirmed its commitment to the Warsaw Pact, calling for the further strengthening of the organization, and hailed the February meeting of the Warsaw Pact foreign ministers as facilitating "the further coordination of the foreign political efforts of socialist states in questions of ensuring European security." In the realm of Warsaw Pact activities, Bulgaria was host to joint maneuvers of Bulgarian, Rumanian, and Soviet forces on 20-27 August.

**Relations with Western Europe.** Bulgarian policy toward Western Europe was directed toward assuring "European security" and promoting a policy of peaceful coexistence with states having different social systems on the basis of the Bucharest declaration of 1966. However, the BCP has emphasized that the problem of European security is one that "must be solved by the European states first and foremost and it must be the international work of the popular masses and of the Communist and workers' parties" (Tsola Dragoycheva, "The October Revolution and Proletarian Internationalism," *Rabotnichesko Delo,* 28 July 1967). In the same spirit, the BCP placed high value on the results of the Karlovy Vary Conference of European Communist and Workers' Parties, stating that it "facilitated the strengthening of fraternal ties between communist and workers' parties and showed the people an attainable perspective of peace and security on the European continent" (Bulgarian-Soviet communique, 13 May 1967).

With regard to the Bonn government's "new Eastern offensive" aimed at normalizing relations with the East European states, Bulgaria showed cautious interest in January but then joined East Germany, Poland, and the Soviet Union in violently condemning the West German policy as an attempt to "split the socialist countries" and to "isolate" the German Democratic Republic.

**Relations with the Balkan States.** Bulgaria has been the most active promoter of a policy of Balkan cooperation. Steps have been taken especially with regard to Greece and Turkey, both on a governmental level, by means of agreements, and through the channel of the Bulgarian Committee for Mutual Understanding and Cooperation in the Balkans. In early 1967 Bulgaria was host to a conference of the Committees of Bulgaria, Rumania, and Yugoslavia; Albania and Turkey did not participate. In an interview with Austrian journalists, Todor Zhivkov went so far as to declare that he supported the idea of treaties with all Balkan countries, regardless of their political systems (*Die Presse,* Vienna, 21 October 1967).

Particularly intensive activity was conducted in relations with Turkey. In May Turkish Foreign Minister Caglayangil made an official visit to Sofia, and the communique following the visit stressed the importance of the contribution of all Balkan countries to peace and security in the area. Economic cooperation between the two countries was exemplified by a Bulgarian-Turkish protocol signed in Sofia on 12 August, providing for improvements in jointly used railway, road, air, and sea transport. Finally, progress was made in the nationality problem when in October Caglayangil announced that Turkey had reached an agreement with Bulgaria on the emigration to Turkey of some 30,000 Turks living in Bulgaria (the agreement pertains only to those Turks having close relatives in Turkey).

Relations between Bulgaria and Yugoslavia continued to be strained over the issue of Macedonia, but in the areas of mutual cooperation and foreign policy the views of the two countries were complementary. The two countries exchanged a number of party, military, and economic delegations highlighted by the visit of Macedonian party leader Krste Crvenkovski to Sofia in March and a visit by Todor Zhivkov to Yugoslavia in June. The 6 June communique following the Zhivkov visit to Yugoslavia declared an "identity or similarity of views on the basic international issues" and noted that, among other topics of discussion, the two countries spoke of their efforts for strengthening peace and friendship among the Balkan people. Both sides also expressed "serious concern" over the situation in Greece.

Bulgarian-Greek relations were strained by reports from Greece that Bulgaria was supporting a force aimed at overthrowing the Greek military junta. The reaction of Bulgaria was to deny such reports and to criticize "anti-Bulgarian propaganda." The Bulgarians, however, continued to reaffirm their decision "to follow readily [the] policy of peace and good-neighborliness in the Balkans and to develop friendship and understanding among all Balkan countries, including the Greek people" (*Otechestven Front*, 19 August 1967).

**Other International Relations**. Bulgaria has continued to condemn, in strongest terms, U.S. "imperialism" throughout the world, and especially in Asia. "The insane American imperialists, obsessed by a mania for world domination, are adding to the fire of aggression in Vietnam, subjecting the Vietnamese land to barbaric bombings and destruction, preparing a new escalation of military actions against the DRV, and threatening Cambodia and other countries of Indochina," declared the Fatherland Front in an official statement (*Otechestven Front*, 8 September 1967). United States imperialism was charged with being behind the major international crises of 1967—the military coup in Greece, the Arab-Israeli war in June, and the crisis on Cyprus.

In accordance with its "socialist" foreign policy, the BCP has given moral and material support to the national-liberation movements, to newly developing countries, and to "progressive" regimes in Africa and Asia in their fight against "imperialism" and "neocolonialism." Bulgaria has repeatedly affirmed that it will support in every possible way the struggle of the Vietnamese people against U.S. "imperialist aggression." The new political program of the National Liberation Front of South Vietnam, published in late summer of 1967, was hailed by the Bulgarians as a "brilliant expression of the invincible desire of South Vietnam to achieve final victory in the liberation struggle against the imperialist invaders." "It is evidence of the deciding role played by the NLFSV as organizer, leader, and inspirer of the liberation struggle of the South Vietnamese people," the Fatherland Front declared (*Otechestven Front*, 8 September 1967). On 20 November the Bulgarian News Agency announced that a permanent mission of the National Liberation Front was to be established in Sofia.

Bulgaria also provided material aid to the North Vietnamese under the terms of new trade and aid agreements with North Vietnam signed in Bulgaria in August. Bulgaria will render Hanoi gratuitous economic and military assistance in 1968 and will grant it a long-term interest-free loan for the purchase of equipment for industrial projects from 1968 to 1970, and an interest-free credit to purchase of goods in 1968. In August 150 young North Vietnamese arrived in Sofia to study at Bulgarian schools.

Bulgaria strongly supported the Arab cause in the Middle East crisis of June 1967. A 29 May official statement (even before the outbreak of hostilities) declared Bulgaria's solidarity with the Arab states, and a second declaration of 6 June placed the responsibility for the outbreak of hostilities completely on Israel, which was said to be backed by the "imperialists" and the "neocolonialists." Todor Zhivkov represented Bulgaria at the Moscow meeting called to discuss the Middle East and signed the 9 June declaration condemning Israel as the aggressor. On 10 June Bulgaria followed the Soviet Union and Czechoslovakia in breaking diplomatic relations with Israel.

In accordance with the Moscow declaration of the readiness of the socialist countries to extend aid to Arab countries, a Bulgarian government delegation led by Deputy Premier Luchezar Avramov visited the United Arab Republic, Syria, Iraq and the Sudan in July-August and signed agreements to strengthen Arab economies which had been seriously weakened by the war.

Throughout the year Bulgaria maintained particularly close contacts with the Arab countries of the Middle East and their communist parties. On 10 February Bulgaria and Iran signed their first trade agreement in Teheran, providing for a volume of $7 million in each direction. A Bulgarian military delegation visited Damascus in May and again in July. On 8-14 September the Minister of Trade and Industry of Kuwait held talks in Sofia with Todor Zhivkov and Bulgarian Trade Minister Ivan Budinov, and on 20-27 September Ismail al-Azhari, President of the Supreme State Council of Sudan paid an official visit to Sofia and concluded agreements on expanding economic and trade relations and scientific-technical cooperation. At the party level, shortly after the Arab-Israeli war BCP leaders met in Sofia with representatives of the Iraqi, Israeli, and Tunisian parties, respectively. On 24 August Todor Zhivkov met in Sofia with Reza Radmanesh, First Secretary of the Central Committee of the Tudeh Party of Iran. The communique affirmed Bulgarian solidarity with the Arab cause.

**The International Communist Movement.** Other consultations between the BCP and foreign parties included a visit to Sofia at the beginning of June by a West German Central Committee delegation headed by First Secretary Max Reimann, followed by a communique affirming a "complete identity of views." On 18-25 June Pedro Saad, Secretary-General of the Communist Party of Ecuador visited Bulgaria; on 15-24 July a Central Committee delegation of the Danish party headed by Politburo member and Central Committee Secretary Ib Nørlund visited Bulgaria at the invitation of the BCP Central Committee. Todor Zhivkov conferred with Secretary-General Waldeck Rochet of the French party and Secretary-General Luigi Longo of the Italian party at the end of July. At the invitiation of the BCP Central Committee, a Central Committee delegation of the Spanish party, headed by Secretary-General Santiago Carrillo, visited Bulgaria on 4-11 October. On 30 October Todor Zhivkov received a visiting Colombian party Central Committee delegation headed by First Secretary Gilberto Vieira, and on 21-25 November a Greek party delegation led by Chairman Apostolos Grozos visited Bulgaria.

The BCP prided itself on being the first party to call for the convening of an international communist party conference at its Ninth Congress in November 1966 and throughout 1967 continued to press for the convening of the conference "at the earliest possible date." On the occasion of the celebration of the Fiftieth Anniversary of the October Revolution, Bulgarian party leaders reaffirmed the "obvious and urgent" necessity for convening such a conference. The aim of the conference, noted the BCP, was to promote the unity of action—to work out a joint strategy—of the communist parties in their struggle against imperialism. Stanko Todorov elucidated the Bulgarian stand in an interview published in the Danish party organ *Land og Folk* on 7 December:

> We want the new conference to be a conference at which no Party is given orders, and at which no Party is condemned. Our discussions there should center on the activities of the imperialists and not on the actions of our party brothers. . . . Naturally enough, we cannot meet without considering our disagreements. These we must try to overcome with new methods such as the power of persuasion, aiming for the greatest possible unity of action.

**Publications.** The most important publications of the BCP are the daily central organ *Rabotnichesko Delo* (Workers' Cause); the monthly organ of the Central Committee *Partien Zhivot*; (Party Life); the theoretical monthly of the Central Committee, *Novo Vreme* (New Times); and two Central Committee biweeklies, *Politicheska Prosveta* (Political Education) and *Ikonomicheski Zhivot* (Economic Life). The organs of the Dimitrov Communist Youth Union are *Narodna Mladezh* (National Youth) and *Mladezh* (Youth).

# BURMA

The Burma Communist Party (BCP) was founded 15 August 1939, under the leadership of Thakin Soe. In 1946, following a dispute over the correct strategy for achieving Burmese independence, Thakin Soe withdrew his faction of the BCP and formed the Communist Party of Burma (CPB), known as the Red Flags, and Thakin Than Tun founded a new Burma Communist Party, known as the White Flags.* While the Red Flags went underground to initiate armed insurrection against the government, the White Flags placed primary emphasis on legal struggle until 1948, when they, too, went underground. Thakin Ba Thein Tin, First Vice-Chairman of the White Flag Central Committee, has described their interim position:

> During this period, though legal struggle was the main form of struggle, our Party had nevertheless simultaneously carried out armed struggle while the whole Party was being taught ideologically that in the event of the enemy's armed attacks, he must be given immediate armed counter-blows. (*Peking Review*, no. 35, 25 August 1967.)

From 1951 to 1963 the White Flags operated in loose alliance with the Red Flags and were joined in July and August 1963 by a group of White Flag Communists who had taken up residence in Communist China. After the breakdown of negotiations in November 1963 between Ne Win's "Revolutionary Government of the Union of Burma" and members of both the White Flags and the Red Flags, however, the Peking-based White Flags joined Thakin Than Tun's group in an attempt to dominate it; and the Red Flags were labeled as Trotskyites by other Communists. While both the White Flags and the Red Flags have resumed their insurgent activities, the Red Flag group, which is the more extreme of the two, appears to have receded into the background. Although most pronouncements and terrorist activities originate from the White Flags, a member of the Red Flags who surrendered in December 1967 revealed that an underground united front between the White Flags and the Red Flags had been formed in the Southern Command in 1966, but that it was dissolved shortly thereafter.

**Party-Government Relationship.** Since the military coup of 2 March 1962 the only legal political party has been the Burma Socialist Program Party, which was established by the government. The "Revolutionary Government of the Union of Burma" holds all legislative, executive, and judicial powers, which are exercised by General Ne Win as Chairman of the Union Revolutionary Council.

**Membership, Leadership, and Organization.** Estimates of White Flag membership range from 2,000 to 5,000. A recent defector put the number at more than 3,000. Reports indicate that several thousand additional supporters could be mobilized if so directed by the White Flags. Red Flag membership is estimated at 200 to 300. Neither group has a significant following, despite the White Flags' close association with the illegal National Democratic United Front (NDUF), founded in 1959 and consisting of a bloc of left-wing and procommunist groups, including the Karen National Unity Party (KNUP), whose leader, Mahn Ba Zan, is also leader of the NDUF; the New Mon State Party; the Kayah Progressive Party; and the Chin Supreme Committee. In addition to the White Flags, who dominate the NDUF, the only other significant element within the Front is the KNUP, whose membership is believed to number several thousand. The population of Burma is 25,246,000 (mid-1966 estimate).

The White Flags have also attempted to unify various religious, ethnic, and political insurgent groups. Although they have successfully infiltrated the ranks of the Kachins and the Shans, two of Burma's largest minority groups, they have not yet succeeded in establishing any formal alliance with

---

*Considerable confusion exists regarding the precise names of the two groups. While the Burma Communist Party (BCP) generally refers to the White Flags and while the Communist Party of Burma (CPB) generally refers to the Red Flags, the two names have frequently been used interchangeably.

them. The White Flags have, however, successfully collaborated with the militant Karen National Defense Organization (KNDO), which claims to have some 7,000 men under arms.

Virtually nothing is known about the leadership and organization of the Red Flags, who operate under the chairmanship of Thakin Soe. The White Flags, under the leadership of Chairman Thakin Than Tun, are directed by a Politburo which includes the Peking-based First Vice-Chairman of the Central Committee, Thakin Ba Thein Tin, and Yebaw Goshal (alias Ba Tin),* Yebaw Htay,* Thakin Chit, Thakin Zin, and Thakin Than Myaing. Besides those in the Politburo, the Central Committee members include Ko Aung Gyi, Bo Zeya (Chief of Staff of the Central Military High Command, who was killed in a clash with government troops on 16 April 1968), and Thakin Pu. Other high-ranking White Flag Communists who participated in the negotiations with the Burmese government in 1963 include Yebaw Bo Soe Maung, Yebaw Bo Pu, and Yebaw Thet Tin. It is not known whether they are still active.

**Internal Party Affairs.** Following the termination of unsuccessful negotiations between the White Flags and the Burmese government on 14 November 1963, a serious split developed in the party between those members who favored continuing the White Flag strategy of armed struggle and those who favored abandoning armed insurrection in favor of legal, political struggle. Although the December 1964 plenary session of the White Flag Central Committee reaffirmed the policy of armed struggle, the issue continued to have repercussions in 1967, particularly in view of Communist China's increasing influence over the White Flags.

In a speech on 1 August commemorating the fortieth anniversary of the Chinese People's Liberation Army on that date, Thakin Ba Thein Tin, First Vice-Chairman of the White Flag Central Committee, stated (NCNA, 14 August): "The history of armed struggle in Burma is one of life-or-death struggles between the military lines of the Marxism-Leninism of Mao Tse-tung on the one hand and the bourgeois military line on the other, and the victory of the former over the latter." Specifically, Thakin Ba Thein Tin declared that within the party and army the Marxism-Leninism of Mao Tse-tung had "battered against the idea that stressed only legal struggle and surrendering arms to the enemy" and against the "revisionist idea of seizing political power peacefully by taking the legal parliamentary road." He further noted that "Chairman Mao's idea of waging a protracted people's war to encircle the cities from the countryside and of establishing Red political power by waging protracted war" and also his idea that the armed struggle waged by Burmese Communists should be a "peasants' war led by the proletariat" had met with fierce opposition in the party and army: "It conflicted with the bourgeois idea of launching an insurrection through general strikes in factories, schools, and ships and of first capturing political power in cities and then spreading to the countryside." In addition there had been a "fierce struggle within the party and army" between on the one hand "Chairman Mao's thinking that imperialism and all reactionaries are paper tigers and that one should despise the enemy strategically and take full account of him tactically" and on the other the "bourgeois military thinking of taking full account of the enemy strategically and slighting him tactically." Finally, Thakin Ba Thein Tin stated that a "fierce struggle" had developed in the party and the army between "Chairman Mao's thinking of waging a revolutionary war on the basis of self-reliance and the bourgeois thinking of relying on outside help in making revolution." In all instances, Thakin Ba Thein Tin emphasized, the "Marxism-Leninism of Mao Tse-tung's thought triumphed."

That the struggle between the two lines had not been completely resolved, however, was indicated by the reports of several White Flag Communists who surrendered to the government during 1967. According to Yebaw Thein Myint (alias Ba Khet), an office superintendent of the White Flag headquarters who surrendered on 9 June, Thakin Than Tun, White Flag Chairman, and Thakin Chit and Thakin Zin, both members of the White Flag Politburo, on 27 April "dismissed" Yebaw Goshal and Yebaw Htay, two of the more moderate members of the Politburo. Yebaw Thein Myint stated that he had no knowledge of what had become of the two "dismissed" Politburo members, but that within the White Flag party the term was synonymous with "liquidated."

Yebaw Thein Myint's reports were supported in mid-August when Bo Saw Lin (alias U Saw Hla), a

*Yebaw Goshal and Yebaw Htay reportedly were dismissed from the Politburo on 27 April 1967.

member of the White Flag Toungoo District Organization Committee, surrendered to government forces. Bo Saw Lin reported that he believed that both Yebaw Goshal and Yebaw Htay had been executed and that a third Politburo member, Thakin Than Myaing, had met the same fate in Communist China for opposing the cultural revolution and advocating the "revisionist line." Other party leaders reportedly attacked by Thakin Than Tun's group included Bo Yan Aung and Ba Khet. Bo Saw Lin also stated that the White Flag leadership had become totally subservient to Peking; that White Flag leader Thakin Than Tun was "a mere figurehead," with the real power wielded by Peking-trained cadres who were directing all White Flag activities; and that area commanders had been issued a party directive calling for the arrest of all those unwilling to subscribe to the Peking line.

Subsequent reports by communist insurgents captured during 1967 suggested that the White Flag leadership was divided from the Central Committee down to the township committees and that numerous veteran party members were being replaced by cadres trained in Communist China, while others were undergoing "ideological reorientation."

**Strategy and Tactics.** In a lengthy statement commemorating the twenty-eighth anniversary of the founding of the BCP, Thakin Ba Thein Tin outlined the party's strategy. "We may make use of bourgeois democracy but we do not have blind faith in it," he said, adding: "To seize political power from the hands of the ruling classes, the oppressed classes can only rely on the gun. Apart from this, there is no other method. . . . Political power can only be won by arms; it is impossible to do so through so-called peaceful development." (Quoted in *Peking Review,* no. 36, 1 September 1967.) At a meeting of White Flag members held on 15 December,* party Chairman Thakin Than Tun reportedly declared: "We stand for the annihilation of all enemies, armed or unarmed . . . . If anybody disagrees with this view he is a pacifist traitor."

Thakin Ba Thein Tin in his party anniversary statement stressed the role of the peasantry:

> It is necessary at the present stage of the revolution to formulate correct peasant policies so as to establish an anti-feudal united front in the rural areas and to carry on a peasant war. Our Party has formulated and put into practice the policy of "relying on the poor peasants and farm laborers firmly uniting with the middle peasants, neutralizing the rich peasants, and concentrating the attack on the landlords." (*Ibid.*)

**Domestic Program and Activities.** Although the Red Flags have been more vitriolic in their condemnation of various Burmese governments and US "imperialists," the Red Flags and the White Flags advocate similar policies, with the principal issue dividing the two groups centering on the long-standing personal animosity between their leaders.

Since coming to power, General Ne Win has carried out the "Burmese road to socialism," a program which has involved the construction of a socialist economy, with particular attention devoted to agriculture and the living standards of the country's large peasant population. All land is state owned, and peasants are provided with holdings to cultivate. Middlemen have been abolished, farmers are provided with loans, and market cooperatives have been established. Within such a context, communist efforts to arouse mass opposition to the government have met with considerable difficulty. Communist statements have accused the Burmese government of "committing a big fraud under the signboard of socialism" and have called on "all the Burmese people to rise up to strive for the complete overthrow of the Ne Win military government and the establishment of a people's democratic and united front government." In foreign affairs, the Burmese communists have attacked the nonaligned position of the Burmese government, charging that the "ideology and program of so-called neutrality is, in practice, serving modern revisionism" and calling on the Burmese people to "struggle against it under all circumstances."

Communist activities in Burma during 1967 consisted of guerrilla attacks on transportation and communication networks, mass attacks on and executions of civilians, disruption of government economic programs and government distribution of food supplies, and agitation and organizational activities among the peasants. In May, White Flag Communists and the "Karen National Defense Organization" launched an armed raid on Gyo Bingauk, Tharawaddy District, in what was reportedly the largest raid since the Ne Win government took power.

*It is not known whether or not this meeting was the Central Committee meeting scheduled for September 1967.

Following Communist China's announcement in June of its open support for the Burmese communists, communist terrorism increased significantly. Reports indicate that during the year the White Flags also started their own "proletarian cultural revolution," with Chairman Thakin Than Tun declaring:

> The great cultural revolution is here in Burma. In this great cultural revolution you young people are "model hard cores." We the elders rely primarily on you young people. . . . All of you dare kill your father; you dare kill your mother. This I firmly believe. On such thought is solidly established the success of the Burmese cultural revolution.

Despite the claim that "guerrilla bases of the Burmese people's forces are set up in all parts of the country," the White Flags insurgents have been active primarily in the Delta area, (where their infrastructure is relatively weak), the Dry Zone west of the Irrawaddy River (from which they can withdraw to the Arakam Yoma or hill country), central Burma, and the southern peninsula, while Red Flag insurgents are concentrated in the Delta area and the Dry Zone. Reports also indicate that in March 1965 a "Marxist-Leninist Training School" was opened in the mountainous Pegu Yoma region of southern Burma, reputed to be the "base area for building Red power."

**White Flag Self-Analysis.** In his address honoring the fortieth anniversary of the founding of the Chinese People's Liberation Army, Thakin Ba Thein Tin hailed the "new great victories" scored by the BCP and added:

> The principal manifestations of this military victory are in the following aspects: (1) The enlargement and consolidation of the base areas. Our base areas and guerrilla zones are scattered all over the north, south, east, and west of Burma. In a word, extensive guerrilla warfare has besieged the enemy. In these base areas, including Burma's major rice producer, the delta area, our party and the people's army control the vast countryside. (2) An increase of 50 per cent nationally in the strength of the armed forces led by our party. (3) Increased frequency of our people's army attacks on enemy strongholds and small and medium towns with many more men involved in the operations. (4) The expansion of fighting zones. There are guerrilla activities in 31 out of over 50 counties in the country, or more than 67 per cent of the total. (5) The close integration of the peasants' economic struggle with the people's war and its continual growth in strength. (NCNA, 14 August.)

In a statement a few days later, Thakin Ba Thein Tin enumerated the same points, adding:

> At the same time we must admit that at present, the enemy has surpassed us, both numerically and in equipment. In order to completely change the balance of forces between the enemy and ourselves, we must take firm hold of Mao Tse-tung's thought and closely integrate it with the practice in our own country. . . .
>
> We may meet with twists and turns in our road of advance and may suffer temporary setbacks, but, viewed as a whole, the Burmese revolution is forging ahead step by step and it is certain that final victory will be won. (*Peking Review*, no. 35, 25 August 1967.)

A lengthy article in the White Flag organ *People's Power*, (broadcast by NCNA, 15 November) outlined a series of tasks facing the White Flags and "revolutionary people" and added:

> The revolutionary armed forces must unite further and fight together hand in hand until the Ne Win military dictator government is crushed. So, revolutionary Burmese people of various nationalities, crush the dirty anti-China plot of Ne Win, further strengthen the comradeship of the revolutionary Burmese people and the revolutionary Chinese, and fight against the Ne Win military dictator government and its master US imperialism. . . .
>
> Fight for the people's struggle for food and eliminate the Ne Win government! Step up the armed struggle being launched by the Communist Party and Ma-Da-Nya-Ta [the National Democratic United Front]! The whole country, unite and struggle for the elimination of Ne Win and for the establishment of a people's democratic government.

Noncommunist sources state that there is no foundation for the White Flag claim that armed struggle is being waged over half of the country, and that a more realistic estimate would be that one-tenth of the population and nearly two-fifths of the country are under communist control.

The position taken by the Burmese government is that communist insurgent activities are an impediment but not a danger. Nevertheless, an October editorial in the official *Working People's Daily* noted:

> The guerrilla campaign of the Communist rebels has sharply increased to the level of 1950 (when every single town except Rangoon had fallen into rebel hands). The reactivation of the civil war is not wholly unsuspected, since the Communists are being incited by unscrupulous elements outside the country.

Communist insurgents captured during 1967 reported that internal disunity and government offensives had caused considerable disruption of White Flag activities and possibly prevented—or at least postponed—a White Flag Central Committee meeting scheduled for September. There is no indication as to whether the meeting was ever held.

**International Views and Activities: Communist China.** The Burmese government was the first noncommunist government to extend diplomatic recognition to the People's Republic of China. A border agreement and a treaty of friendship and nonaggression were subsequently signed, with the Chinese Communists referring frequently to the Burmese as "kinsmen" and hailing relations between the two countries as an outstanding example of Communist China's friendly relations with noncommunist countries. Sino-Burmese cordiality was brusquely terminated in 1967, however, following anti-Chinese riots in Rangoon in late June which were touched off by the refusal of Chinese students in Burma to comply with a ban by the Burmese Ministry of Education on the wearing of Mao Tse-tung badges. Additional government efforts aimed at preventing the Chinese Communists from extending the cultural revolution to the Chinese community in Burma resulted in a series of violent mass demonstrations. On 26 June some 2,000 Burmese reportedly rioted outside the Chinese Embassy and tore down the Chinese emblem. Riots and demonstrations continued for two days, and on 28 June a Chinese staff member was stabbed to death by two Burmese who had climbed over the Embassy walls. That same day, the NCNA broadcast a protest note in which Peking accused the Burmese government of instigating the riots, conniving with the Burmese mobs in insulting Mao Tse-tung, and persecuting the Chinese residents in the country. On 1 July, a statement issued by the White Flag Central Committee on June 28 was broadcast by the NCNA:

> As a result of the cruel persecution by the Ne Win military government, the blood of our Chinese brothers was shed.
>
> This is the most serious crime committed by the Ne Win military government. This is an outrageous insult to the feeling of friendship of the Chinese and the Burmese peoples, which is ardently cherished by the broad masses of the people.
>
> This is by no means an accident. It is a carefully calculated maneuver, executed in close cooperation and coordination with the American imperialists, the modern revisionists headed by the revisionist leadership of the CPSU, other international forces of reaction, and the Chiang Kai-shek bandits. It is an act directly connected with the anticommunist, anti-people policy long pursued by the Ne Win military government in the interests of its own class. By this act, it has revealed its true colors even further.

Demonstrations continued during the summer and early fall. On 17 July the Burmese expelled Yu Min-shen, the NCNA's resident correspondent in Rangoon, for "interfering in the internal affairs of Burma" and for publishing the 28 June statement of the BCP Central Committee. On 4 October Peking called on the Burmese government to accede to a series of demands stemming from the anti-Chinese riots in June. On 6 October the Burmese government responded by saying that after 31 October it would no longer pay the living expenses of Chinese technicians in Burma. On the latter date Peking announced the withdrawal of its economic aid mission in Burma and accused the Ne Win government of "unilaterally, perfidiously, and completely tearing to pieces the Sino-Burmese economic and technical cooperation agreement." (NCNA, 31 October 1967.)

Although Communist China pursued a policy of "peaceful coexistence" with Burma from 1949 to mid-1967, it had at the same time given tacit approval to communist insurgents operating in Burma and maintained close contacts with them. Reports indicate that close to 100 Burmese communists have undergone military training in China and that Chinese advisers have been infiltrating northern

Burma to aid insurgent groups there (*New York Times,* 18 January 1968). Apparently little, if any, material aid has been given directly to the White Flags.

Communist China has given considerable propaganda support to the White Flags. While the Chinese Communists gave no publicity to the BCP's twenty-seventh anniversary, in 1966, they openly hailed the twenty-eighth anniversary of the party:

> The Chinese Communist Party and the Chinese people firmly support the people's revolutionary armed struggle led by the Burmese Communist Party. We regard such support as our bounden proletarian internationalist duty. . . .
>
> Our two parties and the people of our two countries have forged profound friendship in long revolutionary struggle. Let us further consolidate and develop the militant friendship between our two parties and the people of our two countries in the joint struggle to liquidate the counterrevolutionary revisionist line of the top person in authority in the Chinese Communist Party taking the capitalist road.
>
> It is our firm conviction that the Burmese Communist Party headed by Comrade Thakin Than Tun, which persists in the revolutionary line of "to win the war and seize political power," will assuredly further unite the whole party and the people of all nationalities in Burma, overthrow the reactionary Ne Win government, and win complete victory in the revolutionary war in Burma. (NCNA, 14 August.)

The White Flags, in turn, have repeatedly hailed the thought of Mao Tse-tung as the "acme of Marxist-Leninism in our era" and have praised the cultural revolution as having "set a new example for the proletariat of the whole world in solving the question of how to consolidate the dictatorship of the proletariat and prevent the restoration of capitalism—a question of historical importance."

Upon the publication of the Burmese edition of the *Selected Works of Mao Tse-tung,* in 1967, Thakin Ba Thein Tin stated:

> In the present era, one's attitude towards Mao Tse-tung's thought, acceptance or non-acceptance of Mao Tse-tung's thought as Marxism-Leninism of the present era, is the important criterion for judging whether or not one is a real Marxist-Leninist, a real revolutionary. To be a real Marxist-Leninist in the present era, it is not enough to accept Marxism-Leninism in general or just in words; one must recognize that Mao Tse-tung's thought is Marxism-Leninism of the present era and apply it in practice. Facts have fully proved that those who oppose Mao Tse-tung's thought all become traitors to the revolution and the people and are inevitably discarded and thrown on to the garbage dump of history. (*Peking Review,* no. 48, 24 November.)

**The Soviet Union.** White Flag statements regarding the Soviet Union have declared that the "Soviet revisionists are outright renegades to the revolutionary movements in all countries" (quoted, *ibid.,* no. 36, 1 September). The Burmese communists have also accused the "Soviet Khrushchevian revisionists" of working to "undermine" their armed struggle, and "inflicting heavy losses" on their party and armed forces by advocating the abolition of armed struggle and the seizure of power through parliamentary means.

On the occasion of the fiftieth anniversary of the October Revolution, the BCP Central Committee issued a resolution stating:

> Today the clique centered around the renegades Khrushchev, Brezhnev, and Kosygin has destroyed the fruits of the Great October Revolution which belong not only to the people of the Soviet Union but also to the people of the whole world. They have destroyed the dictatorship of the proletariat in the Soviet Union built with the blood of the heroic people of the Soviet Union. They are building capitalism under the cloak of Marxism-Leninism. These traitors have also sabotaged the revolution of the proletariat and other oppressed classes in various countries.
>
> These traitors are denying the universal truth of Marxism-Leninism that the bourgeois state cannot be superseded by the proletarian state (the dictatorship of the proletariat) through the process of "withering away," but, as a general rule, only through a violent revolution; they are trying to substitute in its stead parliamentary means. They are doing

their utmost to blunt the revolutionary spirit of the people of the world and are working to prolong the regimes of all reactionary forces. (Quoted in *Peking Review*, no. 47, 17 November.)

The Soviet response to Communist Chinese support of White Flag activities and to the demonstrations of mid-June was to maintain that Peking was carrying out a "hostile and subversive campaign" against its neighbors. While expressing support for the Burmese government, however, Moscow addressed itself primarily to the Burmese Communists in an attempt to woo the BCP away from Peking. In a Soviet broadcast on 12 July Moscow warned that the Chinese leaders were "plotting to assume the leading role in regions where the national liberation movement flourishes, chiefly in Asia," and added that the "bitter defeats suffered by the progressive forces in Burma, Malaya, and the Philippines over the past twenty years have clearly reflected this point." The following day, a Soviet broadcast noted:

It is because of the policies of the Peking leadership that the Burmese Communist Party has not been able to this day to benefit from the favorable conditions created by the assumption of power by the revolutionary democrats. They have not been able to come out of the forest and take part in the building of a non-capitalist Burma.

**Other International Activities.** Although direct contact between the BCP and other members of the international communist movement have been limited, the Burmese Communists have regularly stressed that the "Burmese revolution is . . . a component part of the world proletarian revolution." During 1967 the BCP hailed the outbreak of what it called "revolutionary armed struggle" in India and sent greetings to the Communist Party of Thailand on the occasion of the twenty-fifth anniversary of its founding (1 December). A delegation of the BCP Central Committee headed by Peking-based Thakin Ba Thein Tin, attended Communist China's National Day celebrations on 1 October.

Although the BCP sent a delegation to the 1960 meeting of communist and workers' parties, it did not send a delegation to the 1957 meeting in Moscow, nor was it represented at the Moscow celebrations of the fiftieth anniversary of the October Revolution or the Budapest meeting in February 1968.

**Publications.** The official publication of the BCP is *People's Power*. Other communist or procommunist publications in Burma include the *China Commercial Times, New China Pao,* and pro-Soviet daily *Socialist* (known as *Botataung*—"Vanguard"— until it was nationalized in September 1964). Additional publications included *Zin Min Pao,* which ceased publication in January 1966, and *Ludu,* an aboveground pro-Chinese daily which ceased publication in July 1967 because of the government's refusal to renew its printing permit. BCP statements and policies are also widely publicized by the Chinese Communist news media.

# CAMBODIA

Although a Committee for a Revolutionary People's Party was founded in Cambodia in 1949, the communist Cambodian People's Revolutionary Party (PRP; Dang Nhan Dan Cach Mang Cao Min) was not founded until 1951. Although its name and statutes were drafted in Vietnamese, they were later translated into Cambodian. Following the 1954 Geneva Agreements on Indochina, Communists in Cambodia sought to escape the label of "Vietnamese puppets" and formed the Pracheachon Party (PP–Khmer People's Party), a front organization through which they operate today. The PRP is illegal and is estimated to have no more than 100 members. On 3 April 1967 Prince Norodom Sihanouk, head of state, estimated the membership of the Pracheachon Party to be "100 or 200," but actual strength is probably closer to 1000, with several thousand sympathizers. The population of Cambodia is 6,320,000 (estimated 1966).

**Organization and Leadership.** During 1967, Sihanouk continued to refer to the Khmer Communists as the "partisans of Non Suon," leading member of the PP who was arrested in 1962 on charges of directing a Communist espionage network in the province of Kompong Cham and whose death sentence was later commuted, and commented on the "partisans of Hu Nim." However, very little is known about the leadership and organization of either the PRP or the PP. Information regarding the leadership of the Cambodian communist movement was revealed following the arrest of 140 people involved in the April 1967 disturbances in the province of Battambang. Local leaders involved in the disturbances admitted that they were Khmer Communists who had acted on instructions from their "chiefs in Phnom Penh," whom they named as Chau Seng, So Nem, Khiev Samphan, Hou Youn, and Hu Nim. Even more deeply implicated were Khiev Samphan, Hou Youn, and Hu Nim, who were accused of being the directing leaders and the authors of numerous tracts and leaflets distributed by the local Communists. Although little information is available regarding these individuals, it is known that Hu Nim, Khiev Samphan, and Hou Youn are deputies in the National Assembly and that So Nem and Chau Seng held the cabinet posts of Minister of Health and Minister of National Economy, respectively, until their dismissals on 11 September 1967. So Nem was also Chairman, and Hu Nim one of the Vice-Presidents, of the Khmer-Chinese Friendship Association, until it was dissolved on 1 September 1967.

In addition to these leaders, Phouk Chhay (also referred to as Put Chay), Secretary-General of the banned Khmer-Chinese Friendship Association and Chairman of the now defunct pro-Peking General Association of Khmer Students, has also been accused of being a "Khmer Red" leader and a Maoist partisan of Communist China. Other leaders reportedly include Khiet Chhon and Keo An.

Cambodian Communist elements have been active through two other organizations, both of which are reportedly financed by the Communist Chinese embassy: The Khmer-Chinese Friendship Association, founded on 1 May 1964 and headed by Leng Ngeth, and the General Association of Khmer Students, headed by Phouk Chhay.

Communist elements in Cambodia also operate through the Vietnamese and Chinese communities in Cambodia, with significant infiltration of the Vietnamese community association, the Viet Kieu.

While the PRP is illegal, its front, the PP, enjoys a status of quasi-legality, in that it is officially legal but is suppressed by the government. For this reason a number of leftist Cambodians have refrained from active association with the Party. In suppressing internal communism, however, Sihanouk has followed a policy of militant "neutrality" in international affairs, thus enjoying the favors of the communist powers. His rationale for such a strategy is that neutrality is a precondition for a noncommunist Cambodia and that alignment with either bloc would result in a loss of "independence, territorial integrity, and peace" for Cambodia. While such a strategy may not prevent a Communist takeover in the long run, Sihanouk appears to believe that it will at least postpone such an event for a few years.

Since 1955 Cambodian politics have been dominated by Sihanouk's People's Socialist Community (Sangkum Reastr Niyum). On 11 September 1966 elections to the National Assembly were held in which the Sangkum ran all the candidates and won all the seats. Of the 82 deputies elected to the National Assembly, which included a handful of well-known leftists, 73 voted to form a right-of-center government under the prime ministership of General Lon Nol. Of the 16 members of the cabinet formed, two were regarded as leftists—So Nem, who was named Minister of Health, and Chan Sing, who was named Minister of National Economy. Reports indicate, however, that the "real left" refused General Nol's invitation to nominate its own candidates and is therefore not represented.

After the elections Sihanouk announced the formation of a "countergovernment," to be known as "her Majesty's Opposition," in honor of the queen, Sihanouk's mother. Prince Sihanouk insists that the countergovernment is a "private organism of the Sangkum" with limited powers which consist mainly of providing semiofficial constructive criticism. The 18-member countergovernment includes a number of leftists, including such "Khmer Reds" as Hou Youn, Khieu Samphan, So Nem, and Hu Nim.

Sihanouk has continually emphasized the need to control and suppress internal communism and has accused the "Khmer Reds" of attempting to organize a government at Prey Chhor, with Hu Nim as president, in opposition to the Sangkum and the royal government. However, he has also said:

> I have often urged the Khmer Communists, or Reds, not to create a civil war like the Laotians, the Thai, and the Vietnamese, for this is not good for us. Despite our ideological differences, we Khmer can solve these differences peacefully. If these Communists do not want to accept any peaceful arrangement, and if the JSRK [Royal Khmer Socialist Youth] and the people accept communism, I will immediately approve of this and offer my resignation. I would rather resign than remain at the post of Chief of State.
>
> Moreover, the Sangkum will not insist on remaining and will also resign if the Communists want to take over power. In fact, I have asked them many times to come and take over the nation. I have also written them letters asking them to take over power. However, they have refused, and some of them do not even bother to answer. (Phnom Penh Domestic Service, 6 April 1967.)

**Domestic Tactics and Programs.** Communist cadres in Cambodia are active primarily in the tightly organized Vietnamese and Chinese communities in Cambodia, with most of their activities focusing on the central and eastern provinces of Kompong Cham and Kompong Thom, the southern province of Kompong Speu, and the northwestern province of Battambang.

Communist tactics in Cambodia have followed the familiar pattern of propaganda and subversion. Numerous precise directives have been outlined in pamphlets and leaflets, such as one "on the struggle to eliminate passivity, timidity and, the adherence to tranquility among our followers, who must prepare a violent revolution," which declared:

> 1. Marxist-Leninist doctrine calls for a revolution to create a society healthy and egalitarian in rights and obligations.
>
> 2. To attain this end there must be a struggle without mercy, a solidarity between the oppressed classes.
>
> 3. The members of the revolutionary party must face up to all trials and to the evils of the imperialists and the ruling class.
>
> 4. These trials are not eternal; the revolution will conquer; one has to act like the Russian Bolsheviks in the days of Marx and Lenin. (*Sangkum,* 13 April 1966, quoted in *Est et Ouest,* 16-30 June 1967.)

Additional instructions noted:

> Today's society is corrupted and won over by the cult of the individual, which we must abolish at all costs. We live in a sick society since the return to peace.

All the courageous and honest children of the fatherland must join the revolutionary party in order to lead the country to socialist communism.

The aim of the revolution is the liberation of the people from the capitalists and feudal elements. In order to succeed, we must resort to force.

As a result of increased domestic activities on the part of local Communists during 1967, Sihanouk delivered an address to the nation on 11 September 1967 in which he noted that Communist subversion had reached a potentially dangerous stage, and that whereas the "Khmer Reds" had previously confined themselves to subversion and propaganda in their efforts to convert the Khmer people to "Chinese Marxism," they "have now passed to the second phase of their plan, to liquidate the Sangkum and Sihanouk and to openly support the local Reds . . . " (quoted in *Est et Ouest*, 16-30 November 1967).

In carrying out their activities the "Khmer Reds" have outlined a number of specific grievances against the national government, accusing it of corruption, of selling the country to the "US imperialists" and the French, of doing nothing in the field of national defense, of failing to make any national progress, and of exploiting the people through unjust government prices for rice harvests.

On 11 March 1967 members of the PP demonstrated in front of the headquarters of the opposition party, demanding the dissolution of the Lon Nol government, a reduction in the prices of consumer goods, and the withdrawal of government troops from Pailin in Battambang, an area in which "pro-Khmer Reds" originating in Thailand are reportedly active. The next day Sihanouk called a special session of the National Assembly, during which he noted the demonstration had been staged by the "Khmer Communist Party, the Pracheachon, in connivance with certain members of the Sangkum to sow dissension among the Khmer people, to overthrow the present Royal Government, and to dissolve the National Assembly." Refuting the "Khmer Reds' " claims that Cambodia was becoming the "lackey of the US imperialists" and their "slanders" against the Lon Nol government and the Cambodian army, Sihanouk replied that although the National Assembly had committed no misdeed, he would not object to its dissolution if the "Khmer Reds" would show up and promise to respect a new National Assembly and royal government. He also warned that there were many "Suhartos" in Cambodia ready to liquidate the Communists in 24 hours, but that he did not want that to happen. He added, however, that they should be careful not to provoke him too much, or he would declare a state of emergency throughout the country.

On 2 April 1967 left-wing elements launched a series of attacks against several provincial guard posts and a model farm run by the Royal Khmer Socialist Youth in the Pailin district of western Battambang. On 3 April Sihanouk delivered a lengthy message to the nation, pointing out:

> In order to remove Mau Say and Duoc Rasy, the Khmer Reds accused these two personalities of being corrupt, rotten, and procapitalist. The other day they forced the Nationalist Assembly to remove them. They thought that once these two were removed, Lon Nol would be compelled to resign. To their disappointment, Lon Nol has not submitted his resignation and has remained in his post. Seeing this, they decided to take stronger action. Thus on 2 April they came to attack their nation, that is, the provincial guards and the Royal Khmer Socialist Youth. (Phnom Penh Domestic Service, 3 April 1967.)

Sihanouk also announced that the "Khmer Reds" had "massacred those who refused to submit to their party," burned a number of houses and bridges, and incited the people to fight against the provincial guards and the Royal Khmer Armed Forces in order to "leave the land for the Vietnamese Viet Minh." He outlined the Cambodian government's response to the disturbances, which reportedly involved some 100 insurgents:

> They launched these attacks because they want to create civil war. The fact that they came to attack the nation and massacre the provincial guards and compatriots . . . has compelled the Royal Khmer Armed Forces and provincial guards to conduct mopping-up

operations to repress this, for when they are using weapons against the state, the nation must reply with force.

Formerly the Khmer Viet Minh only distributed tracts, composed songs, and performed on the stage to criticize the Chief-of-State. Despite this, I refused to take any action against them. But now it is different. They came to attack our posts. From their forests, they launched surprise attacks against us. Thus we are compelled to take action in reply to these attacks. I want to inform the Bonzes [Buddhist monks] and the children that we are now compelled to repress them by launching operations so that this kind of groundless revolution can be put to an end. (Phnom Penh Domestic Service, 21 April 1967.)

Sihanouk warned that additional disturbances would present serious problems for the Cambodian government. In a moment of frankness he admitted that "it is our great friends of People's China, Russia, and France who have given us arms and ammunition to resist these attacks" but at the same time asked, "now that the Khmer Reds have come to attack us, how can we ask China and Russia for ammunition and rifles to fight against the Khmer Reds?" He proposed a number of possible government actions to be implemented, should the need arise; these measures included closing all embassies abroad to make funds available for weapons "to achieve peace and national security," suspending the national Five Year Plan, and suspending the National Assembly and government in order to allow the chief-of-state to assume full powers.

Government concern over Communist-inspired activities was further compounded when on 7 April Sihanouk noted that although they had not yet revolted, the "Khmer Reds" were making plans for insurgent activities in the province of Kompong Cham, which is represented in the National Assembly by Hu Nim and Hou Youn. Additional reports indicated that perhaps the disturbances in Battambang, which has been leftist for years, were meant to be a diversionary action to cover a larger disturbance in Kompong Cham, an area which would be of strategic importance for the Viet Cong. In the same address Sihanouk noted:

Until now I have not ordered the partisans of Non Suon executed, but I have only imprisoned them after offering proof. As for the partisans of Hu Nim, I have obtained proof of their activities and yet I have ordered their release. I have always been kind to them. This time I want to warn them that I can no longer tolerate them. Once they are arrested along with sufficient proof of their acts . . . they will be tried by the military tribunal. If it finds them guilty and sentences them to death, I will not pardon them. This is my warning in advance. (Phnom Penh Domestic Service, 13 April 1967.)

He went on to warn that "if [the Communists] want to avoid death, they have only to flee abroad, for if they remain here they will be executed."

On 22 April Sihanouk disclosed a list of persons named by captured "Khmer Reds" as the leaders of the disturbances in Battambang. Among those named were Chau Seng, So Nem, Khiev Samphan, Hou Youn, and Hu Nim, with most of the accusations centering on the last three. Sihanouk continued to maintain that until they had been tried and convicted of specific offenses, the accused would still enjoy parliamentary immunity and would remain members of the High Council and the National Assembly. On 24 April 1967 Hou Youn and Khiev Samphan took Sihanouk's advice and fled from Cambodia.

The disturbances in the province of Battambang were not without repercussions in the government. On 30 April 1967 Lon Nol resigned on grounds of ill health, and on 2 May 1967 an interim government was formed under the former Deputy Prime Minister Son Sann, with Sihanouk assuming special powers voted to him by the National Assembly. Sihanouk explained that because of the present situation, it was impossible to form a government by normal processes, but added that he expected the interim government to last no more than three months. On 7 August he accused pro-Peking leftists in Cambodia of increased subversive activity and announced his decision to continue the interim government, in spite of his earlier offer to resign. During May he continued to accuse the Cambodian leftists of promoting anarchy in Cambodia in order to "demonstrate loyalty to the ideology of their great Chinese friends" and condemned them for attempting to turn Cambodia into a "lackey of the Viet Minh, the Chinese People's Republic, and the USSR."

On 10 May Leng Ngeth resigned from the presidency of the Khmer-Chinese Friendship Association " . . . because of the improper conduct of certain members of the Association, disregarding the wise traditions observed by the Cambodian community, who have begun to spread subversive propaganda secretly or publicly with the aim of destroying the Khmer spirit of solidarity in such a way that the Association's honor finds itself gravely compromised" (quoted in *Far Eastern Economic Review*, 15 June 1967).

Increased Communist activity in Battambang in April and the fear of Communist subversion elsewhere in Cambodia, however, resulted in Sihanouk's decision on 1 September to dissolve all friendship associations between Cambodia and foreign countries on the grounds that they were becoming propaganda organs aimed at the destruction of the Cambodian national government. He also announced that the associations would be replaced by "national committees," that all privately owned newspapers would be suppressed, and that Peking's New China News Agency would be banned. This dissolution order seemed to be specifically directed at the Khmer-Chinese Friendship Association, the strongest, largest, and best-organized of the associations, particularly in view of the reportedly disorganized state of the Khmer-Soviet and the Khmer-North Vietnamese Friendship Associations. Sihanouk's decision elicited no foreign response except from Peking.

Communist China ignored the order until 4 September, when the Sino-Cambodian Friendship Association in Peking sent a telegram to its counterpart in Phnom Penh expressing its good will and solidarity with the Association and urging it to continue its activities in spite of the decision of the "reactionary" Cambodian government. The result was a near break in diplomatic relations between the two countries. Following publication of the Peking directive in the French-language paper *La Nouvelle Dépêche*, Sihanouk demanded the immediate resignation of two pro-Peking ministers, Minister of Health So Nem, and Chau Seng, Minister of National Economy and owner of the offending newspaper.

During the fall Sihanouk launched a series of attacks on Phouk Chhay and the General Association of Khmer Students, accusing it of being "constituted and directed by a minority of Communists and of Communist and pro-Communist students who apply dictatorship to the 90 per cent composed of non-Communist students" (Phnom Penh Domestic Service, 18 September 1967). In a speech delivered on 30 September in Kompong Cham and later in a press conference held in Phnom Pehn on 5 October, Sihanouk elaborated on the efforts of leftists to communize Cambodia and noted in particular the efforts of Hu Nim and Phouk Chhay, Chairman of the General Association of Khmer Students. He concluded with an order that a military tribunal give full consideration to their cases, warning both Phouk Chhay and Hu Nim to leave the country or face the tribunal.

In a special message to the nation on 7 October, Sihanouk again commented on the state of affairs of the General Association of Khmer Students and the activities of Phouk Chhay, noting that he had received representations from the majority of students protesting the failure of the Association to represent accurately the views of the student body. In response to these representations Sihanouk announced that since the Association did not represent all the students but did include the "Red partisans of Phouk Chhay," a general assembly of students would be held to elect new representatives and form a new national student organization. In elaborating on his decision to form a new association, Sihanouk stated that the General Association of Khmer Students was protesting such plans and denying the government the right to dissolve it. He warned, however, that the "Red Students" would face military trial if they pretended to represent all the students, slandered the present regime, and plotted to turn Cambodia into a satellite of Communist China by importing Communist Chinese doctrine and culture into Cambodia. He also suggested that the "Red Students" might prefer to go to China, since they were no longer Khmers, and again warned that if they insisted on maintaining their illegal association, they would be brought to trial.

On 9 October Hu Nim followed the advice of Sihanouk and disappeared from Cambodia, as Hou Youn and Khiev Samphan had done several months earlier. In commenting on their disappearance, Sihanouk said: "We know that they were ordered to flee by foreigners because they would probably be summoned to answer before a military tribunal and this would naturally implicate some foreign country. They were not allowed to do so." (Phnom Penh Domestic Service, 14 October 1967). Hu Nim, Hou Youn, and Khiev Samphan are still believed to be in China. Phouk Chhay was not allowed to leave after the discovery of Hu Nim's disappearance.

In commenting on Hu Nim's disappearance Sihanouk elaborated on the activities of the General Association of Khmer Students, referring to it as a "Red association" whose members acted as "anti-US agents to please China and not to safeguard Cambodia." He also revealed that "no national, but only Communist, documents were found in the file of the General Association of Khmer Students," and that these documents concerned "the crusade in South America, the communist road, Fidel Castro's theories, and the Chinese cultural revolution" (Phnom Penh Domestic Service, 14 October 1967).

On 30 December the Cambodian National Assembly and the High Council met in a plenary session and unanimously decided to ask Sihanouk to continue in the "presidency of the exceptional government."

**International Affairs.** The PRP and the PP are in the paradoxical position of belonging to a country whose government adheres to the principles of militant "neutrality," thus enjoying the favors of the communist powers while at the same time severely suppressing internal communism. Sihanouk's neutrality, however, has proved somewhat mercurial, with a distinct tendency to favor the communist camp until 1967, when he began to indicate his desire to correct his drift toward the left.

Following Communist disturbances in Battambang, Sihanouk declared on 6 May 1967:

> . . . our independence, our neutrality, and our territorial integrity will be defended against any enemy, be it Viet Minh [North Vietnam] or America.

> As for such socialist countries as the DRV [Democratic Republic of Vietnam], the NLFSV [National Liberation Front of South Vietnam], or the DPRK [Democratic People's Republic of Korea], we support them politically and diplomatically without reservation. But we cannot support certain among them in their efforts to neocolonialize Cambodia and turn it into a satellite by using Khmer Reds as their Trojan horses.

He further commented on Cambodia's relations with the communist powers, noting that

> . . . any friction between us and China, or between us and the Vietnamese, or between us and the Communists could be ascribed to the Khmer Reds, who are jealous of the fact that, although not Red, the Sangkum has been on friendly terms with their masters, and they therefore try all means to sow discord between the Sangkum and their masters. The Khmer Reds have exerted every effort in this direction recently. . . . They think that by insulting Sihanouk, they will make Sihanouk reciprocate. They believe that if Sihanouk insults them—the Khmer Reds—he will shock the Chinese, Russians, and Vietnamese, who are also Red. In their opinion, if Sihanouk hurts the Khmer Reds' honor, the latter will part with him. If this happens, the other Reds will support the Khmer Reds. That is the malicious intention of the Khmer Reds.

> Therefore, I must emphasize that this dispute is only among Khmer, and that we do not want any friction in our relations with the Chinese, Russians, or others. (Phnom Penh Domestic Service, 16 May 1967.)

As expected, Moscow, Peking, and Hanoi have made no reference to Sihanouk's complaints of foreign control of internal subversion in Cambodia. Instead, they have continued to maintain that they fully support the "just struggle of Cambodia against US imperialists and their agents."

**Relations with China.** Despite Sihanouk's statements to the contrary, increased subversive activities during 1967 on the part of the "Khmer Reds," whom Sihanouk accuses of being Maoists and following the instructions of Communist China, resulted in a significant deterioration of Sino-Cambodian relations. This deterioration had already begun prior to the disturbances in Battambang. Although Cambodian support of the Chinese cultural revolution has been reported by Communist China, there is no record that Sihanouk himself has ever expressed support for it. On 1 January 1967, at the Twenty-Third Buddhist Conference in Phnom Penh, Sihanouk dissociated himself from "certain individuals" who are "deeply interested in and even satisfied with the Chinese cultural revolution" (Phnom Penh Domestic Service, 1 January 1967), and on 12 March he pointed out that "the creation of the Red Guards in China has proved to be an erroneous policy which must be stopped . . . ." According to Sihanouk, "Nobody in the world admires the Red Guards; only Cambodia has praised them because we have eaten Chinese rice. As for me, I am obliged to congratulate anyone who has given me rice" (Phnom Penh Domestic Service, 12 March 1967). Cambodia's relations with Communist China were also tarnished by the rather tardy Chinese recognition of Cambodia's frontiers on 12 June, especially in view of the fact that the Soviet Union had extended recognition almost two weeks earlier.

Following the dissolution of all friendship associations in Cambodia on 1 September 1967 and the Communist Chinese telegram of 4 September calling on the Khmer-Chinese Friendship Association to continue its activities in spite of the "reactionary" Cambodian government's decision, Sihanouk severely condemned Communist China, labeled the telegram the "first attack by the PRC [Communist China] on the national regime of Cambodia," and accused the Chinese Communists of interfering in Cambodian state affairs.

On 13 September Sihanouk announced his decision to recall Truong Cang, the Cambodian ambassador to Peking. On 18 September, however, he suddenly cancelled the recall of Truong Cang and the Cambodian embassy staff after "direct overtures" from Chou En-lai to the effect that the incident did not necessitate such a serious reaction and should in fact be forgotten. On 1 November Sihanouk declared that Cambodia should accept "complete reconciliation with People's China."

**The International Communist Movement.** Relations with the rest of the communist world are handicapped by the foreign parties' unwillingness to offend the Cambodian government, as indicated by Communist China's desire to settle its dispute with Cambodia as quickly as possible. There is no evidence that representatives of either the PRP or the PP attended any communist congresses or meetings during the year, although there have been occasional expressions of support and solidarity for the "struggle of the Cambodian people" by such organizations as the Afro-Asian-Latin American Peoples' Solidarity Organization (AALAPSO), and Sihanouk did report finding Cuban documents in the files of the General Association of Khmer Students.

Within the context of the Sino-Soviet dispute, the PRP's pro-Peking position is mirrored by the PP. During 1967 Sihanouk accused Cambodian Communists of "carrying out subversive activities in favor of the Chinese Communists," of "selling their bodies and souls to China," and of attempting to "transform the Khmer people into Communists who will replace Buddhism with Mao Tse-tung's religion" (Phnom Penh Domestic Service, 31 May, 18 September, 19 October 1967). At the same time, however, he accused them of having the Viet Minh and the Viet Cong as their masters and of attempting to turn Cambodia into a "slave of the Viet Minh." Vietnamese Communists, taking directions from the Vietnam Workers' Party of North Vietnam, operating through the National Liberation Front of South Vietnam, are known to have infiltrated the Viet Kieu, the Vietnamese community association, as well as several daily newspapers and schools. In addition, it is reported that the Vietnamese Communists have at least six large bases in Cambodia, with up to 35,000 troops—Viet Cong and North Vietnamese regulars—using Cambodian territory.

**Publications.** Shortly after its formation, following the 1954 Geneva Agreements on Indochina, the PP published four journals, *Mitt Pheap, Ek Pheap, Pracheachon,* and *L'Observateur*. In 1962, the semiweekly official organ of the party, *Pracheachon*, was renamed *Somleeng Apyiakrut*. The official organ of the Vietnamese Communists in Cambodia is the daily *Trung Lap*. In addition to these official publications, Communists in Cambodia have operated through a number of left-wing journals. During 1967 Sihanouk referred to the "Khmer Reds of the journals, *Meatophum, La Nouvelle Dépêche, Sorya,* and *Sochivator*" and accused *Sovanaphum* of being a "pro-Red" newspaper. *Sorya,* a Chinese paper printed in Cambodian, was reportedly subsidized by the Chinese Communist embassy, and *La Nouvelle Dépêche* was owned by Chau Seng. Other newspapers include *Mien-hua Jih-pao* and *Kung Shang Jih-pao,* reportedly subsidized by the Chinese embassy, and *Yuvamitt, Shen Huo Wu Pao,* and *Mekong Pao,* all of which follow the communist line. Cambodian Communists have also published a number of pamphlets and leaflets bearing the name and symbol "Reaksmei Kraham" (Red Light). Following the decision to ban all privately owned newspapers, a number of these papers ceased circulation and the New China News Agency's right to issue local news bulletins was terminated.

# CAMEROUN

Although there is no organized communist party in Cameroun, within a faction of a noncommunist party, the Union des Populations du Cameroun (UPC) there has been formed a "First Marxist-Leninist Group of Cameroun" which has declared its intention to become the nucleus of a new communist party. The UPC, founded in 1948 and banned in 1955, has continued its activities underground and in exile, receiving aid and support from both the Soviet Union and Communist China. After 1960, as a consequence of the death of UPC leader Félix Moumié, the strengthening of the Ahidjo regime in Cameroun, and the split within the international communist movement, the UPC divided into several factions. Some members defected from the party and returned from exile to Cameroun. A faction which calls itself the "Revolutionary Committee of the UPC" is maintaining close ties with the French Communist Party and has a pro-Soviet orientation (although it is not formally a communist party). Still another faction, calling itself the "Provisional Committee of the UPC," has turned to Peking and has created the nucleus of a Marxist-Leninist party. The strength of any faction of the UPC in Cameroun is negligible.

A new phase in the history of the UPC began in 1964 under the leadership of Osende Afana, who was elected Secretary-General of the "Provisional Committee of the UPC." The first plenary session of the Provisional Committee, in May 1965, adopted a 10-point program based on Marxism-Leninism and on the thoughts of Mao Tse-tung and decided that the foundation of its activities was to be the creation of a "first base of revolutionary activity" within Cameroun. In September the vanguard group led by Osende Afana entered the country. The action proved to be a complete failure and Osende Afana was killed in March 1966.

The "First Marxist-Leninist Group of Cameroun," which is the name given to Osende Afana's vanguard group, published the first issue of its journal *Le Communiste* in February 1966, and the second issue in June 1966. It subsequently also published a document "Report of Activity and Orientation Discussed and Adopted 2 May 1966 by the General Assembly of the First Communist Group of Cameroun, Enlarged into Cadres and Advanced Leaders of the UPC." The document, which was a critical and self-critical appraisal of the attempts of Osende Afana to form an armed detachment of partisans and engage in revolutionary activity in Cameroun, declared that the most basic cause for the failure of the attempt was the "lack of the correct direction of the working class, a communist party having a truly political line, and a solid organization." The document outlined three steps to revolution in Cameroun:

Formation of a communist vanguard.

Winning over of the popular masses by this vanguard.

A people's war under the absolute direction of the communist party for the achievement of state power and new democracy. (*Progressive Labor* [New York], February-March 1967; reprinted from *La Voix du Peuple,* 17 June 1966).

In an interview reprinted by *Progressive Labor*, a member of the communist group in Cameroun declared that national democratic revolution cannot fully triumph without the direction of a communist vanguard, and that the building of socialism is impossible without the existence of a Marxist-Leninist party. "Any other concept of socialism is only a bluff to mystify the people," he said. The representative of the Cameroun communist group declared his belief that the creation of a communist party and proletarian revolution was possible in Cameroun despite the small proletarian class. (*Ibid.*)

A declaration of the "General Assembly of the First Marxist-Leninist Group of Cameroun" on the

Great Proletarian Cultural Revolution in China, dated 29 January 1967, hailed the cultural revolution and referred to Mao Tse-tung as the "living Lenin of our time." The declaration also stated:

> The victory of the cause of liberation of peoples in various countries of Asia, Africa, Latin America, and the rest of the world depends absolutely on the direction of the thought of Mao Tse-tung. To study the thought of Mao Tse-tung is the task of primary importance for revolutionaries throughout the entire world and notably the Cameroun revolutionaries. (*La Voix du Peuple*, 7 April.)

The "Provisional Committee of the UPC" has repeatedly sent messages of solidarity to pro-Chinese communist parties and issued declarations condemning the "revisionists" of the Soviet Union for "jointly plotting with the American imperialists." The messages were frequently signed by François Fosso, who identified himself as Secretary of the UPC Provisional Committee. Identifying himself also as Secretary-General of the "Democratic Youth of Cameroun," François Fosso sent a message of solidarity to the pro-Chinese "Communist Youth Movement" of Belgium in which he denounced "collusion between the Soviet Revisionists and the USA" and hailed the cultural revolution in China as raising the level of world revolution (*ibid.*, 12 May). The message was countersigned by the Vice-President of the "Democratic Youth," William Nguembus, who also represented that organization at the Fifth Congress of the Albanian Working Youth in Tirana during June 1967.

In an article in the organ of the pro-Chinese Belgian Communist Party, *La Voix du Peuple* (12 May), the Secretary of the Provisional Committee, Robert Ekwalla, declared that the UPC had decided to continue its attempts to form a national liberation army. Other tasks of the party were to foster the unity of its forces and develop a definitive statement of its ideological orientation, in order to organize a "proletarian leadership" and lead the Cameroun revolution to "definite victory and socialism."

# CANADA

The Communist Party of Canada (CPC) was founded in May 1921. In 1967 it had approximately 2,500 members out of a total Canadian population of 20,014,880 (1966 census). Most of the membership is concentrated among industrial workers, white-collar employees, and students in the urban areas of the provinces of Ontario and British Columbia.

The CPC has never been a significant political force in Canada. No Communist has held a seat in Parliament since 1945 or in a provincial legislature since 1948. In the general election of November 1965 only 4,200 votes were cast for the party, and all twelve communist candidates were unsuccessful. While the party's performance in the election was virtually the same as in 1963, there was some consolation for the Communists in the showing of the New Democratic Party, which polled 17.8 per cent of the total vote and claimed 21 seats in Parliament. Candidates of this noncommunist left-wing party were supported by the CPC in constituencies without communist candidates on the ballot.

Communist candidates have fared best in elections at the municipal level. Winnipeg voters returned a communist alderman and a communist school trustee to office in 1967 with fairly comfortable majorities; their reelection continued the unbroken pattern of some communist representation which has prevailed in the city for more than forty years. While Winnipeg represents the outstanding communist success story, Communists in recent years also have scored in local elections in Vancouver.

**Organization and Leadership.** The CPC is headed by William Kashtan, who was elected Secretary-General in 1965. Tim Buck is the party Chairman, a position which he assumed in 1962 after thirty years as Secretary-General. Working most closely with Kashtan and Buck is the 17-member Central Executive Committee. Prominent members of this committee are Nelson Clarke, Norman Freed, Alfred Dewhurst, Rae Murphy, Alfred Stenberg, Bruce Magnuson, Tom Morris, Sam Walsh, and Jeannette Pratte Walsh. The Central Committee of the CPC is composed of 51 members and 6 alternates.

In spite of its limited membership, the CPC has organizations in all but three of the ten Canadian provinces. Five provinces even have their own party leaders: Bruce Magnuson in Ontario; William Tuomi in Alberta; William Ross in Manitoba; William Beeching in Saskatchewan; and Nigel Morgan in British Columbia. Since 1965 a separate, quasi-autonomous party has been active in Quebec. Known as the Parti Communiste de Quebec (PCQ), its establishment was not due to an ideological split in party ranks, but resulted from an amicable decision to set up a distinct organization within the structure of the CPC. The main reason for the organization of the new party was to take advantage of French Canadian nationalist sentiment and to take a stand in the developing Quebec separatist controversy. Heading the PCQ is Sam Walsh, who had been the provincial communist leader in Quebec from 1962 to 1965. His most important assistants are members of the PCQ National Committee, such as Claire Dasylva, Bernadette Lebrun, Charles-Henry Lutz, Mel Doig, and Jeannette Walsh.

Much party activity centers on efforts to gain new members and support. Communists have been active in the trade unions, especially the United Fishermen and Allied Workers and the United Electrical, Radio, and Machine Workers of America.

**Domestic Policies and Activities.** With major political support derived from the labor unions, the CPC strongly advocates labor rights and admonishes labor to fight for them. The 1967 May Day statement called for a "truly united and truly sovereign trade union movement in Canada" (*Canadian Tribune*, 1 May). Subsequently a "Charter of Labor Rights" was submitted to the

77

government-appointed Rand Commission of Ontario, which was charged with the investigation of labor disputes. The following provisions of the recommended charter are, of course, important to labor interests throughout Canada: the right to consult and negotiate with management collectively through the trade unions on all matters arising out of technological changes before such changes are introduced; the right to gainful employment; the right to strike; the right to leisure and comfortable and secure retirement; and protection of the safety and health of workers. All are listed as requirements by a party which describes itself as "frankly partisan to all people who labor by hand or brain" (*ibid.*, 22 May). In addition to promulgating general demands, the CPC throughout the year worked on more specific problems, such as wage parity with the USA for workers in the Canadian automobile industry and a 40-hour work week for Great Lakes seamen. Repeal of legislation allowing injunctions in labor disputes had been advocated for a long time, but jail sentences meted out to leaders of the United Fishermen's Union in British Columbia made the issue a more famous party cause. Of universal interest to trade-unionists throughout the country was a pamphlet, *Change and Challenge,* written by veteran Communist Rae Murphy; it was widely publicized as dealing with "changes facing the working class and technology demanding new policies and structures."

Reaching the youth of the country and enlisting it in the communist cause is a major effort and a real need of the CPC. The relatively high average age of party members—said to be around fifty years—endangers the party's future unless infusions of new blood can be provided. In the past youth activities were largely locally planned, but now a national Central Youth Commission, headed by party Youth Secretary Alfred Stenberg, has been charged with trying to develop contacts and common action among both communist and noncommunist young people. According to CPC leader Kashtan it is among the young that the "spirit for radical social change is particularly noticeable" (*Viewpoint,* November 1967).

In line with this reasoning, the CPC convened a Youth Conference at Camp Kebeca near Montreal in May 1967 to discuss development of a suitable organization to give voice and direction to the "increasing social awareness of youth" and to "work radically and relevantly to achieve the social changes necessary in this new period" (*Canadian Tribune,* 5 June). For the use of the 75 attendees from all parts of Canada, a list of aims and objectives was prepared, including denunciation of American "aggression" in Vietnam and legislation for limitations of police powers, the ending of discrimination against Indians and Eskimos, Canadian "independence" and equality with the USA. With regard to specific youth interests, the furthering of educational opportunity, job training, and increased contacts with young people throughout the world all were proposed.

Development of the Canadian West—a subject of concern to the rural and farm population—received enthusiastic CPC endorsement at the first "Prairie Conference" of the communist party, held in March 1967 in Edmonton. Here delegates from Manitoba, Saskatchewan, and Alberta endorsed a resolution to support the farmers' unions in their efforts to secure parity prices for farm products. The delegates claimed that the western provinces were "prime targets of US monopolies in their quest for raw materials" and that the "governments of the three provinces were bent on delivering the natural resources to the American interests at the expense of the future needs of Canada." (*Canadian Tribune,* 27 March.)

Not only were labor, youth, and farm problems carefully studied, but the entire CPC party program was subjected to reexamination. A resolution of the party's 19th Convention, in 1966, provided for the program to be "rewritten with an elaboration of [the CPC] position on Canada and its path to socialism" (*WMR,* December 1967) and to be readied for submission to the 20th Convention, early in 1969. The intervening time was to be utilized for the preparation of working papers on a variety of subjects. The list of topics appeared to cover the gamut of CPC interests: US-Canadian oligarchy; Canadian identity and self-determination; the role of the New Democratic Party; the relations of the scientific and technological revolution to social change; structural changes in the working class; the New Left; attitudes to religious phenomena in present social conditions; attitudes to culture and art; the education system in Canada; and the concept of a multiparty coalition. The stated hope was to write a program which would involve not only all party members, but also large numbers of socialist-minded workers and young people. The need was "not formulating a program *for* the Party but a program *of* the Party, a program . . . of concern to all the democratic and progressive forces of our country" (*ibid.*). Presumably, such a program would alter the "false distorted image" that Canadians have of the CPC as "agents of a foreign power" and of communism as an "imported, foreign idea" (*ibid.*, August 1966).

The "peaceful transition to socialism within the framework of the historically evolved Canadian parliamentary institutions" remains the professed all-inclusive communist goal (*ibid.*, December 1967). Canada's Centennial celebrations provided the occasion for CPC advocacy of a "great coalition of conscience," "with the working class at its center and supported by all other patriotic and democratic forces, to meet the challenge of 1967 and win new policies of peace, independence, and equality" (*Canadian Tribune*, 26 June, Centennial Supplement).

The Centennial also presented a logical opportunity for consideration of the complex relationship between English and French Canadians. According to the CPC, these relations "far from being improved, have become aggravated by government and conservative party maneuvers, all directed to maintaining the status quo and the inequality of the French Canadian people"; deterioration can only be stopped by "recognition of the right of both Canadian nations to self-determination, and the embodiment of that right in a new constitution" (*ibid.*, 7 August). The PCQ not only agrees, but goes a step further by urging the adoption of a Quebec constitution which "would make it possible for Quebec to enter into negotiations on a free and equal basis with English Canada to create a new Confederal pact based on the right of both Canadian nations to self-determination up to and including separation" (*Viewpoint*, November).

**International Views and Policies.** Canadian-US relations were, understandably, the most important topic for the CPC in the area of international affairs. Proclaiming that "unity of the two Canadian nations CAN become a shield against the harmful domination by the giant to the south" (*Canadian Tribune*, 10 July), the party stressed the need for "protection" of Canada against the influence of the USA. In repetitive evidence in the communist publications were references to "US imperialism," "US control over the Canadian economy" (to be halted by nationalization of US-owned industries), "American penetration of our country's life and the stifling of our culture and political development," and even the "continuing danger of US absorption of Canada." An open letter sent to members of Parliament by William Kashtan requested support for a "policy of active neutrality for Canada," to be manifested by a "break with the United States alliance," and a decision "not to renew the NORAD agreement" (*ibid.*, 15 May). According to the Communists, the latter involved the "integration" of Canadian forces under US command, for the defense of North America "against the imaginary threat of Soviet aggression," and was to be shunned: "Far from protecting Canada it vastly increases the danger in which our country stands, because it ties us to the aggressive and terribly dangerous policies of those who rule in the United States" (*ibid.*, 1 May).

The USA is also the focus of communist wrath in the Canadian party's assessment of international events further removed from its borders. In Vietnam, according to the CPC, "the US government pursues a policy of genocide and scorched earth," and "its aim is not a just peace but domination of Indo-China and control of Southeast Asia" (*Canadian Tribune*, 1 May). Throughout 1967 the party demanded action in line with the "rising tide of anger against the US murder of the Vietnamese people." The government of Canada was held guilty by association: "Our government out of craven fear of Washington betrays its international responsibilities as a member of the International Control Commission, refuses to speak out against the barbarous American aggression, and continues to allow the sale of more than $300 million worth of armaments for that aggression" (*Horizons*, Summer 1967).

NATO, faring no better than NORAD, was called an "aggressive military pact, which under the leadership of the United States had played a major role in reviving the revenge-seeking West German militarists who have launched two world wars in the 20th century" (*ibid.*). This two-pronged attack was only one of many calling for measures to curb "West German militarism."

Events in Greece and Israel also evoked strong pronouncements by the CPC. For Greece there was complete acceptance of the program outlined by the Communist Party of Greece. Overthrow of the dictatorship, reinstitution of constitutional and democratic freedoms, political amnesty, disbanding of the junta, and free elections sponsored by a government consisting of representatives of all parties were part of the hope for future change.

In the Arab-Israeli conflict the CPC was inclined to be somewhat conciliatory. It urged withdrawal of Israel to its prewar frontiers as a prerequisite for the establishment of peaceful relations "based on mutual respect for the national and social aspirations of both the Israeli and Arab people" (*ibid.*). While declaring that "there can be no peace as long as reactionary Arab spokesmen call for the destruction of the State of Israel" (*Canadian Tribune*, 5 June), the CPC also felt that peace cannot be expected "until Israel comes to terms with the movement of social and national emancipation among the Arab people" (*ibid.*, 12 June).

The CPC expressed its concern and opinions about conditions in virtually every part of the world. It considered as an "essential ingredient" in a new policy for Canada the "refusal to join the Organization of American States as long as it continues to be the instrument of US imperialism" (*Horizons*, Summer 1967). It asked for recognition of the People's Republic of China and the German Democratic Republic. In general it reaffirmed the principle of peaceful coexistence and emphasized the need for world disarmament.

**International Communist Affairs.** Throughout the year the CPC advocated the cohesion and unity of the world communist movement. As in the past, it also firmly adhered to the Soviet line. The war in the Middle East, however, seemed to present a dilemma for the Canadians, who appeared to lag slightly behind other communist parties in their support of Soviet policies. Yet any reservations that may have existed, had obviously disappeared by the time of the Moscow celebrations on the occasion of the fiftieth anniversary of the October Revolution. Not only was the CPC represented by four delegates on that occasion, but there was effusive praise of the example set by the Soviet Union, which was said to give "new inspiration and hope to mankind." (*Canadian Tribune*, 6 November.)

The CPC was openly critical of the "adventurist, sectarian, anti-Soviet and rabidly nationalist line" steered by Communist China (*ibid.*, 16 January), although objection to its policies did not prevent repeated calls for recognition of that country. The CPC clearly stated its position in promulgating its resolution to support a consultative meeting of all communist parties: "Some think the purpose of the conference would be to oust China from the world communist movement. This of course is totally wrong. The main purpose, as we see it, is to achieve cooperation among parties irrespective of differences on some ideological questions." (*IB*, no. 111-112, December 1967.)

Canadian communists in 1967 were frequent visitors at party affairs held in various parts of the world. William Kashtan was a delegate to the congress of the Socialist Unity Party (SED) in East Germany in April and attended the congress of the Communist Party of Great Britain in November. Norman Freed, a member of the Politburo, traveled to Bulgaria in July; Tim Buck headed a group that journeyed to Kiev in April for discussions with the Communist Party of the Ukraine; and a three man delegation of the CPC went to Cuba "at the turn of the year" (1966-67) to participate in the eighth annual celebration of the Cuban revolution. The editor of the *Canadian Tribune*, Rae Murphy, traveled to North Vietnam in October to report on the war.

**Publications.** The *Canadian Tribune* is the official party organ of the CPC. It is published weekly in Toronto. In 1967 some staff changes took place, as Rae Murphy replaced John Boyd as editor of the newspaper. Boyd, in turn, was appointed Canadian representative on the editorial board of the *World Marxist Review.* The *Pacific Tribune*, the West Coast edition of the *Canadian Tribune*, is published weekly in Vancouver, where editorial operations are headed by Tom McEwen. *Horizons*, a quarterly edited by Stanley Ryerson, is the CPC's theoretical journal, issued in both French and English editions. Other party publications are *Scan*, a monthly youth magazine, and *Viewpoint*, a bulletin devoted to political and educational activities. The Communist Party of Quebec has its own monthly official organ, *Combat*, whose editor is Charles-Henri Lutz.

Dissemination of communist views is also promoted by the Montreal Centre for Marxist Research. Its aim is to facilitate the "development of research from the standpoint of scientific socialism" and to "assist those wishing to deepen their knowledge of Marxist theory" (*Horizons*, Summer 1967). Production of material for publication is encouraged, and seminars, colloquiums, and work groups are organized to pursue specific research projects.

The North American edition of the monthly *Problems of Peace and Socialism* (edited in Prague) is printed in Toronto as *World Marxist Review,* a "theoretical and information journal of Communist and Workers' parties." The *Information Bulletin* is its monthly companion publication.

\* \* \*

The Progressive Workers' Movement (PWM), a pro-Chinese Canadian communist splinter group, has been in existence since 1964. Its chairman, Jack Scott, lives in Vancouver, where the organization's main strength (approximately 30 members) is concentrated. Scott and John Wood, a member of the PWM's Central Committee, visited Communist China in 1967. They attended May Day celebrations and toured parts of the country as guests of the All-China Federation of Trade Unions. The PWM's interpretation of the Sino-Soviet dispute can be summarized by quoting from an article in the party's monthly journal, the *Progressive Worker* (August 1967): "The Communists of China have defended Marxism-Leninism against the fierce attacks of the revisionists and given powerful support and inspiration to the revolutionary movements of the whole world and have become the main bulwark of the international Communist movement."

# CEYLON

Marxism was introduced into Ceylon in 1935 with the formation of the Ceylon Equal Society Party (Lanka Sama Samaja Pakshaya; LSSP), a Trotskyist party. Its founders were young, Western-educated, middle- and upper-class intellectuals and professionals, and included N. M. Perera, Colvin R. De Silva, S. A. Wickremasinghe, and Philip Gunawardena. In 1939 the LSSP failed to follow the Stalinist line of the Third International, and a Stalinist group of about 70 members, led by Wickremasinghe, was expelled. This group founded the United Socialist Party, which in 1943 became the Ceylon Communist Party (Lanka Kommunist Pakshaya; LKP). Subsequently, the Trotskyist LSSP split into three factions: the original LSSP, sometimes referred to as the New (Nava) LSSP or the LSSP (Socialist), now led by N. M. Perera; the Revolutionary (Viplavakari) LSSP, led by Edmund Samarkoddy; and the People's United Front (Mahajana Eksath Peramuna; MEP), led by Philip Gunawardena.

A pro-Chinese faction broke away from the LKP in 1963; in 1964 each faction held its own "Seventh Congress of the Ceylon Communist Party," and each has continued to go by the same name since then. During the election campaign of March 1965 a further split appeared in the pro-Chinese LKP between the party's National Organizer, Nagalingam Sanmugathasan, and its General Secretary, Premalal Kumarasiri, which resulted in Kumarasiri's expulsion. During 1967 the party was reported to have had its fifth internal split since its formation in 1964; the party announced removal of the secretary of four trade unions under party control.

All the Marxist parties in Ceylon are legal. Membership in the two communist parties (the LKP and the pro-Chinese LKP) appears to fluctuate significantly but is in any case quite low: estimates range from 1,100 to 2,000 members for the pro-Soviet LKP (hereafter referred to simply as the LKP) and from 200 to 800 for the pro-Chinese LKP. LKP General Secretary Pieter Keuneman in 1967 claimed that his party had a total membership of 17,000; this figure would appear, however, to be considerably exaggerated. The population of Ceylon is 11,500,000 (estimated 30 June 1966).

**Organization and Leadership.** The Trotskyist parties in Ceylon (considered together) have more strength and influence than the two communist parties. In the March 1965 elections the LSSP, the MEP, and the MEP's coalition ally, the National Liberation Front (Jatika Vimukthi Peramuna; JVP) obtained a combined 10.6 per cent of the vote. For the past two decades communist voting strength has remained at about 100,000, which in 1965 amounted to 2.7 per cent of the vote. Of the 157 parliamentary seats, the LSSP won 10 and the LKP won 4. The pro-Chinese LKP has very little electoral strength; it won no seats and polled only 0.2 per cent of the 1965 vote. Communist electoral strength in Ceylon is heavily concentrated in the Colombo urban area along the southwest coast and in a small area in the Southern Province. Nearly all LKP members of the parliament have been from these two regions.

The LKP has a Central Committee of 25 members and 12 candidate members and a Central Control Commission of six members. The leaders of the LKP are S. A. Wickremasinghe, President; Pieter Keuneman, General Secretary; V. A. Samarawickrema, National Organizer; and C. Kumarasamy, Treasurer. Full members of the Central Committee elected in 1964 are I. R. Ariyaratnam, M. K. Arnolis Appuhamy, K. A. E. Britto, Cecil de Silva, U. B. Herath, C. Kumarasamy, P. Kumarasamy, Merenna G. Mendis, S. Nadesan, L. W. Panditha, Pieter Keuneman, J. A. K. Perera, A. Piyadasa, V. Ponnambalam, W. G. Punyasena, H. G. S. Ratnaweera, V.A. Samarawickrema, Sarath

Muttetuwegama, K. P. Silva, S. J. deSilva, U. Saranankara Thero (died November, 1966), B. Tudawe, V. Jayakoddy, S. G. Wanigasekera, and S. A. Wickremasinghe.

Although the pro-Chinese LKP also has an orthodox organizational hierarchy, there is in fact little formal division of function according to office within the leadership. At the pro-Chinese LKP's "Seventh Congress" in January 1964 a Central Committee of 35 members was elected (*Peking Review,* 31 January 1964). Its leading personality and National Organizer is Nagalingam Sanmugathasan, and its President is Watson Fernando. Other important figures in the party are Higgoda Dharmasena, G. K. Jinendrapala, D. N. Nadunge, D. A. Gunasekera, and V. Seenivasagam.

Despite their small size, the Marxist parties have been able to exercise considerable influence in Ceylonese politics through control of much of the trade-union movement and through intermittent cooperation with the Sri Lanka Freedom Party (SLFP), which is the most important party in opposition to the now ruling United National Party (UNP).

**The SLFP and the Marxist Parties.** The SLFP was founded in 1951 by S. W. Bandaranaike. It is not a Marxist party, but represents a wide spectrum of political opinion from populist-socialist to pro-communist, and includes even a small pro-Chinese faction. It has a strong pro-Sinhala orientation, and its major source of support is the rural, largely Buddhist, Sinhalese community. Bandaranaike was assasinated in 1959, and since then the party has been led by his widow. In recent years the SLFP has been the cynosure of left-wing politics in Ceylon. Through electoral agreements with the Marxist parties, the SLFP became the ruling party in the Ceylon government from 1956 to 1959 and again from 1960 to 1965.

The question of cooperation and united-front arrangements with the Marxist parties is a sensitive issue within the SLFP itself, and a substantial portion of the party does not favor cooperation with the Marxists. This has been especially true since the experience of 1964, when cooperation with the Marxist parties in a coalition government greatly polarized the divisions within the SLFP and strengthened the influence of the party's extreme left wing. Numerous measures were introduced to tie Ceylon's economy more closely to the communist countries and to bring the press and judiciary under political controls. At the SLFP's annual conference in 1967, held on 20-21 July at Galle, the SLFP leaders did not allow discussion of the united front, saying that the SLFP Executive Committee would work out an agreement for strengthening the alliance with the LSSP and LKP. Meanwhile, the pro-Chinese LKP was distributing anti-SLFP literature outside the conference, attacking the SLFP for its communal policies.

With its perennial issues relating to language, caste, race, religion, and the endemic personal feuds and splits among party leaders, Ceylon's political climate is most uncongenial to the growth of mass-based secular parties with strong ideological orientations. Marxists in Ceylon are continuously torn between doctrinaire theory and opportunistic practice, between the desire to enhance their strength by united action and personal and factional rivalry.

Thus, for the most part, Ceylonese Marxists have been preoccupied with political maneuvers, alliances, and various united-front tactics at the top of the political structure rather than with mass politics. The most recent attempt to formulate a Marxist united strategy was the establishment of a United Left Front in 1963. This failed when the LSSP abandoned it for the opportunity to participate in the government with the SLFP, and the LKP, fearing political isolation, went along, giving the coalition its reluctant support.

Since then, the principal goal of the LKP has been the "unity of all national progressive forces," meaning primarily unity of action with the SLFP, which the Marxist parties usually describe as the party of the "progressive national bourgeoisie." It was through the coalition government that followed the dissolution of the United Left Front that the Marxists reached the apex of their national influence in 1964 (this led, however, to a revolt of the right wing of the SLFP which brought down the government in December 1964). The manifesto of the LKP in 1960 claimed that the party tried to combine "the principles of scientific socialism with all that is progressive in national traditions." What has generally happened in recent years, however, is that "scientific socialism" has continued to receive vigorous lip service, while the "national traditions" have increasingly become the means with which the Marxists have bought whatever political influence they could. The LKP has thus been forced to adopt "minimum-program tactics" to the point of opportunism, and this was a major, if not the most important, factor in the split with Sanmugathasan's pro-Chinese faction.

The Ceylonese Marxists, with the possible exception of the pro-Peking Communists, appear to have accepted as a fact that they cannot have significant influence in Ceylon, let alone come to power, except by some amalgam of united-front-from-above and coup tactics. Neither direct revolutionary action nor mass electoral appeal seem to the Marxist parties to hold much potential. The LKP, for instance, appears to prefer to forego the attempt to develop a large rural base of support rather than risk alienating the SLFP by competing for its following. Even the "Trotskyist" LSSP has participated in the united front with the SLFP, and its Trotskyism finds expression only in an affiliation with the Trotskyist United Secretariat and the refusal to accept the leadership of either Moscow or Peking. It is by no means certain that even the pro-Chinese LKP is an exception to these generalizations. The pro-Chinese LKP has thus far not been invited to join in the united front arrangements with the SLFP, LSSP, and LKP; although sections of both the SLFP and LSSP are receptive to the idea, exclusion of the pro-Chinese party has been the price of the LKP's cooperation in the front. The strength of the pro-Chinese LKP to date has not been sufficient to induce the other left parties to try to cooperate with it; however, much of the pro-Chinese LKP's support is built on Tamil minority grievances, and the party might well cooperate with other left parties if it became strong enough to be a significant factor in Ceylonese politics.

**Communal Issues.** The most important perennial issues of Ceylonese politics stem from the Tamil-Sinhala cleavage in Ceylonese society. Of a population of more than 11 million, about 2 million are Tamils who are concentrated in the northern part of the island, about 1 million of whom are of Indian nationality. The remaining 9 million are Sinhalese. The LKP now sees the Sinhalese "national struggle" as an irresistable force and takes a strongly pro-Sinhala position, backing the proposal for exclusive use of the Sinhalese language. On this issue, LKP General Secretary Keuneman has declared that "majority rights" must be honored "before settling the minority problems" (*Far Eastern Economic Review,* 20 July 1967). This position constitutes a retreat from the party's more cosmopolitan, secular view of the 1950s, when it advocated reasonable use of Tamil as an official language. By 1960, however, the LKP had come to endorse the Sinhalese position on this question, finding this concession expedient, if not necessary, to stem increasing Sinhala disaffection with the party. In 1966 and 1967, however, the LKP retreated again from an all-out pro-Sinhalese position in the face of the success of the pro-Chinese LKP's aggressive drive for support among the lower-class Tamils.

Both the LKP and the SLFP, in fact, try to take advantage of Tamil grievances, even while giving strong support to the Sinhalese, and the LKP has tried, without notable success, to extend its influence into Tamil radical groups. The pro-Chinese LKP has received the allegiance of some members of the LKP who have been alienated by what they regard as the un-Marxist and opportunistic support of the LKP for the Sinhalese cause. Nagalingam Sanmugathasan is himself a Tamil, and his party has been more successful than the LKP in expanding its support among Tamils and has advocated more vigorously than the LKP anti-caste and anti-untouchability measures. Sanmugathasan has openly declared his intention to build a Maoist-style revolutionary party in Ceylon and has urged the Tamil people not to rule out violent tactics in their political struggle.

**The Labor Movement.** One of the most important sources of the political influence of the Marxist parties is their control of or influence in large segments of the trade-union movement in Ceylon, which has enabled them to call political strikes on numerous occasions in recent years. The LKP controls the Ceylon Federation of Trade Unions. This organization was formed after the 1963 split with the pro-Chinese faction, which gained control of the communist-run Ceylon Trade Union Federation. Watson Fernando, the President of the pro-Chinese LKP, controls the Trade Union Federation. Before the 1963 split this federation claimed 68,000 members; in 1967 pro-Chinese LKP leader Sanmugathasan claimed the support of only 16,000 Federation members (see Kearney, "Communism in Ceylon," and J. M. van der Kroef, "The Many Faces of Ceylonese Communism," *Problems of Communism* March-April 1968). The LKP had won the majority of the former

Federation members to the new Federation of Trade Unions, but the organization of cadres of the old Federation remained with Sanmugathasan's group. The LKP also sponsors a less important Joint Committee of Trade Unions in conjunction with the LSSP. The Marxist parties also have some strength among government employees and exercise significant influence in the Public Service Workers' Trade Union Federation, the largest association of public servants.

Since the accession of the United National Party government in 1965, the Marxists had sought from time to time to engineer a general strike. Prospects for the success of such an attempt in the fall of 1967 did not appear bright, especially since the SLFP neither participated in nor endorsed it, as SLFP leader Mrs. Bandaranaike was in the Soviet Union in November and December. When on 22 November the government devalued the Ceylonese rupee 20 per cent in the wake of the devaluation of the pound, the Marxist parties felt they had an issue over which they could provoke a general strike. The Ceylon Workers' Congress, a large non-communist union of Tamil plantation workers, became involved in a dispute with the government over the government-provided devaluation allowances given to industrial workers to offset economic losses due to the rupee's fall in value. The allowance set for plantation workers was only half that for industrial workers, and the Ceylon Workers' Congress threatened a week-long strike beginning 20 December. Seizing upon this issue, the Marxists made plans to coordinate strikes by their own unions to turn the dispute into a Marxist-led general strike. When the government agreed to raise the devaluation allowance for plantation workers to 75 per cent of that for industrial workers, however, the Ceylon Workers' Congress called off its strike plans, and the Marxist plan collapsed; strikes by individual small unions did not spread. Meanwhile, the Marxist parties were feuding among themselves over leadership of the strike attempt. The LKP wanted to exclude the pro-Chinese LKP's unions from the strike movement, and simultaneously attacked the Revolutionary LSSP for "sordid class collaboration" masked with "ultra-revolutionary phrases." An attempt by the Revolutionary LSSP United Committee of Ceylon Trade Unions to bring all other leftist unions together on 29 December to plan united action met with no response from the other parties.

**The Food Crisis.** Aside from the continuing Sinhala-Tamil problems, the most pressing political issue in Ceylon in the early part of 1967 was the food crisis. On this matter, as on many others, the constraining factors on the behavior of the LSSP and LKP were competition among the Marxist parties themselves and a desire to preserve unity of action with the SLFP. In December 1966 the United National Party government had halved the rice ration under pressure of a drop in imports due to a world rice shortage. Despite the opportunities for agitation over such an explosive issue, the Ceylonese Marxists did not go very far in trying to spark a popular revolt against the government on that occasion. The SLFP had favored a policy of restraint and patience for the opposition parties on the issue. In a speech to an LSSP gathering on 19 December 1966 Mrs. Bandaranaike, while attacking the UNP policy, had urged the people to wait until they could "teach the government a lesson" through the ballot and cautioned the LSSP not to stir up disorder and thereby cause the government to resort to repressive or violent measures against the opposition. Neither the LSSP nor the LKP was prepared to split with the SLFP on the issue by taking to the streets to whip up large-scale "mass struggles." The LSSP in particular, while indulging in much hopeful prophecy about a rising tide of mass struggles, appears to have lacked either the inclination or the strength to bring them about. The Revolutionary LSSP declared, for instance: "The people cannot wait for a general election to obtain relief. What is imperative is the immediate mobilization of the people to oppose and fight the government on this issue" (*Ceylon Daily News*, 12 January 1967). However, both the LSSP and the LKP chose not to push the issue too far. The Trotskyist International Committee of the Fourth International criticized the LSSP's behavior as an example of "revisionist betrayal" (*The Newsletter*, 4 February 1967).

**International Affairs.** The pro-Chinese LKP, dominated by the personality of its leader, Sanmugathasan, pays more attention to international issues than does the LKP. In 1967 Sanmugathasan's strong pro-Chinese views survived even the disputes between the Ceylonese and the Chinese governments. Relations between Ceylon and Communist China were strained throughout 1967, for which Sanmugathasan put the blame squarely on the ruling party. In his party's weekly,

*Red Flag,* Sanmugathasan complained of the anti-Chinese campaign of the Ceylonese government. New China News Agency reported on 28 August that the article said:

> Judging by the frenzy of the anti-China campaign unleashed by the United National Party and by the reactionary monopoly newspapers, the progressive people of this country will have no difficulty in coming to the conclusion that, if China is so disliked and hated by these reactionary forces, then it must be good. It is not difficult for the progressive people of Ceylon to understand that we must support whatever the UNP and the reactionary monopoly press oppose .... Ever since the UNP came to power, its government has been attempting to disrupt the relations between Ceylon and China. Nevertheless, the people will not tolerate this. They treasure the friendship with China and are grateful to her for having proved herself to be their genuine friend.

According to the report, the Sanmugathasan article also included two quotations from Mao Tse-tung.

Early in the year, the Chinese embassy had embarrassed the Ceylonese government by disseminating anti-Soviet propaganda in Ceylon. The government had also become increasingly disturbed by reports of Communist Chinese influence and activities among Tamil radicals. On one occasion in the spring a Chinese embassy official participated in a Tamil demonstration. On 1 May the government banned the importation of communist propaganda and seized many parcels of Chinese publications. Government authorities also confiscated a shipment of several hundred Mao badges alleged by the Chinese to have been for the use of their 35 embassy personnel in Ceylon. On 22 August, at the height of the Chinese interlude of "revolutionary diplomacy," Peking's embassy in Ceylon protested that the Ceylonese government was colluding in a plot to create two Chinas, because Taiwan had been invited to send delegates to an Asian Trainers' Conference sponsored by the Ceylon Association of Girl Guides and to participate in the Third Asian Boxing Championships in Ceylon. The Chinese further remarked that the UNP government had continually maintained "improper connections with the Chiang Kai-shek bandit gang," and that "this is something which the Chinese people will not tolerate" (*Peking Review,* 1 September 1967). In the fall renegotiation of the rice-rubber agreement with China was also used by Peking as an occasion to try to force the Ceylonese government to take a more pro-Chinese international stance, but this attempt so alienated nationalist sentiment in Ceylon that Peking finally backed down (see *China*).

Through it all Sanmugathasan kept his party on a straight pro-Mao line, especially with regard to the question of the leadership of the international communist movement and the necessity of violent revolution. He visited Peking in May and early June and met with Mao on 6 June. Speaking in Peking on 26 May, he declared:

> The era in which we live has correctly been characterized as the era of Mao Tse-tung. It is indeed a joy and an honor for all of us to be able to live in this era in which the invincible thought of Mao Tse-tung illuminates and guides the path of all revolutionaries, an era in which world imperialism is nearing its doom and world socialism is approaching victory. (*Peking Review,* 16 June 1967.)

With regard to China's cultural revolution, Sanmugathasan said: "The Great Proletarian Cultural Revolution will go down in history as the greatest epoch-making event that the world has seen." Finally, regarding Ceylon, he said:

> Inspired and guided by the revolutionary thought of Mao Tse-tung, we are determined to build a revolutionary Party in Ceylon which shall lead the revolutionary movement to success and thus play our part in making world socialism a reality (*Peking Review,* 16 June 1967).

For its part, the LKP followed an equally uncompromising pro-Soviet line on major international issues. On 18-30 August a delegation from the LKP, led by Politburo member M. K. Arnolis Appuhamy, visited the Mongolian People's Republic. *Tass* reported on· 5 September that the Mongolian and Ceylonese parties had signed a joint communique which welcomed the documents adopted by the Karlovy Vary Conference of European Communist and Workers' Parties as "a program of peace and security in Europe which also has great implications for the defense of world peace." The parties agreed further that at present conditions are being created for calling a new international communist conference, that it is necessary to hold a new meeting of communist and workers' parties of the world to ensure its preparation, and that they will continue their efforts toward such a meeting. Earlier in the year LKP General Secretary Keuneman had praised the Karlovy Vary meeting in a statement broadcast on Moscow radio on 30 April. Speaking for the LKP, Keuneman also said: "Our Party thinks that the conditions are ripe now for another world meeting of Communist and workers' parties." Disavowing any anti-Chinese sentiment, he added:

We do not need a meeting to condemn anybody or to try to expel anybody from the movement . . . . The real problem is that since 1960 many new questions have arisen in the world. Six years have gone—seven—and there are a number of problems we have to assess, and we must assess them collectively. This is very important, particularly in some of the newer Asian parties.

However, he did criticize China for obstructing a socialist united front on Vietnam:

We are most deeply concerned with and indignant to see at this stage, in the name of a so-called proletarian cultural revolution, anti-Soviet demonstrations, hostility against other socialist countries, and reluctance to cooperate with the rest of the socialist countries in giving material aid to the heroic fighters in Vietnam.

Both Keuneman and Wickremasinghe delivered speeches at the Fiftieth Anniversary celebrations in Moscow in November and expressed similar sentiments regarding these two important issues. In his speech Keuneman noted:

My Party fully agrees that the time has come to convene a new meeting of representatives of fraternal Communist and workers' parties.

At present, the United States is carrying out aggression in Vietnam because of the split in the international Communist movement caused by the Mao group in China. It is our view that at present it is necessary to attain unity in our forces. This is not only the best way which can cause US defeat and give assistance to all people fighting for independence, but it is also the best way to attain the great objectives of the Great October Socialist Revolution.

On 21 October both the LKP and the pro-Chinese LKP held their own rival Vietnam Solidarity Day celebrations in support of North Vietnam. In their stands on the Arab-Israeli war, the two parties' public statements also followed the line of their respective patrons. The LKP Central Committee declared:

The Central Committee of the Ceylon Communist Party condemns the wanton and criminal aggression that the government of Israel has launched against the UAR and other Arab countries . . . condemns American and British imperialists who have instigated and now support the government of Israel in this aggressive war (*Forward*, 14 June 1967).

The pro-Chinese party said:

The entire Arab world is highly revolted by the dirty role Soviet revisionists have played in the war which cost them dearly in human lives and property . . . . The hands of the Soviet revisionists are stained with the blood of the Arabs who have been killed by the thousands in the war with the Israelis. (*Red Flag*, 15 June 1967.)

A week later, the 22 June issue of *Red Flag* observed: "China was the only major power to declare unqualified support for the Arab cause."

Meanwhile, the LKP was arguing the case for the Soviet Union:

It is precisely because the socialist countries, especially the Soviet Union, have been fighting so energetically to support the Arab states in their just cause that the imperialists have started throughout the world a scurrilous propaganda campaign that the Soviet Union and other socialist states have "let down" the Arabs. What these imperialist propagandists are interested in is only slandering the Soviet Union and the socialist countries, weakening the alliance between the Arab states and the socialist countries and distracting world attention from their own open and secret help to the Israeli government's aggression . . . . It is truly shameful that China should have chosen to join in with this imperialist chorus. (*Forward*, 16 June 1967.)

Criticism of the Soviet Union's role in the Arab-Israeli war was not limited to the pro-Chinese LKP. On 15 June *The Nation,* the English-language weekly of the SLFP, published a commentary critical of Soviet actions during the war and remarked that "it is really painful to see the leading Socialist power playing the game of US imperialism." The 22 June issue carried a defense of Soviet actions by Basil Perera, Vice-President of the Ceylon-Soviet Friendship League. In the article Perera accused critics of the Soviet Union of attempting to "sow discord between the Arab countries and their truest friend in need, the Soviet Union."

**Fronts.** The Marxist parties control many front groups and organizations, and their number has increased significantly in the past two years because of the intense competition among the parties for control of them. Generally, whichever group loses control of an organization starts a rival organization. Among these front organizations is the Samasta Kanka Rajaye Lippikaru Sangamay, an organization of public employees controlled by the LKP and the LSSP which has promoted a boycott of work conducted in English and Tamil. Other LKP- and LSSP-controlled groups are the National Education Front (Jatika Adhapana Peramuna); the Islamic Socialist Front; the Ceylon National Council for Solidarity with Vietnam; and the Women's organization, Lanka Kantha Peramuna. Pro-Chinese LKP fronts include the Ceylon-Vietnam Solidarity Association; the Socialist Bhikku (Buddhist Monk) Organization; the All-Ceylon Peasants' Congress; and the Afro-Asian Solidarity Association of Ceylon.

**Publications.** The LKP publishes a popular daily paper *Aththa* (Truth), which has a circulation of 30,000 to 50,000, and a number of weeklies, including *Forward, Maubhima* (Motherland), *Desabhimani* (Patriot), *Tarunahanda* (Voice of Youth), *Nava Lokaya* (New World), *Kommunist Lokaya* (Communist World), and *Nava Sakthi.*

The pro-Chinese LKP publishes the daily *Kamkaruwa* (Worker), with an estimated circulation of 5,000; A tamil counterpart *Tholilali,* a weekly in English, *Red Flag,* and a Tamil monthly, *Vasantham.* The LSSP daily *Jana Dina* was closed down by the government in January 1967 for allegedly defaming the Prime Minister. The ban was lifted in June, but *Jana Dina* did not immediately resume publication. The LSSP also publishes a weekly *Young Socialist,* the Tamil *Samatharmam,* and a Sinhalese weekly *Sama Samaja* (Equal Society).

# CHILE

The Communist Party of Chile (Partido Comunista de Chile; PCCh) was founded as the Socialist Workers' Party (Partido Obrero Socialista) in 1912. The name Communist Party of Chile was adopted in January 1922.

Since 1958, when ten years of outlaw status were ended, the party has steadily expanded its influence in the popular political realm, using to good advantage its electoral alliance with the Socialist Party (Partido Socialista; PS). The alignment is known as the Revolutionary Popular Action Front (Frente Revolucionario de Acción Popular; FRAP). Although not communist, the PS is a major contending force within the spectrum of the extreme left, which also includes a number of small, violence-prone militant groups.

During 1967 the PCCh recruited about 16,000 new members, bringing its total membership to 50,000. The population of Chile is 8,750,000 (estimated 1966). In the 1965 congressional elections the candidates of the PCCh obtained 12.24 per cent of the votes, increasing the number of Communist deputies from 16 to 18, and senators from 2 to 5 (out of a total of 147 and 45 respectively). In the 2 April 1967 elections for municipal councilmen the PCCh obtained 15.1 per cent of the vote. The total vote obtained by the FRAP was 25.7 per cent in 1965 and 29 per cent in 1967. At present the Communists and Socialists hold 12 Senate and 33 lower house seats. Despite its electoral gains and a pronounced general trend to the left in Chilean political life during 1967, including the ruling Christian Democrat Party (Partido Democrata Cristiano; PDC)—where "rebel" elements acquired control of the party machine in the period July-December—the FRAP continued to be weakened from within by the long-standing rift between Communists and Socialists, a rift that was further intensified in the course of the year.

**Organization and Leadership.** At the Thirteenth Congress of the PCCh, in October 1965, Luis Corvalán was reelected Secretary-General. The Central Committee was increased from 45 to 55 members and alternate members were increased from 10 to 15. The members of the Political Commission of the PCCh are Luis Corvalán, Oscar Astudillo (who replaced José González as Deputy Secretary-General following the latter's death in an airplane crash on 24 November 1966), Orlando Millas, Julieta Campusano, Manuel Cantero, Volodia Teitelboim, Jorge Montes, Alejandro Toro, Mario Zamorano, José Oyarce, Jorge Inzunza, and Samuel Riquelme. Candidate members are Gladys Marín, José Cademartori, Luis Figueroa, José Balladares, and Eugenio Valiejos.

One of the principal sources of support for the PCCh and the FRAP originates in the Single Center of Chilean Workers (Central Unica de Trabajodares de Chile; CUTCh), founded in 1953. The CUTCh is the nearest approach in Chile to a national trade-union organization. At the time of its fourth national congress, in August 1965, the CUTCh had an estimated membership of 300,000. Since then it has incorporated about 80,000 additional workers. An attempt to increase its strength still further was to be made at the CUTCh Fifth Congress (23-27 October 1968) which was to be declared open to nonmembers willing to attend. At the Fourth Congress, the CUTCh leadership was elected from lists which included only Socialist and Communist candidates. The results showed a gain by the Communists, who won twelve posts as against the Socialists' nine. Luis Figueroa (a Communist and former Secretary-General) was elected President, whereas Oscar Núñez (Socialist and former President) was elected Secretary-General. Outside the structure of the CUTCh, Communists and Socialists hold control of such key unions as those of the copper workers, coal miners, and railwaymen. The extreme left wing is thus strongly placed to disrupt the government's economic program by fomenting labor unrest and using its influence to prolong strikes.

The PCCh-affiliated youth movement is called the Communist Youth of Chile (Juventudes

89

Comunistas de Chile; JCC); its Secretary-General is Gladys Marín. At the organization's Fifth Congress (7-13 February 1966) the Central Committee was increased from 25 to 45 members. At the congress Gladys Marín reiterated the underlying PCCh domestic political line by stating that, with regard to the JCC, the "basic pillar of a mass anti-imperialist, anti-oligarchic movement . . . is the unity of the Socialist and Communist youth." This unity, however, has certainly not materialized in the framework of the university student movement. "From 1965 on, the left, with the backing of the Radical Party [Partido Radical; PR] student body, could have controlled the Student Federation of the University of Chile at Valparaíso (Federación de Estudiantes de la Universidad de Chile–Valparaíso; FECh), advancing the overall movement through that triumph," wrote Bernardo Montero in the October 1967 issue of the Chilean leftist review *Plan,* adding: "This year again the left was split because of the positions of the Revolutionary Leftist Movement [Movimiento de Izquierda Revolucionaria; MIR] and of sectors of the Socialist Youth [Juventud Socialista; JS] influenced by the former, who refused to accept Radical support. On their part the Communists, as is usual with them, denied the MIR their recognition as a revolutionary organization." The left is in a minority position also at the University of Chile in Santiago, where on 22 October the Christian Democrats won six positions on the eleven-member local FECh Executive and thus absolute control. Among the remaining five positions the Communists have three, while the extreme left (Socialists, MIR, Revolutionary Communist Party, and Camilo Torres movement) and Radicals have one each. However, the victory achieved by an alliance of militant leftists in the elections held by the Concepción University Federation of Students prompted *Punto Final* (an independent review edited by ex-PCCh member Manuel Cabieses, who follows a general Castroist extreme nationalist line), in its issue of 5 December, to state that the results demonstrated "an about-face by the great majority of university students toward markedly revolutionary positions." The victorious alliance consisted of the Leftist University Movement (Movimiento Universitario de Izquierda; MUI), which includes the MIR, the GRANMA (otherwise unidentified, but possibly named after the daily newspaper of the Communist Party of Cuba), the mass of leftist independents, and the Socialist University Brigade (Brigada Universitaria Socialista; BUS). It won five leadership posts while the Christian Democrat representation was reduced to three voting members and the Radical to one; the Communists failed to elect anyone at all. Notwithstanding the leftist gains at the University of Concepción, the Christian Democrats' control of the Union of University Federations of Chile (Unión de Federaciónes Universitarias de Chile; UFUCh) makes them the dominant force in the organized university-student movement.

**PCCh Assessment of Its Achievements and Failures.** In his report to the PCCh National Conference in September 1967, Secretary-General Luis Corvalán said:

In Ovalle, Valparaíso, San Clemente, Lota, Osorno, and other cities our party organizes the unemployed and heads the struggle for more new jobs. In the countryside it promotes the establishment of peasant trade unions and the intensification of the strike movement of agricultural workers. Communists head twenty-five municipal councils and are represented on more than a hundred. As of June 1967, the party composition was as follows: workers 44.6 per cent, peasants 16.1, office employees 4.1, college-educated specialists 2.2, teachers 1.7, intellectuals 0.1, tradesmen 4.0, industrialists 0.2, housewives 20.9, pensioners 2.8 and other 3.3. . . . In the last two years the party has improved its positions in the countryside. The proportion of peasants in it has grown from 12.4 per cent in 1965 to 16.1. The share of housewives has also increased. Together with working women, they account for 26.5 per cent of the party's membership. The period since our Tenth Congress [held in 1956] has been one of continuous growth of the party. Between June 1965 and June 1967 its membership increased by 28.2 per cent. . . . Thus the general situation of the party is good. But we want it to be better still. We need a bigger and more efficient party. There is an inordinately large gap between the numerical strength and the influence of the party. In the last elections more than 350,000 Chileans voted Communist. Most of these are men and women, predominantly working people, who have been educated by the party and who adhere to its policies. If we succeed in organizing politically only one-third of the people under our influence, we would have an additional 100,000 Communists. A similar gap exists between the number of Communists and the influence the party wields in industrial and mining enterprises, in the public services and in building. There are enterprises employing hundreds of workers, half of whom support our position. But many party cells at these enterprises have not more than a dozen members each. In more serious cases, trade-union leaders are the only Communists or there are no party cells at all. . . . The responsibility for the weaknesses of the party rests primarily with us, its leaders. Therefore, it is necessary first of all to improve the work of the leadership, the methods of guidance. . . . The leading organs of the party must give priority to political work, to organization and orientation of mass movements on the basis of the general line of the party, in conformity with the concrete situation and the problems of the given region. (For the full text of Corvalán's report, see *Documents.*)

**Domestic Views and Policies.** The PCCh is one of the most politically effective communist parties in Latin America and the most prominent champion of the nonviolent electoral approach to political power in the Latin American communist movement. Its declared domestic policy of "united action by all the progressive forces against all the reactionary forces" means in practice a limited amount of congressional cooperation with the Christian Democrat government, while the party attempts to make the FRAP an alliance of radicals broad enough to win power and give the Communists the largest party in the FRAP a strong foothold in the government. This policy was the Communists' response to the election of the reformist President Frei in September 1964, since they felt that all-out opposition to his radical noncommunist reforms would lose the party popular support. Statements by PCCh leaders therefore admit that some progress can be made under the present government. At the same time, the party strives to increase its strength and pacify its own left wing. With this aim in mind it asserts that "reactionaries" and the right wing of the Christian Democrat Party will prevent the government's full program from being carried out, and that those radicals who voted for Frei in 1964 will see their hopes realized only under a Popular Front government. The PCCh's policy of limited cooperation with the government was explained by Secretary-General Luis Corvalán at the Twenty-third Congress of the CPSU (1966): "A little over a year ago the Christian Democrat Party came to power in our country. It is a numerous and heterogeneous party, whose main purpose it is to avert a popular revolution. . . . It is a notable fact that it is using new methods to attain this purpose, working among the masses, suggesting an agrarian reform and other changes. . . . In these circumstances, in a milieu of such varied contradictions, we must deeply examine the new social processes and take them into account. . . . We must support some of the actions by the government and combat others, and promote joint action by all champions of radical change, whatever their present political orientation, and in particular, we must step up the activity of the people on a scale a thousand times greater than the usual, thereby furthering the hegemony of the working class." (*IB*, nos. 74-77, 20 July 1966.)

In January 1967 Communists, Socialists, Radicals, and Nationalists teamed up in the Chilean Senate to deliver the 23-15 vote refusing to grant President Frei permission to visit the USA in early February. In an attempt to counter charges that it was again allying itself with the right wing to obstruct the progress of Chile's reformist government, the PCCh claimed through its organ *El Siglo* that the opposition of the FRAP to the visit was based on "a position of principle" whereas that of the right wing parties and the PR was "opportunist" and reflected only a desire to bring pressure to bear on the government. Following the Senate vote, President Frei submitted to Congress a constitutional reform bill which would permit him to dissolve both houses and call new elections. The PCCh welcomed the prospect of new elections, and announced its support for the constitutional reform bill. *El Siglo* declared on 21 January that the government's decision to seek the dissolution of Congress "opens a way for the participation of the people in the struggle for profound changes."

Meeting in plenary session on 21-23 April, the Central Committee of the PCCh hailed the results of the 2 April municipal elections as a vindication of the policy approved at the party's Thirteenth Congress, and stated that the "proletariat" was beginning to defeat the "bourgeoisie" in the battle for the allegiance of the Chilean masses. Political Commission member Volodia Teitelboim said at the meeting that the rise in the communist vote was greatest in areas where the "mass struggle" had been the most intense; he and other speakers emphasized the importance of party members' working closely together with groups of trade unionists, slum dwellers, and so on, identifying themselves with the aspiration of these persons and helping them with day-to-day problems so that they could come to see the Communists as the most reliable defenders of their interests.

The PCCh's domestic policy stand engendered controversy both within Chile and in the party's relations with external communism, particularly Cuban. The most serious internal controversy has been within the FRAP alliance. The PS, which believes in the inevitability of armed insurrection and is growingly indifferent to the use of parliamentary means for achieving political ends, has been firmly opposed to the attempts made by the PCCh since the defeat of FRAP candidate Salvador Allende in the 1964 presidential elections to widen its electoral appeal by seeking closer association with other parties, and in particular the PR. Strains between Communists and Socialists were increased by the 17 December by-election in the southern provinces of Bio Bio, Malleco, and Cautín. The PS opposed Communist support for Radical candidate Alberto Baltra, who was also supported by the Social Democrat Party (Partido Social Democrata; PSD). Baltra's victory caused consternation among the Socialists and other extremists, who feared that this proof of advancement through elections by Communists and Radicals would weaken support for their own theory of "armed revolution." One of the PS's apprehensions about this election (expressed by a leading member of the party, Clodomiro Almeyda, in an interview with *Punto Final* on 22 November) was that support for a Radical candidate, no matter how leftist he might be, might awaken "illusions" of reviving a popular front (similar to that headed by the Radical president, Pedro Aguirre, in 1938) for the next presidential elections in 1970. The PCCh for its part is opposed to the PS's tendency (especially after that party's November national congress in Chillán) to identify itself more and more with extremist Castroist groups in Chile, a tendency which the Communists cannot accept in view of their declared stand on Castro's theories and tactics. This stand was put forward in an important article on revolutionary unity by Secretary-General Corvalán in *El Siglo* of 2 July (also published in *WMR*, July; for full text see *Documents*). Corvalán conceded that the Cuban experience might be repeated elsewhere, but insisted on each party's right to choose its own strategy, castigating any attempts by some Communists to impose their views on "other detachments of the anti-imperialist movement." He said there were two rival "revolutionary currents" in Latin America: the "proletarian," represented by the communist parties, whose role he fully praised, and that of the "petty bourgeois revolutionaries"–represented, Corvalán implied, by the Cubans and their followers. He stressed that "The revolutionary current arising from a petty-bourgeois basis usually underestimates the proletariat and the communist parties; it is more inclined towards nationalism, terrorism, and at times, it lapses into anit-communism and anti-Sovietism"–a stricture clearly aimed at the Cubans and their supporters. The PCCh is particularly opposed to Castroist insistence on the use of violent tactics, specifically guerrilla warfare, as the sole means of achieving communist aims in Chile. In response to an article in *Punto Final* attacking the PCCh for its refusal to support guerrilla movements in Chile and other countries of Latin America, the party's theoretical organ *Principios* carried an article by José Texier, "The Communist Party and the Revolutionary Process," which said in part:

> It is maintained that the true revolutionary leaders should be trained in the mountains, in the heat of the rifle, in contact with the rigors of the land and the woods, and that the worker-political leader of the revolutionary parties should withdraw from the scene to be replaced with the young guerrilla commander who–they believe it to be preferable–should be of petty-bourgeois extraction. This new doctrine concludes by maintaining that . . . armed struggle is the only feasible course for the Latin American peoples and that military tactics should replace political tactics. . . . Our party maintains that this cannot be the sole form of confronting the reactionary forces, in the conditions under which the struggle of classes is being carried on in Chile and in other countries in this continent. . . . What we maintain is that if the way is closed to the working class to pave the road for a people's government and if the masses choose guerrilla warfare, the party supports them, organizes them, and guides them. Under such conditions, the

Communists do no wait passively. They put themselves at the head of the guerrilla movements. . . . Our conception of the guerrilla movements puts them in their proper place, as an auxiliary means—very important in some cases, but not decisive—in connection with the conquest of political power. . . . What form will the struggle of the masses take on in Chile? . . . The predominant form of struggle cannot be predicted. . . . Revolution is impossible without a strong revolutionary feeling among the people, and this critical moment cannot be created overnight by the working and will of a handful of brave people fighting in the mountains.

The PCCh held a national conference in Santiago on 10-14 September. The main question was the further organizational, ideological, and political consolidation of the party. The previously mentioned report to the conference by Secretary-General Luis Corvalán analyzed the current political situation in the country, the prospects of the struggle by the party for the "consolidation of democracy," and the intentions of the rightists to prevent deep-going economic and social changes—above all, the agrarian and banking reforms.

A plenary meeting of the Central Committee of the PCCh on 8 October, in Barrancas, heard an address by Political Commission member José Cademartori which was highlighted by an appeal for political unity with Radicals and a criticism of the PS's decision not to consent to such an agreement. On 11 October Secretary-General Corvalán summed up the plenum's debates in a speech which stressed that PCCh policy was "the policy of joint action for common goals, of Communist-Socialist understanding, and of the joint action of the FRAP with other anti-imperialist and democratic forces"; that strategic differences among the parties of the left did not prevent joint action; and that, notwithstanding the crisis of the left, reactionaries were mistaken if they believed that the popular movement was "going to the devil." (*El Siglo*, 12 October.)

**Domestic Activity.** In January the Communist Youth of Chile held a national plenum which resolved to undertake a massive campaign for more youth rights, especially the right to vote at the age of eighteen and easier access to universities.

The PCCh marked the 100th anniversary of the publication of Karl Marx's *Capital* and the fiftieth anniversary of the October Revolution by the inauguration 8 August of an Institute of Marxist Studies. Speaking at the inauguration ceremony, Secretary-General Corvalán stated that the creation of the institute answered the "need of the workers' and people's movement . . . for analyzing every problem—primarily the social problem—in the light of Marxism-Leninism, lending valuable assistance to the struggle of our people for freedom." (*El Siglo* 13 August.)

In September a delegation from the PCCh national conference went to the Ministry of the Interior to express the preoccupation of the Communists with the problems affecting the population, especially the "tragedy of unemployment" and the neglecting of "entire provinces" such as Arauco and Aisén.

From 16 October to 20 November the PCCh conducted its Ninth National Financial Campaign with the declared aim of "collecting 885 million pesos in order to have greater material means to support the development of the masses and the organism for the ideological influence of the party."

The Communist-controlled CUTCh gave active support to the December strike of copper miners in El Salvador, Portrerillos, and Barquitos.

**International Views and Policies.** The PCCh follows a firm pro-Soviet line, advocating peaceful coexistence, rejecting the concept of armed struggle, and strongly supporting the Soviet call for a world conference of communist parties.

The PCCh's stand on armed struggle was reaffirmed at the October plenum of the Central Committee in the aforementioned speech by José Cademartori. The speaker was eloquently clear when he said: "We are not going to wage guerrilla warfare. With this we would like to say that if guerrilla warfare provided a genuine and effective solution to existing conditions in our country, then we Communists would not be wasting time on words." Castigating the critics of this policy and those who had abandoned the PCCh in order to establish a more dynamic revolutionary action, Cademartori said: "There are those who say that if the people obtain a few material improvements. they abandon their combative spirit and are lost to the revolution. Basically, those who speak this way are agreeing with the reactionaries who persecute and repress the popular movement."

The doctrinal differences between the PCCh, which is in open disagreement with Fidel Castro's theories and tactics, and its FRAP partner, the PS, which is attracted by the teachings of both Havana and Peking, was publicly manifested before, during, and after the conference of the Latin American Solidarity Organization (OLAS) in Havana on 31 July-10 August. The establishment of a Chilean national committee of the OLAS kept being postponed for months on end because Communists and Socialists disagreed with regard to the committee's composition. While the Socialists wanted to see as broad a representation of the extreme left as possible, the Communists insisted on excluding from the OLAS committee all pro-Chinese and Trotskyist groups and "adventurers" expelled from both the Communist and the Socialist parties. Finally on 16 June, the committee was set up by the Communists and Socialists alone, each party delegating to it four representatives. The Secretary-General of the PS, Senator Aniceto Rodríguez, was elected president of the committee. Other Socialist members were Salvador Allende, Clodomiro Almeyda, and Julio Benítez. The PCCh was represented on the committee by deputies Luis Rascabimo and Jorge Montes, CUTCh President Luis Figueroa, and Carlos Cerda.

The Chilean delegation to the OLAS conference, however, was not identical in composition to the Chilean OLAS committee. It included only four committee members: Jorge Montes, Clodomiro Almeyda, Carlos Cerda, and Julio Benítez. The other four delegates were Socialists Walterio Fierro and Carlos Altamirano, and Communists Volodia Teitelboim and Bernardo Araya. While the Communist members of the delegation were virtually ignored by the Cuban publicity media, the Socialists were interviewed by press and over radio and television, and were given the opportunity to reaffirm their approval of the Castroist thesis on armed struggle. The delegation was, therefore, split equally between supporters of Castro and pro-Soviet Communists who took opposing positions on several resolutions involving Moscow-Havana differences. Since each delegation to the conference had only one vote, the Chileans had to abstain when these resolutions were put to the vote (as in the case of the unpublished resolution condemning Communist financial and technical aid to Latin American countries). Even in his formal address to the OLAS meeting, Communist delegate Volodia Teitelboim had to admit that while Socialists and Communists "make up the vanguard of the Chilean Revolution" and share common principles, there were also "some differences" between them: "On occasion, we argue from different standpoints, as we attempt to interpret social and political phenomena. These may be dialectically opposed attitudes, but they are discussed systematically and in a spirit of fraternity." (*El Siglo,* 5 August.)

The actual disagreement between the PCCh and PS was much deeper. It reached the point where the PCCh members of the delegation refused to sign the final declaration of the conference and took exception to the inflammatory speech made by Socialist delegate Carlos Altamirano, in which he called for guerrilla warfare in Chile. The Communists later denied accusations that the Chilean OLAS national committee was promoting violent insurrection in Chile, and maintained that the committee was solely concerned with offering "solidarity" to similar committees elsewhere in Latin America. Ultra-left groups in Chile lost no time in attacking the OLAS committee as a revisionist organization "likely to become counterrevolutionary" because of the PCCh's stand. Although still professing full support for OLAS, the Chilean Communists have been increasingly outspoken in admitting differences with the Cubans and in expressing opposition to some of the OLAS conference's decisions. In his report to the PCCh National Conference in September, Luis Corvalán attacked the attitude of scorn for the party of the working class, or the idea that it "can be replaced by a caudillo or armed group." (See *Documents.*)

In an editorial entitled "The Situation in the Chinese People's Republic," *El Siglo* launched on 10 January a strong attack against Communist China. Taking an open stand in favor of the USSR, the paper said:

We have seldom expressed our opinion regarding the disagreeable events which have been openly taking place in the Chinese People's Republic during the past two months. We felt that rather than fan the fires of a situation which is extremely harmful to the communist movement, it was more important to initiate efforts to grasp the best possible means of surmounting the crisis. We did forsake this stand only when events became so serious and hateful that to remain silent would have implied a stand on the matter. . . . The CPR's existence as a socialist nation is threatened. This is the bitter result of the violent controversies created by nationalist aggravations and the anxiety for world leadership born of the personality cult. . . . All that can be hoped for is that a true proletarian, socialist spirit will prevail; that the Chinese people as well as the Communist Party may surmount this serious crisis, normalize the construction of socialism, and return to the ranks of the great family of the world communist parties.

On 11 February *Pravda* printed the telegrams sent by the Central Committee of the PCCh to the Central Committees of the Soviet and Chinese parties. The message to the CPSU read: "The Communist Party of Chile most energetically condemns the extreme anti-Soviet actions of the Mao Tse-tung group and voices its complete solidarity with the Soviet Communists and all working people." That to the CCP read: "The Communist Party of Chile brings to your knowledge its most indignant protest against the infamous anti-Soviet provocations typical of ultra-anitcommunists. We assure you that the Chilean working people are alarmed by the dangerous turn of your policy, which objectively facilitates the plans of US imperialism and complicates solidarity with Vietnam. We demand an end to these provocations, which gravely injure the interests of the peoples."

An editorial signed by Pastor Aucapan in *El Siglo* of 22 March was typical of the PCCh's stand on Vietnamese conflict. Discussing the meeting in Guam of leaders of the USA and its four allies fighting in Vietnam, the paper said: "The quintet of death is meeting in Guam. . . . The brains and executioners of the Vietnamese crime are meeting. . . . The agenda is a tragic joke just like all the others which [President Johnson] uses for foreign consumption, namely the pacification and democratization of South Vietnam."

In a public appeal to the Chilean people to participate in the celebrations for the fiftieth anniversary of the October Revolution, the Central Committee of the PCCh declared on 30 October: "Since its very birth, the Soviet state has applied, in a responsible manner, a foreign policy inspired by the principles of peaceful coexistence among states with different economic and social systems. . . The Soviet policy of peace and friendship with all peoples and of disinterested aid to the countries struggling to overcome underdevelopment and dependence arouses the support of all progressive men in the world for the first nation to put an end to capitalist exploitation."

The PCCh's position on the Arab-Israeli war in June, as expressed in a statement by the party's Political Commission, supported the "legitimate right to existence of the State of Israel" and condemned "manifestations of chauvinism by either side." The party statement did not fail to echo the general tenor of communist and Arab propaganda when it blamed the USA for promoting the war in the Middle East. "By obeying US policy in that region, the present-day rulers of Israel jeopardize the interests of their own people" (*El Siglo,* 6 June).

**International Activity and Party Contacts.** From 30 October to 1 November a "Meeting of Solidarity of Latin American Youth with Vietnam" was held in Santiago. The meeting was organized on the initiative of the World Federation of Democratic Youth by a Chilean committee composed of youth organizations of the Communist, Radical, and Christian Democrat parties as well as the CUTCh Youth Department, the UFUCh, and the FECh. According to available information, representatives of student and youth organizations from 14 Latin American countries attended the meeting. Both the World Federation of Democratic Youth and International Union of Students were represented. The opening session was held in the Hall of Honor of the Chilean Congress under a huge banner proclaiming: "Yankee Aggressors Out of Vietnam." Several Chilean newspapers observed that the youth leaders of the Communist and Christian Democrat parties seemed to vie each other in attacking the USA.

The JCC was represented in the UFUCh delegation which took part in the Ninth Congress of the International Union of Students (IUS) in Ulan Bator, Capital of the Mongolian People's Republic, on 27 March-4 April. The main topics on the agenda were (1) solidarity with the Vietnamese people and (2) the "imperialist penetration" into some student organizations, including specifically the UFUCh. The Cuban delegation, joined by delegations of other countries, accused the UFUCh of "pursuing a divisionist and pro-imperialist line," and requested its expulsion from the IUS. Alejandro Yanez Betancourt, a JCC member of the Chilean delegation, proposed that the Christian Democrat-controlled UFUCh should not be dropped from the congress or the IUS, stating his belief that the IUS should remain open to "unions where other forces are temporarily in control" because experience has taught that this policy will "aid the anti-imperialist maturity of the student rank-and-file."

Under the auspices of the Communist-controlled CUTCh, some 2,000 youths marched 90 miles from Valparaiso to Santiago on 8-10 July, "to protest against the Vietnam war, demand the withdrawal of American troops, and call for an end to the criminal economic blockade against Cuba."

In the last week of May, the Secretary-General of the Communist Party of Uruguay, Rodney Arismendi, and the PCCh's Secretary-General, Luis Corvalán, met in Santiago to discuss the need for "common action in defense of the Cuban Revolution and the self-determination of the peoples [of Latin America], and against the aggressive policy of intervention of North American imperialism."

Also in Santiago, representatives of the Central Committee of the Communist Party of Brazil met in early July with members of the PCCh's Political Commission. The joint statement issued at the end of the meeting expressed support for world communist unity and opposition to all factionalism. It pointed out that the two parties were in favor of a new world meeting of communist and workers' parties. The statement resolutely endorsed the Soviet Union's "sustained efforts for peace without annexations" and voiced solidarity with the Arab peoples. (*IB*, no. 103, 1967.)

In another international contact, a delegation of the PCCh headed by Political Commission member Orlando Millas visited East Germany in November to "familiarize themselves" with the experience of the Socialist Unity Party in that country. Representatives of both parties stressed that "the duty of all communists is to fight actively for the unity of the world communist movement." On the question of an international conference of communist and workers' parties, the Chileans and the East Germans expressed their belief that "conditions were ripe" for preparing such a meeting. (*Ibid.*, no. 107.)

A two-man delegation of the Italian Communist Party—Aldo Tortorella (member of the Directorate) and Renato Sandri (Central Committee member and party expert on Latin American affairs)—visited Chile from 22 March to 5 April and met with representatives of the Political Commission, the Secretariat, and some regional and local committees of the PCCh. At the end of the visit, a joint communique was issued (see *Italy*).

**Publications.** The PCCh puts out the following publications: *El Siglo,* edited by Jorge Inzunza Bécquer; *Principois,* a monthly theoretical journal appearing under the editorship of Raúl Araya Bori; *Nuestra Epoca,* a monthly magazine edited by Jorge Soza Egaña; *DEC-67,* a bi-weekly published by communist students of the University of Chile; *El Surco,* an irregular publication of the PCCh's Agrarian Committee; and *Aurora,* a bi-monthly magazine edited by Alfonso González Daguino. All are printed by the Sociedad Impresora Horizonte, of Lira 363, Santiago de Chile. They reflect, without exception, the PCCh's pro-Soviet line. Soviet propaganda, however, has its direct channel for reaching Chileans in their own language. In January the Novosti news agency published the first issue of a monthly magazine called *Enfoque Internacional.* It is the first Soviet propaganda publication of this kind produced for an individual Latin American country. The launching of the new review coincided with the visit to Chile of K. Khachaturov, the head of Novosti's Latin American department.

\* \* \*

**Splinter Groups.** Very little is known about extreme left-wing groups operating outside the ranks of FRAP. It would appear, however, that their membership and following is limited. Prominent among these violence-oriented left-wing extremist groups is the MIR, formed in August 1965. It is the newest of the mirista parties in Latin America and in certain respects it is unique. Unlike the mirista parties of Venezuela and Peru, which have their roots in once reformist and now right-wing parties, Chile's MIR was molded by revolutionary elements of the Communist and Socialist parties and by high-ranking militants of the Trotskyist parties. It was thus Marxist-oriented from its inception. What is more, the Chilean miristas steadfastly oppose the idea of national democratic revolution favored by their Venezuelan and Peruvian counterparts. They are convinced that any collaboration with the national bourgeoisie would be ideologically emasculating, historically unwise, and politically suicidal. Having chosen a guerrilla-oriented revolutionary strategy along Castroist lines, the MIR has brought down upon itself the wrath of other sections of the Chilean left. The Communists and the Socialists ceaselessly attack the miristas, and even the pro-Chinese *Espartaco,* organ of the Revolutionary Communist Party of Chile (Partido Comunista Revolucionario de Chile; PCRCh), misses no opportunity to level charges of adventurism and Trotskyism against the MIR. The miristas are confident that time is on their side and that it militates against the FRAP and Christian Democrats alike. In a statement issued on 13 May, the MIR expressed its "absolute revolutionary solidarity with the Bolivian guerrillas." In a speech on 23 July at a Solidarity-with-Cuba ceremony in Santiago, MIR Secretary-General Dr. Enrique Sepúlveda stressed that the dilemma over whether to attain power peacefully or violently no longer existed: "We are sure that the only alternative is offered by insurrection and armed strategy in Chile."

The PCRCh was formed in May 1966 by the Spartacus (Espartaco) and Insurgent Communist Union (Union Rebelde Comunista; URC). At its first congress, held the same month, the party declared that the only way to "drive US imperialism out of the country and seize power" was through an "armed people's war," and rejected the "peaceful road advanced by the revisionists." (see *YICA,* 1966 pp. 197-98.) In October 1967, following the death of Che Guevara, the PCRCh stated that it applauded the liberation of Cuba and the Second Declaration of Havana, but added: "We cannot accept the present Cuban leadership's position on armed struggle based on a guerrilla nucleus because this isolates the masses; revolutionary war is the struggle of the masses and it can only be carried out by mobilizing them and gaining their support (popular warfare) under the leadership of the proletarian party, represented in Chile by the PCRCh." In May the Central Committee of the PCRCh sent a latter to Mao Tse-tung, expressing the party's "firm support and warm acclamation for China's cultural revolution." The pro-Chinese orientation of the PCRCh was given further expression in an editorial in the November issue of *Espartaco,* which praised Communist China, under the leadership of Mao Tse-tung, as the powerful bastion of world revolution and condemned the Soviet "revisionist ruling clique" for "all-round betrayal of Marxism-Leninism in its domestic and foreign policies."

# CHINA

The First National Congress of the Chinese Communist Party (Chung-kuo kung-ch'an tang; CCP) was held in July 1921 in Shanghai. Of the 12 delegates known to have attended, two, Mao Tse-tung and Tung Pi-wu, are still members of the Political Bureau of the CCP Central Committee.

The People's Republic of China (PRC) was established 1 October 1949. State organs are in all important matters dominated by the party. The 1956 Constitution of the CCP describes the People's Republic of China as "a People's Democratic Dictatorship led by the working class and based on the alliance of workers and peasants." The same document describes the party as "the vanguard of the Chinese working class."

The CCP is the largest communist party in the world. No official CCP membership figures are available for later than 1961; the 1 July 1961 *Jen-min Jih-pao* reported that there were more than 17 million CCP members. This was repeated by *Hung Ch'i* 16 July 1962. Estimates of current membership range from 17 million to 22 million. On the basis of an estimated population of 700 million for mainland China, these membership estimates would give a ratio of party members to population of 2.4 to 3.1 per cent. All of these figures are of questionable significance, however, in view of the current extensive purges of the membership and impending reorganization of the party.

**Organization and Leadership.** In theory, the highest authority in the CCP is the National Party Congress, a body of delegates whose number and manner of election are left to the discretion of the Central Committee. The Congress is elected for a term of five years and is to meet annually; however, the present Eighth National Congress, consisting of more than 1,000 members elected indirectly by lower party congresses, was elected in 1956 and met again only in 1958; thus the Ninth National Congress was six years overdue in 1967. The National Congress elects the Central Committee, which in turn elects the Politburo, the Standing Committee of the Politburo, the Secretariat and the Central Control Commission. The Eighth Central Committee elected in 1956 and 1958 included a total of 99 full members and 96 alternates. As of 1 December 1967, 173 members survived, including 89 full members and 84 alternates.

Effective policy-making power within the party rests at the level of the Central Committee and above, particularly in the Standing Committee of the Politburo. Since the CCP ordinarily does not publish lists of members of the Central Committee or other party bodies and does not usually formally announce new appointments to or expulsions from these bodies, their composition must be inferred from rostrum lineups, incidental information from New China News Agency (NCNA) dispatches, and other unofficial data. Membership of the Politburo and its Standing Committee, in the order given by NCNA in reports of the 1 October 1967 National Day celebrations in Peking, was as follows:

*Standing Committee*:

> Mao Tse-tung
> Lin Piao
> Chou En-lai
> Ch'en Po-ta
> K'ang Sheng
> Chu Te
> Li Fu-ch'un
> Ch'en Yun

Liu Shao-ch'i
Teng Hsiao-P'ing    } Inactive; did not appear 1 October 1967
T'ao Chu

*Other Full Members*:

Tung Pi-wu
Ch'en I
Li Hsien-nien
Hsü Hsiang-ch'ien
Nieh Jung-chen
Yeh Chien-ying

Ho Lung
Li Ching-ch'üan    } Inactive; did not appear 1 October 1967
Liu Po-ch'eng
T'an Chen-lin

*Alternate Members*:

Hsieh Fu-chih
Li Hsüeh-feng
Sung Jen-ch'iung

Po I-po
Ulanfu    } Inactive; did not appear 1 October 1967

Besides those listed above as inactive (all of whom, except for Liu Po-ch'eng, have lost their real power, if not their formal positions, as a direct result of the cultural revolution), not all of the above actually take an active part in top-level policy-making within the party. Chu Te, Liu Po-ch'eng, and Tung Pi-wu are aged and infirm heroes of the revolution (although Chu was also attacked in 1967 for ideological reasons—see below). Of the rest, the important and active members as of 1 January 1968, are: Mao Tse-tung, Lin Piao, Chou En-lai, Ch'en Po-ta, K'ang Sheng, Li Fu-ch'un, Li Hsien-nien, Nieh Jung-chen, and Hsieh Fu-chih. Ch'en I, whose authority as Foreign Minister was eclipsed by left extremists for much of 1967, seems also to have regained his position and power with the help of Chou En-lai. The remainder are of only minor importance in the making of policy at the party-wide, or national level.

Mao's wife, Chiang Ch'ing, although not a member of the Politburo, became an important political figure in 1967.

Lin Piao, Chou En-lai, Li Fu-ch'un, Li Hsien-nien, Nieh Jung-chen, Hsieh Fu-chih, and Ch'en I are, in addition, active members of the State Council, the highest body within the government apparatus of the PRC. Prior to the cultural revolution, this body included Premier Chou En-lai and 15 Vice-Premiers; of these, only the above seven men remain active, and they are thought to have taken on substantially increased responsibility for direction of the state bureaucracy.

The Secretariat, which before the cultural revolution was responsible for carrying out the day-to-day tasks of party leadership in various spheres, such as propaganda, organization, and finance and trade, lost its importance as a body during 1967; its Secretary-General Teng Hsiao-p'ing was Mao's second-most important antagonist during the year. Hsieh Fu-chih indicated that the functions of the Secretariat have been taken over by the Central Committee's Cultural Revolution Group. Originally comprising 10 Secretaries and three Alternate Secretaries, most of the Secretariat membership lost their positions in the course of the cultural revolution. Only four men are known to be active members of this body: K'ang Sheng, Li Fu-ch'un, Li Hsien-nien, and Liu Ning-i.

**The Great Proletarian Cultural Revolution–Objectives.** Both party and government in mainland China in 1967 were convulsed by the continuing Great Proletarian Cultural Revolution. The Great Proletarian Cultural Revolution is both a struggle for absolute control of the party waged by Mao Tse-tung and his supporters, and a nation-wide ideological revival campaign with the objective of assuring that China "will never change its political color." These are simultaneous and interdependent objectives. Mao and his supporters have attempted to use mass political activity in a purposive way as a weapon against regular party and government organizations. Since the inauguration of the Red Guard (*Hung wei ping*) movement in August 1966, Mao and his supporters have been faced with the problem of controlling and directing this mass political activity, as well as with the problem of the seizure of power from the regular government and party apparatus. To utilize the power potential of the masses, Mao must rely both on direct controls and to a certain extent on genuine personal loyalty and commitment to him on the part of the Chinese peasants, workers and soldiers. Thus the Great Proletarian Cultural Revolution has comprehended both a massive, nationwide attempt to inculcate such personal loyalty to Mao, and an attempt to regularize or routinize mass seizures of power by means of new organizational forms. According to the 8 August 1966 decision of the Eleventh Plenum of the Central Committee:

> The cultural revolutionary groups, committees, and congresses should not be temporary organizations but permanent, standing mass organizations. They are suitable not only for colleges, schools and government and other organizations, but generally also for factories, mines, other enterprises, urban districts and villages. (YICA, 1966, pp. 665-673.)

The decision also stated: "These cultural revolutionary groups, committees, and congresses are excellent new forms of organization whereby the masses educate themselves under the leadership of the Communist Party." The Maoist leadership is attempting to create "organs of power" possessing the organizational simplicity and *ad hoc* nature of soviets, that is, organs which will avoid the specialized functions of an ordinary administrative bureaucracy, and at the same time will serve as "transmission belts" for directives from the central leadership down to the grass roots of Chinese society. The words "educate" and "leadership" in the above quotation point to the twin Maoist objectives of the inculcation of personal loyalty to Mao and the imposition of new forms of organizational control.

According to the New Year's editorial in *Jen-min Jih-pao* (see *Documents*), "Carry the Great Proletarian Cultural Revolution Through to the End," the political tasks of 1967 were (1) to carry the cultural revolution to the factories and rural areas, encouraging the people to "grasp revolution and stimulate production"; (2) to encourage students, teachers, and intellectuals to go to the factories and rural areas in an organized way, to integrate themselves with the masses; (3) to mobilize the masses to attack the enemies of socialism and to criticize leading organs and leading cadres at all levels; and (4) to continue mass criticism of the bourgeois reactionary line.

The Great Proletarian Cultural Revolution began in November 1965, with articles in the Shanghai press attacking the play *Hai Jui's Dismissal from Office* as being an antiparty allegory, and quickly reached the proportions of a major purge. From August 1966 to mid-1967 the wall poster campaigns, struggle and criticism movements against leaders, and armed clashes among groups of workers, Red Guards, students, and peasants all reached a peak of intensity and violence. Throughout 1967, but especially during the first half of the year, numerous exhortations and admonitions from Peking stressed the need to keep the cultural revolution within bounds, to avoid unauthorized violence, indiscriminate criticism, unnecessary disruption of production and destruction of state property. Such appeals were sufficiently frequent to indicate that they were largely ineffective. Chou En-lai in a speech on 8 January called for moderation in the criticism of top leaders, including Liu Shao-ch'i and Teng Hsiao-p'ing. On 8 February the Central Committee issued an order to the Red Guards to stop "exchanging revolutionary experiences" and to return to their homes; on 22 February a Red Guard Congress of Peking Universities and Colleges was established in Peking to assist in controlling the Red Guard movement in the capital. On 25 March Chiang Ch'ing called for the cessation of armed struggle, and on 22 May *Jen-min Jih-pao* featured an editorial titled "Immediately Curb Struggle by Force."

Armed struggles in fact continued during the second half of the year, but after August they were generally not so severe or extensive as those of the first half of 1967. Poster criticism, too, followed this general pattern; nearly everyone was criticized on some posters between January and August. Thereafter, poster activity was more restricted and orderly. In September Chou En-lai issued instructions approving the use of posters but warning against posting reports of rumors, gossip, obscenities, and in particular against revealing national secrets. Chou complained that a Japanese agent had sold one poster report abroad for $1,500.

**Attacks on Individual Top Party Leaders—The Struggle for Power.** The nature of the power struggle at the topmost levels of the leadership of the CCP is still not very well understood. A history of sharp divisions of opinion within the Politburo since the Great Leap Forward in 1958-1959 is now evident, but what is not known is whether policy since then has been the resultant of the relative power positions of different factions; just how much political power Mao has had since then; and to what extent there were high-level attempts to sabotage official policy after the Great Leap Forward. Nor is it understood why Liu Shao-ch'i and Teng Hsiao-p'ing, although they were targets of a nationwide criticism campaign and were publicly humiliated and disgraced by crowds, still (as of early 1968) apparently formally retain their posts and are said to draw regular pay. (See Anna Louise Strong, *Letter from China,* 23 September 1967.) At least two factors appear to be important: (1) the existence in Chinese Communist ideology and practice of a particular methodology for dealing with factions within the party, for "inner-party struggle," and for the ideological reform of personal thought and action; and (2) the ambiguous status and power position of secret-police forces in China. The existence of such a tried methodology of personal and organizational rectification has made it possible to conduct extensive "struggle and criticism" against many of China's top leaders without putting them beyond the pale of possible rehabilitation and at least partial reinstatement in their positions. At the same time, Mao, unlike Stalin during the purges of the 1930's, does not appear to have a "trusty hatchet" in the form of a powerful and completely loyal secret-police apparatus that could eliminate his rivals in a more direct fashion. The Ministry of Public Security, headed by Hsieh Fu-chih, is the closest thing to a Maoist secret police, but in early 1967 forces under the Ministry were for a time transferred to the command of the People's Liberation Army (PLA), suggesting that Mao had only limited trust in their loyalty. However, Hsieh Fu-chih is also a member of the Military Affairs Committee, the key military body in China. In addition, there are the Social Affairs Department of the Secretariat and the Ministry of Internal Affairs, headed by Tseng Shan, about which very little is known, but which seem to have some secret police functions.

Nearly all the men who made up the Politburo at the start of the cultural revolution have been subjected to propaganda attacks and criticism of some intensity. The most important targets of attack may be separated into three groups, in descending order of the severity of charges made against them and the severity of treatment accorded them.

**First Group.** Mao has waged his struggle most relentlessly against P'eng Chen (removed from his position as Mayor of Peking in the summer of 1966), and his closest associates within the Peking municipal party organization and the central leadership at large, including Lo Jui-ch'ing (former PLA Chief of Staff), Lu Ting-i (former head of the Central Committee Propaganda Department), and Yang Shang-k'un (former Alternate Secretary of the Secretariat), and others. These men were among the first targets of the cultural revolution, and only this group at this point in the cultural revolution must be considered as totally beyond possible rehabilitation. They are Mao's worst enemies. Accusations of outright treason, specifically and elaborately argued, have been directed against them. They are accused of deliberately sabotaging Maoist policy over the past several years, of attacking Mao personally in the Central Committee meetings, of plotting a military coup, and of betraying state secrets to the Soviet Union. Yang Shang-k'un was accused (probably falsely) of "bugging" Mao's residence and of passing archival information to Moscow. In January P'eng Chen, Lu Ting-i, Lo Jui-ch'ing, and Yang Shang-k'un were named as the chief figures in a plot to overthrow Mao. Lin Piao is reported in January 1967 to have discussed this alleged plot in great detail in a speech to the Central Committee. P'eng Chen was said to be the mastermind of the plot and to have been an old enemy of Mao.

The plotters allegedly met in February 1966 to make their plans and intended to carry out their coup in 1966, perhaps on the occasion of the twentieth anniversary of the proclamation of the Inner Mongolian Autonomous Region. In April 1967 extensive details of the alleged coup plot appeared on wall posters in Peking. By this time Liu Shao-ch'i and Teng Hsiao-p'ing had also come under public attack, and they, along with many lesser figures in the army and in the provinces—particularly Li Ching-ch'üan in Szechwan and Marshal Ho Lung, and eventually including almost everyone of importance but the hard-core Maoists—were also said to have been accomplices to the plot. The strongest attacks, however, were still directed against the original group, whose members were the first to fall from power during the cultural revolution in late 1965 and early 1966. They have not since appeared in public and are variously rumored to have committed or attempted suicide.*

**Second Group.** The second distinguishable group of targets of the cultural revolution among the top leadership of the CCP consists of Liu Shao-ch'i, Chairman of the People's Republic since 1959, Teng Hsiao-p'ing, Secretary-General of the CCP since 1956, and Liu's alleged henchmen or "agents" in various provinces, such as T'ao Chu in South China, Li Ching-ch'üan in Szechwan, Ulanfu in Inner Mongolia, Li Pao-hua in Anhwei, and T'an Ch'i-lung in Shantung. Criticism of this group began in earnest in the fall of 1966, with campaigns against Li Pao-hua, Ulanfu, T'ao Chu, and others, leading up to the campaign which began in late March 1967 against Liu Shao-ch'i. The chief accusations against this group are those of bourgeois mistakes in their work during the early 1960s; they are said generally to have indulged in economism and to have attempted thereby to restore capitalism in China. Ulanfu was also accused of stirring up Mongolian nationalism.

The early 1960s were the years of retrenchment and recovery from the experiments of the Great Leap Forward and the natural disasters of 1959 to 1961, and it is during this period that Mao's role in policy formulation is most obscure. Given the goals of the cultural revolution, Mao in any event would want to dissociate himself from such policies as the encouragement of private plots for peasants, setting output quotas by households, and the slowdown in collectivization, all of which were necessary to restore production in the early 1960s but which violate current Maoist doctrine. Thus, although it is clear that this period saw the apex of Liu Shao-ch'i's personal power, which grew in the aftermath of the failure of the policies Mao himself had advocated, Mao's claims in 1966 and 1967 that he was "never consulted" and had no influence on the course of events during this period cannot be accepted at face value (see *NYT,* 6 January 1967).

All such "rightist deviations" during this period were said to be ultimately the work of "China's Khrushchev," Liu Shao-ch'i. It could not be claimed by the Maoists in 1967 that the whole of the party leadership suddenly became bourgeois in the early 1960s and therefore the sinister influence of Liu, who, together with Teng Hsiao-p'ing, "dreamed only of restoring capitalism," was conveniently detected in every deviation of a provincial leader. An intensive anti-Liu campaign in the party press during 1967 attempted to show that he had always opposed Mao's policies and always advocated collaborating with the bourgeoisie and even with the Japanese invaders during the war. This campaign began with an article in the 31 March issue of *Hung Ch'i* attacking Liu's book *How to Be a Good Communist.* According to the article, the book "advertises the idealistic cultivation of personality. It obliquely advocates bourgeois individualism and slavism and opposes Mao Tse-tung's thought." It was followed by articles criticizing various thoughts, words, and actions of Liu since the late 1920s. He was accused of wartime collaboration with Chiang Kai-shek and of wanting to disband the Red Army after World War II. Liu's wife, Wang Kuang-mei, was said to be thoroughly bourgeois and extravagant and a selfish headline-grabber. Her stay at a commune in 1964 was cited as an occasion on which she displayed irresponsible economism and aversion to labor and to the masses.

Notwithstanding the ferocity of the propaganda barrage against Liu, Teng, and their various "agents" in the provinces, at least some members of this group, including Liu and Teng themselves, although divested of authority, at the end of 1967 still commanded significant political influence and sympathy within the Party. An article in *Hung Ch'i* on 1 August 1967 said with respect to Liu and Teng:

*Lo Jui-ch'ing may have been present at a struggle meeting against him in March, 1968. See 6 March *Jen-min Jih-pao.*

To topple organizationally a handful of Party persons in authority taking the capitalist road is not tantamount of toppling them politically and ideologically, to relieve them of their offices is not tantamount to the complete seizure of power, and to seize power also does not simply mean to relieve them of their offices. Office of course means power, but even without office they still can exercise power. . . . They are not "dead tigers," but are "wounded ones" or even "tigers feigning death."

From the Maoist point of view, their eventual rehabilitation and some degree of reinstatement cannot be ruled out. In the rubric of contradictions, which is used by the Chinese Communists for distinguishing enemies from mistaken or hoodwinked friends, Liu and Teng are said to be separated from the party by "antagonistic contradictions"; but, according to a speech by Hsieh Fu-chih on 14 October, these antagonistic contradictions ought to be dealt with by use of the method for dealing with contradictions among the people—that is, non-antagonistic contradictions—namely, by the process of unity-criticism-unity. Liu, Teng, and some of the others, then, may in the end retain some kind of position within the party, though perhaps only as figureheads and examples of successful self-remolding and the efficacy of Mao's thought. In that same 14 October speech Hsieh went out of his way to note that neither execution nor imprisonment of Liu and Teng were being planned. He also included the "leader" of the Wuhan incident, Ch'en Tsai-tao, and his accomplices among those who were not beyond the pale of redemption.

**Third Group.** The third group of targets consists of central party and government officials who have been criticized, but with relatively less intensity, and who either have not lost their positions or have been promoted since the start of the cultural revolution. Included in this group are the Vice-Premiers Li Hsien-nien, Li Fu-ch'un, Ch'en I, and Hsieh Fu-chih, and the head of China's nuclear program Nieh Jung-chen (Politburo member T'an Chen-lin was in a similar situation until late summer, when he came under intense criticism; he did not appear at the October 1 celebrations and is known to have lost his offices). All these men have been defended by Chou, who said in January that "it is not good to drag them out and struggle against them." According to Chou, these men firmly supported the Mao-Lin line at the Eleventh Central Committee Plenum in August 1966. Also in this category are Sung Jen-ch'iung, Ch'en Yun, Hsü Hsiang-ch'ien, Yeh Chien-ying and Li Hsüeh-feng. While not in the innermost circle of Mao's supporters, all appear to have at least held their own in the power struggles and have been criticized largely by less authoritative sources, such as Red Guard publications and wall posters. Hsieh Fu-chih in particular has become a figure of major importance as head of the Peking Revolutionary Committee and Minister of Public Security; in 1967 he made a number of speeches containing very important, albeit informal, announcements of the Maoist leadership.

**Remaining Politburo Leaders.** Outside of these three groups, the remaining members of the Politburo, Ch'en Po-ta and K'ang Sheng, appear to have been, next to Mao, Lin Piao, Chou En-lai, and Chiang Ch'ing, the most powerful figures among the top party leadership in 1967. They were fourth and fifth, respectively, on the NCNA list of those present on the rostrum at both the May Day and 1 October celebrations. Ch'en Po-ta, since 1958 editor-in-chief of *Hung Ch'i*, the party's theoretical journal, is a former political secretary and speech writer to Mao, having been closely associated with him since Yenan days. K'ang, whose activities are more obscure, is thought to have been a secret police head in the late 1930s and 1940s, and is now believed to be in charge of liaison with other communist parties of the world. Ch'en and K'ang have been the most important members of the Central Committee's Cultural Revolution Group, through which they have directed propaganda campaigns since late 1966. At the end of 1967, however, there were reports that K'ang was the target of criticism campaigns for allegedly supporting extreme leftist criticism of the PLA.

Although not a member of the Politburo, or even of the Central Committee, Chiang Ch'ing, Mao's fourth and current wife, was one of the most prominent personalities in CCP affairs during 1967. Beginning in late 1966 and through much of 1967, Chiang Ch'ing was the spokesman of the Mao-Lin group in the execution of the cultural revolution. As First Deputy Head of the Cultural Revolution Group of the CCP and advisor to the Cultural Revolution Group of the PLA, she led the public criticism of Liu Shao-ch'i and Teng Hsiao-p'ing, as well as the other major targets of criticism during

1967. In August, however, her tone became more moderate, and she referred, for instance, to the burning of the British mission in Peking as a "strange thing." In a speech on 5 September (see *Documents*) she repudiated the slogan "drag out the small handful in the army." She became less conspicuous in the fall of 1967; Chou En-lai told newsmen that comrade Chiang Ch'ing "has worked very hard" during the cultural revolution and that she had been asked to "take a rest for her health."

**The Cultural Revolution Group.** Since the beginning of the cultural revolution Mao has been trying to create a reliable top-level organ that could be used to direct the criticism campaigns against the regular party and government apparatus at all levels. First P'eng Chen, then Liu Shao-ch'i had the responsibility for directing the cultural revolution. Then in July of 1966 the existence of a special group became known, headed by Ch'en Po-ta and in charge of directing the GPCR. This group included T'ao Chu and K'ang Sheng as advisors, and Chiang Ch'ing as First Deputy Head. Eventually fifteen more individuals, most of them veterans of propaganda work, became known as deputy heads and members of the group. Splits and purges within the group quickly developed, however, beginning with the barrage of criticism against T'ao Chu which began in late 1966.

Most serious was the appearance in the spring and summer of 1967 of an extreme left group, known as the 16 May Corps, including Wang Li, Mu Hsin, Lin Chieh, Chao I-ya, and Kuan Feng. This group went very far in promoting criticism campaigns against regional military commanders, local revolutionary committees, and governmental ministers, including Foreign Minister Ch'en I. Ch'en Po-ta and Chiang Ch'ing, if not in active opposition to this faction, at least made a timely retreat from their excesses. It was in *Hung Ch'i*, edited by Ch'en, that the leftist slogan "the small pro-capitalist handful who have infiltrated the army must be crushed," first appeared. Chiang Ch'ing had uttered similar sentiments in public during the spring and summer, but again, her militancy came to a quick halt, and by early September she was making speeches defending the army. Mao Tse-tung, on hearing of this slogan, is said to have personally ordered the purge of the left wing of the Cultural Revolution Group while he was on his tour of five provinces at the end of the summer.

In September Wang Li lost his position as head of the Central Committee's Propaganda Department (in which he had succeeded T'ao Chu); Wang's associates Lin Chieh, Kuan Feng, and Mu Hsin were also dismissed at this time, and extensive public campaigns against Wang began in October. After this purge Chiang Ch'ing's public statements remained very moderate. In December she was quoted as having told a Red Guard conference not to make trouble at foreign embassies or do things that would ruin the reputation of the country. In her 5 September speech (see *Documents*) she said that the 16 May Corps was a "counter-revolutionary organization" and that its leaders were "very bad people" who were opposing Prime Minister Chou En-lai.

There has been much speculation over K'ang Sheng's connection with the leftist group, and he, Ch'en Po-ta, and Chiang Ch'ing must all be regarded as possible targets of campaigns accusing them of collusion with the leftists. In addition to Chiang Ch'ing whose special situation has been explained, Ch'en Po-ta, K'ang Sheng, Chang Ch'un-ch'iao, Ch'i Pen-yü and Yao Wen-yuan were at the end of 1967 the only members of the Cultural Revolution Group who were still active, influential figures and friends of Mao. Chang Ch'un-ch'iao, the Maoist hero of Shanghai, is chairman of the Shanghai Municipal Revolutionary Committee. Yao Wen-yuan, author of many criticism articles, including the first ones written in Shanghai against the P'eng Chen clique in late 1965, is an editor of the Shanghai papers *Wen Hui Pao* and *Chieh-fang Jih-pao* (Liberation Daily), and is said to be a close associate of Chang Ch'un-ch'iao. Ch'i Pen-yü is an assistant to Ch'en Po-ta on the publication *Hung Ch'i*. Like his boss, he in 1967 escaped being criticized for the leftist excesses of Wang Li's group, some of which were published in that journal. He was number 23 on the 1 October Day list, moving up from number 196 in October 1966.*

At the close of 1967 Mao had not yet succeeded in creating a satisfactory high-level party organ to supersede the regular executive apparatus. Members of the Cultural Revolution Group appearing on the rostrum on 1 October were not mentioned together by NCNA, as they were on 1 October 1966 and May Day of 1967. However, according to a Red Guard newspaper of 31 October, Hsieh Fu-chih

---

*In early 1968, however, a campaign of criticism was launched against him, and he dropped out of sight.

said in a speech to University student groups:

> The Cultural Revolution Group is an important part of Chairman Mao's headquarters. . . . It is even more important than the Secretariat. The Cultural Revolution Group has done the important tasks of the Secretariat and the Politburo. We ought to say that this has the highest authority and prestige among the people.

Thus it appears that as of late 1967 Mao had not yet given up hopes that the Cultural Revolution Group might become the nucleus of a renovated and thoroughly "Maoized" party apparatus.

**Lin Piao.** Lin Piao is Vice-Chairman of the CCP, Minister of National Defense, and a Vice-Premier of the State Council. His position as number 2 man in the present hierarchy of power and Mao's heir apparent was carefully and gradually strengthened in 1967. Since 1966 the official press has commonly referred to him as "Chairman Mao's close comrade-in-arms" (*ch'in-mieh chan-yu*). In March 1967 he began also to be commonly referred to in the press by his title of Vice-Chairman of the party. *Peking Review,* for instance, from March on seldom referred to him merely as "Comrade Lin Piao," preferring instead his title of Vice-Chairman. He was very frequently pictured standing next to Mao, often alone with Mao, and as the year wore on, the grouping "Chairman Mao and Vice-Chairman Lin Piao" became more common. Another appelation used for him was "Deputy Supreme Commander" (*fu t'ung-shuai*).

Some time during the summer an unofficial biography of Lin Piao was published by the Branch Detachment of the "Ching-kang-shan Corps," Peking Industrial University. According to this biography:

> At the Eleventh Central General Assembly of the Eighth Session of the Party Central Committee between 1 and 12 August, 1966, Chairman Mao selected and decided upon Comrade Lin Piao as his first successor. We can definitely say that, upon Chairman Mao's selection of Comrade Lin Piao, his most intimate combat partner, as his successor, we can be optimistic over the victory of China's and the world's revolution, as well as that of our cultural revolution. (JPRS 42,503, 7 September 1967, p. 72.)

In an editorial of 12 August *Liberation Army Daily* discussed the importance of the August 1966 Central Committee plenum and said "It is of the greatest happiness to the people of the party and the nation that the meeting confirmed comrade Lin Piao as Chairman Mao's successor."

The high point of the campaign to enhance Lin's status came in late November when the First Congress of Activists in the Study of Chairman Mao's Works in the Navy was held in Peking. On 29 November, Lin, amid great public fanfare, wrote an inscription for the occasion of the congress: "Sailing the seas depends on the helmsman; making revolution depends on Mao Tse-tung's thought." This inscription was immediately hailed throughout the nation as brilliant and inspiring, and everyone was directed to study it conscientiously and carry it out resolutely. This reinforced Lin's position as Mao's "best student" and thus, presumably, the most authoritative interpreter of Mao's thought in the absence of the Chairman. Further, on 1 December the Party Committee of the Navy adopted a much-publicized decision calling on all navy personnel to take Vice-Chairman Lin Piao as their example of loyalty to Mao and as the model of creative study and application of Mao's thought. Most importantly, the decision described Lin as "the closest comrade-in-arms, the best pupil and the 'best successor' of the great leader Chairman Mao":

> He is the deputy supreme commander of the Chinese people. He has always most loyally, firmly, and bravely defended Chairman Mao as the supreme leader, defended Mao Tse-tung's thought and his revolutionary line. With the greatest farsightedness and courage, he has led and organized the movement of vigorous popularization of Mao Tse-tung's thought among the entire party, army, and people of the whole country, ushering in a new era in which hundreds of millions of workers, peasants and soldiers directly master Marxism-Leninism, Mao Tse-tung's thought. (NCNA, 2 December 1967.)

*Jen-min Jih-pao,* however, did not confirm that status of Lin, and the account of the inscription and subsequent Navy Party Committee decision carried in the 8 December *Peking Review* omitted this glowing description of Lin's achievements, nor did it repeat the reference to Lin as "best successor" to Mao.

Lin Piao's wife, Yeh Ch'un, also came into some prominence during 1967. On the rostrum for the 1 October National Day Celebration she was number 24 and was included in the group described by NCNA as "responsible comrades of the Central authorities and from other quarters" who stepped onto the rostrum with Mao; this group consisted mostly of members of the Politburo of the Central Committee. Madame Lin is also a member of the Cultural Revolution Group of the PLA.

**The Ghost of P'eng Te-huai.** Although former Defense Minister P'eng Te-huai was removed from office in 1959, he has, in the eyes of Mao and his supporters, continued to exercise a "sinister influence within the party," and attacks on P'eng and his influence constituted a main theme of Maoist propaganda in 1967. It was P'eng who was the hero of the allegorical play *Hai Jui's Dismissal* written by Wu Han in 1961 with the alleged connivance of P'eng Chen and members of the Peking Municipal Party Committee. The play was attacked by the Shanghai Party press in November, 1965, at the start of the Great Proletarian Cultural Revolution. P'eng Te-huai, who was removed from his post after the Eighth Plenum of the Eighth Central Committee in August 1959, opposed the policies of the Great Leap Forward and favored continued cooperation with the Soviet Union in order to modernize China's military forces. Although Mao prevailed at this plenum, P'eng's viewpoint apparently had the sympathy of many if not the majority of the Politburo.

In 1967 the Maoist-controlled press claimed that P'eng was the head of an antiparty clique at the plenum and released the Central Committee's resolution of the Eighth (Lushan) Plenum, which gave details on P'eng's alleged scheming in an alliance which included Kao Kang and Jao Shu-shih (both of whom had been purged in 1955), as well as the leaders of the Soviet Union. P'eng was portrayed in the resolution and in various articles as an arch-rightist, an "out-and-out big bourgeois warlord, careerist, and conspirator who, with a speculator's mentality of 'investing in a share,' wormed himself into the Party and the army." Further, P'eng's "behind-the-scenes boss" was now said to be Liu Shao-ch'i. It appears that for several years P'eng Te-huai, who was allowed to keep his membership in the Politburo, was the center of opposition to Mao. P'eng Te-huai was said in 1967 to have been defended by Liu Shao-ch'i at an enlarged work conference of the Central Committee in January 1962. At the same meeting P'eng Chen, with his associates in the Peking Municipal apparatus, is alleged to have prepared an elaborate case against Mao and his policies, arguing P'eng Te-huai's point of view. According to an article in the *Kwangming Daily* of 9 August, a protege of P'eng Chen declared: "The present problems are national problems because Chairman Mao and the Party Central Committee have made mistakes of line"; and, "In the history of the party no mistakes of line can be corrected by those who made them." The party press now refers to this as the "Ch'ang Kuan-lou counter-revolutionary incident."

P'eng Te-huai was also strongly attacked throughout the year as the prime source of opposition to Mao Tse-tung's military strategy of the peoples' wars of liberation, which stresses the importance of a guerrilla-oriented people's militia over a modern, technologically oriented military establishment. According to Maoist sources, this conflict in line resolves itself into a question of whether to oppose the enemy "outside the gates" in a bourgeois fashion or to follow Mao's strategy of guerrilla struggle to resist invasion "within the gates." P'eng, along with Lo Jui-ch'ing, was consistently cast as the advocate of the bourgeois military line. Many articles in the press have attempted to show that P'eng had always been a poor general, a coward, and an opportunist, and all opposition to the Mao-Lin military line was depicted as P'eng's work.

From all this it is manifest that P'eng Te-huai had for some years prior to the cultural revolution functioned as a sort of symbol, if not an actual center of opposition to Mao on a whole range of issues, including, but not necessarily limited to, military strategy, Sino-Soviet relations, agriculture, and industrialization.

**Maoist Seizure of Power in Provinces and Local Areas.** The over-all strategic plan of the cultural revolution in the provinces and lower-level local areas is to replace the former party and government organs with new "revolutionary organs of power" formed on the basis of "three way alliances."

The formula of "revolutionary three-way alliances" began to be propagated in February 1967. According to this formula, Maoist seizures of power were to be accomplished by means of an alliance between the army units based in the area, the "revolutionary cadres," and the "revolutionary masses." "Revolutionary masses" were defined to mean workers, peasants, soldiers, and students. Such alliances were to provide the broad base of support needed for successfully seizing and consolidating power from the anti-Maoist party leaders and cadres in the localities.

According to theory, when a three-way alliance has been formed, a revolutionary committee is to be set up. These revolutionary committees are to be established at all levels—in factories, communes, and up to the provincial level. They are to provide the means of bypassing and making superfluous the old party and government organizations which are in Mao's view incorrigibly tainted by revisionist attitudes and practices. At the provincial level, the first step is the formation of a "Preparatory Group," pending formation of the Revolutionary Committee. The Preparatory Group is supposed to take the lead in arranging alliances between the various organizations of the revolutionary masses at lower levels. The People's Liberation Army units in the provinces are supposed to provide support where necessary to maintain Maoist alliances against their opponents, who may be rival organizations not previously in power, or may be the incumbent power holders whom the Revolutionary Committees are to supersede. Finally, when sufficient political support has been mustered for these alliances, and power takeovers at local levels have succeeded so that the provincial group can effectively exercise power, the inauguration of the provincial Revolutionary Committee is to be proclaimed.

Such was the theory. In practice, however, a number of obstacles have arisen. Maoist alliances between and among rival groups and organizations formed to seize power from the incumbent apparatus have not been easy to establish. For instance, the Tientsin Great Alliance Preparatory Group was set up in February 1967, but the Tientsin Revolutionary Committee was not inaugurated until 6 December. At a meeting with representatives of the Preparatory Group on 10-11 October, Ch'en Po-ta and Hsieh Fu-chih complained about the delay. Ch'en said:

> Now Peking has already been set up for more than five months and you in Tientsin have still not managed to get things set up. You have fallen behind. Originally, when the PLA took over the Public Security Bureau the situation was very good. . . . What we cannot understand about you is why you have been going at it so long and still cannot cooperate. . . . The Cultural Revolution Group is very concerned about the Tientsin problem.

The senior partner in these alliances in 1967 was usually the army. In most places the Revolutionary Committee, even when first established, was headed by a military man; the army was the primary means of seizing power from the local apparatus and thereafter continued to exercise it in the name of the Revolutionary Committee. In such cases, the Maoist leadership apparently hoped that new civil organs of power could be formed later, under the army's protection. In other areas, such as the cities of Nanking and Foochow during the summer months the local PLA commanders were reluctant to carry out the instructions of the Military Affairs Committee in Peking and either supported the wrong people or stayed aloof from the contending factions of Red Guards, workers, students, and peasants.

Of Mainland China's 29 administrative regions (21 provinces, 5 autonomous regions, and 3 special municipalities), as of late January 1968, 18 had either full Revolutionary Committees or Preparatory Groups. The remaining nine provinces and two autonomous regions were governed directly by the PLA through the medium of a Military Control Committee for each province. Following is a list of provincial and special municipality Revolutionary Committees formed through January, 1968:

| Administrative Region | Date officially established | Chairman |
| --- | --- | --- |
| Heilungkiang | 1 February 67 | P'an Fu-sheng |
| Kweichow | 14 February 67 | Li Tsai-han |
| Shantung | 23 February 67 | Wang Hsiao-yu |
| Shanghai | 24 February 67 | Chang Ch'un-ch'iao |
| Shansi | 12 March 67 | Liu Ke-p'ing |
| Peking | 20 April 67 | Hsieh Fu-chih |
| Tsinghai | 12 August 67 | Liu Hsien-ch'uan |

| | | |
|---|---|---|
| *Inner Mongolia* | *1 November 67* | *Teng Hai-ching* |
| *Tientsin* | *6 December 67* | *Hsieh Hsüeh-kung* |
| *Kiangsi* | *5 January 68* | *Cheng Shih-ching* |
| *Kansu* | *24 January 68* | *Hsien Heng-han* |
| *Honan* | *27 January 68* | *Liu Chien-hsun* |

Subsequently, eleven more provincial-level revolutionary committees were inaugurated as part of the new year's effort to speed preparations for a Party Congress. *

The problem of consolidating power and of exercising the functions of the former local power-holders after a Maoist takeover is one with which Mao and his supporters have been continually concerned. In mid-January, Chou En-lai and Mao were said to have met and discussed five possible "roads" to take after the seizure of party and government powers in local areas: (1) total reorganization; (2) allowing antirevolutionary leaders to continue to work under supervision after the proletarian seizure of power, but also putting certain checks on them; (3) suspending the leaders from duty but allowing them to cooperate with the revolutionaries; (4) "retiring" the leaders but continuing to make use of them; and (5) retiring the leaders and punishing them after investigation. These "five roads" are neither mutually exclusive nor comprehensive, but they at least make clear that the Maoist leadership has been determined to be very flexible in its approach to handling the local leadership, willing to use them if necessary to maintain order and production, but also determined to enhance control over them by keeping them in a state of uncertainty.

**Shanghai and Wuhan.** Two of the most crucial tests the Maoist leadership faced in its struggle for control of the provinces and special municipalities of China during 1967 were the struggles in Shanghai and in the Wuhan area. Shanghai is the place where the cultural revolution began and in 1967 it was the first major area in which the Maoist-inspired revolutionary masses attempted to seize power from the regular party and government apparatus. Hailing this attempt as the "great January storm" the Maoist-controlled *Jen-min Jih-pao* and *Hung Ch'i* started intense criticism of Tsao Ti-ch'iu and Ch'en P'ei-hsien, respectively Mayor of Shanghai and First Secretary of the party's Shanghai Municipal Committee. Ch'en and Tsao, in order to resist the Maoist attempts to seize power, turned Mao's own tactics against him. They allowed the workers to disrupt production and communications, encouraged them to travel to Peking to "make accusations" to the Central Committee, and set up rival Red Guard co-organizations and revolutionary committees. Chou En-lai spoke to a 10,000-strong rally of such arrivals in Peking on 23 January and said: "A handful of the bourgeois power faction in the party is playing with economism by mobilizing the masses into Peking, while offering them money, train tickets, and food." Chou urged them to return home, while Ch'en and Tsao were subjected to continuing propaganda attacks for being " 'Left' in appearance, but Right in reality." It was clear that Ch'en and Tsao had won the first round of the struggle by 15 January, when Ch'en Po-ta said in a speech, clearly referring to Shanghai: "In an attempt to wreck the social order and the process of production, and thereby make us a laughingstock, they have begun to use another formula, namely, that of withdrawing behind the scene while allowing you to place all the organizations under your control and seizure." This amounted to an admission that the "revolutionary masses" had bitten off more than they could chew. At the same gathering Chou En-lai said: "We must not create the mode of seizure and control as the workers of Shanghai have done. We

---

| | | |
|---|---|---|
| * Hopei | 3 February 68 | Li Hsüeh-feng |
| Hupei | 5 February 68 | Tseng Ssu-yu |
| Kwangtung | 21 February 68 | Huang Yung-sheng |
| Kirin | 6 March 68 | Wang Huai-hsiang |
| Kiangsu | 23 March 68 | Hsü Shih-yu |
| Chekiang | 27 March 68 | Nan P'ing |
| Hunan | 9 April 68 | Li Yüan |
| Anhwei | 18 April 68 | Li Te-sheng |
| Ninghsia Hui A. R. | 10 April 68 | K'ang Chien-min |
| Shensi | 1 May 68 | Li Jui-shan |
| Liaoning | 10 May 68 | Ch'en Hsi-lien |

Of these committees, civilians chair only five: Heilungkiang, Hopei, Honan, Tientsin, and Shanghai.

must establish an organization and see to it that business organizations are truly carrying out business operations." The road of "total reorganization" had thus failed in Shanghai, and Ch'en Po-ta recommended instead the "formula of supervision over the bourgeois reactionary line by the representatives of the masses" (reported in the Tokyo *Sankei,* 17 January 1967).

But Shanghai was still not firmly under Maoist control on 5 February, when the establishment of the "Shanghai Commune" was announced from that city. This sudden appearance of a municipal commune proclaiming itself to be a model of Maoism was plainly embarrassing to Peking. According to the decision of the Eleventh Plenum of August 1966, the new Maoist organs of power were to take the Paris Commune as their model and to elect members to the cultural-revolution groups and committees and delegates to cultural-revolution congresses by means of a system of general elections. In April 1966 the official press had devoted substantial attention to the commemoration of the Ninety-fifth anniversary of the Paris Commune, holding it up as a model revolutionary power seizure. By early 1967, and certainly by the time the Shanghai Commune was formed, Mao saw what a mistake this had been. The official party media referred to the Shanghai Commune only as "the provisional organ of power in Shanghai," and nothing was said of municipal communes. In mid-February there were poster reports that Mao had voiced fears that people's communes in China's cities would drastically weaken central control and turn China into a federal system. Seven months later Hsieh Fu-chih, in a speech on 14 October, drove the final nail into the coffin of the municipal communes by remarking that it was "time to renounce the myth according to which new institutions born of the cultural revolution could be the result of elections similar to those of the Paris Commune." Rather, he said, leaders designated by "mass consultations" would be preferable.

In late February, a measure of stability was achieved in Shanghai and some sort of compromise with the more Maoist-inclined leading party members in the city seems to have been concluded. Chang Ch'un-ch'iao, First Secretary of the party's East China Bureau and member of the Cultural Revolutionary Group, took the leading part in engineering this alliance, which may have avoided an outright Maoist defeat in Shanghai. Chang is said to have earned Mao's personal expression of gratitude and congratulations and was made chairman of the Shanghai Revolutionary Committee which replaced the Shanghai Commune on 24 February.

The crisis in the Wuhan cities occurred in July, when the Maoists were preparing to take power from the local regulars in Hupeh province. The Commander of the Wuhan Military Area, Ch'en Tsai-tao, had earlier proclaimed himself on the side of Mao but now began to interfere with Maoist-sanctioned rebel organizations and to interrupt communications with Peking. Ch'en had also organized his own rival Red Guard organization, the Million Heroes, which was apparently cutting the Maoist-backed group, the Revolutionary Rebels out of the three-way alliance. In mid-July, Hsieh Fu-chih and Wang Li were sent to Wuhan to try to strengthen the position of the Maoists and perhaps to make some kind of deal with Ch'en. Ch'en, however, arrested Hsieh and Wang, and the two men were subjected to personal harrassment by members of "revolutionary organizations" loyal to Ch'en. This presented Peking with a very difficult situation, and in view of the fact that the loyalties of other regional military commanders were much in doubt, brought China to the very brink of true civil war.

Chou En-lai flew to Wuhan and, with the help of a show of naval force consisting of gunboats sent up the Yangtze River from Chekiang, was finally able to secure the release of Hsieh and Wang. Some reports also said that Mao himself had gone to Wuhan at this time (see *NYT,* 10 May 1968).

Once Hsieh and Wang were released, an intense propaganda campaign was started against Ch'en Tsai-tao to erode support for him by bringing him alone into a direct confrontation with Mao. Meanwhile considerable numbers of Ch'en's Million Heroes were welcomed into the Maoist alliance. Subsequently, Ch'en and Chung Han-hua, Political Commissar of the Wuhan Military Area, were dismissed from their posts and replaced by Tseng Ssu-yu and Liu Teng respectively, both of whom are regarded as close supporters of Lin Piao. Whether any kind of a deal was worked out with Ch'en by Chou En-lai is not known; however, despite the seriousness of his actions in July, some months later Ch'en was said by Hsieh Fu-chih to be among those PLA and party leaders who could be reformed and reinstated.

Even after Ch'en's replacement, however, Peking's control over the Wuhan area was still very tenuous. On 10 August Hsieh Fu-chih said that fierce armed struggles were going on in Wuhan, as well as in Hunan and Kiangsi. Three months later, a broadcast of 11 November claimed that revolutionary repudiation campaigns had been successful; whereas, the broadcast noted, three months earlier "class enemies were rampant in Wuhan." Nevertheless, TASS and the Hupeh provincial press continued to report some armed clashes in the province through the end of the year.

**The Cadre Problem.** The Maoist central leadership has shown an active and continuing concern with preserving the position of the cadre as the medium for exercising central leadership at the grass roots level, even while trying to circumvent the degree of autonomy and discretion which that function gives him. On the one hand, the Maoist leadership has attempted to communicate directly with the masses in order to keep the cadre uncertain of his role and its importance; on the other hand, realizing that in so doing they are destroying the most reliable apparatus for controlling the masses, the Maoist leadership in 1967 simultaneously stressed that cadres must not be attacked indiscriminately by the masses, that "the majority of the cadres are good and genuinely want to make revolution," and that when the political. line in question is truly Maoist the masses must follow it faithfully.

The leadership's dilemma was well expressed in an article carried in all Shanghai papers on 13 December titled "Obey or Resist?" which discussed the question of "whether or not subordinates should obey superiors." The central leadership was understandably reluctant to say that final decisions as to whether a particular line was Maoist or not ought to be up to the masses themselves to decide, but such was the unavoidable implication of the campaign to subject the cadres to mass criticism. The article discussed the dangers both of obeying the wrong line and of disobeying the correct line, but finally failed to resolve the dilemma and could give no rule for action other than to be on guard against both kinds of errors:

> We must oppose not only slavishness under the bourgeois reactionary line, but also anarchism under the proletarian revolutionary line. In those units where great revolutionary alliances and revolutionary committees have been established, special efforts must be made to oppose anarchism.

This problem was another manifestation of the central dilemma of the cultural revolution: the Maoist desire for mass political action to be spontaneous and yet controlled. On one hand, Mao and his supporters have truly desired the masses to take the initiative in criticizing the regular apparatus; on the other hand, in the nature of things the masses initiate much that is not in accord with Mao's political goals, and yet the only available means for controlling them (aside from the army) is the experienced cadres backed by the authority of the party. To solve this basic problem the leadership has resorted to turning the whole country into a "great school of Mao Tse-tung's thought," hoping to decrease the importance of formal organizational control.

Pending the ultimate success of the nationwide attempt to inculcate the thought of Mao, the leadership has attempted in 1967 to solve the dilemma of the mass criticism of the cadres by routinizing the cultural revolution. By stressing the importance of the revolutionary three-way alliance (leading members of the revolutionary mass organization, local PLA men, revolutionary leading cadres) the leadership is attempting to bring the course of the cultural revolution under the control of the reliable cadres. Presumably, the cadres will be made to understand the wishes of the Maoist leadership and will be moved to act in accordance with them by the threatened use of the other two parts of the alliance. Although the revolutionary masses and the army cannot provide sustained political leadership, they can, if they are loyal to the center, be used to control the cadres who are able to provide the necessary day-to-day political direction of the sort the Maoist leadership wants. In an article on 1 March 1967, *Hung Ch'i* quoted Mao, "If the masses alone are active without a strong leading group to organize their activity properly, such activity cannot be sustained for long, or carried forward in the right direction, or raised to a high level." The same article also said that "generally speaking, the contradictions between cadres who have committed mistakes in line on the one hand, and the party and the people on the other are contradictions among the people." The prospect of rehabilitation and reinstatement is thus held out to those cadres who might have strayed from the Maoist line, and cadres are encouraged not to become too afraid to do anything at all.

**The Campaign for the Study of Mao Tse-tung's Thought.** One of the most important aspects of the cultural revolution in 1967 was the nationwide campaign to inculcate the thought of Mao Tse-tung as an ideology structuring all human thought and action. This campaign was already well under way by early 1966, but it was in 1967 that it reached the height of a personality cult comparable to or even surpassing that which surrounded Stalin. In addition to the ubiquitous "little red book" of quotations from Mao, published in 1966, large portraits of Mao oversaw nearly all activity in China, and were even carried into the fields as banners by harvesting teams. The explicit aim of this campaign was to turn the entire country into a "great school of Mao Tse-tung's thought." The mind of every Chinese was to become Maoized to the point where he would internalize the values and goals of the party leadership. This meant that each Chinese should maintain: a readiness and a desire to participate in all kinds of political activity except basic decision making; a high level of revolutionary commitment and enthusiasm; an unconditional spirit of sacrifice; and absolute, uncritical loyalty to Mao. This mass campaign, the greatest indoctrination campaign in the history of the PRC, is the means by which the Maoist leadership hopes ultimately to solve the red versus expert dilemma, which is the ultimate source of the danger of China turning to Soviet-style revisionism. Thus there was an intense and continuing effort to show that the thought of Mao itself could make specialized knowledge unnecessary; this, in turn, supplied the rationale for stigmatizing those with specialized knowledge as "bourgeois experts." This campaign was, in other words, an attempt by the Maoists to give technical and specialized knowledge a class character—for instance, to overcome the logical absurdity in such a notion as "bourgeois physics." During 1967 this campaign was carried out at all levels, from the national mass media down to Mao-study sessions within the family. Surgeons, navy commanders, athletes, farmers, oil workers, and many others were all said to have improved their job performance by studying Mao's thought and creatively applying it to their own special problems. The success of China's first hydrogen bomb explosion in June was credited to Mao's genius; Chairman Mao was quoted as saying in 1958 that China could explode a hydrogen bomb within 10 years (*Peking Review*, 23 June 1967).

Besides emphasizing how Mao's thought made expertise unimportant, another aspect of the campaign to inculcate Mao's thought was the promotion of the slogan "fight self-interest and repudiate revisionism," which began to be the predominent slogan from spring on, displacing in prominence the more militant call to "grasp revolution and stimulate production." Under the rubric of this new slogan all deviations from the Maoist line and any flagging of revolutionary enthusiasm, were said to be due essentially to the persistence of selfish attachments. Self-interest in the form of economism, which is to the Maoist the use of material incentives in any form as a means to stimulate production, is incompatible with the thought of Mao because it betrays an attachment to something other than the good of the ongoing revolution and is thus evidence of a bourgeois mentality.

Everyone was urged to study three short pieces by Mao—"Serve the People," "In Memory of Norman Bethune," and "The Foolish Old Man Who Removed the Mountains." These were known as the "three good old articles" (*lao san pien*). Later in the year this list was expanded to become the "five constantly read articles," including "On Correcting Mistaken Ideas in the Party" and "Combat Liberalism." The first three pieces are exhortations to selfless heroism, sacrifice, and patient toil. The other two list types of common liberal or bourgeois deviations and give instructions for correcting such errors. These articles, plus a succession of heroic models of self-sacrifice and devotion to Mao, whose stories were prominently featured by the press and radio (people who smothered fires with their bodies or led daring attacks on Chiang bandit ships), set the tone of the campaign. In general, after March 1967 there was far more emphasis than before on hard work and personal sacrifice and much less on struggling against internal enemies.

In addition to these campaigns in the mass media, the Maoist leadership has also attempted to integrate more formal study of Mao's thought into the daily lives of cadres, students, soldiers, and workers. Various kinds of study schedules were tried. For example, a circular issued in December by the Preparatory Group for the Hunan Provincial Revolutionary Committee specified that in all government organizations, colleges, army units, enterprises, and production units daily study of Mao's thought should be arranged for the first hour of every working day, and a "study day" should be held every Tuesday afternoon. No other activities should be arranged for these times (although the circular also said that "special arrangements" should be made so that daily study will not interfere with production), and telephone communications should be reduced to a minimum. Study should emphasize the "five constantly read articles" plus "On the Correct Handling of Contradictions among the People."

Through the entire campaign in 1967 ran the theme that loyalty to Mao and the study of his thought is the key both to maintaining revolutionary spirit and, in the long run, to increasing production.

**Party Renovation—the Ninth Congress.** Hsieh Fu-chih indicated in a speech in late October that the Ninth Congress of the CCP, which according to the party constitution was due in 1961, would be held in 1968, sometime between May and October. Mao had been quoted as saying in August 1966 that a congress should be held in 1967. Posters appeared in January 1967 predicting this, but nothing came of it. This speech by Hsieh, parts of which appeared in Red Guard publications, was much more specific, although by early 1968 there was still no definite evidence that the congress would actually be held within the year as predicted.

According to the party constitution, "The number of delegates to the National Party Congress and the procedure governing their election and replacement and the filling of vacancies shall be determined by the Central Committee" (Article 30). Delegates to the Eighth Party Congress in 1956 were selected from the bottom up, beginning with the party committees at the county (*hsien*) level. However, in view of the fact that Mao is trying to renovate the entire party apparatus from top to bottom, this procedure cannot be followed for the Ninth Congress.

The Maoist leadership of the Central Committee has done all it could to undercut the authority of the local party committees. By June, in fact, many Central Committee circulars, directives and other documents did not even include the regular party committees among their addressees; instead, at the local level they were sent to the revolutionary committees and preparatory groups, military control committees and mass organizations. Members of the Ninth Congress will be selected rather from the Central Committee level downward (as they were for Congresses preceeding the Eighth), as a first step toward reconstructing the entire party along Maoist lines. Hsieh said frankly:

> To elect representatives first at the central level, then at the provincial level and then at the *hsien* level will result in a Party Central Committee of Chairman Mao with a program of Mao Tse-tung's thought and his revolutionary line which will insure the quality of the party (*NYT*, 14 January 1968).

Mao must confront three major problems in this attempt to consolidate his hold on the party and assure its ideological purity: (1) the relationship of old party members to the members of mass organizations and Red Guard unit members who have, with the PLA, been Mao's principal instruments of power against future revisionist tendencies or any other deviations of the organization from the Maoist line; (2) the rectification of party institutions to guard against future revisionist tendencies or any other deviations of the organization from the Maoist line; and (3) the ideological remolding of veteran party members. All these problems were touched on in several editorials in the Shanghai paper *Wen Hui Pao* in the latter half of November. The young Red Guards and other "proletarian revolutionaries" are overwhelmingly non-party persons, and with the increased participation of such persons in what have heretofore been party functions, the question of who and how many to admit to party membership is not an easy one. The Maoist leadership cannot admit large numbers of such persons to party membership without a fairly long preparatory period. But with the Youth League and other mediating organizations discredited and inactive, Mao has no formal, structured procedure for orderly party recruitment. These organizations must either be reactivated or replaced with new ones. In any case there is bound to be much dissatisfaction among the students, workers, Red Guards and others who suddenly became so powerful and important in the course of Mao's struggle, and who now must be quieted down and denied party membership. The Maoist leadership has all along realized that support from experienced cadres within the party is in the long run indispensable to them, and yet these cadres must be kept ideologically pure. The means to assure this purity must include institutionalized safeguards against the tendencies toward personal cliques, loss of enthusiasm, and other types of bureaucratism inherent in any routinized organization, and also must include ideological safeguards—that is, rectification of the individual's ideological outlook and commitment. The CCP has faced these problems before, notably during the Sino-Japanese war and again during the period immediately after coming to power in 1949, but never with such a serious split among the very top echelons of the party.

**The Army and the Cultural Revolution.** Control of the People's Liberation Army was vital to Mao for carrying out the cultural revolution in 1967. Under Defense Minister Lin Piao, an All-Army Cultural Revolution Group was responsible for maintaining the PLA's loyalty to the Maoist cause, and the cultural revolution greatly thinned the ranks of powerful military leaders in 1967. In January it was announced that Hsü Hsiang-ch'ien was the head of this group, Chiang Ch'ing its advisor, and Hsiao Hua, Yang Ch'eng-wu, and five others Deputy Heads. Nine more members were named, including Madame Lin and *Jen-min Jih-pao* Editor T'ang Ping-chu. This marked the beginning of extensive purges within the army, and the *Chieh-Fang Chün-pao* on 12 January said that it was time to "violently open fire at the powerholders inside the Army who are taking the capitalist road."

Among the casualties of this purge were some members of the Army Cultural Revolution Group itself. The Chairman Hsü Hsiang-ch'ien was removed (although he remained on the Politburo, to which he had been appointed in August 1966); Hsiao Hua, who had for some years worked closely under Lin as his most trusted aide, became acting head of the group. Hsiao Hua himself, however, suddenly disappeared from public view in midsummer; he failed to attend several important army meetings and support-the-army rallies, and was also absent from the National Day celebrations. Others who fell from grace before the end of the summer include Kuan Feng and Hsieh T'ang-chung, who were also members of the CCP Cultural Revolution Group and were said to have been associated with the 16 May Corps. New members of the Army Cultural Revolution Group were Wu Fa-hsien, Commander of the Air Force, and Ch'iu Hui-tso, Director of the Rear Services Department.

The most prominent of the former high military commanders attacked in 1967 were Chu Te and Ho Lung. Both had been active in the PLA from its founding, and Chu Te prior to the cultural revolution had been respected as its cofounder with Mao. Attacks on them in 1967 were part of a concerted attempt to picture the PLA as Mao's personal and exclusive creation. August 1, the anniversary of the Nanchang Uprising in 1927, had hitherto been celebrated as Army Day, and the anniversary of the birth of the PLA. Both Chu Te and Ho Lung took part in this uprising, but Mao did not. Now the origin of the PLA was said to be Mao's organization of armed bands in Hunan in 1927 at the time of the Autumn Harvest Uprising. According to the new line, the reorganization of Mao's forces in the village of San Wan, Kiangsi, in September, 1927, was the "most important date" in the early history of the PLA. Both Ho and Chu were said to have had records of anti-Mao and bourgeois deeds reaching from the 1920s to the present; Ho Lung was even accused of taking credit for discovering a good tabletennis player who had "actually been discovered by Chiang Ch'ing." More seriously, he was accused of supporting P'eng Te-huai elements in the armed forces, including Wang Shang-jung, former army Chief of Operations, and Su Chen-hua, former Political Commissar of the Navy.

The national-level military figures whose status rose most noticeably in 1967 were Yang Ch'eng-wu, acting Chief of Staff and alternate member of the CCP Central Committee;* Su Yu, Deputy Minister of National Defense and member of the Central Committee; Deputy Chiefs of Staff Li Tien-yu and Wang Hsin-t'ing; Wu Fa-hsien, Commander of the Air Force; Ch'iu Hui-tso, Chief of the Rear Services Department; and the two leading figures in the navy, Hsiao Ching-kuang and Li Tso-p'eng. Compared to such figures as Yeh Chien-ying and Hsü Hsiang-ch'ien, these are younger, more active men who are now believed to dominate the working military establishment. As of December 1967, Yang, Su, Hsieh Fu-chih, and Nieh Jung-chen, together with Mao and Lin, comprised the active membership of the Military Affairs Committee, which, because of the role of the army in the cultural revolution, has become one of the most important political bodies in the country.

**The Effect of the Cultural Revolution on Production.** In the New Year's editorial (see *Documents*), the primary political task of 1967 was described as follows:

In accordance with the directive of Chairman Mao and the Central Committee of the

*He was dismissed from his post, however, on 22 March 1968.

party to "grasp the revolution and stimulate production," the Great Proletarian Cultural Revolution should be carried out on a large scale in the factories and rural areas, so as to promote the revolutionization of people's thinking and stimulate the development of industrial and agricultural production.

The editorial reiterated: "Any argument against the carrying out of a large-scale proletarian cultural revolution in factories and mines and the rural areas is incorrect." Thus there was much speculation in the West over whether the cultural revolution might not have a deleterious or even disastrous effect on production. The Great Proletarian Cultural Revolution, in contrast to the Great Leap Forward, the collectivization drive of the mid-1950s, and the Three-anti and Five-anti movements against the bureaucrats and bourgeoisie in 1951 and 1952, was launched with no explicit economic rationale or goal. There are indications, in fact, that the Maoist leadership was willing to make significant economic sacrifices for the sake of the cultural revolution. Chou En-lai said in October:

> Such a world-shaking revolutionary movement of course exacts a certain price in production in certain places and in certain departments. We took this into account in advance. Production is affected to a certain extent, especially in places where disturbances occur, but this is only a transient thing. As soon as disorder is turned into order, production can quickly pick up and rise. (*Washington Post,* 11 October 1967.)

The injunction to "carry the cultural revolution to the countryside" was repeated at various intervals throughout the year, but with what appeared to be halfhearted emphasis. During the spring plowing season in February and March the dominant appeal was for the peasants and rural cadres to stay at their posts in the countryside and to give full attention to urgent agricultural tasks. At this crucial time dependence on the army was again very great; it was used to "arouse the enthusiasm and initiative of rural cadres and peasants." *Jen-min Jih-pao,* on 18 March, for instance, gave the army credit for playing a leading role in the supervision of planting in Shansi province. An eight-point directive had been issued on 23 February and was published in the 26 February *Jen-min Jih-pao,* ordering the members of the armed forces to "act at once to give positive assistance to leadership cadres in rural people's communes and at all other levels so as to enable the latter to grasp spring plowing well."

The major tasks urged on the rural cadres as well as on the PLA at this time were thus organizational and promotional. There was no emphasis on bringing back peasants from the cities or putting aside cultural revolution activities. What apparently worried the party leadership most at this time was not the disruption of the ordinary life of the peasants by cultural revolution activities, but rather the weakening of leadership in the countryside as a result of the turmoil within the party itself, and the possible resultant decline in collective production. Some reports by refugees indicated that once the regular leadership had been confused or frightened by the criticism campaigns against the party apparatus, the peasants became indifferent to collective production and cultivated untilled land for their own benefit. Despite the repeated calls to "carry the cultural revolution to the countryside," serious violence and disruption of production was in 1967 confined mainly to the cities. The relative calm in rural areas, plus the help of the army, and generally very good weather conditions during the year made it possible for agricultural production to be maintained or even to improve slightly over 1966 levels. Actual deliveries to the state, however, may have been significantly below normal, in view of transportation problems and likely increased hoarding of grain at lower levels from provincial authorities. (In China's agriculturally richest province, Szechwan, rail transportation was so poor that even the central leadership said publicly that the situation was "far from what it should be.") Thus, despite good harvests, the party probably found it harder in 1967 to implement Mao's principle of "the whole country a chessboard" in the distribution of produce.

In contrast to the agricultural sphere, appeals to manufacturing and mining production units included exhortations to stay on the job, to make revolution only "after hours" and not to counterpose production and making revolution. There was also far greater emphasis on denunciatons of class enemies deliberately trying to sabotage production. Coal production was one definite problem area. As winter approached, special meetings of coal-industry personnel were held throughout the country, and many calls for increased production were issued. In an editorial of 30

November the *Honan Daily* emphasized that extraction and transportation of coal had become a key problem, and each ton of coal now had very great political and economic significance. The serious disturbances in Shanghai, Canton, and other major cities during the year could not have failed to seriously hurt industrial production in basic areas, including steel and oil. Large-scale absenteeism and suspensions of production were reported, and the customary official reports of new increases in production were lacking. In the absence of reliable statistics, it is impossible to determine the seriousness of this drop in output.

The usual spring and fall Canton trade fairs were both held in 1967, although the opening of the fall fair had to be postponed to 15 November, a month later than usual. Contracts signed at the fairs were below the dollar value of the 1966 fairs, but not by much. Foreign trade was hampered by the bad conditions at the ports and by the waves of both government and Red Guard xenophobia. Despite a 10 per cent decline in turnover with its leading trade partner Japan, China's over all trade did not fall drastically (for the first seven months of 1967, total turnover was down about 13 per cent from the comparable 1966 period); imports from some countries, notably West Germany, Italy, and Australia, were up significantly. For the entire year, Communist China's exports were estimated at $1.97 billion, down 9 per cent from 1966, and imports at $2.2 billion, up 5 per cent (*NYT*, 14 July 1968, p. 6).

**International Fronts.** During 1967, Chinese delegates attended no meetings of major international front organizations. However, two bodies under Chinese control met in Peking in May and in June. The Afro-Asian Writers' Bureau (AAWB) (to be distinguished from the body of the same name under Soviet patronage) held a seminar in Peking to mark the twenty-fifth anniversary of Chairman Mao's "Talks at the Yenan Forum on Literature and Art." An NCNA dispatch 2 June 1967 quoted speakers from various countries in Asia and Africa who praised Mao's talks and who said: "Chairman Mao is the leader and the red sun in the hearts not only of the Chinese people, but of all revolutionary peoples of the world"; "No force on earth can stop the spreading of Mao Tse-tung's thought throughout the world"; and "The revolutionary people the world over, united on the basis of Mao Tse-tung's thought, are capable of defeating the enemy."

Principal Chinese speaker at the seminar was Ch'i Pen-yü, who noted the affinity between China and the Afro-Asian countries and charged that the "Soviet revisionist clique . . . is intensively carrying out cultural infiltration, peddling literature of traitors and advocating capitulation in the Afro-Asian region." He concluded by claiming that "The Asian and African people have now awakened and are waging vigorous revolutionary struggles."

The Fifth Plenum of the Afro-Asian Journalists' Association was held in Peking on 15-17 June. Its Secretary-General, Djawoto, attacked the United States and the "modern revisionists," and praised the worldwide significance of the "people's war in Vietnam." He also attacked Soviet behavior during the Arab-Israeli conflict. The meeting adopted resolutions on the current international political situation, Vietnam, Africa, and the "Arab people's war" which endorsed the main points of Djawoto's opening remarks. At the close of the session the delegates met with Premier Chou En-lai.

**Relations with Other Communist Parties.** The relations of the CCP with other communist parties in 1967 were dominated by the attempt of the CCP to establish the claim that China is now the center of world revolution and that the thought of Mao Tse-tung should be the guide for all communist parties of the world. According to the Communique of the Eleventh Plenum of the Eighth Central Committee on 12 August 1966:

> Comrade Mao Tse-tung is the greatest Marxist-Leninist of our era. Comrade Mao Tse-tung has inherited, defended, and developed Marxism-Leninism with genius, creatively, and in an all-round way, and has raised Marxism-Leninism to a completely new stage. Mao Tse-tung's thought is Marxism-Leninism of the era in which imperialism is headed for total collapse and socialism is advancing to world wide victory.

This amounts to an assertion that all parties which do not follow the Maoist line and strategy of people's wars of liberation are traitors to communism.

It directly follows from this, in the Chinese view, that the leadership of the Communist Party of the Soviet Union is but a bunch of "scabs and revisionists." Sino-Soviet polemics reached such an intensity early in the year that *Pravda* began a lengthy article on 16 February on Mao's anti-Soviet campaign with the following remark:

> During the past half-century our party and our people had to withstand attacks of hostile forces on the first socialist state in the history of mankind. But if we omit the periods of war, the periods of direct armed aggression against the Soviet Union, it will be possible to say that never before has such a fierce campaign been conducted against it as the one launched by the present leaders of China.

The CCP refused to send a delegation to Moscow for the Fiftieth Anniversary of the October Revolution, instead making it the occasion for numerous anti-Soviet speeches and articles by the CCP leadership. The most important of these was the joint editorial of *Jen-Min Jih-pao, Hung Ch'i* and *Chieh-Fang Chün-pao* on 5 November, titled "Advance along the Road Opened up by the October Socialist Revolution" (see *Documents*). Aside from the usual denunciations of the "revisionist" leadership of the CPSU, this editorial carried the claim that, like the October Revolution, "China's Great Proletarian Cultural Revolution is not merely a revolution within national bounds; it is likewise a revolution of an international order." Mao had put forward the "great theory of the continuation of the revolution under the dictatorship of the proletariat" which was said to be of world-wide applicability. This was the strongest claim to date that China had become the center of world revolution.

Toward the Karlovy Vary Conference, the CCP expressed scorn and vehement denunciation, calling it a "counter-revolutionary gangsters' meeting" and its participants "renegades to Marxism-Leninism, scabs of the working class, and enemies of the revolutionary Communist parties." According to the Chinese Communists, the meeting "reaffirmed the capitulationist line of coexistence of the Twentieth Congress of the CPSU in a vain attempt to prop up the tottering rule of imperialism and capitalism." However, the Chinese Communists almost completely ignored the Budapest Conference of Communist Parties scheduled for February 1968. CCP comment prior to the conference was limited to an article in the 12 January 1968 *Peking Review* which printed excerpts from an article in the Albanian paper *Zeri i popullit* which denounced the Budapest gathering as a counter-revolutionary scheme of Soviet revisionism.

Relations remained particularly close with the Albanian Workers' Party, as evidenced by continuous attention in the Chinese press to Albanian affairs, Chinese reports of Albanian attention to Chinese events, and mutual visits (although most of the traveling was by Albanians to Peking, not Chinese to Tirana). However, Albania was the only country which received a visiting Red Guard delegation in 1967; in late June Yao Wen-yuan, a member of the Cultural Revolution Group, led six Chinese youths in a visit to Albania to attend the Fifth Congress of the Working Youth of Albania. Yao, in his speech to the Congress praised the Albanian Workers' Party and its leader, Enver Hoxha, and explained the Cultural Revolution and the role of the Red Guards.

The two main Albanian delegations that visited China were of higher rank. In January, leading Albanian Labor Party Central Committee members Hysni Kapo, Beqir Balluku and Behar Shtylla visited China; both Chinese and Albanians praised each other's recent achievements. A highlight of the Albanians' visit was a meeting with "10,000 commanders and fighters of Chinese PLA's ground sea and air forces [who] had gathered ... to welcome" the Albanians. (*Peking Review*, 20 January 1967.)

The main delegation came to China for National Day celebrations; it was headed by Mehmet Shehu, member of the Albanian Politburo and Chairman of the Council of Ministers; eight others traveled with him. Besides attending ceremonies in Peking and meeting with Chairman Mao Tse-tung, the Albanians visited Tsinan, Taiyuan, Wuhan, and Shanghai where they met with local Chinese leaders.

In Asia China maintained good relations with Communist Parties in Burma, Thailand, Malaya, and the Philippines, as well as with the pro-Chinese Communist organization in Ceylon. The Communist Party of Thailand in late June hailed the explosion of China's first hydrogen bomb, as did the Communist Party of Malaya.

On 8 October the *Jen-min Jih-pao* "Commentator" claimed that "the victories won by the Thai people in their armed struggle are victories of people's wars and of Marxism-Leninism and Mao Tse-tung's thought." "Commentator" further said:

It is precisely in the north-eastern part of Thailand where US imperialist bases are concentrated that the people of Thailand have lit up the torch of armed struggle ... with their guns, the people of Thailand have created an excellent revolutionary situation and set for all oppressed nations and peoples of the world another glorious example of fighting for independence and liberation.

Another article on the importance to Thai wagers of armed struggle of Chairman Mao's thought appeared in *Jen-min Jih-pao,* on 1 December 1967; it was, however, written by a Thai.

When Sino-Burmese relations worsened in mid-summer, and a Chinese was killed in Rangoon, one speaker at a Peking memorial rally for the slain technician was Thakin Ba Thein Tin, First Vice-Chairman of the Communist Party of Burma. Tin praised the slain Chinese worker and condemned the Ne Win government for having planned out the incident "beforehand ... in collusion with the US imperialists, Soviet revisionists, reactionaries of all countries and the Kuomintang bandit gang." He went on to discuss the armed struggle currently developing in Burma:

We ... carry on our fight in accordance with Chairman Mao's theory on protracted war, relying on the countryside as our base area and encircling the cities from the countryside. Our practice has proved that, given a party armed with the thought of Chairman Mao, and given that this party is able to rely first of all on the peasants, protracted war can be carried on even in a small country like Burma. (NCNA 5 July, 1967.)

He also accused "China's Khrushchev," Liu Shao-ch'i, of treating the Burmese Communist Party "badly" and having a "soft-spot for Ne Win."

In mid-August, the CCP hailed the Burmese Communist Party, claiming it:

... has held high the great red banner of Marxism-Leninism Mao Tse-tung's thought, persevered in taking the revolutionary road of using the countryside to surround the cities and seizing political power by armed force; and has led the people of Burma in carrying out a protracted heroic struggle against imperialism, feudalism and bureaucratic capitalism.

On 7 November *Jen-min Jih-pao* carried a statement of Burmese Communist Party Central Committee on the occasion of the Fiftieth Anniversary of the October Revolution.

Hostile sentiments, however, were reflected in exchanges between the CCP and other important Asian communist parties. Japanese party leader Miyamoto Kenji was repeatedly denounced and insulted in CCP media. For their part, the Japanese and other Asian communist parties attacked the Chinese for great-power chauvinism, meddling in the affairs of fraternal parties, and giving invaluable services to the imperialists by their splitting activities. In late January and early February *Akahata,* the Japanese party newspaper, ran a series of articles detailing repeated attempts by the Chinese to force the Japan Communist Party to submit to Mao's line or, failing that, to subvert it. On 24 January *Akahata* said of the Maoist leadership:

The attack on us unmasks the anti-Marxist nature of their political and theoretical position and shows them as trouble-mongers in the international Communist movement, who ignore loyalty to proletarian internationalism and do not hesitate to attack a communist party of another country which is waging untiring struggle leading the people.

In India the Chinese went so far as to alienate even the "pro-Peking" left Communist Party of India (Marxist) by their militant support of peasant uprisings in Darjeeling district; this caused much embarrassment and political difficulty for the Indian left Communists, who were moved in the fall to publish a booklet detailing their policy differences with Peking.

The insistence of the CCP on the strategy of the people's war of liberation as the correct one for all Asian, African, and Latin American communist parties, and their condemnation of all parliamentary participation by communist parties, made the Chinese line particularly unpopular among other parties. The right Communist Party of India accused the Chinese of rank hypocrisy on this point:

The Chinese leaders, who preach revolutionary people's war for everyone else, are themselves extremely flexible wherever their own positions and problems are concerned. Even now they maintain extensive trade with South Africa and Rhodesia, utilizing for this purpose the help of Japan and the Chiang Kai-shek regime. According to official figures published by the South African government, South Africa's trade with China increased ten times in the period 1961-63. Last year the South African government refused publication of trade figures with People's China, saying it would adversely affect the state interests of South Africa. (*New Age*, 27 August 1967.)

In a similar vein, Mao's military doctrine was attacked in the Mongolian party newspaper *Unen* and over Ulan Bator Radio:

Recently Mao Tse-tung and his clique have persistently recommended to the Asian and African peoples the dogma of the "encirclement of the town by the village" as the "only correct road" toward liberation. According to this anti-Marxist "theory," the worldwide "village"—that is, the Asian and African and Latin American countries—must conduct a struggle against the "world city"—the highly developed countries—regardless of whether the latter are socialist or capitalist. The hypocrisy and reactionary nature of this dogma, which has been completely subjected to the designs of the Maoists, is evident. It is aimed at disorienting the revolutionary struggle of the oppressed peoples conducted against imperialism and colonialism, and thus at directing the edge of the struggle against the socialist camp. (*Unen*, 13 December 1967.)

Chinese influence in revolutionary movements in Latin America in 1967 generally declined, with Castroist movements openly critical of the Chinese gaining in relative strength. Anna Louise Strong claimed that there were Chinese-oriented "Marxist-Leninist parties and organizations in more than 12 Latin American countries." (*Letter From China*, 22 February 1968.) The Chinese theory of people's war tended to become overshadowed by the "adventurist" line of guerrilla struggle propagated by the likes of Fidel Castro, Che Guevara, and Régis Debray. The same *Letter From China* said:

In Latin America, now that the revisionists are being exposed and the revolutionaries are turning to preparations for people's war, persons like Régis Debray have come forward to sell what they call revolution. According to them there is no need to organize the masses, to build a party, to build an army, to study theory, to organize a broad front, to make a safe area or prepare for protracted war—all that is needed is to send in a few men with guns. Such notions, if followed, lead to serious reverses for the revolutionary people.

In a speech given in January 1968 and reported in a Red Guard publication Feng Piao, director of the Information Department of *Jen-min Jih-pao*, remarked that "Guevera's line is an adventurist line, but there is contradiction between him and Castro. In any case, this man cannot be called a 'Marxist-Leninist'."

In the face of overwhelming opposition to and criticism of the Maoist line and the cultural revolution, the CCP tried in 1967 to promote pro-Peking parties and organizations among splinter groups wherever they could. These were usually then designated by Peking as the "proletarian revolutionaries" of a given party or organization. Aside from such splinter parties and groups, or puppet organizations such as the Sino-Japanese Friendship Association, favorable reaction to the Great Proletarian Cultural Revolution itself was rare, although a number of parties, especially in Southeast Asia and the Pacific Area, supported Peking's general line as against Moscow's. Besides Albania, exceptions were the Communist parties of New Zealand, the Philippines, and Laos. New Zealand Communist Party Secretary-General Victor Wilcox visited Peking in March and met with Mao. The 1 March issue of the NZCP's weekly, *People's Voice*, carried a resolution of the Political Committee of the New Zealand Communist Party, which claimed that the Great Proletarian Cultural Revolution "is placing the restoration of capitalism forever beyond attainment in China." "All genuine socialists and revolutionary people," the resolution stated, "stand firmly with China, with Chairman Mao, with the cultural revolution. . . . History is marching in the direction of socialism, and China's cultural revolution is giving it a great new impetus." NCNA on 21 May reported a statement of the Politburo of the Philippine party praising Mao's thought as "the highest development of Marxism-Leninism in our era of world socialist revolution," saying it has "lighted up the whole world." The radio of the Patriotic Neutralist Forces in Laos on 9 October wished the CCP all success in carrying out the cultural revolution.

Besides the visit to the Albanian Youth Congress by Red Guards, the only foreign party congress attended by Chinese was that in noncommunist Guinea. Lin Hai-yin led a Chinese government delegation to Conakry and spoke at the Eighth Congress of the noncommunist Guinean Democratic Party. Lin expressed happiness "over the victories and successes gained by the Guinean people under the leadership of the Guinean Democratic Party in the struggle with imperialism and neo-colonialism and in developing the national economy." However, just as Touré, in his speech to the Congress, omitted specific reference to Mao's leadership in China, Lin omitted specific reference to Touré in his address (*Jen-min Jih-pao,* 10 October, 1967).

High-ranking leaders of the following nonruling communist parties visited Peking during the year: South Vietnam, Australia (Marxist-Leninist), Ceylon (Pro-Peking Party), Italy (Pro-Peking Party), New Zealand, and Laos.

**International Relations of the PRC.** At the level of intergovernmental relations, the Chinese Communists in 1967 fared even worse than they did among other communist parties. Only five foreign governments sent delegations to the National Day celebrations: Albania, North Vietnam, Pakistan, Tanzania, and Congo (Brazzaville). Again, the Maoist line of violent revolution was in itself enough to alienate most Asian and African governments; added to this was the provocative behavior of Chinese personnel in other countries and the violent and insulting treatment of foreigners by Red Guards and other left extremists in China, culminating in the sacking and burning of the British mission in Peking on 22 August.

Peking in 1967 became involved in disputes, ranging from minor to very grave, with no fewer than 32 countries:

Afghanistan, Algeria, Bulgaria, Burma, Cambodia, Ceylon, Cuba, Czechoslovakia, Denmark, East Germany, France, India, Indonesia, Iraq, Italy, Japan, Kenya, Mongolia, Morocco, Nepal, North Korea, Portugal (Macao), Singapore, Soviet Union, Sweden, Switzerland, Tanzania, Tunisia, UAR, United Kingdom, Yugoslavia, and Zambia.

The most violent of these disputes were those with India, Indonesia, the Soviet Union, and the United Kingdom. All of these involved embassy violence both in Peking and the foreign capitals as well. In September along the Sikkim-Tibetan border there occurred the most serious Sino-Indian armed clashes since the fighting in 1962. In Indonesia, popular anti-Chinese feeling was very intense during the year, and Indonesian communist guerrilla activity was blamed directly on Peking. The Chinese embassy in Djakarta was attacked and burned, and Chinese personnel beaten up. Mobs of students demanded that the Indonesian government break relations with China, and on 9 October the government announced that relations had been indefinitely suspended.

Chinese students clashed with Soviet police in Moscow in January, leading to several days of demonstrations both in Moscow and Peking; later in the year, Red Guard violence against Soviet personnel in China forced the withdrawal of the Soviet embassy staff.

Among neighboring countries in Asia, aside from Indonesia, Peking's most serious diplomatic setbacks were in Burma and Cambodia. These, too, were direct results of the Chinese efforts to export revolution. Both the Ne Win and Sihanouk regimes had been following a policy of cooperation and political accommodation with Peking. However, Chinese Communist support for armed struggle against the government by the communist parties of Burma and the use of Chinese technical aid personnel to spread Mao badges and propaganda resulted in a popular and governmental anti-Chinese reaction which ended in the withdrawal of Chinese technicians. Similarly, alarmed by Chinese support for subversive groups in Cambodia, Prince Sihanouk on 13 September announced plans to recall the Cambodian ambassador from Peking and warned that Peking was pushing Cambodia into the arms of Washington. In this case, however, Peking was more conciliatory and Chou En-lai expressed regret that "12 years of good diplomatic relations between the two countries" should be interrupted. Peking likewise retreated from its attempt to force Ceylon to take a more pro-Peking diplomatic line by threats not to renew the rice-rubber agreement, which was about to expire; in the face of a firm and vigorous resistance by Ceylon, China finally renewed the agreement in November.

North Korea attempted to steer a course more independent of Peking in 1967. Anti-Peking feeling was also aroused by wall-poster reports appearing in Peking and Canton in January alleging that there had been a military coup against North Korean Premier Kim Il-song.

One of the few Asian countries with which China maintained good relations in 1967 was Pakistan, both being united in opposition to India. Pakistan and China exchanged visits of good will and trade delegations in October and December, and China's National Day was observed with much fanfare in Karachi.

Peking's best friends in Africa were Mali, Mauritania, the Congo (Brazzaville), Tanzania, and Zambia (although, as noted, there were incidental quarrels even with the latter two). Zambian President Kaunda visited Peking in June and announced that Zambia had been granted a $16.8 million interest-free loan. On 5 September Peking announced an agreement to finance and build the projected 1,000 mile Tanzania-Zambia railway.

The conciliatory attitude toward Cambodia and Ceylon in the fall of the year marked a general turn of Peking's diplomacy away from its previous extreme belligerence and antiforeignism. Yao Teng-shan, chargé d'affaires at the Chinese Embassy in Djakarta until his expulsion from Indonesia 23 April, was responsible for the extreme "revolutionary diplomacy" line, which was part of the across-the-board extremism promoted by the 16 May Corps headed by Wang Li. Yao had great influence over the Foreign Ministry from May until late August (when he assumed the position of Foreign Minsiter for a few days), during which time Ch'en I was severely attacked by Red Guards and kept out of power. According to some sources, it was Mao Tse-tung as well as Chou En-lai who decided on the purge of Yao in late August, after which the Ministry gradually returned to the control of Ch'en I's men.

The Chinese Communists saw the Arab-Israeli war as an opportunity both to improve their relations with the Arab countries and to attack the Soviet Union for collusion with the US against Arab interests. Even before the war, on 26 May, NCNA described the arrival of Soviet ships in eastern Mediterranean waters patrolled by the US Sixth Fleet as an example of "US-Soviet collaboration to suppress the anti-American struggle in the Middle East." The Chinese were reported to have sent arms to the Palestine Liberation Organization as early as March 1965; and Israeli forces clearing the Gaza Strip in late June found large quantities of Chinese-made small arms, mines, and chemicals (*Washington Post*, 26 June 1967).

Shortly before the war began, Peking diverted to the United Arab Republic wheat shipments purchased from Australia amounting to at least 150,000 to 200,000 tons, and possibly as much as 2 million tons. Also at this time a $10 million hard-currency loan was extended to Cairo (*Christian Science Monitor*, 16 June 1967).

Some strain was evident in relations between Hanoi and Peking in 1967. Soviet aid shipments to Vietnam were interrupted by the chaos in China's transportation system; also, Vietnam-bound arms were diverted and commandeered by Red Guard groups eager to seize power by armed struggle. Chou En-lai said on 20 September:

> In the months of July and August, throughout the whole country, there were incidents of seizing weapons from the PLA, raiding arsenals, ambushing trains with military aid for Vietnam. . . . Still more important was the looting of military stores destined for Vietnam.

Peking steadfastly opposed the Moscow proposal of a "united front" in support of North Vietnam and urged upon the Vietnamese closer adherence to the Maoist military strategy, which meant less reliance on the kind of military aid that only the Soviet Union could supply. On 21 July, shortly after the death on 6 July of the pro-Maoist line North Vietnamese strategist Nguyen Chi Thanh, *Jen-min Jih-pao* published an editorial emphasizing the differences between the revisionist and the Chinese lines on the Vietnam war:

> On the Vietnam question there has all along been an acute and complex struggle between the two lines in the international arena. The Chinese Communist Party and the Chinese people, together with the Marxists-Leninists and the revolutionary people the world over, persevere in the revolutionary line of Marxism-Leninism, Mao Tse-tung's thought and

firmly support the Vietnamese people in carrying the war against US aggression and for national salvation through to the end until final victory. The Soviet revisionist ruling clique follows an out-and-out counter-revolutionary line, does its utmost to help US imperialism push ahead with its "peace talks" conspiracy, betray the revolutionary interests of the Vietnamese people, and strive to stamp out the Vietnamese people's resistance war so as to bring the Vietnam question into the orbit of US-Soviet collaboration.

The Chinese, in attempting to counter the importance of Soviet aid, placed great emphasis on China's value to North Vietnam as a "dependable rear for the Vietnamese people" and supplied an estimated 60,000 Chinese laborers for construction and repair work. Peking expressed no intention, however, of actually intervening in the war. On 2 June Ch'en I met with a delegation of the Japan Association for the Promotion of International Trade and discussed the war. He said: "At present the Vietnamese people are successfully fighting against the US forces. The Vietnamese people will be able to defeat the US without outside aid. The Vietnamese people whom I have met have convinced me of this." Ch'en further said: "I might as well say that Vietnam is the forefront of the war and that China is a logistic base." (Tokyo *Shimbun,* 3 June 1967.)

In December the Peking mission of the Front for the Liberation of South Vietnam was raised to embassy status on the occasion of the seventh anniversary of the Front's founding. For their part, the North Vietnamese generally tried to avoid antagonizing Peking, and paid due public tribute to the strategy of people's war. However, an article in the North Vietnamese journal *Hoc Tap* on the occasion of Ho Chi Minh's seventy-seventh birthday in May indirectly, but strongly, criticized the Chinese Communist leadership for undermining the principle of collective leadership and weakening the party apparatus by wholesale attacks on the cadres. Anyone who departs from this basic principle, said the article, "cannot keep his leadership role forever."

In the United Nations, the annual proposal to seat Peking and expel Taipei, sponsored by Albania, was voted down on 28 November 58 to 45, with 17 abstentions (in 1966 the vote was 57 to 46). The "important question" resolution requiring a two-thirds vote for Peking's admission passed 69 to 48. There was less debate on this question within the General Assembly than in previous years, and many of Peking's usual supporters appeared to be giving only halfhearted support to the Communist Chinese cause. The 30 November *Jen-min Jih-pao* accused the Soviet Union in particular of betraying the cause of the PRC in the debates:

> With ulterior motives, the Soviet revisionist representative in his statement actually mentioned in the same breath the question of restoring China's legitimate rights and that of admitting the German Democratic Republic as a new member of the United Nations. This is obviously meant to aid and abet the US imperialists in their plot to create "two Chinas" in the UN.

The same article reiterated the Chinese Communist position that, "Frankly speaking, the Chinese people are not at all interested in joining the United Nations."

**Publications.** *Jen-min Jih-pao* (People's Daily), edited by T'ang Ping-chu, is the most authoritative publication of the CCP, *Hung Ch'i* (Red Flag), edited by Ch'en Po-ta, is the theoretical journal of the Central Committee. Originally a semi-monthly, since 1965 it has been published about every 20 days.* *Kwangming Daily,* formerly edited by Mu Hsin, is not officially a party publication and concerns itself primarily with cultural, intellectual, and educational affairs. The following papers have become very important during the cultural revolution: *Chieh-fang Chün-pao* (Liberation Army Daily), and the Shanghai papers *Wen Hui Pao* and *Chieh-fang Jih-pao* (Liberation Daily). *Wen Hui Pao* also publishes a Hong Kong edition; the national daily *Ta Kung Pao* also publishes Chinese and English editions in Hong Kong. *Peking Review* is a weekly publication printed in six foreign languages. Among the most important Red Guard publications during 1967 were the *Hung Ch'i* (Red Flag) of the Peking Aviation Institute and the Tsinghua University *Ching-kang-shan.*

New China News Agency *(Hsinhua)* is the official news agency of the party and government.

*\*Hung Ch'i* suspended publication after its 23 November 1967 issue.

# COLOMBIA

The Communist Party of Colombia originated as the Socialist Revolutionary Party (Partido Socialista Revolucionario) in 1926. In 1928 the party was affiliated to the Comintern, and in 1930 its name was changed to the Communist Party of Colombia (Partido Comunista de Colombia; PCC). This name has been retained, except for a short period from 1944 to 1947 when the party was called the Social Democratic Party (Partido Social Democrático). In July 1965 a schism within the PCC between pro-Soviet and pro-Chinese factions was formalized by the latter's becoming the Colombian Marxist-Leninist Communist Party (Partido Comunista de Colombia Marxista Leninista; PCC-ML).

Both communist parties are legal, but are disqualified from participating in elections under the terms of the National Front Agreement implemented in 1958 and binding until 1974, which states that only members of the Liberal and Conservative parties may hold public office. Membership of the PCC is estimated at 8,000 to 13,000 and that of the PCC-ML at 1,000 to 2,000. The population of Colombia is 18,596,000 (estimated mid-1966).

A number of factors have tended to undermine the influence of the PCC and cause a decline in its membership and following. Among these are the wide appeal of General Rojas Pinilla's opposition group, the People's National Alliance (Alianza Nacional Popular; ANAPO); the Sino-Soviet split, the Soviet Union's ambiguous policy toward Colombia, which includes negotiations with President Carlos Lleras Restrepo*; and the party's hesitating to give full support to the guerrilla movements.

Support for the PCC, in social composition, shows a nearly equal rural and urban distribution. At the party's Tenth Congress, in 1966, according to *Voz Proletaria* (3 February), 48 per cent of the delegates were farmers, compared with 36 per cent for workers and 16 per cent for others from urban environments (students, tradesmen, intellectuals). The social composition of the party, however, only reflects to a certain degree the PCC's influence in the different sectors of the nation. The party's failure to win over the industrial workers has been and remains one of its principal problems. In the *World Marxist Review* (September 1966) Alvaro Delgado pointed out that "organizing work among the proletariat encounters big difficulties" and that among the reasons are the proletariat's "low political level" and the "shortage of revolutionary cadres."

**Organization and Leadership.** The PCC leadership includes its Secretary-General, Gilberto Vieira, and its Central Executive Committee, or Politburo: Alvaro Vásques, Jesús Villegas, Joaquín Moreno, Hernando Hurtago, Manuel Cepeda Vargas, Manlio Lafont, Luis Morantes, Diego Montaña Cuéllar, José Cardona Hoyes, Victor J. Merchan, and César Martínez. (On 17 November 1967 Diego Montaña Cúellar was removed from his position on the Central Executive Committee and expelled from the party.) The PCC Central Committee has 45 full members and 10 alternate members.

The PCC's youth movement, Communist Youth of Colombia (Juventud Comunista de Colombia; JCC) closely follows PCC policy on internal and international questions. The leaders of the JCC are its Secretary-General, Carlos Romero, and Avelino Castro, Gilma Valencia, and Miller Chacón (*Voz Proletaria,* 20 October 1966).

Among students the PCC controls the National University Federation (Federación Universitaria Nacional; FUN). This pro-Soviet control is to a degree handicapped by the pro-Chinese PCC-ML. At the FUN Third Congress (27-29 May 1966) a modus vivendi was reached between the two factions of the JCC by which four of the seven seats on the FUN Executive Committee went to the pro-Chinese

*Diplomatic relations between the two countries were established in January 1968.

and three to the pro-Soviets. Though FUN represents only a minority of Colombian students (out of the 28 Colombian universities, it controls only the National University and a sector of the Free University), it has been very active. Since the army temporarily occupied the National University in June 1967, however, students have been politically inactive.

PCC influence in trade unions is relatively weak. According to Alvaro Delgado (*WMR*, September 1966) one fourth of Colombian wage workers belong to trade unions. Of these, some 180,000 are represented by the communist-controlled Union Confederation of the Workers of Colombia (Confederación Sindical de Trabajadores de Colombia). The remainder are represented by the government-supported Catholic Union of Working People (350,000), the Confederation of Working People (150,000), and other "unions that are under the influence of nascent Christian democracy." While communist labor elements are presumably sympathetic toward the Colombian guerrillas, the unions have in fact demonstrated more concern for the economic interests of their members than for political issues.

**The Colombian Revolutionary Armed Forces.** In April 1966, a number of bandit groups operating in southern Colombia under the leadership of Manuel Marulanda Vélez, alias Tiro-Fijo (Dead Shot), met with the PCC and formed the PCC-controlled Colombian Revolutionary Armed Forces (Feurzas Armadas Revolucionarias de Colombia; FARC). Shortly thereafter the pro-Peking Belgian Communist Party organ *Voix du Peuple* condemned the movement as "mutual blackmail," claiming that the bandits under Marulanda needed the support of a political organization and that the communist party needed contacts with guerrillas as proof of its revolutionary zeal.

Overall leadership of FARC rests with Marulanda, with other top leaders including Ciro Trujillo, Jacobo Arenas, and Isauro Yosa (all three are members of the PCC Central Committee), Ciro Castano, and Januario Valero (alias Oscar Reyes). The PCC's chief liaison officer with FARC is Manuel Cepeda Vargas, who, although an orthodox Communist, is well received in Cuba. While no official comment has been issued by the PCC or FARC, a Colombian armed forces communique of 28 April stated that Marulanda had been relegated to a secondary role and was taking orders from Januario Valero. Guerrilla activities by FARC have centered in the departments of Valle, Choco, and Tolima and in the southwestern departments of Huila and Caqueta.

**Domestic Views and Policies.** PCC domestic policy was outlined at the party's Tenth Congress, held clandestinely in the second half of January and early February 1966. The resolutions adopted at the congress reflected the party's concern about its weakness within the Colombian population and about repercussions of guerrilla activity. While realizing the importance of "utilizing to the maximum degree the legal opportunities" for increasing its influence and consolidating itself with the masses, the PCC was also fully aware that it could not run the risk of denouncing the guerrilla uprising for fear of alienating its own left-wing, already threatened by the pro-Chinese party. The political resolution of the Tenth Congress attempted to resolve this dilemma by declaring that the "most important fact of recent times in Colombia in the sense of a qualitative change is the advent of the Farmer-Guerrilla Movement, constituting a new and superior phase of the revolutionary battle." The resolution added, however, that farmer-guerrilla warfare, although "one of the highest forms of the mass battle," can "consolidate and advance only where it has a mass character." Emphasis on the necessity for mass action was reiterated in the party's call for the formation of a "patriotic front of national liberation" under the leadership of a "powerful mass communist party." Asserting that "armed struggle is each day increasingly becoming the indispensable factor in the Colombian revolution," the PCC declared that its policy should be a "process of organizing the masses which leads them to the conviction of the necessity for armed struggle and opens ways for revolutionary denouements by nonpeaceful paths." (*Voz Proletaria*, 3, 24 February 1966.)

During 1967 the PCC continued to focus considerable attention on the correct strategy to be followed by the party and on the nature of the relationship between the PCC and FARC. An article by Alberto Gomez in the April 1967 issue of *World Marxist Review* declared:

> The Party and the guerrilla detachments are at one; they interweave and are interdependent. By strengthening the Party we strengthen the guerrilla movement. And when the guerrilla detachments gain in influence, so does the Party. . . . Every Communist

in the zone of hostilities is a guerrilla behind the enemy's lines. Whenever a detachment moves into a new locality, provided the conditions are ripe, it lays the groundwork for a new Party organization. Conversely, in areas where guerrilla action has not yet begun but the political base exists, the Party paves the way for the guerrillas to move in. Every zonal, municipal, or district committee in the theater of hostilities works to strengthen the guerrilla movement. Party organizations are as necessary to the guerrillas as the air they breathe; they are a pre-condition of successful operations. *The "secret" of the indivisible unity of the Communist Party and the guerrilla detachments is that the Party and its leadership are in the centre of armed struggle.* (Emphasis in original.)

In further elaborating on the correct policy to be pursued, an article in the 7 December 1967 issue of *Voz Proletaria,* weekly organ of the PCC, stated: "Reality demands combining all the forms of struggle, since the classes and the social groups participating in the democratic, revolutionary movement are different, have various levels of awareness, and use various methods of action." In stressing that all forms of struggle should be utilized by the PCC, *Voz Proleteria* explained that the "combination of all the forms of struggle means being prepared to go rapidly from one form of struggle to another, for example, from the peaceful forms to the nonpeaceful forms, and from these back to the peaceful ones according to the circumstances and the changes in the political situation and the attitude of the ruling classes."

As part of its strategy of calling for the "combination of all forms of struggle," the PCC Central Committee announced that the party would participate in the March 1968 Congressional elections and noted:

There does not yet exist a revolutionary situation which would permit replacing the elections with a better form of struggle at this very moment. Neither is there a situation of sharp weakness in the democratic forces, which makes it very difficult to influence the political development in any way, as happened in the past presidential elections when the Communist Party and the MRL [Revolutionary Liberal Movement; Movimiento Revolucionario Liberal] abstained from voting. (*Voz Proletaria,* 26 October.)

Although the PCC had pursued a policy of "militant abstention" in the May 1966 presidential elections, the PCC now declared:

In Colombia experience has shown that abstention is passive and, therefore, not a form of struggle. That which distinguishes abstention is electoral boycott, meaning the struggle to stop the elections. But now neither the strength nor the political conditions exist for the boycott. The passive character of the abstention will render extremely difficult the bond of the party with the masses, their organization, mobilization, and education. . . . We cannot deduce from this that we must definitely reject elections—only that the people must make better use of them. In our country, experience has shown that communist participation in electoral debates has given positive results, as is proven by certain important debates in Congress which have contributed in stopping certain measures unfavorable to the people. In certain regions, a party has been organized through electoral campaigns. (*Ibid.*)

Since only members of the Liberal Conservative parties may hold public office, the PCC announced that it would support the "MRL del Pueblo," a group of extreme Left-wing dissidents who defected from López Michelsen's Revolutionary Liberal Movement (Movimiento Revolucionario Liberal; MRL) when it reunited with the President's Liberal Party in August 1967.

In spite of PCC theoretical statements reaffirming the correctness of armed struggle in "areas where the government is pursuing a policy of fire and sword," there were indications during 1967 that the party was attempting to call a temporary halt to armed violence. A PCC Central Committee plenum held during the last week of February made no reference to the guerrilla struggle and instead concentrated on the party's preparations for the celebration of the fiftieth anniversary of the October Revolution. In addition, a lengthy article in the February issue of *World Marxist Review* paid considerable attention to the PCC's decision in 1964 to modify its support for armed struggle and cited the success of the government's "acción civica-militar" as the reason for the modification.

On 18 May, Chile's Radio Presidente Balmaceda reported that Gilberto Vieira, Secretary-General of the pro-Soviet PCC, had denied that guerrillas in Colombia were following directives from the Havana Tricontinental Conference or were receiving aid from abroad. Vieira also claimed that although the PCC considered the guerrillas' action justified, it had no links with them. If the radio broadcast is correct, the PCC has adopted an attitude in complete reverse of that which it declared in December 1966 when Gilberto Vieira, in a 15 December 1966 editorial in *Voz Proletaria,* rejected "poisonous" statements that the PCC had withdrawn its support from the Colombian guerrillas because the government had announced its willingness to establish trade relations with the Soviet Union and Eastern Europe. It is entirely possible, however, that the PCC may now be anxious to curtail guerrilla activities and thereby avoid obstructing communist countries' efforts to establish trade relations with Colombia. This would be in accord with President Lleras Restrepo's warnings that Colombia is willing to trade with communist countries only on the condition that they do not interfere in the internal affairs of Colombia and that they keep the Communists under their control out of subversive activities. The PCC may also be reluctant to extend guerrilla activity at a time when extreme left-wing groups in various Latin American countries are hailing it as the only revolutionary path. The fear of being "outflanked" by such movements probably accounts for the delay in making this reluctance public. It is also doubtful whether the PCC is in sufficient control of its own guerrilla movement (FARC) to call at least a temporary halt to armed violence.

**Internal Opposition.** PCC policy regarding armed struggle has not been without internal opposition. In August 1967, Diego Montaña Cuéllar, member of the PCC Central Executive Committee and editor of *Documentos Políticos,* returned from Havana and issued a 30-page document based on resolutions adopted at the OLAS meeting in Havana (31 July-10 August).* In the document, "The Strategic and Tactical Problems of the Revolution in Colombia," Montaña declared that armed struggle is the "only effective way to obtain power for the people" and called for an immediate and violent revolution. In advocating a more militant, Castroist policy, Montaña stated that elections were not a means to power for the people and advocated instead the forming of alliances with existing revolutionary groups in Colombia. In view of the fact that the PCC is already closely connected with FARC, political observers suggest that Montaña may have been agitating for the PCC also to ally itself with the Castroist "National Liberation Army" (see below) or that he favored the formation of a new extreme left-wing party which would be independent of both Moscow and Peking. Montaña also maintained that the PCC could not claim leadership of the workers merely because it existed, and called on it to do more than just call itself communist or Marxist-Leninist in order to truly represent the working class. Finally, Montaña made reference to the theories of the French Castroist Régis Debray contained in the book *Revolución en la Revolución?* which condemned the PCC policy of "armed self-defense" as passive resistance unsuited for Colombia and which Montaña claimed had reduced guerrilla warfare to a tactical role and deprived it of all strategic revolutionary scope. Finally, Montaña criticized the "rightist" tendencies of "some members" of the PCC to ignore party members of "recognized political and intellectual brilliance."

Although the document was prepared in August, the party succeeded in keeping the rift a secret, and party action was postponed until the return of Gilberto Vieira, who was attending the Moscow celebrations of the fiftieth anniversary of the October Revolution. In late October, however, Montaña released his articles to the general press and evoked censure from the PCC Central Committee.

On 2 November an article in *Voz Proletaria* entitled "Is There a Revolutionary Situation in Colombia Now?" indirectly refuted Montaña's call for a more militant policy by stating that conditions for a revolution did not now exist and that there was no growing revolution of the masses against the present situation, as demonstrated by the lack of strikes which had formerly been a regular occurrence. The same article also observed that there had been a "temporary withdrawal" from revolutionary action in Colombia and concluded that the idea that a revolutionary situation existed was an illusion which confused reality with the impatience of militant communists.

In an article in the 9 November issue of *Voz Proletaria* the PCC specifically denied the existence of

*Montaña attended the OLAS meeting on an unofficial basis.

a "dramatic division" in the party and asserted that it was not Montaña's political ideas which were disturbing to the party, but rather his flagrant disregard for party rules:

> The serious thing is not the political viewpoint of any member of the party, but the attitude he assumes, as in the case of Dr. Montaña—that knowing the rules of the party to which he belongs and of which he is a leader, he should ignore them in practice. . . . While the Central Executive Committee was studying the document submitted by Diego Montaña, he expounded his thesis in various places and then distributed the document in mimeographed form to various comrades; this [was] a serious violation of Leninist rules.

According to the article, the PCC leadership had repeatedly asked Montaña to resume his executive duties, which he repeatedly refused to do, displaying an attitude at variance with that expected of a communist leader; further, the Executive Committee had removed him from the editorship of the review *Documentos Políticos* at his own request. While denying that a "dramatic division" existed in the party, the PCC warned that the example of Diego Montaña Cuéllar could not be overlooked: "Under the present difficult circumstances any defection is serious and reinforces the reaction and the anti-party, anti-communist elements." It also cautioned: "Communist activists should be vigilant and cannot accept any theses or doings which go against the general orientation of the party. As long as the majority of the party and its leadership do not pronounce themselves in opposition, the legitimacy of the overall Party line cannot be ignored by any organ or person."

On 16 November *Voz Proletaria* carried the text of an announcement by the PCC Executive Committee which accused Montaña of "developing a public slander campaign," of denigrating the party, and of organizing "groups outside the party framework specifically involving known provocative antiparty elements" with whom he was "publicly in agreement." The announcement concluded:

> . . . In the face of his relinquishing party work for more than one year, in the face of his factional activities, and not because of his divergent opinions, the Executive Committee expanded with members of the Central Committee, decided to retire comrade Diego Montaña Cuéllar from his position of member of the Executive Committee to which he had been elected by a plenary meeting of the Central Committee to which he had been elected by the 10th Congress.

A subsequent statement by the Executive Committee was published as an eight-page special supplement to the 30 November issue of *Voz Proletaria*. The PCC again defended its policy of using all means, legal and illegal, to achieve power and asserted that a revolutionary situation did not exist in Colombia at present. Although not specifically naming Cuba as one of the chief advocates of revolution through armed struggle, the statement declared that the effects of the Cuban revolution on the revolutionary struggle had been exaggerated, and alluded to the "mistaken ideas" of "some revolutionary sectors [which had], by evaluating changes brought about by the Cuban revolution, concluded that a revolutionary situation permeated the whole continent and even the whole world."

Although the degree of support which Montaña commands within the party is uncertain, political observers regard it as representing a growing trend within the Colombian communist movement which seeks to establish the validity of the Castroist theory of armed struggle. Although Cuba refrained from publicly commenting on Montaña's document and his subsequent dismissal from the PCC, the Cuban magazine *Bohemia* did note that a debate was going on within the PCC over the applicability of a strategy of armed struggle to the conditions in Colombia. In commenting on the expulsion of Montaña, however, Secretary-General Vieira warned:

> This is not an isolated incident but rather forms part of an international trend directed toward division and dispersion of the communist movement, on which they have attempted to impose theses which are completely foreign and contrary to Marxism-Leninism. However, this trend is destined for bankruptcy, in spite of the aid which anticommunism in all its diverse manifestations might lend it. The unity of each communist party and the unification of the entire international communist movement are historical necessities of our age which must be imposed in spite of all divisionists. (*Voz Proletaria*, 21 December.)

**The National Liberation Army**. Opposition to the PCC policy of combining all forms of struggle has also come from the National Liberation Army (Ejercito de Liberación Nacional; ELN), a Castroist guerrilla movement which came into existence following a January 1965 attack on the small town of Simacota in the state of Santander in northeastern Colombia.

There are now reportedly two "fronts" of the ELN operating in Santander: the José Antonio Galán front led by Fabio Vásquez Castano and the more recently formed Camilo Torres front led by Ricardo Lara Parada.* Estimates of ELN strength range from 150 to 300.

Considerable information regarding the program and strategy and tactics of the ELN was contained in a series of articles written in February 1967 by Mario Menéndez Rodríquez, director of the Mexican magazine *Sucesos Para Todos* who spent several weeks with the ELN in Santander (*Sucesos Para Todos*, 24 June and 1, 8, 15, 22, and 29 July 1967). In the course of an interview with Menéndez, Vásquez defined the "political-military objectives" of the ELN as the "winning of power for the popular classes" and declared: "Armed struggle must be recognized as the only solution for the nation problem, no matter how difficult and trying for our beloved peoples." Vásquez also outlined the main points of the ELN program, which calls for (1) an "authentic agrarian reform which includes the elimination of latifundism, minifundism, and a single-crop economy"; (2) the "creation of efficient distribution organizations, which will eliminate the speculating and hoarding intermediaries," and (3) "economic and industrial development, housing and urban reform planning, the creation of a popular system of credits, the organization of a national public health program, the drafting of a road program, education reform, the incorporation of the indigenous population into the economy and culture, freedom of thought and religion, independent foreign policy, and the training of a permanent people's army . . . "

Although not a communist movement per se, the ELN has a mission in Havana and from its beginning has shown signs of Cuban aid and training. In his interviews with the above-mentioned Mexican journalist, Vásquez reportedly expressed "absolute disgust" for the "soft-line" pro-Soviet communist parties of Latin America, declaring: "The degree of decomposition that exists in the so-called revolutionary camp is incredible. We admire only Cuba and Fidel Castro, who is a revolutionary of the first order." The ELN also declared support for the position advocated in Castro's 13 March 1967 speech on revolutionary warfare in Latin America in which he stated that the "only correct stand to take against the imperialists is that of being prepared to fight, to confront the enemy with arms." The speech also criticized those socialist states which aid the "oligarchies," claiming that such aid "will only serve to give those in power more resources with which to crush the revolutionary struggle." The ELN also supported the 17 May 1967 statement of the Cuban Communist Party Central Committee which asserted Cuba's right to foment revolution in other countries.

The exact relationship between the PCC and the ELN is unclear. Vásquez told Menéndez that in August 1966 the ELN had made repeated "gestures of friendship" to the PCC-controlled FARC in the hope of coordinating the two forces, but had received from the PCC the "incredible" reply that it was not pleased with the activities of the ELN and that there could be no hope of any amicable relationship between the two groups until the ELN had an "understanding" of PCC policies. A number of simultaneous guerrilla actions by the FARC and the ELN, however, have led some observers to suggest the possibility that past rivalries may have been suspended and that the two groups may be coordinating activities.

Even though some coordination of activities may exist, the ELN position on the PCC has not changed. According to the 4 August 1967 issue of *Le Monde* (Paris), the ELN circulated a clandestine pamphlet during the summer which attacked the PCC position that guerrilla warfare was an erroneous strategy amounting to "adventurism" and which accused Secretary-General Vieira and the PCC of collaborating with the government to crush the guerrilla movements. The pamphlet warned that the time would come when the ELN would apply revolutionary justice to "bourgeois revisionist traitors

*Camilo Torres, a young priest with a large following among students, joined the ELN toward the end of 1965 and was killed in a clash with the army in 1966.

who call themselves Communists."

**Activities during 1967.** The PCC devoted considerable attention to the March 1967 elections. Names that the PCC and the MRL del Pueblo suggested as candidates for Bogotá and Cundinamarca included Gerardo Bernal, Juan de la Cruz Varela, and "other prominent workers and peasant leaders."

During the first part of 1967, communist guerrillas and "extremists and terrorists" launched a series of actions against Colombian authorities. On 10 March government officials responded with mass arrests involving some 200 to 300 "extremists" in Bogotá, Neiva, Ibagué, Cali, Barranquilla, Barrancabermeja, and "other important towns used by the communist leaders for providing aid to the rebels." Those arrested included Gilberto Vieira, Secretary-General of the PCC; Juan Viana, Secretary of the PCC Central Executive Committee; and PCC Central Committee members Manlio Lafont, Gustavo Castro, Manuel Romero, Juan Francisco Mujica, Teodicio Varela, Augusto Lara, Julio Posada, Julio Ernesto Pérez, Roberto Pérez, and Celmira Cruz, Director of the Colombian Women's Communist Party. An official communique issued by the Colombian government commented on the "recent incidents against public order," calling them the "result of a vast subversive action linked to movements of a similar nature in neighbor countries and encouraged from abroad through the training of leaders and the supply of weapons and money."

On 27 April Colombian officials released Vieira, who subsequently declared that the PCC would struggle for legalization and added: "We intend to act more openly than we did before the arrests were made. The country is heading toward a great political crisis from which a change of a democratic nature is bound to result."

In addition to the March mass arrests, government officials succeeded in disrupting a secret "high level" conference of guerrilla leaders held in the Altamizal sector of Colombia. Reports indicate that the purpose of the conference was to analyze plans of action as outlined by the OLAS Conference.

Colombian authorities also took a series of actions against the ELN, whose activities in 1967 spread to the Alto Sinú district and northern and southern sections of the Andes. ELN activities had previously been confined to Santander. Although there are conflicting reports, an army communique signed by Commander-in-Chief Guillermo Pinzón Caicedo claimed that Mario Menéndez Rodríguez, while detained by Colombian officials, had provided pictures and data which had enabled the army to deal a decisive blow to the urban elements of the ELN in Bogotá, Bucaramanga, and Barrancabermeja. Menéndez denied the validity of the communique.

Government analyses at the end of 1967 reported that 85 per cent of the "subversive elements under arms" had been eliminated during the year and claimed that "destruction of the urban nets of the ELN and the FARC" had resulted in "partial neutralization of their subversive activities in the northwest and the southern zones" (*El Siglo*, Bogotá, 22 December). Although both the ELN and the FARC denied that their urban networks had been destroyed, reports from captured guerrillas indicate that both movements were suffering from lack of supplies and equipment.

**International Views and Policies.** PCC statements during 1967 continued to reflect the party's concern for independence, noninterference, and unity in the international communist movement. A joint communique issued by the Central Committees of the Colombian and Venezuelan communist parties following their June 1967 meeting stated:

> . . . The national movements are the ones responsible for formulating their own political line according to the respective national situations prevailing, through proper utilization and an appropriate combination of the various forms of warfare, giving preference to what that same situation would demand on the basis of Marxist-Leninist principles and on the experience gained during the course of revolutionary action. Departing from such considerations, it is not possible to formulate a political line, tactics, and a form of warfare that are alike for all countries. (*Voz Proletaria*, 13 July.)

The PCC further elaborated on this position in an article in *Voz Proletaria* (20 July) which pointed out while the party was not "seeking to impose its political line on those who are struggling or wish to struggle with some other orientation," neither would it accept the "imposition of any other line which would mean renunciation of the theses approved by its congresses and plenums."

In addition to emphasizing the need for each communist party to formulate its own line of action, the PCC also called for "mutual respect and nonintervention in the internal affairs of other parties," noting that "any activity or view that may violate this rule weakens the necessary cohesion and unity between the parties and the formation of a united front against Yankee imperialism and its national agents."

Joaquín Moreno, member of the PCC Central Executive Committee, summarized the party's position on unity of the international communist movement as follows:

> We are firm defenders of the unity of the international communist and workers' movement. We consider that any attitude of no matter what party or person which under any pretext contributes to division in the communist ranks serves not the revolution but imperialism and the reaction, not the cause of peace but of war, which is the imperialistic policy. We reject anti-Sovietism, no matter what cloak it wears. We defend with all our strength international communist unity and we shall do the same on our native soil. (*Ibid.*, 16 November.)

Secretary-General Vieira declared the PCC's support for the convening of a world communist conference:

> The Communist Party of Colombia supports a new world conference of communist and workers' parties, for the purpose of working for the unity of the communist movement and of studying the changes which have occurred since 1960. We believe that the declaration of the 81 communist parties in that year is valid in its basic theses, but that new events demand analysis and united action from Communists throughout the world. Notwithstanding the fact that the Chinese Maoist leaders will not participate in a new conference—as one gathers from their well-publicized statements—and even though certain communist parties for various reasons might remain temporarily outside, the world conference will permit the collective study of burning problems of the current time, will promote the unity of action of anti-imperialist forces, and will be able to contribute to creating the conditions for the future unification of the entire international communist movement. (*Ibid.*, 21 December.)

Vieira also announced his party's support for the consultative conference scheduled to be held in Budapest in late February 1968.

At its February 1967 plenary session the PCC Central Executive Committee condemned the "tragic divisionist activity" of the Chinese Communist Party:

> Our party has at all times attempted to maintain good, friendly, fraternal relations with the Communist Party of China. But, as is natural, the Communist Party of Colombia conditions its relations with other parties, within the spirit of the 1960 declaration, to the attitude that the other party should respect our own autonomy. Relations with the Communist Party of China were not broken by us or by our fault. The Mao leaders believed that they had a right to govern our party in their manner or to break up its unity when they realized that we were inclined to deduce by ourselves and on the basis of an analysis of the conditions of our revolutionary development. This violation of our autonomy as a Marxist-Leninist party that is tied to the community of communist and workers' parties is one of the innumerable demonstrations of great power chauvinism that the Chinese Maoist leaders ordinarily display. In fact, the distortions that the Chinese revolution is undergoing at present show up especially as an intensified nationalism and a semireligious cult of the personality of Mao Tse-tung. All the anti-Soviet hysteria—which ranges from an attempt to take territory away from the USSR to the lowest insults and acts of physical aggression against its diplomatic personnel in Peking—has that origin. And the constant acts of aggression against the Marxist-Leninist parties have the same origin. And the unsuccessful attempt to form—with renegades and expelled members of all kinds—an "international communist movement," completely and absolutely controllable by the Mao leaders for the development of their ultranationalist arrogance, had the same basis. (*Ibid.*, 2 March.)

The PCC Central Executive Committee also condemned the Cultural Revolution as a "grotesque and bloody attack against great conquests of the Chinese revolution" and warned that "its vandal-like operations, supposedly performed in the name of Marxism-Leninism, can only bring discredit to the socialist revolution and accumulate new difficulties to the self-denying effort of the communists all over the world to overthrow imperialism and to liberate the oppressed peoples" (*ibid.*).

In contrast with its condemnation of the current policies of the Chinese Communist Party, the PCC hailed the CPSU as the "most brilliant example for the revolutionaries of the world." On the occasion of the fiftieth anniversary of the October Revolution, the PCC praised the Soviet Union as the "fortress of the socialist system and of the world revolutionary movement" and noted that the "Soviet Union has shown the path which the workers and peasants must take to gain power, to increase the cultural and material levels of the workers constantly, and to transform a backward country into a vanguard of science and planned industrialization."

The PCC also placed considerable emphasis on its relations with other Latin American communist parties. It repeatedly announced support for the "earliest convocation of a meeting of the communist and workers parties of Latin America which would help step up the struggle against Yankee imperialism" and stressed the need for "joint action and solidarity among the communists and other popular groups in Latin America."

The Colombian delegation to the OLAS conference (31 July-10 August) included PCC Central Committee members Manuel Cepeda and Isaias Suárez. In commenting on the conference, *Voz Proletaria* condemned the "adventurers" present at the conference and an editorial (10 August) remarked that the function of OLAS was not the direction of popular revolutionary struggle but rather the promotion of Latin American solidarity. The editorial also warned of various extremists "divorced from Marxism-Leninism" who wanted OLAS to have a directing role. *Voz Proletaria* clearly indicated the PCC's reluctance to surrender control of its activities to OLAS by declaring that the direction of a people's struggle was the responsibility of the "revolutionary vanguard," which should have full autonomy while assimilating the international experience of various communist movements. In his address to the conference, Manuel Cepeda expressed the need for unity in the revolutionary struggle and conveyed the greetings of the PCC and FARC. Fabio Vásquez Castano, leader of the ELN, sent a tape-recorded message to the meeting calling for the establishment of an organization to ensure the necessary solidarity between armed revolutionary movements.

Although the PCC has indirectly criticized Cuba for attempting to impose its strategies on other Latin American communist movements, Secretary-General Vieira stated:

> The Colombian communists consider the Cuban revolution to be the advance guard and beginning of our own revolution. The Cuban revolution has shown that it is possible to break with US imperialism and to defeat it in the political, military, and economic fields. The Cuban revolution has also shown that the Latin American people, uniting their forces against the domination of the oligarchies and imperialism, can count on the effective aid of Socialist countries, especially the Soviet Union. (Gilberto Vieira, *Morning Star,* London, 10 August.)

The PCC has maintained close relations with the Communist Party of Venezuela. In June 1967 delegations from the Central Committees of both parties met to discuss the major issues facing the international communist movement.

Contacts were also maintained between the PCC and the East European communist parties. On 27 August the Yugoslav newspaper *Politika* published an article praising the PCC and FARC for having not yielded to "adventure" or "ultra-leftist" trends. *Politika* rejected the ELN, declaring that it had nothing in common with the ideas of the PCC.

Following its visit to the Soviet Union on the occasion of the fiftieth anniversary of the October Revolution, the PCC delegation, led by Secretary General Vieira, visited the German Democratic Republic, Bulgaria, Rumania, and Czechoslovakia and met with the Central Committees and leaders of their communist parties.

The PCC pledged its support for and solidarity with the "heroic struggle which the Vietnamese people are waging against Yankee aggression" and condemned Israel's "aggression against the Arab countries," calling it a "serious threat to world peace."

**Publications.** The PCC publishes a weekly newspaper, *Voz Proletaria*, and a bimonthly theoretical organ, *Documentos Políticos,* both published in Bogotá. The PCC also publishes a news sheet, *Noticias de Colombia.* The FARC publishes its own organ, *Resistencia.*

\*     \*     \*

The pro-Chinese PCC-ML is a relatively insignificant element in Colombian politics. The party's infiltration within the ranks of the ELN and its virtual control of the Workers', Students', and Peasants' Movements (MOEC) could place it in a strong position in the eventuality of a broadening of the guerrilla movement.

Prominent pro-Chinese communists believed to be in the party's leadership include: Jorge Restrepo, Daniel Díaz, Humberto Salamanca Alba, Napoleón Martínez, Alejandro Soto, and Victor Julio Ramos.

The PCC-ML has its own youth movement, known by the same name as its pro-Soviet rival, Juventud Comunista de Colombia. Late in 1967 the leadership of the PCC-ML launched a small pro-Chinese guerrilla group, the Ejército Popular de Liberacíon (EPL) in the Alto Sinú region. The PCC-ML also controls the Bloque Independiente, a trade union organization which originated in Cali and whose membership is estimated at 2,000.

In internal policy the PCC-ML's position was elaborated at the Fifth Congress of the Albanian Workers' Party: "Our congress [July 1965] pointed out that a peaceful path, under conditions in Colombia, was an opportunistic revisionist fraud, and strongly declared that the path of the Colombian revolution is that of armed struggle." Jorge Restrepo, the PCC-ML's delegate, stated that to further these aims his party had decided at its congress to "transfer the party leadership and its best cadres to the mountains in order to lead the armed struggle by themselves" (Radio Tirana, 4 November 1966).

On 14 January 1967, *Nuova Unità,* the organ of the pro-Chinese Italian Communist Party, carried an unsigned article entitled "Carrying the War by the Colombian People Through to Victory—Extract from the 'Political Conclusions of the Military Front' of the Second Plenum of the Central Committee of the Communist Party of Colombia (M.L.)." The article stated that the plenum (for which no date was given) "clearly brought out" the existence in PCC-ML ranks of 'leftist' deviationist tendencies manifested in the "desire to make people's war an artificial thing, isolated from the masses, to depreciate the struggle (legal, semi-legal, or illegal) by the people in the cities and the countryside, so as to accept the principle of a handful of 'heroes' capable of carrying forward the revolutionary process from the military point of view alone." The article also stated: "A tendency toward pronounced militarism has arisen, which places the rifle above politics, giving precedence to the guerrilla to the detriment of the party and misunderstanding the principles of political democracy, economic democracy, and military democracy in the armed organization."

The article warned: "These deviations have already caused serious prejudice to the construction and development of the communist party (M-L), to the organization armed for the Colombian revolution. At the same time, they have facilitated the strengthening of the antiparty group, deprecating the comrades, and sabotaging the party's official bodies in various ways." In an effort to remedy the situation, the PCC-ML emphasized the party's political line calling for "decisively intensifying the armed struggle of the Colombian people."

On 24 February 1967, *La Voix du Peuple,* the weekly organ of the pro-Chinese Belgian Communist Party, carried a statement by the PCC-ML commenting on its Tenth Congress.

> The Tenth Congress of the party has given the Colombian working class and people a Marxist-Leninist conception of the Colombian revolution, throwing overboard the treacherous positions of revision in Colombia. It has rebutted the treacherous thesis of "peaceful revolution" with the Marxist thesis of "armed revolution." Faced with the bourgeois thesis of the progressive character of the bourgeoisie, it has demonstrated the reactionary, antinational, and "denationalizing" character of the Colombian

bourgeoisie, who are accomplices of imperialism in the bloody task of exploiting and oppressing our people. It rebutted the thesis of the false interpretation of peaceful coexistence, defended by the revisionists, with the thesis of world proletarian internationalism.

In international affairs, at the Albanian congress, the PCC-ML reiterated its pro-Chinese affiliation although emphasis was placed on its solidarity with the Albanians, whose victories were the "best example and stimulation for the Latin American peoples who live under neocolonialism" (Radio Tirana, 4 November 1966).

With regard to the Soviet Union, the PCC-ML declared that "revisionism of our time, headed by the criminal clique at the head of the CPSU, is shamefully occupying the main place in the struggle against the peoples who fight for their freedom" (*ibid.*).

The PCC-ML made no official statements about Cuba and sent no representatives to the Tricontinental Conference.

The PCC-ML has no regular publication. Its two irregular journals, *Tribuna* and *Revolución,* seem to follow the pro-Chinese line.

# COSTA RICA

The Communist Party in Costa Rica was originally founded in 1931 as the Partido Comunista de Costa Rica. The name was changed in 1943 to the People's Vanguard Party (Partido Vanguardia Popular; PVP).

Although the PVP was outlawed in 1948 and is at present illegal, it is able to function to a limited extent. It is usually barred only from presenting its own candidates for public office.

The party's membership, which by 1948 had grown to some 3,000 and included seven Deputies in the National Congress, has now diminished to an estimated 500. There is no evidence of any organized contending factions outside the party's ranks. The population of Costa Rica is 1,510,000 (estimated, January 1967).

Many potential Communists are drawn to the noncommunist left-wing National Liberation Party (Partido de Liberación Nacional; PLN). In the February 1966 elections the PLN won 29 of 57 seats in the Assembly; its Presidential candidate, Daniel Oduber Quirós, obtained 217,514 votes as against 222,012 for the elected President, José Joaquin Trejos Fernández of the National Unification Party.

**Organization and Leadership.** The PVP leadership includes Manuel Mora Valverde, First Secretary; Arnoldo Ferreto Segura, Organizational Secretary, and Political Committee members Luisa González Gutiérrez de González, Alvaro Montero Vega, Humberto Elias Vargas Carbonell, and Mario Solis.

Within the trade-union movement the PVP's principal source of support is derived from the General Confederation of Costa Rican Workers (Confederación General de Trabajadores Costaricenses; CGTC), which represents about 2,500 workers of a total trade-union membership of about 19,000.

In the 1966 elections the PVP tried to gain a political foothold by putting up a front organization, the Socialist Popular Alliance Party (Partido Alianza Popular Socialista; PAPS). Because of alleged international ties, this organization was banned under Article 98 of the Costa Rican constitution.

**Domestic Policy and Activity.** During the year the PVP reiterated the policy lines adopted at the party's Tenth Congress in June 1966 (*YICA*, 1966, pp. 204-205), which pointed out: "The political regime . . . , together with the civic and democratic traditions inherent in the majority of our people, makes possible peaceful development of the revolution today."

At the Third Plenum of the PVP's Central Committee, 16-18 June, the party, while giving full backing to guerrilla movements already in existence, reaffirmed the thesis that the Communist struggle develops in different ways, according to the conditions prevailing in each country, and claimed that the democratic tradition in a number of countries, including Costa Rica, made "mass action" the norm there (*Libertad*, 24 June). The PVP was represented at the conference of the Latin American Solidarity Organization—OLAS—in Havana (31 July-10 August) by a delegation led by Alvaro Montero Vega of the party's Political Committee. In his speech to the conference Montero declared:

> The armed insurrection of the people to overthrow the regime that is oppressing and exploiting them should be the result of a carefully detailed preparation which includes, not only the military aspects, but also all aspects, both objective and subjective . . . . This means, in other words, that we revolutionaries cannot decide capriciously, much less on the basis of our own desires or of anger, upon the moment when an armed uprising should start, or think that armed insurrection is the only possible way to achieve the revolution. (*Libertad*, 19 August.)

Following speculations in the Costa Rican press that as a result of the OLAS conference the PVP would be controlled from Havana and that it would resort to armed struggle, a clarification of the

PVP's stand appeared in the 26 August issue of the party's weekly organ, *Libertad*, in an article by Arturo Jara:

> The political line of the PVP is drawn up by the Central Committee in its meeting and . . . under no circumstances has it permitted an international organization to make decisions for the Costa Rican Communists. Furthermore, one of the issues promoted at the OLAS Conference by our delegates was that said organization should not hold Latin American revolutionary leadership because the revolutionary struggle in each country should be led only by native revolutionaries, who are the only ones capable to conduct it. [In] Costa Rica, the development of a peaceful revolution is possible because of this country's strong democratic traditions, the strength of its institutions, the lack of an army, and many other circumstances. . . . It is therefore the duty of all Costa Rican revolutionaries to explore the possibility of a peaceful revolution. . . . The issue of Communists carrying out their struggle through peaceful means is not a passing tactical attitude, but is, instead, the party's strategic line.

Jara qualified the party's stand with a warning: "If the oligarchy of the country and their imperialist masters obstruct the democratic course of the people to bring about the necessary changes . . . and if the working classes are deprived of their right to carry out social changes, then violence will arise."

The PVP's stand with regard to peaceful revolution was subsequently reiterated elsewhere—in an article by Humberto Vargas in the *World Marxist Review* (September, pp. 51-53); in a speech by Arnoldo Ferreto in San José commemorating the Fiftieth Anniversary of the Bolshevik Revolution (*Libertad*, 11 November), and a further article by Jara, carried by *Libertad* on 21 October.

The PVP organized a number of minor demonstrations during the year. The most publicized of these was a "peace march" in Puntarenas on 22 February. The march ended with a meeting, attended by some 250 people, which was addressed by PVP leaders, including the party's First Secretary, Manuel Mora Valverde.

**International Views and Policy.** In international affairs the PVP continued to adhere to the policy reiterated at the party's Tenth Congress, in 1966: "Our Party has always supported and will continue to support the foreign policy of peace and peaceful coexistence pursued by the countries of the socialist camp headed by the Soviet Union" (*YICA*, 1966, p. 205). Resolutions adopted at the PVP's plenum in June approved the Soviet Union's stand during the Middle East conflict; hailed the "tremendous aid" the Soviet Union and the other socialist countries were giving to the "heroic Vietnamese people"; denounced "disruptive actions of the Mao Tse-tung group"; and reaffirmed the party's position "in support of the unity of the world Communist movement [and jin favor of the convocation of an international meeting of Communist and workers' parties" (TASS, 27 June). First Secretary Manuel Mora Valverde's speech on 5 November in Minsk, at the celebrations of the Fiftieth Anniversary of the Bolshevik Revolution, praised the "heroism of the Soviet people and the role and wisdom of the Party founded by Lenin" and attacked "ultra-revolutionaries" in the form of the Mao Tse-tung group: "[They] are attempting to undermine the unity of the world's Communists and are causing harm to the revolutionary struggle of the peoples. They are assailing the USSR and the CPSU, not hesitating to resort to the most pernicious slander. But by attacking the CPSU they are attacking all Communist Parties . . . "(*IB*, special anniversary issue).

The PVP's relations with Cuba were governed by the party's aforementioned belief in revolutionary diversity. At the June plenum the PVP emphasized the necessity to "settle differences, reestablish harmony, and fix firm bases for unity" at the forthcoming OLAS Conference. It added, furthermore, that interference and "verbal aggression" among parties and groups in Latin America must be stopped. (*Libertad*, 24 June.) Though there were reports (*La Nación*, San José, 6 April) that Castro was supporting a group of guerrilla warfare advocates within the PVP and had criticized the majority of the Party leadership for "inactivity," the PVP continued to stress its solidarity with the Cuban regime (*Libertad*, 24 June).

In an address to the OLAS Conference, the Chairman of the Costa Rican delegation, Alvaro Montero Vega, declared: "We members of the Costa Rican revolutionary organizations, combined with the National Committee for Solidarity, have, in the recent past, defended Cuba's Socialist

Revolution, and will always do so, unconditionally and with unquenchable zeal." He added, however: The social revolution can only be the achievement of the people who need it, and . . . it must develop within the framework of the conditions peculiar to each country. This makes it necessary to respect the forms of warfare which such people and their vanguard detachment select, as well as the individual character that the revolution takes on in a particular country. This does not negate the interrelationships and assistance which some revolutionary movements may offer to others, much less the fact that the revolution which is on the rise in one country helps in winning the revolution in other countries, especially if they are on the same continent, and, what is more, neighbors. Thus solidarity as organized through an international organization such as the OLAS must depart from the principles of respect for the independence of the revolutionary movement in each country and in its revolutionary organizations." (*Libertad,* 19 August.)

The PVP attended a meeting of the communist parties of Mexico, Central America, and Panama, and was a signatory to the meeting's communique (see *Documents*).

The PVP's First Secretary, Manuel Mora Valverde, attended the celebrations of the Fiftieth Anniversary of the Bolshevik Revolution in the Soviet Union.

**Publications.** The PVP publishes a weekly newspaper, *Libertad.*

# CUBA

The Cuban Communist Party (Partido Comunista de Cuba; PCC) was founded in August 1925 and within weeks was driven underground. Some PCC members surfaced in 1937 and joined several non-Communist groups in the Revolutionary Union (Union Revolucionaria). In 1939 all Communists were reunited in the legal Revolutionary Communist Union (Union Revolucionaria Comunista). In 1944 the party was renamed the People's Socialist Party (Partido Socialista Popular; PSP), a name it retained until it merged with Fidel Castro's 26th of July Movement and the small Revolutionary Directorate (Directorio Revolucionario; DR) to form the Integrated Revolutionary Organizations (Organizaciones Revolucionarias Integradas) in 1961. This was followed in 1963 by the unceremonious formation of the United Party of the Socialist Revolution (Partido Unido de la Revolucion Socialista). In October 1965 the party was reorganized along more orthodox communist lines and the name it had originally taken in 1925 was adopted. The 1967 party membership of about 60,000 represented only a small percentage of the total Cuban population, estimated at 7,900,000. It was, however, pointed out by PCC Organizing Secretary Armando Hart on 26 August that any Cubans who willingly gave everything for the revolution, even if they were not already party militants, "must be treated as Communists" (*Granma*, weekly English edition, 3 September).

Real political power in Cuba in 1967 rested primarily in the hands of Fidel Castro by virtue of his personal magnetism and his positions as PCC First Secretary, Prime Minister, Commander in Chief of the Armed Forces, and Minister-President of the National Institute of Agrarian Reform (Instituto Nacional de la Reforma Agraria; INRA). In a speech on 2 January celebrating the eighth anniversary of the revolution, Castro said: "The time should come when we begin to change our slogans. Instead of saying 'Everyone with Fidel!' rather, 'Everyone with the Party!' and 'Everyone with the Central Committee of the Party!' " (*ibid.*, 8 January). In practice, however, with a few exceptions like the May Day address given by Juan Almeida, Castro retained his position as spokesman for the Cuban people. Indeed, in his 13 March address he went so far as to suggest that he would not hesitate to pass judgment on the credentials of anyone in the world who claimed to be a Communist (see *Documents*).

Among persons wielding varying amounts of secondary but not insignificant power were: (1) the members of the eight-man Political Bureau of the PCC, headed by Fidel Castro, and including Deputy Prime Minister and Armed Forces Minister Raúl Castro, President Osvaldo Dorticós, Acting Armed Forces Minister Juan Almeida, Interior Minister Ramiro Valdés, PCC Organizing Secretary Armando Hart, Guillermo García, and Sergio del Valle; (2) the members of the PCC Secretariat, headed by Fidel Castro and including Raúl Castro, Osvaldo Dorticós, former DR leader Faure Chomón, and former PSP members Blas Roca and Carlos Rafael Rodríguez; (3) certain members of the PCC Central Committee, originally composed of 100 persons, including Foreign Relations Minister Raúl Roa, Education Minister José Llanusa, Deputy Minister of the Interior and head of the State Security Department José Abrahantes, Secretary-General of the Confederation of Cuban Labor Miguel Martín, head of the General Direction of Intelligence (Directorio General de Inteligencia; DGI) Manuel Piñerio, head of the Committees for the Defense of the Revolution Luis González, President of the Federation of Cuban Women Vilma Espín (wife of Raúl Castro), Haydée Santamaría (wife of Armando Hart), and Celia Sánchez. The Central Committee itself, heavily weighted with military men, is evidently largely a paper organization which seldom meets and can only affirm decisions or issue declarations made by individuals or groups superior to it.

Some reports indicate that four Central Committee members (Juan Vitalio Acuña, Antonio Sánchez Díaz, Alberto Fernández Montes de Oca, and Eliseo Reyes Rodríquez) were killed with "Che" Guevara in Bolivia. (*The Complete Bolivian Diaries of Ché Guevara and Other Captured Documents*, ed. and intro. by Daniel James, Stein and Day, New York, 1968, 324-25.)

Since February 1959 the Cuban people have lived under a frequently amended Fundamental Law. They were first promised a "socialist" constitution in May 1961, but no such document has yet been presented. On 30 March 1967 Radio Havana reported that Blas Roca, who heads the constitution

136

drafting commission which has been working since October 1965, expected a draft constitution to be completed by July. Either the draft was never completed, or it was finished and found unacceptable, for on 28 September Fidel Castro told the Cuban people that they would not be living under a constitution until 1969 or 1970. He explained that too often revolutionaries write a constitution too quickly and it "becomes a kind of inviolable taboo; it becomes an inefficient intellectual creation, unable to conform to reality." The Cuban Revolutionary Government would not make this mistake, he explained, but would delay producing a constitution until additional experience had taught the party leaders what would best serve their revolutionary purposes (*Granma,* weekly English edition, 8 October).

The difficulty in preparing an acceptable draft constitution may have been one reason for the postponement of the long-awaited first PCC Congress, scheduled for 1967. Other factors behind the postponement were probably the decision first to strengthen the party hold over the state apparatus, much of which has changed little since prerevolutionary days, and Fidel Castro's probable reluctance to look with real favor on any organization or meeting which might tend to obstruct his own freedom of movement and political power.

During 1967 Cuban sources claimed a significant increase in popular participation in two areas of local government. (1) The "people's courts" or "popular tribunals," whose job it was to dispense what Radio Havana (7 July) called "real revolutionary justice," were considerably expanded during the last four months of the year. The judges were "elected" by the people themselves from among their most revolutionary co-workers. They were given ten-day courses by Cuban law students and professors before beginning to hand down sentences, which could not exceed six months' imprisonment or 500 pesos in fines, on issues involving "public order and human relations." The spirit of the courts was revealed by Minister of Justice Alfredo Yabur, who said: "We use first of all Communist workers and afterwards, as an addition, lawyers." (2) Heavy coverage was given, especially during September, to the election of delegates to local administrative (local power) assemblies, in which "militant active membership in a mass organization," the Young Communist Union, or the PCC was the "minimum requirement" for any candidate (*Granma,* 6 September). According to Julio Carranza, National Coordinator of Local Administration, the assemblies were "branches of the party in each locality for confronting and resolving important tasks of politico-social character." Their basic tasks were "community service, commercial service, construction, and handicraft and industrial production." They were expected not only to help the people improve their lives, but also to explain why some desired changes were at present beyond the means available to the government. One delegate was to be elected for each 100 workers in PCC-selected factories, rural areas, and, above all, Committees for the Defense of the Revolution. (Havana radio and television, 30 August; *Granma,* weekly English edition, 10 September.) According to a call issued on 18 September in *Granma,* the official organ of the Central Committee of the PCC, the election of some 20,000 delegates in mid-September represented the "direct intervention of the people through the highest form of democracy . . . grand and true democracy, that which the people practice from below with their word and creative force."

Probably the largest and most active mass organizations in Cuba today are the Committees for the Defense of the Revolution (Comités de Defensa de la Revolución; CDR), headed by Luis González. As described in a *Granma* commentary (26 September), the Committees were founded on 28 September 1960 "in the heat of struggle against the imperialist enemy and its henchmen" in order "to crush enemies, saboteurs and conspirators at home," and their fundamental activity was continuing, being: "defense, revolutionary vigilance against those who hope to throw us back to the past or who break revolutionary laws, attempting to live as parasites or delinquents in a workers' society." In addition to these "internal security" assignments for the PCC, the Committees in recent years have joined or led activities in such fields as public health, education, urban reform, recreation, and local government (Radio Havana, 27 April 1967). On the celebration of the seventh anniversary of their founding Fidel Castro commented that "recently the role of the CDR's as liaison between the masses and the institutions of revolutionary power has come to the fore" (*Granma,* weekly English edition, 8 October).

The Committees played a prominent role in both of the "elections" mentioned above, by providing candidates themselves and by screening individuals nominated by other individuals or organizations. According to a Havana broadcast of 8 December 1966, there were in almost every block some CDR members who devoted their time to informing on their personal enemies "because of some petty in-fighting or unmerited jealousy." Efforts have been made to weed these individuals out. At the beginning of 1967 it was estimated that roughly one-third of all adult Cubans belonged to the Committees. In a communication to the CDR's published in *Granma* on 27 September it was announced that during the year the organization had added some 800,000 new members.

The Young Communist Union (Unión de Jóvenes Comunistas; UJC) held its Third Plenary Session in January, elected a 27-member National Committee, and returned Jaime Crombet to his position as UJC First Secretary. During the year the UJC played an active role in mobilizing tens of thousands of young persons for participation in agricultural and construction work. The Conclusions of the National Committee, reached late in June, said that the Union had adopted the "guerrilla method" in its work in order to eliminate bureaucratic waste and increase responsibility on all levels, adding, however, that in spite of the UJC members' many accomplishments they should have achieved more. In November it was announced that the UJC would merge with (in effect, absorb) the decades-old Havana University Youth Federation, 99 per cent of whose leaders were already UJC members. It was asserted that youth activities would be more effective if coordinated since the two groups had the same objectives in mind for the same students. (*Granma*, 2 December). The UJC membership increased by 50,000 in 1967 to a total of 153,000 (*Juventud Rebelde*, 26 January 1968). UJC Second Secretary Roberto Ogando, who became Regional Secretary of the PCC on the Isle of Pines in September, reportedly said in May that under his direction membership in the Pioneers Union, which brings together children between the ages of seven and thirteen years, had reached 804,000 (84 per cent of that age group in Cuba).

In August the Federation of Cuban Women (Federación de Mujeres Cubanas; FMC) celebrated its seventh anniversary. In a television review of the activities of her organization, FMC President Vilma Espín noted the role of women in Civil Defense units, in work safety and hygiene activities, and in social work and the prevention of juvenile delinquency. The FMC received its widest press coverage during the year for its role in two other activities: the creation (by August) of 231 day nurseries which cared for some 32,000 youngsters between the ages of 45 days and six years, and the organization of more than 50,000 women for agricultural work in the countryside. Radio Havana announced on 4 December that FMC membership had reached upwards of 800,000 women, an increase of some 175,000 during the year.

The August 1966 appointment of 29-year old Miguel Martín, a recent First Secretary of the UJC, as Secretary-General of the Confederation of Cuban Workers (Central de Trabajadores de Cuba; CTC) was intended to inject enthusiasm and dedication into the Cuban labor force. Martín has been a devoted follower of Castro since the 1950's and in his new CTC position has frequently echoed Castro's calls for moral rather than material incentives for workers. During 1967 the CTC was responsible for mobilizing volunteer workers for agricultural work under the slogan, "Industry at the Service of Agriculture" (*Granma*, weekly English edition, 23 April). Its membership, which includes state farm laborers as well as urban workers, was estimated at about 1.5 million.

The Small Farmers National Association (Associación Nacional de Agricultores Pequeños; ANAP), headed by José (Pepe) Ramírez, brings together the roughly 200,000 farmers who still own their own land. Fidel Castro gave one of his longest speeches of the year at the Third ANAP Congress in May. He repeated his earlier promise that the farmers' land would not be nationalized, but urged the "voluntary" sale of land to the state, although it can be sold legally to no one else. He proclaimed that there should and would be more state regulation of planting and selling of crops with the aim of promoting the good of the whole nation rather than the material interests of the few. Coordinated plans for production and sale of products were studied by the ANAP beginning in September with the assistance of the INRA and the PCC (*El Mundo*, 9 September). Probably no important mass organization in Cuba is so torn by contradictions as the ANAP, where Castro's ideological disapproval of private farming runs headlong into his need to rely on the cooperation and produce of these small farms, which occupy 30 per cent of the arable land but have consistently contributed a higher percentage of the country's total agricultural output.*

Most of the important shifts of political power during 1967 resulted in a further decrease in influence for the old communists of pre-Castro days. (1) *Cuba Socialista* ceased publication with the February issue, stating that it lacked the "theoretical background . ... required to enable the magazine to play its role as the official theoretical spokesman of the party in a capable manner." It is possible that the editorial board, which included Blas Roca, whose draft consitution did not appear as expected in July, could not agree on important points. In any event, the suspension of the journal removed some former PSP members (three of the five-man editorial board) from participation in authoritative PCC statements. (2) On 26 May *Granma* announced the dismissal of Aurelio Martinez from his position as director of the Cuban Broadcasting Institute, and the appointment of Major Jorge Serguera, a dedicated advocate of armed revolution. In recent years Serguera has been ambassador to Algeria (under Ben Bella) and to the Congo (Brazzaville). (3) On 5 July Isidoro Malmierca, a former PSP member, was removed from his position as director of *Granma* and reassigned to the National Fishing Institute. The new director was Captain Jorge Enrique Mendoza, formerly chief announcer for the rebel radio station in the Sierra Maestra during the struggle against Batista, and recently a relatively important figure in several administrative posts in the Cuban educational system. (4) On 12 July the First Secretary of the PCC in Oriente Province, Armando Acosta, another former PSP member, was dismissed. (5) On 10 August, in his speech at the closing session of the Latin American Solidarity Organization (OLAS) conference, Fidel Castro launched a heated attack on a "microfaction" in Cuba: a group "systematically opposed to all the concepts of the Revolution, to the deepest, sincerest, purest revolutionary attitudes of the people, to our concepts of socialism, of communism, of everything." The microfaction was pointedly linked up with foreign critics of Castro, including by implication the Soviet Union (*Granma*, weekly English edition, 20 August). Late in the year, reports from generally reliable sources in Havana indicated that a group headed by former PSP official Aníbal Escalante had been arrested for anti-Castro activities (*New York Times,* 22 December). In late January and early February 1968 these reports were confirmed when *Granma* published a series of speeches and documents relating to the arrest and trial of 34 "sectarians" who were sentenced to a total of 277 years' imprisonment. Included were Escalante and two members of the Central Committee of the PCC, José Matar, a former CDR chief and ambassador to Hungary, and Ramón Calcines of the Agrarian Reform Institute, along with the 31 others, who were mostly members of the old PSP. Carlos Rafael Rodríguez, probably the most influential old-guard communist in Cuba today, declared: "Without doubt there are three or four times as many involved in this affair" (*Granma*, weekly English edition, 11 February 1968). The 34 were charged with carrying on systematic attacks and intrigues against Castro, distributing clandestine propaganda contrary to the PCC line on such issues as incentives and economic policies, trying to undermine Cuban relations with other countries, making special efforts to win over old PSP members, working for foreign intervention in Cuban affairs, and many other such acts. Also implicated were foreign communists, including a member of the Central Committee of the Czech Communist Party (Frantisck Kriegel, who in April 1968 was elevated to his party's Politburo), and two Soviet advisers to the Cuban security service. Major Juan Almeida's position as Acting Armed Forces Minister during much of 1967 was probably accounted for at least in part by the fact that Raúl Castro was Chairman of the Revolutionary Armed Forces and State Security Commission of the Central Committee, which played an important role in the investigation of the microfaction.

The basic domestic political policies and activities in Cuba during 1967 were extraordinarily interrelated. They ranged from efforts to strengthen the party and the struggle against bureaucracy to programs of education, the mass employment of "volunteers" in agricultural work, the emphasis placed on moral rather than material incentives, and the veneration of the fallen hero, Major Ernesto "Che" Guevara.

Considerable attention was given to the internal strengthening of the PCC and the extension of party control throughout the Cuban state structure and society. Early in 1967 a document entitled

*According to Castro on 28 September, in some underpopulated areas the state owns more than 90 per cent of the land, whereas in others, like Havana Province, more than half is privately owned (*Granma*, weekly English edition, 8 October).

"Some Basic Party Tasks" (not published until *Granma* released it in installments beginning on 26 October) was circulated among PCC organizations. Proclaiming that "The tasks of the party are the tasks of the revolution," it indicated that these tasks were directed by means of the administrative apparatus, the party's own internal organization, and the mass organizations, and that policies would be proclaimed by the national and provincial party leaders, passed through municipal committees, and set into action by the party cells. In outlining their specific work plans, the cells must consider the problems of organization, direction of production, ideological and political struggle, and political, cultural and technical development.

According to the document, the success of the party organization depended on "the quality and competence of the cadres within it and the development of work plans directly contributing to the promotion of the revolutionary tasks." Pointing out that the vanguard party must be a "shock brigade," not a deliberately intellectual "debating circle," the document declared: "Theoretical knowledge is indispensable, but must come from practice and from the solution of concrete problems, and should be reflected in better daily work."

On 7 April, at a meeting of vice-ministers of state organizations chosen for PCC membership, Armando Hart admitted that many people thought it strange that the party had "taken this long to be organized in the central State apparatus." In the past, "weaknesses and inefficiency" within the party had led to many practical difficulties, which now would be overcome not by formally linking the party and the state apparatus but by creating a "close bond between communists of the various State organisms and those who do not work directly in the central State organizations." (*Ibid.*, 14 May.) Thus during the year an exacting and demanding selection of new party members was called for throughout the state apparatus, the mass organizations, and Havana University. Actual increases in party membership have not been made known.

On 20 February Fidel Castro stated: "Our Party today has two fundamental tasks: the agricultural development of the country and the fight against bureaucracy" (*ibid.*, 26 February). The primary features of the "revolution against bureaucracy"—in many ways resembling those of Mao Tse-tung's "cultural revolution" in China—were the interconnected problems of how to prevent the state and party from becoming self-perpetuating power structures and how to retain (or perhaps even regain) the revolutionary fervor associated with the years of guerrilla struggle. Although Cuban spokesmen sometimes traced the campaign against bureaucracy back to late 1964, the actions of 1967 were without precedent in scope and intensity. The need to avoid bureaucratic stagnation was stressed within PCC ranks at the beginning of the year in "Some Basic Party Tasks," and received its greatest public expression in speeches by major Cuban leaders and in page after page of the official and semiofficial magazines and newspapers.

This problem was treated most systematically in four *Granma* editorials between 27 February and 2 March. Bureaucracy was seen as the creation of the bourgeoisie in capitalist society; its origins were ideological and its outstanding manifestation was an overextension of administrative work with a consequent insensitivity to human beings. Thus bureaucracy was "one of the most unsavory holdovers from the past" in Cuba, its dangers multiplied by the inexperience of the revolutionary leaders and the "introduction of some administrative systems and organizational procedures, copied from countries of the socialist camp, that were weighted down with bureaucracy." *Granma* warned: "If the Party does not win this battle over bureaucracy . . . through the formation of the new man and the application of an unyielding policy, consistent with Marxist-Leninist principles, the party will end by bureaucratizing itself." Even under the best of conditions, *Granma* admitted, "bureaucracy will grow, develop and gain strength during the early years of revolutionary power," at the same time taking on a "new character in its relationship to the means of production and, therefore, to political activity as well"; unless constantly opposed—and eventually eliminated completely under communism—bureaucracy would grow completely out of control and tend to operate as a new class, defending nothing except its own privileged position.

*Granma* continued: "Bureaucracy causes us more damage than imperialism. Imperialism is an open and external enemy. Bureaucracy corrodes us from within and attacks the healthiest, firmest elements of the masses, those who must suffer the most from it." Unrelenting struggle against bureaucracy would have to be waged by a youthful and alert party, which would eradicate the ideological remains of this holdover of petty-bourgeois mentality and would confront functionaries and cadres "directly with problems of production," thus making the state "simple" yet "dynamic." It was necessary that party branches on all levels should participate, from administrative leaders to local work centers, and that city militants should go to the countryside to strengthen the party there. This "veritable revolution within the revolution" would be successful, *Granma* declared, "insofar as it combined the struggle *against* bureaucracy and the struggle *for* self-improvement, technological training, and massive participation in the tasks of production, especially agriculture." (Emphasis in original.)

On 20 February Fidel Castro proclaimed that the revolution was taking the offensive against bureaucracy and that "the Revolution's future advance" would be "gauged by the progressively lower number of administrative employees every year" (*Granma*, weekly English edition, 26 February). On 28 September he proclaimed that though the struggle was not yet over, one could safely say that bureaucracy was "beating a retreat" (*ibid.*, 8 October). Although Castro had promised on 20 February that no family would "be left without an income," he continued:

There will be no blood shed in this battle against bureaucracy but there will be sanctions.

There will be sanctions! And possibly hundreds of administrators will be removed from their posts, their salaries will be reduced and they will be sent to other, nonadministrative jobs.

As a result of the campaign there were reportedly many frightened, puzzled, and angry people in Cuba, above all in Havana. (Radio Havana, 6 March; *Granma,* 22 September). Late in September it was announced that some 31,500 "nonproductive" jobs had been eliminated in the ongoing campaign against bureaucracy, including 21,000 since the beginning of the year. Two-thirds of those fired had worked in the Ministries of Industries, Transportation, Domestic Trade, Education, or Construction, or for the INRA or the National Bank. According to *Granma* on 22 September, about 88 per cent had gone into productive work or study programs, were being retired, or had left the labor force, while some 12 per cent were "sitting idly at home" with a "recalcitrant, parasitic attitude" which could not be tolerated indefinitely. The magnitude of some changes were evident in the 70 per cent reduction in personnel in the Ministry of Foreign Trade (from 4,600 to 1,395) between December 1966 and October 1967 (*Granma,* 30 September).

Not only were "nonproductive" bureaucrats removed from many offices; in a number of instances high-ranking offices were eliminated altogether. For example, Minister of Education José Llanusa abolished five vice-ministries and replaced them with smaller "education advisory groups" (*ibid.,* 15 April). On 20 February Fidel Castro commented that the revolutionaries had "failed in one respect early in the Revolution; and that failure consisted in not doing away with the ministries and in not moving the Capital of the Republic to the town of Guáimaro" (*ibid.,* 26 February).

In 1965 "Che" Guevara wrote that "the education of the new man" was one of the "two pillars of the construction of socialism," ("Notes on Man and Socialism in Cuba," *Che Guevara Speaks,* Grove Press, New York, p.131). On 9 December 1967 Fidel Castro commented: "It is in education that our Revolution has made what is very nearly its greatest and its most significant investment." He pointed out that during the 1966-67 school year 52,834 active teachers had made use of such teaching aids as films, television, radio, and tape recorders. During that year, he added, there was a total of 2,127,000 students, consisting of 1,382,000 in the primary grades, 283,000 at the intermediate level, and 40,000 in the universities, with most of the rest (about 410,000) studying in the Worker-Farmer Education Program. Some 254,000 reportedly received full scholarships, and 151,800 were at semi-boarding schools and day-care centers. (*Granma,* weekly English edition, 17 December.)

At the inauguration of the pilot school project at San Andrés on 28 January, Fidel Castro said that many people complain, suffer, and are miserable because they "have not been prepared for life" (*ibid.,* 5 February). One remedy for this problem, which the Cuban government hoped to have in effect within seven or eight years, would be, as Castro pointed out at the Gran Tierra project on 27 July, to provide for every Cuban "all the necessary facilities for their education from the time they are 45 days old through their graduation from a university." The Prime Minister explained that "up to the sixth grade they will be semi-boarding students"—having breakfast, lunch, and supper at school and sleeping at home—"and in secondary schools the pupils will be full boarding students" (*ibid.*, 6 August). At San Andrés Castro explained that the children's lives would be "perfectly organized": "There will be no opportunity to go astray or acquire bad habits." On 29 April Castro predicted that by 1970 there would be a half million students between the basic secondary (middle) school and the university level and that by 1975 the number would be a million (*ibid.*, 7 May). The existing intermediate school program will be altered, he stated on 26 July, so that one year of compulsory military service would in the future be incorporated in high schools and technological institutes (*ibid.*, 30 July).

About 24,000 of the 40,000 university students in Cuba were enrolled at the University of Havana. According to the Ministry of Education, there had been 20,000 students at the university in 1958/59 after which there was a low of about 12,500 in 1962/63, from which the number rose to about 22,000 in 1965/66. Slightly more than 40 per cent of the students in 1966/67 were in the schools of education, medicine, and dentistry. (*Granma*, weekly English edition, 10 September.) Speaking at a meeting on 14 December to party members in the School of Technology at that university, Armando Hart gave some idea of what Cuban university students can expect in the future. Hart stated that the Communist vanguard must "seek to apply communist methods of leadership throughout the entire University structure" and devote its energies to certain "basic tasks": "ideological development," "scientific training," and active participation in "production and research." They were to improve the currently inadequate "political leadership for the faculty" and "struggle against the superintellectual mentality," while striving for the "total integration of the University into production and the life of the country." (*Ibid.*, 31 December.) The merger of the Young Communist Union (comprising more than 30 per cent of all University of Havana students) and the University Youth Federation was intended to facilitate the achievement in the university of, "in short, the creation of the new man, whose most faithful exponent was Major Ernesto Che Guevara" (*ibid.*, 17 December).

Efforts to make each Cuban youth into a "new man" were not limited to the school classroom. According to a *Granma* editorial of 24 April more than 140,000 junior and senior high school students and teachers participated in the six-week "School Goes to the Countryside" program which was tested in Camaguey in 1966 and extended to all areas of the island in 1967. In essence the program was intended to combine theory and practice actively in the lives of the students. In an interview with *Granma* on 22 September, UJC head Jaime Crombet said that by the end of 1967, in spite of a serious lack of camp supplies and insufficient cooperation from some administrative organizations, there would be 70,000 young people participating for a two-year period in agricultural and construction programs. At the same time he announced that pregraduation activities for the nation's three universities would include two weeks of agricultural labor on the Isle of Pines, for years the most notable Cuban prison camp, which during 1967 was invaded by young "volunteers" and transformed into the "Isle of Youth." (According to the *New York Times* of 24 September, the 40,000 political prisoners in Cuba, about one-fifth of whom were on the Isle of Pines and most of whom were former Castro followers, were being classified in three categories according to their political attitudes and thereby assigned to varying degrees of hard labor and "political rehabilitation.") The UJC was specially praised for its efforts to overcome the "crime" of "employment of young people in bureaucratic, unproductive work" by directing young persons toward studying, service in the Revolutionary Armed Forces (FAR) and, above all, labor in agriculture" (*Granma*, editorial, 2 March).

Cuban efforts to form the "new man," the "communist man," were not, however, limited to young people. In September 1967 the Conclusions of the National Committee of the CTC proclaimed: "The essential task of our Revolution is to form the communist man, and all that does not aid in this objective ought to be eliminated" (*Juventud Rebelde*, 14 September). A *Granma* commentary of 7 September elaborated on how the Communist man was to be formed:

> Through great educational programs; with mass incorporation into production, by including ample sectors of the people in the work of administration and in the solution of community problems; combating narrow, selfish prejudices and giving priority to factors

which promote a sense of revolutionary honor and social responsibility, which stress the heroic nature of the great work of the Revolution (weekly English edition, 17 September).

Thus the Cuban people were asked to "participate" in their government through "people's courts," "local power" assemblies, and mass meetings, while the government allegedly was moving closer to the masses through attacks on bureaucratic stagnation and simultaneous emphasis on greater responsibility for local leaders. Among the most publicized programs were those involving thousands of "volunteers" for work in agriculture. FMC, UJC, and CTC participation in these programs has already been noted. Employees at state organizations in Havana were expected to devote one week every month to agricultural work according to the "Three and One" plan. A special mass mobilization to "celebrate" the Playa Girón (the so-called Bay of Pigs) victory was carried out between 19 March and 2 April and involved more than 300,000 persons. In some places (for example, Matanzas Province) this "Girón Fortnight" actually continued for a full month. At the end of September more than 150,000 "volunteers" spent several days in the Escambray Mountains planting six million coffee-tree seedlings. On 30 October Fidel Castro inaugurated the "Che Guevara Trailblazers Brigade," an agricultural machinery unit led by officers of the FAR and manned chiefly by soldiers. Castro pointed out on 24 December that up to that time the Brigade had "worked mainly at the cleaning of land for new rice fields" (*ibid.*, 31 December). Throughout the year Castro tried to convince the Cuban people that (as he said on 29 April) work would "never again be an ordeal but rather the most enjoyable, noblest, most creative activity of mankind" (*ibid.*, 7 May).

It was pointed out, shortly after the Girón Fortnight, that such mobilizations also had strictly economic motives (*ibid.*, editorial, 9 April). Several years ago Castro predicted that Cuba would produce 7.5 million metric tons of sugar in 1967, and 10 million in 1970. Thus far, however, production has been erratic and has not reached the projected levels. The 1967 harvest yielded 6,128,287 tons (*Granma*, 26 July; later raised to 6,128,917). This amount has been surpassed only twice in Cuban history (in 1952 and 1961); it was slightly above the 1965 total of 6,050,768 tons and considerably above the 4,455,255 tons achieved in 1966.*

Miguel Martín, the Secretary-General of the CTC, has written that "there are three major factors in agricultural development: development of technical knowledge, adequate use of mechanization and efficiency of agricultural workers." One problem in Cuba, according to Martín, is that "agricultural workers do not average more than 5 or 6 hours' work a day, and the total amount of work done in a workday is very low indeed." (*Granma*, 13 September.)

Cuban agricultural difficulties were aggravated by the misuse, poor maintenance, and improper repair of existing machinery, a situation much criticized by the INRA and other government organizations. (*Granma*, 16, 17 and 18 March; *Bohemia*, 12 May). Under these conditions the mass mobilization of "volunteers" appeared to offer a temporary economic solution which at the same time would serve to advance the ideological or revolutionary consciousness of the people; however, although the mobilizations do increase the agricultural manpower, they also put many inexperienced and inefficient workers in the fields and simultaneously disrupt much of the rest of the Cuban economy.

Important among the approaches to developing the "revolutionary consciousness" of the Cuban people during 1967 was the heavy emphasis placed on moral incentives. Although Fidel Castro frequently spoke out on this theme, its most articulate expositor was probably Miguel Martín. In an article in *Granma* on 20 September, Martín wrote that past "socialist competition" in Cuba had been based on "material incentives, glorification of individualism, and bureaucratic methods." The new method, represented by the "Advance Guard Movement," expected the worker to "see his production activity from the social point of view, as his contribution to the collective work of the people for the construction of the Communist Society." Such a worker would be characterized by: "overfulfillment of the production plan, no absenteeism, no payment for overtime, positive attitude toward improvement, voluntary labor, and participation in the social life of the work center."

On 20 February at the Cubana steel plant, during a speech honoring steel workers who had done

*The 1968 yield, in large part as a result of poor weather, is expected to be only slightly above 5,000,000 tons (*Granma*, weekly English edition, 30 June 1968).

outstanding work in the construction of agricultural equipment, Fidel Castro asserted that many technicians, bound hand and foot by their reliance on "laws" and precedents established in the past, did not believe that revolutionary goals could be fulfilled. Citing a department head in an agency concerned with livestock who doubted figures on the number of cows in the artificial insemination program, Castro concluded that this technician, "did not know, nor could he know, that in a Revolution and with revolutionary methods all indices can be broken" (*Granma,* weekly English edition, 26 February). An example of this "revolutionary consciousness" was reportedly shown by the workers at the Nico López oil refinery who, in honor of May Day, allegedly volunteered about 2,500 hours of extra work in 14 days (*Granma,* 28 April). Similarly, on 20 September *Granma* announced that more than 1,600 work centers in Havana Province had proclaimed themselves "Territories Free of Overtime Pay."

Dissatisfaction of many workers with current initiative trends was probably the reason for the defeat of 50 per cent of the incumbent low-level union officials (in whose selection the workers have some choice in spite of PCC supervision) in the CTC election in August. The CTC National Committee remarked about the high voter participation (above 80 per cent), called the election "very interesting," and said that it would need to analyze the outcome to determine the causes of the unusually high turnover of officials. (*Juventud Rebelde,* 14 September.)

On 15 October, Fidel Castro announced over Cuban radio and television that all leaders of the revolution accepted "unanimously and without the slightest doubt" the death in Bolivia of Ernesto "Che" Guevara. On the same day the Council of Ministers resolved that "as many activities be carried out as may be conducive to perpetuating his life and his example in the memory of future generations," and the Central Committee of the PCC established a commission of four (Juan Almeida, Ramiro Valdés, Rogelio Acevedo, and Alfonso Zayas) to orient and direct this effort. In honor of Guevara, the Council of Ministers proclaimed 8 October, the day of Guevara's capture (he died on 9 October), as "The Day of the Heroic Guerrilla." (*Granma,* weekly English edition, 22 October.)

There followed the most concerted idolization campaign in modern Cuban history. Guevara, who had frequently called for the education of the "new man," the "communist man of the future," was himself made the model for all to emulate. His writings were reprinted in *Granma* and other Cuban publications, and praise of this "most complete man of his time" (as Jean-Paul Sartre called him; *ibid.,* 13 December) highlighted all publications and speeches. In a eulogy delivered on 18 October, Fidel Castro asserted: "Che brought the ideas of Marxism-Leninism to their freshest, purest, most revolutionary expression. . . . When an example of a proletarian internationalist is sought, that example, high above any other, will be Che's example! . . . If we wish to express what we want the men of future generations to be, we must say: Let them be like Che!" (*Ibid.,* 29 October.)

In general, Fidel Castro and the Cuban government seem to see their primary successes as being achieved in education, health, defense, and perseverance in the face of difficulties. The Cuban educational program, whether viewed narrowly as dealing with schools or broadly as related to the development of the "new, communist man," is a leading item in the Cuban budget. This program, which has increasingly scorned and turned from the experiences of the Soviet and European communist parties, has been noted already. Efforts to extend hospital care, control infectious diseases, and train medical personnel have also cost a great deal and have received widespread praise (*Granma,* 25 January and 12 December) as well as some severe criticism (*ibid.,* 4 April 1968). The government is particularly proud to have built up, from almost nothing in 1959, what it considers a highly competent military force, capable of carrying out regular and irregular warfare. On 26 July 1967 Fidel Castro asserted: "In case of any aggression [Cuba] is prepared to arm more than a half a million soldiers" (*Granma,* weekly English edition, 30 July). The development of the Revolutionary Armed Forces and other aspects of this military power has been achieved both by direct aid from foreign communist parties, especially the CPSU, and by major allocations from the Cuban budget (which itself is increased by an estimated equivalent of US $1 million a day from the Soviet Union).

On 26 July Castro declared also: "The great lesson of our history [is that] the idea of defeat can never be accepted." Castro and other Cuban officials frequently referred to what they considered to be Cuban accomplishments in the four fields mentioned above, and in agriculture, technology, and so on, pointing out that all of this had been done in the face of the US "blockade" and the political and economic opposition of all Latin American countries (except Mexico). Castro continued to claim that Cuban accomplishments as a whole constituted a further success as a blow against the far-reaching evil of "US imperialism."

Many problems, in any case, remain. On 27 July Castro declared:

> Some people think that it is difficult to make the revolution, that it is difficult to oust the oligarchies, and we tell them: no, that is not the most difficult part. The most difficult part, after you have overthrown the oligarchies which represent reactionary, imperialist interests, will be to oust underdevelopment, to oust poverty, to oust the age-old misery, amid the chaos which is capitalist society in every sense. That is the most difficult problem. (*Ibid.*, 6 August.)

In its struggle to overcome underdevelopment, Castro said on 28 September, the revolution developed by stages:

> the years of ignorance, the years of agony, the years of extremely hard work and the years of triumph ... next year will mark the stage of transition between the years of agony and the years of intensive work, with available resources to carry out this work (*ibid.*, 8 October).

Not denying that the revolutionaries have made many mistakes in the past; Castro has asserted that failures were inevitable for those who were inexperienced in running a government. On 29 April he observed that people might well marvel "at how the revolutionaries, having been a bunch of ignoramuses, did not sink the island" (*ibid.*, 7 May).

Few of the present problems faced in Cuba, however, are said to be the fault of "revolutionary ignoramuses." Instead they are generally either denied or attributed to bad weather, inadequate manpower, counterrevolutionaries, a lingering petty-bourgeois mentality, profiteering by small farmers and businessmen, the CIA and the USA generally, bureaucracy, and even on occasion the influence of certain socialist countries. When admitted, they are followed by promises of a coming utopia.

Promises for the future make up an important part of most of Castro's speeches on domestic affairs. For example, on 18 May he admitted that "the housing problem has not been solved" and went on to say:

> The Revolution has been building homes—not many, unfortunately. Some 7, 8, 10 thousand ... [But] beginning in 1970, 100 thousand families will receive homes every year; in 10 years that will be one million. (*Ibid.*, 28 May.)

On the same day, and on many other occasions as well, he spoke in glowing terms of a future society where there would no longer be any lazy farmers or profiteers, and where all men would work out of habit, not for money but for the good of society. Money, that "vile intermediary between man and man's products," as well as the ration book, a sign of scarcity, would be unnecessary. Fruits, vegetables, milk, and coffee would be free and everyone would have all his needs satisfied.

**International Views and Positions.** Cuban international views and positions in 1967 were enunciated in the speeches of Fidel Castro and some other Cuban leaders, in official PCC statements, usually published in *Granma,* and in the report of the Cuban delegation to the Organization of Latin American Solidarity (OLAS) conference. The writings of "Che" Guevara and Régis Debray also generally reflected the Cuban view on most matters they touched upon.

Fidel Castro is undoubtedly the most unorthodox Communist at present in control in any country. Since his rise to power his actions and words have frequently come into conflict with Marxism as formulated by Marx or Lenin, or by the Soviet or Communist Chinese leaders of today. During some of his years at the head of the Cuban government he has not drawn attention to these differences; during some years he has. In 1967, most emphatically, he openly and forcefully took positions and actions which put him at odds with his most powerful ally, the Soviet Union.

On several occasions Castro attacked many of his foreign comrades (though usually not by name) with the charge that the Communist movement had taken on many of the characteristics of a religion. On 10 August, addressing the OLAS conference in Havana, he said that the literature of the movement often repeats

> the same old clichés, phraseology and verbiage that have been repeated for 35 years .... In what way is this different from a catechism ... a litany ... a rosary? [And] worse than the phrases are the ideas they often encompass. (*Ibid.*, 20 August.)

**Bourgeois and Socialist Revolutions.** Continuing his 10 August address, Castro said that one of the most pernicious ideas in Marxist writings today, as far as Latin America was concerned, was that regarding the national bourgeoisie:

> This idea is an absurdity on this continent; how much paper, how many phrases, how much empty talk have been wasted while waiting for a liberal, progressive anti-imperialist bourgeoisie.

The report of the Cuban delegation to the OLAS conference provided the most systematic critique of this sort during 1967. While admitting that it would be "sectarian and unacceptable" to assert that the bourgeoisie could play no positive role in the struggle against imperialism, the report, nevertheless, concluded:

> The revolution will be led by the working people. In Latin America—and this is at the bottom of the problem—the bourgeois revolution did not occur and ... will not occur. There will be no bourgeois revolution in Latin America.

The report thus was in agreement with the opinion of "Che" Guevara, stated in his April "Message to the Peoples of the World," which attacked such reformers as Chilean President Eduardo Frei: "Either a socialist revolution or a make-believe revolution."

**On Contradictions.** On 11 August, the day after the conclusion of the OLAS conference, Fidel Castro met informally with a few sympathetic Latin American journalists, including one from the Chilean review *Punto Final*. According to the Chilean reporter, the Cuban Prime Minister stated that there were at present two "fundamental contradictions" in the world, the first between "imperialism" and the "socialist camp," and the second between the underdeveloped world and "imperialism." Taking a position wholly at variance with that of orthodox Communists, Castro concluded that the latter contradiction was "the more fundamental." (*Punto Final*, 1-15 September.)

**Peaceful Coexistence.** One widely distributed rejection of a key strategic position of the Soviet Union, that of "peaceful coexistence," was included in the May statement of the Central Committee of the PCC:

> If the concept of peaceful coexistence between States with different social systems does not guarantee the integrity, sovereignty and independence of all countries alike, large and small, it is essentially opposed to the principles of proletarian internationalism. What kind of peace are the Vietnamese enjoying? What kind of coexistence is the United States practicing with that country? (*Granma*, weekly English edition, 21 May.)

The most obvious rejection of peaceful coexistence, however, is the whole thrust of Cuban foreign policy with its emphasis on armed struggle throughout Latin America and the world.

**Guerrilla Warfare and "True Revolutionaries."** The cornerstone of Cuban foreign policy during 1967, enunciated officially by Fidel Castro and unofficially by "Che" Guevara and Régis Debray, was the conviction that sooner or later armed struggle would be necessary for the establishment of socialism in every Latin America country. Working on the assumption that armed struggle would be profitable immediately in most countries, these spokesmen called for the waging of guerrilla warfare throughout the continent. During the year, and in particular at the OLAS conference, the most popular slogan (taken from Castro's 1962 "Second Declaration of Havana") was "The Duty of Every Revolutionary Is to Make Revolution." On several occasions Castro admitted that it would be "dogmatic and sectarian" to insist on the necessity of immediate armed struggle everywhere. In a few countries, the Cuban Report to OLAS noted, peaceful forms of struggle could be revolutionary, but only if the objective was set forth of "supporting the armed struggle that is carried on in other countries and preparing the inevitable revolutionary confrontation in one's own country."

For Castro the "true revolutionary" in Latin America was distinguished by his attitude toward guerrilla warfare and his efforts to move the masses. Thus the true revolutionary either participated in and supported guerrilla warfare in his country and elsewhere, or supported guerrilla warfare abroad while actively preparing for the use of this method at home. The "false revolutionary" (for Castro this designation applied to most of the Communists in Latin America, and in particular the leadership of the Communist Party of Venezuela) opposed, held back, or actively betrayed the guerrilla activities in his country and to varying degrees tried to cooperate with the "oligarchs" and "imperialists." The false revolutionary was satisfied to put off positive revolutionary action until after the masses as a whole had acquired adequate awareness. Castro emphasized the importance of revolutionary initiative in an interview published in an Italian communist weekly when he stated that a true revolutionary could probably start a revolution in a given country even if favorable objective conditions were missing. (In Cuba, he said, not all objective conditions had been favorable.) Conversely, if a country had altogether favorable objective conditions, but lacked true revolutionaries, there would be no revolution. (*Rinascita,* 22 September.)

According to Castro, the guerrilla force, which was bound to be the nucleus of the revolutionary movement, must unite in itself both political and military commands. Above all, political leadership must not be confined to party officials in the cities. Yet, the Cuban Report to OLAS stated clearly:

> The fact that the revolutionary army is organized in the countryside ... does not mean that the leadership of the struggle should not be oriented by the ideology of the proletariat. On the contrary, the ideas of the proletariat, and even its best cadres, should be at the head of this struggle.

On 13 March Castro observed that not all parties of the proletariat had taken their obligations to heart. Thus he warned:

> If in any country those who call themselves communists do not know how to fulfill their duty, we will support those who, without calling themselves communists, conduct themselves like real communists in action and in struggle. For every true revolutionary, who bears within him the revolutionary spirit, revolutionary vocation, will always come to Marxism! ... Many, the immense majority of those who today proudly call themselves Marxist-Leninists, arrived at Marxism-Leninism by way of the revolutionary struggle (*Granma,* weekly English edition, 19 March).

Many of these ideas were treated in detail in Régis Debray's *Revolution in the Revolution?* (published in Havana by the government-backed Casa de las America; English translation published in New York by the Grove Press, 1967). According to the Introduction to the Cuban edition, Debray visited revolutionaries in several Latin American countries and spent more than a year in Cuba just before the book's publication in January 1967. While in Cuba he had access to numerous unpublished documents and talked at length with Fidel Castro and other revolutionary leaders. In the Introduction to the French edition Debray stated that the ideas put forward were, above all, those of Fidel Castro.

Debray's declared aim in this book was to disprove the "dangerous cliché"—which he had once held—that the Cuban revolution could not be repeated. According to Debray, the technical, tactical, and strategic truths of the Cuban revolution provided a revolutionary model for other Latin American countries seeking national liberation. The Cubans had proceeded "by means of the more or less slow building up, through guerrilla warfare carried out in suitably chosen rural zones, of a *mobile strategic force,* nucleus of a people's army and of a future socialist state" (Grove edition, p.24; emphasis in original). Much of the book is devoted to a condemnation of *"imported* political conceptions, disguised as military lines and applied to historic conditions very different from those in which they had their roots. We have in mind: the concept of armed self-defense; a particular way of interpreting armed propaganda and the guerrilla base; and finally, the subjection of the guerrilla force to the party" (pp. 24-25; emphasis in original). According to Debray, Fidel Castro was able to lead the Cuban revolution so effectively because he avoided these "imports," and invented, "on the spot and out of his own experience, principles of a military doctrine in conformity with the terrain" (p. 20), and Latin Americans today should follow his example.

Near the end of his study, Debray concluded:

> The Latin American revolution and its vanguard, the Cuban revolution, have thus made a decisive contribution to international revolutionary experience and to Marxism-Leninism.

> *Under certain conditions, the political and the military are not separate, but form one organic whole, consisting of the people's army, whose nucleus is the guerrilla army. The vanguard party can exist in the form of the guerrilla* foco *itself. The guerrilla force is the party in embryo.* (p. 106; emphasis in original.)

This emphasis on military over political concerns does not imply the total absence of a unified political outlook among the guerrillas, however, for Debray states that, in contrast to Cuba, the ideology of the new guerrilla commands is clearly Marxist (p. 107), and the majority of the fighters come from communist ranks (p. 114). Those whose ideological background is incomplete will learn during the struggle: "The best teacher of Marxism-Leninism is the enemy, in face-to-face confrontation during the people's war" (p. 111). When Debray concludes that "at the present juncture, the principal stress must be laid on the development of guerrilla warfare and not on the strengthening of existing parties or the creation of new parties" (p. 116), he is faithfully stating Fidel Castro's line during 1967.

**"Che" Guevara.** "Che" Guevara wrote two important documents in 1967 relating to the foreign policy of the Cuban government—"Message to the Peoples of the World" (see *Documents*) and his *Diary* (released by the Cuban government in July 1968; authorized Cuban English trans. by Bantam Books, N.Y., 1968; see also James, *Complete Bolivian Diaries*). The "Message" discussed the Latin American role in what Guevara considered the expanding national liberation movement of the world: in order to force the USA to overextend and thus weaken herself, Latin America had as its task "to create a Second or a Third Vietnam, or the Second and Third Vietnam of the world." Guevara saw a need for "international proletarian armies," composed of men who had become "effective, violent, selective and cold killing machines" and were prepared for long and arduous struggles before the ultimate victory. The *Diary* is an impressive account of the complete failure in Bolivia of an inter-American guerrilla band attempting to carry out the policies advocated by Castro, Debray, and Guevara himself.

**Exportation of Revolution.** Before 1967, Cuban leaders argued that revolution could not be exported and refused to acknowledge officially that they were training and in other ways supporting revolutionaries from Latin America and other parts of the world.* On 18 May 1967, however, after several Cubans were found participating in the guerrilla landing on the coast of Venezuela, the Central Committee of the PCC issued a statement which said:

> We are accused of helping the revolutionary movement, and we, quite so, are giving and
> will continue to give help to all revolutionary movements that struggle against imperialism
> in any part of the world, whenever they request it.

The statement argued that the USA was the real aggressor in Latin America and that Cuban help was merely to enable Latin Americans to liberate themselves from imperialism and its puppets. Yet the Guevara-led insurgency in Bolivia was clearly an effort not to aid foreign revolutionaries but to export a revolution from Cuba. In his Introduction to Guevara's *Diary*, Fidel Castro wrote that "Che" wanted beside him a "small nucleus of experienced guerrilla fighters, almost all of whom had been his comrades in the Sierra Maestra." The *Diary* itself shows that much of the time the majority of the guerrillas in Bolivia were Cubans (17 out of about 25 in early June) and that there was no support from the peasants and little from any other group in Bolivia.

**United Nations.** According to the 18 May statement of the PCC Central Committee, the UN had "in general served as an instrument to validate the crimes and villainy of Yankee imperialism." On 28 September, however, Fidel Castro declared that the UN does provide a platform from which to condemn the US leaders to their faces in the presence of many delegates who oppose imperialism.

**Organization of American States.** On 13 October Cuban Foreign Minister Raúl Roa told the UN General Assembly:

> I will not commit the offense of taking the OAS seriously. It would be practically
> impossible to find a more disreputable organization. This would-be regional organism of

---

*According to Carl T. Rowan in the *Washington Post* (18 June 1967), the Cuban General Directorate of Intelligence, which has a staff of Soviet advisors, "is now spending $1.1 million a month to support stepped-up guerrilla warfare in Latin America," and "most of the money is [used] to train insurgents, with some 3,000 latinos already trained in Havana and returned to their native countries since Castro came to power." See also an article by Juan de Onis, *New York Times,* 2 August.

the U.S. was, from its very inception, an instrument of the U.S. Government's foreign policy in Latin America and is today its Ministry of Colonies. (*Granma,* weekly English edition, 12 November.)

On 18 July *Granma* published an editorial on the "yelping dogs" of the OAS and "their masters, Yankee imperialism." Fidel Castro in particular, however, has always been very careful to exclude Mexico from all of his attacks on the OAS member-states.

**Middle East Conflict.** On 7 June the Cuban Revolutionary Government issued a declaration stating:

The United Arab Republic and other Arab nations have been the object of a sneak attack by the Israeli Armed Forces, which, instigated and backed by imperialism, have committed this act of aggression against the liberty and integrity of the Arab countries (*ibid.,* 11 June).

Drawing a lesson from the crisis, a *Granma* editorial stated on 29 May: "The events which have been unfolding show more and more each day that imperialism can only be halted by firmness" (*ibid.,* 4 June). On 3 July the Foreign Minister of Iraq stated before the UN General Assembly that the Arab nations supported the Cuban amendment to the nonaligned nations' draft resolution which called for condemnation of Israel as an aggressor along with her "imperialist accomplices." Although Cuba was critical of joint Soviet-US efforts to arrange a cease-fire through the UN, Castro was quoted in an Italian communist weekly as saying that the Arab society and countries had neither the cohesion and strength nor the real commitment to wage the people's war which could have destroyed Israel. (*Rinascita,* 29 September.) Cuba did not break off relations with Israel.

**Vietnam War.** During 1967 Cuba gave unequivocal support to the forces opposing the South Vietnamese government. On 2 January Fidel Castro said: "The battle in Vietnam is being waged for all humanity, and Vietnam, victoriously and heroically standing up to the most powerful, aggressive and hated imperialists in the world, is also waging a battle for us." He then declared 1967 "The Year of Heroic Vietnam." (*Granma,* weekly English edition, 8 January.) Near the end of the year Foreign Minister Raúl Roa called South Vietnam "the vanguard of the oppressed, subjugated peoples of Asia, Africa and Latin America" (*ibid.,* 24 December). In its editorial on 23 March, the Havana daily *El Mundo* declared that all Cuban people approved the statements on Vietnam by their government. Messages of support for the National Liberation Front of South Vietnam (NLFSV) and North Vietnam were issued throughout the year by Fidel Castro and other government leaders and by groups such as the Cuban Committee of Solidarity with South Vietnam (Melba Hernández, president) and by various mass organizations. Four Cubans testified at the Russell Vietnam Tribunal in Stockholm in May.

Cuban newspapers and magazines gave extensive coverage to events in Vietnam, provided commentary by Vietnamese leaders such as Vo Nguyen Giap (*Juventud Rebelde,* 3 October) and foreign correspondents like Wilfred Burchett (*Granma,* 11 March), and reproduced statements and programs of the NLFSV (*Granma,* 15 and 16 February, 8 September). Articles on the bravery of Vietnamese women appeared frequently in the press; a speech by FMC President Vilma Espín on "International Women's Day" was covered in *Granma* (9 March) in an article entitled "We Will Always Follow the Example of the Vietnamese Women." A sugar cane cutting brigade was named "Heroic Vietnam." "Solidarity with Vietnam" weeks were celebrated in March and December. Frequent assertions that the Cuban people were ready to "shed their blood . . . fighting at the side of the Vietnamese for their full liberation" (*Granma,* editorial, 18 July) were gratefully acknowledged in *Nhan Dan,* the daily organ of the (North) Vietnamese Workers' Party (VWP), (quoted over Radio Hanoi on 22 September), adding: "Large numbers of young [Cuban] men and women are ready to go and fight as volunteers beside the Vietnamese people."

**South Vietnam.** On 30 June *Granma* announced that Cuba had established a diplomatic mission accredited to the Central Committee of the NLFSV. On 22 September Radio Hanoi broadcast a large part of the text of a commentary in *Nhan Dan* on the recently established Cuban-NLFSV relations, including:

Cuba is the first country in the world to accept a permanent mission of the NLFSV, to found a national committee for solidarity with the people of South Vietnam, and to raise the South Vietnam permanent mission in Cuba to the level of an official diplomatic organ. Cuba is also the first country in the world to establish a diplomatic mission and appoint an ambassador to the NLFSV.

On 21 April *Granma* published a message (dated 16 April) from Nguyen Huu Tho, Chairman of the Presidium of the NLFSV, to Fidel Castro and Osvaldo Dorticós, which declared: "The great victory at Playa Girón marked the first and most ignominious defeat for the United States imperialists in Latin America." One NLFSV fighting unit was designated the "Glorious Girón Battalion." A message to Raúl Castro from the commander of this unit indicated that the battalion was launching a movement entitled "Three Months for Magnifying the Victory of Girón," to last from 19 April to 26 July, "commemorating the two historic anniversaries of the heroic Cuban people's armed struggle." (*Granma*, weekly English edition, 30 April.)

Several groups of South Vietnamese visited Cuba during the year, including a delegation of the NLFSV and Vietnamese women in January, a song-and-dance ensemble from the South Vietnamese Liberation Army in July, and a seven-member delegation of observers from the NLFSV at the OLAS conference in August. (See also *Vietnam: Republic of Vietnam.*)

**North Vietnam.** The Cuban news media devoted considerable space to North Vietnamese participation in and analysis of the Vietnam War (e.g., *Granma*, 3 February), and also published some Vietnamese commentary on Latin America (e.g., *ibid.*, 16 February). Ho Chi Minh, Truong Chinh, Pham Van Dong, and other leaders of the VWP sent messages to Cuba on almost all Cuban anniversaries (e.g., Independence Day, Playa Girón, and 26 July), and on special occasions such as the opening of the OLAS conference.

Hoang Quoc Viet, a Central Committee member of the VWP, led a nine-member delegation to the 26th of July celebrations and the OLAS conference. Between 13 and 20 September there was a widely publicized visit by a delegation led by Le Thanh Nghi, a member of the VWP Political Bureau, and including two alternate members of the Central Committee of the VWP, Ly Ban, Vice-Minister of Foreign Trade, and Dinh Duc Thien, Chief of the General Department of Logistics of the People's Army of Vietnam. During their visit they signed a trade protocol for 1968 and other agreements contributing to the "combative solidarity that exists between the peoples of Cuba and Vietnam in their common struggle against US imperialist aggression." (*Granma*, weekly English edition, 1 October). In an interview of 17 September on Havana television, Le Thanh Nghi commented on the Vietnam war, the long-standing Vietnamese-Cuban friendship, and other topics. He said also:

> The struggle of the Latin American peoples—which is becoming stronger each day in Venezuela, Colombia, Bolivia, Guatemala, etc.,—has strong bonds with, gives active support to and is a direct ally of the struggle of the Vietnamese people against the Yankee imperialists (*ibid.*, 24 September).

The North Vietnamese ambassador in Cuba during 1967 was Ngo Mau.

Although no Cuban visitors to North Vietnam in 1967 matched the high-level delegation of November 1966 (which included three Political Bureau members—Dorticós, Raúl Castro, and Del Valle), there were nonetheless several of considerable importance. As General Secretary of the Afro-Asian-Latin American People's Solidarity Organization (AALAPSO), PCC Central Committee member Osmany Cienfuegos led a delegation from that organization to Hanoi in late February and early March. Cienfuegos spoke at the "Week of Solidarity with Vietnam" meeting called by the Tricontinental Organization for Solidarity with Vietnam. The AALAPSO and the Vietnam Committee for Afro-Asian Solidarity issued a joint declaration at the end of the visit. (*Ibid.*, 26 March.) In November a Cuban military delegation headed by Belarmino Castilla Mas, a member of the PCC Central Committee and Chief of Staff of the Cuban Revolutionary Armed Forces, visited North Vietnam and North Korea. On 22 November the VWP daily *Nhan Dan* carried an editorial on the delegation's visit entitled "A Wholehearted Salute to our Cuban Comrades-in-Arms." Among the activities of the delegation was a call at the permanent mission of the NLFSV in Hanoi. (*Ibid.*, 3 December.) The Cuban ambassador in North Vietnam was Major Julio García Olivera. (See also *Vietnam: Democratic Republic of Vietnam.*)

**China, the Soviet Union, and the Sino-Soviet Dispute.** During 1967 the Cuban government carefully maintained a position of neutrality in the Sino-Soviet dispute. Generally the split was not mentioned at all; occasionally, as in Guevara's "Message," it was vigorously condemned for destroying socialist solidarity and thus leaving the underdeveloped world (especially Vietnam) unnecessarily vulnerable in a time of intense "imperialist" activity. Cuban neutrality, however, did not imply a particularly conciliatory attitude toward either of the major communist powers.

**Cuba and China**. The deterioration of Sino-Cuban relations, which had begun in 1965, came into the open with Fidel Castro's speech at the Tricontinental Conference on 2 January 1966. Although the Chinese generally tried to play the conflict down, the Cubans greatly aggravated it by infrequent but severe attacks, most importantly those in Castro's speech on 13 March 1966 and in a full-page article published in *Granma* on 31 August. The latter reproduced many releases from the New China News Agency (NCNA) on the "achievements" of the Great Proletarian Cultural Revolution and the Thought of Chairman Mao, and commented that they had made China the laughingstock of the whole world. Further, *Granma* proclaimed, they even provided information the imperialists could use to ridicule not only China but, however unjustifiably, the very ideas of communism itself.

During 1967, however, China was virtually ignored by the Cuban news media and by all political leaders in their public statements. What little the Cuban people could learn about events concerning China came from radio broadcasts originating outside Cuba (especially the Soviet Union), from occasional comments made by foreign visitors to Cuba which were reported by the Cuban press (for those of a North Korean correspondent see *North Korea*), and from a few noncommunist sources available in Havana.

Although the Chinese ambassador to Cuba was recalled in January, and the Cuban ambassador to China was withdrawn shortly thereafter, modest diplomatic contacts were maintained. The Cuban reception in Peking on the eighth anniversary of the Cuban revolution was attended by a fairly impressive Chinese delegation headed by Vice-Premier Ch'en I (NCNA, 2 January). The Havana reception in honor of the eighteenth anniversary of the People's Republic of China, given by the Chinese chargé d'affaires, was attended by a Cuban delegation led by Foreign Minister Raúl Roa (*Granma*, 2 October). On at least three occasions (4 August, 5 September, and 2 October) the NCNA reported enthusiastic pro-Mao meetings of more than 400 Chinese nationals in Cuba.

Sino-Cuban trade apparently experienced none of the difficulties which were so widely publicized in 1966. On 21 March the NCNA reported the signing in Peking of a new trade protocol which indicated a continuing emphasis on the shipment of Cuban sugar to China and Chinese rice to Cuba.

Although on the surface it might appear that the Chinese and the Cubans would agree in their encouragement of guerrilla wars throughout Latin America, this was not the case. To a certain extent this was because the Chinese alienated Castro by appealing to the so-called Jacobin leftists, whose allegiance the Cuban leader had sought with considerable success in his effort to become the fountainhead of a continental socialist revolution. Also, the Chinese have tried, often successfully, to win support in their dispute with the USSR by splitting off the more belligerent (or merely discontented) members of the existing Latin American communist parties. These splinter groups, however, have played only a limited role in guerrilla struggles, in part because they have taken an overriding interest in their opposition to "Soviet revisionism," and in part (for some of them) because they were aware that they still lacked resources for beginning guerrilla wars against the existing governments. In Fidel Castro's view, however, they appeared to be "sectarians" or even "false revolutionaries."

The disagreement over when and how to engage in guerrilla warfare was made clear by the Chinese reaction to the Guevara-led insurgency in Bolivia. The Chinese published statements by the small, pro-Chinese Bolivian Communist Party during 1967 calling for armed struggle and people's war, but they did not report "Che" Guevara's guerrilla efforts. A Bolivian follower of Guevara claims that the pro-Chinese party even expelled one of its members for actively cooperating with the guerrillas (Inti Peredo in a special supplement to *Tricontinental*, Havana, July 1968). The Chinese and Albanian communist parties were among the few which did not send a message to Cuba after Guevara's death. Guevara's fate was not even reported in China until January 1968, when the Director of the Information Department of the *People's Daily* branded him an "adventurist" (see China). A comment in the

*Ceylon Daily News* (5 November) by the leader of the pro-Chinese Communist Party of Ceylon said that the Cuban theory of guerrilla warfare was "fundamentally the romantic and petty-bourgeois ideology which places its main reliance on a band of swashbuckling 'Three Musketeers' type bravados who are expected to perform miraculous exploits against terrific odds." The first open Chinese comment on "persons like Régis Debray" came in Anna Louise Strong's periodic Peking-supported *Letter from China* (22 February 1968):

> According to them, there is no need to organize the masses, to build a party, to build an army, to study theory, to organize a broad front, to make a safe area or prepare for protracted war—all that is needed is to send in a few men with guns. Such notions, if followed, lead to serious reverses for the revolutionary people.

The Cubans, on the other hand, besides following some domestic policies which have parallels in Mao's "cultural revolution," have found themselves in substantial agreement with China on many important international issues, as in their contempt for the concept of peaceful coexistence in a world where many countries are the victims of "imperialist aggression," criticism of Soviet-bloc willingness to give financial and technical aid to existing Latin American governments, displeasure over Soviet-US cooperation in the UN during the Middle East crisis, and opposition to international agreements on the banning or testing of nuclear weapons.

In sum, the Cubans and the Chinese took similar stands much more often than not, though the Cubans have not drawn attention to this fact. The two countries have been kept apart primarily by: their disagreements over a complex of problems surrounding the waging of guerrilla warfare; Castro's interest in having Cuba be the vanguard of Latin American revolution, as opposed to Mao's efforts to promote his "Thought" and the Cultural Revolution (domestically and internationally), while winning foreign allies in the Sino-Soviet dispute; their relative lack of economic importance to each other; and Cuba's need to keep on good enough terms with the USSR to guarantee the continuation of Soviet economic and military aid.

**Cuba and the Soviet Union.** Soviet visitors to Cuba during 1967 included several CPSU Central Committee members, along with specialists in the peaceful use of atomic energy, architects, maritime officials, and so on. All arrived with little fanfare, however, and carried out their business relatively unnoticed.

The visit of Alexei Kosygin between 26 and 30 June marked the first time a Soviet Prime Minister had been to Cuba. Press coverage and popular reaction to Kosygin's arrival and activities were significant but not overly enthusiastic. (They did not begin to approach the enthusiasm shown for North Korean official Choi Yong-kon when he arrived in November.) Kosygin did not address the Cuban people as Mikoyan had done in 1962 and Gromyko in 1965. According to *Pravda* (1 July), a number of unspecified subjects were discussed by the Soviet leader and his hosts "with complete frankness"—thus suggesting that little agreement was reached. No joint communique was issued after the talks. Press reports indicate that Kosygin's departure was more cordial than his arrival, however, and Castro told an Italian Communist that Kosygin was "a profoundly serious man, a man of principles—not like Khrushchev" (*Rinascita,* 29 September).

Although some Cubans, including an estimated 2,500 students, were in the Soviet Union during 1967, their activities were given almost no attention by the Cuban news media. The only high-level visit planned for the year—the attendance of President Dorticós at the Moscow celebrations of the fiftieth anniversary of the October Revolution—did not materialize. The decision to send José Ramón Machado, the little-known Cuban Health Minister, was evidently made at the last moment and was possibly Castro's reaction to several attacks on the OLAS conference (and indirectly on Cuba) published in *Pravda* by pro-Soviet Latin American Communists Rodolfo Ghioldi and Luis Corvalán. The Cuban ambassador in Moscow, Raúl García Pelaez, even stayed away from N. V. Podgorny's reception in commemoration of the anniversary of the Bolshevik revolution (*New York Times,* 7 and 8 November).

Very little news of events in the Soviet Union was carried in either *Granma* or *Juventud Rebelde*; coverage in *El Mundo* was more extensive, though still limited.

The most revered Russian in Cuban eyes during 1967 was Vladimir Lenin. He was quoted frequently in the *Granma* editorials on bureaucracy. His *State and Revolution* in particular was referred to as profound and essential for understanding such varied subjects as bureaucracy (Armando Hart, *Granma*, weekly English edition, 14 May) and contemporary Cuba (Régis Debray, interview, *ibid.*, 5 February). Although the *Granma* editorial on the fiftieth anniversary of the October Revolution praised the present economic, political, military, and cultural power of the Soviet Union, its main emphasis was on the accomplishments of Lenin. Central Committee member Fabio Grobart, for many years an important agent in Latin America for the Communist International, gave the main address at the Cuban celebration of the October Revolution on the evening of 6 November. He too devoted much time to Lenin, stating that the people in "the vast majority of Latin American countries" now see that

> ... there is no road except revolution, the responding to reactionary violence with revolutionary violence, the road along which Lenin and the Bolshevik party guided the Russian workers to victory just 50 years ago (*ibid.*, 19 November).

Between 23 October and 9 November *Granma* carried a series of excerpts from Lenin's writings, many with particular stress on such passages as "An oppressed class which does not strive to learn to use arms, to acquire arms, only deserves to be treated like slaves" (*ibid.*, 5 November).

On 2 February *Pravda* announced the signing of the 1967 trade protocol with Cuba. The agreement, reached after three months of discussions, called for an increase in trade of some 23 per cent over 1966, to a total value of $800 million.

Cuba and the Soviet Union have had a number of ideological, strategic, and tactical differences since their close contacts began in 1960. Over the years they have succeeded to varying degrees in overlooking or putting up with these differences because each is of such great importance to the other.

During 1967 Soviet-Cuban relations became increasingly strained, though an open dispute was avoided. Castro, for his part, could not afford to break with the USSR, primarily because his survival was dependent on Soviet military and economic support. Military aid, the extent of which is not known precisely, has helped the Cubans to build a military force much larger and more sophisticated than any other in Latin America. Economic aid in 1967 amounted to about $1 million a day. In addition, the Soviet Union buys the bulk of the Cuban sugar crop at a fixed price of 6 cents per pound (three times the average 1967 market price) in spite of the fact that the USSR is the world's leading sugar producer and could easily supply its domestic needs for this product.

The Soviet Union, for its part, recognizes the value of Cuba as the only communist country in the Western Hemisphere and knows very well that a return of Cuba to the noncommunist world would eliminate the hard-won communist presence in the Americas as well as decrease Soviet prestige around the world. Thus in spite of Castro's propensity to bite the hand that is feeding him (discussed below), the USSR continued to pay many of Cuba's bills throughout 1967.*

Soviet-Cuban attacks and counterattacks, which encompassed a wide range of issues in 1967, were almost always indirect. Cuban charges against the USSR, for example, were usually directed at either pro-Soviet parties in Europe or Latin America (usually the latter, and especially the Communist Party of Venezuela) or socialist countries in general. Soviet responses, often made by the same pro-Soviet parties, were most often aimed at "petty-bourgeois nationalists" or "Maoism and related currents."

Fidel Castro's belief that the fundamental contradiction in the world today is between the underdeveloped world and "imperialism,"—an implicit relegation of the Soviet Union and the socialist world to a secondary position—was attacked by a prominent Soviet professor at an international

---

*Some of the charges made against the "microfaction" (discussed above) would suggest that the Soviet Union may have been trying to apply some pressure on Castro from within the PCC. On the other hand, under certain circumstances, Castro's militancy in Latin America may even be beneficial to the Soviet Union. To the extent that the Russians can disassociate themselves from Castro's words and actions, and can follow their own policy of peaceful coexistence toward some countries in Latin America (such as Colombia and Chile), they will gain indirectly in the international field from any harassment of the United States and its allies carried out by the Cubans and those they support. In the end, much Cuban support for Latin American guerrillas is possible only because of generous Soviet aid, and, on occasion, is transmitted with the cooperation of Soviet personnel.

conference held in Baku on 19-22 September. This viewpoint was described as "essentially a bourgeois theory which splits the international alliance of revolutionary forces," and was called a product of "the Mao Tse-tung group." (Radio Moscow, 20 September.) A similar attack on this "Maoist theory" was made in *Pravda* on 25 October by Rodolfo Ghioldi, a prominent member of the Argentine communist party.

In the same *Pravda* article, without naming Cuba, Ghioldi commented on the assertion that (as Guevara put it) there must be "either a socialist revolution or a make-believe revolution":

> Petty-bourgeois nationalists are also stubbornly insisting it is necessary for Latin American countries to proceed directly to socialist revolutions, spurning the preliminary stages of agrarian, anti-imperialist, and democratic revolutions. In the narrow aspiration to prove the "weakness" of invincible Marxist-Leninist positions they are attempting nothing other than to repudiate the basic proposition of the unity of the world socialist system, of the proletarian movement in capitalist countries, and of the national liberation movement in dependent countries.

The primary conflict which developed during 1967 between Cuba and the pro-Soviet parties in Latin America, and thus indirectly with the Soviet Union itself, revolved around the Cuban insistence that their revolution, and in particular their experience with guerrilla warfare, should serve as a model for revolutions throughout the continent. At the Conference of the Communist Parties of Latin America which met in Havana in November 1964 it was agreed, in the presence of Soviet (but not Chinese) observers, that the decision as to the forms of struggle suitable to a given country should be determined by the party in that country. Even though it did not take Castro long to begin his criticisms of the Latin American parties again, the attacks which came in 1967 were more direct and without precedent in their severity and implications.

An increased belligerency in Havana was indicated in January by the publication of Régis Debray's *Revolution in the Revolution?* This was followed by a speech by the Cuban Prime Minister on 13 March (see *Documents*), one of his longest and most violent of the year, directed primarily at the leaders of the Communist Party of Venezuela, who had recently taken a stand against the use of guerrilla warfare at the present time in their country (see *Venezuela*). Castro's target, however, actually included all the communist parties in Latin America, as his comment that "what will define the Communists on this continent is their attitude toward the guerrilla movement" made clear. The call for guerrilla struggle was given a world-wide character by the publication, in April, of "Che" Guevara's "Message to the Peoples of the World" through the Tricontinental (see *Documents*). The importance of this form of struggle for all of Latin America (with the few concessions mentioned earlier) was emphasized at the OLAS conference in August, both in Fidel Castro's speech on 10 August and in the resolutions adopted by the delegates (for several OLAS reports see *Documents*). The cult of the guerrilla reached its peak after "Che" Guevara (who had been appointed honorary president of the OLAS Conference) was reported dead in Bolivia in October.

One of the few times in which Cuban criticism of the Soviet Union was direct came in an interview Castro gave to Herbert Matthews on 16 October:

> I [wrote Matthews] pointed out that the Soviet Union, Hungary, Bulgaria and other Eastern European countries were seeking commercial accords in Latin America.
>
> "We consider this to be a lack of socialist solidarity," he [Castro] said. "They should not be helping governments that are trying to destroy us."
>
> I remarked that this indicated that Russia and East Europe did not agree with Cuban policies in Latin America, especially the guerrilla campaigns. "Yes," he answered wryly, "it does indicate just that." (*War/Peace Report,* New York, December.)

The Soviet Union used several methods to try to bring the Cubans closer to their own position. Prime Minister Kosygin, who visited Cuba on 26-30 June after his trip to the United States, undoubtedly discussed these problems with Cuban leaders though little agreement seems to have been reached. Another effort was made by Rodney Arismendi, the First Secretary of the Uruguayan Communist Party, who played an important role before, during, and after the OLAS conference trying to smooth over differences between Cuba and the pro-Soviet parties.

The Soviets also publicly but indirectly answered most of the charges leveled at them and their Latin American allies. Chilean Communist Party head Luis Corvalán wrote in *Pravda* on 30 July that any Communist who tried to force his views on another was encouraging disunity among anti-imperialist forces. He also warned specifically against overgeneralization on the basis of the Cuban experience. In a broadcast to Latin America on 8 August, Moscow Radio Peace and Progress attacked the "anti-Soviet speeches from representatives of ultrarevolutionary groups" at the OLAS conference. The broadcast mentioned in particular a speech by Venezuelan guerrilla leader Francisco Prada which covered more than half a page in *Granma* on 3 August. The same broadcast quoted at length from an article in the French communist paper *L'Humanité* which stated that it was "easy to recognize the doctrines sustained by Peking" in the "anti-Soviet diatribes" of certain "tiny leftist groups" at the conference.

On 25 October Rodolfo Ghioldi commented in *Pravda* on those who seek to export revolution:

> Maoism and related currents advertise extreme adventurism, adapting the "offensive theory" to any situation regardless of the presence of objective and subjective conditions. They propose that a revolution can be initiated from the outside and artificially stimulated across the borders, considering the nature of revolution isolated from the process of class struggle in the countries involved.

Here Ghioldi was undoubtedly commenting on the Cuban role in exporting revolution in general and on the Guevara-Cuban leadership of the Bolivian insurgency which had been defeated earlier in the month. Castro acknowledged the presence of Cubans in Bolivia in an offhand manner in his speech on 2 January 1968, and openly in his Introduction to Guevara's *Diary* in July 1968. Ghioldi may also have been alluding to the Cubans captured while landing on the coast of Venezuela in May 1967, whose presence was acknowledged in the 18 May statement of the Central Committee of the PCC.

Another issue which caused friction between Cuba and the USSR was the Soviet effort to expand political and economic relations with the Latin American "oligarchs" Castro had committed himself to overthrowing. Castro's disapproval of this Soviet policy, already expressed before 1967, was more intense in his speech of 13 March. The PCV immediately countered with the charge that Cuba was being inconsistent, in view of Cuban trade with Franco's Spain (*Ultimas Noticias,* Caracas, 17 March). Castro responded at great length on 10 August by saying that he had not condemned *trade* with these countries, but only financial and technical aid, which in effect helped to suppress the guerrillas and the revolution. (In fact he had criticized not only aid but also any efforts to improve relations generally.) In *Pravda* on 27 October Chilean Luis Corvalán praised Soviet efforts to expand economic and trade relations which would "help the independent development of national economies." In the meantime the Soviet Union continued her policies as before.

Cuban attacks on pro-Soviet international organizations, which had occurred in 1966 (for instance on the World Federation of Democratic Youth and the World Council of Peace), continued during 1967. One important conflict came at the Ninth Congress of the International Union of Students (IUS) held in Ulan Bator, Mongolia, from 26 March to 8 April. When the Cuban demand for the ouster of the Union of University Federations of Chile (which had boycotted the Latin American Students' Congress in Havana in 1966) was voted down, the Cuban delegates walked out, taking a large percentage of the other Latin American delegates with them (see *IUS*). The Cubans boycotted the Fifth conference of the Building Workers' Trade Union International in May, asserting that the meeting would be directed more toward builders' affairs than the national liberation struggle. For their part, the Cubans sponsored several international and inter-American meetings which were objectionable to the Russians, including the OLAS conference in August and the Tricontinental Cultural Congress, held in January 1968 but in the planning stage during the last six months of 1967.

Soviet efforts to schedule a world conference of communist parties lost Cuban support during the year. The PCC, which had supported such a conference (though unenthusiastically) at the 1965 consultative meeting in Moscow, was not mentioned in a *Pravda* article on 25 October which listed those parties who were urging that such a conference be held in 1968.

As noted earlier, the Cubans have also criticized the Soviet Union and its allies for the "introduction of some administrative systems and organizational procedures" in Cuba which were "weighted down with bureaucracy" (*Granma* editorial, 1 March), and for their growing use of material rather than moral incentives for workers. A dispute over the possible harmful effect of using Soviet manuals for the training of Cuban Communists was reported in the Italian Communist weekly *Rinascita* (31 December 1966); in the January 1967 issue of the review of the Cuban Schools of Revolutionary Instruction, *Teoría y Práctica*, it was announced that in the future only indigenous manuals would be used.

**North Korea.** The excellent relations which existed between Cuba and the Democratic People's Republic of Korea (DPRK) in 1966 continued, or even became better, during 1967. The Cuban press carried long articles from Korean papers like *Nodong Sinmun* (e.g., *Granma*, 8 May) and by DPRK leaders such as President Kim Il-song (*ibid.*, 24 January), and also articles by Cubans in honor of Korean celebrations (*ibid.*, 9 September). A "Month of Solidarity with the Korean People" began on 25 June, the anniversary of the beginning of the Korean war.

The Koreans devoted considerable attention to Cuban affairs, carrying articles on such anniversaries as those of the Second Declaration of Havana, Playa Girón, and the 26th of July. Kim Il-song and other Korean leaders sent messages to the Cuban leadership on all important occasions. Radio Pyongyang announced on 11 August that the publishing house of the Korean Workers' Party (KWP) had published a collection of Castro's speeches entitled "Cuba Is the Vanguard and Example for the Latin American People." The month between 20 July and 20 August was declared a "Month of Solidarity with the Cuban People."

Delegations of Koreans visited Cuba to attend a wide variety of celebrations, ranging from International Children's Day to May Day. Among the prominent guests were Ri Chang-song, DPRK Vice-Minister of Culture, in February; Yun Ki-pak, Minister of General Education, who led a delegation of five to the OLAS conference in August; Yu Song-ui, Vice-Minister of Foreign Trade, in August and September; and Choe Yong-kon, a member of the Political Bureau of the KWP and President of the Presidium of the Supreme People's Assembly, in November. In Choe Yong-kon's delegation were Pak Song-chol, member of the Political Bureau of the Central Committee of the KWP, Deputy Prime Minister, and Minister of Foreign Affairs; Li Min-su, member of the Central Committee of the KWP; Major General Chong O-tae, Assistant Director of the General Bureau for Political Affairs of the People's Army of Korea; and Kim Yun-son, Assistant Director of the Foreign Relations Department of the KWP.

The visit by Choe Yong-kon and other Korean officials between 10 and 17 November was one of the most publicized events of the year in Cuba. *Granma* devoted twice as much space (6 1/2 pages) to Korea on the day the delegation arrived as it did to the Soviet Union during the entire visit of Prime Minister Kosygin. Similarly, the joint report issued on 19 November was in striking contrast to the *Pravda* account of Soviet-Cuban talks. It said:

> The two parties exchanged opinions on problems of common interest and other international questions. They arrived at absolutely identical viewpoints. (*Granma*, weekly English edition, 26 November.)

On 15 November *Granma* published Choe Yong-kon's answers to a number of questions relating to Korea, Vietnam, Latin America, and "US imperialism." The essence of Korean-Cuban harmony was seen in his comment:

> Che Guevara's idea of creating one, two, three, many Vietnams is a revolutionary idea. The more countries that arise and struggle against Yankee imperialism in the world as Vietnam is doing, the better, for this will accelerate the development of world revolution. (Weekly English edition, 26 November.)

An editorial in the KWP daily *Nodong Sinmun* on 16 November emphasized the similarity between Cuban and North Korean views. It noted that while large communist states had normal relations with the "imperialists," the latter were actively trying to "swallow up" small communist countries, and declared that "unprincipled compromise" only made imperialism "more arrogant and outrageous."

Although the Cubans did not attempt to send any delegation to Korea so prestigious as the one which was there in October 1966 (including Political Bureau members Dorticós, Raúl Castro, and Del Valle), several important Cubans made the trip. They included three Central Committee members:

Basilo Rodríguez, who went to the DPRK as Cuban ambassador in April; Ursinio Rojas, who led a delegation of Cuban workers in May; and Major Belarmino Castilla Mas, Chief of Staff of the Cuban FAR, who led a military delegation in November. All three had meetings with DPRK President Kim Il-song and other top leaders.

On 4 September Radio Havana announced the signing of a protocol which called for an "appreciable increase" in trade for 1968. (See also *North Korea.*)

**Southeast Asia.** On 6 January 1967 *Granma* published a full-page interview with Prince Souphanouvong, President of the Laotian Patriotic Front (Neo Lao Hak Xat). Although the Prince commented primarily on events in Laos, he expressed his profound admiration for the Cuban revolution and its position of leadership in the struggle against the USA in Latin America. A delegation from the Patriotic Front, including Central Committee members Sithon Khommandam and Sisana Sisane, attended the celebration of the eighth anniversary of the Cuban revolutionary victory in the same month. Osmany Cienfuegos visited the "liberated" zones in Laos in March. Another delegation from the Patriotic Front, including Central Committee members Saly Vongkhamsao and Khamphay Boupha, visited Cuba to participate in the "Tricontinental Day of Solidarity with the People of Laos" on 12 October.

**Yugoslavia and Eastern Europe.** Cuban attacks on Yugoslavia, which had diminished after the polemics of the first half of 1966, began again with a *Granma* commentary on 22 July 1967. The occasion of the attack was the passage of new laws in Yugoslavia authorizing investment of foreign capital in business interests. According to *Granma,* "All economic and political steps" in Yugoslavia pointed to a "resurrection of the bourgeois parliamentary system and free enterprise." *Granma* spoke of Yugoslavia's having a "great army of the unemployed," criticized its acceptance of US economic and military aid, and charged that Yugoslav foreign policy, though called "positive neutralism," was in fact in line with US policy on all important issues such as the Vietnam War and national liberation movements. The commentary concluded:

> In our opinion, the so-called Yugoslav way is the way of opportunism, the way of conciliation, the way of bungling in the face of imperialism; it is the way of treason to the revolutionary movement and to its own people. (Weekly English edition, 30 July.)

In general, Cuban criticism of other East European countries was included in the indirect attacks on the Soviet Union since the problems regarding trade relations, incentives, and roads to power were essentially the same. Diplomatic and trade relations were the rule with the pro-Soviet parties; even Albania maintained a degree of contact.

Travelers from most East European countries went to Cuba during the year. The most frequent contacts were probably with Czechoslovakia, which provided, along with other assistance, a hundred specialists to help with Cuban mining enterprises. Czech equipment and supervisory personnel were used in setting up at least some of Cuba's six new radio stations, two (in Oriente and Havana provinces) using 150,000 watts (Havana Domestic Radio, 16 February). An especially warm reception was given the Rumanian delegation, headed by Gheorghe Rădulescu, member of the Executive Committee of the Central Committee of the Rumanian Communist Party, which visited Cuba between 20 and 25 November. The two countries agreed to establish a joint commission for economic and technical-scientific cooperation, and signed a trade protocol which according to the Rumanian news agency Agerpres (27 November) represented a "substantial" increase over the previous year. The largest single influx of East Europeans probably came when a group of 489 East German tourists arrived in February.

**Middle East.** In the Middle East crisis of mid-1967, as already noted, Cuba supported the Arab countries and indirectly criticized the USSR both for its apparent failure to assist the Arabs during the war and for its role in arranging a cease-fire through the UN. On the other hand, the Cuban insistence that armed resistance was the only revolutionary position possible for the Arab countries inevitably was turned against those countries when they stopped fighting. On 26 July Castro criticized the Arabs indirectly by saying that if the US were to invade Cuba as Israel had invaded the United Arab Republic, anyone who called for a cease-fire would be considered a traitor. Castro insisted that however serious the losses might be in a struggle against the US, Cuba's attitude would be: "While there is one man with a rifle, there is the nucleus of a guerrilla army!" (*Granma,* weekly English edition, 30 July). In an interview printed in an Italian communist weekly Castro even partly excused the Soviet position in the war by saying that the Arab society and countries had neither the cohesion, strength, nor real commitment to wage the people's war which could have destroyed Israel (*Rinascita,* 29 September).

On 15 June *Granma* published a long editorial praising the Algerian opposition to a Middle East cease-fire. The editorial marked a new high in Cuban-Algerian relations (which had fallen in June 1965 when Houari Boumedienne overthrew Ahmed Ben Bella) and was an implicit attack on both the United Arab Republic and Syria for their acceptance of the cease-fire. *Granma* stated:

> The Algerian Government has thus declared the need to resist and fight the aggressors and to place the struggle of the Arab peoples within the framework of the broader struggle of the peoples of Asia, Africa, and Latin America against imperialism . . . [Their] position on questions of the Arab world is a key point by which to differentiate revolutionaries and pseudorevolutionaries and the enemies of the peoples. (Weekly English edition, 25 June.)

A delegation from the PCC, headed by Central Committee member Major Víctor Dreke, visited Algeria from 28 October to 14 November. In a joint communique signed by Dreke and Bouarfa Mustapha, a member of the Central Board of the ruling Algerian National Liberation Front, it was stated that the two countries had "identical points of view in their evaluation of the world scene." Present at the ceremony was the recently appointed Cuban ambassador to Algeria, Rafael Fernández Moya. (*Granma,* weekly English edition, 26 November.)

Abdel Kader Ben Barka, the brother of El Mehdi Ben Barka (Moroccan President of the International Preparatory Committee of the First Tricontinental Conference who was murdered in the autumn of 1966) arrived in Cuba for a visit on 27 March.

**United States.** On 28 September Fidel Castro declared that the United States was:

> A fount of subversion! the mother of subversion! the State that intervenes everywhere, in every corner of the world . . . the barbarous and brutal State that has constituted the scourge of the continent for a century. (*Granma,* weekly English review, 8 October.)

On 7 January Radio Havana called the US-sponsored Alliance for Progress an anti-guerrilla creation since it was "intended to suppress revolutions." The Peace Corps, according to Radio Havana on 25 January, was "a real army of subversion and espionage." Eight prisoners, allegedly CIA agents, were interrogated in the presence of OLAS delegates in August. According to the 18 May statement of the PCC Central Committee:

> It is seldom taken into account that the people of the United States constitute one of the main victims of Yankee imperialism. It is they who, in large part, pay for the repressive, unjust wars of the imperialists with the sweat of their toil and the blood of their sons. (*Ibid.,* 21 May.)

On 10 August Fidel Castro told the delegates at the OLAS conference, among whom was Stokely Carmichael:

> The revolutionary vanguard within the United States will arise from the most mistreated, the most exploited and oppressed of the Negro sectors . . . not for racial reasons, but for social reasons . . . . The drawing together of the revolutionaries of the United States and those of Latin America is the most natural thing in the world, and the most spontaneous. (*Ibid.,* 20 August.)

Negro militants in the United States were given extensive coverage in Cuban news media during the summer riots in US cities and at the time of the OLAS conference. Interviews with or articles about Stokely Carmichael, Julius Lester, and Rap Brown appeared frequently in *Granma* and *Juventud Rebelde.* Carmichael attended the OLAS conference—at which he was made an "honorary delegate"—and received more attention from the Cuban and foreign press than any other non-Cuban participant. Fidel Castro praised him at length in his speech of 10 August. Carmichael's admiration for "Che" Guevara was repeatedly hailed by Cuban leaders, as were his calls for guerrilla warfare in US cities.

**Africa.** Cuban political and military activities in Africa have generally been clandestine and are thus difficult to document in detail. African guerrillas are thought to have been trained in Cuba as early as 1961 (*New York Times*, 22 November 1967). "Che" Guevara noted in his *Diary* that he had been to the Congo sometime after his departure from Cuba in 1965. Cuban political or military activities, or both, during late 1966 and early 1967 have been reported in (or with nationals from) Algeria, Angola, Cameroun, Congo (Brazzaville), the United Arab Republic, Guinea, Mali, Morocco, and Tanzania (*New York Times*, 23 October 1966; *Washington Evening Star*, 12 January 1967). It was also reported that Cuba and Communist China had agreed to train guerrillas for the Eritrean secessionist movement that has been carrying out a terrorist campaign in Ethiopia (*New York Times*, 3 March).

The most overt Cuban relations with ruling governments were with Algeria, Congo (Brazzaville), and the United Arab Republic.

**Latin America.**\* The Communist Party of Venezuela (PCV) was the object of frequent and severe Cuban denunciations during 1967, notably in Fidel Castro's speeches of 13 March and 10 August, the PCC Central Committee statement of 18 May, and the *Granma* editorial of 5 June. The PCV ordered Castro to stop his interference in Venezuelan affairs and called for a dialogue with the PCC.

Cuban relations with the Bolivian communists, in particular the pro-Soviet party led by Mario Monje, grew increasingly bad during the year due to opposing positions regarding the guerrilla war in Bolivia led by "Che" Guevara. The Cuban government also repeatedly condemned the Bolivian government of President René Barrientos both for its "oppressive" rule in general and for its arrest of Régis Debray in particular.

The joint command formed by the Guatemalan Party of Labor (PGT) and the Rebel Armed Forces (FAR) guerrillas in 1965 brought the Guatemalan communist activities largely into line with the Cuban model. Reports of serious disagreements between the city leaders and the guerrillas during 1967 were confirmed early in 1968 when a formal split was announced and the PGT was relegated to the ranks of the "false revolutionaries" (*Granma*, weekly English edition, 25 February and 3 March 1968).

The Communist Party of Chile (PCCh) has long been a strong supporter of the Soviet Union. The PCCh daily *El Siglo* (26 June) supported the UN cease-fire in the Middle East and criticized those who opposed out of hand any form of negotiated settlement. The *Pravda* article (30 July) by PCCh General Secretary Luis Corvalán on the eve of the OLAS conference, cited earlier, was indicative of the state of Cuban relations with the PCCh during the year. Three Chilean Communists, including PCCh Political Bureau member Volodia Teitelboim, attended the OLAS conference, but received very little attention from the Cuban hosts.

Cuba's closest allies in Chile were members of the Socialist Party (PS). Aniceto Rodríguez, Secretary-General of the PS, led a delegation to Cuba early in the year. Four Socialists, including Senator Carlos Altamirano and Professor Clodomiro Almeyda, attended the OLAS conference in August. Senator Salvador Allende arrived in Cuba late in October to deliver PS condolences to the Cuban people on the death of "Che" Guevara.

Beginning in mid-1967, the Communist Party of Argentina (PCA) became one of the most outspoken Latin American critics of Castro's policies. Ernesto Giúdici, a member of the Central Committee of the PCA, launched an attack on many of the key tenets of the Cuban revolutionary line at an international communist seminar in Prague in June. His critique was widely circulated in Soviet-controlled *World Marxist Review* in August. Shortly after the OLAS conference, which the PCA boycotted, the party's propaganda committee released a leaflet refuting the Castroist line as presented in Régis Debray's *Revolution in the Revolution?*

Cuban relations with the Communist Party of Uruguay (PCU) remained fairly good during the year. Rodney Arismendi, First Secretary of the party, who acted as an intermediary between Castro and the Soviet Union, was widely quoted in the Cuban press. He was prominent among those interrogating alleged CIA agents at the OLAS conference.

\*Cuban relations with the pro-Soviet and pro-Chinese communist parties are discussed in general terms elsewhere in this profile. More detailed accounts of relations with individual parties are found in the profiles devoted to those parties.

According to Fidel Castro, Mexico had the only honorable government in Latin America during 1967—it had defied the OAS and maintained both diplomatic and economic relations with Cuba. Although conflicts have arisen, as in 1966 when a Cuban diplomat in Mexico was ordered home after being implicated in the arming of Guatemalan guerrillas, relations have generally remained relatively cordial. A six-member delegation of leftists and communists attended the OLAS conference just the same, and most of the group supported the belligerent policies proclaimed at that meeting.

Cuba's closest friends in Latin America were the militant groups which were predominant at the OLAS conference. Prominent among them were the National Liberation Army (ELN) in Bolivia, the National Liberation Army (ELN) in Colombia, the Rebel Armed Forces (FAR) in Guatemala, the National Liberation Army (ELN) and Movement of the Revolutionary Left (MIR) in Peru, and the National Liberation Front and Armed Forces of National Liberation (FLN/FALN) in Venezuela. Articles about and declarations by these groups were frequently printed in *Granma* and other publications (e.g., *Granma*, weekly English editions, 19 and 26 March, 2 and 9 April, 21 May, 11 June, 13 August, and 17 September). They often received material or financial as well as verbal support from the Cubans. Recognizing the unpopularity of these policies with the Soviet Union and her allies, Castro commented on 26 July, and on other occasions as well, that the Cuban people would have to become accustomed to the idea of defending themselves, without foreign help, in the event of an "imperialist" retaliation against Cuba.

**Cuban-Sponsored Conferences.** The First Conference of the Latin American Solidarity Organization (OLAS), an organization founded in January 1966 after the Tricontinental conference, was held in Havana between 31 July and 10 August 1967.* Although the planning was done by an organizing committee made up of revolutionary groups in nine countries, the program, choice of participants, and ultimately the resolutions, were largely controlled by the Cubans. Some 550 persons attended, mostly from 27 Latin American countries and territories, and members of the Cuban and foreign press. Castroist delegates predominated, though a number of pro-Soviet Communists were also present. There were a few pro-Chinese participants, though not as official representatives of pro-Chinese parties.

The purpose of the conference was to give expression to the Cuban-advocated line of revolution, and to bring Latin America more actively into the worldwide "struggle against US imperialism." Every effort was made, both in conference meetings and in the Cuban press, to publicize such figures as Venezuelan guerrilla Francisco Prada and US "Black Power" leader Stokely Carmichael. Although there was some opposition to the more militant resolutions from the pro-Soviet delegates, the declarations of the conference were close to what the high-level Cuban delegation had called for in its report. Fidel Castro closed the conference on 10 August with one of his most belligerent speeches of the year. The dominant theme of the meeting was caught in the omnipresent slogan "The Duty of Every Revolutionary is to Make Revolution."

During the second half of 1967 elaborate plans were laid for the International Cultural Congress of Havana, which was held in January 1968. Preparations included an eight-day seminar involving more than 1,400 Cuban "intellectuals," nationwide discussions conducted by mass organizations, and extensive press coverage. A long statement entitled "What Is the Cultural Congress of Havana," which frequently referred to the nineteenth century Cuban national revolutionary hero José Martí, designated the general theme of the Congress as "colonialism and neo-colonialism in the cultural development of the peoples" (*Granma*, weekly English edition, 24 December). The militant spirit of the Congress was more clearly expressed, however, in the Declaration of the seminar and other documents. The Declaration called for the development of the "revolutionary intellectual" throughout the underdeveloped world and proclaimed "Che" Guevara, "in his role of doctor, writer, and revolutionary thinker, but above all in his magnificent role of guerrilla," as the "greatest, most exact, and purest expression of the revolutionary intellectual" (*ibid.*, 12 November). Thus the Cultural Congress was designed to win support for Cuban ideas among intellectuals just as the OLAS conference had been among Latin American political extremists.**

*The OLAS conference is treated in detail in a separate profile.

**The important events of the year were reviewed in special supplements to *Granma* (31 December) and *Juventud Rebelde* (30 December).

**Publications.** *Granma,* which is named after the schooner which carried Castro and his followers to Cuba from Mexico late in 1956, is the daily organ of the Central Committee of the PCC with a circulation of 327,000 in June. Published since 1965, it also appears in weekly editions in Spanish, English, and French. In July, Jorge Enrique Mendoza replaced Isidoro Malmierca as *Granma's* director. The daily evening newspaper *Juventud Rebelde,* circulation 68,000 in June, is controlled by the Young Communist Union. During the year Félix Sautie replaced Miguel Rodríguez as its director. *El Mundo,* with Luis Wanguemert as director, had a daily circulation of 158,000 in June. The monthly theoretical journal of the PCC, *Cuba Socialistsa,* which has an editorial board consisting of Fidel Castro, Osvaldo Dorticós, Blas Roca, Carlos Rafael Rodríguez, and Fabio Grobart, suspended publication with the February issue. *Pensamiento Critico,* a new political magazine aimed at the "revolutionary intellectual," first appeared in March under the directorship of Fernando Martínez. *Casa de las Americas,* with Roberto Fernández Retamar as director, is a monthly socio-political and literary review. *Bohemia,* a weekly magazine with articles on a wide variety of subjects, is under the directorship of Enrique de la Osa. *Verde Olivo* is the organ of the Revolutionary Armed Forces and is under the directorship of Luis Pavón. *Politica Internacional* is a quarterly publication of the Ministry of Foreign Affairs. *Nuestra Industria* is the organ of the Ministry of Industries and *Comercio Exterior* the organ of the Ministry of Foreign Trade. Prensa Latina, the only Cuban news agency, was under the directorship of José Felipe Carneado until March, and then Orlando Fundora López. The Cuban Broadcasting Institute changed its director in May, from Aurelio Martínez to Jorge Serguera. Radio Havana broadcasts in Arabic, West Indian Creole, English, French, Guaraní, Quechua, Portuguese, and Spanish.

# CYPRUS

The Reconstruction Party of the Working People of Cyprus (Anorthotikon Komma Ergazomenou Laou Tis Kiprou; AKEL) is the only well-organized political party on Cyprus, and also the strongest. It was founded as the Communist Party of Cyprus (Kommounistikon Komma Kiprou) in August 1926, outlawed in 1931 with other political parties, and revived under the name AKEL in April 1941. It was outlawed again in 1955 along with all Greek political organizations, but it became legal once again in 1959.

There is a small adjunct to AKEL in Great Britain called the "Union of Cypriots in England" which is the apparent successor to the "Cypriot Branch of the Communist Party of Great Britain" and is estimated to have 1,250 active members. The Union of Cypriots in England maintains close ties with AKEL and follows its line. (See YICA, 1966, pp. 95-96.)

The most recent elections in Cyprus, in 1960, gave AKEL five of the 35 seats reserved for the Greeks in the House of Representatives. This representation was based on a political agreement with the ruling Patriotic Front (Patriotikon Metopon) with which AKEL cooperates, rather than on the election returns, since AKEL did not present its own communist party ticket. The party claims, however, that it can control one-third of the vote of Cyprus (see "Communism in Cyprus," *Problems of Communism,* May-June 1966). AKEL also holds by appointment three of 26 seats in the Greek Communal Assembly.

An anticommunist campaign inspired in 1966 by the right-wing nationalist commander of the Greek Cypriot National Guard, General George Grivas, came to an end in 1967, when Grivas was sent to reside in Greece by the Makarios government.

The only nonruling communist party whose membership constitutes a higher proportion of its country's population is the Italian Communist Party. The strength of AKEL is estimated at between 12,000 and 14,000. Since 1964 AKEL has attempted a policy of mass recruitment, but it is still almost entirely Greek Cypriot in composition, despite concerted efforts to attract members from the island's Turkish minority. (Of the total population on Cyprus — estimated to be 610,000 in March 1967 — 80 per cent are Greek and 18 per cent Turkish.)

**Organization and Leadership.** The constituent parts of the organizational structure of AKEL include: the Presidium which is the supreme directorate; the Central Committee consisting of a Political Bureau, an Organizational Bureau, a Finance Bureau and a Bureau of Education and Enlightment; the Central Control Committee; and the various provincial and urban committees which are composed of the basic party organizations (cells). AKEL is particularly influential among young persons, farmers, and industrial workers. It controls the principal labor confederation, the Pan-Cypriot Workers Confederation (Pankipria Ergatiki Omospondia; PEO), which has approximately 36,000 members out of a total of 130,000 wage earners (including farmers), less than half of whom are organized in labor unions. The PEO has 18 member unions and workers' organizations and is an affiliate of the communist-led World Federation of Trade Unions.

The AKEL-controlled United Democratic Youth Organization (Eniaia Dimokratiki Organosis Neolaias; EDON) claims to have 26,000 members out of 135,000 youths between the ages of fifteen and twenty-nine, but the active membership may be closer to 15,000. A communist, P. Paionidis, is the Secretary-General of EDON. It also has an organization of secondary school students (PEOM), with an estimated 2,000 members, most of whom are also members of EDON. The EDON is a member of the communist-run World Federation of Democratic Youth and holds a seat on that body's executive committee. The strength of the Federation of National Unions of Cypriot Students (FNUCS), and the part AKEL plays in its activities are not known, but the federation is a member of the communist-controlled International Union of Students. AKEL's organization for women, the Pan-Cypriot Confederation of Women's Organizations (Pankiprios Omospondia Gynekon Organosen; POGO), claims 11,000 members, although western estimates place the number at 2,500.

Other AKEL-dominated fronts include the Pan-Cypriot Committee of Peace (Pankiprios Epitropi Erenis; PEE) which is a member of the World Council of Peace and whose Chairman Giagos Potamitis, holds one of the AKEL seats in the Cypriot parliament; the Cypriot-Soviet Club (Kipriosovietikos Syndesmos), and the Cypriot Club for Afro-Asian Mutual Assistance (Kipriakos Syndesmos Afriko-Asiatikis Allilegiys) whose Chairman Vassos Lissaridis, is also an AKEL member of parliament. The total figure for all elements within the AKEL apparatus, including various fronts and allowing for overlapping memberships, is estimated at more than 60,000.

AKEL's strong interest in mass organizations was reflected in the attention given to them at the party's Eleventh Congress in March 1966 (see *YICA*, 1966, p. 93). A resolution of the congress emphasized that the role of the mass movements was "of decisive importance" in the struggle for nationhood and that the party welcomed the creation of the "Coordinating Committee of Cooperative Organizations" or a united front of mass organizations.

The General Secretary of AKEL is Ezekias Papaïoannou (reelected at the 1966 Congress); his deputy is Andreas Fantis. Other leading personalities are Politburo members Pavlos Georgiou, Charalambos (Chambis) Michailidis, Christos Petras, and Yannis Sofoclis and Central Committee members Kostas Partassidis, Georgos Savvidis, and Andreas Ziartidis (the Secretary-General of the PEO). Papaïoannou, Michailidis and Ziartidis hold seats in parliament.

**Domestic Views and Policies.**  AKEL has supported and maintained close relations with the Makarios government since 1960, and this policy was reaffirmed in 1967. At the same time AKEL has reserved the right to offer "constructive criticism" whenever it feels government action is at variance with "the interests of the people." The party's domestic policy also includes: espousal of Cypriot nationalism (with concomitant deemphasis of the purely Greek objective, *enosis*); development of a strong, united "national liberation front" opposed to "imperialism" in order to strengthen the unity and uphold the independence of Cyprus; complete demilitarization of the island; and reconciliation with the Turkish community (*Kharavgi*, 8 December).

For AKEL, the demilitarization of Cyprus means ultimate disbanding of the anticommunist Cypriot National Guard (long a hindrance to achievement of the party's objectives), withdrawal of all Greek and Turkish forces from the island, and the removal of all British and NATO bases. AKEL would entrust peacekeeping to the UN International Peace Force, but states that the "role and authority of the international peace force must not be such as to allow it to become a state within a state" (*ibid.*).

AKEL's attitude toward reconciliation with the Turkish community reflects the preponderantly Greek membership of the party. AKEL has proclaimed: "Our enemies are not the Turkish Cypriots with whom we have lived and will continue to live in peace and fraternity. Our enemies are the imperialists and their chauvinistic organs . . . Greeks and Turks must forget the past and look to the future with faith and mutual confidence." (*Ibid.*) In contrast, party statements made outside Cyprus tend to place the blame for communal strife on the Turkish minority: "The differences between Turks and Greeks in Cyprus have in the main been instigated by the imperialists and are the result of the working out of their divide-and-rule doctrine . . . . It is high time that this is grasped by the Turkish Cypriot leaders who should no longer allow themselves to be used as a cat's paw by the imperialists." (*WMR*, September; see also the speech by E. Papaïoannou at the Karlovy Vary conference, in *IB*, 97-98, June.)

Although the April military coup in Greece came as a shock to AKEL, the party could take comfort in noting that its position in Cyprus seemed, as a result, to become stronger than ever. By the end of the year General Grivas, an implacable opponent of the communists, had not only been forced out of Cyprus, but the Greek soldiers who formed the best-disciplined troops under his command had been returned to Greece. Viewing Grivas' anticommunist attacks as part of an "imperialist plot" to destroy "Cypriot unity," AKEL took the credit for preventing a collision between right and left on Cyprus (*WMR*, May 1968). The proposed *enosis* or incorporation of Cyprus into Greece, previously a troublesome issue for AKEL, lost much of its popularity among Greek Cypriots after the coup. As a mass party attempting to appeal to Turks as well as Greeks, AKEL did not support *enosis* until 1965, and even then only with great reluctance. Knowing the growing coolness of many Greek Cypriots, including President (Archbishop) Makarios, toward *enosis* under the new circumstances within Greece, the party was relieved to let the issue lie dormant.

With Grivas gone, anticommunist military strength ebbing, Cypriot independence assured, and AKEL's position unimpaired, the party could face the future with fewer serious problems than ever before in recent times. On the other hand, AKEL still suffers considerable embarassment domestically from improved Soviet-Turkish relations and from frigid Soviet relations with Greece.

**International Views and Policies.** AKEL loyally supports the Soviet Union. On the occasion of the fiftieth anniversary of the October Revolution, AKEL portrayed the Soviet Union as a "consistent and disinterested supporter of the national independence of the peoples," "devoted fighter against imperialist slavery," and "champion of equality, brotherhood and cooperation among the peoples of the world." At the same time, the party declared:

> The peoples' national-liberation movement cannot defeat imperialism, which is still strong enough on its own, without the all-round support and help of the socialist world system and of the working-class movement of the capitalist countries . . . . The peoples who are fighting for their freedom, for their complete independence, for the social reconstruction of their countries, receive all possible aid from the Soviet Union and the other socialist countries. This aid is all-round and decisive. (*WMR*, October 1967.)

AKEL, as a pro-Soviet party, has opposed the "unfortunate" path taken by Communist China. Although not bitter in its criticism of the Chinese Communists, the party complained of the "peculiar" situation in which the Chinese leaders' "slanderous campaign" against the Soviet Union "surpassed even the propaganda of the imperialists, who have a direct and real interest in splitting the anti-imperialist camp" (*ibid.*).

AKEL has supported the Soviet Union in favoring the convocation of an international conference of communist and workers' parties.

For AKEL the chief danger to Cyprus lies not in the communal problem, but in "imperialism" in the form of NATO, which General Secretary Papaioannou has characterized as the "worst enemy of our people" (*WMR*, May 1968). In a speech at Karlovy Vary, Czechoslovakia, in April 1967 Papaïoannou also stated:

> The West German revanchists and the NATO aggressive circles headed by the US imperialists, which threaten European security, are the same forces which threaten Cyprus too. . . . In 1959, the Anglo-American imperialists, abetted by reactionaries in Ankara and Athens, imposed on Cyprus the Zurich-London Agreement. Through this agreement the British imperialists obtained 99 square miles of Cyprus territory and 32 other sites in various parts of the island as sovereign military bases . . . NATO, and particularly the Anglo-American imperialists, continue to plot against Cyprus, trying to undermine the Cyprus state and its government. They cling to their plan for partitioning Cyprus, and turning it into a NATO base. (*IB*, no. 97-98, June 1967.)

AKEL also maintains that the "fascist coup in Greece" was "basically the work of the American CIA and the Bonn revanchists," whose aim was to solve by "fascist means, not only the internal problems of Greece, but also the Cyprus problem in accordance with the wishes of the Americans" (*ibid.*).

Papaïoannou believes Cyprus to be under a triple attack from the "imperialists." He sees their aims as to break down the Patriotic Front on which the Makarios government is based; to conclude an agreement between Greece and Turkey which would "provide for Turkey to take over Cypriot territory" and for Greece to "take what remains"; and to overthrow the Makarios government, replacing it by puppets who would consent to partition. "This is the three-pronged satanic imperialist plan for the partition and NATO-ification of Cyprus" (Radio "Voice of Truth," 10 September). (The implication of a coup against Makarios underscored fear in AKEL at that time that General Grivas might overthrow the government of Cyprus.)

AKEL saw danger in the bilateral Greek-Turkish talks of 9-10 September which sought a solution to the Cyprus problem. The party opposed the talks as part of the alleged NATO-imperialist plot and was relieved when they failed. When Turkey threatened an invasion of Cyprus after the attacks by Greek Cypriot troops on the Turkish Cypriot towns of Ayios, Theodoros and Kophinou, an AKEL Central Committee proclamation laid the blame on "imperialism, the real instigator of this new tension," adding: "The imperialists, relentless foes of Cyprus, lie in wait and advance their infernal plans for partition and the subjugation of Cyprus to NATO" (*Kharavgi*, 23 November).

AKEL charged that the same "imperialists" who were "plotting" against Cyprus were behind the "aggression" against the "progressive" Arab states in the Arab-Israeli War: "The main aim of the US imperialists in our area is to overthrow progressive regimes in the newly independent Arab countries and to replace them with reactionary regimes which will loyally serve their imperialist interests, particularly those of the oil monopolies. This was their intention in the recent aggression against the Arab countries." (Radio "Voice of Truth," 31 July.)

Papaïoannou represented AKEL at the celebration of the fiftieth anniversary of the October Revolution in Moscow, making a speech at the grand rally on 6 November. He also attended and spoke at the Conference of Communist and Workers' Parties of Europe at Karlovy Vary, Czechoslovakia, in April. Deputy General Secretary Fantis was present at the Seventh Congress of the East German Socialist Unity Party, in Berlin, also in April. Yannis Sofoclis attended the Thirtieth National Congress of the Communist Party of Great Britain in November.

The eighth council meeting of the Afro-Asian People's Solidarity Organization (AAPSO) was held in Nicosia, Cyprus, on 13-16 February and was attended by about 300 delegates from 43 countries. The meeting closed one day ahead of schedule because of clashes between pro-Chinese and pro-Soviet delegates over the question where to hold the fifth AAPSO conference in 1967. After the pro-Chinese representatives of South-West Africa had been expelled and several other pro-Chinese African delegates had walked out in protest, the AAPSO officially picked Algiers as the site for the congress instead of Peking and pledged to fight disruptive tendencies. The part played directly by AKEL at the council meeting is not known, but a resolution on Cyprus supported the right of the Cypriot people to "unrestricted and unfettered sovereignty and independence and fulfillment of the national aspirations of the people" and concluded: "No solution will be accepted except the solution chosen by the people of Cyprus as a whole." The resolution contained no reference to *enosis* but followed the current AKEL (and Soviet) line on Cypriot self-determination.

**Publications.** The central organ of AKEL is the daily newspaper *Kharavgi* (Dawn). The party also publishes a quarterly theoretical review, *Neos Dimokratis* (New Democrat); a monthly journal, *Nea Epochi* (New Epoch); and a weekly, *Neoi Kairoi* (New Times). The PEO labor confederation publishes a weekly newspaper, *Ergatikon Vima* (Workers' Step), and the youth organization EDON a monthly, *Neolaia* (Youth). In addition to these, the Greek party United Democratic Left (EDA), whose program and policies largely coincide with those of the Greek Communist Party and AKEL, prints a daily newspaper in Nicosia, *Dimokratiki Allagi* (Democratic Change).

# CZECHOSLOVAKIA

The Communist Party of Czechoslovakia (Komunistická Strana Československa; CPC) was founded in 1921 and has been in power since 1948. It is the leading force in the Czechoslovak National Front (Národní Fronta), which comprises all political parties and major mass organizations. The CPC has a membership of 1,698,985 (December 1967) out of a total population of 14,240,000 (estimated 1966).

**Organization and Leadership.** The CPC has 46,000 basic party cells and is directed by a 110-member Central Committee. The leading organs of the party include a 10-member Presidium (plus five candidate members), and a six-member Secretariat (plus three candidate members) headed by a First Secretary. Antonín Novotný holds the post of Central Committee First Secretary, as well as Secretary-General of the National Front and President of the Czechoslovak Socialist Republic. The Secretariat includes Jiří Hendrych, Drahomír Kolder, Vladimír Koucký, Štefan Sádovský (elected at Central Committee plenum in February 1967), and Lubomír Štrougal; the members are Miroslav Pastyřík, František Pecha, and Martin Vaculík. The Presidium includes Oldřich Černík, Michal Chudík, Jaromír Dolanský, Alexander Dubček, Jiří Hendrych, Drahomír Kolder, Bohuslav Laštovička, Jozef Lenárt, Antonín Novotný, and Otakar Šimůnek; the candidate members are Antonín Kapek, Miroslav Pastyřík, Michal Sabolčik, Štefan Sádovský, and Martin Vaculík.*

The Communist Party of Slovakia (Komunistická Strana Slovenska) is an integral part of the CPC. The First Secretary of its Central Committee is Alexander Dubček.†

**Domestic Issues.** The tumultuous and frequently sensational events in Czechoslovakia in 1967 concerning the problems of the economic reform, the revolt of dissident writers, youth demonstrations, and the nationality question built up to a crisis in the top organs of the CPC in November and December and finally culminated in the removal of Antonín Novotný from his position as First Secretary at the beginning of January 1968 and his subsequent "resignation" from the presidency of the Republic amidst the process of purging the ranks of the party and state bureaucracy of his supporters.

The CPC's most important concern in 1967, and the basic cause of the personnel and policy changes of early 1968, was its activity in relation to the new economic mechanism which was put fully into force on 1 January 1967.

The Czechoslovak economic model is a far-reaching reform aimed at the rationalization of the national economy; its major characteristic is the decentralization of planning and the coordination of production with market demands. Under the new system individual enterprise managers are responsible for the production and sale of their products, whereas the central planning organs develop only general and long-range goals. The economic functions of prices, profit, and interest are reestablished and consequently effect the extensive use of material incentives in production, the deleveling of wages, and fluctuating prices.

As applied in January 1967, the reform was merely a modified version of the original theoretical

---

*Major changes in the party leadership began 3 January 1968 and continued in subsequent months. Antonín Novotný was removed from all of his three functions. As of April 1968 the party leadership includes First Secretary Alexander Dubček and an 11-member Presidium including František Barbírek, Vasil Bilák, Oldřich Černík, Alexander Dubček, Drahomír Kolder, František Kriegel, Jan Piller, Emil Rigo, Josef Smrkovský, Josef Spaček, and Oldřich Švestka and alternate members Antonín Kapek, Jozef Lenárt, and Martin Vaculík. The Secretariat includes First Secretary Dubček, Jozef Lenárt, Alois Indra, Čestmír Císař, Štefan Sádovský, and Drahomír Kolder. The Premier of Czechoslovakia is Oldřich Černík and the President is Ludvík Svoboda.

†Dubček's successor in 1968 was Vasil Bilák.

plan drawn up at the Economic Institute of the Czechoslovak Academy of Sciences under Ota Šik, and it did not meet with unanimous approval. Dissatisfaction was shown both by those who felt the reform a betrayal of the building of communism and by those who felt that it remained too closely controlled by the party and the old bureaucrats. The progressive members of the Czechoslovak leadership insisted that the new economic model could overcome obstacles only if it were implemented rapidly and argued that "the degree of risk involved in the consistent application of the new system is undoubtedly smaller than the degree of risk involved in the endeavor to retain outdated methods of management, whatever the form in which this is done" (Jiří Kantůrek, "What Progress This Year?" *Kulturní Tvorba,* 5 January 1967).

However, the party leadership, while continuing to urge the implementation of the reform and approving measures aimed at its successful implementation, adopted a middle-of-the-road policy which was most clearly elucidated in Novotný's closing speech to the March Central Committee plenary session.* Novotný declared that administrative pressure, rather than reliance on economic pressures, was to be used in cases where the implementation of the reform was not proceeding smoothly and efficiently, and that the party could not ignore the international political situation or think "that political class viewpoints have ceased to be valid in the management of the society's development." He affirmed the party's aims to speed up the process of implementing the reform and to proceed further in the development of "socialist democracy." He added:

> However, Comrades, I cannot agree that everything we do in the national economy and the life of our society must be weighed and assessed solely according to economic viewpoints. In all our measures, including economic measures, we must proceed so as to keep our political aims in view. As long as economic measures are not in harmony with our political aims and our political program, these measures cannot be accepted by us, no matter how effective they may be.

In practice, the rigid party attitude was demonstrated by continued interference of the central and party organs in the work of the enterprises. This interference was the most important factor in obstructing the implementation of the reform during 1967.

The reports on the progress of the reform showed that the leadership was unable to solve some basic and recurring economic problems, and at the same time was unable to fulfill its promises or respond to the rising expectations of the various interest groups. The party definition of the present stage of development was described as the "penultimate stage of our industrial revolution," that is, "the rounding off of our industrial revolution and simultaneously the beginning of the scientific and technological revolution" (Bohumil Šimon, "The Economic Policy of the Communist Party of Czechoslovakia in Industry," *WMR,* July 1967). However, the Central Committee plenum which met on 3-4 May to discuss economic development in the past two years and further policies toward the solution of the problems of economic equilibrium and the raising of living standards admitted in its resolution that recent developments had "thus far failed to change the serious structural and qualitative problems of the national economy." The major problems were reported as the undesirable growth of the labor force and stockpiles, the large volume of unfinished capital construction and the discrepancy between production and foreign trade. The resolution of the May plenum revised the existing Five Year Plan, and called for the curtailment of capital construction and industrial investments and the full utilization of the "international division of labor;" it adopted a cautious price and wage system allowing increased wages at a slightly more rapid rate than retail prices; it adopted a credit ceiling to curb excessive demand for investments; it provided unemployment benefits and retraining subsidies and called for the full utilization of work shifts and the reduction of the work week in shift-work enterprises in order to deal with the problem of unemployment—even if temporary—engendered by the new economic mechanism.

The directives of the May plenum did not, however, provide a solution to the economic weaknesses, and the same problems were discussed at subsequent Central Committee plenary sessions

---

*The Central Committee met on 23-24 March to discuss measures to improve managerial methods in agriculture and food supply organs. The plenum also discussed the role and function of the national committees and the drafting of an electoral law.

(26-27 September and 19-21 December). The December plenum resolution again called for a slowdown of capital construction in heavy industry, a greater share of investments in nonproductive branches, and an acceleration of the growth rate of the national income from the planned 22 to 24 per cent to 31 to 32 per cent in the period from 1966 to 1970.

Another basic defect in the Czechoslovak economy continued to be the inadequate price system, particularly the wholesale- price system, which lent itself to speculation by individual enterprises. The unexpected rapid rise in the prices of wholesale goods combined with an unanticipated reduction in enterprise overhead alarmed the central planners and resulted in the decision of the state Commission for Finances, Prices, and Wages that by 15 September all enterprises must remit to the state budget "unjustifiably gained funds" from the price reorganization. This measure was followed by a new party study to reorganize the price system. The government reaction was characteristic of the moves to define more sharply and tighten economic ordinances to deal with the unexpected developments. The freedom of individual enterprises to dispose of profits at will, a basic principle of the reform, was thus heavily curtailed.

The insufficient production of goods able to compete on world markets was yet another deficiency of the economy. Oldřich Černík, Deputy Premier and Chairman of the State Planning Commission, warned that enterprise managers were to be judged by world-market standards, and that if an enterprise did not meet the test it would be closed, for the state would not continue indefinitely to support inefficient production (*Rudé Právo,* 25 July 1967).

The development of the economic reform, however, showed positive tendencies, such as an improved situation on the domestic front resulting in a buyers' market for some items, the successful introduction of a shorter work week, an increased tempo in the growth of utilized national income and the elimination of some basic disproportions in its allocation, and an increase in agricultural production. The midyear report of the State Bureau of Statistics showed that in comparison with the same period in 1966, industrial production had risen 5.5 per cent in the first six months of 1967, the gross income had reached almost 48 billion crowns, and the over-all net profitability (the ratio of net profits to costs and expenditures) was nearly 13 per cent in the first six months of 1967, four points higher than the comparable period in 1966.

In the realm of agriculture the party goal was to raise the level of the agricultural workers to that of industrial workers through added incentives and benefits and more favorable legislation for farms. However, the primary need was a significant raise in the productivity of farms through more efficient organization and technological developments. The March plenum of the Central Committee adopted the outline of a program to integrate state and collective farms with the suppliers and purchasing agents. "District agricultural associations" were set up to coordinate the farms with all previous district planning, service, supply, and purchasing functions, giving farms "greater scope for socialist enterprise through various forms of specialization and cooperation." The leadership insisted that the distinction between integration in socialist countries and in capitalist countries was the "voluntary" nature of the association in the socialist state and its "horizontal" formation, in contrast to the "vertical" formation in the capitalist states and the resultant exploitation of the farmer (Jan Havelka, "New Features in Czechoslovak Agriculture," *WMR,* September 1967). A newly created Ministry of Agriculture and Food, which replaced the Ministries of Agriculture and of the Food Industry and the Central Administration for the Purchase of Agricultural Products, was put in charge of the alterations scheduled for approval by the government organs in 1968.

Recognizing that political and social changes would have to be made as a consequence of the economic reform, in late 1966 the Czechoslovak leadership set up an interdepartmental research team at the Czechoslovak Academy of Sciences to develop a model for the course of political and social development. The team worked on a wide variety of problems, such as the nature of politics and the state in socialist society, the development of a representative system, the assertion of various social interests and the development of political policy, sociological studies of the theory of the elite, relations between the individual and institutions, and social engineering. The team is to submit its first report on short-term changes by the end of 1968, but preliminary information on its work indicated that the basic premises for the model were to be the high level of productivity of the socialist society effected by the scientific-technological revolution and the "true democratization" of the political system (see *Rudé Právo,* 6 July 1967 and Jiří Kroupa, "The Development of the Political System in this Country," *Student,* 27 September 1967).

A concrete step in "expanding socialist democracy" was made in 1967 by the development of a new electoral system creating electoral districts with more seats. It called for the registration of more candidates in electoral districts than deputies to be elected and established a system of substitutes to eliminate by-elections except in extraordinary cases. In addition, it provided for elections to national committees at all levels to take place separately from the elections to the National Assembly and the Slovak National Council.

Other measures aimed at the democratization of the nation's political and social life included a new Press Law, stipulating that the press should "provide information promptly and truthfully, presenting as complete and balanced a picture as possible on all domestic and foreign events." The provisions of the law gave journalists the right of access to all information except that which "could harm the interests of the State or society," and required individuals to answer criticism directed at them in the press. However, Article 17 of the Press Law also referred to the new Central Publication Authority set up under Government Ordinance 119 (28 December 1966) to supervise all communications media, which in effect legalizes censorship in Czechoslovakia. Article 17 provided that editors may appeal decisions of the Central Publications Authority to ban an item of information, but also stipulated that the Central Publications Authority can "draw the attention of an editor-in-chief" to any information it deems contrary to "other interests of society."

The Sixth Congress of the Revolutionary Trade Union Movement (31 January-4February) enacted measures to ensure improved methods of worker participation in managing production, particularly in the areas of planning and technical development, and in June measures defining administrative rules of procedure and guaranteeing a number of rights of the citizen *vis-à-vis* the administrative organs was passed. In addition, a new penal code was being formulated.

**Protests by the Czechoslovak Writers.** In the forefront of events in Czechoslovakia during 1967 was the conflict between the central party bureaucracy and the nation's writers and intellectuals. The tension between the party and the intellectuals, particularly those connected with the publications *Literární Noviny* (organ of the Union of Czechoslovak Writers) and *Host do Domu* (Brno literary monthly), has become increasingly acute since 1964 and reached a climax at the Fourth Congress of the Union of Czechoslovak Writers (27-29 June 1967), when a number of writers, many of whom were long-time party members, delivered scathing indictments of the 20 years of Communist rule in Czechoslovakia, demanding the abolition of censorship, the reestablishment of civil rights, and other measures amounting to what the party termed an "opposition political platform."

Playright novelist Pavel Kohout attacked the government's support of the Arab states in the Middle East crisis and drew a historical parallel between the relations of Israel and the Arab world and those of Czechoslovakia and Nazi Germany in 1938. He also read to the congress the May circular letter of the Soviet writer Solzhenitsyn, which called for an end to censorship in the Soviet Union. At this point Jiří Hendrych, who was representing the CPC, reportedly walked out of the congress. Writer A. J. Liehm charged that communist cultural policy has and is experiencing continuous breakdowns, and that culture "must be liberated from the dictates of power and the market." Ivan Klima compared the present Czechoslovak constitution with the constitution of 1867 from the standpoint of freedom of speech. In his closing address Jan Procházka, Chairman of the Writers' Union, affirmed that writers would persevere in their struggle for the right of expression "to the last writer, the last ruler and the last reader in this world," and would refuse to be subordinated "either to doctrines or dogmas." He also declared that "to pass any judgment at the close of this Congress is not only beyond the power of a writer, it is beyond the power of anybody, because already now our Congress . . . is history and subject to deeper and more lasting judgments . . . ."

The most outspoken writer at the congress was Ludvík Vaculík, who both theoretically and with reference to historical examples refuted totalitarianism and a regime based solely on power. With specific reference to Czechoslovakia, he expressed the belief that "citizens" no longer exist, that the constitution does not benefit the people, and that freedom is nonexistent in Czechoslovakia. "It is necessary to understand that in the course of twenty years no human problems have been solved in our country," Vaculík charged.

To add to the explosive atmosphere of the congress, the Slovak contingent of writers walked out when their demand to form an autonomous writers' union was not met.

The final resolution of the congress, even though it was drawn up before the meeting with the aid of the party's Department of Ideology, only cautiously endorsed the resolution on culture adopted by the Thirteenth Congress of the CPC in 1966 and stressed the aspect of the party resolution which repudiated "sectarian and primitive concepts." The resolution was devoted to the discussion of socialist culture and human freedom and made concrete proposals urging that censorship be limited to state defense information, that the Press Law be amended to permit accused authors to defend themselves directly and personally, and that relations be cultivated with those Czechoslovak writers living abroad "whose activity is not directed against the Czechoslovak state."

The crisis in the Writers' Union continued as the congress was unable to elect a leadership acceptable to the party. It was not until October that the Central Committee was able to elect a Presidium, and it remained without a chairman. It was reported by Western sources that the Writers' Union had nominated Jan Procházka, who proved unacceptable to the party, and then offered the chairmanship to Eduard Goldstücker, who declined it.*

The background to Fourth Congress of the Union of Czechoslovak Writers was a series of explosive events, beginning with the introduction on 1 January 1967 of the new Press Law legalizing censorship in Czechoslovakia and setting up an organ to control it under the Ministry of the Interior. Also in January, the Czechoslovak leadership made the fifth change since 1965 in the management of *Literární Noviny,* and a new Ministry of Culture and Information, headed by Karel Hoffmann, was established to coordinate the work of all cultural institutions in the spirit of the party line set out in the Thirteenth Party Congress resolution. On 8-9 February the Central Committee of the CPC met to discuss ideological questions and the unity of the socialist society and heard a lengthy report by Party Secretary Jiří Hendrych. Hendrych stressed that the immediate task was the purposeful shaping of the political and moral unity of the socialist society by strengthening the party role in all spheres of life. He called for a "substantial injection of politics" into cultural educational activity and declared that state media must "present only such works as support socialism and human progress and no works subservient to a philosophical view alien to our society." He then turned to strong criticism of specific ideological deviations by the nation's artists and writers, noting that the issue involves not just different interpretations of socialist views, but a "foreign philosophy which harms our society and its unity."

In March Pavel Auersperg, head of the Ideological Department of the Central Committee, was replaced by František Havlíček, an old party functionary who most recently edited the party's theoretical journal *Nová Mysl.* Western reporters (for example, the *Frankfurter Allgemeine Zeitung,* 3 March 1967) attributed Auersperg's removal to his relative leniency toward the intellectuals and his determination to defend their independence against growing pressure from Berlin and Moscow.

The CPC's reaction to the events at the Writers' Union congress was severe. At the congress itself, Jiří Hendrych presented his scheduled report to the writers, but then he presented a second speech in which he harshly condemned the proceedings at the congress and warned that "the party's patience is at an end." The party stalwarts were then mobilized to address a message to the CPC Central Committee dissociating the Union from the speeches presented by the dissident writers and declaring to the Central Committee that "together with you, Comrades, we intend, in the spirit of the conclusion of the Thirteenth Czechoslovak Communist Party Congress, to develop the greatest possible effort toward eliminating obstacles to the further development of socialist Czechoslovakia and its culture."

The day after the close of the Writers' Union congress, Novotný, speaking at the School of Politics in Prague, harshly condemned the opinions expressed at the congress, in particular those charging that the party has betrayed its mission and that the country is passing through a period of "a second dark

*Eduard Goldstücker became chairman of the Union of Czechoslovak Writers in 1968 and confirmed that he had been offered the post in 1967.

age." Warning that in matters of ideology the party will not compromise, Novotný declared: "We shall not permit any national socialist, reactionary clerical, rightist social democratic or other trend to be revived." Again, in a speech before graduates of military academies on September 1, Novotný emphasized that Czechoslovak democracy is a "class democracy" and its freedom is a "class freedom," and declared that "education and the media acting on the formation of public opinion and the people's way of thinking must be fully in the hands of our socialist state and fully influenced by our Communist Party."

The September plenum of the Central Committee took up the matter of the intellectual ferment, and a wide range of opinion could be heard on how to deal with the dissident writers. However, the report on the Writers' Union congress given by Jiří Hendrych formed the sole basis for the final resolution. Hendrych attacked the speakers at the congress for posing purely political problems, for aiming direct attacks against the party and republic, and for "blind professional interest." He linked the congress proceedings to the "imperialist anticommunist campaigns" and charged that the writers were serving the interests of the imperialists: "This anticommunist drive cannot be left unanswered. And he who has lent himself to this propaganda or who aids it must also count on a hard answer." He also noted that the writers "are trying, by their Europeanism, to eliminate the Soviet Union, its art and culture."

The plenary session voted to expel Ivan Klíma, Antonín Liehm, and Ludvík Vaculík from the CPC and Jan Procházka from candidate membership in the Central Committee. It also put *Literární Noviny* under the Ministry of Culture and Information, and adopted a "series of measures which should strengthen the close comradely ties between the Party and the writers . . . and start the process of the further crystallization of the character of our socialist literature and the entire Czechoslovak culture." One such measure, initiated by Jiří Hendrych, proved to be the "decentralization" of the Writers' Union into "autonomous branches," a move interpreted as a "divide-and-rule" tactic intended to undermine the unique position of the Slovak Union of Writers, formed after the June Writers' Union congress.

The Central Committee administrative action did not succeed, however, in silencing the dissident writers, who continued to express their views through other organs (such as *Kulturný Život,* the journal of the Slovak Union of Writers) and in the foreign press. Thus Ludvík Vaculík defended his position to a *New York Times* correspondent (20 September 1967), and in November Antonín Liehm publically challenged Jiří Hájek, editor-in-chief of *Plamen* (monthly of the Union of Czechoslovak Writers), on the latter's evaluation of the events at the Union of Writers congress.

In contrast to the Union of Czechoslovak Writers, the Union of Czechoslovak Journalists, at its Fifth Congress (19-20 October), disassociated itself from the opinions expressed in *Literární Noviny* and *Host do Domu,* and showed itself a loyal ally of the CPC. Addressed by Jiří Hendrych, the journalists were encouraged to criticize "all distortions in the implementation of the principles of the party and the socialist state and distortions in practice of party and government resolutions." Hendrych also reiterated his condemnations of the writers. The journalists did, however, criticize the fact that the new Press Law was not being observed specifically because journalists were unable to obtain information to which they were entitled under the new law.

The CPC was challenged in other spheres of Czechoslovak intellectual life and reacted as it had to the Writers' Union congress. Three days after the close of the congress three Czech authors went on trial, charged primarily with "subversive activities." Although the trial was to have been open to the press, reporters were unable to gain admittance, and the British lawyer Paul Sieghart, who came as an observer representing the organization Amnesty International, was evicted from the courtroom on the first day and was subsequently expelled from Czechoslovakia. Pavel Tigrid, tried in absentia for subversion, was given 14 years, Jan Beneš was condemned to five years on the same charge (and acquitted on charges of speculation), and Karel Zámečník was acquitted of charges of "damaging the interests of the Republic."

The Czechoslovak leadership was dealt another blow on the cultural front when one of Czechoslovakia's most popular writers, Ladislav Mňačko, made a "protest trip" to Israel, despite official disapproval, and published in *Frankfurter Allgemeine Zeitung* (11 August 1967) a declaration of protest over his country's policies toward Israel. The CPC's reaction was to strip him of party membership and to deprive him of his Czechoslovak citizenship and the numerous honors he had received.

On 3 September a sensational Czechoslovak "writers' manifesto" appeared in the London *Sunday Times.* The manifesto was alleged to have been drawn up and signed by 400 Czechoslovak intellectuals, appealing to the "public and writers of the entire free and democratic world . . . to help to rescue the spiritual freedom and fundamental rights of every independent artist threatened by the terror of the state powers." The question of the authenticity of the document was debated throughout the year, with the CPC calling it a "fraud" and the Union of Czechoslovak Writers dissociating itself from authorship. In November, a man identified only as "Dr. I.P.," reported to be the sole author of the manifesto, was arrested.

The CPC was also challenged on the issue of religion. In October a party secret document (dated 7 August and reportedly circulated to all party organs) was brought to light; in it the CPC called for "appropriate pedagogical and politico-religious measures to increase the instructional efficacy of the fight against the influence of religious ideology." The document was issued following unsuccessful negotiations between representatives of Czechoslovakia and the Vatican on the subject of nomination of bishops. The document, rejected by official Czechoslovak sources but believed authentic by Western diplomats and observers, was viewed as part of the tightening of party controls on culture, and not as a return to the religious persecution of the Stalinist period.

The CPC's conflict with the intellectuals brought widespread repercussions both within the party and from the foreign communist parties. The leadership's methods of dealing with the dissident writers—dogmatic and repressive measures and expulsions of individuals from the party and implemented in a context which was clearly explosive—were regarded by many party members as a demonstration of the CPC's unwillingness or inability to deal "creatively" with new problems. The attitudes and reactions of Jiří Hendrych and Antonín Novotný toward the dissident writers was thus a major factor in their downfall in early 1968. The reaction of some foreign communist parties was noteworthy. An article in the Italian Communist organ *Rinascita* on intellectual life in Czechoslovakia questioned the changes in *Literární Noviny,* the inability of the Writers' Union to elect leading organs, and other moot points: " . . . basically it is incomprehensible that one can still exercise a political censorship over works of art in a socialist society," the author of the article declared, attributing the censorship to deep imperfections and contradictions in this phase of development of Czechoslovak society (Franco Bertone, "Intellectuals and Socialist Power," *Rinascita,* 29 September 1967).

**Youth Protests.** The intellectual ferment in Czechoslovakia overshadowed the continuing problems which the CPC experienced with the nation's youth. Although the February plenum of the Central Committee on ideology was specifically concerned with youth, and the party-controlled Czechoslovak Youth League (Československý Svaz Mládeže) held its Fifth Congress on 5-9 June, the party leadership, when faced with the concrete challenge of student demonstrations in Prague in November, was unable to grasp quickly the situation and offer a successful solution to the crisis.

At the February plenum Jiří Hendrych stressed that one of the party's most important tasks was the intensification and improvement of the ideological education of youth. He noted the "negative phenomena" appearing in the ranks of the youth, including "degeneration" and "passivity," but also deplored a completely negative attitude toward youth, stating that "in reality, young transgressors form only a small part of our boys and girls." Hendrych urged a more objective evaluation of the problems of youth and declared that the duty of the party was "to place young people in their proper place in contemporary life in order that they can gather experience in harmony with the possibilities and needs of socialism, best apply their energy and enthusiasm according to all social interests, and become worthy continuators of our endeavors for social progress."

On 31 October a student demonstration protesting dormitory living conditions elicited severe reaction from the police and during the following weeks escalated in size and content to the point where the students demanded formally that Education Minister Jiří Hájek rectify the errors made in handling the demonstration. In an unprecedented move the government, in a 14 December statement, made some concessions to the students by admitting to "excessively harsh action against individual students" and effecting personnel changes.

It was reported in the Western press and in the Czechoslovak press that the student demonstrators were also expressing political sentiments. An article in *Kulturní Tvorba* (16 November) tried to link the student protests with anticommunist Western propaganda. At a student protest meeting on 21 November the students declared that the 31 October demonstration was the consequence of the "unhealthy situation in this country and the expression of this country's political and economic conditions" (*Frankfurter Allgemeine Zeitung*, 22 November 1967). A UPI dispatch of 22 November reported that, according to Eduard Goldstücker, "the student initiative must be seen for what it is—an effort toward further democratization of our nation."

**Reevaluation of the Party's Role.** The new principles brought into Czechoslovak life by the new economic model, the disaffection of the nation's intelligentsia, the rebellious youth, and the statistical evidence from public-opinion polls of national disunity in all spheres led the party to begin to seriously reevaluate its organization and its role in Czechoslovak life.

The CPC membership figure of 1,698,985 represents 17 per cent of the adult Czechoslovak population, the highest ratio of all communist parties. The most numerous groups are workers, followed by engineer-technicians and economic officials. An analysis in the trend of new party members shows that there has been a decline in the membership of enterprise organizations and organizations on the collective farms, while the number of communists in village and street organizations has increased. This unfavorable trend in the development of the social structure of the party, as well as the fact that workers constitute the "overwhelming majority" of those who are being expelled from the party, has been noted by the party organs. Another membership problem is that in the age structure; the age differences between the oldest and the youngest are increasingly more pronounced, and an especially serious situation exists in the countryside, where 41.1 per cent of the communists are over 60 years of age (*Rudé Právo*, 25 July 1967, and *Rudé Právo*, 14 September 1967).

With regard to the growth of membership, the party has maintained that it does not wish to change its present size. The criterion for size is that the party be large enough to penetrate into all spheres of society and be able to influence them (*Rudé Právo*, 24 October 1967).

The CPC has consequently been greatly concerned with the quality of membership. It has repeatedly criticized "passivity," "irresponsibility," and "breach of party discipline" in the membership and has called for a purge of undesirable members and the training of better party cadres through improved ideological education. Recognizing the implications of the new economic model's emphasis on professionalism and its penetration into other spheres of life, the CPC has demanded unequivocal loyalty from its members. Antonín Novotný summed up his remarks at the March Central Committee plenum with this point:

> I would like to stress, comrades: We must base every organizational or cadre measure on the fact that, for the insurance of the Party's policy, we continue to need firm and resolute communists who are consistent fighters for the aims of our Party and who, regardless of their position, serve the Party and our socialist aims. We need people who fight daily for the Party's policy and who do not let themselves be confused by the various waverings society undergoes and who do not lose their heads whenever shortcomings appear. In this sense it is also necessary to teach and bring up the young people.

The CPC has never raised the question of relinquishing its "leading role" in all spheres of Czechoslovak life. Lengthy press articles devoted to party activities always proceed to the conclusion that the party is at the apex of responsibility for social development and cannot share that responsibility with any other social institution (or party) (see for example the four-part article by Jan Fojtík, "On the Meaning of the Activity of the Communist Party," *Rudé Právo*, 29 June, 7 July, 13 July, and 20 July, 1967). However, during 1967 the methods and form of leadership were being seriously reconsidered and redefined. The CPC, recognizing that the social sciences lag behind the needs of the political leadership, encouraged public-opinion polls, sociological studies, and interdepartmental research (such as the group at the Academy of Sciences mentioned above). It was also active on all levels of its own organization in conducting surveys, studies, and experiments, sociological and otherwise, on basic questions of social development. Discussions in the lower party organs extended to questions which had been previously the prerogative of the Central Committee first to discuss and then to formulate decisions, which were then handed down to the lower organs. The results of the wide-ranging surveys and the conflicts of opinion in the lower party organs were to provide the basis of the discussions at the October Central Committee plenum, which was convened to define the role of the CPC in Czechoslovak life.

On 31 October the Central Committee met to hear a report by Jiří Hendrych on "the position and tasks of the party in the current stage of socialist society" and adopted a "thesis" on the subject. Neither Hendrych's report nor the thesis were published, but it was announced that the thesis was to be distributed to the party membership and then discussed. The press communique on the Central Committee plenum simply reaffirmed that the party was "the leading political force, the ideological center, the cognitive and directing organism of socialist society" and that "it demands full responsibility from state and economic bodies for the operative and perspective management of various spheres on the basis of the set political line." The thesis, according to the communique, also emphasized that the party must penetrate all spheres of public life and that the party leadership must have sufficient room for critically judging the work of state bodies and individual functionaries, and underlined the direct responsibility of party functionaries for implementing the party's economic policy at all levels of management.

The October plenum of the Central Committee, however, was marked by conflicting views of the highest party functionaries and demands by some of their number for a new CPC leadership. Three forces in the highest organs of the party could now be identified: those who wished to treat the party as a synonym of power, those who felt the economic reform must be implemented and then followed by political reform, and finally, those who thought political reform must be made immediately, taking precedence over economic reform (Risto Bajalski, "Party at a Crossroads," *Borba*, Belgrade, 18 November 1967).

The critical decisions on the new party line, and with it the inevitable changes in leadership, which were first raised at the October plenum, continued to be discussed by the Presidium for 10 days at the beginning of December, but again no decision was reached. Rumors became widespread of the resignation of Antonín Novotný from at least his party post and of the resignation of Jiří Hendrych. It was reported that the Presidium, on the initiative of the Slovak members (who had demanded that Slovakia be given equal attention in implementing the new economic mechanism and a larger share in investments), had voted at least to remove Novotný from his party post. But on 8 December Leonid Brezhnev, First Secretary of the Soviet party Central Committee, made an unexpected visit to Prague at the invitation of Antonín Novotný and was able to swing the vote back to Novotný's favor (Brezhnev was unwilling, or unable, to ensure Novotný's position, and could only stabilize the situation temporarily).

A Central Committee plenum was scheduled for 12 December to affix the stamp of approval to the Presidium's decisions, but because of the inability of that body to reach any conclusions, the discussions were continued in the Central Committee which finally met on 19 December. The essentially "open debate" in the plenum on such momentous issues was unprecedented, and once begun, proved uncontrollable by the party leadership. Novotný attempted to hold his position by promising concessions, but the attention of the Central Committee was rather drawn to the proposals for major changes in the policy lines and in party leadership. The most far-reaching proposal, although it was not one which claimed large support, was that of Ota Šik, the author of the new economic mechanism, who called for the right to form opposition groups within the Central Committee and for the creation of commissions of experts to be attached to the Central Committee to direct the economy, with their decisions binding on party officials at all levels (Pavel Tigrid, "How Novotný Fell," *The New Leader,* 29 January 1968).

The Central Committee plenum again proved inconclusive and was postponed until 3 January. However, for the 10 days between the plenary sessions the party and state were ruled by the Presidium, headed by the doyen of the body, Jaromír Dolanský. The presidium was enlarged by 10 party officials from the 10 regions into which Czechoslovakia is divided. The First Secretaries of the parties of these regions were excluded, as they were known to be pro-Novotný (Tigrid, *The New Leader*, 29 January 1968). The 3 January 1968 plenum finally decided Novotný's removal from his post as party First Secretary and replaced him with the First Secretary of the Slovak Communist Party, Alexander Dubček.*

The actual events and controversies at the October plenum and its aftermath have remained partially obscured by official silence and can only be pieced together from a variety of official and nonofficial reports. The reports show that the failure of the Czechoslovak party leadership to handle the events of 1967 was owing in large measure to its inability to tackle "creatively" the new problems and challenges which have arisen in the broad context of the New Economic Model. The party leadership resorted to traditional methods of repression, and finally even to reliance on support from Moscow to handle new problems which also called for new methods of control.

**Relations with the Socialist States.** The foreign policy of Czechoslovakia is based on close friendship and alliance with the Soviet Union and the East European socialist states. On the occasion of the Fiftieth Anniversary celebrations of the October Revolution the Czechoslovak leaders reaffirmed the close ties with the Soviet Union in all respects: "All that we have achieved in the building of socialism, and what we want to achieve for the further development of the socialist community, is unbreakably linked with the international cooperation with the . . . Soviet Union," declared Antonín Novotný at the Prague jubilee celebrations. "It is beyond doubt that for Czechoslovakia, considering its natural and economic conditions, broad cooperation with the Soviet Union and with the other socialist countries is a basic prerequisite if the country is to take the way of socialism" (*Rudé Právo*, 7 November 1967).

Throughout 1967 the CPC continued undeviatingly to follow the Soviet foreign-policy line. On 4-6 February Leonid Brezhnev, accompanied by Yuri Andropov, paid an unannounced visit to Czechoslovakia and held talks with CPC leaders. The joint communique indicated that European security and the German problem were high on the agenda of the talks, and both sides expressed "complete unity of views on questions of the present day international situation and the world communist and workers' movement." Following a visit of Czechoslovak Foreign Minister Václav David to Moscow on 16-25 February for talks aimed at "coordinating and more effectively implementing their respective foreign policies," the joint communique again announced a "complete unanimity on all questions discussed." Novotný again conferred with Brezhnev in the Soviet Union on 5-6 July.

In the sphere of foreign trade Czechoslovakia and the Soviet Union maintain close ties, as Czechoslovakia depends on the Soviet Union for supplies of raw materials. The share of the Soviet Union in Czechoslovak foreign trade amounts to nearly 40 per cent, and the Czechoslovak share in Soviet foreign trade to 10 to 11 per cent.

Czechoslovakia has continued to maintain close ties with its East European neighbors, politically as well as economically, culturally, and militarily. A top-level Czechoslovak delegation headed by Novotný visited Warsaw on 1 March and signed a treaty of friendship, cooperation, and mutual assistance with Poland, replacing a treaty signed in March 1947. On 17 March Novotný signed a similar treaty with the German Democratic Republic in Prague. Both treaties called for the defense of existing European frontiers, declared the Munich agreement invalid from the very beginning, and warned against the revanchist danger from the German Federal Republic. Under the provisions of the treaty the contracting states would develop closer bilateral ties and hold consultations on all important international questions concerning the two countries. Despite the clauses pertaining to West Germany in the respective treaties, and the strong anti-West German attacks expressed at the ceremonies surrounding the signing of the treaties (especially by the East Germans and Poles), Czechoslovakia emphasized that the treaties were not directed against any country and denied Western press comments on the formation of an "iron triangle" in the north. Czechoslovak sources put the treaties into the broader context of "European security."

---

*In early 1968 the Czechoslovak press brought to light an attempt by Novotný to retain power by mobilizing tank units around Prague. This attempted coup was widely publicized following the defection of the top political officer of the Czechoslovak army, General Jan Šejna, who had been implicated in the Novotný plot.

Relations with Hungary were especially cordial, and the joint communique following a visit by János Kádár to Czechoslovakia on 10-14 October noted that Hungarian-Czechoslovak relations are developing in every field in the spirit of "friendship, mutual understanding, and close cooperation." The communique stressed in particular that the introduction of the new systems of management and planning in their respective economies would create further possibilities for developing new and more effective forms of cooperation.

Czechoslovak relations with Yugoslavia were highlighted by a visit by Novotný to Belgrade (11-15 September) at the invitation of Yugoslav President Tito. The talks between the two party and state leaders concerned primarily bilateral relations and the Middle East crisis, on which an agreement of views was expressed. The two leaders noted that all avenues of contacts between the two states had not been developed and urged the future extension of cooperation in all spheres.

Czechoslovakia continued to give strong backing to the Warsaw Pact: "The Czechoslovak Socialist Republic is a firm link of the Warsaw Pact, and we realize that we can rely for our security on the armed forces of all member states of the Warsaw Pact, especially its main force—the Soviet Union and its armed forces," declared Antonín Novotný during a visit to the Soviet Union (*Rudé Právo*, 3 November 1967).

Czechoslovakia has also stressed the need to strengthen and improve the work of COMECON. COMECON member countries accounted for 67 per cent of Czechoslovak exports and supplied 69 per cent of its imports during 1967. In view of the economic processes developing within Czechoslovakia, the efforts of the Czechoslovak representatives in COMECON are directed toward perfecting forms of coordinating plans for technological development and toward pursuing the principles of specialization and cooperation within the organization. The Czechoslovak representatives have also actively urged the development of new institutions within COMECON, such as the International Bank for Economic Cooperation.

A strong case for the "integration" of COMECON countries from a Czechoslovak source was that individually the member states (with the exception of the Soviet Union) could not keep pace with world developments in science and could not attain economic superiority over capitalism in the foreseeable future. A "gradual and differentiated approach" to integration was urged, in contrast to a "global approach" (Josef Lašek,"Thoughts about the Integration of the Comecon Countries," *Rudé Právo*, 14 June 1967).

**Relations with Western Europe**. A leading issue on the foreign-policy agenda was the problem of European security, particularly relations with Bonn. Following the announcement in December 1966 of German Chancellor Kiesinger's new *Ostpolitik*, Czechoslovakia indicated interest in the possibility for the future establishment of diplomatic relations (but drew a specific distinction between diplomatic relations and "normalization" of relations.) However, following the Rumanian step to establish diplomatic relations with Bonn, the subsequent visit by Leonid Brezhnev to Prague (4-6 February), and the Warsaw Pact foreign ministers' meeting (8-10 February 1967), the earlier cautious interest seemed to disappear.

Czechoslovak demands on West Germany before Czechoslovakia could seriously consider Kiesinger's new *Ostpolitik* were declared to be the Bonn government's recognition of German postwar frontiers, the illegality of the Munich treaty from the very beginning, recognition of the German Democratic Republic, and renunciation of nuclear armament.

Czechoslovakia, however, continued to express interest in the general amelioration of relations with Bonn, particularly in the economic sphere. On August 3, after lengthy and difficult negotiations, Czechoslovakia and West Germany signed an agreement in Prague on the exchange of trade missions and an agreement on goods exchange and payments for the period 1967 to 1969. Czechoslovak sources noted the benefit of the treaties to bilateral trade but emphasized that the normalization of trade relations were still a far cry from normalization of political relations (*Rudé Právo*, 5 August 1967).

**The Third World**. Czechoslovakia has given active support, both moral and military, to the national liberation movements of the third world and to developing states "in the spirit of its socialist foreign policy" and in the spirit of Vladimír Koucký's statement: "It is without doubt that the final victory of socialism on a world scale is to a considerable extent dependent on how the third world countries start on the road of progress, and how consistently they proceed along this road" (*Rudé Právo*, 2 November 1967).

In the view of the Czechoslovak leadership the international situation has become increasingly tense owing to efforts by "imperialist circles to reverse the progressive trends in the world." The tension in Cyprus, the anticommunist campaign in Indonesia, the *coup d'état* in Greece, the Middle East crisis, and other political crises of 1967 were attributed to the "imperialist efforts to hold back the forces of progress." However, the focal point in the anti-imperialist struggle was Vietnam. "In the forefront of our international efforts," declared Vladimír Koucký, CPC Secretary in Charge of Foreign Affairs, at the Eighteenth Congress of the French Communist Party in January, "is the struggle against American imperialist aggression in Vietnam." Czechoslovakia offered Vietnam both moral and material aid. It fully endorsed the positions of the Democratic Republic of Vietnam and the National Liberation Front of South Vietnam, the "sole genuine representativies of the South Vietnamese people," as to the settlement of the conflict. On 9 October two economic agreements were signed at Zbraslav Castle near Prague, providing North Vietnam with material assistance, partly free of charge and partly on long-term interest-free credit, and aimed at strengthening North Vietnam's economy and defenses.

**Relations with the Middle East.** Czechoslovak relations with the Arab countries of the Middle East were especially cordial during 1967 and were characterized by the development of military ties. During the week of 3 January an army delegation from the United Arab Republic, headed by Chief of Staff Mohammed Fawzi, conferred in Prague with the Czechoslovak Chief of Staff, Colonel General Otakar Rytíř. The visit was returned by Rytíř in April, and on 14 April an agreement was signed in Cairo on the expansion of cooperation between the Czechoslovak and U.A.R. armies. Details of the agreement were not published, but Prague radio reports declared that the new agreement included provisions for collaboration in combat training, whereas earlier agreements had provided mainly for military education. On 10-17 May Czechoslovak Defense Minister Bohumír Lomský, accompanied by a group of experts, visited Damascus. The visit was returned in October by a Syrian military delegation headed by Defense Minister General Hafiz Assad.

The Czechoslovak government fully supported the Arab cause during the Middle East crisis, despite widespread popular sympathy in Czechoslovakia for Israel. A Czechoslovak Foreign Ministry statement of 25 May and another of 6 June put the blame for the crisis on Israel, which was backed by the "imperialists." Following the emergency meeting of East European communist party and government representatives in Moscow to coordinate action on the Middle East crisis, Czechoslovakia broke diplomatic relations with Israel on 10 June, the first state after the Soviet Union to do so. Czechoslovakia then sent delegations to the United Arab Republic and to Syria headed by Secretary Vladimír Koucký and Deputy Foreign Minister Václav Pleskot, respectively, to assess the situation in the Middle East and examine possibilities of further developing mutual relations.

The Czechoslovak anti-Israel stand was characterized by extreme statements describing the Israeli action as a "treacherous assault" and Israel as "the most militarist state in the entire world" (Jozef Lenárt, speech at the United Nations, 20 June, 1967, and *Pravda*, 18 June 1967). At the same time Czechoslovakia viewed the Middle East crisis as the consequence of efforts of "US imperialism" to hold back the progressive forces of the Middle East and put a barrier between them and the socialist states: "Thanks to the determined opposition by the people, the firm stand of the USSR and the position of the European socialist states, the aggressors did not succeed in overturning the progressive regimes in Syria and the UAR" (joint communique of the CPC and the French Communist Party, *Rudé Právo*, 12 July 1967).

The Czechoslovak leadership's anti-Israel propaganda had strong overtones of antisemitism, despite its claim that "there is no place whatsoever for anti-semitism in the ČSSR, and it will always be suppressed without compromise" (*Rudé Právo*, 15 June 1967), and despite its extensive efforts to present its policy as "anti-zionist," since "zionism" is "a tool of imperialism."* However, following

---

*Rudé Právo* (18-19 July 1967) charged that the Arab-Israeli war resulted from an "unholy alliance" between the "zionist circles" in Israel and the "imperialists."

the Arab-Israeli war Czechoslovak officials cancelled a scheduled celebration of the millenium of Czechoslovakia's Jewish community and even withdrew from circulation a recently issued series of postage stamps commemorating the Jewish museum in Prague.

**Relations with China.** Czechoslovakia played a leading role in the international communist movement as one of the closest adherents to the Soviet party line. The CPC has vehemently supported the Soviet Union against "calumnies" emanating from Peking and has consistently denounced the "adventurous" and "splitting" policies of the Chinese leaders, describing them as "blending petit bourgeois adventurism with big power chauvinism, a policy which runs counter to Marxism-Leninism, which is profoundly opposed to the principles of proletarian internationalism, and which gravely threatens the socialist achievements of the Chinese people" (Alexander Dubček at a mass rally in Bratislava marking the Fiftieth Anniversary of the October Revolution). The attacks of the Chinese leaders against the Soviet state and the party, and the international communist movement, according to Alexander Dubček, objectively help the aggressive policy of American imperialism.

Despite existing difficulties with China, the CPC affirmed its belief that the present actions of the Chinese leaders "cannot pass the test of time" and that the Czech government and the CPC consider cooperation and friendship "right and beneficial" and will "continue to support the people of China who are building socialism to restore friendship and cooperation based on the idea of Marxism-Leninism and proletarian internationalism" (*Rudé Právo,* 28 March 1967 on the occasion of the tenth anniversary of the Sino-Czechoslovak treaty of friendship and cooperation).

**International Meetings.** The CPC helped to organize and was host to the Karlovy Vary Conference of European Communist and Workers' Parties on 24-26 April. In its evaluation of the conference two major points emerged: that the responsibility for peace and security in Europe lies with the communist and workers' parties, and that the conference proved that it is still possible to hold an international communist meeting which can agree on a joint line of action.

The CPC was also host to an international conference "on the historical significance of the Great October Socialist Revolution" (22-24 June 1967). Vladimír Koucký's lecture presented at the conference (reprinted in *WMR,* August 1967) was a comprehensive report of the CPC's views on the unity of the international communist movement. Koucký warned that, despite the growing strength of the socialist forces of the world and the weakening of the imperialistic camp, the socialist forces must not underestimate imperialism's attempts at subversion in the political and ideological fields. It is thus necessary to insist on international solidarity and joint action of all the·anti-imperialist forces in conformity with decisions made by the majority of communist parties and aimed at the strengthening of the international movement as a qualitatively separate entity with sovereign interests. Koucký rejected the views that the domestic achievements of a communist party are a principal contribution to the international movement; he also rejected the view that an individual party could evaluate Marxism-Leninism and make final decisions on what is and what is not beneficial to the movement, and that the "isolated policy of one party" can be put on the same level as "conclusions discussed and agreed upon by fraternal parties." Koucký's lecture concluded with the urgent call for an international conference, embracing a "maximum number of communist parties," which would adopt a platform acceptable to all parties desirous of joint and genuinely international action."*

On 2 November Koucký again called for the convening of an international meeting and stressed that the time was ripe for "concrete preparations." He also indicated that the urgency of the meeting was due to activities of the Chinese leadership:

> We cannot be indifferent to the way the Mao Tse-tung group in the CCP is systematically and intentionally undermining the unity of the socialist community and the world

---

*Vladimír Koucký's lecture had wide repercussions in other socialist states. The Rumanian party deleted the summary of his lecture from the Rumanian edition of the August issue of *World Marxist Review.* In a Radio Belgrade commentary (13 October) Branko Prebićević, professor at the Institute for Political Sciences, challenged Koucký's statement (without defining, however, the specific occasion of the statement) on the right of any one party to evaluate Marxism-Leninism.

Communist movement, and disparaging the ideas of socialism in the eyes of the progressive world public. . . . The historic responsibility for the detrimental consequences of this policy must be fully borne by those who are carrying it out. (V. Koucký, "The World Progresses in the Significance of October," *Rudé Právo,* 2 November 1967.)

The December plenum of the Central Committee passed a resolution officially declaring the CPC's support for the upcoming international communist party meeting to be held in Budapest in February 1968.

The CPC leadership held numerous consultations with foreign party leaders, primarily to discuss the convening of the conference at Karlovy Vary and the convening of an international communist party conference. Before the opening of the Karlovy Vary Conference, CPC representatives met in Prague with leaders of the Belgian party on 18-20 January and the Italian party on 24-28 January. They met with Yugoslav party representatives on three occasions: in Belgrade on 3-6 February and in Prague on 2-6 April and on 20 April. The CPC leaders also met with Rumanian party representatives in Prague on 13 April and with a representative of the Communist Party of Colombia on 19 April. Following the Karlovy Vary Conference, a CPC delegation went to Austria (18-24 May) and to Finland (23-30 May) for talks with the representatives of the respective foreign parties. Talks were held in Prague between leaders of the CPC and the French Communist Party (4-10 July), the Iraqi Communist Party (11-18 July), and the Israeli Communist Party (13 July). A high level CPC delegation traveled to Italy (18-21 July) and conferred with Secretary-General of the Italian Communist Party Luigi Longo, and First Secretary of the East German party Walter Ulbricht conferred in Czechoslovakia with Antonín Novotný in August. Beginning in October, numerous foreign party delegations stopped in Prague en route to and from Moscow to attend the Fiftieth Anniversary celebrations, and held talks with Vladimír Koucký and other CPC representatives. These included First Secretary of the Central Committee of the Communist Party of Colombia Gilberto Vieira (10 October and 6-10 December), Secretary-General of the Australian Communist Party Laurie Aarons (12 October), Secretary-General of the Communist Party of Spain Santiago Carrillo (12 October), Chairman of the Communist Party of Argentina Victorio Codovilla (18 October), Austrian Communist Party Politburo members Friedl Fuernberg and Erwin Scharf (who also met with Antonín Novotný on 20 October), Secretary-General of the Communist Party of Ecuador Pedro Saad (23 October), First Secretary of the Central Committee of the Communist Party of Uruguay Rodney Arismendi (27 October), a delegation of the Communist Party of India headed by Secretary-General Rajeshwar Rao (who also met with Antonín Novotný on 15 November), and a delegation of the People's Party of Panama consisting of Chairman Hugo Victor and Secretary-General Rubén Souza (25 December). At the beginning of December Vladimír Koucký traveled to Budapest for talks with First Secretary of the Central Committee of the Hungarian party János Kádár and Politburo member Zoltán Komocsin.

In addition to hosting the Conference of European Communist and Workers' Parties, Czechoslovakia was also host to other international meetings, such as a symposium held at Marienbad (27-30 April) to discuss the theme "creative activity and freedom in a human society," jointly sponsored by the West German Paulus Society and the Sociological Institute of the Czechoslovak Academy of Sciences, and a conference at Marienbad (17-19 May) of directors of European institutes for the study of international relations to discuss European security. An international symposium was organized in Prague (25-26 October) by the journal *Problems of Peace and Socialism (WMR)* to mark the one hundredth anniversary of the publication of the first volume of Karl Marx's *Das Kapital,* and the fiftieth anniversary of the publication of V. I. Lenin's *Imperialism: The Highest Stage of Capitalism,* and on 4-6 December an international conference of representatives of Marxist cultural-political and literary journals from communist and some West European countries was held in Prague.

**Publications.** The daily central organ of the CPC is *Rudé Právo,* the theoretical biweekly is *Nová Mysl.* The Central Committee biweekly for party functionaries is *Život Strany.* The organs of the Communist Party of Slovakia are the daily *Pravda* and the Central Committee weekly on politics, culture, and economy, *Predvoj.*

# DENMARK

The Communist Party of Denmark (Danmarks Kommunistiske Parti; DKP) was founded 9 November 1920. A legal party, the DKP claims a membership of 6,000; its principal support is in Copenhagen and other major urban centers. The population of Denmark is 4,797,000 (estimated, January 1968). There exists also a politically insignificant Maoist splinter group, the Communist Working Circle (Kommunistisk Arbejdskreds; KAK), established by Gotfred Appel and Benito Scocozza in June 1964, which has a small following (approximately 50 members) among intellectuals and students.

Since the 1945 elections, in which the DKP polled 12.5 per cent of the votes and gained 18 parliamentary seats, due in large measure to the party's favorable resistance record in World War II, support for the DKP has steadily diminished; the party has not been represented in Parliament since 1960. The Socialist People's Party (Socialistisk Folkeparti; SF), founded in 1959 by Aksel Larsen, Chairman of the DKP from 1932 until his expulsion in 1958, has succeeded in siphoning votes from both the Social Democratic Party (Socialdemokratiet) on the right and the DKP on the left. In December 1967 a new socialist party, the Left Socialists (Venstresocialisterne), was formed from the left wing of the Socialist People's Party. It was with notable difficulty that the DKP managed to secure the 15,966 pledges required to place it on the ballot in the special elections of 23 January 1968; its share of the votes (one per cent) showed a slight increase over the 0.8 per cent obtained in the 1966 elections. The SF polled 6.1 per cent, a decline from 10.9 per cent in 1966, while the Social Democratic Party vote dropped from 38.2 to 34.2 per cent. The Left Socialists, on the ballot for the first time, polled two per cent of the votes and took four seats previously held by the Socialist People's Party. Securing a combined 98 of the 179 mandates, three centrist and conservative parties (Conservative, Radical Liberal, and Moderate Liberal) formed a coalition government.

In general, 1967 marked a year of declining fortunes for the left in Danish political life, culminating in the defeat in the January 1968 elections of the Social Democratic Party, which had been in power for 40 years, and in the ouster (after less than one year) of the first socialist majority to govern Denmark. With a margin of two seats over the nonsocialist opposition as a result of the November 1966 elections, the Social Democratic minority government in March 1967 entered into a parliamentary alliance with the SF, under the terms of which the Social Democrats retained all cabinet appointments. It was Prime Minister Jens Otto Krag's failure to gain consolidated SF support on an austerity bill designed to stem inflation following devaluation of the Danish krone which toppled his administration and forced the special election. Passage of the bill was blocked on 15 December by the defection of six SF extremists in defiance of their party Chairman, Aksel Larsen.

Larsen, a partisan of genuine de-Stalinization, critical of Soviet intervention in Hungary in 1956 and sympathetic to the League of Communists of Yugoslavia, was expelled from the DKP for his alleged "revisionism." While claiming ideological adherence to Marxism, the SF maintains that the Danish road to socialism must follow Danish parliamentary-democratic traditions; it asserts an anticapitalist, anti-imperialist, neutralist, and anti-USA political position, calling for total and unilateral disarmament, opposing Danish membership in NATO and any move to join the European Economic Community, and favoring a diplomatic break with Saigon and recognition of Hanoi. (This policy is at variance with that of the Social Democratic Party on such issues—Krag is, for example, strongly pro-NATO—and the Parliamentary alliance of the two parties was intended more as an instrument for the passage of domestic economic measures than as a mutual expression of policy positions.)

Factionalism within the SF, characterized by a "soft" wing supporting Larsen's policy of collaboration with the Social Democrats and a "hard" wing calling for radical policy changes, threatened to produce a split at the extraordinary party congress held in June 1967. Although Larsen, the sole nominee for party Chairman, gained reelection, the congress actually represented a victory for the left wing, which unseated Larsen's principal supporters; all but four of the 31 members elected to the Executive Committee were proclaimed leftists "with different ideas about the proper direction of the party." The split was temporarily staved off, but on December 17 the dissenters walked out of the second party congress of the year (called because of the resignation of the Krag government), and announced the formation of the Left Socialists. In the absence of another candidate, and with almost two-thirds of the delegates abstaining from voting, Larsen was once again reelected to the post of Chairman, but was this time forced to agree to step down after one year.

Throughout the course of these events, the DKP failed to anticipate that the split in the SF would produce a new, fourth labor party, and in *Land og Folk* (24 June) acclaimed the action of the "rebels" ("whose demands are very close to those demands on which we once stood alone") and saw "new hope for uniting the left." But with the declared intention of the Left Socialists to enter the 1968 elections, it became evident that the new party had no plans to join ranks with the Communists, whose reaction was: "However understandable the SF split, it is not necessary to form new parties in order to conduct a new policy" (*ibid.*, 31 December 1967-1 January 1968).

**Organization and Leadership.** Chairman of the DKP is Knud Jespersen; Ib Nørlund is the Secretary-General. Together with Jespersen and Nørlund, the Politburo of the Central Committee includes Poul Emanuel, Ludvig Hansen, S. Nilsen, and Johannes Poulssen. Other Central Committee members are Alfred Jensen, Villy Fuglsang, Gelius Lund, Villy Karlsson, Erik Hansen, Ingmar Wagner, Per Kristensen, Christian Hermann Jensen, Arne Madsen, Inge Nielsen, Kaj Buch, Knud Nyeng, and Luis Chandorf.

**Domestic Policies and Activities.** The DKP favors a "peaceful transition to socialism," and the promotion of a "united front," applying Marxism to "the country's conditions and circumstances" and recognizing the need to "develop more concretely the [DKP] stand against the policy of complete dependence on other nations as well as the hysteria of sectarianism" (*Tiden*, no. 2, 1967). "Peaceful transition to socialism," according to the party, "should be understood as a steadily intensified struggle for major reforms and political measures, and a "period of extreme tension . . . of broad and active mass struggle"; moreover: "the forms of transition to socialism and the institutions through which this will be effected must grow out of specific national conditions" (*WMR*, November 1967). The precise nature of those "forms" and "institutions" prescribed by the DKP for a nonviolent seizure of power and transition to socialism remains obscure. Commenting on this issue, a DKP representative was reported as stating: "It should be by a majority of the people, but not necessarily by means of the ballot" (*SF Bladet*, Copenhagen, no. 19, 8 March).

The DKP continues to follow the program issued at the Twenty-second Party Congress in November 1965, which calls for a united struggle against "monopolistic capitalism" and for the "social and democratic rights of workers." The party accuses the Social Democrats and the SF of betraying the workers and "acting as business managers of the capitalists." In his New Year statement of 1967, DKP Chairman Jespersen stated: "A labor majority in parliament is not synonymous with a socialist majority. . . . The expectations of the workers have not been fulfilled. Big financial powers still have their hands free, and profiteering increases." Calling for "division of the national income 'in a new manner'," he said: "The time is ripe for nationalization of banks and insurance companies, takeover by the state of the large building material monopolies . . . , improvements in housing programs, establishment of a new taxation scale in favor of the working class, expansion of the domestic market's buying power, and raising of the employment level" (*Land og Folk*, 1-2 January).

After the Social Democratic–SF Parliamentary union, the DKP embarked on a concerted campaign against the two parties, directed largely toward Aksel Larsen. Jespersen commented: "The disappointments over the position of the majority and the indignation over the failure of the SF leadership should not lead to passivity. [Rather,] there should be a reinforced effort for a policy with greater democratic reforms, with socialist goals and a steadfast approach to militarism and capitalism. The key to a new development is to continue the breakthrough which led to the 22 November 1966 election." (*ibid.*, 4 April.)

Expressing readiness to "take up tasks [with the SFj upon which we can agree," Jespersen admitted to a reversal of the March 1959 theses of the DKP, which proclaimed that Communists could under no circumstances recognize the (then newly formed) Socialist People's Party as part of the socialist movement in Denmark.

In a speech to the DKP National Conference (Copenhagen, 18-19 November), Jespersen attacked the Government's foreign and military policies, the housing shortage, land laws and their "lack of clarity," and the "compromise policy" of the Government in the area of tax legislation. He claimed that "big capital" had been "used in a general attack against the working Denmark, under the slogan of 'structural rationalization'," and that in the meantime the two parliamentary majority parties had "contented themselves by stating that 'there is no ground for panic'." He went on to say: "Now as before there are two main lines in the labor movement, one revolutionary and communist and one for the existing administrative and reformist line," adding that the Danish Communists had "perhaps not asserted sufficiently" their "independent policy," and that the character of DKP shortcomings was "not one of principle, and was to be found in the weaknesses and defects acquired along the lengthy path following the confrontation with those who wanted to liquidate the party." (*Land og Folk,* 19-20 November.)

**Auxiliary Organizations.** The DKP youth organization, Communist Youth of Denmark (Danmarks Kommunistiske Ungdom; DKU), generally supports the party in both domestic and foreign policy, but seeks to pursue a more "revolutionary" development and a "modernized" ideology which will appeal to youth on a broader front. Gunnar Kanstrup, reelected Chairman of the DKU at its Twenty-seventh Congress (Copenhagen, 21-23 April), has stated: "We will work for socialism . . . but we will not restrict ourselves to discussion—we want action also" (*Land og Folk,* 22 April).

Uniting with other youth organizations, ranging from left-socialist to social democrat, the DKU in 1967 staged numerous demonstrations and propaganda campaigns opposing US policy in Vietnam, the April coup d'état in Greece, and calling for governmental recognition of political opinions as grounds for exemption to military service. The DKU was also vociferous in its condemnation of "neocolonial exploitation" in developing countries.

DKU-DKP relations concerning events in Communist China are openly strained. Although the youth organization, like the DKP, espouses a pro-Soviet stand, it deplores the "lack of objectivity" in the DKP press in "uncritically reporting anti-Chinese articles from Soviet, East European, and bourgeois press bureaus" (*Land og Folk,* 2 February).

A delegation of the South Vietnam Liberation Youth Union visited Denmark in June at the invitation of the DKU. Gunnar Kanstrup was in Moscow for the Fiftieth Anniversary celebrations as the guest of the Soviet youth organization Komsomol.

There exists within the DKP an auxiliary League of Women (Kvindeudvalg), which has negligible political influence. Chairman of the League is Lilian Thomsen. Its National Conference (4-5 March), urged legislation assuring equal pay for equal work, improved health and welfare services, and "voluntary motherhood only."

DKP influence in trade unions is insignificant; the SF, Left Socialists, and DKP together control less than five per cent of organized labor and no national unions (see *World Strength of the Communist Party Organizations,* 1968). Kaj Buch, a member of the DKP Central Committee, is Vice-President of the Permanent Committee of the Workers' Conferences of the Baltic Countries, Norway and Iceland, held annually by trade unionists in Rostock, East Germany, to which the DKP sends delegations. The 1967 meeting took place 12-14 July.

The DKP is influential in a number of "friendship" organizations, including the Denmark-Soviet Union Association, whose Chariman is DKP Central Committee member Alfred Jensen.

**International Views and Policies.** The Central Committee of the DKP in February issued a policy statement reaffirming the party's "adherence to the policy lines drawn up at the international [communist and workers' parties] conferences of 1957 and 1960" (*Tiden,* no. 2, 1967). In his New Year statement, party Chairman Jespersen said: "NATO is singing its final chorus." He advocated initiatives to "bring the world to recognition of the North as a nuclear-free zone." (*Land og Folk,* 1

January). "The key to making Europe a zone of peace," he later stated, is recognition of "existing borders, including the Oder-Neisse border," and of "two German states," together with "negotiations on a collective peace guarantee to replace NATO and the Warsaw Pact" (*ibid.*, 2 May).

Convening on 28 May to discuss the documents issued at the Conference of European Communist and Workers' Parties (Karlovy Vary, 24-27 April), the Central Committee adopted a resolution urging that Denmark declare itself a neutral nation, demand world guarantees for its inviolability, and embark upon a policy of disarmament, adding that "the realization of proposals for the Nordic region as an atom-free zone can be a first step" (*ibid.*, 30 May).

In the Middle East conflict, the DKP "sharply condemned" Israel's "aggression, supported by American imperialism, directed against the UAR, Syria, Jordan, and other Arab countries," and called for Israel's withdrawal to previous borders, and for peaceful negotiations leading to "binding international guarantees for the security and inviolabililty of Israel and of the Arab states" (*Land og Folk*, 24 June).

An "informal" Nordic Socialist Seminar, held 26-27 February by the Socialist People's Party, sought to provide a "positive contribution in the struggle for a reevaluation of the North." The DKP, together with the Norwegian Communist Party, was denied admission (although the Swedish, Finnish, and Icelandic Communists were represented). The DKP reacted vehemently, stating that the meeting could not be considered a "representative expression of the socialist parties and leftist elements in the North." Without a "reevaluation of the North's relations to the socialist world and thereby of the position to state, economic, and cultural relations with the socialist countries," Jespersen claimed, "the North cannot achieve the desired goal." Citing the participation of Finnish Communists in the coalition government of that country, he emphasized that the times demanded a "new cooperation between all socialist forces—in spite of ideological differences and organizational division and without discrimination against the Marxist-Leninist forces." (*Land og Folk*, 26-27 February).

The DKP achieved some measure of success during 1967 in its efforts to align with other movements in a "popular front" on "cross-party" issues, seeking unity of action as a means of creating a "national movement" against NATO, the European Economic Community, and the "American war" in Vietnam. At the National Party Conference, Central Committee member Ingmar Wagner, one of the founders of the Danish "Vietnam Committee," stressed the significance of "cooperation in a broad gathering of the many different initiatives," and added: "The Vietnam work has a span from the most sectarian, who follow Chairman Mao's thought or the Trotskyists, and over to the bourgeois pacifists." (*Ibid.*, 21 November.) In this vein, and in order to exploit the anti-Americanism espoused by "new leftists," the Communists staged a broad-based "Vietnam solidarity meeting" on 29 August, the anniversary of Denmark's liberation from German forces in World War II. Implicit in this timing was a comparison to be drawn between the occupation of Denmark and the situation of the South Vietnamese people.

While there exist within the DKP substantial elements sympathetic to the Chinese position, the higher echelons of the party have assumed an unquestionably pro-Soviet stand in the polemics between the Soviet and Chinese parties. Early in 1967 a DKP statement sharply criticized the Chinese leadership:

> A horribly long leap backwards seems to have taken place in China. Mistakes and backsliding in China are being overcome with the help of new mistakes which are not being corrected when the collective leadership is abolished in favor of an unheard-of personality cult, when the party is replaced by school youths. The struggle against American imperialism has slipped into the background. One hardly hears of it. One cannot say the same about the Mao-people's crazy and warlike attack on the Soviet Union . . . . The latest events . . . are bringing China completely into isolation from all other people and from the whole communist world movement. (*Land og Folk*, 7 February.)

Challenging Mao's ideological motivation, Central Committee member Gelius Lund suggested that the Chinese leader "thought Communism could be realized without an interim phase of socialism." This, Lund wrote, was a "conspicuous break with Marxism." (*Land og Folk*, 17-18 September).

While praising the CPSU's "enduring and consistent efforts to strengthen and develop the international unity" of the communist movement, Politburo member Ib Nørlund blamed China for the threat to unity:

It is exactly those dark clouds which are now appearing in different places on the horizon of the international sky which make the strengthening of the unity of the communist movement an even more meaningful and called-for task. . . . Those who fall behind in this unity serve the gloomiest forces in the struggle of our day. The Mao-wing's activity in China is a warning example of this. (*ibid.*, 5-6 November).

The DKP has not been remiss, however, in its criticism of working conditions of writers in the USSR, and the party leadership renewed its protest against Soviet prosecution of intellectuals:

It is the affair of the Soviet courts to interpret and mete out sentence. But socialism's social system is an international concern, and the picture of socialism as a symbol of humanity's ideals should not be despoiled. (*ibid.*, 21 September).

The DKP favors the convocation of a "thoroughly prepared" international conference of communist parties. Returning from Karlovy Vary, Nørlund commented: "The time is ripe for an international conference which, based on the experience gained in the fifties, will give the unity of the communist movement a decisive forward tug. There is increasing common understanding that the new ideological forms of the anticommunist efforts must be met by joint actions." (*ibid.*, 14-15 May).

The party's position was reaffirmed in joint communiques following meetings with the Bulgarian Communist Party (Sofia, 15-24 July, and Copenhagen, 27 November-4 December), by Knud Jespersen's speech at the fiftieth anniversary celebrations in Moscow, and in the joint communique issued by the CPSU and the DKP following their meeting in Moscow on 11 September. The latter document alleged that the "divisive activities of the Mao Tse-tung group make it compellingly necessary to consolidate all anti-imperialist forces, above all the unity of the Marxist-Leninist parties." (*IB*, no. 108, 1967). This denunciation of "the Mao Tse-tung group" would appear to represent a significant shift from a Central Committee resolution of December 1966 which stressed that "the conference must be a forum which does not pass judgment but serves the restoration of unity of action."

The DKP was represented at the congresses of the French Communist Party (Paris, 4-8 January); the German Socialist Unity Party (Berlin, 17-22 April); the Finnish People's Democratic League (Helsinki, 13-15 May); and the Swedish Communist Party (Stockholm, 13-16 May).

The party also had bilateral contacts with other communist parties. A five-man party delegation, headed by Jespersen, went to Hungary on a "study tour" 25 July-2 August as guests of the Central Committee of the Hungarian Socialist Workers' Party; a Rumanian Party delegation was in Denmark 22-29 September for discussions with the DKP on "European security"; and a French Communist Party delegation visited Denmark 24-26 October.

A delegation of the National Liberation Front of South Vietnam (NLFSV), headed by Nguyen Van Dong, Permanent Representative in the USSR, visited Denmark during "Vietnam Week" (1-7 May) at the invitation of the DKP. On 30 November delegations from the Democratic Republic of Vietnam and the NLFSV, in Denmark for the Russell Tribunal, held talks with the DKP.

**Publications.** The DKP daily organ is *Land og Folk* (Land and People), edited by Villy Karlsson. The party's theoretical organ is *Tiden* (The Times), issued eight times a year and edited by Ib Nørlund. *Fremad* (Forward) is the organ of the DKU.

The Communist Working Circle (KAK) issues weekly a mimeographed bulletin, *Kommunistisk Orientering* (Communist Orientation), edited by Gotfred Appel and Benito Scocozza.

# DOMINICAN REPUBLIC

Internal dissension and fragmentation characterizes communism in the Dominican Republic. There are three principal movements: first, the traditionally pro-Soviet Dominican Communist Party (Partido Communista Dominicano; PCD), which has shown definite signs of adopting a Castroist stance; second, the Dominican People's Movement (Movimiento Popular Dominicano; MPD), which is both pro-Chinese and, to a lesser degree, Castroist; and, third, the Revolutionary Movement of June 14 (Movimiento Revolucionario 14 June; MR-1J4), which though primarily Castroist appears to court Chinese support. Splits have occurred within all three groups, resulting in the creation of several new factions and parties, including the Dominican People's Socialist Party (Partido Socialista Popular Dominicano; PSP), the Orthodox Communist Party (Partido Communista Ortodoxo; PCO), and the Communist Party of the Dominican Republic (Partido Comunista de la Republica Dominicana; PCRD or PACOREDO).

Overall communist membership, which the fragmentation of the Dominican extreme left makes it difficult to ascertain, is estimated as between 1,000 and 2,000 persons. The population of the Dominican Republic is 3,750,000 (estimated July 1966). Western estimates break down the communist membership as: PCD, 300; MPD, 300; MR-1J4, 500; PCO 50; PCRD, 100; and PSP, 50. All of these groups have admitted their weakness. The relative strengths of the left and extreme left parties were apparent in the elections of June 1966. The government's Reformist Party (Partido Reformista), in a coalition headed by its representative, Joaquin Balaguer, obtained 57.4 percent of the votes. Professor Bosch's supporters—the Dominican Revolutionary Party (Partido Revolucionario Dominicano; PRD) and the Social Christian Revolutionary Party (Partido Revolucionario Social Cristiano; PRSC)—representing the left-wing opposition, obtained 39.1 per cent of the poll (36.8 per cent from the PRD and 2.3 per cent from the PRSC). The near totality of the remaining votes went to the supporters of the right-wing candidate, Rafael Bonnelly. The only communist party allowed to participate in the elections under its own ticket was the Revolutionary Movement of June 14; members of other communist parties were limited to expressing support for the participating parties (including the MR-1J4). Support by the MR-1J4, as a party, was offered to Juan Bosch, but was not accepted. The MR-1J4 obtained only 0.3 per cent of the poll and ceased to hold legal status (8 per cent being required for this).

Though the PCD advocated support for Juan Bosch, the extent of PCD participation in the PRD-PRSC vote is impossible to ascertain.

In view of the divisions within Dominican communism, it is difficult to determine which segment of the population supports which party. According to documents seized in Venezuela in 1967 from Fernando de la Rosa (a prominent MPD member) and publicly revealed by President Balaguer (*El Nacional*, 5 February), communist support is to be found among some university and secondary school students and in a segmant of organized labor. The principal source of student communist support is an organization called Fragua, which controls the Federation of Dominican Students (Federación de Estudiantes Dominicanos; FED). The Union of Revolutionary Students (Unión de Estudiantes Revolucionarios), an organization of secondary school students, is also a source of support. Within the trade unions, support comes from the "Foupsa-Cesitrado" and "Fenepia" unions (representing mainly sugar and construction workers and government employees). The Federation of Dominican Women (Federación de Mujeres Dominicanos) also contributes to communist support. The various student and trade union groups were formerly almost solely supported by the PCD. Recently they have either split and aligned themselves with various contending parties or taken an independent position, as with the United Patriotic Committee (Comité Patriótico Unitario; CPU). The

CPU includes communists from the "Foupsa-Cesitrado" and "Fenepia" labor unions and from the FED.

**PCD.** The PCD was founded clandestinely in 1942. It was reestablished openly as the Dominican People's Socialist Party (Partido Socialista Popular Dominicano) in 1946. During the military-civilian revolt in April 1965 the party identified itself once again as the Dominican Communist Party.

The PCD is illegal, but is not repressed. Its activities are tolerated and illegaility is limited to electoral participation.

The PCD has apparently gone through a major ideological and tactical struggle. Due to this and also as a result of the arrest of the prominent PDC leader Narciso Isa Conde (*El Nacional,* 5 September), it is difficult to determine who now represents the leadership. It is believed that Fabio García is still the Secretary-General of the PCD.

**Domestic Views and Policies.** In domestic affairs, the PCD has seemingly repudiated its acceptance of Soviet "peaceful coexistence" as the principal means of establishing socialism and communism. In the last months of 1967, the PCD revealed itself as increasingly pro-Castroist. At the Havana conference of the Latin American Solidarity Organization (OLAS), in August 1967, it supported armed struggle as the principal means to revolution, although other forms were not ruled out (*El Nacional,* 7 August).

Following the death of "Che" Guevara, the PCD issued a communique to the press (*El Nacional,* 16 October) lamenting his demise and stating that it was a serious blow to the Latin American guerrilla movement. The statement claimed that Guevara would live on in the revolutionaries who would now rush to the mountains. It went on to reveal, however, that there was disagreement among the Communists themselves over the advocacy of armed struggle, admitting the existence of "waverers" and of those who would cite the Guevara diasater and denounce the guerrilla path as "adventurism." Such dissent was termed betrayal. On 29 November, Guaroa Ubiñas, the new Secretary-General of the PCD—influenced FED, led a march to the University of Santo Domingo in memory of Guevara (*ibid.,* 30 November).

The PCD communique reiterated the position adopted by the party at the OLAS conference. The Dominican Republic newspaper *El Caribe* on 7 August published a PCD document supporting Cuba against both "ultrarevolutionaries" who said Cuba was not socialist and "pacifists" who called Cuba's material aid to revolutionaries elsewhere "interference in the internal affairs of their countries." This document also set out the position to be taken by the party delegation at the conference, supporting the line that all "bourgeois" governments must be overthrown and that the Latin American path to revolution was armed struggle in nearly every case; further, because the peasantry comprises most of the Latin American population, the countryside would be the principal scene of "revolutionary war," however, this fact would not preclude insurrection or armed action in the cities. In general, the document held that the revolutionary movements should practice all forms of armed struggle, but particularly guerrilla struggle.

Preoccupied with the formulation of this new ideological position, the PCD was not very active domestically during 1967. Most of its efforts were directed toward discrediting other communist factions, such as the PCRD, which it branded as serving the interests of "reactionaries and imperialists" (*ibid.,* 14 August). Even so the wave of terrorism and violence in the streets of Santo Domingo in early May seems to have been fomented partly by the PCD, although it emphatically denied the charge (*ibid.,* 9 May).

**International Views and Policies.** In international affairs the positions taken by the PCD during 1967 reflected its pro-Castroist stand. In January the Central Committee of the PDC made public a document stating its position on the current events in China. It criticized Mao Tse-tung for purging the Chinese Communist Party by means of the Red Guards and endorsed the party's efforts to maintain its organization and existence (*IB,* no. 95, 1967).

Following the Arab-Israeli war in June, the PCD condemned Israel and proclaimed support for the Arab peoples (*El Nacional,* 12 June). After criticizing the Soviet Union for adopting a passive attitude toward the Middle East crisis, the PCD condemned it for accepting peace and "abandoning its solidarity with the Arabs when this was most necessary" (*ibid.,* 17 June).

The PCD's shift toward armed struggle and the Castroist line has not so far had a marked effect on its relations with the Soviet Union. A communique published as a paid advertisement in *El Nacional* (30 October) praised the Bolshevik Revolution on its fiftieth anniversary and denounced the memoirs of Svetlana Alliluieva (Stalin's daughter), stories of Stalin's misgovernment, and accounts of the deficiencies of Soviet rule. A Dominican communist delegation to the anniversary celebrations was reported by the Soviet press to have been led by Fabio García.

**Publications.** The PCD publishes a weekly, *El Popular.* Its declarations also appear as paid advertisements in the independent daily *El National.*

**PCD Dissidents** The PCD's "hard Line" has met considerable opposition from less militant Communists within the PCD. *El Nacional* on 12 October reported a PCD complaint that the brothers Juan and Félix Servio Ducondray, who had been expelled as "rightists," had formed a new party, and that after publishing some issues of a newspaper called *Adelante* they were confusing the public by producing one under the name *El Popular,* the same as that of the PCD's own paper.

The formation of this new communist faction took place in August. An announcement in *El Nacional* (27 August) claimed that Central Committee members, intermediate leaders, and rank and file of the old Dominican People's Socialist Party (PSP; renamed the PCD in 1965), had refused to be carried away by the PCD leadership's "wave of adventurism and anti-Sovietism." They had, therefore, decided to reorganize the party under its old name and would oppose the "left opportunists" who had broken with the Moscow declaration of 1960 on peaceful coexistence.

"Extreme leftists," the statement continued, had weakened the Dominican revolutionary movement: the PDC, MR-1J4, PCRD, and PCO had all contributed to the demoralization of the movement by presenting a deformed picture of communism and discrediting the revolutionary theory of Marx, Engels, and Lenin. The PSP claimed that is was not another sectarian group, but was the true representative of Marxism-Leninism and would correct the errors and disunity of the revolutionary force.

The ultimate aim of the PSP does not seem to differ from that of the parties it condemns: "The supreme object of the PSP is the truimph of the proletarian revolution in order to bring socialism and communism in the Dominican Republic." But it rejects armed struggle and sees the correct path as the formation of a united front of workers, peasants, the middle class, and the national bourgeoisie, to bring about as a first step a "democratic and anti-imperialist revolution." (*Ibid.*)

**MPD.** The PCD's principal communist opponent in the Dominican Republic is the pro-Chinese Dominican People's Movement, formed in Havana in 1956 by a militant wing of the Dominican People's Socialist Party to fight "revisionist" tendencies. The MPD did not attempt to consolidate itself as a formal party until 16-24 August 1965, when it held a "pre-congress" in Santo Domingo (See *Documentos del Primer Pre-Congreso del Partido de la Clase Obrera, Movimiento Popular Dominicano,* 30 September 1965).

Due to extreme internal strife within the MPD—evident in 1966 (See *YICA,* 1966) and continued in 1967—it is not clear who is in control of the party. The most important members appear to be Caonabo Jorge Tavárez, Cayetano Rodríguez, Ramón A. Pinedo, Julio de Peña Valdez, Marino Nazario, Henry Segarra, Otto Morales, Maximiliano Gómez, and Rafael "Fafa" Taveras. After breaking with the MR-1J4, Taveras joined the MPD in December 1966 (*El Nacional,* 13 and 15 July). There are indications that the Taveras "hard liners" are gaining prominence in the party. A number of MPD statements on the party's domestic and international positions in 1967 were signed by Taveras (see, for instance, *ibid.,* 15 May).

The leadership has been dealt severe blows by the apparently effective measures of the National Police in the Dominican Republic. In early May, Ignacio Marte Polanco, a top party member and Cuban-trained espionage agent, was arrested. Balaguer in his 8 May address to the nation noted that this marked the first time that an international communist agent had been captured operating in the Dominican Republic (*ibid.,* 9 May). On 12 July the police reported in a paid advertisement in *El National* that Julio de Peña Valdez, the Secretary-General of the labor organization "Foupsa-Cesitrado," was the main leader of the MPD in labor affairs. Documents concerning plans f communist subversion were seized by the police in De Peña Valdez' home. The police also hav files of a prominent MPD leader, Ramón A. Pinedo, (alias "Monchín"). These files indicated that Caonabo Elpidio Jorge Tavárez was also an important member of the MPD (*ibid.*, 13 July). Subsequently Tavárez was arrested for having traveled to a communist country, being in possession of a false identification card, and violating national law no. 6 on communist activities (Radio Comercial, Santo Domingo, 12 October). Tavárez indicated that Otto Morales and Melvin Manon were also members of the MPD Central Committee.

**Domestic and International Views and Policies.** In domestic and international affairs, the MPD has continued in its pro-Chinese orientation. On 24 November the MPD proclaimed that it "firmly and resolutely" supported the cultural revolution in China (NCNA 25 November). "The remarkable fruits of this great proletarian cultural revolution," said the MPD, "will multiply the spiritual and material force of all oppressed peoples."

"Since the great cultural revolution started in China, there has been an increase in the revolutionary upsurge both inside and outside China," the statement continued. Its influence was "reaching the working masses" in the Dominican Republic, where the revolutionary upsurge was said to be the result of the intensive study of the *Quotations from Chairman Mao Tse-tung* and other writings of the Chinese leader. The statement declared that Chairman Mao's teachings, such as "political power grows out of the barrel of a gun," "no investigation, no right to speak," and the theory of "one divides itself into two" were frequently quoted by the revolutionary workers, peasants, and students.

Referring to specific tasks in the domestic political situation, the statement said that the MPD "plans to organize and direct the revolutionary fight of the people against US imperialism and its lackeys at home, turning to armed struggle as the only way out and taking the countryside as the chief arena of struggle." As a central task, the MPD would stregthen its political work among the peasants and send its best members to the countryside. The fight must also be waged against Soviet "revisionism," the statement added.

In a communique denying MPD participation in the terrorism during early May in Santo Domingo, Rafael Taveras, also asserted the party's pro-Chinese position, hailing the Chinese Communist Party the "vanguard of the world struggle against imperialism" and Mao Tse-tung as the "highest expression of this struggle" (*El Nacional* 15 May).

Although the MPD is primarily a pro-Chinese oriented party, it has sought and received support from Cuba. In a television broadcast on 4 February President Balaguer gave details of subversive plans revealed in documents found on Dominican communists. These documents indicated that the MPD-controlled trade union group "Foupsa-Cesitrado" was receiving funds from the Confederation of Cuban Workers and other foreign communist organizations, (*Ibid.*, 5 February.)

In documents seized from MPD leader Ramón A. Pinedo, it was found that the MPD had received funds amounting to $24,185 from Cuba. The funds were allegedly received by the MPD through Caonabo Elpidio Jorge Tavárez. According to the police, Jorge Tavárez visited Cuba and Communist China after leaving the country on 14 February 1967. He returned on 19 June (*ibid.*, 12 July).

**Publications.** The MPD publishes a weekly, *Libertad.*

**MPD Dissidents.** In the spring of 1966 the MPD split, resulting in the formation of a new pro-Chinese party, the Orthodox Communist Party (Partido Comunista Ortodoxo; PCO), headed by Máximo López Molina, the founder and President of the MPD. López Molina was expelled from the MPD on being found guilty of ideological deviations of a "bourgeois" nature, repeated "violations of communist morals and discipline," rejection of the Marxist-Leninist principles of criticism and self-criticism, and finally, living above his means in Paris on party funds. (*Libertad*, 21 April, 1966; see also *YICA*, 1966.)

On 15 August 1966 the independent weekly *Ahora* published a statement by López Molina revealing the positions taken by the PCO. The crucial difference between the PCO and the MPD, according to the statement, was "the difference between the thinking of Mao Tse-tung, constituting the Marxism-Leninism of our epoch, and the counterrevolutionary line of revisionism headed by the PSU." In connection with specific domestic problems, López Molina declared the PCO to be against oral participation and against cooperation with the liberal bourgeoisie. On democratic centralism, he accused the MPD of using this as an argument to depose him. Also he indicated that the PCO was against cooperation with the PCD. On international affairs, López stated: "At this time the thought of Mao Tse-tung marks the dividing line between the revolution and the counterrevolution, between Marxism-Leninism and revisionism. There is no intermediate line; there is no position of 'neutrality.' " Affirming the party's complete solidarity with Communist China, he declared: "To be on the side of China and the thought of Mao Tse-tung at this time means to be Marxist-Leninist."

Late in 1966 yet another pro-Chinese faction emerged from the MPD as the Communist Party of the Dominican Republic (Partido Comunista de la Republica Dominicana; PCRD or PACOREDO). The faction is, if anything, more extreme than the MPD. Pin Montas, a former leader of the MPD (see YICA, 1966), is one of the prominent spokesmen of the PCRD.

On 13 March Radio Hin, Santo Domingo, reported that the PCRD was calling on youths to disassociate themselves from the PCD student group "Fragua" and to form a new goup, to be called Juventud Comunista (JC), which would rally Dominican youth to carry out Marxist-Leninist doctrine. The statement accused Fragua and other "moderate" communist groups of revisionism and dishonesty and charged the PCD with being the vanguard of North American "imperialism."

The JC has now been banned for two years. Seven of its leaders have been expelled by the Santo Domingo University Council (El Nacional, 27 May 1967). The expulsions followed the JC's action in organizing violence during the student elections of 23 May and refusing to obey a University Council resolution banning the raising of "any foreign flag" above the National Flag on the university building. The JC's action was condemned by both the MR-1J4 and the MPD.

**MR-1J4.** Another sector of Dominican communism is represented by the Castroist "Revolutionary Movement of June 14" (MR-1J4), founded in 1959 as the Political Group of June 14 (Agrupación Política Catorce de Junio; APCJ). Originally it was a nationalist organization incorporating communist elements in its membership. After the death of its founder, Manuel Tavarez Justo, in 1963, the MR-1J4 was torn by a struggle for leadership between nationalists and communists. After expelling the nationalist elements, led by Luis Genao Espaillat, the party was still involved in internal quarrels. Finally, on 8 December 1966, seven members of the leadership, led by Rafael "Fafa" Taveras, left the movement and joined the MPD. In 1967 the Central Committee claimed that this was the MR-1J4's greatest success as far as the party's own affairs were concerned, as these "liquidators" had tried to hold back its ideological development (El Nacional, 21 December). Statements issued by both sides at the time of the split showed, however, that each followed communist policies, while disagreeing with the other over their interpretation.

The split weakened the MR-1J4, whose Central Committee admitted that the movement had to put its house in order. A movement of "self-criticism" was launched to remove "bourgeois" ideas arising from the middle-class background of most members. The leaders claimed great success in adopting a proletarian ideology and expressed hopes for extending it through the mass political action which the movement was trying to organize. (Ibid.)

The MR-1J4 statement did not mention that there had been a second purge. El Nacional of 4 December reported an MR-1J4 statement that Rafael Cruz Peralta had been expelled for offending against "communist ethics" and Enma Tavarez Justo and Ivelisse Acevedo Gautier for "rightist, revisionist attitudes." A few days later Enma Tavarez, the founder's sister, claimed that she had resigned on her own initiative. She also condemned the "adventurism and opportunism" of the MR-1J4 leadership under Fidelio Despradel, which she linked with a trend toward a "Debray type" of guerrilla struggle which denied the need for a party or for political indoctrination. Cruz Peralta, on the other hand, favored the pro-Chinese MPD, which the "Fafa" Taveras faction had joined.

Besides Fidelio Despradel, who seems to command the leadership of the party, other important members of the MR-1J4 have been identified by the military and police of the Dominican Republic: Homero Hernández Vargas, Nelson Morelo Cevallos, José María Pantalion, Nelson Antonio, Juan Pablo Soto Féliz, and Julio E. Montander (El Nacional, 24 July). Internal dissension makes it unclear which positions these men hold.

**Domestic Views and Policies.** Perhaps as a result of its fragmentation and internal disruption during 1966 and 1967, the MR-1J4 has been unable to formulate a definite tactical and ideological position. In domestic affairs it adheres primarily to Castroist lines, although its leaders occassionally espouse pro-Chinese sympathies.

The Dominican national police and military publicly issued a communique (*El Nacional*, 24 July) which revealed the seemingly "opportunist" nature of the MR-1J4. The police maintained that they had possession of documents strongly indicating that the movement was planning to overthrow the government with Chinese and Cuban assistance. The communique added that officials had detailed information about a "badly organized" MR-1J4 plan which would have executed the orders of Mao Tse-tung and Fidel Castro and initiated subversion.

In a paid advertisement in *El Nacional* on 21 December the MR-1J4 Central Committee appeared to definitely follow Castroist lines. It announced that the movement was now following the correct political-military line, in which armed struggle was the central task, and that without armed struggle neither the proletariat nor the masses could establish a viable revolutionary organization or solve any important political problem.

This statement substantiated a communique of 22 July in *El Nacional*, where in the MR-1J4 proclaimed that the Dominican Republic would be "liberated" only after "great, prolonged revolutionary struggle, of both a national and civil character." The MR-1J4 also termed itself the "political vanguard of the working class."

According to Radio Havana on 6 April, the MR-1J4 had declared: "At the head of the entire liberation movement is the glorious vanguard of the Cuban revolution, with its great example lighting the road we must follow." The MR-1J4 has been active in attempting to indoctrinate the peasants and preparing for guerrilla warfare in the interior. For instance, on 28 September three young guerrilla fighters, Octaviano Johannes, Juan Bautista Lajara and Radhamés García were killed by the police in Bonao. The MR-1J4 endorsed the activities of these "guerrilla revolutionaries." (*Ibid.*, 1 October.)

Although these statements indicate a Castroist alignment, other communiques issued by the MR-1J4 reveal support for the Chinese line. In a statement in *El Nacional* on 26 July, Fidelio Despradel and Roberto Duvergé expressed the view that Mao Tse-tung, although he did not have absolute authority over Marxism-Leninism, was its "most correct interpreter."

**International Views and Policies.** In international affairs the MR-1J4 has revealed certain "opportunist" tendencies, vacillating between Castroist and Chinese positions. This uncertainty was reflected in a speech by Gerardo Sánchez, who headed the delegation from the Dominican Republic to the OLAS conference in Havana. Sánchez praised the Cuban revolution for having "opened a new stage in the struggle of the Latin American peoples," in which a "new awakening overran the mountains and valleys, the cities and universities." After quoting the Castroist dictum that "the duty of every revolutionary is to make the revolution," Sánchez declared: "To oppose mass struggle to the guerrilla struggle, or vice versa, is nothing but a set pattern intended to avoid guerrilla struggle as well as mass struggle." The "vanguard," he said, must fulfill its duties in the battlefield as well as in the ideological field.

Sánchez stressed the need to maintain a ceaseless struggle against "imperialistic" forces preventing the Dominican Republic's development. Yet he also emphasized the Chinese theory that the large rural areas would have to be incorporated into the struggle through the method of guerrilla warfare, and his conclusion seemed to indicate a pro-Chinese position: "Even though all forms of mass struggle are necessary, the fundamental method must be the armed struggle, through incorporation of the rural masses into it. The immediate task of all revolutionaries must be the incorporation of those rural masses. . . " (OLAS Conference Documents.)

According to the Communist Chinese news agency NCNA (16 November), in response to the fiftieth anniversary of the Bolshevik Revolution, the MR-1J4 issued a statement denouncing the "Soviet revisionist clique" for its betrayal of Marxism-Leninism, for bringing about the restoration of capitalism in the USSR, and for pursuing a counterrevolutionary program in league with "US imperialism." The statement reportedly asserted that this "clique of renegades" would not succeed in carrying out its program, owing to the "vigilance of the true Marxist-Leninist parties and the revolutionary peoples of the world."

In conjunction with the other communist parties in the Dominican Republic, the MR-1J4 strongly condemned "Israeli aggression against the Arab nations." The movement charged that the Israelis had the "active support of Anglo-American imperialism that is stealing the oil riches of the Middle East." The statement concluded with a call for all Arab nations to increase their efforts and to persist in armed struggle until they gained complete national sovereignty and the definite liberation of their natural resources. (Radio Havana, 15 June.)

**Publication.** The MR-1J4 publishes an irregular newspaper, *1J4.*

# ECUADOR

The communist movement in Ecuador, which originated in May 1926 with the founding of the Socialist Party of Ecuador (Partido Socialista Ecuatoriano; PSE), was represented in 1967 by a number of rival parties and factions, the oldest and largest of which is the pro-Soviet Communist Party of Ecuador (Partido Comunista del Ecuador; PCE), founded in 1931 as an offshoot of the PSE. The most important pro-Chinese faction is the Communist Party of Ecuador, Marxist-Leninist (Partido Comunista del Ecuador Marxista-Leninista; PCE/ML), a Quito-based group which broke from the PCE in 1963. At least one pro-Chinese faction has subsequently split away from the PCE/ML (see below). Castroist support is found in the Socialist Revolutionary Party of Ecuador (Partido Socialista Revolucionario del Ecuador; PSR or PSRE), another offspring of the PSE, founded in 1962, and in the Independent Revolutionary Movement (Movimiento Independiente Revolucionario; MIR) (see below).

The PCE has passed through several periods of legal and illegal status. The party was legal from 1931 until 1946, illegal between 1946 and 1948, legal from 1948 to 1963, and declared illegal again, along with the PSR, in 1963 when a military junta replaced constitutional government in Ecuador. The return to civilian government on 30 March 1966 gave rise to hopes within the PCE and other communist factions that their parties would be legalized. Although this has not happened, the official organs of the various parties were allowed legal publication after May 1966.

The total membership of all the communist factions is estimated at between two and three thousand, with the PCE accounting for some 1,500 members. The population of Ecuador is 5,386,000 (estimated October 1966).

**Organization and Leadership.** The PCE is governed by a permanent Secretariat selected by the Central Committee. The Central Committee is elected at the national party congress which, in theory, convenes every two years; however, there has been no party congress since the seventh held in 1962. The PCE attempts to maintain a provincial committee in each of Ecuador's 19 provinces and local committees where appropriate. In urban areas these local committees are sometimes grouped under a zonal committee to coordinate their work. The basic unit of the PCE is the cell of a few individuals, formed in a factory, office, or other place of work. Party members in nonparty organizations, such as mass fronts, labor unions, and peasant associations, are required to act as a group to promote party goals in these organizations.

The leadership of the PCE includes the party's Secretary-General, Pedro Antonio Saad Niyam (Pedro Saad), and possibly the following members of the Central Executive Committee: Enrique Gil Gilbert (Organizational Secretary and editor of the PCE organ *El Pueblo*, who was the unsuccessful PCE candidate for mayor of Guayaquil in the June 1967 local elections), Alba Calderón, Milton Jijon Saavedra, Elias Muñoz Vicuña, Ricardo Alejandro Paredes, Antonio Ramírez and Gonzalo Villalba Colma.

The Communist Youth of Ecuador (Juventud Comunista Ecuatoriana; JCE) is a PCE auxiliary. Although there are no more than 200 young people in the JCE, it is a member of the Soviet front World Federation of Democratic Youth (WFDY), and was elected to a seat on the Executive Committee of the WFTU at its seventh Assembly, in July 1966. The JCE Secretary-General is René Maugu. Through the JCE, pro-Soviet Communists have managed to maintain a large measure of control in the Federation of University Students of Ecuador (Federación de Estudiantes Universitarios del Ecuador; FEUE) until recent years, but increasing animosity between communist groups has split the FEUE, and at the FEUE's 23rd congress, in Guayaquil in November, the pro-Soviet faction lost control. The delegates voted to expel from the Congress as "deviationists" the

192

chairman of the FEUE Guayaquil branch, Gustavo von Buchwald, a noncommunist, and Enrique Gallegos Arends, the pro-Soviet communist chief of the Quito branch. Gallegos was also expelled from the FEUE. The congress also passed a vote of censure against René Maugu of the JCE. The FEUE had been a member of the pro-Soviet student front organization, the International Union of Students (IUS), until this time, but the 23rd congress voted to suspend its membership indefinitely until the IUS should expel the Chilean affiliate of the IUS, which is objectionable to Cuba.

The 23rd congress adopted an openly revolutionary line. Resolutions approved during the six-day session placed responsibility for the "crisis conditions" in Ecuador on the US, local oligarchs, and feudal landlords, and declared "war to the death against US imperialism and its allies." The FEUE now advocates armed struggle as the clearest road to victory. The congress also reportedly condemned reformists, revisionists, and adventurists, which if true would mean social democrats, the followers of the Soviet line and the Castroists. The leadership chosen at the congress apparently does not completely reflect the hard revolutionary line adopted in the resolutions. The new president is Galo Verdesto; the vice-presidents are Edison Fonseca, Bayardo Tobar, Orlanda Sierra, and Armando Conforme.

The PCE has also been active in youth affairs through the Communist Revolutionary Union of Ecuadorian Youth (Unión Revolucionaria de la Juventud Ecuatoriana; URJE) which it controls. After 1960 the URJE rejected the possibility of achieving power by peaceful means and became strongly Castroist in its orientation. The PCE exerted heavy pressure to maintain control of the URJE and to force adherence to the pro-Soviet position. As a result, URJE membership fell off to the extent that by the mid 1960's URJE influence among Ecuadorian youth had waned.

The PCE maintains control of Ecuador's largest labor organization, the 60,000-member Confederation of Ecuadorian Workers (Confederación de Trabajadores Ecuatorianos; CTE), although in 1966 it fell into pro-Peking communist hands for a time. By December 1966, however, at the Tenth CTE Congress the pro-Soviet faction recovered its ground, removing hard-line Chinese supporters including President Victor Zúñiga. The CTE is a member of the Soviet-controlled World Federation of Trade Unions (WFTU). The PCE also controls the Ecuador Federation of Indians (Federación Ecuatoriana de Indios; FEI). Dr. Bolivar Bolaños, leader of the FEI, is reportedly a member of the PCE (*El Tiempo,* Quito, 5 July).

The PCE, claiming to be the fighting vanguard of the people of Ecuador, offers a six-point basic program which includes "liberation of the country from the imperialist yoke, democratization of the government, true agrarian reform, improved wages and living standards for the working people, independent foreign policy, and complete sovereignty (broadcast, Moscow Domestic Service, 22 May). In practice the weak and faction-ridden PCE has had little success in implementing any part of this program. In private, as at the meeting of the Central Committee PCE in November 1966, the party admits that its propaganda is poor, organization weak, and membership small. While the PCE believes that power can only be achieved through a broad united front of progressive elements, a strong united front has always eluded it in the past, and with communist factionalism and revolutionary militancy in the ascendant, the prospects remain dim for any permanent success of a united front strategy in the immediate future.

During 1967 the PCE supported labor strikes and certain activities of the students, but a considerable amount of the party's energy was absorbed in interfactional strife. As the most conservative of the communist parties, the PCE had difficulty in maintaining its revolutionary image under a barrage of accusations that it had abandoned revolutionary struggle for parliamentarism. Pedro Saad stated his party's case as follows:

> We Ecuadorian Communists. . . believe that our revolution will proceed almost inevitably along nonpeaceful ways, that we shall have to win our liberation through an arduous armed struggle. But we, inspired by the ideas of Marxism-Leninism, do not regard armed struggle as an adventure, as the action of a group of men, but as an armed action of the masses, closely united to the struggle of the masses on all planes. We think that in this action we have to use all forms of struggle, including armed struggle; to be prepared for all forms and to use the most suitable one for each case, and to be ready to move on to

higher forms when it is necessary and possible. (*El Pueblo,* Guayaquil, 9 December.)

**International Views and Policies.** As a pro-Soviet communist party the PCE dutifully follows Moscow in international affairs. The party believes that the "triumphal march of the Soviet Union toward communism" is of "vast importance" and that the "camp of peace and progress"—meaning the Soviet Union and the socialist states in alliance with her—is the "beacon" which directs it and inspires it with "faith in final victory" (broadcast, Moscow Domestic Service, 22 May).

During 1967 the PCE publicly supported Soviet policies on Vietnam and the Middle East and acclaimed Soviet efforts to hold a consultative conference in Budapest in February 1968 in order to settle arrangements for an international meeting of communist and workers' parties. In February the Central Committee of the CPE sent a telegram to the CPSU "supporting the dignified position taken by the CPSU in the face of the chauvinist and anti-Soviet campaign led by Mao Tse-tung and other [Chinese Communist] leaders." According to the contents of this telegram, the CPE "hailed the correct policy line of the CPSU and the government and the people of the Soviet Union aimed at extending effective aid to the Vietnamese people, who are waging a heroic fight against imperialist aggression." A second telegram to the Chinese Communist Party protested China's anti-Soviet campaign as injuring the cause of proletarian internationalism, and asked the Chinese to reconsider their recent attitude in the name of world communist unity, socialist friendship, and victory in Vietnam. (*IB,* no. 93, 10 April.)

PCE Secretary-General Pedro Saad headed a delegation of his party to the fiftieth anniversary celebrations of the October Revolution in the Soviet Union. Saad delivered a short speech in praise of Soviet accomplishments at the grand rally in Moscow on 6 November. Saad also visited Bulgaria in June at the invitation of the Bulgarian Communist Party Central Committee and during his trip to the Soviet fiftieth anniversary celebrations he made a brief official visit to Czechoslovakia.

Central Committee member Villalba was the PCE delegate to the Fifteenth Congress of the Mexican Communist Party in July. The party also held a "fraternal meeting" with the Venezuelan Communist Party in October, when delegates chosen from the Central Committees of the two parties met, probably in Caracas, "to exchange opinions and experiences on the struggle . . . against Yankee imperialism and the cliques in its service." The meeting placed "special emphasis" on the need to restore unity to the international proletarian movement, but reaffirmed the "principle of noninterference in the affairs of fraternal parties." They agreed that the "attempt to impose uniform tactics and the adoption of a specific form of struggle, ignoring national idiosyncracies . . . is inadmissable." Both parties saw the need to continue the ideological battle against "erroneous ideas" which "tend to deny the validity of working class parties" and their vanguard role. (*El Pueblo,* 18 November.) The PCE declined to send a delegate to the Latin American Solidarity Organization (OLAS) conference in Havana in July and August because "certain parties" (i.e., Cuba) had intervened in the affairs of fraternal parties in violation of the principles agreed to at the meeting of Latin American communist parties in December 1964. The PCE also pointed out that there were cases in which fraternal parties had given support to "divisionist groups" in another country, ignoring or undermining the influence of the authentic communist party. (*Ibid.,* 4 August.)

**Publications.** The 1963 split, which divided the PCE, left the pro-Soviet party, based primarily in Guayaquil, in a weak position for publishing and printing since the best facilities available to the communists were in Quito, in the hands of the PCE/ML. The organ of the PCE is the weekly *El Pueblo,* published legally since May 1966 in Guayaquil. *El Pueblo* has an estimated circulation of 3,000.

**The Communist Party of Ecuador, Marxist-Leninist and Other Pro-Peking Communist Factions.** The most important communist rival to the PCE is the pro-Peking PCE/ML headed by Jorge Isaac Arellano. The party is small and riddled by factionalism, but it has caused considerable problems for the pro-Moscow PCE. The PCE/ML has waged a continuous struggle, intensified since the return to civil government in Ecuador in 1966, to seize control of the communist front apparatus. The party did manage to gain the upper hand in the CTE in 1966, but lost control by the end of the year. Its revolutionary line, more strident than that of the PCE, has given it at least temporary success in the activist student front FEUE. Effective control of the FEUE passed to the PCE/ML in November (see above), although it will probably be forced to share power with Castroist groups.

In spite of the strong showing made by the PCE/ML among mass organizations, the party is basically an unstable one. Not only are there ideological differences among its members, but also there is good reason to believe that there has been considerable corruption and peculation in its finances. When Arellano returned from exile in June 1966 after the fall of the junta, he was confronted with a serious situation within the party. It appeared that several high-ranking and trusted members in the Quito organization had been spending large sums from the party's treasury for their own personal purposes. After a long period of investigation, during which time the suspects used every subterfuge to camouflage their activities, they were finally expelled. The amount of the embezzlement was, at the very least, greater than $30,000 and may have been more than twice this sum. The misappropriated funds were largely those received from "international sources," presumably Communist China. The situation came to a head at a party congress held in March 1967, which was designated the Eighth since the PCE/ML claims to be the legitimate Communist Party of Ecuador and hence heir to the seven previous congresses (statement of the PCE/ML, Guayaquil, undated, 1967). The alleged miscreants have now formed a splinter party under the leadership of Rafael Echeverría Flores. Other members of the faction include José María Roura Cevallos, whose financial dealings with the Chinese Communists were a proximate cause of the 1963 split between the PCE and PCE/ML; César Muñoz Mantilla, a former central committee member of the PCE; Mecías Rovalino, Jorge Ron, and Celso Fiallo. Ideologically the Echeverría faction tends toward a more militant position than the PCE/ML and bestows its approval on Havana as well as Peking. A second splinter faction from the PCE/ML may exist under the leadership of Pedro Sorroza, a man who has served on the Central Committee of the PCE/ML.

The PCE/ML has exhibited two major theoretical concerns during 1967. The first is an examination of its own "errors" which allowed men like Echeverría into the party organization. The party states that "inexperience and a lack of a full and precise concept of the new type of party" that was to be established was the root cause of the problem. Party leaders assert they were mistaken in accepting into their ranks "ideologically inconsistent persons who had maintained erroneous and vacillating positions in regard to problems of principle" and that, concerned with numbers to the detriment of quality, they failed to adhere rigidly to their own dictum that "the party is the highest form of organization," the "general staff for combat," of the proletarian class, and that "only the best revolutionaries, the most aware, the most self abnegating, the most dedicated and valiant, those who are prepared to sacrifice all, including their very lives, for the cause of the revolution, should form the ranks of the Party." (*Política,* Quito, March-April.)

The party's second concern was to defend its ideological integrity from attack by "opportunists" and "revisionists" (the PCE), "adventurists" (the Castroists), and their own dissidents (Echeverría *et al.*). Feeling closer ideological attunement to the revolutionary Castroists, the party was particularly chagrined when the pro-Castro weekly *Mañana* published portions of Régis Debray's *Revolution in the Revolution?* which criticized the Chinese Communist line as "adventurism" and were comparatively uncritical of the Soviet position. However, the party reserved its strongest words for the "false party," which, it described as "deserters of the revolution, a group of electoral bill-stickers at the service of the petty bourgeoisie and, at times, the oligarchy" (flyer, PCE/ML, date and place of publication unknown), and for the renegade Echeverría group, "a fraction on the party's edges [which has] decided to destroy its organization," led by men whose attempts to conceal their perfidy "behind appeals for 'democratic centralism' appear as but a miserable fig leaf incapable of hiding the nudity of the immodest perpetrators" (*Política,* March-April).

**Publications.** The PCE/ML publishes an irregular weekly, *Espartaco,* and the journals *En Marcha* and *Política.* In Guayaquil, PCE/ML materials appear in print through Ediciones Liberación.

**Castroist Revolutionary Parties and Organizations.** The principal exponent of Havana's view on revolution, popular primarily among Ecuadorian students, is the Socialist Revolutionary Party of Ecuador (PSR) headed by Dr. Anibal Leonardo Muñoz Quirola (Anibal Muñoz) as Secretary-General. Muñoz has stated that armed struggle is the only possible way for the revolution to succeed in Latin America. The party holds no brief for elections or for the parties which participate in them. It believes only in armed struggle, and that solidarity in Latin America must be achieved by armed uprisings in all countries. The party openly looks to Havana for leadership and inspiration, and eulogized Che Guevara upon his death. It was the PSR that led an Ecuadorian delegation to the first OLAS conference, at Havana in July and August. Muñoz headed the delegation; Jorge Arturo González Moreno of the PSR Executive Committee also attended.

Two other Castroist organizations exist in Ecuador which might properly be classified as student organizations rather than political parties. The first of these, the Independent Revolutionary Movement (MIR) sent a delegate, José Hernández Villegas, to the OLAS conference in the company of the PSR representatives. The MIR believes that it is a possible vanguard for the Ecuadorian people; that is, if the MIR can be the first to begin armed insurrection, the people will flock to its standard and it will lead them on to victory. The second of these is the very small Conquer or Die (Vencer o Morir; V/M) movement, which appears to be in a state of near dissolution.

**Publications.** The weekly *Mañana,* published in Quito, is the chief purveyor of the Castroist point of view in print; another pro-Castro organ is the *El Grito del Pueblo,* printed in Loja in southern Ecuador.

# EL SALVADOR

The Communist Party of El Salvador (Partido Communista de El Salvador; PCES) was founded in 1930. Although the PCES has been confronted with some internal dissidence along pro-Chinese and Castroist lines, there is no evidence that any significant contending communist factions are active outside the party's ranks. The PCES is illegal. Its membership is estimated at 200. The population of El Salvador is 3,037,000 (estimated, July 1966).

The party's influence, which was never very great, has diminished further as a consequence of political and economic progress achieved by President Rivera's administration (1962-1967). In an article analyzing 35 years of communist failure in El Salvador (*WMR,* June 1965), Alberto Gualan, PCES Central Committee member, wrote that when Rivera took office the economy revived, unemployment fell, and the climate for revolution vanished. The PCES, he added, had failed to take into account industrial development and progress and had limited its propaganda to the decreasing numbers of rural craftsmen.

In 1967 the party's views concerning El Salvador's revolutionary potential appeared to undergo some modification. Nonetheless, support for the party remained weak. During the presidential elections held on 5 March 1967 the PCES gave its qualified support to the Renovation Action Party (Partido Acción Renovadora; PAR), whose candidate was Fabio Castillo. Despite Castillo's personal popularity, the PAR won only 14.4 per cent of the votes. Colonel Fidel Sánchez Hernández, Rivera's successor and candidate of the ruling National Conciliation Party (Partido Conciliación Nacional), polled 54.4 per cent of the votes cast.

**Organization and Leadership.** Very little is known of the composition and organization of the PCES leadership. In addition to the party's Secretary-General, José Sánchez, prominent members of the party appear to be Jorgé Roberto Shaflick Handal, Roque Dalton, Bernardo Dominguez, Alberto Gualan, and Jorgé Arias Gomez. José Serpas and Berto Castillo, leading members of the April and May Revolutionary Party (Partido Revolucionario Abril y Mayo), a PCES front organization, are also believed to hold prominent positions within the PCES.

In the field of labor the Communists control the Unitary Trade Union Federation of El Salvador (Federación Unitaria Sindical de El Salvador; FUSS). This organization, however, with less than 5,000 members, has been overshadowed by the principal Salvadoran union, the General Confederation of Trade Unions (Confederación General de Sindicatos; CGS), which has a membership of about 20,000.

The PCES has a certain degree of influence within the student body. All university students belong to a general association (Asociación General de Estudiantes Universitarios Salvadoreños), which the party has used as a forum. On the Executive Committee of this body, however, communists have been outnumbered. Left-wing extremist support is found in such groups as the Revolutionary University Students' Federation (Federación de Estudiantes Universitarios Revolucionarios) and the Vanguard of Salvadoran Youth (Vanguardia de las Juventudes Salvadoreñas), both of which were represented at the Havana conference of the Latin American Solidarity Organization (OLAS), by Osmani Cruz León and Camilo Sierra, respectively.

**Domestic Policy and Activity.** The PCES' principal concern during the first months of 1967 (as it had been a year earlier during the municipal elections) was the participation of the left-wing PAR in the presidential elections. The PAR had, as of 1964, with the election of Julio Ernesto Contreras as its Secretary-General, adopted a radical line considerably to the left of its original policies when it was founded in 1944. The presidential elections on 5 March were preceded by debate over whether PAR was Communist-controlled, and Castillo's candidacy was not officially accepted until 1 March. The PCES, in a declaration issued on 3 March, stated that it had analyzed all party programs, and while it

197

did not wholly agree with the PAR's policies, it publicly sympathized with them. Later in the year Fabio Castillo acknowledged PCES support in an article published in the organ of the Costa Rican People's Vanguard Party, in which he was reported as stating that the movement supporting his program was made up of both Marxists and non-Marxists. Their alliance was not solely an electoral one, but would continue the ideological and political struggle to change the structure of Salvadoran society. The article pointed out that Castillo had emphasized that the loyalty of the Communists to his party, the PAR, deserved to be stressed (*Libertad*, 3 September 1967). In the meantime, the PAR's registration had been canceled on 16 May on the grounds that it had abandoned the policies previously accepted for electoral qualification.

During the year PCES policy lines were elaborated by Roque Dalton in two articles published in the *World Marxist Review.* In a lengthy analysis of the "present phase of the revolutionary movement in Latin America" (*WMR,* May 1967) Dalton appeared to be reiterating the stand adopted in August 1966 by Bernardo Dominguez, who had warned against "adventurism" (*Pravda,* 10 August 1966). Dalton stressed that

> . . . it would be incorrect to assume that revolutionary solutions are always *feasible,* that revolution is *possible* at every stage of social development [italics in original] . Clearly, the solution should be based on an analysis of the deep-going trends and objective laws governing the present stage of the continent's history, on an analysis of the requirements and potentials of the economic and socio-political development.

In his second contribution to the *World Marxist Review* (October) Dalton inserted a statement by PCES Secretary-General José Sánchez:

> The more than thirty years' existence of a military tyranny with its ruthless repression and terror, which has robbed our people of elementary freedoms and brazenly turned elections into a means of prolonging its rule, has convinced our Party and the other democratic forces that our people cannot in the foreseeable future win power by peaceful means. The people, we believe, will have to engage in armed struggle if they want to conquer political power and solve the problems of their democratic, antifeudal and anti-imperialist revolution.

Commenting on Sánchez' assertions, Dalton pointed out:

> Although at present the Party and the masses rely chiefly on nonviolent (legal, semilegal, and illegal) forms of struggle, preparations for employment of other forms is also on the order of the day. But whatever means are used in the struggle for power, victory is unthinkable without the participation of the masses. Our objectives are organization of the masses and struggle for their immediate demands as a means of bringing the masses to a comprehension of the revolutionary tasks.

Dalton went on to quote Sánchez' views as to the timing of the revolution:

> All the objective conditions for our revolution exist. The task of our Party is to provide the subjective conditions for the growth of the revolutionary struggle. We know that there is no need to wait for the maturing of the *maximum* of subjective conditions to accompany the revolution. But we also know that the people must create a *minimum* of subjective conditions if they want the revolution to triumph [italics in original] . We must provide this indispensable minimum of organization and preparation.

Sánchez' apparent adoption of the policy of armed struggle as reported by Dalton appeared inconsistent with an earlier report in the organ of the Communist Party of Denmark, *Land og Folk* (24 August 1967), in which he was quoted as saying:

> The progress of our Party depends not only upon whether we are able to carry out comprehensive work upon the masses, workers and peasants, but also upon whether we are able to secure relations with other progressive circles which stand in opposition to the military dictatorship. There are some revolutionaries who believe that a military dictatorship makes such a political line impossible, and that there is only one way out—to take arms. In reality, the military dictatorship itself is creating the conditions for this line . . . [bringing] to life a powerful opposition in broad segments of the people. These

segments have in our country gathered around a progressive action program and have produced such well-known leaders as the former Rector at the University, Dr. Fabio Castillo (presidential candidate in the elections), whom the people respect. We support these forces in order to arrive at united actions against the military dictatorship's regime.

Answering the query as to whether the way of armed struggle had been abandoned, Sánchez replied:

Naturally not. In the struggle against the military dictatorship our people have more than once taken arms as a response to violence, and in this the CP has played the leading role. In this area we have rich experiences . . . [but] also, because of these experiences, we have learned that the former slogans on armed struggle lead only to passivity and in the end to defeat for the revolutionary movement. Such a policy would in the present situation lead to a splitting of the progressive forces and to a weakening of the united front, which is necessary in order to be able to overthrow the reactionaries and win power for the working people in El Salvador. Instead, our policy is based on strengthening of the united front. It is a very difficult task, which places extraordinarily high demands on the Party and upon individual Communists, but it is that way we must go if we are to succeed.

The PCES' attempts to gain influence within organized labor by means of the Communist-controlled FUSS achieved a certain degree of success in April. A three-day general strike sponsored by both the FUSS and the CGS motivated a temporary joint FUSS-CGS command, and May Day celebrations were an occasion for further FUSS-CGS cooperation, an objective the FUSS had failed to achieve the previous year (*YICA* 1966, p. 221).

**International Views and Policy.** The PCES was represented at the Fifth Meeting of the Communist Parties of Mexico, Central America, and Panama and was signatory to the meeting's communique (see *Documents*). Thus the party reiterated the pro-Soviet stand it had voiced a year earlier at the Twenty-Third Congress of the CPSU (*YICA*, 1966, p. 221). Subsequently a PCES delegation attended the Fiftieth Anniversary celebrations in the Soviet Union.

With respect to China, the PCES had issued a statement in November 1966 analyzing the Eleventh Plenum of the Central Committee of the Chinese Communist Party. It had declared itself "concerned about the fact that on certain international problems the Chinese party leaders have taken a stand fraught with extremely grave consequences," and referred to the Chinese "cultural revolution" as a "distortion of Marxism-Leninism" (*IB*, no. 88, 1967).

Relations between the PCES and Cuba were somewhat ambiguous and reflected the party's apparent indecision concerning its own stand on "armed struggle." The official speech of the Salvadoran delegation to the OLAS Conference in Havana referred to the "strategy of the Continental Revolution," which would necessarily have to reflect both "community and diversity, if we do not wish to doom it to failure." However, José Serpas, a leading member of the PCES front organization, the April and May Revolutionary Party, was reported as stating that "the peoples of Latin America may be sure that we Salvadorans will work to carry our people to triumph by means of armed struggle." He went on to attack the Venezuelan Communist Party for "holding back the guerrilla movement in the country." The Salvadoran delegation voted against an OLAS resolution endorsing guerrilla warfare as the principal means of gaining power. During 1967 Havana Radio broadcasts to El Salvador appeared to indicate that the Cubans remained hopeful of persuading the PCES to adopt their line of revolutionary militancy.

**Publications.** The PCES issues a biweekly clandestine publication, *La Verdad.*

# FINLAND

The Communist Party of Finland (Suomen Kommunistinen Puolue; SKP) was founded in Moscow on 29 August 1918 by exiled members of the Finnish Social Democratic Party; it has been legal since 1944.

Although the party's influence is strongest in the underdeveloped regions in northern and northeastern Finland, the majority of its membership of about 50,000 is in the urban industrial centers in the south. The population of Finland is 4,639,000 (estimated, January 1968).

Traditionally one of the most "Stalinist" communist parties in Europe, the SKP in recent years has undertaken a political and programmatic reassessment; modifications of party attitudes and leadership, evident at the party's Fourteenth Congress (29 January-1 February 1966) were further elaborated during 1967. The formation in May 1966 of a coalition Government in which the communists were represented (Finland's fiftieth government in her fifty years as a republic) marked a significant change in the political life of Finland.

The Finnish People's Democratic League (Suomen Kansan Demokraatinen Liitto; SKDL), formed by the SKP in 1945 as an electoral front organization, succeeded in gaining representation in Finland's first postwar Government. In subsequent elections the SKDL has polled between 20 and 23.5 per cent of the vote and won from 38 to 50 of the 200 seats in Parliament. Its chief supporters, besides Communists, are left-wing socialists; it probably draws a larger share of radical intellectuals than any other party. About a third of the SKDL's estimated 145,000 members are members of the SKP. Other auxiliary organizations of the SKP include the Finnish Democratic Youth League (headed by SKP Politburo member Ossian Sjöman), the Finnish Women's Democratic League, the Finnish Defenders of Peace, and the Finnish-Soviet Society.

The SKP is very active in Finnish trade unions, and controls the largest single union, the 61,000-member Building Workers' Union. The most important areas of Communist penetration within the labor movement have been the Confederation of Finnish Trade Unions (SAK), in which seven members of the 19-man Executive are SKP members, and the Workers Sports League. While the SAK claims a membership of 260,000 in 24 unions (an estimated two-thirds of its members support the SKDL), the social-democratic Federation of Finnish Trade Unions (SAJ) claims a membership of 107,000 in 18 unions. Noncommunist, independent trade-unions affiliated with neither the SAK nor the SAJ have approximately 100,000 members. (*World Strength of the Communist Party Organizations*, 1968.) Since the new government came into power, the SAK and SAJ have both indicated that they would favor the establishment of a new central organization, but negotiations toward this end have been hampered by rivalry between the SAK and SAJ in a contest for control of the new organization and, to an even greater extent, by rumors circulating during 1967 that the SAJ was receiving financial support from the US Central Intelligence Agency (*Washington Post,* 18 October 1967).

**Organization and Leadership.** The SKP's Fourteenth Congress brought to the fore the internal power struggle between hard-line "Muscovites"—called also the "barricade group" for their 1948 abortive coup attempt (See John H. Hodgson, *Communism in Finland* [Princeton, N.J., 1967])—and younger "reformists." The reformists, led by Erkki Salomää, who directs the ideological institute of the party (the Sirola Institute), were appointed to seven of the 14 Politburo posts, and Aimo Aaltonen was replaced as party Chairman by Aarne Saarinen, head of the powerful Building Workers' Union. In a "compromise measure," Ville Pessi, considered by many party members to be an "unrepentant Stalinist," was reelected Secretary-General. The Politburo of the Central Committee consists of Aarne Saarinen, Ville Pessi, Erkki Salomää, Hertta Kuusinen, Anna-Liisa Hyvönen, Inkeri Lehtinen, Jorma Simpura, Ossian Sjöman, Leo Suonpää, Olavi J. Laine, Markus Kainulainen, Taisto Sinisalo, Martti Malmberg, and Erkki Tuominen. The Secretariat of the Central Committee consists of Ville Pessi, Aarne Saarinen, Erkki Kivimaki, Olavi Poikolainen, and Lars Junttila. The Central Committee is made up of 35 full and ten alternate members, more than half of whom are relatively young members, newly elected at the Fourteenth Congress.

The Parliamentary elections in March 1966 saw a resounding victory for the Social Democratic Party, which increased its share of the vote from 19.5 per cent in 1962 to 27.7 per cent, and its seats from 38 to 55. It thus became the strongest political party in Finland, dislodging the Center (formerly Agrarian) Party, which lost some 35,000 votes and four seats (from 53 to 49). The share of the Communists, under the electoral front of the SKDL, dropped from 22 per cent in 1962 to 21.2 per cent, and six of their former 47 seats were lost. The Socialist League (a left-wing splinter of the Social Democratic Party) lost some 40,000 votes, but increased its Parliamentary representation from two to seven seats.

On 27 May 1966 four parties—the Social Democratic Party, the Center Party, the Socialist League, and the SKDL—formed a coalition Government, presided over by the head of the Social Democrats, Rafael Paasio.* The SKDL was apportioned three of the 15 cabinet posts; Deputy Finance Minister (Ele Alenius, Chairman of the SKDL), Deputy Transportation and Communication Minister (Leo Suonpää, member of the SKP Politburo), and Social Affairs Minister (Matti Koivunen, also a party member).

The return of the SKP to the Government after an interval of 18 years was in important event in Finnish and international politics; the SKP was the first communist party in noncommunist Europe to be accepted as part of a coalition government since the beginning of the cold war in 1947-48. In the opinion of SKP Chairman Aarne Saarinen, the most significant implication was the party's "victory" over the long-standing anticommunist posture among the leadership of the Social Democrats. On the other hand, Secretary-General Ville Pessi, together with other "old guardists," faced an immediate challenge from the party's lower ranks—and especially its younger generation—who were pressing for the replacement of many of the present leaders with men they consider more suited to the new role of the party. By the same token, there have been indications that some members of the SKDL, including its Chairman, Ele Alenius, favor emancipation from SKP tutelage. (Alenius, who claims to be a "left-wing socialist" and not a member of the SKP, in 1965 succeeded in defeating Hertta Kuusinen, a prominent member of the old guard, in the election for Secretary-General of the SKDL.) In a bid to offset this trend, the leadership of the SKP, and particularly its new Vice-Chairman, Erkki Salomää, emphasized that the "emergence of the SDKL as an organized group and the drawing-up of its own program did not signify discontinuance or change of ideology," and that the scope of the SKP was sufficiently broad to include all progressive forces—including those who do not call themselves socialists—who seek a "shift in the power structure" (*Kansan Uutiset,* 7 March 1967). On numerous occasions, SKP leaders have raised the question of absorption of the SKDL into the SKP, "with a view to abrogating the need for maintaining separate governing bodies," which in several constituencies actually overlap. However, since the greater number of the SDKL's supporters are not communists, SKP fear of the political consequences of such a move has halted any action.

**Ideological and Programmatic Orientation.** Clearly, the SKP has been attempting to avoid repetition of errors made in its first participation in the Government two decades ago (see *Est & Ouest,* Paris, 16-28 February 1967). The gradual "renewal" process within the party has been charted by (1) the "Program for the Preservation and Development of Democracy," adopted at the party's Thirteenth Congress, in 1963, which stresses adherence to Finnish democratic traditions, including the multiparty Parliamentary system; (2) a document known as the "October Manifesto," published by the Central Committee on 16 October 1965 under the title, "Marxist State Theory and the Finnish Way to Socialism," which advocates rejection of the "dictatorship of the proletariat" formula

*Paasio was replaced following the 1968 elections by Mauno Koivisto, another Social Democrat. Koivisto increased the number of cabinet posts to 16 to accommodate a member of the Swedish People's Party. (*Washington Post,* 28 April 1968.)

as being unsuited to Finnish sociopolitical conditions and replacing it by "workers' rule"; and (3) a "program of action for the immediate future," adopted at the Fourteenth Congress, entitled "The SKP is a Modern Marxist Mass Workers' Party," which reiterates the need for greater cognizance of recent advances in science and technology. Further, a commission was appointed to draft a new program for consideration at the Fifteenth Congress, scheduled for 1969. (The program still officially valid was adopted in 1957 and is only the second in the party's 49-year history.) The draft program, adopted by a plenary meeting of the Central Committee and released for discussion on 10 September 1967, was published in the party organ, *Kansan Uutiset,* in October. Testifying to the growing influence of moderates within the party, it clearly spells out a broad "people's front" strategy, dispensing with any final vestiges of a design for one-party dictatorship, and is aimed at creating, in collaboration with other leftist parties, a "bloc of anti-imperialist, progressive forces." The alliance with the Social Democrats is the pivot of the program.

Stressed in the draft is a peaceful transition to socialism through the parliamentary process:

> [The party] has never directed its criticism of bourgeois democracy toward its democratic nature but toward bourgeois limitations which have given too few rights and benefits to the working classes and too many to those with abundant wealth.... The Communist Party of Finland aims at realizing socialism in a peaceful, democratic way, which means that the steps into socialism would be a series of reforms, predicated on a Parliamentary majority supporting socialist reforms.

In order to appease certain elements, however, it was considered necessary to retain that section of the existing program which anticipates "answering the use of force with force."

Discussing the draft program in a Swedish communist daily, Vice-Chairman Salomää clearly reflected the trend of Finnish Communists toward "Scandinavian communism":

> The working class cannot achieve power in Finland in the same way as it did in Russia in 1917. Nor can power be taken over on the same manner in which it was in a number of countries where socialism triumphed after World War II.... In Finland and in other highly developed, capitalist countries, it is realistic to revise constantly the Marxist theory of the state and adapt it to present conditions. (*Norrskensflamman*, Luleå, 10 July 1967.)

Politburo member Inkeri Lehtinen saw the program as a "two-staged, revolutionary" solution: the democratic stage, aimed against big capital and monopolies, and the stage of the actual socialist revolution. Although a unified process, "these stages should nonetheless not be confused with one another," said Lehtinen, adding: "Equally erroneous would be the assumption that they are completely independent of each other." (*Kommunisti,* no. 11, 1967.)

In spite of the party's efforts, spearheaded by Erkki Salomää, semiprofessional and white-collar workers, who constitute an increasingly important segment of Finnish society, have not been attracted to the SKP. The party's liberalized ideological requirements, according to which candidate members need not be versed in "theoretical and party work" and are assured freedom of religious expression (*Kansan Uutiset,* 5 March), have not had the desired effect of broadening its support. Laborers and agricultural workers still account for 80 per cent of the membership.

**Domestic Policies and Activities.** By the beginning of 1967, the SKP's difficulties in adjusting to participation in a ruling coalition had been compounded by the existence of internal factions, ranging from "revisionists," who see socialism as an automatic process achievable through the parliamentary method with little effort, to "dogmatists," who reject the concept of a gradual reduction of capitalist political power through structural reforms and refuse to support SKDL cooperation with its coalition partners. Also to be reckoned with was the discontent of many younger members who argued that communist influence in the administration had failed to bring about greater economic and social benefits. They were able to point to the adverse effect on workers of the devaluation of the Finnish mark in October 1967, and to a stringent tax increase (both measures enacted in spite of communist opposition), as well as to continued employment and housing problems.

A plenum of the Central Committee (4-5 March), attended by secretaries of regional party organizations and secretaries for propaganda, attested to the need for ideological and political clarification of the party's twofold position as participant in the Government and in the opposition.

Politburo member Hertta Kuusinen later urged the party to "grapple with the current, acute problems of significance to the Finnish people," adding:

> The government coalition of Social Democrats and Agrarians is of the greatest importance for us. We must come up with constructive proposals and activities, not only from the Communists and People's Democrats, but from all parties cooperating in the Government and all groups represented by them. . . . The Communist Party does not endeavor to find solutions alone and looks for cooperation with all forces representing democracy and socialism. (*Kansan Uutiset,* 31 August).

The economic policy program adopted in 1966, which pointed to the continued domination of Finland's economic life by 20 families, claimed to offer a "different, socialist solution" to domestic and foreign policy problems. The SKP leadership has since asserted that the current administration has, in fact, enacted several measures advocated by the Communists, and that this has made it clear that the SKP and other Finnish parties have "common goals." The measures included an increase in child support allowances, sickness compensation, welfare allowances, and old-age pension increases. Enumerating these measures, party Chairman Aarne Saarinen cautioned "dogmatists":

> The party must not unconditionally assume the continued intensification of the class struggle as a prerequisite to the socialist revolution. That concept can easily lead to the mere waiting for the intensification, resulting in passivism, or to artificial intensification, with the consequent danger of sliding into the course of ultraleftism, political adventurism, and alienation from the masses. We must assume that the expansion and development of the class struggle will take place in new forms and at different levels. (*Kansan Uutiset*, 11 June 1967.)

A polemic leveled at the Muscovites came in October from Erkki Salomää, who voiced his concurrence with a frequently used analogy: that the SKP had not yet held its "Twentieth Congress" (referring to the Twentieth Congress of the CPSU in 1956 which initiated the "de-Stalinization" movement in the Soviet Union). Salomää's intimation that the party leadership must "come to terms" with the Stalinist minority could lend credence to reports of the increasing consolidation of this hitherto fragmented faction. The Vice-Chairman asserted that the attitudes of the opposition were "dictated by the struggle for power": "It tries to ride with Marxism-Leninism and canonizes itself as its sole defender. And what is really provocative, it states that only this group supports and maintains good and fraternal relations with the Communist Party of the Soviet Union." (*Kansan Uutiset,* 2 October.)

The principal centers of opposition are Turku (Abo) in the Southwest and Kuopio (Uusimää), in east-central Finland. Its chief organizer is deposed party Chairman Aimo Aaltonen, whose removal was certainly a contributing factor in the acceptance of the Communists as coalition partners by the Social Democrats. Aaltonen has actively pressed for reorganization of the new party leadership, and specifically for the ouster of Vice-Chairman Salomää. His group is allegedly determined to start a new party unless the decisions of the party's Fourteenth Congress are revised and the proposed program, "revisionist in spirit," is rejected (*Neue Zürcher Zeitung,* Zurich, 11 October). Aaltonen's main weapon in this power struggle is his claim that only the Stalinists can maintain good relations between the Finnish and Soviet parties. To the "revisionists," this sounds out of date. They hope to enter the 1970 general election with a new party program and a record in Government free from any Stalinist taint. (*The Economist,* London, 28 October.)

Abandoning attempts to quell the intraparty dissension on a regional level, the party leadership called a special session of the Central Committee and regional secretaries on 9-10 December. In his address to the session, Secretary-General Ville Pessi noted that liberal discussion of the situation "had not led to the desired results," and that the differences of opinion within the party had continued and had "partly even intensified, reaching aspects of sectarianism" which could not, however, "be explained as arising from a single factor." Pessi criticized the "dogmatists" for their continued refusal (1) to support the activities of the SKDL within the administration and (2) to recognize that party tactics must keep pace with technological and social advances if the Communists were to maintain their foothold within the labor movement. He urged "extremists" to exercise moderation in order to avoid "erroneous political lines." According to the Secretary-General, the "main weakness" in the party's operations was not in its policies, but in their implementation. A causal factor, he added, was the attitude of certain members who failed to abide by decisions of the Central Committee and the Politburo even though these had "generally been reached unanimously." (*Kansan Uutiset,* 10 December.) A draft resolution, drawn up by the Politburo and presented to the meeting, reportedly containing a "recommendation of the measures which, in the opinion of the Politburo, ought to be taken," was not adopted. Instead, a committee was set up to examine ways and means of restoring party unity.

With 215 delegates from district organizations, the SKP, the Democratic League of Women, the Socialist Student Union, and the Democratic Youth League, a congress of the SKDL was held in Helsinki on 13-15 May. Foreign parties sending delegations included the Scandinavian communist and socialist parties and the communist parties of the Soviet Union, the German Democratic Republic, Czechoslovakia, and Bulgaria.

Because of his ministerial duties, Ele Alenius declined to stand for reelection as Secretary-General of the SKDL. He was, instead, elected to replace retiring SKDL Chairman K. L. Kulo. Hertta Kuusinen, a member of the SKP Politburo, became Vice-Chairman.

A draft program was adopted by the SKDL Congress which would replace the existing one adopted in 1949. Emphasized were the realization of socialism by peaceful means, and the function of the SKDL as a "mass organization for all progressive forces and organizations, including those which do not recognize socialism," with Finnish traditional democracy as a "starting point." Commented Alenius: "It is highly probable that some will say that the draft is 'more social-democratic than revolutionary,' and the following sentence has therefore been included: 'Those Finnish social democrats who truly wish to take advantage of the peaceful possibilities for transition to socialism can attain this goal only in cooperation with communists and by common force'." (*Land og Folk,* Copenhagen, 13 and 21 October.)

The Finnish Democratic Youth League held its Eighth Congress in Turku on 24-27 March and resolved to apply for affiliation with the SKDL. The application was approved by the SKDL Congress in May.

*Kansan Uutiset* on 28 August hailed the signing of a "joint pact for cooperation and the formation of a joint elective permanent organ" by three socialist university-student organizations: the Socialist Student Union (a member organization of the SKDL), the Social Democratic Union of Student Youth, and the Academic Socialists of Helsinki (left socialist).

**International Views and Policies.** At a plenary meeting of the Central Committee on 21-22 January, SKP Chairman Saarinen reviewed the party's attitude toward the electoral alliance (proposed by the Center Party and subsequently agreed to by the other coalition partners) for the reelection of Urho Kekkonen in the 1968 presidential elections. Saarinen emphasized that the position of the Communists would be "considerably influenced" by the foreign policy objectives of the electoral alliance, and that Communist support would be witheld until the "political aims" of the alliance could be ascertained. Saarinen added:

> [At the moment]there are no sufficiently clear signs of a left-wing policy although the left makes up the majority. Among the tasks of a left-wing policy is that of promoting good and trustful relations between Finland and the Soviet Union, as well as an active effort to safeguard peace, including the demand that the United States stop its aggression in Vietnam, the establishment of a European security system, which implies recognition of the two German states and the present frontiers of Europe, nonproliferation of nuclear arms, the disbanding of military alliances, and gradual disarmament. (*IB,* no. 91, 1967.)

While it would be appropriate for the SKP to "look for" another presidential candidate, said Saarinen, it was "obvious" that no candidate of the Democratic League could expect to receive the backing of the Social Democrats. But, by the same token, he went on, it could also be said that "no one holding a key post in the Social Democratic Party today could, in the sphere of foreign policy, particularly with regard to the Soviet Union, expect to achieve what the present president has achieved." Moreover, the danger of "anticommunist and anti-Soviet" forces gaining the upper hand within the Social Democratic Party would be allayed by that party's support of Kekkonen.* (*Ibid.*)

The party's formal endorsement of Kekkonen came in an announcement by Ville Pessi at the September meeting of the Central Committee: "There is no one at present who qualifies for the post of Finnish President, [and, in consequence,] the current President is the best candidate." (Helsinki radio, 9 September.) The party's procrastination in committing its support to Kekkonen was no more than a political gesture directed toward the Social Democratic Party, then under censure by the Soviet Union for its hesitation in endorsing the President's reelection. According to an interview which Saarinen gave to the Finnish independent weekly *Suomen Kuvalehti* (28 January), *Pravda* was said to have expressed, on at least one occasion, its dissatisfaction that the SKP had itself delayed in "defining its position." Kekkonen's standing endorsement by the Soviet Union—largely due to its approval of the foreign political line developed by Kekkonen and his predecessor, Paasikivi—virtually assures that of the SKP.** Both Presidents have often referred to the 1948 Finnish-Soviet treaty of mutual assistance as the "foremost guarantee of Finnish neutrality and independence." More recently, Kekkonen has become an avid protagonist of the Moscow line advocating "Nordic security," which envisages the establishment of a nuclear-free zone in Scandinavia and the demilitarization of the Arctic regions, which would mean the removal of NATO bases in Northern Norway (*Washington Post*, 12 February). The program of the coalition Government, which Rafael Paasio has himself called a "compromise of compromises," concentrates on social and economic tasks, and pledges to modernize Finland, leaving unchanged the "Kekkonen-Paasikivi" foreign policy.

Kekkonen has urged acceptance by all Finns of the "right" of the SKDL to take part in the Government and "equally with others to influence the course of the state's affairs," adding: "The Finnish nation would be weak if a fourth of the country's inhabitants were an enemy of the homeland" (Helsinki radio, 4 February).

In an address to the Soviet delegation, headed by Soviet President Podgorny, in Helsinki for the fiftieth anniversary of Finnish independence (6 December), Kekkonen stated that "the consolidation of Soviet-Finnish relations on the basis of mutual respect and [the] expansion of fruitful cooperation which takes different forms are irrefutable and concrete facts" (TASS, 7 December). The remarks of Prime Minister Paasio later that month, on the anniversary of Soviet recognition of Finland's independence, were in the same vein, referring to the "common sense" which had taken the "upper hand" in relations between Finland and the Soviet Union," adding: "We can now continue developing our peaceful cooperation to achieve still better results" (TASS, 29 December).

But there is evidence that, with their new role in the Government, the Finnish Communists are formulating bilaterally with the CPSU decisions on policy questions of purely internal concern to the Finnish Government. Speaking in Moscow at the celebrations marking the fiftieth anniversary of the October Revolution, Secretary General Pessi stated that, given the "consistent unanimity of views" between the SKP and the CPSU, and "with Soviet-Finnish relations becoming more versatile [sic], party delegations have delved into problems tabled for settlement at government level" (*WMR*, November).

Attending the Congress of the General Council of the Socialist Internationale in Zurich (November), Erkki Raatikainen, Secretary-General of the Finnish Social Democratic Party, supported the proposal for a commission to assess the "emerging dialogue between Social Democrats and Communists," and spoke of the development of a "friendship policy between Finland and the Soviet Union with an eye to strengthening security in northern Europe." Pointing to the "open proposal for cooperation" made by the communists at Karlovy Vary, Raatikainen continued:

*It should be remembered that for many years (in the period frequently referred to as the "night-frost"), Soviet-Finnish relations were strained because of the firm anticommunist attitude of the Finnish Social Democrats. Despite the mellowing of their position, rumors were current during Premier Kosygin's visit to Finland in June 1966 that the inclusion of Communists was the price Rafael Paasio had to pay to gain Soviet endorsement of his Government. (See *YICA*, 1966; also *Survey*, London, no. 62, January 1967.)

**Commenting on Kekkonen's election to a second six-year term in office in 1962 and on his favorable prospects for reelection in 1968, the *Financial Times* (of London, 28 April) claimed that the Finnish president had been "elected in Novosibirsk."

> The relation between social-democracy and communism is changing to a new basis. For the Social Democratic Party of Finland, the question of this relation in our state life is timely [and] the good-neighbor relations with the Soviet Union are especially of vital importance. . . . We are of the opinion that the deprecatory posture of the Internationale with respect to contacts between socialist parties and communist parties is in need of revision. (*Die Andere Zeitung,* Hamburg, 16 November 1967.)

Aarne Saarinen, Ville Pessi, and Olavi Poiklainen attended the Conference of European Communist and Workers' Parties at Karlovy Vary (24-27 April). Pessi stated in advance: "Every attempt and every step aimed at safeguarding the security of Europe means also national security for the Finnish people." He added that success, the prospects for which were "greater than before," could be achieved not by the Communists alone, but only by cooperation between "all sectors of the labor movement and all progressive forces." (Moscow radio, 22 April.) A plenary session of the Central Committee on 4-5 May approved the conference resolution on European security, the Vietnam war, and the Greek military coup.

**International Communist Movement.** In an interview with *Suomen Kuvalehti* (28 January) Aarne Saarinen asserted: "The Chinese try to get other parties to accept their main line of thought; that, apparently, is their condition for peace. The Chinese, however, are in the minority in the international communist movement, and the opinions of a minority cannot be accepted." A Politburo statement deplored "the measures being taken under the slogan of the 'cultural revolution'" which it said were "ever more openly aimed at splitting the Communist Party of China, the socialist camp and the world communist movement," and expressed hope that "active manifestations of the sound spirit of socialist and proletarian internationalism" would enable the Chinese Communist Party to "emerge" from its difficulties. (TASS, 2 February.)

In a resolution of the Central Committee adopted on 22 January, the party supported the proposal for an international conference of communist parties and stated that experience had confirmed the "correctness of the political line defined by the 1960 meeting [in Moscow]." Even though a joint discussion of "all the important issues" was "impossible at the present stage," the resolution urged that an international meeting be convened to discuss the "most pressing" ones. The Central Committee suggested a "three-point agenda: (1) Unification of all peace forces to stop the war in Vietnam and in Southeast Asia; (2) Support for the national liberation movements and newly free states; the fight against neocolonialism and hunger in the world; and (3) The possibility of averting a third world war; peaceful coexistence, nonintervention in the internal affairs of other states." The purpose of such a convocation should not be "to isolate any one of the parties from the international communist movement"; preparations should be carried out "particularly thoroughly and collectively," and the aim should be the participation of as many parties as possible. (*IB*, no. 91, 1967.) A delegation of the SKP later joined with 17 other parties in "launching preparations" for the new conference.

Fraternal party congresses attended by the SKP or the SKDL, or both, during 1967 were those of the French Communist Party (Paris, 4-8 January), the Socialist Unity Party (Berlin, 17-22 April), and the Communist Party of Sweden (Stockholm, 13-16 May).

Aarne Saarinen and Ville Pessi represented the SKP at the October Revolution anniversary celebrations in Moscow; the SKDL delegation was headed by the SKDL Chairman, Ele Alenius.

The SKDL was represented at the congresses of the Norwegian Socialist People's Party and the Danish Socialist People's Party, and at Nordic Socialist Seminars held in Copenhagen in February and in Oslo in the fall, sponsored by these two parties. Both Nordic Socialist Seminars dealt with the relations of Nordic nations to the European Economic Community and to NATO, and with the proposed revitalization of the Nordic Council.

A delegation of the SKP, headed by Politburo member Olavi Laine, conferred with representatives of the Hungarian Socialist Workers' Party in January, and party Chairman Saarinen headed a second delegation to Budapest in August. A delegation of the Communist Party of Czechoslovakia visited Finland on 23-30 May, and the parties jointly stressed the importance of cooperation with socialists and social-democrats. A six-man delegation, headed by Saarinen and Pessi, held talks in Moscow on 6-7 June with Brezhnev, Suslov, and Ponomarev. In addition to an exchange of viewpoints on current questions, the two parties discussed the "development of friendly relations between the Soviet Union and Finland." (*Land og Folk*, Copenhagen, 11-12 June 1967.)

The Finnish and Yugoslav party leaderships issued a joint communique later in June, after talks in Helsinki. The parties condemned Israel's "acts of aggression" against its Arab neighbors and US "aggression" in Vietnam, and called for an "all-out drive against imperialism, power politics, and interference in the domestic affairs of other countries." According to the communique, the issues "plaguing the international communist movement" required a "deep exchange of views and experiences," and "differences of views arising among some parties should not disturb normal ties." (TANYUG, Belgrade, 28 June.)

The Finnish and Bulgarian parties held talks in Sofia in September and jointly stressed the need for immediate preparations for a world conference. SKP Central Committee member Ossi Nurminen, responsible for municipal questions, and Jalo Lepola, organizational secretary of the SKDL, went to France in October to study the activity of communists in French municipal administrations. During October a Rumanian party delegation visited Finland, and the SKDL sent representatives to Prague at the invitation of the National Front Central Committee. At the invitation of the SKDL's Democratic Youth League, a Komsomol delegation visited Finland in December. Ville Pessi headed a SKP delegation to East Germany in December to discuss the international situation and the development of cooperation between the two parties.

**Publications.** The central organ of the SKP is the daily *Kansan Uutiset* (People's News), edited by Jorma Simpura, a member of the Politburo. It has an estimated circulation of 59,000. The party's theoretical journal, *Kommunisti* (Communist), edited by Politburo member Inkeri Lehtinen, is issued monthly. In addition, the party publishes a number of regional organs, including *Uusi Paiva* in Turku and *Kansan Sana,* the Kuopio district daily.

# FRANCE

The French Communist Party (Parti Communiste Français; PCF) was founded 29 December 1920. It is legal and has claimed a membership for 1967 of "more than 400,000" (*France Nouvelle,* 14 February 1968), a net increase of 12,000 over 1966; 25.5 per cent of the members are women (*ibid.*). Estimates of the true membership vary. It is probably around 300,000. The party refuses to release exact membership figures; it derives approximate figures from the number of blank membership cards sent out by headquarters to federation offices throughout the country, and as party officials admit (Marchais at Eighteenth Congress, cf. *France Nouvelle,* 18 January 1967), this number does not correspond exactly to the actual membership. The population of France is 49,750,000 (estimated March 1967).

The major ideological rival of the pro-Soviet French Communist Party is the French Communist Movement (Marxist-Leninist), which became the new Marxist-Leninist Communist Party of France at a constitutive congress 30-31 December 1967. There are also other active groups such as the *Unir-Débat* group, which are not formally organized into parties (see below).

In the National Assembly elections 5-12 March 1967, the French Communists advanced from 41 to 73 seats (PCF sources speak of 72 deputies and one for the Guadeloupean Communist Party, making the separation to stress the autonomy of this offspring party). Compared to previous National Assembly elections, the more than 5 million communist votes polled in 1967 represented an increase of more than 1 million over 1962, and of more than 2 million over the 1958 election totals. In the cantonal elections of 24 September - 1 October 1967, the PCF almost doubled its seats, advancing from 56 to 97 of the more than 1700 seats open for election. In general, the year 1967 saw marked progress for the French Communist Party in terms of membership, voter support, and acceptance by members of the noncommunist left.

**Organization and Leadership.** At its Eighteenth Congress 4-8 January 1967, the French Communist Party elected a Central Committee of 74 full members (previously 70) and 22 candidate members (previously 23); a Politburo of 17 (previously 14) full members and 2 (previously 4) candidate members. The members of the Politburo are Gustave Ansart, François Billoux, Jacques Duclos, Etienne Fajon, Benoît Frachon, Georges Frischmann, Roger Garaudy, Raymond Guyot, Henri Krasucki, Paul Laurent, Georges Marchais, René Piquet, Gaston Plissonnier, Waldeck Rochet, Georges Séguy, and Jeannette Thorez-Vermeersch; the candidate members are Guy Besse and André Vieuguet. The only addition to the Politburo was Vieuguet, who also was elected to the six-man Secretariat (formerly five members). The other members of the Secretariat are Roland Leroy, Georges Marchais, René Piquet, Gaston Plissonnier, and Secretary-General Waldeck Rochet. The Congress also elected a 10-man Central Commission of Political Control and a five-member Central Commission of Financial Control.

**Auxiliary Organizations.** The most important auxiliary organization of the French Communist Party is the trade union General Confederation of Labor (Confédération Générale du Travail; CGT), the largest trade union in France with a membership of about 1 million. CGT President Bénoît Frachon who until June 1967 was Secretary-General of the CGT, and the newly elected Secretary-General Georges Séguy, are both members of the PCF Politburo. The CGT was very active in 1967 trying to promote unity of action with other trade unions, notably the French Democratic Labor Federation (CFDT). Major strikes organized by the CGT in 1967 were the general strikes of 1 February, 17 May and 13 December, all conceived as demonstrations against political measures of the Gaullist regime. The CGT was also very active in anti-Vietnam war demonstrations and in a number of international activities including exchanges of delegations with trade unions of Hungary, the Soviet

Union, North Vietnam, and the Italian Communist CGIL. Other politically important front organizations of the PCF are the Union of French Women (Union des Femmes Françaises; UFF); the National Council of Writers (Conseil National des Ecrivains), headed by PCF Central Committee member Louis Aragon; the Association of Democratic Lawyers (Association des Juristes Démocrates); the Association France-USSR (Association France-URSS), headed by General Petit; and the Peace Movement (Mouvement de la Paix).

The Movement of Communist Youth (Mouvement de la Jeunesse Communiste; MJC) was active throughout 1967 propagandizing on a number of issues—notably the war in Vietnam and the military coup in Greece. The organization is comprised of four communist youth groups (see below). Total membership (as reported at the Eighteenth Congress of the PCF) is 50,000. The MJC publishes *Nous les Garçons et les Filles*. François Hilsum, since the Eighteenth PCF Congress a candidate member of the Central Committee, is Secretary-General of the National Council of the MJC. The National Council is formed by the National Bureaus of the four member organizations: Union of Young Girls of France (Union des Jeunes Filles de France; UJFF), with Monique Mercieca as Secretary-General; Union of Rural Youth of France (Union de la Jeunesse Agricole de France; UJAF), with Raymond Monteil as Secretary-General; Union of Communist Youth of France (Union de la Jeunesse Communiste de France; UJCF), headed by Roland Favaro; Union of Communist Students of France (Union des Etudiants Communistes de France; UECF), with Secretary-General Guy Hermier and Deputy Secretary-General Jean-Michel Catala (*L'Humanité* frequently spells his name Cathala) both reelected at the Tenth UECF Congress in mid-April 1967. In recent years, internal dissensions have substantially weakened the Union of Communist Students and caused the defection of many of its intellectuals. It took PCF leaders more than three years to regain complete control of the UECF after the formation in 1964 of a strong "Italian" faction within the group's leadership. The elimination of this "revisionist" group in the spring of 1965 was followed by the expulsion of the "Sorbonne-Lettres" group early in 1966. Then at the Ninth UECF Congress in April 1966 a "leftist" faction split off to form the Communist Revolutionary Youth (Jeunesse Communiste Révolutionnaire; JCR) which at the time declared its Fourth International Trotskyist views and by 1967 was also expressing admiration for Castro and "Che" Guevara. The JCR is close to the French section of the Fourth International, the Parti Communiste Internationaliste (PCI), and its Secretary Pierre Frank. It publishes *L'Avant-Garde* and a number of journals at universities throughout France. The JCR held its First Congress in Paris 24-27 March 1967 which not only condemned the UECF, but also requested that its members reject positions within the National Union of Students of France (UNEF) and operate exclusively "at the base" (cf. *Le Monde*, 29 March 1967). At the beginning of January 1967, the UECF group at the French elite school ENS (Ecole Normale Supérieure) in Paris announced they had held a congress 10-11 December 1966 and created the Union of Communist Youths, Marxist-Leninist (Union des Jeunesses Communistes, Marxiste-Léniniste; UJCML), with a pro-Peking orientation.

To understand groups like the UJCML one has to take into consideration the great importance attributed to the Great Proletarian Cultural Revolution in China. Its study fills a large part of the press of these groups. Generally, the views of the so-called "pro-Chinese" are richer and broader than the official PCF's positions. The UJCML publishes a bimonthly theoretical organ *Cahiers Marxistes-Léninistes*, a monthly *Garde Rouge*, and (since mid-1967) a biweekly "militant newspaper" *Servir le Peuple*. A major issue of dissent of the UJCML against the PCF and its student organization UECF is the position on Vietnam. The young Marxist-Leninists push much further; they accuse the PCF of not using the (Maoist) term "people's war" instead of "legitimate defense," of receding from the US nuclear threat, of seeking "political victory" in Vietnam instead of "military victory." The PCF slogan "Paix au Vietnam" is countered by the Maoists' "FLN vaincra" (NLF will win). The UJCML follows an autonomous political line and is not directly associated with the two "pro-Chinese" groups MCF(M-L) or CMLF (see below) with which they disagree on several points. *Le Monde* 2 April 1968 estimated the membership of UJCML at about 1,000.

**Eighteenth PCF Congress.** The Eighteenth Congress of the PCF, held 4-8 January 1967 at Levallois near Paris, was attended by 788 delegates. Prominent foreign guests included Secretary-General of the

Italian Communist Party Luigi Longo; CPSU Politburo member Arvids Pelshe; and Secretary-General of the Spanish Communist Party Santiago Carrillo. Thirty-six delegations represented communist parties from Austria, Belgium, Bulgaria, Canada, Chile, Cyprus, Czechoslovakia, Cuba, Denmark, Dominican Republic, Finland, Germany (West), Great Britain, Guadeloupe, Hungary, Ireland (North), Republic of Ireland, Italy, Jordan, Luxembourg, Lebanon, Martinique, Morocco, Mongolia, Portugal, Poland, Rumania, Soviet Union, Spain, Switzerland, Syria, Tunisia, United States, Vietnam (North), West-Berlin (SED-W), and Yugoslavia. An SED delegation from East Germany, headed by First Secretary Walter Ulbricht, could not attend because the French Government refused to issue visas. Paul Vergès, Secretary-General of the Communist Party of Réunion, allegedly could not obtain Air France passage. In addition to the Communist Party delegations, six delegations from "democratic parties and movements" were present (*L'Humanité*, 5 January 1967): National Liberation Front of South Vietnam, National Revolutionary Movement from Congo (Brazzaville), Democratic Party of Guinea, Sudanese Union R.D.A. of Mali, National Union of Popular Forces of Morocco, Union of the Populations of Cameroun.

Messages addressed to the Congress included one from the CPSU, another from Nguyen Huu Tho, President of the NLF of South Vietnam, and one from the Central Committee of the Workers' Party of Vietnam. The delegates to the Congress addressed to Ho Chi Minh a letter expressing solidarity with North Vietnam. The Congress stressed the importance of solidarity with the Vietnamese people and of the war in Vietnam, which was a major focus of PCF activities throughout 1967. The Congress resolutions also acknowledged certain positive aspects of de Gaulle's foreign policy and denounced both NATO and West Germany. Concerning events in China and the attitude of the Chinese Communist Party, the Congress emphasized the utility and necessity of a world communist meeting of the sort proposed in the opening day report by Waldeck Rochet. Referring explicitly to the CPSU Central Committee session in December 1966, Soviet delegate Arvids Pelshe and many other delegates to the Congress, notably those of the Communist Party of Germany (West) and the Spanish Communist Party, lent support to Rochet's call for a world conference. Italy's Luigi Longo, on the other hand, cautiously opposed a world meeting and stressed the need for a conference of European communist parties. The representatives of North Vietnam and the National Liberation Front of South Vietnam, by their failure to speak out either on China or on a world conference, suggested that they might not attend such a conference.

**Unity Within the PCF.** Politburo member Georges Marchais reviewed the activities of the French Communist Party in optimistic terms, placing strong emphasis on unity within the ranks of the party. In his report to the Congress he set the actual membership increase in 1966 at 11,000, with a total increase of about 50,000 since the Sixteenth Congress in 1961. He reported the age groups of the French Communist Party membership at 9.4 per cent below 25, 33.1 per cent between the ages of 26 and 40, 42.2 per cent from 41 to 60, and 17.3 per cent 61 and older. A remarkable resurgence of party recruitment was reported: 42.1 per cent of the members at the end of 1966 had joined since 1959. The report also stated that since the Seventeenth Congress in 1964, the Central Committee of the PCF had excluded 79 members for activities hostile to the party. Among those excluded were 56 with leanings toward "Marxist-Leninist Circles". Marchais' optimism concerning the unity within the party stands in contrast to his violent attacks on the divisive activities of leaders of the Chinese Communist Party, who were accused not only of splitting the world communist movement, but of openly attempting "to organize the split within the communist and workers' parties." Marchais charged that certain elements, which seem to consist of "only several hundreds of renegades," are in the pay of the Chinese leaders and distribute a weekly (*L'Humanité Nouvelle*) which they cannot sell. While they have no influence among the masses, he said, they are welcomed and acknowledged and their importance exaggerated by the bourgeois reactionaries. In France, said Marchais, there is room for but "a single Communist Party." "For this reason we will continue to combat on the political and ideological level the profoundly erroneous theses of the Chinese Communist Party leaders and the splitting activities of their agents in France." Although several other speakers drew attention to pro-Chinese activities in France, none of them commented at the Congress on the wholesale conversion of the UECF group at the Ecole Normale Superieure (see above) into a new

Marxist-Leninist youth group, although this turn of events was made public by *Le Monde* just before the Congress began.

**Dialogue with Socialists.** In addition to its evaluation of the international scene (which included condemnations of NATO, United States involvement in Vietnam, and the Chinese Communist Party leaders whose attitudes had allegedly made a new world conference necessary), the PCF Congress was primarily occupied with the problem of unity of the left in France. Both Waldeck Rochet's report to the Congress and the main Congress document, "The Political Resolution of the Eighteenth Congress," reflected the political and ideological problems facing the French Communist Party after the election accord concluded 20 December 1966 with the Federation of the Democratic and Socialist Left (FGDS*). This accord (see *Documents*), concluded for the legislative election in March 1967, provided that in the first election round (5 March) each side would have its own candidates, while in the second round (12 March) the strongest candidates of the left would receive joint support from all the left factions in order to improve their chances in a runoff election against Gaullist candidates. Thus the unity expressed in this accord was primarily a unity against the "personal power" regime of de Gaulle. But the differences within the left on such basic foreign policy questions as NATO or the European Economic Community (EEC) seemed to preclude imminent agreement on a joint government program. On 7 January the French Communist Party concluded a similar accord for the March elections with the United Socialist Party (PSU) which specifically declared approval of the 20 December accord between the PCF and FGDS. The second accord was announced to the Eighteenth Congress on 8 January (*L'Humanite*, 9 January 1967; see *Documents*).†

The unity of action with the Socialists raised the issue of "peaceful passage to socialism" and the implications of collaboration with Socialist, Christian and other noncommunist forces. In anticipation of the inevitable charges of "revisionism" from revolutionary and pro-Chinese quarters, the Political Resolution, although it proclaimed the 20 December accord "an event of great importance," insisted that it does not constitute "a renunciation of our fundamental political position. The party remains attached to its proposals of a joint program and will continue to fight for its realization." To meet the question of critics of what will happen to the alliance partners of the Communist Party once the working class has come to power through unity of the left, the Congress stated that since its Sixteenth (1961) and Seventeenth (1964) Congresses the PCF had firmly advocated a "durable collaboration between Communist and Socialist . . . . It has rejected the thesis of a unitary party as [an] obligatory condition for the Socialist Revolution and has spoken out in favor of a plurality of parties." However, the resolution also stated that the workers should not leave to the "exploiters" the possibility of restoring capitalism. The PCF thus remained suspiciously vague on the question of whether it would willingly relinquish power in the face of future unfavorable election returns: "The regime of the workers will take all measures necessary to safeguard and defend the socialist regime which it will install."†† The Congress stressed the importance of increased party work among the rural population, since the alliance with noncommunist forces necessary for a peaceful passage to socialism must include the working peasantry and the middle strata of the cities. Concerning intellectuals and artists, the Congress fully endorsed the position developed at the Central Committee meeting at Argenteuil, March 1966 (see *YICA*, 1966, pp. 107-8).

**Dialogue with Catholics.** A striking feature of the Eighteenth Congress was the relatively slight attention given to relations between the Communist Party and Catholics. Following the position adopted earlier at Argenteuil, the Political Resolution stated that an understanding of "the scientific, social and political realities of our time" are "at the base of the efforts at adaptation by the Catholic Church." The Communists, the resolution stated, appreciate those changes "without overestimating

---

*The Federation de la Gauche Democrate et Socialiste, founded in September 1965, consists of the SFIO (Socialist Party), the Radical-Socialist Party, and the Convention of Republican Institutions.

†PSU and FGDS also concluded an electoral accord 20 January 1967.

††In the Fiftieth Anniversary [of the October Revolution] issue of *World Marxist Review* (November 1967), Waldeck Rochet wrote that for the "new political power of the workers . . . including that in which a plurality of parties is preserved" it is a "basic" requirement that party members "defend the new system of socialist democracy against sabotage by the former exploiting classes aiming to regain power and restore capitalism" (p. 29).

them." While such changes would facilitate joint action on the part of believers and atheist masses, "joint action, with all respect for the conviction of each, does not imply any philosophical convergence or any relaxation of the ideological struggle. The party will develop its policy of the outstretched hand (*la main tendue*) to the Christian workers and to all democratic believers. . . ." The shift in attention away from dialogue with Christians becomes clear when this statement is compared with those of the Seventeenth Congress, which lauded the new thinking within the Church and stated that Communists "should not underestimate the importance of the change." The shift can be explained by the fact that by the end of 1966 the PCF had regained political respectability (as evidenced by the 20 December accord), and the Catholic dialogue had served its function while the dialogue with the Socialists had just entered a new phase. Unlike the Italian Communist Party, the PCF had never made any ideological concessions in the Christian-Marxist dialogue. The ideological position demonstrated at Argenteuil in March 1966 and approved by the Eighteenth Congress seems to have isolated within the ranks of his own party the internationally known contributor to the dialogue, French Communist Party member Roger Garaudy.*

In line with the turning away from Christian-Marxist dialogue and the isolation of Garaudy, was the absence of news in the French Communist press concerning the international Christian-Marxist meeting of the Paulus Society, held in April 1967 in Marienbad (Czechoslovakia), where the PCF was represented by Politburo members Garaudy and Guy Besse and journalist André Moine, who frequently presents the PCF view on religious questions (for instance, Moine's *Après "Pacem in terris": Communistes et chrétiens*, 1965). In fact, the dialogue with Christians had virtually disappeared from the French Communist Party press by 1967, although the party took a permissive attitude toward Garaudy's extra-party pursuit of the dialogue in Europe and America. The appeal to Christians for joint action with Communists and other progressive forces was written into the final statement of the April 1967 All-European Communist Party Conference at Karlovy Vary which was organized mainly by the French Communist Party together with the Polish Communists.

The increasingly cool attitude of the French Communists toward the Church was further reflected in the reception of Pope Paul VI's encyclical *Populorum Progressio* of 28 March 1967. A first editorial in *L'Humanité* (29 March) interpreted the papal statement primarily as an indictment of the capitalist world and even implied that the Pope considered aid from the socialist camp to the underdeveloped world as the only efficient aid. In *L'Humanité* of 4 April, André Moine approached the encyclical more critically, charging that it remained within the moral, i.e., outside the political, realm by its condemnation only of "liberal" capitalism and its acceptance of "ideal" capitalism. The Politburo of the PCF 11 April passed a resolution on *Populorum Progressio* which, with reference to the decisions of Argenteuil, emphasized that moral covergencies between Christians and Communists afford favorable conditions for a dialogue, but philosophic convergence will be beyond reach so long as the Church aims not at the "disappearance of capitalism but at its amendment" (*L'Humanité*, 12 April 1967). In this connection it is interesting that an analysis of the March elections acknowledged the effectiveness of the Christian-Marxist dialogue in the past: an article in *France Nouvelle* (3 May 1967) cited among the reasons for the progress of the Communist Party in the Moselle Department "the patient and persistent fight of our Federation for several years in the direction of that immense mass who are the Catholics." The current position of the French Communist Party was summed up in a paper on "The Christian and the Socialist Revolution" in November 1967 (see text, *France Nouvelle*, 10 January 1968) in which neither the name nor the works of Garaudy are mentioned,

---

*Except for reading a message of the Communist Party of Reúnion, Garaudy did not speak at the Eighteenth Congress; he had not been so silent in many years. Then the French Communist press failed to report the Garaudy interview published in the West German weekly *Der Spiegel* 30 January 1967—for which Garaudy was attacked by an East German paper. Strangely, Garaudy, a good writer and the best philosophical mind in the PCF leadership, rarely contributed throughout the year to party organs. A short preview of the Sixth Marxist Week of Thought appeared in *L'Humanité* 27 October; a letter by Garaudy in reply to Central Committee members Kanapa and Seve who had "corrected" a favorable review of Garaudy's book *Marxisme du XXe Siecle* (1966) in *Cahiers du Communisme* of January 1967 was printed together with the criticism in the July-August issue of the same journal. In the PCF weekly *France Nouvelle* of 26 July 1967 Garaudy's book *Le problème chinois* (1967) was attacked by Central Committee member Courtieu, to whom Garaudy also replied by letter (*ibid.*, 9 August). On *Le problème chinois* see more below. The silence of all other party publications concerning this book was certainly significant in itself.

while due reference is made to the decisions of the Central Committee at Argenteuil. The author, Politburo candidate member Guy Besse, quoted as official and still valid the party position stated by Waldeck Rochet in his speech at Argenteuil — that cooperation between Communists and Socialists and in general between all forces interested in the construction of socialism and socialist democracy is the only means of hastening the arrival of socialism in France. As there are also a number of Christians who aspire to socialism, they will consequently "play their proper role."

**Domestic Activities.** Unity of the left against the Gaullist regime and some sort of international unity against the United States remained the broad goals for French Communists in 1967. The drive for unity of the left found evidence not only in the agreements for the spring and fall elections, but also in a number of other party activities throughout the year. For instance, the trade unions CGT and CFDT jointly organized a general strike for 1 February (agreed upon 11 January 1967, immediately after the first anniversary of the CGT-CFDT collaboration accord). Another general strike took place 17 May, organized by the Communist CGT together with noncommunist trade unions, notably the CFDT, in opposition to the Government's announcement at the end of April that it would ask for "special powers" (under Article 38 of the Constitution) to legislate by decree in the economic and social field. In the same spirit, the PCF Politburo 28 April recommended to the parties of the left a joint "motion of censure" in the National Assembly. Although the motion, supported by the PSU, the FGDS and members of the Democratic Center, failed when it came to a vote three times in May and June, the fact that it could materialize at all was an achievement. Discussing the joint motion at a conference of Communist deputies on 4-5 May, Waldeck Rochet compared in detail the PCF position and the program (of July 1966) of the Federation of the Left. It was primarily in foreign policy that the differences seemed irreconcilable. Joint opposition of the left to the Government's social security plans helped to unite Communists and the left again for the cantonal elections in the fall—after the serious disagreements over the Middle East situation (see below)—and resulted in the general strike of 13 December against de Gaulle's domestic policies. However, an attempt by the Federation of the Left to unite the left in a new motion of censure against de Gaulle's European Economic Community policies shortly before Christmas (i.e., before the parliamentary recess until 2 April 1968) failed because of the Communist Party's support for de Gaulle's stand on the EEC.

One other major factor which helped to rally the French left was the war in Vietnam. Widespread anti-Americanism and resentment of US policy in Vietnam among the French population afforded a chance for the Communist Party, the Communist trade union CGT, the Movement of Communist Youth, and other auxiliary organizations, to appear in a favorable political light. Thus the resolution of the Central Committee, assessing the March elections in its meeting at Aubervilliers 29-30 March, stated that joint action between the Communist Party and the Federation of the Left could be realized in the immediate future on the basis of the 20 December Accord by (a) actions on social and welfare issues, and (b) work for peace in Vietnam. Confirming a Politburo decision of 16 March, the Central Committee then called upon deputies of groups and parties of the left in the (newly elected) National Assembly to coordinate their efforts and find "joint positions on essential questions of national and international life." The extent to which the PCF viewed its domestic activities as a contribution to an anti-American international front was formulated by Waldeck Rochet in a speech 15 October, "What Being a Revolutionary Means in France Today" (see *Documents*). The text of the speech subsequently received wide distribution and publicity as a basic document of the party.

During 1967 the French Communist Party held three Central Committee sessions. The first, at Aubervilliers 29-30 March, was devoted to an analysis of the legislative elections and resumed the discussions of the Eighteenth Congress on unity of the left. In their reports, Waldeck Rochet (see *Documents*) and Georges Marchais confirmed the utility of the 20 December Accord and stressed the party's past efforts to "find appropriate forms of united front"—with a joint government program of the left as a final goal, "for the left must demonstrate not only that it can unite to fight, but also that it can unite to govern." The resolution of Aubervilliers (see *Documents*) listed as basic achievements of the elections (a) the success of the French Communist Party; (b) the advance of the left in general; (c) the setback for Gaullist power; and (d) the voters' condemnation of Lecanuet's Democratic

Center. According to Central Committee Secretary Marchais, the 5,029,808 votes for the PCF in the first round on 5 March were mainly the result of party progress in the big industrial centers, among farm workers and peasants, and among young voters. On the basis of the 20 December and subsequent PSU-PCF and PSU-FGDS accords—which had been applied in 367 of 398 possible districts—the Communists received concerted support from the left for 187 candidates, the Federation of the Left received support for 173, and the United Socialist Party for 7. Marchais emphasized that in 13 cases the Communist Party withdrew candidates in favor of noncommunist candidates of the left who had a better chance of winning. In 16 districts no left candidate reached the second round, so that the 20 December Accord actually was not honored in only 15 districts.

On 28 February Waldeck Rochet had proposed in a letter to François Mitterand that the talks between the PCF and the Federation of the Left be resumed. Mitterand's assent came on 28 April. Leaders of both sides met on 11 May; and on 15 June a joint "working group" was established which would meet regularly and present a report in October on the prospects for strengthened cooperation.

In a report on "Problems of Unity" before the Central Committee at Arcueil 29-30 June, Rochet reviewed the major developments in Communist Party relations with the Federation of the Left from 28 February until the 15 June meeting when disagreements over events in the Middle East shook French left unity. He called the June meeting of leaders of the Communist Party and the Federation of the Left a "pause" in the development of unity of action, because then the two groups found their positions so "absolutely different" that they agreed to abandon further discussion of the Middle East crisis. Echoing the resolution of Aubervilliers, the Secretary-General then declared opposition to US policy in Vietnam to be a factor fostering unity among the forces of the left, and urged continued unity of action "across the struggle," from Vietnam (the Fifty-Sixth Congress [29 June—2 July] of the SFIO Socialists, members of the Federation of the Left, passed a resolution on Vietnam condemning the war and asking for a bombing halt as a minimum requirement for a settlement of the war) to the defense of social security. The Arcueil Central Committee meeting also heard a report by Raymond Guyot on international questions, and adopted a short resolution condemning the military coup in Greece and a long resolution on the international situation in general (text in *Cahiers du Communisme* July-August 1967), in which de Gaulle's views on Vietnam and the Middle East were viewed as "positive."

The Communists failed to persuade the Federation of the Left to apply the rules of the 20 December Accord "automatically" to the second round of the cantonal elections, although they made it widely known that they themselves would do so. However, local election deals were worked out some before and some after the first round (24 September) among the groupings of the Left, and received the blessing of the national leadership. *L'Humanité* 3 October listed by name 173 candidates of the Federation of the Left who, it said, were elected or reelected because of Communist support; it also named 46 Communist candidates elected with the help of the Federation. The Communist Party pointed out that it had made "gifts" in several instances to candidates of the noncommunist left when a Communist Party candidate, although placed ahead, withdrew in favor of a left candidate more likely to win. In six newly districted departments in the Paris region, the Communist Party won 78 of 192 seats. Elsewhere they gained 97 seats against 56 held previously. Voting participation in both rounds was about 57 per cent. The French Communist Party received a country-wide average of 26.36 per cent of all votes cast in the first round (FGDS received 21.55 per cent), thus advancing by about 3.5 per cent over previous elections. The Federation of the Left by and large maintained its strength (see the analysis in *Le Monde* 3 October 1967), while the Gaullists advanced and the Democratic Center lost ground.

The Central Committee meeting at Vitry 17-18 October, convened to examine the elections (report by Central Committee Secretary Plissonnier), reflected the optimism which had fired the French Communist Party and its leaders after the legislative and cantonal elections. The new tasks for party militants, outlined at the meeting by Marchais and stated in the general resolution, are a broadening of the struggle on social matters, manifestations in various forms of solidarity with the Vietnamese people (a preview of the 21 October and 25 November demonstrations), and continued efforts toward a joint government program of the left. A report by Rochet on the international activity of the party gave a general survey of international contacts (those passages of the report were not made public) and made a plea for an international communist conference (see below).

The Communist Party has faithfully pursued those tasks. The opposition to, and mobilization against, the war in Vietnam has picked up momentum, notably with the "Ship for Vietnam" campaign launched by the Politburo 3 November and a nationwide Vietnam demonstration staged 26 November by the Movement of Communist Youth attended by most of the PCF leadership. The "social struggle" produced a joint PCF-FGDS declaration on social security in November and a general strike 13 December. By mid-October the "working group" (study committee) of the French Communist Party and the Federation of the Left, established 15 June, had terminated its work and submitted to the leadership of both sides an account of its findings. This document subsequently was to serve as the basis for the important joint declaration by the PCF and FGDS (24 February 1968) which marked a new phase in the dialogue between communist and socialist forces in France and established a platform for further collaboration.

**International Views and Policies.** Serious barriers to cooperation between the French Communist Party and the left arose in the field of foreign policy. The resolution of the PCF Congress in January stated that divergencies within the capitalist world explain "certain positive modifications" of de Gaulle's politics, such as the improvement of French relations with the Soviet Union, the withdrawal of French troops from an integrated NATO command and revision of the status of US bases in France, and de Gaulle's attitude toward the war in Vietnam. The PCF shared the view of most communist parties that a cessation of the war in Vietnam would first require a complete bombing halt, a recognition of the National Liberation Front as the only true representative of the people of South Vietnam, and a retreat of American and other foreign troops from Vietnam. The Congress further demanded that military blocs in Europe be dissolved and replaced by a "collective security system," and expressed support for a European conference to plan collective security. It warned against West German territorial ambitions and the resurgence of Nazism, and deplored the fact that the Communist Party of Germany remained outlawed. Among points of disagreement with Gaullist foreign policy expressed at the Congress were the French *"force de frappe"* and de Gaulle's refusal to sign the nuclear test ban treaty of 1963; France's continued opposition to recognition of the German Democratic Republic; the colonial status of Guadeloupe, Martinique and Réunion.

In April, the French Communist Party signed the joint statement of the Karlovy Vary Conference which dealt primarily with NATO and West Germany and condemned the military coup in Greece. Speaking at a PCF parliamentarians' meeting in early May, Waldeck Rochet outlined the points of difference between the foreign policy position of the party and that of the Federation of the Left. The main points of friction were (and still are) the European Economic Community, the Atlantic Alliance, and the recognition of East Germany.

**Middle East Crisis.** Events in the Middle East brought some modification of the hard pro-Arab line expressed in an editorial in *L'Humanité*, 24 May. Guy Mollet (SFIO) and FGDS President Mitterand came out clearly in favor of Israel; Mendès-France even issued a personal appeal to Moscow. The French Communist Party immediately softened its tone — probably because of Jewish adherents within its own ranks, and in order to avoid completely alienating intellectuals and the noncommunist left who sided with Israel — and in an editorial in *L'Humanité* 26 May, took the position that the PCF does not question the right to the existence of the state of Israel, although it condemns Israeli leaders as instruments of imperialists and oil interests in the Middle East. In essence this also was the official position as expressed in a Politburo communique of 3 June. When the Mideast fighting began 5 June, the PCF immediately denounced the military action and stressed the need for negotiations. Party propaganda remained pro-Arab, however, and there never was any doubt about the true sympathies of the PCF. In Raymond Guyot's report on the international situation, presented to the Central Committee at Arcueil on 29 June, and in the final resolution of that meeting, the events in the Middle East were interpreted as part of a global US imperialist strategy apparent in Vietnam, Cuba, Congo, Ghana, Dominican Republic, Korea, Greece, and West Germany, as well as in NATO. The meeting expressed concurrence with de Gaulle's view that events in the Middle East are linked to those in Vietnam. In full support of the Soviet position on the Middle East and the decisions of the Moscow meeting in June, the Arcueil resolution stated: "The French Communist Party advocates a durable peace in the Middle East, without humiliation or territorial annexation, founded on the national rights of the Arab peoples, notably the Arab people of Palestine, and at the same time on the right to existence of the people and the state of Israel. It demands the evacuation of the occupied territory by the Israeli troops. . . ." In June a special joint issue of *Le Nouveau Clarté* and *La Nouvelle Critique* was devoted to the theme of Communists and the Middle East.

At a press conference held on 6 September — before the cantonal elections — Waldeck Rochet again outlined the points of disagreement on foreign policy between the PCF and Mitterand's Federation. He particularly stressed points relating to Europe. The Secretary-General also supported the position of the Canadian Communists, who were seeking some sort of autonomy for the French-speaking part of Canada thus making it clear that the French Communists agreed with de Gaulle's controversial stand on this question which he had stated at Quebec at the end of July. In the closing speech at the Sixth Week of Marxist Thought (Semaine de la Pensée Marxiste) on 20 November, Rochet (in a paper entitled "Socialism, Peace, National Liberation" which was subsequently distributed in the form of a pamphlet bound together with "What Being a Revolutionary Means in France Today") summarized the foreign policy position of his party. Following the policy of "peaceful coexistence" (this was the phrase used), the paper (a) demanded a settlement in Vietnam according to previously stated conditions and a political solution of the Middle East conflict (which would have to include "free traffic" in the Gulf of Aqaba and the Suez Canal); and (b) supported the fight of Latin Americans against "fascist and military dictators," although each communist party or progressive movement should have the right to determine its own form of struggle. It further said that NATO should not be renewed in 1969, and that a "supranational government" of the six EEC members would jeopardize French independence, especially vis-à-vis "revanchist" West Germany. Other demands on West Germany followed those expressed in the Karlovy Vary statement (see *Documents*). That the PCF was not willing to compromise on the question of the EEC became clear when the Communist deputies blocked the motion of censure proposed by the Federation against de Gaulle's policy toward British entry into the EEC. This also showed how strong an element the Communist Party had become within the French left, for only a few days earlier, Socialist leader Guy Mollet had said on television that a joint government of Socialists and Communists (i.e., the PCF's goal) would require certain modifications in foreign policy on the Communist side, particularly concerning Europe.

Maintaining its previous attitude on the Sino-Soviet split, the French Communist Party carried its attack against the Chinese leaders to a new height at the Eighteenth Congress in January, charging the Chinese Communist Party with violation of the "general line" of the international communist movement adopted by 81 parties in 1960. Through their opposition to any collaboration between socialist and communist parties, said Waldeck Rochet in his Congress report, the Chinese leaders hold a sectarian view opposed to the 1960 Statement. Because of the "adventurist," "nationalist" and "essentially anti-Soviet" theses of the Chinese leaders, the Congress favored a new international conference which would permit the communist parties to "consolidate, on the basis of Marxism-Leninism and a joint general line, the unity of the international communist movement" (Waldeck Rochet's closing speech at the Congress). A theoretical critique of Maoism by Central Committee member Jean Kanapa, published in *L'Humanité* 6 February 1967 ("Marxism Is Not a Catechism," see *Documents*), was reprinted by several West European communist papers as an authoritative analysis of the problem. Relentless hostility toward the Chinese leaders, often complemented by exaltations of the Soviet Union, recurred throughout the year in articles and resolutions, and was reflected in the tone with which the PCF press reported events in China, as well as in the selection of news. A major charge against the Chinese Communist Party was that it obstructed international communist solidarity with and supplies to North Vietnam.

A new dimension was added to previous anti-Mao arguments by Raymond Guyot and Waldeck Rochet at the Central Committee meeting at Arcueil (29-30 June) when they blamed the Chinese theses for the mistakes of the Indonesian Communist Party in connection with the abortive coup d'état of 30 September 1965. The example of the Indonesian Communist Party, said Waldeck

Rochet, "shows that the leftist phraseology and adventurist slogans of 'armed struggle everywhere' and 'at every moment' render the greatest service to imperialism." In a statement apparently addressed specifically to Politburo member Roger Garaudy, the Secretary-General of the Party said: "I fully agree with the comrades who have underlined the point that Maoism does not represent a special concept of socialism, but an ideology alien to Marxism-Leninism." Garaudy, in his book *Le problème chinois* (1967) in advocating some sort of "dialogue" with the Chinese leaders, had implied that there are not only different roads to socialism, but also different forms of socialism. Central Committee member Paul Courtieu, in *France Nouvelle* 26 July, accused Garaudy shortly after the Arcueil session of holding views contradictory to the decisions of the Eighteenth Congress of the party. Garaudy defended himself (*ibid.*, 9 August) by pointing out that an honest examination of the "Chinese model" would further the discussion of a "French model" of Socialism. "The current discussions with the Socialist Party and with the Federation, as well as the dialogue with the Christians, require that we make this new theoretical effort."

On 14 July *L'Humanité* again dealt with the "Indonesian tragedy" caused by the application of Mao Tse-tung's thought. *France Nouvelle* of 26 July carried an article on the "auto-critique" of the (pro-Chinese) Politburo of the Central Committee of the Indonesian Communist Party (see *Documents*) and condemned the "fundamentally erroneous line" of the Indonesian Communist Party since 1963. The following week *France Nouvelle* (2 August) reported on a pro-Soviet "Marxist-Leninist Group of the Indonesian Communist Party" and its secretly circulated document "On the Correct Road of the Indonesian Revolution," which is highly critical of "ultra-leftist" and "sectarian" (i.e., Chinese) conceptions.* When *L'Humanité* 4 August launched an attack against the OLAS Conference, it suggested that those Peking-inspired "ultra-leftist grouplets" meeting in Havana could have drawn an advantageous lesson from the 1965 events in Indonesia. (Radio Moscow read large portions of this *L'Humanité* commentary on 8 August, thus implying approval of its rigorous anti-Castro position.)

Again on 15 October, in his lecture entitled "What Being a Revolutionary Means in France Today," Rochet cited the Indonesian case as a warning against the Chinese theses. "To be a revolutionary in the France of today" means to gain the majority of the people for socialism, which is similarly true, according to Rochet, for a number of Latin American countries. Those who would impose their views on other countries, on the one hand, seriously threaten the national liberation struggle and, on the other hand, intrude upon the independence and the equal rights of each party to determine its own methods. This admonition was repeated a few days later at the Central Committee meeting at Vitry.

The critique of the OLAS Conference and the alleged pro-Chinese leftists attending it in *L'Humanité* of 4 August (which also contained an outright defense of the Soviet Union) was not an isolated judgement, but fell in line with the PCF general attitude toward Latin American communism. While the PCF never ceased to emphasize its support for the Cuban Revolution, it also stated repeatedly that armed struggle after the Cuban model is not a "panacea" for all Latin American countries. The pro-Soviet line of a number of Latin American communist parties was publicized in the pages of *L'Humanité;* for instance, a long interview with Secretary-General Prestes of the Brazilian Communist Party, was published 16 January; Castro's speech of 13 March was ignored by *L'Humanité* while Secretary-General Jesus Faría of the Communist Party of Venezuela—the main target of Castro's speech—had an interview with the PCF daily only a few days later; and letters and reports from Bolivia, Colombia, Peru, and Venezuela, explained the position of the respective parties vis-à-vis the guerrilla fighting. What these Latin American views had in common was that, while formally backing the guerrillas, they stressed the political base among the masses as their political goal, a goal which coincides with the unity-of-the-left policy of the PCF and the Moscow camp.

*This unsigned document, first published in the pro-communist Indian journal *Mainstream* 11 March 1967, was reprinted in comprehensive excerpts in three May issues of the East German information bulletin *Aus der Internationalen Arbeiterbewegung* from where it has been reprinted in the *Information Bulletin* No. 106 of the *World Marxist Review. L'Humanité* carried excerpts on 9 and 11 December 1967.

It is therefore not surprising that relatively little attention was given in the French Communist press to the arrest on 20 April 1967 of Régis Debray, the French associate and supporter of "Che" Guevara. (Only a few days before the arrest, Guevara's "Message to the Peoples of the World" had been published in Havana [see *Documents*]. He had charged that the socialist countries share the guilt for Vietnam because they failed to make Vietnam a part of the socialist world.) The first, and rather detached, editorial comment by the French Communist Party on Debray came on 30 May in *L'Humanité*. After months of regular but brief reports on the progress of the trial of Debray, *L'Humanité* on 18 November published a dispassionate report on the 30-year sentence handed down by the Bolivian court. The story contrasted sharply with the paper's front-page coverage of the simultaneous trial of the Greek Mikis Theodorakis. In only eight lines the PCF daily on 21 November reported that the party Secretariat had addressed a protest on behalf of Debray to Bolivian President Barrientos. Similarly, there was little warmth or sympathy in the way the PCF reported the death of "Che" Guevara in October, although *L'Humanité* carried a front-page picture of Guevara and Castro, together with a message of Waldeck Rochet to Castro. The French Communist Party indirectly stated its position on armed rebellion in Latin America by reprinting in *L'Humanité* (15 November) an interview from *El Siglo* (Chile) in which a leading Bolivian Communist Party member repudiated any charges that the Communist Party of Bolivia had abandoned the guerrillas and betrayed Guevara.

On international issues the French Communist Party position in 1967 was identical with that of Moscow on questions of both international communism and international politics. The French Communist press served as a forum for the illegal communist parties of Spain, Portugal, Greece, and West Germany; the favorable coverage of the SED and East Germany, combined with demands that France recognize the East German regime, added up to propaganda support for Soviet policy. As in the Soviet propaganda, the rise of the National Democratic Party in West Germany was a constantly-evoked specter. *L'Humanité*, for instance, timed a series of nine full-page articles on "Neo-Nazism" in West Germany to run while the Seventh SED Congress was taking place in East Berlin. Other international activities of the French Communist Party included support for liberation movements in Portuguese Africa through participation of its youth organization MJC in an international solidarity conference in Conakry, Guinea, in April, and by hosting an international conference of national anti-apartheid committees from many countries, 5-6 May in Paris.

**International Party Contacts.** Two main aspects of relations between the French Communist Party and other communist parties were the PCF's active participation in the preparations for the Karlovy Vary Conference in April 1967 (the conference was primarily aimed at orienting communist and "progressive" political forces in Western Europe to Soviet foreign policy goals), and its contribution to the preparations for a new international communist conference (similar to the meetings of 1957 and 1960) which originally was sought by the CPSU in order to rally the communist parties to its side in the Sino-Soviet dispute. The French Communist Party was in a particularly good position to undertake these activities within the international movement after the impressive election results it scored on the home front. Now the French Communists could speak with new authority on international matters.

The PCF also gave more direct support to the CPSU. Not only did a delegation, headed by Secretary-General Rochet, attend the celebrations of the Fiftieth Anniversary of the October Revolution in Moscow; but the French Communist press also was one of the main publicity outlets in Western Europe for news of the celebration. It was promoted in numerous books, pamphlets, special journal issues, article series, and statements. (See, for instance, Waldeck Rochet, "The Greatest Event in Contemporary History," *Pravda,* 11 August 1967, and the PCF Central Committee resolution in honor of the October Revolution, adopted at the meeting at Vitry in October.)

Following the Preparatory Meeting at Warsaw 22-26 February 1967 (see *Karlovy Vary*), at which the French Communist Party was represented by Raymond Guyot and Jacques Denis, *L'Humanité* of 1 March carried some explanations by Guyot to the effect that the meeting of communist parties in Vienna in May 1966 had asked the PCF to go ahead with preparations for a European security conference of all European communist parties, and that Waldeck Rochet's talks with Gomulka in the fall of 1966 and Guyot's trip to Poland at the end of the year were part of those preparations. Guyot had already made known to a press agency at the end of January 1967 (see *L'Humanité*, 1 February) that the PCF had cooperated with the Polish communists in preparation for such a conference. (The French communists would coordinate the West European parties, the Poles the parties in the socialist countries.) However, what the French Communist Party never made public was that on 12 October 1966 it had sent a letter to the West European communist parties inviting them to attend the all-European conference. The date of the letter became known when the Communist Party of the Netherlands, in a Central Committee meeting of 20 March 1967 (i.e., after the Warsaw Preparatory Meeting) decided not to attend the Conference at Karlovy Vary in April. The Netherlands party, in a long letter to the Central Committee of the French Communist Party, explained its reasons for the decision (see *Netherlands*). The letter was published in the Dutch party organ *De Waarheid*, 21 March 1967. A trip by Guyot and Central Committee member Jourdain to Yugoslavia on 14-17 February, a visit of a Yugoslav delegation to Paris on 3-4 April, and Etienne Fajon's trip, together with Central Committee member Jacques Denis, to Rumania on 7-8 April, were all part of an unsuccessful attempt to secure the participation of the Yugoslavs and the Rumanians in the Karlovy Vary Conference. Central Committee Secretary Leroy's talks in Rome on 17-18 April with Italian Communist Party leaders, like Luigi Longo's previous stopover in Paris on his way home from Moscow on 29 March, also was mainly concerned with Karlovy Vary and the ironing out of differences between the two leading West European communist parties. (Longo, at the Eighteenth Congress of the PCF, had advocated an all-European communist party meeting but showed little interest in a world international conference—see above.) The Karlovy Vary Conference was attended by Secretary-General Waldeck Rochet and Central Committee members J. Denis and Jean Capievic.

A new series of high-level talks regarding an international conference began at the end of July. The PCF leadership met with Politburo member Kliszko of Poland in Paris on 26 July and with Ponomarev of the CPSU on 26 to 29 July. Waldeck Rochet visited with leaders of the Bulgarian and Rumanian communist parties at the end of July and in mid-August, respectively; and with the League of Communists of Yugoslavia at the end of August. A Yugoslav delegation in Paris (12-14 October) again discussed problems of the international communist movement. On 25 November the PCF was among the 18 parties to sign the call for an international consultative meeting in Budapest in February 1968. The proposed Budapest meeting was further discussed when Guyot went to Hungary for talks with Biszku and Komocsin 26-28 December, and when Waldeck Rochet met with Luigi Longo and other Italian Communist Party leaders in Rome 28-30 December.

Other international party contacts included one PCF delegation visit to Finland in April and another to the Seventh SED Congress (17-22 April), the visit of an Italian Communist Party delegation 4-13 May and of a Moroccan Communist Party delegation headed by Secretary-General Ali Yata 23-28 May. At the end of May a PCF delegation under Politburo member Plissonnier left for Moscow, while another PCF delegation earlier in the month had gone to Hungary. Two leading members of the Israeli Communist Party (RAKAH) met in Paris with Guyot, Leroy and Denis 9-11 September; in mid-October PCF delegations went to East Germany and Italy. A delegation to the 30th Congress of the Communist Party of Great Britain (25-28 November) was headed by Politburo member Ansart. Early in December a Czech Communist Party delegation came to Paris. From 29 November to 4 December a delegation headed by Guyot were guests of the (noncommunist) Ba'ath Party of Syria. During a visit to Paris 4-7 December, Secretary-General of the Chilean Communist Party Luis Corvalán had talks with Waldeck Rochet and other French Communists.

In addition to official contacts, French communists met with many foreign youth organizations and trade unions during 1967. Because of the high party status of certain participants (for instance, the Secretary-General of the [French] Movement of Communist Youth [MJC] is also a member of the Central Committee of the PCF, and the top leaders of the CGT trade union [President Frachon and Secretary-General Séguy are in the Politburo]), these contacts were of at least semi-official nature.

**Dissident Groups Around the PCF.** In January 1967 a group of PCF dissidents who work more or less in clandestine fashion began the publication of a monthly named *Unir-Débat* which is addressed to French Communists "with or without PCF membership cards." *Unir-Débat* resulted from the merger of two communist opposition journals. One, *Unir pour le Socialisme,* was founded in October

1952 by a group of French communist militants (who remained anonymous) in protest against the PCF's "United National Front" policy and claimed over 6,000 subscription holders in 1966. The other, *Le Débat Communiste,* was published since March 1962 by two former members of the PCF Central Committee, Marcel Prenant and Jean Chaintron, and a group of former PCF members "who remained attached to the Communist principles" (*Unir-Débat,* 10 January 1967). *Le Débat Communiste* claimed 1,046 subscription holders at the end of 1966. *Unir-Débat* refused to be identified with any particular trend. Viewing itself neither as "pro-Chinese" as those charged who wished a total condemnation of the Chinese leaders (that is, the official PCF leadership), nor as "rightist" – an accusation coming from Trotskyists – *Unir-Débat* wished to offer a broad discussion forum for different views on French Communist Party policies and problems of international communism. In this spirit, the *Unir-Débat* group on occasion came to the defense of the Revolutionary Communist Youth, a splinter group with Trotskyist tendencies (see above). According to *Unir-Débat* of 10 January 1968, the pro-Chinese *L'Humanité Nouvelle* had rejected a proposal for a public debate with *Unir-Débat* and treated the latter's representatives as if they were Trotskyists. Mentioning notably PCF Politburo members Duclos and Fajon, *Unir-Débat* characterized as "Stalinist" the PCF policy of lumping together the "monopolist government" and forces to the left of the PCF, warning against a repetition of the errors of the "anti-Yugoslav" era. In this context the journal deplored the fact that the French Communist Party had never undertaken a serious theoretical analysis of the phenomenon of Stalinism. The *Unir-Débat* group criticized the Eighteenth Congress of the PCF for having settled all important issues beforehand, thus reducing the discussion sessions at the Congress to a show of party democracy for the outside world.

Criticism from the left came from a group which publishes *Le Communiste,* a "monthly of the revolutionary tendency of the French Communist Party." This group, which claims to have begun in 1953, persistently criticized the "right-wing leadership" of the PCF. It would be inaccurate, however, to identify it as "pro-Chinese." Although this group "since 1957, approved the broad revolutionary effort of the Chinese Communist Party," the May 1967 issue of *Le Communiste* castigated the Chinese cultural revolution as a "disastrous and absurd error." Aiming at the "revolutionary transformation" of the PCF, *Le Communiste* (September 1967) came out against social democracy in general and the alliance with the Federation of the Left in particular. (It previously had urged the public to vote PCF on both rounds of the 5-12 March elections.) The journal deplored the PCF's total break with China, Albania and Algeria. It gave repeated and favorable publicity to Castro (e.g., his 13 March speech, which was ignored by *L'Humanité*), to "Che" Guevara whose "Message to the World" appeared in a special May issue of *Le Communiste,* and to the OLAS Conference. The leaders of the PCF were also accused of being responsible for the lack of relations with revolutionary movements in the Third World and in the United States, while PCF relations with the Soviet Union, the socialist countries, North Vietnam, Egypt and Syria, were based on ambiguities, according to *Le Communiste.* Quite different from "pro-Chinese" sources, *Le Communiste* (May 1967) considered Karlovy Vary an achievement and some of its objectives (regarding class struggle in Western Europe) as "fair." The same article on Karlovy Vary strictly rejected the idea of peaceful coexistence, a criticism of the Soviet position later repeated in the otherwise favorable appraisal of the CPSU Theses on the Fiftieth Anniversary of the October Revolution in *Le Communiste,* July 1967. Regular contributors to *Le Communiste* are Christian Garcia, Michèle Mestre, and Henri Pezerat, who seem to represent this opposition monthly officially (cf. 14 February 1968 letter of *Le Communiste* to the Central Committee of the Communist Party of Cuba).

**Marxist-Leninist Communist Party of France.** Founded at a constitutive Congress 30-31 December 1967, the Marxist-Leninist Communist Party of France (Parti Communiste Marxiste-Léniniste de France; PCMLF) originated from a pro-Chinese Communist group which had passed through several stages. First, a number of Marxist-Leninist circles, established with the help of the Franco-Chinese Friendship Association in 1963, formed the Federation of Marxist-Leninist Circles (Fédération des Cercles Marxistes-Léninstes) in July 1964. The Federation in February 1965 began the publication of a monthly *L'Humanité Nouvelle* in Marseilles, which later became a weekly and in 1966 moved its editorial headquarters to Paris. At the closed Congress in June 1966, the Federation announced a name change to become the French Communist Movement, Marxist-Leninist (Mouvement Communiste Français, Marxiste-Léniniste; MCF [M-L]). On 23-24 April 1967 a Central Committee meeting of the MCF(M-L) decided to convene a second Congress at the end of 1967 for the principal purpose of reconstructing a "genuine Marxist-Leninist communist party" in France. The MCF(M-L) was legal and so is the new PCMLF created at the end of the year. The constitutive Congress, however, was clandestine, mainly for fear of interference by the pro-Moscow French Communists. The bimonthly cultural journal *L'Opposition Artistique* was launched in December 1967 as an MCF(M-L) organ "on the cultural front."

Membership estimates for this pro-Chinese organization vary. Following the Congress, *L'Humanité* of 3 January 1968 spoke of "fewer than 500 adherents in all of France." Earlier, *Le Figaro* of 29 September 1967 claimed that some people in the PCF were willing to admit a possible membership of up to 7,000 for the new party — which would indeed be large for a grouplet (*groupuscule*) which the PCF pretends to disregard. Michel Legris in *Le Monde* 2 April 1968 gave a membership of about 2,000 for the PCMLF.

Like the Marxist-Leninist Center of France (see below), the new PCMLF kept its connection with the Franco-Chinese Friendship Association (Association des Amitiés Franco-Chinoises) as a liaison body with Peking.* This common link with China, however, does not keep the two pro-Chinese organizations from engaging in violent feuds with each other. The Executive President of the Franco-Chinese Friendship Association, Charles Bettelheim, visited Peking in July 1967 and on 8 July met with Vice-Premier and Foreign Minister Ch'en I. Shortly after, radio reports from Communist China stated that the membership in the organization in France had increased by more than 1,000 since the beginning of 1967.

Major meetings of the French Communist Movement (M-L) during 1967, besides the founding Congress, were the Central Committee meeting on 29 January (dealing with domestic French politics), on 22-23 April (calling for the constitution of a new Marxist-Leninist Party), and on 25 June (two resolutions denouncing the Glassboro talks and "revisionist" influence within the CGT trade union, respectively). An anti-Vietnam war demonstration staged on 5 May apparently was disrupted by activists of the PCF (cf. *L'Humanité Nouvelle,* 11 May 1967).

A major occupation of the MCF(M-L) throughout the year was the fight against the official French Communist Party. The "revisionist" Eighteenth Congress, the alliance with the "false left" of the French Socialists, the support for Moscow's Vietnam policy—all this, in the opinion of the MCF(M-L), testified to the complete ideological bankruptcy of the PCF. *L'Humanité Nouvelle* denounced Podgorny's visit with the Pope and rejected the Karlovy Vary Conference. Domestic and international policies of the Chinese leaders were given full support, including unqualified praise for the cultural revolution. A two-page article in *L'Humanité Nouvelle,* 19 January 1967 defended the cultural revolution and the concept of the dictatorship of the proletariat. (See also the editorial "La Veritable Unité," by Raymond Casas on the ideological differences between the PCF and the MCF(M-L) in *L'Humanité Nouvelle,* 30 November 1967.)

The most prominent leaders of the French Communist Movement (M-L) were Secretariat members Raymond Casas, Claude Combe, Jacques Jurquet (Political Secretary), and François Marty. The philosopher Gilbert Mury who left the PCF in late 1966 and Georges Gauthier are among the members of the Politburo. The editor-in-chief of *L'Humanite Nouvelle,* Régis Bergeron, belongs to the Central Committee. These men apparently continued to play the leading role in the newly formed Marxist-Leninist Communist Party of France, although no details were published after the Congress.

**PCMLF Constitutive Congress.** The constitutive Congress, which was held in the countryside at Puyricard near Aix-en-Provence 30-31 December 1967, was attended by 104 delegates with an average age of 32 who all were full members of the MCF(M-L), according to *L'Humanité Nouvelle,* 11 January 1968. (*L'Humanité,* 3 January 1968, spoke of "not more than thirty" delegates.) The Congress listened to a six-hour report by Jacques Jurquet which, according to *L'Humanité,* was contested by many delegates in the subsequent discussion, while *L'Humanité Nouvelle* said it was adopted unanimously. *L'Humanité Nouvelle* issues in January and February 1968 carried sections of the report. Claude Combe gave the closing address. The statutes of the PCMLF, adopted by the Congress and published in *L'Humanité Nouvelle* 18 January 1968, provide for a Central Committee of 40 (full and candidate) members who elect the Politburo, the Secretariat, and the Central Political Control Commission. The new Central Committee is said to have a "more proletarian" social

*\*La Voix du Peuple,* 28 April 1967, listed in a world-wide survey of pro-Chinese forces for France "notably" the UJCML and the MCF(M-L).

composition than the outgoing one. The Congress issued an appeal to the workers of France to join the new party, and adopted a program (published in *L'Humanité Nouvelle,* 5 March 1968) which calls for "violent overthrow of the entire bourgeois social order" and the establishment of a "revolutionary dictatorship of the proletariat," thus reconfirming the ideological positions and the foreign policy objectives of the French Communist Movement (M-L). The only foreign delegate at the Congress was Ray Nunes, member of the Secretariat of the Communist Party of New Zealand, who was greeted by the Congress "as a symbol of all foreign delegates of the entire world" who for visa reasons or political and security considerations could not come. The new party was greeted in *Peking Review,* 19 January 1968. Messages on the occasion of the Congress were received from the Albanian Workers' Party, the Polish Communist Party (stationed in Albania), the Organization of Communists of Switzerland, the Communist Party of Ceylon (pro-Peking party), the Quito-based (pro-Peking) Communist Party of Ecuador, the pro-Peking Communist Party of Bolivia, the Communist Party of Colombia (M-L), the Marxist-Leninist Party of Austria, the Marxist-Leninist Center of the Netherlands, the Greek Marxist-Leninist Communists, GONG (Guadeloupe), the Marxist-Leninist Committee of Portugal, the Communist Party of Italy (M-L).

**Marxist-Leninist Center of France.** A rival pro-Chinese group in France, the Centre Marxiste-Léniniste de France (CMLF), with a strong neo-Stalinist orientation, attacked the PCMLF in its organ *Tribune Rouge* as a "pseudo-party" which grouped around it a "collection of adventurers" and is nothing but "servile puppets carrying out the directives of those Chinese leaders who had followed the path of counterrevolution" (see *Le Monde,* 7-8 January 1968). The Marxist-Leninist Center of France, founded 18 March 1965 by various Marxist-Leninist groups in the Paris region, in June 1967 changed their monthly *Bulletin d'Information Marxiste-Léniniste* (founded in January 1964 by Claude Beaulieu) into the journal *Tribune Rouge,* with Claude Beaulieu as political director. Beaulieu had been excluded from the PCF in 1963. As President of the Clichy Committee of the Amitiés Franco-Chinoises he (during the May Day celebration in 1964 in Tirana) established contacts with Jacques Grippa, the Belgian pro-Chinese leader. Other leading figures of the CMLF were A. Dupuy and P. Prado. When *L'Humanité Nouvelle* had announced the projected transformation of the MCF(M-L) into a new party, *Tribune Rouge,* No. 4 (November, 1967) violently attacked the "Bergeron-Jurquet clique," to which *L'Humanité Nouvelle* on 16 November replied with the charge that the leaders of the Marxist-Leninist Center were agents of the PCF. CMLF membership size is not known. *Le Monde* 2 April 1968 estimated about 100 members.

**Publications.** The main publications of the PCF are the daily central organ *L'Humanité* with a circulation of 538,806 in September 1967 (*L'Humanité,* 19 September 1967); the central weekly *France Nouvelle;* the monthly theoretical organ *Cahiers du Communisme;* the popular weekend magazine *L'Humanité Dimanche;* the peasant weekly *La Terre* (edited by F. Clavaud); the intellectual monthly journal *La Nouvelle Critique;* the monthly of international affairs *Démocratie Nouvelle;* the literary monthly *Europe;* the bimonthly economic journal *Economie et Politique;* the philosophically oriented bimonthly *La Pensée;* and the historical quarterly *Les Cahiers de l'Institut Maurice-Thorez,* published since 1966 by the PCF's Institut Maurice-Thorez. In addition the party has a number of provincial newspapers. The Communist Youth Movement publishes *Nous les Garçons et les Filles;* the Union of Communist Youth journal is *Le Nouveau Clarté.* For intraparty work the Central Committee publishes *La Vie du Parti,* a monthly dealing with organizational, propaganda, educational and other problems. The French edition of the *World Marxist Review* appears as *La Nouvelle Revue Internationale.*

The Communist Revolutionary Youth (see above) publishes the (irregular) monthly *L'Avant-Garde;* the Union of Communist Youth, Marxist-Leninist, publishes *Cahiers Marxistes-Léninistes,* a bimonthly theoretical organ; *Garde Rouge,* a monthly; and since mid-1967 a bi-weekly "militant newspaper" *Servir le Peuple.*

A dissident French Communist group publishes the monthly *Unir-Débat* (see above). Another dissident PCF group is centered around the monthly *Le Communiste.*

The Marxist-Leninist Communist Party of France publishes the weekly *L'Humanité Nouvelle;* and a bimonthly cultural journal (launched December 1967) *L'Opposition Artistique.* The rival pro-Chinese group, the Marxist-Leninist Center of France, publishes the monthly *Tribune Rouge.*

# GERMANY: GERMAN DEMOCRATIC REPUBLIC

The Socialist Unity Party of Germany (Sozialistische Einheitspartei Deutschlands; SED) was founded on 21 April 1946 in the Soviet occupation zone when the Communist Party of Germany (KPD) and the Social-Democratic Party of Germany (SPD) merged, under Soviet pressure, into a single party. At the constitutive Congress at the end of the same month, 53 per cent of the 1,298,415 SED members came from the SPD and 47 per cent from the KPD. The highest membership so far reached by the SED was 1,786,138 in May 1947. At the party's Seventh Congress a total of 1,769,912 members as of the beginning of 1967 was reported. (Central Committee report, *Neues Deutschland,* 17 April 1967.) The Central Statistical Board of the German Democratic Republic (GDR) puts East Germany's population at 17,093,921 as of mid-1967.

The SED has been a ruling party ever since the establishment of the GDR in October 1949. Leading SED members occupy the key positions in the administration and the armed forces. The First Secretary of the SED, Walter Ulbricht, is at the same time Chairman of the State Council and Chairman of the National Defense Council.

Combined with four minor parties* in the "National Front," the SED presented a slate of candidates on 2 July 1967 for election to the People's Chamber. Of 583 candidates, 434 were to be elected deputies, the remaining 149 to become "substitute candidates" (*Nachfolgekandidaten*). With a voting participation of 98.82 per cent of the electorate, the East Germans overwhelmingly approved (with 99.93 per cent of all votes cast) the candidates proposed by the National Front. Votes cast against the National Front ticket totaled 8,021.

**Organization and Leadership.** The Seventh Congress of the SED, 17-22 April 1967, elected a Central Committee of 131 members and 50 candidates. The new Central Committee on 22 April relected Walter Ulbricht as First Secretary and elected the following 15-member Politburo: Friedrich Ebert, Paul Fröhlich, Gerhard Grüneberg, Kurt Hager, Erich Honecker, Hermann Matern, Günter Mittag, Erich Mückenberger, Alfred Neumann, Albert Norden, Horst Sindermann, Willi Stoph, Walter Ulbricht, Paul Verner, and Herbert Warnke. Six Politburo candidate members were elected: Hermann Axen, Georg Ewald, Walter Halbritter, Werner Jarowinsky, Günther Kleiber, and Margarete Müller. The ten Secretaries of the Central Committee are: Ulbricht (First Secretary), Honecker (listed by *Neues Deutschland,* out of alphabetical order, after Ulbricht), Axen, Grüneberg, Hager, Jarowinsky, Werner Lamberz, Mittag, Norden, and Verner (all Politburo members except Lamberz).

The Central Party Control Commission consists of nine members: Hermann Matern (Chairman), Ernst Altenkirch, Erich Ament, Elli Hempel, Heinz Juch, Helmut Pruss, Otto Sepke, Günther Tenner, and Herbert Wittholz; its five candidate members are Richard Eyerman, Hanny Gläser, Kurt Hausmann, Ewald Munschke, and Erna Warnke.

Political leadership and decision-making authority in the SED rests with the Politburo, which meets about once a week, while the Central Committee Secretariat handles personnel questions and the organizational and technical work of the party (see *Dokumente der Sozialistischen Einheitspartei Deutschlands,* IX, 311). Although officially no special areas are assigned to the individual Secretaries, their activities in the party leadership reveal certain special responsibilities: Honecker (a potential successor to Ulbricht as the party leader), security and military policy; Norden, together with Lamberz, propaganda; Hager, ideological problems; Axen, international party relations; Verner, work in the West (for instance, relations with West Germany's Social-Democratic Party); Mittag, industry and economics; Jarowinsky, trade; and Grüneberg, agriculture.

*Liberal-Demokratische Partei Deutschlands, National-Demokratische Partei Deutschlands, Demokratische Bauernpartei Deutschlands, and Christlich-Demokratische Union.

The most important mass organizations of the SED are the Free German Trade-Union Federation and the Free German Youth, both very active in establishing international contacts and promoting SED views. The Free German Trade-Union Federation (Freier Deutscher Gewerkschaftsbund; FDGB) has about 6,700,000 members and is a member of the World Federation of Trade Unions. A major concern of the FDGB in East German-West German politics is to maintain and develop relations with West German workers below the level of the official trade-union leadership. The Free German Youth (Freie Deutsche Jugend; FDJ) in May 1967 had a membership of 1,401,296 (*Junge Welt*, 11 May 1967), as compared with about 1,300,000 in 1963. At its Eighth Parliament, 10-15 May 1967, the FDJ unanimously elected Günther Jahn, a 37-year-old economist and member of the SED Central Committee, to the post of First Secretary of the Central Council (Zentralrat), replacing Horst Schumann.

Other mass organizations include: the Democratic Women's League of Germany (Demokratischer Frauenbund Deutschlands; DFB), a member organization of the Women's International Democratic Federation (the DFB has been able to enlist only a small number of the women workers and employees in the GDR); the German League of Culture (Deutscher Kulturbund); the Peasants' Mutual Aid Association (Vereinigung der gegenseitigen Bauernhilfe); the German-Soviet Friendship Society (Gesellschaft für Deutsch-Sowjetische Freundschaft; DSF), which is very active in promoting pro-Soviet views (Johannes Dieckmann is President of the DSF); and the "Ernst Thälmann" Pioneers Organization. The last-named organization, officially affiliated with the FDJ, but also directly under the control of the SED, was known until 1952 as the Young Pioneers. At the end of 1964 it had almost two million members, from six to 14 years. Most of the 40 members of the Central Council of this youth organization are members of the SED Central Committee or functionaries of the FDJ.

**Seventh SED Congress.** The Socialist Unity Party of Germany held its Seventh Congress in East Berlin, 17-22 April 1967, with 2,082 voting delegates attending. Foreign parties represented numbered 67, including noncommunist parties such as the radical left PSIUP of Italy, the Arab Socialist Union of the UAR, the Sudanese Union of Mali, the Democratic Party of Guinea, the Afro-Shirazi Party of Zanziber, the Ba'ath Party of Syria, the Neo Lao Hak Xat of Laos, and the Liberation Movement of Portuguese Guinea. The most prominent foreign guest was the Secretary-General of the CPSU, Leonid Brezhnev, who headed a Soviet delegation which among others included CPSU Central Committee Secretaries Andropov and Ponomarev. The other East European delegations were from Poland (led by First Secretary Gomulka), Czechoslovakia (led by Presidium Member Jiří Hendrych), Hungary (led by Politbureau Member Béla Biszku), Rumania (led by Permanent Presidium and Executive Committee Member Chivu Stoica), Bulgaria (led by Politburo Member Stanko Todorov), and Yugoslavia (led by Presidium Member Djoko Pajković). Politburo Member Dugersuren headed the Mongolian People's Revolutionary Party. From ruling communist parties in the Far East came a delegation of the Korean Workers' Party (led by Politburo Member Yi Chu-yon) and a delegation from North Vietnam under Politburo Member Nguyen Duy Trinh; Le Quang Chanh headed a delegation of the National Liberation Front of South Vietnam. The communist parties of China, Albania, and Cuba were not represented. Non-ruling communist party delegations came from West Germany (led by Secretary-General Max Reimann), West Berlin (led by Chairman Danelius), France (led by Marchais), Italy (led by Pietro Ingrao), Spain (led by Secretary-General Carrillo), Finland (led by Salomää), the United States (led by Hyman Lumer), Canada (led by Secretary-General Kashtan), Great Britain (led by Ramelson), Austria (led by Lauscher), Luxembourg (led by Chairman· Urbani), Belgium (led by Levaux), Portugal (no name given), Switzerland (led by Lechleiter), Greece (led by Partsalidis), Cyprus (led by Deputy Secretary-General Fantis), Denmark (led by Fuglsang), Sweden (led by Thunborg), Norway (led by Nettum), Iceland (led by Chairman Olgeirsson), Northern Ireland (led by Chairman Barr), Republic of Ireland (led by Palmer), Turkey (led by Demir), Iran (led by Radmanesh), Syria (led by Faisal), Lebanon (led by Secretary-General Chaoui), Jordan (led by First Secretary Nassar), Iraq (no name given), Sudan (led by Suliman Hamid el Hag), Morocco· (led by Layachi), Tunisia (led by Harmel), Nigeria (SWAFP, led by Otegbeye), Senegal (African Independence Party, led by Secretary-General Diop), South Africa (no name given), India (led by Bhowani Sen), Ceylon (led by Secretary-General Keuneman), Japan (led by Numata), Chile (led by Zamorano),

Argentina (led by Arévalo), Brazil (no name given), Venezuela (led by Secretary-General Jésus Faría), Uruguay (led by Massera), Ecuador (led by Secretary-General Pedro Saad), Peru (led by Reccio Gutiérrez), Bolivia (led by Otero), and Mexico (led by Unzueta).

First Secretary Walter Ulbricht's address on the first day of the Congress (*Neues Deutschland,* 18 April) was mainly devoted to economic, social, educational, judicial, and cultural problems since the last SED Congress in 1963. Ulbricht claimed that in the process of building socialism, the SED was in the period of the "formation of the developed society system of socialism" (cf. Erich Honecker's report on the Congress: "Problems of Building a Highly-Developed Society in the GDR," *World Marxist Review,* September 1967). Internationally the two main problems for the GDR, according to Ulbricht's report, are relations with the socialist countries of eastern Europe (especially in view of West Germany's new policy of "opening to the east") and with West Germany. Ulbricht demanded coordination of East European policies vis-à-vis the West in support of the East German search for recognition as a state. This was a rather clear allusion to Rumania's resumption of diplomatic relations with West Germany earlier in the year. Generally, Ulbricht's views on European Security, NATO, West Germany and West Berlin followed the decisions adopted at the 1966 Bucharest meeting of the Warsaw Pact and the "ten-point plan" proposed by Ulbricht in his 1967 New Year address (*Neues Deutschland,* 1 January), both of which reflect the foreign policy interests of the Soviet Union. A statement by West German Chancellor Kiesinger on 12 April proposing measures to ease restrictions on relations between the "people in both parts of Germany," and an accompanying letter by the leadership of the SPD, sent in advance to the SED Congress delegation, received an answer in Ulbricht's speech and in a declaration of the Congress (*ibid.,* 21 April). One of Ulbricht's conditions for developing relations with West Germany was the legalization of the West German Communist Party. Ulbricht also reiterated the idéa of a dialogue between the SED and the SPD (see *YICA,* 1966, pp. 56-57) and appealed directly to "all Social-Democratic members" for cooperation. The goal of Ulbricht's policy toward West Germany is the "formal recognition" of the GDR and "normal relations" between the two German states. American involvement in Vietnam and the activities of the Communist Chinese leaders received more or less routine reference.

The Central Committee report, presented in written form to the delegates (*ibid.,* 17 April) made specific reference to the Moscow meetings of 1957 and 1960 and emphasized the necessity of convening a new world conference of communist parties. In its condemnation of the "great-power chauvinism" and "adventurism" of the politics of the "clique around Mao" the report referred to the events in Indonesia in the fall of 1965 as an example of the "disastrous" consequences of such views.

Politburo Member Willi Stoph—like Erich Honecker, a potential successor to Walter Ulbricht—spoke on economic problems on 18 April.

Honecker addressed the Congress on 20 April with a speech on "The Function of the Party in the Period of the Completion of Socialism" (*ibid.,* 21 April) which contained the Congress's most detailed statement of the international position of the SED. Hailing the 1957 and 1960 Moscow meetings, Honecker pledged SED adherence to the "general line of the communist world movement," friendship with the Soviet Union as the "most important measure of proletarian internationalism," and support for "national democratic parties of Asia and Africa" and of "national liberation movements." Honecker demanded the end of West Germany's ban on the Communist Party and protested against "anticommunist policies" in West Germany, Spain, Portugal, Greece, Turkey, Venezuela, and Colombia. The Chinese leaders were condemned by Honecker, who called for unequivocal rejection of Chinese "nationalism" by the Marxist-Leninist fraternal parties. In order to elaborate anew the general line of the international communist movement, Honecker in the name of the SED called for a new world conference.

As the first foreign speaker, Leonid Brezhnev on 18 April denounced West German "aggressive policies" and then made a strong plea for convening a new international conference of communist parties to bolster the unity of the movement. Although Brezhnev did not specifically refer to the 1957 and 1960 meetings, his plea, coming on the eve of the Karlovy Vary conference, would seem to be significant inasmuch as CPSU leaders had played down the world conference and stressed the need for regional meetings during talks with Luigi Longo in Moscow at the end of March. Although there was basic agreement between the guest speakers concerning Vietnam, the front against West Germany was not united. Rumania's delegate, who demanded that West Germany accept the existence of two German states, did not follow the SED line, and Hungary gave it only half-hearted support. No agreement among attending parties was achieved on the two major international issues of China and the world conference. Some parties, including those of France, the USA, Hungary, and Bulgaria, followed the Brezhnev-SED line. Max Reimann of the West German Communist Party declared that his party was "uneasy" over China's attitude and saw conditions for a world conference "ripening." Gomulka concentrated his polemics on West Germany and made no reference at all to Karlovy Vary, the international conference, or China. Hendrych, of the Czech Communist Party, favored the preparation for a world conference, but made no reference to China. The Rumanian delegate generally supported unity among communist parties, but warned that nothing should be done which would sharpen the split. Yugoslavia rejected the idea of an international conference. The North Korean delegate simply ignored these issues, while the North Vietnamese delegation leader Nguyen Duy Trinh expressed warm thanks to the Soviet Union, the People's Republic of China and all fraternal parties for their support, thus revealing a view on China's role different from that expressed by Moscow and the SED.

The Congress, which had become a demonstration of Soviet-East German solidarity and of a high degree of party unity behind First Secretary Ulbricht, was given exceptionally broad coverage in the Soviet press. *Pravda,* on 12 April, devoted a full page to the SED, discussing the new economic system of the GDR, the party achievements since the last Congress, and the pre-Congress debate. The Congress, which received messages from both North Vietnam and the National Liberation Front of South Vietnam, issued a declaration condemning US involvement in Vietnam and pledging full support for the people of Vietnam. A protest resolution against the "terror" in Greece was approved on the final day of the Congress (*Neues Deutschland,* 23 April). Following the declaration of the Congress (issued 20 April) on Chancellor Kiesinger's statement and the SPD letter, Politburo Member Albert Norden explained to Social Democratic guests (who had come to the Congress in defiance of the SPD leadership's recommendation not to attend) the passages in Ulbricht's speech concerning the relationship of the SED to the working class and the Social-Democrats in the Federal Republic. A Manifesto of the Seventh Congress addressed to the citizens of the GDR (*ibid.,* 23 April) expressed the hope that someday the working class in West Germany would overcome "imperialism." This eventuality, according to the manifesto, represented the "only possibility for ever attaining reunification of the two German states." That the SED viewed the chances for finding broad popular support for a Socialist restructuring of West German society with little optimism is quite clear from a document which served as an intraparty discussion paper in the preparations for the Seventh Congress. This document ("Concerning Some Fundamental Questions of the International Situation and International Relations") is dated 31 January 1967. It looks at the German situation in realistic terms, admitting that there is so far in West Germany no political force to channel certain tendencies into a progressive mass movement. It regrets the SPD's participation in the coalition government in Bonn and adds: "The SPD holds . . . a strong influence in the West German working class. Large sections of the trade-union movement stand left of the SPD; but trade unions, of course, can not assume the function of a political party." (See *SBZ-Archiv,* No. 8, April.)

The central place given to the discussion of economic problems at the Congress indicated that the SED leaders consider the economic strength of the GDR of no less importance than its international political standing. Under the "New Economic System" in economic planning which was officially adopted in 1963 (at that time a sensational step among the socialist countries, although since then countries such as Czechoslovakia and Hungary have taken the lead in economic reform) the East German economy has made important progress. Following the new orientation expressed at the Seventh Congress, which was reconfirmed by the Third Plenum of the Central Committee in November 1967, emphasis shifted, at least in terms of proposed growth rates, to consumers' goods and light industry. On 26 May the People's Chamber adopted a "Perspective Plan until 1970" (proposed by Director of the State Planning Commission Schürer). The goal of the new plan is the "highest possible growth in actually usable national income" and a "most effective use" of this income. Priority is given to export-related industries and those having a high impact on economic development within the GDR, to automation and means of increasing efficiency, to industries that use domestic raw materials and offer a high value increase in the finished product, and to consumers' goods industries. The determination of the SED leaders to approach economic problems in a more realistic fashion was expressed by Politburo Member Günter Mittag, industry and economics expert among the SED Central Committee Secretaries, in an article in the *World Marxist Review,* January 1968. While the final authority of the party in economic matters is not challenged, a new attempt at increasing management responsibility and improving production techniques is stated as a vital task. The use of computer programming is considered necessary for the rationalizing of production and the introduction of automation: "Computers make planning more dynamic. They rationalize management and all economic work, especially at factory level. We are on the point of embarking on a new state in planning and management, in keeping with the process of socializing labor in conditions of the technological revolution." A Western analysis of the New Economic System (Hans Boehme, "East German Price Formation under the New Economic System," in *Soviet Studies,* XIX, January 1968, pp. 340-358), focusing on changes of attitude toward price functions in a socialist economy, concludes that East Germany has "begun a process of rationalization, and of more intensive theorizing which might eventually spread to other fields, especially since developments during the past 15 years on the whole show increasing flexibility and adaptation of ideology to the requirements of changing economic conditions."

In view of the efforts made by the German Democratic Republic to improve its economy, it is surprising that the volume of trade between the GDR and the Federal Republic of Germany (including West Berlin) dropped in 1967 for the first time since 1962. Since East German trade with foreign countries for 1967 showed an increase, the relative recession in inter-German trade relations is noteworthy (cf. Hans-Dieter Schulz, "Gebremster Interzonenhandel," *Europa-Archiv,* 25 March 1968, pp. 191-200, and M. von Berg, "Innerdeutscher Handel 1967," *SBZ Archiv,* January 1968, pp. 7-10.) The conditions offered by the Federal Republic are very favorable for the GDR, although the GDR, in 1967 as in 1966, imported considerably more from West Germany than it exported there, while the volume dropped below 10 per cent of the total trade of the GDR. Trade with the Soviet Union and other socialist countries is high. (Figures for 1966, based on information from the *Statistisches Jahrbuch 1967 der DDR,* are: with the Soviet Union 41.5 per cent of total GDR trade; with other socialist countries 31.6 per cent.) On 16 November a GDR-USSR trade agreement was signed for 1968 which proposes a total trade volume of 13 billion marks, an increase of some 10 per cent over 1967. The GDR negotiated bilateral trade agreements in 1967 with COMECON member countries and with Cuba, North Korea, North Vietnam, and the People's Republic of China, and also with many Western countries with which the GDR does not have diplomatic relations. Intensive efforts to increase trade relations with Latin America and the Arab countries were motivated more by the political goal of establishing diplomatic relations than by economic considerations. Diplomatic setbacks in the early 1960's led the government of the GDR to shift from trade relations to cultural relations with Latin American states as a means to pursue its goal of achieving recognition of the GDR as a state. To this end the German-Latin American Society was founded in 1961. Its President is SED member Professor Johann Lorenz Schmidt. Diplomatic relations with Cuba were established in 1963.

**Inner-German Relations.** In 1967 almost every issue of the SED daily organ *Neues Deutschland* printed attacks on the leadership of West Germany's Social Democratic Party. The SPD leaders were accused of "anticommunism," of taking a "right-wing" position, of participation in the "Kiesinger-Strauss Government," and so on. The SED propaganda tried to show not only that the Social-Democratic leaders had betrayed the German working class and their own party, but also that there had developed strong opposition within Social-Democratic circles and West German trade unions against this policy. The SED quite openly stated what it considered its primary goal: to free of their "anticommunist clichés" the "progressive non-Marxist forces of the Federal Republic, especially those in the DGB [West Germany's trade union federation] and in the West German Social Democracy, who do not go along with [SPD Deputy Chairman]Herbert Wehner's policy of collaboration with Kiesinger and Strauss." The SED admitted that the overcoming of anticommunism in the "ideology of non-Marxist forces in the West German workers' movement" would be a long and complicated process requiring a different method from the one used to "unmask the anticommunism of imperialists or Social Democratic ministers," which it termed the "fundamental principle of their theory and practice" (Wolfram Neubert, "Probleme der Ueberwindung antikommunistischer Tendenzen bei fortschrittlichen Kräften Westdeutschlands," *Einheit,* No. 8, 1967, pp. 1061-1070). The new approach to be applied to the West Germans would employ subtle propaganda conducted in the Federal Republic directly or indirectly from the GDR. According to West German information, about 2,000 persons are being trained at SED, FDJ, and FDGB schools as agents to be deployed in 1968 in West Germany, especially in the Ruhr area and around Hamburg.

Of the annual budget of about 25 million West German marks and 250 million East German marks which the SED has allotted for communist activities in the Federal Republic, the largest part is spent by the FDGB for "work in the West." This includes the visit of tens of thousands of West German delegates to meetings and discussions per year. A major meeting of this type, for instance, was the twenty-fifth German Workers' Conference, held in Leipzig 10-11 March. East German sources listed more than 800 participants from the West. Themes included the emergency legislation (for years a controversial issue in Bonn's Parliament), the rise of the National-Democratic Party of Germany (NPD) and right-wing extremism in West Germany, and the question of labor's share in management's decision-making (*Mitbestimmung*). Hopes of the FDGB leadership (Chairman Herbert Warnke is a members of the SED Politburo) for unity of action between the FDGB and DGB were expressed in an "open letter of the FDGB to members and leaders of the DGB and its [member] trade unions" (*Neues Deutschland,* 10 March) which expressed a unity of interests between East and West German workers regarding world peace, neo-Nazism, disarmament, European security, and *Mitbestimmung*. The twenty-sixth German Workers' Conference took place in Leipzig 8-9 September. The importance which the SED attributes to the Social Democratic Party in its attempt to win over the minds of the workers of West Germany was stated in the party's Central Committee monthly *Einheit,* which summed up a discussion of the SPD in the words: "Essentially the struggle within West German Social Democracy concerns the problem of on which side of the class front in the big struggle between capital and labor the Social Democratic Party will stand in the future" (Hans Pirsch and Kurt Voigtlander, "Parteien Westdeutschlands in der Krise," *Einheit,* No. 12, 1967, pp. 1530-1540).

The Social Democratic Party on 18 March slightly modified the guidelines for "East contacts" of its members (cf. *Die Welt,* 20 March), but still rejected any organizational or political relations with communist organizations, especially the SED. When Chancellor Kiesinger on 12 April made a declaration in the Bundestag on the Federal Republic's "Germany policy" (*Bulletin des Presse und Informationsamtes,* 14 April) which listed a number of practical steps that could lead to an inter-German detente, the SPD leadership wrote a letter (dated 12 April, text in *Die Welt,* 14 April) to the delegates to the Seventh Congress to explain the West German Government's declaration (which had also been sent to the SED Congress) and to remind the SED leaders that the Social Democrats would in principle be ready to continue the SED-SPD dialogue which in 1966 broke up before it got started. (The reaction of the SED congress to these proposals from Bonn has been discussed above.)

The German Democratic Republic's policy regarding a solution to the German problem found expression in 1967 in a series of proposals, letter exchanges, and polemics, which opened with Walter Ulbricht's New Year's address for 1967 (*Neues Deutschland,* 1 January) outlining a ten-point program that could lead to a confederation of the German states. Ulbricht's New Year's message for 1968 (*ibid.,* 1 January 1968) repeated the essential conditions required by the GDR for "a new beginning" in the relations between the two German states: establishment of normal relations with each other; formal renunciation of the use of force in their mutual relations; recognition of existing frontiers in Europe; renunciation of nuclear weapons; renunciation by West Germany of the claim to be the sole representative of all Germans (*Alleinvertretungsanspruch*). Generally, Ulbricht asked that Bonn accept the treaty on the establishment of normal relations between the GDR and the FRG proposed in a letter by GDR Premier Willi Stoph on 18 September (*ibid.,* 20 September). Previously, Willi

Stoph had replied on 10 May to Kiesinger's declaration of 12 April. Kiesinger's answer came on 13 June; on 27 June the SED sent an open letter (*ibid.*, 27 June) to members of the CDU/CSU, the parties of Kiesinger and Strauss. A GDR memorandum about the normalization of relations followed on 21 July. Chancellor Kiesinger replied to Willi Stoph's letter of 18 September by a letter of 28 September, regarding which the editor-in-chief of *Neues Deutschland* commented on 4 October that Bonn's claim of sole representation and the concept of an inter-German "dialogue" excluded each other. (Three SED Politburo Members discussed this subject in Albert Norden, Hermann Matern, and Friedrich Ebert, *Zwei deutsche Staaten: Die nationale Politik der DDR* [Vienna: Europa Verlag, 1967], which also contains documentation up to the beginning of 1967.) The SED determination not to compromise in its drive to gain diplomatic recognition found expression also in the decision of 2 February to change the name of the GDR State Secretariat for All-German Questions to "State Secretariat for West-German Questions" and in the 20 February law concerning citizenship in the GDR which changed the Constitution and substituted "GDR citizenship" for "German citizenship" and was officially interpreted by the East Germans as an expression of the sovereignty of the GDR. The People's Chamber of 1 December set up a commission, headed by Ulbricht, to work out a new "socialist" constitution for the GDR;* this was a further step to underscore the determination of the SED to pursue a course that would lead to German reunification only under socialist conditions. It should be noted in this context that the SED painstakingly made clear that it does not wish to imply that diplomatic recognition of the German Democratic Republic would render the two German states "foreign countries." Thus, the leading propagandist of the SED Politburo, Albert Norden, was corrected in two *Neues Deutschland* editorials (20 and 21 December) after he had expressed this view at an international press conference on 18 December. The SED organ attempted to blame West Germany for distorting Norden's statement, but left no doubt that Norden himself had not presented the position of the SED leadership.

**International Views and Policies.** The frequent and violent attacks by the SED against West Germany's policy toward eastern Europe, so vigorously pushed by the new government of the Great Coalition since December 1966, together with the unfavorable publicity given by the East German press to the West German controversy over the treaty on nonproliferation of nuclear weapons, were a major part of SED propaganda in 1967. While serving the interests of the GDR, such propaganda also fell in line with the Soviet Union's foreign policy goals in Europe. On every international issue, the SED has linked its anti-West Germany position with a pro-Soviet stand, assuming West German participation in the "global strategy" of "US imperialism."

Motivated by support for Soviet plans in the Middle East as well as hope of furthering its own cause of gaining diplomatic recognition among the Arabs, the SED took a relentless anti-Israel course during the Middle East conflict. SED propaganda likened the Middle East war to Hitler's Blitzkrieg and denounced Israel in every possible way. Solidarity with the Arabs and support for the "anti-imperialist alliance" (i.e., against Israel, the USA, and West Germany) were, for instance, expressed in a GDR Foreign Ministry declaration after the UAR had blocked the Gulf of Aqaba (*Neues Deutschland,* 24 May). Once it became obvious that the Arabs were militarily defeated, the GDR Council of Ministers on 7 June demanded an end to all military actions and the retreat of Israeli troops from the occupied territory. The GDR participated in the Middle East meetings of socialist countries in Moscow (9 June) and Budapest (11-12 July). This extreme partisanship for the Arab side was followed by a more moderate tone from the SED leadership. Like most other Moscow-oriented communist parties, the SED accepted the idea that the state of Israel has a right to exist. An intraparty discussion paper of the SED Politburo (excerpts in *SBZ-Archiv*, No. 18, September) dealt with problems arising from the Middle East conflict and came to the conclusion (like the CPSU leadership) that the nationalism of Arab "progressives" in the long run would be harmful. In general, however, the effects of the conflict were evaluated favorably for the cause of communism in the Middle East. The political and organization weakness of the "progressive forces" among the Arabs

*A draft constitution was presented by the commission on 31 January 1968. After weeks of nationwide discussion and certain changes in the text, a plebiscite in the GDR approved the text of the new constitution 6 April by a 94.54 per cent vote.

were seen as the main reason for the defeat. In the view of the SED, this clearly necessitates the creation of ideologically unified and well-organized political parties based on support from workers and farmers. It is interesting that the internal SED document specifically criticized Rumania, which had refused to sign the Moscow Declaration of 9 June, and praised Yugoslavia because it cooperated and, for the first time since 1957, signed a document together with other communist parties. China–the "clique around Mao"–was charged with having used the Middle East conflict as the basis for a "disgusting defamation campaign against the Soviet Union" and having advocated a continuation of the fighting "until the end," a course which would have caused the end of the present governments in Syria and the UAR. The SED discussion paper also criticized Cuba for "similar hyperradical slogans."

**International Communism.** In the ideological debate among the communist parties the SED firmly sided with the Communist Party of the Soviet Union. The SED not only criticized the Chinese party leaders (see, for instance, "Mao's Squads against Marxism-Leninism," *IB*, No. 91, reprinted from *Einheit*, No. 1, 1967) and denounced them at its congress (see above), but also gave full ideological support to those communist parties in the West who follow the "revisionist" strategy of Moscow. The Latin American communist parties who disagree with Fidel Castro received broad and favorable publicity in the SED press throughout the year. The high attendance of Latin American communist parties at the SED congress equally underscored this closeness of position–while Cuba, significantly, sent no delegation. In spite of trade and cultural relations and all the formal exchanges of greetings and messages, the SED press ignored such events as Castro's quarrel with the Venezuelan party (Castro's speech of 13 March 1967) or "Che" Guevara's "Message to the World" in April. Again, in August, the reports in *Neues Deutschland* on the OLAS Conference were remarkable for their brevity and sparse information. Although a representative of the GDR's Afro-Asian Solidarity Committee was there, *Neues Deutschland* of 4 August limited itself to reporting his declaration that West Germany's "policy of aggression" endangered the "peoples of Asia, Africa and Latin America." When Fidel Castro announced in October the death of "Che" Guevara, *Neues Deutschland* carried a short wire-service note. Two days later it reported on an official CPSU Central Committee telegram of condolence to the Cuban Communist Party. Several days later, Politburo candidate member H. Axen made a visit of condolence to the Cuban Embassy in East Berlin, expressing the feelings of the SED Central Committee and First Secretary Ulbricht to the Cuban party (*Neues Deutschland*, 21 October). More importantly, an indication of the SED position was given in the September issue of *Einheit* ("Die Volker mussen wachsam sein"), which said that the development of revolutionary potentialities in Latin America varied from country to country:

> From the ranks of the conscious workers originated the communist parties which unremittingly fight for social and national liberation. Besides, there exists in Latin America a strong sector of the petite bourgeoisie in which significant groups assume revolutionary positions. The Cuban revolution has also shown that there are in the petite bourgeoisie of suppressed countries revolutionary potentialities of great heroism for the struggle of national liberation and socialism.  .
>
> Between the revolutionary trends coming from the working class and those which originate in the petite bourgeoisie, many differences of views appear as well as points of mutual interest in the struggle. The revolutionary trend of the petite bourgeoisie mostly underestimates the proletariat and the communist parties. It is more susceptible to nationalism and adventurism and is inclined to fall into despair and subjectivism. Communication and collaboration and joint action between the revolutionary proletariat and the revolutionary circles of the petite bourgeoisie form the fundamental problem today in Latin America.

This article stated, in an incidental manner only, that in Latin America an "Organization for Solidarity", with corresponding committees in each country, was developing.

The foreign relations of the GDR on the government-to-government level remained in 1967 largely confined to the socialist countries, mainly in eastern Europe, with which economic and political association was very close through the Council for Mutual Economic Aid (COMECON) and the

Warsaw Defense Pact. Around the world, however, both in those countries which have diplomatic relations with the GDR and in those which have only trade missions, cultural exchanges, or no official relations at all, the SED and the GDR Government engaged in varied activities to promote international recognition of the GDR as a second German state. Communist parties abroad and the governments of the socialist countries fully supported those efforts.

The relations with eastern Europe were dominated by concern over the new West German policy of opening to the east. When Rumania decided on 31 January to resume full diplomatic relations with the Federal Republic of Germany, East German officials criticized this move. *Neues Deutschland,* which throughout January had increased the campaign against West Germany's *Ostpolitik,* in a front-page editorial on 3 February found it "deplorable" that Rumania had not rejected the West German claim to sole representation of all Germans as the Bucharest Declaration of 1966 had demanded. The Rumanian reply came 4 February in the party daily *Scinteia,* which rejected the SED charge and in turn said that the East Germans had failed to see the political gain in the Rumanian resumption of relations with West Germany, namely that West Germany had not insisted on the Hallstein Doctrine (i.e., the principle of not establishing diplomatic relations with any country recognizing East Germany—except the USSR—and breaking off relations with any so doing). A Warsaw Pact Foreign Ministers meeting, scheduled for 6 February in Berlin to deal with the situation, had to be shifted to Warsaw on 8-10 February because of the East German-Rumanian tensions.* A TASS communique stated that the Warsaw meeting was concerned with developments in Europe since the Bucharest meeting of 1966 and was taking place "in full mutual understanding." According to the report, by the GDR delegation, to the State Council session on 16 February (*Neues Deutschland,* 17 February), the interpretation of the Bucharest Declaration and the policy of the socialist countries toward West Germany were an important issue of debate at the Warsaw meeting.

After Poland and Czechoslovakia had signed a treaty of friendship, cooperation and mutual aid on 1 March, the GDR signed similar treaties with Poland (15 March) and Czechoslovakia (17 March). This "iron triangle" against West German detente proposals was, at the same time, a further contribution to the growing bilateral treaty system among the Warsaw Pact countries which could eventually replace the Pact, in the event of an agreement with the West to dissolve both NATO and the Warsaw Pact. Like the 1964 Treaty between the GDR and the Soviet Union, the new treaties with Poland and Czechoslovakia regarded West Berlin as a "separate political unit." Shortly after the signing of the two treaties, a high-ranking SED party and government delegation, headed by Walter Ulbricht, went to Moscow (21-22 March) for talks with Soviet leaders. The talks affirmed the desire on both sides to "fight for the solution of the European problems . . . according to the principles of the Bucharest Declaration and the guidelines elaborated at the Warsaw Pact Foreign Ministers Conference" of 8-10 February (*ibid.,* 25 March). Socialist policy vis-à-vis the German problem again became a major issue at the conference on "European security" at Karlovy Vary, 24-26 April, attended by twenty-four European communist parties. The GDR signed a treaty of friendship, cooperation, and mutual aid with Hungary on 18 May and with Bulgaria on 7 September.

The tenth Baltic Week, held in Rostock on 9-16 July, was an important international event in the SED's campaign among noncommunist forces in the Nordic countries. Begun in July 1958, these annual meetings have developed into platforms for propaganda against West Germany and NATO, and for the Soviet concept of "European security." As in previous years, a number of conferences and meetings of a political nature were held within the framework of the Baltic Week of 1967, such as a seminar for teachers, a seminar for lawyers, a women's forum, a discussion with Nordic Christians, and a parliamentarians' meeting with participants from Denmark, the GDR, Finland, Iceland, Norway, Poland, Sweden, and the Soviet Union. The most significant of these meetings was the tenth Workers' Conference of the Baltic Countries, Norway, and Iceland on 12-14 July, attended by more than 700 trade-union delegates, which discussed the questions of NATO and West Germany. The East German FDGB, with the approval of the World Federation of Trade Unions, was the main organizer.

---

*In a speech to SED functionaries on 13 February, Ulbricht discarded as unfounded speculations by "our enemies" concerning disagreement over time and place of the meeting (*Neues Deutschland,* 16 February 1967).

The SED press carefully presented the Baltic Week and the various meetings in such a manner as to emphasize its ostensibly noncommunist character. There was little information, for instance, in *Neues Deutschland* concerning the presence of communist party leaders from abroad, save those of ruling parties.* The SED leadership was represented on the opening day by Ulbricht, Honecker, Stoph, Mittag, Verner, and others. Hermann Matern met with visitors from West Germany and with members and functionaries of the SPD, socialist youth organizations, and West German trade-unions (*Neues Deutschland,* 16 and 17 July).

**International Party Contacts.** For years the SED press has been the main publicity outlet for the illegal communist party of Germany (KPD; see *Germany: Federal Republic*), as well as for the SED-W of West Berlin (q.v.). The KPD actually operates out of East Berlin.

The SED in 1967 sent party (as distinct from government) delegations only to communist countries and to "national democratic" and developing countries ruled by "progressive parties"; such delegations did not meet with any nonruling communist parties. One reason for this was that SED delegations had to face travel restrictions in Western countries. An SED delegation under Ulbricht to the French Communist Party's congress in January was not granted entry visas. The same happened to an SED Central Committee delegation scheduled to arrive 16 October in Vienna for talks with the Austrian Communist Party. Low-level Central Committee delegation meetings between the SED and ruling parties took place throughout the year. Besides the foreign delegations to the Seventh Congress (see above), high-ranking communist-party visitors from abroad included an Italian delegation in January, a Chilean delegation in September, Chairman Dange of the Indian party on 9-10 October, Secretary-General Vieira of the Colombian party on 19-26 October, Secretary-General Moore of the party of North Ireland on 20 October, a French party delegation on 16-27 October, the Chairman and the Secretary-General of the Communist Party of South Africa 15-20 November, First Secretary Nassar of the Jordanian party on 23 November, a delegation of the Socialist Unity Party of New Zealand under National Secretary Jackson, a Finnish party delegation under Secretary-General Ville Pessi on 12-18 December, and Chairman Hugo Victor and Secretary-General Rubén D. Souza of the People's Party of Panama.

SED international communist party activities included participation in the Preparatory Meeting on 22-26 February at Warsaw for the Karlovy Vary Conference, participation in the Preparatory Commission (Politburo Members Matern and Axen), and attendance at the Karlovy Vary Conference of a delegation headed by Ulbricht to discuss ideological problems. An SED delegation under Kurt Hager visited Moscow on 14-15 March. Ulbricht himself led a top SED delegation to Moscow on 21-23 March and headed the large and high-ranking SED delegation to the celebration of the Fiftieth Anniversary of the October Revolution; he headed also a party and government delegation when the SED leadership met with the leadership of the CPSU on 11-12 December (*Pravda,* 13 December, with text of communique).

At various times during the year the SED advocated a communist world conference (therefore *Neues Deutschland,* reporting on Luigi Longo's address to the French party congress, did not mention that Longo was opposed to an international conference at this juncture). The SED affirmed support of the idea at its Seventh Congress, at the Central Committee meetings of 6-7 July and 23-24 November; and in its theoretical organ *Einheit* (see issue for October-November, article "Der Zusammenschluss der marxistisch-leninistischen Parteien um die KPdSU") listed the tasks of a world conference. The SED also was among the eighteen parties signing the declaration of 25 November calling for the convening of the consultative meeting early in 1968 at Budapest. Judging from the mostly generalized information contained in the published communiques, the high-level party delegations visiting East Germany toward the end of the year all discussed the consultative meeting and questions relating to an international conference.

**Publications.** The official SED publications include the daily Central Committee organ, *Neues Deutschland*; the biweekly Central Committee organ for party questions, *Neuer Weg*; the monthly of

---

*Although the Danish party paper *Land og Folk,* for instance, reported (13 July) that Secretary-General Ib Nørlund and Party Secretary Ingmar Wagner represented the party at the Parliamentarians' meeting during Baltic Week, their presence was not reported in *Neues Deutschland.*

the Central Committee, *Einheit*; the German edition of the *World Marxist Review* (under the name *Probleme des Friedens und des Sozialismus*); an information bulletin on international communism, *Aus der Internationalen Arbeiterbewegung* (different from the *WMR*'s *IB*), which is published twice a month; and the biweekly *Beitraege zur Geschichte der deutschen Arbeiterbewegung,* which is edited by the SED Central Committee's Institute for Marxism-Leninism.

# GERMANY: FEDERAL REPUBLIC OF GERMANY

The Communist Party of Germany (Kommunistische Partei Deutschlands; KPD) was founded in 1918. Outlawed by the West German Constitutional Court in August 1956, the party was declared illegal, and ordered dissolved, and membership in it was prohibited.

During the eleven years that the party ban has been in effect, the KPD has engaged in clandestine activities in West Germany. Underground work is directed from East Berlin, which serves as a base of operations for KPD party officials. The headquarters location in East Berlin also facilitates maintenance of a very close link with the Socialist Unity Party of Germany (Sozialistische Einheitspartei Deutschlands; SED), the ruling party of East Germany. Cooperation of the two parties was an accomplished fact even before the prohibition of the KPD. Since then the SED has provided guidance and major financial support for communist activities in the Federal Republic of Germany (FRG). In 1967 it contributed an estimated 250 million East German marks and 25 million West German marks. It also provides advice and keeps in close touch with the leaders of the KPD. Heading the KPD is Secretary-General Max Reimann. Prominent members of the Politburo are Josef Ledwohn, Max Schäfer, Willi Mohn, Erich Glückauf, and Jupp Angenfort, and alternate member Josef Schleifstein.

Membership in the illegal KPD in 1967 was estimated at approximately 7,000. The population of West Germany is 57,400,000 (estimated 1967). Membership figures showed little change from the previous year, although determined efforts were made to recruit new members and especially to attract the young, who might provide new leadership for the future. This is considered important strategy in view of frequent complaints directed at the inactivity of many old party members, with the implication also that dogmatic attitudes among some current leaders would disqualify them from holding their positions in the future.

The party has its greatest strength in the most highly industrialized areas of the Federal Republic, and especially in the state (*Land*) of North Rhine-Westphalia. According to its Interior Minister, KPD membership in this state alone stood at between 3,000 and 4,000 (*Frankfurter Allgemeine Zeitung,* January 31, 1967), and considerable expansion of activities was noted. In this connection it is noteworthy that, reportedly, more than 2,000 SED members were undergoing training in East Germany in order to be ready to engage in communist propaganda in West Germany in 1968. The main targets for their propaganda were to be the Ruhr miners and the shipyard workers in West German coastal cities (*ibid.,* 29 November).

**Domestic Views and Activities.** The most important KPD party goals have remained relatively unchanged for a number of years. The basic objective remains the transformation of the FRG into a genuine socialist state. Other key points of the program have also been stressed for many years. The following are among them: the fight against "Emergency Legislation" (*Notstandgesetze*); recognition of two separate and equal German states within the existing frontiers; complete abandonment of the FRG's claim of sole representation of the German people; repudiation of the Hallstein Doctrine; reduction of arms expenditures and relaxation of the "policy of force"; institution of effective measures to combat neo-Nazism; conclusion of a nonproliferation treaty; and, above all, the establishment of good relations and peaceful coexistence with the German Democratic Republic (GDR). The KPD's plans for changes in West Germany also cover such economic measures as the nationalization of the iron, steel, coal, chemical, and electrical industries and of banks and the press. The tenth plenary session of the KPD Central Committee in June 1967 authorized preparation of a detailed party program draft; upon completion the program is to be submitted to the population for discussion (*Neues Deutschland,* Berlin, 21 June).

The campaign to regain legal status for the KPD—begun actively in 1966—gained great momentum. Repeal of the ban was urged throughout the year not only by party functionaries, but also by such diverse groups as May Day demonstrators in Munich, strikers in Stuttgart and Mannheim, and miners in Dortmund, and by the "Legalize the Communist Party" conference held in Düsseldorf in May. One of the fundamental arguments advanced at this conference was that the prohibition of the KPD was a "negative political decision which should be seen in close context with the Nazi resurrectionist trend." It was also agreed that repeal of the ban was "central to the defense of democracy" and "necessary in the interests of peace and European security" (*WMR*, December 1967).

The most significant and best publicized effort against the ban was the organization of the "Initiative Committee for the Readmission of the Communist Party" (Initiativausschuss für die Wiederzulassung der KPD) on 15 February. The new committee immediately started to seek public support in many cities and to coordinate its work with various existing groups working along similar lines. The founding members of the initiative committee were Karl Schabrod (Düsseldorf), former leader of the communist group in the Landtag of North Rhine-Westphalia; Franz Ahrens (Hamburg), former editor of the communist party organ *Freies Volk*; Kurt Erlebach (Hamburg), former communist member of the Hamburg Senate; Richard Scheringer (Kösching/Bavaria), member of the KPD Central Committee and former leader of the communist group in the Bavarian Legislature; and Manfred Kapluck (Essen), journalist and, before transferring his residence to West Germany, a member of the KPD Central Committee. By the end of the year a number of regional subcommittees had been formed including those active in Hannover, Mannheim, and Frankfurt. The Initiative Committee also reported having organized 96 public meetings, drawing more than 20,000 attendees. While the number of meetings was not disputed, figures provided by the government put attendance at about 12,000.

In a letter to the federal government, members of the Initiative Committee declared that lifting the KPD ban would be "in line with a policy aimed at an international detente and the promotion of peace" (*WMR*, December 1967). Reaction to the letter's demand for readmission came from the Interior Ministers of the West German states, who rejected the possibility of reestablishment of legal status for the KPD. They suggested as an alternative, however, the founding of an entirely "new" communist party which would not pursue "old" aims and would confine its activities to those permitted under the constitution (*Grundgesetz*) of the Federal Republic. The proposal by the ministers was emphatically rejected by Max Reimann, who insisted that his party "exists" and therefore "need not be refounded" and by Manfred Kapluck, who stated: "We do not want a communist party without teeth," adding that a party that has "no Marxist principles and no communist aims has no right to call itself a communist party" (*Elan*, April 1967).

The fight for legalization was, of course, the fundamental reason for the organization of the Initiative Committee. But the group appeared to become the spokesman for the KPD and identified itself clearly with the party's overall political goals. This was less clearly the case with the so-called Petition Movement (Petitionsbewegung) of a number of regional groups demanding mainly political amnesty and removal of the Communist Party ban.

The KPD never loses sight of its end objective, the imposition of socialism in West Germany; however, the methods tried in pursuing this aim have been somewhat modified in response to changing conditions. In 1967 the Institute of Marxism-Leninism of the SED published a new edition of *Imperialism Today* (*Imperialismus heute*), which included an assessment of the special problems of achieving socialism in the Federal Republic. Direct imposition of socialism was seen as not feasible: only "step-by-step revolution" could lead to the desired "dictatorship of the proletariat." In order to proceed toward that goal, the communists advocated the use of a gradual "process of democratization" and *Bündnispolitik* or the "union of all democratic progressive forces under the leadership of the working class."

"Progressive forces" to be enlisted in a "unity of action" program would include members of the Social Democratic Party (Sozial Demokratische Partei; SPD) who were dissatisfied with their party leadership or the policies of the Grand Coalition government, in which their party participates together with the Christian Democratic Union and Christian Social Union (Christlich Demokratische Union and Christlich Soziale Union; CDU/CSU). This is a less universal approach to the SPD than was attempted in 1966, when an official dialogue between the SED and the SPD was the chosen tool for contact, at least until the move foundered. Nevertheless some dialogue continued and Walter Ulbricht, First Secretary of the SED, stated in February 1967 that it would go on until there was effective united action "over the heads" of the Social Democratic leaders.

"Unity of action" also involves organized labor and specifically the members of the German Trade Union Federation (Deutscher Gewerkschaftsbund; DGB). The Communists support the DGB's opposition to emergency legislation and endorse its demands for *Mitbestimmung,* or labor participation in managerial decision-making. Such "unity of action from below" appeared to be successful in 1967. It was reported that 31,000 members of the DGB—4,000 more than the previous year—had accepted invitations to travel to East Germany for political discussions arranged by the Free German Trade Federation (Freier Deutscher Gewerkschaftsbund; FDGB), the East German counterpart of the DGB. Such travel and contacts were not endorsed by the West German union leadership, whose attitude was expressed in the following quotation: "As fighters for, and defenders of, democracy, the Deutsche Gewerkschaftsbund, and the trade unions united in it, are and will remain resolute adversaries of all communist, fascist, and military dictatorship" (*Neue Zürcher Zeitung,* 12 March).

A modification of tactics used in previous years was discernible in a reduction of KPD attention to some communist front organizations of long standing, such as the German Peace Union (Deutsche Friedens Union), League of Germans (Bund der Deutschen), and the West German Peace Movement of Women (Westdeutsche Frauen Friedensbewegung). Instead, heavier stress was placed on infiltration of independent organizations. To coordinate plans for this purpose, the Central Committee of the KPD formed a special "Friedenskommission" (Peace Commission). Under its guidance, pacifism and neutrality—previously the key motives for the existence of such organizations as the German Peace Society (Deutsche Friedensgesellschaft; DFG), the International of Conscientious Objectors (Internationale der Kriegsdienstgegner; IdK), and the Campaign for Disarmament—Easter March of Opponents of Atomic Weapons (Kampagne für Abrüstung—Ostermarsch der Atomwaffengegner; KfA)—were overshadowed by the more communist-line interests of "European security" and recognition of the Oder-Neisse line. When the German Peace Society celebrated its 75th anniversary during the year, Dr. Martin Niemöller, honorary president, was awarded the Lenin Peace Prize by the Soviet Union.

Increased infiltration of Christian religious organizations was also attempted. At the Christian Peace Conference (Christliche Friedenskonferenz), held in Cologne in November, the inclusion of communist-line proposals was strongly opposed by some moderate leaders and members. The arguments were heated, and in the election of officers several independent pacifist leaders refused to participate or were rejected. On the other hand, for the first time a communist, Walter Diehl, was elected an officer of the organization. A former protestant minister, Heinrich Werner, who has become prominent in the DFU, collected 1,200 signatures of theologians and others active in church affairs for an open letter addressed to members of the *Bundestag* and voicing objections to Emergency Legislation. The subject of "Communists and Christians" was discussed frequently in publications of the KPD and the SED. In material intended for Catholics, the papal encyclical *Populorum Progressio* was interpreted as signifying a turn to socialism.

Youth organizations continued to play an important role in communist plans. Members of the KPD, or young people selected by them, were instrumental in the formation of a number of new clubs. "Elan," "Liberté," "International," and "Humanité," were among clubs set up for the stated purpose of furthering not only social life, but also political discussion.

In June the Socialist Opposition (Sozialistische Opposition; SO) was organized in Frankfurt with the announced hope of uniting all opposition forces in a new socialist party to the "left of the SPD." The KPD was responsible for preventing the founding of a real new party, however, and instead the SO became a less rigid union of several socialist groups under noticeable communist influence. Communist influence was even more obvious in the Democratic Left (Demokratische

Linke), a political group founded in November in Stuttgart. Its program encompassed all the "minimum requirements" of the Communists; its head, Eugen Eberle, was formerly a functionary of the KPD in Baden-Württemberg.

Not a party, but a component of the "new left," is the Socialist German Student League (Sozialistischer Deutscher Studentenbund; SDS), whose radical policies and demonstrations were widely publicized and widely upsetting. They even disappointed the original hopes of the KPD that SDS activities could be steered into channels acceptable to the Communists. By the end of 1967, fears had arisen that the militant radicalism displayed by the SDS, which was antagonizing and frightening the population, might actually jeopardize the KPD's chances of regaining legal status in West Germany. The "anti-authoritarianism" promulgated by the SDS was generally looked upon as a virtual espousal of anarchy. The "series of revolutions" envisioned by the SDS leader Rudi Dutschke were alarming not only to capitalist countries; the inclusion of the "stifling bureaucracies of communism" as targets was also upsetting to the East Germans. (For more on the SDS see *West Berlin*.)

In addition to both overt and clandestine communist activity within the West German borders, direct and "imported" help to the KPD was provided by the SED. Politically motivated visits by party workers from East Germany numbered 1,350 during the year, a slight reduction from 1,430 in 1966. Of this new total, 22 per cent were dispatched to address meetings of communists or communist-leaning groups, and 24 per cent played a role at 118 meetings of democratic organizations. The remainder of the functionaries from East Germany arrived on clandestine missions, to establish wide-ranging contacts. Besides the obviously political assignments, exchanges of ideas were also sought with persons in agriculture, education, communications, and cultural fields of all kinds. Greater regional diversification was noted in these contacts, which in previous years had been centered in North Rhine-Westphalia, Hesse, and Lower Saxony, while in 1967 Bavaria and Baden-Württemberg also received major attention.

**International Policies and Activities.** A capsule view of the KPD approach to international affairs was provided by the Central Committee of the party at its tenth plenary session, in June. The Committee "condemned Israeli aggression against Arab nations and the support it received from US and West German imperialists," "expressed disgust at the escalation of war and all crimes of US imperialism against the Vietnamese people," and "assured the democratic forces of Greece of its fullest solidarity in the struggle against military dictatorship of the monarcho-fascist conspirators" (*Neues Deutschland*, June 21).

The KPD showed unswerving loyalty in its support of East Germany in international or inter-German relations. It quickly welcomed East German Premier Willi Stoph's proposal and draft treaty to conclude an orderly agreement between the Federal Republic and the GDR for the establishment of normal relations: "The realization of these proposals and the conclusion of an appropriate treaty would provide new possibilities for saving democratic rights and freedoms in the Federal Republic and for improving the social position of working people who are endangered, above all, by the reckless arming of the Federal Republic. The GDR premier's proposals are in accord with many demands raised by trade-unionists, SPD organizations, members of the intelligentsia, and youth and women's organizations" (*ADN Domestic Service*, 19 September).

The KPD considers itself a member of the international communist movement. It participated in the conference at Karlovy Vary in April and was a signatory of the "Declaration for Peace and Security in Europe" issued by the conference members. It also signified its intention to be represented at the consultative meeting of communist and workers' parties to be held in Budapest in 1968 to make preparations for a new international conference. In meeting with communist parties of foreign countries the KPD always aligns itself with the CPSU. At a meeting with the CPSU in Moscow in May the KPD directly confirmed its unconditional approval and support of the Soviet party. In keeping with this stance, it publicly criticized developments in the People's Republic of China.

**Publications and Radio.** A number of communist publications are openly printed and distributed in West Germany. Most of them have mainly regional appeal and circulation, but virtually all states are covered. It is estimated that approximately 1.8 million copies of overtly published communist papers and newssheets were issued in 1967. Four of these publications were weeklies, with a circulation of 27,300; those issued twice monthly accounted for 19,500 copies. The list of titles includes *Blinkfüer, meinung, Neues Echo, tatsachen, Tribüne für Frieden, Freiheit und Demokratie, offen und frei, Unsere Zeit,* and *Frankfurter Bote* (since November issued as *Arbeitertribüne-Zeitung für kritische Leser in Rheinland-Pfalz*).

Clandestine publications are printed in East Germany and also in Austria, Sweden, and France, where local communists are enlisted to assist in the preparation and distribution. The most important is the KPD's official party organ, *Freies Volk,* published in 1967 in twelve issues with an average circulation of 15,000. *Wissen und Tat* is the party's journal of political theory for party members; it was issued seven times during the year in an edition of 6,000 copies. Max Reimann's *Informationsdienst* appeared once a month. In addition the press service *KPD-Information* functioned throughout the year. Various "open letters," brochures, and leaflets were also circulated. Most of them were mailed from abroad, but sometimes rockets and parachute drops were used to deposit the material near industrial plants.

Over the air, the *Deutsche Freiheitssender 904* broadcast regularly throughout the year. In October it announced the number of a post office box in Vienna that could be used in addressing mail to the radio station. Thereafter the station daily broadcast the content of letters received and frequently requested the contribution of usable material, especially that dealing with industry and the military service.

* * *

Early in 1967 a few Communists in West Germany founded the Free Socialist Party (Freie Sozialistische Partei). It has since issued a mimeographed newssheet, *Die Wahrheit,* to approximately 30 members. The newssheet contains materials in opposition to the KPD, SED, and CPSU and favorable to the Chinese Communists. Another pro-Chinese publication is *Roter Morgen,* published since July by Ernst Aust, formerly an official of the KPD in Hamburg and editor of the communist weekly *Blink füer.* The KPD considers his defection a disturbing development.

# GERMANY: WEST BERLIN

The Socialist Unity Party of Germany-West Berlin (Sozialistische Einheitspartei Deutschlands-Westberlin; SED-W) was founded 24 November 1962. The SED-W functions as a legal party, since the West German prohibition of the Communist Party of Germany (Kommunistische Partei Deutschlands; KPD) does not apply in West Berlin. The SED-W was established as a party separate from the SED of the German Democratic Republic (GDR) primarily to underscore the communist position that West Berlin constitutes a separate political unit. In the spring of 1967 the SED-W claimed a membership of about 6,400. In spite of its increased vote total in the Senate elections and the admission of 776 new members in 1967, membership during the year increased only "very little, owing to deaths," and in May 1968 was put at 6,500 (Chairman Danelius in an interview with the Austrian Communist Party daily *Volksstimme* 25 May). The population of West Berlin is about 2.2 million. In the elections for the Senate (city government) of West Berlin on 12 March 1967 the SED-W received 29,934 (2.0 per cent) of 1,482,608 votes cast, an increase of almost 50 per cent over the elections of 17 March 1963, when it received 20,929 votes (1.4 per cent).

**Organization and Leadership.** At its First Congress, 21-22 May 1966, the SED-W elected Chairman Gerhard Danelius and a 41-member Parteivorstand (Leadership), which functionally corresponds to a central committee. The ten members of the Secretariat of the Parteivorstand are Dietmar Ahrens, Else Dibbern, Karl-Heinz Kniestedt, Bruno Kuster, Hans Mahle (editor in chief of the party organ *Die Wahrheit*), Emil Redmann (SED-W spokesman on economic problems), Horst Schmitt, Gerhard Stolle, Wilhelm Tesch, and Erich Ziegler.

The party's youth organization, the Free German Youth of West Berlin (FDJ-Westberlin) was founded in April 1947 as part of the Free German Youth organization of the SED. It became a member of the World Federation of Democratic Youth in 1966. Its Chairman is Walter Rudert. Another SED-W front organization, the Society for German-Soviet Friendship-West Berlin (Gesellschaft für Deutsch-Sowjetische Freundschaft-Westberlin), is headed by Rolf Elias (who attended the celebration of the Fiftieth Anniversary of the October Revolution in Moscow in November 1967).

**Domestic Policy and Activities.** In January 1967 the SED-W presented its program for the Senate elections (*Die Wahrheit* 19 January; also in *Neues Deutschland,* 20 January). The main thrust of the program was to offer an alternative to the policy of the Federal Republic of Germany and the City Senate of West Berlin on social issues such as *Mitbestimmung* (workers' participation in management decision-making) and rent regulations, and on international issues such as NATO alignment, recognition of the German Democratic Republic, and the status of West Berlin. The SED-W asked that West Berlin no longer be a "front city" of the cold war, but follow an "independent policy line," establish "normal relations with both German states," and trade with the GDR.

Propaganda among workers, trade-union organizations and students was the activity of the SED-W most important to the East German SED. SED-W support for the East German position on West Berlin and the German problem took the form of the publication of and favorable comment on major East German documents, proposals, and speeches (for instance, Ulbricht's address to the SED Congress in April) relating to the quest for recognition of the GDR. Also, *Die Wahrheit* published listings of radio and television programs broadcast in East Berlin, although it is not allowed to circulate there (instead, SED-W activities and views are reported in *Neues Deutschland*).

Throughout the year, *Die Wahrheit* gave wide and favorable publicity to those noncommunist groups who opposed West German plans for "emergency laws" (see *Germany: Federal Republic*) or demonstrated against US involvement in Vietnam. On various occasions in 1967 pamphlets against the emergency laws were distributed at the gates of West Berlin factories by SED-W activists. Several political factors favored the SED-W's intensified efforts toward a united front of workers, trade unionists, students, and "left forces and democrats": an already widespread opposition to Bonn's emergency legislation plans among trade unionists, intellectuals, and a growing number of students; criticism of the war in Vietnam, of Bonn's attitude toward East Germany, of West German reluctance to support plans for the nuclear nonproliferation treaty; and a general mood of dissatisfaction among many West Germans and West Berliners concerning the political scene after the formation of the great coalition of the Christian Democrats with the Social Democrats (see *Germany: Federal Republic*) late in 1966. Criticism of the influence of newspaper and magazine publisher A. Springer and concern over election successes of the National Democratic Party of Germany (NPD), allegedly fostered and supported by leaders in Bonn, became major issues of joint action on the part of the SED-W, students, and other "anti-establishment" groups.

The participation of the Social Democrats in the coalition in Bonn, and the heavy opposition to this move even within the SPD ranks, especially in West Berlin, made it relatively easy for the SED-W to denounce the "right" SPD leaders as helpers of the "Kiesinger/Strauss government" and to appeal to dissident SPD members for united action against the wishes of the SPD leaders. Like the East German SED, the SED-W charges that the SPD "collaborates" with CDU/CSU leaders, especially on the question of the emergency legislation and on policy toward Eastern Europe under Foreign Minister Willy Brandt. On the latter subject, such criticism by the SED-W was meant as direct support for the GDR; this was made quite clear on 10 September when Chairman Danelius and Secretariat members Tesch and Kuster discussed the unity of left forces and defined as the fundamental political goal the "uniting of all those forces which support normal and reasonable relations with the GDR." The SED-W was, for the first time, officially represented in a noncommunist demonstration against the war in Vietnam on 21 October, when seven SED-W Secretariat members participated. Afterward Danelius stated that the demonstration brought together, "side by side," "young workers and students, friends of peace of both [Catholic and Protestant] denominations, workers' councilors and trade unionists, members and friends of the Socialist Unity Party, Social Democrats, and members of the Free German Youth of West Berlin" (*Die Wahrheit*, 24-25 October). Writing in *Neues Deutschland* (2 December), Danelius said that there was an emerging "alliance between the working class and the intelligentsia based on the identity of interest between workers and students," and added: "The collaboration of all left forces and all democrats develops irrespective of existing ideological differences."*

A new impetus was given to SED-W support for the students of West Berlin, notably at the Free University, by the events of 2 June, when the student Benno Ohnesorg was fatally shot by a police detective during student demonstrations against the Shah of Iran. The SED-W had already taken the side of the students in their quarrels with the faculty and the administration. The 2 June events, however, added a new touch of urgency to the SED-W call for unity of action between students and workers against the government. (*Die Wahrheit* was so preoccupied with the students' affairs, "police brutality," and SED-W expressions of sympathy and solidarity with the students that the events in the Middle East were treated as a matter of secondary importance.) Danelius made a declaration on 7 June "against police terror and emergency [orders]" and characterized steps taken by the City Senate during the student turmoil as typical for the proposed "closer connection" of West Berlin with Bonn, where, he said, "dictatorial powers of authority for Kiesinger and Strauss" were being prepared "with the help of the great coalition" (*Die Wahrheit*, 8 June). At an extraordinary session of the SED-W leadership on 9 June a declaration was issued which attempted to relate the death of Benno Ohnesorg to more general political issues such as Vietnam, NATO, and the emergency legislation, charging that government "violence" against the students was another manifestation of the "reactionary outlook" of West German authorities.

*When asked by *Der Spiegel* (27 May 1968) when the SED had initiated collaboration with groups of the "Extraparliamentary Opposition" (Ausserparlamentarische Opposition), Danelius replied: "The contact has existed already over several years. It intensified and developed further during the democratic actions against US aggression on 21 October 1967 and 18 February 1968, and especially during the preparations for May Day 1968."

After the 2 June events the SED-W made a notable effort to activate discussions and meetings between the students and the party and to propagate the idea of a "unity of interest" between students and workers. Part of this new campaign was a two-page article by Danelius on "The Student and Our Party" in the 29 June issue of *Die Wahrheit*, copies of which were distributed to the students. The SED-W also supported student plans to establish a "critical university." Further, on 14 November Danelius participated in a meeting at the Free University discussing the tasks of the Extraparliamentary Opposition. Speakers at the 18 November convention of the Socialist German Student League (Sozialistischer Deutscher Studentenbund; SDS) of West Berlin criticized members' prejudices against the SED-W and demanded that the SDS reconsider its official position on this whole question. SDS Chairman Rudi Dutschke said that even double membership—so far forbidden by SDS statutes—could become possible. Late in November, the trial of the detective Kurras who shot Benno Ohnesorg on 2 June and that of the leftist student Fritz Teufel offered to the SED-W occasions on which to stress its solidarity with the students.

The resignation of City mayor Heinrich Albertz on 26 September came as a consequence of the students' agitation. The SED-W commented extensively on these problems of the Berlin Senate, and subsequently intensified its attacks against the new mayor, Klaus Schütz, for following an "unrealistic course" vis-à-vis East Germany.

The SED-W remained aware, however, of existing ideological differences between itself and those radical student leaders who worshipped "Che" Guevara and followed the ideas of the philosopher Herbert Marcuse. In East Germany, Harald Wessel on 31 August addressed members of the Free German Youth (FDJ) on the subject of the "false prophet" Marcuse (an elaborated version was later published in the FDJ organ *Forum*, nos. 2-5, 1968). On 29 September the SED-W dealt with Marcuse's theory that the working class no longer was the "subject of revolution" in a supplement to *Die Wahrheit* (Günter Donath, "Zur Diskussion über Herbert Marcuse 'Der eindimensionale Mensch'"). This article dealt with Marcuse in a very cautious way, but clearly rejected his ideas. On 5-6 December *Die Wahrheit* carried a condensed version of an interview with Josef Schleifstein, alternate member of the Politburo of West Germany's illegal communist party, published in *Marxistische Blätter* (November-December; reprinted in *IB*, no. 115) which dealt with Marcuse.

**International Views and Activities.** The SED-W has in its reporting on international events indicated its position on the key issue of unity of the left, endorsing such unity as the proper political line to be followed. *Die Wahrheit* carried frequent reports on statements by Finnish Social-Democrats and Communists declaring themselves in favor of socialist-communist collaboration; even more publicity was given to the developments in France and the successes of the French Communist Party. While agreeing with the SED stance on the German problem, the SED-W is generally in even more emphatic agreement with the SED on other international issues and problems concerning international communism.

*Die Wahrheit* (27-28 May 1967) defended the Arabs' closing of the Gulf of Aqaba and spoke of an "imperialist plot against Arab states." The SED-W viewed Israel as the "aggressor" (*ibid.*, 30-31 May) and supported Nasser's request that the UN troops be withdrawn from Gaza (*ibid.*, 2 June). The party organ of 6-7 June had a front-page article on the military conflict which openly followed the Soviet line in condemning Israel as the aggressor. By this time the SED-W was so preoccupied by the events and consequences of the 2 June students' turmoil in West Berlin that *Die Wahrheit* gave only secondary prominence to reports on the war in the Middle East. On 9 June at an extraordinary party leadership session Danelius stated that the existence of the state of Israel was a reality, but that the SED-W stood "by the side of the Arab peoples and states," especially since behind the Israeli aggression, in the view of Danelius, the "US Imperialists," with help from the "governing circles of West Germany," were working to secure their "oil interests and imperialist position" in the Arab world (*Die Wahrheit*, 13-14 June).

Within the international communist movement, the SED-W, like the SED, sided with the CPSU. The SED-W position vis-à-vis the Chinese Communist Party was reflected in reporting in *Die Wahrheit*; an article in *Pravda* (16 August) "On the Situation in China" was reprinted for "its particular significance." Such a pro-Moscow orientation was evident on every possible occasion: support for the

Soviet stand on the German question, attendance at the Karlovy Vary Conference, rejection of the ideas of the Chinese Communists, attendance at the Fiftieth Anniversary celebration, and support for a preparatory conference in February-March 1968 and for a new communist world conference. On 3 August *Die Wahrheit* published a resolution of the SED-W leadership entitled "Long Live the Great October" (reprinted in *IB,* no. 104). The official SED-W delegation to Moscow for the anniversary celebrations consisted of Chairman Danelius and Secretariat member Ziegler. *Pravda* invited Hans Mahle, Secretariat member and editor in chief of *Die Wahrheit,* to the celebration; Walter Rudert, Chairman of the Free German Youth of West Berlin, and Rolf Elias, Chairman of the Society for German-Soviet Friendship-West Berlin, also attended. A message of the SED-W to the Central Committee of the CPSU (*Die Wahrheit,* 7-8 November) stated that the party has always held the view "that the attitude of a revolutionary is defined by his relation to the Soviet Union."

The Havana conference of the Latin American Solidarity Organization (OLAS) received brief mention in *Die Wahrheit* (3 August) and then a commentary of some length (15-16 August) which criticized the "left-extremist" and "anarchist" view of guerrilla warfare as the only valid form of struggle, remarking that "such declarations [as the OLAS resolutions] by no means further the unity of the revolutionary forces." Although *Die Wahrheit* (13 October) on its front page criticized West Berlin's senator for cultural affairs for allegedly trying to prevent students from sending a telegram to the Afro-Asian-Latin American Peoples' Solidarity Organization on the death of "Che" Guevara, the SED-W paper reported only in a very tiny note on page two (17-18 October) that Fidel Castro considered "Che" Guevara's death a "great loss for all of Latin America." The newspaper repeatedly publicized, on the other hand, the views of Moscow-oriented communist parties in Latin America.

SED-W Chairman Danelius, accompanied by Parteivorstand member Herwig Kurzendörfer, attended the Eighteenth Congress of the French Communist Party (4-8 January). The SED-W was represented at the preparatory meeting in Warsaw 22-26 February. At the Seventh SED Congress, the SED-W was represented by a delegation headed by Danelius. Secretariat member Bruno Küster participated in the session, opening 21 April, of the redactory commission for the Karlovy Vary conference, and together with Danelius and Secretariat member Tesch attended the conference on 24-26 April. Like his address to the SED Congress, Danelius' speech at Karlovy Vary was concerned almost exclusively with the problem of West Berlin. *Die Wahrheit* on 25-26 July reported on a *Pravda* editorial on the unity of the communist movement and on 24 November presented in detail the views of a *Pravda* article (23 November) on the tenth anniversary of the 1957 communist party meeting which advocated a new consultative conference. On 28-29 November the SED-W organ reported on the declaration by 18 parties calling for a consultative meeting, and subsequently it repeatedly carried information about the agreement to attend this conference by various parties. At the ninth session of the Parteivorstand, on 15 December, the SED-W decided to attend the Budapest 1968 consultative conference.

**Publications.** The organ of the SED-W is *Die Wahrheit,* published four times a week. The editor in chief is SED-W Secretariat member Hans Mahle.

# GREAT BRITAIN

The Communist Party of Great Britain (CPGB) was founded in 1920-21 when after two separate conventions the various groups of the extreme left, partisans of the Bolshevik Revolution in Russia and the Communist International, decided to unite.

The CPGB is a recognized political party in Great Britain. Late in 1967 it claimed a membership of 32,562 out of a population of nearly 55,000,000 (estimated 1967). This total was far below the target of 50,000 members set in 1963 and constituted an absolute decline of 1,000 since membership figures were announced in 1965.

Communist party candidates compete in both national and local elections. In the Parliamentary general election of 1966 the party polled 62,112 votes, or 0.2 per cent of all votes cast. Although 57 candidates were nominated, none was elected and all deposits were forfeited. This was hardly an improvement over the election in 1964, when 36 unsuccessful candidates polled 46,532 votes. However, having put up fifty or more candidates, the CPGB was for the first time allowed a party political broadcast.

There have never been more than two communist members at one time in the British House of Commons, and none at all since 1950. In Parliamentary by-elections in 1967, communist candidates polled 6.8 per cent in Pollok, 1.8 per cent in Rhondda, and 1.0 per cent in Gorton; it should be noted that in these elections massive losses of Labour votes to Conservative and Nationalist candidates were recorded.

In the April 1967 elections to the Greater London Council 38 candidates represented the CPGB—at least one nominee in each of the 32 boroughs. They received 66,403 votes in a total poll of 2,185,849, or approximately 3 per cent. In 1964 their total vote was 92,323. None of the party's candidates was successful in either 1964 or 1967, but the communists had hoped for a better showing in 1967, in view of their well-publicized demand for the construction of 100,000 new houses a year instead of the 17,000 actually built in 1966 by the Greater London and borough councils combined.

Candidates in local municipal elections were more successful. There were 552 communist candidates on the ballot for county councils and wards, and 28 were elected, with two additional seats being won later in by-elections. The Executive Committee of the CPGB reported in July that the party held 37 seats in county borough and district councils, and several on parish councils. At the National Congress, in November, it was announced that there were 17 communist councilors in Wales, including seven newly elected in 1967.

With membership figures generally disappointing and falling, the CPGB hopes to broaden the scope and influence of its youth affiliate, the Young Communist League (YCL). Membership in the YCL is not compulsory for young Communists, however,and many dedicated militants refuse to join. A major recruitment drive was started in May 1966 to raise YCL membership from 5,100 to 10,000; late in 1967 claims were limited to "over 6,000." In spite of lagging progress, the party declared that the "militant radical position of important sections of the youth" and the "disillusionment and dissatisfaction" of others provided excellent possibilities for attracting substantial numbers of young people to the party (*Comment*, 9 December).

Simply attracting new members does not appear to solve the entire problem, since the average stay in the YCL is approximately two years. Many who drop out appear to gravitate to extreme left groups such as the Trotskyists, Maoists, or Castroists. Reasons for the rapid turnover or hesitation to join are believed to range from militants' opposition to an increasingly "reformist" party look, continued distrust of ties with the CPSU, and objectionable recollections of the Stalin era and the Hungarian uprising to the strictness of party discipline that demands complete conformity of each member and allows no dissent on any issue.

**Organization and Leadership.** The organization of the CPGB is based on democratic centralism, and elected leaders control the entire party with complete disciplinary powers. In theory the National Congress is the supreme authority and is responsible for policy adoptions. It meets biennially when called by the Executive Committee, but a special congress can be convened under extraordinary circumstances if requested by a third of the branches or a third of the districts. Such special circumstances prevailed in 1957 after the Hungarian uprising.

The National Congress elects the 42-member Executive Committee, which represents the highest authority between congresses; it discusses and formally approves all Congress resolutions, but seldom makes substantial amendments. At its first meeting after a congress has been convened, the Executive Committee elects the party officers and the Political Committee.

The Political Committee holds the real party power; its decisions are never overruled by the Executive Committee. It meets weekly or more frequently, whereas the Executive Committee meets every two months. Thus party control tends to be vested and self-perpetuating in the Political Committee. Its members are mostly full-time paid officials of the party and its newspaper, the *Morning Star*. They control the party's subcommittees and departments. Separate departments have been set up for Press and Publicity, Organization, Industrial, International, Women, Education, Finance, and Election. Below the leadership level, the CPGB is organized into district committees, further subdivided into area and borough committees, and finally into approximately 1,600 branches, of which 600 are based in industrial and professional institutions where Communists are employed.

Party leaders elected after the Twenty-ninth National Congress, in 1965, continued to serve in office throughout 1967. The Chairman was Frank Stanley; the Secretary, John Gollan; and the Assistant Secretary, William Alexander. Helping them with party affairs were such well-known communists as Gordon McLennan, George Matthews, James Reid, William Wainwright, Sidney Foster, Nora Jefferys, Bert Ramelson, and Jack Woddis,—all of them full-time paid functionaries and members of the Political Committee.

Most of these names reappeared on the list of appointments announced by the Executive Committee at its first post-Congress meeting (13-14 January 1968). Noteworthy among the changes was the replacement of Frank Stanley as Party Chairman by Dr. Tony Chater and that of Assistant Secretary William Alexander by Reuben Falber. Following is the complete new list of appointments: Secretary, John Gollan; Chairman Dr. Tony Chater; Assistant Secretary Reuben Falber. Political Committee members: Reuben Falber, Sid Foster, John Gollan, Nora Jefferys, Gordon McLennan, Cyril Morton, George Matthews, Bert Pearce, Bert Ramelson, James Reid, Frank Stanley, William Wainwright, and Jack Woddis. Heads of departments: Press and Publicity, Nora Jefferys; Organisation, Gordon McLennan; Industrial, Bert Ramelson; International, Jack Woddis; Women, Margaret Hunter; Education, Jack Cohen; National Treasurer, Dennis Elwand; Electoral, Vic Eddisford, (*Comment*, 27 January 1968.)

Fifteen of the members of the Executive Committee are trade union leaders. The CPGB derives its greatest strength from and exercises considerable influence in such large unions as the Amalgamated Engineering Union, the National Union of Mineworkers, and the Transport and General Workers Union.

**Party ideology.** By 1967 the CPGB had become as revisionist as a communist party can be without ceasing to be communist at all in the Marxist-Leninist sense. The fundamental objective of the CPGB continues to be the achievement of socialism, but the approach is unorthodox. The party program, *British Road to Socialism* in 1967 revisions declares that political power can be achieved by parliamentary, peaceful means without armed conflict: "Using our democratic rights to transform traditional institutions, Parliament can be transformed into the effective instrument of the people's will." Further foreseen is the possibility of a "plurality of parties" in line with a new-found CPGB belief that "democratically organized political parties will have the right to maintain their organization, publications and propaganda, even if hostile to Socialism." Taken together with a treatise on "Questions of Ideology and Culture" issued by the Executive Committee in March (see *Documents*), the program revisions seem designed to reduce the ideological differences between the

Communists and other forces of the left in Great Britain to a minimum. The basic assumption is that communist and labor parties can work together—a notion that has consistently been rejected by the Labour Party for many years. In fact, the CPGB remains on the Labour Party's proscribed list, ineligible for affiliation.

To further rapprochement with previously disenchanted groups, the March statement was apologetic about the Lysenko case, citing it as an example of the effect of restrictions on scientific investigations and welcoming "the most critical, inquiring and searching spirit among scientists." Art, literature, and culture, according to the document, should reject the concept of a single school or style determined by the party: "Creative artistic activity, experiment and innovation would be encouraged without administrative interference. There would be full support for scientific inquiry in the natural and social sciences. Free confrontation of ideas would be encouraged." There was an added pledge of communist support for complete freedom of religious worship, and dialogue between Marxists and Christians was encouraged. In the latter connection it may be noted that the first dialogue between Marxists and Christians in fact did take place in October 1967, when the Rev. Paul Oestreicher, associate secretary of the International Department of the British Council of Churches, joined in discussion with James Klugman, editor of *Marxism Today*.

The gradualist, nonrevolutionary approach did have its effect. The noncommunist daily *Sun* (28 April) in a review of "Questions of Ideology and Culture" talked about "an astonishing revolution . . . moving across the Communist world" and interpreted the document as indicating that "the Communist Party is really no better, or for that matter no worse, than any other political party in the pack of cards . . . their goal and their methods are pretty much the same as any other political party: peace and plenty." While the flexible tactics brought approval from some ranks, many younger members of the party resent the lack of revolutionary fervor and are veering to the more militant pro-Chinese and Trotskyist groups.

In relation to the international communist movement, the British party pursues a relatively independent course. "Each Communist Party has the responsibility of working out its own policy, its own forms and methods of struggle, based on the conditions, history, traditions, institutions, and circumstances of its own particular country," is part of the resolution adopted by the Thirtieth National Congress of the CPGB in November 1967. The CPGB is distrustful of congresses meeting to hammer out common ideologies and denies the current existence of a "single directing center"; moveover, it believes that such a center can never be reestablished and that communist affairs "can no longer be handled on the basis of international congresses." In spite of this attitude, the CPGB was an early supporter of plans for an international consultative meeting to be held in Budapest early in 1968; in this instance the theme of "anti-imperialism" aroused enthusiasm among British Communists.

The CPGB for years tried to maintain neutrality in the Sino-Soviet split. In 1967 emphasis was placed on the "restoration and strengthening of unity" as British Communists' attitudes turned mixed. The party deplored "the acute differences with the Communist Party of China and the serious divisions in the ranks of the international movement that have made it easier for imperialism to intervene in the affairs of other countries, to step up its aggression and to increase the danger of nuclear war." There was criticism of Communist China, but also hope for future changes was expressed: "The sectarian errors and non-Communist conceptions which are at present afflicting the Communist Party of China can only be a temporary phenomenon" (*Morning Star*, 6 January). On the other hand, delegates to the National Congress were specifically asked to reaffirm "condemnation of the attempts by Mao Tse-tung and his supporters to impose their views on other parties." Their "disruptive activities . . . completely opposed to Communist principles" were severely criticized. At home the suspension and subsequent expulsion from the party of four prominent members, including Reginald Birch, a member of the Amalgamated Engineering Union Executive Council, reflected the communist world split. Birch's pro-Chinese leaning had long been known. Together with the other men that were suspended by the party, he was accused of expressing "revisionist" views in his capacity as a member of the Editorial Board of *The Marxist*. Late in 1967 Birch was trying to organize a new pro-Chinese party.*

Not all problems confronting the international movement were blamed on China: "Some other countries too have shown a tendency to slip into positions of narrow nationalism or to urge leftist and adventurist actions" (speech by William Wainwright, introducing resolution to National Congress, *Comment*, 9 December). Indonesia was named in this context, but other countries appeared to be included.

**Domestic Activities.** During a debate on a "left unity" resolution at the CPGB's National Congress some delegates criticized the party for neglecting industrial activity in favor of efforts to elect communist MPs and other officials. General Secretary John Gollan countered such complaints with the comment that concentration on industrial activity would cast the party in the role of a militant industrial fringe group and prove highly detrimental.

While there was some controversy at the congress, objective observers generally thought that communist activity in industries and in labor unions was very pronounced in 1967. In no way did the party appear to have slackened its efforts or changed from being the "efficient and disciplined apparatus" that Prime Minister Wilson had referred to during the previous year. In October another government spokesman, Minister of Labour Ray Gunther, anticipated "a winter of disruption" by reason of an "unholy alliance" between Communists and Trotskyists for the purpose of weakening the national economy. These forecasts were called exaggerated by some of the British press, although it was generally recognized that frustrations caused by the income policy, unemployment, and misunderstood productivity agreements were providing Communists with opportunities to exploit. Seeking to take advantage of industrial dissatisfaction was the "Liaison Committee for the Defense of Trade Unions" which was considered an "umbrella organization for a network of communist fronts" (*Evening News*, London, 1 March). The London Building Workers' Joint Sites Committee, the London Docks Liaison Committee, and the London Exhibition Workers' Coordinating Committee were part of the network. Their leaders—"dissident, militant trade unionists operating clandestinely in defiance of official union policy"—were generally linked with a number of crippling strikes, such as those on the docks in London and Liverpool, at the Barbican site in London, and at Vauxall Motors (*Daily Mail*, London, 19 October).

Party members themselves appeared satisfied with their achievements in union activities. The *Morning Star* of 18 October had a big headline "Proud Part in Present Revolt," and applauded "all those . . . in revolt against the attack on wages and trade union rights." Bert Ramelson late in 1967 discussed the "struggles" of seamen, dockers, passenger transport workers, motor workers, and many others and expressed his satisfaction that there was "not a struggle in which Party members were not at the center."

The balance of power in the trade union movement shifted significantly to the left in 1967 with the election of Hugh Scanlon as president of the Amalgamated Engineering Union (AEU), the country's second largest union. The election of Scanlon, a former Communist now calling himself a "Left Socialist," was the culmination of a long drive to expand communist influence in the AEU and was hailed by some as a victory that would help to tip the balance of forces throughout industry in favor of a fight against the government and would inflict a terrible defeat on Wilson and his wage-freeze policy.

Communist criticism of the Wilson government was common and virtually covered the gamut of government activities and decisions. It was particularly vocal at the time the British Government decided to reapply for admission to the Common Market. John Gollan used harsh words in his denunciation: "The vital interests of the British people are being surrendered on every major point." He also charged that joining the Common Market would "worsen living standards, lead to additional unemployment, and deprive Britain of the right to decide its own economic policy"; moreover joining the market would be "a move away from genuine European unity and peace," and this "the British people must utterly refuse to associate with it" (*Morning Star*, 3 May.)

*The Communist Party of Britain, Marxist-Leninist, held its inaugural Congress in North London in April 1968. Chairman of the new group was Reg Birch.

Virtually all major domestic problems were discussed in the months preceding the CPGB National Congress. The party called for total opposition to the Government's price and income policy. Restoration of the trade unions' unconditional rights to engage in collective bargaining and the right to strike was demanded. Most of the new and restrictive government regulations were said to have resulted from the "pursuit of imperialist interests" and to have been evolved at the expense of the working class. The "disastrous" consequences of the new policy would have to be counteracted by means of a determined struggle for repeal of the Price and Incomes Act, the introduction of a minimum wage of 15 pounds sterling a week, and the restoration of full employment. (*Comment,* 19 August, supplement.) A resolution on poverty demanded higher pensions and family allowances, and lower rentals and mortgage interest rates. Devaluation of the British pound was the basis for an emergency resolution and a CPGB call for drastic cuts in overseas military spending and capital investments, for import controls, and for the modernization of British industry on the basis of extended nationalization (*ibid.,* 9 December).

A number of resolutions submitted by branches were adopted. They condemned manifestations of racialism and discrimination against colored citizens of Britain, and included the following general recommendations to deal with these problems: the practice of discrimination in employment, housing, insurance, credit, or any other aspect of economic or social life should become a legal offense; the recruitment of colored people into the ranks of trade unions, cooperatives, and tenants' organizations should be stepped up and later their election to shop steward and positions of higher leadership should be encouraged; and the Commonwealth Immigration Act should be repealed immediately. Economically oriented resolutions affirmed opposition to rent increases and the sale of council houses, called for support for higher living standards for students, and urged the establishment of a comprehensive state education system ranging from nursery school to higher education levels.

**International Views and Policies.** Developments in international affairs during 1967 generally produced CPGB reactions strictly in line with the Soviet point of view.

An emergency resolution demanded the dissociation of the British Government from the war in Vietnam, immediate and unconditional cessation of bombing and withdrawal of US and allied forces from Vietnam, and urged the establishment of peace in South Vietnam in accordance with the program of the National Liberation Front. The National Congress promised to respond to the best of its ability in case the Vietnamese people asked for volunteers (*Comment,* 9 December). A joint statement issued by the British and Soviet communist parties following a meeting in Moscow in September assessed the situation: "The flames of war threaten to spread and engulf other lands," and "American imperialism is waging a brutal, unjust, bloody war against the people of Vietnam, but cannot bring the Vietnamese people to its knees" (*Morning Star,* 18 September).

The Arab-Israeli conflict was not only a matter of major concern to the CPGB, but also a cause of dissension as pro-Israeli sentiment clashed with support of the Arabs by CPGB spokesmen: "The war in the Middle East and its consequences have done nothing to bring about a solution between the Arab States and Israel. . . . On the contrary, every problem has been aggravated and seeds sown for future conflict." (*Morning Star,* 16 June.) Part of the blame was placed on the US and British governments, for having "consistently supported" Israel in order to defend their "imperialist and oil interests in the Middle East." While recognizing the state of Israel's right to exist, the British Communists demanded the withdrawal of Israeli troops from the occupied areas as a prerequisite for a just and lasting settlement. They declared, furthermore, that "Israel must recognize the right of the Palestinian Arab refugees to decide whether to return to Israel or chose compensation for the loss of their property." (*ibid.*)

The CPGB had manifold plans for the solution of Europe's problems. It wanted Britain to withdraw from NATO and work for the dissolution of that organization and the Warsaw Pact. In their place there should be established "a system of collective security with the purpose of preventing war in Europe," and this should arise "from a conference of all European governments." The realization of security would require recognition of the existing frontiers and of the German Democratic Republic, and "resistance to all plans to give Western Germany direct or indirect access to nuclear weapons." The Polaris and Britain's other nuclear arms should be scrapped, all American bases in Britain closed, and an international nuclear test ban enforced. The destruction of all nuclear, bacteriological, and chemical weapons was to be accomplished together with "general and complete disarmament." A treaty of friendship with the Soviet Union should be signed. Abolishment of the Special Powers Act in Northern Ireland and the ending of enforced partition of Ireland were additional demands on the list of European "musts."

Additional suggestions asked for independence of all territories still under British rule, the abandonment of the "East of Suez policy," closing of all overseas bases, withdrawal from SEATO and CENTO, and an end to the Smith regime in Rhodesia. British Communists also appealed for support of the "struggles for democracy" of the people of Spain, Portugal, Indonesia, Ghana, and others under "tyrannical regimes," including the national liberation movements "fighting US imperialism" in Latin America. The CPGB condemned the military junta in Greece and the apartheid regime in South Africa, while strongly endorsing developments in Cuba and a fight for the admission of Communist China to the United Nations. (*Comment,* 9 December.)

**Contacts with Foreign Communist Parties.** In 1967 the CPGB attracted a number of visitors from abroad and dispatched its own representatives to participate in some important meetings or discussions. The list of fraternal delegates to the party's National Congress in November was fairly extensive. Not only were most communist-ruled countries of eastern Europe represented, but attendees also came from the USA, Canada, France, Italy, Israel, and Spain; several special guests were from Africa. Messages and greetings were received from many countries around the world. (For complete list see *Comment,* 16 December.)

In January, Jack Woddis attended the Eighteenth Congress of the French Communist Party and subsequently reported in *Comment* on the Left Alliance in France. In April, British delegates went to East Berlin to the Seventh Congress of the Socialist Unity Party (SED), the ruling party in East Germany. Also in April, John Gollan and Jack Woddis were part of the CPGB delegation attending the Karlovy Vary conference. In September John Gollan and George Matthews traveled to Moscow for high-level discussions with the CPSU. In November a group of delegates was again dispatched to Moscow, to attend the celebrations in honor of the fiftieth anniversary of the October Revolution.

In Great Britain the anniversary became an occasion for stepping-up the promotion of pro-Soviet sympathy. A pamphlet entitled "Revolution 1917-67" drew comparisons between "the tumultuous advances in Russia under Soviet power and the stagnation in Britain under capitalism" and praised "the establishment in Russia of a democracy—the rule of the people and not the domination of a minority capitalist class." The CPGB also expressed hopes for Britain to learn from the "clarity of purpose which changed the world in 1917": "The conditions are different, the path will be different, but the aim is the same—to end the rule of a minority and build a society in which the exploitation of man by man is abolished for ever." (*Morning Star,* 7 November.)

**Publications.** The CPGB has made a strong effort to upgrade the quality of its publications and to increase readership. This is particularly true of the official daily party newspaper, which was completely revamped in 1966, when the *Daily Worker* was replaced by the *Morning Star.* The editor of the enlarged *Morning Star* is George Matthews, a member of the CPGB's Political Committee. Since the paper was modernized, the downward trend in circulation of the communist daily has been halted. Actual sales in 1967 were only around 60,000 per issue, however, and fell short of the target of 80,000 copies; late in the year plans were under way to increase the price of the paper in order to prevent a financial crisis.

*Marxism Today* is the CPGB's monthly theoretical and discussion journal. The *Labour Monthly* provides commentary on political events by communist leaders, Labour left-wingers, militant trade unionists, and intellectuals. *Comment* is a communist weekly review edited by Alex McDonald. It carries not only the principal statements of the British party, but also covers news of socialist and progressive movements throughout the world. Advertisements state that you need to read *Comment* "to find your way in the modern world." The Young Communist League has its own monthly publication, *Challenge.* In November 1967 it was given a new look and format and as a result circulation was said to have risen by several thousand to a high of 16,000. In addition, numerous circulars and pamphlets appealing to young people were printed; one of these special publications *Trend*, was issued in a million copies. Special interest groups were served by specialized communist publications, such as those dealing with agriculture, education, or music.

* * *

At the Thirtieth National Congress of the CPGB, Gordon McLennan, National Organizer, declared that Communists had "worked increasingly in association with other left forces." This statement was basically correct in claiming frequent cooperation, but it does in no way reveal the very serious challenge to the CPGB from more extremist groups. Revolutionaries in large numbers have become contemptuous of the allegedly mild tactics and policies of the communist party and have thrown their support to more militant groups. Leading among them are the Trotskyist organizations—the Socialist Labour League and the Young Socialists.

**The Socialist Labour League.** The Socialist Labour League (SLL) by 1967 was clearly the most powerful of all Trotskyist organizations in Great Britain. Claiming to be the only true Marxist group, it quite openly competed with the CPGB for leadership of extreme left forces in industry. In some instances—notably in northern ports and some sectors of the automobile industry—it had actually managed to make its influence predominant.

A great deal about the plans of the SLL can be gathered from a directive issued to supporters in March 1967 by Gerry Healy, the National Secretary and leader of the organization. Instructing SLL members to intensify agitation in the automobile-manufacturing, passenger and goods transport, docks, electrical, and coal-mining industries, the directive stated: "More and more these organizations can be used as a medium for rallying workers in local struggles which in turn prepares them for big national interventions."

The directive also revealed the background for the decision to form an "open" Trotskyist movement in 1959 after twelve years of effort to infiltrate the Labour Party. The decision for an open organization followed the realization that "total entry" was a "political impossibility." But it did not mean a "sectarian attitude towards events in the Labour Party"; "it means that we are, for the time being, turned almost exclusively toward developments in the trade unions, towards which we have directed the activities of the Young Socialists since 1964."

SLL trade-union activity gained momentum in 1967. When the communist Liaison Committee for Defence of Trade Unions called for demonstrations to be held on 21 February against the Labour Government's incomes and price policies, the SLL decided to climb on the bandwagon and to participate fully in what was shaping up as a "national week of protest and campaigns." Before long it was trying to round up support for "real action" instead of the "sham fight" which it claimed the Communists were leading. By the time scheduled demonstrations outside Parliament got under way, the SLL had clearly gained the initiative and could claim credit without ever having risked blame for failure.

The SLL used preparations for the 21 February demonstration also as a pretext for establishment of the "Oxford Liaison Committee for the Defence of Trade Unions." Under the leadership of Reg Parsons, this was clearly a Trotskyist rival organization to the CPGB-controlled National Liaison Committee for the Defence of Trade Unions. Oxford was chosen as the new Trotskyist center because members of the SLL were already holding key shop stewards' positions in the Midlands motor industry. Following its formation on 1 February, the Oxford Committee during the course of the year organized several national conferences without trying to hide their political implications. In fact, the SLL weekly *Newsletter* of 28 October reported that a conference held on 21 October was called for the purpose of extending the Liverpool and London dock strikes into a national stoppage and if possible to involve other sectors of industry. With Trotskyists playing important parts in liaison committees in Glasgow, Birmingham, and Sheffield, geographical dispersion could also aid their activities.

On 3 June the *Newsletter* published "A Programme of Action for Socialism," spelling out objectives of the SLL on the occasion of its Ninth National Congress. These ranged from the nationalization of basic industries, banks, and insurance companies, to demands to "make the Left MP's fight," to work for a Labour Government with socialist policies, and for a United Socialist States of Europe. Suggestions for building additional local liaison committees for defending trade unions also were featured prominently.

The program and congress discussions (*Newsletter*, 3 June) contained major criticism of the CPGB: "The British CP can never act in the revolutionary interests of the British working class. Since its degeneration under Stalin in the 1930's, it must always act in the interests of the foreign policy requirements of the Soviet bureaucracy. . . . The British CP is only useful in so far as it can assist the Soviet bureaucracy to negotiate some form of diplomatic break with the British capitalist government from the overlordship of US imperialism. . . . The possibility of deepening the crisis in the CP, which is forced constantly to discuss the question of Trotskyism as the alternative to its own liquidationist politics, is an historic advance in the struggle for the Fourth International which is the centre of all our work. . . . None of the other leaderships, be they right-wing, the so-called 'lefts' or the Communist Party can do anything other than betray the working class." Perhaps the crowning criticism is found in the following quote: "Over the past few years the Communist Party has made changes that make the Party itself quite indistinguishable from the Labour Party, and in all matters of fundamental policy really indistinguishable from the right wing" (*ibid.*).

Ways and means of developing Marxist cadres for "work in the unions and amongst the youth" were important topics at the SLL congress. Supporters were urged to take advantage of the "development of the political strike" and were instructed to carry out all their activities "from the factories into the arena of the Labour Party" with the "perspective of preparing for power." Delegates were reminded that they were part of a continuous international class struggle and that Trotskyists would "redouble" their efforts to recruit more and more militants and to train leaders capable of acting in the Marxist way. (*Ibid.*)

**The Young Socialists.** Disclosure in the March directive of the SLL that the Young Socialists—who claim to be self-governing—were in fact controlled and directed by the SLL, was a departure from the existing pattern. Actually, the youth organization is believed to be the most important element of Trotskyist operations in Great Britain. In November 1967 the Secretary of the Young Socialists, Sheila Torrance, claimed some 20,000 paying members. Exact figures are not available, but it is generally understood that in membership the Young Socialists dwarf their communist counterpart, the Young Communist League, and that they have grown into the largest British Marxist youth movement ever.

The head of the Young Socialists is Dave Ashby, who in 1964 was dismissed as National Chairman of the Labour Party's youth organization when his Trotskyist penetration efforts became obvious. In 1965 Ashby admitted working for the Labour Party to advance the cause he publicly espoused later: "If we did not openly announce ourselves as Trotskyists when the Young Socialists was part of the Labour Party, that was because we saw Trotskyism not as a debate but as a struggle to build a movement."

Recruiting drives for the Young Socialists have gained in effectiveness during the past two or three years. Social and athletic events are stressed and possible future members are always encouraged to attend. "It's a Sporting Life with the Young Socialists" proclaimed a banner headline in *Keep LEFT* (July/August), the official publication of the Young Socialists. In a discussion of a new branch in Rotherham, the "football organizer" stated that the formation of a team had "helped the branch a lot" and a member confirmed the importance of football teams to the Young Socialists. In spite of the emphasis on athletics, the objectives of the Young Socialists are completely political; in their own words, they aim to "establish the strongest base inside the trade unions" and to provide basic Marxist education and to train young people for positions of leadership.

The importance of union activities for the Young Socialists was very evident at the group's Seventh Annual Conference, held at Morecambe on 18-19 March. Among the speakers were several shop stewards active in engineering and allied industries; the motor sector in particular was heavily represented. The *Newsletter* of 25 March described the trade union activities of the delegates and declared that they were "rapidly being transformed into a hard core of revolutionary socialist leaders inside the Labour Movement."

An "International Youth Assembly" organized by the Trotskyists attracted about 800 young people to the South Coast of England from 29 July to 5 August. Attendees were reported to have come from France, the USA, Greece, Italy, Belgium, Germany, Madagascar, Algeria, Ceylon, and Nigeria. At the conclusion of the Assembly a committee was elected to prepare for an International Youth Conference to be held in 1968.

**Publications.** The major voice of the Socialist Labour League is its weekly journal, *The Newsletter;* its editor, Michael Banda, late in 1967 announced that beginning in February 1968 the paper would appear twice weekly and that he hoped to turn it into a daily newspaper by the summer of 1969. The official publication of the Young Socialists is the monthly *Keep LEFT. Fourth International* is the theoretical journal of the International Committee of the Fourth International. It appears at irregular intervals several times a year, with subscriptions accepted for a certain number of issues rather than a definite time period. On 4 February the first issue of *International Correspondence,* a fortnightly also issued by the International Committee of the Fourth International, made its appearance. The magazine, which has an edition in French, devotes much of its space to an "analysis of the role of the revisionist groups attached to the so-called 'Unified Secretariat' in Paris." Advertisements further state that the magazine "relates this struggle to the training of cadres inside the sections of the Fourth International."

**Additional Extremist Organizations.** There are many other extreme left-wing groups active in Great Britain, but none of them have been able to muster numerically impressive support. Among the more important are the following:

The Revolutionary Workers' Party (RWP) is a Trotskyist group that has been in existence since 1963. It is directed by an international committee set up in Latin America. The aim of the RWP, under the leadership of J. Posadas, is to establish revolutionary groups in industry, but efforts have been concentrated on Midlands automobile workers. In 1966 supporters of the RWP were behind the introduction of a new publication, the *United Car Worker.* The editor of the journal, Brian Lyman, has also been instrumental in trying to establish an international group of automobile industry workers. The RWP has its own journal, *Red Flag,* which got its start in 1964 as a bi-monthly, but has since changed to a monthly and most recently to a fortnightly. John Davis, the editor, has explained the changing of the frequency of editions: "The International leadership have *insisted* on the necessity of *Red Flag* appearing fortnightly so that it can more effectively fulfill its role [in] stimulating and helping to build revolutionary currents and tendencies." (Emphasis in original.)

The International Socialism Group, also known as the "Cliff Group," is a Marxist organization that has its roots in the old Trotskyist movement. Its alternate name is derived from that of its chief theoretician, Tony Cliff (pseudonym for Ygael Gluckstein), who is also a member of the editorial board of *International Socialism.* The avowed aim of the International Socialism Group is "workers' control and international socialism." Its monthly publication, the *Labour Worker,* in 1968 changed its name to *Socialist Worker* and began weekly publication.

The Marxist-Leninist Organization of Britain is a small pro-Chinese group. It originally backed Mao Tse-tung, but has switched to support of his opponents. The group published *Red Front,* a journal "For Working Class Power, For Socialist Britain."

The Committee to Defeat Revisionism for Communist Unity is a breakaway movement from the CPGB. Remaining loyal to Stalin's policies, it claims to be the only genuine communist organization in the country. The journal of the group, *Vanguard,* has as its slogan "Workers of All Lands and Oppressed People, Unite."

# GREECE

The Communist Party of Greece was founded 18-22 November 1918 in Piraeus as the Socialist Workers' Party of Greece (Socialistikon Ergatikon Komma Hellados; SEKE). In 1920 the party voted for affiliation with the Comintern, and in 1924 changed its name to the Communist Party of Greece (Kommounistikon Komma Hellados; KKE). Outlawed during the communist insurgency in December 1947, the party has since maintained its leadership and cadres in the communist states of eastern Europe. The party headquarters is reported to be in Sofia, Bulgaria.

The KKE does not publicize its strength, and the events of 1967 in Greece make estimation of party membership difficult, but 27,000 party members within the country and 10,000 to 15,000 members in exile is probably a reasonable figure. The population of Greece was estimated to be 8,612,000 as of July 1966. The communists had been particularly active among tobacco workers in the province of Xanthi and among factory workers and stevedores in the principal ports. The KKE has a large following among the approximately 100,000 persons who left Greece at the end of the civil war and made their homes in various countries of Europe. This expatriate group has grown larger since the coup of 21 April 1967 and the subsequent establishment of a military regime in Greece.

**Organization and Leadership.** The leading personalities of the KKE include Chairman Apostolos Grozos and Secretary-General Kostas Koliyannis; Koliyannis, Panos Dimitriou, and Dimitrios (Mitsos) Partsalidis until February 1968 formed the three-man Secretariat (see below). The Politburo included Grigorios Faragos (Rigas), Panos Ifantis, Nikolas Kaludis, Panayotis Mavromatis, Leonidas Stringos and Zisis Zografos.

Because the KKE is illegal in Greece, it has had no direct representation in Parliament, but until the April coup the party maintained an active political life through the United Democratic Left (Eniea Dimokratiki Aristera; EDA), a legal political party founded in 1951. The EDA, declared illegal by the junta government on 29 April 1967, held 22 of the 300 seats in Parliament, polling 11.8 percent of the votes in the elections of 16 February 1964.

The Communists insist that the KKE and the EDA are not identical, since the EDA also represents other "democratic forces." The EDA program approximates only the minimum program of the KKE, and party differences exist in statutory provisions and on some tactical questions. EDA membership, by no means entirely communist, is made up largely of communist sympathizers and fellow travellers, including many prominent Greek intellectuals.

In spite of communist inspiration and leadership in the EDA, the two parties have had differences, growing more serious since 1964 and perhaps earlier. Even the military coup of April 1967 and the subsequent proscription of the EDA failed to bring Greek left-wing forces into harmony. The KKE has criticized the EDA for bourgeois parliamentarianism and "softness," while the EDA has always resented the fact that the KKE maintained a clandestine organization within Greece separate from the EDA party organization. Also the EDA, probably quite correctly, has charged that the KKE leaders, in exile for so long, are out of touch with the real situation in Greece.

Yanis Passalidis is the President of the EDA; Ilias Iliou was its parliamentary group leader. The Greek war hero Manolis Glezos was Secretary of the EDA and concurrently director of the party newspaper *Avgi.* The noted Greek composer Mikis Theodorakis, an EDA deputy in Parliament, also headed the EDA's Lambrakis Democratic Youth, which was dissolved together with the EDA and all other party youth groups in April. (The Lambrakis Democratic Youth is a member of the communist-front World Federation of Democratic Youth and holds a seat on its executive committee.)

The outstanding political fact of 1967 for all Greek parties was the military coup of 21 April, in which a small group of army officers overthrew the constitutional government and established a stratocratic regime. Putting into operation a Greek Army contingency plan, developed as a part of a comprehensive NATO plan for use in case of war with a communist country, the conspirators rounded up and imprisoned thousands of persons active in Greek politics, most of whom were KKE or EDA members. The motivation for the coup was army dissatisfaction with the unsettled nature of the Greek political scene and fear that Greece would veer sharply to the left after the elections scheduled for 28 May. The coup, carried out rapidly and efficiently, caught the government and all political parties, as well as US and other foreign representatives in Greece, completely off guard. Its effect on the KKE and the EDA was severe. The KKE, whose headquarters and top leadership had been outside Greece for 20 years, suffered heavy losses in its clandestine organization and among low ranking cadres within the country. The EDA suffered an even more serious blow, since its top leaders, including Iliou, Theodorakis, Glezos, and Leonidas Kirkos, were seized and imprisoned. By August the EDA, too, was operating from exile. Meeting at Frankfurt-am-Main, the "Committee of the EDA of Western Europe" appealed to Greeks in exile for support against military rule, calling for "an end to the dictatorship, dissolution of the junta, reestablishment of democratic liberties, freedom of action for all political parties, liberation of political prisoners, and free elections guaranteed by a government of all parties." The EDA appealed to Greeks in Europe to support the Patriotic Front which was "struggling in Greece for the overthrow of the military regime," and placed the blame for the tyranny in Greece on "the militarists of the junta, American imperialists, the monarchy and the fascists of the right" (*Humanité,* 19 April 1967).

**Domestic Views and Policies.** The basis for the KKE program up to the time of the coup was given in 1956 when the party proclaimed its strategic objective to be the realization of far-reaching national democratic reforms as the first stage in the transition to socialism. The transition was to be realized through a broad united front and was to be peaceful in nature. The party had defined the political situation in Greece as a basic contradiction between the "foreign imperialists and national oligarchy" on the one hand and all other social groups and individuals on the other. The post-coup program for the party retained the broad popular-front feature, but no longer subscribed to the peaceful pursuit of its objectives, claiming that the Eighth Party Congress (August 1961) had stressed that "attention must also be paid to nonpeaceful forms of struggle," adding: "This applies even more in the present conditions of open fascist elitist dictatorship and it is the way proposed by our party in the present situation" (Radio "Voice of Truth," 8 September 1967, quoting Secretary-General Koliyannis in an interview with *Novosti*). Chairman Grozos, delivering his report on the party's situation to the Eleventh Plenum of the Central Committee, in June, criticized the party for not following up its own decision to explore "the other nonpeaceful road." He admitted that "the Central Committee and the Politburo did not do what was necessary for the ideological and political preparation of the party itself and the people in the direction of the nonpeaceful road, and they did not undertake the necessary organizational measures for the formation of the [revolutionary] forces and the work in the army—where literally no attention was paid—in order that the difficulties . . . could be faced more effectively." (Radio "Voice of Truth," 15 July.)

In the months before the coup the KKE, in anticipation of national elections which were to have been the first since those of February 1964, worked for a program of free elections under the supervision of a caretaker government acceptable to all parties, and for a new election law providing for a simple proportional representation system to be presented by the caretaker government and passed by Parliament before the election.* The party also sought the abolition of the law proscribing

---

*The Greek political scene was disrupted completely in July 1965 when King Constantine refused to allow the majority Center Union (EK) party Prime Minister, George Papandreou, to remove an intractable defense minister from office and to assume the portfolio himself. The King forced Papandreou's resignation. The KKE saw the King's act as a "palace coup" and referred to all succeeding governments as "junta governments." The following cabinet was headed by EK dissidents opposed to Papandreou, but it derived its principal support from the right-wing National Radical Union (ERE). The ERE, tiring of the role of maintaining an EK government, withdrew support and the cabinet fell at the end of 1966. The King replaced it with a caretaker cabinet under Ioannis Paraskevopoulos which was to prepare a parliamentary election, but this cabinet fell on 30 March before the election date could be

the Communist party in Greece, and in February petitioned the government to this effect. (The demand for reinstatement was spurned by the government and was supported by no political party except the EDA.) It also sought to ban right-wing paramilitary organizations, to prevent army interference in elections, to make changes in Greek security organizations, to lift restrictions on freedom of movement in frontier areas, and to ensure equal opportunity for all parties campaigning in the election.

KKE propaganda stressed the anomalous character of the Greek government after 1965, and urged a return to "normalcy," which implied the return of government to the hands of Parliament without interference from the Throne, and the free operation of parties from all segments of the political spectrum including, of course, the KKE.

Since the KKE viewed the King's interference in the government in 1965 as a palace coup, the party bitterly opposed every one of the "junta" or "palace" governments which followed. The usual procedure before elections in Greece was for the King to appoint a caretaker coalition cabinet generally acceptable to all the legal political parties. King Constantine's appointment of the minority right-wing National Radical Union (ERE) party under Kanellopoulos to perform this role gave rise to new KKE denunciations of both the King and the new government:

> May the supporters of the democratic parties, all the democrats, set aside other differences, align themselves in a united rank of normalcy, and ask from the leaders of their parties, without exception, for the united action and cooperation of all the forces of democracy and normalcy in the struggle to remove the ERE government before it even goes before Parliament [that is dissolve it before the elections]. Immediate mobilization and struggle of all the people and all their organizations! This is the imperative demand imposed by the interest of the people and the country. Down with the new palace government of violence, forgery, and blood! Caretaker government! Simple proportional representation system! Amnesty! Free elections! Respect for the will of the people!
> This is the call of national interest. The communists participate in this wholeheartedly.
> (*Ibid.*, 4 April 1967.)

When the ERE government dissolved the Parliament and announced a general election for 28 May, paying no heed to the demands of the KKE (and its legal echo the EDA), the KKE again castigated the government: "The ERE government, branded and isolated by the crushing majority of the people, and with the favor of the palace and the American imperialists as its only support, is making every possible effort to hold elections under conditions of violence, corruption, and fascist impudence, in order to obtain a prearranged result: to propel itself back into power." The KKE also voiced criticism of Papandreou's Center Union (EK) party: "By nurturing self-deceptions as to the plans and aims of the reactionary circles the EK rejected the repeated proposals of the KKE and EDA for joint action against this new deviation. It has facilitated, with its whole policy of retreats, compromises, and splitting of the democratic forces, the promotion of the ERE to power and the present dangerous anomaly." (*Ibid.*, 15 April). The party then appealed again for the unity of democratic forces—its last before the coup.

The coup of 21 April caught the KKE completely by surprise. The party's first statement, a proclamation of the Politburo, revealed its confusion: "Greek men and women! The King and the American imperialists—the circles of oligarchy most servile to the foreigners—through their organs, the militarist junta and neofascist ERE, declared today after midnight an open royal-fascist, stratocratic dictatorship. . . . The monarchy, servile to the foreigners, committed a crime . . . placing itself outside the constitution. The neofascist ERE contributed . . . to the treason." (*Ibid.*, 21 April.)

set. The King replaced the Paraskevopoulos government with a second caretaker cabinet representing only the minority ERE under Panayotis Kanellopoulos. It was this cabinet, in office for only three weeks, that became the victim of the military coup of 21 April.

The focal point of KKE interest after the "palace coup" of July 1965 and the resignation of Papandreou was a united front which included the EK. For an outline of the stormy relationship between the KKE and EDA on the one hand and the EK on the other in 1965 and 1966 see *YICA*, 1966, pp. 118-119.

The coup happened to precede by only a few days the meeting of the European communist parties at Karlovy Vary (24-26 April), and the KKE, which attended, was able to use this meeting as a sounding board for its views. On 25 April the KKE issued a new proclamation which outlined its opinion on the causes of the coup and the line to be followed by the party in its struggle to recover the ground it had lost. Taking advantage of the almost universal disapproval among European nations of the junta's "destruction of parliamentary democracy in Greece," the KKE attempted to enlist sympathy and support in Europe, stressing the arrest and imprisonment of noncommunist democratic leaders of the EDA and the EK to emphasize the "fascist and dictatorial" excesses of the military regime. The analogy to Hilter and Mussolini was freely drawn (see, for instance, the speech of Apostolos Grozos at Karlovy Vary in *IB,* no. 97-98, June). American "imperialism" and the NATO Alliance were seen as the backers of the coup and the whole episode as a continuation of the "reactionary" trend set in motion by the King in 1965:

> The upheaval, inaugurated by the 15 July 1965 palace coup, was completed on 21 April 1967 with the naked, bloody, fascist tyranny, which is the work of the dark circles of anomaly, of American imperialism, of the palace, the junta, the extremists of the right, of the local and foreign oligarchy of wealth.
>
> The fascist coup was organized and carried out methodically and diabolically by these dark circles because, in spite of the enormous means used, of the intensification of terror, and of their maneuvers, they were certain that the democratic forces would achieve an impressive victory at the election. . . . [The coup] aims at stifling, through naked fascist violence, the democratic spirit of the people, at intensifying the plundering of the country and exploiting the working people, at further strengthening the positions of American imperialism and of the aggressive NATO in the eastern Mediterranean, the Balkans, and Europe in general. . . . One of the fundamental aims of the coup is to impose a NATO solution on the Cyprus issue and to integrate Cyprus into the system of rocket bases of the Mediterranean, to draw Greece into the dirty war in Vietnam.
>
> . . . .The Greek Communist Party calls upon all patriots, whichever party they belong to, to set up everywhere—at the factories, in the residential districts, in the villages, in the universities, in the public services—groups of democratic resistance, committees of antidictatorial action, with one common purpose: to overthrow the fascist dictatorship and to restore democracy. In that difficult struggle the communists will be, as always, in the front ranks. They will give all their spirit of organization, their boldness, their energies.
>
> . . . Greek men and women, workers, employees, farmers, craftsmen, intellectuals, clerics, patriotic officers, soldiers, sailors, and airmen! Unite . . . in the sacred struggle for the liberties of the people, for democracy, for national independence, for peace and progress! International public opinion stands by our side! (Radio "Voice of Truth," 25 April.)

When on 29 April the new regime banned the EDA and dissolved the youth organizations of all parties, the KKE suffered another blow, but by this time the party was directing all its resources and energy toward forming a popular resistance movement to oppose the government both within and without Greece.* Advocating unity of "the men of the left, the center, and the right," the party belatedly recognized that the ERE was a victim of, and not a party to, the coup: "The integration in the patriotic front of all democratic, patriotic, and antifascist forces is today the supreme duty. This front must unite all civilians and military, without exception, who are opposed to the junta, who want the dictatorship to be overthrown and a normal political life in the country." (*Ibid.,* 24 May quoting Zisis Zografos.) In the last ten days of June the Central Committee of the KKE held its Eleventh Plenum.

---

*An article in *WMR* (February 1968) reported the existence of three resistance organizations: the Patriotic Front, the Defense of Democracy, and the National Democratic Resistance movement, which were "all cooperating," but it recognized the Patriotic Front as the most active. The article claimed communist leadership "in many places."

The plenum stressed that, faced with the great trial which has befallen the people, it is a supreme national necessity for all the parties, political leaders, and militants, all the political forces, to set aside their differences, and to unite their forces in a broad antidictatorship front, on the basis of a common program of struggle, which could be the following: Overthrow of the dictatorship, restoration of the constitution and democratic liberties, freedom of action of all parties and organizations, release of all prisoners, general amnesty, dissolution of the junta, and free elections by the simple proportional system, to be carried out by a government of all parties. (*Ibid.,* 6 July.)*

This seven point program became the basis for KKE action for the remainder of 1967.

The Patriotic Front, in the organization of which the KKE played a role, apparently accomplished little toward the overthrow of the junta in Greece. Activities were limited to a few acts of disrespect and defiance within the country, to which the military regime responded with alacrity and vigor.† Outside Greece, where KKE strength remained intact, the party launched an active antigovernment propaganda campaign. Grozos, Koliyannis, Zografos and others received considerable coverage for KKE views in news media of western as well as eastern Europe. Pressure from European public opinion, in part alerted by KKE propaganda activity, probably ameliorated the treatment of the leading political personalities arrested and confined by the regime. The communist propaganda attack emphasized the continuing isolation of the military regime, the antidemocratic nature of its rule, the persecution of intellectuals and political figures, the purges in the government bureaucracy, the barren nature of cultural life, and, last but not least, the increasing economic problems facing the nation. It tended to exaggerate the unity and effectiveness of the Patriotic Front, seeing great victories in insignificant skirmishes.

The KKE treated King Constantine's abortive countercoup on 13 December as a falling out among thieves. In commenting on the situation a Politburo statement called for immediate overthrow of the junta, but qualified the terms to mean restoration of all constitutional and democratic forms and not a return to the antidemocratic "abnormal" governments which preceeded the April coup. The King found no support or sympathy in the KKE. When the King's countercoup failed, the party described the episode as a crisis of the military regime and attributed it to "the total resistance of the people and the entire political world" and to the international isolation of the junta government (*ibid.,* 14 December).

**International Views and Policies.** In foreign affairs the KKE demanded that Greece withdraw from NATO and annul the "shackling" treaties with the US, particularly the Greek-American agreement of 1953 (*WMR,* December 1967). It described US "imperialism" and NATO as the sinister plotters of the "fascist coup" in Greece and in a larger context as a force bent on destroying the independence of Cyprus and as the instigators of Israeli "aggression" in the Middle East. In the KKE view, the coup in Greece, the Cyprus situation, and the six-day Arab-Israeli war, were linked to a massive US-NATO conspiracy to dominate the eastern Mediterranean area and to suppress the democratic aspirations of the peoples of the region for the continuing benefit of US and West European monopoly capitalism. On the other side of the globe, US "imperialism" was seen in SEATO and in the "aggressive" war in Vietnam, which the KKE condemned in an appeal to the Greek people issued at the Tenth Plenum of the Central Committee in April 1967. (Radio "Voice of Truth," 9 April).

---

*See *Documents* for the Resolution of the Eleventh Plenary Meeting, Communist Party of Greece, which contains an official description of the situation in Greece, an indictment of the equivocal role of the EK, a self-criticism of the left (KKE and EDA), a statement of the party's attitude toward the US and NATO, a declaration of support for the Patriotic Front, and an outline for party action against the military regime. The resolution was drawn largely from Apostolos Grozos' detailed report to the KKE Central Committee at the plenum, which was boadcast by Radio "Voice of Truth" on 12-19 July.

†By mid-October the KKE was reporting confidently the activities of the Patriotic Front within Greece, but by the end of November reliable Western news sources had reported five mass trials of antiregime activists involving more than 100 persons. It was becoming inceasingly clear that resistance organizations were making very little headway in the face of the government's tight police and security controls.

Alleging that the Arab-Israeli crisis was a direct result of Anglo-American imperialist machinations, the KKE attempted to arouse Greek fears that the junta ("the handmaiden of the US imperialists") was preparing to drag the Greek nation into the war on the side of the Israelis or for service against Albania and North Vietnam (*ibid.,* 7-8 June). Evidence of these plans was adduced from the fact that discussions were held in Athens between US and Greek military leaders during the Middle East crisis.

The KKE showed deep concern for the situation in Cyprus and supported the position of the Cypriot Communist party, AKEL (see *Cyprus*). The main theme of party propaganda envisioned a threat to Cyprus's independence in the form of a US-NATO plot, backed by the military regime in Greece, to overthrow the Makarios government and turn the island into a missile base. Talks between the Greek and Turkish government (9-10 September) to settle the Cyprus problem were viewed as an attempt by the junta to repay the US for its support by delivering Cyprus into NATO hands. Like AKEL, the KKE sought to "solve" the Cyprus problem by "safeguarding the total sovereignty, independence and territorial integrity of Cyprus on the basis of the principles of the UN, removing all non-Cypriot soldiers without exception, liquidating foreign bases, demilitarizing the island except for UN troops, banning all foreign interference in the internal affairs of Cyprus, ceasing the arbitrary mediation efforts of Washington and NATO, and ending the Greco-Turkish dialogue" (*ibid.,* 7 December). The KKE indicated no support, however, for *Enosis,* the union of Cyprus with Greece.

Firmly pro-Soviet in the international communist movement, the KKE confirmed its allegiance in a resolution passed at the Tenth Plenum which hailed the coming celebration of the fiftieth anniversary of the October Revolution in the Soviet Union. The resolution characterized the Soviet Union as "the majestic edifice of the new socialist society proceeding to the building of communism," and declared: "The Greek people [consider] the Soviet Union to be a strong supporter, an unselfish great power, which in its very existence, in its social policy, and in its influence over international developments and relations, helps them in their struggle for independence and democracy" (*ibid.,* 12 April).

In another resolution at the same plenum the party criticized the role of the "leading group of the Chinese Communist Party, led by Mao Tse-tung." This group, it said, was motivated by nationalistic and selfish aims and was splitting the world communist movement, hindering support for the "heroic struggle of the Vietnamese people," "alienating itself from the principles of Marxism-Leninism and proletarian internationalism," and "slandering and undermining the CPSU and other Marxist parties." The resolution went on to affirm full support for the Soviet Union in the convening of an international conference of communist and workers' parties. (*Ibid.,* 10 April.)

In April Chairman Grozos led the KKE delegation to the conference of communist and workers' parties of Europe at Karlovy Vary, Czechoslovakia, and Secretary Partsalidis represented the party at the Seventh Congress of the East German Socialist Unity Party (SED) in Berlin. The party was represented at the fiftieth anniversary celebration of the October revolution in the Soviet Union, where Secretary-General Koliyannis delivered a speech at the grand rally in Moscow on 6 November. Koliyannis also represented the KKE at the Thirtieth Congress of the Communist Party of Great Britain, in November.

**Publications and Radio.** Until the April coup, the KKE used EDA (and other front) publications for the expression of its views within Greece. The principal organ of the EDA was the daily *Avgi* ("Dawn"). After the coup the KKE had no means for the publication and distribution of printed material in Greece on a regular basis. The central organ of the KKE, published outside Greece, is *Risospastis*; the theoretical magazine is *Neos Kosmos.* The Party also publishes several newspapers for Greek exiles in eastern Europe and the USSR: *Elefteria* (Bulgaria), *Dimokratis* (Poland), *Laikos Agon* (Hungary), *Nea Zoe* (Rumania), and *Neos Dromos* (Tashkent, USSR).

During 1967 the KKE operated a clandestine radio station called the Voice of Truth from two sites, one in Rumania, and the other in East Germany.

**KKE and EDA Dissidents.** The KKE has a long record of internal discord and factionalism. The followers of Nikolas Zachariadis, expelled under pressure from Moscow in 1956, form one group of dissidents; those of Markos Vafiadis, removed from the party in 1958, comprise another. These factions are the personal followings of two rival communist leaders of the civil war period (1947-49).

New fissures in the party, resulting from differences on more current issues, may soon leave these older splinter groups as mere anachronisms.

Since 1964 there has been a pro-Peking split which has cut across the party lines of both the KKE and the EDA. The pro-Peking group of Greek Marxist-Leninists published a monthly, *Anagennisis,* in Greece until the April coup, it now publishes an official organ, *Laikos Dromos,* from exile somewhere in Europe.

The EDA is also affected by divisions of an ideological nature. Among them, in addition to the Maoists, there are Trotskyists and "Neutralists" who feel that the path to power lies in a war of national liberation. A more important faction, called the "Restorers," or AODA, is headed by Lefteris Apostolos and has been in operation since 1964. Apostolos, a former KKE member, wants the left-wing movement in Greece to break its ties with Moscow. (See Radio Free Europe, *The Left in Greece: A Forest or Some Trees,* 8 May 1967.)

A recent serious split in the KKE took place in February 1968 as a direct result of the events in Greece in 1967 and the growing opposition to Koliyannis's leadership. The proximate cause of this new cleavage was the calling of a Twelfth Plenum of the Central Committee in Budapest, allegedly without inviting the Central Committee members from Greece. Secretaries Partsalidis and Dimitriou and Politburo member Zografos objected strenuously, criticizing Koliyannis for holding a plenum without these comrades. Koliyannis retaliated by removing the three from their positions and dismissing them from the party. Claiming the support of half the Central Committee and declaring the Twelfth Plenum to be invalid, the rebels, headed by Partsalidis, defiantly formed a "Unifying Central Committee of the Greek Communist Party" (Enotiki Kentriki Epitropi Hellinikou Kommounistikou Kommatos) which subsequently received backing from most KKE members in Greece (in and out of prison) and from the EDA, which denounced Koliyannis's high-handedness. There were indications of sympathy for the Unifying Central Committee among the Italian, Czechoslovakian, and Rumanian communist parties; Moscow backed Koliyannis.

# GUADELOUPE

The Guadeloupe Communist Party (Parti Communiste Guadeloupéen; PCG) originated in 1944 as the Guadeloupe Federation of the French Communist Party (Fédération de la Guadeloupe du Parti Communiste Français), which in 1958 was transformed into the present autonomous party. In recent years the PCG has been plagued by conflict and expulsions, and the communist left in Guadeloupe is now represented by several diffuse groups in addition to the PCG.

The PCG is legal, and party membership is estimated at about 1,000. The population of Guadeloupe is 319,000 (estimated 1966). An active participant in the country's political life, the PCG presented three candidates—Paul Lacavé, Hégésippe Ibéné, and Gerty Archimède—in the 1967 elections for Guadeloupe's three seats in the French National Assembly on 12 March, and gained one of the seats. Paul Lacavé received 34,751 votes against 34,170 for the Gaullist "Fifth Republic" candidates, in spite of Gaullist "fraud" and "corruption," in the view of the PCG. The PCG also accused the Gaullists of using every means to prevent the communist victory, including the giving of material support to splinter groups of the PCG. (In the 1962 election, the PCG obtained 22,912 votes, or 36.9 per cent of the poll, and did not win an assembly seat.) In the 1967 cantonal elections, 24 September-1 October, four seats of the eighteen contested were won by PCG candidates (Paul Lacavé, Henri Bangou, Charles Edwige, and D. Geniès). Two former members of the PCG who are now part of the extreme left were also elected: Nicolas Ludger and Césario Siban. The party's representation in the municipal government includes Henri Bangou, a member of the PCG Politubro, who is mayor of Pointe-à-Pitre, Guadeloupe's major city.

**Organization and Leadership.** The present PCG leadership includes: Secretary-General Evremond Gène, and Politburo members Guy Daninthe, Henri Bangou, Gerty Archimède, Hégésippe Ibéné, Hermann Songeions, Serge Pierre-Justin, Georges René, and B. Alexis. Prominent among the Central Committee members are Paul Lacavé (deputy to National Assembly) H. Petilaire, George Tarer, Félix Flemin, Charles Edwige, and Josephe Felsine.

In 1967 the PCG established a new "Union of Communist Youth of Guadeloupe" (Union de la Jeunessee Communiste de la Guadeloupe; UJCG). The constituent congress of the group met on 30-31 December and defined its program in conformity with the PCG's program of autonomy for Guadeloupe. The program emphasized that the UJCG was a "mass organization open to all young people who aspire to autonomy and to a better future" for the country. The UJCG, the program continued, "adopts the proven principles of Marxism-Leninism which it considers the only theory capable of leading to the creation of a new society built on justice and fraternity." (Supplement, *L'Etincelle* 6 January 1968.)

The PCG also has some influence among students, particularly in the Paris-based General Association of Guadeloupe Students (Association Générale des Etudiants Guadeloupéens; AGEG). The AGEG, however, is not communist-controlled, and its communist members tend to be pro-Chinese (unlike those of the General Association of Martinique Students, who are pro-Soviet).

The PCG has strong influence in the country's largest trade union, the General Confederation of Labor (Confédération Général du Travail—CGT), which has some 5,000 members. A severe conflict has developed between the PCG faction in the CGT and the more militant faction led by the Secretary-General of the CGT, Nicolas Ludger, who though formerly a leading member of the PCG is now branded as a "scissionist" by the party. On the occasion of the 1 May celebrations, the three Guadeloupe trade-union centrals united and organized the demonstrations. With a view to maintaining this unity, the trade union leaders decided that an official invitation to the PCG to participate in the demonstrations would be "inopportune." The party deplored what it call an "anticommunist" campaign within the trade unions, declaring that it had never wanted to create communist trade unions or to penetrate into trade unions to subordinate them to communist political interests (*L'Etincelle*, 5 August).

**Domestic Views and Policies.** The program of the PCG, as set out in 1964 in the resolution of the Third Party Congress (the Fourth Congress is scheduled for 13-14 April 1968) was based on the demand for Guadeloupe autonomy within the framework of an alliance with France.

In an article in *Pravda* (5 October) Serge Pierre-Justin explained this to mean redefining relations with France and replacing the policy of subordination and assimilation with relations based on equality and collaboration.

In the political field, the party calls for a local legislative assembly, an executive Guadeloupe organ responsible to that assembly, and a body for cooperation with France. The program emphasizes that autonomy should be carried through in the interest of the most needy section of Guadeloupe working people at the expense of "feudal and colonial" enterprises.

Economically, the PCG program calls for a noncapitalist path of development combining radical agrarian reform, with rationalized industrialization which would involve extensive development of light industry, a total reconversion of foreign and domestic trade, and the development of cooperatives.

PCG pronouncements repeatedly denounce the status of Guadeloupe as a "colony" of France and the subject of "French imperialism." The party has also consistently attacked Guadeloupe participation in the European Economic Community, declaring that as a consequence Guadeloupe, "is not only a French colony, but an appendage to the economy of the imperialist powers, signatories of the Treaty of Rome . . . " In its present position, according to the Communists, Guadeloupe is part of the zone of underdeveloped countries "condemned to sleep in a monoculture agricultural economy" (*L'Etincelle*, 17 June).

The PCG has adopted a united front policy in promoting its aims in Guadeloupe. "The union of the anticolonialist forces is today more than ever the essential objective of the Guadeloupe Communists," declared Evremond Gène (*ibid.*, 14 October). The party invites the support of all those who wish to oppose openly the policy of "departmentalization" and to fight for autonomy within the framework of an alliance with France.

The PCG's endeavors to create a united front included the sponsoring in June 1965 of a "Guadeloupe Front for Autonomy" (Front Guadeloupéen pour l'Autonomie; FGA). The front was beset with conflicting factions from the very beginning, as militant leftists infiltrated it and called for immediate independence and armed struggle.

On 20 March 1967 in Basse-Terre and again on 26-27 May in Pointe-à-Pitre violence erupted with strong racial overtones. The PCG blamed the riots on the "colonial" status of Guadeloupe. "French colonialism *alone* was responsible for the bloody events of 26-27 May," a Politburo declaration stated (*ibid.*, 10 June). A resolution of the Central Committee meeting of 23 July declared that the events confirmed the dissatisfaction of the people with the deteriorating situation in Guadeloupe. It claimed that in the past three years the rising cost of living had wiped out all beneficial legislation. According to the resolution, the failure of economic planning was due to disregard of the basic need: "The transformation of our economy from a colonial type to an economy centered on the satisfaction of the needs of the masses by an agricultural reform, by the establishing of light industry," which the PCG believes would reduce the imbalance of imports over exports and create employment for the large percentage of young people.

The resolution stressed that the Guadeloupe people need the help of all peoples struggling against imperialism and especially the help of the French Communist Party. It therefore condemned all those who during the May riots attacked indiscriminately all white persons. The resolution warned, further, against "leftists" who in recent years have infiltrated the movement for autonomy. The PCG declared that the leftists are encouraged by "imperialists" to sow confusion in the movement and to lead a faction "along the path of adventurism," the object being to swing the Communists to the left and thus deprive the party of its mass base. While the resolution condemned the "imperialist repression" of the riots and said that the PCG would defend the victims, it emphasized that the defense would be conducted "in the light of and on the basis of the party program: autonomy within the framework of a union with France." (*Ibid.,* 29 July.)

The party's aims were damaged by the spring riots. Noncommunist groups charged the Communists with inspiring the riots, and the militant left accused the PCG of denouncing the leaders of the demonstration to the security offices. The party's answer was a declaration by Gène that the events of 26-27 May showed that the situation was "ripe for riots but not yet for revolution," adding: "The Guadeloupe Communist Party will never be one of rioters" (*ibid.,* 17 June).

The PCG has been so plagued by inner conflicts—caused mainly by opposition from those who demand absolute independence of Guadeloupe, those who demand more militant methods, and those who strive to split the party along racist lines—that Evremond Gène in a speech at Basse-Terre, declared that the most current problem was the preservation of the party and its "strengthening on the base of the principles of Marxism-Leninism." Warning against "isolation," he said: "We must be able to count on proletarian internationalism," whose principal criterion he defined as "opposition to imperialism and to racist and chauvinist ideology." (*Ibid.,* 5 August.)

**International Views and Policies.** The PCG has maintained its traditional close ties with the French Communist Party and has followed the policy line of the Communist Party of the Soviet Union in the International Communist movement. H. Ibéné represented the PCG at the Eighteenth Congress of the French Communist Party in Paris in January 1967. In April, Ibéné led a PCG delegation to Europe where he held talks with representatives of the French party and of the Communist Party of the Soviet Union together with representatives of the communist parties of Martinique and Réunion.

In the communique issued following the meeting with Soviet representatives (19 April-5 May), the participants affirmed support for the convening of an international communist meeting and reported "unity of views on all question." Evremond Gène and Central Committee member H. Petilaire represented the PCG at the celebrations of the fiftieth anniversary of the October Revolution, in Moscow in November, and presented a message in which the PCG reaffirmed its position on the convening of an international conference of communist and workers' parties and declared that conditions were ripe for beginning preparations.

**Publications.** The PCG publishes the weekly *L'Etincelle.*

\* \* \*

**GONG.** Many of the "scissionists" and expelled members of the PCG (and also, apparently, some current members of the party) have associated themselves with a small militant group, the "Guadeloupe National Organization Group" (Groupe d' Organization Nationale de la Guadeloupe; GONG), created in 1963 and based in Paris. In 1964 the group openly espoused a pro-Chinese stand, accusing the PCG of "revisionism." It calls for independence for Guadeloupe by means of armed struggle.

Among the GONG Leaders are Henri Delagua, Hebert Khérel, Nicolas Ludger, Yves Leborgne (expelled from the PCG in February 1967), Florent Girard, Siméon René, Arsène Monrose, Paul Tomiche, and Jules Boisel. The GONG presented two candidates in the 1967 elections for the French National Assembly, Yves Leborgne and Nicolas Ludger, but without success.

The GONG played an active part in the Basse-Terre and Pointe-à-Pitre riots. Consequently many of its adherents were arrested and the organization was largely destroyed by repressive measures. The GONG Politburo's resolution of 17 July on the riots at Pointe-à-Pitre in May declared that the events confirmed that the French imperialist policies had not changed, that the "revisionists" were collaborating with the "colonialists" and that "the struggle of the Guadeloupe people for national independence" had "entered a new phase which will lead to victory" (*La Voix du Peuple,* Brussels, 4 August). Henri Delagua, leading the Guadeloupe delegation to the First Conference of the Latin American Solidarity Organization (Havana, July-August) reaffirmed the views of the GONG resolution and declared that the PCG officials had collaborated with the security forces, especially Mayor Henri Bangou, of whom he said: "Someday the people will settle accounts with him." Already, he added, the people of Guadeloupe had "replied to counterrevolutionary violence with revolutionary violence."

The Guadeloupe delegation also hailed the Cuban revolution as "a living source of Latin American revolution" and proof that armed struggle was the only way to defeat "Yankee imperialism."

**Publications,** The organ of the GONG is the monthly *GONG*. Other dissident publications which reflect the views of the GONG are *Verité,* and *Le Progrès Social.*

# GUATEMALA

The first predominantly communist organization in Guatemala was the illegal Socialist Labor Unification (Unificación Obrera Socialista), founded in 1921. This group became the Communist Party of Guatemala (Partido Comunista de Guatemala; PCG) in 1923 and was recognized by the Communist International in 1924. Increasing communist activities among workers during the mid-1920's were cut off by the end of the decade and kept at a minimum under the dictatorship of Jorge Ubico, from 1931 to 1944. In 1947, during the presidency of Juan José Arévalo, the Communists as an organized group reappeared as the clandestine Democratic Vanguard (Vanguardia Democrática). In 1949 the Vanguard took the name Communist Party of Guatemala (PCG). In 1950 communist labor leader Victor Manuel Gutiérrez founded a second and parallel communist party called the Revolutionary Workers' Party of Guatemala (Partido Revolucionario Obrero de Guatemala). The two communist groups merged in 1951 when, after a trip to Moscow, Gutiérrez dissolved his party and joined the PCG. In 1952 the PCG changed its name to the Guatemalan Party of Labor (Partido Guatemalteco del Trabajo; PGT). The PGT was legalized in 1952, but this status was maintained for only two years. The party has been illegal since the overthrow of President Jacobo Arbenz in 1954.

PGT membership is believed to number between 750 and 1000. The population of Guatemala is about 4,650,000 (estimated, December 1966). PGT membership is thought to have fallen slightly during 1967. Guerrillas operating in Guatemala, not all of whom were Communists, also decreased in number so that by December guerrilla forces were estimated at about 100, with about 300 student sympathizers.

**Leadership.** The most important members of the PGT were Bernardo Alvarado Monzón, the Secretary-General, and César Montes, a Politburo member and the commander-in-chief of the Rebel Armed Forces (Fuerzas Armadas Rebeldes; FAR). Also prominent in the activities of the year were Central Committee members Gabriel Salazar and José María Ortiz Vides. The most frequent spokesman for the PGT in international communist circles was José Manuel Fortuny. The party representative in Cuba was Oscar Edmundo Palma.

**Youth.** During recent years the Patriotic Youth of Labor (Juventud Patriótica del Trabajo; JPT) has been the PGT's most successful auxiliary organization. According to a statement in March 1968 by the Central Committee of the PGT, many activists from the party's youth movement have been "promoted to leading posts in the Party and key positions in the armed struggle" (*IB*, no. 122). Among those promoted was César Montes, who first joined the youth organization in 1958. The FAR declaration of 10 January 1968 asserted, however, that at the beginning of the year the JPT was "defunct" (*Granma*, Havana, weekly English edition, 25 February 1968).

Communist influence on the Association of University Students (Asociación de Estudiantes Universitarios) at the University of San Carlos was evidently maintained during early 1967 through Mario Hercules Betzog, who fled to the countryside after a dramatic escape from the government officials at mid-year. Students, not all of them Communists, have for years made up a significant percentage of the guerrilla forces, though the turnover has been considerable and some have served only as "weekend warriors." The PGT statement of March 1968 revealed that such student support had declined during 1967.

**Labor.** The PGT controls the small, clandestine Guatemalan Autonomous Socialist Federation (Federación Autónoma Socialista Guatemalteca), a relatively insignificant labor organization. Although pointing out that the Guatemalan working class has a "noteworthy battle record," the March 1968 statement declared: "Counterrevolutionary terror and demagogy have immobilized the trade union movement, led largely by opportunist elements with a syndicalist outlook."

**Peasants.** The main PGT-supported groups in which there was some peasant participation were the guerrilla forces. In an interview reported on 15 July by the Montevideo office of the Cuban press agency Prensa Latina, most of which appeared in the Montevideo paper *El Sol* (16 July), César Montes said that communication with the peasants was easiest when the guerrillas declared that their movement was a continuation of the 1944-1954 revolution. Montes asserted that the majority of the guerrillas were peasants and that they, led by the working class, constituted the "principal force," the "motive power," of the revolution. Montes admitted, however, that the guerrillas had suffered serious reverses during the year, and the PGT statement of March 1968 claimed that peasant activities were weakened by opposition similar to that faced by the workers.

According to Montes, no organization has had better than limited success in winning the support of the Indians who make up more than half of the total Guatemalan population. The PGT Central Committee called the Indians a "potentially revolutionary force," but also gave a warning: "It would be a mistake to idealize their revolutionary preparedness in the present conditions. Serious and painstaking work must be conducted among them." (*IB*, no. 122.)

**Rebel Armed Forces.** In May 1965 the Central Committee of the PGT stated that it conceived the Rebel Armed Forces as "the organization responsible for directly carrying on armed struggle, under the control of the PGT and such non-Party revolutionaries as accept the fundamental ideas of Marxism-Leninism; not a parallel organization, but an organization centered in the PGT" (quoted in FAR declaration of 10 January 1968; *Granma,* weekly English edition, 25 February). In July 1967, however, César Montes stated: "The FAR is not the armed branch of any party, let alone the PGT. The fact that we have PGT members in the movement does not necessarily mean that the movement is a communist movement" (*El Sol,* Montevideo, 16 July).

Although some of the guerrillas may well have retained their ideological independence, the PGT Central Committee statement of 1965 would quite accurately describe the FAR leadership and ideology in 1967. Most of the important positions in the FAR were held by PGT members, including César Montes, FAR commander-in-chief; Camilo Sánchez, second in command (under Montes) of the centrally important "Edgar Ibarra Guerrilla Front" (Frente Guerrillero Edgar Ibarra; FGEI); Leonardo Castillo Johnson, killed in January 1968, who was believed to be the head of FAR activities in Guatemala City. Prominent PGT members who acted as spokesmen for the FAR, in addition to those mentioned above, included Gabriel Salazar of the PGT Secretariat, José María Ortiz Vides, Pablo Monsanto, and Oscar Palma. In an interview in mid-1967 Camilo Sánchez acknowledged that he and Pablo Monsanto had joined the FAR to make sure it followed a communist line, and that most of the FAR leaders were members of the PGT (*Partisans,* Paris, July 1967). When FAR leaders (mostly PGT members) broke openly with the so-called "right wing, opportunistic, ruling clique" of the PGT in January 1968, they admitted their previous subservience by stating: "The PGT (its leadership clique) supplied the ideas, while the FAR supplied the dead" (FAR declaration of 10 January).

**PGT Leadership Changes.** Following the formation of the Revolutionary Leadership Council in 1965 (composed of members of the PGT, FGEI, and JPT), the PGT began to promote young guerrilla leaders to important positions in the party. The PGT representative in Cuba, Oscar Palma, wrote in *Granma* (6 February 1967), that the party had changed its structure, including its leadership, "abandoning old and narrow ideas, eradicating formalistic and bureaucratic methods, and bringing representatives of the young and vigorous generation of Marxist-Leninists into its Central Committee." According to the PGT, of the five comrades elevated to the Central Committee in June 1967, four "belonged to the FGEI or identified themselves with its position." This, the party declared, was in keeping with the concept of "integrated leadership" favored by the guerrillas. (*IB*, no. 122.) However, according to César Montes in his statement of 21 January 1968, this "rejuvenation" of the Central Committee was merely a "maneuver to neutralize the most radical proposals and swamp the military leaders in an involved disciplinary setup" (*Granma,* weekly English edition, 3 March).* Among the

*Régis Debray, in his *Revolution in the Revolution?* (Grove Press, New York, 1967), praised only one communist party other than the Cuban in all of Latin America—the PGT, which he said had been "renewed and rejuvenated" in 1965 (p. 41). When asked about Debray's book in the July interview cited above, César Montes declared that

Central Committee members killed during the year were Tranquilino López and Gustavo Grajeda Cetina.

**PGT Evaluation of its 1967 Activities.** In February Oscar Palma asserted that the guerrillas were winning the support of the Guatemalan people in both the countryside and the cities (*Granma*, 6 February). By early 1968, however, the PGT admitted otherwise. In its March 1968 statement, the Central Committee acknowledged that during 1967 the party had lost ground among workers, peasants, and students. The general situation was summed up as follows:

> The revolutionary and popular forces, for all that they are right and wield potential strength, find themsleves in a state of stagnation. After more than four years of armed struggle, active participation by the masses and support by the bulk of the people, who remain largely an onlooker rather than a participant in the drama of the revolution, have yet to be secured. While some comrades affirm that we are advancing with a fair wind, maintaining the initiative and striking blow upon blow at the enemy, we must face reality. The principal battles are still fought by vanguard units. Our forces have been hard hit. . . . We have suffered important losses. Discontent and opposition are growing but so far we have been unable to coordinate them and channel them in the direction of the main blow. The split in the revolutionary movement is making the situation still worse. . . . To be sure, this is a temporary state of affairs but it is reality none the less. . . . The balance of forces is still unfavorable to us. (*IB*, no. 122.)

**Domestic Policy and Activities.** The primary reasons for the losses suffered by the PGT and the FAR during 1967 were the existence of a relatively popular reform government headed by President Julio César Méndez Montenegro, the intensified efforts of the Guatemalan military to break up and defeat the guerrilla forces, the rise of a number of right-wing terrorist organizations, and the disputes among PGT members and between the FAR and the PGT.

The main problem faced by the PGT leaders was that of determining the tactics which would unify the party and reverse the fortunes of the revolutionary movement they directed. Not until early 1968 did the extent and consequences of their failure in 1967 become known in any detail.

In an article on PGT domestic policy published in the *World Marxist Review* (February 1967), José Manuel Fortuny quoted from a 10 June 1966 resolution of the party's Central Committee: "The main enemy—North American imperialism—is changing its tactics. Formerly it openly supported the extreme reaction in order to rule the country through the army. Now it is drawing new forces into the administration and using the army to control the government." Fortuny then pointed out that "From this the Party concluded that it was necessary, without changing the general line of its policy and firmly adhering to the strategy of armed action, to 'define the concrete tactics in the present political situation'." According to Fortuny, the basic aspects of these tactics were:

> (1) Despite the meanderings of [Mendez] Montenegro's Revolutionary Party [Partido Revolucionario], it should not be confused with the parties on reaction. Because of its class composition and policy, it plays a specific role, basically seeking to deceive the masses and to win them over by using reformism as a decoy. . . . The immediate task is to combat the reactionary top stratum, to neutralize the opportunists in the middle group, and to win over the rank and file to Left positions.

> (2) Since the government is clearly seeking to pursue a policy different from that which the army would like to impose on it, the Communist tactics towards the two differ. . . . One of the Party's objects is to make it clear to the government that at the given moment its direct adversary is not the Rebel Armed Forces but the official Army.

> (3) Faced with the constant danger of a coup . . . revolutionary tactics consist in alerting the masses and the government to this danger and, in the event of a coup being attempted, in complementary action by the Rebel Armed Forces and rallying the masses to repel the putschists and, in the event of the latter succeeding in seizing power, to wage resolute armed struggle and to build up a broad front to repel the direct intervention

though the French Marxist seemed well informed on the Cuban experience, he evidently knew relatively little about any other guerrilla movement in Latin America. Montes stated flatly: "[Debray]knows little of the Guatemalan experience."

which the US imperialists may undertake.

(4) . . . The Party sees its main task in all-round utilization of the possibilities afforded by the present situation for improving the organization of the revolutionary struggle in three basic areas—the masses, the Rebel Armed Forces and the Party itself . . . "The best reply to the enemy's tactics," our Central Committee pointed out, "is in the final analysis the proper combination of political, armed, economic and social struggle. . . ."

**Intraparty Conflict.** The adoption of both peaceful and violent tactics led to disputes among PGT members themselves, and between leaders of the PGT, the FAR, and the November 13th Revolutionary Movement of Marco Antonio Yon Sosa (see below). PGT Secretary General Bernardo Alvarado Monzón pointed out in 1966 that the unity of the party was then threatened by "the 'left' danger, on the one hand, and the danger of conservatism, on the other" (*WMR*, October). According to the PGT, incorporation of guerrilla leaders into the party Central Committee before and during 1967 was intended to satisfy the guerrillas and to achieve the "integrated leadership" they so persistently advocated. The FAR charge that it was all a plot to dissipate guerrilla influence (see above) was scorned by the PGT statement in March 1968.

A thinly disguised attack on the PGT policy was made by two members of the party's Central Committee (who were concurrently FAR leaders) in March (*Granma*, weekly English edition, 26 March). During the year the dispute became increasingly bitter. According to the PGT statement of March 1968, the split between the PGT and the FAR "became a fact in October 1967" (*IB*, no. 122). The break was made public by FAR leaders early in 1968.

The conflict, which centered on the policy of the PGT, included such issues as the political tendencies within the PGT hierarchy and the role of the party in revolutionary struggle. When Politburo member César Montes announced his withdrawal from the party in his statement of 21 January 1968, he asserted that the dispute was between "two ideas, two attitudes toward the war, toward the Revolution, toward the people, both determined by deep class roots and a historic moment," adding:

On the one side there is the revolutionary idea [of the FAR guerrillas] . . . a radical vision, revolutionary, audacious, young, dynamic. On the other side is the pseudorevolutionary idea [of the "leading clique" of the PGT] . . . a submissive, opportunist, fainthearted, outmoded, passive vision.

He thus saw "two mutually exclusive tendencies in the revolutionary process" and a "struggle between healthy and malignant forces." (*Granma*, weekly English edition, 3 March 1968.)

According to a FAR statement dated 10 January 1968 (the first two signatories for which were Camilo Sánchez and Pablo Monsanto), the PGT, with its "stubborn insistence on 'other forms of struggle'," had "wasted its energy in trying to achieve coordination and partial understanding with other forces" (*ibid.*, 25 February). In a statement dated 1 January 1968 the same FAR leaders asserted: "The PGT's policy has always been to decide which is the main enemy, not in order to concentrate its struggle against this main enemy, but with the aim of making deals with the 'lesser enemies'; this was the policy which they pompously termed 'united-front work'" (*World Outlook*, New York, 8 March). The FAR statement of 10 January charged that the twofold policy of emphasis on "combat activity" and "political activity" only "deepened the contradictions within the movement," and that the "lack of a central authority caused the premature creation of other 'guerrilla foci,' whose purpose was to gain advantages in discussion [for the PGT] and bring about the resolution of our differences from positions of strength."

The 10 January statement denounced the PGT and declared that Guatemala needed an organization which would bring about a "revolutionary change in the national situation," and that this kind of change, "Marx's age-old dream," has been "turned into reality by men such as Lenin, Mao, Ho Chi Minh, and Fidel Castro." This change, it was asserted, could now be achieved in Guatemala only through the development of the guerrilla movement and the people's army. The statement quoted Major Luis Augusto Turcios Lima, former FAR leader and a member of the PGT up to his death in 1966 (see *WMR*, September): "If a Communist Party does not know how to carry out its role, if it becomes neutralized, destroyed, another organization, other revolutionaries with greater insight take up that role; they will come to Marxism-Leninism, they will lead the revolution and will form a true Communist Party." (*Granma,* weekly English edition, 25 February.) The FAR, which merged with the MR-13 early in 1968 (see below), considered itself such an organization.

Predictably, almost every PGT statement during the year emphasized the importance of the party and its leadership role in the Guatemalan revolutionary movement. José Manuel Fortuny quoted Lenin's words that "Repudiation of the Party principle . . . is tantamount to completely disarming the proletariat in *the interests of the bourgeoisie"* (*WMR,* September; Lenin's emphasis). Writing on the Latin American Solidarity Organization (OLAS) conference about to be held in Havana—where the bypassing of communist parties in favor of guerrilla groups was expected to be a major topic—Fortuny and Waldo Atias (of Chile) declared:

> Communists lay no claim to a monopoly of revolutionary ideas or to sole leadership of the revolutionary movement. It is a fact, however, that the Communists, equipped with the Marxist-Leninist teaching, splendidly organized and disciplined, possessing experience and anti-imperialist tempering, are the best equipped of the Left forces to contribute decisively to the revolutionary transformations imperative in our time. Experience bears witness that any attempt to elbow out Communists has an adverse effect on the unity of the anti-imperialist and democratic forces. (*WMR,* July.)

**Ex-Communist Returns.** Carlos Manuel Pellecer, one of the highest-ranking and most competent Communists of the Arbenz years, returned to Guatemala at the end of 1967. In a series of conferences he explained his reasons for breaking with communism. It did not answer metaphysical questions, and it led to the destruction of individual and national independence. In particular he warned students to beware of the superficial appeals of the ideology.

**International Views and Positions.** During the year the PGT maintained friendly relations with the Soviet Union. It signed the statement of communist parties of Mexico, Central America, and Panama (dated May 1967) which proclaimed that "the socialist community headed by the Soviet Union is seen by all mankind as the bulwark of all the peoples fighting for their independence and for world peace" (*IB,* no. 102). José Manuel Fortuny presented a paper in June in Prague at the international theoretical symposium on the significance of the October Revolution (abridged in *WMR,* September). A PGT delegation was present at the fiftieth anniversary celebration of the October Revolution in Moscow.

On the other hand, in the May statement of the conference of communist parties of Mexico, Central America, and Panama the PGT alone refused to pledge support for the proposed world conference of communist and workers' parties, on the grounds that the party Central Committee had not yet decided on the matter. An affirmative decision seems to have been reached by the end of the year, however, and Central Committee member Julio López attended the Budapest consultative meeting in early 1968. PGT leaders were also reluctant to side openly with the Communist Party of Venezuela (and thus with the Soviet Union) in that party's dispute with Fidel Castro (see below).

While publicly condemning the division in the world communist movement, "the main factor encouraging the imperialists to be more aggressive in Vietnam and elsewhere" (*IB,* no. 102), the PGT carefully avoided any open criticism (or praise) of Communist China.

The PGT's main comments on other major international issues were in the joint statement of May cited above. Support was expressed for the "heroic struggle of the Vietnamese people" and a call was made for "more active solidarity with the people of Vietnam." With regard to the Middle East crisis, the statement condemned the "policy of the United States and Britain, which have turned Israel—against the will of the progressive forces of the Israeli people—into a bridgehead endangering the independence and sovereignty of those Arab peoples that are aspiring to an independent and democratic life." (*IB,* no. 102.)

**Latin America.** The divisions within the PGT on domestic policy showed up most clearly in the international realm in statements on revolutionary policy in Latin America. During the year official PGT statements were in line with the resolutions passed at the Havana conference of Latin American communist parties in November 1964 which stated that each party should be free to determine the form of struggle most suitable in its own country. For example, in the joint statement made in May, the PGT agreed that: "in accordance with the conditions prevailing in our countries and with the strategic and tactical concepts developed by the parties concerned, the working-class movement is making progress, using the most diverse forms of struggle, from peaceful ones to armed struggle" (*ibid.*).

Disagreements among PGT members became particularly clear after Fidel Castro's 13 March condemnation of the pro-Soviet Communist Party of Venezuela. The prime example of this came at the end of March when the Cuban paper *Granma* published a long statement of solidarity with Castro's views—allegedly speaking for the "members of the Central Committee of the Guatemalan Workers' Party (PGT) and leaders of the Rebel Armed Forces (FAR)"—signed by two PGT-FAR leaders, Gabriel Salazar, a member of the Secretariat of the PGT, and José María Ortiz Vides, a member of the Central Committee of the PGT. The statement attacked the "sterile, unimaginative, weak, stereotyped, carbon-copy thinking of organizations that call themselves communist" in many Latin American countries, and proclaimed agreement with Castro that "What will define the communists on this continent is their attitutde toward the guerrilla movement." (*Granma*, weekly English edition, 26 March.)

PGT Secretary General Bernardo Alvarado Monzón immediately repudiated the Salazar-Ortiz statement in the name of the party's Politburo, saying that the PGT had not taken any position on the Cuban-Venezuelan dispute (*La Verdad*, San Salvador, El Salvador, 31 March). César Montes, who avoided public polemics with PGT spokesmen until his break with the party in 1968, repudiated the Salazar-Ortiz statement on behalf of the FAR on the grounds that the two did not have enough information to make a judgment (*ibid.*).

**Cuba.** The PGT attitude toward Cuba was one of admiration and respect, and statements such as "Our future is reality in revolutionary Cuba" (*WMR*, September) were not uncommon. In its official declarations, however, the PGT was cautious with respect to the revolutionary tactics advocated by Castro and his followers. José Manuel Fortuny expressed reservations toward the OLAS conference before it was held (*WMR*, July). Oscar Palma attended the conference in August.

**FAR and Cuba.** César Montes stated in the July interview cited above that the Guatemalan guerrillas were inspired and encouraged by Castro and the Cuban example, but that they did not expect the Cuban experience to be repeated in their country. He acknowledged that many guerrillas have been to Cuba, but denied that Cuba had provided men or weapons for the FAR—the guerrillas were all Guatemalans, and they bought or captured their weapons. Outside sources have reported, however, that there have been efforts to send money to the guerrillas through the Cuban Embassy in Mexico City (e.g., *New York Times*, 5 April) for the purchase of supplies of various kinds.

The Cuban-dominated Afro-Asian-Latin American Peoples' Solidarity Organization proclaimed 6 February the "world day of solidarity with the Guatemalan people." Cuba played a significant part in the dispute among Guatemalan revolutionaries both by forcing certain controversial issues on the Latin American revolutionaries as a whole, and by publishing and broadcasting the words of any Guatemalan who would explicitly or implicitly attack the official line of the PGT.

**International Party Contacts.** The PGT attended the conference of communist parties of Mexico, Central America, and Panama which appears to have been held in May. Gabriel Salazar visited North Korea in May and met Premier Kim Il-song. José Manuel Fortuny visited Prague in June. A delegate from the PGT was present at the OLAS conference in Havana in August, and a delegation, headed by Central Committee Member Miguel Rodríguez, attended the fiftieth anniversary celebrations in Moscow in November.

**Publications.** The organ of the PGT is the irregular, clandestine, *La Verdad*. The publication of the Rebel Armed Forces is the irregular, clandestine *FAR*.

**November 13th Revolutionary Movement: MR-13.** The second important guerrilla organization in Guatemala during 1967 was the November 13th Revolutionary Movement (Movimiento Revolucionario 13 de Noviembre; MR-13) led by Marco Antonio Yon Sosa. The MR-13 became separated from both the PGT and the FAR in late 1964 due to substantial Trotskyist influence in its leadership, and because of strategic, ideological, and personal conflicts. After the expulsion of the Trotskyist leaders in mid-1966, Luis Turcios of the FAR took the first step toward the reunification of the two guerrilla groups (*World Outlook,* 1 March 1968).

According to César Montes, one important difference between the two groups was that the MR-13 regarded itself as regional in scope, setting up guerrilla base areas with self-governing communities, not unlike those advocated by Mao Tse-tung. The FAR, however, considered itself national in scope and avoided the establishment of such elaborate regional base areas. (*El Sol,* 16 July.) José Dones of the MR-13 claimed that another difference between the two was the MR-13 goal of a socialist revolution which conflicted with the FAR goal of a national democratic revolution followed by a socialist revolution. (On the goals of the MR-13 see "El Guerrillero," supplement to *Revolución Socialista,* 12 September 1967.) According to Dones, however, "Che" Guevara and the OLAS conference had "raised the banner of socialism over the entire continent" and this point of contention was no longer a factor separating the guerrillas. (*World Outlook,* 1 March 1968.) The MR-13 has consistently denounced any policy of "peaceful coexistence," or any effort to advance the revolutionary cause by nonviolent means.

In a joint communique signed after the death of "Che" Guevara (dated October 1967, but not released until early 1968), César Montes and Marco Antonio Yon Sosa stated:

The death of Major Guevara, as we understand it, is, more than an irreparable loss to the continental movement, a battle cry, a declaration of war—as he himself stated—that must be heeded by all those of us who have taken up arms and are ready to convert these battle cries into clarion calls of victory. A battle cry that obliges us to define positions, to do away with all ambiguity, all vacillation . . .

We believe that armed struggle is the only path by which to achieve the complete liberation and independence of our people, and that this armed struggle must be pursued unrelentingly, no matter what the circumstances, to its final consequences . . .

We feel that the conception of protracted war must be continental is scope. . .

We believe that the principle of proletarian internationalism is fundamental to a revolutionary. . . . The aforementioned points . . . have brought the MR-13 and the FAR closer together, and have made us see even more clearly the need for a firmer and more concrete basis for identification with and development of the revolutionary war in Guatemala. . . . (*Tricontinental,* Havana, no. 4-5, January-April 1968.)

A merger between the MR-13 and the FAR was achieved in February 1968, after the FAR break with the PGT (*Granma,* weekly English edition, 21 April).

**Publication.** The organ of the MR-13 is the irregular, clandestine *Revolución Socialista.*

# GUYANA

The People's Progressive Party (PPP) of Guyana was founded in 1950. Although it is not nominally a communist party, its leadership adheres to Marxism-Leninism, and the party's domestic policy and international alignment indicate communist orientation.

The PPP is legal, and from 1957 to 1964 it was the governing party in former British Guiana. In the elections of 7 December 1964 the PPP obtained 45.8 per cent of the total vote, which gave it 45.3 per cent of the seats in Parliament. The two major opposition parties, the socialist People's National Congress (PNC) and the conservative United Force (UF), obtained 40.5 per cent and 12.4 per cent of the vote, respectively, and 41.5 and 13.2 per cent of the seats in Parliament. L. F. S. Burnham, leader of the PNC, was called upon to form a coalition government with the support of the UF.

The PPP's principal source of support is racially determined. Just over 50 per cent of Guyana's population of 662,000 (estimated, July 1966) is East Indian, and this group has traditionally supported the party. Since the East Indian population is increasing more rapidly than the Negro population (which traditionally supports the PNC), the PPP may win more votes and an absolute majority in the next elections, due by March 1969 and scheduled for October 1968.

**Organization and Leadership.** The leadership of the PPP was elected at the party's Fourteenth Congress on 26–27 August 1967 and consists of Leader Cheddi Jagan, Chairman Cedric V. Nunes, First Vice-Chairman H. J. M. Hubbard, Second Vice-Chairman Ranji Chandisingh, Secretary-General Janet Jagan (Cheddi Jagan's wife), Treasurer Ramkarran, Assistant Secretary Charles R. Jacob Jr., and Organizing Secretary E. M. G. Wilson. In addition, the following were elected to the party's General Council: Ashton Chase, Derek Jagan, Fenton Ramsahoye, Balchand Persaud, Vincent Teekah, Ivan Remington, Mooner Khan, M. Zaheerudeen, Edgar Ambrose, Kamal Harrylall, Bhola Persaud, Joseph Ally, and Janki Persaud. Following the congress, the General Council elected to the Executive Committee Fenton Ramsahoye, Derek Jagan, Mooner Khan, Vincent Teekah, and Balchand Persaud. The General Council also elected Ashton Chase as Deputy Leader and Vincent Teekah as editor of the PPP's monthly organ *Thunder*. The Deputy Leader and other party officers serve on the Executive Committee.

The PPP has its own youth and women's sections, the Progressive Youth Organization (PYO) and the Women's Progressive Organization (WPO). At its Fourteenth Congress the PPP further consolidated the move initiated a year earlier (*YICA* 1966 p. 228) to reorganize the women's and youth sections of the party in order to "bring about better coordination between these sections and ensure that all women and youth are completely integrated within the party's structure....All members of the youth and women's sections will be first of all party members" (*Thunder,* September 1967). The congress further decided to create "associate members between the ages of 11 to 15 years who will be known as 'Pioneers' " (*Thunder,* September 1967).

**Domestic Policy and Activities.** The Fourteenth Congress resulted in the elimination of nearly all moderates from the top posts and General Council of the party. Altogether, a third of the leadership was replaced. Rudy Luck, former Vice-Chairman was not even reelected to the General Council. Other prominent moderates ousted from the General Council included leaders of the East Indian religious communities, Reepudaman Persaud of the Hindu Maha Sabha and Yacoob and Zaman Ally of the Moslem United Sad'r Anjuman. A number of moderates, including Ashton Chase, Fenton Ramsahoye, Rudy Luck, and Reepudaman Persaud, showed their disapproval by absenting themselves from Parliament for two weeks following the congress, returning only after Jagan had reappointed Chase as Deputy Leader of the PPP.

Faced with an imminent general election, the PPP's Leader, Cheddi Jagan, published a declaration prior to the party congress stating: "Inevitably, the national and class struggle is sharpening. Our Congress must carefully work out the positions we must take ideologically, organizationally, etc., to lead this struggle" (*Thunder,* August 1967). Jagan's report to the congress emphasized that

> . . . unity of the working class regardless of race is vital. If we are to go forward, the party must have the backing of the working class, the peasantry and the intelligentsia not of one race, but of all races. . . . It is necessary for the Guyanese people, like other peoples in the other poor third-world countries, to realize that the cause of our poverty is national oppression by imperialism. We need to develop among the masses, our supporters and nonsupporters alike, fuller understanding that it is necessary to have a Marxist, and not a racist, approach to our problems, to fight for a genuine democracy and an anti-imperialist program based on the public ownership of the commanding heights of the economy. (*Thunder,* September 1967.)

Jagan's report, which insisted that the party should "concentrate on quality" rather than quantity and "on building the well-disciplined party," one which should "constantly promote into leading positions comrades armed with the ideology of Marxism-Leninism" (*Thunder,* September 1967), appeared to run counter to resolutions proposed by the party's Greenwich Park Group. The resolutions read: "A) To consider and take positive action in seeking to bring about a Coalition between the major parties, PPP and PNC, in any future government. B) To press the electorate in thinking in such directions by means of public meetings. C) To make unity of the working people an issue at the election campaign, which could only come about through a coalition of the PPP and PNC." (*Thunder,* August 1967.) The Greenwich Park Group's resolutions were referred to the General Council for further examination.

With regard to the party's domestic program, the Fourteenth Congress reiterated its concern with the issues of nationalization (in 1966 the PPP's Thirteenth Congress had resolved that "all capital resources and industries be nationalized by the government") and specified that the party should "take all constitutional steps to have expatriates replaced by Guyanese in all imperialist industries, and in particular in the sugar and bauxite industries, the ultimate objective being the nationalization of the said industries as soon as this may be practicable" (*Thunder,* August 1967; *NYT,* 30 August 1967).

The possibility that the PPP will use violence to achieve its ends is not excluded. The party accepted a place on the Committee to Aid National Liberation Movements, set up in Havana by the Tri-Continental Conference (January 1966), and has declared that the "national-liberation struggle" is now entering a new stage (*IB,* nos. 74–77, July 20, 1966). In 1967 the PPP was represented at the Havana Conference of the Latin American Solidarity Organization (OLAS) by Lall Bahadur, the party's permanent representative in Cuba. In his speech to the conference Lall Bahadur voiced the party's "solidarity with all peoples in arms" (OLAS Conference Documents).

The PPP's domestic activity is to a degree delineated by Cheddi Jagan's official position as Leader of the Opposition. During 1967 one of the primary domestic concerns of the party was that of "exposing" the fact that "the Government had already, secretly, and without informing the Elections Commission, set up the machinery to rig the next election" (*Thunder,* June 1967). In this connection the PPP came out in strong opposition to the enactment of the National Registration Act.

Another area of concern for the party was that of opposing the government's proposals for compulsory arbitration in labor disputes, which the PPP claimed would "take away the workers' hard-won right to strike . . . emasculate the trade unions, and leave the workers without their most vital weapons in the struggle against capitalism and oppression" (*Thunder,* May 1967). The PPP's role in organized labor is, however, handicapped by the party's failure to win over any significant segment. The PPP-controlled Guyana Agricultural Workers' Union has not succeeded in achieving significant influence.

**International Views and Policies.** In matters pertaining to communist affairs, the PPP continued to adhere to a policy of nonalignment with regard to the Sino-Soviet dispute and Castroism. Prior to the party's Fourteenth Congress Balchand Persaud wrote, in an article entitled "The Task Ahead" (*Thunder,* August 1967), that "on issues like the ideological differences among socialist countries we must be able to study these developments. We must not openly take any particular line but must study each side's point of view and apply whatever strategy and tactics that can be applied in our situation."

On other international issues Persaud stressed that the PPP should

> . . . organize to win constant international working-class support and to join in solidarity with all progressive forces throughout the world struggling against imperialism.
>
> On the international scene we must be able to keep our members and supporters informed of what political and economic developments are taking place in the Socialist, capitalist, and Third World countries.
>
> We must keep our contacts in all progressive movements throughout the world and keep those organizations informed of what is taking place in our country . . . .
>
> We must more resolutely carry out our anti-imperialist policy. (*Thunder,* August 1967.)

With regard to the Vietnam war, the PPP continued to express its solidarity with the National Liberation Front and North Vietnam. On 8–16 July the PPP organized countrywide protests "on US aggression in Vietnam" (*Thunder,* July 1967).

During the Middle East crisis the PPP accused the Israelis of having been "driven into a chauvinistic, militaristic fervor, and become the blind tool of imperialism in subjugating the Arab masses" (*Thunder,* July 1967).

Following the death of Ernesto "Che" Guevara in Bolivia, the PPP referred to him as a "symbol of revolutionary struggle" and commented on the "deep, genuine sorrow for the loss of a man respected and loved far and wide for his courageous life and supreme dedication to the liberation of the suffering millions of Latin America" (*Thunder,* October 1967).

In pursuance with its policy of nonalignment with regard to communist affairs, the PPP's commemoration of the Fiftieth Anniversary of the Bolshevik Revolution, which included a special issue of *Thunder* (October 1967), was of a historical nature. The party made no reference during the year to developments in China.

Members of the PPP who traveled outside Guyana included Cheddi Jagan, who attended the Fiftieth Anniversary celebrations in the Soviet Union and also visited England and certain unspecified Eastern European countries; C. V. Nunes, who left "for abroad" in February (he is believed to have visited Eastern Europe); and Lilian Branco, who represented the WPO in Moscow during the celebrations of the International Women's Day, 8 March.

**Publications.** The PPP publishes a daily, *Mirror,* and a monthly, *Thunder.*

# HAITI

The Communist Party of Haiti (Parti Communiste d'Haiti) was first founded in 1930, but it in effect succumbed the following year when its leaders Max Hudicourt and Jacques Roumain were forced to flee the country. Roumain later died in Mexico, but Hudicourt returned to Haiti in 1946 to lead the Popular Socialist Party (Parti Socialiste Populaire; PSP), established in that year. The effective political life of the PSP ended in 1947 after the assassination of Hudicourt. A second self-styled Communist Party of Haiti was formed in 1946 under the leadership of an Episcopal clergyman, Félix d'Orleans Juste Constant. Denied the support of the international communist movement (which the PSP obtained), this new communist party dissolved itself in 1947 after a complete failure in the elections of 1946. All political parties in Haiti were proscribed by law in 1949; no communist party has been legal since. (Robert J. Alexander, *Communism in Latin America*, New Brunswick, N. J.: Rutgers University Press, 1957, pp. 296-298.)

In November 1954 a new communist party called the People's National Liberation Party (Parti Populaire de Libération Nationale; PPLN) was formed and began a clandestine existence. The PPLN broke up in July 1965, reappearing in 1966 as the Party of the Union of Haitian Democrats (Parti d'Union de Démocrates Haitiens; PUDH or PUDHA, or in Creole, Pati Union Demokrat Ayisiin; PUDA) (*Guardian*, New York, 4 May 1968). A second, more vigorous, and, until recently, less radical party, the pro-Soviet People's Party of Unity or Popular Entente Party (Parti d'Entente Populaire; PEP), was formed in 1959. Both parties are Castroist, the PEP having adopted "violent armed revolution" as its official policy line in May 1967. A third, small, pro-Chinese communist party, the Haitian Workers' Party (Parti de Travailleurs Haitien; PTH), was founded in 1966. The PTH is an offshoot of the PPLN, formed from a group called "The Snipers" who left the PPLN in 1964 (*ibid.*, 27 April 1968); it has support among Haitian students living in exile in Europe (see *YICA*, 1966, p. 230).

Under the present dictatorial regime of Dr. François Duvalier, all communists are persecuted rigorously by the government. Hence much of their activity is carried on outside Haiti among exiles in the USA, Europe, and Latin America. The clandestine nature of the parties and the political environment in Haiti make an estimate of their strength difficult. The combined strength of the PEP and the PUDA probably does not exceed 500 active members. The communist movement is weak and divided and has shown no better aptitude for survival in the repressive political atmosphere of Haiti than have other anti-Duvalier groups.

**Organization and Leadership.** The founder and Secretary-General of the PEP, Jacques Stéphen Alexis, died in prison in Haiti. Surviving leaders of the party include Central Committee members Jacques Dorcilien, Saintigène Guillaume, and Manuel Soundiata. Other prominent members, whose positions in the party are not known, include Pierre Jean Claude, Jal Deshomme, Charles Dumont, Edris Saint-Amand, Roger Tilandingue, and Lionel Vieux.

Less is known about the leadership of the PUDA. Roger Gaillard was Secretary-General of the PPLN. Other possible leaders of the movement are Max Chancy, André Feray (also known as Farray, Ferre, and perhaps Faroul), and Gerard Jean Pierre. (The spelling of the names of the members is seldom consistent in print; variations are common.)

The PEP and the PPLN joined together with the National League of Patriotic Resistance Committees (Ligue Nationale des Comités de Résistance Patriotique; LNCRP) in 1963 to form the United Democratic Front of National Liberation (Front Démocratique Unifié de Libération Nationale; FDULN). This front was dealt heavy blows by the government, and was further weakened by internal discord, so that by 1965 it was largely ineffective. According to 1967 reports, however, it has now been reconstituted. The reorganized front includes the PEP and the PUDA, and it has appeared in news media under several names. (*WMR,* February 1968 calls it the United Party of Haitian Democrats, but also refers to it under the old name FDULN. Havana Radio calls it the United Democratic Liberation Front of Haiti.) In any case, it appears to be no more effective than its predecessors. Haitian communists admit the shortcomings and failures of the old FDULN, and declare that it was unsuccessful "precisely because [itⱼ failed to adapt more active forms of struggle called for by the times" and was "unable to rally the masses and become a real united front of all sections of the population anxious for national liberation." They now look forward to recreating the national front "on the basis of the FDULN program and within the framework of an armed organization, which, in present-day conditions, can more effectively than any other rally patriots not belonging to the vanguard." They feel that the Duvalier regime is "abhorred by all the people" and is the "product and instrument of semifeudal and semicolonial domination," and that, therefore, "the masses can be drawn into the revolutionary and national movement through an armed struggle against the dictatorship." They envision the front as "the broadest form of a people's union, including patriots of all trends and having an unequivocal revolutionary line and clearly defined leadership," presumably communist. (*WMR,* February 1968.)

One reason why the Front has failed to attract the cooperation of many noncommunist nationalist and liberation groups is its insistence that it must struggle not only for national liberation, but also against imperialism (i.e., the USA). This identification with the Cuban communist line holds little interest for many noncommunist Haitians.

Adding to the confusion, another liberation front apparently exists in the Dominican Republic. This "Haitian Liberation Front in Exile" (Front Haitien de Libération dans l'Exile; FHALE), calls for all Marxist-Leninists to unite into a single party for the overthrow of the Haitian government. Although FHALE may have connections in and the support of Cuba, there is no indication that it is part of the PEP, the PUDA, or their liberation front organization. Statements from FHALE are signed by its Secretary-General, Joseph Debat.

In line with the policy of armed revolutionary struggle, there are indications that the front and the parties are attempting to develop armed forces for guerrilla warfare. The *Guardian* (4 May 1968) has mentioned the existence of the "Haitian Revolutionary Armed Forces" (FARH), and the PEP, wishing to convert "every Haitian into a slave of the new independence," has called for the immediate establishment of guerrilla centers in Haiti, for armed action in the cities, and for the creation of an "Army of People's Unity," (*Voix du Peuple,* Port au Prince, 8 August).

The Haitian student movement is represented by the National Union of Haitian Students (Union Nationale des Etudiants Haitiens; UNEH) which is a member of the Soviet-dominated International Union of Students (IUS). UNEH members are probably drawn largely from among Haitian students living in exile. The connections of the UNEH with either the PEP or the PUDA are unclear. There also exists a Federation of Haitian Students in Europe (Fédération des Etudiants Haitiens en Europe; FEHE) which publishes a monthly organ, *La Tribune des Etudiants.* The FEHE has been critical of the PEP, tending to be even more radically revolutionary, and it may be most closely allied with the pro-Chinese PTH. It is also possible that the FEHE is one of the constituents of the UNEH.

**Domestic Views and Policies—PEP and PUDA.** The PEP and the PUDA claim to be united in struggle against "terror, poverty, and Yankee Imperialism". Both parties take a realistic view of the geographical, political, cultural, and economic obstacles that confront them in their struggle. The members are under constant and dire threat from the regime; the people of Haiti are desperately poor, 85 per cent illiterate, and for the most part politically inert; and the party members within Haiti are effectively separated from their comrades in exile as well as from direct aid from Cuba and the communist world. (Florient Marrat, "Problems in the Creation of the Haitian Armed Forces of National Liberation," as read over Havana Radio, 13 May 1968.)

Any attempt to distinguish between the PEP and the PUDA is made difficult by the lack of concrete information on either party. Support for the PEP seems to be concentrated mainly among the urban population in and around the capital, Port-au-Prince, while the PUDA claims organization in eight of Haiti's nine provinces. The PEP at a Central Committee meeting in May 1967 accepted the thesis that immediate armed revolution was the only means to achieve victory, and thus was late in moving into the Castro camp, while the PUDA has advocated a consistent line of militant armed struggle on the Castro model since 1963, when it was still identified as the PPLN. Even though the PEP appears to be the more dynamic party at present, it does not have the power to dominate the Haitian communist movement and admits that it must seek PUDA cooperation in organizing the rural masses. Personal rivalry among the leaders of the parties may be a major factor preventing amalgamation.

Since adopting the Cuban line in May the PEP has in some ways become the more militant. For example, it not only sees enemies in Duvalier's "semifeudal and dictatorial regime" and in "US imperialism," but also treats with hostility any noncommunist opposition groups not amenable to communist manipulation. In spite of the PEP's recognition of the necessity for a united front, a great deal of its time and effort is spent in destroying the atmosphere in which an effective united front could be expected to emerge. PEP propaganda continually identifies the "traditional opposition" with US imperialism and the CIA, belittles its efforts at revolution, and openly states that in the event the noncommunist opposition should launch an attack on the regime, the PEP would infiltrate its ranks and struggle to obtain control, at the same time continuing its own independent activities.

In comparison, the PUDA appears to be indulgent. It feels that the communist movement should not become isolated from the bourgeoisie, since it could benefit from their aid, although it should not rely on their participation in a revolution. In the unlikely event of the establishment of a successful noncommunist opposition movement, according to the PUDA the communists should then infiltrate it and take over from within.

Since its conversion to the cause of armed insurrection, the PEP has found that "the objective conditions for revolution in Haiti have matured to a greater extent, perhaps, than in any other country of Latin America," because "the crisis of the regime is affecting both exploited and exploiters." The whole program of the party is built on this premise and is concentrated almost solely on the development of armed struggle in Haiti:

> Recognizing the need for armed struggle as the decisive form for revolutionary action in Haiti, our Party [advances] the following guiding principle: "Greater political work among the masses must be the pivot of the preparations for armed struggle." We must make the most of negligible opportunities for legal work, carry on underground activity as effectively as possible, do everything to strengthen our Party and awaken the political consciousness of as many people as possible. At the same time we clearly realize, that only dynamic actions can overcome the fear and the inertia. (*WMR*, February 1968.)

The party recognizes the need for a people's army, and puts much stock in the development of a "fugitive movement" as in Napoleonic times when slaves fled into the hills, descending into the villages at night to sow the seeds of revolt among their fellows, thus laying the basis for Haitian independence.

The PUDA's position on the problem of armed struggle has been publicized through Cuban broadcasts in Creole to Haiti. It reportedly holds that "armed struggle on a continental scale is the fundamental, essential, and primary means of struggle the people should adopt," adding:

> The armed struggle will be a long, harsh, and bloody one, but the revolutionaries and the Haitian people have no alternative. We do not underestimate other forms of struggle, but we consider them as secondary, as subordinate to the armed struggle. The role of all other forms of struggle is to strengthen the armed struggle of national liberation. (Broadcast, Radio Havana, 2 September.)

Both parties agree that armed struggle in Haiti will depend upon the success of their work in the countryside and that revolution must begin in the sanctuary of rural Haiti, spreading to the towns and cities as it gathers momentum. Statements about the prospects for recruitment among the peasantry appear to be more moderate in the case of the PUDA, perhaps because of its longer experience and because of the setbacks it has suffered in this field. The PUDA appears, however, to be making an attempt to contact and reconstitute its clandestine apparatus in the rural areas, much of which was cast adrift in the party's time of troubles in 1965.

**International Views and Policies—PEP and PUDA.** As small and relatively insignificant communist parties, totally absorbed in the struggle for survival in their own country, neither the PEP nor the PUDA is particularly active in international communist affairs. Both have strong views of the USA, as was evident at the OLAS conference in Havana, July-August 1967, when a joint delegation of the two parties declared:

> Among all Latin American countries, ours is one of the most exposed to immediate menaces of intervention on the part of US imperialism. The enemy, imbued with the strong tensions of the social contradictions, intends to prevent at all costs a possible popular rebellion to maintain the worm-eaten feudal-imperialist regime. For this reason, and contrary to the past, US propaganda in Haiti has been intensified. . . . CIA agents and the members of the Peace Corps [have] dressed up as protestant preachers, and [these] double agents have repeatedly infiltrated themselves in the ranks of the army and of the tontons macoutes [Duvalier's internal security force], as well as in the high levels of the public administration. (Conference documents.)

Identification of the Duvalier regime as an adjunct of US imperialism is a persistent theme of PEP and PUDA propaganda, employed in part to discredit noncommunist revolutionary groups with large numbers of adherents among Haitian exiles in the United States and in part to buttress their Marxist-Leninist image of the US as an imperialist power. The parties do at times, however, recongize temporary "internal disagreements" between the US and the Duvalier regime thus tacitly admitting that Duvalier might not be a mere tool of the US and supported by US policy and action.

Both PEP and PUDA receive encouragement and support from Cuba. The Cubans favor the amalgamation of the two parties, but since this is apparently impossible at present, they are impartial in their treatment of each. Cuba broadcasts regularly to Haiti in Creole and French, and a good deal of PEP and PUDA propaganda material is included in the transmissions. The Cubans applaud the revolutionary approach of the Haitian parties, but call for greater unity of effort, more attention to organization, and a rise in ideological standards. Naturally, Havana seeks revolutionary action along Castroist lines following the example of the guerrilla movements in Venezuela and Bolivia. Cuba advocates joint action between the revolutionaries of Haiti and the Dominican Republic for the liberation of all Hispaniola.

As noted above, the PEP and the PUDA sent a joint delegation to the first Latin American Solidarity Organization (OLAS) conference in July and August. André Feray of PUDA was its president; other members included Gerard Jean Pierre, also of PUDA, and Pierre Jean Claude and Charles Dumont of PEP. At OLAS the two parties put on a strong show of unity which belied the actual cleavages between them. The delegation's speech accented this unity:

> The two important revolutionary organizations of the country, the Popular Entente Party (PEP) and the Party of the Union of Haitian Democrats (PUDA), have agreed on the essential questions of national liberation. Aiming to gather and unite all anti-imperialist sectors, they have reorganized the unified [United] Democratic Front and are busy constituting its bases while working on the intensification of the mass struggle among the farmers, workers, women, youth and other democratic sectors.
>
> The Popular Entente Party and the PUDA have reached an agreement on the tactics to be used by the Haitian Revolution. According to these two parties, in the present conditions of our country, armed struggle constitutes the only road, the basic road which will lead to the triumph of the revolution. And they are making all possible efforts to create the political and technical conditions necessary to wage this struggle. (Conference documents.)

In response to the situation in Haiti and to the PEP-PUDA call to revolution, the OLAS conference passed a resolution on Haiti which recognized Haiti as having the most "dramatic situation" of any Latin American nation: "Yankee imperialism has taken over the resources of the country and, instead of exploiting them thoroughly, it is keeping them as a reserve"—an act responsible for the "abysmal poverty in which the country has sunk." The resolution condemned "the barbarous, regressive dictatorship of Duvalier and his cynical master US imperialism," echoing the PEP-PUDA line, and then went on to "alert the revolutionary organizations of the world and international public opinion to the danger of imminent Yankee military intervention in Haiti . . . " (*Ibid.*)

The PEP also sent a delegation to the fiftieth anniversary celebrations of the October Revolution in the USSR in November, but the names of members were not revealed.

**Publications and Radio.** The PEP claims regular publication of its clandestine organ, the biweekly newspaper *La Voix du Peuple,* printed in or near Port-au-Prince. PUDA has no known publication unless the irregular clandestine journal *Haiti Demain* is still being published jointly in Haiti with the PEP. The PTH may publish a journal, *La Manchette,* in Brussels; it receives space at times in the pro-Chinese Belgian Communist Party organ *La Voix de Peuple* (not to be confused with the PEP paper). The PEP-PUDA-sponsored Liberation Front may still publish the old FDULN organ *Ralliement.*

No Haitian communist party controls radio facilities, but Havana Radio broadcasts 14 hours per week to Haiti: 11 hours in Creole, three in French. These broadcasts are controlled by the Cubans, but carry news of PEP-PUDA activities and generally support both parties.

# HONDURAS

The Communist Party of Honduras (Partido Comunista de Honduras; PCH) was founded in 1927. It disintegrated in 1932 and did not reemerge on the political scene until 1954. In 1961 a minority claiming to be "scientifically Marxist" split off to become the Honduran Revolutionary Party (Partido Revolucionario Hondureño; PRH). Another group of PCH members, who were expelled from the party in January 1967 as "deviationists," continue to operate under the name of Partido Comunista de Honduras. Allied to the PCH and PRH is an independent pro-Castro terrorist organization, the Francisco Morazan Movement (Movimiento Francisco Morazan; MFM).

Estimates of membership vary from 500 to 1,500 for the PCH and from 150 to 300 each for the PRH and the MFM. The population of Honduras is 2,445,000 (estimated 1967).

Although not formally outlawed, communist parties are implicitly proscribed under the 1957 contitution. The communist groups, which though independent follow relatively similar policies, have never achieved any prominence in Honduran politics. Communist influence is to a large extent limited to young persons and a trade-union minority in Tegucigalpa.

**Organization and Leadership.** The prominent representatives of the communist groups appear to be: PCH—Dionisio Ramos Bejarano (First Secretary), Mario Soza Navarro (whose pseudonym is Ricardo Moncada Zavala), Alonso Muñoz; PCH (Dissidents)—Mario Morales, Jorge Díaz, and Carlos Aldana; PRH—Juan Pablo Cardona Padilla, Idelfonso Orellana Bueso, and Inés Alonso Trochez; MFM—Mariano Aquila and Renaldo Oyela. Very little is known of the organizational structure of any of the parties, apart from the names of "leaders," which are, furthermore, often pseudonyms.

The Communist Youth of Honduras (Juventud Comunista de Honduras) is affiliated to the PCH, but is not under the party's complete control. It often follows an independent line, and has its principal ally in the MFM. Communist-oriented university students are organized in the University Reform Front (Frente de Reforma Universitaria; FRU), which is one of the two important student groups in the University of Honduras, and in a minor organization called Socialist Youth (Juventud Socialista).

Communist influence in Honduran trade unions is limited to the small 'Committee of Revolutionary Workers (Comité de Trabajadores Revolucionarios; CTR). Other trade unions are influenced by the policy of the fruit-growing companies, which send promising young men for training in American Federation of Labor schools in the USA. Significantly, in the summer of 1965, when an attempt to instigate a general strike resulted in the arrest of prominent trade-union leaders accused of communism, it was the intervention of American trade unions that obtained their release.

**Domestic Views and Policies.** In January 1967 the PCH held its Second National Conference, which marked "the beginning of a new phase" in the party's internal affairs. The group of "opportunistic, dogmatic and sectarian deviationists," headed by Mario Morales, Jorge Díaz and Carlos Aldana, was expelled from the party, and resolutions were adopted "corresponding to its true concerns, interests, and needs, charting the right way toward the solution of the party's principal problems with regard to leading the struggle of the Honduran people against the ruling national oligarchy and North American imperialism enthroned in our midst." In July 1967, a "General Assembly of PCH Militants Residing in a Foreign Country" approved a resolution "concerning the struggle between divergent groups within the party." The resolution emphatically rejected the attempts of the "small group led by comrades Morales, Díaz, and Aldana to justify the errors and outrages they have committed by invoking alleged 'adventurous, pro-Chinese, and Fidelist deviations' in the policies of our grouping." It also condemned the resolutions adopted by the "so-called Fourth Enlarged Plenum," convened in early 1967 by Morales, Díaz, and Aldana "behind the party's back," and branded the plenum meeting as a "sabotage against the unity of the party." In the same resolution, the PCH militants in exile reaffirmed their "conscientious and unwavering adherence" to the decisions and resolutions of the Second National Conference of the PCH and called for "reorganizing existing party cells and electing a Politburo on the basis of the principles of democratic centralism in order to assist from the outside the integral development of our party inside the country." They also urged the Central Committee, as reconstructed by the Second National Conference, to "carry out in full the resolutions adopted at the conference, establish closer relations with party militants in exile, and arrange for the early convocation of the First Extraordinary Congress of the PCH." (*Abril* August 1967.)

The dissidents led by Morales, Díaz, and Aldana persist in calling themselves members of the PCH and in claiming that they "fight in its ranks, perform political work within its organization, and develop as new men in the course of its activities and in the process of accomplishing its tasks." They do qualify, though, their contention of fighting in the party's ranks: "Fighting is not simply belonging to a cell and attending its weekly meetings for the purpose of hearing reports on the comrades' activities. . . . Our presence in the party must be characterized by our actions, by what we do politically, by the various forms of energetic activity aimed at developing the party, improving it as a communist organization, bringing it closer to the people and awakening the socialist, democratic, and communist conscience of the working masses." (*Trabajo,* 15 July 1968.)

The PCH's domestic policy was outlined by Mario Soza Navarro (writing under pseudonym of "R. Moncada") in an article in *Pravda* (28 February 1966). Stressing the need for a large united front, which would include liberal elements, Soza Navarro stated that one of the difficulties for the communist movement was that the "alliance between peasants and proletariat" was still "rather fragile." He went on to state, however, that the PCH had to fight not only the "imperialist" policy of the Latin American governments, but also the "leftist" bourgeoisie, which contested the communists' claim to leadership of the "national liberation movement." In another article (*WMR,* September 1967), Soza Navarro warned against an additional factor in the ideological struggle within the national liberation movement" in Latin America. "Mention should be made," he wrote, "of the concepts of Mao Tse-tung and his group. While their organized influence on our continent is negligible, their 'theories' are a factor with which we have to reckon." Concerning the means to be used by the PCH for achieving political power Soza Navarro had this to say in the same article: "It is for the parties of the countries concerned to determine whether the objective and subjective conditions are ripe for armed insurrection and to decide on the means of winning political power. In the case of Honduras we believe that the main contradiction of our society will in all likelihood be resolved through force."

The PRH went even farther in this respect when its representatives in Havana stated in a letter to Fidel Castro that conditions for guerrilla warfare already existed in Honduras. The following is the full text of the letter:

> Commander Fidel Castro Ruz, Prime Minister of the Cuban Revolutionary Government:
>
> We have heard and analyzed your speech of March 13, 1967, which represents for us an enlightening lesson, a lesson that places Latin American realities in the right perspective and at the same time charts the true road toward the achievement of revolutionary power, namely armed struggle. We believe that in almost all Latin American countries, and especially in ours, conditions for the development of armed struggle exist, a position we have alway maintained throughout the short time that our young party has been in existence.
>
> In view of that, and guided by the example of the glorious Cuban Revolution, we take the liberty of expressing to you our firm revolutionary resolve and our fullest solidarity with the well-defined proposals and views which you have consistently expounded throughout your entire revolutionary career. Representatives of the Honduras Revolutionary Party (PRH) in Havana; Havana, 17 March 1967 (*Granma,* 31 March).

Whether the PCH and the PRH have actually translated their words into deeds with regard to armed insurrection is not clear. Both communist and government sources are silent about reported guerrilla activity in certain parts of Honduras. According to a dispatch from Tegucigalpa sent in October 1967 by the correspondent of the San Salvador daily *El Diario de Hoy,* Honduran officials are keeping "strict silence about the guerrilla groups which are operating in the Colon Mountains, in the department by the same name, (near the Nicaraguan border), and in some places in western Honduras."

The only significant communist activities on the domestic scene during 1967 seem to have been the FRU's participation in two protest demonstrations. The one was a public rally held jointly with noncommunist members of the Honduran University Student Federation in Las Merced Park in Tegucigalpa on 25 May to protest against the alleged "wave of crimes and assassinations" in the country which culminated in the murder of a leftist student. The other was a violent demonstration aimed at disrupting the official visit in Honduras of Nicaraguan President Anastasio Somoza on 19 October.

**International Views and Activities.** The PCH is a pro-Soviet party which has endorsed Moscow's call for a world meeting of communist parties. The party also apparently maintains ties with Castro, and, together with the PRH and the MRM, took part in the Latin American Solidarity Organization conference held in Havana on 31 July-10 August.

The PCH's stand on major questions of communist ideology and its alignment within the international communist movement are best illustrated by the following excerpts from the previously quoted article by Mario Soza Navarro in the *World Marxist Review*:

> To regard the Leninist thesis on peaceful coexistence . . . as being contrary to the interests of the national liberation movements of our peoples is not only erroneous, it is also dangerous. In practice it engenders a tendency to split the social base of the broad peace movement and to oppose the interests of the national liberation movement to the general interests of humanity. . . . As conscious processes come to play an increasingly important part in the revolutionary activity of the masses, the greater will be the impact of the experience of the October Revolution which not only blazed the trail to the building of socialism but also created the material base for many new exploits by man, the base of the future world revolution. . . . We consider that solidarity is part of proletarian internationalism, that the documents of the 1957 and 1960 Moscow meetings contain norms obligatory for all contingents of the proletariat, battling on different fronts, which make up the great communist family.

As regards to problems in the Latin American communist movement, the position of the PCH is defined in the following excerpt from the May 1967 statement by the Fifth Meeting of the Communist Parties of Mexico, Central America, and Panama, of which the Communist Party of Honduras is a signatory: ". . . Our parties consider that the necessary efforts must be made to strengthen the militant unity of all the parties and the alliance with the Cuban revolution. In this respect they confirm the conclusions of previous meetings regarding defense of the unity of every party and the fight against factionalism, the right of every party to elaborate its own political line in keeping with the specific conditions of the country." (*IB*, no. 102, 1967).

A more pronounced pro-Castro stand was adopted by the chairman of the Honduran delegation to the first OLAS conference, Hector Martínez, who represented the PRH. In his address to the conference he said: "The Honduran delegation, faithful interpreter of the feelings and thoughts of its people, considers that armed struggle is the only way out. . . . We Honduran revolutionaries approve and support the valiant position of the Cuban Revolution, which, a few miles from the brutal monster, stands like a giant, showing us the way to liberation with its glorious example." (Conference Documents).

The other members of the delegation were José Pereda and Raul Castillo of the PCH and Ivan del Puente, leader of the MFM.

**Publications** The PCH puts out clandestinely the following publications: *Abril,* the theoretical review of the Central Committee; *Trabajo* the organ of the Central Committee; *Unidad,* the central propaganda organ; and *Voz Popular,* a weekly information sheet.

It seems that following the Second National Conference of the PCH, *Trabajo* has become the mouthpiece of the Morales-Díaz-Aldana dissident group, although it calls itself the "Organ of the Central Committee of the Honduran Communist Party." In the past *Trabajo* was known as the PCH's "Organ of Internal Propaganda."

# HUNGARY

The Hungarian Socialist Workers' Party (HSWP; Magyar Szocialista Munkáspárt) was founded on 24 November 1918 as the Hungarian Communist Party. On 13 June 1948, following the elimination of the Smallholders' Party in 1947 and the absorption of the Social Democrats, the party was reorganized as the Hungarian Workers' Party. After the October 1956 rebellion the party was again reorganized, this time as the Hungarian Socialist Workers' Party. The HSWP has been the ruling party since 1948. It is the dominant factor in the Patriotic People's Front, a political alliance of the Communists and representatives of various social strata in Hungary. As of November 1966 HSWP membership was 584,849 out of a total population of 10,179,000 (estimated 1966).

The Ninth Congress of the HSWP, held in November 1966, eliminated the category of candidate membership in the party, and as a result, during the first two months of 1967, party organizations screened 37,957 candidate members. The report on this activity in the party monthly *Pártélet* showed that 35,264 persons were found to be eligible for full membership, 2,508 had their membership cancelled or were expelled, 154 resigned or died, and 41 could not be screened for various reasons. The majority of those rejected were denied membership for reasons of "immaturity," or "failure to fulfill obligations and tasks set by the party." The screening of candidates initially slowed down the party growth rate, but by June the number of new members paralleled 1966 figures.

An analysis of the composition of the new membership showed that 50.4 per cent of all new members admitted to the party since November 1966 were workers (November 1966 figures state that working-class members account for 42.5 per cent of total membership), 9 per cent of all new members were workers in collectives (November 1966 figures show 6 per cent of the total membership from the collective farms), 26 per cent of the new party membership was female (compared with 22.9 per cent in November 1966), 82 per cent of the members were under the age of 39 (presently 54 per cent of total membership is under 39), and 32.1 per cent of the members were under 26. With regard to education, the ratio of new members who have not finished eighth grade dropped significantly (from 18 per cent a year ago to 15.8 per cent), and the ratio of those holding a high school or university degree rose (from 34.7 per cent a year ago to 37.5 per cent).

The HSWP expressed its satisfaction with the results of this campaign, noting that the fears of some party members that the abolition of candidate membership would lower the quality of the party ranks had proved unjustified and that the only area in which much work still remained was in recruiting party members from the agricultural collectives (*Pártélet*, June 1967; *Népszabadság*, 6 June 1967).

**Organization and Leadership.** The party has a pyramidical organization, with a base of 18,000 primary party cells headed by a 101-member Central Committee. The Central Committee in turn is directed by an 11-member Politburo and a five-man Secretariat elected from the Central Committee. The entire organization is headed by First Secretary János Kádár. The Secretariat consists of György Aczél (who replaced Lajos Cseterki in April 1967), Béla Biszku, Zoltán Komocsin, Rezsö Nyers, and Arpád Pullai. The Politburo is composed of Antal Apró, Béla Biszku, Lajos Fehér, Jenö Fock, Sándor Gáspár, János Kádár, Gyula Kállai, Zoltán Komocsin, Dezsö Nemes, Rezsö Nyers, and István Szirmai. The candidate members of the Politburo are Miklós Ajtai, Lajos Czinege, Pál Ilku, and Károly Németh.

A 12 April plenum of the Central Committee, held in response to the results of the March elections to the National Assembly and the exigencies of the imminent economic reform, effected a reshuffling of a number of party posts. The plenum accepted the resignation of Central Committee Secretary Lajos Cseterki to allow him to fill his newly elected post of Secretary of the Presidential

Council, replacing him with former First Deputy Minister of Education György Aczél. The April plenum also replaced Chief of the Economic Department of the Central Committee Imre Párdi, who had been elected President of the Planning Bureau, with József Bálint, and it elected Sándor Lakos to the permanent Agitprop Committee of the Central Committee. These party changes, however, were only a reflection of the more important reshuffling of government posts following the National Assembly election. (See below.)

The party also increased its attention in 1967 to the need for higher-quality party cadres and leaders in state organs and mass organizations. A Politburo resolution of 6 April on the work of party schools in the coming school year emphasized measures to train better cadres and propagandists and changed the curriculum to meet present-day challenges. The resolution also effected a transfer of the bulk of nonparty participants to courses sponsored by the mass organizations, particularly the trade unions—a move which alleviated the overcrowded conditions in the party schools and allowed the HSWP to train its cadres more efficiently.

The moral quality of party members was also under close scrutiny, especially after the disclosures at the Ninth Party Congress concerning widespread corruption in party ranks and a directive by the congress for a "more resolute stand" against "manifestations of petty-bourgeois morals, outlook, and way of life, against lack of modesty, greed, the obtaining and acceptance of unjustified advantages, and immoral life." The most widely publicized disciplinary measure for moral deviation in 1967 was the expulsion from the HSWP in May 1967 of György Varga, who had been dismissed in April from his post as president of the People's Control Committee for "misuse of authority," and specifically misappropriation of funds. Other expulsions of party members were reported for violations of the principle of "democratic centralism." Although the HSWP affirmed on numerous occasions that conditions now exist for expression of divergent views and that debate is necessary for the proper functioning of party organs, it warned that there is a time and place for this before resolutions are passed at party meetings; after a resolution has been adopted, the party members must "represent, defend, and carry through party policy" (Jenö Faragó, "Upholding the Banner for Communism," *Népszabadság*, 21 February 1967). The strain on party unity became acute following the Middle East crisis of June 1967, when the Hungarian party and regime's strong support of the Arab states was contested by elements within the party. An editorial in *Népszabadság* on 9 August again defined unequivocally the party policy:

> Incertitude and doubt breed passivity. Everyone's duty deriving from his party membership is to speak his mind. . . . On the other hand, it is unthinkable that the opinion of any party member should deliberately oppose party opinion, and that if a member's opinion differed from those of other members, he would express it not anywhere, but where conditions exist for discussion and clarifying such questions.

The editorial was followed by a *Népszabadság* interview with Laszlo Pataki, First Secretary of the Györ-Sopron county party committee, in relation to the expulsion of 68 party members in his county for breach of discipline in expressing their views outside the confines of party meetings. Pataki spoke of issues which revealed a strain on party unity and discipline—various measures affecting prices and wages in Hungary's new economic mechanism; the issue of the HSWP's role and tasks, particularly the party policy of "alliance"; foreign policy, notably the Middle East crisis; and problems pertaining to the international workers' movement, particularly Chinese events. He stressed that although these matters might be "complicated," they do not justify, as in the case of the Middle East crisis, the refraining of some Communists from acting "against nationalist, anti-Semitic, or even philo-Semitic views revived by the situation." He further noted that the Communists who failed the party during the Middle East crisis had also wavered in their conviction of principle and confidence in the party during the Cuban crisis, and he attributed this to indolence in the HSWP ranks. Pataki also criticized party cells and individuals for willfully distorting party directives to suit their own ends and nurturing personal antagonisms in party work.

The prestige of the HSWP was strengthened, however, by reports that the noted Marxist philosopher György Lukács, who had broken with the party 10 years earlier, had renewed his membership. The Italian Communist organ *L'Unità* reported that in his letter to the HSWP Politburo Lukács declared himself in "full agreement with the political line of the party and that he was adopting it freely and voluntarily"* (*L'Unità*, 9 September 1967).

**Domestic Policies.** In 1966 the Ninth Congress of the HSWP had declared in a resolution that for the next four years the "historic task" of the Hungarian people and party was to be the "complete building of socialism." In this connection the major challenge in 1967 was preparation for enacting a new economic mechanism aimed at raising the standard of living of the Hungarian people. Also of importance in 1967 were the elections to the National Assembly, held on 19 March and conducted under a new electoral law. The new law, approved by the party's Ninth Congress, was hailed as a step toward the "further democratization" of Hungarian life. These and other issues, particularly in the sphere of international events were discussed in Central Committee plenary sessions on 15 February, 12 April, 23 June, and 23-24 November.

**National Assembly Elections.** In the first election held under a new electoral law, the Hungarian people went to the polls to elect deputies to the National Assembly and to seats in the local councils. The new law provided for direct nomination and election of National Assembly deputies in 249 individual constituencies, instead of voting lists for 20 multiseat constituencies. Also, for the first time more than one candidate was to be nominated by each constituency for each seat.

The results of the nomination meetings for the March elections to the National Assembly and local councils did not live up to the expectations engendered by the new election law. Alternate candidates were nominated in only nine parliamentary constituencies and in about 686 (or less than 1 per cent) of the local council seats. In no case was more than one alternate proposed. Central Committee First Secretary János Kádár expressed disappointment over the nomination proceedings and stated his hope that next time there would be more second and third choices. He also admitted that the fact that all candidates stood for election on the program of the Patriotic People's Front and accepted nomination on this basis was not received everywhere with unanimous approval. He conceded: "It is an old problem of ours that we have to be the government party and the opposition at the same time. This is a difficult craft which we still have to learn." He went on to declare, however, that the Hungarian system is more democratic than a multiparty system, because it is "people's power."

The election resulted in a 99 per cent vote in favor of the HSWP National Assembly candidates. In the local council elections, of the 686 constituencies where two or more candidates were on the ballot, 120 alternate candidates were elected and six constitutencies ran runoff elections. The Western press, such as *Le Monde* (21 March), noted further inadequacies to the election system; for those seats which offered alternate candidates on the ballot the party candidate was named first, and if the voter did not indicate his preference by crossing out the other name, the vote automatically went to the first name on the ballot. Nevertheless, the new election system was a step toward the strengthening of the role of the Parliament in Hungarian life. It meant greater independence and added responsibility for members of the Parliament. The stress had been on choosing the best-qualified deputies, on putting "the right man on the right job," and the importance of the government changes following the election was concrete evidence of this endeavor.

At the first session of the new Hungarian Parliament on 14 April 1967, Pál Losonczi, former Minister of Agriculture, was elected President of the Presidential Council, replacing István Dobi, who was released from the post at his own request owing to ill health and advanced age. Imre Dimény was elected Losonczi's successor as Minister of Agriculture. The Secretary of the Presidential Council, Károly Kiss, was replaced by Lajos Cseterki, and former Premier Gyula Kállai was elected President of the new Parliament.

The House then elected the new government. Jenö Fock, a Deputy Premier since September 1961,

---

*György Lukács, in an article in the French Marxist quarterly *L'Homme et la Société* (July-September 1967) and reprinted in the Czech language periodical *Plamen* (October 1967), and later in an interview with the editors of *Népszabadság* (24 December 1967), publicly expressed his views that the situation of Marxism today is very favorable and that there is an urgent need for a "renaissance" of Marxism. He pointed particularly to the new economic mechanism as a step "which makes the renaissance of Marxism possible and necessary, and on the other hand, the return to that which we used to call proletarian democracy in the era of Lenin." He declared that even bourgeois thinkers are turning to Marxism to solve their problems and urged that Communists take advantage of this and participate in this phenomenon.

became the new Premier of Hungary, and two new deputy premiers, Miklós Ajtai and Mátyás Timár, were chosen. The two former Deputy Premiers, Antal Apró and Lajos Fehér, were reelected.

These changes were a response to the exigencies of the economic reform. Imre Dimény, the new Minister of Agriculture, has substantially greater economic expertise than did his predecessor. The new Premier and the four Deputy Premiers are all economic experts: Jenö Fock had earlier held leading posts in the Ministry of Metallurgy and Engineering and then in the National Council of Trade Unions; Antal Apró, an expert on COMECON; Lajos Fehér, agricultural expert; Miklós Ajtai, former Chairman of the State Planning Office; Mátyás Timár, former Minister of Finance.

**Economic Reform**. 1967 was also the year of the final preparations for the enactment of the new economic mechanism. The Hungarian economic reform is in many respects similar to the Czechoslovak reform put into effect a year earlier; it is designed to extend more independence to individual economic units while continuing to maintain a centralized planned economy; economic enterprises will be subject to centrally prescribed long-term tasks but will make their own short-range plans on the basis of market requirements. The process of rationalizing the economy will make widespread use of individual responsibility and material incentives.

The reform was first initiated at the December 1964 Central Committee plenum by Rezsö Nyers, who in December 1966 became the youngest member of the Politburo. The May 1966 party plenum approved directives for laying the groundwork for the transition of the nation's economy. These directives were carefully implemented in 1967, and the 23-24 November Central Committee plenum, satisfied that the directives had been properly fulfilled, decided to put the new economic mechanism into force on schedule, on 1 January 1968.

In connection with the reform there were a number of ministerial reorganizations in 1967, including the Ministry of Domestic Trade, Ministry of Posts and Communication, the Ministry of Agriculture and Food (newly established), the Ministry of Heavy Industry and Light Industry, and Construction and Urban Development. In addition, new agencies were set up in answer to the needs of the new mechanism. At the beginning of 1967 a National Market Institute was established to supply information to industrial and trade enterprises. On 1 July, a Price Control Board was set up by government decree to replace the National Planning Board; revenue boards under the Ministry of Finance replaced the Central Revenue Office, and an Economic Research Institute was established.

In addition to organizational measures, a wide range of resolutions and decrees were passed by the Hungarian leadership, including measures on price policy, investment policy, employment, wages and social allocations, and foreign-trade problems. A new labor code was published in October 1967. The November plenum of the Central Committee approved the most important indices of the 1968 national economic plan. In consideration of the fact that 1968, the third year of the Five Year Plan and the first of the new economic mechanism, is to be a year of "transition," the indices of growth were modest: national income is to increase 5 to 6 per cent, industrial production 6 to 7 per cent, agricultural production 3 to 4 per cent, per capita real income 3 to 4 per cent, real wages 1.5 to 2 per cent, and consumption 5 to 6 per cent. Most important, the publication of the indices was followed in December by a Ministerial Council decree on the readjustment of prices. There is to be a small increase in consumer prices (1 to 2 per cent), and three price categories are to be delineated: 50 per cent of prices are to be fixed, 27 per cent fixed at a maximum, and 23 per cent free prices. The Hungarian regime has thus planned that wages and general income are to rise considerably faster than prices and has put fixed prices on basic consumer commodities in an attempt to prevent inflation.

In implementing the new economic mechanism the Hungarian party and government have had to deal with scepticism and opposition to the reform on the part of various segments of the population. According to Premier Jenö Fock, agreement on the reform had been reached at the highest level following "resolute educational work, passionate but constructive debates, and clashes of opinion which were often acute." However, he stated that in the lower organs there continues to be a great deal of argument and an exaggeration of the inevitable difficulties in implementing the reform (*Társadalmi Szemle*, November 1967).

On the eve of transition to the new mechanism Fock reviewed the status of the reform and urged "complete optimism" for the future. "We possess the political power necessary for its implementation," he said, pointing to the fact that in 1967 the national income and volume of industrial production had increased faster than anticipated, and that the prime costs of production, the earnings of enterprises, and the earnings of the working people had developed better than planned. In response to "the anxious and sometimes alarmed gossip that 'everything will be more expensive under the new mechanism, and this can end only in inflation'," he pointed to the regulation of consumer prices, saying that the price reform would be attained gradually over a period of 10 to 15 years and would be under close scrutiny of the party and government. His answer to the fear of unemployment was that the growth of production will require greater numbers of workers. In reply to the fear that social allowances will be sacrificed to increased enterprise profits, he declared that they will be protected by the local party organizations, the trade-union organizations, and directly by the people themselves, and that the labor code guarantees that social achievements will not be jeopardized and that there is a possibility of a reduction in the working hours. Despite his optimism, Fock did not preclude the appearance of undesirable "negative manifestations." He reported, however, that "safety devices" have been worked into the mechanism at the present time which, if retained, would damage the reform in the long run but are absolutely necessary in launching it. Thus he did not preclude the possibility of direct intervention by the state to regulate the reform by administrative fiat.

The HSWP was also faced with the task of presenting the reform as a socialist reform, in answer to critics who saw "creeping capitalism" in the principles of the new mechanism. Party propaganda on the reform was discussed extensively by János Kádár at the November plenum of the Central Committee. He urged that the HSWP must stress that "profitable production," the basic aim of the reform, does not contradict socialism: "This is a Marxist and socialist reform of our economic guidance. It has socialist goals—to develop socialist production, increase consumption, to raise regularly the working people's living standard, and finally to promote the completion of the building of a socialist society."

Kádár also dealt with the international aspects of the reform. He stressed that trade with capitalist countries is to be based solely on mutual profitability, but that economic ties with the socialist states were of a "superior nature," and that the principles of the economic reform must be presented in COMECON and taken into consideration by other member countries.

Concerning the effect that the economic reform would have on other spheres of Hungarian activity, Kádár remained silent on possible changes in political and social life but called instead for an analysis of the situation in science and culture, which would then be placed on the agenda in about a year and a half (a government resolution on the application of the principles of the new economic mechanism to the cultural sphere was issued in August 1967). Finally, he qualified the goal of the economic reform:

> We used to say that our main goal was a regular increase in the working people's standard of living. This is true, but it does not suffice to proclaim this goal alone. We must strengthen the attitude that the most important thing is to defend our socialist achievements, to ensure the future of our people, to complete the buildup of the socialist society, and to raise the living standard of the working people in the meantime. If our socialist achievements, our system, the security of our people, and their future are endangered, this has a priority to which everything else must be subordinated. In public opinion the interests of the socialist fatherland must rank first and for this we must give everything, even our lives if necessary. (*Társadalmi Szemle,* no. 12, December 1967.)

**Policy of "Alliance."** To fulfill the tasks of "building socialism" in Hungary and to meet the current challenges, particularly that of the successful application of the new economic mechanism, the party has recognized the need for "socialist national cohesion" and has thus reaffirmed and called for the future strengthening of its policy of "alliance"—the rallying of all social strata of the Hungarian population and the cooperation of Communists and nonparty people.

On the basis of a report from the Central Office of Statistics, "Social Stratification in Hungary," which asserted that social stratification is based on the individual's position in the social division of labor and not his relation to the means of production, the Hungarian leadership concluded that there is no longer any class or stratum in Hungary whose interests are opposed to socialism (the study was published in *Statisztikai Időszaki Közlemények,* vol. 90, 1966). The party thus proceeded with confidence in approving the new electoral law and the consequent strengthening of state organs (Tibor Pethö, "New Election System to be Introduced," *Hungarian Review,* February 1967).

The HSWP paid special attention to the Patriotic People's Front, the organizational embodiment of the ideas of the alliance policy, and reflections of the policy were also evident in party attitudes toward mass organizations, the work of rural associations, and state organs.

The party Politburo resolution of 9 May 1967 outlined policy on "the status and development of party cadre work and supervision of state personnel practices," noting the achievements in cadre work in the objective selection of higher-quality personnel. However, deficiencies were also noted, particularly overemphasis on professional skills to the neglect of political considerations, discrimination against or favoritism to nonparty people, overcentralization of discretionary rights, and finally, the weakest area, the training of new staff. Nepotism, discrimination against women and young people, opportunism, and embezzlement were some of the serious shortcomings of the leading officials. The resolution outlined the basic policies of the party concerning cadre work: all key positions are to be filled with leaders willing and able to carry out the tasks which reflect the interests and policies of the party and the working classes, and the principle that nonparty members should have equal opportunity to fill any position (excepting party functions) if they qualify in every respect must be retained. Political, technical, and leadership capabilities are not separable in evaluating candidates for leading positions, and none should have priority over the others. The major leadership positions should continue to come under the jurisdiction of the party organizations.

The Ninth Congress had called for the strengthening of the role of state organs and mass organizations and their responsibility in making and executing practical decisions: "The organizational independence of the mass organizations is promoted by the realization of the principle that Party decisions concern only the members of the Party and the organizations of the Communist Youth League." Congresses were held in most of the major mass organizations at the beginning of 1967—the National Council of the Patriotic People's Front in January, the First Congress of Agricultural Cooperatives on 20-22 April, the Twenty-First Congress of the Hungarian Trade Unions on 3-6 May, and the Seventh Congress of the Communist Youth League on 29 June-1 July. János Kádár hailed the fact that at its January 1967 session the National Council of the Patriotic People's Front had unanimously endorsed the basic theses of the Ninth Party Congress, the program of the complete construction of a socialist society, and called on the entire nation in its election appeal to translate it into reality (election rally speech, 22 February 1967). The resolution of the Agricultural Cooperatives Congress noted that the congresses are to be a political forum whereby peasants could more actively participate in the party and the formulation of state agrarian policy.

At the Trade Union congress in May Kádár reiterated the principle that party decisions on trade questions are mandatory only for party members working in the trade union, and not for the independently elected trade union bodies. Finally, at the Youth League congress he again praised the fact that the earlier congresses of mass organizations had approved Party policy "not only in words, but also in deeds." "I think we can say," he continued, "that the youth congress which is now being held is also going to prove that the Communist Youth League and its membership, and the young people under their guidance, consider the policy of the Party as their own and are ready to work for its realization."

The decentralization of economic enterprises and the stress on professionalism in economic leaders is also related to the party policy of alliance. "It is one of the important and essential features in the introduction of the reform," declared Kádár at the November Central Committee plenum, "that the relationship between the Central Committee and the government on one side and the 200,000 to 300,000 leaders on the other is such that we work with them on the basis of mutual confidence." On numerous occasions the HSWP repeated that there was to be no discrimination against nonparty people in economic enterprises and that ability was to be the major criterion.

The policy of alliance, however, has not met with full understanding and approval in all sectors of Hungarian life, and the HSWP has had to devote considerable attention to explaining the policies and controlling their application. Kádár dealt with this problem extensively in a speech to a mass meeting at the Ganz-Mavag plant on 28 July, declaring that the policy must be understood as serving the attainment of the revolutionary aims of the working class and deriving from the knowledge that neither party members nor the members of the Communist Youth League alone can build a socialist society. "It is an essential feature of our domestic policy that the criterion by which we judge people is what and how much they contribute to building a socialist society," he said, and then specified:

> Those who attack the system, have been, are, and will be appropriately punished. Of course, this is no longer such an important question as it was 10 years ago, but it is nevertheless a question of principle. On the other hand, those who adapt themselves to our system, respect its laws, and work decently are entitled to the greatest respect and esteem; they are not bothered by anybody, but are judged on the basis of their work and attitude. This is the policy we will continue to pursue in the future (*Magyar Nemzet*, 30 July 1967).

Scepticism about the policy of alliance was also evident in the party ranks, as members displayed fears that party membership was beginning to lack meaning and that the HSWP was losing its "vanguard" position in society. Party leaders responded with a sharp denial of such possibilities and the adoption of various measures to "protect" party members. Although the mass organizations and state organs were assured of increased independence, the HSWP put greater emphasis on and provided more intense training for party propagandists and urged them to participate actively in the mass organizations and assume responsibility for the activity of the organization's members. The Politburo resolution on cadre policy in state organs included numerous qualifications in assigning government posts to nonparty people in order to assure the ideological soundness of the candidates. The reorganization of party schools, by which nonparty people were to be trained by mass organizations, was also a measure to differentiate between party and nonparty people.

The economic reform especially aggravated the issue of the role of the party and Communists in Hungarian society. The HSWP consistently emphasized that the economic reform was the task of the entire population, since everyone was to benefit from it. It also emphasized, however, that party members were to be given special positions and special tasks. At the November plenum János Kádár stressed that

> . . . the fact that the Party must be at the head in this instance, that it must lead this trend and also direct it. Speaking about the Party, I mean both the Central Committee and our Party organizations and members. But I must immediately add as the second condition that we should adopt a method of Party guidance which our Party has already worked out and introduced in practice with fair success: that is that there should be on the upper, the middle, and the lower level a correct division of labor between the Party leadership, the state leadership, and the social leadership, that is, trade unions, youth league, and other mass organizations.

Kádár then expressed his expectation that centrally issued party, trade-union, and government decisions would be identical and warned that "it should not happen that the state organ says 'do this' and the Party organ says 'not so,' while the trade union keeps waiting to see which viewpoint will be stronger."

An editorial in *Népszabadság* on 26 November repeated the need for Communist leadership, concluding: "And, just as the Party had led in the solution to the tasks mentioned and the preparation of the reform, the Communists should have the leading role in the realization of the reform." Finally, Jenö Fock, on the eve of the transition to the new economic mechanism, again stressed the duty of Communists:

> The shaping of the conscience, subjective factors, and most of all the steadfastness of communists play a very large role in the success of the reform. . . . What we ask and expect of communists is to work and combine and fuse universal and local interests at all times. As against temporary local interest producing only short-lived results, they should represent and if need be protect the interests of the people's economy and long-term interests, because it is in this way that they serve the real interests of our people as a whole, including those of the smaller local communities. (*Népszabadság*, 31 December 1967.)

**Ideology.** The HSWP has also faced important challenges in the ideological sphere. The relationship of vested interests to "consciousness" (or the interaction of economy and ideology) and of socialist patriotism to internationalism were two outstanding ideological questions on which party propaganda concentrated.

The new economic mechanism, with its emphasis on material profit incentive, has given rise to widespread scepticism, especially among the old Communists, concerning the depth of "socialist awareness" or "socialist consciousness" of the workers today. During 1967 many party officials expounded on the need for stronger Marxist-Leninist propaganda. István Ballo, Deputy Director of the Propaganda Department of the Central Committee, in discussing the curriculum for party schools, declared:

> The reform is not a panacea. In addition to economic issues, the problems of the development and unity of the communist movement, of the international situation and other important issues of our political ideological activities will play important parts in our curriculum. A special place will be reserved for the discussion of the half century of Soviet history, the outstanding achievements of the fraternal Soviet people, and the strengthening of the ties of friendship between our two nations. (István Ballo, "The Growing Role of Marxist-Leninist Propaganda," *Pártélet,* October 1967.)

An article on "the stratification of social consciousness" by Béla Köpeczi, former head of the Central Committee Cultural Department, revealed that despite the "great social changes" in Hungary, there was no "automatic transformation" in the people's way of thought. "Socialism," Köpeczi said, "needs to be consciously disseminated," and he emphasized the role of the intelligentsia as "the most conscious disseminators of socialism." (*Magyar Nemzet,* 27 August 1967.)

In an article in *Népszabadság* on 28 November Jenö Faragó argued that history has shown that a higher living standard and the prosperity of "democracy" have a stimulating and fruitful effect on the development of socialist awareness. He declared that today, with the new system of economic management, the meaning of socialist awareness has changed; instead of a "spectacular declaration of one's political faith and slogans, we must propel the economy forward by raising its technical and technological standard and by more effectiveness and a better profit making capacity." He concluded: "In the final analysis, everything that strengthens our socialist awareness does not stem from abstract ideals, but from the material and spiritual products of the socialist society in our country and, of course, also outside of it." (Jenö Faragó, "Socialist Awareness Today," *Népszabadság* 28 November 1967.)*

The topic of "socialist patriotism" has been avidly debated in the Hungarian press since the publication of ideological guidelines accepted by the March 1965 Central Committee plenum. The Ninth Party Congress resolution defined socialist patriotism as pride not only in the Hungarian past, but specifically in the socialist achievements of Hungarian society, and also pride in cooperation and solidarity with the international working class and communist and workers' parties. However, the term remains ambiguous, and the debates in the press showed that the party had not succeeded in eliminating deep-seated nationalism, racism, irredentism, and anti-Soviet feelings on the one hand, and the phenomena of national apathy and "cosmopolitanism" on the other. Nor was the issue resolved in 1967; rather the prolonged debates and international events exacerbated the problem.

One of the focal points of the debate during the year was the publication of the results of a questionnaire concerning nationalism to 125 secondary school students. The survey showed, among other things, that 83 per cent of the students were categorically proud to be Hungarians and that 45 per cent stated that marriage with a gypsy or a Negro would be out of the question (18 per cent gave conditional answers). Evaluating the results, Vilmos Faragó, who conducted the survey, deplored the evidence of prejudice, hatred, nationalism, and defenseless patriotism ("A Small Country," *Élet és Irodalom,* 7 January 1967). Strong reactions to Faragó's evaluation appeared in the Hungarian press, and József Darvas, for example, declared that the country is in greater danger from national apathy

---

*At the November Central Committee plenum János Kádár took a strong position on the subject of socialist consciousness in declaring that economic achievements are to be subordinated to the goals of building socialism. He noted, however, that, "fortunately," the Fiftieth Anniversary of the Soviet Socialist Revolution strengthened socialist consciousness in Hungary "better than eight decisions could do."

and cosmopolitanism than it is from nationalism (József Darvas, "A Small Country" *Élet és Irodalom,* 7 January 1967). The debate was extended to the question of the relationship of nationalism to internationalism. Thus those who claimed that the strengthening of the international workers' movement was the prerequisite for the strengthening of each socialist country were countered by those who argued that internationalism can be built only on the basis of nationalism.

The Middle East crisis of the summer of 1967 added fuel to the debates on nationalist and racist sentiments, particulary anti-Semitism, in Hungary. It appeared that the few Hungarians supporting the government's anti-Israel position did so for anti-Semitic reasons, just as a large number sided with Israel because of sympathy for the Jews. Hungarian leaders, faced with charges of anti-Semitism for their support of the Arab cause, emphasized that the party policy was based on principle and called on the population not to fall prey to emotions. Gyula Kállai, in a speech to Szombathely city party activists on 15 June, also referred to Hungarians who during the six-day war had hoped for an Israeli victory "simply because [the Israelis] acted in alliance with American imperialism against the progressive forces of the world." Kállai attempted to discredit these people by charging that they were in reality anti-Semites and that after the end of the war they once again resorted to anti-Semitic incitement in Hungary.

**Relations with Soviet Union.** In his 22 February election-rally speech János Kádár spoke at length on the principles of Hungarian foreign policy, stressing that the consistency of Hungarian policy is its greatest strength and that its alliances and commitments have been and will continue to be faithfully fulfilled:

> We must not for a moment lose sight of the fact that the complexity of the given situation will not alter the constant and enduring trends of world politics. Our foreign policy rests on lasting and principled foundations. We cannot improvise, we cannot pursue temporary and hesitant concepts of *ad hoc* expediency, because our task is permanent. We defend our national independence, our country's sovereignty, our people's socialist achievements, and peace. Accordingly, we militantly oppose imperialist aggression of all sorts, and we are fighting shoulder to shoulder with all who—beyond our frontiers and throughout the world—are fighting for peace, independence, and friendship and equality for the peoples.

Hungary thus continued its close friendship and collaboration with the Soviet government and party. A visit by a high-level Hungarian party delegation to Moscow on 25 February-1 March was followed by a joint communique affirming a "complete unanimity of views." On 7 September Hungary and the Soviet Union signed a new 20-year treaty of friendship, cooperation, and mutual assistance in Budapest, a full five months before the expiration of the existing treaty. At the friendship rally following the signing of the treaty Leonid Brezhnev hailed HSWP leader János Kádár as "a true patriot of his country, consistent internationalist, and prominent leader of the world communist movement." Kádár, in turn, emphasized the "complete identity of views between the USSR and the Hungarian People's Republic in every basic international question" and called for the "eternal friendship" of the two countries. He also stressed the fact that alliance with the Soviet Union guarantees national independence and integrity, in answer to what he termed "the state of fright" of smaller socialist and nonsocialist countries who believe that trade and cooperation with the Soviet Union leads to a state of dependence.

Hungarian friendship with the Soviet Union is reinforced by close economic ties, which, the two countries stress, are based on mutual advantage. Hungarian-Soviet trade presently amounts to 1 billion rubles, or one-third of Hungary's foreign trade. Sixty-eight per cent of the imports from the Soviet Union are raw materials; 28 per cent are machines and installations for industrial and agricultural production. Conversely, 50 per cent of Hungarian exports to the Soviet Union are machines and installations. By 1970 trade is to be increased by 68 to 70 per cent over 1965, and the Soviet Union's share in total Hungarian foreign trade is to be around 40 or 42 per cent (Antal Apró, "On Hungarian-Soviet Economic Relations," *Társadalmi Szemle,* November 1967; J. Biró, "The Development of Hungarian-Soviet Economic Relationships, *Közgazdasági Szemle,* November 1967). According to a Hungarian-Soviet trade agreement signed in December 1967, a 20 per cent increase in the exchange of goods is scheduled for 1968.

**Relations with Other Socialist States.** Friendship and cooperation with other socialist states was also a consistent line in Hungarian foreign policy. The report and resolution of the Ninth Congress had emphasized the party's determination to work for more extensive relations with every socialist country, including China and Albania. Any concrete efforts that Hungary might have made toward the improvement of relations with China and Albania brought no public response from the two countries, and Hungary continued to condemn the Chinese cultural revolution and Chinese calumnies against the Soviet Union. Contacts with other socialist states were greatly intensified. Bilateral talks with party and state leaders were followed by communiques affirming identity of views in most cases, and in all cases reaffirming friendship between the respective parties and countries.

Among the most important meetings were a visit of Yugoslav President Tito to Budapest on 2-4 February for an "unofficial friendly visit"; an "unofficial friendly visit" by First Secretary of the Polish United Workers' Party Wladyslaw Gomulka and Central Committee Politburo member and Premier Józef Cyrankiewicz on 8-9 March; the visit of a party and state delegation from East Germany, headed by Walter Ulbricht on 16-18 May, during which Hungary and the German Democratic Republic signed their first 20-year treaty of friendship, cooperation, and mutual assistance; and a visit of a delegation of the Rumanian Communist Party, headed by Secretary-General Nicolae Ceauşescu, on 24-26 May 1967. An especially cordial visit was paid by János Kádár to Czechoslovakia on 10-14 October, after which he reported that the relations between the two countries are an example of the kind of relations that should exist between two socialist states, and expressed satisfaction with the truly "Leninist" nationalities policy adopted by the Czechoslovak regime toward the Hungarian minority living in Czechoslovakia (Radio Budapest, 14 October 1967).

Hungary also continued to proclaim support of the Warsaw Pact as necessary for the maintenance of Hungary's defense. Hungarian Foreign Minister János Péter participated in the Warsaw Pact Foreign Ministers' meeting held in Warsaw on 8-10 February to discuss European security, and in the 19-21 December meeting to discuss the Middle East situation. In June Hungary was host to joint-operational-staff exercises of the Hungarian, Czechoslovak, and Soviet armies. In view of Hungary's needs deriving from the new economic mechanism, Hungary was among the strongest advocates for increased and more efficient economic cooperation among the socialist states through COMECON and was host to the twenty-first session of COMECON on 12-14 December.

**Relations with Western Europe.** With respect to Western Europe, the Hungarian party and government were primarily concerned with the problem of European security. Hungary has been a firm advocate of a conference of European states to deal with European security and was one of the nine supporters of a proposal to put the problem of European security before the United Nations in January. Hungary has also advocated a meeting of European parliamentary deputies. The central problem for Europe, in Hungary's view, is that of Germany. "Without an acceptable settlement of this matter," János Kádár declared in February, "European security is inconceivable" (election-rally speech, 22 February 1967).

The Hungarian regime responded to the West German initiative to establish diplomatic relations by receiving German Foreign Ministry Secretary Rolf Lahr in January and beginning negotiations to establish diplomatic relations with the Bonn government. However, after the Rumanian agreement to establish diplomatic relations with Bonn, the severely negative reaction on the part of the East German regime, and the Warsaw Pact Foreign Ministers' meeting, these negotiations were held in abeyance. In his election-rally speech on 22 February Kádár did not discount the possibility of establishing relations, but he reiterated the conditons to be fulfilled by Bonn to lend credibility to its verbal intentions: (1) the acceptance by West Germany of "European realities"—that is, recognition of present borders and recognition of the German Democratic Republic; (2) rejection of "revanchist endeavors" and renunciation of the desire to possess nuclear weapons; and (3) abrogation of claims to sole representation of the German people. At the end of February János Kádár held talks with Soviet party Secretary-General Leonid Brezhnev on European security; on 8 March Polish party leaders, who were the strongest supporters of the East German stand on the establishing of relations with Bonn, arrived in Budapest on an "unofficial friendly visit." By signing a friendship treaty with the German Democratic Republic in May, Hungary renounced any possibility of establishing ties with Bonn at that time.

**Program for Danubian Cooperation.** Another effort to create a better political atmosphere in Europe was the Hungarian program for Danubian cooperation. "Our aim is to make the Danubian Basin—which was the source of countless conflicts in the past—a factor in European peace and security," declared János Kádár at the 22 February election rally in Budapest. The Hungarian view is that the Danube Basin (which includes Austria, Czechoslovakia, Hungary, Yugoslavia, Rumania, and Bulgaria), in its position on the border between the two social systems, is particularly significant in efforts to promote "European security." Tibor Pethö, chief editor of the Patriotic People's Front newspaper *Magyar Nemzet,* pointed to a more limited configuration of the Danube Valley (Hungary, Czechoslovakia, Austria, and Yugoslavia) as offering the best objective opportunity for the "peaceful coexistence of countries belonging to different economic systems" because military and economic confrontations are least sharp there. He stressed that Danube cooperation is not viewed as any form of federalism or confederalism, but is to be achieved through better bilateral relations (Tibor Pethö, "Modern Forms of Cooperation," *The New Hungarian Quarterly,* Autumn 1967).

**Relations with "Third-World" States.** In accordance with "the principles of Hungarian foreign policy and the essence of its social system," Hungary continued to give support and extend aid to those peoples "fighting for national liberation," to newly liberated peoples, and those fighting "imperialist aggression." Most conspicuous was the demonstration of solidarity with the people of Vietnam in their struggle against "US aggression." In addition to numerous solidarity meetings and declarations of support, the Hungarian government increased its aid to the government of the Democratic Republic of Vietnam.

On 20 March Hungarian and North Vietnamese representatives signed a plan in Hanoi for cultural cooperation and mutual aid for 1967, and in October representatives of both countries held talks and signed an agreement in Budapest on trade for 1968—nonrepayable Hungarian assistance to the Vietnamese people—and on training Vietnamese experts in Hungary. By the terms of the agreement, Hungary will supply Vietnam with various machines, repair equipment, agricultural equipment, and some consumer goods.

The Hungarian reaction to the Middle East events of summer 1967 was to express solidarity with the Arab states as the "victims of Israeli aggression backed by imperialism." The Hungarian assessment of the situation was in line with that of the other socialist states—that the United States and Britain (and West Germany, according to the resolution of the HSWP Central Committee plenum of 23 June) had incited Israel to start the war in order to "change the course of events in the Middle East." The Hungarian leadership propagandized the events as having a close connection with the "imperialist machinations" in Vietnam, Greece, Indonesia, and Santo Domingo.

On 9 June János Kádár and Jenö Fock represented Hungary at the Moscow meeting of eight European communist countries to discuss the Middle East crisis and signed the declaration condemning Israel as an aggressor (the declaration was signed by all countries except Rumania; see *Documents*), and on 12 June Hungary followed the lead of the Soviet Union, Czechoslovakia, and Bulgaria in breaking diplomatic relations with Israel. A Central Committee plenum meeting on 23 June heard a report by Zoltán Komocsin, Central Committee Secretary in charge of international affairs, on the Middle East situation and other topical international problems and unanimously passed a resolution reiterating the basic line of the Hungarian stand on the Middle East events. A further development of the Hungarian and socialist states' attitude to the Middle East situation was expressed at the Budapest meeting of socialist state leaders (minus Rumania) on 11-12 July. The communique of the meeting called for the withdrawal of Israeli troops behind the 5 June border and pledged further political and economic aid to the Arab states. In August a Hungarian economic delegation visited the United Arab Republic and Syria to discuss further expansion of economic and technical cooperation (*Magyar Nemzet,* 16 August 1967).

As prospects for an early solution to the crisis waned, Hungary began to stress the need for peace through negotiations and to show anxiety about the unity of the Arab forces and their "realistic" attitude toward negotiations. Hungary strongly endorsed the mediation efforts of Yugoslav president Tito and welcomed Tito's visit to the Middle East as an attempt to gather a consensus of the Arab states and arrive at a political solution to the crisis (*Magyar Nemzet,* 20 August 1967).

**The International Communist Movement.** The HSWP was a leading participant in the international communist movement both in ideological contributions and in concrete activity. Party Politburo member Gyula Kállai was the author of a pamphlet issued by Problems of Peace and Socialism Press in Prague, entitled "The Communist Movement and International Policy," which defined the "strategy of peaceful coexistence" and the relations among the communist parties. Kállai warned against "absolutizing either the peaceful way or the nonpeaceful way associated with armed struggle and civil war" in bringing about the socialist revolution and emphasized that neither way can lead to the victory of the revolution "if there is no antimonopoly alliance led by the working class. . . . This is the cardinal condition for the victory of the socialist revolution, be it effected by peaceful or nonpeaceful means."

On 17 September 1967 *Pravda* published a significant article by János Kádár, "Internationalism Today," in which he outlined in ideological terms the principles governing relations among communist parties and socialist states. Kádár took a firm stand on the subject of unity of the world communist movement and attacked—implicitly in the case of Rumania and explicitly in the case of China—any activity which hinders that unity: "The unity of the socialist countries has been damaged not by objective causes but by subjective factors, concretely—elements of national separatism and bourgeois nationalism have appeared and currently are manifested in the most serious form by the policies of Mao Tse-tung and his group."

Kádár declared that in the interests of defending the purity of Marxism-Leninism, a party cannot take a "neutral attitude to disputed questions, or refuse to participate in international contacts and exchanges of opinion, advocate its own particular interpretation of the international situation as the only revolutionary one." He also said that proclamations of internationalism must be accompanied by joint statements on concrete issues and concrete actions. Kádár stated that today, when there is no international communist center, and when each party and socialist state determines its own policies, it is even more necessary that the policies of individual parties not contradict the general interest of the international working class and the socialist states. He stated further that a policy that was not internationalist would in fact contradict the domestic interests of the party. In more specific terms, Kádár praised at length the achievement of the Soviet Union and declared the impossibility of "anti-Soviet Marxism-Leninism," "anti-Soviet internationalism," and "anti-Soviet communism."

Kádár then turned to the much-debated question of convening an international communist party meeting, which he felt was the only means of achieving unity and uprooting dissent. He declared that every party has the right not to attend such a meeting, but that every party also has the right to consult with others. The HSWP, just as it participated in the other conferences of 1967, considers it a "moral, political duty, deriving from internationalism" to attend the meeting. The purpose of the meeting, Kádár stressed, should be to achieve unity and create a stronger and broader anti-imperialist front.

Hungarian party activity in the international communist movement was characterized by continued criticism of the events in China, commemoration and participation in the celebrations for the Fiftieth Anniversary of the October Revolution, participation in international communist conferences, and increased bilateral consultations with fraternal parties. The party's position on China has been to distinguish between the Chinese people and a group of Chinese Communist Party leaders around Chairman Mao Tse-tung who are responsible for a domestic and international policy "which has nothing to do with the creative process of building a socialist state and society and which is sharply opposed in more than one respect to the principles and practice of Marxism-Leninism and proletarian internationalism" (*Társadalmi Szemle,* April 1967).

The HSWP, like the other European communist ruling parties, celebrated the October Revolution anniversary by sending a delegation, headed by János Kádár, to the Moscow festivities, and organizing celebrations at home. A Central Committee resolution of 15 February on the celebration of the Fiftieth Anniversary hailed the Soviet Union as the "paragon and mainstay of the forces struggling for human progress, democracy and socialism" and called for the intensification of propaganda on the Soviet Union and Soviet-Hungarian relations as part of the festivities. The HSWP also hailed the importance of the October Revolution to the socialist development in Hungary: "We are convinced that what we have been able to accomplish ... all serve to promote international socialism and realization of the ideas of the October Revolution" (Béla Biszku, "The October Revolution and Social Progress in Hungary," *World Marxist Review*, November 1967).

Contacts with fraternal parties were intensified during 1967. Zoltán Komocsin reported in *Népszabadság* on 24 December that representatives of the HSWP had conducted exchanges of opinion with representatives of about 50 fraternal parties during the year. Among the most important meetings were a visit by a delegation of the Communist Party of Finland headed by Politburo member Olavi Laine to Budapest on 16-25 January, and a second Finnish party delegation headed by Chairman Aarne Saarinen on 26 July-2 August; a visit to Budapest of a delegation of the Belgian Communist Party headed by Politburo member and Central Committee Secretary Albert de Coninck on 10 March; a visit of Shmuel Mikunis, Secretary-General of the Israeli Communist Party to Budapest on 17-21 April; a visit of French Communist Party officials headed by Central Committee Secretary René Piquet on 12 May; a visit of an Italian Communist Party delegation headed by Secretariat member Allessandro Natta on 24 June-1 July; a visit of a delegation of the Progressive Party of the Working People of Cyprus headed by Christos Petas on 29 June-7 July; an Iraqi Communist Party delegation headed by Nazim Ali on 7 July; a delegation of the Communist Party of Denmark headed by Chairman Knud Jespersen to Hungary on 25-31 July; a visit by Max Reimann, First Secretary of the West German Communist Party in August; a visit to Austria by an HSWP delegation headed by Central Committee Secretary Béla Biszku for talks with Austrian party leaders on 4-9 December; and a visit by French Communist Party Politburo member Raymond Guyot on 26-28 December.

The major purpose of the great majority of these interparty contacts was to debate issues in connection with the Conference of European Communist and Workers' Parties held at Karlovy Vary in April and preparations for an international communist party meeting which the CPSU was attempting to organize. Since the Ninth Party Congress in 1966, the HSWP has firmly supported the convening of both conferences. Hungary sent to the Karlovy Vary Conference a high-level delegation consisting of János Kádár, Zoltán Komocsin, Dezsö Nemes, and Frigyes Puja. In his address to the conference János Kádár repeated criticism of the "new East European policy" of the Bonn government and announced that Hungary would sign a friendship and mutual-assistance treaty with the German Democratic Republic "on the initiative of Hungary." He also spoke of the need for all communist parties to profit by the experiences of other parties, even in internal affairs, and noted without criticism the absence of some parties for "various reasons."

The HSWP was among the earliest initiators of concrete proposals for an international communist party conference, and after Hungary was designated as the host country for the consultative meeting, the party intensified its attention to this issue. The HSWP had consistently called for the conference to be convened as soon as possible, regardless of the number of parties which might absent themselves. The subject of the conference was to be the unity of the world communist movement against "imperialism." HSWP leaders expounded "liberal" views on the specific issues of the conference: it was not to condemn or ostracize any party, nor would there be any discrimination against parties not participating in the conference; it would not draw up new principles for the international communist movement to replace those in the 1957 and 1960 resolutions; it would not attempt to draw up a uniform viewpoint for all parties, but would be in the nature of "open-ended discussions," and decisions taken at the conference would not be binding on the communist parties (see Frigyes Puja, "On the International Conference of Communist and Workers' Parties," *Pártélet*, December 1967; Zoltán Komocsin, "The Budapest Meeting," *Népszabadság*, 24 December 1967, in *Documents*).

**Publications.** The daily central organ of the HSWP is *Népszabadság*. The Central Committee theoretical monthly is *Társadalmi Szemle*; the Central Committee monthly dealing with party life and organization is *Pártélet*. The Communist Youth League's publication is *Ifjú Kommunista*.

# ICELAND

The Communist Party of Iceland was formed in 1930 by the secessionist left wing of the Social Democratic Party. In 1938 the Communists absorbed a radical Social Democratic Party splinter group, and the enlarged party adopted its present name, the United Socialist Party of Iceland (USPI). The party is legal, and was represented in coalition governments from 1944-47 and from 1956-58. USPI membership is estimated at 1,000 out of Iceland's total population of 196,549, of which Reykjavik has 78,400 (estimated 1966).

The USPI contests Parliamentary elections through the People's Alliance (Althýdubandalag; AB), an electoral front formed in 1956 between the Communists, the small National Defense Party, and a group of left-wing dissidents. The latest Parliamentary elections on 11 June 1967 resulted in moderate gains for the political left in Iceland, at the expense of the conservative and centrist parties. The Alliance's share of the vote increased to 17.6 per cent from 16.0 per cent in 1963, and it gained an additional seat; it now holds 10 out of the 60 Parliamentary seats. The Social Democrats polled 15.7 per cent, as against 14.2 per cent in 1963, and increased their seats by one, to nine. The largest Icelandic party, the Independence Party (conservative), polled 37.5 per cent, as against 41.4 in 1963, and lost one of its 24 seats, while the Progressive Party (centrist) polled 28.1 per cent, down slightly from 28.2 per cent, and also lost a seat (19 to 18). Iceland is now governed by a Conservative-Social Democratic coalition.

The communists allege that the two "bourgeois" major parties are seeking to transform Iceland's multiparty system into a "bourgeois" two-party system, but they continue to exploit the rivalry between the Progressives and the Independents. Thus, while contending that the predominantly rural Progressive Party is a "bourgeois opportunist party," heavily influenced by the rightists, the USPI cooperates with the Progressive Party in joint control of the Icelandic Federation of Labor (Althýdsamband Islands; ASI), with 34,940 of Iceland's 43,140 organized workers. In the 1966 election of trade-union officers and delegates to the ASI convention, the communists lost slightly.

Hannibal Valdimarsson, who is Chairman of both the People's Alliance and the Icelandic Federation of Labor, and who professes to be a left-wing social-democrat, is increasingly often in conflict with the USPI leadership. He is reportedly determined to pull out of the AB and form his own political party, but has not yet been able to muster sufficient support to make any such move. In the 1967 elections, however, Valdimarsson, together with a minority group of adherents, defied the USPI by withdrawing from the People's Alliance list of candidates in the Reykjavik district and heading his own rival slate, still under the AB label. This move was clearly designed by Valdimarsson to test his strength among the electorate as well as vis-à-vis the USPI leadership. The results revealed Valdimarsson's influence; while the regular AB slate reflected a drop in the percentage of votes (to 13.9 per cent), support for the ticket headed by Valdimarsson (3.7 per cent) resulted in an aggregate gain for the Alliance of 1.6 per cent over 1963 and gave Valdimarsson a Parliamentary seat. Electoral officials ruled that the double slate constituted, in essence, a "voting union" between the two AB factions; thus their votes were combined in the computation of seat allotments by party, increasing the AB total seats to 10.

The USPI has for some time unsuccessfully attempted to convert the People's Alliance into a separate political party. The communist goals are, first, to block Valdimarsson's bid to secede from the AB and take with him substantial trade-union and nonaffiliated leftist support; and second, to form a counterweight to the "bloc politics" of the conservative and centrist parties.

The Chairman of the USPI is Einar Olgeirsson. The Executive Committee of the USPI Central Committee includes Ingi Helgason, Kristin Andersson, Stefan Sigfusson, and Haraldur Steinthorsson. The Central Committee includes also Kjartan Olafsson and Bovar Petursson.

**Domestic Views and Activities.** The USPI program, "Iceland's Road to Socialism," adopted in 1964 by the party's Thirteenth Congress, states that on the basis of an analysis of the specific features of Icelandic capitalism and the experience of the world communist movement, the peaceful way to socialism is possible in Iceland. The program calls for a "struggle to safeguard national independence, against Iceland's participation in the economic blocs of the capitalist countries and the attempts to establish foreign monopoly domination in the national economy, for ending the US occupation and for an independent foreign policy" (*WMR*, February 1965).

The party continues to stress its opposition to the government's economic stabilization program and, specifically, to a comprehensive wage freeze proposed by the government to bolster Iceland's faltering economy. Through the Icelandic Federation of Labor, the party is able to bring considerable pressure to bear on the government in tariff negotiations, and in 1967 succeeded not only in blocking passage of an austerity bill, but even won wage increases for some sectors of industry. The devaluation of the Icelandic kronur in the fall, following the British move, has led to aggravated differences between the two sides of the political spectrum.

Factionalism continues to plague the USPI; while the pro-Moscow group maintains control of the party leadership, reformist elements appear to be gaining strength. Pro-Peking sentiment within the party, though weak, contributes further to factional strife.

**International Views and Activities.** In foreign affairs, the USPI calls for Iceland's withdrawal from NATO and the adoption of a policy of neutrality. The party has exploited anti-American sentiment in connection with the US base at Keflavik, and continues to wage an active campaign for the installation's liquidation.

The USPI has been noncommittal on the issue of an international conference of communist and workers' parties. The party was not represented at the Vienna conference in May 1966 or at the Prague conference in November of that year. In 1967 the party declined to send a representative to the conference of European communist and workers' parties in Karlovy Vary (24-27 April). The party was, however, represented by an "observer" at the Budapest consultative meeting in February-March 1968.

The USPI attended neither the French Communist Party Congress (Paris, January) nor that of the Swedish party (Stockholm, May), but Chairman Olgeirsson went to Berlin for the Socialist Unity Party Congress (17-22 April). Olgeirsson also went to Moscow for the celebrations of the Fiftieth Anniversary of the October Revolution.

Bilateral contacts with other communist parties during the year were few. Swedish party Chairman C. H. Hermansson was in Iceland on 15-21 March. He conferred with the USPI Central Committee, and discussed "organizational forms of the left" at a meeting arranged jointly by the People's Alliance, the USPI, the Socialist Youth Union, and the Radical Student Association. A four-man delegation of the USPI went to Bucharest on 21 August for talks with the Central Committee of the Rumanian party.

Hannibal Valdimarsson represented the People's Alliance at a Nordic Socialist Seminar in Copenhagen on 26-27 February sponsored by the Danish Socialist People's Party and attended also by Finnish and Norwegian left-socialists and by Swedish Communists. (The Norwegian and Danish Communists were denied admittance.) In his speech to the meeting, which dealt with questions of Nordic economic and security cooperation, Valdimarsson asserted that the "economic and national independence of Iceland, with her peculiar position, is threatened by powerful capitalist forces," and that Iceland is so small that a "powerful financial European or American trust or financial institution could conceivably take over the country should Icelandic state powers fail to intervene"; but, he added, the Icelandic people were not entertaining "any such fears from capital [interests] in the Nordic countries" (*Ny Dag*, Stockholm, 3-9 March 1967).

**Publications.** The USPI publishes a daily newspaper, *Thjodviljinn* (People's Will), with a circulation of 11,000 copies; the weekly organ of the AB is *Utsyn* (Outlook).

# INDIA

Indian communist sources give 26 December 1925 as the founding date of the Communist Party of India (CPI) (*New Age,* 9 June 1963). Western scholars usually give the party's founding as December 1928 (see G. D. Overstreet and M. Windmiller, *Communism in India,* Los Angeles, 1959), although there had been regional Marxist groups in various parts of India earlier than this. In the party's early years Comintern direction was exercised through the Communist Party of Great Britain, through which funds, organizers, and agents were channeled.

Since India's independence there have been continual disputes within the party, predating the Sino-Soviet quarrel, over whether the Indian revolution ought to follow the Soviet or the Chinese model or the third option of parliamentary participation, "constitutional communism." Since 1951 the CPI had followed a general line of participation in parliamentary struggle under the direction of Ajoy Ghosh, General Secretary of the party from 1951 until his death in 1962. After Ghosh's death struggle between right and left factions within the party greatly intensified, culminating in a formal split in 1964, when two separate congresses were held, both claiming to be the Seventh All-India Party Congress. Since that time the two parties have existed independently; they are commonly called the "right," or "pro-Soviet," Communist Party of India and the "left," or "pro-Peking," Communist Party of India. They call themselves, respectively, simply the Communist Party of India (CPI) and the Communist Party of India (Marxist) [CPI(M)]. The CPI accuses the CPI(M) of "splittism" under the influence of the Chinese Communists; the CPI(M) denies the charge and explains the schism as a result of CPI revisionism and opportunism.

Both communist parties are legal, although from time to time individual Communist leaders, mostly of the CPI(M) have been arrested or detained under the Defense of India Rules.

Estimates of party membership vary so much that they are of very limited significance. Membership of the CPI is given by the 1967 edition of *World Strength of Communist Party Organizations* as 55,000; a Dutch source, Interdoc, estimates 77,000, and another European source 90,000. The CPI itself claims a membership of 175,000 (*New Age,* 17 December 1967). For the CPI(M) the same sources, respectively, estimate 70,000, 93,000, and 80,000. However, since India's national elections in February 1967 the CPI(M) has reportedly enrolled large numbers of new members in the state of West Bengal through its peasant and labor front organizations. Western journalists have estimated that the CPI(M) has enrolled as many as 400,000 new peasant members and 30,000 to 40,000 new members in the urban Calcutta area (*Washington Post,* 22 August 1967). This could well be only a temporary phenomenon. (India's estimated population in December 1967 was 511 million.)

**Organization and Leadership.** The organizational structure of the CPI consists of a Chairman, Shripad A. Dange; a General Secretary, C. Rajeshwar Rao; a Central Secretariat, which consists of the Chairman, General Secretary, and seven Secretaries; a Central Executive Committee of 25 members; a Control Commission of seven members; and a National Council of 101 members. Each state of India also has its own secretariat and state council. The Central Executive Committee (elected 16 February 1968) consists of S. A. Dange, C. Rajeshwar Rao, G. Adhikari, Z. A. Ahmad, Bhupesh Gupta, Yogindra Sharma, N. K. Khrishnan, S. G. Sardesai, Romesh Chandra, N. Rajesekhara Reddy, Thammareddy Satyanarayana, Phani Bora, Jagannath Sarkar, Indradeep Sinha, C. Achutha Menon, N. E. Balaram, Eknath Bhagwat, Avtar Singh Malhotra, Satyapal Dang, H. K. Vyas, M. Kalyanasundaram, Kali Shankar Shukla, Bishwanath Mukerjee, Indrajit Gupta, and Bhowani Sen (*New Age,* 25 February 1968).

The CPI(M) organizational hierarchy consists of a Chairman, E. M. S. Namboodiripad; a General

Secretary, P. Sundarayya; a nine-man Political Bureau of the Central Committee, State Secretariats and State Committees. The Politburo elected in August 1966 consists of E. M. S. Namboodiripad, P. Sundarayya, M. Basavapunniah, Jyoti Basu, Promode Das Gupta, A. K. Gopalan, P. Ramamurthi, B. T. Ranadive, and H. S. Surjeet. In both parties, but especially in the CPI(M), the state organizations are very important, and a high degree of autonomy in tactics and policies prevails from state to state, especially in matters of election strategy and alliances. The power of leaders in the national organizations is usually based on control of some regional or state party units.

Before the split the CPI directed the political work of numerous front organizations, including the All-India Trade Union Congress, the All-India Kisan Sabha (Peasants' Association), All-India Youth Federation, National Federation of Indian Women, All-India Peace Council, Progressive Writers' Association, Indian People's Theater Association, and Indo-Soviet Cultural Association. At present, however, of these only the Trade Union Congress and the Peasants' Association have much importance to either communist party.

The All-India Trade Union Congress, which claimed more than 600,000 members in 1966, seemed at the end of 1967 to be on the verge of a formal split, as the CPI(M) was organizing rival trade-union groups at lower levels (*YICA*, 1966, pp. 311-312). Denouncing such activity in the state of Andhra Pradesh, the CPI paper said on 12 November: "The present position of the CPI(M) in the Andhra Pradesh Trade Union Congress and the AITUC is only due to the accommodative spirit of the majority in the interest of unity." In West Bengal the CPI(M) also controlled powerful units of the Trade Union Congress, which it was using to recruit party members. The still-united national organization had a left Communist, S. S. Mirajkar, as President, and a right Communist, S. A. Dange, as Secretary-General.

The All-India Kisan Sabha split in 1967; the CPI captured control of this organization during the year and ousted CPI(M) members from its national committee. Charging that the CPI had enrolled several hundred thousand "bogus members" in a plot to oust leftists, the CPI(M) set up its own rival organization. Both organizations planned their own national conferences for 1968.

**1967 National Elections.** India's fourth national elections were held 15-21 February 1967. The most important domestic planks of the CPI "election manifesto" (published 18 December 1966 as a supplement to *New Age*) included expansion of the state sector of the economy, closing speculative markets and exchanges, tax revision aimed against the wealthy, more power and improved benefits for labor, land reform, increased powers for the state governments, and linguistic diversity. On international questions it called for support for North Vietnam, recognition of East Germany, peace with Pakistan along the lines of the Tashkent agreement, a "no-war pact" with China, and India's withdrawal from the Commonwealth.

In the contests for seats in the Lower House (Lok Sabha) of the national parliament the CPI received 7.1 million votes, or 4.8 per cent of the total vote; the CPI(M) candidates totalled 6.4 million votes, or 4.28 per cent of the total vote. The CPI captured 24 seats in the Lower House (including one Uttar Pradesh Communist running under the Republican Party label) and the CPI(M) 19. In the elections for state assemblies the relative positions of the two parties were reversed: the CPI won a total of 122 assembly seats and 4.23 per cent of the total vote, while the CPI(M) took 127 seats and 4.6 per cent of the total vote. In the 1962 Lower House and state assembly elections the then united CPI had received 9.57 per cent of the total vote, although it won only 30 Lower House seats.

The communist parties appeared to view these results with mixed feelings. This was especially true of the CPI, which did not gain as much from the elections as did the CPI(M). Communist satisfaction at the serious electoral setbacks suffered by the ruling Congress Party was tempered by the fact that the right-wing parties, chiefly the Swatantra and the Hindu nationalist Jana Sangh, had benefited more from the Congress Party defeats than had the communist parties. The Swatantra Party, with 44 Lower House seats, replaced the Communists as the leading party in the parliament in opposition to the Congress Party. Moreover, Communist vote as a percentage of the total had actually declined slightly from the 1962 level. In many cases the Communist vote was split by direct contests between the two parties. Only in the state of Kerala and the Union territory of Tripura were the CPI and the CPI(M) able to form electoral alliances. In Kerala the CPI(M) was alloted 61 constituencies and the

CPI 24, and the alliance captured a majority of the state's 133-seat legislative assembly, although the Communist vote in the state was only 35.5 per cent of the total votes cast. The success of this arrangement was due to the leadership of Kerala state CPI(M) Chairman E. M. S. Namboodiripad, a relative moderate among the top leaders of the CPI(M), who became Chief Minister of the new state government. In other states, notably in West Bengal and Andhra Pradesh, similar efforts to arrange electoral alliances between the CPI and CPI(M) were unsuccessful.

Besides losing much of its majority in the Lower House, the Congress Party also lost control of 5 of the 17 state governments: Kerala, West Bengal, Bihar, Orissa, and Madras. Shortly after the elections, the Congress Party lost control of four more states because of state assemblymen's defections in Punjab, Uttar Pradesh, Madhya Pradesh, and Haryana. Except for Madras, where the Tamil nationalist Dravidian Progressive Movement won a majority of seats, these states now became governed by highly unstable coalitions of parties in opposition to the Congress Party. In Kerala and West Bengal the CPI(M) was the strongest partner in coalitions of 7 and 14 parties, respectively. The CPI participated in 5 state coalition governments, although it did not dominate in any: West Bengal, Kerala, Bihar, Punjab, and Uttar Pradesh.

As the new governments assumed office, the opposition coalitions in the states planned to follow the tactic of blaming state troubles, especially the food crisis in Kerala, West Bengal, and Bihar, on the niggardliness of the central government; more generally, they planned to try to capitalize on all disputes between the states and the central government by claiming that the central authorities were not doing enough to help the states, and at the same time by demanding a greater measure of autonomy from New Delhi (see Sundar Rajan, "India's Opposition Scents Power," *The Reporter,* 20 April 1967).

The National Council of the CPI met in Calcutta on 23-30 April to discuss the postelection situation and future tactics, and sharp differences of opinion within the party became quite apparent. Central Secretariat member Bhupesh Gupta, editor of *New Age,* the party's weekly English-language paper, reviewed the Council session in *New Age* on 7 and 14 May, giving what amounted to a semiofficial evaluation of the election results. Gupta heavily emphasized the importance of a united front of all left parties in opposition to the Congress Party. Convinced that the Congress Party's domination of Indian politics was coming to an end, the preponderance of opinion within the CPI National Council was that the two communist parties must unite to become the nucleus of a left anti-Congress united front which could fill the growing political vacuum. According to the 14 May issue of *New Age*: "The results show that if the CPI and the CPI(M) and the SSP [Samyukta Socialist Party] had come to an understanding on a national scale and avoided mutual contests, that alone would have deprived the Congress of its majority in the Lok Sabha. What a great chance had been lost—thanks to disunity and to the splitting of votes." The CPI was particularly disturbed by its poor showing in the states of Uttar Pradesh, Rajasthan, Gujarat, Orissa, Madhya Pradesh, and Haryana, where Communists were outpaced by Jana Sangh and Swatantra candidates. Also, in Tripura [where the CPI and CPI(M) had in fact concluded an electoral alliance] and Andhra Pradesh the leftist parties all did poorly. Gupta observed generally that "the smallest gains out of this collapse of the Congress have come to the CPI and the CPI(M), while other Left and democratic parties have done comparatively well."

Although *New Age* (21 May) denied the widespread reports of "furious controversy" within the National Council, there was clearly serious disagreement over just how far the CPI should go in attempts to form an anti-Congress united front. A spokesman for the Council while it was in session said that the CPI would not adopt a "rigid attitude of political untouchability" toward potential coalition partners and would, under certain conditions, even join in a united front with the Jana Sangh and Swatantra Party. This line, however, made the CPI more vulnerable than ever to charges of "revisionism" and "opportunism," and the procommunist weekly *Link* in its 14 May issue attacked the idea of joining forces even with the Samyukta Socialist Party and the Tamil Dravidian Progressive Movement, let alone the right parties, accusing the CPI leadership of wanting to "make quick political gains by deft maneuvers at the top rather than undertake the seemingly thankless task of sustained mass activity." There was some bite to this criticism by *Link*, inasmuch as the right Communists themselves admitted in several documents during the year that the party's mass base was far from what it should be, especially among the working class.

The CPI insisted that it was not sacrificing principle for expediency, and that all united-front partners would have to agree upon a minimum program of opposition to imperialism, monopoly capital, and feudalism—a program so minimal, however, that in principle it might embrace any party, even the Congress Party itself. On this point Gupta's 21 May review of the Council session was distinctly defensive in tone:

> Our Party stands for not any type of non-Congress government, but only for a non-Congress Democratic government. This completely rules out as far as the CPI is concerned the government being a rightist government. . . . The trouble arises because the National Council does not in advance declare that the Party will have nothing to do with the Swatantra Party and the Jana Sangh . . . we dare say that such an approach would only weaken our hand and play into the hands of reaction and the ruling Congress Party.

Basic to this line of argument was the premise, advanced at the National Council meeting by Chairman Dange and hotly disputed by many party members, that the elections had brought about a "change in the power structure," raising hopes that a "transition to socialism by peaceful means is possible." Dange also told the meeting that this line conformed to the line of peaceful coexistence put forward at the Twentieth Congress of the Soviet Party in 1956 (*Hindustan Standard*, 26 April 1967).

The right Communists were in a very difficult situation. On the one hand, not only had the right-wing parties in 1967 gained proportionately more strength than had the communist parties, but there was danger of a Congress Party coalition with the right-wing parties, which would isolate the communist and other left parties. Gupta warned: "It will be a mistake to underestimate the capacity of the Congress and reaction to maneuver. The National Council has warned the country against the reaction's slogan of 'a national coalition at the center,' in which the Americans are already showing such avid interest." On the other hand, in attempting to head off such a coalition by associating with right-wing parties, the CPI might lose its identity to the more militant CPI(M), which vehemently opposed any cooperation with the right-wing parties. The CPI(M) could better afford this stand, since its strength was primarily concentrated in states where left-wing strength was predominant (West Bengal, Kerala, Andhra Pradesh), whereas the CPI was not a major political force in any single state, although it had some strength in every state.

**Events in West Bengal.** A group of defectors from the Congress Party in West Bengal running for the state assembly under the party name Bangla Congress was responsible for the loss of the Congress Party majority in that state. After the elections 14 opposition parties formed a government in which the CPI(M) was the most prominent party and secured ministerial posts for three of its leading members: Jyoti Basu, Deputy Chief Minister; Harekrishna Konar, Land and Land Revenue Minister; and Niranjan Sen. Ajoy Mukerjee of the breakaway Bangla Congress became Chief Minister, and CPI members Somnath Lahiri and Bishwanath Mukerjee (Ajoy Mukerjee's brother) also had ministries.

Soon after the new government was inaugurated a rash of labor violence broke out in the Calcutta area, where *gherao* , or lock-in, campaigns were extensively used against company personnel. Despite the widespread violence, the united-front government would not allow police to interfere in "labor disputes," and the Communists defended the *gherao* as a legitimate bargaining weapon of labor.

Under such turbulent conditions the Communist-dominated unions in West Bengal found opportunities to increase their influence at the expense of noncommunist unions by taking the lead in violence and intimidation against employers, and against other unions and their leaders as well. In the spring and early summer numerous reports were published of violence and terror by CPI(M) labor organizers and hired "goondas" against members of noncommunist unions. On 4 June General Secretary B. P. Jha of the Colliery Mazdoor Congress, a coal union controlled by the Samyukta Socialist Party, was murdered by an armed band of CPI(M) members in a struggle for the control of the colliery labor. Deputy Chief Minister and CPI(M) Politburo member Jyoti Basu was said to have personally prevented the arrest of Jha's murderers (see the booklet *Mao's Shadow over West Bengal,* Coordinating Committee of Independent Trade Unions, Bombay, 1967). In the rural areas the

CPI(M)-controlled West Bengal All-India Kisan Sabha, whose Secretary-General is Minister Harekrishna Konar, was used to enroll large numbers of peasants in the party.

Despite its continuing instability, the West Bengal united-front government survived the urban disorders and the equally serious peasant uprisings through the summer. The Congress Party powers in New Delhi, who had been seeking an opportunity to recapture governmental power in the state, finally succeeded in bringing about the downfall of the united front when in November P. C. Ghosh, Food Minister and head of the Progressive Democratic Front (the Bangla Congress group) defected to the Congress Party, taking with him 17 Bangla Congress members of the state assembly. This cost the united front its majority, and two weeks later West Bengal Governor Dharam Vira, obviously at the instigation of Congress Party authorities in New Delhi, declared that the front was unable to govern and dismissed it, installing president's rule and moving 60 truckloads of troops into Calcutta. P. C. Ghosh was invited to form a new government and became Chief Minister. The CPI(M) then took its struggle to the streets of Calcutta and called for a two-day general strike, which was successful, to demonstrate the popularity of the united front and the unpopularity of the Congress Party. Rioting and battles between police and pro-united-front students flared for days. When the new Ghosh government opened its first session, the speaker of the assembly declared the session adjourned by reason of the governor's allegedly illegal action in dismissing the united-front government; this prompted a riot in the assembly. Several days later the CPI(M) again paralyzed Calcutta for a day with a general strike, and the crisis persisted into the new year.

**Events in Kerala.** Prospects for the success of the coalition in Kerala were much better than in West Bengal. Although the coalition was indeed heterogeneous, and included even the conservative Muslim League, as long as Namboodiripad of the CPI(M) could maintain the working alliance with the CPI and at the same time stave off an ever-nascent rebellion against his leadership from the left within his own party, the coalition would be secure, since the two communist factions jointly commanded a majority in the legislature. [In West Bengal the CPI(M) and the CPI controlled only 60 of the legislature's 280 seats.] The strains within the alliance in Kerala were great, however. The left wing of the CPI(M) attacked the Kerala state industrial policy as revisionist, the Kerala Industries Minister, T. V. Thomas, being a CPI member. The CPI, meanwhile, attacked the state Food Ministry, under CPI(M) control, and blamed its policies for the food shortage in Kerala. This prompted a lengthy statement in reply from the Joint Secretary of the Kerala State Committee of the CPI(M) which, according to *People's Democracy* (8 October) "thoroughly exposed the disputive game the revisionists are playing." What particularly angered the left Communists was that the CPI had violated the convention of blaming the continuing food crisis on New Delhi: "Before September 11 it was the Center that was responsible for the serious food situation; ten days later it became the CPI(M) and its Food Minister" (*People's Democracy,* 8 October 1967). Finally, a month later, when Industries Minister Thomas returned from a trip to Japan and discussions on possible Japanese technical and financial aid for Kerala industries, he was attacked by the CPI(M) for collusion with Indian reactionaries and helping US imperialists gain control of India. Namboodiripad tried to end the controversy by blaming press distortions of Thomas' views, and on 9 November he claimed that there were no essential differences between the CPI and CPI(M) on the question of foreign aid (*New Age,* 19 November 1967). However, in the 12 November issue of *People's Democracy,* Politburo member B. T. Ranadive, who is left of Namboodiripad within the CPI(M), accused Thomas of belonging to the same class as Morarji Desai, the relatively pro-American Finance Minister of the Union of India, who is a kind of devil figure to Indian Communists.

**The Naxalbari Uprisings.** The Naxalbari peasant uprisings of 1967 were the occasion of a serious crisis for the CPI(M), resulting in a split within the party, loss of Peking's favor, and a falling out with the other parties to the united front in West Bengal.

Naxalbari is a tribal region in the Silghuri subdivision of Darjeeling district in West Bengal; it is only four miles from the Nepal border, in a narrow neck of territory 15 miles wide that connects the state of Assam with the rest of India. This area is strategically important because of its proximity to the disputed border region where Indian and Chinese troop concentrations face each other. All supplies to the Indian forces along this border area must pass through this neck of territory. It is also a politically sensitive area for New Delhi because there are various tribal and hill groups in the vicinity and in neighboring Assam, including Mizos and Nagas, who have been agitating for their own separate states. Since the Sino-Indian border war of 1962, the Communists had reportedly been stocking arms in the area and otherwise preparing for possible insurrection. Probably at least since 1965, the CPI(M) had been actively organizing peasant sharecroppers, promising rectification of landlord abuses and redistribution of land. A New China News Agency dispatch of 27 June 1967 said:

> The revolutionaries of the Indian Communist Party in Silghuri subdivision, who advocate seizure of political power through armed struggle, raised the slogan in 1965 of preparing for armed struggle by arming the peasants and setting up rural bases. In the past two years, they devoted themselves to mobilizing and organizing the peasants.

Between March and May of 1967 there were scores of cases of forcible occupation of land, looting, physical assault, and murder. Bands armed with bows and arrows terrorized the countryside, and insurgent leaders presided over kangaroo courts which passed and executed judgments against landlords, ranging from confiscation of property to death. Local left Communists leading the movement included the Brahmin intellectual Kanyu Sanyal, Jangal Santhal, Khoken Mazumdar, and Charu Mazumdar.

Meanwhile, the left Communists participating in the united-front government had understandably lost much of their earlier interest in armed revolt but could not now control these dissidents. In this embarrassing situation the CPI(M)-dominated government did its best to delay action and avoid taking sides. The West Bengal left Communists, with one eye on the extreme leftists within their own party and the other on the other parties in the united front, sympathized with the peasant complaints against the landlords but dissociated themselves from the armed rebellion and Peking's support for the uprising. Playing for time in the face of demands on all sides for firm action against the rebels, in early June the government sent to the disturbed area a delegation of six cabinet ministers, including Harekrishna Konar and CPI member Bishwanath Mukerjee. Konar promised that excess land holdings long since expropriated by the government but never redistributed would shortly be distributed to the landless. He later conferred with Kanyu Sanyal and an agreement was reached: lawless activities would be suspended, and thereafter land would be distributed and private grain stocks would be dehoarded by government agencies with the advice of the "people's committees" being formed by the insurgents. All wanted persons, including Sanyal, were to surrender by a specific date, and presumably were to be treated with lenience. The agreement was not carried out, however, and in late May and early June violence became much more severe and widespread.

The Congress Party government in New Delhi was at once concerned about the strategic importance of the Naxalbari area and eager to see the West Bengal government in a situation that could cause its downfall. Differences between Chief Minister Mukerjee and Jyoti Basu were threatening to destroy the united front. Basu himself was under pressure from the left; in June he was attacked by leftist students shouting "down with revisionist Jyoti Basu!" as he tried to attend a meeting at the University of Calcutta. It was in this situation that the CPI(M) in the united front finally acquiesced in the use of police against the insurgents. By early August Naxalbari had returned to near normal, and several of the leaders of the movement, including Jangal Santhal, had been captured; Sanyal had fled into hiding.

The CPI(M) attempted to maintain the ideological orthodoxy of its actions by playing down the political significance of the Naxalbari movement, sympathizing with peasant grievances but castigating the leadership of the movement as "adventurist." Said *Desh Hitaisi*, the CPI(M) Bengali weekly:

> A bold and healthy peasant movement which could have made the entire mass movement of West Bengal much wider and stronger if led properly, is in fact helping the reactionary forces most by being led under most adventurist leadership. . . . Local leadership began to haphazardly grab land and produce by completely disregarding the existence of the united-front government and without taking advantage of this government.

At a three-day session in Calcutta in late July the CPI(M) Politburo adopted a resolution criticizing the police action in the Naxalbari area and saying that the issues involved were economic rather than political.

Despite Peking's strident support for the Naxalbari insurgents, the actual extent of Chinese involvement in the uprisings was not clear. Pro-Maoist printed propaganda material was found in the area, but beyond this and the visit by two Chinese consular personnel in Nepal and West Bengal to the border area in late spring, not even investigation teams of right-wing parties claimed to have found solid evidence of actual Chinese participation or large-scale financing. Peking did not confine its verbal support to the Naxalbari insurgents, however, but also hailed the guerrilla activities of the Naga and Mizo peoples in Assam and along the border of Burma. There were strong fears in Delhi and Rangoon that China might support armed uprisings in these areas, perhaps in collaboration with Communists in East Pakistan. In addition, Peking gave warm verbal support to outbreaks of peasant violence in Northern Bihar and in Kerala.

**Purges in the CPI(M).** The backwash of these events within the CPI(M) was very damaging to the party. By late June 19 leading members of the CPI(M) in West Bengal had been purged for advocacy of the "adventurist" line. On 28 June a forcible attempt was made by extreme left elements of the party to occupy the Calcutta office of *Desh Hitaisi,* in the wake of which incident another 13 leading CPI(M) members were expelled. By early September 40 expulsions had been announced by the West Bengal CPI(M), and former Calcutta district committee member Parimal Das Gupta, who was among those purged, claimed that 200 had been expelled (*NYT,* 5 September 1967). Also among the expellees were Sushital Roy Chowdhuri and Saroj Dutt, both members of the West Bengal state committee; Asit Sen, member of the Calcutta district committee; and Niranjen Bose, member of the editorial board of *Desh Hitaisi.* In November the CPI(M) Central Committee announced the expulsion of Shiva Kumar Misra, the Secretary of the Uttar Pradesh state committee, who during September had issued several circulars within the party calling for open defiance of the party line on Naxalbari and named Politburo members Sundarayya and Surjeet as the "two ringleaders of the leading revisionist clique" in the party (*People's Democracy,* 12 November 1967).

Numerous of these CPI(M) expellees and other extreme leftists were widely reported in mid-1967 to have formed a third communist party. P. Sengupta, Charan Mazumdar, and S. R. Chowdhuri were said to be the leading figures in the new movement. There were in fact several extreme leftist groups going by various names, including the Hindustan Socialist Workers' Party (see *Link,* 7 May), the Inner Party Committee for Fighting against Revisionism, and the All-India Coordination Committee of Revolutionary Comrades within the CPI(M). A Press Trust of India report from Bombay on 17 November said that this last group, on behalf of the All-India Naxalbari Krishak Sangram Sahayak Samiti (Agrarian Reforms Struggle Committee), held a week long meeting in Calcutta in early November. The Struggle Committee announced its intent to build a new party which would work to achieve "a people's democratic revolution through building militant rural bases and extending them to encircle the cities" (see also *World Outlook,* 19 January 1968). It appeared at the end of 1967, however, that these groups had not yet succeeded in forming a united party; although Peking spoke of these "revolutionary comrades" in numerous New China News Agency dispatches, none were mentioned by name.

The monthly *Liberation,* claiming to speak for "revolutionary Communists of India," included in its first issue two quotes from Mao Tse-tung: "Therefore, the united front, armed struggle and Party building are the three fundamental questions for our Party in the Chinese revolution. Having a correct grasp of these three questions and their interrelations is tantamount to giving correct leadership to the whole Chinese revolution;" and "An erroneous leadership that endangers the revolution should not be accepted unconditionally but should be resisted resolutely." In an editorial in its first issue, *Liberation* said:

> It is Naxalbari which has given the revolutionary working people of India their rightful place as a contingent of the world revolutionary forces. Naxalbari has also torn the mask off the neo-revisionist clique led by Ranadive, Namboodiripad, Sundarayya, and Company, and spells its doom. The perfidy of these neo-revisionist leaders, like that of the Dangeites, knows no limit . . . the revolutionary forces will no doubt cast them into the dustbin of history and march forward toward people's democracy and socialism . . . .

*Liberation* sends its warmest fraternal greetings to the great Chinese comrades, the valiant Vietnamese comrades, the brave comrades in Burma, Thailand, Laos, Indonesia, Ceylon, the U.S.A., and all other countries, who, guided by the thought of Mao Tse-tung, Marxism-Leninism of our era, are fighting relentless battles for national liberation, world peace and socialism.

**Relations between the Chinese Communist Party and the CPI(M).** Although the CPI(M) is generally referred to as India's "pro-Peking" communist party, 1967 saw the CPI(M) break publicly with Peking's line of armed people's struggle as the proper road for all Afro-Asian communist parties. At the same time, however, the CPI(M) maintained with increased force the Peking view of Soviet leadership as revisionist traitors to communism. The main issue between Peking and the CPI(M) was, of course, Naxalbari. Radio Peking staunchly supported the Naxalbari elements and denounced the left Communists in the united-front government for not supporting this new "people's war." The Chinese Communist Party appeared little better disposed toward the CPI(M) than toward the CPI. In Chinese Communist parlance, the CPI was the "Dange renegade clique" and the CPI(M) comprised "the revisionists in the Indian Communist Party" (although before Naxalbari it had been "the Indian Communist Party"). The expellees from the CPI(M) and the other partisans of violent revolution were "the revolutionaries of the Indian Communist Party."

As the year wore on, and several non-Congress Party coalition governments fell, the Chinese crowed all the louder that all Indian non-Congress governments were simply tools of reaction, and that all communists who participated in them were revisionists. On 3 December the New China News Agency said: "Life in India has more than once proved that it is impossible to set up a 'people's regime' and win 'people's democracy' through majority in the Parliament without using revolutionary violence to demolish the reactionary State apparatus and capture political power." Not even the Kerala government was "red" enough to suit the Chinese; according to the 15 December *Peking Review*:

> The revisionists in the Indian Communist Party have undertaken to benumb the revolutionary will of the people, prevent them from rising up in revolution, and sabotage their revolutionary struggles with the fallacy of "peaceful transition" and the setting up of "non-Congress governments" which are completely in the service of the reactionary ruling clique. There is no difference between their counterrevolutionary revisionist line and that of the Dange renegade clique. Despite their efforts to disguise themselves as opponents of the Dange renegade clique, the revisionists in the Indian Communist Party of whom Namboodiripad is a representative are nothing but twin brothers of the Dange renegades.

On this issue, as on so many others, the CPI(M) was of many minds, and the partial withdrawal from Peking's orbit was clearly carried out with reluctance. On 18-26 August the CPI(M) leadership met in Madurai, Madras, in secret session to discuss the party's line *vis-à-vis* Peking. Of the several resolutions passed at the session, the most important were two documents, "Inner-party Document on Ideological Controversies in the International Communist Movement" and "Divergent Views between our Party and the CCP on Certain Fundamental Issues of Program and Policy." The first document put the CPI(M) firmly on the side of Peking on the question of revisionism in the Soviet party:

> Modern revisionism led by Khrushchev and pursued by the present CPSU leaders has done the greatest damage to the cause of the working class and communist movement in the world. It should be said that the Communist Party of China has rendered yeoman service to the world working class and communist movement in fighting against this menace of modern revisionism and in defense of Marxism-Leninism. (Quoted in *New Age,* 24 September 1967.)

In the second document, however, the CPI(M) complained that the Chinese party was interfering in the internal affairs of a "fraternal party" by insisting that it follow the Maoist line. This document, noting the constant attacks by the Chinese on leaders of the CPI(M), said:

> Such methods strike at the very roots of fraternal relations between Communist parties,

and no party can allow its leaders to be denounced by other parties if it is to continue its independent existence. Similarly, the practice of upholding and encouraging certain individuals and groups against whom disciplinary actions are taken for their anti-Party activities is highly objectionable and disruptive. (Quoted in *New Age,* 24 September 1967.)

In summary, the CPI(M) tried, however inconsistently, to agree with the Chinese Communist Party's principles but to disagree with their application to India.

The CPI drew some satisfaction from the CPI(M)'s predicament. CPI General-Secretary Rao observed in the 24 September *New Age*:

Why wail now? When the leadership of the CCP was attacking our Party and leaders, the CPSU, and scores of other parties in the filthiest possible terms and splitting the Communist parties, they had no objection. Some of them even gloated over it and supported the CCP. Perhaps even now some among them would do the same. Their only request to the Maoist leadership is—"Please do not abuse, do not split our party!"

The criticisms of the CCP by the CPI(M) did not prevent the CPI(M) Politburo from sending a long message of congratulations to Communist China on the occasion of its 1 October National Day celebration. This document, which occupied more than two full pages in the 1 October issue of *People's Democracy,* was a remarkable exercise in tightrope walking. It excused rather than praised the cultural revolution, remarking that it could be understood only "against the background of US encirclement of China" and the treachery of the Soviet revisionists in withdrawing their help in China's economic development. It further remarked, "There have never been, nor can there ever be, revolutions without mistakes, shortcomings, and setbacks. But they are mistakes, shortcomings, and setbacks made in the course of making a revolution." Most important, the document opened with praise for the victory of the Chinese revolution and observed that this victory "was made possible by the unerring application by the Communist Party of China, led by Comrade Mao Tse-tung, of the revolutionary principles of Marxism-Leninism to the realities of the Chinese revolution, a specific feature of which was that from its early days itself it was an armed revolution facing armed counterrevolution." Thus, since there had been no armed counterrevolution in India, the implication was that application of the same "revolutionary principles" to the Indian reality might not dictate a strategy of armed revolution. Expanding on the role of the Chinese revolutionary model, the document continued: "Only revisionists from the Right or Left discard this great revolutionary experience. The former only talk about a parliamentary path, surrender the leadership of the party in the united front of revolutionary classes. The latter equally repudiate the role of the party, discard the alliance of revolutionary classes, and indulge in verbiage about armed struggle." Clearly, some concession was being made to every shade of opinion within the CPI(M).

**Relations between the Soviet Party and the CPI.** The CPI in 1967 faithfully supported Moscow on the question of revisionism, backed the Soviet proposal for a socialist united front on Vietnam, and defended the Soviets against CPI(M) and Chinese charges that the Soviets had betrayed the Arab people by their actions during the Middle East war. The CPI hedged not at all in its attitude toward the Chinese Communist Party. The *Indian Express* quoted Dange on 6 January 1967 as saying that he was "not prepared to believe that China is ruled by a Communist Party. It is ruled by a personal dictatorship which got its lease on life as a result of the failure of the Great Leap Forward which necessitated suppression of the people."

This attitude toward the Soviet party, however, was not at all reciprocated; Moscow's support for the CPI was at best stepmotherly. The Soviet Union continued its policy of strengthening ties with the New Delhi government, stepping up both military and economic aid to India, and relations between Moscow and the Congress Party leaders generally improved through the year. Thus the Soviet party could not have been pleased by the CPI trend in 1967 toward an anti-Congress stand. Also, while supporting the CPI's constant appeals for unity in the Indian communist movement, the Soviet party did not wholeheartedly support the CPI case against the CPI(M). Soviet media continued to refer to the CPI(M) as the "parallel party," despite the CPI(M) attacks on Soviet leadership.

The leading feature in the 5 November *People's Democracy,* devoted to the Fiftieth Anniversary of the October Revolution, was a statement by the CPI(M) Politburo which echoed the Peking line against Soviet leadership and predicted that its anti-Marxist line would soon be defeated by the Soviet people. It is plain, however, that neither the Politburo nor the editorial board of *People's Democracy* was unanimous in such militant opposition to Moscow. On 15 November the Calcutta District Committee held a rally in Calcutta to celebrate the Fiftieth Anniversary, at which General Secretary Sundarayya delivered a speech less strongly critical of the Soviet leadership, and critical of the Chinese as well. Sundarayya's speech was given extensive coverage in the 26 November *People's Democracy*. Although Sundarayya indeed criticized the Soviet leaders, his complaint was that they were not doing enough to help fraternal parties, rather than that they were revisionist traitors to communism:

> The present leaders of the Soviet Union are not carrying forward the legacy of the October Revolution. It should be in the forefront in helping and carrying on the world revolution. It is not doing that. Hence the bourgeois press is loud in praise of them. We have faith in the people of the Soviet Union. They will certainly make them give up their wrong path or remove them from leadership.

Specifically, Sundarayya, heedless of China's proprietary interest in Southeast Asia, called for direct Soviet action in Vietnam:

> The Soviet Union is giving material assistance in various ways to Vietnam, but is that all that it could do for Vietnam, which is fighting monstrous American imperialism? Is it not necessary for the Soviet Union to directly intervene against American aggression?

Sundarayya emphasized that the CPI(M) would not follow directives from either Moscow or Peking, noting that his party had received bad treatment from both:

> The Soviet leadership does not recognize our Party. They invite Mrs. Indira Gandhi, who was responsible for throwing out the Communist-led Ministry in Kerala [in 1959] by unconstitutional means. . . . But we want to say one thing to the Soviet leadership: You may not help us if you do not want and if you want to enjoy the fruits of your Revolution, but please do not praise and help our enemies whom we are fighting.

Noting that Peking was attacking the CPI(M) for betraying the Naxalbari movement, Sundarayya commented further that in 1948 the CPI had supported peasant uprisings in Telagana in Bihar; after the movement had been suppressed by the Congress authorities in Delhi, "Chou En-lai and other Chinese leaders came to India after that and maintained friendly relations with them."

The attention and publicity paid by the CPI to the two Madurai documents of the CPI(M) is similarly understandable as a bid for Soviet support. The CPI claimed that these two documents constituted proof that the CPI(M) was incorrigibly splittist, and that the disagreements between the CPI(M) and Peking were minor and not to be taken seriously. At a meeting in New Delhi on 27-30 September the CPI Executive Committee adopted a formal resolution on the Madurai documents, printed in full in the 8 October *New Age* under the headline "Open War on Common Line of World Communists." The resolution repeatedly emphasized the CPI contention that:

> The CPI(M) leadership has completely broken from the Declaration and Statement of the 1957 and 1960 meeting of the Communist and Workers parties—the common line of the world communist movement. In fact by their latest ideological document, the CPI(M) leadership has declared an open war against the common line. The CPI(M) leadership has ideologically aligned with the dominant Chinese leadership and the leadership of the Albanian Workers' Party.

Calling the CPI(M) disagreements with the Chinese on the Indian situation "unprincipled and illogical," the CPI resolution blamed the 1964 split of the Indian Communists directly on Chinese interference, and tried to undercut any claim of the CPI(M) to a more orthodox Marxist stand on domestic Indian politics:

> The Madurai documents would confirm our contention that the CPI was split by them not primarily over the differences on internal Indian questions but in response by the CPI(M) leaders to the alternative line which the Chinese leadership wanted to impose on fraternal parties and in particular to the Chinese Party's open call to split the Communist Party of India.

At the close of the year, the CPI was making plans for its Eighth Party Congress to be held in Patna, Bihar state, on 7-15 February 1968. On the agenda were the election of a new party National Council, discussion of amendments to the party program, and the discussion and adoption of a political report and an organizational report (*New Age,* 17 December 1967).

**Publications.** Indian Communists have a network of dailies, weeklies, and monthlies throughout the country, in English and in various vernacular languages. The central organization of the CPI publishes the weekly *New Age* in New Delhi; Bhupesh Gupta is its editor. The English-language weekly of the CPI(M) is *People's Democracy,* edited by B. T. Ranadive and published in Calcutta. A US government source (*Communist Propaganda Organizations and Activities in the Near East and South Asia during 1966,* USIA: July 25, 1967) lists over 100 publications of Indian communist parties and front organizations—dailies, weeklies, fortnightlies, monthlies, and quarterlies—in English and other languages. There are several weeklies with large circulation (*Blitz, Patriot, Link, Mainstream, Century,* and others) which, although not official organs of either communist party, are generally procommunist and may be called fellow-traveling journals. Finally, the extreme leftist Communists following a Maoist line in 1967 published a biweekly, *Commune*; a weekly, *Deshabrati*; a monthly, *Liberation*; and several other publications, including *Patriotic Reminiscences, People's Path,* and *Chhautra Fauz* (Student Army).

# INDONESIA

The Communist Party of Indonesia (Partai Komunis Indonesia; PKI) was founded 23 May 1920 when Indonesian social-democratic associations under the leadership of Dutch radicals and Islamic nationalists, meeting at Semarang, in Java, decided to join the Third International.

Following an unsuccessful uprising in November 1926, the PKI was declared illegal. Until 1945 it operated as an "illegal splinter group," with most of its leaders in Moscow or in Yenan, China. Upon the establishment of an independent Indonesian republic under the leadership of President Sukarno, 17 August 1945, the PKI resumed legal activity. In 1946, after an unsuccessful putsch attempt by Tan Malaka, head of a Trotskyist wing (the Partai Murba) which split off from the PKI in 1928, the exiled leaders returned from Moscow and Yenan and assumed direction of the party.

On the night of 30 September 1965,* six of the senior generals of the Indonesian army were abducted and murdered in the course of an attempted coup mounted by a group of air force and army personnel and led by Lieutenant Colonel Untung. The extent of PKI planning and participation in the coup attempt is debatable. It is known, however, that members of the PKI and PKI-directed front organizations, such as the People's Youth and the Women's Movement, supported the coup attempt, describing it as "patriotic and revolutionary" in an editorial in *Harian Rakyat,* the party newspaper (*Harian Rakyat,* 2 October). General Abdul Haris Nasution, Defense Minister and Chief of Staff of the Armed Forces, and Major General (now General) T. N. J. Suharto, commander of the Strategic Reserves, succeeded in escaping and proceeded to crush the insurgency.

On 12 March 1966 the PKI and all its affiliate organizations were banned and a strict ban was placed on the acceptance of former PKI members into existing political organizations. On 5 July 1966, the Indonesian Parliament formally outlawed the studying and teaching of Marxism-Leninism. On 26 March 1967 the PKI was barred from taking part in the general elections scheduled for 1968.†

In a speech on 6 October 1967, Acting President Suharto elaborated on the decision to ban the dissemination and teaching of Marxism-Leninism: "The ban on the dissemination of communism in Indonesia is our own domestic affair; we are merely exercising our sovereign right in determining our way of life as an independent nation. By banning communism, Indonesia does not mean to interfere in the domestic affairs of other countries or take a hostile attitude toward countries which uphold that ideology." (Indonesian Information Service, 7 October.)

**Membership, Leadership, and Organization.** By September 1965, the PKI had become the third largest communist party in the world, claiming a membership of 3,000,000. In addition it controlled a number of front organizations: the People's Youth (Pemuda Rakjat, 2,000,000 members), the Indonesian Farmers' Front (Barisan Tani Indonesia, 8,500,000 members), the Central Labor Organization of Indonesia ("SOBSI," 3,500,000 members), and the Women's Movement (Gerwani, 1,750,000 members). The party controlled also a number of smaller, more or less ephemeral organizations and had a certain degree of influence within the Nationalist Party of Indonesia (Partai Nasional Indonesia; PNI). Probably about a quarter of the total Indonesian population of 105,300,000 (estimated mid-1965) was directly or indirectly affiliated with the PKI. The party's position was further enhanced by President Sukarno's favorable disposition toward it.††

*Although the coup attempt is generally dated 30 September, it actually took place in the early hours of 1 October, possibly with the intent of coinciding with Peking's National Day (1 October) celebrations.

† On 10 January 1968, Acting President General Suharto formally asked Parliament to postpone the general elections, scheduled to be held before 5 July, pointing out that the Parliament had failed to enact a new general election law and that there was inadequate time to prepare for the elections. For the time being, the Parliament has put off making a ruling on the request.

††On 20 February 1967 Sukarno delegated all executive powers to General Suharto and on 12 March the Parliament formalized Sukarno's actions by appointing General Suharto Acting President pending general elections.

The abortive coup of 30 September 1965 was followed by mass arrests and the execution of Communists and members of communist affiliates, with estimates of the number killed ranging from 100,000 to 500,000. The number of PKI members killed is unknown, but thousands reportedly left the party under the threat of death or arrest. Some 100,000 to 150,000 members of the subsequently banned PKI are believed to be still active.

Among those arrested were Dipa Nusantara Aidit, Chairman and chief theoretician of the PKI; Mohammad Lukman, Vice-Chairman of the PKI and reportedly the leader of its pro-Soviet faction; and Njoto, the party's chief propagandist and publications director. Aidit and Njoto were executed shortly after their arrest; although reports vary, Lukman may also have been executed. By the end of 1967 the status of the former PKI Politburo and Central Executive Committee appeared to be as follows:

| POLITBURO | | CENTRAL EXECUTIVE COMMITTEE |
|---|---|---|
| Director: | D. N. Aidit (b) | Chairman: Sudisman (b) |
| Members: | Jusuf Adjitorop (c) | First Deputy Chairman: Jusuf Adjitorop (c) |
| | Lukman (b) | |
| | Njono (b) | Second Deputy Chairman: Pardede Peris (b) |
| | Njoto (b) | |
| | Sakirman (b) | Third Deputy Chairman: Anwar Kadir (c) |
| | Sudisman (b) | |
| | Anwar Sanusi (a) | Members: Anwar Sanusi (a) |
| | Rewang (a) | Djoko Sudjojo (a) |
| | | Njono (b) |
| | | Noer Suhud (a) |
| | | Ruslan Kamaldin (c) |
| | | Sidortojo (c) |
| | | Siswojo (c) |
| | | Sudjono (c) |
| | | Tjugito (c) |
| | | Zaelani (c) |

(a) arrested but not yet convicted.
(b) awaiting execution or already executed.
(c) at large.

Although a high percentage of the members of the Politburo and Central Executive Committee were arrested, Radio Djakarta has reported 56 of the 86 members of the Djakarta Central Committee as being still at large (*Washington Post*, 24 March 1967). During 1967 Djakarta officials also reported the arrest of former Brigadier General Supardjo, one of the suspected leaders of the attempted coup; Kamaruzaman, better known as "Ssam," chief of the PKI Special Intelligence Bureau; and Sukatno, former General Chairman of the Indonesian Communist Youth Movement.

Attempts to reorganize the PKI after the attempted coup have apparently resulted in the splitting of the party into three factions: the Politburo of the PKI Central Committee, the Peking-based delegation of the PKI Central Committee, and the Marxist-Leninist group of the PKI.

**The Delegation of the PKI Central Committee and the Politburo of the PKI Central Committee.** Following the attempted coup of 30 September, Communist China sought to present the Delegation of the PKI Central Committee and Jusuf Adjitorop, who was in Peking at the time, as the only authentic spokesmen of the Indonesian Communists. According to reports, the Delegation of the PKI Central Committee consists of some 700 persons, including Djawoto, the former Indonesian ambassador to Peking, who resigned from his diplomatic post and resumed his duties as Secretary-General of the Chinese-sponsored Afro-Asian Journalists' Association; Hanafi, former ambassador to Cuba; and Sukrisno, former ambassador to North Vietnam. PKI Central Committee member Sidik Kertapati was also in Peking at the time of the attempted coup, as were six Indonesian cabinet members. Kertapati reportedly has been seen in East Java and is operating as chief liaison between Communist China and the underground PKI. Although Jusuf Adjitorop has been frequently referred to as the leader of the Delegation of the PKI Central Committee, reports in 1967 indicated that Djawoto was a major driving force behind the Peking-based group and were confirmed by Baron Sutadisastra, the expelled Indonesian chargé d'affaires in Peking, who stated that Peking had officially designated Djawoto to lead the campaign against the present Indonesian government. Under the leadership of both these men, the Delegation of the PKI Central Committee has stressed the applicability of Mao Tse-tung's theory of armed struggle to the Indonesian situation and denounced the theory of peaceful coexistence advocated by the Soviet "revisionists."

Despite Peking's efforts, however, the appearance of a statement by the Politburo of the PKI Central Committee datelined Central Java, 17 August 1966, and entitled "The Indonesian Communist Party Reviews the Situation and Tasks Facing the Indonesian Revolution" and the subsequent appearance of a document of the Politburo of the PKI Committee entitled "Build the PKI Along the Marxist-Leninist Line to Lead the People's Democratic Revolution in Indonesia: Self-Criticism of the Central Committee of the PKI" (see *Documents*) indicated that a number of PKI members had regrouped and reorganized themselves and were operating in Indonesia. According to the *Voice of Indonesian Youth,* a journal published by the Indonesian Students' Association in China, the party is primarily active in Central Java, where a "people's armed force under the leadership of the PKI" was formed in July 1966 (*Voice of Indonesian Youth,* as reported in *Challenge,* the organ of the pro-Chinese US Progressive Labor Party, February 1967).

The precise relationship between the Delegation of the PKI Central Committee and the Politburo of the PKI Central Committee is unknown. Most reports indicate, however, that the Peking group comes under the direction of the Politburo of the PKI Central Committee and that the two groups are primarily responsible for current communist activities in Indonesia. While the two groups advocate similar strategies, tactics, and programs calling for revolutionary action, the Delegation of the PKI Central Committee places considerably more emphasis on the thought of Mao Tse-tung.

Although the Politburo of the PKI Central Committee has not publicly commented on the nature of its leadership and organization, reports indicate that it operates under the leadership of PKI Politburo member Sudisman, who served as its Chairman until his arrest in October 1966 and is said to be the author of the PKI Self-Criticism, and Hitapia Djudjido, who currently serves as PKI Secretary-General. Other leaders of the group apparently include: Sakirman, arrested in late 1966; B. O. Hutaped, head of the department for "Reorganization of People's and Youth's Organizations"; Robby Sumolong, head of the department for "Distribution of Agitation Documents"; Sjan Sulis, head of the department in charge of "Maneuvering for Infiltration into Army and Government Organs"; Rewang, Chairman of the Central Java District Branch of the PKI; Ruslan Widjajasasastra, Chairman of the East Java District Branch; Supardji, Chairman of the Djakarta District Branch; Suwardinengsih, Chairman of the Southern Sumatra District Branch; and Wikana, Chairman of the West Java District Branch.

**Strategy and Tactics and the Attempted Coup of 30 September.** Major documents of both the Delegation of the PKI Central Committee and the Politburo of the PKI Central Committee have focused on the reasons for the failure of the attempted coup of 30 September and on the future role of the PKI. At the Fifth Congress of the Albanian Workers' Party (November 1966), Jusuf Adjitorop declared that "events in Indonesia have completely disproved the 'theory of a peaceful path' under any form whatsoever and have revealed the danger that this theory represents for the revolutionary movement." Adjitorop also called for PKI members to wage a "principled and serious internal struggle within the party" and outlined three basic tasks: "reconstruction of the Indonesian Communist Party on a Marxist-Leninist basis," preparation for a "long armed struggle integrated with the agrarian revolution of the peasants in the rural areas, and formation of a united front of "all the forces opposing the dictatorship of the right-wing generals led by Suharto and Nasution."

In analyzing the future course of action for the party, PKI members in China stated: "It is essential to shift the center of activity from the cities to the countryside and to engage in armed struggle there to carry out agrarian revolution and establish revolutionary bases. Beginning people's war from the countryside, which forms the weakest link in the country because the reactionary forces are the most vulnerable in rural areas, and fanning out from the rural bases, the people can encircle the cities from the countryside and eventually capture the cities and win victory over the whole country." (NCNA, 24 July 1967).

While both the 17 August 1966 Statement and the PKI Self-Criticism issued in the name of the Politburo of the PKI Central Committee contain a similar assessment of the attempted coup, there is virtually no praise of Chairman Mao in either document, which is a distinctive feature of documents issued by the Peking groups in general and which was voiced in Jusuf Adjitorop's address to the Albanian Workers' Party Congress in particular; and criticism of the Soviet "revisionists" is at a minimum.

The 17 August 1966 Statement specifically criticized the PKI for supporting the "mistaken theory of two aspects in state power," which maintains that the "pro-people aspect" will eventually supersede the "anti-people aspect" by peaceful means, and stressed the party's failure to realize that "the main problem of every revolution is the seizure of state power." In analyzing the strategy and tactics to be utilized by the PKI in the future, the statement specifically remarked:

> The oppressed classes, in liberating themselves from oppression and exploitation, have no other way but to make a revolution—that is to say, to overthrow by force the oppressor classes from state power, to seize state power by force. This is because the state is an instrument created by the ruling classes to oppress the ruled classes. (Quoted in *New Zealand Communist Review,* January-February 1967.)

As noted earlier, the statement also outlined a series of basic tasks to be fulfilled by the PKI while preparing for armed revolution.

The Self-criticism of the PKI Central Committee apparently issued in September 1966, was printed in full in the January 1967 issue of the *Indonesian Tribune*. In outlining the basic weaknesses of the PKI in both the ideological and the political fields, it commented:

> The PKI leadership had been engaged in adventurism. Violating organizational rules, they had easily involved themselves in the September 30th Movement that was not based on the high consciousness or conviction of the masses. And therefore they had caused the isolation of the Party from the masses of the people. On the contrary, after the defeat of the September 30th Movement, the Party leadership carried out a right opportunist line by entrusting President Sukarno with the fate of the Party and the revolutionary movement. These were the climax of the serious shortcomings and weaknesses of the PKI in the ideological, political, and organizational fields.

In enumerating the ideological weaknesses of the PKI, the document charged that the party had failed to establish a "core of leadership that was composed of proletarian elements which really had the most correct understanding of Marxism-Leninism, systematic and not fragmentary, practical and not abstract understanding." Attributing the party's weaknesses to "subjectivism" in general, it also noted three basic weaknesses in particular: (1) failure to develop the tradition of criticism and self-criticism "in a Marxist-Leninist way"; (2) penetration by bourgeois ideology "through contacts with the national bourgeoisie when the Party established a united front with them and [through] the bourgeoisification of Party cadres, especially the leadership, after the Party obtained certain positions in governmental and semi-governmental institutions"; and (3) penetration by "modern revisionism," which began "when the Fourth Plenary Session of the Fifth Congress uncritically approved a report which supported the lines of the 20th Congress of the CPSU and adopted the line of 'achieving Socialism peacefully through parliamentary means' as the line of the PKI."

In the political sphere, the party was criticized for not yet having come to the "clearest unity of minds on the principal means and the main form of struggle of the Indonesian revolution." Specifically noted was the PKI's mistake in having become "bogged down in parliamentary and other forms of legal struggle" and of having "considered this to be the main form of struggle to achieve the strategic aim of the Indonesian revolution." The PKI was accused of strengthening the system of parliamentarism, "instead of using the general elections and parliamentary struggle to accelerate the political obsolescence of parliamentarianism," and of having given "too many concessions to the national bourgeoisie," thus causing the party to lose its "independent role of leadership."

Considerable criticism was also levied against the party for having failed to adopt an independent attitude toward Sukarno and for having failed to keep the leadership of the revolution "in the hands of the proletariat and their Party, the PKI," with the result that "it was not the program of the PKI that was accepted by the bourgeoisie but ... on the contrary it was the program of the national bourgeoisie which was accepted by the PKI and was made to replace the program of the PKI."

After analyzing the mistakes of "right opportunism" in the ideological and political spheres, the document commented:

> When the deviation to the Right had become overall and complete, another tendency that was quite the opposite emerged, namely a 'leftist' tendency. The 'Leftist' tendency manifested itself in the overestimation of the strength of the Party, the working class, and the rest of the working people; the exaggerated appraisals of the results of the people's struggle, and the underestimation of the strength of the reactionaries.

The PKI was also criticized for "blindly seeking" numerical strength in recruitment and failing to realize that the mass character of a party ought to be expressed primarily in its close ties with the masses, not in its numerical strength alone.

On the basis of its analysis of the errors committed by the PKI, the document concluded:

> To achieve its complete victory, the Indonesian revolution must also follow the road of the Chinese revolution. This means that the Indonesian revolution must inevitably adopt this main form of struggle, namely, the people's armed struggle against the armed counter-revolution which, in essence, is the armed agrarian revolution of the peasants under the leadership of the proletariat. ...
>
> All forms of legal and parliamentary work should secure the principal means and the main form of struggle and must not in any way impede the process of the ripening of armed struggle.

Although the primary importance of a strategy of armed struggle was stressed, the document also noted: "While working for the realization of this most principal question, one must also carry out other forms of struggle; armed struggle will never advance without being coordinated with other forms of struggle." The PKI was called on to "return to the correct conception of a revolutionary national united front based on the alliance of the workers and peasants under the leadership of the working class."

**Domestic Activities.** Although the PKI has been left with no effective legal cover, procommunist support apparently is still found in student groups such as the Indonesian Students' Movement (Gerakan Mahasiswa Indonesia, or Germindo), the National Indonesian Students' Movement (Gerakan Mahasiswa Nasional Indonesia), and the Student Association of Bung Karno University in Djakarta. Other sources of support include the Indonesian Afro-Asian People's Solidarity Organization and the Indonesian Students' Association, both based in Peking.

Remnants of the PKI have attempted to infiltrate existing political parties particularly the Indonesian Nationalist Party (Partai Nasional Indonesia; PNI), whose doctrine of Marhaenism is defined as "Marxism to suit the conditions of Indonesia." Although a number of communists were purged from the PNI in late 1966 and the West Java chapter of the PNI issued a declaration on 30 January 1967 stating that it rejected "Marhaenism-Marxism in all its forms and manifestations," Indonesian authorities reported that a "common front" was being formed between the left wing of the PNI and the communists. Official concern over the activities of the PNI during 1967 resulted in the banning of the PNI in Sumatra and East Java and the outlawing of the PNI youth movement in Djogjakarta and Kedu because of reported infiltration by members of the banned communist People's Youth Organization. Similar limitations and temporary bans were placed on branches of the PNI elsewhere in Indonesia.

In addition to the PNI, the communist-oriented Partindo (Partai Indonesia), a radical offshoot of the PNI, appeared to be providing leadership to those trade unions formerly controlled by the PKI.

Communists were active during 1967 in a number of guerrilla organizations operating in Indonesia. Former PKI members reportedly were joining the Sarawak People's Guerrilla Troops (Pertahanan

Gerila Rakyat Sarawak; PGRS), the military arm of the Sarawak Communist Organization, which operates along the Sarawak border with Indonesian Borneo (Kalimantan). According to Indonesian authorities, leaders of the PGRS were trying to establish connections with Java. Other guerrilla organizations include: the "North Kalimantan Freedom Fighters," reportedly led by former pro-Chinese Foreign Minister Subandrio; the "12th November Movement," apparently part of the underground PKI operating in North Sumatra and described as "an underground military movement which is an integral part of the so-called revolutionary guerrilla war whose mastermind is outside the country" (Djakarta Domestic Service, 5 December 1967); the "People's Defense Force," operating in West Borneo and West Java; and the "People's Liberation Front," operating in Central Java and apparently formed by former members of "SOBSI."

During 1967 Indonesian authorities repeatedly warned that in spite of the fact that the communists had been crushed for the time being, PKI remnants were attempting to consolidate themselves in order to stage a comeback. Numerous incidents of communist activity were reported in Sumatra, Java, West Borneo, and Celebes, with reports indicating that some degree of collaboration might exist between members of the various groups.

Communist activities were focused primarily on infiltration of the armed forces and various political and mass organizations, together with the dissemination of PKI propaganda. Numerous armed clashes between communist guerrillas and government forces occurred, resulting in the arrest of a number of former PKI members. In late October and early November, hundreds of Chinese in Pontianak, West Borneo, were killed, reportedly at the instigation of former members of the PKI.

On 3 October Radio Tirana commented on a statement issued by the Politburo of the PKI Central Committee on the occasion of the 47th anniversary of the founding of the PKI (23 May). Although the Albanian broadcast gave few details, it noted that the Politburo had "reached the conclusion that the current situation was relatively better than that a year ago," adding: "The communist party and the Indonesian revolutionary movement are in the process of revival, and, step by step, they are resolutely marching along the road of revolution." According to the broadcast, the Indonesian statement declared: "In the process of reviving the party and the revolutionary Indonesian movement, we are encountering great difficulties and obstacles, as well as constant counterrevolutionary attacks. But however great the obstacles and difficulties and however bitter the fascist attacks, the facts show that they cannot halt the re-creation of the party and the revolutionary Indonesian movement, which have found the correct revolutionary road." Maintaining that the "objective conditions necessary for revolution" were "improving throughout the country," the PKI statement outlined a series of future tasks facing the party:

> Reconstruction of the Indonesian Communist Party, a party that serves the armed struggle and lays stress on the work in villages and on underground work. It should fully eliminate all traces of the opportunist and revisionist mistakes, eradicating their ideological sources and any conditions conducive to their growth. It should struggle against the spirit of individualism and strengthen the spirit of self-denial in the interest of the party and the people.

> The party gives itself the task of consolidating its links with the masses, of making the masses rise up, and of leading their struggle against oppression and exploitation. It considers armed struggle or the people's struggle to be the only road to liberation.

> The Indonesian Communist Party will even more resolutely struggle for the formation of the united revolutionary front of all nations that are struggling against US imperialism and the Indonesian military regime.

> It gives itself the task of uniting the broad revolutionary masses, who are the victims of the revolutionary policy of the fascist regime.

> By resolutely carrying out our tasks . . . we will acquire three main weapons for the victory of the people's democratic revolution in Indonesia: (1) the Marxist-Leninist party, which represents the leading nucleus of the revolution; (2) the party-led armed people's force, representing the main form of organizing the revolution; (3) a party-led united revolutionary front, uniting all the revolutionary forces in Indonesia.

**International Views and Positions; Communist China and the Soviet Union.** While both the Delegation of the PKI and the Politburo of the PKI Central Committee follow a pro-Peking line, the Delegation places considerably more emphasis on the applicability of the thoughts of Mao Tse-tung and the significance of the cultural revolution. An editorial in *Suara Rakjat Indonesia,* the organ of the Peking-based Indonesian Afro-Asian People's Solidarity Organization, praised Chairman Mao as the "first great Marxist-Leninist who has in an all-round and comprehensive manner, systematically and scientifically formulated the Marxist-Leninist military theory which is the most powerful weapon for the oppressed nations and oppressed peoples the world over in their struggle for national liberation," and went on to hail the cultural revolution:

> This unprecedented and great proletarian cultural revolution personally directed by Chairman Mao Tse-tung and illuminated by the infinitely brilliant thought of Mao Tse-tung has destroyed the bourgeois headquarters headed by China's Khrushchev and shattered all the hopes and dreams of the imperialists, revisionists, and reactionaries of all countries for a capitalist restoration in China. (NCNA, 17 November 1967.)

The international significance of the thought of Chairman Mao was stressed by Ibrahim Isa, Secretary-General of the Indonesian Afro-Asian People's Solidarity Organization, who observed:

> Mao Tse-tung's thought and the Communist Party of China constitute the yardstick for sizing up every revolutionary and every genuine revolutionary party. Every revolutionary and every genuine revolutionary party cannot but sincerely and whole heartedly recognize Mao Tse-tung's thought as the acme of Marxism-Leninism in the present era, recognize Chairman Mao as the most outstanding leader of the proletariat in the present era and the greatest and most brilliant genius in the present era, and recognize the Communist Party of China as the vanguard of the international communist movement and world revolution and China as the center and base of world revolution, because all this is the objective reality of history. (*Ibid.,* 13 October.)

Although the 17 August 1966 Statement and the Self-Criticism issued by the PKI Politburo advocated the "road of the Chinese Revolution" as the only way to achieve "complete victory," both refrained from commenting on the cultural revolution and contained virtually no reference to the thought of Mao. However, an NCNA report (13 October) on the statement issued by the Politburo on the 47th Anniversary of the founding of the PKI declared that the Politburo had hailed the cultural revolution as "today's greatest international event of great historical significance."

In turn, Communist China has repeatedly pointed out that

> The Chinese Communist Party and the Chinese people constantly have the fight of the Indonesian Communist Party and the Indonesian people in mind. Our hearts are closely linked with the hearts of our class brothers in Indonesia. We stand unflinchingly on the side of the Indonesian Communist Party, on the side of the Indonesian revolutionary people, and firmly support the Indonesian Communist Party in leading the Indonesian people's struggle to overthrow the Suharto-Nasution fascist regime and establish a completely independent and democratic new Indonesia.

In addition to propaganda support, Communist China reportedly has been providing military training in China for Indonesian communists. On 17 May 1967, Indonesian Foreign Minister Adam Malik stated that some 180 Indonesians were being trained at the Wuhan Military Academy, and on 7 July Hussein Kartasasmita, Chairman of the Defense, Security, and Foreign Affairs Commission of the Indonesian Parliament, announced that China was attempting to send back to Indonesia certain Chinese nationals who had been repatriated to Communist China and trained in subversion. Indonesian authorities also maintained that Peking was sending military equipment to communist terrorists in Indonesia and attempting to infiltrate the Chinese community there.

Sino-Indonesian relations deteriorated markedly during 1967. Following the death of Ning Hsiang-yu, a Chinese national who had been arrested on charges of being a subversive agent, a series of demonstrations broke out in Djakarta which Indonesian authorities declared were "controlled by Peking with the aim of further worsening relations between Indonesia and Communist China." On 24 April the Indonesian government announced that Yao Teng-shan, chargé d'affaires *ad interim* of the

Chinese Embassy in Indonesia, and Hsu Jen, the Chinese consul-general in Djakarta, had been declared *personae non gratae* and ordered to leave the country before 29 April. In retaliation, Indonesia's charge d'affaires in China, Baron Sutadisastra, was declared *persona non grata* by Peking. On 14 September, the Indonesian government expelled two Communist Chinese diplomats who were accused of instigating anti-Indonesian demonstrations on 5 August. On 15 September, Foreign Minister Adam Malik announced that the Indonesian government had ordered its Embassy staff in Peking to return to Indonesia but that Peking had not yet issued the necessary exit visas. On 25 September, China expelled two Indonesian diplomats whom it charged with "activities undermining relations" between the two countries. A third series of demonstrations in early October eventually resulted in the Indonesian government's announcement on 9 October 1967 that it had decided to suspend diplomatic relations. On 25 October, Indonesia announced the closing of its Embassy in Peking and on 28 October China responded by closing its Embassy in Djakarta.

In accordance with their pro-Peking statements, the Delegation of the PKI Central Committee and the Politburo of the PKI Central Committee had condemned the Soviet "revisionists" and the strategy of "achieving socialism peacefully through parliamentary means." In analyzing ideological errors committed by the PKI, the Politburo's Self-criticism stated:

> The experience of the PKI provides us with the lesson that modern revisionism, the greatest danger in the International Communist Movement, is also the greatest danger for the PKI . . . . Therefore, we must not in any way underestimate the danger of modern revisionism and must wage a resolute and ruthless struggle against it. The firm stand against modern revisionism in all fields can be effectively maintained only when our Party abandons the line of "preserving the friendship with the modern revisionists."

PKI elements in Peking accused the Soviet Union of being the "center of counterrevolution" and maintained that "a number of communist parties, such as those of France, Italy, India, and the United States" had "degenerated into Khrushchev's lackeys and revisionist parties."

**The Sino-Soviet Dispute and the Attempted Coup of 30 September.** In addition to analysis by the PKI itself, the events of 30 September 1965 have been given careful consideration by both Communist China and the Soviet Union. Chinese Communist sources strongly endorsed the 17 August 1966 Statement and Self-criticism of the Politburo of the PKI. An NCNA broadcast on 24 October 1967, criticized the Soviet theory of a "peaceful transition to socialism" and stated: "Contrary to the assertion by the leadership of the Soviet revisionists, the Indonesian revolution suffered a serious setback not because it adopted some kind of left deviationist adventurism of Peking. The serious consequences to the Indonesian revolution were the result of the revisionist line of peaceful transition propagated by the Soviet revisionist clique."

A subsequent NCNA broadcast (1 December) declared:

> The Soviet revisionist renegade group has incurred an immense blood debt to the Indonesian revolution. In their rabid betrayal of this revolution, these renegades have worked hand in glove for a long time with US imperialism and the Suharto-Nasution fascist military group in Indonesia to form a counterrevolutionary alliance to suppress the Communist Party and people of Indonesia. The bloodthirsty massacres of the Indonesian Communists and other revolutionary people in the past two years or more were conducted with the very support of the Soviet revisionist renegade group politically and militarily. In these slaughters, the Indonesian fascist military group was provided with arms by the Soviet revisionists.

Soviet analysis of the attempted coup has taken the position that the 30 September movement was "initiated by units of the armed forces, chiefly the ground troops, which had a large element of progressive servicemen" and that therefore "the fact that some members of the Party participated in the September 30 movement is no reason for the *PKI* to be held responsible as an organization for their conduct" (*WMR* October 1967). An article in *Pravda* (28 May) by I. Antonov on the occasion of the 47th anniversary of the founding of the PKI stated:

> Indonesian reaction is attempting for its own political purposes to saddle the Communist Party and all Communists with responsibility for the putsch activity of Lieut. Col.

Untung and the individuals behind him. In reality, what the Communist Party is wholly responsible for is the program that was worked out on the general principles of Marxism-Leninism as applied to their specific country and ratified by the highest organ of the party—its Congress. The nature of the events that occurred on 30 September 1965 directly contradicts the spirit and letter of the PKI program.

The CPSU Central Committee and our party press, expressing the opinion of millions of Communists and the entire Soviet people, have repeatedly condemned the mass repressions and acts of terrorism against hundreds of thousands of Indonesian Communists, who had nothing to do with the events of 30 September 1965, and cannot bear responsibility for them.

No unbiased person who is acquainted with the Communists' strategic and tactical principles can have any doubt that the 30 September putsch had nothing in common with the theory and practice of the Communist movement. Marxism-Leninism categorically rejects adventuristic tactics and individual acts of terrorism. Therefore, attempts like those being made in Indonesia to discredit Marxist-Leninist doctrine, which is followed by the peoples of the socialist countries and substantial numbers of working people in the capitalist countries, cannot but arouse indignation.

The Soviet Union accused the Communist Chinese leadership of having "directly interfered in the internal affairs of the Indonesian Communist Party and forced it to follow their views," adding:

The consequences of this policy were the events of 30 September 1965 in which the progressive forces of Indonesia were repressed during an adventurous *coup d'état* and became the victims of a bloody terrorist campaign lasting many months.

Although the Indonesian communists are in great straits and are facing ruthless repressive measures carried out by their government, the Mao Tse-tung clique has done nothing to protect the communist elements and all the democratic forces in Indonesia. Instead of helping the Indonesian communists closely analyze the causes of their failure and rebuild the communist party in accordance with Marxist-Leninist lines, Peking on the contrary has staged new provocative acts. (Moscow Radio, 12 July.)

**Vietnam.** Although the Politburo of the PKI Central Committee apparently has issued no statements on the Vietnam war, PKI members in Peking have repeatedly declared their support for the "heroic Vietnamese people" and condemned the "aggressive actions of the US imperialists." Numerous statements have also condemned the "Soviet revisionists" for helping to establish "peace and security in Europe" and thereby enabling the United States to shift its troops from Europe to Vietnam, and for attempting to "intimidate the heroic Vietnamese people to lay down their arms."

**International Contacts.** Although the PKI focused most of its attention in 1967 on the ideological and political errors held to be responsible for the failure of the attempted coup, it also placed emphasis on the international aspect of the party's activities, on which the first issue of the *Indonesian Tribune* (November 1966) carried a lengthy statement:

The struggle to overthrow the fascist military regime of Suharto-Nasution, to establish a popular democratic regime and socialism in Indonesia, must be based, in the first instance, on the forces of the Indonesian people themselves. Despite this, the struggle is an integral part of the revolutionary struggle of the people of the world against imperialism and colonialism for the construction of a new world freed of the exploitation of man by man.

While the military fascist regime of Suharto-Nasution dominates the country, the struggle of the Indonesian people and communists enjoys very great solidarity from the revolutionary peoples of the world, particularly from the Marxist-Leninist parties and organizations of various countries. Therefore, the national tasks of the Indonesian communists can never be separated from the consistent achievement of their international tasks, which consist of a firm struggle against the common enemies of the peoples of the world and the establishment in this struggle of a powerful unity of all revolutionary forces.

In an effort to expand its international contacts, the PKI sought to utilize former officials of Indonesian embassies and Indonesian students living abroad. In warning government officials about these attempts, Indonesia's Foreign Minister, Adam Malik, specifically pointed to Albania, Cuba, and Czechoslovakia as centers for such activities and publicly asked the "friendly countries from the socialist bloc not to allow former PKI elements or those against the present new order in Indonesia to operate in their respective countries" (Antara, 16 August).

Although direct contact between the PKI and other communist parties was limited, Communist China frequently sponsored delegations of PKI members to various meetings of international front organizations. On 25 April an Antara reporter visiting eastern Europe reported that Djawoto, Sukrisno, and Adjitorop—members of the Delegation of the PKI Central Committee in Peking—were in Prague, attempting to "exploit PKI-affiliated students in order to carry out political-guerrilla activities abroad." The same reporter noted that a PKI member was in Paris establishing connections with the French Communist Party and that Hanafi, the former Indonesian ambassador to Cuba, was travelling in Europe with a Cuban passport and publishing illegal pamphlets.

Although the PKI sent delegations to the 1957 and 1960 meetings in Moscow, it was not represented at the celebrations of the fiftieth anniversary of the October Revolution, and it did not send a delegation to the Budapest meeting in February 1968.

**Publications.** Following the attempted coup, all PKI publications were banned in Indonesia. Since then, however, several new publications have become known. These include: *Mimbar Rakjat,* a monthly cladestine publication of the Politburo of the PKI Central Committee; *Voice of the Indonesian Youth,* monthly organ of the Indonesian Students' Association, based in Peking; *Suara Rakjat Indonesia,* organ of the Indonesian Afro-Asian People's Solidarity Organization, also in Peking; and the *Indonesian Tribune,* a monthly publication described as the voice of "progressive Indonesia," whose first issue (November 1966) noted that the purpose of the publication was to "contribute to the implementation of the national and international tasks of the Indonesian communists and progressives."

Statements of the Indonesian communists are also publicized by the Chinese Communist press and radio, as well as by East Germany, North Vietnam, and North Korea, all of which have regular broadcasts in Indonesian, and Radio Tirana, which began broadcasting in Indonesian on 16 March 1967.

* * *

**The Marxist-Leninist Group of the PKI.** Although it has been widely assumed that certain elements within the PKI disapproved of the party's decision to adopt a pro-Peking position, no public expression has been given to such dissent. On 11 and 18 March 1967, however, the Indian pro-Soviet weekly, *Mainstream,* carried the text of a document entitled "For a Sound Indonesian Revolution," issued in the name of the Marxist-Leninist Group of the Communist Party of Indonesia and apparently written in the latter half of 1966 (see *Documents*). *France Nouvelle,* the weekly publication of the French Communist Party, published excerpts from the document on 2 August; the *World Marxist Review, Information Bulletin* (no. 106) carried the complete text in November; and *L'Humanité* published the complete text on 11 December.

Although the name "Marxist-Leninist" is characteristic of pro-Chinese splinter groups in many non-communist countries, the "Marxist-Leninist Group of the PKI" is clearly pro-Soviet. Neither the size nor the importance of the group is known. It may be an entirely insignificant group, but it apparently has received Moscow's approval and reportedly is establishing a clandestine organization in Java and Sumatra.

**Analysis of the Attempted Coup of 30 September.** While the primary emphasis of the document issued by the Marxist-Leninist Group of the PKI is on the mistakes committed by the party, "For a Sound Indonesian Revolution" also discusses and evaluates the party's policies and actions immediately preceding the events of 30 September:

> Following the return of our leaders from a trip abroad which also included one of the Asian countries* (July-August 1965) it became known that the party leadership had taken a rash decision to begin preparation for playing the role of a "savior," with or without President Sukarno and other democratic forces. And all this happened at a time when there was no revolutionary situation in evidence, no instability was manifest in the position of the ruling quarters, the broad masses were not prepared for armed action. There was only a danger of a counterrevolutionary plot and there were the diseased kidneys of President Sukarno. Had a revolution occurred it would have been based not on the revolutionary situation or the support of the revolutionary masses, but would have rather hinged on Sukarno's lesioned kidneys. Truly, that was a gamble of the first order which had nothing to do with the Marxist theory of armed uprising.

While the "Party leadership" referred to above corresponds either to the triumverate of D. N. Aidit, Lukman, and Njoto, or to the entire PKI Politburo, composed of five full members and two alternate members, the document specifically points out that other echelons of leadership were consulted, maintaining that the "Party leadership called an expanded meeting" and undertook all "necessary action" in order to "prepare the party for any emergency," in addition to initiating "consultations with the President and left-wing nationalist leaders. In view of this, the Marxist-Leninist Group concludes:

> It is but natural that the revolutionary and progressive forces in Indonesia and throughout the world demand that the leadership of the Indonesian Communist Party be held responsible, for as the 1960 Moscow Statement says, each party is answerable to the workers and the people of its own country, to the international Workers' and Communist movement.

In analyzing the specific events of 30 September, the Marxist-Leninist statement notes:

> The primary cause of the defeat of the September 30 Movement was not that the enemy confronting us was too strong, or that we lacked courage, or that our fighters lacked courage. The subjective causes lie in recklessnesses on the part of some leading Party quarters, in the ideological, political and organizational muddleheadedness which was the objective result of the petty-bourgeois ideology of revolutionism; in excessive revolutionary zeal, a desire to achieve a quick victory; in forcing the development of the revolution which miscarried; in gambling on the balance of forces; in indulgence in adventurist fantasies, etc.

In addition to analysis of the attempted coup, the statement offers an evaluation of the PKI itself:

> The chief reason underlying the failures of the PKI in leading the revolution was that the PKI still lacked the traits characterizing a Leninist party, i.e., it was not a sufficiently bolshevized party, nor did it have a mass nature. In the past the Party had not paid adequate attention to measures aimed at increasing the role of proletarian elements in it or at improving its ideological and cultural level. In the recent past the Party tended to ascribe too much significance to the revolutionary spirit of the peasantry, whereas, without wishing to detract from our view that the peasantry is the staunchest ally of the working class, it should be pointed out that the petty-bourgeoisie is hamstrung by a serious drawback and one to be borne in mind, namely, that it is inconsistent in its actions.
>
> The doors of the Party were flung wide open for the mass admission of petty-bourgeois elements with the result that ideologically, politically and organizationally the Party was flooded with a petty-bourgeois wave, while the fact that the Party leadership was turning bourgeois was completely ignored.
>
> Hence, ideologically the Party was infected with a petty-bourgeois spirit and fell victim to overindulgence in ultra-left slogans and petty-bourgeois nationalism, all of which crippled the spirit of proletarian internationalism, that integral and inalienable part of the

*Presumably this refers to Communist China.

activities of the party of the working class.

Theoretically, there was, on the one hand, an upsurge of dogmatism which found expression in easy acceptance of concepts revolutionary in form but failing to take stock of local conditons. On the other hand, there was an emergence of revisionism which tended to upend the monolithic doctrine of Marxism-Leninism and replace it with "national Marxism" within the framework of the so-called "Indonesification of Marxism-Leninism."

Politically, the Party was not consistent in defending its class positions and engaged in class collaboration with the bourgeoisie; it gave prominence to cooperation within the framework of the NASAKOM,* it lost its freedom of action in strengthening the sacred alliance of the workers and peasants; it demonstrated subjectivism and haste in assessing the situation and in evaluating the balance of forces; it failed to define its tactics, shuttling between adventurism and capitulation; it made absolute its choice of the forms of struggle, tending to take just one aspect of the struggle out of the many forms that a party of the working class must employ.

All of this led to the Party's inability to play the role of leader of the Revolution.

Organizationally, in its internal activities the Party was further deviating from the principles of democracy and collective leadership, it was increasingly falling into the snare of the personality cult, it was demonstrating an increasing lack of internal democracy in the Party, it was stifling initiative coming from the rank and file, it was fettering criticism from below and was not encouraging the development of vigorous self-criticism.

Firm discipline was not strengthened in the Party, liberal attitudes towards the decisions of the Party organization flourished, serious measures to curb bureaucracy in the Party were not taken.

The adventurism of the abortive September 30 Movement and its epilogue proved to be the inevitable result of the accumulation of the Party's past mistakes, its confused ideological, political and organizational line, all of which caused the Party to be punished by the objective development of history.

The Marxist-Leninist group also criticized a "major mistake" committed by the Party after the coup attempt was launched, namely, the "passivity of the panic among the Party leadership in an emergency situation which resulted in surrender of all authority to President Sukarno and his political decision, but not reliance on the strength of the masses."

While concluding that the PKI committed a number of mistakes, "the consequences of which for the Indonesian Revolution and the international communist movement are hard to rectify," the Marxist-Leninist Group of the PKI also focused on the nature of the future tasks of the PKI. In order to correct the ideological errors committed by the party, it would be necessary that the PKI "strengthen the outlook and methods of the working class, strengthen the proletarian elements of the Party, oppose petty-bourgeois nationalism, [and] develop the spirit of proletarian internationalism in conjunction with true patriotism." According to the Marxist-Leninists, the party "should deepen the knowledge of the universal teachings of Marxism-Leninism in conjunction with concrete revolutionary practices in Indonesia; it should free itself from the wrong concept of the 'Indonesification of Marxism-Leninism.'"

A further passage concerned strategy and tactics:

The Party should return to the correct way of creating a united national front. It should value most of all the strengthening of the union between workers and peasants as the basic foundation of the united national front. The Party should step up its work among the peasants on the basis of a revolutionary agrarian program, which can make the peasants a tested ally of the working class and secure correct proportions in the cooperation of the working people with the national bourgeoisie and other democratic elements . . . . The Party should increase its influence in the masses by using all forms of legal or illegal struggle, take into account the requirements and demands of all strata of

*Sukarno's term for cooperation between Indonesia's nationalist, religious, and communist groups.

the working people for improved living conditions, consistently and increasingly carry out mass revolutionary action for democratic rights, higher living standards and social progress.

While pointing out that "there are chances for a peaceful victory of the revolution," the Marxist-Leninists offered cautionary advice:

To follow the peaceful way we must firstly, be sure that this peaceful way is open to us and, acting on this optimistic assumption, prepare all the conditions that will be instrumental in achieving the victory of the revolution by peaceful means; secondly, we should by no means create an illusion that there is no other opportunity, i.e., the non-peaceful way, so as not to weaken ideological, political and organizational vigilance.

In short, it is for the sake of achieving the victory of the revolution by peaceful means that we must be ready for both alternatives and do our utmost to prepare the conditions outlined above.

The Indonesian Marxist-Leninists recommended a number of changes within the PKI. In general, they declared, "the Leninist norms of party organization should be restored; the principles of democratic centralism should be unflinchingly followed, among them the principle of collective leadership criticism and self-criticism should be reborn."

**International Views and Positions.** In analyzing errors committed before, during, and after 30 September 1965, the Marxist-Leninists criticized the PKI for following the "wrong path" by treating as enemies those whom it "believed to be 'revisionists' matching in their viciousness and evil the pillars of world imperialism." Without mentioning the Chinese Communist Party by name, the statement also noted: "Not only did we fail to stand on our own and strengthen our identity, but rather we became even more ideologically, politically, and economically dependent on a certain party. What is more, that party was responsible for turning the Indonesian Revolution into a gaming table for its political gambles."

In addition to commenting on the Sino-Soviet dispute, the pro-Soviet Marxist-Leninists stressed that the "Indonesian Revolution" was "part and parcel of the world revolution," and called on the PKI to adopt the Moscow Declaration of 1957 and the Statement of 1960 as the "guiding principles in solving Party problems." As to the international obligations of the PKI, the group noted:

The banners of proletarian internationalism should be raised aloft, the unity of the International Communist movement should be strengthened, all attempts to split and undermine the alliance and unity of the front of Communists and Workers' parties fighting the common enemy—imperialism led by U.S. imperialism should be frustrated and foiled; the Party should be truly devoted to the letter and spirit of the Moscow Declaration and Statement worked out jointly by all the fraternal parties. Realistic relations should be maintained with all the Communist and Workers' parties on the basis of the principle of independence and equality, without allowing an open attack against each other in the face of the enemy.

Such is the way out of the existing situation.

Although the Marxist-Leninist Group of the PKI is not known to have attended any international communist conference during 1967 or to have established direct contact with any communist party on a bilateral basis, the Marxist-Leninist document in its conclusions expressed expectation of outside support: "Confidence should prevail that the international proletariat, the Communist and Workers' parties of the world, all the progressive and revolutionaries the world over will always demonstrate their solidarity with us . . . "

# IRAN

The Communist Party of Iran, officially named the Tudeh (People's) Party, was founded in October 1941. During World War II it received the support of Soviet troops and officials occupying northwestern Iran, under whose protection it gained in strength and influence. When the Soviet-sponsored puppet republics in Azerbaijan and Mahabad fell in 1946, the party lost prestige and popularity (*World Strength of the Communist Party Organizations,* 1968). In February 1949 the government of Iran banned the Tudeh Party after an attempt on the life of the Shah, but it continued to operate effectively until the fall of Mohammed Mosadeq in August 1953 (*Ibid.*). In 1954 the government all but destroyed the party by arresting many of its members and repressing its activities. Since then it has operated in exile from Eastern Europe; the Central Committee is located at present in East Germany. As a result of these disabilities, the Tudeh Party has exercised little influence in Iran, but it has been active among Iranian students and intellectuals in Europe (a scattered community estimated at 50,000 persons).

Since 1965 there has also been a small splinter Communist group, the Revolutionary Organization of the Tudeh Party (see below).

**Organization and Leadership.** The Chairman of the Tudeh Party is Reza Radmanesh. Other identified members of the Politburo include Iradji Iskenderi, Ardeshir Hovanesyan, and Abd-os-Samad Kambakhsh. Ehsan Tabari is chief of the Central Committee Propaganda Branch. The precise membership of the party cannot be determined, but it is believed to be less than 1,000 (*Ibid.*). Iran's population is 25,781,000 (estimated November 1967).

**Domestic Views and Policies.** The Iranian Communists face a serious problem in adhering strongly to a pro-Moscow line and simultaneously denouncing the Shah's regime in Iran while that government is instituting extensive reforms and a program of modernization which is being given broad support from Moscow and from East Europe. The rapprochement that began between the Soviet Union and Iran in 1966 burgeoned into a series of trade agreements, cultural exchanges, and reciprocal visits by Iranian and European communist dignitaries during 1967. The Shah's government completed a $110 million arms agreement with the Soviet Union in January, under which the Soviet Union will provide trucks, personnel carriers, and antiaircraft weapons to Iran in exchange for natural gas. In March a second trade agreement was signed with the Soviet Union which will amount to $540 million in nonmilitary trade over the next five years. Other agreements for trade, loans, technical cooperation, or purchase of goods were made in 1967 with Bulgaria, Poland, Hungary, Rumania, Czechoslovakia, and Yugoslavia.

Visits of dignitaries and government officials between Iran and the Soviet bloc during 1967 were numerous; on the Iranian side, the Shah, his brother, his mother-in-law, the Prime Minister, the Foreign Minister, and the Chief of Staff of the Iranian Army (who went to Moscow in December) have all visited various European communist states. Distinguished visitors from communist countries to Iran include Deputy Chairman of the Soviet Council of Ministers N. K. Baibakov, Rumanian head of state Chivu Stoica, and the foreign ministers and delegations from the assemblies of several communist nations. This upsurge of contact between Iran and Communist Europe has left the Tudeh Party in an anomalous position, and it is evident that the changing situation has at times caused the party great embarrassment. For example, in commenting on the Soviet-Iranian arms deal in March, the staunchly pro-Soviet Tudeh Party, apparently caught by surprise, denounced the agreement through its clandestine radio in the following terms:

> Now [Prime Minister] Hoveyda has announced in the Majlis [Parliament] that the Iranian
> government will buy $100 million worth of defensive arms from the Soviet Union in

return for Iranian industrial goods and gas. We use the Premier's remarks to make two points: first, what country contemplates attacking another state, while at the same time supplying it with defensive weapons? This exposes the regime's antinational policy of participating in aggressive pacts [CENTO], obeying US and British warmongers, and spending millions of dollars on arms . . . (Radio Peyk-e Iran, 4 March 1967).

The party has since refrained from further comment on the purchase of Soviet arms, and has given unstinting praise to Soviet-Iranian cooperation.

In 1965 the Tudeh Party program called for the overthrow of the "antidemocratic" government; political freedom for parties and organizations; freedom of press, speech, and assembly; withdrawal of Iran from the Central Treaty Organization (CENTO); renationalization of the oil industry and liquidation of oil monopolies; expulsion of US advisers from the country; protection of the national economy of the country against foreign monopoly capital; and development of the economy, with concentration on heavy industry (see WMR, September 1965, pp. 43-49; YICA 1966, pp. 266-269). The rapprochement between the Iranian government and the Soviet Union has caused important modifications of the Tudeh Party stand. Party Chairman Reza Radmanesh now couches Tudeh Party aspirations in terms of "reforms," rather than "overthrow":

The national and democratic aims of the Iranian people can be attained only through democratization, and the process should begin with a general amnesty, release of political detainees, return of political exiles, reestablishment of civil and social freedoms, including freedom of parties, trade unions and other public organizations. Reforms that have no support among the people and are not of a democratic nature are bound to be short-lived and cannot produce the desired and much needed radical changes. (WMR, November 1967.)

In the same article Radmanesh goes on to point out that Iran needs "thorough agrarian reform in favor of the peasants, abolition of monopoly control of the economy, a larger and democratically controlled public sector, restriction of the private sector. . . ." He charts a "socialist" path for Iran in both domestic and foreign policy, but nowhere does he call for revolution or violence.

Because of its isolated position of exile in Europe, the Tudeh Party has had little opportunity to develop or control front organizations in Iran. However, it has been active among the Iranian students in Europe. In December 1966 the Confederation of Iranian Students (CIS), which is under Tudeh Party influence, amalgamated with the Teheran University Students Union. The united body was unanimously admitted to the International Union of Students (IUS) at its Ninth Congress in Mongolia on 27 March-9 April 1967 (Ulan Bator Radio, 27 March 1967). In spite of this apparent success, by the end of 1967 it appeared that the Tudeh Party's hold on the CIS was being challenged by more radical views from unnamed antagonists. A defensive pamphlet entitled "We and the Confederation" was published for student consumption, and answers to such questions as "Why do we defend the Soviet Union?" and "Has the Iranian Tudeh Party made friends with the regime?" indicated that anti-Soviet and "anti-revisionist" views from the left were influencing CIS members.

**International Views and Policies.** In the international communist movement the Tudeh Party remains in very close alignment with the Communist Party of the Soviet Union. At the same time, the party attempts to stress its patriotic motivation and professes nationalist ideals. The resolution of this apparent contradiction occupies a good deal of the intellectual energies of the Tudeh leaders. For example, Iradji Iskenderi states: "For us Iranians, close friendship with the Soviet Union and other socialist countries is more than a matter of ideological communism. It is, at the same time, the supreme expression of our patriotism and is predicated on Leninism and our country's genuine interests. And we have always regarded this friendship as the permanent basis of our policy." (WMR, August 1967.) He goes on to say that "Our party has always held that genuine patriotism must be internationalist, and that internationalism is a profound expression of patriotism." It is not surprising, therefore, that the Tudeh Party has little patience with Maoist theories of independence and reliance on the strength of one's own forces. To the Tudeh Party communist solidarity and proletarian internationalism mean reliance on the CPSU.

During the Arab-Israeli crisis of June 1967 the Tudeh Party gave unreserved praise to the role of the Soviet Union. The party appeared, however, to be somewhat reserved in its support for the Arabs. The Tudeh Party makes it quite clear that Israel has the right to exist: "We believe that the Jewish laboring people have a right to their own free and independent government in their country, Israel. But the present Israeli ruling circle, which is a protegé of the imperialists, has no right to any territorial claims against Jordan, Syria, and the UAR." (Radio Peyk-e Iran, 21 June 1967.) The Tudeh Party considered that Israel was clearly the aggressor.

The Tudeh Party also stands solidly behind Soviet policy on Vietnam, accusing the Chinese Communist Party of "obstructing vital assistance to the heroic Vietnamese people" through its policies of big-nation chauvinism, petit bourgeois adventurism, and the development of the Mao personality cult.

Since the destruction of the CENTO alliance is one of its most important goals, the Tudeh Party followed with great interest the July summit conference of President Ayub Khan of Pakistan and Premier Demirel of Turkey with the Shah and Prime Minister of Iran at Ramsar. The party interpreted the results of the conference and the communique, which failed to mention CENTO, as "obvious proof of the failure of efforts to revive the pact, which is now, more than ever, reduced to a scrap of paper" (Radio Peyk-e Iran, 2 August 1967).

Chairman Radmanesh represented his party at the Seventh Congress of the East German Socialist Unity (Communist) Party (SED) in Berlin on 17–22 April. In October Radmanesh and Kambakhsh attended the Fiftieth Anniversary celebrations of the October Revolution in Moscow, along with, but presumably not in the company of, the Shah's representative, Shoja-od-din Shafa, Cultural Counselor at the Royal Court.

**Publications.**    The Tudeh Party publishes a monthly information bulletin, *Mardom;*    the Azerbaijan, Democratic Party, incorporated into the Tudeh Party since 1960, publishes the newspaper *Azerbaijan.* Both are printed in Eastern Europe; neither is legal in Iran, and they are not distributed openly. The monthly *Payam Novin* (circulation 2,000) is published by the fellow-traveling Iran-Soviet Cultural Relations Society in Teheran. One other little-known organ, *Flame of the South,* was revealed by *Mardom* in October to be the organ of "the southern branch of the Iranian Tudeh Party." *Flame of the South* has published at least 13 issues.

The Tudeh Party operates two clandestine radio stations: Peyk-e Iran (Radio Iran Courier), probably located in East Germany, and Sedaye Melli Iran (the National Voice of Iran). Both stations broadcast in Persian, Azerbaijani, and Kurdish.

The splinter Iranian Communist group, the Revolutionary Organization of the Tudeh Party (ROTP), was founded in 1965 by exiled left-wing members of the Tudeh Party (*YICA,* 1966, p. 267). The existence of the ROTP was not disclosed until the beginning of 1966, when a statement "On the Activities of the Splinter group" was transmitted over Radio Peyk-e Iran and printed in *Mardom.* The ROTP is apparently led by Ahmed Qasimi and Gholamhosein Forutan, expelled Tudeh Party Central Committee members, and Abbas Seghai, former alternate member of the Central Committee. The chief medium for public expression of ROTP views is the Belgian pro-Peking Communist organ, *La Voix du Peuple,* which on 28 January 1966 published a complete text of the ROTP program (*YICA,* 1966, p. 268).

The activities of the splinter ROTP have not received wide publicity in 1967, except for its views on the Soviet-Iranian arms deal of March, which appeared in *La Voix du Peuple* and received further dissemination through Peking's New China News Agency. The article asserted that "the sale of arms by the Soviet revisionists to the regime of the Iranian monarch is in reality a declaration of war on the people, workers, revolutionaries, and Marxist-Leninists of Iran." The article condemns the arms agreement as further proof of US imperialists and Soviet revisionist collusion to control the world. It implies that the Soviet Union has stepped in to sell arms to the Iranian monarchical regime because the US imperialists, tied down by the war in Vietnam, are no longer able to furnish them. It adds ominously: "Through the people's armed forces, the revolutionary movement in Iran will capture these arms from the reactionary army" (NCNA, 14 May 1967).

# IRAQ

The Iraqi Communist Party (ICP) was founded in March 1934. Although it has never been a legal party in Iraq, at times its existence has been tolerated or even encouraged. Since the coups of 1963, however, the party has not been able to operate openly within the country. At present, its Central Committee exists in exile in eastern Europe.

It is not possible to establish the number of ICP members with accuracy. The party is believed to have about 2,000 regular members and 10,000 to 20,000 sympathizers or supporters. In spite of its small size, it is still considered one of the most vigorous of the Arab communist parties. The population of Iraq is 8,338,000 (estimated 1 July 1966).

**Organization and Leadership.** At the third National Conference of the ICP, in December 1967, a new Central Committee was elected (*World Marxist Review,* April 1968). Nazim Ali, the party's leading figure, continues as First Secretary. An active Kurdish branch of the party exists; 31 per cent of the delegates to the National Conference reportedly were Kurds. The Iraqi Communists are active among students abroad, propagandizing on such themes as self-determination for the Kurds, the nature of Israeli "aggression," the threat of imperialism, and the "reactionary" policies of the Iraqi regime. The General Union of Students of the Iraqi Republic (GUSIR), illegal in Iraq, operates as a party front organization among students abroad. Nuri Abdul Razzak Hussein, a representative of GUSIR, is the Secretary-General of the International Union of Students (IUS).

**Domestic Policy and Activity.** A serious split in the ICP, details of which were not publicized, apparently took place in September 1967 with attempts at assassination and kidnapping of Central Committee members (Voice of the Iraqi People, 30 October 1967). The intraparty battle for control resulted in a postponement and change in the projected second National Congress of the ICP. This meeting eventually took place as a National Conference for ten days in December 1967 (*WMR,* April 1968). Billed as the "biggest assembly in party history," the conference was attended by 55 party members. It "decided that all the party organizations and the public should continue the discussion of the draft Party program which will be submitted to the Second Congress" (*ibid.*), which is to meet at a date yet to be determined. The "immediate goal" of the draft program is the formation of a "national democratic political coalition" (*Information Bulletin,* No. 108, 27 November 1967). The ICP proposes to lead this coalition to "overthrow the military dictatorship and to form a provisional (transitional) national democratic coalition government comprising the representatives of all political forces which commit themselves to the program of action" (*ibid.*). The provisional government would be replaced after an elected constituent assembly promulgated a permanent constitution and a constitutional democratic government was chosen. The program of action of the proposed coalition is as follows:

1. To guarantee democratic freedoms, above all the right to organize political parties, and to eliminate the consequences and vestiges of the military dictatorships and state of emergency, especially to liberate the patriotic prisoners and arrested people and to reinstate all dismissed persons.

2. To liberate the Palestinian Arab people and to enable them to decide their own destiny and on the territory of their homeland.

3. To solve the Kurdish problem by acknowledging the national rights of the Kurdish people, including autonomy.

4. To pursue a national oil policy and wrest Iraq's rights from the oil monopoly.

5. To take speedy measures against unemployment and the high cost of living, to raise

the standards of living of the masses, to establish a progressive tax system, to execute the Land Reform Law after canceling all the reactionary modifications introduced into it and safeguard the rights of the workers and improve their living conditions.

6. To follow a progressive Arab policy and a consistent independent foreign policy.

To organize general elections for a constituent assembly on the basis of a democratic electoral law. (*Ibid.*)

The keystone of ICP policy is the projected united front of all the "democratic forces" in Iraq. This policy, enunciated clearly in the draft party program, has been continuous since 1964. The ICP, suffering severe repression at home, its leaders in exile, and standing in opposition to the Abdul Rahman Arif regime in Iraq (which is on good terms with both the Soviet Union and the East European states), is in a particularly weak position for implementing its united front program. The call for a united front against the Iraqi Government took two general forms in 1967: first, a broad appeal in the Arabic language for the unity of all democratic forces in Iraq; and, second, specific radio appeals to the Kurds in the Kurdish tongue to join forces with the Communist Party.

The perennial attempt to draw the Kurdish Democratic Party into a front was marred by periodic denunciations of that party's leadership. In March and April the ICP line was inflammatory, inciting the Kurds to renew their revolt* which had stopped in June 1966. After the Arab-Israeli war the message to the Kurds again stressed unity instead of violence.

On 10 June 1967, at the height of the Arab-Israeli crisis the Central Committee of the ICP issued a strong plea for a supranational Arab coalition in the face of Israeli "aggression." According to this "10 June Statement": "The present ordeal should serve as a new stimulus for rallying all the progressive and democratic forces of the Arab Orient, excluding the reactionary forces and regimes, and resisting them unfailingly as accomplices of imperialism and Israel."

The Committee's call to battle for Iraq proposed the arming of the populace and forming of "people's battalions," reinstatement of progressive army officers (removed in the coups of 1963), withdrawal of all troops from Kurdistan, restoration of freedom to the people, expropriation and nationalization of US and British oil interests, economic reform, and cooperation with the USSR (*IB*, No. 104, 28 September 1967).

ICP criticism of the Iraqi Government followed three consistent themes through 1967: the failure to implement the terms of the 29 June 1966 cease-fire agreement with the Kurds, the continuing persecution of communists and "democratic forces" (a new communist plot was allegedly uncovered by Iraqi secret police in April), and the exploitation of oil resources by foreign "monopoly capitalists." The party constantly appealed to Iraqi nationalism against the oil companies, contrasting Syria's handling of the oil "monopolists" with the softer policy of the Iraqi government. After the Arab-Israeli conflict the ICP attacked the government for its inability and unwillingness to join in the military effort against Israel, pointing out that two-thirds of Iraq's armed forces were in the north, arrayed against their brothers, the Kurds.

**International Views and Policy.** On the Arab-Israeli war the ICP took the attitude that Israel was acting as an agent of "world imperialism":

Israel has always been a cat's paw, a tool of provocation, a springboard and a base of aggression in the hands of the imperialist states. . . . It has always . . . worked for the implementation of its expansionist plans and designs with the direct support and at the instigation of the American, British, and West German Imperialists.

The ICP claimed that the root of the problem lay in the foreign "imperialist oil monopolies," with

---

*In late January 1967 *Pravda* published a series of three articles (15, 18, and 22 January) by the journalist Ye. Primakov, who had visited Iraqi Kurdistan with the sanction of the Arif government. Primakov reported that the "struggle for peace" continued in Kurdistan even after the bilateral cease-fire agreement of June 1966 because there were "extremists in the Kurdish movement, although they had no influence with Barzani." (Mustafa al-Barzani is the leader of the Kurdish Democratic Party.) The articles, conciliatory toward the Iraqi government and the Democratic Party, seemed to reflect a desire on Moscow's part to end the Arab-Kurd dispute in Iraq by peaceful means, continuing the policy adopted at the time of the visit to Moscow, in July 1966, of the Premier of Iraq, Dr. Abdul Rahman al-Bazzaz (*YICA*, 1966, p. 271).

whose designs Israel was "clearly identified": "Today it is the duty of Arab peoples to launch a resolute struggle against the oil companies and other imperialist interests; to struggle to erase and destroy the traces of Israeli aggression against Egypt, Syria, and Jordan ... and to confine Israel, the tool of colonialism, within its borders." The ICP made no comment as to a final disposition of Israel as a nation, although it called for the liberation of the Palestine Arab people from "imperialist and Zionist domination." (From the "10 June Statement" as broadcast by the Voice of the Iraqi People, 22 and 23 July 1967.)

The ICP view of other Arab and neighboring Middle East states is that the United Arab Republic, Algeria, and Syria are progressive revolutionary states, although Syria has been criticized for poor treatment of its Kurdish minority. The party views the revolution in Yemen with approval, but it is impatient with Yemeni republicans for not pursuing it with greater zeal. Comment on other Arab states is derogatory; Jordan, Saudi Arabia, Tunisia, and Morocco, together with non-Arab Turkey, are criticized along with Iraq as ruled by reactionary regimes or as countries which conciliate the "imperialists."

The ICP made a detailed criticism of the Arab Summit Conference of 29 August – 1 September 1967 at Khartoum. It blamed the failure of the conference on "fundamental differences and flagrant contradictions among the regimes in the Arab countries." That the conference would fail was obvious from the start when "progressive" Syria boycotted the meeting. The ICP also noted the absence of Algerian Premier Boumediène. The party used the attack on the conference as the basis for a new plea for the overthrow of "reactionary regimes" in the Arab world so that the "liberated" Arab nations could present a solid front in the "struggle against imperialism and Zionism." The critique specifically attacked the Iraqi Government for its failure to use oil as an effective weapon against the "imperialist nations supporting Israel."

The ICP's policies are closely aligned with those of the CPSU. First Secretary Nazim Ali summarized his party's position in a speech during the celebrations of the Fiftieth Anniversary of the October Revolution when he said: "We deem it an honor to state that the Communist Party of Iraq will always be together with the Party of Lenin, the inspirer, organizer, and leader of the October Socialist Revolution, and to state that our Communists see in your party a loyal ally in the just revolutionary struggle." He went on to give his party's approval to Soviet international policy, to Soviet support for revolutionary movements and for the Arab States in the Arab-Israeli war, and to the Soviet position on Vietnam. Lastly, he said:

> The Iraqi Communist Party highly values the sincere and principled efforts of the Central Committee of the CPSU to strengthen the unity of the world communist and workers' movement. Our party supports those efforts and believes that today conditions are ripe for convening an international conference of Communist and Workers' Parties. (*IB*, special issue on fiftieth anniversary celebration, 1967.)

In contrast, the ICP is highly critical of Communist China and deeply concerned over the rift in the world communist movement caused, in the ICP view, by Mao Tse-tung and the leaders of the Chinese Communist Party. A series of statements and resolutions issued by the Central Committee of the Iraqi party after a plenary session in February deplored the breakdown of communist world solidarity, condemned the Great Proletarian Cultural Revolution as "fanatic nationalism and a movement which would lower living standards, destroy art and culture, cripple democracy, and deify leaders." All of this, the ICP declared, was "contrary to true scientific socialism and Marxism-Leninism." It also condemned China for having "refused to take joint action with the Soviet Union and the other socialist countries to check the American aggression against Vietnam." (Voice of the Iraqi People, 8 February 1967.)

As noted above, the ICP was represented by First Secretary Nazim Ali, together with Central Committee Member Amjad Rashad, at the fiftieth anniversary celebration of the October Revolution in the USSR. An unnamed ICP representative delivered a speech at the Seventh Congress of the East German Socialist Unity (Communist) Party (SED) in Berlin, 17-22 April. The party sent greetings to the French Communist Party on the occasion of its Eighteenth Congress in January, but no representative attended the congress. The student organization GUSIR was represented at the Ninth

Congress of the International Union of Students, at Ulan Bator, 27 March – 9 April. In addition, it appears that the ICP was one of the communist parties represented at the Arab communist meeting of May 1967. No list of parties or individuals who attended has been published, but documents of that meeting place considerable stress on the situation in Iraq (see *Documents*). A delegation of the ICP headed by Nazim Ali visited Bulgaria, Hungary, and Czechoslovakia in late June and early July.

The central organ of the ICP is the monthly *Tariq al-Sha'b*. The party also publishes a monthly journal, *Munadil al-Hizb*; its Bagdhad committee publishes *Tariq al-Ummal*. The organ of the Kurdistan branch of the ICP is *Rezay-e Kurdistan*. All these periodicals are illegal and are distributed clandestinely in Iraq.

The ICP operates a clandestine radio station, the "Voice of the Iraqi People," believed to be based in Bulgaria. The station broadcasts both in Arabic and Kurdish languages.

*     *

A new split in the ICP, noted above, was announced in a Central Committee statement dated 19 September (Voice of the Iraqi People, 30 September 1967). Little detail was given on the scope of the split or on the persons involved, described only as a "handful of people." The statement did not tie the rebels to Communist China. At its Third Party Conference the ICP adopted a resolution condemning splinter groups and viewing the fight against "left sectarian opportunism" as an urgent task of the party. The resolution described a "second smaller group of splitters . . . characterized by its anti-internationalist position [and] by hostility to the strategy of the international communist movement." It would appear that this statement had reference to a small pro-Chinese "Iraqi Communist Party (Marxist-Leninist)," whose Secretary–General is believed to be Baha-Eddin Nuri (*YICA*, 1966, p. 272). These two groups reportedly merged in late 1967 or early 1968 (*WMR*, April 1968, pp. 81-82).

# IRELAND

The Communist Party of Ireland was founded in 1921. The present communist movement in Ireland is divided into two branches: the Irish Workers' Party (IWP), in the Republic of Ireland, and the Communist Party of Northern Ireland (see below), in the Irish part of the United Kingdom. The two parties maintain separate organizations and hold separate congresses, but have complementary programs. A "Joint National Council," composed of representatives from the executive committees of each, has the task of building the two into strong parties "of a new type," which would become "an essential factor in the effective rallying of the forces in both parts of Ireland for progressive governments in Dublin and Belfast, based on the unity of the working people in the fight against monopoly capitalism." In such a development the Joint National Council sees "the end to the separation of the country into two states and the establishment of a Socialist Government in Ireland." (*WMR*, June 1965, p. 79.)

The membership of the IWP is believed to number about 150 persons, out of a total population of 2,880,000 (estimated 1966). The party is insignificant in the country's political life, and in the trade unions as well. In the latest elections to the national legislature (7 April 1965) the IWP put up one candidate and polled 183 votes (0.01 per cent of the total). The party has no seat in the legislature.

IWP leadership is exercised through an Executive Committee, of which Sean Nolan is Chairman and Michael O'Riordan is Secretary.

The program of the IWP, entitled "Ireland Her Own," was adopted at its fourth national conference, in March 1962. Its starting point was that although the Republic of Ireland is independent, it is held in a close grip by British "imperialism." In the communist view, all the main political parties—whether in the government or in the opposition—look to foreign capital to solve Ireland's economic problems. The IWP claims that British imperialism hinders the political, social, and economic development of the country, and that the situation will grow worse as the crisis of British capitalism develops (*ibid.*, p. 77).

The party coutinues to oppose the Irish-British Free Trade Agreement signed in December 1965 (providing for the abolition of all British import duties on Irish goods in 1966 and for the gradual elimination of most Irish duties on British goods), on the grounds that the agreement will "further strengthen the British monopoly capitalist domination" of the country and cause "further unemployment." The party also stands against membership of Ireland along with Britain in the European Common Market, which it considers an "even greater retrograde step in our independence struggle." It claims that entrance into the Common Market would spell Ireland's "industrial destruction by the European monopoly capitalists [and] would mean the abandonment of the vital national principle of neutrality." (*IB*, No. 97-98, 23 June.)

The IWP supports a peaceful transition to socialism. It aspires to form a mass united front under the leadership of the working class, but encompassing nationalists and intellectuals, small farmers, small merchants, and small bourgeoisie. According to the party, the front would work to establish a progressive government based on policies opposed to imperialism and favorable to national independence, democratic rights, and the satisfaction of the needs of the people (*WMR*, June 1965, p. 78).

**International Views and Policies.** In foreign affairs, the IWP considers the Irish "struggle for national sovereignty" to be part of "the international anti-imperialist struggle and the struggle for world peace." At the Karlovy Vary conference of European communist and workers' parties (24-26 April) Michael O'Riordan stated:

Our people have established for themselves a reputation of continuous struggle, over the

328

centuries, for their national liberation, for an end to the domination of the British imperialists. . . . Our peoples' struggle has never been pursued in isolation from the general world fight for freedom and progress. . . . Because of the strong anti-imperialist feelings of our people, the imperialists have never succeeded in winning our state into either the North Atlantic Treaty Organization or a bilateral military alliance. Consistent with this factor the active development of the fight for peace and security in Europe is of vital concern for our people, *(IB,* no. 97-98.)

The IWP confirmed its position as a pro-Soviet communist party in a joint statement with the Communist Party of Northern Ireland dated 3 February, in which the Executive Committees openly placed the blame for the disunity in the world communist movement on the Chinese Communist Party. After offering the hope that the people of China would "correct these developments and . . . bring about the reunification of its powerful revolutionary force with the world socialist movement," the joint statement went on to support Moscow's call for the convening of an international conference of all communist and workers' parties. On other international issues, the two parties took a strong stand on "US aggression in Vietnam," the "revival of Nazism" in Germany, the struggles against "imperialism" in Aden, Angola, and Rhodesia, and "racism" in South Africa. *(IB,* no. 94, 14 April.)

Besides the Karlovy Vary conference, the IWP took part in the fiftieth anniversary celebrations of the October Revolution in the Soviet Union, with Michael O'Riordan representing the party, and the Thirtieth Congress of the Communist Party of Great Britain, 25-28 November, which Sean Nolan attended.

**Publication.** The IWP organ is the *Irish Socialist.*

**Dissident faction.** There also exists a tiny pro-Chinese Communist splinter group in Ireland, The Irish Communist Organization, which publishes an organ called *The Irish Communist.*

\* \* \*

The Communist Party of Northern Ireland is headed by Chairman Andrew Barr and Secretary-General Hugh Moore. It is believed to have about 100 members, in a population of 1,491,000 (estimated, mid-1967).

The party program adopted in 1962 at its Eleventh Congress and entitled "Ireland's Path to Socialism" was readopted unchanged at the Thirteenth Congress, held at Belfast on 7-8 October 1967. Fifty members attended the congress, including the fifteen members of the Executive Committee. The emphasis of the congress, reportedly under the tight control of the Executive Committee, was on the "Unity of Progressives" *(The Newsletter,* London, 14 October). The congress noted that "the Northern Ireland government had fallen totally under the influence of British and other monopolies and called on it [the government] to take urgent steps to combat unemployment. It [the congress] urged nationalizing a number of industries [unspecified] and suggested a democratic reform of the election law." *(IB,* no. 108, 27 November.) Like the IWP, the party opposes British "imperialism" and advocates a peaceful road to socialism.

As on domestic matters, the Communist Party of Northern Ireland followed the lead of the IWP on all matters of international concern, and like its counterpart in the south, it is strongly pro-Soviet. At the Karlovy Vary Conference the party was represented by Hugh Moore, at the fiftieth anniversary celebrations in the Soviet Union by Andrew Barr, and at the Thirtieth Congress of the Communist Party of Great Britain by J. Graham, a vice chairman of the Central Committee, and J. Stewart, an Assistant Secretary).

# ISRAEL

The Palestine Communist Party was founded in 1922. In 1948, after Israel became a nation, the party was renamed the Israeli Communist Party (Miflaga Komunistit Yisraelit; MAKI). In 1965 this party split into two factions, each claiming to be the legitimate party. The cleavage was in no way related to the international communist alignment in the Sino-Soviet dispute, but was entirely due to local issues which resulted in the creation of one basically pro-Jewish and one fundamentally pro-Arab group. Even before the formal split into two party factions in 1965, the issue of Arab versus Jewish interests had threatened to cause a break and only a facade of unity was maintained. One camp represented anti-imperialist Arab socialism, the other the reality of existence of Israel as a sovereign nation. When the formal break occurred, the existing name MAKI was retained by the Jewish wing of the party, whose members had formed the organizational core of the original unified party. The other wing—pro-Arab, though of mixed Jewish and Arab membership—became the "New Communist List" (Reshima Komunistit Hadasha; RAKAH). The name is explained by the fact that the New Communist List was set up not long before the national elections of 1965, when it offered its own "list" of candidates for election to the Knesset (Israel's Legislative Assembly).

Both Israeli communist parties are small. The 1967 membership of the MAKI was estimated at 600, and that of the RAKAH at 1,000 (of whom approximately 700 were Arabs). The population of Israel is 2,678,000 (estimated 1967). These figures show marked changes over 1966 estimates, which put the membership of the MAKI at 1,100 members and that of the RAKAH at 900. The new figures are considered to be a reflection of the impact of the Arab-Israeli war.

The Communists play a marginal role in Israeli politics. In the latest national election (November 1965) they received 41,000 votes, or 3.4 per cent of the total cast. They won four seats in the Knesset out of 120 up for election. Shmuel Mikunis became the sole representative of MAKI, while RAKAH members winning seats were Meir Vilner, Emile Habibi, and Toufik Toubi. All successful candidates were elected by a combination of hard-core Communists and voters protesting against the government.

The four communist members of the Knesset are also leaders in their respective party organizations. Mikunis and Vilner are the heads of their parties, and hold the post of Secretary-General. Other members of the MAKI Politburo are P. Balti, A. Drukman, Mrs. E. Vilenska, Y. Zilber, S. Litvak, and Dr. M. Sneh. Among the Politburo members of the RAKAH are T. Toubi, D. Burstein, D. Henin, Dr. W. Erlich, and S. Hamiss.

Until the crisis and war of 1967 the two rival communist groups shared some objectives, both domestic and international. Each pledged solidarity with Moscow, gave unqualified support to the CPSU in the Sino-Soviet dispute, and in return, received recognition with something verging on impartiality. Each voiced attacks on the "reactionary" Eshkol government of Israel and condemned American, British, and German "imperialists." Up to the outbreak of hostilities each supported a peaceful solution to Arab-Israeli contention. MAKI called for the "withdrawal of Israeli and Arab contingents from the border areas, for abstention from the use of force by both sides, and for strict observation of existing armistice agreements" (*Morning Star,* London, May 29). It called on the Arabs to stop sabotage raids into Israel and on Israel to abandon its methods of reprisal (*Kol Ha'am*, 19 May). The RAKAH asked "all peace-loving forces in Israel for united action to prevent war and safeguard peace" (Central Committee statement of 26 May, *in Comment,* London, 15 June).

In spite of some of the shared interests, the RAKAH group had for some time before the outbreak of war emerged more clearly as the "voice of Arab protest." It praised the Soviet Union for efforts to "frustrate the warmongers" and warned the Israeli government "not to pull the chestnuts out of the

330

fire for the imperialists." It also insisted that Israel's security and well-being demanded the adoption of a new policy: "not with imperialism against the Arab peoples, but with the Arab peoples against imperialism." (Central Committee statement of 26 May, in *IB,* no. 99.) It squarely put responsibility for solution of Arab-Israeli problems on Israel without the necessity of any Arab recognition of Israel's rights. It considered acceptance of demands of the Palestine Arabs and refugees a prerequisite for any relaxation of tensions. With these demands the RAKAH appeared to have made headway and gained some influence among Communists at the expense of the MAKI. The MAKI, on the other hand, had more clearly tried to represent the Israeli national interest and had sought popular front cooperation with the socialist groups of the left. It continued to insist that Arab-Israeli peace could be based only on "mutual recognition of rights." This formula of years' standing was rejected by the pro-Arab Communists as showing "the fallacy of drawing an artificial parallel between a fulfilled right [of Israel to exist] and a denial of rights [to Arab refugees]."

All pretense of unity was abruptly dropped, once the fighting broke out. The RAKAH quickly accused Israel, the United States, and Great Britain of having made long preparations for "aggressive war" in the hope of overthrowing the anti-imperialist regimes of the UAR and Syria, of trying to protect their oil profits in the Middle East, and of breaking the ties between the Soviet Union and the Arab countries. On 5 June, the day hostilities started, two RAKAH members of the Knesset (the third was absent) stood alone in voting against authorization for new war credits and taxes. Meir Vilner, in fact, got up in the assembly to proclaim: "Even when you scream and yell, still this war helps only the interests of the imperialists and stands in direct opposition to the real interests of Israel."

The MAKI stand was almost diametrically opposed. Expressing the Israeli nationalist point of view, MAKI leader Mikunis sent "fervent greetings" to the Israeli forces "fighting for the integrity and independence of our country" (Israel Radio, 5 June). The MAKI also firmly rejected Moscow's accusations and charges of Israeli aggression by stating that "both Egypt and Syria provoked the war against peace-loving Israel" and that "the aim of Israel was to eliminate the permanent menace of its annihilation, to obliterate the menace resulting from the nonrecognition of the Jewish people's right to any part of this country" (*L'Unita,* Rome, 20 June). MAKI leader Dr. Moshe Sneh, a former member of the Knesset who lost his seat in 1965 but remained a frequent spokesman for his party, considered the new military confrontation a continuation of the fight for liberation in 1948 and blamed both on the Arab refusal to recognize Israeli rights to political and national existence.

These are clear-cut nationalistic pronouncements. It must be added, however, that in a burst of awareness of political reality Dr. Sneh added suggestions for settlement of the Palestine refugee problem: "We would like to see in occupied Palestine free elections from which will develop a constituent assembly. This would have to bring about an Arab-Palestine government which in turn would carry out talks with Israel for an agreement which would cover all issues. Today the people of Palestine should be able to choose freely between union with Jordan, or Egypt, independence, or union with Israel."

While there is no question that the RAKAH communists have long been in opposition to the State of Israel in its existing form and were strong advocates of at least equal rights for Arabs and Jews, their stand has not necessarily always been quite as clear-cut as the international communist press made it appear. That "Israel has a right to exist and that any Arab objection to this premise must be rejected" is an opinion advanced by at least two RAKAH spokesmen, Meir Vilner and Politburo member Wolfgang Erlich. Meir Vilner also added that terrorist acts by the Al Fatah organization in Syria could serve as "pretext" for aggression against the Arabs and did grave harm to the Arab cause. (*L'Unita,* 4 July.) This somewhat softer attitude toward Israeli rights did not prevent Vilner from open attacks on the MAKI stance regarding the conflict. He cited his communist opponents for their failure to condemn Israeli aggression, for neglecting to demand a troop withdrawal to the original armistice lines, and for unwillingness to draw distinctions between the various "great powers" (*ibid.,* 19 June).

The last is an obvious reference to relations with the Soviet Union. Without a doubt the divergent behavior of the Israeli factions created a real dilemma for communist parties outside the Middle East.

The Soviet Union and all East European countries—with the exception of Rumania—broke off diplomatic relations with Israel, condemned her aggression, and demanded immediate withdrawal from all occupied territories. The MAKI reacted by expressing regret for the break and hope that it would prove to be temporary, adding: "In our opinion it is due not so much to the sins of Israel as to the defeat of the Egyptian army and the other Arab forces" (*Ma'ariv*, Tel Aviv independent daily, 13 June). On the other hand, MAKI communists readily admitted that the party's decision to oppose Moscow had been a difficult one. Calling Soviet severance of diplomatic relations "unjustified," they expressed the hope that the same course would not be followed by other communist-ruled countries.

Unlike the MAKI, the RAKAH expressed no criticism of the Soviet Union for breaking off relations with Israel; Meir Vilner, in fact, declared that the move should be accepted as a serious warning that Israel should refrain from a policy of military conquest.

Moscow initially tried to bypass acknowledgment of the existence of more than a single communist point of view in Israel. It happily accepted the declaration at the Moscow conference in June that the unconditional support of Arabs against Israel represented the "last word of Marxism-Leninism." There was no public criticism of the MAKI accusation that Moscow was in violation of the basic tenets of communism with their insistence on a policy of coexistence and solution of national conflicts by peaceful means. The first direct criticism appeared in the July issue of *Kommunist*, which referred to the RAKAH as the "progressive" and internationalist forces in Israel and to the MAKI as having "slid on to nationalist positions" and having supported the "aggressive policy of the bourgeois parties of Israel." Disapproval of the MAKI was later given tacit expression by withholding an invitation to the fiftieth anniversary celebrations of the October Revolution. The omission was enhanced by the welcome given to the RAKAH delegates in Moscow.

Many non-Soviet foreign communist publications simply tried to ignore the existence of two points of view among the Israeli Communists or else avoided referring to the pro-Israel faction. Even by the end of the year the international alignment was not very clearly defined. Shmuel Mikunis in an interview reported by the Tel Aviv newspaper *Letzte Nyess* on 11 December, stated that the Communist Party of the Netherlands had identified itself completely with the MAKI position in the Israeli-Arab dispute. Israel Radio on 16 June announced the receipt of a letter from the Secretary-General of the Swiss Communist Party expressing regret that "a great part of the international communist movement had adopted a clearly biased stand in the dispute between Israel and the Arabs by intentionally basing this stand on very partial information." The Norwegian Communist Youth Organization strongly opposed any slogan or call for the liquidation of Israel and said that Israeli ships should have the right of unrestricted passage through the Red Sea and the Suez Canal. Support was expressed further by influential elements among the communist parties of Austria, Sweden, Canada, and the USA.

To complicate the problem of the contradictory voices of communism within Israel, there was evidence that some Communists in the country were refusing to support either extreme and were anxious to pursue a middle way between the MAKI and the RAKAH. Three well-known members of the Central Committee of the MAKI broke away from the party because they could not endorse the "nationalist and Zionist" policies of its leaders. (In another interpretation they were said to have been expelled.) Best known of the three men was Alexander Pen, a poet, writer, and member of the editorial board of the party organ *Kol Ha'am*. "Defecting" with him were Leon Zahavi and Shlomo Shamli, the latter being the secretary of the Tel Aviv-Jaffa party unit. All three men expressed the belief that the "Jewish nationalist deviation" of one communist faction was equally as dangerous as the "Arab nationalist deviation" of the other. Subsequently they expressed the hope that they might function as a bridge to renewed brotherhood between the two parties. They tried to facilitate such a move by emphasizing that both communist factions continued to carry the banner of "revolutionary Marxism-Leninism."

The RAKAH had to cope not only with criticism by its communist opposition; the entire party and individual members also were repeatedly chastised by others for their pro-Arab and anti-Israeli stand in relation to the war and its aftermath. There were shouts of "traitor" in the Knesset on 5 June when Meir Vilner spoke. In several publications editorials and letters to editors demanded that the RAKAH be declared illegal for its negative or hostile attitude toward the state of Israel. Strangely enough, very effective opposition to a suggested ban was expressed in an editorial in *Kol Ha'am* (5 September). It argued "in the name of democracy" against outlawing the party faction, stating that democracy does not allow the equating of legal disqualification and political disqualification. In demanding that democratic means of community action be employed, the editorial added: "We are absolutely confident that the working class of Israel will never accept the way of RAKAH and will never forgive RAKAH for its position in Israel's time of crisis."

The war resulted in some political arrests, and the RAKAH communist faction lodged strong protests. It claimed "police terror" in some towns and objected to the trespassing on the freedom of movement of even communist members of the Knesset. It reported that in Tel Aviv the police searched the homes of communist party members and of a presidium member of the Israel-Soviet Friendship movement. Editors—including several of the party organ *al-Ittihad*—and trade-union leaders were reported detained.

In October an assassination attempt was made on Meir Vilner. He was stabbed in the back by a knife-wielding assailant while walking in a Tel Aviv street. The motive of the man apprehended for the crime was said to be concern "over the plight of Soviet Jewry." (*Israel Radio*, 15 October.) Political murder has been unknown in Israel, and the attempt produced an outcry of condemnation, the loudest from Toufik Toubi of the RAKAH Politburo, who stated "the assault was perpetrated against the background of anticommunist chauvinism, widespread hysteria, and wild incitement against the communist party" (*The Worker*, New York, 17 October).

In spite of the country's preoccupation with Arab-Israeli hostilities, the Communists did not slacken their efforts to gain converts to their cause in 1967. In particular they tried to woo members of the Labor Federation (Histadrut) and the youth of the country, although acceptance of communism by either group has been limited.

Less than three percent of trade-union members belong to either of the communist party factions. In 1967, however, Israeli communists proclaimed the "vital and urgent necessity" to establish the consolidation of the workers through cooperation between the United Workers Party (Mapam), the Communists, and other leftist circles. In addition, party propaganda was mobilized to help workers in industry and agriculture defend their interests. Throughout the country Communists campaigned against dismissals, unemployment, lowering of wages, and higher prices. In the Knesset, Shmuel Mikunis spoke in opposition to the proposed Labor Court and National Insurance Legislation, popularly known as the law for strike prevention. A special pamphlet, "The Economic Program of the CP of Israel against the Economic Policy of the Government" was issued. Draft proposals for a new wage policy for 1968-69 contained demands that the wage freeze be lifted, that cost of living increases be granted, and that the lot of the workers be improved by a variety of pension, health, and other social benefits.

The Israeli Communist Youth League (Banki) is directed by the RAKAH and has Benjamin Gonen as its secretary-general. During the year it issued an appeal to members of the Youth Movement of the Mikunis-Sneh group to work to heal the split in the movement; pointing out that the young generation becomes the first victim in war, it called for the mobilization of youth for the defense of its rights.

**International Views and Activities.** In the interpretation of international affairs unrelated to the Arab-Israeli conflict, both communist parties in Israel followed Soviet views. They condemned US "imperialist aggression" in Vietnam. They were strongly opposed to the policies of the Kiesinger-Strauss government in West Germany and demanded that Bonn make real efforts to combat neo-Nazi activities and an increase in anti-Semitism. They condemned the policies of the Eshkol government and its rapprochement with West Germany. They came out for the restoration of democracy in Greece, for an amnesty of political prisoners there, and opposition to the "militaristic fascist regime." Overall, their international involvement was summarized as follows: "The historical experience of our own people proves that the security of our own real national interests is bound inexorably with our readiness to take up the cause of other peoples in their struggle for progress and anti-imperialism (*Information Bulletin*, MAKI CC, Foreign Affairs Department, January, 1968).

As has been noted, during and after the June hostilities the CPSU virtually ignored the existence of the pro-Jewish faction of the Israeli Communists. Concurrently the leaders of the MAKI found themselves cast in the role of *personae non gratae* in many parts of the world. While Shmuel Mikunis and Dr. Sneh had been welcome visitors in eastern Europe as recently as April of 1967, this was not the case after June. On the other hand, Meir Vilner, Toufik Toubi, David Henin, and Dr. Wolfgang Erlich of the RAKAH traveled extensively. One or more of that group turned up in Moscow, Prague, Sofia, Budapest, Paris, Vienna, and other cities for the sole purpose of publicizing solidarity. Late in the year, the Central Committee of the Israeli Communist Party issued a press release announcing the intention of Israel to participate in the consultative meeting of the communist and workers parties in Budapest in 1968; who the delegates would be was not stated, but unquestionably only pro-Arab representatives would have received an invitation to a function under the sponsorship of the CPSU.*

**Publications.** Best known among the communist publications in Israel is *Kol Ha'am* ("Voice of the People"), the MAKI Hebrew-language daily that is edited by Dr. Sneh. During 1967 *Kol Ha'am* encountered severe financial difficulties, but announced late in the year that its problems had been solved and that cutbacks would no longer be necessary. The RAKAH does not publish a daily newspaper, but in the course of the year changed its Hebrew monthly theoretical journal *Zo Haderekh* ("Our Path") to a weekly newspaper; *Al-Ittihad* ("Unity") is the biweekly party organ published in Arabic. *Der Veg* ("The Way") is a Yiddish weekly issued by RAKAH. The Foreign Relations Department of the MAKI Central Committee publishes its *Information Bulletin* monthly in several languages.

---

*The leader of the delegation in Budapest was David Henin, Secretary and Politburo member of RAKAH.

# ITALY

The Italian Communist Party (Partito Comunista Italiano; PCI) was founded in 1921. By far the largest communist party in Italy, the PCI has been confronted in recent years with marginal competition from a number of small parties and groups adhering to Marxism-Leninism of differing shades of interpretation–pro-Chinese, Trotskyist, and Castroist (see below).

The PCI is also the largest communist party in the West, although membership has been steadily falling and reached a postwar low of approximately 1,534,000 in 1967, a drop of about 40,000 from 1966–a year which had seen a similar decline from 1965 (see *YICA*, 1966, p. 125). The high mark was attained in 1947 with 2,252,000 members. The party's youth movement, the Federation of Italian Communist Youth (Federazione Giovanile Comunista Italiana; FGCI), had approximately 135,000 members in 1967, a drop of about 30,000 from 1966–a year which had seen a decline of about 5,000 from 1965.* The population of Italy is 52,000,000 (estimated 1967).

In the April 1963 general elections for the Senate and the Chamber of Deputies the PCI obtained 6,991,889 votes (25.5 per cent of the total) and 7,767,601 (25.3 per cent) respectively, winning 85 seats in the Senate (out of 322) and 166 in the Chamber (out of 630). The PCI is the second strongest party in the Italian Parliament. The two other major parties are the Christian Democrat Party (Democrazia Cristiana; DC), holding 133 seats in the Senate and 260 in the Chamber, and the United Socialist Party (Partito Socialista Unificato; PSU), with 46 and 95 respectively. The PSU was founded in October 1966 as a result of the merger of the Italian Socialist Party (Partito Socialista Italiano; PSI) and the Italian Social Democratic Party (Partito Socialista Democratico Italiano; PSDI). The government is a coalition of the DC and PSU, together with the small Italian Republican Party (Partito Repubblicano Italiano; PRI), which has 6 seats in the Chamber of Deputies.

In the 11 June 1967 elections to the Regional Assembly in Sicily (90 contested seats) the PCI showed a loss of two seats (from 22 in 1963 to 20), representing a 2.8 per cent decline in its share of the votes (from 24.1 to 21.3). The 21.3 per cent polled by the party, however, was considered favorably by the PCI in the light of the party's severe losses during the 1964 local elections (in communes of more than 5,000 inhabitants), when it had obtained only 17.3 per cent of the vote. Moreover, the PCI commented favorably on the 4.2 per cent won by the procommunist Italian Socialist Party of Proletarian Unity (Partito Socialista Italiano di Unità Proletaria; PSIUP), even though it would appear that the votes obtained by the PSIUP (which, founded in 1964, had not contested the 1963 elections) were primarily at the expense of the PCI.

The PCI is strongest in central Italy and in the industrialized areas of the North. It is weaker and continues to suffer substantial erosion in the South and in the islands of Sicily and Sardinia. Urban workers comprise 40 per cent of the party membership; agricultural laborers, tenants, and small landowners, 25 per cent; and housewives and pensioners, 26 per cent. The membership is aging, and by their own admission (Longo's speech at the Eleventh Party Congress, *Foreign Bulletin of the PCI*, no. 1, 1966, p. 56), the Communists are encountering serious difficulties in recruiting new members from among the young. This problem, evident in the 1967 decline in FGCI membership, was stressed

*Although the PCI usually publishes annual membership figures, this was not the case for 1967. In early 1968, however, the party published current membership figures (membership to the PCI is renewable annually) as compared to 1967. On 14 January *L'Unità* reported that the membership figures at the time were: PCI–1,064,403 (69.38 per cent of 1967); FGCI–63,921 (47.3 per cent of 1967). On 2 February *L'Unità* reported that the figures were PCI–1,024,128 (78.45 per cent of 1967); FGCI–75,094 (55.54 per cent of 1967). Thus the PCI claims two different figures for 1967: PCI–1,534,164 or 1,534,898, FGCI–135,140 or 135,207.

at the PCI National Conference of Section Secretaries (Bologna, 14-16 April 1967). Speakers at the conference also confirmed the inequality in regional distribution of PCI membership and support. The party, according to Directorate member Armando Cossutta, had 11,130 sections and nuclei in 8,084 communes. He pointed out that in the South there was one section per every 9,500 inhabitants; in the Veneto, one per 6,500; in the industrial triangle of Milan-Turin-Genoa, one per 3,000; and in Emilia, one per 2,300. Marked differences could be seen in the cities: Rome and Naples had one per 24,000 and one per 23,000, respectively, while Bologna had one per 5,000 and Siena one per 1,500. In 1,776 communes the PCI had no sections. (*L'Unità*, 15 April.) In the area of municipal government the PCI controls or participates in about 1,000 of the 8,000-odd local governments in the country. The PCI's influence in local government, however, has been increasingly reduced, particularly with the breakdown in collaboration with former PSI members following the creation of the PSU.

**Organization and Leadership.** The party structure corresponds to the principles of democratic centralism. The leadership includes a Central Committee (151 members), a Directorate (31 members), a Political Office (9 members), a Secretariat (6 members), a Central Control Commission (51 members), and a Board of Auditors (5 members). The Secretary-General of the party and Chairman of the Political Office is Luigi Longo. Other members of the Political Office elected at the party's Eleventh Congress (January 1966) were Mario Alicata (died December 1966), Giorgio Amendola, Enrico Berlinguer, Pietro Ingrao, Giorgio Napolitano, Agostino Novella, Gian Carlo Pajetta, and Ugo Pecchioli. In addition to Longo, members of the Secretariat were Paolo Bufalini, Armando Cossutta, Emanuele Macaluso, Giorgio Napolitano, and Alessandro Natta. The Chairman of the Central Control Commission was Mauro Scoccimarro. In July 1967 Emanuele Macaluso was appointed to the Political Office. The PCI's youth movement, the FGCI, is headed by National Secretary Claudio Petruccioli.

Within the labor movement the PCI controls the Italian General Confederation of Labor (Confederazione Generale Italiana del Lavoro; CGIL), whose Secretary-General is Agostino Novella, a member of the PCI Political Office. The CGIL has some 3,500,000 members and is the largest trade-union federation in Italy. The PCI's control of the CGIL, however, is limited by the presence in the union of noncommunist elements.* Following the October 1966 merger of the PSI and PSDI, the PCI was concerned with the possibility of seccession from the CGIL of former PSI members attracted to the social-democratic trade unions. In order to preserve unity within the CGIL, the PCI allowed its CGIL parliamentary deputies to abstain from voting on the Italian five-year economic plan in March 1967 (*L'Unità*, 21 February), and subsequently placed emphasis on asserting the indepedent role of the CGIL. In turn, this trend has brought criticism of the PCI from the party's own left wing, along with accusations of capitulation to "social-democratic reformism."

The PCI controls a number of front organizations concerned with a variety of issues. These include national affiliates of international communist-controlled organizations, such as the World Council of Peace and the Women's International Democratic Federation, represented in Italy by the Italian Peace Committee and the Union of Italian Women, respectively; various "friendship" societies and associations, such as the Italo-Soviet Friendship Association and the Italo-Cuban Friendship Society; and miscellaneous solidarity groups of a short-term "issue" orientation.

**Domestic Views and Policies.** During 1967 the PCI continued in its quest to attain the aims and implement the guide lines set at the party's Eleventh Congress (25-31 January 1966), rendered all the more urgent by the October 1966 merger of the PSDI and PSI. In his opening speech to the congress, Luigi Longo had called for the creation of a "single party of the working class" and stated that a "new majority" could be "formed through joint action between left-wing lay and Catholic forces." He continued: "The unification of the really socialist forces is today more topical than ever, for the following reasons: owing to the failure of the center-left; owing to the decision of the PSI and the PSDI to carry out a hasty merger; owing to the reactions this has aroused among the left-wing forces." Two of the principal axioms of Longo's proposals—the creation of a new party and

*For an analysis of socialist-versus-communist influence within the CGIL see Donald L. M. Blackmer, *Unity in Diversity—Italian Communism and the Communist World*, M.I.T. Press, Cambridge, Mass. 1968. p. 272.

cooperation with Catholics—were elaborated extensively in the speech. The party's policy with regard to the creation of a "new party" was seen in the context of a two-pronged action: "It is directed toward all the left-wing forces; its purpose is to create new forms of cooperation and unity among them: on the one hand, to help create a new unity of popular and democratic forces, and a new parliamentary majority, and on the other, to create a single Party of the working class embracing all really socialist forces." The progress made in the "dialogue with the Catholics," he said, was "of the utmost importance." Longo termed the Vatican Council "an event of major importance in the life of the Church" and saw the "new positions" adopted there as making it "easier to find common ground with Catholic workers and democrats": "We are now witnessing a transcending of the ideological positions of conservatism, which made religious 'ideology' the opium of the people." He declared, furthermore, that the PCI was "against the clerical State" but also "against State atheism," and proposed "an agreement on an immediate program with the Catholics" (*Foreign Bulletin of the PCI,* no. 1, 1966.)

Among the matters of domestic policy considered by Longo was the PCI's role vis-à-vis Italy's other political parties. While attacking the Christian Democrats and the center-left government (which he said had attained a "deep insurmountable crisis"), he appealed to the left-wing forces within the DC to "transcend the internal struggle for power" and "take up a clear position" which would correspond with the "aspirations of the masses." Similarly, he called on left-wing Socialists to oppose the PSDI-PSI merger and praised Lombardi of the PSI for his "firm battle" against it. With reference to the PSIUP, Longo declared: "The establishment of the PSIUP has given life to a new class, socialist forces in favor of unity. . . . We deeply appreciated the PSIUP's policy of unity with our party. From this tribune we state our determination to carry on the fraternal collaboration between our two parties." Longo's proposals were reaffirmed by the PCI's political commission and adopted unanimously by the congress in its "political motion." (*Ibid.*)

The domestic political strategy set forth at the Eleventh Congress combined two different tactical approaches—advocated primarily by Giorgio Amendola and Pietro Ingrao (see *YICA*, 1966, p. 127, and Helmut König\* *Osteuropa,* Stuttgart, May-June 1967, pp. 342-57)—geared toward meeting the threat of political isolation. While Amendola's course of action is oriented toward the creation of a "Unified Party of the Working Class" which would confine itself to parties adhering to Marxist Socialism, Ingrao opposes the merging of the PCI within a larger party, advocating, rather, that the PCI collaborate on specific issues with the left-wing parties and simultaneously encourage "dialogue" between the communist party and left-wing Catholics, both within and outside the DC. During 1967 the controversy apparent in 1966 between the adherents of the two tactical approaches (see *YICA*, 1966) appeared to have abated, while the PCI oscillated between the two strategies. By the end of the year the only notable success for the PCI was the agreement to run joint PCI-PSIUP lists for Senate seats in the 1968 elections. (For PCI commentary on the PCI-PSIUP electoral agreement see *L'Unità*, 15 and 16 December; and for the PCI-PSIUP statement on agreement, *ibid.*, 17 December.)

In contrast to the French Communist Party, which in 1967 appeared to by playing down Christian-Marxist dialogue (see *France*), the PCI continued to emphasize it. Numerous articles on the subject were published in the party press, including a near-complete issue of *Il Contemporaneo* (the monthly cultural supplement to *Rinascita*) on 30 June. The visit of Soviet President Podgorny to the Vatican on 30 January was widely publicized by the PCI. The papal encyclical *Populorum progressio* (28 March), dealing with economic and social problems, was enterpreted by the PCI as an admission by the Vatican of the "crisis in capitalist society" and was favorably received (*L'Unità,* 29 March). In his speech to the aforementioned PCI conference of section secretaries, Luigi Longo claimed that the encyclical opened "major possibilities of dialogue" and confirmed the stand taken at the PCI's

---

\*In his analysis of PCI strategy König states: "In order to meet the threat of isolation, the Italian Communist Party leadership developed a plan for an incredibly skillful counteroffensive featuring two tactical variants which determine the critical point of Communist agitation and propaganda like two alternating attack wedges, depending upon the domestic political situation: the dialogue with the Catholics and the call for the unification of the entire labor movement in a single Socialist unity party."

Eleventh Congress that "one can, even with religious motives, arrive at a condemnation of the inhuman aspects of capitalism and advance toward a socialist consciousness" (*ibid.*, 17 April). Despite no apparent significant success in winning over Catholics to its cause, the PCI continued in 1967 to emphasize what a PCI Central Committee plenum in October (9 to 11) termed a "new unity of lay and Catholic forces of the left to emerge from the Center Left."

Whereas in 1966 the PCI appeared to be disregarding the challenge from the extreme left (pro-Chinese, Trotskyist, Castroist, and "New Left"), in 1967 the attitude was changing, as was evident in the speech by Berlinguer at the joint plenum of the party's Central Committee and Central Control Commission on 16-18 May when he warned against underestimating "certain extremist groups." Most of the speakers at the plenum mentioned the "extremists," whose publications "found suitable ground among youth"—a dangerous factor for the PCI, whose youth movement, the FGCI, witnessed a large decline in membership in 1967.

**International Views and Policies.** While adhering to the policies and views of the Soviet Union on most international issues, the PCI continued in 1967 to follow the line of "Unity in Diversity" advocated by its late Secretary-General Palmiro Togliatti on matters pertaining to relations between communist parties. It would appear, however, that the PCI advocacy of communist unity and its actions in the furtherance of this goal were more evident than in the previous year (see *YICA*, 1966)—partly as a result of the actions and policies of the Chinese Communist Party leadership (see Luigi Longo, *Rinascita,* 20 and 27 October and 3 and 10 November, and *Documents*), which were reflected domestically in the Italian communist movement.

**World Communist Party Conference.** The stand taken by the PCI with regard to the convening of a world conference of communist parties appeared to change somewhat during the course of the year. On 21-24 February the party held a joint plenum of its Central Committee and Central Control Commission. One of the major speeches at the plenum was delivered by Political Office member Enrico Berlinguer (see *L'Unità,* 24 February, and *Documents*). A part of Berlinguer's speech dealt with the convocation of a world conference, and in a subsequent commentary on his views, Luigi Longo, concentrating solely on the conference, ratified Berlinguer's stand (*ibid.,* 25 February). The position of the party, as reflected by Berlinguer and Longo and in accordance with a PCI resolution published before the plenum (*ibid.,* 10 February and *Documents*), stressed the need for "unity ... unity despite and above differences ... in respect to the main line of the fight against imperialism and for peace" (Berlinguer, *ibid.,* 24 February). Berlinguer, however, while accepting in principle the idea of a world conference and agreeing that party members should do their utmost in working to achieve this end through internal discussion and bilateral and multilateral consultation with other parties, indicated that much preparatory work had to preceed the conference and that one could "hardly expect an international meeting to be called before the end of the year" (*ibid*). Moreover, Longo explained:

> We cannot continue to discuss this dilemma as to whether we ought to say yes or no to the conference; we cannot keep up this debate on an abstract and sterile level; first of all, we cannot do this because there has been no formal proposal for summoning a conference; second, we cannot do this because we do not know precisely what this conference will cover. If we were to answer either in the affirmative or in the negative, today, we would be taking a position on an *idea* of a conference whose content we do not as yet know; in other words, we know nothing about the topics, the procedures, and the time schedule, as well as the commitments that we might eventually have to take upon ourselves. Only after these questions have been settled should we tackle the problem of "yes or no." Today, the way the situation looks, the question is still on the level of an overall exchange of opinions on questions of general interest to the movement—questions which might also be tackled through a conference of all the communist parties. (*ibid.,* 25 February).

Thus in February the PCI leadership, while not opposed to the principle of a world conference (Longo in his opening remarks stated: "First of all I would like to remind you that we have—as a matter of principle—never been against such a conference") or to helping to create conditions favorable to the holding of the conference, did not envisage that it could take place in the near future, nor did they wish to commit themselves to attendance.

In late October and early November, in a series of articles published in the PCI weekly *Rinascita,* Luigi Longo appeared to be modifying the party's stand with regard to the world conference. Reviewing the PCI's former reservations regarding the convening of a world conference, Longo stated:

> We believe that our behavior was right; however, we can see today that, with regard to the standings of the Chinese comrades and precisely because of their attitude, things have gone in a different way from what we had hoped. The leaders of the Chinese Communist Party have arbitrarily broken contacts with all communist parties which do not share their point of view. . . . Under the circumstances, the doubts that we had four years ago can no longer exist. The relations with the Chinese party could not be worse, and any prospect of improving them has failed—we must have this clear in mind even if giving up no possible efforts to change the situation. Consequently, communist parties which share the necessity for an exchange of opinions and experiences and for a participation in a collective analysis of the general problems of the movement can no longer undergo the blackmailing made by the Chinese party, which thus increases its action of disgregation and splitting of the international communist world.

Longo went on to add: "Under these circumstances, the problem of calling a world conference becomes very complex. It is no longer a question of deciding whether the conference is timely, but of deciding *which* conference is to be called, in *which* way, for *which* purposes." (Emphasis in original; for full text see *Documents.*)

Although one of the major reservations held by the PCI regarding the convocation of a world communist party conference—that of alienating Communist China—appeared by October-November 1967 to have been set aside, the party's commitment to attending the conference was still highly qualified. While stressing the necessity for unity in the communist movement, the PCI remained equally preoccupied with its adherence to the concept of diversity of views among communist parties. In his *Rinascita* articles Longo stated: "We must acknowledge that the reason for so many hesitations with regard to the world conference is the fear that it might represent a limitation to the autonomy of the individual parties; it is the fear that a party's requirements or conditions or working possibilites might not be properly kept into account." On the nature of the unity that the communist parites should strive for, Longo warned:

> . . . We cannot forget the fact that the closest types of unity which were effective in the past are no longer able to express the different, complex requirements of the movement, as a result of the development and number of problems which the movement has to face. Therefore it is quite clear to us that under the present conditions a real internationalism and unity of action cannot be implemented unless we find different kinds of unity and collaboration, responding to the concrete possibilities of action of the different parties. A democratic centralization, quite valid as far as the organization of each party is concerned, cannot regulate the relations between parties without affecting their autonomy of decision.

Longo went on to elaborate on a number of procedural safeguards for the preservation of the respective parties' autonomy (see *Documents*) that would have to be adhered to for the PCI to be able to accept participation in the conference. Thus, by the end of 1967, although the PCI was one of the eighteen communist parties sponsoring the consultative meeting for a world communist party conference, to be held in Budapest in February 1968, its commitment to the conference was not without qualification.

**Bilateral and Multilateral Meetings.** In accordance with its decision expressed in February (see above) to further the aim of international anti-imperialist unity, the PCI was involved in 1967 in a series of consultative meetings with representatives of other Communist parties.

On 4-8 January, Luigi Longo together with Guido Fanti (member of the Directorate) and Sergio Segre (member of the Central Committee) represented the PCI at the Eighteenth Congress of the French Communist Party. Although there were indications of differing views between the French and

Italian communist parties on the question of the convocation of a world communist party conference (*L'Unità*, 6 January), the congress was given exceptional coverage in the PCI press, with Longo stating (*ibid.*, 15 January): "In recent times our party has intensified its relations and agreements with the French Communist Party." Longo visited Yugoslavia on 20-21 January and he met with Tito before the latter's trip to Moscow. A PCI delegation headed by Emanuele Macaluso and Alfredo Reichlin (members of the Directorate) visited East Germany on 11-23 January. On his return to Italy Macaluso emphasized the need to recognize the two German states (*ibid.*, 31 January).

In February, a PCI delegation headed by Paolo Bufalini (member of the Directorate and head of the PCI's Cultural Commission) visited the USSR, primarily to discuss coordination of celebrations for the fiftieth anniversary of the October Revolution. In preparation for the Karlovy Vary conference (see below) a PCI delegation attended the preparatory meeting held in Warsaw on 22-26 February; the delegation was led by Ugo Pecchioli (member of the Directorate), who was accompanied by Carlo Galluzzi (member of the Directorate) and Guiseppe Boffa (former Moscow correspondent of *L'Unità*).

On 27 March, Longo left for Moscow, where he met with Leonid Brezhnev, returning to Rome on 29 March via Paris, where he consulted with Waldeck Rochet. On 31 March Longo left for Bucharest, remaining there till 6 April. As a result of these meetings three communiques were published. In connection with the visit to the USSR, the PCI-CPSU communique stated:

> The PCI and CPSU see with satisfaction the growing aspiration of the fraternal parties toward the consolidation of their international unity, based on the autonomy of each party, on the principles of proletarian internationalism, on equality and fraternal solidarity. . . . The PCI and CPSU consider that the convocation of the new [world] conference necessitates a considerable amount of preparatory work, both political and organizational, by fraternal parties, in order to provide solutions for the questions involved in summoning the conference and to create the best conditions for its success and the success of the consolidating process toward the unity of the international communist movement. (*Ibid.*, 30 March.)

In the same communique the parties stated: "The PCI and the CPSU attach great importance to the coming conference of fraternal European parties on problems of European security, and express the opinion that participation of all European communist parties in it would conform to the vital interests of the peoples of the continent" (*ibid.*). Thus the communique, released just before Longo's consultative visit with the Rumanians, could be interpreted as an attempt to persuade the latter to attend the Karlovy Vary conference, offering in exchange the temporary shelving of the world conference, which, the PCI and CPSU admitted, would need "a considerable amount of preparatory work." In this connection, the joint communique of the Italian and French communist parties also stressed the importance of the Karlovy Vary conference (*ibid.*, 30 March).

The joint Italian-Rumanian communique published following Longo's visit to Bucharest did not indicate whether the Rumanians would be willing to attend the Karlovy Vary conference. Following ritual resolutions on such matters as solidarity with Vietnam, the menace of West Germany, and also the importance of the "intensification and broadening of economic, political and cultural relations between states regardless of their social systems," the communique stated:

> Unity in the communist movement, given the great diversity of conditions in which the communist parties act, can only be based on constant respect for the autonomy and equal rights of each party, on noninterference by any party in the internal affairs of another party, and on socialist internationalism. For the best reciprocal understanding between fraternal parties and for the reinforcement of international solidarity the Italian Communist party and the Rumanian Communist party recognize the utility and importance that, under these conditions, contacts and consultations between parties can have. . . . . Differences of opinion and policy that may arise must never affect the relations of solidarity and collaboration that must always exist between communist and workers' parties. In this spirit the two parties reaffirm their decision to seek every opportunity of increasing collaboration between fraternal parties and thus of helping to

overcome the existing difficulties in the communist movement and further strengthen the unity and cohesion of the movement. (*Ibid.*, 6 April.)

The Rumanian Communists, presumably in spite of persuasive efforts by Longo, did not send a representative to the Karlovy Vary conference.

A two-man PCI delegation—Aldo Tortorella (member of the Directorate) and Renato Sandri (member of the Central Committee)—visited Chile from 22 March to 5 April at the invitation of the Communist Party of Chile. The joint communique published following the visit voiced "strong criticism and firm condemnation of the splitting activities of the present leadership of the Chinese Communist Party." The two parties also stressed that the unity of the international communist movement should be based on "the autonomy of each party in elaborating its strategy and method of struggle in accordance with the historical and particular conditions it faces in its country" (*ibid.*, 11 April).

The PCI was represented at the Seventh Congress of the Socialist Unity Party in East Germany (17-22 April) by Pietro Ingrao (member of the Political Office), Sergio Segre (member of the Central Committee) and Carlo Cavalli (member of the Central Control Commission). In his speech to the congress, Ingrao stated that the PCI would further the aims of unity in the communist movement by "using all useful and suitable forms of cooperation, from bilateral and multilateral contacts up to conferences at the continental or world level," adding that this should be done on the basis of "the autonomy of each party" (*ibid.*, 22 April).

The "Conference of Communist and Workers Parties of Europe" at Karlovy Vary, Czechoslovakia, on 24-26 April (see *Conference of Communist and Workers Parties of Europe, Karlovy Vary*) was attended by a high-level PCI delegation consisting of Luigi Longo, Gian Carlo Pajetta, Carlo Galluzzi, Sergio Segre, and Giuseppe Boffa. Longo's two speeches at the conference (*ibid.*, 27 and 28 April) reiterated the party's stand on "autonomy"; appealed for cooperation with other forces of the left, including Catholics, to further peace and security in Europe; stressed the need to remove obstacles inhibiting normal relations between European states; and, while regretting the absence of certain parties from the conference, expressed the belief that their absence would not "raise obstacles to the development of fraternal contacts" with them.

An analysis of the significance of the Karlovy Vary conference was presented to a joint plenum of the PCI's Central Committee and Central Control Commission (16-18 May) by Political Office member Gian Carlo Pajetta, who hailed the conference as "an important moment in the work of restoring working-class internationalism, a step along the difficult road to finding new ways and concrete possibilities for a new, ever more effective unity to meet the problems and opportunities confronted today." According to Pajetta, the conference confirmed the correctness of the PCI's policy of "not wanting to await the development of ideal conditions and opportunities, not wanting to make everything depend on the eventual possibility of convoking a world conference of workers' and communist parties." The PCI policy, rather, was:

> ... to contribute, with our presence and concrete action, with confrontation and development of ideas, to promotion of the chances and conditions for such a conference; to labor in the common search not for formulas or general schemes that will hold for all situations, or diplomatic-type compromises, but for common elements of tactics and revolutionary strategy (*ibid.*, 20 May.)

Pajetta's comments on the conference, while in general favorable, included critical evaluation of the prospects of furthering international communist unity:

> The significance of the conference lies especially in the fact that it shows us the difficulties and the work that remains to be completed in order to find the new paths of proletarian internationalism, after long years of a policy that has left more than one negative mark, at a time made more complex by the break with the Chinese Communists, the crisis in their party, and the polemics and problems manifested on other continents. The road we must travel is a long one. It requires sincere interest and determination; it requires the realism of those who reject subterfuges and instead have resolved to intervene as positive elements. It requires renunciation of provincialism and oversimplification, but

also any tendency to nostalgia for outmoded forms of international unity and discipline that have no justification in a new situation.

Commenting on the need for "development and reform" among the Communist parties, Pajetta stated:

> While it must be emphasized that there is a vigorous revival going on in many parties in the socialist countries (aimed at tackling problems of the state and production) and in the capitalist countries (especially with respect to relations between socialists and Catholics), there remains an impression of delays in ideological development and also in clear political definition of problems that are the target of activities already in progress.

During the early summer members of the PCI leadership continued to engage in consultative meetings with representatives of other communist parties. In meetings apparently related to problems of international communist unity, a PCI delegation consisting of Carlo Galluzzi (head of the PCI Foreign Affairs Section) and Franco Ferri (director of the Gramsci Study Institute) visited Yugoslavia in early May; another, headed by Ugo Pecchioli (member of the Political Office), visited France (4-13 May); and between 24 June and 1 July a delegation headed by Alessandro Natta (member of Directorate and Secretariat) visited Hungary. Giorgio Amendola (member of the Political Office) was reported (*L'Unità*, 27 June) as having visited the USSR; he returned to Italy on 26 June (*ibid.*, 27 June).

Following the Arab-Israeli war of June, problems of international communist unity were compounded by varying communist party stands on issues relating to the Middle East (for PCI reactions see below and *Documents*). Luigi Longo's second major trip of the year (leaving at the end of July and returning at the end of August) included visits to Bulgaria, Rumania—where he also met with French Communist Party Secretary-General Waldeck Rochet—and Yugoslavia. Longo's trip was preceded (24-26 July) by a visit to the PCI of a CPSU delegation consisting of Boris Ponomarev and Iurii Pankov. No communique was issued. A report of Longo's so-called "working holiday" *L'Unità*, 3 September)confirmed that one of the major purposes of the PCI leader's meetings with the communist leadership of the above countries was in connection with the events in the Middle East. While Longo was in East Europe, a high-level PCI delegation consisting of Gian Carlo Pajetta (member of the Political Office), Senator Pietro Secchia and Luca Pavolini (editor of *Rinascita*) visited the UAR and Syria from 27 July to 2 August. Reports on the visit, published in *L'Unità* (6 August) and *Rinascita* (11 August), stressed the growing "anti-imperialism" of the two countries, and advocated increased solidarity with them. Gian Carlo Pajetta, accompanied by Alfredo Reichlin (member of the Directorate), visited Algeria on 2-5 October and met with leaders of the National Liberation Front (FLN), including Belkacem and Boumediène. A joint communique expressing the two parties' desire to reinforce ties and multiply contacts was issued following the visit (*ibid.*, 6 October). An FLN delegation led by Belkacem, visited Italy on 13-20 October. Following this visit, Pietro Secchia and Anna Nicolosi Grassi went to Algeria as the PCI delegation to that country's 1 November celebrations. A month earlier, a delegation of the RAKAH faction of the Communist Party of Israel visited the PCI (4-7 September). The two parties agreed that the withdrawal of Israeli forces from all occupied territory was an essential precondition for peace negotiations in the Middle East (*ibid.*, 12 and 14 September).

During this period the PCI was also concerned with African affairs. A party delegation—Ugo Pecchioli (member of the Political Office) and Romano Ledda (member of the Central Committee)—attended the Eighth Congress of the Democratic Party of Guinea, remaining in Conakry from 25 September to 5 October. In his report on the congress Pecchioli pointed out that 54 delegations from "anti-imperialist movements and parties" had attended (*ibid.*, 6 October).

During the last two months of the year the PCI visited and was host to a number of communist and revolutionary parties and groups. The PCI delegation to the fiftieth anniversary celebrations of the October Revolution in the USSR consisted of Luigi Longo, Enrico Berlinguer, Achille Occhetto, Gian Carlo Pajetta, Umberto Terracini, Giacomo Pellegrini, and Pietro Valenza. For the same occasion a Soviet delegation led by CPSU Central Committee member Alexei Rumiantsev visited Italy (3-16 November). A Polish communist party delegation led by Politburo and Secretariat member Ryszard

Strzelecki visited Italy on 13-23 November and had consultations with the PCI. In December a delegation of the Syrian Ba'ath party held consultative meetings with the leadership of the PCI. At the conclusion of their visit (11-18 December) a joint communique was issued which stressed the importance of collaboration between progressive forces in the Mediterranean. The Ba'ath delegation invited the PCI to visit Syria "in order to reinforce the contacts and develop the discussions between the two parties" (*ibid.*, 22 December). Other visits included that of the Secretary-General of the Communist Party of Chile, Luis Corvalán (28 November-4 December); a delegation of the Greek Community Party, consisting of Panayotis Mavromatis and Achileas Petritis (Members of the Politburo and Central Committee respectively), during the last week of December (joint communique, *ibid.*, 2 January 1968); and a visit by the Secretary-General of the French Communist Party, Waldeck Rochet, on 28-30 December.

**PCI Comments on International Communist Affairs. China.** As mentioned above, the PCI's gradual inclination in 1967 toward accepting participation in a world conference of communist parties was partly motivated by its views relating to developments in and policies of Communist China. The PCI's stand vis-à-vis the policies of Mao Tse-tung was spelled out in early 1967 by Enrico Berlinguer in *Rinascita* (13 January) and again at the plenum of the Central Committee and Central Control Commission in February (see above and *Documents*); the PCI Directorate also reiterated this stand in the statement of 10 February (see *Documents*). By the end of the year, as evidenced in the articles in *Rinascita* by Longo (see *Documents*) the PCI had escalated its condemnatory stand regarding the policies of the leadership of the Chinese Communist Party.

**Soviet Union.** In a manner befitting the year of the fiftieth anniversary of the October Revolution, PCI publications devoted considerable space to analyses, generally favorable, of developments in the Soviet Union, and reaffirmed on a number of occasions the fraternal bonds that linked the PCI with the CPSU. PCI commentary on Soviet policy and trends were not entirely laudatory. A series of articles written for *L'Unità* from Moscow by Giuseppe Boffa included critical commentary on Soviet economic reforms and standard of living (issues of 29 June and 14 July). At the time of the Fourth Soviet Writers' Congress (see *USSR*), the PCI disassociated itself from the views expressed by Sholokhov with regard to both Ehrenburg and the Daniel-Siniavsky trial (*ibid.*, 28 May). The Solzhenitsyn case (see *USSR*) was commented on by Adriano Guerra, *L'Unità*'s correspondent in Moscow, who claimed that anti-Soviet propaganda was being helped by those who "want to perpetuate outworn methods which no longer have—if indeed they ever had—any basis in fact." Guerra added: "Those who see nothing but 'dangers of bourgeois infiltration' and 'ideological contraband' are talking as if Marxism today was a besieged fortress and not a movement that is changing the face of the world and a system of thought always on the attack, always conquering new worlds." He appealed for the liquidation of the "fortress mentality" (*ibid.*, 5 July). The sentencing on 1 September of the Soviet writers Bukovsky, Delone, and Kushev was reported by *L'Unità* (2 September). While pointing out that Western journalists were not allowed to follow the trials, and that therefore it was difficult to evaluate the case for the defendants, the accusations against them, and the punishment, *L'Unità* added: "Nonetheless, in our opinion . . . this last penal verdict suggests that a correct relationship between certain sectors—youth, culture, the state, and socialist society—has not yet been achieved in the Soviet Union. Painful and serious episodes, such as the Siniavsky-Daniel case, have clearly not made this fusion easier . . ."

Notwithstanding the above PCI criticisms, Luigi Longo in his speech in Moscow on the occasion of the celebrations of the fiftieth anniversary of the October Revolution had only praises for the Soviet Union and the CPSU—"the true continuer of Lenin's cause" (*ibid.*, 5 November; *IB*, special issue, "Revolutionary Peace Forces Hail October").

**Cuba and Castroism.** In contrast to the line adopted by the French Communist Party (see *France*), the PCI's comments on Castroist revolutionary theory and the controversy engendered by it within the Latin American extreme left appeared, in 1967, to be relatively uncommitted.* An analysis of the

*For PCI discussion on "armed struggle," "guerrilla warfare," and "political action" see Romano Ledda in *L'Unità*, 4 and 6 June.

Havana conference of the Latın American Solidarity Organization, published in *Rinascita* (25 August), included reports on the controversial issues raised—including Castroist attacks on socialist states' trade with Latin American "oligarchies"—but, in the spirit of "Unity in Diversity," did not offer evaluative judgement. Likewise, *L'Unità* reported both Fidel Castro's attack on the Venezuelan Communist party (15 March) and the latter's reply (18 March). Furthermore, the aforementioned joint communique of the PCI and the Communist Party of Chile stressing "the autonomy of each party to elaborate its own strategy and method of struggle," with its implied denunciation of Castroist claims to leadership and intervention in revolutionary strategy, did not prevent the PCI from publishing in summary form (*L'Unità*, 18 April) "Che" Guevara's message to the Afro-Asian Latin American Peoples' Solidarity Organization (see *Documents*) or bemoaning Guevara's death and expressing uncritical views on his activity (*ibid.*, 17 October).

**Other International Issues. Vietnam.** Throughout the year the PCI voiced its strong support of North Vietnam and the National Liberation Front of South Vietnam (NLFSV), expressed through press conferences (e.g., 18 January, on the return from Vietnam of the PCI delegation, which had included Enrico Berlinguer and Carlo Galluzzi), speeches of PCI leaders (see Berlinguer's in *Documents*); publication of the political program of the NLFSV (*Rinascita*, 15 September), hospitality to North Vietnamese visitors—a delegation of trade union members were guests of the CGIL on 15-27 November, and numerous "solidarity" demonstrations and marches, including massive manifestations of solidarity coinciding with the 21 October demonstrations in Washington, D.C. (see *United States of America*).

**Middle East.** In the days preceding the Arab-Israeli war and in the following weeks the PCI, in its central and local organs, published a plethora of communiques, statements, and points of view, which included divergence of opinions as between the PCI headquarters and its subordinate bodies—particularly in Turin and Rome. Though veiled in appeals for peace in the Middle East and for support of the existence of the state of Israel, PCI statements at the end of May (in particular the PCI communique of 25 May and an editorial by Gian Carlo Pajetta on the 26th—see *L'Unità*) appeared to portray enough pro-Arab sentiment and feeling against Israel (as an "imperialist" force) to engender dissension within PCI ranks and accusations of anti-Semitism from other sectors. Defending itself from what it termed "gross falsifications" of its position, the PCI issued a communique (*ibid.*, 31 May), which attempted, by heaping blame for the Middle East crisis on "US imperialism," to repair the damage done by its misjudgment of popular opinion in Italy. During June the PCI reiterated numerous appeals for peace; by July the party's primary concern appeared to be the justification of Soviet actions during the crisis (see Luigi Longo's speech at Central Committee and Central Control Commission plenum of 10-12 July, *ibid.*, 13 July, and *Documents*).

**European Unity and NATO.** A recurrent theme for the PCI during 1967 was the advocacy of a united Europe, independent of the USA, free of "monopoly capitalism," uniting states in both East and West Europe in "collective security," which would exclude arrangements such as the North Atlantic Treaty Organization (e.g., Giuseppe Boffa in *L'Unità*, 26 March). While the PCI concentrated primarily on uttering concerned comments on the role of NATO (comments which following the military coup in Greece and the Middle East crisis tended to emphasize the organization's presence in the Mediterranean), the PCI's trade union, the CGIL, continued to advocate trade union unity, a step toward which was achieved in late May with the opening in Brussels, together with the communist-controlled French Confédération Générale du Travail, of a joint Permanent Secretariat attached to the European Economic Community.

**Publications.** The PCI has a number of publications. The principal ones are *L'Unità*, the daily organ; *Rinascita*, a weekly; *Critica Marxista*, a bimonthly theoretical organ; *Paese Sera*, the organ of the Rome federation of the PCI; the *Foreign Bulletin of the PCI*, a monthly English-language publication of the Foreign Section of the PCI; and *Vie Nuove*, a popular illustrated weekly.

\* \* \*

In 1967 the pro-Chinese element within Italian communism continued to reflect internecine tendencies. Despite the foundation in October 1966 of a regular pro-Chinese party—the Communist Party of Italy—Marxist-Leninist (Partito Comunista d'Italia—Marxista-Leninista; PCI-ML)—by the time of that party's anniversary, unity between the pro-Chinese had not been attained. At the end of 1967 the following appeared to be the most prominent pro-Chinese organizations in Italy:

**The Communist Party of Italy—Marxist-Leninist.** Founded in 1964 as the "Italian Marxist-Leninist Movement," the aforementioned PCI-ML formed itself as a party on 15 October 1966 (see *YICA*, 1966, p. 130). It has an estimated membership of over 5,000.

**Organization and Leadership.** The PCI-ML is believed to have sections in some twelve Regions. Its headquarters, originally in Milan, were moved to Rome at the end of 1967. The party is organized along the lines of democratic centralism. New statutes issued in 1967 provided for: Cells, Provincial Committees, a Central Committee, a National Congress, a Political Office, a Secretariat and a Secretary-General. The party's Secretary-General is Fosco Dinucci, who is also member of the PCI-ML's Secretariat, together with Osvaldo Pesce and Livio Risaliti. The Political Office of the party consists of the Secretariat plus six other members, while the Central Committee consists of the Political Office plus 22 other members.

The PCI-ML set up its own youth movement in 1967, called the "Union of Communist Youth of Italy (Marxist-Leninist)," whose National Secretary is Antonello Obino. (The statutes of the Union were published in *Guardia Rossa*, June 1967).

The PCI-ML controls a "friendship association"—the Italy-China Association (Associazione Italia-Cina), originally set up in Perugia in 1964. It appeared to be inactive until 1967 when it was revived, with headquarters in Milan. It is headed by Professor Enrico Rambaldi. The party also controls a similar Italo-Albanian friendship association, with headquarters in Rome, although primarily active in Calabria.

**Domestic Views and Policies.** During 1967 the PCI-ML appeared to be primarily concerned with combatting both the "revisionism" of the PCI and "leftist opportunism" represented by contending pro-Chinese forces. The party was likewise preoccupied with the growing influence of Castroism and Trotskyism (see *Nuova Unità*, 6 May). The party was also active in proselytizing among the peasantry. An article in the PCI-ML's weekly organ, *Nuova Unità* (14 October) stated: "For the peasants, our choice has been extremely clear: the revolutionary potential for the socialist revolution must be sought among the ravaged masses of the workers of the land who today are the main victims of capitalist contradition—i.e., the poor peasants with or without land, and the farm laborers." The party did not, however, abandon its work among the urban proletariat, and, in January, it sponsored its first Factory Workers' Conference in Milan.

The PCI-ML held its first National Organizational Conference in Rome, 3 to 4 March. (For report on the conference, see *Nuova Unità*, 11 March).

**International Views and Policies.** The PCI-ML is a steadfast adherent to Maoist interpretation of Marxism-Leninism, thus, in May, the party, guided by developments in the Chinese "Cultural Revolution," expressed its own criticisms of Liu Shao-ch'i's book *How to Be a Good Communist*, and called for: "Total struggle against the Chinese Khrushchev. Total struggle against his Black Book" (*Nuova Unità*, 20 May).

A delegation of the PCI-ML, consisting of Osvaldo Pesce and Livio Risaliti, visited Communist China in April; followed by a delegation of the Associazione Italia-Cina, led by Enrico Rambaldi, in July. Another party delegation, led by Arturo Balestri (member of the Political Office) visited Albania in August at the invitation of the Albanian Workers' Party. During its stay in Albania the PCI-ML delegation had consultations with a delegation of the French Communist Movement, Marxist-Leninist, led by its Political Secretary, Jacques Jurquet. The consultations were reported as having been "conducted in a brotherly atmosphere of proletarian internationalism" (*Nuova Unità*, 2 September). Fosco Dinucci visited Albania in September.

**Publications.** The PCI-ML publishes a weekly newspaper, *Nuova Unità*. The Union of Communist Youth of Italy (Marxist-Leninist) publishes a monthly newspaper, *Guardia Rossa*, which appears as an insert in *Nuova Unità*.

**Federation of Marxist-Leninist Communists of Italy.** Formed in July 1966, in Milan, the federation (Federazione dei Comunisti Marxisti-Leninisti d'Italia; FCMLI) has an estimated membership of 1,500. The FCMLI's youth movement is the League of Communist Youth (Marxist-Leninist) of Italy [Lega della Gioventù (Marxista-Leninista) d'Italia] .

The FCMLI held its first National Congress in Milan, 2-3 September 1967, at which time the federation's constitution was approved (seē *Rivoluzione Proletaria,* October 1967). The constitution proclaimed that the federation was "the avant-garde political organization of the Italian proletariat, which has as its objective the construction—in the unity of all Marxist-Leninist militants—of the Marxist Leninist Communist Party of the Italian proletariat." At the congress the federation also adopted a list of theses (*ibid.,* September), which *inter alia* appeared to indicate that the main source of contention between the FCMLI and the aforementioned PCI-ML was in the appropriateness of founding a regular party without due preparation: "Those comrades of *Nuova Unità* were in error when they, overlooking the thought of Mao Tse-tung and the practical experience of the parties of Lenin and Mao, held that the bureaucratic adoption of the party by-laws was adequate and that no qualifying conditions were necessary for this purpose."

The FCMLI's preoccupation with "preparation before action" was demonstrated earlier in the year on an international level when the federation refused an invitation to attend an "International Conference of European Marxist-Leninist movements" (proposed by the pro-Chinese Swiss Communist Party), declaring: "The initiative . . . is insufficiently prepared, politically unqualified, and limited to the formula of invitation" (*Rivoluzione Proletaria,* April/May 1967).

In domestic policy the federation's primary brunt of attack appeared to be against the PCI. FCMLI adherents were warned that "in order to fight against revisionism, criticism, propaganda, the dissemination of the correct ideas of Marxism-Leninism, and the ideological battle simply are not enough. The struggle against revisionism must be a fight to the end" (*Rivoluzione Proletaria,* December 1967). With regard to the 1968 general elections, federation militants were instructed to "drop ballots into the ballot boxes on which they will write the following slogans: 'Political power springs from the muzzle of the rifle. Long live Mao! Long live the proletarian revolution!'" (*ibid.*).

Very little published information is available on the leadership of the FCMLI. It appears to be directed by ex-PCI members Luciano Raimondi, Manlio Donati and Aldo Serafini, who also issue the federation's monthly periodical, *Rivoluzione Proletaria.* Raimondi is also the editor of the organ of the federation's youth movement, the monthly periodical *Gioventù Marxista-Leninista.* The leaders of the FCMLI's Sicilian affiliate—the Sicilian Union of Marxist-Leninist Communists—appear to be Michele Semeraro and Antonio Monteleone (both expelled from the PCI). The Sicilian union issues *Il Proletario* as an occasional insert in *Rivoluzione Proletaria.*

The federation appears to be connected with the Milan publishing house Edizioni Oriente, which publishes pamphlets in Italian of Chinese material, and distributes Peking-printed material in English and French. Edizioni Oriente also publishes a monthly review entitled *Quaderni,* edited by Giuseppe Regis, and a quarterly *Vento dell'Est,* edited by Maria Regis. It has also founded a "Friends of Edizioni Oriente Association," whose publication is the bi-monthly review *Orientamenti.* In November 1967 Giuseppe and Maria Regis visited Communist China and were received by Kuo Mo-jo, Vice-Chairman of the Standing Committee of the National People's Congress.

**League of Marxist-Leninist Communists of Italy.** This small group, centered around the monthly publication *Il Comunista,* is led by Ugo Duse, former editor of the PCI-ML organ *Nuova Unità.* The league is based in Milan, and has a youth movement with its own periodical *Gioventù Rivoluzionaria,* edited by Ugo Duse. The league's influence in 1967 appeared to be waning.

\* \* \*

**The Trotskyist** element in Italian communism is also highly factionalized and represents an even smaller percentage of the communist movement than the pro-Chinese. The principal organization appears to be the movement called the "Revolutionary Communist Groups (IV International)," which adheres to the Fourth International—United Secretariat. Its National Secretary is Livio Maitan. The movement publishes a quarterly entitled *IV Internazionale* and a fortnightly called *Bandierra*

*Rossa,* both edited by Livio Maitan. In November 1967 the movement set up a "Che Guevara Anti-Imperialist Center" in Rome.

**Castroist** influence within Italian communism is primarily represented by a number of publications. In 1967 the two most prominent were the monthly *La Sinistra* (which, in January 1968, became a weekly and then ceased publication in April) and the bi-monthly *Quaderni Piacentini,* which also tends to reflect pro-Chinese views.

# JAPAN

The Japan Communist Party (Nihon Kyosanto; JCP) was founded in 1922. The party is legal and has a membership estimated at 250,000 (*Sankei Shimbun,* 30 December 1967). It has grown rapidly in the mid-1960s and is now the largest nonruling communist party in Asia. However, the gain in official strength appears to represent the formal recruitment of individuals already part of the communist vote (see Robert A. Scalapino, *The Japanese Communist Movement, 1920-1966,* Berkeley, Calif., 1967, p. 292).

The JCP operates on a relatively strong financial basis, having reported an annual income to the government for the past several years second only to that of the ruling Liberal Democratic Party (LDP) (*Far Eastern Economic Review,* 12 January 1967, p. 44). JCP income derives primarily from its publications empire, which includes the official party newspaper *Akahata* and several periodicals (see below).

Like other Japanese political parties, the JCP tends to form cliques or factions around strong individuals, whose personal rivalries are often expressed in doctrinal terms. This factionalism has contributed to the withdrawal or expulsion of several groups from the party. The expelled factions—some pro-Moscow and some pro-Peking—form the several splinter groups which stand as a communist opposition to the JCP. Together, these anti-JCP groups probably command considerably less than 10 per cent of communist allegiance in Japan.

Two significant elections in 1967 served to place the JCP in perspective as a competing party in the Japanese electoral system. In the balloting for the Lower House of the National Diet on 29 January the JCP received 2,190,573 votes, or 4.76 per cent of the total vote cast, as compared with 1,646,477 votes, or 4.01 per cent of the vote, in the preceding Lower House elections of 1963 (Japan's population passed the 100,000,000 mark in 1967).

Only five of the JCP's 123 candidates were elected (an increase of one over the previous Diet), representing the poorest ratio of successful candidates to candidates of any party. By comparison with other small parties, the Clean Government Party (Komeito) ran 32 candidates, of whom 25 were elected, and the Democratic Socialist Party (DSP) ran 60, of whom 30 were elected.

In the nationwide local elections of 15 April the JCP made small gains, primarily, but not exclusively, in the urban prefectures. The Communists' chief cause for celebration was in the victory of Minobe Ryokichi, an independent backed by the JCP and the Japan Socialist Party (JSP), as governor of the Tokyo Metropolitan Prefecture. Minobe is the first "progressive" gubernatorial candidate to carry Tokyo, and observers agree that JCP assistance was instrumental in Minobe's election.

The total number of JCP seats in all prefectural assemblies doubled to 37 (out of 2,553) in the 15 April election. Neither in the National Diet nor in any prefectural legislature does the JCP hold consequential independent strength. Communist splinter groups have no representation at the national level.

In the 1967 elections both the ruling LDP and the chief opposition party, the JSP, lost voting strength and legislative seats. The shift in voter support, however, went not so much to the JCP but to the Komeito (political arm of the Soka Gakkai religious organization) and the right-socialist DSP.

**Party Organization and Leadership.** The JCP Tenth Party Congress (24-30 October 1966) increased the membership of the Central Committee to 87 full members and 49 candidate members. The Presidium of the Central Committee has 11 full and 8 candidate members. The four standing members of the Presidium—Nosaka Sanzo (also Party Chairman), Miyamoto Kenji (also Party Secretary-General), Hakamada Satomi, and Oka Masayoshi—represent the top leadership of the party.

Other full members of the Presidium are Kasuga Shoichi, Kawada Kenji, Kurahara Korendo, Konno Yojiro, Nishizawa Tomio, Matsushima Harushige, and Yonehara Itaru. Within the Party Secretariat, in addition to Miyamoto, there are 17 full secretaries and eight candidate secretaries, among whom eight are full or candidate members of the Presidium.

The Central Audit Committee, responsible to the Party Congress, has seven members with Murakami Yukari as Chairman; the Central Control Commission has five members with Yoshida Sukeharu as Chairman; and the Central Organ Editorial Committee has 14 members with Hama Takeshi as Chairman. These last two committees are under control of the Central Committee.

**Party Auxiliaries and Front Organizations.** Outside the party structure a principal source of JCP strength lies in the communist Democratic Youth League (Minseido), 40 per cent of whose members are also members of the JCP. Minseido membership dropped 40-50,000 in 1967 to about 150,000. Because the party has laid heavy emphasis on increasing Minseido membership, this loss of strength is a problem of deep concern for JCP leaders. The youth movement is the door to the admission of new members to the party, the training ground for young cadres and future party leaders, and a lever for control of Japan's strong student movement. The impatience of young activists with the generally "low-posture" attitude of Minseido leadership reflecting the current JCP policy of nonviolence and parliamentarism, combined with the increasing pressure against Minseido by industry, has reduced interest in joining. However, by paying close attention to the critical situation in the youth movement, the JCP seems to have held its own in controlling, through Minseido, 70 per cent of the volatile National Federation of Student Self-government Associations (Zengakuren).

There are at present two other smaller and more "activist" organizations which also claim the name Zengakuren. Both of these stand in resolute opposition to the JCP. They trace their origins to the major split of Zengakuren into pro- and anti-JCP groups after the exertions of the Japan-US Security Treaty crisis of 1960. The larger of the rival Zengakuren is usually identified as the Three-Faction Coalition; it was formed in December 1966 by the Socialist Student League, the Socialist Youth League, and the Nucleus Faction of the Marxist Student League. The smaller anti-JCP Zengakuren is the Revolutionary Marxist Faction of the Marxist Student League. Completely intransigent, this body is "Trotskyist" in the eyes of the other Zengakuren groups.

At present the Zengakuren mainstream (JCP affiliate) faction follows the party line in supporting the parliamentary process and remaining generally aloof from the violently obstructionist tactics of the more activist Zengakuren splinter groups. All incidents involving violence by Zengakuren students, including the Haneda Airport incidents of 8 October and 12 November (when students attempted to block Prime Minister Sato's visits to Southeast Asia and the United States), are attributable to the anti-JCP minorities.

Communist China praised the Three-Faction Coalition Zengakuren for aiding Chinese Communist resident students in Japan on the occasion of the Good Neighbor Student Dormitory (Zenrin Gakusei Kaikan) incidents of February and March (see below), and certain pro-Peking party factions have given some financial support to anti-JCP Zengakuren groups. However, there is apparently no formal alliance or permanent affiliation between dissident Zengakuren groups and pro-Peking communist elements.

The New Japan Women's Association (Shinfujin), considered by the JCP to be a "basic public organ," is led and supported by the party. Shinfujin has a membership of approximately 50,000, an increase of 17 per cent over 1966. Through Shinfujin the JCP influences, and to some extent controls, the All-Japan Federation of Women's Organizations (Fudanren). There have been defections from Shinfujin as a result of the JCP's split with the Chinese Communist Party, but no rival pro-Peking communist women's organization has yet emerged.

In Japan JCP efforts in the world peace movement are expressed largely through its membership in and effective control of the Japan Council against Atomic and Hydrogen Bombs (Gensuikyo). Gensuikyo's function has been to mobilize national and international participation in annual "world congresses" and to act as a platform for the dissemination of communist propaganda on atomic matters.

Gensuikyo, founded in 1954 as a nonpartisan movement, quickly came under JCP influence and control. Changing JCP attitudes have successively alienated the Soviet Union (whose relations with Gensuikyo may now be on the mend), the JSP, and Communist China, not to mention more conservative bodies. As a result, the Gensuikyo has at present two rival organizations which attempt to express the views of other elements of the political spectrum on nuclear affairs. National Council for the Prohibition of Atomic and Hydrogen Bombs (Gensuikin) is the JSP and Sohyo labor federation contender formed in 1965 when the JSP and its Sohyo affiliate withdrew from Gensuikyo after the JCP refused to protest against the nuclear tests of communist nations. The DSP, the LDP, and the Domei labor confederation support Council for the Prohibition of Nuclear Weapons (Kakkin Kaigi), a more moderate organization.

The three rivals held congresses in late July and early August (Gensuikyo's Thirteenth Annual Congress was in Tokyo on 4-6 August). None drew important foreign participation. Neither the Soviet Union or Communist China sent delegates to Gensuikyo or Gensuikin congresses, although the Soviet Peace Committee did transmit a message to both groups exhorting them to join forces. In 1966 the Soviet Union had attended the Gensuikin meeting. The neutral Soviet attitude in 1967 was not only a serious blow to Gensuikin, but could also be interpreted as a signal to the JCP that the Communist Party of the Soviet Union was seeking a reconciliation.

With regard to organized labor, the JCP exerts its greatest influence in the socialist-controlled General Council of Trade Unions in Japan (Nihon Rodokumiai Sohyogikai, usually abbreviated to Sohyo). Sohyo represents 4.2 million workers and is the largest trade-union federation in the country. Two other large labor groups—the Japan Confederation of Labor (Domei), with 1.8 million members, and the Federation of Independent Unions (Churitsu Roren), with 1.3 million members—are anticommunist. Although the JCP has made a concerted effort to control Sohyo member unions, it has a preponderant influence in somewhat less than 20 per cent of them. A continuing trend to the right among industrial workers, reflecting increased wage scales and personal security benefits, has made JCP efforts to influence the unions more difficult in the past few years (the conservative Domei confederation surpassed Sohyo strength among industrial workers for the first time in 1967).

**Minority Groups, Friendship Associations, and Other Fronts**. The party maintains a close liaison with and obtains some support from the Korean minority population resident in Japan (approximately 600,000 persons), the majority of whom are affiliated with the North Korean Communist-controlled General Federation of Koreans Residing in Japan (Chosen Soren).

The JCP controls a number of foreign friendship associations, such as the Japan-Soviet Friendship Association and the Japan-Korea Friendship Association, some of which have at times played important roles in maintaining relations between the JCP and fraternal communist parties, or in expounding communist views on international or diplomatic problems. Since the 1966 decline in relations between the JCP and Peking, the Japan-China Friendship Association (Orthodox) has broken away from the JCP-controlled Japan-China Friendship Association, and the communist members have aligned themselves with pro-Peking communist splinter groups. During 1967 the Orthodox Friendship Association received vigorous support from Peking, while the rump JCP-controlled faction, still proclaiming everlasting friendship with the Chinese people, has been stripped of any recognition by China.

The JCP also suffered setbacks during 1966 and 1967 in its control over several other front organizations. Until 1966 all the JCP's external front affiliations were with Chinese-sponsored or -controlled movements. As a consequence of the break with Peking and subsequent deliberate pressures from the Chinese Communist Party, the JCP-supported entries in these fronts all have split.

One outstanding example of Chinese Communist success in dissolving a JCP-controlled front was that of the Japan-China Trade Promotion Association, which in good years has handled as much as 40 per cent of all Japanese trade with Communist China. In the fall of 1966 Peking refused to deal with this association or with any of the member firms of which it disapproved. By the end of 1966 a new list of "friendly firms" was approved by Peking; the firms organized themselves into a new Japan Association for the Promotion of International Trade. In February 1967 the new association signed a friendship and trade agreement with Communist China, cutting the JCP out of the China trade picture completely (KCNA, 28 February 1967).

The China Affairs Research Institute, an affiliate of the Japan-China Friendship Association, was captured by a pro-Peking dissident majority on 10 February, when all the pro-JCP elements in it were voted out of office and expelled. Pro-China rebels have successfully split the Japan Afro-Asian Solidarity Organization, the Japanese Conference of the Afro-Asian Writers' Association, and the Japan Congress of Journalists, all Peking-directed front organizations. The splinter groups go under the names Japan Committee for Afro-Asian Solidarity (formed November 1966), the Japanese Committee of the Afro-Asian Writers' Association (formed September 1967), and the Japan Journalists' League (formed November 1966), respectively.

**Domestic Policies and Events.** At its Tenth Party Congress the JCP called for a united front composed of "progressive" elements and parties. In its report to the congress, the Central Committee declared that the congress had "mandatory responsibility for [moving] in the direction of establishing a united democratic people's front by further strengthening the unification of the people to oppose American imperialism and Japanese monopoly capitalism." In accordance with the party congress decision, the JCP made a strenuous effort to implement this directive by forming joint struggles with the JSP, Sohyo, the Komeito, and even the DSP against US "aggression" in Vietnam, US presence in the Bonins and Okinawa, US nuclear vessels entering Japanese ports, expansion of US bases in Japan, and against establishment of a small constituency system for National Diet elections. However, despite the optimism expressed at the Tenth Party Congress (*YICA*, 1966, p. 338), the JCP united-front strategy was a disappointment on the whole; except for the limited electoral successes and some cooperative efforts in short-term struggle movements, the participating "progressive" groups found themselves unable to unite on any permanent basis because of jealousy, suspicion, and widely divergent viewpoints on important issues. The JCP itself was loathe to admit anti-JCP Zengakuren factions into joint struggles, although they were acceptable to the JSP. The JCP was also reluctant to allow joint struggles to redound to the benefit of pro-Peking political groups, including its arch rival, the JSP, which maintains good relations with Peking. On the other side, Sohyo leaders, attempting to draw the labor movement closer together under the Sohyo banner, found it difficult to woo anticommunist labor groups while engaged in joint struggles with the JCP. Finally, the anti-JCP activities of resurgent right-wing factions in the JSP made permanent cooperation between parties almost impossible. The poor showing of the JSP at the polls in January and April was blamed on the JSP's left-wing leaders, who had insisted on cooperating with the JCP in the election. Internal wrangles in the JSP caused a shakeup in party leadership in August, resulting in a more cautious attitude toward cooperation with the JCP.

Despite its public jubilation over the results of the January Lower House and the April all-Japan local elections, the JCP must regard the over-all trend of the 1967 voting with some disappointment. On the positive side, popular vote for the JCP did increase by a small percentage, and some striking individual gains were made. In addition to Minobe's election in Tokyo, in which JCP support was instrumental, the JCP polled 10 per cent of the vote in that city in the Lower House elections and gained a new Diet seat. In Nagano prefecture the small city of Shiokiri elected a Communist mayor, another first. However, the noticeable swing away from the LDP and JSP in the elections was more of an advantage to other parties than to the JCP. In addition, the united-front system upon which the JCP had pinned such hopes proved ephemeral and fell into disarray soon after the election.

During 1967 JCP membership leveled off after several years of steady increase, even though an intensive drive for new members continued. The quality of the recently recruited members is relatively poor and the party finds them less than enthusiastic in devotion to party work or in financial support.

The JCP drive to infiltrate industrial management and key positions in the government bureaucracy seems to have made some headway, but the results have not lived up to expectations because of industry and government countermeasures. The party is still optimistic that a combination of joint political pressure, youth agitation, and management infiltration (especially in the mass-communications field) can shape Japanese public opinion in order to force the abrogation of the Japan-United States security treaty, the return of Okinawa, and realignment of Japanese foreign policy toward neutralism by 1970. The strong anti-United States reaction to the Vietnam war will, the party feels, be of assistance in this effort.

The JCP faces a real problem in the diminution of Minseido influence and in the continuing recalcitrance of a large segment of the Zengakuren. It has also lost partial or complete control over several other front organizations, especially those connected with Communist Chinese international fronts or those whose purpose is the development of close Japan-China relations. Organized labor continues to be wary of the JCP, as increased prosperity of the workers as well as communist internal strife have tended to reduce labor interest in the communist movement.

The JCP's most pressing problem, however, is the possibility that a strong left-wing communist party backed from Peking will emerge. The specter of a new party on the left will continue to haunt the JCP, and the fight against "splittism, flunkeyism and left opportunism" should absorb a good deal of its attention and energy in 1968.

The JCP continues to espouse "peaceful transition" and the "parliamentary road" to revolution,* and it rejects at present the Maoist dictum that "revolutions and revolutionary wars are inevitable in a class society." The party went to great lengths in the January 1967 election campaign to dissociate itself from Maoist theory, Red Guard tactics, and cultural revolution. The relatively mild demonstrations staged by JCP-controlled Zengakuren students in 1967 are further evidence of their current "legal" approach to political power.

The JCP's disinterest in revolutionary violence and people's war found eloquent, though negative, expression in handling news of "Che" Guevara's death. *Akahata* took no notice whatever of the 9 October Bolivian reports that Guevara had been killed. The newspaper's first cognizance of the event was a short article buried on page 3 of the 18 October edition, which reported skimpily Fidel Castro's long radio and television speech of 15 October acknowledging the death of Guevara and eulogizing him as a great Latin American revolutionary hero. *Akahata* ignored most of the eulogy, reporting only the barest outline of the address. On 19 October *Akahata* printed a tiny article edged in black on page 1 which carried the two-line message of condolence delivered to the Cuban Embassy in Tokyo by the Central Committee of the JCP. These two articles were the extent of JCP interest in Guevara and people's war.

**Attitude toward China.** The independent nature of fraternal communist parties, the line underscored in 1966 by the dramatic break in relations with the Chinese party, continued to be the main thrust of JCP activity in international communist affairs. Within the framework of this independent line the year 1967 saw two important developments in the JCP position. First, a further sharp deterioration in relations with Peking, and second, the beginning of rapprochement between the Soviet party and the JCP on what appears to be primarily Soviet initiative (the parties have had no

---

*The Chinese Communist Party has heaped ridicule and criticism on JCP leaders for their lack of revolutionary zeal and for their dependence upon "the parliamentary road." For example: "Kenji Miyamoto is the 'general secretary' of the Japanese revisionists. Putting on a virtuous front, he presents himself as an orthodox 'Marxist-Leninist.' But an examination of him in the light of Mao Tse-tung's thought, the magic mirror that shows up all sorts of demons, shows that he is a real 'hospital orderly for capitalism,' a lickspittle of the Soviet modern revisionists, and a wretched renegade to Marxism-Leninism.

"Our great leader Chairman Mao Tse-tung has taught us: 'Revolutions and the revolutionary wars are inevitable in class society, and without them it is impossible to accomplish any leap in social development and to overthrow the reactionary ruling classes and therefore impossible for the people to win political power.'

"The Kenji Miyamoto revisionist group, however, looks on voting in elections as its lifeline, and turns [its] back on violent revolution as if it is a natural disaster or a monster. It has placed all its hopes on the 'parliamentary road.'

". . . Not daring to fight against the aggressive forces of the US imperialists and the reactionary rule of the Japanese militarists, the Miyamoto group declared, tongue in cheek, that 'with a secure majority in the Diet, it is possible to convert the Diet from an instrument of the reactionary regime into an instrument in the service of the people.'

"*Akahata*, organ of the Japanese revisionist group, in a lengthy and stinking article in April this year . . . raved that 'so long as the reactionary forces do not use violence to block the path of revolutionary, peaceful transition, our party will exert itself to the full to realize the possibility of peaceful transition.' If there is a malady called ballot-mania, then Miyamoto and Nosaka are no doubt among its most serious victims." (NCNA, 16 November 1967.) The same article, toned down considerably, also appeared in *Peking Review,* 15 December 1967.

formal relations since 1964).

The deterioration of relations with Peking is a continuation of the process begun in 1966 (*YICA*, 1966, pp. 338-339). By the end of 1967 all contacts between the two parties had ended, and they now stand in bitter and complete estrangement. The first flareup of the dispute in 1967 came in January, when the *Akahata* representative in Peking reported to Tokyo that a Red Guard wall poster, actually aimed at discrediting Mao's enemies, Liu Shao-ch'i and Teng Hsiao-p'ing, had indirectly charged the JCP with "revisionism." The JCP, by now exceedingly sensitive to any Chinese Communist slight, real or fancied, reacted with an impassioned defense which incidentally exposed to public view conversations hitherto held in confidence between the parties.

It seems, according to the wall poster, that a communique written at the end of the March 1966 conference of the JCP and the Chinese Communist Party had been rejected by Chairman Mao because it failed to attack Soviet "revisionism." The wall poster went on to charge that Liu and Teng had helped draft the communique, and pointed to this act as another example of the perfidy and the bourgeois anticommunist machinations of these "top Party persons taking the capitalist road." The JCP, interpreting the wall poster as an affront to itself, bristled at the charge of revisionism in the JCP, implicit in the accusation against the former Chinese party leaders.

*Akahata*'s reply appeared on 24 January. The JCP not only denied that Liu and Teng had anything to do with the communique draft, but also insisted that the original communique had contained a strongly worded condemnation of modern revisionism. According to *Akahata*, "Comrade Mao Tse-tung demanded that a change be made in the content of the joint communique. The major point of this demand was that a denunciation directed against the *CPSU leadership* be added to the portion dealing with the struggle against modern revisionism, and furthermore, the stand of a united front against the United States *and the USSR* be included in the communique" (italics added; *Akahata*, 24 January 1967). The JCP delegation, headed by no less a figure than Secretary-General Miyamoto Kenji, unwilling to compromise on the principle of a united front including *all* communist parties and reluctant to attack Soviet party leadership specifically as revisionist, refused to agree to Mao's changes. Mao, according to the *Akahata* interpretation, then dismissed the problem by saying that no communique was really necessary.

This heated exchange entered a new phase in February, when the JCP felt constrained to defend itself against an attack by a Peking Red Guard newspaper which characterized Miyamoto as a "leaping little bug emerging from a ditch," and charged the JCP with "conspiring with revisionists" and "colluding with imperialists."

In the meantime, Miyamoto attacked JCP members living in and siding with Peking and expelled them for antiparty acts. Among the casualties of this purge were the widow of Tokuda Kyuichi, former Secretary-General of the JCP, and the noted "pacifist" Saionji Kinkazu, scion of a highly respected Japanese court family whose membership in the JCP had long been one of the party's most cherished secrets.

In a broadcast on Radio Peking, Saionji had warned Japanese voters shortly before the Diet election that relations with China were being obstructed by "certain members" of the left wing and advised them to vote for those who "struggle sincerely for fraternal relations with China." The JCP interpreted this as an "intolerable act of interference in the affairs of a foreign party." Saionji's broadcast was ineffective in reducing the JCP vote and served only to intensify JCP resentment toward Peking.

The first official Chinese Communist attacks on the JCP arose as a result of the Good Neighbor Student Dormitory incidents, which began in late February, when Chinese students housed in the Tokyo dormitory clashed with the pro-JCP faction of the Japan-China Friendship Association whose offices were in the same building. Serious brawls broke out in the early days of March; petty bickering and minor tussles continued through most of that month as the dispute widened to involve members of the Chinese Communist Trade Office in Tokyo (an exchange of trade offices in the two capitals was provided under the terms of the unofficial Liao-Takasaki Trade Agreement of 1964).

As a result, charges and countercharges flew between Peking and JCP headquarters. The JCP and Miyamoto were attacked in *Jen-min Jih-pao* and on Radio Peking. An official campaign against JCP "revisionism" and "the Miyamoto clique" was launched in China (see *Akahata*, 2 April 1967). The JCP, in turn, replied with specific criticism of China's "great power chauvinism" and her "blatant interference in the affairs of the Japanese democratic movement." Thus mutual criticism, previously veiled by Chinese attacks through unofficial organs and Japanese rebuttal addressed to groups without official status, was now elevated to a full-scale interparty polemic. One more important step toward complete estrangement of the two parties had been taken.

As the dispute raged on in the months that followed, Miyamoto continued to consolidate the position of the JCP mainstream by purging from the party those persons with pro-Peking leanings. Prominent among the victims were leaders in the Sino-Japanese trade-promotion movement, particularly those JCP members who had associated themselves with the Japan Association for the Promotion of International Trade.

Party Chairman Nosaka Sanzo, long-time associate of many top Chinese Communist leaders and previously a leading advocate of alignment with Peking, added new fuel to the fires of the dispute on the occasion of the JCP's forty-fifth anniversary celebrations. Nosaka entered the controversy for the first time, making a speech openly denouncing the Chinese "ultraleftists and racists" as the "obstructors of the international communist movement." He went on to oppose "some CCP leaders" who have "tried in a racist manner to force on the JCP and the democratic movement in Japan the line calling for a united front against the United States and the Soviet Union, a revolution solely by violence, and the apotheosis of Mao Tse-tung's thought" (*Akahata*, 16 July 1967).

The final crisis soon followed when the JCP recalled its two remaining representatives in Peking, candidate member of the Presidium Sunama Ichiro and *Akahata* staff correspondent Konno Junichi, both of whom had been subjected to increasingly severe pressure and abuse by Chinese Red Guard groups. Despite the official recall, the Chinese Communist government delayed the departure of the pair for two weeks thorugh a series of bureaucratic obstructions, during which time both men suffered continual harassment and were forced to undergo many personal indignities. Finally, they were allowed to proceed to Peking Airport on 3 August, where they were met by a well-instructed crowd of Red Guards and JCP apostates. Both men were attacked, mauled, and beaten, and were not allowed to leave Peking for Pyongyang until the following day. This Peking Airport incident represented the formal and final break in relations between the two parties.

The circumstances of the break led only to further JCP bitterness and recrimination. The Central Committee of the JCP met on 5 August, and on 21 August an *Akahata* editorial set the tone for the JCP's new stand, making it clear that the JCP had gone over to the offensive. Sparing no one's feelings, *Akahata* called the "Mao clique and the cultural revolution feudalistic, unscientific dogmatism alien to Marxism-Leninism, an indelible stain on the history of the international communist movement." After two more months of mutual vituperation, Nosaka, in a speech (3 October 1967) officially welcoming Sunama and Konno back to Japan, explicitly charged the "Mao Tse-tung clique" with attempting the destruction of the Chinese Communist Party and other world communist parties and with lowering the prestige of Marxism-Leninism. He said that as long as the Mao clique was in power, there was no prospect for change in this abnormal situation. Nosaka's diatribe was followed by a long anti-Mao article outlining in detail the JCP charges against the Maoists and the "anti-party flunkeyists" subservient to Mao ("The Mao Tse-tung Line of Today and the International Communist Movement," *Akahata*, 10 October 1967; see *Documents*). Finally, on 20 October, an *Akahata* editorial directed all party members to read the 10 October article and to "popularize it among the masses."

**Attitude toward the Soviet Union.** In contrast to the high-pitched intensity of the dispute with Peking, the rapprochement between the JCP and the Kremlin proceeded in muted tones. The Soviet party had been alert to the possibility for better relations with the JCP in 1966 as JCP relations with Peking deteriorated. Moscow had in fact made at least one contact with the JCP in the person of Viktor Grishin, Chairman of the All-Union Central Council of Soviet Trade Unions, who had an informal discussion with the JCP on a trip to Tokyo in June of 1966. Further discussions began in May 1967, when Soviet Central Committee Member Ivan Kovalenko met with Nishizawa Tomio of the JCP Central Committee at the Soviet Embassy in Tokyo.

In the meantime, the Soviet party sent a congratulatory message to Nosaka Sanzo on his seventy-fourth birthday. In July, on the occasion of the Forty-fifth Anniversary of the founding of the JCP, the Soviets recognized the event with a warm greeting in *Pravda*: "The CPSU considers its most important task to be the strengthening of the unity of the world communist movement and the unity of all progressive forces in the struggle against imperialism and reaction, and is prepared to cooperate with the JCP to achieve this end" (*Pravda*, 15 July).

The overt JCP response to these feelers took the form of renewed contact with the "revisionist" parties of Eastern Europe. Party leaders or *Akahata* special correspondents were sent to Bulgaria, Rumania, East Germany, and Czechoslovakia. That the JCP was still hypersensitive about its independent status became evident when a high-ranking JCP group visiting Bulgaria in June had a stopover in Moscow cancelled by party headquarters because news of it had leaked to the press. The party also entertained visiting delegations from the communist parties of Hungary and Australia. All these comings and goings, notably lacking in previous years, could only be interpreted as signs of a softening attitude toward Moscow.

The fact that the Soviets sent no representative to the Gensuikin conference in July indicated their willingness to renounce all support to Shiga Yoshio's pro-Moscow Japan Communist Party, Voice of Japan (Nihon Kyosanto, Nihon no Koe; VOJ). The VOJ was a member of Gensuikin, and one manifestation of Soviet support for Shiga was its participation in the 1966 Gensuikin congress. Soviet support for Shiga, who has hewed loyally to the Soviet line ever since the 1964 split, had been one of the main obstacles to an improvement in the JCP's relations with Moscow.

In the midst of the October *Akahata* attack on Peking which signalled the complete and definitive rupture of relations, the JCP announced that it had accepted an offer from Moscow to send a Soviet party delegation to discuss "issues of common interest to the two Parties" (*Akahata*, 13 October 1967). The JCP told Moscow that a November date for the meeting seemed appropriate; however, no meeting was actually held until February 1968.* The delay has been attributed to JCP insistence on clear recognition of its complete independence and to the troublesome issue of the JCP attitude toward convening an international communist party conference. The JCP continued to criticize modern revisionism even after the Soviet overtures in October, and in a move calculated to assert its independence, declined to send a delegation to Moscow for the Fiftieth Anniversary celebration of the October Revolution. On the matter of the Soviet desire for an international communist party conference, the JCP remained adamant. Its stand had been, and remains, to oppose any conference which seeks to set a general line for all parties, although, in consonance with its new attitude toward Peking, it no longer insists that all parties be represented at an international conference. The JCP agrees, however, to a world communist conference which would establish a concrete joint program to oppose US imperialism (*Akahata*, 7 November 1967).

The JCP position *vis-à-vis* Moscow is not as strong as it appears at first glance. The party faces a small but vocal opposition on its left with serious potential for growth and action. Backed as it is by Peking, these anti-JCP fragments could coalesce and appropriate the role of "proletarian revolutionary leadership" from the JCP itself. In the eyes of many observers, this potentially strong opposition backed by Maoist China may eventually force the JCP into full rapprochement with an increasing dependence upon Moscow, in spite of substantial objections to certain Soviet policies.

**Other International Issues.** Although significant steps have now been taken to effect better

---

*Secretary-General Miyamoto met with a Soviet party delegation headed by M. A. Suslov on 31 January-5 February 1968. The results were encouraging to the Soviets, but were by no means a complete success. The joint communique appearing in *Akahata* on 8 February 1968 reads in part: "Both delegations examined the relations between the JCP and CPSU severed since 1964, and in order to normalize them agreed upon joint resolution of mutual problems. Both delegations recognized the importance of adhering scrupulously to the principle of autonomy, equality, and nonintervention in the other's domestic affairs as prescribed by the standards for fraternal parties as laid down in the Statement adopted by the conference of communist and workers' parties of 1960. We have agreed to normalize relations between parties on this basis." This communique does indeed lay the foundation for the rapprochement sought by the Soviets, but with clear concessions to the JCP on party autonomy and on the correctness of the JCP line. The Soviets were forced to sacrifice Shiga and other supporters in Japan for the greater good of political advantage. On the other hand, they failed to wrest any concessions on the international communist party meeting or its preliminary consultative conference. The JCP sent no delegation to Budapest.

relations with the Soviet party, JCP orientation among world communist parties can still be most closely associated with that of North Korea. The Korean Workers' Party has continued to support the JCP in its independent line, and it gave succor to the battered Sunama and Konno upon their withdrawal from Peking. The Democratic People's Republic of Korea has not failed to laud JCP successes during the year, nor has it neglected to heap lavish praise upon JCP leaders on birthdays and anniversaries. It would still appear that the true sympathies of the JCP lie with the Korean Workers' Party.

In spite of rapidly changing relations between the JCP and the two major communist world powers, whose policies toward the war in Vietnam were at considerable variance, JCP opinions on the war were consistent, vehement, and voluminous. The central theme of JCP foreign policy was "oppose imperialism," which translates in this case to anti-Americanism. The Vietnam war provided the JCP with an endless stream of material for the propagation of the anti-American line. The party constantly urged communist unity in the face of "US imperialist aggression," and declared support for a conference of world communist parties dedicated to that end. The major change in the JCP stand during 1966 and 1967 has been from one urging Communist China to collaborate with other world communist parties to one despairing of Chinese Communist participation until the Maoist ruling clique in Peking has been set aside. The JCP line on communist responsibility in Vietnam is well summarized in the party statement of 9 June 1967 on support for North Vietnam:

> The responsibility which the international communist movement bears today is extremely great and serious. All Marxist-Leninist parties in the world ought to stand in the forefront of the people's struggle against the aggression in Vietnam, to achieve effective united action to oppose the US imperialist aggression in Vietnam, and to struggle resolutely on all fronts against US imperialism, while overcoming the thoughts and deeds of various opportunisms and sectarianisms that are obstructing and hindering the international united front against imperialism. By so doing, the international communist movement can sincerely meet the expectations of the Vietnamese people who are struggling with distinguished heroism. (*Akahata,* 10 June 1967.)

**Publications.** JCP publications include the newspaper *Akahata* (Red Flag), the mainstay of the JCP's organ publications (circulation 300,000 daily; 1,100,000 Sunday); *Zen'ei* (Vanguard), the monthly magazine (circulation 90,000); and several journals directed toward specific groups, such as students and intellectuals. During 1967 local elections (prefectural level and below) news publications of the JCP rose sharply, numbering more than 300 by the end of the year. On 17 October *Akahata* announced that the JCP Central Committee would begin publication of a new journal, *Reference Materials on Theory and Policy* (Riron Seisaku Shiryo), "to elevate the political and theoretical level" of understanding and to protect the party from "ultraleft opportunists, big-power splittists and from sectarian and Trotskyist subversive activities."

During 1967 *Akahata* circulation declined sharply, rose again, and now appears to have leveled off, after having enjoyed a steady rise for several years. Should *Akahata* and the JCP publishing enterprises falter, the foundation of the party's financial position will be threatened. JCP income from publications has taken on new significance since 1966, when Communist China forced the "friendly trading firms" to break all links with the "revisionist" JCP. Only those firms which satisfy Peking's stringent ideological requirements can now do business in China, and the JCP can no longer expect to tap the profits as in the past.

\*   \*   \*

**Anti-JCP Communists.** The dissident element in Japanese communism is represented by disparate pro-Peking factions and the remnants of the former pro-Soviet groups. The latter, anathema to the JCP and now abandoned completely by the Soviet party, have fared badly this year. On 5 February 1967 elements from four out of five of such groups amalgamated to form the Communist Workers' Party, but a segment of the Socialist Renovationist Movement and Shiga Yoshio, the leading figure in the Voice of Japan, declined to participate. As a consequence, the infant party emerged stillborn. In

May, by dint of great effort, it selected a Chairman and a Party Secretary but has made little progress since.

The VOJ suffered a serious blow in February 1967, when eight members of its Central Committee and 200 followers left to join the Communist Workers' Party. Its trials did not end there. In October Nakano Shigeharu and Kamiyama Shigeo, two leading VOJ members, bolted the already fractured party in protest over Shiga's one-man rule. Shiga, who lost his Diet seat in the January 1967 election to a regular JCP candidate, is now politically isolated and bereft of power. The VOJ is virtually defunct.

If the situation among the former pro-Moscow anti-JCP communist factions is confused, the pro-Peking groups provide an even more kaleidescopic picture. The primary difference is that the pro-Moscow groups appear to be in the process of disintegration, while the pro-Peking factions display a certain dynamism, growth, and some tendency to unify. The pro-Peking factional movement began in September 1966, when a portion of the JCP Yamaguchi Prefectural Committee sympathetic to the Chinese Communists left the JCP in disagreement over its "revisionist" line. Control of the local party organ *Choshu Shimbun* went to the dissidents, and the Yamaguchi Prefectural Committee (Left Wing) has since become a prominent spokesman for the Mao line in Japan. By the end of 1967 pro-Peking splinter groups had broken away from JCP prefectural committees in Aichi, Saga, Fukuoka, Hyogo, Osaka, Fukushima, Kyoto, and Chiba prefectures, and district and cell defections came to light in five additional prefectures. There is a growing tendency for these groups to merge into a unified, nationwide, pro-Chinese communist party. This move is abetted from Peking through communist members of the Japan-China Friendship Association (Orthodox), who are in contact with both Peking and the local pro-Peking communist factions. Anzai Kuraji, former JCP Central Committee member, leads the drive for unification from his pivotal position in the orthodox Friendship Association. In July the Japan Communist Party (Left Wing) held its first convention. No regular party organization emerged from this meeting, but the representatives decided that they would confer once each month thereafter. At the August meeting it was further decided that the theoretical organ of the Yamaguchi Prefectural Committee (Left Wing), *Kakumei Senshi* (Revolutionary Warrior), would be the theoretical journal for the entire movement. At year end there still was no formal party structure, but efforts toward unification continued.

Another left-wing group, the Thought of Mao Tse-tung Research Society, formed in 1966, is mainly interested in the propagation of the Mao line through discussion and the printed word. Nishizawa Ryuji, son-in-law of the former JCP Secretary-General Tokuda Kyuichi (who died in 1953) is the moving force of this group. In 1967 it reorganized and now publishes a weekly tract, *Jinmin Shimbun* (The People's News). The Research Society works closely with the forces of the Japan Communist Party (Left Wing).

The Japan Communist Party (Liberation Front), founded by Shida Shigeo in 1965 (*YICA*, 1966, p. 341), has split into two factions. The majority group favors working through and exercising influence in the Japan Communist Party (Left Wing), while a small minority advocating an independent course has broken away to form the Japan Communist Party (Marxist-Leninist). The pro-Peking communist factions have had significant success in gaining control or splitting JCP front organs directly connected with Sino-Japanese relations simply because the Chinese Communist Party has refused to recognize any front in which the JCP operates.

# JORDAN

The generally accepted date of the formation of the Communist Party of Jordan (al-Hizb al-Shuyu 'i al-Urdunni; CPJ) is June 1951. The men who formed the new party were Palestinian Arab communists who became subjects of the Hashemite kingdom of Jordan after the predominantly Arab enclave on the west bank of the Jordan River was annexed in May 1948. Communist activity was illegal in Jordan before the formation of the party, and until 1967, except for short periods, the monarchy pressed a vigorous anticommunist policy which forced the CPJ into years of clandestine operation. Fuad Nassar, the First Secretary of the Central Committee of the party since its formation, is the leading figure in the Jordanian communist movement. Other members of the Politburo include Mazin Kamel, Ahmad Sabir, Farid Said, and Rushdi Shahin. Nassar and other party leaders fled Jordan in 1957 and the CPJ headquarters operated for several years from exile in Eastern Europe.

The unprecedented events of 1967, Jordan's loss of the west bank to the Israelis in the Arab-Israeli war, and the visit of King Hussein to Moscow with the subsequent improvement in relations between the Soviet Union and Jordan, have given a new lease on life to the CPJ. Fuad Nassar and other party leaders returned to Jordan in December 1967 without opposition from the Jordanian government and soon joined the CPJ in a broad nationalist front with revanchist aims (see below).

The CPJ probably has about 1,000 members and, since June 1967, a growing number of sympathizers. The strength of the party has always lain in the west bank territory of Jordan, especially among the displaced Palestinian Arab refugees who feel little loyalty to the Hashemite monarchy. The west-bank character of the party, a disadvantage heretofore, has since the Arab-Israeli war conferred certain advantages, as the party can now credibly identify itself with Jordan's nationalist desire to recover the lost lands.* Jordan before the war had a population of slightly more than 2,000,000. Of these, some 650,000 inhabited the west bank, but nearly 200,000 of them have become refugees in east-bank Jordan since the Israeli occupation of the area.

**Domestic Policy and Activities.** The year 1967, as indicated above, saw a reversal of the fortune of the CPJ and presented political opportunities unequalled in the history of the party. In 1966 and the first five months of 1967 the CPJ still chafed under repressive government restrictions (*YICA*, 1966, p. 276). From the safety of East Europe the CPJ leaders retaliated by denouncing King Hussein's government, as when First Secretary Fuad Nassar declared: "In April 1966, the police authorities and secret service arrested hundreds of communists, Baathists, Arab nationalists, and members of the Palestine Liberation Organization. The Jordanian authorities again whipped up the hysteria of enmity against communism, the Soviet Union and other socialist countries. King Hussein and his Prime Minister Wasfi El-Tell personally took part in this campaign." Nassar objected specifically to the attitude of the "rulers of Jordan" toward the uprising of "progressive forces" in Syria in February in 1966, to their support of the Salim Hatoum coup against the new Syrian regime in September 1966, and to the "reactionary" regime's response to the Israeli attacks on the Jordanian west-bank village of Samu in November 1966. Nassar described that incident as an Israeli attempt to strengthen the "reactionary regime in Jordan" by giving it an excuse to repress the Jordanian people who protested the aggression. He ascribed the regime's motivation to its alleged acceptance (along with the rulers of Saudi Arabia and the "Israeli ruling clique") of a "role" devised by US, British, and West German "imperialists" in a scheme to destroy "progressive" Syria, republican Yemen, and the UAR. He accused the Jordanian rulers of perpetrating acts of "sweeping oppression and terror against the opposition inside Jordan itself." According to Nassar, they persecuted underground armed

*It appears that the CPJ, well versed in clandestine organization and operations, has been a primary factor in the development of Jordan's National Front guerrilla operations and raids in the occupied west-bank territories during 1968 (*Est et Ouest*, 16-31 May 1968).

Palestinians, were inimical to the Palestine Liberation Organization (PLO), and did not oppose the rulers of Israel (*World Marxist Review*, March 1967).

After the June war, the CPJ, sensing the new opportunities in the situtation, softened its criticism of the regime and projected a new image of King Hussein. The party saw "Israeli-Anglo-American plans" as comprising two phases: the first was Israel's "dirty war against the Arab nation"; the second was a political solution to the Palestinian problem in the interest of Zionism and imperialism which would impose "insulting and humiliating settlements on the Arab states" and enable "the Zionist octopus . . . to grow and to prey on the wealth of the Arab peoples." The King was portrayed as under attack from the "secret agents" of "US and British imperialism" in the Jordanian Government who are attempting to frustrate Hussein's plans to promote Arab solidarity, release political prisoners, and carry out needed reforms (*Information Bulletin*, no. 105, October 1967). (See also abridged text of the "Statement of the Jordan Communist Party," in *Documents*.)

The CPJ has drastically revised its earlier opinion of the PLO, heaping criticism on its leadership and objectives, and saying, for example: "Jordan's Communists deplore the tactics and actions of the so-called Palestine Liberation Organization and its leader Ahmed Shukeiry and its calls for the extermination of the Jews or their expulsion from Israel" (*IB*, no. 115, March 1968).

**The Communist Party Program.** The CPJ Central Committee, in order to exploit fully Jordan's economic and political situation, drew up a new "Provisional Program of the Communist Party of Jordan" dated August 1967 which is designed to appeal to Jordanian nationalism and anti-Israel sentiment. In the provisional program the CPJ clearly proposed entering a broad national front of "patriotic forces" which excluded neither the King nor his Government.

This provisional program contains a detailed account of the CPJ's current plan of action, which considers the principal struggle in the Arab world to be that betwen the Arab national liberation movement and "colonialism, imperialism, their partner – Zionism – and reactionary agents." In Jordan, says the CPJ, the "imperialists" now face resistance not only from the Jordanian people and patriotic forces, but also from "some elements of the Jordanian ruling circles whose interests are opposed to the interests and endeavors of imperialism-Zionism and its agents . . . "

The current situation in Jordan, according to the provisional program, was brought about by Israel's aggressive invasion, "which was supported, armed and pushed into the conflict by the imperialist states . . . " These supporters of Israel "falsely portrayed the aggression as a defensive measure against Arab military preparations to slaughter and annihilate the Jews." The "aggression" was said to be aimed at weakening the Arab states, expanding Israel at the expense of Jordan, overthrowing "progressive" regimes in Egypt and Syria, forcing a solution to the Palestine problem in Israel's favor, destroying Arab friendship with the Soviet Union in order to isolate the Arab states, and creating tension in the Middle East which would further "imperialist schemes." The program recognizes the war as a defeat for the Arabs and lays heavy blame on Arab disunity, oppression of the "liberation movement" in many Arab states, the schism in the communist world caused by the Chinese, which has had serious repercussions among the Arab states, and the machinations of "imperialist-Zionist plotters." After summarizing Arab and Jordanian losses in the war, the program outlines the present economic and political situation in Jordan and presents the party with the tasks it must face:

> There still are in Jordan many positions and strong influence for imperialism and its agents in the political, economic, military, and cultural fields. There are still many methods, regulations and laws directed against the people and their freedoms, including the anticommunist law, all of which stifle the people and harm the international reputation of Jordan. In addition to this, the ultrareactionary circles continue their feverish activity against democracy and Arab solidarity to obstruct Jordan's relations with the socialist countries, disseminate defeatism and confusion, and portray the imperialists as the saviours of Jordan. . . . The information apparatus and its cadres are not shouldering their urgent tasks necessitated by the critical situation facing the country, and bribery, favoritism, and corruption continue to be widespread in the state apparatus. . . .

What is required for the present stage on the internal level is the unity of all patriotic forces of the two banks in a single broad front based on a single national charter, a front comprising all the groups, organizations, sections, trade unions, or individuals, regardless of their past, or of whether they are in power or outside, as long as they are loyal, honest, and really desirous of resisting the occupation, imperialism, and their schemes.

For the Arab world the program calls for an end to differences within the Arab liberation movement and freedom for all patriotic forces. On the international level the CPJ seeks closer ties with the USSR and other pro-Soviet communist countries. The task of the Arab states, with the cooperation of the socialist countries, is first to reverse the results of aggression, and then to restore the rights of the Palestinian Arabs: "There can be no true peace as long as the legitimate rights of the Arabs in Palestine are violated."

The work program prescribed for the CPJ is laid out in broad terms to appeal to Arab nationalist sentiments and to guide Jordan into a more cooperative attitude toward the Soviet Union:

[We declare] our readiness to unite our efforts with those of every organization, group or patriotic personality, expressing our confidence that national unity can be achieved and consolidated through practice and common struggle to attain all or some or any of the following objectives:

1. The preservation of Jordan with two banks as a regional and political entity and the struggle against all imperialist, Zionist and reactionary schemes and conspiracies aimed at liquidating this entity.

2. The Western bank is an indivisible part of the Jordanian State, and we should struggle by all possible means to liberate it, regain it and evacuate the Israeli occupation forces from it, returning the new refugees to their homes and compensating them. We insist on the Arab character of Jerusalem and are opposed to both its annexation by Israel and its internationalization.

3. Guaranteeing democratic freedom and annulling, without exception, all laws stifling it, deepening the political consciousness of the masses, enabling them to offer their initiatives and participate in the building of Jordan politically and economically, and mobilizing them to defend it, to liquidate the results of the aggression and to defend the nation's independence and march forward on the road to progress and independent development.

4. To rebuild and reorganize the Arab Jordanian Army on the basis of compulsory military service, to arm it with modern, effective weapons from the Soviet Union, and prepare it in a manner guaranteeing the defense of the country and the interests of the Arab nation.

5. Remedying the economic, financial and social difficulties brought about by the aggression, working to put an end forever to imperialist aid and loans on the imperialists' own terms, and relying in the main on assistance and loans from fraternal and friendly countries.

6. Combating provincialism, tribalism, religious fanaticism, bribery, corruption and favoritism, and purging the state apparatus of corrupt elements, agents and spies of imperialism and Zionism.

7. To continue the policy of furthering Arab solidarity, especially with the United Arab Republic, Syria and Iraq, and all the fraternal Arab peoples and states, and to support the Arab struggle against imperialism and the struggle of all peoples for their independence and freedom and for world peace.

8. To consolidate and develop the relations of friendship and cooperation with the Soviet Union and all the socialist states in all spheres, and to exert constant efforts to improve and consolidate relations with the nonaligned states.

9. To pursue an independent foreign policy free from imperialist pressure and interference, and to present our problems to international public opinion in a manner ensuring its comprehension of our point of view, its support for our lawful rights, and its

siding with us in international organizations.

10. The formation of a government of national unity capable of implementing this programme at the present stage, a government enjoying the confidence of the people and capable of rallying around it the people on the Western bank and inspiring them to resist and to defend the unity of the two banks, as well as able to pursue a policy of information that will take into consideration all that has been mentioned above.

Eliminating the vestiges of the aggression, drawing the proper conclusions and lessons from what has happened, and implementing this provisional programme will pave the way for Jordan's march along the road to independent progress hostile to all manifestations of old and new imperialism, for the liquidation of the imperialist heritage of backwardness, poverty, and weakness, and for progress, social justice and Arab unity. (*IB*, nos. 111-112, December 1967.)*

**International Views and Activity**. The CPJ is solidly pro-Soviet in its international outlook and is extremely critical of Communist China. Fuad Nassar reconfirmed his alignment with the Soviet Union in an article on the October Revolution in the *World Marxist Review* (August 1967). In it he praised the CPSU, "the Party of Lenin," for its achievements and its generous support for the Arab cause, while he scorned the "bankrupt Mao Tse-tung group [which] joined the chorus of imperialists, reactionaries and Zionists . . . and started to emit the venom of its chauvinistic spite against the Soviet Union." The Party continues to back the CPSU call for a world conference of communist and workers' parties in 1968.

Fuad Nassar attended the Seventh Congress of the East German Socialist Unity Party, in Berlin, 17-22 April, where he made an address condemning Chinese policy and supporting the CPSU. Nassar also represented his party in the Soviet Union at the celebrations of the Fiftieth Anniversary of the October Revolution. Mazin Kamel, a member of the CPJ Politburo, was given considerable attention in the British communist press as the party's representative at the Thirtieth Congress of the British Communist Party, in December.

The documents of the Arab Communist Meeting, May 1967, say very little about Jordan or the situation there, perhaps indicating that no members of the CPJ were present. Two short references to Jordan appear in one document, entitled "Statement on the Situation in the Arab Countries" (See *Documents*).

**Publications**. The monthly organ of the CPJ, since 1965, has been called *al-Taqaddum* (Progress), formerly *al-Muqawamah al Sha 'biyah* (Popular Resistance). The CPJ has reportedly (*Arab World*, Beirut, 14 December 1967) asked the Jordanian government for permission to resume publication of its long-defunct party newspaper *Al-Jamahir*.

The CPJ has no broadcasting facility of its own, but party statements have on occasion been broadcast by the Iraqi Communist Party clandestine radio "Voice of the Iraqi People," believed to operate from Bulgaria.

*The CPJ program met with some conspicuous successes. For example, the formation of a "National Front," which includes the CPJ, the Baathists, the Social Nationalists, the Independent Socialists and the Moslem Brotherhood, was announced publicly at the end of March 1968. Reportedly, King Hussein himself appeared at the clandestine meeting in Amman which established the front, thus giving something more than tacit consent to its formation. The King's appearance was a daring step to bring the front under his aegis, and it removed the necessity for it to operate clandestinely. (*Est et Ouest*, 13-31 May 1968.) Guerrilla and terrorist operations in the Israeli-occupied west-bank territories began soon after the official announcement of its formation. The President of the National Front is former Prime Minister Suleiman Nabulsi, noted for his pro-Nasser and procommunist views, whom the King removed from office in 1957 for this reason. Thus, the struggle to liberate the west bank by "all possible means" has begun.

King Hussein paid a visit to Moscow on 2-5 October 1967. Upon his return from the Soviet Union he appointed Bahjat al-Talhouni Prime Minister, with a mandate to "remove the traces of aggression," "recover the immortal city of Jerusalem," and "equip the armed forces with the latest and most effective weapons 'from any source' " (*Washington Post*, 8 October). As a result of the King's visit to Moscow, "relations of friendship with the Soviet Union and all socialist states" have taken a positive turn.

In addition, the recent (December 1967) introduction of a conscription system into the army in place of depending on pro-Hashemite Bedouin volunteers was welcomed by the CPJ as a major step in "rebuilding and reorganizing the Arab Jordanian Army." In fact, the system allows west-bank Jordanians into the army for the first time. The Bahjat al-Talhouni Government has not repealed the anticommunist law, but the communists are operating openly in Jordan for the first time since 1957, and the CPJ could announce with satisfaction that all its members who were in jail have been released. (*IB*, No. 115, March 1968.)

# LAOS

Founded secretly in 1946, the communist Laotian People's Party (Pasachone Lao; PsL) was openly founded in 1955. Although it has not been outlawed, it chooses to operate clandestinely* through the Laotian Patriotic Front (Neo Lao Hak Xat; NLHX). The NLHX, founded on 6 January 1956, replaced the Free Laos Front and became a legal party as a result of the Vientiane Agreements of 1957. It is presently the Communist component of the tripartite National Union Government, often referred to by the Communists as the tripartite National Coalition Government, recognized by the Geneva Agreements of 23 July 1962, and previously by the Zürich Agreement of June 1961 and the Plaine des Jarres Agreement of June 1962.

Although the exact membership of the PsL is unknown, a 1964 estimate placed it at about 700. The NLHX, which is controlled by the PsL, is estimated to have between 1,500 and 3,000 members. The Laotian People's Liberation Army (formerly called the Pathet Lao), the military arm of the NLHX, numbers 20,000 to 30,000 and has in addition approximately 2,500 supporters plus the support of some 3,000 dissident neutralists. The population of Laos was estimated in mid-1966 as 2.7 million.

**Organization and Leadership.** Very little is known about the leadership of the PsL, except that it controls, and to some extent overlaps, the Central Committee of the NLHX. The Secretary-General of the PsL is Kaysone Phomvihan, who is also Vice-Chairman of the NLHX Central Committee; he appears to operate mainly from Hanoi and is reportedly the most important person in the Laotian communist movement. The Chairman of the PsL Central Committee, Nouhak Phoumsavanh, is at the same time Secretary of the NLHX Central Committee and High Commissioner of the Vietnam Workers' Party in Laos, and acts as the liaison between Hanoi and Khang Khay, the headquarters of the NLHX Central Committee. Other known members of the PsL include Sithon Khommandam, also Vice-Chairman of the NLHX Central Committee; Phoumi Vongvichit, Secretary-General of the NLHX; General Phoum Sipasat, member of the NLHX Political Bureau; and Khamphouane Tounalom, member of the NLHX Political Bureau. It is also likely that Sinkapo Chounlamany is a member of the PsL. The PsL, which controls the NLHX, is in turn controlled by the Vietnam Workers' Party.

The leadership of the NLHX consists of Phoumi Vongvichit, Secretary-General of the NLHX; Prince Souphanouvong, Chairman of the NLHX Central Committee; and Sithon Khommandam, Kaysone Phomvihan, and Faydang, all Vice-Chairmen of the NLHX Central Committee. Political Bureau members include Kaysone Phomvihan, General Phoum Sipasat, Sithon Khommandam, General Sinkapo Chounlamany, Nouhak Phoumsavanh, Khamphouane Tounalom, and Phoumi Vongvichit. Additional members of the NLHX Central Committee are Maysouk Saysompheng, Tiao Souk Vongsak, Saly Vongkhamsao, Kiao Sik Phaisomphone, Kong My, Sisana Sisane, General Phoune Sipraseuth, Pheng Phang, and Khamphay Boupha.

With four of the 10 cabinet posts in the government (although they have refused active governmental participation since 1963) and benefiting from the discord between their neutralist and

---

*Although the PsL remains clandestine, it has on occasion issued statements and messages in its name and signed by its Secretary-General, Kaysone Phomvihan, rather than that of the NLHX and Prince Souphanouvong, Chairman of the NLHX Central Committee. The December 1966 issue of *Zen'ei*, the official monthly of the Japan Communist Party, carried a message of greetings to the Tenth Japan Communist Party Congress signed by Secretary-General Phomvihan, and on 15 July 1967 Hanoi broadcast a Laotian message of condolence to the Vietnam Workers' Party on the occasion of the death of Nguyen Chi Thanh. This message, dated 8 July 1967, was also signed by Phomvihan.

rightist ruling partners, Laotian Communists enjoy significant advantages. Of greater importance, however, is the fact that they control the northeastern corner of Laos, an eastern fringe through which passes the Ho Chi Minh Trail, and parts of the south. According to Communist claims, two-thirds of the territory and one-half of the population are under NLHX control and administration. Western sources estimate that one-third of the territory and 20 to 30 per cent of the population are under communist control.

The communist position in Laos is further strengthened by the considerable military, economic, and administrative aid which the NLHX receives from the Democratic Republic of Vietnam. It is believed that there are approximately 7,000 North Vietnamese tactical troops and 18,000 logistic experts in southeastern Laos, in addition to an estimated 15,000 North Vietnamese in the northeast who fight either independently or with the Laotian People's Liberation Army. Although the presence of North Vietnamese regulars has been repeatedly denied by the communists, it appears that most of the communist offensives in Laos are led by North Vietnamese and that North Vietnam provides political cadres down to the district level in the communist-controlled provinces of Laos.

In addition to the North Vietnamese, approximately 500 Chinese are reportedly in Laos assisting in the construction of a road from Communist China across northern Laos and into Burma. While the Democratic Republic of Vietnam and the People's Republic of China maintain diplomatic relations with the National Union Government of Vientiane, both countries also maintain missions at Khang Khay in NLHX-controlled territory.

The Laotian People's Liberation Army is headed by Khamtay Siphandone, who is Commander-in-Chief. Other key figures in the army include General Phoum Sipasat and General Sinkapo Chounlamany. Following the April 1964 coup, the Laotian Communists also acquired the military support of the Patriotic Neutralist Forces, whose Commander-in-Chief is Colonel Deuane Sounarath. The Patriotic Neutralist Forces reportedly consist of two groups: one under Colonel Deuane Sounarath and Commandant Thiepat at Khang Khay and a second under General Khamouan Bouppa at Phong Saly. Their effective forces are estimated to be between 2,000 and 3,000 men. At a national congress on 26 August 1964 they unanimously adopted a resolution of complete solidarity with the NLHX. Cooperation between the NLHX and the Patriotic Neutralist Forces was further emphasized in the 13 October 1965 joint communique of the political consultative conference of the two "patriotic forces."

Communist influence is also exercized through a number of mass organizations, the most important of which are the Laotian Workers' Union, the Patriotic Laotian Women's Federation, the Laotian Youth Association, the Laotian Buddhists' Association, and the Laotian Patriotic Cultural Workers' Association and the Laotian Afro-Asian Solidarity Committee (the last two are headed by Phoumi Vongvichit).

**Elections and Party-Government Relationship.** General elections for the Laotian National Assembly were held on 1 January 1967, with the NLHX boycotting them on the grounds that they were "entirely reactionary and illegal" and "nothing but a deceitful trick to mislead public opinion" (Radio Pathet Lao, 1 March 1967). In an interview with a Voice of Vietnam correspondent, Prince Souphanouvong, Chairman of the NLHX Central Committee, pointed out:

> The so-called National Assembly elections organized by the puppet Vientiane administration on 1 January 1967 were nothing but a political trick . . . . The NLHX and the Laotian people resolutely condemn and denounce the so-called National Assembly elections organized by the puppet Vientiane administration. These elections were entirely reactionary and illegal, and this puppet National Assembly is entirely void . . . . The NLHX and the Laotian people resolutely reject it. (Hanoi Domestic Service, 17 March 1967.)

During the first half of 1967 the NLHX continued to denounce Souvanna Phouma as the "chief of an illegal reactionary government" composed of "only pro-American elements who are serving the interests of the Americans and not the interests of the Laotian people," and maintained that "without the participation of the Neo Lao Hak Xat and more than half of the Laotian population, this puppet Assembly constitutes a barrier to the tripartite National Coalition Government," which is the "only legal government in Laos" (Radio Pathet Lao, 26 January 1967, and Prince Souphanouvong in an interview with Prague Domestic Service, 6 May 1967).

On 3 June Souvanna Phouma presented a reorganized cabinet to the National Assembly, which the NLHX and the Patriotic Neutralist Forces branded as "an illegal administrative body—a government which has sold out our nation to the US imperialists" and denounced as an attempt on the party of the "US imperialists" and their "puppet administration" in Vientiane to "deceive the world into believing that the present government is still the National Coalition Government and is following the path of neutrality in accordance with the agreement signed by the three parties of Laos" (Sithon Khommandam, Vice-Chairman of the NLHX Central Committee, Radio Pathet Lao, 16 June 1967).

On 13 June Radio Pathet Lao carried a statement outlining the NLHX policy toward the new government:

> In view of the present situation in the country, which is more serious than ever, the patriotic party in the tripartite National Coalition Government, including the ministers and secretaries of state of the Neo Lao Hak Xat and the Patriotic Neutralist Forces, is firmly determined to carry out its tasks indefatigably in order to maintain and positively execute the policy set forth by the tripartite National Coalition Government.

The official response of the Souvanna Phouma government was to maintain that by following the instructions of North Vietnam the NLHX "has brought war and the enemy to Laos," thus "slowing down . . . national prosperity and development and . . . destroying the unity of the Kingdom of Laos." At the same time, however, the government continued to stress that "in order to maintain internal unity, the government does not want to sever relations with the NLHX. All Ministerial positions are still open to them. They can return to continue their functions whenever they feel that they are also Laotians, and nobody will object to them." (Message from Souvanna Phouma, Vientiane Domestic Service, 14 October 1967.)

**Domestic Policies.** During 1967 the NLHX continued to uphold the validity of the domestic and foreign policies adopted at the Second National Congress of the NLHX, held at Sam Neua on 2-12 April 1964. The party stressed its adherence to the four-point decision and the five-principle resolution for the solution of the Laotian problem, as set forth by the National Political Union Conference of the NLHX and the Patriotic Neutralist Forces in October 1965, as the correct formulation of their domestic and foreign policies. Briefly stated, the four-point decision stresses the following needs:

1. To defend the peace, neutrality, sovereignty, independence, unity, and territorial integrity of Laos on the basis of the 1962 Geneva Agreements, the Tripartite Agreement of Zürich (1961), and the Plaine des Jarres Agreement (1962)

2. To fight all forms of "imperialist intervention and aggression against the people of Laos"

3. To ensure the right of the people of Laos to settle their own internal affairs through peaceful negotiations by the parties concerned without US intervention

4. To persistently work for the implementation of the tripartite National Coalition Government

The five-principle resolution for the solution of the Laotian problem calls for:

1. Withdrawal from Laos of all armed forces, military personnel, covert military organizations, and all weapons and war material introduced into Laos by the "US imperialists and their satellites," as well as the dismantling of all US military bases in Laos

2. Cessation of all "acts of aggression" against Laos by the United States

3. Cessation of all collaboration between the "US lackeys" in Laos, Thailand, and South Vietnam and the use of Thai and South Vietnamese territory as "springboards for intervention in Laos"

4. Conducting tripartite negotiations in earnest and in a spirit of mutual understanding with a view toward solving all outstanding problems between the parties concerned

5. Restoration of the organization structure and the principle of tripartite unanimity of the Laotian National Coalition Government based on the 1961 Zürich Agreement and the 1962 Plaine des Jarres Agreement

In stressing the four-point decision and the five-principle resolution as the "only acceptable program for a basic and just settlement of the Laos problem," the NLHX insisted that a number of specific domestic and military tasks be carried out during the year. On 20 November 1967 the high command of the Laotian People's Liberation Army issued an order containing four sets of tasks to be carried out by all political cadres and military combatants in the regular, regional, and guerrilla forces throughout the country:

1. All units of the armed forces must execute all orders. On the battlefield, they must strive to defeat the enemy and win brilliant victory. They must always be masters of the situation. They must annihilate as many of the enemy as possible. Especially, they must destroy the enemy's mobile and special forces and they must destroy the reactionaries who have committed criminal acts against the people. They must drive the enemy forces into a hopeless situation. They must inflict on them more and bitter defeats.

2. We must educate the people to build up our substructure. We must carry out propaganda to disseminate the Central Committee policy and to make our revolutionary victories known to the people so that the people will contribute to obtaining such victories. We must really apply the policy of solidarity among the ethnic minorities, and we must strictly enforce the army regulations on the troops' behavior toward the population. We must firmly protect the people's life and property. We must serve the interests of the people and aid them in all works. We must guide the people in all domains and we must fail enemy schemes to displace the people.

3. We must make argicultural developments, promote economy, and oppose greedy acts. We must, at any cost, improve the armed forces' living standard.

4. We must endeavor to construct and improve all the units of our armed forces so that they will become effective in the political, military, and administrative areas, and to publicize the true facts of the revolution of our armed forces. We must propagandize in our three armed forces. We must include the duties of struggle and training in the resolutions of the Central Committee in order to strengthen the sentiments of revolution; we must promote the sentiment of confidence; this means we must win final victory.

(Radio Pathet Lao, 20 November 1967.)

Throughout 1967 NLHX statements and Radio Pathet Lao commentaries emphasized a number of domestic tasks, including the need to "develop our agriculture," "improve our economy and promote our cultural affairs to serve our people's war," and "improve the people's standard of living." Emphasis was also placed upon the need to consolidate the liberated zones, to continue the political education of the population in order to raise the masses to a higher ideological and organizational level, to intensify the political struggle of the population, to instill a higher degree of political consciousness in cadres at all levels, and to strengthen and broaden the national united front against the Vientiane government and the "US imperialists." The NLHX also reiterated its readiness to "cooperate with any party or person who genuinely wants to liberate our nation and defeat the US imperialists and protect the peace, sovereignty, and genuine neutrality of our nation." Numerous appeals were issued to "all the monks and religious people, civil servants, policy officers, and military men in the temporarily controlled areas to see clearly and recognize the US imperialists' and rightists' civil and criminal acts and oppose energetically their attacks and mopping-up operations against the liberated territory, cooperate with the patriotic and NLHX forces in order to carry on our struggle to chase the United States out of our country immediately" (Radio Pathet Lao, 19 June 1967, and Radio of the Patriotic Neutralist Forces, 12 October 1967).

In the military sphere, the NLHX, the Laotian People's Liberation Army, and the Patriotic Neutralist Forces hailed the "rapid development" and "limitless capabilities and strength of people's war" during 1967, and outlined a number of specific tasks to be fulfilled by the regular forces, the regional troops, and guerrilla units.

On 21 January 1967 Khamtay Siphandone, Commander-in-Chief of the Laotian People's Liberation Army, issued a lengthy order calling upon the army, the local units and militia, and the guerrilla forces "to develop guerrilla warfare, set a people's war, and annihilate the US imperialists and their lackeys to celebrate the 18th anniversary of the founding of the Laotian People's Liberation

Army." Specifically, the order called on the army to "arouse the people to establish and consolidate the various revolutionary organizations, form revolutionary villages, fighting villages and fighting districts; raise production and practice economy in the spirit of self-reliance, insure good results in army building and in fighting, cultivate the revolutionary spirit, bring into full play the good traditions of the nation and the people's army, deepen their hatred for the enemy, strengthen solidarity with the Patriotic Neutralist Forces, and jointly defeat US imperialism and its lackeys."

The order also cautioned that "the Laotian people's struggle against US aggression and for national salvation is a fierce, complex, and protracted one," but added that, in the final analysis, "victory must belong to the Laotian people" (NCNA, 21 January 1967).

Subsequent directives repeated the above points, and on 12 October, the Twenty-Second anniversary of the Laotian National Day, the NLHX Central Committee issued a statement noting:

> The first and foremost task of the Laotian armed forces and people . . . . is to increase their strength in all fields; to defend, consolidate, and develop the liberated areas in all their political, military, economic, and cultural aspects; and to step up the people's struggle throughout the country to win newer and greater successes (NCNA, 12 October 1967).

The statement further urged people in the "liberated areas" to "strengthen further their solidarity, make positive contributions to the struggle against US aggression and for national salvation, resolutely defend and build the powerful liberated areas, and smash all the vicious maneuvers of the enemy to stamp out the revolutionary struggle of the Laotian people" (NCNA, 14 October 1967).

Considerable emphasis was also placed on the need to combine political study with military training. On 30 November 1967 Radio Pathet Lao carried a long commentary on the subject, pointing out that more attention must be paid to combining these two tasks because " . . . with strict and serious interest in political study, and with the determination of every armed unit and combatant to carry out . . . [its] assignment . . . the supreme command firmly believes that we will certainly attain more and greater victories militarily and politically." Simultaneously, the "liberation forces are to conduct active propaganda among the people; help them in production, education, and in the stabilization of their existence, developing at the same time agricultural production" (Siphandone, representative of the command of the Laotian People's Liberation Army, in an interview with Polish Press Agency, Warsaw, 9 March 1967).

**Domestic Achievements.** On 3-9 December 1967 the NLHX Central Committee held an enlarged conference chaired by Prince Souphanouvong, who delivered a lengthy report on the achievements and successes of the "patriotic forces" during 1967 and on the "direction and meaning of struggle for the future." He noted that the "liberated areas" of Laos had been secured and expanded, that the people's political background had been "elevated and promoted," and that construction, agriculture, manufacture, light industry, education, and public health had scored "great successes." He concluded:

> Armed with revolutionary fire, our armed forces and personnel have improved themselves in politics, revolutionary thought, military tactics, and strategy. They have become the supporting beacon of our revolution which cannot be put down by any enemy. Most important of all is that the National Front for the Liberation of the Laotian People has created more excellent revolutionary situations in our country. Unity among our minority compatriots and coordination between the NLHX and the Patriotic Neutralist Forces have been promoted and improved. (Radio Pathet Lao, 13 December 1967.)

An analysis by the New China News Agency on 1 January also hailed the successful intensification of political and ideological work within the armed forces and the positive response of the "patriotic forces" to the NLHX production campaign for self-sufficiency launched in the organizations and army units in the "liberated areas" during 1967.

At the Central Committee meeting, however, Prince Souphanouvong also cautioned that

> . . . we have failed to take full advantage of these good results and opportunities to inspire confidence in others and to surmount all obstacles to win further victories. Since our

struggle against the enemy has steadily progressed, we must surely fulfill our mission in accordance with the present situation in our country. However, we have always found it impossible to fulfill all our tasks in accordance with the Central Committee's directives. Since we cannot completely fulfill our tasks in order to give confidence to our people and country, we must consider our situation. We must know how to take advantage of the situation in our country and we must set forth working plans to boost our struggle and win further victories. This is our duty and is also the aim of this enlarged conference of the NLHX Central Committee. (Radio Pathet Lao, 14 December 1967.)

As part of the "working plans" to win further victories, the Central Committee called on the Laotian "patriotic forces" to heighten their sense of responsibility and to obey party orders in order to "remain masters of the situation." In a message to the Laotian people Phoumi Vongvichit stressed the need to stengthen the regular, regional, and guerrilla forces and to train all combatants in theory as well as practice. He also called for "all kinds of efforts and sacrifices to develop our agriculture, improve our economy and promote our cultural efforts . . . in order to defeat the US imperialists and their lackeys in our revolutionary war," concluding that "if we can do these things, undoubtedly we will defeat the enemy in no time" (Radio of the Patriotic Neutralist Forces, 9 October 1967).

In spite of these considerations, the Pathet Lao News Agency's analysis for 1967 hailed the year's successes, noting that "enemy losses in lives, aircraft, combat launches, arms and ammunition, and military equipment in 1967 exceeded those in any previous year since 1954." According to this analysis, 1,300 battles were fought, 12,500 enemy government troops were put out of action, 2,500 weapons—as well as hundreds of tons of ammunition and military equipment—were captured, and some 260 US aircraft were destroyed and hundreds of others damaged (Pathet Lao News Agency, 7 January 1968). The following day Pathet Lao News Agency further declared:

This success was possible thanks to the unity and struggle of the people of all strata in Laos and the ever closer cooperation between the NLHX and the Patriotic Neutralist Forces. The success resulted from the solidarity and ardent patriotism of the Laotian people and the correct political line and clearsighted leadership of the NLHX Central Committee headed by Prince Souphanouvong. It resulted from the Laotian Army and people's determination to defeat US aggressors, and the militant solidarity between other peoples in Indochina . . . ., and the Laotian people who have been enjoying vigorous support from the peace-loving and progressive people in the world.

**Foreign Policy.** Throughout 1967 NLHX policy statements attacked the United States as the "arch imperialist" and accused it of having violated the 1954 Geneva Agreements on Indochina. the 1961 Zürich Agreement, the 1962 Plaine des Jarres Agreement, and the 1962 Geneva Agreements on Laos. The NLHX also accused the United States of having destroyed the tripartite National Coalition Government, "the only legal government of Laos," and of having established a puppet administration in Vientiane.

NLHX directives, as well as those of the Laotian People's Liberation Army and the Patriotic Forces, warned that "while encountering serious losses in Vietnam, they [the US imperialists] will surely bring their troops over to southern Laos in order to make that area a new war front" (Radio of the Patriotic Neutralist Forces, 9 October 1967). Numerous analyses of US intentions in Laos were also made, and the general conclusion was:

The US tricks are intended to escalate the war throughout the Indochinese peninsula so as to save the US imperialists from the approaching disaster. They also intend to dispatch their troops and their lackeys to occupy the southern and central parts of Laos. Thus, they can link the battlefield in South Vietnam with their bases in Thailand . . . This is their new risk, and it seriously endangers our country, the Indochinese peninsula, and Southeast Asia. (Radio Pathet Lao, 19 June 1967.)

Military and political spokesmen also lodged protests with the cochairmen of the 1962 Geneva Agreements on Laos, accusing the United States of "bombing and strafing" the "liberated" territories of Laos and of using toxic gas and poisonous chemicals to destroy the lives and property of the

Laotian people. Emphasis was placed on the NLHX position that the Laotian problem is essentially a problem of American "intervention and aggression" and that consequently its solution lies in the termination of US action against Laos and in the observance of the four-point stand and five-principle resolution.

Attacks on the United States were paralleled by attacks on Thailand, with the NLHX accusing it of blindly following instructions from Washington, and of cooperating with the Vientiane "puppet clique," thus making it the "dirtiest US lackey of all." Specifically, the Central Committee of the NLHX condemned the Thai authorities for allowing B-52 bombers to be stationed in Thailand and for "aiding the puppet Laotian authorities in developing the US aggressive war in Laos" by sending troops, military advisers, ammunition, and war material to Laos.

NLHX attacks also focused on SEATO, which was labeled "an instrument for aggression and war expansion of the US imperialists" and on ASEAN, the Association of Southeast Asian Nations, which was condemned as a "tool to promote neo-colonialism and a reactionary alliance rigged up by US imperialism for suppressing the liberation movement in Southeast Asia" (Radio Pathet Lao, 18 August 1967).

During 1967 the NLHX, the Laotian People's Liberation Army, and the Patriotic Neutralist Forces reaffirmed their support for the "Vietnamese people of the two zones" and pledged to tighten further their "solidarity and close cooperation with the Vietnamese people in their common struggle in order to deal with US imperialists and their lackeys a total defeat and to safeguard the foundation of the brilliant victories achieved in the struggle against US aggression and to contribute toward safeguarding peace in Indochina and Southeast Asia."

The NLHX also insisted upon the validity and correctness of the four-point stand of the government of the Democratic Republic of Vietnam and the five-point statement of the National Liberation Front of South Vietnam.

The NLHX position on the Arab-Israeli war was contained in a telegram from Prince Souphanouvong to UAR President Nasser and broadcast by Radio Pathet Lao on 11 August 1967. In the name of the NLHX and the Laotian people, Prince Souphanouvong protested the "aggressive actions undertaken by the reactionary Israelis against the United Arab Republic and against the other Arab countries under the US imperialists' orders" and pledged the support of the Laotian people for the "struggle and solidarity of the Arab people." The telegram also noted that, "confronted by the same enemies, the US imperialists, the Lao people have decided to increase the struggle for national liberation and to support more effectively the legal struggle of the people of the United Arab Republic and other Arab countries."

**The International Communist Movement.** During 1967 the NLHX's contacts with international organizations centered primarily on the Afro-Asian Latin American People's Solidarity Organization (AALAPSO). On 10 March 1967, at the invitation of the NLHX, an AALAPSO delegation arrived in Sam Neua for a visit to the "liberated areas," with the purpose of discovering ways to further tighten the solidarity of struggle among the Asian, African, and Latin American peoples with the Laotian people and to step up support and assistance to the Laotian people's struggle" (Radio Pathet Lao, 23 March 1967).

Contacts between AALAPSO and the NLHX were strengthened when the AALAPSO Executive Secretariat issued a statement calling for the people of Asia, Africa, and Latin America to celebrate 12 October 1967 as the "tricontinental day of militant solidarity with the Laotian people." In response to the AALAPSO decision, the NLHX sent a delegation led by Saly Vongkhamsao, member of the NLHX Central Committee, to meet with the AALAPSO Executive Secretariat in Havana on 6-30 October 1967.

Although emphasizing the support of the socialist countries for the "patriotic forces" of Laos and the fulfillment of its international duties, the NLHX apparently made no reference to the Karlovy Vary Conference held in Czechoslovakia on 24-26 April 1967 or to the Budapest Conference held in February 1968.

**The Soviet Union.** NLHX contacts with the Soviet Union remained limited in 1967, and party statements and directives contained only occasional references to the Soviet Union. On the Twenty-Second anniversary of the Laotian National Day (12 October 1967) the NLHX Central Committee expressed its "most sincere thanks to the Soviet people and government . . . who have sincerely supported us in our struggle against the US imperialists for our national liberation." At the same time, however, considerably more emphasis was placed on North Vietnamese and Chinese support.

On the Fiftieth Anniversary of the October Revolution Prince Souphanouvong sent a telegram to Podgorny and Kosygin noting that "during the past 50 years, under the splendid and intelligent leadership of the Soviet Communist Party, founded by Lenin, the Soviet people have won great victories in all areas. . . ." Souphanouvong also expressed "sincere thanks for the sincere support and great help of the USSR" and wished the Soviet people, under the leadership of the Soviet party and government, "greater victories in construction and in technical spheres in order to contribute to the protection of world peace" (Pathet Lao Radio, 8 November 1967).

**Communist China.** Contacts between the NLHX and Communist China were considerably more extensive than those with the Soviet Union, with the Laotian "patriotic forces" expressing their determination to "fight shoulder to shoulder with the fraternal Chinese people" against the common enemy. Messages of solidarity were exchanged on the anniversaries of the founding of the Laotian People's Liberation Army and the Chinese People's Liberation Army with Khamtay Siphandone hailing the Chinese for providing "a valuable lesson for the Laotian people to follow in struggling against the US imperialists . . ." and noting the determination of the people of Laos to stand by the Chinese people and army in "the struggle to defeat the US imperialists and their henchmen" (Radio of the Patriotic Neutralist Forces, 31 July 1967).

On 1 October, the eighteenth anniversary of the founding of the People's Republic of China, a representative of the Patriotic Neutralist Forces delivered a speech hailing the "Communist Party, the government, and the great Chinese people under the brilliant leadership of Mao Tse-tung," in which he noted that

> . . . the Chinese people and government have not neglected their international duty and have supported and assisted the other people in their struggle for national liberation, in particular our Laotian people in our national liberation struggle against the US imperialists. The Chinese and Laotian people are bound by strong, friendly relations. . . .
>
> All this constitutes a strong friendship and solidarity in our struggle. The Chinese and Laotian people always assist and support each other in the national liberation struggle. The Chinese Government and people have always supported the Laotian people in their national liberation struggle. The Laotian people can never forget the good deeds the Chinese people have done. (Radio of the Patriotic Neutralist Forces, 1 October 1967.)

In an address delivered on 8 October 1967, in preparation for the Twenty-Second anniversary of the Laotian National Day, Phoumi Vongvichit, Secretary-General of the NLHX, continued to praise Communist China by expressing his

> . . . frank and sincere congratulations to the people of the PRC for their construction of socialism and their recent successes in developing the atom bomb; these have been a stimulant for the revolutionary struggle of the Asian people—who provide a rear for the Laotian people's struggle. We wish the Chinese people—under the bright and intelligent leadership of the Chinese Communist Party with Chairman Mao as the respected and beloved leader—success in their cultural revolution, victories in the liberation of Taiwan, which is a part of the Chinese mainland, and success in the unification of China. (Radio of the Patriotic Neutralist Forces, 9 October 1967.)

The Chinese responded with a message of greetings from Chou En-lai to Prince Souphanouvong, and on 12 October 1967 *Jen-min Jih-pao* (People's Daily) carried an article signed "Commentator" praising the successes of the Laotian people and placing particular emphasis on the Laotian People's Liberation Army and its strategy of people's war and protracted struggle (*Jen-min Jih-pao*, 12 October 1967, as reported by NCNA). The Chinese underscored the importance of the Laotian "national liberation struggle" by noting that "the war of aggression being waged in Laos by the US imperialists is second in scope only to the war in South Vietnam" (Radio Peking, 28 December 1967, and *Peking Review,* no. 2, 12 January 1968).

**Democratic Republic of Vietnam.** During 1967 the NLHX maintained its contacts with the Democratic Republic of Vietnam and with the Vietnam Worker's Party. Congratulatory messages were exchanged on the anniversaries of the founding of the North Vietnamese Armed Forces and the Laotian People's Liberation Army and on 16 March, the NLHX Afro-Asian Solidarity Committee, in conjunction with a visiting AALAPSO delegation, inaugurated a week of solidarity with Vietnam. On 24 July 1967, on the anniversary of the signing of the 1954 and 1962 Geneva Agreements, the Central Committee of the NLHX and the Central Committee of the Vietnam Fatherland Front exchanged messages of support and solidarity. As part of the celebrations of the Twenty-Second anniversary of the founding of the Democratic Republic of Vietnam, Secreaty-General Phoumi Vongvichit praised the Vietnam Workers' Party for having "set a good example for the Laotian people and other peoples who have waged people's war elsewhere" (Radio of the Patriotic Neutralist Forces, 2 September 1967).

On 12 October, the Laotian National Day and the "tricontinental day of militant solidarity with the Laotian people," a delegation of the NLHX and the Laotian Afro-Asian Solidarity Committee left for North Vietnam at the invitation of the Vietnam Fatherland Front Central Committee and the Vietnam Afro-Asian Solidarity Committee. The NLHX delegation, headed by Tiao Souk Vongsak of the NLHX Central Committee, and the Laotian Afro-Asian Solidarity Committee delegation, headed by Colonel Deuane Sounarath, met with Hoang Quoc Viet, member of the Central Committee of the Vietnam Workers' Party and the Central Committee of the Vietnam Fatherland Front, and Ton Quang Phiet, Chairman of the Vietnam Afro-Asian Solidarity Committee. At the meeting the Laotian delegations announced the "firm determination of the Laotian people in close solidarity with the Vietnamese people to struggle to the end against the US imperialist aggressors . . ." and Tiao Souk Vongsak noted that although the victories of the Laotian people had been won mainly by their own efforts, they "were at the same time partly due to the wholehearted assistance of the peoples of Indochina, and first and foremost the brotherly Vietnamese people" (Radio Pathet Lao, 12 October 1967; Vietnam News Agency, 12 October 1967).

The NLHX and Radio Pathet Lao also devoted considerable attention to the Laotian government's decision to recall Thao Pheng, the Laotian ambassador to North Vietnam, calling the action a violation of the tripartite National Coalition Government (Radio Pathet Lao, 22 August 1967).

**Other Party Contacts.** On 23 July Secretary-General Phoumi Vongvichit sent an official note to numerous East European, Afro-Asian, and Latin American countries and to the heads of various organizations calling for the leaders of these groups and organizations to (1) make use of their functions and powers to bring the facts of the Laotian situation to the attention of their populations and to unmask and sternly condemn the "real and aggressive face of the US imperialists who have sabotaged the 1962 Geneva Agreements on Laos," (2) "make fully known to world opinion—especially that in Asia, Africa, and Latin America—the criminal acts of the Washington administration," and (3) foster movements which support the Laotian people's "anti-US national-liberation struggle led by the NLHX so that these movements will grow stronger and take on important significance" (Radio Pathet Lao, 24 July 1967).

Apart from the above NLHX statement and a telegram of support from the Central Committee of the Bulgarian Communist Party on the occasion of the Twenty-Second anniversary of the Laotian National Day, most of the NLHX's contacts were with Cuba and a few key Asian parties.

In an article in the September-October issue of *Tricontinental,* the theoretical organ of the AALAPSO Executive Secretariat, Secretary-General Phoumi Vongvichit hailed the "fraternal Cuban nation" as the "vanguard of the Latin American movements for national liberation, a heroic people, led by their Communist Party and their Revolutionary Government headed by Fidel Castro."

On 1 January 1967 an NLHX delegation led by Sithon Khommandam, Vice-Chairman of the NLHX Central Committee, and Sisana Sisane, Director of the Voice of the Pathet Lao and member of the NLHX Central Committee, arrived in Havana to attend the celebrations of the eighth anniversary of the Cuban revolution.

In response to an invitation extended by AALAPSO, an NLHX delegation headed by Saly Vongkhamsao, member of the NLHX Central Committee, arrived in Cuba for a visit on 6-30 October. The delegation included Khamphay Boupa, member of the NLHX Central Committee; Khamsoubinh Thonveunth, General Staff officer of the Laotian People's Liberation Army; high-ranking army officer Koua Keu; Khamphat Saykeo, representing the Patriotic Laotian Women's Federation; and Sithonh Sibounhoung, Phengkhoune Voraphet, and Bounbiend Sysourath. The delegation met with members of the AALAPSO Executive Secretariat, the Cuban Communist Party, and the Revolutionary Armed Forces of Cuba.

On 25 October 1967 Prince Souphanouvong and Phoumi Vongvichit sent messages of condolence on the death of Ernesto "Che" Guevara.

On 6 January, the eleventh anniversary of the NLHX, Nguyen Huu Tho, Chairman of the Presidium of the National Liberation Front of South Vietnam, sent a message of greetings to Prince Souphanouvong (Radio Pathet Lao, 19 January 1967), and on the eighteenth anniversary of the Laotian People's Liberation Army, Tran Nam Trung, representative of the High Command of the Liberation Armed Forces of South Vietnam, sent a message of solidarity to the High Command of the Laotian People's Liberation Army (Radio Pathet Lao, 24 January 1967). In a congratulatory message to Prince Souphanouvong on the Twenty-Second anniversary of the Laotian National Day, Nguyen Huu Tho again emphasized the support of the National Liberation Front for the Laotian people's "national liberation struggle," noting the determination of the South Vietnamese people to "constantly and closely side with the fraternal Laotian people in the struggle against the common enemy" and to "encourage and help each other with a determination to achieve final success for our two peoples" (Hanoi Domestic Service, 13 October 1967).

The NLHX also strengthened its relations with the Democratic People's Republic of Korea. In conjunction with the Korean May Day celebrations, a delegation of the "Laotian committee of trade union founding movement" led by Xom Lat visited North Korea, and the following month the North Korean paper *Minju Choson* carried an article by Xom Lat thanking North Korea for supporting the NLHX's "stand and struggle" and expressing support for the "correct" policies of the party and government under the leadership of Kim Il-song (KCNA, 22 June 1967). On 10 September Prince Souphanouvong sent a message of congratulations to the Democratic People's Republic of Korea on the nineteenth anniversary of its founding, and on 11 October Kim Il-song reciprocated with a congratulatory message to Prince Souphanouvong on the Twenty-Second anniversary of the Laotian National Day, pledging to "actively assist" the Laotian people in their "anti-US national-salvation struggle" (KCNA, 11 October 1967).

Other contacts with Asian communist parties included a Radio Pathet Lao broadcast on 6 September 1967 in which the NLHX noted the successes of the Thai Patriotic Front, the Philippine People's Liberation Armed Forces under the leadership of the Philippine Communist Party, and the Indonesian people under the leadership of the Indonesian Communist Party, who have begun to "improve their forces, increase their counterattacks, and solidify their position in the hamlets and carry on their struggle more and more violently." In addition, the NLHX Central Committee sent a message to the Central Committee of the Thai Patriotic Front hailing its second anniversary as a "great victory for the Thai patriotic forces on their road of revolutionary struggle for the construction of an independent, democratic, peaceful, neutral, and prosperous Thailand."

**Publications.** During 1967 NLHX directives and policy statements were carried over Radio Pathet Lao (clandestine), Radio of the Patriotic Neutralist Forces (clandestine), and Voice of Laos Radio. On 24 December 1967 the Standing Committee of the NLHX Central Committee decided to establish an NLHX news agency to be known as Khaosan Pathet Lao, or Pathet Lao News Agency. According to the Central Committee decision, Khaosan Pathet Lao is to be the official organ of the NLHX and, in addition to its information service at home, will "assume the task of transmitting official documents of the NLHX, news reports, and photos on the Laotian people's struggle against the US imperialists and for national salvation, thus enabling the people of the world to understand better the Laotian situation and the stand and viewpoints of the NLHX on domestic and foreign affairs." According to the Central Committee directive, Khaosan Pathet Lao is to come into being officially on 6 January 1968 and will be headed by NLHX member Sisana Sisane.

The NLHX also publishes two papers, the *Liberation Armed Forces,* and the *Lao Hak Xat.*

# LEBANON

The Lebanese Communist Party (al-Hizb al-Shuyu'i al Lubnani; LCP) was first founded in 1924 as the Lebanese People's Party (al-Hizb al-Sha'b al-Lubnani). Reconstituted as the Lebanese Communist Party in 1930, the party accepted members from Syria and Lebanon, which at that time were both under French rule by authority of a mandate from the League of Nations. At a national congress in Beirut, January 1944, the party agreed to divide into separate Lebanese and Syrian communist parties, retaining joint leadership in a single Central Committee; in July, however, by a decision of the Central Committee, the two emerged as wholly independent parties. Ties between the parties, very strong at first, have tended to weaken over the years, although a substantial bond still remains, due in part to the forceful personality of Khalid Bakdash, the leader of the Syrian party (see *Syria*).

The LCP has not been a legal party since its proscription by the French mandate authority in 1939. In spite of this, it operates on Lebanese soil under the close supervision of government authorities. Although the party cannot place candidates in Lebanese elections, its members speak at labor union, student, and left-wing party rallies throughout the country and often run for office on an individual basis. No communist has ever been elected to Parliament in Lebanon.

The LCP is estimated to have about 6,000 members, of whom some 4,000 are active. The country's population is 2,460,000 (estimated mid-1966). Ethnic minority groups, mainly Kurds and Armenians, account for a high percentage of the party membership. The LCP is unique in the Arab world in that the majority of its members are not from the lower classes, but rather from the middle class with a remarkably high percentage of professional men, literati, and young intellectuals.

**Organization and Leadership.** The leadership situation in the party became confused during 1967 by splits, defections, and the disciplining of high-ranking party members. Nicola Shawi (Chaoui when transliterated into French) maintained his post as Secretary-General in spite of a reported attempt to remove him at the Central Committee plenum in October. Another of the party triumvirs, Secretary Artine Madoyan, also retained his position, but Hasan Quraitem, long-time Secretary and party personality, was removed.* (*Arab World,* Beirut, 4 October.) Other prominent Communists, presumably still in the party hierarchy, include Sharif al-Ansari, Sulayman al-Basha, Georges (Salim) Batal, Muhsin Ibrahim, Muhammad Kashly, and Fuad Salman. Prominent Communists, in addition to Quraitem, known to have been removed from party offices or to have defected, include Amin al-Awar and George Hawi (both of the communist newspaper *al-Nida*), and Sawaya Sawaya.

The LCP is active in the Lebanese student and trade-union movements. In 1967 the Communist-led National Federation of Labor Unions (NFLU) was granted a government license. The NFLU is thus represented on Lebanon's supreme labor council, but it has been relatively isolated by members of the eight noncommunist federations also on the council. The LCP is very active in the Union Nationale des Universités Libanais (UNUL) having succeeded in splitting the movement into left- and right-wing factions in 1965. The UNUL received a change in status from associate membership to full membership in the communist-front International Union of Students (IUS) at the 9th IUS Congress in Ulan Bator, Mongolia, in March 1967. Other organizations that support and work with the LCP are: the Partisans of Peace (Ansar al-Salam), the Society for Cultural Cooperation between Lebanon and the Soviet Union (Jam 'iyat al-Ta 'awun al-Thaqafi bayn Lubnan wal-Ittihad

*The CPSU reported discussions in Moscow with Shawi, Madoyan and a third "Secretary of the Central Committee" of the LCP identified only as Muruwwah, after the celebrations of the fiftieth anniversary of the October Revolution (Moscow domestic service, 22 November). It is possible that Muruwwah succeeded to Quraitem's Secretaryship.

al-Sufiyeti), the Friends of the Soviet Union (Asdiqa al-Ittihad al-Sufiyeti), Farabi's Center (Dar al-Farabi), and the Center of New Thought (Dar al-Fikr al-Jadid).

**Domestic Policies and Activities.** As an illegal party operating under the sufferance of the Lebanese government, the LCP must tread the path to socialism with great care. The party's announced objective is not to establish a socialist or communist system, but rather to check Western influence and "imperialistic" designs on the country and to introduce reforms on the basis of democratic principles.

The thrust of the LCP's domestic political pronouncements and efforts, as exemplified in a long party manifesto printed in *al-Nida* on 30 July 1966, is directed toward the rallying of "all progressive and democratic forces of the Lebanon" in a "broad front of national unity." The main task of the front is to form a government from which all reactionary elements would be eliminated, and which would then proceed to solve the basic social and foreign political problems of the country. The idea of the front is not new: in 1965 the party joined in the formation of the "Front of Patriotic and Progressive Parties and Personalities," which has as its core the LCP, the Socialist Progressive Party, and the Arab National Movement. (The leader of the front is Kamal Jumblat, the president of the Socialist Progressive Party.) The LCP opposes a merger of all the socialist parties and organizations into one political organization. Instead, it feels that its allies should gradually evolve toward accepting the basic theoretical concepts of Marxist-Leninist scientific socialism; the same holds true for all the "revolutionary patriots" with no established ideology of their own. In the present transitional period the aim is not the direct establishment of socialism, but the renunciation of the capitalist path of development.

In accordance with this general political line and approach, the LCP proposes its own specific way to the economic and social emancipation of Lebanon. It has approved some measures taken by the government, but has offered its own plan aiming at more rapid industrialization, expansion of the state sector in the economy, creation of cooperative state farms, agrarian and tax reform, and state control over the purchase and sale of all fruit for export and over foreign investments. The July 1966 party manifesto advocates further measures, such as state control of imports of medical supplies, state control of foreign-supported schools and universities, a reduction of apartment rents, wage and salary increases to correspond with general living costs, and the creation of cooperatives for employees and workers in public and private enterprises.

In February the LCP was active in cooperation with the "Front of Patriotic and Progressive Parties and Personalities" and the NFLU in leading strikes among workers for changes in the rent control law and against the rising cost of living. The party supported in March the strikes of high school students who demanded standardization of textbooks, changes in the school system, and abolition of the tax on government-sponsored public school examinations.

**International Views and Activities.** The LCP in its July 1966 manifesto outlined the foreign policy that it wanted the government of its choice to pursue. Among other things, it called for the "adoption of prompt measures to liberate the country from the policy of pacts" and for Lebanon's "engagement in the struggle against imperialism and Israel, in Arab solidarity, in salutary friendship with the Soviet Union and the socialist countries, and in economic, cultural, and technical cooperation with the USSR and those countries."

Like the parties of the other Arab states, the LCP is a pro-Soviet party and follows the line of the CPSU without deviation. As Nicola Shawi stated: "The October Revolution and its ideas have illuminated the path of the struggle for national and social liberation, for the achievement of full independence, for freedom, democracy, peace, progress, for socialism. . . . The slogan of Arab-Soviet Friendship, which particularly at the present stage is the cornerstone in the struggle of the Arabs for their independence and social progress, has become a major slogan of the Arab liberation movement. . . . The ideas of the October Revolution, the ideas of Marxism-Leninism developed by the Party of Lenin and by the entire international communist movement, have today become a beacon for the entire world revolutionary movement." (*IB,* special issue, "Revolutionary Peace Forces Hail October," Prague, 1968.) The LCP gives full support to the Soviet Union in its effort to convoke an international conference of communist and workers' parties. By the same token the LCP has rejected the stand of the Chinese Communists and criticized the "splitting attitude of the Mao Tse-tung group." The party accused Peking of acting "insolently," of dealing blows to the national liberation movement, of preventing the peoples of the world from taking the road of independent development, and of reestablishing the domination of neocolonialism in newly independent countries. The nonconforming Chinese position on US "aggression" in Vietnam and on the "imperialist-Israeli aggression" in the Middle East was cited in support of these accusations. (*IB*, no. 111-112, December 1967.)

The Arab-Israeli war was quite naturally an event of great concern to the LCP. Indicating that there was no doubt in the minds of LCP members as to where the blame for the war belonged, Shawi stated the party's opinion:

"No Arab patriot and no progressive Arab doubts that the American and British imperialists, by encouraging, supporting and patronizing the Israeli aggression, were out first of all to strike a devastating blow at the Arab countries that are seeking social progress, namely, at Israel's neighbors — the UAR and Syria — and at Algeria, in order to overthrow the progressive regimes in these countries. It is becoming perfectly clear that the imperialists and the Zionists regard the destruction of progressive Arab regimes as a necessary condition for mounting a broad offensive against the independence, sovereignty, and interests of the other Arab countries, including the Lebanon."

The Soviet Union was portrayed as the hero of the six-day war: The Soviet Union backed the Arab countries and helped them. It condemned, exposed, and warned the aggressors, and took resolute steps to force the aggressors to cease fire. . . . All indications are that Soviet-Arab friendship was the most powerful factor which prevented the imperialists and the Zionists from achieving their ends. . . . We trust that today all patriotic and progressive forces in the Lebanon and other Arab countries [are] more aware than ever of the vast importance of promoting the cooperation and solidarity of the Arab peoples with the socialist countries headed by the Soviet Union . . . .

In a further condemnation of Chinese criticism of the Soviet Union during the Arab-Israeli crisis, Shawi said:

[All Arabs are] bound to condemn and reject most emphatically the truly disgusting efforts which the Mao Tse-tung clique and its myrmidons are making to misrepresent and slander the Soviet position toward the Arabs, to defame Arab-Soviet friendship and split the united front of the Arab peoples and the socialist countries. Needless to say the Mao clique is thereby doing a great service to the enemies of the Arabs — the imperialists and Zionists — and tremendous disservice to the vital interests of the Arab peoples.

Shawi then described the task facing the "progressive national forces of the Arabs," which he said would have to take concrete steps to promote the cohesion of the Arabs in order to further their joint struggle, to eliminate all secondary considerations, and to avoid "radical analysis" of events. Then he reaffirmed the LCP objective of attaining a broad united front of all "progressive parties" in Lebanon as the most effective weapon to "remove the effects of the imperialist-Zionist aggression and ensure the Arab peoples' advance along the road of freedom and progress." (*IB*, no. 104, 28 September 1967.)

On the war in Vietnam the LCP holds to the Soviet point of view, criticizing the Chinese for obstructing aid to the "struggling Vietnamese peoples." The party also charged that the US Central Intelligence Agency, "the agency which formulates and discharges the plans of American foreign policy," was responsible for the war (*al-Nida*, 1 February).

The LCP played host to a conference of Arab communist parties in Beirut in May. The parties which attended have never been named, but the representatives engaged in a general discussion of the international situation as it pertained to the Middle East. The conference passed resolutions on (1) the situation in the world communist movement, castigating the "Mao clique" and endorsing Moscow's call for a world meeting of communist and workers' parties; (2) Vietnam, against the "US imperialists' dirty war"; (3) the fiftieth anniversary of the October Revolution, hailing "the unforgettable and glorious period of constant and unselfish assistance and support to [Arab] peoples by the first socialist state"; (4) the Kurd problem in Iraq (see *Iraq*); and (5) the situation in Greece, finding there a "new link in the chain of attacks" by "US imperialism and the NATO top circles" (*IB*, 99-100, July). (A statement of the conference on the situation in the Arab countries is in *Documents.*)

Secretary-General Nicola Shawi represented the LCP at the Seventh Congress of the East German Socialist Unity Party (SED) in Berlin in April, and at the fiftieth-anniversary celebration of the October Revolution in the Soviet Union, where he delivered a speech at the grand rally in Kiev on 5 November. The party was also represented at the Eighteenth Congress of the French Communist Party near Paris in January. The LCP sent representatives (Nicola Shawi, Muhsin Ibrahim, Fuad Salman and Amin al-Awar) to Algeria to participate in the activities of the Algerian Debating Club (Nadwat al-Gaza'er) which met at Kasr al-Umam on 22 May.

**Publications.** The LCP press, which operates in an atmosphere of relative freedom, includes the party daily, *al-Nida* ("The Call"); a weekly, *al-Akhbar* ("The News"); and a weekly labor journal, *al-Thaqafah al Wataniyah* ("National Culture"). The *Ararad* ("Ararat") is a pro-communist daily published in Lebanon in the Armenian language. The communist-front Lebanese Peace Council publishes the journal *al-Tariq* ("The Way"), and the Lebanese League of Democratic Lawyers issues the quarterly journal *al-Haqq* ("Justice").

**Party Dissidents.** There are several identifiable communist political organizations in Lebanon which stand in opposition to Nicola Shawi and the regular LCP organization. One of these groups, led by Nasib Nimr, issues the communist opposition paper *Ila al-Amam*. A second group, the pro-Chinese "Party of Socialist Revolution" was formed in 1964 by communists expelled earlier from the LCP. The chairman of this party is Yusuf Mubarak; the secretary-general is Mustafa Shakir. (See *YICA*, 1966, p. 280). Another group of communists, led by Nakhle Mutran and Edmond Awn, also left the party in 1964.

The year 1967 saw further splits in the regular party organization, in addition to the removal of Quraitem and Sawaya at the October plenum. George Hawi, former editor of *al-Nida*, reportedly was leading a group of dissident communists known as "young revisionists" (*Le Monde*, 19 March 1968). As early as August 1967 it was reported that Amin al-Awar, a colleague of Hawi on the staff of *al-Nida*, was writing articles strongly critical of the Syrian communist leader, Khalid Bakdash, and the LCP leader, Nicola Shawi, in *al-Muharrir* ("The Liberator"), the organ of the Arab Nationalist Movement (*Arab World*, Beirut, 1, 2, 3, and 17 August).

# LESOTHO

The Communist Party of Lesotho (CPL) was founded in November 1961. It operates as a legal party, The number of members is unknown, but western sources have estimated its membership at less than 100 persons out of a total population of 859,058 (1966 census). The CPL Secretary-General is John Motloheloa.

The CPL has no representation in the legislature of the Kingdom of Lesotho (formerly Basutoland). It wields some influence in the labor unions, particularly in the Lesotho Workers' Union and a parent body, the Lesotho Congress of Trade Unions. The country, however, is primarily agricultural, and many of its people work as labor migrants in South Africa. The Communists have not been able to make any serious impact on the working population and their influence in the country as a whole is negligible.

**Domestic Views and Policies.** The CPL program, issued in 1962, calls for struggle against British and white South African "imperialism." The party aims at the creation of a united front of workers, peasants, professional people, businessmen, chiefs, and commoners. It strives for a national democratic revolution and for social reconstruction along a noncapitalist path of development, with a "socialist worker-peasant republic" as the goal. The program advocates the setting-up of cooperatives and collectives, adoption of mechanized farming, and government control of all recruitment of labor. (*WMR,* February 1966.)

In domestic politics the CPL lends support to the Marematlou Freedom Party (MFP), an opposition group resting on an alliance between advocates of modernization and traditionalists. The MFP opposes Lesotho's existing constitution and condemns the state's friendly relations with South Africa. It is reported to have received funds from the Soviet Union over the past few years, but is in no sense a communist organization. The largest opposition party in Lesotho, the Basutoland Congress Party (BCP) enjoys the support of the Communist Party of China and has endorsed Chinese policies, including the Great Proletarian Cultural Revolution (*La Voix du Peuple,* 20 January 1967).

Lesotho political affairs in 1967 were dominated by reactions to the attempted coup on 27 December 1966 at the sacred shrine of Thaba Bosiu and the subsequent arrests of opposition leaders, including M. N. Mokhehle, leader of the BCP, and Dr. Makotoko, leader of the MFP. On 6 January 1967 King Moshoeshoe II signed a statement agreeing never again to convene a public meeting without the consent of the government and to speak only from government-prepared texts. The conflict between the governing Basutoland National Party, led by Premier Leabua Jonathan, and an opposition radical-royalist alliance was ostensibly over the question of land tenure. The Lesotho government, backed by the constitution, was challenging the head of state, King Moshoeshoe, in his exercise of his traditional right of allocating land. The South African Communist Party, which works in close collaboration with the CPL, in its organ *The African Communist* (no. 29, 1967) attributed the clash to resentment on the part of Premier Jonathan against this traditional system. The South African Communists claimed that Jonathan, catering to the interests of South African financiers, was demanding the introduction of the system of private freehold landholding in Lesotho, and attributed the crisis to this and to the government's cadre policy, which involved the removal of many Basotho from official posts and the retention of veteran white officials and the importation of many others from South Africa. According to them, the people were also opposed to Leabua Jonathan's foreign policy, which "followed the *diktat* of the Republic of South Africa to the letter." (These charges were intensified following Jonathan's visit to South Africa in January 1967.) The South African Communists made the following comments concerning the events of 27 December:

> Naturally all this goes against the interests of the vast majority of the people in Lesotho who are totally opposed to the policy of Leabua Jonathan. Represented by the Congress,

the Marematlou Freedom Party, and other opposition groups including the Communist Party of Lesotho, the people gathered at huge mass meetings to condemn the turning of Lesotho into a client state of South Africa. It is with this background that Leabua Jonathan backed by his South African mentors decided to strike against all opposition in the country. The meeting of December 27th, 1966 at the sacred shrine of Thaba Bosiu seemed a favourable opportunity.

At the trials of government opponents held recently all accused except eight have already been acquitted and freed. The remaining eight who include Mr. Ntsu Mokhehle, leader of the Congress Party, and Dr. Seth Makotoko, leader of the Marematlou Freedom Party, are still facing an artificially prolonged and farcical trial whose aim is to ruin the opposition parties financially.

An article in the Communist Party of Great Britain newspaper *Morning Star* (3 January 1967) provided a similar interpretation of the crisis, stating that Jonathan's minority-rule party was seeking to eliminate the Basutoland National Party (including King Moshoeshoe), the Marematlou Freedom Party, the Basutoland Congress Party, and the Communist Party of Lesotho.

The CPL charged that the "imperialist" objective in Lesotho was to "strengthen the old relations of colonial days by ensuring the continued outflow of labor-power from Lesotho to the fascist Republic of South Africa and maintaining capital development across the border." The CPL advocated the unity of "all the anti-feudal and anti-imperialist organizations and people in a common front that would blast to oblivion the dream of keeping Lesotho a satellite state of apartheid," adding:

> The advantage of going on with this now lies in the fact that the ruling class is deeply weakened amongst other things by the divisions in its ranks between supporters of the King, who seeks to establish an absolute monarchy, on the one hand, and those who seek parliamentary rule under the leadership of Premier Chief Leabua Jonathan, on the other. (*IB*, no. 110, 1967.)

The CPL has close links with the South African Communist Party, together with which it seeks collaboration with all "progressive organizations" in South Africa. The CPL demands the cession of certain South African territories to Lesotho.

**International Views and Policies.** In the international communist movement the CPL is aligned with the Communist Party of the Soviet Union. In a statement issued by its Central Committee, the CPL expressed its expectations of benefiting from Soviet economic growth:

> We must now take this opportunity to wish the Soviet people greater successes in their effort to build the material basis of Communism as the only road that would ensure sufficient socialist military and economic power to prevent the imperialists and the South African fascists from putting through their plans of drowning the coming Lesotho revolution in blood in an annexationist venture that may prove genocidal. (Statement of John Motloheloa, Secretary-General, CPL, *ibid.*)

The CPL sent a delegation to Moscow for the celebrations of the fiftieth anniversary of the October Revolution, but the names of the delegates were not revealed.

**Basutoland Congress Party.** There is no pro-Chinese communist party in Lesotho, but the Chinese Communists have expressed strong support for the BCP. As a "national liberation movement" before Lesotho achieved independence in October 1966, the BCP maintained offices in Dar es-Salaam, Accra, and Cairo. On April 1967, the Tanzania government banned the BCP on the grounds that, in view of Lesotho's independence, it was no longer a national liberation movement. The party has also had internal problems. On 2 February, breakaway members of the BCP objecting to the BCP's hostility to South Africa formed the Lesotho Democratic Party.

The BCP was one of the eight African organizations which signed a joint statement condemning the Communist-sponsored October 1966 Cairo seminar on "Africa—National and Social Revolution," from which the BCP had been excluded, and denouncing the "modern revisionists" who organized it. On 8 January 1967 the Peking branch of the Afro-Asian Writers' Permanent Bureau (AAWPB) sent a telegram to the BCP's Cairo office supporting the "anti-imperialist revolutionary struggle" of the people of Lesotho; the telegram was similar in terminology to the resolution on Lesotho adopted at the Peking emergency meeting of the AAWPB in July 1966. In February 1967 the BCP delegation to the Afro-Asian People's Solidarity Organization meeting in Nicosia walked out in protest against the refusal to seat the South-West African National Union (SWANU). [South-West Africa was already represented by the South-West African People's Organization (SWAPO).] Subsequently, the BCP and SWANU issued a joint statement condemning the "Soviet revisionist clique" for "criminally sabotaging and splitting the Afro-Asian people's movement of solidarity against imperialism."

**Publications.** The CPL organ is *Tokoloholo,* which is published in Maseru.

# LUXEMBOURG

The Communist Party of Luxembourg (Parti Communiste de Luxembourg; PCL) was founded 2 January 1921.

The membership of the PCL, which is headed by Chairman Dominique Urbani, has been estimated by Western sources as between 500 and 1,000. The population of Luxembourg is 335,000 (estimated 1966). The small influence that the party has in the country is concentrated in the urban and mining areas of the industrial south. The communist-dominated Free Association of Luxembourg Workers (FLAV), a labor union with an estimated 3,500 members, was merged on 1 January 1966 with the Socialist Trade Union "without discrimination and on an equal footing." The resulting "United Federation of Free Trade Unions" represents two-thirds of all organized workers. The PCL controls several mass movements, including the Luxembourg Democratic Youth, the "Awakening of the Resistance," the National Movement for Peace, and the Union of Democratic Women of Luxembourg.

In the 1964 parliamentary elections the PCL won 5 seats out of a total 56, an increase of two over its previous number. The party polled 12.47 per cent of the votes as against 9.0 per cent in 1959, and in the south received 17 per cent. This was the second strongest show of support for the party in its history. (It obtained 13.49 per cent of the votes in the 1945 elections.)

**Domestic Views and Policies.** The current economic difficulties, the rising inflation, and the possibilities of a recession, coupled with electoral gains in 1964, have given the PCL renewed optimism for the future. At its Eighteenth Congress, in April 1965, the PCL adopted a new program centered on a policy of collaboration with the Socialist Party. The program recognized the possibility of a peaceful transition to socialism in Luxembourg, the desirability of a multiparty system, and the feasibility of carrying out decisive democratic and social reforms before the abolition of capitalism. The party also advocated the independence of public organizations, and of the trade unions in particular. The PCL tries to reach all social strata opposed to the big monopolies. It appeals even to the small and middle businessman, promising that his position would be maintained within a socialist machinery. The party's program calls for the extension of democratic institutions in the country and the granting of social benefits to the workers, including higher wages, pensions, a shorter working day without lowering of wages, and the solving of the housing problem.

The PCL is attempting to achieve in Luxembourg what the French Communist Party achieved in France by the formation of the United Federation of the Left in December 1966. However, in Luxembourg the Communist and Socialist parties have charged each other with maintaining outdated and inflexible policies. While the Socialists argue that the PCL has not changed its position on a "united Europe" and has not abandoned Stalinism, as has the French Communist Party, the CPL argues that the differences between the policies of the Socialist parties in France and Luxembourg are "like night and day." The Luxembourg Socialists, according to the Communists, are more interested in unity with the right than with the left, and their positions on Vietnam and Germany are entirely unacceptable to the CPL (*Zeitung,* 7 February 1967).

Party leader Dominique Urbani analyzed the present situation in Luxembourg at a Central Committee plenum in September 1967. He noted that the rightist coalition between the Christian Social and the Socialist parties was not a smooth relationship and that the disputes were based on personal rivalries and not on ideologies. He also noted the "malaise" within the Socialist Party between its right socialist leadership and the "left-wing" opposition. He went on to point out that whereas the Communists themselves have made a few gains, these are only temporary and cannot be consolidated, because workers are virtually barred from all decision making by the government and the employers and thus exercise no control at all. Urbani noted that even in trade unions, the election of worker representatives by workers themselves is ruled out in some cases. He claimed that in Luxembourg "monopoly capital" was striving to "undermine, curtail, or abolish parliamentray democracy."

Turning to the cooperation of democratic forces in Luxembourg, Urbani noted that the Socialist opposition was weak because of lack of confidence in the working class and because of its distrust of the Communists, adding: "We cannot of course accept that. We need a new and better policy. And we have no use for shifts on the political scene." Urbani insisted that the Communists were striving "openly and honestly" for the unity of all those in Luxembourg desiring to "break with reactionary policies," to achieve "social advancement and democratic progress," and to strive for "independence and peace, for socialism." On the specific tasks of the party, Urbani took a pragmatic stand:

> The decisive thing is, in the long run, how active the Communist party is on the political scene, how many people we succeed in enlisting for our ideas and our program, how many seats we will win at the next elections. The same is true of trade union and political unity. There is no substitute for our party.

Party work, according to Urbani, should be conducted "frankly, clearly, courageously, and consistently," and the party paper, *Zeitung* ("our best and sharpest, and often our only, weapon"), should be actively promoted. He advocated "explanatory work in every form," systematic studies, and extensive contact between party members and other persons.

Noting in conclusion that there had been a shift to the left by Socialist workers and intellectuals and that cooperation by progressive organizations had improved, Urbani emphasized that this was a valuable development, but added: "We must under no circumstances forget that what matters in the final analysis is the number of votes and seats won by our party, and our strength today and tomorrow." (*Zeitung*, 27-28 September.)

**International Views and Policies.** In foreign policy, the PCL defines itself as a "national" party. It professes to stand for the sovereignty, neutrality, and security of Luxembourg. It campaigns for Luxembourg's withdrawal from NATO and denounces the unwillingness of European planners to permit Luxembourg to become the seat of what the PCL refers to as "the so-called European organizations."

A focal point of PCL attacks on the government has been Luxembourg's participation in NATO. The PCL charges that Luxembourg is more closely tied with NATO than are the other member countries, and insists that the Luxembourg government dissociate itself from NATO in 1969, renounce its present military policy, keep out of military alignments, and advocate a policy of peace and security in Europe. "This implies recognition of the status quo and the European state frontiers resulting from the defeat of Hitler fascism, and rejection of both the US policy of war and West German revanchism," declared Chairman Urbani to the September Central Committee plenum (*Ibid.*).

In the international communist movement, the PCL is closely aligned with the Soviet Union and the CPSU, "Today we trust the Soviet Union and the CPSU more than ever before," declared Dominique Urbani after asserting that the Soviet party was the "decisive guarantee of the worldwide fight for socialism and communism" (*ibid.*).

Writing on the October Revolution in *Pravda* (14 October) Dominique Urbani asked: "What would have been the fate of our small nation [if there were no Soviet Union]? Even until today the terror of the Nazi occupation forces would rule in our country. If we, the Luxembourg Communists, like the Communists all over the world, put friendship with the Great Soviet Union and the CPSU above everything else," he continued, "it is because this corresponds to our ideas and traditions."

The PCL has condemned the policies of the Communist Party of China, declaring that its rejection of unity with the other socialist countries on support for the Vietnamese people was dangerous, that the repeated attacks directed against the Soviet Union ran counter to proletarian internationalism, that the Chinese leaders were attempting to found splinter groups voting against the communist parties in capitalist countries, and that the Chinese leaders were elevating themselves to the position of censors of other communist parties. According to the PCL, all splitting maneuvers, no matter how minor, must be exposed and counteracted, because anything that might split the workers' movement would play into the hands of the "imperialists" (*Zeitung*, 6 January).

The PCL has been a firm supporter of the proposal to convene an international meeting of communist parties: "A meeting of the communist parties should completely clear up the issue," declared Dominique Urbani to the September Central Committee plenum, referring to the disagreements with the Peking-oriented parties.

The PCL was represented by Dominique Urbani at the Eighteenth Congress of the French Communist Party, in January, and at the Seventh Congress of the Socialist Unity Party of Germany, in April. Urbani also represented the party at the conference of European communist and workers' parties in Karlovy Vary in April and at the celebration of the fiftieth anniversary of the October Revolution in Moscow in November.

**Publications.** The PCL publishes a daily newspaper, *Zeitung vum Letzeburger Vollek*, under the direction of Jean Kill, and a weekly periodical, *Wochenzeitung*.

* * *

**Luxembourg-China Society.** There exists a small Maoist splinter group of the PCL called the Luxembourg-China Society. At the beginning of November 1966 the Central Committee of the PCL adopted a resolution according to which membership in the Luxembourg-China Society could no longer be reconciled with membership in the party; at the same time, Johan Steichen was expelled for his association with the group. According to Urbani, four members of the society have since resigned and "all that is left is a handful of hopelessly isolated adventurers" (*Zeitung*, 27-28 September 1967).

The 72-year-old Secretary-General of the Luxembourg-China Society, Adolphe Franck, visited China for the third time in September and October 1967 as head of a two-member delegation. According to the NCNA, Franck's policy is: "We support what the imperialists oppose, and oppose what the imperialists support." He is also said to have declared "Chairman Mao Tse-tung is the powerful mainstay of world revolution. The people of Luxembourg will surely triumph if they take the road pointed out by Chairman Mao." (NCNA, 9 November.)

# MALAYSIA

No single, united communist party exists in Malaysia. The party is instead divided into two virtually independent groups: the Communist Party of Malaya, which operates in western Malaysia and Singapore* (see *Singapore*) and the communist movement in eastern Malaysia, particularly in Sarawak, which is believed to be directed by a somewhat nebulous Borneo Communist Party.

The Communist Party of Malaya (CPM) originated in 1928 as the South Seas Communist Party (nan-yang kung-ch'an tang), with headquarters in Singapore. In 1930 the South Seas Communist Party was transformed into the Communist Party of Malaya, an offshoot of the Chinese Communist Party and composed primarily of ethnic Chinese. The CPM's anti-Japanese stand during the Second World War placed the party in a very strong position in 1945, and in 1948 the CPM initiated a campaign of armed struggle that resulted in the government outlawing the party and declaring a state of emergency which lasted from June 1948 to July 1960. As a result of government measures during this period, the CPM was reduced to small scattered underground groups on the Malay Peninsula and along the Thai-Malayasian border, with the party establishing its headquarters on the Thai side of the border, where it exercises varying degrees of territorial control.

**Organization and Leadership.** There is very little information available on the organizational structure of the CPM. The party is estimated to have between 2,000 and 2,500 members, including perhaps 500 to 1,000 who operate along the Thai-Malaysian border, some 1,500 in Sarawak, and close to 100 in mainland Malaysia. A white paper issued by the Malaysian Government in October 1966 stated that the CPM had "been busy giving guerrilla training to youths in the border area" and had "up to 1,000" of them available on short notice (*The Militant Communist Threat to West Malaysia* [Kuala Lumpur, October 1966], p. 5). The population of Malaysia is 9,711,000 (estimated mid-1966), with 8,298,000 in Western Malaysia, 551,000 in Sabah, and 862,000 in Sarawak.

The party's Secretary-General is Chen Ping and its Chairman is Musa Ahmad. The Central Committee is believed to have a maximum of 10 members. It is not known whether the majority of these members are in the border area or are in Communist China. The Politburo consists of Chen Ping and probably two or three close associates, including Li On Tung.

Regional party control is shared by two border committees: the Penang-Kedah committee, which serves the western extremity of the border, and the Kelantan-Perak committee, serving the eastern extremity. The propaganda function of the party, apparently carried on by the border committees, is under the direction of Chen Tien. Other prominent CPM members include Lam Fung Sing, Liew Yit Fun, Chiam Chung Him, Eu Chooi Yip, Lim Chin Siong, Lu Cheng, and Siew Chong, who are probably in China, and Wu Tien Wang, who is believed to be with the Twelfth Regiment of the "Malayan National Liberation Army." Although Chen Ping's presence in the border areas has not been definitely confirmed, reports by surrendered communist terrorists indicate that he is still there.

**Mass Organizations.** The CPM carries out its activities through several illegal organizations. Among these are the Malayan National Liberation Army, the Malayan National Liberation League, and the Partai Persaudaraan Islam.

The Malayan National Liberation Army (MNLA) was founded 1 January 1949, and is officially described as "responsible for the armed struggle" in Malaysia (*The Militant Communist Threat to West Malaysia,* p. 4). Although the MNLA originally consisted of twelve regiments, it presently consists of only three—the Eighth (or Western), the Twelfth (or Central), and the Tenth (or Eastern)

*Singapore's communists belong to the Communist Party of Malaya, which regards Singapore as an integral part of Malaya.

383

regiment—none of which is up to full regimental strength. The Supreme Commander of the MNLA is believed to be Chen Ping.

Although the Malayan National Liberation League (MNLL) reportedly celebrated its eighteenth anniversary on 1 February 1967, observers doubt that the organization has been in existence that long. It is described as "responsible for the constitutional struggle and certain aspects of the illegal or 'militant' struggle" (*ibid.*, p. 4). In February 1965, the MNLL established a mission in Indonesia. Following the abortive communist coup of 30 September 1965 and subsequent action by the Indonesian government, the mission transferred most of its activities to Communist China and, under the leadership of P. V. Sarma, joined other militant communist front organizations there. In early January 1967, four members of the MNLL Central Committee, led by Ibrahim Mohamad and including Eu Chooi Yip, Abdullah Sudin, and Mme Shamsiah Fakeh, were expelled from Indonesia and were granted political asylum by North Vietnam. It is not known why they chose to go to North Vietnam rather than to Peking.

The existence of a communist terrorist organization known as the Partai Persaudaraan Islam (Islamic Brotherhood Party; Paperi) was disclosed in mid-1966. The Paperi was founded 22 April 1965 and is believed to have been established by the Central Department of Malay Work of the CPM.

**Strategy and Tactics**. Members of the CPM stress that it is "imperative to carry out revolution by violence and to take the road of the Chinese revolution, the road of armed struggle. . . . The success of the Chinese revolution has told us a truth: to achieve complete liberation, the oppressed nations and oppressed peoples must arm themselves with the invincible thought of Mao Tse-tung. Perseverance in taking the road of Mao Tse-tung will definitely lead to liberation and final victory." (*People's Tribune,* a Malayan paper published in Singapore, as broadcast by New China News Agency, 28 December 1967.)

A lengthy document serialized in abridged form in *Malayan Monitor* (September-December 1967) devoted considerable attention to the CPM's strategy of armed struggle and explained that because the CPM and the people were "deprived of every nonviolent means of survival," this was the "only way left . . . to save the lives and the national integrity of the people from utter decimation." The same article stated that the decision to pursue a policy of armed struggle was a completely independent one:

> At this point it is necessary to refute the allegation from imperialist sources that the Communist Party of Malaya and Liberation forces decided on armed struggle at the instigation of this or that foreign power, party, or group. The simple truth is, nobody but the Malayan partriots themselves decided on the aims and course of action they were to take. The decision of the Party and the people to take up arms in self-defense and in furtherance of the National Liberation struggle was reached after careful consideration based on their own experience of the struggle. As in all things in life, the experiences of others are always relevant—especially where objective conditions are similar; but other people's experiences are valuable only if they can be tested by one's own, and are found to be applicable to one's own situation. Therefore, it is absurd to say that the Communist Party of Malaya, or any part of the Liberation forces acted on the orders of this or that foreign power, party, or groups.

While maintaining that "only by holding high this shining banner of violent revolution can the oppressed nations and peoples successfully overthrow the rule of violence of the exploiting classes and achieve complete liberation," the CPM has also pursued a policy of infiltrating left-wing opposition parties, primarily the Labour Party of Malaya, which is non-Malay and largely Chinese, and the Partai Rakyat (People's Party), which is largely Malay in membership. These two were joined in a coalition party known as the Malayan People's Socialist Front, which broke up in December 1965 when the Partai Rakyat withdrew "because of ideological differences."

The Labour Party of Malaya, whose constitution is based mainly on that of the British Labour Party, includes among its objectives "common ownership of the means of production, distribution, and exchange." On 6 May 1966, however, the Bureau of the Socialist International announced at its meeting in Stockholm that it had decided to expel the Labour Party of Malaya because "it was indistinguishable from a communist organization and the propaganda that it put out in Malaysia is indistinguishable from communist propaganda."

Suspected links between the Labour Party of Malaya and the CPM were confirmed in August 1967 when Kam Yau-wah, then Assistant Secretary-General of the Labour Party, was released after a month's detention for his role in anti-government demonstrations sponsored by the Labour Party. Following his release on 19 August, Kam Yau-wah condemned the Labour Party and labor unions controlled by procommunist elements for staging illegal demonstrations and admitted that he had been in contact with members of the CPM in southern Thailand. He also admitted that he had received directives and party documents from the CPM, and that he had used his position in the Labour Party to disseminate CPM views and positions.

The Labour Party of Malaya is divided into an extremist militant faction under the leadership of Lim Kean Siew and a more moderate faction led by Dr. Tan Chee Khoon, party Treasurer and a member of Parliament. The split was revealed at a meeting on 24 September in which the extremists condemned the moderate leadership of Dr. Tan and Dr. Win Lu-huang, the party Secretary-General, calling the struggle between the two factions an "antirightist opportunism movement of deep and far-reaching significance."

The Partai Rakyat is basically a party of extreme nationalism advocating the idea of a "Greater Indonesia." Partai Rakyat strategy was disclosed in a document recovered from an Executive Committee member of the party's Perak branch dated 20 March 1965 and subsequently published in a white paper issued by the Malaysian government:

> Strategy: The main thing is the people's actual struggle but parliamentary struggle is not to be abandoned because it may be used to our advantage.
>
> Methods of Struggle: These are: intense struggle or mild struggle, mass struggle or parliamentary struggle, violent struggle or peaceful struggle, illegal struggle or legal struggle, and covert and overt struggle. The application of the method of struggle depends on the reactionaries, the political fervour of the people, and the comparison of strength between the enemy and ourselves. It is necessary to substitute rapidly one method with another in accordance with changes in the objective situation and make flexible use of methods according to necessity . . . [We] should now adopt the violent method of struggle and make sufficient preparations. (*The Militant Communist Threat to West Malaysia,* p. 6.)

**Domestic Program and Activities.** Although the CPM has apparently issued no new party program since 1957, it issued a number of policy statements in 1960 which reaffirmed the basic points of the 1957 program and which stressed various needs:

> (1) Strengthen and safeguard the independent status of our country; pursue an independent and self-determined foreign policy of peace and neutrality; establish diplomatic relations with all countires; oppose war and uphold peace; refrain from joining any military bloc; unite and cooperate with Afro-Asian countries; strive for the reunification of Singapore with the Federation of Malaya.
>
> (2) Foster unity and mutual support among the Malays, Chinese and Indians, etc., with the Malays as the pivot; protect the legitimate rights and interests of the various nationalities in the country.
>
> (3) Safeguard the democratic rights and liberties of the people; release all patriotic prisoners; extend legal status to all political parties and public organizations which pledge loyalty to the Malayan fatherland.
>
> (4) Protect and develop national industries, agriculture and commerce; improve and develop culture; enforce universal education and ameliorate the living conditions of the people.
>
> (5) Terminate the war; repeal the Emergency Regulations and restore internal peace. ("Forward Along the Path toward Complete Independence," statement of 30 April 1960, as quoted in Frances L. Starner, "Communism in Malaysia: A Multifront Struggle" in Robert A. Scalapino, ed., *The Communist Revolution in Asia*

[Englewood Cliffs, N.J.: Prentice-Hall, Inc., 1965] , p. 239.)

Since the formation of the Federation of Malaysia on 16 September 1963, the CPM has vigorously attacked the Federation as a "neocolonialist intrigue" and called for "consolidation and extension of the broad anti-'Malaysia,' anti-imperialist united front on a national scale in Malaya" and the three Borneo states, and has urged the establishment of a "joint operation council or command to coordinate the day-to-day implementation of the common strategy of the anti-'Malaysia,' anti-imperialist campaign throughout the region."

Through the Paperi, the CPM has attacked the Malaysian Constitution as a "creation of the imperialists" and has stressed the need to establish a "democratic [and] free, prosperous, peaceful coalition in the Malay States stretching from Perlis to Singapore."

Replying to the Malaysian government's white paper of October 1966, *The Militant Communist Threat to West Malaysia,* leaflets distributed by communist terrorists in southern Thailand stated: "On 25 October 1966, the Alliance Government issued their so-called Anti-Communist White Paper which contains entirely malicious slanders and poisonous charges thrown against us that are devoid of foundation," adding: "We regard Malaya as not fully independent and that is why we continue the struggle for the independence, democracy, solidarity, peace and prosperity. The target of our struggle is clear—it is against imperialism and its lackeys."

The CPM has stressed that the aim of its strategy is "not to destroy religion," but to destroy "imperialism and its lackeys in the Motherland," and that it does not "deem it necessary to oppose religion in general and Islam in particular":

> We have no need to fight against the Malays and their special rights. That is not the way to gain influence (among the Malays). We are not willing to carry out foolish acts to exacerbate racial sentiments and split the unity of the people merely to gain a little influence from the people. We [would] rather suffer difficulties and hardship than do mean things. We want not only to protect the Malay race, to elevate the position of the Malays and their language, but also to safeguard the interests of the minority races in this country, and to improve the lot of the aborigines because the basic tenet of the national policy of our Party is to unite the whole nation, especially to unite the three major races—the Malays, the Chinese, and the Indians—in Malaya.

In his New Year's message to the nation, Deputy Prime Minister Tun Abdul Razak warned that there was still a "serious threat to the country from communist terrorists and subversion." Several weeks later, when questioned on the easing of relations between Malaysia and the Soviet Union, Prime Minister Tunku Abdul Rahman replied: "I am not anticommunist. I am only against those communists who use violence to change or take away what is good for others." On 24 August the Malaysian government ordered the release of 180 leftist political detainees as a gesture of good will on the occasion of the tenth anniversary of the nation's independence (31 August). Among those ordered to be released were Dr. Raj Kumar, Secretary of the Labour Party.

Domestic activities of the CPM during 1967 centered around a series of riots and disturbances which occurred during June and November, and which were reportedly inspired by the Malayan Labour Party. Demonstrations in June focused on opposition to the Malaysian government's treatment of political detainees, with the government charging that the Communists were responsible for the demonstrations, which the King of Malaysia described as part of a "foreign-inspired plan to create trouble and disorder in Southeast Asia." The King also noted that because of communist activities and because Malaysia had assumed full responsibility for its own security following the withdrawal of British troops from eastern Malaysia, the government had embarked on a program of expansion for its armed forces.

Under the instigation of the Labour Party of Malaya, a second series of demonstrations were staged on 24 November on the island of Penang on the pretext of protesting against the devaluation of the old Malayan dollar. Racial feelings were aggravated when the Labour Party called for the closing of businesses, most of which were Chinese-owned. As a result of the demonstrations, more than 1,600 persons were arrested, including Lim Kean Siew, Vice-Chairman of the Labour Party, and some 60 "noncitizens" were ordered deported. In addition, 16 branches of the Labour Party were declared illegal (nine in Penang, four in Salangor, and three in Malacca). Deputy Prime Minister Razak displayed subversive literature and pictures of Mao Tse-tung allegedly seized in several branch headquarters. On 28 November the Malaysian government declared limited martial law in northwestern Malaysia, and the next day Prime Minister Tunku Abdul Rahman called on "all loyal citizens to help the government track down the communist elements," which he said were responsible for the disturbances in the country.

**CPM Self-Assessment During 1967.** CPM and MNLL commentaries during 1967 continued to declare that the "revolutionary struggle" was "attaining new heights" and was "increasingly active in central and northern Malaya, and especially in the latter region bordering Thailand." A lengthy analysis carried in the December issue of *Malayan Monitor* took note of difficulties:

> More than nineteen years have passed since the Malayan people's armed struggle for national independence began. In that time, the Malayan patriots have faced many hardships and complex situations. Guided by the National Liberation movement and the Communist Party, they have tackled the many and complex problems with great fortitude and resource. By their persistent struggle they have helped greatly to keep intact the fighting units of the National Liberation movement, and imbued the population with a deeper sense of patriotism.

> The setbacks suffered by the National Liberation movement have been due partly to errors of judgment in assessing the strength and the weaknesses of the imperialists and their agents. Such errors have sometimes led to impulsive actions in the field, resulting in losses and enforced retreats. Further self-critical analysis also revealed failures resulting from insufficient attention to the problems and capacities of the various nationalities. This weakness has, in the past, undermined the unity of the Malayan people and provided an opportunity for the imperialists and their agents to extend their policy of "divide-and-rule." This weakness will, no doubt, be painstakingly and methodically overcome.

The same analysis specifically attacked the "treacherous and destructive action of the modern revisionists" as the "main cause of the movement's setback" and concluded: "The task of the Malayan people and their movement for National Liberation is, therefore, a formidable and complex one. While using the most effective and swiftest forms of struggle to attain victory, they are also prepared for a hard and protracted struggle."

**International Views and Activities.** While maintaining that its members were "internationalists as well as national patriots," the CPM also declared:

> The Communist Party is not a national party which takes to narrow-minded chauvinism; it upholds Popular Proletarian Internationalism. If any Communist Party skips this foundation it becomes a national party of narrow racialism; then it no longer remains a Communist Party in name and in fact.

During 1967 the party's international activities and policy statements focused primarily on the international communist movement in general and the Sino-Soviet dispute in particular.

In "The Malayan People's Struggle for National Independence," a lengthy document serialized in abridged form in *Malayan Monitor* (September-December 1967), the CPM praised Stalin as "the man who, in his lifetime, embodied and symbolized all that was militant, uncompromising, and incisively effective in interpreting and enriching Marxism-Leninism and in smashing the attacks and plans of the imperialists." The same document condemned as a "shocking catastrophe for the revolutionary peoples of the world" the "hydra-headed agents of imperialism" who assumed power in the Soviet Union following the death of Stalin, and accused the Soviet leaders of scheming to "destroy the image and the principles of Marxism-Leninism inside the Soviet Union itself" and to "destroy the main pillars of the Socialist Camp—namely, the Sino-Soviet alliance, and destroy the internationalist lines with, and support for, the national liberation movements of the world."

The CPM condemned the Twentieth Congress of the CPSU and termed Khrushchev's de-Stalinization report a "thinly veiled distortion of facts and history [which] disavowed every single principle of Marxism-Leninism on which the international communist movement and National

Liberation struggle were built." It went on to charge the "modern revisionists" with
> (1) [The] wholesale liquidation of the Soviet Union as a militant, Socialist state, and its transformation into a brand of petty bourgeois social democratic state in which capitalism could be restored
> (2) The complete destruction of the Socialist Camp—principally the Sino-Soviet alliance—as a functional bulwark against world imperialism
> (3) The violent disruption of the internal as well as inter-Party relations of every Communist and Workers' Party in the world—with dire consequences to the respective National Liberation movements and fighting units
> (4) The furtive but unmistakable "rehabilitation" of Tito, Titoism, Browderism, Trotskyism, and both rightist and leftist extremism—as agencies of further disruption inside the international Communist movement and the various National Liberation movements [and] as a prelude to the setting up of "suitable" leadership inside these organizations
> (5) The unprincipled agreement—in policy and in action—between the leadership of the modern revisionist camp and the imperialists to attack all Communist and Workers' Parties and all National Liberation movements which refused to accept the "new orientation"

Criticism was also levied against the 1957 "Declaration of the Twelve Communist and Workers' Parties" and the 1960 "Statement of Eighty-one Communist and Workers Parties":
> Having achieved their dominance of several Communist and Workers' Parties, the modern revisionists bulldozed their way towards more disruptive goals by issuing the "Declaration" of 1957 and "Statement" of 1960. These documents sought to establish in legal form, and with a semblance of the "majority" decision of the international Communist movement, the traitorous and slanderous lines "adopted" at the "20th Congress" of the CPSU. What really happened was that the Soviet revisionist leaders took advantage of the widespread confusion and split which they themselves had engineered throughout the international Communist movement to secure a proper "majority" to support these infamous documents. As shown so clearly in the case of Albania, China, Cuba and other regions, the Soviet revisionists even used physical pressure (including military blockade, economic sanctions, political duress and the full scope of the imperialists' state and propaganda machinery) to try and "bring to heel" all those Communist and Workers' Parties, National Liberation movements and individuals who refused to toe their line.

According to the CPM, "in the ultimate analysis, the main cause of the movement's setback has been the treacherous and destructive action of the modern revisionists" and "the earlier lessons provided by the modern revisionists' actions in Albania, China, Cuba, Indonesia, etc., are being daily reinforced in Vietnam, Indonesia, Burma, Malaya, Thailand, and various other regions of the world. So much so, that it has become a fighting axiom that it is impossible to defeat imperialism without fighting modern revisionism at the same time." The CPM specifically accused "Soviet revisionists" of obstructing the Malayan liberation movement: "Instead of helping the people to rid Malaya of foreign armed occupation, the Soviet and other modern revisionists have attacked the Malayan patriots and the Communist Party of Malaya for resorting to 'violence'."

On 14 May the Central Committee of the Malayan National Liberation League issued a statement condemning the Soviet leaders for signing a trade agreement and an agreement in principle to exchange diplomatic missions with Malaysia and noted that such actions showed that "they have slid very far down the path of complete betrayal of the Malayan people's revolutionary cause." The same statement condemned the "Soviet revisionists": "[They] have tried to acquire footholds in all those areas where the flames of the struggle for national liberation are raging so that they can share the role of the imperialists' fire brigade. Wherever they have succeeded in their infiltration they have attempted to extinguish the oppressed people's struggles from within its ranks." Subsequent MNLL statements accused the Soviet Union of entering into "economic, political, and paramilitary alliances or agreements with the most reactionary local regimes and cliques" and helping the "imperialists to extend the splitting of the country into 'Malaysia' and 'Singapore' by giving diplomatic recognition to the imperialist-sponsored breakaway regimes."

On the occasion of the Fiftieth Anniversary of the October Revolution, the CPM issued a statement declaring that the Soviet leaders had "usurped the leadership of the Soviet Party and Government" and "thus strangled the socialist cause of the October Revolution and betrayed the people of the Soviet Union and the whole world." The same statement declared: the "Soviet revisionist renegade clique" had "thoroughly betrayed Marxism-Leninism" while "Comrade Mao Tse-tung, the great teacher and leader of world revolution of the present era," had "resolutely defended and developed Marxism-Leninism with genius and in an all-round manner, raising it to the stage of Mao Tse-tung's thought." The CPM subsequently declared its intention to "unite closely with the great Communist Party of China and other fraternal Marxist-Leninist Parties and fight to the end to overthrow modern revisionism which has the Soviet revisionist renegade clique at its centre." (*Peking Review*, no. 3, 19 January 1968.)

In contrast to its attacks on the Soviet Union, the CPM had praise for the Communist Chinese leadership and party:

> It has been repeatedly proved by experience that Comrade Mao Tse-tung is indeed the Lenin of our time, that Mao Tse-tung's thought is Marxism-Leninism at its highest in the present era, that the Communist Party of China headed by Comrade Mao Tse-tung is the standard-bearer of world revolution, and that socialist China, which upholds the great red banner of Mao Tse-tung's thought, is the centre of world revolution.

The CPM hailed the Chinese cultural revolution as a "supreme example of mass reorganization and counter-attack," making "inestimable contributions to the international communist movement." On the occasion of the eighteenth anniversary of the founding of the MNLL, P. V. Sarma, the chief representative of the MNLL mission in Peking, declared: "The Great Proletarian Cultural Revolution, personally led by the greatest revolutionary leader of our times, Chairman Mao, has ushered in a new epoch in human history." P. V. Sarma declared also that the cultural revolution would "prevent China from becoming a bourgeois dictatorship under the camouflage of the red flag," "guarantee China's new leap in her socialist construction," and "insure her further advance in the correct orientation toward communism," thereby enabling her to "contribute more effectively to the liberation struggle of the oppressed nations and people." (New China News Agency, 2 February 1967.)

**Other International Activities.** Outside the context of the Sino-Soviet dispute, the CPM focused most of its attention on Vietnam and the Vietnam war. Policy statements continued to attack the Soviet "revisionists" for "collusion" with the "US imperialists" and to maintain that it was "absolutely necessary to crush the modern revisionists and refuse to have anything to do with their 'united action'." Malayan Communist statements continued to condemn the Vietnam war as a "war forced upon the people of Vietnam by the US imperialists with the intention to convert South Vietnam into a US colony forever." A typical charge stated: "The war in Vietnam is not isolated, but involves our own future as well . . . We must support the people of Vietnam to the end [and unite] with the people of Asia and the world to fight against the imperialist venture."

In addition to its support of the "struggle of the Vietnamese people," the Central Committee of the CPM devoted considerable attention to the twenty-fifth anniversary of the founding of the Thai Communist Party, which it praised for "defending the purity of Marxism-Leninism" and having "determinedly fought the modern revisionists led by the Soviet Communist Party." The committee announced its determination to cooperate with the Thai Communist Party in the fight against "imperialism, modern revisionism, and all reactionaries." According to the Malaysian Government's October 1966 white paper, the CPM had an "active group in London" to coordinate CPM "activities in the Afro-Asian and other spheres of interest." In January 1967, however, four members of the Malayan National Liberation League's mission in Indonesia were expelled by the Indonesian authorities and were granted political asylum by North Vietnam.

The CPM declared also its support of the "anti-US-British imperialist struggle of the Arab people against the neocolonialist product, Israel." In Kuala Lumpur, left-wing opposition parties called for a boycott of Israeli goods.

**Publications.** The CPM has no regular official publication of its own. Its statements are circulated through numerous pamphlets and by the Communist Chinese press and radio. The *Malayan Monitor*, although not an official CPM publication, publishes CPM policy statements. This is a mimeographed monthly issued in London; founded in 1947, it was reorganized and renamed the *Malayan Monitor and General News* at the end of 1966; the news editor is Choong Wai Koh, of Malaya. Party views and positions are also publicized in *Barisan*, a Malayan journal published in Singapore; the *Malayan Bulletin*, organ of the Malayan National Liberation League mission in Peking; and such publications as *People's Vanguard, National Liberation News, Awakening News*, and *People's Era*, copies of which have been recovered along the Thai-Malaysian border.

\* \* \*

**Communists in Sarawak.** Communist activities in Sarawak are far more extensive than those of the jungle-based CPM and are closely connected with the state's ethnic problems. Sarawak's population of 862,000 (estimated mid-1966) includes more than 30 per cent ethnic Chinese, the largest single racial group; Malays represent only 17 per cent of the population. Chinese economic and educational predominance and cultural ties with mainland China are connected with the problems of minority status within the Federation of Malaysia, resulting in a certain sympathy toward communist anti-Malaysian campaigns.

Organized communism first appeared in Sarawak in the form of an anti-Japanese "Sarawak Anti-Fascist League" during the Second World War. During the postwar period this league formed the basis of a number of communist-oriented groups—such as the "Sarawak Overseas Democratic Youth League," founded in 1957 and later dissolved by the government. Although no precise information is available, reports indicate that a "Borneo Communist Party" (BCP) may have been secretly founded at this time; virtually nothing is known about its organization and leadership. Communist elements in Sarawak, having been declared illegal, went underground and subsequently initiated a program of united front tactics. Numerous front organizations were formed in all sectors of society. The most important was the "Sarawak Advanced Youths' Association" (SAYA) which is believed to be the BCP's youth front. Founded in 1954, SAYA soon absorbed all or most of the other front organizations and by 1956 had become the headquarters for all communist activities in Borneo. A control organization was eventually formed out of the hard-core membership of SAYA. Originally known as the Clandestine Communist Organization (CCO), now the Sarawak Communist Organization (SCO), this multifront organization is believed to serve the purposes of the BCP, which appears to exercise regional responsibility for communist activities in both Sarawak and Sabah.

**Organization and Leadership.** According to reports of the Sarawak government— *The Danger Within* (Sarawak Information Service, Kuching, 1963) and *Subversion in Sarawak* (Council Negri Sessional Paper, No. 3, Kuching, 1960)—the SCO is directed by a Central Committee which operates through four work departments: labor movement, peasantry, students, and political party. A Politburo and an Organization Bureau function within and give directions to the Central Committee. A pyramidal structure moves upward from cells and branches, district committees, and area and town committees to the Central Committee at the top. Very little is known about the SCO leadership. Three former members of the Sarawak United People's Party—Wen Ming Chuan, Bong Ki Chok, and the latter's wife—are believed to be connected with the SCO, although they have been in Communist China since 1962.

Malaysian government officials estimated in early July 1965 that the SCO membership consisted of some 2,000 hard-core effectives who, with the help of noncommunist sympathizers, could field a trained combat force of some 3,500 men supported by approximately 25,000 civilians. More recent estimates in mid-1967, placed the number of insurrectionists along the Malaysian-Indonesian border somewhere between 700 and 1,000. "Active communists" were put at between 1,000 and 1,500 and "front activists" at some 20,000.

**Strategy and Tactics.** Like the Communist Party of Malaya, the BCP advocates a policy of armed struggle and rejects the Soviet theory of peaceful coexistence. Insurrectionary activities are carried out by highly organized armed bands of the SCO, while indirect pressure is exerted through other organizations, such as the illegal Sarawak Farmer's Association. In late 1964, according to the Malaysian government's 1966 white paper, "the so-called 'North Kalimantan National Liberation League' was established in Sarawak as a broad Communist United Front aimed at creating conditions for the establishment of a Communist-controlled coalition government in a 'North Kalimantan People's Republic' " (*The Militant Communist Threat to West Malaysia*, p. 3). In late December 1964 the Malaysian government announced that it had succeeded in smashing the North Kalimantan National Liberation League. Militarily, communist activities in Sarawak are carried out primarily by the Sarawak People's Guerrilla Troops (Pertahanan Gerila Rakyat Sarawak, PGRS), the military arm of the SCO. Led by Jahaj, PGRS activities center along the Sarawak-Indonesian border, where some 700 communist terrorists, the overwhelming majority of which are PGRS members, are known to operate with the support of an estimated 2,000 sympathizers. During the period 1963-1966, a number of Sarawak communists and PGRS members crossed the border into Indonesian Borneo where Indonesian Army officers and Indonesian Communist Party cadres instructed them in guerrilla warfare. Since the end of confrontation in August 1966, however, the Indonesian government has terminated its support for the Sarawak communists and has cooperated with the Malaysian government in joint efforts to eliminate them. By the end of November 1967, 341 PGRS members had surrendered and PGRS leader Jahaj advised those still at large to do the same.

Since most of the groups incorporated into the SCO are illegal, the organization has advanced its aboveground program through several legal labor and political organizations, the most important of which is the Sarawak United People's Party (SUPP). According to Malaysian officers, the SUPP was founded in 1959 for the specific purpose of advancing communist objectives. While the SUPP claims to have some 10,000 non-Chinese in its 24,000 total membership, the party is primarily in Chinese hands and is identified with Chinese interests. Communist infiltration of the party has apparently been extensive enough to split it into a communist-infiltrated, Peking-oriented left wing and a moderate, "social-democratic" right wing. The party's Secretary-General, Stephen Yong, and Chairman, Ong Kee Hui, are not communists, but the party appears to be oriented toward the communist factions's policies, which were enhanced by the secession of Singapore and the failure of Singapore Premier Lee Kuan Yew's concept of a "Malaysian Solidarity Convention," which was supported by Stephen Yong and Ong Kee Hui.

Although its overt leadership is noncommunist, the program and activities of the SUPP closely parallel those of the SCO by rejecting Malaysia as a "colonialist plot" and advocating the establishment of separate political states on the Malay Peninsula and in Borneo, by calling for improved labor conditions, and by espousing trade relations with Communist China and the lifting of controls on Chinese businessmen.

**Domestic and International Activities.** On 31 January 1967 the Malaysian government terminated the amnesty it had extended on 23 July 1966 to dissident elements in eastern Malaysia, and announced that they would subsequently be treated as enemies of the state and, if caught, prosecuted according to the Emergency Regulations. Known as "Operation Harapan," the amnesty produced some useful information regarding the plans and directives of the SCO but evoked little response from the insurgents themselves, with only 34 taking advantage of the amnesty.

Domestic activities during 1967 focused primarily on the "people's guerrilla troops" of the PGRS. Following the end of confrontation and the restoration of diplomatic relations between Malaysia and Indonesia, the Malaysian and Indonesian governments cooperated extensively in seeking to eliminate armed bands of the PGRS, many of whom had settled on the Indonesian side of the border. Documents confiscated as a result of operations by the two governments revealed that the PGRS was attempting to establish connections with communist elements in Java and South Sumatra.

Although the SCO has had no official international contacts, it is believed to be in direct contact with and to have received support and assistance from the Chinese Communist Party and the Indonesian Communist Party. Indonesian support has undoubtedly been limited since the abortive communist coup of 30 September 1965, but considerable Chinese and Indonesian support has been given to the PGRS. Contacts between the Communist Party of Malaya and the BCP appear to be minimal.

**Publications.** The SCO does not publish an official organ. Communist or communist-oriented newspapers known to be circulating in Sarawak as of 1964 included the *Workers' and Farmers' News*, *National Independence,* and the *Masses News.*

# MARTINIQUE

The Martinique Communist Party (Parti Communiste Martiniquais; PCM) was founded in 1957. Communism in Martinique, however, originated as early as 1918 with the founding of a group called the "Friends of Jean Jaurès," which in 1923 became the "Jean Jaurès Communist Group." In 1925 this group joined the French Communist Party. It was disbanded in September 1939. In 1944 communists reorganized themselves as the Martinique Federation of the French Communist Party, and this group in September 1957 became the autonomous PCM.

The PCM is legal and has an estimated membership of 700. The total population of Martinique is 327,000 (estimated 1966).

The PCM's following has declined during the past ten years, partly because one of its leaders, Aimé Césaire, created in 1956 the left-wing noncommunist Martinique People's Party (Parti Populaire Martiniquais; PPM), and partly as a consequence of the PCM's policy of autonomy for Martinique, which does not have mass support. Whereas in 1956 the PCM obtained 62.5 per cent of the poll, in 1967 it received only 16.24 per cent. It was thus unable to obtain any of Martinique's three seats in the French National Assembly which were contested in March 1967. In the October cantonal elections, the PCM candidate, Victor Lamon, won in Macouba (see below).

PCM support exists primarily within the communist-controlled General Confederation of Labor (Confédération Général du Travail; CGT) whose Secretary-General, Victor Lamon, is a member of the PCM Politburo. It also enlists support among student and youth movements, particularly the General Association of Martinique Students (Association Générale des Étudiants Martiniquais; AGEM) and the Organization of Anticolonialist Youth of Martinique (Organisation de la Jeunesse Anticolonialiste de la Martinique; OJAM).

**Organization and Leadership.** The Secretary-General of the PCM is Armand Nicolas. The Politburo includes Georges Mauvois, Victor Lamon, René Ménil, Georges Gratiant, Walter Guitteaud, Mathurin Gottin, Albert Platon, Richard Laverne, and Georges Fitte-Duval; the Secretariat includes Ph. Duféal, Mathurin Gottin, Edouard de Lépine, Albert Platon, and Georges Mauvois. Other leading Central Committee members are Guy Dufond, Sévère Cerland, Pierre Zobda-Quitman, André Constant, Georges Thimotée, Edgard Nestoret, and D. Banidol.

The PCM has its own youth organization, the Union of Communist Youth of Martinique (Union de la Jeunesse Communiste de la Martinique), which closely follows PCM directives and whose Secretary-General is Edouard de Lépine.

Among Martinique mass organizations serving the interests of the PCM, the Front for the Defense of Public Liberties (FDLP) was active especially in 1964-66. The front included, in addition to the PCM mass organizations and the CGT, the PPM and the United Socialist Party (Parti Socialiste Unifié; PSU). The OJAM mentioned above, founded in 1962, follows a more militant line than the PCM and advocates complete independence for Martinique rather than autonomy. The PCM strongly supports the Councils of Parents of Pupils (Conseils de Parents d'Élèves) and contributed to the creation of the Secular Action Trust (Cartel d'Action Laïque), a grouping of thirteen organizations.

**Domestic Views and Policies.** The PCM program, as formulated at the Third Party Congress in 1964, is based on the demand for autonomy for Martinique within a framework of close ties with France. The party claims that the present departmental status has resulted in Martinique's remaining a colony under the double oppression of French colonialism and local capitalism. The party's program of autonomy is considered a means of advancing toward socialism in Martinique. Union with France is to be in the form of an accord based on cooperation and mutual respect and "excluding all colonialist ties." This accord also excludes the present trends toward integration or regionalism.

The PCM aims at implementing its program by creating a united front of "anti-imperialist" forces in Martinique. The party is directing its calls for unity to the working class and small farmers, the middle class, the small capitalists, and the young people, and to the other autonomist political parties, the PPM and the PSU. The party has opted for peaceful means of struggle, although it warns that violence is not excluded for all time.

The major event in Martinique in 1967 was the elections to the French National Assembly in March.

The party's election program reflected its views on autonomy for Martinique. "All the fundamental problems of the Martinique people can be resolved most easily within the framework of a new statute permitting the Martinique people to rule the affairs of their country by themselves within the framework of a union with France," declared the election program. The program envisaged the election of a legislative assembly by universal suffrage and the creation of an executive responsible to the Assembly and of a body to ensure cooperation between Martinique and France. The immediate economic demands called for protecting and favoring the expansion of local production with priority given to workers and small producers in agriculture as well as industry. (*Justice,* 26 January.)

An important feature in this election was that for the first time an accord was reached by the PCM, PPM, and PSU to support only one "anticolonialist" candidate in each electoral district. Heretofore, on several occasions (participation in the Tricontinental Conference in Havana [January 1966], support of the struggle of the Vietnamese people, organization of demonstrations on such occasions as the anniversary of the abolishing of slavery, cooperation with the FDLP) the parties were able to unite in common action. At each election, however, difficulties appeared which limited accords to a sort of "tacit pact of nonaggression." The PCM greeted the 1967 accord with satisfaction, "seeing it as a success of the line of unity which the party has placed at the center of its policy for the past several years" (*Justice,* 9 February). Actually, a general accord including a common program, common candidates, and a common electoral campaign, proposed by the PCM in June 1966, was turned down by the other parties.

In the election itself, the PPM candidate Aimé Césaire was elected on the first round. The other two seats were won by the Gaullist candidates. Georges Gratiant of the PCM received 12,763 votes in the second round, which according to his party was the highest any communist candidate had ever received in an electoral district. The successes of the Gaullist candidates were denounced by the PCM as being the result of fraud and corruption. Analyzing the results of the elections, the PCM renewed its call for greater unity of the anticolonialist forces. According to a resolution of the Central Committee, "All conditions exist for the autonomist movement to move to a new decisive stage: that of elaborating a common platform, a common platform of autonomy, of an organization for the Martinique Front for Autonomy." The PCM resolution suggested that the party direct its efforts at the small landowners, the trade unions, and the youth, intensify its political and ideological work, and strengthen its organization. The unity must develop through support of specific points such as the defense of popular demands, democratic liberties, secularization of education, and consistent opposition to the Gaullist party, the UNR. (*Justice,* 13 April 1967.)

The PCM proposal received the support of the PPM, PSU, CGT, AGEM, REM, and the Antillan Studies Circle (Cercle d'Etudes Antillais) who met on 2-3 September to prepare the first congress of the "Martinique People for Autonomy," scheduled for December 1967. The congress was later postponed until mid 1968, in order to convene following the PCM congress scheduled for April 1968 and to allow representatives from the Martinique colony in France to attend.

The program for a united front was also voiced at the first congress of the CGT on 18-19 February 1967. Having received no response from the leadership of the trade union organization Force Ouvrière (FO) on uniting on the basis of a common program, the CGT urged its members to redouble their efforts toward the rank and file members of the FO to achieve this unity. The CGT also reaffirmed its stand on autonomy, but also declared that it would now take concrete measures within its possibilities to defend this goal.

**International Views and Policies.** The PCM has retained its traditional close ties with the French Communist Party and has remained a faithful ally of the Communist Party of the Soviet Union in the international communist movement. On the occasion of the fiftieth anniversary of the October Revolution the PCM sent a message declaring: "The Martinique communists were always faithful to proletarian internationalism since 1919 when they enthusiastically came to the defense of the young Soviet regime which was invaded by the imperialists. They have always considered that the attitude with regard to the Soviet Union constitutes the touchstone of internationalism." (*Justice*, 9 November.)

The PCM has conducted an active propaganda campaign in defense of the Vietnamese people and condemning the "American imperialist aggression" in Vietnam. The PCM also voiced hope that the Chinese working class would triumph over "present contradictions" in their country and would "play its revolutionary role and give the Vietnamese people positive aid by associating with the other socialist peoples and the other communist parties." (*Justice*, 6 July.)

A delegation of the PCM, headed by Georges Mauvois, visited the Soviet Union on 29 April-22 May and conferred with leaders of the CPSU. The joint communique issued following the talks declared the support of both parties for the convening of an international communist conference and affirmed the two parties' unity of views on fundamental current problems. A PCM delegation consisting of Armand Nicolas and Albert Platon attended the celebration of the fiftieth anniversary of the October Revolution in November.

The Martinique delegation to the first conference of the Latin American Solidarity Organization (Havana, July-August) was headed by Edouard de Lépine. In his speech to the Assembly, de Lépine warned that while attention was being exclusively focused on "American imperialism," "French imperialism" in the Antilles was a potentially dangerous factor for all of Latin America. He also emphasized, referring to the fact that Martinique was still fighting for independence from a "colonialist power," that Martinique was "a century and a half behind times" and that the Martinique revolutionaries must act with the consciousness of their situation and not leap "irresponsibly" over historical stages.

**Publications.** The PCM central organ is the weekly *Justice* and the theoretical organ is *L'Action*. The party also publishes a regional organ, *Le Progrés du Sud*.

# MEXICO

The Mexican Communist Party (Partido Comunista Mexicano; PCM) was founded in September 1919 with the assistance and support of a number of foreigners, including M. N. Roy and Michael Borodin.

The party is legal, but is too small to qualify for registering candidates for public office in national elections. (Mexican law requires an organization to have 75,000 members in order to be eligible to register its candidates.)

From a peak of about 30,000 before World War II, PCM membership has declined to no more than 5,000 at present (*World Strength of Communist Party Organizations,* 1968). Other estimates put the membership as low as 2,500.

There are also a number of pro-Chinese and Trotskyist parties or groups (see below), with a total membership estimated at below 1,000.

The population of Mexico is 45,671,000 (estimated July 1967.)

**Organization and Leadership.** The Party Congress, required by party statute to be convened every four years, elects the Central Committee, which in turn elects from among its own members the First Secretary, the Political Committee (or Praesidium), Executive Commission, and other special bodies. Below the central apparatus there are state and regional committees, although the party organization has never been nationwide. Party strength is concentrated in the Federal District and in the larger municipalities.

The First Secretary of the PCM is Arnoldo Martínez Verdugo. Leading figures in the Central Committee include Arturo Pasos, Román Blas Manrique, Eduardo Montes, Hugo Ponce de León, José Luna, José Luis Sustaita, Encarnación Pérez Gaytán, Juan Rejano, Ramón Ramírez, Máximo Contreras, Juan Céspedes, José Olarte, Gonzalo Villalobos, Gerardo Unzueta Lorenzano, Marcos Leonel Posadas, and David Alfaro Siqueiros. Siqueiros, a famous painter, often acts as public spokesman for the party.

The party has an auxiliary youth organization, the Communist Youth of Mexico (Juventud Comunista de México; JCM). Celso Garza Guajardo is the JCM Secretary-General; Marcos Leonel Posadas is Organization Secretary. Other leading figures in the JCM include Carlos Reyes, Enrique Semo Caleb, Eduardo del Valle, Rubén Valdespino, Arturo Sama Escalante, Samuel Ovilla, and Rolando Maller. There is also a communist-dominated youth organization, the Centro Nacional de Estudiantes Democráticos (CNED), distinct from the JCM but including many of the same individuals.

**Domestic Policy and Activities.** The PCM is not a significant force in Mexican politics. The center-left Institutional Revolutionary Party (Partido Revolucionario Institucional) holds 174 of the 210 seats in the lower house of the federal legislature, and all of the seats in the upper house.

The PCM claims that Mexico needs a "new revolution" to succeed the "bourgeois" revolution of 1910. Under present conditions, the party is not optimistic about Mexico's revolutionary potentialities, however, and adheres to a line giving primacy to peaceful and legal means of revolutionary struggle, but without ruling out limited and judicious use of violence for specific ends.

In past years the PCM attempted to gain a voice in Mexican politics primarily through cooperation with the Socialist People's Party (Partido Popular Socialista; PPS), a left-wing party founded by Lombardo Toledano in 1948. In 1966 PPS membership was estimated at 38,000. At the end of 1966, however, the PPS itself split (see *YICA,* 1966, pp. 235-36), and only the much smaller faction led by Rafael Estrada Villa, a procommunist deputy in the lower house, continued in 1967 to cooperate with the PCM. Early in 1967 Estrada Villa's group took the name National Revolutionary Directorate (DNR). On 19 March Estrada Villa announced that the DNR and the PCM had agreed to nominate joint candidates for the upcoming elections for federal deputies 2 July. The electoral alliance chose 23 candidates. Unable to secure official registration for their candidates, the DNR and PCM planned a public assembly to announce their names, but government authorities forbade the meeting. After the elections, in which Deputy Estrada Villa lost his seat, Estrada Villa's group was reorganized into a new party, the National Organization of Revolutionary Action (Organización Nacional de Acción Revolucionaria; ONAR), with a Central Committee of 52 members. ONAR continued to cooperate with, but was not dominated by, the PCM.

Another political group which the PCM has sought to dominate or to ally with is the left-extremist National Liberation Movement (Movimiento de Liberación Nacional; MLN). The MLN was founded in 1961 following a conference sponsored by the World Council of Peace and presided over by Lázaro Cárdenas. The MLN, however, under the leadership of Heberto Castillo, successfully fought off PCM attempts to control it and since the Tricontinental Conference in Havana in January 1966, ideological differences and personal antagonisms between leaders of the two groups have become more acute. In an interview published in left-wing magazine *Sucesos Para Todos* (Mexico City), 30 September 1967, MLN leader Castillo criticized the PCM and other Latin American communist parties for claiming a monopoly on revolutionary theories and adhering to out-of-date tactics. Castillo declared that the MLN did not believe in orthodox communist organizational methods, or in trying to turn economic organizations into political ones. Rather, the MLN put men into existing organizations to spread its ideas, but not to form identifiable cells. He also said that he did not believe in "socialism in one country," nor did he equate noncommunism with "imperialism." Nevertheless, he declared his support of guerrilla warfare as the sole means of freeing Latin America from "US imperialism." These differences with the PCM had come to a head at the conference of the Latin American Solidarity Organization at Havana in August (see below).

On 11 and 12 February the PCM Central Committee held its ninth plenum and announced the forthcoming Fifteenth Party Congress in June. At the plenum, Martínez Verdugo said that the aim of the Congress would be to bring about the party's transformation into a mass party (*La Voz de México*, 19 February), with the ultimate aim of giving the masses a revolutionary outlook.

The Fifteenth Congress, originally scheduled for 16-20 June, met in Mexico City 18-22 June. Some 1,200 to 1,300 visitors and delegates were reported to have attended. Visitors present included representatives of the communist parties of Spain, Argentina, Chile, and Ecuador. Two representatives of the Communist Party of the USA en route to the Congress were detained and deported by police in Mexico City (*The Worker*, 25 June). According to David Alfaro Siqueiros, this was the first convention of the party to be held "publicly and in full solemnity." (*El Universal*, Mexico City, 26 August.) A report on the work of the Congress was published as a supplement to *La Vox de México* (2 July). The Congress did not alter the long-standing party line which put primary emphasis on legal struggle, without ruling out limited use of armed struggle for specific purposes. The report said that the party's work in the immediate future would be concentrated in three areas: strengthening of the party, reorganization of the labor movement, and working for the union of all "anti-imperialist" forces within a united front. Special emphasis was placed on political work with students, peasants, and workers through the CNED, the peasant front organization Central Campesina Independiente (not to be confused with the pro-government peasant union of the same name), and the women's front organization Unión Nacional de Mujeres. The Congress hedged its support for legal struggle as opposed to armed struggle, however, by noting that the party must formulate its policy:

> ... in accordance with the framework of the present situation and its objective tendencies, which have been pointing for some time, not toward the democratization of the country, but rather toward dictatorial forms of government. One has to foresee, therefore, that legal actions that today are the essential form of struggle for the masses to defend their rights, may give way to armed struggle as the principal revolutionary action.
> (*El Universal*, 24 August.)

The party's youth auxiliary also held a congress during the year. The Second National Congress of the JCM was held 23-26 February in Mexico City, with a reported 250 delegates attending. The

Congress was addressed by PCM First Secretary Martínez Verdugo, who stressed the importance of youth organization in the PCM's future and outlined plans for a large, unified organization which would recruit on a large scale not only students, but also young workers and peasants.

**International Policies and Activities.** The PCM generally follows the Soviet line on international issues, especially those which do not directly concern Latin America. In the report to the June congress delivered by Martínez Verdugo, for instance, the PCM praised Soviet support for the Arab countries in the Middle East war, expressly criticized the "splitting activities of the Mao Tse-tung group" and its "slanderous campaign" against the CPSU, and endorsed the Soviet call for an international conference of communist and workers' parties (*Pravda,* 20 June).

The PCM's biggest problem in the international sphere is how to deal with the Castroist challenge to Soviet leadership of the communist movement in Latin America, and thus to the leadership of pro-Soviet Communists in the various Latin American countries. The party has responded to this challenge by simultaneously affirming the great importance of the Cuban revolution as a model for the rest of Latin America and insisting that revolutionary strategies in each country cannot be dictated from Havana, but must be decided upon independently by the revolutionaries in each country on the basis of the principles of Marxism-Leninism, the experience of the Cuban revolution, and the conditions peculiar to their own country.

The PCM participated in the conference of the Latin American Solidarity Organization (OLAS) in Havana 31 July-10 August. The Mexican delegation to the congress consisted of six members, two each from the PCM (Hugo Ponce de León, Marcos Leonel Posadas), the MNL (Heberto Castillo Martínez, Armando Castillejos Ortiz), and the ONAR (Rafael Estrada Villa, Adalberto Pliego Galicia). Heberto Castillo was chairman of the delegation. The PCM faction found itself in disagreement both with the rest of the Mexican delegation and the conference at large, splitting with them on issues concerning Soviet interests and the Castroist line for Latin America. After the conference, *La Voz de México* (17 September) complained that the non-PCM majority of the delegation had not been willing to seek a position acceptable to the entire delegation. The PCM publicly dissociated itself from certain decisions of the conference which the majority of the Mexican delegation had supported. These included the conference's condemnation of the Communist Party of Venezuela, which had been accused by Fidel Castro in March of "betraying the Venezuelan revolution" and "opposing Cuba" (see *Venezuela*); its censure of the Soviet Union's trade and aid agreements with some Latin American governments; and its endorsement of Castro's call for immediate armed struggle throughout Latin America. (*La Voz de México,* 25 September.)

PCM antagonism to the Castroist line for Latin America was expressed in a long theoretical critique of the views of the French Marxist and friend of Ernesto Che Guevara, Régis Debray. Debray, imprisoned by the Bolivian government in 1967 (see *Bolivia*), had published a book, *Revolution in the Revolution?,* which strongly attacked the Latin American communist parties for failing to take the Cuban revolution as a model and shunning reliance on guerrilla warfare as a basic strategy (see *Cuba*). Gerardo Unzueta Lorenzano, the PCM's chief theoretical writer, at the end of 1967 wrote an essay in rebuttal of Debray which was published in three installments in the newspaper of the Communist Party of Chile, *El Siglo* (21 and 28 January, 4 February 1968). Unzueta's lengthy critique elaborated the basic point that Debray's line was that of a petit-bourgeois adventurist who slighted the role of the masses in making revolution. "Everything seems to indicate," wrote Unzueta, "that Debray proposes the guerilla form of struggle (taken piecemeal and almost arbitrarily from the Cuban model, particularly where technique is concerned) for a period in which the conditions for revolution are not ripe."

In contrast, Unzueta set forth a summary of the PCM line on the role of armed struggle as a tactic under present circumstances:

> It is our belief that certain armed actions can indeed play and are in fact playing an important role in the process of winning the strata and classes which are separated from the dominant class over to the revolutionary program, and in the task of preventing those groups which have already broken away from the leadership of the oligarchs and the imperialists from being led to return to their support by new actions (reforms,

confessions, repression, etc.).

These actions, mainly those which arise from the masses, represent a denunciation of and a response to the arbitrary actions of the regime—resistance to them—and contribute to showing the masses the probable future of their struggle. If these actions do not basically exceed the limitations of what is possible, and if later they proceed to higher stages only in strict relations to oligarchic-imperialist violence, they will become a powerful contribution to the political development of the country. The truimphs won by this means will contribute to leading new sectors to active resistance, which can also lead to higher forms of struggle. (*El Siglo*, 21 January 1968.)

Finally, in a polemical peroration Unzueto summed up the case of the PCM and the other pro-Soviet Latin American Communist parties against Debray and, by clear implication, Castro:

An ideology and some conceptions which propose to liquidate all the instruments which the masses have created in their revolutionary action—and in the first place, the most prized one, the party—cannot lead to anything other than individualism and spontaneous voluntarism. . . . In their totality, Debray's ideology and conceptions are something which attempt to push us back to stages in the labor and revolutionary movement that have already been surpassed, to pre-Marxist stages; to a socialism that is not class socialism. And anyone who in our age proclaims a nonclass and nonsocialist policy deserves to "be exhibited alongside an Australian kangaroo," as Lenin said. (*Ibid.*, 4 February.)

Sometime in the spring of 1967, the PCM and the communist parties of Central America and Panama met, probably in San José, Costa Rica, and jointly reaffirmed their positions on various international issues in a 13-point statement (see *Documents*). The statement noted that the "working-class movement" in various countries was making progress "using the most diverse forms of struggle, from peaceful ones to armed struggle." At the same time, however, it called for greater efforts to strengthen the "militant unity of all parties and the alliance with the Cuban revolution." Regarding world-wide international issues, the statement reaffirmed Soviet hegemony in the international communist movement and endorsed the Soviet call for an international communist conference.

The PCM sent a delegation to the ceremonies marking the fiftieth anniversary of the October Revolution, in Moscow, where Martínez Verdugo delivered a speech which praised Soviet support for the Cuban revolution.

**Publications.** The organ of the PCM is the weekly *La Voz de México*.

\* \* \*

Pro-Chinese communist parties and groups in Mexico represent a small minority and are splintered into several contending factions. Since 1959 a number of small splinter groups have left the PCM and have assumed a more or less pro-Chinese stance advocating immediate armed revolution, and these groups themselves have undergone subsequent splits (see history in *YICA*, 1966, pp. 237-38).

The most active of these groups and the one which appears to have the closest relations with Peking is the Mexican Movement of Marxist-Leninist Antirevisionist Unification (Movimiento de Unificación Marxista y Leninista Antirevisionista Mexicano; MUMAM), led by former PCM member Javier Fuentes Gutiérrez and Federico Emery Valle. This group has a publication, *Chispa*.

MUMAM in 1967 was implicated in an elaborate plot to start a guerrilla warfare movement in the Mexican countryside, revealed when a group of the rebels unsuccessfully attempted to blow up a military truck to obtain arms on 3 July. On 19 July Mexican authorities announced the arrest of 13 members of the group and charged that further raids and bank robberies had been planned to obtain the means for starting a training camp for urban and rural terrorists in the state of Chiapas, near the Guatemalan border. Two foreign guerrilla leaders, one from El Salvador and one from Nicaragua, were also among those arrested. A fourteenth suspect, arrested later, said that an uprising had been planned for 23 September. Fuentes Gutiérrez, named as the leader of the group, was not among those arrested. Government sources said that he and Emery Valle both left Mexico for Peking on 30 June.

The Mexican government charged that the rebel group had very active Chinese backing. Fuentes Gutiérrez was said to have been receiving from the Chinese 600 pounds sterling ($1680) per month; the money allegedly was received through the Mexico City correspondent of the Communist Chinese news agency NCNA, Pien Cheng, until November 1966 when he returned to China and the agency was closed. Fuentes Gutiérrez' book store in Mexico City was said to be the headquarters for distribution of Chinese propaganda material. (*New York Times,* 21 July 1967.)

The Chinese replied to these charges in an NCNA broadcast by Pien Cheng on 1 August. Pien's statement heatedly attacked the Mexican government, saying that the "real purpose" of its charges was to "hamper the dissemination of Mao Tse-tung's thought in Mexico, undermine the friendship between the Chinese and Mexican peoples, obstruct the return of the correspondents of the NCNA branch in Mexico to their posts to carry on their normal press work, and prevent them from exposing the US imperialist policy of aggression against Mexico." With regard to the specifics of the charges, Pien declared that they were "not worth refuting at all," but said: "My colleagues and I have never had any financial dealings with engineer Fuentes nor have we used pounds sterling in defraying our expenditures in Mexico."

Another NCNA broadcast (15 August) declared: "It is out-and-out fabrication that Fuentes, as the 'statement' alleges, 'has made several trips to Peking, where he obtained promises of financial assistance for carrying out subversive activities in Mexico.' Apart from his recent and first visit to China on a trade talk mission, he had never been to China before."

Three months later, *Peking Review* (3 November) carried an article, "Chairman Mao is the Greatest Marxist-Leninist of Our Era,", with the by-line "Marxist-Leninst Movement of Mexico" (very likely Fuentes' group). The article contained no specific reference to the Mexican government, but said: "At present, the militant task of all Communists in Asia, Africa and Latin America is to thoroughly apply the strategy of people's war and use this highest form of struggle to open up new fronts against imperialism."

The Mexican government also accused Rafael Estrada Villa of being involved in the July plot, and charged that he had engaged in subversive activity in the state of Guerrero. Estrado Villa, then in Havana for the OLAS conference, denied the charges and claimed that the government was only trying to put pressure on him for participating in the OLAS conference. Later reports said that he had tried to take asylum at the Cuban Embassy in Mexico City on 6 September.

At the beginning of 1967, other splinter groups with a pro-Chinese orientation included: the Mexican Workers' Party (Partido de Trabajadores Mexicanos), with leader Juan Ortega Arenas, Daniel Martínez, Raúl Contreras, Salvador Martínez, and Carlo Díaz, and an organ, *Lucha Obrera*; the Leninist Spartacus League (Liga Leninista Espartaco), with leaders Camilo Chávez, Tereso González, Martin Reyes, Hipólito Angelez Bautista, Plutarco Galicia Jiménez, and Samuel López, and an organ, *El Militante;* the Revolutionary Spartacus Association (Associación Revolucionaria Espartaco), with leaders Enrique González Rojo, Jaime Sabines, Eduardo Lizalde, Jaime Labastida, J. Refugio González, Edelmiro Maldonada, Augusto Velasco, and Félix Espejel, with an organ, *Espartaco*; and the Bolshevik Communist Party of Mexico (Partido Comunista Bolchevique Mexicano), with leaders Leonel Padilla, Arturo Velasco, Félix González, and Antonio Farfan, and an organ, *El Machete.*

In addition to the pro-Chinese groups, there are a number of Trotskyist elements, such as the People's Revolutionary Movement (Movimiento Revolucionario del Pueblo), led by Victor Rico Galan and Raúl Ugalde; the Revolutionary Workers' Party (Partido Obrero Revolucionario), and the 23 September Movement (Movimiento Veintitrés de Septiembre). Police in January arrested five members of the last group and charged them with planning acts of sabotage and violence.

# MONGOLIA

The Mongolian People's Revolutionary Party (MPRP) was founded in 1921 by two revolutionary groups led by Sukhe-Bator and Choybalsan. The first congress of the MPRP was held in March of that year under the protection of the Soviet Red Army. The MPRP is the governing and sole party in the Mongolian People's Republic (MPR). In April 1966 the party claimed 48,570 members, and Ulan Bator radio on 1 March 1968 said that party membership was "almost 50,000." The population of Mongolia is 1,140,000 (estimated, 1966).

**Organization and Leadership.** The MPRP is organized approximately on the same pattern as the Communist Party of the Soviet Union. The party Congress is in theory the supreme body within the party (the Fifteenth Congress of the MPRP was held in June 1966), but the true locus of political power is the Central Committee (with 75 full members and 51 candidate members), its Politburo (with seven full and two candidate members), and Secretariat (with five members). The government of the MPR is dominated by the party, and over two-thirds of the members of the highest state body, the Council of Ministers, belong to the party's Central Committee (M. T. Haggard, "Mongolia: the First Communist State in Asia," in R. A. Scalapino [ed.], *The Communist Revolution in Asia.* Englewood Cliffs, N. J., 1965, p. 90).

The leadership of the MPRP elected at the Fifteenth Congress includes the following members of the Secretariat: First Secretary Yumzhagiin Tsedenbal; N. Jagvaral, D. Molomjamts, B. Lhamsuren, and T. Dugersuren. Full members of the Politburo are Tsedenbal, Jagvaral, Dugersuren, Molomjamts, D. Maydar, Sonomyn Lubsan, and J. Sambuu; candidate members are N. Lubsanrabdan and B. Lhamsuren. The Chairman of the Control Committee is N. Lubsanrabdan.

The party's youth movement, the Mongolian Revolutionary Union of Youth, has a membership of about 77,000. Its Secretary is C. Purevjav. Often referred to as the "Revsomol," the Union of Youth and its Young Pioneers are modeled after the Komsomol and Pioneer organizations in the Soviet Union.

**Domestic Affairs.** Following the extensive shakeup of the Central Committee membership which took place at the party congress in 1966, the party leadership appeared to have remained stable in 1967, and no purges or additions at the level of the Central Committee or above were reported during the year. A further indication of such stability was the absence in 1967 of accusations of excessive Mongol nationalism against some of the party leadership which were made on numerous occasions in 1966. Rather, the attention of the party leadership was focused primarily on the country's economic difficulties and the continuing attempt to build up an industrial base in the areas of Ulan Bator, Darhan, and Choybalsan.

The current five-year plan (1966-1970), Mongolia's fourth, got off to a poor start in 1966, when both agricultural and industrial production failed to reach target levels, and the situation improved only modestly in 1967 (see Joe Hart, "Mongolia: 20th Year of Economic Planning," *Asian Survey,* January 1968). Blame for these difficulties was placed on faulty management as well as on bad weather and natural disasters. In an interview published in the Budapest newspaper *Nepszabadsag* on 22 January 1967, Tsedenbal was asked what the main tasks of the MPR in 1967 were. He replied:

> When we defined the main tasks of the 1967 plan we proceeded from the necessity of restoring the damage caused by floods, earthquakes, and other natural disasters and the fact that we must fulfill on schedule the directives of the Fifteenth MPRP Congress in connection with the fourth five-year plan. The major provision of the 1967 plan of the people's economy is to assure a normal rate of development in the production of industry, agriculture, and the building industry, and by this to attain a further

improvement of the gross national product and the welfare and cultural standard of the working people.

Tsedenbal also noted that "reestablishing the cattle inventory, which was harmed by the severe winter last year, will be a considerable task."

Thus the leadership in 1967 had to face squarely various aspects of the familiar "red versus expert" dilemma, including the question of whether to give priority to the goal of increasing collectivization or to that of increasing aggregate production. On the whole, the MPRP leadership dealt with these problems by coming down firmly on the side of expertise; while not giving up the longer-range goals of greater collectivization and ideological control, they followed the example of Soviet Union's recent off-again-on-again economic reforms designed to increase production by judicious use of reformed management techniques and material incentives. This trend was evidenced in the measures adopted at the Third Congress of Agricultural Cooperatives, the first such congress since 1959. At a June meeting of the MPRP Central Committee, Tsedenbal reported on the adoption by the Congress of a number of amendments to the existing Model Rules of Agricultural Cooperatives (see *IB*, No. 104). The thrust of these new measures was to decentralize management and party responsibilities and to demand a higher level of specialized competence from party as well as government personnel. According to Tsendenbal's report, the Politburo had recommended to the Congress that there should be no attempt for the present to reduce the allowed number of individually owned livestock. Tsedenbal further said, "The new Rules envisage forms of material and moral stimulation as well as disciplinary measures . . . and bonuses for better performance, for the fulfillment and overfulfillment of plan assignments." The work team, rather than the larger brigade, was specified as the chief unit of organization of labor for livestock raising. Emphasizing the importance of specialized competence, the report scored widespread mismanagement and complained:

> The regional party committees and agricultural organs do not make a deep analysis of the economics of agricultural cooperatives and state farms. One of the reasons for this is the insufficient economic grounding of executives and party functionaries.
>
> This state of things cannot be tolerated any longer. This year the Central Committee made it obligatory for the heads of agricultural enterprises, local party and government officials and agricultural specialists to learn to draw up production and financial plans, statements of account and balance sheets of agricultural cooperatives, to analyze their economic activities to deepen their knowledge of zoo- and agro-techniques, to acquire a minimum of economic knowledge.

On the question of the training of cadres, the message was clearly that politics should not take command. The report dealt forthrightly with the delicate problem of party personnel who felt that their political role was proof against the need for them to acquire technical knowledge or management capability, remarking:

> It stands to reason that political training of cadres is a prime concern of party organizations, which must pay special attention to raising the executives' ideological level and business competence. But it is still incorrectly believed that the party organizations alone should concern themselves with enhancing the knowledge of our cadres. This should be the duty of all party, government, economic, cultural, and public organizations and their heads.

Finally, the report called for imitation of the example of the Soviet Union by setting up "economic analysis councils and groups in the region, agricultural cooperatives, state farms and other economic organizations."

The number of days per year of collective labor required from members of the cooperatives was raised by the Congress to 250, up from 150 in 1959.

**Relations with the Soviet Union**. Aside from its close imitation of the Soviet pattern of economic development, the MPR is heavily dependent on continuing Soviet aid and economic cooperation. Sixty per cent of Mongolia's foreign trade is with the Soviet Union, and nearly all of the rest with other communist countries. For the period of the Fourth Five-Year Plan, 1966-1970, the Soviet

Union had already promised more than $550 million in economic aid. This amount was substantially increased by the terms of a further agreement between the two governments concluded in November 1967 (see below). Mongolia, clearly with Moscow's support, tried in 1967 to broaden the base of its economic support among the communist nations, except China. This attempt was made primarily through the Council of Mutual Economic Assistance (COMECON). Politburo member D. Maydar said on 19 October: "We pay special attention to the development of interstate economic ties, especially to the joint tapping of natural resources and to the joint construction and exploitation of industrial projects. Our country will continue to use the possibilities for expanding economic relations inherent in such an internal socialist organization as COMECON."

Mongolia is the only Asian member of this organization of Communist countries, having been admitted in 1962. The MPR was very active in COMECON affairs in 1967, attending many COMECON meetings and specialized conferences. On 22-27 June Ulan Bator hosted the tenth session on air transport of the COMECON Standing Committee and on 3-7 October the thirty-first meeting of the COMECON Executive Committee was held in Ulan Bator. (The three previous meetings of this body had been held in Moscow.) The Eastern European members of COMECON, with the exception of Rumania, have undertaken to provide some economic aid to the MPR to assist its industrialization plan. An Ulan Bator broadcast of 10 August gratefully acknowledged the importance of aid from the Soviet Union, Czechoslovakia, Poland, Hungary, East Germany, and Bulgaria in the fulfillment of the Fourth Five-Year Plan.

Current Soviet problems centering on the question of how to describe in Marxist terms the nature of the economic systems of backward but non-colonial countries were reflected in the manner in which the MPR leadership described the relationship of Mongolia's economy to that of the Soviet Union. This relationship also provided grist for Peking's attacks on the allegedly un-Marxist character of the economies of both Mongolia and the Soviet Union.

Two questions were at issue: (1) the close integration of the Mongolian economy with those of the other countries of the socialist camp belonging to COMECON; (2) Mongolia's status as an economically backward, or underdeveloped, country. Classical Marxist-Leninist economic theory allows for only "two camps," consisting of capitalist systems, of which backward colonial countries form a part, and socialist systems. Recently, however, Soviet economists have been elaborating an alleged teaching of Lenin on the possibilities of the development of a backward country along the "non-capitalist path," by depending on "leading countries." As it applies to Mongolia, this, in turn, involves an international division of labor within the socialist camp, which, due to the "proletarian internationalism" of the Soviet Union, redounds to the benefit of all countries concerned. Thus the phrase "the non-capitalist path of development," has gained currency among both Soviet and Mongolian economists. (The Soviets also apply this phrase to contemporary India's economic development. See Stephen Clarkson, "Soviet Theory and Indian Reality," *Problems of Communism*, January 1967.) At a conference in Moscow in September, a Mongolian economist, Jatamba, said that "Lenin's teaching on the possibilities of development of backward countries along the non-capitalist path with the assistance of leading countries has been confirmed in our republic." He further said, according to a broadcast of 11 September, that "under the conditions of the international socialist division of labor, the necessity for the development of all branches of production in every country has passed away. This situation has served as the most important economic condition for the rapid creation of the material and technical base of socialism in formerly backward countries."

Tsedenbal headed the Mongolian delegation to Moscow for the Fiftieth Anniversary celebrations. During this time, the agreement with the Soviet Union increasing Soviet aid was negotiated and was signed 13 November. Ulan Bator Radio said on 27 November that after returning from Moscow, Tsedenbal had addressed the Ulan Bator city party and government leaders and had "emphasized the great significance of the agreement signed in Moscow on the further development of economic relations between the MPR and the Soviet Union for the 1968-1970 period." "In accordance with this agreement," the broadcast said, "the Soviet Union will render our country new additional economic aid in the development of industry and in strengthening the material and technical base of agriculture and of other branches of the economy."

Soviet-Mongolian cooperation was evident in 1967 in military as well as economic matters. On the occasion of the Fiftieth Anniversary celebrations in Ulan Bator on 7 November, the largest military parade in Mongolia's history was held. There were widespread reports of significant increases in Soviet military aid and in numbers of Soviet troops stationed in Mongolia. Soviet tank and missile units participated in the parade. It was also reported that the November aid agreement contained provisions for increased military aid to Mongolia. A Reuters dispatch of 2 January 1968 reported that Soviet infantry, tank, and ground-to-air missile units had been stationed in Mongolia. Moscow radio on 17 January 1968 said that the Mongolian People's Army was devoting a month to the study of the fighting experience and traditions of the Soviet army.

**Relations with China.** Relations between Mongolia and Communist China in 1967 went from cool to frigid. In 1960 the two countries concluded a Treaty of Friendship and Mutual Assistance which provided for a $50 million loan to Mongolia for industrial construction; since then there have been no further aid agreements between the two countries, although a border treaty was signed in 1962. Recent agreements have been limited to trade protocols of minor significance.

The causes of the disputes between China and Mongolia in 1967 were of three kinds: (1) specific diplomatic incidents between nationals of the two countries in Peking and Ulan Bator; (2) the ideological questions involved in the Sino-Soviet dispute; (3) the long-standing national and ethnic antagonisms between Mongols and Chinese. All of these were intensified by the high pitch of extremism in China's Great Proletarian Cultural Revolution during 1967.

Most of the incidents between Mongolians and Chinese occurred in Peking in the course of Red Guard excesses of "revolutionary diplomacy." The most serious incident was in early August, when the official car of the Mongolian ambassador was set afire. The driver, Dashonolt, had allegedly stamped on a portrait of Chairman Mao and was beaten up by Red Guards, who also attacked other Mongolian Embassy personnel and besieged the Embassy for several days. A Czechoslovak official news agency (CTK) report on 9 August described the incident as "the gravest ever to occur in Peking against a socialist state." The MPR and the People's Republic of China exchanged protest notes regarding the incident, each demanding the punishment of the other's nationals alleged to have been responsible for the incident. The Mongolian statement of 9 August said: "The facts show most convincingly that for the present Peking leaders and for those elements deceived and driven by them from among the so-called Red Guards there exists no understanding of the norms of human morality nor a sense of responsibility for the provocations against the peoples of socialist countries—the true friends of the Chinese people."

Earlier in the year there had been numerous instances of violence both in Ulan Bator and in Peking between Chinese and Mongolians. In February Mongolian students broke up an anti-Soviet propaganda display at the Chinese Embassy in Ulan Bator. Meanwhile, the Chinese accused the Mongolians of carrying on a concerted anti-China campaign in the press, publishing, by Peking's count, 120 "anti-China articles" within a three-week period in January and February.

On the ideological level, the Sino-Mongolian dispute turned on the question of "revisionism" and the alleged collusion of the Mongolians with the Soviet Union in the restoration of capitalism on an international scale. The Chinese attempted to turn Lenin's theory of imperialism against the Soviet Union by casting the Soviet Union in the role of a nineteenth-century European colonial power and Mongolia in that of a colony. Mongolia's current five-year plan and its dependence on Soviet aid were subjected to long ideological critiques by the Chinese. The Chinese criticisms were sufficiently close to their mark that the Mongolian leadership could not ignore them or attribute them completely to bad faith. Thus, besides countering with charges that Mao's splittism was "un-Marxist adventurism" and "great-nation chauvinism," the Mongolians were at pains to establish the Marxist orthodoxy of their relationship with the Soviet Union and its plan for economic development. The Mongolians also suggested that Mao was peddling Trotskyism. In an editorial entitled "The Fabrications of the Maoists and Reality," reprinted in *Pravda* on 5 December 1967, *Unen* charged that "Mao Tse-tung's adventurist 'theory' borrowed from the Trotskyites and other traitors of the working class, has nothing in common either with Marxism-Leninism or with the interests of the cause of socialism and national liberation."

Even while taking certain aspects of their ideological debate seriously, neither side was above beating the other with any club at hand. "To begin with," remarked a *Peking Review* article of 29 September, "The Tsedenbal revisionist group, renegade to the proletariat, is a pack of national traitors. The policy it pursues has inexorably pushed Mongolia on to the road of becoming a colony." Thus, at the same time Peking was criticizing the Inner Mongolians for their remnants of Mongol nationalism, it was criticizing the Outer Mongolians for their lack of nationalism. This article went on to make the analogy between Soviet-Mongolian relations and imperialist colonial relations as seen by Marx and Lenin. "It is safe to say that Mongolia is the most heavily indebted country in the world," *Peking Review* observed, claiming that the Mongolian debt to the Soviet Union amounted to ten times the value of all Mongolia's livestock. The heart of the Chinese argument was as follows:

A century ago, Marx wrote in his article *The British Rule in India* that the British colonialist intrusion into India gradually "inundated the very mother country of cotton (India) with cottons." Today, a similiar tragedy is being repeated in Mongolia, the very mother country of animal husbandry, now inundated with Soviet-made animal products—leather shoes, woolen fabrics, canned meat, milk powder and what not. These manufactured goods are made from animals raised in Mongolia, with one Mongolian horse equivalent to a pair of Soviet leather boots, a sheep for two tins of meat, and so on. Mongolia must export its animals to import these goods. Take 1963, for example. According to the obviously doctored figures released by official Mongolian and Soviet circles, the total amount of cattle and sheep purchased by the Mongolian government was 114,000 tons, 80 per cent of which, or 88,100 tons were exported to the Soviet Union. As a result, the number of livestock in Mongolia is fast dwindling, while its debt to the Soviet Union is snowballing. Such is the result of the "disinterested assistance" that the Soviet revisionists claim so shamelessly. If this is "paternal concern," then how is it any different from the capitalist world's law of the jungle?

The Chinese Communists also hit a vulnerable spot in their observation that Mongolia in 1956 had 24,470,000 animals, but in 1966, ten years later, had only some 22 million. The article closed with a quote not from Mao but from Lenin: "The slave who drools when smugly describing the delights of slavish existence and who goes into ecstasies over his good and kind master is a grovelling boor."

An article in *Jen-min Jih-pao* (People's Daily) 10 July by an Inner Mongolian Red Guard unit attacked the "internationalist division of labor" as an excuse for Soviet exploitation of Mongolia. The article said:

The Mongolian revisionist clique has the impudence to say that the Mongolian party instead of following a policy of going it alone, has devoted its efforts mainly to the development of light industry and food industry in accordance with the principle of internationalist division of labor. What a claim! Well, since as you say, you have placed your main emphasis on the development of light industry and food industry, why then do you have to import from the Soviet Union leather shoes, tinned food, cloth, daily necessities, and even toys? Why do you have to buy a Soviet-made toy plastic sheep at the price of a live sheep in Mongolia?

The Mongolian answer to such charges is that relations between the USSR and the MPR are governed by the principles of socialist internationalism, equal rights, close cooperation, and mutual aid rather than exploitation. On 23 October in an article in *Pravda* Tsedenbal said:

It is necessary to stress that the striving to build socialism in isolation, based only on one's own forces, and the negation of the necessity and profitability of cooperation with other countries of socialism, can lead to a divorce of individual countries from the world socialist community and inflict great damage on their national interests. . . . The working people of our country are proudly aware that it was the October Socialist Revolution which opened up the possibility for formerly backward peoples to reduce considerably the path of their socio-economic development and to change from pre-bourgeois relations directly to socialism while bypassing capitalism. This law-governed process was precisely formulated by V. I. Lenin on the basis of the experiences of the October Revolution and the entire world revolutionary process.

In a similar vein, Politburo member Dugersuren, speaking at the opening of the new Ulan Bator television station constructed with Soviet aid, said on 25 September:

> Today's socialist Mongolia is a result of the socialist labor of our people and the correct leadership of the MPRP and the result of nearly a half century of aid, fraternal friendship, and close cooperation between the Mongolian and Soviet peoples. That is why the Mongolian people resolutely reject the clumsy attempts aimed at blemishing the Mongolian-Soviet friendship which is the basis of the prosperity and well-being of our country.

With regard to national and ethnic issues and antagonisms, Mongolia's perennial concern over the long-standing (although now dormant) Chinese claim to Mongolian territory (which the Chinese call Outer Mongolia) was intensified in 1967, as was the historical image of the Han people as enemies of the Mongols. On numerous occasions during the year the leaders of the MPR reiterated their view of the present Peking regime as the great-Han chauvinist successors to the Ch'ing dynasty and the Nationalist government. In his speech at the television station, Dugersuren said that the Peking leaders "are conducting toward our people a policy which resembles the policy of the Manchu emperors and Chiang Kai-shek reactionaries." In the MPR government's official statement of 9 August on the Chinese "anti-Mongolian campaign" it was stated: "The modes and methods of the Peking provocateurs are not new and are well known by the Mongolian people," and that Peking's "malicious intentions" toward Mongolia "have been inherited from the Manchu conquerors and the reactionary Chiang Kai-shek clique, as was repeatedly confirmed by public statements by Mao himself and by his supporters regarding the state sovereignty and national independence of the MPR."

Peking continued its vigorous drive against Mongolian nationalism in Inner Mongolia, and during the year staged many protest demonstrations in the Inner Mongolian capital of Huhehot against the MPR leadership. The largest of these demonstrations followed the seige of the Mongolian Embassy in Peking in August. Ulanfu, a Mongol, long the most important Chinese Communist Party leader in Inner Mongolia, fell victim to the cultural revolution in 1967 and was accused of harboring and abetting the growth of Mongol nationalist sentiment in Inner Mongolia. There were also reports that the cultural revolution in Inner Mongolia had caused a significant number of Mongolians there to flee to the MPR.

**International Views and Policies.** The MPR, with its population of slightly more than a million persons spread over an area about four times as great as the state of California, has always followed a policy of maximizing international contacts as a means of bolstering its independence from its two giant neighbors. This policy has generally had Moscow's support, especially since the beginning of the Sino-Soviet dispute. On the diplomatic level, Mongolia in 1967 concluded agreements to exchange representation with Greece (before the April 1967 *coup* there), Ethiopia, the Congo (B), Tanzania, Mauritania, and Syria. After a goodwill trip to the Middle East and Africa by MPR Foreign Minister L. Toiv early in 1967, Mongolia also set up a permanent mission in Algeria. Japan, after consultations with the MPR, announced its agreement in principle to establish relations between the two countries, but did not actually do so, probably out of deference to objections from the Republic of China on Taiwan, which has never renounced its claim to Outer Mongolia. Diplomatic relations were also resumed in 1967 between the MPR and Iraq, having been interrupted several years ago over the issue of Mongolia's support for the Kurdish separatist movement in Iraq and Iran.

Among the COMECON countries, Mongolia also tried to extend its political and economic contacts, and appeared to seize all possible occasions to take a public stand on major international questions, especially those relating to the international communist movement.

On 21 July Mongolia and Bulgaria concluded the first Treaty of Friendship and Cooperation between the two countries, after a visit by a Bulgarian delegation headed by Todor Zhivkov, First Secretary of the Bulgarian Communist Party. In a luncheon speech on 19 July in Ulan Bator, Zhivkov remarked, "I would like to emphasize with satisfaction that the assessments and concepts of our two Marxist-Leninist parties—the Bulgarian Communist Party and the MPRP—regarding the situation in the international communist movement are identical." (*Rabotnichesko Delo*, Sofia, 19 July 1967.)

This sentiment was echoed by Tsedenbal, who said in his own speech on this occasion:

> The unanimity of our goals, the international solidarity, and the particularly profound loyalty of the Mongolian and Bulgarian people to the friendship and unbreakable alliance with the great Soviet Union, the unshakable faithfulness of the MPRP and the Bulgarian Communist Party to the great Marxist-Leninist teachings and to the general line followed by the international communist and workers' movement jointly worked out by the fraternal parties at the 1957 and 1960 Moscow conferences, represent a sound basis for the successful development of the fraternal friendship and the close and all-round cooperation between the peoples of the Mongolian People's Republic and the Bulgarian People's Republic.

In a joint communique issued on 21 July the two parties declared their common views on a wide range of international questions, favoring the calling of an international conference of communist and workers' parties, expressing solidarity with Cuba, praising the Karlovy Vary conference, and urging the conclusion of a treaty on the nonproliferation of nuclear weapons. The text of the treaty was not published, but Tsedenbal said on 21 July that one of its objects was to promote more effective use of Bulgarian technical and economic aid. The two countries were also said to have agreed on "an exchange of officers" of their military forces. It was not clear what substantial interest Bulgaria had in its relations with Mongolia beyond the desire to accommodate Soviet interests by broadening the international standing of Ulan Bator and by supporting Mongolian and Soviet interests against the Chinese.

Mongolia's forty-sixth National Day was celebrated on 11 July. Official greetings were received from all communist countries except China and Cuba. Cuba's omission might not have been intentional, however, since the Mongolian ambassador to Cuba gave a speech over Havana television 12 July recounting the socialist achievements of the MPR. Regarding Cuba, the ambassador said:

> It is with satisfaction that we emphasize that political, economic, and cultural relations between Mongolia and Cuba are progressing successfully to the advantage of our people, who share common ideas and objectives. The Mongolian people sincerely rejoice over the successes of the sister Cuban nation, under the leadership of Comrade Fidel Castro, both in the construction of a new life and in the defense of the revolutionary successes against the imperialist provocations and aggressions, and our people consider them as their own.

Also held in Ulan Bator was the 27 September-3 October convention of the International Union of Students (see *Front Organizations*).

Regarding the Vietnam and Arab-Israeli war, the MPR consistently backed the Soviet position and defended the Soviet Union against Chinese charges of "covert cooperation with the imperialists." The government released an official statement on the Middle East conflict on 12 June and on 29 August regarding the war in Vietnam. The 12 June statement read in part:

> The Mongolian people and their government believe that at the root of the aggressive actions of the Israeli extremist forces against the peoples of the UAR and other Arab countries are the economic and strategic interests of certain Western powers who for their own and avaricious purposes keep fanning hostilities between Israel and the Arab states. The criminal acts of imperialist circles and their Israeli stooges in the Middle East are a component part of a joint conspiracy by world reaction against the freedom, independence, and social progress of the peoples.

On 22 June Ulan Bator radio praised Kosygin's speech to the UN special session discussing the war, saying that "The Soviet Union again showed its resolve and firmness in protecting the legitimate rights and interests of peoples, victims of aggression, and showed its resolve to protect the world against a destructive thermonuclear war."

The 29 August statement on Vietnam denounced the American bombing of North Vietnam, demanded that US troops and weapons be removed from South Vietnam, and that the US "strictly abide by the Geneva agreements on Indochina."

A Mongolian party and government delegation headed by Sonomyn Lubsan paid a friendship visit to North Vietnam 25-29 December. At a reception in Hanoi North Vietnamese Vice-Premier Nguyen

Duy Trinh said that the Mongolian visit was a "splendid manifestation of the militant solidarity of the fraternal Mongolian people with the Vietnamese people." (Vietnam News Agency 1 January 1968.) Lubsan expressed similar sentiments and said that the meetings and talks "manifested the firm solidarity between the Mongolian People's Republic and the Vietnam Workers' Party and the unshakable will of the peoples of our two countries. . . . We believe that this visit will be an event of particular importance in the history of the fraternal relations between the peoples of our two countries." According to the joint communique issued following the meeting, as reported by Vietnam News Agency 2 January 1968:

> The Mongolian delegation stressed: The party, government and people of the MPR resolutely support the four-point stand of the government of the Democratic Republic of Vietnam and the political program of the National Liberation Front for South Vietnam, the only legitimate representative of the South Vietnamese people, and regard these as the correct basis to settle the Vietnam problem in full conformity with the aspirations of the Vietnamese people, with the 1954 Geneva agreements, and with the interests of peace in Asia and in the world.

**Publications.** Ulan Bator radio reported on 2 November 1967 that the MPR had 56 central and local newspapers and magazines with a total circulation of about 1 million copies. The official party daily newspaper is *Unen* (Truth), which published its 10,000th issue on 5 January 1967. Its editor is Tsendijn Namsray. The party's monthly is *Namyn Amdral* (Party Life). The organ of the Mongolian Revolutionary Union of Youth is *Zaluchuudyn Unen.* The official MPR press agency is Montsame.

# MOROCCO

The Moroccan Communist Party (Parti Communiste Marocain; PCM) was founded in 1943 from the communist groups belonging to the "Moroccan region" of the French Communist Party. The party is banned at present, but continues to operate more or less openly.

The PCM membership is estimated at 500 persons out of a total population in Morocco of 13,451,000 (estimated, 1966). Its first secretary is Ali Yata; Abdallah Layachi and Abdelsalam Bourquia are members of the Politburo and Secretariat; Abdelasis Belal is a member of the Politburo and Simon Levy an alternate member.

**Domestic Views and Policies.**The PCM does not play an important role in Morocco. The opposition to the Government is concentrated in the Union Nationale des Forces Populaire (UNFP) and the Istiqlal Party. Since the PCM's Third Congress, in July 1966, the party has been attempting to build a united front of all "national, progressive, and revolutionary forces," among them being the Labor Union (Union Marocaine du Travail; UMT), the UNFP, the Istiqlal Party, and the PCM.* The party also recognized at its Congress that in order to become a significant force in the country the PCM needed to use less doctrinaire methods of party work and to set up a new organization of the party. The Congress resolution also spoke of the need to rename the party as a step toward "renovating it and winning legality."

In 1967 the PCM tried especially to increase its influence in the UMT. Following the arrest and sentencing to three years in prison of the UMT Secretary-General, Mahjoub Ben Sedik, for having addressed a "disrespectful" telegram to the Director General of the Royal cabinet concerning "Zionists" in the administration, Ali Yata sent a series of protest letters to Prime Minister Mohammed Benhima and letters to the UMT expressing the PCM's full solidarity with any action the UMT might undertake to liberate Ben Sedik. Ali Yata also emphasized the full solidarity of the PCM with the UMT's struggles for the defense of workers' rights and for the Arab anti-Zionist and anti-imperialist cause: "We tell you in a fraternal way, dear comrades, that in all these struggles we are with you, without conditions and without reserve." In closing Ali Yata hailed the UMT, and the "unity of all progressive and revolutionary forces" and "all patriotic anti-Zionist and anti-imperialist forces." (*Solidarité à L'Union Marocaine du Travail,* Casablanca, 12 July.) After Ben Sedik's appeal was rejected in November, Ali Yata urged the UMT to undertake mass action instead of relying on formal protests and again pledged the full support of the PCM for any such action the UMT might organize.

**PCM Program.** The new program of the PCM, worked out at the party's Third Congress and developed throughout 1967, is based on the premise of the "failure of capitalist development" in Morocco. Pointing to the serious problems which still exist after 11 years of independence, the PCM charged that the "liberal-capitalist" road of development chosen by the Moroccan regime had prohibited any true reform and that the "feudal system, the large bourgeoisie, and the economic position of imperialism" remained entrenched, while social conditions deteriorated, territorial unity went unrealized, and democracy was non-existent. According to the PCM, the developing countries cannot succeed through "liberalism" in an age when the "stranglehold of the American imperialists, and the competition from the finished products of advanced countries, and the high price of raw materials and agriculture, which result in the world market's being dominated by the same monopolies, prevent any real head start and weaken the possibility of capital accumulation by classic methods."

The PCM thus has called for a radical change to a noncapitalist road of development which would culminate in the construction of socialism in Morocco. The task of the moment, according to the PCM, was not a direct transition to socialism, but a transition to the "noncapitalist road of

*On 11 August 1967 the UNFP and the UMT issued a communique announcing that they had formed a united political bureau.

development," which would create the conditions for the transition to socialism. The tasks of the "national democratic revolution" were described in a party pamphlet as follows:

(1) On the political plane: the expansion of a healthy democracy giving to the people the means of creative political activity and of constructive mobilization, and which, through the effective guarantee of political and trade-union freedoms (press, assembly, association, strike, etc.) and through the elaboration of a constitution which, within the framework of the constitutional monarchy, would recognize the sovereignty of the people and the effective control of the executive by its electors. Concretely and in the immediate future, that implies the struggle for an end to the state of emergency and the election of a constituent assembly.

(2) In the economic domain: placing in the hands of the state, through nationalization, key sectors of the economy (banks, mines, foreign trade, large monopolist industries) and placing the land in the hands of the working peasantry through expropriation of the feudalists, colonists, and other large agrarian capitalists. Thus the national and democratic state would have the means of industrialization.

(3) In foreign policy: the determined struggle for liberation of territories plundered [by Israel] and the most resolute common action of the Arab world against imperialism and Zionism; active solidarity with all peoples struggling for their independence; positive neutralism and resolute friendship with the socialist countries, the natural allies in the liberation of peoples.

(4) In the social and cultural sphere: the struggle against unemployment, constant amelioration of the standard of living, universal and improved education, and effective recognition of the rights of women and youth, which would show the people that their sacrifices are not in vain and would encourage them to further mobilize their energies. (*La Portée Universelle de la Grande Revolution Socialiste d'Octobre,* pamphlet, Casablanca, November 1967.)

The PCM, in its program and policies, has increasingly appealed to the nationalist sentiment of the Moroccan people. The party argues that capitalism is a system imposed on Morocco by the colonialists and remains essentially foreign to the Moroccan mentality and morals. The PCM thus defines capitalism as "antinational" and socialism—"the goal of the workers, peasants, intellectuals, who form the strong majority of the nation"—as "the purest modern expression of patriotism" (*ibid.*).

**International Views and Policies.** The PCM takes a strongly nationalist position on the question of Morocco's frontiers and territories. It demands that Spain relinquish its hold on Ceuta, Melilla, Ifni, Rio de Oro, and Saguiet el Hamra. In a telegram addressed to King Hassan II, the PCM recommended the mobilization of all the Moroccan people to force Spain to withdraw from Morocco, adding: "[We are ready to] assume all our responsibility and put all our forces in the service of the cause of liberation of Moroccan territories occupied by Spain" (*Al Kifah Al Watani,* 26 May 1967). Speaking over Radio Moscow on 3 November on current problems of the national liberation movement, Ali Yata placed the problem of "Moroccan territories occupied by Spanish Francoists" only second to the problem of the guerrilla wars in the Portuguese territories in Africa.

To the south, the PCM claims Mauritania as Moroccan territory and states that the Ould Daddah regime is simply a "puppet government of the neocolonialists."

The Moroccan border dispute with Algeria has put the PCM in the uncomfortable position of attacking a "progressive" regime for nationalist reasons. On the occasion of the visit of Ould Daddah to Algeria, where he received a warm reception interpretable as a gesture of solidarity against Moroccan territorial claims, the PCM expressed its "uneasiness" on seeing a "progressive regime toward which we [i.e. the PCM] feel respect and sympathy, recognize a servant of colonialism and attribute to him qualities totally in contradiction with the despicable role he was assigned [by his colonialist masters] to play." The PCM declared unjustified the Algerian bonds of friendship with a power "which is in contradiction, in essence as well as in form, with the principles and aims of the Algerian revolution." (*Ibid.,* 21 April.) On another occasion the PCM criticized Algerian students who, during a meeting of solidarity with the Vietnamese people, condemned the attempts of "American imperialists" aligned with "Moroccan reactionaries" to encroach on Algerian territory. The PCM agreed with statements as to the threat of imperialism, but termed "erroneous" the Algerian claim that Morocco was "at the mercy of imperialism." (*Ibid.*, 24 November.)

The PCM issued statements on the Arab-Israeli War strongly denouncing the "imperialist-Zionist aggression" and calling for "relentless struggle" to the end. It refused to accept the UN Security Council's resolution in November on the Middle East, which it said fell far short of "satisfying the dignity of the Arabs and responding to their hopes." The PCM advised that the Arabs should "profit from the resolution's positive aspects to consolidate their position, strengthen their prestige, and develop their struggle to attain their goals," which were "to expel the Zionists from the occupied territories and to gain recognition of the rights of the Palestinian people to return to their homes, enjoy an independent national life, and live in peace and security." (*Ibid.*, 1 December.)

The PCM emphasized in its press and at international conferences that the "success" of the Arabs in the June war was due to "generous and sincere aid" from the Soviet Union. In an exchange of telegrams with Leonid Brezhnev, Ali Yata expressed the party's "profound recognition of the aid, moral and political, as well as material" which the Soviet Government and party had rendered the Arabs in June. "We are certain to be able to count firmly on your support for the Arab people in future struggles," he added. (*Ibid.*, 11 August.)

The PCM expressed its approval of the amelioration of relations between Morocco and the Soviet Union as evidenced in the visit made by King Hassan II to Moscow in October 1966. When King Hassan traveled to Washington in February 1967, the PCM took the stand that this was "natural" since Morocco had to "knock at every door" for aid and especially at the doors of those with a large surplus to give. The PCM warned, however, that this course could lead to "foreign exploitation" and "territorial encroachment," and pointed to the US "massacre" of the Vietnamese and the US arms supplied to Israel. (*Ibid.*, 3 February.) After the visit to Washington, however, the PCM criticized its "meager" results, and, comparing them with the results of King Hassan's visit to Moscow, declared that this was proof that the Soviet Union feels friendship for Morocco, while the US "detests Morocco, laughs at it, and does not want to aid it." The visit also proved, according to the PCM, that the US had no desire to see Morocco independent from its "colonial heritage." (*Ibid.*, 24 February.)

**International Communist Movement.** The PCM has consistently stood in close alignment with the CPSU in the international communist movement. The party hesitated, however, in declaring its support of the Soviet policy line denouncing the anti-Soviet calumnies and the deviations from socialism in Communist China, due perhaps to its desire not to alienate any pro-Chinese elements among the Moroccan left. The PCM also delayed in calling for the convening of an international conference of communist parties. The call for such a meeting had been initiated at the Bulgarian Party Congress in November 1966; it was also given some support at the Hungarian Party Congress held later that month. At the Eighteenth Congress of the French Communist Party, in January 1967, the PCM again declined to express its views on developments in China and on the international conference. Instead, Ali Yata called for the unity of the international communist movement and the opening of discussions on the problems facing it, and only indirectly referred to China:

> The debate should therefore be opened. It should be extensive and profound; it should take the forms that circumstances render advisable and remain open until events decide the issue, even if an agreement cannot be reached. Just as we believe it normal and desirable for calm, serene, and fraternal discussion to be initiated, so do we deplore the refusal to engage in discussion, reject the disposition to impose a certain point of view, and, also, denounce the systematic campaigns of slander against the first socialist country—campaigns that in some quarters take precedence over denunciation of the misdeeds and crimes of the number one enemy of all peoples, American imperialism.

In mid-April, Ali Yata traveled to Bucharest and met with the Secretary-General of the Communist Party of Rumania Nicolae Ceauşescu. The lengthy communique issued following the visit emphasized the need to build the widest possible anti-imperialist front and to give support to national liberation movements throughout the world, and particularly to support the Vietnamese people against US "aggression." The communique also mentioned the "need to reestablish the legitimate rights of the People's Republic of China at the United Nations and in other international organizations." The two sides called for the strengthening of the international communist movement and emphasized the principles of independence, equal rights, noninterference in internal affairs, and proletarian internationalism as basic norms for relations among parties. Recognizing the possibility of differences of views among parties, the two sides declared that "differences of opinion must not affect in any way the friendship and solidarity of collaboration among fraternal parties," and added: "Convinced that what is essential and predominant is that which unites the communist parties, the two delegations hold that under present conditions nothing must be undertaken that might aggravate existing divergencies, add new elements of tension, and deepen the danger of a split."

The views of the PCM had further crystallized, however, when Ali Yata made a lengthy contribution to *Pravda* (5 May) on the events in China and concluded the article with a statement of support for the convening of an international communist party conference. Ali Yata carefully analyzed and rejected the Chinese theses concerning war and peace, the theses concerning "the city and the village," and the theses emphasizing human potential over material. He went on to declare that the policies of Mao Tse-tung and his group had "nothing in common with Marxism-Leninism" and that their positions were a clear departure from the communist movement. Referring to his party's delay in publicizing this assessment of events in China, Ali Yata said that "someone" might see "neutralism" in this position, but the PCM, he declared, was undeviating in its adherence to "revolutionary duties" and had no desire to anathematize a party with so many successes behind it. Ali Yata added that the PCM's criticism at this time must be taken "fraternally" and that the PCM was motivated in its criticism by worry over world reaction to developments in China.

Emphasizing the need at this time for joint anti-imperialist activity, Ali Yata called for an international communist gathering "open to all communist and workers' parties, the main aim of which should be joint action in the struggle against imperialism, the establishment and strengthening of the unity of the world communist movement." He emphasized again that this would not be a conference of "judgment or excommunication, but a conference to mark the triumph of unity in the world communist movement."

Ali Yata has often been the chief spokesman for African communist parties at international communist conferences such as the Cairo seminar on the African national liberation movement in October 1966 and the Baku conference on "The October Revolution and the National Liberation Movement of the Peoples of Asia, Africa and Latin America" in September 1967.

In a contribution to *Pravda* (15 November) on the occasion of the fiftieth anniversary of the October Revolution, entitled "October and the Anti-Imperialist Struggle," Ali Yata hailed the effect of the Soviet experience on the anti-imperialist struggle in the Third World. He claimed that the successes of the socialist states had made it clear to the developing nations that their problems could only be solved by the methods of scientific socialism. He also hailed the fact that today the socialist system renders "disinterested" economic, technical, and military aid to countries fighting for their full independence. Noting with regret the refusal of the Chinese Communist Party to participate in a joint program of aid to the Vietnamese people, Ali Yata declared the need for the international revolutionary movement to "work out a current strategy, calling on a single front to stand up against the imperialist counterrevolution," which, while "recognizing the independence of each revolutionary batallion, would base itself on the might of the socialist system, on all the growing forces of the national liberation movement, and on the workers' movement of the capitalist states."

The PCM continued to maintain close ties with the French Communist Party, at whose Eighteenth Congress, in January, Ali Yata declared the PCM's "great satisfaction" with the agreement between the French Communist Party and the Federation of the Left: "We have many lessons to learn from your brilliant example, made on the firm base of a coherent unified policy, of extreme patience and persistence in efforts, methods, and hard work, in a creative style." Ali Yata declared, further: "We will not neglect to use new methods to promote our unifying efforts to renew the confidence of those discouraged by initial failure, or of those who are defecting, conquered by haste and impatience."

On 23-28 May a delegation of the PCM headed by Ali Yata again visited France at the invitation of the French Communist Party and discussed the international situation and the "imperialist threat" to the Middle East with French party representatives.

Representatives of the PCM also met with representatives of the League of Communists of Yugoslavia, including President Tito, in Belgrade on 20 July and representatives of the Bulgarian Communist Party in Sofia on 27 July. Abdallah Layachi represented the PCM at the Seventh Congress of the Socialist Unity Party of East Germany, in April. Ali Yata, as noted earlier, represented the PCM at the Fiftieth Anniversary celebrations in Moscow in November.

**Publications.** The PCM's central organ is the weekly *Al Kifah Al Watani,* excerpts of which appear in a monthly bulletin in French. Although the newspaper is published regularly, the Moroccan Government holds it under close scrutiny and confiscates objectionable issues. In a letter addressed to King Hassan and calling for freedom of the press in Morocco, Ali Yata complained that *Al Kifah Al Watani* had been seized three times in August and twice in September of 1967.

# NEPAL

The Communist Party of Nepal (CPN) was founded in September 1949 in West Bengal, India, by a small number of Nepali members of the Communist Party of India. Banned in 1952, the party was again legalized in 1956. On 25 December 1960 all political parties in Nepal were banned by royal decree. The CPN's Central Committee decided in 1955 to adopt a temporary acceptance of the monarchy, and in consequence the party was faced with a split between supporters of the new line, led by the party's General Secretary, Keshar Jang Rayamajhi, and dissident elements led by Pushpa Lal Shrestha. Following a number of internal crises between the two factions, during which time the leadership of the Pushpa Lal group moved to India, each group "expelled" the other's leadership from the party during the summer of 1962. The Sino-Indian conflict of October 1962 led to a further split in Pushpa Lal's faction. Although not entirely related to this conflict, the split resulted in the formation of two groups, with Pushpa Lal supporting India, and a minority group led by Tulsi Lal Amatya supporting China. When the Sino-Indian war prompted the major noncommunist antimonarchical party, the Nepali Congress Party, to abandon its campaign against King Mahendra, the CPN dissidents lost their noncommunist "allies."

All factions of the CPN appear to maintain close ties, based on personal associations which date back to the 1940s, with the right Communist Party of India, headed by S. A. Dange.

**Organization and Leadership.** The organizational structure of the CPN, officially "disbanded" by the party, includes local cells; village and town committees; district committees; provincial congress; provincial committees (seven), with a provincial secretariat; the All-Party Congress, with a Central Control Commission; a Central Committee of 17 members; a five-man Politburo, whose most important members are Keshar Jang Rayamajhi and Kamar Shah; and a General Secretary, Rayamajhi. Other prominent members of the Rayamajhi faction are S. K. Upadhyaya, Man Mohan Adhikari (the most popular Communist leader, now in prison), D. P. Adhikari, and Shambu Ram Shrestha (both in exile in India).

The left exile faction of the CPN, although itself divided geographically as well as ideologically into groupings centering on Pushpa Lal (in Banaras) and Tulsi Lal (in Darbhanga), maintained a unified party structure in 1967. Tulsi Lal is General Secretary. The nine-member Politburo consists of Tulsi Lal, Pushpa Lal, Hikmat Singh, Devendra Ray Shrestha, Bharat Mohan Adhikari, Jai Govind Shah, Bharat Roy Joshi, Punne Prataya Rana, and Mahesh Kumar Upadhyaya.

**Domestic Policies and Activities.** In any consideration of the relative strength of the CPN it must be remembered that theoretically parties do not exist in Nepal and that communists (technically, "former communists") aligned with the Rayamajhi faction profess to support this status quo. Before the 1960 ban on parties the CPN claimed to have 6,000 full members and 2,000 cadets (*Samiksha*, 11 June 1963); in addition, large numbers of Nepalis were affiliated with various front organizations, such as the Peasant Association (Kisan Sangh), which claimed a membership of 125,000; the Women's Association (Mahila Sangh); the All-Nepalese Students' Federation; and the Nepalese Peace Committee. Estimates of present CPN membership vary widely, but in any case it is not large. *World Strength of Communist Parties* (1968) gives the estimated figure of 8,000. Other unofficial estimates, however, are in the range of 1,000 to 2,000, and a Nepali source estimates that there are no more than 500 currently active CPN members in the country. The exile faction in India probably numbers 300 to 500, with a smaller number of adherents working in Nepal. The population of Nepal is estimated to be about 10,500,000.

There are two representative bodies in the present political system of Nepal: a four-tier Panchayat or council, which includes primary panchayats (village and town) and higher-level panchayats (district, zonal, and national); and a four-tier "class organization" with local, district, zonal, and national committees. In connection with the latter, the population has been divided into six "classes"—peasants, labor, women, students, youth, and children—and a "class organization" has been established for each. The National Panchayat, which has 125 members, functions as a parliament, but with only limited legislative powers and restricted types of control over the Council of Ministers, which is appointed by the King at his own discretion from members of the National Panchayat.

The general tendency in Nepalese politics in recent years, however, has been toward increased royal power, and even among Nepali Communists the proroyalist line has been gaining in strength. The role of the panchayats in the political life of the country has tended to contract, rather than expand. Only the district panchayats, which have the most extensive administrative powers and which supervise development projects at local and district levels, have had significant powers, and even their role has been reduced of late.

The CPN is in a strong position *vis-à-vis* the present "class organizations," owing both to its own organization of social front groups up to 1960 and to King Mahendra's subsequent concentration on disbanding the organizational framework of the Nepali Congress Party (the only other party with significant political potential), while limiting his actions against the CPN. Within the National Panchayat an estimated 15 to 20 per cent of the membership consists of former or present CPN members or sympathizers. Only a minority of these, however, is thought to be currently in active contact with the CPN. (In the May 1967 National Panchayat elections, with about 40 seats at stake, Communist influence held about steady.) Within the Council of Ministers, two "former Communists," Shailendra Kumar Upadhyaya and Khadga Bahadur Singh, held ministerial posts until their dismissal in a cabinet reshuffle on 10 August 1966. CPN General Secretary Rayamajhi is a member of the National Panchayat and of the powerless but prestigious Raj Sabha (Council of State), an advisory body to the throne. Another source of CPN strength is that, as it is virtually the only group with an active (albeit ambiguous) political program, it represents the only alternative, and therefore has attracted many political activists by default.

Despite the fact that the monarchy's policy against the Nepali Congress Party has increased CPN influence, the CPN operates under several handicaps. Its main strength is in the Kathmandu Valley and the Terai strip adjoining India; in the hill areas its influence is limited to a few places, such as Palpa and Dharan. A significant weakness of the CPN is that nearly all the top party leaders are from the three most prosperous high-caste communities in Nepal—the Brahmans of the Terai and Kathmandu, the Vaisya (commercial) castes of the Newar community of Kathmandu Valley, and the Chettri (Kshyatriya, or warrior, now mostly landowning) castes of the Terai and lower hill areas (see Leo. E. Rose, "Communism Under High Atmospheric Conditions," in R. A Scalapino [ed.], *The Communist Revolution in Asia.* Englewood Cliffs, N. J., 1965, p. 362). Caste antagonisms clearly influence and accentuate rivalries within the party. Rayamajhi is a Brahman, while both Tulsi Lal and Pushpa Lal are Newars. Finally, by its monarchical policy, the Rayamajhi faction of the CPN risks alienating radical and "republican" elements, primarily among students and youth.

During 1967 Pushpa Lal moved toward the acceptance of constitutional monarchy for Nepal, coming around to Rayamajhi's position and hoping to infiltrate the panchayats and the class organizations. This shift of position precipitated a new intrafaction dispute, which surfaced at the exile CPN's Central Committee meetings in Banaras on 26 January-3 February and again in November. The Pushpa Lal group, however, appeared to have lost strength in relation to the Tulsi Lal group, and during the year the center of the left party's activity shifted more to Tulsi Lal's headquarters in Darbhanga.

Particularly damaging to the prestige of the Pushpa Lal group in 1967 were the results of the elections of the Nepali Student Federation at Banaras Hindu University. The candidates supported by Pushpa Lal were beaten by a slate of Nepali Congress Party candidates. The erosion of the strength of the Pushpa Lal group within the left CPN may have been a factor in Pushpa Lal's decision to accept Rayamajhi's line. Tulsi Lal has continued to advocate "national democracy" rather than parliamentary democracy within the framework of a constitutional monarchy.

**Relations with China.** The confrontation between China and India in the Himalayan area and Nepal's desire to remain independent of that confrontation are the basic facts of political life in Nepal. Western observers tend to see CPN activity within this context and often stress the growth of Maoist inclinations among Nepali Communists and their collusion with the Chinese (see, for example, *Washington Post,* 26 November 1967), but in fact pro-Chinese elements are a minority of Nepali Communists and are confined mainly to student groups in Nepal and the Tulsi Lal group in Darbhanga. In 1967 the Chinese continued a policy of cordial to friendly relations with Nepal's royal regime while simultaneously giving limited support to the exile antimonarchy CPN group of Tulsi Lal and to left CPN members in Nepal.

The Left CPN faction extended its influence at Kathmandu's Tribhuvan University in 1967. In May all four officers' positions of the University Students' Union were won by pro-Maoist student left CPN members, who defeated the Nepali Congress-backed slate in strongly contested elections. It was widely suspected that King Mahendra himself gave some tacit support to the CPN-backed candidates in the form of judicious and selective police activities, in order to weaken the Nepali Congress Party. The Rayamahji faction apparently played little part in these events.

The pro-Maoist student Tribhuvan University Study Group, which is associated with the left CPN, includes among its leading figures Govinda Roy Joshi, Khrishna Das Shrestha, Nara Devi Natpackho, Bhagwan Ratna Tuladhan, Tirtha Lal Maharjan, and Thamel Triratna, all of whom are Newars and belong to the left CPN. There is an advisory committee to the Study Group consisting of Janardan Acharya (the group's contact with the Chinese embassy), Mohan Pokharel, Nirmal Aryal, and Mohan Chand. There are, in addition, four regional groups established for the areas of the eastern Nepal Terai, eastern Nepal hills, central Nepal Terai and hills, and western Nepal.

Pro-Maoist activity also flared up at the annual fair held in Kathmandu in the summer. On King Mahendra's birthday, 1 July, pro- and anti-Chinese demonstrations occurred in the neighborhood of the Chinese pavilion, which featured a portrait of Mao Tse-tung in equal prominence with that of King Mahendra.

Throughout 1967 the Chinese encouraged numerous anti-American and anti-Indian demonstrations. What part the CPN played in this policy is not clear, beyond the collusion of the left CPN student elements with the Chinese. There were reports that some Nepalese Communists were in touch with the Naxalbari insurgents near the India-Nepal border (*Times of India,* 23 June 1967), and a few members of the left CPN suspected of planning a peasant uprising in Nepal were arrested by the government in this area in November. The Nepalese newspaper *Naya Sandesh* on 27 October reported that Indian government sources in Bihar state claimed that some of the CPN exiles in India were joining with the left Indian Communists to plan uprisings in Nepal.

**Publications.** The procommunist weekly *Samiksha* (Analysis), published in Kathmandu, is edited by a "former Communist" Madan Dickshit, who is a close associate of S. K. Upadhyaya. When the party was legal, until 1960, it had an official organ, *Narayug* (New Age).

# NETHERLANDS

The Communist Party of the Netherlands (Communistisch Partij Nederland; CPN) was founded in 1918 as the Communist Party of Holland; the name was changed in 1936. CPN membership in 1967 was approximately 12,000 out of a population of 12,573,000 (estimated 1967).

The political influence of the CPN has always been limited. In the general election of February 1967, however, the Communists registered fairly significant gains. They received 248,000 votes, or 3.6 per cent of the total cast, and won five seats in the 150-member Second Chamber of the Dutch Parliament. This constituted an overall gain of one seat and 75,000 votes over the previous election in 1963. Most observers gave credit for this improved performance to the growing appeal of the communist program and to effective campaign efforts directed at the broadest possible audience. This included such diverse groups as Roman Catholics, old-age pensioners, small tradesmen, professional people, and students in addition to the more obvious laboring classes. All, presumably, were expected to find some area of appeal in the CPN manifesto issued in January. The Communists distributed a million copies, calling on the government to make more funds available for municipalities, housing, education, and the fight against unemployment. The money was not be be derived from higher taxation, but from a cut of one billion guilders in defense expenditures. In addition, free demonstration rights, nationalization of natural gas and oil resources, and freeing of wage policies, were important points raised. While the program appeared to be well received, analysts attributed the Communists' increase in voting strength in part to a new tendency toward political experimentation among the electorate which favored the more extreme parties. Rising unemployment and economic uncertainty were other important factors benefitting the communists. As in previous elections, they scored most heavily in Amsterdam, Rotterdam, and other large industrial centers in the western part of the country.

**Organization and Leadership.** During the election campaign and most of 1967 the CPN remained under the leadership of Paul de Groot, who held the title of party Chairman. An old-line Stalinist, de Groot was General Secretary of the CPN from the end of World War II until he became Chairman in 1962. A controversial leader, he had to cope with much dissension in the party over the years. When in the fall of 1967 he announced his resignation, he accepted an appointment as an honorary member of the Central Committee. Henk Hoekstra, more pro-Moscow-oriented than his predecessor, moved up to become party head and was instrumental in an extensive restructuring of the party organization. A new Central Committee of 33 members and four deputies, reduced in number from 37 members and 5 deputies and including replacements for 15 former members, was authorized to make all political decisions; it quickly announced that it would convene more frequently in order to be able to provide more intensive guidance. In addition an Executive Committee was chosen to "conduct the practical activities of the party in a business-like manner." The Executive Committee members were Henk Hoekstra, Chairman; Roel Walraven, Organizational Secretary; Joop van Esch, Administrative Secretary; Marcus Bakker, Chairman of the Second Chamber group in Parliament; Joop Wolff, editor in chief of the party newspaper *De Waarheid;* Cees Jimkers, responsible for national municipal-council work; and Ab van Turnhout, deputy editor in chief of *De Waarheid.* Changes in the party organization, it was announced, had made a Secretariat superfluous. (*De Waarheid,* 15 January 1968.)

**Domestic Policies.** The CPN is fundamentally maverick in character. Under de Groot it tried to adhere to Stalinist concepts of communist theory and practice, but insisted on autonomy and emphasized that it must permit itself to be led only by its responsibility to the Dutch people: "Socialism can only be achieved in the Netherlands along a road of its own ... only take shape for us on the basis of Dutch circumstances and traditions" (*ibid.*, 9 June 1967). This road was mapped out by the Twenty-First Congress of the party, in 1964, which proclaimed a "new orientation" policy. Its goal was to be the creation of a unified political party which would concentrate on issues of national importance and demand that Dutch international activity also serve these interests. This approach foresaw not only unity of action between Communists and socialists, but also the possibility and probability of winning the support of Roman Catholic and Protestant Christian circles.

The Twenty-Second Congress, in December 1967, was the most important event of the year for the CPN. Besides reaffirming the "new orientation" policy, the congress served as an occasion to promulgate basic theses that would guide the Communists in the future. On the "struggle for national independence and progress" the party took a strong stand against the present government, which it declared had taken the "first steps toward interference with parliamentary democracy." Under the heading of "democracy and the party system" the CPN rejected "all interference with the existing election system of proportional representation" and called for "reunification of the workers' movement," cooperation between "Communist and socialist workers in the trade-union movement," and unity of action with "progressive Christians." Guarantees against unemployment, substantial wage increases, and a reduction of working hours were demanded. Peace and disarmament were other important topics. In particular, the CPN wanted the Netherlands to practice neutrality, reject nuclear arms, and insist on the removal of nuclear bases, NATO establishments and the German troop installations at Budel. Complete withdrawal from NATO was the ultimate objective. Negotiations and plans for a nonproliferation treaty were rejected as a "fraud."

The strengthening of the party was included in the basic theses as a prerequisite for further progress. It was recognized, however, that new strength would "never result from a spontaneous development," and instead would require "tenacious and persistent work among the masses." "Rightist opportunism and bourgeois inclinations," manifest in "lack of militancy against capitalism" and "failing to understand the significance of democratic centralism," were noted as trends to be opposed. Means advocated to assure improvement included more extensive and efficient work at the factory level and the distribution of more "topical and militant" information and propaganda. CPN ideology, in summary, emphasized "unification of all antimonopolistic forces as a first step toward renewal of society based on Marxist—Leninist ideology." (Discussion program of the Twenty-Second Congress, published in *De Waarheid,* 10 October, and *Politiek en Cultuur,* November 1967.)

This outline of communist tasks for the future showed little divergence from the basic pronouncements of the past. Outgoing Chairman Paul de Groot, in fact, emphasized that the CPN was not in need of reform or rejuvenation, and hailed it as the "most youthful of all parties." Conceivably this was an exhortation to the new leaders not to make major changes in party orientation. Continuation of the existing party line was not only a hope, but appeared to be likely in view of the favorable general election returns, which stilled some voices of criticism in party ranks. The CPN also had scored rather highly in the fall of 1966 when the majority in the Lower House of Parliament voted to permit the admission of communist representatives to the Foreign Affairs and Defense committees. Such participation had been denied since 1948. Lifting of the ban was considered an impressive victory and a credit for CPN policymakers who had advocated pursuit of truly national political goals.

A few communist front organizations, limited in membership though they may be, have played a part in spreading the communist creed in the Netherlands. The most important is the youth organization, Netherlands General Youth Union, (Algemeen Nederlands Jeugdverbond), which is the main communist vehicle for recruiting future members. Other fronts appeal to special interests, such as the peace movement, Netherlands Peace Council (Nederlandse Vredesraad); the organization of former resistance fighters, United Resistance 1940-1945 (Verenigd Verzet 1940-1945); and the Netherlands Women's Movement, *Nederlandse Vrouwenbeweging.*

**International Views and Policies.** For a number of years the CPN managed to remain an apparently neutral preserve practically insulated from the political and ideological pressures of the Sino-Soviet rift. When the CPN could no longer maintain this position, in 1963, it started to perform a tightrope act. For instance, it sided with the CPSU's peaceful coexistence policy, but warned against revisionism. It criticized the Chinese for their attitude toward the Russians, and the Russians for religious repression. Maintenance of the balance was always coupled with ever more emphatic pleas for autonomy. The discomfort of the CPN at the thought of association with any big communist party abroad—the French and Italian parties were also highly suspect—at last was starkly revealed to all in Brussels in 1965. Here, at the meeting of West European communist parties, the Dutch refused to sign the concluding declaration, maintaining that it was impossible for regional conferences to issue binding declarations. It has commonly been assumed that dissension among the CPN delegates was largely responsible for the refusal.

Whatever the motive in 1965, the CPN's action was the beginning of an accelerating move by the party to a position of virtual international isolation. An invitation to the Karlovy Vary conference (24 April-26 April 1967) was refused, with the CPN explaining: "The manner in which the conference is staged is contrary to the most elementary notions of party democracy and normal relations between parties of the working class." The subject of the conference—problems of European security—was criticized as being "very vague": "European security cannot be seen as detached from political developments in Asia and Africa." Further, the point of view outlined in the invitation was said to be "typically revisionist" and thus of a type "most strongly condemned" by the CPN. (*De Waarheid*, 21 March.)

Attendance at Moscow celebrations on the occasion of the fiftieth anniversary of the October Revolution was also ruled out. In general "experience has taught that physical presence at meetings and congresses will be explained as approval of past policies. The Communist Party of the Netherlands will therefore not participate in an international conference which intends to obligate other communist parties to support revisionist standpoints." (*Ibid.*, 8 November.) Similarly an invitation to participate in the consultative conference in Budapest in 1968 drew a negative reply. In this instance objections were raised against the plan for adoption of binding resolutions, in the belief that "the outcome of the consultation has already been decided." (Letter of the Central Committee of the CPN, *ibid.*, 19 January 1968.) The effectiveness of international conferences was also refuted by the new party leader, Henk Hoekstra, at the CPN congress in December 1967: "The problem of combating revisionism and dogmatism is the exclusive concern of each party. The manner in which this is to take place must be determined by each party alone. It cannot come to pass through an international conference. Quite the contrary, under the present circumstances, such a conference would not lead to the solution of a single problem. It would only worsen the situation and could lead to breaks and fractionalism." (*De Waarheid*, 1 March 1968.)

Even the rank and file of Dutch Communists were discouraged from traveling to foreign communist-ruled countries. A resolution was actually passed at the meeting of the party's Central Committee on 20 March 1967 to ban organized vacation trips: "Complaints show that some elements in power are misusing these vacation trips to try to win members of the CPN for their rightist course, to violate the autonomy of the CPN, and to subject our party to their harmful anti-Leninist policies." (*Ibid.*, 1 April.)

The isolation of the CPN was shown to be virtually complete at the time of its own congress in December 1967. Delegations from abroad were conspicuous by their absence. At the previous congress, in 1963, 12 foreign parties were represented and 27 sent greetings. In 1967, salutations were received only from the CPSU, the Hungarian Socialist Workers' Party, and the MAKI faction of the Israeli Communist Party. Even the Rumanian Communists remained aloof, although in September their party—the only one invited—had sent four delegates to a festival staged by the newspaper *De Waarheid*.

Physical isolation, however, did not coincide with refusal to comment on the international scene or to take sides in issues of contention among Communists in various parts of the world. There were repeated CPN demands for US troop withdrawal from Vietnam and an end to Dutch government relations with South Vietnam, together with calls for greater support for the "Help for Vietnam" organization that tries to provide financial assistance for the North. Solidarity with the Greek people and abhorrence of the "fascist regime of the Greek NATO generals" was expressed. In a similar vein, the CPN expressed sympathy and friendship with the Communist Party of Indonesia and opposition to the "illegal and cruel government of the junta of generals which grabbed the power of government with the help of American and Dutch colonialists." In the latter case the CPN requested an end of all assistance for the Indonesian ruling group by the Netherlands, "whether hidden under a hypocritical cloak of development aid or not." (All quotations from *Politiek en Cultuur,* January 1968.) Even the illegal West German communist party was criticized: "As revanchism and re-emerging overt Nazism in the Federal Republic constitute the main threat in Europe today, we must note with bitterness the complete passivity of the communists in West Germany" (*De Waarheid,* 21 March 1967).

Some positive reaction by the CPN to foreign communist party activities was recorded in 1967: "In the international communist movement there is now developing a realistic current of communist parties who want something else and who are looking for a solution to the present problems on the basis of scientific discussions without interference, formation of factions, etc." (Henk Hoekstra, quoted in *De Waarheid,* 8 November). In this type of comment the Dutch embrace the communist parties of Norway, Sweden, Rumania, and a number of unidentified Latin American countries. All are given credit for their pursuit of independence and equal rights for communist parties. Hope for a resumption of friendly contacts with the Communist Party of Cuba and praise for North Korean policies that run parallel with those of the CPN, are additional positive approaches. In view of the Arab-Israeli war, the situation in Israel was the subject of special scrutiny by the CPN. The behavior of the pro-Jewish communist faction in that country (MAKI) received unstinting approval, while the Soviet support of "Pan-Arab chauvinism . . . overtly aimed at the destruction of Israel" was not given the slightest endorsement.

Naturally the actions of the CPSU and the Chinese Communists were a matter of continuous concern to the Dutch party. By 1967 hesitation to state a position bluntly had virtually disappeared: "Even after the removal of the renegade Khrushchev from the leadership of the Russian communist party, friendly relations . . . were made impossible by intervention and intrigues from that side." Dealing with the CPSU was regarded as impossible because it was guilty of "interference and plotting . . . mainly through its accomplices in the GDR and Czechoslovakia." (*De Waarheid,* 20 October.) Predicting change, Paul de Groot stated in a speech on 23 February: "The Soviet working class will definitely put an end to reformistic policies introduced by Khrushchev, and completely restore the principles of Leninism in the country and put them into practice in Europe and Asia." Whatever the developments, the CPN intended to try to remain detached and autonomous: "The manner in which the CPSU chooses to conduct its foreign policy is its own affair; the manner in which the CPN choses to take a stand on foreign policy is equally well its own affair." (*De Waarheid,* 7 November.) Taking such a position the CPN was quite prepared to remark that the "hostile acts committed against the Chinese Communist Party during the Khrushchev government . . . are the source of later fraternal strife" (*ibid.,* 21 March). Yet, putting the blame for the Sino-Soviet rift on the Soviet Union did not automatically clear the Chinese of all wrongdoing. Instead the CPN was willing to issue a reminder that from the beginning it had been against the 1964 "proposal" of the Chinese Communist Party "for a new line" in the international communist movement, adding that it "continues to reject attempts by that party to establish new Marxist-Leninist parties opposing the old communist parties." In spite of such opposition, the CPN stated that it did not "want to participate in the slander directed at the Chinese Communist Party and its acknowledged leadership," objecting to that slander on the ground that it had "assumed the character of a cold war against the Chinese People's Republic." (*Ibid.,* 20 October).

**Publications.** The most important medium of information for the CPN is the party's daily newspaper, *De Waarheid* (Truth), published in Amsterdam. A theoretical journal, *Politiek en Cultuur* (Politics and Culture) is issued monthly. There is also a Dutch edition of the *World Marxist Review,* entitled *Vraagstukken van Vrede en Socialisme* (Problems of Peace and Socialism). *Kontrast* is a party quarterly for young intellectuals and artists. A special election paper, *De Rode Amsterdammer* (The Red Amsterdammer) was issued three times early in 1967 and had a distribution of 20,000 copies each.

\* \* \*

There are some dissident communist groups in the Netherlands. Gerben Wagenaar, a former party Chairman and resistance hero, left the CPN in 1958 in protest against its continued anti-Khrushchevian programs. He founded a revisionist movement called the "Brug" (Bridge) but did not succeed in turning it into a real political force.

In 1967 the party again considered the case of Friedl Baruch, expelled from the CPN in 1966 for his troublesome opposition. Baruch contested his expulsion, and in 1967 a committee of inquiry was set up to investigate the charges. The final conclusion was that Baruch had been guilty of "deliberate and inadmissable deceit" and "sowing distrust of the party's leaders and spreading personal insinuations about them"; consequently his expulsion was "fully justified." (*De Waarheid,* 27 December.)

Of greater concern are the pro-Chinese radical splinter groups that appear to specialize in heavy criticism of CPN policies and leaders. Most important is the Marxist-Leninist Center in Rotterdam, which is headed by Nico Schrevel. Another active group has its base in Amsterdam and is headed by Chris Bischot; it was established to publish a pro-Chinese paper called the *Rote Vlag* (Red Flag). Late in 1966 the Rotterdam group began publishing its own paper, the *Rode Tribune.* Both publications appear to center their efforts less on pro-Chinese propaganda than on criticism of the CPN and its hopes to become a unified national party. Similar trends are apparent in *De Kommunist,* a monthly distributed from Amsterdam. A Marxist-Leninist youth group, the Netherlands Communist Youth League, was founded in 1966 and the next year started to issue *Aktie* (Action), aimed at the "vanguard, the shock troops of the revolutionary youth of the Netherlands."

# NEW ZEALAND

The Communist Party of New Zealand (CPNZ) was founded in December 1920. Almost alone among the established communist parties in the developed countries of the world, the CPNZ has since 1963 followed a pro-Peking line while retaining its name and the major part of its membership. As the present General Secretary of the party has put it: "Our party is unique in the Western World in one respect, in that we refused to be part of the world-wide revisionist betrayal and that the bulk of our membership took a Marxist-Leninist stand and are part of the great new development of Marxism-Leninism" (*New Zealand Communist Review*, July 1967).

There is also a smaller pro-Moscow splinter group, of perhaps 100 members, called the Socialist Unity Party. It is led by the former CPNZ National Chairman, George Jackson, who resigned from the parent party in 1966.

Both the CPNZ and the Socialist Unity Party are legal.

CPNZ strength has never been great, on either the national or the local level. No communist candidate for the New Zealand Parliament has ever been elected. The best showing by such a candidate was made in 1931 by J. H. Edwards, who received 6.15 per cent of the vote of his constituency. In the 1966 national elections the total communist vote was 1,207. Party membership has declined from a high of about 2,000 at the end of World War II to an estimated 300 to 400 at present. The population of New Zealand is 2,712,000 (1967 estimate).

**Organization and Leadership.** The leading organs of the CPNZ include the National Committee, the Political Committee, and the Secretariat of the National Committee, together with district committees and party branches. The General Secretary of the party is Victor G. Wilcox. The party press and other sources provide only fragmentary information concerning the CPNZ leadership. Members of the National Committee include John Foulds, Ralph Hegman, W. McAra, Hugh McLeod, Ray Nunes, H. A. Ostler, and Rita Smith. Nunes is a member of both the Political Committee and the Secretariat; McAra and Hegman are members of the Political Committee. Ostler is the party's Auckland District Secretary. Pat Kelly is a member of the Wellington District Committee.

**Domestic Views and Policies.** The cornerstone of CPNZ domestic views and policies is hostility to "social-democratic ideology," which is seen by the party as the Siren to which all "revisionists" in the world ultimately succumb. In New Zealand "social-democratic ideology" is regarded by the party as the primary obstacle to the development of communist consciousness and a mass communist party; its stronghold is considered to be the Labor Party and the Social Credit Party, which have preempted worker support and robbed the CPNZ of any real hopes for electoral successes.

In response to this situation, the CPNZ, instead of watering down revolutionary goals as communist parties in Australia, Great Britain, and other countries have done, has chosen to break completely with social-democratic movements and to disavow any expectation of a possible transition to socialism through electoral processes. In practice, however, this stance has left the CPNZ with virtually no coherent political program; the party dares not advocate violent revolution, and itself acknowledges that "revolutionary potentialities" in New Zealand are practically nil. Under such circumstances, about all the party can do is agitate over specific grievances against "class enemies" and the government, while maintaining that the capitalist system in New Zealand is heading for inevitable collapse. Lack of direction and low morale within the party are thus more or less constant problems for the leadership, and are frequently the subjects of reports and criticisms by party leaders.

One of the most important continuing subjects of extensive intraparty discussion is the nature and proper role of the party. Two of the most important contributions in 1967 to this continuing discussion and self-appraisal by the party were the reports delivered by General Secretary Wilcox to a meeting of the National Committee in early June and to a meeting of the Political Committee in November. The more important of the two was the November report, lengthy excerpts from which were published in the January-February 1968 issue of the *New Zealand Communist Review*. An indication of the scope and importance of this report was an editorial note which prefaced the published portions: "The Editorial Board regrets that this comprehensive report cannot be published in full, as it mainly deals with internal political and organizational aspects in the building of a Marxist-Leninist Communist Party which it is considered not desirable to make available to the enemies of our party and of the working class. It is, however, considered that the extracts published will be of value." In the published part of this report Wilcox observed: "We in the Communist Party of New Zealand face this problem of how to fully relate our Marxist-Leninist thought to our activity. As you know, we are seriously trying to tackle this, recognizing it as our primary task at this stage, due to having inherited many bad ideas from the past."

With regard to its nature and ultimate goals, the party leadership stresses that it is not trying to build the CPNZ into a mass party, lest it suffer corruption by "trade unionism" and abandon revolutionary objectives. Nor, in the opinion of the present leadership, should the party think of itself as a "'left' subsidiary or 'ginger group' trying to goad the trade union movement into revolutionary action," since such a stance would ultimately lead to "tailism." ("Ginger group" is the phrase used by S. W. Scott to describe the party; Scott is a former General Secretary of the CPNZ who resigned from the party shortly after the intervention in Hungary by the USSR in 1956, and who is now regarded by the CPNZ as a revisionist heretic.) While the party does not totally eschew participation in the elections, it wages a constant campaign against "parliamentary illusions" and probably finds its poor electoral showing a source of embarassment. Wilcox's November report exhorted party leaders as follows:

> We must be clear as to what is our immediate objective when we talk of party building. Do we still think in terms of a mass movement of which our party is a major numerical section? In other words, a mass communist party? I think very often we do, and until we drop this illusion and realize it is one road to "belief in the inevitability of continued legality," to parliamentarianism, to revisionism, we will make no progress along the lines of our political and organizational decisions earlier this year.

With regard to its style of work and activities, the party is constantly criticizing itself for "splashing about in the same old pool," that is, for speaking in generalities and cliches to a narrow audience of already convinced adherents. These criticisms, however, never seem to move successfully to the level of particulars, except to criticize lack of particularity itself and to call for more thought and greater effort in the attempt to apply the general principles derived from a Maoist view of reality. As Wilcox put it in his November report:

> When we have another critical and self-critical look at our work at Political Committee level, we will have to face up to the fact that in many ways all we end up with is general policy, which policy, not particularized to meet specific local or industry conditions, is all that we have to work on. We remain, in fact, far too vague.

The CPNZ goes very far in its advocacy of the thought of Mao Tse-tung, arguing the Chinese point of view that Mao is the greatest Marxist-Leninist in everything from political tactics to philosophy. This theme was treated in Wilcox's reports and speeches and in numerous articles in the party press. The most elaborately argued brief for Mao presented by the party leadership in 1967 was a long article by Ray Nunes, "Some Aspects of Mao Tse-tung's Contribution to Marxist-Leninist Theory," published in the August and September issues of the *New Zealand Communist Review*. According to Nunes (in the August installment), the article was written "to point to some of the most important of Mao's theoretical achievements, to indicate where possible what is new in them, and to consider some of their implications for the practical work of a party striving to be a Marxist-Leninist party in all respects." It is probable, however, that the article was written not so much in the hope of spelling out any specific implications of Mao's thought for party work in New Zealand as in an attempt to justify or rationalize the CPNZ's pro-Peking line in other than tactical or even opportunist terms and, at the same time, to improve the party's already high standing in Peking's eyes by giving the Chinese a

Western defender of the primacy of the thought of Mao. The Maoist premises that Nunes cites as applicable to New Zealand remain quite general: namely, that the struggle against "imperialism," the international class enemy, is irreconcilable; but, in effect, that strategically, "all reactionaries are paper tigers" and that the long-term struggle, in New Zealand and all other countries, will issue in ultimate victory if the "proletariat" perseveres on the right path. Citing the importance of the Maoist "mass line" and of "serving the people," Nunes described the mass line as a "basic, guiding concept for all fields of party work" and the notion of "serving the people" as the proper basis for the ideological remolding of New Zealand comrades. He also linked hostility to "social-democratic ideology" with the Maoist line which stresses that the path of "revisionism" is the high road to capitalism.

The party's heavy stress on the concept of the "mass line" is in part doubtlessly meant to counteract criticism from the group led by George Jackson (which formed the Socialist Unity Party) that the CPNZ had effectively cut itself off from the working class and the masses by its extreme revolutionary line. An anonymous article, "Our Practice and our Mass Work" in the December *New Zealand Communist Review,* made the following remarks about the proper role and nature of the party which appear to be a reply to such "revisionist" critics:

> We differ fundamentally with the revisionists, social-democrats and the economists on the question of the vanguard role of the party, in our attitude towards the vital question of power, on the dictatorship of the proletariat and many other fundamental principles. There can be no compromise on the need for revolution. When these people, because of our lack of compromise on these issues, accuse us of "sectarianism," "narrow outlooks," etc.—their favorite attack—they are only seeking to hide their own utter lack of principle or clear lack of understanding of Marxism-Leninism. Marxist-Leninists have no need of rigidity or inflexibility in tactics in developing united-front work or building unity among the people. We have confidence that people will make revolution, in their own way and own time. Because people do not readily accept in their present time and situation all the ideology we try to present is no reason for departing from that ideology, but only presents the task of developing tactics to enable people to understand more easily and quickly what we mean. Having a "detached," "advanced" ideology, if we are modest in our presentation, consistently work for the interests of the people, does not isolate us from people at all.

At the end of the year, Wilcox issued a public message urging all New Zealand comrades to "place socialism on the agenda." Still struggling with the problem of relating tactics to revolutionary theory, Wilcox's statement asserted that world capitalism was "approaching dissolution" and said: "That is why the Communist party says: 'Fight on all progressive issues and knock back monopoly's plans to reduce living standards while increasing its profits; but do not fail to place socialism on the agenda, for it is the only solution.'" The statement further said that the CPNZ was confident that in 1968 "new and more effective forms of militant action" would be "found and developed" by its followers. (*People's Voice,* 13 December.)

**International Views and Activities.** The position of the CPNZ on international issues is straightforwardly that of Peking. For its part, the Chinese Communist Party gives much prominence to the pro-Chinese articles and statements of the CPNZ and never fails to give New Zealand Communists a most warm reception in Peking. The New China News Agency on 26 October carried extensive excerpts from and favorable comments on Nunes's article, noting with approval that he agreed with the definition of Mao Tse-tung's thought as "Marxism-Leninism of the era in which imperialism is heading for total collapse and socialism is advancing to world-wide victory."

Within the world communist movement, the CPNZ criticizes and repudiates not only the "revisionism" of the CPSU and the parties aligned with it, but also the "centrism" of communist parties which avoid taking sides in the Sino-Soviet dispute. In his June report to the National Committee Wilcox explained:

> By centrists we mean those who are trying to steer a course between Marxism-Leninism and revisionism. Such a trend has developed in Japan and north [*sic*]

Korea, to the joy of both the imperialists and their revisionist allies. This trend is expressed in the policy and actions of both the Korean Workers' Party and the Communist Party of Japan, both of whom were firmly in the Marxist-Leninist camp and in complete opposition to modern revisionism as the main danger to the world Communist movement. But now they lay the stress on the "dangers of dogmatism," inferring that the Communist Party of China is trying to dominate the world movement. These parties speak all the time of preserving "party independence." They support the false cry for "unity on some things," even if basic principles have to be thrown overboard. (The Soviet cry for "joint action on Vietnam" is an example of this.)

If we look back into history we will find that there were many centrists in Lenin's day; and that, almost without exception, they ended up in the camp of social-democracy.

Wilcox claimed that "independence of parties" in this context amounted in fact to subservience to the Soviet party. Singling out the Japan Communist Party for criticism on this point, he said: "It is interesting to note that when the Japanese Party, after their change of position from one of open attack on the Soviet leaders to silence, asked our party to send greetings to their congress [in October 1966], they requested us 'for tactical reasons' to leave out any attack on revisionism. So much for the 'independence of parties!'" (*New Zealand Communist Review,* July.)

At a meeting in February the CPNZ Political Committee adopted a resolution supporting the Great Proletarian Cultural Revolution. The resolution, published in the *People's Voice* (1 March) said that the cultural revolution was an "absolutely essential development for the prevention of any return to capitalism." Claiming that Mao had restored Lenin's teaching that the transition from socialism to communism was a long historical period under the dictatorship of the proletariat during which class struggle continued, the resolution further observed: "It is not surprising that such a development [i.e., the cultural revolution] will meet with opposition internally and externally. Every movement which has advanced the cause of socialism and the liberation of mankind has had to triumph over more or less severe opposition according to the circumstances of the time."

With regard to the question of convoking a world conference of communist parties, the CPNZ Secretariat issued a statement in December supporting Chinese opposition to such a conference. The statement (*People's Voice,* 13 December) said in part that the immediate aim of the Soviet leaders in calling for such a conference was "to line up a number of satellite communist parties—most of which are Communist in name only—in order to denounce China in the name of communism," and added: "Any Soviet sponsored 'world conference' can only be a blow against the great majority of mankind. It can only be a conference to rubber-stamp policies of collaboration with imperialism and betrayal of socialism."

Upon the outbreak of the Arab-Israeli war in June, the CPNZ predictably gave full support to the Arab cause and attacked the Soviet Union for betraying that cause. Wilcox on 14 June issued a statement on behalf of the party declaring that the CPNZ supported the "Arab liberation movement in its struggle against American and British imperialism" and condemning the war waged by the Israelis as an "aggression in the interests of the imperialists." Continuing, the statement said: "[The CPNZ] condemns, too, the false front of support for Arab liberation put up by the Soviet revisionists and their allies, who, from the outset, had no intention of confronting US imperialism, but whose words led the Arab states into believing that they were prepared to intervene." (*People's Voice,* 14 June.)

The CPNZ also suggested that the Israelis were inadvertently helping to foster anti-Semitism and fascism. A prominent article in the 28 June *People's Voice* stated: "In supporting Israel and Zionism, the Jewish people are in reality bolstering those very forces that gave rise to fascism—the rulers of the big imperialist powers who could at a moment's notice produce new Hitlers and new pogroms."

Nothing but protracted struggle in the Middle East was seen by the party as a possibility for the near future. In the CPNZ view, the Arab struggle against Israel is a part of world-wide irreconcilable class struggle, and thus no near-term political solution is even possible, let alone likely. "The Jewish problem will not be solved short of abolishing classes," said the 28 June *People's Voice.*

New Zealand's involvement in the Vietnam war continued to be an important theme for agitation and propaganda by the party in 1967, though less so than in 1966. The party, however, made only occasional references to Sino-Soviet differences over Vietnam, following Peking's relative caution on this point so as not to aggravate any differences with Hanoi. There was some indication that the party leadership found it difficult to maintain party interest in the Vietnam issue. Wilcox in his June report said:

> The Vietnam issue has for us special importance and we will not be correct if, in practice, we allow the central point of the anti-imperialist fight today to drop out for periods while we solely concentrate on the struggle around falling living standards. This won't be done by just bringing the Vietnam issue forward from time to time in these struggles, although it is correct to show the connection between New Zealand's involvement in the aggressive war policies of US imperialism and our falling living standards. It will only be done by consistent party activity both of a direct open nature and through our members who are active in the broader protest movement. To some extent, particularly as far as direct party activity is concerned, we have failed here. Recently a circular was sent out noting this and calling for action, but little has as yet been reported.

CPNZ leading members and delegations visited China on numerous occasions in 1967. General Secretary Wilcox arrived for a visit in Peking on 8 March and met with Mao Tse-tung on 12 March. He visited Canton on 15 March and departed the next day. For the May Day celebrations the CPNZ sent a delegation headed by Ralph Hegman; the delegation toured China and returned to New Zealand on 21 May. Hugh McLeod and Pat Kelly visited China in early July and met with Mao on 2 July. Finally, a five-member delegation headed by National Committee member John Foulds was in China from 27 September to 15 October, attending the 1 October National Day celebrations in Peking. Rita Smith apparently spent much time in Peking in 1967; she was present on several occasions when CPNZ members visited China, but was referred to by New China News Agency simply as being "in Peking" rather than as a member of the visiting delegations.

**Publications.** The weekly organ of the CPNZ is the *People's Voice,* published in Auckland. The party faces a "crisis both around sales and the financial maintenance of the paper," according to Wilcox, who added: "If things continue as they are we will have no *People's Voice* in its present form" (*New Zealand Communist Review,* January-February, 1968). The theoretical monthly *New Zealand Communist Review* is also published in Auckland.

# NICARAGUA

The Socialist Party of Nicaragua (Partido Socialista de Nicaragua; PSN) was founded in 1944. The PSN is a communist party, it is illegal and subject to repression. The number of party members is estimated at 200; the population of Nicaragua is 1,715,000 (estimated, July 1966). There is no evidence that any contending communist party, following either pro-Chinese or pro-Castro lines, is active in Nicaragua. During 1967, however, a guerrilla movement calling itself the Sandinista National Liberation Front (Frente Sandinista de Liberación Nacional; FSLN) came into prominence (see below). Its membership was estimated at no more than 60.

**Organization and Leadership.** There is little published information on the leadership of the PSN. Following the party's Ninth National Conference in November 1966, *Pravda* referred on 26 December to the post of First Secretary as being held by Manuel Pérez Estrada. An article in *World Marxist Review* (February 1968) by PSN Political Commission member Luis Sánchez referred to Alvaro Ramirez Gonzalez as "presently First Secretary of our Party," and there are indications (see below) that there were changes in the party leadership during 1967. With regard to Ramirez, he was reported on 14 December 1967 as having publicly announced his withdrawal from political activity. Prior to his "withdrawal" Ramirez had held a leading post in the PSN's front organization, the Republican Mobilization (Movilización Republicana). Other prominent members of the PSN appear to be Jorgé Isaac Galo Espinoza and Luis Domingo Sánchez Sancho.

Support for the PSN seems relatively insignificant (the party was not even mentioned in a list of Latin American communist parties published in the August 1965 issue of the *World Marxist Review*). The party has some trade-union support. The trade unions, however, represent less than 3 per cent of the working population, and communist influence is confined to an illegal splinter group within the General Labor Confederation (Confederación General del Trabajo), which itself has only 2,500 members and is one of five such groups. The PSN also has some support among students, particularly at the National University, and other young persons. The PSN's youth organization is the Nicaraguan Socialist Youth (Juventud Socialista Nicaraguense).

The PSN's hopes to start a political renewal by exploiting opposition to the presidential candidacy of General Anastasio Somoza in the elections of February 1967 (*YICA*, 1966, p. 239) proved unsuccessful. A meeting of the party's Central Committee in June noted that the PSN "was unable to make the most of the elections to consolidate and extend its contact with the masses with the purpose of bringing pressure to bear on the legal opposition . . . and also in order to promote the establishment of a people's democratic front." Analyzing the failure of the party, Sánchez pointed out that "the Somoza dynasty and Conservative opposition were able to carry out their reactionary designs all the more easily because of the vacillations in the ranks of the democratic forces (and especially in our Party), the lack of firmness and clarity regarding the main tasks, methods of struggle and policy of alliances and also because of the organizational weakness of our movement" (*WMR*, February 1968, p. 31).

**Domestic Policy and Activities.** During 1967 the PSN was confronted with a number of problems engendered by the appearance of the FSLN guerrilla nucleus and the party's desire to take advantage of the opposition to the Somoza regime, which would require the adoption of united-front tactics. Sánchez' article in the *World Marxist Review* indicated that "the Party had to revise its tactics and correct the mistakes which prevented it from becoming a real national political force and the vanguard of the people."

Analyzing the "motive forces of the revolution," Sánchez pointed out that "the character of the revolution determines its social base. Potentially, it is an exceptionally broad one, although the democratic forces are still dispersed and unorganized. Naturally, the social sections most interested in the victory of the revolution are those suffering the greatest exploitation, the working class and the peasantry." With regard to the working class, however, he said that there were "only 40,000 wage workers (out of a gainfully employed population of 600,000)," that the working class was "still in the process of formation," had "not become a 'class for itself'," and that "its trade-union and political organization [was] weak." As for the peasantry, the June Central Committee meeting's resolutions stated: "The absence of a clear Party policy with respect to the peasantry, the assumption that we would be able in one way or another to influence the Agrarian Institute to solve their immediate demands, are among the direct causes of the crisis in the peasant movement."

However, Sánchez referred to the

> ... process of drawing the peasantry into socioeconomic life, [which had] become particularly evident in the last two years. In 1965 the First National Peasant Conference was held, attended by more than 500 delegates representing over 60 organizations. In January 1967 the Confederation of Peasants and Agricultural Laborers was founded. These organizations unite the most active sections of the rural working people under the leadership of our Party .... The peasantry have joined the revolutionary struggle, thereby proving that they are one of the principal motive forces of the revolutionary process in our country, a force acting in close alliance with the working class under the leadership of the Marxist-Leninist party.

With regard to "the other potentially revolutionary forces—the students, intellectuals, petty-bourgeoisie, and some sections of the national bourgeoisie," Sánchez claimed that the situation was "in general terms similar to that in a number of other countries of the continent. The political actions of these sections—although restricted to their vanguard groups—and their support of joint action with the Party speak of the revolutionary possibilities of these sections and groups."

A section of Sánchez' article was devoted to the question "To whom does the vanguard role belong." He referred to the fact that "for a long time this disturbing question was reduced in the Party documents to the formula, widely current on the continent, that since we are the party of the working class, the vanguard role therefore automatically belongs to us, and to us alone." Sánchez pointed out, however, that "other forces, too, lay claim to this role, for example, the revolutionary petty-bourgeoisie, whose most politically articulate spokesman in our country is the Sandino National Liberation Front," and declared that "reality obliged us to reject this convenient and *pretentious phraseology* [italics in original]which concealed political inactivity. We realized that the vanguard role is something that has to be proved and won." Sánchez then added:

> How much effort was needed, however, before the Party realized this simple truth? How many mistakes did we make because of our complacent and dogmatic attitude? For, whereas in words we did not accept that anybody could so much as dispute our vanguard role, in practice we calmly relinquished it to other forces, including even the parties of the bourgeoisie.
>
> Fighting in the ranks of the Nicaraguan revolutionary movement, along with our Party, are the Party of Republican Mobilization, the Sandino National Liberation Front, the Independent Liberal Party and the Revolutionary Action Party (the latter has practically disappeared).
>
> In our policy of alliances we have made some important changes recently. We have rejected the tendency which, while recognizing in words the need for unity in the interests of the revolution, maintained at the same time that this unity must be based on unconditional acceptance of our program (*WMR*, February 1968).

Sánchez emphasized the gradual nature of the PSN revolutionary tactics, whereby the national aspects would precede the international: "At the present stage of the revolutionary struggle the *immediate principal enemy* [italics in original]is the Somoza dictatorship—the direct instrument of imperialist domination." He added, however, that "This does not signify turning over the leadership of the revolutionary movement to the bourgeois or petty-bourgeois opposition. On the contrary, this orientation presupposes a struggle for the hegemony of the consistently revolutionary forces, presupposes imparting to the democratic and anti-regime movement a radical, anti-oligarchy and anti-imperialist content."

On the issues of "the way to revolution and the forms of struggle," Sánchez declared: "We were guided and continue to be guided by the Leninist thesis that Marxism recognizes all forms of struggle." He indicated that the June meeting of the PSN's Central Committee had "called on the Party to prepare concretely for armed struggle." He added, however:

We think it would be wrong mechanically to separate the armed struggle from the mass movement, and to oppose the one to the other. The armed struggle in Nicaragua in its diverse forms should be the continuation of the mass movement; otherwise it would be doomed to failure. On the other hand, as noted in the resolutions of the Central Committee, if the mass movement is to achieve its objectives it must in its development acquire the character of armed struggle. The nature of the existing regime, the methods of its government admit of no other alternative.

As to the "concrete forms" of the armed struggle, he admitted that "these are questions for which we still have no clear answer." He pointed out that "some consider that guerrilla warfare is the only form that should be employed. . . . We think that this is an over-simplified view and one, moreover, that does not take into account the conditions and exigencies of our national life."

Sánchez pointed out that "the greater part of the peasantry is still under the influence of reaction, and it is hard to imagine that they will immediately support the guerrilla detachments. And as we know, this support is absolutely essential." In this connection he referred to "the events associated with the formation of [the FSLN]guerrilla center in the summer of 1967." The policy of the PSN with regard to the peasantry, adopted at the June Central Committee meeting and quoted by Sánchez, included the following:

1. To take immediate measures to reinforce and enlarge the Party branches in the countryside . . . vigorously to support and stimulate the militant spirit of the peasantry, to link, through the practical day-to-day struggle, our general policy of revolutionary transformations with the immediate demands of the peasant masses.

2. To create and consolidate the different legal organizations waging a struggle in defense of the specific demands of the peasants . . . .

3. To develop a propaganda campaign in the countryside under the leadership of the clandestine Party branches . . . .

4. To make the most of existing possibilities for legal work . . . in particular to press for the application of those points of the existing agrarian law which correspond—even though to a limited extent—with the interests of the peasants.

5. To promote the political and ideological education of the peasants—members and sympathizers of the Party . . . .

6. To elaborate an effective self-defense plan in the regions where the circumstances make this necessary; to maintain this form of struggle we must create a powerful system of Party organizations, with deep roots among the masses, that will ensure the material funds for self-defense.

The extent, if any, of the PSN's participation in the FSLN during 1967 is difficult to determine. On 4 November the Costa Rican communist newspaper *Libertad* claimed that the PSN was not taking part in guerrilla activities. On 15 December the Cuban weekly *Bohemia* carried an article by the Salvadoran Communist Roque Dalton which included interviews given to him in Prague by representatives of the FSLN and PSN. The PSN representative who was not named, spoke of a "revolution within the revolution" which had taken place within the party, removing a number of the old party leaders. The new leadership, "composed of young and revolutionary elements," opened "new perspectives for the unity of the Nicaraguan revolutionary forces, especially with the comrades of the Sandinista National Liberation Front." The PSN representative claimed that the FSLN included a number of former PSN members. There was no indication, however that the PSN itself was collaborating with the FSLN.

**International Views and Policies.** The PSN was represented at the Fifth Meeting of the Communist Parties of Mexico, Central America, and Panama, and was a signatory of the meeting's communique (see *Documents*). Thus the party affirmed its pro-Soviet stand, subsequently reiterated at a plenum in October, which sent greetings to "the Soviet people, government, and Communist party on the occasion of the Fiftieth Anniversary of the October Revolution," stating that the Soviet Union "has become a strong bulwark and a consistent fighter for national independence and democracy, for socialism, for communism, and for peace on earth" (Moscow Radio Peace and Progress, 8 October 1967).

The PSN's relations with Cuba, which came out in full support of the FSLN and publicized the latter's criticisms of the PSN (*Granma,* 8 June 1967), appeared to be deteriorating. The PSN was represented at the Havana conference of the Latin American Solidarity Organization (OLAS), but the Nicaraguan delegation was led by Fernando Martinez (possible pseudonym of Casimiro Sotelo Montenegro), representing the FSLN, and the PSN was outnumbered by the guerrilla representatives. The two PSN delegates were believed to have been Jorgé Isaac Galo Espinoza and Luis Domingo Sánchez Sancho. Fernando Martinez was appointed Secretary of the committee responsible for drafting the resolution on the solidarity of OLAS with national liberation movements.

There are no indications that the PSN made reference during the year to events in China.

The PSN was represented at the celebrations of the Fiftieth Anniversary of the Bolshevik Revolution in the Soviet Union. The names of the members of the party's delegation were not disclosed.

**Publications.** The former clandestine PSN weekly *Orientación Popular* was replaced in 1967 by a new organ of irregular clandestine publication called *Tribuna.*

\* \* \*

**Guerrillas.** The FSLN guerrilla movement active in Nicaragua during 1967 was formed during the years 1959 to 1961 under the leadership of Carlos Fonseca Amador. After severe reverses in 1963 the FSLN disbanded and did not start regrouping again before 1965. Its members, according to *Bohemia* (15 December 1967), came "principally from the student movement and the peasantry."

The FSLN operated primarily in the mountainous areas northeast of Managua, near Matagalpa and Jinotega. Following a number of bank robberies in late 1966 and early 1967, the first serious clashes between the FSLN and Nicaraguan government forces occurred in August and continued through October, by which time the original 60-odd guerrilla force had been seriously depleted. By the end of the year nearly all the FSLN leaders had been either killed or captured. Both Silvio Mayorga Delgado, a founding member of the FSLN, and Casimiro Sotelo, believed to have been the leader of the Nicaraguan delegation to the OLAS conference, were killed. Carlos Fonseca Amador is believed to have left the country. The FSLN debacle provoked the Costa Rican People's Vanguard Party to call on Nicaraguans to adopt a new tactical line in accordance with existing conditions and to eschew "pseudo-revolutionary adventurism" (*Libertad,* 23 December, 1967).

# NIGERIA

The Socialist Workers' and Farmers' Party (SWAFP) was founded in 1963 "on the bedrock of the general truths and principles of Marxism-Leninism," in the words of its Secretary-General, Tunji Otegbeye (*IB*, no. 68, 1966). The party has been banned since May 1966, when the new Nigerian head of state, General Ironsi, announced that all parties and political and tribal organizations would be dissolved until January 1969. The present regime under Lieutenant Colonel Yakubu Gowon, which took power on 1 August 1966, banned not only the political organizations but all political activity.

Estimates of SWAFP membership vary greatly. A few years ago, the party claimed to have more than 70 branches and a total membership of 16,000 (*WMR*, November 1965). A Soviet source spoke of 22,000 members and 83 local organizations being represented at the founding congress (*Agitator* [Moscow], no. 6, 1966). Recently a US government source estimated the membership at fewer than 1,000 (*World Strength of Communist Party Organizations*, 1968). The population of Nigeria is 58,600,000 (estimated mid-year 1966).

**Organization and Leadership.** The SWAFP adopted a monolithic structure based on the principles of collective leadership and democratic centralism. At its first Congress, in December 1965, the party's leaders included the 17-member Central Committee, nine-member Politburo, and three-member Secretariat of the Central Committee, with Uche Omo as President and Tunji Otegbeye as Secretary-General. (A leading member of the SWAFP, J.O.B. Omotosho, died in May 1967.) No information is available about the structure of the Party since the time of its proscription.

The SWAFP supports and closely collaborates with the Nigerian Trade Union Congress (NTUC), headed by Wahab Goodluck. (The NTUC is the left wing of the Nigerian trade-union movement, which is split into several groups.) It also lends support to the National Youth Congress (NYC; founded in 1960 by Tunji Otegbeye), whose political work it declares that it has taken over.

For the purpose of guiding all so-called progressive youth groups, the SWAFP and the NYC founded the Federation of Nigerian Youth. The SWAFP was also instrumental in establishing the Patrice Lumumba Institute of Political Science and Trade Unionism, which trains activists of the party, the NTUC, and the NYC.

At its first Congress, the SWAFP declared that the activities of party cadres should be concentrated in the trade unions, and since its proscription the party has continued to conduct political activity within the NTUC. The NTUC operates the Patrice Lumumba Institute and publishes a fortnightly newspaper, *Advance*. In 1967 an "*Advance* Reading Club" was founded to discuss issues raised in the paper and to promote interest in it.

The SWAFP strives for a national democratic revolution through a united front of all progressive forces in order to open the way to socialism. The SWAFP at the same time advocates the maintenance of its "militant unity" and the assumption of the vanguard position in the national democratic forces. The party has pursued this line at the expense of purging its ranks of factions referred to as the "Eskor adventurists," who called for the initiation of a revolution, and the "Kola branch of opportunist renegades." (*IB*, no. 68, 1966.)

The SWAFP has consistently supported all governmental policies for ensuring the unity of Nigeria and protecting the independence of Nigeria from foreign interference. The SWAFP welcomed the military coup of January 1966, which gave power to General Ironsi, on the grounds that the coup represented a patriotic and progressive action on the part of the armed forces in the struggle against tribalism, corruption, and nepotism. The SWAFP also has given at least partial approval to the government of Lieutenant Colonel Yakubu Gowon, who succeeded Ironsi as head of state in August

431

1966. According to Nigerian communists, the coup was reactionary in content, but nevertheless it had numerous "positive" results. The attitude of the Nigerian communists to the Gowon regime was expressed in an open letter to Colonel Gowon by Tunji Otegbeye:

> Your efforts to ensure that Nigeria continues to be an entity [have] the support of all patriotic forces. Your unequivocal declaration on the rights of the minority group to self-determination has been well received by all democratic forces in and outside Nigeria.
>
> But quite frankly, the policy of your government which promised to carry out all the reforms promised by the late Supreme Commander, Major General Aguiyi-Ironsi, ended with proclamations but little or no action.

Otegbeye pointed to the continued economic crisis in Nigeria and regional tension in the country. Declaring that "the tension in Nigeria today emanates from the army to infect the general population," he called on the army first to "heal its own wounds." Otegbeye charged Gowon with responsibility for starting and creating "an atmosphere of equality and fraternity," but added that this could only be achieved with a socialist objective. (*Advance*, 16-22 April 1967.)

Writing before the secession of the Eastern Region from the Nigerian Federation on 30 May 1967, Otegbeye expressed the view that "nobody genuinely wants to secede," and warned that "secession without the mandate of the people in clear terms is treasonable" (*ibid.*). Nigerian communists and trade unionists within the NTUC condemned the secession and creation of the Republic of Biafra as the work of "power-hungry adventurers" around Colonel Ojukwu, who acted without the mandate of the masses. They charged that Ojukwu was inspired to "balkanize Nigeria" by the combined influence of the USA, Britain, Portugal, West Germany, and Israel, who wanted to weaken Nigeria internally and "create a basis for their continued ruthless exploitation of [its] national resources and manpower." According to Otegbeye, however, the main supporter of Ojukwu's rebellion was the US Central Intelligence Agency: "Inciting the Easterners against the British, who hold the highest share in oil exploitation in Eastern Nigeria, the Americans were planning for a big takeover of the oil prospecting backed by the new regime in 'Biafra.' " He denounced the British and US governments' refusal to supply the Federal Government with arms when it declared war on Biafra in July, and praised the supply of arms by the Soviet Union as a "turning point in the Nigeria civil war for unity, against secession," adding: "The Nigerian people regard this gesture as coming from a friend in need." Otegbeye went on to emphasize that the military government was carrying out a patriotic duty to Nigeria by crushing the Ojukwu rebellion and that the war was not against the Ibos, but against a rebellion inspired by neocolonialism. (*Advance*, 26 November-2 December; 10-16 December 1967.) The communists claimed that the working class in the Eastern Region favored national unity and that many have been drawn into the separatist movement under pressure. Wide influence in Biafra was also claimed by the SWAFP and the NTUC. (*WMR*, October 1967.)

Speaking to Nigerian students in Moscow on the Nigerian crisis, Otegbeye dwelt at length on the future tasks of the country's "progressive forces," indicating that ideological work stressing the political entity of Nigeria must be primary: "Close attention must be paid to develop the spirit of proletarian internationalism and of Nigerian patriotism." The need for economic aid and the necessity for revising the constitution were also mentioned. The most difficult task, according to Otegbeye, was to "counter and effectively defeat the neocolonialist forces and their local collaborators" by exposing past activities of the Nigerian government, eliminating "compradore politicians," and exposing "world imperialism" and the "imperialist involvement" in the Nigerian crisis. Otebgeye called for propaganda to convince the people that the USSR and the socialist states were the true friends of Nigeria and that the USSR was an example for Nigeria to follow. He concluded:

> We must bring it home to our people that there would have been no October Revolution without the guiding role of the Bolshevik Party and there could be no Bolshevik Party without the teachings of Marx, Engels, and Lenin. The conscious Proletariat must therefore rally around its Marxist-Leninist Party and ensure the success of the revolution. . . . Those who have built socialism have had to depend on the dedication and heroic leadership of the proletarian party of a new type . . . . We can succeed, we are bound to succeed, under the banner of Marxism-Leninism and proletarian

internationalism. (*Advance,* 10-16 December 1967.)

**International Views and Policies.** The Nigerian delegation to the Moscow celebrations of the fiftieth anniversary of the October Revolution was headed by Tunji Otegbeye. In an interview afterward with *Advance,* Otegbeye stressed that the successes of the Soviet Union had "established for all times the superiority of the socialist system over the capitalist system," and that its "great victories formed the beacon light to all developing countries, showing the path to freedom, democracy and plenty for all." He hailed the "great might" of the Soviet Union and other socialist countries as the "greatest deterrent to aggressive wars by imperialist power." The multi-national Soviet Union, he said also, was "an example of happy fusion of nations based on equality of men and women." (*Advance,* 26 November-2 December.)

Tunji Otegbeye attended the Eighteenth Congress of the Communist Party of France in January, the Seventh Congress of the Socialist Unity Party of Germany in April, and the Thirtieth Congress of the Communist Party of Great Britain in November.

**Publications.** The mouthpiece of the SWAFP is the organ of the NTUC, *Advance,* which appears fortnightly. The newspaper describes itself as "The Nigerian Workers' Own Newspaper." Contributions by SWAFP members are signed without mentioning the party affiliation and Tunji Otegbeye is identified as "a leading Nigerian socialist."

# NORTH KOREA

The Korean Communist Party (Choson Kongsan-dang; KCP) was organized in 1925 but ceased to operate in 1928. Following World War II Communist strength in Korea was minimal, with local Communists paying allegiance to the Central Committee of the KCP, revived in Seoul in October 1945. On 10 October 1945, however, the North Korean Central Bureau of the KCP was formed, placing all Communists in North Korea under its control. In July 1946 the North Korean Bureau of the Communist Party absorbed the New People's Party, formed in March 1946 and headed by returnees from China, and renamed the organization the North Korean Workers' Party. On 24 June 1949 the North and South Korean Workers' Parties merged to form the Korean Workers' Party (Choson Nodong-dang; KWP).

The KWP is the governing party of the Democratic People's Republic of Korea (DPRK), formed in September 1948. According to the DPRK constitution, the Supreme People's Assembly (SPA) is the highest organ of state power and promulgates all laws, which are in turn executed by the cabinet. In reality, however, all political activity is controlled by the KWP and Kim Il-song, its Secretary-General.

Elections to the Fourth Supreme People's Assembly were held on 25 November 1967, a year overdue. At this time 457 delegates were elected to the Assembly, in comparison with 383 elected on 8 October 1962. A breakdown of party strength in the Assembly is not available, but the extent of its control is indicated by the results of the general election in which, according to the Korean Central News Agency, 100 per cent of the electorate participated and in which all 457 of the officially selected single-list candidates received 100 per cent of the votes cast (KCNA, 26 November 1967). On 14 December 1967 the first session of the Fourth SPA was convened, and on 16 December 1967 a new cabinet and SPA Presidium were announced, in addition to the presentation of a new political program by Kim Il-song. The SPA Presidium consists of a President, Choe Yong-kon; four Vice-Presidents, Hong Myong-hu, Pak Chong-ae, Kang Yang-uk, and Yi Yong-ho; a Secretary-General, Pak Mun-kyu; and nine members, Choe Hyon, Ho Pong-hak, Kim Yong-chu, Yi Kuk-chin, Choe Kwang, O Chin-u, Kim Tong-kyu, Pak Sin-tok, and Kim Yo-chung.

According to a 1966 KWP claim, the KWP has a membership of more than 1,600,000. With an estimated population of 12,400,000 (mid-1966), the ratio of party members to population is almost 13 per cent, one of the highest, if not the highest, ratios of party membership in the world.

**Organization and Leadership.** The KWP is organized along highly centralized lines under the leadership of its Secretary-General, Kim Il-song. According to the party constitution, the highest authority within the KWP is the Party Congress, held every four years, and between congresses,\* the Central Committee, which in theory "elects" and approves the decisions of the Political Committee. At the Fourteenth Plenum of the Fourth Central Committee in October 1966 authority was further concentrated by the elimination of the positions of Chairman and Vice-Chairmen, the election of a six-member Presidium within the Political Committee, and the reinstitution of a Secretariat, which had been abolished in 1953.

The exact number of Central Committee and Political Committee members is unknown. The lists announced by the Korean Central News Agency in October 1966 were apparently incomplete, as several members not included in the list have since been listed in North Korean publications and radio broadcasts with their party titles. Known Presidium members include Kim Il-song, Choe Yong-kun, Kim Il, Pak Kum-chol, Yi Hyo-sun, and Kim Kwang-hyop; other full members of the Political Committee include Kim Chang-pong, Pak Song-chol, Kim Ik-son, Choe Hyon, Pak Chong-ae, Nam Il,

---

\*The last KWP congress was held on 11-18 September 1961; an enlarged conference of the KWP Central Committee was held in October 1966.

Yi Chang-ok, Yi Chu-yon, and Yi Yong-ho. Alternate members of the Political Committee are Sok San, Ho Pong-hak, Kim Yong-chu, Pak Yong-kuk, Choe Kwang, O-Chin-u, Yim Ch'un-ch'u, Kim Tong-kyu, Han Sang-tu, Hyon Mu-kwang, and Choe Kyong-pak. The 11-member Secretariat consists of the Presidium of the Political Committee, plus Sok San, Ho Pong-hak, Kim Yong-chu, Pak Yong-kuk, and Kim To-man. Party leaders reportedly purged in 1967 include Hong Myong-hu, Pak Kum-chol, Yi Hyo-sun, Yim Ch'un-ch'u, and Kim To-man.

In addition to being the governing party of the DPRK, the KWP also controls a number of mass organizations. The principal organizations include the Korean Federation of Trade Unions, founded on 30 November 1945 and headed by Chon Chang-chol and Kim Wal-yong; the League of Socialist Working Youth of Korea (formerly known as the Korean Democratic Youth League), founded on 17 January 1946 and headed by Hong Sun-kwon and O Ki-chon; the Korean Democratic Women's Union, founded on 18 November 1945 and headed by Kim Ok-sun; the Korean Peasants' Union, headed by Hwang Won-po; and the Committee for Cultural Relations with Foreign Countries, founded on 3 April 1956 and headed by Kim Kyong-hwa and So Chol. The KWP also exercises its control through the General Federation of Koreans Residing in Japan (Chosen Soren), which focuses on the more than 600,000 Korean residents in Japan and is headed by Han Tok-su.

In addition to these mass organizations, at least two "democratic" parties exist in North Korea, the Korean Democratic Party (Choson Minju-dang), headed by Kang Yang-uk, and the Young Friends' Party of the Chondokyo Sect (Society of the Heavenly Way; Chondogyo Chong-u-dang), headed by Pak Sin-tok. No statistics are available regarding the membership of these parties, and their function is primarily that of enhancing the legitimacy of the United Democratic Fatherland Front.

The United Democratic Fatherland Front (Choguk Tongil Minjujuui Chonson) was created on 27 June 1949 by 71 political and social organizations in both the DPRK and the Republic of Korea (ROK). Official party publications describe it as "a political organization uniting all the revolutionary forces of North and South Korea" whose task is "to consolidate, under the leadership of the Workers' Party of Korea, the united front, liberate South Korea from the colonial rule of the U.S. imperialists, and to realize the peaceful unification and the complete independence of the country" (*Facts About Korea*, Pyongyang, Foreign Languages Publishing House, 1964). The Presidium of the Fatherland Front consists of Kim Il-song, Han Tok-su, Kim Chon-hae, Ko Chun-taek, and Yi Kuk-no. In addition to the control exercised through the United Democratic Fatherland Front, the KWP also exercises control through the Committee for the Peaceful Unification of the Fatherland, established on 13 May 1961 as a result of increased emphasis on the unification of the country and consisting of representatives of the KWP, the "democratic" parties, and the mass organizations.

**Internal Party Affairs.** Leadership changes during 1967 were reflected, or reportedly reflected, in three sectors: the KWP, the Korean Central News Agency, and the Supreme People's Assembly. According to a Seoul report based on comments made by a North Korean reporter at the Two Hundred Fifty-Seventh Plenary Session of the Military Armistice Commission at Panmunjom (7 November 1967), several members of an alleged anti-Kim Il-song faction were removed in a purge begun in March "under the heavy pressure of the military." The purge, reported to have involved more than 100 party members, apparently came in the wake of an intense investigation by the KWP Central Committee in an attempt to eliminate opposition to Kim Il-song's domestic and foreign policies on the eve of elections to the Supreme People's Assembly. Those reportedly purged during the course of the year include Ko Hyok, Vice-Premier in Charge of Ideologies; Yi Song-un, former Chairman of the Pyongyang City Party Committee and Procurator-General; and several members of the Central Committee, including Pak Kum-chol, member of the Presidium of the Political Committee and member of the Secretariat; Yi Hyo-sun, member of the Presidium of the Political Committee, member of the Secretariat, and Director of the South Korean Bureau of the KWP; Yim Ch'un-ch'u, Deputy Chief of the South Korean Bureau of the KWP; Kim To-man, member of the Secretariat and Director of the KWP Propaganda Department; and Ho Sok-sun, Director of the Education Department of the KWP Academy of Science and Director of the KWP Central Committee's Internal Affairs Department. Pak Kum-chol has reportedly been replaced by Kim Yong-chu and Yi Hyo-sun by General Ho Pong-hak.

Seoul reports also linked the purge of party members with the 22 March 1967 defection to the Republic of Korea of Yi Su-kun, one of the Deputy Directors of the Korean Central News Agency, and the subsequent "concentrated scrutiny" of this agency by the KWP from 15 July to 10 September, which reportedly resulted in the purge of its Director, Pae Ki-chun, and a number of other officials. This would also help to explain the reported dismissal of Ko Hyok, Vice-Premier in Charge of Ideologies, and Kim To-man, Director of the KWP Propaganda Department.

Omissions from the cabinet and the Presidium of the Supreme People's Assembly elected on 16 December 1967 tend to confirm the reports from Seoul. The Korean Central News Agency report of 16 December 1967, commenting on elections in the Assembly, makes no mention of Pak Kum-chol or Yi Hyo-sun, former Vice-President and member of the Assembly Presidium, respectively; nor does it mention Ko Hyok, one of the ten Vice-Premiers appointed in December 1966. Yim Ch'un-ch'u was replaced as Secretary-General of the SPA by Pak Mun-kyu, member of the KWP Central Committee and former Minister of Land Administration. In addition, none of the above was present at the opening session of the SPA on 14 December 1967. Also absent from the opening session were Pak Yong-kuk, member of the KWP Secretariat and alternate member of the Political Committee, and Kim To-man.

Although reasons for the changes are not immediately apparent, Seoul reports describe them as being carried out "under the heavy pressure of the military." This would be in accord with the increased military bias of the Political Committee, which resulted when Generals Choe Hyon, Kim Chang-pong, and Yi Yong-ho were elevated to full membership in the Political Committee and when Colonel General Ho Pong-hak, General O Chin-u, General Choe Kwang, and Colonel General Sok San were made alternate members of the Political Committee at the October 1966 party conference.

Although the KWP has not held a party congress since September 1961, a major enlarged conference of the Central Committee was held on 5-12 October 1966, at which the major party lines on domestic and international affairs were outlined. A plenary session of the Central Committee was held on 28 June-3 July 1967, presided over by Kim Il-song and attended by "the Members and Alternate Members of the Central Committee of the Party . . . ; Members of the Central Auditing Commission of the Party; Party workers in the capital and from the provinces, cities, counties, factories, and enterprises; and functionaries of ministries and central organs" (*Nodong Sinmun,* 4 July 1967, as broadcast by KCNA). According to *Nodong Sinmun,* the party daily organ, the plenary session unanimously approved and reaffirmed the correctness of the policies set forth at the October 1966 conference and "set forth concrete militant tasks confronting different domains after a serious discussion of measures for the continuous successful implementation of the resolutions of the Party conference in all spheres." These tasks include pressing ahead with socialist construction on all fronts while "pouring great energy continuously into defense buildup," further enhancing the production growth rate by mobilizing "all reserves and potentialities latent in the national economy," and strengthening the "revolutionary forces" in the northern half of the country by continuously arming the party members and working people with the lines, policies, and revolutionary traditions of the party, thus "accelerating their proletarianization and revolutionization and establishing more thoroughly the unitary ideas in the whole party" (*Nodong Sinmun,* 4-5 July 1967, as broadcast by KCNA).

In addition to the plenary session of the KWP Central Committee, several of the mass organizations controlled by the party held important meetings during 1967. Among these were the General Federation of Koreans Residing in Japan and the League of Socialist Working Youth of Korea. On 24-27 May 1967, the General Federation of Koreans Residing in Japan held its Eighth Congress. Han Tok-su was reelected Chairman of the Central Committee, and resolutions were adopted opposing US actions in Vietnam and South Korea. Messages of solidarity with the North Korean party and state were sent both by the General Federation's Eighth Congress and by a second plenary meeting of its Central Committee, which met on 10-11 November 1967 to discuss the forthcoming Japanese elections and to mobilize the Korean residents in Japan to defend their right of repatriation.

The Central Committee of the League of Socialist Working Youth of Korea held a plenary session on 23-24 August 1967 and discussed its plans and tasks in carrying out the decisions of the KWP Central Committee plenary session. According to the Korean Central News Agency, discussion also focused on how to equip the youth of Korea with the unitary ideas of the party and on how to organize and mobilize the youth in order to bring about a "revolutionary upsurge" in economic construction and defense buildup (KCNA, 25 August 1967).

Although it was not a party meeting as such, reference should also be made to the meeting of the first session of the Fourth Supreme People's Assembly on 14-16 December 1967. On 16 December Kim Il-song addressed the SPA and presented the government's political program, which *Nodong Sinmun* hailed as a "superb Marxist-Leninist document of our times" that "makes a valuable contribution to further enhancing the ideological and theoretical treasure house of Marxism-Leninism and developing and enriching the practical experience of the international Communist movement" (*Nodong Sinmun,* 28 December 1967, as broadcast by KCNA, 29 December 1967). The 10-point program outlines the DPRK's domestic and foreign policies, as well as the tasks facing the KWP itself, and reemphasizes the basic points made by Kim Il-song in his 5 October 1966 speech to the KWP Central Committee.

In evaluating the position of the KWP during 1967, a *Nodong Sinmun* editorial noted:

> The most important success made in the course of the struggle for implementing the resolutions of the Party Conference [October 1966] is that our revolutionary ranks have been consolidated as never before, politically and ideologically. The unitary Party ideas have been all the more firmly established within the whole Party and among the entire people, and the revolutionization of the Party membership and people has been pushed ahead. (*Nodong Sinmun,* 5 October, 1967, as reported by KNCA.)

On the anniversary of the founding of the KWP, *Nodong Sinmun* hailed the KWP for always having been faithful to its national and international duties and for having exerted itself in an effort to strengthen the international solidarity of the Korean revolution and expedited the development of the international revolutionary forces.

In spite of optimistic appraisals, it should be noted that during 1967 both the North Korean party press and the December political program placed considerable emphasis on the need to intensify the ideological revolution, not only among the working class, but among party members as well.

In an editorial dated 10 March 1967, *Nodong Sinmun* noted that

> ... Party members and workers at all revolutionary sentries must be taught to redouble their efforts to produce more and better articles, to take care of state properties, to better manage the state economy, and to bring about a new revolutionary upsurge in socialist construction. ... In order to enhance class education among Party members and workers, the role and responsibility of Party committees at all levels must be improved. These committees must mobilize Party organizations and workers' organizations, schools and teachers at various levels, and all propaganda forces and media to push class education one step higher.

Kim Il-song further emphasized the need to strengthen the role of the party in carrying out the ideological revolution:

> We should, first of all, strengthen the Party, the general staff of the revolution, and build up the revolutionary ranks as firm as granite politically and ideologically. We should turn our revolutionary ranks into a more powerful combat detachment by thoroughly establishing the unitary Party ideas still more on a Party-wide scale, upholding the unity of the Party ranks in ideology, will, and action and constantly strengthening the kindred ties of the Party, people, and people's army. (KCNA, 5 June 1967.)

Subsequent editorials in *Nodong Sinmun* emphasized the need to "proletarize and revolutionize all members of society" and called on the North Koreans to study more thoroughly the works of Kim Il-song, in order to arm themselves with the ideas of the party and assure the successful independent promotion of the North Korean revolution, as well as contributing to the international revolutionary movement itself.

**Domestic Policies.** North Korean statements in 1967 on party policy in both domestic and foreign affairs strongly reflect emphasis on self-reliance, independence, and national identity, or *chuche*. According to the political program, the KWP's ideas of *chuche* are "the most correct Marxist-Leninist ideas of our leadership for the successful carrying out of our revolution and construction and the invariable guiding principle of the government of the republic in all its policies and activities." According to KWP statements, it is by the creative application of the principles of Marxism-Leninism to the objective conditions of Korea that the policy of *chuche* has been formulated, the establishment of which is "a question of key importance on which depends the victory of our revolution . . . " (political program, as broadcast by KCNA, 16 December 1967).

The North Korean economic policy as outlined in the political program focuses on the importance of establishing a self-sufficient national economy, on the theory that "economic independence is the material basis for political independence" and that "without building an independent national economy, it is impossible to establish [the] material and technical foundations for socialism and [to] build socialism and communism successfully." The political program also points out, however, that while continuing to emphasize the need to create a self-sufficient economy, the DPRK "will establish economic relations and develop foreign trade with other countries on the principles of proletarian internationalism, complete equality, and mutual benefit," noting that "in developing foreign trade, we attach prime importance to the world socialist market."

In specific terms, the economic program continued to call for priority to be given to heavy industry, while simultaneously developing light industry, agriculture, transport, and all other branches of the national economy. In early February 1967 *Nodong Sinmun* noted that the Seven Year National Economic Plan, which was extended by three years in October 1966, would be "carried out successfully" (*Nodong Sinmun*, 3 February 1967, as broadcast by KCNA). The July plenary session of the KWP Central Committee continued in the same optimistic vein, stating that production had "risen sharply" in "industry, rural economy, and all other domains of national economy." At the same time, however, the Central Committee underscored the need to enhance the production growth rate by mobilizing all "reserves and potentialities latent in the national economy" and by continuing to follow the *taean* work system and the *chongsan-ni* spirit and method (*Nodong Sinmun*, 4 July 1967, as broadcast by KCNA, and *Nodong Sinmun*, 5 July 1967, as broadcast by KCNA).

Although no concrete statistics are available, a *Nodong Sinmun* editorial of 1 January 1968 noted that as a whole "the national economic plan for 1967 is expected to have been overfulfilled" and that "an increase of over 10 per cent above the rate of growth envisaged in the 1967 plan . . . is expected" (*Nodong Sinmun*, 1 January 1968, as broadcast by KCNA). That all was not well in the economic sector was indicated by the notation in the political program that "our functionaries . . . still fall short of such levels as are required by our Party in their method and style of work. . . . the functionaries of the state and economic organs should rectify their method and style of work decisively." Reports also indicated that during 1967 salaries and consumer goods were limited and the storing of strategic materials was begun.

1967 also saw a continued emphasis on the KWP line of carrying out economic construction in parallel with defense buildup, with defense expenditures accounting for approximately $465,600,000, or 30.2 per cent of the gross national budget. While the KWP economic line aims at providing the material guarantee of the Korean revolution and the revolutionary base necessary for successfully carrying out the reunification of Korea, its defense policy aims at simultaneously "training the army into an army of cadres, modernizing it, placing the entire people under arms, and converting the whole land into a fortress" (*Nodong Sinmun*, 5 December 1967, as broadcast by KCNA). North Korean party publications continued to stress the line of "self-defense in national defense" and emphasized that "communists cannot rely upon the strength of others in the question of national defense . . . " (*Nodong Sinmun*, 5 December 1967, as broadcast by KCNA).

At the July plenary session the KWP Central Committee noted that "a new advance has . . . been made in defense buildup and the implementation of the military line of the party" (*Nodong Sinmun*, 4 July 1967, as broadcast by KCNA). At the same time, however, Pak Song-chol, member of the Political Committee, Vice-Premier, and Minister of Foreign Affairs, commented on the need to "raise our people's army to be a better cadre army which can take care of the enemy 1 to 100" and added that "we must strengthen the worker-peasant red militia units and step up combat and political training" (Pyongyang Domestic Service, 8 September 1967).

KWP domestic activity also centered on the problem of stepping up the ideological and cultural revolution of the working classes, in addition to that specifically required of party members. Both the party press and the political program paid considerable attention to the need to heighten class consciousness and to consolidate the "revolutionary ranks" so as to "cultivate among the working people the collectivist spirit of placing the interests of the organization and the collective above personal interests . . . " (political program). During 1967 North Korea also undertook a massive resident-reregistration campaign in order to identify and eliminate hostile elements, particularly those among the third generation.

During the course of 1967 the KWP significantly intensified its campaign for the "reunification of the fatherland." Party statements and articles described reunification as the "supreme task set before the Korean people," which must be accomplished by the present generation, and stressed as necessary prerequisites a self-sufficient national economy and a continued defense buildup in parallel with economic construction. Continuing emphasis was placed on the need to consolidate a Marxist-Leninist party in South Korea and to form a broad anti-American "national-salvation united front" embracing all "patriotic democratic forces." North Korea also continued to stress the role of the DPRK in achieving reunification, pointing out that the "revolutionary forces in the northern half of the republic are the most important motive power for the Korean revolution as a whole" (political program).

Increased emphasis on reunification of the fatherland was evidenced by a significant increase in armed clashes along the demilitarized zone and North Korean armed infiltrations into the South, as well as by a new shift in strategy. Whereas Western sources reported only 50 cases of armed clashes along the demilitarized zone during 1966, some 575 cases were reported in 1967, and the number of captured armed infiltrators into the South increased from 106 in 1966 to 345 in 1967. In contrast to previous North Korean policy, a significant number of captured agents were regulars of the Korean People's Army rather than party functionaries. Strategically, the North Korean infiltrations were designed to test the possibilities for guerrilla warfare in the South, as well as South Korean receptivity to such a strategy. North Korea explained the increased number of incidents by stating:

> In the past year, revolutionaries, workers, peasants, democratic personages, and patriotic people of all other sections in South Korea have waged a tremendous struggle for the right to existence, democracy, and the self-dependent unification of the country, holding aloft the banner of the anti-US national salvation resistance struggle. They have waged various forms of struggle, including armed struggle in a more active way. They have valiantly fought and are fighting in all parts, underground, in the mountains, and even from behind bars. (KCNA, 30 December 1967.)

While intensifying its call for the reunification of Korea, the KWP also emphasized its independent position, pointing out in the political program that "the question of Korean unification is an internal affair of the Korean people which cannot be settled by any foreign forces."

**Foreign Policy.** As outlined in the political program, North Korea's foreign policy calls for guarding the unity of the socialist camp and the solidarity of the international communist movement and the forces of world revolution; developing friendly relations with the newly emerging states of Asia, Africa, and Latin America and rendering active support to the anti-imperialist national-liberation movements in these areas; opposing the US "imperialists and their policy of aggression and war"; and conducting foreign affairs in general on the principles of complete equality, independence, and mutual respect. North Korea cautioned, however, that "the socialist countries, even if they maintain diplomatic relations with the imperialist countries, should not dissolve their anti-imperialist struggle or weaken it for that reason" (*Nodong Sinmun,* 16 November 1967, as broadcast by KCNA).

As a corollary to increased North Korean emphasis on reunification, attacks on the United States as the "head of the imperialist camp" were also intensified. In a major *Nodong Sinmun* editorial carried on 16 November 1967 the KWP attacked the United States for "openly scheming to ignite another aggressive war in Korea" and labeled it as the "main force of aggression and war," the "international gendarme," the "biggest international exploiter," the "main bulwark of modern colonialism," and the "enemy of the peoples of the whole world" (*Nodong Sinmun,* 16 November 1967, as broadcast by KCNA).

The KWP continued to call on the world socialist countries and anti-imperialist forces to "direct the spearhead of attack against the United States, deal blows to them everywhere and bind them hand and foot so that they cannot ride roughshod" (*Nodong Sinmun,* 11 July 1967, as broadcast by KCNA).

The KWP's policy of supporting the revolutionary forces of Asia, Africa, and Latin America in their "anti-imperialist struggle" was further emphasized in a major article by Kim Il-song in the first issue (July-August 1967) of *Tricontinental,* the theoretical journal of the Executive Secretariat of the Afro-Asian Latin American Peoples' Solidarity Organization (AALAPSO):

> The peoples of Asia, Africa, and Latin America have common interests and their anti-imperialist, anti-US struggles are linked with each other by a relationship of mutual support. . . . Victory on one front against US imperialism will sap its strength that much, facilitating victory on other fronts. . . . Therefore, it is necessary to form the broadest possible anti-US united front to isolate US imperialism thoroughly and administer blows to it by united struggle everywhere it is engaged in aggression. Only by so doing is it possible to disperse and weaken the force of US imperialism to the last degree and lead the people on every front to beat US imperialism with an overwhelming power . . . .

**The International Communist Movement.** KWP statements and publications reiterated the party's independent stand in the world communist movement, as outlined in a 12 August 1966 editorial of *Nodong Sinmun* and reemphasized by Kim Il-song at the October 1966 KWP Central Committee conference. On the occasion of the anniversary of the KWP conference *Nodong Sinmun* hailed the "complete correctness of Comrade Kim Il-song's Marxist-Leninist analysis and the assessment of the international Communist movement given in the report at the Party Conference" (*Nodong Sinmun,* 5 October 1967, as broadcast by KCNA). At the same time the KWP noted that the principles of the 1957 Declaration of the 12 Communist and Workers' Parties and the 1960 Statement of 81 Communist and Workers' Parties were still of "great significance . . . in the activities of the communist and working parties of various countries and in the revolutionary struggle of the peoples the world over" (*Nodong Sinmun,* 10 November 1967, as broadcast by KCNA).

A lengthy article in *Kulloja,* the monthly organ of the KWP Central Committee, stressed that

> . . . flunkeyism and big-power chauvinism are simply unthinkable between socialist countries which establish new state relations of equality, independence, and cooperation based on the principles of Marxism-Leninism and proletarian internationalism.

> There are among the socialist countries big and small ones, developed and less developed ones. But such differences cannot be any criterion defining mutual relations. Complete equality, independence, mutual respect, noninterference in another's internal affairs and mutual cooperation—this is the basis governing the international relations established among socialist countries. Only on this principle can the international friendship and solidarity among these countries be consolidated.

> The servile spirit of cringing before big-power domination and order and seeking others' patronage, flunkeyism is fundamentally contradictory to the revolutionary ideas of *chuche* and self-reliance of the communists . . . .

> The flunkeyist elements usher in big-power chauvinists and become their stooges working for their shady design. The big-power chauvinists, employing the flunkeyists, cause splits in another country, meddle in its internal affairs, and try to realize their own egoistic ambition. History teaches us that flunkeyism leads the country to ruin.

> The communists should adhere to independency under any circumstances, shape their lines and policies in conformity with the reality of their own country, and solve their problems by themselves on their own responsibility in reliance upon the creative might of

their own people. (KCNA, 7 March 1967.)

In the political program Kim Il-song again stressed the independent stand of the KWP in the Sino-Soviet conflict, noting the need to approach matters critically "instead of mechanically imitating or swallowing them whole" and following others blindly. The KWP also continued to hail Kim Il-song's policy of "*chuche* in ideology" as an "outstanding contribution not only to the victory of the Korean revolution, but also to the development of the international Communist movement and the world situation . . . thus serving as a practical model of anti-imperialist struggle" (Pyongyang Domestic Service, 14 December 1967).

North Korea's declared theory on the correct approach to imperialism and peaceful coexistence is that "as long as imperialism exists, the danger of war will not disappear." In his article in *Tricontinental* Kim Il-song further elaborated the KWP strategy toward imperialism and indirectly criticized the Soviet Union:

It is wrong to try to avoid the struggle against imperialism under the pretext that although independence and revolution are important, peace is still more precious. . . . Peace secured through slavish submission is not peace. Genuine peace will not come unless a struggle is waged against the breakers of peace. . . . We are opposed to the line of compromise with imperialism. At the same time, we cannot tolerate either the practice of only talking big of opposing imperialism but in deed being afraid of fighting imperialism. The latter is a line of compromise in an inverted form. Both have nothing to do with the genuine anti-imperialist struggle and will only be of help to the imperialist policy of aggression and war. (*Tricontinental,* July-August 1967.)

He concluded the political program with indirect criticism of China:

What attitude the socialist countries take toward US imperialism is a criterion that shows whether or not they fight earnestly for the advancement of the international revolutionary movement at the present time. The attitude toward US imperialism is a touchstone that distinguishes between the revolutionary position and the opportunist position . . . .

On 16 November *Nodong Sinmun* stated that communists should "pool all their revolutionary forces" and "make every effort for the unity of the socialist countries and solidarity of the international Communist movement" (KCNA, 16 November 1967). Numerous party editorials stressed that

. . . difference[s] in social systems and political ideas can never be an obstacle to the joint struggle and concerted action against US imperialism. No one must be allowed to split the anti-US united front and refuse joint action, attaching the first importance to his own nation's or Party's specific interests. It will only benefit the US-led imperialists and do harm to the revolutionary people. (KCNA, 15 August 1967.)

**The Vietnam War.** Throughout 1967 North Korea's call for a communist united front focused specifically on the internationalist duty of the communist countries toward Vietnam. A lengthy article in *Kulloja* on 12 April 1967 stressed:

Today the attitude toward the Vietnam question is a touchstone for all the communists who distinguish between the Marxist-Leninist internationalist stand of actively supporting the just war and the opportunist national egoist stand. Especially, the communists of socialist countries should take a decided, positive stand in supporting the righteous war of the Vietnamese people.

Our Party . . . is actively assisting morally and materially the fighting fraternal peoples of Vietnam. The Marxist-Leninists should vehemently oppose the unjust war and fight to deal a blow at the imperialist reactionary forces who provoke such war and to hasten their doom. It is imperative at present to unite all the anti-imperialist forces for smashing the US imperialist policies of aggression and war and administer a blow to them with united might. (*Kulloja,* as broadcast by KCNA, 12 April 1967.)

*Nodong Sinmun* (16 November 1967) reiterated the KWP call to the socialist countries to render all possible assistance to Vietnam, to follow and support the stand of the Vietnam Workers' Party, and to regard the Vietnamese struggle as their own.

**The Arab-Israeli War.** During the Arab-Israeli conflict in June 1967 North Korea expressed militant solidarity with and support for the Arab cause and accused Israel of "aggravating the Middle East situation to the extreme at the direct instigation of US imperialism" (KCNA, 6 June 1967). North Korea also announced its determination to do "everything in [its] power to assist the Arab peoples in their just struggle against the aggressors" (KCNA, 7 June 1967). Unlike China, the DPRK did not criticize the Soviet Union by name, and only hinted that the communist states could have helped the Arabs more actively.

**International Activity.** Although emphasizing the need for unity of the socialist countries and solidarity of the international communist movement, the KWP has continued to oppose the idea of an international communist conference and did not attend the Budapest Conference in February 1968. The KWP apparently also refrained from making any comment on the Karlovy Vary Conference of European Communist and Workers' Parties held in April 1967. The North Korean government, however, did send a delegation of observers to the OLAS Conference held in Havana on 31 July-10 August. The delegation consisted of Yun Ki-pak, Choe Chon-nam, and Kam Sol-mo.

During 1967 the KWP participated actively in most of the major international front organizations. A North Korean delegation attended the June-July Emergency Meeting of the Afro-Asian People's Solidarity Organization (AAPSO). Contacts with the Afro-Asian Latin American People's Solidarity Organization (AALAPSO) were strengthened, and representation in the AALAPSO Executive Secretariat was maintained. At the invitation of the Korean Committee for Afro-Asian Solidarity, a delegation of the AALAPSO Executive Secretariat, headed by Carlos Lechuga, arrived in Pyongyang on 11 April and was received by Kim Il-song. In early May a second AALAPSO delegation, led by Bernardo Araya, visited North Korea.

Contacts were also furthered with other international front organizations. In March a delegation of the Korean Democratic Women's Union attended the "extraordinary meeting of the Committee for Solidarity with Vietnam," sponsored by the Women's International Democratic Federation (WIDF) in East Germany, and in October a Korean Democratic Women's Union delegation attended the Council meeting of the WIDF in Prague. In May 1967 North Korea received visiting delegations from the World Federation of Democratic Youth (WFDY), the International Union of Students (IUS), and the International Association of Journalists (IOJ), as well as Mme. Isabelle Blume, Chairman of the World Council of Peace (WCP).

In May a delegation of the World Federation of Trade Unions (WFTU), led by its President Renato Bitossi, visited North Korea, and a North Korean trade-union delegation participated in the thirty-fourth meeting of the Executive Committee of the WFTU in October.

**Relations with China.** Relations with the Chinese Communist Party remained minimal during 1967. On 20 January Red Guard wall posters appearing in Peking reported the arrest of Kim Kwang-hyop, Deputy Premier, member of the Presidium of the Political Committee of the Central Committee, and former Chief of Staff and Defense Minister, by Choe Yong-kon, member of the Presidium of the KWP Central Committee, member of the Secretariat, and President of the Presidium of the Supreme People's Assembly. North Korea indirectly denied the charges by reporting that Kim Kwang-hyop attended a theater performance on 22 January 1967, but following repeated accusations, the Korean Central News Agency issued an authorized statement attacking the Chinese wall posters as "groundless fabrications" and "an intolerable slander against the Party, government, people, and the people's army of our country" (KCNA, 26 January 1967). Frequent appearances by Kim Kwang-hyop during 1967 and his reappointment to the cabinet on 16 December 1967 appear to confirm North Korean denials.

Red Guard attacks on the KWP did not cease, however, and in early February 1967 Chinese wall posters, reportedly signed by Chinese veterans of the Korean War, attacked Kim Il-song as a "fat revisionist" and "Khrushchev's disciple" and accused him of sabotaging the struggle of the Vietnamese people by refusing to send volunteers to Vietnam, of being ungrateful for Chinese aid during the Korean War, and of slandering the cultural revolution.

North Korea did not reply to these charges directly; instead North Korean embassy officials and

Korean Central News Agency representatives in Algiers, Djakarta, New Delhi, Havana, and elsewhere issued statements denying the Chinese accusations and warning China that it would be held responsible for "all possible consequences" resulting from the attacks. Through these spokesmen North Korea asserted that there was no difference between the Red Guards and the Chinese leaders, who had in fact authorized the attacks, and indirectly criticized the Chinese cultural revolution by noting that "it seems that some who like to defame the living conditions in our country and close their eyes to reality do not live better than we do" (Havana Domestic Television Service, 1 March 1967). As for the rationale for the attacks, North Korea asserted:

As to the matter of slandering our Party as being revisionist, they do this because it is they in fact who stand for the revisionist position. Apparently they do not like us to defend the purity of Marxism-Leninism against right- and left-wing opportunism and that we should actively support and bolster the peoples of all nations who fight for their national independence and freedom against imperialism. (KCNA representative in Havana, Havana Domestic Service, 20 February 1967.)

North Korea and Communist China continued their disagreement over the basic questions of whether the unity of the socialist bloc should take precedence over ideological differences, and whether a party can pursue an independent line which is still valid in terms of Marxism-Leninism. North Korea also continued to attack Communist China indirectly for refusing to join in united action toward Vietnam.

Despite deteriorating relations between the two parties, superficial amenities in state-to-state relations continued, as demonstrated by North Korea's observance of the sixth anniversary of the signing of the Sino-Korean Treaty of Friendship, Cooperation, and Mutual Assistance (11 July 1967) and of the fortieth anniversary of the Chinese People's Liberation Army (1 August 1967). The North Korean regime, however, failed to send special representatives to Peking's National Day celebrations on 1 October. Expressions of solidarity and mutual support have virtually disappeared from public pronouncements. Unlike the Soviet Union, North Vietnam, and the National Liberation Front of South Vietnam, China ignored the nineteenth anniversary of the Korean People's Army.

**Relations with the Soviet Union.** In contrast to North Korea's deteriorating relationship with Communist China, relations with the Soviet Union appeared to improve despite continuing KWP criticism of the Soviet adherence to the policy of "peaceful coexistence." Most contacts with the Soviet Union remained on a governmental level, however, and focused on economic, cultural, and technological cooperation.

A high-level Korean delegation led by Kim Il visited the Soviet Union on 13 February-3 March to discuss economic and scientific matters. Although no specific details were disclosed, the negotiations resulted in the signing of a series of agreements on cultural, economic, and technological cooperation, as well as mutual goods deliveries in 1967. The two sides also signed a second agreement providing for "cooperation in further strengthening the defense potential of North Korea." On 5 October 1967 a second North Korean economic delegation, led by Yi Chu-yon, visited the Soviet Union. An agreement was subsequently signed providing for a 30 per cent increase in mutual trade deliveries for 1968, Soviet cooperation in the building of a number of "enterprises," and the establishment of an economic and technological consultative commission to accelerate cooperation.

Additional North Korean contacts with the Soviet Union during 1967 included a delegation from the Soviet All-Union Central Council of Trade Unions on 9 May 1967, two delegations from the Soviet-Korean Friendship Society (23 August and 1 November 1967), and a delegation led by S. K. Romanovskiy, President of the Committee for Cultural Relations with Foreign Countries of the Soviet Council of Ministers, which resulted in the signing on 26 June of the 1967 plan for cultural and scientific cooperation between the DPRK and the Soviet Union. North Korea also responded to the invitation of the Supreme Soviet of the Soviet Union, and on 17 June a delegation of the Korean Supreme People's Assembly arrived in Moscow, led by Yi Yong-ho, Vice-President of the SPA Presidium and member of the KWP Central Committee Political Committee. On 6 July *Nodong Sinmun* hailed the sixth anniversary of the signing of the Korean-Soviet Treaty of Friendship, Cooperation, and Mutual Assistance.

North Korean preparations for the celebration of the Fiftieth Anniversary of the October Revolution began on 10 July, when the Political Committee of the KWP Central Committee adopted a decision on the October celebrations calling on all party members and working people to celebrate the anniversary "significantly and extensively" (KCNA, 11 July 1967). On 13 July a delegation of the League of Socialist Working Youth of Korea left Pyongyang to attend an international youth gathering in Leningrad to discuss the celebration of the Fiftieth Anniversary. On 31 October 1967 party and government representatives left to attend the October Revolution celebrations in Moscow. The delegation included Choe Yong-kon, member of the Presidium of the KWP Political Committee and President of the SPA; Pak Song-chol, member of the KWP Political Committee, Vice-Premier, and Minister of Foreign Affairs; Yi Min-su, member of the KWP Central Committee and Director of one of its departments; Major General Chong O-tae, Vice-Director of the General Political Bureau of the Korean People's Army; and Choe Yong-kim, Vice-Director of a department of the Party Central Committee (KCNA, 31 October 1967). Other delegations included participants in the Korean "national liberation struggle" and the "patriotic war of liberation" led by Lieutenant General Im Chol of the Korean People's Army; a delegation of the Korean-Soviet Friendship Society led by Yi Ki-yong, Chairman of its Central Committee, a delegation of the League of Socialist Working Youth of Korea, led by O Ki-chon, Co-Chairman of its Central Committee; a delegation of the Korean Democratic Women's Union led by Kim Ok-sun, Chairman of its Central Committee; and a delegation of the Central Federation of the Korean Consumer Cooperatives led by Kim Song-kun, Director of its Council (KCNA, 31 October 1967).

**The Third World.** During 1967 North Korea continued to emphasize its active support for and solidarity with the national liberation movements of the third world. Although few, if any, actual party contacts were made, the KWP continued to exert its influence in the Middle East and Africa and exchanged several visits with Middle East and African countries and organizations, including the Congo (Brazzaville), Algeria, the Mozambique National Liberation Front (FRELIMO), and a series of pan-African organizations.

**Asia.** KWP activity in Asia in 1967 continued to focus on its relations with and support for the Japan Communist Party (JCP). Several *Kulloja* and *Nodong Sinmun* editorials hailed the JCP for " . . . consolidating the organization and ideological unity of its ranks and firmly adhering to an independent stand based on the principles of Marxism-Leninism, frustrating the divisive, subversive machinations of the revisionists, dogmatists, flunkeyists, and sectarian elements" (*Kulloja,* as broadcast by KCNA, 13 April 1967). On the occasion of the forty-fifth anniversary of the founding of the JCP, *Nodong Sinmun* praised the JCP for frustrating "antiparty elements" and for "greatly contributing to the development of the international communist movement." The editorial further praised the Japan Communists as "close comrades in arms, tied with indestructible bonds in the long-drawn common struggle" (*Nodong Sinmun,* 15 July 1967 as broadcast by KCNA). During the course of 1967 Sunama Ichiro, alternate member of the JCP Central Committee Presidium, visited Pyongyang and met with Kim Il-song (August-September 1967). Other contacts included the visit of a delegation of the Japan-Korea Association (13 March-15 April) and a delegation from the Japan Council Against Atomic and Hydrogen Bombs (June-July 1967).

The KWP also maintained its relations with the Vietnam Workers' Party and the National Liberation Front of South Vietnam (NLFSV). Kim Il-song telegraphed Le Duan, First Secretary of the Central Committee of the Vietnam Workers' Party on his birthday and praised the Vietnam Workers' Party as a "powerful member of the international Communist movement whose prestige and authority have greatly increased" and whose "anti-US national salvation struggle has become a paragon for the national liberation movement and a great contribution to the struggle for defending the world socialist camp and safeguarding peace in Asia and the rest of the world" (KCNA, 6 April 1967). In May Kim Il-song received and held friendly talks with representatives of the General Federation of Trade Unions of both North and South Vietnam, the NLFSV, and the Vietnam Committee for Afro-Asian Solidarity. Throughout the year the General Federation of Trade Unions, the League of Socialist Working Youth of Korea, the Korean Democratic Women's Union, and the United Democratic Fatherland Front exchanged expressions of support and solidarity with their counterparts in Vietnam.

On 12 June North Vietnam and North Korea signed agreements for cultural cooperation during 1967, and on 11 August the two countries concluded agreements for providing for nonrefundable Korean economic and military aid to Vietnam, as well as a general program governing trade during 1968.

KWP activities in Asia also included the visit of a SPA delegation led by Yi Yong-ho, Vice-President of the SPA Presidium and member of the KWP Central Committee Political Committee, to Mongolia in June 1967 and a series of KWP Central Committee telegrams to the Central Committee of the Neo Lao Hak Xat (NLHX) in support of the Laotian people's struggle. The Korean party press also gave publicity to an article by Xom Lat, the NLHX representative at the Korean May Day celebrations, which stressed KWP-NLHX relations (see Laos).

**Latin America.** The newly formed Havana-Pyongyang "axis" continued to dominate Korean party relations with Latin America. KWP editorials praised the achievements of Cuba and the Cuban people under the Cuban Communist Party, noting that "our Party and our people are guarding the eastern outpost of the socialist camp and the Cuban Communist Party and the Cuban people are standing guard over the Western Hemisphere outpost for the socialist camp" (*Kulloja,* as broadcast by KCNA, 30 January 1967). The extent of Cuban-Korean relations was further defined by the DPRK ambassador to Cuba on 25 June:

> The unshakeable and combative friendship and unity between our two parties, governments, and peoples of our two countries, is developing and growing stronger every day for the good of the revolution of our two countries and of world revolution. Our people are proud to have the courageous Cuban people, who are steadfast and loyal to the revolution, as their comrades in arms. . . . The Korean Workers' Party and the Korean people have supported, support, and will again support the just position of the Cuban Communist Party, which is correctly directing the revolution and the construction of the country behind the standard of the revolution, and which is fighting for the unity and cohesion of the socialist camp and the international communist movement. (Havana Domestic Service, 25 June 1967.)

North Korea not only emphasized its bilateral party relations with Cuba, but also stressed: "It is an internationalist duty of all the revolutionary peoples to fight in defense of the gains of the Cuban revolution. Revolutionary Cuba represents the future of Latin America and its very existence encourages the peoples of this continent in their liberation movement" (KCNA, 15 August 1967).

Individual contacts between North Korea and Cuba during 1967 included a visit to North Korea on 29 June by a delegation of the Cuban Revolutionary Committee, led by Piolino Reimez Mereno, and a trade-union delegation led by Pak Yi-pil and sent by the DPRK to attend the May Day celebrations in Cuba. On 19 June North Korea sent a delegation led by Yun Ki-pak, Minister of Common Education, Chairman of the Korean-Latin American Friendship Society, and Chairman of the Korean-Cuban Solidarity Committee, to attend the First Conference of the Latin American Solidarity Organization (OLAS) held in Havana.

On 20 July a "month of solidarity with the Cuban people" was proclaimed, and on 27 August Yu Song-ui, the DPRK Vice Minister of Foreign Trade arrived in Havana to sign a trade agreement for 1968. On 17 October the KWP Central Committee sent a telegram of condolence to the Central Committee of the Cuban Communist Party on Ernesto "Che" Guevara's death, hailing him as an "outstanding internationalist fighter."

On 10-17 November a top-level North Korean party and government delegation visited Cuba. The delegation was led by Choe Yong-kun, member of the Presidium of the Political Committee and member of the Secretariat and President of the Presidium of the SPA, and included Pak Song-chol, member of the Political Committee, Vice-Premier of the cabinet, and Foreign Minister; Yi Min-su, member of the Central Committee and Director of a department of the Party Central Committee; Chong O-tae, Major General of the Korean People's Army; and Kim Yun-son, Vice Director of a department of the KWP Central Committee, in addition to lower-level party functionaries.

According to the joint communique issued at the end of the visit, the two sides "exchanged opinions on problems of mutual interest and other international questions," "arrived at an absolute identity of views," and confirmed the correctness of the contents of the joint Korean-Cuban communique signed in Pyongyang in October 1966. Talks reportedly focused on economic and cultural considerations, but considerable emphasis was also placed on the need to wage "revolutionary armed struggle" and the correctness of "Che" Guevara's formula of "creating one, two, three, many Vietnams." Choe Yong-kon hailed the "indestructible bonds" between the Cuban and Korean parties and thanked the Cuban party, government, and people for their "active support and aid in the struggle that our people are waging":

> The development and strengthening of the friendly relations between the two countries, Korea and Cuba, mean a great contribution toward achieving the cohesion and unity of the socialist countries and of the international communist movement. They will also strengthen the anti-Yankee and anti-imperialist struggle and defend the peace of the world. Our people greatly appreciate the friendship and unity with the fraternal Cuban people. In the future, we shall also make every effort to strengthen and develop the friendly relations of collaboration between our two peoples. (Havana Domestic Service, 13 November 1967.)

The KWP also strengthened its ties with the rest of Latin America. While in Cuba, Choe Yong-kon hailed the OLAS Conference as having "contributed greatly to the development of the revolution in Latin America" and thus "strengthened the unity and collaboration of the peoples of the area." He also noted:

> The just struggle of liberation waged by the peoples of Latin America against US imperialism and its lackeys is part of the great revolutionary struggle of the international labor class for socialism. We make every effort to strengthen our international solidarity with it. The Korean people actively support and back the struggle of the several Latin American countries that are fighting bravely, weapons in hand, against Yankee imperialism and the dictatorships and for the consolidation of their liberation and national independence. (Havana Domestic Service, 13 November 1967.)

Contacts were also made with other Latin American parties and revolutionary movements. On 10 May Kim Il-song received Gabriel Salazar, member of the Political Committee and Secretariat of the Guatemalan Workers' Party and Major Elías Manuit, Chairman of the Venezuelan National Liberation Front. Numerous expressions of solidarity were also exchanged between the KWP and the Pro-Independence Movement of Puerto Rico.

**Europe.** North Korea's relations with Western and Eastern Europe continued to emphasize cultural, economic, and scientific-technical agreements, as well as mutual exchanges of trade-union, youth-organization, and parliamentary delegations. Specific party contacts also included a KWP delegation to the Seventh Congress of the East German Socialist Unity Party (17-22 April), led by Yi Chu-yon, member of the Political Committee, as well as a visit by a delegation of the French General Confederation of Labor on 9 May, led by Bénoît Frachon, its Secretary-General and member of the Political Bureau of the French Communist Party.

On 24 May a Hungarian military delegation led by Colonel General Lajos Czinege, candidate member of the Politburo of the Hungarian Socialist Workers' Party and Minister of Defense, arrived in Pyongyang at the invitation of the KWP Political Committee. A North Korean communique issued at the end of the visit stated that the Hungarian delegation had conducted negotiations with the leaders of the North Korean Defense Ministry, but further details were not disclosed.

The KWP Central Committee also sent a message of greetings in November to the Thirtieth Congress of the British Communist Party, expressing North Korean solidarity with the British party and the British working people in their "struggle against the aggressive policy of the imperialists, led by US imperialism, and against the British Labour Party's policy of sympathizing with and following the USA" (KCNA, 24 November 1967).

**Publications.** The daily organ of the KWP is *Nodong Sinmun,* which is edited by Chong Chon-ki, with Chong Ha-chon as vice-editor. The theoretical organ of the KWP Central Committee is *Kulloja.* Other KWP publications include *Minju Choson,* a daily organ of the KWP sponsored by the Supreme

People's Assembly and the cabinet; *1st March,* the organ of the Association of the Restoration of the Fatherland; *Chokuk Tongil,* the organ of the Committee for the Peaceful Unification of the Fatherland; *Nodong Ch'ongyon,* the principal publication of the League of Socialist Working Youth of Korea; and *Nodongja Sinmun* and *Nodongja,* the newspaper and monthly journal, respectively, of the General Federation of Trade Unions of Korea. Western-language publications include *Korea,* an illustrated monthly in Russian, Chinese, English, Japanese, and French; *Korea Today,* in English, French, and Japanese; *New Korea,* in Russian and Chinese; and the *Pyongyang Times* and *Pyongyang Daily,* in English.

North Korea's broadcasts are carried primarily by the Korean Central News Agency, as well as by Pyongyang Domestic Service. The Korean Central News Agency broadcasts in English to Southeast Asia, the Middle East, and Africa; in Spanish to Latin America; and in Japanese, Korean, Russian, Chinese and Indonesian. Its Director is Pae Ki-chun, although Seoul reports indicate that he has been purged as a result of the defection of one of the Vice-Directors, Yi Su-kun. Other Vice-Directors include Ho Kang, Han Yong-yon, and Ku Il-son.

On 31 March 1967 a new North Korean clandestine radio station, calling itself the "Radio of the Democratic Union for the Liberation of South Korea," began broadcasting to the south, calling on the people of the Republic of Korea to overthrow their "reactionary" government.

# NORWAY

The Communist Party of Norway (Norges Kommunistiske Parti; NKP) was founded 4 November 1923. The NKP was strongest at the time of its inception and in the 1945 elections, when it gained 11.8 per cent of the votes, but has been a marginal factor in Norwegian politics for many years. Its decline was accelerated by the appearance in 1961 of the left-wing pacifist Socialist People's Party (Socialistisk Folkeparti; SF), formed from the ranks of social democrats and nonaffiliated leftists. Standing midway between the social democratic Labor Party of Norway (Det Norsk Arbeiderparti; DNA), which was in power from 1935 to 1965 and remains the largest single party, and the NKP, the SF presents an increasing threat to the existence of the NKP.

The declining Communist vote finds its most fertile ground in the "sectarianism" of Finnmark, Norway's northernmost province, which, with its economic insecurity aggravated by an arctic climate, trails all other provinces in socioeconomic development.

The NKP claims "between 4,000 and 5,000 paying members" (*Friheten*, 31 September-5 October), but Western sources place the figure at 2,000 to 3,000. The population of Norway is 3,754,000 (estimated, January 1968).

Beset by internal dissension, the NKP was able to participate in only 84 of Norway's 451 communes in the 23 September 1967 municipal election, 30 fewer than in 1965, and gained 1.3 per cent of the popular vote, down slightly from 1.4 per cent. Fifty-nine communes reflected results similar to the 1965 election, while the remainder showed small declines. Small gains were attained by the DNA, the Liberals, and the Center (Agrarian) Party, while the SF vote increased from 6 to 8.3 per cent, at the expense of the extremes in the political spectrum, the Conservatives and the Communists. The ruling coalition parties (Conservative, Liberal, Center, and Christian People's) dropped slightly to 49 per cent of the total vote. The last parliamentary seat held by the Communists fell to the SF in 1961.

As in the 1965 elections, the 1967 NKP losses were attributed by party Chairman Reidar T. Larsen to "internal difficulties" and to "blows directed against the Party through the acute internal discussion and the demise of CC members right in the middle of the election preparations" (*Friheten*, 31 September-5 October). Owing to the high average age of its members (estimated by some observers as 45 to 50), continued regression at the present rate and continued failure to attract young activists could result in the NKP's disappearance from the political scene in the foreseeable future.

Larsen was elected Chairman at the Eleventh Party Congress in March 1965, replacing "Stalinist" Emil Løvlien. The NKP Secretariat includes Just Lippe, Rolf Nettum, and Arne Pettersen. Eleven of the former Central Committee of 31 members resigned in March 1967, and there is no evidence that replacements have been appointed.

The programmatic reorientation of the NKP started in April 1963 with the adoption of a new program which switched emphasis from the DNA to monopolistic capitalism as "principal enemy" and discarded the concept of the "dictatorship of the proletariat" in favor of the "rule of the working class." According to the program, the NKP is an independent, democratic, and national Nordic party, based on the principles of Marxism-Leninism and having as its aim the overthrow of capitalism in Norway through peaceful transition to a parliamentary socialist republic. Larsen has said:

> In all questions we are trying to arrive at opinions and directives which have not been taken mechanically from some other country or some other party, but which are based on our own conditions and our own evaluations. It is quite simply a matter of applying Marxism in Norway. (*Friheten*, 3 February 1967.)

Both Larsen and those "liberals" who seek to emulate the Swedish example commend Swedish party Chairman C. H. Hermansson for having "translated his knowledge of Leninism into Swedish terms and to suit Swedish conditions" (*Friheten*, 3 March). However, Larsen has been less successful than his Swedish counterpart, and in 1967 reiterated his annual call for a "new start" for the NKP. Failure to achieve the "new start" is explained in part by the differing political circumstances in the two countries. While in Sweden the Communists represent the sole established party to the left of the Social Democrats and control a large number of left-wing socialists, in Norway NKP support among this element has been largely preempted by the SF. The Swedish Communist Party has been increasingly successful in aligning with Nordic socialist parties, whereas the NKP is being rapidly excluded from the "active left" of the North.*

The "renewal process" envisages "the gathering of the broadest possible front . . . often cutting across the line between political parties . . . to limit the power of capitalist interests and expand the democratic rights of the people." Larsen has stated:

> The objective basis for a large, unified leftist formation lies in the fact that most of our people are wage earners or small, independent fishermen, farmers, craftsmen, etc. Their most important common interests are threatened, economically and politically, by a small group controlling economic life. Politically, this group represents the forces of reactionary society that are closely connected with aggressive international capitalism . . . . (*Friheten*, 22-28 April.)

Further, it is only through "political struggle" that leftist forces can "break loose and unite."

The formulation of an "updated" working program, the call to youth, and the party organ's broadened editorial policies together constitute a "united-front" tactical orientation and, in practical political terms, a concentrated attempt to identify with the "active left" on significant domestic and foreign-policy issues rather than risk political annihilation as a "revolutionary" party, a fear increasingly justified in direct proportion to the gains of the SF.

Evaluating the NKP's position at the end of the year, Larsen said:

> We had many difficulties to overcome. The negative discussion of several years culminated this year when certain CC members who could not break with old, bad habits withdrew from the CC. The disturbance in this regard contributed to reduce our chances in the municipal elections, but for the Party itself the year was nevertheless consolidating. We set outselves as a goal to make 1967 a year which would mark a "new start" for the Party, and we have achieved the principal goal which we set. (*Friheten*, 29 December 1967-4 January 1968.)

NKP strength in trade unions is limited. The party controls none of the national labor unions, and its membership in the Norwegian Federation of Labor Unions is well below 10 per cent. The NKP directs only a few auxiliary organizations, including a youth organization, which split in 1967. The Baltic Sea Committee, also controlled by the NKP, aims to keep the Baltic Sea an "ocean of peace." To further this aim, the Committee sends large delegations to the annual meetings of Baltic nations held in Rostock, East Germany; the 1967 meeting took place on 12-14 July. The NKP controls various associations for promoting friendship between Norway and other primarily socialist countries, such as the Norway-Soviet Union Association and the Norway-Czechoslovakia Association.

**Domestic Policies.** In domestic affairs the NKP has called for (1) a cut in the defense budget, (2) establishment of industrial zones in high unemployment areas, (3) increased housing construction, and (4) stronger trade-union influence in wage negotiations.

Although the party saw few possibilities for interparty alliances in the 1967 local elections, it has declared that "the situation is ripening for a common action of leftist forces," and that the NKP would in the future seek "an electoral union and other forms of electoral cooperation between left-socialist forces and other progressively oriented people where the situation is favorable" (*Friheten*, 22-28 April). However, the DNA and the SF have not given the NKP reason to suppose that they would be receptive to proposals for such cooperation.

With no voice in the national legislature, the NKP has criticized the government's "wait-and-see

---

*A similar situation prevails in Denmark, where the Danish Communists have also lost much of their following to the Danish Socialist People's Party. Thus at the Nordic Socialist Seminar sponsored by the Danish Socialists (Copenhagen, 26-27 February) both the Danish and Norwegian parties were denied admission, while the Swedish party was invited to send a representative.

position which characterizes its economic policy" (*Friheten,* 22 March). According to the Communists, industry should be diverted from larger urban areas to less populated high unemployment centers, a position also held by the SF. Larsen has promised workers that the NKP would place "the entire spectrum of this question at the forefront of its attention to domestic policy" (*Friheten,* 22 March).

A new party program, to be worked out and presented at the Twelfth Party Congress 15-17 March 1968 (originally scheduled for Fall 1967 but postponed owing to a threat to party unity) is to

> . . . aim at taking up all important problems in Norway and in Norwegian politics, working with a ten-year perspective. . . . The process of transformation is not easy, but it is necessary . . . and will open the door to a far more trusting and meaningful cooperation with other leftist forces in Norwegian politics in the future. (*Friheten,* 15-21 April.)

The new program will hopefully "lead the Party away from general phrase-filled formulations" (*Friheten,* 29 December 1967-4 January 1968).

**Foreign-Policy Program.** No radical changes in foreign policy were advocated by the NKP during 1967. The party seeks to gain support among the "foes of monopolistic capitalism" on the issues of (1) a Nordic nuclear-free zone, (2) withdrawal from NATO, (3) international disarmament, (4) "neo-Nazism" in West Germany, (5) opposition to EEC affiliation, and (6) "solidarity with the victims of imperialist aggression" in Vietnam, Greece, Spain, Mozambique, and elsewhere.

The NKP cautions against "hasty negotiations" for Norwegian affiliation with the European Economic Community, which would "leave the country open to foreign capital interests, and would involve surrender of Norway's national independence." Norway must strive to a higher degree for "Nordic economic cooperation," and for cooperation with "all peoples of the world" (*Friheten,* 22-28 April). The party calls for "reestablishment of Norway's neutrality" and dissolution of all "economic and military bloc formations," with the ultimate goal of a "North of neutral states which have banned atomic weapons from their territories and which unite their forces in work for international disarmament and relaxation of tension" (*Friheten,* 1-7 September).

With respect to the Arab-Israeli conflict, the Central Committee, in a measure designed to placate those critical of the NKP leadership's "failure to take a stand" in international issues without making any commitment that could isolate the party further from Norwegian voters, steered a neutral course and declared that "only a negotiated solution can ensure Israel's existence on a basis which can be recognized by the Arab people" (*Friheten,* 16-22 June).

**Internal Dissension and the Sino-Soviet Dispute.** By the beginning of 1967 conflict among NKP leaders concerning the attitude to be taken in the Sino-Soviet dispute had assumed overwhelming proportions, despite repeated denials by the party Chairman. Pervading every facet of party life, the internal conflict constituted more a question of interpretation of the concept of "democratic centralism" than merely a divergence of views on an important international issue. The first sign that discussion was to be replaced by active opposition had come at the Central Committee meeting in November 1966, which adopted a resolution emphasizing noninterference in the dispute and calling upon both powers to "normalize their relations."

The majority view favors dissociation from the conflict and maintains that the NKP should seek to "develop friendly and comradely relations on the basis of the right of each Party to full self-determination" (*Friheten,* 22-28 April). International events should be discussed, but no resolutions passed, "as in the case of Khrushchev's deposition, or the judgment on Sinyavsky and Daniel." It is "neither necessary nor appropriate" for the party to "pass resolutions concerning conditions in other [communist parties] or in socialist countries, as if we were a provincial organization belonging to one of them." This is a "tradition left over from the time of the Comintern, when [communist parties] regarded themselves as branches of a world Party," and "there are other [parties] that feel the same way on this matter; Sweden and Rumania are examples." (*Friheten,* 24 February.) Larsen's fundamental premise, shared by most of his supporters, is that unless the NKP is able to offer a constructive contribution in international affairs, its primary efforts should be toward internal consolidation and strengthening of its influence in the domestic political arena. As one prominent Communist put it:

Of course the conflict between the Soviet Union and China concerns us, but we cannot untie the knot. As a brother Party, we can only exert our influence when the opportunity arises, [and] the worst part is that activity within the Party is about to be paralyzed by this discussion. Do we not have enough problems in this country that demand our serious attention?" (*Friheten*, 21 January.)

Expressing the frustration which has historically plagued the NKP in its efforts to mollify both Moscow and the Norwegian electorate, Harold Saehle, a frequent contributor to *Friheten*, said: "Possibly politically interested workers would understand us better if, for example, we had not taken a neutral stand on the Soviet intervention in Hungary, if we had supported the sentences of Sinyavsky and Daniel, and if we had done more to counteract propaganda for liberalization" (*Friheten*, 6 January).

The minority faction, led by Secretariat members Henry Hoff and Jørgen Vogt, then editor-in-chief of *Friheten*,* sought outright condemnation of Chinese policies of violence, inasmuch as they are "incompatible" with the statutes of the NKP. Larsen characterized the pro-Moscow minority as having "developed a distorted view of the NKP, its politics, and its development" and charged that participation of some NKP members in "political schools abroad" has had an "unfortunate influence" (*Friheten*, 15-21 April).

On 10 January 1967 Central Committee member Per Svensson revealed that a "large minority" had abstained from voting on the November 1966 resolution (*Arbeiderbladet*). Although Larsen had claimed that the resolution was passed "unanimously," it was in fact adopted only after a draft resolution proposed by Vogt—condemning China and favoring a conference of all communist parties—had been defeated. (*Arbeiderbladet*, 26 January.)

Confronted with this "credibility gap," Larsen alleged that the party leadership contained "a small group which is strongly engaged in forming our statements and our line after a pattern which is set by another party" (*Arbeiderbladet*, 14 January). He accused Vogt of an "insatiable desire to fill columns with negative debate" (*Friheten*, 27 January). "The 'minority' does not lack the courage to characterize the development in China," said Larsen, "but for one reason or another does not have the same courage as far as the Soviet Union is concerned. It seems proper for this minority to mention only those past events that the present leadership of the CPSU is also criticizing." (*Arbeiderbladet*, 27 January.)

This accusation was in turn repudiated by Hoff, who claimed that the party Chairman failed to criticize the leaders of the Chinese Communist Party in the same manner that the party had "on several occasions" criticized the Soviet leadership. Against such a background, he contested, "Larsen's independence is seen in a strange light, and the question can certainly be asked who is fighting for a manifestation of the NKP as an independent and autonomous Party" (*Friheten*, 4 February).

The party organ was filled with an exchange of polemics, and one reader warned that

    . . . the Central Committee can never prevent this conflict from flaring up within our Party by passing resolutions. . . . Such methods will result in the isolation of the leaders from the people, the crumbling of the Party from below, the shrinking of the leadership to a clique that finds its true support in working with other Party cliques until it destroys itself. . . . Without an ideological struggle, there can be no 'peaceful transition to socialism'. (*Friheten*, 14 January.)

Outlining "the Party's problem and the way out of it," Larsen conceded that the discussion "perhaps represented a stage in a process which our Party must go through" but asserted that the effect had been "primarily negative because it has distracted our attention from the problems with which we are confronted in our own country." The party line is based on the recognition that both sides are responsible for the "malignant strife," and that "none of the events in China today have changed this." He insisted that opposition within the Central Committee is not a result of events in

---

*The positions of Larsen and Vogt were at one time reversed; in 1964 Vogt was Acting Chairman and Secretary of the NKP "due to the failing health of Party Chairman Emil Løvlien," and Larsen was editor-in-chief of *Friheten* before his election as Chairman of the party.

China but has existed all along, and people are simply trying to "take advantage of these events in an effort to destroy this line." As for the future, Larsen said: "I am in favor of relaxing our attitude toward anything occurring in other Parties. Quite simply, I think that members of the NKP should become more interested in their own Party and their own tasks." (*Friheten*, 24 February.)

But with the plea of the Oslo NKP for an extraordinary congress to "put the Party into working condition," it could no longer be denied that the dislocation was paralyzing party activity (*Friheten*, 13 March). Other district meetings held during the first four months of the year reflected this conviction and uniformly issued statements—with little or no opposition—in effect upholding "those lines taken up by the Central Committee in November 1966" and calling for an end to "all useless and negative discussion . . . whether it concerns the Party leadership, the Party otherwise, or newspaper discussion" (*Friheten*, 25 February).

*Friheten* ceased daily publication on 31 March and began as a weekly on 15 April. Surrounding the issue of the "new" party organ was the much-discussed question of its editorial policy. Vogt, in addition to having "lowered the standards" of the paper and thus causing a "degeneration of the discussion," was also alleged by the party Chairman to have disregarded directives concerning insertion of Larsen's own article and to have abused his position as editor by monopolizing the columns with the voice of the opposition. At the Central Committee meeting on 18-19 March the dissension and its cumulative impact upon party unity came to a head with a resolution relieving Vogt of his duties (although not removing him from the Central Committee) and naming an "editorial advisory board" comprising Larsen, Arne Jørgensen (formerly news editor under Vogt), and Vogt—in that order. The party leadership chose not to call this move an ouster, but rather a "reorganization called for by *Friheten*'s publication as a weekly." This measure was adopted only after rejection of a minority proposal to strip Larsen of his position as party Chairman and appoint a new Secretariat, since Larsen had "threatened" to resign if Vogt were not officially condemned.

Two days later, the minority of 11 asserted in a communique that

> . . . the question of the Party's position in the international Communist movement is not the most important aspect in the conflict. . . . [It] concerns first and foremost our Norwegian politics and the question of democracy in the Party. . . . [We] do not wish, under the existing conditions, to continue as members of the Party's leadership to have responsibility for the Party's political and organizational activity. (*Arbeiderbladet*, 20 March.)

With this new development, Larsen declared:

> We do not foresee a new rift in the NKP. In the Central Committee, as well as in the Party at large, the prevailing attitude is that the Party must accept differences of opinion in several areas of Party ideology and develop along with these. . . . We have abolished the practice of exclusion of members for their opinions; they must, however, accept democratic rules. (*Friheten*, 20 March.)

Concurrent with this statement was a broad plea for joint action to reaffirm the ideological directives of the party, and in an ensuing series of articles on "combined efforts for the Party's political line" it was made clear that the split had come at a crucial time—with the establishment of the new party press and, most important, while the party was preparing for the September elections.

On 29 March *Friheten* carried the terse announcement: "Jørgen Vogt has requested to be relieved of his duties on the Editorial Board of *Friheten*. A new member will be elected without delay." Announcing *Friheten*'s new editorial policy, Larsen said the paper would provide scope for all left wingers to present their views but would devote itself to problems that concern "our country, our youth, and our people. *There* our tasks lie. . . . I regard the reorganization of the paper as a first link in the new start we are determined to make this year for the Party [and] our paper is turning its back upon all attempts to tie it and the Party to introvert contemplation of problems totally foreign to our people." (*Friheten*, 31 March.)

Although Larsen claimed that Furubotn's* influence had unquestionably been a factor in the

---

*Peder Furubotn, wartime political leader, was expelled from the NKP, together with his supporters, who comprised the majority of the Central Committee, in a Moscow-directed purge during 1949 and 1950. Described as

"unrest prevalent in the Party in recent years," he argued that this influence was now negligible and should, for the sake of Party unity, be discounted by Furubotn's "political heirs":

> We can no longer allow a group to keep on making our small Party into a battleground over the issues in other [communist parties] and in socialist countries. The Party must demonstrate by its own practice that it is not a foreign element in Norwegian politics. If we cannot succeed in doing so, the Party is doomed to a sectarian existence." (*Friheten*, 15-21 April.)

A national conference was held on 8-9 April to discuss the situation in the party, the proposal to hold a congress, the forthcoming local elections, proposals for local programs, and a proposal to plan a new working program. Supporting the action of the Executive Committee in the internal conflict, the conference reaffirmed the 1963 program of principles and declared that "all public debate on the disputed issues must cease" and that "normal Party conditions must be reestablished [and] existing factions must be disbanded at once" (*Friheten*, 22-28 April).

**Youth Organizations.** In sympathy with the minority faction of the NKP, the affiliated youth organization at its Thirty-First Congress 14-15 October advocated a break with the party and was subsequently denounced.

The Norwegian Communist Youth Organization (Norges Kommunistiske Ungdomsforbund; NKU) claims to be a "self-sufficient and independent political youth organization" nevertheless "indissolubly associated with the NKP." The basic reason for the break is its insistence upon the "right and obligation to object openly and clearly when we think the NKP fails to take its proper stand in Norwegian politics" (*Friheten*, 27 January).

Critical of the NKP program, the NKU alleges that it is "neither adequately understood nor made concrete enough" and attacks the NKP for failing to "advocate democratization of all facets of society" and for the attitude of "certain Party comrades" who apparently want to conceal "divergent views" (*Friheten*, 27 January).

Membership figures have not been disclosed, but it is unlikely that the NKU, even before the 1967 NKP split, had a following larger than that of its parent party. The "lack of interest" shown by youth of "undoubted radical attitude" has been attributed to the failure of the NKP to gear its "Party norms" to current conditions in Norway rather than to "those prevailing in Czarist Russia at the beginning of the century" (*Friheten*, 21 January).

At a meeting attended by only 11 of its 21-member Executive the NKU deplored the "unwarranted dismissal" of Vogt, which shows only too clearly that "the demand for increased democracy within the Party is highly justified." In favor of cooperative efforts within the three labor parties, the NKU claimed that the NKP had failed to "pursue politics that might lead to such cooperation." (*Aftenposten*, 8 April.)

As a result of the NKU's "factional relations to the NKP," the Trondheim youth group voted to "consider itself independent until the NKU has held its Congress" (postponed from May to October due to the internal rift), since the NKU was being used as a "negotiating center for the minority in the NKP" (*Friheten*, 15-21 April).

By a vote of 26 to 17, with two abstentions, the youth congress resolved to break with the NKP and reestablish the NKU as a "cross-political" organization. Claiming that its leadership was not representative of communist youth in Norway, and that a political break with the NKP would "remove the fundamental conditions for a Communist youth organization," the 17 in opposition to the break walked out of the congress and formed a new youth organization, Communist Youth (Kommunistisk Ungdom; KU). Its advent was heralded with enthusiasm by one leading Communist, who urged youth to unite behind the KU and declared that the NKU had for a long time "carried on propaganda" against the NKP, and it was therefore "appropriate" that a new organization be formed.

---

"Trotskyists, bourgeois nationalists, and Titoist elements," they were gradually rehabilitated during the "de-Stalinization" of the NKP. Known as the "Furubotn group," his adherents continue to regard Furubotn "with awe," according to Larsen. Following the resignations of Vogt and others, Larsen declared that "the Party appears to have outgrown these problems," although the "renewal process" is not yet completed. (*Friheten*, 31 September.)

"If our movement is to achieve progress in Norway, the foremost condition is that the Party and the youth organization be on good terms with each other" (*Friheten*, 17-23 November).

A KU Interim Committee, charged with the preparation of a constitutional congress, saw as its task the reestablishment of "the good relations which formerly existed between the NKU and the NKP and [the creation of] a powerful youth organization for revolutionary and democratically oriented youth" (*Friheten*, 20-26 October).

**International Affairs**. Larsen's determination to assert the autonomy of the NKP was much in evidence during the year in international affairs.* This was borne out by a Central Committee resolution of 8 January which declared that the NKP would not participate in the February meeting preparatory to the Karlovy Vary Conference or in the Conference itself, but favored instead a "conference of West European [communist parties] devoted to the same theme—European security." With the exception of a brief announcement of the party's nonparticipation—withheld from the party organ until 24 February—there was a noteworthy absence of commentary on the meeting.

Rolf Nettum, member of the NKP Secretariat, and Eivind Rasmussen, Central Committee member, represented the NKP at the Swedish CP Congress (Stockholm, 13-16 May). Just Lippe, member of the Secretariat, attended the Congress of the Democratic League of Finnish People (Helsinki, 13-15 May).

The most significant bilateral contact during 1967 was the visit to Norway of a high-ranking Rumanian party delegation (25-31 August) and the resulting joint communique reaffirming the "conclusions and viewpoints expressed" after the visit to Rumania by an NKP delegation in October 1966 and stressing once again the "importance attached to the elaboration by each Party of its own political line and of its methods of activity based on the creative application of Marxism-Leninism in accordance with the specific conditions prevailing in each respective country." European security and cooperation on the continent were also emphasized, but without specific proposals for a conference (*Friheten*, 8-14 September).

Party Chairman Larsen's attendance on 3 October at the Chinese National Day celebrations at the Chinese embassy in Oslo was also significant, in view of the nature of the dissension within the NKP.

In his speech at the NKP October Revolution celebrations, at which the guest of honor was CPSU Central Committee member G. Romanov, Larsen praised the "revolution which opened the way for humanity" but made implicit reference to the NKP position *vis-à-vis* the Sino-Soviet dispute:

> Lenin and the Bolsheviks pointed the way for Russia's workers and farmers. In the same manner each country's own labor movement must find ways which correspond to its individual conditions and possibilities ... regardless of individual conditions and possibilities which strongly differentiate them from one another and also from the situation which prevailed in Russia. (*Friheten*, 17-23 November.)

**Publications**. The central organ of the NKP is *Friheten* (Freedom), under the direction of an editorial advisory board comprising Reidar Larsen and Arne Jørgensen. As a result of financial difficulties, the paper, formerly a daily, became a weekly in mid-April 1967. There is also a regional organ, *Kontakt* (Contact), edited by Reidar Berge, Committee member of the Rogaland province. Its circulation is believed to be very small.

---

*The NKP decision of 14 January 1968 to send an observer to the Budapest Conference may well constitute a shift in the party's position of strict neutrality in the ideological conflict and of nonparticipation in international communist meetings. Denying any change in policy, Larsen said: "It is not necessary to support a world conference in order to participate in the Budapest meeting. This is a consultative meeting at which the Parties will exchange ideas, [and] the matter will be reconsidered by the Central Committee if the framework of the meeting appears to shift in a new direction. . . . We would oppose any conference if we thought its intention was to condemn any Party and thus further widen the split." (*Friheten*, 19-25 January 1968.)

# PAKISTAN

The Communist Party of Pakistan (CPP) was founded in 1948 from the sections of the Communist Party of (prepartition) India in the areas which subsequently became Pakistan. The Communist Party of India had never been firmly established in these predominantly Moslem areas, except in a few places such as the Punjab (particularly in Lahore), and more important, in the Mymensingh district and Dacca in East Pakistan. Moreover, Communists in these areas were predominantly Hindu or Sikh, rather than orthodox Muslim. The CPP'S first General Secretary was Sajjad Zaheer (or Sahher), now 65 years old and long in exile in India. The CPP was banned in July 1954, and although clandestine party organizations probably exist in both East and West Pakistan, no national party headquarters appears to be active. No CPP delegation appeared at the Fiftieth Anniversary celebrations in Moscow in November 1967.* CPP "members" have been estimated at about 700 in East Pakistan and 750 in West Pakistan (*World Strength of Communist Parties, 1968*).

Communist activity is primarily concentrated in East Pakistan, particularly in Dacca. Pakistani Communists have been divided along pro-Soviet and pro-Chinese lines since 1966; in 1967, judging from reports in the Indian party press, the pro-Soviet faction appeared to control the party's clandestine organization in East Pakistan.

Currently, the main vehicle of political expression for Pakistani Communists is the extreme left-wing, legal National Awami Party (NAP), led by Maulana Bhashani and active primarily, although not exclusively, in East Pakistan. In March 1965, in the first national elections since the 1958 imposition of martial law, the NAP participated in a coalition, the Combined Opposition Party, formed in opposition to the ruling Pakistan Muslim League. Although no NAP candidates were elected, the Combined Opposition Party succeeded in winning 11 seats (10 of which were in East Pakistan), while the Pakistan Muslim League obtained 118 seats of a total of 150 contests.

**Pakistani Communists and the NAP.** The relationship between the NAP and the Pakistani Communists is quite complex. Although the NAP is sometimes called a "front" for the Pakistani Communists, the term "sanctuary" would be more accurate.

There are four important cleavages in left-wing Pakistani politics, especially in East Pakistan, that are relevant to an understanding of the position of Pakistani Communists: (1) a pro-Soviet orientation versus a pro-Chinese and strongly anti-Indian orientation, (2) a Hindu and Sikh versus Moslem antagonism, (3) a strongly pro-united front, anti-Ayub stand versus conditional support of the Ayub regime and rejection of every specific united-front program, and (4) stress on provincial autonomy for East Pakistan versus stress on unification of the country. At the risk of some oversimplification, it can be said that Pakistani Communists generally lean to the first side of each cleavage, while Bhashani and the leading faction within the NAP in 1967 leaned to the second part of each of the above divisions. (It should be kept in mind, however that Bhashani in particular tries to appear to be on both sides of the fence with regard to these issues, especially the third and fourth.)

The Soviet, Chinese, and both Indian communist parties all agree, however, that the NAP is the "most progressive" party in Pakistan. The NAP leader and founder, Maulana A. H. Bhashani ("Maulana" is a title which technically designates a member of the *ulama* with an advanced knowledge of Islamic law, but which may be bestowed on any distinguished Moslem), has never been a member of the CPP; he is a veteran leftist politician from East Pakistan who has been a leader of the Assam Muslim League, the Awami Muslim League, and the left wing of the Awami League. After the CPP was banned in Pakistan in 1954, Communists joined or cooperated with the Azad (Free) Pakistan

---

*Or at the Budapest Conference in February 1968.

Party in West Pakistan, the Ganatantri Dal in East Pakistan, and Bhashani's wing of the Awami League in East Pakistan. Referring to the period immediately following the adoption of the national constitution in 1956, a source published in 1964 by the USSR Academy of Sciences remarks:

> With police terror at a high pitch throughout the country, cooperation with the Azad Pakistan Party, the Ganatantri Dal, and the left wing of the Awami League was virtually the only opportunity the Pakistan Communists had of conducting legal activities among the working people. Making the most of this opportunity, they were able to head many manifestations of the working class, the peasants, and the progressive intelligentsia in 1956. (Y. V. Gankovsky and L. R. Gordon-Polonskaya, *A History of Pakistan*, Moscow, 1964, p. 261.)

In 1957 Bhashani broke with the Awami League over the issues of autonomy for East Pakistan and a strongly "anti-imperialist" foreign policy, both of which Bhashani favored. Bhashani's splinter from the Awami League, with the Ganatantri Dal, and another left party, the National Party, formed the NAP. Its leadership included Bhashani, the late Mian Iftikharuddin, Abdul Ghaffer Khan, and G. N. Sayed.

From a theoretical standpoint, the NAP is regarded by neighboring communist parties as the leader of the national democratic movement of the petty bourgeoisie and national bourgeoisie, a movement which naturally precedes a true proletarian socialist revolution in an underdeveloped, recently independent country, and Bhashani is regarded as one of the foremost spokesmen of that movement. Gankovsky and Gordon-Polonskaya (*A History of Pakistan*, pp. 301 and 292) put it thus:

> The national democratic movement [in 1958] was growing and consolidating its position in the country. All patriotic and progressive forces of the nation were interested in the solution of national problems. That was the basis on which they could unite. The National Awami Party became the nucleus of such a unification. The democratic nature of its program and its determined struggle for the radical change of the whole home and whole foreign policy of the country gained it the support of the broad masses.

.  .  .

> Despite the fact that some of its demands were not sufficiently clearly formulated and that it was not quite consistent in the pursuit of its aims, "the new Party," as A. Ghosh [then General Secretary of the Communist Party of India] wrote, "had immense potentialities. It was the first All-Pakistan party of a mass, progressive character."

In the 1965 elections the NAP espoused a program calling domestically for left socialist measures, including nationalization of banks, insurance, and foreign investments; for agrarian reforms; and for reconstitution of West Pakistan along cultural and linguistic lines (in order to strengthen the autonomy of East Pakistan, which consists of only one province, *vis-à-vis* West Pakistan). The NAP favored a strongly "anti-imperialist" foreign policy, including abrogation of defense agreements with the United States, withdrawal of Pakistan from CENTO and SEATO, and "positive support for liberation movements in colonial and semicolonial countries" (*US Army Area Handbook for Pakistan*, 1965, p. 292).

What are from the communist view point "national" issues continue to overshadow ideological issues in importance within the NAP. These include antagonism among Hindus, Sikhs, and Moslems, language controversies, relations with China and India, and East Pakistan's autonomy movement. Nevertheless, conflicts within the NAP do mirror to some extent the differences which split Soviet and Chinese-oriented communist parties in many other countries. There is a pro-Chinese faction within the NAP, led in 1967 by Bhashani himself; a pro-Soviet faction led by General Secretary Mahumdul Huq Usmani (who is from West Pakistan), part of which split off from the NAP in late 1967; and a third faction led by Mahmud Ali Qasuri, who, unlike Bhashani, strongly favors a united front in opposition to the Ayub regime and a constitutional path toward "socialism." Pro-Soviet and pro-Chinese leanings are, of course, meaningful in the context of Pakistani national interests as well as in an ideological context.

Such pressures and conflicts are expressed in the tactics and line Bhashani uses to maximize his own personal political influence. He generally follows a line which might be described as "extreme-left phrase-mongering," or as "left in appearance, but (relatively) right in reality." He complains that constitutional democracy is not a worthy goal because it amounts only to bourgoise democracy and then uses this as a reason or excuse to support the Ayub regime, rather than advocating any direct revolutionary action. Similarly, although he supports a united front against the regime in principle, he opposes it in practice on the plea that none of the opposition parties is sufficiently "anti-imperialist." On this latter issue Bhashani had a great deal of trouble in 1967 in keeping the NAP united behind his position.* Finally, he has threatened from time to time to lead a mass movement for provincial autonomy for East Pakistan, but he will not go far in this direction because it is incompatible with both his support of the Ayub regime and a pro-Peking line, and because such a movement would benefit other East Pakistani political elements (notably the Awami League and its imprisoned East Pakistani leader, Sheikh Mujibur Rahman, who led such a movement in 1966) more than it would benefit him (see *Far Eastern Economic Review,* November 19, 1967).

**The NAP and the Pakistan Democratic Movement.** The Pakistan Democratic Movement, a united front of five left opposition parties, was formed in the spring of 1967. The NAP Central Working Committee met in Dacca on 19-22 May. Bhashani claimed that the NAP had been excluded from the meeting of the five opposition parties on 25 April and insisted that the program of the Democratic Front was not sufficiently anti-imperialist. Earlier, however, several NAP leaders, including Bhashani, Abdul Huq, and Haji Mohamed Danesh, had expressed the willingness of the NAP to join such a front against the government, and the NAP had participated in a meeting in Dacca on 8 January 1967 with the other five left opposition parties (*Pakistan Observer,* 9 January 1967). Prior to the Central Working Committee meetings, the East Pakistan NAP Working Committee had met on 16-17 May and had voted not to join in a united front with the East Pakistan Awami League. According to the *Pakistan Times* of 19 May, however, there was substantial minority opinion favoring the united front. The resolution opposing the united front passed 21 to 6 and stated the conditions the NAP would require for its adherence to a united front:

> that the main union must be based on an anti-imperialist, anti-feudal and anti-capitalistic struggle; that it must lend full support to the freedom struggle of Kashmiri people and all other peoples of the world who are fighting for the right of self-determination and against imperialist-colonialist domination.

A similar program was announced after the Central Working Committee meeting. It is more strongly left-oriented than the programs of the other left parties in the Democratic Front, which had united on an eight-point program pledging to "restore parliamentary democracy based on the 1956 constitution" (*Far Eastern Economic Review,* 18 May 1967). It thus appeared that, in contrast to the CPP in East Pakistan, the pro-Soviet faction was in the minority among the NAP leadership.

Controversy over this and related issues led to a dispute within the East Pakistan NAP, which in turn led to the split within the party at the end of 1967. In August Altab Ali, Azizul Islam, Kazi Abdul Bari, and two other leading pro-Soviet members in the Mymensingh district were expelled at a district NAP meeting for alleged "antiparty activities." Their cause was vigorously championed by the right Communist Party of India in its organ *New Age* (26 November). The *New Age* account stated that the leadership of the district organization had become pro-Peking since 1963, partly because of the imprisonment of some veteran (and presumably pro-Soviet) NAP leaders in the area. The pro-Peking group appears to have had control of both the district and East Pakistan provincial NAP organizations. On 9-10 October the East Pakistan Provincial Committee held a meeting which confirmed the expulsion of the five members, according to the *New Age* account, "by a three-vote majority with 30 members attending." NAP General Secretary Usmani was reported to have led the minority fight at the meeting of the Provincial Committee. The pro-Moscow group then attempted to fight the decision in a meeting of the full Provincial Council. However, the pro-Peking leadership set

---

*In January 1968 even the section of the party which continued to recognize Bhashani's leadership repudiated his tactic of supporting the Ayub regime.

the meeting for 30 November at Rangpur, where they apparently felt more confident of mustering a favorable majority, rather than at Dacca, as Usmani's faction desired. At the Rangpur meeting the expulsions were again confirmed. This made a split inevitable, and each of the two factions planned its own provincial meeting for February 1968.

The expulsions also provided an occasion for accusations of tacit collusion between Bhashani's faction and the Ayub government at the expense of the pro-Soviet group. On 26 November *New Age* noted:

> . . . while warrants of arrest against some of the most important leaders of the pro-Peking group have been withdrawn and they are allowed to work freely, many leaders and workers of NAP and other mass organizations have been put behind bars. The resolution confirming the expulsions could be passed in the NAP Provincial Committee only because five important members of the Committee, including the Secretary, Senior Vice-President and a Joint Secretary were in jail.

The same issue quoted General Secretary Usmani as having said on 15 October that "those who are now raising the slogan of people's democracy [Bhashani's faction] now do not want parliamentary democracy and are raising that slogan as a camouflage," and commented editorially that "in practice this counterposing by the pro-Peking group amounts to opposition to the popular struggle for democracy."

An important Pakistani Communist leader, Mani Singh, a Sikh from Mymensingh district in East Pakistan, was arrested by the police in November 1967. Mani Singh had been underground for many years and had a history of involvement with Communist-led peasant movements in East Pakistan going back to the 1940s. He appears to have been a leader of the pro-Soviet faction predominating in the clandestine CPP organization in East Pakistan. Petitions for his release were presented to the government by various East Pakistan groups and individuals, including former Chief Minister of East Pakistan Ataur Rahman Khan (see *New Age* 10 December). The more pro-Chinese elements of the NAP and the Indian communists did not join the campaign to free Mani Singh. The left Communist Party of India (Marxist) did not mention his arrest, nor did Bhashani and his faction within the NAP support the petitions to free him. One of the few pro-Chinese NAP faction members who supported Mani Singh, according to *New Age*'s 10 December report, was Mahbudullah, General Secretary of the East Pakistan Student Union.

**Pakistani Communists and the International Communist Movement.** Both Indian communist parties devote attention to the "progressive movement" in Pakistan, especially in East Pakistan, and the right Communist Party of India also gives coverage to the Pakistani Communists as such and supports the pro-Soviet leadership of the CPP in East Pakistan against pro-Peking dissidents. *New Age* of 11 June 1967 described the division within the CPP in East Pakistan as follows:

> A section of Communists, claiming to be followers of the "Peking Line," have left their comrades and are now following a policy which virtually amounts to supporting the anti-people government [of Ayub Khan]. During the Indo-Pakistan armed conflict, they said that it was a "just war" for Pakistan and fully supported the war. During the movement for the Six Points [of the Awami League] when the common people were fighting for their autonomy, those people discovered "CIA conspiracy" behind the movement and opposed it. They hold that Ayub's foreign policy is "anti-imperialist and progressive" and they support it. They are opposed to forming a united front against the reactionary government even on a minimum program, saying that the leaders of various opposition parties (excepting the NAP) are pro-imperialist and there cannot be any united front with them. The Communists of East Pakistan are a small force. But they are the most organized force and are also the most sincere and militant fighters in the democratic movement. The division within the Communists and the pro-Ayub swing of one section have caused serious confusion within the left-democratic camp and weakened it.

It was not clear, however, whether the pro-Peking communists had formed a separate clandestine organization. In 1967 *People's Democracy*, the organ of the left Communist Party of India (Marxist), published no Pakistani anti-Soviet material comparable to the several anti-Chinese statements of the

CPP in East Pakistan which *New Age* reported. The pro-Peking Indian Communists, in fact, seem unenthusiastic about supporting any NAP or Communist faction. Although they support Bhashani over the pro-Soviet NAP group, they were clearly displeased with Bhashani's support of the Ayub regime in 1967 and would prefer to see a militant revolutionary stand on the part of the NAP. An article in the 4 February 1968 *People's Democracy* emphasized the fiery rhetoric of Bhashani and urged a more militant revolutionary line on the NAP. *People's Democracy* paraphrased Bhashani as saying at the Rangpur meeting in November 1967 that the Ayub regime was "a dictatorial regime of Big Business and the feudals with the US imperialists as its faithful ally" and "only establishment of a socialist society free from all exploitation, which is possible only after the overthrow of the present society based on exploitation, can change the fate of the people, and that is what has been adopted by the NAP as its program, the Maulana said." The report said that the five expellees from Mymensingh had been expelled for "trying to infiltrate bourgeois and petty-bourgeois ideologies into NAP." It is noteworthy, however, that the same report commented on the impending formation of a new left-wing Pakistani party by ex-Foreign Minister Ali Bhutto, without expressing any opinion, favorable or unfavorable, on this party's potential merits as a vehicle for Pakistan's "progressive movement." Some Western observers thought Bhutto's party might attract some dissidents from the NAP, from the badly divided Awami League, and from radical student elements (*Washington Post,* 11 January 1968). If this happened, Bhutto's party could easily rival the NAP as a candidate for communist support.

The most important anti-Chinese statement of the East Pakistani Communists in 1967 was carried both in *New Age* (17 September) and in the *Information Bulletin* (Prague, no. 107, 1967). This was a resolution of the Central Committee of the Communist Party of East Pakistan which strongly condemned the Chinese Great Proletarian Cultural Revolution and the cult of Mao Tse-tung. As reported in the *Information Bulletin,* the resolution stated that "the activities now carried on in the People's Republic of China in the name of the 'cultural revolution' are in direct contradiction to Marxism-Leninism." It characterized the "deviations of the present leaders of China" as "petty-bourgeois revolutionism and great power chauvinism."

**Publications**. The CPP does not appear to have any publication. The NAP publishes an English-language weekly, *Janata,* which is controlled by the pro-Peking faction, while the pro-Soviet faction has a Bengali daily, *Sangbad.* Both are published in Dacca.

# PANAMA

The People's Party of Panama (Partido del Pueblo de Panamá; PDP) originated in 1943 from the Communist Party of Panama (Partido Communista del Panamá), which was founded in 1930. The party has been outlawed since December 1953.

The PDP membership has never been large. By 1963 it had fallen to an estimated 150 persons. In 1964, in the wake of the anti-US rioting in Panama City and the Canal Zone, the party grew to about 500 members, but has since declined to some 300. The population of Panama is 1,287,000 (estimated mid-1966). During the January 1964 riots, communist student leaders demonstrated the PDP's capability for exerting influence far beyond its numbers by assuming positions of leadership and by making common cause with nationalists and other anti-US elements over the Canal issue.

Although the PDP has been prohibited from participating in elections since 1953, the party has run candidates on the slates of other parties. Two of the 42 deputies elected in May 1964, one from the Radical Action Party (PAR) and one from the Socialist Party (PS), had lengthy procommunist records.

**Organization and Leadership.** Hugo Victor is Chairman of the PDP; Valerio Sires, Vice-Chairman; and Rubén Dario Souza, Secretary-General; Rubén Castellanos is known to be a member of the Central Executive Committee. Others believed to hold prominent positions within the party are Victor Avila, Roberto Madariaga Montes, Raúl Montaner, Miguel Porcel, Efrain Reyes Medina, Cleto Souza, Vincente Tello, and González Zapato. Dario Pitti, arrested in December 1966 for smuggling dynamite and propaganda into Panama from Costa Rica, is the PDP representative in Chirique Province.

Communist support is primarily concentrated among high school and university students. The Communists retained effective control of the Federation of Students of Panama (Federación de Estudiantes de Panamá; FEP) during 1967 through continuing control of the directorate of the Union of University Students (Unión de Estudiantes Universitarios; UEU). The UEU elections held in January gave the Communist-controlled University Reform Front (Frente Reformista Universitaria; FRU) 52 seats on the directorate of the UEU, compared with a total of 46 seats for the two noncommunist university student groups. Through the Executive Committee of the UEU the Communists can exercise control over the FEP, which combines the UEU and the Union of Secondary School Students (Unión de Estudiantes de Secundaria; UES) into one all-encompassing student organization. The FEP is a member of the world communist front International Union of Students (IUS) and was elected to one of the twelve vice-presidencies on the Secretariat of that organization at its Ninth Congress, in Ulan Bator, Mongolia, in March 1967. Luis Navas Pajaro, the Secretary-General of the FEP, is under indictment for his part in the student riots of 1966 which followed the mysterious death of his brother, also a student activist.

The Communists' influence within the trade union movement in negligible. Their control is limited to the small Trade Union Federation of the Workers of the Republic of Panama (Federación Sindical de Trabajadores de la República de Panamá).

**Views and Policies in 1967.** In domestic affairs the main issue during the year for the Communists turned upon the acceptance of three new treaties concerning the USA's presence and authority in the Panama Canal Zone. The treaties replace the Treaty of 1903 and represent the fruit of three years of negotiation between the Panamanian government and the USA. The PDP, the students' organizations, and Communist splinter groups were all united in condemnation of the treaties. The Communists took the position that it is a "patriotic necessity to recover full sovereignty and control over the canal area and to evict the military occupants" (Henry Giniger, "Pressure of Panamanian Opposition Puts Fate of Canal Treaties in Doubt," *New York Times,* 13 September).

The PDP-controlled FEP organized in Panama City on 12-14 December the "First National Congress of the Federation of Students of Panama in Defense and Recovery of National Sovereignty." The congress was attended by delegates of university and high school student associations from all over the country with fraternal delegates reportedly from the USA, Peru, Costa Rica, El Salvador, Guatemala, Honduras, Mexico, Venezuela and the Latin American Continental Students Organization (OCLAE). The congress approved a resolution calling for the immediate recovery of the Canal Zone and rejection of the new draft treaty. Representatives of several Panamanian political parties including the PDP addressed the congress and explained their position on the treaty issue.

During 1967 the PDP became more or less reconciled to the existence of rival communist factions in Panama, a change from its hostile attitude in 1966 when the party declared that "renegades, dregs of society, traitors, and even agents of the US Central Intelligence Agency were recuited under the patronage of the Chinese leadership with the aim of weakening our Party" (*IB,* no. 89, 27 January). In contrast, the party now states:

> There are two trends in the national movement which, despite their mistakes, should be considered as allies because the aim of both is radically to change the existing order of things. The Leftist trend does not believe in the activity of the masses as a motive force of the revolution. The reformist trend considers that the leadership of the movement should be in the hands of intellectuals. . . . We are pursuing a flexible and patient policy towards these trends, doing our best to resolve our differences in a fraternal spirit and to help them adopt a more consistent revolutionary position. (*WMR,* September 1967.)

As if to underscore this attitude of condescending tolerance, two PDP members (Castellanos and Montaner) attended the first conference of the Latin American Solidarity Organization (OLAS) in Havana, 31 July-10 August, as part of a six-man Panamanian delegation which included members of pro-Castro splinter groups. The speech of the Panamanian delegation dwelled almost entirely on the Panama Canal problem and ended on a fraternal note:

> Our people and its revolutionary vanguard have clearly understood that the fight for the victory of our sovereignty throughout the Continent is closely tied to the fight for our national liberation and the revolutionary taking of local power. Our people understand that all this will only be achieved by patriotic war, and that it will not be possible for us to be liberated through agreements or by fraudulent elections. (OLAS Conference Documents, Havana, August.)

The PDP attended the fifth meeting of the communist parties of Mexico, Central America, and Panama, believed to have been held in San José, Costa Rica, in May. (For joint statement see *Documents.*) Secretary-General Souza led a PDP delegation to the fiftieth anniversary celebrations of the October Revolution in the USSR, delivering a speech at the grand rally in Minsk on 5 November.

Although the PDP is a pro-Soviet party, it refrained from criticizing Communist China in 1967, stressing instead the positive need for renewed unity among fraternal communist parties. Castellanos, the party's chief spokesman in communist organs, wrote:

> UNITY ABOVE ALL. . . . The Communist parties know that any tendency towards national isolation, any split in the revolutionary forces, hinders the development of the liberation movement (and sometimes dooms it to painful defeat) and thereby plays into the hands of reaction and imperialism. We therefore wholeheartedly welcome every effort towards cementing the unity of revolutionaries in irreconcilable struggle against the common emeny. . . . Only through joint quests of unitary solutions according with the real state of affairs can we achieve our common aim—unity and coordination of the practical activities of the Latin American Communist movement and the revolutionary, democratic, anti-feudal and anti-imperialist movement as a whole. (*WMR,* June 1967.)

Again stressing unity of the communist movement as the goal, the PDP endorsed Moscow's call for the consultative conference of communist and workers' parties in Budapest in February 1968.

**Publications.** The PDP issues an irregular, clandestine publication, *El Mazo.*

**Dissident Communist Groups.** There are two significant communist organizations in Panama that do not adhere to the PDP position. The more important of these is the Revolutionary Unity Movement (Movimiento de Unidad Revolucionaria; MUR)—formerly the Reform Unity Movement—led by Floyd Wendell Britton Morrison (Floyd Britton). The MUR is almost completely composed of students or men who claim student status. Britton himself is in his late thirties and is enrolled in the University of Panama, although he seldom appears for classes (Don Bohning, "Panama Keeps a Wary Eye on Castroite College Boy," *Miami Herald,* 12 October). Originally considered a pro-Peking group, the MUR has apparently shifted of late to a Castroist stance. Britton was selected as the president of the Panamanian delegation to the OLAS conference; Gustavo Valle Rojas, one of Britton's lieutenants, was also among the Panamanian delegates. The MUR's hard-core following is apparently very small, but it has had good success at inciting students to riot, especially those in the high schools (*ibid.*). Battles have been fought between MUR student followers and those of the PDP student organization FRU, but their differences were patched up for a show of unity at the OLAS conference and in opposition to the new treaties. The MUR advocates violent revolution on the Castro model and agrees with the Cubans that whoever tries to carry out revolution in Latin America must become an armed vanguard of the people. It states that the only position true revolutionaries can adopt is to take up arms and reply to reactionary violence with revolutionary violence.

An even smaller group, the National Action Vanguard (Vanguardia de Acción Nacional; VAN) is led by Jorge Turner. Turner was the chairman of the Panamanian delegation to the Tricontinental Congress in 1966. The VAN may have been represented at the OLAS conference in the person of one Gilberto Antonio Velazquez. The very small and unstable VAN organization is built around the personality of its leader. Originally thought to be pro-Peking, the VAN, like the MUR, appears now to be Castroist. Turner asserts that the masses have the right to resort to all means necessary, including armed struggle, to obtain independence, and that the VAN is "prepared to take all steps necessary to light the final continental fires of struggle against North American imperialism at the side of its comrades, the revolutionaries of Latin America" (broadcast, Havana Radio, 9 January).

# PARAGUAY

The Paraguayan Communist Party (Partido Comunista Paraguayo; PCP) was founded in 1928. It is illegal and is severely repressed. Of the estimated 5,000 members of the party, about 4,500 are in exile, chiefly in Uruguay, Argentina, and Brazil. In mid-1963 a minority favoring the Chinese Communists in the dispute with the CPSU broke away to form the Paraguayan Leninist Communist Party (Partido Leninista Comunista Paraguayo; PLCP). The PLCP is illegal in Paraguay, although not so severely repressed as the PCP, and is based in Buenos Aires and Montevideo. Its activities within Paraguay are very limited and its membership is not known. The population of Paraguay is 2,161,000 (estimated, June 1967).

In 1965 an apparent majority within the PCP leadership initiated moves to reorganize the leadership of the party and depose its Secretary-General, Oscar Creydt (*YICA*, 1966, pp. 243-244). The anti-Creydt group, backed by the CPSU, appeared to have attained its goals by 1967, although there are indications that in the process some of the "rebels" were in turn deposed. A "Preparatory National Conference for the Third Congress" of the PCP was held in Montevideo, Uruguay, on 7-14 April 1967. The conference expelled from the party Oscar Creydt, Arturo López, and Raúl Ramírez (the latter had been in 1966 one of the prominent representatives of the anti-Creydt group) and elected a new Central Committee, Political Commission, and Secretariat. The names of the new leadership have not been made public; the following PCP members, however, were prominent in the earlier anti-Creydt moves or were representatives of the PCP during 1967, or both: Obdulio Barthe (leader of the anti-Creydt "National Committee for the Defense and Reorganization of the PCP"—see *ibid.*), Agosto Canete, Luis Centurión, Julio Vega Román, Diosmedes Mora, José C. Agosta, Raimondo Ríotorto, Alipio Yegros, José Chilabert, Juan Jara, Calixto Bogado, Dora Frei, Luis Casablanca, Antonio Alcaraz, Victor Alonso, Efrain Morel, Pedro Aguero, Miguel Angel Soler, and Albino Sosa (members of aforementioned "National Committee"); Jacinto Correa, Héctor Gutiérrez, and Hugo Campos (PCP representatives at the Conference of the Latin American Solidarity Organization—OLAS—in Havana); Félix Moreno (PCP representative in Cuba); and Gustavo Corvalán (candidate member of the PCP Central Committee).

Domestic support for the PCP is found chiefly among secondary school and university students. Paraguayan Communists in exile have established a "United Front for National Liberation," with headquarters in Uruguay.

**Domestic Policy.** The April conference held by the new PCP leadership included an assessment of the party's potential and role. In an article in the *World Marxist Review* (September 1967, pp. 73-75) analyzing the conference, PCP member Gustavo Corvalán referred to the "anarchy, disorganization and confusion to which the Party had been reduced," and stated that the party's "organizational work, propaganda and agitation" were "not yet satisfactory":

> Hundreds of members dispersed all over the country do not belong to a branch. Nor are our positions strong in the factories and in the trade unions. A similar situation exists in the rural areas, in the agrarian leagues, student organizations, and also among teachers and professional people generally. Initial success achieved in the fight for the unity of the democratic forces has not been adequately developed.

He noted, however, "such successes as the contact re-established with the big organizations in the capital and in the rural areas," which "provided the basis for forming the leading committees at lower levels and for re-establishing branches in the capital and countryside." Corvalán also claimed that "most of the Party organizations in emigration" had likewise been reorganized.

Corvalán indicated that there was "urgent need for a ramified network of branches deeply rooted in the masses" and that "the national conference [had]instructed the new Central Committee to regard educational work at all levels as one of [its] main tasks." With the consolidation of the PCP the party saw "its main political task as that of expediting the building of a broad national front of the revolutionary democratic and patriotic forces." In the course of "rallying the forces" the PCP would combine "peaceful and non-peaceful forms of struggle and, gradually uniting all progressives in a broad front, [would] pave the way to a people's uprising on a national scale." Corvalán warned, however, that the party must "display the utmost caution and responsibility in tackling the complex tasks arising in the course of preparing this uprising, [and]must take a resolute stand against, and rout, all the adventuristic trends of toying with guerrilla warfare and insurrection." He qualified this apparent adherence to a peaceful revolutionary line by adding: "with equal determination we must combat and defeat those who retreat before the difficulties and sacrifices that the armed mass struggle may involve." He pointed out that the PCP advocated "self-defense groups to resist the violence and terror of the regime, [and]the setting up of the first armed groups of peasants with a view gradually to building a guerrilla movement on a national scale."

The issue of armed struggle in Paraguay was examined by the delegates at the OLAS Conference in Havana. The Chairman of the group from Paraguay, Francisco Méndez (representing a splinter group from the Revolutionary Febrerista Party) declared at a press conference on 30 July that although armed struggle was the only way to overthrow President Stroessner, there was at that time no guerrilla nucleus in Paraguay. Subsequently, in an interview on Radio Havana on 25 August, Méndez denied that a member of his delegation had stated that the appearance of guerrillas in Paraguay was imminent. He portrayed the attitude of the Paraguayan people as one of "latent struggle."

The April conference of the PCP adopted a domestic political platform which stressed the party's preoccupation with a number of economic issues:

> The Party has set the task of intensifying the fight for higher wages, for timely payment of wages, for observance of the law on the eight-hour working day, against victimization, for more jobs and unemployment benefits, for the repeal of the fascist labor code, against police interference in trade union affairs, and for broad trade-union and democratic freedoms.

> The peasants should be urged to step up the struggle for the land, for transferring to them free of charge holdings ranging in size from 20 to 50 hectares in zones adjoining communication lines, against evictions, for long-term low-interest credits, for higher prices for their products and timely payment in cash, not in promissory notes. We should advocate trade with the socialist countries, work to secure the marketing of the entire mass of agricultural products, the sale of farm implements to the peasants on favorable terms and at low prices through the National Bank of Development, annul the peasants' debt to this Bank, and for the right to form agrarian leagues and other peasants' associations.

The party also commented on student affairs:

> Students should be rallied in the fight against high tuition fees and against other obstacles in the way of education, against the so-called "general education" higher school and against the Yankee-Stroessner interference in the affairs of the university, for genuine university autonomy and discontinuation of the dictatorial intervention in the affairs of the student centers and federations.

The conference also called for the promulgation of a "general amnesty without exceptions" and "abrogation of the notorious Law 294, 'On the Defense of Democracy.' " (*WMR*, September 1967, pp. 74-75; see also *IB*, no. 103, 1967.)

**International Views and Policies.** The new PCP leadership, the product of a Soviet-backed "coup," aligned itself steadfastly with the CPSU on general international issues and on those concerning communist affairs. In the latter context, a speech by Hugo Campos was broadcast by "Radio Peace and Progress," Moscow, on 2 August 1967. Campos referred to the PCP's analysis of "the present situation in the world communist movement," which had "correctly assessed the strengthening of the socialist camp, headed by the Soviet Union and the world anti-imperialist movement." He proceeded to elaborate on the PCP's stand with regard to the "divisive, provocative, hysterically anti-Soviet, nationalistic, petit-bourgeois, and Trotskyite activity of the Chinese leaders." The PCP's national conference, whose resolutions Campos was quoting, "approved the Party's active support of the principles and the general line of the world Communist movement collectively adopted in 1957 and 1960 [and] declared for closer unity and cohesion in the movement on the basis of Marxism-Leninism, for a new conference of Communist and Workers' parties, and the formation of a united world front against imperialism, particularly for unity of action to defeat US imperialist aggressors in Vietnam" (*IB*, no. 103, 1967). With regard to the Middle East conflict, Campos' August broadcast referred to the "massive and multiple assistance given by the Soviet Union . . . to the countries which are now victims of Israeli aggression."

On issues concerning Latin America, the PCP published a manifesto in Montevideo on 5 May 1967 which included a section entitled "The National Liberation Movement in Latin America is Growing." After stressing the role played by "the glorious Cuban revolution, led by the Communist Party and its chief, Comrade Fidel Castro," the manifesto declared:

> Due to the constant growth of the socialist camp, the growth of the worker and popular movement in the capitalist countries, the tremendous development of national liberation struggles, the victory and consolidation of the Cuban revolution, and progress in organizing tricontinental solidarity, all the differences of the Latin American peoples with US imperialism become more acute, while huge mass struggles gain momentum throughout our continent. In Uruguay, Argentina, Chile, and other countries, general or partial strikes by the working class succeed one another as well as fierce struggles by peasants, students, and other popular sectors in demand of economic and political improvement. In Colombia, Guatemala and Venezuela the patriots are boldly carrying on guerrilla movements, which are beginning to spread to other countries like Bolivia, Brazil, and so forth. These are battles for the purpose of seizing power from the imperialists and big landowners and for establishing a revolutionary-democratic rule based on the alliance between the working class and the peasants. This is what is making headway and will become invincible in Latin America and our own country.

The PCP's relations with Cuba and its stand with regard to the controversy between the Cuban and Venezuelan communist parties (see *Venezuela*) were ambiguous. Though the aforementioned manifesto in its reference to Venezuela appeared to support the guerrillas, it also spoke of the developments in Chile and Argentina, whose communist parties' stand in 1967 was one of restraint with regard to the Cuban advocacy of continental guerrilla warfare. Furthermore, the PCP's April conference was attended by representatives from the communist parties of Argentina and Chile, in addition to those of the host country, Uruguay. The speeches of the PCP representatives at the OLAS conference were, in this context, of an noncommital nature.

In addition to the OLAS conference, PCP representatives attended the celebrations of the Fiftieth Anniversary of the Bolshevik Revolution in the Soviet Union, and a delegation, which included Hugo Campos, visited the Soviet Union in July, meeting with Mikhail Suslov, Politburo Member and Secretary of the Central Committee of the CPSU.

**Publications.** The PCP publishes *Adelante,* an irregular clandestine monthly; *Unidad Paraguaya,* an irregular periodical published in exile; *Kavichu-i,* a PCP bulletin, and *Lo Mita Sapucai,* the paper of its communist youth organization in exile.

\*        \*        \*

In view of the exile nature of the Paraguayan communist movement, the size and character of communist dissident elements are difficult to determine. Little is known of the pro-Chinese PLCP, except that its leader appears to be Sebastian Querey. The PLCP was not represented at any international pro-Chinese Communist meetings in 1967. The party does not appear to have a regular publication.

With regard to support for Oscar Creydt, there are indications that the new PCP leadership has not succeeded in attaining complete control of the party. Several months after the PCP national conference, accusations against Creydt were being made by the PCP, including a lengthy attack by Campos in a broadcast September 2 on Moscow's "Radio Peace and Progress."

# PERU

The Peruvian Communist Party (Partido Comunista Peruano; PCP) was founded in 1928 as the Peruvian Socialist Party (Partido Socialista Peruano). It took its present name in 1930. A National Conference convened in January 1964 by pro-Chinese elements in the party resulted in the expulsion of the pro-Soviet leadership. The pro-Soviets, in turn, expelled the pro-Chinese. Consequently there are now two contending communist parties, both proclaiming themselves as the original PCP. The split within the PCP accentuates the fragmentation in Peru's extreme left, which comprises numerous contending groups, including Trotskyist and Castroist elements (see below). The internecine controversy between the various revolutionary groups, the major offensive carried out in 1965-66 by the Belaúnde government against the guerrillas (comprising primarily non-PCP members), the resurgence of guerrilla activity in 1967 and subsequent reprisals, and contradictory reports from Trotskyist and Cuban sources have resulted in a fluid situation, making it difficult to determine which segment of Peruvian communism is in ascendancy. Both PCP's have been weakened by their preoccupation with attacking the other instead of developing their own activities and gaining new supporters. As a result, smaller extremist groups such as the Movement of the Revolutionary Left (Movimiento de la Izquierda Revolucionaria; MIR) and the Army of National Liberation (Ejercito de Liberación Nacional; ELN) are gradually becoming the focal point for left-wing extremist action. An evaluation of overall communist strength and influence is at present indeterminate. The pro-Soviet and pro-Chinese PCP's have memberships estimated at 2,000 and 3,000 respectively. No estimates are available for the other groups. The population of Peru is 12,385,000 (estimated June 1967). Generally speaking, communist support originates primarily in the southern regions around the towns of Cuzco and Puno and in Lima. Sociologically, the various communist factions derive their major source of support from students and the professional classes.

Communists are proscribed from electoral participation, but are otherwise tolerated. The pro-Soviet PCP is represented in Parliament by Dr. Genaro Ledesma Izquieta, elected without ostensible party affiliation on a National Liberation Front (Frente de Liberación Nacional; FLN) ticket.

Outside the party structure, one of the areas of PCP influence is the student movement, where its principal competitor has been the left-wing anticommunist Aprista Party. As a consequence of the Sino-Soviet schism, the pro-Soviet PCP's activities among students have been seriously handicapped. In elections for the student governing body of the National University of San Marcos (July 1967), the pro-Chinese candidate, Andrés Gonzáles, won the presidency of the San Marcos University Federation with 4,554 votes. A total of 3,576 votes went to the Aprista condidate, Hugo Valverde. The pro-Soviet candidate was third with a total of 1,106 votes.

The pro-Chinese have also apparently prevailed over the pro-Moscow Communists in the struggle for control of the Federation of Peruvian Students (Federación de Estudiantes Peruanos; FEP). While the two previous FEP Congresses—held in 1964 and 1965, and both referred to as the Tenth Congress—ended in complete disorder, the Eleventh Congress (7-10 November 1966) issued resolutions supporting the Chinese cultural revolution and stressed that political power could be won in Latin America by armed guerrilla struggle. The FEP, however, has apparently ceased to play a dominant role in the Peruvian student movement and many of its functions have been taken over by the student federation of the University of San Marcos. In early 1967, however, Mario Ugarte, Organizational Secretary of the pro-Soviet PCP, noted that "for the youth organization, the basic test is to reconquer positions in the university movement, both in the base federations and in the FEP" (*Ensayos,* January-February 1967).

PCP influence within the trade union movement is strongest in the south, in the Federation of Cuzco Workers (Federación de Trabajadores de Cuzco) and the Federation of Cuzco Peasants (Federación de Campesinos de Cuzco). To a lesser degree, PCP influence is felt among the miners of Central Peru and the drivers and construction workers in Lima.

In the January-February 1967 issue of *Ensayos,* the bimonthly theoretical journal of the pro-Soviet PCP, Mario Ugarte called on the party to concentrate on the trade union movement and to establish a new "General Confederation of Peruvian Workers" (Confederación General de Trabajadores Peruanos; CGTP), whose primary objective would be to gain the support of noncommunist trade-union leaders. As the point of departure for the creation of the CGTP, Ugarte announced the establishment of a "Committee for Trade Union Unity and Defense."

**Leadership and Organization of the pro-Soviet PCP.** The highest organ of the PCP is the party congress. The last (Fourth) Congress was held in August 1962. The principal leaders of the pro-Soviet PCP are Raúl Acosta Sálas, former Secretary-General of the party, and Jorge del Prado, who now holds the position of Secretary-General. Although little is known about the organization of the pro-Soviet PCP, Organizational Secretary Mario Ugarte noted the need to make the political leadership of the party "more nimble" and stressed the necessity of "establishing the operation of the Secretariat of the Central Committee in place of the Secretariat of the Political Commission" so that it could assume responsibility for administrative tasks and thereby free the Political Commission of these tasks. An article in *Unidad,* the weekly organ of the party, commented on the plenary session of the party Central Committee (November 1967) and noted that there was a "revision of the Political Commission," without giving details.

**Domestic Views and Policies of the Pro-Soviet PCP.** In an address carried in the January-February 1967 issue of *Ensayos* under the title "The Construction of a Communist Party of the Masses is the Cornerstone of the Peruvian Revolution," Mario Ugarte, Organizational Secretary of the PCP, outlined the future plans of the party and placed considerable emphasis on the nature of the party and the need to adhere to the Soviet-style Marxist-Leninist theory on the nature and organization of a communist party. The pro-Soviet PCP clearly rejected the concept of a rural-based communist party and instead advocated an urban-based "proletariat party":

> ... The communist party is the party of the working class because of its doctrine and its political line, which correspond fundamentally to the interests of the working class.
>
> A workers' party because of its ideology and its historical objectives, a workers' party because of its composition, as well as because of its location in the principal workers' centers and concentrations. This structure in no way excludes the development of the party among the peasantry, nor among student and intellectual circles, where it is faced with the greatest needs and prospects. It is in the working class, however, that the party acquires strength. It is in the proletariat that the party finds the reason for its existence.

While stressing the working-class nature of the party, Ugarte admitted: "We know that the composition of our party is not worker in origin in its majority, which is a weakness that must be overcome," and added: "This requires that our policy must be eminently proletarian, that is, that it must be directed more toward the working class than to any other social sector or class." Specifically, Ugarte called for "preferential attention" to be extended to the "centers of proletarian concentration," citing Lima, Callao, Chimbote, Cerro de Pasco, Marcona, Toquepala, and Talara as "the places where we must assign cadres devoted to party construction."

In the course of his analysis Ugarte also pointed out a number of problems facing the party. "There is no doubt but that we have advanced," he wrote, "although this judgement cannot be applied generally, since the PCP has lacked "continuity in leadership formation at national and intermediate levels" and has not succeeded in "crystallizing its leadership nucleus." Ugarte also declared that the struggle against the cult of personality had not been "carried out with the necessary depth" in the Party:

> There are cases in the party and in the youth organization of comrades who, because they showed some positive quality—whether of cleverness in work, or of knowledge of certain

problems, or because of their political level—consider themselves to be some sort of gray eminence manipulating the threads of the party and who in practice make light of party organisms.

As a solution, Ugarte called for a "prolonged examination and critique in depth," to be followed by the "immediate restoration of the authority of party organisms," the establishment of collective leadership, the preparation of a "correct cadre policy," and the "strict application" of party statutes.

The same article noted an "inharmonious growth of the party on the national scale" and called for the development of regional leaderships and increased attention to regional problems, with attention to be focused on Lima and Callao, where 70 per cent of the working class is concentrated; Chimbote ("an area of labor concentration which will be our center of activity for the entire northern area"); Cuzco, Runo, and Arequipa ("which will be our center of activity in the south"); and Huancayo ("which will serve as the focus of our acitivity in the central part of the country").

In the ideological sector, Ugarte focused on the problems of sectarianism and schismatism. "There exists in the party, at its various levels, a sectarian conception of our organization," he noted. Although the PCP was "heir to a tradition of permanent struggle in the interests of the exploited masses," members of the party were not the only "fighters" and were not "automatically infallible": "We are not a sect, we are not a handful of 'chosen ones,' we do not live in ivory towers, we are not infallible nor can we grow on our own account, nor is that our objective." Cautioning that the party must learn from the masses, Ugarte added:

> In order to develop the party, we must build bridges toward all political, trade union, and student organizations, etc. . . . Thus, we are interested not only in the strengthening of the party, but also in the consolidation and development of all democratic and revolutionary organizations.

The article devoted considerable attention to factionalists within the party. While the party had "not only maintained but also strengthened its ideological cohesion," it had four groups of factionalists: "a first offshoot, the youth group called the FALN [Fuerzas Armadas de Liberación Nacional]; then the division between 'Sotomayorists' and 'Paredaists;' and finally the group called the 'Albanian' group; and winding up now with the beginning of a new factionalism within the 'Paredaist' group, a coming division that has already begun to be termed an 'inevitable split' within the ranks of the group itself." Ugarte also referred specifically to the "political and ideological orphanhood of the various schismatic groups within the left" and added: "The schismatism which has resulted in neo-Trotskyist and anticommunist organizations—even though they declare themselves to be 'rabid' Marxist-Leninists—no longer has any weight in domestic political affairs. . . . Now the danger that certain comrades could be won over by schismatism as was the case several years ago does not now exist." At the same time, Ugarte cautioned:

> Nevertheless, it is necessary to note that the neo-Trotskyists maintain important positions at the universities. They also retain a significant role in certain peasant zones. And where the party shows weakness, they attempt to go over to the offensive, becoming a serious threat through sowing confusion among the masses.

Finally, Ugarte emphasized the need to "technify" the party's work and accused the PCP of "spontaneity and improvisation," noting specifically:

> (a.) The lack of solidity in political evaluations, which stems from an excessive inclination for changing our points of view and consequently our outlook on work.
>
> (b.) The lack of resolution and determination to take things to the end in spite of any difficulty which might appear.
>
> (c.) The absence of labor discipline, which causes our activity to be excessively anarchical.
>
> (d.) Finally, the absence of planning.

As a solution to the various problems, Ugarte called for the collective preparation of party plans, a clear indication of PCP goals and the various stages of fulfillment, the "technification" of party work and overcoming of "antiquated and oversimplified" methods of work, and the elimination of "subjectivism and excessive enthusiasm."

At the Sixth National Organizational Conference of the PCP (25-26 November 1967), attended by the PCP Central Committee, regional leaders, and leaders of the Peruvian Communist Youth (JCP), Ugarte outlined the PCP's plans for a massive recruitment program and called on the party to "break the barriers of sectarianism and convert itself into a mass organization under the slogan 'Open the doors of the party to the best of our people' " (*Unidad*, 30 November). In outlining plans to extend PCP influence, party regional committees were directed to open local party headquarters immediately, recruit new militants, promote the sale of *Unidad*, create a "Unity of the Left Committee" including the PCP and other political organizations (see below), and collect signatures in order to have the "Unity of the Left" recognized by the electoral registration board.

An additional task set for the party was the establishment of the PCP as a legal, respectable force. While there is no law which excludes the PCP from legal, political existence, the party is proscribed from electoral participation by the 1933 constitution. Although maintaining that legality was not an "indispensable condition" for PCP development, party leaders stressed the reciprocal relationship between the conquest of legality and the development of the party, pointing out that the party will have "new prospects for development to the extent that it wins legality, and vice versa." At the same time, however, legality was not to mean the subservience of the party to bourgeois laws, but the utilization of these laws to further the development of the party.

At its twenty-fifth plenary session (November 1967), the PCP reaffirmed its rejection of guerrilla warfare, which it called the "simple fruit of impatience" and described as "lacking knowledge of the objective processes" being developed in Peru. Guerrilla struggle was seen as "not the most expeditious form of achieving the development of subjective factors," and the plenary session reaffirmed its position that the "most active participation in the political and trade union struggle . . . constitute the basic form of struggle in the present situation, and are the only way of accelerating the development of subjective factors."

The PCP cautioned that the "support of the peasant masses" was not something "to be taken for granted" and that the "support of the urban and proletarian masses" was not produced spontaneously:

> . . . The process of incorporation of the popular masses into the anti-imperialist front and their resolute mobilization for radical transformations are achieved slowly, or are not achieved at all, without the prior work of revolutionary propaganda, of class trade-union organization, and of revolutionary political organization. During the periods which precede the revolutionary situation, the role of the revolutionary party is precisely that of orienting and directing the ever more resolute and extensive actions of the masses, raising their level of awareness, and developing their organization. . . . .
>
> The communist party has repeatedly pointed out its conviction that the conquest of power without armed struggle will not be possible under the conditions of the country, and that armed insurrection is impossible without the existence of a revolutionary situation. It has also indicated that even though the guerrilla struggle could begin prior to the existence of a revolutionary situation, this does not imply that any situation is good for its unleashing, or even less so for its consolidation and development (*Unidad*, 9 November.)

While maintaining that the party organization "must be prepared to face all the requirements of the struggle, including all the 'illegal' forms of revolutionary activity," the PCP labeled the ELN, MIR, and other guerrilla movements as "premature."

In rejecting armed struggle, the PCP has stressed the importance of the coordination of the party with the "organization of the anti-imperialist left." In an effort to extend communist influence beyond the party ranks and to solidify the "anti-imperialist left," the PCP announced in 1967 the formation of the Unity of the Left (Unidad de Izquierda; UDI), consisting of the Social Progressive Movement (MSP), the Frente de Liberacion Nacional (National Liberation Front), the Fuerzas Populares (*People's Forces*), the Union del Pueblo Peruano (Union of the Peruvian People), the PCP, and "nonparty revolutionaries and leftists." UDI statements describe the organization as a "forward step in the aspirations of all the people of Peru to obtain the greatest possible unity of the anti-oligarchy and anti-imperialist citizen sectors with the objective of constituting a decisive force capable of solving grave national problems and defeating the ruling bipartisanship of the Alianza [Alliance] and the Coalición [Coalition]."

In the congressional by-election held in Lima on 12 November the UDI made an impressive showing with the candidacy of Carlos Malpica by winning 13.5 per cent of the total vote, or nearly 106,000 adherents. The UDI hailed the election as having "offered a valuable example of what the unity of the focus of the left can achieve" and declared its intention to participate in the 1969 elections with its own candidates for President of the Republic, the Chamber of Deputies and Senators, and the Municipal Council. Following the elections, the UDI announced that a "National Coordinating Committee" consisting of Carlos Malpica and Francisco Moncloa would be established in Lima, and declared its intention to establish political blocs in the Chamber of Deputies and Senate and in the municipalities with Parliamentarians and Councilmen who "either individually or through the parties to which they belong" would be UDI members.

In analyzing the activities and role of the party, the pro-Soviet PCP characterized the current situation as a "stage of accumulation of strength," a "prerevolutionary" situation marked by the "possibility of intensification of the activity of the masses and of the sharpening of the political crisis, which, impelled by the economic crisis, could give rise to the upsurge of one or more revolutionary situations during the course of the coming years" (*Unidad,* 9 November). Organizational Secretary Ugarte noted that the party was "experiencing a time politically" which urgently required that it "go on the offensive." At the same time, although the party was experiencing a period of accumulation of forces, Ugarte cautioned: "We can in no way forsee a period of regularity, without political surprises, without the danger of coup d'état, without the prospect of regressive shifts. Aware as we are of the characteristics of our country and of all Latin America, our conception of the period of accumulation of forces is, without any doubt, a dialectical appraisal."

**International Views and Policies of the Pro-Soviet PCP.** Within the context of the international communist movement, the pro-Soviet PCP has endorsed the convening of a world conference of communist parties and supported the proposed Budapest meeting of communist parties scheduled for February 1968. In the field of international affairs, the pro-Soviet PCP continued to reiterate its alignment with the CPSU. The party sent a delegation led by Secretary-General Jorge del Prado to the Moscow celebrations of the fiftieth anniversary of the October Revolution, and hailed the CPSU by noting that "to the consistently Leninist position of the Communist Party of the Soviet Union, the international communist movement, the authentic vanguard in the revolutionary struggle in this area of transition from capitalism to socialism, owes the retention of its unity, its invincible strength, and its growing prestige and ascendence" (*Unidad,* 26 October).

The pro-Soviet PCP continued to attack the Chinese Communist Party and the cultural revolution:

> The flood of blood, terror, and confusion that is invading China has been caused by a complete distortion of the scientific postulates of Marxism-Leninism brought about by Mao Tse-Tung and his followers. Socialist legality and democratic centralism have been displaced by arbitrariness and subjectivism, by a personality cult, and by an impatient desire to skip over, at any cost, the necessary steps in social development, within the framework of a society that is laying the foundation of socialism. All this ideological hypertrophy contains a mixture of petty-bourgeois nationalism, of great-power chauvinism, of rashness, and of racism. (*Ibid.,* 12 January.)

In the Latin American context, a Peruvian delegation attended the OLAS meeting in Havana (31 July-10 August). The attitude of the PCP, represented at the conference by Mario Ugarte, was polite, but not enthusiastic. In commenting on the meeting, *Unidad* stated: "The most valuable and real support which the OLAS can offer to the peoples of the continent is in the search for and discovery of common points which will contribute toward the unity of the vast forces which are fighting on a common front." *Unidad* failed to endorse the OLAS theories on revolution and on 10 August reported in detail the attack made by the French communist daily *L'Humanité* against the "anticommunist and anti-Soviet declarations made by some communists."

Two other members of the delegation were not of the same opinion, however. Juan Quintana and Jesús Maza issued a statement in the Cuban paper *El Mundo* calling for the "immediate resumption of armed struggle in Peru" and announced that Peruvian revolutionary organizations "reject all collaboration and peaceful emulation with capitalism."

On the death of Ernesto "Che" Guevara, Jorge del Prado, Secretary-General of the pro-Soviet PCP, stated: "We Peruvian Communists first of all consider that the serious reverses suffered in recent weeks by the Bolivian guerrilla movement, including among them the irreparable loss of the legendary and heroic Major Ernesto 'Che' Guevara, no matter how painful and difficult they are, still do not lead us to the conclusion that the movement is failing." At the same time, however, Jorge del Prado called on the Bolivian guerrillas to "draw up a balance sheet and make a critical and self-critical evaluation of these events."

**Publications.** The pro-Soviet PCP's publications include *Unidad,* the weekly organ of the party, *Ensayos,* its bimonthly theoretical journal; and *Joven Guardia,* the organ of the Communist Youth.

\* \* \*

The pro-Chinese PCP is headed by Saturnino Paredes Macedo, its Secretary-General. Support for the party derives from primarily two sources—the militant wing of the student movements, as exemplified by elections at the University of San Marcos, and from Castroist and Trotskyist elements disillusioned by the pro-Soviet party's lack of support for the guerrilla movement.

Internally, the pro-Chinese PCP appears to be beset by factions within its leadership and discord between the leadership and the regional committees. Controversy was precipitated by the publication of the resolutions of the party's Fifth National Conference (November 1965). According to the party organ, *Bandera Roja* (4 March 1966), the document was "infested with errors of principle and serious errors of formulation" and in no way reflected the "true conclusions and resolutions which should have been drawn from the debates of the Fifth National Conference" of the party. The paper also noted a "profound malaise" which the Fifth National Conference "had not overcome but, to the contrary, had worsened to unbearable limits." Reports during 1967 indicated that there were signs of a power struggle within the pro-Chinese PCP between supporters of Secretary-General Saturnino Paredes and supporters of José Sotomayor.

**Domestic Views and Policies of the pro-Chinese PCP.** The pro-Chinese PCP's theories of armed struggle were clearly outlined in an unsigned article in the January 1967 issue of *Bandera Roja*:

> No people in the world has ever achieved its liberation except by means of violent revolution. All the socialist countries have followed this path, which was blazed by the Great October Revolution. There is no other way. Peaceful transition is an unattainable illusion that only opportunists and revisionists of every stripe are capable of continuing to proclaim. . . .
>
> Making a correct analysis of the national political situation, and taking into account the nature of Peruvian society, our party has determined with great accuracy that the course of our revolution is that of armed struggle—of a prolongation of the armed struggle from the countryside to the city—within the framework of the national democratic, anti-imperialist, and antifeudal revolution,

While advocating armed struggle, the pro-Chinese PCP refused to back the guerrilla violence launched by members of the MIR in June 1965, labeling them "adventurists." This cost the party support in its own ranks and subsequently resulted in a group of students' breaking away from the party to form the Armed Forces of National Liberation (Fuerzas Armadas de Liberación Nacional; FALN).

In outlining the correct course of action to be followed, the article stressed the need for a "party of the proletariat based on Marxism—Leninism and rooted in the masses of the people, particularly the rural masses." The same issue of *Bandera Roja* carried an editorial by the Political Committee of the Central Committee of the pro-Chinese PCP reaffirming the resolution adopted at the Fifth National Conference calling for the organization and working methods of the party to be kept secret. Declaring that "every revolutionary party that is engaged in the difficult and heroic task of winning power must necessarily create a party organization that is strictly secret," the editorial went on to say:

> Otherwise, if it has no strictly secret party organization, the revolutionary party has only two paths open to it: either an ignoble renunciation of revolution, or a helpless and supine surrender to reactionary violence. For this reason, the problem of structuring a party that is strictly secret is a problem of principle; it is a problem of having a consistent proletarian ideological position. If the party really intends to win power, it must structure itself as a secret organization. The situation is clear: a party is revolutionary if it genuinely builds and develops a secret organization

The editorial also announced that *Bandera Roja* would henceforth be a clandestine publication.

In stressing the clandestine nature of the party, the pro-Chinese PCP attacked the pro-Soviet party's attempts to "precipitate the party onto the path of legalism":

> The revisionists restrict their activity to those areas that are tolerated by the laws of the exploiter state. The Marxists do exactly the opposite: they expose this false legality and never place their trust in it.
>
> Now the revisionists are opening local "party" headquarters. They demonstrate thereby their ideological poverty and their extreme weakness, which does not worry the reactionaries in the least. The Marxists, on the other hand, believe that the party *should be felt, not seen.*
>
> The revisionists are trying to stage a revolution by "winning a majority at the polls." The Marxists believe that since the revolution is an action that is not permitted by the exploiters, the latter will not permit the existence of a communist party either, if the party is a genuine revolutionary party. (*Bandera Roja,* January 1967; emphasis in original.)

Pro-Chinese PCP members and "extremist students" at the National University of San Marcos were particularly active during 1967. Entrance examinations to the university were disrupted in late February and early March, and in subsequent disorders pro-Chinese communist student leaders José Carlos Vertiz and Walter Puga Chávez were arrested and quantities of subversive propaganda were found at the headquarters of the Student Federation. In the elections for the student governing body of the National University of San Marcos, the pro-Chinese candidate, Andrés Gonzáles, won the Presidency of the San Marcos University Federation (see above).

Unlike the pro-Soviet PCP, the pro-Chinese PCP urged its members to cast blank ballots in the November congressional by-elections in Lima. While some 35,000 blank votes were registered, it is unlikely that the pro-Chinese PCP's strength is anywhere near that size, as many Peruvians traditionally cast blank ballots as an expression of generalized protest.

**International Views and Policies of the Pro-Chinese PCP.** In international affairs, the pro-Chinese PCP has rejected the idea of "common action," which it considers a "new deception aimed at leading the undecided into joint treachery." The party favors a "joint anti-imperialist front, but one which has no place for modern revisionists, since they are parleying with yankee imperialism and dreaming of sharing the world with them."

On the occasion of the eighteenth anniversary of the founding of the People's Republic of China, the pro-Chinese PCP Central Committee sent a message stating:

> People's China, as the vanguard of the world proletarian revolution and as the basis of world revolution, as the rearguard of the peoples who are fighting wars of national liberation, must be defended to the death by all of us, everywhere, by each and every revolutionary throughout the world, making revolution in each of our countries. The struggles and wars of national liberation mutually support and defend one another. Proletarian revolutions mutually support one another.
>
> We consider it the duty of all revolutionaries to study and assimilate the experience of the proletarian cultural revolution of China, which, under the guidance of Comrade Mao Tse-tung's thought, points the way to a brilliant development of Marxism-Leninsim. By incorporating the great popular masses, the great proletarian cultural revolution is giving an example of how the communists must place themselves at the head of the popular masses to make revolution. The ideas of Marxism-Leninism developed by Comrade Mao

Tse-tung also guide world revolution and when they are planted in the mind of the popular masses they become a force more powerful than nuclear weapons.

**Publications.** The pro-Chinese PCP publishes an irregular, clandestine journal, *Bandera Roja* (Red Flag). The organ of the party's youth movement is *Peru Juvenil*.

\* \* \*

In addition to the two rival communist parties, the extreme left in Peru comprises the Revolutionary Leftist Front (Frente Izquierdista Revolucionaria; FIR), the Peruvian section of the United Secretariat of the Fourth International; the Revolutionary Workers' Party (Partido Obrero Revolucionario,) also of Trotskyist orientation; the National Liberation Front (Frente de Liberación Nacional; FLN), a united front of numerous small Castroist groups; the Armed Forces of National Liberation (Fuerzas Armadas de Liberación Nacional; FALN); the Army of National Liberation (Ejercito de Liberación Nacional; ELN); and the Movement of the Revolutionary Left (Movimiento de Izquierda Revolucionaria; MIR).

In 1961, a splinter group from the youth wing of APRA, known as the APRA Rebelde, adopted its present name, Movement of the Revolutionary Left, and in March 1964, adopted the resolution "Todos al Campo" ("call to the field") in an attempt to reorient their university-urban base. In June 1965 the MIR initated guerrilla warfare under the leadership of the following: Luis de la Puente Uceda, Secretary-General and leader of the Pachacutec guerrilla wing; Guillermo Lobaton, leader of another guerrilla wing, and Máximo Velando, his lieutenant; Gonzalo Fernández Gasco, leader of the guerrilla wing in the north; Elio Portocarrero Ríos; and Héctor Bejar, leader of the guerrilla wing known as the ELN (see below). By the beginning of 1966 de la Puenta Uceda, Lobaton, and Velando were dead, Bejar was in prison, Gasco and Portocarrero Ríos had fled abroad, and the government's countermeasures had succeeded in severely disrupting the guerrilla apparatus of the MIR. In October 1966 the Central Committee of the MIR met clandestinely to discuss future plans. No specific details of the meeting were revealed.

The MIR program for the realization of the "national popular revolution" consists of seven main ponts:

(1) Immediate dissolution of Parliament as an instrument of the oligarchy and imperialism.

(2) General amnesty for political prisoners and punishment for all government and military officials responsible for massacres.

(3) Authentic agrarian reform involving complete liquidation of the latifundia and the free transference of the land to the peasants, excluding the expropriation of middle farmers who work their own land and who are efficient producers; preferential treatment by the State to all aspects of peasant life and work.

(4) Sliding scale of family wages for workers, public and private employees, professionals and technicians.

(5) Urban reform expropriating large real estate interests making the present tenants owners of their dwellings; excepting middle and small property owners.

(6) Immediate recovery of Peruvian petroleum.

(7) Recovery of broad national sovereignty; elimination of treaties and agreements that compromise national independence and establishment of diplomatic and commercial relations with all countries. (James Petras, "Guerrilla Movements in Latin America—I," *New Politics*, New York, Winter 1967, p. 93.)

While not excluding other means of struggle, MIR strategy stresses that "armed struggle is the principal element of the Peruvian revolutionary process." In an interview (February 1967) an unidentified leader of MIR declared:

In the light of our experience and subsequent analysis, we are reaffirming our revolutionary line that there is no alternative open to our people other than revolutionary violence. This path cannot assume a form other than that of armed struggle beginning in the rural areas. It is necessary to combine this basic concept with other forms of people's struggle. The important thing is that we combine other forms of struggle with the principal form, without ever losing sight of which is the principal one . . .

In analyzing the current situation, the same leader maintained that the revolutionary process was a "historic, difficult, long, and painful task thriving on setbacks and victories, and having negative and positive results," and added that the MIR had not died, but was instead undertaking the "necessary task of self-criticism and reorganization."

Despite the movement's optimistic outlook, it is unlikely that there will be any actions on the scale of the 1965 uprising. On 25 May 1967, Peruvian authorities captured Enrique Amaya Quintana, who took command of the Pachacutec wing after the death of de la Puente Uceda and who appears to have succeeded him as Secretary-General of the MIR. Other MIR leaders arrested during the year included Ricardo Gadea Acosta, Eusebio Dant de la Cruz, Carlos Erick, Alfonso Arata, and Oscar Alvarado. Reports indicate that Amaya may have since been killed.

Internationally, the MIR maintains that the movement "adheres, without reservation, to unconditional proletarian internationalism." MIR was represented at the OLAS meeting held in Havana (31 July-10 August) by Jacqueline de Lobaton, and noted "It is necessary that the representatives of the peoples meet, not in a formal act, but to oppose the global strategy of imperialism with a daring strategy of the peoples." The representative also stressed the MIR's international solidarity with the Cuban Communist Party: "[The MIR] shares the recent declaration made by the Cuban Communist Party's Central Committee, which reserved for itself the right to support subversive movements in the continent as much as possible."

The MIR reaffirmed its support for the Bolivian guerrillas, declaring:

> With fraternal, international support goes our revolutionary salute and firm conviction that Bolivia, by opening a new front in Latin America, will weaken the American aggression in Vietnam and also by its geographical situation will encourge, just as Cuba did, rapid emancipation through armed struggle.

On the occasion of the death of Ernesto "Che" Guevara, the MIR commented:

> The death of Che is an immense loss for the revolutionaries of the entire world, and especially for Latin America. He is the symbol of true proletarian internationalism, of the purest theoretical and pracitcal results consistent with the ideas that he professed. His example, which has imposed respect even on declared enemies, must continue guiding the most conscious sectors of the masses and the youth in the struggle for national liberation and socialism. And there is no doubt that many other Che's will arise within a short period. (*Caretas,* Lima, 8 November 1967.)

Peruvian authorities have charged that the Communist Party of Chile has been financing MIR guerrillas.

The organ of the MIR is *Voz Rebelde.* The MIR also issues an irregular, clandestine mimeographed publication, *El Guerrillero.*

The Army of National Liberation, or ELN, is headed by Héctor Bejar Rivera, who is currently in prison awaiting trial. In a March 1967 interview, Bejar commented on the guerrilla setbacks in 1965, maintaining that they were only a tactical defeat: "We were not able to implement guerrilla tactics properly. We were too naive and not sufficiently astute." In the same interview he defined the ELN's goal as the development of a "popular anti-imperialist and antifeudal revolution leading to socialism." Internationally, the ELN has endorsed the guerrilla movements in Bolivia, the OLAS meeting in Havana, and the 13 March speech of Fidel Castro condemning the "traitorous and reactionary stand of the Communist Party of Venezuela" and asserting Cuba's right to foment revolution in other countries. A statement issued by the National Command of the ELN specifically noted: "At this moment when new fronts are being opened up, it is clear that there can only be one road—that of armed struggle," adding: "It is mistaken, if not criminal, to direct the struggle from the cities. . . . Cuba's experience has shown us that the revolution is forged in the mountains." (*Granma,* 9 April 1967.)

The Armed Forces of National Liberation (Fuerzas Armadas de Liberación Nacional; FALN) is a small splinter group of the pro-Chinese PCP. In a declaration issued in April 1967, the FALN National Command outlined its strategy:

> ... We recognize that there are no two ways to revolution. The only way taught us by the Paris commune, the Russian, Chinese, Korean, Vietnamese, and Cuban revolutions is the path of violent revolution.
>
> We believe class struggle is the moving force in the development of all societies divided into antagonistic classes. The class struggle means to us revolutionary, ideological, political, and military struggle. We reject the illusion of a "peaceful transition."

Internationally, the FALN has stressed the "development of an independent policy of revolutionary movements," "fraternal relations and aid with the sister parties," and, at the same time, "struggle for the unity of the international communist movement." The FALN was represented at OLAS by Jesús Maza Paredes, who hailed the meeting as the "great anti-imperialist front for continental liberation, through which the revolutionary movements will coordinate their actions and provide themselves with a strategy." The FALN also reaffirmed its solidarity with the Cuban Communist Party and declared its support for the guerrilla movements in Venezuela, Colombia, Guatemala, and Bolivia, adding: "the best way for our continent to support the heroic people of North and South Vietnam is by developing the war of liberation, although we believe the basic way must be through common action of the socialist camp against bellicose imperialism."

The National Liberation Front (Frente de Liberación Nacional; FLN) was founded by the PCP in 1961. It was defined as a "political organization of popular combatant unity" advocating "economic emancipation and national sovereignty" and standing for "land, liberty, and bread but against oligarchy, imperialism, and the government of peaceful coexistence." Organizationally, a coordinating committee was established consisting of Antonio Peralta, Oscar Olguin, Teodoro Aspilcueta, Ernesto More, Carlos Balarezo Delta, Ezequiel Ramírez Nova, Angel Castro Lavareilo, Teodoro Núñez Ureta, and Genaro Carnero Checa. A steering committee of 25 members was also established, in an effort to represent the "most divergent political sectors, organizations, and activities." Little is known about the activities of the FLA, although it publishes a newspaper, *Frente.*

In late December 1967, Peruvian authorities announced that a new left-wing terrorist group, distinct from the ELN but also known as the "Army of National Liberation," had been crushed. The movement was under the leadership of a twenty-four-year-old university student known as Benavides Caldas and apparently had sought to establish a guerrilla movement in the province of Puno, in southern Peru, which would ultimately coordinate activities with guerrillas operating in Bolivia. As a result of police actions the original leader, Jorge Benavides, was killed, and in subsequent actions Benavides Caldas was arrested, along with ten other members of the group.

# PHILIPPINES

The Philippine Communist Party (Partido Komunista ng Pilipinas; PKP) was founded in November 1930 but was declared illegal by a Supreme Court ruling in 1932. PKP efforts to expand and consolidate its power were relatively unsuccessful until World War II and the Japanese occupation, when, on 29 March 1942, the PKP assumed the leading role in the formation of a "broad coalition of guerrilla resistance organizations" known as the People's Anti-Japanese Army (Hukbong Bayan Laban sa Hapan), commonly known as the Huks, and later renamed People's Liberation Army (Hukbong Mapagpagpalayang Bayan).

In June 1957 the Philippine government acted against the PKP and its supporters by passing the Anti-Subversion Act (Republic Act 1700), which specifically outlaws the PKP, makes membership in it a felony offense, and provides for the deportation of aliens arrested for violation of the Act's provisions.

Although outlawed, the PKP continues to operate clandestinely. In a June 1966 interview Jesus Lava, Secretary-General of the PKP, who was arrested in 1964, noted that "the members of the Philippine Communist Party today are on their own; they are limited to scattered islands of activity" (Justus M. van der Kroef, "Communist Fronts in the Philippines," *Problems of Communism,* March–April 1967). Although no concrete statistics are available, reports indicate that there are some 1,500 to 2,000 PKP members, whose activities include the establishment of PKP front organizations, the infiltration of existing noncommunist organizations, and support for the Huk movement. Jesus Lava also noted that the Philippine Branch of the Chinese Communist Party (CCP), founded in 1930, was still active and involved with the development of front organizations in the Chinese community and liaison operations with the Huks. Lava specifically denied any formal connections between the PKP and the Philippine branch of the CCP, but expressed PKP appreciation for assistance in the "common struggle." Although Lava placed the Philippine Chinese Communist Party membership at 1,500 to 2,000, Western sources place it at 300 to 500 (*World Strength of Communist Party Organizations,* 1968, p. 94). The population of the Philippines is 34,656,000 (mid-1967 estimate).

**Organization and Leadership.** Little information is available regarding the organization and leadership of the PKP. In an article in *World Marxist Review* (November 1965) Jorgé Maravilla commented on government actions against the Huks and the PKP during the period from 1950 to 1956 and noted that "of the original nine members of the Political Bureau of the Party in 1950, all were either killed or captured. The entire Central Committee of the Party in the same period were either killed or have suffered imprisonment, with many still in prison. . . . The Party was left almost without effective cadres to rebuild the movement after the defeat of the armed struggle."

In an article in the July 1967 issue of *Tricontinental Bulletin,* reprinted in the 30 July 1967 issue of *The Worker,* William Pomeroy, an American journalist who joined the Huk movement and has since been released from jail, noted that there were 60 or 70 political prisoners in the Philippines today. Those imprisoned the longest include some 28 leaders who were tried as a group in 1950 in what was known as the "Politburo Case" because several of those tried were known to be members of the PKP Politburo. Among those in prison are Jesus Lava, Secretary-General of the PKP; Federico Maclang, Organizational Secretary of the PKP; Ramon Espiritu, Finance Secretary of the PKP; and Federico Bautista, head of the PKP Intelligence Department.

**Domestic Views and Policies.** Although supporting the "protracted" struggle of the Huks, the PKP has placed primary emphasis on "legal" and "parliamentary" forms of struggle in an effort to form a broad-based national united front. As outlined in *World Marxist Review* (November 1965), " . . . it is crucial for the nationalist forces to shape their own political instrument around which a nationalist united front of workers, peasants, intellectuals, and nationalist bourgeoisie with an anti-imperialist program can be formed. This is the main task in the present stage of the struggle for national freedom in the Philippines."

In a 1 May 1967 statement issued in the name of the PKP Politburo and carried in the 10 May 1967 issue of the *People's Voice,* the weekly organ of the pro-Peking New Zealand Communist Party, it was noted that "in pursuing its anti-imperialist and antifeudal struggle, the Party undertakes nationwide Party rebuilding, development of rural bases and armed struggle, and a national united front under the leadership of the working class . . . . The outlawed situation of the Party dictates clearly that there is no path to national and social liberation except armed struggle." A subsequent statement, issued in November by the PKP Politburo and carried in *Information Bulletin* (no. 110) attacked the 1 May statement, claiming that it "was not authorized by the PKP and does not reflect its true position." The statement further noted:

> As an illegal organization, the PKP recognizes the necessities in the Philippine situation and observes the organization principles of an underground Marxist-Leninist revolutionary party. While it is true that its illegal status should not in any way hamper its leading role in the struggle for national liberation and socialism, the PKP never advertises its strategy and tactics. Thus the so-called statement printed in the New Zealand paper is not only spurious, but represents a serious breach of underground rules and therefore constitutes an act of treason against the revolutionary movement.

The November statement went on to accuse the "antiparty" group which issued the 1 May statement of displaying a "very narrow and constricted view of the national situation in the Philippines" and of grossly ignoring "the ability of the PKP to lead the revolutionary masses in struggle despite its illegal character." In concluding, the November statement noted:

> Armed struggle is a necessity, as the final step in the overthrow of imperialism, not because of the illegal character of the party, but because of the nature of imperialism itself. Moreover, the spurious statement creates the impression of a "call to arms" at this very moment, again ignoring the present state of objective conditions and subjective forces in the Philippines. The correct position, which is the position of the PKP, is to combine dialectically parliamentary struggle and armed struggle, legal and illegal forms of action.

Although no details are available, the conflicting documents issued in the name of the PKP Politburo indicate that a split exists within the party. The exact nature and extent of the split are unknown, but it appears to reflect the issues of the Sino-Soviet split within the international communist movement. While the 1 May statement noted that "all Party cadres shall isolate elements who conspire against Marxist-Leninists and shall prevent the consolidation of any revisionist faction," the November statement stressed that "the small but reckless antiparty group that issued the statement printed in the New Zealand paper in the hope of gaining international recognition, waves the banner of the thought of Mao Tse-tung in a vain attempt to achieve a semblance of authenticity. But revolutionary struggles are not won by mouthing revolutionary ideas and phrases." It is by no means clear, however, what effect, if any, the apparent split will have on future PKP policies, support for the Huk movement, and formation and infiltration of front organizations.

**The Hukbong Mapagpagpayalayang Bayan (Huks).** While the extent of PKP activity within the Philippines is debatable, the relationship between the PKP and the Huks is even more controversial. Most observers believe, however, that any ties between the PKP and the Huks are tenuous at best, for a number of reasons. It is not known whether any significant and effective PKP apparatus capable of coordinating Huk activities exists at this time, and it is unlikely that the Huks, with their own financial and organizational base, would be willing to accept outside direction. In addition, there would appear to be serious ideological differences between the PKP, whose primary emphasis is on united-front tactics, and the Huks, who place considerably more emphasis on the use of violent methods. If, however, the PKP has in fact split, as appears to be indicated by two conflicting PKP statements issued in 1967, the group maintaining that "there is no path to national and social liberation except armed struggle" may seek closer collaboration with the Huk movement.

Huk founder Luis Taruc noted in June 1966 that there were three kinds of Huks: (1) hard-core Communists, whom Taruc referred to as "Stalinists"; (2) noncommunist "radical reformers," the category in which Taruc placed Pedro Taruc, his cousin, and Faustino del Mundo; and (3) "opportunists," who participate in the Huk movement out of self-interest only (Justus M. van der Kroef, "Philippine Communism and the Chinese," *China Quarterly,* no. 30, April–June 1967).

Thus it appears that whereas the Huk movement and leadership may contain members of the PKP, the movement itself is not controlled by the PKP. There is little doubt, however, that the PKP supports the activities of the Huks and will seek to capitalize on their successes whenever possible.

Various international Communist publications and broadcasts, particularly those originating in Peking, have attempted to create the impression that the Huks are under the control of the PKP by referring to the "People's Liberation Army of the Philippines headed by the Philippine Communist Party," and claiming that the "People's Liberation Army of the Philippines has been resolutely implementing the policy of the Philippine Communist Party for developing base areas in the countryside and carrying out armed struggle."

According to Philippine intelligence estimates, the Huk movement commands 156 "regulars" and 136 "part-time" guerrillas in central Luzon, in addition to 1,000 to 1,200 "hard-core" political members of whom 200 are estimated to be members of the PKP. Reports also indicate that the Huks command the allegiance of some 25,000 to 30,000 sympathizers (*NYT*, 16 April 1967). A subsequent report estimated that the number of "part-time" guerrillas had risen to 345 (*Far Eastern Economic Review*, 11 January 1968).

Organizationally, the Huk apparatus is pyramidal in construction. At the base are 25,000 to 30,000 sympathizers who support the movement with financial contributions which are either voluntary or forced. The next level consists of the some 1,000 to 1,200 "hard-core" political members and loyal cadres whose primary task is the collection of dues and the recruitment of new members. This level is also responsible for providing food, transport, and other services for the armed groups. Above this level is the combat-support group or "part-time, 12-hour Huks" who are "peaceful citizens by day and Huks by night." Their primary responsibility is to provide the necessary security for the "regular" Huks operating in and passing through their territory. They are also responsible for punitive assignments, such as kidnapings and assassinations. At the apex of the pyramid are the "regular, 24-hour Huks."

While little concrete evidence is available regarding the training of Huk insurgents, Philippine armed forces intelligence reports in 1965 revealed the discovery of military training centers in Bioc and the Visayas which were run by Chinese Communists. In early 1967 government troops located another training camp near San Fernando in Pampanga province.

Leadership of the Huk organization rests with Pedro Taruc, cousin of Luis Taruc, founder and leader of the movement until his arrest in 1954, and Faustino del Mundo, who operates under the name "Commander Sumulong." Although he is theoretically second in command, intelligence sources report that the real authority behind the Huks rests with del Mundo. Neither Taruc nor del Mundo held a position of power when the movement was at its peak, however, and neither is regarded as having any strong ideological orientation.

The Huks are primarily active in the rural areas of central Luzon, especially in the provinces of Pampanga, Bulacan, Nueva Ecija, and Tarlac, where they have virtually succeeded in establishing an "invisible government." Reports indicate that they exercise varying degrees of control over some 1,400 square miles of territory and approximately 500,000 people. Philippine officials reluctantly admit that the Huks control approximately 176 villages, nearly 1 out of every 12, in the poorest sections of central Luzon. In addition, reports indicate that the Huks have also succeeded in establishing a sound financial base, with official estimates placing their annual collections at $400,000 to $500,000.

A report by the Philippine First Intelligence Zone listed 143 fatal casualties as a result of Huk terrorism during 1967, compared to 83 in 1966 and 14 in 1965. Huk casualties amounted to 24 killed, including such Huk leaders as Zacarias de la Cruz, alias "Commander Dello"; Bernabe Buscayo, alias "Commander Dante" and reportedly number 11 in the Huk hierarchy; Alfredo Yambao, alias "Commander Freddie"; "Commander Dalusong," and Avelino Bagsik, alias "Commander Zaragoza." Those arrested included Dominador Garcia, alias "Commander Ely" and reportedly number three in the movement; Potenciano de Leon; and Jesus Lindingan, alias "Commander Roldan" and apparently number five in the leadership. An additional 33 Huks surrendered to the government en masse on 29 August 1967.

Government attempts to eliminate the Huks have been twofold. On 22 June 1967 President Marcos announced that the Philippine government was considering granting amnesties to the Huks in an effort to facilitate the administration's pacification and redevelopment program in Central Luzon. In an interview published in the 28 July 1967 issue of *The Manila Times* Luis Taruc stated that he still enjoyed considerable influence within the Huk movement, and that if the government granted the Huks a general amnesty, he was confident that he could persuade the Huks, including Pedro Taruc and Faustino del Mundo, to return to civilian life. No general amnesty was granted, however, and subsequent increased Huk terrorism, timed to coincide with the elections, caused President Marcos to intensify the government's campaign against the insurgents and to instruct the armed forces to deploy additional troops, including the Philippine Constabulary Special Forces, in the provinces of Pampanga, Bulacan, and Tarlac in an effort to destroy the movement. On 12 December the Philippine government raised the reward for Pedro Taruc from $25,000 to $32,500 and for Faustino del Mundo from $20,000 to $30,000.

**Front Organizations.** While supporting the protracted struggle of the Huks, Philippine Communists have also placed considerable emphasis on "legal" or "parliamentary" struggle through the formation and infiltration of various front organizations in an effort to "radicalize public opinion and exploit anti-American nationalist sentiment" and thereby form a "united front" with nationalist overtones. Two of the most outspoken and active of the organizations supported by the PKP are the Kabataang Makabayan (KM; Nationalist Youth Movement), which was described in *World Marxist Review* (November 1965) as the "most outspoken and the most active of the new organizations in the Philippine struggle for freedom," and the Lapiang Manggagawa (LM; Labor Party), which merged with three trade-union organizations in May 1967 to form a new Socialist Party of the Philippines (SPP).

The Kabataang Makabayan was founded in 1964 by José Sison and José Lansang, both of whom have demonstrated procommunist sympathies—Sison in his statements in the bimonthly KM-LM organ, *Progressive Review* (Quezon City) and Lansang by his own admission of his one-time belief in the communist cause as the only approach which appeared to be sincere "about land reform, about fighting for true sovereignty for the Filipinos, about doing something positive for the millions of our people who live in misery in the rural areas." In December 1966 a special mission of the Philippine Congress visited Indonesia to investigate KM and LM connections with the Indonesian Communist Party. The findings indicated that such links existed and that José Sison was directly involved.

José Lapuz, the organization's Chief of Propaganda, claims that the movement has a membership of 6,000, but Western observers are more inclined to put the figure at around 5,000.

As outlined in *Progressive Review,* the KM program alleges that the Philippines is in a "semicolonial condition" and that it is the organization's "national democratic mission" to complete the "Philippine revolution, which has been frustrated by a new type of colonialism, American imperialism." The program calls for "invincible unity [of] all national classes [to] push forward the struggle for national liberation," the implementation of a "genuine land-reform program which benefits all segments of the peasantry," a "nationalist industrialization," and a more diversified economic development. The KM program also calls for the end of US military assistance programs to and rights in the Philippines and asserts that the Anti-Subversion Act should be "annulled because it is detrimental to democrary" (*Progressive Review,* no. 6, 1965).

In a subsequent 12-point "action program" put forth by the KM in January 1966, emphasis was placed on the need to abolish US "parity rights," to disband US military bases, to protect civil liberties, to relax the "tight credit squeeze" on Filipino businessmen, to "Filipinize" the educational system, and to establish diplomatic relations with "all countries in the spirit of internationalism."

The KM has apparently received considerable support from Philippine "big businessmen" and entrepreneurs who resent American economic influence and competition, as well as from those elements protesting the war in Vietnam and the presence of Philippine troops there. A number of militant demonstrations against the war have been organized by the KM and LM, with Philippine armed forces intelligence reports claiming collaboration between the Philippine and American communist parties in the financing of these demonstrations.

Although KM officials have repeatedly denied that there are any Chinese in their organization, two former KM members have asserted that the organization has maintained close contact with pro-Peking elements within the Chinese community and that an "informal Chinese section" participates in anti-American demonstrations (Justus M. van der Kroef, "Philippine Communism and the Chinese," *China Quarterly,* April–June 1967).

The Lapiang Manggagawa (LM) was founded in 1962 by a group of radical trade-union leaders. There is considerable overlapping in the leadership of the KM and LM, with José Sison, one of the founders of the KM, serving as Vice-Chairman of the LM and Ignacio Lascina holding the position of Secretary-General. According to Philippine Congressman Fermin Caram, several of the LM leaders served at one time as members of the PKP Politburo and are still in close contact with the party (Republic of the Philippines, *Congressional Record,* Sixth Congress, House of Representatives, 13 May 1966; *Philippine Herald,* 15 May 1966).

The LM contains some 7,000 members, many of whom are also KM members and the majority of whom come from organized labor, particularly the National Association of Trade Unions, (NATU), whose President, Ignacio Lascina, is also the Secretary-General of the LM.

The political program of the LM closely resembles that of the KM. The LM program asserts that "our economy is colonial in structure and orientation" and that the Philippine workers have been alienated from the "centers of power." The LM describes itself as "an effective instrument of reform political action" whose goals include "social justice," "land for the landless," a "truly independent foreign policy," and the "transfer of economic wealth and power to the Philippines" (*Progressive Review,* no. 1, 1963).

On 1 May 1967, following a dispute in which "certain 'pseudo-left intriguers,' " including the editor of *Progressive Review,* were dismissed, the LM merged with three trade-union organizations to form a new Socialist Party of the Philippines (SPP). José Sison and Ignacio Lascina apparently still retain their positions, however. Other positions in the SPP, which claims a membership of 200,000, are held by a number of former leaders of the Congress for Labor Organization, a PKP front organization outlawed in the early 1950s. The working relationship between the PKP and the SPP is still unclear. It should be noted, however, that several SPP leaders visited Peking toward the end of the year and that Secretary-General Lascina is reported to have met with Mao Tse-tung.

In addition to the KM and LM organizations, numerous smaller Communist-supported organizations are also active in the Philippines. Shortly after the formation of the LM in 1962, the Free Association of Peasants (Malayang Samahan ng Magsasaka, commonly known as MASAKA) was formed. The organization is reported to have some 21,000 members and is headed by Felixberto Olalia, a former Huk commander and treasurer of the Congress for Labor Organization. MASAKA is reportedly active in the communist indoctrination of peasants and in the printing and distribution of pro-Peking documents and pamphlets.

In February 1967, a new organization known as the Movement for the Advancement of Nationalism (MAN) was formed. It is primarily an anti-American organization composed mainly of intellectuals and professionals and is also headed by José Sison. A number of small front organizations are also controlled by the KM and LM (now the SPP), such as the Philippine Committee for Freedom in South Vietnam and the Bertrand Russell Peace Committee of the Philippines.

Considerable efforts have also been made by the PKP to infiltrate the Chinese community in the Philippines, particularly the "left radical element" in it, whose views are generally carried in the daily

*Chinese Commercial News.* According to Philippine intelligence reports issued in 1965, approximately 3,000 Chinese "subversives" were suspected of working closely with the Huks, causing Philippine constabulary chief Brigadier General Flavio Olivares to describe the potential threat posed by Communist Chinese infiltrators as more serious than that of the Huks.

Although the programs of the KM and SPP, as well as those of the smaller organizations, are Marxist in nature, and although these organizations apparently contain members of the PKP, there is no concrete information or evidence regarding the nature and extent of PKP influence and control. Equally unclear is the relationship between the "new-left nationalist movement" and the Huk movement operating in central Luzon. What is apparent, however, is that the PKP has adopted a policy of "walking on two legs" by supporting the "protracted strategy" of the Huks and legal "united-front" tactics.

**International Views and Positions.** Although there is little concrete information regarding the position of the PKP in the international communist movement, the May and November documents disclosed some information regarding the PKP's alignment, as did a separate statement issued by the PKP on the occasion of the Fiftieth Anniversary of the October Revolution. The 1 May statement stressed the need to "fight modern revisionism and all forms of opportunism," and noted that the PKP is

> . . . committed to an uncompromising struggle against modern revisionism, spearheaded by the revisionist ruling clique in the Soviet Union. There is no middle road between modern revisionism and the correct revolutionary line.
>
> The Party has sharply observed that centrist opportunism as it departs from a boldly Marxist-Leninist line has always led to an outright revisionist line. Also, a policy of silence on the fundamental questions of the international communist movement is a sure mark of opportunism and breeds revisionsim.

The 1 May document went on to note that the PKP "is committed to the policy of international united front led by the international proletariat," but that it "rejects the slogan of united action raised by the revisionist ruling clique in the Soviet Union," maintaining that " 'united action' is a clever ruse to trap the working class of the world into a collusion with US imperialism . . . . "

In a statement carried in *Information Bulletin* (no. 110) and contradicting the 1 May statement, the PKP refrained from taking sides in the Sino-Soviet dispute but noted that "in the process of rebuilding itself after a prolonged period of suppression, the PKP wages a resolute struggle against Left adventurism and infantilism, even as it guards against Right opportunism. It likewise opposes dogmatism and the mechanical application of universal laws of Marxism-Leninism to the specific conditions of the Philippines. It condemns splittism, careerism, and intellectual dishonesty." The PKP also noted that because of the "particular conditions of struggle in the Philippines during the past years," it was not able to attend or actively participate in any international communist conference. It added, however, that the "PKP has always viewed the world proletarian revolution as an organic unity; it adheres to the principle of proletarian internationalism and considers itself an integral part of the international Communist movement." The PKP also declared its support of the "general line" of the 1957 and 1960 Moscow meetings and added that there "is a need to explore possibilities of restoring world communist unity and to work out a common programme of action on an international scale." The PKP concluded its statement by noting:

> There is an even more urgent need—the need to maintain and strengthen communist solidarity in action against imperialism, in specific areas of struggle for national liberation and socialism. The spirit of proletarian internationalism embodied in the teachings of Marx, Engels, and Lenin should prevail over differences in strategic and tactical perspectives, no matter how important these differences may be and how zealously contending positions may be expounded and defended. It is utterly disturbing to find out that the assistance of socialist states to the raging wars of national liberation, such as that in Vietnam, is being hampered by the present dispute. The PKP calls on the major Communist parties to maintain solidarity in action against imperialism, even as they carry on struggles on the ideological level . . . .

For these reasons and from this standpoint, the PKP publicly declares its support for the forthcoming international conference of Communist and revolutionary workers' parties.

Although the PKP has not attended any international communist conferences and, except for a congratulatory message to the Soviet government and party, has had virtually no contacts with other parties in the international communist movement, it has reportedly received considerable support from other communist parties.

Documents captured in 1964 at the time of Jesus Lava's arrest indicated that the PKP and the Huks were in contact with the Indonesian Communist Party and the Chinese Communist Party and disclosed communist infiltration into the Philippines via Indonesia. With the abortive Communist coup of 30 September 1965 and the subsequent disintegration of the Djakarta-Peking axis, however, Indonesian and Chinese activities in the Philippines were substantially reduced and remained so in 1967. In October 1967 there were reports that 8 million counterfeit Philippine pesos printed in Communist China had been smuggled to the Huks operating in central Luzon.

The Huks have also received considerable verbal support from Peking, with New China News Agency broadcasts hailing the strategy and tactics of "protracted struggle" and noting:

Of course, in the face of US imperialist aggression and rule by Philippine reactionaries, the Philippine people's armed struggle will still have to undergo twists and turns, but the Philippine revolutionary people will certainly win final victory after protracted arduous struggles if, armed with Mao Tse-tung's thought, they fight a people's war, establish revolutionary base areas, and encircle the cities from the countryside.

**Publications.** Although the PKP has no regular publications of its own, PKP positions and views are frequently reflected in *Progressive Review,* a quarterly publication in English, which is the organ of the Kabataang Makabayan and the Lapiang Manggagawa; the daily *Chinese Commercial Review,* and *The Graphic,* a weekly publication in English. In addition, New China News Agency broadcasts to the Philippines in English and Tagalog.

# POLAND

A Communist Workers' Party of Poland was founded in December 1918 and renamed the Communist Party of Poland in March 1925. It was dissolved by the Comintern in 1938, to reemerge in January 1942 as the Polish Workers' Party. After the Communists gained power in Poland and imposed a fusion with the Polish Socialist Party, a new Communist-dominated party was created in December 1948, the Polish United Workers' Party (PUWP; Polska Zjednoczona Partia Robotnicza).* The PUWP controls the political life of Poland through the National Unity Front consisting of the PUWP, two minor parties, and a few "independents." The PUWP describes itself as the "ideological political standard bearer of the National Unity Front" (Ryszard Strzelecki, *Pravda,* 22 August 1967). In the May 1965 elections, in which 98.7 per cent of the vote was for the single list of National Unity Front candidates, the share of PUWP seats in the Parliament was 255 out of 460.

As of 30 June 1967 the PUWP had 1,951,800 members and candidate members, representing about 10 per cent of the adult population in Poland.**

**Organization and Leadership.** The First Secretary of the 162-member PUWP Central Committee is Wladyslaw Gomulka, who is also a member of the Politburo. The 11 other members of this body are Józef Cyrankiewicz (also the Premier), Edward Gierek, Stefan Jedyrchowski, Zenon Kliszko, Ignacy Loga-Sowiński, Edward Ochab (also Chairman of the State Council and thus nominal head of state), Adam Rapacki (also Minister of Foreign Affairs), Marian Spychalski (also Minister of Defense), Ryszard Strzelecki, Eugeniusz Szyr, and Franciszek Wanoilka, and the three candidate members of the Politburo are Mieczyslaw Jagielski, Piotr Jaroszewicz, and Boleslaw Jaszczuk. The Secretariat includes Witold Jarosiński, Boleslaw Jaszczuk, Zenon Kliszko, Artur Starewicz, Ryszard Strzelecki, Józef Tejchma, and Wladyslaw Wicha. There are about 68,000 basic party organizations. On the voivodship party committee level, First Secretary of the Warsaw voivodship committee, Stanislaw Kociolek, was transferred to the parallel post of the Gdansk voivodship and replaced by Józef Kepa on 22 December.

**Party Affairs.** Analysts of the Polish political scene have identified three distinct groups, representing different views, in the PUWP leadership: the so-called "hard liners," headed by Minister of the Interior General Mieczyslaw Moczar and including the members of the leadership who had belonged to the partisans during World War II; the "progressives," or "technocrats" headed by Politburo member and Secretary of the Katowice voivodship committee Edward Gierek and including those who had fled to the Soviet Union during the Nazi invasion of Poland; and the "moderates," centered around Wladyslaw Gomulka, who balance the two forces. A struggle for increased power by the hard-line group became increasingly evident following the Middle East crisis of June 1967. General Moczar became one of the most outspoken critics of elements in the party and populace at large who showed support for Israel despite the official PUWP policy of complete support for the Arab cause. He was also reported to be influential in the purge of Jewish party personnel during the second half of 1967.

In January 1967 Ryszard Strzelecki claimed the support of the entire party membership for the program of the PUWP: "Never before, no matter how far back we look into our history, has a political organization in Poland been able to claim with pride such an extensive social base and such support for its program as the PUWP can claim" (*Trybuna Ludu,* 15 January 1967). However, the alleged unity of the PUWP suffered a severe blow during the Middle East crisis of 1967 when some party members sided with Israel, openly defying the party line condeming Israel and completely supporting the Arabs. On 19 June Wladyslaw Gomulka, addressing the Sixth Congress of Polish Trade

---

*In 1966 the Communist Party of Poland was "reconstituted" in Albania. See below.

**This figure excludes party members of the armed forces and in the diplomatic service abroad. Of the membership, 40.1 per cent are reported workers, 11.8 per cent are peasants, and 42.6 per cent are white-collar workers.

Unions, severely attacked the "Zionist circles" of Polish Jews who had "applauded Israel aggression" against the Arabs and he warned against the creation of a "fifth column" in Poland:

> We cannot remain indifferent toward people who, in the face of a threat to world peace, which is also [a threat] to the security of Poland and the peaceful work of our nation, come out in favor of the aggressor, for the wreckers of peace and for imperialism. Let those who feel that these words are addressed to them, irrespective of their nationality, draw from them proper conclusions.

The fact that widespread popular opposition to the PUWP Central Committee stand had even penetrated party ranks was acknowledged by First Secretary of the Warsaw Party Committee Stanislaw Kociolek (*Trybuna Ludu*, 16 July 1967). Stating that "a number of comrades differ from the views and evaluation of the Central Committee on Israeli aggression," he warned that such a situation "facilitates attack on Party politics and development of a separate political line, alien to the Party." Reference was also made to the party dissidents by Defense Minister Spychalski in speeches on 19 and 20 July to graduates of two military academies. The "pro-Israeli" stand, he warned, was "proimperialist, antisocialist and antinational" and "could not be tolerated." It was also widely reported in the Western press, and in many instances confirmed by the Polish press, that at least four generals had been relieved of their posts because of differences with the government stand. Numerous mass-media commentators and editors were also replaced. On 15 December Leon Kasman, editor-in-chief of *Trybuna Ludu* was replaced by former deputy editor-in-chief Stanislaw Mojkowski. According to Polish sources, Kasman was leaving at his own request to work in the economic apparatus. United Press International indicated, however, that Kasman and other editors and journalists of Jewish origin were removed from their posts owing to pressure from the "hard-line" faction of the party leadership.

Besides the tension in party unity due to the Middle East crisis, the PUWP had been plagued by difficulties in reconciling the various views held by the old party members who had "experienced the oppression of the capitalist system and who fought against the invaders of [Poland]" and the young party members who had grown up in postwar Poland and who "do not remember the prewar years" (Wladyslaw Gomulka, *Trybuna Ludu,* 9 December 1967). The PUWP found it necessary to remind its members repeatedly that their basic duty remained the implementation of the uniform political line of the party.

In November and December the PUWP conducted a campaign involving exchange of party cards. The formal exchange was preceded by a campaign in which 6 to 10 per cent of the party members were interviewed by a special board at the district party level on their ideological, moral, and political attitudes.* It was emphasized that the purpose of these interviews was not "verification" aimed at dismissing "so-called passive party members," but was merely the gathering of views and opinions to strengthen the power and cohesion of the party, promote the personal involvement of all party members, and especially to make more effective the work of the basic party organizations (Teodor Palimaka, *Trybuna Ludu,* 10 June 1967; Zycie Partii, June 1967). Secretary of the Gdansk voivodship committee Jan Ossowski stressed: "It is most important not to pass hasty judgments and not to lose industrious, dedicated, and honest people whose only fault is passivity caused by insufficient knowledge of statutory rights and duties, by a bad atmosphere within the party organizations, or by fear of supervisors" (Boguslaw Holub, "Before the Exchange of Party Cards," *Trybuna Ludu,* 20 September 1967). *Trybuna Ludu* noted on 8 August that special emphasis was given to the present international situation in talks with the party members and to the necessity of increasing political activities of all party members.**

Reviewing the results of the interviews with party members and candidates, Ryszard Strzelecki noted on 9 November that the interviews considerably increased the militancy and commitment to party work, and that those who had been interviewed had even submitted proposals for streamlining party and trade-union activities. He concluded that the interviews demonstrated that passivity was not a result of inability or unwillingness, but quite often resulted from the style and methods

---

*The percentage of those interviewed was 70 to 80 per cent in the Warsaw party organization (*Trybuna Ludu,* 11 August 1967).
**It is likely that the emphasis on the international situation at precisely that time was due to the tension arising from the PUWP's support for the Arab cause.

of activities of the basic sectional party organizations, or simply the absence of any activities. Nevertheless, the results of the interviews also showed that in numerous districts they had been utilized to discipline and sometimes purge party members. *Gazeta Krakowska* noted on 6 July that the exchange of party cards must include the "indispensible process" of purging "opportunists" and passive members.

**Domestic Affairs.** The PUWP seeks to direct all spheres of life in Poland. In the words of Strzelecki, "the Communists are always and everywhere in the vanguard of everything" (*Trybuna Ludu,* 10 November 1967). Among the workers the Communists are active in initiating projects and are the leading force in the trade unions and workers' self-administrative organs. Party organizations in major industrial enterprises are granted the right of political control over the activities of the administration.

The Socialist Youth Union and the Rural Youth Union are responsible for the ideological education of young people and the implementation of party policies among the Polish youth. Andrzej Zabinski, former Chairman of the Katowice voivodship board of the Socialist Youth Union, was elected to his present post of Chairman of its Central Board on 24 February 1967, replacing Stanislaw Hasiak, who asked to be relieved in order to "continue his studies."

A major task of the Socialist Youth Union in 1967, especially following the Sejm Parliament draft law "on the universal duty to defend the Polish People's Republic" (passed 21 November), was the "inspiration" and training of young people in strengthening the defense of Poland. The organs of the Youth Union worked to generate interest in literature and movies on World War II designed to inspire patriotism; they organized sport and recreational activities which included training in defense skills; they established contacts with military youth and military units; and they were active in maintaining contacts with members of the Youth Union in the military. At a plenum of the Central Board of the Socialist Youth Union on the problems of defense, Chairman Andrzej Zabinski, in stipulating the future tasks of the Youth Union in defense work, also emphasized the need for the total consolidation of Polish society and the mobilization of all its forces around the party program (*Sztandar Mlodych,* 25 October 1967).

In 1966 the PUWP began an accountability and election campaign with meetings in basic party organizations and concluded the campaign in the spring of 1967 with the voivodship committee conferences. Reports on the discussions indicated that the major tasks of the party concerned the economy—elimination of shoddy production, laziness, and poor social relations in factories, the assurance that allocations for agriculture were properly utilized, and elimination of the "negative manifestations" in the administrative bureaucracy. The reports also emphasized that ideological education and political work must not be relegated to second place.

**Economic Issues.** The resolution of the Fourth Congress of the PUWP declared that the "national economy is the main front of activities of all organs and Party organizations." In recent years Poland has begun to institute organizational changes in the national economy, including changes in the financial system, to guarantee more independence to individual enterprises. The price system was modified to conform to actual production costs, and investments from the state budget were limited. Greater attention was given to "objective economic laws" and material incentives in production. Another aspect of the Polish reorganization involved turning over some small shops to private entrepreneurs.

In 1967 the party organs worked to improve the organization of production, work discipline, consistency of production, and efficiency of manpower—tasks that had been set forth by the Seventh Plenum of the Central Committee on 27-28 October 1966. In November 1967 Chief of the State Planning Commission Stefan Jedrychowski reviewed the major problems in the Polish economy during the year: shortcomings in food production, gaps in the financial-accumulation-plan fulfillment, the lag in retail sales in proportion to the purchasing power of the population, difficulties in satisfying market demand for meat and various industrial goods, problems in fulfilling the plan for machinery exports to capitalist countries, excessive imports from socialist states, and finally, the low per capita production rate in industry (speech before the Sejm Budget Commission, 17 November).

Problems of production and efficiency were also discussed at the Sixth Congress of Polish Trade Unions on 19-24 June. The congress stressed the need for more leisure time for workers and raised old-age pensions from the previous minimum of 640 to 1,700 zlotys per month, with the increases to be financed by income taxes and increased municipal-transport fares.

The most important area of party economic activity was the further and more rapid intensification of farm production. This problem was discussed at the Ninth Plenum of the Central Committee, the first devoted to agriculture since the party congress in 1964. Specifically, the goal is to produce enough grain and fodder to obviate the need for imports, which are a heavy burden on the national economy. It was recognized that the great disproportions in the production of grain in the individual voivodships must be eliminated. Other agricultural problems raised by the plenum were the lack of qualified staff on the farms, the heavy administrative duties burdening the agricultural experts, and the general inefficiency of state farms. The plenum adopted a program for land consolidation, including a plan that offers increased pensions to farmers willing to turn over their privately owned farms to the state (about 85 per cent of the land is privately owned, the highest percentage in any East European communist country). The plan is aimed particularly at the inefficiently run and unprofitable small landholdings, which lack the resources to increase production on their own.

Another aspect of the agricultural problem was keeping the young people in the rural areas and training them in the most modern forms of agricultural production. At the Ninth Congress of the Polish Teachers' Union in Warsaw (17 March) Premier Józef Cyrankiewicz stressed that the main way of combating the excessive outflow of youth from rural areas was training in agricultural skills and creating a proper milieu and cultural background.

The Tenth Central Committee Plenum also dealt with the problems of the economy, particularly the critical meat shortages. The plenum unanimously adopted a resolution increasing the price of meat on an average of 16.7 per cent and simultaneously lowering the price of other items, including sugar, milk, margarine, and lard. The plenum also accepted directives on improvements in market supplies as the guideline for action by the government and economic administration. A critical meat shortage had plagued the Polish economy since mid-1967. The supply of meat and meat products was inadequate to meet the demand resulting from higher incomes: while the cash income of the population rose by 7.1 per cent during the second half of 1967, according to chief economic planner Stefan Jedrychowski at the Tenth Plenum, meat supplies had increased by only 4.1 per cent. Polish sources attributed this sorry state of affairs to the inefficiency of production, excessive absenteeism, and the violation of labor discipline, combined with increased income from excessive overtime work.

**Ideological Problems.** The PUWP has stressed that economic activity cannot be the sole concern of party organs, but must be related to political activity. In the words of Wladyslaw Gomulka, the party must not restrict itself solely to solving economic problems, but must also "live with the problems of socialist ideology and of the international workers' movement. In its work it must not dissociate itself from the current world situation." (*Trybuna Ludu,* 9 December 1967.)

The Eighth Plenum of the Central Committee, meeting in May, was the first devoted to ideological problems since 1963. The plenum pointed to the need for the continuous formation of the "socialist consciousness" of the working people and noted the obligations of the workers on the ideological front. The main report was presented by Zenon Kliszko, chief ideologist of the PUWP, who spoke of the intensification of efforts on the part of Western nations, and particularly the United States, to apply the policy of "selective coexistence" with socialist states. The purpose of the policy, he felt, was to isolate socialist states from one another and to facilitate ideological subversion within the socialist states, using "in addition to the liberal bourgeois and social democratic tendencies, the nationalist and anti-Soviet tendencies." He warned that Poland was an "especially privileged target" for such activities. Kliszko admitted that although the majority of Poles approved of socialism, there still existed "in the consciousness of certain social strata many nonsocialist, and, at times, outright reactionary, views, old habits, and customs." He charged that these elements were supported by "hostile forces, both internal and external," referring to the "reactionary part" of the Polish ecclesiastical hierarchy and to subversive activity from abroad.

The report called for the improvement of the work of mass media, including the press, radio, television, and films. On the one hand, their ideological and moral content must be strengthened, and on the other, the mass media programs must become more entertaining and attractive. Information on life in the West should not continually publicize the attractive aspects, but should disclose more thoroughly the life of the workers, social conditions, and the struggle against monopoly capital, according to Kliszko, and more attention should be paid to life in other socialist states.

Kliszko warned against mistaking "peaceful coexistence" for ideological coexistence and called for an intensification of the ideological struggle. "No statement, no view, no publication which attacks our ideological foundations and our essential historical and political views can be left without a realistic and well-documented answer," he declared. He also discussed the importance of the role of criticism, but warned that only constructive criticism was to be allowed, and not "criticism which is destructive and demagogic and which blackens our reality by one-sided concentration on negative phenomena." Socialist democracy must be strengthened, Kliszko stated, but he reminded the delegates that socialist democracy means not freedom for the "enemies" of the system, but the "restriction of freedom for the reactionaries for the cause of the genuine freedom of the popular masses."

The resolutions of the May plenum (based on Kliszko's report) were discussed in party organizations and in a number of conferences with representatives of Polish information media. A meeting of the editors-in-chief of the dailies, periodicals, and press, radio, and television agencies took place in Warsaw on 31 May; a conference of voivodship party secretaries in charge of propaganda was held on 26 May. In addition, extensive press coverage and editorial space were devoted to the problems of "developing the socialist consciousness" of the people.

Following the intense church-state conflict in Poland in 1966 during the Polish millenium celebrations, and the conflict surrounding the decision of authorities in December to close four of the 24 Catholic seminaries following a church refusal to admit state inspectors, at the beginning of 1967 church-state relations were relatively calm. For the first time in three years, a mixed Church-State Commission (which had been created in 1956) convened to discuss current problems. In January the Polish government allowed Archbishop Boleslaw Kominek of Wroclaw to make a visit to Rome, the first time permission had been granted a Polish prelate to travel to the West since Polish authorities refused to let Stefan Cardinal Wyszynski attend celebrations of the Polish Christian millenium in Rome in 1966 (*NYT*, 22 January 1967). Archbishop Kominek was received by the Pope on 3 February and reported on the negotiation between the episcopate and state officials in Poland and the events of the millenium year. In February Vatican emissary Monsignor Agostino Casaroli visited Poland to study the religious situation and try to improve Polish church-state relations. While he was there, he attended a conference of more than 60 bishops convened to hear a report on recent church-state talks. His report, however, indicated that Cardinal Wyszynski and other leading ecclesiastics had strong reservations about the amelioration of relations (*Die Zeit,* 17 March 1967).

Throughout 1967 state authorities refrained from interfering in church functions but continued to place obstacles in the path of the celebration of the Polish millenium celebrations, as in Sosnowiéc on 21 May and Lodz on 11 June. The relative calm in church-state relations was broken in September by the Polish government's refusal of a passport to Stefan Cardinal Wyszynski to attend the First Synod of Bishops in Rome and the subsequent refusal of the remaining members of the Polish Bishop's delegation to attend the synod without Cardinal Wyszynski. In a pastoral letter read in all the churches on 24 September the bishops accused the regime of "having violated the Constitution and acting against the principles of human rights." *Zycie Warszawy* declared on 29 September that Cardinal Wyszynski had been denied a passport because of his "unfriendly and disloyal attitude toward the Polish state" during the visit of President de Gaulle. (Actually, despite speculation about a meeting between President de Gaulle and Cardinal Wyszynski during de Gaulle's visit to Poland on 5-12 September, the meeting was not held, and Western observers considered this a concession by de Gaulle to the Polish regime. Cardinal Wyszynski and de Gaulle merely exchanged written notes on the occasion of the visit.)

On another occasion part of the Polish delegation to the Congress on Laymen held in Rome in mid-October was denied passports to attend. The delegation was then complemented by persons who happened to be abroad at that time.

The situation was further exacerbated by the announcement of a telegram from Pope Paul VI to Cardinal Wyszynski expressing sorrow concerning the Cardinal's inability to attend the synod. The telegram did not reach its destination and, according to Vatican sources, had been "stopped at the Polish end" (*Reuter,* 13 October). Although it was later admitted that the telegram had not been sent because of confusion in the Vatican Secretariat, after the first announcement of the Vatican telegram the Polish episcopate issued a communique, read in churches throughout Poland, charging that the Polish authorities were "seriously restricting freedom of religion." Later in the year two more episcopate communiques were read in the Polish churches, one on the "unjust regulations issued by the Polish authorities regarding registration and inspection of religious instructions by officials and inventories of Church property (29 October), and another demanding cessation of the state practice of obstructing church construction by witholding building permits (16 December).

The policy of the PUWP has been to "counter the reactionary policy of the leaders of the episcopate with a policy strengthening the unity of believers and nonbelievers in the building of socialism" (Zenon Klizsko at the Eighth Central Committee Plenum). The party has attempted to isolate the "reactionary leadership" of the Catholic Church in Poland by claiming that it is not participating in the "modernizing" trends in the Vatican. At the May plenum Zenon Kliszko praised recent Papal encyclicals, especially the last encyclical of Pope Paul VI, *Populorum progressio.* He noted that although these encyclicals contain a number of theses on social problems with which communists cannot agree, they nevertheless "represent something new in the development of the social doctrine of the Catholic Church and create a favorable basis for cooperation between Communists and Catholics for ensuring progress, security and peace to mankind."

The Polish regime has declared that it would not interfere in the religious beliefs and activities of the citizens or religious organizations, but that these groups must abide by "the basic condition, and that is that the activities of the churches and denominational groups must not infringe on the laws of the country and must not be contrary to coexistence, obligatory in Poland" (*Życie Warszawy,* 2 November 1967). Polish officials claim that the episcopate leaders want to create a "state within a state," and that their activities "have nothing in common with the defense of church and religious interests" and are "only a result of the antisocialist, political ambitions of the episcopate leadership which would like to shake Polish National unity, to undermine society's confidence in the state."

The PUWP's relations with the Polish intellectuals were exacerbated by the expulsion from the party in late 1966 of a Warsaw University professor of philosophy, Leszek Kolakowski, following a speech at the university in October charging that the promises of 1956 had not been fulfilled. His expulsion was followed by a letter to the Central Committee signed by 21 writers, all members of the PUWP, questioning party policy on writers and intellectuals. The reaction of the party was severe; 13 of the signers were reportedly deprived of party membership, and a number of others resigned. The party also took repressive measures against students who had participated in the discussions of Kolakowski's speech and called for a true democracy in Poland. One student received a one-year suspension from Warsaw University, and 71 others were reportedly expelled from the Socialist Youth Union for defending their expelled colleague.

The Sixteenth Congress of the Union of Polish Writers, meeting in Koszalin on 2-3 June, was uneventful except for the adoption of a proposal by the Catholic writer Stefan Kisielewski to oblige censors to give reasons for their deletions and give authors the right of appeal. The congress discussed problems connected with publishing policies, contacts between Polish writers and foreign writers, and the spread of culture in Poland. Only 100 writers attended the congress, however, in comparison with earlier congresses in Cracow (December 1965) and Lublin (1964), where more than 300 writers had been present.

Another widely publicized incident was the trial, beginning 2 October and held *in camera,* of a young Jewish woman, Nina Karsaw, who was charged with possessing illegal papers and recordings and with preparing to send abroad written material judged harmful to the interests of the Polish state. Among the materials was a brochure by Jacek Kuron and Karol Modzelewski reportedly calling for the overthrow of the Polish government.* On 27 October Nina Karsaw was sentenced to three years'

*Kuron and Modzelewski, philosophy professors at Warsaw University, had been expelled from the party and jailed in 1965 for circulating a letter criticizing the lack of democratic procedures in the party's decisionmaking. They were released from prison in early 1967 and testified at the trial.

imprisonment for "harboring material dangerous to the interests of the state." The following day Warsaw University students staged a demonstration protesting the verdict and demanding abolition of the Small Penal Code of 1946, under which she had been convicted. The trial was given only brief notice in Polish information media, and then only after the verdict. The Polish News Agency reported on 28 October that Nina Karsaw had been convicted of "slander."

**Relations with the Soviet Union.** The cornerstone of Poland's foreign policy is friendship and alliance with the Soviet Union, which, in view of the "threat" from West Germany, is deemed vital to Polish interests.

On the twenty-fifth anniversary of the PUWP party Politburo member Ignacy Loga-Sowiński emphasized the "current fundamental importance" of the Polish-Soviet alliance:

> The international position of every country depends to a considerable extent on its relations with its neighbors, on its alliances. This factor always had, and still has, particular significance for Poland. This will essentially be a matter of life or death for Poland, as long as the mortal enemy of the independence of our nation, German imperialism, exists. (*Trybuna Ludu,* 5 January 1967.)

At the Fiftieth Anniversary celebrations of the October Revolution in Moscow Wladyslaw Gomulka credited the Soviet Union for "paving the way" for Poland "to regain its independence in 1918" and for liberating the Polish people from Nazi occupation and contributing to the rebirth of Poland within the frontiers of the Oder-Neisse and the Baltic. He also hailed the fact that the nuclear "defensive" power of the Soviet Union "constitutes the fundamental factor of the strength of the world socialist system and plays the greatest role in safeguarding world peace from violation by imperialism" (speech to the joint meeting of the Soviet party Central Committee and Supreme Soviet of the Soviet Union, 3 November 1967).

The Soviet Union is Poland's largest trading partner, with almost one-third of its trade in Polish imports and exports. Edward Ochab, Chairman of the Council of State and member of the PUWP Politburo, praised the development of economic relations with the Soviet Union, and noted that "without the support of the USSR's economic might, without supplies of Soviet raw materials, our country would not have been able to reach such a high rate of development." He also noted that, apart from machines and production installations, the Soviet Union supplies Poland with basic raw and other materials frequently very difficult to obtain in other markets. It supplies 80 per cent of Polish iron- and manganese-ore requirements, over 60 per cent of Polish cotton, and 100 per cent of its oil. (*Trybuna Ludu,* 7 November 1967.)

The Polish and Soviet parties maintained close contact during the year. On 17-18 January a top-level Soviet delegation including Secretary-General Leonid Brezhnev, Soviet Premier Alexei Kosygin, Chairman of the Presidium of the Supreme Soviet Nikolai Podgorny, and others made an unannounced visit to Poland to meet with Polish leaders at an unspecified place. The communique on the meeting did not detail the subjects of discussion, referring only to "the full identity of views in the appraisal of the present day international situation and the situation in the world Communist movement." It is believed that the talks concerned West Germany, China, the convocation of an international communist party meeting, and talks with the Vatican.

On 22 September another meeting of top-level Polish and Soviet party delegations, including Wladyslaw Gomulka and Premier Cyrankiewicz and Leonid Brezhnev, Alexei Kosygin, and Nikolai Podgorny, met in Moscow. Official sources reported that the two delegations discussed "current questions of the present-day international situation, the world communist movement, as well as questions of bilateral relations between the CPSU and the PUWP, the Soviet Union and Poland." The talks apparently concerned the convocation of an international meeting of communist parties.

Numerous other consultations between the Soviet and Polish parties and governments were held during 1967: a party delegation headed by Leonid Brezhnev stopped in Warsaw on the way to Berlin to attend the Seventh Congress of the East German Socialist Unity Party (16 April 1967); Zenon Kliszko, head of a PUWP delegation to Hanoi, visited Moscow en route home and held a short talk with Leonid Brezhnev on "matters of interest to both parties" (24 June 1967); Wladyslaw Gomulka and other Polish party leaders traveled to Moscow to discuss the Middle East crisis with East European socialist-state leaders (9 June) and to attend the Fiftieth Anniversary celebrations in November. On 6-8 December Soviet Foreign Minister Gromyko visited Warsaw for talks on a number of problems, particularly the problem of "European security." The communique reported a "full identity of views on all the problems discussed."

Cooperation between the Soviet Union and Poland was further strengthened by an agreement in September between the Polish News Agency and the Soviet News Agency (Novosti) calling for an exchange of information bulletins and press materials on specific subjects and, in case of need, the preparation of materials on certain problems of interest to both sides.

**Relations with Eastern Europe.** Alliance with the members states of the Warsaw Pact was also deemed vital to Poland's interests. In a speech on 22 February President Ochab declared that "in the face of imperialist maneuvers we shall strengthen our own forces and tighten our fraternal alliance with the Soviet Union, Czechoslovakia, the German Democratic Republic, and all the states of the Warsaw Treaty." Poland was host to two meetings of Warsaw Pact Foreign Ministers. The first, held 8-10 February, discussed the German question and the establishment of diplomatic relations between Bonn and Bucharest (although the communique mentioned only the discussion of European problems) and resulted in a failure to agree on policy; the communique referred only to "a friendly exchange of opinion." The second meeting, held 19-21 December to discuss the Middle East situation, was reported by the communique to have taken place "in a spirit of complete unity and close friendly cooperation."

The PUWP maintained close contacts with its socialist neighbors and consulted with them on problems of establishing diplomatic relations with West Germany and the convocation of an international communist party conference. On 12-13 January East German Foreign Minister Otto Winzer visited Warsaw. On 28 February-1 March a top-level Czechoslovak party and government delegation headed by Antonín Novotný, First Secretary of the Czechoslovak party Central Committee, visited Warsaw; on 8-9 March Wladyslaw Gomulka and Józef Cyrankiewicz visited Budapest on an "unofficial friendly visit"; on 14-15 March Walter Ulbricht, Chairman of the Council of State of the German Democratic Republic and First Secretary of the party Central Committee, and Willi Stoph, Chairman of the Council of Ministers of the German Democratic Republic and member of the party Politburo, paid an official visit to Warsaw; on 3-7 April Wladyslaw Gomulka led a party and state delegation to Sofia.

Poland has been one of the strongest supporters of increased cooperation within COMECON and maximum division of labor among the socialist states. It has consistently pressed for improvement in the functioning of COMECON with reference to more information (especially statistical information) on the trade between COMECON member states, for expansion of COMECON activity in cooperating with some "capitalist" states, for "modernizing" the currency and financial system, for raising the declining rate of trade exchange within COMECON (especially in the field of light industry), and for increasing scientific-technical cooperation [see Stanislaw Albinowski, *Życie Warszawy*, 19-20 February 1967; Piotr Jaroszewicz (chief representative to COMECON), *Trybuna Ludu*, 11 May, 6-7 July 1967].

**Relations with Western Europe.** The problem of European security was a priority issue for Polish foreign policy. According to Wladyslaw Gomulka, whereas wars of national liberation or conflicts in other parts of the world do not necessarily lead to a world conflagration, any outbreak of armed conflict in Europe would be disastrous. Thus "the guaranteeing of security and lasting peace in Europe would be of paramount importance for the consolidation of peace all over the world" (speech to Katowice voivodship party committee, 8 February 1967). The problem of European security, however, is intimately connected with the problem of Germany. The solution to the German problem, in Poland's view, could come only upon fulfillment by West Germany of certain conditions: the recognition of the existing frontiers of Europe (recognition of the Oder-Neisse Line as the frontier between Germany and Poland), the recognition of the German Democratic Republic, and the renunciation of nuclear weapons.

Initial Polish reaction to the Kiesinger government's new *Ostpolitik* was one of profound skepticism and developed into hostile attacks on the West German leadership after the establishment of diplomatic relations between Bonn and Bucharest on 31 January; in contrast to the East German press, the Polish press did not criticize Rumania directly, but concentrated on "exposing" the West German intentions. Speaking at the Katowice voivodship party committee conference on 8 February, Gomulka devoted a large portion of the talk to West Germany. He reminded his listeners that only the methods have changed, and the goals of the new Bonn government are the same as those of its predecessor, the Nazi regime, and that in all the basic problems Bonn continues to maintain its "old positions." He charged that the goal of the Bonn government's *Ostpolitik* was to isolate the German Democratic Republic in order "to create more favorable conditions for a systematic long-term activity aimed at annexation of that socialist state by the GDR." Gomulka also repeated the words of the Soviet statement to the Bonn government: "Should anybody attempt to put to test the stability of the GDR frontiers or the frontiers of other socialist countries, he would get a crushing and irrefutable reply."

Although East Germany immediately criticized Rumania for establishing relations with Bonn (*Neues Deutschland*, 3 February), the Poles refrained from public discussion of their stand on the issue. The attitude of the PUWP was presented for the first time at the Karlovy Vary Conference on 24 April, when Gomulka stated that establishing diplomatic relations with Bonn at the present time would not constitute "a step forward toward the normalization of relations in Europe, [but] on the contrary, would be harmful to the cause of peace if such a step were taken by the socialist countries."

In addition to denouncing the West German government, Poland sought to develop a common "socialist" position on West Germany by strengthening ties with socialist-state neighbors. On 1 March the Polish regime renewed a 20-year friendship treaty with Czechoslovakia. On 15 March a similar treaty was signed in Warsaw by Wladyslaw Gomulka and Walter Ulbricht, First Secretary of the Central Committee of the East German party. Both treaties emphasized the inviolability of existing state borders in Europe and pledged to "use all necessary means," including military means, to repel aggression by West Germany or its allies. In the case of the treaty with Czechoslovakia, the Polish side recognized the 1938 Munich agreement as invalid "from the very beginning" and also confirmed the present borders between Poland and Czechoslovakia.

In a further move to solidify Poland's position against the West German initiative, Gomulka led a party and government delegation to Sofia (on 3-7 April). One Polish commentator described the visit as "the last straw for Bonn's heralds and the so-called new Eastern Policy" (J. Winicki, "Frustrated Expectations" *Glos Pracy*, 20 March 1967). During the visit a 20-year treaty of friendship, cooperation, and mutual assistance was signed between the two states, similar to the earlier treaties with Czechoslovakia and East Germany. On 3 April *Trybuna Ludu* welcomed the signing of the treaty as an "important contribution toward the strengthening of socialist unity and a momentous move in the struggle aimed at thwarting the machinations of the enemies of security on our continent."

At the May Central Committee plenum Gomulka presented a report on the international activities of the PUWP and declared that the series of bilateral friendship treaties were "not an accident, but a conscious and agreed-on political move which obstructed and confused the plans of the West German government." The bilateral friendship treaties were evaluated by another party leader as a "considerable addition to the defensive system of the socialist countries—the Warsaw Pact" (Ryszard Strzelecki, *Pravda*, 22 August 1967).

**Relations with China.** The PUWP has strongly and repeatedly criticized the Chinese leadership for splitting the international communist movement and has come to the support of the Soviet Union in rebutting "calumnies" emanating from Peking. "The stand of the Communist Party of China is weakening the cohesion of the anti-imperialist ranks, while the campaign of slander which is being directed against the Soviet Union, the Communist Party of the Soviet Union and other parties, is only emboldening the imperialist aggressors and doing great harm to the international communist and working class movement," declared Ignacy Loga-Sowiński in his address to the Eighteenth Congress of the French Communist Party in January 1967.

**Other International Issues.** The stand taken by the Polish regime on the Middle East conflict of June 1967 was one of strong support for the Arab cause and severe condemnation of Israel as the "aggressor," despite the fact that this policy was not backed by a large part of Polish public opinion (the Israeli embassy in Warsaw reported numerous letters of sympathy from Polish citizens). In addition to the alleged involvement of American and British "imperialism," the PUWP emphasized the role of West Germany and referred to Israeli contacts with "Nazis" in West Germany. *Trybuna Ludu* charged on 11 June that "West Germany played an important role in the unleashing of the Israeli aggression," and *Życie Warzawy* noted on 13 June the supplying of arms to Israel by West Germany, adding that "together with military equipment, the venom of a strictly defined ideology must have been exported to Israel." The collusion of the "imperialists" and Great Britain and the "revanchists" in West Germany was also noted in a communique on 2 September, following talks in Warsaw between Zenon Kliszko and Meir Vilner, Secretary of the Israeli Communist Party Politburo.

Polish representatives participated in the Moscow conference of 9 June and the 11-12 July Budapest Conference of East European socialist state leaders to discuss the Middle East situation and coordinate aid to the Arab states. On 12 June Poland broke diplomatic relations with Israel. "Spontaneous" meetings of solidarity with the Arab states, held throughout Poland in various factories and towns, were widely publicized by the PUWP. Poland also extended material aid to the Arab states. A protocol to a credit agreement, signed in July between Poland and the United Arab Republic, extended credit to the amount of about $20 million (Radio Cairo, 27 July). Poland also gave aid to "victims of Israeli aggression" to the amount of 430 million zlotys, and the Polish trade unions pledged a total of 4 million zlotys in aid to Arab states.

By September, however, more moderate voices on Israeli "aggression" could be heard in Poland. Israel's right to exist was affirmed by some party leaders, and there was disagreement with "reactionary Arab nationalism" which sought the liquidation of the state of Israel. Internally, the party leaders emphasized their rejection and condemnation of all manifestations of anti-Semitism (Stanislaw Kociolek and Józef Kepa at the plenary session of the Central Committee of the Warsaw party committee, 27 September 1967).

The PUWP attacks on "imperialism," especially "US imperialism in Vietnam," continued unabated. Claiming that the forces of imperialism are weakening, party spokesmen emphasized that their aggressiveness is proportionally increasing. The Vietnam conflict, the Middle East conflict, and the *coup d'état* in Greece were all just "links in the chain of imperialist adventures, which bring about a serious threat to world peace." In accordance with the general line of the communist movement, the United States was singled out for attacks as "leader of the imperialist camp," but the role of West Germany as the United States' "closest collaborator" also received attention (speech by Ignacy Loga-Sowiński to Sixth Trade Union Congress, 20 June 1967).

The United States was also charged with trying to penetrate the socialist countries and subvert them from within, "utilizing various forms of ideological diversion" (Ryszard Strzelecki, "The Main Direction in the Fraternal Parties," *Pravda*, 22 August 1967). United States President Johnson's policy of "bridgebuilding" to Eastern Europe was severely condemned by Zenon Kliszko at the May Central Committee plenum: "This policy," said Kliszko, "tries to weaken the unity of the socialist camp and above all drive a wedge between the Soviet Union and the other socialist states."

The PUWP repeatedly affirmed solidarity with the people of Vietnam fighting against "American aggression" and supplied Vietnam with material, political, and military aid. A high-level Polish party delegation headed by Politburo member and Central Committee Secretary Zenon Kliszko paid a month-long visit to North Vietnam in May-June and had talks with Le Duan, First Secretary of the Central Committee of the Vietnam Workers' Party. During his visit Kliszko emphasized: "We are rendering and will be rendering to you material, political, and military assistance. . . . Such assistance is the duty of each communist and workers' party." (Polish News Agency, 25 June 1967.) The joint communique following the visit reaffirmed the PUWP's "support for the heroic people of Vietnam against US aggression and for the four-point stand of the DRV government and the five-point statement of the NLFSV, the only legitimate representative of the people of South Vietnam."

On 1 October, the eighteenth anniversary of the founding of the Chinese People's Republic, the Polish leaders sent a message of congratulations, but addressed it only to the Chinese nation and people, with no mention of their leadership.

Despite strained political relations, a new trade agreement was signed by Poland and China on 30 June, providing for an unspecified increase in the volume of trade over last year.

**The International Communist Movement.** The PUWP held numerous talks with other fraternal parties during 1967. On 26 July Zenon Kliszko met in Paris with Waldeck Rochet, Secretary-General of the French Communist party. Polish sources reported that "full identity of views of the two parties on all important problems was established." A delegation of the Spanish Communist Party headed by party Secretary-General Santiago Carrillo visited Poland on 27 September-4 October, and the communique following talks with Wladyslaw Gomulka likewise reported a "full identity of views in all matters discussed." On 9 October Zenon Kliszko visited Italy, for talks with Italian party Secretary-General Luigi Longo. Official sources reported that "opinions were exchanged on the international situation and current problems of the international workers' movement." In this case an "identity of views" was not reported. The Western reporters speculated that the talks centered on the convocation of an international communist party meeting. The following month, on 13-23 November, an eight-member delegation of the PUWP headed by Ryszard Strzelecki visited Italy and again held talks with Luigi Longo.

The PUWP, together with the French Communist Party, was assigned the task of organizing the Conference of European Communist and Workers' Parties held at Karlovy Vary on 24-26 April and was host to a meeting on 22-26 February of the 19-member preparatory committee which discussed the aims of the Karlovy Vary Conference. In evaluating the results of the conference Wladyslaw Gomulka emphasized that it had adopted the same stand on the problem of Germany and on all other basic problems pertaining to peace and security in Europe as that taken by the Warsaw Treaty member states in the series of bilateral interstate friendship treaties concluded at the beginning of 1967:

> The significance of the Karlovy Vary Conference resides above all in the fact that in the adopted statement all the parties participating in the Conference gave a uniform evaluation of the situation in Europe, pointed in harmony to the forces threatening peace and security on our continent, presented a program for the establishment of lasting peace based on a system of collective security in Europe, and called on all peaceful forces in European countries to act jointly to wage a common struggle in favor of peace (speech at Eighth Plenum of the PUWP Central Committee).

Since the very beginning of 1967, the PUWP had pressed for the convening of an international communist party conference. An article by Ignacy Loga-Sowiński appearing on the twentieth anniversary of the PUWP in the January issue of *Nowe Drogi* (and excerpted on 5 January in *Trybuna Ludu* and Moscow *Pravda*) urged the convocation of a conference "independent of the fact whether the Chinese Communist Party or some other party will participate in it." In a speech to the Eighteenth Congress of the French Communist Party on 5 January Loga-Sowiński declared that "conditions for convening a conference of communist and workers' parties are more and more ripe."

The PUWP strongly advocated that the conference not only serve as a consultation among parties, but also draw up a general line for the communist movement. On 29 October Wladyslaw Gomulka, in a contribution to *Pravda* for the Fiftieth Anniversary celebrations, emphasized:

> Experience has taught us that international conferences of communist and workers' parties are the broadest forum for meetings and discussions, which make it possible to hammer out a common general line on key problems of the struggle for peace, freedom of the peoples, and socialism. We believe that it is time to convene another world meeting which would undertake to strengthen the solidarity of the communists of all countries in the struggle for our common aims.

On 26 November *Trybuna Ludu* called on all parties "to rally together to counter the aggressive actions of imperialism . . . and to counter the nationalist and disruptive trends in the international communist movement." In the editorial the PUWP attacked the "disruptive policy of the Chinese leadership" and urged the convocation of the international communist party conference.

Poland was also active in the training of Vietnamese in Polish schools. Radio Warsaw reported on 22 August that a protocol had been signed that day on the professional training of Vietnamese, and that about 2,000 Vietnamese were either studying or receiving professional training in Poland.

**The Communist Party of Poland (CPP).** In February 1966 Kazimierz Mijal, a former member of the PUWP Central Committee, with the help of the Albanian ambassador in Warsaw, illegally left Poland for Tirana, Albania, where he "reconstituted" the Communist Party of Poland "along Marxist-Leninist lines" and began to publish denunciations of the Polish regime in the Belgian Communist Party (Marxist-Leninist) organ *La Voix de Peuple* and to broadcast denunciations over Radio Tirana.

Polish sources did not publically recognize the existence of the CPP in Tirana until February 1967, when an article appeared in *Życie Warszawy* ridiculing Mijal's escape from Poland and his activities in Tirana ("The Double Life of Mehmet Servetka," *Życie Warszawy*, 5 February 1967). Although the CPP claims the support of "revólutionary workers" within Poland and has publicized letters of support from "a group of communists from Lodz" (Radio Tirana, 31 July) and "a group of revolutionary students of Warsaw University" (Radio Tirana, 12 November 1967), there is no evidence of membership in the party or support for it in Poland itself. The Czechoslovak party organ *Rudé Právo* claims that Mijal remains the CPP's "founding and only member" (*Rudé Právo* 7 February 1967). Other press reports noted that two of Mijal's earlier associates, Stanislaw Lapot and Wiktor Klosiewicz, had followed Mijal to Albania in 1966 (Michael Gamarnikow, "Poland: Political Pluralism in a One Party State," *Problems of Communism*, July-August 1967).

The CPP continued to claim successes and progress in its organizational activities. Following an alleged "plenary session" of a "Provisional Central Committee" in Warsaw in June, the transformation of this temporary body into the Permanent Central Committee of the CPP was announced. In November 1967 the first issue of the party organ *Czerwony Sztandar* was reportedly published in Warsaw. In 1967 the CPP continued to issue "documents," "treaties," and "manifestos," which were published in the European pro-Chinese newspapers *La Voix du Peuple* (Belgium), *L'Humanité Nouvelle* (France), and *Nuova Unità* (Italy) and broadcast over Radio Tirana to Poland. A "manifesto" read over Radio Tirana dated February 1967 attacked Wladyslaw Gomulka as an "opportunistic, rightist, capitalist servant . . . a faithful lackey of US imperialism" and called for the overthrow of this "bourgeois dictatorship" by "revolutionary struggle." The manifesto advocated the "further setting up and organization of revolutionary groups of the Polish Communist Party" and the publication and distribution of propaganda from the CPP "with one's own resources." It also called for all means of support for the "persecuted and arrested communists" (Radio Tirana, 2 May 1967). Another proclamation of the CPP, dated February 1966 but read over Radio Tirana on 19 April 1967, called on the security organs to ignore the orders of the present party leadership and help overthrow it. It referred to the present leadership as "revisionists and Zionist Israeli agents."

Other documents of the CPP included criticism of the new measures adopted by the PUWP for improving the economy, calling for "not bureaucratic administration on the model of American management, but mastery of our industrial enterprises by the workers and their party" (Radio Tirana, 5 January 1967). A manifesto of 19 June called on Warsaw residents to protest the new municipal transport rates, declaring that the new rates are a "further proof of the betrayal of the working class" by the PUWP.

A CPP document "exposed" the establishment in 1966 of a special department in the Polish Ministry of Internal Affairs "to collect material and to follow revolutionary workers and communists" and which uses the most modern equipment "purchased from abroad." The CPP protested the arrests of "revolutionary workers" and called for demonstrations to secure their release, claiming that "on the one hand, the Gomulka regime attempts to maintain silence on the growth of revolutionary activity led by CPP, while on the other, following the example of bourgeois regimes, it is beginning to employ various forms of reprisal and terror against honest workers who have the courage to rise to defend revolutionary rights." The CPP mentioned in particular the arrest of "Comrade Rowinsky of Virrardow" two years earlier and the arrest of militants in Lodz and in Warsaw (*L'Humanité Nouvelle*, 26 October 1967; Radio Tirana, 12 September 1967).

The blatant anti-Semitism of the CPP's broadcasts was greatly intensified after the Middle East crisis. With respect to the PUWP's stand on the Middle East and the subsequent tension in the party ranks, the CPP denounced Gomulka for opposing Zionism "in words" but in actuality not having any intention of waging a struggle against the fifth column "since he himself is the leader of the fifth column." The reported Central Committee plenum in June 1967 urged the "true revolutionaries and the toiling masses" of Poland to "intensify the struggle against the traitors of socialism, against the Trotskyite-Zionist-nationalist fifth column headed by Gomulka, Cyrankiewicz, Ochab, Kliszko, Spychalski and others" (Radio Tirana, 12 November 1967).

The CPP also made reference to its place in the world revolutionary movement. A lengthy treatise dated 10 January 1967 on China's cultural revolution was read over Radio Tirana in installments during February (Radio Tirana, 15, 17, 18 February 1967), hailing its successes and its effect on the world revolutionary movement. The treatise hailed China as "a great socialist power" and "the center and bastion of world revolution." A pamphlet was issued by the publishing department of the CPP Central Committee under the title "Victory through Struggle," recounting the history of the Marxist-Leninist movement in Poland and concluding with the declaration that the CPP, "the vanguard of the heroic Polish working class, is united with the entire renascent Marxist-Leninist movement around the Chinese Communist Party and the Albanian Workers' Party in the struggle against American imperialism and contemporary revisionism, whose center is the CPSU leadership" (Radio Tirana, 23, 25-30 December 1967).

In January 1967 the CPP Provisional Central Committee issued greetings to the "Soviet Marxist-Leninists" on the occasion of their 1966 manifesto calling for the organization of an "all-Union Communist Bolshevik Party" (Radio Tirana, 14 February 1967). On 11 January Mijal sent a telegram to Enver Hoxha on the anniversary of Albania's "liberation and the establishment of the Albanian People's Republic in 1945." A meeting between a delegation of the French Communist Movement (Marxist-Leninist) and "a delegation" of the CPP headed by Kazimierz Mijal was reported to have been held in December 1967 in anticipation of the upcoming congress of the French Marxist-Leninist party (*L'Humanité Nouvelle*, 25 January 1968).

**Publications.** The daily organ of the PUWP is *Trybuna Ludu; Nowe Drogi* is its monthly theoretical journal and *Życie Partii* its journal on party affairs. *Polityka* is the most important party weekly. There are also 16 local party dailies.

The CPP reportedly publishes the journal *Czerwony Sztandar* (Red Banner).

# PORTUGAL

The Portuguese Communist Party (Partido Comunista Português; PCP) was founded in February 1921 and has been illegal since 1926. Under vigorous repression by the government of Premier Antonio Salazar, the party clandestinely maintains a tight organization and continues to operate both at home and abroad.

Within Portugal the Communists work through the underground "Patriotic Front of National Liberation," which, according to them, also includes socialists, liberals, republicans, Catholics, and liberal-monarchists. The party is mainly influential among urban workers in Lisbon and Oporto and among farm laborers in the upper Alentejo area. The PCP also has considerable support among students, many of whom favor legalization of the party and the establishment of a left-wing coalition government.

**Leadership, Membership, and Internal Party Affairs.** Because of the illegal status of the PCP, little is known about the party's leadership and organization. Among the known leaders are Alvaro Cunhal, the Secretary-General of the PCP, and Manuel Rodríguez da Silva and Sergio Vilarigues, members of the party Secretariat. The membership of the PCP is estimated at about 2,000. The population of Portugal is 9,228,000 (estimated, 1966).

During 1967 the PCP devoted considerable attention to problems of party affiliation. After commenting on the "new problems" created for the party by increasing emigration of Portuguese citizens, the PCP noted in a resolution passed at a meeting of its Central Committee in July:

> There are numerous Portuguese abroad who were members of the Portuguese Communist Party at the time they emigrated and others who wish to belong to the Portuguese Communist Party. It has become necessary to arrive at a definite criterion for Portuguese Communist Party affiliation and for continuation of party membership by Portuguese living abroad. Members of the Portuguese Communist Party have a duty to the party as well as to the working class and the people. There is a need for communist activity among the working class and the masses to lead actions against fascism and for freedom. It is, therefore, a duty of every militant *(a)* not to decide to emigrate without first consulting the party and *(b)* other than for cogent reasons, to remain firmly at his combat post, that is to say, in Portugal. ("Radio Free Portugal," Algeria, 1 September.)

The resolution cautioned that "to be a member of the Portuguese Communist Party, one must be prepared to carry out clandestine activity under the fascist dictatorship existing in Portugal," and added a specific warning:

> There can be no justification for carrying out a policy of recruitment abroad for the Portuguese Communist Party of persons who, while in agreement with the program and political line of the party (being ready to belong to party organizations and to help the party financially, and having done service in the ranks of the party in Portugal), are today only interested in belonging to the Portuguese Communist Party outside Portugal to avoid running the risks of clandestine activity under the Salazarist dictatorship, even when they return temporarily for personal reasons. *(Ibid.)*

The resolution concluded by noting that the party position of those emigrating "must be reviewed in each and every case" and that whether or not those emigrating should remain PCP members would depend on the "work demands of the Portuguese Communist Party, the outlook of these comrades under their new conditions of life, and their integration in party work abroad—within the structure and in accordance with the demands of that work in the respective countries."

**PCP Domestic Program and Activities.** The PCP's Sixth Congress, held in September 1965, eight years after the last such general meeting, adopted a new program which took note of what it called an intensified popular struggle against the dictatorship both at home and in the colonies, and which declared that the "fascist regime" in Portugal had "entered the most crucial phase of its existence." A resolution of the congress hailed the unity of working classes, peasantry, and progressive forces and the party's alliance with the people of the Portuguese colonies. The party opposed the view of "some antifascist groups" that the regime could be overthrown by a military coup organized by a handful of officers, and urged the strengthening of the Patriotic Front.

The Sixth Congress characterized Portugal's present stage as one of "national democratic revolution," an intermediate step toward socialist revolution and communist construction. Among the tasks set by the party's program for this stage were: replacement of the present regime by a democratic government; abolition of the power of industrial monopolies; agrarian reform; raising of living standards; democratization of education and culture; liberation of the country from "imperialist" domination; recognition of a right to immediate independence for Portugal's colonies; and development of a policy of "peace and friendship with all peoples." The party envisioned itself as playing the leading role during the entire process of change from national democratic revolution through a coalition government to eventual socialism.

In July the Central Committee of the PCP met to discuss the "present political situation and the immediate tasks of the party." In analyzing the domestic situation, the Central Committee declared that there was "control of all phases of Portuguese life by a reduced number of large monopolies"–a condition which it said was intensifying–and accused the Salazar government of pursuing a "fascist policy" which was "creating serious difficulties throughout the national economy." The Central Committee charged that the national economy was "in pawn to foreign imperialism" and increasingly so owing to the "increasing flow of profits to the great foreign monopolies from Portuguese industry's search for capital, financing, association, and markets." It declared also that the government's "fascist policy of submission to imperialism and the acceptance by the fascists of a subordinate position for Portugal in the European Free Trade Association"–that is, the "elaboration of development plans . . . subordinated to imperialist economic trusteeship" and "industrialization based on export"–were "causing a series of upheavals in the national economy."

In an interview with *Mundo Obrero,* the central organ of the Spanish Communist Party, PCP Secretary-General Alvaro Cunhal commented on the strategy and tactics to be followed by his party and added: "We maintain that in the present conditions, the overthrow of the fascist dictatorship will call for intense revolutionary struggle, or, in other words, that a developed mass struggle will pose the question of a nationwide uprising, an armed popular rebellion." (*Mundo Obrero,* January 1967, as quoted in *IB,* no. 92, 1967.)

Not all members of the PCP agreed with Cunhal's analysis, according to an article in the 3 July issue of *Avante,* the monthly organ of the PCP:

> In democratic circles and even among some elements in our party the question of the growing internal differences in the Portuguese regime is being hotly discussed. From this, the conclusion is drawn that it is necessary to take advantage of the situation, particularly of the discontent and the more or less visible differences in the Salazarist ranks, in order to establish a dialogue and secure openings which would lead to a liberalization of the regime. Some even go so far as to call discontented Fascists "leftwing Fascists."

Sharply criticizing such "new theoreticians of revolution," *Avante* commented, "This strange theory has its rotten roots in the idea that a revolution is not foreseeable in Portugal's immediate future" and stressed that "popular mass struggle is the motive force of revolution."

The July meeting of the PCP Central Committee elaborated on the issue by noting that the "opportunistic concessions of the right" were, "at the moment, the most dangerous tendency in the Portuguese antifascist movement," adding:

> The Central Committee warns the working class and all antifascists against the fascist maneuver of bribing moderate elements of the opposition with the possibility of liberalizing the regime, and even of cooperation for a political change–a maneuver whose chief aim is to corrupt politically, to mislead, to divert from political action, to separate

from the masses, and to divide, neutralize, and paralize the democratic forces by isolating the Communist Party. (Radio Free Portugal, Algeria, 1 September.)

On the subject of strategy and tactics, the PCP Central Committee noted:

The Central Committee considers wrong and dangerous the demands—more or less openly circulated—of a pretended accumulation of forces which would be achieved through a general withdrawal of party activity and the renunciation of mass struggles with the aim of defending the Central Committee apparatus. Such tendencies, if put into practice, would lead to a greater gap between the directorate and the base, and between base and the working class and the masses, and to the worsening of the party defense by the party. (Ibid.)

Although viewing an "armed popular uprising" as the most likely agent of change, the PCP has maintained that the party would "do its utmost" to use any opportunity for peaceful transition that might arise from future political alterations. The July Central Committee meeting specifically noted:

The Central Committee reaffirms the determination of the Portuguese Communist Party to join its efforts to those of all who are ready to fight against fascist policy for the liquidation of the fascist dictatorship, for the conquest of freedom, and for the building of a democratic and truly independent Portugal. . . . The Portuguese Communist Party is ready to cooperate with all groups and sectors supporting antifascist action. The Central Committee calls on all noncommunist antifascists to cooperate with the Communists; it calls for antifascist unity to spur the dissemination and organization of the popular struggle for concrete and immediate objectives. (Ibid.)

**Self-Analysis.** In analyzing the current situation, Secretary-General Cunhal pointed out:

There is no revolutionary upsurge in Portugal at present. Nevertheless, powerful energy is accumulating which will not be long in manifesting itself in big political battles against the fascist dictatorship. The struggle is very difficult and claims—and will continue to claim—great sacrifice. But eventually the Portuguese people will sweep away fascism from their land, win freedom, and accomplish the democratic and national revolution as defined in the PCP program adopted by the clandestine Sixth Congress in 1965. (Mundo Obrero, January 1967, as quoted in IB, no. 92.)

In the communique issued at the end of the July Central Committee meeting, however, it was specifically noted that "shortages and weaknesses of organizations, cadres, and defenses" had "opened up branches to the repressive offensive." The communique stated also:

The Central Committee notes some hesitancy and weaknesses in the workers' struggles: lack of organisms to lead the struggles, the intervention of army committees and the lack of a strong link between these and the masses, the lack of democratic debate between workers who are interested in defining their claims and the methods of action, and tendencies of accepting intervention by the corporative bureaucracy in lieu of insisting on mass actions, are at the root of a certain lack of success. They have limited and cooled off the spread of movements. The Central Committee stresses that, in part, this depends on the lack of correct orientation and organization by the party, as well as the lack of the cadres correcting the leadership of the working-class struggles. The weakness of party organizations in certain sectors, a deficiency in the study of the respective sector's problems, [together with]a lack of attention in new experiments and a bureaucratic and routine tendency in learning about struggle in lieu of intervening in a cooperative and helpful manner—all these constitute weaknesses which must be overcome so as to give impetus to demands on a national scale and to direct them correctly. ("Radio Free Portugal," 31 August.)

In considering the various problems facing the PCP, the communique pointed to "intensification of the anti-imperialist struggle" as a "task of the greatest importance in the present situation" and declared:

The Central Committee believes that the situation requires the democratic forces to reinforce, without losing any time, their unity and all their revolutionary work, to reinforce their organizations, to reinforce their links with the masses, to reinforce their propaganda on the basis of principles, and to mobilize wide popular masses in the struggle for the most varied aims." (*Ibid.*)

**International Views and Positions.** The PCP's foreign policy vis-à-vis Europe was outlined by Secretary-General Cunhal in an address to the meeting of European communist parties at Karlovy Vary in April 1967:

> Just as the other fraternal parties, the Portuguese Communist Party believes that the organization of a European security system calls for the attainment of three chief aims: to free western Europe from US economic, diplomatic, and military tutelage; to check the growth of the revanchist and expansionist forces in Federal Germany; and to prevent the prolongation of the Atlantic Pact in 1969 . . . (*IB*, no. 97-98, 1967.)

Cunhal added that European collective security must be based on the recognition of existing frontiers, on the recognition of the fact of the existence of two German states, and on the normalization of the relations of all states with the German Democratic Republic. He also affirmed the "importance attached to measures to promote a detente in Europe, to eliminate the barriers in the economic relations between the socialist and capitalist countries, and to intensify exchange and cooperation in all forms."

The PCP Central Committee meeting in July condemned the "chauvinistic expansionist, annexationist, and adventuristic policy of the reactionary government of Israel . . . carried out under the instigation of US imperialism," and declared its support for and solidarity with the Arab people, while also announcing its support for the right of the state of Israel to exist. The Central Committee accused the Chinese communist leaders of having "objectively favored the interests of the imperialists" in the Middle East ("Radio Free Portugal," 29 August). The same meeting added:

> The Chinese leaders, driven by their anti-Sovietism, have adopted in connection with the conflict in the Middle East a position aimed at tearing away the Arab peoples from the socialist camp and pushing them onto the road of an adventuristic policy. This position objectively plays into the imperialists' hands. (*IB*, no. 105, 1967.)

During 1967 the PCP continued to attack US involvement in Vietnam and called for increased "demonstrations of solidarity with the people of Vietnam by the Portuguese communists." Considerable attention was also devoted to anticolonial movements in Angola, Mozambique, and Portuguese Guinea and to the "reactionary putsch in Greece."

**The PCP and the International Communist Movement.** The PCP continued to stress that "as a detachment of the international communist movement . . . the Portuguese Communist Party will continue to be guided by the idea of the defense and unity of the international communist movement, and, for its part, it will do everything to reinforce its ties of friendship and cooperation with the fraternal parties of all countries." Considerable attention was also devoted to the problem of unity of the international communist movement. The July communique of the Central Committee declared: "Defense of the unity of the communist movement is an unfailing duty of all fraternal parties and a criterion of their loyalty to the ideals of Marxism-Leninism. The Portuguese Communist Party employs its best efforts to carry out this task honorably." An earlier communique dealing specifically with the international communist movement stated:

> The identity of interests of the whole socialist camp and the working class of all countries in the fight against imperialism is an objective reality which cannot be destroyed, neither by divergencies of an ideological nature nor by the refusal of this or that sister party to unite in a practical action with other parties. The unity of objectives and action of the communists of the world, which was at the basis of the historic victories of socialism, is necessary more than ever today. The barbarous war of aggression of US imperialism against the heroic people of Vietnam particularly demands common action by all socialist countries and all communist parties. The defense of the unity of the international communist movement, the defense of the unity and cooperation of all socialist countries, continues to be a high criterion of loyalty to Marxism-Leninism, to proletarian internationalism, and to the ideals which always have inspired and continue to inspire the

fight of the communists of all countries. ("Radio Free Portugal," 8 February.)

The same communique stated that the PCP had "on several occasions expressed itself in favor of the holding of another world conference," but had "also always stressed the need for extremely careful preparation, taking into account the opinions and suggestions of all the parties, including the reservations that some may make." The PCP specifically pointed out:

> The fear of displeasing those who openly set as their objective a policy of splitting the communist movement must not prevent initiatives for strengthening the friendship, cooperation, and common action of those who insistently defend unity. The possibility must always be kept open for the Chinese Communist Party, when it wishes, to seek in common with all the other parties paths which lead to overcoming the great present difficulties and to a new drawing together. But it would be absurd to grant the splinters the right to prevent, by their disapproval and by their attacks, any initiatives by the sister parties aimed at the strengthening of the unity. (*Ibid.*)

Within the context of the Sino-Soviet dispute, the PCP was closely aligned with the CPSU. On the occasion of the fiftieth anniversary of the October Revolution, the PCP Central Committee adopted a resolution stating: "The struggle of the Portuguese working class and the formation and development of its vanguard, the Portuguese Communist Party, are inseparable from the ideals and victories of the October Revolution, the achievements and experiences of the people and the Communist Party of the Soviet Union." The PCP also sent a delegation led by Secretary-General Cunhal to the anniversary celebrations in Moscow.

The PCP attacked the Chinese cultural revolution as a "cover for a nationalist and chauvinist campaign aimed directly against the international communist movement, and against Chinese communists who dare to defend friendship with the Soviet Union and the sister parties" ("Radio Free Portugal," 8 February). The PCP has also expressed its hope that "within the Communist Party of China, militants loyal to proletarian internationalism and Marxism-Leninism are working to return their party to the correct position of defense of cooperation and friendship with the other socialist countries and with the entire international communist movement." (*Ibid.*)

**Publications.** The PCP publishes abroad a monthly, *Avante,* and issues occasional leaflets and pamphlets on special topics which are distributed clandestinely. Among such publications for selected readerships are *O Militante, O Campones, O Textil, O Corticeiro,* and *O Marinheiro Vermelho.* Domestic propaganda is supplemented by Radio Free Portugal, which broadcasts from Algeria, and by Radio Moscow, which broadcasts daily in Portuguese.

*     *     *

A pro-Chinese splinter group, the Marxist-Leninist Committee of Portugal, was founded in 1964 as a part of the Popular Action Front (Frente de Acção Popular) by Francisco Rodrigues Campos. Formerly a member of the PCP's Executive Committee, Rodrigues was among the communist leaders who broke jail with Alvaro Cunhal in 1960. He left the party in disagreement over the so-called pacifist line. Rodrigues was arrested again by Portuguese secret police in January 1966. Other top leaders of the Marxist-Leninist Committee include Joao Pulido Valente, Sebastiao Capile, Francisco Martins Rodrigues, and Rui Despiney. Rodrigues and Despiney were arrested and charged by government authorities with the murder of one of the party members for reasons of "political fanaticism" and were convicted in November 1967.

The Popular Action Front is described by the Belgian Marxist-Leninist organ, *La Voix du Peuple,* as "the only antifascist organization [in Portugal] preparing to employ revolutionary violence to seize power from the bourgeoisie." Aiding the front in terrorist activities are "Popular Action Groups." The front was virtually inactive during 1967, apparently weakened by a series of arrests in early 1966.

The Popular Action Front publishes *Revolução Popular.*

# PUERTO RICO

Communism in Puerto Rico is represented by the Puerto Rican Communist Party (Partido Comunista Puertorriqueño; PCP) and the Puerto Rican Socialist League (Liga Socialista Puertorriqueña; LSP), of pro-Soviet and pro-Chinese orientation respectively. Membership figures for these two parties can only be estimated very roughly; moveover, a number of party adherents are believed to be in New York City. Total PCP-LSP membership in 1967 was estimated at between 200 and 300. The population of Puerto Rico is 2,700,000 (estimated 1967). Whereas the two Marxist-Leninist parties represent a very small and relatively insignificant political force, there exists in Puerto Rico a considerably more influential and vocal organization, the Pro-Independence Movement (Movimiento Pro-Independencia; MPI), which while disclaiming Marxist-Leninist denotation aligns itself fully with Castroism (see below).

The degree of popular support in Puerto Rico for parties, such as the above, which advocate the severing of relations between Puerto Rico and the United States and an independent status for the island was demonstrated in a plebiscite on 23 July 1967. Of the 1,067,349 registered voters, 66 per cent (709,293) went to the polls. Of these, 60.5 per cent voted for the existing commonwealth status, 38.9 per cent for statehood, and 0.6 per cent for independence. The PCP, LSP, and MPI advocated a boycott of the plebiscite; however, on the basis of previous electoral returns and the fact that two large parties—the Independence and Statehood Republican parties—also advocated a boycott, it appears likely that only some two to three per cent of those who did not vote were supporters of the extreme left parties.

**Puerto Rican Communist Party**. The PCP was founded in 1934, dissolved in 1944, and founded again in 1946. In its message to the Twenty-third Congress of the CPSU the party appeared to have adopted the name "Party for the Liberation of the Working People of Puerto Rico" (IB, nos. 74-77, July 1966, p. 170), but in 1967 it was referred to again, in communist sources, as the Puerto Rican Communist Party (e.g., *The Worker*, New York, 18 July).

The PCP is legal, but has not registered itself in national elections, preferring to give its support to candidates of nationalist and pro-independence parties.

**Organization and Leadership** Very little is known of the leadership and organizational structure of the PCP, except that the party appears to operate both in Puerto Rico and among the Puerto Rican minority in New York City. The Secretary-General of the party is Juan Santos Rivera.

The party's following is difficult to delineate in view of the existence of other communist and pro-communist organizations. The major source of support for the extreme left originates among student groups, but these groups appear to be oriented toward Castroist and pro-Chinese movements rather than the pro-Soviet PCP.

**PCP Views and Policies**. During 1967 the PCP's views were given practically no publicity in the communist press. The party appeared to have been totally eclipsed by the MPI, whose pronouncements and activity were reported in detail, even by such parties as the pro-Soviet Communist Party of the USA (CPUSA), which had hitherto declared its "explicit support" of the PCP (see *YICA* 1966, p. 251).

The PCP's policy regarding the 1967 plebiscite on the status of Puerto Rico and other related matters was outlined in a Central Committee declaration of August 1966 (*IB*, no. 85, December 1966) which supported an "independent and sovereign" Puerto Rico and claimed that the proposed prebiscite was a "US imperialist move to stem the vigorous and massive anticolonial movement." The Central Committee declaration went on to state that it seemed "very doubtful that the anti-colonialist people of Puerto Rico would be defeated," but added: "Should the brute force and criminal violence of imperialism win the upper hand over the intelligence of the Puerto Rican people, this will justify a changeover to guerrilla war as more suited for Puerto Rican conditions." The declaration concluded:

> Depending on new and old factors, we may visualize a period when: (1) The patriotic organizations will form a united bloc to counter the violence of the plebiscite with the defensive violence of the masses; (2) the united youth of Puerto Rico will show extraordinary courage and self-abnegation in accomplishing deeds of exemplary heroism as it combats wars like the one the US Army has imposed on the people of Vietnam; (3) the revolutionary struggle of the working class against greater colonial exploitation by the imperialists will gain in scope; (4) resistance to and energetic struggle against US monopoly and in defense of Puerto Rico's national patrimony will stiffen; (5) the mass of the people—Popular Democrats, neutrals, and even those who advocate the formation of a state—will realize that they must effectively support the revolutionary patriotic struggle of the Puerto Rican people to foil the fraudulent American maneuver, and must insist on recognizing the independence of Puerto Rico.

In the carrying out of its policies the PCP participates with other pro-independence parties and movements in a loose grouping formed in 1962 and called the Conference of Lares (Mesa de Lares). This body has failed so far to coordinate the activities of its members, who continue to act independently of it, or, as was the case in 1967, follow the lead of the MPI. Thus, demonstrations such as the MPI-organized rally on 16 July at the Sixto Escobar Stadium were actively supported by the PCP (see *The Worker*, 18 July).

In international affairs, a PCP delegation attended the celebrations in the Soviet Union of the fiftieth anniversary of the October Revolution. The party was not represented at the Havana conference of the Latin American Solidarity Organization (31 July-10 August).

**Publications.** The principal publication of the PCP is an irregular newspaper, *Pueblo*.

**Puerto Rican Socialist League.** The pro-Chinese element in Puerto Rican communism works in close cooperation with the Progressive Labor Party (PLP) of the USA and is primarily represented by the LSP. This party was formed during 1964-1965 by Juan Antonio Corretjer (a former member of the PCP, expelled in 1948), as a result of the splitting and dissolution of the Marxist-Leninist "Single Patriotic Action" movement (Acción Patriótica Unitaria) founded by Corretjer in 1959.

**Organization and Leadership.** The LSP has legal status, but very little published information is available on its membership (believed to be greater than that of the PCP) or its organization. Besides the party's Secretary-General, Juan Antonio Corretjer, prominent members of the party include José Marcano, Juan José Munoz Matos, Angel Blanco Santano, Pedro Ronda, Gabriel Mezquida, and Milton Urbina. Like the pro-Soviet PCP, the LSP operates also in New York City, where its policies and actions are publicized by the PLP monthly *Challenge/Desafío*. The close relationship between the PLP and the LSP leaderships was evident in a number of joint actions and policy statements during 1967. In 1966, in an evaluation of this cooperation, Corretjer declared: "The obligatory presence of one million Puerto Rican workers on United States soil converts them into an auxiliary force, perhaps decisive for the precipitation of the historic change in the United States." He stated further: "A revolution of such dimensions, were it to occur in the United States, with the taking over of revolutionary power by the American proletariat, would automatically end the colonial status of Puerto Rico. . . . Two organizations (one American, the other Puerto Rican—the Progressive Labor Party and the Puerto Rican Socialist League) [are putting] their efforts together to recruit, strengthen and force to advance an independent and socialist fatherland for both." (*Challenge/Desafío*, 19 April 1966.)

The LSP also cooperates with the Puerto Rican extremist Nationalist Party (Partido Nacionalista; PN), which likewise has close relations with the PLP. At the PN's General Assembly on 12 March 1967 the following were elected to the national leadership: Jacinto Rivera Pérez, President; Julio Pinto Gandiá, Vice-President: Félix Rivera Otero, Treasurer; W. Valentín Cancel, Secretary-General; and Antonio Herrera, Secretary for Foreign Relations (for names of other PN leaders, see *Challenge/Desafío*, May 1967). At the PN assembly Juan Antonio Corretjer, LSP Secretary-General, gave one of the major speeches, and proposals were put forward for the creation of a United Anti-Plebiscite Front (Frente Unido Antiplebiscitario) which would include PN and LSP participation. Both parties appear to have some support within the small Confederation of Independent Puerto Rican Unions (Confederacíon de Uniones Independientes Puertorriqueñas), whose President is Francisco Colón Gordiany, and within the equally small but militant National Union of Socialist Students of Puerto Rico (Unión Nacional de Estudiantes Socialistas de Puerto Rico), whose President is William Pintado. The PN has its own student group, the National Federation of Puerto Rican Students (Federación Nacional de Estudiantes Puertorriqueños), whose President is Felix Juan Feliciano. In contrast to the PCP, the LSP does not cooperate with the MPI, which officially severed relations with the PLP in a letter sent to PLP leader Milton Rosen on 27 May 1966 (*The Worker,* 3 July 1966).

**LSP Views and Policies.** As in the previous year, LSP domestic policy was concerned principally with "exposing the fraud" of the planned plebiscite which took place on 23 July 1967. During the months preceding, the LSP urged its supporters to boycott the plebiscite (see e.g., *Challenge/Desafío,* April 1967). In July the party, sensing that the plebiscite would take place despite its efforts, published the following communique:

Today we are faced with a reality: the plebiscite is going to take place. And for more than any other reason, it will be carried out because today in Puerto Rico there is not one pro-independence organization in condition to confront imperialism in a revolutionary manner. This is true, of course, even of the two conscientious organizations resolved to face the consequences of that fact that a revolution is a violent deed.

These two organizations are (as in Puerto Rico everyone knows): the Nationalist Party and the Puerto Rican Socialist League. For the Puerto Rican Socialist League, in particular, a revolution is not only a violent act, it is specifically, the violent act of one class against another class.

We tell the truth. We will not be converted into miserable provocateurs. But tomorrow is another day. The hazards and fluctuations of political life have today succeeded in keeping from our hands the weapons which Puerto Rico needed us to hold now: the weapons with the bullets to carry out the revolutionary violence which liberates peoples and makes nations independent.

Puerto Rico is a military fortress of imperialism and it must be assaulted from within. Today's is a transitory situation. This is what we believe. This is our truth. We know our enemy and our enemy knows us. We are each looking at the other's hands although it seems that we are looking at each other's face—and Puerto Rico will be free, independent and Socialist. (*El Socialista,* July 1967; reprinted in *Challenge/Desafío,* September and November/December 1967.)

In a commentary subsequent to the plebiscite, Corretjer declared:

The declaration of the Government: "The debate about status has ended," must be answered by our intensifying the debate on a scale never seen before. This means the surpassing of all means used until now in defense of independence, the abandoning of all customary ways of thinking. (*Challenge/Desafío,* September and November/December 1967).

Other issues affecting LSP domestic policy and activity included demonstrations opposing US policy in Vietnam and a number of initiatives to oppose induction into the US Armed Services. With regard to the latter, the LSP continued in 1967 to express "militant solidarity" with LSP Central Committee member Gabriel Mezquida, whose induction refusal in 1966 had resulted in court action.

Internationally the LSP, while adhering to Maoist interpretations of Marxism-Leninism, was, in contrast to its close ally in the United States, the PLP, considerably less vocal in pledging allegiance to the thoughts of Mao Tse-tung. On matters concerning tactical differences in guerrilla warfare and armed struggle, the LSP was critical of Castroist theoretician Régis Debray's theses outlined in *Revolution in the Revolution?* (see Juan Antonio Corretjer *ibid.,* November/December). The party advocated support, however, to a number of Castroist guerrilla groups in Latin America (*ibid.,* July).

The LSP was not represented at the Havana conference of the Latin American Solidarity Organization.

**Publications.** The major LSP organs, which appear irregularly, are *Pabellón,* a bimonthly; *El Socialista,* a monthly; and *Correo de la Quincena,* a fortnightly. Most major LSP statements and reports of party activity are publicized in the monthly organ of the US Progressive Labor Party, *Challenge/Desafío.*

* * *

Within the militant left-wing movements in Puerto Rico, the most prominent and well organized group is the aforementioned MPI, founded in 1959. Although exact membership figures for the movement are not available, the MPI appears to have between 4,000 and 5,000 followers. Its Secretary-General is Juan Mari Bras. The MPI works in close cooperation with the Pro-Independence University Federation (Federación Universitaria Pro-Independencia; FUPI).

The MPI has on numerous occasions denied Marxist-Leninist orientation, but it closely follows Castroist policy and during 1967 its activities and policies were publicized by variously oriented Marxist-Leninist parties and movements, and the MPI in turn expressed solidarity with them, except the strictly pro-Chinese ones.

The MPI, in a delegation led by Juan Mari Bras, was the sole Puerto Rican group represented at the Havana conference of the Latin American Solidarity Organization. It was also represented on the Secretariat of the Havana-based Afro-Asian Latin American Peoples' Solidarity Organization, with Carlos Padilla, former editor of the MPI organ *Claridad,* replacing Narciso Rabell in July 1967. The latter was dismissed from his post by the MPI for advocating, in defiance of party directives, street demonstrations during the 23 July plebiscite in Puerto Rico.

On 26 January 1967 MPI Secretary-General Juan Mari Bras signed an agreement of cooperation with the US Student Nonviolent Coordinating Committee (SNCC), represented by Stokely Carmichael. Like the aforementioned PCP and LSP, the MPI is also active in New York City.

In his speech to the aforementioned Havana conference, Juan Mari Bras offered "concrete solidarity in any form" to "the heroic fighters in Bolivia, Guatemala, Venezuela, Colombia and other countries, who have started guerrilla warfare as the first battle." Mari Bras referred to the creation in Puerto Rico of a "Puerto Rican Patriotic Vanguard," whose action was based on "two parallel objectives: unity of all progressive forces of Puerto Rico in the struggle for sovereignty and national independence, and the mutual solidarity with all the anti-imperialist and revolutionary forces in the whole world that try to defeat US imperialism." (Conference Documents.)

**Publications.** The principal publication of the MPI is the weekly *Claridad.*

# RÉUNION

The Réunion Communist Party (Parti Communiste Réunionnais; PCR) was founded in May 1959 by the transformation of the Réunion Federation of the French Communist Party into an autonomous party which remained, however, closely linked with the French Communist Party.

The PCR is legal. In a fast-growing population of slightly over 400,000 with a high percentage of young people, the membership of the PCR at the time of its Second Congress, 13-15 August 1967, was reported as 3,500 (*L'Humanité,* 4 September).

For the legislative elections of March 1967 the PCR put up its own candidates in all three districts which, under the status of Réunion as an overseas department, send one delegate apiece to the French National Assembly. The party's candidates were eliminated in two districts in the first election round of 5 March. In the remaining district PCR Secretary-General Paul Vergès received 18,515 (46.32 per cent) of all votes cast and thus qualified for the runoff election on 12 March against the Gaullist candidate Gabriel Macé, who had received 15,319 votes. The Federation of the Left had polled 2,154 votes in this district, and an independent candidate 3,982. Voting participation had been 43,177 of 60,675 registered voters. Paul Vergès lost the runoff election with 19,765 votes against Macé who won 23,412 votes. The Communists charged that only massive election fraud by the authorities made this result possible. (Cf. also Paul Vergès' contribution to the round-table debate on "Les problèmes politiques des départements d'outre-mer," *Démocratie Nouvelle* June 1967.) According to *Le Monde* (14 March) a number of irregularities had indeed been noted by observers. An appeal by the PCR to the Constitutional Council was rejected when in July the Constitutional Council validated the contested election of Macé. Controversies over election procedures, followed by charges of election frauds, recurred during the cantonal and municipal elections in September. During the postponed election in Saint-André-de-la-Réunion on 10 December, candidate Paul Vergès was placed under police protection, a measure criticized by the party (see *Le Monde* 13 December 1967).

**Domestic Policy and Activity.** With 250 delegates and guests attending (including 45 women), the PCR held its Second Party Congress at Saint-Paul, 13-15 August 1967. Congress delegates discussed economic problems and the status of the island. Following the position outlined in a meeting with the French Communist Party and the communist parties from Martinique and Guadeloupe in 1966 (see *YICA,* 1966 pp. 320-321), the political goal remained to obtain a status of autonomy for Réunion without losing the benefits of economic ties with France, as would happen if the island became independent. The Congress restated these goals: to elect a legislative assembly by universal and free ballot; to set up an executive branch responsible to the legislative assembly; and to form a permanent body regulating cooperation with France.

**International Views and Policies.** The PCR Congress condemned US aggression in Vietnam and showed concern over French laxity in resisting United States economic and military penetration of the Indian Ocean area. Support was expressed for the people of South Africa and the Negroes in the United States. Among the messages received at the Congress was one from the CPSU and another from Meir Vilner, Secretary-General of the Israeli Communist Party (RAKAH faction). According to the French Communist Party delegate, Central Committee member Victor Joannes, a CPSU delegation was scheduled to attend but was denied entry visas by the authorities. The Party for the Progress of the Independence of Madagascar (AKFM) was represented by a three-man delegation. The Congress report in the French Communist Party organ *L'Humanité* (4 September) depicts the political orientation of the PCR as close to the Moscow line followed also by the PCF itself.

Secretary-General Paul Vergès was scheduled to attend the 18th Congress of the French Communist Party in January 1967, but apparently was unable to secure air transportation (see

*France*). From 26 April to 2 May Vergès attended the Fourth Congress of the AKFM of Madagascar. In November Vergès represented the PCR at the celebrations for the Fiftieth Anniversary of the October Revolution in Moscow.

   **Publications.** The daily organ of the PCR, *Témoignages,* is directed by Bruny Payet.

# RUMANIA

The Rumanian Communist Party (RCP; Partidul Comunist Român) was founded in 1921. After coming to power in 1948, and until 1965, it was called the Rumanian Workers' Party. The RCP presently exercises a monopoly of power through the People's Democratic Front.

**Organization and Leadership.** The RCP has 69,000 basic organizations headed by a Central Committee. The leading organs are a nine-member Secretariat, a nine-member Standing Presidium, and a 19-member Executive Committee with nine alternate members. The Secretary-General of the RCP is Nicolae Ceauşescu, who since December 1967 has also held the post of President of the Republic. The members of the Secretariat are Mihai Dalea, Mihai Gere, Manea Mănescu, Alexandru Moghioros, Paul Niculescu-Mizil, Vasile Patilinet, Leonte Răutu, Chivu Stoica, and Virgil Trofin. The members of the Standing Presidium are Gheorghe Apostol, Alexandru Bărlădeanu, Emil Bodnăraş, Nicolae Ceauşescu, Alexandru Drăghici, Ion Gheorghe Maurer (also the Premier), Paul Niculescu-Mizil, Chivu Stoica, and Ilie Verdet (also First Deputy Premier).

**Domestic Affairs.** On the domestic front during 1967 the RCP formulated and carried out two distinct policies. First, the party passed specific organizational measures aimed at strengthening its "leading role" in all spheres of Rumanian life. Second, it took the first cautious steps toward the "democratization" of Rumanian life and adopted an economic "reform," in the wake of far greater strides taken in this respect by other East European states, especially Czechoslovakia and Hungary.

**Party Membership.** The RCP's role in Rumanian life was strengthened by its rapidly growing membership. The campaign to increase party ranks began at the Ninth Party Congress in July 1965, at a time when the RCP numbered 1,450,000 persons; at the National Party Conference in December 1967 party Secretary Virgil Trofin announced that RCP membership was 1,730,000; Rumania's total population is 19,105,056, (census, 1966).

The composition of the party membership also indicated substantial penetration into all spheres of Rumanian life. The national composition of the party—88.16 per cent Rumanians, 8.22 per cent Magyars, 1.29 per cent Germans, and 2.33 per cent other nationalities—reflects the general composition of the Rumanian population (the March 1966 census showed 8.4 per cent Magyars, 2 per cent Germans, and 1.8 per cent other nationalities) (*Scînteia,* 2 December 1967). It was reported that almost 42 per cent of the party members are workers and 30 per cent are peasants; about 42 per cent of all academicians and persons with doctoral degrees and 54 per cent of all high school teachers and university professors are party members. In addition, the RCP is strong in the armed forces, with 85 per cent of all officers holding party membership (speeches by Virgil Trofin and General Ion Ioniţă at National Conference, 6–8 December 1967).

**Role of the Party.** On 7 May Secretary-General Nicolae Ceauşescu published a definitive article in the party organ *Scînteia* on "the leading role of the party in the stage of the completion of building socialism." He affirmed the desirability of learning from the accumulated experience of other parties, but rejected the "mechanical copying or transportation" of a "foreign system." Thus, in accordance with the specific conditions in Rumania, he called for "socialist industrialization," modernization of agriculture, familiarity with the results of advanced contemporary scientific thought, and artistic creation. He also stressed the need for highly professional party cadres and strengthened "moral fiber," emphasizing that the growth of the leading role of the party depends in the final analysis upon the activities of each party organization and each member in his relationship with the masses. He also emphasized the necessity for party unity according to the principle of "democratic centralism."

**Secret Police.** On 18 July Ceauşescu announced to a meeting of the basic activ of the Ministry of Internal Affairs that the state security organ was to be put under closer party control in accordance with a decision of the June Central Committee plenum. He severely criticized the "Securitate" for past "transgressions of socialist legality," especially those against party and state activists, and stressed that "it must be understood that no kind of secret or conspiratorial matter could then have been or can now be a reason for removing an organ from under the control of party activity." He declared that the Central Committee had decided to take measures "which will enforce strict respect for legality, so that not a single citizen can be arrested without good and proven reason and no party member be investigated or arrested without the approval of the party organs." This sharp distinction between nonparty and party members has placed party members in a strongly privileged and powerful position. Finally Ceauşecu announced that a Council of State Security, answerable to the party and the government, was to be set up within the Internal Affairs Ministry to ensure collective discussion of important problems. The measures taken against the security organs were intended to combat "factionalism" in the party, and were especially directed against Alexandru Drăghici who, although removed from his post as Interior Minister in 1965, continued to wield considerable influence in security matters.

**Administrative-Territorial Reorganization.** Further measures to strengthen the party's role in society were proposed at the 5–6 October Central Committee plenum and were subsequently approved by the National Conference of the party on 6–8 December. The measures concerned simplification of the administrative system and the establishment of closer links between central directing organs and basic units and between cities and rural areas. First, the existing 16 territorial-administrative units are to be modified to about 40 or 45 county units and are to be the sole mediate territorial units through which the party Central Committee and Council of Ministers are to effect policy. Second, and of greater significance, the duplication of tasks in party, government, and mass-organization posts is to be eliminated, and the party and state posts are to become the responsibility of one man. This move necessitated the abrogation of Section B of Article 13 of the party statutes, which prohibited a member from fulfilling more than one leading political function at the same time. A second change in the party statutes was an amendment to Article 48 stipulating that general meetings of basic party organizations be convened every three months instead of every month. As pointed out by Premier Maurer at the National Party Conference in December, this reorganization leads to a strengthening of the RCP's role by virtue of the fact that it is the party which lays down the guidelines for every field of activity, and those who are carrying out responsible functions at a state level are, at the same time, members of the leading party organs.

In the future economic matters are to be placed under the Council of Ministers, with only their general orientation subject to approval by the Central Committee and the party leadership. The Central Committee is to maintain and consolidate its jurisdiction over politicoideological matters, foreign policy, defense, and state security.

This reorganization and reshuffling of posts was effected at the December National Conference and at the subsequent Central Committee plenum and National Assembly session. According to Ceauşescu's recommendations, the Chairman of the Central Council of the General Trade Union Confederation, as well as the Chairman of the National Union of Agricultural Production Cooperatives, became members of the Council of Ministers. The First Secretary of the Union of Working Youth became Minister of Youth Affairs. At the local level, the first secretary of a given county or city party committee was elected chairman of the local people's council, and other party cadres assumed management functions in local administrative bodies. Thus all industrial management boards must now include among their members the secretary of the local party organization in addition to trade-union representatives.

However, the most significant result of the reorganization was the reunification of the positions of Secretary-General of the party and President of the State Council, as had been the case under Gheorghiu-Dej until 1965. The proposal for the merger was made by Chivu Stoica, President of the State Council:

> The carrying out by the same person of the function of Secretary-General of the Party Central Committee and of President of the State Council will ensure the implementation of the unitary leadership by the Party Central Committee of all social and state activity in

our fatherland, and will mean the representation of party and state policy at the highest
level in the international scene.*

**Ceauşescu—Personal Power.** RCP policies in 1967 were largely attributed to the personal efforts of
Secretary-General Nicolae Ceauşescu, who formulated and presented the directives on the entire range
of party policies. "Comrade Nicolae Ceauşescu's personal role in the initiation, carrying out, and
finalization of the studies of the documents now being discussed by the National Conference is no
longer a secret to anyone," declared Premier Ion Gheorghe Maurer at the national conference. He was
seconded by Alexandru Bărlădeanu, who declared: "As a member of the Standing Presidium, I must
stress that this vast work has been carried out under the direct leadership—I would say daily
leadership—of Comrade Ceauşescu." The policies, in turn, served to strengthen Ceauşescu's personal
position, and culminated in his election to the leading party and state posts at the National
Conference.

The subsequent personnel changes in the party and government leadership were a further step in
the consolidation of Ceauşescu's position. Alexandru Drăghici was transferred from the party
Secretariat to the vice-presidency of the Council of Ministers and was replaced by Chivu Stoica in his
party post. Emil Bodnăraş, Alexandru Bărlădeanu, and Gheorghe Apostol were transferred from their
posts as First Vice-Premiers, leaving as the sole Vice-Premier a close associate of Ceauşescu's, Ilie
Verdeţ, who had assumed the post only in January 1967. Petre Blajovici and Roman Moldovan were
removed from their positions as Vice-Premiers. These personnel changes, against the background of
the further extensive changes called for by the National Conference, removed the influence of the "old
guard" in the government organs and allowed Ceauşescu to eliminate any possible existing or
potential opposition in the leading organs. (At the December 1966 Central Committee plenum
Ceauşescu had alluded to opposition to the economic changes; again in the 7 May *Scînteia* atricle he
indicated concern over contacts between members of the party and a "foreign power.")

**Economic Measures.** In addition to steps taken to improve administrative efficiency, measures
were also taken in 1967 to ensure greater economic efficiency. It was repeatedly emphasized that the
territorial-administrative reorganization was not an end in itself, but was intended "to create an
adequate framework of administrative organization for the implementation of measures regarding
improvements in management and planning" (Chivu Stoica, speech to National Party Conference)

The "improvements" (rather than "reform") in the Rumanian economy used some of the
principles employed in economic reforms currently under way in other East European states
(Czechoslovakia, Hungary, Bulgaria), particularly in the utilization of objective economic laws.
However, the Rumanians explicitly rejected any "exaggeration of objective factors" and "any
fetishization of economic laws." At the same time the utilization of the market as the sole criterion in
planning and economic effectiveness was also rejected. (B.Z., "National Conference of the Rumanian
CP," *WMR*, February 1968.) The Rumanian economic measures were to be seen in the context of the
RCP's goal to modernize and streamline the economy without changing its socialist base.

The essence of the economic modernization in Rumania was elucidated by Paul Niculescu-Mizil at
the National Conference: "The great source of the superiority and strength of socialism lies in the fact
that society is able not only to know objective economic laws, but also to use them consciously and
in the general interest by means of planned economic management." He went on to refute the
"advocates of liberalization, who have hastened to confuse their wishes with reality"·

He who does not understand the essence of the socialist system will never understand that
the problem lies not in renouncing the centralized leadership of economic life, but in
using levers of an economic-objective nature within the framework of this centralized
leadership, in the interests of socialism. In our view such measures do not and cannot
have anything in common with liberalism; they are clearly and categorically hostile to the
unleashing of spontaneous forces. The market must be used and its demands known, since
this affords planning elements which are very useful indeed in increasing economic

*The nomination of Ceauşescu by Chivu Stoica was reported to have caused a "certain sensation" among the
delegates at the National Conference. (Radio Prague 12 December 1967.)

efficiency and stepping up the satisfaction of social needs. But the solution of the problems of economic development must not be left to chance or to the domination of the blind spontaneous forces of the "free market"; the solution of those problems is incumbent on the conscious factor.

The measures for improving Rumania's economy were taken even while agricultural and industrial production continued to grow at a substantial rate. Ceauşescu reported at the National Conference that the average growth of industrial production during 1966 and 1967 had been 12.3 per cent; labor productivity had grown 9.3 per cent and national income 8.77 per cent. All growth rates exceeded the plan. The Rumanian economy had been plagued, however, by serious shortcomings. The growth rate was lower than in 1965, the investment plan was not fulfilled, and there were serious delays in putting new plants into operation. Worst of all, Rumanian productivity and the quality control still did not measure up to West European standards (speech by Ceauşescu to the Conference on Foreign Trade Activity, 22 February 1967).

The changes in the Rumanian economic system were tested in 71 industrial enterprises since 7 July 1967 and were formalized in the directives of the Central Committee issued after the October plenum and approved at the December National Party Conference. The directives established greater decentralization in management of industrial production, foreign trade, planning, financing the national economy, wholesale prices, and wage differentials. The basic unit of industrial production was to be an Industrial Central, a form of trust which would consolidate either horizontally or vertically all enterprises engaged in closely related production. There was to be greater contact between producer and consumer and direct contact between the industrial central and foreign clients. Production costs were to be financed by bank loans and incomes of the individual enterprises, and losses were no longer to be covered by the state budget; a new wholesale price system bearing a "true relation" to production costs was to be established, and material incentives would be extensively applied in enterprises. The wage level was to be based on work actually done, and those who failed to fulfill their tasks would be held materially responsible.

An Institute for Market Research and an industrial management-training center were established, the latter under the cosponsorship of the United Nations and the International Labor Organization.

The Central Committee plenum of 27-28 March approved a decision on measures to improve the leadership, planning, financing, and organization of state farms with a view to increasing production and labor productivity at a sustained pace and reducing substantially material and labor expenditures, thus ensuring profitability of all state agricultural units. The following Central Committee plenums, on 26-27 June and 5-6 October, again took up the issue of improving the economy, and the October plenum approved directives which were then discussed and approved at the National Conference. The plenum also approved proposals regarding the improvement of the wages, bonus, and labor norm system. It was decided that the policy of increasing low wages will continue in 1968 and 1969, and that it will extend to all categories of wage earners. This would mean a gradual growth of wages for all categories of wage earners by an average of 12.3 per cent yearly until 1970. In another measure the plenum approved proposals encouraging the building of privately owned dwellings and a measure providing for over-all rent increases.

**The Youth Movement.** As in the other East European socialist countries, a major area of party activity is work among youth. The 29 November-1 December Central Committee plenum discussed and adopted a decision on improvement of educational work in the ranks of the youth and in the activity of the party-controlled Union of Working Youth. The RCP gave the Union of Working Youth unprecedented responsibility and authority in line with the other administrative changes aimed at strengthening the role of the party.

Recognizing the importance of schools in shaping young people, the party called for a "permanent collaboration system" between the Ministry of Education and the Central Committee of the Union of Working Youth in all matters concerning educational work in schools and also decided that the youth organization would be responsible in the future for the military training of all youth. Measures were taken to simplify the organizational structure of the Union of Working Youth by establishing a single organization in each locale to conduct a wide variety of educational, cultural, and sports activities designed to attract the greatest number of Rumanian young people. Admission requirements were also simplified. Finally, the party decided that the Secretary-General of the Working Youth should also hold the government position of Minister of Youth Affairs.

**Social Legislation.** In other spheres of national life steps toward "democratization" were evident, such as more "open" debates in the National Assembly and indications in Ceaușescu's speech at the National Conference that in the future the roles of the State Council and National Assembly would be strengthened. At the National Conference he announced that the "present stage of development" called for changes in the legal structure: "Our legal standards should sanction and protect our people's fundamental gains and provide for the development of public property and the exercise of civil rights and liberties." He also said that new penal, labor, civil, and family codes would be drafted. Earlier in the year, on 26 July, the National Assembly had passed a measure for the protection of citizens, defining rules for court appeals by citizens against "illegal administrative acts"—that is, arbitrary decisions by public bodies.

**International Views and Positions.** A comprehensive formulation of the principles of Rumanian foreign policy was voiced in a *Scînteia* editorial on 28 February and in an article on the present role of the party on 7 May 1967. At the July session of the National Assembly Ceaușescu reported on foreign-policy activities. Despite the extensive attention paid to foreign policy, there were neither changes in principle nor inconsistencies in policy during 1967.

The foreign policy and activity of the RCP proceeds, in the words of Nicolae Ceaușescu, "from the country's needs, the general interests of socialism, the cause of world progress and peace, and are based on the study and knowledge of the realities of international life." The focus is on "fraternal friendship and cooperation with the socialist countries" and efforts aimed at unity of the socialist states and the unity of the international communist and workers' movement. At the same time, the RCP and the government promote an active and diverse policy of expanding contacts and strengthening relations with all countries, "regardless of social system," and with "all peoples." The basic principles of Rumanian foreign policy are "national independence and sovereignty, equal rights, and noninterference in the internal affairs of other states."

The principles of equality and noninterference are also to be observed in the relations among communist parties. "No one can claim to have the last word on any problem or can say that other views are non-Marxist," Ceaușescu declared. "No party can claim to hold a special place, or to have certain privileges in the workers' movement." Should differences of opinion arise, the parties must analyze them in a "comradely and constructive spirit" and search for common points of unity to ensure that differences of views do not harm the normal links between fraternal parties.

Although the RCP gives precedence to the importance of bilateral exchanges of views and experiences, it recognizes the usefulness of international conferences "organized on the basis of consultation between the Parties concerned, and observing the basic standards of interparty relations—independence, equal rights, and noninterference in the affairs of another party." The RCP emphasizes that each communist party has the legitimate right to participate or not to participate in an international meeting and rejects categorically any question of establishing an "international coordinating center" with the aim of setting up compulsory norms of conduct for the communist parties.*

With repeated emphasis on the principle of noninterference in the internal affairs of another party, Ceaușescu declared: "It is inadmissible, under any form, for a Party member to establish or maintain, over the head of the leadership relations with other parties, to supply information, and to participate in actions against the political line of his Party."† Also emphasizing the need for unity in the

---

*Rejection of the principle of democratic centralism in international affairs was clearly stated in the 28 February editorial in *Scînteia*: "Methods and principles of internal party life such as centralism and the submission of the minority to the majority have no place in international relations."

†While this point was widely interpreted as a reference to the Soviet Union (or to China), Rumanian sources did not specify which countries were involved.

international communist movement, Ceauşescu said: "The Rumanian Communist Party deems that what is fundamental is what unites the communist and workers' parties, and this must prevail over any disputes and differences in views" (Scînteia, 7 May 1967).

Thus, although the cornerstone of Rumanian foreign policy remains "friendship and alliance with the socialist states," the country has developed and maintained an independent policy and has expressed disagreement with attitudes common to the other socialist states and communist parties on a number of foreign-policy issues and issues in the world communist movement. During 1967 Rumania avoided polemics in its disagreements with other socialist states and openly countered only direct criticism aimed at its policies. On other issues Rumania either responded by indirect allusions or maintained silence. Although extensive discussions of divergent views were certainly part of the numerous bilateral consultations in which the RCP participated during the year, the communiques were couched in only the most general terms. Statements, official declarations, and articles by foreign party and state leaders were reported (sometimes without comment) in Rumania, and on occasion objectionable parts were censored.

The RCP has reconciled its independent and nationalist policy with the interests of the entire socialist community by insisting that whatever benefits one socialist state benefits the entire socialist system. "The stronger and the more prosperous each socialist country is in increasing its material, political, and military potential, the stronger the entire socialist system becomes," Ceauşescu stated to the National Assembly on 24 July. His view is in direct contrast to the "general line" of the international socialist system. Thus, when Vladimír Koucký (of the Czechoslovak Communist Party) rejected nationalism and advanced the thesis that the international communist movement is a qualitatively separate entity, the RCP omitted his article from the August 1967 Rumanian edition of the World Marxist Review.

**Relations with the Soviet Union.** Despite open disagreement on numerous foreign-policy issues, relations between Rumania and the Soviet Union were outwardly cordial, primarily owing to the tendency of the two states to refrain from direct criticism of each other's policies. At the July session of the National Assembly Ceauşescu emphasized that the Rumanian party and regime are "convinced [that] what united the socialist countries is far more important than the differences of opinions between them." In this spirit, on the Fiftieth Anniversary of the October Revolution he hailed the "friendship, solidarity, and fraternal collaboration" between Rumania and the Soviet Union and expressed the Rumanian people's "sentiments of friendship and esteem for the Soviet people and the Communist Party." The RCP Central Committee resolution on the Fiftieth Anniversary celebrations also declared that "the Rumanian Communist Party, all our people, highly assess the enthusiastic activity of the Soviet people and of their Communist Party in building communism," and paid tribute to the links of friendship between the two countries "based on the ideology of Marxism-Leninism and of socialist internationalism; on the community of systems and goals; on the principle of independence, equal right, mutual esteem, and respect, [which is] in accord with the interests of our peoples, the unity of the socialist countries, and with the interests of peace and mankind's progress along the road of civilization."

Rumania celebrated the Fiftieth Anniversary of the October Revolution at home, sent a delegation headed by Nicolae Ceauşescu to Moscow, and submitted articles acclaiming the occasion to Pravda (17 October) and to the November issue of World Marxist Review. However, in reporting the celebration ceremonies in Moscow, the Rumanian press omitted Leonid Brezhnev's remarks on China, the Middle East crisis, and the proposed international communist party meeting.

The character of the relationship between Rumania and the Soviet Union was exemplified by the communique released following the visit of a Rumanian party delegation headed by Ceauşescu to the Soviet Union on 14-15 December. The communique noted that the two sides, in talks held in a "frank and friendly atmosphere ... exchanged information" on their respective countries and on the development of further cooperation between the Soviet Union and Rumania, on the international situation, and on the international communist movement. Both parties condemned US "aggression in Vietnam," reaffirmed the principles of the Bucharest declaration of 1966, and stressed the need to strengthen the Warsaw Pact and the need for unity in the international communist movement. The issues of Germany, the Middle East, and the international communist party conference, on which their opinions differed, were not mentioned. Also not mentioned was the issue of renewal of the 20-year friendship and mutual-cooperation treaty, which is due to expire in February 1968.(Whereas the other East European states hastened to sign new treaties and renew existing ones far in advance of their expiration dates, Rumania has refrained from the treaty-signing activities).

One item in the communique, however, was interpreted by Western observers to refer to a point of conflict between the two parties: the two sides reportedly discussed economic relations and "exchanged opinions on the progress of fulfillment of earlier signed agreements." Previously, at the National Conference, Ceauşescu had referred to international trade and cooperation, saying:

> In practice sometimes the provisions of the long-term agreements are not fully respected. . . . Yearly revisions of the agreements, and particularly the renunciation by one or another party of undertakings contained in these agreements, have a negative attitude on economic collaboration and cooperation and infringe on long-term planning. . . . It is necessary to make sure that, in the practice of relations between states, the existence of differences of opinion on one problem or another should not affect economic collaboration and cooperation, and should be based effectively on economic principles and criteria.

Rumanian trade with the Soviet Union in 1967 was to be at a level of 730 million rubles, an increase in absolute figures, but a 7.3 per cent decline from 1966 in the Soviet share of Rumanian foreign trade. A trade protocol for 1968 signed in late December envisions a rise in trade to 770 million rubles, but again, this represents an 0.6 per cent decrease in the Soviet share of Rumanian foreign trade for 1968. From 1966 to 1970 Rumanian-Soviet trade is scheduled to increase by 30 per cent, whereas for the same period Czechoslovakia envisions a 43 per cent increase, Bulgaria a 70 per cent increase, and Hungary a 100 per cent increase. One reason given for the apparent stagnation in Rumanian-Soviet trade is that the two countries produce many similar types of goods.

**Relations with Eastern Europe.** The RCP favors the simultaneous dissolution of NATO and the Warsaw Pact. However, Rumania has repeatedly affirmed its intentions to remain a member of the Warsaw Pact and to fulfill its commitments as long as the pact exists. At the same time it has insisted that its activities would proceed from the "principles which govern relations between the socialist countries, from the fact that each country, each army, must be well organized, powerful from all points of view, and have its own command able to answer any call" (Nicolae Ceauşescu to party activists in Brasov, 18 June 1967).

In his foreign-policy address to the National Assembly on 24 July Ceauşescu again pledged that, as a member of the Warsaw Pact, Rumania would do "all in its power to strengthen its defense capacity to be ready, together with the other socialist countries, to make its contribution to rebuffing an aggressor and any imperialist attempt against the revolutionary conquests of the Rumanian people and of those of the other socialist countries." For the first time since 1964 Rumanian armed forces joined those of the Soviet Union and Bulgaria in joint military maneuvers held in Bulgaria on 20-27 August. Rumania also sent representatives to the Warsaw Pact meetings of Foreign Ministers in Warsaw in February and December. (The press releases in both cases however, were compromises with the Rumanian position and did not appear to run counter to Rumanian foreign-policy principles.)

There was continuous stress on the need for developing economic collaboration "on the basis of mutual advantage and comradely mutual aid" with all the socialist states and proposed concrete measures to the other socialist states for extending the "international division of labor" through the development of scientific and economic cooperation. However, Rumania was unwilling to cooperate in a "socialist division of labor" at the expense of its own industrialization program. The RCP stand on economic relations was set forth by Party Secretary Mihai Dalea at the National Party Conference:

> In the view of our party the lasting basis of international economic exchanges can be only the independent development of each national economy. . . . There never existed, nor can there exist at any time, an international interest without a national one, nor can the strengthening of the world socialist system be effected without the strengthening of each country belonging to it.

Thus, although Rumania attributed to COMECON a "positive role in widening economic relations," the absolute volume of trade between Rumania and the other COMECON countries declined, as did their respective shares in Rumania's over-all trade. In the meantime, Rumania continued to develop important economic ties with the West.

**Relations with Western Europe.** Pronounced differences of views between Rumania and the other socialist states were in evidence over the key issues of establishing diplomatic relations with West Germany and the Arab-Israeli war in June 1967. There were also divergent viewpoints on the subject of China and on the convocation of an international communist party conference.

Appealing to the "spirit of the 1966 Bucharest declaration," which urged the strengthening of political relations among all countries, on 31 January 1967 Rumania established diplomatic relations with the Federal Republic of Germany. Following the signing of the recognition agreement, both sides issued separate statements reiterating their respective views on the European situation. Thus Rumania declared that the recognition of the existence of two Germanies is one of the preconditions for the development of cooperation among European nations and for the amelioration of the political situation in Europe but demanded no concessions from the West German government on this point. The Rumanian move elicited strong reaction, particularly from the East Germans, who found it "regrettable" that in recognizing West Germany Rumania had not insisted on rejection by Bonn of its claim to represent the whole of Germany. East Germany noted that the "West German militarists were encouraged by the agreement" (*Neues Deutschland,* 3 February 1967). In turn, the Rumanian press rejected the East German criticism as distorted and at the same time warned that attempts by *Neues Deutschland* "to set itself up as foreign political advisor to another state and to interfere in the internal affairs of another country do not serve relations of friendship and collaboration between socialist countries; on the contrary, they harm these relations" (*Scînteia,* 4 February 1967). Rumania showed its disapproval of the East German reaction by sending the Deputy Foreign Minister in place of the Foreign Minister to the Warsaw Pact meeting called on 8-10 February to consider policy toward Bonn (Foreign Minister Corneliu Mănescu was away on a previously scheduled trip to Belgium on 6-10 February).

It was reported that the ministerial meeting was scheduled to be held in East Berlin but was moved to Warsaw at the insistence of the Rumanian government. The Rumanians also reportedly insisted, as a precondition for their attendance, on a complete ban on criticism of the Rumanian action (*Vjesnik,* Belgrade, 12 February 1967; *NYT,* 10 February 1967; *Christian Science Monitor,* 8 February 1967). The Warsaw Pact Foreign Ministers' meeting issued no communique, and the press report noted only that there had been an exchange of views on questions connected with the efforts of socialist countries to reduce international tension and strengthen peace, security, and cooperation in Europe in an atmosphere of "friendship, cooperation, and complete mutual understanding." No mention was made of the West German diplomatic offensive, which was the primary reason for calling the meeting. Meanwhile, the Rumanians continued to insist that the establishment of diplomatic relations between Bonn and Bucharest served the *détente* and European security and stimulated "realistic political tendencies manifest in Western Europe" (*Romania Libera,* 9 February 1967).

**Relations with China.** In the spirit of friendship with socialist states, Rumania maintained cordial relations with both the People's Republic of China and Albania. In his 24 July speech to the National Assembly Ceausescu remarked: "Our people nurture feelings of esteem and profound respect for the Chinese people, for the heroic struggle carried on under the leadership of the CCP for the defeat of imperialist domination, for the overthrow of the old regime, and for the establishment of people's power and the building of a socialist society."

In addition to visits by Rumanian cultural and scientific delegations to China, it was reported by Western sources (*Lé Monde,* 5 July, 12 July 1967; *NYT,* 5 July 1967; *Die Welt,* 5 July 1967) and by Moscow (*Izvestiia,* 4 July 1967) that Rumanian Premier Ion Gheorghe Maurer visited China at the beginning of July on his way to Hanoi. Maurer had just concluded a visit to Washington, where he held talks with President Johnson on Vietnam, and to Paris, where he held talks with President de Gaulle. It was speculated that Maurer carried a message from President Johnson to Chairman Mao Tse-tung; but the reports were denied by the White House. Maurer's trip was not officially confirmed by Bucharest or by Peking.

On the occasion of Chinese National Day (1 October), a Rumanian group, including Vice-Chairman Costică Alecu of the Rumanian Institute for Cultural Relations, and a delegation of Albanians were the only East Europeans at the Peking celebrations. Another indication of Rumanian-Chinese cooperation was that after the closing of the Chinese embassy and consulates in Indonesia the embassy of the Rumanian Socialist Republic agreed to act on behalf of the Chinese People's Republic in looking after its rights and interests and its nationals in Indonesia.

**Other International Issues.** The RCP did not mitigate its continuing attack on US "imperialism" and its alleged role in political crises around the world. The United States was condemned for its role in Vietnam, for its alleged support for "neo-Nazist and revanchist forces" in West Germany, and for its alleged activities against the Arab states in the Middle East. Although Rumania did not support the Arab cause against Israel, it strongly affirmed support for the "righteous struggle of the Arab nations against imperialism and neocolonialism," and warned that "the use of arms could only serve the aims of imperialism, above all American imperialism." (Declarations of the RCP Central Committee on the Situation in the Near East, 10 June 1967.)

Rumania has repeatedly pledged economic, political, moral, and material support to Vietnam in its struggle against "American aggression." In December the Rumanian delegation at the United Nations was chosen by the National Liberation Front of South Vietnam to distribute its political program to the delegations of UN member countries. On this occasion the RCP hailed the National Liberation Front as the "true representative of the people of South Vietnam and the organizer of the struggle for their sacred national rights and for the country's reconstruction." "The entire unfolding of events," according to the RCP, "confirms the truthfulness and the firm bases of the principles and conclusions of the NLFSV political program adopted a few months ago, a program which is an expression of the basic aspirations of the people of South Vietnam" (Dumitru Tinu, "The Platform of the Struggle in South Vietnam," *Scînteia,* 18 December 1967.) In 1967 Rumanian sources admitted for the first time that military aid was to be given to Hanoi. During a visit of a Vietnamese economic delegation headed by Vice-Premier Le Thanh Nghi agreements were signed covering the nonrepayable economic and military assistance of the Socialist Republic of Rumania to the Democratic Republic of Vietnam in 1968 and the supply of complete industrial plants in 1968 to 1970, as well as a trade and payments agreement for 1968. It was also agreed to postpone the repayment of previous loans by Rumania to North Vietnam (Radio Bucharest, 26 August 1967; *Rumania Today,* October, 1967). At the present time Rumania is receiving essentially no imports from North Vietnam.

A divergence of views evident between Rumania and the Soviet Union and other socialist states was even more sharply defined during the Middle East crisis. Whereas the Soviet Union strongly condemned Israel as the "aggressor" and gave full support to the Arab states, Rumania, while expressing continued support for the Arab states in their struggle against "imperialism and neocolonialism," refused to blame Israel, and remained the only East European communist state not to break diplomatic relations with Israel. Nicolae Ceaușescu attended the hastily called Moscow meeting of party and state leaders on 9 June but did not sign the joint statement condemning Israel as the aggressor and pledging the signatories to do everything to aid the Arab countries to "rebuff the aggressor" and to "protect their lawful rights." In a separate statement on 10 June the RCP demanded the immediate cessation of hostilities in the Middle East and called for negotiations among the parties involved in the conflict. It also called for the withdrawal of Israeli troops from occupied territories and for all troops to pull back to preconflict borders.

Rumanian representatives did not attend the 11—12 July Budapest meeting of East European party and state leaders convened to further discuss the Middle East crisis. Rumania reported an abridged version of the Budapest meeting communique, including a reference to Israeli "aggression" but omitting the statement that by its "policy of conquest" Israel was "defying the peace-loving forces of the whole world." In his foreign-policy speech to the July meeting of the National Assembly Ceaușescu reiterated the Rumanian position on the Middle East events, calling for the immediate withdrawal of Israeli troops from occupied territories, and negotiations among the belligerents. He repeated Rumanian friendship for the Arab people and solidarity with and support for their aspirations for national unity, for economic and social progress, and for national independence. "However," he said, "we want to say honestly to our Arab friends that we do not understand and we do not share the attitude of those circles who are for the liquidation of the state of Israel." However, Rumania did send Foreign Minister Mǎnescu to the Belgrade ministerial-level meeting on 4–6 September, which sought to coordinate aid to the Arab states, and to the Warsaw Pact Foreign Ministers' meeting on 19–21 December convened to discuss the situation in the Middle East.

Consistent with its policy of silence on disputed issues, the RCP published a censored version of the August *World Marxist Review*, eliminating three contributions on the Middle East by K. Doudera of Czechoslovakia, F. Nassar of Jordan, and L. Kin of Israel, respectively.

While relations between Cuba and the East European socialist bloc continued to deteriorate during 1967, Rumania sought to improve its relations with Cuba. Rumanian Central Committee Member Vlater Roman, attending the Havana Conference of the Latin American Solidarity Organization (OLAS) in July and August as an observer, expressed to the delegates Rumanian "solidarity with the struggle of the Latin American people against imperialism and colonialism." In November Deputy Premier Gheorghe Rǎdulescu traveled to Cuba to sign agreements on trade and economic and technical-scientific cooperation. The trade agreement calls for a significant increase in the exchange of goods for 1968. Rǎdulescu termed the visit "a positive step forward in advancing Rumania's political, economic and trade relations" with Cuba.

**The International Communist Movement.** With reference to the proposed international meeting of communist parties, the RCP declared itself "in principle" for the convocation of multilateral meetings among communist parties but insisted that conditions be "ripe" for such a meeting and that it be of a strictly consultative nature (*Scînteia* 28 February 1967). The RCP declined to attend the Karlovy Vary Conference of European Communist and Workers' Parties on 24–26 April (or the earlier preparatory meeting in Warsaw on 22–26 February), despite efforts by other communist parties to ensure Rumanian participation. The officially reported reason for Rumanian absence was that, "inasmuch as in the course of the exchange of opinions and consultations which took place, no agreement could be reached in advance on the character, purpose, and proceedings of the conference, the Rumanian Party is not attending it" (Radio Bucharest, 24 April 1967).

The Rumanians remained silent concerning Soviet efforts to convene an international communist party meeting, but on repeated occasions they emphasized their preference for bilateral talks (see Nicolae Ceauşescu's "The Decisive Victories of Socialism: a Triumph of Marxism-Leninism," *Pravda* 17 October 1967).

Rumania had frequent bilateral consultations with foreign communist parties in 1967 on the grounds that such consultations serve to strengthen the unity of the world communist movement. In the early part of year Ceauşescu met with Soviet party leaders in Moscow on 17–18 March, with Yugoslav representatives in Bucharest on 30 March, with Italian leaders (including Secretary-General Luigi Longo) in Bucharest on 31 March–6 April, with French party representatives on 7–10 April, with Bulgarian party leaders in Bucharest on 17–21 April. RCP representatives met with high-level Yugoslav party representatives in Belgrade on 30 January, with Hungarian party representatives on 13–14 April, and with Czechoslovak party representatives on 13 April. Although the brief communiques or reports on the meetings did not mention the imminent Karlovy Vary Conference, it was quite evident that this conference was an important point in the discussions.

Following the Karlovy Vary Conference, a top-level Rumanian party delegation headed by Nicolae Ceauşescu visited Budapest on 24–25 May for talks with Hungarian party leaders. Although the communique was couched in general terms, mentioning "comradely" talks between the two delegations on the international situation and the international communist and workers' movement, Homeland Radio (Budapest) declared that the talks took place in the spirit of Hungarian party First Secretary Kádár's statement at the Karlovy Vary Conference, in which he said that communists of the socialist countries will cooperate on the most important international issues regardless of whether they participate in the conference. The tone of the meeting was also affected by statements of Hungarian Politburo member Zoltán Komocsin to the effect that each party has "a right to attend or not to attend" an interparty conference, and that discussions at such a conference must not offend the absent parties (*Népzsabadság*, 4 March 1967). Before and after the Warsaw Pact Foreign Ministers' meeting in February, to which Rumania sent a Deputy Minister of Foreign Affairs, Foreign Minister Corneliu Mănescu also consulted with his Hungarian counterpart in Budapest (5 February and 12 February 1967).

Ceauşescu again held talks with a ruling party leader when Todor Zhivkov, First Secretary of the Bulgarian party Central Committee, paid a "friendly visit" to Rumania on 28 September–1 October. The communique mentioned the international situation and the international communist movement only as items on the agenda, and declared that the talks were held "in a warm and comradely atmosphere in the spirit of the traditional friendship uniting the two parties, countries, and peoples." However, considering the intensified efforts of the Soviet Union to convene an international communist party meeting and Bulgaria's initiating role in its convocation, the talks were very likely centered on Rumania's participation in the meeting.

A spate of consultations took place between the RCP and foreign communist parties, especially those which have shown an independent attitude in recent years. The emphasis which Rumania has placed on the importance of mutual exchanges of opinions, the independence of parties to formulate their own policies, and the strengthening of the unity of the international communist movement were reflected in the respective communiques following talks with foreign party leaders, but disputed issues such as the international communist party meeting were not mentioned. Among the most important visits to Bucharest were that of two separate Greek party delegations, on 28 February–3 March and again in late May to early June; Secretary-General Shmuel Mikunis of the Israeli party on 12 April; Secretary-General Ali Yata of the Moroccan party on 13–19 April; a Syrian party delegation on 24 April–4 May; a Chilean party delegation on 3 May; Secretary-General Santiago Carrillo of the Spanish party on 28 May–2 June; Central Committee Chairman Reza Radmanesh of the Tudeh Party of Iran on 4 August; Central Committee First Secretary Waldeck Rochet of the French party on 14–17 August; First Secretary Luigi Longo of the Italian party on 16–17 August; Secretary-General Jesús Faría of the Venezuelan party on 18 August; a delegation of the United Socialist Party of Iceland on 21 August–2 September; a Belgian party delegation headed by Vice-President Marc Drumaux on 20–29 September; Secretary-General Luis Corvalán of the Chilean party on 22–28 November; and a Colombian party delegation headed by Secretary-General Gilberto Vieira on 1–5 December.

High-level RCP delegations traveled to Norway on 25–31 August to meet with Norwegian party Chairman Reidar Larsen, to Denmark on 22–29 September at the invitation of the Danish party, to the Netherlands on 8–14 September to meet with Dutch party Chairman Paul de Groot, to Sweden on 16–21 October, and to Finland on 23–31 October.

Rumania has not only intensified its contacts with "fraternal" communist parties, but has waged an "active" peace policy through contacts with numerous leftist and progressive parties, and through an extraordinary number of contacts and agreements on a government level with noncommunist states. Of great importance to Rumania was the election of Foreign Minister Corneliu Mănescu as President of the Twenty-Second Session of the UN General Assembly. He is the first representative of a communist regime to hold the post.

Contacts with socialist and "progressive" parties included consultations with representatives from the Syrian Ba'ath Party on 14–30 March, the Italian United Socialist Party in July, the French Socialist Party (including Secretary-General Guy Mollet) on 7–8 April, the Norwegian Socialist Party on 13 April, the Guinean Independence Party on 23 July, the African Party for Independence of Portuguese Guinea and Cape Verde Islands (including Secretary-General Amilcar Cabral) on 29 July–1 August, the National Revolutionary Movement from the Congo on 6 September, the Socialist Party of Japan on 20 October, and the Swedish Social Democratic Labor Party on 23 November.

Relations on a government level with countries of Europe and Asia were also strengthened "in the spirit of the Bucharest Declaration" and in the spirit of the Rumanian emphasis on the important role of small states in promoting international *détente*. As noted by Nicolae Ceauşescu in his speech of 24 July to the National Assembly:

The facts do show that the solution of international conflicts can no longer be decided by the big powers alone; in our day such a solution depends on the active cooperation of all the states of the world. Acting with energy and militancy in defense of their legitimate interests and rights, medium-sized and small countries can play a notable part in international life; they can influence the evolution of events to a considerable degree and thus contribute to the safeguarding of peace and security in the world.

On 5 January Rumania established consular relations with Spain in an agreement which marked the Franco regime's first exchange of official representatives with an East European communist regime. On 3 April Rumania established diplomatic relations with Canada, and later in the year announced its intention to establish diplomatic relations with the Ivory Coast. In February 1967 Rumanian Chairman of the State Council Chivu Stoica visited Tunisia and Somalia in an effort to promote relations with African states. Stoica also traveled to Iran on 13–19 May. Rumanian Foreign Minister Mănescu visited Belgium on 6–10 February and Pakistan, Singapore, and Japan from 22 May to 7 June. Premier Ion Gheorghe Maurer visited Holland on 17–21 July, the United States, and France, and reportedly traveled to Peking and Hanoi.

**Publications.** The daily central organ of the RCP is *Scînteia*; the theoretical monthly of the party is *Lupta de Clasă*.

# SAN MARINO

The Communist Party of San Marino (Partito Comunista di San Marino; PCSM) was found in 1922. Though nominally independent (and represented as such at communist party congresses and international meetings), the PCSM in an offshoot of the Italian Communist Party (Partito Comunista Italiano; PCI). In the September 1964 elections for San Marino's sixty-member legislative body (Grand Council), the PCSM obtained 14 seats out of 60. The second-strongest San Marino political party, it stands in opposition to the governing coalition of Christian Democrats (the strongest single party) and Social Democrats, who have 29 and 10 seats respectively. The Socialist Party in San Marino (unlike its counterpart in Italy) has not joined up with the Social Democrats and continues to cooperate with the PCSM on a number of issues. The Socialists have six seats in the Grand Council. The PCSM has an estimated 900 members. Its youth federation has 200 members. The population of San Marino is 18,000 (estimated 1966).

**Organization and Leadership.** The PCSM is directed by a seventeen-member Central Committee, from which a ten-member executive body is chosen. The Secretary-General of the party is Ermenegildo Gasperoni.

**Domestic Views and Policies.** The domestic policy of the PCSM follows closely that of the PCI, at whose Eleventh Congress (January 1966) Gasperoni declared: "This congress ... is followed with great interest by the workers and communists of San Marino in consideration of the fact that your ideological, political, and social battles are battles which, in substance, concern also our party and people" (*Foreign Bulletin of the PCI,* special number, April 1966).

During the course of 1967 the party continued to campaign against what it termed as Italian "tutelage" of San Marino, emphasizing the need for "respect of San Marino's sovereign rights" which would "facilitate its economic, political, social and cultural progress." Like its counterpart in Italy, the PCSM stressed the value of dialogue with Catholics, who, following the Second Vatican Council, had been "freed from the fear of excommunication for political activity." The party also reiterated its advocation of Communist-Socialist unity, which would be the "backbone" of a "broad alliance of democratic forces for a democratic alternative to the present government coalition."

**International Views and Policies.** As in the case of domestic policy, the PCSM's views on international issues mirror those of the PCI. The party was represented at the celebrations of the fiftieth anniversary of the October Revolution in the Soviet Union by Ermenegildo Gasperoni, who also represented the PCSM at the conference of communist and workers' parties of Europe in Karlovy Vary (24-26 April).

**Publications.** The PCSM publishes an irregular newspaper, *La Scintilla.*

# SINGAPORE

The Communist movement in Singapore is theoretically an integral part of the Communist Party of Malaya (CPM), whose headquarters and leaders are located in southern Thailand (see *Malaysia*). It has, however, always retained a certain degree of independence, which has been considerably enhanced by the reduction of the CPM to a group of jungle guerrillas and the separation of Singapore from the Federation of Malaysia in 1965. In view of Singapore's predominantly Chinese population (some 75 per cent), which in many respects identifies itself with the achievements of mainland China, distinction between communist groups and others with similar aims and sympathies is blurred. Hard-core communist party membership in Singapore is estimated at 200. The population of Singapore is 1,914,000 (estimated mid-1966).

**Organization and Leadership**. Being illegal in Singapore, communist activity there has been of a twofold nature: underground and through selected front organizations and parties. Communist clandestine organization is difficult to delineate, as the communists' strict adherence to a policy of virtual elimination of all records and files and the replacement of party organs by "front publications" has enhanced the organization's anonymity. In 1963, the Malaysian Minister of Internal Security acknowledged the existence of a "well-established network of underground cadres in Singapore" (*Straits Times*, Singapore, 4 November 1963). Reports indicated that this network was directed by underground headquarters in the nearby Indonesian Rhio Islands. However, the effects of the abortive communist coup in Indonesia on 30 September 1965 have almost certainly hampered the Singapore communists; the extent, however, is not known.

Leadership of the clandestine movement appears to be split into at least two contending factions. One is identified with Lim Chin Siong,* a prominent Communist and Secretary-General of the Barisan Sosialis front party before his arrest in 1963, who is believed to favor the Soviet Union's "peaceful coexistence" line and is said to have declared that "armed revolution in Singapore has no future" (*Straits Times*, 8 December 1965). Another faction, founded in 1962 as the "Singapore Town Committee of the Communist Party of Malaya" and subsequently known as the People's Revolutionary Party (PRP) advocates violence. The Secretary-General and leader of the PRP was Sim Siew Lin.** Since the PRP's abortive plot to assassinate Singapore ministers and officials (exposed on 26 August 1965), this faction's organizational structure appears to have been completely disrupted.

**Front Organizations**. Singapore communists operate aboveground principally through a front party, the Barisan Sosialis (Socialist Front), founded in 1961 by former members of the People's Action Party (PAP) under the leadership of Lim Chin Siong. The Barisan Sosialis is made up of communists, communist sympathizers, and dissident extremists who left the PAP. Reports indicate that Lim is the "most prominent communist" in Singapore and that he has become "Chen Ping's plenipotentiary and the operating head of the CPM." In the September 1963 elections the Barisan Sosialis polled 33 per cent of the vote, compared to 47 per cent for Prime Minister Lee Kuan Yew's PAP. Since then, support for the Barisan Sosialis has steadily diminished. A split occurred in 1964 between those disagreeing with the Party's "extraparliamentary struggle," those disapproving of the leadership's dogmatic hard-line in the handling of various internal disputes and of the disciplinary action taken against dissenters, and those advocating that the Barisan Sosialis follow more closely the CPM's policy of revolutionary struggle.

*Although Lim Chin Siong has been detained since 1963, he still holds the position, *in absentia*, of Secretary-General of the Barisan Sosialis.

**Sim Siew Lin was released from detention on 25 September 1967, having renounced his previous connection with the CPM.

A year later, the secession of Singapore from the Federation of Malaysia was denounced by the Chairman of the Barisan Sosialis, Dr. Lee Siew Choh, as "another imperialist plot" (Reuter, 9 August 1965), while it was welcomed by trade unions under Barisan Sosialis control (some 30 out of a total of more than 100). Lee Siew Choh's decision to boycott Singapore's Parliamentary sessions divided the party even further (*Straits Times,* 8 December 1966). Four members of Parliament, Kow Kee Seng, Chio Cheng Thun, S. T. Bani, and the Barisan Sosialis leader in Parliament, Lim Huan Boon, were expelled from the party for refusing to follow party directives. Lim Huan Boon declared that many of the Barisan Sosialis's rank-and-file supporters did not accept the "ridiculous thesis" that Singapore's independence was "phony," and added: "The Barisan Sosialis is not interested in working constructively for the good of our people and our country" (*Straits Times,* 6 January 1966). Two of those expelled, Kow Kee Seng and Chio Cheng Thun, are believed to have the backing of 22 of the party's trade unions.

By October 1966 all Barisan members of Parliament had resigned from that body, leaving in it only representatives of the governing PAP. Two members did not fulfill the necessary legal requirements for resignation, and although the government does not officially recognize their resignation, neither of them attends Parliament. In March 1967 by-elections were held for the other vacant seats, with PAP candidates victorious in all districts. For all practical purposes, therefore, the PAP has been the only party represented in Parliament since October 1966.

In declarations to the press Lee Siew Choh reiterated that "as a responsible constitutional party" the Barisan Sosialis had a "duty and responsibility to expose the imperialist and reactionary deceptions and to educate the people and raise their political consciousness." He claimed that Lee Kuan Yew was in league with the "colonialists, imperialists, and fascists" and that secession was part of an "Anglo-American imperialist plot," to which he also attributed the defeat of the Indonesian Communist Party. He advocated a "genuinely independent, democratic, united Malaya, including Singapore." (*Far Eastern Economic Review,* 20 October 1966, p. 123.) Lee Siew Choh did not explain how, without the support of trade unions and with no Parliamentary representation, he intended to further his policy.

Although the Barisan Sosialis has denied any links with the communists, Ong Chang San, a former Singapore assemblyman and the Organizing Secretary of the Barisan Sosialis, declared on 1 April 1967, after being released from five months' detention, that he had been approached by leading officials of the Barisan Sosialis who urged him to start an underground organization to subvert the government. According to Ong Chang San, the officials had been, and still were, corresponding with "well-known Communists overseas," as well as Communists under detention, with the result that Barisan Sosialis policies were "being determined by communist interests rather than Singapore's interests." (Singapore Domestic Service, 1 April 1967.)

The Ra'ayat Party, an insignificant extreme left-wing party, has cooperated with the Barisan Sosialis on various occasions, and additional communist support has come from a number of left-wing trade unions associated with the Barisan Sosialis. By banning several trade unions which were engaged in illegal strikes and by encouraging union members to leave those unions which were known to be procommunist, the government has sought to reduce the influence of left-wing unions and to establish new unions in the pro-government National Trade Union Congress (NTUC). According to a government report issued in July 1967, the NTUC consists of 61 affiliate unions, with some 150,000 members, as compared with 30 affiliate left-wing unions having a membership of 28,000. Reports also indicate that both the number of left wing unions and the membership of the remaining unions have continued to decline.

A further principal source of communist support originated in one of Singapore's two universities, Nanyang University, which has a student body of about 2,100. A white paper issued by the Malaysian government claimed that communist control and influence extended from the "Singapore Chinese Middle School Students' Union to the Nanyang University Students' Union and on to the Guild of Nanyang University Graduates," whose leadership was said to be "dominated by the underground Communist Party of Malaya" (*Communism in Nanyang University,* Kuala Lumpur, 1964). Since 1965, communist influence at Nanyang University has declined, partly as a result of government pressure but also as a result of constructive reforms within the University.

**Domestic and International Activities.** Several factors make it difficult to ascertain present communist policy: the splits within the underground movement and the Barisan Sosialis party; the trade unions' realization that the Singapore economy is to a certain extent dependent on the British military presence; and the overtures by the Singapore government to the Soviet Union, North Korea, and East Europe. Without adopting any specific directives, communist efforts in Singapore appear to be limited to the fomenting of sporadic riots and demonstrations. Communist activities in Singapore during 1967 were marked by the failure of both a general strike called in April and a march on the City Hall in June in protest against the deregistration of three trade unions. Communist activities since April have been primarily restricted to small-scale demonstrations carried out simultaneously in various parts of the city. In contrast with the situation in Malaysia, the devaluation of the old Straits dollar—but not the new Singapore dollar—as a result of the devaluation of the British pound sterling did not result in any demonstrations in Singapore.

On 12 March the Barisan Sosialis held its Second Congress, which adopted the party's political report, elected a new Central Committee, and unanimously adopted 15 resolutions. A press statement released by the Barisan Sosialis declared: "It was a successful congress of unity and struggle. There was complete unanimity of views among the party delegates on all vital issues confronting the party." As announced by the party, the new Central Committee consists of Lee Siew Choh, Chairman; See Cheng Kiong, Vice-Chairman; Lim Chin Siong (under detention), Secretary-General; Koo Yung, Assistant Secretary-General (later detained); Taycheng Kang, Treasurer; Chai Kuen Fak, Assistant Treasurer; and Fong Swee Suan (under detention), Lim Hock Siew (under detention), Poh Soo Kai (under detention), Yang Ya Wu, Chang Tek Suen, Chen Ru Pen, Liang Li Ing, Li Chen Min, and Hsieh Chin Chen, members of the Central Executive Committee.

The resolutions adopted by the Congress condemned "Soviet-American collaboration" and called for active mass struggle. Specifically, the resolutions called for: release of all political detainees; condemnation of all "enemy collaborators"; opposition to the "divide and rule" tactics of the "imperialists"; promotion of a Malayan consciousness; protection of all Malayan languages as equal and "official"; an end to the "societies act" and "national service bill" created by the "US-British imperialists"; support of the "workers' struggle"; and support of the "students' struggle." The resolutions also condemned Malaysia:

> [This] neocolonialist creation of the US-British imperialists [was] imposed on the people against their will and intended to frustrate the national liberation struggles of the people of Malaya (including Singapore) and North Borneo (Kalimantan Utara) through unite-and-rule. To save "Malaysia" from total collapse and to revert to divide and rule, the US-British imperialists, with the active collaboration of their Rahman-Lee puppets, arranged the so-called "separation" of Singapore from "Malaysia" and created the "phony independence of Singapore."

The Barisan Sosialis stressed the need to "continue. . .resolute struggle to crush 'Malaysia,' oppose the bogus 'Republic of Singapore,' get rid of the US-British imperialists and their Rahman-Lee puppets, and form a genuinely united, independent, democratic Malaya (including Singapore)." Commenting on tactics to be used, the resolutions stated:

> We fully support the correct policies and correct line of struggle which are being carried out by the party. We fully support the boycott of elections, the resignation of Barisan M.P.'s from the "Singapore Parliament," and the emphasis on extra-parliamentary mass struggles for the basic democratic rights of the people of Malaya. We call on the people to cast away all illusions about the bogus "parliamentary democracy" and the bogus "parliamentary election" of the reactionaries and unite to struggle for the eight conditions put forward by the party for the holding of genuinely democratic elections in the context of a unified Malaya so that the people may truly elect a government of their own choice.

Rumors of a split within the Barisan Sosialis—between those favoring "Red Guard"-style activities and demonstrations and those favoring more covert methods in order to increase tensions which could then be exploited by the party—were apparently confirmed by a resolution noting the need to "sharpen vigilance against black gang and enemy agents":

We strongly condemn the black gang, including Lin Chao Nan, Pang Siew Foo (alias Pang Siew Fong), Chiang Lian Kuang, Ho Ta Hai, and others who vainly attempt to use the language issue to spread confusion among the party and leftwing unions and split the unity of the leftwing movement.

We also strongly condemn the black gang (including Lee Sit Chuan, Chang Sheng Lai, Lee Chao Lai, and others) who vainly attempt to use the "student movement publication" to confuse, mislead, and split the student movement and indeed the whole leftwing in Malaya. Both these black gangs, in carrying out their antiparty antileftwing, antisocialism, antipeople activities, have waved the red flag to oppose the red flag. They form part of the imperialist attempt to sabotage and destroy the national liberation struggle of the people of Malaya, including Singapore.

We call on the people to maintain sharp vigilance against these enemy agents and freaks and monsters and resolutely carry out sharp ideological struggles against the spurious arguments and the right opportunist line put forward by them.

In international affairs, the Barisan Sosialis resolutions condemned the "anticommunist campaign in Indonesia" and declared the party's "full support of the Vietnamese people in their heroic struggle against US imperialist aggression and for national salvation," adding: "Soviet revisionist leaders' support for the US-British imperialists and their puppets has only further exposed the reactionary nature of all of them. In betraying the struggles of all the heroic peoples, the Soviet revisionist leaders will certainly come to no good end." The party concluded its series of resolutions thus:

The Soviet revisionists, the black gang, enemy agents, freaks and monsters have repeatedly but vainly tried to confuse and mislead the people with wrong slogans, wrong arguments, and the wrong line (right opportunist) of struggle to paralyze their will and determination, and to sabotage their struggle for national liberation. We call on the people to maintain sharp vigilance against new enemy attacks, either open or hidden, always criticize and repudiate the wrong slogans, arguments, viewpoints, as well as the right opportunist line of struggle put forward by freaks and monsters; and constantly study, carry out, propagate, and defend the viewpoints and the correct line of struggle so as to speed up the victory of the Malayan people's struggles for national liberation.

Because the Communist Party of Malaya stresses that its area includes Singapore, no representatives of the Singapore communist movement as such attended any international meetings or party congresses. Communist front leaders have always represented themselves as delegates from a "Malayan" organization.

**Publications.** The underground communist movement has no official publication. Procommunist publications, however, include Chern Shien Pau and Plebian, weekly organs of the Barisan Sosialis, and Rakyat, also put out by the Barisan Sosialis. Procommunist statements are also carried by New Youth and by the Malayan Monitor and General News, a mimeographed monthly which is published in London.

# SOUTH AFRICA

The Communist Party of South Africa, founded in 1921, was the first communist party to be formed on the African continent. The party announced its own dissolution a few days before it was outlawed in 1950. It was reconstituted as the South African Communist Party (SACP) in 1953, and reorganized to enable it to operate under illegal conditions.

The SACP is banned by the Suppression of Communism Act of 1950, and its leaders are in prison or exile. Party members and sympathizers as well as persons whom the government believes to be communists are subject to prosecution. Among those imprisoned is Abram Fischer, an Afrikaner lawyer and one of the leading members of the SACP, whose trial in 1966 aroused the interest of the world press. Communist sources declared that Fischer was active in building an underground party and was acting chairman of the SACP Central Committee at the time of his arrest (*World Marxist Review,* October 1966). In 1967 Fischer was awarded the Lenin Peace Prize.

The government's suppression of the SACP has been thorough, and the party's cadres appear to have been fairly effectively disrupted. Active SACP membership probably does not exceed a few hundred out of a total South African population of 18,296,000 (estimated 1966). The party continues to publish a quarterly journal from London. The party Chairman is John B. Marks, who is in exile.

The SACP has attempted to increase its influence in South Africa by linking up with the anti-apartheid cause in the so-called congress movements, and has been particularly successful in the African National Congress (ANC). Party Chairman John Marks is a member of the ANC Executive Committee, and Communists hold other leading posts in the ANC. (The leader of the ANC, Chief Luthuli, who died in July 1967, was not a communist, but supported the SACP participation in the ANC on grounds that unity of the opposition was more important than any ideological differences.) The ANC was banned in 1960 and its members made subject to prosecution under the Suppression of Communism Act. Other organizations which are partners in the Congress Alliance with the ANC and are endorsed by the SACP include the South African Indian Congress, the Coloured People's Congress, the Congress of Democrats, and the South African Congress of Trade Unions (SACTU). The SACTU is an affiliate of the Afro-Asian Trade Union Federation and the Communist-controlled World Federation of Trade Unions. Although these organizations are technically legal, the SACP charges that "with thousands of members jailed and all known officials subjected to bans, house arrest and surveillance, the formal 'legality' [of these organizations] has been reduced to a farce" (*The African Communist,* No. 29, 1967).

The SACP program, entitled "The Road to South African Freedom," was adopted at its Sixth Congress, in 1962. The program calls for a united front of all progressive forces, struggling for national freedom and the destruction of colonialism, as the key to the future advance toward socialism and to laying the foundations for a classless, communist society.

The creation of a "national democracy" in South Africa, according to the party program, is in the interest of the African people, the other nonwhite groups, and the white workers, middle class, and professional groups, "to whom the establishment of genuine democracy and the elimination of fascism and monopoly rule offers the only prospect of a decent and stable future."

The SACP's program at the present stage of "national revolution" is defined in the "Freedom Charter," which was formulated by the ANC and the other partners in the Congress Alliance in 1955 and to which the SACP has declared its "unqualified support." Although not a program for socialism, the Freedom Charter has some socialist characteristics in its calls for profound economic and social changes, including agrarian reform and nationalization of key industries.

The SACP rejects the possibility of a nonviolent national democratic revolution, declaring that the Vorster regime has left no alternative to armed struggle (in addition to other forms of mass struggle). In its 1962 program the SACP declared:

> The Communist Party considers that the slogan of "nonviolence" is harmful to the cause of the democratic national revolution in the new phase of the struggle, disarming the people in the face of the savage assaults of the oppressor, dampening their militancy, undermining their confidence in their leaders. At the same time, the Party opposes undisciplined acts of individual terror. It rejects theories that all nonviolent methods of struggle are useless or impossible, and will continue to advocate and work for the use of all forms of struggle by the people, including noncollaboration, strikes, boycotts, and demonstrations.

In 1967 the Central Committee of the SACP passed a resolution elaborating on and bringing up to date the party program. The resolution called for the opening of a new front of struggle: "the beginning of guerrilla actions by armed and trained freedom-fighters, backed by revolutionary struggles of the masses of workers and peasants, against the white supremacy state." The resolution emphasized the building and strengthening of the ANC, the SACTU, and the other organizations in the Congress Alliance and reaffirmed the party's support for the Freedom Charter, professing "unqualified readiness to cooperate in measures of united and coordinated action for the achievement of the aims of the Charter." At the same time, the SACP emphasized the necessity of strengthening its own organization:

> The Central Committee points out that the strengthening of the independent organization of the Party itself is a vital and indispensable task of every member. There can be no conflict between these two tasks, for experience has fully demonstrated that the stronger our Party is and the higher the level of consciousness and activity of its members, the greater the contribution we shall be able to make to the common cause.

The SACP called for more effective party work, a drive to recruit new members, the promotion of the party organ, and the establishment of "*African Communist* study circles," both to "strengthen the journal and to act as centers of Marxist-Leninist theory and practice." (*The African Communist,* no. 29, 1967.)

In accordance with its espousal of violent revolution and guerrilla warfare, the SACP gave its full support to the military detachment of the ANC, the Umkhonto we Sizwe (Spear of the Nation). In August 1967 the forces of the Umkhonto we Sizwe and those of the Zimbabwe African People's Union (ZAPU), which had been fighting separately in Rhodesia, joined forces and attempted to infiltrate guerrilla fighters into Rhodesia from bases in Zambia. A joint statement of the ANC and ZAPU, dated 19 August, stated:

> ... As comrades-in-arms, we are facing a common enemy, fighting a common purpose, facing a common fate. Hence, a combined force for a common onslaught against the enemy at every point of encounter as we march down for the liberation of our respective countries (*The African Communist,* no. 31, 1967).

Noting that neither armed struggle nor the concept of an alliance of liberation forces is new to Africa, the SACP declared that the ANC-ZAPU alliance was especially significant because it was "sealed in a bond of brotherhood on the battlefield" and because "above all. . .it is boldly directed against the main bastion of white supremacy and colonialism in Africa" (*ibid.*). (In response to the union of guerrilla forces, Rhodesian and South African police joined to eliminate the partisan units who had succeeded in making their way south of the Zambezi.)

The SACP continued in 1967 its scathing denunciations of the "racist" and "fascist" Vorster regime, conditions in the Transkei (the test case of "separate development" for the Bantustans), South African "imperialism" against its southern African neighbors (especially with reference to the appointment of South African "advisers" to the Lesotho government), the granting of South African aid to Malawi, and the extension of the policy of apartheid into South-West Africa. Campaigning against what it calls the "Bonn-Pretoria axis" and charging West Germany with being a "secret ally of the South African fascists," the SACP pointed to alleged German-South African collaboration in the development of toxic gases to be used for "South African defense," the growth of West German investments in South Africa, and alleged secret military agreements between Portugal, South Africa, West Germany, and Rhodesia (*ibid.*).

**Foreign Policy.** The SACP condemned in strongest terms the American involvement in Vietnam, describing it as a "war of extermination—the most savage in human history, not excluding Hitler's war." The SACP has declared its "admiration, confidence and love" for the Vietnamese people, who, "like all victims of imperialism," were "fighting not only for their own freedom and future but also for [that of the] South Africans." (*Ibid.*, no. 28, 1967.)

The SACP also declared its complete solidarity with the Arab cause in the Middle East conflict of June 1967. In an editorial in *The African Communist* (no. 30) the SACP declared that the Israeli "aggression" had been planned far in advance and was in the service of imperialism, which wished to overthrow "progressive regimes in the Middle East" and to "secure the territorial aggrandisement of Israel and the return to colonialism – or ruthless expropriation – of Arab populations." The SACP also drew attention to weaknesses within the Arab states, such as lack of unity and declarations of "racialist policies," and warned against "confounding hatred of oppressors with racialism."

**The International Communist Movement.** The SACP is closely aligned with the CPSU in the international communist movement. It views as "lamentable" the "breakaway of the leadership of the Communist Party of China from the principles of proletarian internationalism and Marxism-Leninism." (*WMR*, September 1967.) In a resolution on the events in China, the SACP expressed its "gravest anxiety" over the Chinese campaign of "vilification" of the Soviet leaders, the campaign of "irrational glorification of a single person," and the absence of "socialist legality" in China, and went on to accuse the Chinese leaders of endangering the gains of the Chinese Revolution and of weakening the anti-imperialist front: "To a large extent these wrong policies have already been responsible for unnecessary setbacks and reverses. The imperialists have been emboldened and encouraged by the division within the socialist camp to intensify their counterrevolutionary offensive from Vietnam and Indochina to the Congo and Ghana." (*The African Communist*, no. 29, 1967.)

The SACP also issued a statement on the world situation noting a "world-wide counterrevolutionary offensive of imperialism" which "coincides with a relative weakening of the unity of forces for peace and progress, especially of the unity of the socialist countries." Mentioning the "disruptive tactics" of the Mao group in China, the statement declared: "The SACP strongly favors a new meeting of the Marxist-Leninist parties of the world at the earliest possible time to rally and unite the anti-imperialist forces and to face urgent problems posed by the present international situation."

The SACP presented a three-point agenda for the international conference:
(1) US aggression in Vietnam.
(2) The counterrevolutionary offensive of imperialism on a world scale—particularly the attempt to recolonize Africa.
(3) The need for unity of all anti-imperialist forces, to be led by the communist vanguard. (*Ibid.*)

Contacts between the SACP and other communist parties were limited. The SACP sent only messages of greetings to the French Communist Party and the Communist Party of Great Britain on the occasion of their respective Congresses. (The ANC representative in the United Kingdom attended the Thirtieth National Congress of the Communist Party of Great Britain in November.) The SACP was represented, however, at the celebrations of the fiftieth anniversary of the October Revolution, at Moscow in November, sending John Marks, and the ANC was represented by its deputy president Oliver Tambo. A delegation of the Central Committee of the SACP visited East Germany on 15-20 November and had talks with representatives of the Socialist Unity Party. The two sides agreed that the time was now ripe for preparing and holding a world conference of communist parties. The communique also noted the "more and more alarming details about the economic, political and military collaboration between Bonn and Pretoria" and emphasized the necessity for exposing this "conspiracy"—which it said was "being hatched with the help of US imperialism"—through the "unity of all anti-imperialist forces." (*Ibid.*, no. 32.)

There is no organized pro-Chinese communist party in South Africa, but support for the Chinese communist position does come from the Pan-Africanist Congress of Azania (formerly the Pan-Africanist Congress of South Africa, a militant black-nationalist breakaway movement from the ANC). Excluded, together with eight African nationalist organizations, from the communist-sponsored Cairo seminar in October 1966 on "Africa—National and Socialist Revolution," the Pan-Africanist Congress subsequently signed a joint statement condemning the seminar as a "revisionist" plot to suppress revolution in Africa. The SACP published a statement in turn declaring that the Pan-Africanist leaders had "merely appended their signatures to a document prepared elsewhere [evidenced by the fact that it is] full of the hackneyed formulas and swear-words used as a substitute for argument by the Maoist faction which is today wreaking such tragic damage in China itself and throughout the Communist and anti-imperialist world" (*ibid.,* no. 28). The Pan-Africanist Congress is said to be armed with Chinese weapons.

**Publications.** The SACP organ is *The African Communist.* A notice on the inner title-page of each issue states: "[This magazine is] published quarterly in the interests of African solidarity and as a forum for Marxist-Leninist thought throughout our Continent, by the South African Communist Party."

# SPAIN

The Communist Party of Spain (Partido Comunista de España; PCE) was founded 7 November 1921, and has been illegal since 1939. Criminal penalties are provided both for membership in the party and for participation in political activities sponsored by it. Despite vigorous government enforcement of the ban on the party, the PCE maintains an active underground apparatus within Spain.

Western sources commonly estimate PCE membership at 5,000. The population of Spain is 32,140,000 (July 1967 estimate). PCE members are drawn mainly from among urban intellectuals and manual workers, especially in Madrid, Barcelona, and Bilbao, and from among exiles living in France, especially in Paris and Toulouse. PCE activities are illegal in France, but the prohibition is not rigorously enforced.

Besides the PCE, there are two small splinter groups having altogether perhaps several hundred members and both calling themselves the Communist Party of Spain (Marxist-Leninist). They espouse an extreme revolutionary line and advocate violent overthrow of the Franco government. In addition there is a regional communist party, the Socialist Unity Party of Catalonia. In late 1967, reportedly, this party split away from the leadership of the parent PCE which then set up a group known as the Catalan Communist Party. (*Unir-Débat, pour le Socialisme,* Paris, 10 February 1968). (See below.)

**Organization and Leadership.** The exile leadership of the PCE resides in Moscow, Eastern Europe (particularly in Prague), and in France. PCE Chairman is the elderly Dolores Ibarruri ("La Pasionaria" of civil war days), who lives in Moscow; the Secretary-General, Santiago Carrillo, lives in Paris. Carrillo directs an apparatus that includes the Executive Committee of the Central Committee (which often speaks in the name of the party itself); the Central Committee; provincial committees; various intermediate-level committees below the provincial level; and finally, party cells and party groups. The Executive Committee includes López Raimondo, Horacio Inguanzo, Enrique Lister, Juan Gómez, José Moix, Ignacio Gallego, Santiago Álvarez, and Francisco Gutiérrez.

**Domestic Views and Activities.** Under conditions of growing tension between the regime under General Francisco Franco and such elements of the Spanish population as workers, students, professionals and intellectuals, and liberal clergy, the PCE has sought in recent years to maximize its influence and popularity by participating in a broad range of antigovernment causes and activities. In 1967 the party sought in particular to profit from the unpopularity of the attempts by the regime to retreat, in part, from the very limited liberal reforms approved in the "organic law" which was ratified by popular vote on 14 December 1966. Government suppression of student and labor demonstrations throughout the year; restrictive interpretations of the "press law"; a Supreme Court decision on 12 December banning all strikes; a decree law suspending constitutional rights in the Basque province of Vizcaya in April—all these provided occasions for the PCE to associate itself with popular antigovernment causes.

The PCE does not, however, condemn the regime in toto as consisting of irreconcilable enemies of the people. The party makes a distinction between the "ultras" within the regime (including Franco, Alonso de Vega, Manuel Fraga Iribarne, and José Solis Ruiz), who are seen as bent on maintaining a tight, antipopular dictatorship whatever the cost, and the "evolutionists," who are considered to be willing, if only in the face of. overwhelming popular pressure, to make some concessions in the direction of civil liberties and popular control of the government. The ultras themselves, however, must, in the PCE view, be forced to relinquish their rule completely, presumably after Franco's death. The mitigation of the harshness of the dictatorial rule of Franco in recent years is seen by the PCE as essentially the result of pressure from below, an achievement "brought about by the Spanish people—and first of all by the working class."

At the theoretical level, PCE optimism over the prospects for peaceful political change in a democratic direction is grounded in the opinion that the ultra faction is becoming progressively isolated, not only from the Spanish people at large, but also from elements within the National Movement (formerly known as the Falange) itself, and most importantly, from the class interests of the Spanish bourgeoisie. This argument was set forth in detail in an important PCE Executive Committee "Political Statement" published in April in the party organ *Mundo Obrero* (also in *L'Humanité,* Paris, 10 April, and *IB,* no. 102, 1967). Referring to the regime's suppression of the widespread labor and student unrest during the first quarter of 1967, the statement declared:

> The new onset of the ultras is no longer directed against the labor and democratic opposition alone but affects the "evolutionists" as well. The regime is beginning to devour itself.
>
> At bottom, the reason for the ultras' attempt to fall back on a tough policy is that their positions have been shaken so badly that another retreat could result in their being forced out altogether.
>
> On the one hand, the labor and democratic movement has already achieved such a degree of unity, organization and militancy that the ultras are finding it more and more difficult to stay in power. On the other hand, the hegemony of the ultra team in the ruling set-up no longer meets the interests of the big bourgeoisie to the full and is losing support among the middle bourgeoisie. (*IB,* no. 102.)

This analysis gains in strength, in the PCE view, as Spain's economy continues to retreat from the pace of its rapid growth during the early 1960's; fears of economic recession and of unemployment, and continuing inflation (resulting in the devaluation of the *peseta* in November), are seen as progressively weakening the position of the ultras.

In keeping with these views, the PCE is attempting to implement a broadly based recruiting policy aimed at promoting its development into a mass party rather than a "vanguard" party. The growing unpopularity of the regime is seen as the important factor creating favorable conditions for the growth of a mass party.

An article by Eduardo García, "Concerning an Authentic Policy of Recruitment," in *Nuestra Bandera* (no. 53, 1967) called for a more aggressive policy and observed: "Recruiting possibilities occur primarily in the new worker movement and among the liaison groups and enterprise boards that were elected recently [within the official labor unions]." The article also put heavy emphasis on the point that Catholics could be admitted to the party:

> It seems necessary for us to insist on the possibility that those Catholics who accept our policy and our rules of organization can be members of the party. This is very important in Spain, especially with regard to women . . . [Catholics] must be admitted without any kind of reservations, under equal conditions with the other members.

Regarding the organizational problems involved in building a mass, yet illegal, party, García noted: "In a country under a dictatorship and in which the party's organization is persecuted, the mass nature cannot be achieved within very strict and narrow organizational limits. On the contrary, it is absolutely necessary to resort to different and original forms of organization and of coordination of all the possible forces of the party."

In this vein, the exile leadership issued numerous statements throughout the year eschewing exclusive reliance upon clandestine organizations and urging party workers to participate extensively in open organizations among young persons, women, students, and professionals and intellectuals. An Executive Committee resolution broadcast 26 September over Radio Independent Spain called for the strengthening of the Spanish Union of Communist Youth, especially in small towns and rural areas. The resolution also called for more propaganda work within the armed forces, describing its objective as: "to contribute effectively to the enlightenment of the masses of soldiers, of the noncommissioned officers and, in the best of cases, of officers, so that they will understand the righteousness of the struggle of the people for freedom and democracy and so that the army, instead of propping up the oppressive regime, will adopt an ever more decisive position in favor of the hopes of the majority of Spaniards."

Thus, organizationally as well as politically the party is attempting to integrate itself into the broad anti-Franco movement. Said García in his article: "We are thinking about the need for coordinating and articulating the work of the Communists with simple forms that sometimes are rudimentary, around groups of comrades who are more aware and who, without being yet a party committee, gradually go on acquiring the nature of one, without forcing things, step by step." The basic aim, in other words, is to enable potential recruits to join the party "in an almost natural manner and without great changes in their way of life."

Such a recruitment policy implies definite ground rules for the PCE's political posture and program, confining the party to advocacy of "peaceful transition" to socialism by democratic means. Only such a policy can have sufficiently broad appeal and not demand drastic changes in the life of potential party recruits. Regarding the central issue of Spanish politics—the nature of the regime after Franco—the PCE thus declares its willingness even to accept a restoration of the monarchy and insists only that any regime, monarchical or otherwise, be ratified by a duly elected constituent assembly. In its April "Political Statement" the PCE Executive Committee stated the party's position regarding the political future of Spain as follows:

> The Communist Party considers that all opposition forces and all "evolutionists" should promptly meet at the conference table to discuss ways and means of solving the political problem of Spain without recourse to violence and civil war.
>
> The fundamental thing today is to introduce democratic freedoms for all Spaniards. We Communists are willing to cooperate, even without participating in it, with a transitional government that would implement, loyally and without reservations, the program set out in the recent document signed by 565 intellectuals of the most diverse ideological trends. The program provides for the following:
>
> —releasing all prisoners and reinstating them—as well as all victims of repressions—at their work places of educational establishments;
>
> —higher wages and salaries, and a sliding wage scale;
>
> —freedom of trade unions, and the right to strike;
>
> —freedom of assembly and speech;
>
> —political freedoms;
>
> —an amnesty for political prisoners and exiles.

The party affirmed, on the occasion of the Fiftieth Anniversary of the October Revolution, that this adherence to a line of peaceful transition to socialism was fully Leninist. According to the party's statement commemorating the October Revolution (broadcast 3 October over Radio Independent Spain), "nonviolent revolutionary change" is fully in accord with Leninism as practiced by Lenin himself during the revolution. "Until a few days before the uprisings of 7 November," said the statement, "Lenin was trying to make use of every opportunity to carry out a nonviolent revolution, although in those days such opportunities were very small. But in today's Spanish circumstances, we consider that there is a much greater chance for the revolutionary process of our country to be led into a nonviolent channel which will avoid civil war."

The party leadership is often criticized for this policy, not only by the more militantly revolutionary splinter groups, but also by elements within the parent party itself. Tensions are evident between the exile leadership and some of the party's clandestine workers within Spain. Direct and indirect reference was made to the intraparty dissension over its general line by the official organs of the PCE during the year, but the correctness of the general line of "national reconciliation," with which Secretary-General Carrillo is most closely identified, was reaffirmed on numerous occasions. A *Mundo Obrero* article in October, reviewing Carrillo's book *New Views on Problems of the Day,* argued that the ultrarevolutionary line advocated by "some comrades" totally contravened "the reality of Spain" and would transform the party "into a group of loud-mouthed and inflamed men gesticulating in a vacuum." *Mundo Obrero* acknowledged with regard to the line advocated by Carrillo, that "this is not a communist program," but said: "The great majority of Spanish people accept it. Is this a change from our previous policy? Not at all: it is the achievement of the party policy under the present conditions."

The PCE saw the results of the 10 October popular elections for a fifth of the seats in the Cortes (parliament) as a setback for the ultras and a vindication of PCE policy. A PCE statement broadcast over Radio Independent Spain on 21 October claimed that the call by anti-Franco forces, including the PCE, for a boycott of the elections had been heeded. Noting the government's claim that 74 per cent of the electorate took part in the elections, the PCE remarked that this figure implied 6 million abstentions; further, the party charged that widespread vote frauds were used to attain the 74 per cent figure, and that in fact a majority of the Spanish voters had abstained. The statement claimed that "The defeat of the ultras and bureaucrats of the Falange, which this action of 10 October represents, was possible thanks to the convergence of the positions of the Communist Party and of the other opposition forces with the evolutionist sectors. . . . This convergence goes to confirm the justness of the position taken by the Communist Party on the referendum."

Near the close of the year, in a statement released on 16 December, the PCE Executive Committee surveyed recent developments in Spain and claimed that events were bearing out the correctness of the party's policy and had shown that long-term collaboration between communist and Catholic forces, as well as "other socialist and democratic sectors," was feasible. The statement reiterated the PCE minimum program for agreement on a future political alternative for Spain:

> The Communist Party considers that any agreement on the political alternative will have to be based on the following three points: the restoration of political rights without discrimination, general amnesty for political prisoners and exiles, and election of a constituent Cortes which will be called upon to decide the future regime of Spain. The Spanish Communist Party is ready to cooperate with a transitional government, provided it applies these three points in an effective way, without setting up ministerial participation as a condition.

**Workers' Commissions.** The most important organizational means of expanding party influence in 1967 were the so-called workers' commissions (*comisones obreras*). These groups are illegal, informal organizations of worker leaders outside the official government-sanctioned labor unions (*sindicatos*). They describe themselves as a movement rather than an organization. Communists have been somewhat successful in securing leadership positions in these groups and, with the adherents of the Catholic Labor Movement, are said to form the strongest identifiable elements within them. (See "Franco's Restive Workers," *The Reporter,* 4 May 1967.) The commissions have often been successful in getting their own men elected to positions of shop stewards within the official labor organizations. In 1967 the commissions were particularly active in organizing and carrying out May Day demonstrations (*Washington Post,* 2 May). On 27 October they were the leading force in plans for a "day of protest," which was to be marked by work stoppages, demonstrations, and boycotts of public transportation and markets; these plans, however, were largely thwarted by vigorous police action (*NYT,* 28 October).

Although the workers' commissions are not communist creations, Spanish communists, both within Spain and in exile, were quick to take credit for supporting them once their popularity became clear. Beginning as *ad hoc* committees for sparking particular labor actions in the early 1960's, they became permanent leadership organizations in 1964. The commissions came out further into the open in 1967 with the formation of a "National Assembly of Workers' Commissions," for which the commissions in the Madrid area were the organizational nucleus.

It is apparent that the workers' commissions have been a subject of significant intraparty debate. Dissident Spanish Communists throughout 1967 accused the exile leadership of opposing involvement in the commissions until it had become obvious in 1966 that they were successful. According to an article in the organ of the Revolutionary Communist Youth in France, *Avant-garde Jeunesse* (Paris, November-December 1967), the PCE right wing, under the exile leadership, even in 1967 was against the large May Day demonstrations being planned under the commissions' leadership, fearing that they might hurt the party's attempt to win over elements outside the working class. The article claimed that many party workers involved in the work of the commissions were preparing for a conference to prepare their own line in opposition to that of the regular leadership and would make their case at the next PCE congress. This split, reportedly, occurred toward the end of May (*ibid.*). Catalonia and the

Basque regions appear to have been the strongholds of the leftists opposed to the exile leaders. The party leadership is said to have condemned the dissident Socialist Unity Party of Catalonia and to have replaced it with a group known as the Catalan Communist Party. The clandestine leftist Communists appealed to the Central Committee of the CPSU to settle their dispute with the exile leadership under Moscow's patronage, but without success. The latter move allegedly led to the Ardatovsky exchange (see below). According to another report (*Unir-Débat pour le Socialisme,* 10 February 1968), Carrillo gave the workers' commissions "not a chance of success until he came rushing to help them, once they had succeeded."

Carrillo, of course, told it differently. In a speech broadcast over Radio Independent Spain on 3 January 1967, he called the commissions "an extraordinarily original and profoundly democratic form of organization and unity for the struggle of the masses." Speaking of the PCE's role, Carrillo claimed that the party had "provided an orientation for the workers' commissions." He acknowledged disagreement about whether or not the party should become involved with the commissions, although he did not associate himself with the opposition: "It must be said, comrades, that even within our party there were a number of comrades who were not very confident that this line was correct." Nevertheless, Carrillo hinted that a criticism of "adventurism" in connection with the movement had, in fact, been made by the exile leadership, but gave an elaborate explanation that the "real" target of such a criticism was only the danger of possible adventurist errors in the execution of such a line. He further maintained that the party had concluded that the commissions could be a success on the basis "not so much of our own experience" (i.e., experience within Spain, in which Carrillo, as an exile, is deficient) as on the basis of the "experience of the Bolsheviks in the Soviet Union" and of a "careful study of Lenin's teaching."

**PCE-CPSU Relations.** On 12 December the official organ of the Soviet government, *Izvestia,* published an article by V. Ardatovsky on the political future of Spain. Ardatovsky indicated that a monarchist transitional phase after Franco might be acceptable to Spanish Communists as well as to the Soviet Union. A few days later, an editorial in *Mundo Obrero* attacked the article as "strange and confused," and said that Ardatovsky had wrong opinions about the desire of Franco to reinstate the monarchy. *Mundo Obrero* said that "ill-intentioned people" might regard the article: "as an echo of the position of our party, and even worse, as a correction to this position. But it is neither an echo nor a correction. We, ourselves, draw up our own policy." *Mundo Obrero* quoted a statement made by Carrillo in February 1967:

> We would not accept, in addition, a monarchy or any other regime that would be imposed on the people from the top. We consider that the first step to take to arrive at a genuine political change would consist in reestablishing democratic freedoms. The people should then determine freely whether they are for the republic or for the monarchy. That should be the business of a constituent assembly. We Communists would opt for the republic. If, however, the majority of the people should wish for the reinstatement of the monarchy, we would then bow before the will expressed in a democratic manner by the majority. (*L'Humanité,* 23 December.)

On 22 December *Izvestia* published a further reply by Carrillo to Ardatovsky, along with an editorial note approving Carrillo's criticisms. The exchange was reported in *L'Humanité* on 23 December, allegedly on explicit orders from French Communist Raymond Guyot, a former associate of Carrillo (*Unir-Débat pour le Socialisme,* 10 February 1968). Dissident Spanish Communists saw the entire exchange as having been contrived in order to make Carrillo and the rest of the exile leadership appear independent of Moscow and thus to strengthen Carrillo's leadership position within the PCE. Noncommunist Western observers, however, saw the Ardatovsky article as one of numerous moves by the Soviets in 1967 to improve relations with the Franco government; among other things, trade between the USSR and Spain was up significantly during the year, and regular shipping service between Soviet and Spanish ports was inaugurated. (See *NYT,* 1 November 1967.) The two perspectives on the exchange may not be completely incompatible.

**International Views and Policies.** On international issues the PCE generally follows the lead of the Soviet Union, affirming its support for unity within the international communist movement under

Soviet hegemony.

The PCE delegation to the Karlovy Vary conference of communist and workers' parties in April included both Dolores Ibarruri and Carrillo. Chairman Ibarruri delivered a speech at the conference calling for the communist movement to understand and follow with attention the new developments taking place in the Catholic Church and the Catholic world, particularly since the papacy of John XXIII. On 4 May Radio Independent Spain broadcast a statement by Carrillo hailing the work of the Karlovy Vary Conference and its discussion of European security. Asserting that the "revanchist policy of the German Federal Republic" was the most important obstacle to European security, Carrillo remarked that "it will be difficult for the peoples of Europe to live at ease," as long as the Federal Republic "does not have a clear understanding that it must accept the reality of two German states—itself and the German Democratic Republic"; and as long as it "does not recognize the frontiers set up after World War II, does not renounce its militaristic policy and access to atomic weapons."

Regarding the Middle East war, on 8 June Radio Independent Spain broadcast a statement by the PCE Executive Committee charging the USA with collusion in Israel's "criminal aggression." According to the statement, Israel was "the main instrument for putting into effect the imperialist plans against the Arab people." At the same time the PCE declared that a "decisive factor in forcing Israel to stop its military operations was the firm warning issued by the leaders of the socialist countries of Europe, gathered in Moscow, [which] reaffirmed the consistent line followed by the Soviet Union and other socialist countries of full solidarity with the struggle of the Arab countries." Also, Franco was attacked for allowing Spain to be used as a US military base. The statement nevertheless recognized the "rightful existence of the state of Israel," but added that "in the long run this will only be possible with a different policy" on the part of Israel.

The PCE press and radio carried numerous articles and statements in 1967 concerning China and the Great Proletarian Cultural Revolution, all arguing the Soviet position against the Chinese, sometimes with more force than the CPSU itself. Carrillo's article "China through the Maoist Chaos" (*Nuestra Bandera,* no. 63), attacked Mao and his supporters for having carried out an "uprising against the party and against the institutional organs of the socialist state." Carrillo observed that it was only thanks to the strength of the Soviet Union that the cultural revolution had not brought on an American-backed invasion of China by the Nationalist Chinese in Taiwan. More broadly, he suggested that the Great Proletarian Cultural Revolution and its "disastrous consequences" for socialism in China had their roots in the first major error of the Chinese leadership—the repudiation of Soviet leadership at the time of the Chinese "Great Leap Forward" in 1958. Carrillo asked: "Did not the first *coup d'état* of Mao and his group against the entire orientation of the party and of the Chinese revolution occur precisely at that moment?"

The cultural revolution, and more particularly, Mao himself constituted a "serious obstacle to the struggle of the Vietnamese people," in Carrillo's view: "Today Mao's policy toward Vietnam seems to consist in opposing any peaceful solution that will guarantee the rights of Vietnam to independence and unity and in continuing the war to the last Vietnamese."

Dolores Ibarruri and Carrillo headed the PCE delegation to the Moscow celebrations of the Fiftieth Anniversary of the October Revolution. While in Moscow for this occasion, the delegation conferred with Leonid Brezhnev and Boris Ponomarev.

A delegation led by Carrillo paid an official visit to Bulgaria on 4-11 October. The joint communique issued at the end of the visit declared that the delegations of the Spanish and Bulgarian parties "ascertained the full unanimity of the viewpoints of their parties" concerning the international situation and problems of the world communist and workers' movement. The communique also said that the two delegations considered that the "necessity for convening a new international conference of communist and workers' parties" was "becoming more and more imperative," and that they would "spare no strength to prepare it."

**Communist Party of Spain (Marxist-Leninist).** The splinter group whose central organ is *Vanguardia Obrera* was founded 17 December 1964. Another group publishes *Mundo Obrero Revolucionario.* Both groups apparently call themselves the Communist Party of Spain

(Marxist-Leninist), but the latter one does not appear to have such extensive contacts with the "Marxist-Leninist" pro-Chinese groups in Europe as the other. (One source gives the name of the *Mundo Obrero Revolucionario* group as the Revolutionary Communist Party of Spain.)

The *Vanguardia Obrera* group maintains especially close ties with the pro-Chinese Communist Party of Belgium under Jacques Grippa. The Belgian Communist weekly *La Voix du Peuple* frequently carries items reprinted from *Vanguardia Obrera. La Voix du Peuple* 14 July 1967 contained a message of solidarity from the Executive Committee of the Communist Party of Spain (Marxist-Leninist) to Grippa, expressing support for the latter against his Belgian Communist rivals. The statement noted that the Executive Committee of the *Vanguardia Obrera* group "consider the Communist Party of Belgium to be one of the strongest bulwarks in the struggle against imperialism and revisionism in Europe and in the world." The *Vanguardia Obrera* faction also claims ties of solidarity with the Marxist-Leninist Italian Communist Party, the French Marxist-Leninist Movement, and the Marxist-Leninist Center of the Netherlands, and with Albania and China. This group has declared: "Defense of the Chinese revolution and the Albanian socialist state, and the unconditional support of the just struggle of the Vietnamese people, will continue to be the stepping stones for our authentic international proletarianism, based on Marxism-Leninism" (*La Voix du Peuple,* Brussels, 16 December 1966).

Both splinter groups reject the line of "national reconciliation," advocated by Santiago Carrillo and developed in 1960 at the PCE's Sixth Congress, and call for violent overthrow of the government. A statement of the *Mundo Obrero Revolucionario* group, declares: "To formulate and further the demands of the dissatisfied Spanish masses, to make them conscious of their tasks and lead them toward the taking over of political power by means of an armed revolution, this is our party's great task at the present stage of history" (*Marxistiskt Forum,* Uppsala, no. 1, 1967).

Apparently referring to the *Mundo Obrero Revolucionario* group, *Vanguardia Obrera* has commented:

> The adventurist character of the opportunist group which was excluded from the Plenary Reunion [December 1964] has become more and more apparent. We can assure you that their work consists mainly in telling calumnies and lies against our leaders, and they try to fool certain comrades and friends, who do not know their true nature as yet, with organizations that exist only in their minds . . . . They also create confusion by stating party slogans that sometimes coincide with those of the Carrillo revisionists. (*La Voix du Peuple,* 16 December 1966.)

The *Vanguardia Obrera* group in 1967 launched a "campaign of emulation," seeking to stimulate competition among its activist groups throughout Spain in a sales and distribution drive for *Vanguardia Obrera.* In announcing the campaign, the party made an apparent allusion to financial support from abroad. Noting that the publication's deficit had been constant, *Vanguardia Obrera* (January) declared: "We must achieve conditions under which it is our comrades, the sympathizers and friends of the party, who cover the expenses of our publications. This is difficult but not impossible."

In international affairs the *Vanguardia Obrera* group adheres to the views of the Chinese Communist Party. Excerpts from an article in the first issue of *Revolución Español,* "All Revolutionaries Pay Tribute to China's Great Proletarian Cultural Revolution," were quoted in *Peking Review* (9 June 1967), which commented: "China is the base of world revolution. The Chinese Communist Party is the standard-bearer of world revolution. Comrade Mao Tse-tung's thought is Marxism-Leninism of our era. Therefore, China's might adds to the strength of the entire world revolution. Every forward step which China takes towards communism is a step forward for the people of all countries towards their own liberation and a step forward in their own revolution."

**Publications.** The official organ of the PCE is *Mundo Obrero* (Workers' World), published semimonthly. *Nuestra Bandera* (Our Flag) is the party's quarterly theoretical journal. Both are published abroad. Other major PCE publications include the monthly *España Republicana,* published in Havana, and *Realidad,* a monthly journal aimed at intellectuals, published in Rome and edited by Manuel Azcarate. The party's radio station, Radio España Independiente (Radio Independent Spain), broadcasts to Spain, reportedly from Rumania (*World Strength of Communist Party Organizations,* 1968) or from Czechoslovakia, according to other sources.

The apparently dominant faction of the Communist Party of Spain (Marxist-Leninist) publishes *Vanguardia Obrera* (Workers' Vanguard), a monthly, and *Revolución Español* (Spanish Revolution), a quarterly theoretical journal. The other faction going by the same name publishes *Mundo Obrero Revolucionario* (Revolutionary Workers' World).

# S U D A N

The Sudanese Communist Party (SCP) traces its origins to 1944 when Sudanese students in Cairo began to form Marxist circles. In 1946 an offshoot of the communist movement in Egypt was formed in the Sudan and was called the "Sudanese Movement for National Liberation." After independence in 1956 the SCP functioned openly, but in 1958-1964 when the Abboud military junta held power in the Sudan the Communist Party and all other parties were forced underground. In 1964-1965 the SCP, the only legal communist party in independent Africa, was represented in the National Front government. It was banned in December 1965 by the Constituent Assembly; despite the Khartoum High Court's ruling that the Assembly's action was illegal, the activity of the SCP is in effect suppressed (see below).

The SCP experienced an extraordinary growth of influence following the overthrow of the Abboud regime due to its success in infiltrating mass organizations during the previous six years. In 1958 the party polled about 5,000 votes in the general election; in 1965 it polled more than 73,000 votes and received 11 of the 175 seats in the Constituent Assembly (8 of these 11 assemblymen declared themselves to be members of the SCP). The strongest party—the Umma Mahdist—received 76 seats, and the National Unionist Party (NUP) received 53 seats, resulting in the formation of a coalition government between the two parties. The Communists' 11 seats were among the 15 seats in the Assembly allocated to candidates with a higher education; also, one of the Communist representatives was the first Sudanese woman member of the Assembly. When the party was banned in December 1965, the eight declared Communist representatives were expelled from the Assembly. On 12 May 1967, Ahmad Suleyiman, a leading member of the SCP, was elected to the Constituent Assembly for a Khartoum constituency in a by-election caused by the death of the NUP representative. This was the first time that a member of the SCP won a normal territorial constituency (the seats which the Communists won in 1965 were in the graduate constituency). Ahmad Suleyiman took his seat on 1 June without obstruction, despite the Constituent Assembly's ban on the party.

The SCP is influential among the intelligentsia and students and is active among trade unionists, unemployed workers, and agricultural tenants. Communists have played a significant part in the Federation of Sudanese Trade Unions, an affiliate both of the All-African Trade Union Federation and of the communist-directed World Federation of Trade Unions, and have also wielded influence in the Tenants' Union. The party's strength, however, is out of proportion to its membership, which, although no reliable figures are available, is estimated to number between 5,000 and 10,000. In any case, according to the *East African Standard* (19 April 1967), the party is "more a nuisance than a threat." (The population of the Sudan is 14,530,000 [estimated July 1967] ).

The SCP's Secretary-General is 'Abd al-Khaliq Mahjub. According to Sudanese police reports, a document seized in October 1967 listed what is believed to be a newly elected Central Committee numbering 33 persons. Leading communists include Tigani Babiker, Mustafa Ibrahim, Dr. Izzeddin Ali Amir, Muhammed Ibrahim Nugud, 'Usman Mustafa Mekki, Muawiyah Ibrahim Suri, Hasan Zarruq, and Tagglio al-Tigani, the latter two having acted respectively as editor and assistant editor of the SCP organ, *al-Maidan*.

On 15 November 1965 the Sudanese Constituent Assembly approved a proposal to outlaw the Communist Party (by 150 votes to 12, with 9 abstentions), and a week later the Provisional Constitution of Sudan was amended to state: "It shall not be permissible for any person to propagate or to endeavor to propagate communism, be it local or international, or to propagate or to endeavor to propagate atheism and disbelief in the heavenly religions, or to work or to endeavor to work by means of force, intimidation, or any other illegal means to overthrow the Government." On the basis of this amendment the Constituent Assembly passed a law on 8 December 1965 banning the SCP and depriving the Communist deputies of their assembly seats. During 1966 the SCP, through a legally established "National Congress for the Defense of Democracy," contested the constitutional validity of the ban imposed upon it. On 22 December 1966, the Khartoum High Court overruled the constitutional amendment on the grounds that the Constituent Assembly had exceeded its powers. The Assembly then refused to accept the decision of the High Court and filed an appeal. Despite the final court ruling of 18 March 1967 that the dissolution of the SCP was null and void and the dismissal of Communist deputies from the Constituent Assembly unconstitutional, the Government has imposed an effective ban on the Party.

On 28 December 1966, the Sudanese Prime Minister announced the Government's suppression of an attempted coup during the previous night, and subsequently the police arrested about 400 persons, including the SCP Secretary-General, 'Abd al-Khaliq Mahjub, and the Secretary of the Sudan Federation of Workers' Trade Unions, Shafie Ahmed al-Sheikh. Those arrested were released by 3 January 1967 and responsibility for the coup attempt was put on a group of army officers. The Sudanese Communists claimed that the "coup" was actually fabricated by the Government in an effort to discredit those elements contesting its authority and in order to deliver a blow to the revolutionary movement. In a statement defending the policy of the Sudanese party during this crisis, published by the South African Communist Party organ *The African Communist* (no. 29, 1967), Tigani Babiker charged the Government with being "political bandits" and "enemies of democracy and the constitution," and with "political and ideological bankruptcy."

Another action against the Communists was the raid, in October, on two houses in Khartoum, one of which was the house of Muawiyah Ibrahim Suri, the Organizing Secretary of the SCP. According to the Ministry of the Interior, the search disclosed a quantity of explosives and ammunition and "various dangerous documents, including a two-page document consisting of a program for training in warfare, the use of firearms and explosives, and shooting and military tactics, which was prepared by the trainers of the disbanded Communist Party." Following up the information in the documents, the police continued to raid other homes of communists and reportedly seized weapons found there. The SCP denied knowledge of the supposedly discovered arms.

**Domestic Views and Policies**. The principal issue in the Sudan in 1967 was the writing of a permanent constitution. The coalition of the Umma and the NUP supported the adoption of an Islamic constitution which would include a provision banning the SCP. The Southern Sudanese parties and the SCP waged a campaign in opposition. The SCP held that the adoption of an Islamic constitution would establish a "reactionary and backward system" and would endanger the country's unity by encouraging the partly Christian South to secede. The SCP claimed that the constitution, owing to the way it was being drafted, could not win any respect and that the attempt by "reactionary" parties to liquidate the people's "democratic activity" was doomed to failure. Although the Constituent Assembly decided definitely for an Islamic document, the constitution was not written in 1967 and elections were postponed until February 1968.

A second major problem in the Sudan was the struggle between the Government and the Southern Sudanese secessionists. The SCP has consistently called for the unity of the country and a "democratic solution" to the "Southern Question" by granting regional autonomy for the Southern national groupings. The SCP stated that the other parties in the Sudan have finally conceded the correctness of the SCP's policy but in practice still pursue the "old chauvinistic, great-nationality policy towards the South, thus feeding the fire of hatred between conpatriots and serving the interests of colonialism" (Tigani Babiker, "The Sudanese Communist Party Will Survive," *The African Communist,* no. 29, 1967).

The SCP rejects any "reforms" enacted by the present Sudanese leaders as "an attempt to impose the capitalist path of development on the country, and as a means to check the struggle of the working people for radical social and political changes." The SCP strives for a "national democratic revolution" which would prepare the way for socialism. National independence, in the party's view, would be safeguarded by the transfer of political power to the "national democratic forces" in which the vanguard force would be the SCP.

The SCP held its Fourth Congress in October 1967 and adopted a new program. (The Third Congress was held in February 1956, a month after the Sudan won its independence and immediately preceding the Twentieth Congress of the Communist Party of the Soviet Union.) Referring to the new program, a party leader stated:

> What is envisaged is not merely the program of an opposition party, but one that would voice the interests of the working people and would indicate a realistic approach to the solution of their problems, and thereby mobilize them in the fight against reaction and its deceptive policies. What is envisaged, therefore, is a program of a party that presents itself to the people as the alternative to the "traditional" parties and which is earnestly preparing to shoulder the responsibility of government. (Tigani Babiker, "Sudanese Communists Prepare for Congress," *WMR*, May 1967.)

The major issue at the SCP's Fourth Congress was the task of party building and the creation of a "genuinely mass Marxist-Leninist party." The SCP attracted a large number of new members in 1964, but has failed to keep them as active members because of a gap between the leadership and the rank-and-file. A resolution of the Fourth Congress presented a four-point program for the growth and development of the party:

> 1. The "independent and creative application of Marxism-Leninism" in working out a political line and in discovering forms of organization suitable to the conditions in the Sudan.
>
> 2. The creation and building of various modern mass organizations and their closer association with the political movement.
>
> 3. The differentiation of forms of party growth to coordinate growth with the development of different regions of the Sudan.
>
> 4. The basing of party activities on a detailed and concrete study of the various regions and localities of the Sudan.

The Congress resolved to make party building an "independent and permanent task, according to plans realized over fixed periods." "Clarifying the matter of the vanguards, their attitudes and influence," the resolution continued, "places the planning of party building on firm ground and enables us to follow it up as a permanent and independent task on a par with the political and ideological work and the day-to-day activity of the Party. This, undoubtedly, is a turning point, indicating that our Party had indeed entered the stage of maturity . . . " (*WMR*, February 1968.)

On 22 January 1967 the new Socialist Party, composed of intellectuals, workers, and farmers, was formed. The Socialist Party is the only left-wing party in the Sudan besides the now illegal Communist Party, and a number of sources, including the Sudanese pro-Chinese splinter party, have indicated that the SCP was active in its formation (see *Afrika Heute*, Bonn, no. 12, 1967; *New Zealand Communist Review*, March 1967). The new party is headed by Amin al-Shibli, President of the Sudan Bar Association, and is supported by Trade Union leader Shafie Ahmed al-Sheikh. In his inaugural address Amin al-Shibli declared that the party was to "take the essence of Islam and its teachings on social justice from the hands which had stained it on the Sudanese political scene." He said that the party was inspired by the "socialist banner" in Egypt and by the "progressive" regimes of Algeria, Guinea, and Mali.

**International Views and Policies.** The SCP continued its denunciation of the proposed "Islamic Pact," charging that it is an attempt to smash the revolutionary movement on the part of "imperialism," whose vital interests are threatened by the revolution in the Arab world, and of the Arab feudal and capitalist classes, whose interests and privileges are likewise endangered.

According to the SCP ( *WMR*, October 1967), the Arab-Israeli war of June 1967 was instigated by "the imperialists" as the latest attempt to eliminate the revolutionary regimes in the Middle East. Analyzing the military defeat of the Arabs, the SCP pointed to reactionary regimes in some Arab states, the existence of American and British military bases on Arab territory, the control of oil and the economy in some countries by "imperialist monopolies," and, most important, disunity among the revolutionary forces and lack of unanimity among the progressive regimes on a number of basic questions.

The SCP noted that the situation in the Middle East remains tense and did not rule out the possibility of another resort to arms. It declared, however, that "to claim that military action is the sole choice for the Arab countries betrays not only ignorance of the international situation, but also of the ability of these countries to pursue such a course at present."

Discussing the reasons for the failure of the Arab states in the Middle East conflict, the SCP emphasized the need to struggle first for full independence, freeing the economy from the "grip of imperialism," effecting radical social and political changes in the condition of the working people, building up a "revolutionary vanguard party" and relying on the working people:

> The working people really are the backbone of the revolution. This means that they should be organized, enlightened and relied upon to hold posts of leadership and responsibility in the movement. The yardstick for measuring the seriousness of a revolutionary party is the degree to which, in deeds, it carries out such a policy. . . . The absence of a revolutionary vanguard party drawn from the working class and the working peasantry is one of the graver weaknesses in the countries where there are progressive regimes.

To achieve unity of the entire revolutionary movement in the Arab world, the SCP called for contacts among the broadest masses, combined with contacts at state and party levels to attain unity. Also it emphasized the need to grant Communists freedom of activity. Noting that in some ranks of the revolutionary movement Communists were incarcerated or were restricted in their activity, the SCP specifically called for the "releasing of communists and democrats from the prisons in Algeria and Iraq" and "widening the base of the government in Syria."

**International Communist Movement.** The SCP is pro-Soviet in orientation and its views on foreign policy essentially correspond with those held by the CPSU. In a statement on the significance of the October Revolution to the Sudan, Tigani Babiker stated that Sudanese "progressives" were most inspired by the "success of the Soviet Union in solving the national question and the grand achievements registered in the former Tsarist colonies in Central Asia." "To Sudanese progressives," he declared, "the Soviet Central Asian republics symbolized the future of their own country for which they should work." The Soviet Central Asian Republics were an example used repeatedly to show the feasibility of the noncapitalist way of development when the SCP was formulating its program for national democratic revolution. (*WMR*, September 1967).

The SCP came to the defense of the Soviet Union and the socialist states when Communist China charged that the Soviets had refrained from rendering effective aid to the Arab states during the Middle East crisis: "In this respect the Mao group is at one with the imperialists and the Arab reactionaries. Their common aim is to discredit the Soviet Union and to inculcate defeatism among the Arab peoples. . . . The Mao group, by their splitting activities, are rendering an invaluable service to imperialism." (*Ibid.*).

The Sudanese Communists participated to a limited degree in the international communist movement in 1967. The SCP sent greetings on the occasion of the Eighteenth Congress of the French Communist Party, in January, in which mention was made of its intention to attend the Congress; the reason for its absence, however, was not specified. The SCP sent a delegation to the Moscow celebrations marking the Fiftieth Anniversary of the October Revolution, but the names of the delegates were not reported. On 28 August talks were held in Sofia between an SCP delegation and a delegation of the Bulgarian Communist Party under Ivan Dragoev, head of the Administrative Department of the Central Committee of the Bulgarian Communist Party. Sofia Radio reported on 28 August that the two delegations exchanged information on the activities and tasks of the parties and their attitude toward "certain urgent international issues."

**The Revolutionary Communist Party of the Sudan.** A faction of the SCP which did not agree with the line of "peaceful transition" adopted in 1956 was expelled from the party in August 1964. The group established the Revolutionary Communist Party of the Sudan (RCPS) in 1965. The leader of this party is Ahmad Muhammad Jair, who is believed to be at present in Peking.

The RCPS charges that the "modern revisionist Mahjub clique" has "embarked upon the road of collaboration with the semi-feudalist elements [and] agents of foreign monopoly capital and with US neo-colonialism." It claims that during the Abboud regime the SCP participated in the bourgeois opposition coalition "under the pretext of 'working from the inside to expose it'." The SCP, according to the RCPS, openly opposed the October 1964 uprising and joined in only when it realized that the strike was inevitable. With reference to the SCP successes in the 1965 election, the splinter party notes that the SCP won seats only in the graduate constituency where they won the votes of students studying abroad, most of whom are still in the USSR and other East European countries. (*New Zealand Communist Review,* March 1967.)

At the Sixth Congress of Albanian Trade Unions, held in April 1967, the Revolutionary Communist Party of the Sudan was represented by Sadiq al-Digna, who stated in his address to the Congress that his party was "guiding the working class to prepare itself for the seizure of power by revolutionary means and rejecting the parliamentary road" (*La Voix du Peuple,* 19 May). A delegation of the "Sudanese League of Revolutionary Communist Students" attended the Fifth Congress of the Union of Albanian Working Youth held in June. During a third visit by representatives of the party, 27 June to 12 July, a delegation headed by the First Secretary of the Central Committee of the RCPS, held talks with the First Secretary of the Central Committee of the Albanian Workers' Party, on the international situation, the situation in the communist movement, and problems of interest to their two parties.

**Publications.** The central organ of the SCP is the daily *al-Maidan,* which at present is banned. The SCP also publishes a weekly English version of its organ, entitled *Advance.*

The RCPS has no organ, but its program is published by pro-Chinese party newspapers and periodicals such as *La Voix du Peuple* and the *New Zealand Communist Review.*

# SWEDEN

The Communist Party of Sweden (Sveriges Kommunistiska Parti; SKP), founded in 1921, was renamed the Left Party Communists (Vänsterpartiet Kommunisterna; VPK) at its Twenty-First Party Congress in Stockholm on 13-16 May 1967. The party is legal and claims a strength of 20,000 members and 8,000 to 9,000 "associate members" (*Ny Dag,* 12-18 May 1967). The population of Sweden is 7,808,000 (estimated, January 1968).

While the Communists have at no time been an influential factor in Swedish politics and remain isolated by the other parties, support for the party has reflected a small but steady upward trend in recent elections. The latest general election in 1964 gave the Communists 5.2 per cent of the votes, compared with 4.5 per cent in 1960. The largest shares of its votes were in the northernmost province of Norrbotten (16 per cent), Gävleborg in east-central Sweden (10 per cent), and Göteborg in the south (10 per cent) (*World Strength of the Communist Party Organizations,* 1968). The party gained 6.4 per cent in the local elections of 1966, as against 3.8 per cent in 1962. Holding eight of the 233 seats in the second chamber of Parliament (compared with five in 1960), the Communists are now represented in municipal councils of all cities with more than 40,000 residents* (*WMR,* November 1966).

The Social Democratic Labor Party (Socialdemokratiska Arbetarparti; SAP) which has governed Sweden, either alone or in coalition with nonsocialist parties, since 1932, suffered its worst setback in the 1966 local election, when its share of the votes dropped from 50.5 to 42.3 per cent.

Eleven dissidents, constituting the final remnants of a "hard-line" left wing within the VPK, broke with the party at the Twenty-First Congress in opposition to the VPK program. Headed by Bo Gustavsson, who served on the program commission, this group combined with other Maoist elements to form the Communist League (Marxist-Leninists) [Kommunistiska Förbundet (Marxist-Leninisterna); KF.]The KF claims an initial membership of 500.

**Organization and Leadership.** Carl-Henrik Hermansson was elected Chairman of the VPK at the Twentieth Congress in 1964, succeeding Hilding Hagberg, and gained reelection at the Twenty-First Congress in May 1967 by 303 out of 324 votes cast. Vice-Chairman is Lars Werner, and Party Secretary is Urban Karlsson. The Party Executive (*Partistyrelse*)—the name Central Committee was abolished by the Twentieth Congress—has 30 full and 10 alternate members, reduced from 45 and 15, respectively, at the Twenty-First Congress. Also reduced (from 11 to 7) was the Working Committee, whose members are Urban Karlsson, Carl-Henrik Hermansson, Lars Werner, Nils Berndtsson, Tore Claesson, Gunnel Granlid, and Benne Lantz.

A constitutional meeting held by the Party Executive following the Twenty-First Congress appointed Werner Chairman of the Party Executive and member of the Working Committee, while Karlsson was made Chairman of the Working Committee. These appointments represent a significant restructuring and liberalization of the Party Executive, inasmuch as the party Chairman had hitherto headed both the Party Executive and the Working Committee. The newly elected Party Executive consists of John Takman, Jörn Svensson, Börje Svensson, Lars Werner, Gunvor Ryding, Rolf Hagel, Urban Karlsson, Erik Berg, Nils Berndtsson, Allan Johansson, Gunnel Granlid, Inga-Lill Andersson, Lennart Gustavsson, Tore Forsberg, Benne Lantz, Gustav Lorentzson, Tore Claesson, Erik Nordberg, Olof Nilsson, Lars Pettersson, Gösta Andersson, Johan Andersson, Göte Ask, Rune Pettersson, Britta Andersson, Folke Liljesson, Eivor Marklund, Erik Skoog, Olle Fors, and Folke Persson.

The KF represents the consolidation of the Marxist Society, founded in Göteborg in 1966 by Nils

---

*Sweden's Parliament (*Riksdag*) is scheduled to convert to a single-chamber system on 1 January 1971, and the Communists stand to gain substantially in relation to the larger parties.

Holmberg (former Communist member of Parliament), Knut Senander, and the Marxist Forum of Uppsala, headed by Gustavsson. The latter is Chairman of the KF; Vice-Chairman is Frank Baude. The Central Committee includes Holmberg and Per Maunsbach, who also served with Gustavsson on the VPK program commission.

**Domestic Views and Policies.** A proclaimed "revolutionary" party from its inception and until the de-Stalinization of the 1950s, the VPK has for more than a decade advocated, without reservation, a peaceful, parliamentary transition to socialism "according to Sweden's own conditions." The long-debated needs for "renewal" and "rejuvenation" of the party and the inherent question of its position on "democratic centralism" became central issues in 1963, when it was openly acknowledged for the first time that the party was ruled by "aging dogmatists" and had become, in the eyes of Swedish workers, a mere "tool of Moscow." Reshuffles in 1963 and 1964 resulted in the removal of several party leaders oriented either to the right ("Stalinists") or the left ("Maoists") of the proposed reformation policies. (See Åke Sparring, *Från Höglund til Hermansson,* Stockholm, 1967; and Sparring, ed., *Kommunismen i Norden,* Stockholm, 1965.) During 1967 the "remnants" of these extremists were excluded from the Party Executive.

The 1964 congress and the departure of Hermansson as editor of the party organ *Ny Dag* represented, in essence, a compromise between the "old guard" and "reformists" looking for a younger leader, unbound by ties to Moscow, who could initiate a revamping of the theoretical foundation and organizational structure of the party, thereby presenting to the Swedish electorate a "modern, independent, and nationalist" party whose duty was to "rally all forces that are willing to participate in the struggle to break up the power position of the financial oligarchy and to bring about social changes in our country" (*Information Bulletin,* nos. 97-98, 1967). Hermansson's initial popularity was due to his advocacy of free debate—in defiance of the Hagberg leadership—on the Sino-Soviet rift.

The "renewal process" charted by the Twentieth Party Congress was further elaborated at the Twenty-First Congress in May 1967.* A new program and new statutes were adopted, radically liberalizing both political and ideological orientation and membership requirements; the party name was changed to reflect that liberalization; and the constitution of the Party Executive has been reformed. From these indications and from statements of party leaders, the VPK would appear to be en route from a "traditional" communist party to a left-socialist, national party—with a Marxist ideological foundation, but bent on maintaining little more than *pro forma* allegiance to Moscow and to the world communist movement.

A booklet published by the VPK and entitled *Gathering of the Left* (*Samling Vänster*; Stockholm, 1967), carries the entire proceedings of the Twenty-First Party Congress. The new program, called "Socialist Alternative," states:

> [The VPK] is built upon the socialist tradition in the Swedish workers' movement. It stands on the foundation of Marxism ... [and advocates] freedom of opinion, the common and equal right to vote, parliamentarianism, and decisions according to the majority principle. In cooperation with other groups, parties, and organizations, [the party] will defend and expand the rights won, so that the people may determine the development of society.

It is clear from the 39-point document that the "renewed" VPK places greater emphasis on parliamentarianism and less emphasis on fraternal relations with other communist parties. One of the most important changes, according to Hermansson, is that "we align ourselves resolutely on the side of parliamentarianism and the multiparty system, even after the socialist form of government has been established" (*Kansan Uutiset,* Helsinki, 18 February 1967).

No reference is made in the program and the statutes either to Lenin or to "democratic centralism." Hermansson claims that the term "Marxist" will demonstrate a "freer" approach than is generally meant by the designation "Marxist-Leninist" (*Friheten,* Oslo, 2 February 1967). He has also said that "Marxism must not be interpreted merely as a collection of ever-valid dogmas, but also as a

---

*Both the Twentieth and the Twenty-first Congresses were open to the general public.

method of social analysis . . . . [We] do not believe in a decisive victory within the framework of capitalism, but partial reforms are possible." (*Ny Dag*, 15-21 December 1967.)

The "dictatorship of the proletariat" has also been eliminated from the VPK program, since it fails to correspond to "Swedish technological and socioeconomic conditions." Hermansson suggests that "if one thought of adapting the feasibility of the dictatorship of the proletariat to the highly industrialized Soviet Union in order to attain new levels of enthusiasm among the people, it is not certain the thesis would remain long in the program [of the Soviet party]"(*Ny Dag*, 5-11 May 1967). Swedish Communists have not lost their respect for the "epoch-making importance of Marxism-Leninism," according to Hermansson, "but are against copying any ready-made formulas in our party program, because we see in Marxism a ready means of analyzing social relations and development trends in the making, and not an orthodox set of political theses" (TANYUG International Service, Belgrade, 1 February 1967).

The name proposed in the program draft—Socialist Party of the Left—which was adopted by the Party Executive on 30 January, gained little support at the congress and was shelved in favor of the "compromise" proposal adopted—Left Party Communists—which "indicates the position of the party as a part of the left-socialist movement. . . . The new name means both that it is the name of the party of the Communists and that other socialists may join it." (*Land og Folk*, Copenhagen, 21-22 May 1967.)

Reservations to the program ranged from "reformists" who favor intensified wooing of the SAP and consider emerging left-socialist organizations to have a divisive effect (Sven Landin, Rolf Utberg), to "new-left" proponents of closer ties with the radical left wing of the SAP as opposed to formal cooperation with the "administrators of the capitalist society" (Kjell E. Johanson), to "Maoists" (Bo Gustavsson, Per Maunsbach).

Hermansson's "soft line" has been strongly defended by his followers:

> The fact that the VPK believes in and hopes for the possibility of peaceful coexistence and a peaceful road to socialism does not prevent the party from being revolutionary. If one finds a contradiction in this, one gives too limited a meaning to the concept "revolutionary." A revolutionary situation does not exist in Sweden, [and] to lead a doctrinaire, clumsy policy, out of touch with realities, would be to commit political suicide. (*Norrskensflamman*, Luleå, 15 July 1967.)

Gert Petersen of the Danish Socialist People's Party (with which the VPK has excellent relations) calls the program "startling" and an "inspiration" to the Swedish labor movement: "[The program] spells out a clear adherence to traditional Scandinavian democracy and a definite break with the remaining scraps of Stalinism still to be found in Swedish Communist Party theoretical reasoning. . . . It is Marxist in its analysis, critical in its considerations . . . realistic in its premises, and moderate in its suggestions." (*SF Bladet*, Copenhagen, 15 February 1967.)

Charging that the Swedish "class society" is a "hard and bitter reality," and that 35 years of Social Democratic rule have failed to solve this fundamental problem, the party calls for a "structural change under popular control" to do away with the "capitalist organization" of the Swedish economy* (*Ny Dag*, 10-16 November 1967).

The new program alleges that the SAP has "administered the capitalist society," and that "power in economic areas and over important opinion-forming organs and mass media is concentrated in big business, bourgeois class distinctions and bureaucracy in administration, militarism, and police surveillance" (*Samling Vänster* Stockholm, 1967). Since the "mixed economy [i.e., socialist-capitalist systems] has not succeeded in creating favorable conditions in housing, employment, industrial democracy, and equality . . . decisive changes in the present balance of power and ownership are necessary" (*Ny Dag*, 15-21 September 1967).

The party has continued to promote intraparty debate on "means and methods" of electoral

---

*The VPK continues to attack "the Fifteen Families" who control industry and capital in Sweden. When it was disclosed that a bank owned by one of these "monopolists" had made a loan to the VPK, the party's quest for "respectability" was exemplified by Hermansson's assertion that "the party's printing operations periodically require credit just like any other business activity." (*The Economist*, London, 28 October 1967.)

collaboration with the SAP, in spite of repeated rebuffs by the SAP (the Communists have, in fact, unsuccessfully sought electoral amalgamation with the SAP since 1944).

**Domestic Activities.** When, in January 1967, the SAP scheduled an extraordinary party congress for the fall to evaluate its prospects in the 1968 general elections, the move was interpreted by the Communists as an indication that their advances in the last two elections represent a real threat to the SAP. The SAP's "need" for an extra congress was seen as a "mobilization" and as an attempt to activate and inject new power in failing areas, and "positive consequences" for the VPK could be anticipated (*Ny Dag*, 13-19 January 1967).

Spurred by SAP losses in the last election, the VPK resolved to renew its bid of "technical cooperation" with a view to 1968. A proposal, adopted by the Twenty-First Congress and presented to the SAP congress in October, envisaged cooperative electioneering with separate platforms and slates of candidates, under a joint designation such as "labor parties." No offer was made to withdraw in constituencies in which the Communists have no prospects of mandates. However, the SAP congress chose to reject the Communist bid and, in practical political terms, to face a possible defeat in 1968 rather than enter into an alliance with the VPK which could well clinch a combined parliamentary majority and a continuance in power for the Social Democrats.

Following rejection of its proposal, the VPK Party Executive asserted that the preservation of a parliamentary majority of workers' parties is mandatory to the furtherance of progressive policies and to the continued struggle to break the power of the monopolists. Therefore, "in spite of differences of opinions," and although no formal electioneering agreement would be entered into, the party looked beyond the confines of officialdom to "all socialist forces—organizations, groups, and individuals—to submit proposals for common action in the campaign" (*Ny Dag*, 24-30 November 1967).

The intensive debate since the Twentieth Party Congress and the united-front strategy finally advocated by the new program must be viewed against the exigency of avoiding a further splitting of the labor movement through the formation of a "Socialist People's Party" such as those brought about by the socialist left in Norway and Denmark in opposition to both the Communists and the Social Democrats. Expressing this concern, Kjell E. Johanson, VPK Chairman of the Greater Stockholm district, said: "The results are known. In both countries the new parties have been able to assert themselves at the same time as the Communists have been reduced and have lost nearly all influence within the electorate. In Sweden the Communist Party has been able to act in another manner. Conflict and dissension with the new elements have not been sought." (*Ny Dag*, 29 December 1967-4 January 1968.)

Evolving in the early 1960s concurrently with similar trends elsewhere in Western Europe, the "new-left" dialogue in Sweden is focused principally within the SAP; the Social Democratic youth organizations; the VPK; "solidarity" organizations; and journals such as *Zenit, Tidsignal* and *Forum Vänster*. Younger intellectuals form the core of the movement.

In April 1967 some 1,000 "new leftists" from these various groups united to form a political coalition of academic form, the Socialist Alliance (Socialistiska Förbundet; SF), under the chairmanship of Christer Hogstedt, a left-wing Social Democrat. The VPK has been quick to consolidate its ties with the SF. Kjell Johanson and Lennart Ingberg, Vice-Chairman of the Communist youth organization, have gained election to the SF working committee. The Twenty-First Congress of the VPK—to which the SF was invited—expressed its solidarity with the organizational efforts of the new left, in which "there are radical Social Democrats, Communists, and partyless socialists working together"* (*Ny Dag*, 9-15 June 1967).

It is these growing ties with the new left which prompted Hermansson's assertion that "the

---

*The Party Executive is still experiencing difficulty in convincing a right-wing segment with Sven Landin and Rolf Utberg as the central figures (both of whom were excluded from the new Party Executive) of the propitiousness of seeking close alliance with "progressive forces of the new left." This wing spurns any form of cooperation with the SF, which it terms an "extremist" group, totally unoriented in Swedish politics, and seeks instead closer ties with the SAP, viewing favorably the possibilities which a "mixed economy" together with an "activated public opinion" might offer in projecting a socialist direction into socioeconomic reforms.

Communist campaign for a socialist alternative is gaining the increased cooperation of other socialist groups, which are rebelling against the weak line of the Social Democratic government" (*Ny Dag*, 20-26 January 1967), and because "strong left winds have again begun to blow . . . it would not be appropriate to bring our policy close to that of the Social Democratic Party." On the contrary, "important fundamental differences" have come to the fore, and they have brought about an accentuation of the dividing lines *vis-à-vis* the SAP." (Stockholm Radio, 13 May 1967.) The SF terms itself an "independent, cross-political" organization willing to cooperate with "any" socialists, regardless of their affiliation, who seek to shape "that socialist left which is emerging beyond the framework of established party organizations" (*Ny Dag*, 9-15 June 1967).

A major manifestation of the VPK united-front strategy has been the advent of the "nonpartisan, new left" newspaper *Tidsignal*, which is financed largely by the VPK and, according to the Communists, "has given the new elements a chance to unite and hereby mutually cooperate with the VPK." *Tidsignal* and other "initiatives demonstrating the VPK's open and welcoming attitude" will provide for activity within an "established" party (*Ny Dag*, 29 December 1967-4 January 1968). In addition, the VPK underscores the significance of "unaffiliated action groups such as Left Forum, Ban-the-Bomb, Provos, the Vietnam Committee, and Anti-Apartheid," which have interests in common with the "socialist reshaping" of the VPK, and which should be regarded as "stimulants" in the work to win over Swedish public opinion (*Ny Dag*, 24 February-2 March 1967).

While repeatedly rejecting collaboration with the VPK at the polls, the SAP has in many respects displayed a far more conciliatory attitude toward it since the 1966 elections. Prime Minister Tage Erlander has said that a "merger" of the SAP and the VPK, which is unacceptable to the VPK, would not be out of the question. Moreover, the administration withdrew a parliamentary bill to abolish rent controls in the face of long-standing and vigorous pressure from the nonsocialist parties to enact such a measure. Of all parliamentary groups, the Communists alone opposed the bill, and the SAP decision (in December 1967) to kill it was geared to the interests of low-income voters, mainly Social Democrats and Communists.

At the same time, the SAP has vehemently condemned Social Democratic supporters of the SF, declaring membership in that organization to be "fundamentally incompatible" with SAP affiliation (*Ny Dag*, 2-8 June 1967). A number of leading activists, including Göran Therborn, editor of a book entitled *En Ny Vänster* (A New Left), have subsequently relinquished their SAP membership on the grounds that "socialist activity is impossible within the party" (*Ny Dag*, 1-7 September 1967).

Thus, while Communist perspectives will continue to emphasize consolidation with the new left, the party stands to lose by a formal secession en masse of left-wing radicals from the Social Democratic movement.

Throughout the year the VPK pressed for expanded parliamentary control of the activities of the Swedish security police and for the abolition of a "secret register" maintained by the security police and allegedly containing the names of 300,000 "potential security risks." Following a Vietnam demonstration on 20 December, the party demanded government intervention against "police brutality," which the Communists equated with "nazism" and with the "lack of democracy within the police system" (*Ny Dag*, 29 December 1967-4 January 1968). A report released by the Swedish government on 12 January 1968 disclosed that a special parliamentary commission had, in fact, been set up in 1964 to investigate the methods of the security police, following the conviction of Colonel Stig Wennerström for espionage on behalf of the Soviet Union. According to the report, attempts by Communists to obtain key posts in Sweden's defense and police forces have increased. What impact these disclosures will have on the "new image" of the VPK remains to be seen, but Hermansson has charged the commission with having "insulted" him and his party, and he has threatened to take legal action (*NYT*, 15 January 1968).

**Pro-Chinese Splinter Groups.** No apparent attempt was made by the Hermansson majority to suppress the weak but vociferous pro-Chinese KF, either in the precongress period or at the Twenty-First Congress itself. By openly acknowledging the split, the VPK has sought to demonstrate to the public its disencumberment of "undesirable" and "discordant" elements within its ranks. An editorial in *Norrskensflamman* (27 June 1967) referred to the KF as "a bourgeois conception of a revolutionary policy" and emphasized that "the VPK will not be the tumbling ground for anti-Soviet conspiracies."

Close ties exist between the KF and a pro-Chinese student organization, Clarté, of which the Chairman is Gunnar Bylin and which publishes a journal also called *Clarté*. There is some degree of cooperation between the KF and an older pro-Chinese splinter group, the Communist Workers' Association, headed by Sven-Erik Holmsten and formed in 1953 following the expulsion from the VPK of certain pro-Peking "revolutionaries." The Association has an estimated membership of 3,000.

The KF has announced its intention to enter the 1968 elections, and to establish relations with "the new revolutionary underground movements, forbidden by the revisionists, which are beginning to grow in Poland, in the Soviet Union, and elsewhere" (*Ny Dag*, 26 May-1 June 1967). At its first conference, in Stockholm on 23-25 June, the KF adopted documents calling for the "unmasking of Soviet revisionism," for the "rebuilding of a Marxist-Leninist party in Sweden," and for the "advancement of class struggle until a society of Communism without classes is founded" (NCNA, Peking, 12 August 1967). According to the KF, "socialism can be established only by an extraparliamentary struggle of the masses" (*Marxistiskt Forum*, No. 3, 1967), as opposed to the "cooperation of the VPK with the fascists" (*Ny Dag*, 16-21 June 1967).

The fact that the Chinese Communist Party was instrumental in establishing the KF was clearly evidenced by a meeting which took place in Peking only a month before between Holmberg, Baude, and high-ranking Chinese party officials, including Politburo member K'ang Sheng (*Peking Review*, 21 April 1967).

Pronouncements of the VPK congress favoring broader cooperation in specific areas with the administration engendered substantial sentiment within VPK ranks which, though not avidly in favor of Chinese policies, leans toward support of the KF simply because those pronouncements "sounded the death knell" for revolutionary policies of the VPK, which is today "but an appendage to the bourgeois Social Democratic Party. [In evidence of this], agitation against Communism, formerly so common, has died away almost entirely, [and] it will be the task of the KF to lead the pent-up class struggle which will be developed by the Swedish people sooner or later" (*Norrskensflamman*, 29 July 1967).

**Auxiliary Organizations.** Democratic Youth (Demokratisk Ungdom; DU), the affiliated youth organization of the VPK, held its Twenty-Eighth Congress in Stockholm on 16-18 June and, pursuing the united-front policy of its parent party, advocated that the organization seek recognition as "the youth organization of the combined socialist left" rather than "merely as the youth affiliate of the VPK." Again emulating the VPK, a resolution was adopted to change the name of the group to Leftist Youth League (Vänsterns Ungdomsförbund; VUF) as an indication of its broader front and, in practical terms, to seek "concrete cooperation with the Social Democratic youth movement" (*Ny Dag*, 23-29 June 1967). Kjell Johanson declined reelection as Chairman and retired from the youth organization (he is now an alternate member of the VPK Party Executive, Chairman of the Greater Stockholm Communist Party, and a member of the Board of the SF). Anders Carlberg, President of the student organization, Unity Party of the Left, was named to succeed Johanson. The Executive Committee of the VUF comprises Anders Carlberg, Lennart Ingberg (Vice-Chairman), Ulf Ellemark (Secretary), Urban Osby, and Klas-Göran Warginger. The program and activities of the VUF closely parallel those of the Social Democratic youth organizations, which are considerably more radical than the SAP itself. The theme of the youth congress was "international solidarity," particularly on the Vietnam issue.

The VPK's attempts to foster cooperation with the Social Democrats have met with failure at the trade-union level. Communists control no national unions and only about 80 of the approximately 9,000 union locals. Their strength in trade-union locals is largely in building and construction, forestry, and miners' unions (*World Strength of the Communist Party Organizations*, 1968).

Among the "friendship" organizations controlled by the VPK are the Swedish-Soviet Union Association, which claims 7,000 members, and the Swedish-East German Friendship Society.

**International Views and Policies.** Mindful of electoral defeats of the past stemming from the VPK's overt allegiance to Moscow (as, for example, its defense of the Berlin Wall, which resulted in only 3.8 per cent of the votes in the 1962 elections), the Communists now elect to follow a distinctly more "isolationist" line, paralleling on many issues the "neutralist" policy of the Social Democrats. The party calls upon the socialist left in the Nordic countries to "formulate an independent security policy" based on withdrawal from NATO in 1969, the subsequent formation of a "Nordic neutrality union" and a nuclear-free North, nationalization of armaments industries with a view to eventual total disarmament, and recognition of both German states and of existing borders (*Ny Dag,* 3-9 November 1967). In a "package" proposal to Parliament, Axel Jansson, a VPK member of Parliament, said:

> Military defense must be seen as only a part, and a shrinking part, of our country's security policy, while international tasks—assistance to underdeveloped countries, support to freedom movements, measures for nuclear weapon bans and for disarmament, international cooperation at different levels—increase in significance. Swedish neutrality policies should be directed toward the formation of a Nordic defense alliance. A militarily thinned-out żone in the North combined with a demilitarized Germany, together with a disarmed and nuclear-free Central Europe, would constitute an important contribution to international relaxation of tension. (*Ny Dag,* 26 May-1 June 1967.)

The Twenty-First Congress failed to produce agreement on the question of national defense, and two working commissions were charged with the formulation of specific recommendations. Approximately two-thirds of the delegates (190 votes) favored a "tenacious, extensive, and effective partisan struggle in defense of neutral Sweden against an invading power," while 97 votes were cast in favor of "step-by-step total disarmament linked with an international security system, in which guerrilla struggle is not precluded" (*Samling Vänster,* Stockholm, 1967).

As the only Swedish party opposed to affiliation with the European Economic Community, the VPK alleges that the Social Democrats have "succumbed to the pressures of the capitalists" and that "it is quite obvious that the rightists are openly prepared to surrender our country's neutrality for those advantages upon which they could count in the event of EEC affiliation" (*Ny Dag,* 17-23 November 1967). Since the EEC is "a political union," Swedish affiliation would be "incompatible" with neutrality. As an alternative the VPK advocates "initiatives on a Nordic level" to substitute for "bloc making" (*Ny Dag,* 10-16 November 1967), concentrating upon trade with developing countries and with the socialist states in Europe, "where substantial markets await" (*Ny Dag,* 15-21 September 1967). Such joint Nordic measures to promote an "active peace policy" supporting "social-freedom movements" would "diminish tension between the world power bloc and between rich and poor countries."

According to Hermansson, "the burning issue today is Vietnam" (*Ny Dag,* 17-23 November 1967). Participation and sponsorship by the VPK of movements protesting US involvement escalated considerably during 1967, and the party vigorously supports both national and international campaigns. On 18 August the Party Executive called for government "verification of Swedish exports to the USA which that country can use directly or indirectly in its war against the people of Vietnam, and measures to ban the export of such goods" (*Information Bulletin,* no. 105, 1967).

Of a cross-political character, the antiwar movement has been endorsed by the Swedish government, and only modest attribution for its considerable impact is actually due to the activities of the Communists. The central VPK figure in the Swedish Vietnam Committee is John Takman, member of a 1967 Russell Tribunal medical "fact-finding" commission to North Vietnam, whose stature in the party was reflected in his securing the greatest number of votes in the election of the new Party Executive. A VPK declaration of solidarity with the National Liberation Front of South Vietnam stated: "The Russel Tribunal's session in Stockholm in May and the World Conference for Vietnam [International Conference on Vietnam] in Stockholm in July have shown the possibilities that are to be found in uniting peace-loving people of many religious and political leanings in this international movement" (*Ny Dag,* 6-12 October 1967).

The Communists urge pressure by the government, through the United Nations, the European Free Trade Association, and other organs, against Portugal's "oppressive policy in the African colonies," for economic and material support of the liberation movement in Mozambique," and for an official ban on private Swedish investments in these areas (*Ny Dag*, 26 May-June 1967). The administration was also urged to sever diplomatic relations with the "fascist regime" in Greece. Bolivian authorities were condemned for the sentencing of Régis Debray and Ciro Bustos, which would "win over tens of thousands of new freedom fighters" (*Ny Dag*, 24-30 November 1967).

In the Arab-Israeli conflict, the party carefully steered a middle course, upholding the right of Israel to national existence but denying its right to acquisition of new territories. The left is urged not to divide into pro-Israel and pro-Arab groups, but to jointly seek the only "real solution in the Middle East," namely, "peaceful coexistence on the long term" (*Ny Dag*, 9-15 June 1967).

**The International Communist Movement.** According to an interview in the Italian Social Democratic journal *Corrispondenza Socialista* in April 1967, Hermansson is reported to have stated:

> We do not wish to take a position in regard to China and the USSR. For this reason we will not go to Warsaw if an anti-Chinese world conference is called in the Polish capital. The Communist Party of the USSR and that of China are to us only two Communist parties. Neither the CCP nor the CPSU in our opinion has the right to assume a position of leadership—not even in the ideological area. . . . The truth is that today an international Communist movement no longer eixsts. . . . The problem today is not the strengthening of the Communist movement or its unity. . . . The unity of the workers' movement is more important than the unity of the Communist movement . . . .

Although it did not participate in the conferences of European communist parties in Brussels in 1965 and Vienna in 1966, the VPK did dispatch an "observer" (Fritjof Lager) to the Karlovy Vary Conference of European Communist and Workers' Parties on 24-27 April 1967, and Hermansson explained on 20 April that "were the Conference to be limited to an exchange of views between the participants, we would gladly have accepted the invitation [to send a participant]. But now they want to adopt a complete text, including detailed opinions on questions of European security. We feel that it is more normal for each party to formulate its own decisions on such political questions."* He also commented that "developments in the Soviet Union in important aspects do not correspond to what we believe must follow socialism's ideal" (*Ny Dag*, 30 June-6 July 1967).

As has been the case since he became party leader, Hermansson made few official visits during 1967. He was in Iceland on 15-21 March as a guest of the Radical Student Association and had talks with the Central Committee of the United Socialist Party. Visiting Finland on 3-5 April at the invitation of the Academic Socialist Society, he lectured in Helsinki and in Jyvaskyla on "left winds in Sweden." In the Soviet Union for the first time since his accession, Hermansson attended the 1967 International Scientific Conference in Moscow on 11-15 November. However, reiterating the reason for his failure to attend the Twenty-Third Congress of the Soviet party in 1966, he was not in Moscow for the October Revolution festivities owing to the press of "parliamentary work," and Party Secretary Urban Karlsson headed the VPK delegation. In its greetings to the Soviet party the VPK acknowledged and praised the significance of the Revolution for the Soviet Union but viewed it as an "inspiration" for socialist revolution elsewhere rather than as a pattern to be duplicated (*Ny Dag*, 10-16 November 1967).

The VPK participated in Nordic Socialist Seminars in Copenhagen on 26-27 February and in Oslo in the fall, sponsored by the Danish and Norwegian Socialist People's Parties, respectively. Both meetings dealt with the relations of Nordic nations to the EEC and NATO and with the revitalization of the Nordic Council (the Norwegian and Danish Communist Parties were excluded from both convocations). Evert Holm represented the party at the congress of the Norwegian Socialist People's Party held in Oslo in May. Party Executive member Sture Andersson attended the congress of the Finnish People's Democratic League in Helsinki on 13-15 May. A Rumanian party delegation headed by Mihai Dalea, member of the Central Committee, visited Sweden on 16-21 October and had

---

*The VPK did not attend the Budapest Consultative Conference in February 1968, and the brief and detached reportage carried by *Ny Dag* once more reflected the party's stand. *Norrskensflamman* (14 March 1968), on the other hand, hailed the decision to hold a world conference, even though some parties would be absent: "The world political situation is now so serious that waiting for a miracle would be irresponsible and offering passivity in place of unity would benefit only ruthless imperialism."

talks with the Greater Stockholm Communist Party. John Takman represented the Swedish Peace Committee at the International Conference on Vietnam in Stockholm on 6-9 July.

The foreign delegations at the VPK congress were the Communist Party of Finland, the Finnish People's Democratic League, the Communist Party of Denmark, the Socialist People's Party of Denmark, the Communist Party of Norway, and the Socialist People's Party of Norway.

**Publications.** The party press played a significant role in 1967, and a congress resolution which moved to support the socialist left virtually gave the Party Executive *carte blanche* in the matter of appropriations for *Tidsignal* (Time Signal) and other organs of the new left.

The central organ of the party is *Ny Dag* (New Day), issued weekly and edited by Per Francke. The VPK began publication in February 1967 of a quarterly theoretical journal, *Socialistisk Debatt* (Socialist Debate), edited by Lars Herlitz and Jörn Svensson. It is not known whether the theoretical journal *Vår Tid* (Our Times), previously published by the VPK, still exists. Other party organs made no reference to it during 1967, nor was it mentioned in the congress proceedings.

Although it was proposed by the Party Executive on 19 March that publication of *Norrskensflamman* (Blaze of Northern Lights), the 60-year-old organ of the Norrbotten district and the party's sole remaining daily, be discontinued "for reasons of economy," local support, mustered largely by former party Chairman Hilding Hagberg, was so strong that an extraordinary district conference on 17 September, following a successful fund-raising campaign, "practically unanimously" resolved to continue publication of the paper (*Land og Folk*, Copenhagen, 22 September 1967).

*Stormklockan* (Storm Bell), the organ of the VUF, is issued six times a year.

Organs of the KF are *Marxistiskt Forum* (Marxist Forum), published in Uppsala, and *Gnistan* (Spark), published in Göteborg.

The pro-Chinese Communist Workers' Association irregularly publishes a journal called *Revolte*.

# SWITZERLAND

The Swiss Party of Labor (Parti Suisse du Travail/Partei der Arbeit; PdA) was founded in October 1944 by socialist groups and members of the former Communist Party of Switzerland (founded in 1921 and outlawed by the Swiss Government in November 1940). The PdA functions legally and claims a membership of 5,000 (Edgar Woog, PdA Secretary-General, in *World Marxist Review*, December 1966). The population of Switzerland is about six million. Besides the pro-Soviet PdA, there are the Swiss Communist Party (founded as a pro-Chinese splinter in 1963, renamed Swiss People's Party in September 1967) and the Organization of Communists in Switzerland. Two former splinter groups, the Cercle Lénine and the Organisation des Marxistes-Léninistes de Suisse, merged with the Swiss Communist Party in the fall of 1966.

In the last elections to the Swiss National Council (the lower house of Parliament), 28-29 October 1967, the PdA increased its seats from four to five. With five Councilmen the PdA qualified as an independent faction in the Swiss Parliament; provided that the larger parties agree, it is entitled to participate in Parliamentary commissions. (The Social-Democratic Party, the strongest group in the Council, obtained 50 of the 200 seats.)

**Organization and Leadership.** The structure of the PdA follows the political federal structure of the Swiss confederation, the party being divided into cantonal sections. Although the party is in fact highly centralized at the national level, where domestic matters are concerned the national headquarters remains in the background and the cantonal sections ostensibly speak for themselves.

The cantonal sections of the PdA go by a variety of names: Partei der Arbeit in German-language areas (the most important sections are Zurich and Basel-Stadt); Parti du Travail in Geneva; Parti Ouvrier et Populaire in Vaud and some other cantons; Parti Ouvrier et Paysan in the canton of Valais; Partito Ticinese del Lavoro in the Italian-language canton of Tessin. Most members of the national leadership also have sectional party functions, and party sources usually refer to the PdA leadership by their sectional positions, except in the context of international matters.

The Eighth PdA Party Congress, held in Geneva 16-18 May 1964, elected a Central Committee of 50 members and five candidates, and a Central Control Commission of five members; the names of the Central Committee and Central Control Commission members were not made public by the PdA. The congress reelected Edgar Woog Secretary-General. The Central Committee elected a Directory Committee of 16 members: Jean Vincent, Roger Dafflon, Etienne Lentillon, Armand Magnin, Karl Odermatt, Eugénie Tüscher-Chiostergi, and Henri Trüb (all from Geneva); André Muret, and Ernest Décosterd (both from Lausanne); André Corswant (from La-Chaux-de-Fonds), who died in August 1964 and was replaced by Pietro Monetti (from Mendrisio); Frédéric Blaser (from Le Locle); Franz Dübi, and Robert Krebs (both from Basel-Stadt); Edwin Burlet, Jakob Lechleiter, and Edgar Woog (all from Zurich).

The Directory Committee elected a Political Secretariat of four members: Edgar Woog, Franz Dübi, André Muret, and Jean Vincent. Besides the 16 Directory Committee members, Pierre Guéniat and the "chief ideologist" Konrad Farner are Central Committee members.

Auxiliary organizations of the PdA, several of which are again subdivided into cantonal sections, are the Swiss Peace Movement, which tries to infiltrate noncommunist pacifist organizations; the Switzerland-Soviet Union Society (Gesellschaft Schweiz-Sowjetunion); the Swiss "Culture and People" Association (Schweizerische Vereinigung Kultur und Volk); the Free Youth of Switzerland (Freie Jugend der Schweiz); the Swiss League of Women for Peace and Progress (L'Union des Femmes pour la Paix et le Progrès); the Centrale Sanitaire Suisse (CSS); Swiss Committee for Aid to Vietnam (a section of the CSS); the Association of Older People, the Disabled, and Widows and Orphans (AVIVO); the Literature Distribution Center (Genossenschaft Literaturvertrieb/Centre de Diffusion de la Littérature); the Zurich Progressive Student Body (Fortschrittliche Studentenschaft Zürich); the University Trade Union Action (ASUS), with sections in Geneva, Lausanne, Fribourg, and Bern; the Society for the Defense of Tenants (Lausanne); and the Singing Group of Basel-Stadt and Zurich.

As PdA Secretary-General Edgar Woog stated in *WMR* (December 1966), the party's "position in the trade unions is weak." *Vorwärts* of 26 October 1967 deplored the "ideological corruption of a large section of the trade-union functionaries through absolute peace in labor relations and relatively great material concessions."

**Domestic Views and Policies.** In 1967 the PdA followed rather consistently the course laid out by Edgar Woog at the Prague conference of communist parties in November 1966 (cf. *WMR*, December 1966, pp. 40-42). Except for the small, vociferous, dissident communist groups, Communists in Switzerland went along with the united-left approach and made great efforts to persuade the Socialists to join forces for the various elections to be held in 1967. While this communist-socialist dialogue remained by and large unsuccessful, the PdA could consider its overall performance in the elections successful.

At the PdA National Conference, in Lausanne on 27-28 May 1967, the 135 delegates approved four resolutions: "On the International Situation," "For the Return to Liberty and Democracy in Greece," "Against Real Estate Speculation," and "For the Party Press!—For the Elections!" (*Voix Ouvrière*, 31 May).

The Conference also approved a proposal of the Directory Committee to adopt a platform for the national elections entitled "For a New Politics! For a New Switzerland!" The platform, published in the PdA daily *Voix Ouvrière* on 15 July (also in *Vorwärts*, 20 July), traced the "general perspectives of the struggle for the defense and the improvement of the existence of the working class and the Swiss people, as well as for the establishment of a socialist Switzerland." In a long-range discussion of the Swiss political scene, the platform referred to the "Helvetic malaise," meaning a general political unease which it attributed to Swiss banks, monopolies, and private economic organizations who "dictate their class politics to the governing parties"; the platform admitted that there has been a general improvement in Swiss living standards and attributed to this the growing influence of reformist ideas and petty-bourgeois ideology. To the formation of an "alliance of the people, gathering around it ever broadening groups of workers, employees, peasants, intellectuals, and craftsmen," the Social-Democratic Party was designated the chief obstacle and was accused of pursuing a "policy of reconciliation with the bourgeoisie." The "alliance of the people" was foreseen as being able to carry out a "new politics" of taxation, nationalization, and economic control, although the result would not immediately be a "socialist" society. The new course of this phase of development of Swiss society would constitute the "peaceful transition to socialism." The platform closed with a call to all progressive forces in Switzerland to unite with the PdA to "win the New Switzerland." The platform also listed a number of "immediate solutions," a short-range action program for the PdA, which contained the main points of the ten-point "Immediate Program of the Swiss Party of Labor," published later in *Vorwärts* (14 September, reprinted in *IB*, no. 108). This program demanded: measures against inflation, a "progressive" tax and finance policy, lower military spending, "adequate" old-age pensions, better housing legislation, better social insurance, a more effective "infrastructure" (a national development plan for hospitals, road building, universities, land legislation, and so on), women's rights (e.g., suffrage), education and occupational training for young persons, and a foreign policy of "peace" (i.e., disarmament measures, European security arrangements).

In 1967 the PdA participated in a number of elections besides the national elections in October. In the Great Council elections in the canton of Tessin on 12 February the PdA won two seats. In the Cantonal Council elections of Zurich 8-9 April, the PdA was the only party to make progress: it gained 4.5 per cent of all votes cast, compared with 2.7 per cent in 1963, a success which the Communists interpreted as a result of the PdA's being the "only consistent opposition party with a major social alternative" (*Vorwärts*, 6 April). In the Geneva municipal elections, 22-23 April 1967, the PdA was the only party (except for the newly created conservative Vigilants Party) to gain votes, winning a total of 16 seats, a gain of one over 1963, which made it the strongest party in the city legislature. The Socialists lost four seats. In the Geneva communities, the PdA won 28 seats, a gain of six over 1963. The PdA did not do well, however, in the Geneva administrative (executive) elections of 27-28 May and 18 June. For the elections to the National Council on October 28-29, the PdA entered its own candidates in six of the 25 cantons. Except in Başel-Stadt, there was a noticeable increase in PdA votes, which totaled 28,522 (or 2.9 per cent of votes cast), as compared with 22,088 (2.2 per cent) in 1963. In the canton of Valais, the Communists supported the dissident Socialist Karl Dellberg, who won his seat.

The CPSU and the French Communist Party sent messages congratulating the PdA on winning five seats in the National Council. An article in *WMR* (December 1967) speaks of the "striking success of the Swiss Party of Labor, which has won added public confidence." Unlike their counterparts in France, the Communists in Switzerland still operate in relative isolation from the Socialists. PdA offers of election agreements and coordination of lists have generally met an unfavorable response from the Socialists. The prominent reporting in the PdA press on united-left successes in 1967 elsewhere in the world (as in France and the Indian state of Kerala) showed, however, the party's keen interest in this political strategy. Frédéric Blaser and Jakob Lechleiter, both members of the PdA Directory Committee, who accompanied Roger Dafflon as delegates to the Eighteenth Congress of the French Communist Party, 4-8 January, in reports on the Congress published in *Voix Ouvrière* on 14 January and *Vorwärts* on 19 January greatly emphasized unity of the left as the outstanding theme of the French Congress.

Although facing the same task of enlarging the political base of the party as the Communist Party of Austria, the PdA gave comparatively less emphasis to the Marxist-Christian dialogue. There were favorable comments on the papal encyclical *Populorum Progressio* in *Voix Ouvrière* (30 March, 6 April) and also a long article on this dialogue by PdA Central Committee member Konrad Farner in *Vorwärts* (21 September).

At the Central Committee meeting at Lausanne, 1-2 April, Directory Committee member André Muret presented a report on the national situation. Directory Committee member Jean Vincent spoke on international problems (the struggle for peace, European security, and national independence). Directory Committee member Roger Dafflon reported on the revision of the pension system. The meeting approved three resolutions, dealing respectively with the necessity of a "united-left" course for the PdA, government pension payments, and the international situation (concerning particularly the Chinese Communist Party). (*Ibid.*, 5 June.)

**PdA Attempts at Electoral Cooperation.** A number of cantonal meetings and conferences were concerned with election problems and the refusal of the Socialists to participate in election agreements. The cantonal congress of the Geneva PdA section took place 11-12 March. When the Geneva Socialists on 3 May decided to "go alone into battle" for the administrative elections, the PdA issued a declaration "deploring the attitude of the Geneva Socialist Party" (*ibid.*, 5 May). The PdA of Neuchatel (POP Neuchatelois), which in March had invited the Socialists of Neuchatel to work out some agreement for the national elections, held an extraordinary congress on 1 September after the Socialists had, by a slight majority, turned down the invitation. This PdA section subsequently won the important fifth National Council seat. On 8 September the cantonal committee of the Parti Ouvrier et Paysan (POP) of Valais decided to support the Socialist Dellberg if he should be ousted by his party. Although subsequently ousted, Dellberg won, as noted earlier. The congress of the POP of Vaud, meeting at Vevey on 24 September, again discussed the situation resulting from Socialists' refusal to elaborate a "joint governmental program" (congress resolution, *ibid.*, 26 September); other resolutions dealt with the war in Vietnam and with Greece.

**International Affairs.** On issues confronting the international communist movement, the PdA followed a strictly Moscow-oriented line. Directory Committee member Roger Dafflon, at the Eighteenth Congress of the French Communist Party, spoke in favor of following the course outlined by the declarations of 1957 and 1960, rejected the "erroneous and splitting theses" of the leaders of the Chinese party, and supported "all initiatives necessary to strengthen the unity of the international communist movement" (*ibid.*, 10 January). A joint communique following the talks in Moscow on 6 February between Secretary-General Edgar Woog, accompanied by Muret and Lentillon, and Suslov and Ponomarev repeated this position. The communique also declared the "unity of views of the two parties . . . on all problems examined." (*Ibid.*, 7 February.) The PdA Central Committee meeting in April again condemned the Chinese and "judged a world conference of communist and workers parties to be desirable" at an appropriate time (*ibid*, 5 April). At the Seventh Congress of the Socialist Unity Party of [East] Germany, in April, Directory Committee member J. Lechleiter expressed the view of the PdA that the conditions for a world conference had been met.

The PdA participated in the preparatory meeting of European communist parties in Warsaw, 22-26 February, sending Directory Committee member Jakob Lechleiter (*ibid.*, 23 February) and was subsequently represented at the Karlovy Vary conference by Secretary-General Edgar Woog and Lechleiter. Woog signed the statement of the conference (*ibid.*, 27 April).

Besides the rather detailed reporting on China in the PdA daily, Jean Vincent's full-page article entitled "New Reflections on the Events in China" referred to developments in China as deplorable and having "nothing in common with socialism such as we understand it." On the other hand, Vincent (a member of the PdA Secretariat) went into detail to explain that his party was not condemning or "excommunicating" the Chinese Communist Party, but was simply judging the facts. To do this, he emphasized, was not a proof of being "in the Soviet camp." To illuminate further this critique of the Chinese Communist Party, the PdA paper reprinted two lengthy articles from *L'Humanité* on "Marxism Is Not a Catechism" (*Voix Ouvrière,* 11 and 13 February).

The PdA in 1967 gave active support to opposition to the Vietnam war and the military regime in Greece, both in resolutions of the National Conference in May and in resolutions and communiques of cantonal congresses. The Vietnamese and Greek issues were also recognized as welcome common ground with noncommunist groups in Switzerland. For instance, *Voix Ouvrière* on 3 May, published a letter addressed to the Greek Embassy in Bern by the Socialist Youth of Geneva and the "Youth of the Party of Labor."

A PdA declaration on the conflict in the Middle East (*ibid.*, 8 June) linked the crisis there with Vietnam and Greece and demanded a negotiated settlement which would take into consideration both Israel's right to national existence and the legitimate rights of the Arab people. Subsequently the PdA showed its agreement with Moscow's attitude by reporting in detail on the Moscow and Budapest conferences on the Middle East in June and July, respectively. The PdA openly took the side of the Meir Vilner group in the Israeli Communist Party and published many of its statements. Regarding Cyprus, *Voix Ouvrière* on 10 July denounced NATO and the presence of the US Sixth Fleet in the Mediterranean. The OLAS Conference in Havana received only wire-service coverage in the press of the PdA. *Voix Ouvrière* on 4 August 1967 used excerpts from an article in *L'Unità* to give some hints of the disagreement among Latin American communists and to explain why a number of pro-Soviet communist parties in Latin America were not represented at the Havana meeting. This cautious opposition of the PdA to the political line of Fidel Castro is in agreement with the stand of those West European communist parties who do not wish to see their "united left" drives disturbed by those who advance a violent and revolutionary approach as the only valid road to socialism.

The Fiftieth Anniversary of the October Revolution, on the other hand, was given ample publicity. The Central Committee meeting of 1-2 April hailed the coming celebrations of the anniversary and invited all sections of the PdA to prepare for this grandiose commemoration through popular events, publications, and cultural manifestations and to give it all the pomp it deserved (*Voix Ouvrière,* 5 April). A special issue on the anniversary was published by the PdA daily on 4 November. Secretary-General Woog and Central Committee Secretariat members Muret and Vincent attended the Moscow celebrations. Edgar Woog also attended the international conference on the "Fiftieth Anniversary of the October Revolution and the Contemporary Working Class Movement" in Moscow, 11-15 November. On 8-19 November, three Soviet representatives (a Supreme Soviet deputy, an economics professor, and a journalist) visited Switzerland and participated in a number of Fiftieth Anniversary celebrations.

According to official radio information from Warsaw, a PdA delegation headed by

Secretary-General Edgar Woog visited Poland in May at the invitation of the Central Committee of the Polish party. The delegation met on 10 May with Central Committee Secretary Artur Starewicz and other Central Committee members. On 13 May, the Swiss Communists met with Politburo Member Zenon Kliszko to discuss problems of the international communist movement. The delegation departed on 15 May. This visit was not reported by the domestic communist press in Switzerland. Neither did the PdA report on a visit of Secretary-General Woog to an international communist meeting in Hungary at the end of 1967, on which occasion he was interviewed by the Hungarian Communist Party organ *Népszabadság*.

**The Swiss Communist Party.** The Swiss Communist Party (Parti Communiste Suisse/Kommunistische Partei der Schweiz; PCS) with headquarters in Vevey (Vaud) was founded 1 September 1963 as the first pro-Chinese splinter party in western Europe. At its Third Congress, 24-25 September 1966, two previously "autonomous" cells, the Cercle Lénine and the Organisation des Marxistes-Léninistes de Suisse, declared their adherence to the PCS (press communique, *L'Etincelle,* no. 22, September 1966). Secretary-General Gérard Bulliard, founder of the party and former member of the PdA, in an interview with *National-Zeitung* (17 July 1967) gave the membership of his party as "315 members and sympathizers, including 30 intellectuals." The actual membership is probably far less; there are estimates as low as a "handful."

The PCS organ *L'Etincelle* has taken a firm pro-Chinese attitude, defending the cultural revolution against critics among other communist parties; in particular, its January 1967 issue attacked the views of the Twenty-third Congress of the CPSU, held in 1966. A long rebuttal to French Communist Party Central Committee member Kanapa's article "Marxism Is Not a Catechism" (see *Documents*), reprinted in the PdA organ *Voix Ouvrière* appeared in the February issue. Another article in the same issue analyzed the cultural revolution and stated the PCS position as follows: "In our opinion, this [the cultural revolution] should have upon the destiny of mankind a repercussion and an impact of still more importance than the October Revolution itself"—the reason being, according to the article, that the complete transformation of society after the seizure of power by the proletariat requires a continuous revolutionary effort. The March issue advocated the cultural revolution as part of the dictatorship of the proletariat. Along the same line, the April issue carried a major attack against the PdA and its "revisionist" ideology. Claiming to be the only Swiss organization based on Marxist-Leninist principles, the PCS criticized the PdA leadership for its collaboration with the Pope and the "renegade" CPSU. The PCS proposed Mao's thought and the Chinese comrades as guiding examples.

The PCS took a very militant position against religion and the Vatican. "To seek and to sustain the revolution strongly implies the antireligious struggle," said an article on "Vatican maneuvers" (*L'Etincelle,* January 1967). Chinese and Albanian attitudes toward Rome were praised (*ibid.,* February). The March issue of *L'Etincelle* charged the Soviet Union with collaboration with the Vatican, declaring, "one has to fight the churches and ought not to follow the Soviet Union, [whose policies] conserve and now even support religion." Each issue of the party organ also had a special column for attacks upon religion.

Despite these massive efforts to prove itself pro-Chinese and revolutionary, the PCS was unable to establish itself as the official pro-Chinese group in Switzerland with Peking's blessing. This explains the continuous indirect critique of the much smaller Organization of Communists of Switzerland (see below), which *L'Etincelle* at the end of 1966 even suspected of being an agent of the Swiss federal police. In spite of the publicity given by the PCS daily to Marxist-Leninist activities abroad, and in spite of the recommendations of the PCS by other Marxist-Leninist publications (such as *La Voix du Peuple* and *L'Humanité Nouvelle*), the Organization of Communists of Switzerland remained the internationally accepted Marxist-Leninist group.

On international issues, the PCS showed its anti-"revisionist" position when it accused the socialist countries of obstructing revolution in the Third World by not helping to build up revolutionary parties, and by nullifying the conditions for genuine revolutionary struggle (*L'Etincelle,* February). Using the *coup d'état* in Greece as an example, the PCS ridiculed all hopes for a "peaceful road to socialism." Only violent action by progressive forces can bring about a qualitative change of a given historical situation, the PCS claimed (*ibid.,* April). The PCS rejects terrorism, however, as completely alien to the "Marxist-Leninist theory of revolutionary violence" (*ibid.,* May). Viewing the creation of the state of Israel by the UN as the source of trouble in the Middle East, the PCS denounced a PdA declaration, published in *Voix Ouvrière,* together with the politics of "peaceful coexistence" of the revisionists who ask for "negotiations." Similarly, it opposed any negotiation with the United States on Vietnam (*ibid.,* May).

The above description of the ideological stand of the PCS reflects the views expressed in *L'Etincelle* from January to May (5 issues). The May issue, however, was not delivered until July. A single loose page, inserted into this issue explains that, though the issue was ready, it was delayed because of an "extraordinary congress" of the PCS on 29 May. This congress was convened at the request of a third of the members and was focused on a critique of Secretary-General Gérard Bulliard and certain decisions he had made. The members who called for the congress objected to many of Bulliard's activities and demanded his resignation. His "total nonalignment" with the Chinese comrades was discussed. After the congress, the situation in the PCS returned to normal or "almost" normal, according to this loose page. There were no resignations or exclusions. The inserted page, however, stated that comrade Bulliard had accepted an invitation to visit a "great country of people's democracy" (the German Democratic Republic, as became known later). It further announced the decision of the PCS to adapt itself to the actual Swiss situation: "The ideological line remains resolutely favorable to our Chinese comrades. No personality, however, will be deified." The PCS mentioned plans to become broader and to be open to "all sincere progressives, Marxist or not," adding that it could not afford to be a "simple group of romantics" who considered themselves "pro-Chinese."

A communique of 3 August, signed by Gérard Bulliard and André Monachon, stated that the Swiss Communist Party had been dissolved by majority vote of its members and would be reconstituted at a congress on 9 September as the Swiss People's Party (Parti Populaire Suisse; PPS). According to *Neue Zürcher Zeitung* ([*Fernausgabe*], 6 August), the communique explained that the name change was carried out at the demand of the most active militants of the PCS, together with members of the Swiss Party of Labor, the Swiss Socialist Party, the Socialist Youth, and nonorganized trade-unionists and progressives. The communique stated further that the new party would follow as far as possible a neutral position in the Sino-Soviet dispute. Its political orientation, though still strictly revolutionary, would be adapted to Swiss realities. The Swiss People's Party would consider the peoples of both China and the Soviet Union as friends.*

Between the announcement of the dissolution of the Swiss Communist Party in the communique of 3 August and the constitutive congress of the new Swiss People's Party on 9 September, Secretary-General Bulliard traveled to the German Democratic Republic. The next issue of *L'Etincelle*, no. 30 (no date, sent out in October), the first issue prepared after the extraordinary congress in May and the constitutive congress in September, viewed East Germany as a model for a Swiss socialist society: "For us Swiss Communists, the GDR should serve as a guide in the elaboration of the socialist society which we will construct."

Along with the change in name, the party considerably reshaped its ideological outlook. The statutes of the Swiss People's Party speak of a Central Committee of at least 24 members, a Political Bureau of 12 (including the Secretary-General), and a Central Secretariat of seven members. The names of the party officials were not given, except for Bulliard as Secretary-General. According to Bulliard, there were sections in Geneva, Lausanne, Vevey-Montreux, la Gruyere, Fribourg, and in the Tessin. As to the war in Vietnam, *L'Etincelle* no. 30 described the PdA auxiliary organization Centrale Sanitaire Suisse as the only right recipient for contributions. A lengthy editorial in the same issue by Gérard Bulliard outlined the ideological position of the new party. The main reason for changing the name, according to Bulliard, was that in Switzerland the name "communist" still raises fear: "Communists are still viewed with a knife between the teeth, eating children . . . " The name had to be changed because Switzerland is a "superindustrialized and capitalist country." But the

---

*These events within the PCS-PPS were completely ignored by the PdA.

party principles would not change: the party would remain a fervent friend of "the great People's China, its leader Mao, and its entire people." While criticizing the groups which are blindly pro-Chinese, the PPS expressed "great admiration and profound respect" for Mao. It refused, however, to insult the Soviet Union because (in the PPS view) the Soviet people will make their leaders return to the path of Leninism. A cautious concern about the events in China was voiced when Bulliard referred to the people of China and the Soviet Union as "our friends" and declared that errors at the top will be rectified. In the international field, Cuba and Albania were explicitly mentioned as examples of opposition to imperialism. Boumediène in Algeria and the Popular Liberation Movement of Angola (MPLA) were given full moral support.

The modified ideological position is most evident in the approach to collaboration with the PdA. Much less rigid than before, the PPS not only welcomed all "sincere progressives," but also those who might even prefer to remain members of the Swiss Socialist Party or the PdA and continue the fight "within." The PPS intimated that it no longer wants to concentrate on the fight against the PdA, but rather to attack those who "pretend to be socialist leaders."

**Organization of Communists of Switzerland.** The Organization of Communists of Switzerland (Organization des Communistes de Suisse/Organisation der Kommunisten der Schweiz; OCS), a pro-Chinese rival to the Swiss Communist Party, is centered around the trilingual publication *Octobre*, published irregularly since 1964 in Lausanne. It is connected with the Centre Lénine at Lausanne; according to its critics in the PCS/PPS, it occasionally calls itself the "Marxist-Leninist Organization" (*L'Etincelle*, September 1966). The OCS is legal.

One of the OCS leaders, Freddy-Gilbert-Nils Andersson (a Swedish national), was ordered by the Swiss Government to leave the country early in 1967 because of his political activities abroad. Upholding a National Council decision of 6 November 1966, the Swiss Department of Justice rejected an appeal and issued a communique reaffirming that "as a promoter of a Marxist-Leninist organization with pro-Chinese tendencies, Andersson has deployed in Switzerland a political activity which is inadmissible on the part of a foreigner, and which is of a kind that would compromise the relations of Switzerland with other countries" (*Le Monde*, Paris, 11 May 1967). The Politburo of the OCS published in *Octobre* (23 December 1966) a communique which explained that the expulsion of Andersson primarily satisfied the embassies of imperialist and revisionist countries, ultrareactionary circles, provocateurs of the "allegedly Communist Party of Switzerland," and "revisionists of the Swiss Party of Labor" (*Rote Fahne*, no. 71, 1 February 1967). According to *Octobre*, the PdA took the expulsion as a pretext to attack the "methods" of the federal authorities (see *Voix Ouvrière*, 9 January) without informing its readers about Andersson and his activities.

The first issue of a bimonthly German edition of *Octobre* was published 1 March as *Oktober*, with Peter Maag as editor. This edition was mainly to serve the German-speaking area around Biel, where a cell of the OCS had been established. Toward the end of the year, according to *Octobre*, the Biel cell was liquidated when the OCS Central Committee ousted the Biel group—headed by *Oktober* editor Peter Maag—because of "petit-bourgeois, individualistic, dishonest, and anti-Marxist activities" (*National-Zeitung*, 11 December).

The OCS realized that it had to broaden its base if it were ever to have any political significance. An article entitled "Marxism and Opportunism" (*Oktober*, 1 May) attacked "revisionism" as the "most important" variety of opportunism and deplored the developments in Yugoslavia and Eastern Europe (with the exception of Albania) after the seizure of power by the proletariat. Similarly the Swiss situation was regarded as characterized by revisionism in the Social Democratic Party, the trade unions, and the PdA. The criticism, however, was directed only against the leaders, not rank-and-file members. Intending to "create the basis for a new party with a revolutionary goal and with revolutionary tactics," the OCS has rejected the idea of collaboration with the socialist parties and the concept of a peaceful road to socialism. *Octobre* on 25 September launched a detailed critique of the program adopted by the PdA at its National Conference of 27-28 May. According to a statement of the Cantonal Bureau of the POP Neuchatelois (PdA section) published in *Voix Ouvrière* (23 September), a member of the PdA was ousted in September for distributing *Octobre* and engaging in other activities denigrating the PdA.

Because of its extremely small membership, the Organization of Communists of Switzerland is politically insignificant at home. Internationally, however, it appears to be the pro-Chinese group accepted "officially" by other Marxist-Leninist organizations and parties. For instance, on the occasion of the constitutive conference of the Marxist-Leninist Party of Austria, it sent a message of greeting (dated 5 March 1967) signed by Peter Maag and Gilbert Etienne (*Rote Fahne,* no. 74, 15 March). A message from the OCS was delivered at the founding congress of the Marxist-Leninist Party of France, 30-31 December 1967; the message denounced the Budapest meeting scheduled for February 1968 and defended the Chinese cultural revolution against "bourgeois and revisionist misrepresentations." It emphasized the guidance given by the Chinese Communist Party and the Albanian Workers' Party (*Octobre,* 20 January 1967). Through its attendance at the Albanian Party Congress at the end of 1966, OCS established itself clearly as the accepted pro-Chinese group in Switzerland (*YICA,* 1966, p. 156). OCS ideological orientation was again stated in an editorial in *Octobre* (25 November 1967) entitled "The True Successors to the October Revolution," according to which the inheritors of the mantle of Lenin were the Chinese under the leadership of Mao. The editors stressed that Mao was correct in demonstrating that socialism is not really achieved without total victory in three battles: armed revolution, economic revolution, and ideological revolution.

**Publications.** The organs of the Swiss Party of Labor (PdA) include the daily *Voix Ouvrière,* edited by Etienne Lentillon and Henri Trüb, published in Geneva; the weekly *Vorwärts,* published in Basel; and the weekly *Il Lavoratore,* published in Locarno.

The PCS/PPS organ, *L'Etincelle,* is edited by Gérard Bulliard; in 1967 it appeared irregularly with a total of six issues (nos. 25-30). Simultaneously with issue no. 30 of *L'Etincelle,* the first issue of an Italian-language publication, *Falce e Mattello* (Sickle and Hammer), as the organ of the Tessin section of the PPS (Organo della Sezione Ticinese del Partito Popolare Svizzero), was sent out (dated 20 October 1967). Its editor is Ugo Valentini.

The Organization of Communists of Switzerland publishes *Octobre* in Lausanne, and *Oktober* in Biel (see above).

# SYRIA

The Syrian Communist Party (al-Hizb al-Shuyu 'i al-Suriyah; SCP) is an offshoot of the Lebanese Communist Party, which was first founded in 1934 as the Hizb al Sha'b al-Lubnani (Lebanese People's Party). After many vicissitudes, this party became the Lebanese Communist Party in 1930. The party accepted members from both Syria and Lebanon, which at that time were under French rule by authority of a mandate from the League of Nations. The Syrian element in the party became dominant under the leadership of a dynamic Syrian Kurd, Khalid Bakdash, who acceded to the post of First Secretary in 1932, but the SCP did not become a separate entity until July 1944, after Lebanon achieved full independence from French rule. Ties between the two parties, very strong at first, have tended to weaken over the years, although a substantial bond remains.

Until the coup of February 1966, when left-wing extremists of the Ba'ath (Arab Socialist) Party took over the Syrian government, the position of the SCP within Syria was very weak. Immediately following the change in government, however, Khalid Bakdash returned clandestinely from eight years of exile in the USSR and Eastern Europe, presenting the new government with a *fait accompli*. Bakdash's bold move achieved its purpose when the Ba'athists agreed to his remaining in Damascus subject to certain restrictions.

The Syrian government remains in the hands of the Ba'ath Party left wing. Within the ruling group, Major General Salah Jadid, an Assistant Secretary-General appears to be the "strong man"—a *primus inter pares*. The head of state is Dr. Nureddin al-Atassi, the Ba'ath Secretary-General, whose real power is limited; the Prime Minister is Yusuf Zu'ayyin, another Ba'athist. The 20-man Syrian cabinet includes one communist, the Minister of Communications, Dr. Samih Atiyah, who is a member of the SCP Central Committee. Atiyah is the first communist in the cabinet of any Arab nation.

The Syrian government does not recognize the legality of any political party other than the Ba'ath. Atiyah's participation in the government, like that of Ministers from other parties, is, under the Ba'athists' official position, on an individual nonparty basis. Atiyah serves, however, with the full consent of the SCP.

An emergency Congress of the Ba'ath Party in late August and early September 1967 revealed a deep "dove and hawk" cleavage in the party over attitudes toward Israel in general and the Khartoum Arab summit conference in particular. The crisis situation was allayed, but apparently not resolved, when the party reelected al-Attassi as Secretary-General and a new cabinet was formed, again headed by Zu'ayyin (*Christian Science Monitor*, 9 September). The communist Atiyah retained his office. In spite of the fact that the SCP is tolerated by the ruling party, at least in a *de facto* sense, neither party trusts the other and actual cooperation between them is limited by their mutual suspicions. The Ba'ath Party apparently intends to hold the illegal status of the SCP as an "ace in the hole" against a rise in communist popularity or power.

**Organization and Leadership.** The SCP is small. Western estimates of its membership range between 3,000 and 6,000. The lower figure is the more plausible, in view of the fact that many Communists have defected to the Ba'ath over the years. The population of Syria is 5,450,000 (estimated mid-1966). The Secretary-General of the SCP is Khalid Bakdash, who is not only the leader of his own party, but is still influential in the Lebanese Communist Party and also is considered to be the foremost communist figure in the Arab world. He holds the distinction of being the first communist to be elected to an Arab parliament (1954) and the first in the Arab world to launch the slogan of "Alliance with the National Bourgeoisie." Bakdash heads the Politburo of the SCP; others on the Politburo include Yusuf Faisal and Daniel Daud Naameh. Among those known to be members of the Central Committee are Munir Ahmad, Samih Atiyah, Zahir Abdul Samad, Maurice Salibi, Umar Sibai, and Umar Kashshash, some of whom may also serve on the Politburo.

559

**Communist Influence in the Labor Movement.** The Syrian General Federation of Workers Unions cannot be considered a front organization of the SCP, but the party does have considerable influence therein. Khalid al-Jundi, the Federation president presents himself as a Ba'athist who is willing to cooperate with Communists, but his enthusiasm for communist support is generalized as a feeling that "all progressive forces should participate in the government under the direction of the Ba'ath" (*Granma Weekly Review*, no. 9, 26 February). The Syrian Federation of Workers Unions has approximately 200,000 members, mostly manual laborers. Plans are reported for a great expansion to include white-collar workers, professional men, and peasants (*ibid.*). The Federation left the International Confederation of Free Trade Unions to join the communist-dominated World Federation of Trade Unions in 1966 (*YICA*, 1966, p. 287). In January 1967 the Federation sponsored the "Third Conference of Solidarity with Aden" and in March held its annual Congress, which condemned US "aggression" in Vietnam and called for the people of the world to form a solid front against "imperialism" and "international monopoly." The Congress also castigated Jordanian government authorities for persecuting Jordanian labor representatives to the Aden solidarity conference, and expelled certain less radical members of the Federation who had apparently fled to Jordan earlier.

**Domestic Policy and Activity.** The possibility of cooperation between the Ba'ath Party and the SCP was first opened in 1956, when the Ba'athist government of Syria carried out extensive acts of nationalization and held free trade-union elections—measures which won the approval of the SCP and the Soviet Union. Following the coup of February 1966 and the formation of a left-wing Ba'athist cabinet with a strongly "anti-imperialist" and socialist-oriented program, relations between Syria, the UAR, and the USSR appreciably improved. Prime Minister Dr. Zu'ayyin's visit to the Soviet Union and the signing of the agreement on the construction of the Euphrates River dam symbolized the new relationship between Damascus and Moscow.

In spite of the fact that Bakdash and the SCP were able to make what appeared superficially to be an impressive advance in communist fortunes with his return to Syria and with the Ba'athist government's concessions tolerating the SCP in 1966, the party's progress in the Syrian political arena has not been impressive since. This the party admits in its own public statements. For example, the party Central Committee plenum in February 1967 called on the members to "fight on against the intrigues and sallies of the imperialists and other reactionaries who are seeking to subvert Syria's progress and disrupt the cooperation—limited though it is—that prevails at this time between the Left Ba'athists, the Communists, and other progressive groups," thus indicating that the party was dissatisfied with its own position in the political framework of the "progressive" Syrian state (*WMR*, June). At a second plenum, in July, after the Arab-Israeli war, Bakdash took pride in pointing out that "in all fields of work and struggle the communists exemplified sacrifice, courage, and determination," adding: "Their actions at Al-Quanytirah and other front line areas aroused the admiration of the popular masses and all progressive national elements." After recognizing "the enormity and difficulty of the tasks facing our Syrian people," he saw new opportunity for his party in "strengthening the national progressive regime" and urged that "all parties work with a full sense of responsibility and sincerity to secure the unity of action and struggle among all the progressive national forces" and "overcome . . . all the inherited caution and mutual distrust" (Voice of the Iraqi People, 7 September broadcast). Later, however, Bakdash showed annoyance with the Ba'athists for their failure to give the "party of the working classes" the role it deserved in accomplishing the socialist revolution in Syria (see below).

Thus, the role and the position of the SCP remains ambiguous and the Ba'athists, receiving at least nominal support from the SCP, are still intransigent when it comes to accepting the Communists as full partners in the government or in the "revolutionary movement." They have thus far shown no inclination to allow the Communists more freedom of action or power.

Behind the facade of cooperation between the Ba'athists and the SCP there was evidence that relations were not smooth before the Arab-Israeli war. Whether the war served to ameliorate or exacerbate these problems is not yet discernible. The SCP appeared fearful of the tendency in the Ba'ath which favors the dissolution of "progressive parties" and would force SCP members to join the Ba'ath as individuals in order to participate in the "revolution" (a system similar to that already in effect in the UAR). At the time of the coup in 1966 the Ba'athists advocated the unification of progressive "forces," without detailing what they meant by that, and after the anniversary of the revolution in 1967 they stressed the unity of progressive "elements." This shift in nomenclature has apparently disturbed the Communists. (*Neue Zürcher Zeitung,* 12 April 1967.) Party writings stress the necessity for the preservation of the Communist Party and for it to be given a vanguard role as the party of the working class. They also emphasize the united front of all "progressive forces" to accomplish the socialist aims of the "revolution" and, since the war, to carry out the struggle against "imperialist-Israeli aggression."*

Some observers feel that the SCP is attempting to bring a twofold pressure upon the Ba'ath to accept the SCP on a basis other than mere toleration. In view of Syria's greatly increased dependence on Soviet and East European aid, the SCP may be suggesting to the Ba'ath that more liberal treatment for the SCP is a prerequisite for continued good relations with the Soviet Union, and there are signs that the communists may also be attempting a similar but indirect pressure on the Ba'ath through the Soviet Union itself (*ibid.*).

The SCP attempts to project the image of a loyal opposition—forcefully, but in moderate terms—by pointing out the contradictions and fallacies in Ba'athist interpretations of the "objective conditions" in Syria and the Arab world. When the Ba'athists in power split over Syrian policy toward Israel after the June war, Bakdash came out squarely for the "dove" position, arguing that political, not military, action was the key to restitution. He advocated Syrian participation in the Arab summit conference at Khartoum (*Al-Akhbar,* Beirut, 3 September), which in the end the Ba'athists refused to attend. As an orthodox Marxist-Leninist, he considers his party to be the leader of the working class and he is critical of the Ba'athists for not allowing the SCP to exercise what he considers its proper role:

> Scientific socialism considers it illogical that a political party, or a government should declare that it is for socialism and accompany this with excessive caution towards the working class, the most revolutionary social class which stands foursquare for socialism.
>
> ... To date, the working class and its vanguard role is still the subject of debate between us, Marxist-Leninists, and progressive nationalists.
>
> Some progressive nationalists maintain that the vanguard role in the revolution belongs to the peasantry not only at the stage of the struggle for national liberation from imperialism, but also at the stage of the struggle for socialism.
>
> ... It is clear that in conditions of deepening revolutionary process to speak of the peasantry as a class representing one homogeneous mass is to risk seizure of the leadership of this mass by the kulaks.
>
> ... All this talk about the leading and vanguard role of the peasantry in the socialist revolution, in the fight for socialism is not only wrong; it reflects a class attitude which officially declares for socialism but in practice strives toward something that is not socialism. (*WMR,* June 1968.)

It is not surprising, then, that the SCP should be particularly critical of the Ba'athist land-reform program, which in its view tends to favor the "kulak class":

> The agrarian reform, inaugurated by the first reform law nine years ago, is not being enforced thoroughly enough and proceeds very slowly. Some 4,000 big landowners, while they lost land in the reform, still control one-sixth of the land. Only about a third of the confiscated land has been distributed among the peasants. They are given land, but not the title deeds to it. The other two-thirds are let for rent. What this amounts to is that for a number of years the state has merely replaced the dispossessed owners.

---

*On the other hand, Bakdash himself is reported as saying: "We would even integrate as long as it meant the construction of scientific socialism." (*Granma Weekly Review,* 26 February 1967.) In the past, however, Bakdash has always resisted dissolution or integration of his party. This statement to the Cuban weekly may only reflect his confidence that the terms for integration of the SCP with the Ba'athists would never meet his standard of acceptability.

> One reason for the slow distribution of land is that those handling the reform refuse to let peasant representatives have a say in it ... Recent amendments to the reform law are designed to speed matters up but other amendments enable owners of up to 300 hectares to retain their title. (*Ibid.*, June 1967.)

Similar criticisms were leveled at the lack of scientific planning for the national economy, the continuing capitalist nature of the Syrian banking system, and the lack of planning and centralized administration in nationalized factories (*ibid.*). Bakdash views SCP cooperation with the Ba'athists in the following light: "The proposals of our Party are just a sincere attempt ... to create a situation where there will be no crying contradiction between the superstructure and the base at the present stage of Syria's social development. With things being what they are the Syrian Communists do not consider themselves automatically committed to all the government's measures, even though the cabinet includes a Communist minister." (*Ibid.*, June 1968.)

The basic rationalization of the current "objective situation" in the world to Marxist-Leninist theory was stated for the SCP by Bakdash as follows:

> The merging of the national-liberation movement with that for social emancipation, which process we are today witnessing in Syria and in many other countries that have recently freed themselves from colonialism, confirms the Leninist thesis that national liberation is one of the stages on the way to social emancipation. But the new in this process is that the transition from national to social emancipation began before leadership of the movement passed into the hands of the working class. In fact, it is still led by non-proletarian elements. Herein lies one of the cardinal features of our time. In other words, life is making it clear to the non-proletarian elements that the way to political independence lies through social emancipation. However, more than recognition and support of this idea are needed if the problem of transition of the national-liberation movement to the movement for social emancipation is to be solved. And the task of Communists, in our view, is to do more than just support, encourage and applaud this idea. We must try to see the perspective of this process, and the ways of its development, which can be done only given a class approach to the question. (*Ibid.*)

Given this approach to the problem, cooperation with a government recognized as "progressive" becomes a duty incumbent upon the SCP, but the implication is that only the communist party can give a correct scientific interpretation of history's inevitable course and that these "other progressive forces" must one day give way to the superior judgment of the omniscient vanguard party. Conversely, a break between the Communists and the others would become necessary the moment the SCP should deem that today's progressive forces were no longer progressive. "Any manifestation of anti-communism on the part of a member or members of a progressive group can be taken as stemming either from an anti-socialist class bias bent on turning Syria into a land of kulaks and middle bourgeois, or from the effects of reactionary propaganda and intimidation by sheikhs and imperialists" (*ibid.*, June 1967).

The SCP policy of support for the "progressive" Syrian regime continued throughout 1967, even though the party criticized the government's handling of the Arab-Israeli crisis and war, and the generally militant course of the Ba'athist leaders thereafter. Before the Arab-Israeli war the SCP program (at the time of the February plenum) emphasized internal problems: the struggle to control the flow of Iraqi oil across Syria, the construction of the Euphrates dam, acceleration of the agrarian reform, a higher standard of living for workers and peasant, elimination or restriction of private ownership (regarded negative factors in the economy), scientific state planning of the economy, the fight for democratic rights and privileges, the organizing of the masses, and the strengthening of the SCP position in mass movements (*IB*, no. 95, May).

After the war the cooperative attitude toward the government continued, but the emphasis of the party program changed to meet the emergency situation and placed more stress on external factors.

> The political climate in our country must be changed if we are to nip in the bud every attempt by imperialist agents and the reactionaries to profit by the situation resulting

from the aggression, stop the progressive development of the nation and set up a regime subservient to the imperialist power.

It is necessary: 1. To intensify the progressive development of our nation. The people should enjoy complete trust, which should express itself in all progressive and patriotic forces being granted democratic freedoms. This historic period calls for tremendous effort to organize concerted struggle by all patriotic forces on the basis of cooperation and mutual trust.

Besides, every opportunity should be used to raise the efficiency and organization of the armed forces and restore their strength within the shortest possible time, so that they can defend the country.

This course of action will make for greater confidence and a higher morale. It will help to mobilize all forces and enhance the people's determination to continue their grim fight against an inexorable enemy.

This policy line should express itself in the activity of the government, the trade unions and other popular organizations.

2. All-embracing vigilance toward the intrigues of the imperialists and Zionists, who are trying to take advantage of every disagreement among the progressive forces in each country and the Arab world as a whole.

The solidarity and fraternity which the progressive Arab states displayed during the aggression must be resolutely built up. It is necessary to coordinate and combine the efforts of the progressive Arab states in every field—defense, politics and economy. An effort should be made to engage all Arab states in a determined fight for the withdrawal of the aggressors from the territories they occupy and for the elimination of the effects of the aggression.

3. Consolidating the common front of the Arab and the socialist countries against the common enemy, world imperialism, headed by the US imperialists.

It is particularly important to continue strengthening the bonds of friendship and to promote cooperation between Syria and the mighty Soviet Union, as well as with the Arabs' other friends. A cardinal task is to make full use of the opportunities which the Soviet Union and other socialist countries afford to us to strengthen our defenses and promote our economy.

4. We must pursue a wise and far-sighted foreign policy and avoid publicity-mongering, adventurist and unrealistic slogans. This means that we must increasingly isolate Israel in the world and thus expose her aggressive nature. We must refute Israel's contention that she wants peace in the area and that she waged a war of aggression merely to survive. . . .

Such a foreign policy would bring about a favorable international situation in which the Arab peoples could make a determined effort toward eliminating the effects of the aggression and thwarting all imperialist plans of aggression.

5. We must follow an economic policy taking into account the conditions of the current struggle and the growing importance of agriculture, and continuing the implementation of development plans. Our economic policy should concentrate on tasks connected with strengthening our defenses, increasing the national income and raising the capacity of government enterprises producing capital and consumer goods. We must take appropriate measures to supply the people with food.

6. The people's gains—the economic and social changes that have been brought about—must be maintained and consolidated. This means above all conscientiously implementing the land reform, transferring the land to the poor peasants, managing the nationalized enterprises efficiently, organizing imports and exports according to the need to adapt defense measures, increasing production and safeguarding the interests of the masses.

The actual implementation of this policy is a vast historic task to be accomplished by all progressive citizens, by all enemies of imperialism, irrespective of their party allegiances and of whether they are in power or not. (*Ibid.*, no. 107, November.)

Bakdash later asserted that his party's general line was based on three principles: the "continuation of cooperation with the Left Ba'athists and other progressives in and outside the government," "unreserved defense of the interests of the workers and the peasants," and, again stressing the preservation of his party, "vigorous defense of the Party's independent position, of its patriotism and internationalism, particularly in important political matters and fundamental problems" (*ibid.*, June 1968). He outlined his party's tasks as a twofold fight against reaction and "against extreme tendencies advocating risky adventures without taking into consideration their possible consequence to Syria itself and the Arab East as a whole," seeing this as a fight to "preserve and consolidate . . . progressive social and economic changes" through close relations with all progressives, efforts to mobilize "forces. resources and energies," and a strengthened party organization and discipline (*al-Akhbar*, Beirut, 3 September 1967).

**The Arab-Israeli War.** The SCP view of the Arab-Israeli war corresponded closely with that taken by the communist parties of the other Arab states. In its response to the defeat the SCP played heavily on the themes of nationalism and solidarity: "[The Middle East is] an arena where two political forces are locked in bitter conflict. On one side are the forces of imperialism and reaction, trying to put down the national-liberation movement and to halt progress in the Arab countries and on the other, the progressive forces striving to bring about the complete national emancipation of every people, reliably consolidate their freedom and independence and do away with their age-long backwardness." (*IB*, no. 102, August 1967). The war was seen as the result of "criminal imperialist Zionist aggression" which placed before the Arab people a "fundamental task": "to sweep the aggressor's forces away from our land and liquidate the consequences of the aggression." The party termed the war a "painful" but temporary defeat inflicted by a "sudden and treacherous aggression planned by American imperialism and supported by Great Britain and West Germany," and maintained that "in spite of temporary military success, the goals of the aggression were not reached," describing these goals as "the complete elimination of the whole Arab national liberation movement, the ruination of friendly Arab-Soviet relations, and the overthrow of Arab progressive regimes." In the party's critique of the war it reaches the following conclusions: progressive forces must unite in Syria and in every Arab country; there must be a militant unity of the progressive Arab states, coordinating on military and political issues; and the Arab states must cooperate closely with the Soviet Union and other socialist nations (*al-Akhbar*, Beirut, 3 September 1967).

**International Views and Policies.** The foregoing indicates the SCP's orientation in the communist world. The party is aligned with the Soviet Union and the CPSU. It has justified the apparent paradox of intense loyalty to the Soviet Union, including recognition of the CPSU as the leader of the world communist movement, and the need to identify with patriotism and nationalism at home by portraying the Soviet Union as the benefactor of all struggling proletarian patriots throughout the world:

> [The] history of man has never before known such impartial and honorable relations in the interest of persecuted peoples who search for freedom. All peoples of the world who struggle for their liberation and progress, whether in Asia, Africa, or Latin America, can depend on Soviet assistance in the political, economic and military fields. Thus the Soviet Union gives an example of international solidarity to the peoples of the world and the masses of workers, toilers, and strugglers for national liberation everywhere. (Voice of the Iraqi People, 14 October 1967.)

The SCP consistently and unreservedly supported the CPSU call for a consultative meeting of communist and workers parties. The latest statement to this effect was a resolution of the Central Committee at a December plenum declaring "unanimous support" for the preliminary conference planned for Budapest in February 1968. "The fact that more than seven years have passed since the last international conference of the Communist and Workers' parties in 1960 makes the forthcoming meeting an imperatively needed and urgent measure for the elaboration of common positions in the struggle to foil the imperialist counteroffensive" (*IB*, no. 1, 5 February 1968).

Its view is that Maoist activities and attitudes would "ultimately serve the aims of imperialism," charging that Communist China drove the Communist Party of Indonesia into "strange adventures," that China had blocked united support for Vietnam, and that "during and after the [Israeli] aggression the Mao Tse-tung bloc called on the Arab peoples to sever diplomatic relations with the USSR and adopt a hostile attitude toward it," the latter being "exactly what the radios of Israel, Washington, and London had been urging" and "one of the main aims of American imperialism when it planned for the Israeli aggression" (Voice of the Iraqi People, 7 September).

The documents of the Arab communist meeting of May 1967 do not reveal whether or not the SCP was represented. One of the resolutions adopted at the meeting hailed the cooperation between Communists and Ba'athists as yielding "important results" (see *Documents*). Yusuf Faisal represented the SCP at the Seventh Congress of the East German Socialist Unity Party (SED) in Berlin, 17-22 April, which the Ba'ath Party also attended. Faisal made a speech on that occasion calling for the unity of all "progressive forces" among the Arabs. He later went on to visit Bucharest at the invitation of the Central Committee of the Rumanian Communist Party. Both the SCP and the Ba'ath Party joined the celebrations in the Soviet Union for the Fiftieth Anniversary of the October Revolution. Ibrahim Makhous, the Syrian Foreign Minister and a leading figure in the Ba'ath Party, addressed an audience in Moscow on 3 November; Khalid Bakdash spoke also in Moscow, on 6 November.

Although the USSR has always assigned a high priority to exchange programs with the "progressive" Arab states, Syria was singled out for special attention during 1967, especially in the period following the Arab-Israeli war. Syrian resistance to a "political solution" of the Arab-Israeli crisis and its intransigence in calling for armed force against Israel appeared to be of concern to Moscow. The SCP supported all government cooperation with the Soviet Union, however, and there was no indication that the friendly Soviet attitude toward the Syrian regime had caused any appreciable strain on the relationship between Moscow and the SCP.

Syria is one of the countries in the Middle East where Sino-Soviet rivalry has been most evident in the past. The Chinese Communists have shown displeasure over recent close Syrian relations with Moscow but have been unable to prevent the eclipse of their influence. The consistently antagonistic attitude toward them on the part of the SCP may be a factor in China's loss of status with the Syrians, but the geographic position and the economic power of the USSR and positive Soviet support for the Syrian Ba'athists are probably far more important.

**Publications.** The central organ of the SCP is the weekly *Nidal al-Sha'b* ("People's Struggle"), which has the peculiar distinction of being printed clandestinely (in Lebanon), but distributed legally throughout Syria. The party also frequently publishes material in the Lebanese communist daily *al-Nida* ("The Call") and weekly *al-Akhbar* ("The News").

# THAILAND

Although a communist party was formed in Thailand as early as 1929 by the Siam Special Committee of the South Seas Communist Party, which had been founded in 1927, the Communist Party of Thailand (CPT) itself was not founded until 1 December 1942.

**Organization and Leadership.** The CPT is illegal, and little is known about its membership, which has been estimated as 200 to 500 active members. In addition, little is known about its organization or leadership. An analysis of radio broadcasts and CPT policy statements indicates that it is directed from Peking, where it is represented by Nit Phuongdaphet, member of the CPT Central Committee.

Additional names of CPT members were revealed after a series of government arrests from 31 August to 3 September 1967, which were aimed at the hard-core apparatus of the CPT itself. More than 30 members of the CPT were reportedly arrested, including five Central Committee members, two of whom were also members of the Politburo. Those arrested included Thong Jamsri (alias Thavorn Vongsuma), who is believed to be the highest-ranking member in Thailand of the CPT Politburo, the coordinator of all activities of the Communist terrorists in northeastern Thailand, and the liason officer between the CPT and the Chinese Communist Party and the Vietnam Workers' Party, and Pin Bua-orn (alias Chin Buaprasert), member of the CPT Central Committee and Politburo and coordinator and director of Communist terrorists operating south of Bangkok.

The CPT has had little success, particularly among the ethnic Thais, whose adherence to Buddhism and lack of exploitable- grievances (except in certain areas, notably the northeast) make them unpromising recruitable material. In addition, communism in Thailand has been almost entirely an alien movement, based chiefly on Chinese and, more recently, Vietnamese communism. In an attempt to overcome this difficulty, the CPT has endeavored to establish or influence front organizations and tactics and to win over Thailand's ethnic minorities, which include approximately 3 million Chinese and some 30,000 to 40,000 Vietnamese. Thailand has a population of 31,508,000 (mid-1966 estimate).

In July 1964 Peking disseminated a CPT statement calling for the creation of a "patriotic, democratic united front," and in October 1964 the CPT sent a message to the Chinese Communist Party on the occasion of Communist China's National Day elaborating further on its call for united-front tactics. The call for a united front was followed almost immediately by the establishment of the Thailand Independence Movement (TIM) on 1 November 1964, although the Movement was not officially announced until almost a month later. On 1 January 1965 the second major front came into existence, the Thailand Patriotic Front (TPF), but, as was the case with the TIM, its existence was not announced by the Communists until some days later. Both organizations are based in Peking.

The TIM identified itself as a "political organization having as its objective the achievement of solidarity with all patriotic forces loving democracy without distinction of class or wealth" (Voice of the People of Thailand, 8 December 1964). For its part, the TPF claimed to be a "political organization willing to cooperate with all compatriots of both sexes and all ages, professions, political affiliations, and religions who love peace and democracy" (Voice of the People of Thailand, 23 January 1965); its program called for the rallying of all "patriotic and democratic forces" in Thailand to overthrow the "Thanom-Praphat clique," drive the "US imperialists" out of Thailand, and set up a "democratic" National Union Government with a view to building an "independent, neutral, peaceful, and democratic Thailand."

Shortly after the declarations on the establishment of the two fronts, representatives appeared in Peking, with Mongkon Na Nakorn representing the TIM and Lieutenant Colonel Phayom Chulanont representing the TPF. These men eventually emerged as the leaders of their respective organizations. In December 1965 the two organizations merged. New China News Agency reported on 14 December 1965 that the TIM had "unanimously adopted a resolution immediately to affiliate with the Thailand Patriotic Front as a member organization" and that it would "accept the political leadership of the front." Although there were occasional references to the TIM during 1967, its influence is apparently negligible; Communist China did not even bother to observe its third anniversary on 1 November 1967.

The leadership of the enlarged front organization reportedly consists of Mongkon Na Nakorn, Lieutenant Commandant Nai Vattanchi Chayakit Dhives, Amphorn Souvannabon, Mon Vong Phithiyaroth, Mme. Vattanchi Chayakit Dhives, Lieutenant Colonel Phayom Chulanont, Nit Phuongdaphet, Kularb Saipradit, Sainh Marankoul, and Nai Pridi Phanomyong (*Est et Ouest*, Paris, 1-15 February 1967).

Although the two front organizations were established as a result of CPT appeals, there was initially no conclusive evidence of the actual role of the CPT in their subsequent activities, which consisted primarily of a number of sporadic insurgent actions. At the Albanian party congress in November 1966, however, the CPT appeared to claim responsibility for the insurgency in Thailand, as it did in a party statement on 1 December 1966, the twenty-fourth anniversary of the founding of the CPT. On 7 August 1967 Patriotic Front leader Phayom Chulanont acknowledged the CPT's leadership of the "Thai people's armed forces" and subsequently New China News Agency and Voice of the People of Thailand broadcasts referred to the "flames of armed struggle [which] were kindled by the people's armed forces led by the Communist Party of Thailand in northeastern Thailand two years ago." On 23 November Peking Radio broadcast a speech by Phayom Chulanont in which he called himself "a new pupil of Chairman Mao" and declared his support for the 9 November statement of the CPT rejecting the "peaceful and parliamentary path." He noted that "under the correct leadership of the Communist Party of Thailand and with the active support of the mass organizations of revolutionary people, including the Thai Patriotic Front, the Thai Independence Movement, the Thai Federation of Patriotic Workers, the Organization of Patriotic Youth of Thailand, and various patriotic regional organizations, the armed struggle of the Thai people has grown rapidly."

Although the TPF has now lost the normal appearance of a front organization and is clearly subordinate to the CPT, it continues to play an active role in Thai Communist developments, if only for propaganda purposes. It was most likely the failure of the Patriotic Front to gain a widespread following that led to the CPT's assumption of the leading role in Thai Communist insurgent activites. The decision to abandon any pretense concerning the direction of the Patriotic Front may also have been due to Chinese impatience with its halfway measures and limited success.

Other major front organizations are the Thailand Federation of Patriotic Workers, which was established on 1 May 1964 and immediately declared that it would accept the political leadership of the Patriotic Front; the Thailand Patriotic Youth Organization, which was founded on 15 February 1965 and also declared its adherence to the Patriotic Front; and the Thai Afro-Asian Solidarity Committee. Other mass organizations include the Association of Liberated Farmers and Planters, the Patriotic Teachers' Group, the Thai Monks' Group, the Patriotic Combatants' Group, and the Lawyers' Group. Little is heard of them or their activities in Thailand, however.

**Communist Insurgent Activities in Thailand.** Estimates of Communist insurgents operating in Thailand range from a low of 1,300 to a high of 5,000 to 10,000 guerrillas, with the number of Communist sympathizers estimated at anywhere between 10,000 and 50,000. Communist sources claim that "revolutionary armed forces" are operating in 28 of the 71 provinces of Thailand.

In northeastern Thailand, particularly in the provinces of Ubon, Udorn, Loei, Kalasin, Nong Khai, Nakhon Phathom, and Sakon Nakhon, estimates of Thai Communist terrorists range from 500 to 5,000, with the Thai government estimating their strength at 1,700 (*Bangkok Post,* 13 July 1967). According to a Thai government report, leaders of the Communist terrorists in the northeast include Yod Phatisawat, Choy Latisingh, and Kasem, all of whom were reportedly trained in the Democratic Republic of Vietnam. Communist efforts in the northeast also center on the 30,000 to 40,000 Vietnamese refugees living in the northeastern provinces, where a Communist organization with central, district, and village level committees is reported to exist.

Communist terrorists are also active along the Kra Peninsula and in southern Thailand, where some three-fourths of the 800,000 residents are Malayan Moslems and there are serious racial and religious antagonisms. Communist strength in the south is reinforced by some 500 to 1,000 Malayan Communists along the Thai-Malaysian border, who are under the leadership of Chen Ping, Secretary-General of the Communist Party of Malaya. Reports indicate that there are links between the Communist terrorists in the northeast and the south. While there is no concrete evidence that the Malayan Communists have been coordinating their activities with the Thai Communists, there have been reports of courier links between the two groups.

There have been increased efforts to carry the insurgency to central and western Thailand, particularly the provinces of Suphan Buri, Phet Buri, Rat Buri, and Prachuap Khiri Khan, with disturbances in parts of southern Thailand beginning to figure almost as prominently as those in the northeast.

Communist insurgents in Thailand receive considerable aid from Communist China and North Vietnam, as well as smaller quantities of aid from the Pathet Lao-controlled territories of Laos. In addition, reports indicate that Laotian, Chinese, and Vietnamese Communists have at various times infiltrated into north and northeastern Thailand, as have Thai Communists trained at the Thai Communist Party Political and Military School in the province of Hoa Binh in North Vietnam. On 12 July 1967 Lieutenant General Saiyud Kerdpol, Deputy Chief of Staff for the Thai government's Communist Suppression Operations Command, stated that according to Thai intelligence reports, the Chinese Communist Party is the "super command structure" directing the CPT, while the North Vietnamese Communists direct the Communist terrorist operations in Thailand (*Bangkok Post*, 13 July 1967).

Communist insurgent activities in Thailand increased significantly enough in 1967 to cause the Thai Deputy Prime Minster and Army Commander General Praphat to announce on 15 October that the Thai army would assume full charge of Communist suppression in northeastern and southern Thailand. In addition, on 1 December the Thai government announced that martial-law restrictions would be more strictly enforced in the central and southern provinces of Prachuap Khiri Khan, Phet Buri, Rat Buri, Kanchan Buri, and Suphan Buri.

**CPT Program and Tactics.** The "program of struggle" as outlined by the Thai Patriotic Front, consists of six main points:

1. Struggle for national independence. Abolition of all treaties between Thailand and the United States signed under unequal conditions. Expulsion of all imperialist troops and other aggressive forces from Thailand.

2. Struggle for the democratic rights of the people. Overthrow of the fascist and dictatorial government, loyal lackey of US imperialism. Establishment of a government of patriots and democrats. Defense of freedom and the democratic rights of the people.

3. A policy of peace and neutrality. Withdrawal from SEATO. Cessation of intervention in the affairs of neighbor countries. Friendly relations with the peoples of other countries and support for the progress and the struggle for national independence. Opposition to the aggressive provocations of US imperialism. Pursuit of world peace.

4. Development of the national economy and agricultural production. Aid to poor farmers and protection and promotion of trade and national industries. Restriction of foreign investments aimed at plundering the wealth of the country. Establishment of an independent and self-sufficient national economy.

5. Improvement of the standard of living of the people. Execution and severe punishment of the traitors and bureaucrats who oppress the people. Distribution of sufficient land to the farmers so that they may earn a living and establishment of just salaries for workers and officials, service personnel, teachers, soldiers, policemen and professional workers.

6. Development of education and public health. Opposition to the corrupt imperialist culture and development of a national culture. Building of schools to promote education and adoption of measures to improve sanitation and public health throughout the

country. (*Tricontinental Bulletin,* no. 10, January 1967.)

During 1967 the domestic program of the Thai Communists, as outlined by Phayom Chulanont of the Patriotic Front, continued to emphasize these points and called for the overthrow of the "fascist dictatorial government which is the lackey of US imperialism," the termination of martial law, the release of all political prisoners, the abolition of the "constitution of the lackey US imperialists which deprives the people of their rights and freedom," the formation of a government composed of "patriotic, democratic people," and the proclamation of a constitution giving "full freedom and liberty to the people" (NCNA, 23 November 1967).

Thai Communists also repeatedly attacked the Thai government for having increased its assistance to "US aggression in Vietnam," for allowing the United States to "transform Thailand into a huge base for aggression," and for having become the "devoted lackey of US imperialism." They continued to claim that "because of the [Thanom-Praphat] clique's traitorous and corrupt policy, the national economy has sharply deteriorated, national income has decreased, and the people's living conditions have deteriorated" (Voice of the People of Thailand, 1 January 1967). In a major statement on 9 November 1967 the CPT Central Committee reiterated these points and attacked the Thai government's plans for municipal and national elections, as well as its plans for the promulgation of a new national constitution:

We will determinedly wage a people's war. We will annihilate the sham political tactics of the US-Thanom clique. While the puppet Thanom-Praphat clique is selling out our nation to the US imperialists and suppressing democratic parties, causing bitter hardships for the people, it talks about a sham constitution and elections. This is a political tactic of the US revisionists. The aim of the clique is to use this political device to deceive, divide, and annihilate the revolutionary movement and the armed struggle of the people in order to defend its fascist dictatorial regime, so it can go on selling out our nation.

Under the leadership of the Communist Party of Thailand, democratic patriots have determinedly resisted the US aggression and the nation-selling clique which has destroyed the rights and freedom of the people. The piratical Thanom-Praphat clique has not only suppressed the patriotic people, but has . . . wholeheartedly served the US imperialists.

The Thanom-Praphat clique . . . is trying to force the people to fight against it parliamentarily and peacefully. The clique talks of the so-called "constitution, political parties, and the elections" in order to try to sidetrack the unity of the revolutionary people. The clique hopes that the patriotic armed forces will be isolated. It also hopes that our people will abandon their armed struggle and surrender. This depraved tactic will never deceive the people. The people have clearly understood that the parliamentary and peaceful path cannot resolve the problems of the nation and the people. (Voice of the People of Thailand, 16 November 1967.)*

The tactics of the CPT and the Thai Communist insurgents were also clearly stated in the 9 November statement of the CPT Central Committee:

We determinedly insist on armed struggle and on waging people's war. The daily suppression of the US-Thanom clique reveals its true face as aggressor and nation seller. Our Party and the patriotic people will attack and crush the clique and ruin all its depraved tactics. The armed struggle of the people is a very glorious path. The patriotic and democratic struggle of the people is progressive and just. The patriotic people and the revolutionary people are standing by our side and supporting us. The obstacles we are facing now are temporary ones. If we are not afraid of these obstacles, we will win. The US-Thanom pirates are being resisted by all people because their aggressive and nation-selling action is unjust and reactionary. It will undoubtedly come to an end. (Voice of the People of Thailand, 16 November 1967.)

---

*On 5 October 1967 Deputy Prime Minister Praphat announced that the new constitution would not be ready for promulgation until some time in 1968. He emphasized, however, that the Communist terrorist activity was in no way responsible for the delay in the promulgation of the constitution or the holding of general elections.

A *Jen-min Jih-pao* article further elaborated on the tactics of the Communist Party of Thailand:

The people's armed forces led by the Communist Party of Thailand have devoted the principal part of their work to the rural areas. Going deep down into the countryside, they have carried out prolonged, arduous, and patient work to mobilize and organize the peasants, accumulated their strength, and tempered their forces. They can thus gradually build up and expand their base areas, encircle the cities from the countryside through protracted struggle and finally capture the cities and win nationwide victory. (*Jen-min Jih-pao*, 8 November 1967.)

Although the CPT has stressed Mao Tse-tung's theories of people's war and armed struggle, emphasis has also been placed on the use of united-front tactics. In addition, in an apparent effort to counter the planned government promulgation of a new constitution and the holding of new elections, the CPT renewed its call for the formation of a coalition government "which will carry out an independent and democratic policy."

According to a broadcast marking the twenty-fifth anniversary of the CPT, "all revolutionary classes and patriotic units will join and support our armed struggle to drive the US imperialists from the nation, to annihilate the Thanom-Praphat clique, and to form a coalition government with an independent policy and based on genuine democracy, to build up the prosperity, and culture of our beloved country" (Voice of the People of Thailand, 2 December 1967). The broadcast also indicated the nature of the proposed coalition government, however, when it declared that "to strengthen the struggle of the people for democracy is the primary aim. To create a classless Communist society in Thailand for our prosperity is our secondary aim." In analyzing its activities during the course of 1967 the CPT stressed that the "armed struggle" in Thailand was "rapidly expanding" under the "correct leadership" of the CPT. A broadcast at the end of the year gave the following summary of operations:

During the past year the armed struggle of the Thai people has greatly shaken the throne of the US-Thanom clique. In the countryside, both in mountains and paddy areas, under the correct leadership of the Communist Party of Thailand, the Patriotic People's Armed Forces of Thailand are expanding and becoming more powerful. The combat areas have rapidly extended to every part of the country. The people, especially the peasants and brotherly minorities, have taken part and wholeheartedly supported the people's struggle.

In 1967 more than 17 provinces made up the combat areas of the people's armed forces. At present the people's armed forces are operating in 28 provinces. From incomplete statistics, the people's armed forces made 388 attacks against the enemy in 1967. This is double the number of attacks made during the past one and a half years. We destroyed 709 of the enemy and captured a number of weapons. Furthermore, the people's armed forces held 135 mobilizations in many villages and we were warmly welcomed by the people. Various groups have also expanded and have supported armed struggle. (Voice of the People of Thailand, 31 December 1967.)

In spite of CPT claims that "during the past few years the strength of our Party has rapidly increased, as has that of the individual membership," a CPT Central Committee communique dated 1 December 1967 indicated that the party realized the need for more effective leadership and study:

It is necessary for our Party to strengthen the leadership.

On the occasion of the twenty-fifth anniversary of the founding of the Communist Party of Thailand, we call upon all members of the Party, fighters of the people's armed forces, and the revolutionary people to strive to increase their knowledge of Marxist-Leninist theory and Mao Tse-tung's thoughts. Particularly, they must study the work of Mao Tse-tung thoroughly. They must apply Mao Tse-tung's thoughts to the practice of revolution in Thailand, emphasize the principle of self-improvement, improve their ideas in revolutionary style, and use Mao Tse-tung's thoughts as the guide of the Party. In order to achieve the honorable and hard task of waging the people's war, our Party is still facing a tortuous and protracted struggle. The achievement of the Party depends mainly on the belief of all Party members in Mao Tse-tung's thoughts. They must be armed with these great weapons so that they can hold to this honorable task. Some of our men have much experience in working, but experience alone will not be able to carry out Marxism-Leninism and Mao Tse-tung's thoughts. In order to improve their experience and elevate it, they must keep Marxism-Leninism and Mao Tse-tung's thoughts in mind. Therefore people must be interested in education and systematize education meaningfully, apply Mao Tse-tung's thoughts to solve real problems in a revolutionary way, and inculcate revolutionary ideas into the people. (Voice of the People of Thailand, 14 December 1967.)

CPT policy statements also continued to appeal to its "members and cadres attached to the patriotic armed forces of the people to step up the development of the armed forces politically and spiritually" and stressed the need to "mobilize the broad masses throughout the country to join our fight vigorously" and "to expand our patriotic forces to resist the US imperialists and the domestic reactionaries" so as to "achieve a favorable situation, both domestically and internationally." Reports also indicate that arrests made in the summer of 1967 seriously disrupted the party's structure, including communications to insurgents in the northeast.

In addition to stressing the need for more effective leadership and study by the party members, evidence of deep divisions among the Thai Communists, particularly the Thai exiles in Peking, began to appear during 1967. On 21 May New China News Agency's international service broadcast a speech by a Miss Phatthanothai indicating that some of the exiles had come to resist the domineering way in which they were being treated by the Chinese and would prefer to return to Thailand. According to Miss Phatthanothai, some of these "reactionary remnants" have already been expelled from Peking.

There were other indications of "splits" within the Thai communist movement in general. On 9 November the CPT issued a statement attacking the Thai government's plan to promulgate a new constitution, calling it a "fake propaganda campaign" waged by the "US-Thanom clique, with the cooperation of the traitorous revisionists." In a 1 December *People's Army* article by Nit Phuongdaphet, reference was made to the need to study the works of Mao Tse-tung more thoroughly "in order to avoid indulgence in revisionism in our ranks." Finally, a CPT communique dated 1 December and issued by the Central Committee warned that "the book by China's Khrushchev [Liu Shao-ch'i] entitled *Self-cultivation by Party Members* affects our workers; for instance, in producing defeatism and identifying the individual's interest with the public interest."

**International Views and Positions**. The CPT's foreign policy has focused on its denunciation of the "US imperialists and their lackeys" on the one hand, and its support of the Chinese position in the Sino-Soviet dispute on the other. CPT foreign-policy statements have consistently maintained that "US imperialism is the ringleader of the world's reactionary forces. Because of its aggression in Vietnam, it is being denounced at home and abroad. Its position is becoming more and more isolated. The ranks of the imperialist bloc are also disintegrating. The aggressive NATO and SEATO blocs are disintegrating." (Voice of the People of Thailand, 7 January 1967.) The Thai Communists also continued to attack the Association of Southeast Asian Nations (ASEAN) and the Asian and Pacific Council (ASPAC) as "aggressive tools of the US imperialists in Asia."

The party's position on the Vietnam war was outlined clearly in a 7 January 1967 message of the CPT Central Committee:

The armed struggle of the Vietnamese today forms the nucleus of the revolutionary struggle of the world's people. The heroic Vietnamese people in both zones, north and south, have inflicted grave losses on the enemies. The victories of the Vietnamese people have clearly exposed the paper tiger nature of US imperialism and the world reactionary forces. These victories have greatly inspired the fighting spirit of the world's people, including the people of Thailand. The Thai people will resolutely continue to render assistance to the heroic Vietnamese people. (Voice of the People of Thailand, 7 January 1967.)

**Relations with China**. Within the Sino-Soviet context, the CPT has hailed the People's Republic of China as the "bastion of the present world revolution" and has praised the cultural revolution as "unprecedented in human history":

The Chinese people, under the leadership of the Chinese Communist Party and with

Chairman Mao Tse-tung as its head, are continuing to achieve brilliant successes in their socialist construction, including the explosion of nuclear bombs. These successes greatly inspire the revolutionary forces in the world. The Great Proletarian Cultural Revolution taking place in China under the leadership of Comrade Mao Tse-tung is the most advanced step of the Communist Party of China. (Voice of the People of Thailand, 7 January 1967.)

On 1 October, the eighteenth anniversary of Communist China's National Day, the Thai Communists hailed the "brilliant leadership" of the Chinese Communist Party and Mao Tse-tung and praised the "great and decisive victory in the unprecedented cultural revolution." Communist China reciprocated by sending a congratulatory message to the CPT on the twenty-fifth anniversary of its founding, stating in part that "the Communist Party of Thailand, defending the purity of Marxism-Leninism, has taken a firm proletarian internationalist stand and together with other fraternal Marxist-Leninist parties has waged a resolute struggle against modern revisionism, with the leading clique of the CPSU as its center, and has made important contributions to the cause of the international communist movement" (NCNA, 30 November 1967).

While predicting that the "militant friendship cemented by the Chinese and Thai parties and peoples in their protracted revolutionary struggle will certainly be further consolidated and developed in the course of their common struggle in the future," the Chinese Communists hinted that although they firmly supported the Thai Communists, the performance of the CPT had not been up to their expectations: "We are convinced that the Communist Party of Thailand which is persevering in waging a people's war will certainly be able to develop and grow stronger in the struggle, unite the whole Party and peoples of various nationalities throughout the country, and win final victory in the people's war" (NCNA, 30 November 1967).

**Relations with the Soviet Union.** In contrast to its support for the Chinese Communists, the CPT repeatedly attacked the Soviet Union and its leaders. A 7 January Voice of the People of Thailand broadcast charged that the Soviet leadership has "undermined the solidarity of the international Communist movement" by continuing to follow the "revisionist" policies of Khrushchev. "They are conspiring with the colonialists to maintain colonialism and are attempting to revive capitalism in the socialist countries," the broadcast declared. The Soviet leaders have not only "betrayed Marxist-Leninist policy and the principles of international proletarian theory," but have also "betrayed the interests of the great Soviet people and the people of all other socialist countries." In a broadcast on 13 May the Thai Communists again attacked the "Soviet revisionists," accusing them of following a policy of "assisting Vietnam in word but helping the United States in deed to sabotage the just struggle of the Vietnamese people against US imperialism and for national salvation."

On the occasion of the Fiftieth Anniversary of the October Revolution a lengthy statement was broadcast praising the victories of the October Revolution and claiming that "the traitorous Soviet revisionist leaders will never destroy the Great October Revolutionary spirit of the Soviet people":

Now capitalism in the USSR, which is the first socialist country, is being restored in every way. The revisionists led by Brezhnev and Kosygin have seized the power of the Party.

The dictatorial proletariat has become dictatorial capitalism. The Soviet people once again are facing oppression. The revisionist Khrushchev and Brezhnev-Kosygin clique is a traitor which entirely destroys the results of the Great October Revolution created by Lenin and Stalin. They have destroyed the revolution of the people and are urging the revolutionary people to abandon their revolutionary spirit and their armed struggle, which is the only way to liberate oppressed people.

The Soviet revisionist leaders should not be allowed to destroy our dignity or oppress the people any longer. The great Soviet people must rise up against them, take power, and restore the USSR to communism and socialism as indicated by Marxist-Leninist doctrines and Mao Tse-tung's thought. Victory will undoubtedly go to the Soviet people. (Voice of the People of Thailand, 8 November 1967.)

On the occasion of its twenty-fifth anniversary the CPT cautioned that "there is no middle way in fighting modern revisionism. We must keep in mind that if we resist imperialism, we must resist modern revisionism as well."

**Other International Activities.** Apart from the Sino-Soviet dispute, the CPT has confined most of its international activities to the communist parties and national liberation movements of Asia. The CPT did not attend the October celebrations in Moscow, nor did it send a delegation to the Budapest Conference in February 1968, although it did send delegations to the international meetings held in 1957 and 1960.

Throughout 1967 the Thai Communists stressed their determination to "fight shoulder to shoulder with the peoples of Vietnam, Laos, Malaya (including Singapore), Cambodia, and China in their struggle against their common ferocious enemy" (statement by Phayom Chulanont, NCNA, 1 January 1967).

In a *People's Daily* article of 8 October, signed by "Commentator," the Chinese hailed the Thai people's struggle as a "major contribution to the national liberation movement in Asia, Africa, and Latin America."

On the second anniversary of its founding, the Patriotic Front received congratulatory messages from the Democratic Republic of Vietnam and the Vietnam Workers' Party, Prince Souphanouvong, Chairman of the Neo Lao Hak Xat, and Nguyen Huu Tho of the National Liberation Front of South Vietnam, who praised the Thai Communists for making "an important contribution to the cause of peace and freedom of the peoples in Indochina and Asia, a direct and practical support to the South Vietnamese people's resistance war against aggressors for national salvation" and pledged that "the South Vietnamese people will always stand shoulder to shoulder with their Thai comrades in arms . . . . " (Vietnam News Agency, 4 January 1967). At a reception in Peking Phayom Chulanont made special reference to the Chinese Afro-Asian Solidarity Committee, the National Liberation Front of South Vietnam, the Malayan National Liberation League, the Palestine Liberation Organization, the Asian-Pacific Peace Committee, and various Asian, African, and Latin American mass organizations, thanking them for their "unreserved support of the national salvation struggles of the Thai people."

On the twenty-fifth anniversary of the CPT congratulatory messages included those of the Burma Communist Party (White Flag), the Vietnam Workers' Party, the National Liberation Front of South Vietnam, the Malayan Communist Party, the Neo Lao Hak Xat, and the Chinese Communist Party.

**Publications.** Thai Communist policy statements are carried by the Voice of the People of Thailand, a clandestine radio station located somewhere in North Vietnam, in southern China, or in the Pathet Lao-controlled territories of Laos. Statements are also carried in North Vietnamese, Pathet Lao, and Communist Chinese media. On 1 January, the Voice of the People of Thailand announced that it would begin broadcasting in Laotian, the language spoken by the large minority in the northeast. Printed materials are carried in the CPT's irregular clandestine journal *Ekkarat* (Independence). Reports also indicate that the Thai Communists utilize *Siang Phu Rak Chart,* a monthly periodical in Thai.

# TUNISIA

The Tunisian Communist Party (TCP) was founded in 1920 as a part of the French Communist Party and has existed independently since 1934. The party has been banned since 1963 when the Tunisian government outlawed the party, its organ *al-Tali'ah* and the Communist-front newspaper *Tribune du Progrès.*

At present, the only legal party in Tunisia is the Destourian Socialist Party headed by President Bourguiba and most of the important functionaries in the country are members. There is no effective opposition. The Tunisian communists, who have only slight influence in youth and student circles, have no organ or means of propagating their views within Tunisia. Very little is known about the TCP's organization, and the party membership is estimated to number only between 100 and 200 persons out of a total population of Tunisia of 4,457,862 (estimated 1966). The Party's First Secretary is Mohammed en-Nafaa, and Mohammed Harmel is a Secretary of the Central Committee.

**Party Program.** The TCP's attitude toward the ruling Destourian party is critical but not entirely negative. It concedes that there have been some "positive phenomena" in Tunisia and welcomes some of the effects of the program of "Destourian socialism" which was adopted in 1964, such as the extension of the state sector in the national economy and the implementation of social reforms. The Party's principal objection to "Destourian socialism" is the Destourian Party's attempt to counterpose it to "scientific socialism" and Marxism. The Tunisian Party also claims that the basis of "Destourian socialism," which it describes as absolutizing the specific features of developing countries and not allowing for the application of universal laws of the transition to socialism, is derived from the "capitalist west" and the ideological arguments of "bourgeois reformism." (*World Marxist Review,* September 1967.)

The TCP calls for the transition to a "non-capitalist road of development," which it defines as "an alternative to capitalism, a transitional stage for the newly-free countries, in which the non-capitalist methods create the conditions for the transition to socialism and help steer the country towards it" (*WMR,* September 1967). The Tunisian Communists' criticism of the government is that the government refuses to embark on this non-capitalist road of development, refuses to institute an agrarian reform, refuses to allow the participation of workers, peasants and the masses in building the nation and refuses to grant democratic freedoms (including the legalization of the Communist Party).

While the Tunisian Communists' Maghreb brothers in Morocco and Algeria are calling for a "united front" with other progressive parties, the Tunisian Communists are isolated since there is no organized and effective left wing opposition with which to merge. The Tunisian Communists thus search for support among the "broad popular masses" and among the "progressive" members of the Destourian Socialist Party by means of a program modified to appeal to nationalist sentiment. In elucidating the party program to delegates at the French Communist Party Congress in January 1967, Mohammed Harmel did not refer once to "socialism" in Tunisia or a program based on Marxism-Leninism or "scientific socialism." He instead spoke of rallying the masses—the progressive patriotic forces, including those within the Destourian Socialist Party—to exert their weight to force the country "to embark on a road permitting the realization of aspirations of our people for progress, democracy and well-being." These forces are to be pitted against the "most reactionary forces" which want to liquidate the state sector and the "positive gains of the government."

In an article on the October Revolution in *Pravda* on 31 October Mohammed en-Nafaa was more explicit: "Faithful to the education of Marxism-Leninism, the spirit and the meaning of the October Revolution, the Tunisian Communists consistently waged a struggle to carry through the democratic revolution to the end, to insure that national liberation would be followed by profound social liberation, thus opening the road to the non-capitalist and subsequently socialist development."

In the same article the Tunisian Party First Secretary hailed the fact that Tunisia maintains relations with the Soviet Union and other socialist states and noted that the people and the progressive forces wish these relations to develop further. According to en-Nafaa the people do not desire to see Tunisia "locked in a tight circle," a situation which the "imperialists" and "neocolonialists" are striving to achieve. En-Nafaa assured his readers that Tunisia is "tightly bound" to the socialist world. "It is indisputable," he declared, "that the Tunisian people, inspired by the progressive forces will be able to find their road which will surely lead them to socialism."

The TCP, as far as can be ascertained, made no statements about President Bourguiba's controversial foreign policy in 1967. The outspoken conflict between the Chinese embassy in Tunisia and the Tunisian government, each charging the other with "interference in the internal affairs" of its country culminated in the declaration of 23 September by the Tunisian government that the Chinese chargé d'affaires and the entire embassy staff were personae non gratae and in the closing of the embassy on 26 September. President Bourguiba's policy of support for the American action in Vietnam and his moderate stand in the Arab-Israeli conflict also passed without comment by the TCP. The Party noted in *World Marxist Review* (September 1967), however, that "Communists and other progressives" participated in "the recent anti-imperialism demonstrations in Tunis," referring probably to the anti-Jewish riots of 5 June by gangs of young people, after which the Tunisian police made a number of arrests.

**International Communist Movement.** At the French Communist Party Congress, Mohammed Harmel briefly expressed his Party's "indignation" at the "so-called cultural revolution" and the "splitting and anti-Soviet activities" of the Chinese Communist Party leadership, and gave perfunctory endorsement to the idea of convening an international communist party conference. At the conclusion of his address, Harmel stated: "We share your indignation against their [Chinese] splitting and anti-Soviet activity and we support the efforts which you are making together with the Communist Party of the Soviet Union and other fraternal parties to effect the unity of the international communist movement. In this sense, a new international conference of communist parties, carefully prepared, would play an extremely important role."

The TCP has consistently maintained close relations with the Communist Party of the Soviet Union, and has hailed its influence and aid to the progressive forces of the world. The October Revolution, according to Tunisian Party First Secretary should not be copied entirely by the revolutionary forces, but it affords a "valuable example" (*Pravda,* 31 October 1967). This view was also voiced by Mohammed Harmel: "Although our times differ from the days of the victorious October Revolution, and although peoples can take roads different from those taken by the Russian Communists and employ other forms of struggle and other forms of leadership and organization, the basic ideas of October preserve their validity." (*WMR,* September 1967.)

In August 1967, Mohammed Harmel during a vacation in Bulgaria held talks with representative of the Bulgarian Communist Party Boris Velchev on international problems and problems of the international communist and workers' movement. It was reported that special attention was given to the situation in the Middle East "after the Israeli aggression against the Arab countries, which aggression was encouraged and backed by the United States." A complete unity of views on all questions under discussion was also reported.

Mohammed Harmel represented the TCP at the Seventh Congress of the Socialist Unity Party of the German Democratic Republic in April and at the International Theoretical Conference on the Significance of the October Revolution organized in June by the Problems of Peace and Socialism Press in Prague. He addressed the conference and spoke on the concept of the "non-capitalist road of development." Harmel also represented the TCP at the Fiftieth Anniversary celebrations of the October Revolution in Moscow in November.

# TURKEY

The Communist Party of Turkey (Türkiye Komünist Partisi; TKP) was founded in 1920 in Istanbul. Remnants of two other early Turkish communist organizations, one formed in Anatolia, the other from among Turkish emigrés in Soviet Azerbaijan, were absorbed into the party soon after. The TKP has been illegal since 1925 and is severely repressed within Turkey. Consequently, the party has never been able to create a strong organization, and it is not a significant political force in the country. Turkey, with its predominantly peasant social composition and historical animosity toward Russia, has not proved favorable ground for communist recruitment.

The actual strength of the TKP is unknown, but Western estimates generally agree that there are between 1,200 and 2,000 party members. The population of Turkey is 32,901,000 (estimated, October 1966).

**Organization and Leadership.** Overt activity of the TKP is directed from abroad. The Secretary-General of the party is Zeki Bastimar, who goes under the alias Yakub Demir. Most members of the thirteen man Central Committee live in and operate from Moscow, but the party also maintains one Central Committee member (Halis Okan) in Prague on the editorial board of the *World Marxist Review.* Party groups in Sofia and Baku perform liaison between the Central Committee and party members within Turkey.

**Turkish Labor Party.** The TKP has had some success among Turkish intellectuals, and may have to a certain extent infiltrated the Marxist Turkish Labor Party (TLP), many of whose policies parallel those of the Communists. The TLP, however, is wary of identification with the outlawed communist party, and its members claim to be "national communists." The leader and chief spokesman for the TLP, Mehmet Ali Aybar, maintains that his party has no interest in the international communist movement and that the TLP is strictly a Turkish party. (*Frankfurter Allgemeine Zeitung,* 22 March 1967.) There is little evidence at present to support the view that the TLP is under control of any international communist movement or of the TKP.

As a legal party the TLP can participate in Turkish elections, and in the October 1965 lower house elections it obtained 273,683 votes (3 per cent of the total) and 15 seats (out of 450) in the Parliament. In the June 1966 upper house elections, the party received its first seat in that body. The TLP's emergence as a political force is attributed to the normalization of relations between Turkey and the Soviet Union and to the efforts of the Turkish intelligentsia to present solutions for the country's problems different from those provided by the government.

The TLP advocates armed neutrality for Turkey, and calls for the withdrawal of Turkey from NATO, which it says is not a joint defense system, but an alliance to protect the interests of American "imperialism." The party also favors the abrogation of bilateral agreements with the United States and the removal of US bases from Turkey. The TLP opposed the visit of US warships to Izmir and Istanbul in June, but has said nothing about Soviet fleet movements through the straits into the Mediterranean. The TLP was sympathetic to the Arab cause during the May-June Middle East crisis and generally advocates close relations with the Arab states. It protests against the "unjust war" in Vietnam, and Aybar himself participated in Bertrand Russell's international tribunal. On the Cyprus problem, the party opposes the annexation of the island to Greece, but criticizes both the Turkish government's attempts to reach a compromise solution with the Greeks and its efforts to control Turkish nationalist protest demonstrators against Greek Cypriots and the Cyprus government.

In July the National Assembly voted to lift the parliamentary immunity of TLP Assemblyman Cetin Altan, who had written a series of newspaper articles which it considered to be communist propaganda. The constitutional court later reversed the National Assembly decision, sparing Altan from trial on charges which could have resulted in prison sentences totaling 137 years. TLP overtures in September to the liberal Republican People's Party (RPP) to form a "united left-wing front" were apparently rebuffed.

**Domestic Policy.** A TKP party program is not available, but the party expresses views on the domestic situation within Turkey from time to time which serve to reveal its current interests. In February the TKP attacked the Justice Party government under the leadership of Premier Süleyman Demirel as "aspiring to dictatorship" and having more concern for a handful of "rich landlords," "millionaire capitalists" and "foreign US and West German imperialists" than for the broad masses of the Turkish people. It criticized the government's rising expenditures, which according to the TKP were growing at a faster rate than the national income. The party asserted that "soaring living costs" had cut real wages and worsened living conditions for the masses, and that the blame for this condition rested on the government for being "tied to the foreign imperialists and Turkish monopolists who are reaping huge profits." The TKP also assailed the national tax structure: "More than four-fifths of the budget revenue is obtained from taxes paid by the masses of the workers, who have the lowest share of the national income." It specifically attacked the Turkish government budget for 1967 with the charge that funds were being reduced for industrial development in the public sector, for education, and for agriculture, while direct and indirect military expenditures were being increased. The TKP further charged the government with "terroristic and fascist" repression against progressives and with "whipping up anticommunist hysteria."*(Broadcast, "Our Radio," 13 March, from statement of the Central Committee TKP, 25 February.)

While expressing mild approbation for the improvement in Turkish-Soviet relations, the TKP was critical of the fact that the government remained staunchly anticommunist in domestic policy and suspicious in its dealings with the Soviets. Even as Premier Demirel paid an official visit to the Soviet Union in September (in return for Premier Kosygin's visit to Turkey in December 1966), the TKP complained that Demirel's expressions of good will were "mere words" (Broadcast, "Our Radio," 23 September). This attitude of the TKP is a reflection of its dissatisfaction with Turkey's membership in NATO and CENTO and in the bilateral defense arrangements with the United States.

The party attacks the government for allowing the USA to use Turkish soil in its "aggressive" plans against the Soviet Union and the Middle East by furnishing land for nuclear bomber bases and missile sites. It considers it reprehensible that the government permits the USA to sow a "nuclear minebelt" along the Soviet-Turkish border, or "to spy on the Soviet Union with radar." (For example, broadcasts, "Our Radio," 15 August and 29 September.)

The TKP responds quickly to Turkish government efforts to remain on good terms with the USA. It was critical of President Cevdet Sunay's visit to Washington in January, of US-Turkish military talks at the time of the Arab-Israeli crisis, of US attempts to mediate between Greece and Turkey over the Cyprus problem in September, and of the talks in Ankara between US Secretary of Defense McNamara and Turkish Defense Minister Topaloglu in October.

The TKP interprets the current rise in anti-American feeling in Turkey as an "anti-imperialist struggle" waged by "progressive and democratic forces that place national interests above everything else." The appeal to "national interests" is a popular theme for the party, which constantly refers in historical allusion to Ataturk's nationalist movement and the support he received from Lenin and the Soviet Union.

Taking advantage of recent unrest in the Kurdish provinces of eastern Turkey, the TKP criticized the government for "repressive policies" in Turkish Kurdistan. The party advocates abandonment of Turkey's effort to "Turkicize" the Kurds, and it supports the Kurdish "struggle for equal political

*Ankara Radio (30 January) reported a statement by Premier Demirel shortly after Altan and the Turkish poet Husein Korkmazgil were charged with writing communist propaganda in which the Premier said: "I wish to state once again that those who desire to carry out open or secret propaganda in favor of communism in Turkey or those who defend communism are involved in activities that run contrary to our national interests, and they will not be able to escape punishment by the Turkish state." Earlier, in November 1966, the Chief of Staff of the Turkish Armed Forces issued an order which stated that communists were "trying to capture Turkey by revolution" and that the Army must be "careful and alert." This order to "fight against subversive activities" was reportedly being read to all units once each month. (*Milliyet*, Ankara, 23 January; *The Guardian*, London, 2 February.)

rights, freedom from exploitation by feudal landlords," and for schools, newspapers and radio stations using the Kurdish tongue. It professes to view US Peace Corps activities in the Kurdistan region as an "imperialist plot" to subvert the Kurds and to disintegrate the Turkish nation. Party propaganda attempts to link the Turkish and Kurdish peasantry in a common struggle against feudal, capitalist, and imperialist oppression. (Broadcast, "Our Radio," 21 July and 12 October.)

**International Views and Activity.** As a party almost completely dependent upon the Soviet Union for its continued existence, the TKP follows an unswervingly pro-Soviet line.

On the Cyprus issue the TKP supports the popular Turkish position which opposes the union of Cyprus to Greece. The party professes to believe that the antagonism between the majority Greeks and minority Turks on the island is the result of Anglo-American "imperialist machinations," abetted by their "underlings" in Athens and Ankara, and that the two peoples would be able to live in peace and harmony if only the British and the Americans ceased stirring up trouble between them. The TKP opposes the presence of NATO bases on the island and the Acheson plan for the solution to the island's communal problem. But because the TKP view is based upon support for Soviet policy, there are serious contradictions in the TKP position. For example, it shows great sympathy for the Makarios government, which until the April coup in Greece had *enosis* with Greece as its primary objective, and which denies the Turkish community any role in governing Cyprus as an independent nation. The TKP supports AKEL, the communist party on Cyprus, which is almost completely Greek in composition, and it vilifies Turkish Cypriot leaders as spies for the American CIA. (Broadcast, "Our Radio," 3 November.) The party opposes any plan for the partition of the island along communal lines as an imperialist plot to divide and rule, although such a partition is the desire of the Turkish minority, which feels insecure under Greek Cypriot domination.

On balance, the Soviet position on the Cyprus problem, opposing the union of the island to Greece as a "NATO solution" engineered by the British and American "imperialists," has been a fortunate one for Turkish parties of the left. They have been able to capitalize on the Soviet-Turkish rapprochement and on the upsurge of anti-Americanism engendered by the more equivocal US stand. Unfortunately for the TKP, the TLP, as a legal party operating within Turkey, has reaped most of the advantage. In the long run, the TKP may even stand to lose if good relations with the Turkish government become more important to the Soviet Union than continuing support for an exiled and almost impotent Turkish communist party.

The TKP supported vociferously the Arab cause in the May-June Middle East crisis, claiming that Turkey had become a "build-up zone for aggression" as a result of the bilateral agreements "dictated" by the USA. In May, the party asserted that American forces, aircraft, and missiles were being kept ready in Turkey for an attack against the Arab countries. It also accused the Demirel government of abetting the "aggressive plans" of the USA. (Broadcasts, "Our Radio," May.) During the Arab-Israeli hostilities in June, the TKP inferred that US aircraft based in Turkey were being used to support the Israelis, and that the Turkish government was working in collusion with the USA. For the TKP the Arab-Israeli War was a product of "Anglo-American imperialism" and a further example of "US-Israeli aggression." At the time of the ceasefire the party called for a reconciliation between the Arab and Israeli peoples leading to "joint efforts to expel the US imperialists from the Middle East." (*Ibid.*, June.)

Secretary-General Yakub Demir represented the TKP at the Seventh Congress of the East German Socialist Unity Party (SED) in Berlin, 19-22 April, and at the fiftieth anniversary celebrations of the October Revolution in the Soviet Union. The party also agreed to participate in the consultative conference of communist and workers' parties to be held in Budapest in February 1968.

**Press and Radio.** The most effective medium for the dissemination of TKP propaganda in Turkey is the clandestine radio station *Bizim Radvo* ("Our Radio"), which broadcasts from Leipzig in East Germany under the direction of the Turkish communist Fahri Erding. Party declarations and documents appear in special supplements to *Yeni Cag* ("New Age"), the Turkish-language edition of the *World Marxist Review*.

# UNION OF SOVIET SOCIALIST REPUBLICS

The official founding date of the Communist Party of the Soviet Union (Kommunisticheskaia partiia Sovetskovo Soiuza; CPSU) is 1 March 1898, when a small gathering of Russian Marxists met clandestinely in Minsk and formed the first Russian Marxist party (previously only local Marxist groups had existed) under the name of the All-Russian Social-Democratic Labor Party. This meeting, which later became known as the First Congress of the party, also elected a three-man Central Committee (Lenin, under arrest at the time, was not included) and accepted a statute with relatively broad prerogatives for individual members. But the First Congress and its decisions had little influence on the further development of the Russian social-democratic movement. Most of the participants were arrested immediately afterward. Moreover, internal differences between the centralist Leninists and the more moderate and less centralist elements of the party soon took such proportions that the Second Congress, in 1903, resulted in the formal split of the party into Leninist-Bolshevik and Menshevik factions, and in a walkout of the latter along with various splinter groups and the Jewish Bund. Thus it would be more accurate to attribute the foundation of Lenin's party to the congress of 1903.

Officially, however, the feuding parties continued to be called factions of a single Russian Social-Democratic Labor Party. Finally, the adoption of a new name by the Bolsheviks, the All-Russian Communist Party (Bolsheviks), in March 1918, formalized the fact of the fifteen-year-old split.* In 1925 the name was changed to the All-Union Communist Party (Bolsheviks), in accordance with the change of the name of the country to the Union of Soviet Socialist Republics, in which the Russian Soviet Federated Socialist Republic, standing for a territory which more appropriately could be called Russia proper, became one of the constituent republics.

The present name of the party was adopted at its Nineteenth Congress, in 1952. The Communist Party of the Soviet Union is the only legal party in the country.

**Membership.** On 26 September 1967 *Pravda* reported that on the basis of elections in the basic party organizations there were 368,000 party cells throughout the country, with 12,800,000 members and candidates. This amounts to about 5.5 per cent of the total population of some 234 million (estimated 1 January, 1967). The genuine working class element in the party has always constituted a percentage considerably lower than its proportion of the total population; the peasant element is smaller still. Khrushchev's campaign for greater participation of workers and peasants has been continued in the policy of the CPSU, and the proportion of workers has increased from 32 per cent of the total membership in 1957 to 38 per cent in 1967, but meanwhile the proportion of peasants decreased from 17 per cent to 16 per cent, perhaps owing to migration from villages into the towns. In the same period the proportion of the white-collar workers in the party declined from 51 per cent to 46 per cent. Such data, however, do not give a clear picture. The fact is that the social status of party members is registered on the basis of their social origin, rather than their actual work. Thus, a party functionary occupying a full-time administrative position in the party may have been a peasant or an industrial worker at the time of his appointment, and if so would be still registered as such. Of all the peasants who joined the CPSU in 1966, 48 per cent were tractor and combine drivers, agronomists, zootechnicians, and other professionals (registered as peasants) who form an insignificant part of the total rural population ("CPSU in Figures," *Kommunist,* no. 15, October 1967).

* The remaining Mensheviks were persecuted but continued clandestine and semiclandestine activities well into the 1920's. They were last heard of in 1931 when a show-trial of Menshevik economists and technologists, who had played a leading role in the industrialization drive took place.

**Organization and Leadership.** According to the party rules now in use (adopted by the Twenty-Second Congress of the CPSU, in 1961), the regular All-Union party congresses are to meet once every four years; the next one is due in 1970. The party organization is completely centralized. Although all the constituent republics of the Soviet Union except the Russian Soviet Federated Socialist Republic (RSFSR), have their party organizations, these are but local branches of one unified organization. (The Russian republic is directly under the All-Union Central Committee.) Similarly, although considerations of nationality as such have traditionally played a minimal role in the party makeup, it is apparent that, owing to the unitary and centralized nature of the party organization and administration and its urban-oriented Marxist ideology, the party membership has been predominantly drawn from the more urbanized nationalities of the Soviet Union and from among those persons (particularly for all-Union administrative positions) who are fluent in Russian, the only common language of the country. Since the capital, Moscow, is situated in the center of the Russian republic, naturally the majority of the central party offices have been filled by members drawn from the ranks of the RSFSR population.

One important concession is made to local nationalities in party organizations. After Stalin's death (and particularly after Khrushchev's rise to power) the CPSU began to take care to appoint representatives of the local nationalities to lead the republican party organizations, with the sole exception that the second secretaries of the republican Central Committees have continued to be either Russian or Ukrainian, presumably as a safeguard against too much local nationalism.

The All-Union Central Committee that was elected or reelected at the Twenty-third Congress of the CPSU, in 1966, had 195 members, of whom three died in 1967. The same congress elected 165 Central Committee alternate members, of whom two died in 1967. The first secretaries of the republican Central Committees are full members of the CPSU Central Committee by virtue of their position. The Central Committee holds at least two plenary meetings each year, preceding each Supreme Soviet session* and lasting from one to three days each. At these plenums government bills, economic plans, annual budgets, and other major state changes are announced, reported in detail, and approved, whereupon ratification by the Supreme Soviet follows as a matter of course. In the functioning of the state, the Central Committee thus is of greater importance than the formal "parliament" of the USSR, the huge Supreme Soviet. The real governing power, however, is held by the Politburo and the Secretariat of the Central Committee. In 1967 the Politburo consisted of the following:

### Full Members

| | |
|---|---|
| Leonid I. Brezhnev | Secretary-General, Central Committee of the CPSU |
| Andrei P. Kirilenko | Secretary, Central Committee of the CPSU |
| Alexei N. Kosygin | Chairman, USSR Council of Ministers |
| Kirill T. Mazurov | First Deputy Chairman, Council of Ministers |
| Arvids J. Pelshe | Chairman, Party Control Committee |
| Nikolai V. Podgorny | Chairman, Supreme Soviet Presidium ("President of the Soviet Union") |
| Dmitri S. Poliansky | First Deputy-Chairman, USSR Council of Ministers |
| Alexandr N. Shelepin | Chairman, All-Union Central Council of Trade Unions |
| Piotr I. Shelest | First Secretary, Ukrainian Central Committee |
| Mikhail A. Suslov | Secretary, Central Committee of the CPSU |
| Gennadi I. Voronov | Chairman, Council of Ministers of the RSFSR |

* The Supreme Soviet meets in two regular sessions per year, lasting two to three days, during which all government bills are invariably unanimously approved.

## Candidate Members

| | |
|---|---|
| I. V. Andropov | Chairman, Committee for State Security (KGB) |
| P. N. Demichev | Secretary, Central Committee of the CPSU, in charge of Ideological Department |
| V. V. Grishin | First Secretary, Moscow City Party Committee* |
| D. A. Kunaiev | First Secretary, Kazakh Central Committee |
| P. M. Masherov | First Secretary, Belorussian Central Committee |
| V. P. Mzhavanadze | First Secretary, Georgian Central Committee |
| S. R. Rashidov | First Secretary, Uzbek Central Committee |
| V. V. Shcherbitsky | Chairman, Ukrainian Council of Ministers |
| D. F. Ustinov | Secretary, Central Committee of the CPSU |

The Secretariat consisted of the following:

| | |
|---|---|
| L. I. Brezhnev | Secretary-General |
| P. N. Demichev | Secretary |
| I. V. Kapitonov | Secretary, in charge of Party Organizational Work Department |
| A. P. Kirilenko | Secretary |
| F. D. Kulakov | Secretary |
| B. N. Ponomarev | Secretary, in charge of International Department |
| M. S. Solomentsev | Secretary, in charge of Heavy Industry Department |
| M. A. Suslov | Secretary |
| D. F. Ustinov | Secretary |

Of these key personalities in the Soviet leadership the most important ones are those who are simultaneously *(a)* full members of the Politburo and *(b)* Secretaries: Brezhnev, Kirilenko, and Suslov. Although Kosygin is not Secretary, his importance lies in his being the supreme superviser and endorser of economic policies and the chief administrator of Soviet industry; these are his main functions as Prime Minister. While the Politburo is the body where main political decisions are taken and policies are debated and drawn, it is in the Secretariat that the daily business of appointments and removals is carried out and orders and instructions to the lower party echelons are given. Thus it can probably be safely said that, at least in the carrying out or obstructing of decisions and policies, Brezhnev, Kirilenko, and Suslov with the help of the subsidiary secretaries can achieve more than, for instance, Kosygin, who although Prime Minister and a full member of the Politburo, does not participate in the "routine" deliberations of the Secretariat.

The Central Committee has a large number of specialized departments or commissions. Some of these parallel certain of the ministries and specialized standing committees of the Supreme Soviet (which have lately considerably increased both in number and importance). Other party departments or commissions, such as the Ideological Commission of the Central Committee, have no parallel in the state bodies. The differentiation of functions between these party bodies and their government parallels is not clear; probably the former work out principles and control their execution, while the government bodies work out final decisions in detail and implement them.

---

* Every large town has its own city party committee (smaller ones have only regional or district party committees). The Moscow City Party Committee is the most important of them all, as it is always the host to foreign communist delegations and all the communist party conferences that take place in Moscow.

The Central Committee has a number of ideological schools directly attached to it, including: the Institute of Marxism-Leninism, headed by P. N. Fedoseiev since the summer of 1967, the Higher Party School, headed by N. R. Mitronov; and the Academy of Social Sciences, headed by V. N. Malin.

The Institute of Marxism-Leninism is the highest ideological-theoretical institution in the country. The Higher Party School prepares practical party officials or reeducates them in special courses and seminars. The Academy, which is responsible for education in the social sciences in the Soviet Union, prepares party supervisors for the social-sciences faculties of the country and also cadres of lecturers in Marxism-Leninism and related fields who take up posts in educational institutions.

In the republican party organizations the structure and institutions of the central party organization are duplicated, except on a more limited and modest scale. The party congresses of the republics normally take place on the eve of the all-Union party congress. The first secretaries of the party central committees of the republics are:

| | |
|---|---|
| Armenia | Anton I. Kochinian |
| Azerbaidzhan | Velii I. Akhundov |
| Belorussia | Piotr M. Masherov |
| Estonia | Ivan G. Kabin |
| Georgia | Vasilii P. Mzhavanadze |
| Kazakhstan | Dinmukhamed A. Kunaiev |
| Kirghizia | Turdakun U. Usubaliev |
| Latvia | Augustus E. Voss |
| Lithuania | Antanas J. Sniechkus |
| Moldavia | Ivan I. Bodiul |
| Tadzhikistan | Dzhabar D. Rasulov |
| Turkmenistan | Balysh Ovezov |
| Ukraine | Piotr I. Shelest |
| Uzbekistan | Sharaf R. Rashidov |

In the Soviet Union all organizations, societies, clubs, associations, and other organizations, except for religious bodies,* are directly controlled by the CPSU, and their heads are ultimately responsible to the party Central Committee, which is also the final decision-making body in such cases as, for instance, a conflict between the editor of a journal and its censor. Furthermore, it is the explicit purpose of all "social" organizations (as stated in their statutes) to educate their members in communism and to make them "conscientious supporters and promoters" of the party line.

The largest single bloc of so-called social organizations is composed of the trade unions, headed by the All-Union Central Council of Trade Unions. Its total membership is about 86 million, and it is often referred to in the Soviet press (quoting Lenin's words) as "a school of economic management, a school of communism." This well describes the main purpose of Soviet trade unions, which serve as promoters of more efficient production rather than as defenders of the workers in conflicts with management. This function may change in the long run, assuming further development of the current economic reform, with its greater emphasis on autonomous social institutions; so far, there are very few signs of such a change.**

The Komsomol, or Communist Youth League of the Soviet Union, with about 19.5 million members in the age group between 14 and 28 years, is the party's most important youth organization.

* The apparatus of *indirect* but very real party-state interference into religious affairs is the State Committee on the Affairs of Religious Cults, headed by Kuroiedov, who has the rank equivalent to a cabinet minister. Formally, however, the religious bodies are headed only by their religious leaders.

** For information on labor and trade-union questions in the USSR see Robert Conquest, *Industrial Workers in the USSR* (New York, 1967); on unemployment problems see D. Pospielovsky, article in *Osteuropa* (Stuttgart), no. 4, April 1967.

The purpose of the Komsomol is to educate its members in the spirit of communism, to prepare them for party membership, and to serve as a pool of cadres for difficult industrial and agricultural tasks, such as the building of railways, roads, and hydroelectric plants in Siberia and the cultivation of virgin land in Central Asia. It is very difficult to enter a university or other centers of higher education without being a Komsomol member, and expulsion from the Komsomol while at a university very often carries with it an expulsion from the university as well. Retention of membership is not necessarily so crucial once a young person has found a good job upon graduation and established himself as a needed specialist or has gone on to become a valuable research graduate student. Hence there is a discrepancy between the numbers of party and Komsomol members. Most young persons, after their education is completed, cease to be active members of the Komsomol, often leaving the organization formally as well (nonpayment of membership dues is the most common reason for "expulsion" from the Komsomol). It was to increase Komsomol membership that the Twenty-third Congress of the CPSU stipulated that persons between 18 and 23 years of age may enter the party only through the Komsomol. Apparently as a result of this provision, the Komsomol membership has increased more rapidly in the last two years and surpassed 22 million in 1968. The Komsomol's First Secretary is Sergei Pavlov, a protege of Shelepin and Semichastny (see below), who both preceded him in that post.

The children's branch of the Komsomol is the Pioneer Organization, with some 20 million members aged 10 to 14 years. The Komsomol, from among its members, appoints leaders for the Pioneers. It is very hard for a school child to refuse to be a member, although the official organ of atheism, *Nauka i religia* (Science and Religion) often reports cases of school children who have refused to join the Pioneers on religious grounds, the organization being actively and militantly atheistic.

In addition to the Pioneers there is the Soviet organization for children from seven to nine years of age, the Octoberists, with about 14.5 million members.

In the Soviet press in the last few years, complaints have increased about the bureaucratization of the leadership of all three of these communist youth organizations; the issue was also raised at the Komsomol Congress of 1966. Reportedly, the appointment of youth leaders has become a purely formal procedure, and the Komsomol, Pioneer, and Octoberist meetings have tended to be only a formal routine. The main complaint is that the children do not naturally flock around their leaders and that, after fulfilling the obligation of attending meetings, they gather on the streets in gangs with their own leaders, often with hooliganism or even delinquency as a consequence. To ameliorate this situation there has been some experimentation with informal groupings under various names, led by local enthusiasts from the Komsomol who have been accepted or chosen by the children, rather than centrally appointed. In these organizations there is more emphasis on practical work, less on ideology and theory. It is unclear how far this experimental movement has spread and what its relationship is with the formal youth organizations.

**Internal Party Affairs – Leadership Changes.** Alexandr Shelepin, a former head of the secret police and at least until 1967 one of the most important members of the Politburo, lost his position in the Secretariat of the Central Committee when he was appointed chairman of the trade unions at the Thirteenth Plenum of the All-Union Central Council of Trade Unions on 11 July 1967. This shift has been variously interpreted by Western commentators. One interpretation is that the appointment of Shelepin to the trade-union leadership may have been guided by the need to have a strong personality at the head of the trade unions during the current economic reform. Nevertheless, removal from the Secretariat would seem to have been a considerable personal defeat for Shelepin, and his position may have been further weakened by the removal from office of his close associate Nikolai Yegorychev, who held the very important post of first secretary of the Moscow City Party Committee until 28 June. Yegorychev's subsequent assignment has not been made known.

V. Grishin, the former head of the trade unions, was appointed to Yegorychev's post on 11 July. As first secretary of the Moscow City Party Committee, Grishin played host at numerous important international meetings devoted to the fiftieth anniversary of the Bolshevik Revolution (see *Fiftieth Anniversary*). In the past this post has been held by such important figures as Lazar Kaganovich

(1930-35), Nikita Khrushchev (1935-38), and P. Demichev (1959-62).

Another of Shelepin's men to be demoted in 1967 was V. E. Semichastny. On 19 May he was removed as chairman of the State Security Committee (the KGB, or secret police), and appointed First Deputy Premier of the Ukrainian Republic. Like his predecessor Shelepin, Semichastny had moved into the KGB chairmanship from the Komsomol. Semichastny's removal, like Shelepin's, can be explained by the fact that both men helped engineer Khrushchev's dismissal in 1964. For his part, Shelepin was promoted in November 1964 to the full membership in the Central Committee Presidium (called the Politburo since the Twenty-third Congress). Apparently the new leaders, Brezhnev and Kosygin, found it uncomfortable to have next to them such powerful men as Shelepin and Semichastny. Step by step the authority of Shelepin was diminished: first, in December 1965, the Party-State Control Commission, wherein Shelepin as chairman had authority over the vast army of party "controllers" throughout the country, was disbanded; immediately afterward, he lost his post as Kosygin's deputy on the Council of Ministers. When Shelepin's power had been sufficiently neutralized, Semichastny lost the KGB chairmanship. Then Shelepin was removed from the Secretariat of the Central Committee.

Semichastny's successor as head of the KGB was Iurii Andropov, but following this appointment Andropov lost his position in the Central Committee Secretariat, retaining only his alternate membership in the Politburo. This seems to indicate that the present Soviet leadership is reluctant to vest too many powers in the hands of the secret police.

At the time of the Hungarian Revolution of 1956, Andropov was the Soviet ambassador to Budapest, and upon his recall from this post in 1957 he was awarded a decoration and promoted to the position of head of the Central Committee department for "relations with the fraternal socialist countries," which he occupied until his latest appointment. In 1961 Andropov was elected to full membership on the Central Committee, and the following year to the Central Committee Secretariat. It is likely that his KGB appointment was related to the growing "disobedience" of the East European countries, and of Soviet intellectuals as well. Andropov, an experienced diplomat, a better-educated man than Semichastny, and with experience in the East European area in particular, might have been expected to deal more capably with both problems than his predecessor—who is remembered for publicly calling the writer Boris Pasternak a "pig" at the time of the anti-Pasternak campaign—but the recent trials of intellectuals seem to suggest that Andropov has not been any more successful.

Marshal Andrei A. Grechko was appointed Soviet Minister of Defense on 11 April 1967, following the death of his predecessor, Rodion Malinovsky, on 31 March. Previously Grechko was Commander in Chief of the Warsaw Pact Armed Forces, in which post he was replaced on 7 July by Marshal Ivan Yakubovsky, the First Deputy Defense Minister of the Soviet Union. The gap between the appointments has been generally attributed by Western observers to prolonged negotiations within the Soviet government and party and between the Soviet Union and other East European countries as to who should be appointed. Neither Grechko nor Yakubovsky is known for any outstanding military achievement during World War II.

The appointment of Sergei Bannikov as deputy chairman of the Soviet Supreme Court can be directly related to the activities of dissident intellectuals. Before this appointment General Bannikov reportedly had been entrusted by the KGB with "keeping watch on Soviet cultural life, particularly the poets and the novelists who have challenged the dogmatic party line in the recent years." He had often "attended meetings of writers and other artistic groups and lectured them on the party's ideological demands." Further, "cultural figures were summoned to his office if they strayed too far from the authorized line." (*New York Times,* 10 November.)

P. N. Fedoseiev, a Central Committee member and a vice-president of the Academy of Sciences of the USSR, replaced P. N. Pospelov as the Director of the Institute of Marxism-Leninism. Pospelov, an "old Bolshevik," reached the age of 69 years in 1967. During 1966 he had been at least twice in serious difficulties. One instance was caused by the debate on 16 February at the Institute of Marxism-Leninism over Professor A. M. Nekrich's then recently published book, *22 June 1941,* one of the most serious and uncompromising indictments of Stalin's role in World War II. Historians and military specialists took part in the debate and overruled Pospelov's attempt to condemn the book as a "falsification." The other instance was another debate at the Institute, this time over the third draft volume of the multivolume *History of the CPSU,* during which a major indictment of Stalin was voiced by some hundreds of participants—historians, old Bolsheviks, and various important public figures. Incomplete transcripts of both debates were smuggled to the West and published (*Possev,* Frankfurt, 13 January 1967, and *Survey,* London, no. 63, 1967, pp. 159-169). A further cause for conflict with the Central Committee may have been Pospelov's failure to publish the whole *History of the CPSU* for the fiftieth anniversary of the October Revolution as originally promised.

Alexandr Nekrich, the author of *22 June 1941,* was purged from the party in 1967 (*Christian Science Monitor,* 29 July). This seems to indicate that Pospelov's difficulties were not caused by the party's having a more liberal attitude toward Stalin than his own. The smuggling of the transcripts may have been a much more important issue.

Leonid Brezhnev has been enhancing his position by appointing to important positions certain of his former subordinates in Moldavia, where he was first secretary of the republican party from 1950 to 1952. One of the early appointments from Moldavia to Moscow was that of S. P. Trapeznikov, who in 1965 was made chief of the Central Committee department dealing with science, technology, and education. Another "ex-Moldavian" to get a Central Committee appointment in 1965 was K. U. Chernenko, who was made chief of the General Department of the Central Committee. Very important for the strengthening of Brezhnev's position was the appointment in 1966 of his long-standing associate, N. A. Shchelokov, to head the newly-created All-Union Ministry for the Protection of Public Order. This ministry is in charge of the militia (the Soviet police), but otherwise its functions are undefined and it seems to parallel the KGB in some spheres. Brezhnev's decision to build up this ministry on the all-Union level may have been caused by a desire to protect himself from any plots by the KGB like the one which resulted in Khrushchev's dismissal in 1964. Shchelokov, a Ukrainian, was chairman of the Dnepropetrovsk City Soviet Executive Committee when Brezhnev was first secretary of the Dnepropetrovsk regional party committee in 1939. When Brezhnev became first secretary of the Moldavian party in 1950, he took Shchelokov along with him, making him the head of the party's Central Committee department dealing with party, trade-union, and Komsomol organs and then deputy and afterward first deputy chairman of the Moldavian Council of Ministers.

In 1967 Brezhnev moved another of his associates from Moldavia to Moscow, appointing N. F. Lobachev as deputy chief of the Department of Planning and Finance Organs of the CPSU Central Committee.

Khrushchev tried to surround himself with men who once worked with him in the Ukraine (including Brezhnev and Podgorny), and similarly Stalin had many Georgians in his immediate entourage in Moscow. Thus it is not surprising that Brezhnev has brought along some of his associates from Moldavia. The giving of Moscow "jobs" to Russians and Ukrainians who once held key positions in Moldavia may have also a relationship to the feud with Rumania over this annexed territory and might be intended to show that under Soviet rule it is actually managed by Moldavians, as many of the key positions in Moldavia, formerly occupied by Russians and Ukrainians, are now headed by natives.

**The Cult of Personality Issue.** Despite the official opposition of the party leadership to any further critical analyses of the "cult of personality" issue the intellectuals have continued to insist on the necessity of a deep analysis of the issue. According to a set of "underground" documents received in the West (for some of these see *Documents*), at a meeting of the Leningrad "House of the Press" on 5 October 1967, with a selected audience addressed by Zimianin, the editor in chief of *Pravda,* and Fedoseiev, the director of the Institute of Marxism-Leninism, interalia Fedoseiev stated: "The cult of personality was finished with long ago and there is no use to return to it. Let those who are interested in this problem study the cult of Mao or of the Latin-American dictators." That is, Stalin and his role were not to be discussed openly any more.

Khrushchev's name continued to be unmentionable. At the same time, the third volume of the *History of the CPSU,* published on the eve of the fiftieth anniversary of the October Revolution, and other documents of the anniversary demonstrated that there was practically no revision in the labels attached by Stalin to his main communist adversaries, such as Bukharin and Trotsky.

In the course of the search for greater authority for the party leadership, signs have appeared of a certain type of personality cult around Brezhnev. In the May 1967 issue of the Russian-language Dagestani journal *Sovetskii Dagestan* an article by P. Tepun praised Brezhnev as a military-political leader on the North Caucasian front in World War II. Brezhnev was alleged to have "carried out great and many-sided work in the education of soldiers in the spirit of friendship of nations of the USSR . . . ." Khrushchev's cult began with stories in the Soviet press about his outstanding role on the Stalingrad and Kiev fronts, but whereas Khrushchev was hailed as a brilliant military organizer, Brezhnev has been praised as a top army politician, the representative of the party. The fine difference reflects the present "division of powers," under which Brezhnev heads the party but not the government; Khrushchev was simultaneously in charge of both. The fact that the article appeared in a national-minority journal and emphasized the concept of the "friendship of nations" indicates the present greater concern with the national question in the Soviet Union.

**The Party and Government Interrelationship.** The division of power between party and government has been discussed at some length in the Soviet press during the last two years. Many articles have referred to the necessity to enhance the power of the soviets (particularly local, but also republican and federal) and to broaden the prerogatives and activities of the deputies.* A *Pravda* editorial "The Time and Style of Work" (6 February 1967), criticized "petty tutelage and usurpation of the function of economic managers" by party functionaries as "absolutely intolerable in the new [economic] conditions." In the ensuing wide discussion of the subject in the party press, some articles affirmed the harmfulness of such interference while others claimed that the interference was being caused by the inefficiency of the appropriate administrative and economic organs and managements.

Another *Pravda* editorial (9 December) stated that party members in the soviets should act as party agents: "The party organizations must not supplant the soviet organs, but are obliged to develop their activities, initiative, and independent action." In practice, the editorial went on to complain, party organizations ignored the institutional state organizations and their rights, including the soviets themselves. The Central Committee, *Pravda* stated, "obliges all the party organizations to do away with the unnecessary tutelage and petty interference in the activity of the soviets and their executive committees, and thus to guarantee the further development of initiative and independence in the work of the soviets," adding: "the city, district, and regional committees of the party cannot replace the soviet organs, cannot replace by their activities the work of the organs of state administration . . . ."

In Khrushchev's time the "withering away of the state" was interpreted to mean the growth of the functions of the "social" organizations: the party and its affiliated organizations were gradually to take over many of the functions of the state. Now the emphasis is on the "democratic" and mass character of the soviets on all levels, which altogether include about 23 million of the population. (Cf., for instance, A. Plekhov, "Lenin's Theory of the State and the Present Time," *Kommunist vooruzhonnykh sil,* no. 15, Moscow, 1967.)

The Twenty-third Congress of the CPSU, in 1966, called for an increase of the activities of the soviets. At the first session of the Seventh convocation of the Supreme Soviet (August 1966) the permanent commissions of the Supreme Soviet "were increased from four in the Council of the Union and five in the Council of Nationalities to ten in each chamber" (Robert Conquest, *The Soviet Political System,* New York, 1968).

On 8 March 1967 a decree by the Central Committee of the CPSU on "Improving the Work of

*Soviets, or councils, are allegedly the basis of Soviet democracy. They first appeared in 1905, during the First Russian Revolution, as militant strike committees with general left-socialist leanings. The Mensheviks and the Social-Revolutionaries predominated. In 1917 these committees reappeared under the name of "soviets" of workers', soldiers' and peasants' deputies. Soon after the takeover of control by Lenin the role of the soviets began to decline. This process continued throughout the 1920's and soon the federal congresses of the soviets became only a ceremonial, while the real powers passed fully into the hands of the Party Politburo with its Secretary-General, Stalin, at the top. On the regional level the soviets have acted as the executors of the commands of the local party committees.

Village and Settlement Soviets of Workers' Deputies" criticized the soviets for not making full use of "rights at their disposal." It went on to say: "They do not sufficiently influence the affairs of collective and state farms, undertakings, and establishments. There are still many shortcomings in the work of schools, hospitals, kindergartens and nurseries, stores, clubs, and other organizations serving the people, for the results of whose work the responsibility rests upon the village and settlement soviets. The mass organizational work of the village and settlement soviets is still not sufficiently coordinated with solving concrete tasks of economic and cultural construction . . . .Implementation of approved decisions is not well organized. Permanent commissions are not active enough. Not all the deputies participate in the soviets' activities . . . ." (Moscow Radio, domestic service, 10 March.) The party decree was taken as law: "Thus, the Presidium of the USSR Supreme Soviet has begun the practice of calling in the chairmen of *oblast* and *kray** governments to hear their reports on 'what the local soviets . . . have done under the leadership of the party organs in the way of concrete work for fulfillment of the CPSU/CC decree' . . . ." (Dr. A. Boiter, "More Power for the Soviets?" *Research Bulletin,* Radio Liberty, Munich, January 1968.)

The other attempt to enhance the prestige of the soviets has been a study undertaken by the Supreme Soviet of "proposals to allow more than one candidate to run for each legislature seat," as stated at a press conference in Moscow on 29 August 1967 by M. Georgadze, the Supreme Soviet Presidium Secretary (*Christian Science Monitor,* 31 August).

**Marxism and Philosophy.** Besides the fiftieth anniversary of the October Revolution, 1967 saw also the celebration in all communist countries of the 100th anniversary of the publication of the first volume of *Das Kapital.* The general trend of Soviet writing on the relevance of Marxism today, in connection with the anniversary, was: conditions have changed since the nineteenth century and not everything in *Das Kapital* should now be taken verbatim, but the main thesis remains true—the rich are getting richer, the poor, poorer (see, for instance, the article by the economist G. Kozlov in *Pravda,* 2 September). To give credibility to the thesis, Soviet theorists tended to put it in an international context: the rich, developed countries are getting richer in inverse proportion to the worsening impoverishment of the underdeveloped states.

Another "ideological anniversary" was marked by an international conference of Marxists in Moscow on 12-13 April to commemorate the 30th anniversary of the death of the founder of the Italian Communist Party, Antonio Gramsci. This meeting, organized by the Institute of the International Workers' Movement, was addressed to "Leninism and Problems of the International Workers' Movement," but its documents contained no new interpretations.

Articles touching on historical-ideological subjects were frequent during the fiftieth-anniversary year and were mainly of an apologetic character. Kositsyn, the Deputy Director of the Institute of State and Law of the USSR Academy of Sciences, tried to prove that the Soviet Union was not a "totalitarian antidemocratic regime" and that it had used violence only when necessary to defend itself ("Government of the People and for the People," *Izvestiia,* 5 August). According to Kositsyn, the "dictatorship of the proletariat" is in essence democratic, since it has used dictatorial methods only against its enemies.

A. Rumiantsev, a leading Soviet ideologist of a relatively moderate and reformist orientation and the Vice-President of the Academy of Sciences, went to considerable pains to justify Lenin's coup d'état of 1917 (later known as the October Revolution). Rumiantsev blamed General Kornilov's mutiny for Lenin's decision to take over, and argued that the refusal of the Socialist Revolutionaries (the majority party at the time) to accept the dictatorship of the proletariat accounted for Lenin's persecution of them. Rumiantsev also offered a Marxist justification for Lenin's takeover: Lenin realized that the conditions of the liberation struggle had changed since Marx and that, depending on the particular conditions in different countries, socialist takeovers could occur in countries at different times, and not necessarily first in those technically most advanced. ("The Triumph of Creative Marxism," *Kommunist,* no. 14, October.)

While official Marxist philosophy and ideology in the Soviet Union has petrified, interest in

*I.e., *region* and *territory,* respectively.

"nonconformist" philosophies has grown considerably, particularly among young persons. A Soviet publicist, Ye. Bogat wrote in *Literaturnaia Gazeta* (1 March) that books on philosophy were becoming best sellers among young readers, but presumably did not mean the official philosophy, as any visitor to a Soviet bookshop will see stacks of unsold ideological books. Reportedly, the Russian translations of Teilhard de Chardin's *The Human Phenomenon* and of a Polish critical study of St. Thomas Aquinas sold out within hours. Soviet writers have admitted that there is a great interest in existentialism in the USSR, and a number of articles on this school of thought have appeared in *Voprosy filosofii*, the chief philosophical journal.

Soviet ideologists are concerned over the situation. The academician F. Konstantinov, one of the leading Soviet spokesmen on philosophy and Vice-President of the Academy of Sciences, wrote in *Pravda* (24 July): "Neither the religious philosophy of neo-Thomism, which tries to combine science and religion, nor the subjective philosophy of existentialism, which has become quite popular in the capitalist society, can serve as guidelines." Konstantinov assured his readers that the Central Committee of the CPSU had provided all the necessary ideological answers in the Soviet Union, but went on to state: "Attempts are discernible to replace the dialectical and historical materialism by some variety of bourgeois humanism," presumably referring to the revisionist Marxist philosophical schools of Yugoslavia, Poland, Czechoslovakia, and Hungary as well as to the situation in the Soviet Union.

**Ideological Issues in Relations with Other Countries.** The spread of Yugoslav philosophical and sociopolitical revisionism seemed to cause some concern in the Soviet leadership. The strongest indirect attack on the Yugoslav idea of changing the role of the party from that of ruling the state to that of ideological guidance appeared in *Pravda* (20 February) over the signature of I. Pomelov: "Any narrowing of the party's role or restriction of its functions—for example, to the sphere of ideology alone—would be totally inadmissible to the cause of socialism." Pomelov, however, made direct reference only to China (where the weakening of the party's role had resulted in "subjectivism, arbitrariness, the worst forms of anarchism, outrages and mockery of people"). The USSR's relations with Yugoslavia remained friendly throughout 1967 and became particularly close after the Middle East crisis.

The ideological rift with Cuba appeared to be widening. Soviet authors repeatedly criticized the tactics of uncompromising subversion and guerrilla warfare propagated by Cuba, without mentioning Cuba by name. One such attack (*Pravda*, 11 January) was by a Soviet philosopher, I. Krasin, who stressed that the Bolsheviks had used violent means of change only when conditions for revolution were ripe. Krasin said that deviation from Marxism-Leninism either to the left or to the right was dangerous, especially when it took on forms of "nationalism, big-power chauvinism, and hegemony," adding: "The activity of the CPSU in preparing and carrying out the revolution continues to serve today as the model of the correct approach to the basic questions of the revolutionary struggle . . . . The strategy and tactics of Bolshevism were forged in fierce struggle against right and left opportunism." This simultaneously implied criticism of Cuba, Yugoslavia, and China.

Soviet ideologists strove to direct the attention of Soviet citizens to foreign issues, particularly the "struggle against imperialism" and the "fight against neocolonialist exploitation" of the underdeveloped nations in the Middle East, Asia, Africa, and Latin America. Dmitri Shevliagin, head of the International Department of the CPSU Central Committee, wrote in *Pravda* (14 June): "[At present] the popularization, elucidation of ideas, and practice of true socialism in all its variety assumes particular urgency." In order that world public opinion should be won over by "the bright image of socialism," said Shevliagin, there should be a more active propaganda campaign against bourgeois ideology, combined with the wooing of those forces in the capitalist countries which were "spontaneously attracted by socialism, while far from always adhering to Marxist views"; a further task was the "organization of resistance to anticommunism." An editorial in *Kommunist* (no. 7, May 1967) dwelt on the internationalist principles of communism in an appeal for full communist support of the Karlovy Vary conference.

Soviet ideologists have increased their attention to Western Sovietology in the last few years. In 1967 their attacks became particularly frequent because of the numerous Western publications devoted to the fiftieth anniversary of the October Revolution. Soviet ideologists complained that the West had begun to use ideological weapons against the Soviet Union (see, for instance, D. Shevliagin's "Anticommunism and Its Impotence," *Izvestiia,* 21 September 1967). Western, particularly American, institutions studying communist and Soviet affairs received considerable notice. A *Pravda* article (13 July) by two philosophers, G. Kursanov and S. Alexandrov, stated that these study centers specialized in falsifying Soviet history, and listed among the main ones the Russian Center at Harvard, the Russian Institute of Columbia University, and the Hoover Institution.

**The Nationalities Issue.** The raising of the issue of internationalism, the use of the term "great-power chauvinism" in the Soviet anti-Mao campaign, the support declared for national "wars of liberation," and the wooing of "exploited nationalities" by trying to show them how well the nationalities issue has been resolved in the Soviet Union — all these elements of foreign policy would seem also to have a relationship with the reawakening of local nationalist activities in the Soviet Union and the appearance of many articles on the nationality issue in Soviet journals. The claim that Leninism solved the national issue once and for all has been modified, if not quietly discarded, as Soviet ideologists have sought more up-to-date answers to this problem. (Articles on this issue appeared in most Soviet periodicals during 1967, notably in *Voprosy filosofii,* nos. 9 and 10; *Kommunist vooruzhonnykh sil,* no. 15; *Literaturnaia gazeta,* 31 May; *Kommunist,* nos. 10 and 15; and *Kommunist Moldavii,* no. 1. Such articles admitted directly or indirectly the existence of national friction and some elements of nationalism in the USSR.)

**Youth, Ideology, and Education.** A considerable problem to the Soviet ideologists continued to be the attitudes of young persons and the education of the young in fidelity to the official ideology.

F. Tsarev, the editor in chief of the Soviet military magazine, *Sovetsky voin,* complained about insufficient patriotism among Soviet young people and in the youth press, remarking that such leading youth journals as *Smena, Molodaia gvardiia, Selskaia molodiozh, Yunost,* lacked convincing and talented stories on Soviet patriotism. Writing in *Kommunist* (no. 14, 27 October), Tsarev noted that the main youth daily, *Komsomolskaia pravda,* which used to have a regular page on the lives of members of the Soviet armed forces, had ceased to publish regular articles on these and other patriotic themes and that, instead, overtly pacifist articles were beginning to appear in the Soviet press.

On 14 April an All-Union seminar of ideological workers of the Komsomol was held in Moscow to discuss ideological work among young persons. Shortcomings were discussed and it was determined that many were the results of ineffective work, insufficient militancy, and the legacy of the "cult of personality" (*Pravda,* 15 April). On 26-27 December a plenary session of the Komsomol Central Committee discussed problems in the communist education of students by the university sections of the Komsomol and participation of Soviet young persons in the Ninth World Youth Festival, to be held in Sofia, Bulgaria, in 1968.

On the other hand, some educators and other scholars continued to complain that the Soviet school system was too dogmatic and thus was creating "infantilist" young men incapable of independent thinking and decision-making. S. Kaftanov, rector of the Moscow Chemical-Technological Institute, complained, for instance, about the overpaternalistic system of high school education in the Soviet Union. He was also unhappy over the state of instruction in Marxism-Leninism at the colleges and universities, where he declared the teachers were usually of pensionable age, poorly educated and boring, and it was very difficult to find young candidates for their jobs. (*Pravda,* 4 December 1967.) It was noted in the press that young students were increasingly often posing tricky political-ideological questions which the professors were unable to answer. *Pravda* (11 December) reported an instance at the top center of Soviet education and science, the Akademgorodok of the Novosibirsk University and the Siberian Section of the Soviet Academy of Sciences: at a students' seminar, "dangerous" political issues had begun to be discussed, and when one of the participants exposed his own "muddled-up, illogical" theories, "some of the audience began to approve," whereupon the professor present listened silently and afterward applied to the local party organization for ideological help. *Pravda* criticized the professor for his ideological ignorance, pointing out that he ought to have been capable of coping with the dissident students alone. The same article appealed for the renewal of political-ideological work with the intelligentsia, attacking the current view that the intellectuals need no party tutorials.

**Religion.** The relative lull in attacks against churches and believers, noticeable since Khrushchev's downfall, continued in 1967. The main reason was given in the Soviet atheistic press during 1965 and 1966, most importantly in the official organ of Soviet atheism, *Nauka i religiia* (Science and Religion): the forced shutting of churches and religious communities had resulted in increased hostility of believers toward the Soviet government and in the spread of secret religious associations which were less easily subject to control and supervision by the state than the official religious bodies. The Soviet press also stated that in those areas where all the churches had been shut down in the last five years of Khrushchev's rule, the number of believers and the general sympathy of the population to them had increased. Even the campaigns to recruit priests to atheism and persuade them to make strong oral and written anti-Church statements have been criticized for being too costly in effort and not achieving their purpose, since the usual reaction of believers reportedly has been: "So much the better. The more such priests leave, the stronger the Church will be. These renegades used to cheat us, now they'll be cheating you."

Soviet atheist lecturers have been criticized for poor performance, and during 1966 and 1967 a number of special seminars and study conferences of atheist lecturers were convened to work out new and more sophisticated methods of antireligious propaganda. It has also been claimed that many people attend churches for aesthetic rather than purely religious reasons. It is probably partly with this purpose in mind that with some support from the government, the "Society for the Preservation of Ancient Monuments" was launched in 1965, whose proclaimed aim it is to preserve and restore buildings of historical value, particularly the churches and the monasteries, although not as places of public worship, but as objects of art. Hundreds of leading Russian intellectuals have joined the society, among them the pianist Sviatoslav Richter and the writers Leonid Leonov and Vladimir Soloukhin.

In 1967, for the first time since the revolution, an illustrated book of Bible stories for children was published in the Soviet Union. Also published was a book of selections from the Old Testament with "appropriate" atheistic comments and "explanations" by the Polish writer Zenon Kosidowski. Appeals for the publication of the full Bible as a great work of literature appeared in *Nauka i religiia* and other Soviet journals.

In this general field 1967 saw the posthumous publication of M. Bulgakov's *Master and Margarita,* an allegorical novel on the theme of Christ and Antichrist with flashbacks from the Soviet Union of the late 1930's to the last days of Jesus; the shooting of a film on St. Andrey Rubliov, a 15th-Century monk and painter of ikons; and the appearance in *Novy mir* (no. 5) of an essay on St. Sergius of Radonezh by a contemporary Soviet writer and member of the party, Yefim Dorosh.

It was unofficially stated by churchmen in the Soviet Union that between 1965 and 1967 some 400 to 600 churches were reopened each year. The number is still very small, considering that 12,000 churches were shut in the last five years of Khrushchev's rule.

Strict measures have been taken against dissident religious groups, such as those Baptists who defy the authority of the official Baptist Church for its servility to the Soviet government. In 1966 new legislation was adopted making the punishments for religious instruction of the young heavier than before. A number of trials of persons charged with giving religious instruction to their own and friends' children took place in 1966 and 1967.*

**The Party and the Intellectuals.** Special meetings of the intelligentsia and the press, such as the one in Leningrad, referred to above, indicate that the legitimacy of political censorship has continued to be questioned. At that meeting Fedoseiev stated: "Some writers and workers of culture have begun to advance the demand for creative freedom and the liquidation of censorship. Control of the press has always been one of the party's most important concerns. The party has never renounced control of

*For more detailed picture of the Soviet policies toward religion see: Nikita Struve, *Christians in Contemporary Russia,* London 1967; Robert Conquest, *Religion in the USSR,* New York, 1968; M. Bourdeaux and P. Reddaway, "Soviet Baptists Today," *Survey,* no. 66, London, January 1968; D. Ushinin, "Soviet Policy towards Religion since Khrushchev" (in Russian), *Grani,* no. 60, Frankfurt/Main, 1966.

this kind." The public press reflects this view, but does not put it so bluntly. In an article in *Pravda* (4 December) G. Smirnov commented: "There is nothing in common between our [democracy] and the bourgeois democracy . . . .Imperialists madly applaud all the renegades, defectors, and madmen who choose the bourgeois way of life. They try to infiltrate into our country by radio and other means, trying to show that the absence of freedom in our country for antipeople activities is a limitation to democracy. The achievement of bourgeois-democratic liberties at a certain state of development was a positive phenomenon, but [would not be such] for our working people today . . . ." To substantiate his defense of censorship, Smirnov quoted Lenin's letter to Miasnikov of 1921 justifying the suppression of the opposition press in the country. He then referred to the principle of "democratic centralism" whereby discussion takes place until a decision has been reached (at the top) which thereupon becomes law and cannot be criticized; this he called true "people's democracy." The tenor of the article, recognizing the limitations on civil liberties in the Soviet Union and blaming "imperialist encirclement" for the necessity to suppress opposition, could be found generally in published Soviet ideological discourse on the internal ideological subjects during the jubilee year.

The major event in the official cultural life of the country in 1967 was the Fourth Congress of the Union of Writers of the USSR, which met in the Kremlin Palace of Congresses 22-27 May. The preceding congress met in 1959; although the Union Statutes stipulate that the congress shall meet every four years. The Union of Writers has some 6,500 members.

The 1967 congress, originally scheduled for the end of 1963 and then postponed to 1964, may have been delayed by the disastrous harvest of 1963 and the ensuing dissatisfaction with Khrushchev's administration. A further postponement to 1965 was probably a consequence of the deposition of Khrushchev and the preoccupations of the new regime. In 1965 the arrest of the writers Siniavsky and Daniel was the occasion for putting off the meeting yet again. If the show trial of these writers was intended to frighten the intellectual community into obedience, it was a miscalculation, as petitions, protests, and demands of freedom for the defendants and freedom of the press and expression increased in volume and intensity. Delayed again, the congress of the Union of Writers eventually met in 1967 as one of the multitude of jubilee conferences and meetings.

Like other congresses connected with the fiftieth anniversary, it avoided controversial issues—so much so that M. Sholokhov, one of the staunchest supporters of the regime among Soviet writers, voiced open criticism of the Congress:

> I am a bit embarrassed by the undisguised desire of our writers' leadership to carry out a congress at any cost in such a way as to avoid the sharp corners. I don't think this is wholly justified . . . . We haven't met for seven years and we do have some things to talk about . . . .

Sholokhov also complained about the small representation of young writers at the congress (the average age of those attending was nearly sixty years) and berated the older generation for its ignorance of the young "fronde" and unwillingness to come into contact with the newer writers; at the same time he criticized the young for trying to be too smart and individualistic:

> I am personally very saddened by the absence of my old friend, Ilia Ehrenburg . . . . It turns out that he left for Italy on the eve of the Congress. . . . It is also unfortunate that this bad example is contagious . . . . Looking at such independence and ignorance of norms of social behavior demonstrated by Ehrenburg, some overgrown young writers have been performing such tricks as they will be later ashamed of . . . (*Pravda* 26 May).

Sholokhov's remarks countered the various official speakers at the congress who had stated with assurance that there was no generation conflict in the USSR.

Apparently, few of the writers who are best known both in the USSR and abroad attended the congress. Tvardovsky, the editor of the most liberal Soviet journal, *Novy mir,* was present, but was not reported as having delivered a speech or taken part in discussions. Of the 525 elected delegates, 10 per cent did not show up — an unprecedented disobedience. Solzhenitsyn (the author of *One Day in the Life of Ivan Denisovich*), who had not been invited, sent an "open letter" to the congress denouncing the censorship and persecution of writers and other artists in the USSR and charging the Writers' Union with never coming to the help of its persecuted members.

Solzhenitsyn's outburst was followed by a letter of support signed by more than 80 Soviet writers. A further consequence was an unprecedented link-up with intellectuals in eastern Europe. At the subsequent Polish Writers' Congress, to which only 100 writers came, the Solzhenitsyn letter was read and discussed, and a resolution demanding the relaxing of censorship in Poland was drawn up which received the support of more than 90 participants. The Polish congress closed in the midst of an uproar on 3 June. It was followed and paralleled by the Czechoslovak Writers' Congress (see *Czechoslovakia* and *Documents*), where again the Solzhenitsyn letter was read and supported, and a resolution demanding the dissolution of censorship was adopted.

Sholokhov was not completely right in his statement about the lack of controversy at the congress of the Soviet Union of Writers. At least one speech reflected the ideas of Solzhenitsyn's plea. Oles Ghonchar, the normally docile first secretary of the Ukrainian Writers' Union, expressed open, bitter criticism of Soviet censorship. In his speech, published only (in Ukrainian) in the weekly newspaper of the Ukrainian Writers' Union, *Literaturna Ukrayina* (26 May), Ghonchar said: "The strictest editors and even the invisible being with a coloured pencil in his mighty hand, must understand that only the primitive-minded, the bureaucrats, the careerists and stupid dogmatists, who tremble for their jobs, gain from the suppression of the Soviet writers and of the scope of Soviet literature." Among the communist and fellow-traveling writers from 27 foreign countries in attendance at the congress, it does not appear that any left a noticeable imprint.

The issue of censorship of creative art in the Soviet Union was raised in the official press after the congress in an article in *Komsomolskaia pravda* (30 June) over the signature of two leading Soviet journalists, F. Burlatsky (a regular *Pravda* correspondent) and L. Karpinsky. This article bitterly criticized censorship in the Soviet theater as stultifying and virtually demanded its abolition. It was attacked in the same newspaper (8 July) by the Komsomol Central Committee as a "gross ideological error" and later by *Pravda* (26 July). Such a dichotomy between the position of the Komsomol Central Committee and that of its newspaper demonstrates the existence of controversial streams of thought in the Soviet youth organization. Similar conflict appeared in the case of Efros, who was removed as chief producer at the Moscow Komsomol Theater. His experimentalism had turned the Komsomol Theater during the previous two years (1965-66) into one of the most popular and controversial theaters in Moscow, for which he and his productions became constant objects of the wrath of conservatives. Efros went over to the Moscow Dramatic Theater, making it just as controversial.

A politically embarrassing cultural event was the flight to the USA of Stalin's daughter and the subsequent appearance of her book. She was severely attacked by Sholokhov at the Union of Writers' congress, and by the Soviet press in general. Her flight must have dealt a considerable psychological blow to the Stalinists, being the last element in the disintegration of Stalin's immediate family: his wife either committed suicide or was murdered; the elder son rejected Stalin before the war, signed anti-Stalin leaflets as a military prisoner of the Germans during the war, and disappeared either in the German prison (Svetlana Alliluieva's version in her *Twenty Letters to a Friend:* shot by guards) or in the Soviet Union after having been repatriated (a popular rumor in the Soviet Union). Stalin's younger son, the debauching drunkard Vasiliy, died of alcoholism. Finally, Stalin's favorite child escaped to the "capitalist world" and published an indictment of the Soviet system.

An important landmark in the writers' struggle for independence was the letter of the poet Voznesensky to *Pravda,* which although not published in the newspaper found its way to the West (for instance, *New York Times,* 11 August). Voznesensky charged the Union of Writers with lies, bad manners, and contempt for human dignity, particularly of its own members. When the secretariat of the Union of Writers officially denounced the letter, Voznesensky, to clear his name, published in the union's weekly, *Literaturnaia gazeta* (25 October), a series of verses charging the US Central Intelligence Agency and the NTS* with trying to exploit his personal feuds in order to alienate him from his country and society. No such "apology" came from Solzhenitsyn, whose letter to the Union of Writers had predicted that the continued suppression of his works inside the country would sooner

*Narodno-trudovoi soiuz, or People's Alliance of Labor, a Russian emigre anticommunist organization.

or later result in their smuggling and publication abroad. To call the writers to order, *Literaturnaia gazeta* warned Soviet writers that they could be tried for treason for handing over their works, not published in the USSR, to Western publishers (*Washington Post,* 12 October).

The CPSU and the government meanwhile steered a middle course. *Pravda* (27 January, and on a few other occasions) criticized both the liberal journal, *Novy mir,* and the most dogmatic Soviet literary journal *Oktiabr*: the one for presenting Soviet life too pessimistically and the other for untalented, boring presentation and for underestimating developments since Stalin. A policy article by the editor of *Literaturnaia gazeta,* A. Chakovsky, in *Pravda* (26 October) took the same direction. The article, called "Always with the Party," attacked Western ideologists for their alleged claim that artists tend to be always in opposition to established authority. Chakovsky maintained that this was not true of the Soviet Union, but proceeded to discuss understanding in a purely domestic context. Calling for "understanding" as an appreciation of the aesthetic values of an artistic work, even when it conflicted with the ideological values of the party, he cited the example of Lenin, who approved the publication in the USSR of works by Russian emigre writers although he did not tolerate them ideologically. According to Chakovsky, the judgment as to whether a book should be published must be made on the basis of its literary value, even overruling "negative ideological" aspects if the work proved to be of a great literary value. In order to be able to pass such judgement, Chakovsky writes emphatically, the person in question, in other words, the Party ideological leader, must be highly cultured himself.

**Arrests, Trials, and Campaigns against Intellectuals.** The remarkable activization of a "civil rights" campaign in the USSR following the trial and condemnation of Siniavsky and Daniel in 1966 resulted in a wave of arrests which began late in 1966 and continued in 1967, when four young litterateurs were arrested in January for their leading role in assembling, editing, and illegally publishing two mimeographed books, one a "White Book on Siniavsky and Daniel" and the other a collection of poetry, short stories, reports, and articles critical of the regime, entitled "Phoenix 1966." The four persons were:

Alexandr Ginzburg, a poet, editor of the "White Book," who under Khrushchev was twice placed in detention for publishing an illegal student magazine, *Sintaxis*;

Iurii Galanskov, an active "left wing pacifist" (his own description), author of a long poem ("Manifesto of Man") in defense of human rights in the Soviet Union, and editor of the clandestine "Phoenix 1961" and "Phoenix 1966," who spent some years in prisons for having issued "Phoenix 1961";

Alexei Dobrovolsky, a lay religious thinker in his early thirties, and author of articles on religio-philosophic themes, one of which appeared in "Phoenix 1966," he had spent about four years in forced-labor camps under Khrushchev;

Vera Lashkova, a student at the Moscow Theatrical Institute, who was connected with the publication of "Phoenix 1966."

On 22 January (the anniversary of the "Bloody Sunday" demonstration of 1905, which happened to fall on a Sunday in 1967 as well) a demonstration in protest against the arrest of the above persons was staged in Moscow by the S.M.O.G. (a clandestine intellectual youth group in Moscow with, sections, allegedly, in Odessa, the Urals, and Leningrad; the letters stand for "Word, Thought, Image, Depth," in Russian). The demonstration was immediately dispersed by security forces and some of the 50-odd participants were arrested. Reportedly, another demonstration was staged a few days later, demanding the release of the four earlier arrested and those detained on 22 January, and was likewise dispersed, with additional arrests being made.

At least four demonstrators were kept in confinement in preparation for a trial in accordance with the antidemonstration law of 16 September 1966. These were Khaustov, a young poet; Vladimir Bukovsky, a gifted writer of short stories and one of the organizers of S.M.O.G., who under Khrushchev was several times placed in mental hospitals because of his political activities; and Vadim Delone and Yevgeniy Kushev, two very young poets. Khaustov was soon tried in secret and sentenced to three years' imprisonment, the maximum possible under the antidemonstration law. A scheduled secret trial of the others failed to materialize when Gunnar Moe, the chairman of the Norwegian Committee of Solidarity with the Imprisoned Soviet Intellectuals, went to Moscow on the eve of the trial, visited the defendants' relatives, and informed foreign correspondents in Moscow of the approaching trial and its place and date. The three were given a semi-public trial in Moscow between 30 August and 1 September. Bukovsky was sentenced to three years' imprisonment; the other two received conditional sentences of one year each and were allowed to go home. (For Bukovsky's plea see *Documents*.)

A notable aspect of these events was the role of descendants of the late Maxim Litvinov, foreign minister under Stalin and a leading old Bolshevik. Litvinov's daughter testified on Bukovsky's behalf at the trial. Litvinov's grandson, a physical chemist, smuggled a transcript of the trial abroad, together with detailed notes on his own interrogation by the KGB (see *Documents*). (Reports on the Bukovsky affair appeared in: *Christian Science Monitor,* 31 August and 5 September; the *New York Times,* 1 September, 2 September, and 27 December; and the *Washington Post,* 2 September.)

The trial of the litterateurs Ginzburg, Galanskov, Dobrovolsky, and Lashkova were repeatedly delayed, despite written protests by dozens of Soviet intellectuals, including some leading writers, over the illegality of holding them under arrest without trial for more than nine months. (The trial and sentencing occured in January 1968.)

It has become almost impossible for any political arrest and trial to be kept secret in Moscow, owing to the increasing contacts of Soviet intellectuals and young persons with each other and with foreigners, and the young persons' growing daring and disregard for the police. Political life in the provinces, however, is still very difficult to penetrate. The political trials of certain Ukrainian intellectuals in 1966 and 1967 became known only vaguely and after much delay. Very limited evidence has come to light on the arrest, trial, and mass deportation of some 250 Leningrad University students late in 1965 for taking part in underground political and literary activities, possessing an underground printing press, and publishing an underground journal, "The Bell."

Details on the December 1967 Leningrad trial of a group of university professors, scholars, publicists, and research students, are likewise still lacking. In April 1967 there was unconfirmed news of the arrest of some 25 intellectuals in Leningrad. At about the same time four members of the editorial board of the Leningrad literary monthly *Neva* were replaced. Later reports increased the number of persons arrested to 40. In the course of the investigation some were released and eleven were placed in mental hospitals or under police surveillance. At least four are known to have received very heavy sentences for treason, possessing weapons, and conspiring to overthrow the government. Among them were Professor Ogurtsov, a specialist in Tibetan studies at Leningrad University, and Yevgeniy Vagin, a secretary of the board preparing an edition of Dostoyevsky's works, who received prison sentences of 15 years and 13 years respectively. Two unidentified intellectuals were given sentences of 13 and 8 years respectively. One of the two was reported by Western correspondents to have been a member of the editorial board of the academic journal of literary theory *Voprosy literatury*.

Western press agencies reported that some of those arrested in Leningrad belonged to various underground ideological circles, one being a "Berdiayev Circle" devoted to the study of ideological, religious, and philosophical problems in a Christian-socialist context. It was also reported that the Berdiayev Circle had adherents in Sverdlovsk, in the Urals, and Odessa, in the Ukraine, and that it had been connected with Galanskov's "Phoenix 1966," which in turn was very closely associated with the S.M.O.G. literary-oppositionist youth organization. The S.M.O.G., further, had claimed in its clandestine publications (*Sphinx, Sheia, Chu, Smog-Ural,* and others) that there were branch S.M.O.G. groups in Leningrad, the Urals, and the Ukraine besides the main group in Moscow. The geographic distribution of both groups seems to coincide.*

**The Economic Reform and the Party.** Apparently with the aim of making the local party administrators more flexible, more receptive to the economic reform and its new demands, and to the projected broadening of the activities of the local government bodies, a number of courses were organized in 1967 for local party functionaries. Among these was a month's course in Moscow, ending 15 December, for secretaries of the Central Committees of the republican, kray, and oblast

*The most specific accounts of the Leningrad trial are to be found in the Russian-language monthly *Possev*, Frankfurt/Main, January 1968, pp. 9-12. See also *New York Times,* 22 December 1967.

party committees responsible for agriculture in their areas. The curricula included history and policy of the CPSU, Marxist-Leninist philosophy, political economy, and practical implementation of the decisions of the Twenty-third Party Congress and the Party Central Committee plenum decisions of March 1965 and May 1966.

A similar seminar for deputy chairmen of councils of ministers of autonomous republics and Soviets (i.e., deputy leaders of local legislatures) closed ten days later in Moscow. This seminar, too, was devoted to agriculture, the improvement of capital construction, and the development of light and food industries — that is, to the promotion of the current economic reform and of the general trend of the Soviet economy in the consumer's favor. The earlier seminar was concluded with an address by Brezhnev, the latter with an address by Kosygin.

Related to the need to modernize the economy and to make it more flexible and competitive with the world technological progress was the general opening-up of discussions — often touching upon the most basic premises of the official ideology — on economics, management, education, and allied fields. It is in these fields that the clash between pragmatists and dogmatists has become most apparent. The pragmatists insist on maximum curbing of the prerogatives of the central planning organs, maximum development of "free" market forces and subsequent adjustment of production and prices accordingly, and minimum intereference by the administrative apparatus with the workings of the economy. It has even been suggested that agriculture and the small enterprises working directly for the consumer (such as services, repair shops, sewing, and shoe factories) with fewer than 50 employees be totally removed from the control of the planning institutions and turned into genuine independent producers' cooperatives. The dogmatists keep attacking such "extreme" views, maintaining that the economic reform itself is no more than a secondary adjustment and modernization of methods and prices. The continued publication of complaints by factory managers in the Soviet press indicate that the dogmatists — or the inexpert, party-oriented bureaucrats — continue to rule in the ministries and continue to disregard the very prerogatives reserved to the managers of enterprises by the current economic reform.

Briefly, the main elements of the economic reform are: (1) some decentralization of economic decision-making and a reduction of the number of planned indexes coming from the State Planning Agency and the ministries to the individual enterprises; (2) an effort to make prices more relevant to production costs and to market conditions; (3) enhancement of the profit motive to make the personnel of enterprises directly interested not only in quantity of goods produced, but also in their successful sale; (4) increase of material incentives for each individual worker and employee; and (5) some substitution of indirect controls (fiscal, market, and so on) for direct controls (physical targets, administrative measures).

To curtail administrative interference by the ministries and other state departments, it has been suggested that they also be transferred from external to internal economic accountability. I. Pustovalov, in an article in *Pravda* (15 September) pointed out that under such an arrangement, earnings of the employees (presumably including the ministers themselves) would depend on the economic and financial performance of all the factories and other enterprises under the control of each particular ministry. However limited its scope and however slow its advance, the current economic reform has sparked broad discussion, in the course of which many practices and dogmas have been questioned. The existence of unemployment in the USSR, for example, has been acknowledged, although in a veiled way.

A demand for more independence of thought, work, and initiative for Soviet economists was put forth in an article in *Pravda* (9 October) by A. Rumiantsev, a middle-of-the-road ideologist who lost his post as editor in chief of *Pravda* in 1965 for an article demanding less interference of the party in the work of Soviet scholars, and has since become a vice-president of the Academy of Sciences. Soviet economists, he wrote, needed to become more precise and scientific: "We should not blindly follow Western bourgeois prescriptions, but neither should we dismiss them. We must learn from them and accept whatever is positive."

Another ideologist, V. Stepanov, co-editor of *Kommunist,* the chief ideological journal of the CPSU, also demanded greater freedom for economists and technocrats from petty party tutelage

(*Pravda*, 28 December). Tutelage could be justified in the past, wrote Stepanov, closely following the line of argument of Rumiantsev's 1965 article, but there was no longer a need for it. "Our enterprises," he declared, "are headed by very well educated economists." Stepanov praised the economic reform for having given priority to economic considerations and incentives, and, admitting that not all Soviet people appreciated the guiding values of communism, made a plea that sheer force not be applied against the unappreciative, as the proper tools of the party were "persuasion, education, and example."

I. Pustovalov, in an article noted earlier, added to his plea for a greater independence from central control a call for further strengthening of the "Association of Firm Councils." The "firm councils" (where they exist) consist of the directors of firms or associations, the managers of plants included in the firms or associations, and the directors of the research and planning departments of each component; important engineers, foremen, and skilled workers also are often invited to the council meetings. The firm councils have only consultative functions and have no formal powers vis-a-vis the central planning bodies. Pustovalov urged that they receive decision-making powers as well.

The economic reform, which has raised a number of basic socio-ideological questions, was discussed from the sociological point of view in April 1967 at an all-Union sociological conference which brought together some 500 participants at Sukhumi, in Georgia. A. Rumiantsev delivered the report on the interrelationship of sociology and the economic reform; also problems of employment, population, recruitment, migration, and redistribution of the working population — all of great importance for the economic reform — were discussed (*Vestnik statistiki*, Moscow, no. 9, September). The fact that by mid-1968 the proceedings of this conference had not yet been published in full might signify that "difficult" and controversial topics were brought up.

The CPSU Central Committee, responding to appeals of Soviet social scientists for more systematic, intensive, and comprehensive study of the social sciences, issued a decree on 21 August, "On Measures for the Further Development of Social Sciences and on the Increase of Their Role in the Construction of Communism." On the one hand, the decree called for the enhancement of the role of the social sciences and the quality of scholarship in this field, and, on the other, it ordered that the social sciences pursue a partisan course.

**Development of the Economic Reform in Practice in 1967.** Throughout 1967 the gradual switching over of industrial enterprises to the new economic system of greater enterprise autonomy, more decision making on the spot, more material incentives, and reserving for disposal by enterprises of a greater share of the income gained by them has continued. By the end of the year more than 7,000 factories, producing 40 per cent of industrial output and employing 33 per cent of the labor force, had been transferred to the new system. The ratio of their total volume of production to their total labor force shows that in general the more efficient enterprises were being transferred to the new system. Therefore their success was only partly attributable to the reform. However, the rate of growth in industrial output was very healthy in 1967, being surpassed only by that of Japan, and the best for the Soviet Union in the last ten years. Gross industrial output increased by 10 per cent over 1966; gross national income, 6.7 per cent; labor productivity, 7 per cent; and real per capita income, 6 per cent. Personal savings, reaching a total of almost 27 billion roubles, increased by about 19 per cent. With the continuing shortages of many consumers' goods, particularly of consumers' durables, such a high rate of growth of savings indicated a serious build-up of inflationary pressures, because a high proportion of the savings were a result not of abundance, but of the inability of the market to satisfy the demands and the purchasing capacity of the citizens. On the other hand, as the savings are growing particularly in the higher income bracket, the planned dramatic increase in personal car production in the USSR for 1970 and onwards should at least for some time siphon off a considerable part of the inflationary pressure of savings.

Indirect but important evidence that the economic reform had brought vitality into the economy was furnished by an 8 per cent rise in investments during the year (instead of the planned 7.9 per cent), an increase of only 5 per cent in the share of centralized investment (instead of the planned 7 per cent), and the increase of about 20 per cent — an unprecedented figure — in decentralized investment (by enterprises, state farms, and collective farms). (For statistics see the report of the

Central Statistical Agency in *Pravda*, 25 January 1968.)

In the first few months of 1967 the first conversion of a whole branch of industry to the new system was completed. These were all the enterprises, factories, and shops belonging to the Ministry of Machine Building, Automation, and Control Systems. This was followed by gradual conversion of all the chief departments (*Glavki*, the offices in charge of each of the industrial subsections within the ministry) in the Ministry's jurisdiction to the system of internal economic accountancy. This is one of the most-favored ministries, with probably the highest proportion of modern, efficient plants; its average profitability was high under the old system. With the near completion of this conversion, the Minister of Machine Building, Automation, and Control Systems, K. Rudnev, published an appraisal of the reform's implementation in his enterprises in *Pravda* (5 July 1967). Rudnev revealed that not only the professional party-bureaucrats had opposed the reform, but some "old school" industrial managers as well. In the first year of implementation (1966), however, there was practically none of that resistance, as only the most successful and forward-looking enterprises were being switched over. By the same token it may be expected that in 1968, when the reform should have been completed "in the main," the opposition may increase very substantially as unsuccessful enterprises are converted to the new system, unless new incentives for the management are invented, or the management personnel itself is radically purged and replaced by the younger and more daring men.

In agriculture perhaps the greater innovation was the transfer on an experimental basis of the first 400 of the 12,000 Soviet state farms to a system that is an adaptation to agriculture of the current economic reform. State farms have been economically even more inefficient than the collective farms, since workers on state farms have been paid a regular fixed salary irrespective of whether the given farm paid its way or not, whereas the members' incomes on collectives have depended on the total income of the farm. Besides, nearly all the profit earned by state farms went to the central redistribution fund, which was used to finance the deficits of the unsuccessful farms. Thus, while the collective farmers had very little incentives to work well (the wage fund was a residue left after payment of the farm's arbitrary taxes and other obligations to the state), at least the managers of these farms needed some income to make their farms pay their way; the state farms had not even this incentive. The 400 state farms that were switched to the new system have received as broad an autonomy of decision-making as that of the collective-farm managements. Furthermore, these state-farms no longer have to dispose of all their profit; they retain a proportion for investment, additional pay to the workers, building programs, opening their own subsidiary industrial enterprises, and so on. In November 1967 a well-known Soviet liberal economist, G. Lisichkin, reported in *Pravda* that the state farms on the new system had already made profits 60 per cent above the expected level, despite bad weather (*New York Times*, 21 November).

Another important innovation decreed by the Council of Ministers on 25 September, legalizing the subsidiary industrial and artisan enterprises that were organized, run, financed, and controlled by individual collective or state farms. These are the first legal industrial enterprises (however small and primitive) completely outside the central plan system. Since the Twenty-third Party Congress laid it down that such enterprises should be legalized, enterprises of this sort had ceased to be illegal; however, there were many reports of attempts (often successful) by local party and state bureaucrats to shut down such enterprises under various pretexts — mainly on the grounds that the workers earned too much money, that this income was undeserved, and that it upset the state wage funds and increased the inflationary pressures. Now it will be more difficult to curb them.

A decree by the Ministry of Agriculture (explained in detail in the Soviet economic weekly *Ekonomicheskaia gazeta*, no. 48, November 1967) has prescribed the setting-up of a system of legal services at collective and state farms. All regional and district (*oblast* and *raion*) administrators are required to provide a fully paid senior legal adviser (senior economist and claimant), who is to establish and supervise legal services at the collective and state farms.

This decree, for the first time since the forced collectivization of farming nearly forty years ago, creates a system of self-defense for agriculture against arbitrary actions of the local state and party administrators, the supplying and procuring offices, and the industrial managers, who have often been reported to be arbitrarily appropriating fertile farm lands for the building of factories and other industrial objects. It will undoubtedly result in a greater demand for lawyers and could increase the prestige and role of legality in the Soviet Union (and thus assist in educating the average Soviet citizen and the administrator in the respect for law, badly shaken by the Revolution and by the arbitrary methods of state administration still practiced in the Soviet Union). But the positive effect of the decree may be negligible and be restricted only to the very local level if the central administration and planning offices continue to disregard the law and their own decrees themselves. As a case in point may be cited the new 1967 regulations of agricultural state-procurements for 1968 and the remaining years of the Five-Year Plan (1966-70). The March 1965 Party Plenum, the Twenty-third Party Congress, and the Draft Five-Year Plan established fixed, unincreasing norms for agricultural produce to be sold (obligatorily) by the farms to the state in each of the five years of the current plan period. It was also stated that the farms would have more liberty in deciding what exactly to cultivate over and above the fixed proportions of goods required by the state. Yet in 1967 the government, overruling its own earlier decree, increased the norms for obligatory sale of produce to the state in 1968, and *Pravda* (8 December) reported that the Soviet Council of Ministers had decided that the agricultural "procuring organizations" should "make direct contracts with individual farms for each particular individual produce" over and above the volume of produce to be sold to the state as a type of tax-in-kind. It has often been reported that the procuring organizations refuse to accept farm produce on the pretext of a shortage of storage space. With the new decree in force, the procuring organizations presumably will have to bear the consequences for not accepting goods contracted for, and will have to pay the farms the price previously agreed upon.

At the same time, the original generous investments into agriculture promised for the current Five-Year Plan have been cut somewhat, from 41 billion roubles (*Pravda,* 27 March 1965) to just over 35 billion roubles, judging by State Plan Chairman Baibakov's statement that the "Five-Year" agricultural investments are to be 76 per cent above the previous five years (*ibid.,* 11 October 1967). But the actual expenditure on agriculture over the first three years of the Five-Year Plan period suggests that the total outlay will be even smaller than 35 billion. Nevertheless, the rise in agricultural investments has been very large and this sector of the national economy is gradually ceasing to be the stepdaughter of the Soviet planning system.

Ideological controversies over agriculture were primarily concerned with the problem of ownership. Ever since Khrushchev's downfall and the new lease on life given to the private plots and the free farm market, the liberal Soviet economists have argued that land requires a concrete master (*khoziain zemli*), which, they say, cannot be replaced by the abstract idea that land belongs to the people as a whole.

Discussion has never reached the point of open suggestion that land be restored to full private ownership, however, and the main problem has become how to enhance the feeling of personal responsibility for land and its produce without reverting to private ownership. Experiments have been going on since about 1962-63 with a veiled or covert form of the leasing of land by collective or state farms to small informal groups of four to ten highly qualified farmers, and supplying them with the necessary equipment, seeds, and fertilizers. Such a group is responsible only for the final sale of its produce to the parent farm at pre-agreed prices, somewhat below the state price. In the months preceeding the harvest the parent farm was obliged to pay monthly "advances" to the members of the groups, the advances would then be subtracted from the total sum payable by the parent farm to the group at the harvest time. These experiments, first reported on a broad scale toward the end of 1965, were strikingly successful, resulting in incomes for group members far superior not only to farm averages, but even to average industrial wages. This caused a considerable opposition from the bureaucrats, particularly in the state finance departments. When the 1966 harvest proved such a great success, the further spread of the experiment became very difficult, and many reports of arbitrary closures appeared. Meanwhile a high-ranking commission had been set up, headed by Brezhnev, to discuss and prepare a new draft statute for the collective farms, which presumably would have encompassed all the new experiments. It was first promised that an all-union conference of collective farmers and specialists would meet in 1966 to study the draft and endorse it. No such conference took place in 1966, however; promised for 1967, it did not materialize again.

Preparatory local conferences of farmers have been promised for 1968. Thus the situation has remained unresolved, and the poorer harvest of 1967 again resulted in the appearance of articles making a positive assessment of the land-leasing system. (See G. Radov and V. Yakhnevich in *Pravda*, 8 December 1967, and I. Kopysov's article in *Literaturnaia gazeta*, no. 6, 1968.)

Another ideological-economic tenet of Marxism related to agriculture and to natural resources in general presents a problem in the evaluating of land, forests, fisheries, water, and other natural resources, and in pricing them. All these have no value from the point of view of the labor theory of value. Yet their indiscriminate exploitation has lately caused Soviet economists to call for, and to propose various means of reintroducing a pricing system on all natural resources. By 1967 special academic commissions had been set up by the All-Union Agricultural Academy to debate and work out such prices.

**International Views and Policies.*** Soviet attempts at differentiating between party and state functions on the domestic front had considerable international implications. The apparent separation of the two centers of power served to promote the confidence of foreign states in the Soviet role in world affairs while allowing scope for efforts by the CPSU to try to maintain a world communist movement under its direction. The policy of differentiation was especially beneficial in Soviet relations with states of the "Third World" where the communist parties were banned. Following the overthrow of leftists Nkrumah in Ghana and Ben Bella in Algeria in 1966 and the suppression of the attempted communist coup in Indonesia, numerous articles appeared in the Soviet press stating that internal changes need not necessarily affect Soviet relations with the countries involved. In 1967 one such article, by Soviet foreign affairs theorist S. Sanakoyev, emphasized that party relations with a country need not automatically cause a deterioration in state relations. Similarly Sanakoyev argued that even if state relations between socialist states should deteriorate, this would not mean that one of the states was reverting to capitalism. For instance, in China, according to Sanakoyev, a return to capitalism has been prevented by the people's "stubborn resistance to such a plan." (*International Affairs*, Moscow, no. 10, 1967.)

While the new policy benefited the Soviet Union in some areas, such as in relations with the Arab states where communist parties are outlawed and in negotiating trade agreements with China such as the one signed on 27 July 1967, the policy has been subject to criticism from both right and left. At the Havana conference of the Latin American Solidarity Organization (31 July-10 August), Cuba and a number of Latin American revolutionary groups condemned the Soviet Union and other communist countries for their economic aid to "dictators and oligarchic regimes" in Latin America. The Soviet ambassador to Chile replied on 11 August that the Soviet Union wished to have relations with all countries of the world, whatever their social systems (*L'Humanité*, Paris, 12 August).

The major thrust of Soviet foreign activity in 1967 was in Europe, where the Soviet Union attempted to (*a*) work out differences in the East European socialist bloc, (*b*) rally support on a state level for a collective security system in Europe to replace the system of military blocs, and (*c*) rally support among the major East and West European communist parties for the convening of a world conference of communist parties.

An intensified campaign against West German "neo-Nazi," "militarist," and "revanchist" forces was conducted to counter the new West German *Ostpolitik*, by which the Kiesinger government declared its willingness to establish diplomatic relations with the socialist states despite their recognition of East Germany. (The former Hallstein Doctrine, in effect until the end of 1966, made diplomatic relations conditional on nonrecognition of the German Democratic Republic.) The campaign against the North Atlantic Treaty Organization was also intensified in view of the fact that in 1969 signatories to the treaty would be offered the possibility of withdrawal. While the Soviet Union was calling for an end to military blocs, it was actively renewing and expanding its system of friendship and cooperation treaties with the socialist states. The Soviet initiative for a system of collective security in Europe was promoted at the conference of communist and workers' parties of Europe, at Karlovy Vary, Czechoslovakia (24-26 April), which was the first conference to assemble all

*For details of CPSU relations with other Communist parties, see the respective country surveys.

the European communist parties. The Karlovy Vary conference was also a step toward the convening of a world communist party conference. At the fiftieth anniversary celebrations in Moscow in November, the Soviet Union succeeded in obtaining the support of eighteen communist parties for the convening of an "International Consultative Conference of Communist and Workers' Parties" in February 1968 in Budapest. (Communique, *Pravda*, 25 November.)* A *Pravda* editorial of 28 November gave assurance that there would be no excommunications at the forthcoming conference, whose sole aim would be to unify the communist party ranks to withstand the "imperialist offensive" and to prevent such victories of the "imperialists" as the rightist coups in Indonesia and Ghana.

**Relations with Ruling Communist Parties: East Europe.** The enunciation of the new West German *Ostpolitik,* the establishment of diplomatic relations between West Germany and Rumania, and the preparations for a conference of European communist parties stepped up contacts between the Soviet Union and its allies in Eastern Europe.

During the first four months of 1967, the Soviet leaders met with representatives of all the Eastern European communist states (except Albania). The visits reflected the Soviet attempt to strengthen support for the Ulbricht regime in East Germany, which felt that West Germany was trying to isolate it in East Europe. The visits were also aimed at preparing the proposed or contemplated international communist conferences. Leonid Brezhnev traveled to Warsaw (17-18 January) to discuss "questions of Soviet-Polish relations and urgent problems of international politics." When Rumania established diplomatic relations with West Germany on 31 January, the Soviet Union refrained from such direct and harsh criticism as was expressed by the East German regime, and concentrated on preventing other East European states from following Rumania's example. Leonid Brezhnev traveled to Czechoslovakia (4-6 February), and subsequently Czechoslovak foreign minister Václav David traveled to the Soviet Union (16-25 February) and conferred with Soviet Foreign Minister Gromyko. On 25 February-1 March, Hungarian leader János Kádár went to Moscow and had a "detailed exchange of opinions on the building of communism and socialism in both countries and also on problems of European security (*Pravda*, 2 March). Bulgarian Party leader Todor Zhivkov, Rumanian Party leader Nicolae Ceauçescu, and East German leader Walter Ulbricht all traveled to Moscow in March.

At the Karlovy Vary conference Leonid Brezhnev outlined the Soviet views on European affairs, giving particular emphasis to "neo-Nazi" and "revanchist" trends in West Germany, the tension created by the American presence in Europe, and the desirability of continuing the policy of a united front between communists and left-wing parties in the European states. (See *Conference of Communist and Workers' Parties of Europe, Karlovy Vary*.) He urged the end of military blocs in Europe and their replacement by a system of bilateral agreements.

Throughout 1967 the East European socialist states (except Yugoslavia and Rumania) were active in renewing or signing new bilateral friendship treaties. The Soviet friendship treaties with Bulgaria and Hungary were renewed on 12 March and 7 September respectively, although their twenty-year terms were to be fulfilled until 1968. The Rumanian-Soviet friendship treaty, also to be fulfilled in 1968, was not renewed in 1967, but its nineteenth anniversary on 4 February was celebrated by articles in the press of both countries and by special receptions in their embassies. (The treaty was not renewed in 1968 but was automatically extended for the next five years since neither party renounced it.)

The leaders of all the East European states met in Moscow on 9 June to discuss the Middle East crisis and to formulate a common stand (see below).

The second half of 1967 was marked by a series of East European-Soviet consultations to discuss the unity of the socialist states and preparations for an international communist party conference. Leonid Brezhnev on 5-6 July conferred with Czechoslovak leader Antonín Novotný in Moscow; and during September with the Hungarian party leadership in Budapest, with Bulgarian leader Todor Zhivkov in Moscow and with Polish party and state leaders Wladyslaw Gomulka and Józef

*The parties which signed the communique were those of Argentina, Australia, Brazil, Bulgaria, Czechoslovakia, East Germany, Finland, France, Great Britain, Hungary, India, Italy, Mongolia, Poland, Syria, USA, USSR, and West Germany.

Cyrankiewicz respectively. Further consultations with these leaders were held during the celebrations of the fiftieth anniversary of the October Revolution in Moscow. East German party leader Walter Ulbricht held talks with Brezhnev in Moscow on 11-12 December.

Although Soviet relations with Rumania were outwardly cordial, and the Soviet Union exerted great effort to win Rumanian participation in the socialist bloc activities and programs, consultations between the Soviet and Rumanian leaders in March in Moscow failed to persuade the Rumanians to attend the Karlovy Vary meeting. (Consultations between Brezhnev and Ceauçescu in Bucharest in December, followed by conciliatory promises to the Rumanians in the East European press, succeeded in bringing the Rumanians to the consultative conference in Budapest in February 1968, but when Rumanian conditions were not met at that conference the Rumanian delegation withdrew.) Further, the Soviet Union did not succeed in efforts to persuade the Rumanian leaders to refuse diplomatic relations with West Germany, and to join the leaders of other socialist states in their stand on the Middle East crisis and break off diplomatic relations with Israel (see *Rumania.*)

Soviet relations with Yugoslavia also remained cordial despite Yugoslav unwillingness to attend the Karlovy Vary meeting, opposition to an international communist party conference, and unwillingness to halt negotiations for the establishment of diplomatic relations with West Germany. (Diplomatic relations between Yugoslavia and West Germany were established in early 1968.) Yugoslav President Tito made an "unofficial visit" to Moscow on 28-31 January and held talks with Leonid Brezhnev. Soviet news media termed these talks as being held in an "open and friendly atmosphere." The common stand taken by the Soviet Union and Yugoslavia on the Arab-Israeli war served to strengthen the ties between the two states (see *Yugoslavia.*)

In Czechoslovakia, party leader Antonín Novotný a long time friend of the Soviet Union, had only a precarious hold on his position as First Secretary of his country's communist Party. When the political crisis in Prague broke out into the open at the end of 1967, Novotný sought support from Leonid Brezhnev. On 8 December Brezhnev flew to Prague, but refrained from interfering in what he apparently viewed as a palace coup against the unpopular Novotný. Brezhnev returned to Moscow the same day.

The Soviet Union continued to be subject to violent denunciation by Albania, but in most instances did not react to Albania's accusations. (See *Albania.*)

**The Sino-Soviet Conflict.** Soviet relations with Communist China worsened in 1967. On 3 January, Belgrade Radio reported shooting incidents on the Sino-Soviet border, with losses on both sides. The Chinese allegedly had tried to enter Soviet territory. Two days later a repudiation of the report came from Moscow, in which it was said that the Chinese had been guilty of numerous border violations, but that it would be an exaggeration to speak of "armed conflict." According to Western diplomatic sources, the Soviet Union informed its Warsaw Pact allies of plans to withdraw about 50,000 Soviet troops from East Europe to bolster its defenses along the Chinese border (*NYT*, 3 February). On 25 January, TASS reported a constant flow of refugees from China into the Soviet Union. Six months later, Konstantin Simonov, an influential Soviet writer, described how thousands of Chinese commanded by military officers dressed as private citizens had recently attempted to cross into the Soviet Union over the ice of the Amur River (*Pravda*, 19 July).

There were other forms of provocation from the Chinese side. On 25 January a group of Chinese students returning home from European universities via Moscow staged a violent demonstration in Red Square and then blamed the Soviet Union for using violence against them (*Pravda*, 26 and 29 January; *Peking Review*, 3 February). After this the Soviet government cancelled its agreement with China which had allowed citizens to travel freely between the two countries without visas. Peking replied with a similar cancellation.

The action of the Chinese students in Moscow was apparently a deliberate provocation, since on the next day Red Guards started a violent three-day demonstration in front of the Soviet Embassy in Peking. Although the Soviet Foreign Ministry strongly protested in a note to the Chinese Embassy in Moscow (*Pravda*, 29 January), by 31 January new demonstrations had taken place in front of the Soviet and Yugoslav embassies in Peking. In early February, the Soviet Embassy in Peking dismissed all its Chinese employees, who reportedly had gone on strike "in protest against the Soviet treatment of Chinese students in Moscow" (*Friheten,* Oslo, 3 February). Soviet officials and their families were subjected to considerable personal harassment in leaving China.

In August there were three serious incidents of Chinese obstruction of shipping between the Soviet Union and China. Red Guards in the port of Dairen detained and boarded a Soviet ship while local authorities held the vessel's captain on shore. Kosygin intervened, and on 13 August the ship was allowed to leave with the captain aboard. Two other Soviet vessels were prevented from entering the port of Dairen to load and were forced to return to the USSR without cargo.

Other Chinese acts of hostility included: the ignoring, for the first time, of the anniversary (14 February) of the Sino-Soviet Treaty of Friendship, Alliance, and Mutual Assistance; the unprecedented absence of Chinese officials at a reception in Hanoi given by the Soviet military attaché (this was the first absence of the Chinese from any reception in Hanoi given by a socialist country); an attack by the New China News Agency on Kosygin's trip to Britain as "part of a scheme to rescue the US from the war in Vietnam and destroy the Vietnamese revolution" (15 February); and the accusation of the Soviet Union of "capitulation and betrayal" in agreeing to the US proposal to initiate talks on an anti-ballistic missile moratorium.

The Sino-Soviet war of words was particularly intense during the early part of the year. General condemnation of Soviet actions was upheld in a *Jen-min Jih-pao* statement on 21 July which said: "To oppose imperialism it is imperative resolutely to oppose the counterrevolutionary line of the Soviet revisionist clique. There is no middle road in the struggle between the two lines."

Earlier, on 5 February, *Pravda* published a protest note from the Soviet Foreign Ministry to the Chinese government which declared: "What is happening now in Peking exceeds even the actions of the Chiang Kai-shek regime during the grimmest times of its reactionary domination." The note threatened that the Soviet government would take necessary measures to protect Soviet citizens in Peking.

On 8 February Peking Radio dared the Soviet Union to break off relations with China: "Do it quickly. The Chinese people have made all preparations and you will definitely come to a bad end. Graves are awaiting you, traitors." On 16 February an editorial in *Pravda* stated that Mao wanted to provoke the Soviet government to the point of breaking off relations with China, adding that China's policies could no longer be interpreted as an expression of ideological differences with the Soviet Union: now they were nothing but Mao's "great-power chauvinism." Declaring that the purpose of Mao's hate campaign was to divert the attention of the Chinese people from the "privations and difficulties" they were experiencing and from the "numerous mistakes and failures in the domestic and foreign policy of China," *Pravda* said: "Here we are confronted with the old, hackneyed method of all unprincipled politicians suffering backruptcy." The editorial appealed directly to the Chinese people (so far as is known, for the first time), calling on them to overthrow Mao's dictatorship and bring China back into the "Socialist Community."

Ernst Genry, the doyen of Soviet journalists and the leading Soviet journalist-expert on fascism and Nazism wrote in *Literaturnaia gazeta* (5 April): "The Peking dictator is not interested in communism . . . For him, communist ideas merely serve as a camouflage for something diametrically opposite: a plan to create under his hegemony a kind of new racist *Reich* in Asia and even beyond Asia . . . For this man possessed by the itch of hegemony, global war seems to be the shortest possible way toward his mad adventurist goals. We still remember precedents." Later the Soviet press described Mao as a "frightened megalomaniac" (*Izvestiia,* 3 July), and hope was expressed that the Chinese people would one day overthrow his regime and reestablish friendly relations with the Soviet Union (*Pravda,* 16 August).

There were mutual expulsions during 1967. Two Soviet diplomats were expelled from China on 11 March, accused of "persecuting Chinese employees at the Soviet Embassy in Peking." The Soviet Union reciprocated by expelling two Chinese diplomats on 18 March. On 6 May China expelled Valentin Pasenchuk, the *Pravda* correspondent in Peking, for a verbal "attack on Mao and the Cultural Revolution."

The Soviet Union continued formal support for Communist China's entry into the United Nations, but in its broadcast to China on 26 December, the Soviet Radio Peace and Progress stated: "This year many countries which had previously supported the admission of the Chinese People's Republic either voted against it or abstained, [which] again proved that the peoples of the world are against the domestic and foreign policies of the Mao group."

**Relations with Ruling Communist Parties in Asia. Mongolia.** State-to-state relations and those between the Mongolian People's Revolutionary Party and the CPSU remained friendly in 1967. Official and semiofficial visits were frequent. Both countries accused the Chinese of trying to wrest Mongolia from the Soviet Union. In February a Mongolian-Soviet "Commission for Scientific, Economic, and Technical Cooperation" was formed.

**North Korea.** A North Korean government delegation led by Kim Il, First Deputy Premier and member of the Politburo of the Korean Workers' Party, made a visit to the USSR from 14 February to 3 March during which several agreements were signed, including one on "cooperation in further strengthening the defense potential of North Korea" (*China Quarterly*, April-June 1967). Other agreements were concerned with increased economic, scientific, and technical collaboration and mutual goods deliveries. A further detailed agreement on cultural and scientific cooperation between the two countries was signed in Pyongyang on 26 June.

A Korean Socialist Working Youth League delegation took part in the international youth conference in Leningrad. This conference celebrated the fiftieth anniversary of the October Revolution.

**Soviet Relations with North Vietnam and with the National Liberation Front of South Vietnam.** In both public statements and in the press, Soviet leaders assured the Vietnamese communists of their support and continued aid. According to US estimates, Soviet assistance to North Vietnam in 1967 was valued at about $720 million.

On 13-19 March a "Week of Solidarity with the People of Vietnam" was held in the Soviet Union, in accordance with the decision reached by the Afro-Asian People's Solidarity Organization at its meeting in Nicosia. On 5 October an "International Meeting of Solidarity with Vietnam" was held in Moscow and was attended by representatives of trade union federations and organizations from more than 80 countries (*New Times*, Moscow, 13-30 November).

During the year agreements were signed by Moscow and Hanoi on cultural and scientific cooperation for 1967 (March), technical aid to Vietnam and scientific cooperation (September), and increased Soviet military and economic aid and new Soviet credits for trade between the USSR and the Democratic Republic of Vietnam in 1968 (September). Despite the agreements, it was clear that the Soviets and the Vietnamese were not in full accord. When the Soviet Union issued a note of strong protest against continued Chinese obstruction of Soviet military and economic aid to Vietnam, the Vietnam News Agency termed the allegations "sheer fabrication."

**Relations with Nonruling Communist Parties. Asia.** CPSU relations with the Japanese Communist Party (JCP) improved toward the end of 1967, largely on the initiative of the CPSU. There had been no relations between the two parties since 1964, when the JCP chose to follow Chinese Communist leadership. The opportunity for a rapprochement came as the serious break between the JCP and Chinese Communist Party in 1966 widened into a total split in 1967 (see *Japan*). The CPSU-JCP rapprochement is tentative; the JCP has been willing to accept CPSU concessions, but it has offered little in return.

The communist parties in most Southeast Asian nations are generally pro-Chinese, and CPSU influence is evident only in minority factions. In Indonesia there are indications that a pro-Soviet faction survives among the remnants of the once powerful communist movement there, but there is little evidence of direct CPSU contacts.

**Relations with Communist Parties. Middle East and Maghreb.** On 5 June, the day after the outbreak of the Arab-Israeli war, the Soviet government issued a declaration condemning Israel, declaring full solidarity with the Arab cause, and demanding the immediate cessation of hostilities on the part of Israel; it also called on the great powers to make all possible efforts to stop the war and on the UN to act to reestablish peace (*Pravda*, 6 June). Two days later the Soviet government delivered to the Israeli government a statement charging that Israel had disregarded the UN demand for an immediate ceasefire and warning Israel that the Soviet Union was prepared to "implement other necessary measures stemming from Israel's aggressive policy" (*ibid.*, 8 June). On 9 June a conference of European communist leaders met hastily in Moscow on Tito's initiative to discuss the Middle East crisis and what should be done. The resulting belligerently worded communique condemned Israel, openly accused the USA of collusion with Israel to bring on the war, and pledged to do everything necessary to rebuff the aggressor. Rumania refused to sign the declaration. On 10 June the Soviet Union broke off diplomatic relations with Israel (*ibid.*, 11 June).

A second summit meeting of Soviet and East European leaders to discuss the Middle East situation was held in Budapest on 11-12 July. Rumania was not represented. Although a step back from the harsh Moscow communique of 9 June, the declaration of the Budapest summit pledged continuing support for the Arabs, without any clear promise to rebuff aggression, and roundly condemned Israel and Western "imperialism."

Up to the Arab-Israeli war in June, the CPSU managed to maintain friendly relations with both of the rival communist parties in Israel—the predominately Arab RAKAH and basically Jewish MAKI groups. In spite of their differences in approaching Israeli problems, neither the RAKAH nor the MAKI had ever wavered in supporting the Soviet Union in the Sino-Soviet conflict, and the CPSU had reacted with virtual impartiality.

When the war began, the RAKAH firmly espoused the Arab cause and supported the Soviet Union when it broke diplomatic relations with Israel. The MAKI criticized the Soviet move as "unjustified" and gave support to the Israeli government's decisions. Moscow's reaction to the MAKI criticism was not forthcoming immediately, but in the July issue of *Kommunist* the Soviets praised the RAKAH as progressive and internationalist, and castigated the MAKI as aggressive, bourgeois, and nationalist.

For the remainder of the year the Soviet Union ignored the existence of the MAKI. The RAKAH sent delegates to the fiftieth anniversary celebrations of the October Revolution and its leaders were welcomed in East European countries. (See *Israel.*)

More so than in any other area of the world, relations with the Soviet Union affect the status and the effectiveness of the nonruling communist parties in the countries of the Middle East. The peculiar relationship between Middle Eastern pro-Moscow communist parties and the CPSU was accentuated by the Arab-Israeli war.

Soviet foreign policy in the decade of the 1960's has been to court and reassure the nations of the Middle East and the Maghreb. For the Soviet Union this has yielded a mixed result of diplomatic success and expensive involvement. For the nonruling communist parties of the region—which, were they so inclined, might interpret Soviet diplomacy as the pursuit of national interest—this has been a period of frustration and suppression. The UAR, for instance, in spite of vastly increased dependency on the Soviet Union in 1967, still has no recognizable organized communist party at all, its Communists having been absorbed as individual (and anonymous) members of Nasser's noncommunist Arab Socialist Union. In Algeria, a more typical case, the party is illegal and suppressed although the Soviet Union has continued to maintain actively friendly relations with Algeria's ruling party—the National Liberation Front (FLN)—and its government. In Iraq and Syria, where Soviet diplomacy made appreciable gains in securing the bonds of friendship in 1967, communist parties are illegal; in Iraq the party leadership remains in exile, while in Syria it maintains a precarious overt existence under the watchful eye of the ruling Ba'ath Party. In Jordan, where the Soviets engineered a major diplomatic breakthrough, the party remains illegal although the previously strongly anticommunist King Hussein visited Moscow after the Arab-Israeli war and Jordanian communist leaders were able to return after years in exile.

In the non-Arab states of Iran and Turkey, the Soviet Union and East European states followed one diplomatic achievement with another throughout the year, bringing about trade and cultural agreements and a stream of exchange visits between government officials and dignitaries. But none of this ameliorated the condition of the small illegal and intensely pro-Soviet communist parties of these two countries, whose leaderships were in exile abroad and whose adherents were persecuted at home.

**Relations with Cuba.** While seeming to remain friendly on the surface, Soviet-Cuban relations deteriorated in 1967. At a reception given by the Cuban Ambassador in Moscow on 2 January, Shelepin, representing the Soviet Union, praised Cuba, hailing every step of its development as a "new blow to the imperialist system" and welcoming its aid to Vietnam and its emergency in the international arena (*Pravda,* 3 January). Although praise for Cuba was still frequent in the Soviet press (particularly the youth press), it became increasingly evident that the Soviet Union did not welcome the emergency of Castroism as a rival revolutionary doctrine. (For details on Soviet-Cuban relations, see *Cuba*).

**Relations with Other Latin American Communist Parties.** Generally, the main communist parties of Latin America (in almost every Latin American country there are also splinter communist groups, many of them pro-Chinese) had friendly relations with the CPSU and supported Soviet policy, divorcing themselves from the extreme Cuban line. This was particularly true following the Havana conference of the Latin American Solidarity Organization, which confronted both the Soviet Union and the pro-Soviet communist parties in Latin America with a Castroist challenge to revolutionary leadership. (For details see *First Conference of the Latin American Solidarity Organization,* and individual-country surveys for Latin America.)

Articles appeared at the end of 1967 (*Pravda,* 15 December) and in early 1968 (*Rynki Zagranicne,* Warsaw, 23 January) commenting on the increased trade between the Soviet Union and the Latin American countries in 1966 (which had shown a total of 178 million roubles, or 198 million dollars) and foreseeing further increases, yet during 1967 the Soviet Union was expressing support for local Latin American communist parties. The problems that such a policy engendered were exemplified in Colombia, where the arrival of a Soviet trade delegation in March coincided with the arrest by the Colombian government of several communist leaders, including the Secretary-General of the pro-Soviet Communist Party of Colombia, Gilberto Vieira.

**Relations with Communist Parties. West Europe.** The tendency in West Europe of communist parties to join in "united fronts" with other forces of the left, the most striking example of which was the policy of the French Communist Party during the 1967 elections (see *France*), necessitated for these parties a policy that would indicate "independence" from the Soviet Union and emphasize their "national" character. This emphasis on nationalism and autonomy was especially evident in the Communist Party of the Netherlands (see *Netherlands*), which refused to attend both the Karlovy Vary conference of European communist parties, in April, and the celebrations of the fiftieth anniversary of the October Revolution in the USSR, in November. Whereas most of the major communist parties of Western Europe (as opposed to the Maoist, Castroist, Trotskyist and other splinter groups) supported Soviet foreign policy on most issues, they also allowed criticism to be expressed (primarily in the form of letters to the party organs) on general international issues such as the Middle East crisis and, more notably, on those affecting international communist affairs. The stand of "unity in diversity" advocated by the Italian Communist Party (see *Italy*) appeared in general to be gaining a greater measure of acceptance among West European communist parties. Moreover, in an apparent attempt to achieve domestic "respectability" the parties on certain occasions disassociated themselves from domestic policy in the USSR, as in the case of the trials of dissident intellectuals (see above and, e.g., *Italy*).

On a different level, Soviet state-to-state relations with West European governments, which included visits in January by President Podgorny to Italy and the Vatican (the first such official venture by a Soviet head of state) and in February, by Kosygin to Great Britain, were not of an acrimonious nature (except in the case of West Germany). In some instances, such as Podgorny's visit to the Vatican, Soviet policy probably was instrumental in promoting local communist claims to "respectability."

**Soviet Relations with Sub-Saharan Africa.** In Sub-Saharan Africa, an area where organized communist parties are few and of limited membership, Soviet policy was characterized by the expansion of cultural and economic relations and a strong emphasis on extension of Soviet military aid to "progressive" movements and governments. Excluding Rhodesia and South Africa, the Soviet Union directed its efforts for cooperation at almost all the African states, regardless of ideology.

In its foreign aid program the Soviet Union came into direct competition with the former colonial powers. Also, in rejecting a strict ideological and revolutionary position, it was susceptible to Communist Chinese charges of betrayal, especially in countries such as Mali and Guinea where both the Soviet Union and China have strong influence.

Soviet extension of military and technical aid appeared in countries which had been unable to satisfy their needs in the West. It was reported in the Western press that the Soviet Union made serious offers of military assistance to the Congolese government of Joseph Mobutu, even though more than two years earlier Mobutu had banished Soviet diplomats from the Congo for aiding his enemies. When the USA in October refused arms aid to the Nigerian federal government, Czechoslovakia and the Soviet Union provided Nigeria with ordnance, airplanes, and technicians. Soviet influence in Nigeria was also helped by the publication in October of a new Nigerian magazine, *New World,* dedicated to the promotion of economic, educational and cultural cooperation between Nigeria and the Soviet Union. In September, there were negotiations for Soviet military aid to Sudan and the establishment by the Soviet Union of Sudan's first air college. The two countries also agreed to increase mutual trade during 1968-70, to cooperate culturally and scientifically, and to recognize diplomas and degrees awarded by each.

The Soviet Union gave active moral and material support to "progressive" regimes such as those of Mali and Guinea and to "national liberation movements" such as those in the Portuguese colonies and Rhodesia. The announcement of the program for the development of socialism in Tanzania, known as the Arusha Declaration, was hailed by Moscow Radio (8 February) as a "document of historic significance," and the CPSU sent a message to the ruling Tanzanian African National Union wishing it success in implementing the program.

Soviet relations with Ghana, strained since the overthrow of President Kwame Nkrumah in 1966, were exacerbated by the new regime's disclosure on 22 February of details of Nkrumah's subversive activities against the regime and of Soviet involvement in them. Despite insistence by the Soviet news agency TASS that the information was false, the Ghana government subsequently expelled three communist journalists (two Soviet and one Czechoslovak) for conspiring with Nkrumah.

**Publications.** The main organs of the CPSU are: *Pravda,* a daily newspaper; *Kommunist,* a theoretical review, published 18 times a year, and *Partiinaia zhizn,* a journal on internal party affairs, published twice a month. The organs of the Komsomol are: *Komsomolskaia pravda,* a newspaper published six times a week, and *Molodoi kommunist,* a monthly theoretical journal. *Kommunist vooruzhonnykh sil,* is a party theoretical journal for the armed forces, published twice a month.

The Communist Party of Egypt (CPE) was founded in 1922 as the Egyptian Socialist Party, changing its name to "communist" in 1923 in order to comply with the conditions imposed at the Fourth Comintern Congress (November-December 1922) when it petitioned for admission to that body. The party's original membership was drawn largely from foreign middle-class intellectuals residing in Egypt, and this element remained predominant until the late 1940's. At the Fifth Comintern Congress (June-July 1924) the CPE received the recognition of the Comintern in spite of the fact that the party's entire Central Committee was at this time in prison. For all intents and purposes the CPE succumbed in 1925 as a result of government persecution, not to revive until World War II and then only as a movement whose professed communist factions were never welded into a disciplined unified party. In 1955 six of the eight recognizable "branches or tendencies" formed a United Egyptian Communist Party, but this agglomeration was unstable and broke apart despite the efforts of both the Italian Communist Party and Moscow to secure a permanent unification. As late as 1963 the situation in the movement could be described with candor as "utterly confused": "Nobody knows into how many factions the Communist movement in Egypt is split at present. . . . Egypt is now the only country of comparable size without an officially recognized Communist party." (Walter Z. Laqueur in *The Soviet Bloc, China and Africa*, Sven Hamsell and C. G. Widstrand, eds., Uppsala, Sweden, 1964, pp. 64, 70.)

The Communists were persecuted in the early phases of the Egyptain "revolution," when the Naguib regime was described by communist sources as a "brutal, Fascist military dictatorship" (*Warsaw Radio*, 12 September 1952) which, established "with the knowledge and encouragement of the US Ambassador in Cairo" (*Zycie Warszawy*, 20 August 1952), perpetrated "cruel violence against the workers' movements" (*Soviet Encyclopedia*, Vol. XV, 1952), and the Nasser government was said to have "all the characteristics of Fascist régimes with the additional feature of being in the service of Western imperialism" (*L'Unità*, 20 November 1954).

Early in 1964 came a drastic change in the situation, when about 600 Egyptian Communists were released from prison two months before Khrushchev's visit to the UAR in May. In December of that year representatives of the Arab communist parties met, probably in Prague, to discuss a course of "cooperation between progressive parties, organizations and movements in the Arab World." The communique issued after this meeting referred to the "duty of all revolutionaries, Communists or non-Communists, to display fraternal creative initiative in order to create and strengthen the alliance of all revolutionary forces" (*Pravda*, 11 December). Apparently, most Egyptian Communists willingly followed or were forced to follow this Soviet-advocated policy, because in April 1965 it was announced that the "Communist Party of Egypt" had dissolved itself and its members were joining Nasser's ruling Arab Socialist Union (ASU) as individuals (*Al Ahram*, 25 April). There has been no identifiable communist party in Egypt since that time although cooperation between Cairo and Moscow grew to the extent that Kosygin could say in 1966 that relations of coexistence between the two countries were of a "new type combined with the spirit of mutual trust and based on widespread cooperation in all fields" (*Pravda*, 12 May). Since the Arab-Israeli war these ties have strengthened further. In 1967 there was no positively identified activity undertaken independently by native communist groups or factions in the UAR.

An article by Arminio Saviola, appearing on 21 February, in *L'Unità*, the daily newspaper of the Italian Communist Party, hinted that a "secret party" might exist in the UAR:

> . . . All recognize Nasser as the head of the revolution. But of which revolution? The Marxists see in him the leader of a socialist revolution, more and more radical and in

conformity with historical necessity and with the principles of scientific socialism . . . Nasser is no longer just a patriot; he is an advanced socialist who is approaching ever nearer in his actions, and maybe also in his deepest convictions, to a Marxist position, whether he says so or not. Ever since 1961 the socialist orientation of Egypt has been accentuated, and after 1964 the struggle between Nasser and the Communists ended. . . . Thus, the Communists are today among the most convinced and enthusiastic supporters of Nasser. There no longer exist any communist parties in Egypt, but the Communists (or ex-Communists, or "scientific socialists", or Marxists, however you wish to name them) work and struggle for the revolution "as individuals," giving to Nasser a precious contribution of ideas, or analyses, of action. . . . Officially the Union [ASU] is the sole Egyptian party, but is it really? Many contest the fact that it is a party at all. "It is a mass movement," they say, "not a party," and Egypt, they add, "needs a party of cadres, a vanguard party, not monolithic, but strongly united on the basis of a single ideology—scientific socialism." This party, as we have said, exists, at least in its embryonic state. It has already a membership of 2,000 and it wants to raise that membership to 20 or 30 thousand. It is said, but this is only conjecture, that it is divided for organizational reasons in two sectors, one civilian and the other military. Nasser himself, who discussed it in closed session on 16 May 1965 with the deputies of the Socialist Union, dedicates a good part of his time and energies to it. It is he, as always, who has the last word in the choice of militants, on whom are placed many conditions among which is the injunction not to reveal to anyone one's membership in the party. It is, therefore, a secret party, a clandestine party which supports the regime and struggles for socialism while working in the shadows.

If Saviola's article can be given any credence and the "secret party" does exist, it is plain that Nasser himself controls it. If this embryonic party is a vanguard party as described by the communist paper *L'Unità*, then it should include Communists in its ranks, but nothing further has come to light to substantiate the Italian Communists' claim to inside information, and one must conclude until such evidence is produced that there is no effective communist political organization in Egypt, nor any important political organization in which native Communists have a major influence.

# UNITED STATES OF AMERICA

The communist movement in the USA includes a number of rival groups, of greater or lesser importance, embracing policies ranging from violent revolution to Moscow-oriented "peaceful coexistence."

**CPUSA.** The oldest and largest group is the Communist Party, USA (CPUSA), founded in 1919. The party is legal. In November 1965 the party had been found guilty in a Federal District Court of failure to register and file the registration statement as required by the Internal Security Act of 1950 (McCarran Act). This decision was appealed to the United States Court of Appeals for the District of Columbia, which reversed the conviction on 3 March 1967. The court concluded that the Internal Security Act, as applied in this instance, was "hopelessly at odds" with the protection against self-incrimination afforded by the Fifth Amendment: requiring the party to list its members would expose them to prosecution under the Smith Act of 1940 which makes it a crime to belong to an organization advocating violent overthrow of the US government, and under the Communist Control Act of 1954 the party is listed as such. On 3 April the Department of Justice announced that it would not appeal this decision. The Internal Security Act of 1950 was amended by the 90th Congress. Under the amended act the Subversive Activities Control Board can hold hearings to determine whether individuals are members of the party. If the Board so finds, the names of the individuals will be placed on a public register.

In December 1967 the CPUSA claimed to have a membership of between 12,000 and 13,000. The party claims an additional 100,000 "state of mind" members. The population of the USA is 200,000,000 (estimated, 1968).

The CPUSA is not represented politically at either national or local levels. The party's most recent bids for elective office were made in 1966 when it sponsored the candidacies of Herbert Aptheker, the leading party theoretician, who sought election to the US House of Representatives from the 12th Congressional District, Brooklyn, New York, in November, and Dorothy Healey, the Chairman of the party's southern California district, who campaigned for the office of tax assessor of Los Angeles County, in June. Both candidates were unsuccessful. Aptheker polled 2,876 votes (2.4 per cent of the total), and Healey 86,000 (6 per cent). CPUSA reaction to the results was generally favorable (See *YICA*, 1966, p. 171). According to CPUSA National Committee member Gil Green, in an analysis of the Aptheker campaign: "The time had come to win the right of Communists to participate openly and freely in the life of the nation. . . . The ideology of anti-Communism was being challenged on a wider scale than in any period since the cold war began. . . . We learned, too, that people will listen, that the influence of anti-Communism is still great, but not as all-pervasive as yesterday" (*Political Affairs*, January 1967).

**Organization and Leadership.** The CPUSA is organized along the lines of "democratic centralism." Theoretically, authority is to flow from the National Convention (which should be held every two years according to the party's constitution), to the National Committee, to the National Executive Board, to the Secretariat, and then to the districts where the organizations can be set up according to states, counties, sections, and clubs. In some districts, where membership is sparse, the organizational channel runs directly from the district to the club. Clubs can be and are set up on a variety of bases, such as electoral subdivisions, neighborhoods, areas, shops, or industries.

At the party's Eighteenth National Convention (22-26 June 1966) a National Committee of 80 members was elected (the total has since been enlarged to 86) instead of the usual 30 to 60 members. There was no election of a National Executive Board or Secretariat, the convention having adopted changes in the party's constitution which included the provision that state and national officers should be elected by the State and National Committees respectively to which they would be responsible (see *Political Affairs*, April 1967). Following the convention, party officials were referred to as such in the CPUSA press, but no official statement by the party on their election was published, except with regard to Gus Hall, the General Secretary, and Henry Winston, the National Chairman. In addition to Hall and Winston, prominent members of the National Committee include: Herbert Aptheker, Thomas Dennis, Gil Green, Dorothy Healey, James Edward Jackson, Arnold Johnson, Claude Lightfoot, Albert Jason Lima, Hyman Lumer, George Meyers, Roscoe Proctor, Daniel Mortimer Rubin, Carl Winter, and Helen Winter. Leading youth members of the National Committee include: Carl Bloice, Robert Duggan, Michael Eisenscher, Peggy Goldman Frankie, Matthew Hallinan, Donald Lee Hamerquist, Bettina Aptheker Kurzweil, Scarlett Patrick, Jarvis Tyner, Tim Wheeler, and Michael Zagarell.

The CPUSA derives its principal support from the states on the east and west coasts, primarily from the states of New York and California. Within labor organizations the party is insignificant. The party's 1966 draft program – *New Program of the Communist Party, USA (A Draft)* (New York, 1966) – remarked: "The infection of labor's organs with a cold-war virus has served to drain labor of its militancy." In 1967 the party stressed its need to attain some measure of influence in the trade-union movement. An article by James West in *Political Affairs* (October 1967) called for a return to the policy of "concentration" as a means whereby a small party could extend its influence outside its own ranks.

Outside its party structure the CPUSA has no official auxiliary bodies (such as organizations for young persons, women, and so forth). Nonetheless, the party has set up a number of organizations which, though professing independence of the CPUSA, follow CPUSA policy and directives and are composed primarily of party members. One of the principal organizations falling into this pattern is the W.E.B. DuBois Clubs of America, which acts as the unofficial youth movement of the CPUSA and claims a membership of 3,000 (*National Guardian*, 25 November 1967). The W.E.B. DuBois Clubs held a Third National Convention in New York on 8-10 September 1967, at which a 20-member National Executive Committee was elected, including: Jarvis Tyner, National Chairman; Gene Tournour, Executive Secretary; Carolyn Black, Field Director; Carmen Ristorucci, Publication Secretary; and Bob Heisler, Education Director.

**Domestic Policies and Activity.** The CPUSA's domestic policy was elaborated in a 127-page book, the *New Program of the Communist Party, USA (A Draft),* published in mid-February 1966. During 1967 no changes in the program were published.* The introductory chapter to the program sets a general context around which the subsequent individual policies are elaborated, stating (p. 7): "The 1960's have witnessed a resurgence of popular democratic movements in the United States, and with this a new upsurge of the Left. Active involvement of growing numbers of Americans in movements for civil rights, peace and economic advancement has led, among other things, to an increasing revulsion against anti-Communism and a growing interest in the views of the Communist Party of the United States as a current in American life and a participant in these struggles." The program specifies: "We learn from and apply the lessons of world experience, but the course itself is chartered across American terrain, taking its bearings from American realities, traditions and institutions. It may be called the American way to socialism."

While reiterating traditional accusations against the capitalist system and, in particular, monopolies – "everywhere monopoly places its quest for maximum profit above human needs," "everywhere the selfish interest of monopoly conflicts with the public good" (p. 16) – the *New Program* sketches out a three-phase "political path of social progress" (pp. 40-41). The present phase is described as one in which "the focus of the popular mass, democratic movements is on exertion of political pressures, on modification of existing centers of political power so as to make them more amenable to popular pressure." This is followed by a second phase, which represents the "advance from political pressure to the contest for political power" and "will necessitate a new political alignment, in which a popular alliance of all sectors of society that are oppressed by monopoly directly confronts monopoly and its agents in the struggle for political supremacy." The final stage, "growing out of intense, direct conflict between monopoly and the coalition of its antagonists," is seen as the "advance from an attempt to realize the goals and hopes of the people within the constricting bonds of capitalist society to destruction of those bonds, to socialist reconstruction of society," which "will necessitate yet

*In March 1968 the CPUSA published a second draft of the program. In a letter to party members, Hall and Winston pointed out: "The existence of the new draft does not, of course, nullify the status of the first draft" (*The Worker*, 26 March 1968).

another shift in the political alignment, pitting the forces of socialism against the forces of capitalism."

The *New Program* goes on to discuss two major areas of potential support in the elaboration of the party's policies. On the civil rights movement it states (pp. 58, 66): "Of all forces arrayed against corporate monopoly, of all the major political components of a new, progressive political alignment, the freedom movement displays the greatest independence. . . . Challenging the status quo, the Negro freedom movement is reinforced by those who challenge the very basis of the status quo, the Communists first of all." It remarks also that "Mexican-Americans and Puerto Ricans comprise a significant sector of the anti-monopoly forces, whose fight is closely tied to that of the Negro people" (p. 67). The other sector of support emphasized is the "young generation," which "represents a vast potential in the anti-monopoly array" and "must be employed not blindly but with cool calculation of the social forces in contention" (pp. 74,76).

Encompassing the two aforementioned forces, according to the *New Program* (p. 112), is "a most significant political phenomenon of the recent American past": the "emergence of the New Left." The "principal sources of this New Left have been the civil rights movement, the stirring revival of social concern and commitment among the younger generation, and the struggle for peace." The party's views with regard to the "New Left" (pp. 113-116) reflect some concern with tendencies toward "sectarianism" and "adventurism," and with the proposition that the "New Left," while in a general sense sharing the "conviction that existing society must be changed radically," possesses "no common view as to the nature or the manner of the change." The party proclaims its belief, however, that "in the course of common action, in coordinated efforts, in the exchange of views and experiences, in the discussion of differences, the basis can be found for a unity that will become ever firmer." Granting that the end result "may or may not take the form of one united party of socialism," the *New Program* declared: "Even the existence of different political organizations of the left is no unsurmountable obstacle to long range unity, for we do not envision a one-party system as a condition for American socialism."

The concept of a "new people's party" is elaborated extensively in the *New Program*. Declaring (pp. 76-79) that the "present two-party system places a premium upon corruption, cynicism, frustration of the popular will," the CPUSA advocates the creation of a party whose components "will be drawn from the forces arrayed against monopoly: the working class, the Negro people, independent farmers, intellectuals, professionals, small businessmen and other middle strata, youth and other groups." Since "existing political alignments constitute the womb from which any new alignment must emerge" and "any other conception can only produce a sect-like stillbirth," and since an "overwhelming majority of all social groupings that are indispensable components of a new mass party now express themselves electorally through the Democratic Party as a rule," the party finds that the real problem is "to devise a strategy for the confluence of the several streams that historically flow in a common direction into a great river of a new, popular, labor-based, anti-monopoly party." The ultimate aim of the party in this united front strategy is a "political majority for the socialist alternative" (p. 91), and it considers that "the necessary means for securing such political power is a Marxist-Leninist working-class political party" (p. 125).

That the CPUSA's views on the creation of the "new party" allowed for a certain lapse of time was pointed out by Gus Hall: "The forces that would provide the foundation for such a development [are] not ready to take that step. We can't skip stages" (*The Worker*, 11 December 1966).

During 1967 the party's policy and activity corresponded to the general line advocated by the *New Program*. In this context the aforementioned court ruling of 3 March, followed by the Department of Justice's decision 3 April was welcomed by the party. An editorial in *The Worker* (9 April) stated:

> The Communist Party, now freed of the legal hamstringing by the McCarran Act, may be
> counted on to throw even greater resources and energy into helping to break the barriers
> that hamper united struggle by the unions and other people's organizations. Final burial
> of the fraudulent "anti-communism" and consequent cold-war activities can open the
> way to new advances by the people of the United States.

In its bid for a "united-front" strategy the CPUSA underscored the role of sentiment in the country opposing US policy in Vietnam. In an article in *The Worker* (16 April), Gus Hall observed:

The molding of unity in struggle is a process. When the factors on which diverse groupings agree emerge as the dominant influences, it results in a united force in struggle. The mass resistance to the US policy of aggression in Vietnam is rooted in such a dominant factor. What unites the diverse groups is the opposition to the war policy. There are serious differences as to the causes and the cures for the war policy but there is also a growing united opposition to the war. So there is unity and diversity in one and the same process. . . .

Today's actions must serve to create that greater unity through which the American people can change the course of our country from the course of war to peace.

The same issue of *The Worker* carried a statement by the CPUSA which claimed:

The struggle against the war is becoming the most important radicalizing factor in American life. It continuously raises questions in the minds of the people about the very character of our society. . . .

The time has therefore come to discuss political perspectives on the widest scale possible. . . .

The Communist Party strongly favors a course of independent political action leading toward an independent presidential ticket committed to peace and freedom, in 1968. A strategy of grass roots independent political action can place sharply before the country an alternative policy to the war line. It can help expose the hypocrisy and arrogance of the Johnson Administration and thus widen the already existing credibility gap and crisis of confidence.

The CPUSA statement urged "an intensification of the struggle on all levels, including the fight against the war within the old parties themselves," but pointed out that the party placed "special stress on the importance of building a network of independent grass roots political formations *outside the framework* of the two old parties" (emphasis in original).

The CPUSA's advocacy of a third ticket for the 1968 presidential elections was dramatized at the national convention of the National Conference for New Politics (NCNP), held in Chicago (31 August − 4 September). The conference was attended by representatives of some 370 organizations, covering a broad political spectrum from advocates of urban guerrilla warfare to disaffected Democrats and was "planned to be a 'people's discussion' on perspectives for Peace and Freedom" (*New Politics News,* issue distributed at convention, no date). Officially, CPUSA representatives attended only as observers; a number of organizations with delegate status were formed in advance by the party, however, and these represented its views at the convention. Furthermore, representatives of the DuBois Clubs also attended as delegates.

Preceding the convention, an article by Gus Hall in the party's monthly theoretical organ *Political Affairs* (August) referred to the NCNP: "[It is] a young movement with tremendous potential. It opens up the avenue for a political alliance of the different mass streams of struggle, a path that can lead away from separate, fragmented and isolated political movements. It is a movement engaged both in expressing electoral protest and seeking electoral victories. It has a potential of becoming a winning coalition of electoral forces." An editorial in *The Worker* (3 September), distributed at the NCNP convention, pointed to various strategies for getting "rid of Johnson and all he stands for," and added:

It should be remembered that in the crucial election year of 1968 the issues will be placed on the line for millions of Americans who have not yet been involved.

The ballot boxes should not be surrendered to the Johnson hawks, the Republican hawks, or any vultures. The tens of millions who now are challenging the Administration's course in a variety of ways need to be shown how they can join forces in the national electoral fight against the war and reaction.

At the convention, which in its initial preparatory stage had been oriented toward national electoral political organization, there was strong opposition from some representatives of the so-called New Left − in particular, delegates of the Students for a Democratic Society − who advocated NCNP support for local, community organizing. Another issue was raised by a small group of Negro militants, who formed a "Black Caucus" and refused to participate in the convention unless certain of their demands, including 50 per cent of the convention's vote, were accepted by the convention. The issue of the Black Caucus demands was preceded by a vote on NCNP perspectives, with the supporters of local, community organizing winning over the CPUSA-supported third-ticket advocates by two votes (13,519 to 13,517). Following this vote, CPUSA and DuBois Club representatives were prominent in urging the convention's acceptance of the Black Caucus demands. When the demands were accepted and the Black Caucus was given 28,498 votes (equal to the sum total of the convention's votes, excluding 5,341 votes held by Negro delegates), the CPUSA and DuBois Clubs members proposed a motion of reconsideration of the perspectives resolution. The Black Caucus, however, voted against the third ticket proposal advocated by the CPUSA, although an amendment to the adopted perspectives resolution was accepted advocating NCNP support for independent presidential tickets "in those states where local groups and organizations want to run such a campaign and feel that there is a base therefor."

The NCNP convention demonstrated that the CPUSA was able to influence significantly neither the majority of the young New Left radicals nor the Negro militants. In view of the party's advocacy of a broad-based united front of opposition to President Johnson, the convention was a disappointment. An article in *The Worker* (17 September) stated:

> As often happens many of those in the first flush of radicalization did not address themselves to the crucial problem of how to unite with the far greater number who though discontented were not yet disillusioned with either the capitalist or the two party system but who were ready to vote for an alternative to President Johnson or a Republican supporter of his war policy in '68. . . .
>
> It was this failure to look outward beyond those radicalized which bred a pessimistic outlook on the possibilities for a meaningful third ticket in '68.

CPUSA disappointment with the NCNP was further reflected in an article by National Committee member Arnold Johnson in *Political Affairs* (December 1967):

> The fact that the Convention did not take the step of supporting a third ticket nationally must be regarded as a setback for all those who sought this goal. True, our Party was effective in helping to preserve a form of unity in the Convention, which gained us prestige among new forces. True, the moves of those who sought to disrupt the Convention were defeated. But that, though important, was not enough.
>
> Since it is clear that the need for a third ticket cannot be fully met through New Politics, it becomes urgent for those who see it as necessary to seek additional forms. . . .
>
> We have given great emphasis to New Politics. That was necessary and correct. To call for seeing it in perspective is not to downgrade its importance. It deserves much more attention in every area, but at the same time it should not monopolize our attention. Other forms of independence, especially at the grass roots level, must also receive support.

During the year the CPUSA actively participated in and supported a number of demonstrations opposing US policy in Vietnam. Although none of the major demonstrations was officially proclaimed as CPUSA-sponsored, party members had prominent roles in organizing them, and the party organs gave them publicity and support. In this area of activity the CPUSA participated jointly with other Marxist-Leninist parties and movements. The party appeared, however, to be more concerned with united action with noncommunist groups than with communists. Following the 15 April "Spring Mobilization" demonstrations in New York City and San Francisco, Arnold Johnson commented:

> While the Mobilization was all-inclusive, and nobody was excluded from joining the march [in New York City], this did not mean that there were no divisive pulls and strains that had to be overcome, nor that mistakes were not committed. Representatives of small ultra-leftist groupings were a constant irritant, because of their efforts to restrict the march only to participants that would subscribe to the most advanced slogans. . . . In the final days prior to April 15, they made clear they would violate the discipline of the

leading body and march as the "revolutionary contingent" under the banner of the National Liberation Front.

The varied groups of Trotskyites violated all democratic procedures and pursued a practice of packing committees and conferences to get extended speaking time in their attempt to impose, by their numbers, opinions and conclusions that did not represent the body as a whole. They closed the door against more representative leadership, by taking organizational posts, utilizing them for their narrow ends. Such irresponsible practices turned away spokesmen of mass organizations who, singly, represented more than the total membership of all the Trotskyite groups. The net result had a divisive effect on the movement as a whole (*Political Affairs,* June 1967).

Arnold Johnson's criticism of groups "who refused to sponsor or participate in the action for fear they would be compromised by the advanced stand and militant slogans of some Left groups" was of a limited nature and pointed out that organizations such as SANE (National Committee for a Sane Nuclear Policy), while not throwing the "entire organization behind the march. . . did not discourage local committees from participating in whatever way they saw fit" (*ibid.*).

The CPUSA participated again in the mass demonstrations on 21 October in Washington, D.C., which included a march on the Pentagon. Although the party reported extensively on the demonstrations (*The Worker,* 22, 24, 29, and 31 October) there was little commentary on CPUSA participation, in contrast with the reports on the "Spring Mobilization" (*ibid.*, 16, 18, and 23 April).

While the CPUSA appeared to have made some headway in 1967 in its striving to attain "respectability" and be accepted by the general public, increased militancy among young radicals and ethnic minorities, particularly Negroes, confronted the party with increased competition on the extreme Left from other Marxist-Leninist parties and movements (see below), anarchist movements, and "black nationalist" groups.

On the issue of civil rights and violence the CPUSA held a special national conference in mid-October, sponsored by the party's Negro Affairs Commission. Reports on the conference were carried by *The Worker* on 22 October and again on 12 November. Whereas the earlier report appeared to stress a CPUSA view that "there can be no question of the right of black people in the U.S. to use violence to achieve change" (prompting a *New York Times* article on 23 October entitled "U.S. Communist Party Supports Negro Violence"), the subsequent CPUSA November report on the same conference, which included the complete text of a statement made by the party's National Chairman, Henry Winston, emphasized that violence to achieve political objectives should be used "only when reaction has closed off the channels whereby a majority of the people can realize their objectives by peaceful means." Winston's statement added: "As we see it today, the overwhelming majority of the American people, including black people, are not convinced that the system must be changed; much less that it is necessary to do so by armed force. . . . We therefore reject today the organizing of armed uprisings in the black communities." In turn *The New York Times* reported on 12 November that "U.S. Reds Reject Black 'Uprisings.'"

In an attempt to clarify the party's stand on civil rights, Claude Lightfoot, the head of the CPUSA's Negro Affairs Commission, published a pamphlet entitled *Black Power and Liberation: A Communist View* (New York: New Outlook Publishers, 1967). On the issue of violence Lightfoot claimed that the tactical questions involved in the "freedom struggle" were "much more difficult and complex" than a "choice between violent and non-violent struggle." He differentiated between offensive and defensive violence and stated that with regard to the latter the "right of black people to defend themselves even by force of arms should be supported by all in the country who stand against injustice." He pointed out, however, that while "it is one thing to defend oneself from attack by all necessary means, it is another to choose this as the main method of battle," and cautioned against basing tactics on a mechanical, unrealistic application of guerrilla warfare as applied in Cuba and Vietnam to the quite different conditions in the USA: "Our people have fought too hard and too long to reach this point to throw everything away in a suicidal action."

On the issue of "black nationalism" Lightfoot concluded: "At present the main content of black nationalism is of a progressive character. It does not exclude Negro-white unity, but it demands that such unity be meaningful and between equal partners." The chief task of the CPUSA was seen as striving to introduce "a class content into the present wave of black nationalism," struggling against "all separatist tendencies as self-defeating" while respecting the "fears black people have of being assimilated by whites," and fighting for "full power in the ghettos while struggling against tendencies to go overboard in some situations."

The CPUSA's concern with attracting youth to its ranks was expressed in 1967 as in the previous year by a number of appearances of leading party members at college campuses. According to testimony given by the Director of the Federal Bureau of Investigation, J. Edgar Hoover, before the House Subcommittee on Appropriations on 23 February 1968, 54 speaking engagements were fulfilled by CPUSA representatives at colleges in the US during the academic year 1966/67.

The party claims that "more young people across the country are now in the Communist Party than in all other political parties and groups on the Left combined," and that "the Communist Party has a membership under the age of 30 — mainly 18, 19 and early 20s — of about 2,000 members." In its definition of the Left, the CPUSA does not, however, include the Students for a Democratic Society (SDS) or the Student Nonviolent Coordinating Committee (SNCC) (*National Guardian*, 25 November 1967). The CPUSA's attitude toward the New Left and its predominantly young members, including those of the SDS, was expressed in the aforementioned *New Program* and reiterated in the July issue of *Political Affairs,* which carried a speech given by Dorothy Healey in Los Angeles on 2 December 1966:

> One fundamental issue is whether there is a revolutionary Left, committed to a socialist objective and therefore to the struggle for political power as the instrument for such a transformation; or, a rebel Left that harasses, annoys, needles the Establishment, but despite the most radical posture is essentially reformist, because it shuns political power in the belief that all power corrupts.

Healey pointed out, however, that the CPUSA placed "solidarity in action ahead of doctrinal correctness or moral righteousness" and appealed for what she termed "compassionate political solidarity."

**International Views and Policies.** Complementing its apparent resurgence domestically, the CPUSA in 1967 appeared to be reemerging internationally,* continuing a trend which was highlighted in 1966 by a "world tour" undertaken by Gus Hall (see *YICA,* 1966, p. 175).

On matters pertaining to international communist affairs, the party reiterated its alignment with the Soviet Union. Speaking at the celebrations of the fiftieth anniversary of the October Revolution, in Moscow, on 4 November, Gus Hall referred to the "world revolutionary process" and said that "In this process the Soviet Union remains the most revolutionizing element" (*The Worker,* 12 November). The party's November issue of *Political Affairs* was devoted to commemorating the Fiftieth Anniversary and included a number of articles hailing the achievements and policies of the Soviet Union and the CPSU.

The CPSU's stand regarding Communist China was expressed in the January issue of *Political Affairs,* which carried excerpts of a speech delivered by Gus Hall in New York City on 2 December 1966. Prefixing his remarks with the statement that one "should not be unduly smug about the difficulties of building a new society in a country like China," Hall criticized Chinese domestic policy as exemplified by the Big Leap Forward (1958-1959) and the subsequent failure "to recognize a mistake and to correct it." With regard to the policy proposed by the Chinese "to the world liberation forces and to the world Communist movement," Hall claimed that advocacy of "armed struggle" to the exclusion of other tactics had isolated the Chinese Communist Party from "the Communist movement of the world." Noting that the Red Guard movement and Mao Tse-tung's "petty-bourgeois nationalist positions" had "done tremendous damage" both domestically and on a world scale, Hall affirmed his conviction, however, that this was temporary and that "the Marxist cadre, the working-class cadre, of the Chinese Communist Party will emerge victorious."

Gus Hall's views were reiterated by CPUSA National Committee member James E. Jackson in a speech to the Eighteenth Congress of the French Communist Party (4-8 January 1967):

---

*Gus Hall was chairman of one of the sessions of the Budapest Consultative Meeting of Representatives of Communist and Workers' Parties (26 February to 5 March 1968).

Our Party leadership expresses its solidarity with those forces within the Communist Party of China which are opposing the splittism, the anti-Sovietism, the anti-partyism currently being promulgated in the so-called "Cultural Revolution movement," and looks toward the inevitable and urgently needed restoration of tested standards of Communist Party standards and practice that flow from the science of Marxism-Leninism. . .

Jackson affirmed the CPUSA's stand favoring "the convening of an international conference focused on the question of aiding Vietnam as soon as propitious" (*The Worker,* 29 January).

The developments in Latin America, where polarization between advocates of Castroist strategy (as exemplified by Régis Debray's book *Revolution In the Revolution?*) and orthodox communist parties appeared to be increasing, confronted the CPUSA with a dilemma. The appeal of Castroism among younger members of the party, compounded by the attraction of the "revolutionary internationalism" of Ernesto "Che" Guevara among non-communist radicals, raised the possibility that CPUSA alignment with Soviet support of orthodox Latin American communist parties (such as the Communist Party of Chile) would create dissension within the party and alienate potential support of radicals outside the party.

CPUSA reports on the Havana conference of the Latin American Solidarity Organization (OLAS) − 31 July to 10 August − which were carried by *The Worker* (15 and 29 August, and 3 September) concentrated on the views and reactions of the pro-Soviet communist parties. The September issue of *Political Affairs* reprinted an article by the Secretary-General of the Communist Party of Chile, Luis Corvalán, (which had previously appeared in the July issue of *World Marxist Review* − see *Documents*). Following the death of Guevara in October, at a memorial meeting in New York City on 26 October which was attended by representatives of the CPUSA and the DuBois Clubs there was an apparent difference of views between the two groups. Claude Lightfoot (of the CPUSA) expressed his "profound disagreement" with Guevara, while Carmen Ristorucci (of the DuBois Clubs) hailed Guevara's "internationalism" which, she claimed, had "helped set the stage for more Cubas in Africa, Asia, and Latin America" (*The Militant,* 6 November).

The CPUSA, despite Lightfoot's "profound disagreement" with Guevara, did not publicize the reasons for this disagreement, and in contrast with other communist and radical groups in the USA, did not offer any evaluation of Debray's *Revolution In the Revolution?* The party appeared to adopt a somewhat noncommital attitude toward Latin American revolutionary tactics. Its publicizing of the Latin American pro-Soviet communist parties' views (including a lengthy interview with Jorge Kolle, member of the Secretariat of the Communist Party of Bolivia in *The Worker,* 10 December) indicated the CPUSA's alignment. On the other hand, an editorial eulogy of Guevara (*ibid.,* 22 October) stated: "Guevara's martyred blood will water the seed of thousands of new heroes, who will win that historically imperative struggle of the Latin American peoples for independence from imperialism."

The party's fear of alienating its adherents and other sources of support was evident also in connection with the 1967 developments in the Middle East. The party's preoccupation with what it termed the "Jewish question" (*Political Affairs,* December 1966 and January 1967) preceded the Arab-Israeli war in June. A statement by the CPUSA's National Secretariat pointed out that discussion since the party's Eighteenth Convention had "brought to the surface the main ideological differences on the Jewish question and has made evident the sharpness of the divergences on these points." The statement added: "In the heat of the debate, tendencies toward excesses in language and toward political labeling of comrades have appeared. Such tendencies are regrettable and should be corrected" (*The Worker,* 28 February).

According to the CPUSA statement, the discussions "drew attention away from those cardinal points on which there is unanimity," which were "the alarming growth of anti-Semitism in the United States, coupled with the upsurge of neo-Nazism and revanchism in West Germany, and the need to mount an all-out struggle against these threats to the Jewish people and to peace and democracy generally." It added: "Among these, too, is the need to combat the cold-war campaign against alleged 'Soviet anti-Semitism,' inspired by the State Department and Right-wing reaction." The statement did not enter into a discussion of the intraparty differences except to state: "We do not believe it is proper to characterize any of the comrades involved in the debate as 'bourgeois nationalists,' 'national chauvinists,' 'anti-Soviet' on the one hand, or as 'national nihilists' or 'sectarians' on the other. Nor should any comrade be labeled 'irresponsible.' " (*Ibid.*)

Immediately preceding the outbreak of the June war and in the subsequent months the CPUSA carried a number of commentaries on the events in the Middle East. An editorial in the 28 May issue of *The Worker* asserted: "Guilt for the present dangerous crisis in the Middle East rests solely upon Wall Street imperialists, the oil trusts and the Johnson Administration, which is acting as their agent." The editorial differentiated between "the regime in power in Israel" and "the people of Israel." While stating that "Washington has encouraged and inspired anti-Semitism in the Arab countries and sought at the same time to promote the world-wide image of Israel as the victim of anti-Semitism," the CPUSA remarked also that "It must be noted that Egyptian President Nasser gives aid to this Machiavellian scheme of Wall Street when he says that 'Jews are threatening war,' instead of aiming his accusations against the legitimate target, U.S. imperialism and the policies of the Israeli government." The party referred to "the irresponsible threats of provocateurs in the Arab states to destroy Israel," and declared: "The existence of Arab countries and Israel as viable states economically, politically and socially depends upon cooperation. It is in the interest of the Arab and Israeli people that the Arab states recognize the reality of the state of Israel and that Israel accept the present boundaries."

On 11 June *The Worker* underscored "the need for the withdrawal of all belligerent forces, to the positions held before the Middle East war began, as the most essential requisite of a ceasefire." The same issue of *The Worker* carried extracts of a statement by Gus Hall, who reiterated the party's contention that the responsibility for the war rested on US and British "imperialism" and "the leaders of government and sections of the ruling financial circles of Israel," and claimed that the quest for "national independence" had pitted the forces of "imperialism and anti-imperialism," with "the socialist world, and especially the Soviet Union, [taking] its pivotal place in support of the struggles against imperialism." Hall expressed strong support for the "continued existence of the State of Israel," which he said was "of importance not only for the people living within its borders," having a "deep meaning for the entire world but above all for the Jewish people throughout the world." An article by Hyman Lumer in *Political Affairs* (July), however, reprinted Hall's comments on the existence of the State of Israel and added:

> The crisis in the Middle East has also given rise to a terrifying flood of intense nationalism and anti-Arab chauvinism, fed especially by the military victories of the Israeli armed forces. Concern for the welfare of the Jewish people in Israel obliterates every other consideration. That welfare is viewed as attainable only in opposition to and at the expense of the Arabs. And "defense of Israel" is equated with defense of the reactionary policy of its rulers. With such sentiments we most certainly *cannot* associate ourselves. (Emphasis in original.)

The CPUSA aligned itself with the RAKAH faction of the Israeli Communist Party (see *Israel*). A joint communique signed together with the Communist Party of Canada on 9 November in Moscow reiterated the essential elements of the stand expressed by the CPUSA during the year (*The Worker*, 19 November).

On other international issues the party consistently aligned itself with and supported Soviet foreign policy. The party appeared to be primarily concerned with the advocacy of US withdrawal from Vietnam, although, as Gus Hall indicated in a speech in Moscow on 4 November, such withdrawal should not be limited to Vietnam:

> From this rostrum, so draped in the spirit of Lenin's internationalism, allow me to say to the heroic people of Vietnam, to the victims of U.S. imperialist aggression everywhere, that our party will continue to place the struggle against U.S. imperialism as its primary task, until every last U.S. warship, tank, plane, armed forces and corporation has been removed from foreign soil (*The Worker*, 12 November).

**International Party Contacts.** In addition to CPUSA representation (Gus Hall, Henry Winston, James Jackson, and Albert J. Lima) at the celebrations in the Soviet Union of the fiftieth anniversary of the October Revolution, in November, the party sent delegations to a number of foreign countries, including: France, for the Eighteenth Congress of the French Communist Party, 4-8 January (James Jackson); East Germany, for the Seventh Congress of the Socialist Unity Party of Germany, 17-22 April (Hyman Lumer and Dorothy Healey); Mexico, for the Fifteenth Congress of the Mexican Communist Party, mid-June (Arnold Johnson and John Stanford, both deported back to the United States on 20 June, before the conclusion of the Congress); Cuba, for the First Conference of the Latin American Solidarity Organization (OLAS), 31 July — 10 August (Claude Lightfoot and Beatrice Johnson, as press representatives); India, for the International Conference in Support of the Arab Peoples, in New Delhi, 11-14 November (Herbert Aptheker); and Great Britain, for the Thirtieth Congress of the Communist Party of Great Britain, 25-28 November (Albert J. Lima).

**Publications.** The two principal official publications of the CPUSA are *The Worker,* an east coast organ appearing twice a week (Sunday and Tuesday), and *Political Affairs,* a monthly theoretical organ. Other publications following the party's line include: *People's World,* a weekly west coast newspaper; *Freedomways,* a quarterly review addressed to Negroes: *Labor Today,* a bimonthly trade-union magazine; *Jewish Currents,* a monthly; and *American Dialog,* a quarterly cultural magazine. The party publishes a one-page section of *The Worker* in Spanish, calling it *El Trabajador,* which appears in the midweek edition of *The Worker.* Plans to publish a daily paper were discussed at length during the beginning of 1968, but publication was postponed several times.* The national organ of the W.E.B. DuBois Clubs is the bimonthly *Insurgent.*

\* \* \*

One of the major rivals of the CPUSA in influence within the communist movement in the USA, particularly among youth and minority groups, is the pro-Chinese Progressive Labor Party (PLP).

Formed in 1962 following the 1961 expulsion of Milton Rosen and Mortimer Scheer from the CPUSA, the PLP was originally known as the Progressive Labor Movement. Its present name was adopted at a founding convention held in New York in April 1965.

The extent of PLP membership is difficult to ascertain since the party does not publish any figures. Estimates vary between 300 and 1,000 members. The PLP has its principal sources of support among college students and, outside the campuses, it claims support from young Negroes and Puerto Ricans.

The party is not represented at the national or local level. During the 1966 elections it offered its support to "peace" candidates demanding an end to the war in Vietnam and running as "independents."

**Organization and Leadership.** The leadership of the PLP, elected at the 1965 convention, consists of the 20 members of the party's National Committee. Within this committee most decisions are made and implemented by an unofficial steering committee. This group includes: Milton Rosen, the party's Chairman; Mortimer Scheer and William Epton, Vice-Chairmen; and Fred Jerome, Jack Rosen, Levi Laub, Sue Warren, and Walter Linder.

The PLP's most prominent front organization was the May 2nd Movement (M2M), founded in the spring of 1964. The M2M's 12-member National Executive Committee, elected in the summer of 1964, included nine members of the PLP: Levi Laub, Roger Taus, Marc Schleifer, Rick Rhoads, Jeff Gordon, Mike Brown, Albert Maher, Judith Warden, and Phillip Abbott Luce. As the unofficial youth arm of the PLP, the M2M concentrated on furthering the party's aims on college campuses. In early 1966, after acquiring members in some 20 college chapter organizations, the M2M was reportedly dissolved, and it appears that part of the membership formed a new organization, the American Liberation League. Testifying before a subcommittee on the House Committee on Un-American Activities, on 16 August 1966, former PLP leader Phillip Abbott Luce claimed that when M2M was dissolved, "its members were told to infiltrate other youth groups in order to 'radicalize' them." Two such groups, Luce said, were the Students for a Democratic Society and the Student Nonviolent Coordinating Committee (Committee on Un-American Activities, *Annual Report for the Year 1966,*

---

*A "preview issue" of the scheduled *Daily World* appeared 4 July 1968.

Washington, D.C., 1967). There is no evidence that former M2M members are significantly active within SNCC; their role and influence within the politically heterogeneous SDS is difficult to ascertain, despite PLP claims (see below).

**Domestic Policy and Activity.** The aims of the party were enunciated in the preamble to its constitution: "With the birth of our new Party [we] resolve to build a revolutionary movement with the participation and support of millions of working men and women as well as students, artists, and intellectuals who will join with the working class to end the profit system. . . . With such a movement, we will build a socialist U.S.A. with all power in the hands of the working people and their allies" (*Progressive Labor,* March-April 1966).

In early 1967 the PLP published a statement by the Party's National Committee entitled "Road to Revolution — II" and adopted on 17 December 1966, which was announced as a "reaffirmation of the basic political position of the PLP." It consisted essentially of a lengthy attack on "revisionism," with the introductory section stating: "In order for revolutionary socialism to win power, or to hold state power and consolidate it once it is won by its proletarian forces, it is necessary to win the struggle against revisionism. . . . A party only partially infected with revisionism is like a lady who is 'slightly' pregnant. The elimination of revisionism is the main job within the ranks of revolutionaries" (*Progressive Labor,* February-March).

The means advocated by the PLP for attaining party objectives range from electoral participation (Jack Rosen's wife, Wendy Nakashima, was an unsuccessful candidate for the State Assembly in the 69th Assembly District, New York in 1966) to revolutionary violence, such as that advocated by William Epton in the Harlem section of New York City on 18 July 1964:

> We will not be fully free until we smash this state completely and totally. Destroy and set up a new state of our own choosing and our own liking. . . and in the process of smashing this state we're going to have to kill a lot of these cops, a lot of these judges, and we'll have to go up against their army. We'll organize our own militia and our own army.
> (Quoted in Phillip Abbott Luce, *The New Left,* [New York, 1966], p. 105.)

An editorial by Fred Jerome in the PLP's erstwhile weekly organ *Challenge/Desafío* (1 August 1964) proclaimed: "I urge and will continue to urge and attempt to induce and persuade public demonstrations in the streets of Harlem. . . . I advocate precisely that the people disturb the peace. . . . Let us not run and let us not pray — let us fight back. . . . There is no lawful government in this country today. Only a revolution will establish one. If that is civil rebellion, let us make the most of it."

During the summer of 1967 the PLP came out in full support of the "black militant" elements participating in what the PLP called a "new milestone on the road to revolution." Claiming that the "Afro-American population of Newark, Detroit and a dozen more cities" had "entered the armed struggle," the party stated: "We condemn the fascist terror committed by the repressive forces of the U.S. ruling class and its lackeys, the politicians and the press, and we condemn the Uncle Tom traitors who pave their way. The PLP calls on all progressive, militant and fair-minded people to rally in support of the Black fighting people, and condemn the atrocities of U.S. imperialism and its front men" (*ibid.,* August). During the year the party was highly critical of Negro spokesmen such as the Rev. Dr. Martin Luther King, Jr. and Adam Clayton Powell, and appeared also to deride the pro-Chinese, black nationalist Revolutionary Action Movement (RAM). An article by William Epton in *Challenge/Desafío* (July) referred to RAM as an "almost non-existent organization . . . so highly infested with police agents that it is obvious that the government can easily use it as a vehicle to suppress the Black Liberation struggle." Epton claimed that RAM had 16 members and that *The Crusader,* published by RAM's "Chairman in exile," Robert Williams, was "distributed in this country from abroad," adding: "[It] cannot reflect the struggle of the Black people of this country. These *Crusader* pamphlets get way off base because the people here don't run them." Reports in the PLP publications indicated that the party aligned itself on civil rights issues primarily with the militant SNCC.

Although concern with ethnic minority issues appeared to dominate PLP domestic activity, the party's role within the SDS oriented it toward student issues and related questions such as that of opposition to the military draft. PLP membership in SDS was underscored in the PLP press, and party participation in SDS activities was given prominent coverage. In the context of the party's belief that "The U.S. workingclass ain't dead!" (editorial in *Progressive Labor*, July-August), the PLP emphasized the necessity of a worker-student alliance (*ibid.*, February-March). In its aforementioned National Committee statement, "Road to Revolution – II," a section entitled "Combat Revisionism within the Progressive Labor Party" stated: "The main manifestation of revisionism inside our party at the present time is the continued isolation of too many members from the working people."

The PLP supported and participated in the 1967 mass demonstrations opposing US policy in Vietnam. The party, however, was critical of what it termed "the world-wide tactic growing out of the collusion between Washington and Moscow – the new anti-revolutionary axis," exemplified by the 15 April antiwar mobilization, which was "organized around the false issues of 'stop the bombing and negotiate.'" According to the PLP: "During the last few years the overwhelming majority of growing anti-war forces have recognized the only correct demand is for the *U.S. to Get Out of Vietnam Now*!" (*Challenge/Desafío,* April; emphasis in text.)

In contrast with the CPUSA, the PLP voiced its opposition to the National Conference for New Politics, claiming that the organization and its Chicago convention (see above) were "projected as a cynical maneuver of Robert Kennedy. . . and other liberal imperialists who want to save the system" (*ibid.*, September).

**International Views and Policies.** During the year the PLP remained steadfastly pro-Chinese in its alignment, as exemplified by numerous statements in its party organs and the PLP National Committee's "Road to Revolution – II." The latter statement, while claiming that "success for China's Cultural Revolution is a defeat for imperialist," attacked the Soviet Union (under sections entitled "The Soviet Revisionists Have Already Restored Capitalism in the Soviet Union," "Revisionism, Having Destroyed Proletarian Internationalism, Merges Its Foreign Policy With Imperialism's," and "Soviet 'Aid' Is a Trojan Horse Used by Imperialism"), and both the pro-Soviet communist parties and those advocating an "independent" line, such as the Korean Workers' Party and the Japanese Communist Party.

On issues concerning Latin America, the PLP continued to work closely with the Puerto Rican Socialist League (Liga Socialista Puertorriqueña) and the Nationalist Party (Partido Nacionalista) of Puerto Rico, which operate both in Puerto Rico and in New York City. The PLP publicized the views and activities of these organizations, primarily in the Spanish section of its monthly organ *Challenge/Desafío.*

PLP criticism of Castroism, the revolutionary theories of Régis Debray and the Havana conference of the Latin American Solidarity Organization (OLAS) was primarily in the form of reprints of articles from organs of pro-Chinese Latin American communist parties. By the end of the year the PLP had not published any commentary on the death (9 October) of Ernesto "Che" Guevara.

On issues concerning the Middle East war, the PLP, while attacking "Zionist aggression," concluded:

> The Mid East crisis has produced a number of important lessons. It has demonstrated the vulnerability of Soviet and U.S. policies. It has shown more clearly than ever, the collusion between the Soviet Union and the U.S. It has proven that Soviet leaders are the biggest counterrevolutionaries in history. It has again demonstrated that People's War, as developed by Mao Tse-tung, is the best way an oppressed people can defeat imperialism. It shows that any people who seek liberation from imperialism cannot work with the Soviet renegades if they want to win. And the more "aid" they take from the Soviets the swifter and greater will be their set back (*Challenge/Desafío,* July 1967).

**International Party Contacts.** The PLP did not report during 1967 any visits to foreign countries.

**Publications.** The principal publications of the PLP include: *Challenge/Desafío,* a monthly bilingual (English-Spanish) organ for the east coast; *Spark/Chispa,* a monthly bilingual (English-Spanish) organ for the west coast; *Progressive Labor,* a bimonthly national periodical (in 1967 only three issues appeared); and *World Revolution,* called "a quarterly digest of the revolutionary press" (the first issue was dated Winter 1967).

\* \* \*

The oldest and largest of the Trotskyist parties in the USA is the Socialist Workers' Party (SWP). Founded in 1938, the SWP is aligned with the United Secretariat of the Fourth International. Following the characteristic pattern of Trotskyism, both internationally and nationally, the SWP over the years has been faced by a number of splits, defections, and reunifications. Within the USA, splinter Trotskyist parties originating from the SWP are numerous, and difficulties of delineation are compounded by state-level defections (such as the SWP branches in Milwaukee, Seattle, and Detroit, all of which appear to have broken with the national organization during 1966-1967). The three most prominent national Trotskyist organizations that split from the SWP appear to be the Workers' World Party, the Workers' League, and the Spartacist League (see below).

Owing to the fluidity of SWP membership, estimates regarding the party's strength vary considerably. In 1967 the SWP was believed to have some 500 regular members and its youth movement, the Young Socialist Alliance (YSA), perhaps 400 members. Neither the SWP nor the YSA publishes any membership figures.

**Organization and Leadership.** The SWP is led by a National Committee elected at the party's conventions, the most recent of which was the Twenty-Second Convention held in New York during "the latter part of October 1967" — no precise dates given. The National Committee, whose size and membership were not made public, elected the party officers: James P. Cannon, National Chairman; Farrell Dobbs, National Secretary; and Edward Shaw, National Organization Secretary. According to the SWP weekly organ, *The Militant,* (4 December), the convention, which was held in New York was attended by "over 350 delegates and observers."

The SWP's principal auxiliary organization is the Young Socialist Alliance, formed in October 1957 in New York City and founded as a national organization in April 1960. The YSA held its Sixth Convention on 24-25 March 1967 in Detroit, with "an attendance of almost 300 . . . the largest national meeting in the YSA's history." National officers of the organization elected at the convention were Lew Jones, National Chairman; Mary-Alice Waters, National Secretary; and Doug Jenness, National Organizational Secretary (*ibid.,* 17 April; *Young Socialist,* May 1967).

**Domestic Views and Policies.** The SWP's domestic policy and activity in 1967 in many respects paralled that of the CPUSA. In its bid for broad-based tactical coalitions with dissident groups in the United States — particularly with regard to opposition to US policy in Vietnam and on the issue of civil rights — the SWP's own tactics and pronouncements ranged over a broad political spectrum. The party on the one hand presented candidates for the Presidency of the United States (Fred Halstead for President, and Paul Boutelle for Vice-President) and campaigned for election of party members to mayoral and other local posts (in Berkeley, Oakland, Los Angeles, and Minneapolis); on the other hand, its reaction to the summer disturbances in Detroit, Newark and other cities and its comprehensive coverage of and alignment with Castroist theories of revolutionary strategy appeared to indicate a different approach to US politics. An editorial, "The Lesson of Detroit," carried by *The Militant* (7 August) concluded;

> The ultimate social and political consequences . . . and their enormous import are yet to be fully absorbed. In his message to the Tricontinental, Che Guevara said imperialist aggression would be defeated in Vietnam when there are many Vietnams. A big one may be in the making right in the USA.

Aware of the "united front" potentials in the movement of opposition to US policy in Vietnam, the SWP was prominently active in the mass demonstrations related to this issue. *The Militant* in the weeks leading up to 15 April and 21 October carried special sections (*Spring Mobilization News* and *October 21 News*) publicizing the demonstrations announced for those dates. The party's stand in this area of activity was focused around such slogans as "Bring the Troops Home Now!" and was criticized by more extremist groups for its moderation. A lengthy reply to such critics was published in *The Militant* (8 May), in which the party explained that its stand was motivated by the desire to achieve as broad a coalition of forces as possible: the SWP "did not insist that victory for the NLF [of South Vietnam] be the program of the coalition" because such a proposal "could only have meant there would have been no coalition and no giant demonstration against US efforts to crush the NLF."

Although the SWP favored united-front strategy, it did not support the NCNP. A series of articles on the Chicago convention of the NCNP (*ibid.*, 11 and 25 September, 2 and 9 October) reflected the party's primary concern with support for its Halstead-Boutelle Presidential slate.

With regard to the New Left and its principal spokesman, the SDS, the SWP and the YSA while supporting and cooperating in a number of joint activities were critical of the SDS's failure to develop "a viable program for social change." In a speech to the YSA convention in March, Mary-Alice Waters pointed out that "the growth of SDS as an all-inclusive radical student organization is a symptom of the deepening radicalization of American youth," but added: "The national SDS leadership, however, has drawn back from taking initiative or giving leadership to the national massive anti-war protests, after encouraging moves in that direction in calling the March on Washington in 1965" (*ibid.*, 17 April). A series of articles by Farrell Dobbs in *The Militant* (20 March, 3 and 17 April, and 8 May) deplored the New Left's "prejudices" against the US working class and failure to grasp its revolutionary potential. Dobbs reiterated the SWP's call for an "independent labor party."

With regard to civil rights and related issues, the SWP started the year with a series of articles in defense of Adam Clayton Powell (*ibid.*, 9 and 16 January, 13 and 20 March). By the end of the year the party appeared to be oriented toward the ideas expressed by the late Malcolm X, and advocated the formation of an "independent black political party" (*International Socialist Review*, January-February 1968).

**International Views and Policies.** The most significant trend in 1967 was the SWP's alignment with Cuba and Castroism. Ernesto "Che" Guevara's message to the Executive Secretariat of the Afro-Asian Latin American People's Solidarity Organization in April was carried in full by *The Militant* (15 May), and subsequent issues of this organ and the SWP's bimonthly *International Socialist Review* carried numerous articles and commentaries on Castroist revolutionary theories and development in Cuba. In this context the SWP attacked the Soviet Union for "treacherous maneuvers in Latin America" evidenced by its "cynical proffers of technical and financial aid to Latin American military dictatorships participating with all their counterrevolutionary energy in the US blockade of Cuba" (*International Socialist Review*, November-December).

The SWP's attitude toward China was exemplified in an editorial in *The Militant* (16 January) which attacked Mao Tse-tung's "stubborn sectarianism" and "opportunist policy." The SWP, however, depicted the explosion of the Chinese hydrogen bomb as a "substantial counter to Washington's nuclear blackmail" and "in that sense, a contribution toward world peace" (*ibid.*, 26 June).

The party's views on the Middle East and the Arab-Israeli war were stated in *The Militant* (19 June):

> The Israeli masses, if they are to avoid the death-trap being laid for them by Zionist policies, must break with US and British imperialism, break with Zionist colonialization at the expense of the Arabs, and turn toward integration into the Arab revolution for a socialist and united Middle East.

**Publications.** The SWP publishes a weekly, *The Militant,* and a bimonthly review, *International Socialist Review.* The United Secretariat of the Fourth International, with which the SWP is aligned, publishes in the USA the fortnightly *World Outlook* (the name was changed in May 1968 to *Intercontinental Press*). The YSA publishes a monthly, *Young Socialist* (until mid-1967 it appeared as a bimonthly).

\* \* \*

In addition to the CPUSA, PLP, and SWP there are a number of minor organizations in the USA advocating Marxism-Leninism of one form or another. Estimates of their membership vary considerably. Thus, the pro-Chinese "Communist Party of the United States of America (Marxist-Leninist)," led by Michael Laski as General Secretary, claims 1,500 members, while the CPUSA asserts that Laski's organization has only seven members (*The Worker,* 26 June 1966). The organ of the party is the irregular *People's Voice*, published in Los Angeles. The pro-Chinese Communist Party of Belgium in a listing of pro-Chinese parties in the world (*La Voix du Peuple*, 28 April 1967) did not mention Laski's organization; it referred only to the PLP and the Ad Hoc Committee for a Marxist-Leninist Party of the USA, the latter of which is believed to be centered primarily in Chicago (no membership figures are available). Another pro-Chinese group, which appeared in 1967, is known as the Committee of Correspondence. It is active primarily in the states of Washington and California. It appears to be composed of dissidents from the PLP and its membership is believed to be very small.

Within the Trotskyist movement, the aforementioned Workers' League is affiliated with the International Committee of the Fourth International. The group is led by Tim Wohlforth as National Secretary. It publishes a biweekly *Bulletin of International Socialism* (in mid-1968 the name was changed to *Bulletin*). There are no reliable estimates of its membership, although the number is probably fewer than 100. An organ of the International Committee of the Fourth International, the fortnightly *International Correspondence*, published in Great Britain, carries statements of the Workers' League, as does the Committee's theoretical monthly, *Fourth International*, also published in Great Britain.

The Spartacist League, which is a splinter group from the International Committee of the Fourth International, is led by James Robertson (for commentary on the Spartacist League by the International Committee see "The Pragmatism of James Robertson," *International Correspondence*, 14 March 1967). The Spartacist League publishes a bimonthly, *Spartacist*. The party's membership is estimated at fewer than 100.

The Workers' World Party (WWP) is led by Sam Ballan, National Chairman; Dorothy Ballan, National Organizational Secretary; and Vincent E. Copeland. The party has headquarters in New York and branches in Buffalo, Cleveland, Youngstown, and Milwaukee (the latter formed from 1966-67 SWP defectors). Membership is estimated at approximately 90. The youth group of the WWP is Youth Against War and Fascism (YAWF). It appears to have a larger membership than the parent party. Publications of the WWP include *Workers' World* and the organ of the YAWF, *The Partisan*.

On other groups such as the extremist pro-Chinese "black nationalist" Revolutionary Action Movement, and the so-called "Hammer and Steel" group, led by Homer Chase, there is very little reliable information.

These minor groups, though representing a very small segment of American communism, are vocal and militant (the Revolutionary Action Movement allegedly conspired in 1967 to assassinate Roy Wilkins, the Executive Director of the National Association for the Advancement of Colored People, and to place potassium cyanide in the food and drinks of Philadelphia police). Their actions and pronouncements have the effect within the US communist movement of impeding trends toward moderation.

# URUGUAY

The Communist Party of Uruguay (Partido Comunista del Uruguay; PCU) was founded in 1920. The PCU is legal and is the only Communist party in Latin America to have always been legal. Within the spectrum of the Uruguayan extreme left, the PCU represents the most influential faction. Estimates as to PCU membership range from 12,000 to 20,000. There are no reliable estimates as to the membership of the other parties and groups. The population of Uruguay is 2,783,000 (estimated, July 1967).

The PCU's strength is concentrated in Montevideo, which comprises some 45 per cent of the country's population; an estimated 75 per cent of the party's militants originate from the capital. The PCU's rural support is limited to certain labor organizations in the departments of San José, Río Negro, and Paysandú. The workers in the eastern rice fields and the sugar cane workers in the northern part of the country appear to be predominantly under pro-Chinese influence.

Within the basically strong economy and stable political context of Uruguay, where the liberal "Colorado" and "Blanco" parties divide the support of nearly the total electorate, the PCU's influence has been small. Recently, however, the economy has been facing serious problems (in 1967, inflation was in the region of 100 per cent), and the two major parties have appeared to be beset by internal difficulties. These two factors, combined with the PCU's control of a large sector of the urban labor movement, have enhanced the communist party's influence.

General elections were held on 27 November 1966. Of the total 1,231,762 valid votes cast, the Colorado Party (all factions) received 607,633 votes; the Blanco Party (all factions), 496,910; various left-wing socialist groups, 11,559; the Christian Democratic Party, 37,219; the Christian Civic Movement, 4,230; and the PCU's "Leftist Liberation Front" (Frente Izquierdista de Liberación; "FIDEL"), 69,750. In the department of Montevideo, out of a total of 524,457 votes, the Colorado Party received 268,253; the Blanco Party, 167,406; left socialists, 8,123; the Christian Democrats, 19,746; the Christian Civic Movement, 21,198; and FIDEL, 55,854. In 1962, the year it was formed, FIDEL received 40,886 of a total of 1,171,020 votes and 32,658 out of 484,045 in Montevideo, while the left-wing socialists obtained 27,041 votes in all of Uruguay and 19,677 in the department of Montevideo.

From these results it can be seen that the combined leftist vote increased by 13,382 votes, or some 20 per cent, between 1962 and 1966 (from 67,027 to 81,309) and by 5.8 to 6.6 per cent of the total. The communist-socialist vote in Montevideo increased from 10.8 per cent to 12.2 per cent. FIDEL's gains were thus mostly at the expense of the socialists. The PCU's representation in the 99-member Chamber of Deputies was increased from three to six, and in the 31-member Senate the party retained its one representative. (For further details on elections see YICA, 1966, pp. 254-255.)

**Organization and Leadership.** The PCU has national and departmental structures (the latter corresponding to the country's 19 departments). On the national level, the party's congress (made up of delegates from the departmental conferences) elects a Central Committee, Executive Committee, Secretariat, and Control Commission. On the departmental level there is the Departmental Conference, Departmental Committee, Sectional Conference, Sectional Committee, Affiliates General Assembly, and Group ("Agrupacion").

The PCU has a Central Committee of 33 members, within which the following, in 1967, were members of the Executive Committee: Rodney Arismendi (First Secretary), Enrique Pastorino, Jaime Gerschuni Pérez, Rosario Pietrarroia, Enrique Rodríguez, Alberto Suárez, Julia Arévalo de Roche, Alberto Altesor, José Blanco, Leopoldo Bruera, Félix Diaz, José Luis Massera, César Reyes Daglio, Gregorio Sapin, and Eduardo Viera. The first six also composed the Secretariat. Other members of the Central Committee were Ricardo Mario Acosta, Juan Pablo Acuña, Selmar Balbi, Héctor Bentacour, Gerardo Cuesta, Edison di Pascua, Lauro Fernándcz, Hermes Gadda, Armando González, Juan Vicente Mujica, Julio Omar Oldan, Irene Pérez de Acuña, Raúl Tealdi, José Tomasich, Samuel Wainstein, Esteban Fernández Ruggiero, and Eduardo Bleier.

The party's youth organization is the Union of Communist Youth (Unión de Juventudes Comunistas; UJC). Its women's branch is the Women's Union (Union Femenina).

The PCU is one of the leading groups comprising the FIDEL. Other parties and groups within this front are the Uruguayan Revolutionary Movement (Movimiento Revolucionario Oriental; MRO—the name refers to the official name for Uruguay, "República Oriental del Uruguay"), Popular Unitarian Movement (Movimiento Popular Unitario; MPU), Batllist Vanguard Group (Grupo Batllista "Avanzar"; BAV), 26 October Batllist Movement (Movimiento Batllista 26 de Octubre), Maldonado Popular Unitarian Group (Agrupación Popular Unitaria Maldonadense; APUM), and Sandu Unitarian Group (Agrupación Unitaria Sanducera; AUS). In addition to these political groups, the FIDEL includes a number of interest groups, such as the Workers' Committee, which represents the leadership of the PCU-controlled National Workers' Convention (Convención Nacional de Trabajadores; CNT). For further details on FIDEL composition, see *Pensamiento Critico,* Havana, July 1967, pp. 83-109.

The PCU receives strong support from the trade union movement. The Communist-dominated Workers' Center of Uruguay (Central de Trabajadores del Uruguay; CTU) controls directly and indirectly an estimated 70 per cent of organized labor. A congress called by the CTU 28 September-2 October 1966 established a new trade union organization which is to be called the National Workers' Convention (Convención Nacional de Trabajadores; CNT) until its first congress takes a definite decision on its name. According to the PCU daily, *El Popular,* nearly the whole trade union movement will be grouped together within the CNT. There were 435 organizations represented at the congress, which expressed itself in favor of proletarian internationalism and of developing "friendly relations" with similar organizations over the world. The congress also expressed support for guerrilla movements in Latin America and for the Communists in Vietnam, and denounced the Alliance for Progress and Uruguay's traditional parties. (*El Popular,* 28 September to 3 October 1966.)

The PCU's influence among students, even though Communists constitute a small percentage of the student population, is considerable.* Many key positions in the student organizations are filled by members of the PCU. For instance, Barret Díaz Pose holds the post of Secretary-General of the Federation of Uruguayan University Students (Federación de Estudiantes Universitarios del Uruguay; FEUU).

In addition to its role in labor and student organizations, the PCU is the coordinator of the activities of the Solidarity Committee of the Cuban Revolution (Comité de Apoyo a la Revolución Cubana) and a number of similar "solidarity organizations."

**Domestic Views and Policies.** During the year the PCU's stand on domestic issues, particularly with relation to the question of guerrilla warfare as a revolutionary tactic, was partly determined by the party's role of mediator between Cuba and the pro-Soviet communist parties of Latin America. Fidel Castro himself admitted: "[Uruguay] does not have the necessary geographical conditions for armed struggle. It has no mountains and no forests. There a guerrilla movement cannot develop." (*Marcha,* Montevideo, 18 August.) At the same time, the legal status of the PCU allowed the Soviet Union as well as Cuba to use Uruguay as a center for propaganda distribution to other Latin American countries. Furthermore, owing to its control of the trade union movement, the PCU was not ineffectual domestically.

The PCU appeared to follow a policy of using its control of the CNT to disrupt the economy by a series of strikes (see below) directed toward discrediting the government and broadening the base of support for FIDEL. Yet it was confronted by opposition from a number of militant groups, including its ally within FIDEL, the MRO, which attacked the PCU for its adherence to "nonviolent"

*In a speech reported by *El Popular* (2 February 1968), Rodney Arismendi referred to the existence of a "permanent pact" between Communist labor leaders and students.

revolutionary tactics in Uruguay. In two major speeches, on 20 April and 2 June, Rodney Arismendi analyzed the revolutionary process in Latin America and the role of the Uruguayan "progressive" forces. In his first speech, during a ceremony in Montevideo commemorating Lenin, Arismendi declared:

> It is necessary to have a clear revolutionary perspective concerning Latin America and to see the situation in our country clearly: not as adventurers who believe that history can be made independently of the traditions and beliefs of each nation; who scorn the methods of legal struggle, without replacing them by other methods of struggle; who object to the working class making use of parliament, legal forms, requirements, and labor organizations; who renounce, by themselves and not because of enemy action, propaganda and agitation; who give up the possibility of leading the masses in forging their own experiences and who renounce the best conditions under which to form the national liberation front, to prepare the masses to win power, to create the fundamental social force capable of making revolutionary changes. Nor should we adopt the stance of opportunists who do not feel the cause of the movement which is stirring up the continent, or who attempt to keep their country isolated from a continent, which is moving and shaking and in which, as we said, the underground rumbling of the revolution is being felt.

In the second speech, on the occasion of the eleventh anniversary (2 June) of the PCU magazine *Estudios,* Arismendi emphasized that with regard to Uruguay the party favored the "least painful way" toward revolution:

> For Uruguay we want the most favorable conditions to appear when our people, from its own experience and of its own will, wants to change these structures and come to power.

He added, however;

> But we know that we are in Latin America, imperialism threatens us, and the fight of our peoples and the other Latin American peoples will be a hard one. We are not adventurers; we are not irresponsible or blood-thirsty, and yet we have to keep our eyes open to the situation of the continent, to an hour in America that is hard and bloody. And it is evident—without excluding special cases which history may afford and which possibly will increase if big victories for the Latin American revolution are scored in big countries—that the general line of the Latin American revolution as a basic hypothesis will doubtless be armed struggle.

During the year the PCU continued to emphasize the importance of winning rural support. In 1966, at the party's Nineteenth Congress, Arismendi had pointed out that of the 500 delegates to the congress only 4 per cent represented the peasants. Congress resolutions called on local PCU organizations to take up the cause of the peasants and landless laborers and try to organize them into trade unions, so as to strengthen FIDEL (*El Popular,* 10-14 August 1966). Another area in which the PCU felt weak was ideology. An article in *El Popular's* weekly review, *Revista de los Viernes* (2 January 1967), stressed the role of educating the party militants and the "necessary relationship between theory and practical tasks [which] is found in the fundamental directives of the Nineteenth Congress . . . . The basic premise, found in the character of this Congress in its preparatory stages, was that we had not achieved internal success in Party life." A number of solutions were offered, including the setting up of "mobile libraries" and "night schools."

The PCU's control of the CNT, which in turn appears to control some 400,000 workers, or about 90 per cent of organized labor, gives the party influence in the country far exceeding its electoral strength. During recent years strikes and work stoppages, mostly Communist-inspired, have reached an average annual total of 600. In 1967 agricultural crops and livestock were severely hit by drought, frost and floods, contributing to a sharp rise in the cost of living. In addition to claiming wage increase demands, the CNT and its affiliated trade unions provoked a number of strikes for purely political reasons, such as a general strike called by the CNT to protest against the Conference of American Presidents at Punta del Este on 12-14 April.

**International Views and Policies.** The PCU's stand on revolutionary strategy (see above) and its good relations with both the Cuban and Soviet leaderships entrusted the party with the role of mediator between Castroism and the adherents of the "peaceful" line of revolutionary strategy, such as that espoused by the Communist Party of Chile and other major pro-Soviet communist parties of Latin America.

In its quest to attain "unity in diversity" (in a manner very similar to that adopted by the Italian Communist Party—see *Italy*), PCU leaders, particularly the party's First Secretary, Arismendi, traveled extensively during the year. Arismendi was in Europe and the Soviet Union in the spring, summer, autumn, and winter of 1967; in Cuba in the spring and summer (during the latter period to attend the Havana conference of the Latin American Solidarity Organization), and in Chile in May, where he conferred with the leadership of the Communist Party of Chile. A meeting was also arranged, in Montevideo, with the Brazilian Communist Party in July.

In this context, PCU pronouncements during the course of the year included statements of both Castroist and pro-Soviet orientation. The former included a statement of the party's Executive Committee, dated 1 April, expressing "fervent solidarity" with the Bolivian guerrillas (*El Popular,* 2 April), followed by an editorial in the party's newspaper which stated: "Our party, taking as its point of departure the unity of the Latin American revolution, considers that solidarity is not only an international duty, but a strategic task: each advance of the process of revolution in one country helps all the peoples of the continent. Fervent solidarity with the Bolivian guerrillas . . . means also to defend the future of the Uruguayan revolution." (*Ibid.,* 5 April.) With the publication of "Che" Guevara's message to the Afro-Asian Latin American People's Solidarity Organization (see *Cuba*), *El Popular* (21 April) carried an editorial which proclaimed: "The Uruguayan communists, who have been upholding their leaders' conception of revolution on a continental scale, welcome with joy Guevara's appeal to create on our continent a second and a third Vietnam in order to undermine the foundations of imperialism and contribute to its downfall."

The PCU actively promoted participation in the OLAS conference and sent a high-level delegation to Havana, led by Rodney Arismendi. In his speech to the conference Arismendi declared:

> The debate regarding the fundamental path of the Latin American revolution . . . is the expression of a decision that emerges from specific objective factors, from a certain concrete historical situation, with special characteristics. All this makes us think that the principal road of the liberation of the majority of Latin American countries is armed struggle, as the superior and highest synthesis of all the forms of popular struggle.

On the other hand, Arismendi went on to add:

> It would be absurd to believe that Latin America offers a dull and even picture, where a dry formula for liberation can be worked out for each country, or that its historical path can be transformed into a straight line, instead of the colorful map of the various social developments, of the uneven levels of the revolutionary process, of the different political situations, including social psychology. (Conference Documents.)

Unlike other major pro-Soviet communist parties in Latin America, the PCU made no public criticism of the OLAS conference following its conclusion. A PCU resolution published in *El Popular* (19 August) called for "a salute to the first OLAS conference and support for the effort made to promote the objectives that this organization offers for the development of continental solidarity" and affirmed the "militancy" with which the PCU would "promote these ideas, which have been expressed in the strong solidarity of the Uruguayan people with Cuba and with other struggles on the continent." In a speech in Montevideo on 7 September concerning the conference, Arismendi, while admitting that there had been "differences of opinion," claimed that on all essential points the Uruguayan delegation had agreed with the Cubans, and went on to attack the critical reporting of the conference by the French communist daily, *L'Humanité* (see *France*).

Despite its apparent adherence to a number of Castroist views, the PCU's alignment with the Soviet Union was reiterated by the party on a number of occasions. In an article commemorating the forty-seventh anniversary of the founding of the PCU and the fiftieth anniversary of the October Revolution, the PCU declared:

> This is not a mere coincidence of dates; there is something about these dates which has

been the subject of polemics in the most recent times, an argument made especially sharp in recent weeks by some individuals in Uruguay pretending to be the interpreters of OLAS, when from various aspects and sometimes through the most twisted arguments they tried to call into question, into doubt, the very essence of a phenomenon which changed the face of the world—the role of the Soviet Union as protagonist and vanguard in the struggle initiated fifty years ago. . . . Let the truth be told; it appears inconceivable that the USSR can be "questioned" by an authentic revolutionary . . . Whoever denies the revolutionary, socialist, transforming character of the USSR can hardly be considered a complete, modern revolutionary. (*Revista de los Viernes,* weekly supplement of *El Popular,* 22 September.)

The PCU's role of mediator—as between the Soviet Union and Cuba—did not apply to relations with Communist China. While in the previous year PCU criticism of the policies of the Chinese leadership had been relatively moderate, in 1967 its attacks appeared to escalate in vehemence. In January and February the party claimed to be primarily concerned with the fact that Mao Tse-tung's policies were hindering international communist solidarity with Vietnam—which fact, in turn, prompted the PCU to call for the convening of a world conference of communist parties. By March developments in Sino-Soviet relations prompted PCU Executive Committee member José Luis Massera to declare: "From the first differences . . . our communist party unhesitatingly assumed a position and spoke in favor of unity in the international communist movement. Today China is undergoing a new and more serious phase." Referring to the anti-Soviet "propaganda of Mao and his gang," Massera declared: "We cannot stand idly by while a group of leaders draws China away from the international communist movement" (*El Popular,* 3 March). On the anniversary of the founding of the Chinese People's Republic, an editorial in *El Popular* (1 October) claimed that the conduct of the Chinese leadership had "still further isolated the Chinese Communist Party from the international family of communist parties" until "Today its isolation is complete."

The PCU was represented by Rodney Arismendi at the fiftieth anniversary celebrations of the October Revolution in the USSR.

**Publications.** The two major publications of the PCU are its daily newspaper *El Popular* and a bimonthly theoretical review, *Estudios.*

\* \* \*

Partly as a result of the conciliatory policy of the PCU at the OLAS conference, a number of organizations (many of which were not overtly Marxist-Leninist) proclaimed their adherence to Castroist revolutionary strategy. Six of these organizations united in December for the purpose of reactivating the publication of the daily newspaper *Epoca.* A statement published in the subsequent first issue of *Epoca* (7 December) called for the violent overthrow of the government. In response to the call the government on 12 December, banned the six organizations—the Socialist Party, the Uruguayan Revolutionary Movement, the Revolutionary Movement of the Left, the Uruguayan Anarchist Federation, the Uruguayan Popular Action Movement, and the "*Epoca* Independent Group"—and closed down both *Epoca* and the weekly organ of the Socialist Party, *El Sol.*

By the end of the year the revolutionary element in Uruguay adhering to Castroist strategy was in a state of flux. Delineation of the ideological stands of the different groups or the degree of support for them (which, though growing, still appeared to be marginal) was not possible. The principal challenge to the PCU, however, appeared to come from the Uruguayan Revolutionary Movement, whose First Secretary Ariel Collazo had been Vice-Chairman of the Uruguayan delegation at the OLAS conference.

# VENEZUELA

The Communist Party of Venezuela (Partido Comunista de Venezuela; PCV) was founded in 1931. The party's legal status was suspended throughout 1967.

Estimates of party membership range from 5,000 (*World Strength of Communist Party Organizations, 1968*) to about 30,000. Venezuelan Interior Minister Leandro Mora estimated in September 1967 that active Communists of all varieties (a large percentage being PCV members) numbered below 15,000 (*NYT*, 27 September). The population of Venezuela is about 9,350,000 (estimated, July 1967).

The PCV was at a peak of power between 1958 and 1960, immediately after the overthrow of the dictatorship of Marcos Pérez Jiménez. At that time party influence on the press, labor unions, students, and some other groups was considerable. Subsequently, Communist hostility toward the moderate reform government of President Rómulo Betancourt, the leader of the Democratic Action (Acción Democrática; AD) party who was elected in December 1958, together with the influence of the Cuban revolution after January 1959, led the PCV increasingly away from peaceful participation in national affairs. The communist move toward the use of armed struggle was paralleled by that of the Movement of the Revolutionary Left (Movimiento de Izquierda Revolucionaria; MIR), an organization formed in 1960 by left-wing dissidents from the AD. The violence practiced by these two groups, at first primarily in and around urban centers, led in May 1962 to a government decree which "suspended" their activities. Shortly thereafter those groups which wanted to carry out armed opposition to the Betancourt government, primarily the PCV and the MIR, came together politically in the National Liberation Front (Frente de Liberación Nacional; FLN) and militarily in the FLN's military arm, the Armed Forces of National Liberation (Fuerzas Armadas de Liberación Nacional; FALN). After failing to disrupt the December 1963 presidential election, the FALN concentrated primarily on waging guerrilla warfare in the countryside.

In 1965 some PCV leaders began to feel that emphasis on guerrilla warfare was not advancing communist objectives. The retreat from guerrilla warfare which followed took several years to complete and created some conflicts within the Politburo and lower levels of the party. Disputes over advantages to be gained from violent as against peaceful actions, and then over the leadership of the FALN, culminated at the Eighth Plenum of the PCV, April 1967, in the expulsion of a former member of the Politburo from the party and in the official, but supposedly temporary, abandonment of guerrilla warfare. Almost all statements and activities of the Venezuelan Communists during 1967 were directly or indirectly related to this "strategic retreat" of the PCV.

**Organization and Leadership.** For some years the Secretary-General of the PCV has been Jesús Faría. Although he has lived in Moscow since his release from prison in 1966, he was ratified in his position as party leader at the plenum in April 1967. At the same meeting, however, Pompeyo Márquez (who had escaped from prison with Guillermo García Ponce and Teodoro Petkoff in February) was made Acting Secretary-General. Among the members of the PCV Politburo were Márquez, García, Petkoff, Alonso Ojeda Olachea, Pedro Ortega Díaz, Eduardo Gallegos Mancera, and Germán Lairet. Politburo members Gustavo and Eduardo Machado were in prison throughout 1967. Fifty-four members of the Central Committee were present at the plenary meeting in April, including some guerrilla leaders (*El Nacional*, Caracas, 27 April). Douglas Bravo, who had been removed from the PCV Politburo in May 1966, was expelled from the party at the Eighth Plenum. According to Pompeyo Márquez, this action was taken not because Bravo directed a guerrilla front, but because he was "rebelling against the party's discipline, setting up a parallel apparatus, and working to create a split in the party" (see the letter by Márquez to *El Nacional*, 23 April). Reportedly, the party's new

629

line cost it a third of its membership in Caracas (*The Economist,* London, 30 September).

**Youth.** The most successful of the PCV's auxillary organizations in recent years has been the Venezuelan Communist Youth (Juventud Comunista Venezolana; JCV). During 1967 the JCV was strongest at the Central University of Venezuela, in Caracas, whose 24,000 students account for about half of the university population in the country. Long-standing communist control of the Federation of University Centers through a JCV-MIR coalition was formally maintained throughout 1967. During the year, however, dissension between these two groups increased, in line with PCV-MIR conflicts outside the university, and in the student elections at the Central University in January 1968 an alliance of Communists and more moderate leftists which did not include the MIR won a sweeping victory. At the University of Zulia (the second largest in the country, with some 7,000 students), in Maracaibo, the Communists were unable to match the strength of the Social Christian-COPEI youth group. The JCV was placed fourth in a hotly contested election in October at the University of the Andes in Mérida, the victorious MIR candidates getting over four times as many votes as the JCV candidates.

Before December 1966 a policy of university autonomy in Venezuela made it possible for guerrillas and terrorists to seek shelter, store supplies, and plan activities on the seven square mile campus of the Central University. In December the Leoni government moved to neutralize the campus. In February the JCV and other leftist groups staged demonstrations and strikes against the modified Law of the Universities which allowed the government to enforce law and order and prohibit political activity at the university. The demonstrations led to the second closing down of the university in as many months.

The JCV followed PCV policy during the year and publicly deplored the attacks on the PCV by the Castro regime in Cuba, and by the Douglas Bravo faction of the FALN (see below) and the MIR in Venezuela (see, for example, the JCV organ *Joven Guardia,* Caracas, 30 March). On the twentieth anniversary of its founding, in September, the JCV issued a condemnation of Castroism, of the MIR guerrillas, and of other "adventurers." Radio Havana responded on 5 October by declaring: "These so-called youth leaders [of the JCV] seem as old as horse-drawn stagecoaches in the age of space travel."

On 3 April the Federation of University Centers announced that the Soviet Union, Czechoslovakia, Poland, and Hungary had offered seven postgraduate scholarships to students at Central University.

**Organized Labor.** In 1958 the Communists played a prominent role in the Venezuelan labor movement. As PCV policy became more belligerent, the party lost most of its support in the Confederation of Venezuelan Workers (CTV) and was driven to form a splinter union which it could control, the Unitary Confederation of Venezuelan Workers (Confederación Unitaria de Trabajadores de Venezuela; CUTV). The limited influence of the PCV among Venezuelan workers is apparent when the membership of the CUTV (about 30,000) is compared with that of the CTV (about 1.5 million). At its Fifth Congress, September 1967, in a move seemingly inconsistent with new PCV policy (see below), the CUTV replaced its fairly moderate president with one believed to be pro-Chinese in outlook. PCV dissatisfaction with the ineffective CUTV was reflected at the Ninth Plenary session of the Central Committee, February 1968, when the party resolved to work for unification of the CUTV and the CTV.

**FLN-FALN.** Following its formation in the early 1960's, the FLN and its military arm, the FALN, became the most important allied organization in which the Communists had a leading role. By 1966, however, the association with the FLN-FALN was proving very troublesome. When some PCV officials began to propose a tactical retreat from guerrilla warfare, several guerrilla leaders turned against the party, which by exercising control through the FLN was able to apply pressure on guerrillas with whom it disagreed. On 22 April 1966 five guerrilla leaders, including PCV Politburo member Douglas Bravo, met secretly and set up a "Comando Unico" controlling both the FLN and the FALN, and putting the decision-making offices in the hands of the guerrillas themselves. According to documents issued at that time by the new command group, its officers were: Bravo, Pedro Vega Castejón, Gregorio Lunar Márquez, Elías Manuit Camero, Tirso Pinto, Alfredo Maneiro,

Germán Lairet, Francisco Prada, and Fabricio Ojeda (*Confidencial*, Caracas, no. 32, August 1966). Thenceforth there existed two parallel FLN-FALN organizations. One, headed by Bravo (removed from the PCV Politburo in May 1966 and expelled from the party in April 1967), was Castro-oriented and in rebellion against the PCV. The other, loyal to the PCV, was in overall command of increasingly less active guerrilla forces entrusted to Pedro Medina Silva, one of the leading figures in the January 1966 Tricontinental Conference in Havana.

Relations between the PCV and the FALN (Bravo faction) became ever more hostile during 1966 and erupted before the general public in March 1967. Early in that month Dr. Julio Iribarren Borges, a former Venezuelan government official and brother of the Foreign Minister, was kidnapped and murdered. On 6 March the Cuban paper *Granma* carried a statement by Elías Manuit, in which he, as president of the FALN (Bravo), admitted that his organization was responsible for the application of "revolutionary justice" to Iribarren. Both the murder and the Manuit statement were condemned during the next few days by PCV leaders and by the loyalist FALN headed by Medina Silva. Joining Medina Silva in the condemnation were Germán Lairet, Tirso Pinto, and Pedro Vega Castejón, who had been named as officers in the Bravo faction in April but meanwhile had left it (see *El Nacional*, 12 March).*

On 13 March Fidel Castro made the dispute the subject of one of his longest speeches of the year. He quoted a number of documents issued by the contending groups, attacked the PCV concept of "democratic peace," and concluded that the Venezuelan Communists had committed "treason" against the guerrillas (see *Documents*). Thereafter the previously covert Cuban support for the FALN (Bravo) became overt and the dispute took on continent-wide implications. The PCV conflict with the rebel FALN was made an example of what Castro (and Régis Debray in his *Revolution in the Revolution?*) considered the betrayal by a number of Latin American Communist parties of the guerrillas and thus the revolutions in their countries (see below and *Cuba*). Castro did not invite the PCV or the loyalist FALN to send delegates to the conference of the Latin American Solidarity Organization (OLAS) in Havana in August; the FALN (Bravo) and the MIR, independent of but on good terms with the Bravo group, were each represented by at least four delegates (see below). After the OLAS conference Pedro Medina Silva issued a statement on behalf of the loyalist FALN condemning OLAS and charging that the attending FALN delegation was a "usurper" and did not represent the real FALN.

**Domestic Policy and Activities.** In line with its April decision to participate in the 1968 elections (see below), the PCV in October began the promotion of the "Union for Advancement" (Union Para Avanzar; UPA), a vehicle through which the "suspended" communist party and its allies could make their influence felt. The UPA expected to support any alliance of left-wing parties which might be formed in an effort to defeat the more moderate reform candidates of the broadly popular AD and COPEI parties.

In April the PCV leaders openly recognized that the party and the "revolutionary movement" had suffered little but defeats in recent years and that only through a change of policy could they hope to regroup and strengthen their forces. According to Central Committee member Juan Rodríguez (*WMR*, September), the Eighth Plenum recognized that the mass movement was "at low ebb" and that the revolutionary forces were "divided and defeated." Rodríguez applied Lenin's analysis in the 1907 pamphlet "Concerning the Boycott of the Third Duma" to the PCV situation in 1967:

> Now we are at a period of a lull in the revolution when *a whole series of calls* systematically *met with no response among the masses* . . . . Since the accursed counterrevolution has driven us into this accursed pigsty, we shall work there too for the benefit of the revolution without whining, but also without boasting. (Lenin's emphasis.)†

---

*According to the Pompeyo Márquez letter in *El Nacional* (23 April), Alfredo Maneiro had also by then reestablished his position in support of the PCV.

†In at least one major document the PCV justified its "tactical retreat" by extensive quotations from Mao Tse-tung (see below).

The resolutions formulated at the Eighth Plenum (published in *Ultimas Noticias,* Caracas, 17 May), noted the errors which had led to the party's low position in 1967:

(1) We did not understand the true nature of the insurrectional movement against Betancourtist hegemony. We attempted to attribute immediately the characteristics of a "revolutionary national liberation war" to a movement which had not yet reached that point . . .

(2) When the conditions existed for the achievement of important changes by means of a correct combination of the forms of struggle, especially the use of armed struggle, the party did not act coherently, in depth, and with all its forces in the insurrectional action . . .

(3) We committed serious errors of subjectivism in the application of the forms of struggle. These were expressed in the tendencies to adventurism and in the maladministration of our forces. Some of these errors affected the policy of alliances, the participation of the broad popular masses in the struggle, and they led, subsequently, especially after the December 1963 elections, to the isolation of the party and serious defeats. Owing to the situation created within the party by the work of the splinter group, sectarianism went deeper, provoking new reversals which could have been avoided.

(4) . . . We ought to have participated in the [1963] elections, suspended the armed operations, and laid principal stress on a policy of broad alliances to regroup the opposition . . .

(5) After the 1963 elections . . . we did not realize the need to give priority to a policy that would permit the revolutionary movement to regroup its forces . . . . [Instead, the party] adopted an ultraleftist position—as did the other leftist sectors—allowing the policy of the revolutionary movement to be dominated by dogmatism and sectarianism . . .

(6) Guerrilla struggle as a form of popular struggle is, under certain political and military conditions, an unrenouncible resource of great tactical and strategic value. The experience gained by the party in this regard constitutes a wealth of knowledge we must conserve and enrich. However, to rely on the rural guerrillas as the fundamental force for struggle in the present situation in Venezuela constitutes the mechanical transplantation of an experience which has been successful in other countries, but which does not exactly match the peculiarities of Venezuelan reality, in which the principal forces of the revolution and the dominant social antagonisms are found in the cities and the urban areas . . . . The guerrilla mentality deviationists, . . . in assigning an exaggerated and decisive role to the guerrilla movement, are leading it to visible failure, as we are observing at present . . .

(7) The adaptation of the work of the masses to our general line was incorrect. We mistakenly underestimated the mass fronts. In the labor work, especially, we did not understand the requirements imposed by the changes in the political situation, and there was bureaucratism, passiveness, and sectarian guidance by the party.

(8) Initially, the party leadership acted weakly against the maneuvers of the splinter group. The hesitation permitted the antiparty groups to take over certain positions, sow confusion through a campaign of intrigues and slander, and advance a pernicious divisionist campaign which has harmed the prestige and the authority of the party.

(9) The following is present in all the errors we have committed during this period: the influence of individualism, the vacillation typical of the petty-bourgeois mentality, and poor knowledge of Marxist-Leninist ideology and of the national reality . . .

With respect to the existing situation in Venezuela, the resolutions stated:

Erroneous sectarian and pseudorevolutionary concepts, which are causing so much harm by weakening the popular movement, have gone on to constitute the most dangerous of deviations, which threaten the immediate destiny of the Venezuelan revolution, exposing it to isolation and failure. The defeat of the erroneous ideas is indispensible in order to guarantee the development and victory of our party and the revolutionary movement.

In comments published later, concerning the conclusions reached at the plenum, Juan Rodríguez pointed out:

The immediate political objective [for the PCV] is to oust the reactionary leadership of the democratic Action party from power, foil the designs of the Right Social-Christians to come to power, and create conditions for a "progressive nationalist and democratic change."

"In the interests of this national movement," states the resolution, "the Central Committee has decided actively to participate in the coming election campaign under the slogan: NO to continuation of the old policy, NO to Caldera [the Social-Christian candidate], we are for change!" (*WMR*, September.)

Thus the PCV committed itself temporarily to the peaceful road, and pledged itself to work for the reunification of the revolutionary movement, the direction of the "smoldering discontent" of the masses, the expansion of communist influence in the mass movements, and the participation of the PCV in the 1968 elections in an alliance against the AD and COPEI parties, all with the objective of promoting, as the plenum resolutions put it, "the development of a broad national movement in favor of a progressive, nationalist, and democratic change." Juan Rodríguez again quoted Lenin to point out the "essence, spirit, and meaning" of the resolutions (*ibid.*):

The great wars in history, the great problems of revolution, were solved only by the advanced classes returning to the attack again and again—and they achieved victory after having learned the lessons of defeat. . . . In new forms and by other ways, sometimes much more slowly than we would wish, the revolutionary crisis is approaching, coming to a head again. We must carry on with the painstaking work of preparing larger masses for that crisis; this preparation must be more serious, taking account of higher and more concrete tasks; and the more successfully we do this work, the more certain will be our victory in the new struggle.

Even before the Eighth Plenum, however, Pompeye Márquez pointed out that participation in elections did not mean the abandonment of all other forms of struggle (*Tribuna Popular*, Caracas, 13 March). Indeed as one Venezuelan Communist spokesman has stated, it would be wrong to believe that the PCV "deems it possible to carry out the Venezuelan revolution through the ballot-box." This spokesman, Francisco Mieres, added: "Electioneering is a tactical episode and not a substitute for our strategic line" (*WMR*, November). While calling for the temporary adoption of the peaceful road, the plenum resolutions declared: "The Central Committee ratifies the thesis of the Third Congress concerning the nonpeaceful nature of the Venezuelan road to national liberation and socialism." Similarly, Politburo member Teodoro Petkoff stated in an interview at the beginning of 1968:

For us armed action is still the main way, for no revolutionary or democratic change can be attained without it. Our experience in Venezuela teaches us that no revolutionary movement can be victorious without armed struggle. We must therefore remodel and reinforce our apparatus, in order to operate more effectively than before at those critical moments when the objective evolution, our political work and renewed links with the masses create a revolutionary situation. (*WMR*, April 1968.)

The PCV says that it still has two guerrilla units in operation: the "Simón Bolívar" front in the west-central states of Venezuela, commanded by Tirso Pinto, and the "Manuel Ponte Rodríguez" front, in the eastern mountains of Monagas and Sucre states, led by Alfredo Maneiro (Márquez letter, *El Nacional*, 23 April 1967). According to Teodoro Petkoff, however, these units are putting emphasis on a "political offensive while temporarily discontinuing armed action" (*WMR*, April 1968).

**International Views and Policies.** Weighted down with internal problems, the PCV became involved in international affairs only when it was forced to do so. One chain of events in particular forced the PCV into a position of considerable continental importance. As noted earlier, on 13 March Fidel Castro accused the PCV leaders of betraying the Venezuelan guerrillas and thus, in his view, the Venezuelan revolution (see *Documents*). The Cuban Prime Minister made it clear, however, that the failures of the PCV leaders were matched by those of many other Latin American communist leaders, "false revolutionaries" who had allegedly betrayed the revolutions in their countries. By implication, his criticisms even included the Soviet Union (see *Cuba*). On 10 August Castro asserted that the PCV leaders were a "mafia" condemning the Cuban revolution in league with the "imperialists," the Latin American "oligarchs," the "false revolutionaries" of the communist world, and Cuban exiles and counterrevolutionaries (*Granma*, Havana, weekly English edition, 20 August).

The PCV response was to demand that Castro stop his interference in Venezuelan affairs — including both his unsolicited directives and his moral and material support for the guerrillas of the MIR and Bravo-led FALN. Venezuelan communist leaders were particularly critical of Cuban support for the terrorists who murdered Julio Iribarren Borges in March, for the Cuban role in the guerrilla landing on the Venezuelan coast in May, and for holding the "divisionist" OLAS conference in August, which the PCV declared had been dominated by "tiny pseudo-revolutionary and anti-communist groups which followed the personalist orientation of Fidel Castro" (*Ultimas Noticias*, 20 August). At the end of the year the PCV stated that the events of 1967 had shown the "inability of anarcho-adventurist ideas to give the correct lead to the Venezuelan revolution" (*ibid.*, 23 December).

The conflict with Cuba was probably the main reason for the meeting in June of Central Committee members of the PCV and the Communist Party of Colombia. In a joint statement issued at the conclusion of the meeting, the two parties, with obvious reference to Cuba, called for "mutual respect for and non-interference in the internal affairs of other parties," and condemned "every disruptive maneuver aimed under any pretext at undermining the unity of Communist parties and at promoting factionalism and division in the revolutionary movement" (*IB*, no. 104). Another condemnation of "divisionist maneuvers" was issued after a meeting of Central Committee members from the PCV and the Communist Party of Ecuador in October (*Ultimas Noticias*, 8 December).

During the year, prominent leaders of several other Latin American communist parties, notably Luis Corvalán (Chile) and Rodolfo Ghioldi (Argentina), and from some European parties issued indirect support for the PCV and criticism of the Cubans, often in such Soviet organs as *Pravda* and the *World Marxist Review* (see *Cuba*).

At the same time the PCV continued to praise the Cuban revolution and the lessons it allegedly has provided for all Latin American countries (see, for example, *WMR*, November). In December an anonymous member of the PCV Politburo stated that the Venezuelan Communists agreed with Castro that the fundamental path to power in Latin America was through armed struggle. They disagreed primarily on the relative importance of urban revolutionary action and guerrilla warfare in Venezuela, and on the wisdom of trying to oppose a reforming government with violence in an election year. In spite of their differences, the Politburo member said, the Venezuelan Communists hoped that "public polemics" would be abandoned and that they could "reestablish a veritable dialogue with the Cuban leaders." (*Le Monde*, Paris, 7 December.)

**Vietnam War and Other Issues.** The joint statement of the PCV and the Communist Party of Colombia called for "solidarity with the Vietnamese people who are battling courageously against the US aggression" (*IB*, no. 104). Other PCV references to Vietnam were brief and scattered.

In the same joint statement, the Venezuelan and Colombian parties expressed their ardent solidarity with the nations that today suffer most from repression encouraged by the imperialists:

> with the democrats of Greece who are under fascist attack, with the Indonesian people subjugated by a brutal dictatorship, with the peoples of Africa who continue to fight against colonial oppression, and with the nations of the Middle East who are victims of militarist maneuvers by the imperialists. As for Latin America, the two parties voice their solidarity with the patriots who in various parts of the continent, including Colombia and Venezuela, are fighting against US imperialism and reaction in the most diverse forms.

**Sino-Soviet Conflict.** In February 1967 the PCV issued a statement, "On the Anti-Soviet Campaign" (*IB*, no. 95), maintaining that anti-Soviet sentiments were harmful to the world revolutionary movement and declaring: "Our Party sees no valid justification for such campaigns." On the other hand, the Venezuelan Communists, in their rare statements on Sino-Soviet relations, did not openly attack Peking. The PCV has not split into openly pro-Soviet and pro-Chinese factions.

Although some news reports have suggested that the FALN (Bravo) and the MIR are pro-Chinese groups, their orientations are evidently more toward Fidel Castro than Mao Tse-tung.

**Soviet Union.** The Soviet Union has given indirect support to the PCV in its dispute with Castro and has provided a refuge for PCV Secretary-General Jesús Faría and several other exiled PCV leaders. In the November 1967 issue of the *World Marxist Review,* dedicated to the fiftieth anniversary of the Soviet October Revolution, Venezuelan Communist Francisco Mieres wrote: "Latin America is now closer to the Russia of the time of the victory of Leninism than any other region of the world," developing the idea as follows:

The Russian "model" of revolution . . . cannot but reflect certain *specific features of the socialist revolution in a non-fully-developed capitalist country.* It is this that brings the October "model" closer to Latin America and in a greater measure, we believe, than to the current revolutionary processes in countries of the imperialist West or in the majority of the newly free countries of Asia and Africa.

Indeed, the conflicts developing on our continent are, in effect, similar to those that took place in Russia at the time . . . . The bulk of our continent, no longer in the ocean of backwardness, is nearing the coastline of development. This makes for their inherent unity, distinguishes Latin America from other underdeveloped parts of the world, and underscores the specific character of the modern Latin American revolution in general. (Emphasis in original.)

**Communist China.** Although the PCV did not openly attack or praise China in its public statements during the year, it would be incorrect to say that Chinese influence was absent from PCV affairs. As noted earlier, the Communist-controlled workers' union (CUTV) in September elected a president who is apparently pro-Chinese.

Of particular interest is the fact that whereas quotations from Lenin were used in public statements to justify the tactical retreat from guerrilla warfare (as in *WMR*, September), the authority of Mao Tse-tung was sometimes used to try to influence the guerrillas. In December 1966 the Military Secretary of the PCV Politburo Germán Lairet, issued a bulletin to his comrades in the so-called Brigade No. 3 (available in *Confidencial,* no. 38, February 1967), outlining the tactical retreat to be carried out during 1967. Lairet devoted a third of this long bulletin to quotations from Mao and precedents from the war between the Chinese Communists and Nationalists during the 1930's and 1940's. Calling Mao one of the "two greatest revolutionaries in history" (the other being Lenin), Lairet elaborated on the long-term advantages the Chinese Communists gained from concessions to the Nationalists in 1945, and on Mao's defense of the tactical retreat in the face of attacks from "ultra-leftists" in the Chinese Communist Party. In short, the Venezuelan guerrillas were told that they could learn a great deal from Chairman Mao.

Although the Chinese Communists have refrained from commenting on the PCV, some of their followers have not. For example, *L'Humanité Nouvelle,* Paris, on 30 March characterized PCV Secretary-General Faría as a "revisionist" who, from his haven in Moscow, "preaches abandonment of the armed struggle." The organ of the Communist Party of Belgium, Marxist-Leninist, has called the PCV "revisionist" (*La Voix du Peuple,* 24 March).

Jesús Faría represented the PCV at the celebrations for the fiftieth anniversary of the October Revolution in Moscow.

**Publications.** The PCV has a legal weekly, *Que,* which ceased publication temporarily in December 1966, and a clandestine monthly, *Tribuna Popular.* Communist statements are also carried in several non-communist Caracas daily papers, notably *Ultimas Noticias* and *El Nacional.*

\* \* \*

**FLN-FALN (Bravo faction).** Late in 1966, in an interview broadcast by Radio Havana (24 December), Douglas Bravo told Mario Menéndez Rodríguez, editor of the Mexican magazine *Sucesos Para Todos,* that the FALN program was "vast and not sectarian," and that the FALN included not only communists, but also "patriots" from several other Venezuelan parties. He went on, however, to say: "A vast liberation movement like this one . . . needs a disciplined vanguard which is politically and ideologically coherent and has an advanced doctrine." (*Sucesos* carried articles by Menéndez Rodríguez on the rebel FALN in its issues of 10, 17, 24, 31 December, 1966, and 7 January, 1967.) When FALN Political Secretary Francisco Prada was asked, in another interview broadcast by Radio Havana (13 September), why the PCV had not attended the OLAS conference, he replied that it was only the "rightest leadership" of the party which had been excluded. In a major speech at the OLAS conference on 2 August, Prada commented: "I can tell you that the Venezuelan communists were represented in the OLAS delegation .... In Venezuela, the guerrilla struggle is based on Marxist-Leninist principles" (quoted from the complete official transcript of Prada's speech released at the OLAS conference). According to a sympathetic New York paper (*National Guardian*, 28 January), the FALN is made up mostly of communists. Its two top leaders, Douglas Bravo and Luben Petkoff, are among the former PCV officials who led in the break from the "rightest" leadership of the officially recognized communist party.

At least four FALN delegates, including Francisco Prada who held the position of Vice-President, participated in the OLAS conference in Havana in August.

Elías Manuit, who visited North Korea during April and May, and Gaspar Rojo were the leading officials at the permanent FALN mission in Havana.

**Vietnam War and Other Issues.** FALN leaders spoke of the Vietnam war more often and with greater admiration for the National Liberation Front of South Vietnam than did most officials of the PCV. At an interview held in Havana after the OLAS conference, Francisco Prada took the standard FALN position, remarking on the "extraordinary example" being presented by the Vietnamese people:

> They are a people who are resisting the greatest aggression that any people has ever had to withstand. We are convinced that victory will inevitably be theirs. Their struggle constitutes a true inspiration for all peoples.

In the same interview Prada remarked:

> The liberation movement in Latin America, in the entire world, and the movement of the Negroes of the United States are converging toward the same goal, they are fighting the same enemy, they are facing the enemy of humanity with the same courage, and therefore their interests are identical. (*Granma*, weekly English edition, 17 September.)

**Soviet Union and Communist China.** The FALN did not comment directly on the Sino-Soviet split or on the domestic or international policies of the Soviet Union or Communist China. However, the positions taken by the FALN leaders on the importance of guerrilla warfare, the "rightest" activities of many Latin American Communist parties, and other issues, were parallel to those taken by the Cubans and thus were often implicitly critical of the Soviet Union. Soviet leaders recognized this and openly attacked the FALN on a number of occasions, as when Francisco Prada was called one of the representatives from "ultrarevolutionary groups" at the OLAS conference who had given "anti-Soviet speeches" (Moscow Radio Peace and Progress, 8 August). Since their positions were the same, Soviet attacks on the FALN can properly be considered implicit criticism of the Cubans (see *Cuba*).

Some reports have stated that the FALN (and the MIR) included pro-Chinese elements (see, for example, *Este y Oeste,* Venezuelan supplements for February-March and July). The pro-Chinese *La Voix du Peuple* (24 March) in Belgium commented very positively on Bravo and the FALN. The Chinese themselves have mentioned guerrilla fighters in Venezuela on a number of occasions, but without reference to any particular group (see, for example, *Peking Review,* 13 January).

**Cuba.** The Cuban government has given moral and material support to Bravo's rebels. Official FALN statements, and speeches and interviews by FALN leaders, appear frequently in Cuban publications and on Radio Havana. According to a former Cuban army officer, a group of Cuban and Venezuelan guerrillas led by Luben Petkoff infiltrated Venezuela from Cuba in late 1966 (*The Economist,* 30 September). Hundreds of Venezuelan guerrillas, many of whom are present or former members of the FALN, are believed to have been trained in Cuba since the early 1960's.

At the end of 1967 the FALN maintained two guerrilla fronts: "Rafael Urdaneta," under the command of Freddy Carquéz, in the states of Trujillo and Portuguesa, and "Simón Bolívar," headed by Luben Petkoff, in the states of Falcón, Yaracuy, and Lara. Control of the Simón Bolívar front is also claimed by the PCV (see above). By the end of the year, reports from Venezuela indicated that the FALN had been greatly weakened (see, for example, *The Economist*, 30 September). Reviewing the defeats of the FALN during the past few years, PCV Politburo member Teodoro Petkoff stated at the beginning of 1968: "At present, the Bravo group exists chiefly in foreign propaganda reports, though it started as a fairly large force" (*WMR*, April 1968).

*     *     *

**MIR.** The MIR was founded in July 1960 by Domingo Alberto Rangel and other left-wing dissidents from the AD. Rangel withdrew his support for armed struggle in 1963-64, but most in the MIR did not. During the first half of 1967 the MIR Secretary-General was Américo Martín. After Martín was captured on 2 June, evidently on his way to the OLAS conference in Havana, Moises Moleiro became the new Secretary-General (*Izquierda*, Caracas, July; Radio Havana, 28 September).

Late in 1967 the Cuban Book Institute published Moleiro's book *The Venezuelan MIR*, originally written under the Betancourt regime. A new introduction, added in 1967, stated that after hard ideological struggles in recent years, the philosophy of the MIR was now Marxism-Leninism.

Although there were indications that by the end of 1967 a few MIR members were discouraged with armed struggle, the official policy of the group continued to advocate it as the only road to victory (see MIR statement in *Le Monde*, Paris, 31 December).

At the end of the year the MIR maintained two guerrilla fronts: 'Ezequiel Zamora," commanded by Fernando Soto Rojas (alias "Ramírez"), operating in the El Bachiller Mountains of Miranda state, and "Antonio José de Sucre," under the leadership of Carlos Betancourt (alias "Gerónimo"), operating in the eastern mountains of Monagas and Sucre states. The latter front, begun in March 1967, evidently absorbed some former members of the PCV-controlled "Manuel Ponte Rodríguez" front who did not want to retreat even temporarily from guerrilla warfare. Both MIR fronts were relatively inactive by December.

The MIR, under the banners of "Che" Guevara and the late Colombian guerrilla priest Camilo Torres, lost support at the Central University of Venezuela in Caracas during 1967, as was shown in the elections of January 1968. MIR candidates received more votes than those of any other party, however, in the October 1967 election at the University of the Andes in Mérida (see above).

The Cuban government has also given moral and material support to the MIR. In May Moises Moleiro landed on the Venezuelan coast as part of a Cuban-Venezuelan guerrilla force (*Izquierda*, July). When the Leoni government responded to the landing by charging the Cubans with interference in Venezuelan affairs, the Central Committee of the Communist Party of Cuba issued a long statement which read in part: "We are accused of helping the revolutionary movements, and we, quite so, are giving and will continue to give help to all revolutionary movements that struggle against imperialism in any part of the world, whenever they request it" (*Granma*, weekly English edition, 21 May). The MIR sent at least four delegates to the OLAS conference.

**Publications.** *Izquierda* is the official organ of the MIR and *Patria Libre* is a paper published in the state of Monagas. MIR statements, like those of the FALN, frequently appear in the Cuban press and on Radio Havana.

# VIETNAM: DEMOCRATIC REPUBLIC OF VIETNAM

The Vietnam Workers' Party (Dang Lao Dong Viet Nam, often referred to as the Lao Dong Party; VWP) is an outgrowth of the Indochinese Communist Party founded in 1930. In May 1941, party members organized the nationalistic anti-French, anti-Japanese "League for Vietnamese Independence" (Viet Nam Doc Lap Dong Minh), known as the Viet Minh. After the Indochinese Communist Party was nominally dissolved in November 1945, party functions were carried on clandestinely by the "Association for Marxist Studies," under the leadership of Truong Chinh. In February 1951 the supposedly nonexistent party held its Eleventh Congress and the Viet Minh was absorbed into the "United Vietnam Nationalist Front" (Mat Tran Lien Hiep Quoc Dan Viet Nam), better known as the Lien Viet, a front organization created in 1946, in which the communist component was consolidated under the name of the Vietnam Workers' Party. A public declaration to this effect was issued on 3 March 1951. In September 1955 the Lien Viet was absorbed by the Vietnam Fatherland Front (Mat Tran To Quoc Viet Nam).

**Party-Government Relationship.** According to the 1960 Constitution of the Democratic Republic of Vietnam (DRV), the highest organ of state power is the National Assembly, which enacts laws, supervises the enforcement of the provisions of the Constitution and elects the President and Vice-President. The National Assembly is headed by a permanent President, Truong Chinh, and is composed of 455 deputies, of whom 366 were elected on 26 April 1964 and ran as candidates of the Vietnam Fatherland Front. The remaining 89, representing South Vietnam, were reportedly elected in 1946.

As outlined in the 1960 Constitution, the formal government structure of the republic is distinct from that of the ruling Vietnamese Workers' Party. In practice, however, the VWP dictates and supervises the administrative, legislative, judicial, military, cultural, and economic aspects of the government through parallel and separate hierarchical organizations extending to the lowest territorial units.

**Membership.** The latest official estimate of party strength was an April 1966 statement by Ho Chi Minh in which he estimated the VWP membership at 760,000 members, an increase of 300,000 since the party's last congress in 1960. There are no later figures, but party membership presumably increased during 1967. With a population of 19,500,000 (mid-1966 estimate), the ratio of party members to population is not quite 4 per cent. In a 1967 address dealing with party tasks, Ho Chi Minh commented: "The party does not necessarily need a large membership; although a large number is good, the quality of party members is essential" (Hanoi Domestic Service, 5 March).

**Organization and Leadership.** The VWP is a highly centralized, hierarchical party, with committees at all levels of administration. The basic party organization is the *chi bo* (branch or chapter), officially described as the unit responsible for the "task of linking the party with the masses, implementing the party line and policy among the masses, and reflecting the opinions, aspirations, and desires of the masses to the leading bodies of the party." A *chi bo* is established wherever there are more than three regular party members; it is responsible to the party committee of the area in which it is located. A *chi bo* may be divided into cells (*tieu-to*), which have no administrative authority. At the apex of the hierarchy is the Party Congress, held normally every four years and most recently in September 1960. Between congresses, the party Central Committee directs the activities of the VWP, but plenary sessions of the party Central Committee are held only occasionally; it is the party Politburo which actually determines VWP policy and supervises its implementation on behalf of the Central Committee.

Although reports indicate that the VWP Central Committee consists of approximately 100 members, only 43 regular members and 30 alternate members have been officially referred to as Central Committee members (see Table 1). The Chairman of the committee, Ho Chi Minh, also holds the positions of President of the DRV, President of the VWP Politburo, and Chairman of the National Defense Council.

## TABLE 1

### Central Committee Members

Chairman—Ho Chi Minh

| | | |
|---|---|---|
| Hoang Anh | Song Hao | Ha Thi Que |
| Le Quang Ba | Hoang Van Hoan | Bui Quang Tao |
| Nguyen Luong Bang | Tran Quoc Hoan | Chu Van Tan |
| Tran Tu Binh* | Pham Hung | Pham Trong Tue |
| Duong Quoc Chinh | To Huu | Nguyen Chi Thanh* |
| Truong Chinh | Nguyen Van Kinh | Hoang Van Thai |
| Nguyen Con | Nguyen Khang | Ton Duc Thang |
| Le Duan | Ung Van Khiem | Nguyen Thi Thap |
| Van Tien Dung | Nguyen Lam | Le Quoc Than |
| Tran Huu Duc | Le Van Luong | Le Duc Tho |
| Pham Van Dong | Tran Luong | Xuan Thuy |
| Vo Thuc Dong | Chu Huy Man | Nguyen Van Tran |
| Vo Nguyen Giap | Do Muoi | Nguyen Duy Trinh |
| Ha Huy Giap | Le Thanh Nghi | Hoang Quoc Viet |

### Central Committee Alternate Members

| | | |
|---|---|---|
| Ly Ban | Trang Quy Huy | Tran Danh Tuyen |
| Nguyen Thanh Binh | Nguyen Khai | Le Thanh |
| Dinh Thi Can | Nguyen Huu Khieu | Dinh Duc Thien |
| Le Tho Chan | Hoang Van Khieu | Ngo Thuyen |
| Nguyen Tho Chanh | Le Lien | Tran Van Tra |
| Le Quang Dao | Ngo Minh Loan | Bui Cong Trung |
| Tran Do | Nguyen Van Loc | Nguyen Van Vinh |
| Nguyen Don | Nguyen Huu Mai | Nguyen Trong Vinh |
| Tran Quy Hai | Ha Ke Tan | Tran Quang Huy |
| Le Hoang | Nguyen Khanh Toan | Hoang Tung |

The Politburo, which constitutes the "inner core of the power structure," in 1967 consisted of eleven full members and two alternate members: Politburo President Ho Chi Minh, VWP First Secretary Le Duan, Truong Chinh, DRV Prime Minister Pham Van Dong, Pham Hung, Vo Nguyen Giap, Le Duc Tho, Nguyen Chi Thanh, Nguyen Duy Trinh, Le Thanh Nghi, and Hoang Van Hoan, and alternates Tran Quoc Hoan and Van Tien Dung.

The Secretariat of the VWP in 1967 consisted of the First Secretary, Le Duan, and seven members: Pham Hung, Le Duc Tho, Nguyen Chi Thanh, Hoang Anh, To Huu, Le Van Luong, and Nguyen Van Tran.

Although the VWP has been one of the more stable parties in the world communist movement, reports indicate the possibility of divergences, with the divisive issues centering on war tactics and reflecting the Sino-Soviet dispute. Intraparty tendencies reportedly can be divided into three categories: pro-Soviet, pro-Chinese, and a selective combination of pro-Soviet and pro-Chinese policies. The pro-Soviet group is led primarily by Vo Nguyen Giap and includes Pham Van Dong and Pham Hung. It is confronted by the larger pro-Chinese faction reportedly led by Truong Chinh and

*Deceased, 1967; Tran Tu Binh on 11 February, Nguyen Chi Thanh on 6 July.

including Nguyen Duy Trinh, Nguyen Chi Thanh, and Le Duc Tho. The third group, which adheres to a position of "positive neutrality" on party problems is headed by Le Duan and apparently has the backing of Ho Chi Minh. The death of Politburo and Central Committee member Nguyen Chi Thanh, alleged head of the Central Office for South Vietnam and apparent rival of Vo Nguyen Giap, reportedly increased the influence of the pro-Soviet group led by Giap.

Although the VWP may contain several conflicting factions, their differences probably have been related more to inner party problems and war tactics than to ideology, and it seems that these differences are resolved within the party in accordance with Hanoi's interests rather than those of Moscow or Peking.

**Mass Organizations.** The most important mass organization is the Vietnam Fatherland Front, of which the VWP is the leading component. Founded in September 1955, the Vietnam Fatherland Front has continued to advance a program maintaining that Vietnam is indivisible but allowing for different conditions in the North and South. Communist elements still in South Vietnam have been instructed not to identify themselves with the Vietnam Fatherland Front, but to create separate movements with the same objective. According to official publications, the aims and objectives of the Front are:

> To assemble in a broad unity all political parties and groups, people's organizations, armed forces, personalities, religious denominations, races, and sections of the population at home and of the Vietnamese residents abroad, regardless of social standing, political tendencies, age, and sex, with a view to:
>
> Consolidating peace, achieving unity, complete independence and democracy all over the country, building up a peaceful, united, independent democratic, prosperous and strong Vietnam;
>
> Contributing to the safeguarding of peace in Indochina, Southeast Asia, and the world;
>
> Frustrating all US imperialists' and their henchmen's plots to undermine peace, unity, independence, and democracy in Vietnam.

The Chairman of the Vietnam Fatherland Front is Ton Duc Thang (Vice President of the DRV and member of the VWP Central Committee), with Ho Chi Minh serving as honorary Chairman. The front is directed by its Central Committee, composed of the chairmen of the various affiliate organizations, which in turn is represented by a Presidium. Members of the Presidium include Truong Chinh, Nguyen Van Hoang, Tran Dang Khoa, Mme Nguyen Thi Thap, Le Dinh Tham, Xuan Thuy, and Hoang Quoc Viet. Tran Huu Duc is Secretary-General, and Nguyen Thi Luu is Deputy Secretary-General.

The most important organizations affiliated under the Vietnam Fatherland Front are the Vietnam General Federation of Trade Unions, headed by Hoang Quoc Viet; the Vietnam Labor Youth Union, founded in 1930 as the Indochinese Communist Youth League and renamed in 1953, headed by Vu Quang; and the Vietnam Women's Union, headed by Mme Nguyen Thi Thap. Other mass organizations include the Vietnam Students Union, the Vietnam Youth Federation, the Vietnam Peace Committee, and the Vietnam Afro-Asian Solidarity Committee.

In addition to the above mass organizations, two "democratic parties" exist in the DRV and are affiliated with the Fatherland Front: the Vietnam Socialist Party, founded in 1946 and headed by Secretary-General Nguyen Xien, and the Vietnam Democratic Party, founded in 1944 and headed by Nghiem Xuan Yem. No statistics are available regarding the membership of these parties, which have no real power.

**Internal Party Affiars: Leadership Changes.** On 7 July 1967, Hanoi Domestic Service announced that General Nguyen Chi Thanh, VWP Politburo and Central Committee member, had died of a heart attack in a Hanoi hospital on 6 July. Although the DRV has at no time publicly admitted the presence of General Thanh or North Vietnamese troops in South Vietnam, Western sources report that he was also head of the Central Office for South Vietnam (COSVN), thus exercising de facto control over the political and military activities of the communist forces in South Vietnam and serving as a liaison between the Viet Cong and the North Vietnamese military command. These reports, coupled with his absence from all public DRV functions since 1964 and Hanoi's failure to comment on his recent activities, have caused some observers to conclude that he was in fact killed in action in South Vietnam. In September 1967 reports indicated that General Thanh's COSVN post had been filled by Army Major General Hoang Van Thai, Deputy Chief of Staff, Vice-Minister of

Defense, and member of the VWP Central Committee. North Vietnam, however, has neither confirmed nor denied the reports and there is no indication as to whether General Thanh's party positions have been filled.

Leadership changes were also reported in the DRV government sector. Since the formation of the present Government in July 1964 there have been a number of personnel changes, all involving the economic sphere and thus reflecting the mounting economic problems caused by the Vietnam war. As announced by Hanoi's Vietnam News Agency, Nguyen Huu Mai (alternate member of the VWP Central Committee) replaced Vice-Premier Le Thanh Nghi (member of the VWP Central Committee and Politburo) as Minister of Heavy Industry. A second major change was the appointment of Nguyen Van Loc (alternate member of the VWP Central Committee) as Minister of Agriculture in place of Hoang Anh (member of the VWP Central Committee). Other changes included the elevation of Nguyen Con to the post of Vice-Premier, a reshuffling of the State Price Committee in which Do Muoi succeeded Nguyen Thanh Binh as Chairman, and the appointment of Hoang Quoc Thinh as Minister of Home Trade, a post which had previously been vacant.

**Meetings.** Although the party constitution calls for a party congress to be held every four years, the Third VWP Congress, held in September 1960, was the last party congress to be convened. Important party meetings held during 1967 were primarily those of the Vietnam Fatherland Front (VFF).

On 6-8 March the VFF Central Committee held its thirteenth enlarged session in Hanoi under the chairmanship of Ton Duc Thang, President of the Presidium of the VFF Central Committee. Attended by "all members of the Front's Central Committee, representatives of political parties, mass organizations, religious communities, the Vietnam People's Army, the Front committees in various cities and provinces, and heroes and heroines of the army, industry, agriculture, and so forth," the VFF conference reviewed its work during the past year and discussed the new tasks of the Vietnamese people "in the face of the US imperialists' intensified war of aggression." The VFF Central Committee noted that "the northern army and people have outstandingly performed combat and production, smashed the power of the US Air Force, successfully carried out the 1966 state plan, and fulfilled the obligation of the large rear base toward the large front line," and after hailing the "sympathy and support of the fraternal socialist countries, nationalist countries, many democratic and progressive organizations, and the peace-loving people of the world, including the American people, for the Vietnamese people's struggle against US aggression, for national salvation." The Central Committee outlined five major tasks facing the Vietnamese people:

(1.) Intensify political work, strengthen unity and unanimity among the people. . . .

(2.) Mobilize and encourage the people to fight courageously, participate in the building of the all-people national defense, satisfactorily carry out the people's antiaircraft task, learn from the southern troops' and people's determination to fight and win, resolutely crush all escalation steps of the war of destruction of the US imperialists, and at the same time make all necessary preparations for defeating the enemy in all circumstances.

(3.) Mobilize the people to step up the patriotic emulation movement, develop production, practice economy, and successfully fulfill the 1967 state plan.

(4.) Mobilize 17 million northern compatriots to fulfill resolutely the duties of the great rear toward the great front and, under all circumstances, always side with 14 million southern compatriots in order to struggle resolutely for the common revolutionary task of the entire nation.

(5.) Intensify the fulfillment of the international tasks, actively win over the support and aid of the people in socialist countries and the world over, and, at the same time, actively support the revolutionary struggle movements of the world people. (Hanoi Domestic Service, 10 March 1967.)

On 24 March 1967 the Presidium of the VFF held an extraordinary enlarged conference, again chaired by Ton Duc Thang. The conference called on all political parties, mass organizations, nationalities, religions, the army, and members of the VFF to carry out the resolutions of the Front's Central Committee and to mobilize and "organize the entire army and people to make all-out efforts in production, successfully fulfill the 1967 state plan, heighten vigilance, and fight valiantly and determinedly to defeat the US aggressors in all circumstances."

On 7 September an extraordinary enlarged session of the VFF Central Committee met to express the support of the North Vietnamese people for the recently adopted political program of the National Liberation Front of South Vietnam (NLFSV). Although no specific dates were given, the VWP Central Committee Secretariat also held a meeting sometime during the fall of 1967 to discuss the task of "cultivating and strengthening scientific, technical, and economic management cadres" as well as the mobilization of workers and the activities of trade unions.

**VWP Self-Assessment During 1967: Party Affairs.** In spite of DRV emphasis on the "revolutionary enthusiasm and ardent patriotism" of the Vietnamese people, there are indications that the regime is concerned over the extent of its support by the Vietnamese people and that the VWP is not entirely satisfied with the activities of the party and party cadres, particularly at the lower levels. Numerous party statements and directives have stressed the need to "step up further the ideological and organizational tasks and improve the leadership tasks in order to develop to a high degree the masses' spirit of mastership of the community and mobilize the masses to participate in the anti-US national salvation resistance."

In a major article entitled "Big Victory, Great Task" and serialized in *Nhan Dan* and *Quan Doi Nhan Dan* on 14-16 September, Vo Nguyen Giap noted that greater attention should be paid to the need to "streamline" party organizations and mass organizations, improve leadership methods, and heighten the leading role of the party.

On 16 October *Nhan Dan,* the official organ of the VWP, carried an article by Le Quoc Than, member of the VWP Central Committee, in which he indicated that "counterrevolutionaries" still existed in the North and that the public security apparatus did not come up to expectations:

> In some localities and some areas where the fighting has not as yet been fierce and where the activities of the counterrevolutionary elements have switched over to covert and subtle forms and are not brazenly exposed and where the transformation in the outlook of the township party committee has been slow and incomplete, the movement to maintain security and order has not been strong. If we do not bring about a timely change in the outlook of the party committees in these places, then, when the enemy attacks violently or when counterrevolutionary elements brazenly carry out acts of subversion, the countermeasures will be defensive, late, and inescapably inadequate. . . .
>
> . . . In view of the requirements of the new task, the people's public security forces still exhibit many weaknesses: the level of the public security cadre is low in every field, especially at district and township levels; the various professional branches within public security have not yet fully developed their responsibility to the movement; the organization of monitoring the movement is not rigid and permanent. The aforementioned weaknesses and deficiencies have limited the development of the movement to maintain security and order. They are also an important problem which the party committees at all echelons must concentrate on resolving in order to consolidate the dictatorial tool of the party and government, making it very strong politically and sharp professionally with a view to stepping up the struggle against counterrevolutionaries in general and the movement to maintain security and order in particular.

The same article noted, however, that the "key to strengthening party leadership of the movement to maintain security and order" was to "continue to create more profound transformations in the outlook within the various echelons of the party, especially at the township echelon, and bring about a more thorough and universal understanding of the direction and objectives of the movement."

During 1967 the need to improve the quality of the middle and lower-level units as well as the leadership of the party was treated in numerous party publications. In an article in the DRV Army paper *Quan Doi Nhan Dan,* on 2 January, Chu Van Tan, a VWP Central Committee member, noted the need for party chapters at all levels to thoroughly understand party lines and policies, and added:

To solve this problem, it is of primary importance that party committees at various levels have high revolutionary zeal, a stable stand and viewpoint, and sufficient knowledge of local military tasks, and show themselves worthy of being a banner to lead the advance of the masses. War circumstances do not allow leaders at various levels to wait for high-level instructions and to hand down jobs for underwriting by lower echelons; war requires leaders to evolve vigorously to continuously keep abreast of the situation.

It is necessary to struggle resolutely against subjective and rightist views, against the fear of difficulties and sufferings, against sluggishness, and especially against the lack of determination to go on to remote areas. . . .

At present, a number of party members and leading cadres still fail to grasp the enemy situation. Their awareness of the enemy's schemes is sometimes vague. Sometimes they overestimate the enemy, and at other times they underestimate him. This is due partly to their subjectiveness and to their failure to study and understand the actual situation thoroughly. We must endeavor to train ourselves further. We must improve our ideological and political standards and behavior and our leadership over production and combat by studying party lines and policies . . .

Another problem to which we must pay great attention is that of consolidating and perfecting our leadership. Party committees at all levels must have a firm grasp on military organs in all fields and find out their strong and weak points in order to improve them and create conditions for them to develop their efficient staff role, especially under the increasingly violent war conditions.

In the August issue of the party theoretical journal, *Hoc Tap*, To Huu, a member of the VWP Secretariat and Central Committee, stressed the need to "keep a firm hold on the party Central Committee's lines, and to apply them to the situation in each locality," and criticized party cadres for bureaucratic methods and "formalism." To Huu also called on local party officials to "go more deeply into the area and not exercise leadership perfunctorily at their desks at their district headquarters" and stressed the need for a more rational distribution of tasks, noting that "district committee members in charge of leading branches are too numerous while those in charge of leading villages are too few." To Huu's criticisms of party functionaries, however, went beyond charges of poor organization, charging that a "number of villages and cooperatives are weak because cadres there are weak, their work methods are weak, they are corrupt, they violate the people's right of mastership, and there is no internal unity."

An editorial in the same issue of *Hoc Tap* concluded that the strengthening of basic party organizations and the improvement of individual party cadres involved a series of tasks, including:

. . . strengthening basic party organizations and heightening their combativity; improving the leadership and guidance of various echelons, especially the district echelon; training, improving, assigning, and using cadres in accordance with party policies and lines and with the present revolutionary requirements; and improving party habits with the aim of ensuring the principle of democratic centralization, ensuring the sense of discipline and organization, and ensuring solidarity and unanimity inside the party.

North Vietnamese criticism also focused on government as well as party cadres. At the year-end meeting of the DRV Council of Ministers, Ho Chi Minh criticized weaknesses in the performance of state work and "urged state cadres at all levels, from the central level downward, to closely associate themselves with the masses, learn from the masses, realistically meet the masses' requirements in combat, production, and life, and to truly exercise democracy in the cooperatives and in the enterprises and state organs, closely unite with one another, and conduct criticisms and self-criticisms in order to enable one another to make progress." The significance of party concern over these issues, as indicated by the frequency with which party statements and documents discussed them, is heightened by the fact that a large part of the party and government machinery depends on lower level units and cadres for the efficient implementation of decisions made in Hanoi and for the mobilization of necessary resources. In an effort to improve the level of these units and cadres, the VWP has focused on a series of emulation movements.

**Economic Analysis.** As outlined by Pham Hung, Vice-Premier and member of the VWP Central Committee, Politburo, and Secretariat,

> The most permanent task of the North is to produce, to produce in order to meet the requirements of the war throughout the country, to satisfactorily serve the front line, to strengthen the people's force, to ensure victory over the US aggressors, and, at the same time, to continue to build the material and technical base of socialism and to prepare conditions for stepping up the task of industrializing socialism in the future when the war ends (Hanoi Domestic Service, 5 February).

Pham Hung also noted that present DRV economic policy centers on the need to carry out socialist industrialization "with a pace and scale suitable to wartime, to consider the technical revolution a main objective, to follow the motto calling first for rationally developing heavy industry, and, at the same time, to strive to develop agriculture and light industry and to consider agriculture as a basis to develop industry; to pay attention to building economy at the central level along with considering the building of local economy as a main task . . . "

An article in *Quan Doi Nhan Dan* by Nguyen Van Dao, Vice-Chairman of the State Planning Commission, noted: "In the realization of the state plan for 1967, we not only succeeded in maintaining and developing production for the armed struggle and people's needs, but also strengthened our economic and defense potential." Reports during the course of the year, however, indicated that the DRV was faced with severe shortages in nearly every sector of the economy.

In a lengthy speech concerning the 1967 state plan, Vice-Premier Pham Hung noted: "The newly emerging difficulties also impose heavy tasks on us and require us to exert outstanding efforts." Pham Hung specifically outlined four basic problems in the DRV economy:

> (1.) In many provinces, agricultural production, including cultivation and animal husbandry, especially paddy production, is still low and unstable as a result of the fact that the material and technical bases are still weak . . .
>
> (2.) Various provinces are still lagging in the building of local industries. They are unable to firmly hold to the policy and important points in building local industry, nor have they achieved much in local industry to serve agriculture, communications and transport, and the people's livelihood. . . .
>
> (3.) Leadership of the distribution-circulation link is still weak, leaves much to be desired, and is not given proper attention in the working out of the 1967 economic plan. Corruption and waste, serious in some regions, have restricted the labor and revolutionary zeal of the masses. . . .
>
> (4.) The economic control factor is still weak. The masses' labor and achievements are great while the leadership and guidance task is still weak in several respects. As a result, the masses' latent abilities cannot be properly exploited. . . .

Pham Hung placed considerable emphasis on the "struggle to do the utmost to develop agricultural production," with special emphasis on satisfactorily solving the problem of food production. An article in the April 1967 issue of a Vietnamese language economic research periodical stated:

> Agriculture is the foundation for developing industry, but thus far our country's agriculture still does not yet respond to the requirements of industry. Agriculture still cannot yet satisfy the needs for provisions and foodstuffs needed for the workers and industrial regions and for the branches serving industry. The raw materials of farm products supplied to industrial enterprises are insufficient; many factories, because of the lack of raw materials, have not used all of their equipment capacity, and there are even branches that have had to depend primarily on imported raw materials. Capital for partial industrialization must depend on agriculture. But . . . the percentage of agricultural products in the total value of exports is still low. In recent years, the industrialization of the country has been stepped up even more, but agricultural production has not developed correspondingly. Our agriculture is still basically a monoculture one, it is primarily devoted to growing rice and other crops. The total grain productivity has increased, but the output of the land, generally speaking, has not, and labor productivity

represented in terms of products has decreased.

In his article "Big Victory, Great Task," Giap noted:

[We need to] do out utmost and resolutely fulfill the state plan in order to meet the immediate demands of the anti-US national salvation struggle, the demands for building socialism, and the demands of the people's everyday life. We must step up agricultural and industrial production, attach importance to developing local industries, and endeavor to increase the economic potentials and national defense force of our people . . .

There were also other indications that serious agricultural and industrial problems were causing concern in Hanoi. At least three major meetings were convened to discuss labor and economic problems; major speeches on the subject were delivered by Ho Chi Minh and Le Duan; and numerous articles and broadcasts called on the Vietnamese people to "resolutely resolve" problems of production, leadership, and management. Pham Hung also noted that the DRV was faced with considerable manpower problems:

The main difficulties which we have encountered in the recent past in satisfactorily settling the relations between mobilizing maximum manpower and wealth and improving the people's strength have been: the requirement in all fields—especially the requirements of combat—have been great, increased quickly, usually appeared suddenly, and been concentrated in a number of important strategic areas; a large body of young and strong laborers in rural areas have given up agricultural production to engage in fighting or serving combat, in communication and transport tasks, in basic construction and industrial production; the government machinery has become bulkier; millions of people have been evacuated from cities to rural areas; the types of needs have undergone changes; the norms of consumption of a number of varieties of goods have increased.

Meanwhile, the capacity for supplying manpower has been restricted. . . .

Party concern with economic matters centered, in general, on the need to strengthen the mobilization of the economy and the workers in the face of ever heavier demands and the activities of trade unions, and on the role of the party in this effort.

As reported in *Nhan Dan* on 21 January, a VWP Central Committee resolution specifically called on party members to make further efforts to mobilize the masses in order to fulfill the economic tasks set by the 1967 state plan. At a conference held by the Premier's Office in March, emphasis was again placed on the need to further mobilize the masses and meet the goals set forth in the state plan. At the conference, Vice-Premier Le Thanh Nghi, a member of the VWP Central Committee and Politburo and then Minister of Heavy Industry, stressed the need to "mobilize ideologically the leading cadres of all echelons and, at the same time, ideologically mobilize the masses," adding:

It is necessary to take advantage of every hour, every minute in order to fulfill the state plan successfully under all circumstances. Faced with difficulties, it is necessary to develop resolutely the creative spirit of the masses in order to settle the important links, such as communications and transport, basic construction, and technical equipment. Managerial cadres must pay attention to improving the exploitation, management, and supply of technical equipment and create favorable conditions for the worker emulation drive. (Hanoi Domestic Service, 9 March.)

Again, party efforts apparently did not meet expectations, as was indicated by the convening of an enlarged conference of the VWP Secretariat during the fall of 1967 (no precise data given). At the conference, party leaders noted that, "in exercising their leadership, party echelons and responsible branches" had not "carried out correctly and fully implemented the Party Central Committee's resolutions on stepping up the workers' mobilizing task and trade-union activities." A resolution was passed stressing the duty and role of the party in "educating, improving and training the working class."

Specifically, the Central Committee resolution called on the VWP to "strengthen their leadership over trade-union activities" in order to

organize and educate the masses with the aim of satisfactorily implementing the party's policies and line among the workers and public servants and strengthening the relations between the party and workers and turning them into a stable support which the government relies on to strengthen the worker-peasant alliance and make it the core of the national solidarity bloc. Under the party's leadership, trade unions should rally workers and public servants, educate them, organize them, and mobilize them to carry out the three revolutions: revolution of production relations, technical revolution, and ideological and cultural revolution.

The resolution also called on the Labor Youth Union, "which is responsible for teaching the youth communist ideals," to collaborate with trade unions in educating the working class.

**The VWP and the Vietnam War.** The primary domestic concern of the North Vietnamese Party and Government was, of course, the Vietnam war. North Vietnamese statements continued to point out that "the North is the vast rear of the entire country in the anti-US national salvation struggle":

This is our basic viewpoint in the protection and building of the socialist North. All our activities in the North are aimed at serving the war and protecting and building the socialist North—the common base of the entire country—and at most satisfactorily fulfilling the task of the vast rear toward the vast front line in the fight against the US imperialist aggressors. (Hanoi Domestic Service, 5 February.)

According to Pham Hung, Vice-Premier and member of the VWP Central Committee, Politburo, and Secretariat:

For the independence and freedom of the fatherland, we are determined to mobilize all forces of the entire country, to intensify the great patriotic war, and resolutely defeat the US imperialists' war of aggression under all circumstances in order to protect the North, liberate the South, and advance toward the reunification of the fatherland. This is the common political task of the party and people at present. This is the strategic trend of the task of building economy in the North at present. All economic activities must aim at supporting the political task and lead the anti-US national salvation struggle to complete victory. . . .

In the great revolutionary struggle of the nation, the South, the brass fortress of the fatherland and the large front-line of the entire country, has endured many sacrifices and hardships, has fought and is fighting valiantly and marvelously, and has won glorious victories. More than ever the North must move forward with an extraordinary revolutionary vigor to fulfill its vast rear task toward the vast front-line in the anti-US national salvation struggle of our people.

At present, the North Vietnamese people must work with a self-denial spirit, fight valiantly, and be ready to make sacrifices, endure hardships, and contribute men, labor, and material resources to defeating the US aggressors in both zones. The spirit "for the South" and "for the task of liberating the nation and reunifying the fatherland" must be daily forged among all North Vietnamese people and be turned into a strong moving force to urge all people, units, and branches to devote all their morale and strength to carrying out the motto "All for the front line, all for vanquishing the US aggressors." (*Ibid.*) ·

A *Nhan Dan* editorial of 19 December specifically reaffirmed the leading role of the VWP when it noted: "Only the vanguard party of the Vietnamese working class can organize and head our army and people along the correct path of the people's war and bring it to complete victory . . ."

Although North Vietnam has continued to deny its controlling influence in the Vietnam war, a captured VWP document revealed that in 1961 the Vietnam People's Revolutionary Party (PRP), which controls the National Liberation Front of South Vietnam, was a purely VWP organization which was to be known in the South as the PRP for purely tactical reasons. (See *Vietnam: Republic of Vietnam.*) During 1967 a series of captured Vietnamese documents were made public which further clarified North Vietnam's involvement in the war.

One of the documents, "Resolution of the Central Office for South Vietnam," specifically attributed the leadership of the war to the VWP:

The southern branch of the party . . . is closely led by the party CC. . . . As shown by our recent victories, the factors determining our ultimate victory are apparent. We possess a Central Committee which is clear-sighted, revolutionary in theory and experience, and which is headed by Chairman Ho.

While continuing to refer to "the southern branch of the party," the documents also disclosed considerable information on North Vietnam's relations with the Central Office for South Vietnam, which is the highest echelon of the Viet Cong in South Vietnam and is responsible for the Viet Cong's overall political and military direction. As indicated by the documents, COSVN is a covert, combined party-army-NLFSV organization which is controlled by the DRV. Day-to-day political direction of the war from the North is provided by the Reunification Department of the VWP, which receives its directions from the Party Secretariat and Politburo, and by the North Vietnamese Governmental National Reunification Commission, both headed by Nguyen Van Vinh. Although little is known about the organization and leadership of the COSVN, reports indicate that North Vietnamese General Nguyen Chi Thanh, a member of the VWP Central Committee and Politburo, was commander in chief and senior political officer of the "Liberation Army" (Viet Cong Armed Forces) and COSVN chief until his death in July 1967. Although North Vietnam did not acknowledge the presence of DRV Army officers and soldiers in South Vietnam, a captured document quoted Nguyen Van Vinh as saying: "Even if the Americans intensify their air raids, we will still stand firm to protect the North and reinforce the South. The Northern citizens have clearly realized their responsibility with regard to this matter. Therefore, they have provided reinforcements to the best of their ability." In a June issue of *Quan Doi Nhan Dan,* Truong Son (believed to be a pseudonym for Nguyen Chi Thanh) noted that it went without saying that "if the enemy should succeed in severing the relations between Socialist North Vietnam − the big rear − and South Vietnam − the big front-line − and in stopping the moral and material support for the revolution in South Vietnam . . . then he would secure a notable strategic effect" (quoted on Hanoi radio, 2 June 1967).

Reports also indicate that North Vietnamese Army officers in South Vietnam included Hoang Van Thai, Nguyen Don, Chu Huy Man, Le Chuong, Tran Van Tra, Tran Do, Ha Ke Tan, Le Trong Tan, Van Tien Dung, Hoang Quoc Viet, Bay Dung, Ba Tran, To Ky, and Nguyen Chi Thanh. In addition to the North Vietnamese commanders, there were some 50,000 regular troops fighting in South Vietnam (more than 20 regiments). It was estimated in April that nearly half of the Communist forces in the South were North Vietnamese (US Department of State, *Bulletin,* 15 May), as compared with 1,800 North Vietnamese military personnel confirmed in the South in 1959-1960 and 4,400 in 1964. (US Department of State, "Aggression from the North," February 1965). The infiltration of North Vietnamese regulars in 1967 was estimated at some 6,000 per month. As far as can be ascertained, the North Vietnamese regular units do not come under the complete control of the COSVN Military Affairs Committee and the Liberation Army command, but maintain their own exclusive chain of command direct to Hanoi through the (North) Vietnamese Workers' Party Military Affairs Committee set up for this purpose in 1961 under General Giap.

North Vietnamese analyses of the war during 1967 and projections of future tasks and tactics appeared in several long articles and numerous *Nhan Dan* and *Quan Doi Nhan Dan* editorials and reports. The major analysis was contained in the article "Big Victory, Great Task" by Vo Nguyen Giap in *Quan Doi Nhan Dan* and *Nhan Dan,* 14-16 September (English translation published as *Big Victory, Great Task* by Frederick A. Praeger, Inc., New York, 1968). Giap cautioned that the task ahead would be long:

> The anti-US national salvation resistance of our people in South Vietnam must be protracted resistance because our people have to fight the imperialists' ringleaders, that is, the US imperialists, who have large military and economic potentials. Despite their defeats, the enemy is still very obdurate. In the process of their protracted resistance, the longer they fight, the stronger the South Vietnamese people become, while the longer the enemy fights, the greater difficulties he encounters . . . .Therefore, national liberation wars must allow some time, and a long time, to be able to crush the aggressive desire of the colonialist imperialists and to win final victory.

Giap also warned the US against invading the North and hinted that North Vietnam might call on other communist countries should the US undertake such action:

> We have adequately prepared ourselves and are ready to deal destructive blows at the US

imperialists if they adventurously send infantry troops to the North. If they expand the war to the North, the war would become more complex, because by attacking the North, they would be attacking the mainland of a member country of the socialist camp.

Although maintaining that "the southern people, as well as the people in our entire country," were "ready to carry on the resistance for five, ten, twenty, or more years" and were "firmly confident of victory," Giap's analysis of the war seemed more sober and cautious than North Vietnamese assessments of the war made during the spring and summer of 1966. Giap devoted considerable attention to the need to "increase . . . fighting capacity" and saw the "problem of improving troop quality and developing fighting power" as a "task of strategic significance":

> The problem of improving our armed forces' quality must be raised in a comprehensive way, embracing all fields: political, military, logistics, ideology, organization, and efficiency. We must implement this policy in all three categories of troops – regulars, local troops, and self-defense militia men, in all military services and branches, and in all military organs at all echelons . . .

Specific tasks outlined by Giap included: (1) the heightening of political and ideological levels of officers and men, (2) the heightening of the technical and tactical levels of the armed forces, (3) the improvement of organizations and equipment so as to fit them to combat requirements, (4) the streamlining of party and mass organizations, (5) the improvement of the material life of the armed forces, and (6) the further development and improvement of the efficiency of cadres at all levels.

Numerous *Nhan Dan* editorials and Vietnam News Agency broadcasts during 1967 also stressed the need to improve the quantity and quality of the armed forces and warned against being subjective or "satisfied." Emphasis was also placed on the task of more closely associating the national economy with national defense and on the problem of "mobilizing maximum manpower" in view of increasing requirements.

While summarizing the need to make "greater efforts to improve quality and quantity in all fields and develop fighting power," instructions from the Vietnam People's Army Directorate for Political Affairs focused on the theory that "political strength is the basis of military strength" and called on party organizations to play a decisive role in building and consolidating local military units, while at the same time improving their own organization and leadership:

> The party leadership decides the class nature, revolutionary nature, and combat objectives of our armed forces. Thus, the party building task so far has always been the fundamental task in the building of our armed forces. . . . The process of building our armed forces is also the process of building and strengthening party leadership and the process of maintaining and thoroughly applying the principles of party leadership over the armed forces. Making the party steady and strong is the main link of the task of heightening the armed forces' quality. Military successes first of all depend on the party's line and leadership in the war and on the building up of the party in the armed forces. Therefore, to build steady and strong regiments, it is first of all necessary to make regiment party committees steady and strong in all fields. (*Quan Doi Nhan Dan*, 21 September.)

Specifically, party directives called for the streamlining of party and mass organizations, the consolidation of party committees and branches in all fields, the recruitment of more party members, the strengthening of the party leadership, the improvement of party education and ideological leadership, and the development of party ranks and improvement of party members, "even during operations and combat," thus enabling party members to "heighten their political level and increase their ability to mobilize the masses."

During 1967 the DRV and VWP continued to stress the four-point stand as outlined by Prime Minister Pham Van Dong on 8 April 1965 as the only acceptable basis for the settlement of the Vietnam war:

> (1.) Recognition of the basic national rights of the Vietnamese people: peace, independence, sovereignty, unity and territorial integrity. According to the Geneva

Agreements, the US Government must withdraw from South Vietnam all US troops, military personnel and weapons of all kinds, dismantle all US military bases there, cancel its "military alliance" with South Vietnam. It must end its policy of intervention and aggression in South Vietnam. According to the Geneva Agreement, the US Government must stop its acts of war against North Vietnam, completely cease all encroachments on the territory and sovereignty of the DRV.

(2.) Pending the peaceful reunification of Vietnam, while Vietnam is still temporarily divided into two zones, the military provisions for the 1954 Geneva Agreements on Vietnam must be strictly respected: the two zones must refrain from joining any military alliance with foreign countries, there must be no foreign military bases, troops and military personnel in their respective territory.

(3.) The internal affairs of South Vietnam must be settled by the South Vietnamese people themselves, in accordance with the programme of the NLFSV, without any foreign interference.

(4.) The peaceful reunification of Vietnam is to be settled by the Vietnamese people in both zones, without any foreign interference.

**Strategy and Tactics.** North Vietnamese party statements in 1967 stressed the need for "revolution through violence" and emphasized the international obligations and ties of all "national liberation movements" throughout the world. At no time did the North Vietnamese express any support for a policy of "peaceful coexistence." In an article in the North Vietnamese Army paper *Quan Doi Nhan Dan* (22 July) Brigadier-General Le Quang Dao, an alternate member of the VWP Central Committee, declared that the "two main revolutionary forces of the world, the socialist force and the national liberation force," could succeed only through people's wars and armed struggle and that there was in fact no other way for them to liberate themselves.

The VWP and Vietnamese People's Army (VPA) not only advocated people's war, but also claimed to have evolved new tactical methods and thus "developed people's war to an unprecedentedly high degree:"

> The people's war outlook of our party is a new creative development of the Marxist-Leninist ideas of revolutionary violence and revolutionary war. It is the most fundamental concept of our party's military line. It shows the revolutionary quality and legitimacy of the war, the decisive role of the masses of people, and the leadership role of the party in the war. . . .
>
> Being an advanced scientific study in revolutionary wars, our theory on the people's war is clearly superior to any reactionary military "theory" of the bourgeoisie and all misleading concepts. The people's war line of our party has been proved to be very correct by the facts of revolutionary armed struggle in our country.

A subsequent statement by Vo Nguyen Giap, Minister of National Defense and member of the VWP Central Committee and Politburo, noted: "Creatively applying Marxism-Leninism, our party has not only led our people from victory to victory in the anti-US national salvation struggle, but also has contributed to enriching the theoretical treasure of Marxism-Leninism. . . . The party has set forth the invincible and creative people's war line. Our people have invented clever and unique tactics and have surmounted thousands of difficulties to win great victories." (Hanoi Domestic Service, 20 February.)

While stressing the importance of people's war, the North Vietnamese have also focused on the need to "coordinate cleverly" military struggle with political struggle:

> A striking characteristic of the people's war in our country at present is that even within the limited war, the fight against the enemy on all fronts — military, political, cultural, diplomatic, and so forth — is waged at the same time, in which the military and the political struggles are the most basic forms of struggle. The military and political struggles are closely coordinated, assist each other, and encourage each other to develop. This coordination is a law of the revolutionary struggle in our country. It is also an initiative of our people in the process of the protracted revolutionary war. (Giap, "Big Victory, Great Task.")

The July 1967 issue of *Hoc Tap* carried an article by Nguyen Khanh Toan, an alternate member of the VWP Central Committee, which stated:

> Political struggle is inevitable in the preparation for armed struggle. Armed struggle can break out, survive, and develop only on the basis of political struggle. It is precisely through political struggle that the people are gradually enlightened, organized, and trained. Only when both the progressive masses and the intermediary masses feel that they can no longer live their present life and that they are ready to sacrifice themselves for the revolution will there be conditions for waging armed struggle. To reach this level, the masses must pass through political struggle. . . .
>
> When the armed struggle is started, political struggle and armed struggle are associated to weaken and annihilate the enemy's forces and to prevent and develop our own forces. If the effects of political struggle are developed to a high degree along with the high development of the effects of armed struggle, and if these two struggles are cleverly associated, it is possible to maintain and develop the armed struggle under all circumstances, crush all the enemy's plots, and discover ways to efficaciously cope with all tactics, techniques, and weapons of the enemy in order to annihilate him.

The article further elaborated the nature of political struggle, asserting: "The experience of our revolution shows that the united front is the pivotal factor in assuring revolutionary transformations." It continued:

> There must be an extensive and steady national united front and a powerful political force . . . The national united front is one of the decisive factors which dictate the success of the revolution and the people's war in our country. In the revolution and war against imperialism and its lackeys, to be successful the revolutionary forces must be large and strong. Thus, the creation of a widespread and steady national united front becomes very important. The front must be placed under the leadership of the party of the working class and it must be based on the alliance between the workers and peasants. At the same time, it must rally every patriotic force, national minority, religion, and political party and must direct its revolutionary efforts against imperialism and its lackeys. From the front, we organize strong and steady political and armed forces.

In an interview with a correspondent from *Granma,* the central organ of the Cuban Communist Party, Truong Chinh, a member of the VWP Central Committee, pointed out that "to defeat the imperialists and their henchmen, one must create and foster the following factors of victory":

> (1.) There must be a Marxist-Leninist party to give unified leadership to the revolutionary struggle of the people, lead the people from the national democratic people's revolution to the socialist revolution. . .
>
> (2.) To unite all people in a national united front against imperialism and colonialism, this front must embrace all strata of the people, rely on the basis of the worker-peasant alliance, and receive the leadership of a Marxist-Leninist party. . . .
>
> (3.) As they make revolution, to resist imperialism the people must at a certain stage organize people's armed forces, which must be placed under the education and close leadership of a Marxist-Leninist party . . .
>
> (4.) It is necessary to strengthen international solidarity to resist imperialism and win the sympathy, support, and assistance of the socialist countries and the peace-loving and justice-loving people all over the world, including the people in the aggressor country. . . . (Vietnam News Agency, 11 January.)

North Vietnam's combined strategy of people's war and political struggle is also reflected in its attitude toward the role of negotiations, which was outlined in one of the captured documents. As explained by Nguyen Van Vinh,

> . . . Fighting while negotiating is aimed at opening another front with a view to making the puppet army more disintegrated, stimulating and developing the enemy's internal contradictions and thereby making him more isolated in order to deprive him of propoganda weapons, isolate him further, and made a number of people who

misunderstand the Americans clearly see their nature.

. . . Fighting continues until the emergence of a situation where both sides are fighting indecisively. Then a situation where fighting and negotiations are conducted simultaneously may emerge. In fighting while negotiating, the side which fights more strongly will compel the adversary to accept its conditions. Considering the comparative balance of forces, the war proceeds through the following stages: the fighting stage, the stage of fighting while negotiating, negotiating and signing of agreements.

Whether or not the war will resume after the conclusion of agreements depends upon the comparative balance of forces. If we are capable of dominating the adversary, the war will not break out again, and conversely, therefore, fighting while negotiating also represents a principal step in the resolution of the war. Thus a situation where fighting and negotiating are conducted simultaneously emerges . . .

. . . If we conduct negotiations while fighting vigorously, we can also take advantage of the opportunity to step up the political struggle, military proselytizing, and activities in the cities. Thus we will take advantage of the opportunity offered by the negotiations to step up further our military attacks, political struggle, and military proselytizing.

General Vinh also pointed out: "It is possible that the North conducts negotiations while the South continues fighting, and that the South also participates in the negotiations while continuing to fight."

**International Views and Positions.** North Vietnam's relations with other countries are primarily determined by whether or not — as well as to what extent — the individual country and party supports the Vietnam war. During 1967 considerable emphasis was placed on the improvement of North Vietnamese propaganda abroad, and on justifying the right of the Vietnamese to aid from other communist countries by presenting the Vietnam war as a contribution to the worldwide revolutionary struggle and as an example and inspiration to "liberation struggles" elsewhere in the world.

As stated by Le Duan, First Secretary of the VWP,

By fighting against the US aggressors, our people aim not only at recapturing their holy national rights, but also at protecting the entire socialist camp and contributing to stepping up the revolutionary movement of the proletariat and the oppressed people the world over. The US imperialists' defeat in Vietnam will be a very great defeat, causing the bankruptcy of their worldwide strategy.

The same point was given considerable emphasis by Giap in "Big Victory, Great Task," in which he noted: "This struggle is also of great international significance, because it contributes to protecting the socialist bloc and advancing the movement to liberate the peoples and to protect the peace of the world. It is a great contribution of our Vietnamese people to the common revolutionary struggle of the people of the world to oppose imperialism . . . "

Giap also noted international support for the Vietnamese people: "The prestige of our resistance has been increasingly enhanced and the support of the world's peoples for our people has become more and more vigorous. No national liberation struggle in history has ever obtained as much vigorous and comprehensive sympathy and support from the world's peoples as does our people's anti-US national salvation resistance today."

In an interview published 2 July in *Volksstimme,* the central organ of the pro-Soviet Communist Party of Austria, Nguyen Duy Trinh, Deputy Premier, Minister of Foreign Affairs, and member of the VWP Politburo, noted:

The DRV is a socialist country. The American air raids and shelling from the sea constitute an extraordinarily grave challenge to all countries of the socialist camp. In the spirit of proletarian internationalism, the parties and governments of the socialist countries give us — in line with their possibilities — political and moral support as well as material aid, aimed at strengthening the economic potential and the defensive power of our country . . .

The Vietnam Workers' Party, the Government of the DRV, and the entire Vietnamese people appreciate the valuable and effective aid of all socialist countries to an extraordinarily high degree. We consider it a decisive factor for our victory. In order to show themselves worthy of this encouragement and aid, the people of Vietnam vow to wage their resistance struggle against the American aggression and for national liberation until final victory, for they defend not only their independence and freedom, but also the southeastern outpost of the socialist camp.

At the same time, he remarked, the North Vietnamese recognized the need to "uphold the self-reliant spirit while trying to win the sympathy and support of the socialist bloc and the people of the world.":

The revolution of each country is the private affair of the people of the country concerned. However, it cannot be separated from the world revolution. The revolution in our country led by the proletariat is an indispensable element of the international proletarian revolution. Thus, to prosecute the revolutionary war in our country, our people must rely mainly on our own forces, but the support and assistance of the socialist bloc and the world is very vital. However, only when our people fully exploit our own forces can this support and assistance, both spiritual and material, of the people of other countries show its effect.

On 19 July a high-level DRV delegation led by Le Thanh Nghi, Vice-Premier and member of the VWP Central Committee and Politburo, left on an eleven-week visit to various Asian and East European communist capitals to meet with party leaders and to negotiate non-refund military and economic aid agreements for 1968. Agreements were signed with Communist China, North Korea, Rumania, Bulgaria, Cuba, the Soviet Union, Hungary, Poland and Czechoslovakia. In addition, the DRV Ambassador to East Berlin signed an agreement on East German aid, an Albanian delegation visited Hanoi, where aid agreements were signed, and a protocol on goods exchange and payments was signed with Mongolia.*

Virtually no details were disclosed regarding the value of military and economic aid to be provided. Similar agreements were signed last year, with the exception of Mongolia, with which only a protocol on goods exchange and payments was signed, in comparison with last year's agreements which also called for nonrefundable military and economic aid. In addition, the 1967 agreements with Communist China and Cuba made no mention of military aid. Although no details are available, reports indicate that the agreements provided for overall increases over last year's aid. The Soviet Union did, however, disclose a few details on the nature of Soviet aid to the DRV, noting that it would deliver "aircraft, antiaircraft and rocket equipment, artillery and small arms, ammunition and other military equipment, vehicles, oil products, ferrous and non-ferrous metals, foodstuffs, chemical fertilizers, medicines, and other goods necessary for a further increase in defense capacity and for the development of the national economy" (*TASS*, 23 September).

Other multilateral contacts included an appeal issued by the Vietnam Federation of Trade Unions on 12 July, the thirteenth anniversary of the signing of the 1954 Geneva Agreements on Vietnam, calling on the "international working class and all laboring people in the world to step up their struggle for an end to the US war of aggression in Vietnam." Specifically, the appeal called on "workers and people throughout the world" to

(1) Step up their propaganda activities, so as to make known to the workers' and trade-union movement in all countries the monstrous crimes perpetuated by the US imperialists . . . and to make known the just stand, the stand of independence and peace as embodied in the four-point stand of the DRV government and the five point statement of the National Liberation Front of South Vietnam.

---

*The protocol with Mongolia was signed by Nghiem Ba Duc, deputy head of the delegation and DRV Deputy Minister of Foreign Trade. Agreements concluded with Hungary, Czechoslovakia and Poland were also signed by Nghiem Ba Duc, while Le Thanh Nghi led the DRV party delegation to Peking to attend the 1 October National Day celebrations.

(2) Further promote the mass movement to protest against the dirty war of aggression being waged by the US imperialists in Vietnam and to demand the United States end its war of aggression . . .

(3) Launch a wide movement to boycott the loading, unloading, and transporting of US goods and armaments bound for South Vietnam; [stop] the production of goods, arms, and ammunition of the United States in the service of its aggressive war in Vietnam; protest against the governments of other countries which are collaborating with the United States in the war of aggression in Vietnam, and take all other suitable and feasible forms of action beneficial to the just struggle of the Vietnamese people. (Vietnam News Agency, 12 July.)

**International Conferences and Front Organizations.** While stressing that "the Vietnam Workers' Party and the Vietnamese people" were doing their utmost to "contribute to the consolidation and strengthening of the unity and power of the socialist camp" and "to enhance solidarity among the international communist and worker's movement on the basis of Marxism-Leninism and proletarian internationalism," the VWP expressed no support for the convening of a world communist conference. The VWP did not send a delegation to the Budapest conference in February 1968, even though it had sent delegations to the 1957 and 1960 meetings and did send an important delegation to the fiftieth anniversary celebrations in Moscow.

The North Vietnamese responded favorably to the Karlovy Vary conference of European communist parties held in April 1967. A *Nhan Dan* editorial on 28 April stated: "The conference of communist and workers' parties of Europe held in Karlovy Vary on 24-26 April is an important event in the international communist and workers movement." It went on to stress that the appeal of the conference in support of the Vietnamese people's "anti-US national salvation struggle" was a "living manifestation of the militant solidarity binding the European working class and people to [the Vietnamese] working class and people."

The North Vietnamese also expressed considerable support for the first conference of the Organization of Latin American Solidarity (OLAS), held in Havana from 30 July to 10 August. The conference was attended by a North Vietnamese delegation consisting of Hoang Quoc Viet, Chairman of the delegation, member of the VWP Central Committee, and Chairman of the Vietnam Federation of Trade Unions; Tran Chi Hien, Vice-Chairman of the delegation, Vice-Chairman of the Vietnam Workers' Party Foreign Relations Board, and member of the Vietnamese Afro-Asian People's Solidarity Committee; Nguyen Ngoc Truong, Deputy Secretary of the Nam Dinh Municipal Vietnam Workers' Party Committee; Tran Thi Ly; Trin Ngoc Thai; Mo Thanh; Phan Duy Toan; and Nguyen Dinh Bin. On 31 July Ho Chi Minh sent a message of greetings to the conference reaffirming North Vietnam's "complete solidarity with the just struggle of the Latin American people."

Before adjourning, the conference unanimously adopted a resolution declaring that the "heroic struggle waged by the Vietnamese people" constituted a "front-line trench in the world-wide and anti-imperialist struggle, whose successes are a tremendous contribution to the total destruction of imperialism and whose example of heroism and sacrifice is raising the level of consciousness of struggle of the popular masses to the highest places, and effectively encourages the revolutionary struggle of other peoples, especially in Asia, Africa and Latin America."

During 1967 the North Vietnamese received expressions of support and solidarity from virtually all of the communist front organizations. Specific contacts during 1967 included a visit in early February by a delegation of the World Council of Peace, led by Mme Isabelle Blume; a visit in late June by a delegation of the World Federation of Trade Unions, led by Pierre Gensous, Deputy Secretary-General; and a delegation of the Afro-Asian Latin American People's Solidarity Organization led by its Secretary-General, Osmani Cienfuegos. At the invitation of the Afro-Asian People's Solidarity Organization (AAPSO), a week of solidarity with Vietnam was begun on 13 March. For its part, North Vietnam sent a delegation led by Do Van Hien, Secretary of the Vietnam Students Union, to attend the Ninth Congress of the International Union of Students in Mongolia.

**The VWP and the Sino-Soviet Dispute.** The VWP continued in 1967 to assert a policy of nonalignment and independence in the Sino-Soviet dispute. Considerable emphasis was placed on the originality of the VWP in ideological and military matters, with Pham Van Dong, Prime Minister and member of the VWP Politburo, noting:

> . . . Marxism-Leninism is not a dogma. It is a guide for action. The question is how to apply this theory to the concrete conditions of each country. There lies the whole question and it is a terribly difficult thing.
>
> . . . It is up to the revolutionary parties that adhere to the doctrine of Marx and Lenin to use it well to solve their always complex problems. That is what we have been doing all along. That is what we are doing for example at this stage of our history in order to fight and defeat American aggression. That is what we are doing, and are trying to do better to build socialism in our country, according to the concrete conditions in Vietnam and the genius of our people. In this sense, one may speak of originality. . . .
>
> Precisely because it is a guide and method, the theory of Marx and Lenin is more than ever full of life in our epoch of great revolutionary upheavals. It is being incessantly enriched with new contributions, with the gains of the revolutionary struggle of the proletariat and the world peoples. (Interview with *Le Nouvel Observateur,* broadcast by VNA, 18 November.)

In an interview with a Japanese correspondent, Nguyen Duy Trinh, Foreign Minister and member of the VWP Politburo, stated:

> . . . The present division of opinion within the socialist camp is only temporary. I believe the time will come when such a confrontation will be settled. And when that time comes, I believe the socialist camp will be united more strongly than before. I think such confrontation and differences are like a dark cloud hiding the sun temporarily. The sun will appear again. I don't think differences within the socialist camp will lead to the destruction of socialism.

When asked about the ideological issues involved in the dispute, Trinh reaffirmed North Vietnam's support for the 1957 and 1960 declarations and added: "We know well from experience how the lack of unity brings about various difficulties. Therefore, we are determined to unite and firmly believe that the socialist camp will restore its unity."

An unpublicized speech by Nguyen Van Vinh in a captured document, however, pointed out:

> On the one hand, we find that international support is fairly good, and, on the other hand, we are worried. The reason for this is that we are fighting the enemy at a time when there is a lack of unity within the socialist camp. This is a reality. Disunity still exists. We cannot just sit by and wait until the socialist camp is united to achieve decisive victory. . . .
>
> Since the downfall of Khrushchev, the Soviet Union has provided us with much assistance in all fields. Three-fourths of the weapons sent to the South have been received from the Soviet camp. Half of the South's budget has been provided by our camp, mainly China. The quantity of weapons has been so large that we could not transport all of them. . . .
>
> Nevertheless, we are not satisfied in certain respects. If there were no disunity within the socialist camp, our successes would have been greater yet. We also find that if we did not obtain the great assistance from our camp, we would not have been able to achieve such great successes. Our party has evaluated highly the support of the socialist camp. If we do not try to gain the support of the socialist camp, we will be guilty of our duty to our people. We cannot accept the line of this country or that country in order to obtain aid, nor can we accept aid from one country without accepting aid from another, because otherwise we will be guilty before the entire camp, and before our people. . . .
>
> At a time when there is a polemic among various countries, we must have an independent line. We must be confident in no one but our own party. We advocate

opposing revisionism, and, at the same time, we must take precautionary measures against dogmatism and must constantly preserve international solidarity.

Ideological considerations aside, basic facts of geography and economic necessity dictate that the North Vietnamese maintain a delicate balance between Moscow and Peking. Although Hanoi has endorsed the call for a world-wide united front — which China denounced as a Soviet attempt to isolate her — and although Hanoi has refused to join Peking in denouncing the USSR for "revisionism" in domestic and foreign affairs, Communist China has continued to extend military and economic support to North Vietnam. China's aid to the DRV rose from about $110 million in 1966 to about $215 million in 1967, with the military aid portion rising from about $50 million to $85 million; on the other hand, Soviet aid rose from approximately $520 million in 1966 to an estimated $720 million in 1967; military aid figures were approximately $385 million in 1966 and $520 million in 1967 (*New York Times,* 5 November). While still maintaining an independent position in the Sino-Soviet dispute and still master of its own military strategy, it is likely that Moscow's influence in North Vietnam increased to some extent during 1967.

Communist China continued to assert that the Soviet Union was not rendering sufficient aid to North Vietnam and accused the Soviets of sending out-of-date and obsolete pieces of equipment. The Soviet Union countered by charging Communist China with obstructing the transit of Soviet goods and with seizing Soviet shipments for their own purposes. The North Vietnamese commented:

Of late, American and western news agencies have spread fallacious reports on the transit of aid goods from the Soviet Union and other socialist countries to Vietnam through China. VNA [Vietnam News Agency] is authorized to declare that these reports spread by US and western news agencies are sheer fabrications aimed at very wicked purposes. The DRV government has many times stated that China has wholeheartedly helped transport to Vietnam adequately and according to schedule the aid goods from the Soviet Union and other socialist countries. (Vietnam News Agency, 28 February.)

According to informed sources, an agreement was reached in mid-February whereby the North Vietnamese would take "principal control" of Soviet military equipment at the Soviet border, thereby making the subsequent transit of goods a matter of concern for the Chinese and Vietnamese and thus eliminating friction between Moscow and Peking.

Moscow continued to warn its listeners of "the danger of Mao's policy toward neighboring countries." In a 13 July broadcast to the Albanians but obviously intended for the Vietnamese as well, Moscow warned that China was attempting to seize the "leading role in regions where the national liberation movement flourishes." Moscow also reminded Hanoi of the lessons to be learned from Indonesia and Burma and cautioned that China's policies were unreliable and often caused unnecessary loss of life and the weakening and isolation of the communist party.

Moscow Radio in the same broadcast attacked the Chinese attitude toward "progressive forces in neighboring countries":

An analysis of the policies and tactics of the Chinese leaders shows that, without thinking much about it, they are sacrificing the interests of the progressive force in these countries in order to secure for themselves the role of leader of the national liberation movements, particularly in Asia. Their policies and tactics have nothing to do with Marxism-Leninism and proletarian internationalism.

Outside the context of the Vietnam war, government and party contacts between the DRV and Communist China centered primarily on exchanges between cultural delegations, friendship associations, and trade unions. North Vietnam almost completely ignored internal Chinese developments, and the cultural revolution has only been mentioned in those North Vietnamese publications subject to Chinese influence.

Reports indicate that two important North Vietnamese delegations may have visited China in either late January or early February and that DRV Foreign Minister and VWP Politburo member Nguyen Duy Trinh may have visited Communist China on his way to the Seventh Congress of the East

German Socialist Unity Party in East Berlin. The DRV also sent a party and government delegation led by Le Thanh Nghi, Vice-Premier and VWP Politburo member, to attend the National Day celebrations in Peking.

The Chinese Communists evinced considerable concern that the North Vietnamese might abandon the intention to "fight until final victory" and decide to negotiate a solution to the Vietnam war. Various efforts were made by the Chinese to force the North Vietnamese to choose sides in the ideological dispute, as indicated by the demonstration of Chinese students outside the Soviet Embassy in Hanoi on 30 January and by an editorial in the Peking *Jen-min Jih-pao* which coincided with the arrival of Le Thanh Nghi and declared: "The struggle between the two lines on the Vietnam question is the concentrated expression of the acuteness of the international class struggle. To oppose imperialism it is imperative to oppose the counterrevolutionary line of the Soviet revisionist group. There is no middle road in the struggle between the two lines."

Although continuing to maintain an independent stand in the dispute, *Hoc Tap*, the party theoretical journal, carried in its May issue an article which nominally was a theoretical attack on the qualities of communist party leaders, but which in fact appeared to be an attack on Mao Tse-tung and the policies associated with him. *Hoc Tap* warned of leaders who had "lost sight of reality" and who failed to realize that "man makes history not in accordance with his subjective wishes but in compliance with objective rules and in definite historical situations":

> Human society develops according to objective rules. Only by grasping the objective rules of society can man carry out his activities in a voluntary manner, anticipate the evolution of history, and achieve success in his revolutionary task. It is not true that anyone in an oppressed class can identify the objective rules of history. Only leaders who are capable, tested in revolutionary struggle, and clear-sighted can identify these objective rules and lead the masses' struggle to success. If a certain leader, at a certain time, regardless of the objective rules and the objective situation, acts in accordance with his subjective wishes, he will not be able to avoid all failing or falling into a situation in which every move will be in vain like Don Quixote struggling against the windmill.

Although the VWP and DRV have generally avoided commenting on domestic affairs in China and the cultural revolution, the *Hoc Tap* article strongly suggested that the North Vietnamese were extremely critical of Mao's attempt to use the cultural revolution to bypass the normal party apparatus and undermine the position of prominent officials:

> A leader of the working class does not separate the working class from its vanguard, the communist party. The communist party is "the teacher, the leader" of the working class. In the period of resolute revolutionary struggle and in the period of socialist revolution and proletarian dictatorship, the role of the communist party and the party's leading cadres becomes particularly important. In these periods, the communist party and its leading cadres assume heavy responsibilities to organize and exert leadership over millions of people to attack the enemy, overthrow him, and build and protect the new social system. The fact that the revolutionary struggle proceeds in a fierce manner and that the situation constantly changes requires clear-sighted, resolute, and timely leadership of the party's cadres, primarily the party's leaders.

The *Hoc Tap* article also paid considerable attention to the question of the correct leadership of Marxist-Leninist parties and again indirectly attacked Mao:

> Socialist society is built according to plans. This makes it necessary to strengthen the leadership of the communist party and of the state or proletarian dictatorship, especially of the leaders. Correct leadership determines the success of the activities of millions of people. The leadership's errors have serious consequences in the revolutionary task.
>
> To insure correct leadership and prevent and restrict errors, the Marxist-Leninist parties set forth the principle of collective leadership. Only by exerting collective leadership can one-sided and erroneous decisions be prevented . . .
>
> A leader of a Marxist-Leninist party associates himself with the group of the party's leadership organ, obeys this group, fully implements the party's platform and rules, and

strictly complies with the party's principles governing its activities. If a leader commits errors, yet refuses to correct them and insistently maintains them, he cannot keep his leadership role forever. Therefore, a leader of a Marxist-Leninist party always sets examples of self-criticism and listens to the masses' opinions and criticisms.

*Hoc Tap* also criticized the personality cult: "We respect and love our leader, but we do not deify him. Deification of a leader will lower the position of the masses of people and even the leader himself."

Although the article did not specifically refer to Mao by name, it is certainly applicable to him and apparently was written with him in mind. The *Hoc Tap* article did not necessarily indicate, however, that Hanoi might be moving toward closer alignment with the Soviet Union. In North Vietnam's customary manner of attempting to maintain a balance between Moscow and Peking, the same article indirectly criticized elements of the Soviet leadership when it included several quotations from Stalin and noted: "Along with struggling against the erroneous tendency to deify the leader and to deny or lower the role of the masses of people in the revolution, we must also struggle against the anarchistic tendency to deny all his powers and to use the pretext of 'opposing the personality cult' to deny the role of the leader in the revolution."

Although the *Hoc Tap* article may have been meant as a warning to the Chinese it did not prevent the North Vietnamese from hailing China's hydrogen bomb explosion on 19 June as an "important contribution to the struggle of the world's people for peace, national independence, and socialism." The customary messages of congratulations were also exchanged on the forty-sixth anniversary of the founding of the Chinese Communist Party (1 July), the fortieth anniversary of the founding of the Chinese People's Liberation Army (1 August), the twenty-second anniversary of the founding of the DRV (2 September), and the eighteenth anniversary of the founding of the People's Republic of China (1 October).

**Soviet Union.** North Vietnam and the Soviet Union exchanged the customary visits of friendship associations, trade-union organizations, and cultural delegations as well as congratulatory messages on occasions such as the twenty-second anniversary of the founding of the DRV. Reports indicate that top-ranking North Vietnamese leaders secretly visited the Soviet Union in March, in addition to a visit by DRV Foreign Minister Nguyen Duy Trinh while on his way to the Seventh Congress of the German Socialist Unity Party, in April, and a visit to the Soviet Union by a DRV Government and party delegation from 24 September to 10 October.

Both the North Vietnamese government and party devoted considerable attention to the celebration of the fiftieth anniversary of the October Revolution. On 29 March the Central Committee of the VWP and an enlarged session of the Presidium of the Vietnam Fatherland Front established a committee to organize anniversary celebrations. The following day, *Nhan Dan* hailed the Soviet Union, calling it a "powerful and prosperous socialist country now building the material and technical basis of socialism," and noting that "the outstanding achievements recorded in the Soviet Union . . . have greatly inspired the laboring people throughout the world." *Nhan Dan* was careful, however, to balance these statements with praise of Communist China by describing the Chinese revolution as "the event of greatest significance since the October Revolution."

Other North Vietnamese preparations included numerous VWP directions calling on all levels of the party, administration, army, and the people to "celebrate the fiftieth anniversary of the Great October Revolution in a manner worthy of its great significance," and a decision to hold a month-long emulation drive in September to "record achievement in production and fighting in honor of the fiftieth anniversary of the Great October Socialist Revolution."

DRV party and government delegations to the celebrations in Moscow included: (1) a joint government, party, and National Assembly delegation consisting of Le Duan, First Secretary of the VWP and member of its Politburo, as head of the delegation; Vo Nguyen Giap, Vice-Premier, Minister of National Defense, and member of the VWP Politburo; Nguyen Duy Trinh, Minister of Foreign Affairs and member of the VWP Politburo; Chu Van Tan, Vice-Chairman of the Standing Committee of the DRV National Assembly and member of the VWP Politburo; Hoang Tun, editor in chief of *Nhan Dan* and alternate member of the VWP Central Committee; and Nguyen Tho Chanh, DRV

Ambassador to the Soviet Union and alternate member of the VWP Central Committee; (2) a delegation of the Vietnam-Soviet Union Friendship Association led by its Vice-Chairman Mme Nguyen Thi Thap, member of the VWP Central Committee, Vice-Chairman of the Standing Committee of the DRV National Assembly, and member of the Presidium of the Vietnam Fatherland Front Central Committee, and President of the Vietnam Women's Union, whose delegation she also headed; (3) a delegation of the Vietnam Federation of Trade Unions led by its Vice-President, Nguyen Cong Hoa; (4) a delegation of the Vietnam Labor Youth Union led by its First Secretary, Vu Quang; and (5) a delegation of the Hanoi Committee of the VWP and the Hanoi Administrative Committee, led by Tran Duy Hung, Chairman of the Hanoi Administrative Committee.

Le Duan, VWP First Secretary, delivered a major speech at a joint meeting of the CPSU Central Committee and the Supreme Soviet of the USSR and the RSFSR in which he noted that "the October Revolution had such historical significance that no other revolution before or after it could be compared to it." The focus of attention, however, was on an article written for *Pravda* by Ho Chi Minh (see *Documents*).

While paying tribute to the Soviet Union, Ho Chi Minh was careful not to antagonize Communist China. After praising the October Revolution by noting that "there has been no other revolution in the history of mankind of such tremendous and profound importance," he described the Chinese revolution as the next event of "great international importance," followed by the "victories of the national liberation and socialist revolutions in Poland, Bulgaria, the GDR, Hungary, Rumania, Czechoslovakia, Albania, Mongolia, Korea, Cuba, and Vietnam." In addition to listing the seizure of power in other countries in Europe and Asia out of chronological order — they chronologically preceded the Chinese Communist assumption of power — Ho made no reference whatever to Yugoslavia in his enumeration of countries where communism has triumphed, apparently in an effort to avoid antagonizing the Chinese.

Ho Chi Minh also outlined the various lessons to be drawn from the October Revolution, noting that "only the leadership of a party which is able creatively to apply Marxism-Leninism to the concrete conditions of its country can lead the national liberation and socialist revolution to victory." Emphasis was also placed on the need to "unite all revolutionary and progressive forces on a broad front," with Ho concluding that "in the present epoch, the national revolution constitutes an inseparable component of the world proletarian revolution, and the national liberation revolution can be crowned with complete success only if it develops into a socialist revolution." Although only a formulation of already established Marxist-Leninist principles, it was noteworthy that Ho was so explicit in these statements which appeared to undermine the position taken by the National Liberation Front of South Vietnam that the NLFSV is a free agent capable of maintaining its independence from the North in the event of victory.

On 4 November, TASS, the Soviet press agency, announced that Ho Chi Minh had been awarded the Order of Lenin, the highest Soviet decoration. On 14 November, however, Ho announced that he would postpone accepting the award until Vietnam is "liberated." Vice President Ton Duc Thang was also awarded the Order of Lenin.

**Other Party Contacts.** Although most of North Vietnam's attention was focused on the Vietnam war and on relations with the Soviet Union and Communist China, contacts were also maintained with other communist parties and national liberation movements, and with virtually all of these parties and movements declaring their support for the "Vietnamese people's struggle," the four-point stand of the DRV government, and the five-point resolution of the NLFSV.

**Asia.** North Vietnam's activities in Asia have focused primarily on Cambodia, Laos, and Thailand. Reports indicate that the Laotian Neo Lao Hak Xat (NLHX), through which the communist Pasachone Lao (Laotian People's Party) operates, receives considerable economic, military, and administrative aid from the DRV, including some 30,000 to 40,000 North Vietnamese troops reportedly operating in Laos. Although the presence of North Vietnamese regulars has been repeatedly denied by the communists, it appears that most of the communist offensives in Laos are led by North Vietnamese and strengthened by North Vietnamese troops, and that the DRV provides political cadres down to the district level in the communist-controlled provinces of Laos.

During 1967 the DRV continued to maintain its contacts with the NLHX. Congratulatory messages were exchanged on the anniversary of the founding of the DRV, the Laotian National Day, the eighteenth anniversary of the founding of the Laotian People's Liberation Army, and the anniversary of the founding of the Vietnamese People's Army.

On 16 March the NLHX Committee of Afro-Asian Solidarity, in conjunction with a visiting AALAPSO delegation, inaugurated a week of solidarity with the Vietnamese people, and on 12 October, the "Day of International Solidarity with the Laotian People" and the Laotian day of independence, a delegation of the NLHX and the Laotian Afro-Asian Solidarity Committee visited North Vietnam at the invitation of the Vietnam Fatherland Front Central Committee and the Vietnam Afro-Asian Solidarity Committee. Both the NLHX delegation, headed by Tiao Souk Vongsak of the NLHX Central Committee, and the Laotian Afro-Asian Solidarity Committee delegation, headed by Colonel Deuane Sounarath, met with Hoang Quoc Viet, member of the Central Committee of the Vietnam Workers' Party and the Central Committee of the Vietnam Fatherland Front, and Ton Quang Phiet, Chairman of the Vietnam Afro-Asian Solidarity Committee.

An additional NLHX delegation visited Hanoi in November on its way back from a visit to Cuba at the invitation of the Executive Secretariat of AALAPSO.

North Vietnam has also given substantial aid to communist insurgents in Thailand. During 1967 North Vietnam raised its diplomatic representation in Cambodia to ambassadorial level as a result of Prince Sihanouk's decision to extend the DRV de jure recognition following its recognition of Cambodia's borders, and hailed the second anniversary of the Thai Patriotic Front by noting that "the Vietnamese people warmly support the Thai people's struggle for independence, democracy and progress, which is part of the common front of the Indochinese peoples against US imperialist aggression."

Contacts between the Vietnam Workers' Party and the Korean Workers' Party consisted mainly of exchanges between various mass organizations, congratulatory telegrams on national holidays, and expressions of mutual support and solidarity.

In early January 1967, four members of the Malayan National Liberation League, a communist-front organization formerly based in Indonesia, who had previously been granted political asylum by the DRV, called on DRV government officials to express their thanks and "warm support and firm belief in the victory of the Vietnamese people's struggle against US aggression and for national salvation." According to a 7 January Vietnam News Agency report, the "Vietnamese hosts . . . wished victory to Malayan patriots, so that the latter might soon join their people at home in struggling for the liberation of their country."

On 23 May *Nhan Dan* carried an article marking the forty-seventh anniversary of the Communist Party of Indonesia (Partai Komunis Indonesia; PKI) hailing the "great contribution of the PKI to the national liberation movement and the worker's movement in Indonesia" and calling on Indonesian officials to "set free those communists still detained and give up their policy of terrorism and repression against the communists and other patriots in Indonesia." In spite of North Vietnamese attacks on the Indonesian government, however, a new Indonesian Ambassador to the DRV, M. Nugroho, was appointed in 1967 and arrived in Hanoi in August.

Other contacts in Asia were primarily restricted to contacts with the NLFSV. Hanoi attacked the South Vietnamese elections as a "farce . . . staged by the US aggressors and their henchmen [which] will not be able to stabilize the Saigon administration, but will only bring about sharper contradictions among puppets of the United States" (*Nhan Dan,* 1 August 1967). The NLFSV hailed the twelfth anniversary of the Vietnam Fatherland Front, and in turn the DRV and VWP devoted considerable attention to the seventh anniversary of the NLFSV (20 December). The DRV also praised the new political program of the NLFSV, adopted in mid-August 1967, noting in a government statement of 2 September:

> The political program is the manifestation of the most clear-sighted, most sensible lines and policies of the National Liberation Front for South Vietnam to resist the US aggressors and save the country . . .
> The Front's political program is a strong and lofty manifestation of the broad-scale

unity between North and South Vietnam and the iron will to reunify the country.

**Mongolia.** At the invitation of the VWP Central Committee and the DRV Government, a party-government delegation of the Mongolian People's Republic (MPR) and the Mongolian People's Revolutionary Party (MPRP) arrived in Hanoi for a visit from 25 to 29 December. The delegation, led by Sonomyn Lubsan, member of the MPRP Politburo and first Vice-Chairman of the MPR Council of Ministers, included Jambyn Jamiyan, member of the MPRP Central Committee and head of the Mongolian "Committee for Support of the Vietnamese People's Struggle"; Puntsagiyn Shagdarsuren, member of the Central Committee and head of the committee's Foreign Relations Board; Mangalyn Dugersuren, member of the MPRP Central Committee and MPR Minister of Foreign Affairs; and Damdinneren Giyn Batta, Mongolian Ambassador to the DRV. According to the joint communique issued at the conclusion of the visit, the delegation met and had "cordial talks" with Ho Chi Minh and Le Duan, and the two delegations had an "exchange of views on problems that interested both sides." After both delegations "resolutely condemned the criminal war of aggression of the US imperialists in Vietnam," the delegations "underscored the necessity of further strengthening the solidarity of the revolutionary forces, the socialist countries, the international communist and workers' movement, and the democratic and peace forces on the basis of struggling against imperialism headed by US imperialism . . . " (Vietnam News Agency, 2 January 1968).

**Africa.** On 18 February *Nhan Dan* carried an article supporting the Sudanese Communist Party (SCP) and people and demanding that the "Sudanese authorities give up their policy of repression against communist and other progressive forces and respect the democratic rights of the Sudanese people." The article went on to condemn the Sudanese authorities for arresting 'Abd al-Khaliq Mahjub, Secretary-General of the SCP, and "many communist members and other progressive personalities," and for preparing a new decree to ban the SCP.

North Vietnam also stressed its support for the "liberation struggle" of the people of Portuguese Guinea and acclaimed the "Week of Solidarity with the African Peoples" (22-28 May) proclaimed by the Afro-Asian Latin American People's Solidarity Organization, adding:

> [The Vietnamese people] sincerely thank the African peoples for the support they have given to their struggle against US aggression for national salvation. With their sincere sentiments of long-standing comrades in arms of the African peoples in the common struggle against common enemies—imperialism and colonialism — our people wish them ever greater victories in their glorious struggle for the complete liberation of Africa.

Declarations of support for North Vietnam also came from the Politburo of the African Party for the Independence of Guinea and Cape Verde, the Politburo of the Congo (Brazzaville) National Revolutionary Movement Party, the Popular Liberation Movement of Angola, the Zimbabwe African People's Union of Rhodesia, the Mozambique Liberation Front, the Popular Idea Party of Equatorial Guinea, the African National Congress of South Africa, and the Southwest Africa People's Organization.

**Middle East War.** North Vietnamese relations with the Middle East centered primarily on the Arab-Israeli conflict. Although apparently no official DRV statement was issued, Ho Chi Minh sent telegrams to Gamal Abdel Nasser and Nureddin al-Atassi, President of Syria, condemning the "Israeli aggression . . . instigated and helped by the imperialists." A *Nhan Dan* editorial of 6 June pointed out:

> The Vietnamese people fully support the just struggle of the UAR, Syria, and other Arab peoples against the Israeli aggressors, henchmen of US and British imperialism. . . .
>
> By instigating Israel to launch aggression against the Arab countries, the US and British imperialists are carrying out a long-nurtured scheme of using Israel as a tool to provoke war and invade the Arab countries, oppose the national independence movement now developing there, and sabotage peace in the Middle and Near East, with a view to enslaving the peoples in this area and appropriating their rich resources — first of all petroleum.

A *Nhan Dan* editorial of 11 July, by pointedly reminding the socialist countries of their "obligation to support the struggle of the Arab peoples, indirectly criticized the Soviet Union for not rendering more active assistance to the Arab countries.

**Latin America.** In 1967 North Vietnam continued to maintain that

... a salient feature of the present situation in many Latin American countries is that the leading forces of the national and democratic movements have more and more closely realized that revolutionary violence in one form or another must be used to deal with the current forms of revolutionary violence unleashed against the people by US imperialism and its puppet regimes (VNA, 14 February).

Outside of declarations of support for the Vietnam war, including a joint declaration of support by the communist and worker's parties of Guatemala, Honduras, El Salvador, Nicaragua, Costa Rica, Panama, and Mexico, North Vietnam's relations with Latin America focused primarily on Cuba. In an interview with a correspondent from *Granma*, the central organ of the Cuban Communist Party, Truong Chinh, Chairman of the Standing Committee of the DRV National Assembly and VWP Politburo member, stated:

The Vietnamese people and the Cuban people are two shock brigades on the front line against US imperialism — the international gendarme and biggest exploiter of the world's people .... The people in our two countries are comrades in arms and brothers who have always stood shoulder to shoulder and are of one kind. We have encouraged, supported, and assisted each other. Tested and tempered in the flames of struggle against US imperialism, the relations between Vietnam and Cuba are certain to consolidate and strengthen continually, and can be broken by no force on earth. (VNA, 11 January.)

A North Vietnamese delegation led by Hoang Quoc Viet, Chairman of the Vietnam Federation of Trade Unions, member of the Presidium of the Vietnam Fatherland Front Central Committee, and member of the VWP Central Committee, attended the Cuban 26th of July anniversary celebrations of the national uprising of Cuba, and on 21 November a Cuban military delegation led by Major Belarmino Castilla Mas, member of the Central Committee of the Cuban Communist Party and Vice-Minister of the Cuban Revolutionary Armed Forces, visited North Vietnam at the invitation of the DRV Ministry of National Defense.

On the occasion of the death of Ernesto "Che" Guevara (9 October 1967), the Central Committee of the Vietnam Worker's Party sent a message of condolence to the Central Committee of the Cuban Communist Party and a *Nhan Dan* editorial commented:

For the people of Cuba and other revolutionary peoples in the world, Comrade Guevara has set a shining example of high revolutionary ardor, staunch fighting spirit, and genuine proletarian internationalism, and of the devotion to the interests of the revolution. ...

Comrade Guevara's death is a loss to the revolutionary movement in Latin America and to the struggle of the world's people against imperialism [and] for national independence, peace, democracy, and socialism. (Quoted in *Vietnam Courier*, 23 October.)

At the North Vietnamese celebrations of the ninth anniversary of the Cuban revolution, Hoang Tung, Chairman of the Vietnam-Cuba Friendship Association and alternate member of the VWP Central Committee, noted: "The struggle against a common enemy has made our two peoples become kith-and-kin brothers and comrades in the same boat."

**North America and Europe.** While continuing to attack the US as the "main enemy of our people and the world's people," and condemning "US imperialist aggression" against Vietnam, North Vietnam devoted considerable attention to the protest movements in the US. "The American demonstrations,'" a *Nhan Dan* article of 17 April stated, "clearly show that the movement against the aggressive war in Vietnam has become a mass movement which is drawing millions of people into a resolute struggle. It has really become a second front against US imperialism right on US soil."

Mme Le Thi Kuyen, Vice-Chairman of the Vietnam Peace Committee, hailed the summer American race riots as a "second front" and also as an "integral part of the movement for national liberation." An article in *Quan Doi Nhan Dan*, however, made a cautionary comment: "We understand the true value of the demonstrations held by Americans who are against the war. We consider this development to be a good thing for us and the American people, but we are far from overestimating these internal contradictions."

North Vietnam paid considerable attention to the Eighteenth Congress of the French Communist Party, which opened on 4 January and to which it sent a delegation led by Nguyen Van Tran, member of the VWP Central Committee and Secretariat. At the closing session of the congress, the French Communist Party adopted a resolution stressing that the "common task" of all "peace-loving and progressive people in the world" was to increase further their support of the DRV, the VWP, and the Vietnamese people in order to force the US government to cease unconditionally its bombing of North Vietnam and recognize the NLFSV as the sole representative of the South Vietnamese people. North Vietnam also hailed the French general elections, calling them a "great and important political success of the [French] Communist Party and the left-wing forces in France." At the invitation of the French General Confederation of Labor, a delegation of the Vietnam Federation of Trade Unions, led by its Chairman, Hoang Quoc Viet, visited France in September and met with Waldeck Rochet Secretary-General of the French Communist Party, and members of the Politburo.

North Vietnam sent a party delegation led by Nguyen Duy Trinh, DRV Foreign Minister and member of the VWP Politburo, to the Seventh Congress of the East German Socialist Unity Party in April, and a DRV delegation attended the International Conference for Peace in Vietnam, held in Stockholm from 6 to 9 July. North Vietnam also continued to hail the Bertrand Russell International War Crimes Tribunal.

In addition to visits connected with the series of economic agreements signed with various East European countries, a Hungarian military delegation visited Hanoi 15-23 May. In May-June, a delegation of the Polish United Workers' Party (PUWP) led by Zenon Kliszko, member of the Politburo and Secretariat of the PUWP Central Committee, and including PUWP Central Committee Secretary, Artur Starewicz, PUWP Central Committee members Edward Babuich and Józef Czesak, and Bodgan Wasilewski, Polish ambassador to the DRV visited in June; and an Albanian delegation visited Hanoi in October.

**Publications.** VWP policy statements and directives are carried primarily in *Nhan Dan* (People's Daily), the daily organ of the VWP Central Committee, whose editor in chief is Hoang Tun; *Hoc Tap* (Studies), the monthly theoretical organ of the VWP Central Committee; and *Quan Doi Nhan Dan* (People's Army), the daily organ of the Vietnamese People's Army. Other major publications include *Tien Phong* (Vanguard), the organ of the Central Committee of the Vietnam Labor Youth Union; *Lao Dong* (Labor), the organ of the Vietnam Federation of Trade Unions; *Cuu Quoc* (National Salvation), the weekly organ of the Central Committee of the Vietnam Fatherland Front; *Doc Lap* (Independence), the weekly organ of the Central Committee of the Democratic Party of Vietnam; and *To Quoc* (Motherland), the bimonthly organ of the Vietnam Socialist Party. International publications include *Vietnam Courrier,* a political weekly published in English and French by the Committee for Cultural Relations with Foreign Countries, and *Vietnam,* an illustrated monthly published in English, French, Russian, Chinese, and Vietnamese.

Party statements are also broadcast by Vietnam News Agency (VNA), headed by Dao Tung.

# VIETNAM: REPUBLIC OF VIETNAM

Formed from the covert network of communist cadres left behind by the Viet Minh when it regrouped north of the 17th parallel in 1954, the People's Revolutionary Party (Dang Nhan Dan Cach Mang; PRP) was formally established 1 January 1962. Its formation was not announced until 18 January 1962, however, when Radio Hanoi quoted a report carried by Liberation News Agency which noted that a new party had been formed as a result of a "conference of Marxist-Leninists meeting in South Vietnam in late December under the guidance of veteran revolutionaries."

The establishment of the PRP was the outcome of the need to provide more effective leadership and organization to the National Liberation Front of South Vietnam (Mat Tran Dan Toc Giai Phong Mien Nam Viet Nam; NLFSV), founded 20 December 1960. A statement circulated among NLFSV cadres declared:

> The revolutionary movement has become stronger and has developed. But it continues to lack organization and leadership. At the lower levels, especially, the organization is not well formed; nor is their leadership system adequate at the district level. For these reasons, it is required that the Revolution in the South be placed under a unified leadership system. . . . The PRP was established to assure that the Revolution in the South will have proper leadership. . . . The party is the highest organization. It is responsible for the leadership of all other organizations, the liberation associations, the mutual aid associations, as well as for the leadership of all the people who will overthrow the old regime for the sake of the new. The party is the paramount organization. (Quoted in Douglas Pike, *Viet Cong* [Cambridge, Mass.: M.I.T. Press], 1966, p. 140.)

Despite both North and South Vietnamese attempts to present the PRP as an "indigenous southern proletarian revolutionary party," it is in fact the southern branch of the Vietnam Workers' Party (Dang Lao Dong Viet Nam; VWP) of North Vietnam. A document captured in May 1962 noted:

> In regard to the foundation of the People's Revolutionary Party of South Vietnam, the creation of this party is only a matter of strategy; this needs to be explained within the party, and to deceive the enemy it is necessary that the new party be given the outward appearance corresponding to a division of the party [Lao Dong] into two and the foundation of a new party, so that the enemy cannot use it in his propaganda.
>
> Within the party, it is necessary to explain that the founding of the People's Revolutionary Party has the purpose of isolating the Americans and the Ngo Dinh Diem regime, and to counter their accusations of an invasion of the South by the North. It is a means of supporting our sabotage of the Geneva Agreements, advancing the plan of invasion of the South, and at the same time permitting the Front for the Liberation of the South to recruit new adherents and to gain the sympathy of nonaligned countries in Southeast Asia.
>
> The People's Revolutionary Party has only the appearance of an independent existence; actually, our party is nothing but the Lao Dong Party of Viet Nam, unified from North to South, under the direction of the Central Executive Committee of the party, the chief of which is President Ho. . . .
>
> During these explanations, take care to keep this strictly secret, especially in South Vietnam, so that the enemy does not perceive our purpose. . . .
>
> Do not put these explanations in party bulletins.

In addition, the international communist movement does not recognize the independent existence of the PRP and deals directly with Hanoi in matters concerning material aid and supplies.

Since its formation in 1962, the PRP has made no effort to deny its communist nature or its paramount role as a member of the NLFSV, whose activities it controls in addition to controlling the Viet Cong. In the January 1966 issue of *Hoc Tap*, the theoretical journal of the North Vietnamese Vietnam Workers' Party, an article by Hong Vu entitled "The Vietnamese People's Revolutionary Party and its Historic Mission of Liberating the South" stated:

The partisans of Marxism-Leninism are in fact the soul of the NLFSV. . . .

The experiences of the world and our country's revolution have shown that in order to win the greatest success the national democratic revolution must be led by a workers' revolutionary party. . . . The partisans of Marxism-Leninism in the South have clearly noted the need of a thorough revolutionary party to act as a vanguard force for the southern revolution. . . .

The PRP is a revolutionary party of the working class in South Vietnam, a Marxist-Leninist party. It has applied in a creative manner the principles of Marxism-Leninism to the concrete situation of the South in order to set forth correct revolutionary policies, lines, and methods. . . .

The PRP maintains that the revolutionary struggle of the Southern people must necessarily use the revolutionary violence of the masses to . . . advance toward smashing the reactionary government and replacing it by a genuinely revolutionary government. . . . Straying from this path can only lead to failure.

The PRP has denied, however, that it has any official ties with the Democratic Republic of Vietnam (DRV) or the Vietnam Workers' Party beyond the normal "fraternal ties of communism."

Operating as an illegal party, the PRP was estimated in 1962 to have not more than 35,000 members. Estimates in 1966 placed the membership between 85,000 and 100,000. The population of South Vietnam is 16,543,000 (estimated mid-1966).

**Organization and Leadership.** The highest authority in the PRP is the party congress, which theoretically elects the "central level" or Central Committee (Ban Chap Hanh Trung Uong Dang) which in turn elects from among its members a Presidium, Secretariat, and Central Control section, as well as its own officers, a Chairman and an assistant. The number of members of the "central-level" Central Committee is not known and reports indicate that no nationwide meeting of PRP members has yet been convened. Under the Central Committee and its executive agency, the Central Office for South Vietnam (COSVN), comes the "Central Committee of the Interzone" (*xu or bo*), which is basically a liason and administrative echelon necessitated by the fact that geography and security needs prevented the complete centralization of leadership within the Central Committee. In 1966, it had 21 members, with a Presidium consisting of a chairman, Secretary-General, and assistant secretary. The precise relationship between the Central Committee of the Interzone and the higher-echelon central-level Central Committee is not known, except that the latter appears to give directives which are implemented by the former. Regional committees elaborate COSVN directives, support (but do not command) Viet Cong main forces, and administer all subordinate PRP organizations.

Below the Central Committee of the Interzone there is a split along rural and urban lines. The rural chain of command consists of the zone (*khu*), province (*tinh bo*), district (*quan*), village (*xa*), and hamlet branch (*chi bo*), while the urban chain consists of the special zone (*dac khu*), city (*tanh bo*), town or part of a city (*khu pho*), street zone (*kha pho*), and street branch (*chi bo*). Reports indicate that urban organizations below the "special zone" level were reorganized in late 1966. At the bottom in both rural and urban areas is a three-man cell structure (*tien to*). In addition there exists what is called a "single-contact member" (*dang vien don tuyen*), who is found at all levels from the zone to the branch. He is appointed by the central-level Central Committee, who alone know his identity. The various levels of the party appear to be well integrated through the use of overlapping committee membership, with the Central Committee at each level composed in part of top-ranking leaders from the level just below. (See Pike, *op. cit.*,pp. 145-150).

The entire PRP apparatus, however, is controlled by the Central Office for South Vietnam (COSVN), which is the executive field agency of the PRP Central Committee and thus virtually coterminous with the PRP Central Committee. Some individuals in COSVN are secret members of the VWP Central Committee.

Very little is known about the leadership of the PRP. The Chairman of the Central Committee is Vo Chi Cong; although references have been made to a "Nguyen Van Cuc," reports indicate that these are one and the same person. The Secretary-General is Tran Nam Trung, believed to be the pseudonym of Lieutenant General Tran Van Tra, deputy chief of staff of the People's Army of (North) Vietnam and alternate member of the VWP Central Committee; Tran Nam Trung has also been identified as Vice-Chairman of the NLFSV Central Committee and Chairman of the NLFSV Central Committee's Military Committee. Other members of the PRP leadership include Vo Van Hau, Secretary, and Tran Do (believed to be a North Vietnamese Army General), Pham Xuan Thai, and Pham Trong Dan.

The PRP controls two major mass organizations, the People's Revolutionary Party Youth League (Doan Thanh Nien Nhan Dan Cach Mang; PRPYL) and the Vanguard Youth League (Thanh Nien Xung Phong), both formed in 1962.

**Domestic and Foreign Policies.** Initial policy statements issued by the PRP deemphasized the communist element of the party, and PRP cadres were instructed to minimize the socialist-communist theme when necessary. A leaflet widely distributed in the South at the time of the establishment of the PRP described it as follows:

> [The PRP is] a party of the working class and laboring people in South Vietnam. It is also the party of all patriots in South Vietnam. The immediate task of the People's Revolutionary Party is to unite and lead the working class, the peasantry, the laboring people, and all compatriots in South Vietnam in struggling to overthrow the rule of the imperialists and feudalists . . . and liberate Vietnam, and to set up a broad democratic coalition government that will achieve national independence and democratic freedom, improve the people's living conditions, give land to the tillers, develop industry, trade, culture, and education, bring a comfortable life to all the people, and achieve national reunification by peaceful means and contribute to protecting world peace . . . . The PRP warmly supports the declaration and program of action of the National Liberation Front and volunteers to stand in the Front's ranks.

At the same time, however, instructions to PRP cadres stressed: "Our party does not conceal its ultimate objective, which is to achieve socialism and communism. But our party has not ceased pointing out that the path leading to that objective is long and that the objective can be achieved not in a few years but several score years."

In January 1962, PRP policy was outlined in the "Ten-Point Platform":

(1) We will overthrow the Ngo Dinh Diem government and form a national, democratic coalition government.

(2) We will carry out a program involving extension of democratic liberties, general amnesty for political detainees, and abolition of the Special Military Tribunal law and other undemocratic laws.

(3) We will abolish the economic monopoly of the US and its henchmen, protect domestically-made products, promote development of the economy, and allow forced evacuees from North Vietnam to return to their place of birth.

(4) We will reduce land rent and prepare for land reform.

(5) We will eliminate US cultural enslavement and depravity and build a nationalistic culture and education.

(6) We will abolish the system of American military advisers and close all foreign military bases in Vietnam.

(7) We will establish equality between men and women and among different nationalities and recognize the autonomous rights of the national minorities in the country.

(8) We will pursue a foreign policy of peace and will establish diplomatic relations with all countries which respect the independence and sovereignity of Vietnam.

(9) We will reestablish normal relations between North and South as a first step toward peaceful reunification of the country.

(10) We will oppose aggressive wars and actively defend world peace.

In April 1962 the PRP further elaborated on its foreign policy when it declared its support of the NLFSV goals of peace, neutralism, independence, and unification; denounced US "aggression" in South Vietnam; thanked the Soviet Union, Communist China, and other members of the communist bloc for their support; urged international support for the "Vietnamese people's struggle"; called for implementation of the 1954 Geneva Agreements; and hinted that it would call on the Soviet Union and Communist China for aid unless the USA left Vietnam.

The PRP's emphasis on proletarianism subsequently gave way to more orthodox expressions of communism, and the theme of national salvation gradually merged with the goal of creating a collectivist society. During 1967, however, virtually no references were made to the PRP, and the NLFSV political program adopted in mid-August 1967 refrained from any mention of it.

**The NLFSV: Background.** The establishment of the National Liberation Front of South Vietnam (Mat Tran Dan Toc Giai Phong Mien Nam Viet Nam; NLFSV) was formally announced on 20 December 1960 by Radio Hanoi, three months after a resolution of the Central Committee of the VWP called for a national united front in the South to rally "all patriotic forces" to overthrow the Diem government and thereby guarantee the necessary "conditions for the peaceful reunification of the Fatherland."

The NLFSV, described by Liberation Radio as exercising the function of a "people's true state with full power and prestige at home and abroad," has engaged in the establishment of a relatively formal governmental apparatus in the South. The NLFSV network of organizations, whose leadership is provided at all levels by corresponding PRP bodies, was elaborated in a series of resolutions adopted at the Third Congress of the VWP on 5-10 September 1960 which pointed out that the NLFSV was to "unite all patriotic parties and religious movements, as well as all political organizations that struggle against the US-Diem clique."

**NLFSV Leadership and Organization.** Although separate, the PRP leadership structure exists within and controls all the activities of the NLFSV and the Viet Cong. Formally established in December 1960, the initial organizational phase began at least a year earlier in mid-1959. Basing itself on the village, the NLFSV created a large number of nationwide sociopolitical organizations in a context where mass organizations were virtually nonexistent. The NLFSV is represented at the hamlet and village level by the "administrative liberation associations," is composed of "functional liberation associations" and political parties, and is supported and in part represented abroad by other fronts.

(1) The "administrative liberation association" structure resembles that of a layered government organization which is presented to the world as "performing the function of a new, really national, and democratic state." Nominally, authority runs from the NLFSV Central Committee down through a number of administrative levels to the village administrative liberation association. In fact, all command authority and reporting passes vertically through PRP channels. The NLFSV Central Committee has 64 members (some reports say 52), of which at least eleven positions are unfilled. The NLFSV leadership consists of a Chairman, Nguyen Huu Tho, and five Vice-Chairmen: Vo Chi Cong, Dr. Phung Van Cung (also known as Tran Van Cung), Tran Nam Trung (believed to be an alias for North Vietnamese Army General Tran Van Tra), Ibih Aleo, and Huynh Tan Phat, who is also Secretary-General of the NLFSV Central Committee. A sixth Vice-Chairman, Thom Me The Nhme, died in July 1966. The NLFSV Presidium includes the Chairman and Vice-Chairmen, the Secretary-General, and Nguyen Van Ngoi, Dang Tran Thi, Nguyen Huu The, Mme. Nguyen Thi Binh, Pham Xuan Thai, Tran Bach Dang, Tran Buu Kiem, and Thich Thien Hao. The Secretariat of the NLFSV consists of Huynh Tan Phat, Secretary-General; Ho Thu and Le Van Huan, both deputy Secretary-Generals, and Ho Xuan Son and Ung Ngoc Ky. Other members of the Central Committee include Joseph Marie Ho Hue Ba, Huynh Bai, Rochom Briu, Lam Tri Chanh, Le Quang Chanh, Mme. Ma Thi Chu, Huynh Cuong, Vo Dong Giang, Nguyen Van Hieu, Nguyen Hoc, Vo Van Luong, Vo Man

Mon, Le Thanh Nam, Nguyen Van Quang, Le Thi Rieng, Hoang Bich Son, Huy Son, Huynh Van Tam, Le Van Tha, Duong Truong Thanh, Tran Van Thanh, Dang Tran Thi, Le Van Thinh, Nguyen Ngoc Thuong, Mai Van Ti, Nguyen Van Ti, Nguyen Tien, Nguyen Van Tien, Tran Huu Trang, Le Quang Trang, Hu Tu (also known as Nhan Tu and Hong Lien), Phan Tu, Vu Tung, Pham Xuan Vy, and Xat.

Below the NLFSV Central Committee are: three "interzone" headquarters; seven zones, or suboffices, for the interzones; approximately 30 provincial committees; and the lower echelons, represented by the district, town, and village committees and organizations. (For a detailed discussion, see Pike, *op. cit.*, pp. 210-231.) The village and hamlet committees are the chief operational units of the NLFSV. Reports during 1967, however, indicate that the "interzone" level may have been eliminated.

(2) The "functional liberation associations" are mass organizations of a sociopolitical nature, organized horizontally at the village level. They consist of the following: the Farmers' Liberation Association (Hoi Nong Dan Giai Phong), headed by Nguyen Huu The; the Liberation Federation of Trade Unions (Hoi Lao Dong Giai Phong), headed by Pham Xuan Thai; the Women's Liberation Association (Hoi Phu Nu Giai Phong), headed by Mme. Nguyen Thi Binh; the Youth Liberation Association (Hoi Thanh Nien Giai Phong), headed by Tran Bach Dang; the Student Liberation Association or the "Association for the Union of Students and Schoolboys for the Liberation of South Vietnam" (Hoi Lien Hiep Sinh Vien Va Hoc Sinh Giai Phong Mien Nam Viet Nam), headed by Tran Buu Kiem; and the Cultural Liberation Association or "Association of Arts and Letters for the Liberation" (Hoi Van Nghe Giai Phong), headed by Tran Huu Trang.

As far as can be determined, there is no actual public participation in any of these groups. All of them, however, serve a useful common objective by enhancing horizontally the verticle control of the NLFSV command structure, and all of them are affiliated with corresponding international communist front organizations.

(3) In addition to the "administrative liberation association" and the "functional liberation associations," the NLFSV is composed of a number of organizations such as political parties, special interest groups, and externally oriented organizations.

Two political parties in addition to the PRP are represented in the NLFSV: the Radical Socialist Party (Dang Xa Hoi Cap Tien) and the Democratic Party of South Vietnam (Dang Dan Chu Mien Nam Viet Nam). The Radical Socialist Party, founded in July 1962, is headed by Nguyen Van Hieu as Secretary-General and Nguyen Ngoc Thuong as Deputy Secretary-General. Its Chairman is unknown. It is oriented toward intellectuals, particularly teachers and university students, and it claims to represent a noncommunist social element within the framework of the NLFSV. The Democratic Party of South Vietnam, formed on 30 June 1944, is headed by Tran Buu Kiem as Chairman and Huynh Tan Phat as Secretary-General. It has described itself as the "party of patriotic capitalists and the petty bourgeoisie," and also as the "party of intellectuals, industrialists, and tradesmen"; it appeals primarily to the urban population. Both parties are represented by their leaders in the overall leadership of the NLFSV.

The special interest groups include professional associations (*van hoi*), the most important of which is the "Patriotic and Democratic Journalists' Association" (Hoi Nha Bao Yeu Nuoc Va Dan Chu), together with religious and ethnic minority associations and a broad range of minor groups such as the "Association of Families of Patriotic Soldiers" (Hoi Gia Dinh Binh Si Yeu Nuoc) and the "League of Soldiers Returned to the People" (Nhom Binh Si Tro Ve Voi Nhan Dan), among many others.

The NLFSV also is supported by a number of organizations concerned with projecting the front's image abroad. The most important is the "Afro-Asian People's Solidarity Committee" (Uy Ban Doan Ket Nhan Dan A Phi).

Also included in the NLFSV are the headquarters of the Viet Cong, officially known as the South Vietnam Armed Forces of Liberation and renamed the South Vietnam People's Armed Forces of Liberation in early October 1967. Although operating within the framework of the NLFSV, the Viet Cong is in fact controlled by the Military Affairs Committee of COSVN. North Vietnamese generals reportedly directing the Viet Cong include Chu Huy Man, Le Trong Tan, Hoang Van Thai, Le Chuong, Ha Ke Tan, Van Tien Dung, Tran Do, Hoang Quoc Viet, Bay Dung, Ba Tran, Nguyen Don, To Ky, and Nguyen Chi Thanh. The last named was believed to be the head of the

COSVN until his death in July 1967; reports indicate that he has been replaced by North Vietnamese Army Major General Hoang Van Thai. (For a discussion of the North Vietnamese role in the Vietnam War, see *Vietnam: Democratic Republic of Vietnam.*)

**Membership.** Although exact figures of the total membership of the NLFSV are not available, Radio Hanoi has claimed that the NLFSV comprises 30 organizations and some 7,000,000 members. Western sources estimate that the organized communist movement in South Vietnam comprises 75,000 to 80,000 political-military cadres, 35,000 to 40,000 administrative-support cadres, 118,000 regular armed personnel (including an estimated 54,000 North Vietnamese troops), and 70,000 to 90,000 guerrilla fighters. (*World Strength of Communist Party Organizations,* 1968, p. 97.) Western reports in 1967 estimated that the Viet Cong controlled almost 40 per cent of the territory, mostly jungle, and 13.5 per cent of the population (estimated at 16,543,000 in mid-1966), as opposed to an estimated 50 per cent of the territory and 19 per cent of the population as estimated on 1 December 1966. For its part, the NLFSV claims that the "liberated territories comprising four-fifths of the territory and three-quarters of the population (more than 10 million people) under the administration of the NLFSV are consolidating and expanding every day." (Nguyen Nhu, head of the NLFSV mission in Berlin, *Neues Deutschland,* 20 December 1967.)

**Domestic Activities: Party-Government Relationship.** Since the mid-1950's all communist activities have been outlawed in the Republic of Vietnam. The 1956 Constitution, which was suspended on 2 November 1963, maintains that communism is incompatible with its principles, and anticommunist legislation has reinforced its provisions. South Vietnamese governments established since November 1963 have repeatedly reaffirmed their opposition to communism, and the present Constitution, adopted 1 April 1967, prohibits all activity aimed at furthering communism. Earlier security and antisubversion legislation still remains in force.

NLFSV statements and directives during 1967 repeatedly attacked the South Vietnamese Government as a "puppet of the US imperialists" and denounced the Presidential and Senatorial elections scheduled for 3 September 1967 and the elections to the House of Representatives scheduled for 22 October, stating:

> The holding of so-called elections for the President, Vice-President, Senate, and House of Representatives is merely a deceitful political trick of the US imperialists and their lackeys aimed at applying a layer of legal and democratic veneer to the extremely rotten puppet administration; at coping with an increasingly isolated, dispersed, and condemned situation at home and in the world; at strengthening the reactionaries' power; and at serving the US imperialists' policy of continuing to intensify and prolong the war of aggression in order to massacre our compatriots and destroy our country. . . .

> The US imperialists and their lackeys will certainly gain nothing through this election farce. For the South Vietnamese people, the Presidency, Vice-Presidency, Senate, and House of Representatives to be rigged up by the US imperialists and their lackeys through the election farce will be of no value. The inevitable development of the situation will be that the puppet administration will become increasingly rotten and finally will be overthrown, that the US imperialists will meet with shameful failure, and that the South Vietnamese people will certainly win complete victory. (Statement by the NLFSV Central Committee, 24 July 1967, as broadcast by Liberation Radio, 28 July 1967.)

NLFSV statements called for a general boycott of the elections and for increased terrorism in an effort to disrupt them.

In spite of NLFSV and Viet Cong efforts to disrupt the South Vietnamese elections, 4,868,266 persons, or 83.5 per cent of the 5,853,251 registered voters, cast their votes in the September elections for the President and Senate and some 4,270,754 persons, or 73 per cent of the electorate voted in the 22 October 1967 election for the House of Representatives. The NLFSV subsequently declared that it would not recognize the newly elected Thieu-Ky government "under any circumstances" and denounced the newly formed cabinet:

> No matter how the US–Thieu-Ky clique may try to cover up for the new cabinet, it cannot conceal its low quality, nor can it cheat the South Vietnamese people who have

struggled resolutely and taken to the streets to denounce the Presidential and Vice-Presidential elections as fraudulent and illegal.

Everyone knows that the Nguyen Van Loc cabinet is a product of the illegal 3 September election. Being the product of an illegal election farce and a creation of the traitorous Thieu-Ky clique, it is utterly worthless. In the eyes of the South Vietnamese people, this new cabinet has no legal base. In other words, it is an instrument of the US—Thieu-Ky clique to be used in its aggressive and country-selling schemes. The South Vietnamese people will not recognize this puppet cabinet of the puppet clique because it is illegal and represents nobody except the Thieu-Ky clique. (Liberation Radio, 12 November 1967.)

NLFSV and Viet Cong efforts to destroy the existing South Vietnamese Government and replace it with a new government, national assembly, and constitution stress the importance of the strategy of a people's war, declaring: "our people have prosecuted a people's war to a higher, extremely rich, and fully creative extent." At the same time, the NLFSV stresses that "in the present stage, armed struggle has a direct and decisive effect" and is "playing an increasingly important role, but the greatest success can be achieved only if that armed struggle is closely coordinated with the political struggle." NLFSV directives have explicitly pointed out that whereas the long-range objective is a "national, democratic, and popular revolution," the immediate objective is a "neutral, independent, national, democratic regime progressing toward socialism," which they see as a coalition government in which the NLFSV would play the leading role:

To all appearances, it will be a coalition government, but the real power will lie in our hands, and we will follow the Front's political program, the revolutionary line.

... Our Party [the PRP] will exercise overall control over it, and if our agents are firmly established and if they properly carry out the principal lines of action of the Front, [the Party] will lead the revolution to the final objective.

(For a discussion of the role of the DRV in the Vietnam war, see *Vietnam: Democratic Republic of Vietnam.*)

**Domestic Policies: The NLFSV Political Program.** The NLFSV's domestic program was first formulated in the Front's ten-point program broadcast from Hanoi on 4 February 1961. On 31 August 1967, Liberation Radio announced that an "extraordinary congress of the National Liberation Front of South Vietnam" had been convened by the Front Central Committee in mid-August "in the liberated areas to discuss and adopt the political program of the Front."* According to the announcement, the meeting was attended by some 200 delegates, including "members of the NLFSV Central Committee and delegates from various political parties, mass organizations, nationalities, religious groups, the Liberation Armed Forces Command, departments and branches of the NLFSV Central Committee, and Front committees at all levels from Quang Tri to Ca Mau, from the mountainous region to the delta." Major addresses to the congress were delivered by Huyhn Tan Phat, Vice-Chairman of the NLFSV Presidium and Secretary-General of the Central Committee; Phung Van Cung, Vice-Chairman of the NLFSV Central Committee; Phan Xuan Thai, member of the NLFSV Presidium and Chairman of the South Vietnam Liberation Federation of Trade Unions; and Nguyen Huu Tho, Chairman of the NLFSV Presidium. The addresses focused primary attention on the adoption of the political program (See *Documents*) which was described as the "only correct path to complete the national democratic revolution in South Vietnam." Liberation Radio hailed the political program as: "a turning point of great historic significance aimed at further broadening the great national unity bloc and mobilizing more vigorously all our people and armed forces to exert great efforts and to surge forward to achieve complete success; to build an independent, democratic, peaceful, neutral, and prosperous South Vietnam; and to advancing toward achieving peaceful reunification of the fatherland."

Although references are still made to the five points announced by the NLFSV Central Committee

---

*Two previous congresses have been held by the NLFSV, one in March 1962 and the other in January 1964.

on 22 March 1965,[†] the political program has for all intents and purposes replaced it as the NLFSV formulation of domestic and foreign policies. The new political program, which was not released until 1 September 1967, is primarily an expanded and updated version of the ten-point program adopted in 1961, with revisions taking into account the developments since the collapse of the Ngo Dinh Diem regime.

While continuing to maintain that the NLFSV is the "sole genuine representative of the heroic South Vietnamese people," the political program states in its introduction:

> At this juncture, in a spirit of developing the former program, the NLFSV has worked out this political program with a view to further broadening the bloc of great national union, encouraging and stimulating the entire people to rush forward, resolved to fight and defeat the US aggressors, and to build an independent, democratic, peaceful, neutral, and prosperous South Vietnam.

The political program also states that "the NLFSV warmly welcomes all political parties, mass organizations, and patriotic and progressive personalities who broadly rally within and outside the Front." There is, however, no mention of the PRP in the political program; and although it notes that "those functionaries of the puppet administration" and "puppet army" who are willing to serve in the "state machine after the liberation of South Vietnam will enjoy equal treatment," the political program excludes any form of cooperation with the present South Vietnamese administration.

As outlined in the political program, the domestic program of the NLFSV focuses on 14 key points:

> (1) To achieve a broad and progressive democratic regime; to abolish the disguised colonial regime established by the US imperialists in South Vietnam; to overthrow the puppet administration, hireling of the United States; not to recognize the puppet national assembly rigged up by the US imperialists and their lackeys; to abolish the Constitution and all antinational and antidemocratic laws enacted by the US imperialists and the puppet administration.

> To hold free general elections, to elect the national assembly in a really democratic way in accordance with the principle of universal, equal, direct suffrage and secret ballot. . . .

> To set up a national union democratic government including the most representative persons among the various social strata, nationalities, religious communities, patriotic and democratic parties, patriotic personalities, and forces which have contributed to the cause of national liberation. . . .

> (2) To build an independent and self-supporting economy, to improve the people's living conditions. To abolish the policy of economic enslavement and monopoly of the US imperialists. To confiscate the property of the US imperialists and their diehard cruel agents and turn it into state property. . . .

[†]As outlined by the NLFSV Central Committee, the five points declared:

(1) The US imperialists are the saboteurs of the Geneva Agreements, the most brazen warmonger and aggressor and the sworn enemy of the Vietnamese people.

(2) The heroic South Vietnamese people are resolved to drive out the US imperialists in order to liberate South Vietnam, achieve an independent, democratic, peaceful, and neutral South Vietnam, with a view to national reunification.

(At present all negotiations are useless as long as the US imperialists do not withdraw all the troops, weapons, and means of war of the USA and its satellites from South Vietnam and destroy their military bases in South Vietnam; as long as the sacred rights of the South Vietnamese people—rights to independence and democracy—are still being sold by the Vietnamese traitors to the US imperialists; and as long as the NLFSV—true and only representative of 14 million South Vietnamese people—does not have the decisive voice.)

(3) The valiant South Vietnamese people and the South Vietnam Liberation Army are resolved to accomplish to the full their sacred duty to drive out the US imperialists so as to liberate South Vietnam and defend North Vietnam.

(4) The South Vietnamese people express their profound gratitude for the wholehearted support of the people of the world who cherish peace and justice and declare their readiness to receive all assistance including weapons and all other war materials from their friends in the five continents.

(5) To unite the whole people, to arm the whole people, continue to march forward heroically and be resolved to fight and defeat the US aggressors and the Vietnamese traitors.

(3) To enact the land policy, to carry out the slogan "Land to the Tiller." To confiscate the lands of the US imperialists and the diehard cruel landlords—their lackeys. To allot those lands to the landless or land-poor peasants. To confirm and protect the ownership of the lands allotted to peasants by the revolution. . . .

(4) To build a national democratic culture and education, to develop science and technology, to promote public health. . . .

(5) To guarantee the rights and cater to the livelihood of workers, laborers, and civil servants. To promulgate labor legislation. . . . To improve the living and working condition of the workers, laborers, and civil servants.

(6) To build up strong South Vietnam Liberation Armed Forces with a view to liberating the people and defending the fatherland. . . . To strive to raise their quality and increase their fighting capacity with a view to stepping up people's war, defeating the US satellite and puppet troops, and bringing the fight against US aggression for national salvation to total victory. . . .

(7) To show gratitude to the martyrs, to provide for disabled armymen, to reward the fighters and compatriots who have an outstanding record in the fight against US aggression and for national salvation. . . .

(8) To organize social relief. . . .

(9) To put into practice equality between men and women. . . .

(10) To strengthen unity, to practice equality and mutual assistance among nationalities. To abolish all systems and policies applied by the imperialists and their lackeys with a view to dividing, oppressing, and exploiting the various nationalities. To oppose discrimination among and forcible assimilation of the nationalities. . . .

(11) To respect freedom of creed, to achieve unity and equality among the different religious communities. . . .

(12) To welcome puppet officers and men and puppet officials back to the just cause, show leniency and give a humane treatment to rallied armymen and prisoners of war. . . . To severely punish the diehard thugs acting as efficient agents of the US imperialists. . . .

(13) To protect the rights and interests of overseas Vietnamese.

(14) To protect the legitimate rights and interests of foreign residents in South Vietnam.

Considerable emphasis was also placed on the reunification of the fatherland, with the NLFSV maintaining that "the reunification of Vietnam will be realized step-by-step and through peaceful negotiations between the two zones without either side using pressure against the other and without foreign interference" and that "pending the reunification of the country, the people in both zones will jointly resist foreign invasion and defend the fatherland, and at the same time strive to expand economic and cultural exchanges."

**NLFSV Self-Assessment.** In addition to numerous statements and directives, NLFSV analyses of activities during 1967 were undertaken at a series of meetings including the meetings of the NLFSV Central Committee Presidium on 24-26 April and 20-22 October, the NLFSV Central Committee meetings on 7 November and 18 December, and the "extraordinary" congress of the NLFSV held in mid-August. "The revolutionary movement has been developing increasingly" and the "liberated areas have not only become well protected but have also been increasingly enlarged," NLFSV statements declared, and expressed: "great pride and joy over the fact that our people and armed forces, under the skillful and clearsighted leadership of the NLFSV Central Committee, scored unprecedentedly brilliant achievements in all fields of the anti-US, national salvation struggle."

At the 18 December meeting of the NLFSV Central Committee, Chairman Nguyen Huu Tho stated:

We have won great and comprehensive victories, militarily, politically, and diplomatically. Our present position is very firm and is firmer than ever before. Our enemy has fallen into a completely stalemated and passive situation. He has been defeated in a very important phase of his limited war strategy and will certainly suffer complete defeat. The successes achieved by our armed forces and people are the successes of our completely correct political and military lines, mottoes, and policies. Our armed forces and people have developed the successes of people's wars to a high degree and in a very creative manner. . . . The successes we have achieved are the successes of the all-people's great unity bloc and of the Front, which has been consolidated more and more firmly and has been constantly enlarged. . . . The Front's international prestige and influence have been increasingly enhanced. It is obvious that the Front is truly the sole genuine representative of the heroic South Vietnamese people. Our past successes constitute a firm basis for our people to move forward to defeat the US imperialists' war of aggression and to achieve complete success. (Liberation Radio, 19 December 1967.)

A military communique issued by the South Vietnam People's Liberation Armed Forces Command and broadcast by Liberation Radio on 24 December stated:

Our armed forces and people annihilated more enemy troops and destroyed more enemy war means than in previous years. According to still incomplete statistics—December figures are not yet available—since the beginning of 1967 our armed forces and people have annihilated, killed, or wounded about 365,000 enemy troops, including 170,000 US and satellite troops and 195,000 puppet troops. . . . Our armed forces and people have downed and destroyed 3,200 planes and destroyed 8,500 military vehicles of various types, 4,000 armored vehicles, 730 pieces of artillery, more than 200 warships and military boats, 38 locomotives, 101 coaches, 560 bridges and culverts, many ammunition and fuel depots, and so forth. Moreover, our armed forces and people have seized thousands of weapons of various types and a large quantity of military equipment.

These are the biggest achievements we have ever made. Compared to 1965, the number of enemy troops annihilated in 1967 has increased over 50 per cent; the number of US and satellite troops annihilated has increased nine times; the number of armored vehicles destroyed has increased 10 times; the number of planes downed and destroyed has more than doubled. Compared with 1966, the number of enemy troops annihilated has increased more than one-third; the number of US and satellite troops annihilated has increased 3.5 times; the number of warships and military boats destroyed has doubled.

Liberation Radio concluded its analysis by noting: "The achievements of our army and people in 1967 are great and comprehensive and of an extremely important strategic significance, both in the military and political fields." At the same time it declared: "We do not forget that the US aggressors still have many dark and wicked plots. The fight will be fiercer and more complex. The resistance is requiring all of us to make great efforts, to concentrate all our strength, talent, and intelligence to overcome all difficulties and hardships, to score great achievements, and to achieve at all costs the revolutionary objectives set forth by the NLFSV political program."

While hailing the successes of the armed forces, however, Truong Son (believed to be a pseudonym for North Vietnamese Army General Nguyen Chi Thanh) pointed out five basic tasks to be fulfilled by the liberation forces and people: (1) "to be firmly determined to fight and vanquish one million American and puppet troops"; (2) "to extend our 'people's war'—fought by all our people on all fronts—and bring it to a higher stage"; (3) "to push forward our offensive"; (4) "to develop among the fighters and people on each front the sense of being always ready to cooperate with other fronts, to achieve harmonious coordination between all regions"; and (5) "to preserve and expand our bases [and] build our liberated zones into a solid rear area from all the military, political, and economic points of view, and thereby strengthen our bases." (Truong Son, "Vietnam: Five Lessons, One Victory," *Tricontinental*, no. 3, November-December, 1967.)

In spite of optimistic appraisals, captured documents and NLFSV statements during 1967 indicated that the Front was faced with a number of outstanding problems in both the political and military fields.

A captured Viet Cong document dated 20 January 1967 noted: "Shortcomings in various areas "have" created great obstacles that have impeded the execution of our tasks and limited our victories." Specifically, the document (issued by the South Vietnamese Liberation Army Political

Staff Department and approved by the South Vietnamese Military Affairs Committee) criticized the Viet Cong for showing "signs of passive rightism," "fear of hardships and a fierce, protracted war," "escapism and demoralization," "lack of determination to seek and fight the enemy," "overestimating the enemy," "lack of popular viewpoints," "rightist and pessimistic tendencies," and "lack of a sense of discipline . . . and other deficiencies pertaining to individualism."

Subsequent documents noted that recruitment of soldiers had been done without caution, that soldiers and workers had become demoralized, and that there had been a "lack of understanding of the principle of building up and defending the Party's revolutionary forces," with "little emphasis placed on ideological and political instruction."

In an effort to overcome these and other difficulties, NLFSV directives called for: "A political reorientation" program to develop "revolutionary heroism to oppose all tendencies of rightism and losses of revolutionary pride and promote a fervid revolutionary atmosphere in which our whole people shall stand united." An appeal of the NLFSV Central Committee Presidium cautioned, however:

> . . . all of our armed forces and people must firmly grasp the new situation, must not lessen their vigilance in the face of the deceitful peace arguments of the US aggressors and their lackeys, and must surge forward courageously to win resounding victories. They must do this in order to liberate the South, protect the North, proceed toward peaceful reunification of the fatherland, and make a positive contribution toward stepping up the national liberation movement and guarding peace in Indochina, Southeast Asia, and the world.
>
> Let our Liberation Armed Forces, from main force and regional units to guerrilla and people's self-defense militia units, move forward courageously and vigorously with a determination to win, develop their revolutionary heroism to a high degree, and surge forward to attack the enemy very vigorously everywhere. (Appeal of the Enlarged Conference of the NLFSV Central Committee Presidium, 20-22 October 1967, as broadcast by Liberation Radio, 20 October 1967.)

The PRP also faced serious problems in the political field, with various documents stating that political indoctrination "is not sufficiently strong or consistent" and that "ideologically, escapism and rightist tendencies still persist." A document dated 25 August 1967 noted:

> . . . We are still suffering from many difficulties.
>
> . . . Party members are not yet thoroughly conscious of their task of developing weak villages and still lack confidence in the people of villages and hamlets. A majority of them has still failed to stay close to the hamlets and is not yet resolved to educate and lead the people to attack their enemies on three fronts, VT, CT, and VV [military, political, troop proselytizing] . . . .
>
> The leading role of the party chapter has not yet been actively improved in the matter of staying close to the people in the hamlets and the party chapter still fails to take good care of the substantive rights and interests of the people. Specifically, the party members have not yet entered into membership in the popular organizations in the hamlets, especially the Farmers' Organization. The party chapter has not yet helped various branches and circles to assume heavy responsibilities and authority. A special fact is that they have not yet paid attention to guerrilla warfare and the secret self-defense corps, especially on the question of promoting their fighting quality and the farmers-guerrillas that could take care of civilian proselytizing work.

The same document noted:

> . . . the party chapter has to pay attention to overcoming the thoughts of balking at difficulties, being frightened by sacrifices and losing internal unity, and to fighting against the thoughts of rallying and to helping party members recognize their leading role in all the party's works in blocks and hamlets.

In an effort to combat these and other tendencies and to "grasp fast the people who have doubtful political tendencies," "those who are wavering," and those who show signs of "corruption, bribery, and demoralization," a communique of the Presidium of the NLFSV Central Committee stressed these points:

(1) Front committees at all levels and in all localities, echelons, and branches must convene conferences to review the situation, to evaluate their past tasks, to praise the achievement scored, to overcome all shortcomings and weakpoints, and to undertake practical measures for successfully implementing the tasks of the 1967-1968 winter-spring campaign.

(2) A training phase must be organized for cadres at all branches and echelons to further heighten their awareness of the new situation and tasks and to encourage them to make great efforts and develop a steadfast determination to fulfill their tasks.

(3) It is necessary to develop and strengthen education among the combatants of the People's Liberation Armed Forces and our compatriots . . . to improve their awareness of the new situation and tasks and the Front's lines and policies as reflected in the political program. It is necessary to stimulate all people and forces to advance strongly to step up the military and political struggles and win new, great victories. The Front's political program must be disseminated extensively and intensively among all strata of people, ethnic minority people, and religions in the cities, in areas still under temporary enemy control, and in the liberated areas. Propaganda must be carried out among puppet troops and government personnel to make them understand that the Front's political program has provided the most correct way to liberate the people and has created favorable conditions for them to join other compatriots in the anti-US national salvation struggle.

(4) It is necessary to carry out a phase of commending and rewarding localities, units, branches, and individuals for their outstanding achievements in 1967 on the occasion of the seventh anniversary of the founding of the Front. (Liberation Radio, 11 December 1967.)

**International Views and Positions.** As outlined in the political program, the NLFSV advocates a foreign policy of "peace and neutrality" which would guarantee the "independence, sovereignty, unity, and territorial integrity of the country and help safeguard world peace." Specifically, the program focuses on four main points:

(1) Establishment of diplomatic relations with all countries, regardless of their social and political system, on the principles of respect for each other's independence, sovereignity and territorial integrity, without interference in each other's internal affairs, on the basis of equality, mutual benefit and peaceful coexistence.

—Annulment of all unequal treaties the puppet administration has signed with the United States or any other country.

—Respect for the economic and cultural integrity interests of those countries which sympathize with, support or assist the struggle against the US aggression and for the national salvation of the Vietnamese people.

—Acceptance of technical and economic assistance from any country, provided there are no political strings attached.

—Noninvolvement in military alliances; no military personnel or military bases of foreign countries on South Vietnam territory.

(2) Strengthening of friendly relations with all countries which sympathize with, support or assist the struggle against the US aggression and for the national salvation of the Vietnamese people. Strengthening good-neighbor relations with Cambodia and Laos. Unceasing effort to consolidate solidarity and mutual assistance between the peoples of Indochina countries with a view to defending their independence, sovereignty, and territorial integrity against the aggressive and war provocation policy of the US imperialists and their henchmen.

(3) Active support of the national liberation movement of the peoples of Asia, Africa, and Latin America against imperialism and old and new colonialism.

—Active support of the struggle of the American people against the US imperialists' war of aggression in Vietnam.

—Active support of the just struggle of the Negro people in the United States for their fundamental national rights.

—Active support of the struggle for peace, democracy and social progress in all countries in the world.

(4) Effort towards safeguarding world peace, to combat the bellicose and aggressive imperialists headed by US imperialism, and to bring about the dismantling of the aggressive military blocs and foreign military basis of imperialism.

—Unceasing effort to consolidate and develop relations with international democratic organizations and the peoples of all countries, including the American people.

—Work to contribute to the consolidation and broadening of the worldwide peoples' front in support of Vietnam against the US imperialist aggressors, for national independence and peace.

The political program also stresses the international significance of the Vietnam war, noting: "it has a direct bearing not only on the fate of our people at present and all future generations, but also on the interests of the peoples of the world who are fighting for peace, national independence, democracy, and social progress."

Although NLFSV statements during 1967 continued to claim that "in the international arena, the prestige of the NLFSV has been raised even higher," considerable attention was devoted to developing the image of a legal, independent entity to replace the South Vietnamese Government and to obtaining international respectability as a valid political entity. A document issued by the subcommittee for foreign activities of COSVN dated 15 June 1966 and released in April 1967 noted the need to "pay more attention to the propaganda and motivation of the various peoples in the world" and admitted that the Front's propaganda activities "left much to be desired":

We have not yet made clear to world public opinion US neocolonialism, our line and policy of struggle, the assessment of the enemy weakpoints and strongpoints, and his dark design in peace swindles.

A careful study of our past activities reveals that our propaganda themes are still superficial. . . . In addition, we have not set off the role and position of the Front to the world and ruined the diplomatic relations between the Saigon puppet government and various nationalist countries.

Our people's struggle movement is very intensive but we have failed to conduct a systematic propaganda of our military, political, cultural, and economic successes .

. . . we have not appropriately fulfilled the carrying out of international obligations. We have not, in some instances, enlisted the support at home in favor of the friendly countries in response to their backing of our cause. We have not turned our support for friendly countries into the deeds accomplished by the masses.

In formulating information and propaganda tasks, the COSVN document specifically noted the need to (1) place special emphasis on the role of the NLFSV at home and abroad and present it as the "only and genuine representative of the South Vietnamese people," (2) widen the imperialists' differences on Vietnam, and (3) enlist the support and aid of the socialist countries—particularly Communist China and the Soviet Union, the Afro-Asian and Latin American countries, and the American people. Specifically, the document noted the need to "work out a plan to support the national liberation and revolutionary movements in various countries," to "establish contact with newspapers, international democratic organizations, and important personalities of other countries" and motivate their support by "providing them with suggestive documents and information" and by inviting or authorizing "a number of foreign writers, newsmen, cinematographers to visit South Vietnam and use them as propaganda channels . . ."

A major part of the NLFSV's propaganda effort is conducted through its representatives outside Vietnam, which include some 140 individuals located in Algeria, Bulgaria, Cambodia, Communist China, Cuba, Czechoslovakia, East Germany, Hungary, Indonesia, North Korea, North Vietnam, Poland, Rumania, the Soviet Union, and the United Arab Republic. Cambodia, Communist China, Cuba, and North Korea officially recognize the NLFSV representatives and delegations as equal in status to the ambassadors and embassies of foreign countries. Although the NLFSV foreign missions focus primary attention on propaganda activities, reports also indicate that they are involved in the training of local guerrilla units.

**International Contacts.** During 1967 the NLFSV devoted considerable attention to the publicizing of the newly adopted political program. The culmination of these efforts was the circulation of the program among members of the United Nations, under the sponsorship of the Rumanian delegation, in an attempt to gain international recognition of the NLFSV and to project the NLFSV internationally as a viable political entity independent of Hanoi. Virtually all of the communist parties, front organizations, and national liberation movements declared their support of the program, hailing it as "an extremely important event, not only for the entire Vietnamese people at home and abroad, but also for progressive people all over the world."

The NLFSV sent a number of delegations to leftist and communist-sponsored conferences abroad, as well as to individual countries and national liberation movements. Although there is no concrete evidence, reports indicate that members of the various NLFSV delegations are residents of North Vietnam, where entry and exit is easier than in South Vietnam. NLFSV delegates travel abroad on North Vietnamese passports and are sponsored by North Vietnam at international conferences. According to a COSVN document dated June 1966 and released in April 1967, the "bulk of the propaganda and diplomatic activities is assumed by North Vietnam."

Although the PRP does not appear to have issued any public statements on the question of holding an international communist conference, it most likely supports North Vietnam's opposition to the convening of such a meeting, and was not invited to send a delegation to the February 1968 meeting in Budapest.

The NLFSV also continued to strengthen its ties with the various international front organizations. Numerous expressions of support and solidarity were exchanged between the South Vietnam Afro-Asian Solidarity Committee and the Afro-Asian–Latin-American People's Solidarity Organization (AALAPSO), with the permanent secretariat of AALAPSO sponsoring a meeting of the South Vietnam Afro-Asian Solidarity Committee from 30 September to 6 October which was attended by representatives of the NLFSV Central Committee. In early March, Le Tung Son, member of the permanent NLFSV delegation in Peking, met R.D. Senanayake, Secretary-General of the Afro-Asian Writers' Bureau, in Peking and thanked the Bureau for support given to the Vietnamese people and requested further support in the future. A delegation of the South Vietnam Afro-Asian Solidarity Committee also attended the June emergency session of the Afro-Asian People's Solidarity Committee (AAPSO) held in Cairo. On 10 October, a delegation of the South Vietnam Liberation Women's Union led by Le Thi Chi left for Prague to attend the 14-17 October meeting of the Women's International Democratic Federation, and on 21 October a delegation of the South Vietnam Liberation Federation of Trade Unions led by Dinh Ba Thi left for Prague to attend the Thirty-fourth session of the Executive Committee of the World Federation of Trade Unions.

**The Sino Soviet Dispute.** During 1967 the PRP refrained from publicly commenting on the Sino-Soviet dispute and Chinese cultural revolution. In a captured document released in the spring, however, it was noted that, "at present, the deep dissension between Russia and China and the contradiction in anti-American concepts" had "ruined the consistency of action of the pro-Vietnamese socialist bloc." In commenting on the concept of a united front, a major issue on the Sino-Soviet dispute, the same document specifically noted the need to form: "a front of unified action against the imperialists and colonialists whose leaders are the US" and to "try by any means to induce socialist countries to have unity of action to support our struggle in all fields."

In addition to the customary exchange of greetings on the respective founding anniversaries, specific contacts between Communist China and the NLFSV during 1967 included a reported high-ranking NLFSV military delegation which is believed to have arrived in Peking on 20 February, although the Chinese and Vietnamese refrained from commenting on the subject. A NLFSV delegation led by Huynh Van Danh visited Communist China from 29 September to 19 October to attend the celebrations of the eighteenth founding anniversary of Communist China. A delegation of the South Vietnamese Afro-Asian Solidarity Committee led by Nguyen Xuan Long arrived in Peking on 15 December to attend the celebrations of the seventh founding anniversary of the NLFSV.

NLFSV statements during 1967 hailed the Communist Chinese for having "unswervingly . . . rendered wholehearted support and assistance to the Vietnamese people," and while in Peking Nguyen Xuan Long declared: "We know very well [that] our Chinese brothers, keeping to Chairman Mao's teachings, are supporting the Vietnamese people with unflagging effort in which they are sparing no sacrifice. Not one of the victories now being won by the South Vietnamese people, and the Vietnamese people as a whole, can be separated from the great and powerful help given by the Chinese people."

The NLFSV and the Soviet Union also exchanged the customary congratulatory messages, with primary attention focusing on the celebration of the fiftieth anniversary of the October Revolution, to which the NLFSV sent a delegation headed by Dang Tran Thi, member of the Presidium of the NLFSV Central Committee. On 10 October the NLFSV Central Committee issued a communique on the fiftieth anniversary, stressing the significance of the October Revolution for the "liberation movement in Vietnam and throughout the world," and on 7 November the NLFSV Central Committee held an enlarged meeting to celebrate the anniversary.

NLFSV editorials and statements praised "the warm support of the communist party, government, and people of the Soviet Union" which was "increasing the fighting power of the people in both parts of Vietnam." At the same time the NLFSV maintained careful balance in its praise of Soviet and Chinese support.

**The Third World.** In a speech to the first conference of the Organization of Latin American Solidarity, NLFSV representative Nguyen Van Tien stated:

> As for us, we totally support the struggle for national independence that the peoples of Asia and Africa are waging against imperialism, colonialism, and neocolonialism, headed by US imperialism. We will stand shoulder-to-shoulder with the peoples of Latin America in their struggle for national liberation and against our common enemy, Yankee imperialism. We salute the great successes that the Latin American peoples have achieved in their struggle and we consider them an effective aid and a powerful encouragement in our own struggle.

Declarations of support and solidarity, as well as congratulatory messages on respective founding anniversaries and the NLFSV's adoption of a new political program, were received from virtually all of the communist parties and national liberation movements in Asia, Africa, Latin America, and the Middle East, with the North Vietnamese devoting considerable attention to the publicizing of the NLFSV political program and continuing to express its "firm determination" to "stand side by side with their 14 million compatriots and to fight and defeat the US aggressors in order to defend the north, liberate the south, and proceed toward the peaceful reunification of the fatherland."

The NLFSV also furthered its diplomatic position in Asia when its Central Committee announced on 31 May that it would recognize the "territorial integrity of the Kingdom of Cambodia within its present borders." Following the announcement, the NLFSV and Cambodia agreed to establish permanent diplomatic representations and on 17 July the NLFSV appointed Nguyen Van Hien as representative of the Front in Cambodia.

Although contacts with Africa and the Middle East were limited, NLFSV representatives visited the Congo (Brazzaville), the "liberated zones of Portuguese Guinea," and Algiers. NLFSV commentary on the Middle East conflict condemned the aggression of the Israeli "reactionaries" supported by the "US and British imperialists," and on 8 June Nguyen Huu Tho, Chairman of the Presidium of the NLFSV Central Committee sent telegrams of support to President Nureddin al-Atassi of Syria and Gamal Abdel Nasser of Egypt declaring:

> The South Vietnamese people and the NLFSV are determined to push forward their resistance war against the US aggressors for national salvation, thus contributing a valuable part to the victory of the struggle of the peoples of the Arab countries and the world against imperialism for independence, freedom, and peace.

On 12 June the NLFSV Central Committee issued the following statement:

> The South Vietnamese people and National Liberation Front are highly indignant at and vehemently condemn the US and British imperialists for using the Israeli reactionaries to

launch a war of aggression against the Arab countries. The South Vietnam people and the NLFSV resolutely demand that the Israeli aggressive troops withdraw without delay from the territories of the Arab countries, that the United States, Great Britain, and Israel respect the independence, sovereignity, and territorial integrity of these countries.

The NLFSV Central Committee affirms the 14 million South Vietnamese people's firm and constant support for the brotherly Arab people's just struggle against US and British imperialism and their Israeli henchmen and to defend their sacred national rights.

The NLFSV calls on the socialist countries, the anti-imperialist and peace-and-justice loving forces all over the world to take still more active and resolute actions to support and assist the just struggle of the Arab countries.

For their part, the South Vietnamese people and Liberation Armed Forces are resolved to deal the US imperialists still heavier punishing blows and to defeat them completely in South Vietnam, thus contributing an active part to the brotherly Arab people's struggle. (VNA, 13 June 1967.)

Considerable emphasis was also placed on the further development of NLFSV relations with Cuba. On 29 June the Central Committee of the NLFSV announced the establishment of formal diplomatic relations with Cuba and the appointment of Raúl Valdés Vivo as Cuban ambassador extraordinary and plenipotentiary to the NLFSV. In announcing the appointment, the Liberation Press Agency praised the "people, Communist Party, and Government of the Republic of Cuba headed by beloved Premier Comrade Fidel Castro" and thanked them for having "spared no pain to support [the NLFSV] morally, politically, and materially." The agency added: "The South Vietnamese armed forces and people are thoroughly aware that crushing the US imperialists in South Vietnam actively contributes to the defense of the Cuban revolution . . ."

The NLFSV also sent a delegation led by Nguyen Van Tien, member of the NLFSV Central Committee, to the first conference of the Organization of Latin American Solidarity (OLAS), which met in Havana from 31 July to 10 August. At the end of the meeting, delegates to the OLAS conference unanimously passed a resolution hailing the Vietnamese struggle as "a front-line trench in the world-wide anti-imperialist struggle" and noting that the delegates "solemnly proclaim that Vietnam today is blazing the revolutionary trail for the peoples of America to follow," adding: "our slogan will be the creation of two, three, or more Vietnams in the struggle for the total destruction of imperialism." The OLAS resolution concluded by calling on the "peoples of Latin America to intensify their solidarity actions with Vietnam by every possible means, and especially extend their revolutionary struggle, their armed struggle, as the most effective way of expressing their concrete and militant solidarity with this heroic people."

On the death of Ernesto "Che" Guevara the NLFSV Central Committee sent a message of condolence to the OLAS Standing Committee and to the Cuban Communist Party and Government, declaring: "The South Vietnamese people will never forget his attachment and his complete support in their struggle against the Americans and for national salvation, and consider his revolutionary achievements as a noble contribution to the national liberation cause in South Vietnam."

The NLFSV also continued to declare its solidarity with the various revolutionary movements in Latin America, particularly those in Bolivia and Venezuela, declaring that "when a people decide to take up arms and fight, they have already achieved half of their complete victory."

**Europe.** NLFSV contacts with Europe centered on the French, East German, and British communist party congresses, where it participated as an observer/guest along with other national liberation movements, on the various international anti-war conferences held in Norway, Denmark, and Sweden, and the aid to Vietnam committees in various countries. In addition to a message sent by Nguyen Huu Tho, an NLFSV delegation led by Dang Quang Minh, head of the permanent NLFSV representation in Moscow, attended the Eighteenth Congress of the French Communist Party (4-8 January) and expressed "most sincere thanks" to the French Communist Party and people for support and expressions of solidarity. A second NLFSV delegation, led by Le Quang Chanh, member of the NLFSV Central Committee, attended the Seventh Congress of the Socialist Unity Party (East Germany) on 17-22 April. On 22 November, the NLFSV Central Committee sent greetings to the Thirtieth Congress of the British Communist Party, thanking the party for its "resolute stand against aggression in Vietnam" and for demanding that the British government dissociate itself from US policy.

In addition to expressing its support for the Bertrand Russell International War Crimes Tribunal which met in Stockholm, Sweden, from 2 to 10 May and in Roskilde, Denmark, from 20 to 29 November, the NLFSV also noted the importance of the Stockholm Conference on Vietnam, which met from 6 to 9 July and to which they sent a delegation led by Dinh Ba Thi. The NLFSV furthered its bilateral contacts with Norway and Denmark. In late April, an NLFSV delegation led by Nguyen Van Dong arrived in Norway, where it was received by Knut Løfsnes, Chairman of the Norwegian Communist Party, who declared: "We highly value the struggle of the South Vietnamese people, which we consider as a great contribution to our struggle and which is helping us to unite broadly with other anti-imperialist forces in our country." The delegation also met with the Norwegian Committee for Solidarity with Vietnam, and on 30 April the delegation addressed some 300 representatives of the youth organizations of the Norwegian Communist Party, the Socialist People's Party, and the Social Democratic Party.

On 2 May, at the invitation of the Danish Communist Party, the same delegation met with Knud Jespersen, Chairman, and Ib Nørlund, member of the Party Politburo. On 26 June a delegation of the South Vietnam Liberation Youth Union arrived in Denmark at the invitation of the Danish Communist Youth union, which had earlier in the year adopted a declaration at its Central Committee meeting calling on the Danish government to break diplomatic relations with South Vietnam and to recognize the NLFSV as the "sole genuine representative of the South Vietnamese people."

**The United States.** The NLFSV continued to condemn the "US imperialists and their henchmen" for their "aggressive war in Vietnam" and to demand that they accept the DRV's four-point stand, the NLFSV's five-point stand, and the recently adopted political program as the only solution to the Vietnam question. The NLFSV also placed increasing emphasis on the need to support actively the "struggle of the American people against the US imperialists' war of aggression in Vietnam" and the "just struggle of the Negro people in the United States for their fundamental rights."

On 16 October a communique of Liberation Press Agency announced the formation of the South Vietnam People's Committee for Solidarity with the American People:

> The South Vietnamese People's Committee for Solidarity with the American People is founded with a view to meeting the urgent needs of the friendly relations between the South Vietnamese and American people and the close ties between the movement of the American people against the US Government's aggressive war in South Vietnam and the South Vietnamese people's war of resistance for national salvation.

According to the communique, the committee sought to "consolidate and develop the friendship between the South Vietnamese and American people" and to "unite and coordinate with the American people in the struggle for peace, justice, freedom, democracy, and civil rights and in demanding that the US government put an end to its aggressive war in Vietnam." Toward achieving these objectives, the committee stressed the need to establish relations with and render support to "all progressive organizations and individuals in the USA" who were "struggling for peace, justice, freedom, democracy, and civil rights" and who wished to "join the Vietnamese people in demanding that the US government end its war in Vietnam"; all "progressive social organizations, individuals, personalities, and intellectuals in South Vietnam and all those army men and personnel of the Saigon puppet administration" who wished to "acquaint themselves with the American people's struggle"; and "American personnel and army men in South Vietnam" who wished to "acquaint themselves with the struggle of the South Vietnamese and American people."

As announced by Liberation Press Agency, the leadership of the committee consisted of the Chairman, Ho Thu; Vice Chairmen Mme. Nguyen Thi Binh (member of the NLFSV Central Committee), Reverend Joseph Marie Ho Hue Ba (member of the NLFSV Central Committee), Thich Thien Hao (member of the NLFSV Central Committee), Rochom Briu (member of the NLFSV Central Committee), and Thach Thien Chi; and the Secretary-General, Mme. Truong Thi Hue. Members included Mme. Ma Thi Chu, Huynh Phuong Dong, Thanh Hai, Mme. Thanh Loan, Tran Hieu Minh, Vu Nam, Huynh Minh Sieng, Miss Pham Thanh Van, and Mme. Pham Thi Yen. The agency reported that the committee would establish permanent delegations in Prague, Algiers, and Hanoi.

**Publications.** The NLFSV and the PRP publish a number of clandestine newspapers and periodicals. The Liberation Press Agency, founded in 1961 as the official press agency of the NLFSV, claims 40 publications, all of them clandestine. The major ones include *Giai Phong* (Liberation), the organ of the NLFSV Central Committee; *Trung Lap,* ostensibly published by a group affiliated with the NLFSV and dedicated to a "neutral solution to the Vietnam problem"; *Nhan Dan* (People's Daily), the weekly organ of the PRP, patterned after the North Vietnamese organ of the same name; *Tien Phong* (Vanguard), the monthly political and theoretical organ of the PRP; *Quan Giai Phong* (Liberation Troops), the army newspaper; *Phu Nu* (Women); and two irregular NLFSV journals, *Co Giai Phong* and *Thoi Su Pho Thong.* NLFSV policy statements and directives are also broadcast over Liberation Radio, founded in 1962, and are frequently carried by the Vietnam News Agency in Hanoi. Both the Liberation Press Agency and Liberation Radio are believed to be located across the border in Tay Ninh Province of Cambodia. Reports indicate that the actual writing, translation, and publication of NLFSV propaganda is done in North Vietnam by the Foreign Languages Publishing House. A captured document released in the spring of 1967 also noted that a foreign propaganda branch had been established in Phnom Penh "for the purpose of publishing documents to be sent to foreign countries."

# YUGOSLAVIA

The Communist Party of Yugoslavia was founded in June 1920.* At the Sixth Party Congress, in November 1952, the name was changed to the League of Communists of Yugoslavia (Savez Komunista Jugoslavije; LCY). The League of Communists of Yugoslavia is the supreme political institution and the dominant factor in all spheres of official life in the country.

Legally, the LCY is the only party in the country, although there is also a mass front organization, the Socialist Alliance of Working People of Yugoslavia (Socialistićki Savez Radnog Naroda Jugoslavije), with some eight million members. Membership in this organization is virtually automatic; all trade unions, student unions, and communist youth organizations are part of it, as is the LCY itself. The Socialist Alliance is led by Communist functionaries, but according to its statute it can be joined either by individuals or collectively by whole bodies of socialist mass organizations.

On 1 January 1967 the LCY had 1,046,018 members, a net decline of 184 members from 1966. The decrease primarily reflects the purge of the secret-police cadres resulting from the expulsion of Aleksandar Ranković, the former head of the secret police, and his associates from their posts. This net numerical decrease in membership is very small, as according to official party data published in *Komunist* (6 April 1967) 13,488 members were expelled in the course of 1966, of whom 52 per cent were workers and about 15 per cent were peasants. In addition, 7,640 members left the party voluntarily—some 2,000 more than in the previous year; about 53 per cent of these were workers and about 11 per cent were peasants. The population of Yugoslavia is 19,742,000 (estimated, April 1966).

**Organization and Leadership.** The LCY is headed by Josip Broz Tito, now (1968) 75 years old, who is President of the LCY and also Federal President of Yugoslavia and Marshal of the Armed Forces. Tito holds these positions for life and is the only person in the Yugoslav party and state apparatus not subject to rotation (see below). The chief federal party organs since reorganization by the Fifth Plenum (October 1966) is the 35-member Presidium, chaired by Tito and consisting of the chief party veterans. It is supposed to function as a policy-recommending body, but the importance of its members in the party hierarchy points to its key position in party administration. There is also an 11-member Executive Committee, consisting mainly of younger Party functionaries and chaired by Secretary, Mijalko Todorović. This is the decision-implementing organ of the 155-member Central Committee of the LCY. However, as the latter body meets only occasionally and for a few days at a time, the Presidium and Executive Committee are of principal importance in party affairs. In addition to Tito, the leading personalities in the party are: Vladimir Bakarić, member of the Presidium and Chairman of the Croat Communist Party; Krste Crvenkovski, member of the Presidium and Chairman of the Presidium of the Macedonian Communist Party; Ivan Gošnjak, member of the Presidium and Minister of Defense; Edvard Kardelj, member of the Presidium; Lazar Koliševski, member of the Presidium and Chairman of the Socialist Alliance of Working People of Yugoslavia; Dušan Petrović, member of the Presidium and head of the Yugoslav trade unions; Koča Popović, member of the Presidium; Milentije Popović, member of the Presidium and President of the National Assembly (the Federal Parliament); Vladimir Popović, member of the Presidium; Petar Stambolić, member of the Presidium; Mika Špiljak, member of the Presidium and President of the Federal Executive Council (the Prime Minister); Veljko Vlahović, member of the Presidium; and Svetozar Vukmanović-Tempo, member of the Presidium.

*Yugoslav Communists claim as the year of the party's foundation 1919, the year of the founding of the Socialist Workers' Party, which included both communist and noncommunist elements.

All top government officials are also important party members, and nearly all are members of either the Central Committee of the LCY or the Central Committees of the parties of the constituent republics of Yugoslavia or their presidiums.

Government and party executives (with the exception of Tito) are subject to the so-called rotation principle, whereby no officer may occupy an executive position for more than one electoral term (or, under special circumstances, two terms). This principle of the 1963 Constitution began to be implemented in 1966-67. As a result, Kardelj was replaced by Milentije Popović as the Federal Parliament Chairman, and Stambolić was replaced by Spiljak in the position of the Federal Prime Minister.

The largest single sociopolitical organization in Yugoslavia is the Socialist Alliance of the Working People of Yugoslavia, formerly the Popular Front. As mentioned, it has some eight million members. Another mass organization, the Confederation of Yugoslav Trade Unions, has about 2,800,000 members. Although officially the trade unions are supposed to act "in line with the policy laid down by the program of the League of Communists," some leading Yugoslav ideologists have recently urged a greater autonomy of the trade unions from Party control, admitting that the production interests of management may be in conflict with the interests of the workers. Others go so far as to demand the legalization of workers' strikes (Vladimir Bakarić, addressing the Youth League plenum in Zagreb, 7 October 1967; Professor Tadić of Belgrade University in *Politika*, 25 October). Finally, there is the Youth League of Yugoslavia with about two million members, which is meant to serve as the main reservoir for the future party cadres. But mistrust between the party and the youth organization, and between the latter and the young people, has lately been mounting. Such alienation was repeatedly reflected in the Yugoslav press (as, in *NIN*, Belgrade, 29 January, and *Borba*, 9 March). The party was criticized for dictating objectives to the Youth League, which in turn was charged with being an organization *for* youth, instead of an organization *of* youth (*Borba*, 9 March and 25 November).

All these organizations are headed by important party functionaries. Furthermore, although in Yugoslavia there is a clearer division of powers between the state and the party than in any other communist country, Tito and his closest associates control the government as well as the party; Tito is both the head of the party and of the State. Also, the Council of Federation, an institution not clearly defined in the Constitution, in special circumstances seems to play the role of a supergovernment, similar to the one played in the party apparatus by the Presidium. The members of the Council of Federation are elected by the Federal Chamber (the most important chamber of the five-chamber Parliament) "upon the proposal of the President of the Republic, from among federal officers and officials of the republics and from among officials of the socio-political and other organizations" (*The Yugoslav Constitution,* English Version, Belgrade, 1963). In other words, its members are hand-picked by Tito, who can convene it at any time "in order to consider matters of state policy" (*ibid.,* Article 224). Its importance for President Tito and for the smooth implementation of his policies proved itself during the Middle East crisis. On 1 July Tito convoked the very first meeting of the Council of Federation to legitimize his leading role in arranging the summit meeting of East European communist parties on the Middle East on 9 June in Moscow, his decision to participate in it, and his anti-Israel statement of 5 June made on behalf of the Yugoslav government. This meeting took place simultaneously with the Seventh Plenum of the Central Committee of the LCY, whose support for Tito's Middle East policy was only halfhearted (see below). There was speculation that Tito had decided to call the 1 July meeting of the Council of Federation because of insufficient support in the Central Committee. At this meeting an extraconstitutional permanent body was established, to be called the Organizational Commission of the Council of Federation, thus further confusing the issue of real and fictional government bodies and their actual interrelationship. The Organizational Commission, consisting of Tito's six closest associates,* considerably weakens the actual effect of the principles of rotation and the separation of powers.

*Edvard Kardelj, Ivan Gosnjak, Veljko Vlahović, Koča Popović, Svetozar Vukmanović-Tempo, and Vladimir Popović. All these (except Gosnjak, who is Tito's deputy for the armed forces), formally lost all their nonparty positions in the course of rotation of offices earlier in 1967 and in other government reforms.

**April 1967 Elections.** According to Article 81 of the 1963 Constitution, deputies to the Federal Assembly and to the legislatures of the republics and the communal bodies are elected for four-year terms, half the deputies being elected every two years. Only members of the Federal Chamber and the corresponding chambers of the local governments are elected directly. In 1967, 60 deputies were elected to the Federal Chamber and a total of 325 seats were to be filled in the chambers of the six republics. Abstentions and invalidated ballots amounted to 15.7 per cent in the elections to the Federal Chamber in 1967, as compared to 9.2 per cent in 1965 (*World Strength of Communist Party Organizations,* 1968). Something approaching a real electoral campaign was carried on for the first time since the Communist takeover; as a result, nearly 30 per cent of the official candidates to the republican chambers failed to be elected and independent deputies were elected in their places. On the federal level it appears that at least one of the 60 deputies elected was an independent, although the number was probably greater, as at the final voting stage there were 81 candidates to fill 60 vacancies. This was a substantial achievement in view of the fact that there are no organized opposition parties and no independent press in which opposition candidates could publicize themselves or their views, and given the extreme complexity of the Yugoslav electoral procedure. Prospective candidates are registered at public meetings convoked by the local Socialist Alliance branches. As the result of this registration, there were four candidates for each seat (*Borba,* 6 March). The electoral commissions, together with the Socialist Alliance branches, then cut the number of candidates to a "more practical" number. The final selection of candidates from a reduced list takes place at nominating meetings held in each village and in every urban ward. After these screenings, the voters were left with the choice of 428 candidates for the 325 vacancies in the republican legislatures and 81 candidates for the 60 places in the federal legislature.

Radio Belgrade reported on 7 December 1967 that Vojislav Veljković, a lawyer in the city of Niš, was sentenced by the local court to three years' strict imprisonment because "during the last elections he had written various leaflets and sent them out to farming cooperatives throughout Serbia, Montenegro, and Bosnia and Hercegovina" and in the leaflets had "appealed to the electors not to vote for the official candidates of the Socialist Alliance."

**Language Issue.** Another internal event which considerably affected the officially proclaimed "brotherhood and unity" of the peoples of Yugoslavia and the "unshakability" of the Federation—two basic achievements claimed by the LCY—was the nationalist Croat "language declaration," which appeared unexpectedly and without the advance knowledge of the LCY and the Government leadership. It accused the Serbs of trying to impose the Serbian variant of the Serbo-Croatian language upon the Croats. It further proclaimed that in order to put an end to the Serbian linguistic monopoly, the two dialects should be declared separate languages, one to be used in Serbia and the other in Croatia. The declaration appeared over the signatures of practically all the major cultural institutions of Croatia. The difference between the two linguistic variants is no greater than that between American and British English, probably less, aside from the fact that the Serbs use the Cyrillic alphabet, while the Croats use Latin letters. The issue is complicated by the existence of large areas in Yugoslavia where Serbs using either the Cyrillic or the Latin alphabet speak the Croatian variant of the language; there are also Croats in large communities just north of Belgrade who mostly speak the Serbian variant. There are nearly a million Serbs in Croatia proper (almost 30 per cent of the population of Croatia) with keen memories of the mass killings of Serbs by the Croatian nationalist Ustase during the Second World War.

On 2 April there appeared in the Belgrade *Borba* a Serbian writers' response to the declaration. This "Proposal for Reconsideration," signed by 45 Serbian writers, stated that the signatories would not be averse to declaring the two languages separate and proposed that separate schools using the respective languages and alphabets should be established for the large Serbian community in Croatia and for the relatively small Croat community in Serbia.

Tito and the top party leadership reacted violently to both documents. Speaking on 26 March in Pristina, the administrative center of the Albanian minority in Serbia, Tito used the nationalist Croat language-declaration to denounce his internal ideological foes, putting them all into the same "pot": "Former cetniks [the Serbian Royalist resistance in the Second World War], Ustaše and white guards have remained under cover. . . . These and others like them are now again raising their heads and want to destroy our brotherhood and unity, to make it impossible for us to build socialism. . . . They worked in secret, preparing the Declaration and took us by surprise with a stab in the back . . ." (*Yugoslav Facts and Views*, Yugoslav Information Center, New York, no. 21, 13·April.)

For nearly a month the Yugoslav radio carried broadcasts on the language issue. It was also one of the topics of the Seventh Plenum of the Central Committee of the LCY, on 1 July. A number of Croatian and Serbian intellectuals were either ousted from the LCY or left it under pressure for having a part in one or the other of the language documents. The most prominent was Miroslav Krleža, the most famous living Croat writer.

**Role of the LCY.** In recent years criticism of the one-party system has been mounting, with the result that a number of proposals for a drastic revision of the system have been openly expressed. The main proposals fall into three broad categories. (1) The noncommunist masses could be incorporated into political life just as they have been incorporated into economic life by the workers' self-management system. Under this proposal the Socialist Alliance would play the role of a "political force" encompassing everyone, regardless of party allegiance. This concept has been developed by a prominent Belgrade professor, Svetozar Stojanović, who calls it a "socialist pluralism," in which socialist mass organizations, such as the Socialist Alliance and the trade unions, would become political institutions independent of the party and act as quasi-parties. This view has been termed by Western observers the "one-and-a-half party system." (2) A straightforward multiparty system could be contemplated in the possible future development of Yugoslav society, if it should prove impossible to overcome the stagnating forces of bureaucracy by other means. This view has been proposed by a number of prominent Yugoslavs, such as Professor S. Vračar (*Gledišta,* Belgrade, August-September) and Mijalko Todorović, the Secretary of the Executive Committee of the Central Committee of the LCY (Radio Belgrade, 25 January 1968).* (3) As the communist party withers away, a nonparty system based on the decentralized self-management bodies could be allowed to develop (Jovan Marjanović, *Socijalizam,* January 1967).

The "Draft Theses on the Further Development and Reorganization of the League of Communists of Yugoslavia," issued in April 1967, strike a line somewhere between the first and third types of proposals:

> The League's democratic, ideological-political guidance of social development, by means of which the one-party political monopoly is being eliminated and at the same time the ground for a multi-party system denied, can be achieved only through a broad political organization of all social forces which accept the socialist foundations of social order . . . which permit real conflicts of interest and differing ideological attitudes to be expressed freely and settled democratically through direct political activity by the working people with the League of Communists acting as the internal force of this democratic process. ("Draft Theses," Supplement to *Review of International Affairs,* no. 411.)

From this and other parts of the Draft Theses it appears that the Theses, which are to be discussed and implemented by the forthcoming (1968) Ninth Party Congress, do not envisage any withering away of the role of the party. Yet, the discussion of the coming party reform that ensued from the publication of the Theses has revealed unorthodox views on the future of the Yugoslav political system that go much farther. In fact, the Theses have been criticized for superficiality and evasion of certain problems requiring solution. The idea of a nonparty system, with the Socialist Alliance rather than the Communist Party at the core, has been proposed again and again (as, for instance, in a paper presented at a Belgrade symposium on 7 June by Vida Tomsic, member of the LCY Central Committee and Chairman of the Chamber of Nationalities in the Federal Parliament).

Although the LCY continues to have a monopoly of political power, its monopoly has become somewhat less direct in the economy through the extension of the rights of individual managements

---

*Milentije Popović, the top party theoretician and a member of the party Presidium, has stated on at least two occasions that if the Yugoslav model of "direct democracy" should fail, a multiparty solution "will inevitably develop" (*Komunist,* 1 December 1966, and *Socijalizam,* November 1966).

of factories, economic decentralization, and the widening of the role and rights of private enterprise. There appears to be growing pressure from the "technocracy" and other productive forces to attenuate the political monopoly of the LCY as well, so as to protect the economy from political interference by the party bureaucracy. These pressures meet with the support of the intellectuals and some party functionaries (although the aims of these groups may be quite different).

The wide discussion in the Yugoslav press and news media of the Draft Theses for the forthcoming Ninth Congress of the LCY dwelt extensively on the future role, functions, and position of the party and its functionaries. A broadcast discussing these questions stated: "There are still illusions here about the omnipotence of the socialist states ... illusions about a harmonious way of constructing socialism, and also attempts to carry over the social and moral norms from the times of the revolution into our times of peaceful construction ..." (Radio Zagreb, 30 June). Throughout the year there were also numerous complaints in the Yugoslav press that too many industrial workers and peasants have left the party, while the influx of youth has been very low, causing the percentage of these categories in the party to continue to decline.

The arrests, trials, and sentences of Mihajlo Mihajlov (17 April), Professor Vladimir Munša (29 April), sentenced to 22 months' imprisonment for "hostile propaganda," and Vojislav Veljković (10 June; see above) indicate the limits of the current liberalizing trends in the Yugoslav sociopolitical structure. The Mihajlov case is a particularly vivid illustration. The 1963 Constitution of Yugoslavia allows the formation of independent sociopolitical groups and journals as long as they are not antisocialist and do not preach hatred of other peoples (whether Yugoslav or foreign) or advocate war, civil strife, or violent overthrow of the existing regime. Mihajlo Mihajlov, an assistant professor of philosophy at the Zadar Faculty (campus) of Zagreb University, tried on the basis of this constitutional right to start an independent newspaper in Yugoslavia in 1966, but was prevented from doing so by police. On charges that in his articles published abroad he had falsely described and libeled the Yugoslav system, Mihajlov was arrested, tried, and sentenced to one year's imprisonment in September 1966. Retried in April 1967, he was sentenced to four and a half years of strict imprisonment for "dissemination of false propaganda" about the Yugoslav Government. In his articles and statements Mihajlov proclaimed that an independent newspaper and a second party were needed in the country to prevent one-party hegemony, which—so he argued—inevitably and logically leads to Stalinism (or "Rankovićism" in the case of Yugoslavia).

**Economic Reform.** The further development of the economic reform continued to bring revision of some of the basic assumptions of Marxism-Leninism. The most salient of these relates to the question of unemployment. According to Radio Zagreb (8 July), there were 263,000 unemployed in Yugoslavia in June, or 7,000 more than in the same month of 1966. The number of unemployed was growing, according to the broadcast, owing to the progress of the economic reform, with its more intensive use of labor and the closing down of the most inefficient enterprises. To this number must be added the more than 60,000 school and university graduates who had been unable to find employment for over four months (*Vjesnik u srijedu*, Zagreb, 25 October), and the more than 300,000 Yugoslavs working abroad. This situation clearly contradicted the Marxist premise that socialist society guarantees full employment. As a spokesman put it:

> This is a difficult problem of our society. We have decided not to return to the extensive methods of employment. This we have stated through the reform. ... In order to protect [our citizens] from exploitation we have not allowed [private entrepreneurs] to employ more than three, four, or five workers. This I consider to be a slave-like adherence to dogma without consideration for life. There is no greater tragedy for our citizens than to be unemployed. This is super-exploitation. ... We have heard much about the plotters who think that the private sector of the economy is capable of solving the unemployment problem. It cannot; but the socialist sector cannot do it either ...(Čedo Grbić, Deputy Chairman of the Croat Parliament, over Radio Zagreb, 17 December).

The explicit recognition that the socialist economy cannot solve the unemployment problem gave new support to advocates of the expansion of private enterprise prerogatives. In Croatia, the state insurance and pension system has been extended to cover those engaged in private enterprise (Radio

Zagreb, 2 October). The federal law on private enterprise was changed so that private restaurant owners can now sell or even rent for profit these restaurants, while in the past on termination of the owner's direct engagement his shop or restaurant was nationalized. Also, it was promised that in the near future private enterprises dealing with tourism would be freed from the limitation on legal employment of only three hired workers, and that the appropriate legislation was being prepared in the Federal Parliament in Belgrade (Radio Zagreb, 10 March). It was also decided to allow privately owned camping sites (*Borba*, 25 May). Almost 80 per cent of local freight was being carried by privately owned trucks, whose number had grown from 9,000 in January 1966 to 17,000 in May 1967 (Radio Belgrade, 27 May).

But the most significant breakthrough was made in foreign investment. On 15 March the Yugoslav Government announced that foreign capital investment will be allowed to provide up to 50 per cent of the resources for a Yugoslav enterprise. One important undertaking to which this legislation was geared was the negotiations with the West German Volkswagen firm, whose direct investment in an automobile plant to be built in Yugoslavia is to be 49 per cent. Its share of profit would be the same, and its representatives would have a consultative voice on the factory's management board. (*Politika*, Belgrade, 12 February).

Another ideological problem in Yugoslavia relates to the rise in the number of strikes and strikers. Theoretically, there should be no strikes in a socialist country, because factories and all other means of production belong to the workers and are run by a workers' government. Strikes in Yugoslavia present greater embarrassment than in other communist countries, because Yugoslavia claims to have an industry run by workers' councils. Yet, whereas there were "2,500 strikers in the whole of 1966, their number rose to 4,000 during the first seven months of 1967," with corresponding loss of working hours rising from 10,000 in 1966 to 25,000 in the first seven months of 1967 (Radio Zagreb, 22 September). Authoritative voices have been raised demanding that full recognition be given to the workers' right to strike and that the trade unions be made the defenders of the workers' rights against the bureaucracy and the management.

**International Views and Policies.** In international relations 1967 began with some signs of political estrangement from the East European bloc. This, however, did not affect Yugoslavia's growing economic and cultural relations with those countries. There was some activization of friendly relations with Bulgaria, and news about Yugoslav-Bulgarian relations was given prominence by Yugoslav media. A special "section for the development of economic cooperation with Bulgaria" was established at the Federal Chamber of Commerce in Belgrade (Radio Zagreb, 24 May). An agreement for cooperation between Yugoslav and Bulgarian journalist organizations was signed in Sofia on 15 March. A similar agreement for cooperation between the two countries in the spheres of science, education, and culture was signed in April (Radio Belgrade, 14 April). The number of Yugoslav tourists visiting Bulgaria for the 1 May holidays reached the unprecedented figure of 70,000 (Radio Zagreb, 3 May).

Signs of political tension between Yugoslavia and the rest of Eastern Europe were evident in the Yugoslav refusal to participate in the Karlovy Vary conference of the Communist Parties of Europe on 24-26 April. The decision not to participate was preceded by intensive consultations of the top Yugoslav party delegations with the leaderships of other East European parties. The same was true of Rumania, with the difference that Rumania was receiving delegations, while Yugoslavia was sending them. It appeared that other East European parties were attempting to persuade Rumania to participate, while Yugoslavia was concerned lest Rumania take part in the conference and Yugoslavia remain in isolation. In a speech on 17 April Tito reminded the Yugoslavs about his feud with the Cominform in 1948, saying: "This was a most serious and . . . most unjust attack on our party, an attempt to split it and to turn it into a satellite party" (Radio Belgrade, 17 April). Earlier an article in the *Review of International Affairs* had stated: "The Marxist socialist parties can and must identify with the ideology of peace and progress, . . . . [but] they no longer have a monopoly over this ideology. . . . In recent times the attitudes of the League of Communists on some problems have met with a certain lack of understanding, simplistic and false interpretations. This was the case with . . . the idea of convening a world consultation of communist parties, as a campaign is currently being waged demanding of parties to declare themselves for or against the conference." (N. Opačić, "International Cooperation of the League of Communists of Yugoslavia," *Review of International Affairs,* no. 404, February). This theme also characterized the Yugoslav radio broadcasts on the Karlovy Vary conference and on the reasons for the LCY's nonparticipation. In fact, on 26 April Radio Zagreb criticized Walter Ulbricht for his "tactless" criticism of those Communist Parties which had not participated in the conference, and in its criticism of the Soviet pre-Conference press comments Radio Zagreb stated on 24 April: "Only Europe is being mentioned, while nowhere is there even a word about the coexistence policy or about the countries and movements in the world which are carrying out this policy. This is but another political and regional contraction, and the word coexistence itself in its political usage has now been for some months thrown out of the Soviet vocabulary."

On the Soviet side, there was an indirect criticism of Yugoslavia by I. Pomelov in an article, "The Communist Party in a Socialist Society," in *Pravda* on 20 February. Although the article attacked only Communist China by name, "some parties" were strongly criticized for advancing the idea that the party may wither away and that its political leadership may be replaced by purely ideological and educative guidance.

**The Middle East Crisis.** As soon as the Arab-Israeli war began, Tito issued a strong anti-Israel statement on 5 June on behalf of the Yugoslav Government. Four days later he was in Moscow conferring with party and government leaders of the East European states, including Rumania (but excluding Albania). The Yugoslav delegation included Vladimir Popović, Secretary-General of the Presidium of the Central Committee of the LCY. In contrast with all the other East European delegations at the conference, Tito was not accompanied by his Prime Minister, Mika Špiljak, which seems to suggest that Tito's decision was his own and this, his first statement against Israel, was also made strictly on his own initiative.* According to Article 217 of the Yugoslav Constitution, the President of the Republic has no right to take such an independent initiative in international affairs. It was only after Tito's return from Moscow that a joint session of the party Presidium and the party Executive Committee was held on 11 June, at which, in line with his statement, Tito explained that the top Yugoslav party bodies should approve the 9 June Moscow Declaration because it was in full agreement with the stand taken by the Yugoslav Government on the very first day of the "Israeli aggression" (*Borba,* 12 June). Furthermore, Koča Popović, who went to Cairo on 11 June, and the Foreign Secretary, Marko Nikezić, who went to New Delhi on 13 June, were officially sent as Tito's personal emissaries. On 13 June Yugoslavia severed diplomatic relations with Israel.

Subsequently there were signs of disagreement between Tito and the more liberal circles of the Yugoslav leadership on the Middle East issue and on Tito's pro-Moscow line. Tito himself stated on 1 July at the Seventh Plenum: "[It is being said] in our country. . . that Yugoslavia has aligned itself with the Warsaw Pact [as a result of] our participation at the [9 June] Moscow meeting. This is, of course, nonsense." (Radio Zagreb, 1 July.) In fact, most of the other speakers at the plenum were not as strongly anti-Israel as Tito, who claimed that Israel was "an artificial state" and "an instrument of imperialist forces." Kamal Seyfula, a representative of the Turkish minority in the Central Committee, maintained the opposite: that the Arabs should recognize Israel's right to exist and that Arab-Israeli relations should be normalized (*Politika,* 2 July). The speech of Foreign Minister Nikezić was even more moderate and dealt with the Middle East problem only in passing (*Borba,* 2 July). On 11 July Nikezić was attacked in Parliament (an unprecedented event in postwar Yugoslavia) by a member of the Croatian Central Committee, Josip Djerdja (known for his hard-line statements in the past as well), for not having dealt with "the plot in the Middle East" as one which involved direct repercussions for the security of the Mediterranean, including Yugoslavia (Radio Zagreb, 11 July).

The theme of an "imperialist plot" endangering the whole Mediterranean area, including Yugoslavia, was elaborated by Tito and his immediate Central Committee entourage at the Seventh Plenum (*Politika,* 2 July), but apparently was not taken seriously by Nikezić and the other dissenting politicians and economists. The next issue of *Ekonomska Politika* (8 July), the organ of the Executive

*It appears that this was Tito's first personal participation in an international communist gathering since 1945.

Committee of the Central Committee, which consists of the younger reformist Yugoslav communist executives, came out strongly in its editorial against "the concept of a strong-arm policy." To support its arguments, the article quoted a recent "Slovenian public-opinion poll" presented to the plenum, in which "the population at large strongly supported everything considered to be essential [to] democratic development, while only two per cent . . . considered that because of the world situation the role of the State . . . in society should be strengthened." It was apparent that Tito's statements about the "imperialist plot endangering Yugoslavia" and his demand that Yugoslavia's defenses be strengthened hinted at a recentralized "strong-arm policy."

There appeared to be some inconsistency in Tito's pro-Moscow stance on the Middle East issue so soon after his refusal to participate in the Karlovy Vary conference. A partial explanation may be that Tito's refusal to take part in the Karlovy Vary meeting was a concession to the liberals and that he then seized the first opportunity—the Middle East crisis—to prevail over his opponents on the pretext that this was a much more important issue, that the Yugoslav national existence was being threatened, and that in the face of this, his unity with the rest of the European communist countries was justified.

Yugoslavian aid and trade policies became the subject of open criticism in one of the two most important Yugoslav dailies on 4 October. Writing on the very day when Tito stated that Yugoslavia's aid to the underdeveloped countries amounted thus far to $600 million and a day after his statement that Yugoslavia's alliance with the underdeveloped countries was aimed chiefly at creating "a strong moral-political factor in the world," the foreign policy editor of *Politika*, Gustinčić, wrote that before helping Asia and Africa, Yugoslavs should first "put in order the house in which they live." His argument was that if a small country wants to play a great role in world politics it must first become economically strong, and that no one would take Yugoslavia seriously as long as its trade balances with France and West Germany, for instance, were negative. To this he added that it was important for Yugoslavia to have the best possible relations with countries which were "big in the economic sense." For this virtual attack on the basic premises of Tito's foreign policy, Gustinčić himself was attacked by the Yugoslav newspapers (see respectively, *Borba*, 4 and 5 October; *Politika*, 4 October; *Vjesnik*, 8 October; and *Vjesnik u srijedu*, Zagreb, 11 October).

However, although in official declarations and policy statements Tito's "great power" politics have continued to set policy, in practice more pragmatic considerations have not been forgotten. Important political and economic negotiations with West Germany were carried on throughout the year, and the idea of reestablishing formal diplomatic relations between the two countries received considerable support from the Yugoslav news media.*

Tito's pro-Arab efforts appeared to exceed those of the other East European countries, including those of the Soviet Union itself. From early June to the end of August, almost every day Yugoslav news media reported trips of Yugoslav leaders to the Middle Eastern states, and return visits of the Arab leaders and state delegations to Yugoslavia, mutual communiques and declarations, and commercial treaties. Tito himself went to Cairo on 10 August with Kardelj, Vladimir Popović, Kiro Gligorov, and, significantly, Deputy Secretary for Foreign Affairs Mišo Pavićević (and not Nikezić, the Foreign Secretary whose position had been less enthusiastically pro-Arab than that of Pavićević). This was followed by Tito's active personal participation in the 11-12 July Budapest conference of the leaders of East European countries (from which Rumania abstained). The talks were "carried out in accordance with the agreement reached at the Moscow Conference . . . on 9 June, to keep constant contacts with one another on the situation in the Middle East . . . , (See *Documents*.)

In the course of Tito's first visit to Cairo after the Arab-Israeli war, trade negotiations between the Yugoslavs and the Egyptians also took place. The Egyptian press reported that the talks between Nasser and Tito concerned the "liquidation of the repercussions of the war." On 13 August Tito left for Damascus, and on the following day proceeded to Baghdad, where he was present at the opening of the Conference of the Arab Ministers of Finance, Economy, and Oil Industries on 15 August. Tito was officially thanked for his pro-Arab stand by President Abdul Rahman Arif of Iraq. The

*The negotiations culminated in the formal re-establishment of the West German-Yugoslav diplomatic relations early in 1968.

communique on the Arif-Tito talks stated only that the two leaders had "exchanged thoughts on the Middle East crisis, on the world situation, and on the further development of friendly relations and cooperation between the two states," and that both sides had paid "special attention to the problem of liquidation of the aftermath of the Israeli aggression . . . and to the problem of the economic strengthening of the Arab lands" (Radio Belgrade, 16 August). On 16 August Tito went back to Cairo and continued his talks with Nasser, returning to Yugoslavia the next day. A communique issued in Cairo stressed the identity of views of both leaders, their conviction that "the present situation, which is the result of aggression, cannot be tolerated and deeply harms the legitimate rights and interests of the Arab nations and directly threatens the cause of peace, not only in the Middle East but in the whole world." The UN and the nonaligned countries should play the major role in the normalization of the Middle East situation, according to the communique. (Radio Belgrade, 17 August.)

The travels of Tito were given prominence in Yugoslav and Arab media, and were followed by visits to Yugoslavia by Arab government delegations (Syria on 20 August; Jordan on 22 August; Iraq on 24 August). The Khartoum summit conference of the Arab leaders received detailed attention in Yugoslav broadcasts and was termed "a great step forward toward Arab unity."

Tito also received a delegation from the banned Moroccan Communist Party (20-21 July), but the fact that the party was persecuted at home was not mentioned, and reports about this visit were limited. The talks dealt mainly with "the Israeli aggression."

On 4 September Belgrade was the host to a further conference of the European socialist countries on economic cooperation with the Arab lands. This time Rumania took part in the conference, and presumably the presence of the Rumanian delegation affected the tone of the communique issued 7 September, which was relatively moderate and did not mention "Israeli aggression." The communique stated merely that "the participants in the conference expressed their readiness . . . to study together with the Arab countries concrete measures as to the further broadening of economic cooperation and exchanged information on their plans of concrete actions regarding the extension of help [to the Arabs]' (Radio Zagreb, 7 September).

**Relations with Cuba.** Relations between Yugoslavia and Cuba remained unfriendly during 1967, as was evident in a broadcast by Radio Belgrade on 1 August: "As at the last year's Conference of Solidarity of the Three Continents, the organizers [of the First Conference of the Organization of Latin-American Solidarity which began in Havana on 31 July] have again decided to discriminate against Yugoslavia by not inviting her to send observers to the conference, although such invitations were extended to all the other socialist countries." Earlier in the year, one of Yugoslavia's leading commentators, Sundić, stated that Cuba was "heading for Chinese methods" (Radio Zagreb, 16 March). He charged Cuba with ingratitude for Soviet help and with being tactlessly critical in demanding "that the Soviet Union break relations with those Latin American states which are on bad terms with Cuba." Sundić warned Cuba that the Soviet Union might lose patience, as it finally did with China, and withdraw its "generous aid and support." On the eve of the opening of the OLAS Conference, Radio Zagreb (25 July) criticized Cuba and the OLAS for extremism and for advocating guerrilla warfare as the only means of struggle against imperialism. Great prominence was given to the disagreement of the communist parties of Argentina, Brazil, Chile, and Venezuela with this extremist stand, to their feud with the Cubans before the conference, and to the decision of the parties of Argentina, Brazil, and Venezuela not to take part in the conference (Radio Zagreb, 30 July; Radio Belgrade, 1 August).

**Relations with China.** Yugoslavia's relations with Communist China remained at least as bad as in 1966. One of the signs of this was the expulsion of the correspondent Bogunović from China on 16 April. However, the strong anti-Chinese stand of Yugoslavia, the behavior of Cuba, and the Soviet-Yugoslav rapprochement did not result in any change of heart on the part of the Yugoslav party toward the proposed world communist conference, and Yugoslavia did not join with the Soviet policy stand on China. Yugoslav objections to a world communist conference were explicitly outlined in an *Ekonomska Politika* article which stated that in 1962 it was Mao who had insisted on a world conference, hoping that through it he could "turn the workers' movement against the Communist

Party of the Soviet Union," and added: "The Chinese did not succeed; this is why they are now opposing such a conference . . . " Now, the article went on, it was the "compact, united section of the communist movement" which was "engaged in an ideological and political-diplomatic war with another communist section" and wanted a world conference. In other words, in the Yugoslav view, the purpose of any such conference would be either to expel China or to impose general discipline on the communist parties. This would probably cause similar conferences of those disagreeing with the Moscow-type of discipline, and thus the split would only become greater. "Harm can originate from a false international pose of obedience . . . Such obedience has been demanded . . by all world conferences held so far." (Živko Milić, *Ekonomska Politika*, 7 October. Similar articles in *Borba*, 29 September; *Politika*, 15 October, and *Komunist* (Belgrade), 28 September.)

In spite of a totally negative attitude to the Chinese internal and external policies, Yugoslavia has been calling on the communist states to exercise maximum caution and moderation regarding China. At the same time, Yugoslavia has cautioned noncommunist countries to follow a "hands-off" policy toward China. Both aspects of this position were detailed in a *Borba* article (5 February) by Dr. M. Iveković, entitled "China at the Turning Point."

Analyzing the Maoist evolution (or revolution), a prominent Yugoslav journalist, M Draskic, in contradiction to the Soviet view (according to which communist ideology has been disintegrating in China and Mao has been destroying socialism and communism there), stated: "Never, not even now, have the achievements of the victorious [Chinese] revolution been in jeopardy" ("Theses About China," *Review of International Affairs*, Belgrade, 20 October). Draškić concluded: "Mao's efforts from the outset have been directed towards stepping up economic development and transforming Chinese society on socialist principles. It is not these efforts and aspirations which are being disputed. What is controversial is the methods . . . The trouble with China [is] that she is trying to overcome her underdevelopment on the same old underdeveloped foundations and with the same old methods."

**Yugoslavia and Vietnam.** In general terms Yugoslavia's position on Vietnam has not differed from that of the other East European countries, including that of the Soviet Union. However, anti-American pronouncements on the Vietnam issue have been much less prominent and somewhat more moderate in the Yugoslav media.

Tito has repeatedly denounced American "aggression" in Vietnam. In a speech at Priština, he stated that the US was "testing murderous weapons on a defenseless people" in Vietnam. He then gave his reasons for supporting North Vietnam:

> If the people of any country is not satisfied with its regime . . . then that people has the right to overthrow its oppressors . . . . The people of South Vietnam, where the regime was hated, saw that North Vietnam had liberated itself from colonialism, that it had achieved much, that it was going ahead with construction. Therefore, the people in the south rose against its unpopular regime, which then called upon American troops for assistance so that it could maintain its rule, even at the price of decimating its population.
> (*Yugoslav Facts and Views*, 13 April.)

In constructive suggestions on the Vietnamese situation, the Yugoslav communists took a more moderate position, demanding negotiations rather than an unconditional evacuation of the Americans from the Vietnamese territory prior to any negotiations, as demanded by North Vietnam, China, and, although not as emphatically, the Soviet Union: "The range of choice [for the US in Vietnam] is not wide in view of the fact that escalation so far [has] brought matters to a strategic head . . . The only thing that remains is negotiation . . . or transferring total war above the 17th parallel . . . [The latter] obviously involves a whole series of risks [with] no guarantees that the US can win a military victory in Vietnam." (A. Gabelić, "The Critical Point in Vietnam," *Review of International Affairs*, 20 October.)

**Other International Contacts.** The liveliness of Yugoslav foreign relations (with communists as well as noncommunists) has been reflected in a number of top-level visits, both by the highest Yugoslav statesmen going abroad and by foreign leaders visiting Yugoslavia. Soviet President Nikolai Podgorny visited Yugoslavia on his way to and from the United Arab Republic, stopping over on 20 June in Pula, where he was met by Tito, who took him to his summer island residence of Brioni, and again on

24 June in Pula, going with Tito to Brioni for unpublicized talks. On 3 July Mika Špiljak left for Moscow to open a Yugoslav Exhibition. On 23 August Tito received the Secretary-General of the Italian CP, Luigi Longo. A visit by Waldeck Rochet, the French CP Secretary-General, followed on 26 August. The talks with Italian and French party leaders apparently dealt both with the Soviet-proposed world conference of communist parties, opposed by the Yugoslav Communists, and with the Yugoslav proposal to convoke a Mediterranean conference of communist parties and other "progressive forces," allegedly to discuss the danger to this area resulting from the "imperialist aggression" in the Middle East. Czechoslovak President Antonín Novotný paid a five-day visit to Tito beginning 11 September. The commentary on the meeting by Radio Zagreb (15 September) stated that the discussions dealt with the Middle East and that both sides reached complete identity of views on the subject. The Yugoslav Communists also celebrated the Fiftieth Anniversary of the October Revolution both at home and by sending a delegation to Moscow, led by Tito, for the Anniversary. A delegation headed by Radovan Stijačić, Secretary for Internal Affairs, attended the Moscow celebration of the fiftieth anniversary of the establishment of the state security forces on 20 December. Although in his Moscow speeches Tito appeared tactful by not recalling the Yugoslav-Soviet split, he did mention it in a long article, "The October Revolution and the Peoples of Yugoslavia," broadcast by Radio Zagreb, on 13 September. On 6 October the same article was published in *Pravda,* heavily edited; all references to Stalinism (mentioned only by implication in the original article) and to the split between the two countries were deleted. Radio Belgrade in its "University of the Air" series devoted a long talk to "Stalinism as the Negation of the October Revolution," which asserted that Stalinism contradicted Leninism. The interesting point of it was that it ruled out the Khrushchev "personality cult" explanation of Stalinism, maintaining that Stalinism presented a separate movement in socialist development, a movement away from socialist humanism toward "a new form of subjective idealism, a new form of the theory of force." According to the broadcast, this was still the ruling trend in China, and its elements were still being felt in non-Stalinist, socialist-humanist social relations and conditions. The talk implied that potential dangers from Stalinism existed in all socialist countries.

**Publications.** The chief organs of the LCY's Central Committee are *Komunist,* a weekly magazine, and *Socijalizam,* a theoretical monthly. The most important dailies are *Borba* (Belgrade), and *Vjesnik* (Zagreb), organs of the Socialist Alliances of Serbia and Croatia respectively. The organ of the communist youth organization is the weekly *Mladost.*

# INTERNATIONAL COMMUNIST FRONT ORGANIZATIONS

# INTRODUCTION

As of 1921, the year in which he undertook to modify political strategy both within the Soviet Union and in the context of international communism, Lenin devised the formula of "front organizations," which became an integral part of both the tactics and the organization of the communist movement. In view of Lenin's publicly proclaimed realization that communist revolution was not imminent in the West and that the majority of the working class was not won over to the communist cause, it became necessary to find means to modify this situation. One of the prerequisites was that there should be "transmission belts" between the communist parties and the masses. Whereas in 1920 this function was served only by the International Veterans' Union and two rather limited organizations, the International Trade Union Council and the International Women's Secretariat, during 1921 the two latter were enhanced by a definite structure—the International Trade Union Council becoming the Red International of Trade Unions (Profintern)—and a number of additional front organizations were founded. The new fronts included the International Committee of Aid to Soviet Russia, the International Workers' Aid Organization, and the Red Sport International (Sportintern). In 1922 the International Revolutionary Aid Organization ("MOPR") was created, followed in 1923 by the International Peasants' Union ("Krestintern"). In 1927, Willi Münzenberg, who had directed the International Committee of Aid to Soviet Russia, sponsored the creation of the Anti-Imperialist League (later known as the "Congress against War and Fascism").

The importance of front organizations was stressed by the veteran Finnish communist Otto Kuusinen, the only foreign-born secretary of the Communist International between 1921 and 1943 and a member of the CPSU Politburo until his death in 1964. In March 1926, at a meeting of the Comintern executive committee, he advocated "creating a whole solar system or organizations and smaller committees around the Communist Party . . . actually working under the influence of the Party, but not under its mechanical control" (*International Press Correspondence*, Vol. VI, No. 28, April).

Outwardly these organizations did not appear to be of a communist character; emphasis was placed on their humanitarian, cultural, pacifist, or other roles. In practice, communist action within them was dominant for a number of reasons. Their foundation was initiated by communists, key positions were held by communists, and the financial resources of the organizations originated from communist sources. Linked to the Comintern, they faced the same vicissitudes and, in the case of the Profintern and the Krestintern, even preceded it in official dissolution.

The "grand alliance" between communist and democratic forces, in existence on national and international levels during the Second World War and in its immediate aftermath, favored the renewal, under a somewhat modified form, of front organization strategy. Some of the postwar front organizations were created by the reactivation of earlier fronts (the World Federation of Trade Unions, the Women's International Democratic Federation, the World Council of Peace), while others were new (such as the International Association of Democratic Lawyers and the World Federation of Scientific Workers).

During their existence of now more than twenty years, these organizations have undergone transformations and been faced by varied problems—the cold war, the Stalin-Tito schism, the 1956 events, the consequences of the Sino-Soviet conflict and, recently, the increasing rift between the Soviet Union and Cuba. The purpose of the surveys that follow is to outline the origins, organizational structures, official aims, modes of operation, and internal problems of these organizations.

# WORLD COUNCIL OF PEACE

The "world peace" movement headed by the World Council of Peace (WCP) dates from August 1948, when a "World Congress of Intellectuals for Peace" in Wroclaw, Poland, set up an organization called the "International Liaison Committee of Intellectuals." This committee in April 1949 convened a "First World Peace Congress" in Paris. (Part of the meeting had to be held in Prague because the French government refused visas to delegates from communist countries.) The congress launched a "World Committee of Partisans of Peace," which in November 1950 was renamed the "World Peace Council." Originally based in Paris, the World Peace Council was expelled in 1951 by the French government. It moved first to Prague and then, in 1954, to Vienna. When the occupation forces withdrew and Austria regained independence, the "World Council of Peace" (this name having been adopted meanwhile) was permitted to remain on the condition that it would observe Austrian laws. On 2 February 1957 the Austrian Ministry of the Interior announced that the WCP had been banned and its offices closed because it "interfered in the internal affairs of countries with which Austria has good and friendly relations" and its activities were "directed against the interest of the Austrian State" (*The Observer*, London, 3 February). Though invited back to Prague, the WCP remained in Austria and continued its operations from the same address (Estate-Haus, Möllwaldplatz 5, Vienna 4) under the cover of an ostensibly new organization, the "International Institute for Peace" (IIP).

**Structure.** The WCP movement embraces "national peace committees" in some 80 countries. The national committees are supposed to be self-supporting and to contribute to the Secretariat, but no financial accounts have been published.

The WCP has undergone certain modifications in its structure, the most recent having been adopted at its Council meeting in Geneva, 13-16 June 1966. At present the highest authorities of the WCP movement are the Council of the World Council of Peace and its Presidential Committee and Secretariat.

The Council of the WCP, with a membership of about 500 persons, comprises representatives of national peace committees and also of national, regional, and international organizations and movements agreeing with WCP aims and principles. On the basis of the Council's decisions and resolutions the other bodies carry out their work. The 1966 Council session in Geneva was attended by more than 300 representatives from 79 countries and 13 international organizations. Such sessions are scheduled to meet at least every two years.

With the abolition of the posts of President and Vice-President (due to the movement's failure to agree on a successor to WCP President Frédéric Joliot-Curie, who died in 1958), a Presidential Committee was set up in May 1959. The Presidential Committee controls the WCP between sessions of the Council. It is elected by the Council and normally meets twice a year, or oftener in case of emergency. The size of the Presidential Committee, although determined by the Council, is limited only by the "necessity to ensure that the number is not so large as to prevent its effective functioning." The Presidential Committee at present numbers 45. The Committee elects from among its members a Coordinating Chairman and a Secretariat presided over by a Secretary-General.

As the executive body of the Presidential Committee, the Secretariat is responsible both for implementing the directives of the Presidential Committee and for initiating further activities in accordance with those directives. While each Secretary is responsible for specific sectors of work, the Secretariat is collectively responsible to the Presidential Committee.

Isabelle Blume (Belgium) was elected Coordinating Chairman of the Presidential Committee at the Seventh Congress of the WCP (Helsinki, 1965). Romesh Chandra (India) is Secretary-General of the WCP.

The Presidential Committee includes: Georgi A. Andreev (Bulgaria); Richard Andriamanjato (Malagasy Republic); John D. Bernal (Great Britain; Chairman of the WCP from 1959 until ill-health prompted his resignation in 1965); Isabelle Blume; Lázaro Cárdenas (Mexico); Alberto T. Casella (Argentina); Romesh Chandra; Peter A. Curtis-Joseph (Nigeria); Damantang Camara (Guinea); Alfred Dickie (Australia); James G. Endicott (Canada); Yves Farge (France); Walter Friedrich (East Germany); Carlton Goodlett (USA); Raymond Guyot (France); Hirano Yoshitaro (Japan); Kang Yank-uk (North Korea); Laroussi Khelifa (Algeria); Alexandr E. Korneichuk (USSR); Murad Kuwatli (Syria); Diwan Chaman Lall (India); Li Chu-wen (Communist China); Enrique Lister (Spain); Nils Artur Lundkvist (Sweden); Lucio Luzzato (Italy); Josef Macek (Czechoslovakia); John B. Marks (South Africa); Juan Marinello (Cuba); Faruq Masarani (Lebanon); Herbert Mochalski (West Germany); Khaled Mohei el-Din (UAR); Agostinho Neto (Angola); Nguyen Van Hieu (South Vietnam); Oscar Niemeyer (Brazil); Olga Poblete de Espinosa (Chile); Louis Saillant (France); Gordon Schaffer (Great Britain); Reksoprodjo Setiadi (Indonesia); Tikiri B. Subasinghe (Ceylon), and Alberto Valenzi (Italy). In addition, there are representives from Poland and from the "national organizations of so-called Portuguese colonies." Ilia Ehrenburg (USSR), a leading member of the WCP since its inception, died on August 31; Eugénie Cotton, Presidential Committee member (and President of the Women's International Democratic Federation [WIDF]), died on June 16; the North Vietnamese member of the Presidential Committee, Nguyen Duy Thien, died on April 12.

Members of the Secretariat are: Hassan Mohammed al-Amine (Sudan); Yussef Ismail al-Bustani (Iraq); Romesh Chandra (Secretary-General); Yves Cholière (France); Walter Diehl (West Germany); Angel Dominguez (Spain); Felipe F. Freyre (Argentina); Litto Ghosh (India); Li Shou-pao (Communist China; he has not worked in the Secretariat since December 1966); and Stepan Molodtsov (USSR). Although it had been decided at the Geneva meeting to establish a body of 13 members, "a few national peace movements have not yet made a decision about filling their mandate," Chandra told the Hungarian Telegraph Agency (MTI) on 28 January 1967. Jerzy Sawicki (Poland) and Heinz Badner (Austria) participate in the work of the Secretariat as head of research and editor in chief of the WCP *Information Bulletin*, respectively.

The International Institute for Peace (IIP) has its own elected executive body, ostensibly independent of that of the WCP. However, the IIP executive is, in fact, elected by the WCP General Assembly, and most of its officers also hold positions in the parent body. Several are executive officers of that organization; for example, James Endicott, IIP President, is a WCP Presidential Committee member, and Romesh Chandra, WCP Secretary-General, is Director of the IIP.

The IIP Presidium is composed of seven officers: James Endicott: Stepan Molodtsov; Friedrich Scholl (Austria); Romesh Chandra; Jerzy Sawicki; Varuj Salatian (Syria); and Yves Cholière.

The 17 members of the IIP Executive Committee are: Ismail Hussein Abdin (Sudan); Tamas Bacskai (Hungary); Alexandr Berkov (USSR); Goran Eduard von Bonsdorff (Finland); Alberto T. Casella; Walter Diehl; Faiz Ahmed Faiz (Pakstan); Giovanni Favilli (Italy); Georg Fuchs (Austria); Ibrahim Garba-Jahumpa (Gambia); Hirano Yoshitaro; Erwin Kock (Austria); Olga Poblete de Espinosa; Leopold Schaffer (Austria), Ann Synge (Great Britain); Ernest Vollaire (France); and Emil von Wedel (West Germany).

There exists also a Cultural Commission of the WCP, set up in 1951 and charged with arranging cultural activities in liaison with WCP events. The Commission was inactive for several years, but the WCP Congress in Helsinki in 1965 marked the beginning of efforts to revive it. A meeting of the Commission took place during the Council meeting in Geneva, and another was held in Bratislava in December 1966. Chairman of the Cultural Commission is Diwan Chaman Lall, a member of the Presidential Committee.

Other special commissions, functioning under the chairmanship of individual Presidential Committee members, include: the Commission for Relations with other Organizations; the Commission in Charge of the World Peace Foundation; the Latin American Commission; and the Research and Publishing Commission.

**Membership.** The WCP is organized on a national basis; no figure of the total number of members has ever been disclosed, but the Council has members from more than 100 countries, most of them representing national peace committees.

**Publications.** Two monthly publications, *Perspectives* and *Information Bulletin,* were introduced in October 1966 to replace the *Bulletin of the World Council of Peace.* Both are published in English, French, Spanish, and German. Press statements and "information letters" are also issued by the Secretariat. From time to time the WCP publishes pamphlets on specific subjects—for example: *Black Book on US War Crimes in South Vietnam* (1966) and *Saturday 21 October, 1967—International Day of Peace in Vietnam* (Documents of the Stockholm Conference on Vietnam, July 1967).

**Principles and Aims.** The principles and aims of the movement were reaffirmed at Geneva: the prohibition of all weapons of mass destruction and the halting of the arms race, the abolition of foreign military bases, and a general, simultaneous and controlled disarmament; the elimination of all forms of colonialism and racial discrimination; respect for the right of popular sovereignty and independence, as being essential for the establishment of peace; respect for the territorial integrity of states; noninterference in the internal affairs of nations; the establishment of mutually beneficial trade and cultural relations based on friendship between states with different political systems; and replacement of the policy of force by that of negotiations for the settlement of differences between nations.

From its inception, the WCP has defended the policies of the Soviet Union and has attacked those of the Western powers. In turn it has attacked the Marshall Plan, the European Defense Community, the North Atlantic Treaty Organization, and the European Economic Community. In recent years, "American agression in Vietnam" has been the principal target of WCP propaganda and campaigns.

**Congresses.** The WCP has organized seven peace congresses: the First World Peace Congress (Paris and Prague, April 1949); the Second World Peace Congress (Warsaw, November 1950); the Congress of the Peoples for Peace (Vienna, December 1952); the World Peace Assembly (Helsinki, June 1955); the Congress for Disarmament and International Cooperation (Stockholm, July 1958); the World Congress for General Disarmament and Peace (Moscow, July 1962); and the World Congress for Peace, National Independence and Disarmament (Helsinki, July 1965). The eighth congress, to be called the World Assembly of Peace Forces, is scheduled to take place in East Berlin in June 1969.

**Principal Activities.** The principal activity of the WCP has been to organize world-wide propaganda campaigns, coordinated on regional basis by national peace committees and often involving the mass collection of signatures to support appeals. In addition, regional and national campaigns are launched or co-sponsored by individual peace committees.

The major appeals launched by the WCP have been: The Stockholm Appeal (1950), calling for a ban on atomic weapons; the Warsaw Appeal (1950), calling for a five-power conference to settle disputes; the Germ Warfare Campaign (1952), protesting the alleged use of bacteriological weapons by UN forces in Korea; the Negotiate Now Campaign (1952), renewing the Warsaw Appeal; the Vienna Appeal (1955) and the Berlin Appeal (1957), reiterating the Stockholm Appeal; the Further Campaign against Nuclear Weapons (1957), calling for a nuclear truce to halt the spread of radioactivity; and the Second Stockholm Appeal (1960) for a world disarmament conference.

**Views and Activities in 1967.** The dominating theme of WCP propaganda continues to be that of "driving the American aggressors out of Vietnam" and exposing their alleged "war crimes." "European security" and "anticolonialism" also figure prominently in WCP campaigns. In addition, increasing emphasis is being placed on wooing the Arabs, Africans, and Latin Americans.

Convening in Prague on 25-27 February 1967, the Presidential Committee renewed its pledge of "full support for the four-point statement of the DRV [Democratic Republic of Vietnam] and the five-point statement of the NLFSV [National Liberation Front of South Vietnam], which reflect the spirit and the letter of the 1954 Geneva Agreements" (*Perspectives,* no. 4, 1967). "All forms of action" were urged "in order to develop on an ever-wider scale an active campaign of solidarity by the peoples of the whole world with the Vietnamese people" and to "express with all severity their firm condemnation of the monstrous and unjust war which the USA is waging in North and South Vietnam" (TASS, 28 February).

The WCP has increasingly sought the cooperation of international noncommunist organizations in sponsoring and organizing meetings to support its policy, and its Vietnam "peace efforts" have achieved a wide measure of support from among pacifists, internationalists, intellectuals, churchmen, and "idealists" in general. Thus, the WCP has been able to collaborate with various noncommunist international organizations in organizing such major events as the Appeal on Vietnam (1966), commemorating the twelfth anniversary of the 1954 Geneva Agreements, and the 1967 Stockholm Conference on Vietnam.

The Stockholm Conference (6-9 July), originally the initiative of the noncommunist Swedish Peace and Arbitration Society, was, as it turned out, largely "taken over" by the WCP.* Romesh Chandra assumed a key role in organizational and publicity work for the ostensibly nonaligned conference, co-sponsored by the International Confederation for Disarmament and Peace, the War Resisters' International, the International Peace Bureau, the World Council of Peace, the International Fellowship of Reconciliation, and the Christian Peace Conference.

There were seven officially listed WCP delegates to the conference, in addition to which another 37 Council members were present, representing other organizations. By agreement of the delegates, the conference was constituted as a permanent body with a Continuing Committee.† Romesh Chandra and Alexandr Berkov were appointed to the Continuing Committee, the first meeting of which was held in Stockholm in mid-September.

In a letter published July 20 and broadcast by Moscow Radio on July 25, Chandra wrote that it was "unanimously agreed" that the conference had been an "overwhelming success," and that it had "opened new perspectives for the peace movement in the whole world" inasmuch as it showed that a meeting of different peace groups "has the power to exercise an influence on the large areas of opinion which have not until now entered into the movement." Chandra admitted in the same broadcast that "certain suspicions and hostilities prevented that coordination and unity of action among these internationals," which had become "so vital and so necessary in the light of the continuous intensification of the aggressive activities of the US and other governments." Later, at a public meeting organized by the Indian Association for Afro-Asian Solidarity and the All-India Peace Council (New Delhi, 2 August), Chandra expressed confidence that the results of the conference "marked the beginning of the end of the 'cold war' that existed between the various international organizations . . . in pursuit of peace" (*Patriot,* New Delhi, 3 August).

An appeal adopted unanimously by the conference alleged that "American aggression in Vietnam has become nothing less than genocide," and called for a settlement of the war by ending the bombing of North Vietnam, withdrawing all foreign troops unconditionally, and allowing the Vietnamese to "settle their own affairs" according to the Geneva Agreements (WCP *Information Bulletin,* no. 7/8).

It was urged by the WCP at the Stockholm conference that 21 October be declared "Peace in Vietnam Day"†† to coincide with an antiwar march in Washington (sponsored by the National Mobilization Committee to End the War in Vietnam), and that 20 July (anniversary of the signing of the Geneva Agreements), 10 December (Human Rights Day), and 20 December (anniversary of the founding of the NLFSV) be marked as days of mass demonstrations throughout the world by all "organizations and groups working for peace in Vietnam" (IIP Circular Letters, 10 and 12 July).

The marked interest shown by Moscow in the conference was in clear contrast to the Soviet attitude to the Bertrand Russell Tribunal, held a few weeks previously in the same city. The *Arbeiter Zeitung,* Vienna (15 July) stated that the Tribunal had been completely ignored by the East European bloc. According to this same source, there were heated discussions at the conference among "extreme radical opponents of American policy of Vietnam," including delegates from Algeria,

---

*A Swiss newspaper, *Landbote,* asked on May 19 whether Swedish neutrality would not be endangered if the peace movement's usual anti-American demonstrations took place at the conference. It warned that the preparations thus far suggested that the conference would be completely one-sided and be dominated by "communist camouflage organizations."

†Early in 1968 the Continuing Committee was redesignated the International Liaison Committee (ILC) of the Stockholm Conference.

††A special number of the WCP *Information Bulletin* (no. 12), devoted to reports on the 21 October demonstrations, listed 18 countries in which these demonstrations reportedly took place.

Argentina, and Cuba. The delegations from the Soviet Union, East Europe, North Vietnam, and the NLFSV were described as a "rather moderate group." The Swedish newspaper *Svenska Dagbladet* (10 July) reported a "deep division" over the question of Vietnamese representation. Attempts to invite a Buddhist delegation, favored by some delegates, were thwarted by vetoes of the NLFSV and the WCP. Widespread dissatisfaction was registered over the manner in which the steering committee had yielded to the pressures of the NLFSV and the WCP on the grounds that this would create the impression that the conference was "communist-dominated." The Chinese were not represented or mentioned at the conference (see below, "Sino-Soviet Dispute").

The question of European security is occupying an increasingly prominent position in the attention of the WCP and was second only to Vietnam on the agenda of the Presidential Committee meeting in Prague (25-27 February). The delegates to this meeting agreed that

[While there is] no longer the feeling of a powder keg in Europe that could explode at any moment, a direct confrontation between two powerful military blocs nevertheless exists. There is a vast rise in military potential and in the number of foreign military bases and nuclear bases, and an alarming upsurge of neo-Nazism in the German Federal Republic. (*Perspectives*, no. 4.)

A statement adopted at the meeting asserted that the "striving by the Federal Republic of Germany to represent the whole German people" was one of the "most serious of European problems," and that it was "essential for the attainment of a detente" that West Germany recognize both the German Democratic Republic and the existing frontiers. (*Rude Pravo*, 28 February). A message to the 18-nation Nonproliferation Committee in Geneva affirmed WCP support of a nuclear nonproliferation treaty.

Earlier, on 11 February , following its meeting is Budapest, the Secretariat had "condemned and branded the revival of neo-Nazism and revanchism, and the machinations which aim at enabling the Federal German Republic to acquire nuclear weapons" (MTI, 11 February). An IIP circular letter of 19 October, signed by Yves Cholière and Angel Dominguez, appealed to peace forces in every country to undertake "tireless action to revive the hope" of an agreement leading to "peaceful coexistence between the states of different social systems" inasmuch as West Germany, through NATO, could gain access to nuclear weapons. The International Atomic Agency in Vienna, according to the letter, should be responsible for the control of atomic energy for "peaceful purposes, policing, and as an exchange center," and denuclearized zones should be created.

Efforts of the WCP to organize a conference on European security to precede the twentieth anniversary of the NATO treaty in 1969 have so far failed because of difficulties in enlisting "respectable" noncommunist sponsorship, which would have prospects of appealing to a broader front than a WCP-sponsored conference. Renewing the call for a convocation of "representatives of the people of Europe," and declaring the WCP "ready to cooperate towards this with all political and social forces of all European countries," an editorial in *Perspectives* (no. 3) stressed the need for "military disengagement" and the "abolition of pacts" to replace the "arms drive which has brought to Europe the strongest concentration of opposing forces and military build-up, adding: "These developments and ideas tend to win through because the public has increasingly taken them up and because experience has shown that the so-called Soviet aggressiveness has become an untenable heresy."

The WCP Committee on Questions of European Security met in East Berlin October 6-7 to make plans for an international conference. This was followed by a meeting of 22 European peace committee secretaries October 9-10. Isabelle Blume and Romesh Chandra attended both meetings. Angel Dominguez represented the WCP at a European security meeting of the World Federation of Democratic Youth in Warsaw, 18-20 September. Addressing the Leningrad meeting of the Presidential Committee (27-29 October), Chandra said that any conference on European security should be approached and organized in the "spirit of the Stockholm Conference on Vietnam" and in cooperation with "all others who have similar aims." He added: "Those forces which sincerely desire the coming together of all organizations and sectors of opinion interested in European Security are much larger and wider than those which participated in the Stockholm Conference." The conference of European peoples could be "a real platform" embracing the forces in Europe with the greatest influence—Socialists, Christians, Communists, trade unions, pacifists—both organizations and individuals. Forecasting a change in the style of future WCP assemblies, Chandra continued: "The days are gone when most meetings, conferences or congresses were organized only on the initiative of the WCP on a particular issue." From now on the WCP would be "just one of the organizations, individuals, and forces" to sponsor conferences (WCP Documents). Meeting in Düsseldorf, the German Peace Society claimed that "the policy pursued by the Federal Republic so far does not fulfil the preconditions for a peaceful and friendly coexistence of all states in Europe," and urged the "cooperation of all democratic forces in the Federal Republic" (*Perspectives,* nos. 8/9). (Dr Martin Niemöller, who is president of the German Peace Socety and head of the World Council of Churches, in 1967 received both the International Lenin Peace Prize and the WCP Joliot-Curie Peace Medal.)

In the Middle East, several new peace committees have been formed as part of the WCP's drive to expand its activities in that area. These include the Palestine Peace Committee, with headquarters in Cairo, and a peace committee formed by the Liberation Front of Dhofar, calling for the right of self-determination of the people of Dhofar and an end to "the British occupation with its colonial methods of oppression" (WCP *Information Bulletin,* no. 2). When Aden achieved independence, Isabelle Blume and Romesh Chandra assured the South Yemen Peace Committee in a telegram that the WCP would be "watchful of colonialists' plans to violate" their sovereignty and to move military bases to other parts of the Arab peninsula (*ibid.,* no. 13).

The Arab-Israeli war in June provided the WCP with an opportunity to extend its contacts and influence, although serious disagreement within the WCP over the question of "Israeli aggression against the Arab countries" at times threatened organizational unity of the movement. In his report to the Presidential Committee meeting in Leningrad (October), Chandra referred to these disagreements within the movement, and stated that, because of "complacency," few national peace committees had been given advance notice of the WCP line of the crisis and the majority of subsidiary bodies had been restricted to published statements and telegrams. Due to the failure of the WCP and the Sudanese government to agree on a mutually convenient date, it had not been possible to hold an emergency meeting. In any future emergency situation, "the holding of a meeting should be considered more important than its location" (WCP Documents).

According to *L'Humanité* (June 1), the Secretariat of the WCP had called upon all forces of peace to "act with increased vigilance to prevent any development of the conflict and for a return to a situation of detente." Referring to remarks attributed to Israeli leaders concerning their alleged desire for punitive operations against Syria, the Secretariat claimed that the US government, while continuing to cause bloodshed in Vietnam and at the same time assuring the "coup d'état generals" in Greece of their support, was encouraging the actions of the Israeli government. The movements of the US Sixth Fleet in the Mediterranean were represented as a "grave danger" to world peace and to the independence of peoples. With the outbreak of war, Isabelle Blume and Romesh Chandra sent a cable to the UN Secretary-General (7 June), blaming the "provocative policies of the imperialist powers" for "instigating the Israeli government's warlike actions": in addition to its aggression in Vietnam, the USA was now trying to bring about the subjection of the Arabs. U Thant was urged to do his utmost to end the conflict on the basis of a withdrawal of all Israeli troops to their original positions. (*Perspectives,* no. 7.) Enrique Lister (Presidential Committee member) and Hassan Elamin (Secretary) represented the WCP at an emergency meeting on the Middle East called by the Afro-Asian People's Solidarity Organization (AAPSO) in Cairo on 1-3 July. Chandra sent a message of solidarity to the meeting, and on 10 July he and Isabelle Blume issued a joint statement condemning "the recourse to force as a means of controlling international problems" (IIP press release, 14 July).

A consultative meeting of the Presidential Committee was held in Stockholm on July 10 following the close of the Vietnam conference. It was decided to set up a commission of inquiry into "Israeli crimes," hold a special meeting in an Arab country, and send delegations of solidarity to those Arab countries which had been "victims of Israeli aggression" (IIP Circular Letter, 20 July). Plans for the special meeting were forestalled when representatives of the WCP, arriving in Khartoum on August 16 from Stockholm to discuss preparations for the meeting, were advised by the Sudanese government that the WCP could meet only after the Arab summit meeting (Khartoum News Service, 7 August). (Attempts to hold this meeting were later abandoned, and the WCP subsequently turned to India for initiatives on behalf of the Arabs.) Chandra led the commission of inquiry into "Israeli crimes" in Syria, the UAR, and Jordan. In an interview broadcast from Damascus on September 29 Chandra said that, should the UN fail to reach a "just solution" to the crisis, "the only means left to the Arabs of regaining sovereignty over their stolen territories would be to make war for the sake of peace."

In India, the WCP succeeded in aligning with established Afro-Asian groups. An "Indian National Conference in Support of the Arab People" was held in New Delhi on August 10, with Chandra attending. The official conference statement charged that the governments of the USA, Great Britain, and West Germany had "encouraged the warring Israeli government to carry on its aggression," had been the "instigators" of the aggression, and had "aided it in every possible way" (WCP *Information Bulletin*, no. 9). An "International Conference in Support of the Arab People" was organized in New Delhi on 11-14 November by the Indian Association of Afro-Asian Solidarity with strong WCP support and with Afro-Asian, European, and Latin American delegates. The purpose of the conference was to "express support for the Arab peoples and manifest world opinion's solidarity with the Arab struggle to eliminate the effects of aggression" (Afro-Asian News Service, New Delhi, 3 October). A number of committees were formed to consider the "relationship between Israeli aggression against the Arabs and US aggression against Vietnam, and the use of internationally banned tactics and weapons in both cases of aggression, such as napalm bombs and the displacement of civilians." The final plenary session agreed that: an International Day of Solidarity with Arab Countries would be observed on 25 January 1968; an International Conference in Support of the Arab Peoples would be held in a western capital in January 1968; and the Indian Preparatory Committee of the conference should act as a continuing committee and coordinate activities with the WCP, AAPSO, the World Federation of Democratic Youth, and the Women's International Democratic Federation (*Times of India*, 17 November; *New Age*, 19 November).

Chandra attended the tenth anniversary celebrations of the Afro-Asian Peoples Solidarity Organization (AAPSO) held in Cairo from 27 to 30 December. A joint statement issued following talks with Yusuf As-Sibai, Secretary-General of AAPSO, "affirmed the importance of increasing and developing solidarity and unity among all revolutionary and anti-imperialist forces, in view of the deteriorating international situation in Africa and Asia, resulting from a stronger world imperialist strategy" (Cairo Radio, 1 January 1968).

In Cyprus, the WCP laid the groundwork for future activities. After attending the AAPSO Council meeting in Nicosia (13-16 February), Chandra, accompanied by two WCP Presidential Committee members, met with the Pancyprian Peace Council to "explain the WCP's program and its activities in neighboring Arab countries," and to reaffirm the support of the WCP for the struggle of the Cypriot people. They discussed the "need for the development of the campaign for solidarity with the Vietnamese people" and "ways to promote the joint struggle of the peace movements in the Mediterranean countries against military bases and for the establishment of a demilitarized zone in the Mediterranean." (*Haravghi*, Nicosia, 18 February; *New Age*, 26 February.) On 6 December the Pancyprian Peace Council sent a report to the WCP on the situation in Cyprus, seeking its help. Chandra went to Cyprus at the end of December, where he asserted that "the imperialist powers want to destroy the integrity of Cyprus and involve the Cyprus people in the NATO trap" (*Haravghi*, 6 December 1967, 3 January 1968).

The Permanent Committee set up by the first "Conference for the Denuclearization of the Mediterranean" (held in Algiers in July 1964), and including executive officers of the WCP, met in Rome on August 6-7. A communique recommended the convening of a second conference at the end of November,* stating:

> Since [the conference's] meeting in Rome in 1965 the existence of foreign military bases and the spread of atomic arms, which has increased in some Mediterranean countries, threatens peace in that part of the world more than ever. The danger of war has been further increased by the intervention of American imperialism in the internal affairs of

*Plans for this conference were shelved when a similar convocation was organized by a number of left-wing political parties of Mediterranean countries and scheduled to convene in Rome in April 1968.

Mediterranean countries. In Greece, the reliance on the NATO military bases has provoked the setting up of a fascist regime which suppresses all democratic liberty and threatens peace. Cyprus is placed under the same threat. In the Middle East imperialist intervention has encouraged Israeli aggression against the Arab countries and is supporting Israel in her refusal to withdraw troops immediately and unconditionally to the bases used before the hostilities. (*L'Unità*, Rome, 8 August.)

Greece continues to be a frequent theme of WCP actions. The WCP organized broad campaigns throughout the year, protesting the "fascist coup" in Greece and calling for the release of such "Communist heroes" as Manolis Glezos, a WCP member and holder of a Joliot-Curie Gold Peace Medal. Recalling the assassination of the Greek "peace fighter" Gregoris Lambrakis (the trial of his accused assassin was held in 1967), Isabelle Blume demanded an end to "external pressure" on Greek policy, and declared that "the role Greece can play in the transformation of NATO, the dissolution of pacts and blocs, is too closely linked with the exercise of democracy for the World Council of Peace and peace movements everywhere not to support the Greek peace movement at this time of testing" (*Perspectives*, no 1).

The WCP is having little success in increasing its influence in Latin America and has been unable to organize any significant campaign for several years, although several events are planned for 1968. A major reason for its failure has been the Cuban domination of regional meetings held in Latin America and the seizure by Cuba of control of those regional organizations which have been set up. Chtilian Skoubarev (Bulgaria) and Rafat Said represented the WCP at the first conference of the Latin American Solidarity Organization (Havana, July/August).

In Africa (as in Asia,) the WCP hopes to increase its influence through closer cooperation with the AAPSO. A three-man delegation, headed by Romesh Chandra, represented the WCP at the AAPSO Council meeting in Nicosia on 13-16 February. A resolution was approved expressing the support of the Afro-Asian peoples for the "Conference of Solidarity with the Portuguese Colonies, Zimbabwe, South West Africa, and South Africa," to be organized by the WCP and held in Conakry (Guinea) on 15-25 October (but later postponed). The WCP continued its efforts to align with the South West African People's Organization (SWAPO), and with other African "freedom movements."

In Asia, WCP activity continued to be handicapped by the Sino-Soviet dispute, and for that reason was almost exclusively restricted in that area to support of Soviet propaganda on Vietnam. Japan was the scene of several large "peace demonstrations" during the year, a number of which were co-sponsored by the Japan Peace Committee together with communist and socialist groups. Litto Ghosh (Secretary) and Dina Forti represented the WCP at the "22nd Anniversary World Conference Against Atomic and Hydrogen Bombs" organized by the Japan Congress Against A and H Bombs (Gensuikin) in Tokyo on 1-9 August. The Pakistani peace movement, inactive since the mid-1950's, has been revived organizationally, and has resumed limited activities on a national scale, following programs of the WCP Cultural Commission.

There were numerous indications of the WCP's continued allegiance to Moscow. A large delegation of the WCP attended a plenary meeting of the Soviet Peace Committee held in Leningrad on 25-26 October to mark the fiftieth anniversary of Lenin's "Decree on Peace." Isabelle Blume, speaking on behalf of the WCP, said that the words uttered by Lenin half a century ago "have lost none of their topicality and vital importance for all the peoples of the world." Romesh Chandra presented to the Soviet Peace Committee the Joliot-Curie Gold Medal "for years of consistent work for peace and friendship between nations." (*Pravda*, 27 October.)

Convening in Leningrad on 27-29 October, the Presidential Committee adopted documents on Vietnam, the Middle East, and European Security. Although all final decisions were claimed to be unanimous, there were admitted differences of opinion on the Middle East; nor could agreement be reached on the question of the presidency of the WCP or the location of its headquarters. The question of a conference on European security was pursued, but no date fixed. (IIP Circular Letter, 10 November.) Addressing the meeting, Chandra again stressed the necessity of drawing support from among the "millions of people who have grave anxieties about the danger of a world war and about the aggressive actions of the United States and other imperialist powers," [even though these millions] have perhaps an absolutely different understanding of the reasons for the present dangerous international situation than has the World Council of Peace," adding:

> Many of these are finding a way to support certain other international organizations. These organizations, on their part, have also points of view very different from ours. Some of them are religious organizations, others are pacifist organizations. Many of them are neither religious nor pacifist, but deal with particular problems which to them, at this particular moment, appear acute. There are political forces, people adhering to socialist parties in the West, for example, to nationalist movements, nationalist parties in the continents of Asia and Africa who are equally perturbed by the developments in the international situation. They wish also to act in some particular way. (*Perspectives,* no. 11/12.)

**Sino-Soviet Dispute.** The Sino-Soviet dispute continues to disrupt the work of the WCP, but events in 1966 and 1967 seemed to indicate that the Chinese Communists may play a diminishing role in future WCP activities. They declined to send delegations to any meeting of the WCP in 1967, following the refusal of Austrian authorities to grant Secretariat member Li Shou-pao a visa to attend a 1966 meeting of the IIP in Vienna. According to the Swiss newspaper, *Basler Nachrichter* (11 January), Li Shou-pao had not been reelected into the leadership of the IIP, and therefore was held to have no legal justification for remaining in Vienna; his post as Secretary of the WCP would not justify his continued presence in Vienna, since the WCP Secretariat had been expelled from Austria in 1957.

In a letter to the Secretariat (5 January), the China Peace Committee accused the Soviet "revisionists" of devising a "base trick" to prevent their delegate's attendance at the meeting:

> Under the manipulation of their bosses, the Soviet revisionists, and with an ulterior purpose, the leading members of the Secretariat of the World Council of Peace made use of a base trick to prevent the Chinese member of the WCP Secretariat, along with his assistant and interpreter, from renewing their Austrian visas, thus driving the Chinese member out of Vienna and making it impossible for him to exercise his right to work at the Secretariat of the WCP. . . . [This] is by no means an isolated incident. This is a component part of the scheme devised by the Soviet revisionists to step up their all-round cooperation with the USA and to whip up a new wave of anti-China feeling. For many years the World Council of Peace has been pursuing the capitulationist line of the Soviet revisionist leading clique; the line of uniting with the USA, opposing China, opposing Communism and opposing the people. This ignominious act of ousting the Chinese Secretariat member proves that the Secretariat of the WCP is terribly afraid of the voice of truth, a fact which indicates its weakness and exposes it as a paper tiger. This has added another black mark to its most shameful record. . . . In fact, this act of self-deception by the Soviet revisionists and the Secretariat of the World Council of Peace will not deceive anyone else, and will bring them nothing but ill. We would like seriously to warn the Soviet revisionists and their followers in the Secretariat of the WCP: You will have to shoulder the responsibility for this grave act of splitting the world peace movement, and all its results. (NCNA, 6 January.)

*Rote Fahne,* the Vienna organ of the pro-Peking group of Marxist-Leninists, alleged on January 15 that the "common action taken by the revisionists and the capitalist Austrian state machinery is the sad full-step to the history of an institution which—founded and shaped at the time of Stalin—had for many years helped to organize and lead magnificent anti-imperialist mass movements and had thus constituted a powerful weapon . . . for the fight to defend world peace against the imperialist aggressors." The "Khrushchev and Brezhnev revisionists as well as their paid stooges of various nationalities" were blamed for the "degeneration" of the WCP "into a willing tool of the policy of rapprochement with imperialism."

Following the expulsion of the Chinese, the IIP's lawyer in Vienna denied Li Shou-pao's allegations and accused him of having published "inaccurate and tendentious statements" about the IIP. The official reaction of the WCP to the Chinese attack came at a press conference following the Presidential Committee meeting in February. The WCP Secretary-General claimed that current events in China had aroused the "sincere concern and indignation of every decent person," and that "appeals which aimed at inducing people to display intolerance of the worst kind and chauvinism towards other peoples" were "especially dangerous." The WCP was particularly alarmed, Chandra said, by the "premeditated attacks of the Chinese government and its agencies against the Soviet Union and other peace-loving countries"; nothing could cause greater satisfaction to "the forces of imperialism and reaction." Chandra continued: "The WCP demands that the Chinese authorities immediately stop their hostile actions against the Soviet government, which in effect are also against many other governments. The elementary standards of relations between peoples and states must be observed. An end must be put to all actions hindering the joint struggle against American aggression in Vietnam." (TASS, 28 February.)

On April 20 a spokesman of the China Peace Committee, in a statement "authorized by Kuo Mo-jo," Chairman of the committee (and former member of the WCP Presidential Committee), announced Kuo Mo-jo's withdrawal from the Lenin Peace Prize Committee, of which he was Vice-President, and his refusal to attend its meeting in Moscow on April 20. The spokesman pointed out that the "Soviet revisionist leading clique" had arbitrarily changed the Committee's name from Stalin to Lenin International Peace Prize Committee, and had used the Committee to serve its "counterrevolutionary political line." Further, even the "arch-traitor of the world's revolution," Khrushchev, was a winner of the prize, which was a "grave insult to the name of the great Lenin." (NCNA, 20 April.)

**Plans for Future Activities.** A number of organizational decisions were made at Leningrad. These included wide measures to raise funds and decisions to: take immediate steps regarding application for Status C of UNESCO; study the various aspects of nominating a permanent observer at the UN; develop closer contacts with churches and other religious bodies, in particular Pax Christi; and observe 28 April as Okinawa Day, 25 June as Korea Day, and 10 January as Tashkent Agreement Day.

Activities planned by the WCP for 1968, in addition to those already mentioned, include: a joint seminar with the International Confederation for Disarmament and Peace on the theme "NATO must quit Europe"; a meeting of Southern Latin American Peace Committees in Santiago (12-14 January); a meeting of Northern and Central Latin American Peace Committees (including US and Canadian committees) in February (first planned for late 1967 in Mexico); and a seminar on "Neo-Colonialism and World Peace" proposed by the Indian Writers' Committee and to be organized by the WCP.

To celebrate the twentieth anniversary of the foundation of the WCP in 1969, the Hungarian Peace Committee has suggested holding a Second World Conference of Intellectuals at Wroclaw, where the first such conference took place (in 1948) preceding the foundation of the WCP.

# WORLD FEDERATION OF TRADE UNIONS

The World Federation of Trade Unions (WFTU) was set up at the initiative of the British Trades Union Congress (TUC). The TUC convened a preparatory conference in London in February 1945, which was followed by the Foundation Congress held in Paris in October of the same year. Paris also became the first headquarters of the WFTU, but in 1951 the French government expelled the organization for subversive activities. It moved its base of operations to the Soviet sector of Vienna, where it remained until February 1956. At that time the government of Austria, having regained its independence, ordered the expulsion of the WFTU for endangering the country's neutrality (order of the Interior Ministry, 4 February). The headquarters was then transferred to Czechoslovakia, where it continues to be located at Namesti Curieovych 1, Prague I.

In recognition of Britain's leadership in establishing the WFTU, Sir Walter Citrine was elected its first President. At the USSR's insistence—and the actual threat of withholding cooperation—its own nominee, Louis Saillant, was elected Secretary-General. As a full-time official, Saillant quickly became the most powerful individual in the Federation. Although he called himself a socialist, he was dedicated to Stalin's policies and succeeded in bringing the Secretariat and other ruling bodies under communist control. Arthur Deakin, the successor of Sir Walter Citrine as Chairman of the TUC, stated in 1948: "The WFTU is rapidly becoming nothing more than another platform and instrument for the furtherance of Soviet policy." A year later he commented: "We started with an honest intention, but we were not dealing with honest men." In fact, communist control of the WFTU became so much of a bone of contention that the TUC, the American CIO, and the Dutch NVV were instrumental in the withdrawal of noncommunists from the WFTU in January 1949. At their initiative an alternative organization was inaugurated in London in November; headquarters of this new International Confederation of Free Trade Unions (ICFTU) were established in Brussels.

**Structure.** The highest authority of the WFTU is the Congress, held every four years. Congresses have been held in Paris (1945), Milan (1949), Vienna (1953), Leipzig (1957), Moscow (1961), and Warsaw (1965). The Seventh Congress is due to be held in 1969. Each affiliated organization sends delegates, with the number of representatives determined by the size of the membership. At the 1965 Congress there were 527 participants (including 117 observers), who represented "159,114,000 workers of 90 countries, members of national or local trade-union organizations, some affiliated to the WFTU, some not" (*World Trade Union Movement,* no. 6, December 1965). Congresses are too large to transact much specific business, but they do elect the subsidiary bodies, which include the General Council, the Executive Committee, the Executive Bureau, and the Secretariat.

The General Council is supposed to meet every two years. It consists of 165 members—86 full members and 79 deputy members—representing 48 countries and the 11 Trade Union Internationals (TUIs). Because of its size, it does not have any policy-making functions. Policy decisions are made by the Executive Bureau and reviewed and confirmed by the Executive Committee. The Committee comprises 76 regular and deputy members representing 37 countries and the TUIs plus the members of the Secretariat. It meets twice a year. The Bureau consists of the President, 12 Vice-Presidents, and the Secretary-General. It is supposed to meet quarterly, but actually is convened as required, usually in eastern Europe. The Secretariat comprises the Secretary-General, the Deputy Secretary-General and nine Secretaries. It controls the departments of Press and Information, Relations with National Centers, Economic and Social Questions (including the UN), Solidarity, and Administration and Finance.

The Executive Bureau is constituted as follows: President, Renato Bitossi (Italy); Secretary-General, Louis Saillant (France); and Vice-Presidents Benedicto Cerqueira (Brazil), Shripad

Amrit Dange (India), Shafie Ahmed al-Sheikh (Sudan), Bénoît Frachon (France), Alexandr N. Shelepin (USSR), Ignacy Loga-Sowiński (Poland), Mohammad Munir (Indonesia), Enrique Pastorino (Uruguay), Lazaro Peña Gonzáles (Cuba), Karel Polacek (Czechoslovakia), and Herbert Warnke (East Germany), plus a representative from Communist China.

Members of the Secretariat are the Secretary-General, Louis Saillant; the Deputy Secretary-General, Pierre Gensous (France); and Secretaries Chen Yu (Communist China), Edwin Chleboun (Czechoslovakia), Stana Dragoi (Rumania), Ibrahim Zakaria (Sudan), Luis Alberto Padilla (Chile), Viktor A. Podzerko (USSR), Mahendra Sen (India), Sandro Stimilli (Italy), and Setiati Surasto (Indonesia).

The Trade Union Internationals represent workers of particular trades or crafts. One of the main purposes of the TUIs is to recruit local unions which do not, through their national centers, belong to the WFTU itself. Though the TUIs are in theory independent—each has its own offices and officials, holds its own meetings, and publishes its own bulletin—their policies and finances are controlled by the WFTU department which supervises them. The General Council meeting of the WFTU in December 1966 decided to give each TUI its own constitution; this move for intensifying the appearance of independence had the purpose of allowing the TUIs to join international bodies as individual organizations.

A number of subsidiary organizations have in recent years been set up by the WFTU to deal with specific problems. Normally, after initiating or proposing action, the WFTU leaves most of the work in the hands of affiliated or sympathetic organizations. Their particular function is to achieve collaboration with noncommunist trade-unionists. Among the largest and most active of these subsidiaries is the "International Trade Union Committee for Solidarity with the Workers and People of South Vietnam," proposed by the WFTU Executive Committee early in 1963. The inaugural conference was held in Hanoi in October of that year and a second meeting took place there in June 1965. This committee has set up a permanent Secretariat of seven members, headed by WFTU Secretary Edwin Chleboun and issues its own *Information Bulletin.* Interest in developments in Aden in 1963 led to the organization of the "International Trade Union Committee for Solidarity with the Workers and People of Aden" at a conference in Cairo early in 1964 where the International Confederation of Arab Trade Unions played host. At the second conference in Varna, Bulgaria, in 1965, a permanent Secretariat was formed and the WFTU was represented on it. WFTU influence was even more pronounced at the third conference of the committee, in Damascus, in January 1967; on this occasion it was decided to base the Secretariat in Damascus and to operate branches in Cairo and Prague. Another subsidiary is the "World Trade Union Committee for Consultation and United Action Against Monopolies," successor to the "Trade Union Coordination and Action Committee of Common Market Countries." It has held three meetings since 1963 and at the latest—held in Budapest in December 1966—decided to hold a "World Trade Union Conference for the Development of International Trade and Economic Relations." Still another, the "International Trade Committee for Social Tourism," has held three meetings, in Budapest and Prague in 1964, and in Belgrade in 1967; and in the summer of 1967 it organized a Baltic Sea cruise to celebrate the fiftieth anniversary of the October Revolution and the UN's International Year of Tourism. The "Special Commission on UN Agencies" is a very recent addition on the list of subsidiaries; its first meeting was held in September 1967. Its purpose is to try for an expansion of WFTU activities in the UN. Committees less active or completely inactive in recent years have been those concerned with the workers and people of Africa, study and inquiry on East and West Germany, working women, Algerian workers and people, protection of victims of repression against trade unions, and social security.

The WFTU is the only communist front organization that enjoys category A status with the UN's Economic and Social Council (ECOSOC), International Labor Organization(ILO), Food and Agriculture Organization (FAO) and United Nations Educational, Scientific and Cultural Organization (UNESCO). In April of 1967 it was granted consultative status B with the United Nations Industrial Development Organization (UNIDO). In addition the WFTU takes an active part in two UN regional organizations, the Economic Commission for Europe (ECE) and the Economic Commission for Asia and the Far East (ECAFE). The WFTU has five permanent representatives working with the UN and its agencies in New York, Geneva, Paris, and Rome.

There is no doubt that the expenses of the WFTU are very heavy, but no details of finances have been disclosed since 1949. Early in 1965, however, it was announced that economy measures were necessitated by the failure of China and her supporters to pay their affiliation dues. Staff reductions of the Secretariat and cutbacks in editorial activities were planned, but later in the year many of the financial difficulties disappeared. It is generally assumed that the Soviet Union intervened because curtailment of WFTU activities was not in its own best interests.

**Publications and Communications Media.** The most important publication of the WFTU is the illustrated mazagine *World Trade Union Movement.* Normally published bimonthly, it had two extra issues in 1967. English, French, German, Russian, Spanish, Rumanian, Japanese, and Arabic editions appear regularly, and in the past Chinese, Portuguese, and Swedish editions have been available. The circulation of the magazine is estimated at 45,000 with distribution in more than 70 countries. A new editorial board was appointed in 1967. The *Trade Union Press* (or *International Bulletin of the Trade Union and Working Class Press*) is issued twice a month in six languages and sent to 125 countries. *News in Brief* is a monthly news bulletin in English, French, Russian, and Spanish. *TUI Bulletins* are issued separately by each of the internationals. The WFTU also publishes pamphlets, often as supplements to the *World Trade Union Movement,* which deal with topics of federation activity or political interests. Every four years the WFTU publishes its *Report to Congress* covering the interval between Congress meetings. In 1967 a special pamphlet was circulated on "The October Socialist Revolution and the International Trade Union Movement."

The WFTU has a radio editor in charge of its frequent radio broadcasts in twelve languages from Moscow, Prague, East Berlin, and Warsaw. A full-length documentary film, "The Song of the Rivers," has been produced by the WFTU and filmed on five continents. The subject is the exploitation, degradation, and misery of workers—everywhere but in the communist-ruled countries.

**Aims and Policies.** According to its constitution the WFTU exists "to improve the living and working conditions of the people of all lands." More specifically it lists the WFTU's prime purposes: (*a*) to organize and unite within its ranks the trade unions of the whole world irrespective of considerations of race, nationality, religion or political opinion; (*b*) to assist, wherever necessary, the workers in countries socially or industrially less developed in setting up their trade unions; (*c*) to carry on the struggle for the extermination of all fascist forms of government and every manifestation of fascism, under whatever form it operates and by whatever name it may be known; and (*d*) to combat war and the causes of war and work for a stable and enduring peace.

While the avowed aims of the constitution are acceptable to most trade unions around the world, they have in effect been given special interpretation by the communist-controlled leadership. Secretary-General Louis Saillant in his report to the Sixth Congress in 1965 stated: "The function of the WFTU is not merely to be an international working-class propaganda service. The job of the WFTU is to be a permanent organized structure, whose operations go beyond the mere coordination of the international activities of the national centers." Interpretations of this kind have not always received complete endorsement. When the noncommunist unions broke away from the Federation in 1949, the TUC explained this action in a pamphlet, *Free Trade Unions Leave the WFTU,* which stated that the WFTU was "completely dominated by Communist organizations, which are themselves controlled by the Kremlin and the Cominform." There was an added complaint of the misuse of WFTU publications: "The nations of the Western Hemisphere and their governments have been presented . . . as 'warmongers' and 'servile instruments of the capitalist monopolies and trusts'. . . . Never has a word of criticism of Russia been tolerated."

Subservience to the Soviet Union has been the subject of frequent complaints in recent years. The All-China Federation of Trade Unions stated after a meeting of the WFTU General Council in December 1966: "The leaders of the Soviet trade unions have long schemed to split the international trade-union movement, and to expel the Chinese trade unions from the WFTU. This is because the Chinese trade unions have consistently opposed the Soviet revisionists for imposing their line of class capitulation on the WFTU and turning it into a subservient tool of Soviet foreign policy . . ." (NCNA, 30 December). In July 1967, Constantin Dragan, Chairman of the Central Council of Rumanian

Trade Unions (and a member of the WFTU Executive Committee), referred to the rigid control exercised by the WFTU and its organizations: "[They] still tend to isolate or bar different organizations from membership, to disregard the principles of worker democracy, to have the final say and to impose it on others . . ." (Tanyug, 15 July).

Earlier examples of the WFTU's unquestioned support of the Soviet Union are numerous. One of the most significant was the treatment of the Yugoslavs, who were expelled in 1950 at the time of the Stalin-Tito conflict and labeled as "traitors" and "agents of the fascist Tito clique." Moscow changed its opinion after destalinization and in 1956 the WFTU asked the Yugoslavs to rejoin. Since 1961 they have sent observers to WFTU meetings, but so far have refused to reaffiliate. In 1953 and 1956 when East German and Polish workers went on strike for better pay and better conditions the WFTU ignored the appeals of its own affiliates. The WFTU also supported the Soviet repression of Hungary in 1956 and joined in Russian allegations and accusations of "fascist reactionaries" and "counterrevolutionary groups."

Preoccupation with purely political questions is also clearly shown by WFTU protests against American "aggression" in Vietnam and Israeli "aggression" in the Middle East, against nuclear tests by Western powers but not by the Soviet Union, and against "acts of war and piracy by the American imperialists" in Cuba without any mention of the part played by Soviet missiles in the Cuban crisis. Similarly the Marshall Plan and the Atlantic Pact, the European Defense Community, German claims and rearmament, and just plain "colonialism" have repeatedly been attacked. The importance of taking a stand in political matters is not denied even by the highest echelons of the WFTU. Saillant at a meeting in Moscow on 6 November 1967 reviewed the increase in the ranks of trade unionists over a period of fifty years and then stated: "These changes, substantial though they are, are no less significant than the political and moral changes which have taken place in international trade-unionism. Under the conditions of a Socialist society the trade unions have become a school of administration, a school of Communism." Moscow Radio in a broadcast marking the twenty-second anniversary of the WFTU openly credited the organization with fomenting labor unrest in Western countries: "As a class organization of the workers, the Federation is doing a great deal to develop the strike movement, and if the strike movement in capitalist countries has been growing recently, much of the credit must go to the Federation" (comment by Boris Stolpovsky, 3 October). The WFTU has special solidarity funds available to support strikes, national liberation struggles, solidarity committees, and assistance to developing and newly independent countries.

In addition, solidarity with and support for those fighting their own governments or "colonialists" is such an important part of the WFTU program that a number of "solidarity days" are celebrated each year; with the workers of South Africa (7 February), Spain (7-15 June), Korea (25 July), Algeria (30 November), and South Vietnam (20 December).

To assure continuous availability of personnel ready and able to pursue the aims of the WFTU, training schools and courses have been held since the Vienna Congress decided to start such programs, mainly for trade unionists from Asia, Africa, and Latin America. Subsequently, trade-union schools were set up in Moscow, Eastern Europe, and also in Guinea, West Africa. Early courses lasted a maximum of four months, but now training in Europe may last as long as twelve months. The major schools are the International Trade Union College in Moscow, the Trade Union School in Sofia, and the Fritz Heckert Trade Union College in Bernau, East Germany. Regular seminars have been held in Prague, which late in 1967 was also the location for the second and most recent "Consultative Meeting of Trade Union Cadres in Developing Countries." Smaller training schools are active in such places as Algeria, Congo-Brazzaville, the Malagasy Republic, French Guinea, Martinique, Guadeloupe, Mali, and Chile.

**Views and Activities in 1967.** In line with its far-flung membership and political interests, the WFTU in 1967 sent representatives to celebrations, discussions, or investigations around the globe; protested or praised in line with its specific ideologies; and made decisions about its own future and policies at a variety of meetings and conferences.

Secretary-General Louis Saillant's "New Year Appeal for Trade Union Unity" set the tone for the year and encouraged the idea of "many-sided forms of trade-union dialogue, aimed at extending the field of united activity of the trade unions" (*World Trade Union Movement,* January). In spite of such intentions unity continued to be rather elusive, as Saillant's comments a few weeks later indicate. He then declared that "unity will no longer be flouted at WFTU meetings" and that "trade union democracy which defends itself in operation, is at the same time defending the sacred cause of international trade union unity" (*Ibid.,* March). The implied criticism was directed at the disruptive behavior of the Chinese at the General Council meeting in Sofia in December 1966. After the Chinese were banned from participation in the Council sessions, an announcement was made from Peking around the turn of the year of the dissolution of the All-China Federation of Trade Unions, a step that WFTU spokesmen called "extremely detrimental to the international union movement as a whole." The rift seemed inevitable according to WFTU Vice-President Bénoît Frachon, who reviewed the conflicts of the past and accused the Chinese of using every meeting to "spread falsehoods against the USSR" and of sending "a commando of Red Guards" instead of properly accredited delegates to Sofia (*L'Humanité,* 4 January).

The Chinese were not alone in their dissatisfaction with the WFTU. The Secretary-General of the Albanian Central Trade Union Council declared that "as a result of the pro-imperialist, opportunist, liquidating line imposed by the Soviet revisionists, the WFTU is at present passing through a profound crisis which has led to its complete degeneration" (ATA, 25 April, quoting speech of Tonin Jakova). As the year went on, both Chinese and Albanian membership in the WFTU was nominal at best. This was readily acknowledged by Alexandr Shelepin, who commented in October that ties with the Communist Chinese and Albanian trade unions had ceased to exist.

In contrast, satisfactory progress was reported in contacts with non-WFTU organizations. Particularly positive responses to the call for unity were reported from Europe, with France, Italy, and Belgium singled out. "Labor Unity of Action in Western Europe" late in the year was one of the two main topics at a conference in Milan, Italy. The organizers of this conference—the Communist-dominated Italian and French labor federations (CGIL and CGT)—concluded that contacts between WFTU and ICFTU trade affiliates had never been closer than on this occasion and that relations were so improved as to be "breaking down the ideological barriers raised to justify the division."

Claims of cooperation were not limited to Europe. "Many independent national and continental trade union centers now cooperate with the WFTU. The list includes the All-African Trade Union Federation, the Conferation of Arab Trade Unions, the Latin-American Permanent Congress for Trade Union Unity, and also the Trade Union centers of Yugoslavia, Japan, and several other countries not affiliated to the WFTU." (Petr Pimenov, WFTU Executive Committee, in *Afro-Asian Labour Bulletin,* Singapore, February.) Yet the urgency of cooperation was also stressed by Pierre Gensous, who pointed to the "need to strengthen the units of the world's progressive forces in view of the growing aggressiveness of the imperialists as shown especially in the escalation of the war in Vietnam, in the situation in the Middle East and in Greece, and the revanchist demands of Western Germany" (report to Executive Committee meeting, Prague, October).

The WFTU approach to some of the major international events of 1967 is incidentally included in the last statement. Many additional and direct comments, however, were made. The WFTU Secretariat, for instance, issued a comprehensive statement on the Middle East on 25 July. It accused the government of Israel of "trampling underfoot the basic principles of the UN Charter" and of "most seriously endangering world peace," "multiplying provocations and violations of the ceasefire," and "asserting its desire for further conquests." Israeli actions were said to be "part of a scheme hatched by imperialism which . . . is using all means to prevent the evolution of peoples toward progress and is intervening in their internal affairs." Accusations were followed up with a demand for Israeli troop withdrawal from occupied areas, recognition of the rights of the Arab peoples of Palestine, independence for the Arab states and their choice of social and political regimes, although they should "not question the right of the people and the State of Israel to exist" (*Trade Union Press,* September). Late in the year preparations were under way for "a joint meeting of labor organizations in Arab and Socialist countries . . . with a view to condemning the stand of Israel and discussing means for moral and material solidarity with the Arab countries" (*Al Akhbar,* 6 December).

The Vietnam war figured even more prominently as a subject of criticism by the WFTU. In February telegrams were sent to trade-union federations in both North and South Vietnam declaring: "The continuous escalation of the Vietnam war unmasks ever more clearly the aggressive character of the American imperialists and the hypocrisy of their talk about peace" (CTK, 11 March). The Executive Bureau meeting in Prague in April dispatched a message to the Liberation Federation of Trade Unions of South Vietnam pledging that the WFTU would continue to "promote every effort to mobilize the workers and trade unions on every continent in the struggle for more and more effective support of your worthy cause . . . and for the final defeat of criminal American aggression." In June a WFTU delegation led by Pierre Gensous traveled to Hanoi for a four-week stay; the stated purpose for the visit was "to give testimony to the immense determination of the Vietnam people and strengthen international solidarity with their admirable struggle against the American aggressors." A warning was added that the Vietnam conflict might spread to other countries and that this prospect increased the need for moral and military aid from peace-loving forces throughout the world. There was also the announcement that on-the-spot observations and other testimony proved "that in Vietnam the United States Government is perpetrating a deliberate and premeditated crime of genocide for which it is responsible to mankind as a whole" (*Trade Union Press,* August).

WFTU preoccupation with Vietnam was also indicated by its participation in the Stockholm World Conference on Vietnam in July and by the publication of a new quarterly magazine, *The World Federation of Trade Unions and Vietnam.* Issued by the WFTU in Prague, the magazine is printed in Vienna by Globus, the Austrian Communist Party printers.

The WFTU on 26 April sent a message to the workers and people of Greece denouncing the coup, the cancellation of elections, and the ban of trade unions as a "blatant and brutal violation of trade union liberties and the UN Universal Declaration of Human Rights." The WFTU also called on unions throughout the world to intervene with their respective governments and prevent the new Greek ruling group from being recognized as a representative government. (*Trade Union Press,* May.) A month later the WFTU requested that the ILO intervene with the Greek government in order to annul antitrade-union measures. (*News in Brief,* no. 16, 14 June.)

A "Declaration of Principle on the Problem of European Security" was made at the General Council meeting at Sofia. Its major stipulation was that "the utmost be done to prevent West German imperialism from threatening world peace and provoking a new world war." Full and complete recognition of the German Democratic Republic as a sovereign state was also listed as a prerequisite for European security. These ideas were repeatedly affirmed in 1967. During "Baltic Week" in Rostock (East Germany) consideration was given to planning a special trade-union conference on European security, and Viktor Podzerko (USSR, WFTU Secretary) urged the unity of the trade unions and workers of Europe "for the triumph of security on this continent" (*Ibid.,* no. 21, 12 July).

The WFTU also raised objections against the "repressive fascist terror" and "racial discrimination" in South Africa, Rhodesia, and territories ruled by Portugal; against the "antidemocratic manoeuvres and brutal persecution for which British colonialism is responsible in Aden"; against US bases in Japan, "aggressive designs of the American war-mongers," US "spy radio stations" on Cyprus, "American imperialists' attempts to tighten the economic blockade of Cuba" and increasing "provocations" against the Democratic People's Republic of Korea.

The WFTU not only participated in numerous meetings around the globe, but also held its own regular meetings. Most important were the 54th and 55th Executive Bureau meetings in Prague in April and September and the 34th Executive Committee meeting in the same city on 25-27 October. The Executive Bureau concerned itself with the publicity activities of the WFTU and their possible improvement and the progress in tasks outlined at the Council meeting in Sofia. Interest in close contacts with the UN was emphasized by the naming of an expert commission to study WFTU activities in the various UN organizations. The International Labor Organization (ILO) was a focus of attention. "The Development of the Work of the WFTU within the UN and Its Specialized Agencies" was also one of only two topics on the agenda of the Executive Committee meeting, which noted the "positive results which have been obtained through the orientation of WFTU policy within the UN" and reviewed the "profound political, economic, and social changes which have created more favorable conditions for international cooperation in general, and for united trade union action, both national and international, in particular." A resolution was passed to utilize every chance to cooperate with all "progressive forces in the United Nations."

A number of changes took place in the hierarchy of the WFTU. Most important was the selection of Alexandr Shelepin, Chairman of the Soviet All-Union Central Council of Trade Unions, as Vice-President replacing Viktor Grishin. A great deal of speculation centered around a possible replacement for Louis Saillant, who for some time had been in poor health. Pierre Gensous appeared to be the logical choice as successor in the Secretary-General's post, but the Soviet Union was said to be reluctant to approve another Frenchman in this sensitive spot. By the end of the year the question of new leadership appeared to have lost some of its urgency, as Saillant was anxious to retain his job and enjoyed Soviet backing for his stand.

Not all meetings or conferences organized or attended by WFTU delegates were of equal importance. Early in the year interest centered around the Solidarity With the Workers and People of Aden Conference in Damascus and the International Conference of Railroad Workers' Unions in Budapest. Attendance in Damascus was unusually diverse, including delegates from the Middle East, from all East European and a few West European countries, and from Africa, Latin America, China, North Korea, and North Vietnam. Speeches and resolutions were not confined to the declared objective of the meeting, but covered the gamut of world problems. The Budapest meeting attracted eight member organizations of the ICFTU, nine of the WFTU, and an autonomous one and was called "the most important meeting since the international trade union split of 1949."

In the spring Algiers was the site of a conference called for the purpose of considering the training of "militant trade-unionists" from African countries. African trade-unionism also figured prominently at a Pan-African conference in Dahomey in July.

The International Trade Union Assembly convened by the WFTU in Leningrad late in October attracted representatives from 80 countries and was dedicated to the fiftieth anniversary of the October Revolution. The WFTU also joined in the Moscow festivities and in October published a special anniversary issue of the *World Trade Union Movement* in which an editorial assessed the situation in these words: "The glory of the revolutionaries of October 1917 became the reason for glory in the hearts of the workers of the world." It held the aegis of socialism responsible for the trade-union movement's strong and robust growth and credited its power to "international class solidarity, mutually won, and indissolubly uniting the workers of the world with those of the Soviet Union, and the latter, naturally, with the workers of the world."

The World Federation of Democratic Youth (WFDY) was founded in November 1945 at a "World Youth Conference" convened in London by the World Youth Council. At first the WFDY appeared to represent a variety of shades of political opinion, but key posts were taken by Communists. By 1950 most of the non-Communists had left to found their own independent organization, the World Assembly of Youth.

The WFDY headquarters was in Paris until its expulsion by the French government in 1951; since then it has been at Benczur-utca 34, Budapest 6.

According to the constitution of the WFDY, all youth organizations and other organizations which contribute to the safeguarding or the activities of young persons are eligible for membership. A total membership of 101 million in more than 100 countries is claimed. It is known, however, that the number of affiliated groups—at one time exceeding 200—has been reduced in recent years. The vast majority of WFDY members live in communist countries.

**Structure.** The Assembly (formerly called the Congress) is the highest body of the WFDY. It is supposed to convene every three years, and all affiliated organizations are represented at the meetings. The Assembly actually has met only seven times: in London (Foundation Congress, November 1945), Budapest (September 1949), Bucharest (July 1953), Kiev (August 1957), Prague (August 1959), Warsaw (August 1962), and Sofia (June 1966). The Assembly elects the Executive Committee, which is responsible for implementing decisions of the higher authority. The Committee has 59 members, including all the officers, and is supposed to meet at least twice a year. Day-to-day work at headquarters is the responsibility of the Bureau, theoretically under the direction of the Executive Committee. The Bureau meets whenever necessary and controls the Secretariat, the Departments, and the Regional Commissions. Departments have been set up to handle International Solidarity, Peace and National Independence, Youth Rights, Press and Information, Relations with International Organizations, and Finance and Administration. Regional Commissions exist for Africa, Latin America, Europe, North America and Australia, Asia, and the Middle East and Arab countries.

All leaders of the WFDY are officers of the Bureau, which consists of the following: President Rodolfo Mechini (Italy); Secretary-General Francis Le Gal (France); Assistant Secretaries-General Babacar N'Diongue (Senegal) and Paul Contreras (Venezuela); and Vice-Presidents Hamid Osman Bashir (Sudan), Sushil Chakravarty (India), Chia Hsueh-chien (China), Choe Chang-yul (North Korea), G. Margono (Indonesia), Rosendo Rojas Gomez (Chile), Yevgeni Silin (USSR), and Manuel Torres (Cuba). The Treasurer is Josef Varga (Hungary). The Secretaries are Siegfried Diener (East Germany), Alejandro Gomez Roa (Colombia), Teuvo Homppi (Finland), Ivan Ganev (Bulgaria), Nicolai Mancas (Rumania), Sindiso Mfenyana (South Africa), M. Oliveira (Brazil), Behnam Petros (Iraq), Ricardo Rosales (Guatemala), Shimpo Thosio (Japan), Gregorz Sokolowski (Poland), Alexander Szabo (Czechoslovakia), and Pablo Zapata (Argentina). There are additional Bureau members from Australia, the Dominican Republic, Lebanon, Sierra Leone, and Somalia.

A number of organizations are considered subsidiaries of the WFDY. The "International Committee of Children's and Adolescents' Movements" is reported to "enjoy autonomy within the general line of the WFDY," but actually is a firmly controlled subsidiary, depending on the parent organization for financial survival. Its function is to organize international children's camps and film festivals. The "International Bureau of Tourism and Exchanges of Youth" (BITEJ) is charged with planning and supervising work camps, meetings, and conferences for young tourists. An official of the Bureau defined its function thus: "Some youth organizations cannot or do not want to cooperate with WFDY directly and the first steps for bringing them in touch with the international progressive youth movement leads through this very department. . . . BITEJ's activities are in spheres where there are many possibilities of winning new friends and new organizations." (*Mlada Fronta,* organ of the Czechoslovak Youth Union, 2 November 1965.) The "International Sports Committee for Youth" is charged with the organization of events for the World Youth Festivals. The names of the "International Committees of Solidarity" with South Vietnam, with the "Arab Peoples," and with the "Youth and People of the Portuguese Colonies" explain their functions. The most recently established subsidiary is the "International Volunteer Youth Service of Solidarity and Friendship" (IVYSSF), set up in Moscow early in 1967. It seeks to increase WFDY influence in the developing countries. Its activities have been noted as follows by the London *Economist* (10 June): "The Communist answer to the American and other Western voluntary overseas services tries to make up in quality what it lacks in manpower. . . . The Secretariat insists that it does not take on young men who are just looking for cheap adventure. Needless to say, one precondition is that they should be proven followers of the WFDY party line, and it can be safely assumed that they are expected to spread the word in developing countries." The program for 1967 included the dispatch of "young specialists" to such places as Cuba, India, and Mongolia; the planning of future projects; and the organization of instruction for future leaders of voluntary service groups.

The WFDY maintains relations with a number of independent organizations. It works most closely with the International Union of Students (IUS), with which it assumes the part of senior partner. The World Youth Festivals and a number of regional youth conferences have been joint efforts. The WFDY also has close contacts with the World Federation of Trade Unions, particularly in connection with the interests of young workers. The WFDY has supported campaigns of the World Council of Peace and cooperated with the International Federation of Resistance Fighters. It has Category C status with UNESCO, and has applied for consultative Category B. It is on the Register of ECOSOC and is an associate member of the Coordinating Committee for Voluntary Work Camps, which works under the aegis of UNESCO.

The WFDY claims to be financed entirely by affiliation fees. Details are not published, although it is known that most of the funds expended—and these are very considerable—are received from communist countries. At the Assembly meeting in 1966 Secretary-General Le Gal's report of the failure of some affiliates to pay their dues because of disagreement with WFDY policies implied a weakening of the organization's financial position; yet projects meeting with USSR approval always appear to have ample funds available.

**Publications.** The WFDY publishes a quarterly magazine, *World Youth,* in English, French, and German editions; the editorial board of the publication consists of about ten persons, most of whom are permanent WFDY officials. A newssheet, *WFDY News,* appears monthly in English, French, and Spanish editions. *Youth Information* is a monthly news bulletin. *WFDY Diary* is published annually and reports on the organization's activities and the main Communist-run youth events of the year. Special pamphlets are issued for congresses and festivals, and on other important subjects and events. In 1967 the rights of young people in West Germany were discussed in a new pamphlet entitled, *The Emergency of Democracy—The Emergency of Young People.*

**Aims and Policies.**   The official aims of the WFDY have been laid down as follows: (*a*) to contribute to the education of young persons in the spirit of freedom and democracy; (*b*) to raise the living standard of the young; (*c*) to end colonialism; (*d*) to ensure peace and security in the world; (*e*) to promote the active participation of young persons in economic, social, cultural, and political life; (*f*) to ensure in all countries and for all young persons full freedom of speech, the press, religious belief, assembly, and organization; (*g*) to further the spirit of international friendship and support the principles of the UN.

Actual policies and activities of the WFDY bear little relation to the official aims. Unquestioned support of the Soviet Union has been evident since 1949, when a manifesto condemned the "warlike preparations" of the "capitalist countries" led by the Americans, attacked the Marshall Plan, alleged violation of democratic freedom in "imperialist" countries, and appealed to the young to support the "invincible army" of peace partisans "headed by the mighty Soviet Union."

The pro-Soviet and anti-Western stance of the WFDY has never been modified, and politically motivated decisions have abounded over the years. After Stalin and Tito clashed in 1949, for instance, the Yugoslav affiliate was expelled by the WFDY and the Yugoslavs were labeled as "traitors to the cause of peace and democracy, and deserters to the camp of the imperialist warmongers." Even though its headquarters were in Budapest, the WFDY confined itself to regrets for the "tragic events" during the Hungarian uprising in 1956, refraining from any criticism of the Soviet Union. The Sino-Soviet dispute has constituted a real problem and has been the cause of a number of disruptions of WFDY meetings in recent years.

**WFDY Activities around the World.** The best-known and most publicized activities organized by the WFDY are the World Youth Festivals. Eight such summer festivals have been held, all arranged in cooperation with the IUS. The first took place in Prague in 1947 (attendance 17,000), followed by festivals in Budapest in 1949 (10,000), East Berlin in 1951 (26,000), Bucharest in 1953 (30,000), Warsaw in 1955 (30,000), Moscow in 1957(34,000), Vienna in 1959 (18,000), and Helsinki in 1962 (10,800). The Ninth Festival has been scheduled and postponed several times because agreement could not be reached on its location or because political developments and disputes created adverse conditions. In 1965 Algiers was dropped as the festival site because of a change in the Algerian political regime. Ghana was selected as an alternative, but the fall of Nkrumah necessitated another postponement. Sofia is now designated for the Ninth Youth Festival in 1968. The nature of all the gatherings was adequately described by the Polish newspaper *Trybuna Luda* (28 May 1955) in its commentary on the Warsaw festival. "It must be realized that the festival is not only for song and amusement: it is, above all, a political event on a world-wide scale."

In contrast to the Youth Festivals, which are designed to attract the rank and file of young members, the World Youth Forums held in Moscow in 1961 and 1964 were keyed to political indoctrination of youth leaders. Indoctrination has also been the basic purpose of a number of training schools and courses held in East Germany and the Soviet Union. Scholarship grants provided for participants have mostly been awarded to members from the developing countries.

Anniversaries observed by the WFDY are the Day of Solidarity with Youth and Students Fighting against Colonialism (21 February, in conjunction with the IUS), World Youth Week (late March), World Youth Day against Colonialism and for Peaceful Coexistence (24 April, in conjunction with the IUS), International Children's Day (1 June, in conjunction with the WIDF), and World Youth Day (10 November). Solidarity celebrations of days or weeks have also been dedicated to Vietnam, Korea, Greece, Spain, the Arab Peoples, Portuguese colonies, and others; some are continued from year to year.

Major so-called Specialist Conferences were the International Conference in Defense of the Rights of Youth (jointly with the WFTU, Vienna 1953), the First International Young Workers' Conference (Prague 1959), the Seminar on Youth in the Struggle against Colonialism and Neo-Colonialism (Algiers 1963), and the World Youth Conference on Peace and Disarmament (Florence 1964).

In recent years the emphasis in regional meetings has shifted, and Africa has become a focus of attention. Before 1964, meetings in Africa had been an uncommon occurrence, but since then Accra, Dar es Salaam, and Conakry have all served as host sites for solidarity seminars or conferences, and visits by WFDY delegations to African countries have been numerous. In Europe, on the other hand, the WFDY has recorded many failures in attempts to organize meetings in noncommunist countries; applications have drawn negative replies by Western governments. Problems have also plagued efforts in Latin America, where the last WFDY-sponsored conference took place in 1964. Here Cuba's growing opposition has been a major drawback. At the Seventh Assembly (Sofia, 1966), the Cuban delegate strongly criticized the WFDY for the "little importance it attached to national liberation movements" and condemned both the structure of the WFDY and its lack of support for Latin America.

**Policies and Activities in 1967.** The political orientation of the WFDY was clearly apparent in far-flung activities around the globe in 1967. Almost invariably the organization took its cue from the Soviet Union and was steadfast in following the Soviet lead. This was particularly true with regard to the major international issues, such as Vietnam, the Middle East, and European developments.

Vietnam figured prominently in WFDY attention throughout the year. In February the Secretariat issued a statement characterizing the resumption of bombing of North Vietnam as a "cynical action revealing the American aggressors' real face" (MTI, 21 February). According to Secretary-General Francis Le Gal, one of the WFDY's principal tasks was to "promote the strengthening of international solidarity with Vietnam in the country's fight against the aggression of American imperialism"; he added that there had been drawn up "a far-reaching work program for the future" which would enable the "diversified forces and widest strata of Democratic World Youth to make their contribution in closer unity." When Le Gal headed a WFDY delegation to North Vietnam in March he remarked that the "aim of the aggressor was to demoralize, to destroy, and to paralyze life," but that just the opposite had been achieved and that productive work continued. World Youth Day, celebrated by the WFDY on 10 November, was devoted mainly to Vietnam. A Latin American youth meeting of solidarity with Vietnam was held in Santiago, Chile, and the anniversary of the formation of the National Liberation Front of South Vietnam on 20 December was the occasion for a call on all "progressive youth" to stage "bigger demonstrations of solidarity than ever" (MTI, 24 November).

In March a WFDY delegation headed by President Mechini visited the UAR, Lebanon, and Syria. At the Palestinian refugee camp in Khan Jamil, Syria, they endorsed the determination of the young people in the camp to "free their stolen homeland through a war of liberation." When Arab-Israeli fighting erupted in June the WFDY sent a message to U Thant at the UN demanding strong condemnation of "Israeli aggression." In East Berlin a meeting of the Executive Committee was convened for the sole purpose of discussing developments in the Middle East. The Polish representative claimed that "Israel had found an ally in Western Germany and has modeled itself on the Nazis," and that "the Hitler war and the Israeli war" were similar. President Mechini spoke and pledged the WFDY's "full support to the Arab people in their fight for their legitimate rights," while Israel's actions were to be viewed in the context of the policies of the "most aggressive circles of imperialism." The WFDY called for an "international solidarity conference" in an Arab country, a youth control commission to investigate Israeli "war crimes," and medical and other aid to Arab countries, including scholarships for students whose studies had been interrupted by the fighting.

The WFDY approach toward Germany was only implied in the statement about the Middle East, but the "German problem" directly and repeatedly was the subject of WFDY concern. At the "Consultative Meeting on European Security" held by WFDY European affiliates in Warsaw in September there was general agreement among the participants that "the German problem—resistance to the revanchist and militarist policy of Bonn which claims the right to represent the whole of Germany, does not want to recognize the German Democratic Republic, advances territorial claims and strives for thermonuclear weapons—remains very topical," and that as long as the Federal Republic should pursue such a policy, "camouflaging it with the slogan of a new Eastern policy, the peoples and youth of Europe will struggle against Nazism, militarism, and revanchism." The Portuguese representative claimed there was a "close military-political alliance between Lisbon and Bonn," which he called "a threat to European peace and security." WFDY President Mechini supported East German interests by stating that "recognition of the German Democratic Republic and defense of its sovereignty are the basic duties in warranting peace and security in Europe" and that "East Germany's constructive peace policy is the main obstacle to the realization of the West German imperialists' peace-risking policy." These preliminaries led to a final conference appeal for recognition of the GDR, the inviolability of the existing borders between the two German states, special status for West Berlin, and a catch-all "recognition of all other realities on the European continent." The latter would include creation of a nuclear-free zone and substitution of a collective European security system for NATO and the Warsaw Pact.

Events in Greece led to a WFDY declaration of support for Greek youth, an international campaign to secure the release of youth leader and composer Mikis Theodorakis, and a competition for the lyrics to music composed by Theodorakis for the WFDY's children's organization. The Greek Embassy in Budapest received a communique from the WFDY expressing indignation at the coup and "fascist measures" in Greece. According to Radio Budapest, the unofficial Greek reply to the complaint was an "assault" on the WFDY President and the "pouring of despicable invectives and slanders" on the organization (*Mlada Fronta,* 6 May).

The WFDY declared its opposition to "fascist regimes" in Spain and Portugal; Spanish and Portuguese"colonialism" in Equatorial Guinea, Angola, Cape Verde, and elsewhere; the "Fascist dictatorship in Argentina"; and the "dictatorial and tyrannical, undemocratic and pro-imperialist government creating an atmosphere of terror and repression" in Guatemala (*WFDY News*, no. 6).

Controversy that colored WFDY activity during the previous year continued to prevail as a result of the Sino-Soviet dispute. At a press conference in February President Mechini acknowledged that six months earlier the permanent representatives of Chinese youth had left WFDY headquarters and that since then there had been "no contacts with the youth organization of China." He noted that the Chinese Young Communist League had completely disappeared and been replaced by "new youth organizations" which endorsed vigorous anti-Soviet views. "Anti-Soviet tendencies are always indications of being against the forces of peace, progress, independence, and socialism," the WFDY leader declared, adding that the new Chinese policies would "injure the solidarity of the forces of anti-imperialism and aid aggression" (*Sztandar Mlodych*, Warsaw, 10 February). Replying to these accusations, WFDY Vice-President Chia Hsueh-chien protested against the "rabid anti-China outbursts," which "proved once again that the WFDY had completely degenerated into an instrument for carrying out the counterrevolutionary revisionist line of the Soviet leading cliques." He added a warning: "By opposing China you will come to no good end. You must immediately retract your anti-China outbursts and openly acknowledge your guilt before the youth of China and of the rest of the world." (NCNA, 6 March.) Subsequently, as a result of the controversy, the WFDY President was refused permission to travel to Vietnam via Peking and was forced to travel a longer route.

The Chinese were joined in their opposition to the WFDY by the Albanians. At the Fifth Congress of the Union of Albanian Working Youth, in Tirana, both the WFDY and the International Union of Students were labeled "instruments of the treacherous policy of the leaders of Komsomol and Soviet youth" (ATA, 28 June).

Cuban disenchantment had different roots. Cuba made a very determined bid for the selection of Havana as the site of the Ninth World Youth Festival. When Sofia was chosen instead, Cuban reaction exceeded mere disappointment. In fact, it is generally assumed that postponement of the event until mid-1968 was a move made to allow extra time for fence-mending and to persuade the Cubans to abandon their earlier threat to boycott the festival if it were held in Europe.

The hope of extending WFDY influence was the reason for a number of projects of interest to the developing countries. For instance, the topic of a seminar held in Bamako, Mali, in October was "Rehabilitation of National Culture." A campaign against famine in Bihar, aimed at the good will of Indians through the collection of money, food, medicines, clothing, and machines. More significant than any other project was the establishment of the "International Volunteer Youth Service of Solidarity and Friendship" to "stimulate economic, social, and cultural progress." IVYSSF became a new section of BITEJ, with WFDY Secretary Ivan Ganez in charge. Early plans ranged from medical assistance to Angolan refugees, construction of a hospital in Cyprus, and youth centers and labor camps in Japan, Pakistan, the Sudan, Algeria, and other parts of the world to the teaching of agricultural techniques. Because of obvious similarities, the IVYSSF became known in the West as the "Communist Peace Corps." The WFDY organizers of the IVYSSF admitted that they did not mind learning from American mistakes and added: "If our young people find themselves in the same area as young Western people it would be fairly natural for them to mix" and even to swap ideas on "getting the message across" (*The Economist*, London, 10 June).

The fiftieth anniversary of the October Revolution was the occasion for special activities organized by the WFDY. The biggest was the WFDY-supported Youth Rally in Leningrad during the last week of July, in which more than 200 youth organizations from 118 countries participated. Dedicated to the anniversary, the rally was organized on the initiative of the Committee of Soviet Youth Organizations, which characterized it in advance as "one of the most representative youth forums in recent years" (*Komsomolskaya Pravda*, 6 June). The WFDY and the IUS were praised as a "mighty movement of young peace champions, of fighters against fascism," and as "major factors in world public life and an important force of world revolutionary progress" (report by S. P. Pavlov, First Secretary of the Soviet Komsomol). The WFDY President in his speech gave credit to all youth organizations represented, emphasizing the determination of the rising generations and all progressive forces to "isolate imperialism everywhere."

The anniversary of the October Revolution was noted by the WFDY early in the year when the Secretariat issued a lengthy appeal:

> This anniversary is of the utmost significance in the eyes of the world's democratic youth and of all progressive mankind. The great October socialist revolution opened a new chapter in world history and marked the beginning of an era in which the national liberation and socialist movements gained tremendous impetus. . . . The WFDY, which was born from the unity of anti-Fascist forces immediately after the attainment of victory, feels particular gratitude toward the Soviet people. Together with the socialist countries and the powerful democratic and national liberation movements, the Soviet Union is the bastion of peace and ensures the ultimate victory of anti-imperialist forces over every kind of colonial, neocolonial and imperialist rule . . . (*MTI*, 15 March.)

A pledge to continue to support the youth and people of the Soviet Union and help them "fulfill their sacred and difficult tasks" was also issued (WFDY circular, 25 March). On October 30 a "jubilee meeting" was staged in Budapest and congratulatory messages dispatched to the Soviet Union.

**The Ninth World Youth Festival.** Planning for the Ninth World Youth Festival started early in the year and gained momentum in later months. In January an International Preparatory Committee (IPC) meeting in Vienna settled the site controversy by "unanimous" selection of Sofia. By March, planning in Bulgaria had progressed to the point where the festival's purpose was identified as "the voice of our generation, a voice against the USA's aggressive policy, against imperialism, colonialism and neocolonialism, against racism, ignorance and hunger, a voice in defense of rights and interests of youth and students." (BTA, 21 March.) The slogan adopted was "For Solidarity, Peace, and Friendship."

Preparations for the festival—initially estimated to attract 15,000 delegates, but later upped by several thousand—included an extensive building and remodeling program. A new sports hall, blocks of new flats, and the renovation of concert halls, theaters, and athletic facilities were planned. Even the academic year in Bulgaria was rescheduled to facilitate preparations for the 28 July-6 August festival. The Bulgarian planners, in fact, proclaimed the festival "an activity of the entire country and its people" and termed all preparations for it a "political activity" (*Rabotnichesko Delo*, Sofia, 30 December).

The festival program called for 70-80 events a day, distributed among three major groups—political, cultural, and athletic. The IPC announced that the first day of the festival would be "dedicated to heroic Vietnam" and the second to "manifestations of solidarity with youth in countries fighting for national independence, peace, and social progress." Additional days were to be devoted to the Rights of Man, the Struggle for Peace, Protests against Nuclear Threats, and the Victims of Hiroshima and Nagasaki. Cultural events were intended to "bring together young parliamentarians, religious believers, actors, and persons active in culture and the arts." "Gala concerts, dances, and song competitions" would be held. A novel feature would be "meetings of young scientists, cosmonauts, mathematicians and others." The main attraction of the sports program would be a mass competition for a sports badge. Well-known athletes would be enlisted to participate in sports seminars.

The city of Sofia—it was promised—would be "at its best" for the festival. Specialists and artists would be in charge of decorating the city and places of arrival and departure in the country; assembly halls and public buildings would be spruced up. Even a new Bulgarian Press Agency, Sofia Press, was organized to take over the tasks formerly assigned to the Foreign Language Publishing House and the Bulgarian Information Bureau. The publication of books and pamphlets in five languages, the production of several films, and special festival broadcasts were envisaged. A new series of stamps honoring the festival was issued by the middle of 1967. In fact, no details were to be forgotten in order to assure success and that "in line with their interests, hopes and aims, democratic youth would take their activities to a new stage with the Ninth World Youth Festival." (*World Youth*, no. 2.)

# INTERNATIONAL UNION OF STUDENTS

The International Union of Students (IUS) was founded in August 1946 at a "world student congress" in Prague attended by students of all political and religious persuasions, who thought they were founding a "representative organization of the democratic students of the whole world who work for progress," as the constitution put it. Most noncommunists had left the IUS by 1951 as a result of its pro-Soviet activities. For many the decisive factor was the arbitrary expulsion of the Yugoslav Union of Student Youth in February 1950, following the Stalin-Tito quarrel. The noncommunist unions who left the IUS formed the Co-ordinating Secretariat of National Unions of Students (COSEC), with headquarters at Leiden, in the Netherlands. The COSEC organizes the bienniel meetings of the International Students' Conference (ISC).

The headquarters of the IUS are in Czechoslovakia, at Vocelova 3, Prague 2.

Membership in the IUS is open to national student unions, or to other student organizations where no national union exists. Provision is made for full or associate membership. In 1967 the IUS claimed 87 student organizations as members.

**Structure.** The Congress is the highest body in the IUS. Its meetings, supposed to take place every two years, have been held at Prague, August 1946; Prague, August 1950; Warsaw, August 1953; Prague, August 1956; Peking, September 1958; Baghdad, October 1960; Leningrad, August 1962; Sofia, November 1964; and Ulan Bator, March-April 1967. All affiliates and associated organizations send delegates to the meetings. Observers are invited but have no voting rights. At the 1967 Ulan Bator congress some 300 delegates were present.

The Congress elects an Executive Committee, which comprises a Secretariat, a Finance Committee, and ordinary Members. The national student organizations represented are chosen by the Congress, but each such organization selects its own representative. The Executive Committee meets at least twice a year. At the IUS's Ninth Congress (Ulan Bator) the following national unions were elected to the Executive Committee:*

> *Secretariat*—President, Czechoslovakia (Student Council of Czechoslovak Union of Youth; CSM); Vice-Presidents, West Africa (Union des Étudiants de Dakar; UED), Black Africa under Portuguese Colonial Domination (Union Générale des Etudiants d'Afrique Noire sous Domination Portugaise; UGEAN), Bulgaria (National Student Council of Bulgaria; NSCB), China (All-China Students' Federation; ACSF), Cuba (Federación Estudiantil Universitaria; FEU), India (All-India Students' Federation; AISF), North Korea (Korean Students' Committee; KSC), Panama (Federación de Estudiantes de Panama; FEP), Poland (Polish Students' Association; ZSP), Sudan (Khartoum University Students' Union; KUSU), USSR (Student Council of the USSR), and Venezuela (Federación de Centros Universitarios; FCU); Secretary-General, Iraq (General Union of Students in the Iraqi Republic; GUSIR); Secretaries, Argentina (Federación Universitaria Argentina; FUA), Belgium (Vereniging der Vlaamse Studenten; VVS), Ghana (Ghana National Students' Organisation; GHANASO), Hungary (National Committee of Hungarian Student Organizations, NCHSO), Mexico (Federación Nacional de Estudiantes Técnicos; FNET), Morocco (Union Nationale des Étudiants du Maroc; UNEM), Rumania (Union of Students' Associations of Rumania; UASR), South Vietnam (Union des Etudiants pour la Libération du Sud-Vietnam; UELSV); Treasurer, German Democratic Republic (Free German Youth, Student Section; FDJ). *Finance Committee*—Cyprus

*Nomenclature and initials of national student unions are given as referred to by IUS official publications.

(Federation of National Unions of Cypriot Students; FNUCS), Kuwait (National Union of Kuwaiti Students; NUKS), Spain (Sindicato Democrático de Estudiantes de España; SDEE), and the Kurdish Students Society in Europe (KSSE). Ordinary Members, Western and Equatorial Africa (Fédération des Étudiants d'Afrique Noire en France; FEANF), Algeria (Union Nationale des Etudiants Algériens; UNEA), Brazil (União Nacional dos Estudantes do Brasil; UNEB), Burundi (Jeunesse Révolutionnaire Rwagašore, Section Étudiante; JRR), Ceylon (Ceylon National Union of Students; CNUS), Colombia (Federación Universitaria Nacional; FUN), Congo-Kinshasa (Union Générale des Etudiants du Congo; UGEC), Dominican Republic (Federación de Estudiantes Dominicanos; FED), France (Union Nationale des Étudiants de France; UNEF). Greece (National Union of Greek Students; EFEE), Jordan (Union of Jordanian Students; UJS), Cameroon (Union Nationale des Étudiants du Kamerun; UNEK), Kenya (Students' Union, The University College; SUUC), Madagascar (Fédération des Associations d'Étudiants de Madagascar; FAEM), Martinique (Association Générale des Etudiants de la Martinique; AGEM), Mongolia (Union of Mongolian Students; UMS), Mozambique (Uniao Nacional dos Estudantes Moçambicanos; UNEMO), Nicaragua (Centro Universitario de la Universidad Nacional; CUUN), Palestine (General Union of Palestine Students; GUPS), Quebec (Union Générale des Étudiants du Québec; UGEQ), Surinam (Surinam Students' Union; SSU), Uganda (Makerere Students' Guild; MSG), Uruguay (Federación de Estudiantes Universitarios del Uruguay; FEUU), and North Vietnam (Union Nationale des Étudiants du Vietnam; UNEV).

The two leading posts in the IUS are those of President and Secretary-General; in 1967 these were held by Zbyněk Vokrouhlický, Czechoslovakia, and Nuri Abdul Razzak Hussein, Iraq, respectively.

The IUS works closely with the World Federation of Democratic Youth (WFDY), which it assists in running the "World Youth Festivals" and "World Youth Forums." It also regularly supports the activities of the World Council of Peace.

With respect to other international organizations, the IUS enjoyed consultative status with UNESCO from July 1948 until December 1952, when it was relegated to the register (or "Special List"); in June 1962 it was admitted to Category C status, but applications for Category B status have twice been deferred. It has no consultative status with ECOSOC or with any other UN Specialized Agencies.

The IUS still maintains contact with several national student unions which are no longer members, observers being exchanged at conferences. It also tries to keep contact with the World University Service and with religious organizations such as the World Student Christian Federation, and has tried to promote "united action" with the International Students' Conference and its members (see below).

In addition to the activities connected with the World Youth Festivals and Forums, which the IUS cosponsors with the WFDY, the IUS annually awards scholarships, mainly to students from colonial and newly independent countries. The scholarships, more than 300 a year, are arranged through national student organizations in the countries where the scholarships are tenable. Most recipients are Africans, and the main host countries are the Soviet Union, Czechoslovakia, East Germany, Poland, and Bulgaria.

The IUS celebrates the following anniversaries: 21 February, Day of Solidarity with Youth and Students against Colonialism; 24 April, World Student Day of Solidarity; 8 May, Day of Struggle against German Militarism; 17 November, International Student Day; 11-17 November, International Student Week. There are also solidarity celebrations with the students of numerous countries, including: 4 February, Day of Solidarity with the People and Students of Angola; 14 April, Day of Aid to Spanish Youth; 15 May, Day of Solidarity with Palestinian Students and Refugees; 25 June–1 July, Week of Solidarity with Korean People and Students; 20 July, Day of Solidarity with Vietnamese Students and People; 23 September, Day of Solidarity with Puerto Rico; 21 November, Day of Solidarity with the People and Students of Venezuela; and 7 December, Day of Solidarity with Persian Students. The IUS also often calls for ad hoc "solidarity" celebrations on a number of different issues.

Following a resolution of support passed by its Executive Committee in May 1963, the IUS set up a committee called the International Student Committee of Solidarity with the Struggle of the People and Students of Vietnam.

**Aims.** The official aims of the IUS as incorporated in its constitution are to defend the interests of students and strive for ideals directly and indirectly related to this purpose, such as "promotion of national culture," "eradication of all forms of discrimination and, in particular, of racial discrimination," and "realization of the aspirations of students in colonial, semicolonial, and dependent countries struggling against colonialism and imperialism." The IUS's protests and criticisms are invariably directed against the West. The Soviet Union and its allies have as yet to be criticized.

The IUS claims to be financed by affiliation fees and the sale of its publications, although the scale of the organization's activities and commitments makes it seem doubtful that these resources would cover all the costs.

**Publications.** The two principal publications of the IUS are the *World Student News* a monthly in English, French, German, Spanish and Arabic, and the IUS *News Service* bulletins issued fortnightly in English, French, and Spanish and monthly in Arabic.

**Views and Activities in 1967.** The major event of the year was the holding of the IUS's Ninth Congress in Ulan Bator, Mongolia (26 March - 8 April). Attended by some 300 delegates, representatives from 12 international organizations, and a number of observers, the congress adopted 119 resolutions (see *Resolutions of the 9th IUS Congress,* IUS publication, Prague, 1967). With the admission of a number of new member organizations (including the Yugoslav Union of Students, expelled in 1950) the total IUS national union membership reached 87, "the largest number of national student unions the IUS has ever had" (Zbyněk Vokrouhlický, *World Student News,* no. 5-6, 1967). The following countries with membership in the IUS, did not send delegations to the Congress: Communist China, Albania, Burma, Indonesia, Peru, and Réunion.

The congress was preceded by a meeting of the IUS Executive Committee in Prague (13-16 March) attended by 38 of the (pre-Ninth Congress) 45 members of the Executive Committee. Although there were no representatives present from Communist China, whose delegations had on previous occasions disrupted the IUS meetings (see *YICA,* 1966, pp. 496-498), the IUS leadership was faced with controversy provoked by the Cuban delegation, together with the delegations of Puerto Rico, Venezuela, the Dominican Republic, Ecuador, Haiti, and French Guiana. These delegations, prompted by alleged revelations of involvement of the US Central Intelligence Agency (CIA) in student affairs, demanded a discussion on the Chilean student union (Unión de Federaciones Universitarias de Chile; UFUCh), a member of the Executive Committee. They claimed that the UFUCh had been "one of the organizations indirectly financed by the CIA" and that it was "pursuing a program favorable to the imperialist policies of the United States" (*Sztandar Mlodych,* Warsaw, 22 March, as quoted in *Youth and Freedom,* New York, no. 1-2, 1967). When the majority of the Executive Committee refused to consider this issue, the aforementioned Latin American delegations left the meeting.

The UFUCh issue was brought up again at the congress, bringing into focus the broader subject of the overall strategy of the IUS. In an article on the congress (*World Student News,* no. 5-6, 1967), IUS President Vokrouhlický stated:

> [The UFUCh issue] could have led one to believe that this was to be a discussion relating to one of the member organizations of the IUS, but in fact it concerned a problem of principle significance for the character and over-all concept of the International Union of Students. . . . What was the real motivation behind this problem? At first glance it might seem that this was just another argument between some Latin American student unions. . . . But if we go deeper into the whole problem then what immediately comes up to the surface is what is really behind this conflict, which can be grouped into two questions: the first—what is the real character of the IUS, that is to say, which national student unions have a place in it and which do not; and the second—can or cannot the IUS include in its ranks national student unions with different ideological-political views,

with different political convictions; in other words should the IUS be a narrow organization consisting exclusively of vanguard student unions or a broad front of all progressive student forces? Both questions are indissolubly linked, and moreover, both have a basic—a positively vital—importance for the IUS, for its activities, direction and structure.

After two days of debate, the congress voted against the expulsion of UFUCh (44 against, 12 for, four abstentions, and three not participating in the voting). After issuing statements declaring that they would "reexamine their attitude toward the IUS," the following delegations left the Congress: FEU (Cuba), UNEB (Brazil), FED (Dominican Republic), FUPI (Puerto Rico), FEUE (Ecuador), UEG (French Guiana), AGEG (Guadeloupe), UNEH (Haiti), PYO (Guyana), and SSU (Surinam). The split in the delegations of FUN (Colombia) and FCU (Venezuela), which kept them out of the vote on the UFUCH issue, also prevented their total withdrawal; however, parts of the two delegations left. The two other delegations which voted with the minority—KSC (North Korea) and AGEM (Martinique)—remained in the congress (for further details on this subject and on the Ninth Congress see *Youth and Freedom,* no. 3, 1967).

The UFUCh issue was only one of a number of disputes that plagued the congress. An article in the British Communist Party's daily, *Morning Star* (21 April), pointed out:

> There was a temporary walk-out by the delegations of Kenya, Uganda, Burundi, Sierra Leone, Ethiopia, Nigeria, Tanzania, Zambia and the West African Student Union, when it appeared that a representative of the 'National Union of Israeli Students,' who had visitor status, would not be allowed to speak, but they returned when it became clear that he would. However, Ethiopia finally walked out over a resolution on Eritrea, and the Tunisian delegation did the same over a reference to another organization in their country.

There were also disputes as to accreditation of delegations: "Two competing delegations claimed to represent Japan (Zengakuren). One group which has been represented on the IUS Secretariat until now was given delegate status, and the other, supported by Korea, Rumania, and North and South Vietnam, received visitor status and the right to address the congress." (*Ibid.*) The latter of the two groups has the support of the Japanese Communist Party (JCP), whereas the former, composed of the Kakumaru-ha and Sampa Rengo (see *Japan*), take an anti-JCP stand.

Controversy regarding the Venezuelan accreditation reflected the broader issue of Soviet-Cuban relations. One of the two Venezuelan delegates denounced "socialist" countries which maintained trade and diplomatic relations with capitalist countries, and claimed that "the peoples and students of these 'Socialist' countries do not support their governments." The other delegate claimed that the first delegate represented only a minority trend of Venezuelan student opinion. Commenting on the incident, *Komsomolskaia pravda* (2 April) declared that the first delegate echoed "the 'arguments' of the counterrevolutionary rabble," but added that his statements reflected definite tendencies in the international student movement.

Another source of controversy at the congress was initiated by representatives of the French National Union of Students (UNEF), who challenged every national union seeking admission to the IUS to take a stand on the issue of CIA involvement in student affairs and alleged CIA subsidies to the ISC. Commenting on the congress's reaction to the UNEF challenge, the *Morning Star* (21 April) declared: "The vast majority of student unions in the world regard as unacceptable a national union which fails to break with the ISC in view of what is known of its CIA sponsorship."

One of the major themes that dominated the congress was that of opposition to "US aggression in Vietnam." In his appraisal of the congress, Vokrouhlický stated:

> The congress of a progressive and democratic international organization, which the IUS is, could not possibly have avoided discussion on the utterly shameful and escalating aggression by America in Vietnam. Absolutely logically and unanimously [the] Congress condemned the US imperialists and their allies . . . But it is as clear as daylight that right now it is hardly enough just to condemn American aggression. It is more and more evident that *only through broad, coordinated and united activity of all progressive and*

*democratic forces of the world will assistance to fighting Vietnam be effective and contribute to the defeat of the American aggressors.* [Emphasis in original.]

This thought was also the leading motive of the whole Congress which in the general report and particularly in the special commission on Vietnam sought and—what is even more important—drew up a program of the world in support of the struggle of the Vietnamese people. (*World Student News*, no. 5-6, 1967.)

Vokrouhlický added: "It can be said that the IUS now has the necessary prerequisites to successfully develop, as it did in the past and will do in the future, rich and all-embracing activities in support of our brothers in Vietnam . . . And we even maintain that support to the Vietnamese people in their fight against American imperialism and its aggression is one of the most important criteria of the progressiveness of every student, or every student organization." (*Ibid.*)

A number of criticisms of IUS activity were voiced during the congress, directed primarily at the Executive Committee and Secretariat. Delegations were critical of the IUS's failure to show sufficient concern with problems of education and its acceptance of generalities at the expense of national and regional concerns. Questions were raised with regard to deficiencies in the organization's publications and propaganda activity. It would appear, however, that the most serious challenge to the Soviet-controlled leadership of the IUS was the Cuban-sponsored advocacy of militant exclusiveness, which, according to Vokrouhlický (quoting an Italian delegate), would have transformed the IUS into "a kind of 'Jacobin' club" (*Ibid.*). The congress's resolutions and Vokrouhlický́s subsequent statement that "diversity of opinion and variety of methods in solving our problems is not only feasible but is to be expected" (*Ibid.*), seem to indicate that the IUS surmounted this challenge, although it might prove to be at the expense of losing the support of a number of its Latin American affiliates and others supporting Cuba's militant line. During a meeting in Montevideo, Uruguay (5-7 July), sponsored jointly by the Havana-based Continental Organization of Latin American Students (Organización Continental Latinoamericana de Estudiantes; OCLAE) and the Federation of Uruguayan University Students and attended by representatives from Argentina, Brazil, Ecuador, Puerto Rico and the IUS, delegates criticized the IUS, and the Uruguayan representative commented that "many national student unions were considering withdrawal from the IUS" (*Actualidades*, New York, no. 7, 31 July 1967).

On 8-12 February the IUS was a co-sponsor in Halle, East Germany, of the Fourth International Seminar of the Student Press, attended by representatives from 33 countries. The *Information Bulletin* of the World Council of Peace (no. 2, 1967) quoted the seminar's final communique as stating that "the role of the student press is to give an impulse in its publications and in student circles to actions marking a new stage in the solidarity with the just struggle of the Vietnamese people and students against the American aggression."

In connection with the Vietnam war, the IUS organized a "Week of Solidarity with the People of Vietnam", 10-17 November. IUS representatives, according to Roland Demarcy, a member of the IUS special committee on Vietnam, visited Canada, the USA, Panama, Peru, Mexico, Argentina, Japan, India, Ethiopia, Tanzania, Zambia, Mozambique, Senegal, Tunisia, and a number of countries in Europe. Demonstrations and student strikes were planned and carried out (in Western Europe these took place in December), although in the "socialist" countries "days of work for Vietnam," rather than strikes, were held. (*Al Akhbar*, Cairo, 9 November;*Mlada Fronta*, Prague, 10 November.)

In addition to travel connected with the "Vietnam Week," IUS representatives visited a number of countries and attended several student seminars and meetings, including: 5-8 January, Rüschlikon (Switzerland)—European Student Conference; 25-27 January, Vienna—International Preparatory Committee (IPC) meeting for the Ninth World Youth Festival; 8-12 February, Halle—Fourth International Seminar of Student Press (see above); 12-14 April, Cairo—seminar to "discuss the interference of the U.S. Central Intelligence Agency in international student organizations"; 27-28 May, Paris—meeting of Greek students to discuss the situation " produced by the monarcho-fascist coup d'etat"; 1-3 July, Cairo—Emergency Meeting of the Afro-Asian People's Solidarity Organization; 25-31 July, Leningrad—International Youth Rally; 18-20 September, Warsaw—Consultative Meeting on European Security (see *WFDY*); 28-29 November, Sofia—IPC meeting; and 18-22

December, Kampala (Uganda)—International Student Seminar. According to an interview given by Vokrouhlický to *Mlada Fronta* (17 November), the IUS organized the "Second Seminar of Portuguese Students" in Warsaw in August and a "meeting of all Arab student unions" in Beirut in October (to "organize Arab student unions to work toward overcoming the consequences of aggression"), and held seminars on "democratization of education" in Colombia, Panama, and Argentina.

During the year the IUS issued numerous protests, affirmations of "solidarity," and resolutions (for details see IUS *News Service* bulletins). The views expressed by IUS mirrored those of the Soviet Union.

Two of the areas of concern for the IUS during the previous year—relations with the Chinese student representatives and the ISC (see *YICA*, 1966, pp. 494-499)—appeared to have been temporarily settled. With regard to the former there was a complete boycott of Chinese representation. As far as the ISC was concerned, the IUS took advantage of the revelations concerning the CIA to change its strategy from one of courting ISC cooperation to that of attempting to persuade ISC-affiliated student unions to renounce their membership in the ISC and join the IUS. According to an article in *Komsomolskaia pravda* (25 March), "The IUS policy on cooperation and unity in the world student movement was aimed at exposing the activities of these (the ISC) leaders and drawing to the side of the IUS honest forces from the ISC ranks deceived and misinformed by the anti-Communist, pro-imperialist demagogy of the reactionary student leaders and their overseas masters from the CIA."

# WOMEN'S INTERNATIONAL DEMOCRATIC FEDERATION

The Women's International Democratic Federation (WIDF) was founded in Paris in December 1945 at a "Congress of Women" organized by a Communist-dominated organization, the "Union des Femmes Françaises." The WIDF headquarters was in Paris until January 1951, when the organization was expelled by the French government. Since then it has operated from East Germany at Unter den Linden 13, Berlin 108.

**Structure.** The highest organ of the WIDF is its Congress, which is supposed to meet every four years. Comprised of representatives of affiliated organizations plus some individual members, it examines the work of the federation, plans its future activities, selects the President and the WIDF Council, and ratifies any decisions taken by the Council in the interval between meetings. Congress meetings have been held in Paris (November 1945), Budapest (December 1948), Copenhagen (June 1953), Vienna (June 1958), and Moscow (June 1963); the Sixth Congress is scheduled for Helsinki in June 1969.

The WIDF Council meets annually and controls activities between congresses. Each affiliated organization must have at least one representative on the Council, the total number of members being fixed by the Congress. The Council elects the WIDF Bureau and Secretariat and appoints the Finance Control Commission.

The Bureau consists of a President, Vice-Presidents, Secretary-General, and additional members elected by the Council. It meets at least twice a year and implements decisions taken by the Congress and the Council. It is assisted by the WIDF Secretariat, consisting of the Secretary-General, several Secretaries, and a Treasurer.

No new President has been appointed to fill the vacancy created by the death of Eugénie Cotton (France) in June 1967. Mrs. Cotton, a recipient of the Lenin Peace Prize in 1950 and the gold medal of the World Council of Peace in 1961, had headed the organization since its formation in 1945. The Secretary-General is Cecile Hugel (France—appointed 1967); under her are two Assistant Secretaries-General, Marie-Ange Gaubert (France) and Maria Skotnikova (USSR). There are two Honorary Vice-Presidents, Dr. Andrea Andreen (Sweden) and Dolores Ibarruri (Spain). Vice-Presidents are Hiratsuka Raicho (Japan), Aruna Asaf Ali (India), Miluse Fischerova (Czechoslovakia), Seza Nabaraoui (UAR), Margarita Fornasini (Argentina), Nina Popova (USSR), Marie Frances Pritt (UK), Funmilayo Ransome-Kuti (Nigeria), Marie-Claude Vaillant-Couturier (France), Yang Yun-yu (Communist China), Ilse Thiele (East Germany), Freda Brown (Australia), Vilma Espín de Castro (Cuba), Umi Sardjono (Indonesia), and Helga Dickel (West Germany). Secretaries of WIDF are Angelina Acosta (Mexico), Adela Betinelli Taich (Argentina), Kathe Hager (East Germany), Evelyne Helman (France), Beatrice H. Johnson (Poland—ex USA), Florence Mophoso (South Africa), Promila Mohendra (India), Zakhra Rakhimbabaeva (USSR), Elisa Uria (Spain), Isabelle Vicente (Italy), Elena Vilcoci (Rumania), and Helga Dickel (West Germany). The Treasurer is Erzsi Ragyanszki (Hungary).

Membership in the WIDF is open to women's organizations, groups of women, and in exceptional cases to individuals. The Federation claims to have 83 affiliates, contacts with groups and organizations in many countries of the world, and a total membership in excess of 200 million. The Soviet Union, Eastern Europe, and China are most heavily represented among the membership. Few noncommunist groups are affiliated.

The Federation's financial support is said to be derived from affiliation fees, donations, and contributions, but no public accounting is done. Each project is said to be individually financed by a "special fund."

The WIDF publishes a glossy quarterly magazine, *Women of the Whole World,* in English, French, German, Russian, and Spanish editions. In addition it issues a bulletin, *Documents and Information,* and a similar periodical called *Vietnam* (first issued in 1967). A number of radio and press bulletins, circulars, special pamphlets, and brochures are published "as the need arises." One widely circulated brochure, *We Accuse,* dealt with alleged American atrocities in Korea and was translated into 21 languages. A series of pamphlets entitled *For the Defense of Human Rights* concentrates on the subject of solidarity with the people of developing countries.

The WIDF has a number of subsidiary organizations. The most active has been the International Liaison Bureau, which has been in existence since 1960. It has a headquarters in Copenhagen and a Secretariat, run by Emilienne Brunfaut, in Brussels. The basic purpose of the Bureau is to make contact with other groups and thus to gain support for the WIDF. One of the major efforts was the organization of a "World Forum on Children's Education" in Brussels in 1962.

Several committees and commissions have also been active in the past. Normally their function is temporary, keyed to the planning and publicity for a specific conference or campaign. The names of some of the committees readily explain their purpose. In this category would be the International Committee for the Defense of Children, the Permanent International Committee of Mothers, the Permanent Committee for Women's Questions in Colonial Territories, the Committee for Problems of the Child and the Family (Children's Commission), and the International Solidarity Committee with South Vietnam. The last is currently active. When organized in 1964 it had 46 members from 29 countries; members from a few more countries have joined since. Meetings of this committee have been held in Sofia (1964) and East Berlin (1967).

Close relations are maintained by the WIDF with the World Council of Peace (WCP). Several members hold office in both organizations, and the WIDF regularly supports WCP activities and congresses. It was a sponsor of the First World Peace Congress, held in Paris and Prague in 1949. The WIDF has also cooperated with the World Federation of Democratic Youth on the defense of children and the World Federation of Trade Unions (WFTU) on rights of women workers. It supported the "First World Congress of Women Workers" (Budapest, June 1956) and the second (Budapest, May 1964); both were organized by the WFTU.

The WIDF held consultative status with UNESCO from July 1948 to November 1952. It was relegated to the Register, because its activities were "no longer sufficiently in conformity with UNESCO." The WIDF was granted Category C status in 1962 and in 1967 was readmitted to Category B. It also held Category B consultative status with ECOSOC (Economic and Social Council) from 1947 to 1954, was dropped, then reinstated in 1967. Contact is maintained also with other United Nations agencies, such as the International Labor Organization and the World Health Organization.

**WIDF Aims and Policies.** According to its charter, the WIDF seeks to unite the women of the world, regardless of race, nationality, religion, and political conviction, so that they may work together and defend their rights as citizens, mothers, and workers; to protect children; and to ensure peace, democracy, and national independence and establish bonds of friendship and solidarity among women of the whole world. The WIDF draws attention to these aims by its regular annual celebrations of International Women's Day (8 March), International Children's Day (1 June), and the International Day of Solidarity with the People of Vietnam (20 July).

The goals of solidarity have proved elusive at times largely due to the fact that the WIDF normally supports Soviet policies that have not always been universally acceptable. The Sino-Soviet conflict was responsible for the disruptive behavior of the Chinese representatives at the WIDF Congress in Moscow, in 1963, which virtually brought proceedings to a standstill. In October 1965 Kuo Chien, the leader of the Chinese delegation at a Council meeting, declared that "certain leaders of the WIDF" had "betrayed altogether the aims set by the Federation at the time of its founding, and followed the capitulationist and schismatic line of the Khrushchev revisionists and reduce the Federation to an instrument for the enforcement of the foreign policy of one country" (NCNA, 8 November 1965). The Chinese next refused to participate in the WIDF World Conference on the Protection of Children, held in Stockholm in October 1966, on the ground that the conference was "under the exclusive manipulation of the modern revisionists' leading group of the Soviet Union" (*ibid.*, 2 October 1966).

They have not been represented at any WIDF meeting since. Soviet control of the organization also led to the withdrawal of the Union of Italian Women (UDI) from full membership and a shift to associate membership. Unfulfilled demands for greater autonomy and flexibility were the basis of dissension. Yugoslavia's affiliate was expelled at the time of the Stalin-Tito conflict. Although since then the situation changed substantially, the Yugoslav group has made no attempt to rejoin the WIDF.

The latest denouncement of the WIDF occurred in 1967. The Albanian affiliate's president, Vito Capo, in her report to the 6th Congress of the Albanian Women's Union in Tirana, criticized the WIDF as "an appendage of Soviet diplomacy, reflecting the Soviet line with its waverings, with its hypocrisy and half-way nature" and stated that "revolutionary women of the world will never reconcile themselves with the revisionist views of the WIDF" (Albanian Telegraph Agency, 26 October).

A more positive situation was reported concerning Latin America, where the WIDF was said to be seeking, "above all, to revolutionize the peasant masses," and to have been able "substantially to intensify its subversive activities" (*Neue Zürcher Zeitung,* 6 November 1965). More limited success has been attributed to regional activities in the developing countries of the rest of the world. Since a "Seminar on Mother and Child in Africa," at Bamako, Mali, in August 1965, not one meeting of any significance has been held outside Europe.

**Views and Policies in 1967.** While the basic aims of the WIDF do not change perceptibly, the organization is sensitive to events and problems in the world as they occur. Consequently, in 1967 major attention was focussed on Vietnam, the Middle East, and Greece. In February women from 38 countries and all continents gathered in East Berlin for a meeting of the "Women's International Committee of Solidarity with Vietnam." The fighting in Vietnam also figured prominently in discussions at a meeting in Moscow connected with the observance of International Women's Day (8 March) and the symposium of "Women in a Socialist Society" held there a few days later. A communique adopted by the symposium stressed the need for "unity, greater activity, and the pooling of women's forces in the struggle for peace, democracy, progress, and national independence of peoples, and against imperialism, fascism, and racism" (TASS, 16 March). The appeal on Women's Day included a denouncement of "atrocities perpetrated by US and satellite troops in Vietnam, bringing death and mutilation to the children and the entire civilian population," and stated that throughout the world "mothers cannot remain silent in the face of these crimes" (*New Age,* 12 March). The International Day for the Protection of the Child (1 June) concerned itself specifically with the problems of the children of Vietnam. In addition, the WIDF report to the "Stockholm Conference on Vietnam" in July detailed American "war crimes" and declared that in spite of American denials the bombing was "directed at the civilian population" and that "the ones who suffer most are the women and children" (*Women of the Whole World*, no. 2, 1967).

The WIDF repeatedly discussed the problems of the Middle East and "Israeli aggression against the Arabs." The Bureau meeting in Berlin in June sent a telegram to U Thant of the United Nations expressing alarm and indignation at "acts of extermination committed against women and children prisoners in territory conquered . . . by Israeli Government troops of aggression." It requested that the UN demand "withdrawal of Israeli troops to the lines held before the outbreak of the armed conflict . . . and negotiations to promote a peaceful solution to Middle East problems guaranteeing the national sovereignty, territorial integrity, and national independence of all the countries." U Thant was also asked to take action concerning the use of "napalm against the peaceful population in occupied Arab areas by Israeli troops" and against the "obstacles put in the way of the Red Cross rendering help to victims of this aggression in defiance of all international agreements" (*WIDF Press Communique,* 28 June).

"Violation of human rights in Greece" was charged and strongly opposed by the WIDF on several occasions. Solidarity with "patriot-composer Mikis Theodorakis" and all "arrested women" was proclaimed (ADN, 14 September); their "persecution" was protested in telegrams to King Constantine of Greece, U Thant, and the International Red Cross at Geneva. Late in the year the WIDF was trying to set up a commission of inquiry for an on-the-spot study in Greece of conditions faced by the "imprisoned women and children" and those "whose husbands or parents have been put in prison by the military junta that has seized power and instituted a reign of terror in the country."

The WIDF was particularly concerned with European security and debated the feasibility of organizing a special conference dealing with the topic. West Germany's "aggressive territorial claims," "pretensions to sole representation," and "further throttling of democratic freedoms" were said to constitute a threat to the peace of Europe, while its planning of emergency legislation was "in the hands of those who want to change the results of World War II by force and extend their power at the expense of the people"—all amounting to a "serious demolition of democracy" which possessed "frightening similarities with the military coup in Greece" (WIDF press communique, 29 June). On the other hand, recognition of the German Democratic Republic was called a "necessity to peace and security in Europe" (*Neues Deutschland,* 29 August).

The USA was condemned not only for events in Vietnam, but also for the "use of Federal troops to crush the American Negro movement for social justice" (WIDF circular dated 15 August). The "just struggle of the South Korean people for national independence and for the withdrawal of United States troops from their territory" was another area of recrimination (WIDF press communique, 27 June).

**Meetings and Future Plans.** The most important WIDF meeting in 1967 was the Council Meeting held in Prague 14-17 October. Immediately preceeding it was a Bureau meeting. Representatives of more than 60 countries attended. Delegates paid tribute to the memory of Eugénie Cotton, confirmed Cecile Hugel for the post of Secretary-General vacated by the resignation of Rosa Jasovich-Pantaleon (Argentina), discussed preparations for the next World Congress based on the theme of "The Women's Role in Today's World" and world political problems of all kinds. In the report of the Secretariat it was noted that the "increasing authority of the WIDF" had been "underlined by the granting . . . of consultative status by UNESCO and ECOSOC." In line with this new status it was announced that the WIDF would participate in a meeting of the ECOSOC Committee for Women's Rights in Geneva early in 1968. To widen WIDF influence in the Third World, representatives were selected in Prague for the tenth anniversary meeting of the Afro-Asian People's Solidarity Organization (AAPSO), scheduled for Cairo in December.

The Prague Council meeting also focussed attention on WIDF relations with international organizations. It was announced that a growing number of invitations had been received and that the Federation had been represented at meetings and congresses of such organizations as the Open Door International, the Abolitionist Women's Federation, the World Union for the Defense of the Child, the International Conference against the War Danger (New Delhi) the International Union of Students, the International Peace Bureau, the World Council of Peace, the Latin American Solidarity Organization (Havana), the Indian Women's Congress (Lucknow), and many others. Special praise was reserved for the Canadian "Voice of Women" conference in Montreal in June.

Another significant meeting was that of the WIDF Bureau, held in East Berlin on 14-17 June. On this occasion recommendations were made for a series of seminars "enabling a broad exchange of experiences." For instance, the secretariat was instructed to consult national affiliates on the feasibility of holding seminars in Czechoslavakia, Poland, and Hungary on women's education, and to investigate the possibility of holding a seminar in Africa. Action on earlier proposals for two seminars to be held in Latin America—one in Mexico on the status of peasant women, and another in Montevideo on women in public life—was postponed.

Press and financial activities of the WIDF also were topics on the agenda for the Bureau meeting. A determined request was made for national organizations to "make an effort to pay their WIDF dues and collect articles of value for an international bazaar-exhibition of the Federation." Substantially greater activity to increase circulation of the magazine *Women of the World* was also suggested as a means for improving WIDF finances.

A "Plan of Work" for permanent commissions figured most prominently not at a meeting, but in a circular letter issued in August. The "Women's Rights Commission" was to deal with problems of the education of women and hold a seminar that would be the "first important WIDF initiative in Asia in this field." Nepal, India, Ceylon, Afghanistan, and Pakistan were singled out as countries where preparations for the seminar were making progress. The "Children's Commission" was to study the possibility of arranging adoptions and the so-called twinning between towns in developed and developing countries. The "Commission for Peace, Solidarity, and Independence" would plan to participate in the "initiatives of other international organizations" on subjects indicated by the name of the commission.

Late in the year (9 December) the WIDF sent a letter to the UN on the occasion of the nineteenth anniversary of the Declaration of Human Rights. Describing itself as an organization committed to the principles of peace and humanity laid down in the original declaration, the WIDF pledged, "in the name of millions of women of the whole world," to continue its fight for "social justice, progress, independence, democracy, and peace."

The International Organization of Journalists (IOJ) was founded in June 1946 at a congress in Copenhagen. The International Federation of Journalists (IFJ) and The International Federation of Journalists of Allied and Free Countries were both formally disbanded and merged with the IOJ, so that for a time it was representative of world journalists. By 1950 all noncommunist unions had withdrawn from the IOJ in order to refound, in 1952, the IFJ. From 1955 onward the IOJ has made overtures to the IFJ to cooperate and eventually to form a new universal journalists' organization. The IFJ's standpoint on this proposal was summarized in 1955:

> The suggestion that an International could be formed to unite the International Federation of Journalists and the International Organization of Journalists takes no account of recent history. We can say that we played a very considerable part in forming the International Organization of Journalists at Copenhagen in 1946, and it was only because of the persistent use of its forum for political propaganda of a particularly virulent kind that we were forced to conclude that no useful work could be done within its framework. We—that is to say, most of the organizations now represented in the IFJ—left the IOJ for this reason. It is not possible for us to consider reunification until a radical change is effected in the conditions of the Press in those countries which are represented by national organizations in the IOJ (*IFJ Information*, July-September 1955).

The headquarters of the IOJ, originally in London, were moved in June 1947 to Czechoslovakia and are now at Parízká 9, Prague 1.

**Structure.** Eligible for membership in the IOJ are national unions and groups of journalists, and also individuals engaged in journalism. In 1967 the IOJ claimed to have a membership of "more than 130,000 journalists from 108 countries." The IOJ divides its geographical membership into four categories: (1) countries in which the national organization of journalists is affiliated to the IOJ—27; (2) countries in which there is more than one organization or more than one organization affiliated to the IOJ—7; (3) countries in which there are groups of members or committees of the IOJ—13; and (4) countries in which there are individual members of the IOJ—61 (*The Democratic Journalist*, No. 2-3, February 1967). It should be noted, however, that in a number of the countries listed as represented in the IOJ, the IOJ national representatives are not representative of any significant segment of their country's press.

The Congress is the highest body of the IOJ. Its meetings, supposed to take place every four years, have been held at Copenhagen, June 1946 (the foundation congress); Prague, June 1947; Helsinki, September 1950; Bucharest, May 1958; Budapest, August 1962; and East Berlin, October 1966. Representatives of affiliated organizations or groups and individual members attend the Congress, but individual members and representatives of groups with fewer than 20 members may not vote. At the 1966 Congress there were "282 journalists, including 138 delegates, 31 observers, and 113 guests, from 68 countries" (*The Democratic Journalist*, No. 11-12, December 1966).

The Executive Committee is elected by the Congress. It consists of both officers and ordinary members and meets at least once a year. At the end of 1967 the following group (sometimes referred to as the Presidium of the Executive Committee) constituted the leadership of the IOJ: President Jean-Maurice Hermann (France); Vice Presidents Jean-Baptiste Deen (Guinea), Mamadou El Béchir Gologo (Mali), Michal Hofman (Poland), Georg Krausz (East Germany), Olavi Laine (Finland), Renato Leduc (Mexico), Ahmed Baha' El Dine (United Arab Republic), Tsendijn Namsray (Mongolia), Nguyen Van Hieu (South Vietnam), Kang Sang-wi (North Korea), Hernán Uribe (Chile), Ernesto Vera

(Cuba), and Mikhail Zimianin (USSR); Secretary-General Jiří Kubka (Czechoslovakia); Treasurer Norbert Siklosi (Hungary) (*The Democratic Journalist,* No. 11-12, December 1967). In addition to these members, the Executive Committee has an Auditing Commission, which following the Sixth Congress consisted of: Petko Karadelkov (Bulgaria), Aníbal Pineda (Colombia), and Sharavish (Mongolia); and the following ordinary Members: Abdelaziz Belazoug (Algeria), Eduardo Yazbeck Jozami (Argentina), Fernando Siñani Baldivieso (Bolivia), Georgi Bokov (Bulgaria), Jules-Théodore Misam-Han (Cameroun), Leopoldo Vargas (Colombia), Adolf Hradecký (Czechoslovakia), Huang Thung (North Vietnam), Gabriel Greco (Dominican Republic), Alberto Maldonado Salazar (Ecuador), Athanasius Thomas (Gambia), Manolis Glezos (Greece), Herman Singh (Guyana), Jagdish Prasad Chaturvedi (India), Faisal Hassoun (Iraq), Jorge Rebelo (Mozambique), José Ignacio Briones Torres (Nicaragua), Baltazar Aizpurua (Panama), Genaro Carnero Checa (Peru), Nestor Ignat (Rumania), Brian Percy Bunting (Republic of South Africa), Andreas Shipanga (South West Africa), Nagi El Darawsheh (Syria), Carlos Borche (Uruguay), and Eleazar Díaz Rangel (Venezuela). Places are open on the Executive Committee "for the representatives of unions and member groups which have not yet named their candidates, including the following countries: Albania, Bissao (so-called "Portuguese" Guinea), Ceylon, Indonesia, Madagasgar, Uganda, the People's Republic of China and South West Africa (SWANU)" (*The Democratic Journalist,* No. 11-12, December 1966).

An offshoot of the IOJ is the International Committee for Cooperation of Journalists (ICCJ), founded in 1955. It was created in an attempt to bridge differences between the IFJ and the IOJ, and has held three "World Meetings of Journalists": in Finland, June 1956; Austria, October 1960; and aboard the Soviet liner "Litva," September-October 1963. The "Litva" meeting was attended by 260 journalists from 69 countries. The ICCJ has not succeeded in attracting members of the IFJ. Its leadership includes: President Dante Cruicchi (Italy); Head of Secretariat Joao Antonio Mesplé (Brazil); and members of the Executive Committee Edouard Bassil (Lebanon), Robert Butheau (France), Marie Butheau Guilbert (France), Alexandr Efremov (USSR, probably replaced by Pavel Erofeev), Jean-Maurice Hermann (France), and Roger Viguier (France).

The IOJ celebrates 8 September as International Journalists' Solidarity Day. It obtained Category C status with UNESCO in June 1962.

The IOJ claims to be financed entirely by affiliation fees. No accounts are published.

**Aims.** Though the avowed aims of the IOJ include "defense of the right of every journalist to write according to his conscience and conviction," the organization is, in the words of its President, J.-M. Hermann, at the Sixth Congress, "both a political and a trade union organization" (*The Democratic Journalist* No. 11-12, December 1966). This duality, together with an indication of the IOJ's political convictions, was apparent at the time of the Stalin-Tito controversy when the IOJ followed the pattern set by other communist front organizations and expelled its Yugoslav affiliates.

During recent years one of the principal activities of the IOJ has been the establishment of schools for training journalists from developing countries, with particular emphasis on Africa. Two schools, in Guinea and Mali, were established with the cooperation of the Czechoslovak Union of Journalists; an International Center was formally opened in Budapest in 1964; and the IOJ has also assisted in arranging courses for journalists in Prague and in Buckow, East Germany, where a school for African journalists was opened in 1963. In Latin America the IOJ helped to establish a "Commission for Information and Cooperation among Journalists of Latin America" in 1962, with headquarters in Montevideo. In Asia the IOJ supported the holding of an "Afro-Asian Journalists' Conference" in Bandung in April 1963, but this was taken over by the Chinese and Indonesians; the Conference proceeded to set up the rival Afro-Asian Journalists' Association (AAJA).

**Publications.** The IOJ publishes a monthly journal, *The Democratic Journalist,* in English, French, Russian, and Spanish, and a fortnightly *Information Bulletin.*

**Views and Activities in 1967.** As in 1966 the IOJ continued to pursue a policy aimed at consolidating its position in the developing countries, including the continuation of its 1964 three-year plan, which provides support for journalists in these countries. Emphasis on this area of concern, which had dominated the organization's policies in 1966 (see *YICA 1966,* pp. 505-507), appeared to be superseded by the IOJ's commitment to opposition to US policy in Vietnam. An editorial in the January 1967 issue of *The Democratic Journalist* stated

> The central resolution of our congress, concerning the Vietnamese problem, contains a number of concrete tasks. In the first place there was the sponsorship of an International Week of Solidarity by Journalists with Fighting Vietnam. Preparations for this Week were begun with an appeal to all journalists of the world asking them to join our campaign, and urging them particularly during the course of this week to arouse and influence public opinion so that it resolutely and energetically rejects the criminal, imperialistic war of the USA in Vietnam . . . .
>
> At the opening of the Week of Solidarity [15-20 December 1966], among those present . . . was the Ambassador of the Vietnamese Democratic Republic and the Prague representative of the National Liberation Front of South Vietnam. Both of them had high praise for the moral and material contribution of democratic journalists of the world to the struggle of the Vietnamese people and from their addresses it was clear how highly they esteem this aid and what it means to them for the final, victorious conclusion of their self-sacrificing and just struggle.
>
> This makes it incumbent on us in the future not to lose sight for a single second of world problem number one. In our efforts not only must we concentrate on single campaigns but keep in mind day after day that any weakening of this effort plays into the hands of the aggressors, helps them to continue their criminal war and to push through their conditions. We must, therefore, in the future, also make this question the cardinal one. We must, therefore, on the journalistic front, do everything so that the Vietnamese people wage their just battle until final victory.

In accordance with resolutions adopted at the Sixth Congress, in 1967 the IOJ sponsored an "International Week of Solidarity with the Journalists and People of Vietnam" 20-27 July, ending with an "international press conference" in Prague. Earlier in the month, 6-9 July, the IOJ was represented at the Stockholm Conference on Vietnam (see *World Council of Peace*). Commenting on the IOJ's activities during 1967 with relation to the Vietnam issue, the organization's Secretary-General Jiří Kubka stated in an interview given to *The Democratic Journalist* (No. 1, January 1968):

> Not a single day went by last year without the members of our affiliated unions taking some effective steps in support of the fighting people of Vietnam. We, moreover, tried to coordinate joint actions in support of Vietnam with the World Council of Peace. We took part in the world-wide gathering of peace organizations in Stockholm and are making efforts to participate in the organization of an International Information Centre which would truthfully inform the whole world about the fight of the Vietnamese people.

With regard to extending its influence in the developing areas, the aforementioned editorial in *The Democratic Journalist* (No. 1, January 1967) emphasized the importance of "the schooling of young journalist cadres from developing countries," and added, "we must not relax for a minute in this work because the young national press has a long way to go before it will be saturated by enough qualified, trained journalists."

During the year IOJ delegations travelled extensively throughout the world. Commenting on this aspect of the IOJ's activity, Jiří Kubka noted that IOJ Secretary Rodríguez had visited North Korea—"the second hotbed of imperialist aggression in Asia"—and IOJ Vice-President Namsray "and some other colleagues, visited a number of Asian countries to consolidate the influence of our groups and friends in these countries." Kubka pointed out that the IOJ's "aim in Asia remains to muster all democratic and anti-imperialist forces into one single front" (*The Democratic Journalist*, No. 1, January 1968).

With regard to Latin America, Kubka noted that "full attention was focused this year on Bolivia." Referring to the arrest of Régis Debray, Kubka claimed that the IOJ had "encouraged an avalanche of protests against this arbitrary measure of the reactionary regime in Bolivia" (*Ibid.*). The IOJ also cosponsored a seminar of Latin American news agencies in Havana during July and August.

On 15 June the IOJ held an extraordinary meeting of its Secretariat to "discuss Israel's aggression in the Middle East," issuing a statement condemning Israel and calling for the withdrawal of Israeli forces from Arab territory (CTK, 16 June; *The Democratic Journalist*, No. 11-12, December 1967). Referring to the Middle East crisis, Kubka claimed that "the many delegations which the General Secretariat sent to those parts were well received and our sincere support welcomed" (*The Democratic Journalist*, No. 1, January 1968).

Following reports of alleged US Central Intelligence Agency (CIA) subsidies to certain journalist organizations, Kubka declared that the "revelations" were merely the logical explanation of the policy practiced by the IFJ, which, he claimed, was set up under the influence of the "divisive activities of certain Western journalists' circles." He added, however, that in these organizations "there are now tendencies to thaw out the old cold war policy and take a realistic view of cooperation among journalists all over the world" (CTK, 3 March). In pursuance of its policy of "united action" with non-IOJ journalist organizations, the IOJ organized in cooperation with the IFJ an international conference of journalists at Lignano, Italy (11-16 May). According to L.K. Tolkunov, chief editor of *Izvestia* and leader of the Soviet delegation, "although no one would deny that the participants had fundamental ideological differences, the fact that they did not become a stumbling-block in contacts between them testified to the high sense of responsibility for the destinies of European and world peace which they had shown" (TASS, 16 May).

The coup d'état in Greece (21 April) was followed by "practically simultaneous" IOJ reaction, according to Jiří Kubka, who claimed that the IOJ "aroused a truly effective protest movement in all parts of the world" (*The Democratic Journalist*, No. 1, January 1968). The IOJ's concern was accentuated by the arrest of IOJ Executive Committee member, Manolis Glezos, on whose behalf a number of appeals were publicized. An IOJ delegation was reported as having visited Greece "to help in the defense of our persecuted colleagues" (*The Democratic Journalist*, No. 1, January 1968).

On the occasion of the Fiftieth Anniversary of the Bolshevik Revolution, the IOJ devoted an issue of *The Democratic Journalist* (No. 10, October 1967) to its celebration, including an appeal to all IOJ members "to unite even more closely in the interest of the common struggle against imperialist reaction and aggressive wars, for social progress, peace and friendship among nations."

IOJ representatives were present at a number of international gatherings, including the conference of the Latin American Solidarity Organization, Havana (31 July - 10 August), and the Extraordinary Meeting of the Afro-Asian Peoples' Solidarity Organization, Cairo (1-3 July).

During the year the IOJ issued no official statements concerning events in China or on the activities of its rival, the Afro-Asian Journalists' Association (see *Pro-Chinese International Communist Front Organizations*).

# WORLD FEDERATION OF SCIENTIFIC WORKERS

The World Federation of Scientific Workers (WFSW) was founded in 1946 in London at the initiative of the British Association of Scientific Workers. Eighteen organizations of scientists from 14 countries were represented at the inaugural meeting. Although the WFSW purported to be a scientific rather than a political organization, Communists succeeded in obtaining most of the official posts at the start and have retained control ever since. The WFSW headquarters is at 40 Goodge Street, London, W1, but the Secretary-General works out of an office at 10 rue Vauquelin, Paris 5e.

Membership in the WFSW is open to organizations of scientific workers anywhere in the world and to individual scientists from countries where no affiliated groups are active. Total membership estimates, not claimed by the WFSW to be accurate, recently were revised upward to 300,000. Affiliated organizations are found in 25 countries, but the bulk of the membership is derived from 14 groups in Communist-ruled countries. The only noncommunist affiliate of any size is the British Association of Scientific Workers, which has 21,000 members. Scientists of distinction who do not belong to an affiliated organization may be nominated for "corresponding membership"; selection is made by the Executive Council, which has authority to nominate up to 25 corresponding members from any country. Corresponding members in 1967 were residents of 26 countries.

**Structure.** The governing body of the WFSW is the General Assembly, in which all affiliated organizations are represented. It is supposed to meet every two years, but has not always done so. Only eight meetings have been held so far. The first, at Dobris (Czechoslovakia) in 1948 was followed by those in Paris and Prague in 1951, Budapest in 1953, East Berlin in 1955, Helsinki in 1957, Warsaw in 1959, Moscow in 1962, and Budapest in 1965. The Ninth General Assembly was scheduled for St. Cergue (Switzerland) in September 1968.

The Executive Council is theoretically responsible for controlling the activities of the WFSW between assemblies. According to the WFSW constitution the Council should consist of 27 members, of whom 17 are chosen on an individual basis and ten are regional representatives. Meetings are supposed to be held at least once a year, but have at times been hard to arrange. Consequently much of the day-to-day work and a good deal of authority have been delegated to the Bureau; it meets frequently. The Bureau consists of the President, Vice-Presidents and Treasurer, the Executive Council Chairman and Vice-Chairman, the Chairman of the Editorial Board and heads of regional centers.

The President of the WFSW and Chairman of the Executive Council is Professor Cecil F. Powell, a British physicist and Nobel Prize winner. He is the second President of the organization and has held the post since 1958, when he succeeded Professor Joliot-Curie of France. The list of elected officers of the Executive Council includes also the Vice Chairman, Professor Hermann Budzislawski (East Germany), and five Vice-Presidents, Academician I. I. Artobolevsky (USSR), Professor John D. Bernal (UK), Chou Pei-yuan (China), Professor Charles Sadron (France), and Dr. S. H. Zaheer (India). Dr. William A. Wooster (UK) is the Honorary Treasurer. Council offices are filled by appointment. They include the Secretary-General, Professor Pierre Biquard (France), the Assistant Secretary-General, Dr. Mohamed el-Lakany (UAR), and the four Honorary Assistant Secretaries, Dr. Eric H. S. Burhop (UK), Dr. Grigori Kotovsky (USSR), Dr. Theodor Nemec (France), and Miss Anita Rimel (UK). Honorary Secretaries are Chang Wei (China), Dr. Edward G. Edwards (UK), and Academician Ivan Malek (Czechoslovakia). Malek also functions as the appointed Chairman of the Editorial Board, an office that is always filled by a Council member.

Activities of the WFSW are said to be financed by affiliation fees. The last Assembly (1965) recommended the establishment of a Finance Committee, charged with the task of fund raising. At the first meeting of this committee, in August 1966, a number of proposals for coping with financial problems were made. It was also revealed that the 1966-1967 budget was $7,000.

Two committees are considered subsidiary organizations of the WFSW. One is the Nuclear Hazards Committee, set up in 1957. Originally it issued a newsletter and worked closely with the International Institute for Peace, in Vienna, but it has received no recent publicity. The other is the Committee for the Advancement of Science in Developing Countries, which was established in 1966 and is under the chairmanship of Professor Josef Bognar (Hungary). It met in November 1966 in Budapest and in May 1967 in East Berlin.

Ever since the late Professor Joliot-Curie was President of both the WFSW and the World Council of Peace (WCP), the two organizations have been closely linked. The recently retired President of the WCP, Professor Bernal, is a Vice-President of the WFSW, and three other officers of the WFSW—C. F. Powell, Chou Pei-yuan, and Pierre Biquard—are officers of the WCP or its subsidiaries.

The WFSW maintains close working relations with the World Federation of Trade Unions, the World Federation of Teachers' Unions, and the International Union of Students. It also cooperates with the International Radio and Television Organization, with whom it produces the "Science in the Service of Peace" series of broadcasts from eastern Europe.

The WFSW has been a major influence in the "Pugwash Movement of Scientists for Peace." In fact some of its officials played a vital part in organizing the first Pugwash Conference, held in 1957. Recently the WFSW gained an even greater role in the movement—developed as an independent and ostensibly non-aligned international organization dedicated to the exchange of views between scientists of the East and West—when Professor Powell was elected Chairman of the Pugwash Continuing Committee at a meeting held in Rønneby, Sweden, in September 1967.

The WFSW has consultative status B with UNESCO, but no status with ECOSOC. It does, however, exchange information with such UN groups as the ILO and WHO, and it sent observers to the Geneva Conferences on the Peaceful Uses of Atomic Energy in 1955 and 1958.

**Publications.** The official publication of the WFSW is *Scientific World.* It is issued in English, French, Russian, German, Spanish, and Czech and early in 1967 was changed from a quarterly to a bimonthly. The WFSW *Bulletin,* which appears irregularly and gives news of the organization, is issued in English, French, German, and Russian and is made available to members only. "Science and Mankind" is the general title of a series of booklets that have appeared in several languages. Titles published in this series are *Hunger and Food* (1959), *Science and Health* (1961), *Science for a Developing World* (1962), and *Training for Tomorrow* (1964). Special reports cover such events as WFSW Congresses. A number of pamphlets have been issued. *Unmeasured Hazards,* a pamphlet dealing with the dangers of atomic radiation, has appeared in twelve languages since it was first published in 1956.

**Aims and Policies.** Soon after its foundation the WFSW adopted a constitution and a "Charter for Scientific Workers." These are the two basic documents to which all affiliates subscribe. The constitution lists avowed aims as follows: (a) to work for the fullest utilization of science in promoting peace and the welfare of mankind, and especially to ensure that science is applied to help solve the urgent problems of the time; (b) to promote international cooperation in science and technology, in particular through close collaboration with UNESCO; (c) to encourage the international exchange of scientific knowledge and of scientific workers; (d) to preserve and encourage freedom and coordination of scientific work both nationally and internationally; (e) to encourage improvements in the teaching of the sciences and to spread the knowledge of science and its social implications among the people of all countries; (f) to achieve a closer integration between the natural and social sciences; (g) to improve the professional, social, and economic status of scientific workers; (h) to encourage scientific workers to take an active part in public affairs and to make them conscious of, and more responsive to, the progressive forces at work within society. (*Constitution of the WFSW,* 1963.) The charter is a concise statement of the responsibility of scientific workers and of the conditions that must be provided to "safeguard the freedom, the advancement, and the social utility of science" (*Scientific World,* twentieth anniversary number, 1966).

Although the avowed aims of the WFSW are exclusively scientific, the organization has engaged in political activities quite clearly removed from absolute scientific objectivity. A case in point and a clear indication of the political orientation was the expulsion of the Yugoslav affiliate at the time of the Stalin-Tito controversy in 1949. During the Korean War the WFSW called for support of the Communist Chinese against the UN forces; since the beginning of the Sino-Soviet dispute, however, it has condemned the Chinese, who in turn have disrupted and boycotted WFSW meetings and remain as nominal members only. Repeated warnings have been issued by the WFSW against the dangers of nuclear warfare in general and nuclear tests in particular, but its complaints have always been directed at US, British, or French tests and never against Soviet tests. When the Soviet Union conducted its longest and most contaminating series of nuclear tests in 1962, the President of the WFSW wanted to lodge a protest and even threatened to resign, but was overruled. Objections have often been raised to restrictions on the free exchange of scientific material or the movement of scientists; without exception all such objections have been directed at Western countries. At the time of the Cuban crisis in 1962 the WFSW mobilized its members to send collective telegrams to President Kennedy and the UN condemning the American blockade. No telegrams were dispatched to Khrushchev or to Castro, and no mention was made of the installation of Soviet missiles in Cuba. There have been so many instances of partisan intervention in foreign affairs that the French and British affiliates have become critical of them and in 1962 threatened .to leave the WFSW if statements continued to be issued without their approval. Since that time some caution has been exercised for fear of losing the most important Western affiliates.

**Regional and International Programs.** The WFSW has organized several international symposiums in connection with its General Assemblies. They are normally organized by a scientific body in the host country and deal exclusively with scientific topics, although comparisons between scientific achievements of the USSR and the West are not always nonpolitical. Symposiums have been held on "Science and Planning" and "The Training of Students in Science and Technology" (Helsinki 1957), "Science and Underdeveloped Countries" (Warsaw 1959), "Higher Scientific and Technological Education" (Moscow 1962), and "Problems of Science in Developing Countries, and the Role of International Scientific Cooperation" (Budapest 1965). The next symposium is to be held in 1969.

Efforts have been made by the WFSW to develop activities around regional centers, and regional meetings have been held in New Delhi (1955), Prague (1956), Paris (1957), and Cambridge (England, 1961). Establishment of a "Permanent Committee for the Advancement of Science in Asia, Africa, and Latin America" was the subject of discussion and proposals at both the Seventh and Eighth Assemblies. In Asia, however, plans have been handicapped by the Sino-Soviet dispute. The only active regional center has been the one in New Delhi, which in the spring of 1966 supported an Afro-Asian symposium organized by the Indian affiliate. The "Peking Center of the WFSW" which was opened in September 1963 was quickly revealed to have been set up without the knowledge of the WFSW headquarters and in actual rivalry with the organization's efforts. A regional center was opened in Cairo in 1966 to assist in furthering WFSW activities in the Middle East. Hopes for establishment of a regional center in Latin America, on the other hand, appear to have been dashed at least temporarily by a lack of funds.

**Activities and Meetings in 1967.** The biggest event of the year for the WFSW was the twenty-ninth meeting of the Executive Council, in East Berlin on 3-7 May. In attendance were 60 delegates from 20 countries. The decisions and resolutions announced on the occasion seem to have run the gamut of the current and future interests of the organization.

Vietnam figured prominently in the area of international affairs. A resolution was passed condemning US "aggression" and an open letter was addressed to US scientists which stated: "Escalation can only be halted . . . by those doing the escalating, the armed forces of the United States. This is why it appears to us that the main burden and responsibility for averting the threatening catastrophe of world nuclear conflict must rest in the first instance with the American people." Earlier in the year, Prensa Latina, the Cuban press agency, published charges made by the WFSW that the USA was using biological and chemical warfare in Vietnam and that the war was "A violation of international agreements" (6 February). In line with these opinions it was decided in East

Berlin to prepare a "Scientists' Appeal on Vietnam." Details were published later (*L'Humanité* 28 June) after thirteen scientists of world renown—the list included nine Nobel Prize winners—issued a letter to scientific workers appealing for financial aid to promote the work of laboratories, universities, and schools in Vietnam through the purchase of scientific equipment and books for Hanoi University.

The Executive Council passed resolutions condemning West German interest in nuclear weapons and issued a statement demanding the release of arrested Greek scientists and the restoration of democratic liberties in Greece. It also postponed the planned conference on "Scientific Cooperation and Security in Europe" until April 1968. In March 1967 a working group convened in Prague and scheduled this conference for the last quarter of the year, but plans were completed only at the WFSW Bureau meeting in Geneva in December.

In East Berlin additional future meetings were discussed, including a "Conference on the Utilization of Sciences and Technology in Economic Development," to be held in Cairo, which was proposed also as the site for an "International Symposium on the Scientific-Technical Revolution in the Industrial Countries and the Developing Countries with Different Social Systems."

# INTERNATIONAL FEDERATION OF RESISTANCE FIGHTERS

The International Federation of Resistance Fighters (Fédération Internationale des Résistants; FIR) was founded in 1951 in Vienna by its predecessor, the International Federation of Former Political Prisoners (Fédération Internationale des Anciens Prisonniers Politiques; FIAPP), which, founded in 1946, did not include resistance fighters. Since its foundation, the FIR has been mainly composed of communist groups.

Organizations of former partisans and resistance fighters, and of political prisoners and victims of National Socialism and Fascism, can become members of the FIR; individuals are admitted as "associated members." At the FIR's latest congress (Budapest, 9-13 December 1965), the organization's Secretary, Jean Toujas, declared: "Millions of former resistance fighters are rallied in 47 [member] organizations extending to 21 countries. The existence of the FIR is a reminder of the need for learning from the lesson of the past and for preventing a recurrence of Fascist barbarian destruction" (*Népszabadság*, 10 December). The membership of the FIR is drawn from European countries and Israel.

The headquarters of the FIR are at Castellezgasse 35, Vienna 2. A small secretariat is maintained at 10, rue Leroux, Paris 16. Until 1952 the headquarters were in Warsaw.

The avowed aims of the FIR are to keep alive the memory of those who died in "underground" fighting against National Socialism and Fascism, to protect the rights of those resistance fighters who survived, to prevent a reemergence of National Socialism and Fascism, and to ensure world peace. The actual policies of the organization, however, have been primarily directed toward furthering Soviet policy directed against West Germany and its alleged "revanchism."

The activities of the FIR include the sponsoring of annual rallies at former Nazi concentration camps, such as Auschwitz, Buchenwald, Mauthausen, Dachau, and Ravensbruck. The federation also organizes medical conferences to discuss the effects of imprisonment and maltreatment in concentration camps. Its Historical Commission has organized conferences on the history of the resistance, designed to emphasize the role of communist-led resistance groups and extol the efforts of the Red Army.

The FIR has close relations with the World Council of Peace and the International Association of Democratic Lawyers. It has tried to establish a working agreement with the noncommunist World Veterans' Federation, but with little success. It is not represented in the UN.

Though no details are published, the FIR claims to be financed by affiliation fees, gifts, legacies, and other subventions.

April 11 is celebrated by the FIR as the "Day of Solidarity of Former Political Prisoners and Fighters against Fascism." It has designated September 13 as "International Memorial Day for Victims of Fascism," to be followed by "Resistance Fighters Week" (or "International Fight against Fascism Week").

The highest governing body of the FIR is the Congress, which is supposed to meet every three years. It has met in Vienna in June 1951 and November 1954, and again for a first session in November 1958 and a second session in March 1959; at Warsaw in December 1962 and at Budapest in December 1965. The Budapest congress was attended by some 300 delegates from European countries and Israel, together with representatives from the World Council of Peace, the Women's International Democratic Federation, and the World Federation of Democratic Youth.

The Congress, consisting of representatives of the member organizations, elects a Bureau which conducts day-to-day work. The Congress also ratifies members who, nominated by national associations, serve together with the Bureau on a General Council. The General Council is supposed to meet at least once a year between meetings of the Congress. In 1967 there were 119 members of the General Council, of whom 49 were members of the Bureau.

In addition to ordinary members of the Bureau, there are a Bureau President, 12 Vice-Presidents, and a Secretariat. Elected by the Bureau from among its members, the Secretariat has a Secretary-General, Secretary, and Treasurer. The Bureau President also serves on the Secretariat.

The leadership of the FIR in 1967 included the following: President, Arialdo Banfi (Italy); Secretary-General, Jean Toujas (France); Deputy Secretary-General, Colonel Gustav Alef-Bolkowiak (Poland); Secretary, Maurizio Milan (Italy); Treasurer, Theodor Heinisch (Austria); and Vice-Presidents, Jacques Debu-Bridel (France), Albert Forcinal (France), Josef Husek (Czechoslovakia), Wlodimierz Lechowicz (Poland), Alexei Petrovich Maresiev (USSR), Andre de Raet (Belgium), Dr. Josef C. Rossaint (West Germany), Dr. Ludwig Soswinski (Austria), Georg Spielmann (East Germany), Umberto Terracini (Italy), Pierre Villon (pseudonym of Roger Ginsberger, France), and Svend Olaf Wagner (Denmark).

The FIR publishes a journal in French and German, *Resistance Unie (Der Widerstandskämpfer)*, issued ten times a year; an irregular fortnightly bulletin in French and German, *Service d'Information de la FIR (Informationsdienst der FIR)*; and a historical review in French and German, *Cahiers Internationaux de la Resistance (Internationalen Hefte der Widerstandsbewegung)*, which appeared three times a year up to March 1963, but has been discontinued since. The FIR publishes also a number of pamphlets on problems related directly and indirectly to its movement.

**Views and Activities in 1967.** During the year the FIR continued its efforts to intensify contacts with noncommunist resistance movements. These efforts, however, yielded no concrete results.

In contrast to other communist world organizations, the FIR did not join the general communist chorus in the condemnation of Israel in the June 1967 conflict. Only the East German FIR affiliate offered no resistance to Soviet demands to denounce Israel. The stand taken by the FIR on the Middle East question gave rise to serious clashes, just short of a split, at the Secretariat session held in Sofia, Bulgaria, 2-4 June. A pro-Arab declaration proposed by the pro-Soviet leadership was defeated. Faced with strong opposition, the leadership was forced to give in to a compromise resolution which recognized Israel's right to statehood, on the one hand, and advocated the Arab refugees' right of domicile and their (undefined) "vested national interests," on the other.

Propaganda against "West German neo-Nazism," although temporarily overshadowed by the Middle East issue, was at the center of the FIR's activity during 1967. It was the main theme at the Bureau meeting held in Prague on 7-9 April, at an international gathering in Warsaw on 19 April, and at the Bureau and General Council sessions held in East Berlin on 1-2 December and 3-5 December respectively. To mark the twentieth anniversary of the Nuremberg trials the FIR issued a pamphlet in German (which was later to be made available in French and Italian) entitled *Nuremberg 1946 . . . and Today? An Alarming Document.* In addition to reviewing the criminal methods of Hitlerism from 1925 to 1945, and the trials of Nazis from 1945 on, the publication also dealt with the "revival of neo-Nazism and revanchism, especially in West Germany."

The problem of Vietnam was pushed backstage in the course of the year, and precedence over the sending of a fact-finding committee to investigate "US war crimes" (decided upon in April) was given to the call for a European security conference, which has been long propagated by the World Federation of Scientific Workers and the World Council of Peace.

The subject of the "New Resistance" (a movement that manifested itself under the name "Nuova Resistenza" in various large Italian cities in 1962-63), which had not been on the docket since the autumn of 1963, was taken up again with reference to the events in Greece. At the meeting of anti-Fascist resistance fighters held in Genoa, Italy, on 22-23 April 1967, the president of the Italian partisan association ANPI, Arrigo Boldrini, whose organization maintains close ties with the FIR, emphasized the "continuity of yesteryear's resistance and today's struggle for freedom and national independence in Vietnam and Greece," and the necessity for the resistance fighters to establish a "new popular diplomacy to safeguard freedom, human dignity, and independence." (*l'Unita,* 23 April 1967.)

At its December session, the General Council unanimously adopted resolutions on Vietnam, the

Middle East, the "dangers of neo-Nazism" in the Federal Republic of Germany, and the situation of Greek and Spanish resistance fighters. The resolution on Vietnam condemned the "dirty United States war." With a view to the "Israeli aggression against the Arab states" in the Middle East, the FIR declared: "No country has the right to annex territories conquered by force of arms." The resolution on the "dangers of neo-Nazism" in West Germany demanded the outlawing of the National Democratic Party (NPD), adequate punishment of war criminals, lifting of the statute of limitation on (German) war crimes, prohibition of the supply of nuclear arms to the West German armed forces, and the convoking of a conference on European security. The resolution on the situation of the Greek and Spanish resistance fighters contained a proposal to send a delegation to Greece, (*FIR Information Service,* 5 December 1967; *Neues Deutschland,* 6 and 7 December 1967; and *L'Humanité,* 7 December 1967.) The General Council also confirmed that the FIR could attend the International Conference for the Restoration of Civil Rights in Spain, which was to be held in Paris on 10-11 February 1968. This conference was expected to start another phase of the "New Resistance."

# INTERNATIONAL ASSOCIATION OF DEMOCRATIC LAWYERS

The International Association of Democratic Lawyers (IADL) was founded at an "International Congress of Jurists," held in Paris on 24-27 October 1946 under the auspices of a paracommunist organization, the Mouvement National Judiciaire, and attended by lawyers from 25 countries. Although the movement originally included elements of various political orientations, the "leading role was played by the leftist democratic circles of French lawyers" (*Sovetskoe Gosudarstvo i Pravo*, No. 11-12, 1946, pp. 53-54). By 1949 most noncommunists had resigned.

The IADL's headquarters were originally in Paris. Following an expulsion order on 29 July 1950, the IADL moved to Belgium. Its present address is 49, Avenue Jupiter, Brussels 19. Some organizational work has also been carried out from Warsaw.

Membership is open to lawyers' organizations or groups and to individual lawyers. Membership may be on a "corresponding," "donating," or "permanent" basis. At the IADL's latest congress (March 1964), four hundred lawyers from 64 countries were said to have attended, including delegates from IADL member organizations in 61 countries. Lawyers holding membership through organizations or individually are estimated to number about 25,000. The IADL claims to be supported by membership fees and donations. No details of its finances are published.

**Structure.** The highest organ of the IADL is the Congress, in which each member organization is represented. First held yearly, the Congress is now supposed to meet every three years. It has met in October 1946 (Paris), July 1947 (Brussels), September 1948 (Prague), October 1949 (Rome), September 1951 (East Berlin), May 1956 (Brussels), October 1960 (Sofia), and March 1964 (Budapest). At a meeting of the IADL Secretariat in Mamaia, Rumania, on 15-17 September 1967, it was announced that the Ninth Congress would be held during the first half of 1969. The Congress elects a Council, which is supposed to meet yearly and consists of a Bureau, a Secretariat, and a representative of each member organization and of the co-opted members.

In 1967 the President of the IADL was Pierre Cot (France) and the Honorary President was Denis Nowell Pritt, Q.C. (UK). Vice-Presidents were Ali Badawi (UAR), Rudolf Bystrický (Czechoslovakia), Henriques Fialho (Brazil), Dr. Jorge Giles Pizarro (Chile), Professor Hirano Yoshitaro (Japan), I. I. Karpets (USSR), Mahmoud Ali Kasuri (Pakistan), Li Shin-ju (North Korea), Joe Matthews (South Africa), Marian Mazur (Poland), Luis Muñoz García (Argentina), Umberto Terracini (Italy), Ivan Vachkov (Bulgaria), Cabral Vasco (Portuguese Guinea), and Yang Hua-nan (Communist China), with places reserved for Ceylon and UAR. The Secretary-General was Joe Nordmann (France). The Secretaries were Dr. Jenö Benedek (Hungary), Mme. Solange Bouvier-Ajam (France), Ioan Filip (Rumania), V. R. Krishna Iyer (India), Ugo Natoli (Italy), Nasib Nimr (Lebanon), Osny Duarte Pereira (Brazil), Dr. José Sanche Mijares (Venezuela), and Tram Cong Tuong (North Vietnam), with one place reserved for Algeria. The Treasurer was Dr. Heinrich Toeplitz (East Germany). In addition, three council members were members of the bureau: G. F. Basov, Lev Nikolaevich Smirnov, and Alexandr Nikiforovich Yakimenko (all, USSR).

The IADL has close links with the World Council of Peace (WCP). It supported the WCP and the Women's International Democratic Federation in allegations of "war crimes" in Korea, and has supported the World Federation of Trade Unions by protesting the federation's expulsion from Vienna. It has also collaborated with the World Federation of Scientific Workers and the International Union of Students. Although the IADL had consultative status with the United Nations Economic and Social Council (ECOSOC), at the outset, this was rescinded in July 1950. In June 1967, however, the IADL was again granted consultative status by ECOSOC.

The IADL has sponsored several regional meetings of jurists and has established a number of commissions of inquiry. These include the "Commission for the Investigation of the Reemployment of Nazis in the West German Legal System," which was established in 1963, and the "International Commission for the Investigation of American War Crimes in Vietnam," which the IADL decided to organize in January 1963 but which was apparently not established until October 1965. Two other commissions which are no longer active are the "Commission for the Defense of Democratic Liberties," established in 1954, and the "Commission on the Role of Former Nazi Judges in West Germany," established in October 1960.

In addition to the above permanent bodies, several investigating committees have been organized from time to time to emphasize a particular Soviet propaganda theme. These include the "Commission of Inquiry on Korea" (1952), the "Commission on the Karlsruhe Trial" (1954), the "Commission on WFTU Expulsion from Vienna" (1956), the "Commission on Legal Definition of Neutrality" (1959), the "Commission for the Defense of Manolis Glezos" (1959), the "Commission on Neutrality and Aggression" (1960), the "Commission on Algeria" (1960), and the "Commission to Investigate Arrests in Iraq" (1963).

The IADL has also sponsored a number of conferences, including the First Continental Conference of Jurists (Rio de Janeiro, November 1952), the Second Continental Conference of Jurists (Guatemala City, October 1953), the Congress of Asian Democratic Lawyers (Calcutta, January 1955), the International Lawyers' Conference on the German Peace Treaty (East Berlin, November 1961), and the Afro-Asian Lawyers' Conference (Conakry, October 1962).

**Aims and Policies.** The principal avowed aims of the IADL are: to develop mutual understanding among the lawyers of the world; to support the aims of the United Nations, especially through common action for the defense of democratic liberties; to encourage the study and application, in the field of law, of democratic principles conducive to the maintenance of peace; and to promote the independence of all peoples and prevent the placing of any restrictions on this independence through legislation or in practice.

In practice, the IADL has consistently followed the Soviet line in both national and international matters. It has denounced as a "violation of human rights" any prosecution of Communists or communist parties outside the Soviet orbit, while denying or ignoring the existence of any violation of human rights in communist-ruled countries.

**Ideological Orientation.** As a result of the Sino-Soviet dispute, a move was initiated by the pro-Chinese delegates at the Afro-Asian Lawyers' Conference (Conakry, October 1962) to establish a rival organization to the IADL, and a permanent Secretariat which excluded representation from the Soviet Union was subsequently elected. Although it occasionally issues statements, it has had relatively little success in organizing a second conference and has little influence.

At the Eighth Congress of the IADL (Budapest, April 1964), the Chinese delegation challenged the organizers' "undemocratic attitude" in forcing an "illegal agenda" on the Congress in order to push through the "erroneous line" of the Soviet Union. Since the disruption of the Eighth Congress, the Chinese members have not attended any IADL meetings, although they are still enrolled in the organization.

**Publications.** The IADL issues two major publications and a series of pamphlets. The *Review of Contemporary Law* (formerly *Law in the Service of Peace*) is supposed to appear semiannually but does not always do so. It is published in English and French. The editor-in-chief is Pierre Cot. The *Information Bulletin,* also published in English and French, appears on an irregular basis and generally focuses on a particular subject.

**Views and Activities in 1967.** During 1967 two meetings of the IADL were convened. On 20-21 January the twentieth anniversary of the founding of the IADL was celebrated by a meeting at the UNESCO building in Paris. Among the participants were Pierre Cot, D. N. Pritt, and Rudolf Bystrický, together with representatives of national affiliates; also attending were: Claude Lussier, representative of the UNESCO Director General; Maurice Rolland, President of the Amicale des Magistrats Resistants and the Association des Juristes Européens; and Manolis Glezos, honorary member of the International Federation of Resistance Movements (FIR). In protest against the "Soviet revisionists" in the IADL, the Communist Chinese Society for Political Sciences and Law sent a telegram on 15 January announcing the refusal of Chinese lawyers to attend the anniversary meeting. The telegram attacked the "conspiratorial activity of a handful of IADL leaders under the manipulation of the Soviet revisionists" and accused the IADL of "working hand in glove" with the UN by "shamelessly boosting its consultative status in UNESCO" and by "openly inviting" a UNESCO representative to attend the meeting. The telegram also recalled that the Chinese delegation to the IADL Secretariat meeting in Karlovy Vary (May 1966) had explicitly stated that certain IADL leaders had been "following the revisionist line of the CPSU leading clique for a number of years, betraying the IADL's anti-imperialist tradition and defaming its history." In conclusion, the Chinese Communist Society for Political Science and Law warned that "the Soviet revisionists and certain IADL leaders would work in active co-ordination with the US imperialist peace talks at the meeting to sell out the revolutionary interests of the Vietnamese people." (NCNA, 15 January.) In contrast to the Chinese response, the North Vietnamese Lawyers' Association sent a message of good will to the IADL and expressed gratitude for its "persistent support to the Vietnam people's struggle" (Vietnam News Agency, 25 January).

The annual meeting of the IADL Secretariat was held in Mamaia, Rumania, on 15-17 September. The agenda included the tasks of democratic lawyers in "exposing the imperialist aggression in Vietnam, violation of human rights in Greece and Indonesia, and the contribution by lawyers to settling legal issues in the Middle East" (Rumanian Telegraph Agency, Agerpres, 19 September). Preparations for the Ninth IADL Congress were also discussed. At the conclusion of the meeting, the Secretariat adopted a resolution demanding an "immediate, unconditional, and final termination of the bombing of North Vietnam," the recognition of the National Liberation Front of South Vietnam, and the withdrawal of all US forces from Vietnam. The resolution also condemned "Israeli aggression as a most glaring violation of international law and a threat to world peace" and demanded the immediate and unconditional withdrawal of Israeli forces from the captured territories. In conclusion, the resolution denounced the "terror campaign against democratic forces in Greece and Indonesia." (TASS, 19 September.)

Although the IADL had apparently intended to convene a European lawyers' conference on the problem of European security, no mention of such a meeting was made by the Secretariat and the topic was also dropped by other international communist organizations.

During 1967 the IADL devoted considerable attention to the war in Vietnam. Although the IADL initially refused to participate in the Bertrand Russell Vietnam Tribunal, it eventually established a fact-finding commission of its own and sent a delegation to Vietnam in October 1965. In March 1967, Joe Nordmann, IADL Secretary-General, led a second delegation to the country at the invitation of the Association of Vietnamese Lawyers and met with President Ho Chi Minh and Prime Minister Pham Van Dong. On 24 March a joint press conference was held in Hanoi by the IADL delegation and a delegation of the Bertrand Russell Vietnam Tribunal, with the IADL delegation fully endorsing the position of North Vietnam and the National Liberation Front of South Vietnam. The end result of the joint press conference was to associate the IADL more closely with the Vietnam Tribunal than had been its intention. The IADL delegation returned to Brussels via Moscow, and at a press conference given there on 31 March Joe Nordmann remarked: "As lawyers, we consider that the USA has committed in Vietnam the crime of aggression, a crime against peace, war crimes, crimes against the laws of humanity, and that its actions, as escalation of the war proceeds, are acquiring the character of the crime of genocide."

In addition to protesting against the war in Vietnam, the IADL issued a number of protests attacking the trials of "progressive" elements, particularly those in Indonesia following the abortive communist coup of 1965 and in Greece following the military coup of April 1967. The IADL also took considerable interest in the trial of Régis Debray, the French intellectual and journalist held for trial in Bolivia, and issued a statement declaring: "The Secretariat of the IADL opposes the trial of Régis Debray, who was arrested during the exercise of his profession of journalist and brought before the War Council following an investigation carried out under arbitrary conditions contrary to the Universal Declaration of the Rights of Man and the Bolivian Constitution which guarantees the safety of the person and the rights of defense. We request his release." (L'Humanité, 10 October 1967.)

# INTERNATIONAL RADIO AND TELEVISION ORGANIZATION

The International Radio and Television Organization (Organisation Internationale de Radiodiffusion et Télévision; OIRT) was founded in 1946 at a conference in Brussels as the "Organisation Internationale de Radiodiffusion" (OIR). The present form of its name was adopted in 1959. At the outset, countries of differing political orientation participated, but by 1950 most noncommunist radio organizations had withdrawn. In February 1950 the British Broadcasting Corporation took the initiative in setting up a rival body, the European Broadcasting Union (EBU). All leading noncommunist organizations have since left the OIRT, mostly to join the EBU.

The headquarters of the OIRT is at 15, U. Mrazovky, Prague 5.

In contrast to other communist front organizations, the OIRT's membership is one of state organizations. The OIRT has a number of functions, many of which are of purely technical nature; it serves also, however, as a channel of coordination in the implementing of policy between communist states and in furthering their policies toward the "third world."

Membership is open to any national broadcasting or television organization, and there is provision for associate membership. The present members are organizations from all communist countries (excluding Yugoslavia) and from Finland, Mali, Iraq and the UAR. The Yugoslavs have attended meetings as observers. Communist China is still, in theory, a member of the OIRT, but has refused to pay affiliation fees to the Prague headquarters since 1963. The Chinese did not send a delegation to the OIRT's twentieth General Assembly, in December 1965, and have not attended any meetings since.

The General Assembly is the OIRT's highest body. It meets at least every two years, and each member organization is represented in it. The General Assembly elects the Administrative Council, which meets annually and in 1967 had fourteen members. Within the Administrative Council is a Presidium, comprising the President, Vice-Presidents, Secretary-General, Director of the Technical Center, and Chief Editor.

In 1967, the following represented the leadership of the OIRT: Wlodzimierz Sokorski (Poland), President; Jaromir Hrebik (Czechoslovakia), Secretary-General; Racine Kane (Mali) and Jambului Zundui (Mongolia), Vice-Presidents; Mikhail Vasilcvich Yegorov (USSR), Director of the Technical Center; Alex Suchy (Czechoslovakia), Chief Editor; Zherko Zherkov (Bulgaria), Chairman of the Technical Commission; Estrada (Cuba), Vice Chairman; and Reginald Grimmer (East Germany), Karel Hoffmann (Czechoslovakia), Adolf Hradecký (Czechoslovakia), Mikhail A. Kharlamov (USSR), Ramiro Puerta Quiroga (Cuba), and Tso Yin (Communist China), ordinary members of the Administrative Council.

The OIRT publishes a review, mainly technical, called *Radio and Television*, which appears six times a year in English, French, Russian, and German. It also publishes a monthly bulletin, *OIRT Information*, in the same languages.

The OIRT has Category B status with UNESCO and is on the register of ECOSOC. It also has consultative status with the International Telecommunication Union and is an affiliate of the International Film and Television Council. It has professional contact with EBU, with which it negotiates program exchanges.

Though it has no formal links with other front organizations, the OIRT has often supported and assisted them, particularly the World Council of Peace. In 1957, in collaboration with the World Federation of Scientific Workers, it sponsored a series of broadcasts called "Science in the Service of Peace." It has also cooperated with the International Organization of Journalists in conducting training courses in Africa.

No details are published with regard to OIRT finance. Members' dues and the income gained from publishing radio magazines are claimed to provide the funds.

**Views and Activities in 1967.** The activities of OIRT affiliates in 1967 continued to be directed toward the implementation of a resolution adopted at its twentieth General Assembly (Warsaw, 2-7 December 1965) on "the fullest expansion of fruitful ties with radio and television broadcasting organizations in Africa, Asia, and Latin America."

During 1967, the Soviet Union signed agreements with Guinea, Ethiopia and Mali and conducted negotiations on closer cooperation with India and Dahomey. East European communist states also concluded agreements or expanded existing relations: Bulgaria with the UAR, Czechoslovakia with Syria and Algeria, Hungary with Iraq, Poland with Syria, East Germany with the UAR and Syria and so on. In Latin America, East Germany made intensive efforts to spread propaganda over local or regional stations. By the end of July it had scored a major breakthrough in Chile, where the Radio Service of Magallanes, the southernmost and largest province, started broadcasting a weekly 30-minute program produced by the Chilean-East German Cultural Institute. Entitled "Reports and Information on the German Democratic Republic," the series have dealt with political, economic, and cultural problems. (*National Zeitung,* East Berlin, 1 August.)

Relations with West European broadcasting and television services were considerably intensified in 1967 by East European countries. In May alone agreements on cooperation were concluded or renewed between Rumania and Italy, Bulgaria and France, Poland and Luxembourg, Hungary and France, and Hungary and Belgium. Great Britain and West Berlin participated in the OIRT-supported Tenth International Week for Short and Documentary Films held in Leipzig, East Germany, 18-25 November; entries from 29 countries were selected for the competition.

Delegations from Bulgaria, Czechoslovakia, Finland, East Germany, Hungary, Poland, Rumania, and the USSR took part in the four Intervision council sessions held in the course of 1967: at Budapest (February), Kishinev (USSR, June), Warsaw (August), and Leipzig (November). The Intervision council meetings were attended also by representatives of the Austrian and Yugoslav television services, neither of which is an OIRT or Intervision member. Among the main agenda items were the joint programs devoted to the fiftieth anniversary of the October Revolution and preparations for relaying the 1968 Olympic Games in Mexico and winter games in Grenoble.

# PRO-CHINESE INTERNATIONAL COMMUNIST FRONT ORGANIZATIONS

The Chinese Communists' challenge to Soviet leadership in international front organizations started soon after their clash at the Twenty-second Congress of the CPSU in October 1961. Sino-Soviet rivalry was unconcealed at the World Council of Peace conference at Stockholm in December 1961. When the Afro-Asian People's Solidarity Organization (founded in Cairo in 1958 and combining communist influence with Afro-Asian nationalism, but not, technically speaking a "front" organization) met at Moshi, Tanganyika, in February 1963, it was apparent that Peking's objective was to promote rival front organizations under its own control. This was, in fact, the Chinese answer to defeats suffered at the various front meetings. One of the grievances against Moscow listed in the *Jen-min Jih-pao,* after Moshi, was that "certain comrades of the fraternal party" had "repeatedly tried to impose on these international democratic organizations their own wrong line." One Chinese device which drew Soviet protests was the introduction of "geographical" concepts for organizations. The Afro-Asian idea itself suggests geographical boundaries and has been used in attempts to obstruct and even dislodge the Soviet Union. Although the Chinese have not attended any major front meeting since their delegation was forcibly removed from the WFTU General Council meeting in Sofia, Bulgaria, in December 1966, they have not officially withdrawn from any of the world communist front organizations, nor have they been formally expelled. The Chinese do, however, continually denounce as puppets all world communist front organizations controlled by Moscow.

Chinese endeavors to create rival international organizations have, on the whole, proved unsuccessful. A number of organizations have been planned, and some that were founded have remained inactive. Only two, the Afro-Asian Journalists' Association (AAJA) and the Afro-Asian Writers' Permanent Bureau (AAWPB), appear to be operating in a manner comparable to that of the pro-Soviet organizations. Several other fronts, organized or planned to compete with the Moscow-controlled front organizations, have shown little sign of growth or vitality.

Very little information is available on the organizational structure or membership of any of these organizations. The fact that the Chinese have chosen not to terminate their memberships in the Soviet-controlled mass organizations seems to indicate that their own organizations, though not necessarily fictitious, are far from attaining a competitive level. In general, China's preoccupation with the internal problems of the Great Proletarian Cultural Revolution has had a negative effect on Chinese Communist interest in world communist front movements.

**The Afro-Asian Journalists' Association.** The Afro-Asian Journalists' Association was set up in Djakarta in April 1963, with an Afro-Asian press bureau and a permanent Secretariat. Until the autumn of 1965 the AAJA appeared to represent a possible serious rival to the pro-Soviet International Organization of Journalists (IOJ), partcularly in connection with IOJ's activities in developing countries. Then after the attempted communist coup in Indonesia, the AAJA headquarters announced its "temporary withdrawal" from Djakarta to Peking in January 1966, due to the "difficult conditions" in Indonesia and "interference" in its affairs by the Indonesian Journalists' Association. Djawoto, the AAJA's Indonesian Secretary-General, had been serving as Indonesia's ambassador to Communist China. Dismissed from his post by the Indonesian government, he resumed full-time duty as AAJA Secretary-General in Peking, which has since become the permanent seat of AAJA operations.

At the fifth plenary meeting of its Secretariat, on 15-17 June 1967, the AAJA resolved to hold a second conference of Afro-Asian journalists in Peking at some time in 1968. (A previous attempt to get international support for a second conference in Algiers in early 1967 had been unsuccessful.) In a general resolution on the current international political situation, passed by unanimous vote, the

Secretariat proclaimed: "[The AAJA will] continue to hold high the banner of fighting against imperialism, against old and new colonialism, against Soviet revisionism and against all the reactionaries of the world. The AAJA calls on the Afro-Asian Journalists to study and apply Mao Tse-tung's thought, to propagate Mao Tse-tung's thought and help the Afro-Asian people to grasp Mao Tse-tung's thought, so as to promote the revolutionary cause in this area." (*Peking Review,* no. 26, 23 June.) The Secretariat hailed a new upsurge of world revolution drawing inspiration from China. It charged the Soviet Union with sham support and real betrayal in Vietnam, and with "engineering 'peace talks' " there for the US "imperialists." It charged Israel with "brutal aggression" against the UAR, Syria, and Jordan, and criticized the Soviet Union for "forcing the Arab people to surrender." Criticizing the United Nations as a mere tool of US "imperialism," it voiced support for revolutionary movements or "struggles for national independence" in Laos, Thailand, Indonesia, North Kalimantan (Borneo), Malaya, the Philippines, South Yemen (Aden), Oman, the Congo (Kinshasa), Angola, Mozambique, Portuguese Guinea, Zimbabwe (Rhodesia), Azania (South Africa), the Dominican Republic, Ecuador, Venezuela, Colombia, Bolivia, Guatemala, Peru, South West Africa, French Somaliland, Lesotho, Botswana, Swaziland, and Jammu and Kashmir. It also lent its support to "peoples' struggles" in Japan, South Korea, and Cambodia against "vicious" US "imperialism" or "aggression." Finally, in keeping with China's line in her battle for control of international fronts and movements, the Secretariat condemned the "bogus" Afro-Asian Writers' Conference held in Beirut on 25-29 March (see below) and the Afro-Asian Peoples' Solidarity Organization (AAPSO) Council meeting in Nicosia on 13-16 February (see *Cyprus*). (*Ibid.*)

Although the purpose of the AAJA is to compete with the IOJ, the Soviets may be promoting the revival of a "Bandung spirit" AAJA splinter in Djakarta. The Soviet Journalists' Association invited Mahbub Djunaedi of the Indonesian Journalists' Association to Moscow in October and reportedly assured him of support for the efforts of the Indonesian journalists who oppose Chinese attempts to "split the AAJA situated in Djakarta" by setting up a rival in Peking. (NCNA, 1 November.)

Little is known of the AAJA's organizational structure, but the Secretariat, in addition to Djawoto, includes two other Indonesians (Supeno and Umar Said), at least five Chinese (Chang Kuo-ching, Hsiung Ching-chi, Lu Pin, Peng Chi-chin, and Yang I), two Japanese (Sugiyama Ichihei and Kobayashi Yuichi), Said Salim Abdullah (Tanzania), Abdul Rahman Aboukoss (Syria), Minaj Barna (Pakistan), Ahmed Gora Ebrahim ("Azania"—this man may in fact be from Tanzania), Mamadou Gologo (Mali), and D. Manuweera (Ceylon). The AAJA claims members in 53 countries, but this would seem to include individual memberships as well as formal participating organizations.

The AAJA dispatched delegations to many African and Middle Eastern countries during the year. Two separate groups left Peking in December 1966 and returned in January 1967, one of them visiting Syria, the UAR (including the Palestine Liberation Organization [PLO] headquarters in Cairo and its office in Gaza), Yemen, Iraq, Lebanon, Mauritania, and Kuwait, while the other went to Tanzania, Zambia, Ethiopia, and Somalia. Another delegation composed of members of the AAJA Secretariat left Peking in October "to convey the firm support of the journalists in Asia and Africa in their anti-imperialist and anti-revisionist struggles, to further strengthen the militant unity and close cooperation between the AAJA Secretariat and the Arab journalists, and to explain the revolutionary line and working program mapped out at the 5th plenary meeting of the Secretariat" (NCNA, 12 October). The delegation split into two groups, one visiting the UAR and PLO, Syria, and Algeria, the other the UAR, Yemen, Sudan, Iraq, and Kuwait.

There is little to show that the pro-Chinese AAJA has attained any degree of success in winning over the allegiance of IOJ members or member organizations. During 1967, journalists' organizations or governments in only six nations (Algeria, Ceylon, Japan, Pakistan, Somalia and Tanzania) expressed open support for the AAJA Second Conference or indicated indirectly through public statements that they might send delegates to an AAJA conference.

The AAJA conducts journalism courses in Peking for aspiring young people of the Afro-Asian nations. Its third course, which included members from "Azania," South West Africa, Mozambique, Lesotho, "Zimbabwe," and Ceylon graduated in February 1967. The fourth course, with students from Congo (Brazzaville), Congo (Kinshasa) and Guinea, ended in September.

The AAJA issues a biweekly publication entitled the *Afro-Asian Journalist,* an *Afro-Asian Journalists' Association Bulletin,* and pamphlets on specific subjects.

**The Afro-Asian Writers' Permanent Bureau (Afro-Asian Writers' Bureau).** The first Afro-Asian writers' conference was held in Tashkent in October 1958. This conference approved the establishment of a permanent bureau with headquarters in Colombo, Ceylon. The permanent bureau, however, was not actually set up in Colombo until October 1962, after the second Afro-Asian writers' conference in Cairo in February of that year. The Chinese Communists gained control of the organization at an Executive Committee meeting in Bali in July 1963. Although the AAWPB is still, technically speaking, based in Colombo, an Executive Secretariat was established in Peking on 15 August 1966, and the organization operates exclusively from there. The membership strength of the AAWPB is not clear. An AAWPB "emergency meeting" in Peking in 1966 was reportedly attended by 161 writer delegates from 53 countries.

The Secretary-General of the AAWPB is Rathe Deshapriya Senanayake(Ceylon); Ibrahim Isa is the Acting Secretary-General when Senanayake is absent from Peking. The so-called Cairo (or pro-Soviet) faction of the AAWPB was founded in Cairo on 19-21 June 1966 at an "extraordinary meeting" with delegations present from six countries: Cameroun, Ceylon, India, Sudan, the USSR, and the UAR. The Secretary-General of the Cairo faction AAWPB is Yusuf as-Sibai (UAR); the Assistant Secretary-General is Mursi Saad ad-Din.

The pro-Peking AAWPB, which follows a completely pro-Chinese and antirevisionist line, suffered a serious blow in 1967 when the pro-Soviet faction held a relatively successful "Third Afro-Asian Writers' Conference" in Beirut, 25-30 March, while the Peking AAWPB had to postpone its own "Third" conference scheduled for late 1967. This latter conference was first planned for Djakarta in 1964, then postponed to 1965, and later moved to Peking in 1967, only to be postponed in December until "a time when the people of these two continents and of the entire world have entered a completely new era in which Chairman Mao's thought and his theories on literature and art have become a powerful ideological weapon in their fight against imperialism, modern revisionism and world reaction" (*The Call,* December 1967).

Off to a shaky start in 1966, the Cairo AAWPB is now on a relatively firm footing as a result of the Beirut conference. Attending the conference were approximately 150 delegates from 42 countries. The Lebanese Prime Minister, Rashid Karami, opened the proceedings; Kamal Jumblat, president of the left-wing Lebanese Progressive Socialist Party, presided. Possibly the most significant achievement of the conference was the successful establishment of an Afro-Asian Writers' Organization (also referred to as the Afro-Asian Writers' League) which is to hold conferences every three years with the next conference set tentatively for Delhi. The conference also selected an Executive Committee representing 27 member countries, including Communist China (which, of course, took no part in the proceedings) and the USSR. A ten-member Permanent Bureau was also chosen, with members from India, Japan, Lebanon, Mongolia, the Portuguese colonies, Senegal, South Africa, the USSR, Sudan, and the UAR. In spite of complaints from the African delegations about somewhat inferior treatment at the hands of the Lebanese and a general complaint of an overemphasis on politics at the expense of literature, the conference must be viewed a success for the Soviet Union in its rivalry with Peking for the control of fronts.

The Peking AAWPB made a strenuous effort to weaken the impact of the Beirut conference and to draw support for its own conference in Peking by sending a delegation headed by Senanayake himself on a three-month tour of Middle Eastern and African nations (November 1966 to January 1967). This group went first to Pakistan in a body, where it divided, one half under Senanayake visiting Syria, Lebanon, Iraq, Algeria, Guinea, Sierra Leone, and Mali, while the other, led by Hsu Huai-chung of China, toured Tanzania, Zambia, and Somalia. Although the Peking AAWPB laid claim to support from writers' organizations in 40 countries for its "Third" conference, the attempt to hold the conference failed, indicating that the kind of consensus required by Peking for a successful conference was lacking.

The most important public function of the year for the Chinese-controlled AAWPB was the seminar it conducted in Peking from 31 May until 6 June to commemorate the twenty-fifth anniversary of Mao Tse-tung's "Talks at the Yenan Forum on Literature and Art." The 80 delegates, from 34 countries and regions (many of whom are permanent residents of Peking), agreed that Mao's "Talks at the Yenan Forum on Literature and Art" is a work of "great, world-wide, epoch-making significance: It gives the revolutionary and progressive writers and artists of the world the most correct political guidance bases on revolutionary Marxism-Lennism. . . . This great work [is] the beacon light guiding the Afro-Asian writers' movement and the cultural revolution of the peoples of the world." (*Peking Review,* no. 24, 9 June.)

The Peking AAWPB issues a bulletin, *The Call,* at irregular intervals in English, French, and Arabic. The Cairo faction announced that it would publish a news bulletin bimonthly in English, French, and Arabic and also a quarterly magazine and books by Afro-Asian men of letters. (The first issue of the quarterly magazine, *Afro-Asian Writings,* appeared in March 1968.)

**Other Fronts.** Among the other, less active Chinese-sponsored front organizations there is the reactivated Peace Liaison Committee for the Asian and Pacific Regions (PLCAPR) set up under the auspices of the Soviet-front World Council of Peace (WCP) in 1952 but largely dormant until 1962, when there were signs that the Chinese were reviving it as a rival to its parent body. It has not been very active, however, and has issued only occasional statements in support of Chinese policy.

Another Peking front, designed as a rival to the International Association of Democratic Lawyers (IADL), is the Afro-Asian Lawyers' Conference (AALC). The AALC began as a conference of Afro-Asian lawyers in Conakry, Guinea, in October 1962; in this conference Chinese influence was strong. At an Executive Committee meeting in November 1963, the Chinese took firm control by excluding the Soviet Union from the Secretariat and securing a seat for themselves. Efforts to organize a second conference have been unsuccessful, and the organization's activities have been confined to propaganda statements in support of Peking's position.

A third minor pro-Chinese front is the Peking Center of the World Federation of Scientific Workers (WFSW), inaugurated in 1963. It is a rival to the WFSW and not an Asian regional branch as it claims to be. The Peking Center WFSW held an "International Scientific Symposium" in 1964, sponsored a "Symposium on Physics" in July 1966, and plans a second scientific symposium for the summer of 1968.

Attempts to set up a rival to the World Federation of Trade Unions (WFTU) were made by the All-China Federation of Trade Unions and the Indonesian Central Organization of Trade Unions, on whose initiative an "Afro-Asian Workers' Conference" was undertaken in late 1962 without coming to fruition. The attempted communist coup in Indonesia in 1965 effectively postponed realization of this plan, and dissolution of the All-China Federation of Trade Unions during the Cultural Revolution has removed, at least temporarily, any possibility of the establishment of a pro-Chinese international labor front. The Chinese have tried also to establish organizations in the fields of youth and student activities, but, thus far, these have not progressed much beyond the planning stage.

# INTERNATIONAL COMMUNIST
# CONFERENCES AND EVENTS

# CONFERENCE OF COMMUNIST AND WORKERS' PARTIES
## OF EUROPE, KARLOVY VARY (24-26 APRIL)

The Conference of Communist and Workers' Parties of Europe, at Karlovy Vary, Czechoslovakia, on 24-26 April 1967, was the largest communist meeting since that of 1960 in Moscow. Also it marked the first time that communist and workers parties of both East and West Europe met and discussed common problems. The conference's work was aimed toward drawing up a program of "collective security" to replace the system of military pacts now dividing Europe. The 24 participating parties, represented in almost every case by the party head, adopted three documents:

1. An appeal entitled: "Let us Unite Our Efforts and Intensify the Struggle in Support of the Vietnam People."
2. A statement entitled: "For Peace and Security in Europe."
3. A statement entitled: "On the Military Putsch in Greece."

The convening of the Karlovy Vary conference served also as a stepping-stone toward planning a world communist party conference.

**Background.** At a conference of West European communist parties in Brussels, in June 1965, the French Communist Party proposed the convening of an all-European meeting to discuss "European security." The French communists repeated the call at the meeting of West European communist parties in Vienna, in May 1966. The "practical stage" of the preparations began in October 1966 when Secretary-General Waldeck Rochet of the French party met in Poland with Secretary-General Wladyslaw Gomulka of the Polish United Workers' Party, and preparations continued during meetings between representatives of the two parties in late 1966 and up to the opening of the all-European conference in 1967.

On 22-26 February 1967 a formal preparatory meeting for the conference was held in Warsaw. Although all 32 communist and workers' parties of Europe were invited to the preparatory meeting, only 19 were represented. The absentee parties included those of Yugoslavia, Rumania, and Albania among the East European ruling parties, and those of the Netherlands, Norway, Sweden, Iceland, Eire, Northern Ireland, Luxembourg, Turkey, and San Marino. The preparatory meeting decided to hold the conference at Karlovy Vary on 24-27 April and declared that the purpose of the conference was to discuss European security. (Although scheduled for four days, the conference adjourned after three days of debate.) The preparatory meeting did not prepare an agenda and did not submit a draft resolution for the conference, thereby leaving the door open for those parties not participating in the preparatory meeting to join the conference at Karlovy Vary on equal terms. The documents for the conference were later drafted by a 23-member editorial commission which met in Prague on 21 April. The editorial commission included all parties which subsequently participated in the conference except Cyprus.

**Participants.** The 24 communist and workers' parties represented at the Karlovy Vary conference and the heads of their delegations were

### Ruling Parties

Communist Party of the Soviet Union, Secretary-General Leonid Brezhnev
Bulgarian Communist Party, First Secretary Todor Zhivkov
Communist Party of Czechoslovakia, First Secretary Antonín Novotný
Socialist Unity Party of Germany, First Secretary Walter Ulbricht
Hungarian Socialist Workers' Party, First Secretary János Kádár
Polish United Workers' Party, First Secretary Wladyslaw Gomulka

## Nonruling Parties

Communist Party of Austria, Chairman Franz Muhri
Belgian Communist Party, Politburo member Jean Blume
Progressive Party of the Working People of Cyprus, Secretary-General Ezekias Papaïoannou
Communist Party of Denmark, Chairman Knud Jespersen
Finnish Communist Party, Secretary-General Ville Pessi
French Communist Party, Secretary-General Waldeck Rochet
Socialist Unity Party of Germany-West Berlin, First Secretary Gerhard Danelius
Communist Party of Germany, Secretary-General Max Reimann
Communist Party of Great Britain, Secretary-General John Gollan
Communist Party of Greece, Chairman Apostolos Grozos
Irish Workers' Party, Secretary-General Michael O'Riordan
Italian Communist Party, Secretary-General Luigi Longo
Communist Party of Luxembourg, Chairman Dominique Urbani
Communist Party of Northern Ireland, Secretary-General Hugh Moore
Communist Party of Portugal, Secretary-General Alvaro Cunhal
Communist Party of San Marino, Secretary-General Ermenegildo Gasperoni
Communist Party of Spain, Chairman Dolores Ibarruri
Swiss Labor Party, Secretary-General Edgar Woog.

The Communist Party of Sweden sent a member of the Party Executive, Fritjof Lager, as an observer.

The parties not represented at Karlovy Vary were the Albanian Workers' Party, Rumanian Communist Party, League of Communists of Yugoslavia, United Socialist Party of Iceland, Communist Party of the Netherlands, Communist Party of Norway, and the Communist Party of Turkey.

**Rumania and Yugoslavia**. Intense efforts were made in the weeks preceding the opening of the conference to ensure the participation of all the communist and workers' parties, and especially the parties of Rumania and Yugoslavia. Nicolae Ceauşescu headed a Rumanian delegation to Moscow on 17-18 March; the Italian Communist leader Luigi Longo had talks with Ceauşescu during a visit to Bucharest on 21 March-6 April; Rumanian party representatives visited Austria in early April; French party representatives had talks with Ceauşescu in Bucharest on 13 April; two groups of Rumanian party representatives visited Prague and Budapest; and immediately before the conference Bulgarian Party leader Todor Zhivkov visited Bucharest and talked with Ceauşescu. Yugoslav President Tito talked with Luigi Longo at Brioni on 20 January and during the following week paid an unofficial visit to the Soviet Union and talked with Leonid Brezhnev; in mid-February he met with Hungarian party leader János Kádár in Budapest and visited Vienna. Representatives of the Czechoslovak Communist Party and the Bulgarian Communist Party visited Belgrade in February and March respectively, and the Yugoslavs sent representatives to Czechoslovakia and Budapest in April. Meanwhile the Rumanians and Yugoslavs conferred in Belgrade on 30 January, in Bucharest on 11 February, and in Budapest on 30 March.

The Rumanian party on numerous occasions before the conference indicated its disapproval of multilateral conferences and preference for bilateral talks (see *Scînteia,* 28 February), but did not officially declare its decision not to participate until after the conference opened. Radio Bucharest announced on 24 April that Rumania was not going to the Karlovy Vary conference because during earlier exchanges of views and consultations no preliminary joint agreement on the character, aims, and manner of the holding of the conference was reached.

The League of Communists of Yugoslavia expressed its opinion on the Karlovy Vary conference and other international communist meetings of this nature at its January plenum. Following a joint meeting of the Presidium and the Executive Committee of the Central Committee in April, Executive Committee member Nijaz Dizdarević flew to Prague on 20 April and delivered the Yugoslav note of refusal to participate. The Yugoslavs expressed the view that this conference threatened to isolate the communist parties from other "peace-loving forces," all of which could make valuable contributions to European security, and apparently feared that the meeting would be conducted in the manner of the 1957 and 1960 Moscow meetings, which had been completely dominated by the CPSU. (The Yugoslavs refused to sign the joint declaration in 1957 and were not invited to the 1960 conference.)

The Communist Party of the Netherlands and the Communist Party of Norway refused to attend owing to tension in their ranks over the Sino-Soviet split and their wariness of international communist party gatherings which might condemn China or adopt a policy line contrary to their national interests. (The Communist Party of the Netherlands refused to sign the joint communique at the Brussels conference in 1965 and did not attend the Vienna conference of May 1966.)

There was no direct criticism of the absent parties at the Karlovy Vary conference, but several of the parties attending indicated their disapproval of absenteeism in the case of international gatherings. Leonid Brezhnev mentioned that the "spirit of communism does not allow anybody to stand by waiting for the time when unity becomes a reality by itself." Walter Ulbricht asked: "Is it a restriction of the sovereignty and autonomy of a party if, as in the case of our conference, a free exchange of views takes place to solve common problems?" and added that "The fundamental principle of 'Workers of the World Unite!' proceeds from the premise that every party bears a responsibility to the entire communist movement." The Chairman of the Luxembourg Communist Party, Dominique Urbani, stated that his party could not find justification for the absentees' "noncooperation and quasi-isolationist positions." Officially, every effort was made to accommodate the absent parties and allow them to adhere to the conference resolutions.

**Agenda.** Despite the repeated specification that the Karlovy Vary conference would discuss European security problems, there was widespread speculation in the Western press that it was being convened for the purpose of condemning China and of discussing preparations for an international communist gathering. The speeches at Karlovy Vary, however, closely followed the agenda. China was mentioned only by Leonid Brezhnev, who declared that communist aid to Vietnam could be much more effective if China would agree to cooperate. Passing reference to an international communist conference was made by several delegates, but the subject was not mentioned in the conference documents.

The offensive at Karlovy Vary was taken against the alleged threat of West German "militarism and revanchism" and against "American imperialism." Brezhnev, in his speech on the opening day of the conference, took an uncompromising view of "neo-Nazist" and "revanchist" trends in the Federal Republic of Germany. Although not absolutely denying West Germany the possibility of participating in European affairs or improving its relations with the Soviet Union, Brezhnev did not base his proposals for security on this possibility. Turning to the American presence in Europe, Brezhnev declared that the USA was giving encouragement to "West German militarism" and that the existence of NATO was a threat to peace in Europe. He called for the liquidation of American military bases in Europe and demanded the complete withdrawal of the US Sixth Fleet from the Mediterranean. Noting that the question of renewal of membership in NATO was imminent (in 1969), Brezhnev declared that communists and all progressive forces should try to use this circumstance to "develop still more widely" the struggle against "the preservation of this aggressive bloc," and called for the liquidation of both NATO and the Warsaw Pact, urging their replacement with a network of bilateral agreements and treaties. He then called for the widest possible unity of communists, other left-wing parties, and social-democrats. (He criticized the British Labour Party and the West German Social Democratic Party, however, for "clinging" to the NATO policy.)

The other speeches at the conference were variations of the attack on West Germany and the USA, with varying emphasis on particular national problems. The ruling East European parties, in their speeches, concentrated heavily on West Germany and on US "imperialism." Relations with Catholics, state neutrality, and economic relations were discussed by Luigi Longo (Italy), Edgar Woog (Switzerland), and John Gollan (Great Britain), respectively. No disagreements were evident from published proceedings of the conference, although the Soviet press in describing the debates avoided the standard phrase, "identity of views," and referred instead to "various shades of opinion" on the issues discussed. (*Pravda,* 27 and 30 April.) The conference resolutions were adopted unanimously.

The final Statement of the conference, "For Peace and Security in Europe," was based on Brezhnev's speech but the language was modified to accomodate the views of the less militant parties at the conference and in order to appeal to the broadest possible cross-section of the European population. The proposal for creating a system of collective security in Europe largely restated the proposals voiced in the Bucharest declaration of July 1966 and entailed the recognition of the "existing situation" in Europe, specifically the recognition of the inviolability of existing frontiers, the existence of two equal German states, the preclusion of any opportunity for West Germany to gain access to nuclear arms, and the recognition of the 1938 Munich Treaty as invalid from the moment of its signing. (West Germany has declared the Munich Treaty invalid today but has not denied its validity *ab initio.*)

Proposed steps toward a system of collective security included:

(1) Adherence of all European states to a treaty renouncing the use of force or the threat of force in their mutual relations and promising non-interference in each other's internal affairs. (This point was first proposed by Wladyslaw Gomulka in his speech to the conference.)

(2) Recognition of the principles of neutrality and unconditional respect of the inviolability of neutral states. (This and the above point were not included in the 1966 Bucharest Declaration.)

(3) Liquidation of artificially created barriers in economic relations between socialist and capitalist states.

(4) The conclusion of agreements on partial solutions, above all in the sphere of disarmament, which would create a favorable climate for more far-reaching treaties.

The Statement emphasized that the communist parties did not wish to claim a monopoly on efforts toward European security and would support any initiative or proposal pursuing the purpose of achieving a détente and strengthening such security. The Statement also named those groups to which the communist movement appealed—the working class, socialist and social-democratic parties, trade unions, intellectuals, Christian forces, younger generations, women, bourgeois groups, and "all peace-loving forces." (For full text of Statement see *Documents.*)

On the first day of the conference the participants adopted an appeal, "Let Us Unite Our Efforts and Intensify the Struggle in Support of the Vietnam People," condemning the US involvement in Vietnam and expressing their "firm determination to contribute actively to isolating and defeating the "aggressive policy of American imperialism," and to press for the withdrawal of all foreign troops from Vietnam and for the Vietnamese people's right to deal with their internal affairs. The appeal called on "all antiwar forces to intensify common actions for the cessation of the US war in Vietnam irrespective of their ideological and political convictions."

The participants also adopted a "Statement on the Military Putsch in Greece" expressing their "indignant condemnation" of the "putsch" as part of the "reactionary attempt to prevent the relaxation of international tension and the strengthening of European security and peace in the world." The statement protested against the new regime's ban on political parties and what it termed the "terror which was unleashed by this regime," the arrest of "democratic political leaders," "mass repressions," and the "revival of fascism in Greece."

**Significance of the Conference.** The Western press, almost without exception, emphasized the early adjournment of the Karlovy Vary conference and viewed it as a failure and as a demonstration of disunity in the communist movement. The *New York Times* on 2 May in an editorial entitled "Fiasco at Karlovy Vary" commented that the conference had "shown once again—and dramatically—how divided world communism is today." The *Neue Zürcher Zeitung* (28 April) described the conference as "a ritual rich in phrases, but poor in content" and said that the documents of the conference instead of transcending the Bucharest Declaration appeared to "water it down." The London *Economist* (29 April) remarked that the parties represented at Karlovy Vary had managed to achieve unanimous agreement on a Statement which "contained the hoary old hates and no surprises."

The communist press, on the other hand, throughout 1967 reflected the Soviet assessment of the

Karlovy Vary conference as "a major success for the world communist movement" (*Pravda,* 27 April). Considering the difficulties in the communist movement today, the simple fact that the conference was held at all and that agreement could be reached on some issues was recognized by the communist press as an achievement in itself. The significance of Karlovy Vary to the world communist movement was summarized by *Pravda*'s political commentator on 17 May, who indicated its value as a test case for convening other large communist conferences:

> The conference in Karlovy Vary . . . provided an example of communist [parties'] coordination of their positions under conditions of the great diversity of the tasks facing them and of their experience which cannot but bear the stamp of specific national conditions. The conference provided an example of true equality and noninterference of parties in one another's affairs and of their frank and sincere cooperation. Complete party independence was well combined with the striving to achieve utmost results through joint efforts.

The significance of the Karlovy Vary conference in the solution of European problems was also emphasized. According to the communist press, it was logical that, having borne the brunt of the Nazi attack in World War II, the Communists should be in the forefront of the drive for European security, besides being "the only political force active in both parts of Europe, the only force capable of assuming an all-European mission" (*New Times,* 10 May).

The conference decisions, in the view of the Communists, can exert a long-term influence on world affairs, "among other things because they are *not directed against anyone,* because they accord with the interests of *all* the European peoples" (*ibid.,* 31 May; emphasis in original). The fact that the conference Statement was addressed to the broadest possible strata of the European population, calling for a united front of these forces, and the claim that it had formulated a "concrete program of action," to which these forces could adhere, were also emphasized. The international significance of the conference was held to be based on the interrelation of European problems with other world problems and the assumption that the key to easing world tension lies in Europe. Communists could cite the appeal in support of the Vietnamese people as particular evidence of the international significance of the conference.

The Chinese and Albanian press denounced the Karlovy Vary meeting in uncompromising terms. The Peking *People's Daily* (4 May) called it a "counterrevolutionary gangster's meeting . . . symbolic of the utter bankruptcy of Europe's new scabs." The meeting was convened, according to the Peking newspaper, to "engineer further actions against China . . . preparatory to a massive assembly of all the renegades and scabs of the world" and in the hope that it would help the Soviet leaders "restore the 'authority' of the baton of Khrushchev revisionism"; further, it "revealed that although the European modern revisionists 'sleep in the same bed, they all have different dreams,' each having his own axe to grind." The Albanian party organ *Zëri i Popullit* (5 May) declared: "[The Karlovy Vary meeting] exposed before the world public the depths to which the Khrushchev revisionists have degenerated, their complete capitulation to the bourgeoisie and other reactionary forces, and their eventual turning into a handful of social reformists serving capitalism and counterrevolution heart and soul."

# FIRST CONFERENCE OF THE LATIN AMERICAN SOLIDARITY
# ORGANIZATION, HAVANA (31 JULY-10 AUGUST)

The Latin American Solidarity Organization (Organización Latinoamericana de Solidaridad; OLAS) was created in Havana on 16 January 1966.* Its formation was in accordance with the objectives of the so-called Tricontinental Conference, the First Conference of the Afro-Asian Latin American Peoples' Solidarity Organization (AALAPSO), which had met in the Cuban capital between 3 and 15 January 1966 (see *YICA*, 1966, pp. 451-457).

The purposes of the organization, as stated in Article 1 of the Statutes adopted by OLAS in August 1967, are:

(a) To develop and promote the unity of the anti-imperialist movement and organizations in each one of the Latin American countries.

(b) To develop and promote the unity of the anti-imperialist movements and organizations of all the peoples of the continent.

(c) To support, by all means within their power, the peoples of Latin America that struggle against imperialism and colonialism, especially those who are engaged in armed struggle.

(d) To coordinate the struggle against U.S. imperialism to achieve a united answer of the Latin American peoples to its continental strategy.

(e) To promote the solidarity of the Latin American peoples with the national liberation movements of Asia, and Africa and with the progressive movements all over the world.†

The delegates from 27 Latin American republics and territories who attended the meeting on 16 January 1966 agreed to the formation of national committees (see below) and an Organizing Committee made up of delegates from Brazil, Colombia, Cuba, Guyana, Guatemala, Mexico, Peru, Uruguay, and Venezuela. The Organizing Committee was divided into two subcommittees, one in charge of organizing and conducting the preconvention business of the conference scheduled for 1967, and one responsible for publicizing the opening conference and publishing the bulletin *OLAS*. The only two permanent positions on the Organizing Committee, those of the Secretary General and the Press Secretary, were filled, respectively, by Haydée Santamaría, a member of the Central Committee of the Cuban Communist Party, and Miguel Brugueras, of the Cuban Press agency Prensa Latina.

In addition to the activities mentioned above, the Organizing Committee was responsible for issuing all invitations to the 1967 conference. In January 1967 it sent a detailed questionnaire to all

*"Olas" means "waves" in Spanish. Fidel Castro told the delegates to the first OLAS conference in August 1967: "OLAS is the wave of the future, symbol of the revolutionary waves sweeping a continent of 250 million." (*Granma*, weekly English edition, 20 August.) For an official description of the organization see "What is OLAS?" in *Documents*.

†All quotations in this survey from documents and speeches at the 1967 OLAS conference are, unless otherwise noted, from the official English-language translations published during the conference, dated July-August 1967. There are minor differences in some of the translations which appeared in weekly English editions of *Granma*.

national committees, 25 international organizations, and 197 Latin American institutions. The information gathered in these questionnaires about political, social, and economic conditions in Latin America was compiled in fourteen volumes by six special commissions made up of more than a thousand experts and their assistants.

According to the Regulations of the OLAS conference, the Organizing Committee retained its leadership role until the election of the OLAS Presidency at a meeting of delegation presidents early in the 1967 conference.

According to the Statutes adopted at the August 1967 conference, OLAS is composed of three bodies: the Conference, the Permanent Committee, and the National Committees.

The Conference, "the deliberating body and highest authority of the Organization," is comprised of the national committees of member countries and is scheduled to meet every two years.

The Permanent Committee is "the executive body and the highest authority between the Conferences." It is based in Havana and is made up of representatives from one-third of the member countries. Its function is to work for the purposes of OLAS as described in Article 1 of the Statutes (quoted above). It is charged with coordinating and guiding the activities of the National Committees and with controlling their composition. It is responsible for convoking the Conference every two years and has the power to call special continental meetings when it deems them necessary.

The National Committees, according to the OLAS Statutes, represent the "most active, anti-imperialist and deep-rooted people's groups in each one of the Latin American countries." Political organizations that fill certain requirements have the right to be members of the National Committees. They must: "be anti-imperialist, representative, and unitary"; "accept the General Declaration of the Tricontinental Conference and the General Declaration of the First Conference of OLAS"; and "accept the statutes of the Latin American Solidarity Organization." The Statutes state further that "in those countries where revolutionary armed struggle is developing, all organizations and movements that effectively support or participate in this struggle shall be considered anti-imperialist." In particular cases, mass organizations can become part of the National Committees, but only if they fulfill additional requirements. Any National Committee may recommend that changes be made in its own membership, but all final decisions must be made by the Permanent Committee in Havana. The National Committees are expected to work for the achievement of OLAS goals through unifying and coordinating revolutionary forces in their countries.

The First Conference of the Latin American Solidarity Organization was held in Havana between 31 July and 10 August 1967. In attendance were 163 delegates from the 20 Latin American republics and Guadeloupe, French Guinea, Guyana, Martinique, Puerto Rico, Surinam, and Trinidad and Tobago, as well as one honorary delegate from the United States. According to the official list of participants, there were 38 observers from international organizations (AALAPSO, the International Union of Students, the Confederation of Latin Americans in the German Democratic Republic, the Permanent Congress of Trade Union Unity of Latin American Workers, the Continental Organization of Latin American Students, the World Federation of Democratic Youth, the World Federation of Trade Unions, the Women's International Democratic Federation, the World Council of Peace, the Tricontinental Committee for Support to the People of Vietnam, the International War Crimes Tribunal, the International Organization of Journalists, and the Japanese Council Against the Atomic and Hydrogen Bombs), 25 from "socialist" countries (North Vietnam, North Korea, Bulgaria, Czechoslovakia, Hungary, Mongolia, Poland, East Germany, Rumania, and the USSR), and seven from the National Liberation Front of South Vietnam. The Soviet Union sent only two accredited observers, and, though there are indications that they were invited to attend, Communist China and Albania sent none. Yugoslavia was apparently the only communist country to be purposely excluded. Special foreign guests totaled 38. The foreign press was represented by 157 persons from 38 countries, including eight from the USSR and two from Communist China.

Most of the delegates were left-wing extremists and guerrilla fighters, typified by Venezuelan guerrilla Francisco Prada. Some pro-Soviet Communists and their followers were present, though they seem to have been dominant in only a few delegations, most notably the Uruguayan. A few pro-Chinese delegates attended, though not as official representatives of pro-Chinese parties. The fact that most of the delegates were little known in their own countries was noted by Marcel Niedergang in *Le Monde* on 2 August, and by the Yugoslav press agency Tanyug, which asserted on 1 August: "Many delegations consist of quite unknown personalities, representing groups and organizations which have no influence in their own countries."

Cuban domination of the organization and activities of the conference had been clear from the first meeting in January 1966. It was accounted for by the existence in Cuba of the only communist government in the hemisphere, by the popularity of the Cuban example among some Latin American revolutionaries, and by Fidel Castro's determination to foment and lead a continental "socialist" revolution.

Among the Cuban leaders present at the 16 January meeting were six of the eight-man Cuban Communist Party Politburo (Fidel Castro, Osvaldo Dorticós, Juan Almeida, Armando Hart, Guillermo García, and Sergio del Valle). Both permanent positions in the Organizing Committee were given to Cubans. In addition to Haydée Santamaría (wife of Armando Hart), the Cubans on the Committee included, among others, the leaders of all the mass organizations in Cuba.

The 12-member Cuban delegation to the August conference included Armando Hart, Haydée Santamaría, a former director of *Granma*, leaders of mass organizations, and other influential persons. Haydée Santamaría was elected President of the Conference, and Ernesto "Che" Guevara was elected Honorary President *in absentia*.

Three of the four Vice-Presidents of the Conference were Castroist in outlook: Francisco Prada (Venezuela), Néstor Valle (Guatemala), and Gerardo Sánchez (Dominican Republic). The fourth Vice-President was Rodney Arismendi, the Secretary-General of the Communist Party of Uruguay, the only pro-Soviet Communist given such a high position. Arismendi was also the only pro-Soviet Communist to come close to a full endorsement of the guerrilla-oriented line of the conference, and is generally believed to have worked constantly to smooth over differences between Cuba and the USSR (see *Uruguay*).

The official agenda of the conference was divided into four main sections, the first three of which were in turn broken down into thirteen subsections. The four main sections were:

1. The anti-imperialist revolutionary struggle in Latin America.

2. Position and common action against the political-military intervention and the economical and ideological penetration of imperialism in Latin America.

3. The solidarity of the Latin American peoples with the struggles for national liberation.

4. Statutes of the Organization of Latin American Solidarity (OLAS).

Four working committees were set up to discuss and issue statements on the four central topics. Though all meetings were held in secret some delegates told news reporters most of what went on. Making reference to these delegates, Fidel Castro commented on 10 August: "There were indiscretions, and nearly all the things discussed are known more or less" (*Granma,* weekly English edition, 20 August).

Speeches at the conference were given by three different groups of participants: the Cuban hosts, delegates to the conference, and observers from "socialist" countries and international organizations.

Cuban President Osvaldo Dorticós addressed the opening session of the conference on the evening of 31 July. He discussed what he called "an imperialist world strategy against the peoples and the liberation movements, a strategy which daily acquires greater ferocity." The Latin American people, he asserted, were confronted with two alternatives: "to reply with arms to the challenge of imperialist violence or to renounce all hopes of liberation." (*Ibid.,* 6 August.)

Armando Hart, Organizing Secretary of the Cuban Communist Party, serving as Chairman of the Cuban delegation, presented a concise Castroist analysis of the main objectives of the conference, namely, how to draw up a "common strategy for the struggle against Yankee imperialism and against the bourgeois oligarchies and wealthy landowners that have allied themselves with the interests of the United States Government" (*ibid.*, 13 August).

Fidel Castro discussed certain aspects of that "common strategy" in his speech at the closing session of the conference on 10 August (see *Ibid.*, 20 August). He praised US Negro militant Stokely Carmichael, who was present as an "honorary delegate" from the United States, and declared that there was a spontaneous drawing together of US and Latin American revolutionaries. While maintaining that "seizing power by peaceful means" was impossible in any Latin American country, Castro conceded that "no one can be so sectarian, so dogmatic, as to say that, everywhere, one has to go out and grab a rifle tomorrow."

The outstanding characteristic of this closing speech, however, was the emphasis the Cuban Prime Minister placed on those groups which he said were plotting against himself, the Cuban revolution, and the Latin American guerrillas. His condemnations were directed at: (1) the US government, allegedly responsible for sending CIA agents—eight Cubans charged with being such agents were put on display at the conference—to subvert the Cuban revolution and assassinate himself; (2) all Latin American countries (except Mexico) which in the OAS condoned "US aggression" in the hemisphere while condemning "Cuban aggression," most recently in response to charges made in June 1967 by Venezuelan President Raúl Leoni; (3) the Communist Party of Venezuela, which had "betrayed" the Venezuelan revolution and allegedly was spearheading the attack against Cuba; (4) other unnamed Latin American Communist parties whose ideas were so antiquated and dogmatic that they had ceased to be revolutionary; (5) the "socialist" governments (unnamed, but understood to be those of the USSR and eastern Europe) that gave aid to the "oligarchs" in Latin America and thus made more difficult the activities of the guerrilla forces; and (6) a "microfaction" in Cuba which had been "systematically opposed to all the concepts of the Revolution, to the deepest, sincerest, purest revolutionary attitudes of our people, to our concepts of socialism, of communism, of everything." In short, Castro drew a line between those he considered the "true revolutionaries" who were dominant at the OLAS conference, some of whom did not call themselves communist, and the various groups, some of which did call themselves communist, whom he charged with having formed an alliance to attack Cuba and thwart the Latin American revolution.

Prominent among those at the conference who spoke in support of the Castroist line were Francisco Prada of Venezuela, Fabio Vásquez of Colombia (who sent a taped message), and the delegations from the Dominican Republic, Ecuador, Guatemala, and Peru. Among the least enthusiastic were Volodia Teitelboim of the Communist Party of Chile and the delegation from Costa Rica.

Stokely Carmichael, the only delegate from the USA, received more attention, especially from the foreign press, than anyone at the conference besides Fidel Castro himself. In one of the longest speeches delivered at the conference, Carmichael stated on 2 August that "The American city is, in essence, populated by people of the third world" and that the urban guerrilla warfare US Negroes needed to wage in order to win their "liberation" was merely one part of the international struggle between the "third world" and "Yankee imperialism." At a press conference held shortly after the eruption of violence in Detroit and other US cities, he asserted that these US Negro "rebellions" should be linked up with the outside world because "when the [US] has 50 Vietnams inside the United States, and 50 Vietnams outside the United States, that will mean the death of imperialism" (*Granma*, 3 August). While in Cuba Carmichael repeatedly said that US Negroes found Fidel Castro, "Che" Guevara, and the Cuban revolution an unfailing source of inspiration.

Most of the speeches by observers from other countries and international organizations were shorter and less militant, in accordance with their pro-Soviet positions in the Communist world. Notable exceptions were those of the Vietnamese, Korean, and Syrian delegations, as well as the address of the representative of the AALAPSO Executive Secretariat. The first plenary meeting was held on 1 August and proclaimed "in honor of the people of Vietnam." The privilege of speaking first was granted to the Chairman of the eight-member delegation from North Vietnam, and of speaking second to the Chairman of the seven-member delegation from the National Liberation Front of South Vietnam. Messages were read from North Vietnamese President Ho Chi Minh and North Korean

President Kim Il-song, among others.

The long Report submitted by the Cuban delegation clearly reflected the tone and content of the discussions held and resolutions passed by the OLAS delegates. It sought to show that "the duty of every revolutionary is to make the revolution"—above all by guerrilla warfare. It discussed Marx, Lenin, and the international nature of revolution today. Great stress was put on the history of "colonialism" and "imperialism" in Latin America, and on Latin American revolutionaries, beginning with Simón Bolívar and passing through José Martí to "Che" Guevara.

Emphasis on the specifically Latin American nature of the "anti-imperialist struggle," often overriding the Marxist-Leninist element, was evident on many occasions throughout the conference. Cuban President Dorticós gave his opening address before a large picture of Bolívar, and Fidel Castro in closing the conference spoke before one of Guevara. Latin American speakers, beginning with Dorticós, frequently mentioned Bolívar, San Martín, Martí, and other 19th-century heroes and many of the resolutions quoted these men and recounted their achievements. Typical of this nationalistic, or indeed inter-American, appeal for guerrilla war was this passage in the "General Resolution on Item Number One on the Agenda":

> We, revolutionaries of our America, of the America south of the Rio Grande, representatives of our people, successors of the men who gave us our first independence, inspired by the glorious examples of Bolívar, Hidalgo, O'Higgins, Sucre, Sarmiento, San Martín, Dessalines, Morazán, armed with the will to fight alongside our people, having nothing to lose but the chains that oppress us, assert that in Latin America is a situation that enables us to promote guerrilla struggle, the organization of a peoples' army to develop a war of this nature that will bring about destruction of the armies of the oligarchies and puppet governments; and as a consequence of common and victorious military actions by creating and strengthening the peoples' army, will assure establishment and preservation of revolutionary power.

The conference passed resolutions condemning US and OAS activities in Latin America; declaring support for guerrillas in Latin America, Negroes in the USA, the peoples of Asia, Africa, and the Arab world, and the AALAPSO; and hailing the fiftieth anniversary of the October Revolution in the Soviet Union. "Che" Guevara was proclaimed an honorary citizen of Latin America. (For a summary of the resolutions of the four working committees see *Granma*, weekly English edition, 27 August.)

The OLAS General Declaration pointed out: "The main aim of the Conference has been, in short, to tighten the ties of militant solidarity among anti-imperialist fighters of Latin America and to work out the fundamental lines for the development of the continental revolution." It further proclaimed that "the principles of Marxism-Leninism guide the revolutionary movement of Latin America." The twenty points which conclude the General Declaration are a concise review of the major tenets of the essentially Castroist line which was adopted at the conference. (See *Documents*.) The "Resolution on Solidarity with the Cuban Revolution" declared: "For the revolutionary organizations of Latin America, the most important duty of solidarity is the defense of the Cuban Revolution and unrestricted support of the revolutionary armed movement in Latin America." This armed movement was frequently brought into an international context, as in the "Resolution on Solidarity with the Struggle of the People of Viet Nam," which stated: "Viet Nam today points the revolutionary way that the peoples of America must follow, and our slogan will be the creation of two, three, many Viet Nams in the struggle for the total destruction of imperialism."

The conference took two days longer than had been expected, apparently because the Castroist and pro-Soviet members of the working committees could not agree on the wording of some resolutions. In the end the Cuban viewpoint was reflected on American and international issues (see *Cuba*), though some slight concessions were made to avoid an open conflict with the Soviet Union.

One dispute came over an attack on the pro-Soviet Communist Party of Venezuela (PCV) in the "Resolution on Solidarity with Venezuela." With the passage of this resolution by a vote of fifteen to three (El Salvador, Bolivia, and Uruguay opposed), and nine not voting, OLAS condemned the "bungling and opportunistic position of the rightist leadership of the PCV, which, in abandoning the road of armed struggle, betrays the revolutionary principles and serves the interests of imperialism and the oligarchies and all their policy of oppression" (translated from the official Spanish version).

Probably the most bitter dispute was that over the resolution to condemn "certain Socialist countries" for giving credits and technical aid to "oligarchic" governments in countries such as Brazil, Chile, and Colombia. This resolution, aimed at the Soviet Union and several of her East European allies, was passed by the same number of votes (Costa Rica, El Salvador, and Uruguay reportedly were opposed) but was never published. (See *New York Times,* 10 August, and *Le Monde,* 11 August.)

Communist reactions to the OLAS conference were widely varied. Its most enthusiastic Communist supporters were the parties in Korea and Vietnam. Rodney Arismendi, the Secretary-General of the Communist Party of Uruguay and one of the four Vice-Presidents of the conference, was the only pro-Soviet Communist in Latin America who openly and firmly supported the meeting; at the same time he opposed its more extreme anti-Soviet positions. Arismendi had perhaps the most difficult role to play at the conference, one of trying to retain the confidence of all participants and of endeavoring to avoid further dissension between the pro-Castro and the pro-Soviet forces.

Most pro-Soviet communist parties in Latin America were thrown into disarray by the conference. The parties in Argentina, Brazil, Ecuador, and Venezuela sent no representatives at all. Party delegates from Chile and Mexico expressed some reservations after returning from the conference, though they did not repudiate it. The Venezuelan party, in open conflict with the Cubans since Fidel Castro's speech of 13 March (see *Documents*), issued a communique on 20 July which argued that the meeting would only encourage divisionism, contradict Marxist-Leninist principles, and serve as a platform from which the Cubans would try to direct all revolutionary activities in Latin America.

Some pro-Soviet Communists in the hemisphere made indirect attacks on Castro and the conference, such as the one by the Secretary-General of the Communist Party of Chile which appeared in *Pravda* (30 July) on the eve of the conference (see *Cuba*).

No attacks on the conference by any pro-Soviet party were more unrestrained than those in the French Communist Party paper *L'Humanité*. On 4 August, for example, a long article attacked the "violent anti-Communist and anti-Soviet diatribes" of certain delegates (see *France*). Special attention was drawn to speeches by Francisco Prada and Gerardo Sánchez, two of the four Vice-Presidents of the conference and among Castro's most enthusiastic followers. These "ultrarevolutionaries," the paper said, were speaking the same language as Peking.

Although the Soviet press generally gave minimal attention to the conference, publishing only indirect criticisms, some Soviet radio broadcasts to Latin America were openly critical. On 8 August, for example, a Spanish-language broadcast on Moscow Radio Peace and Progress carried excerpts from the 4 August article in *L'Humanité*.

The absence of commentary on OLAS in Chinese publications left the pro-Chinese groups in Latin America uncertain as to how they should react. Most of them were critical of the Cubans for inviting so few of their number to attend the conference, but not all took exception to the decisions reached in Havana. In light of a February 1968 attack from Peking on some "persons like Régis Debray" (see *Cuba*), it would appear that the pro-Chinese Chilean Revolutionary Communist Party interpreted the Chinese stand correctly when it called Castroism a "political force which expressed the ideology and interests of the petty bourgeoisie" (*Espartaco*, September).

# THE SOVIET UNION'S FIFTIETH ANNIVERSARY OF THE OCTOBER REVOLUTION

The festivities surrounding the Soviet Union's observance of the fiftieth anniversary of the October Revolution, on 7 November 1967, were long in preparation. By the end of February some Soviet journalists were already complaining that there was "a danger of inflation of pompous words" and of "striking the big festival bell,. forgetting the needs of daily bread." (A journalists' seminar, 28 February-2 March, as reported in *Zhurnalist,* Moscow, April.)

The main celebrations took place from 2 to 7 November in Moscow and, to a lesser degree, in Leningrad, Kiev, and Minsk, and were imitated throughout the Soviet Union on a more modest scale.

**2 November.** The first official ceremony marking the anniversary was the unveiling on the afternoon of 2 November of a statue of Lenin inside the Kremlin walls. CPSU Central Committee Secretary-General Brezhnev headed the ceremony and delivered the principal speech, in which the dominating theme was that Lenin combined in himself the roles of a great theoretician of the future communist society and of a man of action, practical leader, and inspirer of a revolution. All the other leaders of the CPSU were in attendance at the ceremony and their presence was reported the next day in *Pravda* in the hierarchal order of official Soviet usage, which was preserved throughout the fiftieth anniversary celebrations. Also present were the leaders of all the foreign party delegations then in Moscow, according to the lists given in *Pravda.* In line with usual procedure, a representative of the working class was the next speaker after Brezhnev, then a member of the Academy of Sciences (Ostrovityanov—a Bolshevik since 1916), and finally a university girl, who quoted Mayakovsky on Lenin. The other events of the day included: the presentation of decorations and medals in the Kremlin to participants in the October Revolution and the Civil War, the placing of wreaths by the delegations of the Soviet constituent republics on Lenin's tomb, and in various districts of Moscow, meetings of workers which were addressed by foreign communist leaders.

**3 November.** The major event of 3 November was the opening of a two-day joint session of the Central Committee of the CPSU, the Supreme Soviet of the USSR, and the Supreme Soviet of the Russian Soviet Federated Socialist Republic. The heads of a number of foreign delegations addressed the meeting, alternating with Soviet officials.

The main speaker at this meeting was Brezhnev, whose speech of nearly four hours consisted of a historical, ideological, and political review of the fifty years of communist rule in the Soviet Union. The speech was divided into six sections, as follows.

1. *The Great October Revolution—Triumph of Marxism-Leninism.* This section was primarily devoted to the glorification of Lenin's personality, stating that his approach to theory had always been flexible and that he had no use for dogmatism. Brezhnev also rejected the concept that the Bolshevik Revolution had been a coup d'état, claiming that it had been a mass movement of the whole country.

2. *The Building of Socialism in One Country—a Great Feat of the Soviet People.* This was a review of the 1920's and 1930's. Avoiding all controversial issues, including reference to Stalin, this section apparently set the tone for the rest of the meeting, as no other speaker, Soviet or foreign, mentioned the name of Stalin.

3. *To the New Successes in the Struggle for Communism.* In this section it was pointed out that in the future primary attention would be devoted to heavy industry, while agriculture, consumer industries, and public services would be developed at "accelerated rates."

4. *The Great October Revolution and the World Revolutionary Movement.* In this section brief reference was made to Communist China, where the cause of socialism, Brezhnev declared, was greatly harmed by the "chauvinist and great-power policy pursued by Mao Tse-tung's group." Events

in China, he said, had "fully laid bare the ideological and political degradation of some leaders of the Communist Party of China." He added, however, that the CPSU believed that these events were a "historically transient stage" in China's development: "We believe that despite all difficulties the cause of socialism will triumph in the Chinese People's Republic." Toward the end of this section Brezhnev asserted that the position of the CPSU was shared by the majority of communist parties over the world. He praised the 1957 and 1960 Moscow international communist conferences, claiming that such conferences strengthened the unity of the parties. The Karlovy Vary conference, he said, had also been a very important meeting serving this purpose. "Today," he concluded, "it is perfectly clear that the majority of the fraternal Parties favor the convening of another international conference. Our Party fully supports this idea and is ready to do everything for the success of a new world meeting of Communists."

5. *The Leninist Foreign Policy of the Soviet Union.* Quoting the Resolution of the 1919 Congress of Soviets that "The Russian Socialist Federative Soviet Republic wishes to live in peace with all peoples and devote all its forces to internal development," Brezhnev maintained that this policy of peace has always guided Soviet foreign policy. He added, however:

> Our foreign policy is internationalist because the interests of the Soviet people coincide with those of the working masses in all countries. It is infused with the spirit of solidarity with the revolutionary, progressive forces throughout the world and represents an active factor of the class struggle in the international arena.

Brezhnev appealed for vigilance as far as "imperialist provocations and adventures" were concerned, warning that otherwise a thermonuclear war could erupt. While referring extensively to the peaceful aims of the Soviet Union, he made no use of the term "peaceful coexistence."

6. *The Communist Party—the Militant Vanguard of the Soviet People, the Inspirer and Organizer of Our Victories.* This section traced the historical role of the CPSU, although the only person mentioned by name was Lenin. In an apparent justification, however, of Stalin's purges in the 1930's, Brezhnev referred to the fact that the party "waged a relentless struggle against the Trotskyites, Right opportunists, and other opposition groups whose views mirrored the pressure of bourgeois and petty-bourgeois elements." The adoption of the party's Third Program at the Twenty-second Congress was mentioned but with no reference to the then First Secretary, Khrushchev.

In his concluding remarks Brezhnev declared:

> We Communists often hear arguments to the effect that Marxism-Leninism has become obsolete and lost its significance. Bourgeois ideologists, reformists and revisionists, and petty-bourgeois muddlers keep on asking: how is it possible to be guided in practical activity today by a theory created many decades ago? And we tell such critics that it all depends on what kind of theory it is.
>
> Yes, history knows of dozens and even hundreds of examples of theories, concepts, and whole philosophic systems which claimed they would renew the world not passing that test of time, falling to dust and perishing ignominiously upon coming into contact with life. This is the common lot of all who try to replace Marxism-Leninism with all sorts of cunningly devised falsifications adapted to the interests of the bourgeoisie, or with half-baked, unrealistic, pseudorevolutionary theories.
>
> Theories which are based on dogmas and cannot march in step with social development do become obsolete. But the historical fate of scientific communism has been and will be different. Marxism-Leninism is strong because it rests on revolutionary, materialistic dialectics, which always require a concrete analysis of the concrete situation. ... We preserve as a great achievement of social thinking all the knowledge [which] Marx, Engels, and Lenin have given us. We preserve it not as an archivist keeps old documents, but in a way befitting the heirs of this great theory, boldly employing this priceless treasure of knowledge in political practice, and constantly developing and multiplying the great theoretical wealth that has been handed down to us. We cannot advance unless we carry forward Marxism-Leninism. (*Pravda*, 4 November, and *IB*, no. 109, December.)

**4 November.** The second day of the joint session consisted primarily of speeches by foreign delegates (for listing see *Pravda*, 5 November). The meeting was chaired by Kosygin. Brezhnev gave a short concluding speech. On behalf of the joint meeting a message "To the Soviet People, to all Working People of the USSR" was issued by the Central Committee of the CPSU, the Presidium of the USSR Supreme Soviet, and the Council of Ministers of the USSR (see *Pravda*, 5 November, and *Documents*). Kosygin and Podgorny left for Leningrad to attend celebrations there on 5 November.

**5 November.** The main events of this day (see *Pravda*, 6 November) were the celebrations of the anniversary in Leningrad, Kiev, and Minsk, with various foreign delegates, who had not yet spoken in Moscow, addressing the meetings in these cities. At the same time, in Moscow, meetings were arranged in a number of industrial enterprises and in a military school, at which foreign delegates, accompanied by high-level CPSU and government representatives, gave speeches (see *Pravda*, 8 and 9 November). The head of the Cuban delegation, J. R. Machado Ventura, (Minister of Health and member of Central Committee) spoke at this time, but his speech was not reported in the Soviet press.

**6 November.** In Moscow a meeting took place on 6 November at the Kremlin's Palace of Congresses, sponsored by the Moscow City and Regional Committees of the Communist Party, and the Moscow City and Regional Councils of Workers' Deputies. The presidium of the meeting consisted of the highest Soviet party and government leaders, but without the republican leaders, who had left for their respective capitals to take part in parallel celebrations there. The meeting was addressed by both Soviet and foreign delegates.

**7 November.** The traditional military parade and demonstrations were held on November 7 in Red Square in Moscow. There was a notable emphasis on the historical aspects of the occasion—from the dress of some of the parade participants to the description of the event in *Pravda* (8 November), which portrayed Red Square (for the first time on such an occasion) in historical terms going back to the fourteenth century. The day and the celebrations ended with a banquet in the Kremlin, at which the main speech was given by Brezhnev.

* * *

**Anniversary Speeches.** Of the 74 foreign communist delegations at the anniversary celebrations, 68 made public statements, according to reports in the Soviet press. Considerable care was taken, evidently, to avoid controversial issues, both by foreign and by Soviet representatives. Of the Soviet speakers, only Brezhnev attacked Communist China and appealed for a world communist conference; these subjects were not mentioned by other Soviet speakers. The issue of China was avoided by most foreign delegates (only four joined Brezhnev in his criticism); while direct support for the convocation of a world conference of communist parties was expressed by only 16 speakers (including Brezhnev). Questions regarding the "cult of personality," Stalin, and Khrushchev were avoided by all speakers. Likewise, the term "peaceful coexistence" (associated with Khrushchev and the Twentieth Congress of the CPSU) was only used once—by the Secretary-General of the Italian Communist Party, Luigi Longo. In connection with the Middle East, attacks on Israel were relatively mild, the harshest criticism being voiced by the representative of the Israeli Communist Party (RAKAH), Meir Vilner. Soviet speakers made no reference to Cuba and the Cuban delegates were not invited to speak at any of the major events. Only five foreign delegates were reported as having mentioned Cuba in their speeches.

   **Foreign Representation.** Ninety-five countries were represented by delegations of the "Communist, workers', national liberation and democratic movement" (*Pravda*, 4 November). These in turn represented three categories: (1) the Communist parties, (2) the party-government delegations of Algeria, Congo (Brazzaville), Guinea, Mali, Syria, Tanzania and the UAR, and (3) the opposition parties and national liberation movements representing the extreme left.

   (1) *Communist Delegations.* (a) *Ruling Communist Parties:* Bulgaria—Bulgarian Communist Party (led by Todor Zhivkov, First Party Secretary and Prime Minister), Cuba—Cuban Communist Party (José Ramon Machado Ventura, Party Central Committee member and Minister of Health),

Czechoslovakia–Communist Party of Czechoslovakia (Antonin Novotný, First Party Secretary and President of the Republic), East Germany–Socialist Unity Party (Walter Ulbricht, First Party Secretary and Chairman of State Council), Hungary–Hungarian Socialist Workers' Party (János Kádár, First Party Secretary), Mongolia–Mongolian People's Revolutionary Party (Yumzhagiin Tsedenbal, First Party Secretary and Prime Minister), North Korea–Korean Workers' Party (Choe Yong-kon, Party Politburo member and President of the Presidium of the Supreme People's Assembly), North Vietnam–Vietnam Workers' Party (Le Duan, First Party Secretary), Poland–Polish United Workers' Party (Wladyslaw Gomulka, First Party Secretary), Rumania–Rumanian Communist Party (Nicolae Ceauşescu, Party Secretary-General) Yugoslavia–League of Communists of Yugoslavia (Josip Broz Tito, Party Chairman and President of the Republic).

(b) *Communist Parties of Western Europe:* Austria–Communist Party of Austria (Franz Muhri, Chairman), Belgium–Communist Party of Belgium (Ernest Burnelle, Chairman), Cyprus–Reconstruction Party of the Working People, "AKEL" (Ezekias Papaïoannou, General Secretary), Denmark–Communist Party of Denmark (Knud Jespersen, Chairman), Finland–Communist Party of Finland (Ville Pessi, Secretary-General), France–French Communist Party (Waldeck Rochet, Secretary-General), Germany: Federal Republic of Germany–Communist Party of Germany (Max Reimann, First Secretary), Germany: West Berlin–Socialist Unity Party of Germany-West Berlin (Gerhard Danelius, Chairman), Great Britain–Communist Party of Great Britain (John Gollan, General Secretary). Greece–Communist Party of Greece (Kostas Koliyannis, Secretary-General), Iceland–United Socialist Party of Iceland (Einar Olgeirsson, Chairman), Ireland–Irish Workers' Party (Michael O'Riordan, General Secretary), Ireland (Northern)–Communist Party of Northern Ireland (Andrew Barr, Chairman), Italy–Italian Communist Party (Luigi Longo, Secretary-General), Luxembourg-Communist Party of Luxembourg (Dominique Urbani, Chairman), Norway–Communist Party of Norway (Reidar Larsen, Chairman), Portugal–Portuguese Communist Party (Alvaro Cunhal, Secretary-General), San Marino–Communist Party of San Marino (Ermenegildo Gasperoni, Secretary-General), Spain–Communist Party of Spain (Dolores Ibarruri, Chairman), Sweden–Left Party Communists (Urban Karlsson, Party Secretary), Switzerland–Swiss Party of Labor (Edgar Woog, Secretary-General), Turkey–Communist Party of Turkey (Yakub Demir, Secretary-General).

(c) *Communist Parties of the Middle East.* Iran–Tudeh Party (Reza Radmanesh, Chairman), Iraq–Iraqi Communist Party (Nazim Ali, First Secretary), Israel–Israeli Communist Party, "RAKAH" (Meir Vilner, Secretary-General), Jordan–Communist Party of Jordan (Fuad Nassar, First Secretary), Lebanon–Lebanese Communist Party (Nicola Shawi, Secretary-General), Syria–Syrian Communist Party (Khalid Bakdash, Secretary-General).

(d) *Communist Parties of Latin America:* Argentina–Communist Party of Argentina (Victorio Codovilla, Chairman), Bolivia–Communist Party of Bolivia (delegation not named), Brazil–Brazilian Communist Party (delegation not named), Chile–Communist Party of Chile (Luis Corvalán, Secretary-General), Colombia–Communist Party of Colombia (Gilberto Vieira, Secretary-General), Costa Rica–People's Vanguard Party (Manuel Mora Valverde, First Secretary), Dominican Republic–Dominican Communist Party (Fabio García, believed to be Secretary-General), Ecuador–Communist Party of Ecuador (Pedro Saad, Secretary-General), El Salvador–Communist Party of El Salvador (delegation not named), Guadeloupe–Guadeloupe Communist Party (Evremond Gène, Secretary-General), Guatemala–Guatemalan Party of Labor (delegation not named), Haiti–People's Party of Unity (delegation not named), Honduras–Communist Party of Honduras (Carlos Aldana, Politburo member of one of two rival parties claiming the name Communist Party of Honduras, see *Honduras*), Martinique–Martinique Communist Party (Armand Nicolas, Secretary-General), Mexico–Mexican Communist Party (Arnoldo Martínez Verdugo, First Secretary), Nicaragua–Socialist Party of Nicaragua (delegation not named), Panama–People's Party of Panama (Rubén Dario Souza, Secretary-General), Paraguay–Paraguayan Communist Party (delegation not named), Peru–Peruvian Communist Party (Jorge del Prado, Secretary-General), Puerto Rico–Puerto Rican Communist Party (delegation not named), Uruguay–Communist Party of Uruguay (Rodney Arismendi, First Secretary), Venezuela–Communist Party of Venezuela (Jesús Faría,

Secretary-General).

(e) *Communist Parties of North America:* Canada—Communist Party of Canada (William Kashtan, General Secretary), United States of America—Communist Party of the United States of America (Gus Hall, General Secretary).

(f) *Communist Parties of the Maghreb and Subsaharan Africa:* Algeria—Algerian Communist Party (referred to in the Soviet press as "Algerian Communists"—delegation not named), Lesotho—Communist Party of Lesotho (delegation not named), Morocco—Moroccan Communist Party (Ali Yata, First Secretary), Réunion—Réunion Communist Party (Paul Vergès, Secretary-General), South Africa—Communist Party of South Africa (John Marks, Chairman), Sudan—Sudanese Communist Party (delegation not named), Tunisia—Tunisian Communist Party (Mohammed Harmel, Politburo and Secretariat member).

(g) *Communist Parties of Asia and Australasia:* Australia—Communist Party of Australia (Laurie Aarons, National Secretary), Ceylon—Ceylon Communist Party (Pieter Keuneman, General Secretary), India—Communist Party of India (Shripad A. Dange, Chairman), New Zealand-Socialist Unity Party (George Jackson, First Secretary).

(2) **Non-Communist Party-Government Delegations.** These were listed in the Soviet press as "Party-Government delegations of the Independent National States following the road of social progress" and consisted of: Algeria (led by Ahmed Kaid, member of the Revolutionary Council and Minister of Finance and Planning). Congo—Brazzaville (Claude de Costa, Secretary of the National Revolutionary Movement and Minister of National Reconstruction and Planning), Guinea (Saifoulaye Diallo, Politburo member of the Democratic Party and Minister of Finance and Planning), Mali (Mamadou Madeira Keita, member of the National Committee of the Defence of the Revolution and Minister of Justice and Labor), Syria (Ibrahim Makhous, member of the Ba'ath Party leadership and Deputy Prime Minister), Tanzania (Paul Bomani, Minister of Economy and Planning), United Arab Republic (Ali Sabri, Vice-President of the UAR and member of the Higher Executive Committee of the Arab Socialist Union).

(3) **Opposition Left-wing Parties and National Liberation Movements.** Angola—Popular Movement for the Liberation of Angola (led by Agostinho Neto, Chairman), Ceylon—Sri Lanka Freedom Party (M. Senanayake, Vice-President), Chile—Socialist Party (Salvador Allende, member of the leadership), Finland—Socialist League and Finnish People's Democratic League (Aarre Simonen, Chairman, and Ele Alenius, Chairman), Guyana—People's Progressive Party (Cheddi Jagan, Leader), India—United Socialist Party (S. M. Joshi, Chairman), Italy—Italian Socialist Party of Proletarian Unity and Movement of Autonomous Socialists (Tullio Vecchietti, Secretary-General, and Luigi Anderlini, member of Coordinating Committee), Japan—Japan Socialist Party (Yamamoto Koichi, Secretary-General), Lebanon—Socialist Progressive Party (Kamal Jumblat, Chairman), Mozambique—Liberation Front of Mozambique (Eduardo Mondlane, President), Norway—Socialist People's Party (Finn Gustavsen, member of the Central Committee), Portuguese Guinea—African Party of Independence of Guinea and the Cape Verde Islands (Amilcar Cabral, Secretary-General), Rhodesia—Zimbabwe African People's Union (George Nyandaro, General Secretary), Somali Republic—Somali Democratic Union (Yusuf Osman Samantar, Secretary), South Africa—African National Congress (Oliver Tambo, Deputy President), South Vietnam—National Liberation Front of South Vietnam (Dang Tran Thi, Presidium member), Sudan—People's Democratic Party (Ali Abdul Rahman, Chairman), Venezuela—Revolutionary Party of National Integration (Josef Vincente Rangel, Secretary-General).

\* \* \*

**Chronology of the Main Events in the Soviet Union in 1967 Connected with the Fiftieth Anniversary of the October Revolution.**

*5 January.* At a ceremony awarding the Order of Lenin to the Leningrad Region, M. Suslov, CPSU Politburo member and Secretary of the CPSU Central Committee, declares that the fiftieth anniversary celebrations will be one of the major events of the year.

*8 January. Pravda* publishes the Directives of the CPSU Central Committee on preparation for the anniversary.

*19 January.* The Moscow City officials of the Komsomol meet to discuss questions of ideological work, preparations of the Komsomol of Moscow for the anniversary, and the tasks of young people arising from the decisions of the December plenum of the CPSU Central Committee.

*20-21 January.* Session in Moscow of the Eleventh Plenum of the All-Union Central Council of Trade Unions of the USSR devoted to the subject, "The Tasks of the Trade Unions in the Preparations for the Fiftieth Anniversary of the Socialist Revolution."

*1-2 February.* The Third Plenary session of the Central Committee of the Komsomol is held in Moscow. Agenda includes discussion of measures for the participation of young communists and other young people in the preparations for the anniversary. The major speakers are S. Pavlov, First Secretary of the Komsomol Central Committee, and L. Brezhnev, Secretary-General of the CPSU Central Committee.

*28 February-2 March.* "All-Union Seminar of Publicists" is held. One of the principal topics discussed is the publicizing of the anniversary.

*28-31 March.* An international conference is held in Moscow on "The International Significance of the October Revolution," sponsored by the Soviet Academy of Sciences, the Institute of Marxism-Leninism, the Academy of Social Sciences of the CPSU Central Committee, and the Institute of the International Workers' movement. Some 500 Marxist scholars and foreign guests attend.

*12-15 April.* An international meeting is held in Moscow on the subject of "Leninism and the Problems of the International Workers' Movement," sponsored by the Institute of the International Workers' Movement. The conference centered around the subject of the anniversary and its influence on the workers' movement. Some 60 papers are presented, the policies of the Communist Chinese leadership are repeatedly condemned—more vehemently than is the case later, at the November celebrations.

*22-27 May.* The Fourth Soviet Writers' Congress takes place in Moscow (see *USSR*).

*25 June.* Publication of the theses of the Central Committee of the CPSU on the fiftieth anniversary (sse *Documents,* for section pertaining to international affairs, and *Pravda* 25 June).

*25-31 July.* An international youth meeting in Leningrad is devoted to the subject of the anniversary. Foreign delegations attend from 118 countries. Total number of participants is reported to have been 700, representing 300 youth groups and organizations.

*19-22 September.* An International conference is held in Baku on "The Great October Socialist Revolution and the National Liberation Movement of the Peoples of Asia, Africa and Latin America," with reported participation of more than 300 Soviet and foreign delegates.

*15 October.* Fiftieth-anniversary slogans are published on the front page of *Pravda* and other Soviet papers. The total number of slogans, 57, is considerably smaller than for previous October Revolution anniversaries. There are no appeals to individual countries or their parties; four slogans are addressed to workers in capitalist countries; and nine slogans are addressed to foreign "anti-imperialists," particularly in the developing countries. A slogan which in 1966 hailed the October Revolution as having inaugurated the era of the "establishment of Communism" this time refers to it as having inaugurated "the epoch of general revolutionary transformation of the world, of transition from capitalism to socialism." The Soviet trade unions, which in previous October slogans were greeted with Lenin's epithet of "schools of communism," are (in an apparent reflection of the Soviet economic reform and its needs) given the additional attribute of "schools of management and economic control."

*17 October.* The Central Statistical Agency publishes a report on the fulfillment of economic developments and construction projects for the first nine months of the year, planned for completion for the fiftieth anniversary. At the same time announcement is made of awards to republics, provinces, and regions for their services in development of socialist economy and culture in honor of the anniversary. Awards to industrial enterprises and state and collective farms, winners of a productivity competition in honor of the anniversary, are announced (*Pravda,* 22 October).

*30-31 October.* An "International Solemn Assembly of the World Federation of Trade Unions" is held in Leningrad, dedicated to the fiftieth anniversary.

*2-7 November.* Main celebrations of the anniversary of the October Revolution are held, primarily in Moscow, Leningrad, Kiev and Minsk (see above).

*11-15 November.* An international conference on "Fifty Years of October and the International Working Class" is held in Moscow, organized by the Institute of the International Workers' Movement. Attendance of foreign representatives from "more than 70 countries" is reported (*Pravda,* 12 November). On 11 November a one-day conference of the Komsomol, dedicated to the anniversary, is held in Moscow.

\* \* \*

**Other Fiftieth Anniversaries in the Soviet Union.** In addition to celebrations of the fiftieth anniversary of the October Revolution, 1967 witnessed the commemoration of a number of other events.

*25-26 October.* An international conference, sponsored by the Soviet Peace Committee (an affiliate of the World Council of Peace), is held in Leningrad to mark the fiftieth anniversary of Lenin's peace decree of 26 October (Julian Calendar). The conference is attended by representatives from 39 foreign countries.

*20 December.* An international conference is held in the Kremlin's Palace of Congresses in commemoration of the fiftieth anniversary of the Soviet security forces. The conference is attended by foreign representatives of security forces from all communist countries, except China and Albania. (For full text of the speech delivered by Iurii Andropov, head of the Soviet State Security Committee, see *Documents*).

*21-24 December.* Celebrations are held in Kiev commemorating the creation of the Ukrainian Republic, with the entire CPSU Politburo and the First Secretaries of all the republican communist parties in attendance. The Ukrainian Republic is awarded the Order of the October Revolution.

*29 December.* The establishment of the Soviet diplomatic service is commemorated in the Kremlin's Palace of Congresses, with the entire CPSU Politburo in attendance.

DOCUMENTS

# "LONG LIVE THE GREAT CHINESE PROLETARIAN CULTURAL REVOLUTION"

*Complete Text*
*(Rruga e Partisë,* Tirana, February 1967)

Today the attention of the entire world is focused with interest on the great Chinese proletarian cultural revolution that has taken the Chinese People's Republic by storm. This has given rise to two completely contradictory attitudes. While the communists and people of our country, in unity with the Marxist-Leninists and revolutionary peoples of the world, have expressed sympathy and given full support to this revolution, the imperialists, Soviet-led revisionists, and all reactionaries have condemned and attacked it most vehemently.

This is normal and surprises no one. The great Chinese proletarian cultural revolution is a struggle for the complete triumph of socialism and communism in the People's Republic of China in order to bar the way to revisionism and the return of capitalism; it is at the same time a vital component of the international proletarian revolution of today which has shaken the foundations of imperialism, modern revisionism, and international reaction.

## The Great Chinese Cultural Revolution Is Reaping Victories and Its Enemies Are Suffering Defeats

The Chinese cultural revolution is a bitter class struggle of life and death between two opposing ways, the socialist and the capitalist. It is a powerful movement of hundreds of millions of workers, peasants, soldiers, intellectuals, youth, students, and revolutionary cadres inspired and guided by the great Marxist-Leninist ideas of comrade Mao Tse-tung, a movement directed against all the forces of capitalism, acting openly or in secret, new and old, that are striving to restore capitalism in the People's Republic of China.

After their overthrow and the establishment of the dictatorship of the proletariat in China, the exploiting classes did not surrender their weapons and never ceased their resistance for the return of their "lost paradise." Their methods and the forms of the struggle changed to fit the conditions. After having failed in the armed conflict, they tried to capture the castle from within, secretly, and mostly through the revisionist elements which in some circumstances had gradually infiltrated and seized leading positions in the party and government. "After the annihilation of our armed enemies," stated comrade Mao Tse-tung, "there will still be unarmed enemies, who will never cease waging a life and death struggle against us." *(Selected Works,* Albanian Ed., Vol. 5, p 473.) Comrade Mao Tse-tung later says: "Even after the victory of the socialist revolution in our country there still remains a number of people who dream of bringing back the capitalist order; they continue to oppose the working class on all fronts, including the ideological. On this front the revisionists are their staunchest supporters." *(On the Correct Handling of Contradictions Among the People.)*

Taking advantage of their usurped position, bourgeois and revisionist elements tried to implement their opportunistic, counterrevolutionary, and capitalist policy in all areas and make it the ruling policy of the party, government, and country. They have tried to prevent the spreading of the revolutionary ideas of comrade Mao Tse-tung among communists and the masses, distort the content of these ideas, preach revisionist views in various ways, spread the opportunistic concept of class reconciliation, deny class struggle in a socialist society, and degrade the dictatorship of the proletariat from a revolutionary weapon in the hands of the working masses into a revisionist and counterrevolutionary dictatorship that opposes the masses and serves the restoration of capitalism; they have done all they could to safeguard their positions, privileges, capitalist profits, and other remnants of the exploiting classes, advocated the revisionist method of profit and stimuli for the development of the socialist economy, opposed the principle of self-reliance in the development of a national Chinese economy, denied the proletarian principle of partisanship in cultural and artistic creativity and the class struggle in this area, defended and supported feudal and bourgeois reactionary methods, concepts, and cultural works, favored surrender to bourgeois "authority," tried to restrain the development of the new revolutionary culture of the proletariat, and attempted to stop the armed struggle of the revolutionary peoples against imperialism and other reactionary forces as well as the principled struggle of the Chinese Communist Party and other Marxist-Leninist parties against the treachery of the modern revisionists, especially the revisionist leadership of the Soviet Union.

But they failed to achieve their goals and suffered a great defeat. Revolutionary forces, under the Marxist-Leninist leadership of comrade Mao Tse-tung, unleashed the great proletarian cultural revolution. Bourgeois and revisionist ideas were subjected to vehement criticism of principle in all areas—philosophy, economic policy, journalism, history, literature, the performing arts, etc. An immense movement of millions of workers, peasants, soldiers, and revolutionary intellectuals to study the ideas of comrade Mao Tse-tung as a guide for action and to implement them rapidly developed in the People's Republic of China.

In the process of the cultural revolution, revisionist and counterrevolutionary elements were exposed and were taken to the revolutionary courts of the masses. The revolutionary drive that enveloped all China produced a new form of revolutionary struggle—the movement of the Red Guards and revolutionary workers, etc., who, led by the teachings of comrade Mao Tse-tung and with his direct support and under the guidance of the party, made and are making a valuable contribution to the purging of society of all remnants of the past and all decay and reaction and constitute the vanguard of the struggle for the advancement of the socialist revolution in the People's Republic of China.

It was a great victory for the Marxist-Leninist revolutionary policy of Mao Tse-tung and a hard blow for the enemies of Marxism-Leninism, the revolution, and socialism, states the 11th Plenum of the Central Committee of the Chinese Communist Party. It unmasked and destroyed the revisionist elements who were preparing a counterrevolutionary attack, established the directions for the further development and intensification of the great cultural revolution, and strengthened the stand and determined struggle against imperialism, led by American imperialism, and modern revisionism, centered in the renegade leadership of the CPSU.

But despite these hard blows, the enemies of the revolution refuse to accept defeat, still continue their resistance, and are attempting a counterattack. They tried in various ways and through demagogy and violent acts to restrain and subdue the movement of the revolutionary masses. They tried to arouse the masses against the great cultural revolution and to deceive and corrupt the workers with "economism" by artificially raising wages. They tried to sabotage production, disorganize the supplying of the people with consumer goods, and sow dissatisfaction among the workers.

But even these counterrevolutionary acts completely failed. They received a smashing blow in Shanghai where the revolutionary movement, which spread quickly throughout China, first exploded. The united revolutionary organizations of the working class and revolutionary people of Shanghai threw a powerful counterblow at the bourgeois and revisionist elements and took power into their own hands; they took the newspapers away from the counterrevolutionaries and turned them into effective weapons of the revolution; they resolutely unmasked "economism" and are carrying out comrade Mao Tse-tung's appeal to combine the cultural revolution successfully with production. The events in Shanghai, which were greeted with enthusiasm by all the workers of our country, are vitally important to the great Chinese cultural revolution and mark a new and better era; they show that the heroic working class of China, the decisive force of the socialist revolution, has resolutely risen and directly leads and protects the revolution. In alliance with the working class, the colossal force of hundreds of millions of Chinese peasants has also risen in support of this great cultural revolution. This is the most distinct proof of the total defeat of the bourgeois, revisionist, and counterrevolutionary forces and the greatest guarantee of the total victory of the great cultural revolution in China.

The exposing and defeat of bourgeois and revisionist elements in China and the brilliant victories won by the great cultural revolution are a hard blow, not only against the positions of the bourgeoisie, revisionism, and counterrevolution in China, but also against imperialism, revisionism, and international reaction, against the anti-socialist and anti-Chinese conspiracies of American imperialism, the Soviet revisionist leadership, Chiang Kai-shek's clique, and other reactionaries. Their dreams of undermining the People's Republic of China from within in order to repeat there the revisionist tragedy of the Soviet Union of the post-Stalin era failed shamefully. It was precisely this defeat that forced the traitorous leadership of the CPSU to abandon the "silent strategy" for the aborted Khrushchevite strategy of open attack with the hope of discrediting the great Chinese cultural revolution and the ideas of Mao Tse-tung, isolating the Chinese Communist Party and the People's Republic of China from the world communist movement and the international arena, and frightening and alienating the revolutionary peoples from them. But these hopes were never realized and never will be. The great Chinese cultural revolution has the ardent revolutionary support of the entire world; it has inspired and encouraged peoples to rise up in national liberation wars to overthrow the capitalist, imperialist, and colonial order of exploitation and oppression.

This revolution is a particularly good example for all workers where revisionist cliques are in power of how to rise courageously in a revolutionary war to overthrow the revisionists, seize the power they have usurped, and pass it to the revolutionary people, the followers of true Marxism-Leninism.

## Historical Lessons of the Great Proletarian Cultural Revolution

The great Chinese cultural revolution that is taking place in China illuminated by the teachings of comrade Mao Tse-tung is a precious contribution to the theory and practice of scientific socialism; its experience is of great value to all Marxist-Leninists and world revolutionaries in their struggle for socialism and to lead socialism to its complete and final victory. What are the historical lessons of the Chinese proletarian cultural revolution?

1. It very clearly shows that the class struggle is inevitable, even in a socialist society, and constitutes one of its most important moving forces. It is in fact a struggle between two opposing paths—the socialist and the capitalist—a struggle for the advancement of the socialist revolution and the building of socialism and communism until their complete and final victory and to bar the way to the restoration of capitalism. Because, as has already been proven by the historical development of socialist society, the danger of returning to capitalism through outside agression and armed counterrevolution from within the socialist countries, that is, through counterrevolutionary violence and through "peaceful evolution," through a gradual bourgeois and revisionist deterioration of the socialist order, does exist.

Such a class struggle between the forces of

socialism and capitalism evolves on many fronts and in various forms which in some instances can become ruthless. Of vital importance to the fate of socialism is the class struggle in the areas of ideology and culture. Socialism and communism cannot triumph merely by overthrowing the exploiting classes and establishing the dictatorship of the proletariat or by expropriating the bourgeoisie and other exploiters and reorganizing the economy on a socialist basis. It is equally necessary to subdue and destroy the ideological influences of the exploiting classes inherited from the old society and fed by the various enemies of socialism within the country as well as by the hostile capitalist world; it is necessary to radically transform the people's awareness of the foundations of communist ideology, that is, to carry the socialist revolution into the areas of ideology and culture. In these areas the class struggle is more subtle, more difficult, more complicated, and longer. "The class struggle between the proletariat and the bourgeoisie between various political forces and between proletarian and bourgeois ideologies," emphasized comrade Mao Tse-tung, "will last long, will have its ups and downs, and at times could become ruthless. The proletariat seeks to transform the world according to its own concept and the bourgeoisie according to its own concept. From this standpoint, the question of which will win, socialism or capitalism, has not been completely solved." *(On the Correct Handling of Contradictions Among the People.)*

All the enemies of socialism within or outside a country—the imperialists, the international bourgeoisie, and all counterrevolutionary elements—in their attempt to eliminate the dictatorship of the proletariat and restore capitalism in the socialist countries seek first to sow confusion in the minds of the people, disseminate their poisonous ideology, promote an ideological counterrevolution, prepare the terrain for political counterrevolution, and seize power. This is how the traitorous clique of the Soviet Union acted; this is how the Hungarian counterrevolutionaries acted in 1956; and this is how the bourgeois and revisionist elements acted in China. Therefore, intelligent ideological vigilance and the correct ideological and cultural class struggle are vitally important to the cause of socialism and the promotion of socialism and to barring the way to revisionism and the restoration of capitalism. These are the most important aspects of the great Chinese cultural revolution.

2. The developments of the cultural revolution in China clearly show that, in order to promote socialism and communism successfully and to prevent the deterioration of the socialist order and the return of capitalism, it is strictly necessary for the proletarian party which guides the entire life of the country to take a Marxist-Leninist stand, protect its ranks, and never lose its revolutionary characteristics. This is extremely important. The experience of many years, including the bitter experience of the CPSU, shows that the enemies of the socialist order have directed their blows primarily against the revolutionary proletarian parties by trying to infiltrate their ranks, weaken them from within, and convert them into

counterrevolutionary tools. This experience also proves that there is a danger that during peaceful construction the party and its cadres can fall into bureaucracy and slowly lose their revolutionary features and thus create favorable conditions for bourgeois and revisionist elements to emerge, spread, and usurp the leadership of the party and government.

For this reason, supreme ideo-political vigilance towards all foreign currents and tendencies appearing in the party, a merciless war of principle against every opportunistic deviation in its ranks, whether of the right or of the left, the safeguarding and implementation of the party's Leninist norms and principles, and the purging of the anti-Marxist, revisionist, and bourgeois elements that may have infiltrated or formed in the party's ranks becomes necessary in order to preserve the purity of the party so it can lead the revolution and the building of socialism with a strong hand. One of the fundamental objectives of the Chinese cultural revolution was precisely the purging of the revolutionary party from the bourgeois and revisionist elements who had infiltrated it and were trying to destroy it from within in order to use it as a tool for the restoration of capitalism in China.

3. The experience of the great Chinese cultural revolution, as the previous experiences of socialism, shows that the question of the state regime, the dictatorship of the proletariat, continues to be a basic question in a socialist society because the essence of the class struggle under socialist conditions, including the ideological and cultural struggle, is in fact the struggle for political power, whether for the preservation and consolidation of the dictatorship of the proletariat as the principal instrument for the promotion of the revolution and socialist and communist construction or its degeneration into an antipopular regime and a tool of counterrevolution for the restoration of capitalism. The principal political objectives of the enemies of socialism, whether overt or clandestine, are the political overthrow of the dictatorship of the proletariat through violence or its "peaceful" degeneration and the seizure of power.

Consequently, it is very clear that the struggle to preserve and continually strengthen the dictatorship of the proletariat and to protect it from falling into bureaucracy and becoming alienated from and even in opposition to the masses—the struggle by state organs to continually purge all hostile and anti-socialist elements, revisionists, and bureaucrats who may make their way into them and sometimes succeed in seizing key positions—must always occupy the immediate attention of the Marxist-Leninist proletarian party which must mobilize and lead the broad masses of cities and villages in this vital struggle. The great Chinese cultural revolution, which is directed against the bourgeois and revisionist elements who have usurped leading party and government positions, is nothing less than the bitter struggle of the millions of revolutionary masses under the guidance of the Chinese Communist Party and the enlightened teachings of comrade Mao Tse-tung to remove these enemies from the government, to pass the power of the state into the hands of the revolutionaries, and to further safeguard, consolidate, and revolutionize the dictatorship of the proletariat and its entire apparatus in China.

4. One of the most profound lessons of the great Chinese cultural revolution is that it shows that the revolution and socialist construction can be constantly advanced and that the way to revisionism and the restoration of capitalism can be checked only if the broad masses of the workers are fully aware of the struggle and if they, under the leadership of the Marxist-Leninist party, take the fate of the revolution and socialism into their own hands. And on the contrary, the defeat of socialism and the restoration of capitalism become inevitable if the masses of the people fall into political indifference and apathy, if they are not molded and continue to live with the great ideas of the revolution, if their revolutionary vigilance ceases, and if they are allowed to be fooled by revisionist demagogy.

This makes it necessary for the party of the working class to implement the policy of the masses in the revolution and socialist construction. This requires that the revolutionary party of the working class have confidence in the revolution and socialist construction and in the revolutionary spirit and creative abilities of the working class, rely completely on the masses, encourage them, and unsparingly support their revolutionary movements and actions. Distrust of the masses, fear of their revolutionary drive, and attempts to limit and control their actions from "above" and act as their "guardians" are alien to Marxist-Leninists and greatly harm the cause of socialism since they lead to the emergence of bureaucracy and create the danger of the deterioration of the dictatorship of the proletariat which is the broadest and most complete democracy for the workers and since a government which stands above the people and contradicts them can create favorable conditions for the seizure of power by bourgeois and revisionist elements. By taking an active part in the revolution and in the struggle to build socialism, the masses develop a taste for ideology and self-educate and equip themselves with revolutionary experience. This is quite clearly shown by the Chinese cultural revolution which is an unparalleled example of hundreds of millions of people under the leadership of the communist party and the ideas of Mao Tse-tung carrying out the revolutionary struggle and establishing revolutionary control.

But in order to promote a self-operating revolutionary movement of the broad working masses and make them aware and capable of playing a decisive role in advancing and defending the cause of socialism, it is necessary that they be educated and molded with the ideas of Marxism-Leninism. Thus, once these ideas are available to the masses they can be turned into a colossal material force for the transformation of the world. Equipped with these ideas, revolutionary workers, peasants, youth, and intellectuals will be able to strengthen their political and ideological vigilance and resist and fight successfully the danger of revisionism and the "peaceful" degeneration of the socialist order. The powerful movement of hundreds of millions of people to study and implement the great ideas of Mao Tse-tung and their active participation in the great cultural revolution and in the struggle for the elimination of bourgeois and revisionist elements and their counterrevolutionary ideas are a splendid example.

5. The education of the new generation through their active participation in revolutionary activities is one of the important teachings of the great Chinese cultural revolution. This is the most vital to the progress of socialism, precisely because it is the youth who will carry the baton of the revolution and socialism. The question is whether the young generation is properly trained for this historical mission, inspired and molded by revolutionary ideals, aware of the interests of socialism and the people, and ready to make any sacrifice for the complete triumph of the cause of revolution and socialism in their own country and throughout the world or whether it is infected by bourgeois, petit bourgeois, and revisionist morality and ideology and leans towards egoism, individualism, personal comfort, and profit—upon all these will in the end depend the destiny of socialism, that is, whether in the future it marches with determination on the road of socialism and communism and whether the cause of revolution is carried to total and final victory or whether society will march in reverse towards the restoration of capitalism.

The Red Guard movement, by assimilating and implementing the ideas of Mao Tse-tung and inspired by revolutionary ideals, stands in the vanguard of the great Chinese cultural revolution; it is at war with its enemies who are trying to turn back the clock of socialism in China; it is being molded in a real revolutionary atmosphere and has become a splendid example; it is a worthy generation and a stalwart guarantee that the cause of revolution and socialism in the great People's Republic of China will march unrestrained in the future.

These are some of the key teachings of the great Chinese cultural revolution which have drawn the attention of Marxist-Leninists and all true fighters for the cause of socialism in every part of the world.

The successful development of the great cultural revolution in the People's Republic of China is a great historical victory for the forces of revolution and socialism both in China and throughout the world against the forces of capitalism, imperialism, reaction, and modern revisionism. This is understandable, because China and its glorious communist party led by a great Marxist-Leninist of our era, comrade Mao Tse-tung, is the principal fortress of socialism and a strong pillar of the revolutionary war of all the peoples of the world. This is why the Marxist-Leninists and revolutionary peoples of the entire world have given their full support to the revolution that is taking place in China and hail it with the cry: "Long live the great Chinese proletarian cultural revolution!"

# ON THE FURTHER REVOLUTIONIZATION OF THE PARTY AND REGIME

Speech by Enver Hoxha at a Joint Meeting of Tirana Basic Party Organizations, 6 February 1967

*Excerpts*

We are engaged in a great, continuous, and very successful struggle to further revolutionize the party. The revolutionization of the party means to revolutionize the communists. They should be steel-like militants, politically lucid, courageous, affectionate, frank, sincere, and also harsh when necessary. They should destroy every bad thing and support, organize, and fight in the forefront for the progressive and new.

Our task is to constantly temper the party so that it can always be a militant, dynamic, and vigorous party, free of mistakes and weaknesses. To this end it is essential to bring new blood into the ranks of the party and to accept new members from the ranks of the working class, the toiling peasantry, and the most remarkable revolutionary elements of the intelligentsia. The statute approved at the Fifth Party Congress clearly determines the conditions needed for admission to the party and the measures to be applied for preparation of candidates.

The task of the basic organizations is to explain and to understand these demands and their aims. If the party's directives concerning the admission in the party are properly explained and correctly understood, it would be clear that the new requirements of the statute do not close the party's doors; on the contrary, they open them. But for whom? For the best elements, for the revolutionaries; they should close the doors to those who do not deserve it.

The people admitted to the party come from various classes of our society, from the workers' class, from cooperative farmers, from white-collar workers, from intellectuals, and other strata. But, despite all this, our party is not an arena of classes in which every class, according to its numerical strength, has its own representatives who defend the particular interests of their individual class. No! In our party the hegemony belongs to the workers' class, with its ideology, Marxism-Leninism, regardless of the fact that the percentage of members of workers' origin or with worker status, for reasons which we know, may at the time being be smaller than that of the members of peasant origin.

The organized detachment of the workers' class in our party, that is, our workers' class, is not an arena, either, in which a class struggle in the classic meaning of the word is being waged. It is the party which directs the class struggle. This means that our party is a monolithic party with a steel-like Marxist-Leninist unity of opinion and action which does not tolerate anti-Marxist, revisionist, Trotskyite, liberal, social democrat, and other factions or opposition in its ranks.

The party has determined its strategy and tactics, always based on Marxist-Leninist theory and on the objective circumstances of our country, caused by the particularities and the time, analyzed in the light of dialectical and historical materialism. Thus, tactics of the party, too, can neither evade nor twist these principles. On this basis, the party has determined its own norms for reaching the target, that is, its program of building socialism, a classless society, and communism. This can only be achieved under the hegemony of the workers' class led by its organized Marxist-Leninist detachment, the Communist Party, or in our country, the Workers' Party.

Why are perfect organization, iron discipline, and Bolshevik norms necessary in the party? They are necessary because they are, so to speak, the party's cement. The party is not an accumulation of people without ideology, without criteria, and without goals, or with opposing or confused criteria and goals, who have come together to attend a wedding. No! The Albanian Workers' Party was formed and involved in a struggle so terrific as neither mankind nor our people had ever seen before. The fate of our people was at stake and only a Marxist-Leninist party like ours was capable of saving them, as it truly did.

Therefore, our party was an invincible sharp and sparkling sword in the hands of the workers' class and the Albanian people. This sword has become such because it was forged with Marxism-Leninism and because it was tempered with the struggle and the norms which the party had set itself. Thus, under the leadership of the party, the national liberation struggle was won, our people's revolution was carried out, and socialism is being successfully built today. The party will fulfill its lofty task even when the communist society is constructed in our country and when the proletarian revolution is victorious all over the world.

In the Soviet Union and other countries of the people's democracy many things have happened which have led to the overthrow of the socialist regime and to the degeneration of their parties. Why did these things not happen in our country as well? For the above-mentioned reasons and precisely for these reasons they will never happen in the future, either. Is there not a continuous imperialist-revisionist coalition against the Albanian Workers' Party and socialist Albania? This coalition is certainly in action, but we, too, have been and continue to be on our guard. We have measured with them and have been victorious, and again we will measure with them and be victorious. It will always happen thus. Therefore, in the final analysis, the victory will belong to us, that is, to our people and our party.

Modern revisionists and reaction used to call us

"Stalinists," thinking that by this they abuse us, or at least this was their goal. However, on the contrary, they praised us by this epithet, because we are proud of being Stalinist, and because by being and remaining Stalinists, we cannot and will never be defeated by the enemies.

The party kept its ranks pure, as the ranks of a proletarian party should be, a party which must go through a thousand dangers to achieve its final goal. The party never wavered on this vital question, always bearing in mind that the enemies, in order to subdue the people, had to subdue the party in the first place and, therefore, were continuously waging a coordinated struggle against it inside and outside its ranks.

A Marxist-Leninist party which is respected as such cannot tolerate the existence of two roads within the party. Therefore it cannot tolerate the existence of one or several factions. When things like this manifest themselves, the party cannot and must not tolerate their existence for any length of time. A faction in the party is in contradiction to the Marxist-Leninist principle of unity of opinion and action and tends to turn the party into a social democrat party and a socialist country into a capitalist country.

Relying on the historic decisions of the fifth congress which guide us in our work, and relying on the open letter of the Central Committee of the Albanian Workers' Party and the appeal of the Central Committee and the government, which have become remarkable events in the work of the communists and the broad masses and which produced such great positive results in the revolutionization of all work, allow me to express certain other thoughts in connection with the uninterrupted struggle which we have to wage against bureaucratism and its protagonists.

Bureaucratism, which develops in concrete forms and assumes frightful forms, is inspired by idealistic concepts which develop and take various forms to serve feudalism, the bourgeoisie, and the capitalists, dominating the masses in order to oppress them and exploit them completely. Bureaucratism is then a form of thinking and acting in open contradiction to the people and their vital interests.

Therefore, bureaucratism and the bureaucrats are antipeople and the enemies of the people. The concepts which form bureaucratism and the bureaucrats are idealistic, reactionary, antirevolutionary, and anti-Marxist.

Therefore, bureaucratism and the bureaucrats are the most cunning enemies of the Marxist-Leninist party, whose constant task is to struggle mercilessly and tirelessly against all their manifestations and, above all, to destroy their political and ideological concepts, as well as the organizational or structural system which they have established or which they are trying to keep alive in various forms and means.

The peoples and the masses of the world are educated and directed in two ways: where the revolution has won, the masses are educated in a revolutionary way; where capital is the master, the masses are educated in a bureaucratic way. In the first society, the socialist society, the people are in power, a proletarian dictatorship has been established, and the Marxist-Leninist party is in power—the line of the party and the masses is in force.

Here is to be found profound and real democracy for the broad masses, and here there is no democracy for the reactionary and oppressive minority, the enemy of the masses, which has lost all its force and which, through the struggle of the classes and proletarian dictatorship, should be subjected to a constantly stable pressure and great vigilance. In the countries where capital dominates there is democracy for the capitalists, the oppressors, and exploiters. Here is a state of oppression for the majority, the masses, and the people. These countries are dominated by a bourgeois dictatorship, a fascist dictatorship, subjected to the regime of bureaucracy.

Thus, there are two concepts which can direct us: the antipeople bureaucratic concept and the people's revolutionary concept. The one wages a life and death struggle against the other. Where the revolution is victorious, bureaucratism has lost the first battle, but it has not yet given up its weapons and continues to struggle in other forms which have their source in the traditions of past regimes, for whose old sins we are still paying today. In particular they have their source in the mentality, prejudices, and world outlook of people.

We have shattered to its very foundations the old bureaucratic regime of the feudal bourgeoisie and of fascism and have established the dictatorship of the proletariat and the rule of the people's councils. But we cannot say that in our new people's rule the old method of working will not manifest itself in one form or other. It is a fact that during the past two decades we have modernized our regime, made it more democratic, and brought it much nearer to the popular masses, but still we have to wage a continuous struggle to insure that our regime is democratic not only in its form and structure but primarily in its inner substance.

To be able to struggle successfully against bureaucratism and bureaucrats we must profoundly understand and resolutely implement the party directives, in particular in connection with the principles "the rule belongs to the masses," "as near as possible to the masses," "broad mass democracy," and so forth.

Some comrades think that they understand and implement these principles well, but their practice reveals just the opposite. They believe that the regime is democratic, because there are elections and that this is enough. Elections take place in bourgeois democracies, too, and discussions take place in bourgeois democracies. However, the deputies there not only are not men of the people, although formally they are elected by the people by means of thousands of tricks, but are men of the bourgeoisie, serving the bourgeoisie in order to defend and replenish the safes of the capitalists with the blood and sweat of the people. These deputies legalize repressive means in order to remain in power and to strengthen an antipeople, antidemocratic, and bureaucratic regime. This is a regime of the gallows and rope and of moral and political corruption.

Thus, elections in our country and their elections are diametrically opposed in principle, substance, goals, and actions. In our country their essence is peopleminded and revolutionary; the deputies of the councils and the people's assembly are men of the people, linked with the people, and elected by the people. They make revolutionary laws in the interest of the people and, together with the people, they implement these laws, directives, and the revolutionary socialist norms.

The will of the broad people's masses is sovereign and can abolish these laws and directives, and correct or alter them if they deem them unsuitable, obsolete, or erroneous. The role and task of a deputy in our people's democracy consists not merely in having formal contact with his voters once or twice a year and in implementing in a bureaucratic way the decrees and decisions of the people's assembly; at the same time he is a deputy and member of the great mass of people who not only implement, but also create, decide, discuss, criticize, oppose, and alter.

The bureaucrat is afraid of the masses and of the work with the masses; when he is compelled to go among the masses, he is exigent and shows his power, trying to impress the masses by his power, that is, by the function which he holds. Thus he deforms the democratic and revolutionary essence of the state power and of the laws. He violates democracy, suppresses criticism, and allegedly defends the justice of a directive or a law or the authority of the party and the state. In fact, he does just the opposite: He debases the authority of the party and the state, and, by his dark, hidden, and sometimes even open endeavors, he makes the masses cooler toward the party and detaches them from the party.

How can a Marxist-Leninist party be afraid of the masses, of their voice and their criticism? A party which is afraid cannot be called Marxist-Leninist. It is never the party which is afraid; it is certain individuals, some members of the party, some state officials, and some bureaucrats who are afraid of the masses. They are the ones who hide behind the authority of the party. We must crush these people, and their crushing must be carried out in a revolutionary manner by the party and the masses at the same time.

Comrade communists, comrade workers, must we permit the kind of people, who, under the cover of the name of the party or the cover of their state functions, violate the laws of our proletarian revolution, deform the life-giving and revolutionary norms of the party, and tarnish the proletarian dictatorship with bombastic words which hide bad actions? Certainly not, because then we would have signed the death warrant of our people.

Comrade workers, would we allow ourselves to please such people and harm the great cause of the people? Absolutely not. Can it ever be imagined that the mass of the people, headed by the party, need fear this kind of maggoty people? Can it be imagined that the working class and its glorious Workers' Party need be afraid? Not even for a second can such a thing be imagined. But we must also not think that these people, because they are few, cannot harm us and, therefore, we need not put them in the iron tongs of dictatorship so that they either improve or they disappear.

We must never forget the tragedy of the Soviet Union. Headed by the party and the working class, the people's masses must always be on their feet for anything in order to defend the proletarian dictatorship and its laws, ideology, policy, and achievements. This is the only correct, healthy, and curative path taught by our party, which advises us all without exception to follow it to the end.

There are two roads, that is, either with the party and people, or against them. Therefore nothing should be permitted outside the laws and norms of the party and people. Nothing should escape the vigilant eye of the party and people. No one should be allowed to avoid accounting for his work to the party and people and receive from the party and people what he deserves.

Basic party organizations should end restrained, superficial, and formal criticism. The reason for this is apparent. We say that no criticism is made at the basic party organization because of fear. If this then is the case, it means that the collective of the basic party organization is not in a position to dispel the feeling of individual fear. In this case, let us then shift this responsibility to the collective outside the basic party organization in order to fight successfully for dismissing individual and collective fear in that basic party organization where a malignant thing of this kind prevails.

The current very ridiculous wall newspapers should be abolished and turned into revolutionary wall newspapers to serve a revolutionary education. Editorial boards of those newspapers which are composed of opportunistic editors who defend the honor and the authority of the director presumably of an enterprise and their own, should be dismissed, and thus everybody should fearlessly and in big letters write what he thinks of work and people. It is also said that the authority of the cadres should be protected because if we do not act in this way our cadres will be discredited. This means that those who harbor this kind of thought agree in advance that cadres are infallible and that the masses are wrong in their judgment. To think in this way is to commit a grave mistake. It means thinking not as a Marxist and revolutionary. Nobody can criticize the cadre who does his job properly; on the contrary, he is loved and protected.

Bureaucrats conceal their ignorance through bombastic words and phrases. They use their long tenure in leading posts as personal capital. They reach the conclusion that they have become inviolate and irreplaceable. They think they have built enough of a reputation in their environment about their own ability, and they envisage no risk whatever of being demoted, transferred, or anything of the sort. They think only about being promoted, about nothing else, and they work toward this goal.

Such a nonrevolutionary mentality creates in them a feeling of stability in the post they occupy, and confidence in their infallibility in work and perfection in method and style of work, which results in this state of affairs. Thus they reach a point of following a way of thinking and living in their family and in society like that of a new bourgeois element in our people's democracy.

This is very dangerous. If we fail to stem his views, the bureaucrat, under the cover of his authority, will spread them and infect others as well. Therefore, I think that, in addition to the political and ideological indoctrination of the cadres and masses in general and the numerous forms of the struggle against bureaucratic manifestations, we should study more seriously and implement more correctly the rotation of cadres, because we have cadres who have been vegetating for more than 10 to 15 years at the same place and who willy-nilly have acquired some of the characteristics of the people that I mentioned above. Their replacement by men from the base will benefit the party and regime at the high level and the base, and men who go from an upper position to a lower one will also benefit.

Of course, not all of them will ardently wish to go. But we should be convinced that we are acting properly, because we thus fight the nonrevolutionary views manifested in them. We will cure them. When moving from one place to another, a worker or a cooperative member is not greatly affected. He never fears work and life in general. He is used to difficulties. Wherever he may be, he earns his bread through sweat. But the intellectual and official finds it difficult to move for many reasons. First, because he has created in himself the view of intellectualism and officialdom, and, second, there is the question of salary and the question of financial treatment. These two views, which are not manifested among the workers and peasants, should be fought among the intellectuals and officials.

Knowledge, science, and intelligence are not the property only of people who have special brains or particular virtues, and it is not only they who are in a position to teach and order others to implement. It is the broad masses who create, build, and transform the world and society, and, when they do this, it means that they deserve the credit having placed themselves at the general service of the society. Thus the credit belongs to the masses who work, think, create, and implement, and again think and create.

Therefore, we must fight the view of those who have a certain amount of knowledge but utilize it to impose their ego on others. This is a bourgeois and reactionary view; equally bourgeois and reactionary is the view of officialdom when it is meant to hide what is wrong in man, that is, his anti-Marxist, antirevolutionary and bureaucratic world outlook and actions.

For a worker and peasant it is quite clear that his income is linked with work and sweat, while the functionary links his salary both with work and with his job. Therefore, his willingness or unwillingness to change his place will depend on whether he is promoted or demoted, that is, whether his salary goes up or down through the change.

Of course, it would not be just to pay personal salaries to people who for reasons of work go from higher places to lower ones. However, in the general interests, we would be even more courageous in setting

about diminishing the gap between the wages of workers and employees and between various categories of employees. This is a correct Marxist-Leninist path. It is also Marxist-Leninist that these measures are accompanied by the creation of economic abundance.

All this sets great tasks for the party of further revolutionizing its work. The great success achieved in our party must not intoxicate us so that we close our eyes to the shortcomings and weaknesses which must not be neglected. It would be very harmful if we failed to deepen even more and implement without fear the policy of the masses and the true democracy of the masses, and if we failed to deepen and implement to the end, correctly, and in a revolutionary way, democratic—and not bureaucratic—centralism, Bolshevik criticism and self-criticism, proletarian discipline, and proletarian morality.

To strengthen the party, we must proceed along this correct path so that the head, heart, and body of the party of socialism, and of our people are always free from pain. For this we have every possibility, because our party is strong and forged, and has great revolutionary experience, and because we have courageous and heroic party members and wonderful people closely linked with the party.

# "ALLIANCE OF ANTI-IMPERIALIST FORCES IN LATIN AMERICA"

Article by Luis Corvalán, General Secretary,
Communist Party of Chile

*Complete Text*
*(World Marxist Review,* July 1967)

## 1.

The fight against imperialist domination and against the oppression of local oligarchies, tense and arduous, diverse in form but single in content and ultimate aim, is gaining momentum in Latin America.

Latin Americans are on the road to national and social liberation, democracy and socialism. Their fight for freedom is conditioned by the need for social progress; their ship is sailing before the wind of history.

True, they have to contend with imperialism's aim of maintaining its grip on the continent and with the aim of the oligarchies to perpetuate their privileges. So the inevitable conflict between the two forces is in full swing. The time of grand battles has come, battles which will be won despite all the vicissitudes.

North American imperialism is resorting to undisguised intervention. Its system of military pacts and missions, anti-guerrilla training centers and units of "green berets," "black berets" and Rangers is a form of armed aggression. President Johnson has stated he will stop at nothing to prevent any other country from following Cuba's example. The imperialists are prepared to sow death and destruction in town and village, flouting international law as they did at Playa Giron and Santo Domingo, and as they are doing every day in Vietnam.

The independence of every Latin American country is in jeopardy. The road to salvation, to a happy future, is that of battle.

The Latin American peoples must unite in defense of their sovereignty and right to self-determination. As pointed out by the Thirteenth Congress of our Party, "the supreme task, the task of tasks, is to frustrate the aggressive designs of the imperialists. The fight for revolutionary reconstruction and people's rule blends with the fight against U.S. intervention, for sovereignty, self-determination and peace."

The historical mission of the proletariat is to abolish capitalism and build socialism, while the specific tasks may change in accordance with changes in the international situation. In the 'thirties,' when Hitler Germany was the center of world reaction, the task was to rally all forces against fascism in defense of freedom. Now that U.S. imperialism is the main reactionary force, the task is to enlist all forces against the imperialist policy of war and aggression, for the liberation of colonial, neo-colonial and dependent countries, for peace and peaceful coexistence, fusing these efforts with the fight for the social reconstruction imperative in every country.

One or another specific aspect of the world wide struggle against imperialism comes to the fore, depending on what the adversary is doing in the particular area at the particular moment. Yet every area of battle is part of the single historical movement.

The October Revolution in Russia, the 50th anniversary of which we celebrate this year, marked the beginning of the end of capitalist domination. It ushered in the socialist era, the time of the liberation of the working class and of peoples oppressed by imperialism.

Today, socialism is being built in Cuba on American soil. Social conflicts have engulfed our continent, which is an important theatre in the world wide battle against imperialism, for democracy, peace and socialism. Imperialist plunder, coupled with the tyranny of the feudal oligarchies, is visiting poverty and suffering on millions of Latin American workers, peasants and Indians, and prejudicing the interests of students, white-collar workers, intellectuals, tradesmen and industrialists, who are joining the social struggle in growing numbers. And they will gain in political awareness and extend their anti-imperialist action as they fight in common for common aims against the aggressive interventionist policy of the Yankee imperialists. The fight against U.S. imperialism and the local oligarchies, their common enemy, is bringing the Latin-American peoples closer together. So are the imperatives of solidarity with the other peoples of the world, particularly of Vietnam and Cuba, and with the anti-imperialist and anti-feudal movements on our own continent, especially those forced to resort to armed struggle (in Guatemala, Venezuela, Colombia and Bolivia) or to function underground.

The Latin American wars of independence in the past century were continental wars. When Bolivar, Sucre, San Martin and O'Higgins fought for the independence of their countries they were striving also for the freedom of the other American peoples. No national states and no geographical frontiers existed on our continent in those days. The borders of the various colonial possessions were rather indistinct, and the independence armies fighting for the liberation of their people counted in their ranks officers and soldiers from other colonies.

It was not until independence was won and capitalism began to develop that the national states came into existence. But, as before, the peoples of Latin America had a common destiny, common problems and common enemies. Still, they could not and did not escape the effects of the law of the uneven development of capitalism and capitalist society.

Against the present general setting of backwardness, there are appreciable disparities between the countries in levels of economic, political and social development. This gives the revolutions a national complexion and conditions their variety in form and discrepancy in time.

For this reason, the present situation differs from that of the past century. However, Washington is pursuing its policy of aggression and intervention throughout the continent, which, as the Cuban Communist Party stressed in its statement of May 18, "internationalizes aggressive wars, in which soldiers of different nationalities are engaged, as in the Korean War and now in South Vietnam where North American, South Korean, Thai, Filipino, New Zealand and Australian troops have been committed, and as in Santo Domingo, where soldiers were shipped from Brazil, Costa Rica, Honduras, Nicaragua and Paraguay; furthermore, imperialism is trying through the OAS to build up an international armed force for use against Cuba and the liberation movements on the continent."

This necessitates joint action by the Latin-American peoples and imparts an all-continental complexion of outstanding international importance to their struggle.

Working hand in hand with the local oligarchies, imperialism spurns the principle of non-interference and the sovereignty and frontiers of the Latin American countries. It espouses the so-called doctrine of ideological frontiers, which revolutionaries have to counter with the utmost solidarity. Among other things, this presupposes direct participation in the liberation struggles of fraternal peoples wherever this is warranted by necessity, provided it is done under their leadership.

In some cases, as in the anti-fascist war in Spain, revolutionaries of different nationalities may participate in large numbers, with marked political and historical effect. However, the most important contribution revolutionaries can make to liberation and working-class victory on a world scale is struggle in their own country and their moral and material support to revolutionary battles in other countries.

In the *Communist Manifesto,* Marx and Engels, the founders of Marxism and of proletarian internationalism, stressed that "though not in substance, yet in form, the struggle of the proletariat with the bourgeoisie is at first a national struggle. The proletariat of each country must, of course, first of all settle matters with its own bourgeoisie."

In this national struggle it is the revolutionaries in each country who determine the various aspects and concrete tasks of the revolution. They know the home situation better than anybody else and are in a far better position to define the aims and the methods of attaining them. They may err, but are less likely to do so than others. In any case, revolutionaries in their respective countries are best equipped to assume full responsibility for working out the right course of action after a preliminary review of their own experience, their successes and setbacks. Needless to say, this does not rule out exchanges of opinion and, in some cases, fraternal counsel.

The Cuban revolution is proof of the fact that

reality plays havoc with preconceived assumptions, serving as a reminder of the folly of generalizing the singular features of this or that experience. This is not to say, however, that the specific features of one revolution, say that of the Cuban, will not recur elsewhere (at least in a somewhat different form). We believe, therefore, that in some Latin-American countries revolution may be sparked off by a guerrilla movement, as was the case in Cuba.

For this to happen the courage and determination of a group of revolutionaries, though an important, sometimes even decisive factor, is not enough. Much more essential are favorable general conditions. To be sure, we hold that they need be neither absolutely favorable nor completely mature, but they must be in the process of maturing with a clear prospect of becoming fully ripe.

Certainly, it is not easy to define the place and the exact time for guerrilla or some other form of armed action. Lenin warned against reckless ventures which, as a rule, cause a senseless waste of lives and end in retreat. On the other hand, Leninism has always been creatively bold, infused with the desire to advance the revolutionary cause. It would be wrong therefore both to reject out of hand or blindly accept any specific form of struggle. The main thing is to embark squarely on the path of struggle, size up the situation to the best of one's ability and decide on the most propitious course of action. The revolutionary must be ready to take the offensive at any moment, to retreat when necessary, and to perceive situations favorable for revolution.

## 2.

Many trends—men, women and youth of varying political views and social backgrounds—have joined the liberation struggle. The important thing is to extend the anti-imperialist front and engage against the common enemy all sections of the public, including those who may not be admirers of the Cuban revolution and revolution in general, but who have taken a stand in behalf of Cuba's right to build socialism and the right of all Latin American peoples to opt for the system of their choice.

Any attempt to impose the communist view on the other anti-imperialist forces, and similarly any attempt by the latter to impose their views on others, can but hamper unity of action and narrow the struggle against the common enemy.

This is why the accent should be on the specific tasks that all agree need to be carried out—that is, on what unites, rather than divides, the revolutionary movement. We believe that the Organization for Latin American Solidarity (OLAS) and the respective national committees should concentrate on extending and coordinating international solidarity and joint action. What is needed most is for all revolutionaries, all anti-imperialists and all popular movements on our continent to thrash out a common revolutionary standpoint. This, however, is inconceivable before a certain process of development runs its course. We may accelerate the course, but cannot as yet consider it completed. If, therefore, we were to try and impose a standard approach, entirely unnecessary difficulties would arise. The best way to facilitate unity in defense of the Cuban revolution and the fight against imperialism and its agents is to promote joint action and to accentuate what unites us, while rectifying whatever disunites us.

It is no secret that Latin American revolutionaries have differing viewpoints on some problems. This tendency made its appearance after considerable numbers of new fighters from the less politically developed sections of the proletariat and petty bourgeoisie joined the Latin-American revolutionary movement, and after differences of an international order obstructing the struggle broke out among the revolutionaries.

The allusion here is to problems bred by the development of modern society, the emergence of new extremely complex social phenomena, the disparities between objective conditions from country to country and to the growth of the revolutionary forces.

Lenin pointed out that any growth of the working-class movement and appearance of new fighters and new sections of working people "is inevitably accompanied by vacillation in theory and tactics." And he called attention to the fact that "the yardstick of an imaginary ideal" will get us nowhere and that vacillation should be regarded as "a practical movement of ordinary people."

In other words, what we are dealing with are growing pains that cannot conceivably be removed overnight. But it is also a cogent fact that imperialism benefits from differences arising between the revolutionary forces and especially from differences in the Communist parties. It is our duty, therefore, to prevent differences from obstructing united action against the common enemy. Differences arising between Communist parties should not impede mutual understanding any more than differences between Communists and other revolutionaries should impede their common fight against imperialism.

Experience has shown that open polemics results in senseless name-calling and in arbitrary judgments. It serves no useful purpose and only aggravates the difficulties. Sometimes, it is true, a party has no choice but to express its opinion publicly. We have nothing against this. But we are sure that direct contacts, bilateral and multilateral meetings, a tactful fraternal dialogue and, most important of all, steadfast unity of action, are the best way to further mutual understanding.

### 3.

The driving force of the revolution in Latin America comprises the working class, peasants (the majority of whom in many countries are Indians), students, middle strata and some sections of the national bourgeoisie. There are contradictions between them, but common interests in the fight against U.S. imperialism and the oligarchies predominate. This offers a serviceable basis for unity and calls for closer bonds. Our policy of united action by all anti-imperialist and anti-oligarchic forces builds on the belief that an alliance of workers and peasants, of the

proletariat and the non-proletarian elements is the best possible basis for an enduring and militant united front. To make headway, mutual understanding between proletarian and petty-bourgeois revolutionaries is absolutely essential.

The proletariat, the most powerful social class on our continent, is still growing. As many as 40 million people (of whom one out of every three is a factory or farm laborer), or more than half the gainfully employed population between the Rio Grande and Cape Horn, earn a livelihood by selling their labor power. In five countries, that is, Mexico, Brazil, Argentina, Uruguay and Chile, with nearly two-thirds of the total population of Latin America, the proletariat is relatively strong, and not in numbers only.

Communist parties exist in all Latin American countries. Like the fraternal parties elsewhere in the world, irrespective of their degree of development, they expound ideas that strike terror into imperialism, of which they are the most relentless enemies.

They are the bearers of the finest revolutionary traditions of their peoples and have acquitted themselves splendidly in the important work of disseminating Marxism and socialist ideas, and moulding the scientific socialist outlook of the foremost workers and intellectuals. Cultivation of proletarian internationalism among the working class is one of their accomplishments. In brief, it is they who are forging the class consciousness of the Latin-American proletariat and the anti-imperialist awareness of the peoples.

In all the countries of Latin America the Communists have been subjected to persecution at one time or another. But they have never flinched in face of the terror campaigns. Thousands have seen the inside of prisons and concentration camps, thousands have been manhandled and tortured, and many leaders have paid with their lives for their convictions. Staunch and experienced fighters emerge from this ordeal.

Some Communist parties, entrenched among the masses, constitute an influential and at times even the decisive, political force. Others are still small and lack some of the requisites of a vanguard. However, international experience has shown that small parties can become large revolutionary contingents, at times virtually overnight. Just before the Second World War, for example, the Italian Communist Party numbered only 15,000 members in a country with a population approaching 50 million. Yet after Mussolini's downfall towards the end of the Second World War the Party grew into a powerful force of millions of members. Early in 1958, at the time the Perez Jimenez dictatorship was overthrown in Venezuela, the Communist Party had a mere 300 members; soon, however, its membership numbered tens of thousands, making it in a matter of months the biggest political body in Caracas.

Communists organize the workers in trade unions, fight for the economic and social demands of the people and safeguard working-class unity by inspiring a new, anti-imperialist patriotism.

The most advanced section of the working class

and the best of the Latin-American intelligentsia have joined the Communist parties. These parties have their sources in the proletariat of their respective countries, in the October Revolution, in the victory of Leninism, of revolutionism over reformism.

This consolidation of the Latin-American Communist parties is a great gain of the revolutionary working class. Their path has not been strewn with roses. They have had to withstand the assault of their class adversaries and also to combat anarchism, Trotskyism and other petty-bourgeois trends in their own ranks.

The founding of Communist parties brought about the fusion of Marxism with the working-class movement. This was an historical imperative so that the working class, to use Marx's words, should not be only a class in itself but a class for itself, and that its fight for emancipation should be a conscious fight.

Pernicious tendencies and sectarian views, isolationism, passivity, adventurism, conformism and time-serving occur now and then in the Communist parties regardless of whether they are functioning legally or underground. None of these can be combated effectively, unless a continuous fight is waged for the Party line through criticism and self-criticism and hard daily work among the masses.

These pernicious tendencies, which we Chilean Communists know all too well from our own experience, are a hindrance to party development. But small parties grow into big ones by virtue of their vanguard position in the social struggle, for as the proletarian masses gather experience they range themselves alongside the Communists. This we want to make absolutely clear. However, we should not lose sight of another objective factor, namely, that not only the politically conscious workers but also a considerable section of the petty-bourgeoisie are adopting a revolutionary attitude and fighting for the liberation of our continent with the aim of building socialism. This became doubly evident after the socialist revolution in Cuba.

Some of the petty-bourgeoisie join the Communist parties or became friends and followers, exerting an influence of their own for a certain length of time. However, a more considerable part forms its own parties or joins the Left wing of other movements.

This trend often engenders sectarianism. In Chile, for example, Communists campaigned for a time for the dictatorship of the proletariat and for Soviet power. This approach did not help our Party to grow. (Upon abandoning this sectarian line, we defined the Chilean revolution as a bourgeois-democratic revolution but realized in 1945 that even this non-sectarian definition had been rendered unsound by reason of the worldwide changes—advance of the working class, the content of the new epoch and the decline in the revolutionary ardor of the bourgeoisie.)

In any case, the rise of revolutionary tendencies among the petty-bourgeoisie can be traced to the struggle waged by the proletariat, to the years of work put in by the Communist Parties, to the entire modern development of history, influenced chiefly by the steady growth of the socialist system.

Objectively speaking, the revolutionary mood of the petty-bourgeoisie is a welcome fact. It is a manifestation of progress and should not be regarded as merely a posture or as an act of desperation, an act which the petty bourgeoisie admittedly often commit. Under no circumstances should we under-rate the revolutionary potential of the rural and urban petty bourgeoisie. While the Latin-American bourgeoisie is no longer capable of heading revolutionary processes (though some sections of it may participate in them), the petty bourgeoisie is still a revolutionary force and one that may even play a leading role in countries where the working class is weak numerically and lacks the needed political weight.

The Cuban revolution has demonstrated that the petty bourgeoisie has a potential of revolutionary courage in battling for national liberation and socialism.

There is, then, a distinct bond between the revolutionary trends of the proletariat, on the one hand, and those of the petty bourgeoisie, on the other. There is much that unites them, but also much that divides them. Petty-bourgeois revolutionaries tend at times to under-rate the workers and the Communist parties, to gravitate towards nationalism, recklessness, terror and, at times, even anti-communism and anti-Sovietism. Also, they are more susceptible to despair and subjectivism. But they are revolutionary all the same and the proletariat must put the accent on unity with them rather than on fighting their mistakes. The two trends are competing for leadership of the movement; to a certain extent, their rivalry is ideological. But if anything is done to accentuate this rivalry and precipitate a "fight for the destruction" of either trend, the sole beneficiary will be imperialism. That imperialism and its agents are concentrating precisely on intensifying the rivalry should be enough to bear this out. The national bourgeoisie, too, which seeks to maintain its class positions, is also eager to see the proletariat and the petty bourgeoisie part ways. So today, mutual understanding, cooperation and united action by the proletariat and the revolutionary petty bourgeoisie is a matter of the first magnitude.

The Latin-American Communist parties are aware of the need for understanding with the other Left forces, above all those espousing socialism. However, this does not apply to anti-Party groups and splinter parties, who represent no one and who live off factional activity and dissent.

The militant cooperation of the working class and the revolutionary petty bourgeoisie need not stop short of founding united revolutionary Marxist-Leninist parties wherever they have parties of their own today. In Chile this cooperation has crystallized into socialist-communist unity within the People's Action Front. The Socialist Party, like the Communist, has deep roots in the working class, though those of the Communist Party are deeper. Both wield considerable influence also among the petty bourgeoisie, with the Socialists holding an edge. The petty-bourgeoisie do not comprise a special group in the Communist Party, whose leadership derives chiefly from the working class.

The mutual understanding of Chile's Communists and Socialists comes up against snags from time to time, but the alliance is sufficiently strong to make a split highly improbable. It draws its strength from the will of the people. As Comrade Galo Gonzalez pointed out at the Tenth Party Congress in 1956, whenever Socialists and Communists worked together *"the working class has gained and whenever we parted ways or quarrelled the enemy benefited."* We are strong when we stand together, and weaker when we do not. The people of Chile will not win political power unless Socialists and Communists are allies. Neither Communists nor Socialists can claim sole leadership. We need each other.

Some sections of the petty bourgeoisie and of the working class while gravitating towards revolution have not yet taken a definite stand. Most of them support the Radical or Christian Democratic parties.

However, since the municipal elections last April the more advanced groups in the Radical Party, who gained considerable ground, have been working for an understanding with the Socialists and Communists. Their leader, Alberto Baltra, maintains that *"the objective interests of the proletariat and the middle sections are similar,"* that *"the world is moving inevitably towards socialism"* and that *"a socialized alternative is perfectly conceivable, paving the way to effective planning, replacement of the capitalist system, abolition of the monopolies, decline of imperialist influence and to accumulation and mobilization of the considerable resources required to expand national capital and, hence, the rate of Chile's development."* Baltra described people's unity as *"a process of joint action by Radicals and other Left forces."*

Some deputies and many members of the Christian Democratic Party, too, are calling for "concentrated fire on the oligarchy" and for joint action with the People's Action Front. Most have expressed themselves in favor of socialism.

To be sure, their idea of socialism differs substantially from that of the Socialists and Communists. But the important thing is their desire to reach an understanding with the People's Action Front.

The most important factor in Chile today is the desire for change. Thanks to Communist and Socialist efforts, the people are beginning to realize that the old economic structure must be radically altered. The national bourgeoisie represented by the Christian Democratic Party is acutely conscious of the advances made by the revolutionary working class and of the possibility of a major shift in public sentiment, which could bring the working class to power. Consequently, large sections of the national bourgeoisie have declared themselves in favor of change, offering reformist solutions within the Alliance-for-Progress framework. To stem the tide, the oligarchy, too aligned itself with the Christian Democrats in the 1964 presidential election, thus enabling the latter to win

The 30 months of the Christian Democratic government have been enough to disenchant the people who had believed in bourgeois reformism. Most of them turned to the Popular Action Front and now seek revolutionary change.

Needless to say, this reaction was not spontaneous.

It was brought about by the work of the Communists who have consistently urged joint action by all partisans of change, regardless of whether or not they are against the government.

The shift in favor of the Communists and Socialists was reflected in the results of the April municipal elections. The Communist Party polled 354,000 and the Socialist Party 322,000 votes. Some 120,000 electors who previously voted Christian Democrat sided with the Communists and Socialists, who polled 30 per cent of the vote. Meanwhile, the Christian Democratic Party, which formerly collected 42 per cent, slipped to 36 per cent. The Socialists and Communists are on the upgrade, while the Christian Democrats have entered a phase of decline.

The future of the Radical Party, which represents some 16 per cent of the electorate and consists chiefly of middle class people, will depend on its eventual understanding with the People's Action Front.

In the circumstances, the People's Action Front is becoming a center of contact for all the democratic forces in the country.

The election was a serious setback for the Christian-Democratic Party and for President Frei's administration. It was a setback for the reformist alternative and the Christian Democratic variety of the pilot experiment offered by the U.S. imperialists to some of the Latin American countries. The election also showed that the Communist effort gradually to win over the masses from the Christian Democrats, delivering them from bourgeois influence and rallying petty-bourgeois support for the People's Action Front, is bearing fruit. This Communist policy holds out good prospects for the people's movement in its advance and in combating the enemy on other fronts in the event of Chile being affected by the present epidemic of "gorillism."

Doubtless the situation in the country is a singular one. But elsewhere in Latin America, too, mutual understanding between proletarian and revolutionary petty-bourgeois groups is being forged in various forms, drawing the middle sections into the fight for change with the ultimate aim of sparking off anti-imperialist and anti-feudal revolutions.

It is up to the revolutionaries to find the way to mutual understanding between the proletariat and the petty bourgeoisie. And clearly, in each country the choice rests with the local revolutionary forces, which makes it doubly necessary to disseminate Marxist-Leninist ideas and implant proletarian ideology.

\* \* \* \*

The argument most frequently used by the enemy is that the Communists' united action policy is simply a tactical maneuver to strengthen their hand, to absorb real and possible allies, use them to the fullest and then abandon them and to go on to achieve a Communist one-party empire.

It would be a sheer waste of breath to go into this at length, for it is malicious slander pure and simple. That the Communists will gain in strength is certain, despite all the difficulties. The other progressive forces will also grow in proportion to their contribution to the common struggle, because the march of time favors the exponents of progress, not the reactionaries. In Chile, the cooperation of Socialists and Communists has benefited both parties. They improved their positions in the recent elections, with the Socialists making a somewhat bigger advance this time.

We Communists have always maintained that the working class has two types of allies—permanent and temporary. This is an objective fact. History never stands still. Upon attaining one goal, society begins planning the next. New tasks and contradictions appear, conditioning changes in the political approach, with new alignments, some drifting into the reactionary camp and the majority straining forward. It is not the Communists, therefore, who by malice aforethought part ways with groups that had been their allies.

Imperialist policies of menacing world peace, flouting the right of nations, assailing democratic freedoms and human rights, and prejudicing the interests of all socio-economic groups save those of the monopoly bourgeoisie, evoke the indignation of all social strata, including a large part of the non-monopoly bourgeoisie. On the other hand, the spectacular achievements of the socialist world and its accomplishments, which are in harmony with man's aspirations for freedom, learning, culture and welfare, coupled with its aid to non-socialist countries aspiring to independent development, is making socialism attractive not only to the proletariat, but also to other classes and social strata.

The development of the Cuban revolution into a socialist one and the socialist orientation of some revolutionary processes in Africa and the Middle East could never have occurred other than in the new historical conditions brought about by the October Revolution and then the Soviet victory over Hitler Germany, after which socialism became a world system strong enough to safeguard the new revolutionary states, frustrate imperialist blockades and assist the newly-free countries in their independent development.

In this situation, the problem of our temporary alliances with non-proletarian and non-Communist forces calls for a new approach. Our allies now have much greater opportunities for marching ahead, not of course without vacillation and difficulties. Whatever happens, it is farthest from our minds to use them at some specific stage, only to discard them at another. On the contrary, we could wish for nothing better than to cooperate with them indefinitely.

What we Communists want is a progressive alignment of all champions of democracy and socialism, recognizing the right of every ally to participate in all stages of the revolutionary process and in all governments that the people's struggle may bring into being.

It should be added here that many Communist parties do not consider the one-party system obligatory for socialist society. The matter hinges on specific national conditions and on the existence in many countries of democratic and popular political forces and of objective social realities that condition a multiplicity of progressive trends and parties. The Communist Party of France, for example, does not believe that "the one-party system is essential for the transition to socialism," and the Italian Communists share its opinion.

The Communists in Chile, too, favor a multi-party system. We hold that the Communist and Socialist parties should not only jointly lead the people in the fight against imperialism and the oligarchy but also jointly build the socialist society of the future, and we expect many other groups to participate as well.

The Communist Party of Chile, a working-class party, exercises leadership in cooperation with the Socialist Party, which, as we have noted before, holds strong positions in the country. Many problems faced by our movement are settled by agreement between the Socialists and Communists on the initiative of one of them. We call this joint leadership, which in Chile represents the concrete form in which the Communist Party plays its vanguard role.

It may be that ultimately the Communists and Socialists will form a united party. But so far the question has not arisen, and is not likely to arise in the foreseeable future, and perhaps may never arise.

As for the other Latin-American countries, it appears that the need for united action by Communist parties and other revolutionary forces fits in with the need for cooperation at the level of joint *leadership* by those revolutionary forces which, in a definite sense, share the function of vanguard.

A vanguard cannot conceivably be built by arbitrary or synthetic means around a leader or a few men, who individually, at least in their own opinion, adopt radical standpoints and prepare for revolutionary action. The exceptions to this rule only bear this out.

A vanguard is the result of the fusions of Marxism with the working-class movement, the moulding of revolutionary thought (above all among proletarians) and the application of Marxism-Leninism to the concrete conditions of a country, that is, the result of purposeful activity and of a natural, rather than spontaneous, process.

On the other hand, as Lenin said, it is not enough to call oneself the vanguard or the forward contingent; all other contingents must be convinced that we really are in the van.

The Latin-American Communist parties were founded at different times. They function in different conditions and in different social and political situations. Some are going forward from dissemination of scientific socialist ideas to consolidating their bonds with the masses, to organizing mass struggle, to the phase of intensive social and political work which paves the way to the conquest of power, to the rapid development of the Latin-American parties into the guiding force of the revolutionary movement.

However, the Communists do not consider this the only possible perspective. In the name of the proletariat and on the basis of Marxism-Leninism, they are prepared to raise to the highest possible level cooperation and unity with the other revolutionary forces.

# "A STRONG COMMUNIST PARTY—A GUARANTEE FOR THE PEOPLE"

Report of Luis Corvalán, General Secretary, Communist Party of Chile,
at the National Conference of the CP Chile, September 1967

*Abridged Text*
(*Information Bulletin,* No. 110, 1967)

The Central Committee has convened this Conference to discuss only one question, namely, that of the Party's organizational, ideological and political consolidation.

Factors breeding backwardness and misery continue to operate in the country. The enemies of well-being and progress keep their economic positions virtually intact. Even latifundism lives on and fares well, although 90 per cent of the Chileans have condemned it to death. A greater part of the population lives in poverty and destitution. The scourge of inflation and high cost of living, the low wages, the shortage and unhealthful condition of housing make life a never-ending tragedy. Unemployment brings desperation to thousands of families.

The factory and office workers are stepping up their class battles. The struggle is being joined and strikes are launched by groups of working people who have never done so before. Peasants are rising in struggle throughout the central zone, where big landowners hold sway. The agricultural workers led by the National Federation of Peasants and Indians and the working people who support Demochristian-inspired organizations are acting simultaneously against the employers and fighting for their demands. The influx of agricultural workers into trade unions and their joining in the strike struggle strengthen the positions and intensify the struggle of the entire proletariat, broadening and deepening the anti-imperialist and anti-oligarchy movement of the people.

We are witnessing a re-awakening of the youth. Catholic students have for the first time gone on strike to demand the rejuvenation of their university. The student movement is growing and joint actions are being undertaken by all its federations in the struggle for university allocations, for students' say in the university councils, for more scholarships and better premises. Young Communists, Socialists, Radicals, Demochristians, atheists and believers alike are rallying in acts of solidarity with the glorious people of Vietnam. The march from Valparaiso to Santiago was an eloquent demonstration of the unity and anti-imperialist spirit of our young people.

A Left-inclined leadership has been elected at a conference of the Radical Party. Forces discontented with President Frei's government and intent on attacking the positions of the oligarchy have come out on top at a recent meeting of the Executive of the Christian-Democratic Party and at the congress of that party's youth organization. These facts show what the people want, how profound is their striving for change.

The clans of the oligarchy, which live off the sweat and blood of the people and enjoy the government's protection, are out to bar the country's way to freedom and progress. They are fighting back, sowing anxiety and apprehension among the weak-hearted, intriguing, splitting the popular forces, conspiring and entering into collusion with foreign reactionaries.

U.S. imperialism reiterates its claims to intervene in any Latin American country. With its aid military juntas are concluding regional military agreements. Imperialism and the juntas, aided by a handful of traitors, have organized a campaign against Chile.

The Communist Party appeals to the country: Chile can and must effect the changes it needs, preserve and extend democracy and proceed along its own, independent road in Latin America.

The Communist Party declares to the government of President Frei that the situation demands an end to any procrastination in effecting the reforms which are supported by a considerable majority in and outside parliament, such as the reform of the banking system. The situation demands reconstruction of the countryside, jobs for the unemployed, better conditions for wage earners, including servicemen, and no more explanations to the U.S. State Department and the "gorillas" regarding the establishment of the Chilean committee of the Organization of Latin American Solidarity, because that was a lawful act and no foreign government has the right to interfere. Explanations will not calm down the imperialists and "gorillas," but only make them more insolent.

The Communist Party stands in firm opposition to the government, whose policy is essentially continuist and anti-labor. At the same time the Party considers itself responsible for the development of the country.

There are problems whose solution is in the vital interests of the working class and the entire people. We have in mind above all the need to preserve and develop the democratic system, prevent reactionary seditious activities in Chile and foil the imperialists' plans to push Chile onto the road of fascization. We also have in mind the danger stemming from the utilization by imperialism and the "gorillas" of old disputes with neighboring countries.

In view of this the Communist Party declares that it is doing and will do everything within its power in the interests of democracy, social progress, independent economic development and a dignified, sovereign and realistic foreign policy which would blow up the international conspiracy and frustrate the provocations of the "gorillas." Acting accordingly, we unhesitatingly denounced the seditious activity of the Rightists. Their leaders have in fact remained in the dock, although the judicial authorities have set them free. They are plotting not only against the government but in the final count against the people, against the possibilities for the victorious development of the popular movement, against the agrarian reform and the strike movement of the rural working people, against the rights and gains of all working people. In this as in all similar cases, Communists stand in the way of those who want to reverse the country's development. We champion peaceful and friendly settlement of disputes between neighboring countries. We support any initiative or measure inspired by this principle. National defense must be based not only on effective armed forces. History shows that unity of the people is decisive, and that it can be achieved if the country enters upon the road of progress, if impediments to the development of the productive forces are removed and the well-being of the masses grows. All this, in turn, should be connected with a policy of fraternity among nations.

For the same reason we follow with interest the efforts of other political circles on behalf of the country's progress. We will support their every initiative aimed at satisfying the demands of the working people or implementing anti-imperialist and anti-oligarchy measures.

More active struggle and stronger unity are needed. Satisfaction of the most urgent demands of the masses depends primarily on their action. Popular unity and struggle will frustrate the conspiratorial maneuvers of the Rightists. Imperialism's direct or indirect interference can be prevented if the Chilean people unite in action. Given unity and struggle, it is possible and necessary to overcome the resistance of the reactionaries, effect already now certain anti-imperialist and anti-oligarchy reforms, and advance towards the establishment of a popular government. But words alone cannot isolate the reactionaries and unite the people. This calls for day-to-day persevering work among the masses which is often anonymous, lacking lustre and publicity. We must work with patience, firmness and wisdom to surmount the difficulties and relegate to the background the contradictions existing among the popular forces.

Hence the importance of the role which the Communist Party plays and is called upon to play.

One of the documents of the Political Commission points out: "The development of our Party, its conversion into a still bigger, more militant and ideologically and politically stronger contingent possessing a larger number of militants and broader and stronger links with the masses is becoming a top-priority, decisive task in view of the present situation and its prospects, and in view of the need to foil the anti-democratic plans of imperialism and the oligarchy and to raise to a higher level the solidarity of our people with all the liberation movements in Latin America and the world over."

We wish success to the other forces fighting for the interests of the people and above all to our Socialist allies. Therefore, when giving priority to the development of our Party we are not guided by considerations of narrow proselytism but only strive to discharge in the best way our duty to the people.

We have a strong Party distinguished by internal cohesion, discipline, links with the masses, political seriousness and responsibility, a firm, militant and broad policy line, a high fighting spirit, day-to-day struggle for the interests of the people, comprehension of Chilean realities, an internationalist and at the the same time profoundly national position, collective leadership, and rich experience. Our Party is an indestructible and indivisible force. It has been steeled in many class battles. Forged in the hard conditions of illegality, its nucleus has successfully withstood repressions, prisons, concentration camps and the hate campaign.

Our Party has become an important factor of national life. It is a political and moral force with which everybody must reckon. The Party exists, functions and fights all over the country, from Arica to Tierra del Fuego. It is the principal force in the trade union movement and among the intelligentsia, and second in importance in the student movement and among the youth in general. It is consolidating its positions in the countryside and broadening its links with women as well as with small tradesmen and other groups of the middle strata.

Great responsibility falls on the Party for the destiny of hundreds of thousands of working people and their families. In Ovalle, Valparaiso, San Clemente, Lota, Osorno and other cities it organizes the unemployed and heads the struggle for more new jobs. In the countryside the Party promotes the establishment of peasant trade unions and the intensification of the strike movement of agricultural workers. Communists head twenty-five and are represented on more than a hundred municipal councils. As of June 1967, the Party's composition was as follows: workers 44.6 per cent, peasants 16.1, office employees 4.1, college-educated specialists 2.2, teachers, 1.7, intellectuals 0.1, tradesmen 4, industrialists 0.2, housewives 20.9, pensioners 2.8 and others 3.3 per cent.

The composition of the Party is improving. Undeniably, most housewives and pensioners belong to the working class. The majority of those bracketed as "office employees" also belong to the working class, for many workers are today officially listed as office employees.

Ours is fundamentally a workers' Party, from the rank and file to the leadership. In the last two years the Party has improved its positions in the countryside. The percentage of peasants in it has grown from 12.4 per cent in 1965 to 16.1. The share of housewives has also increased. Together with working women, they account for 26.5 per cent of the Party's membership.

The period since our 10th Congress [1956] has been one of continuous growth of the Party. Between June 1965 and June 1967 its membership increased by 28.2 per cent.

The Party is closely rallied around its political line and its Central Committee. The attempts to impose on us an adventuristic orientation and nationalistic, one-sided and extremist concepts have been utterly unsuccessful. The doubts which one or another Communist may have, quite understandable in view of the magnitude and complexity of the problems, present isolated instances which in no way affect the health and line of the Party. The Party has once again demonstrated its proletarian firmness and its ability to emerge unharmed from the trials now confronting the world Communist movement.

Thus, the general situation of the Party is good. But we want it to be better still. We need a bigger and more efficient Party.

There is an inordinately large gap between the numerical strength and influence of the Party. In the last elections more than 350,000 Chileans voted Communist. Most of these are men and women, predominantly working people, who have been educated by the Party and who adhere to and support its policies. If we succeeded in organizing politically only one-third of the people under our influence, we would have an additional 100,000 Communists.

A similar gap exists between the number of Communists and the influence the Party wields at industrial and mining enterprises, in the public services and in building. There are enterprises employing hundreds of workers half of whom support our position. But many Party cells at these enterprises have not more than a dozen members each. In more serious cases, trade union leaders are the only Communists or there are no Party cells at all.

The bulk of the Chilean proletariat stands out for generally recognized class consciousness and political maturity acquired in the course of numerous battles since the times of the heroic Workers' Federation of Chile. Hence, ample opportunities exist for recruiting new Party members from among the proletariat. Indeed, it has been proved that where we tackle this job in earnest, especially in industry, big estates and residential communities, the Party grows fairly quickly. As we see, the possibilities for Party building are exceptionally great. Why then do we not make full use of these possibilities? Why do we not recruit more new members? Why does the Party fail to assimilate many new members who fall behind and part ways with us? Why do we still wear short breeches and remain a small party in some central and southern provinces? Why have we not restored yet our positions in such important groups of working people as seamen, dockers, copper miners (although we have achieved noteworthy successes there), railwaymen and city transport workers? Why have we not made substantial progress among the middle strata?

These inadequacies, and generally the Party's weaknesses and shortcomings, are not due to a single cause, and therefore cannot be eliminated by a single measure. In different places these problems pose themselves with different degrees of acuteness and stem from different causes. Therefore the following propositions can be useful only as a general orientation for concrete consideration in each particular instance.

1. The Party grows primarily due to its activity, its struggle at the head of the masses. Hence the need for more active and extensive work among the masses.

This is the reason for the existence of the Party, which is not an end in itself but a combat weapon of the proletariat, its vanguard contingent.

No other party is working and fighting as intensely as ours. But it remains a fact that some Party members are not active enough, that not the whole of the Party works with the masses. There are primary organizations which live a listless, more or less passive life, are absorbed in themselves and preoccupied exclusively—or almost exclusively—with domestic, internal tasks.

The responsibility for the weaknesses of the Party rests primarily with us, its leaders. Therefore it is necessary first of all to improve the work of the leadership, the methods of guidance.

We have achieved significant successes in this respect, especially as regards the collectivity of leadership. Besides, the Party has been able to train a considerable number of national, regional and local leaders distinguished by selflessness, tireless activity and fidelity to communism. But on the whole their efficiency is below their capacity because of the alarming spread of administrative methods of leadership in the Party and the limited number of people charged with Party assignments.

As a result, Party activists are in many cases overworked, leading their organizations from one task or campaign to another, having almost no respite, no time for study, for reflection and deep analysis, for planning, for more creative activity.

The leading organs of the Party must give priority to political work, to organization and orientation of mass movements on the basis of the general line of the Party, in conformity with the concrete situation and the problems of the given region. The line of the Party is struggle for the satisfaction of the most immediate demands of the masses and for structural changes. It is directed first and foremost against imperialism and the oligarchy. But holding forth on this general line is not enough. It is necessary to work constantly and everywhere on the basis of this general line. The entire Party must take to heart the permanent and current problems which concern or interest the population. The Party should head the struggle for those anti-imperialist and anti-feudal aims which are on the order of the day—for instance, for the agrarian reform, the bank reform, the nationalization of the Pacific Steel and Chilean Power companies, the coal mines and saltpeter deposits.

This is all the more necessary since there exist points of contact with other circles which make it possible to unite the people and isolate the reactionaries.

2. In some places there has arisen a contradiction between work among the masses and work in the Party. Some comrades are preoccupied solely with work among the masses and forget about Party work, while others busy themselves with Party work alone. A certain degree of division of labor is necessary, of course, but not to such an extent.

This contradiction can only be explained by malpractices which have to be corrected.

The district and local Party committees should always keep abreast of labor conflicts and problems of the mass movement, and discuss them with the participation of the leaders concerned.

3. The cell is the basis of the Party, its vital organ. All Communists without exception should be members of one or other Party cell. The cell is organized at the place of work or residence. In other words, there are industrial and residential cells, and no cells of other types.

However, concrete peculiarities must be taken into account during the establishment and functioning of cells.

For instance, our Rules provide for the formation of cells consisting exclusively of women. It is difficult for housewives to attend meetings in the evening, but they have free time in the afternoon. Besides, some women do not speak freely enough at meetings in the presence of men. Hence the provision for women's cells.

We must display an equally creative approach to problems connected with the organization and activities of primary organizations in industry.

Serious problems arise in large cities. People work in different shifts and different shops and sometimes have to travel scores of kilometres to and from work. Many work overtime. Not all comrades can be met at factory gates after the shift. Housing problems, especially where workers are their own builders, are of more concern to them than trade union affairs (except at times of labor conflict). We must bear in mind this reality, which explains, in part, why 60 per cent of all Party cells are organized at places of residence and only 25 per cent at places of work (the rest are in the countryside), and also why factory cells do not, generally speaking, excel in their activities.

The Party acts primarily through the thousands upon thousands of Communists united in cells, and these cells must command our attention, for they are the chief vehicle for the pursuit of our policy. We must improve mass work in every cell, organizing and directing struggle in the economic, ideological and political fields.

4. There are tens of thousands of different organizations in Chile—workers' and peasants' trade unions, associations of office employees, shop-keepers, specialists, intellectuals, mothers and heads of family, house committees, mutual aid societies, sports clubs, art groups, etc. Communists should be found in all these organizations. Otherwise reformism may prevail in them, people will fall into the habit of limiting themselves to minor things, will strive for minor gains only, get absorbed with minor problems and lose the perspective, forgetting that in the final count the road to the real solution of all minor problems lies through revolution, through major changes.

On the other hand, it is necessary to organize the unorganized, above all the hundreds of thousands of urban and rural working people who do not yet have trade unions, to make more rapid progress in uniting factory and office workers in branches of industry and the services, to improve the coordination of the strike struggle and broaden trade union unity around the Trade Union Center. There is particularly urgent need to organize peasants' trade unions, bearing in mind that a relevant law has been adopted, that the overwhelming majority of the rural working people are not organized, that the ruling bourgeoisie is seeking to organize them under its own control, and that the character of the trade union movement in the countryside will in many respects depend on who will have applied greater efforts and gained the lead.

5. The Party's advance demands overcoming sectarian concepts and routine.

The methods of work which were useful yesterday are not applicable today.

This year, instead of changing Party cards we have been prolonging them, using special stamps.

We must apply new methods also in recruiting new members. We must rectify mistakes and improve the system which we introduced several years ago, when we admitted new members by tens and hundreds, asking every one who responded to the appeal of the Party and approached the recruiting table to sign the admission application. We shall continue the practice of mass admission, but today we can do this better, in a more organized way, not in lots. We have the names and addresses of almost 200,000 people who voted Communist in the municipal elections several months ago. We must work with these lists, analyze them, single out the best, the most active of these people, invite them to a meeting or visit them at home and help them organize a new cell or join the existing one at their place of work or residence.

6. We have been educated in the spirit of the principle that all Party members have equal rights and duties. Is this correct? Is this really so?

Every Party member can and must enjoy all his rights from the moment of entry, but he cannot start performing all his duties right away. He performs them in measure as he is being educated, as he matures politically, as his knowledge, abilities and devotion to the Party cause grow.

To be sure, it is not a matter of every one doing whatever he thinks fit, but of leading the Party in such a way that every one will do what he can. At the same time, everything must be done to raise the political level of Party members, develop their abilities and help them perform their duties more efficiently.

7. Increasing importance attaches to educational work in the Party. The realities of Chile and of the whole world pose before us all kinds of new and complicated problems demanding sober analysis and fuller mastery of theory. Also, the anti-Communist campaign does not pass entirely without effect, if only by sowing doubts regarding this or that matter. In addition, as the revolutionary movement develops some elements of different social origin and political convictions advocate positions which are not ours or are even anti-communist. There are people who pose as Left Leftists or greater Leftists than our Party and call us moderates, because we do not use high-flown language and measure our every step. We Communists are the chief enemies of imperialism, and one form of its struggle against us is to use precisely such labels. "Moderates" and "traditionalists" are terms widely employed by imperialist news agencies with regard to Communists. Hence the need to pay more attention to the political and ideological growth of the entire Party, to strengthen its unity and see to it that all its

members comprehend ever more deeply its political line and fight for it. The consolidation and development of our positions and the growth of the Party itself largely depend on our efforts in this direction.

We must always remember that the educational level of a greater part of our Communists—not through a fault of their own, of course—is fairly low. Most working people have had only two or three years of schooling.

It is clear that educational work should be conducted at other levels, too, at all levels. The establishment of the Marxist Research Institute is proof of our intentions in this respect. We should set up new regional schools for medium-level cadres. All leaders must continue individual and collective studies. No one can be satisfied with his knowledge. He who knows more must study more. There is always that which can be learned. Knowledge is inexhaustible. One does not have to be a monk or an abstinent to be admitted into the Party. What we want is not angels but men, women and youth of the people. It is therefore improper to pay more attention to people's shortcomings than to their merits. It is all the more improper since the Party itself is a school of education.

8. There are many localities where sectarian concepts and methods have taken deep root. The same applies to quite a few Party functionaries and rank-and-file members.

We regard the Party as a Marxist-Leninist revolutionary contingent, as a party of action, a party of firm unity, iron discipline and high consciousness, a party which has no caudillos, admits of no factions and does not tolerate conformism, passivity, frustration or time-serving.

Old methods and old ideas defend themselves. They do not surrender without a struggle. Therefore it is necessary to discuss all ideas and all problems in order to achieve clarity and make further advance.

9. We are conducting a party-building campaign dedicated to the memory of our remarkable comrade, Jose Gonzalez. We call it a campaign of directed recruitment, because we direct our efforts primarily to big industrial and service enterprises, estates and residential communities, especially those where we are weakest.

We want to stress that directed recruitment, i.e., the emphasis on the admission of workers and peasants, in no way signifies disregard for other strata of the population. The doors of the Party are wide open before the finest sons of our people. The Party can and must be joined by more representatives of the middle strata, more specialists and intellectuals. It is well known that the Party highly values intellectuals, and that it does not demand of them adherence to this or that esthetical school. We only want them to work in the interests of the proletariat, enter the Party and strive to be good Communists and ever better writers and artists.

Our Young Communist League is developing as a remarkable school of communism, as a youth organization deeply devoted to the Party. The Party should give greater support to the League. Where there is the Party, there should be the League. As we know, that is not the case everywhere, and the chief responsibility for this rests with us and not with the young people.

The methods and forms of the work of a Party depend on concrete historical conditions, but the fundamental principles of its organization, elaborated and substantiated by Lenin, remain immutable.

The Communist Party is the most patriotic of all political forces. It expresses and consistently defends the interests of the people, the interests of the country. The patriotism of Communists is harmoniously combined with their proletarian internationalism. Loyal to its internationalist duty, the Communist Party tirelessly strengthens friendship among nations. Communists are opposed to national hatred, national strife and national narrow-mindedness, We are internationalists and at the same time most consistent patriots.

The above-said does not mean that other popular parties, which are not genuine proletarian Marxist-Leninist parties or do not possess all their qualities, are outside the revolutionary process or cannot hold leading positions in this or that country or contingency. Nor does this mean that we regard the existence of a single working-class party indispensable for any revolution.

It is known what great importance we attach to Socialist-Communist mutual understanding as the basis of the unity of the working class and the entire people, as the cornerstone of the popular movement and the future government. Moreover, we consider that many aspects of the work of guiding the revolutionary process are, and should be, shared between Communists and Socialists; we allow for the eventuality of a multi-party popular government.

But history has shown that the proletariat is the only consistently revolutionary class and that the existence of a Marxist-Leninist proletarian party is the best guarantee of the success of the revolution and the building of socialism. Therefore we are strengthening our ranks, combating any disparagement of the role of the working-class party or the opinion that it can be replaced by a caudillo or an armed group.

The revolution in Chile cannot be the cause of one party, but the Communist Party must be present, and take part, in the revolutionary process. Its consolidation, its organizational, ideological and political development will bring nearer the day of victory and will be the decisive factor of firmness and consistency in the struggle for national liberation, democracy and socialism.

The debate on power and on the need for revolution is in the center of the political life of the country. Our advance to power will depend on our everyday struggle for the demands of the people and our efforts to isolate the chief enemy, imperialism and the oligarchy. This aim will be achieved if priority is given today to concrete tasks which will mobilize the masses in struggle and promote the growth and gathering of forces for the revolution. Foremost among these tasks is struggle for the further development of the agrarian reform, for the bank reform, for everything that in one way or other restricts the power of imperialism and reaction.

The Communist Party takes a favorable view of the efforts of other political circles in this direction, and it reaffirms its support of the line of its 13th Congress [1965] to ensure the unity of action of the broadest progressive forces. We are witnessing the development of this unity, which creates prerequisites for the unity of the whole people.

# "CARRY THE GREAT PROLETARIAN CULTURAL REVOLUTION THROUGH TO THE END"

*People's Daily* and *Red Flag* Editorial, 1 January 1967

*Complete Text*
(*Peking Review*, No. 1, 8 January 1967)

The emergence of the great proletarian cultural revolution in China in 1966 is the greatest event in this sixth decade of the 20th century. This revolution has taken China's socialist revolution forward to a new stage. It has opened a new era in the history of the international communist movement.

Under the leadership of V.I. Lenin, the Great October Socialist Revolution opened the new era of proletarian revolution. The October Revolution solved the question of the seizure of political power by revolutionary violence and the establishment of the dictatorship of the proletariat, thus setting a great example for the proletariat of the whole world. At that time it was impossible, however, to solve a series of problems concerning who would win in a socialist state—the proletariat or the bourgeoisie—the maintenance of proletarian political power and the consolidation of the dictatorship of the proletariat, and the prevention of a capitalist restoration. Things have gone so far that in the birthplace of the October Revolution modern revisionism has emerged and usurped the leadership of the Party and state, setting the Soviet Union, the first socialist state, on to the road of capitalist restoration. This lesson shows that whether or not the proletariat is able to maintain political power and prevent capitalist restoration after it has seized political power is now a new, central issue for study by the proletariat of the world. This question decides the fate of a state which practices the dictatorship of the proletariat, and the fate of the revolutionary cause of the whole proletariat and all oppressed nations of the world. The great proletarian cultural revolution started and led by Chairman Mao Tse-tung himself has set a new and great example for the whole world proletariat in the solution of this question of great historic significance.

The great proletarian cultural revolution is a new stage in China's socialist revolution. After the basic completion of the socialist transformation of the ownership of the means of production, the bourgeois Rightists in the country and the handful of bourgeois representatives within the Party are not reconciled to the demise of the system of exploitation, so they have launched repeated frenzied attacks on the proletariat in a vain attempt to stage a capitalist restoration. Under the guidance of Chairman Mao's theory on classes and class struggle in socialist society, our Party has led the proletariat and other revolutionary sectors in successful counter-attacks against the challenge of the bourgeoisie. The current great proletarian cultural revolution is an all-round test of strength between the proletariat and the bourgeoisie and its agents in our Party.

Through intense class struggle, China's great proletarian cultural revolution has already begun to win great victories.

In 1963, under the personal guidance of Chairman Mao, the revolution in literature and art was launched in China, marked mainly by the reform of the dramatic arts; this was, in fact, the beginning of the great proletarian cultural revolution.

Since October 1965, the criticism, initiated by Chairman Mao himself, of the anti-Party, anti-socialist opera *Hai Jui Dismissed from Office*, of the counter-revolutionary "Three-Family Village" clique, and of the counter-revolutionary, revisionist leaders of the former Peking Municipal Committee of the Chinese Communist Party served to prepare public opinion and blazed the path for the large-scale mass movement of the great proletarian cultural revolution.

On June 1, 1966, Chairman Mao decided to publish in the press the first Marxist-Leninist big-character poster in the country, posted first in Peking University. This kindled the raging flames of the great proletarian cultural revolution and set in motion the mass movement which has as its main target for attack the handful of persons within the Party who are in authority and are taking the capitalist road. A number of those in authority who took the capitalist road and reactionary bourgeois academic "authorities" were exposed by the masses who struggled against them until their prestige was completely swept into the dust. Political life in our country, the outlook of society, and the thinking of the people has undergone profound changes. A large number of brave, revolutionary pathbreakers have emerged in the course of this great mass movement.

The path of revolution is tortuous. Precisely at the time when hundreds of millions of people were consciously rising to make revolution under the guidance of the proletarian revolutionary line represented by Chairman Mao, one, two or even several responsible people in the work of the Central Committee, in Chairman Mao's absence from Peking, took the opportunity to put forth the bourgeois reactionary line to counter Chairman Mao's correct line. With those responsible persons who firmly carried out the bourgeois reactionary line, they took the reactionary bourgeois stand to enforce bourgeois dictatorship in those spheres which they could reach temporarily, and tried by every means to suppress the vigorous movement of the great cultural revolution of the proletariat. These people reversed right and wrong, juggled black and white, encircled and suppressed revolutionaries, clamped down on different views, practiced white terror and applauded themselves for doing so. They were puffing up the arrogance of the bourgeoisie and vitiating the morale of the proletariat.

At that crucial moment, the Eleventh Plenary Session of the Eighth Central Committee of the Party was convened, presided over by our great helmsman Chairman Mao himself. It drew up the "Decision of the Central Committee of the Chinese Communist Party Concerning the Great Proletarian Cultural Revolution," and penetratingly exposed the bourgeois reactionary line. This reactionary line shielded the handful of persons within the Party who are in authority and are taking the capitalist road and played a part in their vile actions in suppressing the revolutionary mass movement and opposing the revolutionary masses. In the final analysis, it wanted to lead China towards a capitalist restoration.

The Eleventh Plenary Session of the Eighth Central Committee of the Party proclaimed the victory of the proletarian revolutionary line represented by Chairman Mao and the failure of the bourgeois reactionary line, thus guiding the great proletarian cultural revolution on to the correct path. This marked a great new victory of Mao Tse-tung's thought in the course of the socialist revolution.

After the Eleventh Plenary Session the proletarian revolutionary line represented by Chairman Mao has been integrated with the revolutionary enthusiasm of the broad masses. Hence the mass criticism and repudiation of the bourgeois reactionary line and the new upsurge of the great proletarian cultural revolution. An important sign of this upsurge has been the Red Guard movement and the extensive exchange of revolutionary experience.

The Red Guards are something new that has emerged in the course of the great proletarian cultural revolution. When the Red Guards first appeared in June and July they consisted of only several score people and were smeared as a "reactionary organization" by those who put forth the bourgeois reactionary line; they were attacked and assaulted from all sides. However, the great proletarian revolutionary Chairman Mao perceived the boundless vitality of the Red Guards the instant he discovered the new—the Red Guards. He sang the praise of the Red Guards for their proletarian revolutionary rebel spirit and gave them firm and warm support. Chairman Mao's voice was like a clap of spring thunder. In a very brief time, Red Guards developed in schools all over the country, in many factories and rural areas, and became an enormous and powerful cultural revolutionary army. The struggle [to overthrow those persons in authority who are taking the capitalist road], the criticism and repudiation [of the reactionary bourgeois academic "authorities" and the ideology of the bourgeoisie and all other exploiting classes] and the transformation [of education, literature and art and all other parts of the superstructure that do not correspond to the socialist economic base] in the schools have been extended to the whole of society. The revolutionary Red Guards have destroyed the "four olds" of the exploiting classes on a large scale and extensively fostered the "four news" of the proletariat. They are in the van in the criticism and repudiation of the bourgeois reactionary line. They have served as the vanguard.

The extensive exchange of revolutionary experience is also something new that has emerged in the course of the great proletarian cultural revolution

and has been supported and promoted by the great proletarian revolutionary Chairman Mao. The extensive exchange of experience by revolutionary students and teachers on a nationwide scale has linked the great proletarian cultural revolutionary movement throughout the country. The extensive exchange of revolutionary experience has spread Mao Tse-tung's thought, propagated Chairman Mao's proletarian revolutionary line and organized the proletarian revolutionary ranks all over the country and greatly battered the bourgeois reactionary line.

However, the very few persons who stubbornly persist in the bourgeois reactionary line are not reconciled to their defeat. The bourgeois reactionary line has its social base, which is mainly the bourgeoisie, and those landlords and rich peasants, counter-revolutionaries, bad elements and Rightists, who have not reformed themselves sufficiently. The bourgeois reactionary line has a certain market within the Party too—among cadres whose world outlook has not been remolded, or not been remolded sufficiently. The very few persons who stubbornly persist in the bourgeois reactionary line are stirring up trouble by making use of its social base and its influence inside the Party. They resort to a variety of tricks in their dual tactics to resist the proletarian revolutionary line and to sabotage the criticism and repudiation of the bourgeois reactionary line by the revolutionary masses.

The most important plot and scheme of the very small number of persons who stubbornly persist in the bourgeois reactionary line is to incite the masses to struggle against each other. They have secretly organized and manipulated some people and mass organizations, whom they have hoodwinked, to suppress the revolution, protect themselves, and to provoke conflicts in which coercion or force are used in a vain attempt to create confusion. They spread rumours, turned black into white and shifted the blame for the evil they had done behind people's backs on to the proletarian revolutionaries, labelling the latter with the "bourgeois reactionary line." They have continued to vainly attempt to direct the spearhead of the attack against the revolutionary masses, the proletarian revolutionary line and the proletarian revolutionary headquarters.

When our Party was organizing the proletarian cultural revolutionary ranks in accordance with Chairman Mao's class line, this very small number of persons who stubbornly cling to the bourgeois reactionary line made use of the slogan "A hero's son is a real man! A reactionary's son is no damn good!" to bewilder a number of students, create factions and confuse the class fronts. This slogan was first put forth by some naive young people. Because of certain onesidedness in their methods of thinking, and proceeding from the correct premise of opposing the discrimination against and attack on the sons and daughters of revolutionary cadres, workers and peasants by the handful of persons within the Party who are in authority and taking the capitalist road, these young people have moved to another extreme. Towards these naive youngsters, the proper thing to do is to patiently give them correct guidance. This was what the Party did at the time. However, those who stubbornly persist in the bourgeois reactionary line have made use of this slogan and have ulterior motives for deceiving a very small number of students (among whom are some cadres' sons and daughters who have not been properly educated), trying to lead them on to the wrong path and to create antagonism between these and other students. The slogan "A hero's son is a real man! A reactionary's son is no damn good!" has thus been turned into something in opposition to the proletarian revolutionary line. It should be pointed out that the way those people with ulterior motives have made use of the slogan is in essence to advertise the exploiting classes' reactionary "theory of family lineage." This is exactly the same as the lineage theory spread by the feudal landlord class that "a dragon begets a dragon, a phoenix begets a phoenix, and those begotton by rats are good at digging holes." This is out and out reactionary historical idealism.

The very small number of persons who stubbornly persist in the bourgeois reactionary line not only refuse to make a self-criticism before the masses, to reverse the verdicts passed on those of the revolutionary masses who have been branded "counter-revolutionaries," "anti-Party elements," "pseudo-Leftists but genuine Rightists," "self-seeking careerists" and so on and so forth, and to publicly burn the material they have compiled against some of the revolutionary masses. On the contrary, they have been loudly publicizing "the theory of settling accounts after the autumn harvest," and declaring that some of the revolutionary masses will be dealt with as "Rightists." This means that they are going to counter attack and settle their accounts with the revolutionary masses. The proletarian revolutionaries are not afraid of settling accounts. The "theory of settling accounts after the autumn harvest" can in no way intimidate the revolutionary masses. Those who spread such talk have contracted a new debt to the Party and the revolutionary masses who are sure to settle accounts with them.

These maneuvers of the very few persons who stubbornly persist in the bourgeois reactionary line serve precisely to expose them. The greater the disturbances they make, the clearer the masses understand what is meant by the bourgeois reactionary line and the more they see that it is absolutely necessary to rise up and expose, criticize and repudiate it.

Why were these persons who persist in the bourgeois reactionary line able to hoodwink some people for a time? They made use of the high prestige enjoyed by Chairman Mao and the Party among the masses; they arrogated to themselves the credit of the Party, describing themselves as the personification of the Party, their words and actions as the expression of the Party leadership and the people's faith in the Party as faith in them. They also made special efforts to spread the idea that people should obey the leadership of their immediate superiors unconditionally and in disregard of principle. Such an idea in essence advocates blind obedience and slavishness, and is opposed to Marxism-Leninism, Mao Tse-tung's thought.

As early as during the rectification campaign in 1942, when the question of the Wang Ming line was solved ideologically, Chairman Mao pointed out:

*"Communists must always go into the whys and wherefores of anything, use their own heads and carefully think over whether or not it corresponds to reality and is really well founded—on no account should they follow blindly and encourage slavishness."*

Chairman Mao has often taught us that *erroneous leadership, which brings harm to the revolution, should not be accepted unconditionally but should be resisted resolutely.* In fact, in the course of the current great cultural revolution, the masses of revolutionary students and teachers and revolutionary cadres have put up wide resistance to erroneous leadership.

It is both a political and organizational principle of a proletarian political Party armed with Marxism-Leninsim, Mao Tse-tung's thought, resolutely to accept and carry out correct leadership by Marxism-Leninism, Mao Tse-tung's thought, resolutely to resist wrong leadership that brings harm to the revolution, and resolutely to oppose slavishness. All true Communists should act in accordance with this principle resolutely, wholly and fearlessly, and undertake to propagate it correctly to the masses. Once this principle is grasped by the revolutionary masses and the masses of revolutionary cadres, those persons who stubbornly persist in the bourgeois reactionary line and the handful of persons within the Party who are in authority and are taking the capitalist road will be disarmed.

More than four months have passed since the Eleventh Plenary Session of the Eighth Central Committee of the Chinese Communist Party. Chairman Mao and his comrades-in-arms have done much political and ideological work with regard to those comrades who have committed errors of line, and the revolutionary masses have criticized and educated them. Some comrades have already corrected their errors and others are now correcting them, and this should be welcomed. As for those persons who still refuse to correct their errors, we should sharply tell them: pull back before it is too late! If they continue to cling to the bourgeois reactionary line and use two-faced tactics towards the Party and the masses they will be wallowing in the mire with those persons who are in authority and are taking the capitalist road, or prove themselves to be, in fact, persons in authority who are taking the capitalist road.

This struggle between the two lines is a very deep-going one. The mass movement carried out in the past few months to criticize and repudiate the bourgeois reactionary line has scored tremendous achievements and enabled hundreds of millions of people to understand the essence of the struggle. The proletarian revolutionary line represented by Chairman Mao aims to boldly arouse the masses, overthrow the handful of persons within the Party who are in authority and are taking the capitalist road and the bourgeois reactionary academic "authorities," and eradicate all vestiges of the exploiting classes. On the other hand, the bourgeois reactionary line aims to suppress the masses, protect the handful of persons within the Party who are in authority and are taking the capitalist road and the bourgeois reactionary academic "authorities" and defend all vestiges of the exploiting classes. One wants to carry the socialist revolution through to the end while the other wants to preserve the old capitalist order. One wants to revolutionize while the other wants to preserve. This is the essence of the struggle between the two lines.

As the mass criticism and repudiation of the bourgeois reactionary line grows deeper, the masses are further grasping the proletarian revolutionary line of Chairman Mao and a new situation has developed in China's great proletarian cultural revolution. The main features of this new situation are the following:

Vast numbers of workers and peasants have risen. They are breaking through all obstacles to establish their own revolutionary organizations and they have plunged into the movement of the great proletarian cultural revolution.

The forces of the revolutionary students have grown greatly and become much stronger, and their level is much higher. A number of revolutionary students have gone to factories and villages and have begun to integrate themselves with the worker-peasant masses.

The revolutionary cadres in Party and state organizations have risen to revolt against those persons holding responsible posts who are subbornly clinging to the bourgeois reactionary line.

The mass movement has grown in scope. The content of struggle has grown richer. More revolutionary path-breakers have appeared among workers, peasants, students and cadres. The handful of persons within the Party who are in authority and are taking the capitalist road have beome more isolated.

All cultural revolution movements in contemporary Chinese history have begun with student movements and led to the worker and peasant movements, to the integration of revolutionary intellectuals with the worker-peasant masses. This is an objective law. This was true of the May Fourth Movement which marked the beginning of China's contemporary history of revolution and is true also of the great proletarian cultural revolution which has brought the country's socialist revolution to a new stage. In 1967, China's great proletarian cultural revolution will continue to develop in line with this objective law.

1967 will be a year of all-round development of class struggle throughout China.

It will be a year in which the proletariat, united with other sectors of the revolutionary masses, will launch a general attack on the handful of persons within the Party who are in authority and are taking the capitalist road, and on the ghosts and monsters in society.

It will be a year of even more penetrating criticism and repudiation of the bourgeois reactionary line and elimination of its influence.

It will be a year of decisive victory in carrying out the struggle [to overthrow those persons in authority who are taking the capitalist road], the criticism and repudiation [of the reactionary bourgeois academic "authorities" and the ideology of the bourgeoisie and all other exploiting classes] and the transformation [of education, literature and art and all other parts of the superstructure that do not correspond to the socialist economic base].

The main political tasks confronting the whole Party and all revolutionaries in the country for 1967 are:

*First,* in accordance with the directive of Chairman Mao and the Central Committee of the Party to "grasp the revolution and promote production," the great proletarian cultural revolution should be carried out on a large-scale in the factories and rural areas, so as to stimulate the revolutionization of people's thinking and promote the development of industrial and agricultural production.

The great proletarian cultural revolution in the factories and rural areas must follow the 16-point decision of the Party's Central Committee concerning the cultural revolution and firmly adhere to the line of letting the masses educate themselves, liberate themselves and rise up and make revolution by themselves. No one should take everything into one's own hands. The "four clean-ups" movement is to be incorporated into the great cultural revolution in which the question of the "four clean-ups" and the question of re-checking the results will be solved.

The great proletarian cultural revolution in the factories and rural areas is of the utmost importance. The workers and peasants are the main force in this revolution. The worker-peasant masses must be boldly aroused to struggle against and overthrow the handful of persons in the Party who are in authority in the factories and mines and in the rural areas and who are taking the capitalist road and root out all vestiges of capitalism and revisionism. Only in this way can the roots of capitalist restoration be eliminated.

In the early period of the War of Resistance to Japanese Aggression, Chairman Mao said: *"only by mobilizing the masses of workers and peasants, who form 90 per cent of the population, can we defeat imperialism and feudalism."* Likewise, only by *"mobilizing the masses of workers and peasants, who form 90 per cent of the population,"* will it be possible today to defeat the handful of persons within the Party who are in authority and are taking the capitalist road and to settle the question of who will win, the proletariat or the bourgeoisie.

The great proletarian cultural revolution must go from the offices, schools and cultural circles to the factories and mines and the rural areas so that all positions are captured by Mao Tse-tung's thought. If the movement is confined to offices, schools and cultural circles, the great proletarian cultural revolution will stop half way.

Any argument against the carrying out of a large-scale proletarian cultural revolution in factories and mines and the rural areas is erroneous.

Some muddle-headed people counterpose the revolution to production and think that once the great cultural revolution starts, it will impede production. Therefore, they take hold of production alone and do not grasp the revolution. These comrades have not thought through the question of what is the purpose of farming, weaving, steel making. Is it for building socialism, or is it for building capitalism? The historical experience of countries under the dictatorship of the proletariat tells us that only when the great proletarian cultural revolution is carried out successfully can the advance of our economic construction along the road of socialism and communism be ensured. Many instances during the great proletarian cultural revolution show that production makes great headway wherever the cultural revolution is successful. Revolution can only promote the development of the social productive forces, not impede it. This is a Marxist-Leninist truth, a truth of Mao Tse-tung's thought.

There are also an extremely small number of persons who use the taking hold of production as a pretext to repress the revolution. They appear to be interested in production, but, in point of fact, they are interested in their own posts and the preservation of old bourgeois things; they are afraid that the revolution may turn against them. They go to such lengths as abetting the section of people who, for a time, are hoodwinked by them, to halt production and take action against the revolutionary masses when the masses rise to make vigorous revolution. Some of them even collude with landlords, rich peasants, counter-revolutionaries, bad elements and Rightists to engage in underhanded activities. This only exposes them as pursuing the bourgeois reactionary line, or worse still, that they are, or are on the point of becoming, persons in authority taking the capitalist road.

The mass movement in factories and mines and the rural areas in the great proletarian cultural revolution is an irresistible historical trend. Any argument or person standing in the way of this trend will be swept on to the rubbish heap by the revolutionary masses.

*Second,* with regard to the great proletarian cultural revolution in the schools and every cultural sphere, the idea should be energetically advocated that revolutionary students, teachers and intellectuals should go to the factories and rural areas in a planned and organized way, to integrate themselves with the worker-peasant masses.

In *The May 4th Movement* and *The Orientation of the Youth Movement,* both published in 1939, Chairman Mao pointed out:

*"The intellectuals will accomplish nothing if they fail to integrate themselves with the workers and peasants. In the final analysis, the dividing line between revolutionary intellectuals and non-revolutionary or counter-revolutionary intellectuals is whether or not they are willing to integrate themselves with the workers and peasants and actually do so."*

*"The young intellectuals and students throughout the country must unite with the broad masses of workers and peasants and become one with them, and only then can a mighty force be created. A force of hundreds of millions of people! Only with this huge force can the enemy's strongholds be taken and his last fortresses smashed."*

Here, Chairman Mao stated a universal truth. Integration with the worker-peasant masses is the orientation for the youth movement in both the period of the new democratic revolution and the period of the socialist revolution.

It is still true today that *"in the final analysis, the dividing line between revolutionary intellectuals and non-revolutionary or counter-revolutionary intellectuals is whether or not they are willing to integrate themselves with the workers and peasants and actually do so."* Only by integrating himself with the workers and peasants can the intellectual establish a truly proletarian world outlook and become a proletarian intellectual in the true sense.

It is still true today that young intellectuals and students must go to the factories and the countryside, integrate themselves with the workers and peasants and become one with them. Only then can a mighty hundreds of millions strong force be organized to take by storm the positions held by the handful of persons within the Party who are in authority and are taking the capitalist road and to win final victory in the great proletarian cultural revolution.

Going to the factories and the countryside should be rationally arranged in relation to the tasks of struggle, criticism and repudiation, and transformation in a given unit. The necessary summing up of the struggle in the previous period in the unit has to be done, so as to further clarify the essence of the struggle between the two lines in the great cultural revolution, distinguish right from wrong on cardinal issues, and adopt a correct attitude and get a correct understanding in the matter of going to the factories and rural areas.

Having gone to the factories and rural areas, we should learn modestly from the worker and peasant masses and be their willing pupils, join together with them to work, study and discuss the problems in the cultural revolution, propagate the proletarian revolutionary line of Chairman Mao, and criticize and repudiate the bourgeois reactionary line. We must direct our eyes downward, undertake thoroughgoing investigation and study, integrate ourselves with the revolutionary mass organizations in the factories and rural areas, guard against the idea of our being always right and avoid taking everything into our own hands.

An important condition in carrying out the tasks of struggle, criticism and repudiation, and transformation within a given unit is that its members should go to factories and rural areas. When students and other young intellectuals plunge into the heat of the mass movement of the workers and peasants so that their ideology will be remolded, they will be able to struggle more powerfully against the handful of persons within the Party who are in authority and are taking the capitalist road, and to differentiate more clearly between right and wrong in the big debate. Only when the great proletarian cultural revolution in the factories and rural areas is carried out thoroughly can the revolution in the schools and cultural circles, which belong to the superstructure, be completely accomplished. Only when the actual conditions in the factories and rural areas are understood and the voice of the workers and peasants is heard, can the system and content of education and the method of teaching be changed in a practical way and our cultural bodies and cultural work be transformed effectively so that they will serve the workers, peasants and soldiers truly and completely.

*Third,* fully develop extensive democracy under the dictatorship of the proletariat. This extensive democracy means mobilizing hundreds of millions of people under the command of Mao Tse-tung's thought to launch a general attack on the enemies of socialism and, at the same time, criticize and supervise leading organs and leading cadres at all levels. Fostering such a social atmosphere of extensive democracy is of great, far-reaching significance for the consolidation of the dictatorship of the proletariat and the prevention of the restoration of capitalism.

Extensive proletarian democracy is a new development of Chairman Mao's mass line and a new form of the integration of Mao Tse-tung's thought with hundreds of millions of people. This extensive democracy is the best way for the masses to educate and liberate themselves. In the course of this movement for extensive democracy, the masses are taking Mao Tse-tung's thought as their weapon to draw a line between the enemy and themselves and distinguish right from wrong. This extensive democracy is the best school for learning Mao Tse-tung's thought.

Chairman Mao teaches us: *"Democracy sometimes seems to be an end, but it is in fact only a means."* What we aim to achieve by means of extensive democracy is the carrying out of the great proletarian cultural revolution and the development of the cause of socialism. If we depart from the interests of the proletariat and other laboring people, from socialism and from the proletarian revolutionary line represented by Chairman Mao, we shall not be able to have extensive proletarian democracy, and the result can only be the oppression of the revolutionary masses by a small number of persons.

The extensive democracy we advocate is under the centralized guidance of Mao Tse-tung's thought. Different opinions among the masses should be debated under the guidance of Mao Tse-tung's thought by presenting facts and reasoning things out; it is impermissible to use coercive measures to make others submit. Among the people, it would be against the principle of extensive proletarian democracy if only one himself is allowed to express opinions while others are forbidden to air different opinions. A very few bad eggs with ulterior motives are instigating those of the masses whom they have hoodwinked to carry out struggles by force and coercion in an attempt to suppress the revolution. They are sabotaging extensive proletarian democracy, the great proletarian cultural revolution and the dictatorship of the proletariat.

Chairman Mao teaches us that there should be democracy within the ranks of the people and dictatorship over the reactionaries. The dictatorship of the proletariat is the safeguard for the implementation of extensive proletarian democracy. Extensive proletarian democracy in turn is aimed at consolidating the dictatorship of the proletariat. Without extensive proletarian democracy, there is the danger that the dictatorship of the proletariat will turn into the dictatorship of the bourgeoisie. Without the dictatorship of the proletariat there can be no proletarian democracy. There cannot even be democracy on a small scale, let alone extensive democracy. In the course of the great proletarian cultural revolution, our organs of proletarian dictatorship must resolutely and unswervingly guarantee the democratic rights of the people and guarantee that free airing of views, the posting of big-character posters, great debates, and the large-scale exchange of revolutionary experience proceed in a normal way. Where there is clear evidence of cases of murder, arson, poisoning, traffic accidents created with murderous intent, maintaining traitorous relations with foreign countries, theft of state secrets and sabotage, the counter-revolutionaries concerned must be subjected to dictatorship and punished according to law. All revolutionary people must assist and supervise our state organs of the dictatorship in carrying out their task of safeguarding extensive proletarian democracy. As for Rightists who are reactionary-minded but have not done anything against the law, the masses should struggle against them by presenting facts and reasoning things out.

*Fourth,* continue to carry out mass criticism of the bourgeois reactionary line.

It is by no means accidental that the bourgeois reactionary line has appeared in the great proletarian cultural revolution. Since China entered the stage of socialist revolution, struggles have existed between the proletarian revolutionary line represented by Chairman Mao and the bourgeois reactionary line, and over the issue of whether to build socialism or capitalism. Those who have put forward the reactionary line in the great proletarian cultural revolution only further exposed their bourgeois reactionary stand.

A great deal of intensive and careful work still has to be done in order to get rid of the bourgeois reactionary line and stamp out its effects in the factories and mines, in rural areas, in primary and middle schools, in colleges and universities, in cultural circles, in Party and government institutions and in all other spheres so that people can really get to the ideological root in solving this question. We must soundly understand this point.

Great efforts must be made henceforth to destroy the bourgeois reactionary line and establish Chairman Mao's proletarian revolutionary line in the movement among the workers, peasants and students, and on a variety of fronts in the great proletarian cultural revolution. This is the key to carrying the great proletarian cultural revolution through to the end.

Revolutionary cadres in the Party and government institutions must break with outmoded rules and regulations and conventions which shackle the revolution. They must go among the masses and, together with the workers, peasants and revolutionary students, criticize and repudiate the bourgeois reactionary line and struggle against the handful of people within the Party who are in authority and are taking the capitalist road. Through the mass movement of the great proletarian cultural revolution, we shall realize the thorough proletarian revolutionization of our Party and government institutions.

During the criticism and repudiation of the

bourgeois reactionary line, those comrades who commit errors of line must be treated in accordance with Chairman Mao's instructions: *"In the spirit of 'learning from past mistakes to avoid future ones' and 'curing the sickness to save the patient,' in order to achieve the twofold objective of clarity in ideology and unity among comrades."* As for the very few double-dealers who refuse to correct themselves, stick to their errors and feign compliance while acting in opposition, the masses will surely overthrow them and they will have only themselves to blame.

The Chinese Communist Party is great, glorious and correct. Those in the Party who are in authority and are taking the capitalist road amount to just a handful of people. The overwhelming majority of Party members and cadres are good and want revolution. Through the testing and tempering of the mass movement in the great proletarian cultural revolution, they will become still stronger.

The revolutionary Left should make great efforts to study and apply Chairman Mao's works creatively, raise their level and readjust their ranks in the struggle to criticize and repudiate the bourgeois reactionary line. The ranks of the revolutionary Left must strengthen their unity on the basis of Mao Tse-tung's thought. They should make greater efforts to study and grasp the strategic and tactical concepts of Chairman Mao and be good at winning over and uniting with the great majority so as to isolate the diehard enemy to the greatest possible extent. In the struggle, a strict distinction must be made between ourselves and the enemy and those among the people. "The strictest care should be taken to distinguish between the anti-Party, anti-socialist Rightists and those who support the Party and socialism but have said or done something wrong or have written some bad articles or other works," and "to distinguish between the reactionary bourgeois scholar despots and reactionary 'authorities' on the one hand and people who have the ordinary bourgeois academic ideas on the other." By the end of the movement we shall achieve unity of more than 95 per cent of the cadres and more than 95 per cent of the people.

It is certain that the handful of people within the Party who are in authority and are taking the capitalist road and those very few diehards who stick to the bourgeois reactionary line will play new tricks and continue to make trouble. Like all other reactionaries, *"in the last analysis, their persecution of the revolutionary people only serves to accelerate the people's revolutions on a broader and more intense scale."* To be sure, like all other reactionaries, they too are paper tigers. We must do as Chairman Mao teaches us: despise them strategically and take full account of them tactically, and wage an unremitting struggle against them.

In the great proletarian cultural revolution, we should take as the key link the class struggle between the proletariat and the bourgeoisie, the struggle between the two roads of socialism and capitalism and the struggle between the proletarian revolutionary line and the bourgeois reactionary line, and, in conjunction with the free airing of views, big-character posters and great debates, develop more fully the mass movement for the creative study and application of Chairman Mao's works in response to the call of Comrade Lin Piao who is holding high the great red banner of Mao Tse-tung's thought, and temper and strengthen the highly proletarianized and militant revolutionary ranks to win one new victory after another.

Under the banner of the great thought of Mao Tse-tung,

Let the working class unite,

Let the working class unite with the poor and lower-middle peasants and other laboring people,

Let all laboring people unite with the revolutionary students, revolutionary intellectuals and revolutionary cadres,

Let the people of all nationalities unite,

Unfold class struggle in an all-round way throughout the country,

And carry the great proletarian cultural revolution through to the end!

Long live the great teacher, the great leader, the great supreme commander and the great helmsman Chairman Mao!

# "ON THE PROLETARIAN REVOLUTIONARIES' STRUGGLE TO SEIZE POWER"

*Red Flag* Editorial, No. 3, 1967

*Complete Text*
(*Peking Review,* No. 6, 3 February 1967)

Proletarian revolutionaries are uniting to seize power from the handful of persons within the Party who are in authority and taking the capitalist road. This is the strategic task for the new stage of the great proletarian cultural revolution. It is the decisive battle between the proletariat and the masses of working people on the one hand and the bourgeoisie and its agents in the Party on the other.

This mighty revolutionary storm started in Shanghai. The revolutionary masses in Shanghai have called it the great "January Revolution." Our great leader Chairman Mao immediately expressed resolute support for it. He called on the workers, peasants, revolutionary students, revolutionary intellectuals and revolutionary cadres to study the experience of the revolutionary rebels of Shanghai and he called on the People's Liberation Army actively to support and assist the proletarian revolutionaries in their struggle to seize power.

Chairman Mao's great call received an immediate enthusiastic response from the revolutionary masses and the commanders and fighters of the People's Liberation Army. The proletarian revolutionaries who have formed a mighty force are capturing one citadel after another in certain places and units, where the handful of persons within the Party who are in authority and taking the capitalist road have been entrenched, and are then consolidating these captured positions one by one. The storm of the "January Revolution" is now sweeping the whole country.

The ranks of the handful of persons within the Party who are in authority and taking the capitalist road have been badly battered. However, like all reactionaries, they will never be reconciled to their own extinction. And like all reactionaries, they *"will never lay down their butcher knives ... they will never become buddhas."*

*Chairman Mao has pointed out: "Make trouble, fail, make trouble again, fail again ... till their doom; that is the logic of the imperialists and all reactionaries the world over in dealing with the people's cause, and they will never go against this logic."* This is also true of the handful of persons within the Party who are in authority and taking the capitalist road. We must *"cast away illusions, prepare for struggle"* in accordance with Chairman Mao's teaching.

The experience of the city of Shanghai, Shansi Province and other places tells us that in the course of the struggle to seize power, we must pay great attention to the following questions:

## 1.

When they were in power, the handful of persons within the Party who were in authority and taking the capitalist road always used their power to counter the proletarian revolutionary line represented by Chairman Mao and to suppress the revolutionary masses. When they are stripped of power by the revolutionary masses, they still do their utmost to stage a counter seizure of power in a vain attempt to counter-attack in revenge and to recapture their lost power.

In some places, these reactionary elements are reorganizing their reactionary ranks. They are gathering together landlords, rich peasants, counter-revolutionaries, bad elements and Rightists, and collecting the dregs of society to stage counter-attacks against the proletarian revolutionaries and seize power from them.

In some places, these reactionary elements have resorted to the method of worming their way in [to the ranks of the revolutionaries] and pulling people out [of the revolutionary ranks] in a vain attempt to split up the great alliance of the proletarian revolutionaries, and usurp the leadership of the revolutionary rebel organizations. In this way they hope to shift the general orientation of the struggle.

In some places, these reactionary elements instigate their collaborators who still hold the leadership of a factory, a workshop, a unit, or a production brigade to sabotage production, disrupt communications and transport and destroy state and collective property, in a vain attempt to disturb the economic life of the state so as to achieve their political aim of staging a counterseizure of power against the proletarian revolutionaries.

*Chairman Mao teaches us: "Strategically we should despise all our enemies, but tactically we should take them all seriously."* The handful of persons with the Party who are in authority and taking the capitalist road will never succeed in their schemes, which are doomed to failure. We should despise them. However, we must deal with them seriously, and must never treat them casually or lightly.

Proletarian revolutionaries must fully understand that the struggle to seize power and counter-seize power between us and the handful of persons within the Party who are in authority and taking the capitalist road is a life-and-death struggle between the proletariat and the bourgeoisie. It is a contradiction between ourselves and the enemy.

The general orientation for proletarian revolutionaries is to form an alliance and seize power from the handful of persons within the Party who are in authority and taking the capitalist road. All revolutionary comrades should take this general orientation as their starting point and adhere to it in considering and handling all matters. If not, they will embark on the wrong road and may go over to the opposite side.

In places and organizations where the great proletarian cultural revolution has been vigorously carried out for more than half a year, the revolutionary masses have become clear as to who are the chief figures among those in the Party who are in authority and taking the capitalist road. In the struggle to seize power, the proletarian revolutionaries must focus on their target and deal the enemy heavy blows. A strict distinction must be made between contradictions between ourselves and the enemy and those among the people. We must not treat contradictions among the people as contradictions between ourselves and the enemy and blast away indiscriminately. Otherwise, the struggle to seize power from the handful of persons within the Party who are in authority and taking the capitalist road will be hindered and errors on questions of orientation will be committed and will be used by the class enemy.

## 2.

Resolutely build the great alliance of the proletarian revolutionaries and unite the broad masses. This is the most important condition for victory in the struggle to seize power from the handful of persons within the Party who are in authority and taking the capitalist road.

Now that the great proletarian cultural revolution has reached the stage of the struggle to seize power in an all-round way from the handful of persons within the Party who are in authority and taking the capitalist road, it is essential for revolutionary mass organizations to forge a great alliance. Without a great alliance of proletarian revolutionaries, the struggle to seize power cannot be completed successfully; even if some power has been seized, it may be lost again.

To form and consolidate the great alliance of proletarian revolutionaries, it is necessary to study and apply Chairman Mao's works creatively in the course of struggle, to straighten out the ranks ideologically and organizationally and strengthen the proletarian sense of organization and discipline. It is necessary to use Mao Tse-tung's thought as the weapon to correct such erroneous tendencies as departmentalism, "small group" mentality (considering the interests of a particular group rather than the overall interest), excessive decentralization, the disregard of organizational discipline, ultra-democracy, liberalism, subjectivism and individualism in people's minds and in their organizations. All of these ideas and actions that run counter to Chairman Mao's teachings and hamper the great alliance of the proletarian revolutionaries are an expression of the bourgeois world outlook, a reflection of the current acute class struggle in the revolutionary ranks. These questions fall within the category of contradictions among the people, which must be solved in line with the policy of "learning from past mistakes to avoid future ones" and "curing the sickness to save the patient" and the formula of unity-criticism-unity, all of which Chairman Mao has always advocated. Do more self-criticism, and don't attack one another. The erroneous, non-proletarian ideas and actions cited above must not be allowed to develop or they will be made use of by the class enemy. If anyone clings to these erroneous ideas and persists in taking these erroneous actions and lets them develop, the non-antagonistic contradictions can turn into antagonistic ones.

Once the revolutionary mass organizations have seized power in a particular department, their own position alters. At this time, the bourgeois ideas and petty-bourgeois ideas in the minds of certain comrades easily come to the fore. We must be highly vigilant. We must rid ourselves of all selfish ideas and personal considerations and make a revolution to the depth of our souls. Everything must proceed from the fundamental interests of the proletariat. We must attach the utmost importance to the interests of the whole instead of concerning ourselves with personal prestige and position. We must firmly respond to Chairman Mao's call to *"practice economy in carrying out revolution"* and not show off, spend money without measure and waste state property. We must not fall victim to the "sugar-coated bullets" of the bourgeoisie.

Revolutionary mass organizations which have seized power and the leaders of these organizations should adopt the principle of unity towards the masses and the mass organizations holding different views. They should win over the majority instead of excluding the majority. This helps to isolate to the maximum the handful of persons within the Party who are in authority and taking the capitalist road and deal them blows and it helps to establish the new proletarian revolutionary order.

Everyone, in the course of the struggle to seize power and after coming to power, has to undergo new tests. We hope that the revolutionary path-breakers who come to the fore during the movement will always be loyal to the proletariat, to Chairman Mao, and to the proletarian revolutionary line represented by Chairman Mao, and that they willl become politically mature in the course of time rather than be like those who just flash across the stage of history. The only way one can live up to this hope is to study Mao Tse-tung's thought conscientiously, to integrate oneself with the masses of workers and peasants and to make serious efforts to remold one's own non-proletarian world outlook. There is no other way.

## 3.

Adequate attention must be paid to the role of revolutionary cadres in the struggle to seize power. Leading cadres who have firmly adhered to the proletarian revolutionary line are the treasure of the Party. They can become the backbone of the struggle to seize power and can become leaders in this struggle.

Such leading comrades have, for quite a long time in the past, waged struggles within the Party against the handful of people in authority taking the capitalist road. They have now stepped out before the masses and have proclaimed to the masses that they stand on the side of the proletarian revolutionaries and will integrate themselves with the revolutionary masses and fight together with them. The workers, peasants, revolutionary students and revolutionary intellectuals should trust them. A clear distinction must be drawn between those in authority who belong to the proletariat and those who belong to the bourgeoisie, between those who support and carry out the proletarian revolutionary line and those who support and carry out the bourgeois reactionary line. To regard all persons in authority as untrustworthy is wrong. To oppose, exclude and overthrow all indiscriminately runs counter to the class viewpoint of Marxism-Leninism, Mao Tse-tung's thought.

When the revolutionary leading cadres rise up to join the masses in seizing power from the handful of persons within the Party who are in authority and taking the capitalist road, the revolutionary mass organizations should support them. It must be recognized that they are more experienced in struggle, they are more mature politically and they have greater organizational skill. The seizure and retention of power will be helped immeasurably by their inclusion in the core of leadership.

Cadres who have made errors should be treated correctly and should not be overthrown indiscriminately. All those who are not anti-Party, anti-socialist elements, and do not persist in their errors or refuse to correct them after repeated education, should be allowed to correct their errors and be encouraged to make amends for their crimes by good deeds. To learn from past mistakes to avoid future ones and to cure the sickness to save the patient is a long-standing policy of the Party. Only thus can those who commit errors submit willingly; and only in this way can the proletarian revolutionaries get hearty support from the great majority of the people and remain invincible. Otherwise, there is great danger.

The overwhelming majority of the ordinary cadres in the Party and government organizations, enterprises and undertakings are good and want to make revolution. The proletarian revolutionary rebels among them are the vital force for seizing power in these organizations. This is the point which must not be neglected.

Cadres at all levels have to undergo the test of the great proletarian cultural revolution and make new contributions to the revolution. They should not rest on their past achievements, think that they are so wonderful and lightly regard the young revolutionary fighters who have now come to the fore. The following concepts are completely wrong and must be corrected: to see only one's own past merits but not the general orientation of the revolution today and to see only the shortcomings and mistakes of the newly emerged young revolutionary fighters, but not to recognize the fact that their general orientation in the revolution is correct.

### 4.

The current seizure of power from the handful of persons within the Party who are in authority and taking the capitalist road is not effected by dismissal and reorganization from above, but from below by the mass movement called for and supported by Chairman Mao himself. Only in this way can the leading organizations of our Party and state, enterprises and undertakings, cultural organizations and schools be regenerated and the old bourgeois practices be thoroughly eradicated.

Experience proves that in the course of the struggle for the seizure of power, it is necessary, through exchange of views and consultations among leading members of revolutionary mass organizations, leading members of local People's Liberation Army units and revolutionary leading cadres of Party and government organizations, to establish provisional organs of power to take up the responsibility of leading this struggle. These provisional organs of power must *"take firm hold of the revolution and promote production,"* put the system of production into normal operation, direct the existing set-ups in administrative and professional work (they should be readjusted where necessary) to carry on with their tasks, and organize the revolutionary masses to supervise these set-ups. These provisional organs of power must also shoulder the task of giving unified direction in suppressing counter-revolutionary organizations and counter-revolutionaries. Such provisional organs of power must be set up; this is essential and extremely important. Through a period of transition, the wisdom of the broad masses will be brought into full play and a completely new organizational form of political power better suited to the socialist economic base will be created.

A number of units, where a handful of persons within the Party who are in authority and taking the capitalist road have entrenched themselves over a long period, have become rotten. There these persons have been exercising bourgeois dictatorship, not proletarian dictatorship. The Marxist principle of smashing the existing state machine must be put into practice in the struggle for the seizure of power in these units.

In summing up the experience of the Paris Commune, Marx pointed out that the proletariat must not take over the existing bourgeois state machine but must thoroughly smash it. Practice in the international communist movement has proved this to be a great truth. Since a number of units, in which a handful of persons within the Party who are in authority and taking the capitalist road have entrenched themselves, have been turned into organs for bourgeois dictatorship, naturally we must not take them over ready-made, resort to reformism, combine two into one and effect peaceful transition. We must smash them thoroughly.

The great mass movement to seize power from the handful of persons within the Party who are in authority and taking the capitalist road has begun to create and will continue to create new organizational forms for the state organs of the proletarian dictatorship. Here, we must respect the initiative of the masses and boldly adopt the new forms, full of vitality, that emerge in the mass movement to replace the old practices of the exploiting classes and in fact to replace all old practices that do not correspond to the socialist economic base. It is absolutely impermissible to merely take over power while letting things remain the same and operating according to old rules.

On June 1 last year, Chairman Mao described the first Marxist-Leninist big-character poster in the country, which came from Peking University, as the Manifesto of the Peking People's Commune of the sixties in the 20th century. Chairman Mao showed his wisdom and genius in predicting even then that our state organs would take on completely new forms.

To arouse hundreds of millions of people from below to seize power from the handful of persons within the Party who are in authority and taking the capitalist road, to smash the old practices within the Party who are in authority and taking the capitalist road, to smash the old practices and create new forms, opens up a new era in the international history of proletarian revolution and in the international history of the dictatorship of the proletariat. It will greatly enrich and develop the experience of the Paris Commune, greatly enrich and develop the experience of the Soviets, and greatly enrich and develop Marxism-Leninism.

## 5.

The struggle by the proletarian revolutionaries to seize power from the handful of persons within the Party who are in authority and taking the capitalist road is being carried out under the dictatorship of the proletariat. In the course of the seizure of power, the dictatorship of the proletariat must be strengthened. This is an indispensable condition for the establishment of the new proletarian revolutionary order.

In the present stage of the decisive struggle being waged by the proletariat against the bourgeoisie and its handful of agents within the Party, the landlords and rich peasants, who persist in their reactionary stand, the bourgeois Rightists, bad elements, counter-revolutionary revisionists and the U.S.-Chiang Kai-shek special agents all emerge. These ghosts and monsters spread rumors to confuse the people, and deceive and mislead those who are not aware of the true facts into forming counter-revolutionary organizations to carry out frenzied counter-revolutionary activities. For example, the so-called "Worker-Peasant Red Flag Army of China," "Rong Fu Jun," "United Action Committee" and a number of other organizations set up by the revisionists, which call themselves "revolutionary" but are actually royalist organizations, are reactionary organizations of this kind. The majority of the masses in these organizations have been duped and should be won over by education. However, the handful of ringleaders of these reactionary organizations have schemed and used every kind of trick to bombard the proletarian revolutionary headquarters, to seize power from the proletarian revolutionaries and raid the

revolutionary mass organizations. They have stabbed the revolutionary people in the back, bought over workers and staff, halted production, interrupted communications and transport, wrecked and looted state property. They have stirred up trouble to serve their own ends and have been indulging in vain hopes of a come-back. Some of these organizations are carrying out counter-revolutionary activities on the orders of those in authority who persist in taking the capitalist road. These counter-revolutionary organizations are built on sand. Once the masses see through them, they immediately collapse, and the handful of ringleaders are dragged out by the masses.

It is a very good thing that all the ghosts and monsters come out into the open. This provides us with an opportunity for a good spring-cleaning to *"sweep away all pests."*

We must be firm in exercising dictatorship over these counter-revolutionaries.

*In his noted treatise "On the People's Democratic Dictatorship," Chairman Mao says that in dealing with the reactionaries, we must "enforce dictatorship . . . suppress them, allow them only to behave themselves and not to be unruly in word or deed. If they speak or act in an unruly way, they will be promptly stopped and punished."*

*"Revolutionary dictatorship and counter-revolutionary dictatorship are by nature opposites, but the former was learned from the latter. Such learning is very important. If the revolutionary people do not master this method of ruling over the counter-revolutionary classes, they will not be able to maintain their state power, domestic and foreign reaction will overthrow that power and restore its own rule over China, and disaster will befall the revolutionary people."*

All revolutionary comrades must firmly bear in mind these teachings of Chairman Mao. For the reactionaries, even limited democracy is not allowed, not to speak of extensive democracy, not one iota. Towards them, only dictatorship should be carried out!

A group of ghosts and monsters have now come out to set up counter-revolutionary organizations and carry out counter-revolutionary activities. These counter-revolutionary organizations must be resolutely eliminated. Counter-revolutionaries must be dealt with in accordance with the law without hesitation.

*Chairman Mao has called on the People's Liberation Army to actively support and assist the genuine proletarian revolutionaries and to oppose the Rightists resolutely.* The great People's Liberation Army created by Chairman Mao himself has heartily responded to his call. The People's Liberation Army is making new, great contributions to the cause of socialism in the great proletarian cultural revolution. This is the glorious task of the People's Liberation Army.

In certain places, the counter-revolutionary organizations have been fully exposed. It is entirely correct that the P.L.A. units stationed there, the revolutionary masses and the public security bodies in the hands of the proletarian revolutionaries take action to suppress these counter-revolutionary organizations. The handling of the reactionary "Rong Fu Jun" in Harbin by the P.L.A. units stationed there, the revolutionary masses and the committee for taking over the municipal public security bureau has provided useful experience. Immediately after encircling the "Rong Fu Jun," they launched a political offensive which awakened those who had been hoodwinked, and turned the scene of this counter-revolutionary incident into a meeting place for accusing the counter-revolutionaries. Those who had been deceived then handed over their chieftains and the "Rong Fu Jun" quickly disintegrated. All this dealt heavy blows to the counter-revolutionaries who are extremely few in number, and won over those who were duped.

In suppressing counter-revolutionary organization and counter-revolutionaries, the instruments of dictatorship must work closely with the revolutionary masses. For counter-revolutionaries, this is an escape-proof net.

All revolutionary mass organizations and all revolutionary comrades must increase their revolutionary vigilance to prevent counter-revolutionaries from sneaking in to make trouble. They must co-ordinate with the instruments of dictatorship under a unified command to safeguard the proletarian dictatorship.

As the War of Liberation entered the stage of a general counter-offensive against the Chiang Kai-shek reactionary clique, Chairman Mao issued a call to the whole Party, the whole army and the people of the whole country when he said: *"The army advances, production increases. When our sense of discipline is strengthened, we are ever-victorious in the revolution."*

Today, when the great army of the proletarian revolution is seizing power from the handful of persons within the Party who are in authority and taking the capitalist road, and is launching a general counter-offensive against the bourgeoisie and its agents in the Party, we must also take firm hold of the resolution and promote production, and strengthen our sense of discipline. In this way, we shall also be ever-victorious in the present struggle.

*"But now that the cock has crowed and all under heaven is bright."* Let us heartily welcome the decisive victory of the great proletarian cultural revolution!

# "ON THE REVOLUTIONARY 'THREE-IN-ONE' COMBINATION"

*Hung Ch'i* Editorial, No. 5, 1967

*Complete Text*
(*Peking Review,* No. 12, 17 March 1967)

*Chairman Mao has pointed out that in those places and organizations where power needs to be seized, the policy of the revolutionary "three-in-one" combination must be carried out in establishing a provisional organ of power that is revolutionary and representative and has proletarian authority. This organ of power should preferably be called a revolutionary committee.*

This policy is the political and organizational guarantee for the victory of the proletarian revolutionaries in their struggle to seize power. The proletarian revolutionaries should understand this policy correctly and implement it correctly.

The revolutionary "three-in-one" provisional organ of power should be formed by leaders of revolutionary mass organizations that truly represent the broad masses, the representatives of the People's Liberation Army units stationed in the area and revolutionary leading cadres. None of these three bodies can be excluded. It is wrong to overlook or underestimate the role of any one of them.

As a result of the vigorous mass movement of the great proletarian cultural revolution during the past half year and more, the masses have been fully mobilized, and large numbers of up-and-coming representatives of the revolutionary masses have emerged. The revolutionary masses are the base of the proletarian revolutionaries' seizure of power from the handful of persons in the Party who are in authority and taking the capitalist road. They are the base of the revolutionary "three-in-one" provisional organ of power.

True proletarian revolutionaries and up-and-coming representatives of the revolutionary masses have performed immortal exploits in the great proletarian cultural revolution. They are the new rising forces nurtured by Mao Tse-tung's thought and they embody the general orientation of the revolution.

This struggle to seize power from the handful of persons in the Party who are in authority and taking the capitalist road is a mass movement from below under the leadership of the Central Committee of the Chinese Communist Party headed by Chairman Mao. In the revolutionary "three-in-one" provisional organ of power, it is imperative to give full play to the role of leaders of the revolutionary mass organizations and to take full account of their opinions, and never regard them simply as secondary, because they are the representatives of the broad revolutionary masses. If their role is not recognized or if it is underrated, in effect, the revolutionary masses as well as the great proletarian cultural revolution are negated. If they are excluded or regarded as secondary, it is impossible to establish a provisional organ of power that is revolutionary, representative and has proletarian authority; it is impossible to have a revolutionary "three-in-one" combination.

In all great revolutionary mass movements, it is scarcely avoidable having shortcomings and making mistakes. It is necessary to see clearly the essence, the mainstream and the general orientation of the revolution. In this great proletarian cultural revolution, the shortcomings and errors of the leaders of revolutionary mass organizations who truly represent the masses are a question of one finger among ten, and a problem that arises in the course of progress. As proletarian revolutionaries, we should recognize that their general orientation is correct, that they have many strong points and we should learn from them modestly. As for their shortcomings and errors, we should warmheartedly, patiently and painstakingly help them. It should also be noted that many revolutionary mass organizations have pointed out themselves the wrong tendencies existing in their own organizations and have proposed ways of correcting them as a result of their creative study and application of Chairman Mao's works. Such revolutionary consciousness and initiative is praiseworthy. It is precisely the revolutionary masses themselves who have proposed eliminating self-interest in their own thinking while seizing power from the handful of persons in the Party who were in authority and taking the capitalist road.

In the final analysis, the question of one's attitude towards leaders of revolutionary mass organizations that truly represent the masses taking part in the "three-in-one" provisional organ of power is a question of one's attitude towards the masses, towards the mass movement itself. It is also an important indication of whether the proletarian revolutionary line represented by Chairman Mao can be carried out or not. We must at all times remember *Chairman Mao's teachings: "The masses are the real heroes," "the masses have boundless creative power," "the people, and the people alone, are the motive force in the making of world history."* If alienated from the revolutionary masses, it is certain that no organization or individual is able to carry out the proletarian revolutionary line represented by Chairman Mao.

The vigorous mass movement of the great proletarian cultural revolution of more than the last half year has been a severe test for the ranks of our cadres. The handful of persons in the Party who were in authority and taking the capitalist road has been exposed. At the same time, the majority of our cadres have proved to be good or comparatively good. The concept of excluding and overthrowing all cadres is absolutely wrong. It is necessary to point out that the masses are not to be blamed for this. To exclude and overthrow all cadres indiscriminately is the view advocated by those several people who put forth the bourgeois reactionary line, and this was precisely what they did. The poisonous influence has not been wiped out of the minds of certain comrades, and therefore they have, to a certain extent, committed similar mistakes without being conscious of them.

In every place, department, enterprise and unit there are great numbers of revolutionary cadres. This is also true even for some places or departments where those in authority taking the capitalist road have been entrenched, but the revolutionary cadres there were suppressed over a long period. We must be aware of this.

The role of the revolutionary cadres in participating in the "three-in-one" provisional organ of power must be given full consideration. They should and can play the role of nucleus and backbone of the organ. Of course, they can do this only by integrating themselves with the masses and by following the mass line in work.

Provided those cadres who made mistakes criticize their own mistakes and correct them, draw a clear-cut demarcation line between themselves and the handful of persons in the Party who are in authority and taking the capitalist road, between themselves and the bourgeois reactionary line, and really stand on the proletarian revolutionary line represented by Chairman Mao, they should be united with in accordance with the principle of "early or late, all who make revolution merit equal treatment," proper jobs should be arranged for them and many of them can be allowed to participate in the provisional organ of power.

However, those who persist in their mistakes, and who do not draw a clear-cut demarcation line between themselves and the people in authority taking the capitalist road, between themselves and the bourgeois reactionary line must not be imposed on the masses and arbitrarily pushed into the "three-in-one" provisional organ of power. Otherwise, this would not be the revolutionary "three-in-one" combination, to say nothing of the seizure of power from the handful of persons in the Party who are in authority and taking the capitalist road; a new reversal would occur and those in authority taking the capitalist road who had been overthrown might even regain power.

We must be vigilant against those who distort the principle of revolutionary "three-in-one" combination and, on the pretext of forming "three-in-one" combination, carry out eclecticism, conciliation and the combining of two into one, and furthermore, in a hundred and one ways, pull in the persons in the Party who are in authority and taking the capitalist road. This is trying to fish in troubled waters, usurp the fruits of the great proletarian cultural revolution and carry out counter-revolutionary restoration. All revolutionary masses and all revolutionary cadres must resolutely resist, oppose and smash the conspiracy of the class enemy.

The great People's Liberation Army is the mainstay of the dictatorship of the proletariat. Chairman Mao's call on the People's Liberation Army to actively support the masses of revolutionary Left is a matter of great strategic significance.

Experience proves that participation by representatives of locally stationed People's Liberation Army units in the revolutionary "three-in-one" provisional organ of power has played an extremely important role in successfully accomplishing the task in the struggle to seize power.

With the participation of cadres of the People's Liberation Army in the "three-in-one" combination in which P.L.A. cadres take part the most. They try by every means to manufacture rumors and fabricate stories in a vain attempt to sow dissension between the revolutionary masses and the People's Liberation Army, and to incite those among the masses who do not know the truth to direct the spearhead of their struggle against the People's Liberation Army. Such class enemy intrigues must be fully exposed and firmly smashed.

The Chinese People's Liberation Army is an extremely revolutionized army of the proletariat, unmatched in the world. Chairman Mao Tse-tung has said: *"The sole purpose of this army is to stand firmly with the Chinese people and to serve them wholeheartedly."* It is precisely because of this that all revolutionary mass organizations and revolutionary masses have faith in the People's Liberation Army and warmly support the participation by representatives of the local army units in the revolutionary "three-in-one" provisional organ of power. At various levels, in those departments where power must be seized, representatives of the armed forces or of the militia should take part in forming the "three-in-one" combination. This should be done in factories and rural areas, in financial, trading, cultural and educational departments (universities, middle schools and primary schools), in Party and government organizations and in people's organizations. Representatives of the armed forces should be sent to the county level or higher and representatives of the militia should be sent to the commune level or lower. This is very good. If representatives of the armed forces are not sufficient, their posts can be left vacant for the time being and filled in the future.

The attitude towards the People's Liberation Army is actually the attitude towards the dictatorship of the proletariat and it is an important criterion for distinguishing whether a person is of the genuine revolutionary Left or not.

In certain places, some comrades in the local army units may commit temporary mistakes in giving their support because of the intricate and complex conditions of the class struggle. When such problems occur, the genuine revolutionary Left should explain, with good intentions and in the proper way, the conditions and state their views to the leading members of the army units. They should absolutely not adopt an openly antagonistic attitude and still less should they direct the spearhead of their struggle against the People's Liberation Army. Otherwise, they will commit gross mistakes and do things which sadden our friends and gladden our enemies, and they will be used by the class enemy.

The People's Liberation Army has made important contributions in supporting the proletarian revolutionaries in their struggle to seize power. All commanders and fighters must follow Chairman Mao's teachings, closely rely on the broad revolutionary masses, learn from them modestly, be their students before acting as their teachers, be good at discussing matters with them, and carry on deep-going and careful investigations among them. In doing so, they will be able to give the proletarian revolutionaries very powerful support in their struggle to seize power and bring still closer ties between the army and the people and, on their part, the army units will get new tempering and improve in the course of the struggle.

The "three-in-one" provisional organ of power must be revolutionary, representative and have proletarian authority. This organ of power must resolutely carry out the proletarian revolutionary line represented by Chairman Mao and firmly oppose the bourgeois reactionary line. It must not be "combining two into one" or eclectic. Only thus, can this organ be representative and speak for the broad revolutionary masses and revolutionary cadres. Only thus, can it have proletarian authority, exercise powerful centralized leadership on the basis of the most extensive democracy, impose effective dictatorship on the class enemy, and smash every kind of scheme for counter-revolutionary restoration on the part of the handful of persons in the Party who are in authority and taking the capitalist road and the ghosts and monsters in society.

A big question now confronting the people of the whole country is whether to carry the great proletarian cultural revolution through to the end, or to abandon it half-way. All revolutionary comrades must keep a cool head and not get confused. *"With power and to spare we must pursue the tottering foe and not ape Hsiang Yu the conqueror seeking idle fame."* At present, we should especially keep this teaching of Chairman Mao's in mind.

# LIU SHAO-CHI'S CONFESSION
## AT THE PEKING CIVIL ENGINEERING COLLEGE, 9 JULY 1967

*Complete Text*

Warriors of the new 1 August Battle Corps of the Peking Civil Engineering College: all revolutionary teachers, students, personnel and workers of the Peking Civil Engineering College:

On the evening of 4 July Comrade Wang Tung-hsing, the Director of the General Office of the Central Committee informed me that it was the view of the Central Committee that I should write an examination. This examination is appended below.

### I

At the end of July 1966 our great leader, great teacher, and great helmsman, Chairman Mao called upon all responsible comrades of the Central Committee, together with all responsible comrades who had come to Peking, to take a personal part in the proletarian Cultural Revolution in Peking schools and institutes so that they could acquire both feeling and knowledge. Thus it was that in response to this call of Chairman Mao's that on 1 August last year I went to Comrade Li Hsüeh-feng, to study with the comrades of the new Municipal Committee the question of which school I should go to. After study it was unanimously decided that I should go to the College of Civil Engineering. Comrade Li Hsüeh-feng also decided to go with me. Since the Ministry of Building Materials had reverted to the leadership of the State Capital Construction Commission, Comrade Ku Mu also came to the college to take part in the Cultural Revolution. At the time I informed the Cultural Revolution Sub-Committee that they should send somebody to take part and they sent Comrade Ch'i Pen-yü. At the time none of us had the intention of creating experience to propagate throughout the whole country.

On the evening of 2 August we came and attended your rally here and the above mentioned comrades also came. Apart from this there was also Liu Lan-tao and other comrades from outside Peking. They had decided to come on the spur of the moment and I knew nothing about it.

In the main we attended your rally of 2 August in order to hear various divergent opinions which were current amongst you. At the very end I said a few words.

On the evening of 3 August Li Hsüeh-feng, Ku Mu, Ch'i Pen-yü and I came to the college again. We first had a talk with the representative of the "1 August Corps" and then with the representative of the "Revolutionary Corps." Again it was in the main a case of listening to opinions. At the end I gave an account of a few points of view of my own to the two representatives separately.

On the evening of 4 August I sought out the responsible comrade of the work team in the Chung Nan Hai for a talk, in the main to enquire after the situation, but I also said a few words at the end.

On 5 August Chairman Mao's big character poster "Bombard the Headquarters" appeared. Only then did I realize that I had committed serious errors in the proletarian Cultural Revolution. At this stage I felt that I could no longer enquire into the affairs of the Civil Engineering College. The same afternoon, I told Comrade Li Hsüeh-feng by telephone that from then on I would not go to the Civil Engineering College nor would I take any interest in the affairs of the college. I was unaware of Comrade Li Hsüeh-feng's speech of 5 August and of Wu Hsing-feng's later activities at the Civil Engineering College. After 5 August I received letters from several students in the college as well as a few simple reports. I replied to none of them. Some I gave to Comrade Li Hsüeh-feng, some were dealt with.

The above is a simple account of my experience in taking part in the proletarian Cultural Revolution in the Peking Civil Engineering College.

### II

On 1 June last year (1966) following Chairman Mao's minutes to the effect that the big character poster of Comrade Nieh Yuan-tzu and seven others in Peking University should be published throughout the whole country, the Cultural Revolution unrolled thunderously in Peking and throughout the whole country. However, in the fifty or more days that followed 1 June last year I made errors of line and direction in my direction of the Cultural Revolution. I should bear the major responsibility for these errors. Despite the fact that other comrades also had a definite responsibility, for example other leader comrades of the Central Committee in Peking, certain leading comrades of departments of the State Council, leading comrades of the new Peking Municipal Committee, leading comrades of certain of the work teams, leading comrades in certain areas and others, I am the person who should bear the major responsibility. I only started to realize the mistakes I had made after the publication of Chairman Mao's big character poster "Bombard the Headquarters." Before this I did not realize that I had made such serious mistakes.

Chairman Mao was not in Peking in the period preceding 18 July last year and the daily work of the Central Committee was overseen by myself. The situation in all aspects of the Cultural Revolution in Peking was reported at conferences of the Central Committee presided over by myself. Some mistaken decisions were taken at these report conferences which approved or agreed some mistaken suggestions.

For example:

—the dispatch of large numbers of work teams to universities, middle schools and some organs in Peking;

—the restriction of the revolutionary activities of the masses, e.g. the difference between internal and external, forbidding the masses to demonstrate in the streets and the prohibition of big character posters in the streets;

—the issue to all Party Committees of simplified Report No. 9 on the Cultural Revolution in Peking University which described the revolutionary actions of the revolutionary students and teachers as counter-revolutionary;

—the issue of several Central Committee appreciations on the great proletarian Cultural Revolution together with records of discussion.

In many schools in Peking there was a so-called "away with control by cadres" struggle. In the Civil Engineering College this struggle became the so-called "grab the swimming fish" struggle, although in fact I had had no previous knowledge of it at all and had never heard of it at Central Committee conferences. Because of these struggles under the leadership work teams, in many of the schools struggles broke out between students. Illegal activities, such as limiting the personal freedom of people, and other actions such as surrounding the revolutionaries suppressing people of different opinions and even the labelling of various students as "counter-revolutionaries," "rightists," "false leftists" and "drifters" all took place. All these things for a certain period of time distorted the general direction of the struggle and in quite a few schools these actions created an atmosphere of terror which was reactionary and was an atmosphere of white terror.

When the work teams first went to each school they were generally welcomed by the masses but different opinions very quickly formed among the masses. Among these different opinions some included criticism of and doubt about the leadership of the work teams or about certain members of the teams. Some of the masses even criticized and doubted the opinions of several of the Party leaders. Because the vast majority of the work teams attempted to replace the mass movement and to act on its behalf and because they laid down all sorts of restrictions, this naturally aroused the dissatisfaction and suspicion of the masses. This led to some excessive expressions being used which, however, were appropriate to the spirit of daring to think, daring to say, daring to struggle and daring to rebel. Of course, a small minority of rightist expressions also appeared. This was a perfectly normal phenomenon. At this critical point, sufficient time should have been allowed to permit different ideas to be fully expressed and to allow a clear and complete debate. However, the Central Committee report meeting continued to send those mistaken directives which I have mentioned earlier. In the fifty days after the work teams were sent out, I was in direct charge of the work and in this way increased the possibility and seriousness of errors on the part of the work teams. The vast majority of the responsible persons in the work teams did not understand the great proletarian Cultural Revolution

and had not properly learned from the masses. From the very beginning they wished the masses who had been aroused by them to act in accordance with the plans and measures thought up by them and by me. In this way they ran counter to the laws of the development of revolutionary mass movements and many serious incidents took place. In fact, they went over to the standpoint of the reactionary bourgeoisie, implemented a dictatorship of the bourgeoisie, struck at the blossoming Cultural Revolution, confused truth and error, pretended black was white, greatly encouraged the bourgeoisie and disillusioned the proletariat. At this point I was not conscious of the situation and was not aware that the situation was developing abnormally. This was gravely harmful to the Cultural Revolution, to the Party and to socialism. This was an error of line of right opportunism. Although this only lasted for fifty days the harm and influence stemming from these errors was really extremely great. The consequences of these actions have still not been completely eliminated even to the present time. In some places they have become even more serious so that the masses have come out in opposition to each other. This error of mine was a violation of Mao Tse-tung's thought and was a violation of the theory, line, direction and policies embodied in the notice on the Cultural Revolution of the 16th of May, 1966.

### III

During the period when Chairman Mao was not in Peking, Chairman Mao and the Party Central Committee entrusted me with the direction of the day to day work of the Central Committee. Since before the 5th of August last year I did not understand that idea, committed errors of line and direction in the Cultural Revolution. When I made several speeches at the College of Civil Engineering I did not take the initiative in accepting responsibility. I did not speedily proclaim to the whole body of teachers and students at the College that I should accept the main responsibility for the errors which had been committed during the early period of the Cultural Revolution in the College and did not lighten the responsibility for these errors which had fallen upon other leading comrades in Peking in the Central Committee in the new Peking Municipal Committee, the Ministry of Building Materials and in the work team. At the time I merely said briefly that the work teams in your college had committed mistakes and that the responsibility for the mistakes should not be entirely placed upon the work teams. The Party Central Committee and the new Peking Committee were also responsible for these errors. You are aware of the mistakes made by the work teams in your school and you can discuss them. You can also discuss the mistakes of the Central Committee and of the new Peking Municipal Committee as well as who made the mistakes and who was responsible. At this point I did not make it clear that I should bear the major responsibility nor did I make it clear that at the time the Central Committee was without Chairman Mao who was not in Peking, and that I took charge of the day to day working of the Central Committee. This confused the problem of who should have borne the major responsibility for the mistakes made. At the time the way I spoke was incorrect.

When I attended your discussion meeting on the evening of 2 August I heard arguments between two differing points of view. In addition to this some students sent me notes putting forward a third differing view. Although these differing views included some questions of principle and direction I considered them to be fundamentally a problem of internal contradictions among the people and that they should achieve unity through normal discussions and argument, distinction between right and wrong, support for the correct, and correction of errors. This is because the Cultural Revolution can only be carried out properly by relying on revolutionary students, teachers, personnel and workers and uniting all that is possible to unite. The Cultural Revolution in schools should be carried out by relying mainly on the students. I believe that the sort of unity starting from an aspiration of unity itself and undergoing sufficient discussion and argument, distinguishing between right and wrong, supporting truth and correcting errors was what was required at the time and that it could not be said that this kind of unity was "two into one." Of course I should make an examination of myself here and say that in talking of this problem at the time there were places where I was neither sufficiently complete nor sufficiently accurate.

The result of listening to various views on 2 and 3 August and listening to the leading comrades of the work team on 4 August was that gradually in my mind the following impression began to form: that is, the main direction of the struggle of the "1 August Battle Corps" was correct, they were vigorously opposing the erroneous leadership of the original college Party Committee and the work team, and their proletarian revolutionary make-rebellion spirit as good. Whereas, "the revolutionary corps" although it said that there were failings and errors in the leadership of the Party Committee and the work team, were, because they were misled, in fact fundamentally protecting the college Party Committee and work team. The spearpoint of their struggle was not directed in the main against the Party Committee and work team but against the "1 August Corps" thus the general direction of their struggle was incorrect. This view of mine was precisely similar to that of the new Municipal Committee. However, I did not have time to put this view to the teachers, students, personnel and workers of the college. I merely sought out the comrades of the work team on 4 August and gave them a glimpse of this idea but it was far from being all-round and complete.

Apart from this, in my contacts at all levels I discovered that the Party and Youth League Organization of the college was still being run by its original members, not only had there been no re-elections, activity had not stopped as well. Thus the activities of the Party and Youth League Organization frequently upheld the old order and opposed revolutionary action and the spirit of revolutionary rebellion. I therefore suggested that the Party and League Organization should be re-elected. If this came to nothing then temporary appointments could be made. Generally speaking, Party and League members should not hold secret meetings. During meetings non-members should attend. The aim of this suggestion of mine was to prevent the great proletarian cultural revolutionary movement being manipulated by the original Party and League Organization, thus putting obstacles in the way of its development. Whether or not this suggestion of mine was later carried out, and whether in being carried out it brought about attacks on the majority of cadres in the college I do not know. If later in implementing this suggestion of mine it so happened that the majority of cadres in the College came under attack, then I should bear the major responsibility.

In several speeches I mentioned the following problems:

1. Do not be afraid if people make trouble and oppose the Party Committee and work teams; you should support them, even if a few bad elements creep in you should not be afraid because the great majority are good and protect the Chinese Communist Party, socialism and Chairman Mao. The bad elements are very few. If you fear people making trouble and prevent them from opposing us then that is definitely an error of direction. However, in explaining this problem I spoke too much, even going to the extent of saying "do not be afraid of bad people getting into control, there is some good in this, you can only kill a snake when it comes right out of its hole." This was entirely erroneous and should be refuted.

2. In several speeches I emphasized the need to unite the majority, to unite all those people who could be united, but I did not state clearly the need to make the proletarian revolutionaries the nucleus, to unite all those who could be united and implement revolutionary unity and the revolutionary triple alliance on the premise of unanimity of direction. I did not state clearly that without the proletarian revolutionaries as a nucleus, without unanimity of direction, neither revolutionary unity nor the revolutionary triple alliance would be realized and even if they were they could not be consolidated.

3. In several speeches I quoted Marx's dictum "the proletariat can only achieve liberation of itself by liberating the whole of mankind." In explaining the constituent parts of mankind I first pointed out that it included workers, peasants and other laboring people, students and intellectuals. This was the great majority but it also included those landlords, rich peasants, counter revolutionaries, bad elements, rightists, capitalists and their families who had not yet been done to death—they should all be remolded. Remolding them would require a lot of work, thus in speaking of the remolding of the remnants of these exploiting classes I spoke too much and with excessive emphasis. This led people to feel that I was putting the cart before the horse. This was also erroneous.

I would be grateful if comrades would freely reveal and criticize the mistakes I made at the college and their evil influence.

I would be grateful if comrades would freely reveal and criticize my erroneous ideas on leadership and their evil influence in the early stages of the Cultural Revolution.

I would be grateful if comrades would freely reveal and thoroughly criticize any other words and actions of mine which are not in accordance with the thought of our great leader, Chairman Mao.

Finally, I wish to humbly apologize to those revolutionary teachers, students, personnel and workers who were suppressed and harmed by the erroneous line represented by myself. In the early states of the great proletarian Cultural Revolution those revolutionary teachers, students, personnel, workers and the broad mass of work team personnel who were hoodwinked by the erroneous line, committed varying degrees of error and their responsibility is very small—my responsibility is great. They suffered from the erroneous line and I wish to humbly apologize to them as well.

I hope that in their criticism and uncovering of my errors comrades will create great revolutionary unity and a revolutionary triple alliance with the proletarian revolutionaries as a nucleus, thus making the Peking Civil Engineering College into a Red school for Chairman Mao's thought.

Carry through the great proletarian Cultural Revolution to the end!

Long live the dictatorship of the proletariat!

Long live the revolutionary make-rebellion spirit of the proletariat!

Long live the great and glorious and correct Communist Party of China!

Long live the invincible thought of Mao Tse-tung!

Long live our great teacher, great leader, great commander, great helmsman Chairman Mao!

(signed) Liu Shao-ch'i
9 July, 1967

# SUMMARIES OF SPEECHES MADE BY MEMBERS OF THE CENTRAL CULTURAL REVOLUTIONARY GROUP AT AN ENLARGED MEETING OF THE PEKING REVOLUTIONARY COMMITTEE, 1 SEPTEMBER 1967

(From Red Guard Newspapers)

### Speech by Chiang Ch'ing

Yesterday, together with the Premier, I heard about the Szechwan situation, which is very good. Even cadres also say it is very good. In the year or more that has now passed is it conceivable that the situation should get worse and worse? I am of the opinion that Peking should take the lead in making a good job of struggle, criticism and transformation, and of the great unity. It should get on with the struggle, criticism and transformation within individual units, we ourselves should make a good job of it. Does not Peking have one or two schools which are test points? One must be resolute and not fear to talk of "right wing," one must get on with struggle, criticism and transformation within individual units and carry out the criticism even more fully than in the times of Trotsky. This is a big job. It is a glorious task. One must oppose anarchism and once again bring about a great liaison, this is altogether different from last year. Last year it was a matter of blowing the spark into fire. This year there is a factional struggle and when mistakes are made they are not realized. The PLA was formed and is led personally by Chairman Mao and Vice Chairman Lin Piao. Where in the world is there any Army like it? When someone strikes they do not strike back, when someone curses they do not curse back. You must believe in the Army, it is only a small number who are bad. The broad masses of Commanders and fighters are good. Indeed there are very few people like Ch'en Tsai-tao, and even fewer like Chao Yung-fu. Of the several millions in the armed forces very few are bad. And the slogan of going everywhere to pluck out a small group of individuals within the Army is mistaken. Making trouble among our own Army is just like tearing down the Great Wall. The important thing is for Peking to get on with struggle, criticism and transformation, the great unity, and the triple alliance, and to stop violent struggle. The small group of bad men who stir up violent struggle must be exposed to the broad light of day and we must put a stop to the evil wind of beating, seizing and breaking. I can tell you I shall never forget the three years of rectification in Yenan. There we had self-criticism, establishing oneself and then negating oneself and then establishing oneself again. It was not like you, who won't even make a self-examination and do not let people criticize or quietly consider problems.

### Speech by Ch'en Po-ta

The Cultural Revolution is once again at an important turning point. The Party Central Committee has issued an important appeal, and you must resolutely act in accordance with the directives of the Party Central Committee and Chairman Mao and thoroughly discuss the speech by Chiang Ch'ing. There are a number of students who, at present, have fallen into an extremely serious state of anarchy and a genuine revolutionary is not permitted. At the beginning of the Cultural Revolution many Peking students went off in all directions to fan the spark into flame and accomplished great things, but you exaggerated as if nothing could succeed without you. You tried to monopolize things and when you went off to some place you claimed to represent the Red Guard Congress. I have never been in favor of this sort of thing... Resolute left-wingers must be tried in a long period of storm and turmoil. The whole country watches Peking, therefore, we must put on a good show. All those on liaison outside must return, everyone except those sent by the Central Committee. Everyone must return *before the 11th.* Peking should get on with the great unity, the triple alliance and struggle criticism and transformation. We must put on a good show. We must not allow factionalism to dominate anything. What is superior to every other consideration is the Proletarian Party, Mao Tse-tung's Thought and the interests of the people. Does ransacking constitute a revolutionary act? There are a minority of students and some workers who are muddleheaded. In them the factional element is higher than everything else instead of Mao's Thought. In this serious class struggle, you should look out for people who get themselves up in all sorts of guises, some of them extreme leftists and some of them extreme rightists, who throw into confusion Chairman Mao's strategic disposition. You must take care to cherish Chairman Mao's strategic dispositions as if you were taking care of your own eyes... *Our line in foreign relations is laid down and led by Chairman Mao's Headquarters and implemented by Premier Chou. The foreign relations line of Liu and Teng was one which sold out the country. It has been negated by Chairman Mao.*

### Speech by K'ang Sheng

The political questions raised by Chiang Ch'ing, Chun Chiao and Ch'en Po-ta are a way of passing on Chairman Mao's strategic dispositions. They are questions of general direction. You should not treat them as off-the-cuff remarks. Mao and Lin have said that bad things can be turned into good things. The appearance of Ch'en Tsai-tao was a bad thing but when the revolutionary line of Chairman Mao was published to the masses of that city, the situation immediately changed and the bad thing became a good thing. But it is not all bad things which become good things. There are certain conditions.

1. The most important condition is to have the leadership of Chairman Mao and the Proletarian Headquarters headed by Chairman Mao.

2. You must have the PLA created by Chairman Mao and directed by Lin Piao. Comrades see that the PLA is the mainstay for protecting the dictatorship of the proletariat. Therefore a most important condition for protecting the victory of the Cultural Revolution is to believe in and rely on the PLA, under the leadership of the Central Committee headed by Chairman Mao and the Cultural Revolution Group. The situation in the Cultural Revolution is very good. This year on October 1 a great many Marxist-Leninists from the Party and all over the country want to come and see the achievements of the Cultural Revolution, particularly the achievements in Peking. Peking should be a model for the whole country and we should propagate to the whole world the Cultural Revolution created by Chairman Mao which is unparalleled in history, and the Red Guard movement. We must resolutely cherish the Party Central Committee headed by Chairman Mao, cherish the Chinese People's Army and respect the Central Committee's directives. In the great Cultural Revolution on no account must class enemies be forgotten. As for imperialism, modern revisionism headed by Soviet revisionists, reactionaries in all countries and Chiang Kai-shek reactionaries, the present juncture is not advantageous to them. But the enemy will not willingly accept failure. In the past the enemy tried to encircle us and now the Soviet Revisionists and the Mongolian Revisionists openly aid U.S. Imperialism, in forming an encirclement, while on the Eastern side, there is the Japanese Imperialists—what was the Foreign Minister of the Japanese Imperialists up to when he went to see the Soviet Revisionists recently? And think how many Communists were slaughtered by the Indonesian reactionaries and yet the Soviet Revisionists still help them.

### Speech by Premier Chou

Some of you have a wrong assessment of the situation. The Red Guards were born last August and the revolutionary great liaison spread like wildfire. You should remember this achievement. For a year the whole country has been alight. There was no province, city or district where the fire did not catch. *Now in the second year it is the year for grasping victory.* The revolutionary masses throughout the country are all rising up to grasp victory. Of course victory may come sooner or later. But as with liberation one relics upon oneself so for victory one can also rely upon oneself. People must go back to their own unit and grasp victory in their own unit. Point the spearhead at Liu, Teng and Tao. Unite your unit in struggle, criticism and transformation, grasp revolution and boost production. *Now it is the year for grasping victory. The third year is for winding up, then after an interval of a few years we will start again.* The Cultural Revolution was personally launched and

led by Mao, we must stick by Chairman Mao and not make subjective assessments of the situation. If a Chao Yung-fu appears, then pluck him out. If a Ch'en Tsai-tao appears, pluck him out. With regard to Chairman Mao's directives, resolutely implement those that you understand and also resolutely implement those you do not understand. Mao's strategic dispositions cannot be left to small skirmishing. If you are going to strike, then strike on the large scale, and when you assess the situation, unite the Chinese revolution with the revolution of the whole world. Consider carefully every question and ask for instructions, otherwise you will influence the overall situation. The second year is the year of victory. The main thing is self-reliance. Do not go interfering. Supporting the Army and loving the people is Chairman Mao's great slogan. The PLA are a marvellous army without an equal in the world. The majority of leaders in the Army are good. People like Chao Yung-fu and Ch'en Tsai-tao are extreme individualists. Once the task of the "3 supports" and the "2 military duties" was undertaken, some mistakes were made because for many years they have not done mass work and lack experience, *but this was not part of the Liu-Teng reactionary line.* It only needed the Chairman to say "you are wrong" and the majority of them very readily changed their ways. You should certainly write open letters and support the PLA. We do not want to pull down our Great Wall *and make imperialists, revisionists and reactionaries laugh at us.* The Peking Revolutionary Committee and the Garrison District have provided sufficient accommodation for the masses from outside. All you Red Guards, stopping violent struggle is at present an important task and to carry on doing it you must take steps strictly to prevent bad men from worming their way in. This year every unit should get on with the great unity and three-way alliance, otherwise how can we have any results?

### Speech by Hsieh Fu-chih

Workers, peasants and students should all get on with the great criticism and do so for a fairly long period of time. That is to say, the thorough and complete criticism on the political, ideological and theoretical plane of Liu, Teng, Tao, Peng, Lu, Lo and Yang. Even more important you must make a good job of struggle, criticism and transformation within your own unit. To make a good job of your own unit is the greatest support of the whole country. All Red Guards should undertake new accomplishments. When they began they made a contribution but it is no use stopping on ones laurels. Everybody including myself must make new contributions in the struggle of criticism and transformation. Consolidating and developing the revolutionary great alliance is the general directive. All revolutionaries in Peking should raise high the flag of revolutionary great alliance, oppose civil war, avoid splitting into factions. We emphasize unity, we cannot have people bringing about splits. We must step up new accomplishments in the revolutionary great criticism and revolutionary great alliance. Stop violent struggle, put an end to this evil wind. The main reason for violent struggle is those

814

going the capitalist road and bad people who are
provoking it. But one day the masses will come to
their senses and drag out those who provoke violent
struggle. The study of Mao's works, the great criticism,
great unity and triple alliance in all cases act in
accordance with Mao's instructions and do not let
your minds get overheated.

# SPEECH OF CHIANG CH'ING (MME. MAO TSE-TUNG) TO REPRESENTATIVES OF MASS ORGANIZATIONS IN ANHWEI PROVINCE VISITING PEKING, 5 SEPTEMBER 1967

*Complete Text*

I reckon that the situation of the Cultural Revolution throughout the whole country is excellent. Of course if you look at the situation in isolation in some individual areas don't you feel that it is rather serious, but in fact this is not so. We should look at the situation as a whole and from the historical point of view there is a great difference between the situation this time last year and the present time. This time last year those in authority in the Party going the capitalist road and their minions in the Provinces had a certain amount of freedom of action. Now they are paralyzed and have been overthrown by revolutionary young generals. The fact that they are paralyzed is no bad thing because the "small handful" cannot move. Some areas have set up Revolutionary Committees. At present the Central Committee is solving the problems in one Province after another and in one city after another. From last year to this year there has been a big change in the situation and we are carrying on the large-scale criticism of the top person. We are now gradually expanding this criticism throughout the whole country and we should open fire on the top person on each front and thoroughly criticize him and make him stink. You must do this so that every household knows of it, so that he will stink even more than Trotsky in the Soviet Union. In this way China will never change color.

At present we do not want clashes. In clashes people always get hurt and bad elements smash up State property. Why do they want to harm State property? On the question of "a peaceful response to an armed attack" we should not forget the class content nor lose sight of the circumstances and the conditions. When you return both sides should "resist by peaceful means" and put out an olive branch and not go round waving cudgels.

To sum it all up, I feel that the situation is excellent. We have tempered the young people and tempered the young generals, tempered the revolutionary cadres and tempered the older generation.

In some areas the situation is complicated but this is quite normal. Besides it is also rather uneven but this again is perfectly normal. In general the situation is developing favorably. To ensure this you need certain factors. These are the leadership of the Central Committee headed by Chairman Mao. This is the most important aspect. You also need the pillar of the proletarian dictatorship, the People's Liberation Army, to protect the proletarian Cultural Revolution. It is essential to set up gradually local Revolutionary Committees and to get on with revolutionary alliances and revolutionary triple alliances so that we can carry out struggle, criticism and reform and coordinate the large-scale criticism movement throughout the whole country.

First of all you have the people in authority going the capitalist road. Apart from them you also have landlords, rich peasants, counter revolutionaries, bad elements and rightists in society together with American, Soviet, Japanese and Nationalist agents. All of these are trying to carry out sabotage. It is easy for you to see whose black hands are hidden behind all these people. It looks as if they come out in the guise of either extreme "leftists" or rightists who oppose the Central Committee headed by Chairman Mao. This is quite impermissible and they are doomed to failure. At present if you take Peking as an example you have this kind of thing. I call it a thing because it is a counter-revolutionary organization. It is really called the "16th May" group. They don't have a very large membership. On the surface they are young people and these young people have been misled. They are a minority of bourgeois elements and are filled with hatred against us; but these are only individuals. The vast majority are young people and they are using the instability of young people's ideology. *The real manipulators behind the scenes are very bad people.* This "16th May" group appeared first of all under the guise of extreme "leftists." They concentrated their aim against the Prime Minister and in fact they collected material about us to send abroad. Naturally we are not scared. Why should we be frightened by this? You can go and sell it if you like. If you have had a good meal and feel like doing something and don't want to do revolution, no matter what you do, we are not scared. From the point of view of the rightists, at the end of January and February there was an atmosphere of opposition to the proletarian Cultural Revolution. At present this atmosphere is one of "leftism." They are opposing the Central Committee. This is the guise of extreme "leftists" *who are opposing the Prime Minister.* This is absolutely typical. The "16th May" group is a counter-revolutionary organization and we must raise our vigilance against agents from this organization as well as American, Nationalist and Soviet agents and the "five bad elements." They are never frank and sincere and they are bent on carrying out their death struggle. In that case we must raise our vigilance and see through them. We must undertake propaganda among the masses so that the masses see the light. We must isolate them so that they become an insignificant handful. This means that they are opposing the Central Committee leading group headed by Chairman Mao from the points of view of extreme "leftism" and rightism. I advise comrades to raise their vigilance on this problem.

Another problem is the problem of the Army.

Earlier some mistaken slogans appeared such as "pluck out a small handful in the Army." These people went about everywhere demanding that a "small handful" in the Army be plucked out and even went as far as to steal weapons from our conventional forces. Comrades should use their brains and consider whether we could come to the Hall of the People for this talk if we did not have the Army. What if our Field Armies were sabotaged? We can never permit this. So don't be deceived. These slogans are mistaken. No matter whether they are in the Party, the Government or the Army they are all under Party leadership. You can only refer to the people in authority going the bourgeois road in the Party and *you cannot refer to other people.* That would be unscientific. As a result *almost all the Military Regions throughout the country have been attacked.* No matter what the rights and wrongs are, no matter what we think of a minority of comrades in the Army, even those who have committed serious mistakes, we still cannot do this. The Army was founded by Chairman Mao personally and is directly controlled by Vice-Chairman Lin Piao personally. Wherever in the whole world do you have such a good Army. You dare to steal their weapons, beat them and criticize them and yet they keep silent and do not retaliate. Is there such another Army in the world like them (answer: No). So now you should not be deceived by the enemy and go around plucking out the "small handfuls" to your heart's content. I have already spoken of this problem to young generals in Peking. The mistake has been that you have rushed out to other areas. Last year was the period for lighting the fires of revolution. New great liaison activities have begun again. This is a hindrance rather than a help. It means you have miscalculated the situation and have been deceived by other people. Why? Young people like to be active, they like to be energetic. Struggle, criticism and reform is a bit hard. They don't want to sit down and read articles and afterwards use their brains. This is pretty difficult. Young people are all right. They like to be active. You might go somewhere but once you get there you don't understand the local situation. The moment you poke your nose into it you make a mistake. You should believe the masses in that area and you cannot try to act on their behalf in the same way as we cannot do your revolution for you. We can only discuss things with you and assist you and talk things over with you. Slogans such as "pluck out the small handful in the Army" are mistaken. They have produced some unfortunate results. At present this tendency is only just beginning and we can put a brake on it.

If people have not been able to keep up with the situation in the Cultural Revolution, have made mistakes, said a few wrong things, done a few wrong things, as long as they do a self-criticism comrades should allow them to correct their mistakes. They should follow the Chairman's teachings and let them wipe out past mistakes by present endeavors and cure the sickness to heal the patient. But as for things like attacking our Field Armies, this is quite wrong and we don't want to start on that road. Our Field Armies are good and our troops are good. Just think, the vast majority of the Commanders and troops come from poor and lower middle peasants or worker families and are faithful to the proletarian revolutionary line of the Central Committee headed by Chairman Mao. *At first they did not intervene but afterwards they intervened.* Of course, they did not really get the hang of things but this is inevitable. You try and think if you were in their place whether or not you would have made mistakes. What I mean to say is it is easy to make some ordinary mistakes in what you say or to make some mistakes in what you do; these are not errors of line. This is a question of principle. *But you cannot steal weapons from the Army in this way.* On the National Defense Front we are going to lay down a death penalty. The Central Committee has already passed it. I want to warn soldiers if anyone wanted to take away my weapons I would certainly retaliate. Of course opening fire would be wrong. I am that sort of person and I know whether you are a good person or a bad person, if you come to steal my weapons.

We should become revolutionaries for Chairman Mao's thought, not members of the Chang or the Li groups. Factionalism is a characteristic of the petty bourgeoisie and is mountain-topism, departmentalism and anarchism—very serious anarchism. If both sides would do a self-criticism, I think this is a method. For example, if you oppose me I should go to your place and do a self-criticism. Naturally you would feel a bit ashamed. I would seek out my own mistakes and do another self-criticism. In this way we could cool down and have a chat.

When you seek harmony there are small problems. What is harmony? Harmony is togetherness, it is revolution. It is the Cultural Revolution. Are you on the side of the proletarian Cultural Revolution led by Chairman Mao or on the side of the people in authority going the capitalist road? This is a big problem of right and wrong. On the basis of this principle, if you both want to struggle against the handful in the Party whatever reason is there for not uniting? Why do you act according to your own factionalism? You are not for revolutionary alliance. I think it is because you are not revolutionary but are out for yourselves. You are not acting for the people or for the proletariat. If you are a revolutionary then first of all you should have a spirit of self-criticism. You must strictly ask yourself and make strict demands on yourself and not make heavy demands on other people and then afterwards quarrel, fight, indulge in violent clashes and steal weapons. If you do that then you will certainly not keep a cool head and you won't know the difference between right and wrong.

If your basic premise is the same then this means you are on the same side. If there are differences in small issues or in methods or in some of your view points this can exist. (K'ang Sheng: a person often struggles against himself.) When you write an essay you want to change it. This means that you are struggling against yourself. This kind of thing does happen. You oppose yourself sometimes so you quarrel with yourself. It is easy to carry out a revolution against yourself. This is because in your own mind there are dark patches and bright patches. The dark patches lead you towards petty bourgeois or bourgeoisie things. If you don't get rid of these you inevitably change and will inevitably go over to the opposite side. If selfish individualism becomes stronger in your mind, you go over to clique-ism and departmentalism. It can reach such a stage that you will not listen to anyone so that you even want to attack our Field Armies which have excellent organization, excellent equipment and are first class in political work. This is not you, it is the bad elements. They hope to achieve their aims of splitting you, and you must be careful not to be deceived by them. You must keep your minds clear and be cool. You must be good at seeing through whether a person is an enemy or a friend . . . You must strive for revolutionary unity, and afterwards for revolutionary "tripartite alliances." Then you can have leadership. If you don't have leadership it is impossible to carry out revolution.

I want to discuss the third question of setting up a Revolutionary Committee. This is a provisional organ of command which has been gradually evolved. There is a bad atmosphere at present and a tendency towards not only attacking the Central Committee headed by Chairman Mao or the PLA, i.e., "plucking out the small handful" but also attacking the Revolutionary Committees. Inevitably members of the Revolutionary Committee have made mistakes and have shortcomings. It is even more inevitable that some bad elements should sneak in. The Revolutionary Committees are new-born things which were produced on the basis of the masses. At present there is this tendency to demand that the Central Committee annul all the Revolutionary Committees which they have sanctioned. Is it not a case of some people with ulterior motives creating splits? Comrades, do you know about this or not? (Yes) In the future when you gradually evolve a Revolutionary Committee there, you should keep up your vigilance about this problem. Naturally we are not scared if the problem is a bit complicated.

In the present excellent situation you should be vigilant about three things. This is that people from extreme "leftists" to extreme rightists are sabotaging the Central Committee headed by Chairman Mao, the PLA and revolutionary committees. Not only are the people in authority going the capitalist road behind them but they also have landlords, rich peasants, counter-revolutionaries, bad elements and rightists as well as American, Nationalist, Soviet Revisionist and Japanese agents on their side. We have some material on them and we have done some criticism.

Demarcate the boundaries between the reactionaries and the revolutionaries, expose the plots of the reactionaries, bring this to the attention of the revolutionaries, raise your own morale, destroy the prestige of the enemy and then you can isolate the reactionaries, fight on to victory and we shall either beat them or kick them out.

# SPEECH OF LIN PIAO AT THE RALLY CELEBRATING THE 18TH ANNIVERSARY OF THE FOUNDING OF THE PEOPLE'S REPUBLIC OF CHINA

Complete Text
(*Peking Review*, No. 41, 6 October 1967)

*Comrades and friends,*

Today is the 18th anniversary of the founding of the People's Republic of China. On this glorious festive occasion, on behalf of our great leader Chairman Mao, the Central Committee of the Party, the Government of the People's Republic of China, the Military Commission of the Party's Central Committee and the Cultural Revolution Group Under the Party's Central Committee, I most warmly salute the workers, peasants, commanders and fighters of the People's Liberation Army, the Red Guards, the revolutionary cadres and revolutionary intellectuals and the people of all nationalities throughout the country, and extend a hearty welcome to our comrades and friends who have come from different parts of the world!

We are celebrating the 18th anniversary of the founding of the People's Republic of China at a time when tremendous victories have been won in the great proletarian cultural revolution and an excellent situation prevails both in China and in the whole world.

The great proletarian cultural revolution movement initiated and led personally by Chairman Mao has spread to the whole of China. Hundreds of millions of people have been aroused. From the capital to the border regions, from the cities to the countryside, and from factory workshops to workers' homes, everyone, from teenagers to grey-haired old folk, concerns himself with state affairs and with the consolidation and strengthening of the dictatorship of the proletariat. Never before has a mass movement been so extensive and deep-going as the present one. The broad masses of workers and peasants, commanders and fighters of the People's Liberation Army, Red Guards, revolutionary cadres and revolutionary intellectuals, gradually uniting themselves through their struggles in the past year, have formed a mighty revolutionary army. Under the leadership of the Party's Central Committee headed by Chairman Mao, they have badly routed the handful of Party persons in authority taking the capitalist road headed by China's Khrushchov, who have collapsed on all fronts.

Frightened out of their wits by China's great proletarian cultural revolution, U.S. imperialism, Soviet revisionism and all reaction hoped that this great revolution would upset our national economy. The facts have turned out to be exactly the opposite of the wishes of these overlords. The great proletarian cultural revolution has further liberated the productive forces. Glad tidings about the successes in our industrial production keep on coming in. In agriculture, we are reaping a good harvest for the sixth consecutive year. Our markets are thriving and the prices are stable. The successful explosion of China's hydrogen bomb indicates a new level in the development of science and technology. What is even more important, the great cultural revolution has educated the masses and the youth, greatly promoted the revolutionization of the thinking of the entire Chinese people, enhanced the great unity of the people of all nationalities and tempered our cadres and all the P.L.A. commanders and fighters. Our great motherland has never been so powerful as it is today.

China's great proletarian cultural revolution has won decisive victory. In the history of the international communist movement, this is the first great revolution launched by the proletariat itself in a country under the dictatorship of the proletariat. It is an epoch-making new development of Marxism-Leninism which Chairman Mao has effected with genius and in a creative way.

In response to the great call of Chairman Mao, we must not only thoroughly destroy the bourgeois headquarters organizationally, but must also carry out more extensive and penetrating revolutionary mass criticism and repudiation so that the handful of Party persons in authority taking the capitalist road headed by China's Khrushchov will be completely overthrown and discredited politically, ideologically and theoretically and will never be able to rise again. Such mass criticism and repudiation should be combined with the struggle-criticism-transformation in the respective units so that the great red banner of Mao Tse-tung's thought will fly over all fronts.

At present, the most important task before us is, in accordance with Chairman Mao's teachings and his theory, line, principles and policy for making revolution under the dictatorship of the proletariat, to hold fast to the general orientation of the revolutionary struggle pointed out by Chairman Mao, to closely follow his strategic plan and, through the revolutionary mass criticism and repudiation combined with the struggle-criticism-transformation in the respective units, to consolidate and develop the revolutionary great alliance and revolutionary "three-way combination" and make a success of the struggle-criticism-transformation in these units, thus carrying the great proletarian cultural revolution through to the end.

Chairman Mao has recently instructed us that *"it is imperative to combat selfishness and criticize and repudiate revisionism."* By combating selfishness, we mean to use Marxism-Leninism, Mao Tse-tung's thought to fight selfish ideas in one's own mind. By criticizing and repudiating revisionism, we mean to use Marxism-Leninism, Mao Tse-Tung's thought to combat revisionism and struggle against the handful of Party persons in authority taking the capitalist road. These two tasks are interrelated. Only when we have done a good job of eradicating selfish ideas, can we better carry on the struggle against revisionism through to the end. We must respond to the great call of Chairman Mao and, with the instruction *"combat selfishness and criticize and repudiate revisionism"* as the guiding principle, strengthen the ideological education of the army and civilian cadres and of the Red Guards. Various kinds of study classes should be organized both at the central and local levels and can also be run by the revolutionary mass organizations, so that the whole country will be turned into a great school of Mao Tse-tung's thought. These studies will help our veteran and new cadres and young revolutionary fighters to study and apply Mao Tse-tung's thought in a creative way, liquidate all sorts of non-proletarian ideas in their minds, raise their ideological and political level and perform new meritorious deeds for the people.

We must respond to the great call of Chairman Mao and *"take firm hold of the revolution and promote production,"* energetically promote the development of our industrial and agricultural production and rapidly raise our scientific and technological level.

We must respond to the great call of Chairman Mao and unfold a movement of *"supporting the army and cherishing the people."* We must strengthen the dictatorship of the proletariat and resolutely suppress the sabotaging activities by class enemies, domestic and foreign.

The great proletarian cultural revolution is a movement that integrates Mao Tse-tung's thought with the broad masses of the people. Once Mao Tse-tung's thought is grasped by hundreds of millions of people, it turns into an invincible material force, ensuring that the dictatorship of the proletariat in our country will never change its color and enabling our socialist revolutionary and socialist construction to advance victoriously along the road of Mao Tse-tung's thought!

Proletarian revolutionaries, unite, hold high the great red banner of Mao Tse-tung's thought and carry the great proletarian cultural revolution through to the end!

Workers of all countries, unite; workers of the world, unite with the oppressed peoples and oppressed nations!

Down with imperialism headed by the United States!

Down with modern revisionism with the Soviet revisionist leading clique at its center!

Resolute support to the Vietnamese people in their great war against U.S. aggression and for national salvation!

Resolute support to the revolutionary struggles of the peoples of Asia, Africa and Latin America!

Resolute support to the revolutionary struggles of all peoples!

We are determined to liberate Taiwan!

Long live the great unity of the people of all nationalities of China!

Long live the People's Republic of China!

Long live the great, glorious and correct Communist Party of China!

Long live great Marxism-Leninism!

Long live the ever-victorious thought of Mao Tse-tung!

Long live Chairman Mao, our great teacher, great leader, great supreme commander and great helmsman! A long life, a long, long life to him!

# SPEECH OF CHOU EN-LAI AT WUHAN MASS RALLY TO WELCOME ALBANIAN PARTY AND GOVERNMENT DELEGATION, 9 OCTOBER 1967

*Abridged Text*
(*Peking Review*, No. 43, 20 October 1967)

Dear Comrade Mehmet Shehu,

Dear Comrade Ramiz Alia,

Dear Comrades of the Albanian Party and Government Delegation,

Revolutionary people of Wuhan municipality, commanders and fighters of the People's Liberation Army, Red Guard comrades-in-arms, comrades:

The Albanian Party and Government Delegation headed by Comrade Mehmet Shehu, bringing the profound revolutionary friendship of the heroic Albanian people, is now making a friendly visit in China. Taking different routes, members of the delegation have visited Tsinan and Tsingtao, and Tachai, Taiyuan and Yenan in the past few days and they have now come together in Wuhan. Once again we extend to them the heartiest and warmest welcome.

Comrades, comrades-in-arms!

I want to tell you a piece of very good news. Comrade Shehu, Comrade Alia and the other comrades of the Albanian Party and Government Delegation have come to Wuhan at the special invitation of our great leader Chairman Mao. Chairman Mao invited them to see for themselves the great proletarian cultural revolution movement in Wuhan. Comrade Shehu and Comrade Alia themselves wanted very much to see this great movement here. This shows the greatest concern and gives the greatest encouragement and support to Wuhan's proletarian revolutionaries and revolutionary masses.

Wuhan is a city with a glorious revolutionary tradition. On a number of occasions, our great leader Chairman Mao has swum the Yangtse River here, braving the wind and waves. The proletarian revolutionaries in Wuhan have always followed Chairman Mao in advancing through storms and waves. They have weathered new tests in the great proletarian cultural revolution which has no parallel in history. The proletarian revolutionaries in Wuhan are today holding a big rally here to welcome the Albanian comrades-in-arms who have come from the forefront of the anti-imperialist and anti-revisionist struggle. We feel that they are specially close to our hearts and we are overjoyed.

The glorious Albanian Party of Labor headed by Comrade Enver Hoxha consistently holds aloft the great red banner of Marxism-Leninism and resolutely opposes imperialism, modern revisionism and all reaction.

Revisionism in a new form emerged in Europe after the end of World War II. The first to make its appearance was the Tito renegade clique in Yugoslavia. Following this, the Khrushchov revisionist clique cropped up in the Soviet Union, which had the glorious tradition of the Great October Revolution. Leaders of the Communist Parties of many countries have degenerated into modern revisionists. The Albanian Party of Labor was the first to raise the great anti-revisionist banner in Europe. Undaunted by force and violence, fearing no difficulties or isolation, firm and unyielding, it has waged uncompromising, tit-for-tat struggles against modern revisionism with the Soviet revisionist leading clique at its center and against the Tito renegade clique.

While the Soviet Union and a number of other socialist countries have changed or are changing their political color, the Albanian Party of Labor has stuck to the dictatorship of the proletariat and the socialist road. To prevent the growth of revisionism and to deal with encirclement by imperialism, modern revisionism and reaction, the Albanian Party of Labor has of late adopted a series of revolutionary measures of tremendous significance: to oppose bureaucracy; propagate atheism; emancipate women; advocate moral incentives; reduce the wage gap; reduce private plots and private livestock; achieve all-round agricultural co-operation; develop the mountainous areas and strive for self-sufficiency in grain; adopt the system of functionaries taking part in physical labor; adopt the system of rotating functionaries; establish militia units in all parts of the country; bring guns and picks on to the stage, and so forth. In the movement of revolutionization, the Albanian comrades do what they say, and what they do, they do with all their will and might. This is, in many ways, worthy of our study.

U.S. imperialism is the most ferocious enemy of the people of the world. The people of the world have the common task of ending aggression and oppression by U.S. imperialism. Fighting at the forefront of the armed struggle against U.S. imperialism, the Vietnamese people have tied down a considerable part of the forces of U.S. imperialism, hitting hard at its aggressive arrogance. To isolate U.S. imperialism to the maximum and hit it hard, we must establish the broadest international united front to oppose U.S. imperialism and its lackeys. This united front cannot include modern revisionism with the Soviet revisionist leading clique as its center, which is working hand in glove with U.S. imperialism in selling out the interests of the people of all countries. But it should unite all anti-U.S. forces that can be united. Provided we continuously consolidate and expand the anti-U.S. united front and persist in struggle, the day will soon come when the people throughout the world defeat U.S. imperialism, no matter how much modern revisionism serves it.

Comrades, comrades-in-arms!

The great proletarian cultural revolution initiated and led personally by our great leader Chairman Mao has already won decisive victory. Hundreds of millions of people have been truly aroused. Mao Tse-tung's thought has been popularized on an unprecedentedly gigantic scale. The handful of Party persons in authority taking the capitalist road headed by China's Khrushchov have been dragged out. The power they usurped has come back into the hands of the proletariat. An excellent revolutionary situation prevails throughout the country.

An excellent situation prevails in the Wuhan area, as in other parts of the country. More than two months ago, dark clouds scudded across the sky as our class enemies acted in a frenzy. The enemy has now disintegrated and the proletarian revolutionaries are triumphantly advancing, riding the wind and waves. The revolutionary situation in the Wuhan area provides vivid proof of the wisdom and correctness of Chairman Mao's statement that *"disturbances thus have a dual character"* and *"bad things can be turned into good things."*

It can be clearly seen now that wherever disturbances occur, they are instigated by a handful of Party persons in authority taking the capitalist road or by landlords, rich peasants, counter-revolutionaries, bad elements and Rightists who have not really reformed, or enemy special agents who make trouble clandestinely. At the same time, the existence and influence of all sorts of bourgeois and petty-bourgeois ideas provide the soil for the class enemy to cause splits and instigate incidents. We do not approve of disturbances, but if the class enemy is bent on making them, this is nothing to be afraid of. When they act in this way, they are lifting a rock only to drop it on their own feet. Our class enemies fully reveal themselves in their true colors through such disturbances. By negative example this enhances the class consciousness of the proletarian revolutionaries and arouses their greater indignation, makes misled people see more clearly and mobilizes the masses more fully.

Where disturbances are great, the enemies themselves are in fact in great trouble, while the masses are tempered better. This makes for a more thorough solution of problems. The situation in the Wuhan area fully proves this point. The vicious intrigues of the class enemy have been defeated. A handful of capitalist roaders in authority hidden within the Party have been dragged out. Proletarian revolutionaries and the revolutionary masses were educated and tempered and became stronger in the course of this severe class struggle; their ranks have been expanded. The establishment of new revolutionary order has become the conscious demand and course of action of the revolutionary masses. The great proletarian cultural revolution in the Wuhan area has entered a new stage. This is a great victory for Chairman Mao's proletarian revolutionary line.

Naturally, certain conditions are needed to turn bad things into good things. We have the great thought of Mao Tse-tung and Chairman Mao's wise leadership and high prestige. We have the masses who can be trusted and relied upon. We have the People's Liberation Army that can be trusted and relied upon. We have the great majority of cadres who can be trusted and relied upon. What is more, the Liberation Army is an organized and disciplined armed force of the working people which has a militant tradition formed through long years of revolution and is armed with the thought of Mao Tse-tung, and, therefore, it is the most reliable mainstay of the great proletarian cultural revolution. Precisely because we have these most fundamental conditions, it does not matter if the class enemy tries to make disturbances which are severe and last for some time.

At present, the most important task confronting the proletarian revolutionaries and the revolutionary masses throughout the country is to follow Chairman Mao's great strategic plan closely, to take firm hold of the general orientation of the revolutionary struggle, to carry out revolutionary mass criticism and repudiation well and to realize revolutionary great alliances and "three-in-one" combinations. It is a very arduous task to throughly repudiate and completely discredit the handful of Party persons in authority taking the capitalist road and to carry to success the struggle-criticism-transformation in the respective units; the latter task, especially, it can be said, has not in the main begun yet. The realization of the revolutionary great alliance is a very important key to the successful accomplishment of these tasks.

Chairman Mao teaches us: *"There is no fundamental clash of interests within the working class. Under the dictatorship of the proletariat, there is no reason whatsoever for the working class to split into two big irreconcilable organizations."*; *"the revolutionary Red Guards and revolutionary student organizations should realize the revolutionary great alliance. So long as both sides are revolutionary mass organizations, they should realize the revolutionary great alliance in accordance with revolutionary principles."* In the Wuhan area, through the severe struggle between the two classes, the two roads and the two lines in the preceding stage, cardinal issues of right and wrong have been recognized, the bad elements have been isolated and the conservative organizations disintegrated. Thus the proletarian revolutionaries and the revolutionary mass organizations have conditions for forming revolutionary great alliances. Now you have united to hold the National Day celebrations and to welcome and play host to the Albanian Party and Government Delegation headed by Comrade Shehu. This is a good beginning for forming revolutionary great alliances. I hope that you will continue to make efforts, overcome all obstacles on the road of advance and form revolutionary great alliances and "three-in-one" combinations still better and faster on the principled basis of Mao Tse-tung's thought and by taking *"combat self-interest and criticize and repudiate revisionism"* as the key.

To promote the revolutionary great alliance, the various revolutionary mass organizations should seriously study Chairman Mao's works and his supreme instructions, conduct open-door rectification, do more self-criticism, pay more attention to other people's strong points, learn from and complement each other, strengthen proletarian Party spirit and overcome petty-bourgeois factionalism. If there are some people in a revolutionary mass organization who sabotage the great alliance based on revolutionary principles, then we should rely on the revolutionary masses in that organization to expose and deal with them. Other organizations must not interfere. The People's Liberation Army units stationed in the Wuhan area and their leading organizations should do more ideological and political work so as to help promote the great alliance of the mass organizations.

United and forming a mighty revolutionary army, the proletarian revolutionaries will be better able to carry out revolutionary mass criticism and repudiation of the handful of Party people in authority taking the capitalist road headed by China's Khrushchov on a still broader scale and in still greater depth, carry out struggle-criticism-transformation in the respective units well, realize revolutionary "three-in-one" combinations and carry the great proletarian cultural revolution through to the end.

The great proletarian cultural revolution has given an impetus to the development of our country's socialist construction. It is already clear that there will be another bumper harvest in agriculture this year. Within the space of less than one year, we have conducted three more nuclear tests, including a guided missile nuclear weapon test and a hydrogen bomb test. Such a world-shaking revolutionary movement of course exacts a certain price in production in certain places and in certain departments. We took this into account in advance. Production is affected to a certain extent, especially in places where disturbances occur. But this is only a transient thing. As soon as disorder is turned into order, production can quickly pick up and rise. The revolutionization of the thinking of the people is bound to be transformed into a tremendous material force. We believe that through this great cultural revolution, a new high tide in the development, by leaps and bounds, of our country's socialist construction will inevitably be brought about.

To take a firm hold of revolution and to promote production vigorously and to achieve new successes in fulfilling the state quotas with greater, faster, better and more economical results is the aim that proletarian revolutionaries ought to have and it is their glorious task. We should respond to Chairman Mao's great call and resolutely implement the strategic policy of *"taking firm hold of the revolution and promoting production."* Every revolutionary mass organization should meet the test in production. We are confident that the vast numbers of revolutionary workers and staff members and members of people's communes will act in this way and can achieve this.

The present great cultural revolution is an overall examination of and a rigorous test for cadres at all levels. The movement over the past year or more has brought to light a handful of bad people, discovered large numbers of good cadres and also revealed the shortcomings and errors in the ranks of our cadres. Some of our cadres, who have risen to high positions, have assumed arrogant airs, thinking that they are somebody and becoming fond of telling people off, and have thus become seriously estranged from the masses; this is very dangerous. This state of affairs is the result of the pernicious influence of the bourgeois reactionary line pushed by China's Khrushchov. At present, we should especially intensify education of cadres, carry out Chairman Mao's mass line still better and improve relations between the cadres and the masses.

The overwhelming majority of our cadres are good or relatively good. As for those who have committed mistakes or even serious mistakes, still, the majority can be taught to rectify these. We should let them make up for their mistakes or crimes by winning merit in the great cultural revolution, and, by the method of *unity—criticism and self-criticism—unity,* teach them and help them to see and correct their mistakes and enable them to return to Chairman Mao's revolutionary line, unless they are anti-Party, anti-socialist elements who persist in their mistakes and who refuse to correct them after repeated education. We believe that, after being criticized and helped by the masses, a large number of cadres should and can be emancipated.

Cadres at all levels should conscientiously accept examination and criticism by the masses. We should adopt an attitude of welcome, not of resistance or even antagonism, towards exposure, criticism and repudiation by the masses. From above, we should seek guidance from Chairman Mao, just as Vice-Chairman Lin Piao, close comrade-in-arms of Chairman Mao, has repeatedly taught us, study Chairman Mao's writings, follow his teachings and act according to his instructions. From below, we should seek advice from the masses, go to them and be their willing pupils. Only in this way can we win the understanding and trust of the masses and win new merit serving the people.

Our great leader Chairman Mao issued the great fighting call to us to *"combat self-interest and criticize and repudiate revisionism"* at a time when the great proletarian cultural revolution is developing victoriously. This is the basic program of the great proletarian cultural revolution whose fundamental goal is to energetically destroy the bourgeois world outlook and foster the proletarian world outlook. "Self-interest" is the core of the bourgeois world outlook and the ideological basis for the existence and growth of revisionism. Only by completely removing "self-interest" from people's minds is it possible to dig out the roots of revisionism, establish the absolute authority of Mao Tse-tung's thought and be better able to carry the anti-revisionist struggle through to the end. The broad masses of workers and peasants, commanders and fighters of the People's Liberation Army, young Red Guard fighters, revolutionary cadres, revolutionary intellectuals and all proletarian revolutionaries must strive to transform their inner, subjective world while transforming the objective world. We are determined to follow Chairman Mao's latest instruction, and, by using Marxism-Leninism, Mao Tse-tung's thought, struggle against "self-interest" in our own minds and against the handful of Party persons in authority taking the capitalist road, and turn the whole country into a great, red school of Mao Tse-tung's thought.

# "ADVANCE ALONG THE ROAD OPENED UP BY THE GREAT OCTOBER SOCIALIST REVOLUTION"

by the Editorial Departments of *People's Daily*, *Red Flag* and *Liberation Army Daily*, 6 November 1967

*Complete Text*
(*Peking Review*, No. 46, 10 November 1967)

Full 50 years have passed since the Great October Socialist Revolution.

The October Socialist Revolution led by Lenin, great teacher of the proletariat, for the first time translated into reality the theory of the dictatorship of the proletariat advanced by Marx and Engels and established the first state of the dictatorship of the proletariat in the history of mankind over one-sixth of the globe.

A new epoch began in the history of mankind.

A new era of world proletarian revolution and the dictatorship of the proletariat began.

A new era of the oppressed nations' struggle for liberation led by the proletariat began.

Comrade Mao Tse-tung, the greatest Marxist-Leninist of our time, has made a most penetrating exposition of the great historic significance of the October Socialist Revolution. He points out:

*"The first imperialist world war and the first victorious socialist revolution, the October Revolution, have changed the whole course of world history and ushered in a new era."*

*"The October Revolution has opened up wide possibilities for the emancipation of the peoples of the world and opened up the realistic paths towards it; it has created a new front of revolutions against world imperialism, extending from the proletarians of the West, through the Russian revolution to the oppressed peoples of the East."*

*"The road of the October Revolution is, fundamentally speaking, the bright common road for the progress of all mankind."*

Under the guidance of the great banner of Marxism-Leninism and the illumination of the October Revolution, the world has undergone earth-shaking changes in the last 50 years. The flames of the October Revolution are now raging throughout the world.

The great People's Republic of China under the dictatorship of the proletariat stands like a giant in the East. Aroused and led by our great leader Chairman Mao himself, the 700 million people of China are carrying out a great proletarian cultural revolution such as has never been known before in history. This great revolution which has a vital bearing on the future of China and the destiny of mankind has won decisive victory.

The Albanian Party of Labor headed by the great Marxist-Leninist Comrade Enver Hoxha has led the Albanian people in persevering with proletarian heroism in the socialist revolution and the dictatorship of the proletariat, thus raising a bright red banner of socialism in Europe.

Valiantly resisting the wanton U.S. imperialist aggression, the 31 million people of Vietnam have scored brilliant victories and set a great example of anti-U.S. armed revolutionary struggle for the people of the whole world.

The people of Laos, Burma, the Philippines, Thailand, India, Indonesia and other countries are embarking on or persisting in the road of revolutionary armed struggle. The national-democratic revolutionary movement is unfolding vigorously in the vast areas of Asia, Africa and Latin America.

The proletariat of Western Europe, North America and Oceania are awakening and plunging into the struggle against U.S. imperialism and monopoly capital in their own countries.

In short, under the banner of Marxism-Leninism, Mao Tse-tung's thought, the international communist movement is cleaning up all the mire of Khrushchov revisionism, and the revolutionary Communists and the broad masses of revolutionary people the world over are fighting, along the road of the October Revolution, to create a new world without imperialism, without capitalism and without the exploitation of man by man.

Under the leadership of Lenin and Stalin, the people of the Soviet Union, with revolutionary initiative, smashed the old state machine in the dark world of capitalist rule by means of violent revolution, established the dictatorship of the proletariat, and thus erected a radiant beacon. In the subsequent years, following the road of the October Revolution, the Soviet people won great victories in defeating the White Guard rebellion and the armed intervention of 14 countries, in smashing the opportunist line of Trotsky, Bukharin and company, counter-revolutionary representatives of the bourgeoisie who had wormed their way in the Party, in carrying out socialist transformation and socialist construction, and in waging the anti-fascist war. All these glorious exploits were made at the cost of oceans of the sweat and blood of the heroic sons and daughters of the October Revolution, and they shine with the brilliance of the revolutionary heroism and lofty internationalism of the Soviet proletariat.

Today, in commemorating the 50th anniversary of the Great October Socialist Revolution, the Chinese people and Marxist-Leninists and revolutionary people of all countries deeply cherish the memory of Lenin, the great creator of the October Revolution, and his successor Stalin. We shall never forget the indelible historic feats of the glorious Bolshevik Party and the great Soviet proletariat in opening up the road of the October Revolution and establishing the dictatorship of the proletariat.

However, the first great socialist state, the Soviet Union, which was the pride of the Soviet and the world proletariat and was thriving at the time of Lenin and Stalin, has now changed its political color as a result of the usurpation of Party and state leadership by the handful of top persons in authority taking the capitalist road within the C.P.S.U., as represented by Khrushchov. Under the reactionary rule of the notorious Khrushchov and the revisionist clique headed by his successors Brezhnev and Kosygin, the powerful red bastion, which was once regarded as the light and hope by the people throughout the world, has become the center of modern counter-revolutionary revisionism and another headquarters of world reaction.

The renegades Brezhnev, Kosygin and company now have the impudence to style themselves successors to the cause of the October Revolution and to engage in demagogy, flaunting the banner of "commemorating" the 50th anniversary of the October Revolution. What a monstrous insult to the great Lenin, to the Great October Revolution and to the great Soviet people! You renegades to the October Revolution, by what right do you commemorate the October Revolution? The only place for you is in the dock of history to be tried by the Marxist-Leninists and the hundreds of millions of revolutionary people all over the world!

It is you renegades who have trampled underfoot the great banner of Leninism, betrayed the cause of the dictatorship of the proletariat and, under the signboard of the "party of the entire people" and "state of the whole people" turned the Communist Party of the Soviet Union founded by Lenin into a bourgeois party, turned the dictatorship of the proletariat set up by the Soviet people at the cost of their blood and lives into a dictatorship of the bourgeoisie which suppresses the laboring masses, and turned the Soviet state born amidst the storm of the October Revolution into a revisionist and bourgeois state. The Soviet people have been denied the right to be their own masters and are again under oppression and enslavement by a group of despicable scabs—a new privileged bourgeois stratum.

It is you renegades who have discarded the banner of socialism, strangled the socialist cause of the October Revolution and, under the cloak of "building communism," replaced the socialist planned economy and the principle of "to each according to his work" by the capitalist principle of profit-seeking and free competition, causing enterprises owned by the whole people and collective farms to degenerate into enterprises of a capitalist nature and a kulak economy.

It is you renegades who, under the cover of "culture of the entire people" energetically advertise reactionary revisionist ideas, the decadent bourgeois way of life and ugly "Western culture." Bourgeois ideology dominates all spheres of ideology and culture in the Soviet Union today. The socialist culture fostered by the October Revolution has been trampled underfoot. The communist morality personally nurtured by Lenin and Stalin is being submerged in the icy waters of egoism.

It is you renegades who have betrayed proletarian internationalism and the revolutionary cause of the world proletariat, made "peaceful coexistence," "peaceful competition" and "peaceful transition" the general line of foreign policy, prostrated yourselves before U.S. imperialism and formed a new "Holy Alliance" with all the most reactionary forces in the world against communism, against the people, against revolution, and against China. You are everywhere peddling the opium of revisionism, trying to paralyze the masses of the people, selling out the interests of the revolution and undermining revolutionary struggles, with the result that Communists and revolutionary fighters have been massacred in their tens of thousands by imperialism and its lackeys.

You renegades have committed heinous crimes against the Soviet people and the people throughout the world. You are the sworn enemy of the Soviet people as well as the common enemy of the revolutionary people of the world.

Comrade Mao Tse-tung has often told us: *It is only through repeated education by positive and negative examples, and by making comparisons and contrasts, that revolutionary Parties and revolutionary people can temper themselves, reach maturity and gain assurance of victory. Those who belittle the role of teachers by negative example are not thoroughgoing dialectical materialists.*

The usurpation of state power by the modern revisionists and the gradual emergence of an all-round capitalist restoration in the Soviet Union and other socialist countries have provided the Marxist-Leninists and revolutionary people of the whole world with a very profound historical lesson: After seizing state power, the proletariat may still lose it and the dictatorship of the proletariat can still revert to a dictatorship of the bourgeoisie. Not only must the proletariat guard against armed subversion of state power by its enemies at home and abroad. What is more important, it must be vigilant against usurpation of Party and state leadership from within by persons of the Khrushchov type and against the taking of the path of "peaceful evolution." In betraying the cause of the dictatorship of the proletariat, the Khrushchov revisionists serve the world proletariat as first-rate teachers by negative example. In this sense, Khrushchov deserves a one-ton "medal."

Comrade Mao Tse-tung, the great and valiant standard bearer of Marxism-Leninism, and the Communist Party of China headed by him are leading the 700 million Chinese people, along with the Marxist-Leninists and revolutionary people the world over, in waging with dauntless proletarian revolutionary spirit a great powerful struggle against modern revisionism with the Soviet revisionist renegade clique as its center. They have won brilliant victories internationally and will surely continue to win still greater victories.

Comrade Mao Tse-tung's greatest contribution to the international communist movement is his systematic summing up of the historical experience of the dictatorship of the proletariat in China and of the dictatorship of the proletariat in the world since the October Revolution; he has summed up not only the positive but also the negative experience, and, in particular, the grave lessons of the all-round restoration of capitalism in the Soviet Union; and he has comprehensively and thoroughly solved the cardinal issue of our time, the issue of carrying on the revolution and preventing capitalist restoration under the dictatorship of the proletariat. This is a great epoch-making development of the Marxist-Leninist theory of the dictatorship of the proletariat.

The theory of the dictatorship of the proletariat was founded by Marx and Engels. The proletariat of Paris made the first heroic attempt to seize political power. The Paris Commune failed but, as Marx said, *"the principles of the Commune are perpetual and indestructible."*

In his *Critique of the Gotha Programme*, Marx advanced the well-known thesis summing up his entire revolutionary theory, that *"between capitalist and communist society lies the period of the revolutionary transformation of the one into the other. There corresponds to this also a political transition period in which the state can be nothing but the revolutionary dictatorship of the proletariat."*

In his struggle against the revisionism of the Second International, Lenin inherited, defended and developed the Marxist theory on proletarian revolution and the dictatorship of the proletariat, solved a series of problems of the proletarian revolution in the era of imperialism and solved the question of the possibility of the victory of socialism in one country, thus developing Marxism to a new stage, the stage of Leninism.

After the October Revolution, Lenin pointed out on many occasions that acute and complex class struggles and the possibility of capitalist restoration still existed under the dictatorship of the proletariat. He said:

*"Class struggle, . . . after the overthrow of capitalist rule, after the destruction of the bourgeois state, after the establishment of the dictatorship of the proletariat, does not disappear (as the vulgar representatives of the old socialism and the old social-democracy imagine), but merely changes its forms and in many respects becomes fiercer."*

*"The transition from capitalism to communism takes an entire historical epoch. Until this epoch is over, the exploiters inevitably cherish the hope of restoration, and this hope turns into attempts at restoration."*

Lenin made a penetrating analysis of why, under the dictatorship of the proletariat, the overthrown bourgeoisie still has immense strength and is in the position to resist and carry out activities for a restoration, and he explained the necessity for consolidating and strengthening the dictatorship of the proletariat. He stated:

*"The dictatorship of the proletariat means a most determined and most ruthless war waged by the new class against a more powerful enemy, the bourgeoisie, whose resistance is increased tenfold by their*

overthrow (even if only in a single country), and whose power lies, not only in the strength of international capital, the strength and durability of their international connections, but also in the force of habit, in the strength of small-scale production. Unfortunately, small-scale production is still wide spread in the world, and small-scale production engenders capitalism and the bourgeoisie continuously, daily, hourly, spontaneously, and on a mass scale. All these reasons make the dictatorship of the proletariat necessary."*

Lenin also took note of the seriousness of the class struggle in the ideological sphere. He explicitly pointed out:

*"Our task is—to defeat all the resistance of the capitalists, not only military and political but also ideological, which is the deepest and the most powerful."*

These brilliant ideas and these great scientific predictions of Lenin's have tremendously developed the Marxist theory of the dictatorship of the proletariat and are of immense practical significance today for all Marxist-Leninists who adhere to the road of the October Revolution.

The modern revisionists Khrushchov, Brezhnev, Kosygin and company have completely betrayed these ideas of Lenin's. Comrade Mao Tse-tung, while fighting against the modern revisionists and explaining the necessity for persevering in the dictatorship of the proletariat, has invariably taught us not to forget these statements of Lenin's.

Comrade Mao Tse-tung has comprehensively inherited, defended and developed Marxism-Leninism, he has creatively put forward the great theory of the continuation of the revolution under the dictatorship of the proletariat, and he has personally initiated and led the great practice of the first great proletarian cultural revolution in the history of mankind. This is an extremely important landmark, demonstrating that Marxism has developed to a completely new stage, the stage of Mao Tse-tung's thought.

The essentials of Comrade Mao Tse-tung's theory of the continuation of the revolution under the dictatorship of the proletariat are as follows:

One. It is necessary to apply the Marxist-Leninist law of the unity of opposites to the study of socialist society. Comrade Mao Tse-tung points out: *"The law of the unity of opposites is the fundamental law of the universe."* *"Contradictions exist everywhere,"* *"contradictoriness within a thing is the fundamental cause of its development."* In socialist society, there are *"two types of social contradictions—those between ourselves and the enemy and those among the people themselves."* *"The contradictions between ourselves and the enemy are antagonistic contradictions. Within the ranks of the people, the contradictions among the working people are non-antagonistic."* Comrade Mao Tse-tung tells us: It is necessary to *"distinguish contradictions among the people from those between ourselves and the enemy"* and *"correctly handle contradictions among the people,"* so that the dictatorship of the proletariat can become increasingly consolidated and strengthened and the socialist system developed.

Two. *"Socialist society covers a fairly long historical stage. In this stage, classes, class contradictions and class struggle continue, the struggle between the socialist road and the capitalist road continues and the danger of capitalist restoration remains."* After the basic completion of the socialist transformation of the ownership of the means of production, *"the class struggle is by no means over. The class struggle between the proletariat and the bourgeoisie, the class struggle between the different political forces, and the class struggle in the ideological field between the proletariat and the bourgeoisie will continue to be long and tortuous and at times will even become very acute."* In order to prevent capitalist restoration and "peaceful evolution," it is imperative to carry the socialist revolution on the political and ideological fronts through to the end.

Three. The class struggle under the dictatorship of the proletariat is in essence still a matter of political power, in other words, the bourgeoisie tries to overthrow the dictatorship of the proletariat while the proletariat strives to consolidate it. *The proletariat must exercise all-round dictatorship over the bourgeoisie in the field of the superstructure, including the various spheres of culture. "Our relation with them can in no way be one of equality. On the contrary, it is a relation of one class oppressing another, that is, the dictatorship of the proletariat over the bourgeoisie. There can be no other type of relation, such as a so-called relation of equality, or of peaceful coexistence between exploiting and exploited classes, or of kindness or magnanimity."*

Four. The struggle between the two classes and two roads in society is inevitably reflected within the Party. *The handful of Party persons in authority taking the capitalist road are the representatives of the bourgeoisie within the Party.* They *"are a bunch of counter-revolutionary revisionists. Once conditions are ripe, they will seize political power and turn the dictatorship of the proletariat into a dictatorship of the bourgeoisie."* In order to consolidate the dictatorship of the proletariat, we must take great care to see through the *"persons like Khrushchov"* *"who are still nestling beside us,"* fully expose them, criticize and repudiate them, overthrow them, make it impossible for them ever to rise again, and we must firmly recapture for the proletariat the power they have usurped.

Five. It is of the greatest importance for the continuation of the revolution under the dictatorship of the proletariat that *the great proletarian cultural revolution* should be carried out.

*"In the great proletarian cultural revolution, the only method is for the masses to liberate themselves." "Let the masses educate themselves in this great revolutionary movement."* In other words, *this revolution is boldly arousing the masses from below by means of extensive democracy under the dictatorship of the proletariat and, at the same time, is forging the great alliance of the proletarian revolutionaries and the revolutionary "three-way alliance" of the revolutionary masses, the People's Liberation Army and the revolutionary cadres.*

Six. *"Fight self, repudiate revisionism"* is the *fundamental program of the great proletarian cultural revolution in the ideological field. "The proletariat seeks to transform the world according to its own world outlook, and so does the bourgeoisie."* Therefore, *the great proletarian cultural revolution is a great revolution that touches peoples to their very souls and aims at solving the problem of their world outlook.* We must criticize and repudiate revisionism politically, ideologically and theoretically, use proletarian ideology to overcome bourgeois egoism and all non-proletarian ideas, transform education, literature and art and all other parts of the superstructure that are not in correspondence with the socialist economic base, and thus uproot revisionism.

In putting forward the above theory of the continuation of the revolution under the dictatorship of the proletariat, Comrade Mao Tse-tung has creatively and with genius developed the Marxist-Leninist conception of class struggle in the period of the dictatorship of the proletariat and has developed with genius the conception of the dictatorship of the proletariat. This is of epoch-making significance and represents the third great milestone in the history of the development of Marxism.

Fifty years ago Lenin stressed that *"only he is a Marxist who extends the recognition of the class struggle to the recognition of the dictatorship of the proletariat. This is what constitutes the most profound difference between the Marxist and the ordinary petty (as well as big) bourgeois. This is the touchstone on which the real understanding and recognition of Marxism is to be tested."* We may now say that only he is a genuine Marxist-Leninist who extends the recognition of the dictatorship of the proletariat to the recognition of the need to continue the revolution under the dictatorship of the proletariat. This is the touchstone on which the real understanding and recognition of Marxism-Leninism are to be tested.

The Great October Socialist Revolution opened the way for the proletariat to seize political power. The fundamental experience of the October Revolution expresses the universal law for making revolution in the era of imperialism and proletarian revolution. China's great proletarian cultural revolution has opened the way for the consolidation of the dictatorship of the proletariat, for the prevention of capitalist restoration and for the advance to communism. The fundamental experience of the cultural revolution expresses the universal law of class struggle in the historical stage of the transition to communism following the establishment of the dictatorship of the proletariat. Various new problems may arise in the future and there may be difficulties and twists and turns; nevertheless, with the triumph of China's great proletarian cultural revolution, *"the important thing is that the ice has been broken—the road is open and the path has been blazed,"* as Lenin said in appraising the significance of the October Revolution.

Stalin said: *"The October Revolution should not be regarded merely as a revolution 'within national bounds.' It is, primarily, a revolution of an international, world order."* Like the October Revolution, China's great proletarian cultural revolution is not merely a revolution "within national bounds"; it is likewise a revolution of an international order. This great revolution has won the enthusiastic support of the proletariat and revolutionary people throughout the world. Its great victory has opened a new era in the international communist movement and will assuredly have a far-reaching influence on the course of human history.

Advanced revolutionary theory always spreads far and wide along with the great victory of the revolutionary struggle which it guides. The October Revolution 50 years ago very greatly stimulated the dissemination of Marxism-Leninism so that the world revolution took on an entirely new look. With the victory of the Chinese revolution in 1949 under the guidance of Comrade Mao Tse-tung, the world has undergone a further radical change. In the short space of over a year, China's great proletarian cultural revolution has crushed the bourgeois headquarters led by China's Khrushchov, and utterly discredited the exploiting classes in every respect. This great mass mobilization has shaken the world, and has brought the understanding of Mao Tse-tung's thought on the part of the people of the world forward to a new and higher level, making it far richer and more profound than ever before.

The revolutionary people of the world have come to understand more and more clearly that Comrade Mao Tse-tung is the greatest teacher and most outstanding leader of the proletariat in the present era and that Chairman Mao is indeed the Lenin of our time. Mao Tse-tung's thought is Marxism-Leninism at its highest in the present era, it is Marxism-Leninism that strikes terror into the hearts of the imperialists, revisionists and reactionaries of all countries, and is the most powerful ideological weapon of the proletariat and the masses of revolutionary people.

With the dissemination of Mao Tse-tung's thought, the revolutionary people are better able to draw a strict line between Marxism-Leninism and modern revisionism. When they look back at the dung hill in the backyard of the workers' movement and see the old wares which Khrushchov and his followers have been trying to peddle, people can now more clearly distinguish the fragrant flowers from the poisonous weeds, distinguish the road of the October Revolution from the road which runs counter to it. The Khrushchov revisionist buffoons who clamor for a "party of the entire people" and a "state of the whole people" and have cast the dictatorship of the proletariat to the four winds are finding it more and more difficult to deceive the people with the signboard of "all-round communist construction." Those parliamentary cretins who don the cloak of Marxism are finding it more and more difficult to prevent the proletariat from rising in arms to seize political power.

The world has now entered a revolutionary new era, with Mao Tse-tung's thought as its great banner. France was the center of revolution in the late 18th century, and the center moved to Germany in the mid-19th century when the proletariat entered the political arena and Marxism came into being. The center of revolution moved to Russia early in the 20th century, and Leninism came into being. The center of world revolution has since gradually moved to China and Mao Tse-tung's thought has come into being. Through the great proletarian cultural revolution, China, the center of world revolution, has become more powerful and consolidated.

Chairman Mao says: *"The Chinese people have always considered the Chinese revolution a continuation of the Great October Socialist Revolution and have looked upon this fact as a great honor."* The great proletarian cultural revolution in which we are now engaged is precisely the continuation of the October Revolution in a higher stage under new historical conditions. The best way for the Chinese people to commemorate the 50th anniversary of the October Socialist Revolution today is to hold aloft the great banner of the October Revolution and the great banner of Marxism-Leninism, Mao Tse-tung's thought, carry the great proletarian cultural revolution resolutely through to the end, firmly support all the revolutionary Marxist-Leninists of the world and the people of all countries, and, together with them, carry the struggle against imperialism, modern revisionism and all reaction through to the end.

When commemorating the 40th anniversary of the October Revolution, Comrade Mao Tse-tung pointed out: *"The socialist system will eventually replace the capitalist system; this is an objective law independent of man's will. However much the reactionaries try to hold back the wheel of history, sooner or later revolution will take place and will inevitably triumph."*

And in 1962 Comrade Mao Tse-tung said: *"The Soviet Union was the first socialist state and the Communist Party of the Soviet Union was founded by Lenin. Although the leadership of the Soviet Party and state has now been usurped by the revisionists, I would advise comrades to remain firm in the conviction that the masses of the Soviet people and Party members and cadres are good, that they want revolution and that rule by revisionism will not last long."*

The all-round restoration of capitalism in the Soviet Union is only a brief interlude in the history of the international communist movement. We are firmly convinced that the genuine Soviet Communists and the great Soviet people, who have been taught by the great Lenin and Stalin, who have the glorious tradition of the October Revolution and who were tested and tempered in the anti-fascist war, will not tolerate for long the renegade clique of the Soviet revisionists riding roughshod over them. They are now waging struggles against the Soviet revisionist renegade clique in a variety of ways. They will certainly unite under the banner of the Great October Revolution, carry forward the behests of Lenin and Stalin, persevere in prolonged struggle, break through the heavy darkness and make the red star of the October Revolution shine forth again, and shine still more brilliantly.

The great truth of Marxism-Leninism, Mao Tse-tung's thought, is irresistible. More than 90 per cent of the world's population are invariably for revolution. The masses of the people will eventually

828

triumph. The world revolution will eventually triumph. Under the great revolutionary banner of Mao Tse-tung's thought, the great cause of the dictatorship of the proletariat pioneered by the October Revolution will certainly advance in more gigantic strides, and communism is sure to win final victory throughout the world.

# SPEECH OF LIN PIAO AT THE PEKING RALLY COMMEMORATING THE 50TH ANNIVERSARY OF THE OCTOBER REVOLUTION

*Complete Text*
(*Peking Review*, No. 46, 10 November 1967)

*Comrades, Young Red Guard Fighters and Friends:*

Today the Chinese people join the proletarians and revolutionary people throughout the world in grand and solemn commemoration of the 50th anniversary of the Great October Socialist Revolution.

The October Revolution led by the great Lenin was a turning point in human history.

The victory of the October Revolution broke through the dark rule of capitalism, established the first state of the dictatorship of the proletariat in the world and opened a new era of the world proletarian revolution.

For more than one hundred years since Marx and Engels formulated the theory of scientific socialism, the international proletariat, advancing wave upon wave and making heroic sacrifices, has been waging arduous struggles for the great ideal of communism and has performed immortal exploits in the cause of the emancipation of mankind.

In his struggle against the revisionism of the Second International and in the great practice of leading the October Socialist Revolution, Lenin solved a series of problems of the proletarian revolution and the dictatorship of the proletariat as well as the problem of victory for socialism in one country, thus developing Marxism to the stage of Leninism. Leninism is Marxism in the era of imperialism and proletarian revolution. The salvoes of the October Revolution brought Leninism to all countries, so that the world took on an entirely new look.

In the last fifty years, following the road of the October Revolution under the banner of Marxism-Leninism, the proletariat and revolutionary people of the world have carried the world history forward to another entirely new era, the era in which imperialism is heading for total collapse and socialism is advancing to worldwide victory. It is a great new era in which the proletariat and the bourgeoisie are locked in the decisive battle on a worldwide scale.

Led by the great leader Chairman Mao, the Chinese people have followed up their victory in the national-democratic revolution with great victories in the socialist revolution and socialist construction. Socialist China has become the mighty bulwark of world revolution. Adhering to the road of the October Revolution, the heroic people of Albania have raised a bright red banner in Europe. By their war against U.S. imperialist aggression and for national salvation, the Vietnamese people have set a brilliant example of struggle against imperialism for the people of the whole world. The movement of national-democratic revolution in Asia, Africa and Latin America is developing vigorously. The ranks of the Marxist-Leninists are growing steadily, and a new situation has emerged in the international communist movement.

Compared with half a century ago, the world proletarian revolution today is far deeper in content, far broader in scope and far sharper in its struggle. The new historical era has posed a series of important new problems for Marxist-Leninists. However, in the final analysis, the most fundamental problem remains that of seizing and consolidating political power.

Chairman Mao says: *"The aim of every revolutionary struggle in the world is the seizure and consolidation of political power."* This is a great Marxist-Leninist truth.

The struggle between the Marxist-Leninists and the revisionists always focuses on this fundamental issue. The modern revisionists, represented by Khrushchov and his successors, Brezhnev, Kosygin and company, are wildly opposing the revolution of the people of the world and have openly abandoned the dictatorship of the proletariat and brought about an all-round capitalist restoration in the Soviet Union. This is a monstrous betrayal of the October Revolution. It is a monstrous betrayal of Marxism-Leninism. It is a monstrous betrayal of the great Soviet people and the people of the world. Therefore, if the proletariat fails to smash the wanton attacks of the modern revisionists, if it does not firmly defend the road of the October Revolution opened up by the great Lenin, continue to advance along this road under the new historical conditions and thoroughly solve the question of how to seize and consolidate political power, it will not be able to win final victory, or will probably lose political power even after seizing it, and, like the Soviet people, will come under the rule of a new privileged bourgeois stratum.

It is our good fortune that because Comrade Mao Tse-tung has comprehensively inherited and developed the teachings of Marx, Engels, Lenin and Stalin on proletarian revolution and the dictatorship of the proletariat, the most fundamental issue of the world proletarian revolution, that is, the road to the seizure and consolidation of political power, has been brought to a higher stage in theory and in practice. Our great leader Chairman Mao has developed Marxism-Leninism and raised it to an entirely new peak. The ever-victorious thought of Mao Tse-tung is Marxism-Leninism in the era in which imperialism is heading for total collapse and socialism is advancing to worldwide victory.

In the course of leading the great struggle of the Chinese revolution, Chairman Mao has with genius solved a whole series of complicated problems concerning the seizure of political power by force of arms. Under his leadership, the Chinese people went through the most protracted, fierce, arduous and complex people's revolutionary war in the history of the world proletarian revolution and founded the red political power, the dictatorship of the proletariat.

The way the Chinese people seized political power by force of arms under Chairman Mao's leadership may be summarized as follows: Under the leadership of the political party of the proletariat, to arouse the peasant masses in the countryside to wage guerrilla war, unfold an agrarian revolution, build rural base areas, use the countryside to encircle the cities and finally capture the cities. This is a great new development of the road to the seizure of political power by force of arms indicated by the October Revolution.

Chairman Mao has said: *"As a rule, revolution starts, grows and triumphs first in those places in which the counter-revolutionary forces are comparatively weak."* Since in our time all the reactionary ruling classes have a tight grip on the main cities, it is necessary for a revolutionary political party to utilize the vulnerable links and areas of reactionary rule, fully arouse the masses, conduct guerrilla warfare, establish stable revolutionary bases and so build up and temper their own forces and, through prolonged fighting, strive step by step for complete victory in the revolution. Hence, reliance on the masses to build rural revolutionary base areas and use the countryside to encircle the cities is a historic task which the oppressed nations and peoples in the world today must seriously study and tackle in their fight to seize political power by force of arms.

Not only has Comrade Mao Tse-tung creatively developed Leninism on the question of the seizure of political power by the proletariat, he has made an epoch-making creative development of Leninism on the most important question of our time—the question of consolidating the dictatorship of the proletariat and preventing the restoration of capitalism.

From the first day of the victory of the October Revolution, Lenin paid close attention to the consolidation of the new-born Soviet state power. He recognized the sharp and protracted nature of the class struggle under the dictatorship of the proletariat, pointing out that *"the transition from capitalism to communism takes an entire historical epoch. Until this epoch is over, the exploiters inevitably cherish the hope of restoration, and this hope turns into attempts at restoration."*

The biggest lesson in the history of the international communist movement in the last fifty years is the restoration of capitalism in the Soviet Union and other socialist countries. This harsh fact has strikingly brought the Marxist-Leninists of the world face to face with the question of how to consolidate the dictatorship of the proletariat and prevent the restoration of capitalism.

It is Comrade Mao Tse-tung, the great teacher of the world proletariat of our time, who in the new historical conditions, has systematically summed up the historical experience of the dictatorship of the proletariat in the world, scientifically analysed the contradictions in socialist society, profoundly shown the laws of class struggle in socialist society and put forward a whole set of theory, line, principles, methods and policies for the continuation of the revolution under the dictatorship of the proletariat. With supreme courage and wisdom, Chairman Mao has successfully led the first great proletarian cultural revolution in history. This is an extremely important landmark, demonstrating that Marxism-Leninism has developed to the stage of Mao Tse-tung's thought.

The victory of the great proletarian cultural revolution has opened up in China, which has a quarter of the world's population, a bright path for consolidating the dictatorship of the proletariat and for carrying the socialist revolution through to the end. The proletariat and the revolutionary people of the world who are fighting imperialism, modern revisionism and all reaction resolutely support our great proletarian cultural revolution. They find in the victory of this revolution tremendous inspiration, bright prospects and greater confidence in victory.

The imperialists headed by the United States and their lackeys the modern revisionists and all the reactionaries have taken great pains to curse and vilify our great proletarian cultural revolution. This proves by negative example that our victory has dealt the enemy a very heavy blow and that they are nothing but a bunch of vampires that are bound to be destroyed.

The world is moving forward. And theory, which reflects the laws of the world, is likewise developing continuously.

Mao Tse-tung's thought is the banner of our era.

Once Mao Tse-tung's thought—Marxism-Leninism at its highest in the present era—is grasped, the oppressed nations and peoples will, through their own struggles, be able to win liberation.

Once Mao Tse-tung's thought—Marxism-Leninism at its highest in the present era—is grasped, the countries that have already established the dictatorship of the proletariat will, through their own struggles, be able to prevent the restoration of capitalism.

Once Mao Tse-tung's thought—Marxism-Leninism at its highest in the present era—is grasped, the people of those countries where political power has been usurped by revisionists will, through their own struggles, be able to overthrow the rule of revisionism and re-establish the dictatorship of the proletariat.

Once Marxism-Leninism, Mao Tse-tung's thought is integrated with the revolutionary practice of the people of all countries, the entire old world will be shattered to smithereens.

Comrades, young Red Guard fighters and friends:

The fifty years since the October Revolution have been years of fierce struggle between socialism and capitalism and between Marxism-Leninism and modern revisionism, with the former winning one victory after another. The imperialist system resembles a dying person who is sinking fast, like the sun setting beyond the western hills. The emergence of Khrushchov revisionism is a product of imperialist policy and reflects the death-bed struggle of imperialism. Although imperialism and revisionism will go on making trouble in collusion with each other, the reactionary adverse current can, after all, never become the main current. The dialectics of history is irresistible. Henceforth, the proletariat and the revolutionary people of the world will raise still higher the great red banner of Marxism-Leninism, Mao Tse-tung's thought, and march forward in giant strides along the road opened up by the October Revolution!

Those who betray the October Revolution can never escape the punishment of history. Khrushchov has long since fallen. In redoubling its efforts to pursue the policy of betrayal, the Brezhnev-Kosygin clique will not last long either. The proletariat and the working people of the Soviet Union, with their glorious tradition of revolution, will never forget the teachings of the great Lenin and Stalin. They are sure to rise in revolution under the banner of Leninism, overthrow the rule of the reactionary revisionist clique and bring the Soviet Union back into the orbit of socialism.

Comrades, young Red Guard fighters and friends!

The situation in our great motherland is excellent. Under the guidance of the latest instructions of the great leader Chairman Mao, the great proletarian cultural revolution is forging ahead victoriously.

We must raise still higher the great banner of the October Revolution and the great banner of Marxism-Leninism, Mao Tse-tung's thought, and carry the great proletarian cultural revolution through to the end.

We must build our great motherland into a still more powerful base for world revolution.

We must give ever more vigorous support to the revolutionary struggles of the proletariat and people of all countries.

We must, together with the revolutionary people everywhere, carry through to the end the struggle against U.S.-led imperialism and against modern revisionism with the Soviet revisionist renegade clique as its center.

We must intensify our efforts in studying and mastering Mao Tse-tung's thought and disseminate it still more widely throughout the world.

These are glorious tasks entrusted to the people of our country by history, and they are our incumbent internationalist duty.

Our great leader Chairman Mao has given the call: *"Let the Marxist-Leninists of all countries unite, let the revolutionary people of the whole world unite and overthrow imperialism, modern revisionism and all reaction. A new world without imperialism, without capitalism and without exploitation of man by man will surely be built."*

Let us fight with courage for the realization of this great call of Chairman Mao's!

Long live the Great October Socialist Revolution!

Long live the great proletarian cultural revolution!

Workers of all countries, unite!

Workers of all countries, unite with the oppressed peoples and oppressed nations!

Long live the invincible Marxism, Leninism, Mao Tse-tung's thought!

Long live the great teacher, great leader, great supreme commander, great helmsman Chairman Mao! A long, long life to him!

# "BASIC DIFFERENCES BETWEEN THE PROLETARIAN AND BOURGEOIS MILITARY LINES"

Written by "Proletarian Revolutionaries" in the Offices
of the Headquarters of the General Staff of the People's Liberation Army

Complete Text
(*Peking Review*, No. 48, 24 November 1967)

To seize and consolidate political power and carry its revolutionary struggle to complete victory the proletariat *"need[s] a correct Marxist military line as well as a correct Marxist political line."* Without the guidance of a correct political line, it is impossible to have a correct military line; without a correct military line, it is also impossible to implement and carry out a correct political line.

However, *"correct political and military lines do not emerge and develop spontaneously and tranquilly, but only in the course of struggle. These lines must combat 'Left' opportunism on the one hand and Right opportunism on the other. Without combating and thoroughly overcoming these harmful tendencies which damage the revolution and the revolutionary war, it would be impossible to establish a correct line and win victory in this war."*

Within our Party and army, in recent decades and in all historical stages of the development of the Chinese revolution, there has always been a sharp and acute struggle between two diametrically opposed military lines. One is the proletarian military line represented by Chairman Mao, the other is the bourgeois military line advocated by opportunists of the "Left" and Right. Chairman Mao's proletarian military line has been gradually developed and perfected in the course of this struggle against the bourgeois military line.

Our great leader Chairman Mao has created with genius the greatest, most comprehensive and scientific proletarian theory on military affairs. In the Kutien Congress Resolution, which was drawn up by him in 1929, and in a series of other military writings, Chairman Mao has formulated the most correct proletarian military line. This is the highest peak of the Marxist-Leninist concept of military affairs. It is the sharpest and most powerful weapon of the proletariat and revolutionary people the world over for defeating imperialism, modern revisionism and all reaction.

The great victory of the Chinese people's revolutionary war was a great victory for Chairman Mao's proletarian military line, for the thought of Mao Tse-tung.

Comrade Lin Piao, Chairman Mao's closest comrade-in-arms and our deputy supreme commander, has always most faithfully, resolutely and thoroughly implemented Chairman Mao's proletarian revolutionary line and military thinking. At every major historical juncture in the last forty years, Comrade Lin Piao has invariably, unequivocally and resolutely upheld Chairman Mao's correct line, safeguarded Mao Tse-tung's thought, waged an irreconcilable struggle against the wrong lines in the Party and the army, and made outstanding contributions.

China's Khrushchov and his agents, Peng Teh-huai and Lo Jui-ching, have persistently opposed Chairman Mao's proletarian military line and frantically pushed their bourgeois military line. After Peng Teh-huai had been exposed at the Lushan Meeting of the Party in 1959, Lo Jui-ching became the foremost champion of the reactionary bourgeois military line. He formed a conspiratorial anti-Party clique with Peng Chen, Lu Ting-yi and Yang Shang-kun and, protected and supported by China's Khrushchov, worked desperately to usurp military power on behalf of the bourgeois headquarters. In co-ordinating the cultural and military fronts, they were preparing to unleash a counterrevolutionary coup and subvert the dictatorship of the proletariat at an opportune moment.

Throughout the period of socialism, the struggle between the two military lines is in essence a struggle for military power between the proletariat and the bourgeoisie. It is an important component of the struggle, waged under the dictatorship of the proletariat, between the bourgeoisie attempting a come-back and the proletariat opposing such an attempt.

## Whether to Give Prominence to Proletarian Politics or Not Is the Focus of the Struggle Between Chairman Mao's Military Line And the Bourgeois Military Line in Building Up Our Army

In the last forty years, the struggle between Chairman Mao's line and the bourgeois line in army building has always focussed on the fundamental question of whether to put politics or military affairs first, whether prominence should be given to politics or to military affairs.

The very essence of Chairman Mao's thinking and line on army building is the putting of proletarian politics to the fore in building a people's army. It is, first and foremost, to build an army politically.

In the Kutien Congress Resolution, a document of great historic significance which was drawn up by Chairman Mao himself and adopted at the early period after the founding of our army, Chairman Mao pointed out that *"military affairs are only one means of accomplishing political tasks"* and that *"the*

*Chinese Red Army is an armed body for carrying out the political tasks of the revolution.*" He correctly explained the relationship between military affairs and politics, that is, military affairs must be subordinated to politics and politics must command military affairs.

The representatives of the bourgeoisie like Peng Teh-huai and Lo Jui-ching, who wormed their way into the Party, always opposed Chairman Mao's thinking and line on army building. They always opposed giving prominence to proletarian politics and, instead, advocated giving first place to military affairs, to technique.

During the War of Resistance Against Japan, two fundamentally antagonistic lines took shape on the question of how to deal with correctly the co-operation between the Kuomintang and the Communist Party and with the united front.

The proletarian revolutionary line represented by Chairman Mao advocated that our policy is *"one of independence and initiative within the united front, a policy both of unity and of independence."* It upheld *"the principle of absolute leadership of the Eighth Route Army by the Communist Party."*

The capitulationist line represented by Wang Ming and China's Khrushchov, advocated handing over the leadership of the anti-Japanese united front to the Kuomintang. With servile flattery, China's Khrushchov lauded Chiang Kai-shek as a "revolutionary banner" and wanted to hand over the army led by the Communist Party and place it under the leadership of the "national government."

To meet the needs of the capitulationist line, Lo Jui-ching issued a book entitled *Political Work in the Anti-Japanese Army*. In this book, instead of dealing with class struggle and the proletarian seizure of political power, he did his utmost to blow the trumpet for the Kuomintang's reactionary politics. He even asked the political commissars to "guarantee absolute obedience of the troops" to the command of Chiang Kai-shek, and he wanted to hand over the guns of the proletariat to Chiang Kai-shek.

During the War of Liberation, in a report on "How to Strengthen Political Work in the Army," Lo Jui-ching listed political, military, rear-service and other work as being on an equal footing, and opposed putting political work in first place. He said: "It is wrong to favor over-emphasis" of political work. Actually, what he meant by not over-emphasizing political work was to do away with proletarian politics and replace it with bourgeois politics.

Comrade Lin Piao, our deputy supreme commander, has always held high the great red banner of Mao Tse-tung's thought. After he took charge of the work of the Military Commission of the Central Committee of the Party, he personally supervised the formulation of "The Decision on Strengthening the Political-Ideological Work in the Army" on the basis of Chairman Mao's ideas on army building and the historical experience of our army.

He creatively advanced the ideas of the "four firsts"[1] and a series of policies, principles and important measures for putting proletarian politics to the fore, creatively studying and applying Chairman Mao's works, upholding the "four firsts," promoting the "three-eight" working style,[2] practicing democracy in the three main fields,[3] and launching the "four-good" company movement.[4] These policies, principles and measures carried forward the building of our army to an entirely new stage.

Chairman Mao has pointed out: *"The 'four firsts' is good; it is an invention. Since Comrade Lin Piao put forward the 'four firsts' and the 'three-eight' working style, the ideological-political work of the People's Liberation Army, as well as its military work, has developed remarkably, has become more concrete and at the same time has been raised to a higher theoretical plane than in the past."*

To put politics to the fore is to put Mao Tse-tung's thought to the fore, to arm commanders and fighters with Mao Tse-tung's thought and establish the absolute authority of Mao Tse-tung's thought. The great thought of Mao Tse-tung is the soul of our army, the corner-stone in building our army and the basic guarantee that our army will never change color.

Dominated by personal ambition and his reactionary class instinct, Lo Jui-ching mortally feared and hated Mao Tse-tung's thought. He consistently opposed Comrade Lin Piao, who always holds high the great red banner of Mao Tse-tung's thought. He opposed him for actively promoting the mass movement to creatively study and apply Chairman Mao's works throughout the army, the Party and the country.

At the same time, he reverenced and respected the book on "self-cultivation" written by China's Khrushchov, and personally issued the order making this book compulsory reading for the whole army.

His purpose was to use this revisionist "self-cultivation" to corrupt the soul of our army, make us lose our orientation and depart from Chairman Mao's proletarian line on army building, and make us forget classes, class struggle and the dictatorship of the proletariat. His was a vain attempt to change the proletarian nature of our army fundamentally.

Lo Jui-ching used contests in military skill to obstruct politics and disrupt the study of Chairman Mao's works.

Vice-Chairman Lin Piao promptly corrected this mistake and again issued instructions to put politics to the fore. But Lo Jui-ching still resisted desperately and talked such nonsense as: "Military training itself is politics, the biggest politics." This argument which puts politics and military affairs on a par and replaces politics with military affairs is an out and out bourgeois military viewpoint.

Chairman Mao teaches us: *"Politics is the commander, politics is the soul of everything. Political work is the life-blood of all work."*

By spreading his revisionist fallacies, Lo Jui-ching wanted to subordinate politics to military affairs, to make military affairs command politics, deprive our army of its soul and turn our proletarian army into a bourgeois army.

In a society where there are classes and class struggle, no sphere of society exists in a vacuum. It is under the guidance either of proletarian ideology or of bourgeois ideology. The army is a tool of class struggle. Either it serves proletarian politics or it serves bourgeois politics. There has never been and never will be an army that is separate from politics.

All Khrushchovites who want to seize political power from the proletariat and restore capitalism seek to corrode the army ideologically, usurp military power, seize the gun. This is a very important step they want to take. Therefore, whether to put proletarian politics to the fore or not, whether to work for the revolutionization of people's minds or not has a vital bearing on whether the proletarian army will degenerate or not, on whether the gun is in the hands of the proletariat or the bourgeoisie. In the final analysis, it has a vital bearing on whether or not the proletariat can consolidate its political power after seizing it.

### Whether to Fight a People's War or Not Is the Dividing Line Between Chairman Mao's Military Thinking and Bourgeois Military Thinking

Chairman Mao's great theory on people's war has developed Marxism-Leninism creatively and with genius. It not only points out the correct way for the Chinese people to win country-wide victory but also indicates the road to thorough emancipation for the oppressed nations and oppressed classes throughout the world.

In seeking their own emancipation, the most important thing for all oppressed nations and oppressed classes is to arm themselves with Chairman Mao's theory on people's war, to smash the old state apparatus with arms, to overthrow imperialism and its running dogs by force of arms and with arms to transform the entire world.

Whether one intends to fight a people's war or not, whether one dares to fight a people's war or not is the dividing line between Chairman Mao's military thinking and bourgeois military thinking, between Marxism-Leninism and revisionism, between genuine and sham revolution.

Chairman Mao teaches us: *"The revolutionary war is a war of the masses; it can be waged only by mobilizing the masses and relying on them."* *"Rallying millions upon millions of people round the revolutionary government and expanding our revolutionary war, we shall wipe out all counterrevolution...."*

Chairman Mao's thinking on people's war is built on the ideological basis of fully trusting and relying on the masses.

As with all opportunists, the military thinking of Lo Jui-ching is founded on the theory that weapons decide everything. He does not trust the masses at all and does not rely on them. He opposes arming the masses, opposes the people's militia system and opposes Chairman Mao's great strategic idea of a people's war.

China's Khrushchov maintains that technique has pride of place, and that technique decides everything. Lo Jui-ching maintains that with new technical equipment, "any invading enemy can be annihilated on the sea, in the air or at the base from which it launches its attack." They use the theory of winning victory by superior weapons to oppose arming the masses, and dealing with imperialist aggression by people's war. They vainly hope that the enemy can be defeated by relying purely on technical equipment. This is typical bourgeois military thinking.

Is it true that under modern conditions, there is no need to rely on the masses in war, no need to wage a people's war? No, it is not. *"The contest of strength is not only a contest of military and economic power, but also a contest of human power and morale. Military and economic power is necessarily wielded by people."* Regardless of how developed modern weapons and technical equipment may be, how complicated the operations of modern warfare, victory in war is still decided by the support and assistance of the masses, by the struggle of the masses. In the final analysis, it depends on people's war. This is the most important and reliable guarantee for the defeat of the enemy.

Our great leader Chairman Mao has fully and most profoundly explained the importance of arming the masses. After country-wide victory, Chairman Mao told us time and again: *"The imperialists are bullying us in such a way that we will have to deal with them seriously. Not only must we have a powerful regular army, we must also organize contingents of the people's militia on a big scale. This will make it difficult for the imperialists to move a single inch in our country in the event of invasion."* *"Should the imperialists dare to unleash an aggressive war against our country, then we will turn the whole nation into soldiers; the militia will co-operate with the People's Liberation Army and at any time replenish it to crush the aggressors utterly."*

Vice-Chairman Lin Piao points out: People's militia work is fundamental to the building up of China's national defense, an important part of the strategic program and a concrete application of the Party's mass line in warfare. Combining the building of a modern revolutionary armed force with organizing contingents of the people's militia is the concrete application of the principle of "walking on two legs" in the building up of China's national defense. It is an important development of Chairman Mao's concept of people's war under modern conditions.

The people's militia has always been an important component of our armed forces, a solid basis for the waging of a people's war, and an instrument of our proletarian dictatorship. In fact, whether to have a militia or not is a major issue which affects the weakening or strengthening of the dictatorship of the proletariat.

China's Khrushchov and his agent Lo Jui-ching consider that the militia organized in accordance with Mao Tse-tung's thought is a main obstacle to their usurpation of Party and army leadership and to their realization of a capitalist restoration. They used a hundred and one ways to undermine the building of the militia and to oppose arming the masses. In building the militia, they also tried to spread purely military viewpoints and opposed putting proletarian politics to the fore. They vainly attempted to remold our militia with a bourgeois world outlook and so turn it into a tool for realizing their personal ambitions.

Chairman Mao teaches us: *"This army is powerful because of its division into two parts, the main forces and the regional forces, with the former available for operations in any region whenever necessary and the latter concentrating on defending their own localities and attacking the enemy there in co-operation with the local militia and the self-defense corps."*

After the winning of nationwide victory, Chairman Mao repeatedly gave instructions that *great efforts should be made to strengthen the building of regional forces. In addition to building themselves up ever more effectively, the regional forces should, in ordinary times and in co-operation with the local authorities, strengthen their mass work and do a good job in building the people's militia to reinforce and expand their ranks and fight the enemy.*

China's Khrushchov and his accomplice Lo Jui-ching, while opposing the militia system, did their utmost to oppose the building of the regional forces. China's Khrushchov said: "Should we or shouldn't we have some (regional forces)? They leave farm production part of the time and return home in the busy farming season." This absurd statement altogether negates the regional forces.

In accordance with his master's intentions, Lo Jui-ching for five years tried to keep secret Chairman Mao's instructions on strengthening the building up of the regional forces and refused to carry them out. Later on, although outwardly compliant he did not actually give in and repeatedly discounted them. In a hundred and one ways he attempted to undermine the building of the regional forces.

Vice-Chairman Lin Piao points out: "Our army consisted of local forces as well as of regular forces; moreover, it energetically built and developed the militia, thus practicing the system of combining the three military formations, i.e., the regular forces, the local forces and the militia."

The system of combining these three military formations brings into play the enthusiasm of hundreds of millions of people. A militant whole can thus be organized and the power of people's war can be brought into full play. If imperialism invades us, the militia are not only an inexhaustible reservoir for our army but can also lead the broad masses in waging widespread guerrilla warfare. The regional forces are the backbone in regional struggle against the enemy. They lead the vast militia in co-operating energetically with the main forces and continuously expand and are themselves transformed into main forces. This ensures the latter's growth and expansion.

With the regional forces and the vast militia fighting in co-operation with them, the main forces have their hands freed. They can form powerful "fists," seek and create favorable opportunities for battle, maintain their mobility and concentrate their strength to fight battles of annihilation.

China's Khrushchov and Lo Jui-ching wanted to cut out the militia as well as the regional forces. They opposed arming the masses and the use of people's war in dealing with an imperialist war of aggression; they staked the future of the country on technical equipment, fundamentally negating the concept of people's war. If we followed out Lo Jui-ching's

theories, the fruits of victory we have won in hard struggle would be lost and the whole proletarian revolutionary cause would be lost.

## Active Defense and Passive Defense Are Two Diametrically Opposed Principles of Strategic Guidance Between Chairman Mao's Military Line and the Bourgeois Military Line

Active defense is Chairman Mao's consistent strategic concept, and the fundamental guiding principle by which we have successfully fought revolutionary wars and dealt with imperialist aggression. It is also the correct guilding principle for the winning of victories in revolutionary wars by the peoples in other countries.

Chairman Mao teaches us: *"Active defense is also known as offensive defense, or defense through decisive engagements. Passive defense is also known as purely defensive defense or pure defense. Passive defense is actually a spurious kind of defense, and the only real defense is active defense, defense for the purpose of counter-attacking and taking the offensive."*

Whether one adopts the strategic principle of active defense or of passive defense is a fundamental question of strategic guidance which has a vital bearing on the outcome of a revolutionary war.

Active defense is founded on the ideological basis of the proletariat's thoroughgoing revolution and complete annihilation of the enemy forces. Its essence is to fight wars of annihilation. Only by fighting a war of annihilation, is it possible to constantly deplete and weaken the enemy forces, develop and strengthen our own forces and finally defeat the enemy. Waging a war of annihilation is the basic guiding thought in our conduct of war. This guiding thought must be impelemented whether guerrilla or mobile warfare is the primary form of warfare being waged, whether strategic guidance or battle operations are involved.

The history of the Chinese people's revolutionary war proves that only by firmly implementing our great supreme commander Chairman Mao's strategic principle of active defense, will we be sure to win battles and enable the revolutionary cause to develop successfully. Otherwise, we will lose battles and the revolutionary cause will suffer setbacks.

Comrade Lin Piao, our deputy supreme commander, has always most faithfully, resolutely and thoroughly defended and followed Chairman Mao's correct principle of active defense and opposed the wrong principle of passive defense. He has repeatedly called on us to study Chairman Mao's great strategic concept earnestly and resolutely ensure thorough implementation of Chairman Mao's strategic principle of active defense.

Lo Jui-ching has always opposed Chairman Mao's strategic concept and stood for passive defense. As early as the War of Resistance Against Japan, he followed Peng Teh-huai in opposing Chairman Mao's correct policy of boldly arousing the masses and starting up guerrilla war independently in the enemy's rear, of building anti-Japanese base areas and of developing the people's anti-Japanese armed forces. They had the presumption to concentrate the main forces of the Eighth Route Army for a war of attrition with the Japanese invaders. This caused serious setbacks to the development of the north China anti-Japanese base areas and our army there. In fact, these people supported and helped the Kuomintang. After usurping an important position in our army, Lo Jui-ching did his utmost in advocating the wrong policy of passive defense to meet the needs of the class capitulationist and national capitulationist line of China's Khrushchov. China's Khrushchov said: "Hold the enemy back" and "it will be bad if the enemy comes in." Lo Jui-ching also said: "Now conditions are different," and that the only method to be used was that of "blocking the water." Such absurd statements are nothing new, they are simply the same trash of passive defense, of "engaging the enemy outside the gates," which was criticized by Chairman Mao as early as the thirties.

Acting according to this wrong policy would inevitably lead to the building of defensive works eveywhere and wide dispersal of forces to man them. In that way, we would always be in a passive position and this would lead finally to the wreck of the proletarian regime. This is the psychology characteristic of the successors to the Khrushchov revisionism of submission to imperialism and the fear of war.

The Chinese people are a great people armed with Mao Tse-tung's thought. In order to annihilate the enemy forces in large numbers, they dare to lure the enemy in deep, concentrate superior forces and annihilate the enemy forces when circumstances favor our victory. In the final analysis, it is only by annihilating the enemy's effective strength, that it is possible to maintain positions.

They clamored that "the conditions are different." What conditions are different? The imperialists do indeed have atomic bombs and nuclear weapons. But this is not so terrific! Marxists have at all times held that no matter what changes take place in technical equipment the basic laws of revolutionary war will never change.

*"Weapons are an important factor in war, but not the decisive factor; it is people, not things, that are decisive."* Final victory or defeat in war is determined by the ground forces in fighting successive battles, by the political consciousness and courage of the people and their spirit of sacrifice, by fighting with rifles, hand-grenades and bayonets, by hand-to-hand engagements, night fighting and fighting over a range of tens of meters. In combating an imperialist war of aggression, no matter what weapons the enemy may use, if they dare to go deep into our country, we will enjoy the maximum initiative, give full play to our strong points and advantages, use various methods to deal them blows, vigorously demonstrate the magic power of people's war and make sure that the aggressors will never go back alive.

China's Khrushchov and Lo Jui-ching frenziedly opposed Chairman Mao's strategic principle of active defense and made every effort to push the strategic principle of passive defense for no other purpose than that of meeting the political needs of imperialism and modern revisionism. Utterly betraying the cause of the proletarian revolution, they acted completely against the basic interests of the Chinese people and the peoples of the world.

On the eve of the great proletarian cultural revolution initiated and led by Chairman Mao himself, the counter-revolutionary revisionist Lo Jui-ching's plot to oppose Chairman Mao, Mao Tse-tung's thought and Chairman Mao's military line and to usurp the army leadership and oppose the Party, went completely bankrupt. The reactionary bourgeois military line pursued by him, and he also, were cast off by the commanders and fighters of the whole army.

Holding high the great red banner of Mao Tse-tung's thought, the revolutionary masses of the entire country are now bringing about an upsurge in revolutionary mass criticism and repudiation to overthrow and completely discredit the handful of top Party persons in authority taking the capitalist road, headed by China's Khrushchov. We must vigorously destroy the bourgeois military line and thoroughly wipe out their poisonous influence. We must establish the absolute authority of Mao Tse-tung's thought and of his military line in a big way, keep proletarian politics always to the fore, take further steps to promote the revolutionization of the ideology and organization of the whole army, ensure that the guns are held firmly in the hands of the proletariat at all times and defend the dictatorship of the proletariat so that our impregnable state of the proletariat will never change its political color!

*(Written by proletarian revolutionaries in the offices of the Headquarters of the General Staff of the Chinese People's Liberation Army.)*

## NOTES

[1] "Four firsts": this means giving first place to man in the correct handling of the relationship between man and weapons; giving first place to political work in the correct handling of the relationship between political and other work; giving first place to ideological work in the correct handling of the relationship between ideological and routine tasks in political work; and giving first place to living ideas in the correct handling of the relationship between ideas in books and living ideas in ideological work.

[2] "Three-eight" working style: "three" refers to three mottoes: keep firmly to the correct political orientation, maintain a plain, hard-working style, and be flexible in strategy and tactics; and "eight" refers to the eight characters which mean unity, alertness, earnestness and liveliness.

[3] Democracy in the main fields: this refers to political democracy, economic democracy and military democracy.

[4] A "four good" company is a company good in political and ideological work, good in the "three-eight" working style, good in military training and good in making arrangements for daily life.

# SPEECH OF 13 MARCH 1967 BY FIDEL CASTRO AT THE COMMEMORATION OF THE 10TH ANNIVERSARY OF THE ATTACK ON THE PRESIDENTIAL PALACE

*Complete Text*
(*Granma,* Havana, 19 March 1967, English edition)

Comrades Professors and University Students:

All present here:

In these ceremonies commemorating the glorious assault of March 13, 1957, just 10 years ago today, it has become a tradition for us to take up some essential aspect of a theme that interests the Revolution and the people. These themes may be extremely varied, but on these occasions we have generally analyzed, when circumstances have demanded it, a subject of international character. And today circumstances again demand that we treat this type of theme. (APPLAUSE) We refer to the problems in Venezuela, the problems of the Venezuelan revolutionary movement, the accusations the Venezuelan puppet government has made against our Revolution and the charges of the rightist official leadership of the Communist Party of Venezuela.

For several days a tremendous campaign against our country has been carried on by the government of that country and by the Yankee news services, following the death of an ex-functionary of the Venezuelan government. And for several months in the clandestine and semi-clandestine press, even in the legal press of that country, and at different international events, the rightist leadership of the Communist Party of Venezuela has been making similar charges against our Party. The pro-imperialist oligarchy says that we interfere in the internal affairs of Venezuela; and the rightist Party leadership that we interfere in the internal affairs of the Party in Venezuela. This is not at all a strange coincidence between reactionaries and rightists!

We have had to bring along a good number of papers, including numerous dispatches from various news agencies. And, following chronological order as much as possible, we are going to read the most important items appearing in these dispatches, which give a better idea of the sequence of events.

This first dispatch is datelined "Caracas, March 1 (AFP): Dr. Julio Iribarren Borges, former Social Security Director and brother of Foreign Minister Ignacio Iribarren Borges, was kidnapped here this morning. The kidnapping was perpetrated by three extremist elements armed with pistols who forced him into a vehicle which then drove off at full speed.

"Police authorities," the dispatch says further on, "presume the extremists to be young members of the so-called Armed Forces of National Liberation. The authorities have reinforced security measures to draw a tighter ring around the kidnappers, who may be hidden somewhere in the city."

Naturally, I am not reading the complete text of these dispatches, but rather paragraphs containing the essential items; many of the cables merely repeat the news, more or less, in one way or another.

"Caracas, March 1 (AP): A well-known Venezuelan public figure, Julio Iribarren Borges, brother of the Minister of Foreign Relations, disappeared today in mysterious circumstances.

"Julio Irribarren Borges is one of the most controversial figures of Venezuela due to the fact that he recently increased the Social Security tax. Beginning January 1, workers and employees have been paying a considerably higher contribution, while the promised expansion of social services has not gone into effect.

"A television commentator said that if the extremists did this, it is easy to imagine why they kidnapped Iribarren Borges, perhaps the most hated man in Venezuela at this time. They would prefer to kidnap him rather than a more appealing public figure." This is what the AP dispatch says.

Now: "Caracas, March 3 (AP): Julio Iribarren Borges, who disappeared Wednesday morning, was found dead about 24 kilometers from Caracas, police sources reported tonight.

"The police sources said that the body of Iribarren Borges, found near the Venezuelan Scientific Institute, had three bullet wounds in the back. Many leaflets, signed by the so-called Armed Forces of National Liberation (FALN), reading 'We have three other political leaders on the list,' were found near the body."

"Caracas, March 4 (UPI)." Referring to the burial of Iribarren Borges, this dispatch contains a statement of the former Minister of the Interior of the government of Venezuela, which reads as follows:

" 'This is Cuban Prime Minister Fidel Castro with his methods in Venezuela,' former Interior Minister and present leader of the parliamentary fraction of the government party, Accion Democratica, Carlos Andres Perez, declared to United Press International. 'The time has come for Venezuela and all the countries of Latin America to decide to do something about Cuba,' he added."

### They are Trying to Involve Cuba

"Caracas, March 4 (AP): Forty-eight hours after reestablishing constitutional guarantees, the government decided today to suspend them again following the assassination of Julio Iribarren Borges, outstanding public figure and brother of the Foreign Minister, who was found dead near Caracas last night.

"The decision, taken in a Cabinet meeting held after noon today, was announced this evening by

Reinaldo Mora, Minister of the Interior. This measure will serve to restrain the excesses committed under the stimulus of foreign ideas promoted from abroad by the dictatorship that took power in Cuba."

"Caracas, March 4 (AFP): Hector Mujica, member of the Central Committee of the Communist Party of Venezuela, energetically condemned today the assassination of Dr. Julio Iribarren, who died sometime between last Wednesday and Friday.

"Mujica, a lawyer and professor at the Central University of Caracas, referred to the crime, affirming that his Party categorically and unequivocally condemns this method of struggle, since it has nothing to do with either the revolution or the defense of the popular cause. He added that he had wired condolences this morning in his own name and in that of his family to Foreign Minister Ignacio Iribarren Borges, brother of the victim."

"Caracas, March 5 (AFP): Communist Party leaders Pompeyo Marquez, Guillermo Garcia Ponce, and Teodoro Petkoff, who made a rocambolesque escape through a tunnel from the fortress of San Carlos in this capital last February 6, condemned the assassination of Dr. Julio Iribarren Borges.

"In a document sent to the national press as an official declaration of the Communist Party of Venezuela, the fugitives declared that personal assaults and methods of struggle considered characteristic of anarchy and terrorism not only are unrevolutionary, but damage the cause, and therefore merit repudiation."

"On Monday, March 6, 1967, the daily GRANMA carried declarations by Major Elias Manuitt on the execution of Iribarren in Caracas. The headline read, and we quote: 'Declarations of Major Elias Manuitt on the execution of Iribarren in Caracas.'

"The text of the declaration reads as follows: 'The government of Raul Leoni, in a new demonstration of its growing weakness and fear produced by the numerous blows received from the revolutionary forces, has just decreed a new suspension of constitutional guarantees, using as a pretext the recent execution of Julio Iribarren Borges.

"Recently, on the occasion of the disappearance and assassination of the revolutionary leaders Andres Pasquier and Felipe Malaver by the AD (Accion Democratica) Government, the National Command of the FLN-FALN of Venezuela issued a communique stating that, for every combatant of the revolutionary movement assassinated by the government, the patriotic forces would answer with the application of revolutionary justice to three government personages, accomplices of the repression and misery prevailing in our country, governed by traitors in the service of the Yankees.

"In the cases of various missing members of the revolutionary movement, later proven to have been assassinated by the government, nothing has come of appeals to the regular courts of justice of our country, or of requests for information on their whereabouts, or of declarations to the press made by the mothers and wives of the missing persons.

"For these reasons, as the broadsides circulating in Caracas proclaim, our movement decided to apply revolutionary justice to Julio Iribarren Borges, important government figure and accomplice in the deceit and excesses committed against the workers of Venezuela through the obligatory Social Security, which Iribarren directed until a few days ago and from where, moreover, he worked as a spy and an informer for DIGEPOL. Many innocent Social Security employees and functionaries have been imprisoned as a result of the espionage and informing carried on by Iribarren Borges in that body as one more DIGEPOL agent.

"With each application of revolutionary justice, the assassins of the tyrannical government find no lack of echo to their laments among their followers and even among those who pretend to be neutral or in the camp of the opposition. But the people support and hail each one of these actions.

"We will continue to fight a war to the death against the enemies of our people, whether they are directly or indirectly implicated in the situation existing in Venezuela.

"None of Leoni's repressive measures, the new suspension of constitutional guarantees, the arrests, the tortures, and the assassinations will be of any avail. The people of Venezuela are no longer helpless; they have an armed vanguard, firmly consequent and decisive, that will protect them at all times, avenge their dead and lead them to final victory, which is no other than their definitive and total independence.

"Fight until Victory or Death!"

"Major Elias Manuitt Camero, President of the National Command FLN-FALN of Venezuela, Havana, March 4, 1967."

### Leoni Attempts to Accuse Us

"Caracas, March 6 (AP): Today the investigations seeking to throw light on the assassination of Julio Iribarren Borges are continuing, and it is stated that one student and a key figure in the case have been arrested. A version is also circulating to the effect that Iribarren was friendly with an individual connected with certain ring-leaders of a right wing coup plotted from the Ramos Varde garrison last October. According to that version, the friend informed Iribarren Borges of the plot, and the latter denounced it. A police source stated that it is reasonable to assume that groups of this sector wanted vengeance."

"Washington, March 7 (AP): Caracas news sources announced tonight that the government of President Raul Leoni has arrived at the conclusion that the plans for the assassination and other acts of terrorism against the people of Venezuela, committed in the country with the full support of the Cuban government, constitute a flagrant violation of international morality and order."

"Caracas, March 7 (AP): The Minister of the Interior, Reinaldo Leandro Mora, directly accused Cuba today of the kidnapping and assassination of a Venezuelan public figure. He added that the government may begin diplomatic action within the Organization of American States.

"The criminal acts of political terrorism are prepared, directed and financed in the Cuba of Fidel

Castro,' said Leandro Mora.

"Yesterday, in Havana, the Venezuelan leader of the so-called Armed Forces of National Liberation, Elias Manuitt Camero, said in a public communique that the FALN assumed full responsibility for the kidnapping and assassination of Iribarren Borges.

" 'This reveals,' declared Leandro Mora today, 'that the participants are not only delinquents, but are protected as well by a delinquent government.'

"The Minister made his declarations moments before entering a routine Cabinet meeting in the Presidential Palace of Miraflores.

"The Minister was asked if Venezuela is considering the possibility of making new charges against the Castro regime in Havana within the Organization of American States. 'It is possible that the current Cabinet will consider such a possibility,' replied Leandro Mora."

"Caracas, March 7 (AP): President Raul Leoni and his Cabinet decided today to begin diplomatic action against Cuba for aid to and instigation of acts of violence against Venezuela, and will perhaps take the matter to the United Nations.

"The decision, announced by Manuel Mantilla, Presidential Secretary, is related to the kidnapping and assassination of Julio Iribarren Borges, brother of the Minister of Foreign Relations.

" 'The matter must be taken before the United Nations, since Cuba does not belong to the Organization of American States,' stated Prieto Figueroa. The charges are based on the fact that the official news organ of Cuba published a communique of the so-called Armed Forces of National Liberation, in which these assumed responsibility for the kidnapping and assassination of Iribarren Borges.'

"Prior to the meeting, Reinaldo Leandro Mora, Minister of the Interior, had charged Cuba directly with the crime and expressed the possibility that Venezuela might decide to take diplomatic action against Cuba."

"Caracas, March 8 (ANSA): While the government wages an intense battle to wipe out terrorism in the country, both through security measures within the nation, and through action abroad before international organizations, according to announcements made yesterday by members of the government of Venezuela, terrorists have also stepped up their activities. As a sequel to the spectacular kidnapping and assassination of the Foreign Minister's brother last week, for which responsibility has been assumed by members of the extremist organization, Armed Forces of National Liberation, new episodes took place today."

And it goes on to relate several incidents. Referring to some of them, it says:

"According to police reports six men armed with machine guns appeared at the home of an Army guide who had been sentenced to die by the armed groups which operate in the mountains of Bocono. Detachments of police and anti-guerrilla command forces of this region have been sent to the foothills of the Bocono mountains in search of the armed groups.

"Finally, there is the disappearance of an official of the Defense Ministry's Organization and Liaison Command, a fellow worker of Dr. Alfredo Seijas, the Police Counselor who was assassinated three weeks ago by terrorists in Caracas."

## An Accusing Document

"Caracas, March 8 (AP): Apparently Venezuela will launch a diplomatic offensive against the Government of Fidel Castro in the United Nations, on grounds of aggression. Evidently, this diplomatic action will be taken up within the Organization of American States and then extended to individual countries.

"It is logical to assume that we will submit this matter to the United Nations, but it should be remembered that Venezuelan foreign policy is based on the proposition that regional organization should be strengthened,' a high government official declared to the Associated Press today.

" 'The diplomatic offensive will be three-pronged: through the OAS, bilateral contacts, and last, but not least, Venezuela will submit the matter to the United Nations.

" 'Obviously, we do not expect much more from the OAS than an official condemnation. That would only have a moral value,' said the high government official, 'but remember that morality is a weapon invented by weak nations.'

"The same official said that the OAS has already done everything that can be done in connection with the Cuban case. 'The case of Cuba is closed in the OAS,' a Foreign Ministry source said. 'Remember that Cuba no longer is a member of the Organization. Besides, Havana laughs at anything the OAS may do.'

"It was stated that, among these bilateral contacts, some are friendly nations and others are not.

"Venezuela will apply pressure mainly on the United Arab Republic to have this nation suspend all official contacts with the Tricontinental Conference, which will possibly be held next year at Cairo."

"According to a high-ranking government source, 'Venezuela will try to force the Egyptian Government to define its position: whether it wishes to maintain relations with Latin America in general, or with Cuba in particular.'

"The Tricontinental Organization consists of a General Secretariat and eight secretaries, one of them a United Arab Republic Government official. Venezuela holds this is an untenable position. The UAR will be asked to renounce its affiliation with the Tricontinental Organization which pledged in Cuba last year to continue helping the Venezuelan insurrectionists. The UAR will also be requested to withdraw its petition that the next conference be held in Cairo, according to a high-level Venezuelan spokesman. On a bilateral basis, diplomatic measures will be taken with respect to Mexico, the United States, Great Britain, the Soviet Union, and the other four nations that met in Bogota last August, that is, Colombia, Chile, Ecuador and Peru.

"Venezuela will request a demonstration of solidarity from Mexico. The Venezuelan government is dissatisfied with Mexico's refusal to break diplomatic relations with Havana even after the OAS had condemned Cuba and requested all its members to suspend relations with Fidel Castro's regime.

"Venezuela will probably ask Washington's help in bringing pressure on the countries the Venezuelan government wishes to persuade. For example, it could request the State Department to inform the Soviet Union as to Venezuela's position. In addition, it could ask Washington to bring pressure upon Great Britain, through credit guarantees, to persuade the British to cease helping Cuba with offers such as the construction of a petrochemical complex.

"The AP was informed that Venezuela expects to have a Soviet Embassy in Caracas in the hope that Moscow will place more value on a doorway to Latin America than on a blind alley in Havana. Contact could be established with the Soviet Union's representatives in the United Nations or in Washington."

Apparently, the only thing these gentlemen overlooked was to ask South Viet Nam and North Viet Nam to cease their fight against the Yankee imperialists. (APPLAUSE)

"Caracas, March 9 (AFP): The Communist Party of Venezuela disclaims the statement of Elias Manuitt Camero who, in the name of the so-called National Liberation Forces, credits that organization with the murder of Dr. Julio Iribarren Borges.

"A document of condemnation, signed by Dr. Hector Mujica, member of the Political Bureau of the Communist Party of Venezuela, reads: 'Manuitt Camero's statements were as shocking as the abominable crime itself.' It adds that it is deplorable that GRANMA, the organ of a fraternal Party, should lend itself to the publication of such bombast.' "

"The document adds that anti-Cuban feelings never existed among the people of Venezuela and that now the enemies of the Cuban Revolution are taking advantage of the opportunity to introduce such feelings among them.

"The document emphasizes an unequivocal repudiation of the crime against the brother of the Venezuelan Minister and of the ranting declarations of an ex-militant who was publicly expelled from the ranks of the Communist Party for divisionist activities and slackening of his political position. The same action was applied to Douglas Bravo. (APPLAUSE), Gregorio Lunar Marquez, Freddy Carques, Francisco Prada and others using the name of the national movement of liberation.

### The "Indispensable" Yankee Intervention

"The document ends exhorting the democratic movement not to fall into confusion or be swayed by the imperialist provocation against Cuba in this new offensive that divisionists and adventurers expelled from the Communist Party will take against Cuba."

"Miami, March 9 (AFP): 'At what point will the patience of the governments of America with the abuses of Castro run out?' writes the *Diario de las Americas* today about the death of the brother of Venezuela's Foreign Minister.

"This newspaper, the most important published in Spanish in the United States, devotes today's editorial

to the death of Julio Iribarren Borges, under the title of 'A New and Greater Monstrosity Every Time.'

"The editorial affirms that as long as the crimes of the Castro-Communist dictatorship against the Cuban people and the citizens of other American countries do not meet their proper international punishment, it can be said that this chain of crimes will increase considerably in number and in intensity."

"Caracas, March 9 (UPI): Foreign Minister Ignacio Iribarren Borges consulted today with foreign diplomats on the formal complaint that the Venezuelan government plans to lodge against Communist Cuba before the Organization of American States and possibly before the United Nations.

"The Venezuelan government accused Cuba of surreptitiously promoting the resurgence of terrorism in that country.

"President Raul Leoni and his Cabinet stated yesterday that they were studying the possibility of presenting the complaint before international bodies.

"Iribarren Borges had an interview yesterday with U.S. ambassador, Maurice M. Bernbaum, and stated that he would discuss the matter with other accredited diplomatic delegations.

"The decision to present formal accusations against Cuba arose from the kidnapping and assassination of Julio Iribarren Borges, ex-director of the Social Security Institute and brother of the Foreign Minister.

"According to information from Havana early this week, the Armed Forces of National Liberation (FALN) boasted that they were the authors of the assassination.

"After the 30-minute interview with the Foreign Minister, Bernbaum confirmed that one of the subjects discussed was the case of Venezuela against Cuba.

"We are against aggression, no matter where it comes from, declared the U.S. ambassador."

"Bogota, March 9 (UPI): Juan Oropesa, new Venezuelan ambassador, stated on his arrival last night that his country will formally bring charges in an international organization against Cuban complicity in the recent assassination of Julio Iribarren Borges, brother of the Venezuelan Foreign Minister."

"Caracas, March 10 (AFP): President Raul Leoni today announced that he would denounce Cuba's participation in the assassination of Julio Iribarren Borges before international organizaions.

"The announcement, included in a message to Congress, is in reply to declarations of Venezuelan guerrilla, Captain Elias Manuitt Camero, which were published in GRANMA, official news organ of the Cuban government.

"In avenging the death of the Venezuelan Foreign Minister's brother, the Chief of State added that he would not request concrete sanctions, very unlikely to be approved in the present international situation, but rather the moral satisfaction of adding one more charge to the record of despotism enthroned in the Land of Marti, as viewed by the public conscience of America.

"Waxing implacable as regards international communism, something he did not do in his former messages to Congress nor in his speeches before the nation, Leoni attributed the sharpening of violence in

Venezuela which culminated last week in the kidnapping and assassination of Julio Iribarren Borges, former director of Social Security and brother of Foreign Minister Ignacio Iribarren Borges, to agents of Mao-Soviet-Castro communism.

"Despite his attacks against the communists of Red China, the Soviet Union and Castro's Cuba, during his speech to the National Congress, President Leoni proposed no concrete plan for bringing charges in international organizations, such as the Organization of American States, on a continental level, and the United Nations, on a world level, where approval would be sought for new sanctions against the government of Fidel Castro.

### Cuba is Held Responsible for Everything that Happens on This Continent

"However, he said that Venezuela, an orderly country, will appear before international organizations to denounce the unheard-of fact of participation by the government of Cuba in the murder of a citizen in Venezuela, referring to the death of Julio Iribarren, as was revealed in a statement published in the Cuban government's official newspaper, undoubtedly a reference to GRANMA.

" 'Venezuela will not request concrete sanctions, which are unlikely to be agreed upon given the present international state of affairs, but rather the moral satisfaction of adding a new and shocking charge to the record of despotism enthroned in the Land of Marti as viewed by the public conscience of America.' "

The dispatch continues: "Political circles were deeply impressed by the direct reference made by the President of Venezuela to Red China and the Soviet Union as bearing the responsibility along with Communist Cuba for the worsening of terrorist activities in Venezuela that led to the suspension of constitutional guarantees on December 14, the raiding of the Central University, and the suspension of citizens' rights again on March 14."

It is curious to observe that on the 4th, long before any statement had appeared in GRANMA, they were already accusing us, ending up by directly accusing China and the Soviet Union. It is even more curious if we take into account that on January 1, New Year's Day—even though no diplomatic relations existed between the Soviet Union and Venezuela—the news agencies announced that the Soviet ambassador had very cordially attended the New Year reception given by the Embassy of Venezuela in Washington. The dispatch ends by saying that "the government receives under benefit of inventory the reports on Communist Party dissidence from the hard tendencies within the Party and another Marxist organization. It is incumbent upon the Communist Party," Leoni pointed out, "to offer unequivocal and reiterated demonstrations of its sincerity in rectifying its mistaken behavior and in its desire to return to democratic legality."

See with what contemptuous coin Sr. Leoni repays the statements made in the name of the Communist Party!

And finally, one of the most recent dispatches:

"Caracas, March 11 (AFP)," it says, "Ex-naval captain Pedro Medina Silva, leader of the 1962 Puerto Cabello military uprising, for some time considered the commander of the National Liberation Armed Forces, announced in a clandestinely-circulating document that the people's justice will be applied to the assassins of Dr. Iribarren Borges. The Medina Silva document, signed also by guerrilla leaders German Lairet, Tirso Pinto and Pedro Vega Castejon, stated that 'those who usurp the name of the combat organization led by us become provocateurs and accomplices of the enemies of the people.' "

Of all the many happenings on this uneasy continent, there is not one that does not lead to the immediate and familiar accusation against Cuba.

A few weeks ago, at the time of the Nicaraguan electoral contest, Somoza's gangs carried out a massacre of the opposition party. At once, logically—despite the fact that it was a question of a party bearing the name of "Partido Conservador"—Cuba turned out to be guilty of promoting that clash, that bloodshed.

Any happening anywhere: in Colombia, blame Cuba right away; in Guatemala, Cuba is at fault. If there is a military uprising in Santo Domingo that leads to the intervention of Yankee troops, troops that even now remain stationed in that sister nation, the inevitable justification is Cuba. There is hardly anything that happens in this continent that is not blamed on Cuba. But Cuba is to be blamed for just one thing: for having made a Revolution and for being ready to carry it forward to its final, ultimate consequences! (APPLAUSE)

And that is Cuba's responsibility. We assume that responsibility! (APPLAUSE)

### Reviewing the Struggle in Venezuela

But what does that mean? How can we explain the insinuations of the oligarchies, and those of the Venezuelan oligarchy in particular, blaming Cuba for revolutionary actions in their countries? And the insinuations made by the rightist leadership of the Communist Party of Venezuela? What preceeded it and what gave rise to it? How can it be explained? It is necessary to make a brief resume of the history of the revolutionary struggle in Venezuela.

First: a few months prior to the triumph of the Cuban Revolution, there was a formidable popular movement in Venezuela, that overthrew the Perez Jimenez regime. Participating in this movement were ample popular forces, among them the Communist Party of Venezuela. And a young newspaper man was especially outstanding: Fabricio Ojeda (APPLAUSE), who was President of the Patriotic Council that ousted Perez Jimenez. However, that victory of the people of Venezuela was frustrated, because from that moment the Partido Accion Democratica which at one time had played a certain revolutionary role, a certain role in the anti-imperialist struggle, that had mass support, not in the capital (because naturally the most advanced sectors had majority support in the capital), this party had particularly broad support in extensive regions of the interior of the country, and began to act as a fundamental factor in hindering the maturing and development of the Venezuelan revolutionary movement.

Betancourt won some elections, coming up with a ridiculous minority in the capital and getting his majority in the interior of the country—similar to what sometimes happened in our country. And from the moment it was sworn in, that government dedicated itself to developing a clear policy of conciliation, kowtowing to imperialism, and defending imperialist interests in Venezuela. Naturally, it became one of the instruments of U.S. policy.

There began to be repression of the revolutionary movement; repression of the workers, of the students, of the revolutionaries. Those repressions became more and more brutal, and the first massacres of students and the general population took place in Caracas. Betancourt felt a deep resentment toward the people of the capital; he could not pardon that lack of support, the affront he had been given by the population of Caracas.

We remember when, in the early days of the Revolution, we visited this sister nation. In the Plaza del Silencio there we spoke at a gigantic assembly of 300,000 people. When we mentioned the name of Betancourt—as was our courtesy obligation to the president-elect—a great hiss came up out of that great mass. Since we were visitors in the country, this put us in a rather embarrassing situation and I even felt compelled to protest, saying that I had not mentioned a man's name so that people would boo him, but that it was simply my duty to make official reference to him who was about to assume the presidency as a result of elections. In this way, the people of Caracas demonstrated themselves furiously anti-Betancourtist. And this feeling of scorn in the capital of Venezuela, which was the vanguard in the struggle for the overthrow of Perez Jimenez was shown thus. This, naturally, contributed in no small way to the extraordinary hate Betancourt felt for the popular masses of the capital of Venezuela.

And soon, just as soon as the repression had become intolerably brutal, supporters of the armed struggle arose. One of the first of these was the Movement of the Revolutionary Left, organized by a group of progressive leaders who had broken off from the official party, Accion Democratica, and organized this movement. They began to prepare for armed struggle. Similarly, the Communist Party began to prepare for armed struggle.

At first, it was thought that the extreme right-wing elements in the army would surely overthrow Betancourt; and at first these organizations set about their preparations with the idea that the struggle would have to be against a reactionary military government. But the sharpening of repression, which increasingly characterized Betancourt's policy, made these organizations cease to regard their efforts as directed against the Betancourt regime itself, which was becoming increasingly repressive and brutal in its dealings with the people.

## Setbacks are the Revolutionaries' Greatest Teachers

And so the first moves began. The Third Congress of the Communist Party of Venezuela approved the road of armed struggle for the revolution in Venezuela. Other dissident forces from different parties also began preparations for armed struggle. Among these was a sector of the political party to which Fabricio Ojeda belonged. And Fabricio Ojeda, friend of Cuba, friend of our Revolution—like so many other Venezuelans—one day resigned his position as member of Parliament and went into the mountains to organize a guerrilla movement.

Several years passed. Undoubtedly the Venezuelan revolutionaries, as in all revolutions in every part of the world made a number of errors in their conception of the struggle, a number of errors of a strategic and of a tactical nature. Different factors contributed to these errors. One of these was the fact that the revolutionary movement was very strong in the capital, and on the other hand—as has or had happened in many other countries in Latin America—and for this the Communist Parties are to blame—the revolutionary movement was weak in the country. Why? Because the Marxist parties concentrated their attention mainly on the city, on the workers' movement, which is, of course, quite correct. But in many cases—for naturally all these generalities have their excpetions—they greatly underestimated the importance of the peasantry as a revolutionary force.

As the official party of Venezuela was strong in the countryside and the parties of the left were weak there, although strong in the capital, for a long time the leadership of the Venezuelan revolutionary movement overestimated the importance of the capital and the struggle in the capital and underestimated the importance of the guerrilla movement.

But not only this. Venezuela was one of the countries—or *the* country in recent times—where the revolutionary movement had the greatest influence in the ranks of the professional army. Many young Venezuelan army officers openly showed their sympathy for the revolutionary movement, even in its most radical form, inspired in Marxist concepts. So the force of the revolutionary movement was strongly felt in the ranks of the army. And this led to another conceptual error: to a downgrading of the guerrilla movement in favor of great hopes in a military uprising.

They accuse us of promoting subversion, they accuse the Cubans of directing the armed revolutionary movement in Venezuela. And if we Cubans had had anything to do with the leadership of that revolutionary movement, we would never have fallen, and that revolutionary movement would never have fallen, into those two major conceptual errors. (APPLAUSE) Why? Because it is the revolutionaries, they and only they, who decide, who are able to determine their general strategy and their specific tactics. And the revolutionaries always do that, always! In Venezuela, in all other countries, their criteria—and these criteria may often be mistaken—are only rectified as a consequence of the process itself, of the experience of the process itself, of the blows received in the process. It is not we, the Cuban revolutionaries or leaders, who tell them what they must do; it is their own experience. And the best teachers of revolutionaries in every country of Latin America—as it was in Cuba—the best teachers, the great teachers, were the setbacks.

And naturally the Venezuelan revolutionary movement suffered many setbacks, as revolutionary movements in all parts of the world have always suffered setbacks, and Latin America's movement logically had to go through a long apprenticeship. Today it can be affirmed that that movement has learned a great deal, not from Cuba, but from its own experience, from the blows it has received. And therefore that more experienced revolutionary movement is growing and consolidating itself, and the rulers are showing themselves unable to crush it. They are impotent to crush it in Guatemala, unable to crush it in Colombia, unable to crush it in Venezuela.

But reverses always take a toll; they frequently take a toll in desertions from the revolutionary ranks by the weakest, the least tenacious, the least persevering, in a word, the least revolutionary.

## Directing the Guerrillas from the City an Absurdity

Apart from erroneous strategic conceptions in themselves, these erroneous conceptions in turn gave rise to serious errors of a practical nature: the guerrillas found themselves abandoned and deprived of the most elementary resources. The revolutionary leadership of the Party was trying to direct the guerrillas from the city, from the capital. What ought to have been done was not done—what a daring and truly revolutionary leadership would have done, what the leadership of the great and historic contemporary movements that have triumphed have done,—that is, go up to the mountains with the guerrillas to lead the war from the battlefield, to lead the war from the mountains. (APPLAUSE) It is absurd and almost criminal—we don't call it a hundred per cent criminal because it is a question of ignorance more than of willful fraud—to try to direct guerrillas from the city. The two experiences are so different, so utterly distinct, the two settings so completely dissimilar, that the greatest insanity—a painfully bloody insanity—that can be committed is to try to direct guerrillas from the city. And the guerrillas were not really seen as a force that could be developed to take revolutionary power in countries such as ours, but rather as an instrument of agitation, a tool for political maneuvering, for negotiation. Underestimation of the guerrillas led to the errors committed subsequently.

And in Venezuela the guerrillas were constantly being ordered to cease fire, and that is madness! A guerrilla contingent that agrees to a truce in fighting is one condemned to defeat. (APPLAUSE)

A guerrilla contingent can agree to a truce of one or two days as we did on some sectors of our front to return prisoners to the Red Cross. As a matter of principle, a guerrilla contingent must never agree to a truce of any other kind. The men get used to the quietude of the camp, a weakening and demoralization of forces sets in. But the commanders of the city-led guerrillas constantly received orders to make truces, more and more truces. That was happening in Venezuela.

And naturally, as a result of an inept leadership, blows and setbacks followed in succession. Nevertheless, in spite of the errors in leadership, in spite of the conceptual errors, the government could not eliminate the guerrillas. Yet what the repressive and pro-imperialist forces of Betancourt and Leoni could not achieve was very nearly achieved thanks to the ineptness of the revolutionary leadership.

The leaders of the Communist Party of Venezuela began to speak of a democratic peace. "What is this about democratic peace?" many people asked. "What is this about democratic peace?" we, the leaders of the Cuban Revolution, asked ourselves. We did not understand. We did not understand, but, nevertheless, we wanted to understand. "What does this mean?" we asked some Venezuelan leaders. As a reply we received the same old worn-out and elaborate theory of a tactic, a maneuver—by no means an abandonment of the war; No! No! It was only a maneuver to broaden the base, to destroy the regime, to weaken and undermine it.

And, of course, we by no means considered this a correct point of view. Nevertheless, we had hope and confidence, in spite of the fact that a democratic peace seemed absurd, ridiculous. For only a revolutionary movement that is winning the war can speak of peace, because then it can begin to mobilize national opinion in favor of a peace that can only be won by winning the revolution. Then one can mobilize people's spirits, public opinion, the people and their desire for peace on the only possible foundation; the defeat of the tyranny and of exploitation. But to speak of peace when the war is being lost is precisely to concede peace by defeat.

In the history of revolutionary movements, the words *democratic peace* were mentioned for the first time after the victory of the Bolshevik Revolution in 1917. The new Revolution launched a campaign for a democratic peace, that is, peace in the midst of World War, a peace without annexations or conquests of any type. And the new Soviet power launched this campaign and struggled for a peace without annexation or conquests: a victorious revolutionary power that did not want to continue participating in that imperialist slaughter.

## In Silence, We Have Withstood a Campaign of Defamation

So the slogan of democratic peace was launched. And we asked ourselves: "What similarity can there be between that historic situation, between that victorious proletariat in the first socialist revolution, and the situation of a revolutionary leadership that has been unable to lead the armed struggle to victory?"

However, in reality, behind their explanations, lay deceit. Deceit! They told us that their democratic peace was a maneuver, but that the struggle would be stepped up, guerrilla warfare would be stepped up. Nevertheless, they were lying. In reality the intention was to abandon the armed struggle and they were simply preparing the way.

How did we learn about these things, these truths? How did we confirm them? We would have preferred not to air this matter publicly; as a matter of fact, during many weeks and months we have silently borne a defamatory campaign waged by the rightist leadership of the Communist Party of Venezuela, which voiced accusations against us in various Communist Party congresses, and sent letters to various Latin American Communist Parties, accusing Cuba of interfering in their internal affairs and of supporting and fomenting fractionalism.

We would have preferred not to discuss this matter; however, it has become unhappily impossible to avoid doing so. In order to answer the imputations of pro-imperialist oligarchies and of renegade communists, since both are intimately related, we find ourselves obliged to clarify and answer these charges, reserving the right to do this at the opportune moment and in a more detailed form, in a document which our Party will draw up when it deems convenient. Recent events in Venezuela have made this necessary.

### A Letter from Fabricio Ojeda

I have mentioned Fabricio Ojeda's name, his clean record, his participation in the overthrow of Perez Jimenez, the rarely-seen phenomenon of his resignation from office when he gave up his parliamentary immunity, relinquished his parliamentary privileges, to go into the mountains. A rare case in a politician in our America. Fabricio was ignominiously assassinated on June 21, 1966. Sixteen days earlier, on June 4, 1966, Fabricio wrote a letter, the letter was addressed to me and was probably one of the last things he ever wrote. And that letter, which I have kept without knowing that I would need to reveal its contents one day, goes as follows:

"My dear friend:

"Here, all of the time, as always, attempting to overcome the burden of temporary difficulties in order to wage the struggle on a more serious and precise basis; we have made some advances toward this end. The fundamental step has been that of going directly to the solution of the problems of leadership, the structuring of our national organizations, such as the FLN Executive Committee and the Executive Command of the FALN; starting points for a general re-organization of the movement's entire structure. To this end we are working intensely. We intend to hold a national FLN-FALN conference as soon as possible which, as a constituent power, will devote itself to a study and analysis of the situation, to establishing strategy and tactics, political and military lines and to defining the effective constitution of our directing organism at all levels. In this way the liberation movement will break out of its present state of stagnation, overcome differences, and clarify its historic potential, in addition to consolidating the factor indispensable to further progress, revolutionary unity of the revolutionary forces.

"Our project of restructuring the struggle on new bases has forced us to define certain important questions. The first of these is the provisional restructuration of the present directing organism of the national FLN-FALN. In this regard, we have decided to increase the number of nuclei in the existing leadership, which has produced a critical situation within the Communist Party of Venezuela. This includes the sanctioning of comrade Douglas Bravo by the majority of the Political Bureau of the Party, who have removed him from this organism, accusing him of an attitude of anti-Party fractionalism.

"The second question of importance is the decision to confront any circumstance whatsoever in order to bring all revolutionary forces together with the purpose of incrementing the war of national liberation as the only means of advancing toward the conquest of power and the achievement of national independence, taking into account the objective conditions prevailing in the country and the peculiarities of the Venezuelan process.

"In both areas we have made advances. Steps are being taken to set up a unified FLN-FALN command. This will be led by myself as President in charge of the FLN, together with the First Commander of the FALN, Douglas Bravo. A leader from the MIR will join us this week as Secretary General.

"The General Command of the FALN now includes the commanding officers of the guerrilla fronts. This new form was arrived at after an analysis of the present situation of these organisms, since it was considered that a nucleus of three-members of the FALN General Command who were still active was insufficient for general military leadership, since the other members of the Command have either been taken prisoner or are abroad. In relation to the unification of the revolutionary forces for the purpose of advancing the war of national liberation, a unified commission will be designated to study and draw up the theoretical material on strategy, tactics and the political and military line of the movement to be presented for discussion in the coming FLN-FALN national conference.

"The incorporation of the MIR into the directing organizations and the preparatory work for the conference are steps of great significance, since in this way a period of internal discussion on present differences will begin replacing polemic diatribe in our talks, and opening up truly democratic roads for the ideological and political unity of the revolutionary movement.

"Nonetheless, a new breach has been opened in our ranks by the disciplinary measures taken by the majority of the Political Bureau of the Communist Party of Venezuela.

"In respect to this new problem, I have been informed that the intermediate and basic sectors, including those in the Central Committee itself, have been reacting against the sanction imposed on comrade Douglas.

## A Change in Course and Tactics

Already certain documents have been circulated which expressly state this reaction. In my opinion, the disciplinary measures taken by the majority of the Political Bureau correspond to problems of a truly ideological and political nature, to profound questions, which they have attempted to cover-up by talking of methods or supposed errors on the part of comrade Douglas and other comrades whose ideas on strategy and tactics of our revolutionary process coincide with his. The fact is that within the Communist Party of Venezuela two important currents are being debated.

"One of these is held by a minority in the base of the Party but is very prevalent among the members of the Political Bureau and the Central Committee. Its essence is as follows: Present developments permit the revolutionary movement to take the initiative on the political front. Nonetheless, the FALN must order the guerrillas and the UTC (Tactical Combat Units) to fall back. It does not mean simply another truce but rather something more profound; it means diverting the form of struggle. That is, a new tactical period begins, which in place of combining all forms of struggle, would suspend guerrilla and UTC operations. The guerrillas and the UTC should make an orderly retreat and the revolutionary movement introduce a change in tactics. Several conditons are indispensable, to maintain unity and internal cohesion, to maintain iron discipline, and to support and aid the directing nucleus. To achieve these ends the Party and the Young Communists must act in the two ways. First, employ persuasion, using every kind of reasoning and political arguments in support of the new tactical changes, discussing matters calmly with all who must be convinced. Second, carry on an active campaign against adventurist tendencies and provocations. (This is a synthesis of two documents presented to the organization by prominent members of the Political Bureau.)

"The other, held by a majority of the base of the Party, but with little support among members of the leadership of higher organizations, is headed up by comrade Douglas Bravo, who not only opposes the alteration of plans and the changes in tactics, but who presents strong criticisms of the way that the revolutionary struggle has been carried out.

"It is quite obvious that the crux of these differences is the question of armed struggle, which a group of leaders within the Communist Party of Venezuela have opposed since the very beginning.

"There is no doubt that the sanctioning of comrade Douglas is the beginning of these alterations, and that these are designed to eliminate, by means of disciplinary actions, any who oppose a new tactical period which rather than combining all forms of struggle would choose to suspend all action by the guerrillas and the Tactical Units.

"In a situation like this, the decision to enlarge the integral organizations of leadership by incorporating the most responsible and firm cadres, is a step forward of great magnitude.

"The majority of the Political Bureau has opposed this measure and has proceeded to repudiate us publicly, denying the validity and legitimate nature of the groups already formed.

"We have, however, remained firm and we have been pleased to note that a great body of opinion has formed in support of our cause, in the guerrilla fronts and in the intermediate organizations, as well as at the base of the Communist Party of Venezuela. In addition, some members of the Central Committee, parties within the FLN and urban units of the FALN have lent their support.

"A period of clarification of ideology and definition of the revolutionary road has begun. There is one unfavorable transitory factor involved in this situation and which places us in a rather difficult spot. That is the problem of economic resources, since it has been the Political Bureau which has exercised control over this sector.

## Economic Strangulation of Guerrilla Zones

"Until now all funds for the revolutionary movement have been centralized in that organization and used to further their policies—that is, snuff out guerrilla centers by economic means." The letter ends as follows:

"Our guerrilla fighters have maintained a high state of morale and there is gigantic resolution in our movement. We are conscious that the present picture is full of difficulties but we are sure that these will be overcome within a short time. Truth will be borne in on the skeptics and then a bright future will appear on our horizon. Not one step backward, not even to gain speed!" "The bearer can give more details and better explain some things.

"We go forward, toward victory. To fight until victory. A warm embrace from your friend, Fabricio Ojeda." (APPLAUSE)

Sixteen days later Fabricio is arrested and vilely assassinated by the henchmen of the tyranny oppressing Venezuela, precisely when these steps for organization and restructuration which he speaks about in his letter were being taken.

One can say, well, this was the opinion of a respected, worthy, valiant comrade, but is it proof? Is this enough to guarantee his words? Of course, for us who knew Fabricio well, there is no doubt: the integrity with which this letter is written, its serenity, are guarantees of its author's honesty. But, in addition, some documents which came to our hands verified what Fabricio had said, one hundred percent; documents which were distributed among the militants of the Communist Party of Venezuela for discussion; documents which, without any doubt, indicate and at the same time explain the policy followed in recent times by the government of Venezuela.

One of the documents is written by Pompeyo Marquez, Teodoro Petkoff, and Freddy Munoz and in essence says the following in its main lines:

"First. Some changes have taken place which force the revolutionary movement to revise certain aspects of its tactics in a fundamental way regarding the armed struggle.

"In broad outline the situation is the following: The armed struggle has suffered several blows and has weakened. The revolutionary movement at present is not in a condition to continue the frontal and open attacks on its enemies. The armed apparatus of the Party has been severely damaged; a bloody and brutal repression is effecting the ability of the revolutionary movement to organize, unify and mobilize the broad masses and give an adequate riposte to government policy.

"Due to the continual reverses and blows suffered, to its own weakness which impede successful actions, the armed struggle, by not taking appropriate measures to safeguard its instruments, could lose the role it has played in the recent past, in which it offered a perspective of revolutionary transformation to the masses. In reality, it is not playing this role at present and its future depends on the measures we take today.

"The weak armed operations which do nothing but repeat similar former operations, without attaining progress of true significance, are:

"a) making political action difficult and impeding the regrouping of forces against the Betancourt 'gorillas';

"b) letting the Betancourt 'gorilla' clique maintain its alliances;

"c) acting as a brake and preventing the rapid decomposition of its broad base;

"d) wiping out convictions, faith in the correct general strategy of the revolutionary movement, whose basis was set down in the 3rd Congress of the CPV and was later strengthened in the successive plenaries of the CC.

"Second. Consequently, the Party must undertake a retrenchment on the military front and recommend the suspension of armed actions in favor of proceeding to a regrouping of its forces and their preparation for a new revolutionary stage which must be qualitively superior to those existing up to now.

"Until recovery has been attained in a fundamental sense, and until some advance is achieved in the promotion of new forces and the regrouping of nationalist sectors, all operations of the FALN must cease.

"This military retrenchment must be accompanied by a political offensive which will permit us to cover the retrenchment, alleviate the pressures of repression and recover the political initiative.

"In short, it is not a new truce, but something deeper;"—textually what Fabricio explained—"it is a temporary about-face in the forms of struggle, that is, suspending the actions of the guerrillas and the UTC and giving political initiative priority."

### Another Document From the Communist Party of Venezuela

This is, in essence, the position taken in this document by Pompeyo Marquez, Teodoro Petkoff, and Freddy Munoz. At the same time, other leaders sent a similar document to the Party, this time signed by Guillermo Garcia Ponce and other leaders. It is, in essence, the same with some slight variations. They themselves explain these differences in the introduction.

It reads: "Document enclosed. We present this to you, comrades, in order to arrive at opinions in a more collective way. However, you will receive not one, but two documents—this one and another.

"As you will note, the resolutions and conclusions are the same: retrenchment of the guerrillas and of the UTC, as well as a change of tactics toward an emphasis on political acts. There are, therefore, no differences on fundamental decisions; there is full unity on the essence of the problems. The motivations, the reasons for the change in forms of struggle for a specific period are also the same. Nevertheless, there is one shade of difference: our document places prime importance on political motivations and secondary importance on setbacks conceived as a reason for change.

"For the other comrades this order is reversed. First: the blows received constitute a very important factor, but we should not change our tactics for this reason. Setbacks help us to become aware of the changes that we ought to introduce, but they form part of a concrete and principally political reality which has forced us to make a certain change in course. The truth of the matter is that we should have retrenched before receiving the blows."

In other words, and in essence, Pompeyo, Teodoro, and Freddy Munoz speak of retrenchment because of receiving blows. And they say: Yes, Yes, very well, we're in agreement. There is only one fundamental difference: We should have retrenched even before receiving the blows.

"Second, upon giving prime importance to political elements, we emphasize one of the peculiarities of the present situation; namely, while the guerrillas and the UTC are in retrenchment, the revolutionary movement can take the offensive on the political front, where all militants, organizations, etc. of the Party and the UTC can place the weight of their activity in a high combative spirit, free of all passivity and terrorist attempts."

Further on, the document reads: "The need for a retrenchment of the FALN. The events transcurring permit the revolutionary movement to take the initiative on the political front; nevertheless, it will be necessary for the FALN to order a retrenchment of the guerrillas and the UTC. This will not be a new truce, but something deeper: an attempt to change the forms of struggle, that is, to open a new tactical period in which, instead of combining all forms of struggle, guerrilla and UTC actions will be suspended. Prime importance will be taken by political events; a grouping of the leftist organization; promotion of new forces of struggle against "Betancourtism"; unity, organization and mobilization of the popular masses; alliance with nationalist sectors of the Armed Forces; action by the workers on behalf of their demands; struggle against repression; etc."

The only thing they didn't put in was the colloquy, the electoral struggle, which they obviously did not insert here because they intended to insert it later on.

"As long as no new political situation occurs and while material conditions improve, the guerrillas and the UTC should retrench." Retrenchment meant disappearance, dissolution, since they had kept them retrenched practically all the time.

The document contines: "In this sense, it should be recommended that the FALN publish a manifesto giving the political reasons for the retrenchment of the guerrillas and the UTC." And finally, the worn-out litany, the classic cliche, the glib phrase, the diatribe.

"In particular it is necessary to watch the uncontrollable groups—the difficult, the bellicose, the rebels—and also to defend actively the policy, tactics, and leadership of the Communist Youth and the Communist Party from the attacks of the anarcho-adventurist MIR group."

If only they had as much imagination for revolutionary action as they have for glibness and diatribe! (APPLAUSE) "In order to prevent tactical changes from being presented in an adulterated form by U.S. and 'Betancourtist' policies, and to prevent the enemy from taking advantage of any insufficiently formulated proposal or excess of information, it will be necessary to pay special attention to propaganda and, in general, to all written matter."

### Violation of Agreements

The Communist Party was not the only one constituting the FALN; at least two or three other organizations were also members. One of them was the Movement of the Revolutionary Left (MIR), which was one of the first organizations to initiate the struggle. The FALN also included the forces represented by Fabricio Ojeda which came from—if I remember the name correctly— the **Partido Union Republicana** as well as the Communist Party and several organizations of fighting-men.

Notice how these allies are not mentioned in the two documents; rather they are mentioned, but only to accuse them of adventurism, anarcho-adventurism. Not one word is said about the sector represented by Fabricio Ojeda. No! They do not recognize the right of other organizations to participate in the formulation of policy; they launch the policy, and publish it as an order. Not only do they violate the agreements taken in a Party Congress, which should be inviolate, but they also refuse to recognize the forces that in all loyalty had been fighting side by side with the Party.

They not only disregard the agreements adopted by the Congress, they disregard their allies, the militants, the combatants, and the guerrilla fighters and begin talking of discipline and imposition of discipline.

And what happened? The principal guerrilla chief—among them the most respected one, who from within the Communist Party from the very beginning, since 1959, was in charge of the military section, organizing cadres for armed struggle, who remained in the mountains for years and fought many victorious battles, not great ones but hard-fought ones, to the extent of his own forces and this while harassed by continuous orders of truce and more truce—and along with him a large number of guerrilla commanders reacted against that line. We can see how Fabricio and

his followers rejected that conception. The MIR and with them the fighters of El Bachiller front, rejected that defeatist conception. And the Party's best men, the most courageous, the most experienced men, those who had carried the heaviest load in the struggle, refused to accept such a defeatist conception.

That was the state of affairs. Out of three organizations, two remained in the struggle. Some of the first leaders of the MIR deserted, but the majority, represented by Saez Merida, who upon being taken prisoner was replaced by Americo Martin—who now heads the MIR fighters at El Bachiller—maintained their position in favor of armed struggle and continued their ideological line until he died. And Douglas and the most respected guerrilla commanders maintained theirs. On what basis can we be accused of fomenting divisionism within the Venezuelan Party? What can be used as a base to blame Cuba for problems resulting only and exclusively from an inefficient political leadership?

### We Have the Right to Express Our Solidarity with the Fighters

From the point of view of principles, revolutionary theory, revolutionary dignity, and our revolutionary experience, could we ever accept the theses of official leadership, the theses expounded in these documents? No! Never! Because had we been men with little faith in the Revolution we would have given up the fight following our first setback at the Moncada garrison (APPLAUSE), or when our little army landed from the Granma only to be dispersed three days later, and only 7 of us were able to reunite. Thousands, or rather millions of reasons could have been used as a pretext to say that we were wrong and that those who said that it was impossible to fight that army, those great forces, were right. However, three weeks later, on January 17, we who at the end of December had barely reunited our forces, carried out our first successful attack on an army post killing its occupants. Five days later we were fighting again; this time against the parachutists.

These two first successful actions were followed by intense persecution and several cases of treason that came close to bringing about our destruction. Twenty men, practically isolated from the rest of the country, pursued by thousands of soldiers. Even under such conditions of hardship we maintained our faith in carrying our fight to victory. And—as many of you may recall—when during the April Strike our movement was dealt a disastrous blow we would have had plenty of reasons, similar to these, to give up our struggle.

Many letters were written. One of them, entitled "A Letter to a Patriot" urged us to give up the fight. However, that crisis in the revolutionary movement was overcome in less than four months when 10,000 soldiers armed with cannon were sent against 300 guerrilla fighters only to meet a disastrous defeat. They were defeated due to our experience because we had lived through a revolutionary struggle from its very inception. How could we docilely accept the defeatist pronouncements of those guilty of the faulty development in the revolutionary movement, of those who were incapable of leading that armed struggle?

The only correct thing to be done by those who had failed, by those who did not have the capacity to lead, was not to court-martial and expel those who had shown the capacity to defeat the enemy in the field of battle, but rather to resign. It was the only honest, correct thing to do: to take the responsibility for defeat and to turn the leadership of the Party over to those who had proved their capacity to carry on the war.

Why should we be forced to accept such a theses? It is not incumbent upon us to decide the problems of strategy or tactics in the Venezuelan revolutionary movement. Nobody has ever asked us to make any decisions on such problems nor have we ever attempted to do so. But we do have an inalienable right, and that is the right to think, the right to have an opinion, the right to express our sympathy and solidarity with the fighters. And it was not possible that we, revolutionaries—having to choose between capitulators, between defeatist, and men determined to convert to reality the watchword of "make our country free or die for Venezuela", (APPLAUSE) men who were not a group of theorizing charlatans, but a group of combatants—it was impossible for us, as an elemental question of revolutionary principle and morality, to do other than express our solidarity with those combatants.

Our history, the history of our country, a history full of beautiful examples, tells us of an unforgettable episode from our wars of independence when, in 1878, after 10 years of war, a great many—even the majority—of the leaders of the revolutionary movement decided to ask for a truce, and the Peace of Zanjon was signed after ten years of heroic struggle. Our most brilliant general refused to accept that peace and drew up the famous Protest of Baragua. (APPLAUSE)

### Douglas Bravo Has Voiced a Sort of "Baragua Protest"

How many things our history has taught us! Are there many things more admirable from the pages of Cuba's history than that rebellious and noble gesture, full of greatness and dignity with which Antonio Maceo asked for an interview with Martinez Campos and declared that he would not accept peace with the Spaniards? (APPLAUSE) In a gesture which won him immortality in the eyes of past, present, and future generations, immortality before world opinion, after ten years of war!

How can we consider Douglas Bravo a common divisionist, a common adventurer, a commonly ambitious person, if Douglas Bravo has made within the sector of the revolutionary movement deriving from the Party, has declared, a kind of Protest of Baragua against the Peace of Zanjon which defeatist leadership wanted to impose on the Party? (APPLAUSE)

For this reason he has our support and solidarity. And we have the unalienable right to express with all honesty what we think and what we feel. He did not side with the capitulators; he sided with the combatants. Acceptance of the capitulationist theory would have meant that we, as well, would have had to deny our solidarity to Americo Martin and the combatants of the MIR who are fighting in mountains of El Bachiller (APPLAUSE); it would have meant denying our solidarity to Fabricio Ojeda and his comrades. Proof that the capitulators were wrong and proof that their theory amounted to handing the revolutionary struggle of Venezuela to the pro-imperialist government of Leoni on a silver platter is that, in spite of this virtual treason, the pro-imperialist government of Leoni, aided by Yankee officials, supported by and supplied with Yankee weapons, has not been able to crush the heroic and unvanquished guerrillas that fight in the western mountains of Venezuela and in the mountains of El Bachiller. (PROLONGED APPLAUSE)

It was on November 7, 1965, that the defeatists signed the document that I read to you before; we are already in mid-March, 1967. If the defeatists had been right, the government of Venezuela would not have found itself obliged to take desperate suppressive steps in view of the upsurge of the guerrilla movement, and it would long since have wiped out the last fighter. In this case, then, it will not be necessary to wait for time to prove the fighters right; time is already proving them right. Any one of those fronts, in the western mountains or in El Bachiller, has at least as many, or more, men and weapons as did our columns when they were considered invincible in the Sierra Maestra.

And the sell-out, traitorous oligarchy that rules Venezuela will not be able to crush those fighters; that is why it is so frantically seeking guilty parties and advocating aggressions against Cuba, against the revolutionary example constituted by this country.

In the name of what revolutionary principles, reasons or fundamentals were we obliged to say that the defeatists were right, to say that the rightist, capitulationist current was right? In the name of Marxism-Leninism? No! We would never have been able to say they were right in the name of Marxism-Leninism. In the name of the international communist movement? Were we perhaps obligated by the fact that it was a question of the leadership of a communist party? Is this the conception we are supposed to have of the international communist movement? To us the international communist movement is in the first place just that, a movement of communists, of revolutionary fighters. And those who are not revolutionary fighters cannot be called communists! (APPLAUSE)

We conceive of Marxism as revolutionary thinking and action. Those who do not possess a truly revolutionary spirit cannot be called communists.

### There are Some Who Call Themselves Revolutionaries Who Are Not Revolutionaries at All

Anyone can give himself the name of "eagle" without having a single feather on his back. (LAUGHTER) In the same way, there are people who call themselves communists without having a communist hair on their head. The international communist movement, to our way of thinking, is not a church, it is not a religious sect or a Masonic lodge that obliges us to hallow any weakness, any deviation, that obliges us to follow the policy of a mutual admiration society with all kinds of reformists and pseudo-revolutionaries.

Our stand regarding communist parties will be based on strictly revolutionary principles. The parties that have a line without hesitations and capitulationism, the parties that in our opinion, have a consistent revolutionary line, will receive our support in all circumstances; but the parties that entrench themselves behind the name of communists or Marxists and believe themselves to have a monopoly on revolutionary sentiment—what they really monopolize is reformism—will not be treated by us as revolutionary parties. And if in any country those who call themselves communists do not know how to fulfill their duty, we will support those who, without calling themselves communists, conduct themselves like real communists in action and in struggle. (APPLAUSE) For every true revolutionary, who bears within him the revolutionary spirit, revolutionary vocation, will always come to Marxism! It is impossible for a man, travelling the road of revolution, not to arrive at Marxism! And every revolutionary on the continent who is deserving of the name will arrive at the Marxist conception of society! What is important are the revolutionaries, those who are capable of making revolutions and developing themselves in revolutionary theory.

Many times practice comes first and then theory. Our people too, are an example of that. Many, the immense majority of those who today proudly call themselves Marxist-Leninists, arrived at Marxism-Leninism by way of the revolutionary struggle. To exclude, to deny, to reject a priori all those who from the beginning did not call themselves communists is an act of dogmatism and unqualified sectarianism. Whoever denies that it is the road of revolution which leads the people to Marxism is no Marxist although he may call himself a communist.

This will be our line of conduct. It is the line that has guided our conduct in relations with the revolutionary movements.

At the Tricontinental Conference in Havana representatives of revolutionary organizations of the three continents met. Some called themselves communists and others did not. What defines a communist is his attitude toward the oligarchies, his attitude toward exploitation, his attitude toward imperialism; and on this continent, his attitude toward the armed revolutionary movement. What will define the communists of this continent is their attitude toward the guerrilla movement, toward the guerrilla movement in Guatemala, in Colombia, and in Venezuela. No one who claims to call himself communist will support the rightist official leadership opposing Douglas Bravo. Communist Parties must differentiate between the guerrillas who are fighting in Venezuela and the defeatists who wish to renounce the struggle, who in practice wish to give up the guerrilla movement. And this will be a dividing line, for we are arriving at the time of definitions, not by anyone's whims, but by the force of the process itself,

of historical events themselves.

Those who condemn the guerrillas for the simple reason of sect or dogma, in the spirit of freemasonry, cannot consider themselves revolutionaries.

One must ask the revolutionary guerrillas in Guatemala, Colombia or any other country, who in their opinion are the revolutionaries; who in their opinion, are those who show them solidarity, who are their real supporters: the Venezuelan guerrillas or the defeatists? For those who fight in Venezuela, those who force the imperialists to use up part of their resources against them, who bear their share of imperialist bombs, aid those who are fighting in Guatemala or Colombia. Those who fight in the mountains of Venezuela are the only real and possible allies of those who are fighting in the mountains of Colombia and in the mountains of Guatemala.

### Revolutionaries do Well to Avoid Procedures That May Serve As An Instrument For the Enemy

What have those official representatives made out of the death of Iribarren Borges. And, first of all, what do we think of his death? How are we to analyze this event? This must be analyzed both in the light of the government's position and the light of the reactionary and rightist leadership.

First of all, we have no previous knowledge of Iribarren Borges. We have no information except that published by AP and other imperialist news agencies. We do not know who killed Iribarren Borges.

The FALN representation in Cuba issued a declaration. What can be deduced from that declaration—when it says: "For these reasons, as broadsides that circulate in Caracas proclaim . . ."—is that the FALN representation in Havana had no news of the events other than what appeared in dispatches saying that FALN leaflets were found beside Iribarren's body. In other words, On March 6, when the FALN representatives made this declaration, they had no means of knowing what had happened, other than the wire services.

What attitude must we revolutionaries assume before any revolutionary deed? We may disagree with a concrete method, with a concrete deed; it is possible to disagree with the method of liquidating this former government official. As I said, we know nothing about him—whether he was hated, as the AP says, or not; whether or not he was responsible for measures taken against the revolutionaries.

Our opinion is that revolutionaries must avoid procedures which may give the enemy ammunition: killing a man who has been kidnapped. We never did this sort of thing no matter how great our outrage at the ferocity of the enemy. And in combat, we knew how to deal with prisoners with serenity.

Revolutionaries must avoid procedures which are similar to those of the repressive police. We do not know the circumstances of this death, we do not know who were responsible; we do not even know whether or not it was produced accidentally, whether or not it was really an act of revolutionaries. Our sincere opinion—and to give one's sincere opinion is a right of any revolutionary—is that, if it was the revolutionaries, we consider it to have been a mistake. It was a mistake to use this type of procedure that the enemy can use to full advantage before public opinion, that may remind the people of enemy procedures.

The entire world knows the behaviour of the Revolution, knows that we have revolutionary laws, and severe ones. We have never mistreated a prisoner. We have made strict laws, and our revolutionary courts sentence serious offenders against the Revolution and our nation to capital punishment, but not once has a man been found dead on a highway, in a ditch, or in a park.

The Revolution acts within given revolutionary forms and respects those forms. Even in dealing with people who have committed heinous crimes, we have always insisted upon proper procedure. This is our criterion.

It is perfectly legitimate for a revolutionary to disagree with a deed, a method, a concrete aspect. What is immoral, what is unrevolutionary, is to make use of a given deed in order to join the hysterical chorus on the reactionaries and imperialists to condemn the revolutionaries. (APPLAUSE) If revolutionaries are responsible for this deed, we may give our opinion, but we may never join the hysterical chorus of the hangmen who govern in Venezuela, in order to condemn the revolutionaries.

What has the official leadership of the Communist Party of Venezuela done in this instance? What have they said officially? Just what we read here: "The Communist Party of Venezuela disowns Elias Manuitt, who, in the name of the so-called Armed Forces of National Liberation, claimed his organization had assassinated Dr. Julio Iribarren Borges." ..."Elias Manuitt is an ex-militant who was publicly expelled from the ranks of the Communist Party for divisionist activities and slackening of his political position. The same action was applied to Douglas Bravo, Gregorio Lunar Marquez, Freddy Carques and others using the name of the national movement of liberation."

The declaration concluded by practically accusing the guerrilla commanders of this act. It implicated Douglas Bravo, Gregorio Lunar Marquez, Freddy Carques, Francisco Prada and other heroic guerrilla fighters who in the mountains of Venezuela are facing legions of soldiers who are trying to wipe them out and are defending the worst kinds of interests.

## Anyone Might Think That the Revolutionaries Are the Murderers While Leoni's Regime Personifies "The Prince of Peace"

And what does the official leadership do? It places charges against the guerrilla combatants, via the most repugnant opportunism, thus playing into the hands of Leoni's pro-imperialist puppet government. They do little less than ask for the head of Douglas Bravo, besides implying that they hold him responsible for the death of Iribarren.

And this position, with respect to the men who are waging a heroic combat and upholding the banner of the Venezuelan Revolution, is tantamount to demanding their heads for what they have done; it is just one short step from this to asking Leoni for a rifle

to exterminate Douglas Bravo.

Mention has been made here of another supposed declaration of Pedro Medina Silva. It has been a long time now since any revolutionary combatant recognized the leadership of Pedro Medina Silva. It is said that other guerrillas such as German Lairet signed the declaration. We know German Lairet, and we know that he has never even paid a visit to a guerrilla camp.

A torrent of declarations! What kind of attitude is this? A cowardly, opportunistic and repugnant attitude, an adherence to the chorus of counter-revolutionary and anti-Cuban hysteria.

What good are the words of this gentleman when he says, "There has never been any anti-Cuban sentiment among the Venezuelan people, and now the enemies of the Cuban Revolution are taking advantage of this opportunity to instill such sentiments."

Who, if not they, are the accomplices in this plan? Who are the accomplices in this imperialist campaign, if not those who have been charging us with meddling in the internal affairs of the Venezuelan party? In what way do these charges differ from those made by the CIA, the State Department, the counterrevolutionaries? The only difference is that one bunch charges us with meddling in the internal affairs of Venezuela and the other with meddling in the internal affairs of the Party.

And why all of this? Because we have maintained a principled stand, and because we have not withheld our sympathies and solidarity from the revolutionary combatants. And in these declarations of cowards and opportunists, that can never be declarations of revolutionaries, for a revolutionary can criticize, he can disagree with something, but never fall into this shameful attitude. One would say that the assassins are the revolutionaries and the Leoni regime is the "prince of peace"; that the ferocious and bloody clique that has assassinated hundreds of combatants is a flock of docile lambs. It is cowardly not to accuse the real offender! It is cowardly not to take advantage of the circumstances in order to demand punishment for the thugs who have assassinated so many Venezuelans!

It is all well and good to make any criticisms considered necessary. But those criticisms must be made with a revolutionary spirit; they must be made standing up to the enemy and not in his corner; against the enemy and not with him: and the enemy is the assassin of hundreds of combatants, scores of heroic militant communists. If any Latin American government in recent times has murdered communists, it has been the Venezuelan government, first under Romulo Betancourt and later under Leoni. And here there is not a single word condemning the killers, not a single word condemning the regime that has let loose the repression, that has let loose violence in Venezuela, that has forced the students and the revolutionaries in general to take up arms as the only way to free their people, to free their country from the clutches of the oligarchy and imperialism.

It was logical for them to join in the chorus, to accuse the Cuban Revolution; that does not matter to us. Our Revolution has had to keep itself unblemished in the midst of lies and calumny ever since it came into being, even before it came into being. When we attacked the Moncada garrison, the next day the newspapers reported that the revolutionaries had slaughtered the patients in the hospital. We are familiar with those tricks so dear to imperialism and reaction. All the worst iniquities are attributed to the Revolution by the reactionaries and the imperialists.

They will not give up that system, that campaign. Therefore, the calumnies and imputations of the gorillas, of the imperialists and their lackeys, do not matter to us; such accusations will never move us to withhold our sympathy and solidarity from revolutionary fighters.

## We Proclaim Our Sympathy With the Guerrilla Fighters of the Western Mountains and El Bachiller

And in the midst of the campaign of hysteria, in the midst of threats, denunciations and agreements; in the midst of that ferocious campaign, where betrayal of Country joins hands with betrayal of the Revolution, at the moment when the defeatists who call themselves communists and the pro-imperialist oligarchy let loose their campaign against the Venezuelan revolutionaries and against Cuba, we once again proclaim our sympathy and our unwavering solidarity with the guerrillas fighting in the western mountains, with the guerrillas fighting in the mountains of El Bachiller, with the combatants who, in the cities, defy the repression and the fury of the tyranny. (APPLAUSE)

Our policy is clear. We recognize only revolutionaries as representatives of the peoples. We do not consider any of those oligarchic and traitorous governments that broke with Cuba, following orders from the Yankee embassy, as representatives of their peoples. Only one of those governments, which is not a socialist government, but whose international position deserves our respect—only one of those governments deserves such respect—and that is the Government of Mexico. (APPLAUSE)

What is our diplomatic position with the other governments? We will not re-establish diplomatic relations with any of those governments that obeyed imperialist orders; we have no interest in doing so; we have no desire to do so. (APPLAUSE) We will only establish diplomatic relations with revolutionary governments in those countries; and, therefore, with governments that show they are independent. Re-establish relations so that they can break them the day after tomorrow following a simple indication from the State Department? No. We do not like to waste our time on such foolishness. Economic relations with those oligarchies, when they were the ones that broke with us? We are not interested in re-establishing relations until there are revolutionary governments leading those countries.

We will not give financial aid to any oligarchy to put down the revolutionary movement with blood. (APPLAUSE) And whoever, no matter who, aids those oligarchies where guerrillas are fighting will be helping to suppress the revolution, for repressive wars are carried on not only with weapons but also with the millions of dollars used for purchasing the weapons and for paying the mercenary armies.

An unmistakable proof of the lack of independence of those governments is to be found in the recent case of Colombia, where at 6 a.m. a few days ago, because of a guerrilla attack against a train, they arrested the General Secretary of the Communist Party of Colombia and all the leaders of that Party who were found in their customary places. They did not hesitate a bit because at that very moment a delegation of high Soviet officials were present for the signing of a commercial, cultural and financial agreement with the Lleras Restrepo government; that same day, it was said there was to be an interview between Lleras Restrepo and the high Soviet officials. And that same day not only did they arrest the Communist leadership but they also attacked, according to the wire service dispatches, the offices of the news agency TASS. What a friendly spirit those oligarchies have! What an independent spirit those puppets have! There is reciprocity for you! That is a proof of the lack of independence, of the hypocrisy of the international policy of those puppet governments.

## We Will Never Renew Relations With the Regime That Has Killed More Communists Than Any other Regime in This Hemisphere

You see how the Venezuelan puppets talk, with their demands that the U.S.S.R. withdraw from the Tricontinental Organization, that the U.S.S.R. do no less than virtually break with Cuba, the "dead-end street," to enter through the wide, expansive and friendly door of the Venezuelan government, the government that has slaughtered more communists than any other on this continent!

As for us, we are Marxist-Leninist; let others do as they please. We will never re-establish relations with such a government!

They have broken relations with us, we have not broken relations with anyone. The German Federal Republic even broke with us because we recognized the German Democratic Republic. But we did not waver; as a matter of principle, even though it affected our economic interests, we recognized the German Democratic Republic. All is not rose-colored in the revolutionary world. Complaints and more complaints are repeated because of contradictory attitudes. While one country is being condemned for reopening relations with Federal Germany, there is a rush to seek relations with oligarchies of the sort of Leoni and company. A principled position in everything, a principled position in Asia, (APPLAUSE) but a principled position in Latin America, too.

Let us condemn the imperialist aggression against Viet Nam, let us condemn the crime that the Yankee imperialists are committing today against Viet Nam and let us condemn it with all our might and all our heart! But let us condemn starting right now the future Viet Nams in Latin America, let us condemn starting right now the future imperialist aggressions in Latin America! (APPLAUSE)

What would the Vietnamese revolutionaries think if we were to send delegations to South Viet Nam to deal with the Saigon puppet government? What would those who are fighting in the mountains of America think were we to seek close relations with the puppets of imperialism on this side of the continent, with the puppets of the future Yankee aggressions and interventions in this continent?

The Leoni of today, the Lleras Restrepo of today, will be the Ngo Dinh-Diem and the Cao Ky of tomorrow; they will be on the string of governments that have passed through South Viet Nam just to justify the imperialist aggressions, just to legalize the interventions of the Yankee marines.

And all of them, imperialists and puppets, join in a conspiracy against our revolutionary, socialist nation, which is as it is not because we have imported revolution from any other country, but rather because we have generated it on our own soil and under our own skies.

There are some who speak of supposed cases of fatalism, but there is no fatalism that can hold back this Revolution, not the 90-mile fatalism, or any other kind of fatalism! This Revolution that sprang from nothing at all, this Revolution that years lived in conditions of encirclement by the enemy, where nothing could get through, is a Revolution which has its own particular right to exist. It is a Revolution—understand this well, all puppets, oligarchs, and shilly-shalliers and pseudo-revolutionaries of all stripes—it is a Revolution which no one or nothing will be able to crush or halt! (PROLONGED APPLAUSE) And this Revolution will maintain its position of absolute independence, that kind of independence to which all people capable of fighting for it are entitled, that kind of independence all honorable people are entitled to have.

## This Revolution Will Follow Its Own Ideological Line and Will Never Be Anybody's Puppet

We proclaim it to the world: This Revolution will hold true to its path, this Revolution will follow its own line, this Revolution will never be anybody's satellite or yes-man. It will never ask anybody's permission to maintain its own position either in matters of ideology, or on domestic or foreign affairs; proudly and courageously our people are ready to face the future, whatever that future may hold. (APPLAUSE)

Today we work with feverish enthusiasm, with more enthusiasm than ever before; and we are advancing in our national development, in the development of our economy more impetuously than at any other time in the past eight years. Great ideological battles are being won on all fronts, in all respects; and we will confidently hold true to our ideological path, with the confidence of true revolutionaries, with confidence in our people and in our masses.

Perhaps, if it had not been necessary to deal with the subjects I have been concerned with tonight, it would have been necessary to talk about this profound, incredible revolution that is taking place in the awareness of our people. We look to the future serenely and confidently, as we face any eventuality. We are aware that this struggle will not and cannot be easy, that we live on a continent in full revolutionary ferment, in the midst of a score of peoples who are waking up to reality, who are already fighting or are getting ready to do so. We realize that threats of all kinds will be hurled at us, and conspiracies will be organized against us, and possibly even aggressions by the dozens will be launched against us. Very well, from this very moment, we declare ourselves invincible. (APPLAUSE)

An invasion of this country ... and this is practically what Senor Leoni proposes or insinuates. He does not now call for sanctions because of the international situation, but he wishes to start building up his dossier; in short, it is perfectly clear that once they are through in Viet Nam it will be time for them to ask for sanctions and war against us. No wonder the first person he talked with was "His Highness" the Yankee ambassador in Caracas. Very well: now or at any other time, while they attack Viet Nam or after they are defeated in Viet Nam—because they will be defeated, they are going to be defeated in their aggression against the heroic people of North Viet Nam and they are going to be defeated in their aggression against the heroic people of South Viet Nam, led by the National Front of Liberation, whose position and policy the Cuban Party supports without any vacillation; (APPLAUSE) there is no doubt whatsoever that they will defeat the imperialists—if they think they will find a pushover here, let them know that they will find at least one Stalingrad here plus 3.6 Viet Nams; (APPLAUSE) and, besides, half a dozen more Viet Nams in the rest of the continent. Let them take note of that as of now! And as far as we are concerned, we base ourselves on mathematical calculations, on numbers of men, on the volume of fire, and on a fire that burns hotter than that of arms; the fire in the hearts and the fire of the valor of an entire people! (APPLAUSE)

## It Is Ridiculous to Try to Make Cuba Responsible for What Other Revolutionaries Do

Plots and threats do not worry us; we don't care about the sins and transgressions they try to pin on us. It does not matter to us! It is ridiculous to want to blame Cuba for what revolutionaries do, for their strategy, for their tactics. We know how revolutionaries and revolutionary organizations operate; how in all revolutionary processes there are always different forces, and within each revolutionary movement there are different centers of authority. In our own Cuban experience, when we went to attack Moncada no other revolutionary organization knew it; when a group of patriots went to attack the Goicuria military garrison, other organizations did not know about it; when the comrades of the Directorio Revolucionario attacked the Presidential Palace on March 13, we in the mountains found out about it from the radio news bulletins. Within our own organization, the men of the plains never knew what we in the mountains were going to do and the men of the mountains did not know what those in the cities were going to do, because it cannot be supposed that the revolutionaries are connected by radio or telephone systems. No. In the revolution, within the revolution, there are different organizations; within each organization there are different spheres of decision; and the organizations that operate in the underground are considered autonomous, in each town.

One cannot put the responsibility on revolutionary organizations—not all of them or even one—for any individual act that might occur; and it is even more absurd, ridiculous, idiotic to attempt to make such a charge against the Revolutionary Government of Cuba.

But who are those who have let loose this campaign? What government? One of the most repressive, sanguinary governments this continent has ever seen, characterized by deeds written in blood and brutal repression, is the sole agent of the bloody deeds in Venezuela. It is the Leoni clique who bear the principal responsibility for the death of Iribarren Borges, for they are the ones who unleashed repression and violence. They, who at the service of their Yankee masters are turning over the wealth of Venezuela for the few crumbs that are left them; they, who have assassinated so many of their compatriots while serving their imperialist master, bear the chief responsibility.

The list of Venezuelan combatants who have fallen victim to the repression of the Betancourt and Leoni regimes is long indeed. In collusion with Batista henchmen, for example, they assassinated young Livia Gouverneur. In the very heart of Caracas, in El Silencio, a police bullet killed Alberto Rudas Mezones, whose only crime was that of having shouted "Viva Cuba!" The following day his body was secretly taken from his home by the Betancourt police in order to avoid the demonstration of public mourning and protest that would have marked his funeral.

From August, 1959, to March, 1963, hundreds of Venezuelan patriots were murdered by Betancourt and Leoni henchmen. That terror began when a demonstration of the unemployed was machine-gunned, causing the death of Juan Francisco Villegas, Rafael Simon Montero and Rafael Baltazar Gonzalez.

Betancourt later had the effrontery to state in one of his speeches, referring to these deeds, that the streets were not for the people but for the police.

After Ricardo Navarro defeated Betancourt—sponsored union leaders in an election, this oil workers' leader was assassinated by government armed bands at a union meeting where seven workers were wounded.

In Barquisimeto, Julian Torres was arrested, tortured and later murdered when a bullet was fired into his abdomen. The Venezuelan police resorted to the old saw that the "prisoner had tried to escape."

Jose Gregorio Rodriguez was barbarously tortured by DIGEPOL agents and later thrown from a four-story building to give the appearance of suicide. This crime was confirmed by a commission of the Chamber of Deputies whose report was never made public.

When Leoni became president, no change whatsoever occurred in the repressive policy of the Venezuelan government. The young high school student, Rafael Urdaneta, was tortured, horribly kicked and knifed and then riddled with bullets by DIGEPOL agents in Jaroa.

The National Guard officer, Pena Pena, arrested and tortured a number of peasants in the State of Miranda. Three of the prisoners, including the peasant leader, Trino Barrios, and the youth leader, Victor Ramon Soto Rojas, and Jesus Maria Hernandez, were thrown from a helicopter over the mountains of Miranda in the presence of ten of their arrested comrades who were then shot for refusing to talk.

A student at the Maracaibo Technological School, just 14 years of age, was assassinated when the police fired on a demonstration which was organized precisely to demand an end to police repression.

Pedro Rojas, after having been arrested by DIGEPOL, was hanged in a concentration camp at Cachipo.

Alberto Lovera was arrested by the DIGEPOL and savagely tortured until the moment he died. His body was found with a heavy chain around his neck, and an autopsy revealed that his vertebrae had been crushed.

## The DIGEPOL Is Leoni's Instrument for Murder and Torture

World public opinion was stirred by the assassination in prison of the revolutionary leader Fabricio Ojeda. President of the FLN-FALN General Command.

Ramon Pasquier was arrested on the Yaracuy highway, tortured and mutilated, and his body was never found.

Making off with the victims' bodies is the systematic practice of the repressive agents of Betancourt and Leoni. They did this recently with FLN-FALN urban commandos Andres Pasquier and Felipe Malaver, Donato Carmona, Angel Guerra, Domingo Sanchez and many other Venezuelan patriots.

On three different occasions, Congress has been obliged to carry out investigations of the DIGEPOL, and in every instance, it has been proved that this agency has committed assassinations and torture.

The list of victims of Betancourt's repressive police is very long. A wide river of blood runs between the Venezuelan people and the imperialist lackeys in power.

To mention just a few of the names: Samuel Sanchez Alvarez, Andres Coba Casas, Luisa Maria Cazola, Isabel Acosta, Alexis Rivero, Jose del Carmen Chavez, Natalia Ghinaglia, Santos Chauron, Rosario Mujica, Antonio Mogollon, Pedro Anian, Jose Montesinos, Luis Adrian Gonzalez, Francisco Losada, Edgard Gonzalez, Francisco Velazquez, Alejandro Montiel, Isidro Espinosa, Livia Gutierrez, Victor Cesari, Amadeo Sifoni, Jose Rodriguez, Alirio Mendez, Juan Gomez, Hector Trujillo, Leonidas Rojas, Alfredo Tirado, Pedro Ramos, Juan Osirio Magallanes, Miguel Arviaca, Ernesto Alvarez, Concepcion Orta, Alfredo Carmona, Isaac Velazquez, Ana Lourdes Pacheco, Anibal Gimenez, Justo Camacho, Carlota de Ochoa, Simon Caghualga, Esther Flores, Olga de Hernandez,

Ramon Guevara, Rodolfo Garcia, Rafael Hurtado, Pilar Ponce, Santiago Figueras, Emilio Dos Santos, Armando Sanchez, Elias la Rosa, Martin Palacios, Ernesto Alvio, Antonio Diaz, Jose Zurita, Alberto Manzanares, Luis Saavedra, Francisco Rosales, Valentin Araujo, Daniel Matute, Aquiles Bellorin, Alvaro Ruiz, Manuel Infante, Rafael Guerra, Enrique Perez, Eduvigis Colorado, Eulalia Fuenmayor, Angel Linares, Julio Manzano, Jose Vazquez, Esteban Padilla, Carlos Novoa, Enrique Leal, Rafael Villegas, Manuel Cachutt Sahoudala, Alfonso Rodriguez, Jesus Osuna, Omar Ramones Prieto, Jesus Manuel Rojas Figueroa, Luis Martinez Anez, Vivian Hernandez, Elvina de Morales, Rafael Clemente Acosta, J. Pfeifer, Ignacio Diaz Nino, Carlos Martinez, Alejo Celis, Alejandro Sandoval, Eduardo Mirabal Machado, Ivan Alfredo Cordero, Jesus Alberto Trujillo, Ramon Jimenez, Humberto Mendez Figueredo, Antero Mendoza Angarita, Francisco Barreto, Manuel Antonio Mujica, Efrain Cordero, Carmelo Mendoza, Luis Vicente Garcia, Hector Beltran Diaz, Nancy Alvarado Palma, Luis Rafael Tineo Gamboa, Rafael Antonio Briceno, Ivan Daza, Alijo C. Paredes, murdered in the presence of his mother, and an endless list of patriots, of combatants, all basely assassinated. I do not by any means refer to those who have died fighting like heroes against the hangmen or soldiers of the tyranny. These names are the names of so many other Venezuelans, the victims of shootings, torture, and murder.

This is the history of Venezuela during the last few years! This is the history of Betancourt's crimes! This is the history of Leoni's crimes, of the crimes for which Leoni and Betancourt will have to account for before History! These are the crimes they are trying to conceal! This is the reason for the smoke-screen leading to pure fabrication and to crude maneuvers which are an attempt to place the responsibility for Iribarren's death on Cuba.

And they will have to answer for these crimes somewhere, everywhere in fact. And if they wish to take it to the United Nations, that's even better! If they wish to take it to the United Nations, that's fine! But let them be prepared to discuss their crimes, their outrages, their acts of treason to Venezuela, and answer for the thousands of millions of pesos which they hand over to Yankee imperialism and for the rivers of blood they are responsible for. (APPLAUSE)

**Venezuela Too Will Some Day Assemble and Recall Its Heroes and Martyrs**

They are the ones who will be placed on the dock. The above charges do not include the brutal repression, the exploitation to which the people of Venezuela are subjected, the suspensions of constitutional guarantees and the violations of university autonomy. If that vile filth is what they call democracy, I ask them: Why is it that they cannot hold a meeting with the university students? We meet here today precisely to commemorate that glorious date, that heroic date when, as in Venezuela, some fought heroically and others—entrusted with other missions—were killed, in some cases fighting a patrol car, like Jose Antonio Echevarria, while in other cases, they were wounded, imprisoned and then murdered.

We meet tonight after having lived through experiences similar to those the Venezuelan people are living through today. We gather here to recall our glorious combatants in the same way that some day in the future Venezuelans too will meet to recall their heroes and martyrs. Moreover, there will be a day in Venezuela when many places in the country and many factories and plants will bear the names of those heroes who were murdered by the henchmen of the tyranny. (APPLAUSE)

However, we challenge "democrat" Leoni, traitor to his people, betrayer of his country, imperialist henchman, and repressive agent of Yankee imperialism, to try to go into the University of Venezuela. It is traditional and accepted throughout the world that the purest sentiments are found among the youth; that the most pure, the most idealistic, the best of any people is found among its youth. And the best of Venezuela—its youth—is found among the students, the same as in many other countries.

And how does Leoni treat that rebel, heroic, worthy, combative part of Venezuela's people? At the point of a gun! Who enters the university? Tanks, henchmen and policemen!

Traitors, henchmen and murderers will never be able to inter-mix with Venezuela's youth. We challenge Senor Leoni to go into the university, meet with the people, explain his policy. Because only where there is no contradiction between people and government, only in the midst of a revolutionary process in which the unity of all the people is forged from the working masses, from the peasant masses, from the masses of young people, from the masses of intellectuals. No longer in the midst of the sirens of that heroic March 13, nor in the midst of shots, but in the future, of revolutionary awareness, of patriotism, we, the leaders of this people, can meet here with the students as we do in the mountains with the peasants and with the workers in the factories.

Because the Revolution is that. We, too, lived through a past laden with abuses, with shootings, expulsions, massacres, murders; our university also knew what heroic demonstrations meant; face to face with the fire trucks, the clubs, the shots, but there was perseverance, struggle and victory was won. Our university won the right to build its future, it achieved the right to occupy a worthy place in the world, to be truly free, to be truly independent.

And so we are sure that Venezuela also, will have these things, and that their heroic watchword, "Make our country free or die for Venezuela!" will be fulfilled, and that watchword is like our own of PATRIA O MUERTE! VENCEREMOS! (OVATION)

# MAJOR ERNESTO "CHE" GUEVARA'S "MESSAGE TO THE PEOPLES OF THE WORLD," APRIL 1967

*Complete Text*
(*Granma*, Havana, 23 April 1967, English edition)

Twenty-one years have already elapsed since the end of the last world conflagration; numerous publications, in every possible language, celebrate this event, symbolized by the defeat of Japan. There is a climate of apparent optimism in many areas of the different camps into which the world is divided.

Twenty-one years without a world war, in these times of maximum confrontations, of violent clashes and sudden changes, appears to be a very high figure. However, without analyzing the practical results of this peace (poverty, degradation, increasing exploitation of enormous sectors of humanity) for which all of us have stated that we are willing to fight, we would do well to inquire if this peace is real.

It is not the purpose of these notes to detail the different conflicts of a local character that have been occurring since the surrender of Japan, neither do we intend to recount the numerous and increasing instances of civilian strife which have taken place during these years of apparent peace. It will be enough just to name, as an example against undue optimism, the wars of Korea and Viet Nam.

In the first of these, after years of savage warfare, the Northern part of the country was submerged in the most terrible devastation known in the annals of modern warfare: riddled with bombs; without factories, schools or hospitals; with absolutely no shelter for housing ten million inhabitants.

Under the discredited flag of the United Nations, dozens of countries under the military leadership of the United States participated in this war with the massive intervention of U.S. soldiers and the use, as cannon fodder, of the drafted South Korean population. On the other side, the army and the people of Korea and the volunteers from the People's Republic of China were furnished with supplies and technical aid by the Soviet military apparatus. The U.S. tested all sorts of weapons of destruction, excluding the thermonuclear type, but including, on a limited scale, bacteriological and chemical warfare.

In Viet Nam, the patriotic forces of that country have carried on an almost uninterrupted war against three imperialist powers: Japan, whose might suffered an almost vertical collapse after the bombs of Hiroshima and Nagasaki; France, that recovered from that defeated country its Indo-China colonies and ignored the promises it had made in harder times; and the United States, in this last phase of the struggle.

There have been limited confrontations in every continent although in Our America, for a long time, there were only incipient liberation struggles and military coups d'etat until the Cuban Revolution sounded the alert, signaling the importance of this region. This action attracted the wrath of the imperialists and Cuba was finally obliged to defend its coasts, first in Playa Giron, and again during the October Crisis.

This last incident could have unleashed a war of incalculable proportions if a U.S.-Soviet clash had occurred over the Cuban question.

But, evidently, the focal point of all contradictions is at present the territory of the peninsula of Indo-China and the adjacent areas. Laos and Viet Nam are torn by civil wars which have ceased being such by the entry into the conflict of U.S. imperialism with all its might, thus transforming the whole zone into a dangerous powder keg ready at any moment to explode.

In Viet Nam the confrontation has assumed extremely acute characteristics. It is not our intention, either, to chronicle this war. We shall simply remember and point out some milestones.

In 1954, after the annihilating defeat of Dien-Bien-Phu, an agreement was signed at Geneva dividing the country into two separate zones; elections were to be held within a term of 18 months to determine who should govern Viet Nam and how the country should be reunified. The U.S. did not sign this document and started maneuvering to substitute the emperor, Bao Dai, who was a French puppet, for a man more amenable to its purposes. This happened to be Ngo Dinh Diem, whose tragic end—that of an orange squeezed dry by imperialism—is well known by all.

During the months following the agreement, optimism reigned supreme in the camp of the popular forces. The last redoubts of the anti-French resistance were dismantled in the South of the country—and they awaited the fulfillment of the Geneva Agreements. But the patriots soon realized there would be no elections—unless the United States felt itself capable of imposing its will in the polls, which was practically impossible even resorting to all its fraudulent methods. Once again fighting broke out in the South and gradually acquired full intensity. At present the U.S. invading army has increased to nearly half a million troops, while the puppet forces decrease in number and, above all, have totally lost their combativeness.

Almost two years ago the United States started systematically bombing the Democratic Republic of Viet Nam, in yet another attempt to overcome the resistance of the South and impose, from a position of strength, a meeting at the conference table. At first, the bombardments were more or less isolated occurrences and were represented as reprisals for alleged provocations from the North. Later on, as they increased in intensity and regularity, they became one gigantic attack carried out by the air force of the

United States, day after day, for the purpose of destroying all vestiges of civilization in the Northern zone of the country. This is an episode of the infamously notorious "escalation."

The material aspiriations of the Yankee world have been fulfilled to a great extent, despite the unflinching defense of the Vietnamese anti-aircraft artillery, of the numerous planes shot down (over 1,700) and of the socialist countries' aid in war supplies.

This is the sad reality: Viet Nam—a nation representing the aspirations, the hopes of a whole world of forgotten peoples—is tragically alone. This nation must endure the furious attacks of U.S. technology, with practically no possibility of reprisals in the South and only some of defense in the North—but always alone.

The solidarity of all progressive forces of the world with the people of Viet Nam today is similar to the bitter irony of the plebeians urging on the gladiators in the Roman arena. It is not a matter of wishing success to the victim of aggression, but of sharing his fate; one must accompany him to his death or to victory.

When we analyze the lonely situation of the Vietnamese people, we are overcome by anguish at this illogical fix in which humanity finds itself.

U.S. imperialism is guilty of aggression—its crimes are enormous and cover the whole world. We already know all that, gentlemen! But this guilt also applies to those who, when the time came for a definition, hesitated to make Viet Nam an inviolable part of the socialist world; running, of course, the risks of a war on a global scale—but also forcing a decision upon imperialism. The guilt also applies to those who maintain a war of abuse and maneuvering—started quite some time ago by the representatives of the two greatest powers of the socialist camp.

We must ask ourselves, seeking an honest answer: Is Viet Nam isolated, or is it not? Is it not maintaining a dangerous equilibrium between the two quarrelling powers?

And what great people these are! What stoicism and courage! And what a lesson for the world is contained in this struggle! Not for a long time shall we be able to know if President Johnson ever seriously thought of bringing about some of the reforms needed by his people—to iron out the barbed class contradictions that grow each day with explosive power. The truth is that the improvements announced under the pompous title of the "Great Society" have been poured down the drain of Viet Nam.

The largest of all imperialist powers feels in its own guts the bleeding inflicted by a poor and underdeveloped country; its fabulous economy feels the strain of the war effort. Murder is ceasing to be the most convenient business for its monopolies. Defensive weapons, and never in adequate number, is all these extraordinary Vietnamese soldiers have—besides love for their homeland, their society, and unsurpassed courage. But imperialism is bogging down in Viet Nam, is unable to find a way out and desperately seeks one that will overcome with dignity this dangerous situation in which it now finds itself. Furthermore, the Four Points put forward by the

North and the Five Points of the South now corner imperialism, making the confrontation even more decisive.

Everything indicates that peace, this unstable peace which bears the name for the sole reason that no world-wide conflagration has taken place, is again in danger of being destroyed by some irrevocable and unacceptable step taken by the United States.

What role shall we, the exploited people of the world, play? The peoples of the three continents focus their attention on Viet Nam and learn their lesson. Since imperialists blackmail humanity by threatening it with war, the wise reaction is not to fear war. The general tactics of the people should be to launch a constant and a firm attack on all fronts where the confrontation is taking place.

In those places where the meager peace we have has been violated, what is our duty? To liberate ourselves at any price.

The world panorama is of great complexity. The struggle for liberation has not yet been undertaken by some countries of ancient Europe, sufficiently developed to realize the contradictions of capitalism, but weak to such a degree that they are unable either to follow imperialism or to start on their own road. Their contradictions will reach an explosive stage during the forthcoming years—but their problems and, consequently, their solutions are different from those of our dependent and economically underdeveloped countries.

The fundamental field of imperialist exploitation comprises the three underdeveloped continents: America, Asia and Africa. Every country has also its own characteristics, but each continent, as a whole, also presents a certain unity. Our America is integrated by a group of more or less homogeneous countries and in most parts of its territory U.S. monopoly capital maintains an absolute supremacy. Puppet governments or, in the best of cases, weak and fearful local rulers, are incapable of contradicting orders from their Yankee master. The United States has nearly reached the climax of its political and economic domination; it could hardly advance much; any change in the situation could bring about a setback. Its policy is to maintain that which has already been conquered. The line of action, at the present time, is limited to the brutal use of force with the purpose of thwarting the liberation movements, no matter of what type they might happen to be.

The slogan "we will not allow another Cuba" hides the possibility of perpetrating aggressions without fear of reprisal, such as the one carried out against the Dominican Republic, or before that, the massacre in Panama—and the clear warning stating that Yankee troops are ready to intervene anywhere in America where the established order may be altered, thus endangering their interests. This policy enjoys an almost absolute impunity: the OAS is a suitable mask, in spite of its unpopularity; the inefficiency of the UN is ridiculous as well as tragic; the armies of all American countries are ready to intervene in order to smash their peoples. The International of Crime and Treason has in fact been organized. On the other hand, the national bourgeoisies have lost all their capacity to oppose imperialism—if they ever had it—and they have become the last card in the pack. There are no other alternatives; either a socialist revolution or a make-believe revolution.

Asia is a continent with different characteristics. The struggle for liberation waged against a series of European colonial powers resulted in the establishment of more or less progressive governments, whose ulterior evolution has brought about, in some cases, the reaffirming of the primary objectives of national liberation and in others, a setback towards the adoption of pro-imperialist positions.

From the economic point of view, the United States had very little to lose and much to gain in Asia. The changes benefited its interests; the struggle for the overthrow of other neocolonial powers and the penetration of new spheres of action in the economic field is carried out sometimes directly, occasionally through Japan.

But there are special political conditions, in Asia, particularly in Indo-China, which create certain characteristics of capital importance and play a decisive role in the entire U.S. military strategy.

The imperialists encircle China through South Korea, Japan, Taiwan, South Viet Nam and Thailand, at least.

This dual situation: a strategic interest as important as the military encirclement of the People's Republic of China and the penetration of these great markets—which they do not dominate yet—turns Asia into one of the most explosive points of the world today, in spite of its apparent stability outside of the Vietnamese war zone.

The Middle East, though geographically a part of this continent, has its own contradictions and is actively in ferment; it is impossible to foretell how far the cold war between Israel, backed by the imperialists, and the progressive countries of that zone will go. This is just another of the volcanoes threatening eruption in the world today.

Africa offers an almost virgin territory to the neocolonial invasion. There have been changes which, to some extent, forced neocolonial powers to give up their former absolute prerogatives. But when these changes are carried out without interruption, colonialism continues in the form of neocolonialism with similar effects as far as the economic situation is concerned.

The United States had no colonies in this region but is now struggling to penetrate its partners' fiefs. It can be said that following the strategic plans of U.S. imperialism, Africa constitutes its long-range reservoir; its present investments, though, are only important in the Union of South Africa and its penetration is beginning to be felt in the Congo, Nigeria and other countries where a sharp rivalry with other imperialist powers is beginning to take place (non-violent up to the present time).

So far it does not have great interests to defend there except its assumed right to intervene in every spot of the world where its monopolies detect the possibility of huge profits or the existence of large reserves of raw materials.

All this past history justifies our concern over the possibilities of liberating the peoples within a moderate or a short period of time.

If we stop to analyze Africa we observe that in the Portuguese colonies of Guinea, Mozambique and Angola the struggle is waged with relative intensity, with particular success in the first and with variable success in the other two. We still witness in the Congo the dispute between Lumumba's successors and the old accomplices of Tshombe, a dispute which at the present time seems to favor the latter, those who have "pacified" a large area of the country for their own benefit—though the war is still latent.

In Rhodesia we have a different problem: British imperialism used every means within its reach to place power in the hands of the white minority, now in control. The conflict, from the British point of view, is absolutely unofficial; this Western power, with its habitual diplomatic cleverness—also called hypocrisy in plain language—presents a facade of displeasure before the measures adopted by the government of Ian Smith. Its crafty attitude is supported and followed by some Commonwealth countries, but is attacked by a large group of countries belonging to Black Africa, even by some that are still docile economic vassals of British imperialism.

Should the efforts of Rhodesia's black patriots to organize armed rebellion crystallize and should this movement be effectively supported by neighboring African nations, the situation in that country could become extremely explosive. But for the moment all these problems are being discussed in such innocuous organizations as the UN, the Commonwealth and the OAU.

Nevertheless, the social and political evolution of Africa does not lead us to expect a continental revolution. The liberation struggle against the Portuguese should end victoriously, but Portugal means nothing in the imperialist field. The confrontations of revolutionary importance are those which place at bay all the imperialist apparatus, though this does not mean that we should stop fighting for the liberation of the three Portuguese colonies and for the deepening of their revolutions.

When the black masses of South Africa or Rhodesia start their authentic revolutionary struggle, a new era will dawn in Africa. Or when the impoverished masses of a nation rise up to rescue their right to a decent life from the hands of the ruling oligarchies.

Up to now, army putsches have followed one another; a group of officers succeeds one another or replaces rulers who no longer serve their caste interests and those of the powers who covertly manage them—but there are no great popular upheavals. In the Congo these characteristics appeared briefly, generated by the memory of Lumumba, but they have been losing strength in the last few months.

In Asia, as we have seen, the situation is explosive. The points of friction are not only Viet Nam and Laos, where actual fighting is going on, but also Cambodia, where a direct U.S. aggression may start at any time, Thailand, Malaya, and, of course, Indonesia, where we cannot assume that the last word has been said, despite the annihilation of the Communist Party of that country carried out by the reactionaries when they took power. And also, naturally there is the Middle East.

In Latin America armed struggle is underway in Guatemala, Colombia, Venezuela and Bolivia and the first uprisings are appearing in Brazil. Other foci of resistance appear and are later extinguished. But almost every country of this continent is ripe for a type of struggle that, in order to achieve victory, cannot be content with anything less than establishing a government of a socialist nature.

On this continent, for all practical purposes, only one tongue is spoken (with the exception of Brazil, with whose people those who speak Spanish can easily make themselves understood, owing to the great similarity of both languages). There is also such a great similarity among the classes of the different countries, that an identification exists among them, as an "international American" type, much more complete than that of other continents. Language, customs, religion, a common foreign master, unite them. The degree and forms of exploitation are similar for both the exploiters and the exploited in many of the countries of Our America. And rebellion is ripening swiftly.

We may ask ourselves: how will this rebellion come to fruition? What type will it be? We have maintained for quite some time now that, owing to the similarity of national characteristics, the struggle in Our America will achieve, in due course, continental proportions. It will be the scene of many great battles fought for the liberation of humanity.

Within the overall struggle on a continental scale, the battles which are now taking place are only episodes—but they have already furnished their martyrs, who will figure in the history of Our America as having given their necessary quota of blood in this last stage of the fight for the total freedom of Man. These names will include Major Turcios Lima, the priest Camilo Torres, Major Fabricio Ojeda, Majors Lobaton and Luis de la Puente Uceda, all outstanding figures in the revolutionary movements of Guatemala, Colombia, Venezuela and Peru.

But the active mobilization of the people creates new leaders; Cesar Montes and Yon Sosa raise the flag of battle in Guatemala; Fabio Vazquez and Marulanda in Colombia; Douglas Bravo in the western half of the country and Americo Martin in El Bachiller direct their respective fronts in Venezuela. New uprisings will take place in these and other countries of Our America, as has already happened in Bolivia; they will continue to grow in the midst of all the hardships inherent to this dangerous profession of the modern revolutionary. Many will perish, victims of their errors; others will fall in the hard battle ahead; new fighters and new leaders will appear in the heat of the revolutionary struggle. The people will produce their fighters and leaders in the selective process of the war itself—and Yankee agents of repression will increase. Today there are military "advisers" in all the countries where armed struggle exists, and the Peruvian army, trained and advised by the Yankees, apparently carried out a successful action against the revolutionaries in that country. But if the foci of war grow with

sufficient political and military wisdom, they will become practically invincible, obliging the Yankees to send reinforcements. In Peru itself many new figures, practically unknown, are now tenaciously and firmly reorganizing the guerrilla movement. Little by little, the obsolete weapons which are sufficient for the repression of small armed bands will be exchanged for modern armaments and the U.S. military "advisers" will be substituted by U.S. soldiers until, at a given moment, they will be forced to send increasingly greater numbers of regular troops to ensure the relative stability of a government whose national puppet army is disintegrating before the attacks of the guerrillas. It is the road of Viet Nam; it is the road that should be followed by the peoples of the world; it is the road that will be followed in Our America, with the special characteristic that the armed groups may create something like Coordinating Councils to frustrate the repressive efforts of Yankee imperialism and contribute to the revolutionary cause.

America, a forgotten continent in the world's more recent liberation struggles, which is now beginning to make itself heard through the Tri-continental in the voice of the vanguard of its peoples, the Cuban Revolution, has before it a task of much greater relevance: to create a Second or a Third Viet Nam, or the Second and Third Viet Nam of the world.

We must bear in mind that imperialism is a world system, the last stage of capitalism—and it must be defeated in a great world confrontation. The strategic end of this struggle must be the destruction of imperialism. Our part, the responsibility of the exploited and underdeveloped of the world, is to eliminate the foundations of imperialism: our oppressed nations, from which they extract capital, raw materials, cheap technicians and common labor, and to which they export new capital—instrument of domination,—arms and every kind of article, submerging us in absolute dependence.

The fundamental element of this strategic end is, then, the real liberation of all peoples, a liberation that will be brought about in most cases through armed struggle and will, in Our America, almost certainly have the characteristic of becoming a Socialist Revolution.

In envisaging the destruction of imperialism, it is necessary to identify its head, which is no other than the United States of America.

We must carry out a general task which has as its tactical purpose drawing the enemy out of his natural environment, forcing him to fight in places where his living habits clash with the existing reality. We must not underrate our adversary; the U.S. soldier has technical capacity and is backed by weapons and resources of such magnitude as to render him formidable. He lacks the essential ideological motivation which his bitterest enemies of today—the Vietnamese soldiers—have in the highest degree. We will only be able to triumph over such an army by undermining its morale—and that is accomplished by causing it repeated defeats and repeated punishment.

But this brief scheme for victory implies immense sacrifice by the people, sacrifice that should be demanded beginning today, in plain words, and which perhaps may be less painful than what they would have to endure if we constantly avoided battle in an attempt to have others pull our chestnuts out of the fire.

It is probable, of course, that the last country to liberate itself will accomplish this without armed struggle and that people may be spared the sufferings of a long and cruel war against the imperialists. But perhaps it will be impossible to avoid this struggle or its effects in a global conflagration and the last country's suffering may be the same, or even greater. We cannot foresee the future, but we should never give in to the defeatist temptation of being leaders of a nation that yearns for freedom but abhors the struggle it entails and awaits its freedom as a crumb of victory.

It is absolutely just to avoid all useless sacrifice. For that reason, it is necessary to study carefully the real possibilities that dependent America may have of liberating itself through peaceful means. For us, the answer to this question is quite clear: the present moment may or may not be the proper one for starting the struggle, but we cannot harbor any illusions, and we have no right to do so, that freedom can be obtained without fighting. And the battles will not be mere street fights with stones against tear-gas bombs, nor pacific general strikes; neither will they be those of a furious people destroying in two or three days the repressive superstructure of the ruling oligarchies. The struggle will be long, harsh, and its battle fronts will be the guerrilla's refuge, the cities, the homes of the fighters—where the repressive forces will go seeking easy victims among their families,—among the massacred rural population, in the villages or cities destroyed by the bombardments of the enemy.

They themselves impel us to this struggle; there is no alternative other than to prepare it and decide to undertake it.

The beginnings will not be easy; they will be extremely difficult. All of the oligarchies' power of repression, all of their capacity for brutality and demagoguery will be placed at the service of their cause. Our mission, in the first hour, will be to survive; later, we will follow the perennial example of the guerrilla, carrying out armed propaganda (in the Vietnamese sense, that is, the propaganda of bullets, of battles won or lost—but fought—against the enemy). The great lesson of the invincibility of the guerrillas will take root in the dispossessed masses. The galvanizing of national spirit, preparation for harder tasks, for resisting even more violent repressions. Hatred as an element of struggle; relentless hatred of the enemy that impels us over and beyond the natural limitations of man and transforms us into effective, violent, selective and cold killing machines. Our soldiers must be thus; a people without hatred cannot vanquish a brutal enemy. We must carry the war as far as the enemy carries it: to his home, to his centers of entertainment, in a total war. It is necessary to prevent him from having a moment of peace, a quiet moment outside his barracks or even inside; we must attack him wherever he may be, make him feel like a cornered beast wherever he may move. Then his morale will begin to fall. He will become still more savage, but we shall see the signs of decadence begin to appear.

And let us develop a true proletarian internationalism, with international proletarian armies; let the flag under which we fight be the sacred cause of redeeming humanity, so that to die under the flag of Viet Nam, of Venezuela, of Guatemala, of Laos, of Guinea, of Colombia, of Bolivia, of Brazil—to name only a few scenes of today's armed struggle be equally glorious and desirable for an American, an Asian, an African, or even a European.

Each drop of blood spilled in a country under whose flag one has not been born is an experience for those who survive to apply later in the liberation struggle of their own countries. And each nation liberated is a step toward victory in the battle for the liberation of one's own country.

The time has come to settle our discrepancies and place everything we have at the service of the struggle.

We all know that great controversies agitate the world now fighting for freedom; no one can hide it. We also know that these controversies have reached such intensity and such bitterness that the possibility of dialogue and reconciliation seems extremely difficult, if not impossible. It is useless to search for means and ways to propitiate a dialogue which the hostile parties avoid. But the enemy is there; it strikes every day, and threatens us with new blows and these blows will unite us, today, tomorrow, or the day after. Whoever understands this first, and prepares for this necessary union, will earn the people's gratitude.

Because of the virulence and the intransigence with which each cause is defended, we, the dispossessed, cannot take sides with one or the other form of manifestation of these discrepancies, even if we at times coincide with the contentions of one party or the other, or in greater measure with those of one part than with those of the other. In time of war, the expression of current differences constitutes a weakness; but as things stand at this moment, it is an illusion to hope to settle these differences by means of words. Time will erase them or give them their true explanation.

In our struggling world, all discrepancies regarding tactics and methods of action for the attainment of limited objectives should be analyzed with the respect that the opinions of others deserve. Regarding our great strategic objective, the total destruction of imperialism via armed struggle, we should be uncompromising.

Our aspirations to victory may be summed up thus: total destruction of imperialism by eliminating its firmest bulwark: imperialist domination by the United States of America. To carry out, as a tactical method, the gradual liberation of the peoples, one by one or in groups; forcing the enemy into a difficult fight far from its own territory; liquidation of all of its sustaining bases, that is, its dependent territories.

This means a long war. And, we repeat once more, a cruel war. Let no one fool himself at the outstart and let no one hesitate to begin in fear of the consequences it may bring to his people. It is almost our sole hope for victory. We cannot elude the call of this hour. Viet Nam is pointing it out with its endless lesson of heroism, its tragic and everyday lesson of struggle and death for the attainment of final victory.

There, the imperialist soldiers encounter the discomforts of those who, accustomed to the vaunted U.S. standard of living, must face a hostile land, the insecurity of those who are unable to move without being aware of walking on enemy territory, death to those who advance beyond their fortified encampments, the permanent hostility of an entire population. All this provokes internal repercussions in the United States and propitiates the resurgence of a factor which was attenuated in the full vigor of imperialism: class struggle even within its own territory.

What a luminous, near future would be visible to us if two, three or many Viet Nams flourished throughout the world with their share of death and their immense tragedies, their everyday heroism and their repeated blows against imperialism obliging it to disperse its forces under the attack and the increasing hatred of all the peoples of the earth!

And if we were all capable of uniting to make our blows more solid and more infallible so that the effectiveness of every kind of support given to the struggling peoples were increased—how great and how near that future would be!

If we, those of us who, on a small point of the world map, fulfill our duty and place at the disposal of this struggle whatever little we are able to give: our lives, our sacrifice, must some day breathe our last breath in any land, not our own yet already ours, sprinkled with our blood, let it be known that we have measured the scope of our actions and that we consider ourselves no more than elements in the great army of the proletariat, but that we are proud to have learned from the Cuban Revolution, and from its maximum leader, the great lesson emanating from Cuba's attitude in this part of the world: "What do the dangers or the sacrifices of a man or of a nation matter, when the destiny of humanity is at stake?"

Our every action is a battle cry against imperialism, and a call for the peoples' unity against the great enemy of mankind: the United States of America. Wherever death may surprise us, it will be welcome, provided that this, our battle cry, reach some receptive ear, that another hand be extended to take up our weapons and that other men come forward to intone our funeral dirge with the staccato of machine guns and new cries of battle and victory.

# SPEECH BY LUDVIK VACULIK AT THE FOURTH CONGRESS OF CZECHOSLOVAK WRITERS, 27–29 June 1967

*Complete text*
*(IV Sjezd Svazu Ceskoslovenskych Spisovatelu. (Protokol), Prague, 1968)*

On this occasion I want to express something that you know without my telling you; however, I have a few objective suggestions to make.

According to the draft of the Resolution, it is the purpose of the Socialist order to bring about the re-integration of man whose status as a citizen is to be guaranteed.

"Citizen," this used to be a glorious, revolutionary term. It denoted a person over whom no one could rule in an uncontrolled fashion without in a skillful manner creating the impression in him that he almost ruled himself. To create this impression in those who were ruled used to be the aim of a demanding specialized job called politics. In actual fact the notion of a citizen ruling himself was and will be a myth.

Marxist analysis of power brought to light formerly unexplored relationships between the ruling power and the ownership of the means of production. This discovery, along with the interpretation of the history of mankind as the history of class struggles, prepared the socialist revolution from which a solution of the age-old problem of power was expected. Although the social revolution has succeeded in our country, the problem of power continues to exist. Although we took "the bull by the horns," and hold him, some one still kicks our backside and does not stop kicking. It seems that power, whoever exercises it, is subject to its own unbreakable laws of development and conduct. Power is a peculiar human phenomenon based on the fact that someone must command in any group of people and that even in a society solely composed of noble minds someone has to summarize knowledge derived from discussions and to formulate the necessary. Power is a specific human situation. It embraces those who rule and those who are ruled alike and it is unhealthy for both of them.

Thousands of years of mankind's experience have prompted man to try and find certain rules for controlling power, some kind of traffic regulations; this is what the system of formal democracy means, with all its feedbacks, control switches, and time limits. However, the interests of people endowed with power based on the possession of capital, on the force of arms, on favorable family connections, on a monopoly of production, etc., intervene in the clearly defined mechanism of government. Thus, the rules do not prevent the malady and a slight distortion of this statement can be easily used by others to make the vulgar claim that it is the rules of formal democracy which are the cause of the malady. Yet, the rules as such are neither capitalist nor socialist, they do not determine what ought to be done, but merely outline the manner in which decisions are made about what ought to be done. This is a human invention which,

essentially, renders governing more difficult. This invention favors those who are ruled, but it also saves the rulers from being shot when their government falls. This formal system of democracy does not produce too firm a government, but only the conviction that the next government might be an improvement on the preceding one. Thus, the government falls but the citizen is renewed. And vice-versa, wherever the government remains in power forever or for a long time, the citizen falls. Where does he fall? I shall not please our enemies and claim that the citizen falls at a place of execution. This fate is only in store for some dozens or for a few hundred citizens.

However, our enemies know that this suffices, because then follows the fall of the whole nation into fear, political indifference and civil resignation, petty everyday worries and small wishes, into dependence on lesser and lesser masters; in a word, it falls into vassalage so novel that it defies any explanation one might wish to give to a visitor from a foreign land. I believe that citizens no longer exist in our country. I have my reasons for this belief, reasons founded on my long experience working for newspapers and radio. I want to dwell on one recent example: this congress was not convened after the members of this organization had decided to meet but only after the master, having considered his problems, graciously gave his consent. In exchange he expects, as he has been accustomed to for thousands of years, that we will render tribute to his dynasty. I suggest that we should not. I suggest that we should examine the text of the Resolution and delete everything that smacks of the spirit of a vassal. In those countries which developed their culture by criticizing the regime, the writers must not forget this tradition and upbringing. I suggest, that every one who is to speak from this rostrum should always make his own proposals about solutions to matters which worry him. So, let us play this game of citizens, since we have been given permission to play it and to use this playground. And let us act for three whole days as if we were adult and had come of age.

Here I speak as a citizen of a state which I shall never renounce but in which I cannot live contentedly. I am thinking of civil affairs but I am in a tricky position; I am, at the same time, a member of the Communist Party and therefore I am not supposed to discuss Party affairs here, and I also would not wish to do so. But it so happens that in our country there is almost nothing left which does not become a Party matter at some stage of the debate. What am I to do when both—my Party and my Government—have done everything to fuse their affairs? In my opinion, this is a disadvantage for both of them. Moreover, it renders difficult the position of the citizens assembled here. Party members are bound to refrain from discussing crucial aspects of most questions in front of non-members and the latter have no access to meetings where, alone, one can seriously discuss these crucial problems; thus both Party members and non-members are limited in their basic civil freedom—to speak with one another as equals. This may even contravene Article 20 of the Constitution. However, I am disciplined and I withdraw to the civil field, and I shall confine my remarks to the Government; however, in those cases in which this term does not fit, and then alone, I shall refer to "ruling circles." This is a tested and older term which in spite of its seeming vagueness, is more precise than many other terms can be. From time immemorial it has connoted those who actually rule regardless of the function they exercize in a democratic stage setting, those whose power has its source off stage, in wealth, influential connections, a monopoly of production of services, the possession of arms, etc. This term also encompasses government from behind the scenes, sudden messages sent by special courier in the middle of the night, and pacts and laws voted on before they have been submitted to Parliament. Both our nations were, through history, prepared for socialism. And after the last war this state was restored as a political organism which had nothing else to do but to organize this socialism. I do not want to go into details, although these also are important; however, a different program really did not exist after 1945. One of the attributes postulated for this new regime was the unity of those ruled and of the rulers, and, in reality, their identity. The people and the government are one.

Now I would like to revert to my thoughts about the character of every power: its development and conduct are governed by inherent laws which can be changed neither by the person in power, nor by any class in power, since these are laws governing human conduct in a certain situation: laws for those in power. The first rule of power is that it wishes to continue to exist. It reproduces itself in increasingly precise reflections of its own image. Secondly, it becomes increasingly homogeneous, expelling all alien bodies until every part of it is a likeness of the whole, until every part is interchangeable, with the result that even a cell on the periphery of power can practically replace the whole of the center, and the individual cells can be interchanged without any peripheral consequences and without preventing the apparatus of power from functioning as before. This is because the apparatus of power is essentially designed not to react to a change of environment, to changes in altitude, to changes in the composition of the population, etc., but it is always designed to react to the same thing: to mold the environment to suit its own purposes, to make it uniform, permitting the apparatus always to use the same, very simple pattern. Thus power becomes more independent—and this is another law of its conduct—it does not canvass support but relies on itself, the center on the periphery and vice versa, with one being able, completely, to rely on the other, which they also are compelled to do since they form a

circle. No one can be eliminated from this circle, nor will it release anyone. Internal disagreements and transgressions also are liquidated internally.

Then comes another phase which I have termed "dynastization." At a favorable moment the ruling power convokes the legislative assembly and instructs it to embody its independent position in the Constitution. From then onward, the ruling power acts in accordance with the Constitution, whatever it does. And, since it does not put any undesired point on the agenda for 10, 20 or 50 years and, according to the Constitution, no one else can put it on the agenda, and (again according to the Constitution) no one else can convoke another legislative assembly, a dynasty is founded via the Constitution. This is a dynasty of a historically new type, because it preserves one important democratic principle: those who wish, may jump on its bandwagon. Thus the dynasty cannot become extinct on the male or on the distaff side.

From our point of view the most interesting aspect is one internal law of power, a very particular law of history which has been described in literature a thousand times over and which always concerns itself with the same way of treating people. The regime prefers people whose internal makeup is similar to its own. But because there are too few of them, it has to use others whom it molds to its own requirements. It is *natural* that those are most suitable for serving the regime who themselves lust for power, those who are obedient by nature, and those who have a bad conscience, people whose longing for wealth, profit, and advantages knows no moral limits. One can condition people who have to care for large families, those who were previously humbled and who then trustingly accept an offering to their new-found pride, and those who were born stupid. For a certain time under certain conditions and for certain purposes, various types of moral absolutists also can be used, as can unselfish but ill-informed enthusiasts such as myself. Essentially old-fashioned means are used to condition people: physical or psychic temptation, threats, compromising situations, denunciations, unjustified accusations, which they try to refute by demonstrating their loyalty; people can also be induced to form undesirable associations from which they are then saved in a hypocritical manner. The seeds of general distrust are sown. Trust is classified as trust of the first, second, or third degree—and it is assumed that the mass of people does not deserve trust. Information also has its grades of quality; on pink, green, or yellow paper, or in ordinary newsprint.

What I have said about the character of power is meant in the most general terms; I do not even necessarily have a socialist state in mind for I combine the concept of socialism with scientific direction. And the scientific theory of socialism could not be envisaged without the psychology of power: just as it cannot do without philosophy, political economy, or sociology, it cannot do without the psychology of power which applies the knowledge gained in individual and social psychology, in psycho-analysis, and in psycho-pathology.

I have left aside the questions of the class character of power, because it appears as part and parcel of the problem of power in general.

In our country too, we have witnessed the selection of men on the basis of their usefulness to the ruling power. Confidence was given to the obedient, to those who made no difficulties, to those who asked no questions which were not raised by the regime itself. At every stage of selection, the average man came out best. From the scene disappeared the more complex individuals, people with personal charm and above all those, who, because of their qualities and work used to constitute a silent and undefined standard of decency and public conscience. From political life disappeared people endowed with a sense of humor and with their personal ideas. The combination of words "politician–thinker," has lost its meaning; the word "movement" has a hollow sound if nothing moves. The fabric on which rests the intangible structure and personal culture of such human communities as parishes, plants, workshops was torn. Nothing was permitted to bear the stamp of a person's own work, the term of workshop was only kept in rare cases, principals of schools were sacked who were working on their own methods of education, managers of tile factories were dismissed who expressed a critical opinion about the surroundings of their factory. Cultural and sports clubs and societies with a good reputation were dissolved, institutions which, for some people, represented the whole scale of continuity in their parish, region and state.

Benjamin Klička, in his work *Wild Daja* said: "Remember, ability is an insult to your superior and therefore pretend to be as dumb as a doornail, if you want to live a long life and enjoy it in this land of ours." This quotation is forty years old and it was coined for a society prior to the social revolution. Yet, it seems to me that it only acquired its full validity in our country after this revolution and that every one has found out for himself how true it is. You may have noticed that all of us, Czechs and Slovaks, are inclined to feel that in our various jobs we are led by men less capable than ourselves. But all we do is to complain. The whole situation is obnoxious because the incapable, the absolute good-for-nothings, and the people with limited intelligence complain along with those who may have a reason to do so. The former also say that they must not do this or are not allowed to do that. In other words, a false and damaging unity has grown up between people who by no means belong together. We are all united by the most miserable connecting link one might think of—our common disgust despite our different motives.

The practical people have found an alternative field of activity, the impractical are wearing the halos of martyrs. In literature depression, nihilism, and spiritual decay are the fashion. An orgy of snobs. Even the intelligent are growing dumb. From time to time the instinct of self-preservation asserts itself—people feel like lashing out to left and right. But when they look up and see what is above them and then look down and see that there are people ready to stamp on them, they must ask themselves: "My God, for whom are we doing this?" And now let us remember that those had the greatest success in the past 20 years who

offered the weakest resistance to all demoralizing influences which power produces. Let us also remember that those whose conscience does trouble them find no support in the ruling power, nor recourse to the laws which, according to the letter, ought to protect them. According to the letter, it might appear as if a code of rights and duties really existed in our country which "ensures the free and general development and assertion of the personality of the citizen, and, at the same time, the consolidation and development of socialist society." (Article 19 of the Constitution.) I have found in my work in newspapers and radio that in actual fact citizens rarely invoke their constitutional rights because anyone, even at the periphery of power, can attach conditions to the exercise of these rights, conditions which are not included in the Constitution and which, in common decency, cannot be written into it.

Often of late I have read the Constitution and have arrived at the conclusion that it is badly compiled and perhaps because of this, has lost the respect of citizens and authorities alike. As far as style is concerned the Constitution is wordy, but is very vague in many of its important provisions. To quote an example which bears on the sphere of thought and work chiefly connected with our Union, Article 16 reads: "The entire cultural policy of Czechoslovakia, the furthering of knowledge, education and teaching, will be conducted in the spirit of the scientific world view of Marxism-Leninism and in close connection with the life and work of the people." Aside from the fact that every good educator will regard it as a matter of course and that the term "education" implies a connection with work and life, it is not clear which agency, or perhaps which court, is to decide if a certain opinion is scientific, inasmuch as the term "science" implies a movement and change of opinions in keeping with the progress of knowledge and inasmuch as this flexibility is contrary to the immutable and unequivocal nature of the concepts required by every legal norm. This contradiction in terms could only be reconciled if "scientific world view" were to be interpreted as a mere collection of phrases; on the other hand, this would give rise to the question whether our state ought to be regarded as a state governed in a doctrinaire, rather than in the scientific manner which our legislators most certainly envisaged. Another example which is connected with my own subject:

Article 28 reads: "In harmony with the interests of the working people, freedom of expression is guaranteed for all citizens in all branches of society's life, especially freedom of speech and of the press." In my opinion, these freedoms are in themselves in the interest of the working people and therefore I regard this passage as superfluous and even directly misleading, because the interpretation of that which represents the interests of the working people is left to each individual. I believe that if a specialist found it necessary to use this wording, he would regard it as necessary to specify that which represents, and that which does not represent, respectively, the interests of the working people, and I also believe that a provident legislator would equally eschew an illustrative list and would insist on an enumeration. Personally, I would prefer a succinct formulation whose validity could not be called into question. A clear and brief formulation alone endows the laws with the weight of a generally known proverb which is eventually accepted as a generally valid rule; if this is the case, the general consciousness of right and wrong functions to a degree almost permitting one to dispense with courts to find that which is right. The prolix language and the fuzzy ideas of the Constitution render it impossible to enforce. In this manner the supreme legal norm becomes a program and an expression of good intentions, rather than a legal guarantee of the rights of the citizens. Moreover, in my opinion, the Constitution must have the same function as any other legal norm and, in addition, it is the supreme norm, no other norm of a lower rank, whether ordinance, statute, decree, or operative order, should restrict its validity or detract from its clarity.

I have explained my views about the character, development, and behavior of every ruling power and tried to show that the control mechanisms, which should check it, fail, so that the citizen loses his respect for himself and objectively loses also his status as citizen. If this state of affairs lasts as long as it has in our country it is only natural that it becomes deep-rooted in the minds of many people, in the philosophy of life especially of the youngest generation. The latter has not learned in the course of its studies or through practical experience, that there is a certain continuity in human efforts to achieve a more perfect democracy. If this state of affairs were to continue any longer (and if the natural defensive reactions of men did not work simultaneously against it) the character of our nation would change in the next generation. Instead of a cultural community possessing the power of resistance, an amorphous mass of people would arise, which could be easily dominated, and which would be child's play to govern even for foreigners. If we were to allow this to happen the thousand years of our resistance would have been in vain.

In the belief that none of us was born to be easily dominated, I propose that the Union of Writers, perhaps in cooperation with the Union of Journalists and other similar associations, take the initiative and ask the Czechoslovak Academy of Sciences for its expert analysis of the Constitution. Should it prove necessary, the Union could begin a movement for changes in the Constitution, for example by recommending that members visit election meetings during the next election campaign, ventilate these problems there, and see to it that the elected deputies are aware of them. But perhaps every one of us should visit his deputy even sooner and ask him to take up this theme in the National Assembly.

When I stand here and talk I do not have by any means the feeling of freedom which a man should have when he says freely what he wishes to say. I have rather the feeling that I am exploiting somewhat cowardly a kind of armistice between the citizen and the regime, that I am trespassing against the "closed season" extended to writers and artists. How long it will last I do not know—till the winter or perhaps only till tomorrow. Just as I do not believe that the citizen and power can be identical, that the ruled and the rulers can sing the same song, I do not believe that art and power can ever feel well together. They never will; they cannot; they are different; they do not match. What is possible and what gives us hope for the success of our efforts is that both sides will become aware of the situation and will work out decent rules for mutual contacts. The writers are people, and the ruling circles are also made up of people. If any one of us should by any chance find himself in a body wielding political power he will find himself exposed to its internal organization and will worry about himself. A freedom-loving person who is also a little egoistic and thinks about his own cleanliness a tiny little bit more than about the dirt of the world, a person who realizes how complicated matters are but who madly desires that they be simple, such as a poet or a musician, will never join the state power. A poet-minister is nothing more than a gracious bow made by power when it is in a good mood. I am talking about incompatibility and do not refer to hostility.

I shall recount to you an incident about which I have been repeatedly thinking during the past two days. As a member of the editorial board of *Literární Noviny* I attended in March last year a conference at the ideological department of the Central Committee of the Party. The conference did not take a favorable turn for us. I was seated at the table exactly opposite to the secretary of the Central Committee, Comrade Jiří Hendrych, and so I had the opportunity of observing face-to-face the features of a man older than myself—when I was a boy they used to tell me at home to greet people so much older than I—the face of a man who, until now more an institution than an individual, has his personal, professional, and perhaps other worries, certainly greater than my own, and has had to stick it out for much longer than I. I was not very smart at the conference. I wanted to talk with absolute frankness but I was frightened, I kept backing down, I thought that they misunderstood my motives. They whispered something among themselves; I succumbed to a feeling of hopelessness. I felt humiliated and the result was that I lost my temper. On my way home, apart from some rather confused thoughts, a completely new idea crossed my mind in connection with the conference, a rather disquieting apprehension which confused the division of everything into two clear fields, "WE and THEY." I felt that I was touched by a breeze coming from the unknown, that I was beginning to grasp human distress caused by a certain situation not covered by those concepts so frequently used in our country, like "class viewpoint," "opposition," etc. These are battle terms. Naturally, I had to help myself by taking a firm stand, if only a temporary one, in order to be able to act at all, and I said to myself that the distress is part of the game. It is so because he wants it, although he does not have to, and I want to be part of the newspaper board. But it provided me with a new impulse, it made me think about power as a human situation. I shall end this digression and shall continue where I left off. Writers are human, and ruling circles are also composed of people. The writers do not want anarchy; they too wish to live in pleasant towns, they too would like to have nice apartments, and wish the same for others. They wish for prosperous industries and trade, and all this is impossible without the organized activities of the government.

Art cannot give up the theme of government, for governing means making continuous direct and indirect decisions, through administrative acts, involving the life of man, his well-being, and his disappointments, everything he thinks about and which cannot be decided. And the activity of power overlaps the activity of art, especially in what cannot be decided and yet decisions have to be made. Therefore art must not give up its criticism of the government because governments, whatever their nature, whatever their customs may be, are the product of the culture of their nations.

Our government pleases the artists when it praises them for having, for instance, designed a good pavilion for the World Exposition. The government certainly likes to do this and such declarations also have a political aspect. And perhaps the government actually means it. However, the artists need not be pleased with the government. Such a pavilion which enjoys, in a certain sense, the rights of cultural extraterritoriality only shows what the same creative workers could do at home if they were allowed to do so, if they carried the same weight in their own land. Thus I must ask myself whether we all do not serve an illusion when we build beautiful pavilions representative of our culture? When we know that our best work is unwanted, that we do everything only by the grace of God, that our time is running out and we don't even know the date. Everything that our culture has achieved, everything good that men have done or created in our country, all the good products, the good buildings, the well conceived ideas from our laboratories and institutes, all this has been achieved rather despite our government's behavior. It was done literally in spite of them. But I don't want to be unjust; I am convinced that even in the best movement within these ruling circles, every attempt to improve the style, has to be paid for dearly, requires sacrifice, and when it has a visible result this has to be won by persistence.

Well then, what direction and what leadership? I see only a brake. Not for decades after reading one of their expositions have I felt like: "Look, what a splendid idea which has never occurred to anyone." On the contrary, I have often said to myself gloomily: "So what, everybody knows it anyway!" And most often have I asked myself how I should save my own ideas, how I could outfox them when I cannot persuade them, because I never see them. I see and hear how power gives way only when it sees too strong an opposition. No arguments convince it. Only failure, repeated failure when it wants to do things the old way. Failure which costs us all money and tries our nerves. I see a continuous will and also a continuous danger that the bad old days may return, for what is the purpose of telling us that we have the Union, the "Litfond", the publishing houses, and the newspapers? A threat that they would take them away from us if

we did not behave. If I were to admit that this was their right I would be saying what my sister used to say: he gave—he took. But are they really the masters of everything? And what do they leave to the authority of others? Nothing? Then we need not exist. But they should say so. Then it should be perfectly clear that basically a handful of people wants to decide about the existence or non-existence of everything, about all that should be done, thought, or felt. This demonstrates the position which culture has in our country; this, and not the exhibited individual works, shows the position achieved by the culture of the nation.

Recently we have often had the opportunity of hearing that the ruling circles recognize a certain degree of autonomy for culture in its own field. But culture should not be annoyed, they say, if it is reproved as soon as it ventures into the field of politics. They accuse us of breaking our own rule that each kind of work should be carried out by specialists. It is true that politics should also be made by specialists, but how are we to be certain who the specialists are? I doubt it and I prefer to describe the reason for my doubts figuratively. A doctor is certainly a specialist. He is more capable than we of diagnosing our illness, he is able to give us expert treatment, but he can certainly not say that he knows better than we ourselves how we feel under his treatment. But only a doctor who is grossly inexpert in his field would carry out a dangerous operation on us without having obtained our permission. Autonomy of art and culture? This is nothing more than a slogan and a frequently used tactic. Today one thing is valid, tomorrow another; they seem to differ but one does not have to be an expert to see that it is one and the same thing coming from the same barrel equipped with two taps.

Just as I do not feel very secure in a cultural-political situation which the regime apparently can drive to a state of conflict, neither do I feel safe as a citizen outside this room, outside this playground. Nothing happens to me, and nothing has happened. That sort of thing is not done any more. Should I be grateful? I don't want to. I am afraid. I see no firm guarantee. It is true that I see better work in the courts but the judges themselves do not see any hard and fast guarantees. I see that better work is done by the public prosecutor's office, but do the public prosecutors have guarantees and do they feel safe? If you like, I should be glad to interview some of them for the newspapers. Do you think it would be published? I would not be afraid to interview even the Prosecutor General and ask him why unjustly sentenced and rehabilitated people do not regain their original rights as a matter of course, why the national committees are reluctant to return to them their apartments or houses—but it will not be published. Why has no one properly apologized to these people, why do they not have the advantages of the politically persecuted, why do we haggle with them about money? Why can we not live where we want to? Why cannot the tailors go for three years to Vienna and the painters for thirty years to Paris and be able to return without being considered as criminals?

Our Parliament obviously has a legal maxim: *Nullum crimen sine lege,* no crime without law. It implies that it can produce for the state as many criminals as it pleases. Why aren't those people, who don't like it in our country, allowed to go to Hell and why don't those people, who do not wish to see the democratic reforms, now in their initial stage, brought to a conclusion, leave?

True enough, some new and better laws have been passed. It is also true that others are pending. It is also true that the new press law has made a clean sweep of matters. Also an amendment of the laws concerning other civil freedoms is in the preparatory stage—the freedom of assembly and association. The draft is being prepared by the Ministry of the Interior—but an article concerning it and already set by *Literární Noviny* was confiscated. I see no guarantees.

What guarantees? I do not know. And here I stop because at this point I am in great doubt, whether the ruling circles themselves, the government and its individual members possess those guarantees of their own civil rights without which it is impossible to create, even to create a policy. At this point my characterization of internal affairs this evening closes and I can only refer to the formulation already used by others—about the millstones which sometimes grind even those who set them in motion in the first place.

The measure of the real cultural level which a country has attained is the manner in which organized actions of the state are carried out. It is, therefore, more a question of the cultural level of politics than of a good cultural policy.

Where the policy of the politicians is cultural the writers, artists, scientists, and engineers need not weaken themselves by a tug of war for their working rights, rank rights, sectoral rights, club rights, union rights. They don't need to stress the specifics of their work. They do not need to rouse the antagonism of other citizens, the workers, the peasants, the officials, who have the same rights as they but have no way of forcing their thoughts through the sieve of censorship, and who cannot present their sorrow or their moral pathos in an artistic construction, color, aphorism, or in a poem or musical work. Uncultured politics, not bad cultural politics, evokes centers of struggle for freedom and yet it is offended when one talks about it. It does not understand that freedom only exists in places where ones does not need to speak about it, and is annoyed because people talk about what they see. Yet, instead of changing what people see, it wants to change their eyes. And in the meantime we are losing what alone is worth all the pathos, namely the dream of a government identical with the citizen, the dream of a citizen who governs himself almost alone. Is this dream realizable?

We have achieved some partial successes on the way to this dream which has been the aim of the nation since the beginning of history. One of these successes was the rise of an independent Czechoslovakia, a gain made by progressive popular forces and progressive politicians, which has not been so far expressed in the draft of the resolution and I propose that it be done. A stage was formed which, despite the imperfections present in the historical category of regimes existing at that time, brought with it a high level of democracy, did not accumulate any aversion to speak about the ideas of socialism in the minds and thoughts of its citizens, to the socialism which was realizable only in the second stage of the state's development. The continuity of the conception of a social state changed after the war into a program of socialism. The special conditions under which socialism began to be implemented, and above all the position of socialism in a country where it already existed and the level of knowledge of socialism at that time, resulted in certain deformities occurring in our country in the course of its realization. Certain events took place which were not solely explicable by the climate in this country and which stem neither from the character of the people nor from its history.

When we talk about this period and seek explanations as to why we lost so much morally and materially, why we are economically backward, the ruling circles say that it was necessary. I believe that from our point of view it was not necessary. Perhaps it was necessary for the spiritual development of the organs of the regime, of the organs which compelled all the supporters of socialism to experience this development with them. It is necessary to understand that in the course of twenty years no human problem has been solved in our country—starting with elementary needs such as housing, schools, and economic prosperity and ending with the finer requirements of life which cannot be provided by the undemocratic systems of the world, for instance the feeling of full value in the society, the subordination of political decisions to ethical criteria, belief in the value of even less important work, the need for confidence among men, development of the education of the entire people. I fear that we have not risen to the world stage and I feel that the name of our republic has lost its good reputation. I see that we have not given humanity any original ideas and any good inspirations, that we do not have e.g. our own ideas on how to produce and not to be suffocated by the results of production, that we follow apathetically the dehumanized civilizations of the American type, that we repeat the errors of the East and West, that our society has not an organ which would be charged with looking for a short cut in the ramshackle and foggy development of the modern style of life.

By this I do not wish to say that we have lived in vain, that none of this has any value. It has value. But the question is whether it is only the value of forwarning. Even in this case the total knowledge of mankind would progress. But was it necessary to make a country which knew precisely the dangers for its culture into an instrument for this kind of lesson? I suggest that in the resolution we should state what progressive Czechoslovak culture already knew in the thirties, or at least what it sensed.

I have recently met many extraordinarily fresh people, several individuals and some collectives, both work and interest collectives. Their resistance was remarkable by which they demonstrated that they have withstood the influence of power and follow the natural principles of better people—to work hard, keep one's word, not betray, not let oneself be poisoned. To these altogether classical qualities of better people a new quality has been added, namely a lack of the sense of distance between the subordinates and the superiors, between those holding lower and those holding higher positions. Strangely enough this revolting quality of today's slackers, when added to the classical good qualities, has the effect of a new trait of man not obliged to humiliate himself in order to earn his daily bread.

Finally, I should like to express what has certainly been made clear throughout my speech, namely that my criticism of power in this state is not a criticism of socialism because I am not convinced that such a development was necessary here and because I do not identify this power with the concept of socialism in the way in which this power tries to identify itself with it. Not even its fate need be identical. And if the people who exercise this power—I relieve them for a little while of this power and appeal to them as to individual people with their private feelings and thoughts—were to come here and ask us the question whether this dream is realizable they would have to take the following answer as the expression of our goodwill and at the same time of our supreme civic loyalty: "I do not know."

# COMMUNIQUE OF THE PLENARY SESSION OF THE CENTRAL COMMITTEE OF THE COMMUNIST PARTY OF CZECHOSLOVAKIA, 26-27 SEPTEMBER 1967

*Excerpt*

(*Rudé Právo,* 28 September 1967)

Together with topical questions of the further development of economy and socialist democracy, the Central Committee also dealt with certain problems in the ideological sphere. These negotiations were brought about by the course and results of the Fourth Congress of the Czechoslovak Writers' Union, particularly the statements of several congress participants, which supplied food for anticommunist propaganda and naturally called forth the justified concern of the party and the broad public. The Central Committee proceeded from the position that the Writers' Congress reflected to a certain extent many contemporary problems in the entire field of ideology, education, and culture, and the strong pressure exerted, from abroad as a result of the sharpening of the international situation. It was a signal indicating what any weakening of the party's leading role in this field and any inconsistency in the realization of the party policy could lead to.

The party's conscious endeavors toward an all-round upsurge in our society in the recent years also gave scope to the upsurge of esthetic values in arts and literature. Important works of art were created and, together with the new names of the emerging writers' generation, they testify that the development of our literature has progressed. However, the differentiation of creative opinions was joined by ideological differentiation, and various creative groupings were formed some of which had power ambitions. Some of the writers who had bound their whole lives to the policy of the party manifested insufficient preparedness; they became dominated by uncertainty and insufficiently evaluated the new processes now taking place in our society. They began to give scope to ideological adversaries; in this situation the writers' union did not rely consistently in its activity on the resolution of the 13th party congress on the further development of socialist culture and gave outlet to individuals who formulated their own cultural-political platforms, removed from or completely foreign to socialism. In this negative process an unpropitious active role was also played by certain party members; a special role was played by the editorial board of *Literárni Noviny* which for some time polarized bearers of standpoints contradictory to the policy of our party. Only thus could the fourth congress of the Czechoslovak Writers' Union partly become the scene of opinions foreign to the party and the republic and be misused against the will of the majority of the writers present for the expression of trends foreign to the socialist system and the basis of our policy.

The party Central Committee unambiguously rejected the antiparty, incorrect, and confused opinions debasing the 20 years of work by the party and the people, idealizing the situation during the pre-Munich republic, depriving ideas of freedom, democracy, and humanism of their socialist content, making light of the importance of the basic class conflict in the world, and introducing chaos into the relations of culture, ideology, and politics. The Central Committee differentiated carefully between this approach and the positive approach of the great majority of writers to the solution of the interests of our literature and the development of our society, especially because only a small part of the writers took part in the disparagement of the writers in the eyes of the public.

At the same time we must not permit the function and import of literature and its creators to be confused with the writers' organization. The party regards the whole writers' community as its close aktiv which plays an important role in the accumulation of knowledge by the party and the society and in the forming of socialist human relations, socialist ethics, and morals. The party respects the specific nature of arts, the laws governing their development, and the freedom of creators. It respects real art as an ally which helps form the complete socialist man, and it respects the creators of such art. The cooperation and unity of politics and culture and politics and literature is not a relationship of subordination; culture and literature are not dictated by politics. Both these spheres of human activity are linked in our society by a single ideology and single aim; this forms their unity, their dialectical unity and cooperation, which contains discussion, polemies, and confrontation. However, discussions must always be permeated by the realization of the uniform aim and the Marxist ideological basis on which the road toward this aim is built.

The party Central Committee has approved of a series of measures which should strengthen the close comradely ties between the party and the writers, establish the necessary prerequisites for the development of creative work and its implementation without any narrow group or even ideologically foreign influences, and start the process of the further crystallization of the character of our socialist literature and the entire Czechoslovak culture.

The Czechoslovak Communist Party Central Committee expelled I. Klima, A. J. Liehm, and L. Vaculík from the ranks of the party for procedure incompatible with party membership. The Central Committee removed J. Procházka from the function of candidate member of the Czechoslovak Communist

Party Central Committee for political errors. Since, despite the patient endeavors of the party organs, *Literární Noviny* was completely out of the control of the Czechoslovak Writers' Union and became the platform of oppositional political views, the Czechoslovak Communist Party Central Committee advised its transfer into the sphere of the Ministry of Culture and Information.

The Central Committee adopted concrete resolutions on the questions under discussion. It also approved of the party's foreign political activities.

At the conclusion of the session the main tasks of the party and the topical political questions were dealt with by Comrade Antonín Novotný.

# ON THE PARTY PROGRAM

Speech of Aarne Saarinen, Chairman,
Communist Party of Finland,
at the June 1967 Meeting of the Central Committee
(Abridged from *Kansan Uutiset,* Helsinki, 12-13 September 1967)

The first socialist state came into being fifty years ago in a comparatively underdeveloped country. The socialist or proletarian revolution was accomplished at a moment when factory and office workers made up less than 20 per cent of the population (17 per cent in 1913). Two years ago, factory and office workers accounted for 70 per cent of the population of Finland, but we do not yet have the political prerequisites for a socialist revolution. Despite this tremendous difference, we tend to think only in terms of the pattern of the October Socialist Revolution. That is an ideological tradition which is preserved in the thoughts and sentiments of Communists by virtue of strong solidarity and of the situation that obtained in the working-class movement for a long time.

For many decades, the international and internal position of the Soviet Union, and the situation in the working-class movement in other countries were such that Social Democrats regarded Communists as their chief enemy. On the other hand, Communists were very careful not to adopt a Social Democratic view on practically any issue. It was considered vitally necessary to draw clear-cut demarcation lines. This state of things ruled out any fruitful discussion between the main trends of the working-class movement and schematized Marxist thought also within the Communist movement.

As a result, one Social Democratic party after another departed from socialist objectives or abandoned them for good. Gradually they became citadels of anti-communism, champions of bourgeois policy, and their leaders turned into loyal managers of capitalist affairs. They departed from socialism so far that we Communists would be prepared to hail even the re-emergence of Kautskian ideas in the Social Democratic movement.

The impression now is that the time of the "major discord" in the Finnish working-class movement is past, we hope for good. But we must also overcome the "minor discord." Naturally, the after-effects of that period are still strongly felt on both sides. Distrust, fear and caution still hamper fruitful cooperation and prevent the victory of socialist ideas. We must strive to overcome them precisely because the return of the Social Democratic Party to a socialist policy is essential for a socialist Finland.

An indispensable condition for winning over the majority of the working class and Social Democrats for Socialism is that no one should have any doubts left as to the desire of the Communist Party to achieve socialism in a peaceful and democratic way.

The natural exception are the extreme rightists, whose political existence directly presupposes their disbelief in this.

The proposition that our program should envisage two alternatives—peaceful and non-peaceful—is inconsistent and is not substantiated by concrete arguments. Our program must indicate all the *prerequisites* which we think are necessary for the peaceful transition to socialism. If we fail to indicate them, we must work out a program of non-peaceful transition. But we should not appear as double-faced, with two programs, for no one would know by what means we actually intend to achieve socialism. The matter concerns the program of *our* Party, the *will* of our Party and its view of the *conditions* in which we would think it possible to accomplish a peaceful and democratic transition to socialism. All "ifs" and "buts" are harmful and reflect on our will and our views. This is not the way to win new supporters of socialism.

Some may say that the exclusion of the second alternative could incapacitate our Party if the situation changed, and that it would be dangerous to lull Party members with the belief in the possibility of a peaceful transition only. Reference is readily made to Greece. But here again the history of Greece, its economic, social and political conditions are mechanistically applied to Finland. There are many essential differences between Greece and Finland. If we are to prepare for a situation such as obtains, for instance, in Greece today, we should set about creating illegal organizations side by side with legal ones, setting up armed groups, etc.

We are drafting our program with due regard to the present-day conditions—Finnish conditions and not those existing in Greece or any other country and considerably differing from ours. At the same time we proceed from the possibility of averting a third world war.

Programs grow obsolete quite soon. Therefore we should bear in mind that this program, too, is not being worked out for a very long period. Should radical changes occur, the program must be revised.

Of vital importance are definition and characterization of the transitional period, the question of gradual development and development by leaps, the question of transition from quantity to quality. We find ourselves in a difficult position as soon as we begin searching for an answer to the question when feudal society became capitalist, or whether "capitalist reforms" were effected within feudal society, when the nobility and the clergy held political power.

The transition from capitalism to socialism is undeniably a more profound process than the transition from feudalism to capitalism. It is a fact, however, that the beginning of this last transitional stage was particularly violent and bloody, as the history of Britain and France shows.

In Finland, where the transition from semi-feudal to capitalist society took place much later, the transitional period was comparatively long and peaceful. Capitalist development started in our country at the beginning of the 19th century, and the capitalist "break-through" did not occur until the end of the century. But the changes in the political superstructure which accorded with these economic changes were first effected in 1906, when our parliamentary institutions were reformed. Before that, political power was wielded, in addition to the tsar, by the nobility, the clergy, the peasantry and the nascent bourgeoisie. Thus, political power was exercised by forces representing an outgoing society.

As you know, the reform of parliamentary institutions went further than envisaged by capitalism and the bourgeois power. But that was because the working class had strengthened its positions and organized to an extent enabling it to make a major contribution to the reform.

It appears that the question of what socialist and non-socialist reforms are holds pride of place in theoretical debates. We must take a realistic, practical-policy view of this. In any case, it is a fact that Big Business and its political spokesmen are very uneasy about the increasing independent and direct participation of the state in investment, production and foreign trade. I do not think they are sounding the alarm over "contraband socialism" for no reason at all.

We can in any case speak of creating prerequisites for socialism. It is an essential condition for building a socialist society that the socialist forces should hold political power. There is hardly any disagreement on this point. But before this becomes possible there can already be a considerable number of "socialist elements" in the material basis of society and in the organizations adjoining it.

Indisputably, the discussion of the program and its final adoption will play a very important role in the life and development of our Party. Our opponents and enemies, as well as shady individuals and anti-Communists in the working-class movement look forward to serious controversies during the discussion. Whether their hopes come true or not will be a test of our maturity.

# FOUR DOCUMENTS OF THE FRENCH COMMUNIST PARTY ON THE GENERAL ELECTIONS

A. JOINT COMMUNIQUE BY THE PCF AND THE FGDS, 20 DECEMBER 1966*
B. JOINT COMMUNIQUE BY THE PCF AND PSU, 7 JANUARY 1967*
C. 30 MARCH RESOLUTION OF THE CENTRAL COMMITTEE, PCF**
D. REMARKS BY WALDECK ROCHET AT THE CENTRAL COMMITTEE MEETING**

*Complete Text; **Abridged Text
(A. Le Monde, 22 December 1966; B. L'Humanité, 9 January 1967;
C. L'Humanité, 1 April 1967; D. L'Humanité, 3 April 1967.)

## A. JOINT COMMUNIQUE BY THE PCF AND FGDS, 20 DECEMBER 1966

The delegation of the Federation of the Democratic and Socialist Left and the delegation of the French Communist Party have examined the conditions under which the struggle of the forces of the Left against "personal power" and for an authentic democratic regime should be carried out.

The delegation of the French Communist Party upheld the proposals of its Central Committee according to which "the elaboration of a joint majority and government program between the parties of the Left, and the conclusion of an agreement of reciprocal withdrawal on the national level in favor of the candidate of the Left who is placed best in the first electoral round, would constitute the best means to eliminate "personal power" and to establish a true democracy satisfying the interests of the workers, the people and the nation. It [the CP delegation] regretted that its proposal of a joint program—a goal that the Communist Party still adheres to—was not accepted. It declared that "the Communist candidates will not withdraw in favor of candidates of the Right and that they will remain on the ballot in the second round against both Gaullist candidates and any other reactionary candidate."

The delegation of the Federation of the Democratic and Socialist Left set forth the decisions of its Executive Committee according to which "the assertion of the character of the Federation based on the program of the 14th of July corresponds to the interests of democracy, whereas the elaboration of a joint program would presuppose that all differences existing within the Left had been resolved." Confirming that the withdrawal [of the lesser placed Left candidate] has priority for the Left, it [the Executive Committee] recalled that "in order to assure the defeat of the Gaullist candidates when no candidate of the Left is in the position to win, it would be necessary not to exclude withdrawal in favor of a Republican resolutely hostile to 'personal power.' "

The two delegations agreed that on these points the two organizations which they represent reserve their freedom of evaluation and action.

For the first electoral round, the two delegations confirmed that each group would enter the battle with its own program and candidates.

For the second round, in all the districts where the Left is in a position to win, the two groups will call on the voters to assure the success of the best placed candidate of the Left by universal voting. In order to apply this rule and to study the particular cases, they [the two groups] will examine together the situation the day after the first round.

The two delegations have, however, stated important points of convergences between the goals of their organizations.

Priority among their joint goals is given to the struggle against "personal power." The Gaullist Regime must be eliminated. It is incompatible with democracy and constitutes the major obstacle to an expansion of liberties, to economic and social progress, and to the enactment of a consistent policy of peace and disarmament. Its disappearance would imply the defining of joint perspectives made possible through the establishment of points of convergence between the programs of the two organizations and the recognition of joint goals allowing the citizens to determine in full clarity in the second electoral round the reasons for their choice of the candidate of the Left.

The two delegations deem necessary a revision of the Constitution in terms of the removal or revision of the articles used by the President of the Republic to impose "personal power." They agree to guarantee and develop individual and collective liberties: independence of the judiciary; freedom of information and a democractic status for the ORTF [French Radio and Television]; a protection of the powers of local communities; removal of the limitations of the right to strike; recognition of the role of the trade union sector in enterprises; broadening of the competence of enterprise committees; material and moral promotion of women; annulment of legislative texts against contraception.

The two delegations affirm that there can be neither true democracy nor a happy future for France as long as those investments are not considered primary which would enable the country to participate effectively in the peaceful competition between nations and to give to all French citizens the means to satisfy their most legitimate needs. For this reason, the two delegations oppose to the priority given to nuclear armament the fundamental priorities of the right to housing, public health, and, above all, national education and scientific research. The interests of the nation demand, in effect, equal opportunities for the young who will receive the means to prepare their future by the democratic reform of the instruction system and by making available to the national educational system the necessary funds, with due respect to the principles of the undenominational character of the State and the schools.

Denouncing the delays accumulated by the Gaullist Regime in all fields of economic activity and social life, the two delegations consider indispensable a policy of expansion and progress. Such a policy should be based on an economic and social plan democratically elaborated and decided, destined to replace the Fifth Plan and having as essential points: nationalization of armament industries and business banks and the democratic management of national enterprises; the revaluation of wages, salaries, pensions and retirement pay, in conformity with the increase in productivity; defense of laws assuring social protection; full employment; the right for a happy old age and the progressive lowering of the retirement age; a fiscal reform foreseeing the taxation of large incomes and an easing of the taxes hitting wage earners and the less privileged groups; a policy of land management taking into account human needs and regional realities; an agricultural policy based on cooperation, modernization of agriculture, the improvement of the conditions of rural life and a just remuneration of peasant labor.

The delegations do not conceal their differences on important points of foreign policy. But they declare themselves in favor of all initiatives leading to general, simultaneous and controlled disarmament (notably through France's return to the Conference in Geneva); to the development of peaceful coexistence and political, economic and cultural relations with all countries; to a negotiated settlement of international conflicts. They consider necessary the immediate cessation of American bombing of North Vietnam and the return of peace to this area through the application of the Geneva Agreements. They proclaim their fundamental hostility to the "force de frappe," and their will to work toward France's signature of the Moscow agreement and to oppose the manufacture and proliferation of nuclear arms. Hostile to Germany's access to nuclear armament, they support the establishment of European and international collective security, and the recognition of the Oder-Neisse line.

This confrontation of viewpoints in a cordial atmosphere permitted the affirmation of important points of convergence and a basis of joint action for the realization of joint goals in the struggle against "personal power" and for democracy. Thus it opens up perspectives favorable to the French people.

## B. JOINT COMMUNIQUE BY THE PCF AND PSU, 7 JANUARY 1967

The delegations of the French Communist Party (PCF) and the United Socialist Party (PSU) met to examine the conditions in which the Left must fight to eliminate the de Gaulle regime and establish a political and social democracy opening the way to socialism.

The two parties regard the agreement concluded on December 20 between the Federation of the Democratic and Socialist Left (FGDS) and the French Communist Party as an important and positive move creating a new situation and strengthening the Left opposition.

The two parties have agreed on the following measures in view of the forthcoming general election:

–In the first round each party will go into action with its own program and its candidates.

–In the second round, the two parties will, on the basis of the agreement concluded between the PCF and the FGDS, call on the voters in all electoral districts where the Left can win to ensure the success of the Left candidate who has polled the greatest number of votes.

–In the other electoral districts the two parties will prevent a return to the disastrous alliances of the past by jointly casting their votes for the Left candidate who has polled the greatest number of votes, and at the same time against the Gaullist and other reactionary candidates.

To implement these measures and study specific cases concerning them, the two parties will examine the situation after the first round.

The two parties are agreed that the elaboration of a common majority and government program by the two Left-wing parties remains the best means of strengthening the trend for popular unity and of establishing a democracy meeting the interests of the working people and the nation.

After the general election the two parties will carry forward the work they have begun with a view to overcoming existing differences and to increasing their contribution to the common program of the entire Left.

## C. 30 MARCH RESOLUTION OF THE CENTRAL COMMITTEE, PCF

The results of the general election constitute a major political victory for the French Communist Party and the Left parties generally. The election creates favorable conditions for new gains by the alliance of democratic forces, so that they can defeat the present regime and establish a genuinely democratic government.

The main features of the March election are the following:

1. Within the framework of a general advance of the Left, the PCF registered a gain of more than a million votes. The number of Communist deputies increased from 41 to 72 plus a deputy from the CP of Guadeloupe. By confirming the CP as the principal democratic force of the country, over five million voters approved its democratic program of social progress and peace. They endorsed the Communists' unflagging effort for the alliance of all democratic and national forces on the basis of a common government program.

2. The overall success of the Left parties is

indicative of the electorate's approval of the alliance formed by them, particularly of the agreement concluded between the Communist Party and the Federation of the Democratic and Socialist Left (FGDS) on December 20, 1966.

On March 12 the common candidates nominated in line with the agreement obtained, as a general rule, the votes cast for the Left parties in the first round. Indeed, they exceeded that number in many constituencies. This proved that the alliance of the Left parties is a decisive factor in uniting all republicans. It enables them to rally the majority of the population for action on their side in the near future.

3. The Gaullist regime suffered a telling reverse. Despite enormous spending on propaganda, its candidates in the first ballot marked time, polling 38 per cent of the votes. In the second ballot they plainly retreated in comparison with the 1962 election. Reduced to a minority in France, the Gaullist deputies retained a precarious majority in the National Assembly due only to the overseas mandates tainted by widespread frauds.

The working people and the democrats condemned the government's anti-democratic policy, a policy of social retrogression.

4. The Democratic Center, hoping for a reactionary succession to the de Gaulle regime and oriented toward subservience to the U.S. imperialists, was condemned by the electorate.

With the general election over, it remains the goal of the democratic forces to end monopoly power and replace it by genuine democracy. This calls for the early winning of the majority by the forces of progress.

With the general election over, it is possible to prepare for a democratic succession to Gaullism by drawing up a common government program to be applied by a stable government of democratic alliance capable of defeating every reactionary maneuver and of embarking on a policy of peace and social progress meeting the interests of the people and the nation.

With this aim in view, the CC PCF renews the proposals it made to the FGDS before the first ballot for a common government program that would become the contract of the majority of tomorrow.

To win the confidence of those Frenchmen who waver or are still influenced by the Gaullist regime, the Left parties should show that they are resolved to fight in common, not only in order to end the regime of personal power, but also to rule the country in the interest of the people.

The Communists are willing to assume every responsibility to the cause of democratic and national renovation, including those at the government level.

In the near future, account will have to be taken of the more favorable situation that has shaped since March 12 and at the same time of the fact that the Gaullist regime will try to continue, in one form or another, the anti-social and anti-democratic policies of the capitalist monopolies.

The Central Committee of the PCF calls on all Communists and Democrats to contribute their utmost to the development of united action by the Left in and outside parliament.

United action by the PCF and FGDS can be carried out on the lines laid down in the agreement of December 20, 1966, particularly for the near future, with a view to:

—supporting the movement for the working people's demands, for a readjustment of wages, salaries and pensions;

—stopping the U.S. bombings of the DRV, and restoring peace in that area by implementing the Geneva agreements.

Since the success of the Left parties is bound to enhance the importance of parliament, the Central Committee approves the decision of the Political Bureau instructing the PCF group in the new National Assembly to work for agreements among the Left groups and parties on the main national and international issues.

A delegation of the PCF group in parliament will meet with its FGDS counterpart with a view to coordinating their common activity in the National Assembly.

At the same time the parliamentary group and the Communist deputies will from the moment parliament reconvenes uphold the more urgent demands of all social strata suffering from the current policy.

The upsurge of the struggle of the workers, peasants and other working people in the country speaks of the deterioration of their living conditions and of a higher morale inspired by the success of the democratic forces in the general election.

The crying injustice of the present electoral system stresses the need to assure fair representation of the urban centers, which are systematically underrepresented. It lends force to the democratic demand for the return to proportional representation in all elections.

On the international scene, the steady intensification of the U.S. aggression in Vietnam makes it the duty of Communists to contribute actively to increased action by the French peace forces in order to isolate the aggressors, impose an end to the bombings of the DRV and guarantee the Vietnamese people peace and independence.

Everywhere—in the enterprises, neighborhoods and rural communities—the task is to bring about unity of action in support of the economic and social demands of the working people, for greater democratic freedoms, for disarmament and peace.

The clarity and correctness of the PCF policy of alliance, and the cohesion and power of its organizations were the main reason for the Communist success in the general election. They earned the PCF widespread support among the youth, who can look on the Communists as the staunchest champions of the demands and aspirations of the young people.

The March victory can and should be followed by an increase in Communist influence and a strengthening of the Party. The Communists should work for a wider circulation of the Party press, first of all *L'Humanité and L'Humanité-Dimanche.* Public meetings should be held everywhere to ensure that the new members of the Party who joined the Party during the election campaign, including numerous young people, are followed by thousands of others and that numerous new Party cells are formed.

The 1967 general election was a landmark in the progress of the French democratic forces. The French Communist Party will do everything to carry on successfully the great battle for the unity of the working class, for the victory of the democratic and progressive forces of the country.

## D. REMARKS BY WALDECK ROCHET AT THE CENTRAL COMMITTEE MEETING

The most important aspect of the recent presidential elections was the broad republican unity achieved under the aegis of the alliance of the Left, with the Communist Party in the front ranks.

Two of the more important reasons for the Communist gains were the following:

1. Millions of working people and democrats voted Communist because they regard the Communists as the most active defenders of the working people's interests, that is, as those who devote the greatest attention to social problems without forgetting, however, about the defense of democratic freedoms, peace and national interests.

2. Millions of working people and democrats voted Communist because they see the Communist Party as the best architect of working-class and democratic unity of action, of the alliance of the Left against one man rule and for democracy.

Appreciating the gains of the PCF, our Central Committee noted with satisfaction that these gains fit into the context of a general advance of the Left. Indeed, you know that while our Party won more than a million votes, the Federation of the Left, for its part, polled about 500,000 additional votes. These results show that when the Left parties rally together they gain to the detriment of the reactionary forces.

The alliance of the Left parties is henceforward a great force that must win the majority in the country and replace, at a more or less early date, the de Gaulle regime by a government of democratic alliance. It is with a view to hastening this democratic change, which our people are looking forward to, that the Communist Party advocates unity of action of the Left parties both in parliament and on a national scale.

The Communist deputies, who support the present struggles of the working people, will, on taking office, submit draft laws on the more pressing social problems. Foremost among these problems are a readjustment of wages and salaries, guaranteed employment and shorter working hours without pay cuts.

At the same time the PCF group in parliament will search for a basis for joint action with deputies from the other Left parties on all fundamental national and international issues.

The December agreement on unity comprises many objectives which in the near future can provide conditions for numerous joint actions both in and outside parliament. At the same time, however, these objectives are guidelines for a common program. If the December agreement is to become a common government program it should be complemented and,

above all, specified in terms of the means and time limits of attaining the objectives it envisages.

We are thinking, in particular, of ways and means likely to prevent attempts by big finance to impose its will under the threat of sabotaging the economic and social activity launched by the government of democratic alliance. For there is no question of entering the government and, submitting to the demands of the capitalist monopolies. The task is to pursue a policy of economic and social progress, peace, and national independence with popular support.

To this end it is necessary to free the state from the grip of big finance and at the same time effect a massive reduction of unproductive spending, such as the expenditure on the so-called strike force, in order to curb inflation. To free the state from the grip of big finance, our program puts forward a certain number of economic and financial reforms prominent among which are:

—gradual nationalization of the biggest banks and most powerful monopolies;

—replacing the Gaullist Fifth Plan by an economic and social development plan guaranteeing full employment, economic progress and a higher standard of living;

—a genuine tax reform, and measures against financial profiteering and the outflow of capital.

To be sure, the scope and time limits of these reforms are open to debate, but we suggest that they be examined along with the proposals to be advanced by the Federation and by other Left groups.

At any rate, we believe that as a result of the December agreement it is now possible to draw up a real common government program to be carried out by a Left majority and a government of democratic alliance.

As the end of Gaullism draws near it is important for the Left parties to concern themselves with carefully clearing the ground for the takeover by a strong government of democratic alliance ready to foil all reactionary maneuvers and capable of carrying out a policy of economic and social progress and of peace meeting the interests of the people and the nation.

We Communists believe that to win the confidence of numerous Frenchmen who still waver the Left parties must show that they are resolved to fight in common, not only to end the regime of personal power but also, and above all, to rule successfully and lastingly on the basis of a well-considered common program, in the interests of the people and the nation.

We hardly need to repeat that, given agreement on a common program, the Communists will be ready to contribute—in particular at the government level—to the democratic and national renovation to be undertaken.

The Communists are not making any unreasonable demands. They merely insist on being treated on an equal footing with the other Left groups. And provided they share the responsibilities with the other Left parties on the basis of a common democratic program, they will scrupulously honor commitments made in common, nor will they expect the other Left parties to do more than honor their commitments.

This line of action will enable the Communists to continue upholding the interests of the working class, the people and the nation unfailingly and effectively.

While the goal is to end the regime of personal power and establish genuine democracy, we should not forget that the de Gaulle regime is still there and is determined to do all it can to stay in power. This means that the most pressing task in the near future will be to maintain, strengthen and expand the alliance of the working-class and democratic forces so as to defeat the new moves of the regime of personal power and to create favorable conditions for the advance to real democracy.

Having been defeated, the Gaullist leaders say they are now going to follow a bold social policy to do away with discontent and the opponents of their regime. But this is not the first time the holders of personal power have made such a declaration, and we know that the facts have always given them the lie.

Actually, it is only when they are forced by the struggle of the masses and by the fear of losing their power that the big trusts and the present government, which is in their service, give in and make this or that concession. Besides, we must not forget that even when they are compelled to yield ground they do not give up the idea of eventually taking back with one hand what they had to let go with the other.

In these circumstances it is essential that unity of action be established first of all in the country, through the working people's economic and social struggles, through their fight to safeguard democratic freedoms and win their extension and to promote peace.

Furthermore, at a time when the Americans are intensifying their war of aggression against the Vietnamese people, we must not forget that for us Communists the fight for peace and national independence is a primary task. This is why our Party, which fully identifies itself with the people of Vietnam, fighting for their freedom and independence, proposes in the weeks to come to contribute actively to the preparation of a conference for peace in Vietnam and to the setting up of numerous committees for peace in Vietnam associated with the peace movement.

Lastly, within the framework of our fight for democracy, we plan a vigorous campaign for the application of the principle of proportional representation in all elections. Had the proportional system been there, the Gaullists, who collected only 38 per cent of the votes, would have no majority in the National Assembly. The republicans should insist on the proportional system enabling each party to be represented according to the number of votes polled, so that a democratic majority can be elected.

The Central Committee consider that the most important aspect of the elections is the republican unity brought into being under the aegis of the Left alliance, with the Communist Party in the front ranks. But this unity did not arise spontaneously or without difficulties. It was a result of persevering effort for unity and alliance carried on over a long period.

Politically, we have in recent years witnessed a considerable growth of opposition to the regime of personal power. This mounting opposition to the anti-social and anti-democratic policies of the Gaullist regime has unquestionably provided the objective basis for increasing the influence of the working-class and democratic forces.

This is not to say, however, that this opposition was bound to lead to Left alliance. We must remember that in recent years we have seen numerous maneuvers designed to maintain the division of the Left parties and to channel toward reactionary solutions the discontent of certain social strata which legitimately turn away from Gaullist power.

If we want to make a deep analysis of our united front policy, we need something more than repeating that it is correct. We must stress the different forms this united front has taken according to the period and the objectives concerned. For the search for these different forms and their application required a daring and creative approach by our Party, an approach from which we must now learn every lesson.

I recall, for instance, that during the 1962 referendum the Socialists and Communists urged a "no" vote. Yet the conditions at that time were not entirely favorable for the Socialists and Communists to call in common for a "no" vote. The relations between the two parties were not good.

It was then that, to promote a Socialist-Communist rapprochement, our Party advanced the slogan, "Let us march shoulder to shoulder and strike jointly at the common enemy." This slogan undoubtedly helped to bring the Socialists and Communists closer together in the subsequent general election, and to launch joint and parallel actions in the country by Socialists, Communists and other republicans.

It must be said that we largely took account of that experience to shape our tactics in the presidential and the recent general elections.

In the case of the general election, we renewed our proposal for a common program. But the Federation leaders refused to go beyond the December agreement.

After that the important question arose: must we renounce the December agreement on unity under the pretext that it did not yet imply the adoption of a common program? Of course not. That would have been a bad mistake.

It is now clear to anyone, I imagine, that the agreement on unity did not lead away from a common program but brought us nearer to it by providing favorable conditions for a genuine alliance of the Left parties.

The efforts we have made to find suitable forms of a united front meeting every situation are inseparable from our efforts in the ideological field.

It is beyond question, for example, that the new theses advanced by the 16th, 17th and 18th congresses of our Party on the possibility and conditions of a peaceful transition to socialism under a multi-party system have led to closer links between Communists and Socialists, and we think the continued Communist-Socialist dialogue may make it possible to overcome certain differences and promote joint Socialist-Communist action.

To sum up, an important lesson of the varied

experience of applying the united front policy is that if we want to advance we must at one and the same time stand firm on principle and eschew all formalism, dogmatism and hidebound routine.

Our united front policy has consistently followed the fundamental idea that the Party's independent activity among the masses is inseparable from its unrelenting effort for unity and alliance.

While stressing the vast importance of the December agreement on unity, we combated all tendencies toward effacing the role of the Communist Party by calling on the electorate to vote massively for the Communist candidates, beginning with the first round. We insisted again and again that France can have no genuine Left nor a policy of social progress without the Communists and that, consequently, the Communist Party should occupy the place it is entitled to alongside the other democratic parties and, in the event of a Left victory, in the government of democratic alliance.

It is quite certain that had we not stated, beginning with the first ballot, all the reasons for voting Communist, and had we let the tendency to efface the role of the Communist Party develop on the pretext of not wanting to impede unity, our Party would not have won a million votes more nor strengthened its position of foremost party of the Left.

And it is just as true that our Party would have been unable to grow and to increase its influence among the masses by retreating into its shell in sectarian fashion and by slackening its efforts for unity and alliance.

We must not forget that the Communist Party, while absolutely irreplaceable, does not exist for its own sake and has a raison d'etre only to the extent that it effectively serves the interests of the working class and the people today and will do so in the future. This means that our Party should boldly pursue its unitary policy clear of dogmatism, sectarianism and Rightist opportunism.

Our Party is emerging from the battle stronger and bigger than ever. Its policy has won the approval of more than five million French men and women. Our Party has never been more closely united around its Central Committee which has gained in prestige. More than ever before, it expresses the hopes of the French people. This makes the recruitment of numerous new members, in particular young working people, a prime task. The election campaign showed, in fact, that the younger generation is looking more and more to the Communist Party, and this is a promising development.

The fact that after the elections the Communist Party is a force growing and developing vigorously will increase its opportunities of winning over the younger generation.

Our Party has just registered a great political victory because it has unremittingly fought from the outset against personal power, because it has a program meeting the aspirations of the people and the nation, and lastly, because it has done everything to unite the working-class and democratic forces for action.

Nevertheless, we must not indulge in self-satisfaction, for there are new and big battles ahead.

By implementing in a spirit of initiative the unitary line defined by our 18th Congress, and by steadily improving its work, our Party will win new important victories in the fight it is waging against personal power, for genuine democracy and, beyond that, for socialism.

# "MARXISM IS NOT A CATECHISM"

Article by Jean Kanapa, Member of the Central Committee,
French Communist Party

*Complete Text*
(*l'Humanité*, Paris, 6 February 1967)

Everyone knows that whatever is done in China, at least by the "Red Guards" and the "Maoists," takes place with reference to a collection of quotations from Mao Tse-tung. All the wisdom of the world and all revolutionary science would seem to have been concentrated in that collection.

This prompts a first comment: the very *idea* of this procedure is a striking proof that the "Maoists" have *broken* with Marxism and scientific socialism. Indeed, it is unthinkable for a Marxist and Communist that one book, whatever its merits, could constitute the bible of Marxism. Speaking of even the *Communist Manifesto* of Marx and Engels, a real turning point in the history of the working-class movement and in modern history, no Communist would ever say that one had only to read and memorize the Manifesto to know Marxism in all its richness and continuous development. The notion that there can exist a prayer-book of scientific socialism is contradictory terminologically, and is foreign to the *scientific* character of socialism. It stems from religiousness.

It leaps to the eye that the collection in question is a hodgepodge of quotations dating from vastly different periods. No historical reference sheds light on their context, the historical conditions of struggle at the given moment, the forces at work, and so on. Thus circumstantial estimations and guidelines formulated in situations as different for China as those of the '20s and the '60s are all given out to be non-temporal and hence eternal truths. And this is most typical of dogmatism.

## CARICATURE OF MARXISM

This is all the more striking because the quotations are very short, being generally made up of two or four sentences, and sometimes of only a few words. The purpose is evident—the reader is invited to use them as both prayers and recipes. And this means representing revolutionary theory as something oversimplified to the point of obscurantism.

Marxism is a (scientific) world outlook. It is not a catechism.

Marxism is also a "guide to action." But it is not a travel guide.

Incidentally, the level of this Mao bible is more than elementary.

It is hard to see what good could come of memorizing (and reciting as an incantation), say, the precept which is supposed to furnish the best method of defeating imperialism. "Strategically," it says, "We are not afraid of taking a meal—we can cope with it. In

practice we eat mouthful by mouthful. We could not swallow the whole meal at once. This is known as solving problems one by one." Is it, then, these kind of aphorisms that are the last word in revolutionary theory and the acme of Marxism? Is it this "theoretical rigor," this "doctrinal fertility," that inspires suddenly and in a rather unexpected manner observers who were never before known to be so drawn to socialism? In fact, is it not obvious that this caricature of socialism offered by "Maoism" plays into the hands of the opponents of socialism?

## SOCIALIST DEMOCRACY DOES NOT GIVE PREFERENCE TO REPRESSION

The collection of quotations from Mao provides, in effect, evidence condensed to a digest that the very peculiar theses the "Maoist" leaders would like to impose on their people and the international working-class movement have decidedly nothing to do with Marxism-Leninism, with our doctrine and our policy.

Here is, for example, how the functions of the "people's democratic dictatorship led by the working class and based on the worker-peasant alliance" are defined: "Its *first* function is to exercise repression inside the country with regard to the reactionary classes and elements, as well as on the exploiters opposing the socialist revolution, etc. The dictatorship has a second function, that of defending our country against subversive activity and eventual aggression from without." These are the only functions the collection assigns to the dictatorship of the proletariat (the "people's democratic dictatorship" being no more than a form of the latter, according to Mao).

This is a far cry from Lenin, from the concept of the dictatorship of the proletariat upheld by the world Communist movement, including our own Party. In Lenin's view, and in ours, coercion is only *one* of the functions (a temporary function) of the dictatorship of the proletariat, nor is it the primary function. At the recent congress of our Party, Waldeck Rochet stressed that the two functions of the new political power of the working people are: "(1) ensuring the great possible democracy for all working men and women and the people as a whole in order to enlist their participation in socialist construction and in managing government affairs in various forms; (2) defending the new regime of socialist democracy against the acts of sabotage organized by the former exploiter classes with a view to recapturing power and restoring capitalism." *To give preference to the repressive function of socialist power runs counter to Leninism.* True, Stalin maintained such an idea (and practice). But this does not excuse Mao. On the contrary, since Stalin's mistakes in this respect were disclosed for the enlightenment of all the Communists of the world, this aggravates Mao's responsibility.

## MAO'S "THEORY OF VIOLENCE"

To be sure, another quotation concedes that one of the "methods" of the proletarian dictatorship should consist in "enabling the people to participate in political activity." The very wording is condescending and restrictive in respect of the Leninist principle according to which socialist power should ensure the *greatest* democracy for the people. It will be noted, moreover, that Mao no longer speaks here of the "functions" of working-class power but of its "methods." The difference is appreciable. It is no longer a question of the nature of this power but merely of its "style."

Let us take another example.

"Every Communist," Mao contends, "should learn the truth that 'power grows out of the barrel of a gun'." Nothing is said before or after this—the sentence is presented as it stands, in isolation. In other words, it is no longer just a guideline given in definite circumstances to the People's Liberation Army of China in 1938 and valid in *that* context. It becomes something much more important—a non-temporal truth valid at all times and everywhere. Yet as such it is in glaring conflict with one of the central theses of Marxism. Exactly 90 years ago Engels devoted a whole section of *Anti-Duehring* to disproving this oversimplifying theory which says that violence is the origin and basis of political domination.

It may be argued that perhaps Mao has in mind another aspect of the matter, the one Marx stressed by saying that violence, too, plays a revolutionary role in history, the role of midwife "of the entire old society which bears a new one in its womb." But, first of all, Marx said that about past history, the history of the bourgeoisie to be precise. Secondly, it was amply demonstrated years ago that neither Marx, Engels, nor Lenin ever held that the proletarian revolution, the assumption of power by the working people, must *necessarily* take on the form of armed violence. Yet armed struggle is what Mao maintains on every page as the only possibility. The idea that "power grows out of the barrel of a gun" is spelled out in the following quotation: "The central task and highest form of the revolution is to win power through armed struggle, to *solve the problem through war.* This revolutionary principle of Marxism-Leninism is valid everywhere, in China as in other countries." No, this is not a principle of Marxism-Leninism, which stresses, on the contrary, the need to use different forms of struggle depending on time and place. The principle advocated by Mao is a principle prompting adventurism. The Communists by no means consider civil war indispensable in every case to the victory of the socialist revolution. Indeed, they consider it highly desirable to dispense with it if possible.

## WAR AND POLITICAL STRUGGLE

The collection under survey suggests, in effect, that to Mao violence and war is the predominant solution to every fundamental problem. He shifts *political* struggle, the Communists' main weapon, to the background. He even regards it as above all a curious moral and psychological action, a rather puerile form of education. To him, war is the key to everything.

That is why we are presented with the dogma: "War can be abolished only through war. If there are to be no more guns, one must take up a gun." In other words, while assuring us that the imperialists are "paper tigers," they regard them nevertheless, as absolute masters of war and peace who cannot be prevented from unleashing war. They also tell us that war has an advantage, for it will make it possible to bury war. Let us dismiss this sophistry. Things become particularly serious when put plainly, for in 1967 the war in question would not be waged with rifles. Thus the inference should be: "If there are to be no more atom bombs one must use the atom bomb." This may "abolish" war. It is certain to abolish civilization in a large part of the planet. What, then, will one gain through this method of "abolishing war"?

Even more serious is the fact that this thesis essentially underestimates the political might of the popular movement of the world. This might is increasingly becoming capable of making the imperialists respect world peace, that is, peaceful coexistence—*Provided everything is done to promote, extend and stimulate still more this political struggle of the masses for peace.* The Chinese leaders, however, are doing the exact opposite. They are trying to undermine and demoralize this struggle. To them war is a *necessity.*

What we, all the peoples, regard as a necessity—and what we must make a necessity for the imperialists—is peaceful coexistence. We do want to abolish war, but not by taking up the rifle. We want to do it by beating guns into ploughshares, by fighting unrelentingly and consistently to impose disarmament on imperialism.

## UNDER COVER OF A REVELATION

One could cite any number of examples. All of them would confirm that it is a question of ideas entirely at variance with genuine historical progress. Most of the theses do not even appear to be departures from a fundamental allegiance to Marxism, but the fruit of an ideology totally alien to scientific socialism.

It is understandable that those propositions are now coming up against serious resistance in China itself.

Besides, how can one trust this primitive prayer-book? While it assures that "our principle is that the Party commands the rifles and it is impermissible for the rifles to command the Party," the Chinese press and radio tell us that the Army is being used to enable heaven knows what "revolutionary rebels" to "seize power," operating against the established bodies of the Communist Party of China.

It is well known that one can always do anything under cover of a revelation.

# "WHAT BEING A REVOLUTIONARY MEANS IN FRANCE TODAY"

Paper Delivered by Waldeck Rochet, Secretary-General, PCF
at the Maurice Thorez Institute, October 1967

*Abridged Text*
(*Information Bulletin*, No. 93, 1967)

The immense merit of the October Socialist Revolution is that it opened the era of socialism. A bitter ideological and political struggle has been going on for fifty years now over the legacy of the October Revolution and its estimation.

The right-wing opportunists and revisionists question the fact that the experience of the first victorious socialist revolution is largely of universal value. They readily speak of a purely "Russian," or even an "oriental" development lacking in value as an example for the Western world and the industrially developed capitalist countries.

On the other hand, the left-wing revisionists, or dogmatists, would like the masses in the France of 1967 to be led to the socialist revolution along exactly the same road as the Russian Communists followed in 1917.

We French Communists consider that Marxism is not a dead dogma but a guide to action, and we fight both the Right opportunists and the Left opportunists, or dogmatists, for they all turn their backs on Marxism and the socialist revolution.

This is the point we want to make in answering the question: "A revolutionary: What does it mean in France today?"

Speaking of the revolution, Lenin always stressed the existence of universal laws of the socialist revolution and socialist construction, on the one hand, and the necessity for knowing how to apply these fundamental principles in the specific conditions of the country and period concerned, on the other.

"All nations will arrive at socialism," he wrote, "this is inevitable, but all will do so in not exactly the same way, each will contribute something of its own to some form of democracy, to some variety of the dictatorship of the proletariat, to the varying rate of socialist transformations in the different aspects of social life." (*Collected Works,* Vol. 23, p. 69.)

Maurice Thorez was prompted by the same idea when, more than twenty years ago, in an interview given to *The Times,* he said that each people naturally chooses a different road and that the French people, in particular, who possess an original tradition, would find their own road to socialism. In view of the new balance of forces in the world and in France, this road could be peaceful, as Thorez saw it.

These precepts now are rejected by the "leftist" groupings advocating "Maoism." In doing their disruptive job, these demagogues use and abuse that excellent word, *revolution.* As they lose all hope of gaining at least some little influence among the French workers, they are trying flattery to win over a small,
politically inexperienced fraction of the student youth, as the Russian Trotskyists did at one time.

Lenin always stressed that the "leftists'" adventuristic vacillations reflect petty-bourgeois instability. In "The Revolutionary Phrase," an article he wrote in February 1918, he showed that there was not a whit of revolutionary common sense in the "leftists'" attitude.

"We must fight against the revolutionary phrase," he pointed out, "we have to fight it, we absolutely must fight it, so that at some future time people will not say of us the bitter truth that 'a revolutionary phrase about revolutionary war ruined the revolution'." (*Collected Works,* Vol. 27, p. 29.)

Lenin traced the social origins of left-wing opportunism to the peculiar position of the petty bourgeoisie, which easily switches in words to extreme "revolutionism" but lacks firmness, organization, discipline and staunchness, all of which are qualities of the proletariat.

"By revolutionary phrase-making we mean the repetition of revolutionary slogans irrespective of objective circumstances at a given turn in events, in the given state of affairs obtaining at the given time." (*Ibid.,* p. 19.)

In this way Lenin warned that tactics should be deduced not from general truths, but from an analysis of events as they present themselves.

The only genuinely scientific approach to problems is accurately to estimate the actual situation and the balance of class forces, to discern and foresee new trends in time, and to determine the right policy line on this basis.

When we try to apply these recommendations and to approach from a scientific standpoint the problem of the revolution, which is still the fundamental problem, now as in 1917, we are struck by the fact that the single revolutionary process has become diversified in fifty years.

New and original situations have developed, and the world has undergone deep changes. The formation of the socialist system has weakened imperialism, which, on the other hand, has lost its colonial empires.

Inside the imperialist countries the development and consolidation of state-molopoly capitalism are creating objective conditions for a very broad anti-monopoly unity encompassing every class and every stratum suffering from the domination of the financial oligarchy.

The obvious conclusion to be drawn is that the *forms* of the fundamental content of our epoch are changing and becoming diversified. The fundamental content of our epoch is the transition from capitalism to socialism, but the forms of this transition vary.

The October Revolution revealed the existence of universally valid general principles of the socialist revolution. It is a question, among other things, of the need for the working class to win political power in close alliance with other working people—victims of capitalism—of a temporary dictatorship of the proletariat, the promotion of socialist democracy, socialization of the major means of production, the building of a socialist economy serving the peoples, and the necessity for a party that really would be the revolutionary vanguard of the working class.

We know that from the outset the partisans of reformism and the adherents of Social Democratic parties in various countries took a stand against the October Revolution. By so doing they made a mistake, all the more so because subsequently they were unable to bring about socialist changes, or even to undertake such changes, anywhere, in any country.

In numerous countries the Right Social Democratic leaders, striving to adapt the working-class movement to the requirements of capitalism and to reconcile the working class and the bourgeoisie, have virtually renounced the idea of building socialism. Some of them, such as Harold Wilson, continue to play the role of spokesmen of the bourgeoisie among the working people.

By and large, Social Democratic governments have operated within the framework of capitalism, without ever setting themselves the task of abolishing this system in favor of socialism.

Now, while Communists and Socialists have been following different roads, the main problem today is whether the radical changes which have occurred in fifty years in favor of socialism can lead, proceeding from present-day reality, to rapprochement between Communists and Socialists and so to working-class unity, which is indispensable for the victory of socialism.

I mentioned a little earlier the universally valid lessons of the October Revolution. I must repeat, however, that the form of the socialist revolution is not linked to any one pattern.

Any Marxist-Leninist who would be worthy of the name should base his political activity on a concrete analysis of the given situation and not on conclusions drawn in the past from a different situation.

This means that while the model provided by the October Revolution is still valid in its general features, it cannot be copied in its every aspect, for a common goal and a common class position presuppose a multiplicity and diversity of forms and means, and not uniformity.

To be a Marxist and a revolutionary means, therefore, using different methods and different forms of struggle when the historical conditions for action are different.

The French Communist Party is operating in a country and at a time when the rallying of the middle classes in town and country behind a united working class can impose the establishment of genuine democracy capable of creating favorable conditions for the struggle for socialism.

It was with due regard to these circumstances that the latest congresses of our Party formulated theses which were widely echoed among the working class and all democrats, especially the Socialists.

Concerning the diversity of ways of transition to socialism, we stressed that it is inconsistent with our doctrine to present the Communists as people advocating at all costs the seizure of power by force, through an armed rising.

As a matter of fact, Communists have never regarded violence as an end in itself, for they consider, on the contrary, that the working class has every interest in accomplishing the socialist revolution by peaceful means.

The use of force has never been a result of preference by the working people. It depends on the forms of struggle which the exploiters and oppressors use against the people.

Lenin said in 1915 that it was wrong and absurd to oppose the democratic to the socialist program.

"The proletariat," he wrote, "cannot be victorious except through democracy, i.e., by giving full effect to democracy and by linking with each step of its struggle democratic demands formulated in the most absolute terms . . . We must *combine* the revolutionary struggle against capitalism with a revolutionary program and tactics on *all* democratic demands . . ."(*Collected Works,* Vol. 21, p. 408.)

We think in a country like France, where the existence of several parties is part of the nation's democratic tradition, a peaceful transition to socialism can be effected despite the existence of many parties, provided Communist-Socialist cooperation firmly asserts itself in the struggle for democracy and socialism.

To insist on the possibility of a peaceful and democratic transition to socialism does not at all mean that socialism can be achieved without class struggle, without mobilizing the working class and its allies, the working peasantry and the urban middle classes, for action.

Indeed, we should proceed from the Marxist idea that the big bourgeoisie will never relinquish power of its own free will. It follows that the transition to socialism can be effected peacefully only if a united working class rallies all democratic, progressive and national forces, that is, the majority of the people, behind it and on its side, that the big bourgeoisie, being isolated, cannot use arms against the people, cannot resort to civil war.

This means that the transition to socialism under a multi-party system does not depend on the options of the Communist Party alone. But it implies, first of all, that the Socialist Party must discard its policy of class cooperation with the bourgeoisie to pursue, alongside the Communists, a policy of effective struggle for democracy and socialism.

Naturally, the new political power of the working people must protect and defend the cause of socialist construction, which must be continued under socialist laws and democracy, against the resistance of one-time exploiting classes trying to restore capitalism and their own rule.

The Marxist concept of the dictatorship of the

proletariat expresses this function, which is as necessary as it is temporary, since it must end with the disappearance of class antagonisms.

This is why the primary function of the new working people's power is steadily to extend socialist democracy, with working men and women and the people as a whole taking an increasingly effective part in the building of socialism and the management of public affairs in various forms.

In short, by striving today to bring about greater political and economic democracy, to curb monopoly power and to promote unity of action by all working-class and democratic forces, we are doing a revolutionary job.

It is through joint struggle by the working class and large sections of the population for increasingly far-reaching democratic reforms and for the overthrow of monopoly domination that the majority of the people can, as a result of increased political consciousness, be brought to realize that radical solution of the problems of our epoch can be achieved through a struggle for "democracy to the finish," that is, for a socialist transformation of society.

The 1960 Statement tells us that the main distinction between Communists and reformists is not that the reformists are the only ones to advocate reform, for they are not. The distinction lies in the fact that, to the reformists, reforms under capitalism are an end in itself, which makes them renounce the struggle to abolish capitalism, whereas the Communists fight resolutely for immediate reforms attainable within the framework of capitalist society but, never give up the fight for the ultimate goal, socialism.

Having specified this, we say that those who think the revolution can be carried out in present-day France only through an armed uprising actually lack confidence in the working class, in its political intelligence and skill, in its ability to unite the majority of the people with a view to fighting for both their immediate and their future interests. Their solutions would be solutions suggested by despair had they not been purely verbal and fictitious. Their refusal to distinguish between opportunist reconciliation of the classes and the revolutionary theory of using peaceful forms to win power merely proves their incapacity for dialectical thinking and their intellectual sclerosis.

What is true is that the peaceful road is historically relative and conditioned by specific circumstances. The working class should therefore be prepared to change forms of action according to the situation. Marxism, said Lenin, differs from all primitive types of socialism in not linking the movement to a definite form of struggle. It recognizes the most diverse forms of struggle, nor does it invent these forms but borrows them from life—they are suggested to it by this or that relationship of class forces.

"Under no circumstances," wrote Lenin, "does Marxism confine itself to the forms of struggle possible and in existence at the given moment only, recognizing as it does that new forms of struggle, unknown to the participants of the given period, *inevitably* arise as the given social situation changes."

(*Collected Works*, Vol. 11, p. 213.)

The "leftist" adventurers who advocate "Maoism" do not share this view. They would like to impose on the working class of all countries one and the same form of action—armed struggle.

Yet one must not give priority beforehand to one form of struggle to the detriment of others, since the situation varies from continent to continent and from country to country.

Obviously, the situation in Asia, Africa and Latin America is not the same as in various West European countries, and to resort to the same forms of struggle in all these continents and countries would mean heading inevitably to defeat.

The Vietnamese people, for instance, have no choice but to use arms in resisting the American invaders. Their liberation struggle has the unqualified support of the French Communist Party.

We realize that armed and guerrilla struggle, combined with the movement of the masses, is necessary to the revolution in this or that country of Latin America, where military fascist dictatorships subservient to U.S. imperialism are in power.

It is for the Communist parties and the revolutionary and progressive movements of the countries concerned to decide on the forms of struggle to be used, taking into account national conditions, peculiarities and potentialities.

We have repeatedly and fully identified ourselves with the Cuban revolution, and we identify ourselves with all the Latin American peoples fighting against Yankee imperialism, with all revolutionary movements, whatever their form.

But the present Chinese leaders are no less wrong for claiming that only armed struggle can everywhere ensure the victory of socialism, and for ruling out every other form of struggle.

Unfortunately, the recent experience of Indonesia showed that the use of armed force is not in itself sufficient to guarantee success. Quite the contrary, to the extent that this form of struggle was out of keeping with conditions and circumstances, its application led the Indonesian revolutionary movement to failure and retreat.

This means that the revolutionary character of a struggle is not determined essentially by the form it takes but by its content, linked with the use of appropriate methods of action.

The fight against imperialism today is being carried on simultaneously by the socialist system, the national liberation movement and the working class of the capitalist countries.

The system of socialist countries and the international working class are at the head of the revolutionary process.

Undoubtedly, it is not the community of socialist states that accounts for the revolutionary movement in the capitalist countries, but the internal contradictions in these countries, which make the working class and the mass of the people fight against exploitation and oppression. Nevertheless, the existence and development of the socialist countries plays the role of a great revolutionary force by showing, for example, that socialism is ultimately the only positive solution to which the working class is striving to fight its way.

At the same time, the economic, social and cultural achievements of the socialist countries are steadily changing the general balance of class forces in the world to the detriment of imperialism and in favor of socialism.

The growing might of the socialist system, coupled with the mounting national liberation movement, the struggle of the working class in the capitalist countries and the growth of other peace forces, is making it possible to prevent a new world war, provided all anti-imperialist and peace-loving forces rally against imperialism, above all against American imperialism.

Engels wrote to Kautsky on September 12, 1882, that the victorious proletariat in this or that country could not presume to bring happiness to another people against the latter's will, without thereby undermining its own victory. In the same letter, however, he added that the force of example of victorious socialism would be tremendous.

Bearing that in mind, Lenin said that the working people of the Soviet Union must demonstrate in practice the superiority of the new social system over capitalism, its economic advantages.

There is no doubt any longer that the great economic achievements of the Soviet Union and other socialist countries are enhancing the appeal of socialism in the eyes of the working people of the capitalist countries, stimulating their struggle.

No amount of imperialist slander can conceal the truth or prevent the example of victorious socialism revolutionizing the minds of the workers, peasants and intellectuals, contributing to the growth of socialist consciousness and inspiring the masses in their fight against big capital and imperialism.

The Mao Tse-tung group's attacks and false accusations against the Communist Party of the Soviet Union and other parties will prove just as futile.

One of the inventions of the present Chinese leaders is that the Soviet Union is restoring capitalism by raising the people's standard of living. This sounds as if the Communist Party of China had not signed the 1957 Declaration, which says in black and white that one of the general, universally valid laws of the socialist revolution is planned economic development aimed at improving the working people's standard of living, and as if the object of the revolution were egalitarianism and asceticism! Primitive egalitarianism, which Marx and Engels criticized so scathingly, has nothing to do with the ideology of the working class. It is a relapse of the ideology of the lumpen-proletariat and the declassed strata of paupers.

The present Chinese leaders also caricature communism by pushing the personality cult—rightly condemned by the Communist Party of the Soviet Union—to monstrous extremes.

The opponents of Marxism have alleged over and over again that communism is a big barracks flouting the diversity of tastes and aspirations and the wide range of human requirements.

In reality, however, Marxists do not propose to level tastes and material needs, put spiritual life on a barracks footing, or slavishly squeeze people's minds

into the bounds of a collection of quotations from prominent individuals, such as the "little red book."

Communism in our view, has the historic mission of freeing everyone from social inequality, from every form of oppression and exploitation. Its object is to ensure "*full* well-being and free, *all-round* development for *all* the members of society." (*Lenin, Collected Works,* Vol. 6, p. 54.)

Mao Tse-tung and his followers would like to nullify the main lessons of October, the main precepts of Marxism.

In their own country, they are trying hard to weaken the positions of the working class, the mass organizations and the Party itself in favor of such fanatical groups as the "Red Guards," who were called into existence for the express purpose of fighting the Communists who refuse to toe the erroneous line of the Mao group.

The Mao group's efforts are also aimed at disrupting the alliance of the international working class and the national liberation movement by opposing them to each other.

That is why they have advanced the fallacious theory of the "town" being encircled by the "countryside" on a world scale, a theory designed to justify the present Chinese leaders' chauvinism and inordinate nationalist ambitions.

To be sure, the national liberation movement is a component of the world revolutionary process and one of the decisive factors in that process. This cannot, however, make us forget that the October Revolution awakened the East and brought the colonial peoples into the general stream of the world revolutionary movement.

Nor can there be any question that the forces of world socialism, primarily the Soviet Union, have rendered, and continue to render, decisive assistance to the liberation struggle of the peoples of the colonial and dependent countries.

It is a fact, for example, that the aid which Vietnam receives from the Soviet Union and other socialist countries is playing an increasing role.

According to recent U.S. estimates, the Soviet Union has supplied Vietnam with more than 10,000 guns and mortars. The ground-to-air rockets and the MIGs which are taking an increasing toll of raiding aircraft are of Soviet make.

According to General Wheeler, Chairman of the U.S. Joint Chiefs of Staff, the Soviet Union last year shipped 1,500,000 tons of supplies to Vietnam, and this year deliveries will amount to 2,000,000 tons, or roughly 60 per cent of the total aid being rendered by the socialist countries.

In the light of these facts, one really cannot help being outraged by the crude calumnies of the present Chinese leaders, who claim without batting an eye that the Soviet Union sides with the American imperialists on the issue of Vietnam.

It is perfectly natural, of course, that the Soviet Union and other socialist countries are extending ever greater assistance to the courageous people of Vietnam, as well as increasing their support of all the peoples fighting for their independence.

To establish unity of action between the struggle

of the working class for socialism and the national liberation struggle of the oppressed peoples is one of the important conclusions of the Leninist theory of the October Revolution that is as valid as ever. Hence every attempt to minimize the role of the international working class and the socialist system runs counter to Marxism and, indeed, to the entire evidence of modern history.

Like it or not, the facts show that the working class is in the focus of the epoch marked by the October Revolution.

And since the French Communist Party is the party of the French working class inspired by the great principles of Marxism-Leninism, it is, in France, the only revolutionary party in the true sense of the term.

The French Communist Party has always openly declared itself to be the party fighting for the overthrow of capitalism and the transition to socialist society as a result of the winning of political power by the working class and its allies.

We have advocated these great ideas ever since 1920 and are happy that they have been gaining ground.

However, it is one thing to be convinced of the necessity of the socialist revolution and another to imagine that it will materialize in the same forms under any circumstances.

What is true is that the transition from capitalism to socialism invariably implies vigorous struggle by the people, militant unity of the working class, and unity of the middle class of town and country behind the working class and on its side.

To work for the advent of socialism does not mean uttering big words. It means striving with due regard to reality to win the majority of the people for socialism. And this is what being a revolutionary in France today implies.

The peoples are becoming more and more aware that the threat of a new world war cannot come from the Soviet Union, which steadfastly champions peace. That threat stems from the U.S. imperialists' aggressive policies.

Whether it is a question of the criminal war against the glorious Vietnamese people, of provocations against Cuba, foreign military intervention in the Dominican Republic, the coups in Greece, the Congo, Ghana and elsewhere, or of the war in the Middle East, we see U.S. interference behind every conflict. Again, it is the U.S. leaders who encourage the West German revanchists' claims, which is a major obstacle to organizing European security.

In these circumstances it is necessary to expose imperialist plans and mobilize all popular forces to safeguard and maintain world peace and the independence of the peoples.

The French Communist Party, which is aware of its responsibility to the French people and all other peoples, takes a clear stand. Prompted by solidarity with all the working people of the world, it has always supported, and supports without qualification, the democratic forces of every country and the liberation struggle of all the peoples oppressed by imperialism.

We consider that in the present international situation France can make an active contribution to peace and international cooperation. We therefore think it is in the best interest of France to keep out of blocs borne of the cold war and to take an active part in elaborating a system of collective security and mutual assistance between all the countries of Eastern and Western Europe.

This being so, how could we fail to side with the Soviet Union, knowing as we do of its role in the great battle for world peace, for peaceful coexistence, in support of the peoples fighting for their independence, for European and world security?

Thus it is the vital interests of our country and the common interests of all the peoples concerned with heading off a new world war that prompt us to strengthen the bonds of friendship linking France, the Soviet Union and other socialist countries.

Indeed, more than ever before the fight for peace and the fight for socialism are inseparable; it is through the worldwide victory of socialism that the International will embrace the human race.

# "QUESTIONS OF IDEOLOGY AND CULTURE"

Statement adopted by the Executive Committee,
CP of Great Britain, 11 March 1967

*Complete Text*

In no earlier phase in man's history has the world presented such striking contrasts as it does today. Science, technology, man's capacity to control nature leap ahead at breakneck speed, yet the greater part of mankind still lives in poverty and hunger. The same science can immeasurably improve man's conditions of life or be used for destruction. The epoch we live in is one of revolutionary change, of transition from one social system to another, from capitalism to socialism. To speed and to lead that change, and so to help open out a new era in man's history, is the role of Communist Parties throughout the world.

We live in a world of struggle. The great social transformation, now on the order of the day, is neither an easy nor a spontaneous process. Men of monopoly and Empire do not lightly surrender. And the struggles—economic, political, social—are reflected in the realm of ideology. Ideas of war, of race, of self-enrichment, of despair and self-destruction do battle, consciously and unconsciously, in the service of the old, dying system of capitalism.

## Marxism

For many people all seems confused, uncertain; established beliefs fade, established outlooks are questioned. In the turmoil of contrast and change they can see no future, no purpose or direction. In this situation it is natural that many are now turning to Marxism precisely because it points the way forward to a socialist and communist society; it shows how the vast potentiality of science can be put to the service of man, how culture can be freed from the degrading commercialism of capitalist society, and because Marxism can give men a sense of confidence in their own capacity to change the world.

Among those turning to Marxism in interest and hope are many who raise questions about the attitude of the Communist Party, concerned as it is, with bringing about the socialist transformation of society, to issues of great importance for humanity—questions of science, culture, religion, democracy. It is good and welcome that they do so. For Marxism too must itself continuously face up to the new problems of the mid-twentieth century, must continuously develop, shed dogmatism, overcome deficiencies, listen to critics and clarify its attitudes.

We regard the clarification of our attitudes to such questions of ideology and culture as of first importance at this critical moment in world history. But we cannot here attempt to define the attitude of Communists to all the issues raised by these questions. Rather we wish to state our approach to the nature of the work of scientists, artists and others today under socialism and to indicate, as clearly as possible, the grounds for joint discussion and action in the achievement of socialism. We believe that these issues are of interest, not only to scientists and artists themselves, but to wide sections of the people, including industrial workers, who are deeply interested in and closely affected by developments in the sciences and the arts.

## SCIENCE

Marxist philosophy is based on the study of reality through the use of scientific method, by which theories are tested in practice. Just as the laws of nature are derived from scientific study and practice, so Marxism attempts to penetrate the nature of social evolution and establish its laws by use of scientific method. Marxism, therefore, bases itself on science and cannot be separated from science. It points to the need for the spread of scientific education on a wide scale so that all may have the means of understanding natural and social phenomena.

The twentieth century is a period of extremely rapid scientific advance. Scientists are investigating ever more thoroughly the complexities of nature and, for the first time, discovering the nature of life itself. Vast sources of power are opening up, space is subject to human exploration, while new particles of matter are being discovered.

Communists welcome this advance. We see the task of the scientist as that of exploring nature, society, man, of enriching man's knowledge of every aspect of the universe, and of taking part in the application of this knowledge for the benefit of man.

Under capitalism, the development of science and technology is restricted and distorted. This is inevitable when much of it is influenced, or even controlled, by monopoly and other big private profit interests, and when half this country's research and development spending is for military purposes involving one in four scientists and technologists.

Universities, Technical Colleges and Research Institutes are not accorded the resources they need for the development of effective research, while the vital importance of science itself, of scientific organization and planning are insufficiently recognized. In addition to this, immense social problems have arisen as a result of the productive potentialities of the new automation and computer techniques. These problems cannot be solved by capitalism, but only in a socialist system.

Science must serve the people, and the battle for this end begins *now*, under capitalism. Socialist society

885

will, we consider, provide the conditions for the massive development of scientific enquiry.

The extent of resources to be made available for science must be determined by the community as a whole through its democratic institutions. Careful planning of the use of these resources is, of course, essential—priorities must be determined in the light of social needs as well as the state of science itself. In deciding these priorities scientists can make their special contribution through scientific organizations, universities and research institutes as well as government bodies, so influencing the direction of scientific investment and advance. Although at particular times special attention will have to be paid to particular fields, all scientific research should be encouraged, including pure research carried through without concern for its immediate practical application.

### Against dogmatism

The Communist Party, therefore, welcomes the most critical, enquiring and searching spirit among scientists, whose function, we recognize is to explore all aspects of phenomena and to avoid going into enquiry with a fixed notion of the result. The development of science requires the free confrontation of different scientific theories, and, where necessary, prolonged debate. We recognize, first, that only experiment and testing in practice can decide which of any two or more theories is valid, and, secondly, that theories and hypotheses that provide an adequate explanation of phenomena at one date will most probably be modified later and sometimes even be replaced by new and more complete theories.

We recognize that when attempts have been made in a dogmatic way to limit the scope of scientific investigation, to determine as foregone conclusions theories that could not be established as a result of research, debate and experiment, as in the case of Lysenko, the result has been extremely harmful for science, for scientists and for Marxism itself. The Communist Party, therefore, does not and will not attempt to "lay down a line" on science, to forecast the results of scientific research, or decide questions still under investigation. It considers that this is the field of scientists themselves and encourages the confrontation of conflicting approaches as an integral part of science. Above all, we will encourage the study of nature and of society in all its complexity and contradictions. For the more freely men explore nature the more effectively can they control it in the interests of man; the more they understand society the more they will fight to develop and change it.

### ART

A fundamental aim of the Communist Party is to bring into being a society where art and culture flourish and where all may participate in artistic activity. We recognize the debasement and perversion of art and culture today resulting from commercialism. Art to no small extent has become a commodity sold for profit. Yet under even capitalism

art is far from subdued, and creative artists in every field resist its encroachments and degradation. The struggle goes on in art as in politics.

Communists will fight against all restrictions of art imposed under capitalism, seek to defend its free development and extend its availability.

We do not think that, under socialism, painting, sculpture, literature, music must comply with a single standard, congenial to all, or immediately comprehensible without effort and study, but that society, through education and the facilities it provides, must make both the enjoyment and the practice of one or other field of artistic activity easily available to all sections of the people. By this means a free choice can be made as to which branch or branches of culture may be enjoyed and practiced.

Marxist historians and critics have made a considerable contribution to the study of the history of culture—its relations to society, to the struggle of classes—and to understanding how it arose and the role it has played. Marxism can assist the analysis and disclose the relations between works of art and the social and political conditions which gave rise to them. We recognize, however, that much difficult but exciting work lies ahead for those who are making a Marxist approach to the problem of artistic values, and we welcome the most extensive discussion in this field.

Communists know that art exercises a deep influence on people's thoughts and attitudes and lives, and that art can move people to progressive or reactionary ends. We welcome artists in every field who lend their talents in their own particular way to the struggle for peace, freedom and socialism.

### Innovation

But the Communist Party, during the fight for and under socialism, does not see its task as being to direct what should be written, painted or composed—either in terms of subject or of style; it does not see its role as laying down laws governing literary and artistic creation. We reject the concept that art, literature or culture should reflect only one (official) school or style. On the contrary, we look on innovation in art as part of its very heart and nature. Not every innovation will lead to positive results, but without it culture will be stifled and stultified. We think it probable that art under communism will change its nature more than we can today foresee.

The history of culture shows that many of its greatest innovators and protagonists have drawn deep inspiration from the people and their struggles, from the progressive classes and forces of their day. At certain periods, cultural work has played directly a part of great importance in progressive political struggles; today, for instance, the novel, drama, poetry, music, song can give a powerful stimulus to the struggle for an end to United States aggression in Vietnam, against racialism, for peace and socialism.

But at the same time the direct political struggle, past and present, is not, in any sense, the only subject of art. We recognize that artists convey their views of reality, their dreams and passions, in a multitude of ways.

## Artists and politics

We welcome, therefore, the widest variety of artistic approaches, subjects and styles, and encourage our members freely to express their views. We welcome creative workers who, in their work, or as part of it, speak clearly on the urgent issues of the day, and help to win people for the struggle for peace and socialism. But this does not mean, in any sense, that *all* artistic work can or should, play a direct political role.

Above all we know that creative workers who are committed to the struggle of peace, socialism and communism will, in one way or another, express these ideals in their work. While creative workers must have the conditions freely to develop their work, as well as opportunities and means of publication and exhibition, we see our task as being to win their political conviction, to inspire them with opposition to capitalism and confidence in socialism, and so to practical activity in the different facets of the struggle. There can be no doubt that progressive artistic activity, expressing confidence in man and his future, can be a great force in developing a socialist consciousness; but this can only be achieved to the fullest possible extent if artistic creation is carried out in conditions of freedom.

## RELIGION

The Communist Party welcomes the discussion taking place in many religious groupings around the great social, political and moral issues of our time, the turn of many people of different religions towards progressive causes and struggles, the efforts of many churches to come to terms with the discoveries of science and modern technique.

We welcome especially the developing dialogue between Christianity and Marxism, the genuine attempts being made on both sides to get rid of false conceptions of each other, the beginnings of personal contact and friendship, the shedding of older sectarian approaches, the frank discussion of our fundamental differences as well as all points of contact and co-operation.

One of the conditions for fruitful dialogue is complete sincerity with each other, a recognition of our differences of approach and philosophy as well as our points of agreement and co-operation.

We do not seek for a moment to disguise that as Marxists our philosophy is based on science and that we do not believe in the supernatural or in personal gods. We do not conceal our criticism, which is shared by many religious people, of the reactionary role so often played by religious establishments and institutions, nor the fact that religion has at times been used to secure obedience and acceptance of unjust and evil rule. But we do not make the mistake of reducing religion to this aspect of its existence. We know equally that religious faith has also inspired men and women to courageous action and sacrifice for progressive causes.

We recognize that there can be much common ground in our faith in the future of man, in our joint concern for moral values, and in the striving for a world where men can live as brothers and human individuality be expressed; we recognize also that there are many urgent issues for common effort; the preservation of peace, opposition to racialism, the fight against all forms of discrimination, servitude, indignity. Examination of this common ground as well as the means of joint action would be fruitful for both sides.

Communists have confidence in the future of mankind; in man's ability through struggle and effort to transform society, increasingly to gain control of nature and so to open up new vistas for humanity. We hold that human nature is not fixed; that men and women in the course of ending class exploitation, injustice, war, in the course of changing society, will change their own nature and fit themselves for the future society, in which human personality can develop to the full. The history of man will be a continuous, never-ending exploration of nature and man.

Such is the Marxist perspective; in the meantime it is evident that there is a great need as well as a firm basis for common contact and work between Marxists, atheists, agnostics, and those who hold a religious faith.

## Religious freedom

To facilitate this we wish to make it clear that the Communist Party will fight now under capitalism, and work in the future under socialism, for complete freedom of religious worship, for the right of all faiths to worship in their own churches with their own sacred books and for making available the resources necessary for ritual articles. We consider that both under capitalism and socialism, religious and non-religious views should freely contend. Finally we wish to make it clear that the Communist Party welcomes people of any religious faith including those who are ministers, not only working side by side with Marxists in common causes, but as members of the Communist Party, provided they accept the political program of our party. We have never made, nor will we, acceptance of religious beliefs a bar to membership of our party.

## DEMOCRACY

The Communist Party is sometimes asked, what is its attitude to the transition to socialism? How do we envisage the change from capitalist democracy to socialist democracy?

With the publication in 1951 of our program, *The British Road to Socialism,* we have shown how, in our opinion, this transformation may be brought about.

The aim of the Communist Party in the first place is to win socialism, when political and economic power pass out of the hands of the capitalist class into the hands of the working class. We hold that this involves a revolutionary change—a socialist revolution. Revolutionary change does not necessarily involve violence and bloodshed—it can take different forms; essentially, revolutionary change involves a fundamental change in political power. Any attempt by reactionaries to use force or illegal means to resist or obstruct the socialist legislation of the elected government of the people will have to be firmly rejected. To secure and defend the revolution, the rule of the working people is essential. Given the unity of the working class, as well as leadership and clarity of purpose, the people can be strong enough to hold their gains. We believe that the possibility now exists of achieving socialism through our traditional democratic institutions including Parliament by struggle but without armed conflict and civil war. It is this perspective which is held out in our program and which forms the basis of our policy.

Monopoly capitalism is at present vigorously attacking all the achievements of democracy. It is our aim to defend these achievements and to develop them to the maximum extent. The freedom of the trade unions, freedom of the press, of meeting, the freedoms embodied in our democratic institutions, the jury system, local government, parliament, were won in the struggle of the working class and its allies in the past. Their defense and extension is an essential aspect of the advance to socialism, as is the ending of all forms of racial discrimination, and the recognition of national rights for Scotland and Wales.

The more effectively these freedoms are now defended and extended, the more easily will the transition to socialism be brought about.

### The British Road

Communists see socialist democracy as both a continuation and a qualitative extension of all that is best in democracy under capitalism. What has been won must be kept, but the essential limitations of capitalist democracy—ownership by a small minority of capitalists of the key sources of wealth, their domination of the machinery of state, and of the institutions of education, culture, the press and opinion formation—must be ended, and in different forms pass into the hands of the majority.

In *The British Road to Socialism* we make clear that we do not envisage the advance to socialism as the work of a single party, but as the work of a broad front in which the Communist Party, the socialists of the Labor Party and Labor movement, industrial and professional workers and intellectuals, participate together in common struggle inside and outside Parliament.

We stand for a plurality of parties, including those that do not accept, or oppose, the advance to socialism. Naturally all parties will be expected to obey the laws of the land passed by the democratically elected socialist majority.

Socialist ideas and socialist leaders will be strengthened by the daily contest of ideas and attitudes that this will necessitate. We stand for taking away from such parties the special class privileges, based on the ownership of private property, that they enjoy today. But we aim to defeat parties defending specific class privileges by the strength of socialist ideas, the success of a socialist economy, culture and administration, and by the mass struggle of the people

led by the working class. Only if such parties themselves undertake violent or illegal activity will they invoke against themselves measures of law. But such is not our aim.

### HUMANISM

We, who are Marxists, claim to be the most consistent humanists of our time. One cannot be a genuine humanist in words alone.

We stand for a classless, communist society, where all men and women, freed from the divisions of class, from national and racial hostilities, can develop to the full their human potentialities. But to reach such a society men and women must struggle now against war, against colonialism, against the exploitation of man by man, against the dehumanization that capitalism inevitably involves both for the majority of ruled and the minority of rulers.

Modern technique is beyond individual control; it cannot be fitted into the framework of capitalist firms or even national frontiers. Science and technique, the results of long-term collective activity, require a new social organization for their full potential development. Such technique can remove from mankind the sordid cares of hunger, disease, monotonous, repetitious labor, drudgery in all its forms, and take away the fears of insecurity. The achievement of socialism and still more, communism, will speed the day when science and technique can so develop that the age-old division of mental and manual labor will be brought to an end.

In such a society the individual can really blossom, develop to the full his "slumbering powers." In such a society, man can begin to live a fully human existence, bringing to an end his alienation from the products of his activity and so from society, and entering into a direct relation with his fellow men.

For Communists the aim and purpose of all our action and struggle is not only a world where exploitation and oppression is ended, where the full resources of science and technique are released and put in the service of man, where the fear of war is ended, but a society—a communist Britain and a communist world—where the individual can freely develop his many-sided talents.

### THE COMMUNIST PARTY

It is for this end that Communists all over the world have lived, fought, sacrificed, and sometimes died. Whether man today is on the threshold of a new society, or whether mankind fails even to survive to reach this society, depends to no small extent on what we do today. Never has any generation held to this extent posterity in its hands!

For technique can be used for destruction as well as for construction; if the bombs begin to fall, the survivors, if any, might regret their survival.

Millions, as we know, can starve in a world of surplus, redundancy can reduce families to fear and misery when the machines are brought to a halt. In this world of contradictions many seek a road, a direction, a purpose, "a strategy for struggle."

Without it, some will accept the system; others, bewildered, come to despair and passivity.

Marxism does not replace the labour of scientists nor the creation of artists, yet it gives them an approach to an understanding of the world in all its complexity, and indicates how they can help so to change it that their inventions and creations are turned to the joy and welfare of man.

The weakness of the great working-class movement of this country, with all its strength and traditions of organization and struggle, has been above all a lack of theory and perspective. This is what reformism's boasts of pragmatism mean. For the adaption to circumstances, rejection of theory, means acceptance of the capitalist outlook and of capitalist society.

We welcome all those who have come in one way or another to appreciate the importance of Marxist approaches in different fields of research. We hope to work closely in discussion and co-operation with them. But we feel that a consistent, logical application of Marxism to the world today, above all to problems of changing it, of ending imperialism, capitalism, and building socialism and communism demands Marxist political organization—the Communist Party.

We appeal, therefore, to all to deeply consider this question and to join our ranks. As Marx wrote the point is not just to interpret the world, but to change it. If there is to *be* a world to be *interpreted* it will have to be *changed*.

# RESOLUTION OF THE 11TH PLENARY MEETING, COMMUNIST PARTY OF GREECE

*Complete Text*
(*Information Bulletin,* No. 104, 1967)

1. The fascist military dictatorship, the product of the coup of April 21, is the dictatorship of the ultra-reactionary servile circles of the Greek plutocracy. It was established with the connivance and direct support of the more aggressive circles of U.S. imperialism and NATO. Behind it stand foreign monopolies, predominantly American ones.

The dictatorship is inimical to the entire nation, to its supreme interests, its honor and dignity. The democratic movement has been dealt a severe blow. The democratic gains of the Greek people, won at the cost of many years of hard struggle and sacrifice, have been abolished.

A new seat of tension and provocation has been created in the Eastern Mediterranean and the Balkans. New grave trials have fallen to the lot of the Greek people, and the prospect before them is one of grim struggle.

The dictatorship's internal-policy aims are to destroy the powerful democratic movement for the renovation of Greek society, settle the problems of the country in an anti-popular way, to depose the Cypriot government in a coup and hasten the settlement of the Cyprus problem in the interests of NATO, to turn the people of Greece into a defenseless object of ruthless exploitation by foreign and domestic monopolies. In the field of foreign policy, it intends to strengthen the position of the imperialists and NATO in Greece, to use the country as a base for imperialist gambles in the Balkans and the Middle East, to hit the liberation and democratic movements so that fascist regimes could be installed in other countries of Europe, and to stem the important movement for mutual understanding and cooperation of states and for the establishment of a European collective security system.

2. Although the governments that succeeded one another following the coup of July 1965 relied on the Right forces and reaction strengthened its positions in the army and in key government posts, they were unable to contain mass actions and break up the democratic movement. The people and the political forces continued to move towards democracy. The influence of the CPG and other Left forces was on the uprise. Serious openings toward democracy developed in the Center Union.

The anti-constitutional and anti-democratic policy and activities of the royal court, which is the pole of concentration of reaction, and of the Right forces before and after July 15, 1965, were paving the way for the establishment of military dictatorship.

Two trends were taking shape among the reactionaries: to achieve their ends either through an electoral coup or through an open military dictatorship.

The formation of the Kanellopoulos government was a victory for the trend to enter upon an anti-democratic road behind the smokescreen of parliamentarism, through rigged elections in conditions of violence.

But the more reactionary internal and external forces, the junta and the U.S. and NATO militarists would not be satisfied even with that solution, i.e., the holding of such elections by the Kanellopoulos government, for they saw that even if the elections yielded the expected results they would be unable to subdue the powerful democratic movement and free their hands for the realization of their anti-popular, anti-national plans.

Such were the causes that led to the coup and the establishment of the military-fascist dictatorship.

The recent aggravation of the international situation resulting from the global aggressiveness of U.S. imperialism, especially the preparation for aggression in the Middle and Near East, was an important factor that speeded the putschists' hand.

3. In a situation characterized by the active interference of the Americans in our internal affairs, the strong positions held by the military and the concentration of the Right forces in the ERE party and around the royal court, only unity of action and strong organization of the democratic forces could stop the process of fascization, foil the plans for the establishment of an open dictatorship and clear the way to democratic development.

Although the reactionaries managed to consolidate their positions in the recent period, their plans could have been foiled and the coup prevented if the democratic forces, in face of the direct threat of dictatorship, had fought in common, as the Left suggested.

The historic responsibility for the fact that democratic unity failed to materialize rests with the Center Union leadership.

The anti-unity stand of the Center Union leadership, its concessions to and compromises with the rightists, its anti-communism and fear of the popular movement, its refusal to purge reactionaries from the army, the security organs and the administrative apparatus, to repeal the emergency measures and clean the General Confederation of Labor and other trade union organizations of agents of the monopolies and stooges of the rightists hampered the movement towards democracy and made that movement extremely painful. Finally, the resignation of the Center Union government in July 1965, when the reactionaries had mounted an offensive, and its compromises with the rightists in 1966-67 weakened the unity of the democratic forces and objectively facilitated the reactionaries' plans.

4. Throughout these years of the fierce offensive of reaction and fascism the Communist Party and other Left forces were in the van of the struggle as consistent champions of democracy and the interests of the people.

In keeping with their policy of democratic cooperation, they fought in the front ranks together with other democrats and patriots for the freedoms and democratic rights of the Greek people.

The CPG and other Left forces pursued a correct policy of mobilizing the broadest possible democratic forces in a struggle for a democratic way out of the political crisis in Greece. They advocated support of the Center Union government in 1963 and backed its every positive step so that its promises could be carried out. The CPG and the EDA supported the Center Union government in August 1964 to ward off the direct threat of a fascist coup. Owing to the unitary policy of the CPG and the EDA the reactionaries found themselves in isolation, and there was increasing democratic unity of action among the lower- and middle-level activists, which helped intensify the resistance of the people to the reactionaries' plans.

In February 1966, when the menace of dictatorship assumed even more concrete forms, the EDA submitted to all political forces opposed to lawlessness a five-point program which could serve as a real basis for joint action and agreement to foil the conspirators' plans and ensure normal democratic development.

5. In the hard struggle for the solution of the problems facing the people and the country campaigning against the plans of the reactionaries and for a democratic way out of the political anomaly, the CPG and the EDA were not free from weaknesses, shortcomings and mistakes which could not but affect this struggle.

The CC and the Political Bureau did not make a proper analysis of some new factors, such as the growing interest in Greece the imperialists showed in their strategic plans, especially following the outbreak of the serious crisis in NATO, the ever greater dependence of the Greek army on the imperialists and NATO, and the increasing role of the military.

The CPG was correct in stating that a severe political crisis broke out in July 1965 and that the people were faced with a choice between fascism and democracy. But later on it failed to take stock of all data testifying to consolidation of the reactionaries' positions. It did not see clearly that the contradictions between the centrists and the rightists were growing in acuteness as a result of the popular resistance, that the reactionaries' attempts to base their policy on a compromise of the centrists with the rightists were falling through, and that the more reactionary elements were increasingly urging an open fascist dictatorship.

Although the Party had repeatedly warned against the danger of a fascist putsch, in the recent period it underestimated this danger and tended to orient itself on resistance to an electoral coup. This is one more reason why the events of April 21 caught us somewhat unawares.

Along with weaknesses, shortcomings and mistakes of a rightist nature, in implementing its unitary tactics the Party sometimes displayed a rather narrow-minded approach to problems, which certainly affected the struggle for democratic unity.

The Party proved inadequately prepared ideologically, organizationally and technically to act properly in the new situation. This was chiefly due to the highly unsatisfactory implementation of the decisions adopted by the 8th Congress and other Party organs after the 6th Plenary Meeting. As a result, the functionaries were not properly trained in the ideological, political and organization respects for successful struggle in any contingency.

On the other hand, the illusions in our ranks that the situation would develop more or less normally further complicated the ideological, political and organizational preparation of the Party and the masses generally for combating the danger of dictatorship.

Another serious omission was that the Party did not pay attention to the Army and conducted no work in it.

The grave responsibility for all these omissions, shortcomings and mistakes in the work of the Party rests with the Political Bureau, the Secretariat and the entire Central Committee.

6. Although the junta came out on top and received every support from its foreign patrons, its power is insecure. The Greek people are definitively opposed to the dictatorship, loathed also by the country's political world and a large part of the army officers, who feel humiliated by the colonels, puppets of the foreigners.

The junta is opposed by world public opinion, especially in Europe, for whom the newly-installed dictatorship in Greece signifies that fascism is knocking at their door. A number of Western statesmen, even governments of NATO countries and some inter-governmental organizations have expressed their negative attitude toward the coup.

There are contradictions within the dictatorship itself, especially between the junta and the royal court and among the putschists themselves. The instability of the national economy and the grave difficulties suffered by it following the coup aggravate these contradictions and the dictators' instability.

Contradictions also exist between the imperialist forces which directly or indirectly support the present regime.

The dictators' attempt to camouflage the nature of the regime and assuage incensed world public opinion by promises of a new Constitution and a return to parliamentarism is a dangerous maneuver which must be exposed and resisted. The new Constitution will in all probability be nothing more than the charter of the fascist dictatorship.

7. On the day of the coup the Communist Party urged the people to unite in the broadest possible national movement, the broadest possible front of all parties, organizations and leaders irrespective of their political positions, from Left to Right, which would act to overthrow the dictatorship and restore democratic order, to enable the people to solve the

problems of the country without foreign interference. The Party has been working to build this front, to mobilize the people against the dictatorship.

The establishment of the Patriotic Front by some Left, Center and Right leaders is a positive development. The Communist Party considers that at a time of grave trials that fell to the lot of the Greek people and threaten the destiny of the country, supreme national interests demand that all democratic forces should leave aside their political differences and coordinate and unite their efforts on the basis of a common program of struggle which could envisage the following: *deposition of the dictatorship; restoration of constitutional and democratic freedoms; freedom of action for all parties and organizations; release of all detainees; general political amnesty; dissolution of the junta; free elections according to a simple proportionate system, to be conducted by a government of all parties.*

There exist, of course, other serious problems which concern the people and the democratic world, such as a revision of the Constitution and the problem of the monarchy. The CPG considers, however, that the different attitudes of the parties toward these problems should not prevent coordinated and united action of all anti-dictatorship forces, on the basis of a common program for one immediate aim—sweeping away the dictatorship.

Action against the dictators should assume most diverse forms, from the distribution of leaflets and the issue of slogans to strikes, demonstrations and open nationwide struggle. The form of the latter will be determined in its process.

The greater the unity of action of the working class, the main force in the struggle against the dictatorship, the greater the strength of the Patriotic Front. Progressive organization against the dictatorship and the struggle of the working class can impart strength and magnitude to the entire anti-dictatorship movement and struggle. In the labor movement, the front can materialize in most varied forms, such as unitary committees in factories and offices, among ship crews, in any branch where the struggle for immediate economic demands will be combined with the struggle against the dictatorship. Work in the trade unions, cooperatives, all organizations of the people is of the utmost importance.

The Communist Party thinks very highly of the assistance given to the anti-dictatorship struggle by world public opinion and the Greek emigrants. It believes, however, that the outcome of the struggle will be decided by the unity and actions of the people, by the efforts of all the anti-dictatorship forces in Greece herself.

8. The plenary meeting regards it as a top-priority task of the Party to ensure independent formation of Party branches on the principles of underground work, vigilance and strict decentralization. All Communists must unite in illegal Party organizations. An influx of new members, especially from among the youth, is of vital importance for the Party. The Party branches must exert every effort to set up an underground technical apparatus which should be strictly decentralized and discharge its specific functions.

Exceptional importance attaches to our work in the army, the security organs and the entire state apparatus. It is necessary to assign suitable forces to carry on this work, to conduct propaganda in the army with the help of all the means the Party possesses.

Special attention should be paid to the Party's work among emigrants, students and all Greeks residing abroad, as well as among seamen. It is necessary to improve our work among political emigrants and especially among young people, so as to ensure their stronger links with the movement in Greece and their greater contribution to the struggle of our people. Serious work should be conducted among the Party rank and file and functionaries to enhance vigilance and improve the security of the Party. These matters assume special urgency today.

In the difficult conditions of dictatorship the need is particularly great for the unity of the Party, for the cohesion of its members and activists on the basis of the Party's line and decisions.

The plenary meeting considers that along with reconstructing their organizations Communists should help reconstruct the organizations of the EDA and all popular organizations.

Aware of the existing difficulties, the 11th Plenary Meeting of the CC CPG calls upon all Communists, all activists, members and supporters of the Party to apply themselves with optimism to the hard struggle and, marching, as always, in the front ranks, to become ardent propagandists, tireless organizers and courageous fighters in the anti-dictatorship patriotic front against the monarcho-fascist tyranny and for the victory of democracy.

# "THE BUDAPEST MEETING"

Article by Zóltán Komocsin, Member of the Politburo,
Hungarian Socialist Workers' Party

*Complete Text*
(*Népszabadság*, Budapest, 24 December 1967)

Both in the international Communist movement and in the general world situation we concurrently notice great events and serious difficulties. The forces of socialism, national independence, and peace are developing and rushing forward throughout the world. It is a compulsory consequence of this social and historical progress that the authority and influence of Marxist-Leninist ideas and of Communist parties are increasing on all continents. The most important difficulty along with the successes of the Communist parties, is that there has been no unity in the international Communist movement for a long time. All progressive forces feel the resulting damage, while the imperialists are encouraged by this lack of unity in the international Communist movement. This explains why the imperialist forces of exploitation and repression have become more aggressive during the past few years, although the general formation of the world situation creates favorable conditions for the forces of socialism, international independence, peace, and progress. In the imperialist international policy, upheaval, military putsch, and even military aggression have been emphasized as the example of Vietnam shows.

It is obvious, if we consider historical experience and the correlation of forces, that the imperialists' successes are only temporary and local. Gigantic forces are opposing the imperialists throughout the world and are waging a selfless struggle to curb and repress aggression. Hence it is more important for the main forces in the struggle against imperialism, the Communist and workers' parties on all continents, to wage a campaign to reestablish the unity of our international movement and to strengthen it.

Every fraternal party can do much to unify the international Communist movement and to increase its strength and striking power. The individual Communist and workers' parties will primarily serve both the cause of their fatherland and the common cause of international progress by pursuing a correct and useful policy in their own country and in the international arena. Any party, whether large or small, whether powerful or not, will also contribute by its own achievements within its national limits to the successes of our international movement This is a most important factor by which we can strengthen and develop the international Communist movement.

The fraternal parties, however, have collective tasks in the common interest. Consider the following interconnection: the independent activities of individual parties promoted the multiplication of strength in the entire international movement, and, on the other hand, collective, common, and combined efforts create a more favorable situation for the more successful struggle of the individual parties within their national limits.

Nothing is more obvious in the present situation than what would be most important to the individual Communist and workers' parties and also for our entire international movement: Eliminating all the ideological-political contradictions existing between the CCP and the great majority of the fraternal parties.

Eliminating them would lead to a new unity producing an extraordinary increase in the strength of the international workers' movement. It is obvious, however, from the generally known events, that this main contradiction, the worst hindrance to unity, cannot be shortly liquidated. All this, however, does not mean that we can do nothing, that we must resign ourselves to a passive role and wait infinitely. Until total unity is reestablished on problems of ideology and policy, of strategy and tactics, the fraternal parties can and do make efforts to create unity of action on most important and urgent issues. The present situation of the international Communist movement demands that we reject the slogan "everything or nothing," and that we not rely only on the passing of time; we should instead find possible methods to do the most for our common cause. These methods include the increasingly frequent bilateral and multilateral meetings and exchanges of opinion among fraternal parties.

It would be wrong to consider such bilateral and multilateral meetings only as a compulsive and temporary form produced by the unfavorable nature of the present situation, by the disintegration of our unity. It is certain that we found in them a method and form of relations among the fraternal parties which will become even more frequent in the future. Such bilateral and multilateral meetings facilitate a mutual and thorough study of experiences gained by the Communist and Workers' parties, but they are also an expression of the independence and self-reliance of the individual parties.

Social progress on individual continents, and even more in individual countries, comprises—in addition to the general characteristics, or within these—a great many individual moves and various intricate and divergent conditions. It is primarily the task of the communists of a given country to consider and analyze both identical and different social phenomena and problems. This demands not only that the parties possess theoretical alertness and adopt Marxism-Leninism in a flexible manner, but also that they develop their work methods and forms of relations with fraternal parties and progressive forces.

In this respect the future will certainly pose even greater demands to us and will certainly bring even more changes.

The greater frequency of bilateral and multilateral meetings is to the advantage of the entire international Communist movement. Realizing this, representatives of our party have conducted useful bilateral exchanges of opinion with the representatives of about 50 fraternal parties during the year. Last April our party sent its representatives to Karlovy Vary to the conference of the European Communist and Workers' parties; in July 1966 our party-government delegation took part in the Bucharest conference of European socialist countries, and last June at their Moscow conference, and then in July at the Budapest meeting. We also approved of bilateral and multilateral meetings of the other fraternal parties at which no representatives of our party took part, for example, the conference of the West European Communist and workers' parties in May 1966 and even earlier, that of the Latin American Communist and Workers' parties.

Adopting on principle and practically utilizing the method of bilateral and multilateral party meetings, together with the majority of the Communist and Workers' parties, we advocate holding an international conference of fraternal parties. Just as it would be a mistake to disregard the positive role played by bilateral and multilateral meetings, it would also be incorrect to oppose these to large-scale international conferences. We need both approaches; one cannot replace or substitute for the other.

Our own and unmistakably approving viewpoint does not prevent us, however, from understanding the debate about the great international conference, and, after all, we consider this natural.

The debate on whether the Communist and workers' parties should or should not hold an international conference to include the entire movement, or at least the majority of the parties—this debate shows that the individual fraternal parties approach today's great problems of the international situation and Communist movement differently, as questions requiring answers and solutions, and with regard for their own special position. This is precisely why we must not disregard any argument prompted by common interests, goals, and responsibilities, regardless of what attitude individual fraternal parties finally assume on the international conference. The essence of our viewpoint is that our Central Committee will support any initiative and exchange of opinions for a better understanding and unity. We believe that an international conference of Communist and Workers' parties would promote this. For our part we—and we are sure that most of the fraternal parties agree—want an international conference promoting better understanding and unity among all Communist and Workers' parties, including those who probably feel that they cannot take part in the common effort at the present time.

Past and present debates reveal that we must liberate the idea of an international conference of Communist and Workers' parties from two kinds of phobia, one following from the fact that the communists, partly by themselves, and partly duped by bourgeois-propaganda, are trying to guess, among endless dramatic tirades, what would happen if the conference should take place and certain parties were not present. What would happen, what would the world say? We must certainly not neglect the foreseeable factual difficulties, but we should not allow these thoughts to paralyze us. We will act correctly if we realistically envisage all problems and make maximal efforts for the benefit of our common cause without being self-centered, disregarding considerations of prestige.

It is another phobia if people think that holding an international conference would mean a turning point in world history. Historical turning points are produced by social struggles. The Communist movement is the heart of the worldwide class struggle and of historical development regardless of bilateral or multilateral exchanges of opinion and international meetings.

We must consider the idea of an international conference of Communist and Workers' parties in connection with present realities. We must accustom the international Communist movement, ourselves, the progressive forces which are our allies, and even our enemies to the fact that, if necessary, and in addition to other methods, we will occasionally avail ourselves of the benefits furnished by an international conference.

The success of an international conference of Communist and Workers' parties depends to a great extent on the goals we set for it, on the tasks we will try to solve thereby, and on the manner in which we prepare and conduct it, if it materializes at all. Those fraternal parties which so far have advocated holding an international conference unanimously state that their goal is to strengthen unity. This goal determines the topic of the conference and the method for its preparation and conduct.

In view of the present situation, an international conference would serve our unity most successfully if we exchanged opinions on the most important topic for all Communist and Workers' parties—the present tasks in the anti-imperialist struggle. Each fraternal party separately is almost continuously dealing with this problem in bilateral and multilateral exchanges of opinion. While realizing that this is important in the struggle against imperialism, we must emphasize that all this cannot replace collective experience and wisdom on this basic issue—an experience contributed to by all continents. We must solve this problem: Are the Communists capable, on the basis of a comradely exchange of opinion, of collective evaluation and deduction, of making more thorough analyses, determining the tasks and goals more forcefully, and on this basis taking more effective countermeasures? It is our conviction that the Communist and Workers' parties of the different continents are certainly capable of this, and an international conference cannot be replaced by anything else.

The international conference of Communist and workers' parties will be totally worthwhile if it solves the most urgent problems of today's struggle for the national liberation movement and for peace. After all, this task is closely related to the struggle against imperialism. We also think that an international conference would be an opportunity to disclose the current possibilities for united activity by all anti-imperialist forces and to show the road to cohesion and unity and to increase the strength of the communists and all anti-imperialist forces struggling for peace.

We entered a new period in our efforts to convene a great international conference after the statement of the 18 fraternal parties published on 25 November. As is known, the 18 fraternal parties undertook to convene a consultative meeting concerning a great international conference of Communist and Workers' parties. By agreement among the fraternal parties, this consultative meeting will take place in Budapest in February 1968. Our Party Central Committee will make every possible effort to comply with this honorable international assignment.

Preparations for the Budapest meeting have begun. As a first step, our Party Central Committee sent invitations to the Central Committee of all fraternal parties whose representatives took part in the 1960 Moscow international conference of Communist and Workers' parties.

It is clear that a consultative meeting is not tantamount to a great international conference. It also follows from the consultative nature of this meeting that on this occasion the topic of a great international conference will not be discussed because it will be precisely the task of this meeting to plan this collectively. In Budapest in 1968 the participants primarily will exchange opinions on convening a great international conference of Communist and Workers' parties. The Budapest meeting will collectively implement what so far the fraternal parties have pursued in bilateral exchanges of opinion. Individual delegations will express the standpoints of their parties freely and democratically on all issues connected with the international conference and probably also other problems they think it necessary to discuss at that time.

Our party thinks that the prime condition for the success of the consultative meeting and the international conference is for all interested fraternal parties to take part democratically and collectively in their preparation and conduct.

We must insure both at the Budapest and the subsequent large conference a comradely exchange of opinion concerns the issues jointly placed on the agenda, and that there be no interference in the internal affairs of any party. We must prevent any party from being the recipient of epithets, and we must in particular prevent fraternal parties from being divided into camps, condemned, or excluded from our international conference unlike decisions made by the leading organs of individual parties, mandatory for party members concerned—cannot be mandatory and must be considered as directives to be implemented by the appropriate leading organ of each party, according to the peculiarities of its situation. Last year's bilateral exchanges of opinions with the representatives of fraternal parties showed that the great majority of the Communist and Workers' parties expressed the same opinion as our party about norms for relations among parties, that is, the method for preparing and holding international meetings and conferences.

The appeal of the 18 fraternal parties to hold a consultative meeting was followed by interested and for the most part approving comment. So far, about 30 fraternal parties have accepted the appeal and stated that they will take part in the Budapest meeting. We would like every invited fraternal party to send its representativies to the February consultative meeting in Budapest. Each fraternal party will of course decide by itself whether it wants to take part or not in one or the other preparations or in the international conference itself. We on our part will do everything to insure the best possible conditions for all participants at the Budapest meeting. We are also prepared to hold bilateral talks with the representatives of any fraternal party—even up to February—either about the preparations or the manner in which we imagine that the meeting should be run.

Owing to democratic and collective efforts, the Budapest consultative meeting of Communist and Workers' parties will be able to cope with its task successfully. It will be able to promote better understanding and strength unity, and it will be able to help the great conference to be prepared in a manner acceptable to all fraternal parties. If this is the case it is sure to be useful for the international Communist movement and for the forces throughout the world struggling for national independence and freedom, and for peace.

# "BUILD THE PKI ALONG THE MARXIST-LENINIST LINE TO LEAD THE PEOPLE'S DEMOCRATIC REVOLUTION IN INDONESIA"

Self-Criticism of the Political Bureau of the Central Committee
of the Indonesian Communist Party (PKI)

*Complete Text*
(*Indonesian Tribune*, Vol. 1, No. 3, January 1967)

In the Statement of the Political Bureau issued in commemoration of the 46th anniversary of the founding of the Party, it was stated among other things that "the fact that counter-revolutionary forces within a short time have succeeded in their attacks and inflicted such a great damage to the PKI demands from us, who are still capable to continue the revolutionary struggle, to make criticism and self-criticism as the only correct way to find our shortcomings and mistakes in the theoretical, political and organizational fields, in order to correct them."

The disaster which has caused such serious losses to the PKI and the revolutionary movement of the Indonesian people after the outbreak and the defeat of the September 30th Movement has lifted up the curtain which for a long period had hidden the grave weaknesses of the PKI. The PKI leadership had been engaged in adventurism. Violating organizational rules they had easily involved themselves in the September 30th Movement that was not based on the high consciousness and conviction of the masses. And therefore they had caused the isolation of the Party from the masses of the people. On the contrary, after the defeat of the September 30th Movement the Party leadership carried out a Right opportunist line, by entrusting president Sukarno with the fate of the Party and the revolutionary movement. These were the climax of the serious shortcomings and weaknesses of the PKI in the ideological, political and organizational fields.

The Political Bureau is aware that it has the greatest responsibility with regard to the grave weaknesses and mistakes of the Party during the period under review. Therefore, the Political Bureau is giving serious attention to and highly appreciates all criticisms from cadres and members of the Party given in a Marxist-Leninist spirit, as well as honest criticism from Party sympathizers that have been expressed in different ways. The Political Bureau is resolved to make self-criticism in a Marxist-Leninist way, putting into practice the teaching of Lenin and the example of Comrade Musso in unfolding Marxist-Leninist criticism and self-criticism. Lenin has taught us that "the attitude of a political party towards its own mistake is one of the most important and surest ways of judging how earnest the Party is and how it in *practice* fulfills its obligation towards its *class* and the toiling *masses.* Frankly admitting a mistake, ascertaining the reasons for it, analyzing the conditions which led to it, and thoroughly discussing the means of correcting it—that is the earmark of a serious party; that is the way it should perform its duties, that is the way it

should educate and train the *class,* and then the *masses.*" (V.I. Lenin, *"Left-Wing" Communism, An Infantile Disorder.*)

In August, 1948, Comrade Musso set an example in the Political Bureau of the Central Committee on how to conduct criticism and self-criticism in a free, Marxist-Leninist way, against the serious mistakes and weaknesses of the PKI in the years of the August Revolution of 1945. Thanks to the merciless criticism and self-criticism against the weaknesses and mistakes, a way-out was found so as to reestablish the PKI as the vanguard of the Indonesian working class, restore the good tradition of the PKI in the period before, during and after the World War II, and enable the PKI to wrest the hegemony in the leadership of the revolution. (The New Road for the Republic of Indonesia, Resolution of the Political Bureau of the CC PKI, August 1948.)

The internal Party struggle which took place during the rebuilding of the Party after the heavy blow of the "Madiun Provocation" and during the realization of "The New Road" (Resolution of the Political Bureau of the CC PKI, August 1948), brought into being the new Political Bureau in 1951. The experience of the Party until the outbreak of the September 30th Movement has shown that the Political Bureau which was elected in 1951 and re-elected by the Central Committee of the Vth and the VIth Congresses not only had failed in implementing the Great Correction of Comrade Musso that was stated in "The New Road," but had committed serious deviations from Marxism-Leninism. As a result, the PKI was unable to fulfill its historical mission as the vanguard of the working class and leader of the liberation struggle of the Indonesian people.

In view of the seriousness of the weaknesses and mistakes involving the whole Party, the Political Bureau considers it necessary to make a complete analysis, to enable every Party member to make the most thorough study of them, so that the recurrence of the same weaknesses and mistakes in the future can be avoided. However, under the situation where the most vicious and cruel white terror is being unleashed by the Nasution-Suharto military dictatorship of the right-wing army generals, it is not easy to make as complete criticism and self-criticism as possible. To meet the urgent necessity, we consider it necessary to point out the main mistakes and weaknesses of the Party in the ideological, political and organizational fields, in order to facilitate the study of the weaknesses and mistakes of the Party during the current rectification movement.

With all modesty and sincerity the Political Bureau presents this self-criticism. The Political Bureau expects all members to take an active part in the discussions of the weaknesses and mistakes of the Party leadership, critically analyze them, and do their utmost to improve this self-criticism of the Political Bureau by drawing lessons from their respective experiences, collectively or individually. The Political Bureau expects all members to take firm hold of the principle: "unity–criticism–unity" and "learning from past mistakes to avoid future ones, and curing the sickness to save the patient, in order to achieve the two-fold objective of clarity in ideology and unity among comrades" (Mao Tse-tung, *Our Study and the Current Situation*). The Political Bureau is convinced that, by holding firmly to this correct principle, every Party member will take part in the movement to study and surmount these weaknesses and mistakes with the determination to rebuild the PKI along the Marxist-Leninist line, to strengthen Communist unity and solidarity, to raise the ideological, political and organizational vigilance, and to heighten the fighting spirit in order to win victory.

### The Main Weaknesses in the Ideological Field

"The New Road" Resolution, in pointing out the main cause of the principal mistakes made by the PKI in the organizational and political fields during the period of the August Revolution, states: "The Political Bureau considers that these principal errors are mainly caused by the ideological weaknesses of the Party."

The serious weaknesses and mistakes of the Party in the period after 1951 certainly had as their source the weaknesses in the ideological field, too, especially among the Party leadership. The source of these ideological weaknesses is the petty-bourgeois class origin and the lack of knowledge of Marxism-Leninism among the Party leadership. Lenin has taught us that "without a revolutionary theory there can be no revolutionary movement" and that "the role of vanguard fighter can be fulfilled only by a party that is guided by the most advanced theory." (V. I. Lenin, *What is to Be Done?*) The experience of the Indonesian Communists fully testifies to the truth of Lenin's teaching. The serious weaknesses and mistakes which had made the PKI unable to fulfill its role as the vanguard of the Indonesian working class had been caused not only by the failure of the Party leadership to integrate revolutionary theories with the concrete practice of the Indonesian revolution, but also by the adoption of the road which was divorced from the guidance of the most advanced theories. This experience shows that the PKI had not succeeded as yet in establishing a core of leadership that was composed of proletarian elements, which really had the most correct understanding of Marxism-Leninism, systematic and not fragmentary, practical and not abstract understanding.

The ideological weaknesses of our Party have a long historical root. The source of these weaknesses is subjectivism. The social basis for this subjectivist ideology is the petty-bourgeois class. Indonesia is a country of the petty-bourgeoisie, where small-owners'

enterprises, in particular individual farms, are found in great number. Our Party is surrounded by a large petty-bourgeois class, and many Party members have come from this class. Inevitably, petty-bourgeois ideas and habits are brought into the Party. The petty-bourgeois method of thinking in analyzing problems is subjective and one-sided. It proceeds not from objective reality, nor from objective balance of forces among classes, but from subjective wishes, subjective feelings and subjective imagination. Subjectivism is the ideological root of dogmatism and empiricism in the theoretical field, of Right or "Left" opportunism in the political field, and of liberalism or sectarianism in the organizational field; these are diseases that have afflicted our Party.

During the period when we were implementing "The New Road" resolution, an internal struggle took place within our Party against subjectivism. But as it turned out, the struggle did not succeed in completely eradicating this ideology of subjectivism. This was shown by the Vth National Congress of the Party. During the Congress, sharp criticisms were directed at subjectivism which constituted a stumbling block in the implementation of "The New Road" resolution. But at the same time, the Congress committed the same mistake by adopting the Manifesto for General Elections of the PKI which put forward the program for the establishment of a people's democratic power through the general elections. This was a simultaneous manifestation of "Left" and Right opportunism. Viewed as a program that went too far and beyond the reach of the existing objective conditions, it was a "Leftist" error. But viewed from its line of thinking that a people's democratic power could be achieved through general elections, thus by peaceful means, it was a rightist error.

During the period after 1951, subjectivism continued to grow, gradually became greater and greater and gave rise to Right opportunism that merged with the influence of modern revisionism in the International Communist Movement. This was the black line of Right opportunism which became the main feature of the mistakes committed by the PKI in this period. The rise and the development of these weaknesses and errors were caused by the following factors:

*First,* the tradition of criticism and self-criticism in a Marxist-Leninist way was not developed in the Party, especially among the Party leadership. One of the many examples was the revocation of the Manifesto for General Elections of the PKI. After it was discovered that the Manifesto was erroneous, it was then withdrawn and replaced by another program, the Program for a Government of National Coalition. But this measure was not followed by an extensive and profound criticism and self-criticism concerning the ideological root of the mistake, merely because "the prestige of the leadership must be safeguarded." Consequently, the substitution of the Manifesto for General Elections by the Program for a Government of National Coalition had failed in thoroughly eradicating the opportunist stand towards the general elections in the framework of bourgeois democracy. We will deal more with this problem later.

The rectification and study movements which from time to time were organized in the Party were not carried out seriously and persistently, their results were not summed up in a good manner, and they were not followed by the appropriate measures in the organizational field. Study movements were aimed more at overcoming certain weaknesses among the rank-and-file, and never at unfolding criticism and self-criticism among the leadership. Criticism from below, far from being carefully listened to, was even suppressed.

The failure to promote the tradition of criticism and self-criticism in a Marxist-Leninist way in the Party, especially among the Party leadership, on the one hand, and the low theoretical level of Party cadres in general on the other hand, had blunted the critical power and the ideological vigilance of Party cadres in general, and of leading cadres in particular.

*Second,* the penetration of the bourgeois ideology along two channels, through contacts with the national bourgeoisie when the Party established a united front with them, and through the bourgeoisiefication of Party cadres, especially the leadership, after the Party obtained certain positions in governmental and semi-governmental institutions. The increasing number of Party cadres who occupied certain positions in governmental and semi-governmental institutions, in the center and in the regions, created "the rank of bourgeoisiefied workers" and this constituted "the real channels for reformism" (V. I. Lenin, *Imperialism, the Highest Stage of Capitalism*). Such a situation did not exist before the August Revolution of 1945.

*Third,* modern revisionism began to penetrate into our Party when the Fourth Plenary Session of the Central Committee of the Vth Congress uncritically approved a report which supported the lines of the 20th Congress of the CPSU, and adopted the line of "achieving Socialism peacefully through parliamentary means" as the line of the PKI. This "peaceful road," one of the characteristics of modern revisionism, was further reaffirmed in the VIth National Congress of the PKI which approved the following passage in the Party Constitution: "there is a possibility that a people's democratic system as a transitional stage to Socialism in Indonesia can be achieved by peaceful means, in a parliamentary way. The PKI persistently strives to transform this possibility into a reality." This revisionist line was further emphasized in the VIIth (Extraordinary) National Congress of the PKI and was never corrected, not even when our Party was already aware that since the 20th Congress of the CPSU, the leadership of the CPSU had been following the road of modern revisionism.

In facing the modern revisionism of the CPSU leadership, the PKI leadership who had been tightly bound by the alliance with the national bourgeoisie took an unprincipled stand. The main consideration for such a stand did not start from the independent interests of the proletariat, but rather from the need to save the alliance with the national bourgeoisie. Though in later years the PKI leadership criticized the various modern revisionist lines of the CPSU leadership and, thanks to this stand, the PKI earned a respectable position in the ranks of the world Marxist-Leninists, they nevertheless continued to maintain their good relations with the leadership of the CPSU, and the influence of modern revisionism in our Party was by no means eradicated.

The experience of the PKI provides us with the lesson that by criticizing the modern revisionism of the CPSU leadership alone, it does not mean that the PKI itself will automatically be free from errors of Right opportunism, the same as what the modern revisionists are doing. The experience of the PKI provides us with the lesson that modern revisionism, the greatest danger in the International Communist Movement, is also the greatest danger for the PKI. For the PKI, modern revisionism is not "a latent but not an acute danger" (D. N. Aidit, *Be a Good and Still Better Communist*), but a concrete danger that has brought great damage to the Party and serious losses for the revolutionary movement of the Indonesian people. Therefore, we must not in any way underestimate the danger of modern revisionism and must wage a resolute and ruthless struggle against it. The firm stand against modern revisionism in all fields can be effectively maintained only when our Party abandons the line of "preserving the friendship with the modern revisionists."

It is a fact that the PKI, while criticizing the modern revisionism of the CPSU leadership, also made revisionist mistakes itself, because it had revised Marxist-Leninist teachings on class struggle, state and revolution. Furthermore, the PKI leadership not only did not wage a struggle in the theoretical field against other "revolutionary" political thoughts which could mislead the proletariat, as Lenin has taught us to do (see Lenin, *What is to be Done?*), but had voluntarily given concessions in the theoretical field. The PKI leadership maintained that there was an identity between the three components of Marxism: materialist philosophy, political economy and scientific socialism, and the so-called "three components of Sukarno's teachings." They wanted to make Marxism, which is the ideology of the working class, the property of the whole nation which includes the exploiting classes hostile to the working class.

### The Main Errors in the Political Field

The mistakes of Right opportunism in the political field which are now under discussion include three problems: (1) the road to People's Democracy in Indonesia, (2) the question of state power, and (3) the implementation of the policy of the national united front.

Right opportunism in the political field reveals itself first and foremost in the choice of the road to be taken (the "peaceful road" or the road of revolution) to achieve people's democracy in Indonesia as a transitional stage to the Socialist system. One of the fundamental differences and problems of disputes between Marxism-Leninism and modern revisionism, both classic and modern, lies precisely in the problem of choosing the road to Socialism. Marxism-Leninism teaches that Socialism can only be achieved through the road of proletarian revolution and that in the case of colonial or semi-colonial and semi-feudal countries like Indonesia, Socialism can only be achieved by first completing the stage of the people's democratic revolution. On the contrary, revisionism dreams of achieving Socialism through the "peaceful road."

Along which process had those mistakes in the political field grown and developed?

For full fifteen years since 1951, the PKI had conducted a legal and parliamentary struggle. Legal and parliamentary form of struggle is a method that must be used by a revolutionary proletarian party in a definite situation and under certain conditions, as Lenin explained in his work, *"Left-Wing" Communism, An Infantile Disorder*. It is a mistake refusing parliamentary struggle when it is needed, and to play with revolution when the conditions are not yet ripe.

The parliamentary struggle as a form of legal struggle carried out by the Party in 1951 was in the main correct, and in accordance with the objective conditions existing at that time. The objective conditions at that time were as follows: the revolutionary tide was at the low ebb, the driving forces of the revolution were not reawakened as yet, and the great majority of the people who had never enjoyed political independence before the August Revolution still cherished great hopes in the bourgeois democracy.

During the initial years of this period, our Party had achieved certain results in the political struggle as well as in the building of the Party. One important achievement of this period was the formulation of the main problems of the Indonesian revolution. It was formulated that the present stage of the Indonesian revolution was a new-type bourgeois democratic revolution, whose tasks were to liquidate imperialism and the vestiges of feudalism and to establish a people's democratic system as a transitional stage to Socialism. The driving forces of the revolution were the working class, the peasantry and the petty bourgeoisie; the leading force of the revolution was the working class and the principal mass strength of the revolution was the peasantry. It was also formulated that the national bourgeoisie was a wavering force of the revolution who might side with the revolution to certain limits and at certain periods but who, at other times, might betray the revolution. The Party furthermore formulated that the working class, in order to fulfill its obligation as the leader of the revolution, must forge a revolutionary united front with other revolutionary classes and groups based on worker-peasant alliance and under the leadership of the working class.

However, there was a very important shortcoming which in later days developed into Right opportunism or revisionism, namely that the Party had not yet come to the clearest unity of minds on the principal means and the main form of struggle of the Indonesian revolution. The Central Committee of the Party had once discussed this problem in broad lines, but in the subsequent period had never discussed this problem intensively so as to reach the most correct single understanding, as a prerequisite to reach the most correct single understanding of this problem in the whole Party.

It is a great mistake for a Party with a historical mission to lead a revolution like the PKI not to make the question of the principal means and the main form of struggle of the Indonesian revolution a problem which concerned the whole Party, but rather a problem that concerned a few persons among the leadership and certain cadres in the Party. Consequently, the minds of the majority in the Party were rendered passive with regard to this most important problem of the revolution.

Though the leadership of the Indonesian revolution is the working class, its principal mass supporters are the peasantry. In view of the small number of the working class in Indonesia, the method of struggle typical to the working class, such as general strikes which are intended to lead the awakening of other driving forces of the revolution and which will develop into an armed insurrection, as in the case of the Russian bourgeois democratic revolution of 1905 (See Lenin, *Lecture on 1905 Revolution*, English Edition, FLPH, Moscow), can never become the main form of struggle or the method of the Indonesian revolution.

The Chinese revolution has provided us with the lesson concerning the main form of struggle of the revolution in colonial or semi-colonial and semi-feudal countries, namely, the people's armed struggle against the armed counter-revolution. In line with the essence of the revolution as an agrarian revolution, then the essence of the people's armed struggle is the armed struggle of the peasants in an agrarian revolution under the leadership of the working class. The practice of the Chinese revolution is first and foremost the application of Marxism-Leninism to the concrete conditions of China. At the same time, it has laid down the general law for the revolutions of the peoples in colonial or semi-colonial and semi-feudal countries.

To achieve its complete victory, the Indonesian revolution must also follow the road of the Chinese revolution. This means that the Indonesian revolution must inevitably adopt this main form of struggle, namely, the people's armed struggle against the armed counter-revolution which, in essence, is the armed agrarian revolution of the peasants under the leadership of the proletariat.

The agrarian revolution which is the essence of the present stage of the Indonesian revolution is not an agrarian reform according to the bourgeois fashion that will only pave the way for the development of capitalism in the countryside. This revolution will liberate farm laborers, poor peasants and middle peasants from the feudal oppression by foreign or native landlords, by confiscating the lands of the landlords and freely distributing them to farm laborers and poor peasants individually to be their private property. Such a revolution will be victorious only when it is carried out by force of arms under the leadership of the working class. This revolution cannot be enforced from without. It will break out on the basis of the high consciousness and conviction of the peasants themselves obtained through their own experience in the struggle and through the education by the working class.

It is clear that in a situation where the conditions for a revolution have not existed as yet, the task of the PKI should be directed at educating Party members, the working class and the peasantry, through political work, agitation and propaganda, as well as through organizational work, with regard to the main form of struggle of the Indonesian revolution.

All forms of legal and parliamentary work should serve the principal means and the main form of struggle, and must not in any way impede the process of the ripening of armed struggle.

The experience during the last fifteen years has taught us that starting from the failure to reject the "peaceful road" and to firmly hold to the general law of revolution in colonial or semi-colonial and semi-feudal countries, the PKI gradually got bogged down in parliamentary and other forms of legal struggle. The Party leadership even considered this to be the main form of struggle to achieve the strategic aim of the Indonesian revolution. The legality of the Party was not considered as one method of struggle at a given time and under certain conditions, but was rather regarded as a principle, while other forms of struggle should serve this principle. Even when counter-revolution not only has trampled underfoot the legality of the Party, but has violated the basic human rights of the communists as well, the Party leadership still tried to defend this "legality" with all their might.

As has been stated before, the "peaceful road" was firmly established in the Party when the Fourth Plenary Session of the Central Committee of the Vth Congress in 1956 adopted a document which approved the modern revisionist line of the 20th Congress of the CPSU. In such a situation, when the revisionist line was already firmly established in the Party, it was impossible to have a correct Marxist-Leninist line of strategy and tactics. The formulation of the main lines of strategy and tactics of the Party started from a vacillation between the "peaceful road" and the "road of armed revolution," in the process of which the "peaceful road" finally became dominant.

Under such conditions, the General Line of the PKI was formulated by the VIth National Congress (1959). It reads, "to continue the forging of the national united front, and to continue the building of the Party, so as to accomplish the demands of the August Revolution of 1945." Based on the General Line of the Party, the slogan "Raise the Three Banners of the Party" was decided. These were: (1) the banner of the national front, (2) the banner of the building of the Party, and (3) the banner of the 1945 August Revolution. (D.N. Aidit, "Report to the Second Plenary Session of the Central Committee of the VI Congress.") The General Line was meant as the road to people's democracy in Indonesia.

The Party leadership tried to explain that the Three Banners of the Party were the three main weapons to win the people's democratic revolution which, as Comrade Mao Tse-tung has said, were "a well-disciplined Party armed with the theory of Marxism-Leninism, using the method of self-criticism and linked with the masses of the people; an army under the leadership of such a party; a united front of all revolutionary classes and of all revolutionary groups under the leadership of such a Party." (Mao Tse-tung, *On the People's Democratic Dictatorship*.)

Thus the second main weapon means that there must be a people's armed struggle against armed counter-revolution under the leadership of the Party. The Party leadership tried to replace this with the slogan "Raise the Banner of the 1945 August Revolution." It is true that they had explained that "the banner of the August Revolution establishes the importance of using the experiences of the struggle during the August Revolution of 1945," and that "in defending the sovereignty of Indonesia, the role of guerrilla warfare is of the utmost importance" (D.N. Aidit, *Raise High the Banner of Revolution*), yet in practice not a single effort was made in this direction.

In order to prove that the road followed was not the opportunist "peaceful road," the Party leadership always spoke of the two possibilities, the possibility of a "peaceful road" and the possibility of a non-peaceful road. They held that the better the Party prepared itself to face the possibility of a non-peaceful road, the greater would be the possibility for a "peaceful road." In fact, such statements show precisely the existence of dualism concerning the road followed by the Party leadership. By doing so the Party leadership cultivated in the minds of Party members, the working class and the masses of the working people, the hope for a peaceful road which in reality did not exist.

In practice, the Party leadership did not prepare the whole ranks of the Party, the working class and the masses of the people to face the possibility of a non-peaceful road. The most striking proof of it was the grave tragedy which happened after the outbreak and the failure of the September 30th Movement. Within a very short space of time, the counter-revolution succeeded in massacring and arresting hundreds of thousands of Communists and non-communist revolutionaries who found themselves in a passive position, paralyzing the organization of the PKI and the revolutionary mass organizations. Such a situation surely would never happen if the Party leadership did not deviate from the revolutionary road.

The Party leadership declared that "our Party must not copy the theory of armed struggle abroad, but must carry out the Method of Combining the Three Forms of Struggle (D.N. Aidit, *Raise High the Banner of Revolution*). The three forms of struggle according to this theory were guerrilla warfare in the countryside (especially by farm laborers and poor peasants), revolutionary action by the workers (especially transport workers) in the cities, and intensive work among the enemy's armed forces. The Party leadership criticized some comrades who, in studying the experience of the armed struggle of the Chinese people, were considered seeing only its similarities with the conditions in Indonesia. On the contrary, the Party leadership put forward several allegedly different conditions that must be taken into account, until they arrived at the conclusion that the method typical to the Indonesian revolution was the "Method of Combining the Three Forms of Struggle."

Adopting the experience of other countries dogmatically is a mistake. But refusing to use another country's experience whose truth as the theory of people's revolution has already been tested, is equally a mistake. Lenin has taught us that "a movement that is starting in a young country can be successful only if it treats the experience of other countries critically and tests it independently." (V.I. Lenin, *"What is to be Done?"*)

Facts have shown that the "theory of the Method of Combining the Three Forms of Struggle" was not the result of treating the experience of another country critically and linking it with the concrete practice of Indonesia, so as to create a revolutionary theory typical to Indonesia. In any case, this is not a method typical to Indonesia. The Russian revolution of 1905, as Lenin explained in his "Lecture on the 1905 Revolution," was a combination of strikes by the workers, anti-feudal struggle by the peasantry in the countryside and mutinies by the army, among which the strikes by the workers served as the vanguard. The Chinese revolution also combined the revolutionary agrarian war, the work in the countryside and in the cities under enemy occupation and the work among the enemy's armed forces, with the revolutionary war as the main form.

The "three forms of struggle" that should be combined, instead of having been led along the road of revolution, each was led along the "peaceful road." The struggle of the peasants against the exploitation and suppression by the vestiges of feudalism, if given the correct leadership by the PKI, would develop into its highest form; namely, the agrarian revolution to liberate the peasants from the oppression by the landlords. This struggle would only gain its complete victory if it had been waged by arms under the leadership of the PKI. But the Party leadership did not concentrate its leading work on the ever higher development of the peasants' struggle, and did not prepare the Party in the face of any eventuality.

When the peasants began to rise in direct unilateral actions against the native landlords, these actions were not encouraged to develop into a higher form, but were diverted along different lines and transformed into various actions that were not directed against the landlords, such as the "New Culture Movement," the "One Thousand-and-One Campaign" to raise production, the "Rat extermination Campaign," and the like. Naturally, it is not wrong for a revolutionary peasant movement to launch campaigns to increase production, to exterminate pests and to raise the cultural level of the peasants. But all of this should serve the main objective of the revolutionary peasant movement, namely, the anti-feudal agrarian revolution. Therefore, such campaigns should not be evaluated far too highly, so much so that the revolutionary peasant movement was diverted from its correct orientation and became a reformist movement.

In the cities, despite the increasingly heavy burden in the life of the workers, actions by the workers that had political significance gradually disappeared, because they lacked proper leadership. It is true that there were apparently big actions by the workers that had great political significance, such as the take-over of the enterprises belonging to the Dutch, British and Belgian imperialists. But the actual results of these actions were beneficial only for a handful of bureaucrat-capialists and could by no means improve the living conditions of the workers concerned. Besides, since the Party leadership considered the former imperialist-owned enterprises that were controlled by the government as a national property, further actions by the workers were restrained. On the contrary, far too manny activities were organized directly by the trade unions or through the Enterprise Councils aimed at increasing production, raising the working efficiency of the enterprises, improving the economy, etc. which did not improve the living conditions or heighten the revolutionary spirit of the workers.

Proceeding from the erroneous view that "the armed forces of the Republic are not reactionary armed forces" (D.N. Aidit, *Raise High the Banner of Revolution*), the problem of "working within the enemy's armed forces" was interpreted as "integrating the important organs of the state with the people," or "strengthening the relations between the people and the armed forces." It plainly means integrating the instrument of violence of the oppressing classes with the oppressed classes. Such a grave error could occur because the Party leadership had deviated from the Marxist-Leninist teachings on state. They considered the Indonesian Republic not a bourgeois state and the armed forces of the Republic not an instrument of the bourgeois state. The Party leadership forgot the reality that the armed forces of the Republic, as a whole, despite the fact that they were brought into being by the August Revolution, had beome the organ of rule in the hands of the classes which ruled the state, since the time when the revolution failed and the state power fell entirely into the hands of the reactionary bourgeoisie. In view of their class origin as sons of workers and peasants, the rank-and-file of the armed forces might indeed constitute elements who would take the side of the people. But this could not in any possible way alter the position of the armed forces as a whole as an organ of the state which served the interests of the ruling classes.

To fulfill its heavy but great and noble historical mission, to lead the people's revolution against imperialism, feudalism and bureaucrat-capitalism, the Indonesian Marxist-Leninists must firmly reject the revisionist "peaceful road," reject the "theory of the Method of Combining the Three Forms of Struggle," and hold aloft the banner of armed people's revolution. Following the example of the glorious Chinese revolution, the Indonesian Marxist-Leninists must establish revolutionary base areas; they must "turn the backward villages into advanced, consolidated base areas, into great military, political, economic and cultural bastions of the revolution" (Mao Tse-tung, *The Chinese Revolution and the Chinese Communist Party*).

While working for the realization of this most principal question we must also carry out other forms of struggle; armed struggle will never advance without being co-ordinated with other forms of struggle.

\* \* \*

The line of Right opportunism followed by the Party leadership was also reflected in their attitude with regard to the state, in particular to the state of the Republic of Indonesia. Marxism-Leninism has taught us that "the state is an organ of class rule, an organ for the oppression of one class by another;" that "the forms of bourgeois states are extremely varied, but their essence is the same: .... the dictatorship of the bourgeoisie;" and that "the supersession of the bourgeois state by the proletarian state" (in Indonesia through the people's democratic state, Politbureau), "is impossible without a violent revolution." (V.I. Lenin, *State and Revolution.*)

Based on this Marxist-Leninist teaching on state, the task of the PKI after the August Revolution of 1945 failed should have been the education of the Indonesian working class and the rest of the working people, so as to make them understand as clearly as possible the class nature of the state of the Republic of Indonesia as a bourgeois dictatorship. The PKI should have aroused the consciousness of the working class and the working people that their struggle for liberation would inevitably lead to the necessity of "superseding the bourgeois state" by the people's state under the leadership of the working class, through a "violent revolution." But the PKI leadership took the opportunist line that gave rise to the illusion among the people about bourgeois democracy. The development of this opportunist line with regard to the state is as the following:

In implementing the tactics of drawing the national bourgeoisie back to the national united front, the PKI supported the Wilopo Administration (beginning of 1952) and other administrations that followed—with the exception of the Burhanuddin Harahap Administration that was led by the Masjumi party—which had relatively progressive programs. By this policy, the PKI was able to draw the national bourgeoisie in a united front and prevent the formation of reactionary administrations. But subsequently, the PKI followed such practices which abandoned its position as a proletarian party that had to take an independent attitude towards a bourgeois government. The PKI failed in totally discharging its task to expose the bankruptcy of bourgeois democracy. Worse still, the PKI, instead of using the general elections and parliamentary struggle to accelerate the political obsolescence of parliamentarism, had even strengthened the system of parliamentarism.

The PKI took part in the first parliamentary general elections with a program for the establishment of a Government of National Coalition, a united front government of all democratic elements, including the Communists. With such a program, the PKI had committed the same error as the petty-bourgeois democrats and opportunists who, according to Lenin, "instill into the minds of the people the false notion that universal suffrage 'in modern state' is really capable of ascertaining the will of the majority of the toilers and of securing its realization." (V. I. Lenin, *State and Revolution.*)

This demand for the establishment of a Government of National Coalition became the tactical program of the PKI, which subsequently assumed the form of a demand for the establishment of a Cooperation cabinet with the Nasakom as the core. By making the establishment of a Government of National Coalition the principal political demand, the illusion was spread that [under?] the rule of bourgeois dictatorship, where the armed forces under the leadership of the Party did not exist, it would be possible to set up a united front government of all democratic elements, including the Communists, in accordance with the people's sense of justice, that would facilitate the accomplishment of the strategic aims. The campaign to demand the establishment of a Co-operation cabinet with the Nasakom as the core had relegated to the background the propaganda for a people's democratic state, and in that way hampered the development of the revolutionary consciousness of the working class and the rest of the working people.

The climax of the deviation from Marxist-Leninist teaching on state committed by the Party leadership was the formulation of the "theory of the two aspects in the state power of the Republic of Indonesia." Since the birth of the "two-aspects theory" Marxist-Leninist doctrines were maintained only when discussing the state in general terms. But in the discussions about the state in a concrete sense, that is to say about the state of the Republic of Indonesia, Marxist-Leninist doctrines on state were completely abandoned.

The "two-aspects theory" viewed the state and the state power in the following way:

"The economic structure (basis) of the present Indonesian society is still colonial and semi-feudal. However, at the same time there is the struggle of the people against this economic system, the struggle for a national and democratic economy" (D. N. Aidit, *Raise High the Banner of Revolution*).

"The realities of the basis are also reflected in the superstructure, including in the state power, and especially in the cabinet. The forces that are against the colonial and feudal economic system, and the forces that defend imperialism, the vestiges of feudalism, bureaucrat-capitalism and the compradors, are both reflected in the state power." (D. N. Aidit, *Raise High the Banner of Revolution.*)

"The state power of the Republic, viewed as contradiction, is a contradiction between two opposing aspects. This first aspect is the aspect which represents the interests of the people (manifested by the progressive stands and policies of President Sukarno that are supported by the PKI and other groups of the people). The second aspect is the aspect that represents the enemies of the people (manifested by the stands and policies of the right-wing forces and die-hards). The people's aspect has now become the main aspect and takes the leading role in the state power of the Republic." (D. N. Aidit, *Raise High the Banner of Revolution.*)

The "two-aspect theory" obviously is an opportunist or revisionist deviation. It denies the Marxist-Leninist teaching that "the state is an organ of the rule of a definite class which *cannot* be reconciled with its antipode (the class opposite to it)." (V. I. Lenin, *State and Revolution.*) It is unthinkable that the Republic of Indonesia can be jointly ruled by the people and the enemies of the people.

No one will deny that in Indonesian society there are forces fighting against the colonial and semi-feudal economic system. These forces are the working class, the peasantry, the petty bourgeoisie and, to a certain degree, also the national bourgeoisie. But to consider that these forces have a common concept for a "national and democratic economy" is erroneous. In this case, there are two different concepts, the concept of the national bourgeoisie and the concept of the proletariat. Whether it is wrapped in beautiful names like "national and democratic economy," "guided economy," etc. this concept of the national bourgeoisie has no other demand but the full development of capitalism in the country.

The concept of the proletariat is to create a people's democratic economy, which means: the nationalization of all capital and enterprises belonging to the imperialists, compradors and other reactionaries, and the free distribution of lands confiscated from the landlords to the peasants. This will be the transitional economic system to Socialism that can be realized only after the establishment of the people's democratic dictatorship, namely, the joint power of all anti-imperialist and anti-feudal classes under the leadership of the proletariat. In the people's democratic economy, the socialist sector, namely, the vital enterprises owned by the people's state, takes a leading position in all the economic life of the country.

Prior to the establishment of a people's democratic power, the struggle of the people in the economic field will never possibly give birth to a people's democratic economic structure. The take-over of imperialist-owned enterprises and the existence of old-type state-owned enterprises did not mean the birth of the socialist sector in economy, because these state-owned enterprises did not belong to the people and were not managed by the people's state, but had fallen into the hands of the bureaucrat-capitalists. Similarly, the Basic Agrarian Law could by no means liberate the peasantry from the oppression and exploitation by the vestiges of feudalism.

Disregarding the differences between the economic concept of the national bourgeoisie and the economic concept of the proletariat, and lumping them together in the formulation of "national and democratic economy," without discussing the necessity to establish first the people's democratic power, were tantamount to abandoning the proletarian class stand and capitulating to the bourgeoisie. Obviously, the birth of economic concepts like the "Economic Declaration" did not mean that the forces of the working class and the rest of the working people who fought against the colonial and semi-feudal economy were already reflected in the state power. People's democratic elements will never grow in a state power which represents the interests of imperialism and the vestiges of feudalism.

Contradiction did take place in the state power of the Republic, namely, the contradictions between the comprador and landlord elements who represented the interests of imperialism and the vestiges of feudalism on the one hand, the national bourgeoisie who, to a certain extent, took an anti-imperialist and anti-feudal stand, on the other. But the position of the national bourgeoisie could not in any way be interpreted as representing the interests of the people, and that is why it could not be called the "people's aspect" in the state power. Such contradictions would never lead to the fundamental transformation of the class nature of the state power.

Even when Party leaders assumed certain functions in the government, both in the central and in the regional administrations, it could not be interpreted that the quality of the national bourgeoisie aspect in the state power had changed into a "people's aspect," because, the joint forces of the national bourgeoisie and the proletariat were led not by the proletariat but by the national bourgeoisie. The position of the Party leaders in the government that gave them no real power was offered as a political concession from the national bourgeoisie who needed the support of the people in their contradictions with the comprador-bourgeoisie and, to a certain extent, also with the imperialists.

With the support of the masses of the people who were led by the PKI, the national bourgeoisie could, to a certain extent, undermine the position of the comprador-bourgeoisie in the state power. The situation was shown by a series of policies adopted by the government such as the abrogation of the Round Table Conference Agreement, the liberation of West Irian, the enactment of the Basic Agrarian Law and the Law of Crop Sharing, the liquidation of the armed forces of the counter-revolutionaries including the Darul Islam and the "PRRI-Permesta," the acceptance of the Political Manifesto, the Economic Declaration, the anti-imperialist foreign policy, etc.

The Party leadership who wallowed in the mire of opportunism overestimated far too highly these developments and claimed that the "people's aspect" had become the main aspect and taken the hegemony in the state power of the Republic. It was as if the Indonesian people were nearing the birth of a people's power. And since they considered the forces of the national bourgeoisie in the state power really the "people's aspect," the Party leadership had done everything to defend and develop this "people's aspect." The Party leadership had altogether merged themselves in the interests of the national bourgeoisie.

It is clear that the Party leadership applied in a subjective way the theory of contradiction in the state power. Furthermore, by considering the national bourgeoisie the "people's aspect" in the state power of the Republic, and president Sukarno the leader of this aspect, the Party leadership erroneously recognized that the national bourgeoisie were able to lead the new type democratic revolution. This is contrary to historical necessity and historical facts.

The Party leadership declared that the "two-aspect theory" was completely different from the "theory of structural reform" of the leadership of the revisionist Italian Communist Party. (The leadership of the Italian Communist Party holds that the dictatorship of the proletariat in Italy can be established, not through a proletarian revolution to smash the bourgeois state machine, but through the gradual reforms in the state structure by making use of the Italian Constitution and by parliamentary means.) However, the fact is, theoretically or on the basis of practical realities, there is no difference between the two "theories." Both have for their starting point the "peaceful road" to Socialism. Both dream of a gradual change in the internal balance of forces in the state power. Both reject the road of revolution and both are revisionist in character.

The anti-revolutionary "two-aspect theory" glaringly exposed itself in the statement that "the struggle of the PKI with regard to the state power is to promote the pro-people aspect so as to make it bigger and dominant, and the anti-people force can be driven out from the state power." (D. N. Aidit, *Raise High the Banner of Revolution*.)

The Party leadership even had a name for this anti-revolutionary road; they called it the road of "revolution from above and below." By "revolution from above" they meant that the PKI "must encourage the state power to take revolutionary steps aimed at making the desired changes in the personnel and in the state organs." While by "revolution from below" they meant that the PKI "must arouse, organize and mobilize the people to achieve the same changes." (D. N. Aidit, *Raise High the Banner of Revolution*.) It is indeed an extraordinary fantasy! The Party leadership did not learn from the fact that the concept of president Sukarno on the formation of a Co-operation cabinet (the old-type Government of National Coalition), eight years after its announcement, had not been realized as yet. There were even no signs that it would ever be realized, despite the insistent demands. Let alone a change in the state power!

It is true that Lenin once showed the possibility of "actions from above," that is to say when there was the possibility to take part in the provisional revolutionary government on the eve of the Russian Revolution of 1905. Then, the period of political upheavals and revolutions had begun. If there was no possibility to act from above, according to Lenin, a pressure must be exercised from below, and for this purpose the proletariat must be armed.

Clearly there was a great difference between the situation described by Lenin where the conditions for the possibility of "actions from above" as well as the conditions for "actions from below" existed, and the situation and the conditions in Indonesia for a "revolution from above and below" meant by the Party leadership. The first was put forward in a revolutionary situation, while the latter in a relatively peaceful condition. Furthermore, the latter was also put forward in an opportunist way.

The "two aspect theory" is similar to Kautsky's distortion of Marxist doctrines on state. Kautsky theoretically does not deny that the state is an organ of class rule. What he loses sight of and glosses over is that "the liberation of the oppressed class is impossible not only without a violent revolution, *but also without the destruction* of the apparatus of state power which was created by the ruling class . . . ."

(V. I. Lenin, *State and Revolution*.)

To clean itself from the mire of opportunism, our Party must discard this "theory of two-aspect in the state power" and reestablish the Marxist-Leninist teaching on state and revolution.

One of the serious mistakes criticized in "The New Road" resolution was the neglect of fostering the national united front during the August Revolution of 1945. The Communists neglected the establishment of the national united front as a weapon in the national revolution against imperialism. (See, *The New Road for Republic of Indonesia*, Resolution of the Political Bureau of the CC PKI, August 1948.)

In the period after 1951, the question of establishing the national united front was decided as one of the most important tasks of the Party. The Vth National Congress of the PKI went even further by deciding that the building of a national united front constituted the foremost and urgent task of the Party. This line was maintained in the VIth National Congress of the Party and thereafter. The national united front was put in the primary place in the "General Line" of the Party and became the first banner of the Three Banners of the Party. All this shows how the Party leadership evaluated the national united front. From "neglecting" it in the second half of the forties, they swung to another extremity by regarding the national united front as the number one question.

The Vth National Congress of the Party in the main had solved theoretically the problem of the national united front. It formulated that the worker-peasant alliance was the basis of the national united front. With regard to the national bourgeoisie a lesson had been drawn on the basis of the experience during the August Revolution that this class had a wavering character. In a certain situation, the national bourgeoisie took part in the revolution and sided with the revolution, while in another situation they followed in the steps of the comprador-bourgeoisie to attack the driving forces of the revolution and betrayed the revolution (as shown by their activities during the Madiun Provocation and their approval of the Round Table Conference Agreement). Based on this wavering character of the national bourgeoisie, the Vth National Congress of the Party formulated the stand that must be taken by the PKI, namely, to make continuous efforts to win the national bourgeoisie over to the side of revolution, while guarding against the possibility of its betraying the revolution. The PKI must follow the policy of unity and struggle towards the national bourgeoisie.

Nevertheless, since the ideology of subjectivism in the Party, particularly among the Party leadership, had not yet been eradicated, the Party was dragged into more and more serious mistakes, to such an extent that the Party lost its independence in the united front with the national bourgeoisie. This mistake had led to the situation in which the Party and the proletariat were placed as the appendage of the national bourgeoisie.

The process along which the mistakes in carrying out the national united front had developed can be briefly traced as follows:

In the course of the work to rebuild the Party in 1951, efforts were simultaneously made to win the national bourgeoisie over to the side of the people. By utilizing the contradictions between the national bourgeoisie and the comprador-bourgeoisie, the Party succeeded in gradually winning the national bourgeoisie over to the side of the people. This process was started during the struggle against the August razzia launched by the Sukiman Administration and for the replacement of this administration. This struggle was successful and the Wilopo Cabinet was reformed. At that time and in the following years the Party was still weak and the alliance of the workers and the peasants was not established as yet. So the united front with the national bourgeoisie was not formed and did not grow up upon strong foundations, namely, the alliance of the working class and the peasantry under the leadership of the working class.

The Party leadership highly appraised the establishment of the united front with the national bourgeoisie and considered that it "opened up possibilities for the development and the building of the Party and for the realization of the immediate tasks of the Party, namely, the formation of the alliance of the working class and the peasantry against feudalism." (D. N. Aidit, "Lessons from the History of the PKI," Speech at the 40th anniversary of the founding of the PKI.) This appraisal gave rise to the formulation that the fostering of the national united front was the first and most urgent task of the PKI. This formulation clearly indicated that by the national united front the Party leadership meant first and foremost the united front with the national bourgeoisie.

In a situation in which a strong alliance of the working class and the peasantry was not yet formed, why could the united front with the national bourgeoisie be maintained? There were two reasons. Firstly, because the national bourgeoisie, in their contradictions with the comprador-bourgeoisie, needed the support of the working class. Secondly, because the Party gave the needed support without arousing the apprehensions of the national bourgeoisie that their position was in any way threatened.

The formation of the united front with the national bourgeoisie resulted in the formation of those administrations which, to a certain extent, pursued an anti-imperialist policy and gave little freedom of action to the PKI and the revolutionary mass organizations. No doubt this situation was rather favorable to the work of Party building, especially in the countryside, in order to establish the worker-peasant alliance. Furthermore, the formulation of the revolutionary agrarian program provided the political prerequisite necessary for the welding of the alliance between the working class and the peasantry.

However, in the course of the co-operation with the national bourgeoisie, the ideological weaknesses in the Party, in particular among the Party leadership, grew and were influenced by the bourgeois ideology through that co-operation. The growth of the ideological weaknesses in the Party gradually deprived the Party of its independence in the united front with the national bourgeoisie. The Party gave too much concessions to the national bourgeoisie and lost its independent role of leadership.

A manifestation of this loss of independence in the united front with the national bourgeoisie was the evaluation and the stand of the Party leadership towards Sukarno. The Party leadership did not adopt an independent attitude towards Sukarno. They had always avoided conflicts with Sukarno and, on the contrary, had greatly overemphasized the similarities and the unity between the Party and Sukarno. The public saw that there was no policy of Sukarno that was not supported by the PKI. The Party leadership went so far as to accept without any struggle the recognition of Sukarno as "the great leader of the revolution" and the leader of the "people's aspect" in the state power of the Republic. In many articles and speeches, the Party leaders frequently said that the struggle of the PKI was based not only on Marxism-Leninism, but also on "the teachings of Sukarno," that the PKI made such a rapid progress because it realized Sukarno's idea of Nasakom unity, etc. Even the people's democratic system in Indonesia was said to be in conformity with Sukarno's main ideas as expressed in his speech "The Birth of Pantjasila." (See D. N. Aidit, "Report to the IVth Plenary Session of the Central Committee of the Vth National Congress.") Thus the Party leadership did not educate the working class and the rest of the working people that the leadership of the revolution must be in the hands of the proletariat and their Party, the PKI.

The Party leadership boasted that the birth of the Political Manifesto meant that the persistent struggle of the Indonesian people led by the PKI had successfully brought the broad masses to recognize the correctness of the PKI's program. And therefore, "to implement the Political Manifesto in a consistent manner is the same as implementing the program of the PKI." (D. N. Aidit, *Raise High the Banner of Revolution.*)

The formulation of a common program for the united front is indeed a good thing, and in this sense, the birth of the Political Manifesto, too, was a good thing, because to a certain extent it could serve to unite the mind of the various anti-imperialist classes and groups, with regard to certain parts of the problems of the Indonesian revolution. However, it is not true that the birth of the Political Manifesto and its further elaboration meant that the broad masses recognized the correctness of the PKI's program, because, only certain parts of the Party program were in common with the Political Manifesto.

The Communists must not be naive and consider that other classes who do not belong to the driving forces of the revolution could easily accept the program of the PKI. They accepted only those parts of the Party's tactical program which were not detrimental to their own interests. While those parts which are contrary to their interests, such as on the leading role of the working class, on the revolutionary agrarian reform, etc. were rejected by them. As for those parts of the Party's program which they accepted, there was no guarantee that they would be implemented. Meanwhile, the reactionaries who assumed a dominating position in the state power accepted hypocritically the Political Manifesto, in an effort to adjust themselves to the prevailing situation. Therefore, no matter how consistent the Political Manifesto would be implemented, it could never be the same as the program of the PKI. Consequently, saying that consistently implementing the Political Manifesto meant implementing the program of the PKI could only be interpreted that it was not the program of the PKI that was accepted by the bourgeoisie, but that, on the contrary, it was the program of the national bourgeoisie which was accepted by the PKI, and was made to replace the program of the PKI.

The abandonment of principle in the united front with the national bourgeoisie had developed even further in the so-called "General Line of the Indonesian Revolution" that was formulated as follows: "With the national front having the workers and peasants as its pillars, the Nasakom as the core and the Pantjasila as its ideological basis, to complete the national democratic revolution in order to advance towards Indonesian Socialism." (D. N. Aidit, "Report to the Fourth Plenary Session of the Central Committee of the VIth Congress," May, 1965.) This so-called "General Line of the Indonesian Revolution" had not even the faintest smell of the revolution. Because, from the three preconditions to win the revolution, namely, a strong Marxist-Leninist party, a people's armed struggle under the leadership of the Party, and a united front, only the united front was retained. Even then, it was not a revolutionary united front, because it was not led by the working class, nor was it based on the alliance of the working class and the peasantry under the leadership of the working class, but on the contrary it was based on the Nasakom. It was said that without the Nasakom as the core, "the national united front will be like a wheel without an axis; it certainly will not be able to revolve" (D. N. Aidit, "General Report to the VIIth (Extraordinary) National Congress of the PKI," 1962).

The Party leadership said that "the slogan for national cooperation with the Nasakom as the core will by no means obscure the class content of the national united front." (D. N. Aidit, *Raise High the Banner of Revolution*.) This statement is incorrect, because apart from the working class party, there were political parties in the Nasakom representing mainly the interests of the national bourgeoisie, the compradors, the bureaucrat-capitalists and the landlords. Ever since the banning of the comprador parties like the Masjumi and the PSI, the compradors and landlords were seeking admittance in other political parties and organizations of nationalist or religious trends. Thus, the class content of the Nasakom was the working class, the national bourgeoisie, and even elements of compradors, the bureaucrat-capitalists and the landlords. Obviously, putting the Nasakom in the core not only meant obscuring the class content of the national united front, but radically changing the meaning of the revolutionary national united front into an alliance of the working class with all other classes in the country, including the reactionary classes, into class collaboration.

This error must be corrected. The Party must throw to the dustbin the erroneous "General Line of the Indonesian Revolution" and return to the correct conception of a revolutionary national united front based on the alliance of the workers and peasants under the leadership of the working class.

The abandonment of principle in the united front with the national bourgeoisie was also the result of the Party's inability to make a correct and concrete analysis of the concrete situation. In the article "The Indonesia Society and the Indonesian Revolution" (adopted by the Fifth Plenary Session of the Central Committee of the Vth National Congress in July, 1957, as a textbook used in Party schools), it was said that overthrowing imperialism was the primary of the two urgent tasks, the overthrow of imperialism and the liquidation of the vestiges of feudalism. This line was also found in different variations in other documents of the Party, such as "the spearhead today must be directed at the principal enemy, namely, imperialism" (D. N. Aidit, Speech at the First National Party Conference on the Work Among the Peasants), or, "the main contradiction in Indonesia today is the contradiction between the Indonesian people on the one hand, and the imperialists on the other hand" (D. N. Aidit, *Raise High the Banner of Revolution.*). From such erroneous views on the concrete situation, came the slogan of "placing class interests under national interests" (D. N. Aidit, "Report on the Second Plenary Session of the Central Committee of the VIth Congress"). This was a dogmatic copy of the correct slogan of the Chinese Communist Party raised up for the mobilization of resistance against the aggression by the Japanese imperialists.

This error rendered it impossible for the Party to build a strong and consolidated alliance of the workers and peasants, despite the spreading influence of the Party in the rural areas. Because, under the erroneous slogan of "overthrowing imperialism is the primary task," all contradictions among the classes within the country, including the contradictions between the landlords and the peasants must be subordinated to "the main contradiction..., the contradiction between the Indonesian people and imperialists."

Ever since the failure of the August Revolution of 1945, except in West Iran, the imperialists did not hold direct political power in Indonesia. In Indonesia, political power was in the hands of compradors and landlords who represented the interests of imperialism and the vestiges of feudalism. Besides, there was no imperialist aggression in Indonesia taking place. Under such a situation, provided that the PKI did not make political mistakes, the contradiction between the ruling reactionary classes and the people, would develop and sharpen, constituting the main contradiction in Indonesia. The primary task of the Indonesia revolution at the present moment is the overthrow of the rule of the reactionary classes within the country who also represent the interests of the imperialists, in particular the United States imperialists. Only by fulfilling this task, can the real liquidation of imperialism and the vestiges of feudalism be realized.

By correcting the mistakes made by the Party in

the united front with the national bourgeoisie it does not mean that now the Party need not unite with this class. So long as the economic structure of Indonesia is still colonial and semi-feudal in nature there will always be some strata of the bourgeois class who suffer from the oppression by imperialism and the bounds of the vestiges of feudalism. These strata of the bourgeois class are the national bourgeoisie who are, to a certain extent, opposing imperialism and the vestiges of feudalism. On the basis of the worker-peasant alliance under the leadership of the working class, our Party must work to win the national bourgeois class over to the side of the revolution.

* * *

Those were the main mistakes of the Right opportunism in the political sphere committed by the PKI which had developed into revisionism and reached their climax on the eve of the September 30th events. When the deviation to the Right had become overall and complete, another tendency that was quite the opposite emerged, namely, a "Leftist" tendency. The "Leftist" tendency mainfested itself in the overestimation of the strength of the Party, the working class and the rest of the working people, the exaggerated appraisal of the results of the people's struggle and the underestimation of the strength of the reactionaries.

The political situation in the country at that time indeed began to reveal the existence of tensions. Political victories crowned the actions launched by the people, including the boycott of American films, the expulsion of the U.S. "Peace Corps," the closing of the American Motion Pictures Association in Indonesia and the deportation of its director, Bill Palmer, the banning of the reactionary Cultural Manifesto, the take-over of the British-owned enterprises, the dissolution of the so-called "Body for the Promotion of Sukarnoism" and the Murba party, the actions against U.S. aggression in Vietnam, etc. Such actions enjoyed broader and broader support from the people. In some districts the peasants started unilateral actions to win their demands for reduction of rents. Reacting to the victories of the people's struggle, the domestic reactionaries in collusion with the U.S. imperialists were also intensifying their activities, creating provocations against the workers and peasants, spreading forged documents, etc.

The "Thesis on the 45 Years of the PKI" stated on the one hand that "the bureaucrat-capitalists not only are worsening the present economic conditions in Indonesia, but are also trying to seize political power through a coup d'etat." On the other hand it stressed that "the growing resistence of the Indonesian people against imperialism, feudalism and the forces of counter revolution in the country shows that today an increasingly mounting and ripening revolutionary situation develops in our country."

According to Lenin, a revolutionary situation or a revolutionary period is a period "when the old 'superstructure' has cracked from top to bottom, when open political action on the part of the classes and masses who are creating a new superstructure for themselves has become a fact . . . ." (V. I. Lenin, *Two Tactics of Social Democracy in the Democratic Revolution.*) In comparison to what Lenin said, the political situation in Indonesia at that time, even with the take-over of the British-owned enterprises and the anti-imperialists and anti-bureaucrat-capitalist demonstrations which took place in rapid succession in the capital and other big cities, could not yet be called to have reached the stage of a revolutionary situation, let alone "an increasingly mounting and ripening revolutionary situation." The demands raised in the actions that reached their climax in the demonstrations were essentially still in the framework of partial demands or reforms. Meanwhile, the actions by the peasants, the main force of the Indonesian revolution, had not yet reached the higher stage nor were they widely spread. What were alleged as thousands of actions a day in the rural areas were delusive, because such activities as submitting written petitions, repairing irrigation ditches, etc. were counted as peasant actions. Real actions that were directly aimed against the native landlords were not many nor widespread.

The conclusion on the "ever ripening revolutionary situation" was nothing but the result of a method of thinking which regarded subjective wishes, feelings and imagination as reality. The Party leadership were afraid to see realities that differed from their subjective wishes. The Party leadership were displeased when the regional committees or other Party organizations reported that the degree of the development of the mass actions still fell short from the conclusion drawn.

As a result, to please the subjective wishes of the Party leadership, exaggerated assessments were made on the mass actions, in particular the peasant actions.

The Party leadership attempted to push forward the "ever ripening revolutionary situation" to become "a revolution." This was stressed in the Statement of the Political Bureau of the Central Committee of the PKI on August 17, 1965.

The Statement called on the Communists to work harder in order "to push the present revolutionary situation forward to its climax," so that the people "can achieve not only ever greater victories, but also fundamental victories." This was the climax of the other mistake, the "Leftist" mistake, which dragged the Party leadership into adventurism that has brought such a great disaster to the Party and the revolutionary movement in general.

# FOR A SOUND
# INDONESIAN REVOLUTION

*Complete Text*
*(Information Bulletin, No. 106, 1967)*

The attempt by the September 30 Movement to engineer a counter-coup failed. The counter-revolutionaries have succeeded in gaining control of the situation and consolidating their forces. A ruthless campaign of white terror ensued which transgressed all the limits of inhumanity. Hundreds of thousands of progressive revolutionaries and innocent people ranging from babies to old men lost their lives in this unprecedented massacre. Hundreds of thousands of activists from progressive organizations were thrown into prisons and concentration camps. The top Party leadership, including such prominent men as Comrades D. N. Aidit, M. H. Lukman and Njoto, also fell victim to the terror campaign. In fact, the Communist Party of Indonesia (PKI) and other mass revolutionary organizations were paralyzed. The Indonesian Revolution suffered a major setback. Counter-revolutionaries rejoiced in their victory.

The failure of the September 30 Movement has greatly harmed the cause of the national Indonesian Revolution and the international front of anti-imperialism and peace.

Naturally, deep in their hearts all progressive people and revolutionaries in Indonesia and in the entire world began to ask themselves how it could have happened that a small group of leaders of the Communist Party of Indonesia, a Party seasoned by a heroic 45-year-long struggle, a Party that demonstrated its strength during the celebrations of its 45th anniversary, a Party that commanded admiration among friends and fear among foes, got themselves involved in the September 30 Movement, which was of a purely adventuristic nature, and was used by reaction to strike a blow at the Party, a blow that has stunned it and left it unconscious for a long time. Where does our main mistake stem from? Or has it been pre-ordained that such a tragic fate should have befallen us? Did we have to pay for the Revolution so dearly and in vain?

It is but natural that the revolutionary and progressive forces in Indonesia and throughout the world demand that the leadership of the Indonesian Communist Party be held responsible, for as the 1960 Moscow Statement says, each party is answerable to the workers and the people of its own country, to the international Workers' and Communist movement.

## 1.

A correct assessment of the Party's success in the sphere of ideology and administration in the past, and an analysis of serious mistakes, which are the reverse side of this success, committed especially during the PKI's recent development—will give us objective guidance in the work of rebuilding the Party in the future; it will show us what we must strengthen and consolidate, and what must be removed from the Party's body.

The objective and subjective factors which have been influencing or determining the course of the Indonesian Revolution may be listed as follows:

A. International factors;

B. National factors;

C. Subjective factors operating within the PKI.

It is, obviously, very useful for the Party and the revolutionary progressive masses in Indonesia always to remember the importance of making a correct estimate of the degree of mutual influence of international and national factors.

In other words, on an international scale, the might of the socialist camp is not merely an external condition which affects the course of events, but, in conjunction with other forces combating imperialism, it determines the main content, direction and individual trends of the historical development of human society in our times.

The *international factors* which have played no small part in pushing Indonesian policies to the left are as follows:

1. The emergence of the socialist camp which has become the bastion of the struggle of nations against imperialism, for peace and freedom. At the present time the socialist camp towers high above the imperialist camp in all spheres of human endeavor and the life of society.

2. The force of example set by socialist countries in improving living conditions and raising living standards.

3. The progressive trends of foreign policies pursued by socialist countries, i.e., peaceability, peaceful coexistence and *unconditional* support of all national-liberation movements in the world.

4. Economic and cultural cooperation between socialist and developing nations, meetings of statesmen and various international forums of all prominent fighters for peace and the independence of nations held on a non-governmental level.

5. Fraternal militant solidarity of the international proletariat and progressive nations of the world with our struggle in Indonesia.

The *national factors* which have objectively catalyzed the revolutionary process in Indonesia are as follows: the existence of strong revolutionary traditions among the Indonesian people; polarization—on the one hand, the impoverishment of the working people and, on the other, the emergence of a rich stratum alongside the comprador bourgeoisie and landowners— which has revolutionized the

908

Indonesian working people and caused a rapproachement between the national bourgeoisie and the people which, in turn, has fertilized the soil for the establishment of a united national front; and, finally, the rallying of the peasantry around the Party.

*Subjective factors*—the existence of the Party of the working class—the PKI—which has been a vital stimulating force in the development of the revolutionary situation in Indonesia.

The working class and its Party—thanks to their experience in effecting the August 1945 Revolution and due to making their knowledge of Marxism-Leninism more profound and through borrowing ideas from other fraternal parties—demonstrated their ideological, political and organizational maturity, succeeded in providing answers to the crucial questions of the Indonesian Revolution and in laying the correct strategic and tactical foundation for the victory of the Revolution. This foundation was laid at the Fifth National PKI Congress and further developed at the Sixth National PKI Congress.

The Party correctly concluded that Indonesian society at the present stage of development is a semi-feudal and semi-colonial society (or more mildly, not yet fully independent and semi-feudal); the enemies of the Indonesian Revolution are the class of the comprador bourgeoisie, landowners and capitalistic bureaucrats; because of the geographic factors which determine the uneven development of the Indonesian Revolution, its progress has taken a long time and has had a complex nature, while to lead this lengthy and complex Revolution the PKI had to follow gradual and cautious tactics in the revolutionary struggle, fighting two tendencies at the same time, i.e., a tendency to surrender and a tendency to adventurism, both tendencies being based on the instability of the petty bourgeoisie, with the PKI having to carry out a well-planned ruthless struggle against both these dangerous tendencies; as regards its essence the Indonesian Revolution was a bourgeois-democratic revolution of a new type, or a popular-democratic revolution, i.e., a revolution of the broad popular masses led by the proletariat; the leadership of the Revolution should be effected by the working class while its driving force is the working class and peasants, the petty bourgeoisie outside the peasantry, and other democratic elements; these classes, together with the national bourgeoisie represent a revolutionary force in Indonesia; the prospect of the Indonesian Revolution is socialism; a government of people's democracy will assume the form of a united national front and will be a joint government of all anti-imperialist and anti-feudal classes. This government will lean heavily on the popular masses and will effect changes of a democratic, not socialist, nature. It will secure national independence and the development of the nation, along democratic and progressive lines; a people's democracy in Indonesia can be attained by peaceful means—a possibility which we must do our best to turn into reality, simultaneously increasing our vigilance toward our political enemies and bearing in mind that the class of the bourgeoisie will strive to foist upon us a non-peaceful way of attaining this end; the way out lies in changing the balance of power between the imperialists, the class of landowners and the comprador bourgeoisie, on the one hand, and the forces of the people on the other, it lies in arousing, mobilizing and organizing the masses, workers and peasants first and foremost.

It was on the basis of the above conclusions that the general strategic line of the Revolution was determined, i.e., a line of a united national anti-imperialist front based on union between workers and peasants, a line of building up a party on a nationwide and mass scale, a party fully consolidated ideologically, politically and organizationally.

The working class must make up the vanguard of the people's struggle. To reach this end, the working class must heighten its activity, educate itself and become a large and conscious force able to render help to the struggle of other classes. The working class must help the peasants in their struggle to obtain land, it must help the intelligentsia in the struggle it is waging for its rights, it must help the national bourgeoisie in its struggle against foreign competition, it must help the entire people of Indonesia in the struggle for national independence and democratic freedoms. The people cannot achieve victory unless the working class of Indonesia becomes a free, conscious and politically mature force, well organized and able to lead the struggle of the nation, unless the people see in the working class their undisputed leader.

To win the peasants over to their side, the immediate target for the Indonesian Communists was the elimination of the vestiges of feudalism. The first step in conducting work among the peasants was to give them assistance in their everyday needs, in formulating their demands. This implies the organization and education of the peasants, so that they might reach a higher level in their struggle. This is the basis for the creation of a union of workers and peasants as the foundation for a powerful united national front.

As was officially recognized, on the national scale the strength of the Party began to grow after it had succeeded in winning a major victory at the elections to the Council of People's Representatives (DPR) and the Constituent Assembly, a fact that made it the fourth biggest party in Indonesia. It was this particular basis which enabled President Sukarno, for the first time, to put forward the concept of "mutual cooperation" (Pemerintah Gotong-Rojong) according to which the Communists had to participate in the work of not only legislative but also of executive organs, both on a central and on regional levels.

If we give prominence to the great successes of the Party achieved during the 1954-1960 period, it does not mean that there were no bad symptoms already then.

—Lack of order in the admission of new members. It can be said that each of the rules determining the admission of new members into the Party (Party Statute, Part 2) was violated. According to Lenin, the Party can play its vanguard role only when it comprises the best elements of the working class. However, as a result of the subjective assessment of a mass party as one which has a large membership, the Party admitted new members without sufficiently rigorous selection, so much so that there was little difference between admission to the Party and to various mass organizations. This resulted in the Party becoming oversaturated with petty bourgeois ideology; the organizational purity and quality of the Party dropped. This was further aggravated by the inactivity, or simply lack of groups and primary Party organizations in villages, which led to a situation where ideological education in the Party within the framework of strengthening the views and methods of the working class, could not be carried out as it ought to have been.

—In primary Party organizations and in the revolutionary peasant organization (BTI) leadership was in the hands of rich peasant elements and petty bourgeoisie of non-peasant origin (employees, village headmen, teachers).

—The figures contained in the reports and bearing on the plan were impressively high, although the number of people versed in Marxist-Leninist ideology was rather slender.

As a result, the Party organism began to be infected with bourgeois ideology. That was the reason why after the most trying of ordeals—the third white terror—many primary Party committees embarked on the road of disbanding their Party organizations—something entirely without precedent in other countries or in the history of our own Party even at the period of terror which occurred during the "Madiun Affair." The main reason was crystal clear: our Party with its large membership had not yet developed into a true Leninist party.

We often talk about the strength of our Party as the largest party beyond the borders of the socialist camp, because the PKI had 3,000,000 members, while mass revolutionary organizations had the following membership: SOBSI 3,500,000; BTI 3,000,000; GERWANI 1,500,000 and Pemuda Rakjat 2,000,000 members. The flouting of these figures of strength, supported by various inspiring acts such as mass meetings, demonstrations, etc., produced a good effect in the sense that it boosted the Party's prestige both within the country and abroad, and proved the best attraction for the masses which were still hesitating about whether or not to join the Party.

However, this advertising of strength did more harm than good. The enemy learned too much about it and acted with greater caution, whereas we were not vigilant enough. Our closest allies, the intermediary forces, did not trust us and were afraid lest we should dominate them and take the helm of the Revolution into our own hands.

The greatest damage, however, has been done to us. We let down our guard and overestimated our strength. We were sure that our real strength was as great as we had vaunted it to be. Miscalculations in the assessment of the balance of forces could lead to political steps fatal to the Party and the Revolution, which actually was the case during the September 30 Movement.

Another obvious drawback in the implementation of the plan for Party building was the failure to reach the targets in collecting membership dues. Thus, the Party had no firm financial footing, which ought to have been provided by membership dues received from the Party masses, but rather was supported by donations from Party sympathizers from among high social quarters, private owners, etc.

Undoubtedly, this limited the Party's political freedom with regard to national private owners and some bureaucrats.

The period of the Party's development prior to the outburst of the September 30 Movement was marked by the flourishing of these negative tendencies, all extremely dangerous to the safety of the Party and the Revolution. These tendencies are as follows:

1) Increasing penetration of bourgeois ideology into the Party organism and the shifting of the Party's policy on to an adventuristic footing;

2) Increasing symptoms of the Party leadership turning bourgeois, which made them lose the Party identity, caused them to sink down even deeper into the bog of self-conceit and bureaucracy, and become drunk with their achievements.

All this affected the Party's political activities which produced a paradoxical impression. On the one hand, there was an overindulgence in leftist phraseology, such as "our determination is stronger than hunger," "crush all the imperialists and revisionists," "let us turn Indonesia into the revolutionary beacon for Asia, Africa and Latin America," etc., while, on the other hand, we tended to depart still further from stepping up mass revolutionary action, engaged in class collaboration with the bourgeoisie and thus were steadily losing our political freedom.

The Party made quite a few gains from cooperation with Sukarno. But this cooperation was also fraught with some negative symptoms. Not infrequently, when analyzing our political successes it was hard to see which of them were the result of our own struggle and which we achieved by borrowing from the President's prestige. Moreover, the Party was being increasingly misled by illusions with regard to Bung Karno which resulted in the loss of its political independence, the inexorable gravitation toward ideological prostitution, and the alignment of its theory and practices with those of Bung Karno. This, in turn, led to utter confusion in interpreting Marxism-Leninism—and to complete departure from it.

The Party's cardinal mistake in the field of theory was the thesis of "subordinating class interests to national interests" ("Madju terus menggempur imperialisme dan feodalisme"/Forward to the victory over imperialism and feudalism/, D.N.A., J.P. 1961, p. 18). Compliance with this thesis would make it appear that, allegedly, class interests contradict national interests. In actual fact this was a deviation from Marxism-Leninism which teaches us that the interests of our class encompass the best interests of the entire nation.

It is thus clear that the thesis of the priority of national interests over class interests, the attempts to subordinate the Party Program to the Political Manifesto, the United National Front to the Nasakom Alliance, the attempts to "make Marxism the property of the nation"—all this is but a reflection of how deeply petty-bourgeois ideology became rooted in the body of our Party.

The Chinese comrades were not averse to capitalizing on the positive and negative characteristics of President Sukarno, while in doing so they aligned themselves with our Party's leadership to ensure the victory of their petty-bourgeois concepts of political hegemony in Asia and Africa and to replace the policy of the international anti-colonial front and struggle for peace with the "Djakarta-Peking axis."

Petty-bourgeois political views and nationalism have resulted in an inability to correctly understand the burning issues of today, and this crippled the anti-imperialist struggle and the fight for peace on an international scale, and it hurled Indonesia into the catastrophe of the September 30 Movement.

## 2.

As a doctrine, which is not dogmatic but creative, Marxism-Leninism is constantly being enriched with the latest experiences of the international workers' and Communist movement as summed up in such militant documents as the Moscow 1957 Declaration and the Moscow 1960 Statement. Both of these historic documents should become the common guiding principles in solving Party problems in each individual country, aimed at achieving the victory of the revolution, and in fighting the common enemy, international imperialism led by the United States of America.

In this common cause we are united first and foremost by devotion to Marxist-Leninist principles and proletarian internationalism.

The Indonesian Revolution is part and parcel of the world revolution of mankind in its struggle for socialism and eternal peace. Likewise, the theories of the Indonesian Revolution were elaborated by us through combining the general precepts of Marxism-Leninism with concrete revolutionary practices in Indonesia. However, these theories of the Indonesian Revolution should constantly be put to the test in the process of the development of our Revolution so as to see to what degree they truly reflect the fundamentals of the universal Marxist-Leninist theory. That is why it is by no means permissible to believe that our revolutionary theories are the only correct ones and are not liable to reconsideration.

In the past few decades Marxism-Leninism has gone through an ordeal of major discussions in the international Communist movement aimed at blazing the best trail to follow in its effort to expedite the historical mission of the proletariat. Our true devotion to Marxism-Leninism and proletarian internationalism is gauged by our disinterested service to the spirit and the letter of the documents elaborated and agreed upon by all Marxist-Leninist parties, i.e., the Moscow Declaration of 1957 and the Moscow Statement of 1960.

As a member of the international Communist movement, the PKI, which has already demonstrated its maturity, at first held a position from which *a priori* it neither accused nor justified any side in its earnest desire to make a critical study of all the materials and arguments that issued from the already-mentioned major discussion. It also strove to make a contribution of its own to the reunification of the international Communist movement in accordance with the ideas of proletarian internationalism, having no intention whatsoever of taking a middle-of-the-road position.

Further developments demonstrated, however, that in reality a deviation did manifest itself in the policy of our Party from the above approach. Not only did we fail to become more critical of ourselves, we succumbed to sentimentality and *a priori* justified one side while we preached alienation toward the other. Not only did we fail to elevate the principle of holding discussions and consultations in search of the contradictions in the international Communist movement, but we used the slogan, "Let us turn the major discussion on the international Communist movement into a Marxist-Leninist university on an international scale," to support the idea of an open and broad discussion of internal issues in the international Communist movement before the very eyes of the enemy. Although, officially, our relations remained good and friendly, in actual fact we followed the wrong path by treating as our enemies those whom we believed to be "revisionists" matching in their viciousness and evil the pillars of world imperialism. Each critical thought or argument which failed *a priori* either to justify or accuse the sides was increasingly strongly condemned as "an inconsistent class position reeking of revisionism," to be, naturally, exorcised from the Party. Not only did we fail to stand on our own and strengthen our identity, but rather we became even more ideologically, politically and economically dependent on a certain party. What is more that party was responsible for turning the Indonesian Revolution into a gaming table for its political gambles.

## A. ON THE MAIN CONTENT AND THE CHIEF CONTRADICTIONS OF OUR EPOCH

At the beginning we expressed our full agreement with the thesis of the Moscow 1960 Statement to the effect that the chief contradiction of our epoch is the contradiction between socialism and imperialism.

However, the Second Plenary Meeting of the PKI which took place after the 7th Party Congress,* had drastically changed the Party's stand on this score by declaring that the chief and decisive contradiction of our time is the contradiction between the national liberation movements in Asia, Africa and Latin America on the one hand, and imperialism on the other. This change was caused by a new orientation, from which it followed that the center of world storms, the center of revolutionary explosion in the modern world lay not in imperialist and capitalist countries but in Asia, Africa and Latin America.

It is quite obvious, and it is correct to assert, that the flames of the Revolution are burning bright in Asia, Africa and Latin America, and in the past few years they are especially hot in Vietnam, although this is by no means proof of the fact that the main contradiction in the world today has changed into the contradiction between the oppressed nations and imperialism. The chief world contradiction of our time, a time of transition to socialism, a time of the world revolution, is still the contradiction between the proletariat and the bourgeoisie in general and the contradiction between the new victorious social system (socialism) and the moribund social system (capitalism) in particular, between the proletarian states and the bourgeois imperialist states.

Recognition of the fact that "in our epoch world development is detemined by the course and results of the competition between two diametrically opposed social systems" means that:

1) For the international Communist movement, for Communist and Workers' parties the prime duty is to strengthen the cohesion of the countries of the socialist system, guarding it as the apple of their own eye, and to oppose any actions that may undermine the authority and unity of the world socialist system.

2) For the proletariat in the countries where it is in power, for socialist states, the prime duty is continuously to increase the economic and defense potentials of these states and see to it that socialism preserves its leading role in the field of science, technology and culture, retaliates to any imperialist outrages, thus augmenting socialism's possibilities in the implementation of the tasks of proletarian internationalism, acting as the tried and tested friend of the peoples fighting for their freedom.

All this indicates that making the strengthening of the world socialist system its cornerstone by no means implies that the revolutionary struggle in Asia, Africa and Latin America should be treated as a bastard child. On the contrary, the strengthening of the socialist system creates more favorable conditions for the growth of solidarity with this struggle to which it renders moral and material support, giving the peoples of Asia, Africa and Latin America economic, cultural, armed and other types of assistance, so that their struggle may end in the victory of the revolutions of Asia, Africa and Latin America at their first and second stages.

## B. ON THE STRUGGLE
## FOR INTERNATIONAL PEACE
## AND PEACEFUL COEXISTENCE

In later documents of the Party there is not a single paragraph refuting the task of the Communists to struggle for world peace and peaceful coexistence between the two different social systems. However, a point of view has been expressed recently, and has developed into the Party line. This point of view boils down to antipathy toward the struggle for peace and peaceful coexistence.

Thus, it was pointed out that:

—talking of peace, and especially of disarmament, when imperialism is still in existence is simply a waste of words;

—only then does the struggle for peace acquire any sense when it is a struggle against colonialism and imperialism and, in particular, against the imperialism of the United States;

—the correct slogan is this: "We love peace, but more still we love independence." Peaceful coexistence has a meaning solely for the settlement and the preservation of relations between socialist and imperialist states and cannot be extended to the struggle going on in colonial nations. There can be no peaceful coexistence between imperialism and the oppressed peoples;

—the struggle for peace and peaceful coexistence is, in effect, only a poisonous concoction paralyzing the revolutionary energies of the oppressed nations who are in a state of revolutionary upsurge, and serves to adorn the facade of imperialism, making it look as if the U.S. loves peace too;

—making peaceful coexistence task No. 1 means to deviate from the highest principle governing relations between socialist countries and fraternal parties, i.e., the principle of proletarian internationalism while, in fact, it implies surrender to the nuclear imperialist blackmail.

Chiefly, this line was readily toed only by the hot-headed petty-bourgeois revolutionaries, but it could not be taken for granted by the proletariat armed with the theory of scientific socialism and thinking along more realistic lines. If a thorough analysis is made of this issue, it will turn out that the relations between its many aspects are impaired, which results in these questions falling short of the mark.

*Firstly,* it is necessary to have a clear idea that the struggle for peace and peaceful coexistence is an alternative to destructive thermonuclear war between different social systems, a war which would inevitably push all countries and peoples of the world on to a road of disaster. Thus, it cannot be an alternative to the revolutions of liberation of the oppressed peoples in their struggle against imperialism. It can by no means make imperialism look more attractive, but rather heightens the vigilance of the peoples and fully exposes the nature of imperialism and all its cunning tricks. The struggle for peace and peaceful coexistence does not imply class collaboration but on the contrary creates more favorable conditions for a class struggle in all spheres. The principle of peaceful coexistence should by no means be considered an Aladdin's lamp which would bring wealth and happiness to humankind without a struggle, for it is in conditions of peaceful coexistence that we are expected tirelessly to mobilize the broad popular masses to form a peaceful front against imperialism.

On all these questions the Moscow Statement clearly pointed out the following:

To fight for peace today means to maintain the greatest vigilance, indefatigably to lay bare the policy of the imperialists, to keep a watchful eye on the intrigues and maneuvers of the warmongers, arouse the righteous indignation of the peoples against those who are heading for war, organize the peace forces still better, continuously intensify mass actions for peace . . .

"The struggle of the peoples against the militarization of their countries should be combined with the struggle against the capitalist monopolies connected with the U.S. imperialists."

It is further pointed out: "Peaceful coexistence of

states does not imply renunciation of the class struggle as the revisionists claim. The coexistence of states with different social systems is a form of class struggle between socialism and capitalism. *In conditions of peaceful coexistence favorable opportunities are provided for the development of the class struggle in the capitalist countries and the national liberation movement of the peoples of the colonial and dependent countries. In their turn, the successes of the revolutionary class and national liberation struggle promote peaceful coexistence.* (Author's emphasis).

*Secondly,* it is necessary to combat an opinion, which, *although revolutionary in form, in essence signifies the lack of trust in one's own strength* of rendering imperialism unable to unleash a new world war for many years to come. We must realize that although imperialism still exists in some parts of the globe, and although wars are always concomitant to the system of capitalism in conditions of the present-day balance of forces and the ever-changing conditons in favor of the socialist camp, the mighty front of the peoples of the world will prevent imperialism from madly gambling on war, and if it does take this crazy step, it will doom itself to destruction.

*Thirdly,* as regards the slogan that "we love peace, but more still we love independence," it should be pointed out that this is indeed a true slogan and there is no need to counterpose it to the slogan that it is necessary to raise high the banners of peace. For in case imperialism does wage its aggressive war in Asia, Africa and Latin America, or if it attacks one of the socialist-camp countries, hard-headedly pitting itself against peaceful public opinion, there can be no doubt that we shall have to launch a counter-offensive and deal imperialism a resolute blow. We are not pacifists or saints and we do not believe in non-resistance to violence.

*Fourthly,* it should be remembered at the same time that the world struggle for peace and peaceful coexistence contains lofty humane traits, which are instrumental in mobilizing mighty forces and attracting the progressive and humanistic-minded intelligentsia, of which we had ample proof during our own experience of stepping up the peace movement in Indonesia.

*Fifthly,* a distinction should be made between peaceful coexistence and proletarian internationalism. The Moscow Declaration and Statement when dealing with the question of peaceful coexistence, always pointed to the character of relations between countries with different social systems. In other words, relations between socialist countries and imperialist states, e.g., between Britain and the Soviet Union, or relations between socialist countries and independent non-socialist states, e.g., relations between the Soviet Union and Indonesia. Due to the triumph at the Bandung Conference of the principles of peaceful coexistence they are in fact followed in state relations by the countries in Asia and Africa.

Even though the Declaration and the Statement lay such a heavy stress on the principle of peaceful coexistence this does not mean at all that these documents want to extend these principles also to relations between socialist states, between socialist states and the nations fighting for their freedom, to relations between fraternal parties.

Unity of the international Communist movement would indeed be durable and strong if all parties (including the PKI) showed true mutual respect in the implementation of all these principles which they themselves had jointly formulated. But it is a great pity, a thousand times great pity, that there were some parties which violated these principles, with the result that the rift in the international Communist movement grew steadily wider to the obvious advantage of the enemies of revolutionary progress.

The line pursued by the PKI leadership in relations with the CPSU prior to the 7th Congress of our Party was materially and morally manifest in our firmly advocating the idea of friendship, we highly valued what the Moscow Statement said about relations between fraternal parties, although even then different points of view on this issue had already emerged. A year later, however, our relations were rather of a formal nature and had departed from the standards of relations between fraternal parties.

The stand taken by the 7th Congress of the PKI on the successes of socialist construction, the acme of which is the construction of communism in the Soviet Union and which was hailed with applause by the entire gathering, was later abruptly denounced by the CC of the PKI without any reason whatsoever.

The weakening and disappearance of friendship between the two major parties, while the advantages of this friendship had been tested over decades, caused serious damage to our movement due to the fact that we were forced to subscribe to a lopsided point of view. This is what led us to the 1965 tragedy.

While considering in its entirety the chief problem of the international Communist movement, it is possible to define the international duties of the PKI as follows:

1) The need to pursue a consistent anti-imperialist and anti-colonial foreign policy and to defend world peace and peaceful coexistence;

2) The need to raise aloft the banners of proletarian internationalism, consolidate the unity of the international Communist movement and remain truly faithful to the letter and spirit of the Moscow Declaration and Statement.

## C. THE PROBLEM OF A PEACEFUL AND NON-PEACEFUL WAY OF REVOLUTION

Many a classical statement has been made to defend the point of view that the revolution can be effected by violent means, i.e., an armed revolution against an armed counter-revolution. On the other hand, there is weighty proof that Marx, Engels and Lenin did not believe that the revolution should necessarily develop along military lines; they insisted that it can also be effected by peaceful means, although in their lifetime the chances for this were very slender indeed and the idea lacked practical confirmation. It would be out of place to discuss this problem *per se* in this work. It is sufficient to draw your attention to what is in concert with our consensus as laid down in the Moscow Declaration and Statement, which was that under present historical conditions, especially after the emergence of the world socialist system, *there are chances* for a peaceful victory of the revolution. Whether revolution can develop peacefully or not depends largely on concrete historical conditions in each individual country.

The Statute of the PKI points out in this connection that since it is we ourselves who are concerned, our way should be that of the least possible sacrifices, i.e., the way of peace. The Indonesian experience teaches us that to use this best of opportunities, i.e., to follow the peaceful way, we must:

*firstly,* be sure that this peaceful way is open to us and, acting on this optimistic assumption, prepare all the conditions that will be instrumental in achieving the victory of the revolution by peaceful means;

*secondly,* we should by no means create an illusion that there is no other opportunity, i.e., the non-peaceful way, so as not to weaken ideological, political and organizational vigilance.

In short, it is for the sake of achieving the victory of the revolution by peaceful means that we must be ready for both alternatives and do our utmost to prepare the conditions outlined above.

Later, however, this point of view underwent some changes and turned into its opposite, i.e., into the belief that the revolution could be victorious solely if effected by force of arms while pessimism was expressed as to the peaceful way of revolutionary development.

The subjective opinion that revolution can be victorious solely if brought about by force of arms had a hypnotizing effect upon us and drastically changed the course of our Revolution pushing it on to the wrong path. This revisionist leftist point of view was instrumental in paving the theoretical way for the gamble known as the September 30 Movement.

### 3.

An analysis of the facts demonstrates that the September 30 Movement was triggered off by several units of the Indonesian Republic's Armed Forces, the Army in particular, comprised of the most progressive servicemen. The Movement concentrated in Djakarta. In other words, it was an action started in the center, in the hope that it would extend to all the regions of the Motherland.

The following goals were pursued:

1) To foil the plot of the Generals' Council and purge the Armed Forces of the conspirators.

2 To set up a "Revolutionary Council" as an organ of assistance to NASAKOM which would be a precursor of a people's democracy, a body that would consistently have to implement the five principles (Pantja Azimat) of the Indonesian Revolution.

It is quite clear that the September 30 Movement was a movement spearheaded against the coup, a movement that overthrew the Generals' Council and was at the same time a revolutionary movement aimed at the establishment of a state power that would be a harbinger of a people's democracy. In reality, this Movement developed into a military adventure, and was foiled.

The primary cause of the defeat of the September 30 Movement was not that the enemy confronting us was too strong, or that we lacked courage, or that our fighters lacked courage. The subjective causes lie in recklessness on the part of some leading Party quarters, in the ideological, political and organizational muddleheadedness, which was the objective result of the petty-bourgeois ideology of revolutionism, in excessive revolutionary zeal, a desire to achieve a quick victory, in forcing the development of the revolution which miscarried, in gambling on the balance of forces, in indulgence in adventurist fantasies, etc.

These chief mistakes set off a chain reaction of other serious errors committed during the Movement.

Let us now consider the political situation which obtained on the eve of the September 30 Movement, so as to see whether there had been any subjective and objective conditons for a revolutionary explosion in Indonesia then.

Lenin taught us that revolutions are not made to order. A revolution must needs be preceded by a revolutionary situation.

The objective symptoms of a revolutionary situation are as follows:

—the inability of the ruling classes to hold power in it old form;

—usually, it is not enough for a revolution to occur when the lower classes do not want to live as before, what is needed is that the upper classes, too, cannot live as before;

—the unprecedented aggravation of the impoverishment and the sufferings of the oppressed classes, which is fraught with extreme intensification of spontaneous action by the masses.

Lenin also said that the existence of such a revolutionary situation does not automatically lead to revolution. Added to this should be subjective conditions, i.e., the ability of the revolutionary class to wage a courageous and self-sacrificial struggle and the presence of an experienced revolutionary party which effects *strategically and tactically correct leadership*.

The Fourth Plenary Session of the CC of the PKI (May, 1965) made the following conclusions:

At the present time Indonesia finds herself in an ever-increasing and maturing revolutionary situation which has the following characteristics:

1) The popular masses are actively fighting for changes that could be instrumental in improving their living conditons.

2 Anti-popular aspects of political power are increasingly replaced by popular aspects, while the government's policies are increasingly adapted to the demands of the people.

3) Mass popular actions are broadening, which results in the ever-growing role of the popular masses and their decisive importance in the life of society and state politics.

Our task at the present time is "to step up the revolutionary offensive, continue to develop the revolutionary situation bringing it to a state of maturity."

Let us test the correctness of the above conclusions by the realities of the economic and political situation in our country.

## In the Field of Economics

The economic crisis which had afflicted Indonesia was growing increasingly worse; setbacks in all the key sectors of the economy had worsened the living standards of the people; prices of foodstuffs and clothing were inexorably rising.

The luxury in which the upper stratum of the population was wallowing was becoming ever more apparent against the background of intolerable suffering of the people and the flourishing of capitalist bureaucrats, who were plunging their claws ever deeper into the body of the Indonesian economy, their interests being interlocked with those of the imperialists, while the latter were using these capitalist bureaucrats as their mainstay; this "economic dynasty" had caused great damage to the public sector of the economy, aggravated the living conditions of the working people and brought to bankruptcy private enterprises which were not the property of capitalist bureaucrats.

The progressive revolutionary forces of Indonesia had time and again tried to find a way out of these economic difficulties, but their efforts had proved futile due to the following causes:

a) Sabotage on the part of internal reactionaries holding key positions in the major branches of Indonesia's economy, assisted by the subversive economic actions of the imperialists;

b) The sky-rocketing state budget within the framework of confrontation with Malaysia and the squandering of public funds on major uneconomical projects and all kinds of government political activities.

Failure to cope with the economic difficulties had both given rise to general dissatisfaction among the progressive revolutionary circles in Indonesia and been used by the internal reaction as material to discredit Sukarno's regime—a campaign which had affected the sentiments of the broad masses still lacking sufficient political consciousness.

## In the Field of Politics

The revolutionary and progressive forces, the PKI and its mass revolutionary organizations were becoming even stronger. They put forward the demand that the Gotong-Rojtong Cabinet be formed:

—in the process of crystallization of the middle-of-the-road forces, they were cleaning their house of right-of-center elements;

—the hardheaded elements were consolidating themselves and emerging as a new group comprised of the right-wing old-timers (former Masjumi—PSI) and new right-wingers (capitalist bureaucrats and Trotskyites), plus the right wing of the Centrist forces kicked out of the nationalistic parties;

—the number of mass actions by the people rose abruptly and aimed at the following major targets:

1) crushing the city devils (capitalist bureaucrats, corruptionists and embezzlers of public funds);

2) crushing the village devils;

3) take-over of U.S. imperialist enterprises.

The President's deteriorating health started speculations in Indonesia's political circles. Playing on President Sukarno's illness, the new right-wing trio, Sukarni-Hatta-Chairul, attempted to engineer the seizure of state power in Indonesia. This attempt backfired, as a result of which the Murba party was banned and its leader, Sukarni, arrested.

Simultaneously, the conspirators from the Generals' Council and their braintrust (Hatta-Nasution) were taking more and more concrete steps towards thorough and well-planned actions which were hard to expose since they were not known beyond a group of topmost officers of the Armed Forces and in a number of regions. Nevertheless, Subandrio and his central intelligence organ, the BPI, got wind of these actions, reported them to the President and informed the Party.

As soon as they received word of the danger of the generals' conspiracy the high party leadership called an expanded meeting and drew conclusions, then took preventive steps which boiled down to the following:

—necessary action was undertaken to prepare the Party for any emergency in case the Generals' Council dared carry out their dastardly plan;

—consultations with the President and left-wing nationalist leaders were held in the event of possible complications that could set in in connection with the danger presented by the Generals' Council.

Had a consensus been reached at that period by the joint front acting against the Generals' Council to destroy the conspiracy, great political progress within the country could possibly have been achieved, Indonesia's progressive forces could have been consolidated and the Gotong-Rojong Cabinet—the objective of a long drawn out struggle—could probably have been formed. At that time, even President Sukarno himself was already more resolutely inclined to renovate his Cabinet along the lines of the Gotong-Rojong Cabinet, in spite of strong pressures brought to bear on him by the Generals' Council. Reports had it that in the Generals' Council itself there was no unanimity as to the timing of their actions: some believed that the anniversary of the Armed Forces should be the date (October), others were inclined to fix a later date in the belief that Armed Forces Day should be turned into a show of force, so as to prevent the formation of the Gotong-Rojong Cabinet.

Following the return of our leaders from a trip abroad which also included one of the Asian countries (July-August 1965) it became known that the Party leadership had taken a rash decision to begin preparation for playing the role of a "savior," with or without President Sukarno and other democratic forces. And all this happened at a time when there was no revolutionary situation in evidence, no instability was manifest in the position of the ruling quarters, the broad masses were not prepared for armed action. There was only a danger of a counter-revolutionary plot and there were the diseased kidneys of President

Sukarno. Had a revolution occurred it would have been based not on the revolutionary situation or the support of the revolutionary masses, but would have rather hinged on Sukarno's lesioned kidneys. Truly, that was a gamble of the first water which had nothing to do with the Marxist theory of armed uprising.

Lenin taught us to be successful, an uprising should rest not upon a conspiracy of any one party, but on the progressive class. That is the first precondition. An uprising must be based on the revolutionary wave of a popular upsurge. That is the second precondition. An uprising should coincide with the most tense moment in the history of a revolution, which sets in when the activities of the vanguard of the people reach their peak and when instability in the enemy ranks and among the weak and inconsistent allies of the revolution is at its highest. That is the third precondition. The existence of these three preconditions in posing the question of an uprising differentiates Marxism from Blanquism.

The PKI made the final analysis and algebraically formulated the power balance in Indonesia at the time as follows:

center forces + right wingers are greater than the leftist forces
center forces + leftists are greater than the right-wing forces

That meant that in taking action that could lead to the instability of the center forces and their tendency to make common cause with the Right-wing, the situation was very disadvantageous for the Party and the whole affair would have fizzled out.

It is necessary to bear in mind at the same time that the formula:

Left-wingers + centrists are greater than the right-wingers

is justified within the framework of an anti-imperialist struggle, although it cannot be applied as easily against the General's Council due to the following factors:

The reactionary forces had acquired considérable additional strength from the Right-wing of the Center forces which were ousted from the Marhaenis Front as a result of the increasing crystallization of the center forces.

The religious parties were more sympathetic toward the Generals' Council which they tended to see as a savior of religion from atheism.

That was the root of the difficulty of preserving NASAKOM intact in the duel with the Generals' Council especially at a time when part of the PKI leadership were behaving like fighting cocks.

We often said that at least thirty per cent of the Armed Forces are the followers of the Hammer and Sickle. However, we often also mistakenly forgot what measure of the thirty per cent were loyal to the Party and President Sukarno. One can say with certainty that when the Party and Bung Karno were united these thirty per cent of the Armed Forces would pledge back their hearts and souls to them. When, however, they had to choose between the Party and President Sukarno it is a good guess that the majority would demonstrate greater devotion to Sukarno; at best they would occupy an unstable position. That is why the factor of President Sukarno had to be seriously borne in mind.

Let us now analyze the subjective factors bearing upon ourselves, factors which, scientifically speaking, determine the success of the revolution, namely: the readiness of the vanguard class for a struggle under the leadership of the Party armed with the correct strategy and tactics.

Actions aimed at taking over U.S. imperialist enterprises did not imply any physical clashes because they were fully supported by the government. The workers, at the same time, had a bitter experience that these actions failed to give them clear advantages, while the enterprises were falling into the hands of capitalist bureaucrats.

The actions aimed at crushing the city devils were still at the level of demonstrations and demands that government officials take resolute steps against the city devils, i.e., there was no immediate physical contact with the devils themselves. Only the onesided actions of the peasants aimed at crushing the village devils went through the stage of physical clashes with the armed forces and resulted in the loss of human life. However, these one-sided actions were later checked by the Party and directed along the lines of reason and negotiations (mushavarah). It is becoming ever clearer that we were not sufficiently seasoned in non-peaceful action, that we did not want to quarrel with Sukarno who had extinguished the revolutionary actions of the peasants.

As a result of the disease of self-conceit, bureaucracy and the cult of the personality that flourished in the Party (see Chapter 2) many functionaries and rank and file were unable to train themselves ideologically and organizationally to act according to the maxim: "Do not cry over broken pots and cut knuckles."

During those tense days the Party, having given its support to Colonel Untung's actions, committed the following political mistakes:

a) The organizers of and immediate participants in Untung's actions failed to take into consideration the need to draw the masses to their side in order to secure the support of progressive forces within the country. After the successful seizure of Radio Republic of Indonesia (RRI), they did not offer their people a positive socio-economic platform, nor did they call upon peasants and workers to watch for the danger of the conspiracy of the Generals' Council.

Instead of issuing a decree for the creation of people's armed forces, a decision was made to give a fresh boost to the military. Following all this, it was hard to count on the support of the masses for the September 30 Movement.

b) When all the political leaders denied their participation in the Revolutionary Council the leadership of the Party made a belated statement to the effect that it was wrong to believe that the Party had taken part in the September 30 Movement. However, the Party leadership did not refute allegations that it had supported the purge carried out by Untung and his followers.

Western Java, as a region where the influence of the Party was relatively small, ought to have received primary attention from the Party leadership during the preparatory stage. In actual fact it was treated as an orphan up to the defeat of the September 30 Movement in Djakarta. In Western Java neither the situation nor plans for future actions were known.

Within twenty four hours the Party leadership in the provinces and in the Kebupaten (countries) were arrested by the authorities on a large scale and practically without resistance. In the following days, under the influence of dissatisfaction with the leadership and despondency resulting from mass surrender to the reactionary authorities, statements were made on the dissolution of Party committees, accompanied with accusations against the Party leadership. On the other hand, those who still continued to fight attacked the Party leadership from the left, which explains the fact why two diametrically opposed tendencies emerged in Western Java: shameful mass surrender was going on parallel with the flourishing of the ultra-leftists. Both stem from the one and same source: general disillusionment with the political leadership of the Party.

Heated debates had taken place in the Party leadership about whether the Party should obey the President's orders or continue the struggle and repulse the onslaught of reaction. It was decided to issue a statement in support of a political solution by the President, to attend the full Cabinet meeting so as to bring pressure to bear upon the President during that meeting, to recognize the Generals'·Council and agree to the formation of the NASAKOM Cabinet; if this failed—to continue resistance.

In this lies the following major mistake committed by the Party: the passivity of and panic among the Party leadership in an emergency situation which resulted in surrender of all authority to President Sukarno and his political decision, but not reliance on the strength of the masses.

While the Party depended on President Sukarno's actions aimed at finding a political solution, which was long in coming, reaction was not idle. Persecution of progressive revolutionary elements began. Mad white terror was unleashed which knew no limits of inhumanity. Hundreds of thousands of the Party rank and file and the functionaries of progressive revolutionary organizations together with their innocent families were plunged into a blood bath and became victims of mass killings. Hundreds of thousands of others were thrown into prisons or concentration camps. Even the Party's top leaders failed to avoid the terror, among them Comrades D. N. Aidit, Lukman and Njoto.

Counter-revolutionaries came to power and the revolutionary tide began to ebb. Such is the sad fate of the September 30 Movement resulting from suicidal leftist policies for which the Revolution paid a dear and unnecessary price. That was the mistake the consequences of which for the Indonesian Revolution and international communist movement are hard to rectify.

## CONCLUSIONS

An analysis of the entire development and activities of the Party in the past few years and during the September 30 Movement yields the conclusion that:

1) The chief reason underlying the failures of the PKI in leading the revolution was that the PKI still lacked the traits characterizing a Leninist party, i.e., it was not a sufficiently bolshevized party, nor did it have a mass nature. In the past the Party had not paid adequate attention to measures aimed at increasing the role of proletarian elements in it or at improving its ideological and cultural level. In the recent past the Party tended to ascribe too much significance to the revolutionary spirit of the peasantry, whereas, without wishing to detract from our view that the peasantry is the staunchest ally of the working class, it should be pointed out that the petty-bourgeoisie is hamstrung by a serious drawback and one to be borne in mind, namely, that it is inconsistent in its actions.

The doors of the Party were flung wide open for the mass admission of petty-bourgeois elements with the result that ideologically, politically and organizationally the Party was flooded with a petty-bourgeois wave, while the fact that the Party leadership was turning bourgeois was completely ignored.

Hence, ideologically the Party was infected with a petty-bourgeois spirit and fell victim to overindulgence in ultra-leftist slogans and petty-bourgeois nationalism, all of which crippled the spirit of proletarian internationalism, that integral and inalienable part of the activities of the party of the working class.

*Theoretically*, there was, on the one hand, an upsurge of dogmatism which found expression in easy acceptance of concepts revolutionary in form but failing to take stock of local conditions. On the other hand, there was an emergence of revisionism which tended to upend the monolithic doctrine of Marxism-Leninism and replace it with "national Marxism" within the framework of the so-called "Indonesification of Marxism-Leninism."

*Politically*, the Party was not consistent in defending its class positions and engaged in class collaboration with the bourgeoisie; it gave prominence to cooperation within the framework of the NASAKOM, it lost its freedom of action in strengthening the sacred alliance of the workers and peasants; it demonstrated subjectivism and haste in assessing the situation and in evaluating the balance of forces; it failed to define its tactics, shuttling between adventurism and capitulation; it made absolute its choice of the forms of struggle, tending to take just one aspect of the struggle out of the many forms that a party of the working class must employ.

All of this led to the Party's inability to play the role of leader of the Revolution.

*Organizationally*, in its internal activities the Party was further deviating from the principles of democracy and collective leadership, it was increasingly falling into the snare of the personality cult, it was demonstrating an increasing lack of internal democracy in the Party, it was stifling initiative coming from the rank and file, it was fettering criticism from below and was not encouraging the development of vigorous self-criticism.

Firm discipline was not strengthened in the Party,

liberal attitudes towards the decisions of the Party organization flourished, serious measures to curb bureaucracy in the Party were not taken.

2. The adventurism of the abortive September 30 Movement and its epilogue proved to be the inevitable result of the accumulation of the Party's past mistakes, its confused ideological, political and organizational line, all of which caused the Party to be punished by the objective development of history.

The alternative facing the Communist and Workers' movement in Indonesia at the present time is this: whether to stick to the old erroneous position and continue adventurist policies, failing to see the real state of affairs, and upholding organizational sectarianism, which signifies a divorce from the masses, or to completely give up pseudo-revolutionary concepts and take to the right path again, to be devoted to the Statutes and the Program of the Party adopted by the Fifth Congress of the PKI and supplemented at the Sixth Congress, to enjoy the love and sympathies of the broad masses and to make the Party play the role not just of the vanguard, but of leadership of the Revolution.

*Ideologically*, it is necessary to strengthen the outlook and methods of the working class, strengthen the proletarian elements of the Party, oppose petty-bourgeois nationalism, develop the spirit of proletarian internationalism in conjunction with true patriotism. The Party should deepen the knowledge of the universal teachings of Marxism-Leninism in conjunction with concrete revolutionary practices in Indonesia, it should free itself from the wrong concept of the "Indonesification of Marxism-Leninism."

The Party should return to the correct way of creating a united national front. It should value most of all the strengthening of the union between workers and peasants as the basic foundation of the united national front. The Party should step up its work among the peasants on the basis of a revolutionary agrarian program, which can make the peasants a tested ally of the working class and secure correct proportions in the cooperation of the working people with the national bourgeoisie and other democratic elements. The Party should increase its influence in the masses by using all forms of legal or illegal struggle, take into account the requirements and demands of all strata of the working people for improved living conditions, consistently and increasingly carry out mass revolutionary action for democratic rights, higher living standards and social progress.

3. The building of a bolshevized and mass party should continue, a party that would be spread through the entire country, giving priority in it to the admission to the party of workers, without, however, slamming the doors in the faces of the best sons of other strata of the working people, especially the poor peasants and agricultural laborers in accordance with the norms and standards of the party Statutes bearing on party membership.

The Leninist norms of party organization should be restored, the principles of democratic centralism should be unflinchingly followed, among them the principle of collective leadership; criticism and self-criticism should be reborn.

4. For the sake of preserving true unity within the Party and for the sake of the renovation of the Party, a clear line of division should be drawn with those who still stand on positions of advocating ultra-leftist and sectarian principles, those who in the past unambiguously pushed the Party to adventurism and opposed cohesion in the international Communist movement.

5. Under the prevailing conditions, it is important to remind the Party of the need always to heighten Party vigilance, enforce firm discipline among the Party members, effect the division of labor in concert with the abilities and growth of professional Party cadres; it is necessary to remember the need to encourage initiative from below, the wise and flexible use of all the forms and methods of work in legal organizations, even though they may be of the most reactionary sort.

6. To provide for the victory of the August 1945 Revolution the immediate target task of the Party today is to forge a united Left-wing front, progressive, democratic and patriotic in nature, a front able to carry on a consistent struggle against pro-imperialist and anti-democratic reaction and thus deal it a crushing blow, as before to concern itself with keeping Indonesia in the camp of anti-imperialism and peace and preserve the good relations of the Republic of Indonesia with the Socialist-bloc countries.

7. In the sphere of international activities the Party should continue to pursue a consistent anti-imperialist and anti-colonial foreign policy, continue to defend peace and peaceful coexistence.

8. The banners of the proletarian internationalism should be raised aloft, the unity of the international Communist movement should be strengthened, all attempts to split and undermine the alliance and unity of the front of Communists and Workers' parties fighting the common enemy—imperialism led by U.S. imperialism—should be frustrated and foiled, the Party should be truly devoted to the letter and spirit of the Moscow Declaration and Statement worked out jointly by all the fraternal parties. Realistic relations should be maintained with all the Communist and Workers' parties on the basis of the principle of independence and equality, without allowing an open attack against each other in the face of the enemy.

Such is the way out of the existing situation.

Confidence should prevail that the international proletariat, the Communist and Workers' parties of the world, all the progressive and revolutionaries the world over will always demonstrate their international solidarity with us, as was the case during the time when Indonesia's progressive and revolutionary forces went through an ordeal similar to the present one, and we drew on their support and sympathy. Experience demonstrates that life itself ruthlessly condemns those who, instead of gratitude, flaunt evil prejudices by alleging that there are fraternal parties which, while saying they are concerned, in fact do no more than shed crocodile tears.

To the fallen victims, who number hundreds of thousands of Communists and their followers, who have shed their blood for the escutcheon of the

Motherland as a result of the recent atrocities of the white terror, and in token of our gratitude for fervent international solidarity, we can give but one answer: to forge ahead along the new correct way, along the Marxist-Leninist way toward the final victory of our national democratic Revolution.

Long live the PKI, the vanguard of the working class!

Long live the unity of the international Communist and Workers' movement!

Eternal condemnation to the assassins of the hundreds of thousands of Communists, workers, peasants and intelligentsia—the true sons of Indonesia!

Long live the Indonesian people and the Indonesian Revolution!

*The Marxist-Leninist Group of the PKI.*

# THREE DOCUMENTS OF THE COMMUNIST PARTY OF ISRAEL

### A. SPEECH BY MEIR VILNER IN THE KNESSET, 22 MAY 1967
### B. STATEMENT OF THE CENTRAL COMMITTEE, CP OF ISRAEL, 26 MAY 1967
### C. DECISIONS OF THE CENTRAL COMMITTEE 16TH PLENARY SESSION, 22 JUNE 1967

*Complete Texts*
*(Information Bulletin,* Nos. 99-100, 102, 1967)

## A. SPEECH BY MEIR VILNER IN THE KNESSET, 22 MAY 1967

Speaker of the Knesset, Honorable Knesset.

The Prime Minister's statement confirms the fact that tension in our area has reached serious dimensions. In all walks of life people ask anxiously: what will the next day bring, how is it possible to avoid slipping into a war? The Prime Minister's statement gave no answer whatsoever to this question and contributed nothing towards quietening down the anxiety.

The Premier tried to explain the latest developments which brought about the present tension. But his explanation was very far from being objectively presented and showing realism.

Until the month of April this year, during some months, the northern borders (with Syria) were relatively quiet. The Israeli-Syrian armistice commission held several special meetings, on the proposal of the UN Secretary-General, in order to try to find a peaceful solution and come to agreement about tilling the soil in the demilitarized zone. Suddenly, and without considering the interests of peace, the interests of quiet borders and the security of the border settlements, the government decided, at its meeting on April 2nd, to till the disputed plots in the demilitarized zone. It is nearly impossible to think that the government, in taking this decision, did not take into consideration possible chain reactions, including the bombing of settlements. This proves *that this decision was taken for political reasons.*

On April 7th, the Israeli air force was put into action and its planes reached even Damascus.

Instead of taking the proper political initiative there came a new wave of threats of military action against Syria. In an interview published on the 10th of May, 1967, in the organ of the army *Bamahaneh,* the Prime Minister said: "Israel has the right to act in self-defense according to the circumstances." And at the meeting of Mapai speakers on the 11th of May, the Prime Minister said openly: "It may be that we shall be forced to take steps not less serious than those we took on April the 7th." (The air attack on Syria.)

On May 14th the Chief of Staff said again in an interview published in the daily *Hayom:* "One action is not enough to bring about the change in the Syrian government's policy concerning the acts of sabotage." In the same interview the Chief of Staff talked of the "Instability of Syria." These statements caused concern in world public opinion. The French, British, American and West German press reported in those days that the only point Israel is debating is *"how* to invade Syria, and not *if* it is necessary." (STA press agency report, May 13th, 1967.)

The Israeli press even published articles on the kind of action to be taken. According to *Yediot Ahronot,* it would have to be forceful and quick, so as not to enable Egypt and the Soviet Union to interfere and stop it.

Some states which are interested in peace in our region, and first of all the Soviet Union, officially warned the government that to threaten Syria with military actions meant playing with fire and was contrary to the national interests of Israel. But the government did not listen to this warning and this friendly advice. The Prime Minister's statement today gave an untrue description of the stand taken by the Soviet Union. The sole aim of the Soviet Union is that peace in the area be kept.

Even American sources are forced to admit in public today, after consulting with Soviet spokesmen, that "the Soviet Union has shown great interest in ensuring peace in the Middle East, and it opposes any use of force."

On the other hand, the government listened to the advice of the rulers of the USA and Great Britain, who are interested in raising the tension in the region, even at the cost of the blood of our sons.

The government is pursuing an unrealistic policy. All its reckoning was upset by the events of these days. It had believed that the anti-imperialist Arab states would split, and had thought that a repetition of the events of April 7th would be possible. But events took a different course.

The experience of the last 18 years proves that the official policy was a serious failure and was not able to reach peace and security. In these fateful days we emphasize again that there is a road to peace, but to take this road means altering the official policy entirely. We must do two main things: first, become independent from the Western colonial powers, and secondly, recognize the legitimate national rights of the Arab people of Palestine, above all the rights of the Arab refugees. Such a change in the Israeli policy would lead to the recognition of the national rights of Israel by the Arab states, including the right of free navigation.

Therefore, for the security of Israel, we must find a common language with the Arab people, with the Arab anti-imperialist forces. Experience proves that peace can only be established through mutual recognition of national rights. We have no need for preaching peace but for a policy of peace. No international law whatsoever recognizes as self-defense military action on the territory of other states.

MK Ben Gurion sought to prevent the debate in the Knesset. In 1956 too, when he was Prime Minister, he used to act behind the back of the sovereign Knesset. And as Mr. Anthony Eden did in the British Parliament, so Mr. Ben Gurion did in the Knesset by withholding the truth from us. Anthony Nutting's revelations, which we published recently, are very enlightening. Ben Gurion declared then that Israel never would be the first to start war. But only two weeks later she started a war in conformity with the governments of France and Britain. Is it not possible that, one or two years hence, we shall learn that we did not today hear the whole truth from the Prime Minister, especially concerning regional cooperation between the Israeli government and the governments of the USA, Great Britain and other colonial powers?

We propose that the Prime Minister close—in case he is really concerned with lessening the tension—the "open notebook" in which he pencils down military operations across the border. Instead he should open a new book, a book of peace and a different policy, which would serve the security of Israel and not foreign interests.

In 1956 the world forces of peace, progress and socialism prevented an aggravation of the war, and stopped it before it grew into a major conflagration. In 1967 there are reliable prospects for preventing war in our region by the common effort of the peace forces in Israel, the Arab countries and the whole world.

We call on all who are really concerned with the well-being of our sons and daughters, with the security of Israel and her taking root as a recognized state in the region, to mobilize in unity against being pushed into war and military adventure, for peace.

We propose deciding to return permanently to the Israeli-Egyptian and Israeli-Syrian armistice commissions, according to the advice of the UN Secretary-General.

Let us defend peace with all our might, for peace assures the security of Israel.

## B. STATEMENT OF THE CENTRAL COMMITTEE, CP OF ISRAEL, 26 MAY 1967

A dangerous and explosive situation has developed now in the Middle East in consequence of American and British imperialist plots supported by the Israeli government, disregarding Israel's security and true national interests. The Israeli air attack on Syria on April 7th and repeated threats by the Israeli Prime Minister and Chief of Staff about new large-scale military action against Syria were a prelude to the present dangerous escalation. The main aims of the imperialists and their henchmen are to overthrow the Syrian anti-imperialist regime, weaken Aden and the South Arabian national-liberation struggle and safeguard oil concessions and bases.

The Communist Party of Israel condemns the Al Fattah acts of sabotage in Israel and declarations against the right of the State of Israel to existence, which harm the political struggle of the Palestine Arab people for their legitimate national rights and are exploited by the imperialists and their henchmen as a pretext for military intervention against anti-imperialist Arab regimes.

Israel's right to free passage in the Red Sea should be ensured only by political means and agreement with the states concerned, and not through war.

The Communist Party of Israel calls for a peaceful settlement of the Israeli-Arab conflict and of the Palestine problem.

The Communist Party of Israel demands that the Israeli government recognize the legitimate national rights of the Palestine Arab people and above all the right of Arab refugees to choose repatriation or compensation. Such recognition will lead to recognition by the Arab states of the State of Israel and its legitimate national rights, including free navigation.

Israel's security and well-being demand the adoption of a new policy: not with imperialism against the Arab peoples, but with the Arab peoples against imperialism.

The Communist Party of Israel calls on all peace-loving forces in Israel for united action to prevent war and safeguard peace. The Communist Party of Israel calls on the Israeli government to adopt an independent peace policy, not to pull chestnuts out of the fire for the imperialists, not to take any military steps beyond the armistice lines, and return to the armistice commissions with Syria and Egypt.

The Communist Party of Israel highly values the policy and endeavors of the Soviet Union and other peace forces aimed at frustrating the warmongers and safeguarding peace and people's independence, a policy serving the interests of both the Israeli and the Arab peoples.

The Communist Party of Israel calls on all forces interested in maintaining peace and preventing war in the Middle East to condemn the imperialist plots and maneuvers in our region, demand the withdrawal of the United States Sixth Fleet from the Mediterranean and stay the hand of those who want to kindle the flames of war.

## C. DECISIONS OF THE CENTRAL COMMITTEE 16TH PLENARY SESSION, 22 JUNE 1967

### "The Struggle Against Aggression And For Peace"

The Central Committee of the Communist Party of Israel holds that the war which was started by the Eshkol-Dayan-Begin government on June 5, 1967, has caused the most serious harm to the national interests of the State of Israel and its international position. The war has not strengthened the security of Israel but has shaken it even more; it has not brought Israeli-Arab peace nearer but has put it off still further.

The war which was started by the Eshkol-Dayan-Begin government is an aggressive war, which was planned beforehand, together with the governments of the USA and Britain and with the support of the West German government.

The war has brought death, destruction and ruin.

The principal aim of the war was to bring about the fall of the anti-imperialist regimes in Egypt and Syria, to sever the connections of the Arab countries with the Soviet Union and the other socialist countries, and to protect the concessions of the foreign oil monopolies and the strategic bases of the Western colonial powers in our region.

The Central Committee warns: The security and future of the State of Israel demand an end to the aggression and to the plots with the American oil and armament magnates, whose hands are stained with the blood of the peoples of Vietnam and other countries.

The Communist Party of Israel has repeatedly warned the leaders of the Arab national movement that the declarations against the right of existence of Israel and the acts of terror on Israeli territory only serve the imperialists and Israeli militarists as a pretext to execute their aggressive plans against the anti-imperialist Arab countries, and cause harm to the anti-imperialist struggle and the struggle for the legal rights of the Palestinian Arab people.

The struggle of our Communist Party has been and continues to be directed against the policy of the rulers of Israel, which is an adventurous anti-national policy in the service of imperialism, endangers peace in our region and the whole world, and is apt to lead the State of Israel to a catastrophe. A positive plan for the solution of the Palestinian problem, acknowledging the legal rights of the two peoples of Palestine, promulgated by the Arab national movement, would strike at the root of imperialist plots and would assist in the isolation of the militarist ruling circles of Israel.

The Communist Party of Israel is fighting for liquidating the aggression and for the retreat of the Israeli Army to the armistice lines. Liquidation of the aggression is the necessary precondition for the creation of the possibility for the attainment of permanent peace.

The new bitter experience has shown again that the Israeli-Arab conflict can only be solved by peaceful means and agreement on the basis of recognition of the rights of all peoples concerned.

The disentanglement of the State of Israel from dependence on the imperialist powers and the recognition by the State of Israel of the national rights of the Palestinian Arab people, and first of all the rights of the refugees, is the road to Israeli-Arab peace, and to the Arab countries' recognition of Israel and her national rights, including freedom of sea passage.

The Central Committee declares that all proposals for peace negotiations by the rulers of Israel under the conditions of continued Israeli occupation of Egyptian, Syrian and Jordanian territories are empty, demagogic proposals. These proposals, including the proposal for autonomy or the establishment of a Palestinian protectorate in the occupied territories, are not directed towards a peaceful solution but to the continuation of occupation.

The Central Committee condemns the acts of oppression, serious infringement of the rights of the civilian Arab population, the expulsion of tens of thousands of people from their homes, the cold-blooded destruction of towns and villages, the acts of pillage and looting of the property of civilians in the occupied territories. These are in fact crimes of war which should be condemned and fought against for the sake of saving Israel, for the sake of the future of Israeli-Arab relations.

The Central Committee calls upon all people of conscience in Israel to protest against these cruel acts perpetrated in the occupied territories, damaging the soul of our youth and poisoning Israeli society with racialist microbes.

The Central Committee points out with concern that the aggressive war and the widening of the coalition government to include RAFI (Ben-Gurion's party) and GAHAL (Herut-Liberal bloc) brought in their wake the trampling underfoot of democratic rights, terror against those in places of work that are opposed to war, a wave of discriminatory arrests of Communists and other fighters for peace, and an intensification of the oppression of the Arab population in Israel.

The Central Committee warns against the danger of a military dictatorship in Israel. Only a united and militant struggle of all democratic forces can prevent the victory of fascism in Israel.

The Central Committee points out with concern the worsening of the economic condition following the war.

The Central Committee points out with concern the difficult conditions, in particular of the Arab workers and peasants who were detached from the source of their living and face a regime of military and police oppression in the Arab districts.

The Central Committee calls for a united struggle of the Jewish and Arab workers in defense of their interests, against oppression and national discrimination, for equal national rights.

The Central Committee expresses its regret over the severance of diplomatic relations with Israel by the socialist countries—USSR, Czechoslovakia, Bulgaria, Poland, Hungary, Yugoslavia, and also by democratic Guinea. All the responsibility for this severance of Israel's relations with the socialist world falls on the Eshkol-Dayan-Begin government which launched an aggressive war.

The Soviet Union was and remains a faithful friend of the people of Israel and of all peoples. The severance of relations is not directed against the State of Israel, but against the policy of the government of Israel, which sacrifices the real national interests of Israel at the shrine of the interests of the Anglo-American oil companies in our region.

The Soviet Union did everything in order to prevent war in the Middle East. Now the Soviet Union acts with all its might to liquidate the results of aggression and to safeguard peace and security in the region.

The experience of the period between the first and the second world wars proves that every capitulation to aggression, every appeasement of the aggressor, will only increase his appetite, spread the flames of war and increase the danger of world war. The American imperialists who, with the help of their local agents, kindled the flames of war in Vietnam and the Middle East, are pushing towards a third world war. The cause of peace and people's independence, the cause of preventing a third world war, demands the liquidation of imperialist aggression everywhere.

The people of Israel are interested in peace in our region and in the world. The people of Israel are deeply interested in friendly relations with the USSR and all socialist and peace-loving countries.

The Central Committee warns against the danger to Israel emanating from the irresponsible national policy of its rulers, and calls for the withdrawal of the Israeli army to the armistice lines, for an end to the policy of force which relies on the imperialist powers for support.

### "Stop the Arrests and the Police Terror, Release the Political Prisoners"

The Central Committee protests strongly against the arrest of persons opposed to the war, against the arrest of leaders and members of the Communist Party of Israel and others.

Immediately after the opening of the war, many administrative arrests were made. Some of the arrested were released after 14 days. The arrest of others was prolonged and more were arrested. Other Arab citizens, who are known to be against the war, were arrested too.

The government introduced new regulations against the freedom of movement of Arab citizens, and even trespassed on the freedom of movement of Communist members of the Knesset. The imprisoned are not given the right to contact their relatives and even their lawyers are denied the right to see them. In some places, like Taibeh and Kufr-Yassif, police terror reigned.

In Tel Aviv and other Jewish towns, the police searched the homes of comrades of our Party, the home of a presidium member of the Israel-Soviet Friendship Movement, the homes of trade union activists, in order to terrorize and to instigate hatred amongst the population.

The Central Committee points with satisfaction to the courageous stand of the members of the Party, of the members of the Young Communist League and of many sympathizers, Jews and Arabs, shown in these days of trial. No terror and threats whatsoever, no arrests and cruelties are able, or ever will be able, to hinder Communists from defending peace or fighting against aggression, from defending the national interests of Israel or fighting against imperialist intrigues and the anti-national policy of the government.

The Central Committee of the Communist Party of Israel demands the immediate release of all political prisoners, an end to the acts of terror and provocation, and respect for the democratic freedoms and rights of the citizens.

The Central Committee calls on all democratic forces in Israel to raise their voice in protest against the infringement of the democratic freedoms and rights of the citizens and to demand the release of all political prisoners.

The Communist Party of Israel calls on democratic and peace-loving public opinion in the world to organize solidarity actions for the release of political prisoners and to demand a stop to the police terror in Israel.

# "NEW UNITED EFFORTS BY COMMUNIST PARTIES NEEDED"

Resolution of the Leadership of the Italian CP on the Events in China
and Problems of the World Working-Class Movement

*Complete Text*
(*L'Unità,* 10 February 1967)

The Leadership of the Italian Communist Party had a meeting, presided over by Comrade Luigi Longo, to discuss Comrade Natta's report on the internal political situation and the activity of the Party and Comrade Berlinguer's report on the international activity of the Party. The Leadership decided to put these questions on the agenda of the CC meeting to be held on February 15 through 17, and to instruct all Party organizations to step up the fight against the policy of the present government. The impotence and contradictions of the Center-Left majority and government further aggravate the acute problems facing the country whose solution calls for a new upsurge of all democratic and Left forces and the mobilization of the masses for unitary actions. To confront the Moro government with a crisis, to open the way to a new policy and to a new government—such is the imperative national and democratic necessity.

The Leadership also reviewed the present alarming development of the situation in China, characterized by the fury of an unheard-of campaign of hate and violence directed against the Soviet Union. This is a campaign whose most probable aim is to suppress the fairly widespread and strong resistance and discontent caused among the Chinese people and in the Communist Party of China itself by the absurd policy of break-off with the USSR pursued by the group now centered around Mao Tse-tung. The outrageous character this policy has assumed in recent days cannot but evoke among all Italian Communists not only grave alarm but also feelings of indignation and disapproval. All this seriously harms first and foremost the cause of socialism in China, and its international authority. The disagreements and misunderstandings of the past can in no way justify the anti-Soviet aberrations of the Chinese leaders and the provocative and insulting attacks on the Communist Party and government of the Soviet Union organized by them on an ever broader scale, all the way to trampling underfoot the most elementary norms of diplomatic representation.

The Soviet Union is the country of the October Revolution, the first and biggest socialist state. The Communist Party of the Soviet Union has played and continues to play a role of intransient historic importance in the struggle for the liberation of the peoples and for socialism all over the world. The role of the USSR in the defense and consolidation of peace, the tremendous gains the Soviet Union has made owing to socialism are seen in increasingly bolder relief by the broad masses, also and especially in Italy.

The high sense of responsibility the Soviet government displays with regard to the events in China is highly appreciated by all democrats and working people today. The Italian Communists repudiate the anti-Soviet campaign launched by the Chinese leaders, denounce the grave dangers with which it is fraught, and reaffirm their pledge to do their utmost for the sake of achieving the unity of the international Communist movement, while paying due regard to the autonomy of every party and rejecting the dangerous theses of the present Chinese leaders.

The Leadership of the ICP also discussed questions connected with the preparation of the conference of the Communist parties of Europe and with the holding, on a broader plane, of consultations and meetings between Communist and Workers' parties. This is demanded by the growing complexity and urgency of the problems facing the Communist movement and calling for joint discussion. To reveal these problems—which pertain primarily to the development of international relations and the prospects of the struggle against imperialism, for peace in Vietnam, for peaceful coexistence—and to discuss them thoroughly in all possible forms and at all levels is necessary also for creating conditions for a world conference of the Communist parties and its success.

Efforts should be made to ensure that more and more Communist parties contribute to this work for unity on the basis of guaranteed independence of every party. It is in this direction that the ICP will develop its initiative and make its contribution.

# "THE FIGHT FOR PEACE AND FREEDOM IN VIETNAM, TASKS OF THE ICP IN THE STRUGGLE FOR WORLD COMMUNIST UNITY"

Report to the CC, Italian CP by Enrico Berlinguer

*Abridged Text*
(*L'Unità*, 24 February 1967; reprinted in *Information Bulletin*, No. 94, 1967)

With the resumption of the U.S. bombing of the DRV—an extremely grave step because it was decided on after the Vietnamese side had affirmed that discontinuance of the bombing would pave the way for talks—the war has resumed its inexorable course.

The bombing has done severe damage to North Vietnam. Nevertheless, the Americans have not succeeded either in destroying or in seriously disrupting the economic and defense potential of the DRV.

The attempt to intimidate and demoralize the population has failed completely. Air defense is becoming ever more effective, as the 1,700 U.S. aircraft shot down over North Vietnam testify. (The U.S. has admitted the loss of 2,273 aircraft and 973 helicopters in North and South during the last two years. This figure is close to the number of military aircraft manufactured in the U.S. in the same period.) A great deal has already been said on other occasions of the calm, discipline and courage inspiring the resistance of those people, one of the rarest examples of collective heroism ever seen. The unity of the whole people around the government and the Party is most solid. Besides, the Vietnamese have already taken a series of measures to prepare themselves politically, militarily and organizationally for an eventual change in the nature of the war. This change could result from an intensification of massive bombing or from a direct attack on the North by land and sea.

As regards the reaction of world opinion, it is becoming increasingly unfavorable to the leading imperialist groups of the United States. The American aggression is condemned more widely, and solidarity and sympathy for the people of Vietnam have grown. Lastly, there is greater awareness of the danger the continuation of the conflict spells for world peace.

The main factors for these changes are, first of all, the fight of the Vietnamese people, who have shown that they are upholding a just cause and that the Americans cannot win the war; secondly, the valuable and decisive economic, military and political assistance of the socialist countries, above all the Soviet Union. Lastly, there is the vast impact of the solidarity struggles and movements organized by the Communist parties and progressive forces in many countries, as well as the many political actions and initiatives taken by political and governmental forces of various trends in the capitalist countries and the third world, and by authoritative international personalities.

Account should also be taken of the substantial value of the diplomatic offensive the Vietnamese comrades launched early in January to show everyone that they really are willing to seek a reasonable peaceful settlement of the conflict on the basis of the Geneva agreements. The United States, by contrast, has never made a proposal for solving the problem. The Vietnamese proposals, above all the statement that unconditional discontinuance of the bombing of the North was the only condition for starting talks, were met with widespread approval everywhere. They were seen as the famous "signal" which the American leaders had said so many times they were awaiting to call a halt to their raids and start talks.

It is particularly interesting to note that the Vietnamese comrades want national reunification to be achieved by the people of North and South Vietnam autonomously and peaceably, on the basis of the Geneva agreements. The Vietnamese leaders of North and South alike have made it perfectly clear that since there exists in the North a socialist system and a state which is part of the socialist community even though it is not committed to any military alignment, while in the South the task is to form a government of democratic and national unity committed to a neutral policy, unification does not have to be effected by annexing the South to the North. It can come about gradually, through a process that may take many years and forms affording every guarantee of respect for democratic principles and of a stable peaceful equilibrium in that region of Southeast Asia.

Naturally—and this is a fundamental aspect of the Vietnamese position—the National Liberation Front should participate as a decisive representative and autonomous force of the people of South Vietnam in any discussion regarding a settlement in South Vietnam.

We know that U.S. leaders have replied by rejecting the Vietnamese proposals out of hand, ignoring even the appeal to merely prolong the bombing pause, and resuming the raids. Does it follow that the matter may be regarded as closed? We do not think so. The prospects and signs of a peaceful solution seemed too near for the aggression to be viewed as inevitable. But first we must try to understand why attempts to bring about talks have so far failed.

Among the reasons for U.S. intransigence are not so much strategic and political considerations relating to the defense of America's positions in that area of Asia, as the resolve to make clear to the peoples of that region and other parts of the world that the United States is determined to resist the advance of liberation movements by every means.

The U.S. is having to wage an increasingly costly war in Vietnam. While it is true that powerful industrial groups are making huge profits out of the conflict, it is just as true that in recent months financial and monetary difficulties have increased enormously, compelling the U.S. to give up important economic plans and initiatives at home and abroad, and that the economic consequences of the war have begun to tell in a new way. (Almost half the American merchant shipping is taken up with carrying troops and supplies to Vietnam.) The political and ideological rifts caused in American society by the continuing aggression are becoming increasingly grave, and perhaps no postwar American government has seen its prestige sink lower than the Johnson administration has. Internationally, this is affecting the relations with the neutral countries and an important section of America's own allies, and leading to serious isolation from ever larger sections of public opinion.

Thus there are many weighty reasons for which the U.S. leaders should have begun to search for a way out of the war. Why, then, do they persist in the war? There are two reasons that may account for this. One is the differences among the socialist countries resulting from the Chinese position, and the aggravation of these differences to the point of rupture. The Chinese leaders' rejection of every form of unity and coordination in rendering material and political aid to Vietnam has encouraged the Americans.

Besides, the events in China may have aroused in the U.S. leaders the hope that in the long run there may occur a more radical and favorable turn in the Chinese situation and policy which could reinforce their resolve to keep a war near the Chinese frontier going. This war seems to have already become—owing also to the absurd Chinese refusal to help restore, if only in the fight against this aggression, the solidarity of all the socialist countries—an important cause of the tension that has developed in China and the Communist Party of China.

The second cause is that the political and moral isolation of the United States in the world, while becoming increasingly serious, has not yet advanced far enough to put the American leaders in a politically impossible situation. The U.S. can still count on substantial support, not only from the ultra-reactionary governments of Far Eastern and Pacific countries, but from such governments as the Japanese, West German, British and unfortunately, even the Italian. We must add that the positions and actions of other major national and international forces, including the Catholic Church, while prompted by a fundamental desire for peace, and fairly effective at certain moments, have not always been sufficiently consistent and resolute. Lastly, it has to be admitted that even the popular movement and the trend of public opinion in all countries of the world, including the U.S., has yet to reach the degree of mobilization which at present is both necessary and possible.

The situation is so critical that we must not rule out the possibility of a more or less rapid intensification and extension of the war. However, a steady if partial change in one of the fundamental aspects of this situation could open up the prospect of a reverse process. This makes the direction in which our activity should develop quite clear. The main lever to be used is growing mobilization of the masses, encouragement of all the peace forces and pressure on the governments. The task is to stop the U.S. aggression and bring about talks leading to recognition of the rights of the Vietnamese people and to peace. Each step toward a just settlement of the conflict may influence all other factors in the international situation. It may make for the development of new relations of peaceful cooperation among nations, further the progress of the working-class and liberation movements and even influence the situation in China and, China's attitude. Conversely, if no headway is made along these lines every aspect of the international situation will become aggravated. In short, Vietnam is something more than the battlefield of a vast national-liberation fight. It is also the main pivot and turning point of the international situation.

This implies that the only correct strategy for us to use in this struggle should be one inspired by the great principles of peaceful coexistence, that is, what we have always maintained—a struggle to establish international relations ruling out the prospect of atomic conflict, foil every attempt at resorting to the policy of aggression, and create that atmosphere of peace and detente that is particularly favorable, as the experience of the past two decades has shown, to the advance of the liberation movements and to democratic progress.

Efforts today should be devoted above all also to isolating the extremist imperialist groups of America still further. Important steps in this direction can and must be made throughout the capitalist world to set new large segments of public opinion in motion.

We reject the theses contradicting this strategic objective. One of them calls for "counter-escalation," and we consider it absurd. It is absurd because it reveals the tendency to see only the military aspects of imperialism and its material strength, forgetting that imperialism is also a political system, a system of alliance and hegemonies having a foothold among the masses. Anyone who forgets or underestimates these elements is virtually renouncing the struggle, which is difficult, of course, but indispensable for defeating the policy of imperialism, and in the final analysis is laying the whole burden of the struggle on the socialist countries.

That means also declining the principal request the Vietnamese comrades are addressing to their friends all over the world, asking them to press forward the political movement aimed at increasingly isolating the extremist groups of U.S. imperialism and at stripping them of the support they are getting from governments and various political and social forces. In practice, all application of the theory of "counter-escalation" is sheer folly because its end result could be nothing but an atomic world war.

Another erroneous thesis is that so long as the imperialist aggression in Vietnam goes on every initiative to improve the relations between the socialist and capitalist countries and ease tensions in other parts of the globe, including Europe, should be given up. Those who uphold this thesis are trying to conceal the fact that the Soviet position on this issue is perfectly clear, for it maintains that Soviet-American relations can begin to develop on a new basis only if the U.S. abandons its war of aggression against Vietnam. This line in no way conflicts with the search for international agreements, such as that banning the military uses of outer space, or the agreement on nuclear non-proliferation, which has now become so essential and urgent. Such agreements are intended to make it ever more difficult to unleash an atomic world war. As regards the Soviet policy in Europe, it is striving for two objectives which are particularly important for the struggle against the aggressive trends of imperialism and for peace. One is to combat the danger of West German revanchism and the other is to promote every advance and every process that can bring nearer the prospect of a Europe which will be peaceful, increasingly united and at the same time more independent of the United States. This policy, which is providing more favorable conditions for the independent development and advance of the working-class and democratic movements in Western Europe, is a substantial contribution to the entire world-wide struggle against the forces of aggression and war.

Imperialism and reaction have succeeded in delivering telling blows to the liberation movements and revolutionary forces in various Asian, African and Latin American countries, especially in Indonesia and Brazil. But even in those areas the situation varies from country to country. In many countries the liberation movement resists imperialist attack and pressure, and there are signs of an awakening of national and revolutionary forces. Worthy of note was the meeting of a group of Central African countries in the Congolese capital, which adopted a common program of struggle against colonialism and neocolonialism. Also worthy of note, and highly important, is the electoral success scored by the Communists and the Left in India.

Major gains have been registered by the Communist parties of Europe in election campaigns and in unitary policy (France, Finland). The democratic struggle is entering a new stage in Spain.

The chief drawback is that the Communist parties and other sectors of the anti-imperialist front have been unable to join forces to resist the American aggression in Vietnam. Indeed, it is in these years that the split with China has gone deeper. And this is the most serious fact. The harm which the Chinese position is doing to the advocacy and spread of socialist ideals is enormous. To top it all, there is the concern about the evolution of the situation in China itself.

Three big problems arise here. We must try to understand better what goes on in China. Secondly, we must study and carry out measures aimed at limiting the adverse repercussions of the situation in China and the Chinese position. Lastly, there is a problem which will hardly become pressing for some time to come but which certainly cannot be dismissed, and that is the problem of overcoming the break with China and the CPC.

As regards analysis of the Chinese situation, some elements can be established. First of all, there is a rather sharp and tense struggle going on in the CPC and the whole Chinese society. It is so confused and chaotic that it cannot be explained by a "rational plan" of the group leading the "cultural revolution."

The second element is the political and ideological substance of the position upheld by a group which cannot be said to be leading China in the full sense of the word but which at the moment is at the head of China and speaks for it.

All this undoubtedly has its roots in growing serious difficulties arising from the internal development and international position of China. First to blame for these difficulties is the policy of the U.S. imperialists, a policy of threats, provocations, and isolation based on the criminal attempt to make the Chinese people renounce the historical national and social gains of their revolution, and to prevent full recognition of the international rights of People's China. The struggle against this policy remains therefore an important point of our entire orientation.

And yet China's internal and international position would not cause so much concern if the CPC leadership had not made serious, fundamental mistakes in recent years.

It is clear, for instance, that the policy and prospect of "changing the face of China in a few years of hard work" have failed. The attempt to forge ahead to communism by skipping a whole phase of economic and social development has proved illusory, even though there is no denying some great historical achievements of the revolution and people's power.

Ever since a certain juncture there has predominated a trend marked by voluntarist and subjectivist errors. The forced rate of growth prompted by this trend had grave consequences, as in agriculture, in the years when all national resources were concentrated on effecting the "Big Leap" in industry. In the international field, the policy which enabled China to play a vastly important role both in the socialist community and among the new independent countries (witness the Bandung Conference) has radically changed. The prospect of peaceful coexistence has been replaced by the advocacy of a strategy opposing the oppressed peoples of the third world to the rest of the world. The conflict with India was pushed further, and then came the anti-Soviet propaganda of today. Now developments have shown that this line has led to the failure of the very same goals the Chinese leaders had set themselves.

These failures were one of the main reasons for deep and widespread discontent among the masses which, in turn, gave rise to attempts to reconsider and review things in the Party and the leading group. It is significant that at the CC, CPC meeting last summer many comrades stressed the need of a united anti-imperialist front against the policy of U.S. imperialism and the aggression in Vietnam.

It is also indicative that the Chinese press and leaders are continually referring to widespread "economist" trends, which we may presume urge a more correct consideration of the objective and material factors in economic development.

In the light of these facts, the "cultural revolution" seems to be an attempt to avoid, block or prevent every trend toward rectifying the policy pursued so far, and at the same time to mount some major diversions so as to turn popular discontent in that direction.

The struggle is in full swing. Resistance to the Mao group appears to be growing. It would hardly be wrong to regard this struggle as a great contest for "power," which means not only a struggle between individuals or groups, but a struggle to ascertain the organized and social forces on which power in China should lean for support. Are these to be the Communist Party, the working class and its organizations or the Army, or some other forces?

The turns that the situation may take cannot be foreseen. They might be very serious, such as a sharpening of the situation, division and strife between autonomous bodies and, in the long run, a gradual polarization of reactionary forces around one of the warring factions. On the other hand, it is legitimate to believe that a Communist party like the CPC will hardly allow things to take such a headlong course. It is therefore right to carry on our work always bearing in mind the prospect of a straightening out of the situation.

Be that as it may, there remains the necessity for laying down a line that would make it possible to limit and overcome the adverse effects of the positions and actions of China's present leaders. We therefore reject—as we have always done—every tendency to defer judgment. While reaffirming our pledge to combat U.S. imperialist policy in Asia and toward China, and our solidarity with the Chinese people in this struggle, we renew our severe criticism and condemnation of the present Chinese stand. This has been our position from the outset. It has been absolutely firm and unambiguous even though we have always distinguished between our criticism and the anti-Chinese campaigns carried on by the reactionaries, including those in our country.

What we now regard as particularly serious is the Chinese leaders' rejection of every proposal for united action against the U.S. aggression in Vietnam and Asia, and their present absurd and slanderous campaign of anti-Soviet provocation. In this way the Chinese leaders are reducing their opposition to imperialism to hollow, pointless utterances. To go as far as to consider the Soviet Union the chief enemy of the Chinese people means rendering a service to imperialism which could derive a new stimulus for its policy of war out of a further deterioration of Sino-Soviet relations. It also means raising more obstacles to the very search for a negotiated and peaceful settlement of the Vietnam conflict. It neither meets the national interests of Vietnam nor promotes peace.

For all these serious reasons—apart from the fact that it reflects on the ideas of socialism—we criticize and reject the Chinese position. This is not to say, of course, that we are launching an anti-Chinese campaign, for we always remember that the common enemy on whom the full fire must be concentrated is U.S. imperialism. However, we openly dissociate our line from that of the Mao group. At the same time we must reaffirm and give an ever higher estimation to the policy and role of the Soviet Union, which is proving itself, also in the present international situation, as the main bulwark of the struggle of all peoples for freedom and peace.

The Italian working-class movement and our Party have a solid and long-standing internationalist tradition that has never been lost. The principle and practice of autonomy to which we firmly adhere have never been regarded or applied by us as renunciation of the general vista of the common and permanent general interests of the world proletariat, or of deep and militant solidarity with the working people and revolutionary forces of all countries or with the socialist countries. The supreme document expressing the thought and line of our Party on these issues—Comrade Togliatti's "Memorandum," which so emphatically stressed that the autonomy of each party has now become a requisite for its political development, and which so precisely underlines the need to bear in mind, with regard to internal relations in our movement and to the initiatives it takes, the diversity of situations and concrete political positions corresponding to the position and degree of development of each country—is wholly inspired by concern for the unity of the working-class and Communist movement, and by the desire to show the ways and means of upholding and promoting this unity and solidarity.

That has been, and is, the invariable axis of our policy line toward the working-class and Communist movement. In the present situation and at this particular moment we consider in fact, that the problem of restoring and promoting the unity of our movement is of special and increasing importance. The attitude to the issue of unity of the Communist movement and the anti-imperialist forces is becoming the touchstone of the internationalist spirit and line of the various parties. It is no longer enough to swear allegiance to Marxism-Leninism. The experience of recent years and the position of the Chinese comrades, who keep on declaring that they are the most loyal and consistent supporters of Marxism—Leninism, show, in effect, that declarations are not enough to prove that one is combatting imperialism by deeds and not merely by words. The position on the issue of unity is now acquiring the value of significance of a real discriminant.

Unity today—unity despite and above differences—can mean only unity in respect of the main line of the fight against imperialism and for peace.

Differences do exist and they are serious and to a certain extent inevitable, and we are as agreeable as ever to any effort to lessen and overcome them, in particular through open discussion and an objective confrontation of positions. Experience has shown, however, that the tendency to exacerbate differences on the pretext of combating so-called "modern revisionism," to the point of slander and rupture, is bound to lead to renunciation of the indispensable solidarity in struggle against the common imperialist enemy.

It goes without saying that the unity of the working-class and Communist movement should manifest itself and find specific expression in forms and methods corresponding to different situations. One of the most important and difficult problems facing our movement today is precisely to choose and test new forms of unity corresponding to the present period.

There can no longer be a question of reconstituting an international organization that would lead the entire Communist movement by centralized methods, or of reverting to the concept and practice of leader party and state (however, the Chinese comrades may be thinking of this). The unity we should seek should therefore recognize and take into account the different conditions of work and struggle, as well as the particular points of view of each party. It should guarantee the autonomy which today is a condition, not only for the development of each party, but for the strength and progress of the movement as a whole.

But reaffirmation of these immutable positions, now widely recognized—and the arduous effort to determine the method of inter-party relations meeting these requirements—should by no means assign a secondary place to the fundamental issue of unity and struggle for unity. In fact, this issue is becoming particularly important now. We therefore oppose and criticize every tendency, coming from anyone, to minimize the importance of the issue of unity so as to bring to the fore particularist and narrow-minded concern for one's own national or party interests.

What we actually need today is to reaffirm the unity of our movement in political terms, that is, in terms of the fundamental objectives of the struggle against the aggressive policy of imperialism and for peace. It is for these reasons that the Party Leadership stated, in its resolution published on February 10 last that we must work to "create conditions for the convening and success of a world conference of the Communist parties." We would expect the conference to have this characteristic and to set itself this principal aim. We would expect every effort to be made at it, with ourselves actively participating, to surmount the difficulties and solve the complex problems arising from this initiative.

To achieve that we must, of course, take into account certain things and provide adequate conditions. The first problem is that of the character and content of the meeting. We think it would be wrong in the present situation to look forward to a meeting that would try to answer and bring system into all the various and difficult questions facing the Communist movement and specific parties. We must work on these questions, but the method to use if we are to make progress in dealing with these questions should be rather bilateral and multilateral meetings and conferences, as well as public discussions making it possible to tackle each question from time to time in concrete terms. A general meeting of the Communist parties should be mainly political and should bear on the main current issues of the fight against imperialism and for peace. We must therefore

make a proper estimation of the political impact such a meeting would have in the actual international situation in which it would be held or, in other words, its impact on the enemy and on the masses and the revolutionary forces of the world.

Closely linked with this question is that of the parties that will or will not be able to attend. The number of participants is neither the only nor the most important question. Besides, it is clear that the convening of an eventual meeting can no longer be made conditional on the participation of CPC delegates, which in the present situation is apparently out of the question. There are, however, other major parties which are against attending a meeting that would be called at present. Obviously, the attitude of these parties toward the meeting, and their eventual non-participation are estimated very carefully and with a sense of responsibility, in particular and precisely in view of the important role they play in the fight against imperialism. For these reasons we think there is a need for thorough discussion and serious effort to bring the positions of these parties on the contemplated meeting closer together. This is not excluded also in view of eventual new developments in the international situation and in the relations between parties. We ought also to consider the possibility of the meeting being attended by observers from certain parties and labor and progressive movements of the capitalist countries and countries in the third world. In preparing for and holding the meeting, we should use a method corresponding to the present composition of our movement and taking into account the requirements of the various parties. What I mean is not only the necessity for extensive and manifold consultations making it possible to ascertain, compare and specify the positions and proposals of the various parties, but other aspects as well. It would be right, for example, to begin with bilateral and multilateral exchanges and confrontations of views on every question relating to the date of the meeting and the method of preparing for it, including the nature and content of the documents to be adopted in conclusion.

The points and reservations we made when, between 1963 and 1965, the question of a new meeting came up for discussion were not due to fundamental opposition (we have never adhered to such a line) but to political considerations and doubts as to the opportuneness of a meeting in the conditions prevailing at the time. We are convinced that the line we followed was correct. The facts have shown that a meeting held in those conditions would not have benefited the unity and struggle of our movement, nor the struggle of the movement as a whole against the position of the Chinese comrades. The conditions obtaining today are largely new and different. It is becoming increasingly necessary to counter the disruptive processes of division, centrifugal trends, and the dangers of disintegration with a reverse process, by strengthening and carrying forward the cohesion of our movement in the common fight against imperialism and for peace. Consequently, the situation has to be re-examined.

We must strive, however, to avoid possible false

steps if we are to surmount existing difficulties and advance to a meeting that would really promote the objectives we all seek. In any case, it is clear that since we can hardly expect an international meeting to be called before the end of this year whereas there is a pressing need for the parties to cooperate on various urgent international problems, the next few months and the whole of this year should be devoted to intense and manifold international efforts to strengthen unity, with the collective participation of the greatest possible number of parties. These parties should take the initiative of carrying on vast struggles and joint campaigns, and of holding bilateral and multilateral meetings aimed at a thorough study of burning issues, such as problems of collective security (with which the first meeting preparatory to a conference of the European Communist parties is concerning itself in Warsaw these days), meetings of the Communist parties of the capitalist countries and the liberation movements to formulate a common program of struggle against imperialism, colonialism and neocolonialism, and theoretical conferences (for instance, on the changes that have occurred in almost all the socialist countries due to the reforms effected in recent years).

The important thing—and the conclusion we must draw from our entire assessment of the present situation in the Communist movement—is that our whole Party, being fully aware of its international responsibilities, should now begin working earnestly and on a large scale to make an effective contribution to the struggle for freedom and peace in Vietnam, to every struggle against imperialism and for peace, to the unity of the working-class and Communist movement all over the world.

# STATEMENT OF LUIGI LONGO, GENERAL SECRETARY OF THE ITALIAN CP, AT A MEETING OF THE CENTRAL COMMITTEE AND CCC IN JULY 1967

*Abridged Text*
(*L'Unità*, 13 July 1967; reprinted in
*Information Bulletin*, No. 103, 1967)

Activities aimed at securing a peaceful settlement of the conflicts in the Middle East have been and remain the cornerstone of our position. Proceeding from the recognition of the right of the State of Israel to existence and the recognition of the legitimate rights of the Arab peoples, we condemn the war started by Israel and resolutely criticize the political course of the Tel-Aviv leaders. Nothing can justify the unleashing of this war.

If the Israeli government had complaints and denunciations to make, there is a legal establishment which it could have addressed: the United Nations Organization. Having resorted to the force of arms, to a preventive attack and war, it automatically became the guilty party. The chief problem immediately resulting from the aggression was the problem of halting it. Therefore, when a ceasefire was demanded, we found this to be a just demand and supported it. It became necessary to take the initiative to stop the invasion. Today Israel has big military trumps with the help of which it intends to blackmail the Arab countries, jxstify its annexationist aims and keep the Arab countries under a constant threat to prevent them from eliminating the consequences of the aggression and reorganizing their national life. Obviously, in these conditions Israel will strive to exploit to the full its military success without giving the Arabs a moment's respite. Israel's aggressive actions should be condemned, on the political and diplomatic plane, by actions of states friendly to the Arab states, by the pressure of democratic public opinion.

We must fight for the attainment of these principal objectives: (1) liberation of occupied territories; (2) refusal to encourage any aggression; (3) solution of still outstanding problems, in the first place the problem of the refugees. These problems are not easy to solve. There exist contradictions between different imperialist countries. An independent stand has been taken only by France. Other countries have also dissociated themselves from the United States, as the results of the voting in the UN show. In effect, Italy, along with Iceland, was the only UN member which sided with the United States in all General Assembly votes.

On the other hand, many countries joined the Soviet Union and the socialist states in condemning and exposing at the General Assembly the aggression against the Arab countries. The Israeli aggression has dealt a serious blow at the Arab liberation movement and created a grave danger. But there is the reverse side of the medal. The defeat has put into motion a positive process of unification of the Arab movement and anti-imperialist actions in the third world.

In any case, it will not be easy for the Arab movement to overcome the state of weakness in which it has found itself. It is the duty of the states friendly to the Arab countries, the duty of every movement of public solidarity with the national-liberation movement to prevent the isolation of the Arab movement, to frustrate Israel's expansionist and annexationist plans.

To this end it is necessary to launch extensive and varied actions, to help a reappraisal of the real situation and intentions even among those who succumbed to the wave of anti-Arab propaganda and who are beginning to have doubts regarding the role of Israel and U.S. imperialism in all these events.

In appraising the events in the Near East we should stress the importance and significance of the popular demonstrations which compelled Nasser to withdraw his decision to resign. These demonstrations testified to the depth and magnitude of the national-liberation movement among the Arab peoples. Far from resulting in the break-up of the movement, the military defeat has given a powerful stimulus to closing the ranks. Taking into consideration all possible consequences of the military defeat for the alignment of the political and social forces in the various Arab states, I think it can be definitely said that the result has not been one expected by the aggressor and hoped for by some people, namely, the break-up of the Arab movement, the fall of the anti-imperialist governments of Egypt and Syria and the resurgence, on capitulationist positions, of the reactionary forces. This means also that the resistance and struggle of the Arab peoples continue, although in more difficult conditions also because the victory-dizzy Israel intends not only to annex the occupied territories but to proceed to the end in its expansionist policy, the policy of economic, political and military domination in the entire Middle East.

Much has been and is being said about the role the Soviet Union has been playing in all the events in the Middle East. I must note, nevertheless, that one cannot limit one self to the events of recent months, however indicative they may be, for a precise definition of all aspects of the Soviet Union's peace policy, also in connection with the Israeli aggression. The first absolutely clear element is the fact that the

Soviet Union has never fanned the smouldering fire in the Middle East. On the contrary, it has consistently, energetically and persistently worked for peace. Consequently, the assertions heard over the recent weeks, also from Social-Democratic leaders, that the Soviet Union favored the opening in the Middle East of a kind of "second front" (after Vietnam) are entirely false.

This is a lie for at least two reasons: first, as is recognized on an ever broader scale, and as the Israeli Prime Minister admitted a few days ago, it was Israel that launched hostilities on the morning of June 5; second, Soviet foreign policy is based on the affirmation the world over of a policy of peaceful coexistence, a policy recognizing and respecting the right of all peoples to freedom and national independence. Thus, Soviet policy is aimed at settling the existing conflicts and above all the Vietnam conflict by peaceful means, for the Soviet Union, aware of its responsibility, realizes, as Comrade Kosygin declared at the U.N. General Assembly, that "the continuation of the war in Vietnam aggravates the danger of the military conflict expanding beyond that region and is fraught with the grave danger of this conflict developing into a large-scale military clash of powers."

Consequently, the Soviet Union lays emphasis on peaceful settlement of existing conflicts, not on the creation of new ones. This is the main point of principle which we must be fully aware of at all times in order to counter U.S. interventionist policy manifesting itself today in many regions of the world with a vigorous intensification of struggle. There are sufficient testimonies and documents bearing out the correctness of our affirmation.

It is perfectly obvious that it is imperialism and not the Soviet Union that is responsible for the tension in the Middle East. In addition, it is well known that the Soviet Union has always favoured peaceful settlement of the conflicts in the Middle East, a settlement which would at once respect the right of Israel to existence and the legitimate rights of the Arab peoples. "Every people has the right to set up its own independent national state," Comrade Kosygin declared in the United Nations. "This is one of the fundamental principles of the Soviet Union's policy."

"We proceeded precisely from this when we determined our attitude towards Israel as a state by voting in 1947 for the U.N. resolution to establish on the territory of the former British colony Palestine of two independent states—Jewish and Arab." Also, following this the Soviet Union established diplomatic relations with the new State of Israel.

It is not my intention to review the entire Middle-Eastern policies of the postwar period. But I want at least to remind you what was the decisive element in 1957, soon after the aggression of Great Britain, France and Israel against Egypt. The Soviet Union contributed then decisively to nipping the aggression in the bud.

In face of the obvious intention of Israel and the United States to impose by force the hegemony which they had failed to establish by other means in the Middle East, it was the Soviet Union's duty of solidarity to help the Arab peoples ensure their own defense, all the more so since it was clear that Israel and the imperialists were not sitting back but were preparing the aggression both militarily and politically, as the facts clearly testify today.

The Soviet Union and other socialist countries did help the Arab peoples organize their defense by supplying them large amounts of modern arms. When military defeat began to loom large, the Soviet Union acted in defense of the Arab peoples. It took the initiative to force a ceasefire and thus prevent an extension of the Israeli invasion. Then it severed diplomatic relations with Israel. In addition, the Soviet Union launched extensive activities in the UNO and among world public opinion and undertook demarches before a number of governments to make Israel withdraw troops behind its frontiers and to expose its annexationist and expansionist aims. I do not think there are grounds to criticize in any way the main lines of the policy which the Soviet Union and the socialist countries pursued in this instance.

The Soviet Union invariably informed Nasser and the Arab countries directly concerned about all its steps in the UNO, and acted with their full agreement. Consequently, the Soviet Union's actions in this case were absolutely clear and straightforward. In its policy the Soviet Union invariable guided itself by the interests and needs of the Arab peoples who were attacked and suffered military defeat in the first hours of the aggression. To appraise correctly the various stages of the Soviet Union's actions, one must keep this important factor in mind. No doubt, the Israeli aggression caused great damage to the Arab peoples. And once again the socialist states headed by the Soviet Union pledged to render maximum diplomatic, military and economic assistance to the Arab countries to eliminate the grave consequences of the surprise aggression. But we should not forget what this assistance costs the Soviet Union and the socialist countries.

As before, these countries bear the brunt of international solidarity. This is a point to ponder for those who hasten to criticize the Soviet Union and the socialist countries. Everything can be achieved given maximum unity of the progressive and socalist forces. It seems to me, judgments are often passed on complicated and difficult events and moments appraised with too much lightness and superficiality. This is by no means the best way of forming one's own opinion of them and helping public opinion to understand them.

I believe that in such cases it would be more rational and useful to proceed, pending more ample information and analyses, from a favorable attitude and not from an inimical and mistrustful preconception.

I think that for the fifty years of its existence and revolutionary activity the Soviet Union deserves at least trust, not mistrust. I consider that when complicated and involved situations arise, one should regard the Soviet Union's position with trust, for it is a socialist state possessing great weight and rich hsitorical experience, and because in the many years of its existence the Soviet Union has proved its ability and striving constantly to uphold the cause of the working people, the cause of peace and socialism, and that in any case, especially when serious international matters are in question, the Soviet Union possesses more ample elements of information and analysis than we can have to take our bearings and pass our judgment with confidence.

Whenever tension and difficulties arise in the struggle against imperialism one can hear—also in our own ranks—words of doubt and criticism with regard to the policy of peaceful coexistence which the Soviet Union has pursued with exceptional persistence in the past 12-13 years and which is supported by the international Communist and working-class movement. In the first place, it will be recalled that the policy of peaceful coexistence is an important ideological and political gain of the working-class and democratic movement which has never impeded but, on the contrary, has been promoting the advance of the national-liberation movement and generally facilitating the successes of the struggle of the broad masses for peace and socialism.

In confirmation of this, it suffices to recall that precisely the past 12-13 years have witnessed major successes in the struggle for national liberation, from the birth of the Democratic Republic of Vietnam to the victory of the Cuban revolution, the victorious war for the national liberation of Algeria, the emergence in Asia and Africa of more than thirty independent states, the respect for the independence of Cuba imposed upon the United States, thwarting the designs of West German imperialism and revanchism to thrust back the borders of socialist countries, the development of profound progressive social transformations in the direction of socialism as is happening in a number of Arab and African countries.

The attitude of China has generated weaknesses and divisions both among the socialist forces, the progressive forces of the world, and among the population of countries that have recently freed themselves from colonial oppression. The United States is taking advantage of this situation to employ its traditional means of struggle—military bases, corruption, coups.

We must not forget that the policy of peaceful coexistence is a struggle and a gain, a long, complicated and many-sided process. We must continue this struggle, waging it in close conjunction with the struggle for national liberation in various parts of the world, putting the accent on the main front—the struggle against the aggressive policies of U.S. imperialism.

We are advocating peaceful coexistence because we are fighting for peace. This struggle is the political aspect of our struggle against the concrete policy of war pursued by imperialism. This struggle cannot and must not lead to tolerance, to passivity in face of the attempts of the imperialist groups to realize their intentions. On the contrary!

It should serve as the basis not only for exposing these attempts but for rebuffing, on the same battlefield, the imperialist and reactionary provocations and acts of aggression.

# LUIGI LONGO ON THE INTERNATIONAL COMMUNIST MOVEMENT

Four Articles by the Secretary-General
of the Italian Communist Party

*Complete Texts*
(*Rinascita,* Rome, 20 October, 27 October, 3 November,
10 November 1967; *Foreign Bulletin* [CC, PCI—Foreign Section],
September-December 1967)

## THE UNITY OF THE WORKING CLASS AND COMMUNIST MOVEMENT
### (20 October 1967)

Undoubtedly, the international situation is becoming more serious. The present escalation in Viet Nam, the aggression against the Arab countries, and the U.S.' heavy imperialistic presence in Latin America, are the most recent evidences of the aggressiveness of imperialism and of the expanding method of "local wars."

We must say immediately that this increased aggressiveness, despite its temporary and partial successes, does not indicate that the U.S. government has a stronger control over the international situation. On the contrary, it indicates only the difficulties, we could even say the impossibility, for it to solve the problems of power and economic direction which have been brought about by the development of the situation.

Actually, the aggression against Viet Nam is keeping a huge war organization swamped in the Vietnamese jungle and marshes with no prospect of coming out of it unhurt. The attack against the Arab countries, despite its quick success, has strengthened the Arabs' anti-imperialistic tendencies and has brought to·light the necessity to make certain political and social choices to face the imperialistic pressure and aggressiveness. In Latin America, the peoples' hostility against the United States is growing and taking the more definite forms of an armed fight. In the United States itself the Negroes' rebellion and progressive movements sharply criticize Johnson's social and war policy.

It is a fact that the United States is becoming more isolated, with regard to the world public opinion, because of the brutal policy carried out everywhere, including Europe, and because of the dangers for freedom and independence of the peoples, democracy and peace, brought about by this policy.

It is also a fact that in front of these dangers not only the working-class and communist forces but also the popular and progressive forces in every country tend to gather and to act united, although so far too timidly and insufficiently.

It is also a fact that the socialist countries, and the Soviet Union first, tend to present, politically and diplomatically, a united front, and to give the threatened countries a concrete economic and military aid beside full moral and political solidarity to strengthen their capacity of resistance and their economic and civil development.

However, it is also a fact that precisely among socialist countries and among working-class and communist forces so many difficulties exist today to co-ordinate the efforts against imperialism, whereas it is obvious that these efforts will find the necessary drive and intensity only in this co-ordination, not only to defeat the imperialist attack but also more resolutely to bring forward the movement of emancipation of the peoples and of socialist transformation of the society.

On the contrary, even in front of these increased dangers not only the existing differences and splits are not smoothed away, but unfortunately on many sides they are often exasperated to the extent of rejecting any type of collaboration and understanding. As a result, the anti-imperialistic, democratic and progressive forces only partially, and not always, succeed in carrying out the necessary co-ordination of their strifes, and therefore they cannot bear a thorough weight on the contrasts arising in the world and even among the "Western" countries as a result of Washington's policy.

Here lies the difficulty for the most advanced forces to find, under the present circumstances, new possibilities to continue, in new ways, that unitary action which in the past was successful in the strife for peace, against fascism, nazism, colonialism and for the national liberation of the peoples.

This situation concerns all those who care for the destiny of the working-class and progressive struggles. The unity of the working-class and communist movement cannot but concern us who have always pivoted our policy upon international unity and solidarity.

Already comrade Togliatti noticed, in his memorandum from Yalta, that "the danger exists of the parties' isolation one from the other and therefore of a certain confusion." Undoubtedly this danger has grown. The actual implementation of agreements and collaboration among parties is today difficult. We can see it also from the difficulties encountered, and not completely overcome, in the occasion of the conference at Karlovy Vary. It is not only the question of the absurd, exasperated positions of the Chinese Communist Party. The tendencies to stress the elements of differentiation instead of the necessity for unity and collaboration prevail also in other parties.

As comrade Togliatti wrote in his memorandum,

"we must fight" against the dangers of isolation of one party from the other. In our mind, it is necessary to stop the existing centrifugal process and to stress the need for international solidarity and for a larger collaboration and unity of action. It is necessary to oppose these centrifugal tendencies through a process of strengthening and development of the unity of our movement in a joint action against imperialism and for peace. In this sense we have recently stated at a Central Committee of the PCI that the attitude concerning the question of the unity of the communist movement and of anti-imperialistic forces is today the touchstone of the international spirit and struggle of the different parties.

We are aware of the difficulties which we must still overcome to bring forward this process of international strengthening and collaboration. There are objective difficulties which arise from the very development of the working-class and communist movement under the present conditions of struggle. However, we know that international collaboration can develop and take shape in the course of the struggles, with the help of frank discussions about the problem and duties arising from life.

We are persuaded that these difficulties will not be overcome unless a new type of relations is established among communist parties: these relations should rigidly guarantee the autonomy of each party; should not impose compulsory tendencies and lines; should not demand hostile attitudes against those parties which do not agree with the common decisions.

We consider that, in this regard, the conference at Karlovy Vary meant a significant step forward, on account of its procedures, of the statements made and of its outcomes.

A principle unanimously accepted today is that the autonomy of each party is necessary for its political and organizational development. Of course, autonomy cannot and must not mean being detached from a general sight of the common problems and of the general interest of the working-class movement. The requirements for autonomy must by no means put aside the fundamental need for an active international solidarity, or the communist movement will be degraded to a social-democratic level.

This is why we criticize all tendencies, however justified, to neglect the international and unitary requirement of the working-class movement and to stress the individual, limited view of one's own national and party interests. In our mind this is the worst way to defend these interests, in a world which is so interdependent and where reactionary and exploiting forces are united in a close coalition under the leadership of American imperialism.

The autonomous, national requirements and the international, unitary requirements are not in contradiction. On the contrary: they can and must be integrated, in a concept of "unity in diversity," as comrade Togliatti said. Only in this way the existing centrifugal tendencies will be overcome.

It must be clear to everybody that the alternative to these tendencies is not a return to monolithism, to a lead party and State, already condemned and rejected by the 20th Congress of the Soviet Communist Party itself; or to something that in some other way would re-establish some kind of political and organizational centralization. The new type of unity must be articulate and fit for the concrete possibilities existing in the different situations, that is to say it must allow for the different conditions of work and life of each party.

It is from these objectively different conditions that the divergencies among communist parties often arise, concerning the way to conceive and fulfill their duties; these divergencies are therefore partially unavoidable but they can be overcome and they must not prevent the understanding and collaboration on basic questions, as all communist parties work for the interest of the working classes and have peace, freedom and socialism as their constant goals. It is clear, in any case, that every possible effort must be made to smooth away and overcome these divergencies through a fraternal discussion, exchange of experiences, and with a view to achieve the maximum understanding and collaboration.

## THE QUESTION OF THE WORLD CONFERENCE
### (27 October 1967)

We must recognize that much has been done, by several parties, in the last three years, to overcome the existing contrasts and to find a mutual understanding and the maximum unity possible. Contacts between the different parties and exchanges of delegations have increased; plurilateral meetings have taken place: all this has allowed a useful exchange of ideas and experiences on problems of orientation and the realization of agreements of struggle and action.

Let us recall:

—the Convention of communist parties from European capitalist countries, held in Brussels in June 1965, which dealt with solidarity with Viet Nam, and the strife for European security against fascist systems and for democracy;

—the study Convention on contemporary European capitalism (Rome, June 1965), sponsored by the Gramsci Institute, in which outstanding economists, sociologists and members of communists parties from capitalist and socialist European countries took part;

—two French initiatives dealing with State capitalism and the experience of the Popular Front;

—the international convention held in Moscow in October, 1965, on the occasion of the 30th anniversary of the Comintern's 7th Congress. Thirty-seven parties from Europe, America, Asia and South Africa took part in it;

—the seminar of North-European communist parties, held in Finland in November, 1965;

—the first three-continents solidarity conference of Asian, African and Latin-American peoples in which participated the representatives from the revolutionary organizations of about 80 countries;

—the Conference of communist parties from European capitalist countries (Vienna, May 1966), to deal with "The experiences and present possibilities to unite democratic and popular forces in the struggle against monopolies, for democracy and social progress," attended by 15 parties;

—the meeting of the Preparatory Committee to the Conference of European communist parties, to deal with European security, attended by 20 parties (Warsaw, February 1967);

—the Conference at Karlovy Vary (April 1967) to deal with European security attended by delegations from 24 parties and one "observer" from the Swedish party;

—the OLAS Conference at Havana, (August, 1967) dealing with solidarity among Latin-American peoples, in which took part the representatives and personalities from communist groups and national liberation movements in Latin America.

Undoubtedly, all these initiatives, however different, have helped to overcome the chopping of an international action by the working-class and communist movements. These initiatives and their outcome—however limited—and, on the other side, the greater aggressiveness of imperialist forces, stress the fact that an understanding and collaboration among the different sections of the communist and working-class world are possible, and that they are the condition for their strength, and the decisive element to defeat imperialism.

"It is a time of unity." This necessity was pointed out in several occasions by many parties. To this aim, the idea was prospected to call a world conference of communist parties in which the parties which so desire and, according to somebody's viewpoint, also all progressive forces should take part.

The aim of this conference—it is to be stressed—would not be that of exasperating contrasts; on the contrary, it would be that of creating a favorable atmosphere to overcome them, of examining the present conditions of strife of the society and the present struggle against imperialism to give it more unity or possibly, even to elaborate a common strategy.

The question of the conference has been largely discussed by each party; we have discussed it at the Central Committee meetings, at the meetings of the Political Bureau and in several articles.

In these occasions we have recalled that three-four years ago, when the question of the conference was first ventilated during the hottest polemic time with the Chinese comrades, we expressed some doubts as to its usefulness, and we tried to avoid it as it could make worse or even break the relations with the Chinese Party; we recommended instead, as Togliatti had indicated, to hold less ambitious meetings and conferences on particular issues and for limited areas, which in fact was done as it appears from the above-mentioned list of meetings.

We believe that our behavior was right; however, we can see today that, with regard to the standings of the Chinese comrades and precisely because of their attitude, things have gone in a different way from what we hoped. The leaders of the Chinese communist party have arbitrarily broken contacts with all communist parties which do not share their point of view. They have systematically refused every proposal for collaboration and joint action with the other socialist countries and communist parties in helping

the heroic Vietnamese people. They keep on carrying on a denigration and disgregation campaign of communist and working-class parties.

Under the circumstances, the doubts that we had four years ago can no longer exist. The relations with the Chinese Party could not be worse, and any prospect of improving them has failed—we must have this clear in mind even if giving up no possible efforts to change the situation.

Consequently, communist parties which share the necessity for an exchange of opinions and experiences and for a participation in a collective analysis of the general problems of the movement, can no longer undergo the blackmailing made by the Chinese Party which thus increases its action of disgregation and splitting of the international communist world.

However, under these circumstances, the problem of calling a world conference becomes very complex. It is no longer a question of deciding whether the conference is timely, but of deciding *which* conference is to be called, in *which* way, for *which* purposes.

Our party has never been opposed not only to contacts with other parties but also, in principle, to world conferences which have been always generally recognized as a useful means to elaborate collectively and to co-ordinate the action of the individual parties.

Even in his memorandum from Yalta, in which Togliatti expressed his doubts as to the usefulness of a world conference under the existing circumstances, it was however clearly said that "a right definition of the common tasks of our movement cannot be reached without a serious collective elaboration" and that "to this aim, the question could be examined of calling an international conference which could really represent a new stage for our movement, and its real strengthening on new and right positions."

As to the proposal which was made at that time, to hold a preparatory meeting to the conference, Togliatti said: "we shall definitely take part in the preparatory meeting to express our standings and viewpoints." Actually a delegation from the PCI attended the meeting held in March, 1965. At the meeting—as the final communique says—the delegations "expressed their belief that what communist parties had in common was stronger, for the moment, than that which divided them;" consequently "an active preparation of a new world conference and the calling of such conference at a timely moment corresponded to the interest of the international communist movement."

In his memorandum from Yalta, comrade Togliatti stressed the importance of an international meeting called by Western parties and attended by representatives from the democratic countries in the Third World to elaborate a concrete line of co-operation and aid to these movements.

It is in recalling that indication that we work today to organize an international meeting of working-class and communist parties, as well as progressive parties from the Mediterranean countries, to examine the situation that has arisen in the Mediterranean after the Israeli aggression, to co-ordinate the action for freedom and independence of the peoples against imperialism, and to bring about a lasting peace in the Mediterranean.

## TO BE PROTAGONISTS
## INSTEAD OF OUTSIDE ADVISERS
### (3 November 1967)

The international communist and progressive movements are facing today very urging problems: South East Asia, Middle East, Mediterranean, Latin America.

These problems are characterized by the U.S.' increased aggressiveness; but they also indicate the necessity for the working-class movement to oppose, to what is called "the imperialistic global strategy," a broad unitary front, an "anti-imperialistic strategy" so to say, which according to the different local possibilities and conditions would convey all working-class, progressive, democratic forces (parties, organizations, peoples, States) to a common anti-imperialistic struggle.

From here the necessity arises to tackle a series of questions which have not yet been fully examined and discussed. Namely: the struggle for peace and peaceful co-existence under the present circumstances; the relations between the main representatives of the anti-imperialistic struggle—socialist countries, working-class movement, "Third World"; the action of communist parties with regard to other progressive forces in their countries—socialists, Catholics, national liberation movements; different kinds of anti-imperialistic struggle in different areas and continents.

A lack of clarity in these questions gives rise to the ideological and political confusion existing in some sectors of the working-class and communist movement which takes away the necessary drive from the anti-imperialistic struggle. It is our task to reach such clarity. This task cannot be accomplished just through bilateral or multilateral meetings, between delegations from communist parties, and—in our opinion—not even through meetings of communist parties alone, but through the participation, in some way or the other, of all the forces connected with these questions.

There are several questions to be solved; however, they need not be solved all at the same time, or in the same way, or in one convention. Actually, this would possibly lead only to generic statements and maybe to a greater confusion. Besides, experience teaches us that very important questions can be tackled through meetings, seminars, round table conferences, having different participants and different formalities or aims. We believe that this method should be employed and further enlarged.

We recommended this method, during all recent meetings, as a way to prepare broader conferences and even a world conference of communist parties. We believe that we must secure successful prospects for such a conference if we want to avoid that it might become a further element of tension among parties. The conference should be prepared—not only in the sense of technical and organizational preparation, but in the sense of starting debates inside each party on the various issues.

During these debates, both at the preparatory stage and at the conference itself, the existence of differences and even contrasts on some issues must not make a collective discussion impossible; if an agreement cannot be reached, we cannot consider every disagreement a reason to break off. Formal condemnations of dissenting parties must be avoided as well as the attempt at imposing one's position on other parties which cannot accept it. The persistence, after the debate, of differing viewpoints must only lead to the conclusion that a further examination and a further discussion are necessary.

In our mind, the debate must aim at clearly pointing out agreements and disagreements, possibilities and difficulties to implement a concrete co-ordination of actions; concerning these actions, however, the party must always be free to decide autonomously.

Only thus can the recognition be carried out of the autonomous responsibility of each party in establishing its own political line and the necessity to reach understanding and collaboration not only among communist forces but also with all democratic and progressive forces.

We must stress once again that we do not consider the communist movement as an ensemble of different rigidly closed compartments. Exchange of experiences, circulation of ideas, discussions are essential to the development of the movement, both at the national and international level. We believe that also criticism must not be avoided, if the criticism is made fraternally and without becoming an interference in the other parties' life.

Only imperialistic and reactionary forces—rigidly united under the control of the U.S. State Department and of the different military alliances—are interested in discrediting and opposing all tendencies to a collaboration among anti-imperialistic forces. They know that such unity and collaboration may bring their plans to a failure, make them pay for their aggressions and compel them to leave the attacked countries. It is astonishing that this reactionary, anti-imperialistic campaign might be joined at times by groups which—with a false leftist air, while practically aiding the social-democrat propaganda—claim to be concerned with popular and progressive interests.

We must acknowledge that the reason for so many hesitations with regard to the world conference is the fear that it might represent a limitation to the autonomy of the individual parties; it is the fear that a party's requirements or conditions or working possibilities might not be properly kept into account.

This fear must be dispelled in the preparation of the conference itself. In our mind, we should not begin—as it has been done so far—from the preliminary elaboration of a document which the parties should discuss afterwards: on the contrary, we should start from the elaboration and the clarification of the individual positions of each party on the question to be examined, to draw from them—through a debate at the conference—the indications and possible common conclusions.

As far as we are concerned, we consider these very articles as a way to help the debate which should precede the decision to call a conference. This debate has already started. We have discussed this question in the various talks which we had with leaders of brother parties; we shall discuss in this sense in all those meetings which will deal with the calling and the preparation of a new conference of the communist and working-class parties.

We intend to help, in the best possible way, solve the questions concerning the necessity and timeliness of a conference, the choice of the subjects to be discussed, the system of discussion, and the possible engagements to be taken; still believing, however, that it would be useful to leave the maximum freedom for the participants in the conference to decide the agenda and working methods.

Concerning this problem of the unity of the communist and working-class movement and of an international conference, we carry on the same line adopted to face all ideological, political and theoretical debates, even with non-communists; that is to say, to keep into account also other ways in which some problems are seen.

Concerning all the problems directly or indirectly related to the communist world and its unity, we cannot be just advisers or critics from outside; we want to be interlocutors in each debate, ready to take into consideration the points of view of other parties and the possibilities of understanding with everybody.

We know that many of the existing differences are based on real difficulties and requirements. We intend to work for the overcoming of these differences, in a close collaboration with all brother parties. To us, discussion does not mean a denial of unity, but, on the contrary, a way to reach unity and consolidate it.

## NEW FORMS OF UNITY
## AND INTERNATIONAL COLLABORATION
### (10 November 1967)

One might deduce from the preceding articles that the unity of struggle is in our concept something very small. Let us recall that in the conclusions made by the 81 parties conference in 1960 was said: "when they deem it useful, the communist parties call conferences to discuss problems, to exchange experiences, to be informed of respective standings and viewpoints, to elaborate a common line through consulting and coordinating their activities within the struggle for common goals." These conclusions underline particularly the information, co-ordination and consultative aspects which an international conference of communist parties should have.

On the other hand, we cannot forget the fact that the closest types of unity which were effective in the past are no longer able to express the different, complex requirements of the movement, as a result of the development and number of problems which the movement has to face. Therefore it is quite clear to us that under the present conditions a real internationalism and unity of action cannot be implemented unless we find different kinds of unity and collaboration, responding to the concrete possibilities of action of the different parties. A democratic centralization, quite valid as far as the organization of each party is concerned, cannot regulate the relations between parties without affecting their autonomy of decision.

Actually, in the struggle against imperialism, for peace, to break the predominance of monopolies, to reject all kinds of neo-capitalism and neo-colonialism, a common tactics or even rigidly common strategy are not absolutely necessary.

So much so that we deem it possible to convey forces of different ideal origin to a unitary action according to the different situations and conditions of strife. This indication comes from our most valid experience in the struggle against fascism, in which we gathered several different political and social forces thanks to a policy of unity.

Of course, it is quite often possible and necessary to promote international discussions, at a scientific level, on many problems of theoretic elaboration and analysis. But it is our opinion that these problems can be more usefully and freely dealt with at a scientific level through meetings of cultural organizations and of scholars, while it is best to leave the dealing of more engaging problems to meetings of party representatives, who are politially responsible.

Naturally, in a time when events develop very rapidly, the necessity is often felt of consultations and understanding among forces which are interested in the same goals. Consequently, the way these consultations are made should become less solemn, more articulate and more concrete.

To be more precise: it is not necessary for each meeting to be concluded by a formal document. The consultative character that these meetings should have at an international level would allow a larger participation of parties and an easier co-ordination of actions concerning those issues which find a common agreement. The non-participation in the meeting would not then appear as a breaking off in itself, because of this consultative character of the meeting.

Fraternity among parties is consolidated through frank discussions, through the overcoming of too formal, too diplomatic relations, and through the liquidation of any appearance that a party is interfering upon another. The diversity existing in the communist movement is a result and an element of its strength and breadth, if it is accompanied by a common will to struggle for common goals.

The dialectic of the movement will make it possible to overcome the existing diversity which at the same time, represents a precious patrimony which must neither be hidden nor underestimated, also on account of its value with regard to the democratic public opinion continuously urged by a propaganda which tends to show communist parties as dogmatic, undifferentiated, opposed to debate, ready to excommunicate the others.

Precisely the reality of this diversity should advise us to hold an open debate for each question, aimed not at crystallizing differences but at overcoming them through the search for what we have in common in connection with respective intersts and goals. Within this framework we believe it necessary to have public debates, not only because we want to show the party members and the public opinion the problems which need to be solved and how we intend to solve them, but also because this is the only way to make a dialectic possible.

In this way every position is submitted to the judgement of the movement and of public opinion; briefly, we really make the party "responsible with regard to the working-class, the workers of its own country and the whole international communist movement," as we read in the declaration made by the 81 parties in 1960.

We certainly cannot fear public opinion's checking of our debates and decisions which are concerned with the present and future of the working masses and of the peoples.

The real problem to solve, now, is that of finding new kinds of unity. We think of new kinds of unity among all those forces which are fighting for socialism, peace and progress; new kinds of unity among the socialist countries themselves, between the socialist countries and the Third World countries, and between them and the working-class democratic movements in the capitalist countries.

Facts show that an absolute uniformity of socialist countries concerning the problems to be faced is not possible. Much the less is such uniformity possible among the Third World countries, or among the communist parties which struggle in different countries and conditions. Therefore unity and collaboration among them cannot be reduced to one formula or much the less can it be found by re-establishing leading centers and some kind of monolythism which would only make differences worse.

Unity and collaboration can only be found in the sense, indicated by Togliatti, of unity in diversity. Already in a Soviet declaration from 1956 was stressed "the necessity to allow for the historical past and the particular conditions of each country which is building a new society."

It is our opinion that if this problem is not fully tackled, the discussion remains around more or less abstract formulas.

To accept the concept of unity in diversity means to recognize that every kind of unity or collaboration must respect the right and duty of each party to take autonomous decisions concerning each question, including that of unity or collaboration itself; namely that each party may or may not—or may partially—accept the decisions collectively taken with no splitting consequences upon the parties' relations. For instance, to agree or not to agree on the question of the international conference, or to have doubts as to certain problems, cannot injure the friendship and solidarity among communist parties.

From all what we have said it appears that an international conference can be successful depending on the questions to be dealt with, the preparation of the conference, the commitments that the participants in the conference will be asked to take, and the relations which will be established between the different parties attending or non-attending the conference.

As to us, we shall take part in an international conference because we want to be active interlocutors, to support, through an open exchange of opinion, the necessity to search for every possible common action and agreement among all communist parties, between them and the democratic movements in each country, in the strife against imperialism, for peace and freedom of the peoples, for progress and socialism.

# "THE MAO TSE-TUNG LINE OF TODAY
AND THE INTERNATIONAL COMMUNIST MOVEMENT"

*Excerpts*
(*Akahata,* Tokyo, 10 October 1967)

## Chapter I: The Mao Tse-tung Faction as the Anti-Marxist-Leninist Group

With all their policies and activities both at home and abroad, the ultraleft opportunist and big-power chauvinist elements in the CCP recently have been demonstrating evermore clearly that they are the anti-Marxist-Leninist group undermining the international communist movement and the cause of socialism and communism.

As our party pointed out in the 21 August *Akahata* editorial, "A clear-cut answer to underminers: Smash the antiparty subversive activities of the Mao Tse-tung faction as an ultraleft opportunist group as well as the treacherous antiparty elements who are blindly following them," while acclaiming Mao Tse-tung as the "greatest Marxist-Leninist in our times," the Mao Tse-tung faction in the CCP is pressing forward its demand for unconditional obedience both at home and abroad to Mao Tse-tung's ultraleft opportunist and splittist line. It is waging unwarranted attacks against every individual and every party who disobey such a demand by regarding all of them as the enemy, and is promoting a lunatic plot to wreck the CCP, which is honored with great revolutionary traditions, and to openly split the international communist movement. Especially against our Japan Communist Party, they have come to openly call for "smashing" and "overthrowing" our party, which is honored with glorious revolutionary traditions, by slandering our party as the "revisionist Miyamoto group" and by supporting and encouraging a handful of treacherous antiparty elements and Trotskyists who blindly follow them.

All this indicates that in order to safeguard the independent development of the revolutionary and democratic movements in Japan and to achieve Marxist-Leninist solidarity for the international communist movement, it is necessary for our Party to expose before the Japanese people the counter-Marxist-Leninist reality and true nature of the theories and practices of the ultraleft opportunist and big-power chauvinist group with Mao Tse-tung as its nucleus in the CCP. Also, it is necessary to strengthen more inclusive, systematic, open criticisms against their ultraleft opportunist, big-power chauvinist, and sectarian line and deed which run counter to Marxist-Leninist principles and proletarian internationalism.

1. "In order to protect the independence of the revolutionary and democratic movements in Japan."

2. "The Mao Tse-tung faction aims at making the CCP its private property."

What has taken place in the CCP today is, no doubt, a typical monopolization and control of the party by a group with a specific individual as its core. According to the CCP regulation, as adopted at its Eighth Congress in 1956 the party congress, which is the highest organization of the Party, is to hold elections every five years. Also, it is to meet every year. According to the party regulation, the term of the Eighth CCP Congress should have expired six years ago. And, the Ninth and 10th congresses already should have been convened, since 11 years have elapsed since the Eighth congress in 1956. Notwithstanding, no CCP Congress has ever been convened during this period. No Party organization, except for the Party Congress, can revise the Party line once it is decided upon at a Party congress. Nevertheless, the reports to the Eighth Congress and, its resolutions have been all but denied as the "Chinese version of Khrushchev's revisionism" and the "bourgeois reactionary line" by the Mao Tse-tung faction in its attacks against Liu Shao-ch'i and Teng Hsiao-p'ing who, on behalf of the CCP Central Committee, delivered the reports to the Eighth Congress.

The CCP regulation stipulates that the CCP Central Committee, which is the highest leading organ while the Party congress is in recess, holds a term of five years and convenes a plenum at least twice a year. Actually, however, this regulation was observed only until the eighth Central Committee plenum in August 1959. After that, the regulation was openly ignored because the ninth plenum was held in January 1961, the 10th plenum in September 1962, and the 11th plenum in August 1966. In an extreme case like the 11th plenum, it was convened for the first time in several years. Supreme decisions on internal and international problems began to be adopted by Mao Tse-tung-headed conferences other than regular party Central Committee meetings, such as Party activists' conferences.

Particularly when the 11th Central Committee plenum was held in August last year for the first time in four years in the midst of the cultural revolution, the number of regular and alternate members of the Central Committee who attended the plenum was not announced. This was quite unusual. As made clear by the communique, furthermore, the plenum was attended not only by the members of party organs in Peking and local districts but even by the representatives of "Red Guards," who were given the title of "representatives of revolutionary teachers and students at metropolitan universities and colleges." This was quite an abnormal plenum.

After the 11th plenum, attack by a certain group headed by Mao Tse-tung on Party cadres and organizations have been totally expanded and the Central Committee and Party's collective guidance based on the Party regulations have been virtually dissolved, thereby being actually transformed into "guidance" only by Mao Tse-tung's group. It is a well-known fact that the "thought," speech, and behavior of a person named Mao Tse-tung, who has been deified to the utmost extent, have been placed before any decisions adopted by Party congresses and Central Committee meetings and that the sole highest standard is whether a person is faithful to even one word mentioned by Mao Tse-tung.

The "guiding" group headed by Mao Tse-tung is denying the unconditional observance of party regulations as principle of becoming slaves. At the same time, however, this group is using violence to force the people to be unconditionally subservient to Mao Tse-tung. It is replacing party regulations with slavish "loyalty" to a certain group headed by Mao Tse-tung.

The group also is instigating the "rebel" struggles aimed at dissolving party organizations which are not blindly subservient to the group and at destroying party regulations, while severely suppressing the "rebellion" against the group itself. Furthermore, the group is developing the "power seizure" struggle, which is aimed at depriving Party committees and people's committees of their authoritative rights, on a nationwide scale by using the Liberation Army and other military powers as its background and also by monopolizing propaganda organs, such as newspaper and radio broadcasts. As a result, the dissolution of the Party has been spread throughout the country. This is nothing but an attempt to make the Party the private property of the ultraleft opportunist group headed by Mao Tse-tung.

It is quite ridiculous, therefore that the Mao Tse-tung faction, which dared to dissolve Party organizations in order to dominate and monopolize the Party, is accusing our party, which has consistently adhered to the democratic centralization system and collective guidance, by saying that our party is nothing but a "revisionist group headed by Miyamoto."

3. "In order to safeguard the principles of Marxism-Leninism and to attain the unity of the international communist movement."

Another important reason why our Party has found it necessary to openly criticize the Maoist faction by name is that the faction's subversion activities against our Party and the democratic movement in our country have become more ferocious. The faction, preposterously deifying Mao Tse-tung, has come to call Mao Tse-tung's thought the "acme of Marxism-Leninism," thereby forcing the international communist movement to accept such an unpardonable distortion and impairment of Marxist-Leninist principles. The faction has openly embarked on division of the international communist movement.

It is true that the CCP played a considerably important role in the struggle against modern revisionism led by Khrushchev—especially in its early stage. The Maoist faction, however, soon committed the mistake of making the "struggle against revisionism" serve its own selfish interests, in disregard of the overall interests of the international struggle against U.S. imperialism and of the liberation struggle of the people of the whole world. Also, overemphasizing its role, the faction now has the audacity to call Mao Tse-tung a genius equal or even superior to Marx or Lenin. It is trying to win him the highest position in the international communist movement. The faction is pushing ahead with the most flagrant ultraleft opportunist racist, and divisionist plot by trampling underfoot Marxism-Leninism and proletarian internationalism.

The Maoists discuss the CPSU and U.S. imperialism in the same light and regard both of them as enemies. They have proposed an "anti-U.S. and anti-Soviet international front" by systematically excluding the CPSU, thereby splitting the international united action of the anti-imperialist democratic forces against the U.S. imperialists' ferocious aggression in Vietnam and thus encouraging the U.S. imperialists.

They are trying to popularize the theory of "people's war," the theory of "violent revolution," and other such ultraleft adventurist ideas unreasonably developed from their particular experiences. Also, by trying to give an absolute value to "Mao Tse-tung's thought," they are forcing the revolutionary movements and national liberation movements in various countries of the world to accept their view, thereby dealing a serious blow to the revolutionary struggles of various nations.

They call those parties which do not accept their ideas "revisionists" or "accomplices of U.S. imperialism." Holding high the banner of anarchism and party-dissolutionism and shouting "rebellion is justified," they interfere in the domestic affairs of other communist parties, support antiparty elements and the Trotskyists, and encourage them to subvert the revolutionary movements in other countries. They claim that the Soviet Union and some other socialist countries have already degenerated into capitalist countries. Under "overthrow fascist dictatorship!" and other Trotskyist and counterrevolutionary slogans aimed at undermining the socialist countries, they are openly advocating the overthrow of the parties and governments of those socialist countries.

They shout divisionist slogans, such as "One is divided into two" and "This is an era of great polarization, and of reorganization," thereby openly seeking to split the international communist movement and to place the movement under their faction.

All these words and deeds of the Maoist faction clearly reveal that Mao Tse-tung's current line is anything but the "acme of our day of Marxism-Leninism" and has nothing in common with Marxism-Leninism. It is outright hostile to Marxism-Leninism and proletarian internationalism.

Chapter II: "True situation and nature of the 'great proletarian cultural revolution.'"

1. "The 'great proletarian cultural revolution' has nothing in common with Marxist-Leninist cultural revolution."

2. "The main objective of the 'great cultural revolution' is to establish the Mao Tse-tung faction's dictatorship.

If the "great proletarian cultural revolution" has nothing to do with the cultural revolution or Marxism-Leninism, what is the nature of the situation which was "created" by Mao Tse-tung in late 1965 and is being developed under the name of the "great proletarian cultural revolution?" It can be concluded that it is nothing but a political struggle systematically launched by the Mao Tse-tung faction. The faction, which was dissatisfied with the situation in China because it took an undesirable course for the faction, launched the struggle in order to establish a dictatorship, which is based on the deification of Mao Tse-tung and is not restricted by the party and state, by resorting to emergency measures. This is clearly proven by the factual process of the recent situation.

In the first place, in the process of promoting the "great proletarian cultural revolution launched and led by Chairman Mao himself," the Mao Tse-tung faction has stepped up the deification of Mao Tse-tung by taking advantage of the Chinese people's affection and respect for Mao Tse-tung, who was the leader of the Chinese revolution.

The absolute character of Mao Tse-tung's thought and respect for Mao Tse-tung have been promoted by Lin Piao and the Liberation Army throughout the country particularly since 1959 when Lin Piao was appointed National Defense Minister. *People's Daily* and *Red Flag* also cooperated in launching an extensive campaign to achieve this objective. Under the "great proletarian cultural revolution," the absolute character of Mao Tse-tung's thought and respect for Mao Tse-tung have finally created the crazy deification of Mao Tse-tung by taking a fantastic and abnormal course.

Furthermore, the "Quotations From Chairman Mao Tse-tung," which is just a collection of what Mao Tse-tung said in the past, has been made a sacred book which everybody must carry all the time and memorize accurately. At present, the ceremony of reading this sacred "Quotations" must be held before any activity, such as sports events, business transations, and theatrical performances. It even occurred before the collective terrorism against comrades Sunama and Konno. There is no other religion in the world whose respect for its sacred book can match the cult of the "Quotations From Chairman Mao Tse-tung" and its ceremonial reading. Moreover, even foreign tourists are being indiscriminatingly forced to respect this "Quotations" at hotels, in airplanes, and on trains.

Needless to say, such deification of Mao Tse-tung and the cult of Mao Tse-tung completely ignore the scientific spirit of Marxism-Leninism.

The current CCP regulations were adopted, after some revisions, by the first conference of the Eighth Congress in 1956. One of the important revisions made at this time was to establish the organizational guarantee against errors—such as the deification of an individual and the cult of an individual—in the Party regulations by learning lessons from the errors of the cult of Stalin, which was made clear by the 20th CPSU Congress. From this point of view, new regulations, such as "the existence of any conduct of elevating an individual above the Party groups should not be permitted" and " there cannot be any political party or individual that has no defect or makes no mistake in carrying out activities," were inserted in the general platform of the party regulations. Furthermore, the regulation adopted by the Seventh Congress in 1945 stipulating that "Mao Tse-tung's thought" is the milestone of the Party activities, was changed into a regulation to the effect that "the milestone of the CCP's activities is Marxism-Leninism."

At the Eighth Party Congress, Teng Hsiao-p'ing made a report on the revision of the Party regulations on behalf of the Party Central Committee and stated the following about the significance of the revision: "One of the important achievements of the 20th CPSU congress is that it taught us the serious and harmful effects of deifying an individual. Our party has believed that there is neither a party nor an individual that has no defect when engaging in activities. This point is clearly mentioned in the general platform of our Party's draft regulations. It can be said, therefore, that our Party stipulated that the deification of an individual has nothing to do with us."

This regulation is the highest CCP rule. Every CCP member should strictly observe it, since no revision has been made to it since the Eighth Party Congress. Nonetheless, the Mao Tse-tung faction has hated and scrapped the party regulation, as well as its spirit, which was approved at the Party Congress, with the Mao Tse-tung faction itself participating. The faction has mobilized all mass propaganda media to press forward the cult of Mao Tse-tung, and even the worship for him as a divinity, far beyong the cult of Stalin.

Secondly, as it declared in its "resolution" of the 11th CCP Central Committee plenum last August that the "main target" of the "great proletarian cultural revolution" is the "Party persons in authority taking the capitalist road," the Mao Tse-tung faction has promoted a "struggle" to overthrow, expel, and smash many hostile Party organizations and Party cadres both in the center and at the local level. It has done so by mobilizing the "Red Guards" and the so-called rebels with the armed forces, whose central command is under Lin Piao, supporting them from behind.

According to the Mao Tse-tung faction, these cadres are either the "Party persons in authority taking the capitalist road" or the "representatives of the bourgeois reactionary line." They are the "antiparty, antisocialist, and counterrevolutionary" forces which have transformed the mechanism of proletarian dictatorship and have, instead, promoted bourgeois dictatorship during the past 10 years and more, while consistently following, consciously and systematically, the counterrevolutionary plot to revive capitalism in China.

However, such accusations are not based on objective facts or on scientific analysis. This can be guessed from the Mao Tse-tung faction's way of making such unfounded slanders as calling foreign parties and communists "counterrevolutionaries" and "traitors" only because these parties and communists refuse to unconditionally follow its views, including the deification of Mao Tse-tung. If the Mao Tse-tung faction's accusations are pertinent, we can only conclude that during the past more than 10 years since the founding of the CPR the representatives of the counterrevolutionary bourgeois line have elaborately promoted the policy of reviving capitalism in China by seizing such top posts as State head, party vice chairmen, Political Bureau, and Secretariat, as well as other important offices both in the government and the party. This is a ridiculous conclusion which actually contradicts the history of the socialist construction in China and its achievements to date. And if such accusations are pertinent, Mao Tse-tung himself should be charged most seriously for allowing the rise of a situation running counter to the cause of socialism, since he has been CCP chairman, or the highest person in charge of the party. In truth, the basic direction of the "criminal" line, which the Mao Tse-tung faction today criticizes as manifesting the bourgeois reactionary line of the "power faction," was approved together with the report and resolutions at the Eighth CCP Congress in 1956 with Mao Tse-tung himself participating.

The Mao Tse-tung faction flung every slander at the so-called representatives of the counterrevolutionary bourgeois line, or the cadres whom it calls the "party persons in authority taking the capitalist road," and judged that the contradictions between the Mao faction and the power faction are those "between the revolutionaries and counterrevolutionaries"and those "between our side and the irreconcilable foe" (August 1966 *Red Flag* editorial, "Long Live the Great Proletarian Cultural Revolution.") Yet it has been unable to produce any concrete fact to date indicating the power faction's counterrevolutionary links with the bourgeois.

In addition, one of the peculiar characteristics of the so-called "great proletarian cultural revolution is that, notwithstanding its self-appraisal of its own promotion of "great democracy," the Mao Tse-tung faction has never published the opinions or counterarguments of the so-called power faction, including Liu Shao-ch'i and Teng Hsiao-p'ing, while heaping serious accusations upon them. Also, it has never made clear at all the genuine controversial points of view with them concerning the policy line at home and abroad. Therefore, we are consequently unfamiliar as yet with the view of those who have been condemned as the "power faction."

However, according to the materials published by the Mao Tse-tung faction and the "Red Guards" under its command, what was wrong with those cadres after all can be boiled down to the fact that they have maintained more or less an indecisive attitude toward the deification of Mao Tse-tung, or that they held different views with those of the Mao Tse-tung faction on various questions. From the very beginning of its open attacks against the "Party persons in authority" last year, the Mao Tse-tung faction itself has emphasized over and over again that the biggest crime of the so-called power faction, in fact, lies in the fact that they did not unconditionally aline themselves with the deification of Mao Tse-tung and the Mao Tse-tung faction's line, and that the attitude toward Mao Tse-tung and Mao Tse-tung's "thought" is the highest criterion to distinguish between the "revolutionaries" and the "counterrevolutionaries."

"The attitude toward Mao Tse-tung's thought—whether to recognize it or reject it, protect it or oppose it, cherish it or show hostility to it—is the dividing line and the testing stone for distinguishing between genuine revolution and fake revolution, between revolutionaries and counterrevolutionaries, and between Marxism-Leninism and revisionism" (7 July 1966 *Liberation Army Daily* editorial, "Mao Tse-tung's Thought Is the Telescope and Microscope of Our Revolution").

The above editorial plainly confesses that the main objective of the struggle to overthrow the so-called power faction is not at all to secure the cause of socialism from the counterrevolutionary elements who plot the revival of capitalism. Instead, it is to eradicate all the forces which do not act in unconditional concert with the deification of Mao Tse-tung and the Mao Tse-tung faction's view, as well as those which in one way or another cannot please the Mao Tse-tung faction, branding them the class enemy or the bourgeois counterrevolutionary elements, and to eventually establish the Mao Tse-tung faction's boundless dictatorship in China.

Thirdly, in the process of the so-called great proletarian cultural revolution, the Mao Tse-tung faction has neglected the party regulations and has promoted on a large scale the dismantling and monopolization of the organization of the CCP, the highest leadership corps of the Chinese revolution.

Article 2 of the CCP regulations adopted by the Eighth Party Congress in 1956 stipulates that "strict observance of the party regulations and the nation's law" is the duty which all party members are without exception required to assume, "regardless of their meritorious deeds or ranks." Its preface emphasized the importance of observing the party regulations: "The party is comprised of united militant organizations which are linked with the rules and regulations that must be observed by all party members. Without rules and regulations, the party can never lead the nation and people to defeat strong enemies and realize socialism and communism."

Since last year, however, the faction headed by party Chairman Mao Tse-tung has taken the initiative in openly violating party rules and regulations. It has promoted arbitrary conduct to destroy the CCP, which a large number of Chinese communists and people have guarded and nurtured at the risk of their own lives. It has put the army headed by Lin Piao before the Party. It has attacked the Party organizations and cadres that refused to unconditionally cooperate with the Mao Tse-tung faction, by mobilizing a large number of "Red Guards" and "rebel groups" which are outside the Party, and also by monopolizing and taking advantage of *People's Daily, Red Flag,* central and local newspapers and broadcasting stations, and other propaganda media. It has openly asked for the "revolutionary" overthrow of these Party organizations and cadres. It is crystal clear, in the light of the organizational principle of a Marxist-Leninist party, that this is the worst conduct aimed at destroying the unity and rules and regulations of the Party.

Furthermore, it began to clearly divide the Party organizations, which must be "united militant organizations linked with rules and regulations that must be observed by all party members" (according to the CCP regulations) into two kinds—organizations which are faithful to the Mao Tse-tung faction and organizations which are not blindly subservient to the Mao Tse-tung faction. It also began to denounce the unconditional observance of the Party rules and regulations for adopting the "principle of becoming slaves."

According to the Mao Tse-tung faction, in places where its influence is not prevailing, the party organizations have already become the "organs of bourgeois dictatorship" and the party rules and regulations have changed into "counterrevolutionary rules and regulations"; thoroughly destroying such a situation is the duty of "proletarian revolutionary fighters."

Since this January, the Mao Tse-tung faction, which is adhering to the above requirement, has deprived party committees of all their rights by adopting emergency measures in the cities of Shanghai and Peking and the provinces of Heilungkiang, Shantung, Shansi, Kweichow, and Tsinghai. It has begun to carry out the so-called power seizure struggles aimed at transferring the authoritative power to "rebel factions" and the Liberation Army. This is aimed at unilaterally dissolving the regular CCP organizations without going through regular procedures stipulated by party regulations, at finally destroying the party organizations, and at concentrating all authoritative rights in the hands of th Mao Tse-tung faction. In other words, the Mao Tse-tung faction has finally reached the point of the most arbitrary and open dissolution of Party organizations in order to realize its dictatorial domination of the party.

In the fourth place, the Mao Tse-tung faction has not only tried to dissolve the party organizations but has attempted to violently destroy the various organs and laws and orders of the socialist nation, which were established by the Chinese people themselves through their revolution. In places where the "power-seizure struggles" were successfully carried out, not only party committees but also people's committees, which are authoritative power organs representing the people, were deprived of their rights. It was declared that "revolutionary committees" and "general command of rebel organizations"—temporary power organs headed by PLA units which are under the control of the Mao Tse-tung faction—have "all power, such as party rights, political rights, financial rights, and cultural rights."

It is crystal clear that this "power-seizure struggle" of the Mao Tse-tung faction is destructive conduct aimed at illegally dissolving the regular state organ of a socialist nation. As clearly mentioned by the CPR constitution, People's committees in various classes are elected by people's congresses representing people in various districts, and only the people's congresses have the right to dissolve the people's committees. The Maoist faction also has virtually disbanded the labor unions , which are the largest organizations of China's working class, the Young Communist League, which had a membership of more than 20 million, and several other mass organizations which constituted the main prop of the proletarian dictatorship of China.

The fact that, amid the "great cultural revolution," which stresses its "proletarian" nature, the "proletarian cultural revolution" depends not on the workers and their organizations but mainly on the "Red Guards" of college and high school students and also on PLA troops sheds much light on the anti-Marxist-Leninist nature of the Chinese "great cultural revolution."

In addition, the law and order dictated by the constitution of the Chinese People's Republic are virtually nonexistent today. All constitutional provisions have been scrapped since the initiation of the "great proletarian cultural revolution." As a result, the "Red Guards" and "rebels" have illegally arrested leaders and perpetrated outrages against them. All conceivable violations of national laws have been reported.

### Chapter III: "The Anti-Marxist-Leninist Nature of the Mao Tse-tung Line Today."

1. "Big-power chauvinists forcing 'Mao Tse-tung's thought' on the whole world."

2. "Mao Tse-tung's thought, its past and present."

All these facts clearly reveal that the "great proletarian cultural revolution" in China is anything but a great revolution which will lead socialism to victory. It is an antisocialist, anti-Marxist-Leninist "scheme" which is aimed solely at allowing the Maoist faction to establish and strengthen an absolute dictatorial system based on a morbid deification of Mao Tse-tung. As a result, the order and discipline of the party and the state have greatly been impaired, the achievements of the Chinese revolution which have gone down in the history of Asia and of the world have been nullified, and the CCP and the state structure of China have virtually been dissolved.

The very fact that the Maoist faction is arguing that "Mao Tse-tung's thought is the present-day acme of Marxism-Leninism" and is demanding that the revolutionary movement of the world accept it as the highest "guiding theory" proves that "Mao Tse-tung's thought" is anything but the "acme." It has degenerated into something hostile to Marxism-Leninism. The Maoists' arguement is utterly unscientific and dogmatic.

It may be true that Mao Tse-tung's works published during the Chinese people's struggle for liberation have played a great role in the Chinese revolutionary movement. However, this does not prove that Mao Tse-tung's works and statements are of universal significance as a "guiding theory of the world revolution."

The works which Mao Tse-tung wrote in the past and which have played a positive role in the Chinese revolution, as Mao Tse-tung himself has repeatedly stressed, are the results of his "application of the principles of Marxism-Leninism in the practice of the Chinese revolution." The works have been able to function as a "guiding theory" since they have taken the concrete characteristics of the Chinese revolution into consideration and have appropriately applied the various principles of Marxism-Leninism into the concrete conditions of China. Thus, these works have made a considerable contribution to the development of Marxism-Leninism. But, no matter how successful they have been as the guiding theory of the Chinese revolutionary movement, it is wrong to try to regard them as a "universal truth" which can be applied to the revolutionary movements in all countries.

The Maoist faction and its blind followers, insisting on the universality of "Mao Tse-tung's thought," stress that "Mao Tse-tung's thought" is something that has "connected the principles of Marxism-Leninism to the practice of the Chinese revolution" and has also "connected Marxism-Leninism to the practice of the world revolution." This also is an unfounded dogmatic argument.

The reason that the theory of Marxism-Leninism, which Marx, Engels, and Lenin created, is of universal significance as the guiding theory of world revolution is that not only did Marx, Engels, and Lenin analyze the situations of their own countries and study the experiences of the revolutionary movements in their own countries, but they conducted detailed scientific studies in all aspects of the political and economical relations of world capitalism and in all aspects of the experiences of all countries of the world before they established their Marxist-Leninist revolutionary theory.

Meanwhile, what Mao Tse-tung set forth in the works which he published in the course of the Chinese people's liberation struggle were mainly problems of the Chinese revolution. Under the guidance of the general theory of Marxism-Leninism, Mao Tse-tung tried to solve the "theoretical and tactical problems of the Chinese revolution."

The four-volume *Selected Works of Mao Tse-Tung* is different from any works by Marx or Lenin in that Mao Tse-tung's works contain no systematic study or theory on economy or socialist economic construction. There is no relevent work on the general analysis of the politics or economics of world capitalism. There also is no single systematic work on the problems of the revolutionary movements in other countries. The problems of the revolutionary movements in the advanced capitalist countries are not discussed at all in the four volumes, except for a few remarks here and there. How is it possible for a "thought" or "theory" to be significant or capable of being the "guiding theory" of world revolution without including any systematic study or giving any clear-cut conclusion on today's complicated political, economic, social, and cultural problems, problems of the revolutionary movements outside China, and especially problems of democratic revolutions or socialist revolutions in the advanced capitalist countries? There is no doubt that Mao Tse-tung's thought has no universal significance.

The insistence of those who strongly contend that "Mao Tse-tung's 'thought' is the summation of the experiences of revolutions in the world" is nothing but an anti-Marxist-Leninist standpoint. It absolutely regards the experience and theory of the Chinese revolution as a universal principle for any revolution in the world and mechanically introduces the experience and theory into any revolutionary movement in the world by ignoring the different concrete situation in each country.

Also, the Mao Tse-tung line of today, which the CCP ultraleft opportunist and big-power chauvinist elements believe to be absolutely correct as Mao Tse-tung's thought," is fundamentally different from the past insistence and theory of Mao Tse-tung, which played a leading role at the time of the Chinese revolution. For example, in the revolutionary theory of Mao Tse-tung when he guided the Chinese revolution, the theory and policy of the united front held quite an important position. Especially, at the time of the war against Japan he correctly analyzed the fact that Chiang Kai-shek's Kuomintang was promoting a reactionary "two-faced" policy against Japan and against communism. He posed the "revolutionary two-faced policy" to cope with it and helped develop the anti-Japan national united front through the formation of Nationalist-Communist cooperation. In this, he provided an excellent application of the Marxist-Leninist united front policy of uniting all integral forces in order to overthrow the main enemy of the times.

However, this united front policy has been totally discarded in the Mao Tse-tung line today. The Mao Tse-tung faction's argument on the "united front against the United States and the Soviet Union," which demands rejection of the CPSU leadership from the international anti-imperialist front, flatly runs counter to the principle of the anti-Japan national united front which Mao Tse-tung called for and promoted in the past. It is a sectarian policy which pleases U.S. imperialism—the common archenemy of the peoples the world over. This is crystal clear and needs no further illustration.

Also in his past works, Mao Tse-tung emphasized over and over again that the "people's war" formula of developing a long-term armed struggle, with farm villages as its basis, is the "characteristic strong point of the Chinese revolution," and is inapplicable in other capitalist countries. Nonetheless, scrapping Mao Tse-tung's caution against the unwarranted generalization of the "people's war" formula in China, the Mao Tse-tung faction is trying to press forward the formula as the universal principle of the revolutionary movement in the world under the name of "Mao Tse-tung's thought."

On the pretext of the single phrase "rebellion has its reasons," the Mao Tse-tung faction is contradicting the Marxist-Leninist organizational principle, which has been tested and established through the whole of experiences in the world communist movement, as well as the basic Marxist-Leninist principle—the importance of which Mao Tse-tung himself once emphasized. Thus the Mao Tse-tung faction today is openly trying to justify not only its violation of the party regulations and dismantling of the Party organization at home but also such unprecedented big-power chauvinist intervention in the revolutionary movements abroad as its efforts to wreck and subvert the JCP by instigating antiparty blind followers of foreign influence in Japan.

Actually, the slogan "rebellion has its reasons" is derived from Mao Tse-tung's speech at the celebration in Yenan to mark Stalin's 60th birthday in 1939. At that time, Mao Tse-tung said: "Although Marxism has various reasons, it can be boiled down to a single phrase, 'rebellion has its reasons.'"

As is well known, the concept that the people have the right of rebelling against any antipopular political system is not at all peculiar to Marxism alone. For example, as is clearly stated in the U.S. Declaration of Independence of 1776, this phrase is a "rationale" recognized by all democratic-minded people concerning the bourgeois revolution. Mao Tse-tung's phrase, which has reduced the entire logical system of scientific Marxist socialism into such a commonplace and simple "rationale," is a typical example of his vulgarization and crude simplification of Marxism.

In the meantime, when he mentioned the "rebellion" in Yenan, he meant, of course, a revolution to overthrow the imperialist or reactionary regime—and not at all a "rebellion" within the Communist Party. Yet the phrase has been given a new meaning and a new role in the Mao Tse-tung line today, which have nothing to do with its origin more than 20 years ago. In other words, it is used not as a call for a people's revolution to oppose an imperialist or reactionary regime but a pretext to justify, under the name of Mao Tse-tung, the rebellion against the Communist Party and its discipline, as well as the violation of Party regulations.

What has exposed the counter-Marxist-Leninist nature of the Mao Tse-tung line today in its extremity is the Mao Tse-tung faction's argument on the so-called revolution under the proletarian dictatorship. According to the joint editorial in *Red Flag* and *People's Daily* entitled "Great Historic Documents": 1) even after the establishment of the proletarian dictatorship, the bourgeois representatives will smuggle themselves into the leading organizations of the party and government and will try to subvert the proletarian dictatorship and change it into a bourgeois dictatorship; 2) therefore, even under the conditions of the proletarian dictatorship, it is necessary to conduct a "revolution" in order to prevent the revival of capitalism, and the main targets of this "revolution" are the bourgeois representatives within the structure of the proletarian dictatorship—or, in other words, the party persons in authority taking the capitalist road; and 3) this revolution will be incomplete if it is only accomplished once, for it should be conducted over and over again through an extremely long period of history until ultimate victory of communism can be attained.

The ultraleft opportunist and big-power chauvinist elements in the CCP deem Mao Tse-tung's solution of the problem of "revolution under the proletarian dictatorship" as his "largest contribution to the international proletariat in the phases of theory and practice." They emphasize that with this, Marxism has been enhanced to the third new developing stage, "the stage of Mao Tse-tung's thought," above Leninism. According to them, this has been an unsettled basic problem of the proletarian revolution which neither Marx nor Engels could solve at that time, with which Lenin could not survive until its practical solution, and which was brought to Stalin's awareness only one year prior to his death. They assert that the fact that Mao Tse-tung solved this problem is "the most important landmark indicating that Marxism has developed into quite a new stage."

However, the contents of the "theory" on "revolution under the proletarian dictatorship," which has been made the most essential basis to play up "Mao Tse-tung's thought" sky-high as the third stage of Marxism, above the stage of Leninism, can be called nothing more than a patchwork theory to rationalize the Mao Tse-tung faction's disintegrationist and antisocialist deeds of dismantling and monopolizing the CCP as well as the organizations of the proletarian dictatorship only in order to establish its own unlimited dictatorship.

In the previous chapter, we clarified in detail the counter-Marxist-Leninist realities of the "great proletarian cultural revolution" under Mao Tse-tung. In addition, on the pretext of the necessity of a struggle against the danger of modern revisionism and the revival of capitalism, the Mao Tse-tung faction's theory justifies in the name of "revolution" its dismantling and monopolization of the Marxist-Leninist party and socialist government organizations, which are the indispensable insurances of victory for socialism. It calls for repeating such a "revolution" over and over again.

Such a theory by no means indicates a new developing stage of Marxism-Leninism. It fundamentally denies the Marxist-Leninist theories on socialist revolution, on socialist construction, and, above all, on the theory and practice of proletarian dictatorship—one of the cores of Marxism-Leninism. It has nothing in common with Marxism-Leninism at all. Neither Marx and Engels nor Lenin and Stalin brought about such a counter-Marxist-Leninist "theory."

It should be noted in this connection that Mao Tse-tung's "theory" is, theoretically speaking, another version of Trotsky's notorious theories on "eternal revolution" and "the second supplementary revolution."

The Mao Tse-tung line today, which demands acclámation and worship of "Mao Tse-tung's thought," has basically changed into something heterogeneous with Marxism-Leninism. It is self-evident to any Marxist-Leninist that he cannot call this counter-Marxist-Leninist Mao Tse-tung line today the "acme of Marxism-Leninism of the present age" or the "guiding thought for a world revolution." That is, of course, he cannot do so unless he takes the stand of blind big-power chauvinism, of worshiping the works and views of the leader of his country as the highest theory in the world and pressing these forward in the international arena, or unless he holds to the stand of blind and base flunkyism to such chauvinism.

# STATEMENT BY THE JORDANIAN COMMUNIST PARTY

*Abridged Text*
*(Information Bulletin,* No. 105, 1967)

Jordan and the other Arab countries have been subjected to a savage aggression reminiscent of the barbarous crimes committed by Hitler during his invasion of Europe. Backed and helped by the U.S., Britain and other imperialist powers, Israel resorted to Nazi methods in destroying towns, villages and houses with their inhabitants, using napalm bombs, which are internationally banned, to kill people and burn their crops and other property, taking the life of thousands of victims—children, old people and women—and mutilating thousands of others. Tens of thousands of people were turned out of their houses, whole towns and villages reduced to ruins, many young people arrested, murdered or taken away to unknown places. War prisoners were treated in a most savage manner, many of them were killed and others manhandled.

With the help and support of world imperialism, Israel executed the first part, the military, of its foul conspiracy against our Jordanian people and the other Arab peoples, by occupying the Western bank of the Jordan, the Gaza strip, the Tiran Straits and the Syrian border area as a result of its dirty war against the Arab nation, a war which had been planned for a long time and which was executed in complete concert with the imperialists.

Aggressive Israel is now cooperating with all the criminal imperialist forces which supported it and instigated it to commit aggression, making feverish efforts to carry out the second, political part of its conspiracy by exploiting the military gains achieved through treachery and aggression. The U.S. and British imperialists and their aggressive agent, Israel, have many criminal projects and plans all aimed at definitively eliminating the Palestinian problem in the interests of Israel and imperialism, at imposing insulting and humiliating settlements on the Arab states and enabling the Zionist octopus, a creation of imperialist monopolies, to grow and to prey on the wealth of the Arab peoples, to deal a blow at their political, economic and social gains.

The most dangerous of these Israeli-Anglo-American plans is the one which is to be carried out in case the aggressors and their supporters do not succeed in subjugating the Arab states and in imposing final general solutions upon them. It is the plan which is being brandished by the Zionist aggressors and their partners in Washington, London and Bonn and which is evident from the behavior of the Zionist assassins on the Western bank and in the Gaza strip, as well as from the behavior and the moves of a handful of traitorous agents who are collaborating with the enemy in order to establish an artificial entity on the newly usurped land under the spears of the barbarous invaders, conclude a unilateral peace with that entity, and achieve mutual recognition in an attempt to mislead and deceive world opinion and make it believe that the Palestinian question has been settled by agreement with its "people" and that no other side, Arab or non-Arab, has anything to do with the Palestinian question any longer.

To achieve this, the Zionists and their traitorous agents have resorted, and continue to resort to persecution, terror, injustice and discrimination, used by successive governments against the population.

Today, with the western bank of the Jordan and Gaza occupied and Palestine with its natural frontiers under Israeli control, the imperialists, Israel and the reactionary circles think this is the time to achieve what they were unable to achieve in the past, by establishing the false and artificial Palestinian entity in the occupied areas of Jordan and Gaza. The plotting agressors realize that this would inevitably contradict the existence of the Jordanian state as an independent and sovereign state and a UN member and that international laws, principles and practice do not allow any part of its territory to be taken by force of arms. That is why the second part of their conspiratorial plans is to destroy and eliminate Jordan as a state and as an entity, which would enable Israel to swallow the western bank of the Jordan and Gaza. If they do not succeed in liquidating the Jordanian state, their alternative would be to destroy the forces opposing the Israeli and imperialists' plans in the country and to put in power those willing to conclude a separate peace with Israel, to submit to any settlement or to conspire to tear off the eastern bank and annex it to a reactionary state, thus eliminating the Jordanian state.

That is the reason for the furious activities of the open and secret agents of U.S. and British imperialism who are everywhere in the state apparatus of Jordan, and of the Arab ultra-reactionaries and their agents in Jordan, as well as of the imperialist circles and their agents in Jordan, of the pressures, rumors and dubious contacts resorted to by the American, British and West German embassies in Jordan. It explains the attacks made on King Hussein and the forces supporting him in the government with a view to diverting them from the new Arab policy line of Jordan, to instigate the anti-national elements opposed to the policy of Arab solidarity, against King Hussein's initiative of concluding a mutual defense agreement with the UAR, against his effort to promote Arab solidarity, release political prisoners and give all Jordanians at least some opportunity of working hand in hand in order to regain the western bank and undo the effects of the imperialist and Zionist aggression against our country.

The fundamental task facing our people and the brother Arab peoples today is to defeat all imperialist and Israeli plans and eliminate all the effects of the treacherous aggression territorially, militarily and economically. It is therefore necessary inside the country to rally the mass of our Jordanian people with all their national forces and organizations, official or otherwise, which are opposed to imperialism and Israeli occupation, to fight as one man and unrelentingly for the preservation of the eastern bank of our country and the recovery of every inch of our country on the western bank, to be fully vigilant in the face of imperialist agents and Israeli spies in the country, to bar the way of all conspirators and adventurers, to consolidate and strengthen the trend which is loyal to the country and to Arab solidarity within the state apparatus, and to resist all trends towards conspiracy and collusion with imperialism and Zionism and their criminal projects.

Realization of this sacred task requires, in our opinion, the convening of a general national conference, on the initiative of King Hussein as the first responsible official who can pave the ground for this meeting and contribute effectively to its success. This meeting should be attended by representatives of the different popular and patriotic forces, the elements known for their hostility to imperialism and Zionism, and all loyal and patriotic elements in the government, both civilians and military men. The meeting should exchange opinions with a full sense of responsibility and in all frankness in order to formulate a national charter defining the mottoes and aims at the crucial stage that Jordan and our entire Arab homeland are passing through.

To contribute to the success of this national conference, we propose, with full responsibility and modesty as a basis for discussion, the following points, which can be changed or modified for inclusion in the above-mentioned charter:

1. To preserve the territorial and political existence of Jordan as a basis for regaining our occupied territory and for resisting any attempt to encroach on the eastern bank of the Jordan.

2. To struggle for the recovery of the western bank as an integral part of the Jordanian state.

3. To rebuild our armed forces and equip them with efficient up-to-date weapons.

4. To unite all forces hostile to Zionist occupation and imperialism in a broad front grouping all loyal elements among the people and in the government.

5. To resist and foil all imperialist and Israeli plans, and to eliminate all the effects of the aggression.

6. To mobilize, train and arm the people, and to foster their political consciousness.

7. To solve the economic, financial and social problems resulting from the aggression.

8. To insist on the return of the refugees to their homes and on the payment of compensation for damage to state and private property.

9. To persevere in the policy of promoting deep solidarity with the UAR, Syria, Iraq and all other brother Arab states against imperialism and Israel, defeating all imperialist and Zionist plans, and regaining all the Arab territory occupied by Israel.

10. To establish the best of friendly political, economic and cultural relations with the Soviet Union and the other socialist countries and friendly states.

It is proposed that a coalition government be formed on the basis of the above program.

We are fully confident that the Arab peoples will finally triumph over all their enemies in the just battle they are engaged in, that our people in Jordan will succeed in regaining every inch of national soil, set out again to rehabilitate Jordan, use their resources in the interests of their sons, and work shoulder to shoulder with the brother Arab countries for the future progress and unity of the Arab nation and for the recovery of all the usurped rights of the Arabs in Palestine.

# "ON THE CURRENT TASKS IN THE POLITICAL WORK OF THE PARTY"

Report of Zenon Kliszko, Secretary of the Central Committee,
Polish United Workers' Party, 16 May 1967

*Abridged Text*
(*Trybuna Ludu*, Warsaw, 17 May 1967)

The building of socialism in Poland is a part of the world-wide process of the struggle and rivalry of two systems: the socialist system and the capitalist system. The course of this struggle exerts a major influence on the political climate in our country, on the moods and views of our people.

The deep conviction about the political, economic and moral superiority of socialism over capitalism, about the inevitable victory of the new system on a world scale constitutes the basis of socialist consciousness. The main task of our Party in shaping socialist consciousness is to disseminate among the whole nation the truth about the superiority of socialism over capitalism, the truth in favor of which speaks in our times not only scientific theory, but above all the practical results of the fifty-year march of socialism in the world, the experience of the dynamic development of the economy and culture of the socialist states, the experience of the liberation struggle of colonial nations against colonialism and of the working class against monopoly capital. Only the consciousness of participation in the universal process of progressive transformations, encompassing nations and continents, can give our working class, our intelligentsia and the entire community a proper criterion for appraising current political events and the feeling, indispensable to each man, that his daily toil serves more general and noble social aims, that he is participating in creating the future of his own nation and that of mankind.

The struggle between the two systems—the socialist system and the capitalist system—has in recent years entered a new phase. It is becoming increasingly obvious that imperialism has lost the chance of a military victory not only in a global war. It is no longer able also by way of local interventionist wars to prevent a further advance of socialism and of the national liberation movement.

The policy "from positions of strength" pursued by the United States and its Atlantic allies in the course of the long years of the cold war against the Soviet Union and other socialist states, has proved ineffective. It has been unable to halt economic, technical and social progress in socialist countries, to stifle the national liberation and anti-imperialist movement in the countries of the third world, or to check the growing tendency toward peaceful coexistence with the capitalist world in the governing circles of many capitalist states, particularly in Europe.

The consistent peaceful policy of the socialist states has shattered among broad sections of public opinion the myth about the alleged threat of "communist aggression." It has thereby deprived the system of imperialist military pacts, and above all the core of that system—the Atlantic Pact, of political cement. Many west European countries feel today threatened not because of the policy of the socialist states, but because of the expansion of American capital, because of the adventurous and aggressive policy of the United States, a policy which could draw them into conflicts which have nothing in common with the real interests of Europe. This could be seen most clearly in connection with the United States war in Vietnam.

The prospect of political and economic hegemony of the United States over a so-called united Western Europe under its baton, a Western Europe in which the first fiddle would be played by the strongest and most aggressive American partner—Federal Germany, arouses growing opposition in France and also among the leading circles and public opinion in a number of other European countries. There is a growing tendency in Western Europe to get rid of the tutelage of the United States, and at the same time a desire to establish good neighborly relations with the socialist countries.

As the policy from positions of strength was breaking down and the crisis in NATO grew, American imperialism was compelled to modify its strategy in the struggle against socialism. Not giving up by any means its preparations for a world war in the long run and continuing to intensify the arms race, the United States is counting above all on centrifugal tendencies within the socialist camp, on the deepening of the rift between the Soviet Union and China, and would like to weaken the unity and cohesion of the Warsaw Treaty member-states. These aims are to be served by the notorious policy of "building bridges to Eastern Europe," proclaimed by president Johnson three years ago, and intensified psychological warfare against the socialist countries. This policy aims at weakening the unity of the socialist camp, and above all at driving a wedge between other socialist countries and the Soviet Union—the main anti-imperialist force and barrier to the aggressive plans of imperialism.

The real objectives of the Johnson policy of "building bridges" have been commented upon with a fair dose of cynicism, by one of the well known American theoreticians of anti-communism, State Department adviser, Zbigniew Brzezinski: "Whenever a country increases the scope of its external independence from Soviet control, it should be rewarded; whenever a country appreciably liberalizes its domestic system, it should be rewarded. And similarly whenever an opposite trend develops, the United States should be prepared to discontinue its assistance, withdraw special privileges, such as the most-favored-nation clause and should not hesitate to indicate the political motivations involved." ("Alternative to Partition," New York 1965.)

While practicing this peculiar "selective coexistence," the United States would want to isolate some socialist countries from others, carry out political penetration and internal subversion by playing on both liberal-bourgeois and social-democratic tendencies, and nationalist and anti-Soviet tendencies. American imperialism would like to coexist better with some socialist states and worse with others, and to wage a "local" war against still others, in order to gain in this manner a free hand to impose *pax americana* on the rest of the world.

This United States policy in Europe is matched by the so-called new eastern policy of the German Federal Republic. The essential aims of this policy were defined long before the present Bonn coalition government came into being. "American-German cooperation," wrote in 1965 the already quoted Z. Brzezinski, "is the point of departure of the eastern policy. Essentially, the aims of the Americans and Germans are identical . . . The task of the West is to penetrate Eastern Europe and at the same time to isolate eastern Germany." (*Die Zeit,* March 19, 1965.)

Bonn's whole tactic with regard to socialist countries is, in its newest edition, calculated on weakening the position of the German Democratic Republic which, in alliance with the Soviet Union, with Poland and other socialist countries, constitutes a pillar of peace in Europe and a barrier to the implementation of the aggressive plans of imperialism.

The socialist countries of Europe, united by the Warsaw Treaty, expressed last year in the Bucharest Declaration their solitary stand with regard to this policy of American imperialism and West German militarism.

To strengthen the common anti-imperialist front, Poland and other fraternal socialist countries concluded this year treaties of friendship, cooperation and mutual assistance with the German Democratic Republic, and renewed analogous treaties concluded between themselves directly after the war and aimed at the defense of their security in face of the aggressive aspirations of the West German revanchists.

The conference of Communist and workers' parties in Karlovy Vary put forward a constructive program for the consolidation of peace and security in Europe, demonstrating the internationalist unity of the socialist forces in the East and West of Europe in the struggle against imperialism and the danger of war. The prospect of replacing the opposed military blocs in Europe by a system of collective security, based on the recognition of the existing frontiers and of the two German states, constitutes an alternative to the policy of imperialism and creates a suitable platform for common action of Communists with all peaceful, democratic and progressive forces on our continent.

While applying the tactic of "selective coexistence" with regard to the socialist countries, American imperialism continues to appear in the role of a gendarme of capitalism and reaction, clinging convulsively to the bankrupt "policy of strength." It even intensifies it through brutal intervention and

aggression against nations which want to free themselves from the yoke of exploitation and foreign colonial dependence, against the revolutionary and democratic strivings of the popular masses which could lead in one country or another to socialist transformations. In their struggle against socialism the ruling circles of the United States attach more and more importance to psychological warfare against the socialist countries, as well as against the communist and socialist movement all over the world.

The lessening of tension in Europe has by no means resulted in a weakening of the anti-communist propaganda offensive of the United States. On the contrary, the latter has even intensified its sharpness and, in a more elastic fashion, has directed it toward supporting and instigating all reactionary forces, toward conducting political subversion. The tremendous propaganda apparatus has been expanded with this aim in view. This apparatus is made up of dozens of specialized official and so-called private agencies. The most important positions among them are occupied by the United States Information Agency (USIA), the Central Intelligence Agency (CIA), as well as such institutions as the "Free Europe Committee," and also dozens of propaganda, scientific and pseudo-scientific institutions. Allies of the United States, particularly West Germany, have been drawn into the psychological warfare and subversive activities against the socialist countries.

Radio propaganda occupies a central place in the arsenal of psychological warfare. The Information Agency alone had at its disposal last year a network of 110 radio stations broadcasting in thirty-six languages for almost 900 hours weekly, of which about 200 hours of programs were broadcast to the socialist countries.

The channels of "Free Europe" and its anti-Soviet branch *Svoboda* (Liberty) are the main instruments of the psychological warfare. From the territory mainly of the German Federal Republic and with the support of anti-communist emigres from various socialist countries, they are conducting a broad radio and publishing propaganda campaign, and also activities of the intelligence and subversion type. "Free Europe" has at its disposal 32 radio stations and broadcast programs during 450 hours per week.

Owing to her importance in the camp of socialism, Poland is a particularly "privileged" target of this hostile action. In addition to "Free Europe," dozens of institutions financed by government and intelligence agencies of Western states–above all by the United States and the German Federal Republic–such as for example the "Congress for the Freedom of Culture," various anti-communist and revisionist periodicals, publications and institutes, are engaged in the organization of propaganda aimed against Poland, against socialism. This propaganda concentrates the main fire of its attack on our Party, attempts to vilify and discredit it, undermine the authority of its leaders and confidence in its policy.

Imperialist propaganda takes advantage of every error of ours and every difficulty, it utilizes every voice of opposition, even the least important incident which can be exaggerated and presented as a manifestation of struggle against our policy and the socialist system. It is constantly attacking the foundation of our security—the Polish-Soviet alliance, it attempts to feed distrust and nationalist prejudices with regard to our neighbors, to undermine the faith in the strength and dynamism of socialism, in its great mission of defending peace and the freedom of nations.

This deceptive propaganda which is resorting to any and all demagogic means advertises capitalism, attempting to fascinate our society with the consumption model of life of some of the wealthiest countries which have grown fat on colonial exploitation and taking great pains to conceal the truth about the injustices and misery, unemployment and undernourishment, to which—outside the realm of the socialist world—the tremendous majority of nations is still condemned.

The main aim of the psychological warfare is not confined to whitewashing imperialism and attacking the socialist policy. Its objective is cooperation with definite political tendencies in our country, both those which attack socialism and people's power from openly hostile and reactionary positions and those which hit out at the leading role of the Party, at socialist democracy and at our international alliances from revisionist and liberal-bourgeois or nationalist positions. Every orientation and every small group, irrespective of its political character, is good for the political subversion carried out by imperialism if only it opposes the policy of our Party.

Our Party should be fully aware of this intensified hostile activity from abroad, it should remain vigilant with regard to it and immunize our community against its influence. For there is a close connection between the ideological and political struggle against the internal foes of socialism and its external enemies.

The process of identifying with socialism the civilizational advance of Poland and the achievement of her national interests is already so advanced in social practice that the overwhelming majority of the nation consciously or instinctively understands that any questioning of the socialist system would be bound to signify the questioning of the foundations of Polish statehood.

This does not mean that the problem of transforming the consciousness of our society in a socialist spirit has been fully solved. The process of shaping social consciousness is particularly complicated in a period of transition from one social formation to another. Historical experience teaches us that, as a rule, many decades were needed in post revolutionary periods before the question of "who will win"—a question which had already been settled in favor of the working class on the field of battle for political power and social-economic relations—had found its final solution in the consciousness of the society.

Despite the fact that the overwhelming majority of the nation approves of socialism, a good deal of non-socialist, at times outright reactionary views, old habits and customs have remained in the consciousness of certain social strata. These vestiges and accumulated layers of old traditional mentality are being cultivated and exploited by hostile forces, both internal and external.

If we evaluate the present political relations in our country, in their entirety, we find that the influence of the adversaries of socialism and their own possibilities of influencing the attitude of various social strata are quite limited. They are in no position to threaten on their own the socialist system and the direction of development of our country. This does not signify, however, that we can treat lightly their activity and weaken the political struggle of the Party against them. We must always bear in mind that our political work and our struggle against the adversaries of socialism is not taking place in isolation from the rest of the world, that imperialism, using all means at its disposal, is constantly intervening on behalf of the anti-socialist forces.

Four years ago, at the 13th Plenum of the Central Committee we took up the struggle against tendencies to carry over the principles of peaceful coexistence from the sphere of relations between states with different systems to the sphere of ideology. The experience of recent years has proved beyond doubt that there is not and cannot be any peaceful coexistence in ideology, that the progressing detente between capitalist and socialist countries, the direct contacts, the growing scientific, cultural and tourist exchange, etc., that all that has not weakened in the least the struggle between the capitalist and socialist ideologies. On the contrary, it has even intensified it in a certain sense. As I said before, our class enemies as well as various centers of ideological and political subversion have intensified the pressure and aggressiveness with regard to various groups, turning the offensive in the sphere of social consciousness, "psychological warfare," into an organic part of the struggle against socialism. Those who do not perceive this and declare that political divisions have supposedly come to an end, that the new generations will not "get into the rut of this political orthodoxy and of ideological dogmas" and that, therefore, this will not be a generation of struggle, but a "generation of coexistence"—are victims of dangerous delusions.

The forces of the old world, pervaded with hatred for the new system, for the idea which it brings to mankind, will not admit defeat, will not give up any means available to them in order to stem the advance of socialism. This we know from the experiences of our times. We should closely observe the contemporary world, take from friends and also from enemies, everything that might promote the welfare and growth of the forces of our country, but we should not for a moment relax our vigilance and lose sight of the realities.

We are deeply convinced that the young generation which was born in People's Poland and is entering life in great numbers, will be spared the misfortunes and horrors of war, which we had to experience. But no one will make them a gift of this. The young generation must fight to win this great chance of lasting peace; they must fight on the front of economic, technical and scientific progress which, in the final account, determines the relation of forces between socialism and capitalism; they must fight in the sphere of ideology against anti-communism, the

952

cold war and reaction, against that which could disarm
us politically, weaken the spirit of patriotism and faith
in the socialist prospect of the country.

# STATEMENT ON THE ESTABLISHMENT OF DIPLOMATIC RELATIONS BETWEEN THE RUMANIAN SOCIALIST REPUBLIC AND THE GERMAN FEDERAL REPUBLIC

*Complete Text*
(Agerpres, 1 February 1967)

In compliance with its consistent policy of peace and of promotion of international cooperation, Rumania campaigns actively to develop relations in the economic, cultural, scientific and political-diplomatic fields with all countries, irrespective of their social systems. Intensification of cooperation based on equality, strengthening of political relations among all states, including the establishment of normal relations with both German states, is emphasized in the declaration on the strengthening of security in Europe, which was endorsed by the socialist countries participating in the Bucharest meeting of July 1966, as one of the important ways of developing cooperation among the European states. In this spirit, the Government of the Rumanian Socialist Republic has reached an agreement with the Government of the German Federal Republic on the establishment of diplomatic relations between the two countries, at embassy level.

This act, which places diplomatic relations between the two states on a normal basis, is the outcome of the evolution of their economic technical and cultural-scientific relationships. It constitutes a step forward toward development of mutual understanding and serves the interests of both sides. At the same time it serves the creation of a climate of trust and rapprochement between the European states and corresponds to the interests of insuring security and peace.

In connection with the Bundestag statement made on 1 February 1967 by Chancellor Kurt Georg Kiesinger, the Rumanian Government deems it necessary to reassert its well-known stand, according to which one of the fundamental realities imposed on Europe as a result of World War II and of the subsequent evolution of events is the existence of two German states—the GDR and the German Federal Republic. Acknowledgement of this reality is one prerequisite for the development of cooperation between the European countries and improvement of the political climate on our continent.

The Rumanian Government is convinced that the establishment of diplomatic relations between the Rumanian Socialist Republic and the German Federal Republic means a contribution to the strengthening of security on our continent, international detente, and development of conditions favoring peace.

# "THE LEADING ROLE OF THE PARTY
# IN THE STAGE OF THE COMPLETION OF BUILDING SOCIALISM"

Article by Nicolae Ceauşescu,
Secretary-General of the Rumanian Communist Party Central Committee

*Excerpts*
(*Scînteia*, 7 May 1967)

### The Rumanian Communist Party--An Active Detachment of the International Communist and Workers' Movement

As in domestic affairs, the party sets the guiding political line of state foreign policy and directs Rumania's entire activity in the world arena. The foreign policy and activity of our party proceed from the country's needs, the general interests of socialism, and the cause of world progress and peace and are based on the study and knowledge of the realities of international life.

The foreign policy of the Rumanian Communist Party focuses on fraternal friendship and cooperation with the socialist countries, on channeling efforts toward the defense and consolidation of the unity and cohesion of the socialist countries and of the international communist and workers' movement. At the same time, proceeding from the fundamental desiderata of contemporary international life, the party and state promote an active and diverse foreign policy, expand and intensify Rumania's relations with all countries regardless of social systems, and contribute to expanding interstate cooperation and strengthening confidence and friendship among peoples.

The aspiration of broad circles of public opinion for the establishment of a climate of peaceful coexistence among peoples and for the abolition of the policy of inequality between countries and interference in the affairs of other states is asserting itself evermore strikingly in the contemporary world. But the principles of national independence and sovereignty, equal rights, and noninterference in internal affairs in the international arena still meet strong opposition from the reactionary forces.

The efforts to strengthen security in Europe and the world, at eliminating the vestiges of the cold war, and at developing trust and cooperation among peoples conflict with the stubborn opposition of the imperialist circles, primarily U.S. imperialism. But these foreign policy principles, these advanced aspirations, comply with objective necessities of contemporary international life. That is why, despite resistance and opposition, they are being imposed with increasing force in interstate relationships and are gaining more and more supporters throughout the world. In fully supporting the establishment of a realistic policy in international life and actively and untiringly working to promote the principles of independence and sovereignty in the world arena, the Rumanian Communist Party and the government proceed from the principle that what is new and accords with the requirements of life develops and imposes itself, despite any obstacle.

The development of contemporary history reveals that a main characteristic of the present epoch is the continuous increase in the role of the communist and workers' parties in the revolutionary struggle of the exploited and oppressed peoples, in the implementation of the aspirations for peace, democracy, and social progress of the masses, and in the entire development of international life. This puts increased responsibilities upon communists everywhere and creates the imperative necessity for strengthening the unity and cohesion of the international communist and workers' movement, on which depend decisively the solidarity of the entire anti-imperialist front and the victory of the struggle for foiling a new war and safeguarding the peace and security of the peoples.

Ever since its beginning, the Rumanian Communist Party has carried on its activity in close connection with the fight of the entire communist and workers' movement, honorably fulfilling its role as an active detachment of the huge army of communists, and manifesting its internationalist solidarity with the international working class and progressive forces everywhere. In this context, our party devotes particular attention to steadily developing links with the communist and workers' parties.

Our party will continue to broaden and intensify comradely contacts with communist and workers' parties and with democratic and progressive organizations in the interest of strengthening relations of internationalist solidarity with all detachments of the working class and the advanced forces of the contemporary world in the interest of the cause of socialism, peace, and progress.

Life today shows that unity in the communist and workers' movement must be achieved by proceeding from the existence, as an objective factor, of a great diversity of conditions and circumstances under which communist parties are carrying on their activity, and of tasks and preoccupations which differ from country to country and from party to party. The respective communist party is the only one which can know best the concrete realities under which it is waging its fight; and that is why shaping its own political line, revolutionary tactics, and strategy is its inalienable right.

As an outcome of social development, new

problems which must be solved have emerged in the communist and workers' movement. The Rumanian Communist Party considers that discussion of these problems is an imperative necessity on which the progress of the revolutionary movement depends. The debating of all problems must be carried out in a climate of principled objectivity, without resorting to labeling and invectives. In the framework of discussions, all opinions must be heard.

Nobody can claim to have the last word on any one problem or that other views are non-Marxist. No party can claim to hold a special place, or to have certain privileges in the workers' movement. The correctness of a thesis must be proved from the point of view of principle, theory, and practice and not by invoking a certain authority.

It is the firm conviction of our party that any controversial problem arising in the communist and workers' movement must be analyzed in a comradely, constructive spirit of mutual respect between the fraternal parties, seeking and bringing to the fore the common standpoint, displaying receptiveness to the opinions of others, and allowing outstanding questions to be solved by life. This is the only correct, principled, and efficacious way of solving differences of views in compliance with the interests of unity. It is of essential importance that differences of views should not harm, in any way whatsoever, the normal links between the fraternal parties. This is even more important when relations between government parties are involved. Any discordant views between them must have no repercussion on relations between socialist countries.

Considering that direct contacts between parties and bilateral exchanges of views and of experience are of the highest importance for strengthening unity, our party also holds that multilateral meetings of communist and workers' parties and international conferences may take place, organized on the basis of consultations between the parties concerned, and observing the basic standards of interparty relationship—independence, equal rights, and noninterference in the affairs of another party.

Each communist party has the legitimate right to participate in an international meeting if it considers it necessary and useful, just as it has the legitimate right not to participate. Internationalist solidarity is not a conference. It has a much more profound content, which is manifest in the identity of cooperation and mutual assistance among them, and in the common struggle for the cause of socialism, peace, and social progress. The representatives of communist parties who uphold that nonparticipation in a conference must not affect, in any way whatsoever, the comradely relations between parties, the development of cooperation between them, the subsequent consultations, and common actions are perfectly correct.

Such an approach to the problem contributes to eliminating old practices of linking interparty relations to the acceptance or nonacceptance of a point of view and of exerting pressure in one form or another, all of which result in sharpening divergencies in the communist movement.

Life has shown that the normal development of the communist movement and the assertion of each communist party as a vanguard political force of the working class and its people are incompatible with the existence of an international coordinating center, with the practice of setting compulsory norms of conduct for the communist parties, norms which, perforce, cannot take into account the concrete conditions under which they are carrying on their activity or the tasks and targets peculiar to each party.

Almost a century ago, referring to the history of "the league of the communists," Engels pointed out:"The international movement of the European and American proletariat has now become so powerful that not only its first, narrow form—the secret league—but even its second, infinitely more embracing form—the international association of workers, a legal association—has become for it a chain. The simple sentiment of solidarity which is based on an understanding of the identity of the class situation is sufficient to unite the workers in all countries."

Furthermore, in 1943 the decision to dissolve the Third International proceeded from a realistic acknowledgement of the fact that due to the deep differences between the historic roads of development in various countries, between the character of their social order, and between the rhythm and level of their political, economic, and social development, the existence of an international leading center raises insurmountable obstacles to the activity of communist parties.

Studying the complex social realities within which they have been carrying on their activity, mobilizing the working class and the broad masses of the people to fight against exploitation and oppression for socialism, democracy, and peace, communist and workers' parties have tempered and matured politically, strengthened their organizational force, and are fulfilling better and better the lofty mission entrusted to them by history.

In the discussions with the representatives of a number of fraternal parties, the problem has been raised as to whether it is admissible for a party member, without the approval, and over the head, of the leadership, to establish relations with the representatives of another party, whom he would inform on the activity in the ranks of the party to which he belongs, and to participate in actions against the political line of his own party.

The answer to this can only be: It is inadmissible, under any form, for a party member to establish or maintain, over the head of the leadership, relations with other parties, to supply information, and to participate in actions against the political line of his party. In the light of the ideological and organizational principles of the new-type party, such acts are incompatible with the statutory obligations of a communist having the status of party member.

Proletarian internationalism requires that principled relations of cooperation and mutual assistance exist among communist and workers' parties. These relations must unfold in an organizational framework, from party to party, from leadership to leadership. An attempt by a party to establish relations with members or groups within another party outside the organized framework means an encroachment upon the principle of proletarian internationalism, an action splitting the unity of that party. Any support given by a party, regardless of the reasons submitted, to members or groups within another party signifies interference in its internal affairs, disregard of the norms which must govern the relations between communist parties, leading to weakening the unity of the party, and entailing serious consequences to the class struggle it is waging and—in the socialist countries—to the work of building socialism. Under such circumstances, each party is fully entitled to take every measure it considers necessary to insure its political and organizational unity and to implement its political line.

Under today's international conditions, when the communist and working class movement is playing an increasingly important role in the life of the peoples, the unity of each communist party is an objective necessity, on which victory in the fight for world socialism and peace depends. Proceeding from the responsibility of all parties for the world communist movement, it can be clearly seen how important is the steady growth of the fighting capacity of each contingent of the huge army of the proletariat. The unity of the world communist and workers' movement is contingent upon the unity existing within each communist and workers' party. That is why any action which weakens the political and organizational unity of a party is, at the same time, directed against the interests of the international communist and working class movement and the cause of socialism and peace throughout the world.

The Rumanian Communist Party deems that what is fundamental is what unites the communist and workers' parties, and this must prevail over any disputes and differences in views. It is the essential duty of each party not to undertake anything which might aggravate the divergencies in the communist and workers' movement, which might further deepen the abyss of division. Any constructive action of a nature contributing to the restoration of the principled climate in the communist movement, to the establishment of normal relations between parties, and to the normalization of relations within the socialist system would be hailed with deep satisfaction by communists in all countries and by progressive forces everywhere.

Henceforth, our party shall spare no effort to contribute to strengthening the unity of the socialist countries and the communist and workers' parties, and it shall do everything in its power, everything which depends on it, to contribute to the cohesion of the international communist movement and of all forces of the great world front in the fight for socialism, for peace and social progress.

## Raising To an Ever Higher Level the Party's Role of Leading Force of the Nation

The new phase, which the process of accomplishing the socialist construction in Rumania has entered, increases even more the responsibilities of the Communist Party. The party is becoming more and more organically integrated with the country's whole social life and is strengthening even more its ties with the broad masses of the people. The increasingly intensive attraction of citizens to the discussion and the working out of the important decisions and measures concerning the country's domestic and international policy contributes to the constant strengthening of the unity between the party and the people. In the process of accomplishing the socialist construction and perfecting socialist democracy there is an ever stronger affirmation of the party's role of leader of our society's whole life, and of its nature of principal force of socialist democracy.

This fundamental principle of our system must be embodied by reality, by the concrete forms of work and activity of the Communist Party. From its capacity as government party of socialist Rumania, from the Rumanian Communist Party's role of leading force of society—written in the country's constitution—derive a number of consequences which receive concrete form in the whole social life. This basic attribute imposes on our party a great responsibility for everything being done in the country, for everything that the Rumanian people's future makes incumbent, and requires it to adopt all the necessary political-organizational measures which are necessary for the implementation of its program adopted by the whole nation.

The question arises: How will the role and the attributes of the Rumanian Communist Party evolve in the perspective of the development of socialist society and the transition to communism? Will the accomplishing of socialist society and the creation of conditions for the construction of communism lead to a decrease or to an increase in the party's leading role in society? Experience to date in social development demonstrates that increasing the party's role in the process of forging the new system is a mandatory requirement, an objective law.

There is no doubt that the party's role as the motive force of the entire social development is increasing in direct proportion with the perfecting of the socialist production relations, with the gradual elimination of the essential differences involving workers, peasants, and intellectuals, the merging of the social classes, the strengthening of the unity of all the members of society, and the creation of a unique society of working people. The party has the task of conscientiously leading and directing this ample social process, of insuring uninterrupted progress on the road of forging a communist society. In these conditions there is a constant broadening of the party's ranks with the most advanced members of society, there is an increase in and a perfecting of the forms of collaboration of the party with the broad masses of the people, there is public discussion of its political line and of the program of economic and cultural construction, of making society flourish comprehensively.

The party's existence is becoming more and more closely and more organically interwoven with the life of all the citizens of the homeland. From the party emanate the advanced ideas and the plans which envisage the constant improvement of the people's life and the enriching of their material and spiritual life. The citizens go to the party with their joys and their troubles, they confer with the party when they do something decisive for their life. All that is more creative and valuable, more advanced and daring in society relies on the party and from its strength draws strength and energy. Through its members—workers, peasants, intellectuals of all categories, and leadership cadres in the economy—the party speaks out in absolutely all realms of material and spiritual life in the most competent and authoritative way, and is acting directly in every sector of activity.

An objective necessity in the current phase is for socialist law to mirror the new structure of socialist reality in our country and strikingly show the leading role—inscribed in the constitution, the country's fundamental law—which the Communist Party has in socialist society. Historic experience shows that in all societies the laws have crystallized on the basis of social practice, through a system of norms aimed at protecting the respective production relations and social system. The norms of law in our country must correspond better with the requirements of today's reality, with the interests of defending the basic values of socialism, with the development of public property, and with the constant strengthening of the socialist system, and at the same time must insure the unhampered exercise of civic rights and freedoms.

The constant growth of the party's leadership role in society requires adoption of appropriate organizational forms in the relations between the party and state organs, insuring the merging of the effort of all the collectives and cadres in responsible posts in every sector for the implementation of the party's political line and of the decisions of the party and the state, and the adoption of efficient means of control and of forms of clear-cut responsibility in the whole public and communal life.

Nothing within the sphere of our people's life and work must be alien to the party organs. They have the task of working out solutions for the country's economic and social development, of carrying out intensive organizational work—mobilizing the efforts of all the creative forces of the people—for the implementation of the policy of building socialism, and of exercising guidance and control in all the fields of activity. Party organs must not, however, supersede other social organs; they must not do the work which is the province of other collectives or persons, thus absolving them of their responsibilities. It still happens sometimes that in practice there is a waste of parallel forces for the achievement of life tasks. The effect of this state of affairs is the diminution of the responsibility of certain cadres in the sectors with which they are dealing: the adoption of a waiting attitude because they expect the solution of the problems by the party organs. We must eliminate the phenomenon of parallelism so that every party and state aktivist may be directly responsible for the implementation of the tasks entrusted to him personally.

Perfecting the socialist production relations and the development of society leads to an increase in the role of the mass and public organizations and, as such, makes necessary the crystallization and ever more clear-cut regulating of their activity and terms of reference in accordance with the requirements of the new society. The more and more effective manifestation of the mass and public organizations in social life depends on the improvement and the diversification of their forms and methods of work, on increasing their functions and responsibility.

In the same order of ideas it is worth stressing the ever greater role of the creative unions in stimulating and orienting cultural-artistic life so that the message of ideas transmitted by socialist art may correspond with the Rumanian people's aspirations and the ideals of socialist society—ideals of happiness, prosperity, and well-being for all. History shows that everything which has remained lasting and great in the heritage of national and universal culture bears the message of a humanist philosophy and was inspired by the problems of social existence. Socialist humanism, the militant philosophy of our epoch, is fostering confidence in man's ability to carve for himself a better fate, in his ability to improve himself, in his noble sentiments and virtues, and in the victory of the struggle for the happiness of mankind. Creating works imbued with this bright philosophy, the always present artistic talents of the Rumanian people undoubtedly will be able to create a new brilliant era in the history of our national culture.

The analysis of the requirements of social life shows that, to the extent of accomplishing socialism and going over toward communism, the party's role not only does not gradually weaken and disappear of its own accord but, on the contrary constantly increases. Naturally, the party's activity and its organizational forms change constantly in accordance with the new phase and the new political tasks.

The gradual achievement of the objectives of the program established by the Ninth Congress require the Rumanian Communist Party to directly lead activity in every sector of society and to exercise the responsibility entrusted to it by the people also in the economy, foreign policy, and culture and art.

Its great responsibilities in its capacity of leading force of society require that the party insure the gradual raising of the broadest masses to the level of social consciousness and responsibility of its members and carry out activity which will lead to transforming every citizen into an active militant for society's progress, for the homeland's prosperity. The process of the party's disappearance which will be achieved in the complete communist society mandatorily passes through its strengthening and development to the utmost degree of its role of leader in society. This process is closely linked with the ideological improvement of all the citizens, with the final merging from the conscience point of view of the nonparty members with the party members. This will be tantamount to a qualitative leap in the development of society.

I have referred to some aspects of the most important problem of our party's life and activity—the increase in its role of leader in society during the period of accomplishing the construction of socialism.

The Rumanian Communist Party has received the people's unanimous mandate to lead the country's destiny. For almost half a century since its creation our party has affirmed itself as the most faithful exponent of the aspirations of the Rumanian people as the only social force able to bring to life the centuries-old dreams of our predecessors and to achieve the bright future ardently wished for Rumania and for which whole generations have fought. During the years of socialist construction, the policy of the party, whose gigantic transforming force has been fully verified, has become the policy of all the working strata of society.

Life imposes as an imperative necessity the thorough studying of all the new phenomena which appear in the process of the social development of our homeland in order to find in all circumstances the most appropriate answers and solutions in order to insure the uninterrupted perfecting of the party's activity, of all its organs and organizations, of all society.

Only in this way are we going to achieve the constant triumph of the noble principles of our party's policy, make our socialist democracy develop and flourish, and make the blessings of socialist civilization and humanism penetrate more and more deeply in the whole life of society, in the existence of all the working people.

Successfully fulfilling the historic mission which it has assumed before the Rumanian people, and constantly enriching its experience as leader of socialist society, the Rumanian Communist Party at the same time is making its contribution to the development of the Marxist-Leninist teachings, of revolutionary theory and practice. Conscious of its high responsibility, our party is constantly perfecting the ways in which it is exercising its role of leader in socialist society and in the Rumanian people's struggle to accomplish the building of socialism and the general transition to communism.

Our party is followed by the whole nation with endless love and confidence and is recognized by all the working people as the tested leader of Rumania's destiny. The duty of all the communists, of our whole party, is to stint nothing for society's progress, for the prosperity and the greatness of our beloved homeland, socialist Rumania.

# RESOLUTION OF THE NATIONAL CONFERENCE
## OF THE RUMANIAN COMMUNIST PARTY

*Complete Text*
(Agerpres, 9 December 1967)

Between 6 and 8 December 1967, the National Conference of the Rumanian Communist Party discussed the measures on the perfecting of the management and planning of the national economy and improvement of Rumania's administrative-territorial organization. The Conference noted that in the period that has elapsed since the Ninth Congress of the Rumanian Communist Party, big successes were obtained in all domains of social activity in our homeland - which are the outcome of the enthusiastic, heroic work of the entire people, of the consistent implementation by the broad mass of the people of the Marxist-Leninist policy of the Party which, united and strong, ably and consistently directs the destinies of socialist Rumania. The Conference expresses its full adherence to the work carried on by the Central Committee in the conduct of socialist construction, and to the measures adopted in the course of these years.

The National Conference of the Rumanian Communist Party fully approves the report delivered by Nicolae Ceausescu, General Secretary of the Central Committee of the Rumanian Communist Party, and the principles and measures contained in this report, which are a synthetisation of experience in the direction of the construction of socialism in Rumania, a creative materialisation of the directives of the Ninth Congress.

The conference endorses the directives on the perfecting of management and planning of the national economy conducive to the enhancement of the role of the economic-financial factors in the entire economy, to the liquidation of the phenomena of excessive centralism, to the widening of autonomy, to the increase of the powers and competence of the production units in the planning, organization and running of economic activity, to the better use of the internal resources of the enterprises and of all branches of the national economy, to the development of the creative initiative of the working people's collectives.

The National Conference approves the principles of improvement in Rumania's administrative-territorial organization and the development of rural localities, on account of which enhancement will be ensured of the role and attributions of the towns and communes—the basic units of the entire economic, political and social-cultural activities of the citizens—and counties will be created; the efficiency of the local bodies' activity will increase and their initiative will rise; and the central leadership will be more closely linked to the basic echelons of State administration. This will ensure a favourable setting for the rational distribution of the productive forces

for the rational distribution of the productive forces on the country's territory, for the harmonious economic and social-cultural development of all areas, and will contribute to the faster penetration of the elements of modern civilization to the countryside, the acceleration of the process of the gradual coming closer [together] of village life and town life—one of the main conditions of building communist society.

The conference approves the measures for bettering the methods of organization and conduct of social life, of improving the work of the Party and State bodies, of eliminating duplications and overlappings in their activities, in compliance with the growing leading role of the Party in society; measures which have regard to the intensified participation of the mass organizations in the running of State affairs, to the steady growth and strengthening of our socialist democracy.

The National Conference considers that all these measures fully conform with the present stage of economic and social development of our country, with the requirements of the rapid advance along the road of completing socialist construction, of the progress and prosperity of Rumania, of raising the living standards of the mass of the people—the basic aim of the entire policy of the Rumanian Communist Party. Their translation into reality will determine a further powerful increase in the country's productive forces, in the development of the technico-material base of the socialist society, will contribute to the perfecting of the social relations of production, to the increase of economic efficiency, to an even greater encouragement of creative initiative and the participation of the mass of the people in running State affairs.

The National Conference empowers the Central Committee to take all requisite economic, political and social measures for the carrying out of the decisions adopted, for the perfecting of the Party and State apparatus and the entire machinery of our system, for raising the development of the socialist society in our homeland to a higher level. Furthermore, the Conference entrusts the Central Committee with the mandate of applying in Party work the measures emanating from the administrative-territorial reorganization, and the necessary changes in the Party rules are to be submitted to a future congress.

The National Conference assesses highly the international activity carried on by the Party and State leadership, and Rumania's foreign policy which was focused and continues to be focused on friendship, alliance and co-operation with all socialist countries, on striving for the steady strengthening of the forces and cohesion of the world socialist system, of the solidarity of the international communist and working-class movement, of the unity of the entire anti-imperialist front. The National Conference considers that the efforts made by our country for the development of all-round collaboration and co-operation with all States, irrespective of their social systems, is a contribution to an international detente, to the cause of democracy and social progress. The Conference assesses [that it is] a high duty of our Party and State to manifest themselves in the future, too, as active factors in the struggle for the triumph of the ideas of socialism, for the strengthening of the revolutionary and progressive forces, for the cause of freedom and national independence of the peoples, against the aggressive actions of imperialism and reaction, for international understanding and co-operation, for peace and security in the world.

Confident as it is that the measures endorsed open up wide prospects of creative work, of successes and satisfaction for the entire people, the National Conference of the Rumanian Communist Party calls upon the broad mass of workers, peasants and intellectuals, all laboring folk, regardless of nationality, to put their entire energy and working capacity, talent and knowledge at the service of the implementation of this inspiring programme of economic and social construction, on which depend the raising of our homeland to even higher summits of civilization and well-being, the steady flowering of our nation, of the Socialist Republic of Rumania, the increase of its contribution to the cause of socialism and peace in the world.

# POLITICAL STATEMENT BY THE EXECUTIVE COMMITTEE, CP OF SPAIN

*Complete Text*
*(Information Bulletin,* No. 102, 1967)

These past months have been months of great tension. The ultras were still noisily celebrating the outcome of the referendum when workers and students, backed by large sections of the nation, launched mass actions greater in scale and militancy than had ever been seen under the Franco regime. The events in Madrid on January 27, in Asturias on February 1, in Barcelona on February 17, and the nationwide strike of students were the highlights of these actions, which at some moments drew 400,000 workers and students.

The Franco regime, far from clearing the horizon through its "Operation Referendum," is up against an even more critical political and economic situation.

In the streets and at various public meetings, the most diverse segments of Spanish society say no to the dictatorship and demand freedom. This is undeniable rejection of the results of the December 14 farce.

The international position of the regime shows no improvement. The dirty water of the referendum was not the best for washing off the stigma of fascism that still makes negotiations with the Common Market difficult. The obstacles to normal relations with the socialist countries persist. Owing to its regime, Spain remains the "poor relative" in the international community.

## Ultras and "Evolutionists"

The contradictions between the ruling groups have increased since the referendum. Even in the government there are increasingly sharp clashes between the ultras (Alonso Vega, Solis and Fraga, with Franco at their head), on the one hand, and the partisans of an "evolutionary" policy, of a certain loosening, who regard the present fascist structure as harmful, on the other. Their differences find vivid expression in the press.

Measures of a fascist nature follow one another: virtual repeal of the press law through the reform of the criminal code; the decision to refer to military courts cases of participation in the movement of workers and students; persecution of the Workers' Committees and their leaders, of students, professors and intellectuals; the confiscation and suspension of newspapers; mounting pressure on foreign press representatives; amendments restricting the draft law on freedom of conscience; and to top it all, there are the drafts of a new electoral law and a law on the Movement. The latter draft has given rise to heated argument because it is intended to maintain the political monopoly of the General Secretariat of the Falange while virtually denying every opportunity to other groups still moving in the orbit of the regime.

The new onset of the ultras is no longer directed against the labor and democratic opposition alone but affects the "evolutionists" as well. The regime is beginning to devour itself.

At bottom, the reason for the ultras' attempt to fall back on a tough policy is that their positions have been shaken so badly that another retreat could result in their being forced out altogether.

On the one hand, the labor and democratic movement has already achieved such a degree of unity, organization and militancy that the ultras are finding it more and more difficult to stay in power. On the other hand, the hegemony of the ultra team in the ruling set-up no longer meets the interests of the big bourgeoisie to the full and is losing support among the middle bourgeoisie.

At a time when Spain is apparently heading for an economic crisis—in a capitalist Europe in which the signs of a recession are multiplying—and when the miscarriage of the regime's economic policy is evident, the continuation of the dictatorship, the nefarious policies and repressive measures of the ultras will undoubtedly lead to an aggravation of political and social tensions. The immediate task is to foil the attempt at returning to fascist forms of repression and at the same time demand an amnesty for all political prisoners and exiles. To remove the ultras and the Movement bureaucrats from key government posts is a national necessity today. Most sections of society would welcome this.

Workers, students and intellectuals show the way—strikes, collective protests, meetings, street demonstrations and collective documents are the best reply to rabid fascists. Recent weeks have been eventful in this sense. The firmness and calm displayed by the foremost participants in the labor and popular movement, the prompt and vigorous reply to each repressive measure, and the participation in the protest movement of men and women belonging to every segment of society and every trend suggest that the ultras have been unable to attain their aim—intimidation—and that the situation is favorable for pushing back the ultras and for promoting the democratic movement.

Resistance to repressions becomes stronger when closely linked with economic, social, cultural and political demands. There will be no setback if each segment of the population bears this in mind and acts accordingly. To this end it is advisable to strengthen and extend the unity of the mass movement while respecting their democratic and autonomous development.

The mass movement will never return to the catacombs.

The new working-class movement must not cede any of the legal positions it has won. Firm resistance, accompanied by counterattacks at various levels and posing the real and urgent problems of the working people should be the answer to the bosses of the vertical unions who are trying to oust the genuine representatives of the workers from these positions. It is these bosses from the "command" that must vacate the posts to which they were never elected.

The fight for trade union freedom, against the attempts of Solis and his men to draft a law maintaining the monopoly rights of the vertical union bosses, provides a broad basis for agreement and opens the prospect of bringing the mass of the working people into the movement. The working people are already tackling the decisive problem of forming new trade unions of their own. By pushing on along these lines we will defeat the vertical union bosses and arrive through union meetings and congresses at creating a great trade union federation—a unitary, independent and democratic class federation.

### Resist Layoffs, Uphold the Working People's Demands

The working class, which had to pay the bill of the stabilization plan and the imbalances caused by neo-autarchic and inflationist growth, is now threatened with the effects of the current recession and the economic crisis the latter heralds. Layoffs are beginning, and unless they are vigorously resisted they will assume dangerous proportions. Overtime is being abolished and workers' incomes are dwindling. There are more and more signs of crisis. The industrialists of Biscaya want the working day reduced by half for six months. Some employers have sent their workers on the annual holiday earlier than usual. In Asturias pits are closing and the miners are fired. "Concerted action" is beginning to tell on steel workers and miners. The government has ordered the enterprises to reject every demand of the working people.

At a time when the high cost of living has considerable reduced real wages, which were inadequate as it was, the workers are denied what they most legitimately demand—a minimum wage of 250 pesetas a day and a sliding wage scale. The employers' offensive is complemented by repressions by the government and the vertical union bosses against prominent labor leaders. This offensive is aimed at making it impossible for the workers to defend themselves, and so compelling them to swallow the effects of the crisis and the regime's harmful policy.

But the working people's reply is far more resolute than on previous occasions. Strikes, demonstrations and other forms of protest have mobilized hundreds of thousands of workers for simultaneous action. Such struggles as that of the workers discharged from the Laminacion de Bandas in Frio plants in Echevarri or that of the eleven miners who shut themselves up in the depths of the Llamas pit shook the whole country.

Proletarian solidarity is resurging with tremendous force. In some cases action ended in important partial gains.

### New Level of the Labor Movement

The struggles today are characterized by organization and unity. They show that the working people are able to provide themselves with effective leadership. The Workers' Committees, combining underground activity with utilization of the opportunities afforded by the elective posts in the vertical unions, have set up a complex system of highly efficient organizations.

The facts give the lie to the smear misrepresenting the new working-class movement, whose activity it viciously describes as "collusion" or "conspiracy." How can anyone speak of "conspiracy" when it is a question of struggles carried on in broad daylight and mobilizing the masses in various cities, struggles that have assumed national dimensions?

The new working-class movement and its leaders have no intention of withdrawing underground or into secrecy. They are convinced that by acting openly they are exercising a right, even though the Establishment refuses to recognize it. Theirs is a noble and lofty cause. Far from injuring the country, this cause serves it.

We Communists are not, nor do we claim to be, the only ones who are active within the labor and democratic movement. Also active in it are numerous Catholics and people of socialist and syndicalist leanings, as well as others who have not yet opted for any party or political trend but are aware of their rights and ready to wrest them.

In noting the vast participation of Catholics in the labor and democratic movement, which brings them reprimands and sanctions from the integralist Church leadership trying to continue taking advantage of the people's religious sentiments for their own reactionary political purposes, we reaffirm our desire for an end to the sectarianism and dogmatism of the past, on the basis of respect for one another's convictions. The growing cooperation of Communists and Catholics, who courageously protest against the present state of affairs and strive to change it, is a most encouraging aspect of the situation. We declare most emphatically that we want to march with the Catholics (and other forces) against the dictatorship, toward political and social democracy, toward socialism.

### Alliance of the Forces of Labor and Culture

A characteristic of the present situation is the numerous links that are naturally becoming established between the various movements and tend to develop into a single front of action.

The Spanish countryside is the scene of struggles involving both the rural proletariat and the peasants. These struggles have met with sympathy and solidarity among the mass of the population. Peasants in some areas already resort to strikes and demonstrations after the example of the working class. But these early struggles, while important, reflect no more than a tiny part of the peasants' enormous discontent. Besides, account must be taken, in the case of agricultural workers, of the grave problem of seasonal unemployment.

All this shows that solution of the problems of the countryside must be regarded as an urgent national task. We need a deep-going agrarian reform on the principle "the land for those who till it," a reform socially eliminating the non-productive and parasitic class of big landowners and making it possible to effect the technological and economic changes agriculture needs. If faced with the mass action extending to the countryside, the regime would be virtually powerless.

The students' campaign for their rights, for a university reform and for democracy is gaining in scale and strength. To all intents and purposes, there already exists a democratic student union in different phases of organization.

Today the Spanish university is, despite its class character, a stronghold of democratic national consciousness and a bulwark of progress due to the action of students and part of the academic staff. There are fundamental points of agreement between the struggle of the university and the new labor movement.

Spanish intellectuals, for their part, have shown great civic courage by supporting the workers' action. The free professions, too, take actions of vast importance, including actions by doctors, lawyers and teachers, and the democratic organization of technologists.

The Workers' Committees, the peasant opposition, the democratic student union, the various associations of intellectuals and professional people, the youth and women's movements, and progressive Catholic groups are all establishing links among themselves that are informal at times but effective nevertheless. We are advancing to more and more conscious and explicit coordination. A broad alliance of the forces of labor and culture is in the making.

Without trying to anticipate the forms that it may eventually take, we note that this alliance, led by the working class, already is a real and growing force opposing the fascist political order. These links and this extensive coordination in the course of the most diverse partial actions are bringing near the prospect of a great civic demonstration against the dictatorship, of what we call a national strike.

In the future, the alliance of the forces of labor and culture will become the foundation of Spanish democracy.

## The Option

In view of the present dilemma—reactionary fascist dictatorship or democracy—the ultras' offensive is confronting the "evolutionists" with an option: remaining powerless and ridiculed hostages of the ultra group who must share with it the responsibility for isolating and discrediting Spain internationally, or fighting against this group undeterred by the possibility of their attitude coinciding with that of the opposition. The facts indicate that under the present regime there is no third, liberal way. Freedom is indivisible in the face of the ultras: either there will be freedom for all, or everyone will remain at the mercy of the ultras, to be treated as the ultras please.

The Communist Party considers that all opposition forces and all "evolutionists" should promptly meet at the conference table to discuss ways and means of solving the political problem of Spain without recourse to violence and civil war.

The fundamental thing today is to introduce democratic freedoms for all Spaniards. We Communists are willing to cooperate, even without participating in it, with a transitional government that would implement, loyally and without reservations, the program set out in the recent document signed by 565 intellectuals of the most diverse ideological trends. The program provides for the following:

—releasing all prisoners and reinstating them—as well as all victims of repressions—at their work places or educational establishments;

—higher wages and salaries, and a sliding wage scale;

—freedom of trade unions, and the right to strike;

—freedom of assembly and speech;

—political freedoms;

—an amnesty for political prisoners and exile

Another outstanding issue is the travesty of elections which the government is preparing with a view to introducing so-called family representation in the Cortes. We call on all opposition forces, on all who are against the policy of the ultras, to reach agreement and to act by abstaining from the vote. It is urgent that an end at all costs be put to the sad picture presented by Spain under Franco, Alonso Vega, Solis and Fraga.

We, for our part, will continue to appeal to the workers, peasants, students and intellectuals—to the whole people—to combat the present situation with increasing energy, to come out into the streets and demonstrate their resolve to end the dictatorship.

# STATEMENT BY THE POLITICAL BUREAU
# OF THE CENTRAL COMMITTEE, SYRIAN CP

*Abridged Text*
*(Information Bulletin,* No. 102, 1967)

As a result of the barbarous aggression committed by Israel against the UAR, Syria and Jordan, a portion of Arab territory finds itself in the hands of the invaders, and the situation in the Middle East and the rest of the world has sharply deteriorated.

In this period of stress for the Arab nation, the progressive forces of the world have been rendering great support to our people. The Soviet Union is in the van of these forces. Being the closest and most loyal friend of the Arabs, it exerted tremendous efforts for an end to the aggression. When the aggression was launched the Soviet Union did all in its power to stop it. It took the initiative of convening in Moscow a conference of the leaders of the Communist and Workers' parties and the heads of government of socialist countries which adopted a statement demanding the immediate discontinuance of the aggression in the Middle East and the restoration to the Arabs of the areas taken away from them. There were also other steps taken in defense of the Arab countries.

It is not mere chance, therefore, that the imperialists are trying to deal their main blow at Soviet-Arab friendship, tested in action and consolidated in the course of grim trials.

The official propaganda conducted by Peking against the Soviet Union in this situation, which is so hazardous for peace, helped rabid imperialists headed by the United States to carry out their nefarious designs.

Friendship and close unity with the Soviet Union and other socialist countries is the most powerful weapon of the Arab people against the reactionary forces and imperialist conspiracies. It is in the best interest of the Arabs to maintain and further this friendship. It alone will help them eliminate the effects of the Israeli aggression and overcome their present difficulties.

The Middle East today is an arena where two opposed political forces are locked in bitter conflict. On one side are the forces of imperialism and reaction, trying to put down the national-liberation movement and to halt progress in the Arab countries, and on the other, the progressive forces striving to bring about complete national emancipation of every people, reliably consolidate their freedom and independence and do away with their age-long backwardness.

The Arab peoples must strengthen the bonds of friendship with the forces of progress foremost among which is the Soviet Union. They must seek complete unity of the progressive forces in each country and throughout the Arab world. This is the sacred duty of every Arab who wants to follow the road of freedom and progress.

# SPEECH BY LEONID I. BREZHNEV IN GORKY ON 13 JANUARY 1967

*Excerpts*
*(Pravda, 14 January 1967)*

The complexity of international life and the rapid development of events in the international scene make it imperative for us to devote constant and unflagging attention to foreign policy questions. Recently, as you know, the question of the international policy of the USSR and the struggle of our Party for cohesion of the world communist movement was discussed at a Plenary Meeting of the Central Committee.

The Plenary Meeting noted the further consolidation of the international positions of the Soviet Union. It reaffirmed the determination of our Party and the Soviet Government to continue to follow the foreign policy set forth in the decisions of the 23rd CPSU Congress. Our policy has been and will remain that of strengthening the might and unity of the world socialist system, of active support for the liberation movement of peoples, of uniting all revolutionary and progressive forces in the struggle against imperialism and reaction, for peace and international security.

The most burning problem of world politics today is that of Vietnam. You know, comrades, from press and radio reports and from the Soviet Government's statement about the new criminal acts of American imperialism in Vietnam. American planes recently made a number of raids on the capital of the Democratic Republic of Vietnam, bombing Hanoi's residential districts. Words fail to express in full measure the indignation felt over this new act of aggression.

Washington politicians spared no effort to convince world public opinion of their "love of peace" and their readiness to sit down at a conference table. Now they have shown their real face once again. Who will believe the calls for peace if these calls are accompanied by provocative actions which aggravate the situation and create new obstacles in the way to the settlement of the conflict.

The Americans have amassed an enormous number of troops and military equipment in Vietnam. The forces of the United States, its satellites and Saigon puppets in Vietnam now exceed 1,170,000. But even the American generals admit that they see no prospects in the venture they started. The actions of the American imperialists in Vietnam are, probably, the most disgraceful page in the history of the United States, a page which all honest Americans are ashamed of.

We are firmly convinced that the Vietnamese people who have the sympathy of all progressive mankind, will win in their just struggle for the independence of their country. Whatever difficulties may have to be overcome on the way to this victory, resistance to American aggression will go down in the annals of the peoples' struggle for freedom and social progress as an example of valor and heroism.

In its decision the Plenary Meeting of the CPSU Central Committee fully endorsed the policy of the Party and the Soviet government on the Vietnamese question, and stressed the need for continued support and aid to the heroic Vietnamese people in their struggle against American imperialist aggression.

In a situation when imperialism is organizing dangerous provocations against the forces of peace and democracy, the consolidation of the world system of socialism, the cohesion of fraternal countries and their united action on the international scene acquire particular importance.

Our Land of Soviets has reliable allies and loyal friends. We spare no effort to consolidate our cooperation with the fraternal countries of socialism, our unity in the struggle for our common aims and against our common enemy.

The Warsaw and Bucharest meetings of the Political Consultative Committee of the Warsaw Treaty member-states marked an important stage in the joint struggle of the socialist countries for peace and against the imperialist policy of aggression and war. As you know, these meetings gave much attention to the questions of European security. And this is quite understandable. Big military forces of two worlds—socialism and imperialism—confront each other in Europe. It is in Europe that the revanchist circles of West Germany are growing more and more active. The West-European place d'armes holds a central place in American imperialism's strategic plans.

In Bucharest, the socialist states put forward a comprehensive program of a European settlement on a democratic and peaceful basis: from recognition of the immutability of the existing frontiers to the establishment in Europe of conditions of trust and cooperation of all states, big and small, on the basis of equality. This program is contributing to the activization of the European peoples' struggle for a peaceful future of their continent.

The beginnings of a new approach to European problems are now evident almost everywhere in Europe. These new tendencies are particularly evident in the improved relations between France and the Soviet Union. Our cooperation with that country is developing in many areas to the mutual advantage of both France and the Soviet Union. We value the relations that are developing between us and France, and for our part shall do everything possible to further and deepen them.

Of great importance are our relations with Italy, in the development of which favorable trends have been observed of late. We can also say with satisfaction that good relations are being established between us and several other European states.

Of course, there are quite a few obstacles on the road to guaranteeing the European peoples' security The question of the danger of West German revanchism is still very acute.

The development of the situation in Europe, and throughout the world, is obviously unfavorable for the designs of West German militarists and revanchists. Their policy is going through a deep crisis, an expression of which is the recent change of leaders in the Bonn Government.

The new government has already made public its program. What can be said about this program? First of all, it contains ample evidence that the goals of West German imperialism unfortunately remain unchanged. We hear again the FRG's claims to represent "the whole of Germany." This means a continued policy of "non-recognition" of the GDR, which in effect is a policy of absorbing this socialist state. Again Bonn lays claim to West Berlin, although the latter has no relation to the FRG. As before, the FRG Government maintains a dangerous stand on the question of the post-war frontiers in Europe, the frontier between the FRG and the GDR included. Nor has the FRG Government abandoned its ambitions to gain access to nuclear weapons.

True, the new government of the FRG speaks of its desire to contribute to a relaxation of tension in Europe. Chancellor Kiesinger said, specifically, that his government would "strive to promote mutual understanding and trust" between the FRG and the Soviet Union in order to "create prerequisites for future successful meetings and talks." But so far these are mere words. And these words, by the way, conflict with other statements in the program of the new government of the FRG.

Naturally, we shall support everything that is sensible and useful for peace in Europe, including appropriate steps by the FRG, should such steps be taken. But we will not for a moment relax our struggle to bar completely to West German imperialism any access to nuclear weapons, without which it is difficult to think of the problem of peace in Europe. Together with our allies, with all peace-loving forces we shall defend with all our might the frontiers that took shape in Europe after World War II. And he who would like to violate these frontiers will get a most crushing and final rebuff.

The Soviet Union is firmly convinced that unconditional recognition of the German Democratic Republic as a sovereign independent state is in our time one of the basic prerequisites for real normalization of the situation in Europe. No one can shake our friendship with the German Democratic Republic, our solid alliance with it. The establishment of the GDR is a great achievement of the German working people and of all peace forces in Europe in general.

Needless to say, the question of a European security system is worrying not only the peoples of this continent. A stable peace in Europe would make an important contribution to the prevention of another war, to the cause of peace throughout the world.

Way back at the dawn of Soviet power Vladimir Lenin said: "We have an international alliance, an alliance which has nowhere been registered, which has never been given formal embodiment, which from the point of view of 'constitutional law' means nothing, but which, in the disintegrating capitalist world, actually means everything" (Coll. Works, vol. 40, p. 243, Russ. Ed.). This is what Lenin said about our alliance with the working class the world over. The international working class, the peoples fighting for their liberation are now acting in close alliance with the world socialist system. This is a wonderful proof of the justice of Lenin's words. Militant cohesion of the revolutionary forces is the best guarantee that working mankind will overcome imperialism and reaction and emerge on the wide road of progress and freedom.

This year, Communists and progressives throughout the world will celebrate with us the 50th anniversary of the Great October Revolution. They rightly regard this date as not only the national holiday of the Soviet people but also as a big holiday of the working class of the whole world, of all the revolutionary forces, all progressive mankind.

If in the world there are now not one but 14 socialist countries with a population exceeding one third of mankind, this is the result of social development started by the October Revolution. If in place of the former colonial empires over 70 independent states have come into existence in the world, this is, in the final count, also the result of the influence of world socialism. If the working class in the capitalist countries has succeeded in gaining solid positions and the communist movement has developed into the biggest political force of our time, this achievement can also be traced to the October days of 1917.

For 50 years the communist movement has been developing under the invincible banner of the ideas of the October Revolution. It is quite understandable, therefore, that while marking this momentous anniversary the fraternal Parties review the results of the path they have covered, sum up the gigantic experience they have accumulated in the revolutionary struggle. Communists the world over have something to be proud of and they are confidently looking to the future. They have a collectively elaborated and truly Leninist program of struggle for the vital interests of the working class.

The communist movement, and the revolutionary movement as a whole could have scored much greater successes if not for the splitting, disorganizing activities of the present leadership of the Communist Party of China.

The decisions of the Eleventh Plenary Meeting of the CPC Central Committee and the political campaign that is going on in China in the guise of the "great cultural revolution" show that the great-power, anti-Soviet policy of Mao Tse-tung and his group has entered a new dangerous phase. This policy is directed not only against the Soviet Union, our Party and the people. The splitting policy of the Chinese leaders is harming the unity and cohesion of all Communist and Workers' Parties. It is damaging the interests of fighting Vietnam, preventing, as it does, the establishment of a united anti-imperialist front. One cannot but see how damaging the present course of Mao Tse-tung and his group is to the interests of the Chinese people themselves—the workers, the peasants, the intellectuals—what a blow it is to the Communist Party of China. It is a big tragedy for all real Communists in China, and we express our deep sympathy to them.

The Communist Party of the Soviet Union will continue to follow unswervingly the course of friendship and internationalist solidarity with the Communist Party of China, with the People's Republic of China. By exposing the ideology and policy of the present Peking leaders which have nothing in common with Marxism-Leninism, we are struggling not against the CPC, not against China, but for the Communist Party of China, for bringing it back to the road of internationalism, for its unity with all fraternal Parties on the principled basis of Marxism-Leninism, on the general line of the communist movement.

The striving for united action in defense of common goals, for stronger cohesion is, probably, the most characteristic feature of the communist movement in our days. In the present situation the Communists of the world face quite a few problems which have to be considered and solved jointly. These problems are connected with the process of the development of the world system of socialism and with the new phenomena in the international working class movement, in the national-liberation struggle of peoples and, of course, with the aggressive policy of the imperialists.

Of late, many fraternal Parties have pointed out with ever growing insistence that the conditions are ripe for a new international meeting of Communists. Most of the Parties have already expressed themselves in favor of such a meeting. Our Party supports this idea. Naturally, such a meeting must be preceded by intensive preparatory work, broad consultations and creative discussions of the pressing problems of our time.

We all know that a principled Marxist-Leninist line and a firm and flexible foreign policy are needed to protect the interests of our country in the international arena, the interests of world socialism and peace. These are questions to which the Central Committee and the Soviet Government are giving much attention.

The main source of our strength and international prestige is the economic and defense might of our country, the ideological and political unity of the people, the monolithic strength of Soviet society. And all this is created by the effort, knowledge, will and the political activity of our workers, collective farmers, intellectuals.

The mighty support of the Party and the entire Soviet people makes our foreign policy invincible, helps us emerge with honor from all trials, overcome the intrigues of all enemies. This support is the main guarantee of new successes in our struggle for peace, freedom and happiness of the peoples.

# STATEMENT OF THE SOVIET GOVERNMENT ON THE FEDERAL REPUBLIC OF GERMANY

*Complete Text*
*(Pravda, 29 January 1967)*

The attention of the peoples and governments of European countries, and not only European, is again focussed on the activities of the forces of nazism and militarism in the Federal Republic of Germany. All this shows that though more than two decades have passed since the adoption of the historic Potsdam decisions, the criminal past of Hitlerism has not by far been done away with in the FRG, that the nazi spirit there has not died, that it lives on.

Meetings, demonstrations and torch processions bearing a striking likeness to the nazi gatherings of the thirties are held in many West German cities. Numerous organizations, unions and groups which actually preach fascism and try to poison broad sections of the West German population with neo-nazism and which in Bonn are indulgently called "right radicals," or "extremists" play a mounting role in the political life of the country. "Historical studies" on Hitler, Goering and Goebbels are published as well as the letters of Hess and diaries of Ribbentrop, with the help of which the top leaders of the Third Reich are eulogized. Hardly a day passes without some nazi or anti-semitic outbursts. Numerous fascist leaflets are distributed and swastikas are again appearing on the walls in FRG cities. The new-fangled nazis threaten to make short work of progressive personalities in the country, all those who dare to come out for peace and good relations with other peoples, for turning the FRG policy towards realism.

The revival of nazism in the FRG is a manifestation of a fatal malady which undermined and destroyed the foundations of the Weimar Republic, and brought into being the Hitler regime with its monstrous crimes against peace and humanity. The FRG Ministry of the Interior itself admits in a published official report that neo-nazi parties and organizations are advocating what are "composite parts of national-socialist ideology."

Let us take, for example, the program of the so-called National Democratic Party whose representatives were seated in the Hessen and Bavarian landtags as a result of the recent elections. It is permeated with a spirit of undisguised chauvinism, a striving for revenge, seizure of foreign territories, and a desire to re-establish the Third Reich and make it "Europe's first state." According to statements by the National Democratic Party, the piratic Munich collusion of 1938 "remains in force," and the Sudeten region "belongs to areas Germany has the right to claim." In effect, this is a return to the demands for "lebensraum," to the notorious slogan of "Deutschland Über Alles."

Members of this party are waging a campaign for the complete rehabilitation of nazism, they seek to justify the crimes of nazi war criminals and to represent them almost as national heroes. Maidanek, Oswiecim, Buchenwald, the scores of other death camps, the mass executions of peaceful civilians, the razing of towns and villages, the destruction of cultural monuments—all these countless crimes, which have been exposed a thousand times and sternly condemned by the International Tribunal at Nuremberg, are cynically declared by the neo-nazis to have never existed. More than that, demands are made for "presenting a bill to other peoples and powers."

The neo-nazis are urging the unrestrained militarization of the FRG, equipment of the West German army with rockets and nuclear weapons, the revival of the general staff. Making use of the country's economic difficulties and resorting to fascist demagogy to win the sympathy of different sections of the population, these Hitlerite offspring are campaigning to end the "cramped position" of the FRG in the international arena, demanding the lifting of all restrictions on German militarism, and complete "independence" for the FRG revanchist policy, and at the same time urging all West European states and the USA to march in step with this West German political course.

Voices of sound forces demanding effective measures against the increasingly rampant neo-nazis are also heard in the FRG.

The attempts to belittle the danger of the growing activity of the neo-nazi forces in the FRG in many ways resemble the soothing statements made in the past when the National Socialist Party was worming its way into the state life of Germany. Then, as now, the nazi threat was underestimated, they were said to be few in number and to play no important part in the public and political life of the country. The consequences of this for Europe are well known.

Parallel to the rampage of the neo-nazi forces in the FRG, the growing influence of militarism is also in evidence. The West German militarists who have learned nothing and drawn no conclusions from the catastrophe that befell the nazi Reich are carrying out an extensive program of war preparations with blind stubbornness.

The Soviet Government has already called the attention of states and peoples to the secret work now under way in the FRG to develop a material and technical foundation for a nuclear and rocket industry of its own. It is common knowledge that the key sections of the government machinery—all kind of departments, committees and commissions—have now merged with the country's biggest concerns and research centers to form a single rocket-nuclear cartel. The spending on rocketry and atomic research has increased dozens of times in recent years and runs,

968

even by official figures, into something like 1,000 million marks.

Under cover of talk on the need "to keep abreast in technical progress" and taking advantage of the fact that opportunities for peaceful and military uses of the latest achievements of atomic, rocket and space technology are closely interwoven, the FRG military circles are engaged in large-scale military research in these fields.

While laying emphasis on the development of far-reaching nuclear research, the FRG ruling circles are also trying to gain "independence" in the sphere of means of delivery of nuclear weapons. In the recently adopted so-called rocket memorandum the leading West German monopolies openly proclaimed a line of developing production of most up-to-date arms, of developing rocketry by their own efforts and actually demanded that the entire economy of the country be subordinated to meet the steadily growing demands of Bonn brass hats.

But not so much time has passed between former Chancellor Adenauer's "solemn assurances" that he is "against the rearmament of the FRG," "against the creation of a new German Wehrmacht" and Bonn's demand for access to rocket-nuclear weapons and the establishment of a powerful West German Bundeswehr reared in the spirit of revanche and aggression against other states. Only ten years ago the armed forces of the FRG were practically non-existent. Today, however, the Bundeswehr, headed by former Hitler officers and generals, has become one of the big armies and claims the role of the main striking force of the NATO military organization in Western Europe.

How can all this be brought in line with the Potsdam agreement which solemnly prescribed that most resolute measures be taken "permanently to prevent the revival of reorganization of German militarism and nazism"? Does not this agreement concern the Federal Republic of Germany?

It is no accident that people in many countries are now asking: what road is the Federal Republic of Germany following? Why have the forces of nazism and militarism in the FRG survived and gained in strength to such an extent that it is now becoming a source of concern and alarm in Europe, and not only in Europe? The reply to these questions is provided by the conditions prevailing in the social and political life of the FRG, by the policy of its ruling circles.

Who does not know that a process of enlisting former active nazis into administration of the state, including provision of posts in the government and the Bundeswehr command, has been going on since the very inception of the Federal Republic of Germany. Active nazis in the FRG have enjoyed most touching care: those who were not appointed to high posts received generous pensions. In 1965 a law was adopted in the FRG on the strength of which nearly all nazi criminals were actually pardoned.

At the same time democratic and progressive organizations were and are still being persecuted in the FRG. The Communist Party of Germany, known for its glorious traditions in the struggle against nazi fascism, has been outlawed for over ten years and the entire police machine in the FRG is used to stifle its

courageous voice. A number of other mass organizations coming out against war, for peace, have also been banned. Progressives are quite often put on trial only because they call nazis nazis and remind the war criminals of their crimes.

It is no secret that neo-nazi forces began to rear their heads precisely when a clear turn was made in the FRG toward the practical preparation of military and political prerequisites for a revision of the results of the past war. Demands for a revision of existing European frontiers and for access to nuclear weapons, militarization of the country, a striving to aggravate international tension in Europe, development of aggressive military-strategic conceptions, a hostile attitude to the GDR, and cultivation of hatred toward peoples on whom territorial claims are made—all this provides a climate that is more than suitable for the national-chauvinistic, racialist activities of pro-fascist elements. Who can guarantee in these conditions that some new Hitler will not appear in the FRG, and armed with nuclear weapons to boot? Nobody can give such a guarantee.

Political activity has its logic. No matter what subjective motives guided the leaders of the Federal Republic of Germany in the past, the present growth of the neo-nazi, pro-Hitler trend and the rampage of militarism in the FRG is the outcome of their policy, a voluntary or involuntary result precisely of their efforts. An attentive analysis shows that in the final count there are quite a few common features in the political orientation of neo-nazis of different shades and the official revanchist-militarist course of the FRG ruling circles.

It is impossible, of course, not to see also that the present situation in West Germany is also a product of the policy of certain powers who have gone back on their commitments under the anti-Hitler coalition in order to collude with the West German aggressive forces, going so far as to support their revanchist strivings and nuclear ambitions.

Unfortunately, the first steps of the new FRG Government which was set up with the participation of the Social-Democratic Party do not warrant the conclusion that FRG policy is being brought into line with the spirit of the time and the actually existing conditions in Europe.

There is ample evidence to show that whatever shades of opinion may be represented in the new cabinet it has not only retained a sympathetic memory of its predecessors but also seems to have inherited to a considerable degree the essence of their policy. True, the Government's key-policy statement mentions a desire to help relieve tension and improve relations with the Soviet Union and other socialist countries. At the same time the statement contains also the revanchist aims of the old governments. One can find in it the FRG Government's absurd claim to speak on behalf of the whole German people, territorial claims to other states, a striving for nuclear weapons, provocative designs vis-a-vis West Berlin and the like. What we see is an attempt to reconcile the irreconcilable and do no more than just modify the looks of FRG policy without making any meaningful corrections in its essence.

A constructive approach to the strengthening of peace and security in Europe and throughout the world is only possible on the basis of existing reality, and above all on recognition of the existence of two German states—the German Democratic Republic and the Federal Republic of Germany. Equal participation of both German states in efforts to develop and strengthen European cooperation in various spheres will enable their population to make their contribution, along with other European peoples, to the cause of progress and peace. The division of these sovereign states, which resulted from the rout of Hitler's Reich and post-war developments over a long period, came about on the socio-class basis, and nobody can alter this situation.

Immutability of frontiers and inviolability of the socialist German state, the German Democratic Republic, is one of the mainstays of enduring peace and the security of peoples in Europe. Any attempts to put pressure upon or blackmail the GDR, as well as plans of hostile penetration into the socialist German state, are senseless and hopeless. Only incorrigible adventurists can hope for a forcible change in post-war European frontiers. An inexorable shattering retribution awaits anyone who would attempt to test the strength of the borders of the GDR and other socialist states.

The FRG continues to press for nuclear weapons. The NATO decisions to set up new NATO nuclear planning bodies with the participation of the FRG were hailed by the West German militarists and revanchists only as encouragement of their nuclear ambitions. Apart from claiming "special influence" for the FRG in matters of applying nuclear weapons, the FRG Government also began talking of setting up a so-called European nuclear force in which, it claimed, the FRG must directly participate.

The Soviet Government proceeds from the fact that the development of good-neighborly relations among all European states to improve the situation in Europe and promote mutual confidence and respect would meet the interests of peace. The Soviet Union and other socialist countries put forward in the Bucharest Declaration a broad program for strengthening peace and security in Europe. Proceeding from this program, the Government of the USSR will continue to work consistently and unswervingly for real improvement of the political climate in Europe, promotion of cooperation between the European states of East and West including, of course, the Federal Republic of Germany. But the Soviet Government cannot and will not close its eyes to the danger to peace in Europe and throughout the world from the neo-nazi and militarist forces of the Federal Republic of Germany.

In the historic days of the collapse of the nazi Reich, millions of people in the world who were fighting to the death for their freedom and independence believed that an end had been put to German nazism and German aggression forever. The peoples longed for durable and lasting peace, complete disarmament and demilitarization of Germany so that she "never again will threaten her neighbors or the peace of the world." They received with relief and hope the decision of the powers of the anti-Hitler coalition to wipe the nazi party off the face of the earth, to destroy "its affiliated and supervised organizations, to dissolve all nazi institutions, to ensure that they are not revived in any form."

Expressing the will and determination of the peoples who had held out in a mortal struggle against fascism, the Nuremberg Military Tribunal denounced Hitler's party as the center of a conspiracy for crimes against peace, war crimes and crimes against humanity.

German nazism, acting as enslaver of other peoples, had brought much suffering to the German people themselves, carried away or crippled the life of millions of Germans. It is only natural that within the German people themselves a resolve has arisen to do away with all traces of fascism, and an understanding has grown that a resolute and uncompromising rupture with the militarist past and national-chauvinist ideology with all its perversions, and a rebuilding of public and state life along democratic lines was to them a matter of life and death.

Yet, the facts go to show that realistic conclusions have been drawn from the lessons of the past only in the German Democratic Republic, where the Potsdam decisions on the eradication of nazism, demilitarization and a democratic reorganization of society have been fully carried into life. The socialist German state has taken upon itself a noble mission, that of doing all in its power to ensure that the threat of a new war should never again come from German soil. This mission has earned the German Democratic Republic the confidence and respect of all peace-loving peoples.

German nazism played a leading part in preparing and unleashing World War II, which did not stop at European borders but brought devastation to and claimed numerous sacrifices also from peoples in other regions of the world. That is why the Soviet Government considers it its duty today to appeal to the governments, parliaments and peoples not only in Europe, but in all other continents to display utmost vigilance and in face of the facts showing the increased activity of the militarist and neo-nazi forces in the FRG to do everything in their power so that these forces may never threaten world peace.

The peoples have not forgotten and never will forget that fascism means war. The very mention of the word fascism conjures up visions of Europe in the smoke of fires, the countless ruins of cities, the torment and death of millions of people. No, this tragedy must not happen again. To permit the shadow of the swastika to fall on the world again would be to betray the memory of those who gave their lives in the struggle against fascism, to jeopardize the future of the present and coming generations.

The Soviet Union proceeds from the assumption that the powers of the anti-Hitler coalition, by their commitments under the Potsdam and other international agreements, continue to bear responsibility for preventing the resurgence of German militarism and nazism. To forget this responsibility would mean to encourage the forces of militarism and nazism which are today ever higher rearing their heads in the FRG.

The Soviet Government draws attention of the Government, political parties, public forces and the entire population of the Federal Republic of Germany to the need to block the way to neo-nazism, to put an end to the policy of militarization and, together with other European peoples, direct their efforts to ensuring durable peace and security in Europe.

The peoples yearn for peace and hate war. They know what lies behind the West German militarists' efforts to obtain rockets and nuclear bombs and rightly demand that mankind be protected from the forces of reaction and destruction.

The Soviet people, the peoples of other socialist countries and, it can be said with conviction, other peace-loving peoples will direct all their anger, all their might against those who, in a blind striving for revenge, would foist on mankind the calamities of another war.

The Soviet Government, guided by interests of ensuring peace and security of the nations, is closely following the intrigues of the neo-fascist and militarist forces, and is ready, in accordance with its commitments under the Potsdam and other international agreements, to take, if need be, together with other peaceful states, all measures that may be required by the situation.

\* \* \*

The above Statement of the Soviet Government was delivered by the USSR Ministry of Foreign Affairs to the embassies of the United States, Great Britain and France in Moscow on January 28, this year, with appropriate brief accompanying notes.

The Soviet Government's Statement was also forwarded to the Embassy of the FRG in Moscow with an accompanying note saying that the Soviet Government expected the Government of the FRG to take appropriate measures to curb the activities of neo-nazi and militarist forces in the FRG, which are dangerous to peace, in accordance with the commitments arising for the FRG from the Potsdam and other allied international agreements.

# "ON THE ANTI-SOVIET POLICY OF MAO TSE-TUNG AND HIS GROUP"

*Complete Text*
(*Pravda*, 16 February 1967)

During the past half century our Party and our people had more than once to withstand vehement attacks of hostile forces on the first socialist state in the history of mankind. But if we omit the periods of war, the periods of direct armed aggression against the Soviet Union, we can say that never before has such a fierce campaign been conducted against it as the one launched by the present leaders of China.

The aggravation of Soviet-Chinese relations, brought about by the policy of the leading grouping of the Communist Party of China, has its own history. It is well known to the socialist countries, to the fraternal Parties, to world public opinion as a whole. Also widely known is the stand of our Party and the Soviet Government on this important question. We consistently and steadfastly adhered to the line of normalizing relations with China, and striving to secure a return to the road of friendship and cooperation, we did everything possible to promote united action of our two countries and Parties in the struggle against imperialism, and, above all, in giving support to the Vietnamese people heroically repelling American aggression.

Therein lay the gist of the numerous proposals and initiatives of the CPSU Central Committee and the Soviet Government on concrete measures to develop Soviet-Chinese cooperation in politics and economy, on talks and meetings, which could pave the way to improving relations both along state and Party lines. This is the gist of our policy, invariably aimed at safeguarding the lawful interests of the People's Republic of China in the international arena, at ensuring the most favorable conditions for the building of socialism in China, as in the other socialist states. This, finally, is the reason for the restraint and patience manifested by our Party, why for a long time we unilaterally refused to engage in open polemics, even when confronted with obviously hostile demarches on the part of the Chinese leadership.

It is common knowledge, however, that peace and accord require the good will of both sides and not of one alone. What was the will of Mao Tse-tung and his grouping? It is generally known that all the proposals of our Party and Government, aimed at improving relations, were constantly rejected in an ever ruder and increasingly impertinent form. The policy of Peking assumed an ever more hostile nature. Even where internationalist duty and the entire logics of events dictated the need of putting the differences aside and uniting for joint action against imperialism, a struggle was whipped up for all sorts of far-fetched reasons, and sometimes without any reason at all, inside the socialist community and the communist movement, a struggle spearheaded against the CPSU and the Soviet Union. The Mao Tse-tung group openly steered a course of systematically thwarting the steps taken by the Soviet Union in the international arena together with other socialist nations to safeguard the interests of world socialism, the revolutionary movement, universal peace, a course of splitting the communist and liberation movements and the international democratic organizations. Furthermore, Peking began to make ever more persistent attempts to conduct subversive activity against the socialist countries and the Communist Parties, interfering in their internal affairs and organizing its split-away groups in a number of Parties.

The time has long passed when the policy of Mao Tse-tung's group could seem to be an expression of ideological differences, discussions within the framework of the communist movement. This group did not confine itself to attacking the line of the CPSU and other fraternal Parties, it went over to open political struggle against our country, against our Party and our people. After the 11th Plenary Meeting of the CPC Central Committee, held last summer, and at the outset of the so-called cultural revolution, this struggle entered a new, even more dangerous phase. As is known, it reached particular intensity lately.

One of the main directions of the Mao Tse-tung leadership's anti-Soviet activity is slanderous propaganda. It maliciously distorts every foreign policy step of the Soviet State, every step dictated by concern for the interests of peace and socialism. The press and broadcasting stations of China are trying might and main to fling mud at our people and their Party. Furthermore, Chinese propaganda has been calling on the Soviet people for months on end to overthrow the existing system, to hoist the "banner of Mao Tse-tung in Red Square," to establish in the USSR a "new order" modeled after the one now being imposed by Mao Tse-tung in China.

Matters are not, however, confined to mendacious propaganda which in tone and filthy methods exceeds anything the enemies of our Party and of our people had ever dared to undertake. The Chinese leadership has embarked upon the road of direct anti-Soviet actions and provocations. The Soviet Embassy in Peking has become their permanent target. A fresh orgy, lasting for more than a fortnight, was recently staged at its walls, creating absolutely intolerable conditions for the work of the Embassy personnel. The Chinese authorities go to such lengths in their shameless violations of the existing norms and customs of international law which even the most reactionary imperialist governments have rarely permitted themselves.

At present the "geography" of such provocations has been considerably expanded. Mao Tse-tung and his entourage are obviously endeavoring to carry out their adventurist threat to introduce "Red Guards" methods of political hooliganism into the international arena. The Chinese representatives, acting on instructions from Peking, tried to stage anti-Soviet rioting in Hanoi, Paris, Bagdad, Algiers, Pnompenh, and other cities. Furthermore, Moscow was selected as the venue for one such provocation, and in Moscow—such a sacred place for all working people as Red Square and the Lenin Mausoleum.

This list of outrages is being augmented by new ones every day. Suffice it to recall such facts as the unprecedented outrages of "Red Guards" at the Peking Airport during the departure for home of the families of Soviet citizens, the vicious acts against Soviet train crews servicing railway trains on the Moscow-Peking line. The Soviet personnel, passing through China to Vietnam to assist in the heroic struggle of the Vietnamese people, are becoming the target of Chinese provocations and insults.

The present leaders of China are trying to create the impression of "popular indignation" by drawing scores of thousands of people into anti-Soviet manifestations, deceiving them by cock-and-bull stories about "bloody assaults in the USSR," fabricated by Mao's retinue. All the propaganda machine of China is today concentrated on this goal. It daily incites passions with tales about "unprecedented atrocities" allegedly perpetrated against Chinese citizens in Moscow, directly instigates crowds of teenagers and youth with the slogan "blood for blood," threatening to demand "payment of the blood debt." But the true organizers of provocations, who control and direct the actions of the young people, and who, therefore, bear full responsibility for them, will not be able to hide behind the backs of the "Red Guards" and "rebels."

\* \* \*

Many people all over the world, who are following the anti-Soviet campaign launched by the Chinese leaders, cannot take in the fact that its organizers and inspirers are this time not imperialists, not a capitalist state, but politicians who call themselves Communists. This indeed is amazing and can hardly be conceived. The more important it is, therefore, to analyze the reasons of this monstrous Peking paradox.

What, in fact, do the organizers of this hate campaign against the Soviet Union seek to achieve?

The facts show that the people, who today direct the policy of China, have set themselves the aim not only of bringing up the Chinese people in a spirit of enmity towards the USSR, but of aggravating Soviet-Chinese relations to the limit and, in the final count, of bringing them to a complete rupture. However, fearing responsibility for the consequences of such a step, they dare not act openly, and strive to provoke the Soviet Union to break off these relations in order to deceive world public opinion, to deceive the Chinese people, to convince them that it is our country allegedly and not the Mao Tse-tung group that bears the guilt for aggravating Soviet-Chinese relations. This, specifically, was the essence of the speeches of Chou En-lai and Chen Yi at the anti-Soviet meeting held in Peking the other day.

Another question arises in this connection: Why does the Mao Tse-tung group need such aggravation and what goals does it pursue? The answer to this question should be sought in the entire nationalistic, great-power policy of the present Chinese leadership.

It was already obvious a few years ago that this policy inevitably prods the Mao Tse-tung group to aggravate relations with the Marxist-Leninist Parties, and primarily with the CPSU. Having embarked upon the nationalist, great power course, this group tried hard to subject the socialist camp and the world revolutionary movement to its interests, to impose its political line upon them, signifying a break with Marxism-Leninism.

The great international prestige of our Party, its consistent struggle for Leninist relations in the communist movement, based on equality and fraternity, this is what made the Chinese leaders regard the CPSU as the main obstacle to their great-power goals. Naturally, in its endeavor to subject the other socialist countries and fraternal Parties, the entire revolutionary and liberation movement to its nationalistic, great-power interests, the Chinese leadership banked on discrediting at all cost the Soviet Union and our Leninist Party.

Nor is there any doubt that one direct reason for the anti-Soviet policy and propaganda of the present Chinese leadership is a desire to divert the attention of the Chinese people from the privations and difficulties they are experiencing, from the numerous mistakes and failures in the domestic and foreign policies of China. Here we are actually confronted with the old, hackneyed method of all unprincipled politicians suffering bankruptcy. If matters steadily deteriorate, if their political actions suffer one failure after another, the only way out, for such people, is to place the blame at the door of the "enemies," both "internal" and, especially, "external." This precisely is the principle applied today by the Peking leaders.

It is by no means accidental that they fired their first shots in the political war against the Soviet State and the CPSU shortly after the collapse of the ill-starred course of the "big leap" and "people's communes." As the scope of setbacks in domestic policy and the failure of the foreign policy line pursued by the CPC leadership, which led the country to isolation, became clearer, the intensity of the anti-Soviet campaign grew more and more. The farther it departed from the principles of scientific socialism, the louder and more persistent was the outcry of the Peking propaganda that this departure was allegedly being effected by the Soviet Union, that our country "was betraying the interests of the revolution," "restoring capitalism." Soon Chinese propaganda began to ring of pure nationalism and even racialism. By advancing territorial claims to the Soviet Union, the leadership of the CPC set before itself the goal of further inciting chauvinistic moods in the Chinese people. The slanderous propaganda began to be augmented more and more extensively by various anti-Soviet acts and provocations. By creating, in every way possible, the impression in the Chinese people that they are surrounded by enemies on all sides, the Peking rulers seek to rally them together on nationalistic lines, to distract the masses of working people from the actual problems confronting the country and to justify the military-bureaucratic dictatorship of Mao Tse-tung and his stooges.

Yet another important motive of Peking's anti-Soviet policy is lately increasingly coming to the fore. The essence of the domestic political course which is being insistently and stubbornly promoted by Mao Tse-tung and those who think like him is now obvious. Actually, it is a frontal attack against the socialist gains of the Chinese people during which the very ideals of socialism are being shamelessly distorted and trampled underfoot. It was precisely to cover up and "ideologically" to substantiate this policy that the Peking rulers had need to launch the fierce attacks against the countries where socialism is being really built and the smear campaign against the Parties which are really following the teaching of Marxism-Leninism, the ideals of scientific socialism. In the atmosphere of tense struggle inside the Party and the people, Mao Tse-tung's group needed this slander precisely in the interests of the struggle for power. Mao Tse-tung simply could not have remained in power without such slander, for the Soviet Union's successes in communist construction and the successes in socialist construction in other countries expose his apostasy and the bankruptcy of his political line.

It is an obvious fact, for instance, that as a result of Mao Tse-tung's economic ventures, the Chinese leadership had in effect to abandon the plans of China's economic development, abandon the build-up of the material and technical basis of socialism and to openly renounce the course of raising the living standards of working people. In these conditions the Peking rulers could think of nothing better than to try to make a virtue of need, and to declare economic development and concern for improving the people's living conditions as something "anti-socialist" and "bourgeois." In the field of theory they had little trouble substantiating this idea by firing against Marxist-Leninist science another broadside of Mao Tse-tung's quotations ("In production to strive for high indices and in life to stick to a low level," "Poverty is good," "It is terrible to think of the time when all people will be rich," etc.). But since the practice of world socialism fully contradicts such directives and notions of socialism, the Chinese leaders started a slander campaign against the USSR and other socialist countries declaring their struggle for economic progress, for raising the living and cultural standards of the people as "revisionism," "economism" and even "restoration of capitalism." For the greater the economic successes of the Soviet Union, the better the life of the Soviet people, the greater is the fear of Mao Tse-tung and his group for the destinies of their special line, the stronger the opposition to this line in China itself. Thus, the more vicious the slander against the Soviet Union, the more reckless the anti-Soviet provocations.

The same applies to other problems the CPC leaders come up against. Meeting with mounting opposition to their policy, they launched a fierce campaign of repressions and mass reprisals of those who think otherwise. Obliging "theoreticians" from

Mao Tse-tung's entourage have tried to declare lawlessness, arbitrariness and coercion against their own Party and the broad masses of workers, peasants and working intelligentsia, "genuine" dictatorship of the proletariat, "genuine" socialism. But this, too, required slandering of the Soviet Union and other countries of socialism which are consistently advancing along the Leninist road—the road of developing socialist democracy, consolidating legality, expanding the participation of working people in the settlement of all public and state affairs.

The entire practice of the CPSU and the other Communist Parties, which are consistently developing the Leninist norms of inner-Party life, strengthening principles of collective leadership and strictly adhering to democratic principles in the activities of all Party organizations from top to bottom naturally creates a danger to Mao Tse-tung and his power, for Mao Tse-tung's group has long been attacking its own Party. The most elementary norms and principles of inner-Party life—electivity of Party bodies, responsibility of leaders to the Party and Party organizations, publicity in the discussion of the Party line, etc., have been trampled underfoot in China. The Mao Tse-tung personality cult has reached the absurd, has become nothing less than idolatry. Lately, under the flag of the "cultural revolution," Party organizations are being consistently routed, Party cadres persecuted and annihilated by detachments of Mao Tse-tung's storm troopers, with the support of the army and security bodies. To justify all this and silence the Chinese Communists who cannot but compare happenings in China with the practice of other Communist Parties, the Mao Tse-tung group had to smear the CPSU's Leninist line and to level the absurd charges of "revisionism" against it.

The Mao Tse-tung group has similar motives when organizing the slander campaign against the foreign policy of the Soviet Union and the other socialist countries. It has broken with the cardinal principles and objectives of socialist foreign policy—internationalism, a readiness to support other socialist countries and to struggle jointly with them against imperialism, a striving to defend peace, struggle for the prevention of a world war, establish good-neighborly relations with all peaceloving countries and especially with countries which have freed themselves from the colonialist yoke. It is not surprising that the Chinese leadership has found it necessary to attack these Leninist principles and objectives of foreign policy, declare them revisionist and to slanderously state that the policy of the socialist countries is a policy of "collusion" with imperialism, of "surrender to the class enemy."

The history of the working class movement shows that renegades from Marxism have always nurtured a blind hatred for the banner which they had betrayed. The Mao Tse-tung grouping is no exception in this respect. One of the main objectives of the anti-Soviet hysteria now whipped up is to keep the Chinese people away from genuine Marxism-Leninism, from the experience of world socialism. In the present conditions this experience is not only alien to the Chinese leaders but is dangerous to them, because a knowledge of this experience would only show the Communist Party and people of China how far their leaders had departed from the interests of the revolution and socialism. That is why the Chinese leadership had need to isolate their country, erect a "Chinese Wall" to keep their people away from the socialist community, from the entire progressive world public.

We are witnessing precisely such self-isolation. Peking is conducting a hostile policy not only against the Soviet Union but also against other socialist countries. All fraternal Parties, the entire communist movement, the international democratic organizations and movements have become the target of the splitting intrigues of Mao Tse-tung's group. The subversive activities of this group are directed also against the young national states, against the forces in Africa, Asia and Latin America struggling for national liberation.

Mao Tse-tung's fallacious policy has led the country into an impasse. Seeing no way out, the Chinese leadership plunges from one venture to another. Its anti-Sovietism is precisely one such venture.

*  *  *

The anti-Soviet campaign of the Chinese leaders is effected in the most outrageous, truly hooliganistic forms. But this seeming offensiveness should not delude anyone. In effect, the actions of Mao Tse-tung's grouping are dictated not by their power but by their weakness, by their fear of their own Party and their own people. The latest events showed that the Peking leaders have sufficient grounds for such fear. The "cultural revolution" has brought out the great scope of the dissatisfaction of workers, peasants and intelligentsia, dissatisfaction that has spread even to the army and the youth on which Mao Tse-tung's group is staking. The events which had started under the flag of the "cultural revolution" have actually developed into a fierce struggle for retention of power by Mao Tse-tung and his followers. Their policy shows that for the sake of power they are ready to sacrifice everything—the interests of socialism, the interests of their people and the interests of the revolution.

This is vividly illustrated by the transition of Mao Tse-tung's group to the positions of rabid anti-Sovietism. This course signifies first of all a blow at the Chinese Communist Party itself, at the Chinese people. At all stages of the Chinese revolution, the Soviet Union's fraternal aid and support have been an important source of the victories of the Communists and all working people of China. Friendship and cooperation with the Soviet Union and other fraternal countries have helped the Chinese people to start building socialism and to achieve considerable successes in this difficult cause. Alliance with our country has always created for China a reliable guarantee against imperialist intervention and aggression. By disrupting these historical ties and becoming heralds of anti-Sovietism the Peking rulers are dooming China's working people to serious additional difficulties, and isolating their country from its natural allies and friends. The conclusion suggests

itself that Peking is now looking for new allies.

In this world public opinion today rightly sees an important source of the anti-Soviet campaign started by Mao Tse-tung's group, since hatred for the Soviet Union has always been the common ground that united the enemies of socialism. And it is not fortuitous that interest in China has grown so much in imperialist reactionary quarters where the prospects and possibilities of rapprochement with that country are being discussed with growing persistence. Many facts show that these intentions are meeting with a response in Mao Tse-tung's group. A re-orientation of China's economic ties from the socialist to the capitalist world has been underway for quite a few years now. Peking's political contacts with imperialist powers, including the USA, are becoming increasingly more frequent and regular.

But the main thing is that already today Mao Tse-tung and his entourage are by their policy rendering an incalculable service to the imperialists. This group has actually substituted the struggle against imperialism by a struggle against the Soviet Union, the other socialist countries and against the communist movement. Thereby, it is weakening the front of anti-imperialist forces and aggravating the entire political situation in Asia. All this is, above all, a stab in the back of the heroic Vietnamese people in their struggle against the American aggressors.

Imperialist quarters fully approve of this line of Mao Tse-tung's grouping. The *Washington Post* wrote that officials in Washington believe that Mao serves American interests and therefore even think of cultivating Maoism as a means of bringing pressure to bear on Moscow. The *United States News and World Report* magazine directly wrote in this connection that the United States is banking on Mao and that American officials are inclined to prefer victory of Mao Tse-tung in his struggle to destroy the more moderate elements, because this would mean more trouble for Soviet Russia.

Such is the reaction of imperialist quarters to Mao Tse-tung's policy which Peking propaganda is presenting as the latest in "revolutionarism." Such praise by the class enemy is yet another proof of the extent to which the domestic and foreign policies of Mao Tse-tung and his group contradict the interests of socialism, the interests of the revolution, and plays into the hands of imperialism, above all United States imperialism.

*  *  *

The latest events confirm once again the high degree of political maturity and self-control of our Party and the entire Soviet people. These events have again demonstrated the lofty internationalist traits of our people, who with bitterness and pain witness the present events in China and who sincerely sympathize with the Chinese people, the Communist Party of that country, now living through such a tragedy.

At the same time the latest events reaffirmed the unanimous support given by all Communists, by all working people of our country to the line of the CPSU Central Committee and the Soviet Government and the decisions of the December Plenary Meeting of the Central Committee, as well as their determination to administer a crushing rebuff to all splitters and provocators.

These days the hearts of Soviet people are full of wrath and just indignation. Firm warnings to the Chinese provocators have been voiced at numerous meetings in towns and villages. The Soviet people unanimously support the position of their Government outlined in the statements of February 4 and 9, containing a principled appraisal of the latest actions of the Chinese authorities.

Persisting in its anti-Soviet policy, Mao Tse-tung's group will only further lay bare the depth of its fall, show the extent which its political regeneration has reached. The international isolation of Mao Tse-tung's grouping is increasing virtually every day, the world communist movement and upright people in all countries are more and more indignant over Peking's adventurist course and its anti-Soviet position.

Needless to say, Mao Tse-tung's grouping will not be able endlessly to deceive the Chinese people and Chinese Communists. As was rightly stated by Moscow workers in their protest resolution presented to the Chinese Embassy in Moscow, "Mao Tse-tung and his clique will have to answer in full to the Chinese people and the Chinese Communists, to entire progressive mankind for their shameful, criminal actions aimed at undermining the friendship of the Chinese and Soviet peoples.

The entire international communist movement now asks: where is Mao Tse-tung's group heading?

Everything goes to show that it is preparing the People's Republic of China for further adventuristic actions in both domestic and foreign policies, not excluding fresh provocations against the Soviet Union either.

Having replaced the struggle against imperialism by the struggle against the Soviet Union, against the entire socialist community, against the international communist and liberation movements, Mao Tse-tung's group is inflicting great damage to the cause of world socialism, to the Chinese people themselves and the cause of building socialism in China. The anti-Leninist, adventurist policy of this group holds out for the Chinese people only the prospect of still greater economic difficulties, falling living standards, a worsening of the international situation and the prospect of China's complete isolation from the socialist community.

But the Chinese people, the People's Republic of China, the Chinese Communist Party have, objectively, also another prospect. This is the prospect of improving relations with the CPSU and the Soviet Union, with all socialist countries and Communist Parties, the prospect of joint struggle in the ranks of the socialist community against imperialism, the prospect of economic development and rectifying previous errors in agriculture and industry, and the raising on this basis of the people's living standards, the prospect of asserting Marxist-Leninist norms in the life of the Chinese Communist Party and the establishment of socialist legality in the People's Republic of China. In other words, the prospect of developing along the road outlined by the Eighth Congress of the Communist Party of China, by the documents of the international meetings of Communist and Workers' Parties. This Marxist-Leninist prospect meets the vital interests of the Chinese people, People's China and the Chinese Communist Party.

The Communist Party of the Soviet Union, all Soviet people want precisely this prospect to triumph, want the People's Republic of China to take this correct road.

# "ON THE POLICY OF THE SOVIET UNION IN CONNECTION WITH THE ISRAELI AGGRESSION IN THE NEAR EAST"

Resolution of the Plenary Meeting of the CPSU Central Committee, Adopted 21 June 1967

*Complete Text*
*(Pravda,* 22 June 1967)

Having heard and discussed the report of L. I. Brezhnev, General Secretary of the CPSU Central Committee, "On the Policy of the Soviet Union in Connection with the Israeli Aggression in the Near East," the Plenary Meeting of the CPSU Central Committee resolves:

*fully to approve the political line and practical activities of the Politbureau of the Central Committee aimed at cutting short Israeli aggression, at supporting the United Arab Republic, Syria and other Arab states subjected to attack, and at averting the dangerous consequences of aggression to the cause of universal peace.*

The Israeli aggression is the result of a collusion of the most reactionary forces of international imperialism, primarily the United States, against one of the detachments of the national-liberation movement, against the advanced Arab states which have embarked upon the path of progressive social and economic transformations in the interests of the working people, and which pursue an anti-imperialist policy.

In the conditions when the United States is continuing its predatory war in Vietnam the Israeli aggression in the Near East constitutes another link in the common chain of the policy of the belligerent imperialist circles which are trying to stop the historical advance of national independence, democracy, peace and socialism.

The Soviet Union, the other socialist countries and all progressive anti-imperialist forces are with the Arab peoples in their just struggle against imperialism and neo-colonialism, for the inalienable right to themselves decide all questions of home and foreign policy. Expressing the will of Soviet Communists and all Soviet people, the Plenary Meeting of the Central Committee vigorously condemns the Israeli aggression and declares its solidarity with the peoples of the UAR, Syria, Algeria and the other Arab countries.

The Plenary Meeting notes that the quick, resolute and joint actions of the Soviet Union and the other socialist states played an important role in stopping the military operations in the Near East. The position of our Party and the Soviet Government and their practical steps in connection with the events in the Near East have the full support of all Soviet people.

The Plenary Meeting of the Central Committee states with satisfaction that at the important point in the development of international events the fraternal socialist states that signed the Statement on June 9, 1967, acted together, shoulder to shoulder. It has been confirmed once again that the joint actions of the socialist countries are a powerful factor in the struggle against the aggressive intrigues of international imperialism.

The Plenary Meeting of the Central Committee fully approves the Statement of the Central Committees of the Communist and Workers' Parties and Governments of the Socialist Countries of June 9 this year and confirms that the Soviet Union, together with the other socialist countries, will do everything necessary to help the peoples of the Arab countries vigorously to repulse the aggressor, to protect their lawful rights, to abolish the hotbed of war in the Near East and to restore peace in that area.

The chief task today, when the forces of imperialism and neo-colonialism, taking advantage of the situation created by Israeli aggression in the Near East, encroach on the independence and territorial integrity of the Arab states, is to prevent the aggressor from profiting from the results of his treacherous actions, to get the interventionist troops withdrawn immediatley and unconditionally behind the armistice line and have the aggressor pay for the damage caused to the UAR, Syria and Jordan.

In accordance with the basic aims of the policy of our Party laid down by the 23rd CPSU Congress and confirmed by the 1966 December Plenary Meeting of the CPSU Central Committee, it is necessary to continue the struggle against the bellicose forces of imperialism and their policy of interference into the internal affairs of other countries, continue to pursue the line of support of the Arab states in their struggle for freedom, independence, territorial integrity and social progress.

It is necessary in the future, too, to consolidate friendship and cohesion between the Soviet Union and Arab states, resolutely to rebuff imperialist scheming, expose its real, anti-popular aspect, conduct the struggle against the slanderous campaign and splitting activities of the Mao Tse-tung group aimed at disuniting the anti-imperialist forces, undermining confidence between the peoples of the Arab nations and the peoples of the socialist countries.

The Plenary Meeting of the CPSU Central Committee considers that the developments in the Near East emphatically stress the need of unity of action of the Communist and Workers' Parties, the international labor movement and the national-liberation movement of the Afro-Asian and Latin American peoples, all peaceloving and progressive forces, all who hold dear the cause of peace and independence of peoples, the cause of the struggle for world peace.

The Communist Party of the Soviet Union, translating into life the decisions of the 23rd Congress, will continue to conduct unflaggingly the struggle against the aggressive forces of imperialism, to maintain high vigilance of the Soviet people, to consistently implement the Leninist line of peaceful coexistence of states with different social systems, to fulfill its internationalist duty—to give all possible support to the peoples fighting for their freedom and national independence for social progress. Joint actions of the forces of peace, democracy and socialism, of the national-liberation movement can bridle the aggressor and avert a new world war.

The Plenary Meeting of the CPSU Central Committee calls upon Party organizations, all working people of the Soviet Union to exert fresh labor efforts aimed at the building of communism, at the further consolidation of the economic and military might of the country, to mark the glorious 50th anniversary of the Great October Socialist Revolution in a worthy manner.

# "THE GREAT OCTOBER SOCIALIST REVOLUTION AND THE WORLD REVOLUTIONARY PROCESS"

Section III of the Theses of the Central Committee of the CPSU
on the Fiftieth Anniversary of the Great October Socialist Revolution

*Complete Text*
*(Pravda,* 25 June 1967)

The Great October Revolution marked the beginning of the revolutionary transition from capitalism to socialism on a world scale. During the past 50 years the world revolutionary process has been developing uninterruptedly, drawing in more and more countries and peoples. From the outset this development proceeds in struggle with imperialism, which tenaciously resists the forces of revolution and mounts counter-offensives wherever it can. At the same time the world revolutionary movement encounters internal difficulties, due to its rapid growth and the heterogeneity of the social forces participating in the anti-imperialist struggle. However, the main trend of mankind's historical development, charted by the October Revolution, has asserted itself firmly: its main content, direction and features are now determined by the world socialist system, by the anti-imperialist forces fighting for the socialist reorganization of society.

*16. The experience of the 50 post-Revolution years has borne out the conclusion of revolutionary theory that capitalism is doomed.*

Imperialism has strikingly revealed the anti-popular substance and intrinsic vices of the modern capitalist system. It precipitated two world wars, taking a toll of 60 million lives, and now it threatens to unleash another world war that would involve missiles and thermonuclear weapons. Local wars and punitive expeditions against the national-liberation movement (the US imperialist aggression in Vietnam, the Israeli invasion of Arab countries), the militarization of the economy, the onslaught on democracy and the striving to establish terroristic fascist regimes (the most recent example being the reactionary coup in Greece) are the most obvious expressions of the reactionary nature of imperialism.

The conclusion of Marxist-Leninist theory that capitalist relations have become an obstacle preventing the productive forces from developing in the interests of the peoples, in the interests of the working people has been fully confirmed. This is demonstrated by the terrible economic crisis of 1929-33, by the stagnation of production in the subsequent years, the cyclic crises in a number of countries after the Second World War, the general instability of capitalist economy, constant undercapacity of industry and the growing uncertainty of the working people in their future. Imperialism with its policy of plunder, its promotion of colonialism and neo-colonialism, is responsible for the economic and technological backwardness of dozens of Asian, African and Latin American countries.

The positions of imperialism in world economy and politics have been considerably undermined. Imperialism is resorting to every means to prolong its existence. Modern capitalism is, first and foremost, state-monopoly capitalism, which adapts itself to the coexistence and struggle between the two world systems. In face of the modern level of the productive forces, the specific features of the class struggle, the successes of the socialist countries and the intensification of class battles within the capitalist world, the imperialists are maneuvering in an effort to curb such highly destructive and socially dangerous phenomena as anarchy of production, economic crises and mass unemployment. They widely resort to state regulation of the economy, introduce new and better camouflaged, but essentially no less ruthless, methods of exploitation and increasingly take recourse to social demagogy.

However, no innovations can change the exploiting essence of capitalism, no maneuvers can heal it of its basic vices and remove its incurable contradictions. The scientific and technological revolution, the increasing state-monopoly regulation and, on this basis, a certain growth of production inevitably lead to a greater socialization of production in the imperialist countries, to an aggravation of class contradictions, to substantial changes in the alignment of the social and political forces. This creates objective conditions for the further growth of anti-imperialist forces called upon to effect the revolutionary transition from capitalism to socialism under the leadership of the working class.

*17. The revolutionary rejuvenation of the world, begun by the October Revolution and embodied in the triumph of socialism in the USSR, has been continued by the triumphant socialist revolutions in other countries. The emergence of the world socialist system is the most important historic event after the Great October Socialist Revolution.*

A number of countries embarked on the socialist road immediately after the Second World War and in later years was a striking confirmation of the Marxist-Leninist theory about the inevitable triumph of the new social system. The building of socialism proceeds in those countries in more favorable conditions: from the very beginning they were able to rely on the support of the socialist community, on the Soviet Union. True to its internationalist duty, the country of the October Revolution rendered and continues to render extensive support to the fraternal socialist countries. The Communist and Workers'

Parties are able to draw upon the rich experience of building socialism in the USSR. In turn, the progress made by a large group of countries along the road blazed by the October Revolution facilitates the building of communism in the Soviet Union.

The example of many peoples has demonstrated that there are a number of general laws governing the transition from capitalism to socialism which first became manifest in the course of the socialist transformations in the USSR. The fact that every nation injects many new features into the forms and methods of this transition has also been confirmed. The experience gained by the socialist countries has given both a fuller understanding of how these general laws operate and how the diverse forms and methods of socialist construction are applied in specific conditions.

Within a short period most of the socialist countries that had a low economic level in the past have become highly developed states with a high standard of living and rapidly developing science and culture. The socialist countries are outstripping the capitalist states in economic growth rates. In 1966 their industrial product was approximately ten times that of the same territory in 1937, while in the capitalist world industrial output rose only 3.6-fold in the same period.

The successful development of socialist economy, influenced by the profound changes being wrought by the scientific and technical revolution, presupposes a constant improvement of economic management and of the scientific basis of planning, the strengthening of cost accounting principles, and greater moral and material incentives for the working people in developing production. The economic reforms now under way in many socialist countries have the aim of raising the effectiveness of social production, of utilizing the reserves of socialist economy, of creating conditions for further successes of socialism in the economic competition with capitalism.

As a result of the struggle of the working people under the leadership of Marxist-Leninist Parties, the foundations of socialism have been built in most countries that have taken the socialist road, and a society of working classes has been formed in which the socio-political and ideological unity of the whole people is asserting itself. The consolidation of the new system and the unfolding of all its potentialities are promoted by the extension of socialist democracy and the enlistment of the masses into active participation in political life and in the solution of all social issues.

*18. The victories and achievements of socialism spring directly from the formation and development of the new, socialist international relations based on principles of equality and national sovereignty, all-sided mutually advantageous cooperation and fraternal reciprocal assistance of the socialist countries.*

The rapprochement of the countries that have embarked on the socialist road and their consolidation in the socialist community falls in with the fundamental interests of the peoples; it is based on the fact that they have a socio-economic and political system of the same type, a single Marxist-Leninist ideology, and identical tasks in the struggle against imperialism, for peace, democracy and socialism. The idea of proletarian internationalism, which has always been the leading principle of the communist movement, has found a new vivid embodiment in the cooperation of the sovereign socialist countries, guided by the working class and its Marxist-Leninist Parties, in the economic, political and military fields.

The formation of international relations of a new type is a complex and manifold process linked up with overcoming the grim heritage left by the age-long rule of the exploiting classes—national exclusiveness, strife and mistrust. The differences in the levels of economic and social development, class structure, historical and cultural traditions inherited from the past give rise to objective difficulties in the fulfillment of such essential tasks as the establishment of comprehensive cooperation and the organization of a system of socialist international division of labor.

All these gigantic tasks have to be carried out by the Communist Parties for the first time in history. And while the formation of socialist international relations is still in progress it would be hard to overestimate the importance of what has been achieved in the twenty years of the world socialist system's existence. A sound foundation has been laid for the community of socialist countries, various forms have been created for their economic, political and military cooperation (the Council for Mutual Economic Assistance, the Warsaw Treaty Organization, bilateral treaties, and so on), and considerable experience has been accumulated in the joint action of socialist nations in the world arena.

Devotion to Marxism-Leninism and proletarian internationalism is an earnest of the successful development of the world socialist community, the growth of its influence on world developments. At the same time, any deviation from Marxism-Leninism, from proletarian internationalism is fraught with dire consequences to the cause of socialism, to the genuine national interests of the peoples. The situation in China testifies to this.

In the first years following the triumph of the revolution, which inflicted a heavy blow on imperialism, the Chinese people secured major success in the social transformation of their country, in the development of its economy and culture. This success was, to a great extent, due to the comprehensive political, economic, military and cultural cooperation of the Chinese People's Republic with the socialist community, with the Soviet Union.

At the end of the fifties the CPC leadership adopted a new line in foreign and domestic policy, which was a deviation from Marxism-Leninism and flagrantly contradicted the principles of proletarian internationalism and the basic laws of socialist construction. The Mao Tse-tung group took up a policy which combined petty-bourgeois adventurism with great-power chauvinism disguised by "Left" phraseology; it openly set out on a course intended to undermine the unity of the socialist community and to split the world communist movement.

The adventurist line of the Mao Tse-tung group seriously weakened the positions of the Communist

Party and the Chinese working class and gave a free hand to petty bourgeois and anarchist elements. It seriously threatens the socialist achievements in China.

The Soviet people have always considered the great Chinese people a friend and ally in the struggle for the revolutionary transformation of society. The CPC's rupture with its present ruinous policy and the strengthening of relations between the Chinese People's Republic and the Soviet Union and other socialist countries would promote the interests of world socialism and, primarily, those of China herself.

True to Lenin's behests, the CPSU consistently upholds the jointly worked-out standards and principles of relations between socialist countries and opposes all violations of these principles. Greater political and economic cooperation among the socialist countries and their further consolidation clear the road for new successes, ensure the growing might of the world socialist system and the enhancement of its influence on social development.

Being in the forefront of the struggle against imperialism, for peace and social progress, the socialist community makes a decisive contribution to the development of the revolutionary process.

*19. The Great October Socialist Revolution dealt a crushing blow to the whole system of imperialist colonial rule, and gave a mighty impetus to the spread of the national liberation movement.*

The triumph of the October Revolution triggered the crisis of the colonial system of imperialism. The Soviet Republic, which gave a practical example of the fusion of the socialist revolution with the national-liberation movement, became a model for and a reliable bulwark of the liberation struggle.

In keeping with Lenin's behests, the Soviet Union has, throughout its history, consistently conducted a policy of giving every assistance to the national-liberation forces in their struggle against imperialism, for freedom and social progress.

After the Second World War, at a time when imperialism had grown weaker, the world socialist system emerged and there was a powerful upswing of the working-class and democratic movement; the capitalist system of colonial oppression collapsed under the impact of anti-imperialist national-liberation revolutions. More than 70 independent national states were formed on the territory of the former colonies.

The imperialists seek to keep their former colonies in economic and social dependence, to fetter their social and cultural progress. However, the peoples refuse to remain objects of imperialist exploitation. They strive to strengthen and consolidate their independence, look for a road of economic and social development that would enable them to solve the complicated problems facing them in the shortest possible time. They have before them the example of how the national border regions of Russia, once oppressed by czarism, relying on the support of the victorious proletariat of Russia, succeeded in eliminating economic and cultural backwardness in a short period, and achieved remarkable successes in all fields of social life. This may be seen in the example of the Mongolian People's Republic, which is successfully building socialism.

The revolutionary-democratic forces of some newly-free countries have directed the development of their countries along the non-capitalist road and are now implementing far-reaching practical steps to that effect. The revolutionary-democratic parties are expanding their ties with the international working-class and communist movement, and are evincing greater interest in the ideology of scientific socialism. The achievement of unity between the national-democratic and all progressive forces in the struggle for social reform is a major condition that will enable these countries to develop successfully and overcome the serious difficulties in domestic and foreign policies.

In many young national states the division between the social forces fighting for progressive social development and the reactionary circles entering into collusion with the imperialists is becoming more pronounced. Imperialism, notably US imperialism, was and continues to be the main enemy of the national liberation movement. Relying on internal reaction, it organizes plots and coups, sows strife between nations, fosters reactionary nationalism and beguiles newly-free states into territorial disputes.

The world socialist system actively supports the courageous struggle of the peoples of the former colonial and semi-colonial world against imperialism, colonialism and neo-colonialism and renders them political and economic assistance and, if necessary, helps to strengthen their armed forces and defenses. The union of the forces of socialism and the national-liberation movement is an important condition for the success of the struggle against imperialism for freedom, national independence and social progress.

*20. The revolutionary transformation of the world initiated by the October Revolution has created new conditions conducive to the struggle of the international working class for its immediate and ultimate aims. The organization and international bonds of its various contingents have strengthened. The triumph of the October Revolution has made the working class a pivotal factor of the modern epoch.*

The consolidation of the forces of socialism increasingly influences the correlation of the class forces in the capitalist world. Objective material prerequisites for the socialist revolution have been formed within bourgeois society. Subjective conditions for a revolutionary transition to socialism are also taking shape under the impact of mounting class contradictions. The astute tactics of the bourgeoisie, the concessions it was forced to make, could not prevent the process of revolutionizing the masses.

The October Revolution opened up greater possibilities for the masses in the capitalist countries to acquire class, socialist consciousness. They see the advantages of socialism in its practical achievements. The fact that the position of the working man has radically changed under socialism has given the proletarians new stimuli in their struggle. The working people in the West won their most important gains under the direct impact of the October Revolution and the successes of socialist and communist construction in socialist countries. These successes, the example set by socialist countries are a powerful factor intensifying the class battles, now acquiring ever new forms.

Under state-monopoly capitalism, when the proletariat in the economic sphere is directly confronted not only by individual industrialists and their associations but also by the bourgeois state, the economic struggle of the working people is bound to become political in nature. The working class is advancing direct political demands with growing insistence, fights against monopoly rule and against the aggressive and reactionary policies of imperialist governments and for democracy and social progress.

In 50 years the participation of the working class in the economic and political life of the capitalist countries has grown substantially. The progressive trade unions that have appeared and grown strong in the capitalist countries are now playing an important role in the working-class struggle against the offensive of the capitalist monopolies for the economic, social and political rights of the working people. The international unity of the trade unions in the fight against imperialism, for peace and social progress is becoming more solid.

The working class of the capitalist countries is stepping up militant action against the rule of the monopolies and their governments. And if thus far it has not succeeded in realizing its socialist ideals, this is largely due to the split in its ranks. Today more favorable conditions are being created for overcoming this split. The successes of socialism have convincingly demonstrated that the working class's ultimate aims can be achieved only through a radical reorganization of society. At the same time history has proved the futility of the reformist way. In no country have the Social-Democratic governments done anything to shake the foundations of capitalist rule. Workers supporting the Social-Democrats, the Catholic parties and the trade unions, are becoming more and more aware of the necessity to approach social problems from class positions and to cooperate with Communists in finding solutions to these problems.

The changes in the balance of class forces in individual countries and on a world scale witnessed in the fifty years since the October Revolution, have broadened the possibilities for effecting the transition from capitalism to socialism and have brought to life new means of struggle for socialist revolution.

At a time when the united anti-monopoly front is consolidating and expanding, when the working class and its allies are gaining ever greater political weight in society, they can make wider use of their hard-won democratic rights and institutions in the struggle against monopoly rule. The democratic reforms, expressing the interests of the working class and the non-proletarian sections of working people, which are being enforced under pressure of the masses, result in the consolidation of the positions of the progressive forces, and expand the bridgehead for launching a decisive offensive against capitalist positions. The movement to win greater rights for the people in the bourgeois countries is an important aspect of the class battles and an integral part of the struggle for socialism.

Worked out by the 20th-23rd Congresses of the CPSU and the Moscow Meetings in 1957 and 1960, the Marxist-Leninist thesis on the possibility of applying peaceful and non-peaceful forms of struggle in the transition to socialism, depending on the specific relation of class forces in a country, on the organization and political maturity of the working class, on the authority and ability of its vanguard, on the degree of resistance offered by the ruling classes, and on the world situation is becoming particularly important.

In our time the working class of any country can rely in its revolutionary struggle on the support of the victorious contingents of the working-class movement—the working people of the socialist countries—and can draw upon the experience of the socialist countries and, primarily, of the country of the October Revolution, whose enormous achievements inspire and help the working people and their revolutionary vanguard. This is an expression of the organic bonds linking the struggle of the proletariat in the capitalist countries with the gains of the October Revolution, and the achievements of the world socialist system.

*21. The triumph of the socialist revolution in Russia marked the birth of the contemporary international communist movement, which is developing under the banner of the ideas of the October Revolution.*

The October Revolution has shown the world proletariat how much it needs a Party of a new type, a Party of revolutionary action, armed with Marxist-Leninist theory, a Party standing in the vanguard of the masses.

The Communist International, organized on Lenin's initiative, had played a great role in establishing and strengthening the Communist Parties. It was their revolutionary headquarters, a school of Marxism-Leninism, a center for the creative development of Marxism-Leninism in the new conditions, a school spreading communist ideas among the masses, a school of internationalism. The Communist International had played an important role in educating many outstanding leaders and militant cadres of the communist movement.

In 50 years the communist movement has developed into an enormous force. It has become a world movement in the true sense of the word. There are Communist Parties practically in all countries where there is a working class.

Communists are the most consistent spokesmen of the interests of all the exploited and oppressed, and selflessly champion the vital interests of the peoples. It is for this reason that the vanguard of the international working class spreads its influence on ever broader sections of the working people, and is one of the most important factors altering the balance of forces in the world today in favor of peace, democracy, national independence and socialism.

The experience of the past fifty years has demonstrated that the strength of the communist movement rests on its loyalty to Marxism-Leninism. There can be no communist movement outside the orbit of scientific communism. Elaborating its strategy and tactics, the communist vanguard of the working class of the socialist countries, of the advanced capitalist countries and of the newly-free states develops and enriches the heritage of the October Revolution. The creative result of the joint, collective work of Marxist-Leninists is their general line, formulated in the Declaration and Statement of the Moscow Meetings of 1957 and 1960.

The most urgent task of the international communist movement is to ensure its unity on the basis of Marxist-Leninist principles. At the present stage, this unity is being achieved by finding joint solutions to common tasks, by holding bilateral and multilateral meetings between Parties, comradely exchanges of views, and by mutual study of experience. The Conference of the European Communist and Workers' Parties at Karlovy Vary, at which problems of peace and security in Europe were discussed, has played a major role in strengthening the unity of Communists throughout the world. International conferences of Communist and Workers' Parties are a tested form of collective discussion of the most urgent problems and for working out a common program of action.

Particularly significant in modern conditions is a correct combination of the national and international tasks of the huge army of Communists. International obligations cannot be fulfilled outside the struggle for the solution of national tasks, or in disregard of the vital interests of the working masses of every country. At the same time the national tasks cannot be fulfilled without active participation of every detachment of the communist movement in the solution of general problems. The faithfulness to proletarian internationalism is one of the most important lessons to be drawn from the 50-year-long experience of the communist movement since the October Revolution.

The international unity of Communists was tempered and grew stronger in the struggle against imperialism, against all kinds of opportunism and sectarianism and against bourgeois nationalism. The CPSU has always fought and will continue to fight against Right and "Left" deviations, the danger of which to the cause of the revolution has been proved by the history of the communist movement. Events have demonstrated that deviations from the Marxist-Leninist line become particularly dangerous when they are coupled with manifestations of nationalism, great-power chauvinism and hegemonism.

The CPSU works tirelessly and consistently to strengthen the unity of the international communist movement on the basis of Marxist-Leninist principles. The unity of Communists, the international solidarity of the working class and the working people of the world with the country of the October Revolution has been an important condition of the historic victories achieved by the Soviet peoples in the field of battle and in labor.

Our Party, all Soviet people, express their deep gratitude to the working people of all countries, their communist vanguards, for their fraternal international solidarity and for the support they have rendered and are rendering to the country in which socialism had first triumphed.

*22. The October Revolution has precipitated radical shifts in the entire system of international relations, thrown imperialist foreign policy into a deep crisis and proclaimed principles of peace and international security, equality, friendship and cooperation between peoples. The struggle between socialism and imperialism has become the pivot of world politics.*

By its emergence, the Soviet country had limited the maneuvers of the imperialists in the world arena. In all its doings the bourgeoisie has to reckon with the Soviet Union. Today there is not a single important international question that can be solved without the participation of the Soviet Union and the other fraternal countries. Further successes of the world socialist revolution will create more and more ground for asserting the principles of the national sovereignty, the right of nations to self-determination, the equality of all countries, both large and small.

After the October Revolution the working masses, the working class, began to play an increasingly greater part in solving fundamental foreign political problems.

There has been a radical change in the role played by the former colonial and dependent countries in international relations. In our days progressive national states which are conducting an independent foreign policy actively work for peace and for democratic solutions to key international problems.

The militant union of the socialist countries and all anti-imperialist forces is an important factor in international politics. Imperialism no longer dominates the world arena. By vigorous, coordinated action the peoples can now prevent a new world war.

However, there will always be a threat of predatory wars breaking out as long as imperialism continues to exist. This is borne out by the U.S. aggression in Vietnam, Israel's aggression against the freedom-loving Arab peoples, inspired by imperialism, the unceasing provocations against Cuba. All the peace-loving forces and peoples must redouble their vigilance and mobilize their forces in order to be ready to repel the aggressive actions of imperialism, to curb international reaction, to stop it from plunging mankind into a new world holocaust.

Consistently defending peace and international security, the Soviet Government has maintained and will maintain its defense potential at the highest level. Our Armed Forces possess all types of modern weapons, including missiles and nuclear arms. Large funds are spent on defense, but Soviet people understand such outlays are necessary. The socialist revolution, as Marx and Lenin had said, must be capable of defending itself, and must confront the aggressive actions of the class enemy with invincible military force. The strength of the Soviet Union and of the socialist countries creates a real counterweight to the aggressive forces of imperialism, and is an important factor in the struggle to avert a new world war and to preserve peace. The defense potential must be strengthened in every way and the questions of defense given the utmost attention—such is one of the principal conclusions to be drawn from the experience of the past five decades.

The foreign policy of the socialist countries plays a key role in the struggle for peace, against imperialist aggression. It is aimed at consolidating all anti-imperialist peace-loving forces in the struggle against the forces of reaction and war. The course of peaceful coexistence of countries with different social systems, which is an integral part of this policy, is aimed at preventing the imperialists from unleashing a new world war, instigating international provocations and exporting counter-revolution. At the same time its purpose is to create favorable conditions for the peoples to exercise their sacred right of choosing their own road of development and to promote mutually advantageous economic, scientific and technological cooperation, and cultural exchange between all countries.

Condemning predatory imperialist wars, Marxist-Leninists support and regard as just the wars which are waged to defend the peoples' gains against imperialist aggression, national-liberation wars, and wars fought by the revolutionary classes to repel the attempts of the reactionary forces to perpetuate or re-establish their rule by force of arms. The Soviet people decisively support the Vietnamese people in their heroic fight against the criminal aggression of U.S. imperialism. They firmly believe that the just cause of the Vietnamese people will triumph. The Soviet people fully support the just struggle of the Arab peoples against Israeli aggression, against Israel's imperialist benefactors.

Fulfilling Lenin's behests, the Soviet people and the Communist Party during the past 50 years have consistently pursued a policy of proletarian internationalism, in line with the principle of the indivisibility of the international and national tasks of the country where socialism had triumphed.

The great aim of the Soviet people, the building of communism, is also its chief internationalist cause. Working heroically the Soviet people have transformed their country into an invincible citadel of socialism which is exerting growing influence on world affairs. The establishment of a new social system, and the constant growth of its economic and defense potential are decisive factors further altering the balance of forces in the world today to the detriment of imperialism and reaction, and strengthening the material, political and ideological prerequisites for the victory of the socialist revolution on a world scale.

The principal aim of Soviet foreign policy is to ensure favorable conditions for building communism. The Communist Party and the Soviet Government are doing all that is necessary to strengthen the unity and cohesion of the socialist countries, to support the struggle of the peoples for national and social emancipation, to develop cooperation with the young sovereign states, to consistently implement principles of peaceful coexistence of countries with different social systems, and to deliver mankind from the threat of a world thermonuclear war. The achievement of these aims fully corresponds to the interests of all revolutionary and democratic forces and all peoples.

The aim of the international policy of the Communist Party of the Soviet Union is to achieve an all-out strengthening of the links and fraternal cooperation with the Communist and Workers' Parties of all countries, to consolidate the ranks of the world communist movement. Throughout its history our Party and our people, in the face of difficulties, always rendered extensive assistance to the fighters for the cause of freedom and national independence, for the cause of the revolution. The international working class knows that there has not been a single considerable revolutionary action that was not supported by the CPSU and the whole Soviet people. The CPSU, the Party of Lenin, considers rendering support to international revolutionary forces as an integral part of its activity.

*Holding aloft the torch of socialism, lit by the Great October Socialist Revolution, the Soviet people, the Leninist Party have opened a new epoch in world history. Socialism, which in the nineteenth century had turned from a dream into a science, became the socio-political practice of millions of working people in the twentieth century, following the victory of the Great October Socialist Revolution.*

*We are marching along the right road to our goal, that of building communism, which was paved by the development of Soviet society over the past fifty years.*

*We are armed with an advanced scientific theory—the Marxist-Leninist teaching, and we rely on the rich experience of the revolutionary struggle and socialist construction.*

*United in a single international detachment we are marching together with the international working class, with the fraternal socialist countries, with the forces of the national-liberation movement in the struggle against imperialism, for peace, democracy and socialism, national independence, and the security and freedom of peoples.*

*The strength of communism is inexhaustible, on its side is the truth of life. Only communism can solve the fundamental problems of social development, deliver mankind from oppression and exploitation, from hunger and poverty, from militarism and war, and establish on our planet democracy, peace and friendship between peoples, a life that is in keeping with the dignity of man.*

*The ideas of the October Revolution, the ideas of communism, are the leading ideas of our time, the great creative force of contemporary history.*

*Future years will bring new victories to the teaching of Marx, Engels and Lenin, to the cause of communism.*

# LETTER BY A. I. SOLZHENITSYN TO THE CONGRESS OF THE UNION OF SOVIET WRITERS

*Complete Text*
*(Posev,* Frankfurt-am-Main, no. 8 [August] 1968)

To the Presidium of the Congress and the Delegates
To the members of the Union of Soviet Writers
To the editors of literary newspapers and periodicals

Not having access to the Congress rostrum, I beg the Congress to discuss the following:

1. The further intolerable oppression to which our artistic literature has been subjected decade after decade by the censorship, an oppression which the Writers' Union can no longer tolerate.

Not stipulated in the constitution, and therefore, illegal, nowhere publicly named, under the vague name of "Main Literature Administration" this censorship weighs over our literature and enables literary illiterates to exert their arbitrary rules over the writers. A vestige of the Middle Ages, it has dragged its archaic terms almost into the twenty-first century! Perishable, it tries to assume the aspect of imperishable time: to choose among worthy and unworthy books.

Our writers are not presumed to have the right to express advanced views on the moral life of man and society, interpret in their own manner the social problems or historical experience so deeply experienced in our country. Works which could express a matured popular idea and promptly and healingly influence our spiritual realm or the development of social awareness are banned or distorted by the censorship for petty and egotistical considerations, shortsighted from the point of view of the life of the people. Excellent manuscripts by young authors, names still totally unknown, are now being refused by editors only because "they will not pass." Many members of the Union and even delegates to this Congress know how they themselves have yielded to censorship pressure in the structure and intent of their books, replacing chapters, pages, paragraphs or sentences, giving them pale titles only for the sake of having them published, thus distorting them irrefutably. By virtue of the nature of literature all these distortions ruin the works of talent and have no effect whatever on the mediocre ones. It is precisely the best part of our literature that is published in a distorted manner.

Yet, the censorship labels themselves ("ideologically harmful," "depraved," etc.) are of short duration, shifting, changing under our very eyes. At a given time even Dostoyevsky, the pride of world literature, was not published in our country (he is not published in his entirety still today); he was deleted from the school curricula, made inaccessible to the reader, defamed. How many years was Yesenin considered "counterrevolutionary" (and possession of his books meant even a jail term)? Was not Mayakovsky considered "an anarchic political hooligan?" For decades the unfading verses of Akhmatova were considered anti-Soviet. The first shy publication of the brilliant Tsvetayeva, ten years ago, was proclaimed a "gross political error." It is only after a delay of 20 or 30 years that we were given back Bunin, Bulgakov and Platonov. The turn has irreversibly come from Mandelshtam, Voloshin, Gumilev and Klyuyev. One day, Zamyatin and Remizov will not fail to be "recognized." There is a dividing point: the death of an inconvenient writer, following which, sooner or later, he is given back to us with "explanations of errors." Was it so long ago that one could not even mention Pasternak's name? Yet he died and his books are being published and his poetry is being cited even on formal occasions.

Surely, Pushkin's words are coming true:
They can love only the dead!

However, the posthumous publication of books and the "permission" of mentioning names does not restore the social or artistic losses suffered by our people as a result of such distorted delays or the oppression of the artistic consciousness. (There were, among others, writers in the 20's such as Pilnyak, Platonov and Mandelshtam, who quite early pointed out the birth of the cult of personality and Stalin's particular characteristics. However, they were destroyed and suppressed instead of being listened to.) Literature cannot develop as classified into "will pass — will not pass," "this is possible—this is not." A literature which does not breathe the air of its society, which does not dare transmit to the society its aches and alarms, adequately warning of the threatening moral and social dangers could not be even called a literature. It could be considered no more than a whitewash. Such a literature loses the trust of its own people and it is used not as reading material but as scrap.

Our literature has lost the leading position in the world which it held by the end of the Nineteenth century and at the beginning of this century as well as that experimental brilliance which distinguished it in the 1920's. In the eyes of the entire world, the literary life of our country is incomparably poorer, worse and lower than it is in fact, than it would be had it not been restricted or locked in. This is to the detriment of our country in terms of the world of public opinion and to the detriment of world literature: placing at its disposal all the unrestricted fruits of our literature, it would become deeper with the help of our spiritual experience. The entire artistic development of the world would take a different course than it has taken. It would acquire a new stability, it would even reach a new level of art.

I submit to the Congress to adopt the requirement and achieve the elimination of all – open or hidden – censorship over works of art, to free the publishing houses from the obligation to seek a permit for every printed sheet;

2. Obligations of the Union concerning its members. These obligations are not clearly formulated in the bylaws of the Soviet Writers' Union ("protection of authorship rights" and "measures for the defense of other writers' rights"); yet, it has become distressingly clear that in one-third of a century neither the "other" nor the authorship rights of the persecuted writers have been protected by the Union.

During their lifetime, many authors have been subjected, in the press and from various rostrums, to insults and slander and were deprived of the physical possibility to answer them. Furthermore, they were subjected to individual restrictions and persecution (Bulgakov, Akhmatova, Tsvetayeva, Pasternak, Zoshchenko, Platonov, Alexandr Grin, Vasiliy Grossman). The Writers' Union not only did not yield the pages of its publications for their answer and justification, not only failed to undertake their defense, but even the leadership of the Union invariably showed itself in the first ranks of the persecutors. The names which embellish our Twentieth century poetry were in the list of those expelled from the Union or even not given Union membership! Furthermore, the leadership of the Union pusillanimously left in the lurch those whose persecution ended with exile, concentration camp or death (Pavel Vasilyev, Mandelshtam, Artem Veselyi, Pilnyak, Babel, Tabidze, Zabolotsky and others). We have to add to this list the words "and others": we learned, after the Twentieth Party Congress, that they numbered over 600 – entirely innocent writers at a time when the Union obediently surrendered them to a destiny of jail and concentration camp. However, the list is even longer and its end cannot be read nor will it ever be by us: it includes the names of young prose and poetry writers whom we accidentally met personally and whose talent perished in the camps unblossomed, whose works did not go beyond the state security offices, in the times of Yagoda, Yezhov, Beriya, and Abakumov.

The newly elected leadership of the Union has no historical obligation to share with the former leadership the responsibility for the past.

I submit the need for a clear formulation, in paragraph 22 of the Bylaws of the Soviet Writers' Union, of all the protection guarantees which the Union offers its members subjected to slander and unfair persecution, so that a repetition of lawlessness may become impossible.

In the case that the Congress does not indifferently bypass what I have said above, I beg to direct its attention to the interdictions and persecutions I have experienced:

1. My novel *V kruge pervom* (The First Circle) (35 author's sheets) has been taken from me for almost two years by the state security, thus preventing any further moves toward publishing it. On the contrary, even during my own lifetime and despite my wishes or even my knowledge, this novel has been "published" in an unnatural "closed" edition for reading by a selected unnamed circle. My novel has become accessible to the literary officials and is being concealed from most writers. I am unable to obtain the open discussion of the novel in the writers' sections and prevent misuse or plagiarism.

2. Together with my novel, my literary files assembled in the course of 15 to 20 years, consisting of items not aimed at publication, have been taken away. Now tendentious excerpts from these files have been "secretly" "published" and disseminated among that same circle. My play in verse *The Feast of the Victors*, written in the concentration camp where I was only a four-digit number (when, doomed to death by starvation, we had been forgotten by society and no one outside the camps opposed the repressions), a play long abandoned, is being ascribed as my most recent work.

3. For three years an irresponsible slander has been disseminated against me who spent the entire war as a battery commander who was awarded combat orders: that, allegedly, I was serving time as a criminal or had surrendered (I have never been a prisoner of war), that I had "betrayed the motherland," or "served the Germans." That is the interpretation given of the eleven years I have spent in concentration camps and exile for criticizing Stalin. This slander is disseminated in closed instruction meetings and gatherings of people holding official positions. I have tried in vain to put an end by appealing to the Board of the Writers' Union of the RSFSR and to the press! The Board has not even answered. Not a single newspaper printed my answer to the slanderers. Conversely, the slander from official places directed against me has intensified and increased during the last year. Twisted data is being used, confiscated from my files. Yet, I am deprived of the opportunity to answer such slanders.

4. My story "The Cancer Ward" (25 author's sheets), approved for publication (first part) by the prose section of the Moscow Writers' Organization can be published neither in individual chapters (rejected by five periodicals) nor in its entirety (rejected by *Novyi mir* (New World), *Zvezda* (Star), and *Prostor* (Space).

5. The play "The Deer and the Sparrow" accepted by the "Sovremennik" Theater in 1962 has still not been issued a staging permit.

6. The movie script "The Tanks Know the Truth," the play "The Light Which is In You," and the short stories ("The First Cluster," and the "Tiny Stories" series) have found neither a director nor a publisher.

7. My stories published in *Novyy Mir* have not been reissued as a book once. They have been rejected everywhere ("Sovetsky pisatel," Gospolitizdat, and the "Ogonek" series), thus remaining inaccessible to the wide public.

8. I am forbidden to have any other contact with the readers: public readings of excerpts (in November 1966 nine out of eleven such readings already agreed upon were banned) or readings on the radio. Simply giving a manuscript to someone "to read and copy" is banned in our country as a crime (500 years ago this

was allowed to the old Russian copy clerks!).

Thus my work is totally suppressed, silent and twisted.

With such a gross violation of my authorship and "other" rights, will or will not the Fourth Congress undertake my defense? It seems to me that this choice is not unimportant to the literary future of anyone among the delegates.

I am certain, of course, that I shall fulfill my duty as a writer under any circumstances, even more successfully and unquestionably from the grave than while alive. No one can obstruct the path to truth, and to promote it I am ready to accept even death. But perhaps at last the many lessons we have learned will teach us, once and for all, not to stop the writer's pen while he is alive.

This practice has never as yet made our history more attractive.

# "TO THE SOVIET PEOPLE, TO ALL WORKING PEOPLE OF THE USSR"

Message of the Central Committee of the CPSU,
the Presidium of the USSR Supreme Soviet,
and the Council of Ministers of the USSR, 4 November 1967

*Complete Text*
(*Pravda*, 5 November 1967)

Dear comrades!

The Central Committee of the Communist Party of the Soviet Union, the Presidium of the Supreme Soviet of the USSR and the Council of Ministers of the USSR warmly congratulate the workers, collective farmers, Soviet intelligentsia, servicemen in the Soviet Army and Navy, all working people of the Union of Soviet Socialist Republics on the occasion of the 50th anniversary of the Great October Socialist Revolution—the national holiday of the people.

Half a century ago the Russian proletariat, in alliance with the toiling peasantry, led by the Bolshevik Party and under Lenin's guidance, carried out the triumphant Socialist Revolution and established the power of the Soviets. The working class became master of the plants and factories. The peasants received land. The oppressed nations took to the road of freedom and equality. The Revolution had pulled the country out of the imperialist war and delivered it from national catastrophe.

THE VICTORY OF THE OCTOBER REVOLUTION WAS THE GREATEST TURNING POINT IN WORLD HISTORY. IT CREATED CONDITIONS FOR THE BUILDING OF SOCIALISM IN THE LARGEST COUNTRY IN THE WORLD AND MARKED THE BEGINNING OF THE LIBERATION OF MANKIND FROM EXPLOITATION AND OPPRESSION. The glorious anniversary of the October Revolution is being celebrated together with us by the peoples of the socialist countries, by the fraternal Parties, the international working class and all progressive mankind.

The October Revolution lit the flame of enthusiasm in the hearts of millions of people; it was the beacon and hope for the oppressed, for all fighters for freedom.

The ten days of October shook the world and the half a century has changed it.

In October 1917, Soviet Russia was the first to take the road of socialism. Today, many states and nations are following this road. The world system of socialism has become a mighty factor of historic progress.

The world communist movement was in its infancy in October 1917. Today it is a mighty political force, uniting in its ranks millions of Communists, who are fighting under the banner of Marxism-Leninism and proletarian internationalism.

Most of the world was enmeshed in the chains of colonialist oppression in October 1917. The mighty hurricane of the national-liberation revolutions swept away the centuries-old colonialist system, and the previously oppressed peoples started out on the road of national renaissance and social progress.

October 1917 wrought radical changes in world politics. For 50 years, beginning with Lenin's Decree on Peace, our socialist State has consistently opposed the imperialist policy of oppression and aggression, international provocations and military ventures, interference in the domestic affairs of other states, and championed peaceful cooperation and international security, freedom and independence of nations. The Communist Party and the Soviet Government are doing everything necessary to secure peaceful conditions for communist construction in our country, preserve and strengthen peace throughout the world, promote the unity of the socialist countries, and support the struggle waged by the nations for national and social liberation.

The Leninist Party, the working class of our country, the Soviet people have shown by their revolutionary experience how the working people can achieve liberation, have given a practical answer to the question what is socialism and what it brings the toiling people.

In five decades the Soviet Union has become a mighty socialist power, it is building a communist society, and is marching in the vanguard of social progress. The ideas of Marx, Engels and Lenin, the aims and tasks which our Party and our people have set themselves are being successfully implemented.

WE POSED AS OUR GOAL THE DESTRUCTION OF EXPLOITATION OF MAN BY MAN. AND WE HAVE ACHIEVED THIS.

Socialism is a society of working people. It has no exploiters and no exploited. Labor has become the sole source of material wellbeing, a sacred right and an honorable duty of all members of society. For the first time in history the labor of the worker, of the peasant, the work of man has received supreme social recognition.

WE SET OURSELVES THE TASK OF CREATING SOCIALIST PRODUCTION. AND WE HAVE ACHIEVED IT.

A highly developed modern industry has been created in our country by the heroic labor of the people. Large-scale technically well-equipped collective-farm and state-farm agriculture has succeeded small-scale peasant farming. Planned socialist economy is developing at a high and stable rate.

WE SET OURSELVES THE TASK OF ENDING NATIONAL STRIFE AND OPPRESSION. AND WE HAVE ACHIEVED THIS.

Socialism has established the fraternal unity of the peoples of our multinational Motherland. No alloy in the world is more durable and solid than the friendship of the peoples of the USSR. This friendship was born in the years of the Revolution and Civil War. It was strengthened in the day-to-day work during the five-year plans and steeled in the flames of the Great Patriotic War. The indestructible fraternity of the USSR nations is the most valuable gain of socialism, the earnest of our coming victories.

WE SET OURSELVES THE TASK OF IMPLEMENTING THE SOCIALIST PRINCIPLE: "FROM EACH ACCORDING TO HIS ABILITY, TO EACH ACCORDING TO HIS WORK." AND WE HAVE ACCOMPLISHED IT.

Poverty, unemployment, and exploiter parasitism have been liquidated in our country. Socialist production has been made to serve the interests of the people, to satisfy the needs of the working people. The right to work and leisure, to free education, medical services and pension are inalienable features of the Soviet way of life. Steady improvement of the material wellbeing of the people is law in socialist society.

WE SET OURSELVES THE TASK OF CREATING A NEW SOCIALIST STATE, A NEW SOCIALIST DEMOCRACY, WHICH WOULD BE THE EMBODIMENT OF THE POWER OF THE PEOPLE AND FOR THE PEOPLE. AND WE HAVE FULFILLED THIS TASK.

The socialist democracy born of the October Revolution has drawn broad masses of the people into managing state and public affairs, and has provided a broad field for the application by the toiling people of their abilities, knowledge and talents. For the first time in history a state has been created whose strength is contained in the consciousness and organization of the masses. The makers of life—those who mine the ore and coal, smelt steel, till the land, fathom the secrets of the atom and outer space, who create all the material and spiritual wealth—have become its masters.

THE REVOLUTION ADVANCED THE GOAL OF EDUCATING THE WORKING PEOPLE IN A SPIRIT OF LOFTY SOCIALIST CONSCIOUSNESS. TODAY, WE MAY PROUDLY SAY: GENERATIONS OF WONDERFUL FIGHTERS FOR THE GREAT COMMUNIST CAUSE HAVE GROWN UP IN OUR COUNTRY.

Socialism has done away with ignorance and obscurantism, has liquidated mass illiteracy. Knowledge and culture have become the property of the people. Socialist ideology is a mighty creative force for the development of social consciousness. The achievements of socialist culture and the successes of Soviet science constitute a tremendous step forward in the spiritual progress of mankind.

The 50 years of the Great Revolution are an embodiment of the great road traversed by a great people. It is the life, labor and the feats of the working class, the toiling peasantry and the intelligentsia, who have been elevated by the October Revolution, by the Party of Communists, to conscious creative activity, to building a new life.

The 50 years of the Great Revolution stand for continuity of the links of the glorious generations of fighters and builders of the new society—of those who together with Lenin had built up our Party, stormed the citadels of czarism and capitalism, who defended the young Republic of Soviets with arms in hand, those who developed the industrial might of the socialist power, organized collective and state farms, upheld the freedom and independence of the socialist Motherland in the years of the Great Patriotic War, those who rehabilitated the economy of the country and are now building a communist society.

The greatest selflessness and courage of the Soviet people, their loyalty to the revolutionary ideals, and their conscious discipline, evoke admiration everywhere in the world.

While feeling justifiable pride and profound satisfaction at the magnificent successes of socialism, we clearly see how complex was the path traversed. In building the new society, the Party and the people have never been daunted by the difficulties met on unknown paths. We have passed through grim trials and have known both the joy of victories and the bitterness of losses, drawing lessons from the temporary setbacks and errors. The fine characteristics of our people, their revolutionary consciousness and selflessness, proletarian internationalism and boundless loyalty to the socialist homeland and to the ideals of communism have unfolded most fully at a time of both triumph and severe trials.

Dear comrades,

Socialism has brought new life to our country, it has brought the happiness of free labor and the inexhaustible energy of purposeful creative endeavor. The economic and the socio-political results of socialist construction open up before us the majestic prospects of transition to communism.

WE HAVE SET OURSELVES THE GOAL OF BUILDING A COMMUNIST SOCIETY. AND WE SHALL BUILD IT.

By their labor and struggle the Soviet people are translating the ideals of communism into a practical reality. The Leninist Party has evolved in its program, in the decisions of the 23rd Congress, the main ways of building communist society. Our people are confidently marching towards the triumph of communism under the banner of the great Lenin, under the leadership of the Communist Party.

To build communist society, it is necessary to accomplish the main economic task—to create the material and technical basis of communism. We must ensure—on the basis of all-round utilization of the achievements of science and engineering, the industrial development of all social production, its increased effectiveness and higher labor productivity—a steady growth of industry and agriculture and, thereby, obtain a further improvement in living standards, and a more complete satisfaction of the material and cultural needs of all Soviet people.

To build communist society, it is necessary persistently to improve socialist social relations; consistently to implement the measures directed at removing the essential distinctions between town and countryside, and between workers by brain and by hand; to develop the economy and culture of the nations and nationalities, securing even closer fraternal cooperation and mutual assistance among them; to strengthen the political foundations and the material basis of the alliance of the working class and the peasantry; to strengthen the Soviet State and develop socialist democracy, to improve planning and economic management.

To build communism, it is necessary to persistently educate all members of society in a spirit of lofty consciousness, and a communist attitude to labor and public property, in the spirit of Soviet patriotism and internationalism; to draw all citizens into management of public affairs, develop criticism and self-criticism, enhance the organization and discipline of the working people; to strengthen in every possible way the standards of socialist communal life; to use free time for the spiritual enrichment of the person; to improve secondary and higher education; develop as much as possible scientific research, and raise the educational role of literature and the arts.

We express the confidence that our heroic working class, scientists, engineers, technicians, designers, all workers in industry will, in the future too, work indefatigably for further engineering progress and the implementation of the economic reform. The raising of labor productivity, improvement of the quality of goods, emulation for fulfilling production plans and socialist pledges, for saving of raw materials, and the strengthening of state and labor discipline are all most important conditions for the further growth of the economic might of our State, for accelerated progress towards communism.

We express our confidence that our glorious collective-farm peasantry, the men and women working on state farms, the specialists in agriculture, will continue, in the future too, constantly to raise the standards of crop farming and animal husbandry, to cut down expenditure of labor per unit of output, persistently to improve the economic indices in their work, and to manage their farms ably and intelligently. Upon this depends the increase of production of grain, meat, milk, and other agricultural produce, the strengthening of the economy of the collective and state farms, the constant improvement of life in the countryside and the wellbeing of the entire Soviet people.

We express the confidence that workers in science and culture, teachers, doctors, and our entire Soviet intelligentsia, will continue, in the future too, with honor to fulfill their duty to the people, to give their strength and knowledge to the great cause of communist construction, to persistently develop science and engineering, to bring culture to the masses, and to help educate the younger generation in the spirit of communism.

Today, we appeal to you, our dear Soviet women. The Great October Revolution changed your destinies radically, opened a broad and radiant road towards a new life. By your selfless labor and care in bringing up the children you are making your wonderful contribution to our common cause.

The Communist Party and the Soviet State will continue to do everything necessary to provide for women in our country still greater opportunities for developing their creative abilities and talents.

We appeal to you, young men and girls, our glorious Soviet youth. Loyal sons and daughters of the country, you are giving it your energy of youth, selflessly working together with the older generations at industrial enterprises, in collective and state farm fields; you are studying, exploring outer space, and tapping mineral wealth. The future of the Motherland is in your hands.

We feel confident that you will be worthy continuers of the great cause of Lenin, that you will courageously uphold the ideals of the October Revolution, and, if need be, defend with arms in hand the honor and independence of the socialist Motherland.

Servicemen in the Soviet Army and Navy! Together with the armies of the other socialist countries you are standing guard over the gains of the October Revolution, the gains of socialism, you are standing guard over international security and universal peace. Persistently master the military equipment and arms, perfect your military and political training, reliably guard the borders of the Soviet Union, heighten your vigilance, and strengthen the defense potential of our country.

Our people are firmly convinced that the glorious Soviet Armed Forces are reliably defending their peaceful labor.

Comrades—men and women workers, men and women collective farmers, specialists in industry and agriculture, workers in culture and science, servicemen of the Soviet Army and Navy!

THE 50-YEAR ROAD OF OUR DEVELOPMENT IS MOST VIVID PROOF OF THE UNBREAKABLE UNITY OF THE WORKING PEOPLE AND THE COMMUNIST PARTY.

The Party has awakened in the masses of the people an awareness of their strength, faith in the possibility of building a new and better world on earth. Today, we may say with pride that the cause for which the Communist Party fought, the cause of the working class, has become the cause of the entire people. The Soviet people have displayed great confidence in our Party as the ruling Party of the first socialist state in the world. Our Party prizes this faith. It has no interests other than the interests of the people.

The Soviet people may rest assured that Communists shall always be in the vanguard of the national efforts to promote our great cause. Our Party, armed with the most advanced theory and very rich political experience, is charting the right course which leads to the triumph of communism.

DURING THIS GREAT HOLIDAY, THE SOVIET PEOPLE ARE SENDING WORDS OF SINCERE GRATITUDE TO THEIR BROTHERS ABROAD.

We remember and shall never forget the exploits of the soldiers-internationalists who fought shoulder to shoulder with us in the trying times of the Civil War.

We remember and shall never forget the fraternal support accorded our Motherland in the unforgettable years of the rehabilitation of our economy and the heroic first five-year plans.

We remember and shall never forget our common struggle in the years of war against fascism.

We express to you, dear foreign comrades and friends, our heartfelt gratitude for your internationalist feelings for the world's first country of socialism, for your unselfish and selfless support.

THE SOVIET PEOPLE, ENTERING THE SECOND 50-YEAR PERIOD OF THE GREAT REVOLUTION, ARE CARRYING HIGH THE IDEAS OF COMMUNISM, THE IDEAS OF THE GREAT OCTOBER REVOLUTION. We rely on the successes already achieved in socialist construction. We are armed with the immortal teaching of Marxism-Leninism, the truth of life is with us, and our forces are countless. Marching shoulder to shoulder with us are the peoples of the fraternal countries of socialism, the forces of the international communist movement, the forces of democracy and national liberation. No one and nothing can halt our progress along the road towards the realization of our ultimate goal—the construction of a communist society.

We wish the Soviet people, each and every Soviet person, fresh successes in work, studies, happiness in personal life, success in the struggle for the triumph of our great communist cause.

Long live the Great October Socialist Revolution!

Long live our beloved Motherland—the Union of Soviet Socialist Republics!

Long live the fraternal countries of socialism!

Long live the unity of all revolutionary and progressive forces in the struggle against imperialism, for democracy and socialism!

Long live peace and friendship among the peoples!

Long live the great Soviet people—the creator of the new society!

Under the banner of Marxism-Leninism, under the tried leadership of the Communist Party—forward, to complete victory of communism!

# "FIFTY YEARS ON GUARD OF THE SOVIET UNION'S SECURITY"

Report by I. V. Andropov, Chairman of the State Security Committee (KGB)

*Abridged Text*
(*Moscow News,* Supplement to issue 52 (887), 1967, and *Pravda,* 21 December 1967;
portions in brackets were omitted from the English version in *Moscow News* Supplement.)

Comrades,

We all are deeply moved by the message of greetings we have recieved from the CPSU Central Committee, the Presidium of the Supreme Soviet and Council of Ministers of the USSR. Appreciation for the work done by state security bodies is also reflected in the orders and medals of the Soviet Union that have been awarded to a large group of security workers. On behalf of the state security personnel permit me to express our warm gratitude to the Party and Soviet Government for their trust and high appraisal of our work and to assure them that Soviet security men will spare no effort in accomplishing their duty to our great Motherland.

This year is noteworthy for the series of remarkable dates, each being an important landmark in the history of the Soviet state. Following the 50th anniversary of our militia and of the Soviet judicial system, today we are celebrating the half-century of our security bodies; two months from now we shall hold celebrations in honor of our heroic Soviet Army.

All these glorious dates in the biography of the Soviet state are closely interconnected and profoundly meaningful. During its earliest days the young Soviet state began to build up institutions essential for the defense and preservation of the gains of the world's first victorious revolution of workers and peasants. Vladimir Lenin used to say that "No revolution is worth anything unless it can defend itself." The half-century development of the Soviet state has clearly confirmed the truth of this statement. During this time, our people were not only building a new, socialist world, but had also to manifest the greatest possible vigilance, heroism and self-sacrifice in defending their state against internal and external foes. Soviet power was won by the working class, by all the working people of our country in struggle against the old world. It was consolidated, it grew and scored tremendous victories largely because the Leninist Party taught the working masses how reliably to protect and defend their gains.

Soviet people have covered a heroic road. The state security bodies have made this road together with the people. On December 20, 1917, the All-Russian Extraordinary Commission for Combatting Counter-Revolution and Sabotage (Cheka) was founded on Lenin's initiative. The Cheka men were commissioned by the Party and the people to defend the gains of the October Revolution. That was the beginning of the militant activity of the Extraordinary Commission which became the shield and sword of the October Revolution in the full sense of the word. The state security bodies have performed their difficult and honorable duty ever since.

Comrades, the Bolsheviks came to power experienced in class struggle and equipped with the most progressive and the only scientific theory of social development, namely Marxism-Leninism. It stands to reason that no experience of prerevolutionary struggle, however valuable, and no theory, however profound, gave or could provide answers to all the questions arising in the process of the country's revolutionary remaking. We had to experiment, search and in a number of cases redo what had already been done. We had to return again and again to matters that seemed to have been settled. However, one thing was plain to the Bolsheviks and this was that the working class would not be able to discharge its historic mission of building socialism without a strong political authority. This power, which Karl Marx termed the dictatorship of the proletariat and which was established in our country as a result of the victorious socialist revolution, had to become, and did indeed become that main lever which enabled the working class and all toiling people of Soviet Russia to hold out in bitter battles against the old world and to build a new socialist world.

Vladimir Lenin repeated time and again that the prime objective of the dictatorship of the proletariat is the task of construction. The main and decisive trends of the stupendous crusade for socialism launched over the boundless expanses of our Motherland were to build up a socialist industry and a socialist agriculture, effect a cultural revolution and reorganize the entire system of social relations along socialist lines. However, in our country this had to be started in the midst of cruel battles with the class enemy, with armed counter-revolution and intervention.

The Cheka was established to guard the Revolution from enemies and to discharge the function of suppressing exploiters who came out against the people. The work of the Cheka conformed to the entire democratic spirit of Soviet power and was wholly subordinated to the working people's interests, to the tasks of the struggle for socialism.

Lenin clearly defined the cardinal principles of the activity of the Cheka: selfless devotion to the cause of the Revolution, the closest of bonds with the people, unshakable allegiance to the Party and to Soviet power, firmness in the struggle against class enemies, and lofty proletarian humanism. These democratic principles have been and remain the basis of the activity of the men of the Cheka.

Attaching especial significance to guarding the gains of the October Revolution, the Party Central Committee sent tried and tested men to work in the

Cheka. Its first Chairman was Felix Dzerzhinsky, a prominent Party leader and staunch Leninist who had gone through the grim school of underground activity, czarist jails and hard labor camps, a man infinitely devoted to the Revolution and ruthless towards its enemies. At different times there worked for the Cheka such splendid personalities of our Party as V.R. Menzhinsky, M.S. Uritsky, Y.Kh. Peters, M.S. Kedrov, I.K. Ksenofontov, V.A. Avanesov, M.J. Lacis, I.S. Unschlicht, S.G. Uralov and Y.Y. Buikis—to mention only a few—who formed the Bolshevist core of the Cheka bodies.

In 1918 the Cheka smashed a counter-revolutionary organization headed by well-known Social-Revolutionary terrorist Boris Savinkov linked with the British and French intelligence services. The same year the Lockhart plot was laid bare and rendered harmless. Lockhart tried to bribe Kremlin guardsmen for engineering a counter-revolutionary coup. A year later the so-called National Center in Moscow linked with the Denikin army and then the spying "Tactical Center" in Petrograd were also liquidated. Counter-revolutionary forces and their foreign patrons suffered many setbacks in their duel with Soviet power and its militant organ—Cheka, from the ill-starred "ambassadors' plot" to the complete rout of various White Guard organizations.

Staunch Cheka men inspired by the October Revolution's ideals grew up and became steeled in the struggle against the enemies of Soviet power. It is with these men's activities that the image of the Cheka man is linked in people's memories. He is an ardent revolutionary, of scrupulous honesty and great personal bravery, irreconcilable in the struggle against enemies, stern in duty, and humane, ready for self-sacrifice in the name of people's cause to which he devotes his life.

The transition from the Civil War to peace necessitated a substantial reorganization of work of all Party and Government organizations. The work of the security organs was also reorganized. Cheka men and special units of servicemen were still fighting, arms in hand, banditry, counter-revolutionary sorties in Tambov region, revolts by kulaks in Siberia, as well as armed Basmachi gangs in Central Asia. Much effort was also required to expose and render harmless the espionage activities carried out by imperialist powers.

At the same time organs of Cheka and later on OGPU got down directly to the solution of some pressing economic and social problems. They actively participated in the struggle against hunger, dislocation, transport difficulties; helped to combat epidemics of typhus and assisted in procuring food and fuel.

The struggle to overcome the problem of homeless children is an unforgettable page in Cheka-OGPU history. This task was challenging in its difficulty and at the same time of stupendous nationwide significance. Soviet power inherited from the war a host of homeless, starving, orphaned children, many of whom had fallen under bad influences.

Extraordinary commissions as organs of the proletariat's dictatorship, said one of Cheka circulars, should "help in every way Soviet power in its work to protect and accommodate children. Care for children," said the circular further on, "is the best means of combatting counter-revolution."

Cheka men saved many thousands of children from death of starvation. Hundreds of children's homes, orphanages and reformatory schools were set up in the country on the Cheka's initiative where children who had had no homes were surrounded with attention and solicitude and became conscientious Soviet citizens.

Recalling this and many other events from Cheka history, we think again of humanistic prime sources of Soviet state security organs' activity. Now the situation is different and the tasks are, naturally, not the same. But active, purposeful communist humanism and the realization by every Cheka man that his work is to protect the Soviet people, their peaceful work, tranquility and security, have been and remain the rock-firm basis for the entire activity of the state security organs.

As the foundations of socialism strengthened in our country, the conditions were gradually created for changing the nature of the security bodies' activities. After the liquidation of the hostile classes, they began increasingly to go over from struggle against internal class enemies to struggle against external enemies. In the prewar period the state security bodies had no more important task than to cut short the intelligence and other subversive activities of fascist Germany and militaristic Japan. The enemy failed to disorganize our rear and to undermine the fighting capacity of the Soviet Union—and a big credit for that goes to the state security bodies.

In the years of the Great Patriotic War, the state security service concentrated on the struggle for the victory over the fascist invaders. Our frontier guards were the first to oppose the enemy, they inscribed many heroic pages in the chronicles of the war and showed many stirring examples of self-sacrifice. With the help of the high command of the Soviet Army, political organs of the Soviet Army and Navy, the military counter-intelligence officers successfully guarded our armed forces from enemy spies, saboteurs and terrorists and did all to prevent enemy eyes from seeing the plans of the Soviet command.

Soviet intelligence officers operating in the enemy's rear fearlessly fought against the enemy. The feats of the famed Soviet intelligence officers, Heroes of the Soviet Union N.I. Kuznetsov, I.D. Kudrya, V.A. Molodtsov, V.A. Lyagin, S.I. Solntsev, F.F. Ozmitel and many others, who operated in the enemy rear, have become legendary. The heroic and courageous raids of the partisan units commanded by Cheka men, Heroes of the Soviet Union D.N. Medvedev, K.P. Orlovsky, M.S. Prudnikov, N.A. Prokopyuk are forever inscribed in our history.

While fulfilling their sacred duty to the Motherland and fighting her enemies, many Soviet Cheka men lost their lives. But their names live and will always live in the people's hearts.

Comrades, the state security bodies have traversed a long and difficult road. They have contributed to the cause of defending the Revolution's gains, to the cause of building socialism. Today we are legitimately proud of the glorious deeds of those to whom the Party and the people entrusted the security of our Soviet state.

As we trace the history of the Soviet security bodies, we see clearly that all their successes have always been connected, above all, with the strictest observance of Leninist principles. It is only on this basis, only under the leadership of our Party, that we can accomplish successfully tasks involved in defending the socialist state.

We have no right to forget the times when political adventurers, who managed to climb to top positions in the NKVD, tried to remove the state security bodies from the control of the Party and to isolate them from the people, and violated the laws, thus seriously injuring the interests of our state, the interests of the Soviet people and the state security bodies themselves.

In the last few years our Party has done a tremendous amount of work to strengthen socialist legality. The distortions in the operation of the state security bodies were removed, daily Party and state control over their activities was established, and reliable political and legal guarantees of the observance of the socialist laws introduced.

Thus, our Party has shown with utmost clarity that any recidivism to violations of the socialist laws is ruled out. The state security bodies are guarding and will continue to guard the interests of the Soviet state and the Soviet people's interests.

Comrades, in determining the security tasks at the present stage, the Party proceeds from both the international and internal conditions of the development of the Soviet state.

Substantial changes have taken place in Soviet society over the last few years. Having healed, in a short span of time, the wounds inflicted by the war, our country has made tremendous headway in all economic, social and cultural spheres. The successes achieved in building a developed socialist society and in the transition to communism have increased the might of the Soviet state and strengthened its democratic foundations.

The time is long past when our country was in the capitalist encirclement, surrounded by hostile states. The formation of the world socialist system, the growth of its might and influence, the successes of the international workers' and national-liberation movement have radically changed the balance of forces on the world arena in favor of socialism and progress.

As a result of all these historic gains capitalism has lost any social base inside our country, while on the world arena the forces of imperialism are weakened and have lost their once dominating positions.

However, the threat to the security of the Soviet Union and other socialist countries has not disappeared.

Life shows that as long as imperialism, with its economic and military might, exists, a real danger remains to the peoples of our country and other socialist countries, to all the progressive forces, and to world peace. Evidence of this is the dirty war of American imperialism against the heroic Vietnamese people, the imperialists' vigorous support for the Israeli aggression against the Arab countries, and constant United States' interference in the affairs of Latin America, Asia and Africa.

Our Party and the Soviet Government firmly uphold the policy of peaceful coexistence of states with different social systems. But the Soviet people do not forget that the better the security of our Motherland, the more reliably the borders of the Soviet Union are sealed against imperialist agents and the more energetically and firmly we rebuff the enemy, the more effective this policy will be.

[In his speech devoted to the Fiftieth anniversary of the October Revolution, Comrade Brezhnev has formulated the chief aim of the Soviet foreign policy: "To defend the conquests of the October Revolution, to shatter the imperialist intrigues against the fatherland of socialism, to secure the necessary external conditions for the construction of the communist society."

The organs of state security are among those actively participating in implementing this aim. The members of the organs are aware of the fact that peaceful coexistence is a form of class struggle, that this is a cruel struggle, a persistent [struggle] on all the fronts: the economic, the political, and the ideological. In such a struggle it is the duty of the state security organs to fulfill their specific duties precisely and unerringly.

Under present conditions, it is difficult for the imperialists to think of being able to overcome socialism by frontal attack. The leaders of the imperialist states are endeavoring to draw lessons from their defeats, to adapt themselves to the new situation in the world. They are employing any, the most cunning, the most insidious means to carry out their policy.

At this time when the struggle on the world arena has acquired a vividly-expressed class character and become more complex, the scale and boundaries of the intelligence and subversive activities of the imperialists change. The intelligence centers of certain Western powers, in the first place the United States, exert considerable influence on the foreign policy of their respective states.

It should be mentioned that the imperialists, for their own purposes, are making ever more extensive use of the chauvinistic and splitting policy of the Mao Tse-tung group which has started an outrageous campaign of calumny against our Party and the Soviet people, against the entire communist movement.

Our Party and the Soviet Government organize resolute and timely resistance to the imperialists' subversive activities in all fields. Where specific conditions of struggle demand their action, the state security agencies also play their part.

Recently, state security bodies have exposed and rendered harmless a number of agents of the imperialist intelligence services and emissaries of foreign anti-Soviet organizations; besides, many channels of criminal contact between enemy agents and the intelligence centers abroad have been cut off, and quite a few subversive operations planned by the enemy have been torpedoed.

Our borderguard troops have big and responsible tasks. Of course, today the situation on our borders is much different from what it used to be. Our neighbors on vast areas are now fraternal socialist countries and other friendly states. However, there are still quite a few sectors where we have to be particularly vigilant.

The fact that most of the out of the ordinary occurreces on our country's frontiers do not go further than attempts to violate the Soviet border can be attributed solely to the enormous and persistent effort, heroism and great vigilance of the borderguards who stand watch there. They do a splendid job in carrying out their difficult service.

Comrades, a guarantee of successful work by the state security agencies, a reliable guarantee of a correct approach to fulfilling the tasks put before them is the consistent implementation of Leninist principles, an unswerving observance of the directives and instructions of the Communist Party, a strict observance of the laws of the socialist state, constant and the closest possible contacts with the working masses.

. . . we still have facts of crimes committed against the State and individual cases of hostile anti-Soviet actions, which are often committed under the hostile influence from abroad. . . . As far as individuals are concerned, who from time to time fall into the nets of the CIA and other subversive centers, such renegades do not by any means reflect the feelings of the Soviet people. Of course, even in the period of the formation of new communist relations it is possible to dig out individual human samples, who for certain reasons of personal character, or under the influence of hostile propaganda from abroad, become favorable objects for the enemy intelligence services.

But . . . not one of such people has not been and will not be able to gain any considerable degree of support. Sooner or later all those victims of the "soul-hunters" from the CIA, the NTS,* and other imperialist intelligences become unmasked with the help of the Soviet people. . . . In the conditions of the all-people socialist state the links of the KGB with the toilers particularly strong. Only our enemies, who have all the reasons to fear and hate the "chekists," portray the Soviet state security service as a "secret police" of sorts. In actual fact the security service has been created by the society itself for its self-protection from the intrigues of the imperialists and other hostile forces. It constructs its work on the principles of socialist democracy, it remains under the constant supervision of the people, its party and the Government.]

*NTS (Narodno-trudovoy soyuz), or the Labor Alliance of Russian Solidarists, is an emigre organization seeking and in some cases achieving strong links with the dissident elements in the Soviet Union. See *Union of Soviet Socialist Republics.*]

# OPEN LETTER FROM SOVIET SCIENTIST PAVEL M. LITVINOV

Sent to four Soviet newspapers and to *L'Humanité* and *L'Unità,* newspapers of the French
and Italian Communist parties
(Text of the plea by author Vladimir I. Bukovsky at his trial in Moscow, 1 September 1967, was attached
to the letter.)

*Excerpts*
(*The New York Times,* 27 December 1967)

## Litvinov Letter

I regard it as my duty to make public the following:
On Sept. 26, 1967, I was summoned by the Committee of State Security [K-G-B] to appear before Gostev, an official of the K.G.B. Another officer of the K.G.B., who did not give his name, was present during our conversation.

After this talk was over, I wrote it down immediately and as fully as I could remember. I vouch for the accuracy of the substance of what was said between the representative of the K.G.B. and me.

Gostev: Pavel Mikhailovich, we have knowledge that you together with a group of other people intend to reproduce and distribute the minutes of the recent criminal trial of Bukovsky and others. We warn you that if you do that, you will be held criminally responsible.

I: Irrespective of my intentions, I cannot understand what the criminal responsibility for such an action might be.

Gostev: The court will decide that, and we wish only to warn you that if such a record should be spread through Moscow or other cities or appears abroad, you will be held responsible for this.

## 'Know the Laws Well'

I: I know the laws well and I cannot imagine what particular law would be transgressed by the composition of such a document.

Gostev: There is such an article. 190-I. Take the criminal code and read it.

I: I know this article very well and can recite it from memory. It deals with slanderous fabrications which would discredit the Soviet social system and regime. What kind of slander could there be in recording the hearing of a case before a Soviet court?

Gostev: Well, your notes will be a biased distortion of facts and a slander of the court's actions, and that would be proved by the agency competent to handle such cases.

I: How can you possibly know this? Instead of starting a new case, you yourself should publish the record of this criminal trial and in this way kill the rumors circulating in Moscow.

Gostev: And why do we need to publish it? It is an ordinary criminal case of disturbance of the peace.

I: If so, it is all the more important to give information about it, to let all the people see that it is really an ordinary case.

## Newspaper Cited

Gostev: *Vechernaya Moskva* [a Moscow newspaper] of Sept. 4, 1967, gives all the information about the case. All that has to be known about that trial is in there.

I: In the first place, there is too little information: The reader who had heard nothing previously about this case simply would not understand what it is all about. In the second place, it is false and slanderous. Rather the editor of *Vechernaya Moskva* or the person who gave such information should be charged with slander.

Gostev: Pavel Mikhailovich, the news report is absolutely correct. Remember that.

I: It says there that Bukovsky pleaded guilty. Yet I, who was interested in this case, know perfectly well that he did not plead guilty.

Gostev: What does it matter whether he pleaded guilty or not? The court found him guilty. Consequently, he is guilty.

I: I am not talking now about the court's decision; nor did the newspaper have it in mind. And confession of guilt by the defendant represents a completely independent judicial concept. In general, it would be a good idea to tell more about Bukovsky; for example, how he was arrested while reciting poetry on Mayakovsky Square, brought to the police station and beaten up.

## Beating Is Denied

Gostev: This is not true. It could not be.

I: His mother said so.

Gostev: Who cares what she said?

I: She did not tell it to me—I do not know her—but to the court, and nobody interrupted her or accused her of slander.

Gostev: She should rather have told you how she was summoned and warned about the conduct of her son. We can summon your parents too. And in general, Pavel Mikhailovich, have in mind: *Vechernaya Moskva* has printed all that the Soviet people *should know* about this case and this information is completely true and we warn you that if not only you, but your friends or anybody makes this record, you specifically will be held responsible for it. You understand very well that such a record can be used by our ideological enemies, especially on the eve of the 50th anniversary of Soviet power.

I: But I do not know of any law that would

prohibit the dissemination of a nonsecret document only because it might be misused by somebody. Much critical material from Soviet newspapers might also be misused by somebody.

### Warning Is Given

Gostev: It should be clear to you what we are talking about. We are only warning you, and the court will prove the guilt.

I: It will prove it, I have no doubt. The trial of Bukovsky makes that clear. And how about my friend Alexandr Ginzburg? Is he imprisoned for the same kind of actions that you are warning me about?

Gostev: Well, you will learn what he did when he is put on trial. He will be acquitted if he is innocent. Could you possibly think that now, in the 50th year of Soviet power, a Soviet court would make a wrong decision?

I: Then why was Bukovsky's trial closed to the public?

Gostev: It was not.

I: Yet it was impossible to get in.

Gostev: Those who had to get in got in. There were representatives of the public and all seats in the hall were taken. We did not intend to rent a club [auditorium] because of this case.

I: In other words, the public nature of legal proceedings was violated.

Gostev: Pavel Mikhailovich, we have no intention of arguing with you. We simply warn you. Just imagine if people would learn that the grandson of the great diplomat Litvinov [Maxim M. Litvinov, former Foreign minister] is busy with such doings, this would be a blot on his memory.

I: Well, I do not think he would blame me. Can I go?

Gostev: Please. The best thing for you to do now would be to go home and destroy all that you've collected.

I know that a similar kind of conversation was conducted with Alexandr Ginzburg two months before his arrest.

I am asking you to publish this letter so that in case of my arrest the public would be informed about the circumstances which preceded it.

P. M. Litvinov.
*Assistant in the Faculty
of Physics in Moscow,
Institute of Precision
Chemical Technology*

Oct. 3, 1967
Moscow, 8 Alexei Tolstoy
Street, Apt. 78

### Bukovsky Plea

In preparation for this trial, I anticipated that the proceedings would completely reveal all the motives for the actions charged, and would deal with the legal analysis of the case. The court has done nothing of the kind. It engaged in character defamation—whether we are good or bad is irrelevant to the case.

I expected the prosecution to present a detailed analysis of the "disturbance" which we made on the square: who hit whom, who stepped on who's foot. And this did not follow either. The prosecutor in his speech says: "As I see it, the danger of this crime lies in its insolence."

But I have here before me the text of the Soviet Constitution: "In accordance with the interests of the workers and with the aim of strengthening the Socialist system, the citizens of the U.S.S.R. are guaranteed by law . . . the right of street processions and demonstrations." Why is such an article included? For May Day and October [revolution anniversary] demonstrations? But it is not necessary to include such an article for demonstrations that the government organizes—it is clear that no one will disperse these demonstrations.

### Right to Protest

We do not need freedom "pro" if there is no freedom "anti." We know that protest demonstrations are powerful weapons in the hands of the workers; this is an inalienable right in all democratic states. Where is this right denied? In Madrid, there was a trial of the participants of a May Day demonstration. They were tried under a new law recently passed in Spain that provides imprisonment from one and a half to three years for participation in demonstrations. I see a disturbing identity between fascist Spanish and Soviet legislation.

Judge: Defendant, you are comparing things that cannot be compared: the actions of the rulers of Spain and those of the Soviet state. In court, the comparison of Soviet policy with the politics of foreign bourgeois states is intolerable. Stay closer to the substance of the indictment. I object to the abusiveness of your words.

Bukovsky: You do not have the right to interrupt me. I have not departed from the essence of my case.

In our country, the organs of state security play a police role. What democracy can there be to speak of when we are being watched? Let them catch spies! Why are we being questioned about our acquaintances, about what we were doing two or three years ago and such things? I recognize the important role of the organs of the K.G.B. in the fight for state security. But what is their business in this case? There were no external enemies involved here. Perhaps they had internal ones in mind. There were no grounds for the interference of the state security organs. Now, let's take a look at how our case was conducted. Why did they have to drag it out for a period of seven months? I see one explanation: to trump up some means of covering the traces of this unseemly business. When stalling finally became impossible, the proceedings about us were made so secret that nobody would be able to penetrate and convince oneself of their illegality. Although the investigation of our case had been started by the prosecutor's office, the decree on my arrest was signed by the K.G.B. Captain Smelov. By the fourth month, our case had been transmitted from the prosecutor's office to the K.G.B. This is a violation of proceedings.

Judge: Defendant Bukovsky, this is of no interest to us—keep closer to the indictment. What significance does everything you are saying essentially have to do with the resolution of your case?

Bukovsky: I have already said that you have no right to interrupt me. The significance is quite simple: There have been breaches of the law in the conduct of the investigation, and it is my duty to speak out about them, so now I am speaking out.

We demonstrated in the defense of legality. It is incomprehensible why the office whose responsibility it is to safeguard the citizens' rights sactions such actions by the Druzhinniki [civilian auxiliary police] and the K.G.B. We did not come out against laws. We protested against an unconstitutional decree. Was this really an anti-Soviet demand? Not we alone find the decree unconstitutional. A group of representatives of the intelligentsia have presented a similar demand to the Presidium of the Supreme Soviet of the U.S.S.R.

Isn't the Constitution the basic law of our country? I shall read the full text of Clause 125:

"In accordance with the workers' interests and with the aim of strengthening the Socialist system, the citizens of the U.S.S.R. are guaranteed by law: A. Freedom of speech; B. Freedom of the press; C. Freedom of gatherings and meetings; D. Freedom of processions and demonstrations on the street. These rights of the citizens are secured by making available to workers and their organizations printing facilities, supplies of paper, public buildings, streets. . . . "

Yes, streets, citizen prosecutor!

". . . means of communication and other material conditions, necessary for their realization."

### Need for Revision

Now, about Article 70. We demanded its revision because it is subject to too wide an interpretation. Here is its text:

"Agitation and propaganda conducted with the aim of subverting or weakening Soviet authority or with the aim of committing particularly dangerous crimes, dissemination with the same aim of slanderous statements, discrediting the Soviet state and social system as well as dissemination or preparation and possession, with the same aim, of literature of the same character, will be punished by imprisonment for a period of six months to seven years or by deportation for a period of two to five years."

Article 70 refers to such different things as agitation and propaganda aimed at particularly dangerous state crimes, and, on the other hand, slanderous statements against the Soviet system.

Judge: Defendant Bukovsky, we are lawyers here, and all those present in the courtroom have also been through grammar school. We realize that you have recently become exposed to problems of the law and have become interested in them. We applaud this interst, but it is unnecessary to discuss them at such length here. We must decide the question of your guilt or innocence, decide your fate. Possibly you will enter Moscow University as a student of law. There, at the seminars, you shall discuss these questions on a higher level.

Bukovsky: No, I won't enter it. I object to the prosecutor accusing us of legal illiteracy and lack of seriousness. I do know the laws, and speak of them seriously. If, however, what I'm speaking about is so well known, it is even more incomprehensible why the prosecutor sees criticism of the law as a crime.

Freedom of speech and of the press is, first of all, freedom for criticism. Nobody has ever forbidden praise of the Government. If in the Constitution there are articles about freedom of speech and of the press, then have the patience to listen to criticism. In what kinds of countries is it forbidden to criticize the Government and protest against its actions? Perhaps in capitalist countries? No, we know that in bourgeois countries Communist parties exist whose purpose it is to undermine the capitalist system. In the U.S.A. the Communist party was suppressed. However, the Supreme Court declared that the suppression was unconstitutional and restored the Communist party to its full rights.

Judge: Bukovsky, this does not have any relevance to the accusations in your case. You must understand that the court is not competent to decide the questions you are talking about. We must not judge the laws; we must execute them.

Bukovsky: You are interrupting me again.

Judge: I declare a five-minute recess.

Bukovsky: I did not ask for one. I will soon end my final statement. You are destroying the continuity of my final statement.

[The judge declares a recess.]

Judge [after the recess]: Defendant Bukovsky, continue your last speech, but I warn you, that if you continue to criticize the laws and the activities of the K.G.B. instead of giving an explanation about the case at hand, I will have to interrupt you.

Bukovsky: We are accused of criticizing the laws. This gives me the right and the foundation for raising these fundamental critical questions in my final statement. But there is also another aspect. The question of honesty and civic integrity. You are judges. You are supposed to embody these qualities. If you actually embody honesty and integrity, you will make the only possible sentence in this case—a verdict of "not guilty." I understand that that is very difficult.

Prosecutor: I direct the attention of the court to the fact that the accused is abusing the right for a final statement. He criticizes the laws, discredits the activities of the organs of the K.G.B., he is beginning to insult you. A new criminal act is being perpetrated here. As a representative of the prosecution, I must stop this and I call upon you to require the defendant to talk only about the substance of the charges against him. Otherwise one may listen without end to speeches here with all kinds of criticism of the laws and of the Government.

Judge: Defendant Bukovsky, you have heard the prosecutor's remarks. I will permit you to speak only on the substance of the indictment.

Bukovsky [to the prosecutor]: You accuse us of trying, by our slogans, to discredit the K.G.B., but the K.G.B. has discredited itself to such a degree that we have nothing to add. [To the court] I shall speak about the charges. But what the prosecutor would like to hear from me, he won't hear. There is no criminal act in our case. I absolutely do not repent for organizing this demonstration. I find that it accomplished what it had to accomplish, and when I am free again, I shall again organize demonstrations, of course with complete observation of the law, as before. I have finished my statement.

# DOCUMENTS ON THE A.I. SOLZHENITSYN CASE

A. Letter from the Union of Soviet Writers to A.I. Solzhenitsyn
B. Reply by Solzhenitsyn to the Secretariat of the USSR Writers' Union
C. Remarks by Pravda Editor M.V. Zimianin at The House of the Press, Leningrad, 5 October 1967
D. Letter from Pavel Antokolsky to P.N. Demichev

(Radio Liberty dispatch, 29 January 1968)

### A. Letter from the Union of Soviet Writers to A. I. Solzhenitsyn

On September 22, the Secretariat of the Board of Directors of the Union of Soviet Writers discussed your letter. You had an opportunity to learn from this discussion the attitude of the community of USSR writers toward you and your literary activities. At that time no resolution was adopted. It was believed that you would think this discussion through and make your decision accordingly. The secretariat would like to know what decision you have come to.

Secretary K. Voronkov

### B. Reply to the Secretariat of the USSR Writers' Union

I am unable to understand from your (letter) No. 3142 of November 25, 1967:

1) Does the secretariat intend to defend me against the slander (calling it unfriendly would be an understatement) which has been going on without interruption for three years in my homeland? (New facts: on October 5, 1967 at the House of the Press in Leningrad at a very crowded assemblage of listeners, the editor-in-chief of *Pravda*, Zimianin, repeated the tiresome lie that I had been a prisoner of war, and also tried out the old trick used against those who have fallen from grace by announcing that I am a schizophrenic, and that my labor camp past is an obsessive idea. The MGK [Ministry of State Control] set forth new false versions to the effect that I allegedly "tried knocking together in the army" either a "defeatist" or a "terrorist" organization. It is incomprehensible why the military collegium of the Supreme Court did not detect this in my case).

2) What measures did the secretariat take to nullify the illegal ban on the use of my published works in libraries and the censorship decree prohibiting any mention of my name in critical articles? (*Voprosy Literatury* applied this ban even to . . . a translation of a Japanese article. At the University of Perm, sanctions were enacted against a group of students who sought to discuss my published works in their academic review).

3) Does the secretariat wish to prevent the unchecked appearance of *Rakovyi Korpus (The Cancer Ward)* abroad or does it remain indifferent to this menace? Are any steps being taken to publish excerpts from the novel in *Literaturnaya Gazeta,* and (to publish) the whole novel—in *Novy Mir*?

4) Does the secretariat intend to appeal to the Government to permit our country to join the International Copyright Convention? Doing so would enable our authors to obtain reliable means for protecting their works from foreign pirating and a shameless commercial negotiation's race.

5) In the six months since I sent my letter to the Congress, was the distribution of the unauthorized "edition" of excerpts from my archive discontinued and has this "edition" been destroyed?

6) What measures did the secretariat take to return to me the archive and the novel, *In the First Circle,* which they impounded besides giving public assurances that they allegedly returned them (Secretary Ozerov, for instance)?

7) Has the secretariat accepted or rejected K. Simonov's proposal to publish a volume of my stories?

8) Why is it that, to date, I have not received for my perusal the September 22 stenographic report of the meetings of the secretariat?

I would be very grateful to have an answer to these questions.

A. Solzhenitsyn

C. Remarks by the editor-in-chief of Pravda, M. V. Zimianin, on October 5, 1967, at the House of the Press in Leningrad

Recently there has been a great deal of slander in the Western press against several of our writers whose works have played into the hands of our enemies. The campaign by the Western press in defense of Tarsis ended only when he went to the West where it became evident that he was not in his right mind.

At the moment, Solzhenitsyn occupies an important place in the propaganda of capitalistic governments. He is also a psychologically unbalanced person, a schizophrenic. Formerly he was a prisoner and justly or unjustly was subsequently subjected to repressions. Now he takes his revenge against the government through his literary works. The only topic he is able to write about is life in a concentration camp. This topic has become an obsession with him. Solzhenitsyn's works are aimed against the Soviet regime in which he finds only 'sores and cancerous tumors. He doesn't see anything positive in our society.

I have occasion to read unpublished works in the course of my duties and among them I read Solzhenitsyn's play, "The Feast of the Conqueror." The play is about repressions against those returning from the front. It is very genuine anti-Soviet literature. In the old days, people were even put into prison for works of this kind.

Obviously we cannot publish his works. Solzhenitsyn's demand that we do so cannot be honored. If he writes stories which correspond to the interests of our society, then his works will be published. He will not be deprived of his bread and butter. Solzhenitsyn is a teacher of physics; let him teach. He very much likes to make public speeches and often appears before various audiences to read his works. He has been given such opportunities. He considers himself a genius of a writer.

Among the other names which come up quite often in the Western press, one must not forget Yevtushenko and Voznesensky. We have beautiful poetry and a great many poets who write wonderful poems. But in the West they basically recognize only these two because they find passages in their works worth using in their propaganda. We, of course, cannot consider the works of these poets to be anti-Soviet like those of Solzhenitsyn. They write good patriotic works, too. They are not that young any longer although everyone thinks of them as being young; their works, however, lack the necessary political maturity. That is why they sometimes play into the hands of our enemies. I know them and have spoken with them about this. But they also consider themselves geniuses.

Take Yevtushenko. Recently during a closed meeting, Pavlov, the Secretary of the Central Committee of VLKSM (Komsomol) criticized him. So Yevtushenko replied in words which were four times more powerful, ten times more powerful. He made fun of him in a poem.* In this way, he branded him forever.

Then there is the tale of Voznesensky. Last year he went to the USA; he read his poetry there in front of large audiences. He had a great success and also profited financially. He was getting ready to go on a tour of American cities again this year. His trip was already arranged; it was publicized in the USA and his visa was reserved at the American Embassy. At this time the war in the Middle East broke out. Our relations with the USA deteriorated. The board of administration of the Writers' Union clearly hinted to Voznesensky that it would be better for him not to go to the USA at this time. Simultaneously, the administration told the American Embassy that the poet was ill.

What did Voznesensky do? I came to the office on Monday morning and I glanced through my mail. There was a letter from Voznesensky accusing the Writers' Union. I telephoned him at home. I was told that he had left and that his destination was unknown. I telephoned the Central Committee. They answered that they too had received a letter from Voznesensky and that they also telephoned him at home but could not locate him. One day went by, then another. No Voznesensky. Then suddenly I learn that the BBC has broadcast Voznesensky's letter to *Pravda*. He appeared only a week later. Apparently he was sitting it out at a dacha in the outskirts of Moscow. I invited him to come to see me. He denied having given the letter to Western journalists.

I told him that he might get off with a reprimand the first time. But if he ever did it again, he would be ground to dust. I myself would see to it that not a trace of him remained.

Some thought that we should have published his letter and given him an answer. But why make this sordid story a topic of general discussion?

*The poem in question is entitled "Pismo Eseninu." Yevtushenko read this poem at a meeting of young people at which Sergei Pavlov was present.

### D. Letter from Pavel Antokolsky to P. N. Demichev

Comrade P. N. Demichev Secretary of the Central Committee of the CPSU [head of the Ideological Commission of the CC CPSU]

Dear Pyotr Nilych!

Like other delegates to our congress, I have also received the famous letter written by Alexandr Isayevich Solzhenitsyn and it has filled me with excitement, as it has several other comrades.

As an old writer and as a Communist, I feel obliged to share my feelings with you.

I consider Alexandr Solzhenitsyn to be a writer endowed with a rare talent, the growing hope of our realistic literature, an heir of the great and humanistic traditions of Gogol, Leo Tolstoy and Alexey Maximovich Gorky. We ought to cherish such contributors to our culture. Criticism of those works by Solzhenitsyn which have been published has shocked me because it is biased, unjust and unconvincing.

The ban on Solzhenitsyn's manuscripts, described in detail in his letter, strikes one as an incredible occurrence, unworthy of our socialist society and our Soviet state. It is all the more dreadful given the fact that the same thing happened several years ago to the manuscript of the second part of the novel by the late Vasily Grossman.

Is it possible that such reprisals against the manuscripts of our writers threaten to become a custom in our country sanctioned by law?

This cannot and must not happen!

Such savagery toward works of art is incompatible with our fundamental laws and unthinkable in any normal human community.

If Solzhenitsyn's works contain controversial and unclear elements, if political mistakes have been discovered in them, they should be submitted to the public for open discussion. Writers have many opportunities to do this.

I have worked in the field of literature for 50 years. I have written many books and lived out my life, a life full of vicissitudes. I experienced periods of burning anxiety for the fate of our entire literature, and sometimes for various comrades—Bulgakov, Pasternak, Titsian Tabidze—I recall the names of those who were close to me.

Having lived out my life, I would never have thought that such anxiety would recur in the evening of my days, and on the eve of our great and glorious anniversary!

If a Soviet writer is compelled to turn to his fellow writers with a letter like Solzhenitsyn's, this means that we are all morally responsible to him and to our own readers. If he cannot tell readers the truth, then I too, old writer that I am, have no right to look straight into the readers' eyes.

# "THE INTERNAL SITUATION AND THE COMMUNIST PARTY"

Statement by the Political Bureau of the Central Committee,
CP of Venezuela, January 1967

*Complete Text*
*(Information Bulletin*, No. 94, 1967)

The year 1966 is just over, with a plainly adverse balance for the national interests. Among the more salient facts characterizing the situation early in 1967 are the suspension of constitutional guarantees—a move aimed at ensuring the establishment of a virtual state of emergency—the brutal eruption into Central University, the arrest of more than 700 students, massive raids on numerous neighborhoods, accompanied by violence and detentions, and lastly, the bloody repressions carried out by SIFA, Digepol, and the already notorious State Security Corps, set up on the initiative and under the guardianship of the CIA (this has resulted in more assassinations and in an increased number of people who are said to have "disappeared" and whom their relatives look for desperately and fruitlessly in every prison). In other words, the year 1967 is beginning in the atmosphere of the abolition of civil liberties, the frank suppression of freedom of speech, a rapid decline in the people's standard of living due to a telling increase in the prices of necessities, greater domination of every area of public life by the gorilla-Betancourt camarilla, and the brazen intensification of the process of handing over our natural resources to the imperialist monopolies.

In view of so grave a situation, the Political Bureau of the Central Committee of the Communist Party of Venezuela considers it necessary to acquaint public opinion with its estimations.

The gorilla offensive, supported by the Pentagon, the oil companies and the big bourgeoisie, has scored new gains, as we had foreseen and pointed out. Once again the government has been forced to its knees and made to jettison some of the surviving outward elements of token democracy.

The occupation of the university campus by the Army and police, with all its implications—the violation of university autonomy, mass arrests, evidence forged by servile investigators and their police masters to justify the encroachment on culture and legality that has been committed—was merely the culmination of the pressure which the State Department brings to bear throughout the Latin American continent to crush the student movement.

However, the gorillas refuse to content themselves with imposing their terms on Leoni. Nor are they appeased by the government's major concessions to the oil companies and the oligarchy they represent. Their leaders continue to exert increasing pressure to ensure that terror is stepped up and that there is complete surrender to the demands of reaction. In November 1966 we clearly stated the political outlook as follows:

"In this grave political situation there are two alternatives equally injurious to the interests of the people: either the government will again yield to the pressure of imperialism and home reaction, intensify the terroristic regime established since the beginning of Betancourt's term in office, and comply with the gorillas' demand for curtailing university autonomy and declaring a state of emergency, suspending the Constitution and taking harsher repressive measures in town and country; or it will be removed through a military coup, with the result that the tatters of democracy long used by the Democratic Action and Republican Democratic Union parties will be cast away."

Recent developments have fully borne out our forecasts, for terror has gained in intensity, university autonomy has been violated and constitutional liberties suspended. But the two alternatives indicated by us are still there: either the government will make even greater concessions to the gorillas and the Betancourt group on all points, or the Supreme Command of the armed forces will proceed to establish the regime of force aspired to, in the same way as this was done in Brazil and Argentina.

Thus the country is still faced with the prospect of a new crisis at the top to which the democratic sections of the nation cannot remain indifferent.

Tortures, shootings and "disappearances" are the order of the day again. These facts shocked and aroused the nation, especially when last year the monstrous assassination of our dear comrade, Alberto Lovera, revealed the criminal background of the repressive policy of the present regime. The names of those sentenced to death by the police agencies have now been added to the long list of people who were kidnapped or "disappeared." It includes Comrades Rafael Guerra Ramos and Domingo Sanchez (members of the National Leadership of our Party), Rafael Celestino Chavez, Hector Gimenez and many others whose whereabouts are unknown in spite of the numerous inquiries made in government quarters by relatives and friends, and even by such official bodies as the Municipal Council of the Federal District. Most of the revolutionary leaders have been entered in the list of those sentenced to immediate physical destruction.

All this is a tangible reality which the most hypocritical declarations of Leoni and other spokesmen of the regime cannot conceal from public opinion. The reason why the gorillas have imposed restrictions on press and radio information that are still in force is precisely that they want to commit these crimes, and others planned long ago, with greater ease and behind the back of the nation, as well as to let the assassination of Alberto Lovera, Donato Carmona, Soto Rojas, Burguillos and many more go unpunished.

What is befalling the revolutionaries today is bound to happen tomorrow to all other democrats who refuse to be reconciliated to the present state of affairs. To call a halt to this spate of bloodshed and brutal persecution is, therefore, the bounden duty of all who sincerely champion respect for human life and human rights, which the gorillas today trample underfoot.

The new stage of the development which reached its climax in December was preceded by a well-coordinated campaign of the most reactionary elements of the country whose most characteristic spokesmen are Carlos Andres Perez, a Betancourt man, and Edecio La Riva, the ultra-reactionary of the Christian Social (COPEI) Party. It was they who singled out the university as an immediate target. But Washington and the local reactionaries were supplied with the best pretext they could have wanted by the acts of terrorism committed by factionalist adventurists and other Leftist groups in various parts of the capital in the weeks preceding the suspension of constitutional guarantees.

In this connection we declare emphatically that individual terror has nothing in common with the methods we Communists use to achieve the liberation goals we have set ourselves. Such methods are completely alien to revolutionary tactics. They contradict Marxism-Leninism and are extremely harmful to the popular movement. This is why our Party vigorously condemns and firmly rejects them. Decades ago Lenin, in keeping with the dialectical method typical of genuine revolutionaries, demonstrated the negative aspect of terrorism. " We cannot kill the system by killing the tsar," he said. "They can always find a worse tsar."

Leninism teaches us that those who try to create artificial stimuli in order to set the masses in motion from the top, solely through vanguard actions, are denying, in practice or in theory, that the masses have sufficient reason to rise, being daily plundered and humiliated by their masters and the landowners. They are denying that real revolutionary work consists in providing political and organizational conditions, both objective and subjective, for bringing the masses into the fight against the iniquities they suffer from inasmuch as more or less daring individual actions supply no solutions whatever to the problems of the working class and the people as a whole. If we act in close unity with the masses, we can and must use every form of struggle until we bring the masses to victory.

When, last November and December, the Communist Party fought together with other democratic forces for amnesty, against the terror exercised by the regime, it helped to put the puppet government in a difficult position and won widespread support. In that way the revolutionary forces surrounded themselves by friends and allies while neutralizing major intermediate groups and steadily isolating the enemy by pillorying him for his crimes, repeatedly proved by public opinion. On the other hand, the adventurous actions of the Leftists created a situation unfavorable to the interests of the revolution. Friendly individuals and groups are compelled to keep silent, the masses are confused and cowed, the wavering and the neutral are giving in to the government, and the latter is finding it easier to strike at the popular movement. When the enemy attacks the democratic camp without any justification, this angers and brings protests from the bulk of the population, and enables us to rally the most diverse progressive groups and to take the offensive with a fair chance of success. But when the enemy uses arguments like those we have indicated and which carry weight with certain segments of the population that have not grasped the essence of the problem, the exact reverse occurs. Terror, it should be remembered, has two sources. On the one hand, it is used by the government to suppress democrats and revolutionaries, nullify the gains of the masses and stamp out mounting popular discontent. On the other hand, terror is resorted to by those who have lost faith in themselves, in their ability to carry on a protracted struggle, such as the national-liberation movement calls for.

For all these reasons, the Political Bureau, expressing the opinion of the Central Committee of our Party, says without beating about the bush to the Venezuelan people and, in particular, to our allies and friends that that absurd form of struggle weakens the revolutionary movement instead of reinforcing it, and is bound to lead to defeat. This specification of our position does not mean that we renounced our policy line of offering armed resistance to government violence. It is a necessary reaffirmation of those principles of our doctrine which regard individual terrorism as ineffective and harmful, and direct action in isolation from the masses as contrary to the interests of the revolutionary movement.

The definitive establishment of gorilla terror in our country and complete subservience to foreign monopoly are not fatally inevitable, and we wish to stress this for the benefit of those who are at one with us in the desire to regain and consolidate democratic freedoms. In the new situation that has been created, with the prospect of new gorilla advances and of even a coup d'etat, of new outrages and assassinations, with the imminence of a second phase of Operation Trap that will carry the blood-bath into the rural areas where the guerrillas are heroically resisting the troops trying to close in on them, there is only one way. It is that of joint mobilization of all democratic and nationalist forces, of those members of the opposition parties who want real progress for the people, and lastly, of those members of the government parties who disagree with the activity of the gorillas and are likely to be hard hit by them sooner or later.

This exceedingly grave situation does not affect the Communists alone. While the offensive today is spearheaded against us, there can be no doubt that it is directed also against the democratic interests of the nation and against the parties and groups vitally concerned with maintaining these interests. The best proof of this affirmation is what happened in Central University, the house raids against such distinguished Venezuelan intellectuals as Rector Bianco and Dr. De Vananzi, as well as the affront to the Association of University Professors, not to speak of numerous other cases. All those who sincerely desire a radical change in the situation must therefore take prompt action against the new dangers looming on the political horizon.

To unite this front, which is what the situation imperatively demands, the Political Bureau of the CC, CPV addresses this appeal for united action, to be aimed above all at:

1. Fully restoring constitutional guarantees, including freedom of the press and the principle of inviolability of the home.

2. Ending the bloodbath being carried on by the repressive agencies, ranging from SIFA to the recently established State Security Corps.

3. Immediately investigating the increasingly numerous "disappearances" of fair-minded citizens, who afterwards turn out to have "committed suicide under mysterious circumstances" in the dungeons of some repressive agency, thrown into the sea, as was the case with Alberto Lovera, or buried in an out-of-the-way spot in the mountains.

4. Immediately releasing the prisoners, in particular the student leaders and other persons unlawfully arrested on the university campus; stepping up the fight for an amnesty, which is a prerequisite for any attempt to pacify the country.

5. Restoring university autonomy, consolidating the university, and providing conditions for the proper maintenance of its rights against new encroachments, which are bound to be attempted as long as the present team, represented by the reactionary camarilla of Betancourt and his followers, is in power.

6. Coordinated action by the democratic forces to thwart the plans of the gorillas aimed at strengthening their rule and stepping up terror.

We submit these proposals to the masses and the democratic groups and leaders interested in real progress of the nation, for we believe them to meet the serious exigencies of the present critical situation in our country.

# POLITICAL PROGRAM OF THE SOUTH VIETNAM NATIONAL FRONT FOR LIBERATION

Adopted by the Central Committee, Mid-August 1967

*Complete Text*
(Hanoi, Vietnam News Agency International Service,
1 September 1967)

In 1960, the South Vietnam National Front for Liberation came into being with its ten-point program aimed at uniting the entire people against the U.S. imperialists and their lackeys. Since then, the Front has achieved a broad union of the various sections of the people, the political parties, organizations, nationalities, religious communities, and patriotic personalities with a view to jointly fighting against U.S. aggression, for national salvation. It has successfully consolidated its base among the broad masses of the people; at the same time, it has achieved joint action with many political and religious forces and won over many industrialists and traders, many officials and functionaries of the puppet administration, and many officers and men of the puppet army.

The Front has constantly enjoyed wholehearted encouragement and assistance from our compatriots in the north and abroad. It has also enjoyed ever stronger approval and support from the peoples of neighboring Cambodia and Laos, from the peoples of the socialist, nationalist, and other countries in the world, including progressive people in the United States.

Under the leadership of the NFLSV, our people in the south have gone from victory to victory. The prestige of the Front has been unceasingly enhanced at home and abroad. The South Vietnam National Front for Liberation has become the sole genuine representative of the heroic South Vietnamese people.

These great achievements have proved that the line and policy of the front are correct, and that the strength of our people's unity and struggle is invincible.

At present, despite heavy defeats, the U.S. imperialists are still unwilling to give up their aggressive designs against Vietnam. They are stepping up the war, trampling upon the south, and intensifying the bombing of the north of our country. The monstrous crimes of the U.S. imperialists, however, have only served to deepen our people's hatred and increase their indomitable will. The people of South Vietnam, regardless of social standing, and even a number of persons in the puppet army and administration, have seen through the true features of the U.S. imperialists and their lackeys, hate them, and want to contribute to the struggle against U.S. aggression, for national salvation.

Never before in our nation's history has the mettle of our entire people united for the fight to wipe out the enemy and save the country been so strong as now. Our people are in a victorious, initiative, and offensive position. The U.S. imperialists and the lackeys have been increasingly driven into passivity and embarrassment; they are in an impasse and are sustaining defeats.

At this juncture, in a spirit of developing the former program, the NFLSV has worked out this political program with a view to further broadening the bloc of great national union, encouraging and stimulating the entire people to rush forward, resolved to fight and defeat the U.S. aggressors, and to build an independent, democratic, peaceful, neutral, and prosperous South Vietnam.

## I. Unite the Entire People, Fight the U.S. Aggressors, Save the Country.

1. During 4,000 years of their history, the Vietnamese people have united and fought against foreign invasion to preserve their independence and freedom. Ever since our country was conquered by the French colonialists, our people have fought unremittingly for their liberation. In 1945, our people from north to south rose up, successfully carried out the August revolution, seized political power from the Japanese militarists and their lackeys, and founded the Democratic Republic of Vietnam.

When the French colonialists came back to invade our country once again, our entire people heroically fought for nearly nine years, brought our sacred resistance to the great victory of Dien Bien Phu, smashing the aggressive schemes of the French colonialists and the interventionist policy of the U.S. imperialists.

The independence, sovereignty, unity, and territorial integrity of Vietnam were formally recognized by the 1954 Geneva conference. Since then, our compatriots in South Vietnam together with the people all over the country, should have been living in peace and building a free and happy life. However, the U.S. imperialists have sabotaged the Geneva agreements, ousted the French colonialists, set up in South Vietnam an extremely cruel puppet regime, and tried to turn the southern part of Vietnam into a neocolony and a military base in an attempt to prolong the partition of our country, conquer the whole of Vietnam, and impose their domination throughout Indochina and Southeast Asia.

The U.S. imperialists have shrunk from no cruel method to carry out their dark design. Defeated in their special war, they have switched to a local war, using over half a million U.S. and satellite troops, along with more than half a million puppet soldiers, for aggression against South Vietnam. At the same time, they have undertaken a war of destruction against the northern part of our country. They have also stepped up their special war in Laos and carried out continual provocations aimed at wrecking the independence and neutrality of Cambodia.

The U.S. imperialists are daily causing untold sufferings and mourning to our compatriots throughout the country! They have resorted to all kinds of modern war means and weapons, including strategic aircraft, napalm bombs, toxic chemicals, and poison gas to massacre our fellow countrymen. They have launched repeated operations, again and again sweeping many areas, carrying out the kill all, burn all, destroy all policy to raze villages and hamlets to the ground. They have herded the population, grabbed land, and set up a no-man's land and fascist-type concentration camps dubbed strategic hamlets, prosperity zones, resettlement areas, and so on. In the north, they have wantonly bombed and strafed streets, villages, industrial centers, and heavily populated areas. They have even struck at dikes, dams, schools, hospitals, churches, and pagodas.

Obviously the U.S. imperialists are the most ruthless aggressors in history, the saboteurs of the 1954 Geneva agreements, the saboteurs of the peace and security of the peoples in Indochina, Southeast Asia, and the world—the enemy number one of our people and of mankind.

Over the past few years, the U.S. imperialists have continually escalated the war, yet they have unceasingly clamored about peace negotiations in an attempt to fool the American and world people.

The Saigon puppet administration has sold out South Vietnam to the U.S. imperialists. It has oppressed and exploited our southern compatriots in an extremely ruthless way. It has forced South Vietnam youth into the army to serve the United States in massacring our fellow countrymen. In a demagogic bid, it has also staged the farce of working out a constitution and holding elections. It is only a clique of traitors, an instrument for the U.S. imperialists to enslave the South Vietnamese people, prolong the partition of our country and further the U.S. war of aggression.

2. The U.S. aggressors and their lackeys think they can intimidate our people by the use of force and deceive them by means of tricks. But they are grossly mistaken. Our people definitely will never submit to force, never let themselves be deceived! Bringing into play our nation's tradition of undauntedness, our 31 million compatriots from the south to the north have resolutely stood up and united as one man to fight against the U.S. aggressors and save the country.

On the frontline of the fatherland, our southern fellow countrymen have over the past 13 years shown marvelous heroism. Irrespective of age, sex, political tendencies, religious beliefs, and no matter whether they live in the plains or in mountain areas, our people of all strata and all nationalities have resolutely fought shoulder to shoulder to liberate the south, defend the north, and proceed toward the reunification of the fatherland.

Since 1959-1960, our compatriots in the South Vietnamese countryside have carried out successive, simultaneous uprisings, destroyed a series of concentration camps and prosperity zones of the U.S. imperialists and the puppet administration and liberated vast rural areas. Our armed forces and people then rushed forward, destroyed thousands of strategic hamlets, liberated millions of people, and defeated the U.S. special war.

Since 1965, although the U.S. aggressors have brought in hundreds of thousands of U.S. expeditionary troops for direct aggression against South Vietnam, our armed forces and people have repeatedly won big victories, smashed two successive U.S. dry-season strategic counteroffensives, defeated over one million enemy troops—U.S., puppet, and satellite.

The liberated areas have continuously expanded and now make up four-fifths of the South Vietnam territory with two-thirds of its population. In these liberated areas, a national and democratic power is taking shape and a new life is blossoming. In addition to big military victories, we have also recorded important successes in the political, economic, cultural, and diplomatic fields.

In the beloved northern part of the fatherland, our 17 million compatriots are heroically defeating the U.S. imperialist's war of destruction, maintaining and boosting production, and wholeheartedly encouraging and helping the cause of liberating the south, thus fulfilling the obligations of the great rear toward the great front.

In the world, the peoples of the socialist, nationalist, and other countries, including the progressive people in the United States, are sternly condemning the U.S. imperialist's war of aggression, and are giving their approval, support, and assistance to our people's struggle against U.S. aggression and for national salvation.

Facts have clearly shown that the more the U.S. imperialists obduratly intensify and expand their war of aggression against our country, the more they sustain bitter defeats and are driven into isolation; on the other hand, our people win greater victories and get more friends.

3. The most dangerous enemies of our people at present are the U.S. imperialist aggressors and their lackeys—the traitorous puppet administration.

The tasks and objectives of the South Vietnamese people in the struggle for national salvation are now as follows: To unite the entire people, resolutely defeat the U.S. imperialist's war of aggression, overthrow their lackey puppet administration, establish a broad national union and democratic administration and build an independent, peaceful, neutral, and prosperous South Vietnam, and proceed toward the peaceful reunification of the fatherland.

The force that guarantees the fulfillment of the above task of fighting against U.S. aggression and saving the country is our great national union. The NFLSV constantly stands for uniting all social strata and classes, all nationalities, all political parties, all organizations, all religious communities, all patriotic personalities, all individuals, and all patriotic and progressive forces, irrespective of political tendencies, in order to struggle together against the U.S. imperialists and their lackeys, wrest back our sacred national rights, and build up the country.

The NFLSV is prepared to invite and welcome all patriotic forces and individuals who oppose the U.S. aggressors to join its ranks, and to shoulder together the common duties. It proposes that any force which, for one reason or another, does not adhere to its ranks, take joint action against the common enemy—the U.S. aggressors and their lackeys.

The NFLSV pledges itself to strive, shoulder to shoulder with the Vietnam fatherland front, to fulfill gloriously the common task of fighting against U.S. aggression to liberate the south, defend the north, and proceed toward the peaceful reunification of the fatherland.

While fighting for their sacred national rights, the people of South Vietnam actively accomplish their internationalist duty. Their resistance war against U.S. aggression is an integral part of the revolutionary struggle of the people all over the world.

The NFLSV undertakes to stand within the united bloc of the Indochinese peoples to fight against the U.S. imperialists and their lackeys, to defend the independence, sovereignty, unity, and territorial integrity of Vietnam, Cambodia, and Laos.

The NFLSV pledges to take an active part in the common struggle of the world's people against the bellicose and aggressive imperialists headed by U.S. imperialism, for peace, national independence, democracy, and social progress.

4. The cruel U.S. aggressors are trampling upon our homeland. We, the people of South Vietnam, must stand up to make revolution and wage a people's war with a view to annihilating them, driving them out of our borders, and wresting back national independence and sovereignty.

Having experienced over 20 years of war, our southern compatriots eagerly want to live in peace and rebuild our war-devastated country. But the U.S. imperialists have trampled underfoot this legitimate aspiration. That is why our people have to fight against them to win peace in independence. Nothing is more precious than independence and freedom. Only when real independence is secured can we have genuine peace!

The enemy of our nation is ruthless and obdurate. But our entire people are determined to fight and to defeat the U.S. aggressors and their lackeys. So long as the U.S. imperialists do not end their war of aggression, withdraw all U.S. and satellite troops from our country, and let the South Vietnamese people settle themselves the internal affairs of South Vietnam without foreign intervention, our people will resolutely fight on until total victory. The South Vietnamese people's liberation war is a long and hard one, but it is sure to end in victory.

Our people rely mainly on their own forces; at the same time they strive to win the sympathy, support, and assistance of the world's peoples.

To defeat the U.S. aggressors and their lackeys, our people do not spare any sacrifice. They enthusiastically contribute manpower, material resources, and talent to the national liberation war in the spirit of doing everything for victory.

The NFLSV undertakes to develop the Liberation Armed Forces comprising the main force units, the regional troops, and the militia and guerrilla units, with the aim of promoting people's war, combining guerrilla with regular warfare, wiping out as many live enemy forces as possible, crushing the enemy's will for aggression, and winning the final victory.

The front undertakes to build and develop the political forces of the masses, promote the movement of political struggle, and combine armed struggle with political struggle and agitation among enemy troops, thus forming three converging prongs to defeat the enemy.

The NFLSV undertakes to encourage all strata of the population in the towns and rural areas still under enemy control to unite and struggle in every possible form to break the grip of the U.S. aggressors and their lackeys, destroy the Phuong (corporations) and strategic hamlets, demand democratic freedoms, national sovereignty, and a better life, oppose the pressganging of troops and forcible labor draft, struggle against enslaving and depraved culture, and march forward, together with the entire people, to overthrow the enemy's rule and seize political power.

At the same time, the Front undertakes to encourage all strata of people in the liberated areas to unite closely, to build the people's self-management system, to achieve step by step a local national democratic administration, to build base areas, to strive to produce and fight against U.S. aggression and for national salvation, to proceed with a good settlement of the agrarian question, to build the new economy and culture of the liberated areas, to foster the people's forces with a view to insuring supplies for the frontline and carrying the resistance war through to complete victory.

## II. Build an Independent, Democratic, Peaceful, Neutral, and Prosperous South Vietnam

The people of South Vietnam are determined to defeat the U.S. aggressors and their lackeys, and to devote their might and main to build a political system that guarantees the independence and sovereignty of the nation and the freedom and happiness of the people, to heal the wounds of war, to liquidate the social evils left over by the U.S. puppet regime, to restore moral life and build an independent, democratic, peaceful, neutral, and prosperous South Vietnam.

To achieve these objectives, the NFLSV lays down the following concrete policies:

1. To achieve a broad and progressive democratic regime:

To abolish the disguised colonial regime established by the U.S. imperialists in South Vietnam, to overthrow the puppet administration, hireling of the United States, not to recognize the puppet national assembly rigged up by the U.S. imperialists and their lackeys, to abolish the constitution and all antinational and anti-democratic laws enacted by the U.S. imperialists and the puppet administration.

To hold free general elections, to elect the national assembly in a really democratic way in accordance with the principle of universal, equal, direct suffrage and secret ballot. This national assembly will be the state body with the highest authority in South Vietnam. It will work out a democratic constitution which fully embodies the most fundamental and most eager aspirations of all social strata in South Vietnam and guarantee the establishment of a broad, progressive, democratic state structure. To guarantee the immunity of the deputies to the national assembly.

To set up a national union democratic government including the most representative persons among the various social strata, nationalities, religious communities, patriotic and democratic parties, patriotic personalities, and forces which have contributed to the cause of national liberation.

To proclaim and enforce broad democratic freedoms—freedom of speech, freedom of the press and publication, freedom of assembly, trade union freedom, freedom of association, freedom to form political parties, freedom of creed, freedom to demonstrate.

To guarantee to all citizens inviolability of the human person, freedom of residence and lodging, secrecy of correspondence, freedom of movement, freedom to work and rest, and the right to study.

To enforce equality between man and woman and equality among the various nationalities.

To set free all persons detained by the U.S. imperialists and the puppet administration on account of their patriotic activities.

To dissolve the concentration camps set up in all forms by the U.S. imperialists and their lackeys.

All those people who have had to seek asylum abroad because of the U.S. and puppet regime, have the right to return to the country to serve the fatherland.

To severely punish the diehard cruel agents of the U.S. imperialists.

2. To build an independent and self-supporting economy, to improve the people's living conditions. To abolish the policy of economic enslavement and monopoly of the U.S. imperialists. To confiscate the property of the U.S. imperialists and their diehard cruel agents and turn it into state property. To build an independent and self-supporting economy. To rapidly heal the wounds of war, to restore and develop the economy so as to make the people rich and the country powerful. To protect the right to ownership of the means of production and other property of the citizens under the laws of the state.

To restore and develop agricultural production. To improve farming, animal husbandry, fish rearing, and forestry.

The state will encourage the peasants to unite and help one another in boosting production, grant them loans at low interest for the purchase of buffaloes, oxen, farming implements, agricultural machines, seeds, fertilizers, etc., help them develop irrigation works, and apply advanced techniques in agriculture. To guarantee outlets for agricultural products.

To restore and develop industry, small industries and handicrafts. To guarantee to the workers and employees the right to take part in the management of enterprises.

The state will encourage the capitalists in industry and trade to help develop industry, small industries and handicrafts. To enforce freedom of enterprise to the benefit of nation-building and the people's welfare; to apply a customs policy designed to encourage and protect home-production. To restore and develop communications and transport. To encourage and step up economic exchanges between towns and country, between the plains and the mountain areas. To give due consideration to the interests of the small traders and petty shopkeepers. To set up a state bank. To build an independent currency. To apply a fair and rational tax policy. The state will adopt a policy of granting loans at low interest to encourage production, and will prohibit usury. To develop economic relations with the north; the two zones will help each other so that Vietnam's economy may prosper rapidly.

In accordance with the front's policy of neutrality and on the principle of equality, mutual benefit and respect for the independence and sovereignty of the Vietnamese nation, trade with all countries will be expanded, and economic and technical assistance from foreign countries will be accepted, regardless of political and social systems.

3. To enact the land policy, to carry out the slogan "Land to the Tiller." To confiscate the lands of the U.S. imperialists and the diehard cruel landlords—their lackeys. To allot those lands to landless or land-poor peasants. To confirm and protect the ownership of the lands allotted to peasants by the revolution.

The state will negotiate the purchase of land from landlords who possess land upward of a certain amount, varying with the situation in each locality. It will allot these lands to landless or land-poor peasants. The recipients will receive the lands free of charge and will not be bound by any condition whatsoever. In areas where the required conditions for land reform do not yet obtain, land-rent reduction will be carried out.

To entrust the lands belonging to absentee landlords to peasants for cultivation and enjoyment of the produce. Adequate steps will be taken on this subject at a later stage in consideration of the political attitude of each landlord. To allow landlords to offer land to the Liberation Peasants Association; the state will allot these lands to landless or land-poor peasants. To encourage the owners of industrial crops or fruit-tree plantations to keep their farms going. To respect the legitimate right to ownership of land by the churches, pagodas, and holy sees of religious sects. To carry out a fair and rational redistribution of communal lands. To guarantee the legitimate right to ownership of reclaimed lands to those who reclaim them.

Those compatriots who have been forced into strategic hamlets, or concentration camps in any other form, will be free to return to their former villages.

Those who have been compelled to evacuate or to change abodes and who wish to go on living there, will enjoy recognition of their ownership of the lands and other property which have resulted from their labor, and will be helped to continue earning their living in the same place; those who wish to return to their native places will also receive help.

4. To build a national democratic culture and education, to develop science and technology, to promote public health. To fight against the American-type enslaving and depraved culture and education now adversely affecting our people's fine, long-standing cultural traditions. To build a national democratic culture and education, to develop science and technology in service of national construction and defense. To educate the people in the Vietnamese nation's tradition of struggle against foreign invasion and its heroic history. To preserve and develop the fine culture and good customs and habits of our nation.

To raise the people's cultural standards: to liquidate illiteracy, to promote complementary education, to open new general education schools, higher learning establishments, and vocational schools. To make an all-out effort to train and foster a contingent of scientific workers, technicians, and skilled workers. To use the Vietnamese language as the teaching medium in higher learning establishments. To reduce school fees for pupils and students. To exempt poor pupils and students from school fees, or grant them scholarships. To reform the system of examinations.

The state will give every possible help to those youth and children who have rendered services to the fight against U.S. aggression and for national salvation, to the children born into the families who have rendered services to the revolution, and to other outstanding youths so as to enable them to study and develop their capabilities.

Every citizen is free to carry out scientific and technological research, to indulge in literary and artistic creation, and to participate in other cultural activities. To encourage the intellectuals, writers, artists, and scientists and to afford them the required conditions for research work, creation, and invention in the service of the fatherland and the people. To afford opportunities to those cultural workers, writers and artists who have been persecuted by the U.S. imperialists and their lackeys for their patriotic activities. To develop health service and the movement for hygiene and prophylaxis. To attend to the people's health. To control epidemics. To do away with dangerous diseases left over by the U.S. and puppet regime. To develop the movement for physical training and sports. To develop cultural relations with the north; the two zones will help each other to raise the people's educational level and the (development) of qualified people. To promote cultural relations with foreign countries on the basis of equality and mutual benefit.

5. To guarantee the rights and cater to the livelihood of workers, laborers, and civil servants. To promulgate labor legislation. To put into practice the eight-hour working day. To provide for a regime of rest and recreation. To set up a rational system of wages and bonuses for increased productivity. To improve the living and working conditions of the workers, laborers, and civil servants. To apply a policy of adequate remuneration for apprentices. To provide jobs to the workers and the poor people in the towns. To make every effort to do away with unemployment. To put into practice a policy on social security to care for and assist workers, laborers, and civil servants in case of disease, incapacitation, old age, or retirement. To improve living conditions in working people's residential quarters.

To settle disputes between employers and employees through negotiations between the two sides and mediation by the national democratic administration. To strictly prohibit the beating of workers and laborers, to strictly prohibit fines deducted from wages and unjustified sacking of workers.

6. To build up strong South Vietnam Liberation Armed Forces with a view to liberating the people and defending the fatherland. The South Vietnam Liberation Armed Forces—comprising the main force units, the regional troops, and the militia and guerrillas—are the children of the people, and are boundlessly loyal to the interests of the fatherland and the people, and are duty-bound to fight shoulder to shoulder with the entire people to liberate the south, defend the fatherland, and make an active contribution to the defense of peace in Asia and in the world. To pay due attention to the building of the Liberation Armed Forces. To strive to raise their quality and increase their fighting capacity with a view to stepping up people's war, defeating the U.S. satellite, and puppet troops, and bringing the fight against U.S. aggression, for national salvation to total victory. To strengthen the political work with a view to enhancing the patriotism and determination to fight and to win of the Liberation Armed Forces, enhancing the sense of discipline, and continuously tightening the "fish and water" relations between the army and the population. Officers and men of the Liberation Armed Forces have the right to vote and eligibility to stand for election, and are entitled to own land and to all other rights of citizens.

7. To show gratitude to the martyrs, to cater for disabled armymen, to reward the fighters and compatriots who have an outstanding record in the fight against U.S. aggression and for national salvation. The entire people are grateful to, and constantly bear in mind the memory of the martyrs who belonged to the Liberation Armed Forces or to various services and revolutionary organizations, and those who laid down their lives in political struggles. Their families are catered for and assisted by the state and the people. Armymen and compatriots disabled in the course of the armed and political struggle are cared for and helped. To reward in a worthy manner all fighters and compatriots who have an outstanding record in the struggle against U.S. aggression and for national salvation. The entire people are grateful to and help the families who have rendered services to the revolution.

8. To organize social relief. To give relief to the compatriots—victims of the war of aggression unleashed by the U.S. imperialists and the puppet regime. To attend to orphans, old folks, and invalid

people. To organize relief for the areas affected by natural calamities or bad crops. Consideration is also given to disabled puppet armymen and to the families of puppet armymen killed in action, who are poor and forlorn. To help those people driven to desperation by the U.S. imperialists and their lackeys, to rebuild their lives and serve the fatherland and the people.

9. To put into practice equality between man and woman, to protect mothers and children. To pay utmost attention to raising the political, cultural, and vocational standards of women in a manner fitting with their merits in the struggle against U.S. aggression and for national salvation. To develop the Vietnamese women's traditions of heroism, undauntedness, loyalty, and aptitude to shoulder every responsibility. Women are equal to men politically, economically, culturally, and socially. Women who do the same job receive the same salary and allowances, and enjoy all other rights as men. Women workers and civil servants enjoy two months maternity leave with full pay before and after childbirth.

To put into practice a policy of actively helping perfecting and training women cadres. To promulgate progressive marriage and family regulations. To protect the rights of mothers and children. To develop a network of maternity homes, creches, and infant classes.

To do away with all social evils brought about by the U.S. imperialists and their lackeys, which are harmful to women's health and dignity.

10. To strengthen unity, to practice equality and mutual assistance among nationalities. To abolish all systems and policies applied by the imperialists and their lackeys with a view to dividing, oppressing, and exploiting the various nationalities. To oppose discrimination among and forcible assimilation of the nationalities. To develop the long-standing tradition of unity and mutual assistance among the various fraternal nationalities with a view to defending and building the country. All nationalities are equal in rights and obligations.

To implement the agrarian policy with regard to minority peasants. To encourage and help them settle down in fixed residences, to improve their lands, to develop economy and culture, to raise their living standards so as to keep abreast of the general level. The national minorities have the right to use their own spoken and written languages, to develop their own culture and art and to maintain or to change their customs and habits.

To strive to train minority cadres so as to quickly bring about conditions for good management of the local affairs by the concerned minority itself. In the areas inhabited by big communities of a specific minority and where the required conditions exist, autonomous zones will be established within independent and free Vietnam.

11. To respect freedom of creed, to achieve unity and equality among the different religious communities. To fight against all maneuvers and tricks of the imperialists and their lackeys who use a number of persons under the cloak of religion to oppose our people's struggle against U.S. aggression and for national salvation, to sow dissension between believers

and nonbelievers and among different religious communities, and to harm the country, the people, and the religion. To respect freedom of creed and worship. To preserve pagodas, churches, holy sees, temples. All religions are equal and none is to be discriminated against. To achieve unity among believers of various religions and between believers and the entire nation for the sake of the struggle against U.S. aggression and their lackeys to defend and build the country.

12. Welcome puppet officers and men and puppet officials back to the just cause, show leniency, and give a humane treatment to rallied armymen and prisoners-of-war. To oppose the U.S. imperialists and the puppet administration's attempts to pressgang mercenaries to serve the U.S. aggressors against the fatherland and massacre the people. To severely punish the diehard thugs acting as efficient agents of the U.S. imperialists. To afford conditions for puppet officers and puppet officials to come back to the just cause and join the people's fight against U.S. aggression to save and build the country.

Those individuals, groups, or units of the puppet army and administration who render services to the cause of fighting against U.S. aggression for national salvation will be rewarded and entrusted with responsible jobs. Those who sympathize with and support the struggle against U.S. aggression for national salvation or those who refuse to carry out orders of the United States and puppets to harm the people will have their merits recorded.

Those individuals, groups, or units who have broken away from the puppet army and voluntarily apply to join the Liberation Armed Forces for fighting against the United States to save the country are welcomed and enjoy equal treatment. Regarding those individuals or units who have broken away from the puppet army and administration and risen against the U.S. aggressors to save the country, the front stands ready to join actions with them in the fight against the U.S. aggressors on a basis of equality, mutual respect, and assistance so as together to protect the people and liberate the fatherland.

Those functionaries of the puppet administration who volunteer to serve the country and the people in the state machine after the liberation of South Vietnam will enjoy equal treatment. Those in the puppet army and the puppet administration at any level who have committed crimes against the people but are now sincerely repentant will be pardoned. Those who redeem their crimes by meritorious deeds will be rewarded accordingly. Captured officers and men of the puppet army will enjoy humanitarian treatment and clemency.

Those in the U.S. Army and its satellite armies who cross over to the people's side will be given kind treatment and helped to return to their families when conditions permit. Captured U.S. and satellite troops will be treated as captured puppet troops.

13. To protect the rights and interests of overseas Vietnamese.

To welcome the patriotism of overseas Vietnamese and highly value all their contributions to the resistance to U.S. aggression for national salvation of the people. To protect the rights and interests of overseas Vietnamese. To help those overseas Vietnamese who wish to return to take part in the building of the country.

14. To protect the legitimate rights and interests of foreign residents in South Vietnam. To welcome those foreign residents who have contributed to the Vietnamese people's resistance to U.S. aggression for national salvation. All foreign residents living in South Vietnam must respect the independence and sovereignty of Vietnam and obey the law of the national democratic administration. To protect the legitimate rights and interests of all foreign residents who do not cooperate with the U.S. imperialists and their henchmen in opposing the Vietnamese people and who do not harm the independence and sovereignty of Vietnam. To give adequate consideration to the rights and interests of those foreign residents who have directly or indirectly supported the Vietnamese people's resistance to U.S. aggression for national salvation.

To resolutely oppose and abolish all policies of the U.S. imperialists and their henchmen aimed at sowing discord between the Vietnamese people and Chinese residents in South Vietnam and exploiting, repressing, and forcing Chinese residents to adopt Vietnamese citizenship. To punish the diehard agents and secret agents of the imperialists and the South Vietnam puppet administration.

### III. To Restore Normal Relations Between North and South Vietnam, Proceed Toward Peaceful Reunification of the Fatherland

Vietnam is one. The Vietnamese people are one. No force can divide our fatherland. Reunification of the country is the sacred aspiration of our entire people. Vietnam must be reunified.

The policy of the NFLSV consists of the following:

1. The reunification of Vietnam will be realized step by step and through peaceful means on the principle of negotiation between the two zones without either side using pressure against the other and without foreign interference.

2. Pending the reunification of the country, the people in both zones will make joint efforts to oppose foreign invasion and defend the fatherland and at the same time endeavor to expand economic and cultural exchanges. The people in both zones are free to exchange letters, to go from one zone to another, and to choose their place of residence.

### IV. To Apply a Foreign Policy of Peace and Neutrality

The NFLSV applies a foreign policy of peace and neutrality, a foreign policy which guarantees the independence, sovereignty, unity, and territorial integrity of the country and helps safeguard world peace. In more concrete terms this policy consists of the following points:

1. To establish diplomatic relations with all countries regardless of their social and political system on the principle of mutual respect for each other's independence, sovereignty, and territorial integrity, on the principle of mutual respect for each other's independence, sovereignty, and territorial integrity, without infringement upon each other, without interference into each other's internal affairs, territory, equality, mutual benefits, and peaceful coexistence. To abolish all unequal treaties which the puppet administration has signed with the United States or any other country. To respect the economic and cultural interests of those countries which sympathize with, support, or assist the struggle against U.S. aggression for national salvation of the Vietnamese people. To accept technical and economic assistance from any country without political conditions attached. To join no military alliance, to accept no military personnel or military bases of foreign countries on South Vietnam territory.

2. To strengthen friendly relations with all countries which sympathize with, support, or assist the struggle against U.S. aggression for national salvation of the Vietnamese people. To strengthen relations of good neighborhood with Cambodia and Laos. To unceasingly consolidate solidarity and mutual assistance between the peoples of the Indochinese countries with a view to defending their respective independence, sovereignty, and territorial integrity against the aggressive and war-provocation policy of the U.S. imperialists and their henchmen.

3. Actively support the national liberation movement of the peoples in Asia, Africa, and Latin America against imperialism and old and new colonialism. Actively support the struggle of the American people against the U.S. imperialists' war of aggression in Vietnam. Actively support the just struggle of black people in the United States for their fundamental national rights. Actively support the struggle for peace, democracy, and social progress in all countries of the world.

4. Actively struggle to contribute to the safeguarding of world peace, oppose the bellicose and aggressive imperialists headed by U.S. imperialism. Demand the dissolution of the aggressive military blocs and foreign military bases of imperialism. Unceasingly consolidate and develop relations with international democratic organizations and the peoples of all countries including the American people. Actively contribute to the consolidation and development of the world people's front in support of Vietnam against the U.S. imperialist aggressors, for national independence and peace.

The struggle against U.S. aggression, for national salvation of our people is an extremely hard but glorious cause. It concerns not only the destiny of our people at present and all our future generations but also the interests of the peoples in the world who are struggling for peace, national independence, democracy, and social progress. In order to accomplish that glorious cause, our people, already united, must unite still more closely and broadly!

The NFLSV warmly welcomes all political parties, mass organizations, and patriotic and progressive personalities who broadly rally within and outside the front in order to defeat together the U.S. aggressors and their henchmen.

The struggle against U.S. aggression, for national salvation of our people is a just cause. Our people throughout the country are of one mind to fight and defeat the U.S. aggressors and their henchmen. The sympathy, support, and assistance of the people of the socialist countries, the Asian, African, and Latin American countries, and peace-loving, justice-loving people all over the world, including the progressive people in the United States, are becoming deeper and stronger day by day. We are willing and will surely win complete victory.

No matter how frenzied, brutal, obdurate, and perfidious the U.S. imperialists may be, they will inevitably meet with bitter failure in their criminal schemes.

In the supreme interests of the fatherland, let our entire people in South Vietnam strengthen their solidarity, millions as one, and rush forward shoulder to shoulder in the impetus of our victories to completely defeat the U.S. aggressors and their stooge administration, and together with our northern compatriots to fulfill the great and glorious cause of liberating the south, defending the north, and proceeding toward the peaceful reunification of the fatherland.

The NFLSV pledges to be always worthy of the confidence of our compatriots and our friends on the five continents. The Vietnamese people will surely be victorious! The U.S. aggressors and their henchmen will certainly be defeated! The NFLSV program for liberation is sure to materialize! Fighters and compatriots throughout South Vietnam, under the glorious banner of the NFLSV, march forward heroically!

# "THE GREAT OCTOBER REVOLUTION SHOWS THE PEOPLES THE ROAD TO LIBERATION"

Article by Ho Chi Minh on the Occasion of the
50th Anniversary of the October Revolution

*Complete Text*
(*Pravda*, 28 October 1967)

Together with the Soviet people and the working people of the whole world, the Vietnamese people celebrate with pleasure and enthusiasm the 50th anniversary of the Great October Revolution in Russia.

Waging a struggle against the United States to save the motherland, filled with determination to smash the American aggressors and to continue the building of socialism on their soil, the Vietnamese people are turning their eyes with feelings of gratitude and trust to the Soviet Union, the motherland of the great Lenin and of the glorious October Revolution.

Like a sun, the October Revolution illuminates with its light all the five continents of the world, awakening millions of oppressed and exploited masses. There has been no other revolution in the history of mankind of such tremendous and profound importance.

The October Revolution was the first victory of Marxism-Leninism. Moreover, in such a tremendous country as the Soviet Union, which occupies one-sixth of the globe, it was the greatest victory of the proletariat, the working people, and the oppressed masses under the leadership of the working class and its vanguard, the party of Bolsheviks. By revolutionary force the October Revolution overthrew the rule of the capitalists and estate owners, set up the rule of the working people, and built a new society which has no place for exploitation of man by man.

The October Revolution showed the peoples and all mankind the road to liberation. It opened a new epoch in history, the epoch of the transition from capitalism to socialism on a universal scale.

Lenin wrote about the historical importance of the October Revolution: " .... We are proud that it has been our share to *begin* the construction of the Soviet state, to *begin* this new epoch of world history, the epoch of the rule of a *new* class suppressed in all capitalist countries and advancing everywhere toward a new life, toward victory over the bourgeoisie, toward the dictatorship of the proletariat, toward the liberation of mankind from the yoke of capital and from imperialist wars."

After 50 years the world situation constitutes a clear confirmation of this brilliant assessment of Lenin. Truly tremendous revolutionary transformations have taken place in the world since the October Revolution.

The Soviet Union, as the first state of the dictatorship of the proletariat, demonstrated its extraordinary might. Having just been born, it not only smashed the internal counterrevolution; it also victoriously repelled the armed intervention of 14 imperialist states. Almost 30 years later it smashed the German and Japanese fascists and not only defended the Soviet state but also made a tremendous contribution to the liberation of other countries and saved mankind from fascist slavery.

Despite the tremendous destruction caused by the war and tremendous losses (20 million dead, 1,710 destroyed towns, and over 30,000 enterprises put out of operation), the Soviet Union was able, thanks to the correct leadership of the party and the heroic efforts of the people, within a few years to heal the wounds inflicted by the war, to successfully build socialism, and to tackle the creation of the material-technical base of communism. The Soviet Union has been transformed into a great industrial power with a most progressive science and technology, and it became the first state to open the path for the conquest of the cosmos.

After the October Revolution in Russia, the victory of the revolution in China was of great international importance. It was a new, great victory of Marxism-Leninism, won in a semicolonial and semifeudal country with 650 million inhabitants led by the CPR. In less than 20 years the Chinese people, in a backward agrarian country subject to merciless oppression and exploitation by foreign imperialists, local bureaucratic bourgeoisie, and feudal estate owners rose to win and strengthen their national independence, build socialism, and transform China into a great country with modern industry, developed agriculture, and progressive science and technology.

Of tremendous historical importance were also the victories of the national liberation and socialist revolutions in Poland, Bulgaria, the GDR, Hungary, Rumania, Czechoslovakia, Albania, Mongolia, Korea, Cuba, and Vietnam.

As a result of all these victories the world socialist system emerged which now extends from Central Europe to Southeast Asia and which has its first outpost in Latin America. The formation and strengthening of the socialist camp is a factor which determines the development of the world revolution and the bright future of mankind.

Thanks to the mighty impetus given by the October Revolution and by other socialist countries, and thanks to their assistance, the movement of the working class in the capitalist countries and the national liberation movement is today in a mighty upswing and has reached unprecedented scope. Everywhere, in Asia, in Africa, and in Latin America, the movement for national liberation is like a hurricane smashing the colonial system of imperialism and is opening to millions of people the path for freeing themselves from the chain of slavery, the path to independence and freedom.

The forces of the socialist camp, of the working class of the capitalist countries, and of the revolutionary movement for national liberation of oppressed peoples—these three grandiose forces, united,—have an insurmountable might and are dealing continuous blows against the fortresses of imperialism headed by American imperialism. Under the present correlation of forces all over the world, the forces of the revolution and peace are superior to the forces of war, imperialism, and reaction. On the whole, the world revolution is on the offensive, its forces are continuously growing, and it is winning ever new victories. On the other hand, imperialism and reaction are on the defensive, losing their strength, suffering one defeat after another, and are approaching their ultimate doom.

After the Great October Revolution, socialism and communism were transformed from beautiful dreams of mankind into social reality. Their tremendous force of attraction draws millions of people to the path of revolutionary actions in the name of peace, national independence, democracy and social progress.

The great victory of the October Revolution gave the working class, the working people, and the oppressed peoples of the whole world many valuable lessons which insure the victory of the cause of the full liberation of the working class and all mankind. The working class and the entire people of Vietnam realize with growing awareness the importance of Lenin's instructions and the lessons of the October Revolution:

—It is necessary that leadership be exercised by a truly revolutionary party of the working class which serves the people with all its heart and thoughts. Only the leadership of a party which is able to creatively apply Marxism-Leninism to the concrete conditions of its country can lead the national liberation and socialist revolution to victory.

—It is necessary to implement the alliance of the working class and the peasantry, which constitutes the most reliable guarantee for the victory of the revolution. When there is an alliance of the working class and the peasantry under the leadership of the working class it is possible to achieve a final and full smashing of the counterrevolutionary forces, to win and safeguard the rule of the working people, and to fulfill the historical tasks of the national democratic revolution in order to embark upon the path which leads to socialism.

—It is necessary under the leadership of the working class and on the basis of the alliance of the working class and the peasantry (this alliance must grow stronger with the degree of the development of the revolution) to unite all revolutionary and progressive forces on a broad front and to achieve action unity of all these forces in the most different forms in the struggle against the common enemy.

—It is necessary in the irreconcilable struggle against the class enemies and the enemies of the nation to oppose counterrevolutionary violence with revolutionary violence, to take the power into one's hands and strengthen it.

—It is on the basis of a concrete analysis of a given historical situation that it is necessary to determine the corresponding forms of the revolutionary struggle, to correctly utilize and skillfully combine the armed struggle with the political struggle for achieving the victory of the revolution.

—*It is necessary to continuously strengthen the dictatorship of the proletariat.* After having assumed power, the working class must above all strengthen the dictatorship of the proletariat in order to conclude the historical tasks of the revolution, completely destroy the regime of exploitation of man by man, establish socialist production relations, build socialism, and advance toward communism.

—In a merciless struggle between the working class, the working people, and the oppressed peoples on one side and the imperialists, their lackeys, the betrayers of the nation, feudalists, estate owners, and reactionary bourgeoisie on the other, the peoples must demonstrate *revolutionary determination,* must always carry high the banner of revolutionary heroism, must not shrink from any difficulties and sacrifices, and must finally and stubbornly wage the struggle for national independence, freedom, and socialism.

—*It is necessary closely to combine patriotism with proletarian internationalism* both in the national liberation and the socialist revolutions. In the present epoch the national liberation revolution constitutes an inseparable component of the world proletarian revolution, and the national liberation revolution can be crowned with complete success only if it develops into a socialist revolution. The victory of the peoples in the struggle for independence and freedom is closely connected with the support and active assistance of the countries of the socialist community and the workers movement in the capitalist countries.

"Proletarians of all countries and oppressed peoples unite." This most sacred appeal by Lenin, which we constantly keep in mind, obliges us to do all that is necessary to preserve and strengthen the unbreakable unity of the revolutionary forces in the interests of the working class and of all mankind.

This in brief is also the practical lessons of the Vietnamese revolution.

A Vietnamese adage says: "When drinking water, one thinks of the spring." The more the working class and the Vietnamese people think of their difficult, humiliating, slavish past of the various stages of their agonizing and selfless struggle, which at the same time was filled with glorious victories, the more deeply they realize all they owe to Lenin and the October Revolution.

Before the October Revolution, the Vietnamese people, whom the colonizers and imperialists forced to live in darkness, knew nothing of Marxism and had not heard about Lenin. Thanks to the victory of the October Socialist Revolution which shook the whole world, Marxism gradually spread in Vietnam. In early 1930 the Communist Party of Indochina (now the Vietnam Workers' Party) was born and took into its hands the leadership of the revolution. A mighty revolutionary upsurge emerged which attained its climax in the period of the creation of the Ngean and Khatinya Soviets (1930-31). Since that time, the Vietnamese working class and people have determined the road of their liberation.

In August 1945, exploiting the victory of the heroic Soviet Army over German and Japanese fascism, the Communist Party of Indochina led a nationwide uprising, took power into its hands, and formed the DRV. The August revolution in Vietnam was the first victorious national-democratic people's revolution in Southeast Asia. Hardly a month had passed when the Vietnamese people, lacking the necessary time to organize and strengthen their forces and chiefly armed with spears, were forced to begin a prolonged and difficult war against the French colonizers, who relied on the support of American imperialism. Finally the people completely liberated North Vietnam after the great victory of Dien Bien Phu.

The Geneva agreements signed in 1954 officially recognized the sacred rights of the Vietnamese people: independence, sovereignty, unity, and territorial integrity. Since 1954 the Vietnamese revolution has been faced with two strategic tasks—on the one hand, the implementation of socialist transformation and the building of socialism in the north, and on the other hand, the patriotic struggle for the liberation of the south of Vietnam from the domination of American imperialism and its lackeys and to realize the reunification of the country.

The socialist revolution in the north of Vietnam achieved brilliant successes. After the successful implementation of the agrarian reform, the Vietnam Workers' Party led the struggle of the Vietnamese people for the socialist transformation of agriculture, industry and trade, including retail trade, for the establishment of new production relations, and for the elimination of the exploitation of man by man. Step by step, the material-technical base of socialism is being created, agriculture and industry are developing steadily, and the people's living standards are rising continuously. In the field of culture, illiteracy has been eliminated and the national education system is rapidly expanding.

Through all these years our compatriots in the south of Vietnam did not bow their heads to the new colonizers despite terror and mass murders organized by the American imperialists and the puppets—the betrayers of the nation. Quite on the contrary, with even greater determination they are heroically waging the political and armed struggle.

The people in the south of Vietnam have won a victory over American imperialism and its stooges in a "special war." They are now inflicting defeats on them in a most violent "local war," in which the aggressors are using more than 1 million soldiers, including 500,000 Americans and more than half a million soldiers of the puppet regime and the satellite countries, thousands of aircraft, hundreds of military vessels, millions of tons of modern weapons, and the most barbaric means of waging war—poisonous chemical substances, toxic gases, napalm, fragmentation bombs, and so forth.

Exceeding in atrocity even the Hitler fascists, these modern vandals everywhere pursue their policy under the slogan: "Burn everything, destroy everything, and annihilate everybody." Trying to extricate themselves from the quagmire in South Vietnam, the American imperialists, with the help of the air force and navy, are waging a war of growing intensity and brutality against North Vietnam. They are bombing communications, industrial complexes, densely populated city districts, villages, hospitals, schools, churches, pagodas, dams, and so forth. They think that with their shower of bombs and shells they can shake our patriotic feelings and wreck the sacred combat solidarity of our people in both parts of Vietnam. But the 31 million-strong Vietnamese people have closely rallied to the independence and liberty of their fatherland; they are over fulfilled with determination to *struggle until victory against the American aggressors for the salvation of the homeland.*

Great victories have been won on the fronts of South Vietnam in the war of resistance waged by our people against the United States for the salvation of the homeland. During the last two so-called dry seasons alone (the dry season extends over seven months; it begins in October and ends at the end of April the following year) 290,000 enemy soldiers have been put out of action, of whom 128,000 were American soldiers and mercenaries of satellite countries. During the first campaign of 1965-66 the liberation army and the partisans of South Vietnam put out of action 114,000 of the 700,000 U.S. soldiers, soldiers of the puppet regime, and soldiers of the satellite countries. During the second campaign of 1966-67, 175,000 of the 1.2 million enemy soldiers were put out of action.

More than 2,450 U.S. aircraft were shot down over North Vietnam in the period between August 1964 and October 1967. It is quite evident that the more new troops are sent by American imperialism to Vietnam, the heavier are its losses. In spite of the numerous losses and privations, the Vietnamese people are becoming stronger in the course of the battles and will inevitably win complete victory.

Why has the Vietnamese revolution won such great victories? Why will the Vietnamese people inevitably defeat the American aggressors, who possess considerably more powerful armaments?

*This is insured by the correct leadership of the Vietnam Workers' Party and the NFLSV.* In working out its political line, the Vietnam Workers Party has always striven to combine the universal truths of Marxism-Leninism with the practice of the Vietnamese revolution and to study the valuable experience of the fraternal parties. Our party has invariably ascribed tremendous importance to educating the cadres, members of the party, and all the people in a spirit of selfless heroic struggle and in the name of the supreme interests of the working class and the nation. Our party has always maintained close ties with the masses. This is why it bases itself on the confidence, the love, and the support of the masses, which display tremendous enthusiasm in implementing the line and the policy of the party.

Our party has succeeded in creating *a united national*

*anti-imperialist front on the basis of the alliance of the working class and the peasantry.* This front encompasses all democratic parties, people's organizations, religious sects, and national minorities which, under the leadership of the Vietnam Workers' Party, wage a joint struggle to implement the general program of the Front, the Front which stands for a peace-loving, united, independent, democratic, and flourishing Vietnam.

Our party has succeeded in utilizing those forms of revolutionary struggle in keeping with the given concrete situation, and in particular, *to combine armed struggle with political struggle, waging a protracted, persistent, and heroic people's war to crush the aggressors.*

Our party always educates cadre workers, party members, and the people in a spirit of true patriotism and proletarian internationalism; it always strengthens solidarity and friendship with the Soviet Union, the CPR, and the other fraternal countries. Proceeding from the realization that it is above all necessary to rely on one's strength, our party at the same time strives to obtain the active support and assistance of the fraternal socialist countries and the peoples of the whole world who are struggling for peace and justice, including the progressive forces of the American people.

Relying on its own experience, the Vietnamese people are firmly convinced that under present conditions, which are propitious for the revolutionary movement of our epoch, any people, small in numbers as they may be, can vanquish any imperialist aggressors, including American imperialism, if these people are united and are fully determined to struggle on the foundation of a correct political and military line, and if they rely on the support and the active assistance of the socialist community and the revolutionary peoples of the world.

Marching along the road pointed out by the great Lenin, on the road of the October Revolution, the Vietnamese people have won tremendous victories. It is precisely because of this that they harbor such deep feelings of attachment and gratitude for the glorious October Revolution, for the great Lenin, and for the Soviet people.

The Vietnamese people will never forget that their victories are inseparable from the tremendous assistance of the Soviet Union, the CPR, and progressive people of the whole world.

On behalf of all of the people of Vietnam, I express on the occasion of the 50th anniversary of the glorious October Revolution our profound gratitude to the party of Lenin and the fraternal Soviet people, who are giving us cordial assistance in our war of resistance against the United States for the salvation of the homeland.

Sharing the joy of the working class, the working people, and the oppressed peoples of the whole world on the occasion of the 50th anniversary of the Great October Revolution, the Vietnamese people wish the fraternal Soviet people even more remarkable successes in building the material-technical base of communism and in enhancing their role in the struggle of the peoples of the whole world against imperialism, for peace, national independence, democracy, and socialism.

Long live Marxism-Leninism!

Long live the fraternal solidarity of the Vietnamese and the Soviet peoples!

Long live the fraternal solidarity of the great family of socialist countries and the international communist movement!

# "CONCLUSIONS FROM THE JULY 1 PLENUM OF THE CENTRAL COMMITTEE OF THE LEAGUE OF COMMUNISTS OF YUGOSLAVIA ON CURRENT INTERNATIONAL PROBLEMS"

*Complete Text*
(*Review of International Affairs,* Belgrade,
5-20 July 1967)

1. The Central Committee of the League of Communists of Yugoslavia unanimously lends its support to the positions assumed and action undertaken by this country relative to the aggression against the United Arab Republic and other Arab states. At the same time, the Central Committee gives its full approval to the conclusions adopted and the activities pursued by the Presidency and Executive Committee of the Central Committee of the League of Communists of Yugoslavia on the occasion of the Near East crisis, the Declaration made by President Tito in connection with the aggression, the intensive activities undertaken by Yugoslavia in the international sphere, in collaboration with the UAR, India, Algeria and other non-aligned, socialist and other countries and in the United Nations; it also fully approves the measures and steps taken by the Federal Assembly, the Federal Executive Council and all other organizations and institutions in Yugoslavia. The working people of this socialist community have offered united and determined support to these positions and steps, reflected among other things in the mass nation-wide demonstration of solidarity with the Arab nations and countries.

The talks held and conclusions reached by representatives of socialist countries and Communist parties in Moscow have had a positive influence on developments in the Near East. Determined support for the Arab countries, condemnation of Israel's aggression and demands for urgent and decisive help and support by the socialist countries and progressive forces in the world for the purpose of preventing further aggression and eliminating its consequences were attended by concrete efforts to implement comprehensive assistance.

President Tito's participation in the Moscow meeting reflects the principled positions of this country's foreign policy and its implementation in the present situation, as well as the need for cooperation among socialist, non-aligned and other peace-minded countries and all progressive and democratic forces in the world in resisting aggressive imperialist actions. Such broad-based cooperation is the most effective means of action against the policy of aggressive pressure and the use of force.

2. The true meaning and dimensions of the emergency in the Near East cannot be grasped without perception of the link between the events there and similar imperialist undertakings, particularly the war in Vietnam, as parts of the planned and long-range offensive strategy of imperialist forces in the world, particularly the USA, directed against countries, peoples and movements in Africa, Asia and Latin America which are fighting to consolidate their independence and assure development in peace and security, a strategy which also poses a threat to the security of the nations and states of Europe, and to the whole world.

The most reactionary circles in the world are making an attempt to disrupt the growing front of resistance to their policy. They are endeavoring to frustrate joint actions by the forces of peace and progress, to isolate certain developing countries and progressive movements. In doing so, they are striving to exploit and exacerbate internal difficulties, instability and the economic underdevelopment of emerging countries, and local conflicts as well, in order to impose their domination upon others.

The same purpose is also served by the arms race, the maintenance and expansion of military bases on foreign territories, and the strengthening of contingents. As this represents a special threat, it provokes justified protests and demands from peaceminded countries and forces that such activities be stopped, that military bases on foreign territories be abolished and that the arms race cease.

3. Faced with the fact that outright and direct confrontation between the two biggest powers would inevitably lead to a general nuclear catastrophe, the imperialist forces are trying to achieve their hegemonistic goals in other ways, to apply economic, political and military pressure for putting a brake on the process of emancipation, independent development of countries and peoples and the consolidation of their independence and equality.

The realities of the contemporary world are such that the USA and USSR bear a special responsibility for the maintenance of world peace; at the same time these realities make it important and indispensable for all countries to participate on a footing of equality in the solution of problems concerning their interests or the maintenance of peace and international cooperation.

4. The most recent international developments unequivocally demonstrate that the efforts of certain aggressive circles in the world to expand their hegemony through the medium of local wars are in the final analysis doomed to failure and lead to the increasing isolation of such circles.

The continuation of such a policy of pressure, putches and local wars can lead to a world-wide conflict with disastrous consequences. This danger multiplies with each fresh provocation of such wars and crises. It is for this precise reason that each nation must be unified and ready in offering resistance to aggression and that all peaceminded forces must demonstrate their solidarity, in action, with the victims of aggression; these forces must also persevere in fighting implementation of the policy of local wars, aggressive pressure and violence as means for achieving hegemonistic goals. Each act of aggression is an attack on the policy of coexistence and non-alignment; as such it stands as a threat to the independence of individual nations and world peace. More than ever before, the world is indivisible, peace is indivisible, the material and social progress of mankind is indivisible.

5. The continually widening gap between the developed and the underdeveloped countries is an increasingly dangerous source of conflicts and crises.

The present state of international economic relations operates above all against the interests of the emerging countries and wields a negative influence on the economic development of the world as a whole, exacerbates the relationships of dependence that already exist and prevents these countries from taking a greater part in world economy on a footing of equality. Their accelerated economic development is therefore in the interests both of the world economy and the industrialized countries themselves.

There is a growing conviction that the solution of this acute problem requires the comprehensive engagement of the entire international community; in this respect, socialist and progressive forces should take the lead in providing initiatives for the establishment of new practices and the hammering out of acceptable solutions.

6. The aggression against the Arab countries has reaffirmed that the struggle for assertion of the policy of peaceful coexistence and non-alignment is not and cannot be a policy of reconciliation with imperialist violence but rather the chief and most successful form of action against imperialism and violence against nations, and for the independence and equality of nations large and small.

The significance and role of the policy of non-alignment and active peaceful coexistence have made the emerging countries and non-aligned states the chief target of attack by imperialist circles throughout the world, and particularly by US imperialism.

A growing number of countries, movements and people in the world are grasping the fact that the policy of peaceful coexistence alone can surmount the state of affairs in which peace is constantly hanging in the balance, and render possible the successful solution of outstanding international problems.

After strong pressure had been brought to bear on certain emerging countries, especially those which had won their independence only recently, some non-aligned states showed a tendency to stagnate in their activities along these lines. It has been demonstrated in this dangerous emergency, however, that the non-aligned countries in the United Nations are determinedly opposed to aggression and that they are pursuing with full responsibility the struggle against the policy of force. They have therefore reasserted themselves as a powerful political factor in the United Nations and in international relations generally.

This indicates that aggressive imperialist plans are running up against mounting pressure from all progressive peoples and forces in the world. This has been confirmed by the unity of the masses of the people in the Arab countries at a moment of serious crisis when they were faced with enemy military forces on their territory, and by the readiness of those people to defend their independence and the achievements of their progressive development.

In fighting imperialism and hegemony, and in struggling for independence and equality among nations, we must be aware of the growing expansion of the joint interests binding together the nations of the contemporary world. Activities directed toward rapprochement and democratic cooperation, and toward the joint solution of the problems besetting the present-day world are therefore a component part of the struggle against imperialism and all forms of violence against peoples.

Intensification of the tendency to consolidate independence and gradually transcend the bloc divisions in the world, attended by simultaneous expansion of international cooperation, is causing the maneuvering space of the most reactionary imperialist forces to dwindle.

The uncritical attitude toward Israeli aggression or the direct support extended to it by certain leaders and leading groups in socialist parties is increasingly being shown up as untenable in view of the fact that the aggressiveness and danger inherent in Israeli policy at present are becoming clearer as time goes on. In the interests of peace and social progress, relations and cooperation with these forces must continue to be developed, all the more so as it is to be expected that further developments will lead to an evolution in their positions on the Near East crisis.

Possibilities, and awareness of the need, for taking joint action and activating to the maximum all forces in the world willing to strive for peace, security, independence of nations and social progress, have waxed rather than waned. Circumstances confirm the significance of action by progressive forces and socialist countries in a joint front with the non-aligned countries for the purpose of strengthening national independence and the equality of emerging countries, which also makes the greatest possible contribution to the further assertion of the most progressive strivings and aspirations of numerous countries and peoples throughout the world.

7. Socialist Yugoslavia, and the League of Communists of Yugoslavia, consistent with their international policy, will exert the greatest possible efforts to make a full contribution in the new circumstances to increasing the possibilities for affirmation of the policy of non-alignment and active peaceful coexistence.

The Central Committee of the League of Communists of Yugoslavia stresses the importance of taking all the indispensable measures to implement with consistency the positions adopted by the Central Committee, the decisions of government bodies and political organizations in the country relevant to support and assistance for the struggle of the Arab countries to preserve their independence and national integrity.

In this respect, the Central Committee attributes particular importance to the further development of all inter-state relations, and of the international relations of our community generally and to activities by socio-political organizations.

8. The Central Committee of the League of Communists of Yugoslavia concludes that under the circumstances it is necessary to develop Yugoslavia's bilateral and multilateral cooperation with socialist, non-aligned and all other countries, for which new and broader possibilities are arising, on the basis of respect for independence, equality, common interests and non-interference. On this basis, Yugoslavia will strive for intensification of still more comprehensive European cooperation and the development of relations with European, and especially with the neighboring states.

Towards the same goal, the Central Committee of the League of Communists of Yugoslavia will undertake the measures necessary for developing further the activities of the League of Communists in the international working class movement and its cooperation with all progressive and peaceminded forces throughout the world.

In its international activities, Yugoslavia will make a special effort, particularly through the United Nations, to accelerate the economic and social development of emerging states, particularly the newly-liberated ones, to eliminate the present points of conflict and to ameliorate the consequences of aggression in the Near East.

The Vietnamese war, the most flagrant example of aggressive US policy, stands as a permanent threat to world peace. Unless it is settled, there can be no possibility of achieving a lasting stabilization of international relations. Yugoslavia will continue with even more determination to offer full support to the righteous struggle of the Vietnamese people for freedom and independence.

9. The international activities of this socialist country are fully in keeping with the realities of the contemporary world and the possibilities for its own further development. This policy is grounded in the social realities of this country, it reflects the needs and interests of all working people; upon it depends the further successful development of our socialist system of self-government.

This country's persevering struggle for active peaceful coexistence and the policy of non-alignment has so far been and will continue to be a factor of significance in the continuing consolidation of the internal unity and strength of this community, of its defensive forces and security.

By striving for peace, independence and equality of peoples and countries and for social progress in the world, our country is consolidating its international position, contributing to friendship and solidarity among nations, and thereby also bolstering its own security.

In order to protect the independence, freedom and socialist development of this country, the League of Communists of Yugoslavia, as the leading political force, is also acting along the lines of strengthening defensive forces. Toward that end, the League of Communists will support the further development of the Yugoslav Army. It is the duty of Communists not only to lend their full support to all necessary measures along these lines but also to take the initiative in engaging the entire community, all working collectives, communes, representative bodies and socio-political organizations to increase the country's security.

# "THE DUTY OF EVERY REVOLUTIONARY IS TO MAKE REVOLUTION"

Call to the First Conference of Solidarity
of the Peoples of Latin American (OLAS),
15 February 1967

*Complete Text*
(*Granma*, Havana, 26 February 1967, English edition)

The similar past history, common enemy and common destiny of the peoples of Latin America oblige them to join forces in an analysis of their current struggle to strengthen the bonds of militant solidarity and outline a global strategy that will make social redemption, on which the entire continent's hopes are poised, a reality.

The peoples of Latin America must study the experiences of their common struggle, the hopes that these experiences engender, and the organization of their inexorable battle against imperialism. Hunger, poverty, disease, unemployment and death by starvation are the common lot of millions of Latin Americans who, when they refuse to resign themselves to this fate, must confront a monstrously implacable wave of terror, that leaves its wake of blood and death throughout our America.

The generator of this reality is U.S. imperialism, which is joined by its indefatigable and bloody henchmen, the native oligarchies. The enemy is united on all fronts—military, political, cultural, and financial. It elaborates joint programs, marshals the action of its mercenary armies, of its repressive forces, schooling them in crime and abuse in the new Washington-sponsored "scientific" academies, thus consolidating and making even more intolerable the chains that oppress our countries.

Despite widespread popular protest and the vacillation of its own irresolute allies, the U.S. government, in collaboration with the native oligarchies, attempts to enforce the Permanent Inter-American Force program, or plans new plunder of our riches and prepares broad "common" markets to facilitate new monopoly capital investments through the treacherous Alliance for Progress and Latin America Economic Integration Programs. Washington also plans to wield its complete control in the OAS in order to organize a conclave of Latin American governments that will permit it to carry out its policy of absolute domination, backed up by continent-wide repression.

We, the peoples of Latin America, are the heirs and standard-bearers of an heroic legacy. From the original natives, from Tupac Amaru, and later, Bolivar, Marti, Tiradentes, Artigas, Juarez, San Martin and Sandino, flow the combative spirit that spurs us on to struggle for the total independence of our countries. By their example, numerous martyrs such as Luis de la Puente Uceda, Camilo Torres, Fabricio Ojeda, Luis Augusto Turcios Lima, have shown us the way. The recent history of Latin America is the life of its liberators.

Always present, as a reminder of our duty to unite ourselves in struggle, is the persistent violation by imperialism of our sovereignty. Although imperialism is unable, in the end, to thwart our decision to fight for our rights, for the inevitable rich future that is ours, it will never give up the struggle—except in defeat—to impose upon us its program of supremacy and death. But it is necessary for the Latin American peoples' representatives to come together, not simply for a formal conclave where we verbally express our collective disagreement with the status quo, but this time to oppose the enemy's global strategy with the daring strategy of the peoples.

There are struggles today in many parts of our America, and much valuable experience for mutual interchange arises from these struggles. It is our duty to carry out the resolutions of the Tricontinental Conference, which proclaimed the peoples' right to oppose the violence of imperialism and reaction with revolutionary violence. It is necessary to unite, to coordinate and stimulate the battle of all the exploited peoples of Latin America.

Today, in Venezuela, Guatemala and Colombia, the peoples have taken up arms, and in other countries we see the awakening of great forces ready to win their liberty. The call to the hour of struggle against imperialism resounds throughout the world. The example of Cuba, a short distance from the monster, sustains the banners of dignity, inspiring all anti-imperialist men and women of this continent. The glorious people of Viet Nam, who are battling the Yankee imperialists, deserve our active, militant and material support. Solidarity with all the struggling peoples, brotherhood among all revolutionaries, a stimulus to that which unites and binds us, must be developed to defeat imperialism and its lackeys.

As the Second Declaration of Havana states, "each year that the Latin American revolution is hastened will mean the lives of millions of children saved, millions of minds will be saved for culture; the people will be saved from infinite suffering." It is therefore urgent to speed up this process. The Second Declaration of Havana, source of revolutionary teachings, speaks also of the importance of the present for us, the Latin Americans, stating: "The epic of Latin America's independence struggles was great, and that fight was an heroic one. But today's generation of Latin Americans is summoned to write a greater epic, one even more decisive for humanity."

To better fulfill this historic destiny, which falls to the present generation, the Latin American

Organization of Solidarity (OLAS) resolves to call for the holding of the First Conference of Solidarity of the Peoples of Latin America to begin next July 28, under the slogan: "The Duty of all Revolutionaries is to Make Revolution."

This great assembly of our peoples will be the best response to the maneuvers of the enemy. This assembly will permit us to know each other better. This meeting will unite efforts and channel energies onto the path of revolutionary unity of all the peoples of Latin America.

We expect great battles in 1967. Yankee imperialism, savage enemy of all mankind, is growing fat on Latin America. Military dictatorships and reformist governments join to impoverish and massacre the people. In the face of all this, our anti-imperialist unity is a duty and an urgent need.

We call on all the national committees of OLAS, and on the Latin American revolutionary movement in general, to offer their broad and vigorous support to the First Conference of Solidarity of the Peoples of Latin America, to meet in Havana, Cuba, Free Territory of America, from July 28 to August 5.

"The duty of all revolutionaries is to make revolution."

THE ORGANIZING COMMITTEE OF OLAS.

# "WHAT IS OLAS?"

Pamphlet Published by the Organizing Committee
of the Latin American Solidarity Organization
24 May 1967

*Complete Text*

## FOUNDATION AND PURPOSES

The anti-imperialist delegations of the 27 Latin American nations that attended the First Tricontinental Conference founded the Latin American Solidarity Organization (LASO) on January 16, 1966, in Havana, Cuba.

As stated in its constitution, its aims are to unite, coordinate and give impetus to the struggle waged by all the exploited peoples of Latin America against U.S. imperialism.

## AALAPSO AND LASO

AALAPSO, the Afro-Asian-Latin American Peoples' Solidarity Organization, was created by the First Tricontinental Conference, whereas LASO was created at a special, exclusive meeting of Latin American delegations taking part in its debates.

They are two different and totally independent organizations. Neither is organically or functionally subordinate to the other. Although they were established almost at the same time and at the same place and set up their headquarters in the same country, they could have been established at different times and places and could have chosen different headquarters sites.

The international climate created by the global strategy of U.S. imperialism and that of other colonialist powers for dominating all the backward countries of the world by fire and sword, and the need for the underdeveloped, colonized, and dependent peoples to help each other effectively, to coordinate their efforts in the national liberation struggle, to support liberated countries, and to give a united reply to imperialist aggression and defeat its aims—all this made necessary and possible the creation of these two organizations.

AALAPSO seeks to unite, coordinate and give impetus to the struggle against imperialism and colonialism in the sphere of three continents. LASO seeks the same thing on one single continent: Latin America. Therefore the relations between the two are those of fraternal support and cooperation.

## THE ORGANIZING COMMITTEE

On January 16, an organizing committee was appointed, made up of the delegations from Brazil, Cuba, Colombia, Guyana, Guatemala, Mexico, Peru, Uruguay, and Venezula. Its basic tasks are to orient the work of the new organization in cooperation with the national committee of each country, and to organize the First Latin American Peoples' Solidarity Conference.

The internal structure of the Organizing Committee is not based on permanent secretariats, but rather on working groups that exist only until the tasks assigned them are accomplished. Immediately thereafter, new groups are created to carry out new tasks. Only the General Secretariat, headed by the representative of the Cuban National Committee, Haydee Santamaria, and the working group for the LASO bulletin are permanent.

The Organizing Committee holds a weekly plenary meeting at which the decisions of the working groups are approved, disapproved, or modified. It is attempted to obtain unanimous resolutions at all times, but if this is not possible, a resolution may pass with a two-thirds majority. Thus far it has not been necessary to apply this rule for basic decisions.

The Organizing Committee has accomplished the following tasks, among many others:

Early this year it modified the composition of the national committees of the great majority of the organization's member countries and consulted them as to the date of the Conference, the criteria to be followed in creating and revamping the national committees, the topics on the agenda, and other proposals they might make.

On this basis, it selected the month of July 1967 for the First Latin American Peoples' Solidarity Conference, and it has prepared the draft agenda and regulations for the Conference and draft statutes for the Organization.

It has promoted investigation of the economic, social, political, and cultural conditions of the continent, for the purpose of providing the Conference with sufficient information for making judgments. This investigation is to be conducted by the national committees to the best of their ability.

## THE NATIONAL COMMITTEES

The national committees represent the anti-imperialist sectors that are most active and that have the most extensive and deepest roots among the people of each Latin American country. They are composed of one or more truly anti-imperialist, representative, and unitary organizations that accept the General Declaration of the First Tricontinental Conference and the organic bases of LASO.

The starting point for the formation of each national committee was established by the

1023

International Preparatory Committee of the First Tricontinental Conference. Thus, in principle, the national committee of a specific country is composed of the organizations that were invited to participate in that conference.

## THE DYNAMISM OF THE NATIONAL COMMITTEES

However, some important organizations were not invited to the First Tricontinental Conference, and some others that did not meet the entry requirements may have been invited. It is also true that some political forces that were taken into account have ceased to exist and that additional ones may follow that course. Some organizations merged, and others may do so in the future, and new popularly supported anti-imperialist movements have appeared.

These realities have determined the dynamic character of the composition of the national committees. No organization may belong in perpetuity to the national committee if it loses the qualities that made possible its admission. Moreover, organizations that acquire those qualities must be admitted. The national committees must always represent the most active anti-imperialist sectors, and those with the most profound and extensive roots among the people in each of the Latin American countries.

The dynamic character of the national committees is also a characteristic of LASO and is its contribution to the international revolutionary institutions.

The first review of the national committees was carried out in accordance with this basic criterion. Today their composition is determined by the results of that work and no longer only by the decisions of the International Preparatory Committee of the First Tricontinental Conference.

## ADMISSION TO THE NATIONAL COMMITTEE

Any anti-imperialist organization wishing to form part of the national committee of its country presents its application for admission simultaneously to the national committee concerned and to the Organizing Committee of LASO. In its application, it indicates that it meets the requirements for admission. Once this application is received, the national committee, after verifying the applicant's qualifications, informs the Organizing Committee as to whether or not it favors its admission.

If the national committee's opinion on the applicant is unanimously favorable, the Organizing Committee, after making its own determination of the applicant's qualifications for admission, recognizes the addition of the new organization as a member of the national committee. If there is a difference of opinion, the Organizing Committee decides for itself.

The same procedure is followed for expelling an organization that no longer meets the necessary requirements for belonging to the National Committee. Request for such action must come from the organizations making up the national committee or from the Organizing Committee itself.

## POLITICAL ORGANIZATIONS, OR MASS ORGANIZATIONS?

Basically, the national committees are made up of anti-imperialist political organizations, since they are organizations that now perform political functions and will continue to do so.

In particular cases, however, mass organizations may belong to the national committees when, besides meeting the requirements for admission, they include essential sectors of the population, contribute toward attracting new political forces to the national committee, and help to develop and consolidate the unified bases of work of the organizations that compose it.

## ACTIVITIES OF THE NATIONAL COMMITTEES

The fact that political organizations basically make up the national committees does not in any way limit the work of these committees. When they hold public meetings, demonstrations, conferences, and round tables, and when they issue publications, or conduct other activities, they act in the same way as regular political organizations. They take advantage of the influence that each of them has in mass organizations to promote their work. Solidarity campaigns are organized directly by the national committee, separately by each of the organizations that composes it, or by the mass organizations in which they have influence. Likewise, they establish solidarity committees or other forms of organization to achieve their objectives, all in accordance with the existing situation of the anti-imperialist organizations in each country. The difference between the national committee and the organizations through which it does its work is the same as that between the political organizations and the mass organizations.

From an organizational standpoint, the national committee is also flexible. When possible, it functions through periodic meetings of the delegates of each of the various organizations that make it up. But also, when the situation of clandestineness or repression obstructs organic functioning, it functions through contacts or liaison with the member organizations.

## FOUNDING COUNTRIES OF LASO

The agreement to establish the Latin American Solidarity Organization (LASO) was adopted by the national committees of the following countries: Argentina, Bolivia, Brazil, Colombia, Costa Rica, Cuba, Chile, Ecuador, El Salvador, Guadaloupe, Guatemala, Guyana, French Guiana, Haiti, Honduras, Jamaica, Martinique, Mexico, Nicaragua, Panama, Paraguay, Peru, Puerto Rico, the Dominican Republic, Trinidad and Tobago, Uruguay, and Venezuela. Surinam (Dutch Guiana) joined later.

## PROSPECTS FOR LASO

The Latin American Solidarity Organization (LASO) and the National Committees that make it up conduct and must conduct in the future an intensive campaign for the unity of the anti-imperialist movements in each of our countries. They must prevent sectarianism from causing the havoc that is familiar in Latin America and division between anti-imperialist organizations from flourishing. With their practical activity, they must instill the conviction that only the firmest unity will make the anti-imperialist movement in each country strong.

But also, they must demonstrate with their policy that only by unifying, coordinating, and giving impetus to the anti-imperialist struggle in all the Latin American countries, and giving each other mutual support and solidarity—especially to the peoples engaged in armed struggle—can an effective reply be given to the hemisphere-wide strategy for domination on the part of U.S. imperialism.

By getting to know each other, helping each other, coordinating and giving impetus to scattered efforts in the anti-imperialist struggle, our peoples will find the road to victory.

If the Latin American Solidarity Organization (LASO) and the National Committees that make it up progress in the fulfillment of these tasks, the prospect for our struggle is a future of joint struggle and solidarity, a future of success for our present efforts.

# STATEMENT OF THE COMMUNIST PARTIES AND GOVERNMENTS ON THE SITUATION IN THE MIDDLE EAST, 9 JUNE 1967

*(Complete Text)*
*(Pravda,* 10 June 1967)

On June 9, this year, leaders of the Communist and Workers' Parties and of the Governments of the socialist countries gathered in Moscow: from the People's Republic of Bulgaria–Todor Zhivkov, First Secretary of the Central Committee of the Bulgarian Communist Party, Chairman of the Council of Ministers of the People's Republic of Bulgaria, Zhivko Zhivkov, Member of the Politbureau of the Central Committee of the Bulgarian Communist Party, First Vice-Chairman of the Council of Ministers of the People's Republic of Bulgaria; from the Hungarian People's Republic–Janos Kadar, First Secretary of the Central Committee of the Hungarian Socialist Workers' Party, Jeno Fock, Member of the Politbureau of the Central Committee of the Hungarian Socialist Workers' Party, Chairman of the Council of Minsters of the Hungarian People's Republic; from the German Democratic Republic–Walter Ulbricht, First Secretary of the Central Committee of the Socialist Unity Party of Germany, Chairman of the Council of State of the German Democratic Republic, Willi Stoph, Member of the Politbureau of the Central Committee of the Socialist Unity Party of Germany, Chairman of the Council of Ministers of the German Democratic Republic, Hermann Axen, Alternate Member of the Politbureau of the Central Committee of the Socialist Unity Party of Germany, Secretary of the Central Committee of the Socialist Unity Party of Germany; from the Polish People's Republic–Wladyslaw Gomulka, First Secretary of the Central Committee of the Polish United Workers' Party, Jozef Cyrankiewicz, Member of the Politbureau of the Central Committee of the Polish United Workers' Party, Chairman of the Council of Ministers of the Polish People's Republic; from the Soviet Union–L. I. Brezhnev, General Secretary of the CPSU Central Committee, A. N. Kosygin, Member of the Politbureau of the CPSU Central Committee, Chairman of the USSR Council of Minsters, N. V. Podgorny, Member of the Politbureau of the CPSU Central Committee, President of the Presidium of the USSR Supreme Soviet; from the Czechoslovak Socialist Republic–Antonin Novotny, First Secretary of the Central Committee of the Communist Party of Czechoslovakia, Jozef Lenart, Member of the Presidium of the Central Committee of the Communist Party of Czechoslovakia, Chairman of the Government of the Czechoslovak Socialist Republic; from the Socialist Federative Republic of Yugoslavia–Josip Broz Tito, Chairman of the League of Communists of Yugoslavia, President of the Socialist Federative Republic of Yugoslavia, Vladimir Popovic, Member of the Presidium of the Central Committee of the League of Communists of Yugoslavia.

They studied the situation that has taken shape in the Near East as a result of Israel's aggression which is the outcome of a conspiracy against the Arab countries by certain imperialist forces, above all the United States. The participants in the meeting exchanged views on measures required to cut short the aggression and to avert its consequences which would be dangerous to the cause of universal peace.

The participants in the meeting deem it necessary to draw conclusions from the fact that Israel did not comply with the decision of the Security Council and did not stop military actions against the Arab states. The Israeli occupation of the territory of Arab states would be used to restore a foreign colonial regime.

On June 9, despite the cease-fire statement by the Government of Syria, Israeli troops started a new offensive on Syria's border, subjecting Syrian towns to barbaric bombing.

Struggling against imperialism for their freedom and independence, for the integrity of their territories, for the inalienable sovereign right to decide for themselves all questions of their domestic life and foreign policy, the peoples of the Arab countries are upholding a just cause. The peoples of the socialist countries are completely on their side.

The peoples of the UAR and several other Arab countries have scored historic victories in recent years in the winning of national independence and freedom. Important social transformations in the interests of the working masses were carried out.

We express confidence that these gains will be preserved, that progressive regimes will be consolidated despite the difficulties in the way of the Arab peoples.

At a difficult hour for the states of the Arab East, the socialist countries declare that they are in full and complete solidarity with their just struggle and will render them aid in repelling aggression and defending their national independence and territorial integrity.

The states participating in this meeting demand that Israel stop immediatley military actions against the neighboring Arab countries and withdraw all its troops from their territories behind the truce line.

It is the duty of the United Nations Organization to condemn the aggressor. If the Security Council does not take the proper measures, grave responsibility will rest with those states which failed to fulfill their duty as members of the Security Council.

Resolute concerted action by all peace-loving and progressive forces, by all those who treasure the cause of freedom and independence of peoples, are necessary today as never before.

If the Government of Israel does not stop the aggression and withdraw its troops behind the truce line the socialist states which signed this Statement will do everything necessary to help the peoples of the Arab countries administer a resolute rebuff to the aggressor, to protect their lawful rights, to extinguish the hotbed of war in the Near East and restore peace in that area.

The just struggle of the Arab peoples will triumph!

# GENERAL DECLARATION OF THE FIRST CONFERENCE
# OF THE ORGANIZATION OF LATIN AMERICAN SOLIDARITY

*Complete Text*
*(Conference Document, Havana)*

The First Conference of the Organization of Latin American Solidarity met in Havana, capital of the Republic of Cuba, from July 31 to August 10, 1967.

This Conference constituted a brilliant stage in the revolutionary struggle which the peoples of our continent are waging in mountains and cities for definitive and total national and social liberation. For the first time in the history of Latin America the true representatives of its exploited, starved and oppressed masses met together to discuss, organize and advance revolutionary solidarity, interchange experiences, coordinate their activities on an ideologically firm basis and, in the light of what their revolutionary past and the present conditions have taught them, the people will confront the global counter-revolutionary strategy of imperialism and the national oligarchies.

The main aim of the Conference has been, in short, to tighten the ties of militant solidarity among anti-imperialist fighters of Latin America and to work out the fundamental lines for the development of the continental revolution. This great assembly has opened up possibilities for an ample and profound discussion of old problems of revolutionary strategy and tactics as well as an interchange of opinions regarding the role of different classes and social strata within the present historical process of the continent. The interchange of opinions, the agreement on a common line and the creation of a permanent body of solidarity constitute an important step toward the encouragement and the promotion of the revolutionary struggle in Latin America. Revolutionary armed struggle triumphant in Cuba and already started in Venezuela, Colombia, Guatemala and Bolivia will not end until the bureaucratic and military apparatus of the bourgeoisie and the landholders is destroyed and the revolutionary power of the working people is established confronting at the same time the internal counter-revolution and Yankee intervention, to inexorably eliminate imperialist domination at its roots.

The struggle undertaken will end only with the victory of the true descendants of those who formed the heroic and self-sacrificing hosts of liberators. We are already living under the promising sign of the second war for independence.

One and a half centuries have elapsed since the peoples of our America took up arms to crush the colonial power that subjugated, exploited and humiliated them, shaking the whole continent with their valiant deeds and sacrifices. The revolutionary struggle which culminated in the overthrow of Spanish domination in almost all of America was led by capable, resolute and undaunted men, the majority of them coming from those groups of wealthy intellectuals educated in the theory of bourgeois liberalism and the ideals of the French Revolution, with a clear perspective of the continental character of the struggle, thus, with a perfect understanding of their duties as Latin American revolutionaries. Simon Bolivar, the highest personification of the liberators of his time, said, "For us, homeland is America." These men, who constituted the revolutionary vanguard of the emancipating movement, not only realized that the struggle was one from the American Septentrional to Patagonia but together, they set out to liberate the common homeland with common actions that extended beyond the frontiers of the viceroys and captaincies, to deprive the enemy of its territorial base for ulterior attacks against the peoples who had gained independence. In accordance with such concepts, objectives and methods, the vanguard of the liberators forced from the onset a united political and military leadership and marched always at the head of the revolutionary armies, organizing and guiding the peoples along the only path that would lead to victory: armed insurrection. The objectives pursued determined the nature of the struggle. In the face of reactionary violence, the essence of the colonial regime, there was no alternative for the winning of independence, sovereignty and dignity, than revolutionary violence. History does not list a single case of class domination that has graciously given up power. On the contrary, history shows that the oppressed and exploited must wrest power from their oppressors and exploiters.

Then, as now and as always, there were some who had little faith and rejected the effectiveness of the path undertaken, adopting pro-colonialist positions or passing openly over to the side of the enemy. They were, obviously, pseudo-revolutionaries, incapable of facing the test by fire, able only to mask their tendencies to conciliation, inaction and treason with long winned [sic] pseudo-revolutionary rhetoric, the typical weaklings to whom Jose Marti alluded. In ostensible contrast to conformists, failures and cowards, the combatants of the liberating vanguard always sustained a burning confidence and absolute security in the inevitable victory of their major undertaking. The most fruitful lesson given by this militant vanguard to posterity is that when the peoples are determined to win or die, and have the benefit of an audacious, firm and enlightened leadership, the result of that determination is always victory, despite the odds and the enemy's might.

But that vanguard went even further, when, at the Panama Congress called at the request of Bolivar, it tried to include its solidary [sic—ed. note, solidarity] decision to contribute to the emancipation of Cuba and Puerto Rico, the last footholds of Spanish domination on the continent. The plot hatched by the government of the United States against such an intention exposed its early ambitions to seize Cuba and Puerto Rico and exercise its control over our America, as already included in the Monroe Doctrine presented when the armies of the peoples of the continent were the masters of the Andes and the brilliant glory of Ayacucho was rising above the horizon.

The first war of independence waged by the peoples of our America was, in fact, reduced to a formal transfer of political sovereignty and a replacement of the chiefs of the revolutionary movement by the native minority that retained both the status quo of land ownership and its leadership. The colonial flags had been lowered, but the weak and backward economic structure of colonial society, characterized by its slow rate of technical and capitalist development, remained intact, and therefore, the regime of oppression and exploitation against which the peasant masses, the slaves, Indian and manual laborers had rebelled, remained. Never had an epic yielded such poor results for its true, heroic and anonymous protagonists, nor have its great feats been so completely ignored.

The conditioning factors of the colonial regime—latifundia, commercial monopoly, ideological misoneism, scientific backwardness, social stratification, religious yoke, political oppression—explain the tardy development of the future nations of Latin America and, likewise, the frustration, shortly after becoming independent from the mother country, of a capitalist development free of ties and the formation of a national bourgeoisie. The radical discrepancy between the ideas that inspired the struggle for independence and the reality on which the new republics were based was evident. A fully developed capitalist bourgeois regime did not arise from this gigantic battle. This process was contrary to the one that took place in the United States which rapidly became the most dynamic, powerful and aggressive form of capitalism at first, and then of criminal and aggressive imperialism.

With the increase in economic growth during the years following independence, certain favorable conditions for the independent development in Latin America of capitalism and the bourgeoisie were created; but this development was paralyzed, deviated and deformed when imperialist penetration broke in on the scene. However, the organic weakness of the Latin American bourgeoisie to break up the latifundia—which was indispensable for the extension of agricultural production and of the internal market—and the interconnection of their class interests with the class interests of the landowners, forced the bourgeoisie to form a closely united oligarchy with the landowners—directly linked to the caste which controlled the professional army—in whose hands the decisive levers of political power were concentrated.

It would be absurd to suppose that, under such conditions, the so-called Latin American bourgeoisie could develop political action independent of the oligarchies and imperialism in defense of the interest and aspirations of the nation. The contradiction in which it is objectively caught is, by its nature, unsurmountable. The weakness of such a structure explains with complete clarity its incapacity to face the brutal assault which universal imperialist expansion implies. And it also explains its immediate subordination to the foreign interests and the framework of underdevelopment in which it stagnates, with its corresponding class relations, privileges and hierarchies and its economic, political, social and cultural corollaries.

The economic influence of the European colonial powers was swiftly shifted, starting from the Spanish-Cuban-U.S. war, and replaced by the growing colonial domination of the United States, ever more voracious, harsh and expanding, propped up by the oligarchies and the apparatus of force of the puppet governments, which, for many years, presented to the world the tragicomedy of a falsely free continent which had the banner, the anthem and a color on the map as formal attributes of their so-called sovereignty and of their subjected economy.

It is well known that U.S. imperialism controls in Latin America almost all the mechanisms of foreign trade, the banking system, the most fertile land, the mines, the public services, the principal industries and the propaganda media. The vast natural resources of this continent—tin, zinc, lead, manganese, cobalt, graphite, iron, copper, nickel, vanadium, beryllium, sulphur, oil—are subjected to a systematic draining, in detriment to the development of the peoples that, with their work and sweat, extract those riches from the heart of a land that is theirs in name only. Latin America appears at the head of the underdeveloped regions of the world in the field of investments of U.S. capital, which are concentrated especially in mining, oil, commerce and industry. In the period from 1956 to 1965 those investments reached the amount of 2893 million dollars, obtaining a profit of 7441 million dollars. For every dollar invested, U.S. imperialism has plundered nearly three dollars from our peoples. These key figures do not include, of course, the interests and benefits obtained from loans, by the associated capital, by the various forms of penetration it uses, the looting and the plunder violating bourgeois pseudo-legality. Its objective, already achieved, is to take over our internal market and to transform the Latin American economy into a complementary economy of that of the U.S., condemning to disappearance—or, at best, to a stagnant life—those branches of national industry that can compete with U.S. products. The scope of action of national capital is necessarily limited to commerce and manufacture dependent on the foreign monopolies. The consequences of this process of absorption and hegemony are obvious: plunder of the resources, ruin of national industries, distortion of economy, a permanent deficit in the balance of payments, low wages, chronic unemployment, increasing inequality, technological backwardness, massive malnutrition, massive illiteracy, insanitary conditions on a great scale, a very high mortality rate, social serfdom, racial discrimination, political instability, an ever sharpening of class contradictions, and criminal violence as the essence of power.

To these forms of economic penetration of imperialism we may add the thousand forms of ideological penetration and the comparative rates of demographic expansion with the increase of the internal gross product *per capita*, and the unequal redistribution of the national gross income, and we get a vivid picture of the dramatic situation that our people are facing.

The tremendous political gravitation that this entails is self-evident. The same contradictions between the Latin American bourgeoisie and U.S. imperialism are developed under conditions of such subordination and subjection that they never take on an antagonistic character. The impotence of the Latin American bourgeoisie is absolute.

There has not been a single act of direct or indirect imperialist intervention in our countries—since the past century—that has not been justified or supported by the bourgeoisie. It is intrinsically unable to face the imperialists. Furthermore, it is their obedient servant and their profiting intermediary. The problems caused by this complex and condensed structure of anti-popular, and anti-national and anti-historic interests, based on the exploitation of man by man, maintained by force—and mainly for the benefit of Yankee imperialism, which generates and conditions it—cannot be solved through academic "structural reforms" and "the effective exercise of representative democracy." The only real way to solve them is through the revolutionary struggle of the peoples.

The interventionist policy of the United States in Latin America that was initiated with the Monroe Doctrine is emphasized and defined with the "doctrines" of the "ripe fruit" and of "manifest destiny," with the pillage of a vast part of Mexican territory, the filibuster adventures of William Walker in Central America, the imposition on Cuba of the Platt Amendment and the leasing of the territory occupied by the Guantanamo Naval Base, the shameful occupation of Puerto Rico, the dirty maneuvers in connection with the control of the Panama Canal, the cynical Roosevelt Corollary to the Monroe Doctrine, the unfair loans, the brazen interventions in Nicaragua, Panama, Mexico, Haiti, Colombia, Guatemala and the Dominican Republic, and the creation in Bogota of the so-called Organization of American States, mere cover of the old and discredited Pan-American Union, whose devious intentions were denounced and fought by José Marti, who foresaw before anyone else, with keen political insight, the inception of the imperialist phenomenon in the United States, identifying it by name—in a letter to Manuel Mercado in the eve of his heroic death.

The pseudo-legal machinery set up in the OAS by Yankee imperialism in order to legalize its economic expansion, political domination and military aggression in Latin America is completed with the so-called Inter-American Treaty for Mutual Assistance, an instrument for the application of its repressive policy on the continent.

The peoples of Latin America have not remained with their arms folded in face of their executioners and exploiters. They have stood up to them repeatedly in unequal battle against the oligarchies and imperialism, sometimes obtaining certain benefits and the temporary respect of elementary rights. They have resorted to all forms of struggle, from popular demonstrations and political strikes to sporadic uprisings, and on no few occasions have been victims, due to the desperate way of life in which they live, of the illusion of demagogic movements led by parties at the service of the oligarchies and imperialism. But the most important thing has undoubtedly been their unwavering attitude of resistance and rebellion against oppression, poverty, plunder and humiliation, with no other support than the moral strength that originates from the principles of conscience and dignity. In the course of their struggles against the oligarchies and Yankee imperialism, the Latin American people have accumulated revolutionary energy, have raised their political level, have strengthened their cadres and have promoted militant solidarity beyond their frontiers. They have not obtained any political or economic advantage that was not wrested from the exploiters by sheer force and that is why they have gained a clear perception that only the defeat of the oligarchies of the puppet governments and of imperialist domination could definitely and totally liberate them and place in their own hands their right to lead their own lives.

The triumph and consolidation of the Cuban Revolution made clear that armed insurrection is the true way to the seizure of power by the working people and, at the same time, that professional armies can be destroyed, oligarchies vanquished, Yankee imperialism defeated and socialism—as a national way of life—developed and strengthened in spite of economic blockade, subversion, aggression, blackmail, harassing, pressure and counterrevolution.

The first fundamental consequence of the Cuban Revolution was the rise of the anti-imperialist movement and the resulting radicalization and demarcation of the clashing forces. The polarization of these becomes clearer and sharper all the time: on the one hand, closely united, fighting militantly for its liberation, defending and promoting the Cuban Revolution with its concrete actions; the urban working class, the agricultural laborers, the peasants, the students, the most progressive middle strata, the underemployed, the unemployed, the Indians, and the Negroes; on the other hand, the oligarchies, the puppet governments and Yankee imperialism, trying to suffocate it.

Yankee imperialists have tried to isolate Cuba from America, so that its example doesn't spread throughout the continent. But Cuba has never been more united with the rest of the peoples of America. The imperialists have raised the issue that Cuba wants to impose an extracontinental ideology on the continent. The peoples of America, however, have felt the Cuban Revolution to be closely linked to their own revolution.

The strangers to Latin America are the Yankee imperialists and their reactionary ideology. In Cuba the aspirations and ideals of all the peoples of Latin America are defined and summed up. They attempted to isolate it and with this attitude they have succeeded in tightening even more the bonds of indestructible unity between the Cuban people and the other peoples of America—that constitute one big family facing a common enemy, the principal enemy of all humanity: Yankee imperialism.

The submission and surrender of the oligarchies and puppet government reached extremes starting with the Conference of the OAS which took place at Punta del Este in 1961 and 1962, where they openly plotted, following the dictates of Washington, to isolate Cuba diplomatically and economically from the rest of Latin America, unleashing, at the same time, a brutal repression against their peoples, crudely exposing the counterrevolutionary and pro-imperialist nature of the gorilla regimes as well as that of the reformists of "representative democrats." Incapable of solving the problems posed by underdevelopment and imperialist penetration; increasingly harassed by the growing demands of the workers, the peasants, the students and the unemployed; terrorized by the growing tide of the revolutionary war; they see in the aid, the alliance and the intervention of imperialism—with its anti-guerrilla centers, its Green Berets, its marines and its Inter-American Peace Force—the only guarantee to their survival and the only force capable of defending their interests. Yankee imperialism, on the other hand, fruitlessly attempting to thwart the revolutionary drive and smear the image of the Cuban Revolution in the minds of the Latin American masses, plotted the fraud of the Alliance for Progress, aimed at tying them even closer to their policy of enrichment, exploitation and repression. Its failure has been so complete that even the Inter-American Committee, under its direction, has been forced to point out the fraud contained in this Alliance for Backwardness.

In the present circumstances in Latin America, there are conditions for the development and triumph of the Revolution that emancipate it from the structure of the oligarchic-imperialist power which holds back its independence, progress and welfare. These conditions exist because in the rural areas there are thousands of peasants and agricultural workers subjected to sub-standard living conditions and to an extraordinary regime of labor exploitation and an incredible concentration of land, because in the cities the luxury and excessive spending of the dominant classes dramatically contrasts with the overcrowdedness, sordidness and poverty in which millions of workers and unemployed have to live. This shows the antagonistic nature of the interests of the exploiter and exploited classes. The increasingly clear and firm class awareness created through the development of capitalism in some regions of the continent; the existence of a progressive intellectual class and particularly of a student body with great traditions of struggle which form part of the left; the strong position of the oligarchies, the puppet governments and Yankee imperialism—which resort to torture and murder to oppose every people's demand and also to the most cruel and stupid methods in their war against the masses and their revolutionary vanguards, contributing also to develop militant consciousness and clear understanding of the road of political, economic, social and cultural changes. To the counterrevolutionary violence we must oppose revolutionary violence—already exemplified by the Cuban Revolution and by the success of the guerrilla forces.

The revolutionary conditions existing in Latin America are also in force in other underdeveloped countries of Africa and Asia, continents that with Latin America form part of the same historic anti-imperialist trend. As in Russia and China in the years before the revolution, said conditions show that the development of revolution is possible. In the context of the Latin American revolutionary struggle these conditions set forth the development of the task with a bold, decided and valiant revolutionary vanguard, forged in the people's war and closely linked to the peasant and proletariat masses, and who, uniting the political and military leadership, can and must turn into the center of political, ideological, and revolutionary action, that by facing and defeating the professional armies do away with oligarchies, puppet governments and imperialist domination. In Latin America, the Revolution of the working people is the first item on the agenda. Conditions are ripe to begin this Revolution with confidence, determination and prospects of success. Viet Nam teaches us that victory of the Latin American peoples is possible.

This Conference, after deeply and attentively analyzing the conditions existing in the Continent and after having made clear in the ideological field the essential problems of the revolutionary movements, has arrived at the following conclusions:

In Latin America there exists a convulsive situation, characterized by the presence of a weak bourgeoisie that, indissolubly united to the landowners, constitutes the oligarchy which dominates our countries. A greater submission and an almost absolute dependency of this oligarchy on imperialism determine the intense polarization of forces on the continent; the oligarchic imperialist alliance on the one hand, and, on the other hand, the peoples.

The peoples have a tremendous revolutionary power which is only waiting to be channeled by a correct leadership, by a revolutionary vanguard, in order to develop or to initiate the fight.

That power is the power of the proletarian masses, of workers of city and country, of a super-exploited poor peasantry, of the young intellectuals, of students with a great tradition of struggle, and of the middle classes, all joined together by the common denominator of the exploitation to which they are subjected.

In the face of the crisis of the whole structure of the economic, social and political system throughout the continent, and the growing rebelliousness of the peoples, imperialism has designed and developed a continental strategy of repression that tries unsuccessfully to hold back the tide of history. The survival of the colonial and neocolonial systems of exploitation and domination are the aims of U.S. imperialism.

This situation determines and demands that revolutionary violence be unleashed and developed in answer to reactionary violence.

Revolutionary violence as the highest expression of the peoples' struggle is not the only path, but it is the most concrete and the most direct way to defeat imperialism.

The peoples as well as the revolutionaries have confirmed this reality and consequently realize the need to initiate, develop and conclude armed struggle in order to destroy the bureaucratic-military apparatus of the oligarchies and the power of imperialism.

In many countries the special conditions prevailing in the countryside, the favorable topography and a potentially revolutionary social base in addition to the special adaptation of technical methods and the professional armies to repress the peoples in the cities with their inability to adapt themselves to an irregular war, mean that guerrilla warfare is the fundamental expression of armed struggle, the best school for revolutionaries and their indisputable vanguard.

The revolution, already underway in some countries, an imperative necessity in others and a future prospect in the rest, has a well-defined anti-imperialist character within its anti-oligarchic aims.

The principal objective of the peoples' revolution on the continent is the seizing of power by means of the destruction of the bureaucratic-military apparatus of the State and its replacement by the armed people in order to change the existing economic and social regime. The said objective can only be achieved through armed struggle.

The development and the organization of the struggle depend on the site on which to carry it out and the most adequate methods of organization.

The lessons of the Cuban Revolution and the experiences accumulated by the revolutionary movement in recent years throughout the world and the presence in Bolivia, Venezuela, Colombia and Guatemala of an ever-growing armed revolutionary movement show that guerrilla warfare as a genuine expression of the people's armed struggle is the most effective method and the most adequate form for waging and developing revolutionary war in most of our countries and, consequently, on a continental scale.

In this particular situation the unity of the people, the identity of their aims, the unity of their views and their disposition to unite in carrying out the struggle are the elements characterizing the common strategy that must be opposed to that which imperialism develops on a continental scale.

This strategy requires a precise and clear expression of solidarity, whose most effective character is the revolutionary struggle itself, which extends across the continent and whose vanguard detachments are the guerrilla and liberation armies.

We, the representatives of the peoples of our America, conscious of the conditions which prevail on the continent, aware of the existence of a common counterrevolutionary strategy directed by U.S. imperialism,

**PROCLAIM**

1. That making the Revolution constitutes a right and a duty of the peoples of Latin America.
2. That the Revolution in Latin America has its deepest historical roots in the liberation movement against European colonialism of the 19th century and against imperialism of this century. The epic of the peoples of America and the great class battles that our peoples have carried out against imperialism in earlier decades constitute the source of historical inspriation of the Latin American revolutionary movement . . .
3. That the essential content of the Revolution in Latin America is to be found in its confrontation with imperialism and the bourgeois and landowner oligarchies. Consequently, the character of the Revolution is the struggle for national independence, emancipation from the oligarchies, and the socialist road for its complete economic and social development.
4. That the principles of Marxism-Leninism guide the revolutionary movement of Latin America.
5. That armed revolutionary struggle constitutes the fundamental course of the Revolution in Latin America.
6. That all other forms of struggle must serve to advance and not to retard the development of this fundamental course, which is armed struggle.
7. That, for the majority of the countries of the continent, the problems of organizing, initiating, developing and crowning the armed struggle at present constitutes the immediate and fundamental task of the revolutionary movement.
8. That those countries in which this task has not yet been undertaken nevertheless *will regard it as an inevitable sequence* in the development of revolutionary struggle in their countries.
9. That the historic responsibility of furthering revolution in each one of these countries belongs to the people and to their revolutionary vanguards in each society.
10. That the guerrilla is the nucleus of the liberation armies, and guerrilla warfare constitutes the most effective method of initiating and developing the revolutionary struggle in most of our countries.
11. That the leadership of the Revolution demands, as an organizational principle, the existence of a unified politico-military command, as a guarantee of success.
12. That the most effective solidarity that the revolutionary movements may practice among themselves, is the furthering and the culmination of their own struggle in their respective countries.
13. That the solidarity with Cuba and the collaboration and cooperation with the armed revolutionary movement is an undeferrable international duty of every anti-imperialist organization of the continent.
14. The Cuban Revolution, as a symbol of triumph of the armed revolutionary movement, constitutes the vanguard of the Latin American anti-imperialist movement. The peoples that develop the armed struggle, as they advance along this road, put themselves in the vanguard.
15. That the peoples who have been directly subjected by colonialism of the European countries, in order to achieve their liberation, must have an immediate and basic objective: that of struggling for independence, and uniting with

the general struggle of the continent as the only means of avoiding being absorbed into U.S. neocolonialism.

16. That the Second Declaration of Havana, that expresses the beautiful and glorious revolutionary tradition of the past 150 years of American history, constitutes a document outlining the program of the Latin American Revolution which has been confirmed, deepened, enriched and made more radical by the peoples of this continent during the last five years.

17. That the peoples of Latin America have no differences with any other peoples in the world and extend their hand of friendship also to the peoples of the United States, whom they exhort to undertake the struggle against the repressive policy carried out by imperialist monopolies.

18. That the Latin American struggle strengthens its ties of solidarity with the peoples of Asia and Africa and those of the socialist countries, the workers of the capitalist nations, and especially with the Negro population of the United States which suffers class exploitation, poverty, unemployment, racial discrimination and the denial of their most elementary human rights, and which constitutes an important force within the revolutionary struggle.

19. That the heroic struggle waged by the people of Viet Nam gives invaluable aid to all revolutionary peoples who are fighting imperialism, and constistutes an inspiring example to the peoples of Latin America.

20. That we have approved the Statutes and created the Permanent Committee, in Havana, of the Organization of Latin American Solidarity, which constitutes an inspiring example to the peoples Latin American peoples.

We, the revolutionaries of our America, the America south of the Rio Bravo, successors of the men who gave us our first independence, armed with an undaunted will to fight, and with revolutionary and scientific guidance, and with nothing to lose but the chains which oppress us,

ASSERT

That our struggle constitutes a decisive contribution to the historic struggle of humanity to liberate itself from slavery and exploitation.
THE DUTY OF EVERY REVOLUTIONARY IS TO MAKE THE REVOLUTION.

# FOUR DOCUMENTS OF THE CONFERENCE OF EUROPEAN COMMUNIST AND WORKERS' PARTIES ON PROBLEMS OF EUROPEAN SECURITY HELD IN KARLOVY VARY, CZECHOSLOVAKIA, APRIL 24–26, 1967

### A.  OPENING COMMUNIQUE
### B.  SPEECH BY LEONID I. BREZHNEV
### C.  STATEMENT, "FOR PEACE AND SECURITY IN EUROPE"
### D.  FINAL COMMUNIQUE

*Complete Text*
*(Information Bulletin*, Nos. 8-10, 1967, Prague edition)

## A.  OPENING COMMUNIQUE

The Conference of European Communist and Workers' Parties on Problems of European Security opened in Karlovy Vary on Monday, April 24, at 10 a.m.

The delegations of the following fraternal parties are taking part in the conference: the Communist Party of Belgium, the Bulgarian Communist Party, the Communist Party of Czechoslovakia, the Communist Party of Denmark, the Communist Party of Finland, the French Communist Party, the Irish Workers' Party, the Communist Party of Northern Ireland, the Italian Communist Party, the Progressive Party of the Working People of Cyprus, the Communist Party of Luxembourg, the Hungarian Socialist Workers' Party, the Socialist Unity Party of Germany, the Communist Party of Germany, the Socialist Unity Party of Germany—West Berlin, the Polish United Workers' Party, the Portuguese Communist Party, the Communist Party of Austria, the Communist Party of Greece, the Communist Party of San Marino, the Communist Party of the Soviet Union, the Communist Party of Spain, the Swiss Party of Labor, the Communist Party of Great Britain. The Conference is attended by a representative of the Communist Party of Sweden.

The Conference was opened by Comrade Antonin Novotny, First Secretary of the CC of the Communist Party of Czechoslovakia. He proposed a draft order of business, which was unanimously adopted. Then the chair was taken by Comrade Wladyslaw Gomulka, First Secretary of the CC of the Polish United Workers' Party.

At the morning session the participants in the Conference unanimously adopted an Appeal calling for solidarity with the struggle of the Vietnamese people.

The Conference also adopted a Statement concerning the military coup in Greece.

The first speakers in the debate at the morning session were Waldeck Rochet, General Secretary of the French Communist Party, L. I. Brezhnev, General Secretary of the CC of the Communist Party of the Soviet Union, and F. Muhri, Chairman of the Communist Party of Austria.

During the first part of the afternoon session, presided over by Waldeck Rochet, the Conference was addressed by Antonin Novotny and Wladyslaw Gomulka.

Alvaro Cunhal, General Secretary of the Portuguese Communist Party, was in the chair during the second half of the afternoon session. The speakers were Knud Jespersen, Chairman of the Communist Party of Denmark, Max Reimann, First Secretary of the Communist Party of Germany, Ville Pessi, General Secretary of the Communist Party of Finland.

## B.  SPEECH BY LEONID I. BREZHNEV

Dear Comrades, allow me to convey fraternal greetings from the C.C. of the Communist Party of the Soviet Union and the many millions of Soviet Communists to the participants in this Conference. In your person we greet all Communists, the proletariat and other working people of Europe and all the European fighters for peace and socialism.

The delegation of our Party expresses sincere thanks to the Central Committee of the French Communist Party for their extensive and fruitful work in preparing our Conference.

We heartily thank the Central Committee of the Communist Party of Czechoslovakia for their cordial hospitality and for the fine conditions they have created for the work of the Conference.

Our Conference has been convened on the initiative of the Vienna Meeting of West-European Communist Parties. From the very outset this initiative has had the support of the CC CPSU. We fully appreciate the view of our comrades in the capitalist part of Europe that in order to settle the problem of security in our continent the efforts of the socialist countries must be concerted with the actions of all peace-loving forces in the West-European countries. In this light, special significance attaches to the activity of the working class.

Security in Europe is not the business only of governments. In the settlement of this problem a tremendous role is played by broad masses, the proletariat and progressive forces who are untiringly working for peace, and opposing the aggressive forces of imperialism and their preparations for another war. That is why we subscribe to the opinion voiced here that the initiative of the Communist Parties, participants in our Conference, can and must greatly benefit the common actions of all political forces championing security in Europe. This fully conforms to the aims of the Communist parties and the role they are at present playing in European politics.

## 1. The International Situation and the Struggle For European Security.

Comrades, in going over to the substance of the problems on the Conference agenda, we should like to emphasize first of all that our Party does not regard the strengthening of peace in Europe as something isolated from the world-wide struggle of the peoples against imperialism, from the struggle for peace, national independence and social progress. Today the situation in any part of the world cannot be examined in isolation from the general processes of international development. Similarly, the situation in Europe is inseparable from the entire international situation.

At their Meetings in 1957 and 1960, Communists drew important conclusions on the main trends of contemporary world development. The period that has elapsed has confirmed the correctness of these conclusions.

Far be it from us to assess the international situation in a simplified way. We put on record confidently that in the years since the Moscow conferences contingents of the revolutionary movement have advanced to new positions and continue, though perhaps not so fast as we all would like them to, their movement forward. The world socialist revolution is a complicated process in the course of which hard battles have to be fought and some stages of which are not free from difficulties.

Important positive processes are under way in the socialist system. The majority of the socialist countries are thoroughly changing the forms and methods of management of the national economy, striving to make more effective use of the inherent possibilities of socialism and acquire fuller mastery of the laws of development of the socialist economy. Ever greater attention is paid by the Communist parties of the socialist countries to perfecting socialist democracy, to the further development of the political activity of the masses, to securing their participation in the guidance of all aspects of social life. An intensive and interesting quest in this field is to be observed everywhere. Cooperation of the socialist countries in the economic, political spheres and in defense also goes on improving and becoming more and more regular and comprehensive. In many respects this cooperation is rising now to a new, higher level.

It stands to reason that in appraising the situation in the socialist world system we cannot lose sight of such a serious fact in its development in the recent years as the well-known positions of the leadership of China and the disruption of the cooperation of the CPC and PRC with the other fraternal parties and socialist countries. A discussion of this problem is not on the agenda of our Conference, but nevertheless the problem exists and negatively influences the Communist and the entire liberation movement.

The national-liberation movement continues to grow in scope and depth. The sixties have witnessed the victory of the Algerian revolution, the consolidation of the positions of the democratic forces in the United Arab Republic, Syria's entry upon the road of social progress, the laying of the foundations of socio-economic development in a number of countries of the so-called third world. This road is not free from acute conflicts, as, for instance, the events in Ghana and Indonesia show. It is natural that after the former colonies and semi-colonies have acquired state independence the reactionary elements in them, supported by the imperialists from without, are seeking to push these states onto the road of capitalist development and cooperation with the forces of international reaction. In view of this the forces of progress, above all Communists, should display even greater perseverance and flexibility.

The wave of the revolutionary movement against imperialism and local reaction is rising ever higher in the Latin-American countries. Important changes are taking place in the working-class movement of the developed capitalist countries. As a result of the active work of the Communist and Workers' Parties and the operation of the intrinsic laws of capitalism, anti-monopoly sentiments are running high among broad sections of the people; the masses are clearly veering towards the Left. This is giving rise to new possibilities for the unity of the working class and all progressive forces and in the struggle for socialism. It goes without saying that the comrades from Western Europe present at this Conference know these problems much better and we shall therefore confine ourselves to general remarks about these changes.

The imperialist leaders realize that their positions have grown weaker and are aware of the strength of the revolutionary contingents opposing imperialism. In recent years they have made a tremendous effort, in line with this new situation, to improve their class strategy both on a national and international scale, and to devise new ways and means of combating world socialism and the revolutionary and liberation movement. Imperialism is counting more and more on a division among the socialist countries and on the split in the liberation movement.

The most sinister expression of the predatory nature of imperialism and its main force—U.S. imperialists are waging shameful and hopeless war in that country. They will never conquer a people that has been for more than twenty years heroically fighting for its freedom and independence. Relying on the many-sided assistance of the socialist countries and the support of the progressive forces of the whole world, the patriots of Vietnam are successfully resisting the interventionists. They are therby dealing telling blows at the positions of U.S. imperialism as a whole, and not only because nearly half a million U.S. soldiers, a large fleet and a sizeable portion of the U.S. Air Force are tied down in Southeast Asia. Another point is that this aggression in Vietnam is seriously undermining the prestige and political position of the USA in the whole world.

This aggression in Vietnam has set millions upon millions of people against the USA. It is arousing the hatred of the Asian peoples for the American interventionists. This is a factor that the U.S. leaders will have to face for many years to come. The dirty U.S. war in Vietnam has aggravated the contradictions among the U.S. allies, many of whom are reluctant to have anything in common with it.

It is known that socialist countries, including the

Soviet Union, are actively helping fighting Vietnam by giving it political, economic, and military support. It could not be otherwise for here we are confronted with imperialist aggression against a socialist country—the Democratic Republic of Vietnam. I can assure you, comrades, that we, Soviet Communists, shall continue fulfilling our internationalist duty to fighting Vietnam and rendering her all the aid she requires.

At present the war in Vietnam is the most serious threat to world peace. In all continents huge numbers of people of different classes, religion and convictions demand that the USA stop bombing the Democratic Republic of Vietnam and end its aggression in Vietnam. This is equally true of Europe, where opposition to U.S. aggression is steadily mounting. I think you will all agree that the struggle in this sector is also an important contribution to European security.

Lastly, the developments in Vietnam bring to the fore the vital importance of strengthening the unity of the world Communist movement in the present situation. It is quite obvious that if we had the possibility to act in defense of Vietnam in agreement and jointly with China, the task of ending U.S. aggression would have been considerably easier. Allow me to repeat here what we declared at the Congress of the Socialist Unity Party of Germany, namely, that the CC CPSU and the Soviet Government are prepared to take joint action with China in planning and rendering aid to fighting Vietnam. We are prepared for such unity of action on the broadest possible scale.

Comrades, such are some of the international factors that we have to take into consideration when we discuss European security.

When we assess the present situation in Europe we base ourselves mainly on the changes that have taken place here after the Second World War. One of the key social and political factors of the post-war period is that here in Europe—i.e., the part of the world where capitalism emerged, where it developed into a social system that for many centuries determined the course of world events—the positions of capitalism have been enormously undermined.

This is mirrored in the downfall of capitalism and the triumph of socialist revolutions in eight countries in Eastern and Central Europe. Moreover, this is mirrored in the fact that to a large extent the bourgeoisie has been able to retain its supremacy over the rest of Europe solely with the support of U.S. military, political and economic might.

That West European capitalism could emerge from the sharp crisis in which it found itself directly after the Second World War was only thanks to U.S. support, to the possibilities given it by the combination of the power of monopolies with that of the governments, and also to the scientific and technical revolution, and to its maneuvers in the sphere of social relations and politics. Naturally, this does not in the least signify the restoration of the former political might of European capitalism. Its basic weaknesses remain.

The new balance of social and political forces in the continent is reflected in the foreign policy of the leading European capitalist powers. The main contingents of European capitalism, whose interests frequently come into sharp collisions, are doing their utmost to avoid methods and forms of struggle with each other that might threaten the foundations of capitalism with further upheavals.

Having restored their economic potential, some European capitalist countries are now inclined to implement a more independent policy. No small role is played in this by the growing contradictions between the interests of European and U.S. magnates. The pro-American concepts of policy are being swept away more and more by concepts whose object is to turn capitalist Europe into a force that would be independent of the USA and able to play its own role in the world.

It is perfectly obvious to us Communists that these concepts are designed to strengthen European capitalism and its international positions. But it is also apparent that these plans are breaking the united front of world capitalism and that this is opening fresh possibilities of the European and world working-class movement to struggle for peace and security in Europe and throughout the world.

Comrades, the Draft Statement which our Conference is discussing underlines that European security is not simply a regional problem, not an internal affair of the European peoples that does not concern the rest of the world. What makes us draw this conclusion? We cannot forget that two world wars broke out in Europe, and that today, as well, one of the most dangerous hotbeds of international tension is situated in this continent. If another war breaks out in Europe it may develop into a thermonuclear war and envelop the whole world. European security is a key condition for averting a world nuclear conflict.

But that is not all. Already today the struggle for peace in Europe is to some extent paralyzing the aggressive forces of the imperialists and obstructing their actions to crush the liberation movement in the other parts of the globe. It is, comrades, after all a fact that despite its dogged efforts the USA has failed to inveigle its European NATO allies into the Vietnam adventure, as had been the case during the war in Korea. This is a result of the struggle of the Communist Parties, the working class of the whole world, of all peace-loving forces.

To incapacitate the forces of imperialism in Europe and frustrate their aggressive plans means not merely to narrow down the radius of action of the aggressive policy of imperialism, although that in itself is important, but also to inflict on this policy a defeat that would have world-wide reverberations. This would also be real assistance to the liberation struggle of the peoples in all the other continents. I think, comrades, that I shall be expressing your common opinion if I say that by showing concern for the interests of European security we are fulfilling our internationalist duty to the people of the whole world.

## 2. U.S. and West-German Imperialism—Main Threat to Peace in Europe

We may be asked: is the threat of war in Europe so grave today that we have to pose this question so sharply?

Yes, comrades, there are grounds for these apprehensions. We do not wish to exaggerate the danger of war, but neither do we wish to belittle it. Where and in what do we today see the threat to European security?

Our reply is: peace in Europe is threatened by the aggressive forces of U.S. and West German imperialism. What underlines the ever closer partnership of these forces? For U.S. imperialism agreement with the West German rulers is the basic, most convenient and, in fact, not very expensive means for preserving its military and strategic positions in Europe. This gives the USA powerful levers for bringing pressure to bear on the policy and economy of the West European countries. As regards the West German politicians, they reckon that their partnership with the USA will give them real possibilities for carrying out their revanchist designs.

The aggressive policy of German imperialism has caused enormous suffering for many European nations. This is well known not only to the peoples of the Soviet Union but also to the peoples of Poland, Yugoslavia, Czechoslovakia, France, Britain, Belgium, the Netherlands, Norway, Denmark and other European countries. Soviet people have not forgotten, nor will they ever forget, that 20 million citizens of our country gave their lives for victory over nazism. We had to exert tremendous efforts in order to heal the war-inflicted wounds and rebuild thousands of towns and villages that had been razed to the ground.

The Soviet people who are today engaged in peaceful creative endeavor will not allow their gains and the gains of the other socialist countries to be threatened again. Today we are recalling the lessons of war not because we seek retribution for the past, but because we are concerned about the future. The vital interests of all the European nations demand that aggression by German imperialism, alone or in alliance with any other country or countries, must be excluded once and for all.

The principles of the post-war arrangement in Europe were defined in the Potsdam Agreement, whose main demand was the uprooting of militarism and nazism, so that Germany could never again threaten her neighbors or world peace. This demand holds good today and for the future.

The Potsdam principles have been fully implemented in the German Democratic Republic. But they are ignored in the Federal Republic of Germany, where German militarism is alive and German nazism is being galvanized. The fact that the germs of nazism have not been exterminated in West Germany, as required by the Potsdam Agreement is no news to anybody. But today when the neo-nazis have come out openly on the political scene the matter is much more serious.

The danger is becoming particularly grave in view of the fact that the FRG rulers have made their revanchist demands a pivot of their official state policy. It is not only some irresponsible tub-thumpers and extremists from the soldiers' unions or refugee organizations but also the Government of West Germany that comes forward with the absurd claim to the right to speak on behalf of the entire German people, refuses to recognize the present frontiers in Europe, puts forward claims to West Berlin and seeks loopholes for West Germany's nuclear armament. If to all this we add the fact that the Bonn authorities are maintaining a ban on the Communist Party and suppressing other progressive forces, what we get is a whole set of political and ideological means of preparing for a war of revenge.

The West German Government now in office likes to speak of its peaceableness. But the point is that in so doing it seeks all sorts of elastic formulas in order to avoid any renunciation of revanchist objectives. Consequently, how can any one believe that the peaceable statements of the West German rulers are sincere? Is it not clear that in this way the new Government desires only to delude European public opinion in order to emerge from isolation and thereby secure stronger positions for its plans?

The Soviet Union by no means considers that the European nations should cold-shoulder West Germany; a road lies open before her, as before all the other countries to equitable international cooperation and participation in European affairs. We know that there are considerable forces in the FRG that are opposed to the aggressive reactionary policy of West German imperialism. The class clashes involving the miners of the Ruhr, the metal-workers of Stuttgart and the chemical workers of Mannheim have shown that the movement against militarism and nazism is growing in West Germany itself. Thousands of people have taken part in peace marches and in meetings protesting against the war in Vietnam, and this shows that the working people in West Germany cherish peace like any other nation does.

For our part we have repeatedly declared and declare once more that the Soviet Union is not opposed to improving relations with the Federal Republic of Germany and that it is prepared to do everything in its power to achieve this improvement. If the present FRG Government adopts a sober approach to the present situation in Europe, if it refrains from encroaching upon the interests of other countries and peoples and in its actions demonstrates its desire to strengthen peace in our continent, we shall be among the supporters of such a policy.

But both we and all those who cherish peace and the security of nations have never agreed, and never will agree, to compromise at the expense of this peace and security. The more tenaciously the FRG leaders cling to their revanchist doctrines, the stronger will be the rebuff they will encounter from the Soviet Union and all the European nations.

Facts show that the present war threat from German imperialism is very real indeed.

In the course of the past ten years the FRG has built up one of the largest armies in Europe, nearly half a million strong, and now has a sufficient number of regular officers to enable it to mobilize huge armed forces at short notice as had been the case on the eve of the Second World War.

The West German imperialists are, of course, unable to achieve their revanchist goals. The Soviet Union and other socialist countries have sufficient military power to deal an aggressor a crushing blow, should he dare to start a war. But the revanchists can plunge the European countries and then the entire world into the abyss of war. This danger must be clearly apprehended.

U.S. military presence in Europe encourages West German imperialism and increases the menace to European peace. The hundreds of thousands of U.S. troops stationed in Europe, the U.S. war bases, the U.S. aircraft carriers and nuclear submarines in the seas washing the continent, and U.S. bombers flying in the European skies with their nuclear loads are creating a constant and real threat to the security of the European peoples.

NATO has been and remains the main instrument of U.S. policy in Europe. From the very beginning this bloc has rested on the artifically created myth of "communist aggression" and "the threat from the East." This myth has been exploded by the peace-loving policy of the Soviet Union and other socialist countries and by the entire course of events in Europe and the rest of the world. Today everybody sees that the "hand of Moscow," which imperialist propaganda has used as a bogey to intimidate nations, has held and continues firmly to hold aloft the banner of peace, peaceful coexistence and friendship among nations.

Today the conditions have become more favorable for improving the situation in Europe and arranging mutually advantageous cooperation among the European states. This, in turn, means that there are more favorable conditions for the activity of the Communist Parties as well, for uniting the efforts of all who are working for peace and security in Europe. That is our common achievement.

In this situation the acute question confronting the peoples of the NATO countries and their Governments is: Why is this bloc in existence and what is the price for participating in it?

In the period that NATO has been in existence, its European members have spent a sum exceeding 3,000,000 million dollars on military preparations. This expenditure painfully hits the interests of the working people, hinders economic development and adversely affects progress in science and culture.

The United States is taking advantage of the situation to drain Western Europe of many of its talented scientists. In some countries this phenomenon has been aptly called the "brain drain."

We are not concealing the fact that the building up of the NATO war machine is compelling the Soviet Union and other socialist countries to increase their defense capacity and allocate considerable funds for defense purposes.

U.S. tutelage over the policy, economic development and armed forces of a number of West-European countries and the penetration of Americanism into all pores of social and cultural life are becoming increasingly intolerable to those who cherish national dignity and peace.

The West-European peoples do not wish to put up endlessly with the fact that vast regions of their countries have been set aside as permanent quarters for American expeditionary forces. The more than 20 years' old U.S. military, economic and political presence in Western Europe has become a burden even for some monopoly circles, which have gained enough strength to compete with their overseas rivals. The demand that European problems should be settled without the interference of the overseas power but solely by the strength and intelligence of the Europeans themselves is winning more and more supporters throughout Europe.

In recent years numerous plans have been advanced in the West for "modernizing" NATO and arguments have been devised with the aim of preserving this "holy alliance" of U.S. and European reaction at all costs. They have gone so far as to maintain that NATO can play a positive role in the promotion of East-West contacts. It would be difficult to find a more absurd argument. It turns out that an organization specially set up for struggle against the socialist countries and which has foisted upon its members a thousand and one prohibitions and restrictions as regards economic and commercial relations with the socialist countries is now made to appear as an instrument of peaceful relations and cooperation between the West and the East. Who will believe it?

Experience shows that political, commercial, economic and cultural relations between the European socialist and capitalist countries are promoted faster where our Western partners base themselves on national interests and act in defiance of the NATO Council's recommendations and of its discriminatory measures with regard to the socialist states.

In these conditions the Communists consider it to be their duty to propose to the peoples and governments of Europe constructive measures that can, in our view, lead to the elimination of the war threat, basically improve the situation in the European continent and lay the foundation for broad reciprocally advantageous cooperation between countries.

## 3. Road to Security in Europe

The present international situation offers real possibilities for implementing such measures. We are convinced that it is possible and necessary to build up a Europe in which the security of each state, of each people, would simultaneously be the security of all. Our confidence rests not only on an understanding of the deepest aspirations of the European peoples, but also on a realistic appraisal of the forces which oppose the policy of military gambles and the preparation of aggression.

The community of socialist states is a factor of primary importance in postwar Europe. What makes their foreign policy strong is that its fundamental aims coincide with the vital interests of the broad masses in all the countries of our continent.

At their meeting in Bucharest, it will be recalled, the socialist states united in the Warsaw Treaty

Organization took the initiative in sponsoring a program of security and peaceful cooperation in Europe. This program finds ever more supporters among European and world public opinion.

The Warsaw Treaty countries specifically have advanced the idea of convening an all-European conference of states to examine problems of safeguarding security in Europe and arranging all-European cooperation. This proposal has met with a favorable response among many West European states.

The central question of European security is the inviolability of the frontiers of European countries in the way they were shaped as a result of and after the Second World War. Any attempt to break up these frontiers would bring immeasurable calamities to the peoples. This also applies in full measure to the frontiers of the Federal Republic of Germany in the east and the west, in the north and the south.

Recognition of the real fact that two German states with different social systems exist, is a major prerequisite for the security of Europe. The shortsighted policy of "non-recognition" of the German Democratic Republic, which in effect meets solely the interests of the West German revanchists, irreconcilably conflicts with European reality and is a serious source of international tension. The German Democratic Republic has been in existence and making progress for nearly 20 years now. Both the Soviet Union and the other European socialist countries regard it as an important aim of their policy to contribute in every possible way to the strengthening of the international positions of the German Democratic Republic.

In the atomic and missile age new problems related to the safeguarding of European security have arisen. The peoples of Europe are well aware what the placing of nuclear weapons in the hands of a state clamoring for the recarving of European frontiers would mean. That is why prevention of the further proliferation of nuclear weapons is not only a world-wide problem but also one of the focal issues of European security.

Negotiations are now under way concerning the conclusion of an international treaty on the non-proliferation of nuclear weapons. The Soviet Union and other socialist countries are exerting efforts to get this work successfully consummated and to have a treaty on the non-proliferation of nuclear weapons open for signature to all states of the world.

Weighing the possibilities opened up by new developments in Europe, we cannot ignore the fact that in two years from now the governments of NATO countries will have to decide whether to prolong the North Atlantic Treaty or not. In our opinion, it is absolutely right that the Communists and all progressive forces are trying to utilize this circumstance for further extending the struggle against the preservation of the aggressive bloc.

In response to the creation of the NATO bloc, the European socialist countries were forced to set up the Warsaw Treaty Organization to safeguard their security. This organization, which is not only a military but also a political alliance of a part of the socialist states, has for many years been successfully discharging its mission. The aggressive aspirations of the West German imperialists and their American patrons are compelling us constantly to work for the utmost strengthening of all-round cooperation among the Warsaw Treaty member countries. However, the socialist countries have never favored a division of Europe into military blocs. We have put forward our alternative to such a policy. At the Bucharest Conference its participants once again declared that if the activities of the North Atlantic alliance were to cease, the Warsaw Treaty would also lose its force and that they should be replaced by a system of European security. Considering the fact that the governments of the NATO states so far do not agree to such a radical solution, the participants in the Bucharest Conference put forward a new proposal: to reach understanding already now on the liquidation of the military organizations of these groupings.

For a number of countries, including North European ones, neutrality could become an alternative to their participation in military-political power groupings. The CPSU acts on the principle that a great deal depends on the initiative of the neutral states, on their good offices in strengthening European peace. The Soviet Union would readily meet halfway an undertaking promoting this aim.

To eliminate the division of the world and Europe into military blocs or alliances is part of the common struggle of all the peoples for the reduction and ultimate stopping of the arms race, for curbing militarism, for purifying the political atmosphere in Europe and the world over. From this angle, considerable importance would attach to partial measures for a military detente on the European continent, beginning with the establishment of atom-free zones in separate areas of the continent to the closing of foreign military bases.

There is no justification whatsoever for the constant presence of the U.S. navy in seas washing the shores of Southern Europe. The question arises, what grounds are there, 20 years after the end of the Second World War, for the Sixth U.S. Fleet to cruise in the Mediterranean, to use military bases, ports and refuelling stations in a number of Mediterranean countries. After all, this is fraught with a grave threat to the independence of all maritime countries. The time has come for the demand to remove the Sixth U.S. Fleet from the Mediterranean to resound in full force.

Europe has not only military bases of the USA, there are also bases of a different kind. These are the subversive, espionage and sabotage centers, radio stations and various organizations set up by the Americans in the Federal Republic of Germany and other West European states, which are conducting slanderous propaganda against the socialist countries. It is high time to raise the question of ending the activity of all the poisonous centers on European soil which vitiate international relations.

The development of bilateral relations between countries of our continent could be an important prerequisite for strengthening European security. The existing trends towards a detente on the European continent are largely a result of the improvement in bilateral relations between the states of the East and the West.

As for the Soviet Union, our policy in future too will be aimed at developing mutually advantageous relations with the European capitalist countries on the basis of the principles of peaceful coexistence, in the interests of a stable peace and the security of the nations. The Soviet Union is prepared to exchange opinion on the drafting of bilateral treaties and agreements with the governments of European states which, for their part, want to develop relations with our country.

There is one more important and highly promising trend in the efforts of European peoples and states which has a direct bearing on solving the problems of consolidating European peace. It is cooperation in the economy, science, technology and culture both on a bilateral and an all-European scale.

A beginning has already been made here, but we consider it merely the beginning. The scientific and technological revolution now in swift progress, the growing desire to strengthen national independence and get rid of the dictation of the dollar are suggesting to European states many ways and undertakings in the most diverse areas—from the building of gas pipelines across the continent to the introduction of a common color television system for all of Europe.

The peaceful use of atomic energy too is arousing interest in many countries. We are ready to reach agreement with European states on assistance in nuclear research and the application of nuclear energy for peaceful purposes. A realization of this offer will enable states, which renounced the production and acquisition of nuclear weapons, to enjoy all the advantages the peaceful energy of the atom brings mankind.

Joint work on such matters as purification of the waters of European rivers and seas washing the shores of Europe, the pooling of effort by states in combating diseases like cancer, cardio-vascular and other ailments, are also important spheres for all-European cooperation.

Each of the European nations has made its contribution to the treasure-house of world culture. Each European state has its history and national features. We, Communists, consider it our mission to devote our revolutionary energies to the struggle for preserving the cultural heritage of the European nations, for the further development of Europe as one of the most important seats of world civilization, historical and social progress.

### 4. The Peoples are the Decisive Force in the Fight for European Security

In questions of war and peace, just as on many other issues, the interests of the people of Eastern and Western Europe coincide. Here the divide does not pass along geographical frontiers and not even along the frontiers between the social systems—it passes between broad popular masses that are striving for the security of their continent and lasting peace, on the one hand, and the small "party of war" leaning on the overseas forces that are alien to Europe, on the other. There are no reasonable arguments to prevent all European peoples who are safeguarding peace from uniting their forces and forming a united front in defense of their vital interests. The broader and the stronger this front becomes, the faster the demons of war will be bridled.

Obviously, our friends from the capitalist countries know best what particular measures have to be taken for common actions by the different peace-loving forces in their countries. On our part, we are prepared to contribute to the solution of this important task.

In this connection I should like to dwell on the important question of the unity of the working class.

Europe is the cradle of the organized working-class movement. It was here that its militant traditions of struggle against militarism, against aggression, and for peaceful relations between peoples were forged in sharp class battles.

Today the working class is the most powerful social force in Europe. It is in power in the socialist countries. It exerts vigorous influence over social life in the capitalist states. The working class is called upon to play an important part in the struggle for strengthening European security. And the stronger its unity, the better it will fulfill this mission.

The split in the working-class movement has not yet been healed in Western Europe, where alongside the Communists—the militant vanguard of the working class—the Social-Democrats too speak in the name of the working class. It has been said on more than one occasion that united action by Communists and Socialists could sharply change the entire political situation in Western Europe and create a serious obstacle in the way of reaction and aggression. This is why the CPSU appreciates the policy of the fraternal Parties aimed at overcoming the split in the working class.

The striving of the masses for unity is growing. Regretfully, the leadership of many Socialist and Social-Democratic parties are still in the thralls of anti-Communist ideology which is alien to the working class. Some leaders of Social Democracy have so closely allied themselves with NATO policy that they are clinging to it despite the evident crisis which has gripped this military bloc. A case in point is the British Labor Party leadership. Being in power, they are not only reluctant to utilize the available possibilities to obstruct imperialism's aggressive policy, but, on the contrary, are helping promote it. European peace, as well as the interests of the British people themselves, demand that the shackles of the so-called Atlantic solidarity be thrown off at last, and that the Labor Party leadership prove by deeds its desire to promote peace.

In this connection mention has to be made also of the Social-Democratic Party of Germany, whose leaders have for years rejected an independent line in foreign policy matters and take their cue from the Christian Democratic Union—the party of the German monopolists. Today representatives of the Social-Democratic Party of Germany are in the government and have considerably more chances to influence West Germany's foreign policy in favor of peace and security of the peoples. Unfortunately, there are no indications thus far that they have undertaken any serious measures towards this end.

Under the pressure of broad sections of the working class a tendency is maturing in some European Socialist and Social-Democratic parties to discard the ballast of the cold war and to join the search for constructive measures to strengthen European security. We see these new tendencies. They show that now more favorable conditions are taking shape for expanding contacts with the Social-Democratic movement with a view to promoting the joint struggle of the Communists and the Social-Democrats against the division of Europe into military blocs, for peace and social progress.

The CPSU for its part is prepared to develop contacts with those Social-Democratic parties that wish to join us in the struggle against the aggressors and for peace and European security.

We believe that in the struggle for European security it is possible to achieve unity of action with other political forces in Europe, too. They include trade union movements of all trends and peasant parties and associations. We know about the fruitful work of the fraternal parties to establish closer contacts with the working people belonging to various Christian parties and organizations.

We Communists by no means consider that we have the monopoly of elaborating programs of action for the European peace-loving forces. The proposals that our Conference will advance will undoubtedly be a good stimulus for discussions and an important contribution to the formulation of a common platform which could unit all those who want the consolidation of peaceful relations in Europe.

At present the movements against the war danger are gaining momentum in Western Europe. They are represented by dozens of organizations. Some sectors of European public opinion consider it expedient to convene a Congress of the Peoples of Europe on the broadest possible basis to discuss problems connected with the struggle for peace and for European security. The convocation of such a congress could possibly give fresh impetus to the development of the mass movement for peace and security in Europe.

Dear comrades, Communists are active supporters of the unity of action of all democratic and peace-loving forces. But this can be achieved only if we ourselves set an example of unity in thought and action. Our Conference is the first meeting in history of the Communist parties of both parts of Europe—those which are the ruling parties in the socialist countries and those which are waging a selfless struggle for the working-class cause in the capitalist states. Its convocation convincingly manifests the growing desire for unity of the world Communist movement, for concerted joint action of the Marxist-Leninist parties.

All our parties are united by the common Marxist-Leninist ideology and common ultimate goals. We know that there are certain disparities in the tactics of the fraternal parties arising out of the specific conditions in which they are working. But all this does not prevent our parties from closely cooperating, working out agreed positions and achieving unity of action in the struggle for our common goals. And we are convinced that the solidarity of the Communists will continue to strengthen. In this sense, our Conference is the best reply to those bourgeois politicians who allege that the Communists have taken to their national quarters.

Our Party is deeply convinced that the necessary conditions exist for achieving—by concerted efforts, in a short period of time—solidarity in our ranks. This is our unfaltering belief, and we are doing everything—together with other fraternal parties—to put this idea into practice.

If this task is tackled with the energy and principled approach typical of Marxist-Leninists, the differences can be overcome. Of course, this will require efforts and goodwill on the part of all the parties without exception. The duty of a Communist does not allow any one of us to stand aloof from this, waiting for unity to come of its own accord.

Joint efforts by the Communist and Workers' parties are imperative in our times and accord with the fundamental interests of the entire revolutionary movement. The strength of every Communist party and the effectiveness of every national contingent of Communists is determined not only by its influence in its own country, but also by its ability to act together with other contingents of the Communist movement.

The historical goal of our movement is socialism and communism.

We are sure that sooner or later the working class and the peoples of Western Europe will take the socialist road. The Communist parties are selflessly struggling precisely for this, the only correct road, which guarantees the triumph of democracy and peace, and full growth of the creative forces of every nation. Communists realize that this can only be a result of class struggle during which the working class becomes conscious of the role it plays in society and of its fundamental interests. That is why the Communist parties are working tirelessly to see to it that their policy consolidates the socialist, Marxist-Leninist orientation of the working-class movement, and actively and purposefully to create favorable conditions for the triumph of socialism.

If we were to look at the questions which we are discussing from this point of view—and we consider that for the Communists it is the principal and decisive position—we cannot but arrive at the following conclusion *European security is not only a problem of foreign policy but also a most important social problem*. Our Party advances this thesis on the basis of practical experience which has been accumulated in Europe in the post-war decades.

What can be learned from this experience? It teaches, in particular, that the cold war climate, the confrontation of military blocs and the atmosphere of war threats seriously handicaps the activity of revolutionary, democratic forces. In conditions of international tension, reactionary elements in the bourgeois countries step up their activity, the military rear their heads and anti-democratic tendencies and anti-Communism become more pronounced.

Conversely, recent years have demonstrated with

particular force that when international tensions relax the hand of the political barometer swings to the left. The certain improvements in the relations between Communists and Social-Democrats in some countries, the perceptible abatement of the anti-Communist hysteria and the increased influence of West-Europe Communist parties are directly connected with a certain easing of tension on the European continent.

One of the fundamental tenets of Communist strategy that the struggle for peace does not contradict the struggle for socialism is being repeatedly confirmed. If it is true that the struggle for peace helps the struggle for socialism, it is no less true that the struggle against imperialism and reaction, for democracy and social progress is an important condition for strengthening peace and international security. It can be said that militarism and reaction are twins, and therefore an improvement of the European situation is inseparable from a vigorous struggle aginst fascist and semi-fascist regimes which still exist in some capitalist countries of Europe. Speaking from this rostrum, we declare once again our solidarity with the heroic struggle of the Communists and democrats in Spain and Portugal. We believe that the crucial task of the European working-class movement is to fight against the persecution of democratic and peace-loving forces in the FRG and primarily for lifting the ban on the Communist Party of Germany.

On the very eve of our Conference came the disturbing news of the military coup in Greece. The Greek reactionaries are trying to establish a fascist dictatorship in the country. Thousands of the finest sons of the Greek people have been put into prison.

The exchange of views which is taking place at our Conference, and the Statement which we will adopt will play a major role in the development of the struggle against the policy of imperialist aggression and for strengthening European security and universal peace.

Permit me, comrades, on behalf of the CPSU, once again to underline that we are supporting the program of struggle for European security which is outlined in the draft Statement of our Conference. We all realize that in order to have it fulfilled we Communists will have to carry out extensive work among the masses.

We are for a diversity of forms in the struggle against the war danger. All roads should lead to a lasting peace in Europe and they will lead to it, provided the Communists and all progressive forces mobilize the masses for a determined struggle for European security.

Comrades, soon the Soviet people and their friends throughout the world will celebrate the 50th anniversary of the Great October Socialist Revolution. It will be opportune to recollect that on the very next day following the storming of the Winter Palace, the Congress of Soviets appealed to peoples and governments to end the war immediately. Lenin's Decree on Peace contained a special appeal to the conscious workers of the major West European states and expressed conviction that by their resolute, selfless and vigorous activity West European workers would help consummate the cause of peace and help revolutionary Russia complete the liberation of the working people.

For half a century already we have felt the fraternal solidarity and support of the international working class, of the progressive and democratic forces of Europe and the world. The Soviet Communists have already considered it their sacred duty to do everything to promote the struggle of the working class, of the democratic forces in Europe and other continents for peace, democracy, national independence and socialism.

We Soviet Communists have always regarded the struggle for peace and social progress as the internationalist duty of all Communist parties. The Marxist-Leninist parties in the West-European countries have covered a long and difficult road of struggle for the working-class cause. Our comrades from the fraternal parties in the capitalist countries have gone through many years of heavy trials, defeats and victories in class battles against the old world, against exploitation and oppression. The enormous experience of work among the masses which our comrades have acquired in the movement for a united popular front, for resistance to fascism and Hitlerite aggression in the Second World War, and in their current struggles, has become a valuable asset of the Communists of the whole world. Drawing on this experience, we Communists who are in power in our countries, and our comrades who are fighting for the victory of socialist revolution, can say with confidence of this Conference that we are capable of solving the grandiose but fully realistic task, that of uniting the broad popular masses in the struggle for peace and curbing the forces of reaction and war.

Let us strengthen the solidarity and unity of the Communist movement for the purpose of achieving these lofty aims.

## C. STATEMENT, "FOR PEACE AND SECURITY IN EUROPE"

We representatives of European Communist and Workers' parties gathered in Karlovy Vary realize our responsibility for the future of our peoples and the cause of the international working class and believe that preservation of peace is the most important question for all the peoples of our continent. We met to discuss the present situation, to exchange experience and jointly work out ways and means of helping unite all forces of peace and progress in the struggle for European security.

### I

The experience of recent years has borne out the correctness of the Communists' thesis that world war is not inevitable and that it can be averted by the joint efforts of the world socialist community, the international working class, the national-liberation movement and all states opposed to war, all peace forces. These forces have grown considerably, but the aggressiveness of American imperialism has also increased.

The United States, the main force of aggression and reaction, is trying to reverse the march of history and wipe out the right of the peoples to decide their destinies themselves. It is grossly interfering in the home affairs of countries in Latin America, Asia and Africa and is extending its war of aggression against the Vietnamese people, a war which represents today the most serious danger to world peace.

In this situation the struggle against the imperialist forces acquires special significance in Europe. Every success in this struggle means not only a step toward a stable peace in this part of the world but also a new blow at the policy of strength and the system of interconnected aggressive military pacts with which imperialism has girdled the globe.

Europe, which has experienced two world wars, remains a troubled region where the main forces of the imperialist camp and the socialist community confront each other. An armed conflict between them could grow into a total nuclear war. This danger is hanging over the entire life of the European peoples, it retards social and economic progress, vitiates international relations and involves tremendous wastage of material means in an arms race. Military intervention by some European states to suppress the national-liberation movements also creates seedbeds of tension and imperils peace.

After the Second World War the imperialist countries, headed by the United States, concluded the North Atlantic Pact, spearheaded against the socialist states, and also against the democratic movements in the capitalist countries. This brought about the division of Europe into counterposed military blocs. Having remilitarized the Federal Republic of Germany and supported its unlawful claims to represent all Germany, the imperialists assigned it the role of an advanced anti-communist bastion which became a seat of tension and which threatens peace and security in Europe as a whole. The Bonn state, where revenge-seeking and militarist forces have come to power, has become the mainstay of United States global strategy in Europe. The growing strength of the Bundeswehr, which is commanded by former Hitler officers, testifies to increasing military preparations. The Communist Party has been banned in the FRG, while other democratic and peace-loving organizations are subjected to repressions. Broad scope is being given at the same time to extremely reactionary and neo-fascist forces whose growing influence deeply alarms the European public, which knows from painful experience that fascism is always accompanied by aggressive militarism.

The cold war has become for the monopolies of all the European capitalist states an instrument of waging an offensive against democracy, for exerting pressure on the working people with a view to suppressing their struggle for better conditions, for restricting their social gains, a means of shifting the growing burden of armaments on the masses.

The cold war concept, the myth of the menace of "communist aggression" used by the United States to justify its hegemony in Europe have failed. The aggressive course of imperialism was undermined by the active foreign policy of the socialist states which are consistently implementing the principle of peaceful coexistence, a policy which has been carried through on an evergrowing scale, especially since the 20th Congress of the CPSU. The aggressive course was also undermined by the struggle of Communist and Workers' parties, the actions of the masses, the activity of broad sections of the West European public. The joint defensive might of the socialist states, deriving from the technical and scientific achievements of the Soviet Union, is an obstacle barring the way to war.

The Atlantic bloc has entered a stage of open crisis. The rulers of some Western countries challenge the value and expedience of the policy of military alliance with the United States or participation in the NATO joint armed forces, which threatens to embroil their states in war and which has nothing in common with their national interests. Tendencies towards emancipation from the political and military trusteeship of the United States are growing in the European capitalist countries. At the same time anxiety is growing over the increasing penetration of American capital.

The contradictions have also been aggravated between the national interests of West European states and the expansionist aims of the Federal Republic of Germany, its desire to occupy a dominating position in NATO, in the Common Market and in Euratom.

The German Democratic Republic, which has carried out the Potsdam agreements, has strengthened its sovereignty as a state and its international prestige. Its growing strength and constructive peace policy are a barrier to the plans of West German imperialism. Recognition of the GDR and defense of its sovereign rights have become one of the main tasks in the struggle for European security. The existence and development of a peace-loving socialist German state has great implications not only for the German people but also for peace throughout Europe.

The crisis of the cold war policy has opened up new opportunities for the democratic and progressive forces in West Germany, forces that sincerely demand a radical change in foreign policy and deserve every support. The change of government in Bonn was brought about precisely by this crisis. However, there are no signs that the new goverment of the so-called grand coalition has abandoned the imperialist aims of its predecessors. On the contrary, despite assurance of peaceful designs, it upholds claims to represent all Germany, continues to persist in its striving to swallow up the GDR, to restore Germany within the frontiers of 1937, refuses to recognize the unlawfulness of the Munich diktat, continues to advance provocative claims to West Berlin and wants access to nuclear arms.

Serious changes are taking place in public opinion. Awareness of the fruitlessness and the danger of the imperialist policy of splitting Europe is growing. Ties of cooperation, specifically, in the fields of economy and culture, are developing between the countries with differing social systems. In the course of establishing relations representatives of the governmental and public circles of socialist and capitalist countries are carrying out a useful exchange of views on problems of European security.

The constructive proposals for the strengthening of security and peaceful cooperation in Europe, set out by the socialist countries in the Bucharest Declaration of the Warsaw Treaty states, and the proposals of the Communist parties of the capitalist countries put forward at their meetings and in their decisions provide a realistic basis for strengthening peace and security in Europe.

New and positive trends toward an international détente and cooperation with Communists are appearing in the Socialist and the Social-Democratic movement in some West-European countries. New trends are emerging in Christian circles as regards problems of progress and peace. New possibilities have arisen for contacts and cooperation between various trade union and other democratic organizations. Cooperation of Communists with Socialists and believers in European security can promote the cause of peace on our continent.

The people of Europe do not want another war: "They want neither the cold war nor the 'balance of terror' which leads to a still more intensive arms race and increases the risk of a deliberate or accidental conflict."

It is high time to achieve new relations in Europe, resting on a genuine relaxation of tension and mutual confidence.

We Communists operating in different national conditions will spare no effort to build a system of collective security, to establish such relations between states which would preclude any possibility of aggression and ensure enduring peace in Europe and throughout the world. This is a difficult but feasible task.

The Communist and Workers' parties of Europe submit for consideration by public opinion and by all the political and public forces concerned a program in the interests of creating a system of collective security, based on peaceful coexistence. This requires, primarily, that all states should recognize the existing situation as it has developed in Europe in the post-war period. This means:

—recognition of the inviolability of the existing frontiers, in Europe, particularly on the Oder and the Neisse, and also of the borders between the two German states;

—recognition of the existence of two sovereign and equal German states, the German Democratic Republic and the Federal Republic of Germany, which requires of the latter renunciation of its claim to represent the whole of Germany;

—preclusion of any opportunity for the FRG to gain access to nuclear arms in any form, either European, multilateral or Atlantic;

—recognition of the Munich Treaty as invalid right from the moment of its conclusion.

The European working-class movement and all democratic forces are faced with the task of ensuring the development of peaceful relations and cooperation among all European states on the basis of respect for their sovereignty and equality. With these aims in view it is necessary to work for the realization of a number of aims which can be achieved in the new situation, namely:

—conclusion by all European states of a treaty renouncing the use of force or the threat of force in their relations and interference in internal affairs; a treaty guaranteeing the solution of all disputes by peaceful means only, in accordance with the principles of the UN Charter;

—normalization of relations between all states and the GDR, as well as between the two German states and between the GDR and West Berlin as a separate political entity;

—consistent defense and development of democracy in the FRG—the right to demand this is given to the peoples by law, historical experience and postwar international agreements. This envisages universal support for the struggle of the FRG progressive forces for banning neo-nazi organizations and all revenge-seeking propaganda, annulment of the emergency legislation, freedom of activity for the democratic and peace loving forces, lifting the ban on the Communist Party of Germany;

—conclusion of a non-proliferation treaty as an important step towards halting the arms race.

The system of European security must contain recognition of the principle of neutrality and unqualified respect for the inviolability of neutral states. A more active peace-loving policy by these countries and their contribution to disarmament would help establish such a system.

Ending the artificially created barriers in economic relations between the socialist and capitalist states of Europe would be of particular importance for all states and would be conducive to fruitful cooperation, including broad agreements in the sphere of production and scientific research.

Striving to open up the prospect of European security and cooperation, we are resolutely for the conclusion of agreements on partial solutions, above all, in the sphere of disarmament, which would create a favorable climate for more far-reaching treaties. All proposals in this area advanced by governments, parties, public organizations, political leaders and scientists deserve thorough examination. Particularly topical among these proposals are those which refer to the withdrawal of foreign troops from the territory of European states, dismantling foreign war bases, establishing denuclearized zones in Central Europe, in the Balkans, the territory of the Danube countries, in the Mediterranean and in Northern Europe, and also zones of thinned-out or frozen armaments and, in general, zones of peace and cooperation in various regions of the continent. These and other steps would check the tendency towards intensifying the arms race.

The twenty-year period of validity of the Atlantic Treaty expires in 1969, and this heralds a clear alternative: a Europe without military blocs.

No efforts should be spared in order to develop a broad movement of the peace-loving forces of our continent against extension or modification of the Atlantic Treaty. This movement is favored by the constructive attitude of the Warsaw Treaty member-states, which have repeatedly stated and solemnly confirmed in the Bucharest Declaration their readiness for the simultaneous abolition of both military alliances. We second the moves of these states regarding an immediate agreement on abolishing the military organizations of the Atlantic Treaty and the Warsaw Treaty.

We express readiness to support any initiatives or proposals pursuing the aim of achieving a détente and strengthening the security of the peoples of our continent.

We fully support the proposals for a conference of all European states on the question of security and peaceful cooperation in Europe. The proposal for a conference of representatives of all the European parliaments also merits support.

Consolidation of security and peace will open up before the peoples of our continent new prospects for progress and prosperity.

The peoples of Europe are faced with important social, economic and cultural problems. A Europe rid of the arms race, which consumes tremendous economic resources and the fruits of labor of workers, engineers and scientists, will be able not only to ensure higher living standards to its population, but also to make a valuable contribution to man's further development.

The struggle for this Europe is closely associated with the struggle for genuine national independence, for democracy, against reactionary and fascist dictatorships such as exist in Spain, Portugal and Greece. The fact that the governments of Spain, Portugal and Greece assist American imperialism in building atomic bases in exchange for U.S. support for these discredited regimes shows the grave danger they are to Europe. European Communist and Workers' parties express complete solidarity with and support the struggle that is now being waged by the united front of Spanish workers and democratic forces, and all peoples fighting against reactionary regimes, for freedom and democracy.

The Communists, who have always fought against imperialism, colonialism and neocolonialism, will strengthen their solidarity with the peoples still fighting for national liberation. They will act for the development of new relations with the countries of Asia, Africa and Latin America, relations based on respect for national independence, sovereignty, non-interference in internal affairs, mutually advantageous economic cooperation and effective aid by industrial developed countries to the newly free countries now taking the road of socio-economic and cultural progress.

## II

The Communist and Workers' parties of Europe are ready to dedicate all their strength to the realization of these tasks, serving the cause of peace, progress and democracy.

Our movement, which this year is marking the 50th anniversary of its great victory—the Great October Socialist Revolution—has become a mighty political force exerting a decisive influence on the development of all mankind.

Each Communist Party, in the specific conditions in which it works, is responsible to the working class and the working people of its country, to the people in general. At the same time each party is aware of its international responsibility for safeguarding peace, for forming new international relations conforming to the needs of our time.

This sense of responsibility requires of us, the Communist parties of Europe, that we pool our efforts for the solution of these problems. The stronger the unity and solidarity of the Communist and Workers' parties in Europe and all over the world, the more effective our struggle.

This sense of responsibility obliges us to address primarily the working class, the main producer of material values, the most conscientious and progressive class in modern society. We address the close ally of the working class, the peasantry, and also the middle strata, which are vitally interested in peace and prosperity. The workers and other working people in Europe, combining patriotism with international fraternal solidarity, are capable of playing a decisive role in the struggle for peace and European security, for democracy and social progress on our continent.

We address the Socialist and Social-Democratic parties which exert a big influence on the European working class and take part in the governments of a number of European countries. The experience of decades has shown that joint action by Communists and Socialists enables the working class to exert a decisive influence on political life and rally around themselves sections of the public that are interested in peace and in democratic social changes.

We address the trade unions of Europe, which for the past 100 years have been the biggest mass organizations of the working class, defending its material and social interests. We call upon the trade union organizations to use their authority and influence in the struggle for a peaceful Europe.

We address scientists, writers, workers of art, all European intellectuals, whose finest representatives have always defended human rights and freedom, the independence of the people, and have supported international cooperation and peace.

We address the Christian forces, Catholics and Protestants, believers of all denominations, whose striving for peace and social justice is motivated by religious conviction.

We address the young generation in Europe whose future is inseparably bound up with victory of the idea of collective security and peace. The place of the youth is in the first ranks of the fighters against the policy of war, against reaction and fascism, for freedom and progress, for friendship of the peoples.

We address the women, whose role in social life is growing all the time and whose participation in upholding peace and the security of mankind is so important.

We address the bourgeois groupings displaying a realistic approach to modern reality, who realize the danger of a nuclear war, who wish to rid their countries of dependence on the United States and are ready to support the policy of European security.

We call upon all the peace-loving forces to rally and launch broad campaigns in their countries and on a continental scale to expand direct actions for collective security. We urge support in every possible way of the proposal to hold a conference of European nations.

The Communists of Europe are deeply convinced that by defending peace and security on their continent against the forces of aggression and war they are promoting the interests of democracy, social progress and national liberation, the interests of the peoples of the whole world.

The present historical period requires courage and initiative. We urge all people of good will, irrespective of political convictions and party affiliation, nationality and religion to use all their influence and exert every effort to achieve our common goal—peace. By overcoming all that divides us, we shall be able to create a mighty force, capable of triumphing over war and uncertainty about the future, of paving the way to lasting peace and prosperity for the peoples.

The European peoples are capable of deciding themselves the questions of peace and security on their continent. Let them take the destinies of Europe into their own hands!

## D. FINAL COMMUNIQUE

A Conference of European Communist and Worker's Parties on Questions of Security in Europe was held in Karlovy Vary on April 24 to 26, 1967. It was attended by the delegations of the following fraternal parties: the Communist Party of Austria, the Communist Party of Belgium, the Bulgarian Communist Party, the Communist Party of Great Britain, the Hungarian Socialist Workers' Party, the Socialist Unity Party of Germany, the Communist Party of Germany, the Socialist Unity Party of Germany—West Berlin, the Communist Party of Greece, the Communist Party of Denmark, the Irish Workers' Party, the Communist Party of Northern Ireland, the Communist Party of Spain, the Italian Communist Party, the Progressive Party of the Working People of Cyprus, the Communist Party of Luxembourg, the Polish United Workers' Party, the Portuguese Communist Party, the Communist Party of San Marino, the Communist Party of the Soviet Union, the Communist Party of Finland, the French Communist Party, the Communist Party of Czechoslovakia and the Swiss Party of Labor. The Conference was attended by a representative of the Communist Party of Sweden.

European problems and measures necessary to safeguard security in Europe, which is of great importance for the strengthening of world peace, were examined in a free and broad discussion and fraternal cooperation, in the spirit of internationalism, which distinguished both the preparatory work and the Conference itself.

The Conference adopted a Statement emphasizing the danger created by the collusion between American imperialism and West German militarism and also the significance of specific peace initiatives, prompted by the situation in Europe.

The program of action contained in the Statement opens up to the peoples a real prospect of peace, proposing that antagonistic military blocs be replaced by a system of collective European security, resting on the principles of peaceful coexistence between states with a differing social order.

The Statement supports the ideal of convening a conference of all European states with the object of studying problems of security and development of European cooperation, and also other initiatives in this direction.

It is with a sense of high responsibility that the Conference addresses the working class, the Socialist and Social-Democratic parties, trade union organizations, believers of all creeds, intellectuals, the rising generation, women and all peace forces. The Conference urges them to unite and unfold in each country and on the entire continent broad campaigns, mass actions, directed at safeguarding collective security in Europe, at ending the ruinous arms race and defeating the war forces.

The participants in the Conference are convinced that the program of struggle for collective security in Europe drawn up in Karlovy Vary could be the basis for joint actions by all Communist and Workers' parties in Europe.

The Conference adopted an appeal calling for the rallying of forces, wider development of struggle in support of the Vietnamese people; it denounced the barbarous United States aggression emphasizing that this aggression constitutes a danger to universal peace.

The Conference called on all who cherish freedom to step up joint actions to secure an end to the American intervention and ensure to the heroic Vietnam people the right to independence.

The Conference also adopted a Statement condemning the military coup d'etat in Greece. It called for the organization of a broad movement of solidarity with the Greek people.

The participants in the Conference in Karlovy Vary are deeply convinced that their meeting helped strengthen the fraternal ties among the Communist and Workers' parties, helped rally the peace-loving and anti-imperialist forces in Europe and throughout the world.

# STATEMENT BY THE FIFTH MEETING OF THE COMMUNIST PARTIES OF MEXICO, CENTRAL AMERICA AND PANAMA, MAY 1967

*Complete Text*
*(Information Bulletin,* No. 102, 1967)

1. Continuing the tradition of holding meetings to exchange experience gained in struggle, the Communist parties of Mexico, Central America and Panama held their fifth meeting in an atmosphere of growing unity and brotherhood.

2. The speeches of delegates from the parties attending the meeting showed that in all these countries the working class and the people as a whole are stepping up their fight against imperialism and home reaction, for a higher standard of living, for democracy. As this fight goes on our parties are showing themselves more and more to be the principal revolutionary force mobilizing the working people and large segments of the population.

3. The exchange of experience showed that in accordance with the conditions prevailing in our countries and with the strategic and tactical concepts developed by the parties concerned, the working-class movement is making progress, using the most diverse forms of struggle, from peaceful ones to armed struggle.

4. Analysis of the general course of international development shows that the world socialist system, the revolutionary movement of the working class in the capitalist countries and the anti-imperialist movement are on the rise and are, moreover, improving their positions. The imperialists' provocations and policy of intervention aimed at changing the present balance of forces and at stopping the upsurge of the world revolutionary movement have fallen flat. There can be no doubt, however, that the danger of a third world war has increased. The U.S. imperialists are creating new hotbeds of war in various parts of the world through their policy of interference in the affairs of other countries. The Arab-Israeli conflict is the latest hotbed of this kind. But in view of the war menace there is a growing world movement for peace, extending to the American people. Against this background, the socialist community headed by the Soviet Union is seen by all mankind as the bulwark of all the peoples fighting for their independence and for world peace.

5. The division of the world Communist movement is the main factor encouraging the imperialists to be more aggressive in Vietnam and elsewhere. Our parties consider that in these circumstances a world meeting of Communist and Workers' parties to promote unity and intensify the struggle against imperialism on a world scale would play a most positive role. Regarding this point it is noted that as far as the convening of an international meeting of the parties is concerned the Guatemalan Party of Labor still withholds its opinion because that is a question to be decided by the Central Committee of the Party at one of its coming plenary meetings.

6. As for the problems that have arisen in the Communist movement of Latin America, our parties believe that proper efforts should be made to strengthen the militant unity of all parties and the alliance with the Cuban revolution. In this sense, there is confirmation of the conclusions of previous meetings, calling for maintenance of the unity of each party and for resistance to factional activity, and acknowledging the right of each party to work out its own policy line according to the actual conditions in its country. Having examined the issue of solidarity in view of the conference to be held in Havana, this meeting recommends to each party to do all it can, in keeping with its own policy line, to extend moral and material support to and show solidarity with all the peoples fighting against imperialism, for their independence and sovereignty.

7. In the face of new threats of invasion and aggression against Cuba, the Communist parties of Mexico, Central America and Panama call on the parties and peoples to redouble their vigilance and their solidarity with the Cuban revolution. The parties reaffirm their resolute support of the heroic struggle of the Vietnamese people for independence, against the U.S. aggression, and express their support of the four points advanced by the Democratic Republic of Vietnam and the five points advanced by the National Liberation Front of South Vietnam. At the same time they urge more active solidarity with the people of Vietnam, insisting on the unconditional and definitive discontinuance of the bombing of North Vietnam and on the withdrawal of U.S. troops from South Vietnam as prerequisites for peace in that country.

8. In view of the Middle East crisis, which threatens to become a hotbed of world war, the meeting resolved to identify itself with the struggle of the Arab peoples against colonial and imperialist rule. It condemns the policy of the United States and Britain, which have turned Israel—against the will of the progressive forces of the Israeli people—into a bridgehead endangering the independence and sovereignty of those Arab peoples that are aspiring to an independent and democratic life. Both old and new colonialism must be torn up by the roots in the Middle East in the interest of world peace and in the national interests of the Arab peoples and the Israeli people themselves.

9. The meeting calls on the peoples of Mexico, Central America and Panama to conduct an active campaign of solidarity with the Guatemalan people, who are fighting against the dictatorship of an army serving the U.S. imperialists. It is the imperialists that openly direct the struggle against the revolutionary

forces led by the Guatemalan Party of Labor and against the insurgent armed forces. The meeting urges resolute exposure of and counteraction to the campaign of reactionary terror being waged against the people of Guatemala.

10. The meeting points out once again the need to intensify the campaign for the release of political prisoners and imprisoned trade unionists in Mexico, Guatemala, Honduras, Nicaragua, Panama, Venezuela, Colombia, Peru, Paraguay, Bolivia and Haiti, and to continue the fight to end encroachments on human rights in these countries. The meeting has resolved, in particular, to demand the release of Ramón Danzos Palomino, the Mexican peasant leader, member of the Presidium of the CC, Communist Party of Mexico, who was recently kidnapped by the Mexican authorities and is in danger of losing his life. A struggle will also be carried on to end repressions against the labor movement in all our countries and to secure the return of political exiles to their countries, on the understanding that their lives and their freedom will be guaranteed.

11. The meeting calls on all the democratic and revolutionary forces of these countries to fight with the utmost determination against the growing military and police penetration of American imperialism, which is taking place through the Central America Defense Council (CONDECA) and the Council for Security Matters, two bodies set up to put down the struggle of our peoples for progress and prosperity, flouting the national sovereignty of our countries.

12. Having examined the actual results of the fulfilment of plans for the economic integration of Central America, the meeting came to the conclusion that, as our parties had predicted, integration has in fact helped the North American monopolies to establish even more rigid control over the Central American economy in furthering their interests, and has made it easier for a handful of home capitalists in the service of these monopolies to grow richer still.

13. The Communist parties of Mexico, Central America and Panama express their admiration and respect for the people of the Soviet Union and its glorious Communist Party on the occasion of the fiftieth anniversary of the Great October Revolution. This event marked the beginning of a new era for mankind, the era of freedom and social justice for all peoples, for all men and women irrespective of racial origin.

*Mexican Communist Party*
*Guatemalan Party of Labor*
*Communist Party of El Salvador*
*Communist Party of Honduras*
*Socialist Party of Nicaragua*
*Party of the People's Vanguard of Costa Rica*
*People's Party of Panama*

# TWO DOCUMENTS OF THE ARAB COMMUNIST MEETING, MAY 1967

## A. STATEMENT ON THE SITUATION IN THE ARAB COUNTRIES
## B. RESOLUTION ON THE SITUATION IN THE WORLD COMMUNIST MOVEMENT

*Complete Texts*
*(Information Bulletin,* No. 99-100, 1967)

### A. STATEMENT ON THE SITUATION IN THE ARAB COUNTRIES

The Communists of the Arab countries, meeting in May 1967, discussed the present situation in the Arab countries, and the course of the struggle going on on the main front between imperialism, reaction and Zionism, on the one hand, and the Arab national-liberation movement, on the other. They also exchanged information on the peculiarities and perspectives of the development of the actual situation in the various Arab countries. In connection with all this the meeting also discussed the problems of links and unity between the Arab patriotic, progressive and revolutionary forces.

The meeting believes that the present situation in the Arab world is characterized by the extension and intensification of the national struggle against colonialism and neocolonialism, and by a deepening of the content of the national liberation movement. Large sections of the Arab peoples and influential social forces are increasingly becoming attracted to the slogan of socialism, which is the right way of development for our countries, for them to build their independent economies and do away with their backwardness.

The participants in the meeting note with satisfaction that the struggle of their parties over a long period, the sacrifices they have made and the light of socialist ideas, which have triumphed in the socialist world, have been, and will be, the most important factor in this development.

In such new states as the United Arab Republic, Syria and Algeria, where deep-going social and economic changes have been effected, the Communists and other progressives see it as their task to uphold, consolidate and extend these gains, and to complete the job of providing the necessary political and social prerequisites of their countries' advance to socialism.

The Arab peoples are stepping up their fight against imperialism and its plans, against reaction and Zionism. Cooperation and solidarity between the newly-free Arab countries are becoming closer. Their policy of liberation and their progressive achievements play an important part in intensifying the struggle of the Arab peoples for freedom and progress and in carrying it deeper.

The national revolution of the peoples of Aden and the occupied south of Arabia against the British imperialists, for freedom and independence is gathering momentum. This sacred revolution involves the working class and all other patriotic forces. It is supported and assisted by all progressive and patriotic forces in the Arab countries and throughout the world.

The people of the UAR and their revolutionary, progressive and patriotic forces are increasing their resistance to the American and other imperialists, who are intent on changing the progressive policy line of the country. The UAR continues to develop its independent economy and to build important economic projects, first of all the Aswan Dam. It continues to extend fraternal support and assistance to the Yemen, which is defending its revolution and its republican system.

The Arab people of Syria have, thanks to the cooperation of their progressive forces, won an important victory over the oil monopolies in seeking higher royalties. Syria foils all the conspiracies and threats of imperialism, Zionism and reaction directed against it, which intensified above all after February 23, 1966, and after Syria began to extract its oil by itself and to build economic projects of its own, primarily the Euphrates Dam.

In Algeria the main trend is to fight imperialism, and Algeria is carrying on this fight together with other newly-free Arab and African countries, in the face of attempts on the part of the reactionaries backed by the imperialists to do away with the political, economic and social gains of the Algerian people. However, the social forces opposing the road chosen by the people and trying to abolish the people's achievements have not laid down arms yet. To foil the schemes of the imperialists, defeat the home reactionaries, maintain and consolidate the gains of the revolution and raise the creative enthusiasm of the masses so that they may overcome the political difficulties facing the country by peaceful and democratic means, it is necessary for the revolutionary, progressive and patriotic forces, both those participating in the present government and those not participating to achieve unity and wage a joint struggle in accordance with the aspirations of the people.

In Jordan, after Israel's aggression against the village of Sumu, the people took vigorous patriotic action against the imperialists and the policy of the pro-imperialist regime. This action is evidence of the great revolutionary potentialities of the Arab people of Jordan and of their progressive and patriotic forces fighting for a national system that would side with the free area of the Arab world and ensure freedom and democracy to the people.

The Lebanese people are intensifying their fight against imperialism and reaction. By rallying their patriotic and progressive forces, they have succeeded in preventing a visit by the U.S. Sixth Fleet, which is used as an instrument of conspiracy and intimidation against the Arab liberation movement.

In Iraq the patriotic forces and the masses generally are fighting with increasing resolve to establish a democratic system opposing imperialism and its oil monopolies, taking steps to settle the Kurd question and leading the country to liberation and to social and economic progress.

We support the people of Iraq, the Iraqi Communist Party and the progressive forces of that country in their struggle and their effort to secure the release of thousands of Communists and other progressives who are tortured in Iraqi jails. The continued detention of these fighters for freedom, progress and socialism is a violation of human rights and a challenge to Arab public opinion and to the progressive forces.

In Saudi Arabia, the isolation of the feudal reactionary puppet government is increasing, and the struggle of the masses and their progressive forces against this regime and the American monopolies which plunder the people of their riches is growing in breadth and depth.

The people of Bahrein are opposing the imperialists and the oil monopolies. By consolidating their revolutionary front they are fighting for liberation and independence, against the British colonialists' plans for setting up a new military base in that country.

New steps are being taken in an increasing number of Arab countries toward cooperation and mutual support of the progressive, revolutionary and patriotic forces. There are objective and subjective conditions for this cooperation to become closer and to develop into a broad front in each Arab country, in keeping with the actual situation there, and in the Arab world as a whole.

In the Syrian Arab Republic, the Communists and Left Baathists are engaged in cooperation that yields important results. It is in the interest of progress in Syria to promote this cooperation.

In the Lebanon the front of the progressive and patriotic parties, forces and political leaders, which furthers the popular movement and influences developments in the country, is going from strength to strength.

In the Sudan the progressive and patriotic forces are closing their ranks. These forces are in the van of the mass struggle in defense of democracy and the Constitution, against the reactionaries and the Rightists, who are trying to abolish democracy and the Constitution, taking advantage of the attempt to dissolve the fraternal Sudanese Communist Party.

It is a legitimate historic aspiration of the Arab peoples to achieve unity. A new conception of the idea of Arab unity is evolving, a conception prompted by the interests and the will of the masses, the new social content of the national liberation movement, objective conditions, the free expression of the will of each Arab country on an equal footing, and solidarity and cooperation against imperialism and reaction, for social progress. The experience of the struggle for Arab unity has helped to ascertain this new content, and our Communist parties have enriched it.

Relations between the newly-free Arab states and some other Arab countries, on the one hand, and the socialist countries, particularly the Soviet Union, the cradle of the Great October Socialist Revolution, a true friend of the Arab peoples, a bulwark of world peace, on the other, are growing and strengthening. These friendly countries render vast disinterested assistance to our countries in every field, which makes for the consolidation of their political independence and helps them to build up their independent economies and to combat backwardness.

The struggle of the progressive forces for full-fledged diplomatic relations with the friendly German Democratic Republic is gaining in scope. Imperialist and reactionary attempts to restore the relations between the Arab countries and the Federal Republic of Germany, which backs Israel, participates in supplying it with all that is needed for aggression, takes a provocative stand against the cause of liberation of the Arab countries and helps neo-colonialism to strengthen its positions in the Arab world, fall through.

The imperialists, particularly the American imperialists, do all they can to prevent the progressive liberation movement in the Arab world from growing, to stop and eliminate it, to maintain their positions and privileges, to continue plundering the Arabs of their riches, regain lost positions, and penetrate into various Arab countries by neocolonialist methods. The imperialists continue their feverish activity in support of the plan for a so-called Islamic pact, which is plainly intended to camouflage their criminal schemes in the Arab world. They bribe the home reactionaries in the Arab countries and help them to gather strength in the hope of re-establishing their rule in those countries.

The reactionary puppet rulers of Saudi Arabia and Jordan not only carry on subversion against any joint Arab action against imperialism and Zionism but try, on the instructions and according to the plans of the Anglo-American imperialists, to aggravate the situation in the area and to divide the Arab countries. They encourage Zionist aggression and reactionary conspiracies as they clear the ground for open imperialist intervention. The rulers of Saudi Arabia are continuing and extending their military intervention against Yemen to restore a medieval regime in that new republic. They are in open collusion with the imperialists against the revolution of the Arab people in Aden and in the occupied south of the Arabian peninsula. As for the rulers of Jordan, they bribe and mobilize mercenaries from among Syrian exiles and train them for hostilities in Syria with a view to undermining the progressive gains of the Syrian people and to replacing the progressive national system there by a reactionary Rightist regime that would suit its activity to imperialist plans.

The progressive patriotic forces are subjected to brutal repressive measures in both countries. Nineteen patriots were executed in Saudi Arabia. The prisons are filled with those who oppose reaction and American domination in the country. In Jordan the reactionary rulers have arrested Communists and other progressives, and hold rigged election to impart a semblance of legality to their rule and to continue their policy of conspiracy.

The imperialists arm Israel, supply it with all that is required for aggression, and support its efforts to usurp the legitimate rights of the Palestine Arabs in their own country. They incite it to continuous sorties in the Arab border area aggravating the situation in that area and endangering peace. Israel committed its latest act of aggression against Syria last April. It showed itself once again to be a tool and the main base of imperialism in the area. The imperialists use Israel to combat the Arab liberation and progressive movement, to back reaction and rotten reactionary regimes, and to prevent the Arab peoples from using their riches and other resources to develop their countries.

In northern Iraq (Kurdistan), where the Kurd question has yet to be settled, the Iraqi rulers are committed to a policy which does not in fact lead to meeting the Kurd people's lawful demand for autonomy. The imperialists and reactionaries are trying to aggravate the situation in Kurdistan by refusing to recognize the legitimate rights of the Kurds, thwarting the armistice agreement and resuming the civil war.

In the Lebanon the imperialists instigate and encourage the reactionaries to provoke religious discord with an eye to establishing a reactionary regime that would take its cue from the imperialists and the Arab reactionaries against the interests of the Lebanese people and the newly-free Arab states, primarily against fraternal Arab Syria.

The imperialists try to take advantage of border disputes between Arab states to aggravate the relations between them and to exhaust their strength.

In North Africa—in Tunisia, Algeria, Morocco—and particularly in the relations between Algeria and Morocco, the interests of the two brother peoples require that the two states should do all in their power to avoid violence and the use of arms, to make earnest efforts toward settling their disagreements through direct peaceful, fraternal talks. In this connection it is necessary to note that to bring about such a settlement, the progressive and revolutionary forces in both Arab countries must play a decisive role in the interest of uniting the Maghreb as an important step toward the unity of the whole Arab world.

The U.S. Sixth Fleet cruises in the Mediterranean and in Arab territorial waters, endangering the Arab national liberation movement and supporting Israel.

The military coup carried out in Greece according to the plans and instructions of U.S. intelligence agencies and directed against the vital interests of the Greek people should not be viewed in isolation from the conspiracies the U.S. imperialists hatch in the Mediterranean and the Arab world.

In a number of Arab countries whose rulers do not—primarily because of the struggle of the progressive forces—play the role played by the rulers of Saudi Arabia and of Jordan, the imperialists try to reinforce the reactionary elements and to crush the Communist, progressive and patriotic forces. They strive to establish territorial regimes there whose entire activity would serve imperialist interests and plans.

Everywhere the imperialists are out to undermine or prevent cooperation between Communists and other progressive and patriotic forces.

All this imperialist activity is aimed at undermining the regimes existing in the newly-free Arab countries, deliver a blow to the Yemeni revolution, thwart the revolution in Aden and the occupied south of the Arabian peninsula, prevent the liberation and progress of other Arab countries, check the upward trend of the national democratic movement in the Arab world and strike hard at the whole liberation movement of the Arabs, so as to strengthen the shaken position of the imperialists and to regain those of them that were lost, assure the continued plundering of our countries of their riches, first of all of their oil resources, and perpetuate the backwardness of our countries.

The meeting, exposing the plans of the imperialists, Zionists and Arab reactionaries and their acts of aggression, wants to reveal the immense danger threatening the Arab national liberation movement today, to contribute its share to the definition of the objects of the movement and to the planning of actions necessary for staving off this danger and to defeat those from whom it emanates. We are certain that there is every opportunity of achieving this lofty goal.

In view of the fundamental contradiction existing in the Arab world, where the imperialists, Zionists and reactionaries are at one pole and the peoples of the Arab countries, their patriotic, progressive and revolutionary forces supported by the forces of liberation, progress and socialism throughout the world, and above all by the Soviet Union, at the other pole, we consider that the chief method of countering the impending danger is to promote the solidarity and cooperation of these forces, join their efforts together in each Arab country and throughout the Arab world despite certain differences, which should not be an obstacle to joint action on the principal agreed issues.

The Communist, revolutionary and patriotic forces must cooperate to beat off the furious attacks of the imperialists and reactionaries on the Arab peoples, to eliminate colonialism and neo-colonialism in the Arab world, mobilize the masses against all imperialist intrigues, conspiracies and blocs, and bring about the withdrawal of the U.S. Sixth Fleet from the Mediterranean. They must cooperate to support the struggle of the Arab countries to establish national anti-imperialist and progressive regimes leading these countries along the road to progress and prosperity.

The progressive and revolutionary forces must cooperate to maintain the progressive achievements and changes won or being won in the newly-free Arab countries, to strengthen these countries and develop them with a view to encouraging the initiative of the masses and to drawing them into the creative endeavor in those countries. They must cooperate to curb the enemies of progress who are operating and gathering strength and are supported from without, and to close all the loopholes in the policies and the economies of these countries that may be used by imperialist and reactionary conspirators. They must cooperate to ensure that the Arab peoples have all their natural resources, particularly oil, put at their complete disposal, and that these resources are used wisely for developing the Arab countries and doing away with their backwardness. They must cooperate to give the fullest moral and material support to the revolution in Aden and the occupied south of the Arabian peninsula, to support and strengthen the Yemeni Republic and end all interference by the imperialists and by Saudi Arabia aimed at re-establishing the hated monarchic regime there. They must cooperate to step up the fight against continual acts of aggression on the part of Israel, to identify themselves with all progressive and patriotic groups and organizations fighting courageously in those countries whose governments submit to an imperialist diktat, and to fight for an end to terrorism and repression in those countries.

The Communists of the Arab countries are inspired by the ideas of creative Marxism-Leninism. They are inspired by a high morale in the fight against the imperialists and reactionaries, and are carrying on a selfless struggle for social progress. Ever since their parties came into being the Arab Communists have been fighting for the triumph of socialism and for the deliverance of the masses from backwardness and exploitation, and they have always put the interests of their peoples above everything else. They earnestly and sincerely call on all patriotic, progressive and revolutionary forces in the Arab countries irrespective of the parties or trends they may belong to, to rally together against imperialism, Zionism and reaction in order to fight for the complete liberation of the Arab world, for progress and the elimination of backwardness in any political, economic and cultural field, for a radiant future for their peoples, for Arab unity on a sound basis.

The road to these cherished aims and aspirations of the Arab masses lies through close relations between these forces, relations ruling out all discrimination against this or that trend and based on mutual respect, on fraternal, frank and principled exchanges of views. All this will make for an atmosphere of mutual confidence without which no cooperation can be fruitful.

The imperialists and reactionaries raise the banner of anti-communism as they strive to prevent the unity of the patriotic, progressive and revolutionary forces. Hence every attempt to split the progressive forces, bring confusion into their ranks, ignore or attack the Communist parties serves, as the sad experience of the past has shown, none but the interests of the imperialists and reactionaries and injures the national liberation movement and progress, that is, the cause of the whole Arab people.

In the interests of the fight against imperialism, for progress, for the unity and cooperation of the progressive forces, all progressives must strive for the release of imprisoned Communists and other revolutionaries and champions of progress in Iraq, Algeria, Jordan or any other Arab country. Meeting this demand will go a long way toward closer links and cooperation between all progressive forces.

A very important task in this respect is to foster cooperation between the newly-free Arab countries and to promote their relations with other Arab countries through the fight against imperialism. This will weaken the positions of reaction and strengthen the progressive and patriotic forces of various trends.

The nature of the struggle going on in a number of Arab countries against continued imperialist influence and reactionary domination calls for the cooperation of the revolutionary and progressive forces and all other patriotic forces and for the rallying of all sections of the people interested in complete emancipation from imperialism.

Our parties believe that at a time when semi-feudal regimes and the rule of the big bourgeoisie are being abolished and when society is advancing to a socialist future, it is necessary to realize the increasingly important role of the working class, which has nothing to lose in the fight for socialism but its chains. It is necessary to respect its rights and democratic freedoms, provide conditions for it to display initiative, and enable it to take part in production management and in the implementation of reforms. This has been confirmed by the experience of the socialist countries.

The Communists have been and will remain an indispensable and effective force in the fight against imperialism with all its old and new methods, for the provision of prerequisites of the transition to the socialist stage of development.

That is why it is in the interest of liberation and progress to increase and deepen the present cooperation between the Communist parties and other progressive forces and parties and to launch this cooperation where it is still lacking.

The unity, solidarity and consolidation of the Communist parties of the Arab countries are highly important. They contribute to the unity of the progressive forces in the Arab world, to the maintenance of democracy and freedom for the people, to the struggle of the Arab peoples against imperialism, for progress and socialism.

We believe in the future of our countries, in their inevitable victory over the enemy—imperialism and reaction. The potentialities of our countries, of their patriotic, progressive and revolutionary forces, are very great, particularly if there is unity, cooperation and mutual support between them.

The world forces supporting us are mighty. We have on our side the socialist camp and its chief force, the Soviet Union. We have on our side the international working class and all the peoples of the "third world" who are fighting for freedom and progress.

## B. RESOLUTION ON THE SITUATION IN THE WORLD COMMUNIST MOVEMENT

The events that have taken place in the world during the year that has passed since the last meeting of the Communist parties of the Arab countries confirm the fact that the general line of the world revolutionary and Communist movement is a line of unity and cohesion, of new victories in every field. The economic and military power of the Soviet Union and other socialist countries is growing steadily and so is their international prestige, and their positions in the economic competition with capitalism are becoming stronger. The Communist and Workers' parties in the capitalist countries have registered new gains in class battles against capital and monopoly domination, in their effort to promote close unity of the democratic and other Left forces. In Asia, Africa and Latin America the Communists have, together with other forces of liberation and progress, scored new successes in the struggle against colonialism and neocolonialism, for liberation and for economic and social progress. The relations of cooperation and solidarity between the socialist community and the national-liberation movement, between the Communist parties and other progressive parties, movements and forces in Asia, Africa and Latin America, including the Arab countries, have become closer.

This period has seen a number of meetings of Communist and Workers' parties reflecting the growing unity and cohesion of the world Communist movement on the basis of creative application of the principles of Marxism-Leninism and proletarian internationalism. The Karlovy Vary Conference of European Communist and Workers' Parties, which outlined a specific program for maintaining peace and security in Europe, was a new important step in this direction. This program is very important for world peace and security.

The entire course of development during this period has proved the Marxist-Leninist general line of the Communist movement, jointly formulated at the Moscow meetings of the Communist and Workers' parties in 1957 and 1960, to be perfectly correct.

On the other hand, there have been attempts during this period to step up the offensive of imperialism and reaction on a world scale, which expressed itself in the continuation and extension of the U.S. aggression in Vietnam, in reactionary coups in a number of countries, in increased pressure and terrorism against Communists and other patriotic and progressive forces in various countries, in greater activity aimed at splitting the revolutionary movement. It is now more obvious than ever before how very urgent is the need for world Communist unity, for the unity of the socialist countries, for united action by all patriotic and revolutionary forces to repel and thwart this furious offensive of imperialism and reaction.

The situation reveals the vast extent of the responsibility of the Mao Tse-tung group of renegades for their subversive and disruptive activity. It is already clear that the so-called "cultural revolution" is aimed at radically reshaping the superstructure in China by eliminating the cadres of the Communist Party of China that went through the revolution and are devoted to Marxism-Leninism, by routing the Party, the trade unions and other mass organizations, as well as the government apparatus, by establishing a military dictatorship in the country. This has created a serious threat to the existence of the Communist Party of China, to the achievements of the Chinese working class and the people as a whole, to the future of socialist construction in China.

This activity, in the course of which the Mao group went as far as to deny the role of the Party and to liquidate it, is a natural result of the dogmatism underlying this deviation. The group, which lyingly and slanderously accuses other Communist parties of revisionism, has in the end arrived at extreme revisionism and liquidationism.

Our Communist parties, which have condemned the Mao group for its departure from the general line of the world Communist movement and for its renunciation of Marxist-Leninist principles, will always adhere to the documents of the 1957 and 1960 meetings of the Communist and Workers' parties. They will steadfastly uphold the purity of these principles against the danger of bourgeois nationalist deviations, revisionism and dogmatism.

The Mao group has replaced the fight against imperialism by a fight against the Soviet Union and other socialist countries, against the world Communist movement, the national-liberation movement, the revolutionary movement as a whole. It has openly declared the Soviet Union, the first socialist country, a bulwark of the freedom and security of all peoples, to be Enemy Number One.

In carrying on its disruptive and subversive activity, the Mao group now links up in many respects with the American and other imperialists by coming out against the interests of the people. The most striking proof of this is the group's attitude toward Vietnam and its refusal to cooperate with the Soviet Union and other socialist countries in joint efforts directed against the U.S. aggression, as well as the fact that the group obstructs the delivery of Soviet arms and other kinds of Soviet assistance to Vietnam.

These disgraceful events, which have been taking place in China under the flag of the "cultural revolution," have not only confirmed the Mao group's break with Marxism-Leninism but have exposed its far-reaching and dangerous home and foreign policy plans.

However, the objectives of the Mao group have lately been laid bare. On the international scene the group finds itself completely isolated in the world Communist movement, the national liberation movement and other spheres, since those who formerly misjudged the group have been turning away from it in increasing numbers. Inside the country the group is meeting with widespread resistance—verging on civil war—on the part of Party organizations, workers, peasants and other sections of the people. This is why we are certain that the Chinese people and their working class will maintain their achievements and weather the severe trial to which the Mao group has put them. We are also certain that the Chinese Communists, loyal to the principles of Marxism-Leninism, will under all circumstances bring their party back into the world Communist movement.

The Communist parties of the Arab countries, realizing the gravity of the situation in China, have taken a stand in common with the world Communist movement by condemning the Mao group for its apostasy from Marxism-Leninism and for all its activities in and outside the country.

During the past year the Communist parties of the

Arab countries have come to know many new facts showing how Mao Tse-tung's emissaries and hirelings carry on their subversive policy in the Arab world and how this policy links up in many respects with imperialist plans in the Arab countries.

The Mao group is making feverish attempts to poison the relations of friendship, cooperation and solidarity between the new Arab states and the Soviet Union and other socialist countries, to undermine the relations between the Arab countries themselves. It concentrates on combating the Communist parties of the Arab countries as it continues its fruitless attempts to split their ranks. It tries to foil efforts toward cooperation between the revolutionary and progressive forces throughout the Arab world and in each particular Arab country, and makes futile attempts to strengthen adventurist trends in the Middle East, playing by its activity into the hands of the imperialists and of Israel.

In the light of the foregoing, the participants in the meeting reaffirm the determination of their parties, which are loyal to the principles of Marxism-Leninism and the general line of the world Communist movement, to continue the fight against the splitting and subversive activity of the Mao Tse-tung group, for closer unity and cohesion of the world Communist movement on the basis of Marxism-Leninism and proletarian internationalism.

The participants in the meeting declare that their parties unanimously support the idea of convening a new world meeting of the Communist and Workers' parties and are convinced that the conditions are already ripe for beginning the necessary preparations for such a meeting. This is needed for the unity of the world Communist movement. Besides, in the seven years that have passed since the 1960 meeting of the Communist and Workers' parties, life has posed numerous new problems that must be examined and assessed. Experience has shown that such meetings are the best form of discussing common problems facing the Communists, for exchanging views and experience and for promoting unity in the fight for the victory of the cause of peace, liberation, socialism and communism.

# CHRONOLOGY

# JANUARY

| | |
|---|---|
| Cuba | Régis Debray's *Revolution in the Revolution?* a study of guerrilla warfare in Latin America, is published in Havana. |
| Honduras | The Communist Party of Honduras holds its Second National Conference. Its major decision is to expel from the party a group of "deviationists" headed by Mario Morales, Jorge Díaz, and Carlos Aldana. |
| 1 China | A New Year's Day editorial in *Jen-min Jih-pao* calls for the extension of the cultural revolution to the countryside and predicts: "1967 will be a decisive year for the cultural revolution." |
| 1 Czechoslovakia | A new press law, passed in late 1966, is put into effect. The press law legalizes censorship in Czechoslovakia but puts legal limitations on censorship. It is subsequently announced that censorship is to be placed under the control of the Ministry of the Interior. |
| 4 USSR | CPSU Secretary-General Leonid Brezhnev in Moscow and CPSU Secretary M. A. Suslov in Leningrad begin a series of leadership reports to party actives on Sino-Soviet tensions as discussed at the December 1966 CPSU Central Committee plenum. |
| 4-8 France | The French Communist Party holds its Eighteenth Congress. |
| 4-11 China | Revolutionary groups in Shanghai seize power from regular party and municipal authorities. |
| 5 China/ USSR | The Soviet Union begins jamming Chinese broadcasts, suspended since October 1964. |
| 5 Rumania/ Spain | Spain and Rumania sign an agreement establishing for the first time since the Spanish Civil War official consular and commercial relations between Spain and a European communist country. |
| 10 USSR/ Yugoslavia | The sixth plenum of the Central Committee of the League of Communists, concerned over a December CPSU letter which criticized Yugoslav policies, admits foreign communist "misunderstandings and reserve" about Yugoslav reform, rejects foreign (i.e. Soviet) interference in Yugoslav affairs, and takes a strong stand against an international communist meeting, labeling it as an "out of date" concept of leading the international movement "from a single center" and "enforcing a signed-by-all joint general line document." |

| | |
|---|---|
| 10-13 February<br>Albania/<br>China | An Albanian military delegation headed by Beqir Balluku, member of the Politburo of the Central Committee of the Albanian Workers' Party, Vice-Chairman of the Council of Ministers, and Minister of Defense, and including Hito Cako, member of the Central Committee of the Albanian Workers' Party and Chief of the Political Department of the Albanian People's Army, pays a "friendly visit" to China. During the same period, a high-level Albanian party delegation, including Politburo member and Secretary of the Central Committee, Hysni Kapo, and Behar Shtylla, member of the Central Committee, visits China at the invitation of the Central Committee of the Chinese Communist Party. The two delegations meet with Chairman Mao Tse-tung on 3 February. During the visit, the Albanian Workers' Party fully endorses for the first time the Chinese Great Proletarian Cultural Revolution and the Red Guard movement. |
| 11<br>Italy | The Italian police break up an alleged plot by pro-Chinese communists to dynamite a US consulate and NATO installations in Italy. Six are arrested, including Maria Regis, owner of the publishing house Edizioni Oriente, founded in 1964 as the first pro-Chinese center in Italy. |
| 12<br>China | The existence of a Cultural Revolution Group within the People's Liberation Army becomes known upon the occasion of its reorganization. Hsü Hsiang-ch'ien is appointed head of the group, with Chiang Ch'ing as its adviser. |
| 15-16<br>Germany: German<br>Democratic Republic/<br>USSR | Secretary-General of the CPSU Leonid Brezhnev, Chairman of the Council of Ministers Alexei Kosygin, and Chairman of the Supreme Soviet of the USSR Nikolai Podgorny pay an unofficial visit to the German Democratic Republic. |
| 15-18<br>Syria/<br>World Federation of<br>Trade Unions (WFTU) | The "Third International Trade Union Conference for Solidarity with the People of Aden," sponsored by the WFTU and attended by some 50 delegations, is held in Damascus. |
| 17-18<br>Poland/<br>USSR | By invitation of the Central Committee of the Polish United Workers' Party, a top-level Soviet party delegation, headed by Leonid Brezhnev, visits Poland and meets with Polish party leaders. The communique reports that bilateral relations and international affairs were discussed and that the two sides affirmed "complete identity of views." |
| 18<br>Mongolia/<br>Tanzania | A Mongolian delegation traveling in Africa arranges the establishment of diplomatic relations between Mongolia and Tanzania. |
| 20<br>China/<br>North Korea | Red Guard wall posters appearing in Peking report the arrest of Kim Kwang-hyop, Deputy Premier, member of the Presidium of the Political Committee of the Central Committee of the Korean Workers' Party (KWP), and former Chief of Staff and Defense Minister, by Choe Yong-kon, member of the Presidium of the KWP, member of the Secretariat, and President of the Presidium of the Supreme People's Assembly. |

| | |
|---|---|
| 20-21<br>Italy/<br>Yugoslavia | Luigi Longo, Secretary-General of the Italian Communist Party, pays an unexpected visit to Yugoslavia, where he consults with President Tito shortly before the latter's visit to the USSR. |
| 20-22<br>China/<br>International<br>Association of<br>Democratic Lawyers<br>(IADL) | The Communist Chinese Society for Political Science and Law, although a regular member of the International Association of Democratic Lawyers (IADL), refuses to participate in an IADL conference in Paris on the occasion of the twentieth anniversary of the association. The Chinese accuse leading IADL officials of "conspiratorial activity for Moscow" and particularly attack the IADL for its efforts to establish contacts with UNESCO. |
| 22<br>China | *Jen-min Jih-pao* calls for the Shanghai power seizure to be emulated throughout China. |
| 23<br>Ivory Coast/<br>USSR | The Ivory Coast and the USSR announce the establishment of diplomatic relations. |
| 24<br>Ethiopia/<br>Mongolia | A Mongolian delegation traveling in Africa arranges the establishment of diplomatic relations between Ethiopia and Mongolia. |
| 24-31<br>Italy/<br>USSR/<br>Vatican | Chairman of the Presidium of the Supreme Soviet of the USSR Nikolai Podgorny pays the first official visit of a Soviet head of state to Italy and the Vatican. |
| 25<br>China/<br>USSR | Chinese students demonstrate in front of Lenin's tomb in Moscow. |
| 26<br>China/<br>Mongolia/<br>USSR | A three-week seige begins outside the embassies of Mongolia and the Soviet Union in Peking. |
| 26<br>China/<br>North Korea | The Korean Central News Agency issues an authorized statement denying the Peking wall posters (20 January) which reported that Kim Kwang-hyop had been arrested by Choe Yong-kon. The news agency calls the wall posters a "groundless fabrication" and an "intolerable slander against the party, government, people, and people's army of our country." |
| 26<br>China/<br>USSR | Communist China and the Soviet Union exchange protests over an incident the previous day between Chinese students and Moscow police in Red Square. Peking radio carries the text of the Chinese Foreign Ministry which attacks the Soviets as fascists and calls for revolution in the Sovet Union. |
| 28<br>China/<br>Yugoslavia | The Chinese government protests to Yugoslavia against the "connivance" of Yugoslav authorities with ruffians in smashing news display cases in the Chinese Embassy in Yugoslavia on 20 January. |

| | |
|---|---|
| 28<br>Rumania/<br>Venezuela | Venezuela and Rumania restore diplomatic relations, broken off in 1945. |
| 28-31<br>USSR/<br>Yugoslavia | President Josip Broz Tito of Yugoslavia pays an unofficial visit to the USSR, where he has consultations with representatives of the CPSU, including Secretary-General Leonid Brezhnev. |
| 29<br>Japan | Elections are held for the Lower House of the Diet, with the Japan Communist Party polling a record 2,190,573 votes (4.76 per cent of the total vote cast) and receiving five seats. |
| 29-30<br>China/<br>Yugoslavia | About 200 demonstrators besiege the Yugoslav Embassy in Peking protesting the breaking of a show window of the Chinese Embassy in Belgrade and shouting "crush the Dog's Head of Tito." The demonstrators burn an effigy of Tito on the Embassy walls and plaster the Yugoslav Embassy walls with anti-Tito posters. |
| 31<br>Congo (Brazzaville)/<br>Mongolia | A Mongolian delegation traveling in Africa arranges for the establishment of diplomatic relations between the Congo (Brazzaville) and Mongolia. |
| 31<br>Germany: Federal<br>Republic of Germany/<br>Rumania | Rumania and the Federal Republic of Germany establish diplomatic relations. The agreement involves no concessions from either side on policy. Rumania is the first East European country to establish diplomatic relations with the Federal Republic. |

# FEBRUARY

| | |
|---|---|
| 1<br>China | The Heilungkiang Revolutionary Committee is established. It is the first such committee at the provincial level. |
| 1<br>China/<br>North Korea | Chinese wall posters, reportedly signed by Chinese veterans of the Korean War, attack Kim Il-song as a "fat revisionist" and "Khrushchev's disciple" and accuse him of sabotaging the struggle of the Vietnamese people by refusing to send volunteers to Vietnam, of being ungrateful for Chinese aid during the Korean War, and of slandering the cultural revolution. |
| 2-4<br>Hungary/<br>Yugoslavia | Yugoslav President Tito pays an unofficial visit to Budapest. |
| 3<br>Germany: Federal Republic of Germany/<br>Germany: German Democratic Republic/<br>Rumania | A *Neues Deutschland* editorial deplores the Rumanian move to establish diplomatic relations with Bonn and finds it "regrettable" that in recognizing the Federal Republic of Germany, Rumania did not insist on Bonn's rejecting its claim to represent the whole of Germany. The editorial declares that "West German militarists" were encouraged by the agreement. |
| 4<br>Bulgaria/<br>Colombia | Bulgaria and Colombia agree to open consulates in Bogota and Sofia respectively. |
| 4<br>Germany: Federal Republic of Germany/<br>Germany: German Democratic Republic/<br>Rumania | *Scînteia,* organ of the Rumanian Communist Party, rejects the German Democratic Republic's criticism of Rumania's decision to recognize the Federal Republic of Germany as distorted and warns that attempts by *Neues Deutschland* to "set itself up as foreign political adviser to another state and to interfere in internal affairs of another country do not serve relations of friendship and collaboration between socialist countries; on the contrary, they harm these relations." |
| 4-6<br>Czechoslovakia/<br>USSR | Secretary-General of the CPSU Leonid Brezhnev pays an unannounced "friendship visit" to Prague at the invitation of the Central Committee of the Communist Party of Czechoslovakia. The joint communique indicates that European security and the German problem were key issues discussed. Both sides expressed "complete unity of views on questions of the present-day international situation and the world communist and workers' movement." |
| 6<br>Albania | First Secretary of the Central Committee of the Albanian Workers' Party Enver Hoxha delivers a speech to a joint meeting of basic party organizations of several enterprises and the Tirana University in which |

he calls for a further revolutionization of the party and regime. Hoxha demands a more profound understanding of party policies from the basic organizations, higher quality membership, and a more creative implementation of party directives. The speech and the subsequent editorial in *Zeri i Popullit* (8 February), the organ of the Albanian Workers' Party, launches a "cultural revolution" in Albania similar to the Chinese Great Proletarian Cultural Revolution.

| | |
|---|---|
| 6<br>Venezuela | Three members of the Central Committee of the Communist Party of Venezuela (Pompeyo Márquez, Guillermo García Ponce, and Teodoro Petkoff) escape from a Venezuelan jail. |
| 6-13<br>Great Britain/<br>USSR | Alexei Kosygin, Chairman of the Council of Ministers of the USSR, pays an official visit to Great Britain. |
| 8-10<br>Poland | A meeting is held in Warsaw by the foreign ministers of the Warsaw Pact countries to discuss European security and the new West German *Ostpolitik*. The Warsaw Pact countries are represented by their Foreign Ministers, with the exception of Rumania, which is represented by Deputy Foreign Minister Malita. |
| 9<br>China/<br>Japan | *Akahata,* daily organ of the Japan Communist Party, publishes the party's first direct attack on the Communist Chinese leadership, declaring that their attempt to spread the thought of Mao is "an intolerable interference" in the affairs of other communist parties. |
| 12<br>Austria | The Marxist-Leninist Party of Austria is founded by a conference of the organization of the Marxist-Leninists of Austria and is welcomed by *Peking Review* as a party which will, "together with the Chinese Communist Party, the Albanian Party of Labor, and other Marxist-Leninist Parties, fight against imperialism and revisionism." |
| 13-16<br>Afro-Asian Peoples'<br>Solidarity Organization<br>(AAPSO) | The eighth council meeting of the Afro-Asian Peoples' Solidarity Organization convenes in Nicosia, Cyprus, and is attended by 300 delegates from 43 countries. After clashes between pro-Soviet and pro-Chinese groups, it is decided to hold the Fifth AAPSO Conference in Algiers in 1967 instead of Peking. |
| 13-18<br>Austria/<br>Yugoslavia | President Josip Broz Tito of Yugoslavia pays an official visit to Austria. |
| 13-3 March<br>North Korea/<br>USSR | Kim Il, member of the Presidium of the Political Committee of the Korean Workers' Party, leads a delegation to the Soviet Union to discuss economic and scientific-technical matters. Agreements are signed providing for economic, cultural, and scientific-technical cooperation and mutual goods deliveries in 1967. An agreement is also signed providing for "cooperation in further strengthening the defense potential" of North Korea. |
| 14 | The Chinese Communists openly attack the Japan Communist Party for |

| | |
|---|---|
| China/<br>Japan | the first time; previous attacks were indirect and muted. |
| 14<br>China/<br>USSR | For the first time Communist China ignores the anniversary of the Sino-Soviet Treaty of Friendship, Alliance, and Mutual Assistance. |
| 15<br>Albania/<br>USSR | Radio Tirana announces the formation in the Soviet Union of the "Marxist-Leninist All-Union Communist Bolshevik Party." |
| 15<br>Germany: Federal<br>Republic of Germany | The "Initiative Committee for the Readmission of the Communist Party," a major effort to obtain legal status for the West German Communist Party, is organized. |
| 15-21<br>India | In the fourth Indian national elections, the two communist parties win a total of 43 seats in the Lower House. The Communist Party of India (Marxist) becomes the strongest member of state coalition governments in Kerala and West Bengal. |
| Mid-February<br>China/<br>USSR/<br>Vietnam: Democratic<br>Republic of Vietnam | Western sources report that an agreement is reached whereby the North Vietnamese will take "principal control" of Soviet military equipment at the Soviet border, thereby making the subsequent transit of goods a matter of concern for the Chinese and the Vietnamese, thus avoiding friction between Moscow and Peking. |
| 20<br>China/<br>USSR/<br>Yugoslavia | Pomelov's article in *Pravda* on the role of the party dismisses both the "purely ideological" role proposed by Yugoslavs and the undermining of the party as now practiced under Mao Tse-tung, and claims that the "masses need" a strong political leader and guide. |
| 22<br>Colombia/<br>Poland | Colombia and Poland sign a $33 million trade agreement and agree to commence consular relations as of 1 March. |
| 22-26<br>Poland | A nineteen-member preparatory committee for the meeting of European communist and workers' parties meets in Warsaw. The committee drafts and discusses the documents to be submitted to the meeting. Also discussed are organizational matters connected with the meeting, which is scheduled for Karlovy Vary, Czechoslovakia on 24-27 April. |
| 23<br>China | The Shantung Revolutionary Committee is established. |
| 24<br>China | The Shanghai Revolutionary Committee supersedes the Shanghai Commune. |
| 24<br>USSR<br>World Federation<br>of Youth (WFDY) | The formation of a communist version of the US Peace Corps, to be called the "International Volunteer Youth Service of Solidarity and Friendship," is announced at the end of the Moscow session of the WFDY Tourist Bureau. |

| | |
|---|---|
| 25-1 March<br>Hungary/<br>USSR | First Secretary of the Central Committee of the Hungarian Socialist Workers' Party János Kádár heads a high-level Hungarian party-government delegation to Moscow and confers with Soviet party leader Leonid Brezhnev on European security. The joint communique following the talks affirms a "complete unity of views." |
| 26-27<br>Denmark/<br>Finland/<br>Iceland/<br>Norway/<br>Sweden | The Finnish, Swedish, and Icelandic communist parties participate in a socialist-sponsored "Nordic Socialist Seminar" in Copenhagen. The Danish and Norwegian parties are denied admittance. |
| 27-2 March<br>Cuba | *Granma,* organ of the Cuban Communist Party, publishes four long editorials condemning bureaucracy in an intensified campaign in Cuba. |
| 28<br>Rumania | A *Scînteia* editorial presents a comprehensive formulation of the principles of Rumanian foreign policy and reaffirms the principles of "national independence and sovereignty, equal right, and noninterference in the internal affairs of other states." |
| End February<br>Austria/<br>Belgium | First Secretary of the Marxist-Leninist Party of Austria Franz Strobl meets with Jacques Grippa, First Secretary of the Marxist-Leninist Communist Party of Belgium. |
| 28-1 March<br>Czechoslovakia/<br>Poland | Czechoslovak President and Party leader Novotný heads a party-government delegation to Poland to sign a bilateral Treaty of Friendship, Cooperation, and Mutual Assistance. |

# MARCH

**1**
**Czechoslovakia/**
**Poland**

The second twenty-year Treaty of Friendship, Cooperation, and Mutual Assistance is signed in Warsaw by Poland and Czechoslovakia during a visit by a top-level Czechoslovak party-government delegation headed by Antonín Novotný. The treaty concerns primarily the problem of European security, particularly the case of West Germany. Article 6 of the new treaty declares that the Munich agreement of 1938 was "invalid from the very beginning." In addition, the treaty contains provisions for closer economic and cultural contacts.

**1**
**Hungary/**
**USSR**

Hungarian party leader János Kádár and his top Politburo aide Béla Biszku, as well as Deputy Foreign Minister Erdelyi, return from a "friendly and unofficial" visit to Moscow.

**2-4**
**Venezuela**

Constitutional guarantees (suspended in December 1966) are restored on 2 March. Following the slaying by Castroist guerrillas of Julio Iribarren Borges, a former director of social security and the brother of the Venezuelan Foreign Minister, on 3 March, the guarantees are once against suspended on 4 March.

**3**
**USA**

The United States Court of Appeals, District of Columbia, reverses conviction against the Communist Party of the USA for failure to register as required by the Internal Security Act of 1950 (the McCarran Act). On 3 April the Justice Department announces that it will not appeal this decision.

**5 and 12**
**France**

French Communist Party wins 73 seats to the National Assembly, an increase of 32 from the last General Elections in 1962.

**8-9**
**Hungary/**
**Poland**

First Secretary of the Polish United Workers' Party Wladyslaw Gomulka and Central Committee member and Premier Józef Cyrankiewicz pay an "unofficial friendly visit" to Budapest to discuss the political situation in Europe. A "full identity of views on all matters discussed" is reported.

**8-16**
**China/**
**New Zealand**

V. G. Wilcox, General Secretary of the Communist Party of New Zealand, visits China. He is received by Mao Tse-tung on 12 March.

**10**
**Colombia**

Colombian authorities launch a series of mass arrests which reportedly involve some 200 to 300 persons. Those arrested include Gilberto Vieira, Secretary-General of the pro-Soviet Communist Party of Colombia; Juan Viana, Secretary of the Central Executive Committee of the pro-Soviet Communist Party of Colombia; and Manllo Lafont, Gustavo Castro, Manuel Romero, Juan Francisco Mujica, Teodicio

Varela, Augusto Lara, Julio Posada, Julio Ernesto Pérez, Roberto Pérez, and Celmira Cruz, all members of the Central Committee of the pro-Soviet Communist Party of Colombia.

**11, 18**
**India/**
**Indonesia**

In two installments the Indian pro-Soviet weekly *Mainstream* carries the text of a document titled "For a Sound Indonesian Revolution," issued in the name of the pro-Soviet Marxist-Leninist Party of Indonesia. This is the first indication that such a party exists in Indonesia.

**12**
**China**

The Shansi Revolutionary Committee is established.

**13**
**Cuba/**
**Venezuela**

Fidel Castro publicly and at great length attacks the "rightist" and "traitorous" leadership of the pro-Soviet Communist Party of Venezuela.

**13**
**Germany: German**
**Democratic Republic/**
**Poland**

A twenty-year Treaty of Friendship, Cooperation, and Mutual Assistance is signed in Warsaw during a visit to Poland by Walter Ulbricht, First Secretary of the Central Committee of the Socialist Unity Party and Chairman of the Council of State of the German Democratic Republic and Willi Stoph, member of the Socialist Unity Party Politburo and Chairman of the German Democratic Republic's Council of Ministers. The treaty provides for guaranteeing the Oder-Neisse line and the territorial integrity of the German Democratic Republic, and refers to Berlin as an "autonomous political unit."

**13-15**
**Bulgaria/**
**USSR**

By invitation of the Central Committee of the Communist Party of the Soviet Union, a Bulgarian party delegation headed by First Secretary of the Central Committee Todor Zhivkov visits the Soviet Union.

**17**
**Czechoslovakia/**
**Germany: German**
**Democratic Republic**

A twenty-year Treaty of Friendship, Cooperation, and Mutual Assistance is signed in Prague by the German Democratic Republic and Czechoslovakia during a visit by a top-level German Democratic Republic party-government delegation headed by Walter Ulbricht. The treaty primarily concerns the problem of European security and the West German "threat."

**17-18**
**Rumania/**
**USSR**

A top-level Rumanian party-government delegation headed by Nicolae Ceauşescu pays a "friendly visit" to the Soviet Union at the invitation of the Central Committee of the Communist Party of the Soviet Union and the Soviet government. The two sides exchange opinions on questions of Soviet-Rumanian relations and on urgent international problems including European security. A "sincere, friendly atmosphere" is reported, but not a unity of views.

**18**
**Sudan**

The Khartoum High Court issues its final ruling that the dissolution of the Sudanese Communist Party, ordered by the Constituent Assembly, is null and void and that the dismissal of communist deputies from the Constituent Assembly is unconstitutional.

**19**
**Hungary**

Elections to the National Assembly are held under a new electoral law. The new law provides that National Assembly Deputies be nominated and elected directly in 249 individual constituencies instead of voting by lists in 20 multiseat constituencies. Also, for the first time, more than one candidate is to be nominated by each constituency for each seat. The election results in a 99 per cent vote for the communist candidates.

20
Norway

Eleven members of the Central Committee of the Communist Party of Norway resign because of the refusal of the majority of the party to condemn the Chinese Communist Party.

21-23
Germany: German
Democratic Republic/
USSR

A German Democratic Republic delegation led by party chief Ulbricht and including party Secretaries Honecker and Mittag, as well as Premier Stoph, Foreign Minister Winzer, and State Planning Commission Chairman Schürer, visits the USSR and holds talks with leading Soviet officials on "all important current problems."

23
Bolivia

Initial clash between Bolivian troops and a guerrilla group led by Ernesto "Che" Guevara takes place at Nancahuazú, northwest of Camiri. Following the encounter, the guerrillas proclaim themselves (on 25 March) the National Liberation Army of Bolivia (Ejercito de Liberación Nacional de Bolivia).

25
USSR/
Uruguay

A meeting is held in Moscow between First Secretary of the Communist Party of Uruguay, Rodney Arismendi, and Secretary-General of the CPSU, Leonid Brezhnev.

25-30
Afro-Asian Writers'
Permanent Bureau
(Cairo) (AAWPB)

The Afro-Asian Writers' Permanent Bureau (Cairo) holds the Third Afro-Asian Writers' Conference in Beirut. The conference is attended by 150 delegates from 42 countries.

26
Indonesia

The Indonesian parliament formally bars the Communist Party of Indonesia from taking part in the general elections scheduled for sometime in 1968.

26-6 April
Cuba/
International Union
of Students (IUS)
Mongolia

The International Union of Students holds its Ninth Congress in Ulan Bator, Mongolia. The Congress is marked by controversy, including the walkout of Cuban and other Castroist-oriented delegations.

29
France/
Italy/
USSR

Returning from talks with leaders of the Communist Party of the Soviet Union, Luigi Longo, Secretary-General of the Italian Communist Party, stops in Paris to discuss matters with Waldeck Rochet, Secretary-General of the French Communist Party, and other leaders of the party.

31
China

A nationwide official propaganda campaign against Liu Shao-ch'i begins with an article in *Hung Ch'i* attacking Liu's book, *How to Be a Good Communist*.

31

A new North Korean clandestine radio station calling itself the "Radio

North Korea

of the Democratic Union for the Liberation of South Korea" begins broadcasting to South Korea.

31
USSR

TASS reports the death from cancer of USSR Minister of Defense R. Ya. Malinovskiy.

End March
Cuba/
Guatemala/
Venezuela

Venezuelan Communists demand that Castro cease his interference in their domestic affairs. Bernardo Alvarado Monzón, Secretary-General of the Guatemalan Party of Labor, and César Montes, Commander-in-Chief of the Rebel Armed Forces, repudiate a statement made earlier in the month by two prominent members of their organizations in support of Castro's 13 March attack on the Communist Party of Venezuela.

East Europe/
Israel

Secretary-General of the Israeli Communist Party (MAKI), Shmuel Mikunis, tours East Europe.

South Africa

The Central Committee of the South African Communist Party issues a statement calling for the creation of a new front of struggle: "the beginning of guerrilla actions by armed and trained freedom fighters, backed by revolutionary struggle of the masses of workers and peasants against the white supremacy state."

Venezuela

The Eighth Plenum of the Communist Party of Venezuela ousts guerrilla leader and former Politburo member Douglas Bravo from the party. The plenary meeting notes that the revolutionary movement in Venezuela is at a "low ebb," calls for a "strategic retreat" from guerrilla warfare, and proclaims its intention to participate in the 1968 presidential elections.

31-6 April
Italy/
Rumania

Luigi Longo, Secretary-General of the Italian Communist Party, visits Bucharest and holds talks with his Rumanian counterpart Nicolae Ceauşescu. The communique declares that communist unity can be based only on respect for the independence and equal right of each party and noninterference in its internal affairs.

# APRIL

| | |
|---|---|
| 3<br>Malaysia/<br>USSR | Malaysia and the USSR sign their first bilateral trade agreement and agree in principle to establish diplomatic relations. |
| 3-7<br>Bulgaria/<br>Poland | A Polish party-government delegation, headed by First Secretary of the Central Committee of the Polish United Workers' Party Wladyslaw Gomulka and Polish Premier and member of the Politburo of the Party Józef Cyrankiewicz, pays an official visit to Bulgaria at the invitation of the Bulgarian Communist Party and the Council of Ministers. A twenty-year Treaty of Friendship, Cooperation, and Mutual Assistance is signed during the visit. |
| 7<br>Yugoslavia | The Yugoslav Federal Assembly adopts amendments changing the provisions of the Yugoslav constitution of 1963, increasing the role of the Council of Nationalities, abolishing the offices of Vice President and Deputy Supreme Commander of the Armed Forces, reducing the membership of the Federal Executive Council, limiting federal authority in investments, and increasing the authority of the republics over state security and justice. |
| 7-14<br>Paraguay | A majority group within the Paraguayan Communist Party holds a "preparatory national conference" for the Third Congress of the party, in Montevideo, Uruguay. In a Soviet-supported move, the conference expells PCP Secretary-General Oscar Creydt and elects a new Central Committee, Political Commission, and Secretariat. |
| 12<br>Bolivia | In response to the appearance of guerrilla activity in southern Bolivia, the government outlaws the pro-Soviet and the pro-Chinese Communist Parties of Bolivia, both factions of the Trotskyist Revolutionary Workers' Party, and the Revolutionary Party of the Nationalist Left. |
| 14<br>Hungary | At the first session of the new Hungarian parliament, important changes are made in top government personnel. Former Premier Gyula Kállai is elected Speaker of the House and Jeno Föck becomes the new Premier of Hungary. Hungarian President of the Presidential Council István Dobi resigns and is replaced by Pál Losonczi. |
| 14-16<br>Argentina | The Communist Party of Argentina holds its Seventh National Conference clandestinely. |
| 16<br>Cuba/<br>Afro-Asian Latin<br>American People's | Osmany Cienfuegos, Secretary-General of AALAPSO, releases a document addressed to the "peoples of the world" and signed by Ernesto "Che" Guevara, calling for the creation of "two, three, many Vietnams." |

Solidarity Organization
(AALAPSO)

| | |
|---|---|
| 16<br>Norway | Due to threatened party unity, the National Conference of the Norwegian Communist Party moves to postpone the Twelfth Party Congress, scheduled for October 1967, until March 1968. |
| 17<br>Vietnam: Democratic Republic of Vietnam | An article in *Nhan Dan,* organ of the Vietnam Workers' Party, declares that antiwar demonstrations in the USA "clearly show that the movement against the aggressive war in Vietnam has become a mass movement which is drawing millions of people into a resolute struggle [and] has really become a second front against US imperialism right on US soil." |
| 17-21<br>Bulgaria/<br>Rumania | Bulgarian party and state leader Todor Zhivkov heads a party-government delegation to Bucharest, where he confers with Rumanian party leader Nicolae Ceaușescu. The final communique affirms the desire of the two parties to establish closer economic and technical collaboration. It also stresses the principle of noninterference in the internal affairs of each state. |
| 17-22<br>Germany: German Democratic Republic | The Socialist Unity Party holds its Seventh Congress, which is attended by 67 foreign delegations, including a Soviet delegation led by the Secretary-General of the CPSU, Leonid Brezhnev. |
| 19<br>Morocco/<br>Rumania | In a lengthy communique following a week-long visit by Moroccan Communist Party Secretary-General Ali Yata to Bucharest for talks with Rumanian party leader Nicolae Ceaușescu, the two sides emphasize the principles of independence, equal right, noninterference in internal affairs, and proletarian internationalism as basic norms of relations among parties. Recognizing the possibility of differences of views among parties, the two sides declare that "differences of opinion must not affect in any way the friendship and solidarity of collaboration among fraternal parties," and add: "Convinced that what is essential and predominant is that which unites the communist parties, the two delegations hold that under present conditions nothing must be undertaken that might aggravate existing divergencies, add new elements of tension, and deepen the danger of a split." |
| 20<br>Bolivia | Jules Régis Debray, French author of *Revolution in the Revolution?* is captured shortly after leaving a guerrilla group led by Ernesto "Che" Guevara. On 17 November he is sentenced to thirty years' imprisonment. |
| 20<br>China | The Peking Municipal Revolutionary Committee is established. |
| 21<br>Greece | Officers of the Greek army carry out a military coup, overthrowing the constitutional government of Greece and establishing a stratocratic regime. During the execution of the coup, thousands of members of the clandestine Communist Party of Greece and the legal fellow-traveling party, the United Democratic Left, together with members of various |

communist splinter groups, are arrested and imprisoned.

**22**
**Germany: Federal**
**Republic of Germany**

The pro-Chinese Free Socialist Party, with a monthly Central Committee organ known as *Die Wahrheit,* is founded.

**23**
**China/**
**Indonesia**

Yao Teng-shan, Chinese Communist chargé d'affaires in Djakarta, returns to Peking after being expelled by the Indonesian government.

**24-26**
**Czechoslovakia**

A "Conference of Communist and Workers' Parties of Europe" is held in Karlovy Vary, Czechoslovakia. The conference is attended by representatives of 24 parties. Notable absentees include the Rumanian Communist Party, the League of Communists of Yugoslavia, the Communist Party of the Netherlands, the Norwegian Communist Party, and the United Socialist Party of Iceland.

**24-27**
**Albania**

The Sixth Congress of Albanian Trade Unions is held in Tirana. The congress is attended by representatives of 23 countries. In the main report, Tonkin Jakova, Chairman of the Albanian Trade Union, urges a renewed struggle against bureaucracy and a strengthening of the worker-peasant alliance. He denounces "US-Soviet collaboration" and praises China's aid to Albania. He also hails the strengthening of a new Marxist-Leninist trade union movement.

**27**
**Colombia**

Gilberto Vieira, Secretary-General of the Communist Party of Colombia, is released from jail following his arrest on 10 March.

**29**
**Greece**

The military government of Greece dissolves the left-wing United Democratic Left, which had acted as a spokeman for the Greek Communist Party and the youth organizations of all parties.

**30**
**China**

Ulanfu is dismissed from his post as First Secretary of the Inner Mongolian Autonomous Region Committee of the Chinese Communist Party.

# MAY

| | |
|---|---|
| Central America/<br>Mexico/ | A meeting of representatives of the communist parties of Mexico, Central America, and Panama is held. |
| China/<br>Vietnam: Democratic<br>Republic of Vietman | The May issue of *Hoc Tap,* theoretical journal of the Vietnam Workers' Party, carries an artilce which, in the form of a theoretical criticism of the qualities of communist party leaders in general, appears to be an attack on Mao Tse-tung and the policies associated with him. |
| Lebanon | The Lebanese Communist Party hosts a conference of Arab communist parties in Beirut. Resolutions are passed on the situation in the world communist movement, Vietnam, the fiftieth anniversary of the October Revolution, the Kurds in Iraq, and the military government in Greece, and a joint statement is prepared on the situation in the Arab countries. |
| 1<br>Philippines | A statement issued in the name of the Politburo of the Philippine Communist Party and carried in the 10 May issue of *People's Voice,* the weekly organ of the pro-Chinese New Zealand Communist Party, declares that the "outlawed situation of the Party dictates clearly that there is no path to national and social liberation except armed struggle." |
| 1-6<br>Syria/<br>Iraq/<br>USSR | Chairman of the Presidium of the Supreme Soviet of the USSR, Nikolai Podgorny, visits Syria. On 3 May he leaves for Iraq, where he stays till 6 May. |
| 6<br>Hong Kong | Communist agitation and violence begins in Hong Kong with a labor dispute in an artificial flower factory. |
| 6-7<br>Germany: Federal<br>Republic of Germany | An international conference is held in Düsseldorf on the problem of the outlawing of the West German Communist Party, with participants attending from eight West European countries and West Germany. |
| 8<br>Cuba/<br>Venezuela | A Cuban-Venezuelan guerrilla force lands on the Venezuelan coast. The Organization of American States meets on request of the Venezuelan government and in September issues a condemnation of Cuban subversion. |
| 9<br>China | Li Ching-ch'üan is dismissed from his posts as First Secretary of the Southwest Bureau of the Chinese Communist Party and First Political Commissar of the Chengtu Military District. |
| 10<br>Albania/ | First Secretary of the Albanian Workers' Party Central Committee Enver Hoxha receives Franz Strobl, First Secretary of the Austrian |

| | |
|---|---|
| Austria | Marxist-Leninist Party. |
| 10-13<br>Bulgaria/<br>USSR | CPSU Secretary-General Leonid Brezhnev heads a party-government delegation to Bulgaria to sign on 12 May a twenty-year Treaty of Friendship, Cooperation, and Mutual Assistance. |
| 12<br>Bulgaria/<br>USSR | The Soviet Union and Bulgaria sign a new twenty-year Treaty of Friendship, Cooperation, and Mutual Assistance in Sofia following three days of talks between Leonid Brezhnev and Todor Zhivkov. The treaty is an extension of an existing one signed in 1948. In a speech following the signing, Todor Zhivkov declares: "The past, the present, and the future, our feelings and ideas, our interests and aspirations—everything unites our peoples and nothing separates them." |
| 12-16<br>Austria/<br>Hungary | Franz Muhri, Chairman of the Communist Party of Austria, pays an "unofficial" visit to Hungary and meets with János Kádár, First Secretary of the Hungarian Socialist Workers' Party. |
| 13-15<br>Finland | The Finnish People's Democratic League, the communist electoral front organization, holds its congress and adopts a draft program. |
| 13-16<br>Sweden | The Swedish Communist Party holds its Twenty-first Congress and adopts a name change and a new party program. |
| 18-21<br>Germany: German<br>Democratic Republic/<br>Hungary | The German Democratic Republic and Hungary sign a twenty-year Treaty of Friendship, Cooperation, and Mutual Assistance, in Budapest, during the visit of a top-level party-state delegation from the German Democratic Republic led by Walter Ulbricht. |
| 18-20<br>Bulgaria | The First Congress of Culture is held in Sofia and is attended by 1,800 delegates and by delegations from abroad. |
| 19<br>USSR | V. E. Semichastny is replaced as Chairman of the State Security Committee by I. Andropov. On 25 May Semichastny is appointed First Deputy Chairman of the Council of Ministers of the Ukrainian Soviet Socialist Republic. |
| 20-24<br>Germany: Federal<br>Republic of Germany | A West German Communist Party delegation, headed by First Secretary Max Reimann, visits the Soviet Union. Talks are held with Soviet party leaders. |
| 22<br>China | *Jen-min Jih-pao* publishes an editorial appeal titled "Immediately Curb Struggle by Force." |
| 22-27<br>USSR | The Fourth Congress of the Union of Writers of the USSR meets in Moscow. The issue of censorship is raised by a letter addressed to the congress by A. Solzhenitsyn. |
| 23-28<br>France/<br>Morocco | A Moroccan Communist Party delegation, led by Secretary-General Ali Yata, visits France and meets with French Communist party leaders. |

| | |
|---|---|
| 24-26<br>Hungary/<br>Rumania | A top-level Rumanian Communist Party delegation headed by Nicolae Ceauşescu visits Budapest and holds talks with Hungarian party leaders. The communique declares that talks were held concerning the international situation and the international communist and workers' movement. |
| 25<br>Peru | Peruvian authorities capture Enrique Amaya, who took command of the Pachacutec wing of the Movement of the Revolutionary Left (MIR) after the death of de la Puente Uceda and who appears to have succeeded him as Secretary-General of the MIR. |
| 26<br>Ceylon | Nagalingam Sanmugathasan, leader of the pro-Chinese Ceylon Communist Party, speaks in Peking while on a visit to China and declares his intention to build a Maoist-oriented revolutionary party in Ceylon. |
| 26-27<br>Guadeloupe | Violent riots take place at Pointe-à-Pitre over trade-union demands, after which numerous members of the pro-Chinese organization, the Guadeloupe National Organization Group (GONG), are arrested. |
| 28-2 June<br>Rumania/<br>Spain | Santiago Carrillo, Secretary-General of the Communist Party of Spain, visits Rumania. |
| 30<br>Afghanistan/<br>USSR | Soviet President Podgorny begins an official four-day visit to Afghanistan. |
| End May—early June<br>India | Uprisings in Naxalbari reach the peak of intensity and violence. |
| 31-6 June<br>Afro-Asian Writers'<br>Permanent Bureau | The Afro-Asian Writers' Permanent Bureau (Peking) conducts a seminar in Peking on the twenty-fifth anniversary of Mao Tse-tung's "Talks at the Yenan Forum on Literature and Art," which is attended by 80 delegates from 34 countries. |

# JUNE

| | |
|---|---|
| Colombia/<br>Venezuela | Delegations of the Central Committees of the Communist Party of Colombia and the Communist Party of Venezuela meet to discuss the major issues facing the international communist movement. |
| 1-4<br>Bulgaria/<br>Germany: Federal<br>Republic of Germany | Max Reimann, First Secretary of the Central Committee of the West German Communist Party, leads a party delegation to Sofia for talks with Bulgarian party leaders. The joint communique affirms a complete identity of views between the two parties on all questions discussed. |
| 2<br>Venezuela | Américo Martín, Secretary-General of the Movement of the Revolutionary Left and prominent guerrilla leader in Venezuela, is captured by government forces. |
| 4<br>Albania | The last Roman Catholic church in Albania is closed, in the course of the "cultural revolution" in Albania. The Albanian press declares that the young people of Albania have "created the first atheist state in the world." |
| 5<br>Israel | As Arab-Israeli fighting starts, Israeli Communist Party (RAKAH) members of the Knesset vote against the authorization of new war credits and taxes. On the other hand, Israeli Communist Party (MAKI) leaders encourage Israeli forces to fight for the integrity and independence of Israel. |
| 5-6<br>Bulgaria/<br>Yugoslavia | A high-level Bulgarian party-government delegation headed by First Secretary of the Central Committee of the Bulgarian Communist Party Todor Zhivkov visits Yugoslavia. The communique issued following the visit declares an "identity or similarity of views on the basic international issues." |
| 6-7<br>Finland | Finnish Communist Party chairman Aarne Saarinen and Secretary-General Ville Pessi hold talks in Moscow with Brezhnev, Suslov, and Ponomarev on the development of Finnish-Soviet relations. |
| 7<br>Bolivia | To combat guerrilla activity, the Bolivian government declares a state of siege. A number of politicians and labor leaders are arrested. |
| 9<br>East Europe/<br>USSR | East European party and state leaders meet in Moscow to discuss the Middle East crisis. Rumania refuses to sign the statement issued at the conclusion of the meeting. |
| 9-12<br>Australia | The Twenty-first Congress of the Communist Party of Australia is held in Sydney. |

| 10<br>Austria | The Austrian Communist Party holds a party conference to discuss the political orientation of the Austrian Communist Party vis-à-vis the Socialist Party of Austria. |

10
Israel/
USSR

The USSR breaks diplomatic relations with Israel, followed by the other signatories of the Moscow Declaration.

11-16
France

The communist General Confederation of Labor (CGT) holds its Thirty-sixth Congress and elects Georges Séguy Secretary-General.

16
Chile

After a long controversy between Communists and Socialists over its composition, the Chilean national committee of the Latin American Solidarity Organization is established.

16
France/
USSR

Premier Alexei Kosygin confers with General De Gaulle.

18-22
Mexico

The Mexican Communist Party holds its Fifteenth Congress.

18-25
Bulgaria/
Ecuador

Pedro Saad, Secretary-General of the Communist Party of Ecuador, visits Bulgaria at the invitation of the Central Committee of the Bulgarian Communist Party.

21
Germany: Federal
Republic of Germany

The tenth plenary session of the Central Committee of the West German Communist Party authorizes the preparation of a detailed party-program draft to be presented to the population for discussion.

21-24
United Arab
Republic/
USSR/
Yugoslavia

USSR President Podgorny visits Cairo and confers with Tito on his way to and returning from Cairo.

21-30
Greece

The Central Committee of the Communist Party of Greece, exiled in eastern Europe, convenes an eleventh plenum to determine the program for its struggle against the new military government in Greece. The seven-point program, based on the strategy of a broad united front, calls for the overthrow of the dictatorship, restoration of liberty, freedom of action for all parties, release of all prisoners, general amnesty, dissolution of the junta, and free elections.

22-24
Czechoslovakia

The Communist Party of Czechoslovakia hosts an international conference on the "Historical Significance of the Great October Socialist Revolution."

23-25
USA/
USSR

President Johnson and Soviet Premier Alexei Kosygin hold "useful" talks on a wide range of issues at Glassboro, New Jersey during Kosygin's visit to the US to address the United Nations on the Middle East situation.

| | |
|---|---|
| 25<br>China/<br>Sweden | Leaders of a pro-Chinese splinter group form the Communist League (Marxist-Leninist) in Sweden following talks in Peking with officials of the Chinese Communist Party. |
| 25<br>Germany: Federal<br>Republic of Germany | The West German Communist Party issues an open letter to all Social-Democratic militants, urging unity of action against the federal government. |
| 26-29<br>Albania/<br>China | A delegation of Red Guards, led by Yao Wen-yuan, attends the Fifth Congress of the Union of Working Youth of Albania. This is the first time that a Red Guard delegation has traveled abroad. |
| 26-30<br>Cuba/<br>USSR | Soviet Premier Alexei Kosygin visits Cuba and confers with Fidel Castro. |
| 27-29<br>Czechoslovakia | The Fourth Congress of Czechoslovak Writers is held in Prague. The congress is the scene of outspoken indictments by dissident intellectuals of the twenty years of communist rule in Czechoslovakia. The writers demand the abolition of censorship, the reestablishment of civil rights, and other measures amounting to what the party terms an "opposition political platform." Jiří Hendrych, representing the communist party at the congress, warns the writers that "the party's patience is at an end." |
| 28<br>India | Attempts by extreme left elements of the Communist Party of India (Marxist) to seize the editorial offices of the party's Bengali newspaper, *Desh Hitaisi,* results in their expulsion from the party. |
| End June<br>Cuba/<br>Vietnam: Republic<br>of Vietnam | Cuba becomes the first country to accept a permanent mission of the National Liberation Front of South Vietnam, to found a national committee of solidarity with the people of South Vietnam, and to raise the permanent mission of the National Liberation Front of South Vietnam in Cuba to the level of an official diplomatic organ. |

# JULY

| | |
|---|---|
| Argentina/<br>Brazil/<br>Chile/<br>Uruguay | Bilateral meetings are held between the leadership of the Brazilian Communist Party and the leaders of the communist parties of Chile, Argentina, and Uruguay. |
| 1-3<br>Syria/<br>USSR | Soviet President Podgorny visits Syria. |
| 3-4<br>Iraq/<br>USSR | Soviet President Podgorny visits Iraq. |
| 3<br>Czechoslovakia | The trial of three Czechoslovak intellectuals opens in Prague. On trial are Jan Beneš, Karel Zámečník, and Pavel Tigrid (in absentia), all charged with subversion. |
| 5-6<br>Czechoslovakia/<br>USSR | First Secretary of the Communist Party of Czechoslovakia Antonín Novotný confers with Secretary-General of the Communist Party of the Soviet Union Leonid Brezhnev in the Soviet Union. The talks concern bilateral as well as international affairs. The official communique reports a "complete unity of views" on all questions discussed. |
| 7<br>USSR | Marshal Ivan Yakubovsky is appointed Commander-in-Chief of the Warsaw Pact Armed Forces. |
| 7<br>Vietnam: Democratic Republic of Vietnam | Hanoi Domestic Service announces that General Nguyen Chi Thanh, member of the Politburo of the Vietnam Workers' Party, died of a heart attack in a Hanoi hospital on 6 July. Although the Democratic Republic of Vietnam has at no time admitted the presence of North Vietnamese troops in South Vietnam, western sources report that Nguyen Chi Thanh was also head of the Central Office of South Vietnam (COSVN), thus exercising *de facto* control over the political and military activities of the communist forces in South Vietnam and serving as a liaison between the Viet Cong and the North Vietnamese military commands. |
| 11<br>USSR | Alexandr Shelepin loses his post on the Secretariat of the CPSU Central Committee. He is appointed Chairman of the All–Union Central Council of Trade Unions, replacing Viktor Grishin, who becomes First Secretary of the Moscow City Party Committee. |
| 11<br>Yugoslavia | The Yugoslav Federal Assembly adopts legislation amending eight laws, thus permitting the investment of foreign capital in Yugoslavia. Foreign |

participation is limited to 49 per cent, although exceptions are possible.

**11-12**
**East Europe/**
**Middle East**

Party leaders and heads of state of seven East European countries meet in Budapest to discuss means for reestablishing peace in the Middle East. The communique of the meeting charges Israel with "aggression" and violation of the basic principles of the UN Charter and of international law. The communique also pledges "further use of appropriate means corresponding to the interests of the struggle against aggression and the restoration of peace in the Middle East." Rumania is not represented at the meeting.

**12**
**Albania/**
**Sudan**

A delegation of the Sudanese Communist Party (Marxist-Leninist), led by First Secretary Muhammad, meets with the First Secretary of the Albanian Workers' Party Central Committee Enver Hoxha.

**18**
**Albania**

Albanian Foreign Minister Nesti Nase presents a report to the Albanian National Assembly titled "On the International Situation and the Foreign Policy of the Albanian People's Republic Government," in which he declares that the struggle against "American imperialism" and against the "Khrushchevite revisionists" is today the "most imperative duty of all the revolutionary peoples and forces of the world," but affirms a gradual improvement in state relations between Albania and other governments.

**18-23**
**Bulgaria/**
**Mongolia**

A Bulgarian party-government delegation headed by First Secretary of the Central Committee of the Bulgarian Communist Party and Premier Todor Zhivkov and Chairman of the Presidium of the National Assembly Georgi Traykov visits Ulan Bator, Mongolia. During the visit, Bulgaria and Mongolia sign a twenty-year Treaty of Friendship, Cooperation, and Assistance.

**19**
**China/**
**Cuba/**
**East Europe/**
**Mongolia/**
**North Korea/**
**Vietnam: Democratic**
**Republic of Vietnam**

A high-level North Vietnamese delegation led by Le Thanh Nghi, Vice-Premier and member of the Politburo of the Vietnam Workers' Party, leaves on an eleven-week visit to various Asian and East European communist capitals to meet with party leaders and to negotiate non-refundable military and economic aid agreements for 1968. Agreements are signed with China, North Korea, Mongolia, Rumania, Bulgaria, Cuba, the Soviet Union, Hungary, Poland, and Czechoslovakia. In addition, the North Vietnamese Ambassador to East Berlin signs an agreement on East German aid and an Albanian delegation visits Hanoi where aid agreements are signed.

**20**
**Italy/**
**Rumania**

Italian Communist Party leader Luigi Longo and Rumanian Communist Party leader Nicolae Ceauşescu issue a joint communique in Bucharest following talks on European security and the international communist movement.

**21**
**China**

*Jen-min Jih-pao* publishes an editorial detailing the differences between the respective lines of Communist China and the Soviet Union regarding the Vietnam war.

**21**
**China**

Hsieh Fu-chih and Wang Li, sent by central party authorities in Peking to Wuhan to help establish central control over the area, are detained by forces loyal to Ch'en Tsai-tao.

**22**
**Cuba/**
**Yugoslavia**

*Granma,* the official organ of the Communist Party of Cuba, attacks the new policy of the government of Yugoslavia which allows for foreign capital to be invested in that country. In an editorial entitled "The So-Called Yugoslav Way Is the Road to Opportunism and Betrayal," the Cuban Communist Party claims that the newly approved law allowing foreign investments in Yugoslavia is another indication that "economic dependency on Yankee imperialism has made Yugoslav foreign policy, disguised as 'positive neutralism,' agree with the policy of the US."

**25-31**
**Denmark/**
**Hungary**

A delegation of the Communist Party of Denmark, headed by Chairman Knud Jespersen, visits Hungary.

**26-2 August**
**Finland/**
**Hungary**

A delegation of the Communist Party of Finland led by Chairman Aarne Saarinen visits Hungary.

**28**
**Bulgaria/**
**Italy**

First Secretary of the Bulgarian Communist Party Todor Zhivkov confers with Luigi Longo, Secretary-General of the Italian Communist Party, during his visit to Bulgaria.

**30**
**Bulgaria/**
**France**

First Secretary of the Bulgarian Communist Party Todor Zhivkov confers with Waldeck Rochet, Secretary-General of the French Communist Party, during his visit to Bulgaria.

**31-10 August**
**Cuba**

The First Conference of the Latin American Solidarity Organization meets in Havana under Cuban sponsorship. Its adopted slogan is "The duty of every revolutionary is to make revolution."

# AUGUST

| | |
|---|---|
| Albania/<br>Austria/<br>Belgium/<br>France/<br>Italy | Representatives of pro-Chinese communist parties and movements from Austria, Belgium, France, and Italy visit Albania. In addition to conferences with the leadership of the Albanian Workers' Party, bilateral meetings are held between the visiting parties. The Austrian and Belgian delegations are led by their respective First Secretaries, Franz Strobl and Jacques Grippa. |
| Jordan | The Communist Party of Jordan draws up a new provisional program designed to appeal to Jordanian nationalism and anti-Israel sentiment. The program calls for a broad coalition of all patriotic forces and appeals to the revanchist spirit rampant in Jordan after the Arab-Israeli war. |
| 3<br>Japan | The representative of the Japanese Communist Party and the correspondent for the party newspaper *Akahata* are attacked by Red Guards and Japanese residents in China at the Peking International Airport, precipitating the final act in the split between the Japanese and Chinese communist parties. |
| 4<br>Iran/<br>Rumania | The President of the Central Committee of the communist Tudeh Party of Iran, Reza Radmanesh, visits Rumania. |
| 8<br>Chile | The Communist Party of Chile marks the 100th anniversary of the publication of Karl Marx's *Das Kapital* and the fiftieth anniversary of the October Revolution by the inauguration of an Institute of Marxist Studies. |
| 10<br>Cuba/<br>Venezuela | Fidel Castro, in an address at the closing session of the conference of the Latin American Solidarity Organization, severely attacks "counterrevolutionaries" around the world, in particular a "microfaction" in Cuba and the pro-Soviet Communist Party of Venezuela. |
| 10-17<br>Iraq/<br>Syria/<br>United Arab<br>Republic (UAR)/<br>Yugoslavia | Yugoslav President Tito makes a tour of the Middle East and confers with UAR President Nasser (10-13 and 16-17), Syrian President al-Atassi (13-14), and Iraqi President Arif (14-15) on matters concerning the Middle East crisis. |
| 12<br>China | The Chinghai Revolutionary Committee is established. |
| 13-15<br>Réunion | The Communist Party of Réunion holds it Second Party Congress. |

| | |
|---|---|
| 14-17<br>France | Secretary-General of the French Communist Party Waldeck Rochet visits Rumania, where he holds talks with Rumanian First Secretary Nicolae Ceauşescu on questions of European security and the international communist movement. |
| Mid-August<br>Vietnam: Republic of Vietnam | An "extraordinary congress" of the National Liberation Front of South Vietnam is convened in the "liberated areas" to discuss and adopt the political program of the front. |
| 16-17<br>Italy/<br>Rumania | Secretary-General of the Italian Communist Party Luigi Longo visits Rumania and meets with party leaders. |
| 18<br>Czechoslovakia/<br>Germany: German Democratic Republic | East German party and state leader Walter Ulbricht meets with Czechoslovak President and party leader Novotný in Prague. |
| 18<br>Rumania/<br>Venezuela | Jesús Faría, Secretary-General of the Venezuelan Communist Party, visits Rumania and meets with Rumanian party leaders. |
| 18-26<br>India | The Communist Party of India (M) leadership meets in Madurai, Madras, and passes resolutions detailing differences betwen the Communist Party of India (M) and the Chinese Communist Party, and setting forth party views on the international communist movement. |
| 19<br>Rhodesia/<br>South Africa | The military detachment of the South African National Congress (ANC), the Umkhonto we Sizwe, joins forces with the Zimbabwe African People's Union (ZAPU) of Rhodesia and begins an "armed struggle for liberation" in Rhodesia. The South African Communist Party declares that the ANC-ZAPU alliance is significant because the alliance is "sealed in a bond of brotherhood on the battlefield" and is "boldly directed against the main bastion of white supremacy and colonialism in Africa." |
| 20-27<br>Bulgaria/<br>Rumania/<br>USSR | Warsaw Pact joint maneuvers are held in Bulgaria and in the western Black Sea. Ground and naval forces of the Soviet Union, Bulgaria, and Rumania participate. This marks the first time in three years that Rumania has participated in the joint military exercises of the Warsaw Pact. |
| 21<br>Uruguay/<br>USSR | A communique is published in Moscow following talks between Soviet party leaders, including Secretary-General Leonid Brezhnev, and leaders of the Communist Party of Uruguay, including First Secretary Rodney Arismendi. |
| 22<br>China | The British Legation building in Peking is set afire by Red Guards. |
| 25<br>Argentina | A law is promulgated providing for the registration of Communists in Argentina and imposing severe restrictions on their activities. |

| | |
|---|---|
| 25-29<br>France/<br>Yugoslavia | During a visit to Yugoslavia, Secretary-General of the French Communist Party Waldeck Rochet meets twice with President Tito. |
| 26<br>Rumania/<br>Vietnam: Democratic<br>Republic of Vietnam | The Democratic Republic of Vietnam and Rumania sign economic and military aid agreements in Bucharest. This marks the first time that Rumanian sources have declared that military supplies are being sent to North Vietnam by Rumania. |
| 26-27<br>Guyana | The communist-oriented People's Progressive Party (PPP) holds its Fourteenth Congress. Most moderate elements in the party are eliminated from the leadership. In his report to the congress, PPP leader Cheddi Jagan declares that the party should "constantly promote into leading positions comrades armed with the ideology of Marxism-Leninism." |
| 30<br>China/<br>France | A delegation of the French Communist Movement (Marxist-Leninist) is received in Peking by K'ang Sheng. |

# SEPTEMBER

| | |
|---|---|
| 3<br>Czechoslovakia | A "Thousand-Word Manifesto of Czechoslovak Writers to the World Public," allegedly signed by some 300 Czechoslovak intellectuals and smuggled out of Czechoslovakia, is printed in the London *Sunday Times*. The manifesto, which calls on world opinion for moral support of Czechoslovak writers against censorship and repression, is denounced by official Czechoslovak sources as a fabrication. On 3 December, a man is arrested in Czechoslovakia and accused of being the sole author of the manifesto. |
| 4-6<br>East Europe | Deputy Premiers of the Soviet Union, Bulgaria, Hungary, the German Democratic Republic, Poland, Rumania, Czechoslovakia, and Yugoslavia meet in Belgrade to discuss the question of expanding economic cooperation with Arab countries and to decide on the most effective forms of assistance to be given to them. |
| 5<br>China | Chiang Ch'ing delivers a speech to representatives from Anhwei revolutionary organizations and calls for moderation of the revolutionary struggle. |
| 5-7<br>Albania/<br>Italy | A delegation of the Communist Party of Italy—Marxist-Leninist, headed by Secretary-General Fosco Dinucci, visits Albania. |
| 7<br>China/<br>India | Fighting breaks out between Indian and Chinese troops on the Sikkim-Tibet border. |
| 7<br>Bulgaria/<br>Germany: German<br>Democratic Republic | Bulgaria and East Germany sign a twenty-year Treaty of Friendship, Cooperation, and Mutual Assistance in Sofia during a four-day visit by the First Secretary of the Central Committee of the Socialist Unity Party of East Germany, Walter Ulbricht, and the President of the German Democratic Republic Council of Ministers, Willi Stoph. |
| 7<br>Hungary/<br>USSR | Hungary and the Soviet Union sign a new twenty-year Treaty of Friendship, Cooperation, and Mutual Assistance in Budapest, five months before the expiration of the existing treaty. |
| 10<br>Finland | The Communist Party of Finland's Central Committee adopts the draft of a new party program. |
| 10-14<br>Chile | The Communist Party of Chile holds a national conference in Santiago. |
| 11-15 | Czechoslovak party and state leader Antonín Novotný visits Belgrade |

| | |
|---|---|
| Czechoslovakia/<br>Yugoslavia | and holds talks with his Yugoslav counterpart, Josip Broz-Tito. The communique following the talks notes that all avenues of contact between the states have not been developed and urges the future extension of cooperation in all spheres. |
| 13<br>Great Britain/<br>USSR | John Gollan, General Secretary of the Communist Party of Great Britain, leads a delegation to the USSR and meets with CPSU Secretary-General Leonid Brezhnev. |
| 15<br>Bulgaria/<br>USSR | First Secretary of the Central Committee of the Bulgarian Communist Party Todor Zhivkov meets with Soviet party leader Leonid Brezhnev in Moscow during an unannounced visit. A "unanimity of views" on all questions discussed is reported. |
| 19<br>Iraq | The Iraqi Communist Party in exile in East Europe acknowledges that a serious split occurred in the party ranks during September. The intraparty disturbance is apparently accompanied by physical violence between the protagonists. |
| 19<br>Rumania | Rumanian Foreign Minister Corneliu Mănescu is elected President of the twenty-second session of the United Nations General Assembly. This marks the first time that a representative of a communist country has been elected to this post. |
| 22<br>Poland/<br>USSR | First Secretary of the Central Committee of the Polish United Workers' Party Wladislaw Gomulka and Premier Józef Cyrankiewicz confer with Soviet leaders Leonid Brezhnev, Alexei Kosygin, and Nikolai Podgorny. |
| 25<br>China | Radio Peking announces that Mao Tse-tung recently visited parts of North China, South-Central China, and East China to "investigate the state of the cultural revolution." |
| 26-14 October<br>Albania/<br>China | An Albanian party and government delegation headed by Mehmet Shehu visits China and attends the celebrations of the eighteenth anniversary of People's Republic of China. The joint communique published following the visit and talks with Mao Tse-tung specifies that both sides "reaffirmed the principles and stand set forth in the Joint Statement of China and Albania dated 11 May 1966." It also states that "today the attitude toward China's Great Proletarian Cultural Revolution is the touchstone to distinguish Marxist-Leninists from revisionists, and genuine revolutionaries from counterrevolutionaries." |
| 27-4 October<br>Poland/<br>Spain | A delegation of the Spanish Communist Party, led by party Secretary-General Santiago Carrillo, visits Poland. |
| 28-1 October | Todor Zhivkov, First Secretary of the Central Committee of the |

Bulgaria/
Rumania

Bulgarian Communist Party and Chairman of the Council of Ministers of the Bulgarian People's Republic, visits Rumania and holds talks with Nicolae Ceauşescu, Secretary-General of the Rumanian Communist Party. The joint communique states that the talks were held "in a warm and comradely atmosphere in the spirit of the traditional friendship uniting the two parties, countries, and peoples."

| | |
|---|---|
| Ecuador/<br>Venezuela | Members of the Central Committees of the Communist Party of Ecuador and the Communist Party of Venezuela meet to discuss the international communist movement and issues facing the two parties. |
| Guatemala | César Montes, Commander-in Chief of the Guatemalan Rebel Armed Forces, and Marco Antonio Yon Sosa, leader of the 13 November Revolutionary Movement, sign a joint statement—which is not made public until early 1968—on the death of "Che" Guevara. The statement calls for closer cooperation among Guatemalan guerrillas. |
| Guatemala | The break between the Rebel Armed Forces and the Guatemalan Party of Labor becomes a fact, though it is not made public until January 1968. |
| Sudan | The Sudanese Communist Party holds its Fourth Congress, eleven years after the Third Congress. The major issue at the congress is the task of party building and the creation of a "genuinely mass Marxist-Leninist party." |
| 3-10<br>Albania/<br>Ceylon | The Secretary-General of the pro-Chinese Communist Party of Ceylon, Nagalingam Sanmugathasan, visits Albania. |
| 4-11<br>Bulgaria/<br>Spain | A delegation of the Communist Party of Spain, headed by Secretary-General Santiago Carrillo, visits Bulgaria. |
| 5<br>North Korea/<br>USSR | A North Korean economic delegation led by Yi Chu-yon visits the Soviet Union. Negotiations result in an agreement providing for a 30 per cent increase in mutual trade deliveries for 1968, for Soviet cooperation in the building of a number of enterprises, and for the establishment of an economic and scientific-technical consultative commission to accelerate cooperation. |
| 8<br>Bolivia/<br>Cuba | Ernesto "Che" Guevara is captured at the head of an international guerrilla force in Bolivia. He dies on 9 October, and on 15 October Fidel Castro proclaims 8 October as "The Day of the Heroic Guerrilla." |
| 9<br>China/<br>Indonesia | The governments of Indonesia and China announce suspension of diplomatic relations and subsequently withdraw their respective diplomatic missions. |
| 10<br>Colombia/ | Gilberto Vieira, Secretary-General of the Communist Party of Colombia, holds talks in Prague with Vladimír Koucký, Secretary of the |

| | |
|---|---|
| Czechoslovakia | Central Committee of the Communist Party of Czechoslovakia. Czechoslovak sources report that the representatives from the fraternal parties exchanged information on current problems of party policy and questions of the international communist movement. |
| 10<br>India/<br>Germany: German Democratic Republic | S. A. Dange, Chairman of the pro-Soviet Communist Party of India, leads a delegation to the German Democratic Republic and meets with First Secretary Walter Ulbricht. |
| 10-14<br>Czechoslovakia/<br>Hungary | A Hungarian party-government delegation led by János Kádár, First Secretary of the Hungarian Socialist Workers' Party, visits Prague at the invitation of the Communist Party of Czechoslovakia and the Czechoslovak Socialist Republic. The communique states that talks between the two parties concerned mutual relations, international problems, and the world communist movement and showed "complete identity of views on all questions discussed." The two sides express support for the convening of an international communist conference and also agree to conclude a new Treaty of Friendship, Cooperation, and Mutual Assistance before the expiration of the existing treaty on 16 April 1969. |
| 13<br>Japan/<br>USSR | *Akahata,* the organ of the Japanese Communist Party, announces the acceptance of an offer from the Communist Party of the Soviet Union to dispatch a delegation to discuss issues of interest to the Soviet and Japanese parties, thus signaling a willingness to improve relations between the two, which had been virtually broken off since 1964. |
| 15<br>Israel | Meir Vilner, leader of the Israeli Communist Party (RAKAH), is the object of an unsuccessful assassination attempt. |
| 16<br>USA<br>Vietnam: Republic of Vietnam | Liberation Press Agency issues a communique announcing the formation of the "South Vietnam People's Committee for Solidarity with the American people." According to the communique, the committee seeks to "consolidate and develop the friendship between the South Vietnamese and American people" and to "unite and coordinate with the American people in the struggle for peace, justice, freedom, democracy, and civil rights and in demanding that the US government put an end to its aggressive war in Vietnam." The communique also announces that the committee will establish permanent representations in Prague, Algiers, and Hanoi. |
| 19-26<br>Colombia/<br>Germany: German Democratic Republic | A delegation of the Colombian Communist Party, led by its Secretary-General Gilberto Vieira, visits the German Democratic Republic. |
| 20<br>Germany: German Democratic Republic/<br>Northern Ireland | Hugh Moore, General Secretary of the Communist Party of Northern Ireland, confers with members of the Socialist Unity Party of East Germany. |

26-27
Czechoslovakia

A plenum of the Central Committee of the Communist Party of Czechoslovakia hears a report by Central Committee Secretary Jiří Hendrych on the Fourth Congress of Czechoslovak Writers and decides to expel several dissident writers from the party and put the organ of the Writers' Union, *Literární Noviny*, under the Ministry of Information and Culture.

30
Bulgaria/
Colombia

A visiting Colombian Communist Party delegation led by Secretary-General Gilberto Vieira meets with Bulgarian party leader Todor Zhivkov in Sofia.

End October
USA

The Trotskyist Socialist Workers' Party holds its Twenty-second Convention in New York City "during the latter part of October."

# NOVEMBER

**Philippines**

A statement issued in the name of the Politburo of the Philippine Communist Party attacks the 1 May statement that "there is no path to national and social liberation except armed struggle," and claims that it was issued by an "antiparty group" and therefore "was not authorized by the Philippine Communist Party and does not reflect its true position."

**2-7**
**USSR**

Main celebrations of the fiftieth anniversary of the October Revolution are held in Moscow, Leningrad, Kiev, and Minsk. Delegations from 95 countries are present, including representatives of 74 communist parties. (For further details and chronology of major events in the USSR in 1967 connected with the fiftieth anniversary, see *The Soviet Union's Fiftieth Anniversary of the October Revolution.*)

**4**
**USSR,**
**Vietnam: Democratic Republic of Vietnam**

TASS, the Soviet press agency, announces that Ho Chi Minh has been awarded the Order of Lenin, the highest Soviet decoration. On 14 November Ho announces that he will postpone accepting the award until Vietnam is "liberated."

**7**
**North Korea**

South Korean reports state that a high-level purge of the Korean Workers' Party is being conducted "under the heavy pressure of the military." The purge reportedly began in March 1967 and has affected more than 100 members of the party.

**13-17**
**Austria/**
**Yugoslavia**

A delegation of the Communist Party of Austria, led by its Chairman, Franz Muhri, meets with members of the League of Communists in Yugoslavia.

**15**
**China**

The fall Canton Trade Fair opens after being postponed for one month because of disorders in Canton.

**16**
**Colombia**

*Voz Proletaria,* organ of the Communist Party of Colombia, announces the expulsion of Diego Montaña Cuéllar, member of the Central Executive Committee of the Communist Party of Colombia.

**21-25**
**Bulgaria/**
**Greece**

A Greek Communist Party delegation led by Chairman Apostolos Grozos visits Bulgaria.

**22-28**
**Chile/**
**Rumania**

The Secretary-General of the Communist Party of Chile, Luis Corvalán, visits Rumania and meets with Rumanian party leaders.

**24**

The Soviet and Malaysian governments decide, on the basis of

| | |
|---|---|
| Malaysia/<br>USSR | negotiations held in April 1967, to exchange diplomatic missions at the embassy level. |
| 25<br>North Korea | Elections are held for the Fourth Supreme People's Assembly, a year overdue. |
| 25<br>USSR | *Pravda* publishes a communique signed by eighteen communist parties inviting all communist parties to a "consultative" meeting in Budapest in February 1968. |
| 25-26<br>Peru | The pro-Soviet Communist Party of Peru holds its Sixth National Organizational Conference in Lima. |
| 25-28<br>Great Britain | The Communist Party of Great Britain holds its Thirtieth National Congress. The party program *British Road to Socialism,* revised for the occasion, advocates the achievement of political power through parliamentary means. A reduction of ideological differences between Communists and others in Great Britain is suggested in the new *Questions of Ideology and Culture.* |
| 28<br>China | The proposal to admit Communist China to the United Nations and to expel Nationalist China is rejected by a vote of 58 to 45, with 17 abstentions. |

Brazil

The pro-Soviet Brazilian Communist Party holds its Sixth Congress. A number of leading members of the party, including Castroist Carlos Marighella, former member of the Executive Committee, are expelled.

Iraq

The Iraqi Communist Party holds a National Conference somewhere in East Europe in lieu of the planned Second National Congress which was postponed due to a split in the party during the month of September. The conference, attended by 55 top party members, decides upon a new draft program.

Jordan

Fuad Nassar, First Secretary of the Communist Party of Jordan, returns to Jordan after more than ten years in exile, without opposition from the government. Still illegal, but now tolerated, his party joins a broad national front dedicated to recoup Jordanian losses in the Arab-Israeli conflict.

1-5
Colombia/
Rumania

Secretary-General of the Communist Party of Colombia Gilberto Vieira visits Rumanian party leader Nicolae Ceauşescu.

4
Finland/
USSR

Nikolai Podgorny, Chairman of the Presidium of the Supreme Soviet of the USSR, goes to Finland for the celebrations of the fiftieth anniversary of the Finnish Republic.

4-7
Chile/
France

Luis Corvalán, Secretary-General of the Communist Party of Chile, visits France and meets with Waldeck Rochet, Secretary-General of the French Communist Party.

6-10
Colombia/
Czechoslovakia

A delegation of the Communist Party of Colombia, headed by Secretary-General Gilberto Vieira, visits Czechoslovakia at the invitation of the Communist Party of Czechoslovakia and holds talks with Czechoslovak party leaders Jiří Hendrych, Vladimir Koucký, and Oldřich Kaderka. The joint communique affirms that a "full identify of views on all questions" was reached. Both sides affirm their full support for the convening of an international communist party conference.

8
Czechoslovakia/
USSR

Secretary-General of the CPSU Leonid Brezhnev pays an unannounced visit to Prague. The communique specifies that talks were held concerning bilateral relations and the international communist movement. Subsequent events indicate that Brezhnev was personally invited by Antonín Novotný for support in his struggle to retain leadership of the Communist Party of Czechoslovakia.

10

First Secretary of the Socialist Unity Party and Chairman of the State

| | |
|---|---|
| Germany: German Democratic Republic/ USSR | Council Walter Ulbricht departs for Moscow. |
| 12 Poland | According to a report over Radio Tirana, the first issue of the organ of the Central Committee of the pro-Chinese Communist Party of Poland appeared in November. An editorial in the journal declared that the organ would play the role of mass agitator and organizer of the working masses and that its task was to "mobilize the working class for the struggle for socialism, to take over authority from the hands of the treacherous revisionist clique now in power in Poland." |
| 12-18 Finland/ Germany: German Democratic Republic | A delegation of the Communist Party of Finland, headed by Secretary-General Ville Pessi, visits East Germany and confers with East German party leader Walter Ulbricht. |
| 14-15 Rumania/ USSR | Nicolae Ceaușescu heads a top-level party delegation to the Soviet Union and holds talks with Soviet party leaders. The joint communique published after the visit declares that the two sides "exchanged information" in a "frank and friendly atmosphere," and does not mention points on which the two parties disagree, such as the Middle East crisis, West Germany, or the issue of an international communist conference. |
| 14-16 North Korea | The first session of the Fourth Supreme People's Assembly convenes. On 16 December, a Cabinet and Presidium of the Assembly are elected and a new political program is presented by Kim Il-song. |
| 16-17 Belgium | The Eighteenth Congress of the Belgian Communist Party is held in Brussels. |
| 19-20 Germany: German Democratic Republic/ Panama | A delegation of the People's Party of Panama, led by Hugo Victor, Chairman of the party, and Rubén Dario Souza, Secretary-General of the party, visits the German Democratic Republic. |
| 19-21 Czechoslovakia | A plenary session of the Central Committee of the Communist Party of Czechoslovakia is held following a one-week postponement. The meeting is not reported until 21 December in the Czechoslovak press. Official reports declare that economic policy and the upcoming international communist and workers' party meeting in Budapest were on the agenda. Subsequent events show that the real issue was problems of party personnel and the question of Novotný's retention of his party position. The plenum was inconclusive and adjourned for the holidays. It reconvened on 3 January 1968 and replaced First Secretary Antonín Novotný with Alexander Dubček. |
| 19-21 East Europe/ USSR | The Foreign Ministers of the Warsaw Pact member countries meet in Warsaw to dicuss the situation in the Middle East. The communique reports that talks were held "in a spirit of complete unity and close friendly cooperation." |

| | |
|---|---|
| 22-24<br>Netherlands | The Twenty-second Congress of the Communist Party of the Netherlands reaffirms a "new orientation" of policy. Isolation of the party is obvious, as no foreign communist parties are represented. |
| 23<br>Nicaragua | *Libertad,* organ of the Costa Rican (communist) People's Vanguard Party, reports that most of the leaders of the Castroist guerrilla movement in Nicaragua—the Sandinista National Liberation Front—have either been killed or are in hiding. |
| 24<br>Laos | The Central Committee of the Neo Lao Hak Xat (NLHX) decides to establish a NLHX news agency to be known as Khaosan Pathet Lao (KPL). According to the Central Committee's decision, Khaosan Pathet Lao will be the official organ of the NLHX and will begin broadcasting on 6 January 1968 under the directorship of Sisana Sisane. |
| 28-30<br>France/<br>Italy | Secretary-General Waldeck Rochet of the French Communist Party visits Italy and meets with Luigi Longo, Secretary-General of the Italian Communist Party. |
| 30-31<br>France | The French Communist (Marxist-Leninist) Movement holds a Congress at which it constitutes itself as the Marxist-Leninist Party of France. |

# BIBLIOGRAPHY

# RULING COMMUNIST PARTIES

*China*

Asia Research Center (Hong Kong). *The Great Cultural Revolution in China.* Rutland, Vt., Charles E. Tuttle, 1967. 507 pp.

—————. Vol. 1, *Men Atop Tien An Men*; Vol. 2, *Diary of the Cultural Revolution*; Vol. 3, *The Enigma of China.* Tokyo, Ashahi Shimbun, 1967.

Barnett, A. Doak. *Cadres, Bureaucracy, and Political Power in Communist China.* New York, Columbia University Press, 1967. 563 pp.

—————. *China After Mao.* Princeton, N. J., Princeton University Press, 1967. 287 pp.

Bechtholdt, Heinrich. *Die Allianz mit der Armut.* Frieburg, Rombach Verlag, 1967. 348 pp.

Berton, Peter; Wu, Eugene. (Koch, Howard Jr., Ed.) *Contemporary China: A Research Guide.* Stanford, Hoover Institution on War, Revolution and Peace, 1967. 695 pp.

Bloodworth, Dennis. *The Chinese Looking Glass.* New York, Farrar, Strauss & Giroux, 1967. 432 pp.

Boorman, Howard; Howard, Richard. *Biographical Dictionary of Republican China.* Vol. I. New York, Columbia University Press, 1967. 483 pp.

Chen, Hsi-en. *The Chinese Communist Regime: Documents and Commentary.* New York, Frederick A. Praeger, 1967. 344 pp.

Chen, Nai-Penn. *Chinese Economic Statistics: A Handbook for Mainland China.* Chicago, Aldine Publishing Company, 1967. 539 pp.

Donnithorne, Audrey. *China's Economic System.* New York, Frederick A. Praeger, 1967. 592 pp.

Dutt, R. Palme. *Whither China?* New York, New Outlook, 1967. 42 pp.

Elliot-Bateman, Michael. *Defeat in the East: The Mark of Mao Tse-tung on War.* London, Oxford University Press, 1967. 270 pp.

Fairbank, John K. *China: The People's Middle Kingdom and the U.S.A.* Cambridge, Mass., Harvard University Press, 1967. 145 pp.

Feuerwerker, Albert; Murphy, Rhoades, & Wright, Mary C. (Eds.) *Approaches to Modern Chinese History.* Berkeley, University of California Press, 1967. 356 pp.

Franke, Wolfgang (trans. by R. A. Wilson). *China and the West.* Columbia, S. C., University of South Carolina Press, 1967. 165 pp.

Garaudy, Roger. *Le problème chinois.* Paris, Seghers, 1967. 300 pp.

Geoffroy-Dechaume, Francois. *China Looks at the World.* New York, Pantheon, 1967. 237 pp.

George, Alexander L. *The Chinese Communist Army in Action: the Korean War and its Aftermath.* New York, Columbia University Press, 1967. 255 pp.

Gittings, John. *The Role of the Chinese Army.* New York, Oxford University Press, 1967. 331 pp.

Goldman, Merle. *Literary Dissent in Communist China.* Cambridge, Mass., Harvard University Press, 1967, 343 pp.

Granqvist, Hans. *The Red Guard: A Report on Mao's Revolution.* New York, Frederick A. Praeger, 1967. 159 pp.

Griffith, Samuel B. *The Chinese People's Liberation Army.* New York, McGraw-Hill, 1967. 398 pp.

Hevi, Emmanuel J. *The Dragon's Embrace: The Chinese Communists and Africa.* London, Pall Mall, 1967. 152 pp.

Houn, Franklin W. *A Short History of Chinese Communism.* Englewood Cliffs, N. J., Prentice-Hall, Inc., 1967. 245 pp.

Karol, K. S. *China: The Other Communism.* New York, Hill & Wang, 1967. 474 pp.

Li, Tien-yi (ed.). *Selected Readings in Chinese Communist Literature.* New Haven, Yale University Press, 1967.

Liu, William T. (ed.). *Chinese Society Under Communism: A Reader.* New York, Wiley, 1967. 496 pp.

Meisner, Maurice. *Li Ta-Chao and the Origins of Chinese Marxism.* Cambridge, Mass., Harvard University Press, 1967. 326 pp.

Moseley, George. *A Sino-Soviet Cultural Frontier: The Ili Kazakh Autonomous Chou.* Cambridge, Mass., Harvard University Press, 1967. 163 pp.

Peng, Shu-tse; Frank, Pierre; Heinson, Joseph; Worack, George. *Behind China's 'Great Cultural Revolution.'* New York, Merit, 1967. 63 pp.

Portisch, Hugo. *Red China Today.* New York, Fawcett Crest, 1967 (rev. ed.). 384 pp.

Roper, Erich. *Geteilites China. Eine Volkerrechtliche Studie.* Mainz, Hase & Koehler, 1967. 320 pp.

Salisbury, Harrison E. *Orbit of China.* New York, Harpers, 1967. 204 pp.

Schram, Stuart R. *Mao Tse-tung.* New York, Simon & Schuster, 1967. 351 pp.

Schurmann, Franz; Schell, Orville (Eds.). *The China Reader: I-Imperial China,* 322 pp.; *II-Republican China,* 394 pp.; *III-Communist China,* 667 pp. New York, Random House, 1967.

Schwartz, Benjamin I. *Chinese Communism and the Rise of Mao.* New York, Harpers, 1967 (sec. ed.). 259 pp.

Spitz, Allan A. (ed.). *Contemporary China.* Pullman, Wash., Washington State University Press, 1967. 56 pp.

Steinhaus, Fritz C. *Rot-Asien 1985.* Wurzburg/Marienburg, V. H. O. Holzner, 1967. 326 pp.

Taruc, Luis. *He Who Rides the Tiger.* New York, Frederick A. Praeger, 1967. 188 pp.

Teiwes, Frederick C. *Provincial Party Personnel in Mainland China 1956-1966.* New York, Columbia University Press, 1967. 114 pp.

Townsend, James R. *Political Participation in Communist China.* Berkeley, University of California Press. 1967. 233 pp.

Trotsky, Leon. *Problems of the Chinese Revolution.* Ann Arbor, University of Michigan Press, 1967. 432 pp.

Vidal, J. E. *Ou va la Chine?* Saint-Armand, Ed. Sociales, 1967. 284 pp.

Wu, Chun-hsi. *Dollars, Dependence, and Dogma.* Stanford, Hoover Institution on War, Revolution and Peace, 1967. 231 pp.

Wu, Yuan-li. *The Spatial Economy of Communist China.* New York, Frederick A. Praeger, 1967. 367 pp.

*Mainland China in the World Economy.* Hearings Before the Joint Economic Committee Congress of the United States. Washington, D. C., U. S. Government Printing Office, 1967. 248 pp.

## Cuba

Lockwood, Lee. *Castro's Cuba, Cuba's Fidel.* New York, MacMillan, 1967. 288 pp.

Suarez, A. *Cuba: Castroism and Communism, 1959-1966.* Cambridge, Mass., M.I.T. Press, 1967. 266 pp.

Zeitlin, Maurice. *Revolutionary Politics and the Cuban Working Class.* Princeton, N. J., Princeton University Press, 1967. 306 pp.

## Czechoslovakia

Mnacko, Ladislav. *The Taste of Power.* New York, Praeger, 1967. 235 pp.

## German Democratic Republic

Hornsby, Lex (ed.). *Profile of East Germany.* New Jersey, A. S. Barnes and Barnes, 1967. 120 pp.

Koch, Hans-Gerhard. *Luther's Reformation in kommunistischer Sicht.* Stuttgart, Quell Verlag, 1967. 262 pp.

Kroeger, Herbert. *"Neue" Ostpolitik in Bonn?* Berlin, East Germany, Staatsverlag der DDR, 1967.

Nawrocki, Joachim. *Das geplante Wunder, Leben und Wirklichkeit im anderen Deutschland.* Hamburg, Chr. Wegner Verlag, 1967.

Norden, Albert; Matern, Hermann; and Ebert, Friedrich. *Die Nationale Politik der DDR.* Vienna, Europa Verlag, 1967.
Schulz, Eberhard. *An Ulbricht führt kein Weg mehr vorbei.* Hamburg, Hoffmann und Campe, 1967. 271 pp.
Woitzik, Karl-Heinz. *Die Auslands-Aktivitat der Sowjetisch-Besetzten Zone Deutschlands.* Mainz, V. Hase und Koehler Verlag, 1967. 283 pp.

## Hungary
Laszlo, E. *The Communist Ideology in Hungary: Handbook for Basic Research.* New York, Humanities Press, 1967.
Tökés, Rudolph L. *Béla Kun and the Hungarian Soviet Republic.* New York, Praeger, 1967. 292 pp.

## North Korea
Cho, M. Y. *Die Entwicklung der Beziehungen Zwischen Peking und P'yongyang 1949-1967.* Weisbaden, O. Harrassowitz, 1967. 175 pp.
Suh, Dae-sook. *The Korean Communist Movement 1918-1948.* Princeton, N. J., Princeton University Press, 1967. 406 pp.

## Poland
Bromke, Adam. *Poland's Politics: Idealism vs. Realism.* Cambridge, Mass., Harvard University Press, 1967. 304 pp.

## Rumania
Fischer-Galati, Stephen. *The New Rumania: From People's Democracy to Socialist Republic.* Cambridge, Mass., M.I.T. Press, 1967. 126 pp.
Montias, John M. *Economic Development in Communist Rumania.* Cambridge, Mass., M.I.T. Press, 1967. 377 pp.

## Union of Soviet Socialist Republics
Aboltin, V. I. (ed.). *Mezhdunarodnyi Ezhegodnik. Politika i ekonomika.* Moscow, Politizdat, 1967. 320 pp.
————.*Politika gosudarstv i razoruzheniie.* Moscow, Nauka,1967.
————.*Sotsialisticheskaia revolutsia i sovremennyi kapitalizm.* Moscow, Mysl, 1967.
*Aktualnyie ekonomicheskiie problemy kommunisticheskovo stroitelstva.* USSR, Minsk, 1967.
Alliluyeva, Svetlana: *Twenty Letters to a Friend.* New York, Harper & Row, 1967, 246 pp.
Ami, Ben. *Between Hammer and Sickle.* Philadelphia, Jewish Publication Society of America, 1967. 307 pp.
Anderson, Thornton. *Russian Political Thought: An Introduction.* Ithaca, N. Y., Cornell University Press, 1967. 444 pp.
Armstrong, John. *Ideology, Politics and Government in the Soviet Union.* New York, Frederick A. Praeger, 1967. 173 pp.
Avrich, Paul. *The Russian Anarchists.* Princeton, N. J., Princeton University Press, 1967. 303 pp.
Blinov, L. P. *Effektivnost kapitalnykh vlozhenii v selskoe khoziaistvo.* USSR, Kazan, 1967. 147 pp.
Bor, Mikhail. *Aims and Methods of Soviet Planning.* New York, International Publishers, 1967. 255 pp.
Brezhnev, Leonid Iliich. *Piatdesiat let velikikh pobed sotsializma.* Moscow, 1967. 40 pp.
Brzezinski, Zbigniew K. *Ideology and Power in Soviet Politics.* New York, Frederick A. Praeger, 1967. 291 pp.
————. *The Soviet Bloc: Unity and Conflict* (rev. and enl. ed.), Cambridge, Mass., Harvard University Press, 1967. 599 pp.
Bunyan, James. *The Origin of Forced Labor in the Soviet State, 1917-1921.* Stanford, the Hoover Institution, 1967. 276 pp.
Carr, E. H. *The Bolshevik Revolution 1917-1923.* New Orleans, Pelican, 1967.

Chambre, Henri. *Union Soviétique et développement économique.* Paris, Aubier-Montaigne, 1967. 430 pp.

Conolly, Violet. *Beyond the Urals: Economic Development in Soviet Asia.* New York, Oxford University Press, 1967. 420 pp.

Conquest, Robert (ed.). *The Politics of Ideas in the USSR (1967 Annual).* New York, Frederick A. Praeger, 1968. 175 pp.

————.(ed.). *Industrial Workers in the USSR.* New York, Frederick A. Praeger, 1967. 203 pp.

Daniel, Norman. *Marx and Soviet Reality.* Chester Springs, Pa., Dufour, 1967.

Daniels, Robert V. *Red October: The Bolshevik Revolution of 1917.* New York, Scribners, 1967. 269 pp.

Deutscher, Isaac. *Stalin: A Political Biography.* (2nd rev. ed.), London and New York, Oxford University Press, 1967. 661 pp.

————. *The Unfinished Revolution: Russia 1917-1967.* Oxford, Oxford University Press. 1967. 115 pp.

*Dokumenty i materialy po razvitiiu sovetsko-polskikh otnoshenii,* Volume 5. Moscow, Nauka, 1967. 612 pp.

Dragilev, M. S. Mokhov, N. T. and Kashutin, P. A. *Sovremennyie voprosy politicheskoi ekonomii kapitalizma,* Moscow, Vysshaia shkola, 1967. 424 pp.

*Ekonomicheskaia zhizn SSSR.* (2 volumes, 2nd ed.), Moscow, Sovetskaia entsyklopedia, 1967. Vol. 1, 439 pp., Vol. 2, 441 pp.

Ellenstein, Jean. *La Révolution des Révolutions—A propos de l'histoire de la révolution soviétique.* Paris, Ed. Sociales, 1967.

Eudin, Xenia J. and Slusser, R. M. (eds.). *Soviet Foreign Policy, 1928-1934.* (Vol. 2). University Park, Pennsylvania State University Press, 1967.

Farnsworth, Beatrice. *William C. Bullitt and the Soviet Union.* Bloomington, Indiana University Press, 1967. 244 pp.

Fay, Victor (ed.). *La Révolution d'Octobre et le Mouvement ouvrière européen.* Paris, E.D.I., 1967. 231 pp.

Feiwel, George R. *The Soviet Quest for Economic Efficiency.* New York, Frederick A. Praeger, 1967. 420 pp.

Ferro, Marc. *La Révolution de 1917. La Chute du tsarisme et les origines d'Octobre.* Paris, Flammarion, 1967. 606 pp.

Field, Mark. *Soviet Socialized Medicine.* New York, Free Press, 1967. 231 pp.

Fischer, George (ed.). *Science and Ideology in Soviet Society.* New York, Atherton, 1967. 176 pp.

Flechtheim, Ossip K. *Bolschewismus 1917-1967. Von der Weltrevolution zum Sowjetimperium.* Wien/Frankfurt, Europa Verlag, 1967. 255 pp.

Fletcher, William C., and Strover, Anthony J. (eds.). *Religion and Search for New Ideals in the USSR.* New York, Frederick A. Praeger, 1967. 135 pp.

Fomin, V. G. *Biudzhet vremeni nauchnovo rabotnika.* Moscow, Nauka, 1967.

Foner, Philip S. *The Bolshevik Revolution: Its Impact on American Radicals, Liberals and Labor.* (A Documentary Study.) New York International Publishers, 1967. 304 pp.

Frachon, Bénôit. *Léopoée d'un peuple maitre de son destin. L'ascension de l'Union Soviétique et ses causes.* Paris, Ed. du Pavillon, 1967. 50 pp.

Frankland, Mark. *Khrushchev.* New York, Stein and Day, 1967. 213 pp.

Garaudy, Roger. *Karl Marx.* New York, International Publishers, 1967. 223 pp.

Gehlen, Michael P. *The Politics of Co-existence: Soviet Methods and Motives.* Bloomington, Indiana University Press, 1967. 334 pp.

Getman, V. S. and Kurochkina, O. I. (eds.). *Ob Oktiabrskoi revolutsii,* Moscow, Politizdat, 1967. 319 pp.

Getzler, Israel. Martov: *The Political Biography of a Russian Social Democrat.* Cambridge, Cambridge University Press, 1967. 246 pp.

Ginzburg, Eugenia Semionovna. *Journey into the Whirlwind.* New York, Harcourt, Brace and World, 1967. 418 pp.

Grey, Ian. *The First Fifty Years: Soviet Russia 1917-1967.* New York, Coward McCann, 1967. 558 pp.

Griffith, William E. *Sino-Soviet Relations, 1964-1965.* Cambridge, Mass., M.I.T. Press, 1967. 504 pp.

Gruber, Helmut. *International Communism in the Era of Lenin.* Ithaca, New York, Cornell University Press, 1967, 512 pp.

Hartl, Hans and Werner, Marx. *Fünfzig Jahre Sowjetische Deutschlandpolitik.* Bopparch, Harald Boldt Verlag, 1967.

Hendel, Samuel (ed.). *The Soviet Crucible 1917-1967.* Princeton, N. J., Van Nostrand, 1967. 458 pp.

Hingley, Ronald. *Russian Writers and Society.* New York, McGraw-Hill, 1967. 256 pp.

Iakovlev, A. N. *Ideologiia amerikanskoi "imperii".* Moscow, Mysl, 1967. 463 pp.

Institute of Marxism-Leninism attached to the CPSU CC. *K. Marx, F. Engels, and Revolutionary Russia* (K. Marks, F. Engels i revolutsionnaia Rossiia). Moscow, Politizdat, 1967, 816 pp.

Juviler, Peter H. and Morton, Henry (eds.). *Soviet Policy Making.* New York, Frederick A. Praeger, 1967. 274 pp.

Kahn, Jean-Francois and Durand, Pierre. *Tout commence à Petrograd.* Paris, Ed. Fayard, 1967.

Karcz, J. F. (ed.). *Soviet and East European Agriculture.* Berkeley, University of California Press, 1967. 445 pp.

Kaser, Michael (ed.). *Soviet Affairs: Number Four.* New York, Oxford University Press, 1967.

Katkov, George. *Russia 1917: the February Revolution.* New York, Harper and Row, 1967. 489 pp.

Kolkowicz, Roman. *The Soviet Military and the Communist Party.* Princeton, N. J., Princeton University Press. 1967. 429 pp.

Kool, Fritz and Oberlander, Erwin (eds.). *Arbeiterdemokratie oder Parteidiktatur.* Freiburg, Walter Verlag, 1967.

Kovalenko, D. A. (ed.). *Sovety v pervyi god proletarskoi diktatury. Oktiabr 1917—Noiabr 1918.* Moscow, Nauka, 1967. 419 pp.

*KPSS o profsoiuzakh.* Moscow, Profizdat, 1967. 665 pp.

Kroll, Hans. *Lebenserinncrungen eines Botschafters.* Cologne/Berlin, Keipenheuer und Witsch, 1967. 611 pp.

Krotkov, Yury. *I am From Moscow: A View of the Russian Miracle.* New York, E. P. Dutton, 1967. 213 pp.

Laloy, Jean. *Le Socialisme de Lénine.* Paris, Desclée de Brouwer, 1967. 319 pp.

Laquer, Walter. *The Fate of the Revolution: Interpretations of Soviet History.* London, Weidenfeld Nicolson, 1967. 216 pp.

Laski, Harold J. *"The Communist Manifesto": An Introduction with the Original Text and Prefaces by Marx and Engels.* New York, Pantheon, 1967. 179 pp.

Laszlo, Ervin. *Philosophy in the Soviet Union:* A Survey of the Mid-Sixties. New York, Frederick A. Praeger, 1967. 208pp.

Lebeel, A. I. and Schulz, H. E. (eds.). *Who's Who in the USSR 1965-1967.* Munich, Olderbourg, 1967. 1189 pp.

*V. I. Lenin i sovetskiie vooruzhonnyie sily.* Moscow, Voienizdat, 1967. 448 pp.

Lewytzkyj, B. *Die Kommunistische Partei der Sowjetunion.* Stuttgart, Ernst Klett, 1967. 312 pp.

. *Die Rote Inquisition: Die Geschichte der Sowjetischen Sicherheitsdienste.* Frankfurt, Societats-Verlag, 1967. 395 pp.

Lockhart. R. H. Bruce and Keep, John. *The Two Revolutions: An Eye-Witness Account of Russia, 1917.* London, The Bodley Head, 1967. 144 pp.

Lyons, Eugene. *Workers' Paradise Lost: 50 Years of Soviet Communism: A Balance Sheet.* New York. Funk and Wagnalls, 1967. 387 pp.

Maslow, P. P. *Sotsiologia i statistika.* Moscow, Statistika, 1967. 334 pp.

Matskevich, V. V. *Sotsialisticheskoie pereustroistvo selskovo khoziaistva.* Moscow, Znanie, 1967. 62 pp.

Mazour, Anatole G. *Soviet Economic Development, Operation Outstrip: 1921-1965.* Princeton, N. J., Van Nostrand, 1967. 191 pp.

McNeal, R. H. (comp.). *Stalin's Works: An Annotated Bibliography.* Stanford, Hoover Institution on War, Revolution and Peace, 1967.

Mchedlov, M. P. *Evolutsia sovremennovo katolitsyzma.* Moscow, 1967.

*Metodologicheskie osnovy ekonomicheskoi otsenki zemli.* Moscow, Ekonomika, 1967. 200 pp.

Mickiewicz, Ellen Propper. *Soviet Political Schools: the Communist Party Adult-Instruction System.* New Haven, Yale University Press, 1967. 190 pp.

*Mir sotsialiszma v tsyfrakh i faktakh,* 1966. Moscow, Politizdat, 1967. 144 pp.

Moscow Institute of the International Workers' Movement. *Velikii Oktiabr i mirovoi revolutsionnyi protsess (50 let borby rabochevo klassa no glave revolutsionnykh sil sovremennoi epokhi).* Moscow, Politizdat, 1967. 464 pp.

Moshensky, M. G. *Marxova teoria pribavochnoi stoimosti i sovremennost.* Moscow, Znanie, 1967. 48 pp.

Munby, Lionel M. and Weingermann, Ernst. *Marxism and History.* London, Lawrence and Wishart, 1967. 62 pp.

Nettl, J. P. *The Soviet Achievement 1917-1967.* New York, Harcourt, Brace and World, 1967. 288 pp.

Pantskhava, I. D. *Chelovek i ievo zhizn i bessmertiie.* Moscow, 1967.

Payne, Robert. *The Fortress.* New York, Simon and Schuster, 1967. 448 pp.

Pearlstien, Edward (ed.). *Revolution in Russia!* As Reported by the N. Y. Tribune and the N. Y. Herald, 1894-1921. New York, Viking Press, 1967. 297 pp.

Perrault, Gilles. *L'Orchestre rouge.* Pars, A Fayard, 1967.

Planty-Bonjour, Guy. *The Categories of Dialectical Materialism: Contemporary Sovet Ontology.* New York, Frederick A. Praeger, 1967. 182 pp.

Pomeroy, William J. *Half a Century of Socialism: Soviet Life in the Sixties.* New York, International Publishers, 1967. 125 pp.

Rauch, George von. *A History of Soviet Russia.* New York, Frederick A. Praeger, 1967 (rev. ed.). 530 pp.

Reed, John. *Ten Days that Shook the World.* New York, International Publishers, 1967.

*Reshenia partii i pravitelstva po khoziaistvennym voprosam. 1917-1967.* Moscow, Politizdat, 1967.

Rodionov, P. A. *Kollektivnost–vysshyi printsyp partiinovo rukovodstva.* Moscow, Political Literature, 1967. 285 pp.

Romensky, Serge. *L'URSS à 50 ans, les révisionistes conservateurs.* Paris, Editions du Seuil, 1967.

Rosenberg, Arthur. *A History of Bolshevism from Marx to the First Five Years' Plan.* New York, Doubleday, 1967, 282 pp.

Royal Institute of International Affairs. *The Impact of the Russian Revolution: The Influence of Bolshevism on the World Outside Russia 1917-1967.* New York, Oxford University Press, 1967. 357 pp.

Salisbury, Harrison (and staff of the *New York Times*). *The Soviet Union: The Fifty Years.* New York, Harcourt, Brace and World, 1967. 484 pp.

Schaffer, H. G. (ed.). *The Communist World; Marxist and Non-Marxist Views.* New York, Appleton-Century-Crofts, 1967. 558 pp.

Schapiro, Leonard. *The Government and Politics of the Soviet Union.* (rev. ed.). London, Hutchinson University Library, 1967 176 pp.

—— and Reddaway, Peter (eds.). *Lenin: The Man, the Theorist, the Leader.* New York, Frederick A. Praeger, 1967. 317 pp.

Sharpe, Myron E. (ed.). *Reform of Soviet Economic Management.* White Plains, N. Y., International Arts and Sciences Press, 1967.

Shukman, Harold. *Lenin and the Russian Revolution.* New York, Putnam, 1967. 224 pp.

Simmonds, George W. (ed.). *Soviet Leaders.* New York, Crowell, 1967. 405 pp.

Smith, Edward Ellis. *The Young Stalin: the Early Years of an Elusive Revolutionary.* New York, Farrar, Strauss and Giroux, 1967. 470 pp.

Soria, Robert. *Les 300 Jours de la Révolution russe.* Paris, Ed. Robert Laffont, 1967.

Stokke, Baard Richard. *Soviet and Eastern European Trade and Aid in Africa.* New York, Frederick A. Praeger, 1967. 326 pp.

Stroyen, W. B. *Communist Russia and the Russian Orthodox Church.* Washington, Catholic University of America Press, 1967. 161 pp.

Struve, Nikita. *Christians in Contemporary Russia.* New York, Scribners, 1967. 464 pp.

Tatu, Michel. *Le pouvoir en URSS de Khrouchtchev à la direction collective.* Paris, Editions Bernard Grasset, 1967. 604 pp.

Taubman, William. *The View From Lenin Hills.* New York, Coward-McCann, 1967. 249 pp.

Tompkins, S. R. *The Truimph of Bolshevism.* Norman, Okla., University of Oklahoma Press, 1967. 331 pp.

Toynbee, Arnold J. (ed.). *The Impact of the Russian Revolution, 1917-1967.* Oxford, Oxford University Press, 1967. 357 pp.

Treadgold, Donald W. (ed.). *Soviet and Chinese Communism: Similarities and Differences.* Seattle, University of Washington Press, 1967. 452 pp.

Trotsky, Leon. *Stalin: An Appraisal of the Man and His Influence.* New York, Stein and Day, 1967. 516 pp.

Velikovich, L. N. *Krizis sovremennovo katolitsyzma.* Moscow, 1967.

Williams, Albert Rhys. *Through the Russian Revolution.* New York, Monthly Review Press, 1967. 311 pp.

Wolfe, Bertram D. *The Bridge and the Abyss.* New York, Frederick A. Praeger, 1967. 180 pp.

Wynne, Greville. *The Man From Moscow.* London, Hutchinson and Company, 1967. 222 pp.

Yegorov, V. N. (ed. and collector). *Kratkii bibliograficheskii spravochnik, 1964-1966.* Moscow, Mezhdunarodnyie otnosheniia, 1967.

Zaleski, Eugene. *Planning Reforms in the Soviet Union, 1962-1966.* Chapel Hill, University of North Carolina Press, 1967. 203 pp.

Zeitlin, I. M. *Marxism: A Reexamination.* Princeton, N. J., Van Nostrand, 1967. 170 pp.

## Democratic Republic of Vietnam

Bain, Chester. *Vietnam: The Roots of Conflict.* New Jersey, Prentice Hall, 1967. 184 pp.

Buttinger, Joseph. *Vietnam: A Dragon Embattled.* New York, Frederick A. Praeger, 1967.

Fall, Bernard. *Last Reflections on a War.* New York, Doubleday, 1967.

———. (translator). *Ho Chi Minh on Revolution: Selected Writings.* New York, Frederick A. Praeger, 1967. 389 pp.

Giap, Vo Nguyen, *Big Victory, Great Task.* New York, Frederick A. Praeger, 1967. 120 pp.

Lacouture, Jean, *Ho Chi Minh.* Paris, Les Editions de Seuil, 1967.

Rupen, Robert and Farrell, Robert, *Vietnam and the Sino-Soviet Dispute.* New York, Frederick A. Praeger, 1967. 120 pp.

Swearingreñ Rodger and Hammond, Rolph, *Communism in Vietnam.* Chicago, American Bar Association, 1967. 195 pp.

Zagoria, Donald S. *Vietnam Triangle.* New York, Pegasus, Division of Western Publishing Company, 1967. 286 pp.

## Yugoslavia

Campbell, John E. *Tito's Separate Road: America and Yugoslavia in World Politics.* New York, Harper and Row, 1967. 180 pp.

Djordjevic, Jovan. *La Yugoslavie.* Paris, Librairie Général de Droit, 1967. 482 pp.

## Communist Europe—General

Blanc. A., George, P., and Smotkine, H. *Les Républiques socialistes d'Europe centrale.* Paris, Press Universitaires de France (PUF), 1967. 295 pp.

Daim, Wilfred. *Der Vatikan und der Osten kommentar und Dokumentation.* Vienna, Frankfurt,

Zurich, Europe Verlag, 1967.

Domes, Alfred (ed.). *Osteuropa und die Hoffnung auf Freiheit.* Cologne, Verlag Wissenschaft und Politik, 1967. 269 pp.

Ionescu, Ghita. *L'Avenir Politique de l' Europe Orientale.* Paris, S.E.D.E.I.S., 1967. 387 pp.
    *The Politics of the European Communist States.* New York, Praeger, 1967. 303 pp.

Lembeig, Eugen. *Reformation im kommunimus?* Stuttgart, E. Klett Verlag, 1967.

Starr, Richard. *The Communist Regimes of Eastern Europe.* Stanford, Hoover Institution on War, Revolution and Peace, 1967. 387 pp.

Wolff, R. L. *The Balkans in Our Time.* New York, Norton, 1967. 618 pp.

Zsolnay, Vilmos v. *Die Wissenschaft in Osteuropa.* Mainz, v. Hase und Koehler, 1967. 230 pp.

## NON-RULING COMMUNIST PARTIES

### Africa

Attwood, William. *The Reds and the Blacks.* New York, Harper and Row, 1967. 341 pp.

Hooker, James R. *Black Revolutionary: George Padmore's Path from Communism to Pan-Africanism.* New York, Praeger, 1967. 168 pp.

Hunter, Guy. *The Best of Both Worlds? A Challenge on Development Policies in Africa.* New York, Oxford University Press, 1967. 132 pp.

Stahn, Eberhard. *Kommunistische Modelle für Afrika? Ghana und Guinea.* Hannover, Verlag für Literatur und Zeitgeschenen, 1967. 192 pp.

Taylor, Sidney (ed.). *Reuters' Guide to the Contemporary History of Emergent Africa and its Leaders. The New Africans.* New York, G. P. Putnam's Sons, 1967. 504 pp.

### Asia

Allworth, Edward. *Central Asia: A Century of Russian Rule.* New York, Columbia University Press, 1967. 552 pp.

Australian Institute of Political Science. *Communism in Asia.* Sidney, Angus and Robertson, 1967. 206 pp.

Grant, Bruce. *Indonesia.* Baltimore, Penguin Books, 1967. 247 pp.

Gulick, J. M. *Malaysia and its Neighbors.* New York, Barnes and Noble, 1967. 194 pp.

Hughes, John. *Indonesian Upheaval.* New York, David McKay, 1967. 304 pp.

Kavic, Loren J. *India's Quest for Security.* Berkeley, University of California Press, 1967. 263 pp.

Leifer, Michael. *Cambodia: The Search for Security.* New York, Frederick A. Praeger, 1967.

Masani, M. R. *The Communist Party of India.* Bharatiya Vidya, 1967.

Milne, R. S. *Government and Politics in Malaysia.* New York, Houghton Miflin, 1967. 259 pp.

O'Ballance, Edgar. *Malaya: The Communist Insurgent War, 1948-1960.* England, Faber and Faber, 1967.

Rudolph, Lloyd and Suzanne. *The Modernity of Tradition: Political Development in India.* Chicago, University of Chicago Press, 1967. 306 pp.

Scalapino, Robert A. *The Japanese Communist Movement, 1920-1966.* Berkeley, University of California Press, 1967. 412 pp.

Vittachi, Tarzie. *The Fall of Sukarno.* New York, Frederick A. Praeger, 1967. 191 pp.

Ward, Robert E. *Japan's Political System.* Englewood Cliffs, N. J., Prentice-Hall, 1967. 126 pp.

Wilmott, William E. *The Chinese in Cambodia.* Vancouver, University of British Columbia, 1967.

### Europe

Cammett, John M. *Antonio Gramsci and the Origins of Italian Communism.* Stanford, Stanford University Press, 1967. 306 pp.

Dulles, Eleanor Lansing. *Berlin: The Wall is Not Forever.* Chapel Hill, N. C., University of North Carolina Press, 1967. 245 pp.

Evans, Robert H. *Coexistence: Communism and its Practice in Bologna, 1945-1965.* Notre Dame, Indiana, University of Notre Dame Press, 1967. 225 pp.

Fejtö, François. *The French Communist Party and the Crisis of International Communism.* Cambridge, Mass., M.I.T. Press, 1967. 225 pp.

Gorz, André. *Le Socialisme Difficile.* Paris, Seuil, 1967. 249 pp.

Hodgson, John H. *Communism in Finland: A History and Interpretation.* Princeton, N. J., Princeton University Press, 1967. 261 pp.

König, Helmut. *Lenin und der Italienische Sozialismus, 1915-1921.* Cologne, Böhlau Verlag, 1967. 240 pp.

Planck, Charles R. *The Changing Status of German Reunification in Western Diplomacy, 1955-66.* Baltimore, Johns Hopkins University Press, 1967. 65 pp.

Renard, Claude. *Octobre 1917 et le mouvement ouvrier belge.* Bruxelles, Editions de la Fondation Jacquemothe, 1967. 132 pp.

Rochet, Waldeck. *Qu'est-ce qu-un Révolutionnaire dans la France de Notre Temps?* Paris, Ed. Sociales, 1967. 110 pp.

Tarrow, Sidney G. *Peasant Communism in Southern Italy.* New Haven, Yale University Press, 1967. 389 pp.

Trotsky, Leon. *Le Mouvement Communiste en France (1919-1939).* Paris, Ed. de Minuit, 1967. 724 pp.

Volensky, M. S. *"Vostochnaia" politika FRG.* Moscow, Nauka, 1967. 427 pp.

Weber, Hermann (ed.). *Völker hört die Signale: Der deutsche kommunismus, 1916-1966.* Munich, Deutscher Taschenbuch Verlag, 1967. 411 pp.

Willard, Claude. *Socialisme et Communisme Français.* Paris, Colin, 1967. 158 pp.

## Latin America

Aguilar, Luis E. *Marxism in Latin America.* New York, Knopf, 1967. 271 pp.

Debray, Régis. *Revolution in the Revolution?* New York, MR Press, 1967. 126 pp.

Guevara, Che. *Che Guevara Speaks.* New York, Merit, 1967. 159 pp.

Jagan, Cheddi. *The West on Trial: My Fight for Guyana's Freedom.* London, Michael Joseph, 1967. 127 pp.

Lipsett, Seymour Martin and Solari, Aldo. *Elites in Latin America.* New York, Oxford University Press, 1967. 531 pp.

## GENERAL ON COMMUNISM

Allen, R. V. *et al. Democracy and Communism, Theory and Action.* Princeton, N. J., Van Nostrand, 1967. 520 pp.

Baerwald, Helmut and Scheffler, Herbert. *Partisanen ohne Gewehr.* Köln, Verlag Wissenschaft und Politik, 1967. 139 pp.

Bennett, E. M. *Polycentrism: Growing Dissidence in the Communist Bloc?* Pullman, Washington, Washington State University Press, 1967. 63 pp.

Braunthal, Julius. *History of the International, Vol II: 1914-1943.* New York, Praeger, 1967. 596 pp.

Davis, H. B. *Nationalism and Socialism.* New York, Monthly Review Press, 1967. 258 pp.

Dinerstein, Herbert S. *Intervention Against Communism.* Baltimore, Johns Hopkins Press, 1967. 53 pp.

Ebenstein, W. *Today's Isms.* Englewood Cliffs, N. J., Prentice-Hall, 1967 (5th ed.). 262 pp.

Kallai, Gyula. *Problems of the World Communist Movement and the International Political Scene.* Prague, Peace and Socialism Publishers, 1967.

Lachs, J. *Marxist Philosophy.* Chapel Hill, University of North Carolina Press, 1967. 327 pp.

Lichtheim, George. *The Concept of Ideology and Other Essays.* New York, Vintage, 1967. 327 pp.

Lobkowicz, N. (ed.). *Marx and the Western World.* Notre Dame, Indiana, Notre Dame University Press, 1967. 444 pp.

McNeal, Robert (ed.). *International Relations Among Communists.* New York, Prentice-Hall Spectrum, 1967. 181 pp.

Meyer, A. G. *Communism.* New York, Random House, 1967 (3rd ed.). 237 pp.

Meyer, F. S. *The Moulding of Communists.* New York, Harcourt, Brace and World, 1967. 214 pp.

Petrovic, Gajo. *Marx in the Mid-Twentieth Century.* New York, Doubleday, 1967. 237 pp.

Ponomarev, B. N. *et al. World Revolutionary Movement of the Working Class.* Moscow, Progress, 1967. 483 pp.

Prpic, G. J. *Fifty Years of World Communism, 1917-1967.* Cleveland, Ohio, John Carroll University, 1967. 180 pp.

Ramundo, B. A. *Peaceful Coexistence: International Law in the Building of Communism.* Baltimore, Johns Hopkins University Press, 1967.

Sanger, Robert Harlakender. *Insurgent Era: New Patterns of Political, Economic, and Social Revolution.* Washington D. C., Potomac Books, 1967. 231 pp.

Shaffer, H. G. (ed.). *The Communist World.* New York, Appleton, 1967. 558 pp,

Tanham, G. K. *Communist Revolutionary Warfare.* New York, Praeger, 1967. 166 pp.

INDEXES

Aaltonen, Aimo, 200, 203
Aarons, A., 21
Aarons, Eric, 21, 26; quoted, 23
Aarons, Laurie, 21, 25, 179, 768
Abakumov, Viktor A., 986
Abboud, Ibrahim, 537, 541
Abdin, Ismail Hussein, 697
Abdul Rahman, Tunku, see Rahman, Tunku Abdul
Abdul Razak, Tun, see Razak, Tun Abdul
Abdullah, Said Salim, 748
Abid, Said, 13
Aboukoss, Abdul Rahman, 748
Abrahantes, José, 136
Acevedo, Rogelio, 144
Acevedo Gautier, Ivelisse, 189
Acharya, Janardan, 416
Acheson, Dean, 578
Acosta, Angelina, 726
Acosta, Armando, 139
Acosta, Isabel, 853
Acosta, Ricardo Mario, 625
Acosta Salas, Raúl, 468
Acuña, Juan Pablo, 625
Acuña, Juan Vitalio, 136
Aczél, György, 282, 283
Adenauer, Konrad: quoted, 969
Adhikari, Bharat Mohan, 414
Adhikari, D. P., 414
Adhikari, G., 297
Adhikari, Man Mohan, 414
Adjitorop, Jusuf, 309, 310, 317; quoted, 310
Adriazola Veizaga, David, 44
Afana, Osende, 75
Agosta, José C., 463
Agosti, Héctor Pablo, 16
Aguero, Pedro, 463
Aguirre, Pedro, 92
Ahidjo, Ahmadou, 75
Ahmad, Munir, 559
Ahmad, Musa, 383
Ahmad, Z. A., 297
Ahmed, Kaid, 14
Ahrens, Dietmar, 239
Ahrens, Franz, 235
Aidit, Dipa Nusantara, 309, 318; quoted, 898, 900-906
    passim; cited, 900, 905, 908, 917
Aizpurua, Baltazar, 732
Ajtai, Miklos, 282, 285
Akhmatova, Anna, 985, 986
Akhundov, Velii, 582
Albertz, Heinrich, 241
Albinowski, Stanislaw: cited, 491
Alcaraz, Antonio, 463
Aldana, Carlos, 278, 279, 281, 767, 1057
Alef-Bolkowiak, Gustav, 740
Alenius, Ele, 201, 204, 206, 768; quoted, 204
Aleo, Ibih, 666
Alexander, Hal, 21
Alexander, Robert J.: cited, 273
Alexander, William, 244
Alexandrov, S., 589

Alexis, B., 259
Alexis, Jacques Stéphen, 273
Ali, Altab, 457
Ali, Aruna Asaf, 726, 820
Ali, Bachir Hadj, 12, 13
Ali, Nazim, 294, 324, 326, 327, 767; quoted, 326
Alia, Ramiz, 3, 32, 33; quoted, 4
Alicata, Mario, 336
Alleg, Henri, 12, 12n; quoted, 13, 14
Allende, Salvador, 92, 94, 159, 768
Alliluieva, Svetlana, 187, 592
Ally, Joseph, 270
Ally, Yacoob, 270
Ally, Zaman, 270
Almeida, Juan, 136, 139, 144, 760
Almeyda, Clodomiro, 92, 94, 159
Almeyra, Guillermo Marcello, 20
Alonso, Victor, 463
Alonso de Vega, Camilo (Camilo Alonso Vega), 529,
    961, 963
Altamirano, Carlos, 94, 159
Altan, Cetin, 576-77, 577n
Altenkirch, Ernst, 223
Altesor, Alberto, 624
Alurralde, Antonio, 43
Alvarado, Oscar, 475
Alvarado Monzón, Bernardo, 263, 266, 268, 1068
Alvarado Palma, Nancy, 854
Alvarez, Ernesto, 853
Alvarez, Santiago, 529
Alvio, Ernesto, 854
Amatya, Tulsi Lal, 414, 415, 416
Amaya Quintana, Enrique, 475, 1074
Amazonas, João, 49
Ambrose, Edgar, 270
Amendola, Giorgio, 336, 337, 342
Ament, Erich, 223
al-Amine, Hassan Mohammed, 697
Amir, Izzeddin Ali, 537
Amphorn Souvannabon, 567
An, Keo, 67
Anderlini, Luigi, 768
Andersson, Britta, 542
Andersson, Freddy-Gilbert-Nils, 557
Andersson, Gösta, 542
Andersson, Inga-Lill, 542
Andersson, Johan, 542
Andersson, Kristin, 295
Andersson, Sture, 549
Andreen, Andrea, 726
Andreev, Georgi A., 697
Andriamanjato, Richard, 697
Andropov, Iurii, 175, 224, 581, 584, 770, 1073;
    abridged text of his report on guarding Soviet
    security, 992-95
Angelez Bautista, Hipólito, 400
Angenfort, Jupp, 234
Anh, Hoang, 639, 641
Anian, Pedro, 853
al-Ansari, Sharif, 373
Ansart, Gustave, 208, 219

Antokolsky, Pavel: text of his letter to Demichev on Solzhenitsyn case, 1002
Antonio, Nelson, 189
Antonov, I.: quoted, 315-16
Anzai Kuraji, 357
Apostol, Gheorghe, 508, 510
Apostolos, Lefteris, 258
Appel, Gotfred, 180, 184
Appuhamy, M. K. Arnolis, 82, 86
Apró, Antal, 282, 285; cited, 290
Aptheker, Bettina, see Kurzweil, Bettina Aptheker
Aptheker, Herbert, 609, 610, 618
Aquila, Mariano, 278
Aquinas, Saint Thomas, 588
Aragon, Louis, 209
Araoz, Angel, 16
Arata, Alfonso, 475
Araujo, Valentin, 854
Araya, Bernardo, 94, 442
Araya Bori, Raúl, 96
Arbenz, Jacobo, 263, 267
Archimède, Gerty, 259
Ardatovsky, V., 533
Arellano, Jorge Isaac, 194, 195
Arenas, Jacobo, 123
Arévalo, Juan José, 263
Arévalo, Oscar, 16, 225
Arévalo de Roche, Julia, 624
Arias Gomex, Jorge, 197
Arif, Abdul Rahman, 325, 325n, 688-89, 1081
Arismendi, Rodney, 96, 154, 159, 179, 624-28 passim, 760, 763, 767, 1067, 1082; quoted, 626, 627
Ariyaratnam, I. R., 82
Arjones, Armando, 16
Arnedo Alvarez, Gerónimo, 16
Artigas, José Gervasio, 1021
Artobolevsky, I. I., 735
Arviaca, Miguel, 853
Aryal, Nirmal, 416
Ashby, Dave, 250
Ask, Göte, 542
Aspilcueta, Teodoro, 476
Assad, Hafiz, 177
Astudillo, Oscar, 89
Atanassov, Georgi, 54
al-Atassi, Nureddin, 559, 660, 677, 1081
Ataturk, Kemal, 577
Atias, Waldo: quoted, 267
Atiyah, Samih, 559
Aucapan, Pastor: quoted, 95
Auersperg, Pavel, 170
Aung Gyi, Ko, 61
Aust, Ernst, 238
Avanesov, V. A., 993
Avila, Victor, 460
Avramov, Luchezar, 59
al-Awar, Amin, 373, 376
Awn, Edmond, 376
Axen, Hermann, 223, 230, 232, 1026
Aybar, Mehmet Ali, 576
Ayub Khan, Mohammad, 323, 455-59 passim

Azcarate, Manuel, 535
al-Azhari, Ismail, 59

Ba, Joseph Marie Ho Hue, 666, 679
Ba, Le Quang, 639
Ba Khet, see Thein Myint, Yebaw
Ba Thein Tin, Thakin, 61, 66; quoted, 60-65 passim, 117
Ba Tin, see Goshal, Yebaw
Ba Zan, Mahn, 60
Babel, Isaac, 986
Babiker, Tigani, 537; quoted, 538, 539, 540
Babuich, Edward, 662
Bacon, E. A., 21
Bacskai, Tamas, 697
Badawi, Ali, 742
Badner, Heinz, 697
Bagsik, Avelino (alias "Commander Zaragoza"), 480
Bahadur, Lall, 271; quoted, 271
Bahia, Sabino, 45
Bai, Huynh, 666
Baibakov, N. K., 321, 598
Bajalski, Risto: cited, 174
Bakarić, Vladimir, 681, 682
Bakdash, Khalid, 373, 376, 559, 560, 561, 565, 767; quoted, 560-64 passim
Bakker, Marcus, 417
Balaguer, Joaquin, 185, 187, 188
Balaram, N. E., 297
Balarezo Delta, Carlos, 476
Balbi, Selmar, 625
Balestri, Arturo, 345
Bálint, József, 283
Balladares, José, 89
Ballan, Dorothy, 623
Ballan, Sam, 623
Balló, István, 289; quoted, 289
Balluku, Beqir, 3, 7, 116, 1058
Balti, P., 330
Baltra, Alberto, 92; quoted, 785
Ban, Ly, 639
Banda, Michael, 251
Bandaranaike, S. W. R. D., 83
Bandaranaike, Mrs. Sirimavo R.D., 83, 85
Banfi, Arialdo, 740
Bang, Nguyen Luong, 639
Bangou, Henri, 259, 261
Bani, S. T., 522
Banidol, D., 393
Bannikov, Sergei, 584
Bao Dai, 855
Barbírek, František, 166n
Bari, Kazi Abdul, 457
Bârlădeanu, Alexandru, 508, 510; quoted, 510
Barna, Minaj, 748
Barr, Andrew, 224, 329, 767
Barreto, Francisco, 854
Barrientos, René, 159, 218
Barrios, Trino, 853
Barthe, Obdulio, 463
Baruch, Friedl, 421

al-Barzani, Mustafa, 325n
Basavapunniah, M., 298
al-Basha, Sulayman, 373
Bashir, Hamid Osman, 713
Basov, G.F., 742
Bassil, Edouard, 732
Bastimar, Zeki, *see* Demir, Yakub
Basu, Jyoti, 298, 300, 302
Batal, Georges (Salim), 373
Batista, Fulgéncio, 139, 853
Batista, Miguel, 45
Batta, Damdinneren Giyn, 660
Baude, Frank, 543, 547
Bautista, Federico, 477
Bautista Lajara, Juan, 190
Baxter, Joe, 20
al-Bazzaz, Abdul Rahman, 325n
Beaulieu, Claude, 222
Beeching, William, 77
Begin, Menachem, 921, 922
Bejar Rivera, Héctor, 474, 475; quoted, 475
Belal, Abdelasis, 409
Balaúnde Terry, Fernando, 467
Belazoug, Abdelaziz, 732
Belkacem, Chérif, 342
Bellorin, Aquiles, 854
Beltran Díaz, Héctor, 854
Ben Barka, Abdel Kader, 158
Ben Barka, El Mehdi, 158
Ben Bella, Ahmed, 12, 13, 14, 139, 158, 599
Ben Bella, Hadj, 14
Ben Gurion, David, 921, 922
Ben Sedik, Mahjoub, 409
Benavides, Jorge, 476
Benavides Caldas (Peruvian), 476
Benedek, Jenö, 742
Beneš, Jan, 171, 1078
Benhima, Mohammed, 409
Benítez, Julio, 94
Bentacour, Héctor, 625
Bento, Augusto, 45
Benzine, Abdelhamid, 12
Berg, Erik, 542
Berg, M. von: cited, 227
Berge, Reidar, 454
Bergeron, Régis, 221, 222
Bergstein, Jorge, 16
Beriya, Lavrentiy P., 986
Berkov, Alexandr, 697, 699
Berlinguer, Enrico, 336, 338, 342, 343, 344, 924; quoted,
     338; abridged text of report to Italian CP, 925-30
Bernal, Gerardo, 128
Bernal, John D., 697, 735, 736
Bernbaum, Maurice M., 840
Berndtsson, Nils, 542
Bertone, Franco: quoted, 172
Besrodnik, Felipe, 16
Besse, Guy, 208, 212, 213
Betancourt, Carlos (*alias* "Gerónimo"), 637
Betancourt, Rómulo, 629, 632, 637, 842, 843, 846,
     847, 850, 853, 854, 1003, 1004

Betinelli Taich, Adela, 726
Bettelhcim, Charles, 221
Betzog, Mario Hercules, 263
Bhagwat, Eknath, 297
Bhashani, Maulana A. H., 455-59 *passim*
Bhutto, Ali, 459
Bianco, Jesús María, 1005
Bilak, Vasil, 166n
Billoux, François, 208
Bin, Nguyen Dinh, 653
Binh, Nguyen Thanh, 639, 641
Binh, Mme. Nguyen Thi, 666, 667, 669
Binh, Tran Tu, 639, 639n
Biquard, Pierre, 735, 736
Birch, Reginald, 245-46, 246n
Biró, J.: cited, 290
Bischot, Chris, 421
Biszku, Béla, 219, 224, 282, 294, 1065; quoted, 294
Bitossi, Renato, 442, 706
Black, Carolyn, 610
Blackmer, Donald L. M.: cited, 336n
Blajovici, Petre, 510
Blanco, José, 624
Blanco Santano, Ángel, 503
Blas Manrique, Román, 396
Blaser, Frédéric, 551, 553
Bleier, Eduardo, 625
Bloice, Carl, 610
Blume, Isabelle, 442, 653, 696, 697, 700, 701, 703;
     quoted, 701, 703
Blume, Jean, 34, 36-37, 754
Bocaj, Sadik: cited, 4
Bocka, Vangjo: cited, 4
Bodiul, Ivan I., 582
Bodnăraş, Emil, 508, 510
Boehme, Hans: quoted, 227
Boeynants, Paul Vanden, 35
Boffa, Giuseppe, 340, 341, 343, 344
Bogado, Claixto, 463
Bogat, Ye., 588
Bognar, Josef, 736
Bogunović, Branko, 689
Bohning, Don: cited, 462
Boisel, Jules, 261
Boiter, A.: quoted, 587
Bokov, Georgi, 732; quoted, 56
Bolaños, Bolívar, 193
Boldrini, Arrigo, 740; quoted, 740
Bolívar, Simón, 762, 781, 1021, 1028; quoted, 1028
Bomani, Paul, 768
Bonev, Vladimir, 51
Bong Ki Chok, 390
Bong Ki Chok, Mme., 390
Bonnelly, Rafael, 185
Bonsdorff, Goran Eduard von, 697
Bora, Phani, 297
Borche, Carlos, 732
Borodin, Michael, 396
Bosch, Juan, 185
Bose, Niranjen, 303
Boukhali, Larbi, 12, 14-15; quoted, 15

Boumediène, Houari, 12, 13, 13n, 14, 158, 326, 342, 557
Bounbiend Sysourath, 371
Bound, M., 21
Bourdeaux, M.: cited, 590n
Bourguiba, Habib, 574, 575
Bourquia, Abdelsalam, 409
Boutelle, Paul, 621, 622
Bouvier-Ajam, Solange, 742
Boyd, John, 80
Branco, Lilian, 272
Bravo, Douglas, 629-37 *passim*, 840, 844, 845, 848, 849, 850, 858, 1068; quoted, 635-36
Braz, Marcel, 45
Brezhnev, Leonid I., 14, 55, 65, 174, 175, 176, 207, 224, 225, 226, 290, 291, 340, 490, 513, 534, 572, 580, 581, 584, 585, 586, 595, 598, 600, 601, 704, 753, 754, 755, 764-65, 766, 769, 824, 825, 831; 977, 994, 1026, 1034, 1057, 1058, 1060, 1061, 1064, 1067, 1070, 1073, 1075, 1078, 1082, 1085, 1092; quoted, 55, 755, 764, 765, 994; excerpts from speech on Soviet foreign policy, 965-67
--speech at Karlovy Vary conference, 755, 756; résumé, 755; text, 1034-42
Briceno, Rafael Antonio, 854
Briones Torres, José Ignacio, 732
Britto, K. A. E., 82
Britton, Floyd, 461, 462
Briu, Rochom, 666, 679
Brown, Freda, 21, 726
Brown, Mike, 618
Brown, Rap, 158
Brown, W. John, 21; quoted, 22
Brown, William J., 21
Bruera, Leopoldo, 624
Brugueras, Miguel, 758
Brunfaut, Emilienne, 727
Brzezinski, Zbigniew, 949; quoted, 949-50
Buch, Kaj, 181, 182
Buchwald, Gustavo von, 193
Buck, Tim, 77
Budinov, Ivan, 56, 59; quoted, 56
Budzislawski, Hermann, 735
Bufalini, Paolo, 336, 340
Buikis, Y. Y., 993
Bukharin, N. I., 586, 823
Bukovsky, Vladimir, 343, 593, 594, 996, 997; text of his plea at Moscow trial, 997-99
Bulgakov, Mikhail A., 590, 985, 986, 1002
Bulgaranov, Boyan, 51, 53; quoted, 54
Bulliard, Gérard, 555-58 *passim*; quoted, 555, 556, 557
Bunin, Ivan A., 985
Bunting, Brian Percy, 732
Burchett, Wilfred, 149
Burguillos (Venezuelan), 1004
Burhop, Eric H. S., 735
Burlatsky, F., 592
Burlet, Edwin, 551
Burnelle, Ernest, 34, 37, 767; quoted, 36
Burnham, L. F. S., 270

Burstein, D., 330
Buscayo, Bernabe (*alias* "Commander Dante"), 480
al-Bustani, Yussef Ismail, 697
Bustos, Ciro, 549
Butheau, Robert, 732
Butheau Guilbert, Marie, 732
Bylin, Gunnar, 547
Bystrický, Rudolf, 742, 743

Cabieses, Manuel, 90
Cabral, Amilcar, 518, 768
Cachutt Sahoudala, Manuel, 854
Cademartori, José, 89, 93; quoted, 93-94
Cahualga, Simón, 853
Caglayangil, Ihsan Sabri, 57, 58
Cako, Hito, 1058
Calcines, Ramón, 139
Caldera, Rafael, 633
Calderón, Alba, 192
Caleb, Enrique Semo, 396
Camacho, Justo, 853
Camara, Damantang, 697
Campos, Daniel, 42
Campos, Hugo, 463-66 *passim*
Campusano, Julieta, 89
Can, Dinh Thi, 639
Cancel, W. Valentin, 503
Canete, Agosto, 463
Cang, Truong, 73
Cannon, James P., 621
Cantero, Manuel, 89
Capievic, Jean, 219
Capile, Sebastiao, 501
Capo, Vito, 728
Caram, Fermin, 481
Carcani, Adil, 3
Cárdenas, Lazaro, 397, 697
Cardijn, Jozef, 35
Cardona Hoyes, José, 122
Cardona Padilla, Juan Pablo, 278
Carlberg, Anders, 547
Carmen Chávez, José del, 853
Carmichael, Stokely, 158, 160, 505, 761; quoted, 761
Carmichel, L., 21
Carmona, Alfredo, 853
Carmona, Donato, 853, 1004
Carneado, José Felipe, 161
Carnero Checa, Genaro, 476, 732
Carques, Freddy, *see* Carquéz, Freddy
Carquéz, Freddy, 636, 840, 850
Carranza, Julio: quoted, 137
Carrillo, Santiago, 59, 179, 210, 224, 494, 518, 529-35 *passim*, 1074, 1085, 1087; quoted, 533, 534
Carvalho, Apolonio de, 45
Carvalho, Benedito de, 49
Casablanca, Luis, 463
Casaroli, Agostino, 488
Casas, Raymond, 221
Casella, Alberto T., 697
Castano, Ciro, 123
Castellanos, Rubén, 460, 461; quoted, 461

Castelo Branco, Humberto, 45
Castilla Mas, Belarmino, 150, 157, 661
Castillejos Ortiz, Armando, 398
Castillo, Berto, 197
Castillo, Fabio, 197, 198, 199
Castillo, Raul, 280
Castillo Johnson, Leonardo, 264
Castillo Martínez, Heberto, 397, 398; quoted, 397
Castro, Alfredo, 45
Castro, Avelino, 122
Castro, Fidel, 30, 50, 72, 92, 94, 118, 127, 134, 136-
    61 passim, 190, 209, 217, 218, 220, 230, 242,
    266, 267, 268, 275, 279, 344, 352, 370, 398,
    399, 407, 465, 475, 554, 630, 633-34, 635,
    678, 737, 760-63 passim, 837-41 passim, 1066,
    1068, 1077, 1081, 1087; quoted, 42, 43, 136,
    137, 139-49 passim, 152, 154, 158, 625, 758n,
    760, 761
—speech on Cuban CP's conflict with CP of Venezuela,
    154, 268, 475, 633, 1066, 1068; text, 837-54
—See also Castroism, Castroists
Castro, Gustavo, 128, 1065
Castro, Raúl, 136, 139, 150, 156
Castro, Mrs. Raul, see Espín, Vilma
Castro Lavarello, Ángel, 476
Catala, Jean-Michel, 209
Cathala, Jean-Michel, see Catala, Jean-Michel
Cavalli, Carlo, 341
Cazola, Luisa Maria, 853
Ceauşescu, Nicolae, 37, 291, 411, 508-18 passim, 600,
    601, 754, 767, 959, 1066, 1068, 1070, 1074,
    1079, 1082, 1085, 1092, 1093; quoted, 508,
    509, 512-19 passim; excerpts from his article
    on role of Rumanian CP, 954-58
Celis, Alejo, 854
Centurión, Luis, 463
Cepeda Vargas, Manuel, 122, 123, 130
Cerda, Carlos, 94
Cerland, Sévère, 393
Cěrnik, Oldřich, 166, 166n, 168
Cerqueira, Benedicto, 706
Cerro, Severo, 16
Césaire, Aimé, 393, 394
Cesari, Victor, 853
Céspedes, Juan, 396
Chacón, Miller, 122
Chade, Calil, 49
Chai Kuen Fak, 623
Chaintron, Jean, 220
Chairul (Indonesian), 915
Chakovsky, A., 593
Chakravarty, Sushil, 713
Chan, Le Tho, 639
Chancy, Max, 273
Chand, Mohan, 416
Chandisingh, Ranji, 270
Chandorf, Luis, 181
Chandra, Romesh, 297, 696-705 passim; quoted, 697-
    705 passim
Chang Ch'un ch'iao, 104, 107, 109
Chang Kuo-ching, 748

Chang Sheng Lai, 524
Chang Tek Suen, 523
Chang Wei, 735
Ch'ang Kuan-lou, 106
Chanh, Lam Tri, 666
Chanh, Le Quang, 224, 666, 678
Chanh, Nguyen Tho, 639, 657-58
Chankov, Velcho: cited, 53
Chao I-ya, 104
Chao Yung-fu, 812, 813
Chaoui, Nicola, see Shawi, Nicola
Chase, Ashton, 270
Chase, Homer, 623
Chater, Tony, 244
Chaturvedi, Jagdish Prasad, 732
Chauron, Santos, 853
Chávez, Camilo, 400
Chávez, Rafael Celestino, 1003
Chay, Put, see Chhay, Phouk
Chen Ping, 383, 384, 521, 568
Chen Ru Pen, 523
Chen Tien, 383
Chen Yi, see Ch'en I
Chen Yu, 707
Ch'en Hsi-lien, 108n
Ch'en I (Chen Yi), 99, 103, 104, 120, 121, 151, 221,
    973; quoted, 121
Ch'en P'ei-hsien, 108
Ch'en Po-ta, 98, 99, 103, 104, 121; quoted, 107, 108,
    109; summary of speech to Revolutionary Com-
    mittee, 812
Ch'en Tsai-tao, 103, 109, 812, 813, 1080
Ch'en Yun, 98, 103
Cheng Shih-ching, 108
Chermont, Abel, 45
Chernenko, K. U., 585
Chhay, Phouk (Put Chay), 67, 71, 72
Chhon, Khiet, 67
Chi, Le Thi, 676
Chi, Thach Thien, 679
Ch'i Pen-yü, 104, 104n, 808; quoted, 115
Chia Hsueh-chien, 713; quoted, 717
Chiam Chung Him, 383
Chiang Ch'ing (Mme. Mao), 99, 100, 103-4, 113, 812,
    1058, 1084; summary of speech to Revolu-
    tionary Committee, 812; text of speech to
    representatives of mass organizations, 815-17
Chiang Kai-shek, 102, 111, 118, 602, 774, 833, 945.
    See also Chiang Kai-shekists
Chiang Lian Kuang, 524
Chilabert, José, 463
Chin Buaprasert, see Pin Bua-orn
Chinh, Duong Quoc, 639
Chinh, Truong, 150, 638, 639, 640, 650; quoted, 650
Chio Cheng Tun, 522
Chit, Thakin, 61
Ch'iu Hui-tso, 113
Chlehoun, Edwin, 707
Choe Chang-yul, 713
Choe Chon-nam, 442
Choe Hyon, 434, 436

Choe Kwang, 434, 435, 436
Choe Kyong-pak, 435
Choe Yong-kim, 444
Choe Yong-kon, 152, 156, 434, 442, 444, 445, 446,
    767, 1058, 1059; quoted, 446
Choliere, Yves, 697, 700
Chomon, Faure, 136
Chon Chang-chol, 435
Chong Chon-ki, 446
Chong Ha-chon, 446
Chong O-tae, 156, 444, 445
Choong Wai Koh, 390
Chou En-lai, 73, 98-104 passim, 108, 109, 115, 120,
    306, 369, 812, 973; quoted, 108-9, 114, 119,
    120; summary of speech to Revolutionary Com-
    mittee, 813; abridged text of speech welcoming
    Albanian delegation, 820-22
Chou Pei-yuan, 735, 736
Chowdhuri, Sushital Roy, 303
Choy Latisingh, 567
Choybalsan (Mongolian), 401
Chu, Mme. Ma Thi, 666, 679
Chu Te, 98, 99, 113
Chudik, Michal, 166
Chung Han-hua, 109
Chuong, Le, 647, 667
Churchward, Lloyd: quoted, 25
Cienfuegos, Osmany, 150, 157, 653, 1069
Cisar Cestmir, 166n
Citrine, Sir Walter, 706
Claesson, Tore, 542
Clancy, Pat, 21
Clarke, Nelson, 77
Clarkson, Stephen: cited, 403
Claude, Pierre Jean, 273, 276
Clavaud, F., 222
Clemente Acosta, Rafael, 854
Cliff, Tony (pseud. of Ygael Gluckstein), 251
Coba Casas, Andres, 853
Codovilla, Victorio, 16, 20, 179, 767; quoted, 17-18,
    18-19
Cohen, Jack, 244
Colendsky de Fanjul, Dora Ida, 20
Collazo, Ariel, 628
Colon Gordinay, Francisco, 504
Colorado, Eduvigis, 854
Cols, Jean-Claude, 37
Combe, Claude, 221
Con, Nguyen, 639, 641
Conforme, Armando, 193
Cong, Vo Chi (alias Nguyen Van Cuc), 665, 666
Coninck, Albert de, 34, 294
Conquest, Robert: cited, 582n, 590n; quoted, 586
Constant, Andre, 393
Constantine, King of the Hellenes, 253n, 254, 254n,
    255, 256, 728
Contreras, Maximo, 396
Contreras, Paul, 713
Contreras, Raul, 400
Cooke, John William, 18, 20
Copeland, Vincent E., 623

Cordero, Efrain, 854
Cordero, Ivan Alfredo, 854
Correa, Gentil, 45
Correa, Jacinto, 463
Corretjer, Juan Antonio, 503-4; quoted, 503, 504
Corswant, Andre, 551
Corvalan, Gustavo, 463; quoted, 463-64
Corvalan, Luis, 89-96 passim, 152, 155, 159, 219,
    343, 518, 616, 634, 767, 1090, 1092; quoted,
    90-94 passim, 155
—article on anti-imperialism in Latin America, 92;
    text, 781-86
—report on CP of Chile, 94; quoted, 90, 94; abridged
    text, 787-92
Cossutta, Armando, 336
Costa, Claude de, 768
Costa e Silva, Artur da, 45
Cot, Pierre, 742, 743
Cotton, Eugenie, 697, 726, 729
Courtieu, 212n, 217
Coussement, Urbain, 34
Creydt, Oscar, 463, 465, 466, 1069
Crombet, Jaime, 138, 142
Cruicchi, Dante, 732
Cruz, Celmira, 128, 1066
Cruz, Zacarias de la (alias "Commander Dello"), 480
Cruz Peralta, Rafael, 189
Cruz Varela, Juan de la, 128
Crvenkovski, Krste, 58, 681
Cseterki, Lajos, 282-83, 284
Cuc, Nguyen Van, see Cong, Vo Chi
Cuesta, Gerardo, 625
Cung, Phung Van (also Tran Van Cung), 666, 669
Cung, Tran Van, see Cung, Phung Van
Cunhal, Alvaro, 497, 498, 501, 754, 767, 1034; quoted,
    498, 499, 500
Cuong, Huynh, 666
Curthoys, G., 21
Curtis-Joseph, Peter A., 697
Cyrankiewicz, Jozef, 57, 291, 484, 487, 490, 491, 496,
    600-601, 1026, 1065, 1069, 1085
Czesak, Jozef, 662
Czinege, Lajos, 282, 446

Daddah, Moktar Ould, see Ould Daddah, Moktar
Dafflon, Roger, 551, 553; quoted, 533-54
Dalea, Mihai, 508, 549; quoted, 514
Dalton, Roque, 197, 429; quoted, 198
"Dalusong, Commander," 480
Dan, Pham Trong, 665
Danelius, Gerhard, 224, 239-42 passim, 754, 767;
    quoted, 240, 240n, 241
Danesh, Haji Mohamed, 457
Dang, Satyapal, 297
Dang, Tran Bach, 666, 667
Dange, Shripad Amrit, 232, 297, 298, 300, 303, 304,
    414, 706-7, 768, 1087; quoted, 300, 305
Danh, Huynh Van, 676
Daniel, Yuli, 343, 450, 451, 591, 593
Daninthe, Guy, 259
Dant de la Cruz, Eusebio, 475

"Dante, Commander," *see* Buscayo, Bernabe
Danzos Palomino, Ramón, 1048
Dao, Le Quang, 639, 649; quoted, 649
Dao, Nguyen Van, 644; quoted, 644
El Darawsheh, Nagi, 732
Darvas, József, 289-90
Das Gupta, Parimal, 303
Das Gupta, Promode, 298
Dashonolt (Mongolian), 404
Dasylva, Claire, 77
David, Václav, 175, 600
Davis, John: quoted, 251
Dawson, D., 21
Dayan, Moshe, 921, 922
Daza, Ivan, 854
Deakin, Arthur, 706; quoted, 706
Debat, Joseph, 274
Debray, Jules Régis, 18, 44, 118, 125, 145-48 *passim*,
    152, 153, 154, 159, 189, 195, 218, 264n-265n,
    398, 399, 504, 549, 616, 620, 631, 733, 744,
    763, 1057, 1070; quoted, 147-48
Debrouwere, Jan, 34
Debu-Bridel, Jacques, 740
De Coninck, Albert, *see* Coninck, Albert de
Décosterd, Ernest, 551
Deen, Jean-Baptiste, 731
De Gaulle, Charles, *see* Gaulle, Charles de
De Groot, Paul, *see* Groot, Paul de
Delagua, Henri, 261; quoted, 261-62
Delgado, Alvaro, 123; quoted, 122
Dellberg, Karl, 553
"Dello, Commander," *see* Cruz, Zacarias de la
Delogne, M., 37
Delone, Vadim, 343, 593
Demarcy, Roland, 724
Demichev, P. N., 581, 584; text of P. Antokolsky's
    letter to, on Solzhenitsyn case, 1002
Demir, Yakub (*alias of* Zeki Bastimar), 224, 576, 578, 767
Demirel, Süleyman, 323, 577; quoted, 577n
Denis, Jacques, 218, 219
Dennis, Thomas, 610
De Raet, Andre, 740
Desai, Morarji, 301
Deshomme, Jal, 273
De Silva, Cecil, 82
De Silva, Colvin R., 82
deSilva, S. J., 83
Despiney, Rui, 501
Despradel, Fidelio, 189, 190
Dessalines, Jean Jacques, 762
Deuane Sounarath, 363, 370, 679
Dewhurst, Alfred, 77
Dharmasena, Higgoda, 83
Diallo, Saifoulaye, 768
Dias, Giocondo, 45
Díaz, Antonio, 854
Díaz, Carlo, 400
Díaz, Daniel, 131
Díaz, Félix, 624
Díaz, Jorge, 278, 279, 281, 1057
Díaz Nino, Ignacio, 854

Díaz Pose, Barret, 625
Díaz Rangel, Eleazar, 732
Dibbern, Else, 239
Dickel, Helga, 726
Dickie, Alfred, 697
Dickshit, Madan, 416
Dieckmann, Johannes, 224
Diehl, Walter, 236, 697
Diem, Ngo Dinh, 663, 665, 670, 852, 855
Diener, Siegfried, 713
al-Digna, Sadiq, 541
Dimeny, Imre, 284, 285
Dimitriou, Panos, 252, 258
Dimitrov, Georgi, 9
Dimitrov, Mircho: quoted, 54; cited, 54
el-Din, Khaled Mohie, 697
ad-Din, Mursi Saad, 749
El Dine, Ahmed Baha', 731
Dinucci, Fosco, 10, 345, 1084
Diop, Mahjmout, 224
Dixon, Richard, 21, 26
Dizdarević, Nijaz, 754
Djawoto (Indonesian), 115, 309, 310, 317, 747, 748
Djerdja, Josip, 687
Djudjido, Hitapia, 310
Djunaedi, Mahbub, 748
Do, Tran, 639, 647, 665, 667
Dobbs, Farrell, 621, 622
Dobi, Istvan, 284, 1069
Dobrovolsky, Alexei, 593, 594
Docker, N., 21
Dodbiba, Pirro, 6
Doig, Mel, 77
Dolansky, Jaromir, 166, 174
Dominguez, Angel, 697, 700
Dominguez, Bernardo, 197, 198
Don, Nguyen, 639, 647, 667
Donath, Günther: cited, 241
Donati, Manlio, 346
Dones, José, 269; quoted, 269
Dong, Huynh Phuong, 679
Dong, Nguyen Van, 184, 679
Dong, Pham Van, 24, 150, 639, 648, 744; quoted,
    648-49, 654
Dong, Vo Tuc, 639
Dorcilien, Jacques, 273
Dorosh, Yefim, 590
Dorsimond, Roger, 34
Dorticós, Osvaldo, 136, 150, 152, 156, 161, 760,
    762; quoted, 760
Dos Santos, Emilio, 854
Dostoyevsky, F. M., 594, 985
Doudera, K., 517
Dragan, Constantin, 708-9; quoted, 709
Drǎghici, Alexandru, 30, 508, 509, 510
Dragoev, Ivan, 540
Dragoi, Stana, 707
Dragoycheva, Tsola, 51; quoted, 57
Draškić, M., 690; quoted, 690
Dreke, Víctor, 158
Drukman, A., 330

Drumaux, Marc, 34, 518
Duan, Le, 444, 493, 639, 640, 645, 657, 658, 660, 767; quoted, 651, 658
Duarte Pereira, Osny, see Pereira, Osny Duarte
Dubček, Alexander, 166, 166n, 175, 178, 1093; quoted, 178
Dübi, Franz, 551
Dubovsky, Robert, 27, 31
Duc, Nghiem Ba, 652n
Duc, Tran Huu, 639, 640
Duclos, Jacques, 208, 220
Ducondray, Félix Servio, 187
Ducondray, Juan, 187
Duféal, Ph., 393
Dufond, Guy, 393
Dugersuren, Mangalyn, 660
Dugersuren, T., 224, 401; quoted, 406
Duggan, Robert, 610
Dumont, Charles, 273, 276
Dung, Bay, 647, 667
Dung, Van Tien, 639, 647, 667
Dupuy, A., 222
Duse, Ugo, 346
Dutschke, Rudi, 237, 241
Dutt, Saroj, 303
Duvalier, François, 273-76 passim
Duverge, Roberto, 190
Dzerzhinsky, Felix, 993

Eberle, Eugen, 237
Ebert, Friedrich, 223, 229
Ebrahim, Ahmed Gora, 748
Echevarría, José Antonio, 854
Echeverría Flores, Rafael, 195
Eddisford, Vic, 244
Edelman, Fanny J. de, 16
Eden, Anthony, 921
Edwards, Edward G., 735
Edwards, J. H., 422
Edwige, Charles, 259
Efremov, Alexandr, 732
Efros, Anatoly, 592
Ehrenburg, Ilia, 343, 591, 697
Eisenscher, Michael, 610
Ekwalla, Robert, 76
Elamin, Hassan, 701
Elias, Rolf, 239, 242
Ellemark, Ulf, 547
Elliot, E. V., 21
Elwand, Dennis, 244
"Ely, Commander," see Garcia, Dominador
Emanuel, Poul, 181
Emery Valle, Federico, 399
Enders, Guido, 49
Endicott, James G., 697
Engels, Friedrich, 7, 187, 482, 765, 823, 825, 829, 878, 879, 883, 913, 945, 946, 984, 988; quoted, 782, 955
Epton, William, 618; quoted, 619
Erdelyi (Hungarian Deputy Foreign Minister), 1065
Erding, Fahri, 578

Erick, Carlos, 475
Erlander, Tage, 546
Erlebach, Kurt, 235
Erlich, Wolfgang, 330, 331, 334
Erofeev, Pavel, 732
Escalante, Aníbal, 139
Escalante, Arturo Sama, 396
Esch, Joop van, 417
Escobar, Federico, 42
Eshkol, Levi, 330, 333, 920, 921, 922, 932; quoted, 920
Espejel, Félix, 400
Espín, Vilma (Mrs. Raúl Castro), 136, 137, 149, 726
Espín de Castro, Vilma, see Espín, Vilma
Espinosa, Isidro, 853
Espiritu, Ramon, 477
Estrada (Cuban), 745
Estrada Villa, Rafael, 396, 397, 398, 400
Etienne, Gilbert, 558
Eu Chooi Yip, 383, 384
Ewald, Georg, 223
Eyerman, Richard, 223

Faisal, Yusuf, 224, 559, 565
Faiz, Faiz Ahmed, 697
Fajon, Etienne, 208, 219
Fakeh, Mme. Shamsiah, 384
Falber, Reuben, 244
Fanjul, Angel Lazaro, 20
Fanti, Guido, 339
Fantis, Andreas, 163, 165, 224
Faragó, Jenö, 289; quoted, 283, 289
Faragó, Vilmos, 289
Faragos (Rigas), Grigorios, 252
Farfan, Antonio, 400
Farge, Yves, 697
Faria, Jesús, 217, 225, 518, 629, 635, 767-68, 1082
Farner, Konrad, 551, 553
Faroul, Andre, see Feray, André
Farray, Andre, see Feray, André
Fava, Athos, 16
Favaro, Roland, 209
Favilli, Giovanni, 697
Fawzi, Mohammed, 177
Faydang (Laotian), 362
Fedoseiev, P. N., 582, 584, 585; quoted, 585, 590-91
Fehér, Lajos, 282, 285
Feliciano, Felix Juan, 504
Felsine, Josephe, 259
Feng Piao: quoted, 118
Feray, André (also André Farray, Ferre, perhaps Faroul), 273, 276
Fernández, Lauro, 625
Fernández, Gasco, Gonzalo, 474
Fernández Montes de Oca, Alberto, 136
Fernández Moya, Rafael, 158
Fernández Retamar, Roberto, 161
Fernández Ruggiero, Esteban, 625
Fernando, Watson, 83, 84
Ferrari, Alberto: quoted, 17
Ferre, André, see Feray, André

Ferreira, Camara, 45
Ferreira, Manoel, 49
Ferreto Segura, Arnoldo, 133, 134
Ferri, Franco, 342
Fialho, Henriques, 742
Fiallo, Celso, 195
Fierro, Walterio, 94
Figueras, Santiago, 854
Figueroa, Luis, 89, 94
Figueroa, Prieto: quoted, 839
Filip, Ioan, 742
Fischer, Abram, 525
Fischer, Ernst, 30
Fischerova, Miluse, 726
Fitte-Duval, Georges, 393
Flemin, Félix, 259
Flores, Aldo, 40
Flores, Esther, 853
Fock, Jenö, 282, 284-85, 286, 292, 1026, 1069;
    quoted, 285-86, 288
Fojtik, Jan, 173
Fong Swee Suan, 523
Fonseca, Edison, 193
Fonseca Amador, Carlos, 430
Forcinal, Albert, 740
Fornasini, Margarita, 726
Fors, Olle, 542
Forsberg, Tore, 542
Forti, Dina, 703
Fortuny, José Manuel, 263, 265, 267, 268; quoted,
    265-66, 267
Forutan, Gholamhosein, 323
Fosso, François, 76
Foster, Sidney, 244
Foulds, John, 422, 426
Frachon, Benoît, 208, 446, 707, 710
Fraga Iribarne, Manuel, 529, 961, 963
Franck, Adolphe, 382
Francke, Per, 550
Franco, Francisco, 155, 519, 529-34 passim, 961, 963
Frank, Pierre, 209
Frankie, Peggy Goldman, 610
"Freddie, Commander," see Yumbao, Alfredo
Freed, Norman, 77, 80
Frei, Dora, 463
Frei, Eduardo, 91, 146, 785, 787
Freyre, Felipe F., 697
Friedler, Josef, 31n
Friedrich, Walter, 697
Frischmann, Georges, 208
Fritz, Heinrich, 31
Fröhlich, Paul, 223
Fuchs, Georg, 697
Fuenmayor, Eulalia, 854
Fuentes Gutiérrez, Javier, 399, 400
Fuglsang, Villy, 181, 224
Fundora López, Orlando, 161
Fürnberg, Friedl, 27-31 passim, 179
Furubotn, Peder, 452, 452n-453n, 453

Gabelic, A.: quoted, 690

Gadda, Hermes, 625
Gadea Acosta, Ricardo, 475
Gaillard, Roger, 273
Galan, Victor Rico, 400
Galanskov, Iurii, 593, 594
Galicia Jiménez, Plutarco, 400
Gallagher, N. L., 25
Gallego, Ignacio, 529
Gallegos Arends, Enrique, 193
Gallegos Mancera, Eduardo, 629
Galluzzi, Carlo, 340-44 passim
Galo Espinoza, Jorge Isaac, 427, 430
Galo González (Chilean): quoted, 785
Gamarnikow, Michael: cited, 495
Gandhi, Indira, 306
Ganev, Ivan, 713, 717
Gankovsky, Y. V.: quoted, 456
Garaudy, Roger, 208, 212, 212n, 217; quoted, 217
Garba-Jahumpa, Ibrahim, 697
Garcia, Christian, 220
Garcia, Dominador (alias "Commander Ely"), 480
Garcia, Eduardo: quoted, 530, 531
Garcia, Fabio, 186, 187, 767
Garcia, Guillermo, 136, 760
Garcia, José María, 16
Garcia, Luis Vicente, 854
Garcia, Radhamés, 190
Garcia, Rodolfo, 854
Garcia Olivera, Julio, 150
Garcia Pelaez, Raúl, 152
Garcia Ponce, Guillermo, 629, 838, 846, 1062; quoted,
    846-47
Garza Guajardo, Celso, 396
Gáspár, Sándor, 282
Gasperoni, Ermenegildo, 520, 754, 767; quoted, 520
Gaubert, Marie-Ange, 726
Gaulle, Charles de, 208, 210, 211, 214, 215, 216, 259,
    488, 515, 872-76 passim, 1076.   See also
    Gaullism, Gaullists
Gauthier, Georges, 221
Genao Espaillat, Luis, 189
Gene, Evremond, 259, 261, 767; quoted, 260, 261
Genies, D., 259
Genry, Ernest, 602; quoted, 602
Gensous, Pierre, 653, 707, 710, 711, 712; quoted, 710
Georgadze, M.: quoted, 587
George, P., 21
Georgiou, Pavlos, 163
"Gerónimo," see Betancourt, Carlos
Gerschuni Pérez, Jaime, 624
Ghaffer Kahn, Abdul, 456
Gheorghiu-Dej, Gheorghe, 509
Ghinaglia, Natalia, 853
Ghioldi, Orestes, 16
Ghioldi, Rodolfo, 16, 152, 154, 634; quoted, 19, 154, 155
Ghonchar, Oles, 592; quoted, 592
Ghosh, Ajoy, 297; quoted, 455
Ghosh, Litto, 697
Ghosh, P. C., 301
Giang, Vo Dong, 666
Giap, Ha Huy, 639

Giap Vo Nguyen, 149, 639, 640, 642, 647, 648, 657; quoted, 645-51 *passim*
Gibson, Ralph, 21
Gierek, Edward, 484
Gifford, C., 21
Gil Gilbert, Enrique, 192
Giles Pizarro, Jorge, 742
Giménez, Aníbal, 853
Giménez, Héctor, 1003
Giniger, Henry: quoted, 460
Ginsberger, Roger (*pseud.* Pierre Villon), 740
Ginzburg, Alexandr, 593, 594, 997
Girard, Florent, 261
Giúdici, Ernesto, 16, 19, 159; quoted, 18
Gläser, Hanny, 223
Glaser, Hugo, 27
Glezos, Manolis, 32, 252, 253, 703, 732, 734, 743
Gligorov, Kiro, 688
Glineur, Georges, 34, 37
Glückauf, Erich, 234
Gluckstein, Ygael, *see* Cliff, Tony
Goebbels, Joseph, 968
Goering, Hermann, 968
Gogol, Nikolai V., 1002
Goldstücker, Eduard, 170, 170n; quoted, 173
Gollan, John, 244, 246, 248, 754, 755, 767, 1085; quoted, 246
Gollan, W. E., 21
Gologo, Mamadou El Béchir, 731, 748
Gomez, Alberto: quoted, 123-24
Gómez, Juan (Spaniard), 529
Gómez, Juan (Venezuelan), 853
Gómez, Maximiliano, 187
Gómez Roa, Alejandro, 713
Gomulka, Wladyslaw, 57, 218, 224, 226, 291, 484-85, 490-96 *passim*, 600, 601, 753, 756, 767, 1026, 1034, 1065, 1069, 1085; quoted, 485, 487, 490, 492, 494
Gonçalves, Ari, 49
Gonen, Benjamin, 333
Gonsaga Travassos, Luis, 45
Gonzáles, Andrés, 467, 473
Gonzales Moscoso, Hugo, 43
González, Armando, 625
González, Edgard, 853
González, Félix, 400
González, J. Refugio, 400
González, José, 89, 791
González, Luis, 136, 137
González, Luis Adrian, 853
González, Rafael Baltazar, 853
González, Tereso, 400
González Alberdi, Paulino, 16
González Daguino, Alfonso, 96
González Gutiérrez de González, Luisa, 133
González Moreno, Jorge Arturo, 196
González Rojo, Enrique, 400
González Zapato, Hilbert, 460
Goodlett, Carlton, 697
Goodluck, Wahab, 431
Gopalan, A. K., 298

Gordon, Jeff, 618
Gordon-Polonskaya, L. R.: quoted, 456
Gorender, Jacob, 45
Göring, Herman, *see* Goering, Hermann
Gorky, A. M. (Maxim Gorky), 1002
Gorky, Maxim, *see* Gorky, A. M.
Goshal, Yebaw (*alias* Ba Tin), 61, 61n, 62
Gošnjak, Ivan, 681, 682n
Gostev (Soviet state security official): text of Pavel Litvinov's open letter on interrogation by, 996-97
Gottin, Mathurin, 393
Goulart, João, 45, 48
Gouverneur, Livia, 853
Gowon, Yakubu, 431, 432
Grabois, Alcira, 49
Grabois, Mauricio, 49
Graham, J., 329
Graindorge, Michel, 37, 38, 39
Grajeda Centina, Gustavo, 265
Gramsci, Antonio, 587
Granlid, Gunnel, 542
Grassi, Anna Nicolosi, 342
Gratiant, Georges, 393, 394
Grbić, Čedo: quoted, 685
Grechko, Andrei A., 584
Greco, Gabriel, 732
Green, Gil, 609, 610; quoted, 609
Grimmer, Reginald, 745
Grin, Alexandr, 986
Grippa, Jacques, 10, 32, 33, 37, 38, 222, 535, 1064, 1081; quoted, 38
Grishin, Viktor V., 354, 581, 583, 712, 1078
Grivas, George, 162, 163, 164
Grobart, Fabio, 161
Gromyko, Andrei, 152, 491, 600
Groot, Paul de, 417, 418, 518; quoted, 420
Grossman, Vasiliy, 986, 1002
Grozos, Apostolos, 252, 255, 256, 256n, 257, 754, 1090; quoted, 253
Grüneberg, Gerhard, 223
Gualan, Alberto, 197
Guéniat, Pierre, 551
Guerra, Adriano, 343; quoted, 343
Guerra, Angel, 853
Guerra Ramos, Rafael, 854, 1003
Guevara, Ernesto "Che," 14, 20, 30, 40, 42, 42n, 43, 44, 117, 136, 139, 142-48 *passim*, 151, 154, 155, 156, 159, 160, 186, 196, 209, 218, 220, 230, 241, 242, 269, 272, 344, 347, 352, 371, 398, 445, 446, 472, 475, 616, 620, 621, 622, 627, 637, 661, 678, 760, 761, 762, 1067, 1069, 1070, 1087; quoted, 141, 146; text of his "Message to the Peoples of the World," 855-60
Guevara, Ramón, 854
Guillaume, Saintigène, 273
Guitteaud, Walter, 393
Gumilev, Nikolai S., 985
Gunasekera, D. A., 83
Gunawardena, Philip, 82
Gunther, Ray: quoted, 246

Gupta, Bhupesh, 297, 299, 307; quoted, 299, 300
Gupta, Indrajit, 297
Gupta, Parimal Das, *see* Das Gupta, Parimal
Gupta, Promode Das, *see* Das Gupta, Promode
Gustavsen, Finn, 768
Gustavsson, Bo, 542, 543, 544
Gustavsson, Lennart, 542
Gustinčič, Anton, 688; quoted, 688
Gutiérrez, Francisco, 529
Gutiérrez, Héctor, 463
Gutiérrez, Livia, 853
Gutiérrez, Victor Manuel, 263
Guyot, Raymond, 208, 214, 216, 218-19, 294, 533, 697
Gyaurov, Stoyan, 51

Hababi, Emile, 330
el Hag, Suliman Hamid, 224
Hagberg, Hilding, 542, 543, 550
Hagel, Rolf, 542
Hager, Kathe, 726
Hager, Kurt, 223, 232
Hai, Thanh, 679
Hai, Tran Quy, 639
Hájek, Jiří, 171, 172
Hakamada Satomi, 348
Halbritter, Walter, 223
Hall, Gus, 609, 610, 615, 615n, 617, 768; quoted, 610n, 611, 612, 615, 617
Hallinan, Matthew, 610
Halstead, Fred, 621, 622
Hama Takeshi, 349
Hamerquist, Donald Lee, 610
Hamiss, S., 330
Hamsell, Sven: cited, 607
Han Sang-tu, 435
Han Tok-su, 435, 436
Han Yong-yon, 447
Hanafi (Indonesian), 309, 317
Hansen, Erik, 181
Hansen, Ludvig, 181
Hao, Song, 639
Hao, Thich Thien, 666, 679
Harahap, Burhanuddin, 902
Harbi, Mohammed, 14
Harmel, Mohammed, 224, 574, 575, 768; quoted, 574, 575
Harmel, Pierre, 35n
Harrylall, Kamal, 270
Hart, Armando, 136, 760; quoted, 140, 142, 760-61
Hart, Mrs. Armando, *see* Santamaría, Haydée
Hart, Joe: cited, 401
Hasiak, Stanislaw, 486
Hassan II, King of Morocco, 410, 411, 412
Hassoun, Faisal, 732
Hatfield, Henry, 21
Hatoum, Salim, 358
Hatta, Mohammad, 915
Hau, Vo Van, 665
Hausmann, Kurt, 223
Hauwaert, Arnold, 37, 39

Havelka, Jan: cited, 168
Havlíček, František, 170
Hawi, George, 373, 376
Healey, Dorothy, 609, 610, 618; quoted, 615
Healey, Gerry, 249
Hegman, Ralph, 422, 426
Heinisch, Theodor, 740
Heisler, Bob, 610
Helfert, Stefanie, 32
Helgason, Ingi, 295
Helman, Evelyne, 726
Hempel, Elli, 223
Hendrych, Jiří, 166, 170-74 *passim*, 224, 226, 864, 1077, 1089, 1092; quoted, 170, 171, 172, 1077
Henin, David, 30, 330, 334, 334n
Herath, U. B., 82
Herlitz, Lars, 550
Hermann, Jean-Maurice, 731, 732; quoted, 732
Hermansson, Carl-Henrik, 296, 448-49, 542, 543, 546, 549; quoted, 543-49 *passim*
Hermier, Guy, 209
Hernández, Jesús María, 853
Hernández, Melba, 149
Hernández, Olga de, 853
Hernández, Vivian, 854
Hernández Vargas, Homero, 189
Herrera, Antonio, 503
Hess, Rudolf, 968
Hidalgo, Miguel, 762
Hien, Do Van, 653
Hien, Nguyen Van, 677
Hien, Tran Chi, 653
Hieu, Nguyen Van, 666, 667, 697, 731
Hill, E. F. (Ted), 25; quoted, 25-26
Hilsum, François, 209
Hirano Yoshitaro, 697, 742
Hiratsuka Raicho, 726
Hitler, Adolf, 229, 381, 425, 527, 716, 781, 786, 947, 968, 969, 970. *See also* Hitlerism, Hitlerites
Ho Chi Minh, 121, 150, 210, 266, 638, 639, 640, 645, 647, 653, 658, 660, 663, 744, 762, 1090; quoted, 638, 643, 653, 658, 660
--article on influence of October Revolution, 658; text, 1014-17
Ho Kang, 447
Ho Lung, 99, 102, 113
Ho Pong-hak, 434, 435, 436
Ho Sok-sun, 435
Ho Ta Hai, 524
Hoa, Nguyen Cong, 658
Hoan, Hoang Van, 639
Hoan, Tran Quoc, 639
Hoang, Le, 639
Hoang, Nguyen Van, 640
Hoc, Nguyen, 666
Hoekstra, Henk, 417, 419; quoted, 419, 420
Hoff, Henry, 451; quoted, 451
Hoffmann, Karel, 170, 745
Hofman, Michal, 731
Hogstedt, Christer, 545
Holm, Evert, 549

Holmberg, Nils, 542-43, 547
Holmsten, Sven-Erik, 547
Holt, Harold, 24
Holub, Boguslaw: cited, 485
Homppi, Teuvo, 713
Honecker, Erich, 223, 225, 232, 1066; quoted, 225
Hong Myong-hu, 434, 435
Hong Sun-kwon, 435
Hoover, J. Edgar, 615
Horn, Karl, 31, 31n, 32
Horn, Otto, 27
Hoxha, Enver, 3-6 *passim*, 9, 10, 31, 32, 116, 496, 820, 823, 1061-62, 1072, 1079; quoted, 3-6 *passim*, 9-10
—speech on revolutionizing Albanian Workers' Party, 3; excerpts, 777-80
Hovanesyan, Ardeshir, 321
Hoveyda, Amir-Abbas, 321-22
Hradecký, Adolf, 732, 745
Hrebick, Jaromir, 745
Hronek, Helmut, 31n, 33
Hsiao Ching-kuang, 113
Hsiao Hua, 113
Hsieh Chin Chen, 523
Hsieh Fu-chih, 99, 101, 103, 104, 109-13 *passim*, 1079-80; quoted, 105, 109, 112; summary of speech to Revolutionary Committee, 813-14
Hsieh Hsüeh-kung, 108
Hsieh T'ang-chung, 113
Hsien Heng-han, 108
Hsiung Ching-chi, 748
Hsu Huai-chung, 749
Hsu Jen, 315
Hsü Hsiang-ch'ien, 99, 103, 113, 1058
Hsü Shih-yu, 108n
Htay, Yebaw, 61, 61n, 62
Huan, Le Van, 666
Huang, Yung-sheng, 108n
Hubbard, H. J. M., 270
Hue, Mme. Truong Thi, 679
Hugel, Cecile, 726, 729
Hughes, A., 21
Hughes, J. R., 21
Hung, Pham, 639, 644; quoted, 644-45, 646
Hung, Tran Duy, 658
Hunter, Margaret, 244
Huq, Abdul, 457
Hurtado, Rafael, 854
Hurtago, Hernando, 122
Husek, Josef, 740
Hussein, King of Jordan, 358, 359, 361n, 604, 947, 948
Hutaped, B. O., 310
Huu, To, 639, 643; quoted, 643
Huy, Tran Quang, 639
Huy, Trang Quy, 639
Huysmans, Marthe, 37
Hwang Won-po, 435
Hyon Mu-kwang, 435
Hyvönen, Anna-Liisa, 201

Ibarruri, Dolores, 529, 534, 726, 754, 767
Ibéné, Hégésippe, 259, 261
Ibrahim, Muhsin, 373, 376
Ibrahim, Mustafa, 537
Ifantis, Panos, 252
Iftikharuddin, Mian, 456
Ignat, Nestor, 732
Iliou, Ilias, 252, 253
Ilku, Pál, 282
Illia, Arturo U., 16
Im Chol, 444
Indra, Alois, 166n
Infante, Manuel, 854
Ingberg, Lennart, 545, 547
Ingrao, Pietro, 224, 336, 337, 341; quoted, 341
Inguanzo, Horacio, 529
Inzunza Bécquer, Jorge, 89, 96
Ioniță, Ion, 508
Iribarren Borges, Ignacio, 837, 840, 841
Iribarren Borges, Julio, 631, 634, 837-41 *passim*, 849, 850, 853, 854, 1065
Ironsi, Aguiyi, 431, 432
Isa, Ibrahim, 314, 749; quoted, 314
Isa Conde, Narciso, 186
Iscaro, Rubens, 16, 17
Iskenderi, Iradji, 321; quoted, 322
Islam, Azizul, 457
Ismail Nasiruddin Shah, King of Malaysia, 386; quoted, 386
Iveković, M., 690
Iyer, V. R. Krishna, 742

Jackson, George, 232, 422, 424, 768
Jackson, James Edward, 610, 615-18 *passim*; quoted, 616
Jacob, Charles R., Jr., 270
Jagan, Cheddi, 270-71, 272, 768, 1083; quoted, 271
Jagan, Derek, 270
Jagan, Janet, 270
Jagielski, Mieczyslaw, 484
Jagvaral, N., 401
Jahaj (Malaysian), 391
Jahn, Günther, 224
Jair, Ahmad Muhammad, 10, 540, 541, 1079
Jakova, Tonin, 1071; quoted, 710
James, Daniel: cited, 42n, 136, 148
Jansson, Axel: quoted, 548
Jao Shu-shih, 106
Jara, Arturo, 134; quoted, 134
Jara, Juan, 463
Jarosiński, Witold, 484
Jaroszewicz, Piotr, 484; cited, 491
Jarowinsky, Werner, 223
Jasovich-Pantaleon, Rosa, 729
Jaszczuk, Boleslaw, 484
Jatamba (Mongolian): quoted, 403
Jayakoddy, V., 83
Jedyrchowski, Stefan, 484, 486, 487
Jefferys, Nora, 244
Jenness, Doug, 621
Jensen, Alfred, 181, 182

Jensen, Christian Hermann, 181
Jerome, Fred, 618; quoted, 619
Jespersen, Knud, 181, 182, 184, 294, 679, 754, 767, 1034, 1080; quoted, 181-82, 183
Jha, B. P., 300
Jijon Saavedra, Milton, 192
Jiménez, Ramón, 854
Jimkers, Cees, 417
Jinendrapala, G. K., 83
Joannes, Victor, 506
Jocha, Alfred, 31n
Johannes, Octaviano, 190
Johanson, Kjell E., 544, 545, 547; quoted, 545
Johansson, Allan, 542
John XXIII, Pope, 534
Johnson, Arnold, 610, 618; quoted, 613-14
Johnson, Beatrice H., 618, 726
Johnson, Frank, 25
Johnson, Lyndon Baines, 32, 95, 493, 515, 612, 613, 617, 781, 856, 926, 934, 949, 1076
Joliet-Curie, Frédéric, 696, 735, 736
Jonathan, Leabua, 377, 378
Jones, Claude, 21
Jones, Lew, 621
Jørgensen, Arne, 452, 454
Joshi, Baharat Roy, 414
Joshi, Govinda Roy, 416
Joshi, S. M., 768
Jourdain, Henri, 219
Juarez, Benito Pablo, 1021
Juch, Heinz, 223
Jumblat, Kamal, 374, 749, 768
al-Jundi, Khalid, 560
Junttila, Lars, 201
Jurquet, Jacques, 10, 33, 221, 222, 345

Kabin, Ivan G., 30, 582
Kádár, János, 30, 176, 179, 282-94 passim, 517, 600, 753, 754, 767, 1026, 1064, 1065, 1073, 1087; quoted, 284, 286-93 passim
Kaderka, Oldřich, 1092
Kaftanov, S., 589
Kaganovich, Lazar, 583-84
Kaid, Ahmed, 768
Kainulainen, Markus, 201
Kállai, Gyula, 282, 284, 290, 293, 1069; quoted, 290, 293
Kaludis, Nikolas, 252
Kalyanasundaram, M., 297
Kam Sol-mo, 442
Kam Yau-wah, 385
Kamaldin, Ruslan, 309
Kamaruzaman (Indonesian; alias Ssam), 309
Kambakhsh, Abd-os-Samad, 321, 323
Kamel, Mazin, 358, 361
Kamiyama Shigeo, 357
Kanapa, Jean, 212n, 216, 555; text of his article "Marxism Is Not a Catechism," 878-79
Kane, Racine, 745
Kanellopoulos, Panayotis, 254, 254n, 890
Kang Sang-wi, 731

Kang Yang-uk, 434, 435, 697
K'ang Chien-min, 108n
K'ang Sheng, 98, 99, 103, 104, 547, 816, 1083; summary of speech to Revolutionary Committee, 812-13
Kanstrup, Gunnar, 182; quoted, 182
Kantůrek, Jiří: quoted, 167
Kao Kang, 106
Kapek, Antonín, 166, 166n
Kapitonov, I. V., 581
Kapluck, Manfred, 235; quoted, 235
Kapo, Hysni, 3, 7, 116, 1058; quoted, 8
Karadelkov, Petko, 732
Karami, Rashid, 749
Kardelj, Edvard, 681, 682, 682n, 688
Karlsson, Urban, 542, 549, 767
Karlsson, Villy, 181, 184
Karpets, I. I., 742
Karpinsky, L., 592
Karsaw, Nina, 489-90
Kartasamita, Hussein, 314
Kasem (Thai), 567
Kashly, Muhammad, 373
Kashshash, Umar, 559
Kashtan, William, 77, 79, 80, 224, 768; quoted, 78, 79
Kasman, Leon, 485
Kasuga Shoichi, 349
Kasuri, Mahmoud Ali, 742
Kaunda, Kenneth, 120
Kautsky, Karl, 883, 904. See also Kautskyism
Kawada Kenji, 349
Kaysone Phomvihan, 362, 362n
Kedrov, M. S., 993
Keita, Mamadou Madeira, 768
Kekkonen, Urho, 204, 205, 205n; quoted, 205
Kelly, Pat, 422, 426
Kennedy, John F., 737
Kennedy, Robert F., 620
Kepa, Józef, 484, 493
Kertapati, Sidik, 309, 310
Keuneman, Pieter, 82, 87, 224, 768; quoted, 84, 87
Khachaturov, K., 96
Khai, Nguyen, 639
Khalfa, Boualem, 12
Khamouan Bouppa, 363
Khamphat Saykeo, 371
Khamphay Boupha, 157, 363, 371
Khamphouane Tounalom, 362
Khamsoubinh Thonveunth, 371
Khamtay Siphandone, 363, 365; quoted, 365-66, 369
Khan, Mooner, 270
Khang, Nguyen, 639
Kharlamov, Mikhail A., 745
Khaustov (Soviet poet), 593
Khelifa, Laroussi, 697
Khérel, Hebert, 261
Khider, Mohammed, 13n
Khiem, Ung Van, 639
Khieu, Hoang Van, 639
Khieu, Nguyen Huu, 639
Khoa, Tran Dang, 640

Khrishnan, N. K., 297
Khrushchev, Nikita S., 65, 152, 304, 315, 387, 420, 442, 450, 572, 579, 580, 584, 585, 586, 590, 591, 593, 598, 607, 654, 691, 704, 705, 737, 765, 766, 820, 824, 825, 827, 831, 940, 941, 1061. *See also* Khrushchevism, Khrushchevists; Liu Shao-ch'i ("China's Khrushchev")
Kiao Sik Phaisomphone, 362
Kiem, Tran Buu, 666, 667
Kiesinger, Kurt-George, 9, 176, 225-29 *passim*, 240, 333, 492, 599, 953; quoted, 966
Kill, Jean, 382
Kim Chang-pong, 434, 436
Kim Chon-hae, 435
Kim Ik-son, 434
Kim Il, 434, 443, 603, 1062
Kim Il-song, 38, 120, 156, 157, 268, 371, 434-46 *passim*, 762, 1061, 1093; quoted, 437, 440, 441
Kim Kwang-hyop, 434, 442, 1058, 1059
Kim Kyong-hwa, 435
Kim Ok-sun, 435, 444
Kim Song-kun, 444
Kim To-man, 435, 436
Kim Tong-kyu, 434, 435
Kim Wal-yong, 435
Kim Yo-chung, 434
Kim Yong-chu, 434, 435
Kim Yun-son, 156, 445
Kin, L., 517
King, Martin Luther, Jr., 619
Kinh, Nguyen Van, 639
Kirilenko, Andrei P., 580, 581
Kirkos, Leonidas, 253
Kisielewski, Stefan, 489
Kiss, Károly, 284
Kivimaki, Erkki, 201
Klaus, Josef, 29, 30
Kleiber, Günther, 223
Klička, Benjamin: quoted, 863
Klíma, Ivan, 169, 171, 868
Kliszko, Zenon, 219, 484, 487, 488, 493, 494, 496, 555, 662; quoted, 487, 488, 489, 493
—report on tasks of CP in Poland, 487-88; abridged text, 949-52
Klosiewicz, Wiktor, 495
Klugman, James, 245
Klyuyev, Nikolai A., 985
Kniestedt, Karl-Heinz, 239
Ko Chun-taek, 435
Ko Hyok, 435, 436
Kobayashi Yuichi, 748
Kochinian, Anton I., 582
Kociolek, Stanislaw, 484, 493; quoted, 485
Kock, Erwin, 697
Kodicek, Egon, 27
Kohout, Pavel, 169
Koivisto, Mauno, 201n
Koivunen, Matti, 201
Kolakowski, Leszek, 489
Kolder, Drahomír, 166, 166n
Koleka, Spiro, 3

Koliševski, Lazar, 681
Koliyannis, Kostas, 252, 256, 257, 258, 767; quoted, 253
Kolle Cueto, Jorge, 40, 42, 616; quoted, 42
Kominek, Archbp. Boleslaw, 488
Komocsin, Zoltán, 30, 179, 219, 282, 292, 294, 517; text of his article on 1968 Budapest meeting, 893-95
Konar, Harekrishna, 301
Kondor, Valerio, 45
Kong May, 362
König, Helmut: cited, 337; quoted, 337n
Konno Junichi, 354, 356, 942
Konno Yojiro, 349
Konstantinov, F., 588; quoted, 588
Koo Yung, 523
Köpeczi, Béla, 289; quoted, 289
Koplenig, Johann, 27-30 *passim*; quoted, 29
Kopysov, I.: cited, 599
Korkmazgil, Husein, 577n
Korneichuk, Alexandr E., 697
Kornilov, Lavr G., 587
Kosidowski, Zenon, 590
Kositsyn (Soviet academician), 587
Kosygin, Alexei N., 25, 32, 65, 152, 154, 157, 205n, 369, 407, 490, 572, 577, 580, 581, 584, 595, 602, 605, 766, 824, 825, 831, 1026, 1058, 1062, 1076, 1077, 1085; quoted, 607, 932
Kotovsky, Grigori, 735
Kotsev, Venelin, 51
Koua Keu, 371
Koucký, Vladimír, 166, 177, 178n, 179, 513, 1087, 1092; quoted, 176-79 *passim*
Kovalenko, Ivan, 354
Kow Kee Seng, 522
Kozlov, G.: cited, 587
Krag, Jens Otto, 180, 181
Krasin, I., 588; quoted, 588
Krasucki, Henri, 208
Krausz, Georg, 731
Krebs, Robert, 551
Kreisky, Bruno, 27-28, 29
Kriegel, František, 139, 166n
Krishna Iyer, V. R., *see* Iyer, V. R. Krishna
Kristensen, Per, 181
Krleža, Miroslav, 684
Kroupa, Jiří: cited, 169
Ksenofontov, I. K., 993
Ku Il-son, 447
Ku Mu, 808
Kuan Feng, 104, 113
Kubadinski, Pencho, 51
Kubitschek, Juscelino, 47-48
Kubka, Jiří, 732, 733; quoted, 733, 734
Kudrya, I. D., 993
Kulakov, F. D., 581
Kularb Saipradit, 567
Kulo, K. L., 204
Kumar, Raj, 386
Kumarasamy, C., 82
Kumarasamy, P., 82

Kumarasiri, Premalal, 82
Kunaiev, Dinmukhamed A., 581, 582
Kuo Chien, 727; quoted, 727
Kuo Mo-jo, 346, 705
Kurahara Korendo, 349
Kuroiedov, Vladimir, 582n
Kuron, Jacek, 489, 489n
Kurras (West German), 241
Kursanov, G., 589
Kurzendörfer, Herwig, 242
Kurzweil, Bettina Aptheker, 610
Kushev, Yevgeniy, 343, 593
Kuster, Bruno, 239, 240, 242
Kuusinen, Hertta, 201, 204; quoted, 203
Kuusinen, Otto, 695
Kuwatli, Murad, 697
Kuyen, Mme. Le Thi, 661; quoted, 661
Kuznetsov, N. I., 993
Ky, Nguyen Cao, 668, 669, 852
Ky, To, 647, 667
Ky, Ung Ngoc, 666

Labastida, Jaime, 400
Lacavé, Paul, 259
Lacerda, Carlos, 47
Lacis, M. J., 993
Lacquer, Walter Z.: quoted, 607
Lafont, Manlio, 122, 128, 1065
Lager, Fritjof, 549, 754
Lahiri, Somnath, 300
Lahr, Rolf, 291
Laine, Olavi J., 201, 206, 294, 731
Lairet, Germán, 629, 631, 635, 841, 850; quoted, 635, 841
el-Lakany, Mohamed, 735
Lakos, Sándor, 283
Lall, Diwan Chaman, 697
Lam Fung Sing, 383
Lam, Nguyen, 639
Lamberz, Werner, 223
Lambrakis, Gregoris, 703
Lamon, Victor, 393
Landin, Sven, 544, 545n
Lansang, José, 480; quoted, 480
Lantz, Benne, 542
Lapot, Stanislaw, 495
Lapuz, José, 480
Lara, Augusto, 128, 1066
Lara Parada, Ricardo, 127
La Riva, Edecio, 1004
La Rosa, Elias, 854
Larsen, Aksel, 180-81
Larsen, Reidar T., 448-54 passim, 518, 767; quoted, 448-54 passim
Lascina, Ignacio, 481
Lašek, Josef: cited, 176
Lashkova, Vera, 593, 594
Laski, Michael, 622, 623
Laštovička, Bohuslav, 166
Laub, Levi, 618
Laurent, Paul, 208

Lauscher, Josef, 27, 30, 224
Lava, Jesus, 477, 483; quoted, 477
Laverne, Richard, 393
Layachi, Abdallah, 224, 409, 412
Leal, Enrique, 854
Leborgne, Yves, 261
Lebrun, Bernadette, 77
Lecanuet, Jean, 213
Lechin Oquendo, Juan, 41
Lechleiter, Jakob, 224, 551, 553, 554
Lechowicz, Wlodimierz, 740
Lechuga, Carlos, 442
Ledda, Romano, 342; cited, 343n
Ledesma Izquieta, Genaro, 467
Leduc, Renato, 731
Ledwohn, Josef, 234
Lee Chao Lai, 524
Lee Kuan Yew, 391, 521, 522, 523
Lee Siew Choh, 522, 523; quoted, 522
Lee Sit Chuan, 524
Lefebvre, Fernand, 37
Le Gal, Francis, 713, 714, 716; quoted, 716
Legris, Michel, 221
Lehtinen, Inkeri, 201, 207; quoted, 202
Lenárt, Jozef, 166, 166n, 1026; quoted, 177
Lenin, V. I., 7, 8, 28-29, 68, 76, 145, 152-53, 179, 187, 266, 284n, 343, 346, 349, 369, 403, 404, 405, 425, 454, 482, 531, 533, 543, 558, 572, 577, 579, 586n, 587, 591, 617, 626, 635, 654, 703, 705, 762, 764, 765, 769, 770, 782, 783, 786, 793, 823-31 passim, 878-83 passim, 896-99 passim, 904, 941, 945, 946, 981-84 passim, 988, 989, 992, 1004, 1014, 1015, 1017, 1042, 1059; quoted, 153, 267, 399, 405, 582, 631, 633, 783, 825, 826, 830, 880-83 passim, 896, 897, 901, 902, 904, 907, 909, 913, 914, 916, 992, 1004, 1014, 1015
Lentillon, Etienne, 551, 554, 558
Leon, Potenciano de, 480
Leoni, Raúl, 630, 637, 761, 838-43 passim, 848-54 passim, 1003; quoted, 841
Leonov, Leonid, 590
Lépine, Edouard de, 393, 395; quoted, 395
Lepola, Jalo, 207
Leroy, Roland, 208, 219
Lester, Julius, 158
Levaux, Marcel, 34, 224
Levy, Simon, 409
Lhamsuren, B., 401
Li Chen Min, 523
Li Ching-ch'üan, 99, 102, 1072
Li Chu-wen, 697
Li Fu-ch'un, 98, 99, 103
Li Hsien-nien, 99, 103
Li Hsüeh-feng, 99, 103, 108n, 808
Li Jui-shan, 108n
Li On Tung, 383
Li Pao-hua, 102
Li Shin-ju, 742
Li Shou-pao, 697, 704
Li Te-sheng, 108n

Li Tien-yu, 113
Li Tsai-han, 107
Li Tso-p'eng, 113
Li Yüan, 108n
Liang Li Ing, 523
Liehm, Antonín J., 169, 171, 868; quoted, 169
Lien, Hong, *see* Tu, Hu
Lien, Le, 639
Liew Yit Fun, 383
Lightfoot, Claude, 610, 614, 616, 618; quoted, 614, 615
Liljesson, Folke, 542
Lim Chin Siong, 383, 521, 521n, 523
Lim Hock Siew, 523
Lim Huan Boon, 522; quoted, 522
Lim Kean Siew, 385, 386
Lima, Albert Jason, 610, 617, 618
Lima, Firmino de, 45
Lin Chao Nan, 524
Lin Chieh, 104
Lin Hai-yin, 119
Lin Piao, 98-106 *passim*, 113, 799, 812, 813, 816, 822, 832, 833, 835, 942; quoted, 834, 835; text of speech on Communist China's 18th anniversary, 818-19; text of speech on October Revolution, 829-31
Lin Piao, Mme., *see* Yeh Ch'un
Linares, Angel, 854
Linder, Walter, 618
Lindingan, Jesus (*alias* "Commander Roldan"), 480
Lippe, Just, 448, 454
Lisichkin, G., 597
Lissaridis, Vassos, 163
Lister, Enrique, 529, 697, 701
Litvak, S., 330
Litvinov, Maxim, 594, 997
Litvinov, Pavel M., 594; excerpts from his open letter on interrogation regarding Bukovsky affair, 996-97
Liu Chien-hsun, 108
Liu Hsien-ch'un, 107
Liu Ke-p'ing, 107
Liu Lan-tao, 808
Liu Ning-i, 99
Liu Po-ch'eng, 99
Liu Shao'ch'i ("China's Khrushchev"), 37, 38, 99-106 *passim*, 117, 314, 345, 353, 571, 812, 813, 818, 821, 822, 827, 832-36 *passim*, 940, 943, 1067; quoted, 835, 836; text of his confession, 808-11
Liu Shao-ch'i, Mme., *see* Wang Kuang-mei
Liu Teng, 109
Lizalde, Eduardo, 400
Llanusa, José, 136, 141
Lleras Restrepo, Carlos, 122, 125, 851, 852
Lo Jui-ch'ing,, 101, 102n, 106, 813, 832-36 *passim*; quoted, 833, 834, 836
Loan, Ngo Minh, 639
Loan, Mme. Thanh, 679
Lobachev, N. F., 585
Lobaton, Guillermo, 474, 858
Lobaton, Jacqueline de, 475; quoted, 475

Loc, Nguyen Van (North Vietnamese), 639, 641
Loc, Nguyen Van (South Vietnamese), 669
Lockhart, R. H. Bruce, 993
Lockwood, Rupert, 25
Løfsnes, Knut, 679; quoted, 679
Loga-Sowiński, Ignacy, 484, 492, 493, 494, 707; quoted, 490, 492, 494
Lombardi, Riccardo, 337
Lomský, Bohumír, 177
Long, Nguyen Xuan, 676; quoted, 677
Longo, Luigi, 59, 179, 210, 219, 225, 232, 335-44 *passim*, 494, 517, 518, 691, 754, 755, 766, 767, 924, 1059, 1067, 1068, 1079, 1080, 1082, 1094; quoted, 336-40 *passim*; abridged text of statement on Middle East, 931-33; texts of four articles on international communist movement, 934-39
López, Arturo, 463
López, Julio, 267
López, Samuel, 400
López, Tranquilino, 265
López Michelsen, Alfonso, 124
López Molina, Máximo, 188-89; quoted, 189
López Raimondo (Spaniard), 529
Lora, Guillermo, 43
Lorentzson, Gustav, 542
Losada, Francisco, 853
Losonczi, Pál, 284, 1069
Lourdes Pacheco, Ana, 853
Lovera, Alberto, 853, 1003, 1004, 1005
Løvlien, Emil, 448, 451n
Lu Cheng, 383
Lu Pin, 748
Lu Ting-i (Lu Ting-yi), 101, 813, 832
Lubsan, Sonomyn, 401, 408, 660; quoted, 408
Lubsanrabdan, N., 401
Luce, Phillip Abbott, 618; quoted, 618; cited, 619
Luck, Rudy, 270
Ludger, Nicolas, 259, 261
Lukács, György, 283-84, 284n; quoted, 284, 284n
Lukman, Mohammad H., 309, 318, 908, 917
Lumer, Hyman, 224, 610, 618; quoted, 617
Lumumba, Patrice, 857
Luna, José, 396
Lunar Márquez, Gregorio, 630, 840, 850
Lund, Gelius, 181, 183; quoted, 183
Lundkvist, Nils Artur, 697
Lungarzo, José Oscar, 20
Luong, Le Van, 639
Luong, Tran, 639
Luong, Vo Van, 666
Lussier, Claude, 743
Luthuli, Albert, 525
Lutz, Charles-Henry, 77, 80
Luu, Nguyen Thi, 640
Luzzato, Lucio, 697
Ly, Tran Thi, 653
Lyagin, V. A., 993
Lyman, Brian, 251
Lysenko, Trofim D., 245

Maag, Peter, 557, 558
Macaluso, Emanuele, 336, 340
McAra, W., 422
Macdonald, A., 21
McDonald, Alex, 248
Macdonald, K. T., 21
Macé, Gabriel, 506
Macek, Josef, 697
Maceo, Antonio, 848
McEwan, Tom, 80
Machado, Eduardo, 629
Machado, Gustavo, 629
Machado, Ramón, see Machado Ventura, José Ramón
Machado Ventura, José Ramón, 152, 766
Maclang, Federico, 477
McLennan, Gordon, 244; quoted, 249
McLeod, Hugh, 422, 426
McNamara, Robert, 577
Madariaga Montes, Roberto, 460
Madoyan, Artine, 373, 373n
Madsen, Arne, 181
Magallanes, Juan Osirio, 853
Magnin, Armand, 551
Magnuson, Bruce, 77
Maharjan, Tirtha Lal, 416
Mahbudullah (Pakistanian), 458
Mahendra, King of Nepal, 414, 415, 416
Maher, Albert, 618
Mahjub, 'Abd al-Khaliq, 537, 538, 660
Mahle, Hans, 239, 242
Mai, Nguyen Huu, 639, 641
Maitan, Livio, 346, 347
Makarios III, Archbishop, 162, 163, 164, 257, 258
Makhous, Ibrahim, 565, 768
Makotoko, Seth, 377, 378
Malaver, Felipe, 838, 853
Malcolm X, 622
Maldonada, Edelmiro, 400
Maldonado Salazar, Alberto, 732
Malck, Ivan, 735
Malhotra, Avtar Singh, 297
Malik, Adam, 314, 315, 317
Malin, V. N., 582
Malinovsky, Rodion Ya., 584, 1068
Malita (Rumanian Deputy Foreign Minister), 515, 518, 1062
Maller, Rolando, 396
Malmberg, Martti, 201
Malmierca, Isidoro, 139, 161
Malone, P., 25
Malpica, Carlos, 471
Man, Chu Huy, 639, 647, 667
Mancas, Nicolai, 713
Mandelshtam, Osipo E., 985, 986
Maneiro, Alfredo, 630, 631n, 633
Mănescu, Corneliu, 518, 1085
Mănescu, Manea, 508, 515
Manon, Melvin, 188
Manov, Emil, 54, 54n; quoted, 54n
Mantilla, Manuel, 839

Manuit Camero, Elías, 446, 630, 631, 636, 838, 839, 840, 850
Manuweera, D., 748
Manzanares, Alberto, 854
Manzano, Julio, 854
Mao Tse-tung, 5, 7, 18, 19, 25-26, 37, 39, 43, 48, 56, 61, 64, 65, 73, 75, 76, 86, 87, 95, 97-120 passim, 129, 134, 140, 151, 152, 154, 178, 183-90 passim, 194, 225, 230, 245, 251, 257, 266, 269, 279, 293, 304, 305, 310, 314, 316, 323, 326, 343, 346, 352n, 353, 354, 361, 369, 375, 382, 384, 389, 398, 400, 404, 405, 406, 412, 416, 423-26 passim, 459, 471, 473-74, 478, 481, 483, 504, 515, 527, 534, 535, 540, 555, 557, 558, 565, 567, 570-71, 572, 585, 589, 602, 603, 615, 620, 622, 628, 631n, 635, 655, 656, 657, 677, 689, 690, 748, 749, 750, 764, 773, 774, 793-837 passim, 878, 879, 883, 924, 928, 940, 966, 967, 977, 980-81, 994, 1053, 1054, 1058, 1062, 1063, 1065, 1072, 1074, 1085; quoted, 110, 303, 352, 352n, 773, 775, 795-807 passim, 819-36 passim, 878, 879, 897, 900, 901, 945, 946, 974; excerpts from Akahata article on his policies and his faction, 940-46; text of Pravda editorial on his and his group's anti-Soviet policy, 972-76. See also Maoism, Maoists
Mao Tse-tung, Mme., see Chiang Ch'ing
Maranhao, Olga, 45
Maravilla, Jorge, 477; quoted, 477
Marcano, José, 503
Marchais, Georges, 208, 210, 213, 214, 224; quoted, 210
Marcos, Ferdinand, 480
Marcuse, Herbert, 241
Marek, Franz, 27, 33
Maresiev, Alexei Petrovich, 740
Margono, G., 713
Mari Bras, Juan, 505; quoted, 505
Marianetti, Benito, 16
Marighella, Carlos, 45-46, 1092
Marin, Gladys, 89, 90; quoted, 90
Marinello, Juan, 697
Marischi, Vicente, 16
Marjanović, Jovan: cited, 684
Marklund, Eivor, 542
Marko, Rita, 3
Marks, John B., 525, 527, 697, 768
Márquez, Pompeyo, 629, 631n, 633, 838, 845, 846, 1062; quoted, 629, 845-46
Marrat, Florient: cited, 274
Marte Polanco, Ignacio, 187
Martí, José, 160, 762, 1021, 1028
Martín, Américo, 637, 847, 848, 858, 1075
Martín, Miguel, 136, 137, 143; quoted, 143
Martínez, Aurelio, 139, 161
Martínez, Carlos, 854
Martínez, César, 122
Martínez, Daniel, 400
Martínez, Fernando (Cuban), 161

Martínez, Fernando (Nicaraguan; *possible pseud. of* Casimiro Sotelo Montenegro), 430
Martínez, Hector, 280; quoted, 280
Martínez, Napoleón, 131
Martínez, Salvador, 400
Martínez Anez, Luis, 854
Martínez de Campos, Arsenio, 848
Martínez Verdugo, Arnoldo, 396, 397, 398, 767
Martins, Walter, 49
Marty, François, 221
Marulanda Vélez, Manuel (*alias* Tiro-Fijo), 123, 858
Marx, Karl, 7, 68, 93, 145, 179, 187, 266, 482, 587, 654, 762, 765, 802, 823, 825, 829, 878, 879, 883, 889, 913, 941, 945, 946, 983, 984, 988, 992, 1081; quoted, 405, 782, 810, 825
Masarani, Faruq, 697
Masherov, Piotr M., 581, 582
Massera, José Luis, 225, 624; quoted, 628
Massoz, Maurice, 37
Matar, José, 139
Mateev, Pavel, 53-54; quoted, 54
Matern, Hermann, 223, 229, 232
Matsushima Harushige, 349
Matthews, George, 244, 248
Matthews, Herbert: quoted, 154
Matthews, Joe, 742
Matute, Daniel, 854
Mau, Ngo, 150
Maugu, René, 192, 193
Maunsbach, Per, 543-544
Maurer, Ion Gheorghe, 508, 509, 510, 515, 519; quoted, 510
Mauvois, Georges, 393, 395
Mavromatis, Panayotis, 252, 343
Mayakovsky, Vladimir V., 764, 985
Maydar, D., 401; quoted, 403
Mayorga Delgado, Silvio, 430
Maysouk Saysompheng, 362
Maza Paredes, Jesús, 471, 476; quoted, 471-72
Mazumdar, Charan, 303
Mazumdar, Charu, 302
Mazumdar, Khoken, 302
Mazur, Marian, 742
Mazurov, Kirill T., 580
Mchedlov, M. P., 28
Mechini, Rodolfo, 713, 716, 717; quoted, 716, 717
Medina Silva, Pedro, 631, 841, 850; quoted, 841
Medvedev, D. N., 993
Mekki, 'Usman Mustafa, 537
Mendès-France, Pierre, 215
Méndez, Alirio, 853
Méndez, Francisco, 464
Méndez Figueredo, Humberto, 854
Méndez Montenegro, Julio César, 265
Mendis, Merenna G., 82
Mendoza, Carmelo, 854
Mendoza, Jorge Enrique, 139, 161
Mendoza Angarita, Antero, 854
Menéndez Rodríguez, Mario, 127, 128, 635, 636
Menesse, Luis, 45
Ménil, René, 393

Menon, C. Achutha, 297
Menzhinsky, V. R., 993
Mercado, Manuel, 1030
Merchan, Victor J., 122
Mercieca, Monique, 209
Merida, Saez, 847
Mero, Agim, 3
Mesplé, Joao Antonio, 732
Mestre, Michele, 220
Meyers, George, 610
Mezquida, Gabriel, 503, 504
Mfenyana, Sindiso, 713
Miasnikov (Russian), 591
Michailidis, Charalambos (Chambis), 163
Mieres, Francisco: quoted, 633, 635
Mihajlov, Mihajlo, 685
Mijal, Kazimierz, 495
Mikhaylov, Ivan, 51
Mikoyan, Anastas I., 152
Mikunis, Shmuel, 294, 330-34 *passim*, 518, 1068; quoted, 331
Milan, Maurizio, 740
Milić, Živko: quoted, 689-90
Millas, Orlando, 89, 96
Minh, Dang Quang, 678
Minh, Tran Hieu, 679
Minobe Ryokichi, 348
Mirabal Machado, Eduardo, 854
Mirajkar, S. S., 298
Miranda Pacheco, Mario, 41
Misam-Han, Jules-Théodore, 732
Misra, Shiva Kumar, 303
Mitchell, J., 21
Mitronov, N. R., 582
Mittag, Günther, 223, 227, 232, 1067; quoted, 227
Mitterand, François, 214, 215, 216
Miyamoto Kenji, 117, 348, 349, 352n, 353, 354, 355n, 940, 941
Mňačko, Ladislav, 171-72
Mobutu, Joseph, 606
Mochalski, Herbert, 697
Moczar, Mieczyslaw, 484
Modzelewski, Karol, 489, 489n
Moe, Gunnar, 593-94
Moerehout, A., 37
Moghioros, Alexandru, 508
Mogollon, Antonio, 853
Mohamad, Ibrahim, 384
Mohendra, Promila, 726
Mohn, Willi, 234
Moine, André, 212
Moix, José, 529
Mojkowski, Stanislaw, 485
Mokhehle, Ntsu M., 377, 378
Moldovan, Roman, 510
Moleiro, Moises, 637
Mollet, Guy, 215, 216, 518
Molodtsov, Stepan, 697
Molodstov, V. A., 993
Molomjamts, D., 401
Mon, Vo Man, 666-67

Mon Vong Phithiyaroth, 567
Monachon, André, 556
Moncada, R., *see* Soza Navarro, Mario
Moncada Zavala, Ricardo, *see* Soza Navarro, Mario
"Monchín," *see* Pinedo, Ramón A.
Moncloa, Francisco, 471
Mondlane, Eduardo, 768
Monetti, Pietro, 551
Mongkon Na Nakorn, 566, 567
Monje Molina, Mario, 40-43 *passim*, 159; quoted, 41
Monrose, Arsène, 261
Monsanto, Pablo, 264, 266
Montaña Cuéllar, Diego, 122, 125, 125n, 126, 1090; quoted, 125
Montander, Julio E., 189
Montaner, Raúl, 460, 461
Monteil, Raymond, 209
Monteleone, Antonio, 346
Montero, Bernardo: quoted, 90
Montero, Rafael Simon, 853
Montero Vega, Alvaro, 133, 134; quoted, 133, 134-35
Montes, César, 263-69 *passim*, 858, 1068, 1087; quoted, 264, 265n, 266, 269
Montes, Eduardo, 396
Montes, Jorge, 89, 94
Montesinos, José, 853
Montiel, Alejandro, 853
Moore, Hugh, 232, 329, 754, 1088
Mophoso, Florence, 726
Mora, Diosmedes, 463
Mora, Reinaldo Leandro, 629, 838, 839; quoted, 838-39
Mora Valverde, Manuel, 133, 134, 135, 767; quoted, 134
Morales, Elvina de, 854
Morales, Mario, 278, 279, 281, 1057
Morales, Otto, 187, 188
Morantes, Luis, 122
Morazán, Francisco, 762
More, Ernesto, 476
Morel, Efrain, 463
Morelo Cevallos, Nelson, 189
Moreno, Félix, 463
Moreno, Joaquín, 122, 129; quoted, 129
Moretti, Florindo A., 16
Morgan, Nigel, 77
Moro, Aldo, 924
Morris, Tom, 77
Morrison, Floyd Wendell Britton, *see* Britton, Floyd
Mortimer, Rex, 21
Morton, Cyril, 244
Mosadeq, Mohammed, 321
Moshoeshoe II, King of Lesotho, 377, 378
Moss, J., 21
Motloheloa, John, 377; quoted, 378
Moulin, Gaston, 34
Moumié, Félix, 75
Mu Hsin, 104, 121
Mubarak, Yusuf, 376
Mückenberger, Erich, 223
Muhammad Jair, Ahmad, *see* Jair, Ahmad Muhammad

Muhri, Franz, 27-31 *passim*, 754, 767, 1034, 1073, 1090; quoted, 28
Mujica, Héctor, 838; quoted, 840
Mujica, Juan Francisco, 128, 1065
Mujica, Juan Vicente, 625
Mujica, Manuel Antonio, 854
Mujica, Rosario, 853
Mukerjee, Ajoy, 300, 302
Mukerjee, Bishwanath, 297, 300, 302
Müller, Margarete, 223
Mundo, Faustino del (*alias* "Commander Sumulong"), 479, 480
Munir, Mohammad, 707
Múniz, Roberto, 20
Muñoz, Alonso, 278
Muñoz, Anibal, *see* Muñoz Quirola, Anibal Leonardo
Muñoz, Freddy, 845, 846; quoted, 845-46
Muñoz García, Luis, 742
Muñoz Mantilla, César, 195
Muñoz Matos, Juan José, 503
Muñoz Quirola, Anibal Leonardo, 195, 196
Muñoz Vicuña, Elias, 192
Munša, Vladimir, 685
Munschke, Ewald, 223
Münzenberg, Willi, 695
Muoi, Do, 639, 641
Murakami Yukari, 349
Muret, André, 551, 553, 554
Murphy, Rae, 77, 78, 80
Muruwwah (Lebanese), 373n
Mury, Gilbert, 221
Musso (Indonesian), 896
Mussolini, Benito, 255, 783
Mustapha, Bouarfa, 158
Mutran, Nakhle, 376
Muttetuwegama, Sarath, 82-83
Myftiu, Manush, 3
Mzhavanadze, Vasilii P., 581, 582

Naameh, Daniel Daud, 559
Nabaraoui, Seza, 726
Nabulsi, Suleiman, 361n
Nadesan, S., 82
Nadunga, D. N., 83
en-Nafaa, Mohammed, 574; quoted, 574-75
Naguib, Mohammed, 607
Nakano Shigeharu, 357
Nakashima, Wendy, 619
Nam Il, 434
Nam, Le Thanh, 667
Nam, Vu, 679
Namboodiripad, E. M. S., 297-304 *passim*
Namsray, Tsendijn, 408, 731, 733
Nan P'ing, 108n
Napolitano, Giorgio, 336
Nase, Nesti, 7-10 *passim*, 1079; quoted, 7, 8, 9
Nassar, Fuad, 224, 232, 358, 361, 517, 767, 1092; quoted, 358, 361
Nasser, Gamal Abdel, 361n, 368, 604, 607-8, 617, 660, 677, 931, 932, 1081
Nasution, Abdul Haris, 308, 310, 314, 315, 316, 896, 915

Natoli, Ugo, 742
Natpackho, Nara Devi, 416
Natta, Alessandro, 294, 336, 342, 924
Navarro, Ricardo, 853
Navas Pajaro, Luis, 460
Nazario, Marino, 187
N'Diongue, Babacar, 713
Ne Win, 60-64 passim, 117, 119
Nekrich, Alexandr M., 584, 585
Nem, So, 67-71 passim
Nemec, Theodor, 735
Nemes, Dezsö, 282, 294
Németh, Károly, 282
Nestoret, Edgard, 393
Neto, Agostinho, 697, 768
Nettum, Rolf, 224, 448, 454
Neubert, Wolfram: quoted, 228
Neumann, Alfred, 223
Ngeth, Leng, 67, 71; quoted, 71
Nghi, Le Thanh, 150, 516, 639, 641, 645, 652, 652n, 656, 1079; quoted, 150, 645
Ngoi, Nguyen Van, 666
Nguembus, William, 76
Nhme, Thom Me The, 666
Nhu, Nguyen: quoted, 668
Nicolas, Armand, 393, 395, 767
Niculescu-Mizil, Paul, 508, 510; quoted, 510-11
Niedergang, Marcel, 760
Nieh Jung-chen, 99, 103, 113
Nieh Yuan-tzu, 808
Nielsen, Inge, 181
Niemeyer, Oscar, 697
Niemöller, Martin, 236, 701
Nikezić, Marko, 687, 688
Nilsen, S., 181
Nilsson, Olof, 542
Nim, Hu, 67-72 passim
Nimr, Nasib, 376, 742
Ninavia, Justiniano, 42
Ning Hsiang-yu, 314
Nishizawa Ryuji, 357
Nishizawa Tomio, 349, 354
Nit Phuongdaphet, 566, 567; quoted, 571
Njono (Indonesian), 309
Njoto (Indonesian), 309, 319, 908, 917
Nkrumah, Kwame, 599, 606, 715
Nol, Lon, 68, 69, 70
Nolan, Sean, 328, 329
Nordberg, Erik, 542
Norden, Albert, 223, 229
Nordmann, Joe, 742, 744; quoted, 744
Nørlund, Ib, 59, 181, 184, 232n, 679; quoted, 184
Nosaka Sanzo, 348, 352n, 354, 355; quoted, 354
Nouhak Phoumsavanh, 362
Novella, Agostino, 336
Novoa, Carlos, 854
Novotný, Antonín, 30, 166, 166n, 167, 170-76 passim, 179, 491, 600, 601, 691, 753, 767, 868, 1026, 1034, 1064, 1065, 1078, 1082, 1084-85, 1092, 1093; quoted, 167, 170-76 passim
Nugroho, M., 659

Nugud, Muhammed Ibrahim, 537
Numata Hidesato, 224
Nunes, Cedric V., 270, 272
Nunes, Ray, 222, 422, 423, 424; quoted, 423
Nuñez, Oscar, 89
Núñez Ureta, Teodoro, 476
Nuri, Baha-Eddin, 327
Nurminen, Ossi, 207
Nushi, Gogo, 3
Nutting, Anthony, 921
Nyandaro, George, 768
Nyeng, Knud, 181
Nyers, Rezsö, 282, 285

O Chin-u, 434, 435, 436
O Ki-chon, 435, 444
Obino, Antonello, 345
Occhetto, Achille, 342
Occhipinti, Juan, 16
Ochab, Edward, 484, 490, 496; quoted, 490, 491
Ochoa, Carlota de, 853
O'Day, Gerald Patrick, 25
Odermatt, Karl, 551
Oduber Quirós, Daniel, 133
Oeste, Lincoln, 49
Oestreicher, Paul, 245
Ogando, Roberto, 138
Ogden, M., 21
Ogurtsov (Soviet professor), 594
O'Higgins, Bernardo, 762, 781
Ohnesorg, Benno, 240, 241
Ojeda, Fabricio, 841-48 passim, 853, 858, 1021; text of his letter to Castro, 844-45
Ojeda Olachea, Alonso, 629
Ojukwu, Odumegwu, 432
Oka Masayoshi, 348
Okan, Halis, 576
Olafsson, Kjartan, 295
Olalia, Felixberto, 481
Olarte, José, 396
Oldan, Julio Omar, 625
Olgeirsson, Einar, 224, 295, 296, 767
Olguin, Oscar, 476
Olivares, Flavio, 482
Oliveira, M., 713
Omo, Uche, 431
Omotosho, J. O. B., 431
Ong Chang San, 522
Ong Kee Hui, 391
Onganía, Juan Carlos, 16
Onis, Juan de: cited, 148n
Opačić, N.: quoted, 686-67
Orellana Bueso, Idelfonso, 278
O'Riordan, Michael, 328, 329, 754, 767; quoted, 328-29
Orlovsky, K. P., 993
Oropesa, Juan, 840
Orta, Concepcion, 853
Ortega Arenas, Juan, 400
Ortega Díaz, Pedro, 629
Ortiz Vides, José María, 263, 264, 268; quoted, 268

Osa, Enrique de la, 161
Osby, Urban, 547
O'Shea, C. L., 25
Ossowski, Jan: quoted, 485
Ostler, H. A., 422
Ostrovityanov, Konstantin V., 764
O'Sullivan, Herman Edward, 25
Osuna, Jesús, 854
Otegbeye, Tunji, 224, 431, 432, 433; quoted, 431, 432-33
Otero, Ramiro, 40, 41, 224; quoted, 41-42
Othar, Irma Carmen, 16
Ould Daddah, Moktar, 410
Overstreet, G. D.: cited, 297
Ovezov, Balysh, 582
Ovilla, Samuel, 396
Oyarce, José, 89
Oyela, Renaldo, 278
Ozerov (Russian), 1000
Ozmitel, F. F., 993

Passikivi, Juho, 205
Paasio, Rafael, 201, 201n, 205, 205n; quoted, 205
Padilla, Carlos, 505
Padilla, Esteban, 854
Padilla, Leonel, 400
Padilla, Luis Alberto, 707
Pae Ki-chun, 436, 447
Pahlavi, Mohammed Reza, Shah of Iran, 240, 321, 323
Paionidis, P., 162
Pajetta, Gian Carlo, 336, 341, 342, 344; quoted, 341-42
Pajković, Kjoko, 224
Pak Chong-ae, 434
Pak Kum-chol, 434, 435, 436
Pak Mun-kyu, 434, 436
Pak Sin-tok, 434, 435
Pak Song-chol, 156, 434, 438, 444, 445; quoted, 438-39
Pak Yi-pil, 445
Pak Yong-kuk, 435, 436
Palacios, Martin, 854
Palimaka, Teodor: cited, 485
Palma, Oscar Edmundo, 263, 264, 265; quoted, 264
Palmada, J., 21
Palmer, Bill, 907
Palmer, Geoffrey, 224
P'an Fu-sheng, 107
Panditha, L. W., 82
Pang Siew Fong, see Pang Siew Foo
Pang Siew Foo (alias Pang Siew Fong), 524
Pankov, Iurii, 342
Pantalion, José María, 189
Papaïoannou, Ezekias, 163, 164, 165, 754, 767; quoted, 164
Papandreou, George, 253n, 254, 254n
Paraskevopoulos, Ioannis, 253n, 254n
Párdi, Imre, 283
Paredes, Alijo C., 854
Paredes, Ricardo Alejandro, 192

Paredes Macedo, Saturnino, 469, 472
Parsons, Reg, 249
Partassidis, Kostas, 163
Partsalidis, Dimitrios (Mitso), 224, 252, 257, 258
Pascua, Edison di, 625
Pasenchuk, Valentin, 602
Pasos, Arturo, 396
Pasquier, Andrés, 838, 853
Pasquier, Ramón, 853
Passalidis, Yanis, 252
Pasternak, Boris, 584, 985, 986, 1002
Pastorino, Enrique, 624, 707
Pastyřík, Miroslav, 166
Pataki, Laszlo, 283; quoted, 283
Patilinet, Vasile, 508
Patolichev, Nikolai, 56
Patrick, Scarlett, 610
Paul VI, Pope, 212, 221, 488, 489, 555
Pavicević, Mišo, 688
Pavlov, Sergei P., 583, 769, 1001, 1001n; quoted, 717-18
Pavlov, Todor, 51
Pavolini, Luca, 342
Pavón, Luis, 161
Payet, Bruno, 507
Pearce, Bert, 244
Pecchioli, Ugo, 336, 340, 342
Pecha, František, 166
Pellecer, Carlos Manuel, 267
Pellegrini, Giacomo, 342
Pelshe, Arvids J., 210, 580
Pen, Alexander, 332
Peña, Alcira de la, 16
Pena Gonzáles, Lazaro, 707
Pena Pena (Venezuelan police officer), 853
Peña Valdez, Julio de, 187
Peng Chi-chin, 748
Peng Teh-huai, see P'eng Te-huai
P'eng Chen, 101, 103, 813, 832
P'eng Te-huai, 106, 113, 812, 832, 833, 835
Peralta, Antonio, 476
Pereda, José, 280
Peredo, Inti, 151
Peredo Leigue, Guido, 44
Pereira, Osny Duarte, 742
Perera, Basil, 88; quoted, 88
Perera, J. A. K., 82
Perera, N. M., 82
Pérez, Carlos Andrés, 837, 1004; quoted, 837
Pérez, Enrique, 854
Pérez, Julio Ernesto, 128, 1066
Pérez, Roberto, 128, 1066
Pérez de Acuña, Irene, 625
Pérez Estrada, Manuel, 427
Pérez Gaytán, Encarnación, 396
Pérez Jiménez, Marcos, 629, 783, 841, 842, 844
Peris, Pardede, 309
Peron, Juan, 18. See also Peronism, Peronists
Persaud, Balchand, 270; quoted, 271-72
Persaud, Bhola, 270
Persaud, Janki, 270

Persaud, Reepudaman, 270
Persson, Folke, 542
Pesce, Osvaldo, 345
Pessi, Ville, 200-207 *passim*, 232, 754, 767, 1034, 1075, 1093; quoted, 203-6 *passim*
Péter, János, 291
Peters, Y. Kh., 993
Petersen, Gert: quoted, 544
Pethö, Tibor, 292; cited, 287; quoted, 292
Petilaire, H., 259, 261
Petit, Ernest, 209
Petkoff, Luben, 636, 637
Petkoff, Teodoro, 629, 637, 838, 845, 846, 1062; quoted, 633, 637, 845-46
Petras, Christos, 163, 294
Petras, James: quoted, 474
Petritis, Achileas, 343
Petros, Behnam, 713
Petrović, Dušan, 681
Petruccioli, Claudio, 336
Pettersen, Arne, 448
Pettersson, Lars, 542
Pettersson, Rune, 542
Petursson, Bovar, 295
Pezerat, Henri, 220
Pfeifer, J., 854
Phat, Huynh Tan, 666, 667, 669
Phatthanothai, Miss (Thai), 571
Pheng Phang, 362
Phengkhoune Voraphet, 371
Phiet, Ton Quang, 370, 659
Phoum Sipasat, 362, 363
Phoumi Vongvichit, 362, 363, 367-71 *passim*; quoted, 367, 369, 370
Phoune Sipraseuth, 362
Pien Cheng, 400; quoted, 400
Pierre, Gerard Jean, 273, 276
Pierre-Justin, Serge, 259, 260
Pietrarroia, Rosario, 624
Pike, Douglas: cited, 663, 664, 667
Piller, Jan, 166n
Pilnyak, Boris, 985, 986
Pimenov, Petr: quoted, 710
Pin Bua-orn (*alias* Chin Buaprasert), 566
Pineda, Aníbal, 732
Pinedo, Ramón A. (*alias* "Monchín"), 187, 188
Piñera, Arnoldo, 16
Piñerio, Manuel, 136
Pintado, William, 504
Pinto, Tirso, 630, 631, 633, 841; quoted, 841
Pinto Gandía, Julio, 503
Pinzón Caicedo, Guillermo, 128
Piquet, René, 208, 294
Pirsch, Hans: quoted, 228
Pitti, Dario, 460
Piyadasa, A., 82
Platon, Albert, 393, 395
Platonov, Sergei F., 985, 986
Plekhov, A.: cited, 586
Pleskot, Václav, 177

Pliego Galicia, Adalberto, 398
Plissonnier, Gaston, 208, 214, 219
Po I-po, 99
Poblete de Espinosa, Olga, 697
Podgorny, Nikolai V., 28, 152, 205, 221, 337, 369, 490, 580, 585, 605, 690-91, 766, 1026, 1058, 1059, 1072, 1074, 1076, 1078, 1085, 1092
Podzerko, Viktor A., 707, 711; quoted, 711
Poh Soo Kai, 523
Poikolainen, Olavi, 201, 206
Pokharel, Mohan, 416
Polacek, Karel, 707
Poliansky, Dmitri S., 580
Pomelov, I., 588, 687, 1063; quoted, 588
Pomeroy, William, 477
Ponce, Pilar, 854
Ponce de Léon, Hugo, 396, 398
Ponnambalam, V., 82
Ponomarev, Boris N., 30, 207, 219, 224, 342, 534, 554, 581, 1075
Popoff, Emil: cited, 54
Popov, Ivan, 51
Popova, Nina, 726
Popović, Koča, 681, 682n, 687
Popović, Milentije, 681, 682, 684n
Popović, Vladimir, 681, 682n, 687, 688, 1026
Porcel, Miguel, 460
Portocarrero Ríos, Elio, 474
Posada, Julio, 128, 1066
Posadas, J., 251
Posadas, Marcos Leonel, 396, 398
Pospelov, P. N., 584, 585
Pospielovsky, D.: cited, 582n
Potamitis, Giagos, 163
Poulssen, Johannes, 181
Powell, Adam Clayton, 619, 622
Powell, Cecil F., 735, 736
Prada, Francisco, 155, 160, 631, 636, 759, 760, 761, 763, 840, 850; quoted, 636
Prado, Jorge del, 468, 471, 472, 767; quoted, 472
Prado, P., 222
Praphat Charusathian, 566, 568, 569, 569n, 570
Prebićević, Branko, 178n
Prenant, Marcel, 220
Prestes, Luis Carlos, 45, 46, 48, 217; quoted, 46-47, 48
Pridi Phanomyong, Nai, 567; quoted, 567
Primakov, Ye., 325n; quoted, 325n
Pritt, Denis Nowell, 742, 743
Pritt, Marie Frances, 726
Procházka, Jan, 170, 171, 868-69; quoted, 169
Proctor, Roscoe, 610
Progsch, Josef, 30
Prokopyuk, N. A., 993
Prudnikov, M. S., 993
Prunov, Ivan, 51
Pruss, Helmut, 223
Prybyla, Jan S.: cited, 7
Pu, Thakin, 61
Pu, Yebaw Bo, 61
Puenta Uceda, Luis de la, 474, 475, 858, 1021, 1074

Puente, Ivan del, 280
Puerta Quiroga, Ramiro, 745
Puga Chávez, Walter, 473
Puja, Frigyes: cited, 294
Pulido Valente, Joao, 501
Pullai, Arpád, 282
Punyasena, W. G., 82
Purevjav, C., 401
Pushpa Lal, see Shrestha, Pushpa Lal
Pustovalov, I., 595, 596

Qasimi, Ahmed, 323
Qasuri, Mahmud Ali, 456
Quang, Nguyen Van, 667
Quang, Vu, 640, 658
Que, Ha Thi, 639
Quintana, Juan, 471; quoted, 471-72
Quraitem, Hasan, 373, 373n, 376

Raatikainen, Erkki, 28, 205; quoted, 205, 206
Rabell, Narciso, 505
Radmanesh, Reza, 59, 224, 321, 322, 323, 518, 767,
    1081; quoted, 322
Radov, G.: cited, 599
Rǎdulescu, Gheorghe, 157, 517; quoted, 517
Ragyanszki, Erzsi, 726
Rahman, Ali Abdul, 768
Rahman, Sheikh Mujibur, 457
Rahman, Tunku Abdul, 386, 387, 523; quoted, 386,
    387
Rahman Khan, Ataur, 458
Raimondi, Luciano, 346
Raindorf, René, 37, 38
Rajan, Sundar: cited, 299
Rakhimbabaeva, Zakhra, 726
Ramamurthi, P., 298
Rambaldi, Enrico, 345
Ramelson, Bert, 224, 244, 246; quoted, 246
"Ramírez," see Soto Rojas, Fernando
Ramírez, Antonio, 192
Ramírez, José (Pepe), 137
Ramírez, Ramón, 396
Ramírez, Raúl, 463
Ramírez González, Alvaro, 427
Ramírez Nova, Ezequiel, 476
Ramkarran, B., 270
Ramones Prieto, Omar, 854
Ramos, Pedro, 853
Ramos, Victor Julio, 131
Ramos Bejarano, Dionisio, 278
Ramsahoye, Fenton, 270
Rana, Punne Prataya, 414
Ranadive, B. T., 298, 301, 303, 307
Rangel, Domingo Alberto, 637
Rangel, Josef Vincente, 768
Ransome-Kuti, Funmilayo, 726
Rao, C. Rajeshwar, 179, 297; quoted, 305
Rapacki, Adam, 484
Rascabimo, Luis, 94
Rashad, Amjad, 326
Rashidov, Sharaf R., 581, 582

Rasmussen, Eivind, 454
Rasulov, Dzhabar D., 582
Rasy, Duoc, 69
Ratnaweera, H. G. S., 82
Rǎutu, Leonte, 508
Rayamajhi, Keshar Jang, 414, 415, 416
Raynov, Bogomil, 54; quoted, 54
Razak, Tun Abdul, 386, 387; quoted, 386
Razzak Hussein, Nuri Abdul, 324, 721
Rebelo, Jorge, 732
Reccio Gutiérrez, Evaristo, 225
Reddaway, P.: cited, 590n
Reddy, N. Rajesckhara, 297
Redmann, Emil, 239
Regis, Giuseppe, 346
Regis, Maria, 346, 1058
Regubaldo Moyano, Roque, 20
Reichlin, Alfredo, 340, 342
Reid, James, 244
Reimann, Max, 59, 224, 226, 234, 235, 238, 294,
    754, 767, 1034, 1073, 1075; quoted, 235
Reimez Mereno, Piolino, 445
Rejano, Juan, 396
Remington, Ivan, 270
Remizov, Alexei M., 985
Remy, Emile, 37
René, Georges, 259
René, Siméon, 261
Restrepo, Jorge, 131; quoted, 131
Rewang (Indonesian), 309, 310
Reyes, Carlos, 396
Reyes, Martin, 400
Reyes, Oscar, see Valero, Januario
Reyes Daglio, César, 624
Reyes Medina, Efrain, 460
Reyes Rodríquez, Eliseo, 136
Rhea, Humberto, 41
Rhoads, Rick, 618
Ri Chang-song, 156
Ribbentrop, Joachim von, 968
Ribeiro, Iracama, 45
Richter, Rudolph, 31
Richter, Sviatoslav, 590
Rieng, Le Thi, 667
Rigo, Emil, 166n
Rimel, Anita, 735
Ríotoro, Raimondo, 463
Riquelme, Samuel, 89
Risaliti, Livio, 345
Ristorucci, Carmen, 610, 616
Rittenberg, Sidney, 38
Rivera, Julio Adalberto, 197
Rivera Otero, Félix, 503
Rivera Pérez, Jacinto, 503
Rivero, Alexis, 853
Roa, Raúl, 136, 148, 151; quoted, 148-49
Robertson, Alec, 21, 26
Robertson, James, 623
Robertson, M., 21
Roca, Blas, 136-37, 139, 161
Rocha, Jorge, 17

Rochet, Waldeck, 59, 208, 210, 213-19 *passim*, 340, 342, 343, 494, 518, 662, 691, 753, 754, 767, 878, 1034, 1067, 1080, 1082, 1083, 1092, 1094; quoted, 211n, 216, 217, 878-79; abridged text of remarks on French general elections, 875-77; abridged text of paper on role of French CP, 880-84
Rodrigues, Felipe, 45
Rodrigues, Francisco Martins, 501
Rodrigues Campos, Francisco, 501
Rodríguez, Alfonso, 854
Rodríguez, Aniceto, 94, 159
Rodríguez, Basilo, 157
Rodríguez, Carlos Rafael, 136, 139, 161; quoted, 139
Rodríguez, Cayetano, 187
Rodríguez, Enrique, 624
Rodríguez, Irene F., 16
Rodríguez, José, 853
Rodríguez, José Gregorio, 853
Rodríguez, Juan, 631, 633; quoted, 633
Rodríguez, Miguel (Cuban), 161
Rodríguez, Miguel (Guatemalan), 268
Rodríguez da Silva, Manuel, 497
Rodríguez Martínez, Marco Tulio, 733
Rojas, Leonidas, 853
Rojas, Pedro, 853
Rojas, Ursinio, 157
Rojas Figueroa, Jesús Manuel, 854
Rojas Gomez, Rosendo, 713
Rojas Pinilla, Gustavo, 122
Rojo, Gaspar, 636
"Roldan, Commander," *see* Lindingan, Jesus
Rolland, Maurice, 743
Roman, Vlater, 517
Romanov, G., 454
Romanovskiy, S. K., 443
Romao, Lucas, 45
Romero, Carlos, 122
Romero, Manuel, 128, 1065
Romero, Ricardo, 42
Ron, Jorge, 195
Ronda, Pedro, 503
Rosa, Fernando de la, 185
Rosales, Francisco, 854
Rosales, Ricardo, 713
Rose, Leo E.: cited, 415
Rosen, Jack, 618
Rosen, Mrs. Jack, *see* Nakashima, Wendy
Rosen, Milton, 504, 618
Ross, E., 21
Ross, William, 77
Rossaint, Josef C., 740
Roura Cevallos, José María, 195
Rovalino, Mecías, 195
Rowan, Carl T.: quoted, 148n
Rowinsky (Pole), 495
Roy, M. N., 396
Rua, Dulfredo, 43
Rubin, Daniel Mortimer, 610
Rubliov, St. Andrey, 590
Rudas Mezones, Alberto, 853

Rudert, Walter, 239, 242
Rudnev, K., 597
Ruiz, Alvaro, 854
Rumiantsev, Alexei, 342, 587, 595, 596; quoted, ⸢
Ruschitzka, Alfred, 27; cited, 30n
Ryding, Gunvor, 542
Ryerson, Stanley, 80
Rytíř, Otakar, 177

Saad, Pedro, 59, 179, 192, 194, 225, 767, 10⸢ quoted, 193-94
Saad Niyam, Pedro Antonio, *see* Saad, Pedro
Saarinen, Aarne, 200-207 *passim*, 294, 1075, 108 quoted, 203, 204, 206; abridged text of spee⸢ on Finnish CP program, 870-1
Saavedra, Luis, 854
Sabines, Jaime, 400
Sabir, Ahmad, 358
Sabolčik, Michal, 166
Sabri, Ali, 768
Sádovský, Štefan, 166, 166n
Sadron, Charles, 735
Saehle, Harold: quoted, 451
Sahher, Sajjad, *see* Zaheer, Sajjad
Said, Farid, 358
Said, Rafat, 703
Said, Umar, 748
Saillant, Louis, 697, 706-12 *passim*; quoted, 708 709-10
Sainh Marankoul, 567
Saint-Amand, Edris, 273
Saionji Kinkazu, 353
Saiyud Kerdpol, 568
Sakirman (Indonesian), 309, 310
Salamanca Alba, Humberto, 131
Salatian, Varuj, 697
Salazar, Antonio, 497, 498
Salazar, Gabriel, 263, 268, 446; quoted, 268
Salibi, Maurice, 559
Salman, Fuad, 373, 376
Salmon, Malcolm, 21, 24
Salomää, Erkki, 200-203 *passim*, 224; quoted, 201, 202
Saly Vongkhamsao, 157, 362, 368, 371
Samad, Zahir Abdul, 559
Samantar, Yusuf Osman, 768
Samarawickrema, V. A., 82
Samarkoddy, Edmund, 82
Sambuu, J., 401
Samphan, Khiev, 67-72 *passim*
Sanakoyev, S., 599
Sanche Mijares, José, 742
Sánchez, Armando, 854
Sánchez, Camilo, 264, 266
Sánchez, Celia, 136
Sánchez, Domingo, 853, 1003
Sánchez, Gerardo, 190, 760, 763; quoted, 190
Sánchez, José, 197; quoted, 198-99
Sánchez Alvarez, Samuel, 853
Sánchez Díaz, Antonio, 136
Sánchez Hernández, Fidel, 197

Sánchez Sancho, Luis Domingo, 427, 430; quoted, 427-28, 428-29
Sandino, Augusto César, 1021
Sandoval, Alejandro, 854
Sandri, Renato, 96, 341
San Martín, José de, 762, 781, 1021
Sanmugathasan, Nagalingam, 10, 82-86 passim, 1074, 1087; quoted, 86
Sann, Son, 70
Santamaría, Haydée (Mrs. Armando Hart), 136, 758, 760, 1023
Santarén, Héctor, 16
Santhal, Jangal, 302
Santos, José, 45
Santos Rivera, Juan, 502
Sanusi, Anwar, 309
Sanyal, Kanyu, 302
Sapin, Gregorio, 624
Sardesai, S. G., 297
Sardjono, Umi, 726
Sarkar, Jagannath, 297
Sarma, P. V., 384; quoted, 389
Sarmiento, Domingo Faustino, 762
Sartre, Jean-Paul: quoted, 144
Sato, Eisaku, 349
Satyanarayana, Thammareddy, 297
Sautie, Félix, 161
Savinkov, Boris, 993
Saviola, Arminio, 607, 608; quoted, 607-8
Savvidis, Georgos, 163
Saw Hla, U, see Saw Lin, Bo
Saw Lin, Bo (alias U Saw Hla), 61-62
Sawaya, Sawaya, 373, 376
Sawicki, Jerzy, 697
Say, Mau, 69
Sayed, G. N., 456
Scalapino, Robert A.: cited, 348, 385, 415
Scanlon, Hugh, 246
Schabrod, Karl, 235
Schäfer, Max, 234
Schaffer, Gordon, 697
Schaffer, Leopold, 697
Scharf, Erwin, 27-31 passim, 179; quoted, 29
Scheer, Mortimer, 618
Scheringer, Richard, 235
Schleifer, Marc, 618
Schleifstein, Josef, 234, 241
Schmid, Johann, 31
Schmidt, Johann Lorenz, 227
Schmitt, Horst, 239
Scholl, Friedrich, 697
Schrevel, Nico, 421
Schulz, Hans-Dieter: cited, 227
Schumann, Horst, 224
Schürer, Gerhard, 226, 1067
Schütz, Klaus, 241
Scoccimarro, Mauro, 336
Scocozza, Benito, 180, 184
Scott, Jack, 81
Scott, S. W., 423
Secchia, Pietro, 342

See Cheng Kiong, 523
Seenivasagam, V., 83
Segarra, Henry, 187
Seghai, Abbas, 323
Segovia, Maria, 45
Segre, Sergio, 339, 341
Séguy, Georges, 208, 219, 1076
Seijas, Alfredo, 839
Šejna, Jan, 175n
Seman, Elías, 20
Semeraro, Michele, 346
Semichastny, V. E., 583, 584, 1073
Sen, Asit, 303
Sen, Bhowani, 224, 297
Sen, Mahendra, 707
Sen, Niranjan, 300
Senanayake, M., 768
Senanayake, Rathe Deshapriya, 676, 749
Senander, Knut, 543
Sendy, John Alan, 21; quoted, 24
Seng, Chau, 67, 70, 71, 73
Sengupta, P., 303
Sepke, Otto, 223
Sepúlveda, Enrique, 97; quoted, 97
Serafini, Aldo, 346
Sergius, Saint, 590
Serguera, Jorge, 139, 161
Serpas, José, 197, 199; quoted, 199
Setiadi, Reksoprodjo, 697
Seve, Lucien, 212n
Seyfula, Kamal, 687
Shafa, Shoja-od-din, 323
Shaflick Handal, Jorgé Roberto, 197
Shagdarsuren, Puntsagiyn, 660
Shah, Jai Govind, 414
Shah, Kamar, 414
Shahin, Rushdi, 358
Shakir, Mustafa, 376
Shamli, Shlomo, 332
Sharavish (Mongolian), 732
Sharma, Yogindra, 297
Shaw, Edward, 621
Shawi, Nicola (Nicola Chaoui), 224, 373, 373n, 375, 376, 767; quoted, 374, 375
Shchelokov, N. A., 585
Shcherbitsky, V. V., 581
Shehu, Mehmet, 3, 4, 7, 116, 820, 821, 1085
al-Sheikh, Shafie Ahmed, 538, 539, 707
Shelepin, Alexandr N., 580, 583, 584, 604-5, 707, 710, 711, 1078; quoted, 604-5
Shelest, Piotr I., 580, 582
Shevliagin, Dmitri, 588; quoted, 588; cited, 589
al-Shibli, Amin, 539; quoted, 539
Shida Shigeo, 357
Shiga Yoshio, 355, 355n, 356, 357
Shimpo Thosio, 713
Shipanga, Andreas, 732
Sholokhov, Mikhail, 343, 591, 592; quoted, 591
Shrestha, Devendra Ray, 414
Shrestha, Khrishna Das, 416
Shrestha, Pushpa Lal, 414, 415

Shrestha, Shambu Ram, 414
Shtylla, Behar, 7, 116, 1058
Shukeiry, Ahmed, 359
Shukla, Kali Shankar, 297
Sibai, Umar, 559
as-Sibai, Yusuf, 702, 749
Siban, Césario, 259
Sidortojo (Indonesian), 309
Sieghart, Paul, 171
Sieng, Huynh Minh, 679
Sierra, Orlanda, 193
Siew Chong, 383
Sifoni, Amadeo, 853
Sigfusson, Stefan, 295
Sihanouk, Prince Norodom, 67-73 *passim*, 119, 659;
    quoted, 68-73 *passim*
Šik, Ota, 167, 174
Siklosi, Norbert, 732
Silin, Yevgeni, 713
Silva, K. P., 83
Sim Liew Lin, 521, 521n
Šimon, Bohumil: quoted, 167
Simonen, Aarre, 768
Simonov, Konstantin, 601, 1000
Simpura, Jorma, 201, 207
Šimůnek, Otakar, 166
Siñani Baldivieso, Fernando, 41, 732
Sindermann, Horst, 223
Singh, Herman, 732
Singh, Hikmat, 414
Singh, Khadga Bahadur, 415
Singh, Mani, 458
Sinha, Indradeep, 297
Siniavsky, Andrei, 343, 450, 451, 591, 593
Sinisalo, Taisto, 201
Sinkapo Chounlamany, 362, 363
Siqueiros, David Alfaro, 396, 397
Sires, Valerio, 460
Sisana Sisane, 157, 363, 370, 373, 1094
Sison, José, 480, 481
Siswojo (Indonesian), 309
Sithon Khommandam, 157, 362, 370; quoted, 364
Sithonh Sibounhoung, 371
Sjöman, Ossian, 200, 201
Skoog, Erik, 542
Skotnikova, Maria, 726
Skoubarev, Chtilian, 703
Smart, W., 21
Smelov (Soviet state security official), 997
Smirnov, G., 591; quoted, 591
Smirnov, Lev Nikolaevich, 742
Smith, Ian, 248, 857
Smith, Rita, 422, 426
Smrkovský, Josef, 166n
Sneh, Moshe, 330-34 *passim*; quoted, 331
Sniechkus, Antanas J., 582
So Chol, 435
Soe, Thakin, 60, 61
Soe Maung, Yebaw Bo, 61
Sofoclis, Yannis, 163, 165
Sok San, 435, 436

Sokolowski, Gregorz, 713
Sokorski, Wlodzimierz, 745
Soler, Miguel Ángel, 463
Solis, José, *see* Solis Ruiz, José
Solis, Mario, 133
Solis Ruiz, José, 529, 961, 963
Solntsev, S. I., 993
Solomentsev, M. S., 581
Soloukhin, Vladimir, 590
Solzhenitsyn, Alexandr I., 169, 343, 591-92, 1073;
    text of his letter to Soviet Writer's Congress,
    85-87; text of letter from Union of Soviet
    Writers to, and reply by, 1000; text of
    Zimianin's remarks concerning, 1001; text of
    P. Antokolsky's letter concerning, 1002
Somoza, Anastasio, 280, 427, 428, 841
Son, Ho Xuan, 666
Son, Hoang Bich, 667
Son, Huy, 667
Son, Le Tung, 676
Son, Truong (*possible pseud. of* Nguyen Chi Thanh);
    quoted, 647, 672. *See also* Thanh, Nguyen Chi
Songeions, Hermann, 259
Sorroza, Pedro, 195
Sosa, Albino, 463
Soswinski, Ludwig, 740
Sotelo Montenegro, Casimiro (*possible pseud.*
    Fernando Martínez), 430
Soto, Alejandro, 131
Soto Féliz, Juan Pablo, 189
Soto Rojas, Fernando (*alias* "Ramírez"), 637
Soto Rojas, Victor Ramón, 853, 1004
Sotomayor, José, 469, 472
Soundiata, Manuel, 273
Souphanouvong, Prince, 157, 362-71 *passim*, 573;
    quoted, 363, 366-67, 368, 369
Souvanna Phouma, Prince, 363, 364; quoted, 364
Souza, Cleto, 460
Souza, Rúben Dario, 179, 232, 460, 767, 1093
Souza Vieira, Mario Alves de, 45
Soza Egaña, Jorge, 96
Soza Navarro, Mario (*pseud.* Ricardo Moncada Zavala;
    R. Moncado), 278, 279; quoted, 279, 280
Spacek, Josef, 166n
Spahiu, Xhafer, 3
Sparring, Åke: cited, 543
Spielmann, Georg, 740
Špiljak, Mika, 681, 682, 687, 691
Springer, A., 240
Spychalski, Marian, 484, 485, 496; quoted, 485
Ssam, *see* Kamaruzaman
Stalin, Joseph, 7, 8, 101, 111, 187, 243, 250, 251,
    387, 571, 580, 585, 586, 586n, 592, 593, 594,
    657, 695, 704, 705, 706, 709, 715, 720, 728,
    732, 737, 764, 765, 766, 823, 824, 827, 829,
    831, 879, 942, 946, 986; quoted, 826. *See also*
    Stalinism, Stalinists
Stalin, Vasiliy, 592
Stambolić, Petar, 681, 682
Stanford, John, 618
Stanley, Frank, 244

Starewicz, Arthur, 484, 555, 662
Starner, Frances L.: cited, 385
Staykov, Encho, 53
Steichen, Johan, 382
Steinthorsson, Haraldur, 295
Stenberg, Alfred, 77, 78
Stepanov, V., 595-96; quoted, 596
Stewart, J. 329
Stijačić, Radovan, 691
Stimilli, Sandro, 707
Stoica, Chivu, 224, 321, 508, 509, 510, 510n, 519; quoted, 509-10
Stojanović, Svetozar, 684
Stolle, Gerhard, 239
Stolpovsky, Boris: quoted, 709
Stoph, Willi, 223, 225, 228-29, 232, 237, 491, 1026, 1066, 1067, 1084
Stoyanov, Atanas: quoted, 53
Strauss, Franz-Josef, 227, 228, 229, 241, 333
Stringos, Leonidas, 252
Strobl, Franz, 10, 31, 31n, 32, 33, 1064, 1072, 1081
Stroessner, Alfred, 464
Strong, Anna Louise: cited, 101; quoted, 118, 152
Strougal, Lubomír, 166
Struelens, Stéphane, 37, 38
Struve, Nikita: cited, 590n
Strzelecki, Ryszard, 343-43, 484, 485, 494; quoted, 484, 486, 492, 493
Su Chen-hua, 113
Su Yu, 113
Suárez, Alberto, 624
Suárez, Isaias, 130
Subrandrio (Indonesian), 313, 915
Subasinghe, Tikiri B., 697
Suchy, Alex, 745
Sucre, Antonio José de, 762, 781
Sudin, Abdullah, 384
Sudisman (Indonesian), 309, 310
Sudjojo, Djoko, 309
Sudjono (Indonesian), 309
Sugiyama Ichihei, 748
Suharto, T. N. J., 308, 308n, 310, 314, 315, 316, 896; quoted, 308
Suhud, Noer, 309
Sukarni (Indonesian), 915
Sukarno, Achmed, 308, 308n, 311, 312, 318, 319, 319n, 896, 898, 903, 904, 905, 909, 910, 911, 915-16, 917. See also Sukarnoism
Sukatno (Indonesian), 309
Sukhe-Bator (Mongolian), 401
Sukiman (Indonesian), 905
Sukrisno (Indonesian), 309, 317
Suleyiman, Ahmad, 537
Sulis, Sjan, 310
Sumolong, Robby, 310
"Sumulong, Commander," see Mundo, Faustino del
Sunama Ichiro, 354, 356, 444, 942
Sunay, Cevdet, 577
Sundarayya, P., 298, 303, 306; quoted, 306
Sundić (Yugoslav), 689; quoted, 689

Sung Jen-ch'iung, 99, 103
Suon, Non, 67
Suonpää, Lec, 201
Supardji (Indonesian), 310
Supardjo (Indonesian), 309
Supeno (Indonesian), 748
Surasto, Setiati, 707
Suri, Muawiyah Ibrahim, 537, 538
Surjeet, H. S., 298, 303
Suslov, Mikhail A., 30, 207, 355n, 465, 554, 580, 581, 768, 1057, 1075
Sustaita, José Luis, 396
Sutadisastra, Baron, 310, 315
Suwardinengsih (Indonesian), 310
Svensson, Börje, 542
Svensson, Jörn, 542, 550
Svensson, Per, 451
Švestka, Oldřich, 166n
Svoboda, Ludvík, 166n
Synge, Ann, 697
Szabo, Alexander, 713
Szirmai, István, 282
Szyr, Eugeniusz, 484

Tabari, Ehsan, 321
Tabidze, Titsian, 986, 1002
Tadić (Yugoslav professor): cited, 682
Tadioli, Pedro, 16
Taft, Bernard, 21
Takman, John, 542, 548, 549
al-Talhouni, Bahjat, 361n
Tam, Huynh Van, 667
Tambo, Oliver, 527, 768
Tan Chee Khoon, 385
Tan, Chu Van, 639, 642, 657; quoted, 643
Tan, Ha Ke, 639, 647, 667
Tan, Le Trong, 647, 667
T'an Chen-lin, 99, 103
T'an Ch'i-lung, 102
T'ang Ping-chu, 113, 121
Tao, Bui Quang, 639
T'ao Chu, 99, 102, 104, 813
Tarer, George, 259
Tarsis, Valery, 1001
Taruc, Luis, 479, 480
Taruc, Pedro, 479, 480
Taus, Roger, 618
Tavares de Sa, J. B., 45
Tavárez, Caonabo Elpidio Jorge, 187, 188
Tavarez Justo, Enma, 189
Tavarez Justo, Manuel, 189
Taveras, Rafael "Fafa," 187, 188
Taycheng Kang, 523
Tealdi, Raúl, 625
Teekah, Vincent, 270
Teilhard de Chardin, Pierre, 588
Teitelboim, Volodia, 89, 91-92, 94, 159, 761; quoted, 94
Tejchma, Józef, 484
Teles, Jover, 45

El-Tell, Wasfi, 358
Tello, Vincente, 460
Teng Hai-ching, 108
Teng Hsiao-p'ing, 99-103 *passim,* 353, 812, 813, 942, 943; quoted, 942
Tenner, Günther, 223
Tenorio de Lima, Luis, 45
Tepun, P., 586; quoted, 586
Terborn, Göran, 546
Terfve, Jean, 34
Terracini, Umberto, 342, 740, 742
Tesch, Wilhelm, 239, 240, 242
Teufel, Fritz, 241
Texier, José: quoted, 92-93
Tha, Le Van, 667
Thai, Hoang Van, 639, 640-41, 647, 667, 668
Thai, Pham Xuan, 665, 666, 667, 669
Thai, Trin Ngoc, 653
Tham, Le Dinh, 640
Than, Le Quoc, 639, 642; quoted, 642
Than Myaing, Thakin, 61, 62
Than Tun, Thakin, 60, 61, 62, 65; quoted, 62, 63
Thang, Ton Duc, 639, 640, 641, 658
Thanh, Duong Truong, 667
Thanh, Le, 639
Thanh, Mo, 653
Thanh, Nguyen Chi (*possible pseud.* Truong Son), 120, 362n, 639, 639n, 640, 641, 647, 667-68, 672, 1078. *See also* Son, Truong
Thanh, Tran Van, 667
Thanom Kittikachorn, 566, 569, 570, 571
Thant, U. 701, 716, 728, 920, 921
Thao Pheng, 370
Thap, Nguyen Thi, 639
Thap, Mme. Nguyen Thi, 640, 658
Thavorn Vongsuma, *see* Thong Jamsri
The, Nguyen Huu, 666, 667
Thein Myint, Yebaw (*alias* Ba Khet), 61, 62
Theodorakis, Mikis, 218, 252, 253, 716, 728
Thero, U. Saranakara, 83
Thet Tin, Yebaw, 61
Thi, Dang Tran, 666, 667, 677, 768
Thi, Dinh Ba, 676, 679
Thiele, Ilse, 726
Thien, Dinh Duc, 150, 639
Thien, Nguyen Duy, 697
Thiepat, Commandant (Laotian), 363
Thieu, Nguyen Van, 668, 669
Thimotée, Georges, 393
Thinh, Hoang Quoc, 641
Thinh, Le Van, 667
Tho, Le Duc, 639, 640
Tho, Nguyen Huu, 150, 210, 371, 573, 666, 669, 678; quoted, 150, 371, 573, 671-72
Thomas, Athanasius, 732
Thomas, T. V., 301
Thomsen, Lilian, 182
Thong Jamsri (*alias* Thavorn Vongsuma), 566
Thorez, Maurice, 880; quoted, 17
Thorez-Vermeersch, Jeannette, 208
Thornton, E., 21

Thu, Ho, 666, 679
Thunborg, Karsten, 224
Thung, Huang, 732
Thuong, Nguyen Ngoc, 667
Thuy, Xuan, 639, 640
Thuyen, Ngo, 639
Ti, Mai Van, 667
Ti, Nguyen Van, 667
Tiao Souk Vongsak, 362, 370, 659
Tien, Nguyen, 667
Tien, Nguyen Van, 667, 678; quoted, 677
al-Tigani, Tagglio, 537
Tigrid, Pavel, 171, 1078; cited, 174, 175
Tilandingue, Roger, 273
Timár, Mátyás, 285
Tineo Gamboa, Luis Rafael, 854
Tinu, Dumitru: quoted, 516
Tiradentes (Joachim José da Silva Xavier), 1021
Tirado, Alfredo, 853
Tiro-Fijo, *see* Marulanda Vélez, Manuel
Tito, Josip Broz, 9, 176, 291, 293, 340, 388, 413, 601, 604, 681-91 *passim,* 695, 709, 715, 720, 728, 732, 737, 754, 767, 820, 1018, 1026, 1059-62 *passim,* 1076, 1081, 1083, 1085; quoted, 683-84, 686, 687, 690. *See also* Titoism, Titoists
Tjugito (Indonesian), 309
Toan, Nguyen Khanh, 639, 650; quoted, 650
Toan, Phan Duy, 653
Tobar, Bayardo, 193
Todorov, Ivan, 52
Todorov, Stanko, 51, 55, 59, 224; quoted, 53, 55, 59
Toeplitz, Heinrich, 742
Togliatti, Palmiro, 338, 928, 934-35, 936, 939; quoted, 934, 936
Toiv, L., 406
Tokuda Kyuichi, 353, 357
Tokuda Kyuichi, Mme., 353
Toledano, Lombardo, 396
Tolkunov, L. K., 734; quoted, 734
Tolstoy, Leo, 1002
Tomasich, José, 625
Tomiche, Paul, 261
Tomšić, Vida, 684
Topaloglu, Ahmet, 577
Tordorović, Mijalko, 681, 684
Toro, Alejandro, 89
Torrance, Sheila, 250
Torres, Camilo, 127, 127n, 637, 858, 1021
Torres, Julian, 853
Torres, Manuel, 713
Tortorella, Aldo, 341
Toska, Haki, 3, 6
Toubi, Toufik, 30, 330, 333, 334; quoted, 333
Toujas, Jean, 739, 740; quoted, 739
Touré, Sékou, 119
Tournour, Gene, 610
Tra, Tran Van (*probable alias* Tran Nam Trung), 639, 647, 665, 666. *See also* Trung, Tran Nam
Tran, Ba, 647, 667

Tran, Nguyen Van, 639, 662
Trang, Le Quang, 667
Trang, Tran Huu, 667
Transky, Slavcho: quoted, 55
Trapeznikov, S. P., 585
Traykov, Georgi, 1079
Trejos Fernández, José Joaquin, 133
Trifaux, Jacques, 37, 39
Trinh, Nguyen Duy, 224, 226, 407-8, 639, 640, 651,
    654, 655, 657, 662; quoted, 408, 651-52, 654
Triratna, Thamel, 416
Trochez, Inés Alonso, 278
Trofin, Virgil, 508
Troise, Emilio, 16
Trotsky, Leon, 586, 812, 815, 823, 946. See also Trot-
    skyism, Trotskyists
Trüb, Henri, 551, 558
Trujillo, Ciro, 123
Trujillo, Héctor, 853
Trujillo, Jesús Alberto, 854
Trung, Bui Cong, 639
Trung, Tran Nam (probable alias of Tran Van Tra),
    371, 665, 666. See also Tra, Tran Van
Truong, Nguyen Ngoc, 653
Tsao Ti-ch'iu, 108
Tsarev, F., 589
Tsedenbal, Yumzhagiin, 401-7 passim, 767; quoted,
    401-2, 405-6, 407
Tseng, Shan, 101
Tseng Ssu-yu, 108n, 109
Tshombe, Moise, 857
Tso Yin, 745
Tsolov, Tano, 51
Tsvetayeva, Marina A., 985, 986
Tu, Hu (also known as Nhan Tu; Hong Lien), 667
Tu, Nhan, see Tu, Hu
Tu, Phan, 667
Tudawe, B., 83
Tue, Pham Trong, 639
Tuladhan, Bhagwan Ratna, 416
Tulsi Lal, see Amatya, Tulsi Lal
Tun, Hoang, 657, 662
Tung, Dao, 662
Tung, Hoang, 639, 661; quoted, 661
Tung Pi-wu, 98, 99
Tung, Vu, 667
Tuomi, William, 77
Tuominen, Erkki, 201
Tuong, Tram Cong, 742
Tupac Amaru, 1021
Turcios Lima, Luis Augusto, 266, 268, 858, 1021;
    quoted, 266-67
Turf, Jef, 34
Turner, Jorge, 462
Turnhout, Ab van, 417
Turnhout, von (Belgian), 37
Tüscher-Chiostergi, Eugénie, 551
Tuyen, Tran Danh, 639
Tvardovsky, Alexandr, 591
Tyner, Jarvis, 610

Ubico, Jorge, 263
Ubiñas, Guaroa, 186
Ugalde, Raúl, 400
Ugarte, Mario, 467-71 passim; quoted, 467-71 passim
Ulanfu, 99, 102, 406, 1071
Ulbricht, Walter, 179, 210, 223-32 passim, 236, 239,
    291, 491, 492, 600, 687, 753, 767, 1026, 1066,
    1067, 1073, 1082, 1084, 1087, 1093; quoted,
    225, 755
Unschlicht, I. S., 993
Untung, Colonel (Indonesian), 308, 315-16, 916
Unzueta Lorenzano, Gerardo, 225, 396, 398; quoted,
    398-99
Upadhyaya, Mahesh Kumar, 414
Upadhyaya, Shailendra Kumar, 414, 415, 416
Uralov, S. G., 993
Urban, Maria, 27
Urbani, Dominique, 224, 380-81, 382, 754, 755, 767;
    quoted, 381, 382, 755
Urbina, Milton, 503
Urdaneta, Rafael, 853
Uria, Elisa, 726
Uribe, Hernán, 731
Uritsky, M. S., 993
Ushinin, D.: cited, 590n
Usmani, Mahumdul Huq, 456, 457, 458; quoted, 458
Ustinov, D.F., 581
Usubaliev, Turdakun U., 582
Utberg, Rolf, 544, 545n

Vachkov, Ivan, 742
Vaculík, Ludvík, 169, 171, 868; quoted, 169-170; text
    of speech at Czechoslovak Writers' Congress,
    861-67
Vaculík, Martin, 166, 166n
Vafiadis, Markos, 257
Vagin, Yevginiy, 594
Vaillant-Couturier, Marie-Claude, 726
Valdés, Ramiro, 136, 144
Valdés Vivo, Raúl, 678
Valdespino, Rubén, 396
Valdimarsson, Hannibal, 295, 296
Valencia, Gilma, 122
Valenti, Ugo, 558
Valenza, Pietro, 342
Valenzi, Alberto, 697
Valero, Januario (alias Oscar Reyes), 123
Valiejos, Eugenio, 89
Valle, Eduardo del, 396
Valle, Néstor, 760
Valle, Sergio del, 136, 150, 156, 760
Valle Rojas, Gustavo, 462
Valverde, Hugo, 467
Van, (Miss) Pham Thanh, 679
Vananzi, de (Venezuelan), 1005
Vanden Boeyants, Paul, see Boeyants, Paul Vanden
Van den Branden, Frans, 34
Van der Kroef, Justus M.: cited, 84, 477, 479, 481
Vanderlinden, Jules, 37, 38, 39
Van Geyt, Louis, 34

Varela, Alfredo, 16
Varela, Teodicio, 128, 1065-66
Varga, György, 283
Varga, Josef, 713
Varga, Viktor, 31, 32
Vargas, Leopoldo, 732
Vargas Arze, Amadeo, 43
Vargas Carbonell, Humberto Elias, 133, 134
Vasco, Cabral, 742
Vasilev, Stefan, 51; quoted, 53
Vasilyev, Pavel, 986
Vásques, Alvaro, 122
Vásquez Castano, Fabio, 127, 130, 761, 858; quoted,
    127
Vattanchi Chayakit Dhives, Mme., 567
Vattanchi Chayakit Dhives, Nai, 567
Vazquez, José, 854
Vecchietti, Tullio, 768
Vega Castejón, Pedro, 630, 631, 841; quoted, 841
Vega Roman, Julio, 463
Velando, Máximo, 474
Velasco, Arturo, 400
Velasco, Augusto, 400
Velazquez, Francisco, 853
Velazquez, Gilberto Antonio, 462
Velazquez, Isaac, 853
Velchev, Boris, 51, 575
Velikovitch, L. N., 28
Veljkovic, Vojislav, 683, 685
Vera, Ernesto, 731
Vercheval-Verwoort, Jeanne, 37
Verdesto, Galo, 193
Verdet, Ilie, 508
Vergès, Paul, 210, 506-7, 768
Verner, Paul, 223, 232
Vertiz, José Carlos, 473
Veselyi, Artem, 986
Viana, Juan, 128, 1065
Vicente, Isabelle, 726
Victor, Hugo, 179, 232, 460, 1093
Vieira, Gilberto, 59, 122, 125-30 passim, 179, 232,
    518, 605, 767, 1065, 1071, 1087, 1088, 1089,
    1092; quoted, 126, 128, 129, 130
Viera, Eduardo, 624
Viet, Hoang Quoc, 150, 370, 639, 640, 647, 653, 659,
    661, 662, 667
Vieuguet, André, 208
Vieux, Lionel, 273
Viguier, Roger, 732
Vila, Jorge, 45
Vilarigues, Sergio, 497
Vilcoci, Elena, 726
Vilenska, Mrs. E., 330
Villa, Hugo, 20
Villalba Colma, Gonzalo, 192, 194
Villalobos, Gonzalo, 396
Villegas, Jesús, 122
Villegas, Juan Francisco, 853
Villegas, Rafael, 854
Villon, Pierre (pseud. of Roger Ginsberger), 740

Vilner, Meir, 30, 330-34 passim, 493, 506, 554, 766,
    767, 1088; quoted, 331; text of speech on Arab-
    Israeli crisis, 920-21
Vincent, Jean, 551, 553, 554
Vinh, Nguyen Trong, 639
Vinh, Nguyen Van, 639, 647; quoted, 647, 650-51,
    654
Vira, Dharam, 301
Vlahović, Veljko, 681, 682n
Vogt, Jørgen, 451, 451n, 452, 453, 453n
Voigtlander, Kurt: quoted, 228
Vokrouhlický, Zbyněk, 721, 724, 725; quoted, 722-25
    passim
Vollaire, Ernest, 697
Voloshin, Maxmilian A., 985
Voronkov, K., 1000
Voronov, Gennadi I., 580
Vorster, B. J., 526
Voss, Augustus E., 582
Voznesensky, Andrei A., 592, 1001
Vračar, S., 684
Vu, Hong: quoted, 664
Vukmanović-Tempo, Svetozar, 681, 682n
Vy, Pham Xuan, 667
Vyas, H. K., 297

Wagenaar, Gerben, 421
Wagner, Ingmar, 181, 232n; quoted, 183
Wagner, Svend Olaf, 740
Wainstein, Samuel, 625
Wainwright, William 244; quoted, 246
Walker, William, 1030
Walraven, Roel, 417
Walsh, Jeannette Pratte, 77
Walsh, Sam, 77
Wang Hsiao-yu, 107
Wang Hsin-t'ing, 113
Wang Huai-hsiang, 108n
Wang Kuang-mei (Mme. Liu Shao-ch'i), 102
Wang Li, 104, 109, 120, 1079-80
Wang Ming, 795, 833
Wang Shang-jung, 113
Wang Tung-hsing, 808
Wanguemert, Luis, 161
Wanigasekera, S. G., 83
Wanoilka, Franciszek, 484
Warden, Judith, 618
Warginger, Klas-Göran, 547
Warnke, Erna, 223
Warnke, Herbert, 223, 228, 207
Warren, Sue, 618
Wasilewski, Bogdan, 662
Waten, J., 21
Waters, Mary-Alice, 621; quoted, 622
Wedel, Emil von, 697
Wehner, Herbert, 227-28
Wen Ming Chuan, 390
Wennerström, Stig, 546
Werner, Heinrich, 236
Werner, Lars, 542

Wessel, Harald, 241
West, Franz, 27, 33; cited, 30n
West, James, 610
Wheeler, Earle G., 883
Wheeler, Tim, 610
Wicha, Wladyslaw, 484
Wickremasinghe, S. A., 82, 83, 87
Widjajasasastra, Ruslan, 310
Widstrand, C. G.: cited, 607
Wikana (Indonesian), 310
Wilcox, Victor G., 118, 422-26 *passim,* 1065; quoted, 422-26 *passim*
Wilding, R., 21
Wilkins, Roy, 623
Wilopo (Indonesian), 902, 905
Wilson, E. M. G., 270
Wilson, Harold, 246, 881
Win Lu-huang, 385
Windmiller, M.: cited, 297
Winicki, J.: quoted, 492
Winston, Henry, 609, 610, 617; quoted, 610n, 614
Winter, Carl, 610
Winter, Helen, 610
Winzer, Otto, 491, 1067
Wittholz, Herbert, 223
Woddis, Jack, 244, 248
Wohlforth, Tim, 623
Wolff, Joop, 417
Wood, John, 81
Woog, Edgar, 551-55 *passim,* 754, 755, 767; quoted, 552
Wooster, William A., 735
Wright, T., 21
Wu Fa-hsien, 113
Wu Han, 106
Wu Hsing-feng, 808
Wu Tien Wang, 383
Wyszynski, Stefan Cardinal, 488, 489

Xat (South Vietnamese), 667
Xavier, Joachim José da Silva, *see* Tiradentes
Xavier, Julius Relecom, 37
Xien, Nguyen, 640
Xom Lat, 371, 445

Yabur, Alfredo: quoted, 137
Yagoda, Genrikh G., 986
Yakhnevich, V.: cited, 599
Yakimenko, Alexandr Nikiforovich, 742
Yakubovsky, Ivan, 584, 1078
Yamamoto Koichi, 768
Yambao, Alfredo (*alias* "Commander Freddie"), 480
Yan Aung, Bo, 62
Yanez Betancourt, Alejandro, 96; quoted, 96
Yang Ch'eng-wu, 113, 113n
Yang Hua-nan, 742
Yang I, 748
Yang Shang-k'un, 101, 813, 832
Yang Ya Wu, 523
Yang Yun-yu, 726
Yao Teng-shan, 120, 314-15, 1071

Yao Wen-yuan, 104, 116, 1077
Yata, Ali, 219, 409-13 *passim,* 518, 768, 1070, 1073; quoted, 409-12 *passim*
Yazbeck Jozami, Eduardo, 732
Yegorov, Mikhail Vasilevich, 745
Yegorychev, Nikolai, 583
Yegros, Alipio, 463
Yeh Chien-ying, 99, 103, 113
Yeh Ch'un (Mme. Lin Piao), 106
Yem, Nghiem Xuan, 640
Yen, Mme. Pham Thi, 679
Yesenin, Sergei, 985
Yevtushenko, Yevgeniy, 1001, 1001n
Yezhov, Nikolai I., 986
Yi Chang-ok, 435
Yi Chu-yon, 224, 435, 443, 446, 1087
Yi Hyo-sun, 434, 435, 436
Yi Ki-yong, 444
Yi Kuk-chin, 434
Yi Kuk-no, 435
Yi Min-su, 156, 444, 445
Yi Su-kun, 436, 447
Yi Yong-ho, 434, 435, 436, 443, 445
Yim, Ch'un-ch'u, 435, 436
Yod Phatisawat, 567
Yon Sosa, Marco Antonio, 266, 268, 269, 858, 1087; quoted, 269
Yonehara Itaru, 349
Yong, Stephen, 391
Yosa, Isauro, 123
Yoshida Sukeharu, 349
Youn, Hou, 67-72 *passim*
Yu Min-shen, 64
Yu Song-ui, 156
Yun Ki-pak, 156, 442, 445

Zabinski, Andrzej, 486
Zabolotsky, Nikolai A., 986
Zachariadis, Nikolas, 257
Zaelani (Indonesian), 309
Zagarell, Michael, 610
Zahavi, Leon, 332
Zaheer, S. H., 735
Zaheer, Sajjad, 455
Zaheerudeen, M., 270
Zahouane, Hocine, 13
Zakaria, Ibrahim, 707
Zámečník, Karel, 171, 1078
Zamora Medinacelli, Oscar, 42, 43
Zamorano, Mario, 89, 224
Zamyatin, Yevgeni, 985
Zangalis, G., 21
Zapata, Pablo, 713
"Zaragoza, Commander," *see* Bagsik, Avelino
Zarruq, Hasan, 537
Zayas, Alfonso, 144
Zbiri, Tahar, 13
Zeneli, Hajro: quoted, 11
Zeya, Bo, 61
Zherkov, Zherko, 745

Zhivkov, Todor, 9, 51-59 *passim*, 406, 518, 600, 753, 754, 766, 1026, 1066, 1070, 1073, 1075, 1079, 1080, 1085-86, 1089; quoted, 54, 55, 57, 406, 1073
Zhivkov, Zhivko, 51, 1026
Ziartidis, Andreas, 163
Ziegler, Erich, 239, 242
Zilber, Y., 330
Ziller, Armando, 45
Zimianin, Mikhail V., 585, 732, 1000; text of his remarks on Solzhenitsyn and other writers, 1001

Zin, Thakin, 61
Zobda-Quitman, Pierre, 393
Zografos, Zisis, 252, 256, 258; quoted, 255
Zoshchenko, Mikhail M., 986
Zu'ayyin, Yusuf, 559, 560
Zundui, Jambului, 745
Zuñiga, Victor, 193
Zurita, José, 854

# INDEX OF SUBJECTS

Listed below are: (1) all communist parties and their splinter groups; (2) certain noncommunist political parties; (3) countries, regions, and cities referred to substantively throughout the book; (4) international organizations; (5) international conferences; (6) titles of books, pamphlets, documents, and periodicals other than party organs; and (7) certain ideological topics (e.g., Castroism, Trotskyism).

National organizations and associations, national communist front organizations, party organs, press agencies, and radio stations are generally not given; references to them can be found by looking up specific communist party profiles. These profiles are indexed under the official names of the individual communist parties (e.g., Communist Party of Austria, Bulgarian Communist Party, League of Communists of Yugoslavia).

Abolitionist Women's Federation, 729
Academic Socialists (Finland), 204, 549
Ad Hoc Committee for a Marxist-Leninist Party of the USA, 31, 623
Aden, 329, 560, 701, 711, 748, 921, 1049-52 *passim*
Afghanistan, 119, 729, 1074
AFP (Agence France Presse): dispatches quoted by Castro, 837-41 *passim*
Africa, 10, 13, 14, 15, 58, 76, 115, 118, 119, 149, 158-59, 165, 225, 230, 248, 368, 370, 406, 412, 419, 439, 440, 444, 447, 526, 527, 528, 564, 573, 588, 605, 634, 635, 653, 660, 674, 677, 688, 698, 702, 703, 704, 707, 712, 713, 715, 721, 729, 732, 737, 745, 746, 748, 758, 762, 786, 823, 856, 857, 882, 910-13 *passim*, 927, 933, 975, 979, 994, 1012, 1013, 1014, 1018, 1031, 1033, 1043, 1045, 1049, 1053, 1082; communist parties in, 117, 400, 412, 605, 1053. *See also* Afro-Asia; Central Africa
African Independence Party (PAI) of Senegal, 224
African National Congress (ANC) of South Africa, 525-28 *passim*, 660, 768, 1082
African Party for the Independence of Portuguese Guinea and Cape Verde Islands, 518, 660, 768
Afro-Asia, 115, 370, 385, 389, 657, 702, 703, 747, 748, 977; communist parties in, 304
Afro-Asian Journalists' Association (AAJA), 115, 309, 732, 734, 747; profile, 747-49
Afro-Asian Journalists' Conference (1963), 732
Afro-Asian-Latin American Peoples' Solidarity Organization (AALAPSO), 73, 150, 242, 268, 368, 370, 371, 442, 505, 622, 627, 653, 660, 676, 702, 758-62 *passim*, 839, 851, 858, 1023, 1069
Afro-Asian Lawyers' Conference (AALC), 743, 750
Afro-Asian People's Solidarity Organization (AAPSO), 165, 379, 442, 653, 676, 701, 702, 703, 724, 729, 734, 747, 748, 1062
Afro-Asian Solidarity Association of Ceylon, 88
Afro-Asian Trade Union Federation, 525
Afro-Asian Writers' Bureau, *see* Afro-Asian Writers' Permanent Bureau
Afro-Asian Writers' Permanent Bureau (AAWPB; *also* Afro-Asian Writers' Bureau [AAWB]): Cairo branch (pro-Soviet), 115, 747, 749, 1067; Peking branch, 115, 378-79, 676, 749-50, 1074
Afro-Shirazi Party (Zanzibar), 224
*Akahata* (Japan Communist Party newspaper), 356
—anti-Mao article in, 354, 1062; excerpts, 940-46
Albania, 32, 39, 43, 56, 57, 116, 119, 121, 132, 157, 220, 257, 291, 317, 388, 495, 496, 515, 516, 535,
555, 557, 600, 601, 652, 658, 662, 687, 710, 722, 728, 732, 757, 759, 770, 820, 821, 1014, 1058, 1061-62, 1071, 1075, 1079, 1084, 1085, 1087; profile, 3-11; abridged text of Chou En-lai's speech welcoming delegation from, 820-22
—Hoxha's speech on revolutionizing party and regime in, 3, 1061-62; excerpts, 777-80
Albanian Party of Labor, *see* Albanian Workers' Party
Albanian Trade Unions, Congress of, 5, 10, 32, 541, 1071
Albanian Workers' Party (AWP), 31, 32, 116, 118, 131, 132, 151, 222, 224, 306, 310, 311, 345, 496, 541, 558, 567, 753, 754, 757, 820, 821, 823, 1058, 1062, 1072, 1079, 1081; profile, 3-11; text of pro-Peking article in party journal, 773-76; abridged text of Chou En-lai's speech welcoming delegation of, 820-22
—Hoxha's speech on revolutionization of, 3, 1061-62; excerpts, 777-80
Algeria, 10, 119, 158, 159, 220, 251, 326, 342, 375, 376, 406, 410-11, 444, 501, 539, 540, 574, 599, 604, 675, 699, 707, 709, 715, 717, 743, 746, 748, 749, 766, 768, 933, 977, 1018, 1035, 1049, 1051, 1052; profile, 12-15
Algerian Communist Party (PCA), 12, 15, 574, 604, 768
Algiers, 677, 679, 973, 1062
All-African Trade Union Federation, 537, 710
All-China Federation of Trade Unions, 81, 708, 710, 750
All-India Peace Council, 298, 699
Alliance for Progress, 158, 625, 785, 1021, 1031
America, Americans, *see* United States
American Federation of Labor, 278
American Motion Pictures Association, 907
Amnesty International, 171
Anglo-America, 164, 191, 257, 359, 522, 578, 922, 1050
Angola, 49, 159, 329, 500, 717, 721, 748, 857
Angola Popular Liberation Movement (MPLA), 557, 660, 768
ANSA (Agenzia Nazionale Stampa Associata): dispatch quoted by Castro, 839
*Anti-Duehring*, 879
Anti-Imperialist League, 695
Antilles, 395
Anti-Semitism, 177, 283, 290, 333, 344, 425, 493, 496, 616, 617
AP (Associated Press), 849; dispatches quoted by Castro, 837-40 *passim*

Apartheid, 218, 378, 526

Après "Pacem in terris": Communistes et chrétiens, 212

Aqaba, Gulf of, 216, 241

Arab Communist Meeting, 327, 361, 375-76, 565, 1072; text of statement on situation in Arab countries, 1049-52; text of resolution on world communist movement, 1052-54

Arab-Israeli crisis and war, 8, 13, 14, 15, 19-20, 23, 24, 30, 32, 36, 38, 49, 51, 58-59, 80, 87-88, 95, 115, 120, 134, 149, 152, 157, 158, 159, 165, 169, 176, 177n, 178, 183, 186, 213-16 passim, 229, 230, 240, 241, 247, 256, 257, 267, 272, 283, 290-93 passim, 305, 322-23, 325-26, 330-34 passim, 342, 344, 358, 368, 375, 398, 407, 411, 420, 425, 442, 450, 465, 484, 485, 493, 496, 500, 527, 534, 539-40, 549, 554, 560-65 passim, 575-578 passim, 588, 601-7 passim, 616, 617, 622, 660, 677-78, 682, 687-89, 691, 701, 702, 709, 710, 716, 728, 740, 741, 766, 824, 931-32, 934, 947-48, 964, 1018, 1019, 1026-27, 1047, 1075, 1081, 1092; texts of Israeli CP (RAKAH) documents on, 920-23; abridged text of statement by CP of Jordan on, 947-48; text of CPSU resolution on Soviet policy concerning Israeli aggression in, 977-78. See also Arab states; Budapest conference on the Middle East; Israel; Middle East; Moscow conference on the Middle East

Arab Socialist Party of Syria, see Ba'ath Party

Arab Socialist Union (ASU) of the United Arab Republic, 224, 604, 607, 608, 768

Arab states, 8, 14, 15, 20, 24, 30, 32, 36, 38, 49, 58, 59, 80, 87, 88, 96, 115, 120, 130, 149, 157, 158, 165, 169, 177, 183, 186, 191, 207, 215, 216, 227, 229-30, 237, 241, 247, 267, 272, 283, 292-93, 305, 325, 326, 359, 360, 368, 374, 375, 376, 389, 398, 407, 410, 411, 425, 442, 450, 484, 485, 485n, 493, 500, 516-17, 527, 534, 539-40, 554, 561-65 passim, 575, 576, 578, 599, 603, 604, 607, 617, 622, 660-62, 677, 678, 687, 688, 689, 698, 701-2, 703, 710, 713, 715, 716, 725, 728, 734, 740, 741, 762, 920, 921, 922, 931-34 passim, 947, 948, 964, 977, 979, 983, 984, 994, 1018, 1019-20, 1026, 1027, 1047, 1072; communist parties in, 607, 1052, 1053-54, 1084; text of statement of Arab Communist Meeting on situation in, 1049-52. See also Arab Communist Meeting; Arab-Israeli crisis and war; Arab Summit Conference; Belgrade conference on economic cooperation with Arab states; and individual countries

Arab Summit Conference (Khartoum), 326, 561, 689

Arabs, see Arab-Israeli crisis and war; Arab states; Israel; Palestinian Arabs

Argentina, 49, 463, 465, 700, 717, 724, 725, 783, 1003, 1024, 1082; profile, 16-20

Argentine University Federation (FUA), 17, 720

Armed Forces of National Liberation (FALN) of Peru, 469, 472, 474, 476

Armed Forces of National Liberation (FALN) of Venezuela, 160, 629, 630-31, 634, 635, 837-41 passim, 844-50 passim, 853; profile, 635-37

Army of National Liberation (ELN) of Peru, 467, 470, 474, 475

Arusha Declaration, 606

ASEAN, see Association of Southeast Asian Nations

Asia, 9, 10, 58, 66, 76, 115, 118, 119, 149, 158, 206, 225, 230, 368, 370, 389, 408, 419, 420, 439, 440, 444, 518, 564, 571, 573, 588, 602, 635, 653, 655, 658, 674, 677, 688, 702, 703, 704, 709, 713, 729, 733, 737, 746, 748, 758, 762, 823, 851, 856, 857, 882, 910-13 passim, 927, 928, 933, 975, 979, 994, 1012, 1013, 1014, 1018, 1031, 1033, 1035, 1043, 1045, 1053; communist parties in, 117, 370, 400, 1053. See also Afro-Asia; Far East; Southeast Asia

Asian and Pacific Council (ASPAC), 571

Asian-Pacific Peace Committee, 573

Association Belgique-Chine, 37

Association France-USSR, 209

Association of Southeast Asian Nations (ASEAN), 368, 571

Association of Vietnamese Lawyers (North Vietnam), 744

Atlantic Pact, see NATO

Australia, 115, 713, 782; profile, 21-26

Australian Communist Party (Marxist-Leninist) [ACP (ML)], 21, 119; profile, 25-26

Austria, 238, 292, 334, 696, 704, 706, 746, 1062; profile, 27-33

Austrian-Soviet Society, 27

Avant Guard Party, 12. See also Popular Resistance Organization (ORP) of Algeria

Azania, see South Africa


Ba'ath Party (Syria), 219, 343, 518, 559-65 passim, 604, 768, 1050

Baghdad, 973

Bahrein, 1050

Baku, 576

Balkans, 9, 57-58, 255, 890, 1044

Baltic nations, 449

Baltic Sea, 449

Baltic Week, 231-32, 232n, 711

Bandung Conference, 913, 927

Baptist Church, Baptists: in Soviet Union, 590

Barisan Sosialis (Socialist Front) of Singapore: profile, 521-24

Belgium, 251, 519, 710, 746, 901, 1037; profile, 34-39

Belgium Communist Party (PCB), 39, 179, 210, 224, 294, 518, 535, 754, 767, 1034, 1046, 1093; profile, 34-37

Belgrade conference on economic cooperation with Arab states, 517, 689, 1084

"Bell, The," 594

Berlin, 170, 1066. See also East Berlin; West Berlin

Berlin Wall, 548

Bertrand Russell International Tribunal, see Russell International War Crimes Tribunal

Biafra, 432

"Big Victory, Great Task," 642, 647; quoted, 645-51 *passim*

Bissao, *see* Portuguese Guinea

*Black Power and Liberation: A Communist View*, 614; quoted, 614, 615

Blitzkrieg, 229

Bolivia, 97, 136, 148, 150, 151, 155, 159, 218, 276, 398, 465, 472, 475, 476, 505, 549, 627, 678, 733, 744, 748, 858, 859, 1024, 1028, 1032, 1048, 1067, 1069, 1070, 1075, 1087; profile, 40-44

Bolshevik Communist Party of Mexico, 400

Bolshevik Revolution, 243, 764, 843

Bolsheviks, 8, 68, 153, 432, 454, 533, 579, 588, 824, 992, 1014

Bonin Islands, 351

Borneo, 391. *See also* Indonesian Borneo; North Borneo

Borneo Communist Party (BCP), 383; profile, 390-92

Botswana, 748

Brazil, 463, 465, 724, 758, 763, 782, 783, 858, 859, 927, 1003, 1023, 1024; profile, 45-50

Brazilian Communist Party (PCB), 19; profile, 45-49

Britain, British, *see* Great Britain

British Association of Scientific Workers, 735

British Broadcasting Corporation (BBC), 745, 1001

*British Road to Socialism, The*, 887, 888, 1091

*British Rule in India, The*: quoted, 405

Browderism, 388

"Brug" (Bridge) movement of the Netherlands, 421

Brussels meeting of Western European Communist Parties (1965), 419, 753, 755, 935

Bucharest conference of European socialist countries (1966), 894, 965, 1038, 1039

Bucharest Declaration of 1966, 231, 513, 515, 518, 756, 950, 970, 1044

Budapest conference on the Middle East, 229, 493, 516, 554, 604, 688, 894, 1079

Budapest Consultative Meeting of Representatives of Communist and Workers' Parties (1968), 10, 29, 31, 66, 116, 179, 219, 232, 237, 242, 267, 294, 296, 317, 334, 334n, 339, 355n, 368, 419, 442, 454n, 455n, 461, 471, 549n, 558, 564-65, 573, 578, 601, 615n, 653, 676, 895, 1091, 1093; text of Zóltan Komocsin's article on, 893-95

Buddhism, Buddhists, 70, 73, 566, 700

"Build the PKI along the Marxist-Leninist Line to Lead the People's Democratic Revolution in Indonesia," 310; text, 896-907

Building Workers' Trade Union International, conference of, 155

Bulgaria, 9, 30, 80, 119, 130, 154, 231, 292, 321, 327, 333, 342, 361, 403, 406-7, 491, 492, 510, 514, 518, 600, 652, 658, 675, 686, 718, 721, 746, 759, 922, 1014, 1026, 1061, 1069, 1070, 1073, 1075, 1079, 1082-87 *passim*, 1090; profile, 51-59

Bulgarian Communist Party (BCP), 184, 194, 204, 207, 210, 219, 224, 226, 355, 370, 406-7, 411, 412, 517, 518, 534, 540, 600, 600n, 753, 754,

766, 1034, 1046, 1066, 1070, 1075, 1076, 1080, 1085-86, 1089; profile, 51-59

Burma, 117, 118, 119, 304, 363, 388, 655, 722, 823; profile, 60-66

Burma Communist Party (BCP), *see* White Flags

Cairo Seminar on Africa (1966), 378, 412, 528

Cambodia, 9, 58, 119, 120, 573, 658, 659, 674, 675, 677, 748, 857, 1006, 1007, 1008, 1012; profile, 67-74

Cameroun, 159, 749; profile, 75-76

Camilo Torres Group (Argentina), 20

Camilo Torres movement (Chile), 90

Canada, 216, 519, 724; profile, 77-81

*Cancer Ward, The*, 986, 1000

Cape Verde, 717

*Capital*, see *Kapital, Das*

Castroism, Castroists, 17, 19, 20, 40, 45, 46, 49, 90, 92, 94, 118, 125, 126, 127, 159, 185, 186, 187, 190, 193, 195, 196, 243, 271, 273, 275, 276, 278, 335, 338, 343-44, 345, 347, 398, 462, 467, 472, 474, 502, 504, 505, 605, 616, 620, 621, 622, 627-31 *passim*, 760-63 *passim*, 1065, 1067, 1092, 1094

Catalan Communist Party (Spain), 529, 533

Catholic Church, 17, 28, 211-12, 337, 488-89, 534, 555, 926, 962

Catholic-Marxist dialogue, *see* Christian-Marxist dialogue

Catholics, 17, 28, 35, 211-13, 236, 240, 336-37, 337n, 338, 341, 342, 418, 488-89, 520, 430, 532, 755, 787, 962, 963, 982, 1045, 1075

CENTO (Central Treaty Organization), 248, 322, 323, 456, 577

Central Africa, 927

Central America, 1030, 1047, 1048

Central America Defense Council (CONDECA), 1048

Central Asia, *see* Soviet Central Asia

Central Europe, 548, 1014, 1036, 1044

Central Labor Organization of Indonesia, *see* Indonesian Central Organization of Trade Unions

Central Office for South Vietnam (COSVN) in North Vietnam, 640, 646-47, 664-68 *passim*, 675, 676, 1078

Central Treaty Organization, *see* CENTO

Ceuta, 410

Ceylon, 119, 120, 251, 304, 729, 732, 748, 749; profile, 82-88

Ceylon Communist Party (LKP), 22, 224, 768; profile 82-88 *passim*

Ceylon Communist Party, pro-Chinese (pro-Chinese LKP), 10, 119, 152, 222, 1074, 1087; profile, 82-88 *passim*

Ceylon Equal Society Party (LSSP; *also* New LSSP *or* LSSP [Socialist]), 82-88 *passim*

Ceylon National Council for Solidarity with Vietnam, 88

Ceylon-Vietnam Solidarity Association, 88

*Change and Challenge*, 78

Chiang Kai-shekists, 56, 64, 86, 406, 774, 803, 804, 813

*Chieh-fang Chün-pao* (*Liberation Army Daily*; Communist Chinese newspaper), 121
—joint editorial on October Revolution, 116; text, 823-28

Chile, 28, 153n, 465, 709, 746, 763, 783-86 *passim*, 839, 1024; profile, 89-97; abridged text of Luis Corvalán's report on CP of Chile and people of, 787-92

Chilean-East German Cultural Institute, 746

China, People's Republic of, *see* Communist China

China, Republic of, *see* Taiwan

China Peace Committee, 704

Chinese Afro-Asian Solidarity Committee, 573

Chinese Communist Party (CCP), 3, 377, 378, 455, 793-836 *passim*, 879, 883, 906, 924-29 *passim*, 934, 936, 980-81, 1035, 1053, 1063, 1071; profile, 98-121; excerpts from *Akahata* article on, 940-46; text of *Pravda* article on anti-Soviet policy of, 972-76
—relations with communist parties of: Albania, 5, 7, 116, 118, 119, 773-76, 820, 823, 1058; Arab states, 1053-54; Argentina, 18, 19; Australia, 24, 25, 26; Austria, 29-33 *passim*, 1062; Belgium, 36-39 *passim*; Bolivia, 43; Brazil, 48, 50; Bulgaria, 56; Burma, 61-66 *passim*, 116, 117; Cambodia, 70, 71, 72; Cameroun, 76; Canada, 80, 81; Ceylon, 86, 87, 116, 1074; Chile, 94-95, 97; Colombia, 129-30, Costa Rica, 134; Cyprus, 164; Czechoslovakia, 178-79; Denmark, 182, 183, 184; Dominican Republic, 186-90 *passim*; East Germany, 224, 225, 230; Ecuador, 194, 195; El Salvador, 199; Finland, 206; France, 210, 211, 216, 217, 220, 221, 222, 878-79, 883, 1083; Great Britain, 245-26, 251; Greece, 257; Guatemala, 267; Hungary, 283, 291, 293; India, 117, 297, 303-6 *passim*, 1082; Indonesia, 309-317 *passim*, 318n, 320, 565, 901, 911; Iran, 323; Iraq, 326, 327; Ireland, 329; Italy, 338-46 *passim*, 924-29 *passim*, 936; Japan, 117, 349-57 *passim*, 603, 940, 941, 946, 1062, 1081; Jordan, 361; Laos, 118, 119, 369-70; Lebanon, 375; Luxembourg, 380, 382; Malaya, 116; Malaysia, 384, 389, 390, 391; Martinique, 395; Mexico, 398, 400; Mongolia, 118; Morocco, 411, 412; Nepal, 416; Netherlands, 419, 420; New Zealand, 118, 423-26 *passim*, 1065; Nicaragua, 430; North Korea, 441, 442-43; North Vietnam, 655-57, 1072; Norway, 451-52, 454, 1067; Pakistan, 458-59; Panama, 461; Paraguay, 463, 465, 471, 473-74; Philippines, 116, 118-19, 477, 479, 482, 483; Poland, 493, 494, 496; Portugal, 500, 501; Rumania, 515-16; South Africa, 527, 528; South Vietnam, 119, 676-77; Soviet Union, 95, 101, 106, 115-16, 134, 326, 490, 513, 773, 774, 820, 827, 941, 945, 967, 972, 976, 1036; Spain, 534, 535; Sudan, 540; Sweden, 547, 549, 1077; Switzerland, 553-58 *passim*; Syria, 565; Thailand, 116-17, 566-73 *passim*; Tunisia, 575; United States, 305, 615-16, 620,

622; Uruguay, 628; Venezuela, 634-35; West Berlin, 241, 242; West Germany, 237, 238; Yugoslavia, 687, 689-90.
—*See also* Sino-Cuban conflict; Sino-Soviet conflict

Chinese Communist Party (CCP), Philippine branch, 447

Chinese cultural revolution, *see* Cultural revolution

Chinese Red Guards, *see* Red Guards

Ch'ing dynasty, 406

Christian Democrat Party (PDC) of Chile, 89, 90, 91, 95, 97, 785

Christian Democratic Union and Christian Social Union (CDU/CSU) of West Germany, 229, 236, 340, 1040

Christian-Marxist dialogue, 28, 212, 217, 245, 337, 337n, 520, 553, 887

Christian Peace Conference, 699

Christians, 217, 236, 418, 538, 1045. *See also* Baptist Church, Baptists; Catholics; Protestants

CIA, *see* U.S. Central Intelligence Agency

Clandestine Organization of the Algerian Revolution, 12n-13n

"Cliff Group," *see* International Socialism Group

Colombia, 150, 153n, 225, 465, 476, 505, 605, 634, 725, 748, 758, 763, 781, 839, 841, 843, 849, 851, 858, 859, 1021, 1023, 1024, 1028, 1030, 1032, 1048, 1061, 1063, 1065-66; profile, 122-32

Colombian Marxist-Leninist Communist Party (PCC-ML), 122, 123, 222; profile, 131-32

"Combat Liberalism," 111

COMECON (Council for Mutual Economic Assistance), 6, 176, 227, 230, 286, 291, 403, 406, 491, 515, 980

Cominform (Communist Information Bureau), 686, 708

Comintern (Communist International), 82, 153, 243, 297, 308, 450, 484, 607, 695, 935, 955, 982

Commission for Information and Cooperation among Journalists of Latin America, 732

Committee for the Defense of The Revolution (Algeria), 12n-13n

Committee of Correspondence (United States), 623

Committee of Soviet Youth Organizations, 717

Committee to Defeat Revisionism for Communist Unity (Great Britain), 251

Common Market, *see* European Economic Community

Commonwealth, The, 298, 857

Communist China, 5, 8, 10, 24-25, 29, 36, 39, 48, 62, 75, 80, 81, 94-95, 97, 130, 183, 188, 226, 237, 246, 248, 306, 311, 329, 339, 350, 351, 359, 369, 383, 384, 388, 411, 412, 414, 420, 425, 454, 471, 473, 476, 496, 512n, 527, 534, 535, 554, 556, 557, 568, 571, 573, 599, 602-3, 615, 622, 628, 636, 675, 676-77, 690, 691, 700, 704, 705, 708, 710, 712, 717, 722, 725-28 *passim*, 732, 734, 737, 743, 745-50 *passim*, 755, 757, 763-66 *passim*, 769, 770, 878, 879, 882, 899, 900, 901, 924-28 *passim*, 933, 942-46 *passim*, 972-76 *passim*, 980, 981, 1014, 1031, 1035, 1053, 1057-63, 1066, 1070, 1072, 1073, 1079-80, 1081, 1084, 1085,

1090, 1091; profile, 98-121; texts (complete and abridged) of Communist Chinese documents on, 793-836
—relations with: Afghanistan, 119; Africa, 819, 975; Albania, 7-8, 9, 115, 119, 516, 820, 1058, 1071, 1076, 1085; Algeria, 14, 119; Arab states, 120, 375, 540, 565, 1053-54; Asia, 602, 819, 975; Bulgaria, 56, 119; Cambodia, 70-74 passim, 119, 120; Ceylon, 85-86, 119, 120; Congo (Brazzaville), 119, 120; Cuba, 151, 152, 159; Czechoslovakia, 119, 178; Denmark, 119; East Germany, 119, 227; France, 119; Ghana, 119; Great Britain, 104, 119, 1082; Guinea, 119, 605-6; Hungary, 291, 293; India, 119, 120, 298, 301, 302, 303, 306, 414, 416, 456, 927, 1084; Indonesia, 119, 120, 314-15, 483, 516, 899, 911, 1071, 1087; Iraq, 119; Italy, 115, 119, 341, 343; Japan, 102, 115, 118, 119, 350-56 passim, 813, 815, 817, 1062-63; Kenya, 119, 1062-63; Korea, 855; Laos, 363, 369-70; Latin America, 118, 159, 279, 819; Macao, 119; Malaysia, 390, 391; Mali, 120, 605-6; Mauritania, 120; Mexico, 400; Middle East, 230, 375, 1074; Mongolia, 119, 403-7 passim, 813, 1059; Morocco, 119; Nepal, 119, 416; North Korea, 26, 119, 120, 226, 652, 652n, 655-56, 667, 668, 1017, 1063, 1079; Pakistan, 119, 120; Poland, 494; Portugal, 119; Rhodesia, 118; Rumania, 515-16, 519; Singapore, 119, 521; South Africa, 118; South Vietnam, 121, 654, 666, 675, 677; Southeast Asia, 306; Soviet Union, 101, 326, 353, 599, 602, 793, 815-20 passim, 827, 831, 967, 972, 975, 976, 981, 1036, 1059, 1063; Sweden, 119; Switzerland, 119; Syria, 565; Taiwan, 118, 774, 803, 815, 817, 819; Tanzania, 119, 120; Tunisia, 119, 575; United Arab Republic, 119, 120; United Kingdom, 119; United States, 29, 183, 305, 369, 461, 515, 774, 803, 813-20 passim, 830, 831, 857, 927, 928, 941, 945, 975, 1053; Vatican, 555; Venezuela, 841; Vietnam, 120-21, 323, 375, 381, 395, 412, 426, 443, 534, 565, 677, 690, 755, 819, 929, 936, 966-67, 975, 1017, 1036, 1053, 1079; West Germany, 115; Yugoslavia, 119, 601, 689-90, 1059, 1060; Zambia, 119, 120
—See also Chinese Communist Party; Cultural Revolution; Red Guards; Sino-Cuban conflict; Sino-Japanese War; Sino-Soviet conflict
Communist Chinese Society for Political Science and Law, 743-44, 1059
Communist International, see Comintern
Communist League (Marxist-Leninist) [KF] of Sweden, 542-43, 546-57, 550, 1077
Communist Manifesto, 878; quoted, 782
Communist Parties of Mexico, Central America and Panama, Fifth Meeting of, 135, 199, 267, 268, 399, 430, 461, 1072
—statement, 661; quoted, 267-68, 280, 399; text, 1047-48
Communist Party (Marxist-Leninist) of Belgium, 38. See also Communist Party of Belgium, Marxist-Leninist

Communist Party of Argentina (PCA), 48, 49, 159, 179, 225, 397, 465, 600n, 634, 689, 763, 767, 1069, 1078; profile, 16-20
Communist Party of Australia (CPA), 26, 179, 355, 422, 600n, 768, 1075; profile, 21-25
Communist Party of Austria (KPÖ), 31, 31n, 32, 33, 179, 210, 224, 232, 294, 332, 553, 711, 754, 767, 1034, 1046, 1073, 1076, 1090; profile, 27-31
Communist Party of Belgium, Marxist-Leninist (PCB-ML), 10, 32, 33, 123, 131, 222, 277, 323, 495, 535, 635, 636, 1064, 1081; profile, 37-39
Communist Party of Bolivia (PCB), 159, 217, 218, 225, 767, 1069; profile, 40-42
Communist Party of Bolivia, pro-Chinese (PCB-II), 10, 40, 151, 222, 1069; profile, 42-43
Communist Party of Brazil (PCdoB), 45, 96, 217, 225, 600n, 627, 689, 763, 767, 1078, 1092; profile, 49-50
Communist Party of Britain, Marxist-Leninist, 246, 246n
Communist Party of Burma (CPB), see Red Flags
Communist Party of Canada (CPC), 210, 216, 224, 248, 332, 617, 768; profile, 77-81
Communist Party of Chile (PCCh), 48, 49, 159, 210, 219, 224, 232, 341, 343, 344, 397, 465, 475, 518, 616, 627, 634, 689, 763, 767, 784-85, 786, 1076, 1078, 1081, 1084, 1090, 1092; profile, 89-96; abridged text of Luis Corvalán's report on, 787-92
Communist Party of Colombia (PCC), 19, 59, 179, 217, 232, 518, 605, 634, 767, 851, 1065-66, 1071, 1075, 1087-92 passim; profile, 122-31
Communist Party of Czechoslovakia (CPC), 30, 37, 204, 207, 210, 219, 224, 226, 258, 268, 355, 600, 600n, 601, 753, 754, 767, 861-67 passim, 1034, 1046, 1061, 1076, 1077, 1078, 1087-88, 1089, 1092, 1093; profile, 166-79; excerpt from its communique on Czech Writers' Congress, 868-69
Communist Party of Denmark (DKP), 59, 210, 224, 232n, 294, 296, 449n, 518, 549, 550, 679, 754, 767, 1034, 1046, 1064, 1080; profile, 180-84
Communist Party of the Dominican Republic (PCRD; PACOREDO), 185-89 passim
Communist Party of Ecuador (PCE), 59, 179, 194, 195, 225, 397, 634, 763, 767, 1076, 1087; profile, 192-94
Communist Party of Ecuador, Marxist-Leninist (PCE/ML), 192, 194, 222; profile, 194-95
Communist Party of Egypt (PCE), 607
Communist Party of El Salvador (CPES), 767, 1048; profile, 197-99. See also Communist Parties of Mexico, Central America and Panama, Fifth Meeting of
Communist Party of Finland (SKP), 179, 183, 210, 219, 224, 232, 241, 294, 550, 600n, 754, 767, 1034, 1046, 1064, 1075, 1080, 1084, 1093; profile, 200-7; abridged text of Aarne Saarinen's speech on program of, 870-1
Communist Party of Germany (KPD; West Germany), 59, 210, 215, 218, 224, 225, 226, 232, 238, 239, 294, 420, 600n, 754, 767, 969, 1034, 1037,

1042-46 *passim*, 1063, 1072-77 *passim*; profile, 234-38

Communist Party of Great Britain (CPGB), 28, 80, 165, 210, 219, 224, 249, 250, 251, 257, 297, 329, 361, 378, 422, 433, 446, 527, 600n, 618, 678, 754, 767, 885-89, 1034, 1046, 1085, 1091; profile, 243-49; text of its statement on ideology and culture, 885-89

Communist Party of Greece (KKE), 59, 165, 218, 224, 343, 518, 754, 767, 1034, 1046, 1070-71, 1076, 1090; profile, 252-58
—resolution on situation in Greece, 256n; text, 890-92

Communist Party of Honduras (PCH), 1048; profile, 278-81. *See also* Communist Parties of Mexico, Central America and Panama, Fifth Meeting of

Communist Party of Honduras (PCH-Dissidents), 278, 279, 281, 767, 1057

Communist Party of India (CPI), 117, 179, 224, 232, 315, 414, 455, 457, 458, 600n, 768, 1063, 1088; profile, 297-307

Communist Party of India (Marxist) [CPI(M)], 117, 455, 458, 459, 1063, 1077, 1082; profile, 297-307

Communist Party of Indonesia (PKI), 32, 216, 217, 371, 391, 419, 480, 483, 522, 565, 659, 857-58, 1067; profile, 308-20; text of statement of self-criticism, 896-907; text of document by Marxist-Leninist Group of the PKI on, 908-19

Communist Party of Israel, *see* Israeli Communist Party; New Communist List

Communist Party of Italy—Marxist-Leninist (CPI-ML), 10, 33, 119, 131, 222, 535, 1081, 1084; profile, 345

Communist Party of Jordan (CPJ), 210, 224, 232, 604, 767, 1081, 1092; profile, 358-61; abridged text of its statement on Arab-Israeli conflict, 947-48

Communist Party of Lesotho (CPL), 768; profile, 377-79

Communist Party of Luxembourg (PCL), 210, 224, 753, 754, 755, 767, 1034, 1046; profile, 380-82

Communist Party of Malaya (CPM), 116, 391, 521, 521n, 522, 524, 568, 573; profile, 383-90

Communist Party of Nepal (CPN): profile, 414-16

Communist Party of the Netherlands (CPN), 32, 219, 332, 421, 518, 605, 753, 754, 755, 1071, 1094; profile, 417-20

Communist Party of New Zealand (CPNZ), 31, 118, 222, 478, 1065; profile, 422-26

Communist Party of Northern Ireland, 210, 224, 232, 328, 329, 753, 754, 767, 1034, 1046, 1088; profile, 329

Communist Party of Norway (NKP), 183, 224, 296, 420, 518, 549, 550, 679, 753, 754, 755, 767, 1064, 1067, 1070, 1071; profile, 448-54

Communist Party of Pakistan (CCP): profile, 455-59

Communist Party of Poland (in Albania), 10, 32, 222, 484n, 1093; profile, 495-96

Communist Party of Quebec (PCQ), 77, 80

Communist Party of San Marino (PCSM), 753, 754, 767, 1034, 1046; profile, 520

Communist Party of Slovakia, 166, 179

Communist Party of the Soviet Union (CPSU), 144, 203, 218, 229, 306, 401, 455, 544, 747, 753, 755, 764, 765, 766, 769, 770, 824, 880, 898, 935, 942, 981, 983, 984, 992-95 *passim*, 1034, 1039-43 *passim*, 1046, 1057, 1063; profile, 579-606; text of its resolution on Soviet policy concerning Israeli aggression, 977-78; text of Section III of its Theses on October Revolution, 979-84; text of joint party-government message to Soviet people, 988-91
—relations with communist parties of: Albania, 7-10 *passim*, 773, 774, 775, 820; Algeria, 14, 15; Argentina, 18, 19; Australia, 22, 25; Austria, 29-33 *passim*; Belgium, 36, 37, 38; Bolivia, 42; Brazil, 48, 50, 96; Bulgaria, 51, 54, 55, 57, 600, 1066, 1085; Burma, 64, 65-66, 117; Cameroun, 76; Canada, 80; Ceylon, 84, 87, 88; Chile, 93, 96, 159, 616; Colombia, 130, 132; Communist China, 95, 101, 106, 115-16, 134, 326, 490, 513, 774, 820, 827, 941, 945, 967, 972, 976, 1036; Costa Rica, 134, 1048; Cuba, 94, 95, 97, 139, 144, 145, 152-56 *passim*, 159, 388, 399, 588, 605, 628, 634, 636; Cyprus, 164; Czechoslovakia, 170, 171, 174, 175, 178, 600, 601, 1061, 1078, 1092; Denmark, 180, 183, 184; Dominican Republic, 186-87, 188, 190; East Germany, 224, 225, 226, 229-32 *passim*, 601, 1070; Ecuador, 194, 195; El Salvador, 199, 1048; Finland, 203-7 *passim*, 1075; France, 208-9, 210, 215-20 *passim*, 605, 883; Great Britain, 243, 247, 248, 1085; Greece, 257, 258; Guadeloupe, 261; Guatemala, 267, 1048; Guyana, 272; Honduras, 1048; Hungary, 289-94 *passim*; India, 304, 305-6; Indonesia, 310, 311, 315-16, 603, 898, 913; Iran, 322-23; Iraq, 326; Israel, 330-34 *passim*, 604; Italy, 338-44 *passim*, 605, 924, 928, 932-33, 1067; Japan, 350-56 *passim*, 425, 603, 1088; Jordan, 360, 361; Laos, 369; Latin America, 605, 616; Lebanon, 373n, 374, 475-76; Lesotho, 378; Luxembourg, 380; Malaysia, 387-89, 391; Martinique, 394-95; Mexico, 398, 399, 1048; Mongolia, 603; Morocco, 411; Netherlands, 418-19, 420, 605; New Zealand, 424, 425; Nicaragua, 430, 1048; Nigeria, 432-33; North Korea, 441, 443-44; North Vietnam, 657-58, 660, 1017; Norway, 451, 452n, 454; Pakistan, 458; Panama, 461, 1048; Paraguay, 463, 464, 465; Peru, 471; Philippines, 482, 483; Poland, 490-91, 492, 496, 600-601, 1058; Portugal, 501; Réunion, 506; Rumania, 513-14, 517, 601, 1093; Singapore, 521, 523, 524; South Africa, 527; South Vietnam, 603, 677; Spain, 533-34; Sudan, 540; Sweden, 543-49 *passim*; Switzerland, 553-57 *passim*; Syria, 561, 564, 565; Thailand, 572; Tunisia, 575; United Arab Republic, 607; United States, 615-22 *passim*; Uruguay, 625, 627, 628, 1067, 1082; Venezuela, 635, 636; West Berlin, 241-42; West Germany, 237, 238, 1073; Western Europe, 605; Yugoslavia, 687, 820, 1057
—*See also* October Revolution; October Revolution,

Fiftieth Anniversary of; Sino-Soviet conflict
Communist Party of Spain (PCE), 59, 179, 210, 218, 224, 248, 397, 494, 518, 535-36, 754, 767, 1034, 1046, 1074, 1085, 1087; profile, 529-34; text of its political statement on Spain, 961-63
Communist Party of Spain (Marxist-Leninist) [*Mundo Obrero Revolucionario* group], 529, 536; profile, 534-35
Communist Party of Spain (Marxist-Leninist) [*Vanguardia Obrera* group], 31, 529, 536; profile, 534-35
Communist Party of Sweden (SKP), 183, 184, 206, 224, 296, 332, 420, 448-49, 449n, 450, 454, 542, 544, 753, 754, 1034, 1046, 1064. *See also* Left Party Communists (VPK) of Sweden
Communist Party of Thailand (CPT), 66, 389; profile, 566-73
Communist Party of Turkey (TKP), 224, 604, 753, 754; profile, 576-78
Communist Party of the Ukraine, 80
Communist Party of the United States of America, *see* Communist Party, USA
Communist Party of the United States of America (Marxist-Leninist), 622-23
Communist Party of Uruguay (CPU), 48, 49, 96, 159, 179, 225, 465, 628, 760, 767, 1067, 1078, 1082; profile, 624-28
Communist Party of Venezuela (PCV), 19, 128, 130, 147, 153, 154, 159, 160, 194, 199, 217, 225, 230, 267, 344, 398, 465, 518, 636, 637, 689, 761, 762-63, 767, 783, 1062, 1066, 1068, 1075, 1081, 1082, 1087; profile, 629-35; text of its statement on terrorist regime in Venezuela, 1003-5
—Castro's speech on conflict between Cuban CP and, 154, 268, 475, 633, 1066, 1068; text, 834-57
Communist Party, USA (CPUSA), 210, 224, 226, 248, 315, 332, 397, 502, 600n, 618, 622, 768, 998, 1065; profile, 609-18
"Communist Peace Corps," *see* International Volunteer Youth Service of Solidarity and Friendship
Communist Vanguard Party (Argentina), 20
Communist Workers' Association (Sweden), 547, 550
Communist Workers' Party (Japan), 356-57
Communist Working Circle (KAK) of Denmark, 180, 184
Communist Youth Movement (Belgium), 37, 76
Communist Youth of Denmark (DKP), 182, 679
*Communiste, Le*, see *Le Communiste* group
*Complete Bolivian Diaries of Che Guevara and Other Captured Documents, The*, 42n
"Concerning the Boycott of the Third Duma": quoted, 631
Confederation of Arab Trade Unions, 710
Confederation of Latin Americans in the German Democratic Republic, 759
Conference of the Arab Ministers of Finance, Economy, and Oil Industries, 688
Conference of Chiefs of State of Members of the OAS, *see under* Organization of American States

Conference of Communist and Workers' Parties of Europe, *see* Karlovy Vary conference
Conference of Communist and Workers' Parties of Latin America (1964), 19, 154, 267
Conference of the Latin American Solidarity Organization, *see* OLAS Conference
"Conference of Marxist-Leninist Unity of Great Britain, Preparatory Committee," 33
Conference of Solidarity with the Portuguese Colonies, Zimbabwe, South West Africa, and South Africa, 703
Congo, 39, 159, 215, 527, 857. *See also* Congo (Brazzaville); Congo (Kinshasa)
Congo (Brazzaville), 10, 119, 120, 159, 406, 444, 677, 709, 748, 766, 768, 1060
Congo (Kinshasa), 606, 748, 884
Congress against War and Fascism, 695
Congress for the Freedom of Culture, 950
Congress on Laymen, 488
Conquer or Die (V/M) movement of Ecuador, 196
Continental Organization of Latin American Students (OCLAE), 461, 724, 759
Convention on European capitalism (1965), 935
Co-ordinating Secretariat of National Unions of Students (COSEC), 720
Costa Rica, 461, 761, 763, 782, 1024; profile, 133-35
Council for Mutual Economic Assistance, *see* COMECON
Council for Security Matters, 1048
*Crisis of Modern Catholicism*, 28
*Critique of the Gotha Programme*: quoted, 825
Cuba, 12, 16, 49, 80, 95-96, 97, 127, 130, 132, 134-35, 186, 215, 248, 262, 274, 317, 370, 445, 475, 476, 557, 588, 605, 614, 625, 634, 636, 658, 675, 678, 700, 714, 715, 717, 724, 737, 758-63 *passim*, 781-86 *passim*, 855, 858, 860, 933, 983, 1014, 1021, 1023, 1024, 1028-32 *passim*, 1064, 1080, 1081, 1087; profile, 136-61; text of Castro's speech on conflict with Venezuela, 837-54
—relations with: Albania, 9, 157; Algeria, 14, 158, 159; Angola, 159; Arab states, 149, 157, 158; Bolivia, 44, 159, 160; Cameroun, 159; Chile, 159, 193; Colombia, 841; Communist China, 151, 152, 159; Congo (Brazzaville), 159; Czechoslovakia, 157; Dominican Republic, 841; East Germany, 157, 227, 230; Ethiopia, 159; Great Britain, 840, Guatemala, 159, 160, 841; Guinea, 159; Israel, 149; Laos, 157; Latin America, 19, 147, 148, 148n, 152-56 *passim*, 398, 399, 445, 625, 634, 689, 703, 760-63 *passim*, 837, 840, 851, 1021, 1030-31, 1032, 1047; Mali, 159; Mexico, 145, 149, 160, 839-40, 851; Morocco, 159; Nicaragua, 841; North Korea, 156-57, 445-46; North Vietnam, 150, 652, 661, 852, 1079; Rumania, 157, 517; South Vietnam, 149-50, 852; Soviet Union, 144, 145, 148n, 151, 152-56, 157, 158, 160, 388, 588, 599, 604-5, 689, 695, 709, 723, 760, 761, 766, 840, 851, 855, 886, 1077; Spain, 155, 848; Syria, 158; Tanzania, 159; United Arab Republic,

158, 159, 839; United States, 130, 145, 149-50, 158, 215, 622, 709, 711, 737, 781, 782, 851, 855, 856, 884, 933, 1029, 1030, 1031; Uruguay, 625, 627; Venezuela, 637, 761, 837-54; Vietnam, 150, 852, 1077; West Germany, 851; Yugoslavia, 157, 689, 1080
—*See also* Cuban Communist Party; Sino-Cuban conflict
Cuban Committee of Solidarity with South Vietnam, 149
Cuban Communist Party (CCP), 127, 264n, 265n, 760, 766, 782, 1064; profile, 136-61; text of Castro's speech on conflict with CP of Venezuela, 837-54
—relations with communist parties of: Argentina, 19, 159; Bolivia, 42, 159; Brazil, 48, 49, 50; Bulgaria, 407; Cambodia, 73; Canada, 80; Chile, 92, 94, 97, 159; Colombia, 130, 160, 634; Costa Rica, 133, 134-35; Dominican Republic, 186, 188, 190; East Germany, 224, 230; Ecuador, 194, 195, 196, 634; El Salvador, 199; France, 210, 217, 218, 220, 343, 882; Great Britain, 248; Guadeloupe, 262; Guatemala, 159, 160, 268, 1068; Haiti, 274-77 *passim*; Honduras, 279, 280; Hungary, 283, 293; Indonesia, 317; Italy, 343-44; Japan, 352; Laos, 157, 370-71; Latin America, 153, 154, 761, 1047; Mexico, 398, 399; Mongolia, 407; Netherlands, 420; Nicaragua, 430; North Korea, 156-57, 445-46; North Vietnam, 150, 661; Panama, 462; Paraguay, 465; Peru, 160, 475, 476; Rumania, 157; South Vietnam, 149-50, 678, 1077; Soviet Union, 94, 95, 97, 139, 144, 145, 152-56 *passim*, 159, 230, 388, 399, 588, 605, 628, 634, 636; Switzerland, 554, 557; United States, 622; Uruguay, 159, 627, 628; Venezuela, 19, 159, 160, 230, 267, 268, 398, 465, 475, 630-37 *passim*, 761, 763, 837-54, 1066, 1068, 1081; West Berlin, 242
—*See also* Sino-Cuban conflict
Cultural revolution (in China), 5, 99-121 *passim*, 140, 152, 377, 404, 406, 747, 750, 804, 812-22 *passim*, 826-27, 830, 831, 1053, 1058, 1085; text of *Rruga e Partisë* article on, 773-76; text of Liu Shao-ch'i's confession concerning, 807-11; summaries of speeches made by Cultural Revolutionary Group, 812-14
—editorial in *Jen-min Jih-pao* and *Hung Ch'i* on, 100, 113; quoted, 113-14; text, 793-99
—as viewed by communist parties of: Albania, 7, 655, 773-76, 1058, 1085; Australia, 24-25; Austria, 31, 31n; Belgium, 37; Brazil, 48, 50; Bulgaria, 56; Burma, 62; Cambodia, 72; Cameroun, 76; Ceylon, 86, 87; Chile, 97; Colombia, 129-30; Cuba, 151, 152; Dominican Republic, 188; El Salvador, 199; Finland, 206; France, 209, 220, 221; Hungary, 291; India, 305; Indonesia, 314; Iraq, 326; Italy, 345, 928; Japan, 352, 354, 941-44; Laos, 369; Malaysia, 389; New Zealand, 118, 425; North Korea, 442, 443, 1061; North Vietnam, 655, 656; Pakistan, 459; Peru, 467, 471, 473; Poland, 496; Portugal, 500; South Vietnam, 676; Soviet Union,

602, 966, 974, 975; Spain, 534, 535; Switzerland, 555, 558; Thailand, 571-72; Tunisia, 575; United States, 616, 620, 830
Cypriot Club for Afro-Asian Mutual Assistance, 163
Cypriot-Soviet Club, 163
Cyprus, 29, 58, 177, 255, 256, 257, 554, 576, 577, 578, 702, 703, 711, 890; profile, 162-65
Czechoslovak Union of Journalists, 732
Czechoslovak Writers' Congress, 169-71, 172, 592, 1077, 1089; text of Ludvík Vaculík's speech at, 861-67; excerpt from Czech CP's communique on, 868-69
Czechoslovakia, 30, 52, 53, 59, 119, 130, 157, 194, 226, 231, 291, 292, 317, 321, 327, 334, 403, 420, 491, 492, 508, 510, 514, 536, 588, 600, 606, 630, 652, 652n, 658, 675, 691, 706, 721, 729, 746, 759, 922, 1014, 1026, 1037, 1057, 1061, 1064, 1065, 1066, 1077, 1078, 1079, 1082, 1084-85, 1088, 1089; profile, 166-79; text of Ludvík Vaculík's speech on civil affairs in, 861-67

Dahomey, 746
*Danger Within, The*, 390
Danubian countries, 292, 1044
"Decree on Peace, 988, 1042; international conference on fiftieth anniversary of, 703, 770
*Deer and the Sparrow, The*, 986
Democratic Action (AD) of Venezuela, 629, 637, 837, 838, 841-42
Democratic Party of Guinea, 119, 210, 224, 342, 768
Denmark, 119, 231, 678, 679, 1037; profile, 180-84
Denmark-Soviet Union Association, 182
Dhofar, 701
*Diario de las Américas* (U. S. Spanish-language newspaper), 840; quoted, 840
*Diary of Che Guevara, The*, 42, 148, 155, 159
Dominican Communist Party (PCD), 189, 210, 767; profile, 185-87
Dominican People's Movement (MPD), 185, 189; profile, 187-88
Dominican People's Socialist Party (PSP), 185, 187
Dominican Republic, 215, 274, 276, 292, 748, 761, 781, 782, 841, 855, 856, 884, 1024, 1030; profile, 185-91
"Duty of Every Revolutionary Is to Make Revolution, The": text, 1021-22

East Berlin, 232, 234, 239
East Germany, 9, 29, 30, 36, 56, 57, 80, 119, 121, 130, 157, 175, 176, 204, 215, 218, 234-41 *passim*, 247, 257, 291-92, 294, 298, 317, 321, 323, 340, 403, 420, 491, 492, 500, 515, 534, 548, 556, 599, 600, 652, 658, 675, 700, 707, 709, 711, 715, 716, 721, 729, 746, 756, 759, 851, 950, 953, 966, 969, 970, 1014, 1026, 1037, 1039, 1043, 1044, 1050, 1058, 1061, 1066, 1067, 1073, 1079, 1082, 1084, 1088, 1092-93; profile, 223-33
"East of Suez policy," 248
Eastern Europe, 8-9, 125, 154, 157, 175-76, 177, 182, 225, 229, 230, 231, 240, 248, 256, 272, 294, 321,

323, 325, 332, 334, 344, 358, 370, 446, 491, 493, 508, 511, 514, 517, 523, 529, 548, 557, 561, 584, 600, 601, 604, 662, 686, 687, 688, 690, 699, 700, 709, 712, 726, 736, 761, 950, 1036, 1040, 1068, 1075, 1076, 1079, 1085; communist parties in, 130, 599, 686, 753, 755

Economic and Social Council (ECOSOC) of the United Nations, 707, 714, 721, 727, 729, 736, 742, 745

Economic Commission for Asia and the Far East (ECAFE) of the United Nations, 707

Economic Commission for Europe (ECE) of the United Nations, 707

*Economist* (London): quoted on Karlovy Vary Conference, 756

Ecuador, 724, 748, 761, 839, 1024; profile, 192-96

EEC, *see* European Economic Community

Egypt, *see* United Arab Republic

Eire, *see* Ireland

El Salvador, 461, 762, 763, 1024; profile, 197-99

*Enfoque Internacional*, 96

*Epoca* Independent Group (Uruguay), 628

Equatorial Guinea, 717

Eritrea, 159, 723

Ethiopia, 159, 406, 724, 746, 748, 1059

Euratom (European Atomic Energy Community), 1043

Europe, 36, 37, 55, 57, 86, 164, 175-79 *passim*, 183, 184, 204, 206, 212, 215, 216, 225, 228, 229, 231, 235, 236, 237, 246, 247, 250, 253, 255, 256, 291, 292, 316, 321, 322, 328, 329, 340, 341, 344, 380, 381, 419, 420, 454, 491, 492, 494, 500, 515, 518, 534, 535, 549, 553, 599, 600, 658, 687, 698, 700-705 *passim*, 710-17 *passim*, 724, 729, 734, 737-41 *passim*, 744, 753-57 *passim*, 823, 857, 873, 884, 890, 891, 927, 934, 936, 947, 949, 950, 953, 954, 955, 961, 965-71 *passim*, 1018, 1020, 1032-42 *passim*, 1053, 1061, 1064, 1065, 1066, 1079, 1082; communist parties in, 24, 144, 153, 210, 218, 292, 535, 753, 820, 927, 1034, 1038, 1041, 1044, 1045, 1046; text of Karlovy Vary conference statement on peace and security in, 1042-46. *See also* Central Europe; Eastern Europe; Mediterranean area; Northern Europe; Western Europe

European Broadcasting Union (EBU), 745

European Defense Community (EDC), 698, 709

European Economic Community (EEC), 29, 35, 183, 206, 211, 213, 215, 216, 246, 260, 328, 344, 450, 548, 549, 698, 961, 1043

European Free Trade Association (EFTA), 498, 548

European Student Conference, 724

*Evolution of Modern Catholicism, The*, 28

FAO, *see* Food and Agriculture Organization

Far East, 926

Fascism, Fascists, 28, 56, 255, 425, 497, 498, 499, 526, 547, 549, 607, 703, 709, 716, 717, 718, 728, 739, 740, 756, 781, 890, 891, 968, 969, 970, 991,
1014, 1016, 1042, 1045, 1059. *See also* Neofascism

Al Fatah organization, 331, 921

*Feast of the Victors, The* (also *The Feast of the Conqueror*), 986, 1001

Federation of the Democratic and Socialist Left (FGDS) of France, 211-17 *passim*, 412, 873-76 *passim*; text of joint communique by French CP and, 872-73

Federation of Dominican Students (FED), 185, 186, 721, 722, 723

Federation of Marxist-Leninist Communists of Italy (FCMLI), 1058; profile, 345-46

Federation of National Unions of Cypriot Students (FNUCS), 162-63, 721

Federation of Students of Panama (FEP), 460, 461, 720

Federation of University Centers (FCU) of Venezuela, 630, 720, 722, 723

Federation of University Students of Ecuador (FEUE), 192-95 *passim*, 722, 723

Federation of Uruguayan University Students (FEUU), 625, 721, 724

*Financial Times* (London), 205n

Finland, 28, 231, 518, 745, 746, 870-1, 927, 1075, 1092; profile, 200-7

Finnish People's Democratic League (SKDL), 184, 200-7 *passim*, 296 454, 549, 550, 768, 1073

Finnish-Soviet Society, 200

*First Circle, The*, 986, 1000

First Marxist-Leninist Group of Cameroun: profile, 75-76

First World Peace Congress (1949), 698, 727

Food and Agriculture Organization (FAO) of the United Nations, 707

"Foolish Old Man Who Removed the Mountains, The," 111

"For a Sound Indonesian Revolution" (also "On the Correct Road of the Indonesian Revolution"), 217, 217n, 317-18, 1066; quoted, 318, 319, 320; text, 908-19

Fourth International: International Committee, 85, 251, 623; International Secretariat (Posadas movement), 20; Parti Communiste Internationaliste (PCI), 209; United (or Unified) Secretariat, 43, 84, 251, 346, 474, 621, 622

France, 9, 9n, 12, 13, 28, 69, 70, 119, 207, 238, 241, 251, 259, 260, 261, 334, 373, 380, 393, 394, 395, 506, 519, 529, 553, 559, 662, 688, 696, 706, 710, 713, 726, 737, 746, 827, 855, 871, 880-84 *passim*, 920, 921, 927, 931, 932, 935, 949, 965, 971, 993, 1006, 1016, 1037, 1065, 1076; profile, 208-22; texts (complete and abridged) of documents on general elections in, 872-77

Francisco Morazan Movement (MFM) of Honduras, 278, 280

Franco-Chinese Friendship Association, 220, 221

Francoists, 410

*Frankfurter Allgemeine Zeitung*, 171

Free Europe Committee, 950
Free German Youth (FDJ; East Germany), 224, 228, 720
Free Socialist Party (West Germany), 238, 1071
French Communist Movement, Marxist-Leninist (MCF [M-L]), 10, 33, 208, 209, 221, 221n, 222, 345, 496, 535, 1081, 1083, 1094. *See also* Marxist-Leninist Communist Party of France
French Communist Party (PCF), 12, 14, 15, 28, 30, 32, 59, 75, 155, 177, 183, 184, 206, 221, 222, 224, 226, 232, 241, 242, 248, 260, 261, 294, 296, 315, 317, 326, 337-43 *passim*, 376, 380, 382, 393, 394, 409, 411, 412, 413, 419, 433, 471, 494, 506, 517, 518, 527, 540, 553, 574, 575, 600n, 605, 615, 618, 627, 662, 678, 691, 753, 754, 763, 767, 786, 872-84 *passim*, 1034, 1046, 1057, 1065, 1067, 1073, 1080, 1082, 1083, 1092, 1094; profile, 208-20; texts (complete and abridged) of its documents on French general elections, 872-77; abridged text of Rochet's paper on role of, 880-84
French Guiana, 1024
French Revolution, 1028
French Somaliland, 748
Friends of the Soviet Union (Lebanon), 374
*50 [Fünfzig] Jahre. Die Sozialistische Oktober-revolution und Österreich*, 29

Gaullism, Gaullists, 394, 872-76 *passim*
General Association of Guadeloupe Students (AGEG), 259, 723
General Association of Martinique Students (AGEM), 259, 393, 394, 721, 723
General Confederation of Labor (CGT) of France, 208-9, 213, 219, 344, 446, 662, 710, 1076
General Union of Students of the Iraqi Republic (GUSIR), 324, 326-27, 720
Geneva Agreements, 24, 407, 648-49, 663, 670n, 699, 873, 874, 924; (of 1954), 73, 408, 649, 666, 698, 699, 855, 1006, 1007, 1016; (of 1962), 362, 367, 370
German Democratic Republic (GDR), *see* East Germany
German-Latin American Society, 227
German Peace Society, 236, 701
German-Soviet Friendship Society, 224
Germany, 169, 175, 176, 183, 228, 229, 234, 241, 242, 251, 291, 329, 330, 380, 490, 491, 494, 514, 515, 548, 700, 709, 716, 721, 741, 781, 786, 827, 873, 968, 969, 970, 993, 1014, 1016, 1037, 1043, 1044, 1061. *See also* East Berlin; East Germany; West Berlin; West Germany
Germany, Federal Republic of (FRG), *see* West Germany
Ghana, 215, 248, 527, 599, 600, 606, 715, 884, 1035
Glassboro meeting, 32, 221, 1076
Gramsci Institute, 935
Great Britain, 8, 20, 30, 87, 104, 119, 163, 164, 216, 267, 292, 322, 325, 328-31 *passim*, 358, 359, 375, 377, 386, 389, 425, 432, 493, 523, 539, 564, 565, 578, 602, 605, 617, 622, 660, 677-78, 701, 702, 711, 737, 746, 839, 840, 857, 871, 901, 907, 913, 920, 921, 926, 932, 947, 971, 993, 1037, 1047, 1050, 1062, 1082, 1091; profile, 243-51. *See also* Anglo-America
Great Leap Forward, 101, 102, 106, 114, 305, 534, 615, 927, 973
Great Proletarian Cultural Revolution, *see* Cultural revolution
Greece, 29, 30, 32, 39, 49, 57, 58, 79-80, 163, 164, 165, 177, 182, 206, 209, 215, 225, 226, 237, 248, 251, 292, 333, 344, 376, 406, 419, 450, 493, 500, 549, 553, 554, 555, 576, 577, 578, 634, 701, 703, 710, 711, 715, 716, 724, 728-29, 734, 738, 740, 741, 744, 753, 756, 870, 884, 979, 1034, 1042, 1045, 1046, 1051, 1070-71, 1072, 1076; profile, 252-58; text of Grek CP's resolution on situation in, 890-92
Greek Marxist-Leninist Communists, 222, 258
Guadeloupe, 215, 709, 759, 1024, 1074; profile, 259-62
Guadeloupe Communist Party (PCG), 208, 210, 261, 506, 767, 873; profile, 259-61
Guadeloupe National Organization Group (GONG), 222, 1074; profile, 261-62
Guatemala, 150, 159, 160, 461, 465, 476, 505, 717, 748, 758, 761, 781, 841, 843, 849, 858, 859, 1021, 1023, 1024, 1028, 1030, 1032, 1047, 1048; profile, 263-69
Guatemalan Party of Labor (PGT), 159, 446, 767, 1047, 1048, 1068, 1087; profile, 263-69. *See also* Communist Parties of Mexico, Central America and Panama, Fifth Meeting of
Guinea, 119, 159, 539, 605-6, 709, 732, 746, 748, 749, 759, 766, 768, 922
Guinean Independence Party, *see* National Independence Front of Guinea
Guyana, 758, 759, 1023, 1024; profile, 270-72

*Hai Jui's Dismissal from Office*, 100, 106, 793
Haiti, 1024, 1030, 1048; profile, 273-77
Haitian Liberation Front in Exile (FHALE), 274
Haitian Workers' Party (PTH), 273, 274, 275
Hallstein Doctrine, 231, 234, 599
"Hammer and Steel" group (United States), 623
Han people, 406
Hanoi, 679, 973. *See also* North Vietnam
Havana Declaration, *see* Second Declaration of Havana
Hiroshima, 718
Hispaniola, 276
*History of the CPSU*, 585
Hitlerism, Hitlerites, 425, 740, 968, 969, 970, 1016, 1042, 1043
Holland, *see* Netherlands
Honduran Revolutionary Party (PRH), 278, 279, 280
Honduras, 461, 782, 1024, 1048; profile, 278-81
Hong Kong, 1072
Hoover Institution, 589
*How to Be a Good Communist*, 102, 345, 1067
Huks, *see* People's Liberation Army ("Huks") of the Philippines

*Human Phenomenon, The*, 588

*L'Humanité* (daily of the French Communist Party), 155, 217, 218, 222, 471, 627, 763

*L'Humanité Nouvelle* (weekly of the Marxist-Leninist Communist Party of France), 222, 635

*Hung Ch'i* (*Red Flag*; Communist Chinese journal), 121; texts of editorials on proletarian revolutionaries, 800-807

—joint editorial on cultural revolution, 100, 113; quoted, 113-14; text, 793-99

—joint editorial on October Revolution, 116; text, 823-28

Hungarian Peace Committee, 705

Hungarian Socialist Workers' Party (SWP), 30, 31, 179, 184, 206-7, 210, 219, 224, 226, 355, 411, 419, 446, 517, 600n, 753, 767, 894, 895, 1034, 1046, 1073, 1074; profile, 282-94

Hungary, 30, 52, 154, 176, 180, 208, 226, 231, 243, 321, 327, 334, 342, 403, 423, 451, 491, 508, 510, 514, 518, 555, 584, 588, 600, 630, 652, 652n, 658, 662, 709, 715, 729, 726, 759, 775, 922, 1014, 1026, 1061, 1064-69 *passim*, 1073, 1079, 1080, 1084, 1088; profile, 282-94

Iceland, 231; profile, 295-96

Ifni, 410

*Imperialism: The Highest Stage of Capitalism*, 179

"In Memory of Norman Bethune," 111

*In the First Circle*, see *First Circle, The*

Independent Revolutionary Movement (MIR) of Ecuador, 192, 196

India, 28, 39, 66, 119, 120, 403, 414, 416, 456, 458, 553, 702, 714, 717, 729, 746, 749, 823, 927, 1018, 1063, 1074, 1084; profile, 297-307

Indian Association for Afro-Asian Solidarity, 699

Indian Ocean, 506

Indian Women's Congress, 729

Indian Writers' Committee, 705

Indochina, Indochinese, 58, 79, 367, 368, 370, 407, 527, 573, 640, 659, 674, 855, 857, 1006, 1007, 1008, 1012

Indochinese Communist Party, 638

Indonesia, 31, 39, 49, 119, 120, 177, 216, 217, 225, 246, 248, 292, 304, 371, 384, 388, 389, 391, 420, 483, 516, 521, 524, 599, 600, 634, 655, 659, 673, 675, 722, 732, 744, 747, 748, 813, 823, 857-58, 882, 927, 1035, 1067, 1071, 1087; profile, 308-20; text of PKI's statement on its role in, 896-907; text of document by Marxist-Leninist Group of PKI on PKI's role in, 908-19

Indonesian Afro-Asian People's Solidarity Organization, 312, 314, 317

Indonesian Bornea (Kalimantan), 313, 391, 748

Indonesian Central Organization of Trade Unions (SOBSI), 308, 313, 750

Indonesian Journalists' Association, 747, 748

Indo-Soviet Cultural Association, 298

Inner Mongolia, 102, 405, 406

Inter-American Peace Committee, 1031

Inter-American Treaty for Mutual Assistance, 1030

International Association of Democratic Lawyers (IADL), 695, 739, 750, 1059; profile, 742-44

International Atomic Agency, 700

International Bank for Economic Cooperation, 176

International Committee of Aid to Soviet Russia, 695

International Committee of Solidarity with the Arab Peoples, of the WFDY, 714

International Committee of Solidarity with South Vietnam: of the WFDY, 714; of the WIDF, 727

International Committee of Solidarity with the Youth and People of the Portuguese Colonies, of the WFDY, 714

International Confederation for Disarmament and Peace, 699

International Confederation of Free Trade Unions (ICFTU), 560, 706, 710, 712

International Conference against the War Danger, 729

International Conference for the Restoration of Civil Rights in Spain, 741

International Conference in Support of the Arab Peoples, 618, 702

International Conference of Communist and Workers' Parties (1957 and 1960), *see* Moscow conference of 1957; Moscow conference of 1960

International conference of Communist and workers' parties, Soviet-proposed convocation of, 10, 19, 36, 59, 86-87, 93, 96, 129, 134, 155, 164, 178, 179, 184, 206, 207, 210, 218, 225, 226, 237, 261, 280, 293, 294, 326, 329, 338-39, 340, 355, 355n, 356, 361, 374, 375, 382, 398, 399, 407, 411, 412, 419, 425, 442, 471, 483, 490, 491, 494, 513-18 *passim*, 527, 534, 549n, 554, 575, 599, 600, 601, 628, 676, 686-91 *passim*, 894-95, 924, 929-30, 939, 1054, 1088

International conference of European Marxist-Leninist movements, proposed, 346

International Conference of Railroad Workers' Unions, 712

International Conference on Fifty Years of the October Revolution and the International Workers' Movement, 554, 770

International Conference on the Historical Significance of the October Revolution, 178, 267, 575, 769, 1076

International Conference on the October Revolution and the National Liberation Movement of the Peoples of Asia, Africa, and Latin America, 412, 769

International Conference on Vietnam, 548, 550, 662, 679, 699, 699n, 700, 711, 728, 733

International Control Commission, 79

International Cultural Congress (Havana, Jan. 1968), 160

International Day of Solidarity with the People of Vietnam, of the WIDF, 727

International Federation of Journalists (IFJ), 731, 732, 734

International Federation of Resistance Fighters (FIR), 714; profile, 739-41

International Fellowship of Reconciliation, 699

International Film and Television Council, 745
International Institute for Peace (IIP), 696, 697, 700, 704, 736
International Labor Organization (ILO), 511, 707, 711, 727, 736
International Meeting of Solidarity with Vietnam, 603
International Organization of Journalists (IOJ), 442, 745, 747, 759; profile, 731-34
International Peace Bureau, 699, 729
International Radio and Television Organization (OIRT), 736; profile, 745-46
International Revolutionary Aid Organization ("MOPR"), 695
International Seminar of the Student Press, 724
International Socialism Group ("Cliff Group") of Great Britain, 251
International Student Committee of Solidarity with the Struggle of the People and Students of Vietnam, 722
International Student Seminar, 725
International Students' Conference (ISC), 720, 721, 723, 725
International Telecommunication Union, 745
International Trade Union Committee for Solidarity with the Workers and People of Aden, 707; Damascus conference, 560, 707, 712, 1058
International Trade Union Committee for Solidarity with the Workers and People of South Vietnam, 707
International Union of Students (IUS), 45, 95-96, 155, 163, 193, 274, 322, 324, 327, 373, 407, 442, 460, 653, 714, 715, 717, 729, 736, 759, 1067; profile, 720-25
International Volunteer Youth Service of Solidarity and Friendship ("Communist Peace Corps"), 717, 1063
International War Crimes Tribunal, see Russell International War Crimes Tribunal
International Week of Solidarity with the Journalists and People of Vietnam, 733
International Workers' Aid Organization, 695
International Youth Assembly, 251
International Youth Rally, 717-18, 724, 769
Iran, 59, 406, 519, 604, 721; profile, 321-23
Iran-Soviet Cultural Relations Society, 323
Iraq, 59, 119, 149, 406, 540, 562, 604, 688-89, 743-49 passim, 948, 1050, 1051, 1052, 1072, 1081; profile, 324-27
Iraqi Communist Party (ICP), 59, 179, 224, 294, 361, 604, 767, 1050, 1085, 1092; profile, 324-27
Iraqi Communist Party (Marxist-Leninist), 327
Ireland, 248; profile, 328-29
Irish-British Free Trade Agreement, 328
Irish Communist Organization, 329
Irish Workers' Party (IWP), 210, 224, 753, 754, 767, 1034, 1046; profile, 328-29
Islamic Pact, 539, 1050
Israel, 8, 20, 24, 30, 32, 38, 49, 58, 59, 79, 80, 87, 95, 120, 130, 149, 157, 158, 169, 171-72, 177, 177n, 183, 186, 191, 207, 215, 216, 229, 237, 241, 247, 248, 256, 257, 267, 272, 290, 292, 323-26 passim, 342, 344, 358, 359, 360, 361n, 363, 374, 375, 389, 390, 407, 420, 425, 432, 442, 450, 465, 484, 485, 493, 495, 500, 516, 517, 527, 534, 549, 554, 556, 559, 561, 563, 565, 575, 578, 601, 603-4, 617, 622, 660, 677-78, 682, 687, 689, 701, 702, 703, 709, 710, 716, 728, 733-34, 739, 740, 741, 744, 748, 766, 857, 920-23, 931, 932, 936, 979, 983, 984, 994, 1018, 1026-27, 1050-54 passim, 1075, 1076, 1079, 1081; profile, 330-34; abridged text of statement by CP of Jordan on aggression of, 947-48; text of CPSU resolution on Soviet policy concerning aggression of, 977-78. See also Arab-Israeli crisis and war; Palestine; Palestine Liberation Organization; Palestinian Arabs; Zionism, Zionists
Israeli Communist Party (MAKI), 179, 294, 419, 420, 518, 604, 1068, 1075; profile, 330-34
Israeli Communist Party (RAKAH), see New Communist List
Israel-Soviet Friendship Movement, 333, 923
Italian Communist Party (PCI), 14, 29, 59, 96, 162, 179, 210, 212, 219, 224, 232, 248, 258, 294, 315, 346, 419, 494, 517, 518, 520, 600n, 605, 607, 608, 691, 754, 767, 783, 786, 903-4, 927-30 passim, 935-39 passim, 1034, 1046, 1059, 1067, 1068, 1079, 1080, 1082, 1094; profile, 335-44; abridged text of Berlinguer's report to, 925-30; abridged text of Longo's statement on Middle East at meeting of, 931-33
Italian General Confederation of Labor (CGIL), 209, 336, 344, 710
Italian Socialist Party of Proletarian Unity (PSIUP), 224, 335, 337, 768
Italo-Albanian Friendship Association, 345
Italo-Cuban Friendship Society, 336
Italo-Soviet Friendship Association, 336
Italy, 9, 115, 119, 251, 605, 710, 740, 746, 903-4, 924, 926, 928, 932, 965, 1058, 1059; profile, 335-47
Italy-China Association, 345
Ivory Coast, 519, 1059

Jacobin leftists, 151, 724
Jamaica, 1024
Jammu and Kashmir, see Kashmir
Japan, 102, 115, 118, 119, 301, 436, 519, 595, 703, 710, 711, 717, 724, 748, 749, 813, 815, 817, 855, 857, 926, 940, 945, 946, 993, 1006, 1014, 1016, 1060; profile, 348-57. See also Sino-Japanese War
Japan Afro-Asian Solidarity Organization, 351
Japan Association for the Promotion of International Trade, 121, 350, 354
Japan-China Friendship Association, 350, 351, 353
Japan-China Friendship Association (Orthodox), 350, 357
Japan-China Trade Promotion Association, 350
Japan Committee for Afro-Asian Solidarity, 351
Japan Communist Party (JCP), 117, 224, 356, 357, 362n, 424, 425, 444, 603, 620, 723, 1060,

1062-63, 1081, 1088; profile, 348-56
—anti-Mao article in party newspaper, 354, 1062; excerpts, 940-46
Japan Communist Party (Left Wing), 357
Japan Communist Party (Marxist-Leninist), 357
Japan Congress against A and H Bombs, *see* Japan Council for the Prohibition of Atomic and Hydrogen Bombs
Japan Council against Atomic and Hydrogen Bombs (Gensuikyo), 349-50, 759
Japan Council for the Prohibition of Atomic and Hydrogen Bombs (Gensuikin), 350, 355, 703
Japan-Korea Friendship Association, 350
Japan Peace Committee, 703
Japan Socialist Party (JSP), 348, 350, 351, 518, 768
Japan-Soviet Friendship Association, 350
Japan-United States Security Treaty, 349, 351
Japanese Committee of the Afro-Asian Writers' Association, 351
Japanese Conference of the Afro-Asian Writers' Association, 351
*Jen-min Jih-pao* (*People's Daily*; Communist Chinese newspaper), 121
—joint editorial on cultural revolution, 100, 113; quoted, 113-14; text, 793-99
—joint editorial on October Revolution, 116; text, 823-28
Jerusalem, 361n
Jews, 24, 30, 36, 38, 178, 215, 290, 323, 333, 359, 425, 484, 485, 575, 616, 617. *See also* Anti-Semitism; Israel; Zionism, Zionists
Jewish Bund, 579
Jordan, 14, 15, 183, 323, 326, 331, 560, 689, 702, 748, 922, 964, 977, 1049, 1050-51, 1081, 1092; profile, 358-61; abridged text of statement by CP of Jordan on Israeli aggression in, 947-48

Kalimantan, *see* Indonesian Borneo
*Kapital, Das*, 93, 179, 587, 1081
Karlovy Vary conference, 10, 29, 30, 32, 36, 51, 57, 86, 87, 115, 164, 165, 178, 179, 183, 205, 206, 212, 215-21 *passim*, 225, 226, 231, 232, 237, 242, 248, 255, 257, 294, 296, 328, 329, 340, 341, 368, 382, 407, 419, 442, 454, 492, 494, 500, 517, 520, 534, 549, 554, 588, 599-600, 601, 605, 653, 686, 687, 688, 765, 894, 934, 935, 936, 950, 983, 1053, 1063, 1071; profile, 753-57; text of opening communique, 1034; text of Brezhnev's speech at, 1034-42; text of final communique, 1046
—final statement, "For Peace and Security in Europe," 756, 757, 1042, 1046; text, 1042-46
Karlsruhe trial, 743
Kashmir, 457, 748
Kautskyism, 870
Kenya, 119
Khmer-Chinese Friendship Association, 67, 71, 73
Khmer-North Vietnamese Friendship Association, 71
Khmer-Soviet Friendship Association, 71
Khrushchevism, Khrushchevists, 8, 10, 38, 65, 102, 117, 314, 345, 421, 571, 727, 757, 774, 818,

821, 822, 823, 827, 830-36 *passim*, 940, 1079
Komsomol (Communist Youth League) of the Soviet Union, 182, 207, 401, 582-83, 589, 592, 606, 717, 769, 770
Korea, 9, 156, 215, 438, 439, 476, 658, 705, 709, 715, 721, 727, 742, 743, 855, 1014. *See also* Korean War; North Korea; South Korea
Korea, Democratic People's Republic of, *see* North Korea
Korea, Republic of, *see* South Korea
Korean Committee for Afro-Asian Solidarity (North Korea), 442
Korean-Soviet Friendship Society (North Korea), 444
Korean War, 442, 737, 782, 855, 1036
Korean Workers' Party (KWP), 156-57, 224, 226, 268, 356, 371, 425, 620, 659, 763, 767, 1058, 1090; profile, 434-47
Koreans, in Japan, 350, 435, 436
Krestintern (International Peasants' Union), 695
Kuomintang, 117, 833, 836, 945
Kurdistan, Kurds, 324, 325, 325n, 326, 373, 376, 406, 577-78, 1050, 1051, 1072
Kuwait, 59, 748

Labor Alliance of Russian Solidarists, *see* People's Alliance of Labor
Labour Party (Great Britain), 29, 243, 250, 384, 446, 755, 1040
Laos, 157, 304, 445, 568, 573, 658-59, 674, 748, 823, 855, 857, 859, 1006, 1007, 1008, 1012; profile, 362-72
Laotian Afro-Asian Solidarity Committee, 363, 370, 659
Laotian Patriotic Front (NLHX), 157, 224, 445, 568, 573, 658, 659, 1094; profile, 362-72
Laotian People's Liberation Army (*former* Pathet Lao), 362-71 *passim*, 659
Laotian People's Party (PsL), 118, 119, 658; profile, 362-72
Latin America, 9, 10, 14, 19, 20, 45, 46, 49, 76, 92, 94, 96, 118, 127, 132, 134, 145-60 *passim*, 186, 190, 195, 196, 199, 216, 217, 218, 227, 230, 242, 251, 262, 265n, 267-68, 272, 279, 343, 344, 368, 370, 395, 397, 398, 439, 440, 445, 446, 447, 462, 465, 467, 471, 475, 504, 517, 564, 573, 588, 599, 605, 616, 622, 625, 626, 627, 634, 635, 636, 653, 661, 674-78 *passim*, 689, 698, 702, 703, 712, 713, 715, 728, 733, 746, 758-63 *passim*, 823, 837-43 *passim*, 851, 852, 855-59 *passim*, 882, 910-13 *passim*, 927, 936, 937, 975, 977, 979, 994, 1003, 1012, 1013, 1014, 1018, 1021-25 *passim*, 1028-35 *passim*, 1043, 1045, 1053, 1057; communist parties in, 19, 91, 96, 117, 125, 130, 147, 151, 153, 154, 159-60, 217, 230, 242, 280, 397-400 *passim*, 420, 461, 554, 585, 605, 616, 620, 625, 627, 631-36 *passim*, 737, 761, 763, 783-86 *passim*, 842, 844, 894, 1047, 1053; text of article by Luis Corvalán on anti-imperialism in, 781-86. *See also* Central America; South America
Latin America Economic Integration Programs, 1021

Latin American Continental Students Organization, *see* Continental Organization of Latin American Students

Latin American Permanent Congress for Trade Union Unity, 710

Latin American Solidarity Organization, *see* OLAS; OLAS Conference

Latin American Students' Congress, 155

*Le Communiste* group (France), 220, 222

League of Communists of Yugoslavia (SKJ), 14, 179, 180, 207, 210, 219, 224, 226, 230, 413, 517, 753, 754-55, 767, 1057, 1071, 1091; profile, 681-91; text of its conclusions on international problems, 1018-20

League of Marxist-Leninist Communists of Italy, 346

League of Socialist Working Youth of Korea (North Korea), 435, 437, 444, 447, 603

Lebanese Communist Party (LCP), 210, 224, 559, 565, 767, 1072; profile, 373-76

Lebanon, 559, 565, 716, 748, 749, 1049-50, 1051; profile, 373-76

Left Party Communists (VPK) of Sweden, 518, 767; profile, 542-50. *See also* Communist Party of Sweden

Leipzig, 578

Lenin Peace Prize, 236, 525, 701, 705, 726

Lenin Peace Prize Committee, 705

Leninist Spartacus League (Mexico), 400

Lesotho, 526, 748; profile, 377-79

*Letter from China*: quoted, 118, 152

Liao-Takasaki Trade Agreement, 353

*Liberation Army Daily*, see *Chieh-fang Chün-pao*

Liberation Federation of Trade Unions (South Vietnam), 667, 711

Liberation Front of Dhofar, 701

Liberation Movement of Portuguese Guinea, 224

London, 389

Luxembourg, 746; profile, 380-82

Luxembourg-China Society, 382

Macao, 119

Madagascar, 251, 732

Maghreb, 13, 604, 1051

Malagasy Republic, 709

Malawi, 526

Malaya, 66, 522, 523, 524, 573, 748, 857. *See also* Malaysia

Malayan National Liberation League (MNLL), 383, 384, 387-90 *passim*, 573, 659

Malaysia, 521, 522, 523, 568, 915, 1069, 1090-91; profile, 383-92

Mali, 120, 159, 539, 605-6, 709, 732, 745, 746, 749, 766, 768

Manchus, 406

Maoism, Maoists, 18, 67, 72, 84, 100-120 *passim*, 129, 153, 154, 155, 180, 209, 216, 243, 258, 303, 304, 307, 322, 345, 352, 354, 356, 357, 416, 423, 424, 504, 528, 542, 543, 544, 565, 605, 690, 878, 880, 882, 975, 1053, 1054, 1074

Marshall Plan, 698, 709, 714

Martinique, 215, 709, 759, 1024; profile, 393-95

Martinique Communist Party (PCM), 210, 261, 506, 767; profile, 393-95

"Marxism Is Not a Catechism," 216, 554, 555; text, 878-79

*Marxisme du XXe Siècle*, 212n

Marxist-Leninist All-Union Communist Bolshevik Party (Soviet Union), 32, 496, 1063

Marxist-Leninist Center of France (CMLF), 209, 221; profile, 222

Marxist-Leninist Center of the Netherlands, 31, 222, 421, 535

Marxist-Leninist Committee of Portugal, 222, 501

Marxist-Leninist Communist Party of France (PCMLF), 208, 209, 222, 558, 635; profile, 220-22

Marxist-Leninist Group of the Communist Party of Indonesia (pro-Soviet), 217, 603, 1066; profile, 317-20; text of document by, 908-19

Marxist-Leninist international movement, 10-11

Marxist-Leninist Organization of Britain, 251

Marxist-Leninist Party of Austria (MLPÖ), 10, 27, 222, 558, 704, 1062, 1064, 1072-73, 1081; profile, 31-33

Marxist-Leninist Party of Indonesia, *see* Marxist-Leninist Group of the Communist Party of Indonesia

*Master and Margarita*, 590

Mauritania, 120, 406, 410, 748

*May 4th Movement, The*: quoted, 797

Mediterranean area, 14, 120, 255, 256, 343, 344, 554, 687, 701, 701n, 702-3, 691, 755, 890, 921, 936, 937, 1039, 1044, 1051

Meeting of Solidarity of Latin American Youth with Vietnam, 95

Melilla, 410

"Message to the Peoples of the World," 146, 148, 151, 154, 218, 220, 230, 344, 622, 627, 1069; quoted, 146, 148; text, 855-60

Mexican Communist Party (PCM), 194, 225, 399, 618, 763, 767, 1068, 1076; profile, 396-99. *See also* Communist Parties of Mexico, Central America and Panama, Fifth Meeting of

Mexican Movement of Marxist-Leninist Antirevisionist Unification (MUMAM), 399-400

Mexican Workers' Party, 400

Mexico, 145, 149, 160, 461, 724, 729, 758, 761, 783, 839-40, 851, 1023, 1024, 1030, 1047, 1048; profile, 396-400

Middle East, 8, 24, 29, 158, 191, 194, 215, 216, 229, 247, 331, 358, 375, 406, 412, 444, 527, 539, 556, 577, 588, 604, 617, 622, 634, 660, 682, 688, 701, 703, 712, 713, 715, 728, 737, 744, 786, 857, 858, 890, 920, 921, 922, 937, 964, 1067, 1054, 1079; communist parties in, 604; Warsaw Pact meeting of Foreign Ministers on situation in, 291, 491, 514, 517, 1093. *See also* Arab-Israeli crisis and war; Arab states; Budapest conference on the Middle East; Israel; Moscow conference on the Middle East; Near East

*Militant Communist Threat to West Malaysia, The,* 383, 385, 386, 389, 391; quoted, 383, 385

Mongolia, 56, 57, 119, 445, 603, 652, 652n, 658, 660, 714, 749, 759, 813, 981, 1014, 1058, 1059, 1060, 1079; profile, 401-8

Mongolian People's Revolutionary Party (MPRP), 22, 86, 118, 210, 224, 600n, 660, 767; profile, 401-8

Monroe Doctrine, 1029, 1030

Montevideo, 729

Moroccan Communist Party (PCM), 210, 219, 224, 518, 574, 689, 768, 1070, 1073; profile, 409-13

Morocco, 119, 159, 326, 574, 1051; profile, 409-13

Moscow, 529, 973

Moscow conference of 1957, 66, 182, 225, 482, 573, 653, 755, 765, 982, 1035, 1053. *See also* Moscow Declaration of 1957

Moscow conference of 1960, 66, 182, 206, 225, 482, 564, 573, 653, 755, 765, 938, 982, 1035, 1053, 1054. *See also* Moscow Statement of 1960

Moscow conference on the Middle East, 58-59, 177, 215-16, 229, 292, 493, 516, 534, 554, 600, 604, 682, 687, 688, 894, 964, 1018, 1075;

—Statement (or Declaration), 59, 230, 292, 332, 604, 687, 964, 977, 1075, 1076; text, 1026-27

Moscow Declaration of 1957, 10, 280, 294, 306, 320, 388, 440, 553, 755, 883, 911, 913, 914, 918, 983, 1053; quoted, 939

Moscow international convention of 1965, 935

Moscow Statement of 1960, 10, 216, 280, 294, 306, 318, 320, 355n, 388, 440, 553, 882, 908, 911-14 *passim*, 918, 983, 1053; quoted, 912-13

Movement of Autonomous Socialists (Italy), 768

Movement of the Revolutionary Left (MIR) of Chile, 90, 96-97

Movement of the Revolutionary Left (MIR) of Peru, 96, 97, 160, 467, 470, 472, 1074; profile, 474-75

Movement of the Revolutionary Left (MIR) of Venezuela, 96, 97, 629, 630, 634, 635, 636, 842, 844, 847, 848, 1075; profile, 637

Mozambique, 49, 450, 500, 549, 748, 857

Mozambique National Liberation Front (FRELIMO), 444, 660, 768

Munich Pact, 175, 176, 492, 756, 968, 1043, 1044, 1065

Nagasaki, 718

National Action Vanguard (VAN) of Panama, 462

National Awami Party (NAP) of Pakistan; profile, 455-59

National Democratic Party of Germany (NPD; West Germany), 218, 223n, 228, 240, 741, 968

National Federation of Student Self-Government Associations (Zengakuren) of Japan, 349, 352, 723

National Front (Czechoslovakia), 166, 207

National Independence Front of Guinea (Portuguese Guinea), 518

National Liberation Army (ELN; ELNB) of Bolivia, 44, 160, 1067

National Liberation Army (ELN) of Colombia, 127, 128, 131, 160

National Liberation Army (ELN) of Peru, *see* Army of National Liberation (ELN) of Peru

National Liberation Front (FLN) of Algeria, 12-13 *passim*, 342, 604

National Liberation Front (FLN) of Peru, 474, 476

National Liberation Front (FLN) of Venezuela, 160, 446, 629, 630-31, 635, 838, 844, 845, 853

National Liberation Front of South Vietnam (NFSV), 18, 58, 72, 73, 121, 149-50, 177, 184, 210, 215, 224, 226, 247, 272, 344, 368, 371, 408, 443, 444, 493, 516, 548, 573, 603, 621-622, 636, 642, 646, 647, 649, 652, 658-65 *passim*, 698, 700, 716, 733, 744, 759, 761, 763, 768, 852, 925, 1016, 1047, 1077, 1082; profile, 666-80; text of political program adopted by, 1006-13

National Liberation Movement (Argentina), 20

National Revolutionary Movement (Congo-Brazzaville), 210, 518, 660, 768

National Union of Algerian Students (UNEA), 12, 721

National Union of Haitian Students (UNEH), 274, 722, 723

National Union of Popular Forces (UNFP) of Morocco, 210, 409

National Union of Students of Brazil (UNE; UNEB), 45, 721, 723

National Union of Students of France (UNEF), 209, 721, 723

National Union of Students of Vietnam (UNEV; North Vietnam), 640, 721, 723

National University Federation (FUN) of Colombia, 122-23, 721, 723

Nationalist China, 635. *See also* Taiwan

Nationalist Party (PN) of Puerto Rico, 503-4, 620

NATO (North Atlantic Treaty Organization), 29, 30, 36, 37, 38, 79, 163, 164, 165, 180, 182, 183, 205, 206, 210, 211, 215, 216, 225, 231, 239, 240, 247, 253-57 *passim*, 296, 329, 344, 376, 381, 418, 419, 450, 500, 514, 548, 549, 571, 576, 577, 578, 599, 697, 700, 702, 703, 705, 716, 755, 890, 891, 949, 970, 1036-45 *passim*, 1058

Nazis, Nazism, 39, 49, 215, 235, 329, 381, 420, 490, 492, 493, 546, 716, 739, 740, 743, 757, 947, 968, 969, 970, 1037. *See also* Neo-Nazism, Neo-Nazis

Near East, 660, 890, 1018, 1019, 1020, 1026, 1027; text of CPSU resolution on Soviet policy concerning Israeli aggression in, 977-78. *See also* Arab-Israeli crisis and war; Middle East

Negroes, American, 10, 39, 158, 506, 611-15 *passim*, 618, 619, 622, 623, 636, 675, 679, 729, 761, 762, 934, 1033

Neo Lao Hak Xat (NLHX), *see* Laotian Patriotic Front

Neo-fascism, 971

Neo-Nazism, neo-Nazis, 29, 218, 228, 234, 333, 450, 516, 599, 600, 616, 700, 740, 741, 755, 968-71 *passim*, 1037

Neo-Stalinists, 222

Neo-Trotskyists, 469

Nepal, 119, 729; profile, 414-16

Netherlands, 29, 519, 901, 1037; profile, 417-21

Netherlands Communist Youth League, 421

*Neue Zürcher Zeitung*: quoted on Karlovy Vary conference, 756
New Communist List (RAKAH) of Israel, 30, 59, 219, 342, 493, 506, 554, 604, 617, 767, 1088; profile, 330-34; texts of its documents on Arab-Israeli crisis and war, 920-23
*New Program of the Communist Party, USA (A Draft)*, 610, 610n, 615; quoted, 610-11
*New Views on Problems of the Day*, 531
*New World* (Nigerian journal), 606
New York City, 502, 503, 505
*New York Times*: quoted on Karlovy Vary conference, 756
New Zealand, 782; profile, 422-26
Nicaragua, 782, 841, 1024, 1030, 1048; profile, 427-30
Nigeria, 251, 606, 857; profile, 431-33
NLHX Afro-Asian Solidarity Committee, 370, 659
*No Puede Haber Revolución en la Revolución*, 18
Nonproliferation Committee, 700
NORAD (North America Air Defense), 79
Nordic Council, 206, 549
Nordic nations, 183, 206, 231, 296, 449, 450, 548, 549. *See also* Northern Europe; Scandinavia
Nordic Socialist Seminars, 183, 206, 296, 449n, 549, 1064
North America, 79, 96, 189, 265, 278, 462, 713, 781, 782, 823, 1048
North Atlantic Treaty Organization, *see* NATO
North Borneo (Sabah), 383, 390, 523
North Korea, 26, 72, 119, 120, 150, 156-57, 227, 317, 350, 356, 371, 420, 523, 603, 636, 652, 675, 711, 712, 733, 759, 761, 855, 1058, 1061, 1062, 1067-68, 1079, 1087, 1091, 1093; profile, 434-47
North Vietnam, 9, 10, 24, 29, 36, 58, 72, 73, 80, 87, 119, 120, 121, 150, 177, 180, 184, 209, 210, 216, 220, 226, 227, 257, 272, 292, 298, 317, 344, 356, 363, 364, 368, 369, 370, 384, 389, 407-8, 419, 426, 442-45 *passim*, 476, 490, 493, 515, 516, 519, 548, 567, 568, 573, 603, 663-68 *passim*, 670n, 675, 676, 680, 690, 698, 699, 700, 711, 712, 716, 733, 744, 759, 761, 840, 852, 855, 873, 874, 925, 933, 1012, 1016, 1036, 1047, 1063, 1078, 1079, 1083; profile, 638-62
Northern Europe, 205, 548, 1039, 1044; 1965 seminar of communist parties in, 935. *See also* Nordic nations; Scandinavia
Northern Ireland, *see* Ireland
Norway, 205, 231, 678, 1037; profile, 448-54
Norway-Czechoslovakia Association, 449
Norway-Soviet Union Association, 449
Norwegian Committee for Solidarity with Vietnam, 679
Norwegian Communist Youth Organization (NKU), 332, 453-54
November 13th Revolutionary Movement (MR-13) of Guatemala, 267, 268-69, 1087
Novosibirsk, 205n
Nuremberg trials, 740, 968, 970

OAS, *see* Organization of American States
OAU, *see* Organization of African Unity
Oceania, 823. *See also* Pacific area
October Revolution, 8, 15, 65, 87, 116, 178, 242, 268, 280, 294, 306, 374, 389, 405, 432, 454, 472, 501, 531, 540, 549, 555, 572, 574, 575, 587, 635, 657, 658, 677, 712, 718, 764, 769, 781, 784, 786, 793, 820, 870, 880-84 *passim*, 966, 988-94 *passim*, 1045; conferences on, 178, 267, 412, 554, 575, 769, 770, 1076; speech by Lin Piao on, 829-31; text of Section III of CPSU Theses on, 979-84; text of article by Ho Chi Minh on influence of, 1014-17
—joint editorial of Communist Chinese publications on, 116; text, 823-28
October Revolution, Fiftieth Anniversary of: celebration of, outside Soviet Union, 25, 29, 30, 55, 59, 95, 124, 130, 153, 175, 178, 187, 190, 272, 289n, 293, 305-6, 375-76, 395, 404, 412, 444, 454, 513, 554, 583, 585-86, 589, 603, 615, 627-28, 635, 657, 677, 691, 707, 712, 717, 718, 734, 746, 762, 966, 1014, 1017, 1042, 1048, 1072, 1081
—celebration of, in Soviet Union: 14, 25, 29, 30, 37, 42, 49, 55, 66, 80, 87, 116, 130, 134, 135, 152, 165, 182, 184, 194, 199, 206, 218, 239, 242, 248, 257, 261, 267, 268, 272, 277, 293, 296, 317, 323, 326, 329, 332, 340, 342, 343, 355, 361, 373n, 376, 378, 382, 395, 399, 403, 413, 419, 430, 433, 444, 455, 461, 465, 471, 490, 491, 501, 503, 507, 513, 520, 527, 734, 540, 549, 554, 565, 573, 575, 578, 600, 601, 604, 605, 615, 617, 628, 635, 653, 657-58, 677, 691, 712, 978, 988, 994, 997, 1042, 1090; profile, 764-70
—CPSU Theses on, 220, 769; text of Section III, 979-84
Oder-Neisse line, 9, 183, 236, 490, 491, 873, 1044, 1066
Okinawa, 351, 705
OLAS (Latin American Solidarity Organization; *also* LASO), 16, 19, 46, 94, 130-35 *passim*, 628, 678, 729, 787, 1020-21, 1076; profile, 758-59; text of pamphlet on and published by, 1023-25
OLAS Conference, 16, 18, 29, 30, 40, 46, 48, 94, 125, 125n, 128, 130, 139, 145, 146, 147, 152, 154, 155, 158, 159, 160, 160n, 186, 190, 194, 196, 199, 217, 220, 230, 242, 261, 267-71 *passim*, 276-77, 280, 344, 395-400 *passim*, 430, 442, 445, 446, 461-65 *passim*, 471, 475, 476, 503, 505, 517, 554, 599, 605, 616, 618, 627, 628, 631, 634, 636, 637, 653, 677, 678, 689, 703, 734, 758, 936, 1023, 1080, 1081; profile, 759-63; text of call to, 1021-22
—General Declaration, 759, 762; text, 1028-33
Olympic Games, 746
Oman, 748
*On Contradiction*, 25-26
"On Correcting Mistaken Ideas in the Party," 111
*On Practice*, 25-26
"On the Correct Handling of Contradictions among the People," 112; quoted, 773, 775

"On the Correct Road of the Indonesian Revolution," *see* "For a Sound Indonesian Revolution"

"On the People's Democratic Dictatorship": quoted, 803

Open Door International, 729

Order of Lenin, 30, 658, 768, 1090

Organization of African Unity (OAU), 857

Organization of American States (OAS), 80, 148-49, 160, 761, 762, 782, 838-41 *passim*, 856, 1021, 1030, 1072

—conferences at Punta del Este: in 1961 and 1962, 1031; in 1967, 626

Organization of Communists of Switzerland (OCS), 31, 222, 346, 555, 558; profile, 557-58

Organization of Latin American Solidarity, *see* OLAS

*Orientation of the Youth Movement, The*: quoted, 797

Orthodox Communist Party (PCO) of the Dominican Republic, 185-89 *passim*

Outer Mongolia, *see* Mongolia

Pacific area, 926; communist parties in, 118. *See also* Oceania

Pakistan, 9, 119, 120, 298, 519, 703, 717, 729, 748, 749; profile, 455-59

Palestine, 331, 359, 360, 921, 922, 947, 948

Palestine Liberation Organization (PLO), 120, 358, 359, 573, 748

Palestine Peace Committee, 701

Palestinian Arabs, 24, 216, 247, 324, 326, 330, 331, 358, 359, 360, 411, 710, 716, 721, 740, 920-23 *passim*, 948, 1051

Pan-Africanist Congress of Azania, 528

Panama, 724, 725, 856, 1024, 1030, 1047, 1048; profile, 460-62

Panama Canal, 460, 461, 1030

Panama Congress, 1028

Pan-American Union, 1030

Pan-Cypriot Committee of Peace (Pancyprian Peace Council), 163, 702

Paraguay, 782, 1024, 1048; profile, 463-66

Paraguayan Communist Party (PCP), 767, 1069; profile, 463-66

Paraguayan Leninist Communist Party (PLCP), 463, 465

Paris, 973

Paris Commune, 109, 476, 802, 803, 825

Parti Communiste de Quebec, *see* Communist Party of Quebec

Parti Communiste Internationaliste (PCI), *see* under Fourth International

Party for the Progress of the Independence of Madagascar (AKFM), 506, 507

Party of Labor of Argentina, 20

Party of the People's Vanguard of Costa Rica, *see* People's Vanguard Party (PVP) of Costa Rica

Party of the Revolutionary Left (PIR) of Bolivia, 40

Party of Socialist Revolution (Lebanon), 376

Party of the Union of Haitian Democrats (PUDA; also PUDH or PUDHA): profile, 273-77

Pathet Lao, *see* Laotian People's Liberation Army

Patriotic Neutralist Forces (Laos), 119, 363-69 *passim*

Paulus Society, 179, 212

Pax Christi, 705

Peace Corps, 158, 276, 578, 717, 907

Peace Liaison Committee for the Asian and Pacific Regions (PLCAPR), 750

Peking Center of the World Federation of Scientific Workers (Peking Center WFSW), 737, 750

People's Action Front (Chile), *see* Revolutionary Popular Action Front

People's Alliance of Labor (NTS; Russian emigre organization), 592, 592n, 995, 995n

*People's Daily*, see *Jen-min Jih-pao*

People's Democratic Party (Sudan), 768

People's Liberation Army ("Huks") of the Philippines, 371, 477, 480, 482; profile, 478-80

People's Party of Panama (PDP), 179, 232, 767, 1048, 1093; profile, 460-61. *See also* Communist Parties of Mexico, Central America and Panama, Fifth Meeting of

People's Party of Unity (Haiti), *see* Popular Entente Party

People's Progressive Party (PPP) of Guyana, 768, 1083; profile, 270-72

People's Revolutionary Movement (Mexico), 400

People's Revolutionary Party (PRP) of Cambodia, 67, 72, 73

People's Revolutionary Party (PRP) of Singapore, 521

People's Revolutionary Party (PRP) of South Vietnam, 119, 646, 666-70 *passim*, 673, 676, 680; profile, 663-66

People's United Front (MEP) of Ceylon, 85

People's Vanguard Party (PVP) of Costa Rica, 430, 767, 1048; profile, 133-35. *See also* Communist Parties of Mexico, Central America and Panama, Fifth Meeting of

*People's Voice* (weekly of Communist Party of New Zealand), 426, 478

Permanent Congress of Trade Union Unity of Latin American Workers, 759

Permanent Inter-American Force, 1021

Peronism, Peronists, 17, 18

Persians, *see* Iran

Peru, 461, 722, 724, 748, 758, 761, 839, 858, 1023, 1024, 1048, 1074; profile, 467-76

Peruvian Communist Party (PCP; pro-Chinese), 467; profile, 472-74

Peruvian Communist Party (PCP; pro-Soviet), 217, 225, 273, 473, 767, 1091; profile, 467-72

Philippine Committee for Freedom in South Vietnam, 481

Philippine Communist Party (PKP), 116, 118, 371, 1072, 1090; profile, 477-83

Philippines, 66, 748, 782, 823; profile, 477-83

Phnom Penh, 973

"Phoenix 1961," 593

"Phoenix 1966," 593, 594

Pioneer Organization (Soviet Union), 401, 583. *See also* Komsomol

Plaine des Jarres Agreement, 362, 364, 367
Platt Amendment, 1030
Poland, 9, 53, 56-57, 175, 231, 321, 403, 547, 588, 600, 601, 630, 652, 652n, 658, 675, 709, 721, 729, 746, 759, 922, 1014, 1026, 1037, 1063-66 *passim*, 1069, 1079, 1084, 1085, 1093; profile, 484-96
—Kliszko's report on CP's tasks in, 487-88; abridged text, 949-52
Polaris weapons system, 248
Polish United Workers' Party (PUWP), 120, 212, 218, 219, 224, 226, 291-92, 342-43, 495, 496, 555, 600, 600n, 601, 662, 753, 767, 1034, 1046, 1058; profile, 484-95
—Kliszko's report on tasks of, 487-88; abridged text, 949-52
Polish Writers' Congress, 489, 592
*Political Work in the Anti-Japanese Army*, 833
Popular Entente Party (PEP) of Haiti, 767; profile, 273-77
Popular Front, 935
Popular Idea Party (Equatorial Guinea), 660
Popular Movement for the Liberation of Angola, *see* Angola Popular Liberation Movement
Popular Resistance Organization (ORP) of Algeria, 15; profile, 12-14
*Populorum Progressio* (papal encyclical), 28, 212, 236, 337, 489, 553
Portugal, 39, 49, 119, 225, 248, 432, 527, 548, 716, 717, 857, 1042, 1045; profile, 497-501
Portuguese Africa, 218, 410, 548-49
Portuguese colonies, 498, 606, 711, 715, 749
Portuguese Communist Party (PCP), 210, 218, 224, 754, 767, 1034, 1046; profile, 497-501
Portuguese Guinea, 49, 500, 660, 677, 732, 748, 857, 859
Posadas movement, *see under* Fourth International
Potsdam Agreement, 969, 970, 971, 1037
Pracheachon Party (PP—Khmer People's Party), 67, 72, 73
Prague, 529, 679
*Pravda*: text of editorial on anti-Soviet policy of Mao and his group, 972-76
*Problème chinois, Le*, 212n, 217
Problems of Peace and Socialism Press, 575
*Problems of Peace and Socialism/World Marxist Review*, 179, 517
Profintern (Red International of Trade Unions), 695
Progressive Labor Party (PLP) of the United States, 503, 504, 505, 623; profile, 618-20
Progressive Party of the Working People of Cyprus, *see* Reconstruction Party of the Working People of Cyprus
Progressive Workers' Movement (PWM) of Canada, 81
Pro-Independence Movement (MPI) of Puerto Rico, 446, 502; profile, 505
Protestants, 240, 418
Provisional Committee of the UPC (Union of the Populations of Cameroun), 75, 76
Puerto Rican Communist Party (PCP), 767; profile, 502-3

Puerto Rican Socialist League (LSP), 502, 620; profile, 503-5
Puerto Ricans, in U. S., 502, 503, 611, 619
Puerto Rico, 721, 724, 759, 1024, 1028, 1029, 1030; profile, 502-5
Pugwash Movement of Scientists for Peace, 736

"Questions of Ideology and Culture," 244, 245, 1091; text, 885-89
Quotations from Chairman Mao Tse-tung, 5, 11, 188, 878, 879, 942

Radical Party (PR) of Chile, 90, 91, 92, 95, 785
Radical Student Association (Iceland), 296, 549
Radio Free Europe, *see* Free Europe Committee
Rankovicism, 685
Rebel Armed Forces (FAR) of Guatemala, 159, 160, 263-69 *passim*, 1068, 1087
Reconstruction Party of the Working People of Cyprus (AKEL); *also* Progressive Party of the Working People of Cyprus), 210, 224, 257, 294, 578, 753, 754, 767, 1034, 1046; profile, 162-65
Red Cross, 728, 843
*Red Flag*, see *Hung Ch'i*
Red Flags (Burma), 60-63 *passim*
Red Guards, 5, 7, 7n, 72, 100-20 *passim*, 186, 352, 354, 404, 405, 442, 443, 601, 602, 615, 710, 774, 776, 794, 812, 813, 818-22 *passim*, 829, 830, 878, 883, 940-44 *passim*, 973, 1058, 1077, 1081, 1082
Red Sea, 332, 921
Restorers (AODA) of Greece, 258
Réunion, 215, 722; profile, 506-7
Réunion Communist Party (PCR), 210, 212n, 261, 768, 1081; profile, 506-7
*Revolution in the Revolution? (Revolución en la Revolución?)*, 18, 44, 125, 154, 159, 195, 264n, 398, 504, 616, 631, 1057, 1070; quoted, 147-48
Revolutionary Action Movement (RAM) of the United States, 619, 623
Revolutionary Brazilian Communist Party, 45
Revolutionary Ceylon Equal Society Party (VLSSP), 82, 85
Revolutionary Communist Groups (IV International) of Italy, 346-47
Revolutionary Communist Movement (MCR) of Argentina, 16-17, 20
Revolutionary Communist Party of Chile (PCRCh), 90, 97, 763
Revolutionary Communist Party of Spain, *see* Communist Party of Spain, (Marxist-Leninist) [*Mundo Obrero Revolucionario* group]
Revolutionary Communist Party of the Sudan (RCPS), 10; profile, 540-41
Revolutionary Leftist Front (FIR) of Peru, 474
Revolutionary Leftist Movement (MIR) of Chile, *see* Movement of the Revolutionary Left (MIR) of Chile
Revolutionary Movement of June 14 (MR-1J4) of the Dominican Republic, 185, 187; profile, 189-91
Revolutionary Movement of the Left (Uruguay), 628

Revolutionary Organization of the Tudeh Party (ROTP) of Iran: profile, 323

Revolutionary Party of National Integration (Venezuela), 768

Revolutionary Party of the Nationalist Left (PRIN) of Bolivia, 41, 1061

Revolutionary Peronist Movement (MRP) of Argentina, 20

Revolutionary Popular Action Front (FRAP) of Chile, 89-97 passim, 784, 785

Revolutionary Spartacus Association (Mexico), 400

Revolutionary Unity Movement (MUR) of Panama, 461-62

Revolutionary Workers' Party (Mexico), 400

Revolutionary Workers' Party (POR) of Bolivia, 40, 43, 1069

Revolutionary Workers' Party (POR) of Peru, 474

Revolutionary Workers' Party (RWP) of Great Britain, 251

Rhio Islands, 521

Rhodesia, 118, 248, 329, 526, 527, 605, 606, 711, 748, 857, 1082

Rio de Oro, 410

Rruga e Partisë (Albanian monthly): text of article on cultural revolution, 773-76

Rumania, 9, 10, 30, 56, 57, 130, 157, 176, 225, 231, 257, 291, 292, 293, 321, 332, 342, 403, 491, 492, 536, 585, 600, 604, 652, 658, 675, 676, 686-89 passim, 746, 759, 956-58, 1014, 1057, 1060-66 passim, 1070, 1074, 1075, 1079-86 passim; profile, 508-19; text of statement on establishment of diplomatic relations between West Germany and, 953; text of Rumanian CP's resolution on improving conditions in, 959-60

Rumanian Communist Party (RCP), 30, 37, 157, 178n, 179, 184, 207, 210, 219, 224, 226, 230, 258, 291, 296, 340-41, 355, 411, 419, 420, 450, 454, 549-50, 565, 601, 686, 753, 754, 767, 1068, 1070, 1071, 1074, 1079 1082, 1086, 1090, 1092, 1093; profile, 508-19; excerpts from Ceaușescu's article on role of, 954-58; text of its resolution on improving conditions in Rumania, 959-60

Russell International War Crimes Tribunal, 149, 184, 548, 576, 662, 679, 699, 744, 759

Russell Vietnam Tribunal, see Russell International War Crimes Tribunal

Russia, Tsarist, 453, 454, 540, 827

Russian Center, Harvard University, 589

Russian Institute, Colombia University, 589

Russian Orthodox Church, 590

Russian Revolution of 1905, 899, 901

Sabah, see North Borneo

Saguiet el Hamra, 410

Samyukta Socialist Party (India), 299, 768

Sandinista National Liberation Front (FSLN) of Nicaragua, 426-30 passim, 1094; profile, 430

San Marino: profile, 520

Santo Domingo, see Dominican Republic

Sarawak, 313, 383, 390-92

Sarawak Communist Organization (SCO), 313; profile, 390-92

Sarawak People's Guerrilla Troops (PGRS), 312-13, 391

Saudi Arabia, 326, 358, 1050, 1051, 1052

Scandinavia, 28, 202, 204, 205. See also Nordic nations; Northern Europe

SEATO (Southeast Asia Treaty Organization), 248, 256, 368, 456, 568, 571

Second Declaration of Havana, 97, 146, 1033; quoted, 1021

Second International, 8, 825, 829

Selected Works of Mao Tse-tung, 65, 945

Self-Cultivation by Party Members, 571

Seminar of Portuguese Students, 725

Seminar on Mother and Child in Africa (1965), 728

Senegal, 724, 749

"Serve the People," 111

SHAPE (Supreme Headquarters of the Allied Powers in Europe), 38

Sierra Leone, 749

Singapore, 119, 383, 383n, 385, 391, 519, 573; profile, 521-24

Sino-Cambodian Friendship Association, 71

Sino-Cuban conflict, 50, 119, 145, 151-52

Sino-Indian conflict, 119, 120, 301, 302, 303, 414, 416, 927, 1084

Sino-Japanese Friendship Association, 118

Sino-Japanese War, 102, 796, 833, 835-36, 906, 945

Sino-Soviet conflict, 19, 25, 29, 43, 56, 73, 81, 86, 95, 115-16, 119, 121, 122, 129, 134, 150-51, 152, 164, 178, 183, 194, 218, 230, 245, 271, 291, 304, 305, 315, 316, 320, 330, 353, 354, 361, 375, 387, 388, 398, 404, 406, 407, 411, 418, 419, 420, 424, 425, 426, 441, 442, 450, 451, 454, 463, 465, 467, 478, 482, 492, 500, 501, 527, 534, 540, 543, 549, 556, 565, 571, 575, 588, 589, 601-3, 604, 605, 628, 634-35, 636, 639, 654-55, 656, 676, 689-90, 695, 703, 704-5, 708, 710, 715, 717, 727, 737, 743-44, 747-50 passim, 755, 764-65, 766, 773-76 passim, 813, 824, 829, 831, 883, 924, 927, 928, 941, 945, 949, 964, 966, 967, 981, 994, 1053, 1057, 1059, 1063, 1079; text of Pravda article on, 972-76

Sino-Soviet Treaty of Friendship, Alliance, and Mutual Assistance, 602, 1063

Social Democratic Labor Party (SAP) of Sweden, 518, 542-48 passim

Social Democratic Party (Finland), 201-6 passim, 241, 870

Social Democratic Party of Norway, 449, 679

Social Democratic Party (SAP) of Sweden, see Social Democratic Labor Party (SAP) of Sweden

Social Democratic Party (SPD) of West Germany, 225-28 passim, 232, 235, 236, 240, 755, 969, 1040-41, 1077

Socialist Forces Front of Algeria, 12n-13n

Socialist Front (Singapore), see Barisan Sosialis

Socialist German Student League (SDS) of West Berlin, 237, 241

Socialist International, 205, 206, 384

Socialist Labour League (SLL) of Great Britain, 250, 251; profile, 249-50

Socialist League (Finland), 201, 768

Socialist Party of Nicaragua (PSN), 767, 1048; profile, 427-30. *See also* Communist Parties of Mexico, Central America and Panama, Fifth Meeting of

Socialist Party (PS) of Chile, 89, 92-96 *passim*, 159, 768, 784-85, 786, 1076

Socialist Party (SFIO) of France, 211n, 214, 215, 217, 518

Socialist Party (Uruguay), 628

Socialist People's Party (SF) of Denmark, 180-83 *passim*, 206, 296, 449n, 544, 545, 549, 550

Socialist People's Party (SF) of Norway, 206, 296, 448, 449, 450, 518, 545, 549, 550, 679, 768

Socialist Progressive Party (Lebanon), 374, 768

Socialist Revolutionary Party of Ecuador (PSR; PSRE), 192, 195, 196

Socialist Tali'ah Party (Algeria), 12. *See also* Popular Resistance Organization (ORP) of Algeria

Socialist Unity Party (New Zealand), 232, 422, 424, 768

Socialist Unity Party of Catalonia, 529, 533

Socialist Unity Party of Germany (SED; East Germany), 30, 80, 96, 165, 179, 183, 204, 206, 207, 210, 218, 219, 234-42 *passim*, 248, 257, 291, 296, 326, 355, 361, 376, 412, 433, 446, 491, 527, 554, 565, 575, 578, 600n, 601, 618, 662, 678, 753, 767, 1034, 1036, 1046, 1070, 1088, 1093; profile, 223-33

Socialist Unity Party of Germany—West Berlin (SED-W), 210, 224, 232, 754, 767, 1034, 1046; profile, 239-42

Socialist Workers' and Farmers' Party (SWAFP) of Nigeria, 224; profile, 431-33

Socialist Workers' Party (SWP) of the United States, 1089; profile, 621-22

Society for Cultural Cooperation between Lebanon and the Soviet Union, 373-74

Society for German-Soviet Friendship—West Berlin, 239

Sofia, 252, 576, 715, 717, 718

Somali Democratic Union, 768

Somalia, 519 748, 749

South Africa, 118, 248, 329, 377, 378, 506, 605, 709, 711, 748, 749, 857, 1068; profile, 525-28

South African Communist Party (SACP), 224, 232, 377-78, 768, 1068, 1082; profile, 525-28

South America, 72

South Arabia, 10, 921, 1049-52 *passim*

South Korea, 435, 436, 439, 447, 729, 748, 782, 855, 857, 1068

South Vietnam, 8, 58, 72, 95, 121, 149-50, 177, 180, 183, 215, 247, 364, 367, 370, 389, 407, 419, 444, 476, 493, 516, 573, 638, 640, 646, 647, 649, 651, 653, 659, 660, 662, 690, 709, 711, 782, 840, 851, 852, 855, 857, 925, 965, 1016, 1047, 1077, 1078, 1088; profile, 663-80; text of political program adopted by NFLSV for, 1006-13

South Vietnam Afro-Asian Solidarity Committee, 667, 676

South Vietnam Armed Forces of Liberation, *see* Viet Cong

South Vietnam Liberation Youth Union, 182, 679

South Vietnam People's Armed Forces of Liberation, *see* Viet Cong

South Vietnam People's Committee for Solidarity with the American People, 679, 1088

South Yemen Peace Committee, 701

Southeast Asia, 10, 79, 206, 306, 346, 367, 368, 386, 447, 640, 663, 673, 937, 1006, 1007, 1014, 1016, 1035; communist parties in, 118, 603

Southeast Asia Treaty Organization, *see* SEATO

South-West Africa, 165, 379, 526, 732, 748

South-West African National Union (SWANU), 379

South-West African People's Organization (SWAPO), 379, 660, 703

Soviet Central Asia, 540, 583, 993

Soviet-Korean Friendship Society, 443

Soviet Peace Committee, 350, 703, 770

Soviet Union, 9, 10, 19, 26, 28, 29, 50, 65, 80, 95, 96, 116, 129, 146, 164, 169, 182, 190, 202, 218, 225, 231, 236, 242, 248, 306, 330, 338, 350, 377, 378, 381, 387, 388, 389, 398, 412, 420, 425, 430, 433, 454, 464, 471, 493, 512n, 521, 533, 540, 544, 546, 549, 556, 557, 564, 572, 615, 620, 630, 636, 675, 698-709 *passim*, 712-18 *passim*, 721-28 *passim*, 737, 743, 746-50 *passim*, 755, 764-66, 768-70, 793, 803, 820, 823, 824, 829,839, 843, 851, 870, 880, 883, 884, 913, 928, 932-33, 934, 939, 949, 950, 972-76 *passim*, 979-84 *passim*, 988-91, 996-1002 *passim*, 1014-18 *passim*, 1026, 1031, 1038, 1039, 1047, 1048, 1052, 1063, 1073, 1078, 1082, 1091; profile, 579-606; excerpts from Brezhnev's speech on Soviet foreign policy, 965-67; text of statement on West Germany, 968-71; text of CPSU resolution on Soviet policy concerning Israeli aggression, 977-78; text of joint party-government message to Soviet people, 988-91; abridged text of Andropov's report on guarding Soviet security, 992-96

—relations with: Afghanistan, 1074; Africa, 115, 564, 605; Albania, 8, 56, 116, 388, 601, 728, 777, 779; Algeria, 12, 14, 15, 604, 977; Arab states, 87-88, 120, 186, 326, 331, 359, 375, 376, 411, 425, 442, 516, 534, 540, 564, 565, 603, 604, 660-61, 688, 748, 922, 932, 933, 964, 977, 984, 1027, 1050-54 *passim*, 1084; Asia, 115, 420, 464; Austria, 30; Bulgaria, 54-57 *passim*, 407, 514, 600, 1073; Cambodia, 70-73 *passim*; Chile, 96; Colombia, 122, 122n, 125, 605, 851; Communist China, 101, 326, 353, 599, 602, 793, 815-20 *passim*, 827, 831, 967, 972, 975, 976, 1036, 1059, 1063; Congo (Kinshasa), 606; Cuba, 144, 145, 148n, 151, 152-56, 158, 160, 388, 588, 599, 604-5, 689, 695, 709, 723, 760, 761, 766, 840, 851, 855, 884, 1077; Cyprus, 165; Czechoslovakia, 175, 176, 514, 600, 1061, 1078; Dahomey, 746; East Germany, 9, 226, 227, 231, 600, 950, 966, 1039, 1058, 1067, 1093; Ethiopia, 746; Europe, 229, 316, 420; Finland, 204-7 *passim*, 1092; France, 215, 884, 965, 1076; Ghana, 606; Great Britain,

248, 524, 602, 605, 913, 1062; Greece, 164, 257; Guinea, 605-6, 746; Hungary, 180, 289-94 *passim*, 423, 451, 514, 584, 600, 709, 1064, 1065, 1084; Indonesia, 315-16; 388, 813, 913; Iran, 321-22, 323, 604; Iraq, 325, 325n, 604, 1072; Israel, 24, 59, 177, 292, 330, 331-32, 516, 604, 922, 923, 932, 1076; Italy, 605, 924, 965, 1059; Ivory Coast, 1059; Japan, 354, 813; Jordan, 358, 360, 361n, 604, 948; Korea, 855; Laos, 369; Latin America, 130, 152, 153n, 154, 155, 398, 605, 622, 625, 635, 689, 759, 762, 763; Lebanon, 374; Malaysia, 386, 388, 1069, 1090-91; Mali, 605-6, 746; Mediterranean area, 620, 576; Middle East, 8, 115, 120, 134, 152, 158, 177, 186, 194, 215, 229, 322-23, 344, 465, 564, 617, 920, 921, 922, 931-32, 1076; Mongolia, 402-7 *passim*, 603; Morocco, 411; Nigeria, 432, 606; North America, 79; North Korea, 26, 442, 443, 603, 1062, 1087; North Vietnam, 120, 121, 226, 603, 652-58 *passim*, 1063, 1079, 1090; Poland, 9, 490-91, 600, 951, 1085; Rhodesia, 605; Rumania, 513-14, 516, 585, 600, 601, 1066; Singapore, 523; South Africa, 605; South Vietnam, 654, 666, 675; Spain, 533; Sudan, 606; Syria, 560-65 *passim*, 604, 977, 1072, 1078; Tanzania, 606; Tunisia, 575; Turkey, 164, 576, 577, 578, 604; United Arab Republic, 604, 607, 977, 1076; United States, 8, 38, 50, 76, 120, 121, 149, 152, 190, 315, 323, 389, 425, 523, 524, 572, 577, 602, 620, 704, 748, 755, 813, 820, 824, 840, 855, 883, 920, 927, 949, 975, 1001, 1071, 1076; Vatican, 28, 221, 337, 490, 555, 605, 1059; Venezuela, 840, 841; Vietnam, 18, 38, 56, 121, 134, 194, 221, 306, 323, 326, 426, 572, 605, 690, 703, 748, 883, 925, 932, 965, 973, 984, 1014, 1017, 1036, 1053, 1079; West Germany, 8-9, 57, 492, 605, 755, 927, 950, 966, 969, 1037; Western Europe, 605, 927, 965, 1040, 1042; Yugoslavia, 588, 600, 601, 689, 690-91, 709, 715, 728, 732, 737, 1057, 1060, 1076

—*See also* Communist Party of the Soviet Union; Glassboro meeting; October Revolution; October Revolution, Fiftieth Anniversary of; Russia, Tsarist; Sino-Soviet conflict

Soviet Writers' Congress, *see under* Union of Soviet Writers

Spain, 39, 155, 225, 248, 410, 450, 519, 709, 715, 717, 741, 782, 848, 927, 997, 1028, 1042, 1045, 1057; profile, 529-36; text of political statement by CP of Spain on conditions in, 961-63

Spanish-American War, 1029

Spartacist League (United States), 621, 623

Sportintern (Red Sport International), 695

Sri Lanka Freedom Party (SLFP) of Ceylon, 83, 84, 85, 88, 768

Stalingrad, 852

Stalinism, Stalinists, 28, 82, 172, 200, 203, 220, 380, 417, 448, 479, 543, 544, 592, 685, 691, 778; de-Stalinization, 180, 203, 387, 453n, 543, 709. *See also* Neo-Stalinists

*State and Revolution*, 153

Stockholm Conference on Vietnam, *see* International Conference on Vietnam

"Strategic and Tactical Problems of the Revolution in Colombia, The," 125, 126

Student Nonviolent Coordinating Committee (SNCC) of the United States, 505, 615, 618, 619

Students for a Democratic Society (SDS) of the United States, 612-22 *passim*

*Subversion in Sarawak*, 390

Sudan, 59, 606, 660, 701-2, 717, 748, 949, 1050, 1066; profile, 537-41

Sudanese Communist Party (SCP), 224, 540, 541, 660, 768, 1050, 1066, 1079, 1087; profile, 537-40

Sudanese Union R.D.A. (Mali), 210, 224

Suez Canal, 216, 332

Sukarnoism, 907

Surinam, 759, 1024

*Svoboda*, 950

Swaziland, 748

Sweden, 119, 231, 238, 449, 678, 699n; profile, 542-50

Swedish-East German Friendship Society, 547

Swedish-Soviet Union Association, 547

Swiss Committee for Aid to Vietnam, 551

Swiss Communist Party (PCS), 551, 556n, 557, 558; profile, 555-56. *See also* Swiss People's Party

Swiss Party of Labor (PdA), 210, 224, 332, 555-58 *passim*, 754, 767, 1034, 1046; profile, 551-55

Swiss People's Party (PPS), 551, 557, 558; profile, 556-57. *See also* Swiss Communist Party

Switzerland, 119; profile, 551-58

Switzerland-Soviet Union Society, 551

Synod of Bishops, 488

Syria, 14, 15, 59, 158, 177, 183, 220, 230, 292, 323, 325, 326, 331, 342, 358, 359, 360, 370, 375, 406, 540, 604, 660, 689, 701, 702, 716, 746, 748, 749, 761, 766, 768, 920, 921, 922, 931, 947, 948, 964, 977, 1026, 1035, 1049, 1050, 1051, 1072, 1078, 1081; profile, 559-65

Syrian Communist Party (SCP), 210, 224, 373, 518, 600n, 604, 767, 1050; profile, 559-65; abridged text of its statement on Arab-Soviet unity, 964

Taipei, *see* Taiwan

Taiwan, 86, 118, 121, 369, 406, 534, 815, 817, 857, 1091. *See also* Chiang Kai-chekists; Nationalist China

"Talks at the Yenan Forum on Literature and Art," 115, 750, 1074

Tanganyika Workers' National Union, 10

Tanzania, 119, 120, 159, 378, 406, 606, 724, 748, 749, 766, 768, 1058

Tanzanian African National Union (TANU), 606

Tashkent agreement, 298, 705

Thai Afro-Asian Solidarity Committee, 567

Thailand, 116-17, 304, 364, 367, 368, 371, 383, 385, 386, 388, 521, 658, 659, 748, 782, 823, 857; profile, 566-73

Thailand Patriotic Front (TPF), 371, 566-69 *passim*, 573, 659

Third International, *see* Comintern

Third World, 15, 176-77, 220, 412, 444, 555, 599, 729, 761, 936, 937, 939, 1052
Thought of Mao Tse-tung Research Society (Japan), 357
*Times* (London): Czechoslovak "writers' manifesto" in, 172, 1084
Titoism, Titoists, 388, 453n
Trades Union Congress (TUC) of Great Britain, 706, 708
Treaty of Rome, 260
Tricontinental Committee for Support to the People of Vietnam, 759
Tricontinental Conference (1966), 125, 132, 151, 271, 394, 397, 689, 758, 759, 849, 935, 1021, 1023, 1024
Tricontinental Cultural Congress, 155
Tricontinental Organization, *see* Afro-Asian-Latin American Peoples' Organization
Tricontinental Organization for Solidarity with Vietnam, 150
Trinidad and Tobago, 759, 1024
Trotskyism, Trotskyists, 20, 40, 41, 43, 60, 82, 84, 85, 94, 97, 183, 209, 220, 245-51 *passim*, 258, 268, 308, 335, 338, 345, 346, 349, 388, 396, 400, 404, 453n, 465, 467, 472, 474, 496, 605, 614, 621, 623, 765, 777, 784, 880, 915, 940, 942, 1069, 1089. *See also* Neo-Trotskyists
Tudeh Party (Iran), 224, 518, 604, 767, 1081; profile, 321-23
Tunisia, 119, 326, 519, 723, 724, 1051; profile, 574-75
Tunisian Communist Party (TCP), 59, 210, 224, 768; profile, 574-75
Turkey, 9, 57-58, 163, 164, 165, 225, 257, 326, 604; profile, 576-78
*Twenty Letters to a Friend*, 592
23 September Movement (Mexico), 400
*22 June 1941*, 584-85

Uganda, 732
UNESCO (United Nations Educational, Scientific, and Cultural Organization), 705, 707, 714, 721, 727, 729, 732, 736, 743, 744, 745, 1059
Union of Albanian Women, 5, 728
Union of Albanian Working Youth, 3-7 *passim*, 10, 11, 76, 116, 119, 541, 717, 1077
Union of Cypriots in England, 162
Union of Czechoslovak Writers, *see* Czechoslovak Writers' Congress
Union of Italian Women (UDI), 336, 728
Union of Polish Writers, *see* Polish Writers' Congress
Union of the Populations of Cameroun (UPC), 75, 210
Union of Soviet Socialist Republics, *see* Soviet Union
Union of Soviet Writers, 591, 592, 985, 986, 1001; text of its letter to Solzhenitsyn and his reply, 1000
—Congress of, 343, 591-92, 769, 1000, 1002, 1073; text of Solzhenitsyn's letter to, 985-87
Union of Students for the Liberation of South Vietnam (UELVS), 667, 720, 723

Union of University Federations of Chile (UFUCh), 90, 95-96, 155, 193, 720, 722, 723
*Unir-Débat* group (France), 208, 219-20, 222
United Arab Republic (UAR), 9, 15, 59, 87, 119, 120, 149, 157, 158, 159, 177, 183, 220, 229, 230, 292, 323, 326, 331, 332, 342, 358, 359, 360, 368, 375, 407, 493, 537, 539, 560, 604, 660, 675, 688, 689, 702, 716, 745-49 *passim*, 766, 768, 839, 920, 921, 922, 931, 932, 947, 948, 964, 977, 1018, 1026, 1035, 1049, 1076, 1081; profile, 607-8
United Democratic Left (EDA) of Greece, 32, 165, 252-58 *passim*, 891, 892, 1070-71
United Kingdom, 119. *See also* Great Britain
United Nations, 8, 15, 19, 121, 148, 149, 152, 157, 159, 241, 248, 291, 407, 411, 412, 511, 518, 548, 556, 602-3, 676, 689, 702, 705-12 *passim*, 716, 721, 728, 736, 737, 739, 743, 744, 748, 839, 840, 841, 854-57 *passim*, 931, 932, 1018, 1019, 1020, 1026, 1076, 1085, 1091
United Nations Charter, 710, 1044, 1079
United Nations Economic and Social Council, *see* Economic and Social Council
United Nations Educational, Scientific, and Cultural Organization, *see* UNESCO
United Nations Industrial Development Organization (UNIDO), 707
United Nations International Peace Force, 163
United Nations Universal Declaration of Human Rights, *see* Universal Declaration of Human Rights
United Socialist Party (India), *see* Samyukta Socialist Party
United Socialist Party of Iceland (USPI), 183, 224, 518, 549, 753, 754, 767, 1064, 1071; profile, 295-96
United Socialist Party (PSU) of France, 211, 211n, 213, 214; text of joint communique by French CP and, 873
United Socialist Party (PSU) of Italy, 335, 518
United States, 10, 38, 39, 80, 88, 115, 129, 153n, 156-60 *passim*, 178, 180, 194, 212, 215, 220, 240n, 248, 251, 256, 262, 320, 323, 344, 352n, 353, 355, 381, 409, 411, 440, 441, 446, 482, 496, 505, 516, 563, 571, 592, 661-62, 676, 699, 699n, 704, 711, 714, 718, 722, 724, 737, 740, 748, 755, 756-57, 820, 823, 839, 856, 859, 860, 883, 884, 911, 912, 918, 932, 933, 934, 937, 941, 945, 949-50, 954, 955, 964, 971, 977, 981, 994, 1001, 1018, 1019, 1035, 1042-43, 1058, 1065, 1070, 1079; profile, 609-23
—relations with: Africa, 857, 994, 1018, 1043; Albania, 8, 1079; Algeria, 13, 375, 411; Arab states, 20, 49, 165, 241, 389, 425, 539, 617, 660, 678, 701, 1026, 1050, 1051; Argentina, 49; Asia, 58, 571, 857, 928, 994, 1018, 1035, 1043; Balkans, 255; Brazil, 49; Burma, 62, 64, 117; Cambodia, 58, 69, 72, 857, 1007; Canada, 78, 79; Central America, 1048; Chile, 91, 97, 787; Communist China, 29, 183, 305, 369, 461, 515, 774, 803, 813-20 *passim*, 830, 831, 857, 927, 928, 941, 945, 975, 1053; Congo, 215, 857, 884; Cuba,

130, 145, 149-50, 158, 215, 622, 709, 711, 737, 781, 782, 851, 855, 856, 884, 933, 1020, 1030, 1031; Cyprus, 58, 163, 165, 256, 257, 577, 711; Czechoslovakia, 886; Dominican Republic, 188, 215, 292, 781, 782, 841, 855, 856, 884; Ecuador, 193; Europe, 164, 255, 344, 600, 755, 934, 950, 1036, 1038, 1039, 1043, 1045; Far East, 926; France, 213, 215, 874, 931, 1016; Ghana, 215, 884; Great Britain, 840, 926; Greece, 30, 49, 58, 164, 215, 253-57 passim, 292, 376, 493, 577, 701, 884, 890, 1045, 1051; Guatemala, 266, 1047; Haiti, 274-77 passim; Honduras, 278; Iceland, 296, 931; India, 301; Indochina, 58, 79, 367, 659, 1006, 1007; Indonesia, 49, 292, 315, 420, 906, 907, 915, 916; Iran, 322, 323; Iraq, 325; Israel, 20, 49, 87, 95, 183, 237, 247, 256, 267, 290, 292, 325, 368, 375, 411, 442, 565, 575, 604, 660, 677-78, 701, 702, 921, 922, 947, 977, 1026, 1047, 1051; Italy, 926, 931; Japan, 349, 351, 354, 711, 857, 926; Jordan, 358, 359, 947; Korea, 215, 440, 727, 855; Laos, 363-71 passim, 855, 1007; Latin America, 14, 130, 148, 149, 150, 156, 160, 248, 395, 397, 446, 465, 634, 661, 758-62 passim, 781, 782, 783, 787, 852, 856, 858, 882, 890, 920, 921, 922, 934, 994, 1003, 1018, 1021-25 passim, 1028-33 passim, 1043, 1048; Malaysia, 522, 523; Mediterranean area, 120, 255, 256, 701, 702-3, 1039, 1051; Mexico, 400; Middle East, 30, 49, 58, 120, 152, 177, 229, 241, 247, 256, 330, 331, 344, 368, 493, 516, 564, 565, 578, 617, 660, 884, 890, 931, 932, 947, 1047; Mongolia, 813; Morocco, 411; Near East, 890; Nepal, 416; Nigeria, 432, 606, 857; North Korea, 439-40, 711; North Vietnam, 641, 646, 647-48, 661-62; Pacific area, 351, 926; Pakistan, 456, 458, 459; Panama, 460, 461, 856; Paraguay, 464; Peru, 858; Philippines, 480, 481, 483; Poland, 495; Portugal, 1045; Puerto Rico, 502-5 passim, 1029; Rumania, 519; Saudi Arabia, 1050; Singapore, 523; South Africa, 527, 857; South Korea, 435, 436, 439, 857; South Vietnam, 364, 367, 647, 649, 653, 659, 666-79 passim, 855, 857, 1006-13 passim; Southeast Asia, 79, 1006, 1007, 1035; Soviet Union, 8, 38, 50, 76, 120, 121, 149, 152, 190, 315, 323, 389, 425, 523, 524, 572, 577, 602, 620, 704, 748, 755, 813, 820, 824, 840, 855, 883, 920, 927, 949, 975, 1001, 1071, 1076; Spain, 534, 1045; Sudan, 541; Sweden, 548; Syria, 358, 375; Taiwan, 857; Thailand, 117, 364, 367, 368, 566-71 passim, 659, 857; Third World, 761; Turkey, 576, 577; United Arab Republic, 358, 375, 607; Venezuela, 838, 840, 842, 847, 848, 852, 853, 854; West Germany, 49, 215, 493, 516, 527, 755, 884, 926, 949, 950, 1037, 1038, 1039; Western Europe, 500, 949, 965, 1036, 1037, 1038; Yemen, 258; Yugoslavia, 6, 1080
—role in Vietnam, 8, 9, 18, 24, 26, 29, 30, 36, 38, 56, 58, 78, 79, 87, 95, 96, 121, 130, 146, 150, 156, 157, 177, 182, 183, 204, 207, 211-15 passim, 225, 226, 237, 239, 247, 256, 272, 292, 306, 316, 323,

326, 329, 333, 344, 351, 356, 367, 370, 375, 389, 395, 407, 411, 412, 419, 425, 426, 436, 441, 444, 465, 475, 493, 500, 503, 504, 506, 513, 515, 516, 524, 527, 548, 556, 560, 569, 571, 572, 575, 602, 612, 613, 617-22 passim, 634, 640-54 passim, 659-79 passim, 690, 698-702 passim, 705, 709, 711, 716, 723-24, 728, 729, 732-33, 737, 741, 743, 744, 748, 756, 781, 819, 820, 823, 840, 851, 852, 855-56, 860, 873, 874, 876, 883, 884, 886, 907, 922-28 passim, 934, 941, 965, 975, 977, 979, 983, 984, 994, 1014-21 passim, 1035, 1036, 1046, 1047, 1053, 1070, 1088; text of political program adopted by NFLSV, with emphasis on, 1006-13
— See also   Anglo-America; Glassboro meeting; Negroes, American; North America
U.S. Central Intelligence Agency (CIA), 145, 158, 159, 164, 200, 276, 375, 432, 458, 461, 578, 592, 722-25 passim, 734, 761, 849, 950, 995, 1003
U.S. Declaration of Independence, 946
U.S. Information Agency (USIA), 950
U.S. News and World Report, 975
U.S. Peace Corps, see Peace Corps
U.S. Sixth Fleet, 120, 554, 701, 755, 921, 1039, 1050, 1051
U.S. State Department, 787, 840, 849, 850, 937, 1003
Universal Declaration of Human Rights, 711, 744
University Students Federation (FEU) of Cuba, 155, 193, 720, 722, 723, 1067
UPI (United Press International): dispatches quoted by Castro, 837, 840
Uruguay, 463, 465, 724, 758, 759, 762, 763, 783, 1023, 1024; profile, 624-28
Uruguayan Anarchist Federation, 628
Uruguayan Popular Action Movement, 628
Uruguayan Revolutionary Movement, 628

Vatican, 28, 172, 337, 488, 489, 490, 555, 605, 1059
Vatican Council, 337, 520
Venezuela, 148, 150, 155, 225, 276, 398, 461, 465, 476, 505, 678, 721, 748, 758, 761, 762, 781, 783, 858, 859, 1021, 1023, 1024, 1028, 1032, 1048, 1060, 1062, 1065, 1068, 1072, 1075; profile, 629-37; text of Castro's speech on conflict between Cuba and, 837-54; text of statement by CP of Venezuela on terrorist regime in, 1003-5
Venezuelan MIR, The, 637
Vienna, 706, 742, 743
Vienna meeting of Western European Communist Parties (1966), 753, 755, 894, 935-36, 1034
Vientiane Agreements of 1957, 362
Viet Cong (South Vietnam People's Armed Forces of Liberation), 70, 73, 640, 647, 664-74 passim, 678, 1010, 1011, 1078
Viet Minh, 69-73 passim, 638, 663
Vietnam, 9-10, 14, 18, 22-26 passim, 29, 31, 35-39 passim, 49, 56, 67, 69, 72, 73, 87, 95, 115, 120-21, 130, 146-51 passim, 156, 177, 183, 184, 194, 206-10 passim, 214-18 passim, 221, 226, 240, 247, 255, 267, 292, 304, 305, 306, 316, 323, 326, 340, 356, 368, 370, 375, 376, 380, 381, 388,

389, 394, 395, 408, 411, 412, 425, 426, 441-46 *passim*, 450, 476, 481, 482, 493, 500, 516, 524, 527, 534, 535, 546, 547, 548, 553, 554, 556, 565, 566, 567, 571, 573, 576, 602, 603, 605, 614, 616, 621, 625, 627, 628, 634, 636, 640-80 *passim*, 698-703 *passim*, 710, 711, 715-16, 718, 721, 724, 728, 733, 737-38, 740, 744, 748, 755, 756, 757, 761, 762, 781, 787, 819, 823, 851, 852, 855-60 *passim*, 874, 876, 882, 893, 911, 924, 925, 926, 930-36 *passim*, 965, 966-67, 973, 984, 1006-14 *passim*, 1015-17, 1018, 1020, 1031-37 *passim*, 1046, 1047, 1061, 1069, 1072, 1090. *See also* North Vietnam; South Vietnam; United States: role in Vietnam
Vietnam, Democratic Republic of, *see* North Vietnam
Vietnam, Republic of, *see* South Vietnam
Vietnam Afro-Asian Solidarity Committee (North Vietnam), 150, 370, 444, 640, 659
Vietnam-Soviet Union Friendship Association, 658
Vietnam War, *see* North Vietnam; South Vietnam; United States: role in Vietnam; Vietnam
Vietnam Workers' Party (VWP) of North Vietnam, 73, 149, 150, 210, 224, 226, 362, 362n, 370, 408, 441, 444, 566, 573, 663, 664, 665, 763, 767, 1015, 1016-17, 1070, 1072; profile, 638-62
Voice of Japan (VOJ), 355, 356, 357
"Voice of Women" Conference, 729
Volkswagen plant, in Yugoslavia, 686

Walloon Communist Party, 37, 38
War Resisters' International, 699
Warsaw, 549
Warsaw Consultative Meeting on European Security, 716, 724
Warsaw Pact, 37, 57, 176, 225, 247, 291, 492, 494, 513, 514, 584, 601, 687, 716, 755, 950, 965, 980, 1038-39, 1044, 1045, 1078, 1082
—meetings of Foreign Ministers: February, 57, 231, 291, 491, 514, 515, 518, 1062; December, 291, 491, 514, 517, 1093
—*See also* Bucharest conference of European socialist countries; Bucharest Declaration of 1966
Warsaw Treaty Organization, *see* Warsaw Pact
*Washington Post*, 975
Week of Solidarity with the African Peoples, 660
Week of Solidarity with the People of Vietnam: in Soviet Union, 603; sponsored by International Union of Students, 724
West Berlin, 225, 227, 231, 716, 746, 966, 969, 1037, 1043, 1044; profile, 239-42
West Germany, 8-9, 10, 29, 30, 49, 57, 79, 115, 164, 175, 176, 204, 210, 215, 216, 218, 225-32 *passim*, 239, 240, 241, 248-49, 291, 292, 294, 325, 333, 340, 358, 381, 418, 420, 432, 450, 490-93 *passim*, 500, 515, 516, 626-27, 534, 548, 564, 577, 599, 600, 601, 605, 616, 688, 688n, 700, 701, 702, 707, 710, 711, 714, 716, 729, 738-43 *passim*, 755, 756, 851, 884, 920, 921, 926, 927, 933, 947, 949, 950, 966, 1037-46 *passim*, 1050, 1060, 1061, 1065, 1066, 1072, 1077; profile, 234-38; text of statement on establishment of diplomatic relations

between Rumania and, 953; text of Soviet statement on, 968-71
Western Europe, 57, 176, 218, 220, 256, 344, 446, 500, 511, 545, 605, 710, 711, 724, 746, 823, 882, 927, 949, 965, 1034-44 *passim*, 1072; communist parties in, 219, 454, 599, 605, 1034, 1035, 1040-44 *passim*. *See also* Brussels meeting of Western European Communist Parties; Vienna meeting of Western European Communist Parties
Western Hemisphere, 580
"What Being a Revolutionary Means in France Today," 213, 216, 217; abridged text, 880-84
"What Is OLAS?": text, 1023-25
"White Book on Siniavsky and Daniel," 593
White Flags (Burma), 116, 117, 573; profile, 60-66
WHO, *see* World Health Organization
Women's International Committee of Solidarity with Vietnam, 728
Women's International Democratic Federation (WIDF), 336, 442, 676, 695, 702, 739, 742, 759; profile, 726-30
Workers' Conference of the Baltic Countries, Norway, and Iceland, 182, 231
Workers' League (United States), 621, 623
Workers' Party—Trotskyist (Argentina), 20
Workers' World Party (WWP) of the United States, 621, 623
World Assembly of Youth, 713
World Conference against Atomic and Hydrogen Bombs, 703
World Conference of Intellectuals, 705
World Council of Peace (WCP), 155, 163, 336, 397, 442, 653, 695, 714, 721, 726, 727, 729, 733, 736, 739, 740, 742, 745, 747, 750, 759, 770; profile, 696-705
World Federation of Democratic Youth (WFDY), 95, 155, 162, 192, 239, 252, 442, 700, 702, 721, 727, 739, 759, 1063; profile, 713-19
World Federation of Scientific Workers (WFSW), 695, 745, 750; profile, 735-38
World Federation of Teachers' Unions, 736
World Federation of Trade Unions (WFTU), 162, 193, 224, 231, 442, 525, 560, 653, 676, 695, 714, 727, 736, 742, 747, 750, 759, 770, 1058; profile, 706-12
World Health Organization (WHO), 727, 736
*World Marxist Review*, see *Problems of Peace and Socialism/World Marxist Review*
World peace congresses, 698. *See also* First World Peace Congress
World Student Christian Federation, 721
World Union for the Defense of the Child, 729
World University Service, 721
World Veteran's Federation, 739
World War II, 585, 586, 683, 729, 757, 970, 1039, 1042
World Youth Festivals, 589, 714-21 *passim*, 724
World Youth Forums, 715, 721

Yemen, 326, 358, 748, 1049-52 *passim*
Young Communist League (Communist China), 717

Young Socialists (Great Britain), 249; profile, 250-51
Yugoslav Union of Student Youth, 720
Yugoslavia, 6, 9, 52, 53, 57, 58, 119, 130, 157, 176, 220, 291, 292, 321, 342, 557, 588, 600, 601, 709, 710, 715, 728, 732, 737, 745, 746, 759, 760, 820, 922, 1018, 1019, 1020, 1026, 1037, 1057-62 *passim*, 1069, 1075-85 *passim*; profile, 681-91

Zambia, 119, 120, 526, 724, 748, 749
Zengakuren, *see* National Federation of Student Self-Government Associations

Zimbabwe, *see* Rhodesia
Zimbabwe African People's Union (ZAPU) of Rhodesia, 526, 660, 768, 1082
Zionism, Zionists, 20, 177, 177n, 326, 332, 359, 360, 361, 375, 409, 410, 411, 425, 485, 495, 496, 563, 564, 620, 622, 947, 948, 1049-52 *passim*
Zurich-London Agreement of 1959, 164
Zurich Tripartite Agreement of 1961, 362, 364, 367
*Zwei deutsche Staaten: Die nationale Politik der DDR*, 229